GW01393224

Irish Income Tax

2017

Formerly *Judge: Irish Income Tax*

Irish Income Tax

2017

Formerly *Judge: Irish Income Tax*

Tom Maguire
FITI (Chartered Tax Advisor) MBA FCCA

Original text by
Norman E Judge

Bloomsbury Professional

Bloomsbury Professional
An imprint of Bloomsbury Publishing Plc

Bloomsbury Professional Ltd
The Fitzwilliam Business Centre
26 Upper Pembroke Street
Dublin 2
Ireland

Bloomsbury Professional Ltd
41–43 Boltro Road
Haywards Heath
RH16 1BJ
UK

Bloomsbury Publishing Plc
50 Bedford Square
London
WC1B 3DP
UK

www.bloomsbury.com

BLOOMSBURY and the Diana logo are trademarks of Bloomsbury Publishing Plc

First published 2017

British Library Cataloguing-in-Publication Data

A catalogue record for this book is available from the British Library.

ISBN: PB: 9781526501547

Typeset by Pica Publishing Services
Printed and bound Great Britain by
CPI Group (UK) Ltd, Croydon, CR0 4YY

Foreword

This text is based on Finance Act 2016 which was signed into law by our President on 25 December 2016. It is a short act containing important amendments regarding the reduction of the Universal Social Charge together with extensions to important reliefs such as interest deductions on rental properties and the EII scheme. The extension of the self-employed tax credit is to be welcomed also. These are important reliefs but when it comes to the taxation of the entrepreneur this author would suggest that there is much to do in this area given the changes being brought to bear in the area of international tax. Now is the time to focus on the indigenous taxpayer to ensure that indigenous growth can continue into the future. Further, there have been a number of the Appeal Commissioners decisions published since the previous edition of this book and they are referred to where appropriate.

Once again I would like to thank Bloomsbury for the opportunity to contribute to what has always been a remarkable text and hope that my contributions will add to the income tax debate into the future. My thanks also to my partners and colleagues in Deloitte for their support in this project.

My thanks to Deirdre, Kay and Paddy for all they have done and continue to do for me; nothing is possible without them. would like to continue to dedicate this text to my mom Carmel Maguire who passed away far too soon. She is and will always be very sadly missed by myself and Deirdre. She and John look after us now.

Tom Maguire

31st January 2017

Extract from Foreword to the First Edition

In writing the original book, I endeavoured to provide a complete analysis of the principles and practice of income tax in the Republic of Ireland. My aim was to produce a definitive textbook which will be of everyday practical use to accountants, solicitors, tax consultants and other practitioners interested or involved in tax matters, as well as to students of taxation and to business men and others who have to consider the impact of income tax on their transactions or activities.

The system and rules contained in the Tax Acts which, even to tax practitioners, inspectors of taxes etc who are used to applying or studying them, are frequently difficult to interpret. I have endeavoured, so far as possible, to explain the principles involved in a relatively simple manner in straightforward language. In general, my approach has been to provide first an explanation of each technical point and then to give an example with narrative and figures showing how the point in question would be dealt with in practice. Clearly, the limitations of space and time do not permit examples to be given of every point, but I trust that the reader will find that most of the more important matters have been adequately illustrated.

As a tax practitioner myself, I have found that there is a tendency for tax books to beg some of the more difficult questions and to leave it to the reader to research the matter further to find his own solution. Since for the tax practitioner in particular, if not for the average student who may not always require the more advanced treatment, it is on the difficult points that guidance is needed, I have, for the most part, sought to face up to the difficult issues and have endeavoured to provide solutions. I should emphasise however, that there may well be more than one possible interpretation of, or solution to some of these difficult issues and I can give no guarantee that my view would necessarily prevail on the facts of a particular case in practice.

I wish to say a very special thank you to my wife, Mary, without whose understanding, encouragement and help over a number of years during which I was researching and writing the original version of this book, it would never have been possible for me to complete it. My sincere thanks to Mary, Gordon, Moira, Stephen and Sophie.

A special word of appreciation is due to the partners in KPMG for permitting me to take a substantial amount of time away from my normal professional activities, both during the period of writing the original work and then in dealing with the subsequent updates.

NORMAN E JUDGE

DUBLIN

October 1985

About the Authors

Tom Maguire FITI (Chartered Tax Advisor) MBA FCCA

Tom Maguire is a Tax Partner in Deloitte and leads its tax policy and technical services team. He has been referred to by counsel in his most recent text *Ireland's General Anti-Avoidance Rule and the Rule of Irish Law* (launched by Ireland's former Attorney General) as one of this country's pre-eminent tax commentators. An award winning presenter at various tax conferences and seminars Tom contributes regularly to *Irish Tax Review* and sits on its editorial board. He has authored leading texts on Anti-Avoidance as above and *Taxing GAAP & IFRS* while co-authoring two others: *Taxing Financial Transactions* and *Irish Tax Policy in Perspective*. He represents the Irish Tax Institute on TALC's technical/capital taxes committee and at Main TALC, and is a regular contributor to the Sunday Independent on tax matters.

Professor John Ward (1950–2014)

From 1996 to 2012 the late Prof John Ward led the team of authors at McAvoy & Associates that made *Irish Income Tax the pre-eminent authority on the law and practice of income tax in Ireland.* He was a founding principal and director of McAvoy and Associates, a chartered accountant and fellow of the Irish Taxation Institute. While recognised as the foremost academic in the field of Irish taxation, he also had an expert command of UK taxation and was a fellow of the UK Institute of Taxation.

In addition to his work in the academic field John also worked for more than forty years as a specialist tax adviser to a cross-section of individuals, partnerships, trusts and corporates on Irish, UK and international tax matters. Throughout this time he displayed extreme generosity of spirit in helping friends and colleagues alike irrespective of whether the work involved extreme complexity or relatively mundane matters. He was Professor of Taxation at the University of Ulster and throughout his career contributed scholarly articles on tax issues to all of the major professional journals in the UK and Ireland.

Norman Judge

Norman Judge was until his retirement from practice in 1993 a partner in KMPG Chartered Accountants. He obtained first place and the Arthur H Muir Memorial Prize in the final examination of the Institute of Chartered Accountants in Ireland in November 1956. He was president of the Institute of Taxation in Ireland in 1991–92 and was Chairman of the Leinster Society of Chartered Accountants for the year 1972–73 and is the author of Value Added Tax in Ireland (1972). In November 1986, he was made a Fellow of the Institute of Taxation in Ireland in special recognition of *Irish Income Tax*.

Contents

Table of Cases

D

E

F

G

I

K

L

M

T

Y

Z

Table of Statutes

Division 1 General Background

1.1 Statutory Framework

1.101 Introduction

This book is primarily concerned with the system of income tax (which is imposed by the Income Tax Acts) in the Republic of Ireland. These Acts use the term 'the State' to denote the territory of the Republic of Ireland and this practice is, in general, followed throughout this book. However, where it is necessary to refer to matters affecting income tax (or any other tax) in the State by way of contrast with taxes in other countries, the term 'Ireland' or 'Irish' may be used. Any such reference has no application to taxation in Northern Ireland.

Income tax is, in principle, payable by individuals and other non-corporate persons on their respective incomes; such persons are also liable to capital gains tax on 'chargeable gains' realised on the disposal of assets. Companies and other bodies of persons with corporate status do not, in general, pay income tax or capital gains tax (there is an exception in the latter case for certain 'development gains'); they are instead chargeable to a separate corporation tax levied on their income and chargeable gains. However, there are special rules relating to the liability of foreign companies to income tax, corporation tax and capital gains tax in respect of Irish source income and certain capital gains.

One important point should be made initially regarding the interrelationship of income tax and corporation tax. Although a company or other body corporate is not normally chargeable to income tax, the rules of income tax are applied – subject to certain modifications on certain matters – in computing the income of a company for the purposes of charging it to corporation tax. Further, many of the rules in the Income Tax Acts relating to the assessment, collection and administration of income tax are applied by the Corporation Tax Acts, with some necessary modifications, for the assessment, collection and administration of corporation tax.

In order to set the scene for the more detailed discussion in the following parts, some of the main principles of income tax are summarised briefly in **Division 1**, where a number of the main exemptions from tax are listed.

In addition to the matters just mentioned, this part sets out to provide a general background to the taxation of income. Firstly, an outline is given of the statutory framework – ie the relevant Tax Acts, regulations, etc, containing the law dealing with income tax. Secondly, the principles which apply to the interpretation of tax statute (including double tax agreements) are discussed. The implications of the Constitution and of EU law are also considered as part of this discussion.

Thirdly, a brief summary is given in **Division 1** of the persons responsible for the administration of income tax and for the implementation of the administrative procedures for the assessment, collection, etc of income tax (discussed in more detail in **Division 2**). Finally, the important questions of 'residence' and 'domicile' for tax purposes and their effect in imposing certain 'territorial limits' on the chargeability of Irish income tax is discussed in **Division 1**.

1.102 The Tax Acts

The laws of the State have since 1922 been made by the Oireachtas (the Irish parliament) consisting of two houses, Dáil Éireann ('the Dáil') and Seanad Éireann ('the Senate'). All Acts of the Oireachtas, including those dealing with taxes, start off as Bills introduced in the Dáil by the Government of the day. After being passed by the Dáil with any such amendments as may have been incorporated during their passage, Bills are sent to the Senate for debate and approval, after which they become law as Acts on being signed by An t'Uachtaráin (the President). The date of the presidential signature, which must be shown on the first page of every Act, is the date on which it becomes law.

The enactments under which income tax and corporation tax are levied are referred to collectively as 'the Tax Acts' and comprise the Income Tax Acts and the Corporation Tax Acts (TCA 1997, s 1(2)). The Income Tax Acts are defined as the enactments relating to income tax contained in the Taxes Consolidation Act 1997 (TCA 1997) and in any other enactment (TCA 1997, s 2). The Corporation Tax Acts are defined as the enactments relating to Corporation Tax contained in TCA 1997 and in any other enactment, together with the Income Tax Acts in so far as they apply to Corporation Tax (TCA 1997, s 1(2)).

Prior to the enactment of TCA 1997 (with effect from 6 April 1997) the 'Income Tax Acts' were defined as the Income Tax Act 1967 (referred to throughout this book as 'ITA 1967') and every other enactment relating to income tax (ITA 1967, s 3). The 'Corporation Tax Acts' were the Corporation Tax Act 1976 ('CTA 1976') together with the Income Tax Acts so far as those Acts apply for purposes of corporation tax and every other enactment relating to corporation tax (CTA 1976, s 155(1)).

The Taxes Consolidation Act 1997, which was enacted on 30 November 1997, consolidated with effect from 6 April 1997 virtually all the previous legislation dealing with income tax, corporation tax and capital gains tax (the exceptions include certain provisions of the Waiver of Certain Tax, Interest and Penalties Act 1993, the Provisional Collection of Taxes Act 1927 and the Diplomatic Relations and Immunities Act 1967). The previous income tax legislation had consisted of the prior consolidation act, the Income Tax Act 1967, together with subsequent Finance Acts and other enactments dealing with income tax. As part of the pre-consolidation process, virtually all provisions relating to income tax contained in enactments other than Finance Acts were imported into the income tax legislation. The pre-consolidation process also encompassed the deletion of much obsolete material and a general tidying up of the legislation. The 1997 Act itself has employed a more uniform and logical style of drafting than was previously the case and has generally purged the statutory language of its most grievous archaisms and obfuscations. The Act also embodies a logical structure, grouping together related provisions, and thereby represents a huge improvement over the jungle of cross-referential law which it replaces. Some of the benefit of this latter improvement may be diluted as a result of the relentless tide of amendments which are already being introduced by subsequent Finance Acts.

The Income Tax Act 1967 consolidated, with effect from 6 April 1967, virtually all of the previous legislation dealing with income tax that had remained in force up to that date, including an additional tax on the income of individuals known as 'surtax'. The

previous legislation had consisted of the Income Tax Act 1918, as amended by the UK Finance Acts 1919 to 1922, which Acts were adopted for Irish taxation purposes on the formation of the Irish State in 1922, and which had also been amended by the subsequent Finance Acts passed by the Oireachtas from 1923 to 1966. The law regarding surtax was repealed by the Finance Act 1974 which substituted the higher rates of income tax applicable in the case of individuals only to the higher levels of taxable income.

The present system of taxing companies was introduced by the Corporation Tax Act 1976. Previously, companies had been liable to two separate taxes on their profits – the same income tax (but excluding surtax) that applied to individuals and a separate tax known as corporation profits tax (referred to in short as 'CPT'). CPT had been introduced by the UK Finance Act 1920 and had, as amended by subsequent Finance Acts up to 1976, applied to form a separate code of tax law known as 'the Corporation Profits Tax Acts'. These latter Acts were repealed with effect from 6 April 1976 by the Corporation Tax Act 1976.

The Tax Acts are subject to regular amendments, usually made by the annual Finance Act which turns into law the Government's budgetary proposals announced initially in the annual Budget Statement. The amendments in the Finance Act may either take the form of altering the wording of the main charging Acts for income tax, corporation tax or capital gains tax or the Finance Act may itself contain new charging or relieving sections or other provisions relating to any of the taxes. A provision in a Finance Act may also amend the wording in a previous Finance Act. Occasionally, a second Finance Act or another Act containing new provisions related to the taxes may be passed in the same year.

If a section in a new Act amends the former law as to income tax, that section is taken as being part of the Income Tax Acts. Similarly, if such a section amends a provision related to corporation tax, or an income tax provision which also applies to Corporation Tax, it becomes part of the Corporation Tax Acts.

Each annual Finance Act (and any other Act relating to taxes) contains a section entitled 'short title, construction and commencement'. The title indicates the term by which the Act is to be cited (for example, 'the Finance Act 2014'). The section then indicates that, so far as the provisions in the Act relate to income tax, those provisions are to be construed together with the Income Tax Acts (ie with TCA 1997, previous Finance Acts and any other Acts dealing with income tax).

This in effect links together all the relevant Acts which contain provisions dealing with income tax so that, unless there is any provision to the contrary in any Act, the new provision in the latest Act has to be construed together with all provisions on the same matter in previous Acts (except to the extent that the previous Acts have since been amended or repealed). Similarly, any provision in any new Finance Act dealing with corporation tax has to be construed together with the existing Corporation Tax Acts.

The provisions in any Finance Act, whether amending any previous Act or introducing completely new rules affecting any tax, are stated in the 'short title, etc' section as coming into force as and from a stated date. In the case of changes in income tax law, this date is frequently specified as being the commencement of the tax year in which the Finance Act is passed, but it is open to the government to propose (and the Oireachtas to pass) a Finance Act which provides for a particular part of the Act to come into force on any other date.

Normally, a change in the income tax law is not made effective earlier than the date on which the Minister for Finance introduced his Budget Statement in Dáil Éireann in the year in question. However, it is possible that a change in the law may be made effective from an earlier date, but this is usually only done in exceptional circumstances. Any such backdating normally only occurs if the Minister for Finance has previously indicated the government's intention to change the law on the particular matter. The author is aware of one eminent senior counsel who has opined that it would be very difficult to successfully challenge retrospective tax legislation on constitutional grounds.

The passing of the TCA 1997 with effect from 6 April 1997 required a series of special provisions in order to allow a seamless transition from the body of old law (now repealed) to the new Act (TCA 1997, Pt 49; Sch 32). FA 1998, s 136 and Sch 9 also effected a number of minor drafting amendments to the Act with effect from 6 April 1997.

In general, all references in this text will be to the provisions of TCA 1997 and subsequent Finance Acts. However, it will on occasions be necessary to set out the history of a particular provision, in which case the statutory antecedents of TCA 1997 will be referred to as appropriate.

1.103 Relevance of case law

The respective Acts charging each of the taxes make provision for appeals by the taxpayer against the inspector's assessments and, unless the matter in dispute is settled at an earlier stage, it may ultimately be determined by the courts. While a minute percentage of all tax assessments reach the courts for decision, those that do usually contain difficult points of law the proper interpretation of which has not been clear from the wording of the relevant Act dealing with the matter.

The decisions of the courts on tax matters brought before them constitute an important element of tax law. While case law cannot overrule anything in the Tax Acts, it does represent an authoritative exposition and, in some cases, an amplification of the statutes. The relevant principles of interpretation are discussed in **Division 1**. Any decision by a court in the State on a point in any Act becomes part of the law on the point in question unless and until that decision is either overruled by a decision on the same point or is reversed by a subsequent change in the law included in a new Act. A lower court may not overrule the decision of a higher court but it may overrule the decision of a court of equal status (although this will be a relatively unusual occurrence). As discussed in **1.410**, in certain cases a point of law may (or must) be referred to the European Court of Justice.

Before any disputed tax assessment can give rise to a case on a point of law in the High Court, it must first have been heard by the Appeal Commissioners (see **2.202**). There is then a procedure under which the taxpayer, if dissatisfied with the determination of the Appeal Commissioners on the matter, may apply to have the case reheard by a judge of the Circuit Court.

Any decision by either the Appeal Commissioners or by the Circuit Court judge on a question of fact cannot be upset by the High Court (nor by the Supreme Court), but either the taxpayer or the Revenue Commissioners are entitled to appeal to the High Court against any decision of either the Appeal Commissioners or the Circuit Court judge on a point of law. A further appeal is then open to either party to the Supreme Court against the High Court's decision on the point of law. The decision of the Supreme Court on the law is final.

A significant part of the Irish tax laws are similar in principle, although they may vary in detail in various respects, to the tax laws of the UK. Consequently, many of the decisions of the UK courts on tax matters are directly relevant to the interpretation of the corresponding Irish statute. Such decisions may have greater or less persuasive value (depending, for example, on the eminence of the Judge(s) involved, or the extent to which the decision has been subsequently followed by later Judges) but do not form precedents as such. However, where a UK decision has been expressly followed by an Irish court, the principles underlying that decision are likely to carry much the same weight as any other Irish precedent.

References are made in the text to the leading decisions in tax cases in Ireland and the UK and, where appropriate, in other jurisdictions. Further, since the judgments in the cases in question frequently contain helpful commentary, giving a better insight into the issues involved, quotations from those judgments are added, where considered helpful.

The judgments in tax cases decided in the High Court and Supreme Court in the State are published in *Irish Tax Reports* (published by Bloomsbury Professional) with annual updates. These volumes include some important, previously unreported, cases.

Historically, the decisions of the Appeal Commissioners (and normally those of the Circuit Court) have not been reported and were not available to the public. However, TCA 1997, s 944A provides that the Appeal Commissioners may arrange to publish their determinations as they consider appropriate. In effect, these will be decisions which the Appeal Commissioners consider to have some precedential value. A number of such decisions are located on the Appeal Commissioners' website. (www.appealcommissioners.ie).

The main source of reference to UK tax case decisions is the Reports of Tax Cases, reported under the direction of the Board of Inland Revenue (with notes of argument supplied by the Incorporated Council of Law Reporting). These reports have been published over many years and continue to be issued on a regular basis. Another source of UK tax case judgments is Simon's Tax Cases published by LexisNexis (previously Butterworths).

1.104 Statutory instruments

The Tax Acts may authorise the Revenue Commissioners to make regulations with respect to particular matters contained in the Acts where this may be necessary to implement the carrying out of any particular provisions in the Acts. Regulations made under these powers are referred to as statutory regulations and are made by way of an order laid before and approved by Dáil Éireann in the manner prescribed in the relevant Act. Any regulation made under such an order may normally be revoked by a subsequent order laid before and approved by the Dáil. The fact that the Revenue Commissioners are given power to make regulations about a specified matter does not necessarily mean that they will do so.

The constitutional position of regulations is discussed at **1.409**. Regulations which exceed the limits laid down by the enabling statute will be ultra vires and void as a consequence (see *R v IRC ex parte Woolwich Equitable Building Society* [1990] STC 682; *Purcell v Attorney General* IV ITR 229).

In some cases, particular provisions of an Act are stated only to take effect on the making of a ministerial order, often from a date to be specified in the order itself (typically in circumstances where the provision is subject to clearance by the European Commission).

The statutory regulations and ministerial orders are published in the form of statutory instruments referred to by a number and by the year in which it was issued. For example, SI 559/2001 was issued in that year and is entitled the Income Tax (Employments)

(Consolidated) Regulations 2001 and deals with the operation of PAYE in respect of employment income. The Revenue Commissioners issued these regulations under a power given to them by TCA 1997, s 986.

In some cases EU Directives may be incorporated in the first instance in Statutory Instruments to permit them to take domestic effect expeditiously even though as a result they effect the substantive tax laws. This procedure was held to be constitutional by the Supreme Court in *Meagher v Minister for Agriculture* [1994] ILRM 1.

1.105 Double taxation agreements

The Tax Acts impose their respective taxes *inter alia* on the worldwide income of resident persons and, in most instances on the Irish source income accruing to non-resident persons (the full territorial scope of Irish income tax is discussed at **Division 1**). A resident person in receipt of foreign source income may also be subject to income tax in the country in which the income arises. Similarly, a non-resident person taxed on Irish income may be subject to tax in his own country in respect of the same items.

In order to avoid so far as possible this form of double taxation of income by the State and by another country, the Tax Acts authorise the Government to enter into arrangements with the governments of other countries to provide relief from double taxation and, as a complementary object, to prevent the evasion of taxation in the respective countries. Arrangements of this type are known as double taxation agreements or conventions, but are frequently referred to more shortly as 'tax treaties'.

There are a number of double taxation agreements in existence between Ireland and other states. The subject of double taxation treaties generally and their effects on the taxation of resident and non-resident persons are discussed in detail in **Division 14**. At this stage, it may be noted that the terms of a tax treaty may modify Irish tax law in certain respects, but only to the extent that a person or transaction is eligible under the relevant treaty. The interpretation of double tax treaties is discussed in **1.411**.

1.106 Other legislation

Apart from the Acts specifically dealing with income tax, it is relevant to mention two other Acts which affect this tax. The Interpretation Act 1937 (as amended by Interpretation (Amendment) Act 1993) contains rules for the interpretation of any Act of the Oireachtas including the Tax Acts up to 31 December 2005. The Interpretation Act 2005 repealed the 1937 Act in its entirety, and came into operation on 1 January 2006. While many of its provisions are of a technical nature, or restate the provisions of the earlier Act, there are also some potentially significant innovations. The Act contains, *inter alia*, pre-existing rules in relation to the meaning and construction of particular words and expressions which may be contained in any Act. Thus, eg the word 'land' is stated to include 'messuages, tenements, and hereditaments, house and buildings of any tenure' (and note also the discussion of the meaning of the term 'person' in **1.302**). These definitions however will not apply to the extent that a contrary intention appears from a reading of the relevant statute.

The Interpretation Act also provides that in construing any other Act, any word importing the singular shall, unless the contrary intention appears, be taken as importing the plural (see, for example, *SW Ltd v McDermott* II ITR 661, where such a contrary intention was found to exist, and note also *Dawson v IRC* discussed at **15.303**; an important discussion of the topic is also contained in *Floor v Davis* [1979] STC 379). This Act also contains certain rules regarding the form of Acts of the Oireachtas, their date of passing and of their commencement, and other related matters (see *State v Ryan* [1934] IR 13, *O'Leary v Revenue Commissioners* IV ITR 357).

Major changes from the pre-existing legislation include the following:

1. The provisions of the Interpretation Act will apply to an Act or Statutory Instrument unless a contrary intention appears in the Interpretation Act itself or in the relevant Act or Statutory Instrument or in the Act under which a Statutory Instrument was made (Interpretation Act 2005, s 4).
2. In construing any provision which is obscure or ambiguous, or where a literal interpretation would be absurd, or would fail to reflect the plain intention of the Oireachtas, that provision is to be interpreted so as to reflect the intention of the Oireachtas where that intention can be ascertained from the Act as a whole. This does not apply in the case of a provision which imposes 'a penal or other sanction' (Interpretation Act 2005, s 5). Arguably this approach does not alter the correct approach to the interpretation of tax law, although it may check the tendency of some judges to apply an overly strict and literalistic analysis (see **1.406**). This is on the basis that tax statute as such does not generally impose a penal or other sanction although of course it does contain many administrative provisions which are penal in nature (see in particular **2.7**) where a strict approach to interpretation will be appropriate. Having said this, as discussed at **1.405**, **1.406**, ascertaining the overriding intention of the Oireachtas may be particularly difficult in the context of tax statute. It may be noted that s 5 only permits recourse to the act as a whole and not to the proceedings of the Dáil (in contrast to the UK decision in *Pepper v Hart* [1992] STC 898, [1994] IJOT 40: see **1.404**).
3. A judge when construing any provision of an Act or Statutory Instrument may make allowances for changes in the law, social conditions, technology, the meaning of words used in the provision and other relevant matters which have taken place since the date of enactment, but only in so far as the text, purpose and content of the relevant provision permit (Interpretation Act 2005, s 6).
4. In situations covered by ss 5 and 6 above, but not otherwise, a judge may look at any notes in the text of any act in the version as signed by the President. This will bring in for consideration, for example, the description of sections in the margins of printed legislation (Interpretation Act 2005, s 7; s 18(9)).
5. Legislation will be permitted to contain examples, if identified as such, which may extend rather than limit the meaning of a provision (Interpretation Act 2005, s 11).

The Provisional Collection of Taxes Act 1927 provides that a resolution passed by Dáil Éireann imposing a specified new tax or increasing, reducing or otherwise varying or abolishing a specified existing permanent tax, or renewing (with or without modification) a specified temporary tax shall, if the resolution so declares, have the force of law. This Act gives statutory effect to the annual 'budget resolutions' when passed by the Dáil on Budget day to implement any tax changes announced in the Budget statement of the Minister of Finance that are required to operate immediately. Any resolution passed under this Act ceases to have statutory effect if a Bill containing provisions to the same effect is not given a second reading by the Dáil within 30 business days on which the Dáil sits. In any event, a budget resolution ceases to be effective four months after the date on which it was expressed to take effect or, where no such date was expressed, from the date of the passing of the resolution by the Dáil. It follows that the provisions of any such resolution must be incorporated in an Act of the Oireachtas which is passed and comes into operation within that four-month period. If any taxes are collected or repaid as a result of a resolution having statutory effect under the Provisional Collection of Taxes Act 1927, and if the required Act is not enacted within the four-month period, a refund must be made or the tax recollected.

1.107 Revenue practice

The application of tax law requires an understanding not only of tax law (as enshrined in the legislation and amplified by case law) but also of tax practice. The Revenue Commissioners' views on the effect of particular legislative provisions do not have the force of law, but have great significance in practice. A knowledge of the Revenue position affords tax advisers the assurance that the tax analysis of a particular transaction, which might otherwise be problematic, will be accepted by the tax authorities. The taxpayer, of course, still retains the option of challenging the Revenue view where he believes this is mistaken, but this can sometimes be a costly and uncertain process. The Revenue Commissioners also operate a number of so-called extra statutory concessions, where the strict letter of the law is not applied, in order to avoid perceived hardship or unfairness. The Revenue Commissioners were for many years somewhat reticent about disclosing their practices and concessions. However, in recent years they have become much more proactive in disseminating such information, primarily through Statements of Practice, their periodical *Tax Briefing* and regular e-briefs. All relevant material published is reflected in the text of this book.

The Freedom of Information Act 1997, s 16(1) (as amended by the Freedom of Information (Amendment) Act 2003) (both now repealed by the Freedom of Information Act 2014) requires the Revenue Commissioners to prepare and publish the 'rules, procedures, practices, guidelines and interpretations used by [them]', as well as an index of any precedents kept by them 'for the purposes of decisions, determinations and recommendations under any enactment administered by them'. The Act also requires the Revenue to publish appropriate information in relation to the manner of administration of such enactments. In compliance with their obligations under the Act, the Revenue Commissioners set out their rules and practices on the Revenue Commissioners' website.

The Revenue Commissioners are generally reluctant to give advance rulings on proposed or prospective transactions, although in certain cases they may be prepared to do so. Their current practice in this respect is set out in Revenue operations manual 37.0.40 being 'Large Cases Division: Opinions/Confirmations on Tax/Duty Consequences of a Proposed Course of Action' – September 2016. This practice was supplemented by eBrief No 08/2017 for rulings which were held for more than five years.

The Freedom of Information Act 2014 was signed on 14 October 2014. The Act provides for people to make 'requests' for access to records, amendment of records or reasons for a decision of a public body.

The legal status of Revenue practices and rulings is considered in **2.206**.

1.108 Other taxes

Although not 'income tax' as such, the pay-related social insurance (PRSI) contributions payable by persons in insurable employments and by their employers under the Social Welfare Acts and PRSI contributions payable by self-employed persons and certain other persons with investment income are also covered in the text, alongside the Universal Social Charge (USC) introduced from 2011 onwards.

Pay-related Social Insurance (PRSI) and the USC are collected in the same manner as income tax – ie either under PAYE in respect of employment income or by assessment on non-PAYE income. These are in effect further taxes on income, (although PRSI contributions may confer entitlement to certain social welfare benefits). The rules relating to self-employed PRSI and the USC are broadly explained in **3.4**. The corresponding rules relating to employers' and employees' pay related social insurance (PRSI) and the USC are covered in **11.2**.

The Domicile Levy was introduced from 2010 and applies to individuals meeting certain conditions. It is also explained in **Division 3.4**.

1.2 Administration of Taxes

1.201 The Revenue Commissioners

The general administration and control of taxes is vested in the Revenue Commissioners. The Board of Revenue Commissioners consists of three Commissioners appointed by the Taoiseach. They are subject to the control of the Minister for Finance, being bound to obey all orders and instructions issued by that Minister (Revenue Commissioners Order 1923, Pt 11). The powers and duties of the Commissioners are, as are those of the other officials appointed for the administration of the taxes, given in TCA 1997 in relation to income tax. Those powers and duties, together with most of the other administrative provisions, were first defined for income tax, but they have been extended as appropriate to apply also for corporation tax and capital gains tax by the Acts introducing those taxes.

The Revenue Commissioners are authorised to do all such acts as may be deemed necessary and expedient for raising, collecting, receiving and accounting for income tax and, unless the Minister for Finance otherwise directs, to appoint such officers and other persons for these purposes as are not required to be appointed by some other authority (TCA 1997, s 849).

1.202 Collector General

The Revenue Commissioners are required to appoint from their officers a person to act as Collector General, to hold office at their will and pleasure. The duty of the Collector General is to collect and levy income tax charged in assessments. The Collector General also collects income tax deducted from emoluments under the PAYE procedure (see **Division 11**) without the making of any assessment. The Revenue Commissioners are also empowered to nominate persons from their officers or employees to exercise powers of collection on behalf of the Collector General. In fact, the whole tax collection function is now handled centrally through the office of the Collector General. The Revenue Commissioners may delegate any or all of the powers and functions conferred by the Tax Acts on the Collector General to a nominated person acting on his behalf ('on his behalf and at his direction', prior to 10 May 1997).

1.203 Inspectors of Taxes

The State is divided into a number of tax districts each of which is set up in charge of an inspector of taxes. Under the Revenue organisational structure, these districts have been subsumed into four regional divisions (Border Midlands West, Dublin, East & South East and South West) under an ongoing process of integration and rationalisation. Individuals dealt with at district level will be assigned by reference to a district on the basis of their place of business if self-employed or by reference to their place of residence if PAYE employees; company directors will be assigned to the same district as the company in which they hold their main directorship. A special section, Large Cases division, will deal with large businesses and high income individuals on a national basis. This division also contains an anti-avoidance unit specialising in direct taxes. Finally, a dedicated Investigations and Prosecutions division deals with certain tax investigations and the prosecution of cases involving tax evasion.

The Revenue Commissioners are seeking to promote a compliance culture by incentivising large businesses to enter into dialogue with them, to consult with them before entering into doubtful tax schemes or structures and to institute continuous compliance monitoring frameworks internally. The Revenue Commissioners have indicated that the frequency and intensity of audits will be influenced by evidence of a strong commitment to self-regulated compliance and a constructive and cooperative attitude to Revenue contacts. They have recently also pioneered a regime of self-review for certain industrial sectors (see **2.704**). Inspectors of taxes are appointed by the Revenue Commissioners. Inspectors of taxes, as well as all other officers or persons employed in the execution of the Tax Acts, are required to observe and follow the orders, instructions and directions of the Revenue Commissioners. The Revenue Commissioners are also empowered to revoke any appointment made by them, Inspectors of taxes who were appointed by the Minister for Finance prior to 27 May 1986 under previous legislation are deemed to have been appointed by the Revenue Commissioners (TCA 1997, s 852).

The inspector of taxes in charge of a tax district is responsible for issuing return forms, examining returns, preparing and making tax assessments, and for agreeing the liabilities of taxpayers within his district. The inspector in charge of a district may be assisted by one or more qualified inspectors of taxes, depending on the size of the district, and in all districts he has a staff of other tax officials to help him discharge his responsibilities.

The Criminal Assets Bureau Act 1996 provides for officers of the Revenue Commissioners to be seconded to the Criminal Assets Bureau (along with members of the Garda Síochána and officers of the Department of Social Welfare). While such officers will continue to exercise their powers and perform their duties under tax statute, they fall under the direction and control of the chief Bureau officer. The Act also makes provision for additional duties and powers to be vested in Bureau officers. The Bureau's objects include (broadly) the seizure of criminal assets and the full imposition of tax on the proceeds of criminal activities.

TCA 1997, s 858 provides for identity cards for officers of the Revenue Commissioners authorised to exercise powers and duties under specified provisions of the Taxes Acts. The cards include inter alia particulars of the provisions in question. Where an officer provides his card this will be taken as evidence of authorisation under these provisions and will satisfy any requirements under those provisions which require the officer to produce authorisation on request (TCA 1997, s 858(2)/SI 212/1998).

1.204 Appeal Commissioners

Appeal Commissioners are appointed by the Minister for Finance with authority to execute such powers and to perform such duties as are assigned to them by the Income Tax Acts (TCA 1997, s 850). The main function of the Appeal Commissioners is to hear appeals by taxpayers dissatisfied with income tax assessments made upon them (TCA 1997, s 933). The procedure for hearing tax appeals and the rights of taxpayers and inspectors of taxes to appeal further against decisions of the Appeal Commissioners on income tax matters are discussed in **Division 2**.

The Appeal Commissioners are also required, where necessary, to hear appeals by taxpayers against decisions of inspectors of taxes and other officers of the Revenue Commissioners on various other matters. These include decisions in relation to claims

Q

for exemptions, reliefs and allowances under the Tax Acts and on claims for repayment of tax.

F(TA)A 2015, s 38, removes this section from the TCA and inserts a new TCA 1997, Pt 40A which is reviewed in **Division 2.2** of this text.

1.205 Obligations of secrecy

Inspectors of Taxes, the Appeal Commissioners, the Clerk to the Appeal Commissioners and the Collector General are all required to make statutory declarations upon taking office (TCA 1997, s 857(1); Sch 27). It should be noted that the definition of 'Clerk to the Appeal Commissioners' in TCA 1997, s 2 was deleted by F(TA)A 2015 as it is not used in that Act (SI 110/2016 appointed 21 March 2016 as the day on which the Finance (Tax Appeals) Act 2015, came into operation). The declarations are to the effect that the person making the declaration will carry out his duties under the Acts properly, without favour, etc and that he will not disclose to any unauthorised person any matter contained in any schedule, statement, return or other document delivered to him regarding any tax charged under the provisions relating to Sch D of the Income Tax Acts. Information may, however, be disclosed to other persons acting in the execution of the Acts where such disclosure is necessary for the purposes of the Acts. It is not clear why the wording of s 857 and Sch 27 has not been amended to include references to Sch E or Sch F. F(TA)A 2015 (SI 110/2016 appointed 21 March 2016 as the day on which the Finance (Tax Appeals) Act 2015, came into operation) replaces TCA 1997, Sch 27 in its entirety, see **2.207** for a discussion of that Act.

TCA 1997, s 872(1) entitles the Revenue Commissioners to use information obtained for the purpose of any tax under their care or management for the purposes of any other such tax. Further, the Revenue Commissioners (or any of their officers) may also use, or produce in evidence, any returns, correspondence, schedules, accounts, statements or other documents or information to which they (or any of their officers) have had lawful access for the purpose of any tax, duty or levy under their care and management for any purpose in connection with the assessment and collection of income tax (TCA 1997, s 872(2)).

The Official Secrets Act 1963 generally binds the Revenue Commissioners and their officers to secrecy regarding the affairs of a taxpayer. The Official Secrets Act 1963, s 4 only permits Revenue officers to disclose official information if authorised to do so or in the course of their duties or when it is his duty to do so in the public interest. Special collectors appointed under the Waiver of Certain Tax, Interest and Penalties Act 1993, are however not permitted to disclose information regarding negotiations or settlements under the Act to any other person (except other special collectors: s 7). The Revenue Commissioners are also relieved of their obligations concerning secrecy and disclosure of information in relation to the issue of notices of attachment (TCA 1997, s 1002(15)). In addition, TCA 1997, Sch 19 para 19 expressly permits the Revenue Commissioners to disclose certain details regarding offshore funds to any person who appears to them to have an interest in the matter (see **17.405**).

The Revenue Commissioners may also disclose details contained in an application by a film company when consulting with third parties by virtue of TCA 1997, s 481(2B): see **18.4**. Under Companies (Amendment) (No 2) Act 1999, s 44 the Revenue Commissioners are entitled to pass on information to the Registrar of Companies concerning certain companies absolved from the requirement to have at least one Irish resident director (as defined). The Revenue Commissioners are also obliged to compile an annual list of certain heritage items, including descriptions and valuations, in respect of which tax relief has been granted under the section and include this in their annual report: see **18.303**.

The Revenue Commissioners or any of their authorised officers may disclose information to any authorised officer of the government of another country with which arrangements for the avoidance of double taxation are made. In such a case, the disclosure may be of such information as is permitted or required to be disclosed by the terms of the particular tax treaty or as a result of requests made by parties to any Protocol to the Convention on Mutual Administrative Assistance in Tax Matters (TCA 1997, s 826(7)). For a fuller discussion see **14.222**.

Information may be transferred by Revenue Commissioners to the Minister of Social Welfare under the terms of the Social Welfare (Consolidation) Act 1993, s 222. Information may be disclosed to the Ombudsman for the purposes of an examination or investigation being carried on by him under the Ombudsman Act (TCA 1997, s 1093). TCA 1997, s 1086 requires the Revenue Commissioners to publish a list of tax defaulters, as defined (see **2.204**). This requirement overrides any obligations to secrecy under the Taxes Acts, or under the Official Secrets Act 1963.

The Revenue Commissioners are also empowered to disclose to the competent taxation authorities of any other EU Member State any information which they are required to disclose by the EU Directive on Mutual Assistance (Council Directive no 77/799/EEC of 19 December 1977). The power to make any disclosure required by the EU Directive is provided for in the European Communities (Mutual Assistance in the Field of Direct Taxation) Regulations 1978 (SI 1978/334). These regulations were made by the Minister for Finance (and approved by the Oireachtas) under the European Communities Act 1972.

The EU Directive requires the competent taxation authorities of each of the EU Member States to exchange between each other such information as may affect a correct assessment of taxes on income and capital (as well as of value added tax). For the purposes of the Directive, the Irish taxes on income and capital (in respect of which disclosure may be required) are stated as being income tax, corporation tax and capital gains tax. The Directive contains certain limits to the information which a Member State may be required to disclose. It also requires that any information disclosed by one Member State to another must be kept secret by that other Member State in the same manner as information it may receive in relation to taxes under its own domestic legislation. Under the European Communities (Mutual Assistance for the Recovery of Claims relating to Certain Duties, etc) Regulations 2002 (SI 462/2002), the Revenue Commissioners are *inter alia* required to provide information to another EU Member State in respect of tax liabilities (including income taxes) arising in that State using the powers which would be available to them in relation to a similar claim arising in Ireland. There is an exemption from the requirement where disclosure would be detrimental to commercial, industrial or professional secrets.

TCA 1997, s 826(1)(b) permits the government to enter into agreements with other states for the purposes of preventing or detecting tax evasion; such agreements will have the force of law notwithstanding any other enactment.

The Revenue Commissioners are authorised to transmit information to the fiscal authorities of other jurisdictions provided to them by paying agents under the provisions of the European Savings Directive under TCA 1997, Pt 38, Ch 3A.

The Disclosure of Certain Information for Taxation and Other Purposes Act (DCIA) 1996, s 1 inserts a new Criminal Justice Act 1994, s 63A. This section provides that where, on the basis of information received, the Revenue Commissioners have reasonable grounds for:

(a) suspecting that a person had derived profits or gains from an unlawful source or activity; and

(b) holding the opinion that they have information likely to be relevant to an investigation within the Criminal Justice Act, s 63(1) and which should be released in the public interest,

then they must release the relevant information to the appropriate law enforcement officer. The latter is, in effect, either a member of the Garda Síochána, at the rank of chief superintendent or above, or the head of the Criminal Assets Bureau or any member of the Bureau nominated by the head thereof.

The Revenue Commissioners may authorise any of their officers at the level of principal officer or above to discharge their obligations under the Act (DCIA 1996, s 1(3)(a)). Where the Revenue Commissioners (or an authorised officer) sign a certificate certifying that the information contained therein (or access thereto) has been provided to an appropriate law enforcement officer, this will be conclusive evidence of both the matters covered by the certificate and the signature itself, unless the contrary is proven (DCIA 1996, s 1(3)(c)). This obligation overrides any other obligations as to secrecy, or other restrictions on the disclosure of information, imposed by any other statute. There is, however, a saving in the case of restrictions on the use of information imposed under the terms of a double tax treaty (unless the treaty partner agrees otherwise).

In December 2012 the Irish and US Governments signed an agreement on the implementation of FATCA (Foreign Account Tax Compliance Act). Under this agreement and TCA 1997, s 891E, Irish banks and similar institutions report details of accounts held by US persons to the Irish Revenue who pass this information on to the IRS.

The Freedom of Information Act 1997 (FIA 1997) now repealed by the Freedom of Information Act 2014 (signed on 14 October 2014) (FIA 2014), provides a right of access to any record held by or under the control of a FOI body (includes a public body or a prescribed body FIA 2014, s 7), including the Revenue Commissioners (FIA 1997, s 6 now repealed by FIA 2014, s 11). A record includes:

(a) a book or other written or printed material in any form (including in any electronic device or in machine readable form);

(b) a map, plan or drawing;

(c) a disc, tape or other mechanical or electronic device in which data other than visual images are embodied so as to be capable, with or without the aid of some other mechanical or electronic equipment, of being reproduced from the disc, tape or other device;

(d) a film, disc, tape or other mechanical or electronic device in which visual images are embodied so as to be capable, with or without the aid of some other mechanical or electronic equipment, of being reproduced from the film, disc, tape or other device; and

(e) a copy or part of any thing which falls within paragraph (a), (b), (c) or (d),

and a copy, in any form, of a record shall be deemed, for the purposes of this Act, to have been created at the same time as the record (FIA 2014, s 2(1) which repealed FIA

1997, s 2(1)). There are a number of restrictions on the right of access. Thus, eg FIA 2014, s 35 previously FIA 1997, s 26, generally denies access to information obtained in confidence and where disclosure would be likely to prejudice the future provision of such information (unless the public interest outweighs these considerations) and to information obtained under a statutory duty of confidence. This exclusion does not generally apply to records prepared for the body concerned by an employee or independent contractor in the course of their work. FIA 2014, s 37 previously FIA 1997, s 28 provides that 'personal information' may not be disclosed unless the public interest outweighs the right to privacy of the individual affected. 'Personal information' includes information 'required for the purpose of assessing the liability of the individual in respect of tax or duty or other payment owed or payable to the State … or for the purpose of collecting an amount due from the individual in respect of such a tax or duty or other payment'. Companies are not covered by this section. The Information Commissioner has held that in some circumstances it may be necessary to encroach upon taxpayer confidentiality in order to determine the Revenue Commissioners' interpretation or application of tax law (Tax Fax 20/5/02).

While an individual may thus be entitled to request details concerning himself and his affairs held by the Revenue, as well as background information on decisions made by the Revenue in relation to himself, this right is not unrestricted. Thus, FIA 2014, s 30 which repealed FIA 1997, s 21 inter alia exempts records where access thereto could reasonably be expected to prejudice the effectiveness of inquiries or audits carried out by a FOI body or would disclose the negotiating position (or negotiation criteria) of any such body unless the public interest outweighs these considerations. FIA 2014, s 32 which repealed FIA 1997, s 23 exempts records access to which could be reasonably expected to prejudice or impair the enforcement of, compliance with or administration of any law or which could lead to the revelation of the identity of a person who has given information in confidence in relation to the enforcement or administration of the civil law.

FIA 2014, s 36 which repealed FIA 1997, s 27 exempts records which contain trade secrets, or other financial, commercial or scientific/technical material disclosure of which could lead to financial loss or which contains information which could prejudice the outcome or conduct of contractual or other negotiations. The exemption does not apply where the public interest outweighs the above considerations. Further, the records in question may be disclosed inter alia if the person to whom the information relates consents thereto or information of the same kind as that contained in the record is available to the general public in respect of persons generally or of a significant class of persons.

FIA 2014, s 40 which repealed FIA 1997, s 31 also inter alia exempts records where access thereto could reasonably be expected to result in an unwarranted benefit to a person or class of persons (unless the public interest outweighs these considerations). It is clear therefore for example that the Revenue will not permit access to files in relation to ongoing audits or investigations (see *Tax Briefing 31*).

A useful guide to the procedures for obtaining access to information under the old Act and for exercising rights of review or appeal is provided in [1998] ITR 284, and see also Fennell, *Freedom of Information Act* – Part I [1999] ITR 45.

TCA 1997, s 851A provides a statutory basis for taxpayer confidentiality and imposes modest fines of up to €3,000 on summary conviction or €10,000 on indictment on Revenue officers, or any person to whom taxpayer information is disclosed, for unauthorised disclosure, grant of access or use of 'taxpayer information'.

Taxpayer information is defined as information of any kind and in any form relating to one or more persons which is either (a) obtained by a Revenue officer for the purposes of the Acts; or is (b) prepared from information so obtained. The definition excludes information which does not directly or indirectly reveal the identity of the person to whom it relates. The Acts covers all the legislation under the care and management of the Revenue Commissioners together with any related Statutory Instruments. As might be expected, the duty of confidentiality does not apply either to criminal proceedings or to legal proceedings relating to the administration or enforcement of tax legislation. Over and above this, a Revenue officer is also permitted to disclose taxpayer information to a professional accounting body where he is satisfied that the work of an agent does not meet the professional standards of a professional body, albeit such information may only be used for the purposes of any investigation by that body. Strangely, the bodies concerned are limited to those within the remit of the Irish Auditing and Accounting Supervisory Authority (or the Authority itself) or the Irish Taxation Institute and with effect from 21 December 2015 (date of passing of FA 2015) the Law Society of Ireland. This is an unsatisfactory element in these provisions, which represents a potentially prejudicial exposure for clients of firms under the aegis of those bodies. Where Revenue has sought expert third party advice, for example with property valuations, the legislation has been expanded to subject these third parties to the same confidentiality requirements as Revenue officers.

1.206 Legal advice privilege

Legal professional privilege provides that communications between a lawyer and a client may not be disclosed without the permission of the client. Legal professional privilege has two sub-heads, legal advice privilege and litigation privilege. Litigation privilege applies to communications between a lawyer and a client in connection with litigation. Legal advice privilege applies to communications passing between a client and its lawyers in connection with the provision of legal advice.

Legal advice privilege does not attach to communications between a client and their tax adviser and only applies to communications between a client and their lawyer. This ruling was found in UK Supreme Court in the case of *R (on the application of Prudential plc and another) v Special Commissioner of Income Tax and another* [2013] UKSC 1.

While the decision is not binding in Ireland it is likely to be followed by the Irish courts unless otherwise provided for in legislation.

The facts of this case were that PwC had devised a marketed tax avoidance scheme which under the UK equivalent of our mandatory disclosure regime (see **2.618**) it was required to disclose to HMRC. The scheme was adapted by PwC for use by the Prudential group of companies. The inspector dealing with the tax affairs of Prudential decided to enquire further into the transactions and to this end issued two notices to Prudential under Taxes Management Act 1970, s 20 seeking documents relating to the scheme. The UK case of *R (on the application of Morgan Grenfell & Co Ltd) v Special Commissioner of Income Tax* [2002] STC 786 had earlier held that the provisions of s 20 could not be invoked to force anyone to produce documents to which legal advice privilege applied. Relying on the decision in the *Morgan Grenfell* case Prudential wished to claim privilege over the documents sought by the inspector on the grounds that they related to the seeking of legal advice by them and the receipt of that advice from PwC in connection with the tax-avoidance scheme. HMRC refused privilege and Prudential issued an application for a judicial review of the validity of the notices issued on the grounds that the documents related to the seeking (by Prudential) and the giving (by PwC) of legal advice in connection with the transactions.

The then UK legislation (Taxes Management Act 1970, s 20) gave HMRC power to request the production of documents of the tax payer and of any other person. Taxes Management Act 1970, s 20A empowered an inspector to seek documents from a tax accountant. Taxes Management Act 1970, s 20B set out the conditions of the powers that can be exercised, specifically:

Taxes Management Act 1970, s 20B(8) provided that a barrister, advocate or solicitor was not obliged to produce a document in respect of which 'a claim to professional privilege could be maintained'.

Taxes Management Act 1970, s 20B(9) provided that a tax adviser did not have to deliver up 'relevant communications' defined as:

> communications between the tax adviser and –
> (a) A person in relation to whose tax affairs he has been appointed or
> (b) Any other tax adviser of such a person
> the purpose of which is the giving or obtaining of advice about any or those tax affairs.

Taxes Management Act 1970, s 20B(11) limited the tax advisers exemption so that it did not apply to documents containing explanations for any information, return, accounts or other documents that the tax adviser assisted the taxpayer in preparing for or making returns to HMRC. Prudential argued that this was too restrictive and that legal advice privilege should apply generally to the seeking and giving of legal advice on tax matters from accountants.

Charles J in the High Court said that legal professional privilege was a 'common law principle'. He had to apply the law as it had developed under common law, and as such this privilege couldn't extend to tax advisers.

In the Court of Appeal, Prudential argued that legal advice privilege should pertain to the function being given (giving of legal advice) as opposed to the giver (whether a lawyer or not). Whether or not legal advice privilege should apply should depend on the nature of the advice being given rather than on who is giving the advice so that legal advice privilege should apply to advice given by an accountant where if that advice were given by a lawyer legal advice privilege would apply. The court felt this would require legislation as opposed to a court decision.

The Supreme Court appeal by Prudential was dismissed by a majority of five to two. The view of the court was that while it would seem logical that legal advice privilege should be extended to advice on tax law given by accountants, the court was not willing to extend it in this manner. The court held that where a common law rule was valid in the modern world but had an aspect or limitation which seemed to be out of date it was not always right for the courts to remove the aspect/limit. In such circumstances the court had to consider whether removal of the aspect/limit would give rise to other problems and on this basis if it would be more appropriate for the matter to be dealt with by Parliament in legislation. In this case the court decided that it would be more appropriate for Parliament to legislate for change on the following grounds:

(1) If the courts were to extend legal advice privilege in this case this would result in making something which is currently very clear becoming uncertain, ie the present rule is that legal advice privilege only applies to advice given by lawyers. If legal advice privilege were to be extended to legal advice given by members of a profession which ordinarily includes the giving of legal advice (advocated by the dissenting Judge Lord Sumption) this would raise questions

about who could be regarded as being a member of a profession and what professions include the giving of legal advice as an ordinary part of their profession.

(2) It is only in exceptional circumstances that the courts should create a new right for citizens or extend an existing right beyond what is currently understood by everyone including Parliament. Parliament had already legislated on the issue and declined to extend it to tax advisers. In the circumstances the extension of legal advice privilege was a policy issue best left to Parliament.

1.3 Principles of Income Tax

1.301 The income tax year

Up to 5 April 2001, income tax was charged or assessed annually by reference to the income tax year which commenced on 6 April in one calendar year and ended on 5 April in the following calendar year. With effect from 6 April 2001, the income tax year became the calendar year. As a result, there was a short tax 'year' running from 6 April 2001 to 31 December 2001. The tax years up to 5 April 2001 were referred to in the form for example 1999–00, indicating the tax year ending on 5 April 2000. The tax 'year' running from 6 April 2001 to 31 December 2001 is referred to as the Tax Year 2001, subsequent tax years will be referred to as the Tax Year 2002, etc. The income tax year is referred to in the Tax Acts as 'the year of assessment', which expression is used interchangeably in this work with the phrase the 'tax year'.

1.302 Persons liable

The Income Tax Acts normally impose tax on a 'person', and not simply an 'individual'. A trustee (whether an individual or a company) is clearly a 'person', but is not subject to income tax on trust income in his own right. Thus, in the case of an individual trustee, trust income is not added to his own income in arriving at his total income, nor may he offset allowances and reliefs to which he is entitled as an individual against any trust income assessable on him; similar considerations apply to the personal representatives of a deceased individual (*Aplin v White* [1973] STC 322, 375). TCA 1997, s 15(2) makes clear that individuals acting in a fiduciary or representative capacity are in fact taxable at the standard rate only. The taxation of trustees and personal representatives is discussed in **Division 15**.

A company is also clearly a 'person', but in most cases its income is subject to corporation tax rather than income tax. The taxation of companies in the income tax context is dealt with below. It may be noted at this point that an Irish resident company, while generally liable to corporation tax, remains liable to income tax in respect of income which it receives as a trustee.

A 'person' is defined by the Interpretation Act 2005, s 18(c) as importing (ie denoting), not only an individual and a body corporate, but also an 'unincorporated body of persons'. However, as always, this definition only applies where the contrary intention does not appear. TCA 1997, s 1044(1) which provides that 'every body of persons shall be chargeable to tax in like manner as any person' appears to be a charging section (see eg *American Foreign Insurance Association v Davies* 32 TC 1, and the dissenting speech of McCarthy J. In *Revenue Commissioners v ORMG* III ITR 28, the issue not being addressed by the other two Supreme Court judges; note also the reasoning in *Curtis v Old Monkland Conservative Assoc* 5 TC 189 and contrast the decision in *Frampton v IRC* [1985] STC 186, criticised in *Ward* [1990] ITR 295).

It would follow that the meaning of 'person' in income tax charging provisions does not generally include a 'body of persons' (since otherwise a 'body of persons' would be chargeable in any event, and TCA 1997, s 1044(1) would be superfluous). It also follows that for a 'body of persons' to be liable to tax it would have to fall within the income tax definition of 'body of persons' in TCA 1997, s 1044(1). The position seems to be confirmed for Sch D purposes by virtue of TCA 1997, s 52, which states that tax is to be charged thereunder on the 'persons or bodies of persons receiving or entitled to the relevant income' (it is not clear why TCA 1997, s 52 refers explicitly to bodies of persons in view of the existence of TCA 1997, s 1044(1), but a degree of overlap and obscurity is a hallmark of the 1842 Income Tax Act, from which these provisions derive).

In *Alex Burns v Hearne* III ITR 553, Costello J suggested that TCA 1997, s 1044(1) was not a charging provision, on the basis that it had not been invoked in order to assess a company receiver in *IRC v Thompson*. However, this provision was in fact not an issue in the latter case since the receiver was taxable in any event as a 'person'. It seems clear that TCA 1997, s 1044(2) which renders the treasurer, auditor or receiver of a body of persons answerable for doing all acts as are required for the purposes of assessing the body and for paying tax, does not impose a personal tax liability on the treasurer, etc (*ITC v Chatani* [1983] STC 477).

The definition of 'body of persons' in TCA 1997, s 2(1) is of ancient origin and is somewhat narrower than the meaning of the term in everyday usage. A 'body of persons' is defined by the section as 'any body politic, corporate or collegiate, and any company, fraternity fellowship and society of persons whether corporate or not corporate'. The income tax definition of 'body of persons' is not apt to include either a set of trustees or a partnership. In general, this does not impact on the taxation of trustees since it seems that they are taxable jointly as 'persons': *Dawson v IRC* [1989] STC 473 (the singular 'person' includes reference to the plural 'person', unless the contrary intention is indicated: Interpretation Act 2005, s 18(a)). It may be noted that the court's conclusion in *Dawson* was based on the assumption that the trustees were not taxable as a 'body of persons' (the case is discussed more fully at **15.303**). However, the fact that a trust is not taxable as a single entity may give rise to significant tax consequences where the trustees are resident in different jurisdictions (see **15.302**). Again, there is also a special tax regime for partnerships under which each partner is taxed separately on his share of partnership profits (see **4.503**). The treatment of both trusts and partnerships, in the context of double tax treaties which refer to 'bodies of persons' can still give rise to difficulties.

The income tax definition of 'body of persons' should however generally cover any unincorporated association, defined in *Conservative and Unionist Central Office v Burrell* [1982] STC 317 by Lawton J in the context of UK tax law as:

> two or more persons bound together for one or more common purposes, not being business purposes, by mutual undertakings, each having mutual duties and obligations in an organisation which has rules which identify in whom control of it and its funds rests on and on what terms, and which can be joined or left at will.

(See also *Carnoustie GCC v IRC* 14 TC 498 and *Blackpool Marton Rotary Club v Martin* [1988] STC 823.)

However, the decision in *Revenue Commissioners v ORMG* III ITR 28 indicates that associations consisting of two members (and possibly more than two members) cannot qualify as a 'body of persons' (ie either under the everyday meaning of the term, or under TCA 1997, s 2(1)). As pointed out by McCarthy J in the *ORMG* case, this leaves unclear the basis for taxing the income of unincorporated associations which, because of their small size, fall outside TCA 1997, s 1044, and in respect of which it is not possible to identify any person(s) to whom the income of the association accrues either beneficially or as trustee(s) (see Rowlatt J at first instance in *Shanks v IRC* 14 TC 249). In the case of individuals who are jointly entitled to income, that income should normally be capable of being apportioned between them as a question of fact (see *Shanks v IRC* 14 TC 249, in the Court of Appeal). In the simplest case, two individuals jointly owning an Irish rental property in equal shares would normally each be taxable on 50 per cent of the net rentals arising under Sch D Case V.

To add to the confusion, there may be cases where the specific context requires that the definition of 'body of persons' in TCA 1997, s 2(1) will not apply. Thus, for example, in TCA 1997, s 1094, a partnership is clearly treated as a 'person' which can hold a licence and which may therefore be required to apply for a tax clearance certificate.

A person, etc resident in the State, other than a company chargeable to corporation tax, is in principle liable to income tax on his worldwide income, unless and to the extent that the income is exempted or excluded from tax by specific provision in the Income Tax Acts. Exemption from income tax or partial exemption may arise in connection with certain bodies, for example, charities.

A non-resident person is liable to income tax on income arising in the State, except where a double taxation agreement with his country of residence provides otherwise. A non-resident company is liable to income tax on any income from sources within the State, but only to the extent that the income is not chargeable to corporation tax. The circumstances in which an individual is treated as resident in the State for tax purposes are discussed in **1.502–1.503**, while the rules for determining the tax residence of a company are dealt with in **1.504**.

An individual who is not resident, but who is ordinarily resident, is taxed as if he were a resident in respect of his overseas investment income (subject to a '*de minimis*' exemption of €3,810 per annum) and in respect of certain overseas trading and employment income. The relevant rules are discussed fully in **Division 13**.

1.303 Income chargeable

Income tax is an annual tax charged on income in respect of all profits or gains in the nature of income. There is no statutory definition of income, but 'total income' is defined as 'total income from all sources as estimated in accordance with the provisions of this Act' (TCA 1997, s 3(1)). This definition introduces the principle that income flows from a source and that before there can be a charge to income tax there must be a source of income. It does not, however, state precisely what constitutes income for tax purposes. Consequently, where doubt arises in any particular instance, it may be necessary to seek guidance from decisions reached by the courts in interpreting the statutory provisions in a previous tax case related to the matter under consideration.

An analogy frequently used is to liken income to the fruit taken from a tree where the tree is the source from which the income flows. Income is often contrasted with capital and capital gains, with only the income being subject to income tax. However, income can arise from sources other than capital, for example, from an individual's personal services for an employer or in his own business. The Income Tax Acts use the phrase 'annual profits or gains' in a number of places to denote income. This phrase does not normally include gains on the sales of capital assets, (which may be taxed separately under the Capital Gains Tax Acts) in the absence of specific provisions to the contrary.

See eg the taxation of certain capital gains on the disposal of land or assets deriving their value from land at **12.310**.

The courts have also concluded that because there cannot be income in the absence of a source, income which arises in a tax year where there is no underlying source is not subject to tax, see eg *Bray v Best* [1986] STC 96. In many instances, this general principle has been overridden by specific statutory rules; thus, the decision in *Bray v Best* has since been countered (see **10.108**). It may also be noted that payments to past holders of offices or employments are subject to a special tax charge, even though the source has ceased (see eg *Nichols v Gibson* [1996] STC 1008). It may also be noted that all Sch D Case III sources are deemed to constitute a single source (TCA 1997, s 70(1)).

The sources of income that are chargeable to income tax are detailed in the Income Tax Acts in four Schedules, Schs C, D, E and F. Only sources of income described in these Schedules are taxable, but as Sch D Case IV charges to tax 'any annual profits or gains not falling under any other Case of Sch D and not charged by virtue of any other Schedule', it may be appreciated that the tax embraces many different types of income. In fact, over the years a number of exceptions have been legislated into the Acts and the charging provisions of the four Schedules have to be read subject to any exception which exempts or relieves, in whole or in part, a particular type of income from the tax.

While the Income Tax Acts frequently refer to 'annual profits and gains', the better view seems to be that 'annual' means 'in the current year, occurring in the year of assessment to taxation' (per Pollock MR in *Martin v Lowry* 11 TC 297, endorsing the views of Rowlatt J in *Ryall v Hoare* 8 TC 521, discussed in **8.201**; and note also *McClure v Petre* [1988] STC 749; however, in *Jones v Leeming* 15 TC 333, Lord Buckmaster did express some reservations on this issue (which is therefore not wholly free from doubt).

1.304 Basis of assessment

Each Schedule and each separate Case within Sch D has its own rules for calculating the amount of income liable to income tax. The 'current year' basis of assessment applies for taxing all income assessable under the different Schedules and Cases. In general, this means that it is the income earned or received in the tax year which is charged to the tax.

However, trading income (Case I) and income from a profession (Case II) generally are taxed on the profits arising for a 12-month period of accounts ending within the tax year. For the exceptions in the case of a commencement or cessation of the trade or profession and in certain other circumstances, see **4.205–4.208**.

1.305 Rates of income tax

TCA 1997, s 15 charges income tax for the tax year 2015 at the 'standard rate' of 20 per cent. For a person liable to income tax other than an individual, all the taxable income is charged at the standard rate only.

In addition, TCA 1997, s 15 provides that an individual (other than one acting in a fiduciary or representative capacity) is to be charged to income tax at the higher rate of 40 per cent on that part of his taxable income for a tax year which exceeds a stated amount (with his taxable income up to the stated amount being taxed at the standard rate). The part or 'band' of an individual's taxable income which is charged at the standard rate is generally referred to as the 'standard rate band'.

The table which sets out the tax rates and the amount of the standard rate band, for the tax year 2015, is given in **3.106**. It is to be noted that there are different standard rate bands for single persons, single parents and married couples/civil partners who are jointly assessed (in the latter case the amount of the band will vary depending on the amount of income (if any) received by the spouses (see **3.502**)).

An individual (or any other person), who is chargeable to income tax in respect of any income receivable in a fiduciary or representative capacity (for example, as a trustee of a settlement or an executor of a will) is, however, only chargeable in respect of such income at the standard rate and the higher rate does not apply irrespective of the amount of income so chargeable. As an exception, if an individual is chargeable in the capacity of guardian or trustee of an incapacitated individual (for example, an infant), the higher rate is applicable to any part of the infant's taxable income which exceeds the standard rate band (TCA 1997, s 1045); a further exception apparently applies to certain trustees of non-residents (see **15.302**).

1.306 Exempted income

The general principle that income tax is chargeable on any income from any source mentioned in the Schedules applies unless the income is of a type specifically exempted from tax under any provision in the Income Tax Acts. The Acts provide that some forms of receipts which might otherwise be classified as income are to be exempted in all circumstances and are not to be treated as income for any purpose and should not, therefore, be included in any return of income made by any person. Other provisions provide an exemption for certain purposes or for receipts up to certain amounts and may require the items in question to be disclosed in the recipient's income tax return.

It must always be borne in mind that in certain cases, the provisions dealing with the limitations of reliefs for high income individuals may reduce the benefit of an exemption: see **3.111**.

1.307 Exempted bodies

The under-mentioned bodies are specifically exempted from income tax but, in some of the cases, subject to certain conditions:

(a) harbour authorities situate within the State to the extent of income arising from the provision of harbour facilities and accommodation for vessels, goods and passengers (TCA 1997, s 229);

(b) any agricultural society, ie a society or institution established for the purpose of promoting agriculture, horticulture, livestock breeding or forestry in respect of income from any exhibition or show applied solely for the purposes of the society (TCA 1997, s 215), see **18.209**;

(c) any approved body of persons established for the sole purpose of promoting athletic or amateur games or sports in respect of all income that is or will be applied for such purposes (TCA 1997, s 235), see **18.206**;

(d) a lottery licensed under the Gaming and Lotteries Act 1956 in respect of the profits from any lottery (TCA 1997, s 216);

(e) any registered trade union meeting certain conditions in respect of interest and dividends taxable under Schs C, D and F if applicable and applied solely for the purpose of paying provident benefits (TCA 1997, s 213), see **18.208**;

(f) bodies established for charitable purposes only in respect of certain income applied only for such purposes and the Charities Regulatory Authority (TCA 1997, ss 207, 207A, 208), see **18.202–18.205**;

(g) any body of persons having consultative status with the United Nations Organisation or the Council of Europe with the sole or main object of promoting human rights, and which is precluded by its rules or constitution from providing any gifts or benefits, directly or indirectly, to any of its members (entitled to claim the same exemption as that available under TCA 1997, s 207 to charitable bodies) (TCA 1997, s 209);

(h) local authorities, the Health Service Executive, vocational education committees and committees of agriculture (TCA 1997, s 214);

(i) the trustees of 'the Great Book of Ireland Trust' in respect of income arising to the trustees from the sale of the Great Book of Ireland; and related payments by the trustees to Clashganna Mills Trust Ltd or Poetry Ireland Ltd (TCA 1997, s 210);

(j) specified non-commercial state-sponsored bodies in relation to income otherwise taxable under Sch D Cases III, IV or V (TCA 1997, s 227);

(k) certain friendly societies: see **18.208** (TCA 1997, s 211); and

(l) qualifying trusts where the trust funds were raised by public subscriptions solely on behalf of individuals who are permanently and totally incapacitated from maintaining themselves: see **18.210** (TCA 1997, s 189A(2)).

1.308 Exemptions for diplomats, EC officials

Exemption from liability to income tax in the State in respect of the earnings of certain diplomatic personnel, officials of the United Nations and certain other international organisations, as well as for the earnings of persons working in the service of the European Community (EC) are provided in certain conventions, etc adopted into law in the State otherwise than through the Tax Acts. A brief reference here to the relevant provisions may be useful. The exemptions apply notwithstanding that the individuals concerned are resident in the State and would otherwise be fully subject to Irish tax on the exempt income.

The Diplomatic Relations and Immunities Act 1967 adopts, and gives the force of law in the State to, the provisions of the Vienna Convention on Diplomatic Relations made on 18 April 1961 and the Vienna Convention on Consular Relations made on 24 April 1963. It also adopts certain provisions relating to the taxation of officials of the United Nations and of the International Court of Justice. Among the provisions given the force of law in the State in relation to diplomatic personnel and to officials of those organisations are the following:

(a) the head of a diplomatic mission of another country to the State, or a member of the diplomatic staff of that mission, is exempted from Irish income tax in respect of all his income from his position as well as on any other non-Irish source income (but remains liable to Irish tax on any private income from any Irish source);

(b) members of the families of the head of the diplomatic mission and of members of the diplomatic staff of that mission are, if forming part of the respective households of such persons, given the same exemption as in (a);

(c) members of the administrative and technical staff of such a diplomatic mission, together with members of their families forming part of their respective households, are given a similar exemption from Irish income tax (but, in this case. only if they are not Irish nationals and not permanently resident in Ireland; the term 'permanently resident' is not defined: see the discussion in Morris [1996] British Tax Review 207);

(d) similar exemptions are given to the head of the consular post of a foreign country in the State, as well as to other consular officers, consular employees, and members of their families in a corresponding way to that mentioned respectively under (a), (b) and (c) above, whichever is relevant;

(e) judges of the International Court of Justice are exempted from income tax in the State in respect of their emoluments received by them in that capacity; and

(f) officials of the United Nations and of the specialised agencies (for example, the World Bank) are exempted from income tax in respect of the salaries and emoluments paid to them by the United Nations or the relevant specialised agency.

The European Communities Act 1972 (as amended 2 November 2012) adopted, and gave the force of law to a number of treaties governing the European Communities, including the treaty establishing the European Coal and Steel Community (signed in Paris on 18 April 1951) and the treaty establishing the European Community (the 'Treaty of Rome' signed in Rome on 25 March 1957). The Protocol on the Privileges and Immunities, attached as an annexe to the Treaty of Rome, includes among its provisions (in Art 12) an exemption from the national taxes of the Member States of the EC in respect of the salaries, wages and emoluments paid by the EC to officials of the Community and to other persons working for it.

This article provides that those officials and other employees of the Community are liable to a separate tax payable to the Community on their salaries, wages and emoluments. This tax, which is payable for the benefit of the Community, is in lieu of any Irish income tax that might otherwise be chargeable on the individual concerned in respect of his EC remuneration, even if he is resident in the State. This exemption from Irish income tax does not, of course, extend to income from other sources for which the individual may be chargeable under the normal income tax rules.

1.4 Interpretation and Application of Tax Statute

1.401 General principles of interpretation

There is substantial authority for the proposition that the normal canons of statutory interpretation apply to tax statute. Thus, in *Revenue Commissioners v Doorley* V ITR 539, Kennedy CJ cited with approval the words of Lord Russell in *Attorney General v Carlton Bank* [1899] 2 QB 158, where the latter had stated that:

> … I know of no authority for saying that a tax Act is to be construed differently from any other Act. The duty of the court is … in all the cases the same … namely to give effect to the intention of the legislature as that intention is to be gathered from the language employed having regard to the context in connection with which it is employed (emphasis added).

Thus, it is sound interpretative practice to construe words and phrases in the light of the statute taken as a whole, taking into account the general legal and factual background against which it is designed to operate (see eg *East Donegal Co-Op v Attorney General* [1970] IR 317; *Maunsell v Olins* [1975] AC 373).

Nevertheless, in applying these principles, the courts are influenced by the fact that tax law is founded on statute. There is no such thing as a recognised common law of taxation in contrast to other branches of the law, such as criminal law or the law of tort. Accordingly, any tax charge must be justified by reference to the terms of the relevant statutory provisions. In the *Doorley* case, Kennedy CJ proceeded to observe:

> A taxing Act (including of course any other Act or part of an Act incorporated in it by reference) of its own proper character and purpose, stands alone, and is to be read and construed as it stands upon its own actual language. The duty of the Court, as it appears to me, is to reject any a priori line of reasoning and to examine the text of the taxing Act in question and determine whether the tax in question is thereby imposed expressly and in clear and unambiguous terms, on the alleged subject of taxation, for no person or property is to be subjected to taxation unless brought within the letter of the taxing statute ie within the letter of the statute as interpreted with the assistance of the ordinary canons of interpretation applicable to Acts of parliament so far as they can be applied without violating the proper character of taxing Acts to which I have referred.

The observations of Kennedy CJ echo a long line of similar admonitions, of which perhaps the most often-quoted is that delivered by Rowlatt J in *Cape Brandy Syndicate v IRC* 12 TC 358:

> In a taxing Act one has to look merely at what is clearly said. There is no room for any intendment. There is no equity about a tax. There is no presumption as to a tax. Nothing is to be read in. Nothing is to be implied. One can only look fairly at the language used.

The above dictum of Rowlatt J underlines that a judge must not come to a tax statute with any background assumptions in favour of either the Revenue or the taxpayer. Rowlatt J had made this point forcibly in an earlier passage of his judgment, when he said:

> … in a taxing act clear words are necessary in order to tax the subject. Too wide a fanciful a consideration is often sought to be given to that maxim, which does not mean that words are to be unduly restricted against the Crown or *that there is to be any discrimination against the Crown in these Acts* (emphasis added).

In particular, the courts must not trespass outside the 'letter' of the statute in order to extend its scope to transactions which they believe fall within its 'spirit' or 'intendment', or which they believe fairness demands should be covered. In *IRC v Herbert* [1913] AC 26, Viscount Herbert observed succinctly in the context of a tax statute:

> The duty of a court of law is simply to take the statute it has to construe as it stands, and to construe its words according to their natural significance. While reference may be made to *the state of the law, and the material facts and events with which it is apparent that Parliament was dealing*, it is not admissible to speculate on the probable opinions and motives of those who framed the legislation, *excepting in so far as these appear from the language of the statute* (emphasis added).

In *Revenue Commissioners v O'Flynn* [2011] IESC 47, the Supreme Court approved the House of Lords' decision in *Barclays Mercantile v Mawson* [2004] 3 WLR 1383 and affirmed that the same principles applied to tax statutes as applied to all other non-criminal statutes.

In *Mayes v HMRC* [2011] EWCA Civ 407 the Court of Appeal dismissed HMRC's appeal and referred extensively to *Barclays Mercantile v Mawson* [2004]. This case concerns a tax avoidance scheme which sought a deduction for both income tax and capital gains tax. The Special Commissioners regarded two of the steps involved in the scheme as 're arranged, self-cancelling steps with no commercial purpose' and therefore disregarded those causing the scheme to fail. The Court of Appeal had a different approach to the interpretation stating

> that he considered the essence of the court's role to interpreting statutes was to give a statutory code a purposive interpretation 'in order to determine the nature of the transaction to which they were intended to apply' and then to ascertain whether the actual transactions under review (in this case those constituting the third and fourth steps of Mr Mayes's arrangements) answered this statutory description.

This passage just cited emphasises an important distinction between the statutory purposes, as inferred from the statute itself, and the conjectured purposes of the legislature in enacting the statute. Thus in *McGrath v McDermott* III ITR 683, the Supreme Court had refused to treat an avoidance scheme as a nullity for tax purposes, despite its complete lack of any economic substance. McCarthy J observed:

> The first canon of construction of statutes is that words are to be given their ordinary meaning; applying that canon … it seems beyond question but that the scheme operated here came within … the Act. To rule otherwise requires looking to the intent of the Act, deduced not from its words, but from what may be termed equity, … if the scheme succeeds, then what is not a loss will be treated as a loss for tax purposes.

In *Revenue Commissioners v O'Flynn*, the Supreme Court was at pains to emphasise that the standard purposive approach to be adopted in construing fiscal statute was implicit in the decision in *McGrath v McDermott*. It also alluded to the particularisation of much tax statute which can makes it difficult to infer an overarching purpose or wider logic to the provisions under review, noting that 'In other cases the provision may be so technical and detailed that no more broad or general purpose can be detected …'. See **17.302** for a discussion on general anti avoidance legislation and the *O'Flynn* case.

There is a danger in taking admonitions such as those of Kennedy J in *Doorley* or of Rowlatt J in *Cape Brandy Syndicate* over-literally. Over the years, the courts have inevitably had to flesh out the bare statutory bones of the tax system in order to make it a workable and (relatively) coherent entity. This has led to the evolution of a number of judge-made 'fiscal principles' which do in fact need to be 'read in' to tax statute. Notable examples include the doctrine of the source, which has many significant ramifications (see **1.303**) and the principle that trading losses may not be anticipated (see **5.102**). A further example is the distinction between an 'application' of income and a 'diversion' of income, illustrated by the decision in *O'Coindealbhain v Gannon* III ITR 484, discussed at **1.403** below. In addition, there are a number of interpretative presumptions both of a general legal nature as well as some which are specific to tax statute, which must always be taken into account (see **1.405**). For a fuller discussion see Ward, 'A Comparative Study of the Interpretation of Tax Statutes in the UK and Republic of Ireland' [1994] British Tax Review 42; 147.

1.402 The statutory context

In *Ramsay v IRC* [1981] STC 174, Lord Wilberforce observed:

> The subject is only to be taxed on clear words, not on the intendment or equity of an Act … but what are clear words is to be ascertained on normal principles. These words do not confine the courts to literal interpretation. There may, indeed should, be considered the context and scheme of the Act as a whole, and its purpose may, indeed should, be regarded.

At first sight, Lord Wilberforce's rejection of a literal approach to the interpretation of tax statute seems to contradict to the prohibition against taxing by reference to 'equity or intendment'. However, this contradiction is apparent rather than real, and arises from the fact that the term 'literal interpretation' is used in at least two distinct senses.

'Literal interpretation' in a positive sense denotes judicial adherence to the terms of the statute, honouring the 'letter' over the alleged 'spirit' of the law. Given that the State's right to levy tax is founded exclusively on legislative enactment, literal interpretation in this sense receives a proper emphasis in the fiscal context.

'Literal interpretation' in its negative sense (the sense in which it was used by Lord Wilberforce) denotes an interpretative style which concentrates on the grammatical sense of the words under consideration, without reference to the wider context in which they appear.

However, as Stamp J said in *Bourne v Norwich Crematorium Ltd* 44 TC 164:

> English words derive colour from those which surround them. Sentences are not mere collections of words to be taken out of the sentence, defined separately by reference to the dictionary or decided cases, and then put back into the sentence with the meaning which you have assigned to them as separate words …

The relevance of the statutory context was explicitly acknowledged by Lord Russell in *Attorney General v Carlton Bank* (as approved by Kennedy CJ in the *Doorley* case (see **1.501**)).

In *IOT v Kiernan* III ITR 19, Henchy J observed:

> A word or expression is a given statute must be given meaning and scope *according to its immediate context*, in line with the scheme and purpose of the particular statutory pattern as a whole, and to an extent that will truly effectuate the particular legislation or a particular definition therein (emphasis added).

A strong example of a 'contextual' construction is provided by *McCann Ltd v O'Culacháin* III ITR 304, where the issue was whether or not the artificial ripening of bananas constituted manufacturing for the purposes of CTA 1976, Pt IV, which exempted profits from the export sales of goods manufactured in Ireland. McCarthy J, delivering the only judgment in the Supreme Court, observed:

> One must in aid of the construction of the particular word as used in the Statute look to the scheme and purpose as disclosed by the Statute …
>
> The scheme and purpose of the relevant part of the statute appear to me to be the very context within which the word is used and the requirements of which must be examined in order to construe it. It is manifest that the purpose of … the Act … was, by tax incentives, to encourage the creation of employment within the State and the promotion of exports – naturally outside the State – objectives of a proper social and economic kind which the State would be bound to encourage. Employment is created by labour intensive processes and exports by the creation of saleable goods. The operation described in the case stated clearly comes within both categories; in my judgment, it is then a matter of degree, itself a question of law, as to whether or not what the company had done to the raw material makes it goods within the [statutory] definition.

It has to be said that it is by no means clear how McCarthy J inferred from the statute itself that relief was targeted at 'labour intensive' processes. It was evident from a reading of the provisions that their immediate statutory purpose was to stimulate exports. However, the fact that one of the macroeconomic benefits to be expected from a growth in exports was increased employment, hardly justifies a finding that the statute was intended to stimulate only those export activities which would make a significant contribution to creating employment.

In *Revenue Commissioners v O'Flynn* [2011] IESC 47, the Supreme Court observed that the question to be posed in relation to the relief should be not what was it's general purpose but the specific purpose of the particular scheme.

McCarthy J adopted a more restrictive approach in *Texaco (Ireland) v Murphy* IV ITR 91, where the taxpayer had incurred expenditure on unsuccessfully exploring for oil. It claimed relief for this expenditure under ITA 1967, s 244 (now TCA 1997, ss 763–765), which effectively granted relief for capital expenditure on scientific research. 'Scientific Research' was defined within s 244 as 'any activities in the fields of natural or applied science for the extension of knowledge. Section 245 of the Act granted relief inter alia for capital expenditure incurred on mineral exploration, but, in effect, only where a workable mine was discovered as a consequence. In addition, the Finance (Taxation of Profits of Certain Mines) Act 1974 granted relief for exploration expenditure on an abortive search for certain minerals, but excluding oil.

It was held at first instance by Carroll J that in the light of the total statutory context, the Dáil could not have intended the term 'scientific research' to include abortive expenditure on non-scheduled minerals. The generality of the term 'scientific research' was therefore held to be cut down by reference to the purpose of the legislation as inferred from its overall scheme.

In the Supreme Court, McCarthy J delivering the only judgment, rejected this conclusion. He said:

> The legal principle appears clearly to be that if the claim for allowance falls within the express wording of the permitting section, it must be upheld. Arguments based upon the application or otherwise of other sections, proximate or not, appear to me to be unsound in law.

If the learned judge was putting forward the suggestion that individual sections must be read in isolation, and out of context, then this would be hard to support; indeed it would contradict his own approach in the *McCann* case. However, the learned judge's observations need to be viewed in the light of the particular circumstances of the *Texaco* case, where no clear statutory purpose could be inferred from the melange of overlapping and fragmented provisions. For a discussion of the present tax regime for scientific research expenditure, see **6.501**.

The learned judge was also less willing to engage in macro-economic speculation when *Texaco* was heard. He stated:

> It may well appear desirable that the general taxpayer should not have to bear the burden, indirectly, of what is essentially the cost of the search for oil, unless the search is successful; on the other hand it may well be national policy to encourage search, successful or otherwise, by tax incentives. That is not a matter for the courts, whose functions is to determine whether or not, in a case of this kind, the expenditure falls within the relevant allowance provisions.

It is suggested respectfully that this demonstration of judicial restraint seems preferable to the approach adopted in the *McCann* case (compare *McNally v O'Maoldhomhanaigh*, discussed at **1.404**).

A more straightforward example of a reference to the statutory context as justification for circumscribing widely-drawn language occurred in *JBO'C v PCD & A Bank* III ITR 153. In that case, an inspector of taxes had issued a summons claiming an order against a bank under a provision equivalent to TCA 1997, s 908(2). The conditions for the making of the order required that the inspector should form an opinion either that a taxpayer's account(s) with the bank concerned had not been disclosed to the Revenue, or that the books of the bank were likely to indicate that the taxpayer had made materially false returns. The order could cover two categories of information, namely:

(a) 'full particulars of all accounts' maintained by the taxpayer; and

(b) 'such information relating to the financial transactions of the taxpayer as was recorded in the books of the bank concerned, and which would be material *inter alia* in determining the correctness of the taxpayers returns.

Murphy J made the following *obiter* comments:

> While I have no doubt that the words 'full particulars of all accounts' could be interpreted so as to include payments in to and withdrawals from an account, it seems to me that, in the particular context, those words should be given a restricted meaning. In the first place, the distinction between the two classes of information seems to me to reflect the different opinions which the authorised officer may form as a condition precedent to making an application to the court under the section ... The provision of basic information in relation to accounts would be sufficient to confirm the opinion of the authorised officer as to the existence of any suspected account. Again, however, it is significant [category (b)] information as opposed to ... [category (a)] information ... is carefully circumscribed. The financial transactions of which information may be sought is, as I have already pointed out, limited to those transactions which are recorded in 'the books of that institution' and which 'would', not 'might', be material in determining the correctness or otherwise of the statements and returns made by the person concerned. As the primary information which a financial institution would have recorded in its books in relation to the affairs of its customer would be lodgements to and withdrawals from the account and the dates of such transactions, it would seem to me surprising if the information was to be divulged in pursuance of the requirement to furnish particulars of accounts requirement to furnish particulars of accounts – a classification which does not enjoy the same protection rather than the information as to financial dealings, which is the more appropriate description of the same transactions.

Leading UK cases where words of seemingly restricted scope were linked by reference to their context include *Bulmer v IRC* 44 TC 1 (see **Division 15**) and *O'Rourke v Binks* [1992] STC 703, a capital gains tax case.

As emphasised by McCarthy, J in *McGrath v McDermott* in the passage cited above (see **1.401**):

> The first canon of construction of statutes is that words are to be given their ordinary meaning.

However, again the 'ordinary meaning' of words or phrases is their ordinary, (ie natural) meaning in the given context. This is not necessarily the same as the most common or everyday meaning of a word or phrase.

An example of an instance where the context made absolutely clear that a word was not being used in an everyday sense can be found in the VAT case of *Diners Club Ltd v Revenue Commissioners* III ITR 680. There, the provision under review referred to the 'reimbursement' of a person 'in respect of the supply by him of goods or services in accordance with a credit and … scheme'. Per Johnson J:

> The use of the work 'reimbursement' in the statutory instrument is not the happiest of choices insofar as technically it would mean repaying someone for that which they had expended … whereas quite clearly a retailer is not reimbursed in that sense by the price of goods which he sells for that also includes a profit not merely his expenditure). However, the parties agreed that the ordinary sense in his case of the word should be taken as meaning 'a paid for' and therefore I think we can deal with the case on the basis of 'services provided to a person under arrangements which provide for the payment of a person in respect of the supply by him of goods or services in accordance with a credit card … scheme'.

In *EG v MacShamhrain* II ITR 352, Teevan J had to interpret the meaning of the word 'settlor' in the context of The word 'settlor' is not defined for the purposes of this provision, but the term 'settlement' was defined by a provision equating to TCA 1997, s 794 as including inter alia 'any disposition trust, covenant, agreement or arrangement….'

The learned judge commented as follows:

> I find that the legislature intended to embrace things other than settlements in the ordinary accepted meaning of the word in property dealings. Now if such things are embraced there must be a settlor in regard to each category. Otherwise the section breaks down at once save in regard to what I may refer to as true settlements and the extended definition of settlement … becomes meaningless. Not infrequently statute law has been found inoperative from inherent defect, but the interpretation here sought, if accepted, would amount to this: that I must say the legislators wrote in these various categories of transactions but did not intend that the section should ever apply to them; that while extending the meaning of settlement in the lawyer's meaning of that term they did not intend the section to apply to such extended meanings.
>
> I must endeavour to ascertain the legislative intention and for that purpose ascribe a meaning to the legislative language. Then I have to question whether the meaning – ie the intention – applies to a given case.
>
> If transfers, dispositions or contracts are to be treated as settlements I would think that the transferors, disposers or contractors as the case may be must be regarded as settlors ….

1.403 The wider fiscal context

The 'ordinary' meaning of words must also be established in the light of the context of tax law as a whole and not just that of the statute under consideration. In particular, certain terms may have acquired a specialised meaning for tax purposes as a result of judicial interpretations over time.

Thus, in *Edwards v Clinch* [1981] STC 617 Lord Wilberforce (although not all of his fellow judges) took the view that the term 'office' had acquired a specialised meaning through accumulated case law, which applied only for tax purposes. However, Lord Wilberforce simultaneously argued that this 'fiscal' meaning had to be modified in the light of contemporary circumstances. This gave him the best of all worlds allowing him to ignore the 'dictionary' definition of the term, without having to adhere fully to the definition established by case law.

A similar issue arose in *Cronin v Youghal Carpets* III ITR 229, where it was held that the phrase 'total income brought into charge to corporation tax' had to be construed as being analogous to the phrase 'profits or gains brought into charge to tax' in the Income Tax Acts. The latter phrase had been subject to extensive judicial interpretation over the years and had been held to denote 'profits … actually assessed to tax'. The Revenue had argued that the ordinary meaning of the words denoted income before general deductions (eg in respect of charges and loss relief). The court was reinforced in its rejection of the Revenue's argument by reference to what are now TCA 1997, s 4(2) and s 76(1), provisions which indicated that income tax principles were to apply to corporation tax.

In *O'Coindealbhain v Gannon* III ITR 484, the main issue was the interpretation of the word 'received'. The taxpayer had ceased to practise as a barrister following his appointment as a High Court Judge. He then formed a wholly owned company which subsequently issued shares to his relatives. He next wrote to client solicitors, indicating that he did not wish to receive any outstanding fees but that, 'if they wished' they could pay his fees to the company instead. The Revenue sought to charge the taxpayer (under what is now TCA 1997, s 91, the 'post-cessation receipts enactment' – see **5.605**) as having 'received' all such sums paid to the company.

Barrington J at first instance, observed there was 'no room for any intendment', but that 'a fair and reasonable construction must be given to the language without leaning to one side or the other'. The learned judge concluded that the transactions concerned were in reality dispositions by the taxpayer in favour of the company of money due to him 'in law or in honour which would otherwise have been paid … [to him]'. on this basis, the learned judge applied the dictum of Lord Hanworth M in *Dewar v IRC* 19 TC 561 that 'you cannot by the use which you make of a sum which has been received or which has come into your disposal escape tax'. The learned judge rejected the taxpayer's contention that what is now TCA 1997, s 91, when, construed literally, failed to catch the transaction, not being expressly extended to cover 'constructive' receipts. Barrington J concluded:

> Under these circumstances and despite the strict canon of literal interpretation to be applied to revenue statutes, it appears to me to be unreal to suggest that these sums were not 'received' by [the taxpayer] …

The decision, which in principle is clearly correct, reflects the fact that (as already discussed in **1.402**) the courts have evolved fundamental principles in respect of tax law, which form an integral part of the statutory context. One such principle is the distinction between the 'application' and the 'diversion' (or alienation) of income. The manner in which income is applied does not affect the tax liability of the individual who receives or is entitled to such income.

In *Revenue Commissioners v Doorley* V ITR 539, the substantive issue was the correct construction of the Stamp Duties (Ireland) Act 1842, which provided an exemption for legacies applied in support of any charity in Ireland or for any charitable purpose. This exemption replaced a previous exemption which was expressed to apply to legacies given applied in support of any charity, irrespective of its location, or (again) for any charitable purpose. It was reasonably clear that under the earlier exemption no territorial limitation could be inferred in relation to the charitable purposes concerned (ie there was no requirement that they had to be Irish charitable purposes). The taxpayer argued that accordingly this constituted evidence in support of his argument that there was no implied territorial limitation in respect of the exemption for legacies applied for charitable purposes under the 1842 Act.

Kennedy CJ took the view that because a priori reasoning was not permissible in relation to tax law (see **1.401**):

> It is not, in my opinion, legitimate for a court, when interpreting a taxing Act, to use … antecedent legislation … for the purpose of deducing an intention to impose or not to impose a tax upon a particular subject.

It is highly arguable that the generally accepted judicial practice of relying on antecedent legislative history to resolve an interpretative doubt could in fact have been properly and usefully applied in the instant case. For an example of a judge applying just such an approach in the context of a tax case, see *Action Aid v Revenue Commissioners* V ITR 392. It is submitted that the rejection of an a priori approach implies that no there should be no background assumption in favour of, or against, taxability not that an unduly restrictive approach should be adopted towards the wider fiscal statutory context.

1.404 The 'mischief rule'

The statutory purpose may not only form part of the statutory context but may also be invoked to resolve interpretative doubts (the so-called 'mischief rule'). In *McGrath v McDermott*, Finlay CJ observed:

> The function of the courts in interpreting a statute of the Oireachtas is … strictly confined to ascertaining the true meaning of each statutory provision, resorting in cases of doubt or ambiguity to a consideration of the purpose and intention of the legislature to be inferred from other provisions of the statute involved, or even of other statutes expressed to be construed with it.
>
> The courts have not got a function to add or to delete from statutory provisions so as to achieve objectives which the courts appear desirable.

This observation again points up clearly the distinction between the statutory purpose, to be discerned from a reading of the statute itself (set in its legislative and factual background); and the 'equity' or 'intendment' of the statute, reflecting the court's concept of 'fair play' or what it conjectures to be the ulterior motives of the legislature (see also the non-tax case *Howard v Commissioners of Public Works in Ireland* [1994] 1 IR 101).

In *Cronin v Youghal Carpets* (discussed above in **1.403**) the court held that the meaning of 'total income' adopted there was consistent with the purpose of the Act to grant both export sales relief and group relief. This was on the footing that it had the practical result of ensuring that group relief would not dilute the benefits of export sales relief. It is respectfully suggested that, in fact, it is unconvincing to infer from the fact that legislation provides for two separate reliefs that one must not be meant to interact with the other. Such reasoning does appear to assume what it sets out to prove.

In *IOT v Kiernan* III ITR 19, the Supreme Court held that the term 'cattle' in the ordinary meaning did not include 'pigs' in the context of ITA 1918, Sch D Case III rule 4. The decision in *Kiernan* is diametrically opposed to that in *Phillips v Bourne* 27 TC 498, a case dealing with the equivalent UK legislation. This divergence however is not evidence of a fundamental discrepancy between the interpretative principles adopted by the Irish and UK courts.

In *Phillips v Bourne*, Atkinson J referred to the edition of the New English Oxford Dictionary current in 1947. This apparently stated that the term 'cattle' was usually confined to bovine animals, but that the wider usage, which would include pigs, also existed. In *Kiernan*, Henchy J relied on the edition of the Oxford Dictionary published at the end of the 19th century which he stated 'clearly confirms the meaning is restricted to bovine animals'.

In *Kiernan*, Henchy J claimed that Atkinson J had been led into error in *Phillips v Bourne* by allowing himself to be influenced by decisions on the meanings of the term 'cattle' in the context of different statutes, which were inapplicable to the present case. In fact, Atkinson J merely looked to these other cases as further evidence that the term 'cattle' was capable of a wide meaning which would include pigs. He then proceeded to apply the 'mischief rule' – ie he chose between the wider and narrower senses of the word 'cattle' in favour of the sense which (as he perceived it) best fulfilled the purpose of the legislation: viz, to tax the profits of dealing in animals, as opposed to taxing the mere occupation of land.

The different results in the two cases are therefore attributable to different views as to the ordinary meanings of a particular word. This shows, amongst other things, that the 'ordinary meaning' of a word or phrase is itself not beyond debate. Words can have, or can be argued to have, more than one 'ordinary meaning': many English words and expressions are capable of bearing different nuances or shades of meaning, each of which might be claimed to reflect 'ordinary' usage. Atkinson J did in fact adhere in principle to the presumption in favour of applying an 'ordinary' meaning, since according to his lights he was faced with a choice between two alternative ordinary meanings. Atkinson J did, however, accept that he was opting for the less usual over a more usual meaning. His decision therefore depended on taking the view that the purpose of the provisions under review were clearly discernible, and that the fulfilment of that purpose was advanced by the adoption of a less usual, but nevertheless 'ordinary', meaning.

Where a tax provision has a clear economic rationale, then reliance on statutory purpose to resolve ambiguities may prove less controversial. In *McNally v O'Maoldhomhanaigh* IV ITR 22, the taxpayer claimed an investment allowance under FA 1971, s 22 in respect of plant with a 94 per cent rate of usage in designated areas, as defined by the Industrial Development Act 1969, s 6. FA 1971, s 22(1) required that for plant to be eligible for the allowance it should 'be provided for use in any designated area'. The Revenue argued that the words 'provided' for use could only mean 'provided exclusively for use', while the taxpayer argued that it meant 'provided substantially for use'. O'Higgins CJ observed:

> The provision of the section is not unambiguous and to construe it properly the court must have regard to the objective of the section. The definition of designated area in s 22(1) by virtue of the direct reference to the meaning attributed to that phrase in the Industrial Development Act 1969 (IDA Act) clearly and unequivocally identifies the objective of the statute as being an allowance intended to further and support the objectives of the IDA Act in relation to designated areas. Section 33 of that Act contains the provision in relation to designated areas …
>
> The clear objective of the IDA Act and of s 22 in relation to designated areas is to encourage economic activity and in particular employment. An interpretation of s 22 which permits the granting of an investment allowance in respect of the provision for use as to 94 per cent of

> its time in designated areas and to be used by a plant hire firm employing persons resident in the designated area is compellingly more in accordance with the objective of the section than would be an interpretation disallowing such allowances by reason of the use of the machinery or plant to the extent of 6 per cent of its time outside the designated area.

The draftsman's failure to specify a measure of usage meant that some qualification had to be applied to the words, so that in this case there was an undeniable choice of meanings. O'Flaherty J, in a concurring judgment, expressly stated that 'substantial' use was what was contemplated by the legislature.

It may be seen that in contrast to *McCann v O'Culacháin* (discussed in **1.402**) the statute itself provided evidence of its purpose to stimulate employment.

Administrative provisions may also lend themselves with greater ease to considerations of statutory purpose. In *The State (Multiprint Label Systems Ltd) v Neylon* III ITR 159, statutory purpose was invoked in order to assist in resolving an ambiguity. What is now TCA 1997, s 941 (as extended by TCA 1997, s 943) obliges a party who wishes to appeal against a determination of the Circuit Court to declare his dissatisfaction 'immediately' after the determination. In this case, the appellant (in fact, his agent) overlooked the need to declare dissatisfaction at the end of the appeal but rectified the omission as quickly as he could on the following day.

The word 'immediately' can arguably bear either the narrow sense of 'without any delay whatsoever' or the wider sense of 'with all reasonable speed in the circumstances' (see eg *In re Coleman's Depositories Ltd and Life and Health Assurances Associations* [1907] 2 KB 798, a decision cited in the judgment). In the High Court, Finlay P opted for the latter meaning on the basis that:

> the only conceivable purpose of [the provision] might be to put the Commissioners, or where the matter arises before the Circuit Court Judge, upon notice that at some time in the future and to be confirmed within 21 days, he may be required to state a case in order, presumably, that he should take the necessary precautions to preserve documents or exhibits concerned in the determination of the appeal. I can see no other reason for the requirement ...

The courts have in recent decades evidenced a greater readiness to draw on official pre-parliamentary materials in order to assist them in resolving interpretative doubts. In *McLoughlin v Minister for the Public Service* [1985] IR 631, the Supreme Court referred to an explanatory memorandum which set out the purpose of the relevant legislation. Interpretation Act 2005, s 7, overriding s 18(9) of the Act, provides that in the cases of obscurity, ambiguity or doubt or in making allowances for modern developments, but not otherwise, a judge may look at all matters which accompany and are set out in the text of an Act, *viz* including marginal notes, headings, etc (but not generally explanatory memoranda). In *Pepper v Hart* [1992] STC 898, [1994] IJOT 40 the House of Lords expanded the scope of the 'mischief rule' in the UK (for a critique of the decision, see Ward: *Pepper v Hart* [1992] STC 898, [1994] IJOT 40). In cases of interpretative doubt, the courts in the UK may now refer to Hansard (the record of parliamentary proceedings) in order to ascertain the nature of the mischief at which the statute was aimed and/or the precise manner in which it was intended to tackle the mischief (note also the limitations on the approach applied, perhaps rather questionably, in *Willoughby v IRC* [1995] STC 174). This approach has not (as yet) been generally followed by the courts in Ireland, as discussed in Hunt, 'Statutory Interpretation, *Pepper v Hart* – The Irish Situation' (1996) 8 Irish Tax Review 17. In *Breathnach v McCann* III ITR 113, McWilliam J took the view that he was not entitled to take into account UK pre-parliamentary materials in relation to a statute based on a UK statute.

However, some *dicta* in *DPP v McDonagh* SC [1996] seemed to have clouded the issue somewhat. Costello J (adopting the line he had taken as a High Court judge in *Wavin Pipes Ltd v Hepworth Iron Co Ltd* [1982] FSR 32) stated:

> It has long been established that a court may, as an aide to the construction of a statute or one of its provisions, consider its legislative history, a term which includes the legislative antecedents of the provisions under construction as well as pre-parliamentary material and parliamentary material relating to it. Irish statutes frequently and for very good reasons adopt with or without amendment the provisions of statutes enacted by the UK in dealing with the same topics and so the legislative history of Irish statutes may well include the legislative history of the corresponding enactment of the UK parliament. It was urged on the appellant's behalf that the court should not consider the legislative history of s 2 of the 1981 Act because the court can only do so when construing a section which is ambiguous, which this section clearly is not. I cannot agree with this submission; our courts do not and should not adopt such a rigid exclusionary rule (see, eg *Bourke v Attorney General* [1972] IR 36 in which the Supreme Court not only used the European Convention on Extradition to assist in the construction of the Extradition Act 1965 but also its travaux preparatoires) and it seems to me that the court should have regard to any aspect of the enactment's legislative history which may be of assistance.

Despite these somewhat strong assertions (which taken at face value, seem to go even further than the decision in *Pepper v Hart*) the learned judge seems to have confined himself in fact to consideration of pre-parliamentary materials; further, that consideration does not appear to have led to an interpretation contrary to the wording of the Act. It is difficult to reconcile the assertions of Costello J with the approach of the majority in the Supreme Court in *Howard v Commissioners of Public Works* [1994] 1 IR 101 and the traditional view appears to have been firmly reasserted, at least for the time being in *Crilly v T & J Farrington* [2002] 1 ILRM 161. Murray J observed:

> Having regard to the respective roles of the Oireachtas and of the courts and all the considerations which I have mentioned, I am not satisfied that it has been shown that recourse to ministerial statements as an aid to the construction of statutes is sufficiently neutral useful or efficient to outweigh, from a judicial policy point of view, the disadvantages or possible inconveniences of abolishing or modifying the exclusionary rule. I do not in this case consider it necessary to go so far as to say that this should be decided as a matter of principle.

Denham J observed:

> … speeches made by ministers in the Dáil and Seanad when introducing legislation have not been admissible in court when the court is construing statutes. I am not persuaded that good reason has been indicated in this case for changing or developing the common law in this jurisdiction.

As discussed at **1.106**, Interpretation Act 2005, s 5 restates the traditional view that the purpose of a statute is to be derived from consideration of the statute *itself* taken as a whole.

In *Revenue Commissioners v O'Flynn* [2011] IESC 47, the Supreme Court considered the legislative background to TCA 1997, s 811 in some depth and declared that it was of considerable importance in construing that enactment.

The special interpretative considerations which apply to constitutional provisions, to matters falling within the ambit of EU law, and to international treaties are discussed at **1.409**, **1.410** and **1.411** respectively below.

1.405 Interpretative presumptions

Presumption against 'absurdity'

The general presumption against 'absurdity' is often described as 'the golden rule' (although this term has been employed much less in recent times).

The classic statement of the golden rule was made by Lord Blackburn in *River Wear Commissioners v Adamson* [1877] 2 AC 743, where he said:

> I believe that it is not disputed that what Lord Wensleydale used to call the golden rule is right, viz that we are to take the whole statute together, and construe it together, giving the words their ordinary significations, unless when so applied they produce an inconsistency, or an absurdity or inconvenience so great as to convince the court that the intention could not have been to use them in their ordinary signification, and to justify the court in putting on them some other signification, which though putting on them some other signification, which though less proper, is one which the court thinks the words will bear.

Finlay CJ alluded to the golden rule in *McGrath v McDermott* when he said:

> In rare and limited circumstances words or phrases may be implied into statutory provisions solely for the purpose of making them effective to achieve their expressly avowed objective.

As Finlay P's observations indicate it must be possible to state with a reasonable degree of certainty the additional words which could have been inserted to give effect to the obvious intention of the legislation, ie it is akin to a process of spelling out what is necessarily implied, but not actually stated, in the relevant provision (see *IRC v Hinchy* 38 TC 625, discussed in *Ward* [1993] ITR 628 and *IRC v Trustees of John Aird* [1983] STC 700).

The golden rule will be relevant, therefore, in the extreme situation when applying any of the natural ('ordinary') meanings of a word or phrase would defeat the clearly discernible purpose of the legislation. Given that the purpose of the legislation has to be gleaned from the language of the statute itself, this will be a rare occurrence, and will usually be the result of a more or less obvious drafting blunder.

This was in fact the position in *Kellystown v Hogan* III ITR 56, where the issue was the correct interpretation of the changing provisions of the Corporation Profits Tax Act (since repealed). Section 53(2) of that Act stated, inter alia, that:

> … profits shall include all profits … received in the accounting period, not being dividends … received from a company liable to be assessed to corporation profits tax in respect thereof.

The taxpayer company had received dividends paid out of capital profits, such profits themselves not being liable to Corporation Profits Tax. The taxpayer argued that the dividends which it had received were not taxable as 'not being dividends received from a company liable to be assessed to corporation profits tax in respect thereof'. This argument firstly involved treating the word 'thereof' as referring to dividends in general; and, secondly it assumed that the paying companies would not be liable to Corporations Profits Tax on dividends (this assumption in fact seems to be rather circular).

Henchy J, delivering what was in effect the majority opinion, commented as follows:

> I accept that if the … [section] is read literally in the way suggested it could lead to the result contended for or by [the taxpayer]. But I consider that such a reading would be contrary to the true legislative intent. I have no doubt that the object aimed at was to ensure that profits received by Company A from Company B in the form of dividends would not be liable to be assessed to corporation profits tax if they were already liable to such assessment in the hands of Company B. The interpretation contended for by … (the taxpayer] while it may

> have the merit of literalness, is at variance with the purposive essence of the proviso. Furthermore, it would lead to an absurd result, for moneys which are clearly profits would escape the tax and, indeed, the tax would never be payable on dividends on shares in any Irish company. I consider the law to be that, where a literal reading gives a result which is plainly contrary to the legislative intent, and an alternative reading consonant with the legislative intent is reasonably open, it is the latter reading that should prevail. If the words 'in respect thereof' are read as referring to the moneys represented by the … dividends … referred to earlier in the sentence, the resulting meaning will accord with common-sense and with the legislative intent. I have no doubt that this is what the draftsman intended.

It can be seen that Henchy J's application of the 'golden rule' involved 'reading in' words which is his view were necessary to prevent the clear statutory purpose being stultified.

It is perhaps more contentious whether considerations of absurdity, in the sense of general unfairness or unreasonableness, are legitimate in the context of tax statute, where there is no room for 'equity or intendment'. It may well be the judges would consider that an interpretation of a tax rule which would give to wholly arbitrary or manifestly unjust consequences is indeed absurd. In *Rank Xerox Ltd v Lane* [1979] STC 640 it was held that the exemption from capital gains tax attaching to the disposal of rights arising under a covenant, applied only to gratuitous promises and not to all agreements under seal. According to Lord Russell, this interpretation avoided the 'wholly capricious outcome of exclusion or non-exclusion from chargeable gains depending on the chance of an unnecessary seal'.

In *Rahinstown v Hughes* III ITR 517 Murphy J commented:

> It is possible to envisage cases in which an apparent interpretation of a section or sections of an Act would lead to a result *which was so unjust* or manifestly absurd that there would be good reason for seeking an alternative if less obvious interpretation of the statute which would lead to a more reasonable solution.

However, the court found that the legislation under review did not in fact give rise to injustice or absurdity.

In *Luke v IRC* 40 TC 630, the point at issue was the correct interpretation of the UK equivalent to what is now TCA 1997, s 119(1), which provides an exemption from a Sch E benefit-in-hand charge for 'any expense incurred … in the acquisition or production of an asset …'.

The Inland Revenue argued that the exception did not cover landlords' repairs and improvements.

The majority in the House of Lords rejected the Revenue argument. Lord Dilhorne said:

> … while the effect of [such] expenditure may last for several years, the whole cost has on [the Revenue's] interpretation to be regarded as taxable income for the year in which it was spent. I cannot believe that it was the intention of Parliament to treat the cost of carrying out repairs which is to both [the landlord's] … and the tenant's advantage, as a benefit in kind to the tenants. I think having regard to this context that this phrase (ie 'production of an asset') should not be narrowly construed if it is [so] understood the result will be manifestly unjust (emphasis added).

Lord Reid also took the view that not only was the outcome of the Revenue interpretation 'absurd and capricious', but also that the references to 'benefits' in the legislation indicated that it was not part of the statutory purpose to tax items which did not in fact benefit the employee. In his opinion, the 'mischief' aimed at the section was to curb the 'growing practice of expense accounts and the like'. The intention of the statute accordingly was merely to tax 'sums which can be regarded as representing income in a broad or popular sense'. On this view, the Revenue contention was not merely unjust, but also contradicted the inferred purposes of the statute.

Lord Reid accepted that the expression 'production ... of an asset' would not in any of its natural or ordinary senses cover repairs or improvements to an asset. However, he proceeded to observe:

> To achieve the obvious intention and produce a reasonable result, we must do some violence to the words ... it is only where words are absolutely incapable of a construction which will accord with the apparent intention of the provision and will avoid a wholly unreasonable result that the words of the enactment must prevail.

Lord Reid's approach was approved, by Henchy J in the leading (non-tax) case of *Nestor v Murphy* [1979] IR 326, where words were 'read in' to the relevant statutory language in order to avoid what the court regarded as an 'absurd' result, and one which clearly exceeded the purposes of the statute. *Luke v IRC* III ITR was also followed in *IRC v Berrill* [1981] STC 784 discussed in **15.407**.

It may be that considerations of justice will be more readily applied in the context of administrative provisions, since concepts of procedural fairness are largely universal in nature. In The *State (Multiprint Label Systems Ltd) v Neylon* III ITR 159 the court had to consider the meaning of what is now TCA 1997, s 941 in so far as it provided that 'immediately after the determination of an appeal ... the appellant or the inspector if dissatisfied with the determination ... may declare his dissatisfaction to the Commissioners'. Finlay P, construing the word 'may' as permissive rather than mandatory, observed:

> It would seem to me to be an insupportable injustice so to construe the statute unless I was obliged to do so as to make the obligation to express verbally dissatisfaction immediately at the termination of the proceedings a mandatory obligation, default of which would obviate the entire of this appeal mechanism.

Finally, it must be borne in mind that, in some cases, the perceived injustice involved may be on a scale or of a kind to call the very constitutionality of the statute into question. This aspect is discussed at **1.409** below.

The limits of the 'golden rule' were lucidly set out by Lord Reid in *IRC v Hinchy* 38 TC 625, a case concerning a provision which imposed a penalty for under-declaration of income equivalent to 'the sum of twenty pounds and treble the tax which (the taxpayer) ought to be charged under this Act'. The Revenue contended that this formula was geared to the tax charged on the taxpayer's total income for the relevant year of assessment. This contention clearly led to harsh and anomalous results – a minor under-declaration of income would attract the same penalty in absolute terms as a complete non-declaration of income.

The House of Lords unanimously upheld the Revenue's interpretation. Lord Reid commented:

> What we must look for is the intention of Parliament, and I also find it difficult to believe that Parliament ever really intended the consequences which flow from the Crown's contention. But we can only take the intention of Parliament from the words which they have used in the Act, and therefore the question is whether these words are capable of a more limited construction. If not, then we must apply them as they stand, however unreasonable or unjust the consequences and however strongly we may suspect that this was not the real intention of Parliament ...

One is entitled and indeed bound to assume that Parliament intends to act reasonably and therefore to prefer a reasonable interpretation of a statutory provision if there is any choice. But I regret that I am unable to agree that this case leaves me with any choice.

In *Saatchi and Saatchi Advertising v McGarry* V ITR 376, the court was concerned with a relieving provision which was expressed in terms of unlimited retrospective effect. However, a pre-existing provision in the same Act prevented the taxpayer from taking full advantage of this retrospection. This was because the latter provision imposed a general time limit for claims for relief by reference to the dates on which assessments had become final (at which time the taxpayer could not have known that the relieving provision would be enacted). Barr J declined to disregard the clear words of the pre-existing provision, even though it was clearly inconsistent with the rationale behind the relieving provision (note also *O'Connell v Fyffes Banana Processing Ltd* VI ITR 131, where the court refused to overrule unambiguous wording even in the face of what appeared to be an oversight on the part of the draftsman. The Supreme Court, rather unconvincingly, found that the provisions were in fact ambiguous and construed them against the taxpayer: see **1.406** below) (SC 24.7.00). The Interpretation Act 2005 (see **1.106**) gives formal recognition to the 'golden rule'. It remains to be seen what the impact of the Act will be in practice.

Presumption against double taxation

There is a very powerful presumption against double taxation (in the domestic sense – ie the subjection of the same income more than once to Irish taxation) which can probably be displaced only by words incapable of bearing an alternative meaning. Indeed, the courts would generally regard double taxation as form of 'absurdity' to be avoided if at all possible. In any event, the constitutional legitimacy of a measure imposing double taxation may well be highly questionable (see **1.409**). In *Birch v Delaney* I ITR 515, Fitzgibbon J said:

> Now it is clear that as there is only one tax, if the tax be charged upon the property or the profits or gains comprised in one Schedule, it cannot also be charged upon the property profits or gains comprised in another Schedule, for that would lead to double taxation in respect of the same subject matter.

This principle was extended in *Bird v IRC* [1988] STC 312 by Lord Keith, holding that the same profit could not be liable to both income tax and capital gains tax, in these words: 'In general, I am of opinion that it is not open to the Revenue to subject a taxpayer to two different charges in respect of the same receipt'. It must be correct that the Revenue cannot sustain two different tax charges based on contradictory assumptions.

It is necessary to be clear what exactly is denoted by 'double taxation'. In *Barnes v Hely Hutchinson* 22 TC 655, Lord Wright said:

> Whatever the precise scope of the rule against double taxation it must at least involve that it is the same income, that it is the same propositus [taxpayer] in respect of the same piece of income that is being doubly taxed whether directly or indirectly, and that the double taxation is by British assessment.

Lord Wright's assertion that it is the same taxpayer who must be taxed twice reflects the fact that 'income' in the hands of one taxpayer is not the same 'income' once it has legally transferred to another taxpayer. The classic example is the distribution of corporate income; the company pays corporation tax on its profits and the shareholder then normally pays income tax under Sch F on his dividends. This is a case of 'economic' double taxation, as opposed to legal or fiscal double taxation. The legislature has for many years recognised and alleviated the economic double taxation involved by imputing part of the corporate tax burden to the shareholder by means of a tax credit, although the imputation system in fact no longer applies after 5 April 1999 (see **Division 9**).

In *IRC v Willoughby* [1995] STC 143, the Inland Revenue argued that the taxpayer was liable on the underlying income attributable to an investment bond (imputed to him under the equivalent of TCA 1997, s 806) (see **Division 17**) as well as being liable to a special income tax charge on the realisation of the bond. The Court of Appeal accepted that in such a case 'double taxation was possible'. However, the income attributable to the bond and the proceeds of realising the bond were different receipts (albeit that the latter derived from the former) so that 'double taxation' in the strict sense arguably did not apply. In the event, the court found that the investment income was not taxable under the UK equivalent to TCA 1997, s 806.

A number of tax provisions also deem the income of one person (A) to be the income of another person (B) or other persons (B) and (C). Such provisions generally spell out that the income in question ceases to be regarded as income of (A) (see, for example, TCA 1997, s 795 – discussed at **Division 15**). Problems can arise however where A's income is deemed to be that of say B and C but there is no mechanism for apportioning that income between B and C. In such a situation, to impute all of the income to both B and C would undoubtedly be a form of double taxation. Addressing just this situation, in the context of TCA 1997, s 806 (discussed at **Division 17**) Viscount Dilhorne said:

> The income of each individual to whom the section applies must be deemed to include the income of [A]. There is no question of the income being taxed more than once.

It is worth noting that TCA 1997, s 811, which purports to enable the Revenue to reallocate income in whatever manner they consider is just and reasonable in order to counter a 'tax advantage' – (see **Division 17**), expressly provides that:

> Where the Revenue Commissioners make any adjustment or do any act they shall afford relief from any double taxation which they consider would, but for this paragraph, arise by virtue of any adjustment made or act done by them pursuant to the foregoing provisions of this subsection.

A transaction in respect of which the taxpayer is denied a deduction for his expenditure but is taxable on the income arising does not give rise to fiscal double taxation (see *Forbes v Dundon* II ITR 491).

In *Speyer Bros v IRC* [1908] AC 92, a stamp duty case, it was held that where an instrument was chargeable under two different categories, the Revenue were entitled to impose tax once only, but that they could choose the category which generated the higher tax charge. Thus, for example, if the same receipt were to be potentially liable under two or more provisions of Sch E, or Sch F, or the same case of Sch D, the principle in *Speyer Bros* would apply. Similarly, if the same charging provision is capable of being applied in more than one way (which would be a relatively rare occurrence) the Revenue may choose the basis which is most favourable to them: see *IRC v Park Investments* 43 TC 200.

The principle would generally apply equally where the same receipt was potentially liable under two different cases of Sch D (see *Liverpool & London Globe Insurance Co v Bennett* 6 TC 327, discussed at **5.210**). However, it has been long established that a foreign trade is assessable only under Sch D Case III and not under Sch D Case I, so that no overlap is possible in that instance (*Colquhoun v Brooks* 2 TC 490). It may also be noted that a receipt which is taxable under Sch D Case I or II by definition does not represent 'pure income profit' and thus cannot also fall within Sch D Case III (see **2.302**, and note the decisions in *British Commonwealth International Newsfilm Agency*

Ltd v Mahony 40 TC 550 and *Purchase v Stainer's Executors* 32 TC 367, discussed at **5.605**). This apparently does not apply to interest, because there is no requirement that it should be pure income profit as such (see *Liverpool & London Globe Insurance Co v Bennett* 6 TC 327 and the other cases discussed at **5.210**). However, it will normally be the case that interest income will be regarded as arising from a separate source, distinct from the trading activities of the taxpayer (see *Northend v White and Leonard* [1975] STC 317, discussed at **16.202**).

Income which is taxable at source must normally be taxed as such under Sch D Case IV (TCA 1997, s 74 and note also TCA 1997, s 261(c)(i)). Thus, such income will fall outside Sch D Cases I & II, even if under general principles it could be regarded as trading income (see also the decision in *Bucks v Bowers* 46 TC 267).

Income which falls under Sch D Case IV on general principles is defined *inter alia* as that 'not falling under any other case of Sch D' (TCA 1997, s 18(2)). In this connection, an income profit on a purchase and resale of an asset can fall only within Sch D Case I and not Sch D Case IV (see *Jones v Leeming* 15 TC 333). For a summary of the statutory extensions to the scope of Sch D Case IV, see **8.202**.

In general, each of the Schedules contain rules governing their relationship with the other Schedules (see eg TCA 1997, ss 18(1)(b), (2), 20(2)). However, it is always necessary to look at the precise statutory rules referable to any particular item. Thus, for example, TCA 1997, s 436(2) arguably excludes certain benefits provided by a close company, but which fall within Sch E, from a potential charge under Sch F (see the discussion at **9.101**).

Similarly, certain income may fall within both Sch D Case I and Sch D Case V (see eg the discussion of conacre lettings at **12.102**); however, TCA 1997, s 641 excludes rent and certain amounts treated as rent under TCA 1997, s 98 from the computation of the Sch D Case I profits of a land dealer or land developer.

Presumption against retrospective effect

The general legal presumption against retrospectivity is also one of some weight. In *Connolly v Birch* I ITR 583, Hanna J observed:

> It is submitted that a statute is not to be read as having a retrospective operation unless it is clearly made so by the statute or statutes in question. This is a well-established proposition.

However, it is again necessary to define terms clearly. In the income tax context, the courts have equated retrospectivity to the imposition of a charge on the income for a year of assessment, as a result of a change in the law enacted in a subsequent year of assessment. Thus, in the *Birch* case, income was brought into charge for the first time on a prior year basis. The fact that the income would not have been taxable in the year or assessment in which it actually accrued was held not to amount to retrospective taxation.

Similarly, when income is to be brought into charge for the first time in a particular year of assessment, this will not be regarded as retrospective, even though the transactions generating the income were carried out prior to that year of assessment (see *Customs & Excise v Thorn Electrical* [1975] STC 617; *Boote v Banco de Brazil* [1997] STC 328). Thus, in *Warnock v Revenue Commissioners* III ITR 356, it was accepted that TCA 1997, s 806, which expressly applied to income attributable to the transfers of assets prior to 6 April 1974, was not retrospective in effect. The court also held that what is now TCA 1997, s 808 which enables the Revenue to seek information regarding relevant transfer of assets, but which is not expressly stated to apply to transactions carried out prior to 6 April 1974, applied to such transactions.

There may well be constitutional issues in relation to legislation which is truly retrospective see **1.409** and note the ECJ decision in *Stichting 'Goed Wonen' v Staatssecretaris van Financien* (Case C–376/02), discussed at **1.410**.

Presumptions against extra-territorial jurisdiction

There is a general legal presumption that Irish enactments do not have extra-territorial effect (see *Hamilton v Hamilton* [1982] IR 446). However, the income tax charging provisions generally specify their territorial scope (see **1.502**). As a result, it is not normally necessary to imply any territorial limits into their operation. This point was made forcefully by Lord Herschell in *Colquhoun v Brooks* 2 TC 490 when he rejected an attempt by the taxpayer to 'read in' a further limitation to the scope of the income tax charging provisions:

> Reliance was placed upon the decisions under the Legacy and Succession Duty Acts, which have imposed a limit upon the broad language of the enactments, subjecting legacies and successions to taxation. But it must be remembered that it was necessary to put some limit upon these general terms in order to bring the matters dealt with within our territorial jurisdiction. Without such a limitation the Legacy Duty Act, for example, would have been applicable although neither the testator nor the legatee, nor the property devised or bequeathed, was within or had any relation to the British dominions. A construction leading to this result was obviously inadmissible. The Income Tax Acts, however, themselves impose a territorial limit, either that from which the taxable income is derived must be situate in the UK or the person whose income is to be taxed must be resident there.

In fact, this famous dictum, which was founded on the wording of the equivalent of TCA 1997, s 18(1)(a), apparently overlooked that the wording of the equivalent of TCA 1997, s 18(1)(b) fails to lay down any express territorial limits. Paradoxically, Lord Hailsham, delivering the majority verdict in *National Bank of Greece SA v Westminster Bank Exor & Trustee Co* 46 TC 472, relied on Lord Herschell's dictum as authority for limiting the scope of the equivalent to TCA 1997, s 18(1)(b) (see also the comments of Hanna J in *Exors & Trustees of AC Ferguson v Donovan* I ITR 183). Nevertheless, Lord Herschell's dictum has been generally accepted as authority for the general principle that a non-resident can only be taxed in respect of Irish source income.

The position in this respect was in fact always a little more subtle than Lord Herschell's dictum might suggest. Thus, the effective definition of 'Irish Source' income is sometimes more restrictive in the case of a non-resident than it is in the case of a resident. For example, a trade or profession which is carried on partly in the State by an Irish resident will be taxable in full under Sch D Case I or II as appropriate (see **13.103**); however a trade or profession carried on partly in the State by a non-resident is generally taxable under Sch D Case I or II only to the extent that it is carried on within the State (see **13.602**); similar considerations apply in the case of Sch E employments (**13.607**).

The position has, moreover, become more complicated since Lord Herschell delivered his dictum. A number of supplementary charging provisions have been grafted on to the basic charging provisions and in some cases, these lay down their own territorial criteria (see, eg *Nichols v Gibson* [1996] STC 1008, discussed at **Division 10**). Further, in a number of cases, anti-avoidance provisions deliberately override the territorial limits of Income Tax Acts (see eg TCA 1997, s 806, discussed at **Division 17**).

Territorial limits may also have to be implied into widely-worded administrative provisions (see *Clarke v Oceanic Contractors* [1983] STC 35 where the novel concept of 'tax presence' was applied in the context of the obligation to operate PAYE).

The courts have held that the territorial limits laid down by the Taxes Acts govern the term 'income' so that it refers only to 'income' which is chargeable to Irish tax, unless the statute clearly provides to the contrary (see *Whitney v IRC* 10 TC 88; and also *Astor v Perry* discussed in **15.403**).

Presumptions regarding the scope of deeming provisions

The Income Tax Acts make frequent use of 'deeming provisions' which require a given set of facts to be treated as if they were a different set of facts. The approach to interpreting such provisions was stated by the UK Court of Appeal in *Marshall v Kerr* [1993] STC 360, following *IRC v Metrolands* 54 TC 679 as follows:

> I take the correct approach in construing a deeming provision to be to give the words used their ordinary and natural meaning, consistent so far as possible with the policy of the Act and the purposes of the provisions so far as such policy and purposes can be ascertained; but if such constructions would lead to injustice or absurdity, the application of the statutory fiction should be limited to the extent needed to avoid such injustice or absurdity, unless such application would clearly be within the purposes of the fiction. I further bear in mind that because one must treat as real that which is only deemed to be so, one must treat as real the consequences and incidents inevitably flowing from or accompanying that deemed state of affairs, unless prohibiting from doing so.

Marshall v Kerr was approved and followed by the Supreme Court in *In the Matter of G O'C and A O'C* V ITR 346. *IRC v Metrolands* was approved and followed in the context of Capital Gains Tax in *O'Connell v Keleghan* VI ITR 201, 497.

In *Hammond Lane Metal Co Ltd v O'Culacháin* IV ITR 187 Carroll J refused to restrict the operation of a deeming provision in order to defeat what she described as a tax avoidance scheme. In *de Rothschild v Lawrenson* [1995] STC 623, a capital gains tax case, it was held that the operation of a deeming provision had to be restricted by reference to its clear purposes. In this case, the court was assisted in reaching its conclusion by the fact that failure to restrict the provision in this way would have lead to grossly anomalous results (see Ward [1994] British Tax Review 250).

Where a deeming provision is expressly stated to be for the purposes of a particular section, then it will normally be the case that the deemed state of affairs will apply only in respect of that section (*Erin Executor and Trustee Co v Revenue Commissioners* V ITR 76, a VAT case). This proposition may however need to be qualified where the section in question controls the operation of other sections.

Presumption re Consolidation Acts

The Irish courts recognise a rebuttable presumption that a consolidation act does not alter the pre-existing law (see, eg, *Harvey v Minister for Social Welfare* [1990] ILRM 185). Thus, the court will look at the pre-consolidation statutes and the surrounding case law in order to ascertain the pre-consolidation position. The UK courts have diluted the force of this presumption. In *Farrell v Alexander* [1977] AC 59, Lord Wilberforce stated:

> … self-contained statutes, whether consolidating previous law, or so doing with amendments, should be interpreted, if reasonably possible, without recourse to antecedents, and that the recourse should only be had when there is a real and substantial difficulty or ambiguity which classical methods of construction cannot resolve.

Thus, it is generally only where there is ambiguity (ie interpretative doubt) that reference can be made to the presumption that a consolidating act is not intended to alter the law. However, the UK courts have not applied this principle rigidly. Thus, they have taken into account the special tax meaning of a term established over a long line of previous cases (see eg *Edwards v Clinch* [1981] STC 617 discussed in **1.503**) and have also stated that it would be unrealistic to disregard very recent decisions (see *NAP Holdings UK Ltd v Whittles* [1994] STC 979). In many cases, the fact that a provision which has been reproduced in a consolidation act has been the subject of previous litigation will imply in any event that there is a real interpretative doubt to be resolved. Thus, for example, the UK Courts routinely refer to prior case law in resolving the question of whether or not a particular receipt arises 'from' an employment (see **10.104–10.111**). Aston takes the view that in any event the Irish Courts are unlikely to follow the principle set out in *Farrell v Alexander* (see [1997] ITR 545).

When the Oireachtas re-enacts a statutory provision which has been the subject of a judicial decision, there is no presumption that the Oireachtas thereby endorses the correctness of that decision. In *IOT v Kiernan* III ITR 19, Henchy J, cited with approval the following dictum of Lord Denning in *Royal Crown Derby Porcelain Co Ltd v Russell* [1949] 2 KB 417:

> I do not believe that whenever parliament re-enacts a provision of a statute it thereby gives statutory authority to every erroneous interpretation which has been put upon it. The true view is that the court will be slow to overrule a previous decision on the interpretation of a statute when it has long been acted on and it will be more than usually slow to do so when parliament has, since the decision, re-enacted that statute in the same terms. But if a decision is, in fact, shown to be erroneous, there is no rule of law which prevents it being overruled.

Presumption re reliefs and allowances

It is generally accepted that, in absence of any statutory direction, taxpayers may claim reliefs and allowances in the manner which is most beneficial to them (see eg *Sterling Trust v IRC* 12 TC 868; *Ellis v BP Oil Northern Ireland Refinery Ltd* [1987] STC 52 and note *Commercial Union Assurance Co v Shaw* [1999] STC 109).

Presumption re subsequent legislative amendments

The UK courts have taken the view that where there is genuine interpretative doubt ('ambiguity') then, this may be resolved, if appropriate, by reference to subsequent amendments to the statute in question. However, where an amendment is made which reflects an incorrect view of the meaning of a statute, such an amendment will carry no interpretative weight (*Kirkness v Hudson* 36 TC 28; *Featherstonhaugh v IRC* [1984] STC 261). By way of contrast, in *Cronin v Cork & County Property Co Ltd* III ITR 198, Griffin J commented as follows:

> the court cannot in my view construe a statute in the light of amendments that may thereafter have been made to it. An amendment to a statute can, at best, only be neutral, it may have been made for only one of a variety of reasons. It is however for the courts to say what the true construction of a statute is, so that construction cannot be influenced by what the Oireachtas may subsequently have believed it to be.

1.406 Strict construction

In *IOT v Kiernan* III ITR 19 Henchy J observed:

> when a word or expression is used in a statute creating a penal or taxation liability, then if there is looseness or ambiguity attaching to it, it should be construed strictly so as to prevent the fresh imposition of liability from being created unfairly by the use of oblique or slack language. See Lord Esher in *Tuck & Sons v Priester* [1887] 19 QBD 629, Lord Reid in *DPP v Ottwell* [1970] AC 642 and Lord Denning MR in *Farrell v Alexander* [1977] AC 59.

The so-called doctrine of 'strict construction' can be applied with varying degrees of rigidity. At its most extreme, it would mean that any verbal doubt would be decided in favour of the taxpayer. Thus, in *Tuck and Sons v Priester* (a non-tax case) Lindley LJ declined to construe the word 'unlawfully' as meaning 'without consent' (which would have resulted in imposing criminal liability on the defendant) even though he accepted that in the context this was 'the probable meaning … almost the certain meaning'. The learned judge decided that the court 'ought to keep on the safe side and say that the words 'unlawfully made' are sufficiently ambiguous to enable the defendant to escape … from the penalty'… A much less rigid version of the principle of strict construction is to be found in *DPP v Ottwell* where Lord Reid observed that the principle:

> only applies where after full inquiry and consideration one is left in doubt. It is not enough that the provision is ambiguous in the sense that it is capable of having two meanings. The imprecision of the English language (and, so far as I am aware, of any other language) is such that it is extremely difficult to draft any provision which is not ambiguous in that sense.

It is indeed this latter approach which Henchy J himself followed in *Kellystown v Hogan*. Clearly the application of a rigid principle of strict construction would not permit the adoption of an 'unnatural' interpretation in preference to a natural interpretation in order to impose a tax charge. This very point was made forcibly by Hederman J in his dissenting speech in *Kellystown v Hogan* when he said:

> In the interpretation of statutes generally, not infrequently the courts have found it necessary to limit the effects of words contained in an enactment or a section and sometimes to depart not only from their primary and literal meaning, but also from the rules of grammatical construction in cases where it seems highly improbable that the words used in the section actually express the real intention of the legislature. Courts have disregarded the more natural meaning of words in a section where it would lead to an unreasonable result and have adopted that interpretation which leads to a reasonably practical result, as was held by Romer LJ in *Fry v IRC*. The court … when faced with two possible constructions of legislative language, is entitled to look to the result of adopting each of the alternatives respectively in its question for the true intent of Parliament. However, when construing penal statutes, or statues imposing tax liabilities a stricter approach is necessary.

In *O'Dwyer v Dublin United Transport* II ITR 115, Black J commented as follows in respect of two competing interpretations of an ambiguous provision:

> In my view the language of the rule does not in itself clearly identify which [interpretation] is intended and is reasonably compatible with either of these interpretations, unless the context suffices to justify the preference of either interpretation to the other. If the words by themselves alone leave the court in hopeless doubt as to which of two possible meanings was intended, then, where a taxing statute is concerned, I think it is in accordance with principle that the benefit of the doubt should be given to the contention of the party on whom the pecuniary burden authorised by the statute is sought to be imposed …. *One is always reluctant to have recourse to this principle, save as a last recourse, but in this case I should be prepared*, if necessary, to treat it as turning the scale in favour of the contention of the respondents. I think, however, that a consideration of the policy underlying the material provision may be invoked to show that the interpretation urged by the respondents is probably the one intended by the legislature (emphasis added).

A further complication arises in that the courts do not give the 'benefit of the doubt' to taxpayers when it comes to exemptions and reliefs – in fact, the reverse holds true. As Kennedy CJ observed in *Revenue Commissioners v Doorley* V ITR 539 (in a passage cited by McCarthy J in *Texaco (Ireland) v Murphy* IV ITR 91):

> If it is clear that a tax is imposed by the Act under consideration, then exemption from the tax must be given expressly and in clear and unambiguous terms within the letter of the statute as interpreted with the assistance of the ordinary canons for the construction of

> statutes. The court is not, by greater indulgence in delimiting the area of exemptions to enlarge their operation beyond what the statute *clear and without doubt* and in express terms excepts … [emphasis added].

This approach is consistent with that of Cohen LJ in *Littman v Barron* 35 TC 373, where he said:

> … the principle that in case of ambiguity a taxing statute should be construed in favour of a taxpayer does not apply to a provision giving relief in certain cases from a section clearly imposing liability.

(Note also *O'Connell v Fyffes Banana Procession Ltd* VI ITR 131.)

It should be noted however that the very concept of 'giving the benefit of the doubt' to the taxpayer is not without its difficulties. This is because a particular interpretation might benefit some taxpayers but penalise other taxpayers. Thus, for example, in *Pepper v Hart* [1992] STC 898, [1994] IJOT 40, the choice was between calculating the Sch E charge on benefits in kind on a 'marginal cost' or an 'absorption cost' basis. While a marginal cost basis would have favoured most taxpayers, this would by no means inevitably have been the case. In *Van Arkadie v Sterling Coated Metals* [1983] STC 95, it was said in a case where the result of a particular tax treatment could have produced widely differing results:

> The burden of establishing a claim for relief cannot fluctuate with the rate of exchange or with changes in the state of the taxpayer's trade.

In *O'Sullivan v Revenue Commissioners* V ITR 570, a stamp duty case, the Revenue Commissioners put forward opposing interpretations in relation to a charging provision; the Revenue interpretation would have resulted in a higher rate of duty applying. In the Supreme Court, Maguire CJ stated that even if both interpretations were reasonably open, the Revenue's interpretation would be rejected since the legislation had failed to impose the alleged (additional) duty in clear terms. Black J held that where both interpretations were reasonably open, the statute should be interpreted in favour of the taxpayer. While both judges arrived at the same conclusion, it may be seen that Maguire CJ applied a 'default rule' while Black J relied on the traditional doctrine of strict construction. The case is also of interest in that it demonstrates that judges may sometimes disagree as to whether or not there is real interpretative doubt. Thus, O'Byrne J regarded the Revenue's interpretation as 'practically unarguable', whereas Black J held that both interpretations were 'reasonably open'.

The term 'strict construction' may also be sometimes used in apparent contradistinction to the concept of equitable interpretation (see **1.401**). Thus, in *Erin Executor and Trustee Co v Revenue Commissioners* V ITR 76, Barron J in the Supreme Court held that the restriction of the deeming provision there to the purposes for which it was expressly stated to apply was in 'accord with the principle of the strict construction of taxing statutes'. In effect, however, what the court did was simply to refuse to extend the clear words of the statute in the absence of any justification to be derived from the statute itself. In *Kearns v Dilleen* V ITR 518, Barron J expressed the view that strict construction meant 'that the courts will be stricter in their endeavours to find a literal interpretation than they might be in other forms of legislation'. This dictum may simply involve a recognition that in other branches of statute law there is often a wider legal and factual background, as well as a more easily identifiable statutory purpose, which may more readily justify a departure from the ordinary meaning of a provision.

In *Harris v Quigley & Anor* VI ITR 839 (discussed at **2.104**), the court stated:

> While, as far as possible, a taxing statute should be interpreted in the same way as any other statute and should not be interpreted, if at all possible, as to create an absurdity, nevertheless there is a countervailing principle that where there is an ambiguity a taxing statute will be interpreted in favour of the taxpayer.

This dictum harks back to the more expansive concept of strict construction adopted by Black J in the *O'Sullivan* case. However, the court had regard in fact to the general scheme of the Act concerning appeals and overpayments of tax and declined to cut down the clear meaning of words which in the event gave the taxpayer a right to a repayment. It is therefore not clear whether the invocation of the doctrine of strict construction was really pertinent to the conclusion of the court.

It is certain that judicial consistency in applying the principles of interpretation is sadly lacking and that at times the invocation of these principles appear to be rather *ad hoc* in nature, selected in order to rationalise the end result.

It is submitted that it may be preferable to move away from a doctrine of strict construction which likens the tax system to the administration of criminal justice, other than in the case of administrative provisions incorporating civil or criminal sanctions. It is, after all, now generally accepted that paying a fair share of taxes represents the discharge of a social responsibility rather than a depredation by the State. A more neutral 'default rule' would still protect the taxpayer's right to a reasonable degree of certainty in his financial affairs. Under this kind of rule, where there was unresolvable doubt as to whether a provision imposed a charge or granted a relief or exemption, then such a provision would simply be regarded as having no effect. This approach, which also avoids the practical difficulties of applying a 'benefit to the taxpayer' approach does in fact seem to be close to the principles expounded by Kennedy CJ in *Doorley*, and appears to be consonant with the principles on interpretation set out in Interpretation Act 2005, s 5 (see **1.106**).

It appears also to have been endorsed by the Supreme Court in *Revenue Commissioners v O'Flynn* [2011] IESC 47 which favoured a purposive over a 'narrow and literalist' approach to the interpretation of tax statute.

1.407 Form over substance

As explained in **1.401**, no weight can be given to 'equity' or 'intendment' in the interpretation of tax statute. Accordingly, where a tax charge is imposed by reference to the legal nature of a particular transaction, such charge cannot be extended to cover a different legal transaction, even though it gives rise to similar economic consequence.

The doctrine of 'form over substance' was upheld unequivocally in the seminal case of *IRC v Duke of Westminster* 19 TC 490. In that case, the Duke paid annuities to certain employees on the firm understanding that they would forego an equivalent sum in wages while they were employed by him. The Revenue argued that the annuities were 'in substance' wages, and that the relevant tax provisions should be applied accordingly. The overall arrangement involved was certainly 'economically equivalent' to the payment of wages, at least while the recipients remained employees of the Duke. Lord Russell identified the 'substance over form' argument as essentially an appeal to the 'equity' of the statute. In a famous passage he observed:

> The Commissioners and Mr Justice Finlay took the view that looking at the substance of the thing the payments were payments of wages. This simply means that the true legal position is disregarded and a different legal right and liability substituted in the place of the legal right and liability which the parties place of the legal right and liability which the parties

> have created. I confess that I view with disfavour the doctrine that in taxation cases if, in accordance with court's doctrine that in taxation cases the subject is to be taxed if, in accordance with court's view of what it considers the substance of the transaction, the court thinks that the case falls within the *contemplation or spirit of the statute*. The subject is not taxable by inference or by analogy, but only by the plain words of a statute applicable to the facts and circumstances of his case (emphasis added).

The doctrine of 'form over substance' was undoubtedly breached when, provoked by the burgeoning so-called 'tax avoidance industry', the House of Lords in the UK initiated the 'new approach' in *Ramsay v IRC* [1981] STC 174. The tax avoidance scheme in *Ramsay* was, taken in the round, economically equivalent to nothing happening at all – by definition, it was self-cancelling. By treating it as such for tax purposes, the House of Lords undoubtedly departed from the principles laid down by their forerunners in *Westminster*. In *Furniss v Dawson* [1983] STC 549, it was held that steps inserted into a preordained series of transactions for the sole purpose of avoiding tax would be denied any intermediate effect; only the legal end results (if any) flowing from those steps would be taken into account.

In *McGrath v McDermott* III ITR 683, the Irish courts rejected even the relatively limited 'equitable' incursion into the doctrine of 'form over substance' represented by the 'new approach'. Finlay CJ observed:

> … it was contended that the real, as distinct from what is described as the artificial, nature of the transactions should be looked at by the court, and that if they were, the section could not apply to them. I must reject this contention … In those circumstances, for this court to avoid the application of the provisions of the Act … to these transactions could only constitute the invasion by the judiciary of the powers and functions of the legislature, in plain *breach of the constitutional separation of powers* (emphasis added).

An example of the doctrine of form over substance being applied is to be found in *O'Grady v Laragan Quarries Ltd* IV ITR 269. There, a company, L, which was engaged in selling quarry materials, entered into arrangements with various lorry-drivers under which the drivers agreed to purchase the materials from the producer, H, and to sell the goods to L. The sales were effected by the delivery of the goods to L's customers at prices which varied according to the distance travelled. Murphy J held that the lorry drivers were not engaged in the 'haulage for hire' of the materials since they owned the materials up to the time of delivery. Accordingly, their activities fell outside what is now TCA 1997, s 531, so that L was not required to withhold subcontractors' tax from the payments to the drivers. Murphy J observed:

> The word 'hire' ordinarily connotes the payment to be made for the temporary use of a thing. Use in the context of s 17 is extended to the action of 'haulage' which implies the process of moving a load in a vehicle which in turn involves the services of a driver L takes advantage of the services of both the lorry owners and their lorries but the parties have deliberately and effectively arranged that the relationship between them should not in law constitute a hiring to L by the lorry owners of their services as vehicles. It is not open to a court of law to hold that merely because the arrangement is commercially unusual or practically unnecessary that its terms and effects should be ignored and be replaced by a more conventional agreement which would have substantially the same *effect but would fall within the provisions of s 17* (emphasis added).

An important application of the doctrine of form over substance is the respect given to the separate legal personality of entities such as companies and trusts. An example of the court's refusal to 'lift the veil' in an administrative context, can be found in The *State (Melbarien Enterprises) v Revenue Commissioners* III ITR 290. The government had decided that any persons tendering for public contracts would be required to produce a tax clearance certificate from the Revenue Commissioners, indicating that they were not in default with their tax liabilities. The plaintiff (M) had been refused a certificate on the basis that its director/shareholders had previously been the director/shareholders of a company which had gone into liquidation owing money to the Revenue. Hamilton P issued an order of mandamus, directing the Revenue to deal with the issue of the certificate solely on the basis of M's record. He observed:

> They were not entitled to take into account in reaching their decision any factors other than the prosecutor's liability for payments due to them. It is quite clear that in reaching their decision to refuse the necessary certificate, they took into account the liabilities of a separate company. In my opinion, they were not entitled to do so …

It is possible for the courts to uphold the principle of separate legal personalities while inferring at the same time that a company is operating merely as an agent for its shareholder(s), ie it is carrying on business not on its own benefit but on behalf of those shareholders. The practical effect of this inference in the income tax context would be to attribute the income of the company to its shareholders. The inference of agency is fairly exceptional, although it may be more likely where the controlling shareholder is a company (for a full discussion of the case law, readers are referred to standard works on company law, such as Courtney, *The Law of Companies* (3rd edn, Bloomsbury Professional, 2012); Keane, *Company Law* (4th edn, Bloomsbury Professional, 2007); or Forde and Kennedy, *Company Law* (4th edn, Round Hall, 2007) – see also Ward, 'The Separate Legal Personality of Companies' [1993] IJOT 33).

In *Firestone Tyre & Rubber Co v Llewellin* 37 TC 111, A Inc, a multinational company, arranged that its wholly-owned UK subsidiary, B Ltd, which manufactured tyres under A Inc's brand name, should sell tyres to A Inc's distributors at a price agreed between A Inc, and the distributors. B Ltd was entitled to receive only cost price plus 5 per cent on the sale of the tyres, the balance of the sale price being accounted for to A Inc. It was held that the profits made by A Inc on these transactions arose from a trade carried on in the UK by A Inc through B Ltd as its agent. Given that A Inc found the customers, set the prices, and most significantly of all, took the profits (bar B Ltd's 5 per cent commission), this was a finding which could be justified without regard to A Inc's control over B Ltd. Indeed, no reliance at all seems to have been placed by the court itself on the mere fact of A Inc's control. It is true to say that the arrangements undertaken would hardly have been feasible had A Inc not controlled B Ltd. However, it is one thing to say that A Inc had exercised its control in order to create an agency relationship, and quite another to say that A Inc's control was in itself indicative of agency.

It must be borne in mind also that it is open to the legislature to overrule the strict legal analysis of transactions by enacting specific anti-avoidance measures. A classic example is TCA 1997, s 806 (see **Division 17**) which can deem the income of a non-resident trust or a non-resident company to be that of an Irish resident individual. This measure clearly negates the principle of separate legal personality where it applies. The constitutionality of provisions of this kind is considered at **1.409**.

Following the decision in *McGrath v McDermott* III ITR 683, the legislature has enacted TCA 1997, s 811, a blanket anti-avoidance provision, discussed at **Division 17**. It is relevant to note that TCA 1997, s 811(5) gives the Revenue the power to reallocate income or gains between any persons in order to withdraw the benefits of tax avoidance. The exercise of this power may evidently lead to wholesale 'lifting of the veil'.

TCA 1997, s 811 also directs the Revenue to look to the 'substance' as well as to the 'form' of transactions in deciding whether or not they have been undertaken to avoid tax. it is not clear whether this means for example that a controlling shareholder or controlling shareholders must be treated as being 'in substance' the same person as 'his'/'their' company. TCA 1997, s 806 (discussed above) includes a provision that in deciding whether or not a taxpayer obtains (broadly speaking) an economic benefit for the purposes of that section, one must look to the 'substance' of the matter. In *Lord Vestey's Executors v IRC* 31 TC 1, Lord Normand took the view that a benefit received by a company could be imputed to controlling shareholders only where they exercised complete control over the company. However, even where complete control exists, the identity between a company and shareholder is far from complete in terms of economic substance, (most importantly, the debts of the company cannot as a rule be recovered from the shareholders).

In *Ransom v Higgs* [1974] STC 539 a number of companies controlled by the taxpayer (H) and his wife, the H group, undertook a pre-planned avoidance scheme. The H group firstly sold land at undervalue to a partnership in which H's family trust (T) had an interest. T subsequently sold its interest in the partnership to the promoter of the scheme. This sale effectively realised the difference between the cost of the land and the estimated development value, less a fee for the scheme promoter. It was hoped that this gain would be treated as capital in nature, on the basis that it had transmuted a disposal of land into a disposal of a partnership interest. Following the sale, C, a development company owned by H, effectively developed the land on behalf of the promoter.

The Revenue argued that H had engaged in trade and that the trust was taxable on the basis that they had received the profits of this trade. As noted above, the courts will not 'look through' companies for tax purposes as a matter of principle. Therefore, the proposition that H was the trader could not succeed once it was accepted that none of the entities involved in the scheme were acting as his agents. The fact that H had procured those entities to play their part in the scheme was insufficient. As Lord Wilberforce commented:

> In the whole course of these transactions [H] bought nothing, sold nothing and ventured nothing.

Instead the scheme was an 'artificial transaction in land' (within what is now, in Ireland, TCA 1997, s 643: see **Division 12.4**).

However, all of the Law Lords in *Higgs* felt justified in looking at the scheme there as a whole, even though there was no legal link between the various transactions. Lord Wilberforce said:

> I accept that it is legitimate to consider the scheme as a whole where there is evidence as there is here, that each separate step is dependent on others being carried out but the question remains whether this organisation and contest of a complex process can possibly constitute trading.

It must always be borne in mind that the doctrine of 'form over substance' would in fact be better expressed as being one of the doctrine of 'legal substance over economic substance'. Accordingly, the taxpayer cannot overrule the true legal effect of what he has done by the use of misleading labels (see *Scoble v Secretary of State* 4 TC 618). Thus, for example, in *O'Coindealbhain v Gannon*, discussed in **1.403**, what was described as a waiver of his fees by the taxpayer, was held by Barrington J to be in law the grant of a licence by him to his solicitor clients to dispose of his fees. The reasons underlying this conclusion are discussed in **1.408**.

Similarly, in *Ridge Securities v IRC* 44 TC 373 sums described as interest were paid in the course of a tax avoidance scheme. They reflected a rate of return in excess of 400 per cent pa. The court observed:

> Here the ratio of interest to principle is such that it seems … impossible to attribute to the payment the character of interest … I have been reminded of the *Westminster* case, but here the description 'interest' is … merely a label which inaccurately describes the transaction as it appears upon the terms of the transaction read in the light of surroundings circumstances.

The principle that it is the true legal nature of the arrangements under consideration which must prevail was restated emphatically by Kenny J in *O'Sullivan v P* II ITR 464, as follows:

> Although liability to tax is to be determined by reference to the legal rights of the parties to the transaction, the court has to decide in each case what the rights are having regard to legal ideas and concepts and so that the words used by the parties do not necessarily determine what the rights are.

(See also the non-tax case, *Irish Shell & BP Ltd v John Costello Ltd* [1987] ILRM 66, discussed in Ward, 'Form over Substance' [1994] ITR 1106; and *McCabe v South County Investment* V ITR 107.)

In *Kearns v Dilleen* (a CGT case) an option was granted, as part of a tax avoidance scheme, to acquire shares in consideration for a sum equating to more than 98 per cent of the price of the shares. Barron J said:

> The reality of a transaction is not governed by the word used to describe it. The word 'option' involves choice. No one would pay over 98 per cent of the price of property for the choice to pay less than a further 2 per cent to acquire the property or give up the over 98 per cent already paid and have neither the money nor the property.

Barron J indicated that in his (obiter) view the transaction would be viewed in equity, not as the grant of an option but as a disposal of an interest in the shares; Murphy J indicated strong support for this view. The principle that the courts can reject the characterisation of a transaction, which so flies in the face of reality that it is unsustainable in the circumstances, is also illustrated in *Darngavil Coal Co Ltd v Francis* 7 TC 1, discussed below.

Another form of mislabelling arises where a taxpayer seeks to present a transaction as if it were separate and distinct, when in law it actually forms part of a larger contractual arrangement. In *Diners Club Ltd v Revenue Commissioners* III ITR 680, the taxpayer was a credit card company. It had agreed with its client retailers that it would buy from them all debts incurred by their customers who used its card. The debts were to be acquired at their face value, less a discount. The taxpayer argued that its business was accordingly that of debt factoring and not the supply of services rendered to persons who received payments from customers under the terms of a credit card scheme.

Johnson J, rejecting this contention, stated:

> … I am of opinion that the utilisation of a credit card may involve three individual agreements but all of these are part of an implementation of an overall agreement between the company, the retailer and the purchaser that they shall conduct business in this fashion, and all three agreement cannot be taken as being independent but are mutually dependent on the overall agreement.

(Note also *T & E Homes v Robinson* [1979] STC 351.)

A more controversial, example of a court looking at the legal substance of a series of transactions 'in the round' can be found in the stamp duty case of *Viek Investments v IRC* IV ITR 367 (for a critical view see *Walsh* [1993] IJOT 74).

Despite its significance, it must always be borne in mind that the doctrine of form over substance is only relevant to the extent that the tax charge is actually determined by the legal nature of a transaction. Thus, for example the determination of whether or not a particular activity, or set of activities, amounts to trading will involve a wide-ranging review of the surrounding circumstances, including possibly the subjective purposes of the participants (see **Division 4**).

The 'label' principle has also been invoked on occasions as a justification for overriding the purported allocation of consideration in a composite transaction (see, in particular, the comments in *Vestey v IRC* 40 TC 112 at p 115). It is probably more logical to regard these cases as applications of the 'sham' doctrine, in so far as the allocation is treated as being incorrect in law in such cases. The doctrine of the sham is traditionally invoked in cases of deliberate deceit; however, as discussed in **1.408**, for tax purposes at least, it appears that there may also be 'innocent' shams.

Thus, in *Darngavil v Francis* 7 TC 1, the court held that what were conventionally described as rental payments under a hire purchase agreement included an element of consideration for the option to purchase (the option price in this case being purely nominal). It is sometimes suggested that this decision disregarded the form of the transaction in favour of its substance. However, the decision in *Darngavil* may be justified on the basis that, as a matter of necessary inference, some part of the rental in *Darngavil* had to represent consideration in law for the purchase option (accordingly, the purported allocation represented a mislabelling of the transaction).

It should be emphasised that the parties to a contract have a legitimate latitude within which to agree the allocation of consideration between different assets, particularly if there is not an active market in the kind of asset which is the subject of the contract. Failing evidence of a deliberate agreement to manipulate valuations so that the allocation is in fact a 'sham' in the traditional sense (see **1.408**), the courts will therefore usually only overturn an allocation which is unsustainable in all of the circumstances. In *O'Connell v Fleming* VI ITR 453, the High Court held that an allocation of consideration in a document must be taken at face value in the absence of fraud, sham or any other vitiating circumstance.

For examples of 'sham' allocations in the traditional sense, see the non-tax cases of *Elmdene Estates v White* [1960] 1 All ER 306 and *Saunders v Edwards* [1987] 1 WLR 55. In *Coren v Keighley* 48 TC 370, a capital gains tax case, it was suggested that the reduction of sale consideration and the concurrent inflation of interest charges on the unpaid balance of such consideration would be a 'sham' designed to 'evade' taxation (note also the comments of the court in this connection in *West London Syndicate v IRC* (1898) 2 QB 507, a stamp duty case).

In a capital gains tax case, *Booth v Buckwell* [1980] STC 598, the court held that the parties to a composite bargain, but not necessarily the Inland Revenue, were automatically bound by their allocation. There seems, however, to be no justification for imposing a form of estoppel on the taxpayer, preventing him from invoking the correct legal analysis of his transaction, at least where there is no dishonesty on his part. This analysis is supported by the approach of the court in *Reade v Brearley* (see **1.408**). The court's comments in the *Booth* case may be explicable on the basis that the capital gains tax code allows any 'necessary' apportionment to be made (see TCA 1997, s 544(5)).

This reluctance of the court to overrule the terms of a genuine bargain cuts both ways. *IRC v Fleming & Co* 35 TC 57 provides an illustration of an apportionment which, despite looking distinctively odd from a commercial perspective, was upheld by the court. This was to the considerable disadvantage of the taxpayer, who had argued that tax should be levied on the basis of the commercial substance of the arrangements under consideration (for an example in the Irish context of the doctrine of 'form over substance' working against the taxpayer, see *McCall v IRC* I ITR 28; note also *Lamport & Holt Line v Langwell* 38 TC 193).

In particular cases, statute may expressly give the Revenue authority to rewrite an apportionment of consideration agreed by the parties to a composite transaction (see, eg the treatment of the sale of assets which have qualified for capital allowances, discussed at **6.106**). Where the parties simply agree a global sum, an apportionment may be made by the tribunal of fact (Appeal Commissioners or Circuit Court judge, as appropriate): see eg *Tilley v Wales* 25 TC 136; *Mairs v Haughey* [1993] STC 569; *MacDaibheid v SD* III ITR 1).

In *Paterson Engineering v Duff* 25 TC 43, the taxpayer made two successive agreements for the rights to use patents and trademarks and to receive details of secret manufacturing processes, drawings and related advice. Under the first agreement, the consideration for these rights was expressed as a royalty of £2,000 per annum. Under the second agreement the consideration was expressed as a royalty of £100 per annum in respect of the patent rights and £1,900 per annum in respect of the remaining rights. The issue arose whether or not the sum of £1,900 was paid 'in respect of the user of a patent' (see **2.309**). MacNaghten J held that some or all of the remaining rights might in fact be merely incidental to the use of a patent. Accordingly, it was an issue of fact (to be decided by the Appeal Commissioners) to what extent the sum of £1,900 should be attributed to the user of the patent. The fact that the taxpayer had labelled only the sum of £100 as relating to the 'user of the patent' could not override the true legal nature of the arrangements. It may be noted that this is not a case where the court held that the allocation of the consideration agreed by the parties should be set aside.

1.408 Extrinsic evidence and shams

In many cases, it will be necessary to establish the legal rights and obligations created by a transaction in order to establish its tax consequences. This process will often involve the interpretation of documents such as contracts, trust deeds and wills. This brief discussion will concentrate on the interpretation of contracts, since these will be the legal documents most commonly encountered by tax practitioners.

It should firstly be borne in mind that evidence of the objective facts and circumstances surrounding a contract ('extrinsic evidence') will generally be admissible in determining its legal effect. In *O'Neill v Ryan* [1992] IR 166, Costello J approved the approach of Lord Wilberforce in *Prenn v Simmonds* [1971] 1 WLR 1381, where the latter observed:

> the time has long passed when agreements … were isolated from the matrix of facts in which they were set … We must … inquire beyond the language and see what the circumstances were with reference to which of the words were used and the object appearing from these circumstances which the person using them had in view.

Thus, Murphy J's analysis of the true legal effect of the arrangements in *O'Coindealbhain v Gannon* (discussed in **1.407**) involved recognition of the general legal background to the arrangements: if the taxpayer's letter had been truly intended as a waiver, then the solicitor clients concerned could not have demanded the fees from their own clients. It would then have been impossible for them to pay anything to the taxpayer's company.

The following passage from a speech of Lord Wilberforce in *Reardon Smith Line Ltd v Hansen-Tingen* [1976] 3 All ER 570 was approved by Griffin J in *Rohan Construction Ltd v Insurance Corp of Ireland* [1988] ILRM 373:

> When one speaks of the intention of the parties to the contract, one is speaking objectively the parties cannot themselves give direct evidence of what their intention was and what must be ascertained is what is to be taken as the intention which reasonable people would have had if placed in the situation of the parties. Similarly, when one is speaking of the aim, or object or commercial purpose, one is speaking objectively of what reasonable persons would have had in mind in the situation of the parties. What the court must do must be to place itself in thought in the same factual matrix as that in which the parties were.

However, under the so-called 'parol evidence' rule, extrinsic evidence may not be invoked to 'add to, vary or contradict' the term of a written instrument (*Jacobs v Batavia & General Plantations Ltd* [1924] Ch 287). There are a number of exceptions to the 'parol evidence' rule, a detailed discussion of which can be found in the leading texts on contract law (see eg Clark, *Contract Law in Ireland* (3rd edn, Round Hall, 2004) pp 105–111).

Some of the more significant exceptions to the rule in the present context are set out below. It should be noted, however, that as a general rule, evidence of preliminary negotiations or of the subjective purposes of the parties are not admissible in any circumstances (see *Prenn v Simmonds*):

(a) Extrinsic evidence may be admitted to show that a document is a 'sham', ie that the professed legal rights and obligations do not correspond with the true legal position. Thus, for example, the transaction reflected in the legal documents may simply not have taken place at all (see *Rahman v Chase Bank (I) Trust Co* [1991] JLR 103 in which a 'trust', where the 'settlor' retained full control over the trust assets, was set aside and note also in *Re Sugar Distributors* V ITR 225). Alternatively, the transaction reflected in the legal documents may be different to that which has actually taken place (see *Reade v Brearley* below). For these purposes, evidence of the conduct of the parties to the transaction subsequent to the execution of the document is admissible. Generally, evidence of subsequent conduct is otherwise excluded unless it demonstrates that the parties had implicitly agreed to vary the terms of their contract.

    The concept of a 'sham' is traditionally associated with a common intention to deceive third parties (as in *Snook v London and West Riding Investments Ltd* [1967] 1 All ER 578). In *R v Charlton & Ors* [1996] STC 1418, an offshore 'invoicing' company was held to be a sham, designed to defraud the Inland Revenue. The court does not however appear to have distinguished in this case clearly between transactions designed solely to avoid tax and transactions which are devoid of reality (note the discussion in [1996] *Taxation 329*); see also *Johnson v Jewitt* 40 TC 231, where artificial transactions designed solely to avoid tax were treated as shams, although this conclusion may be open to question on the facts) and compare *Hitch & Ors v Stone* [1999] STC 431.

    However, it would seem that there may also be 'innocent' shams. In *Revenue Commissioners v Moroney* V ITR 589, an individual had purported to grant a lease to his sons in consideration of a substantial sum of money. On his death, the Revenue claimed the sum still apparently due to him should be included as an asset in his estate. Extrinsic evidence was admitted to show that in fact the parties had never intended that any consideration should pass, and that accordingly there was no asset to be included in the death estate. A further example of an 'innocent' sham may be found in *Reade v Brearley* 17 TC 687, in which the taxpayer acted as the headmaster of a school established by a congregation of secular priests, of which he was a member. The congregation had agreed that none of their members should receive any personal remuneration. Subsequently, new government regulations required that all teachers should be employed under written contracts. As a consequence, an agreement was executed, formally appointing the taxpayer to the headmastership at an annual salary. In the accounts of the school, the salary was charged as an expense, but a corresponding amount was entered as a donation to the congregation; no cash was actually paid to the taxpayer. The court rejected the Revenue's contention that the taxpayer had received a taxable salary and had subsequently applied it for the benefit of his congregation. It was held that the agreement was purely cosmetic and that the 'salary' always belonged to the congregation.

A transaction may simply contain elements of sham, without being a total sham (see eg *IRC v McGuckian* [1994] STC 888). It may be that where one party to a transaction signs a document without caring what it contains, the transaction may still be a sham in the traditional sense if the other party intended to deceive third parties (*Midland Bank v Wyatt*, a UK case, unreported).

(b) Extrinsic evidence may be admitted to show that the document forms a part only of a larger transaction some of the terms of which were not committed to writing. In *IRC v Mallaby-Deeley* 23 TC 153, the taxpayer had undertaken in writing to pay a lump sum by instalments in order to finance the completion of a reference book by a publisher. Subsequently, he entered into a deed of covenant binding himself in effect to pay the unpaid balance of the lump sum over seven years. The deed of covenant incorporated no reference to the lump sum, but the written undertaking was handed over to the taxpayer in exchange for the deed of covenant.

Lord Greene MR commented:

> it … appears to me that the only inference open was that the deed was executed in consideration of a release by the [publisher] of the [taxpayers] obligations …
>
> It is said in the present case that, when you look at the deed you find, upon its face, nothing save a covenant to make annual payments. It contains no reference to a lump sum. It contains no reference to a pre-existing debt, and it must be taken at its own face value … I am unable to take that view. It appears to me that for the application of the principle, which I have stated in quite general language, it is not merely legitimate, but necessary, to examine *what the true legal position was*, and *what the true legal transaction was* of which the execution of the deed … formed part. It is not legitimate to isolate that element in that legal transaction and to pay attention to that alone. It seems to me quite impossible to say that because the parties … the bargain, which is the true consideration for H's covenant to be inferred from their actions and the letter, the previously existing legal relationship and the true nature of the transaction ought to be ignored (emphasis added).

A similar approach was adopted in *Viek Investments v IRC*, noted in **1.407**.

(c) Extrinsic evidence may be admitted to show that separate documents should be construed as a whole in order to ascertain the true contractual arrangements. This approach was implicit in the decision in *Diners Club Ltd v Revenue*

Commissioners discussed in **1.407**. A more sophisticated example of this approach, on this occasion in the context of a complex tax-avoidance scheme, may be found in *CIR v Europa Oil (NZ) Ltd* [1971] AC 760 (see also *Chinn v Collins* [1981] STC 1, where it was held on the facts that a sale agreement expressed to be for an unspecified block of shares in a private company necessarily related to shares held by the taxpayers). Where documents are executed contemporaneously or within a short interval, the nature of the transaction may be such that the documents are treated as representing a single transaction (*Smith v Chadwick* [1882] 20 Ch D 27 and note *Prendergast v Cameron* 23 TC 122).

(d) Extrinsic evidence may be admitted to show that there is consideration for a transaction which is not stated in the relevant document. In *Pritchard v Arundale* 47 TC 680, the taxpayer had agreed to give up his senior partnership in a firm of accountants and to become managing director of a company on the footing that the principal shareholder of the company would transfer shares to him. A clause incorporated into the taxpayer's service agreement expressed the transfer to be 'in consideration of the taxpayer's undertaking to serve the company'. Megarry J took the view that this form of wording was not conclusive on the question as to whether or not the shares were received as a 'reward for services'. The learned Judge noted (amongst other points) that extrinsic evidence was admissible to show that the consideration given by the taxpayer consisted in part of the relinquishment of his partnership interest. The case is discussed more fully at **Division 10**.

(e) Extrinsic evidence may be admitted to identify the true nature of the consideration being provided. In *Vestey v IRC* 40 TC 112, the taxpayer agreed to sell shares for a price of £5.5 million payable over 125 yearly instalments. He argued that the full price should be treated as a capital receipt. Evidence established that the shares had been valued at £2 million and that the annual payments were calculated to reflect an agreed rate of interest on the outstanding balance of this account. The court approved the conclusions of the Appeal Commissioners, who had held that a proportion of the payments should be treated as interest, saying:

> Looking then at the legal effect of the agreement and at the surrounding circumstances we have to determine the true nature of the payments we consider it well settled that the label that parties choose to attach to their payments is not conclusive of their character for the purposes of income tax. Moreover, the unusual terms of the bargain of themselves almost irresistibly lead to the necessity of dissecting the annual payments in order to make plain … the real nature of the consideration.

The 'parol evidence' rule is a creature of the general law. However, the correct application of tax law may well raise issues beyond the correct legal analysis and classification of a particular transaction. In resolving such issues, all extrinsic evidence is potentially admissible, so long as it is relevant to the issue at hand. Thus, in *IRC v Church Commissioners* [1976] STC 339, the taxpayers had sold their interests in properties in exchange for the receipt of rent charges over a fixed term of years. There was no pre-existing legal agreement to sell their interests for a lump sum (the presence of such an agreement would have clearly marked the payments as 'capital' in nature, as in *IRC v Mallaby-Deely*). In seeking to classify the contract for tax purposes, the court looked for indicators both from the terms of the contract but also from evidence of the pre-contract negotiations (compare *Clarke v United Real (Moorgate) Ltd* [1988] STC 273, discussed in Ward, 'Form over Substance' [1994] ITR 1106).

In *IRC v Botnar* [1998] STC 38, tax counsel had drafted a settlement as part of a tax planning exercise. He subsequently drew up a memorandum setting out the intention behind the creation of the settlement for the benefit of the protector of the settlement. In the High Court, Evans-Lombe J refused to admit the memorandum as evidence of the meaning of the provisions of the settlement, since it was not concerned with objective external facts, but rather with indications of the personal intentions of the draftsman. However, the memorandum was properly received by the Special Commissioners as evidence of the taxpayer's actual purpose to use the settlement as part of a series of steps designed to minimise tax by (a finding not at issue before the High Court).

Rectification

Oral evidence may also be cited where a document contains a mistake, so that it does not currently express the original agreement of the parties concerned. In this case, the remedy of rectification may be available so that the legal document is in effect amended to bring it into line with the terms of the original agreement.

The remedy is an equitable one, so that the court may exercise its discretion in deciding whether or not to grant rectification (see Delany, *Equity and the Law of Trusts in Ireland* (3rd edn, Round Hall, 2003) ch 15). Where the courts decline to grant the remedy, then the agreement as established in the document will remain legally effective. It seems that the courts will not deny the remedy merely because the document was designed to avoid tax in a legal manner (see *Lake v Lake* [1989] STC 865).

In *Nolan v Nolan* [1958] 92 ILTR 94, a couple entered into a deed of separation, having previously agreed that the wife should receive a fixed weekly sum free of tax. The wording of the deed was subsequently amended, so that the wife was stated to be entitled to receive the weekly sum 'after the deduction of tax at the standard rate'. It was accepted that the effect of the deed might be to debar the husband from claiming the benefit of any tax refunds obtained by the wife in respect of the weekly sums (see **15.404**). It was held that since the wife knew that the expression of the original agreement was incorrect, she could not deny that there was a mutual mistake (see also *Lucey v Laurel Construction Co Ltd* 18 December 1970, HC).

In *Racal Group Services Ltd v Ashmore* [1995] STC 1151, a deed of covenant was drafted with the result that it was not operative for a sufficient period of time to be tax effective. The court held that it was not sufficient for the parties to establish merely that they had both intended that the covenant should be tax effective; rather they had to show that it had been intended that the covenant should have been operative for a particular period of time (which would then have entitled the parties to claim the appropriate tax benefits).

Rectification may only be granted where there is an 'issue' between the parties. The Court of Appeal in the *Racal* case accepted that the question of whether or not tax should be deducted at source under a deed of covenant could be regarded as such an issue, even though both payer and payee sought rectification. It may be noted that there is generally a 'heavy burden' of proof on the party(ies) seeking rectification (see *Irish Life Assurance Co Ltd v Dublin Land Securities Ltd* [1989] IR 253). The court in *Racal* (see above) held that this burden of proof had not in fact been discharged on the facts of that case.

The question of whether rectification has retrospective effect for tax purposes is open to doubt. In *Morley-Clarke v Jones* [1985] STC 660 (discussed at **15.404**), it was held that the retrospective variation of a court order did not alter the tax treatment of payments made prior to the variation. This was because the tax treatment reflected correctly the legal position at the time when the payment were made (note also *Dodsworth v Dale* 20 TC 283, where, in a case where a marriage was annulled *ab initio*, it was held that there was no justification for re-opening earlier years of assessment in which the taxpayer had been assessed as a married man). It may be argued however that rectification is a process whereby the true legal agreement between the parties is restored retrospectively and that the tax treatment should also be brought back into line with the 'true' position. Interestingly, *Morley-Clarke v Jones* was distinguished from *Spence v IRC* 24 TC 311 in *Hilldown Holdings v IRC* [1999] STC 561. In the *Spence* case, a sale of shares were set aside on grounds of fraudulent misrepresentation, and the defendant was ordered to account for the dividends he had received as a result of the sale transaction; the court there held that the plaintiff was liable to tax on the dividends in question since the court order was regarded as recognising and declaring what had in fact been the true legal position *ab initio*. It is thought that the Revenue Commissioners may well be sympathetic to such an approach.

1.409 Constitutional issues

Article 15.4.1° of the Constitution states that 'the Oireachtas shall not enact any law which is in any respect repugnant to this Constitution or any provision thereof'. Article 15.4.2° proceeds to provide that 'every law enacted by the Oireachtas which is in any respect repugnant to this Constitution or to any provision thereof, shall, but to the extent only of such repugnancy, be invalid'.

In the case of statutes enacted after the present constitution came into force in 1937, there is a presumption of constitutionality. This presumption is a strong one, probably to be displaced only by clear words which are unable to bear a constitutional construction. Thus, it appears that broadly speaking a version of the 'golden rule' can be invoked in order to preserve the constitutionality of a statute (for a recent example of the presumption being applied see *Purcell v Attorney General* IV ITR 229). There is also a presumption that any powers or discretions under post-1937 statutes are to be exercised only in a manner which is compatible with the Constitution (*East Donegal Co-Op v Attorney General* [1970] IR 317). For the position on pre-1937 statutes, see Hogan and Whyte, *JM Kelly: The Irish Constitution* (4th edn, Bloomsbury Professional, 2003) p 2143 *et seq*.

The presumption of constitutionality seems to be particularly weighty in the case of tax statutes, as explained by O'Hanlon J in the High Court in *Madigan v Attorney General* III ITR 127, where he observed:

> … it has been recognised both in our jurisdiction and in the United States, where the constitutional guarantees are closely analogous to those provided by the Irish Constitution, that tax laws are in a category of their own, and that very considerable latitude must be allowed to the legislature in the enormously complex task of organising and directing the financial affairs of the State.

The Supreme Court was at pains in *Madigan* to emphasise that it lies beyond its competence to consider the wisdom or effectiveness of fiscal policy choices made by the Government (see also in this regard *MhicMhathuna v Ireland* [1995] ILRM 69, where the court held it was not competent to determine what would be an acceptable level of state support for families, but note also the discussion of this decision by Professor Dermot Walsh at [1994] IJOT 29).

Nevertheless, the presumption of constitutionality has been rebutted in a number of cases covering tax cases. In *Murphy & Murphy v Attorney General* V ITR 613, the prevailing system of taxing married couples was held to be repugnant to Art 41, under which the State pledged to afford special protection to the constitution of marriage. The constitutional defects were rectified by FA 1980, s 8, with effect from 1980–81 onwards. A similar outcome occurred in *Hyland v Minister for Social Welfare* [1990] ILRM 69, in the context of certain social welfare provisions which favoured cohabiting couples over married couples (contrast *MhicMhathuna v Ireland* [1995] ILRM 69, where provisions of income tax law and social welfare law which favoured single parents were upheld; this distinction can be justified on the basis that the economic circumstances of a single parent are likely to be more disadvantageous than those of a couple).

In *Brennan v Attorney General* IV ITR 229 the rating system for agricultural land was held to be repugnant to Art 40.3.2°, under which the State is pledged to protect the property rights of its citizens from unjust attack. The rating system was based on a set of land values which was long out of date and which lacked any internal consistency. O'Higgins CJ commented as follows:

> In the assessment of a tax such as a county rate reasonable uniformity of valuation appears essential to justice. If such reasonable uniformity is lacking the inevitable result will be that some ratepayer is required to pay more than his fair share ought to be. This necessarily involves an attack upon his property rights which by definition becomes unjust. The plaintiffs have established such injustice in this particular case.

In *Daly v Revenue Commissions & Ors* V ITR 213, it was held that FA 1990, s 26(1) was repugnant to Art 40.3.2°. The effect of FA 1990, s 26(1) was that tax withheld from professional fees under FA 1987, Pt III in one tax year was credited against the tax liability on the fees of the following tax year (see **2.506**). The purpose of the enactment was to prevent taxpayers obtaining a full refund of one year's tax on the switch from the prior year basis to the current year basis. However, the effect was to impose a form of double taxation since the taxpayer had to pay income tax in the normal way, and also suffer the withholding tax, on the same income in the same year of assessment. The credit for withholding tax suffered in the preceding year of assessment was insufficient compensation where profits were increasing.

Costello J observed:

> … legislative interference in property rights is commonplace and no constitutional impropriety is involved unless the claimant can show that these rights have been subject to 'an unjust attack'. He can do this by showing that the law infringing his rights has failed to pass a proportionality test, a concept formulated *in Heaney v Ireland* [1994] 2 ILRM 420) as follows:
>
> The objective of the infringed provision must be of sufficient importance to warrant over-riding a constitutionally protected right. It must relate to concerns pressing and substantial in a free and democratic society. This means chosen must pass a proportionality test. They must:
>
> (a) be rationally connected to the objective and not be arbitrary, unfair or based on irrational considerations;
>
> (b) impair the right as little as possible; and
>
> (c) be such that their effects on rights are proportional to the objective (see *Chaulk v R* [1990] 3 SCR 13.3 1335–1336).
>
> … The object of [FA 1990, s 26] was to deny a windfall gain to established taxpayers arising from the change in the basis of assessment from the preceding year basis to a current year

> basis. If the means chosen to achieve that end fail to pass a test of proportionality then the Court must conclude that the infringement with the applicant's constitutionality protected rights is impermissible. In applying the test the court must take into account the context in which the amendment was made in the light of the other provisions of the regime.

In the event, the learned judge held that FA 1990, s 26 failed the proportionality test on two counts. Firstly, it was manifestly unfair and created undue hardship. Secondly, the section was designed to deal with a transitional situation but in doing so imposed a permanently unfair method of collecting tax; furthermore, this method was imposed on new taxpayers who were unaffected by the changeover to the current year basis.

Thus, while the courts will not interfere with the fiscal policy decisions of the Oireachtas, they will, it seems, be prepared to examine the actual tax measures adopted and see whether *inter alia*:

(i) they are unjust or arbitrary; or

(ii) if they are out of proportion to the objectives which they are designed to achieve.

It remains to be seen whether test (ii), which could be a potent weapon for taxpayers, will be applied in practice to substantive as well as to procedural measures (see the discussion by Professor Dermot Walsh in [1995] IJOT 41).

The striking successes just described are counterbalanced by a number of failures on the part of taxpayers. In *Madigan & Madigan v Attorney General* III ITR 127, the Supreme Court rejected a challenge to the constitutionality of aspects of the residential property tax (see **Division 3**). The court approved the following observations of O'Hanlon J at first instance:

> ... I do not find it offensive to principles of justice or fair play that a tax should be imposed on occupiers of residential premises or that it should be measured by reference to the market value of such premises rather than by reference to poor law valuation or that exemption from the tax should be given to occupiers of premises whose market value falls below a certain figure.

It is undoubtedly the case that a number of anti-avoidance provisions which transfer the liability to pay tax on income to a person other than the person who received the income in question, without any right of recovery on the part of the latter, may be open to constitutional challenge (see eg FA 1974, s 57 discussed at **Division 17**). For a wide-ranging discussion of the possible constitutional infirmities of the tax code see Kenny, Constitutionality, Proportionality and Certainty [1996] ITR 8.

In was held by the High Court in *Browne & Ors v Attorney General, Minister for Finance & the Revenue Commissioners* IV ITR 323 that what is now TCA 1997, s 121, charging a benefit-in-kind on cars under Sch E, was constitutional. The plaintiffs, who were employed as travelling sales representatives argued that TCA 1997, s 121:

(a) effectively taxed what was a tool of the sales representative's trade, ie his car, and accordingly it infringed his right to earn a livelihood, such a right being one of the unspecified personal rights contained in Art 40.3 of the Constitution;

(b) that the tax, being ill-targeted, and arbitrary, was an attack on the plaintiff's property rights which were protected by Art 40.3.2º of the Constitution;

(c) that because the tax operated more unfairly in the case of sales representatives, they were not being held equal before the law, as was their right under Art 40.1 of the Constitution; and

(d) that the availability of a motor car had been thrust upon them.

Murphy J dealt with each of the arguments in turn. He stated that it is not the business activity of the plaintiffs that is taxed; it is not the car that is taxed; it is not the business use that is taxed, it is not even the private use that is taxed. TCA 1997, s 121 instead taxes the availability for private use of an employer's motor car. In response to argument (c) he stated, citing *Brennan v Attorney General* [1984] ILRM 355 that Art 40.1 which deals with the rights of citizens to be held equal before the law:

> … Deals only with the citizen as a human person, and requires for each citizen as a human person, equality before the law.

Murphy J dealt with argument (d) by stating that the plaintiffs were not obliged to accept the availability for private use of the car; they could opt to provide their own car and claim appropriate allowances; or they could avail of TCA 1997, s 121(7), which provides that cars forming part of a 'car pool' (ie available to several employees as and when required) are not subject to the benefit in kind legislation (see **10.210**).

In a line of cases, the taxpayer has failed to establish that a tax measure breaches Art 34(1), of the Constitution, which reserves the power to administer justice to the courts alone. In *State (Calcul International & Solatrex International) v Appeal Commissioners* III ITR 577, Barron J held that the powers of the Appeal Commissioners did not amount to the administration of justice, saying:

> … their essential function is to decide whether the assessment raised by the tax inspector should be reduced or increased. They do not have power to enforce their decision nor to impose liabilities. Essentially, their decisions are enforced by the institution of legal proceedings to recover the amount of tax determined by them as being payable. Equally in those cases where penalties may become payable proceedings must be instituted before they can be recovered. Nor do the Appeal Commissioners determine the amount of or impose such penalties. It is the statute which does so.
>
> The essence of a tax assessment is the determination of the amount of tax to be paid by the taxpayer. It is the particular proportion of this taxable income which is required by the tax code to be paid by way of tax. Undoubtedly, questions of fact and law require to be decided to determine taxable income. I am sure that a spectator to a hearing before the Appeal Commissioners will see no material difference between the conduct of the hearing and the conduct of many hearings in the courts. In each case, there will be an adversarial procedure with each side seeking to establish the law and the facts to suit its own case.
>
> This however is not the test. This lies in the orders which the Appeal Commissioners are empowered to make. Such orders obviously impose liabilities upon the taxpayer concerned, but they do not deprive him of anything nor impose penalties nor limit his freedom of action. They declare his liability for tax upon the basis of the facts as found by them. Having declared this liability, they have no power to enforce their decision.

The concept that the role of the Appeal Commissioners is merely to declare a tax liability rather than to adjudicate on a justiciable dispute is also found in other jurisdictions and may be difficult to dislodge (see the criticism of this concept in David Gwynn Morgan, *The Separation of Powers in the Irish Constitution* (Round Hall, 1997), and note the comments below). It may be noted however that in *Navan Carpets Ltd v O'Culacháin* III ITR 403, the Supreme Court, in a different context, treated an appeal heard by the Appeal Commissioners as effectively relating to a dispute inter partes.

Barron J also held in the Calcul International case that, even if his conclusion was erroneous the powers of the Appeal Commissioners fell within Art 37 of the Constitution which permits 'the exercise of limited functions and powers of a judicial nature in matters other than criminal matters by anybody of persons authorised by law to exercise such functions and powers …'. The learned judge observed:

> … the decision of the Appeal Commissioners undoubtedly affects the fortune of the taxpayer concerned. Any taxpayer appearing before the Appeal Commissioners either seeks to establish that he has no tax liability or a tax liability less than that for which the tax inspector contends. In reality, the decision has no effect on the fortune of the taxpayer since the Appeal Commissioners do no more than decide the amount for which the taxpayer was always liable. Their decision may well affect the particular taxpayer adversely since he may be found liable to pay a sum for which he believes he was not liable. But this does not have far-reaching effects. The payment of customs duty or value added tax is related proportionately to the value of the goods concerned, whereas the payment of income tax and corporation tax is related proportionately to the relevant taxable income. Such payment cannot have far-reaching effects on the fortune of the taxpayer as contemplated by the authorities since in each case the liability is relative, being proportionate either to his income or to this turnover as the case may be.

The notion that the Appeal Commissioners merely declare a liability that was somehow 'always there' is clearly unreal. Firstly, the extent of any liability will depend on the findings of fact by the commissioners; it is the position, however, that there is often a range of alternative findings open to the commissioners, none of which will normally be overturned by the courts, so long as the commissioners are not regarded as acting unreasonably (see **2.204**). Further, the commissioners may be required to resolve issues of statutory interpretation, a process which most certainly does not consist of arriving scientifically at a species of objective truth. It may also be objected that an argument that income tax is proportionate to the taxpayer's income (and therefore does not have far reaching effects on him) is inherently flawed; this is because income tax is levied proportionately to taxable income, which may be quite different to a taxpayer's income in say the accounting sense or to his cash flows, To take a simple example, the denial of a capital allowances claim could turn a project with a positive return into a loss-making project, with potentially far reaching economic repercussions.

In *Kennedy v Hearne* III ITR 590, it was held that the Revenue Commissioners' power to raise and enforce estimated assessments of an employer's PAYE liability under FA 1968, s 7 was constitutional. The Supreme Court held that the determination of the collector that tax remained unpaid did not impose a liability on the taxpayer or affect any of his rights. If (as was the case) the collector's determination was incorrect, any proceedings which ensued would be a nullity. Furthermore, FA 1968, s 7 (now TCA 1997, s 989(1)) did not in any way oust the jurisdiction of the courts, which could set aside any invalid proceedings and compensate the taxpayer for any loss suffered (see also *Deighan v Hearne* III ITR 533 and the discussion of judicial review at **2.206**).

In *Orange v Revenue Commissioners* V ITR 70, Geoghegan J held that the provisions of what is now TCA 1997, s 1002 (notice of attachment proceedings) did not involve the administration of justice, since they concerned the collection of a liability which had already been admitted. He also took the view that while the provisions themselves were constitutional, it was conceivable that in certain circumstances it was conceivable that service of a notice under the provisions might constitute an unjust attack on property rights.

The above analysis is open to criticism on two grounds. Firstly, it again incorporates the notion that the Appeal Commissioners merely declare a pre-existing liability that was 'always there'. This notion is unreal, since the 'facts' on which the liability will be founded will depend on the exercise of judgement by the Appeal Commissioners, which so long as it is not exercised wholly unreasonably, cannot generally be challenged (see **2.204**). Furthermore, the Appeal Commissioners will often decide on issues of interpretation where the question of liability must wait on the resolution of those issues.

In *Kennedy v Hearne* III ITR 590, it was held that the Revenue Commissioners' power to raise and enforce estimated assessments of an employer's PAYE liability under what is now TCA 1997, s 989 was constitutional. The Supreme Court held that the determination of the collector that tax remained unpaid did not impose a liability on the taxpayer or affect any of his rights. If (as was the case) the collector's determination was incorrect, any proceedings which ensued would be a nullity. Furthermore, TCA 1997, s 989 did not in any way oust the jurisdiction of the courts, which could set aside any invalid proceedings and compensate the taxpayer for any loss suffered (see also *Deighan v Hearne* III ITR 533 and the discussion of Judicial Review at **2.206**). In *Orange v Revenue Commissioners* V ITR 70, the attachment proceedings under what is now TCA 1997, s 1002 were held not to involve the administration of justice; this followed because the sum to be attached consisted of an admitted liability.

The constitutionality of delegated legislation (usually in the context of tax law, in the form of regulations made by the Revenue Commissioners) also raises some significant issues. Article 15.2 of the constitution reserves the power to make laws to the Oireachtas alone. In *Cityview Press v AnCo* [1980] IR 381, it was held that in order to conform with Art 15.2, delegated legislation must do not any more than give effect to principles and policies which are contained in the statute itself.

In *McDaid v Sheehy* IV ITR 162, the Imposition of Duties Act 1957, s 1, which purported to empower the government to 'impose vary or terminate any excise, customs or stamp duty by order, was held at first instance to contravene Art 15.2. When the case came to the Supreme Court, it was held (McCarthy J dissenting) that the issue of constitutionality should only be considered if the case could not firstly be determined on other grounds. The court in fact held that the particular order being challenged had been incorporated into statute law by FA 1976, s 46 and that the taxpayer in question was not affected by the operation of the order prior to that enactment.

In recent years, the courts have increasingly leaned towards the so-called 'harmonious' approach in construing the provisions of the Constitution. This approach is akin to the 'teleological schematic' approach adopted by the ECJ in the context of EU legislation. For a fuller discussion of the principles of constitutional interpretation, see Byrne and McCutcheon, *The Irish Legal System* (5th edn, Bloomsbury Professional, 2009) ch 15; Hogan and Whyte, *JM Kelly: The Irish Constitution* (4th edn, Bloomsbury Professional, 2003).

1.410 The European context

The impact of European law is keenly felt in the tax domain. The original Art 29.4.3 of the Constitution paved the way for the European Communities Act 1972 and subsequently for the Single European Act in 1987 and the Maastricht Treaty in 1992 (see now Arts 24.3–24.6).

The interpretation of EU legislation is based on somewhat different principles to those normally adopted by Irish courts in the context of purely domestic law. The ECJ will normally look firstly at the literal meaning of the relevant provision, bearing in mind that where the provision is authentic in several languages, the meaning which is common to the different language versions will be taken as the literal meaning: see *Wendelbar v LJ Music* [1985] ECR 457).

However, the court will normally only uphold a literal interpretation (however clear and unambiguous this might be) where it is consistent with a schematic or teleological approach to the interpretation of the provision in question. A schematic approach looks at the legislative plan or system of which a particular treaty article, directive, etc forms a part, avoiding, where possible, any interpretation which would lead to disharmony or inconsistencies in the legislative framework.

The teleological approach (which may often overlap with the schematic approach) is based on consideration of the purpose and object of the legislation. In this context, it should be noted that Art 253 of the EC Treaty requires that EU regulations, directives and decisions 'shall state the reasons on which they are based and shall refer to any proposals or opinions which were required to be obtained pursuant to this treaty'. Again, the teleological approach may lead to the rejection of a literal wording of a provision in favour of an alternative interpretation which is consistent with the underlying objectives of that provision (see eg *Franz Grad v Finanzamt Traunstein* [1970] ECR 825). It is suggested that this approach goes much further than would be permitted under the 'golden rule' and is more akin to the 'equitable' method of interpretation which has been the subject of particular judicial disapproval in the tax context (see above), (note the comments to this effect of Keane J in *Revenue Commissioners v Young* [1996] ITR 61 (a capital acquisitions tax case)).

In *Buchanan & Co v Babco Ltd* [1977] QB 208, Lord Denning said of European judges:

> They adopt a method which they call in English by strange words – at any rate they were strange to me – the schematic and teleological method of interpretation. It is not really so alarming as it sounds. All it means is that the judges do not go by the literal meaning of the words or by the grammatical structure of the sentence. They go by the design or purpose which lies behind it. When they come upon a situation which is to their minds within the spirit – but not the letter – of the legislation. They solve the problem by looking at the design and purpose of the legislature – at the effect which it was sought to achieve. They then interpret the legislation so as to produce the desired effect. This means that they fill in gaps, quite unashamedly, without hesitation. They ask simply: what is the sensible way of dealing with this situation so as to give effect to the presumed purpose of the legislation?

However, when the *Buchanan* case went on appeal to the House of Lords, the Law Lords rejected the use of the schematic and teleological approaches to interpretation in the context of UK domestic law.

Nevertheless the Irish courts have on occasions tended to conflate the relatively conservative 'golden rule' with the more expansive 'teleological/schematic' approach, treating them as indistinguishable. As already noted, the decisions in *Kellystown v Hogan* and *Nestor v Murphy* like that in *Luke v IRC* (see **1.405**) seem to reflect the restrictions inherent in the 'golden rule' under which a departure from an ordinary meaning is allowable only in order to avoid an absurdity and only where the words are capable of bearing an alternative construction. These limitations do not apply in the case of full-blooded 'teleological/schematic approach'.

The ECJ also recognises a number of general legal principles, such as the presumption against retrospective effect (see eg *Kloppenburg v Finanzamt Leer* [1984] ECR 10750) and the need for legal certainty, ie clarity and predictability. In *Stichting 'Goed Wonen' v Staatssecretaris van Financien* (Case C–376/02), a VAT case, the European Court of Justice pronounced on the use of press releases to flag up forthcoming changes in the law the effect of which be backdated to the date of the release. The court stated:

> The principles of the protection of legitimate expectations and legal certainty did not preclude a Member State, on an exceptional basis and in order to avoid the large-scale use, during the legislative process, of contrived financial arrangements intended to minimise the burden of value added tax that an amending law was specifically designed to combat, from giving that law retroactive effect when, in circumstances such as those in the instant case,

> economic operators carrying out economic transactions such as those referred to by the law were warned of the impending adoption of that law and of the retroactive effect envisaged in a way that enabled them to understand the consequences of the legislative amendment planned for the transactions they carried out.

The doctrine of proportionality, whereby the interpretation which least restricts the rights of individuals is preferred, has assumed considerable importance (see eg the *Bachmann* case discussed below). The thinking behind the doctrine has also become influential in the context of Irish constitutional law (see the discussion at **1.409**). The doctrine of 'legitimate expectation', which has again influenced the development of Irish law in the field of judicial review (see **2.206**), is also significant: see *Carbery Milk Products v Minister for Agriculture* IV ITR 492. The court also generally favours a strict construction of exceptions and exemptions, placing priority on the preservation of original principles and rights (see *Stichting Utivoering Financiel Acties v Staatsecretaris Van Financien* [1991] 2 CMLR 429.

Article 234 of the EC treaty provides that where a domestic court or tribunal is required to interpret EU law (usually a treaty provision or a directive), that court may request the ECJ to give a ruling thereon, if it considers that it is necessary to do so. There is generally an obligation on a court to obtain such a ruling where there is no right of appeal against the decision of the court under domestic law (as, for example, in the case of Supreme Court decisions). A referral to the ECJ may only be made while a case is still being heard by the appropriate Irish court or tribunal, and not after the decision has been delivered (*McNamara v An Bord Pleanála* [1996] IEHC 60). There is however no such obligation to refer to an issue to the ECJ in cases of an '*acte clair*' (ie where the interpretation of community law is obvious or where that particular issue has already been determined by the ECJ). Furthermore, no reference is required where a decision on EU law is not necessary in order to decide the case (see eg *Doyle v An Taoiseach* [1986] ILRM 693).

In strictness, the ECJ will rule only on issues of interpretation, although the facts of a particular case may in practice be crucial (see for example the discussion of *Werner* below). Under Art 177, the ECJ does not make any declaration as to the compatibility of specific national statutes with EU law. However, it will normally provide the national court with all relevant guidance as to the interpretation of EU law, with a view to enabling the national court to evaluate the compatibility of the relevant domestic statutes (including the provisions of double tax treaties, which themselves form part of domestic law) with the EU treaty provisions, etc. In practice, the ruling of ECJ will often make the ultimate finding of the national court inevitable.

Where an Irish court interprets EU law (ie in order to ascertain whether an Irish provision is consistent therewith) it must apply EU interpretative principles in so doing; similar principles apply when interpreting domestic legislation specifically designed to implement EU directives, regulations, etc (see for example, *Lawlor v Minister for Agriculture* [1990] 1 IR 356 and the UK decision in *Lister v Forth Dry Dock* [1989] 1 All ER 1134).

Where an Irish statute is not enacted in order to implement a directive, the Irish courts are nevertheless obliged to interpret it, where possible, in a manner which is consistent with the obligations imposed on the State by virtue of the EC treaty and/or EU directives (see *Marleasing SA v La Commercial Internacional de Alimentacion SA* [1990] ECR 1–4135) and note also *ICI v Colmer* [1999] STC 1089.

In *Murphy v Bord Telecom Éireann* [1989] ILRM 53, Keane J was faced with statutory provisions which, although not specifically designed to implement EU legislation, were in conflict with what was then Art 119 of the EC treaty (which has 'direct effect': see below). The learned judge observed:

> The [Irish] Act is presumed to be constitutional until the contrary is shown and it is a necessary corollary of that presumption that the Oireachtas is presumed not to legislate in a manner which is in breach of rights protected under community law. Those rights already existed in our domestic law by virtue of s 2 of the European Communities Act 1972 when the Act was passed by the Oireachtas. In the present case, in the light of the ruling of the Court of Justice of the EC, this court should seek *if possible* to adopt a teleological construction of the relevant sections of the Act … [that is] one which looks to the effect of the legislation rather than the actual words used by the legislature (emphasis added).

In the event, Keane J inserted additional words by reference to the clear objectives of Art 119 of the EC treaty. The principle in *Marleasing* was also invoked in *Byrne v Conroy* [1995] HC, where it was held that an ambiguity should be resolved in favour of the construction which was consistent with the EC treaty.

Where it is not possible to interpret domestic legislation so that it conforms with EU law, taxpayers may be able to rely on the doctrine of 'vertical direct effect' in order to assert their rights under EU law against the state. In *Van Gend en Loos v Nederlandse Belasting Administratie* [1963] ECR 1, the European Court of Justice held that the provisions of the EC treaty were capable of having a 'vertical direct effect', ie they could be enforced by taxpayers in the national courts of any Member State. In the *Van Gend en Loos* case, the ECJ held that Art 12 of the EC treaty (which prohibited the introduction of new import taxes) could be raised by an individual taxpayer in the Dutch courts against the Dutch government.

It is also the case that certain provisions of the treaty may also have horizontal direct effect (discussion of which is outside the scope of this text). The doctrine of vertical 'direct effect' may also apply to the provisions of EU directives whose implementation date has already passed (see for example *McDermott & Cotter v Minister for Social Welfare (No 1)* [1987] ILRM 234).

In order for a directive or treaty provision to possess 'direct effect' it must be:

(a) clear and precise;
(b) unconditional; and
(c) of a nature such that no further action is required by the community institutions or Member States, nor must be there any substantial latitude or discretion granted to the Member States in implementing it.

These criteria have been applied somewhat flexibly in practice by the ECJ. Where a provision has 'direct effect', it overrides any domestic legislation which is incompatible with that provision (see *Administrazione delle Finanze dello Stato v Simmenthal* [1978] ECR 629). This principle extends to overruling previous decisions of superior courts which are no longer compatible with EU law.

In *Pubblico Ministero v Ratti* [1971] ECR 1629, the ECJ held that a Member State which has not implemented (or has not fully or adequately implemented) a directive cannot rely against individuals on its failure to perform the obligations which the directive requires. In effect, a form of estoppel operates against the defaulting Member States (see also *Marshall v Southampton & SW Hampshire AHAT* [1986] 2 All ER 584). Thus, only the taxpayer and not the Revenue Commissioners can rely on the doctrine of direct effect in these circumstances.

An individual who relies on direct effect might also seek to persuade the Commission to instigate Art 226 proceedings against a Member State which has failed to implement a directive adequately (or at all) in domestic law (see for example the *Bachmann* case discussed below where both the taxpayer and the Commission had brought proceedings). The Commission may also bring proceedings under Art 226 where a state has failed to repeal provisions which are incompatible with EU law (see *EC Commission v Luxembourg* [1995] STC 1047).

EU law does not oblige the Members States to harmonise their direct taxation systems. However, Art 10 provides that the Member States shall, acting unanimously, issue directives 'for the approximation of such laws, regulations or administrative provisions … as directly affect the establishment or functioning of the common market'.

The only substantive direct tax directives issued to date have been concerned with the tax treatment of dividends paid by a subsidiary resident in one Member State to a parent company resident in another Member State (Council Directive 90/435 EEC) the tax treatment of international mergers (Council Directive 90/434/EEC), the tax treatment of interest and royalty payments between associated companies resident in different Member States (Council Directive 2003/49/EC) and the European Savings Directive (see **2.604**). However, the fact that it is left to each Member State generally to decide upon its own income tax rules does not entitle a Member State to adopt measures which are inconsistent with EU law (*EC Commission v United Kingdom* [1991] ECR 1–4585).

The following Articles have direct effect and therefore may impinge on domestic tax provisions:

Article 39:	guaranteeing freedom of movement of workers within the EU. Art 48(2), in particular prohibits discrimination based on nationality between workers of Member States as regards, inter alia their remuneration.
Article 43:	guaranteeing freedom of establishment within the EU.
Article 49:	guaranteeing freedom of provision of services within the EU.
Article 73b:	guaranteeing freedom of capital movements within the EU.
Article 6:	of the EEC treaty prohibits discrimination on the grounds of nationality. This principle is upheld by Art 39 and Art 43 in the context of freedom of movement of workers and freedom of establishment. Thus, if a domestic law is compatible with Arts 39 or 43, it will also be compatible with Art 6 (see eg *Werner v Finanzamt Aachen-Innenstadt* [1996] STC 961).
Articles 39:	and 43 are based on the same principles both as regards discrimination against individuals on the grounds of nationality and the right to pursue economic activities in other Member States (see *Asscher* discussed below). Article 220 which (*inter alia*) directs Member States to enter into negotiations so far is necessary in order to abolish double taxation does not have direct effect (*Gilly v Directeur des Services Fiscaux du Bas-Rhin* [1998] STC 1014).

In *Biehl v Luxembourg* [1991] STC 575 a Luxembourg statute provided that overpayments of the equivalent of PAYE tax were not refundable to individuals who were not resident in Luxembourg for the whole of the relevant tax year. The ECJ held that this provision was unable to work particularly against nationals of other EU states, and was thus a form of covert discrimination against non-nationals. Luxembourg attempted to justify the provision under challenge or by reference to the need for what is now termed 'fiscal coherence' (often mistranslated as 'fiscal cohesion'). This was on the basis that a taxpayer who was resident in another EU state in the same tax year could spread his liability between that other state and Luxembourg and thus escape the higher rates of tax in Luxembourg. This argument was rejected on the grounds that the provision would result in unequal treatment of a non-resident taxpayer who in fact received little or no income in the other Member State (ie so that all or virtually all of his income arose in Luxembourg).

The court also rejected an argument that discrimination did not arise in practice since non-residents had a non-contentious right of appeal against the bar against refunds of overpaid PAYE. The ECJ held that an administrative procedure of this kind was insufficient, since it did not bind the Luxembourg authorities to remedy the potentially discriminatory consequences of the provision under challenge in all cases (see also to similar effect, *Finanzamt v Schumacker* [1995] STC 306).

In *Bachmann v Belgium* [1994] STC 855, the taxpayer was a German national who worked in Belgium. Under Belgian tax law, he was not entitled to deduct contributions in computing his taxable income towards sickness, invalidity and life insurance made with (broadly speaking) non-Belgian institutions. The ECJ held that the Belgian tax rules in question restricted the free movement of workers and the freedom to provide services, since it was likely that the rule could impact particularly on non-nationals coming to work in Belgium. However, it was held that the rules were justified by the need to ensure the coherence of the Belgian tax system, since the sums ultimately paid out by the insuring institutions would not be taxable in Belgium. Furthermore, the rules passed the text of 'proportionality' (see above) since the tax rules could not have secured the same result by means of less restrictive measures (a proposition which is perhaps open to question).

In *Werner v Finanzamt Aachen Innenstadt* [1996] STC 961, the taxpayer was a German national who resided in the Netherlands but who worked in Germany, where he had also obtained his professional qualifications. The ECJ held that the German fiscal authorities were entitled to deny the taxpayer certain deductions (and the right to the favourable 'income splitting' regime available to resident married couples) by reference to his non-resident status. This was because the only factor which took the case out of a purely internal domestic context was the fact that the taxpayer lived outside the state where he worked.

The court said:

> Article 43 of the EEC treaty does not preclude a Member State from imposing on *its* nationals who carry on their professional activities within its territory and who earn all or almost all of their income there … a heavier tax burden …

The discussion in *Werner* accordingly would have differed if the taxpayer had been a non-German national (or a dual Dutch/German national on which see the judgment of the ECJ in *Gilly v Directeur des Services Fiscaux du Bas-Rhin* [1998] STC 1014; it also seems that if, for example, he had obtained his qualifications outside Germany the outcome might well have differed also.

The *Werner* decision seems to focus on the particularities of the case under review. The general effect of the tax provisions under challenge was clearly to discriminate covertly against non-nationals who worked in Germany (contrast the approach of the court in *R v IRC ex parte Commerzbank* [1993] STC 605; there it was held that a rule which generally denied interest on overpaid tax to non-residents was discriminatory even though the overpayment in the particular circumstances was attributable to an exemption granted only to non-residents). Further, the distinction made in *Werner* between a national of State A who works in State A and who chooses to go to live in State B, as opposed to one who lives in State B and who then decides to work in State A seems rather unreal. It is arguable that the decision in *Werner* might be different now in the light of EU Directive 90/364 (providing a general right of residence in Member States, irrespective of whether or not any economic activity is being pursued).

In *Finanzamt v Schumacker* [1995] STC 306, the taxpayer was a Belgian national who was resident in Belgium but who worked in Germany. He and his wife enjoyed virtually no other income apart from his German earnings. Under Art 15 of the Belgium/Germany Double Tax Agreement, Germany was given sole taxing rights over the taxpayer's earnings. However, the German tax system denied various reliefs to non-residents, in particular, the taxpayer was not entitled to attribute half of his income to his spouse (thus mitigating the impact of the progressive German tax rates). The taxpayer succeeded before the ECJ in a claim that these provisions were contrary to Art 48 of the EU Treaty.

The ECJ firstly confirmed its holding in *Biehl v Luxembourg* [1991] STC 575 that the prohibition against discrimination in respect of workers' remuneration under Art 48(2) extended to discriminatory provisions in domestic tax systems. Secondly, the ECJ held that domestic tax provisions which discriminated against non-residents would in practice mainly disadvantage nationals of other Member States. Accordingly, such provisions represented indirect discrimination on the basis of nationality. Thirdly, the ECJ asserted that discrimination only arose where different rules were applied to comparable situations, or where the same rules were applied to different situations. In general, the situations of residents and non-residents were not comparable, because the income in the state of source generally constituted only a part of a non-resident individual's total income. Correspondingly, the state of residence was generally the place where the individual's total income should be aggregated and his personal circumstances taken into account in determining his ability to pay. However, this general rule did not apply where, as in the present case, a taxpayer received the major part of his taxable income and almost all of his family income in the state of source. In such a case, the situations of non-resident and a resident were comparable, since the non-resident could not obtain tax reliefs for his personal and family circumstances in his state of residence (note also *Zurstrasser v Administration des Contributions Directes* [2001] STC 1102).

In the *Schumacker* case, an argument was raised that the coherence of international tax systems in general required that individuals should only be entitled to full personal allowances, etc in the State where they were resident (and in which their worldwide income was taxable). The ECJ rejected this argument saying:

> That argument cannot be upheld. In a situation such as that in the main proceedings, the State of residence cannot take account of the taxpayer's personal and family circumstances because the tax payable there is insufficient to enable it to do so. Where that is the case, the Community principle of equal treatment requires that, in the State of employment, the personal and family circumstances of a foreign non-resident be taken into account in the same way as those of resident nationals and that the same tax benefits should be granted to him.

It may be seen that the taxpayer's overall (or 'global') position in the two Member States was taken into account by the ECJ in arriving at its conclusion. The *Schumacker* case is technically distinguishable from that of *Werner* (where the facts were strikingly similar) on the basis that (a) the taxpayer in *Schumacker* was a non-German national; and (b) he had exercised his freedom of movement by deciding to work in a State other than the State in which he resided. As noted above, the decision in *Werner* is probably best regarded as an oddity, and is unlikely to be a persuasive precedent. In contrast to the decision in *Biehl*, the court's finding was that the provision in question was not discriminatory per se but only in cases where the taxpayer's income arose wholly or principally in the State of employment. The potential relevance of the *Schumacker* case to the Irish tax treatment of cross-border workers is discussed in **13.610**.

In *Wielockx v Inspecteur der Directe Belastingen* [1995] STC 876, the taxpayer was a national and resident of Belgium who derived all his income from his profession, which he carried on in the Netherlands. Under Dutch tax law, a non-resident (unlike a resident) was not entitled to deduct pension contributions in computing his taxable income. The ECJ held (following *Schumacker*) that a non-resident who received all, or almost all, of his income in the State where he works is in an objectively similar position as a resident of that State who does the same work there. As in the *Bachmann* case, the tax authorities argued that the discrimination involved was justified on the basis of fiscal coherence, since the taxpayer would not be liable to Dutch tax on his future pension entitlements by virtue of the Netherlands/Belgium double tax treaty. The ECJ rejected the Dutch argument and distinguished *Bachmann*. While it accepted that the taxpayer's situation lacked coherence, this arose only because the Netherlands had deliberately waived its rights to levy tax on his pension rights under a double tax treaty. The Netherlands had to accept the loss of tax which followed from this concession and could not rely on it as a justification for discrimination.

In *Asscher v Staatssecretaris Van Financien* [1996] STC 1061, the taxpayer was a Dutch national who carried out duties as a director of two companies, one based in Belgium and the other in the Netherlands. The taxpayer had previously moved residence from the Netherlands to Belgium, although this did not involve any alteration in the pattern of his duties. The Netherlands imposed a higher rate of tax on the taxpayer by reference to his status as a non-resident. The taxpayer's income from his Dutch duties were exempt from tax in Belgium (by virtue of the Belgium-Netherlands Double Tax Treaty) but was taken into account for the purposes of calculating the higher rates of tax there on his Belgium income.

The ECJ held that the taxpayer, by virtue of the fact that he had pursued economic activities in both his State of residence and his State of origin, had exercised the rights and liberties recognised under Art 52 of the treaty. Accordingly, he could rely on the treaty (compare the decision in *Werner*). The ECJ again held that the taxpayer's global tax position must be looked at. Accordingly, the Netherlands could not argue that the higher rate of tax imposed on non-residents compensated for the fact that non-residents escaped the normal progressive rates of Dutch tax (ie because only their Dutch, and not their worldwide income, was liable to Dutch tax). The taxpayer remained liable to progressive taxation in Belgium (taking into account his Dutch income), and his position was therefore comparable to that of a Dutch resident. It followed that the Dutch tax authorities were seeking to apply a different tax rule to a non-resident than to a resident, although both were in comparable situations; accordingly, such a rule was discriminatory.

In *Gilly v Directeur des Services Fiscaux du Bas Rhin* [1998] STC 1014, the taxpayer was a French resident with dual French/German nationality who worked as a teacher in Germany. Her husband who was also French resident worked in France (his earnings represented 45 per cent of the couple's joint income). Under the terms of the France-Germany Double Tax Treaty, residents of one state who worked in the public service of the other state, or who did not the hold the sole nationality of the other state, were liable to tax on their earnings in the latter state. Mrs Gilly was accordingly taxable in Germany (on both counts) as a single person. However, while she was entitled to a credit for the tax which she paid in Germany, this exceeded the amount of tax due on her earnings in France (where she and her husband were taxed jointly). The court distinguished the

Schumacker case on the basis that the total income of Mrs Gilly and her husband was taxed in France and only part of that income was taxed in German. Accordingly, Germany was entitled to tax her less favourably than a married couple who were both resident in Germany and all of whose income was totally liable to German tax.

In *Gschwind v Finananzamt Aachen* 2001 [STC] 331, the taxpayer was resident in the Netherlands but was employed in Germany; his German earnings represented 58 per cent of the total income of himself and his wife. Under German tax law, a non-resident married individual was taxed as a single person unless inter alia 90 per cent of the couple's income was subject to German tax. The ECJ held that the German rules were consistent with European law, since they only operated in circumstances under which the taxpayer had sufficient income to enable his state of residence to grant him allowances based on his personal and family circumstances. This conclusion may perhaps be doubted as being strictly accurate in all cases; however, the decision makes clear that it is not sufficient for a taxpayer merely to show that he is worse off than he would have been if he had been taxed as a resident in the employing jurisdiction. It would appear therefore that where a taxpayer is fully taxable in his Member State of residence, he may legitimately be taxed as a single person in the Member State of employment, since the residence state will be in a position to give him full allowances. In such cases, the taxpayer will generally be entitled to credit for the tax paid in the employing state on his earnings against the amount of his liability on those earnings in the residence state; this will be the position for individuals resident in Ireland. The fact that a taxpayer may incur additional, non-creditable tax in the Member State of employment does not per se appear to be incompatible with European law.

In *Marks & Spencer plc v Halsey* (Case C–446/03), the ECJ held that a discriminatory provision denying group relief for losses incurred by non-resident subsidiaries of a UK resident parent against the profits of its UK-resident subsidiaries could be generally justified on grounds of the public interest, namely:

(a) ensuring the balanced allocation of taxation powers between states, ie the group should not have a free choice as to which jurisdiction in which to obtain tax relief for losses (this is a new concept);

(b) preventing the possibility of obtaining relief in both jurisdictions; and

(c) preventing opportunities for tax arbitrage and tax avoidance, ie group companies in low-tax jurisdictions offsetting their losses against profits made by other group companies in high-tax jurisdictions.

However, a blanket prohibition on group relief for the losses of non-resident subsidiaries was held to be excessive and disproportionate in a situation where the non-resident company had no possibility of obtaining relief for its losses in its state of residence; in these circumstances only, the public interest justifications cited above in effect no longer applied and the blanket prohibition would not be effective. The case shows again that it is the overall position of the taxpayer in the two Member States concerned which must be considered; the decision may perhaps indicate that the ECJ will in future be more receptive to arguments based on the principle of fiscal coherence.

In *Egon Schempp v Finanzamt Munchen v European Court of Justice* (Case C–403/3), a German resident, individual was making maintenance payments to his ex-wife, who was resident in Austria. If she had been resident in Germany, he would have been entitled to a tax deduction for the payments. However, under German tax law a German resident can only claim a deduction for maintenance payments made to a non-resident if the payments are taxed in the recipient's state of residence. Maintenance payments are disregarded for all tax purposes in Austria so that the individual's ex-spouse was not in fact taxed there on the payments. The ECJ held that this treatment was not discriminatory under Art 12, since the basis for the disallowance was that the receipt of the payments was no longer taxable, ie there was a lack of tax symmetry within the EU taken as a whole. They also held that the treatment did not breach the right of free movement of the taxpayer under Art 18 since it was his ex-spouse and not he who had moved. This seems a trifle disingenuous since at the end of the day a tax disadvantage was imposed as a direct result of an individual relocating within the EU.

In *'D'* (Case C–376/03). In this case, a German resident was subject to Dutch wealth tax on his assets located in the Netherlands. If he had been a Belgian resident, he could have claimed the benefit of the Netherlands/Belgium tax treaty and had the benefit of a tax free allowance. The ECJ held that the Netherlands was not obliged to extend the benefits of a treaty with one Member State to the residents of a different Member State. In effect, Member States are entitled to apportion the tax base between each other on a one-to-one basis under bilateral double tax treaties even if this leads to effective discrimination between non-residents of different Member States; this is of course a pragmatic decision, allowing Member States to carve-up their competing tax claims between them without undue distortions arising as a result of intervention by the ECJ. Again, it may perhaps signal a more passive approach in the future by the ECJ in the sphere of domestic tax law.

Discrimination may also arise in cases where the tax position of the taxpayer in his State of residence is not a material factor. Thus, for example if the taxpayer's business profits are generally subject to the same tax regime as resident of the source country, it would be discriminatory to refuse him tax credits available to residents (*EC v France* [1968] ECR 273 and note also *Saint Gobain* (Case C–307/97). It might be argued that the taxpayer in the *Wielockx* case should have succeeded regardless of the proportion of his income arising in the source State. This is because the right to deduct pension contributions arose only in respect of business income and accordingly such contributions were in effect business-related expenses.

In *R v IRC ex parte Commerzbank* [1993] STC 605, the ECJ held that the UK was not entitled to deny the benefit of interest on overpaid tax to non-resident taxpayers (notwithstanding that the overpayment there arose only by virtue of the non-resident status of the taxpayer).

In *Futura Participations SA and Singer v Administration des Contributions* [1997] STC 1301, the ECJ considered two measures of Luxembourg tax law which related specifically to non-resident taxpayers carrying on business through a permanent establishment in Luxembourg. The first of these measures provided that relief could only be claimed for losses to the extent that these referred economically to the generation of income by the permanent establishment in question. The ECJ held that this measure, based on the accepted principle of fiscal territoriality, was not in itself discriminatory (the position would of course have differed if more favourable treatment had been granted to residents). The second measure provided that loss relief could only be claimed if separate accounting records for the permanent establishment were drawn up under Luxembourg law and held in Luxembourg. This measure was held to be discriminatory even though a similar requirement applied to resident companies. The point was, however, that the taxpayer was not in a like position to a resident company, since it only had a branch in Luxembourg and already drew up its full accounts under the laws of its state of residence. The ECJ also held that while discrimination could be justified by the need to ensure effective fiscal supervision, the means in this case failed to meet the test of proportionality; this was on the basis that Luxembourg could instead have merely imposed a broad requirement that non-residents should demonstrate clearly and precisely their entitlement to loss relief.

For discussion of the potential implications of the *Cadbury Schweppes* (Case C–196/04) see **17.202**.

1.411 Interpretation of double tax treaties

Double tax treaties are incorporated into Irish law by virtue of TCA 1997, s 826(1) which provides that a treaty will have the force of law 'notwithstanding anything in any enactment'. However, the relevant treaty does not thereby forfeit its status as an international agreement.

In *McGimpsey v Ireland* [1990] ILRM 441, Barrington J stated:

> An international treaty has only one meaning and that is its meaning in international law. Its interpretation cannot be coloured by reference to the Constitution ... for guidance on this subject one must look to the general principles of international law and in particular to the rules of interpretation set out in Article 31 of the Vienna Convention on the Law of Treaties. Ireland, admittedly, is not a party to that convention, but Article 31 is acknowledged to have codified the relevant principles of interpretation.

Articles 31 of the Vienna Convention reads as follows:

(1) A treaty shall be interpreted in good faith in accordance with the ordinary meaning to be given to the terms of the treaty in their context and in the light of its object and purpose.

(2) The context for the purpose of the interpretation of a treaty shall comprise in addition to the text, including its preamble and annexes:

- (a) any agreement relating to the treaty which was made between all the parties in connection with the conclusion of the treaty;
- (b) any instrument which was made by one or more parties in connection with the conclusion of the treaty and accepted by the other parties as an instrument related to the treaty.

(3) There shall be taken into account, together with the context:

- (a) any subsequent agreement between the parties regarding the interpretation of the treaty or the application of its provisions;
- (b) any subsequent practice in the application of the treaty which estimates the agreement of the parties regarding its interpretation;
- (c) any relevant rules of international law applicable in the relations between the parties.

(4) A special meaning shall be given to a term if it is established that the parties so intended.

Article 32 of the treaty supplements Article 31 in the following terms:

> Recourse may be had to supplementary means of interpretation, including the preparatory work of the treaty and the circumstances of its conclusion, in order to confirm the meaning resulting from the application of Article 31, or to determine the meaning when the interpretation according to Article 31:
>
> (a) leaves the meaning ambiguous or obscure; or
>
> (b) leads to a result which is manifestly absurd or unreasonable.

In *Murphy v Asahi Synthetic Fibres Ltd* III ITR 246, O'Hanlon J, distinguishing the UK case of *Collco Dealings v IRC* 39 TC 509, took the view that the words 'notwithstanding anything in any enactment', meant that the treaty overrode any conflicting domestic provisions enacted at a later date. O'Hanlon J also took the view that Art 29 of the

Constitution would preclude the enactment of legislation which conflicted with an international agreement. Their views were obiter, since on the facts of the case, it was held that there was no inconsistency between the treaty and domestic law. Furthermore, O'Hanlon J's views appear to be inconsistent with other judicial dicta in this area (see, eg Re *O'Laighleis,* discussed in Hogan and Whyte, *JM Kelly: The Irish Constitution* (4th edn, Bloomsbury Professional, 2003)).

TCA 1997, s 826 is stated to apply *inter alia* to 'arrangements … made in relation to affording relief from double taxation in respect of income tax … and any taxes of a similar character imposed by the laws of the State or by the laws of [the other treaty] territory' (emphasis added). These are words of limitation so that eg it is generally accepted in Ireland that this means that a treaty cannot be used to justify the imposition of a greater liability to tax than would be the case under domestic law (and note the decision in *Boake Allen Ltd v HMRC* [2006] EWCA Civ 25).

The various double tax treaties entered into by Ireland have generally been influenced to a greater or lesser extent by the particular version of the OECD Model Double Tax Convention which was current at the time when each particular treaty was being negotiated. Three versions of the Model Convention have appeared, in 1963, 1977 and 1992 respectively. The 1992 version, unlike its predecessors, is 'ambulatory', ie it is a 'loose-leaf' document due to be updated on a regular basis. Each of the versions includes detailed explanatory material ('the commentaries') in respect of each of the Articles contained in the Convention. It has been updated in 1994, 1995, 1997, 2000, 2003, 2005, 2008, 2010 and 2014.

As noted above Art 31(1) of the Vienna Convention requires a treaty to be interpreted in the light of [the treaty's] object and purpose. In the case of a tax treaty the declared object is usually stated as the elimination of double taxation and counteraction of tax evasion, which may be of limited use in construing the detailed articles of a particular treaty. In *Memec v IRC* [1996] STC 1336, Robert Walker J suggested that the object of a tax treaty meant that it should be interpreted if possible in a way that achieved symmetry between the allocation of taxing rights and the arrangements for granting credit relief. However, the Court of Appeal subsequently rejected the judge's view that this broad brush approach could justify overriding the specific language of the treaty [1998] STC 754.

Because the wording of double tax treaties is much wider, and far less detailed, than that of the typical tax statute, this suggests that a broader brush, less technical, approach may be more appropriate when interpreting such treaties.

In *James Buchanan & Co Ltd v Babco Forwarding & Shipping (UK) Ltd* [1978] AC 141, Lord Wilberforce stated that treaties should accordingly be interpreted a manner:

> unconstrained by technical rules of English law, or by English legal precedent, but on broad principles of general acceptation.

In construing double tax treaties the UK courts have in practice striven to ensure that none of the terms of the treaty are rendered meaningless or ineffective. In *Avery-Jones v IRC* [1976] STC 290, Walton J observed:

> … I think the courts would always be very slow to refuse to give any meaning at all to a provision in an agreement made between two governments if any sensible construction at all could be placed on it.

Thus, in *IRC v Exxon Corporation* [1982] STC 356, Goulding J departed from the 'ordinary' meaning of the words in a treaty in order to give it practical effect (this resulted in the same word being given two different meanings in consecutive sentences).

This approach is in effect an application of the 'golden rule' (discussed at **1.505**). However, as in the case of the 'golden rule', the UK courts are prepared to give the words of the treaty an unusual meaning but not to give them a meaning which they are not capable of bearing (see, eg *Avery-Jones v IRC* [1976] STC 290).

As Art 32 of the Vienna Convention indicates, '*travaux prepatoires*' (ie preparatory works such as reports or possibly, draft agreements) and indeed other supplementary material (eg learned commentaries or the case law of other jurisdictions) may be consulted either to confirm the meaning of a treaty provision or in order to resolve cases of ambiguity/absurdity, etc (see, eg the reference to '*travaux prepatoires*' in the non-tax case of *Bourke v Attorney General* [1972] IR 36).

In *IRC v Commerzbank*, Mummery J, (relying on the approach of House of Lords in the non-tax case of *Fothergill v Monarch Airlines Ltd* [1981] AC 251) observed that the use of supplementary aids of this nature is discretionary, not mandatory, depending for example on 'the relevance of such material, and the weight to be attached to it'. He also noted that the persuasiveness of the decisions of foreign courts 'depend for their authority on the reputation and authority of the court'.

The issue also arises as to what extent the commentaries which accompany the Model Conventions (and which in the case of the 1992 version will reflect the 'ambulatory' nature of that version) should be taken into account when interpreting the terms of a Double Tax Treaty (ie by reference to the principles stated in Art 31 of the Vienna Convention). The commentaries which are in force at the time a treaty is concluded may be regarded as being in the nature of '*travaux preparatoires*'. Nevertheless, they do not form part of the process of negotiation of the treaty and may therefore be needed to be regarded with some caution.

The OECD's Committee on Fiscal Affairs states in the introduction to the 1992 Model Convention that the commentaries are not designed to be annexed to the treaties concluded by OECD members, since the treaties alone constitute legally binding agreements. However, the Committee also states that the commentaries 'are of great assistance in the application and interpretation of treaties'. The commentaries were in fact used as an aid to the interpretation of a specific Double Tax treaty in *Sun Life Assurance Co v Pearson* [1986] STC 335 (see also the Australian case *Thiel v FCT* [1990] 90 ATC 4717 an approach approved by the High Court in *Kinsella v The Revenue Commissioners* [2007] IEHC 250).

The position is more complex where a new Model Convention was issued following the conclusion of a particular treaty, or where, under the 1992 Model Convention, the commentaries have been updated subsequently. The question is: should a court consult only the commentaries as they stood at the time the treaty was concluded or can they (or should they) take into account changes and revisions to the commentaries made subsequently?

The OECD Fiscal Committee in its introduction to the 1992 Model Convention recommends that it is the latest version of the commentaries which should be consulted. It is unclear whether this approach is consistent with Arts 31 and 32 of the Vienna Convention (see Avery Jones, 'Article 3(2) of the OECD Model Convention, etc' [1993] European Taxation 252). This issue remains to be addressed by the UK (or Irish) courts.

1.412 European Convention on Human Rights Act 2003

The European Convention on Human Rights Act 2003 (ECHRA 2003) incorporates certain provisions of the European Convention on Human Rights into Irish law, subject to the provisions of the Constitution, with effect from 31 December 2003. The principal effects of the Act are:

(i) The courts must so far as possible interpret and apply any statutory provision or rule of law in a manner compatible with the State's obligations under the Convention, subject however to the rules of law relating to such interpretation and application (ECHRA 2003, s 2). This requirement is similar to that applicable in respect of statutory interpretation in the context of European law as established in the *Marleasing* case: see **1.410**. Thus, where the statutory language is not capable of an interpretation in conformity with the Convention, no relief is available: see *R v IRC ex parte Wilkinson* [2005] UKHL 30.

    The courts must also take judicial notice *inter alia* of the judgments and other pronouncements of the European Court of Human Rights and take due account of the principles enshrined therein when interpreting and applying the provisions of the Convention (ECHRA 2003, s 4). This does not mean that the relevant judgments, etc must be accepted as binding precedents but they will clearly generally possess persuasive force. The requirements above do not apply to tribunals.

(ii) The High Court and the Supreme Court may make a declaration in the course of proceedings that a statutory provision or rule is incompatible with the State's obligations under the Convention (ie where it is not possible to interpret or apply the relevant provision in a manner that is thus compatible) (ECHRA 2003, s 5(1)); this will not affect the validity of the provision thus impugned (ECHRA 2003, s 5(2)) but the government may make a discretionary payment for compensation in respect of any injury or loss suffered as a result of the incompatibility (ECHRA 2003, s 5(4)). The government is likely to, but is not bound to, amend the offending provision or rule.

(iii) Every organ of the State (including the Revenue Commissioners and the Appeal Commissioners) must perform its functions in a manner compatible with the State's obligations under the convention (ECHRA 2003, s 3(1)); a person who has suffered injury, loss or damage may bring proceedings to recover damages in respect of any contravention of this requirement if no other remedy in damages is available by an organ of the state (ECHRA 2003, s 3(2)).

Article 1 of Protocol 1 of the Convention (protection of property) provides that:

> Every natural or legal person is entitled to the peaceful enjoyment of his possessions. No one shall be deprived of his possessions except in the public interest and subject to the conditions provided for by law and by the general principles of international law.

However, it adds:

> The preceding provisions shall not, however, in any way impair the right of a State to enforce such laws as it deems necessary to control the use of property in accordance with the general interest or to secure the payment of taxes or other contributions or penalties.

Notwithstanding this rider, it is clear that even tax laws must accord with the general principles embodied in the convention, namely that tax must be levied on the basis of the rule of law, must be levied in the public interest and must be levied in a proportionate manner. However, this would seem to add little to the existing constitutional rights already enjoyed in this regard by individual taxpayers: see **1.409**.

Article 6 of the convention grants the right to a fair trial, inter alia, as follows:

> 1. In the determination of his civil rights and obligations or of any criminal charge against him, everyone is entitled to a fair and public hearing within a reasonable time by an independent and impartial tribunal established by law …
>
> 2. Everyone charged with a criminal offence shall be presumed innocent until proved guilty according to law …

The European Court of Human Rights has consistently held that Art 6 has no application to ordinary tax proceedings, most recently in *Ferrazzini v Italy* 2001 STC 1314, where the taxpayer unsuccessfully invoked Art 6 in the context of a delay in excess of 10 years in resolving a tax appeal. The court stated:

> The court considers that tax matters still form part of the hard core of public authority prerogatives, with the public nature of the relationship between the taxpayer and the tax authorities remaining predominant.

The court also stated:

> Bearing in mind that … [Article 1/1], which concerns the protection of property, reserves the right of States to enact such laws as they deem necessary for the purposes of securing the payment of taxes … the court considers that tax disputes fall outside the scope of civil rights and obligations, despite the pecuniary effects which they necessarily produce for the taxpayer.

The decision in *Ferrazzini* looks questionable (particularly as it excludes honest taxpayers from Art 6 whereas those who commit criminal misdemeanours may rely upon it: see below) and as indicated above the Irish courts are not bound to follow it. However, it would be unwise to depend on the Irish courts declining to do so.

In any event, proceedings for the recovery of overpayments of tax or recovery of assets seized by the Revenue may in some circumstances fall within Art 6 as being in the nature of private law actions (see eg *National & Provincial Building Society v UK* [1997] STC 1466).

Criminal proceedings in relation to tax fraud or other tax offences clearly fall within the ambit of Art 6. Furthermore, civil penalties levied for breaches of tax law may be regarded as criminal for the purposes of the Convention depending on the nature of the breach and/or the severity of the penalty (see eg *Customs & Excise v Han & Yau* & Ors [2001] STC 1188, where stringent civil penalties for tax evasion were treated as criminal matters and also *AP, MP and TP v Switzerland* (App No 19958/92) concerning tax-geared fines for tax evasion). In *King v UK* Ect HR 13881/2004, (heard in the UK High Court as *King v Walden* [2001] STC 822), the European Court of Human Rights held that tax-geared penalties could not be regarded as merely compensation for costs incurred by the taxpayer's actions and that their objective was to pressurise taxpayers into compliance and to punish breaches of tax law; accordingly, they were criminal in nature for the purposes of the Convention.

The protections provided explicitly or implicitly by the Convention in relation to criminal matters include the following:

(a) the requirement that proceedings should be completed within a reasonable time frame (see *King v Walden* [2001] STC 822);

(b) the right to a hearing (see *JJ v the Netherlands* (App No 21351/93);

(c) the right to silence and to non self-incrimination, ie freedom from coercion or inducements to disclose self-incriminating information, at least where it is clear that proceedings of a criminal nature are in contemplation (see *JB v Switzerland*

[2001] Crim LR 748 and note the comments of Lord Hutton in *R v Allen* [2001] STC 1537);

(d) the presumption of innocence (but note the qualified approach of the UK courts in *King v Walden*); and

(e) personal liability to charges (ie penalties of a criminal nature cannot be imposed after the death of the offender: see *AP, MP and TP v Switzerland* (App No 19958/92), as conceded in *e-brief 15/2008*).

Somewhat anomalously, Art 6 does not exclude ordinary proceedings in relation to social security contributions (*Schouten and Meldrum v the Netherlands* (App No 19005/91)).

1.5 Residence and Territorial Limits

1.501 Territorial limits

The income assessable under the Tax Acts, whether to income tax or corporation tax, is in the case of a resident person income derived from both domestic and foreign sources, but the Tax Acts generally only seek to assess a non-resident person on his income from sources within the State (some of the exceptions to this general principle are discussed at **1.405**: Presumptions against extra-territorial jurisdiction). The area of the State for this purpose consists of the Republic of Ireland, its islands and its territorial seas, but the Government's taxing rights are extended by TCA 1997, s 13 to permit the taxing of specified types of income arising from certain activities on the Irish section of the Continental Shelf.

TCA 1997, s 821 has also extended the scope of income tax to cover non-resident but ordinarily resident individuals who are in receipt of certain types of foreign income (generally foreign investment income). It should also be noted that resident individuals who are domiciled outside the State are taxed only to the extent that they remit income or capital gains from foreign sources into the State.

The application of the principles of territoriality to the imposition of taxation requires the classification of persons, whether individuals, other non-corporate persons or companies, into residents and non-residents, and distinguishes between income from sources situated within and without the State, ie domestic and foreign source income. In addition, the question of ordinary residence and domicile will be of relevance to individuals. Since the point occurs throughout the book, it is appropriate at this stage to discuss the rules under which persons are classified as resident, ordinarily resident and non-resident. Similarly, the principles applied in establishing an individual's domicile are also discussed below. The various rules for distinguishing different categories of income between domestic and foreign sources are dealt with in **Division 13**.

1.502 Residence of individuals: 1994–95 onwards

Significance of residence and ordinary residence

The concept of 'residence' and the question of whether or not an individual is 'resident' in the State is important since a resident individual is, in principle, generally liable to Irish income tax in respect of his worldwide income, whereas an individual who is not resident is generally liable to Irish income tax only in respect of his Irish source income (and may be exempted by a double taxation agreement from Irish tax on certain types of Irish source income).

A second and related concept is that of 'ordinary residence'. Most individuals who are resident in the State for a tax year are also 'ordinarily resident' for the same tax year. However, in certain circumstances, an individual may be resident in the State for a tax year without being ordinarily resident or he may be ordinarily resident in a tax year without also being resident for the same year.

The question of whether an individual is ordinarily resident in the State for any tax year in which he is not resident is extremely significant as the result of TCA 1997, s 821. This is the section which make an individual who is not resident, but who is ordinarily resident in the State in a tax year, liable to Irish income tax (broadly speaking) on investment income from foreign sources in excess of €3,810 (see **13.504**).

TCA 1997, Pt 34 (ss 818–825C) lays down the rules for determining when an individual is resident or ordinarily resident in the State for tax purposes and, in addition, contains other rules regarding 'split year' residence (see **13.503–13.504**), a deduction for certain income earned outside the State (see **10.306**, **13.302**) and certain other matters affected by residence or ordinary residence.

Prior to the tax year 1994–95, the rules for determining whether or not an individual was resident and/or ordinarily resident in the State in any tax year were based on long-standing case law and administrative practice (the 'old law'). There were virtually no statutory provisions in the fiscal legislation for defining residence or ordinary residence.

TCA 1997, s 818 *et seq* provide definitive statutory rules for income tax purposes to determine when an individual is resident in the State and when he is ordinarily resident.

'Residence' defined

Since income tax is an annual tax, it is necessary to consider the question of an individual's residence separately for each tax year in which it is sought to tax him as a resident. Alternatively, if an individual wishes to avoid income tax on foreign source income for any tax year on the grounds of non-residence, the individual must establish that he is not resident in that tax year.

TCA 1997, s 819(1) prescribes two alternative tests for determining an individual's residence for tax purposes for any tax year. Thus, an individual is resident in the State either:

(a) if he is present in the State for 183 days or more in that tax year (the 'current year' test); *or*

(b) if he is present in the State for 280 days or more days in that tax year and the preceding tax year taken together.

For the purposes of (b), periods of presence which do not in total exceed 30 days in a tax year are disregarded. One effect of this rule is that an individual present for 30 days or less in a tax year will not be resident for that year.

For the tax year 2001, the number of days under (a) was reduced from 183 to 135 and the number of days under (b) was reduced to 244 days. Further, for the tax year 2001 the 30 days disregard rule became a 22 day disregard rule. For the year 2002, the number of days under (b) was again reduced to 244.

In applying either test, an individual is only regarded as present in the State for any day if he is physically present therein at any time during the day for tax years 2009 onwards or at the end of that day, ie at midnight for tax years prior to 2009. (TCA 1997, ss 818, 819(4)). Counting the number of days presence or absence in applying both tests, there is no distinction, between workdays, holidays, days of illness or others and it does not matter whether the days presence come together or are spread between a number of different periods during any tax year. However, from 2009 onwards, certain days of presence will be disregarded in practice by the Revenue Commissioners, as set out in *e-*

brief 03/2009, In the practical operation of the new rule, Revenue will apply the following treatment:

1. Individuals in transit

   An individual will not be regarded as being present in the State for any period during which he or she arrives in, and departs from, the State and throughout which he or she remains 'airside' – that is, remains throughout the period in the State in a part of an airport or port not accessible to members of the public (unless, of course, such members of the public are arriving in, or departing from, the State).

2. '*Force majeure*' circumstances

   Where an individual is prevented from leaving the State on their intended day of departure because of extraordinary natural occurrences (for example, sudden and severe adverse weather conditions) or an exceptional third party failure or action (for example, the breakdown of an aircraft or a labour strike) – none of which could reasonably have been foreseen and avoided – the individual will not be regarded as being present in the State for tax residence purposes for the day after the intended day of departure provided the individual is unavoidably present in the State on that day due only to 'force majeure' circumstances.

Example 1.502.1

Mr Brown intends to depart from the State at 6 pm on 20 January 2017. However, due to unanticipated and severe adverse weather conditions, his flight is delayed until 4 pm on 21 January. In this instance, Mr Brown will be treated as present in the State on the 20th but will not be treated as present in the State on the 21st.

Ms Black intends to depart from the State at 6 pm on 10 February 2017. However, due to unanticipated technical difficulties with the plane, her flight is delayed until 4 pm on 11 February. In this instance, Ms Black will be treated as present in the State on 10 February but not 11 February.

In the further examples shown herein, it is assumed that the application of *e-brief 03/2009* is not in point.

Example 1.502.2

Mr CD Pickwick, a management consultant working for an international firm of accountants, arrived in the State on 1 September 2016 to work on a number of short term assignments on behalf of the firm's Irish branch.

Apart from a return visit to his home in New York for Christmas, leaving on the afternoon of 20 December and returning on the evening of 29 December, Mr Pickwick remained continuously in the State until his departure on 18 June 2017.

The actual days of his presence in the State are as follows:

2016:	*Days*
1/09/2016 to 20/12/2016	111
29/12/2016 to 31/12/2016	3
2017:	114
1/1/2017 to 18/6/2017	169
	283

Although Mr Pickwick has less than 183 days in the State in 2017 (and would not be a resident under the current year rule), he has a total of 283 days in the State when his days in the preceding year (2016) are aggregated with his days present in the current year (2017). He is therefore resident for the year 2017.

Mr Pickwick was not resident in 2016 as he did not meet any of the tests of residence.

Example 1.502.3

Same facts as in **Example 1.502.2** except assume that Mr Pickwick returned home on 10 December 2016 instead of 20 December 2016. His days present in the State in 2017 and the preceding year were therefore as follows:

	Days
In tax year 2016:	
1/09/2016 to 10/12/2016	101
29/12/2016 to 31/12/2016	3
	104
In tax year 2017:	
1/1/2017 to 19/6/2017	169
	273

Since he was not present in the State for 183 days in the current year (2017), and as he has not had 280 or more days in the State in 2017 and 2016 combined, Mr Pickwick is not resident in the State for 2017. As in the previous example, he was not resident for 2016.

Example 1.502.4

Dr Oscar Twist, who has been resident in the State since 2006, leaves the State for a temporary work assignment in Zambia on the afternoon of 30 January 2016 and does not return at all until the evening of 9 September 2017 (from when he is present in the State continuously).

Dr Twist's days present in the State in 2016 and 2017 are as follows:

	Days
In tax year 2016:	
1/1/2016 –30/1/2016	30
In tax year 2017:	
9/9/2017 to 31/12/2017	114

Although present in the State for all of 2015 (365 days), the look back test is not satisfied for residence in 2016 because Dr Twist is not present in the State for *more than* 30 days in that year.

He is not resident either for 2017 as his 114 days present are again less than the 183 days (current year test). Since the number of days present in 2016 are only 30 (not in excess of 30), they would not be counted when applying the look back test in relation to residence in 2017. Clearly, the look back test does not make Dr Twist resident for 2017.

Ceasing to be ordinarily resident

TCA 1997, s 820(2) expressly provides that an individual who is ordinarily resident in the State for a tax year shall not cease to be so ordinarily resident until after that individual has had three consecutive tax years in which he was not resident in the State.

The position concerning individuals who were ordinarily resident in 1993–94 under the 'old law' may be open to doubt in some cases.

Example 1.502.5

Mr Vole arrived in the State on 6 June 1992 intending to remain based there indefinitely. He was therefore resident and ordinarily resident in the State for 1992–93 and 1993–94 under the 'old law'. Mr Vole, who travels extensively, established the following history of residence for the tax years 1994–95 to 1996–97:

1994/95: Non-resident

1995/96: Resident

1996/97: Resident

The Revenue Commissioners take the view (see *Tax Briefing 17*) that the application of the rules in TCA 1997, s 820(2) has the result that Mr Vole continued to be ordinarily resident from 1994–95 to 1996–97 since he did not achieve three consecutive years of non-residence prior to 1994–95. Indeed, on this view, Mr Vole will not have ceased to be ordinarily resident at the earliest until he was non-resident for the years 1997–98 to 1999–00 inclusive, with effect from 2000–01.

The alternative view is that TCA 1997, s 820(2) provides the definition of ordinary residence which applies from 1994–95 onwards. Thus, one must determine for each tax year from 1994–95 onwards whether an individual was ordinarily resident under the 'three year residence rule'. On this view, Mr Vole would have been non-ordinarily-resident for 1994–95 to 1996–97 inclusive since he would not have satisfied the 'three year residence rule' in respect of any of those tax years.

Election for residence

TCA 1997, s 820(1) entitles an individual, who is not resident for a tax year under either of the current year or look back rules, to elect to be treated as resident in the State for that tax year if the individual can satisfy an authorised officer of the Revenue Commissioners that he is in the State:

(a) with the intention; and

(b) in such circumstances;

that he will be resident in the State for the next tax year.

This election for residence may be made by the individual 'at any time'. It does not have to be done in advance or even during the tax year for which the election is to apply. The Revenue Commissioners require the election to be in writing and (in the case of an individual arriving in the State) to be accompanied by documentary evidence of the individual's intention to be resident in the next tax year (eg contract of employment, evidence of purchase or long term letting of a residence). In the absence of such evidence, the Revenue Commissioners will review the position at the end of the tax year following the tax year of arrival. If the individual was in fact resident for that year the Revenue Commissioners will accept the election at that point. The effect of this approach is to extend the right of election to an individual who did not initially intend to become resident in the tax year following the tax year of arrival, but who actually does so. The election will most commonly be relevant to individuals who are arriving in the State. However, the election would be equally open to an individual living in the State who spends sufficient time abroad in a particular tax year to fall outside the TCA 1997, s 819 tests of residence for that year.

Clearly before making an election to be treated as resident, the individual should consider the tax consequences. One possible reason would be to obtain personal allowances and any other reliefs for the tax year which are not, or which may not, be available to a non-resident individual. On the other hand, a reason for not making the election could be the fact that the individual's income from sources outside the State will be taxed for the year for which the election is made (subject to the possible availability of the 'split year treatment'; see **13.503** and the availability of relief under a relevant Double Tax Treaty: see **14.2**), whereas such income would not be taxed if he did not make the election so as to remain non-resident for that year. Another possible reason for not making the election is that the year in question consequently be counted for the purposes of ascertaining the individual's ordinary residence status (see below).

Becoming ordinarily resident

TCA 1997, s 820(1) provides that an individual becomes ordinarily resident in the State for a tax year after he has been resident in the State for three consecutive tax years. The individual then continues to be treated as ordinarily resident for subsequent tax years unless and until he ceases to be ordinarily resident under the rule of TCA 1997, s 820(2) (see below). It is to be noted that the individual becomes ordinarily resident for the fourth year, whether or not he is actually resident in the fourth year. Rules apply to a donor of a gift to the State which was accepted under the State Property Act 1954 and which was made prior to 4 February 2010. The donor and/or his spouse will be regarded as non-ordinarily resident from the date he leaves the State for permanent residence abroad, so long as he is taxed on a worldwide basis in his new state of residence in respect of his income, capital gains and gifts or inheritances.

1.503 Residence of individuals: up to 1993–94

For tax years up to and including 1993–94, there were no statutory rules comparable to FA 1994, ss 150, 151 for determining whether an individual was resident and/or ordinarily resident for a tax year. The issues were determined by the administrative practice of the Revenue Commissioners based on the results of various judicial decisions and dicta in the courts. The pre-FA 1994 position is set out in the 2001 edition of this book.

1.504 Residence of companies

This is a topic which is primarily of relevance in the sphere of corporation tax. A detailed discussion of the relevant issues will be found in Feeney, *Taxation of Companies* (Bloomsbury Professional, 2014). A comprehensive discussion of the principles involved can be found in the UK case of *Wood & Anor v Holden (Inspector of Taxes)* [2006] EWCA Civ 26, where the Court of Appeal held (in the context of a tax planning arrangement involving the use of offshore companies) that in seeking to determine where central management and control of a company incorporated outside the UK lies, it is necessary to distinguish between situations where management and control of a company is exercised through its own constitutional organs and cases where such functions are effectively usurped so that management and control is exercised independently of, or without regard to, those constitutional organs. In situations within the former class, it is essential to distinguish between the role of an 'outsider' in proposing, advising or influencing the decisions which the constitutional organs take and the role of an outsider who dictates decisions which are to be taken. Furthermore, a management decision did not cease to be such because it was made on the basis of insufficient information: ill-informed decisions by directors remained management decisions.

1.505 Domicile of individuals

Apart from having a residence for tax purposes, an individual has also a domicile which may, or may not, be in the same country as that of his residence. The concept of domicile is a much more permanent one than that of residence.

Domicile is a concept of general law which is relevant for certain tax purposes. It is more important in connection with taxes on capital such as gift and inheritance tax (capital acquisition tax) than in connection with the taxes on income or capital gains. Its primary relevance to income tax is in relation to the treatment of certain foreign source income of an individual who is resident in the State but who has a domicile in a foreign country (see **13.401**).

An individual can have a domicile in a country or state that has its own separate system of laws. For example, an individual could be domiciled in the Republic of Ireland, in Northern Ireland, in England and Wales, in Scotland, in France or, say, the State of North Carolina (USA). Each state of the US has its own separate legal jurisdiction and, therefore, confers its own separate domicile on its permanent residents.

In any question for any of the Irish taxes as to whether an individual has an Irish or a foreign domicile, it is the Irish law on the subject, and not that of the foreign country, that is relevant. Under Irish law, every individual is regarded as acquiring a domicile of origin on his birth. He automatically assumes on birth a domicile of origin. This is the domicile of his father, unless either his father had died before his birth or he was an illegitimate child. In either of these latter events the individual takes the domicile of his mother. Since 1986, the above rules are modified in the case of the child of a couple who are living apart (see below).

An individual normally retains his domicile of origin until he comes of age. However, an individual's domicile may change during his infancy, as a result of his father (or, in some cases, his mother) acquiring a new domicile of choice. The individual will retain the parent's domicile of choice (known as 'domicile of dependency') up to the time that he comes of age. If he subsequently abandons that domicile of dependency then his domicile of origin automatically revives, unless (and until) he acquires a new domicile of choice: *Gulbenkian v Gulbenkian* [1937] 158 LT 46.

A child has no say in his own domicile while he is still a minor. After he comes of age, he may by his own actions acquire a new domicile referred to as a 'domicile of choice' (see below). In order to establish a new domicile of choice, an individual who has reached the age of majority must move to a new country, with the intention of making a permanent home there.

In order to acquire a domicile of choice, the individual must physically reside in the new country. It is not necessary for him to cease residence completely in the country of origin, but the new country must be the chief place of residence (*Earl of Iveagh v Revenue Commissioners* I ITR 259; *Plummer v IRC* [1987] STC 698).

Where an individual abandons his domicile of choice, then his domicile of origin automatically revives unless (and until) he acquires a new domicile of choice. A mere intention to return to the country of origin will not revive the domicile of origin unless it is accompanied by a change of residence (*Rowan v Rowan* III ITR 572).

In *M v M* [1988] ILRM 456, the taxpayer, who had been UK domiciled, became resident in the State in order to avail of exemption under what is now TCA 1997, s 195 (the 'artists' exemption – see **Division 5**). The taxpayer intended to remain based in Ireland so long as tax rates in the UK remained prohibitive. Barr J referred to the onerous burden of proof placed on a person who asserted a change in the domicile of origin. He observed:

> Although the British tax regime in 1979 may have been crippling for the husband, he would have anticipated that the situation was not necessarily a permanent one and that there would be a radical improvement in the fiscal and economic climate in the UK in the medium term which would enable him and his family to adopt their first chose and take up permanent residence again in their native land.
>
> It does not follow from the fact that the husband decided to accept the tax and other advantages which Ireland offered, that the setting up of a family residence here for an indefinite period established *per se* an intention on his part to make his permanent home in Ireland and to abandon his domicile of origin. It seems to me that there is an important distinction between setting up home for an indefinite period in a particular place and setting up a permanent home there. The latter implies that this situation thus created is intended to continue for the foreseeable future and may be altered only in the event of a change in circumstances which is not then in contemplation or anticipated as being likely to happen at a future date (but excluding consequences such as the inevitability of old age and natural changes in family circumstances which are not anticipated in the short or medium term). On the other hand, a home which is established in a particular place for an indefinite period may depend upon the continuance of certain circumstances which are in themselves indefinite as to likely duration. In my view a home set up on the latter basis does not have the element of permanence as so defined which is an essential indicator of a change in domicile.

The UK courts have tended to use the terms 'permanently' and 'indefinitely' interchangeably. However, the essential point in *M v M* seems to have been that the taxpayer always intended to return to the UK on the happening of a future event which it could be reasonably anticipated would occur in time (ie the reduction of UK tax rates). In *PL v An t'Ard Chlaraitheoir* [1995] 2 ILRM 241, Kinlen J observed that the reference to an 'indefinite' period in *M v M* should be construed as reference to a period of residence contingent on the happening of a certain event.

In *IRC v Bullock* [1976] STC 409, an individual with a Canadian domicile or origin, married an English wife and settled in the UK. He intended to return to Canada in the event that his wife predeceased him. The court held that he had retained his Canadian domicile of origin, observing:

> … is there a sufficiently substantial possibility of the contingency happening to justify regarding the intention to return as a real determination to do so on the contingency occurring rather than a vague hope or aspiration? In the present case, in my opinion, that question should be answered affirmatively.

The court added:

> No doubt, if a man who has made his home in a country other than his domicile of origin has expressed his intention to return to his domicile of origin or to remove to some third country on an event or condition of an indefinite kind (for example, 'if I make a fortune' or 'when I've had enough of it'), it might be hard, if not impossible, to conclude that he retained any real intention of so returning or removing.

In *Re Fuld (deceased) No 3* [1965] 3 All ER 776, Lord Scarman said that in establishing the acquisition of a domicile of choice, it was necessary to show that the individual intended to reside indefinitely (ie permanently) in the country in question, saying:

> If a man intends to return to the land of his birth upon a clearly foreseen and reasonably anticipated contingency, for example, the end of his job, the intention required by law is lacking; but, if he has in mind only a vague possibility, such as making a fortune (a modern example might be winning a football pool) or some sentiment about dying in the land of his fathers, such a state of mind is consistent with the intention required by law.

In Re *Furse* [1980] STC 596 the taxpayer was a US domiciled individual who came to live with his family on a farm in the UK. He lived in the UK for forty years up to his death. There was evidence that he visited the US regularly and retained a property there. After some initial indecision, the taxpayer had ultimately decided not to return to the US 'so long as he was capable of leading an active life on his farm'. The taxpayer clearly enjoyed his lifestyle in the UK and had become fully integrated into his local community.

The court held that the taxpayer had died domiciled in the UK saying:

> It seems to me that, from the manner in which he expressed his intentions, the testator's hope was that he could go on living his accustomed and very pleasant life at West Hoathly to the end of his days. It was his good fortune to achieve that. The only circumstances on the happening of which he expressed any intention of leaving England was if he was no longer able to live an active physical life on the farm. Apart from that, he intended to remain in England all his life.
>
> But that contingency is altogether indefinite. It has no precision at all. A man's idea of an active physical life is likely to contract with the years. At the age of 80, after 40 years in England, the testator was still living at West Hoathly and, although he had been ill, he had no firm plans at all for leaving England.
>
> The testator's expressed intention it seems to me, depended entirely on his own assessment of whether an ill-defined event had occurred. I think it really amounted to no more than saying 'I will leave England when I feel I want to leave England'.
>
> It seems to me that the intention of the testator was indeed to continue to reside in England for an unlimited period.

In *MT v NT* [1982] ILRM 217, the Supreme Court held that the fact that an individual had come from the UK with his family in order to take up employment here and had lived here for two years was too meagre a basis on which to infer the acquisition of an Irish domicile of choice. Interestingly, the court noted that 'freedom of movement and mobility of employment are the order of the day under the [EU] treaty'.

In *DT v FL* [2002] 2 ILRM 152, a matrimonial case, an Irish domiciled individual moved to Holland with his wife to take up work there. He and his wife integrated into Dutch society and became fluent Dutch speakers but after about five years the marriage broke up and his wife returned to Ireland. The High Court held that the individual retained his Irish domicile of origin, observing:

> I can never foresee the possibility that the respondent would remain in Holland come what may and even if he were without employment. In my view he has not satisfied the positive element of the (domicile test). No more do I consider that he had formulated any intention of abandoning Ireland as his domicile of origin. The only evidence, which is consistent with this intention, was the sale of the family home and the cancelling of his membership with clubs.
>
> If one weighs these factors against the evidence that he returned to Ireland for summer holidays, that he visited his family in Ireland on a number of occasions that he arranged for his wife to return to Ireland when difficulties arose in the marriage, in my view it is clear beyond doubt that he never abandoned his domicile of origin.

The above cases illustrate that in practice it is likely to be particularly difficult to establish a change in the domicile of origin. This is because it is necessary to show that the taxpayer has clearly decided to remain in the new country of residence. If he intends to return to the country of origin on the happening of an definite event which has a reasonable chance of occurring, then he is likely to retain his domicile of origin. Furthermore, the intention to stay for an uncertain or contingent period (as in *M v M*) is not sufficient to establish the required degree of permanence.

Where an individual has acquired a domicile of choice but then leaves the country of domicile of choice than his domicile of origin will automatically revive unless he acquires a new domicile of choice. It follows that where an individual acquires a domicile of choice, but then returns to live in his country of domicile of origin, his domicile of origin is liable to revive if he has only a vague intention to return to the country of domicile of choice. Where the intention to return is relatively concrete, then the domicile of choice will be retained (*Proes v Revenue Commissioners* V ITR 481). This is the position of many foreign nationals who come to live in the State, particularly those sent to work here on a foreign assignment.

The burden of proof in respect of any change of domicile rests with the person who asserts the change. It is sometimes asserted that the burden is stricter in the case of a domicile of origin. While many of the earlier UK cases reflect a presumption against a change of domicile of origin this tendency is less marked in more recent cases, which seem to reflect a similar approach to that adopted by the Irish courts. Nevertheless, a change of domicile of any kind is not to be lightly inferred. As noted above, the factual matters which need to be established to show abandonment of a domicile of origin may tend to militate against such a finding.

It may be noted that in *M v M*, Barr J placed no weight on a declaration by the taxpayer that he was Irish domiciled. The taxpayer had in fact only made the declaration based on a misunderstanding that it would assist his Irish tax position. In *Rowan v Rowan* III ITR 572, Costello J held that a deceased individual's declaration that he was Irish domiciled was 'a conclusion of law' on his part, and could not override the contrary inference of fact, drawn from the objective evidence. However, in *PL v An t'Ard Chlaraitheoir* [1995] 2 ILRM 241, Kinlen J stated that an uncontradicted declaration of intention which was consistent with a person's actual conduct might be regarded as evidence of acquisition of a domicile of choice.

In *Proes v Revenue Commissioners* V ITR 481, the taxpayer had to establish that she had a UK domicile of choice in order to establish a claim for the remittance basis under ITA 1967, s 76(2) now TCA 1997, s 71(3): see **13.401**. This in turn required her to establish:

(a) that she had acquired a domicile of choice in the UK after leaving Ireland; and

(b) that she had not abandoned that domicile of choice on returning to Ireland.

Thus, in this case the terms of the statute placed the onus of proof on the taxpayer to show that there was not a change of domicile of choice.

It had been thought that under the Irish law of domicile, a woman automatically assumed the domicile of her husband on her marriage, regardless of their respective residences. It followed from this that only on her husband's death had the woman a clear power to acquire a new domicile of choice, but until she took steps to do so, her domicile remained that of her late husband. The Domicile and Recognition of Foreign Divorces Act 1986 (DFDA 1986) purported to abolish, with effect from 2 October 1986, the rule of law under which a woman acquired the domicile of her husband upon their marriage and was incapable of having any other domicile during the marriage. A married woman's domicile was stated to be determined separately from that of her husband by reference to the same factors as are applied in the case of any third person capable of having an independent domicile. However, in *JW v JW* IV ITR 437, the Supreme Court held that the domicile of dependence of a married woman was repugnant to Art 40(I) of the Constitution, which guarantees that 'all citizens shall as human persons be held equal before the law'. Accordingly, the concept of domicile of dependency did not in fact survive the enactment of the Constitution.

DFDA 1986 also deals with the domicile of a minor (an individual under 18) in the case where his father and mother are living apart. In such a case, the minor is regarded as having the domicile of his mother (which may or not be the same as that of his father) at any time if:

(a) the minor has at that time his home with his mother *and* has no home with his father; or

(b) the minor has at any time taken his mother's domicile as a result of rule (a) and has not since that time had a home with his father.

In any case where a minor has had his mother's domicile under either of rules (a) or (b), and if his mother subsequently dies, the minor continues to have the same domicile as his mother had at her death, provided that the minor has not since her death had a home with his father. None of these rules alters the rule that a minor takes the domicile of his father in the case where his mother and father are married and living together.

Citizenship or nationality does not determine a person's domicile, although in a case where the position otherwise is uncertain it may be a factor to be considered. However, it is possible for an individual to retain a foreign citizenship or nationality but to be domiciled in the State, if he makes his permanent home there. Conversely, an Irish citizen living permanently abroad is capable of having a foreign domicile which need not be upset by temporary visits back to the country, for example, for holidays, to visit relatives, etc.

In *Earl of Iveagh v Revenue Commissioners* I ITR 259, it was held by the Supreme Court that the question of domicile is a question of fact to be decided, primarily by the Appeal Commissioners (or, if appropriate, the Circuit Court judge). Where their decision is one which is erroneous as a result of a misconception of the law, or is one which no reasonable tribunal of fact could reach, it will be reversed by the court (*Proes v Revenue Commissioners* [1998] 4 IR 176), and see **2.204**.

A recent UK High court case, *Perdoni v Curati* [2011] EWHC 3442 (Ch), considered the issue of domicile. The case was not a tax case but was concerned with an individual's will. The case explored the interpretation of an individual's life history in the context of determining his domicile. It is likely that this case will have an impact on how the Irish Revenue Commissioners address the question of an individual's domicile.

This case concerned an Italian individual who had moved to the UK in 1955 'to improve his economic situation'. He married a British citizen, of Italian descent, and lived in the UK until he passed away in 2008. During the later years of his life he expressed a desire to return to Italy but due to circumstances of his wife's ill health and him suffering a stroke he died in England.

He was held to have an English domicile of choice based on the following factors:

(a) he married a British citizen and his marital home was in the UK;

(b) he was gifted a restaurant in London by his wife's parents and this restaurant was the centre of his business activities for many years;

(c) when the couple sold this restaurant the proceeds were invested in UK property;

(d) he held investment properties and holiday homes in Italy, however none of these were deemed to have been a permanent or a marital home in Italy and as such were insufficient to prove an intention to return to Italy to live;

(e) while he did have a burial plot in Italy and his will stated that he wished to be buried in Italy, he did not have an intention to return to Italy 'upon a clearly foreseen and reasonable anticipated contingency';

(f) the deceased always referred to England as his home even though he would speak about wishing to be buried in his family plot in Carpeneto, Italy.

It was held in this case that the deceased acquired a domicile of choice in the UK and the fact that the couple established their sole marital home in England which remained their primary marital home even after they acquired the properties in Italy was a deciding factor in the case.

In the author's view, the importance of this case is that it would appear to be easier to acquire a domicile of choice than was previously thought. Greater consideration should be given to this issue by individuals who assert that they have not acquired a domicile of choice.

Division 2 Assessment and Collection of Tax

2.1 Self Assessment for Income Tax

2.101 Introduction

This division deals with the administration of the taxes on income, the principles and methods of assessing and collecting the taxes and the powers conferred on the Revenue Commissioners to assist them in enforcing the taxes. It also details the main penalties which may be imposed on taxpayers if they fail to comply with the tax return requirements and other obligations imposed on them by the Tax Acts.

In principle, three main methods of collecting the taxes on income may be distinguished, namely:

(a) collection by assessment on the taxpayer in receipt of income (other than the emoluments of offices and employments taxed under the PAYE system);

(b) collection by deduction at source from certain other types of payment made by certain persons (for example, annual payments made by individuals and others, interest on deposits paid by banks and building societies – dealt with here in **2.3, 2.4** and **2.5**); and

(c) collection by deduction from the emoluments of offices and employments taxable under Sch E and paid over to the Collector by employers under the 'Pay as you earn' or PAYE system (see **Division 11**).

For 2012 and previous years of assessment TCA 1997, Pt 41, ss 950–959, contained the main rules for the collection of the taxes on income by assessment (method (a)). The collection by assessment is referred to as 'self assessment'. These sections were amended extensively by FA 2001, s 78, the principal effect of which was to introduce a 'pay and file' regime providing for a common tax return filing and tax payment deadline for self-assessed income. FA 2012, s 129 and Sch 4 deleted TCA 1997, Pt 39 (Assessments), ss 918–931, and TCA 1997, Pt 41 (Self Assessment), ss 950–959, and replaced them with Pt 41A (Assessing Rules Including Rules for Self Assessment), ss 959A–959AV, with effect for the year of assessment 2013 and subsequent years of assessment. Part 41A was introduced in order to simplify and streamline the assessing rules for direct taxes. Many of the provisions contained in Pts 39 and 41 are reproduced in Pt 41A but are set out in a more logical and simplified manner. The new Pt 41A provides for the move to a full self assessment system, thus some of the provisions relating to the issue of assessments have become obsolete and are not included in the new Pt 41A. The principles of self assessment are described in the rest of **Division 2**. The law is stated below as it applies from 1 January 2013, however significant differences between the law pre- and post-1 January 2013 are highlighted. The law as it applied up to 31 December 2012 is covered in previous editions of this text.

Division 2.2 deals with the conditions and procedures in making appeals against assessments to income tax. It also covers the rules for the payment of any additional tax becoming due as a result of the determination of an appeal. It then goes on to describe the procedure in appeal hearings before the Appeal Commissioners, rehearings by the Circuit Court judge and appeals (on points of law) to the High Court and the Supreme Court, as well as the remedy of Judicial Review. Finally, it deals with the rules for appeals against determinations of officers of the Revenue Commissioners other than by assessments.

Division 2.3 outlines the rules for the collection of income tax by deduction at source, ie where persons who make certain annual and other payments are required to deduct tax and to account to the Revenue for the tax deducted, so that the payee receives the relevant item of income net of income tax. It also deals with the rules of TCA 1997, Pt 18 Ch 2, whereby principal contractors are obliged to deduct tax when making payments to subcontractors for work done on 'relevant contracts', but which excepts from this requirement payments to 'certified subcontractors'. This division deals with the rules of Sch C under which persons entrusted with the payment of interest, or dividends out of the public revenue (other than excepted dividends) must deduct income tax and pay it to the Revenue Commissioners. This division also explains the broadly similar rules under which banks and other persons collecting foreign dividends on behalf of recipients in the State are required to deduct income tax and pay it to the Revenue Commissioners.

Division 2.4 deals with the deposit interest retention tax which banks, building societies and other financial institutions are required to deduct when paying or crediting interest on 'relevant deposits' to their depositors.

Division 2.5 covers the professional services withholding tax which Government departments, semi-State companies, medical insurers and certain other bodies are required to deduct when paying fees or other payments for professional services.

Division 2.6 outlines the wide range of powers available to the Revenue Commissioners to enforce collection of all the taxes, to obtain information and generally to follow up persons suspected of failing to comply with their obligations to make tax returns, pay tax, etc.

Division 2.7 describes the main penalties which may be imposed, if legal proceedings are taken to enforce these penalties, for non-compliance with the requirements to make returns, etc (but excluding the late return surcharge dealt with specifically in **2.110**). Also dealt with in this division is an outline of what is involved in a back duty investigation.

2.102 Self assessment: important definitions

This division deals primarily with the self assessment rules as they apply to income tax (together with, to the extent these are integrated into the self assessment system, self-employed PRSI contributions on 'reckonable income': see **3.402**, **3.403** and the Universal Social Charge on relevant income see **3.404**, ie so far as not collected through the PAYE system). The self assessment procedure for the collection of tax is expressed as applying to chargeable persons for chargeable periods. Any person, who is a chargeable person in respect of any tax for a given chargeable period, is required to make a return to the inspector of taxes of income and other particulars for the tax concerned for that chargeable period and to pay the appropriate amount of tax in accordance with the self assessment described in this division.

The explanation of the legislation begins with the definition of the terms 'tax', 'chargeable period' and 'chargeable person', as these terms are applied for the rules of self assessment contained in TCA 1997, Pt 41A as follows:

Tax

'Tax' is defined in s 959A. From the point of view of an individual and self assessment, in addition to income tax it includes any other levy or charge which under the 'Acts' is placed under the care and management of the Revenue Commissioners. The 'Acts' is defined in s 959A and includes the Income Tax Acts, Pt 18C (Domicile Levy) and Pt 18D (Universal Social Charge); F(TA)A 2015, s 39 (SI 110/2016 appointed 21 March 2016 as the day on which the Finance (Tax Appeals) Act 2015, came into operation) adds TCA 1997, Pt 18A – Income Levy into the Act's definition. The Income Tax Acts mean the enactments relating to income tax in TCA 1997 (TCA 1997, s 1(2)). TCA 1997, s 849 provides that income tax, corporation tax and capital gains tax shall be placed under the care and management of the Revenue Commissioners. TCA 1997, s 531AK provides that the domicile levy is under the care and management of the Revenue Commissioners and TCA 1997, s 531AAC provides that the universal social charge is under the care and management of the Revenue Commissioners. From the point of view of individuals, and self assessment, 'tax' therefore means income tax, domicile levy and universal social charge.

The Social Welfare Consolidation Act 2005, s 23(4) provides that self-employed PRSI shall be assessed, charged and paid in all respects as if it were an amount of income tax. Thus in applying the rules of self assessment to individuals (but not other persons liable to income tax) self-employed PRSI not collectible under the PAYE system is deemed to be, and is treated in the same way as, income tax. TCA 1997, s 531AAA(b) provides that Pt 41A shall apply, with any necessary modifications, to universal social charge as it applies to income tax. References to 'income tax' in Pt 41A should therefore be taken to mean income tax, self-employed PRSI and universal social charge. Unless otherwise stated, the term 'income tax' in this Division should be interpreted as including universal social charge and self-employed PRSI.

Chargeable period

For income tax purposes, a 'chargeable period' is a tax year ending on 31 December and future references will be to tax years accordingly.

Chargeable person

TCA 1997, s 959A defines 'chargeable person', in relation to a tax year, inter alia as any person who is chargeable to tax for that tax year, whether on his own account or on account of some other person (but see below for persons excepted from this definition as respects income tax). The spouse (or civil partner) of a chargeable person is not a chargeable person in respect of their income: *Gilligan v Criminal Assets Bureau* V ITR 424.

In applying this definition of a chargeable person, 'chargeable' is taken to mean having any income or profits for the tax year in respect of which income tax is chargeable. The fact that the income in any tax year may be covered by deductions (for example, losses) or reliefs or that any liability is covered by tax credits does not prevent a person being a chargeable person for the tax concerned for that tax year. In most cases there will in any event be a *prima facie* liability to tax until any such reliefs and credits are the subject of a formal claim.

The Revenue Commissioners have expressed the debatable view in a precedent that the very act of their raising an assessment on a potentially chargeable person renders such a person a chargeable person pending discharge of the assessment. It may be noted that TCA 1997, s 959O(2) provides *inter alia* that a certificate may be issued by an officer of the Revenue Commissioners certifying that he has examined the relevant records (the scope of which is not defined) and that it appears therefrom that a named person is a chargeable person for a tax year and that a tax return has not been received from that person by the relevant specified return date. In this case, the certificate shall be evidence of the facts stated therein until the contrary is proved (TCA 1997, s 959O(3)).

Consequently, an individual or other person chargeable to tax who has any income for a year of assessment (say the tax year ending 31 December 2015) is a chargeable person for that year (2015) for tax purposes, subject to the exceptions noted under the next subheading.

TCA 1997, s 128(2A) additionally provides that where a person realises a gain on the exercise, assignment or release of a share option which falls to be taxed under Sch E by virtue of TCA 1997, s 128, then that person will always be a chargeable person for the tax year in which the taxable event occurs, unless that person has been excluded from the obligation to make a return under TCA 1997, s 959B (see below). This overrides the effect of a previous determination by the Appeal Commissioners subsequently upheld in the High Court in *Crowley v Forde* HC 2004. The concept of a chargeable person is also extended in the case of certain high income individuals with restricted specified reliefs: see **3.111**, a person liable to tax in relation to the conversion of specified employment-related securities (see **10.113**), a person in receipt of certain relevant payments from a Collective Investment Undertaking exempted from withholding tax (see **8.401**) and any person who obtains or seeks to obtain a tax advantage from a disclosable transaction (see **2.618**).

TCA 1997, s 895(6) (see **2.605**) provides that where an individual resident in the State opens a foreign deposit account the individual will be deemed for that tax year to be a chargeable person. TCA 1997, s 896(5) (see **2.605**) provides that where an individual acquires certain offshore products the individual will be deemed for that tax year to be a chargeable person. In either of these cases this would mean, for example, an individual whose only source of income is salary from which PAYE is deducted, who opens a foreign deposit account or acquires certain offshore products is required to file a tax return under the self assessment system. It should be noted however that an individual who is deemed to be a chargeable person under TCA 1997, s 895 or s 896 is only a chargeable person for the purpose of Ch 3 of Pt 41A, ie ss 959I–959Q which deal with the obligation to file a return, thus an individual who is a chargeable person only by reason of these sections does not have an obligation to pay preliminary tax.

A chargeable person for income tax may be an individual, a trustee, the personal representative of a deceased person or any unincorporated body of persons chargeable to income tax. A non-resident person with income from sources in the State is a chargeable person subject to the exceptions noted below (unless that income is exempted from Irish tax by any provision in the Tax Acts).

An individual who is not resident in the State but who is ordinarily resident is a chargeable person for income tax in respect of certain foreign income (as well as in respect of Irish source income) (see **13.504**).

Bodies such as charities, friendly societies, trade unions, etc are not chargeable persons for any tax year for which their only income is excluded by a tax exemption (see **Division 18**), but if such a body has income not so exempted, it is a chargeable person in respect of the latter income.

A non-resident company may be a chargeable person for income tax if it has any Irish source income (other than from a trade carried on through a branch or agency in the State where a liability to corporation tax arises), unless such income is exempted under any provision, or is completely relieved from Irish tax by a double tax treaty (see **Division 14**).

A person may be a chargeable person in more than one capacity and, if so, he (or, if a company, it) must fulfil all the obligations of a chargeable person in each such capacity (TCA 1997, s 959A). For example, a person may be chargeable to tax in his or its own right and may also be chargeable as a personal representative or trustee of another person.

A person who is not a chargeable person for one tax year may be a chargeable person for another tax year. For example, an individual may not be a chargeable person for 2014 because his only income for that year is Sch E emoluments from an employment taxed under PAYE, but may, for example, become a chargeable person for 2015 on becoming a director during that year (see Directors below).

Exceptions

TCA 1997, s 959B provides certain exceptions to the definition of 'chargeable person'. None of the following persons is a chargeable person for a year of assessment (and is not, therefore, liable to be assessed or to pay tax under self assessment for that year):

(a) an individual (other than a company director or the spouse or civil partner of a director taxed jointly, subject to the exceptions outlined below) whose total income for the year consists solely of Sch E emoluments subject to the PAYE procedure (see **Division 11**);

(b) an individual (other than a company director or the spouse or civil partner of a director taxed jointly, subject to the exceptions outlined below) whose only source or sources of income refer to Sch E emoluments subject to PAYE; for these purposes, this will also include a person with other sources of income where that other income does not exceed €3,174 (€5,000 for 2016 and subsequent years of assessment) in total and is either taken into account in arriving at his tax credits and standard rate cut-off point for PAYE purposes for the year or is interest from which DIRT has been deducted.

Before FA 2014 was passed, TCA 1997, s 959B(1)(a) did not specify that the individual's non-PAYE income could not exceed €3,174 in order for the individual not to be regarded as a chargeable person. However in practice before this change Revenue would not adjust tax credits and standard rate cut-off points for individuals where net taxable non-PAYE income exceeded €3,174. In addition in practice Revenue will not adjust tax credits and standard rate cut-off points for individuals where other income (excluding legally binding maintenance payments and social welfare payments) computed before deductions, losses etc exceeds €50,000 (*Tax Briefing 62*) and such individuals will be regarded as chargeable persons). For the purpose of determining whether or not to adjust an individual's tax credits and standard rate cut-off point for other income, Revenue may have regard to the person's income from other sources for the tax year in question or for previous tax years (TCA 1997, s 959B(1)(a));

(c) a person who, for that year of assessment, has been excluded by a Revenue officer, by reason of a notice given under TCA 1997, s 959N, from the requirement to make a tax return, typically in a case where there is insufficient income to give rise to a tax liability; and

(d) a person who is chargeable to tax for the year by reason only of having made annual payments or other payments from which he is entitled or required to deduct income tax under TCA 1997, s 237 or s 238 (see **2.3**).

An individual, who is not a chargeable person under exception (a) or (b) and who is paying all his tax under PAYE in any tax year, may become a chargeable person should he start to have any income in that year which is not taxable under Sch E and/or is not deducted from his PAYE tax credits, etc. Such an individual then has the responsibility of filing a self assessment tax return for the tax year in which the change occurs (and subsequent years unless the new income is deducted from the PAYE tax credits).

Directors of companies

A director of a company (other than a director of certain companies referred to as an 'excepted company' in this commentary) is always a chargeable person for income tax, notwithstanding that his total income may consist solely of Sch E emoluments subject to the PAYE procedure or may consist only of Sch E emoluments and other income deducted in arriving at his tax-free credits, etc for PAYE (TCA 1997, s 959B(1)).

Similarly, the spouse or civil partner of a director of a company (other than an excepted company) is a chargeable person for any tax year in which both individuals are assessable jointly under TCA 1997, s 1017 or s 1031C. However, for any tax year for which a spouse or civil partner of a director is assessed as a single person, the spouse or partner is not a chargeable person for income tax if he has no income other than income within the PAYE system (and is not a director himself).

The inclusion of directors (and jointly assessed spouses or civil partners) as chargeable persons is designed to ensure that every director (other than a director of an excepted company) makes a self assessment tax return, notwithstanding that his total income may consist only of Sch E income within the PAYE system. The Revenue Commissioners consider it necessary to be able to review the tax position of company directors each year.

However, there are certain exceptions. A director of an excepted company (or the jointly assessable spouse or partner of such a director) is not a chargeable person, provided that he is not a chargeable person for any other reason (for example, through having income other than Sch E income falling within the PAYE system). For this purpose, an excepted company is one in respect of which, during the three years ending on 5 April (this date has not been amended in line with the change in the tax year end to 31 December) in the tax year for which the exception is to apply, the following three conditions are met:

(a) the company was not entitled to any assets other than cash or money on deposit not exceeding €130 (but a company the only assets of which were cash and/or deposits in excess of €130 does not meet this condition);

(b) the company did not carry on a trade, business or other activity including the making of investments; and

(c) the company did not pay any charges on income within TCA 1997, s 243.

It may be seen that the exclusion from being a chargeable person for the director of an 'excepted company' is limited to the case where the company is a dormant one. There is no exclusion in law, for example, for a director of a charitable company or for the director of a sporting club incorporated as a company. The requirement for a director of a company to make a self assessment tax return (and, if necessary, to pay preliminary tax) therefore applies in almost all cases, even if he does not have any fees, emoluments or remuneration of any kind from the company.

For the purpose of the foregoing rules, a 'director' is defined in the way set out in TCA 1997, s 116 for the purposes of the benefit in kind rules (see **2.201**) as meaning:

(a) in relation to a body corporate the affairs whereof are managed by a board of directors or similar body, a member of that board or similar body;
(b) in relation to a body corporate the affairs whereof are managed by a single director or similar person, that director or person; and
(c) in relation to a body corporate the affairs whereof are managed by the members themselves, any member of the body corporate.

Further, any person in accordance with whose directions or instructions the directors (as just defined) of a body corporate are accustomed to act is deemed to be a director, except if the directors are accustomed to act in accordance with such directions or instructions by reason only that they are taking advice given by the person concerned in a professional capacity (see **2.201**).

The most significant aspect of the treatment of a director and, if relevant, his jointly assessed spouse or civil partner, as a chargeable person relates to the calculation of the late return surcharge if he fails (or if the spouse or civil partner fails) to file his tax return for any year of assessment on or before the specified return date.

However, the Revenue Statement of Practice, IT/1/93, states that returns need not be filed automatically and that consequently the surcharge will not be applied in the case of non-proprietary directors, all of whose income is taxed directly or indirectly under PAYE, and who are not otherwise chargeable persons. A proprietary director is defined as one who (on his own or with his spouse or civil partner) beneficially owns, or is able either directly or indirectly to control, more than 15 per cent of the ordinary share capital of the employing company.

2.103 Principal features of self assessment

Stages in self assessment

The stages in self assessment are as follows:

(a) the chargeable person is required to make a payment of 'preliminary tax' in respect of his liability for the tax concerned at the latest by 31 October in the relevant tax year (ie 31 October 2015 in relation to his 2015 tax liability);
(b) the chargeable person is required to complete and deliver to the Collector General a tax return giving details of his (or its) income and other required information in respect of the tax year at the latest by 31 October following the tax year, termed the 'specified return date' (ie 31 October 2016 for tax year 2015). Except in the case of individuals who file a paper return early, the chargeable person's return must include a self assessment setting out details of his income and tax; and
(c) the chargeable person is also required to pay the balance of tax due for a tax year (ie net of preliminary tax already paid for that year) at the latest by 31

October following the tax year (ie 31 October 2016 for tax year 2015), if the preliminary tax paid exceeds the net tax payable (after deducting credits and reliefs against tax), the amount of the excess is repayable to the chargeable person, with interest if appropriate.

The effect of these rules is that, under the self assessment 'pay and file' regime, taxpayers are obliged on or before 31 October in any tax year to have filed their tax return for the preceding tax year and to have paid any balance of tax due for that year (after taking credit for the preliminary tax already paid). By the same date, taxpayers are also obliged to have paid their preliminary tax for the current tax year. In the case of taxpayers filing their 2015 return and paying both their preliminary tax for 2016 and their balance of tax due for 2015 electronically under the Revenue Online Service (ROS), the deadline is likely to be extended beyond 31 October 2016 to mid November in line with the practice of previous years. This concession also applies to Partnership Tax returns where all the partners therein use ROS and qualify for the extended deadline.

Because chargeable persons are generally required to include a self assessment in the self assessment return (see **2.106**), with effect from 1 January 2013 the Revenue Commissioners are no longer required to raise an assessment on the taxpayer in order to establish the legal liability of the taxpayer to pay the tax charged for the year. Revenue may make an assessment to tax on a taxpayer but can only do so by the specified return date at the earliest (ie 31 October 2016 for tax year 2015) unless the return is filed before that date when an assessment can be raised at any time thereafter (eg if the return for 2015 is submitted on 31 March 2016, an assessment could issue at any time from 1 April 2016 onwards). Whether or not a taxpayer makes a self assessment or Revenue raise an assessment taxpayers will still be obliged to 'self assess' the net tax payable and pay the tax due by 31 October. Where a taxpayer files his returns and makes payments electronically under the ROS system, the Form 11 return includes a self assessment section which must be completed by the taxpayer before the return can be filed – ROS will not accept a return in which the self assessment section has not been completed. In addition by completing the Form 11 form produced by ROS an instantaneous calculation of the taxpayer's tax liability is provided.

Self assessment also contains rules for dealing with a chargeable person who, for any relevant tax year, fails to file a tax return with Revenue. In such cases, Revenue is empowered to make an estimated assessment for the tax Revenue thinks ought to be paid. Also, if not satisfied that a tax return made by a chargeable person is a full and correct one, Revenue may make a similar estimated assessment (see **2.106**).

Amendments of assessments

For tax returns filed for the tax year 2013 and subsequent tax years, subject to the exception for taxpayers who file paper returns early, taxpayers are required to include a self assessment in their self assessment return. Revenue will not in general issue an assessment following the filing of a return unless the return does not contain a self assessment. If a subsequent review of the return by Revenue shows that the assessment based on the chargeable person's return has understated or overstated his or its proper liability to the tax concerned, Revenue will amend the self assessment to show the correct net tax due (or repayable). Alternatively the taxpayer may file an amended return with an amended self assessment (see **2.105**). Any tax underpaid is then demanded from the chargeable person or, if the amendment is to reduce the net liability, the tax overpaid is refunded to that person (see **2.108**).

Appeals against assessments

A chargeable person, who disagrees with the amount of the relevant tax included in an assessment or in an amendment of an assessment, may appeal against the assessment or amended assessment, but subject to certain conditions and limitations. The rules related to appeals against assessments are discussed more fully in **Division 2.2**. At this point, it may be noted that a chargeable person is not entitled to appeal against a self assessment or against any Revenue assessment calculated by a Revenue officer based on the data contained in the chargeable person's own tax return.

Interest on tax

Interest is chargeable on any tax underpaid or on any tax paid late (ie not paid on or before the due date for the tax in question). The rules for interest on tax (other than in cases of fraud or neglect) are discussed in detail in **2.107**, **2.109** and **2.203**. Where tax is underpaid in cases of fraud or neglect, interest is charged at a penal rate as a form of penalty for tax years up to and including 2004: see **2.702**.

Obligations of chargeable person

It is to be emphasised that a chargeable person's obligations to make the minimum preliminary tax payment required by the facts of his/its circumstances and to make the tax return for each tax year exist whether or not Revenue sends him/it any notice to pay preliminary tax or to make a tax return. Failure by the chargeable person to meet his obligations by the required dates is likely to result in liability for interest on the tax ultimately found to be payable and a surcharge for the late filing of the return.

The date for the payment of preliminary tax and the specified return date, as well as the other rules for preliminary tax and the making of tax returns, are discussed in more detail respectively in **2.104** and **2.105**.

TCA 1997, s 876 requires any person chargeable to income tax for any year of assessment to notify an inspector of taxes that he is so chargeable if he has not been sent a return of income to complete under either TCA 1997, s 877 (persons liable to income tax) or TCA 1997, s 879 (individuals liable to income tax) or if he has not made a return of income for that year of assessment. The person must give this notice to the inspector no later than one year after the end of the year of assessment for which he is chargeable. For example, an individual liable to income tax for the year 2015 must notify the inspector that he is chargeable for that year no later than 31 December 2016 if he has not been sent a tax return for 2015 or has not otherwise made a return of his total income for the year 2015 before that date.

Failure to comply with this rule renders the person concerned liable to a penalty of €3,000 (TCA 1997, s 1052). In the context of self assessment, TCA 1997, s 959I goes beyond TCA 1997, s 876 by imposing on every 'chargeable person' (see **2.102**) the obligation to make a full tax return in accordance with s 879 to the Collector General, whether or not the Revenue is previously aware of the chargeable person's existence (see **2.105**). TCA 1997, s 876, however, remains applicable to chargeable persons under the self assessment regime.

2.104 Preliminary tax and overpayments of tax generally

TCA 1997, s 959AN provides that every person who is a chargeable person for income tax as respects any relevant tax year is liable to pay the amount of preliminary tax appropriate to that tax year in respect of the tax concerned. TCA 1997, s 959AO sets out the due dates for payment of income tax, including the rules regarding the payment of preliminary tax.

By way of exception, up to the tax year 2013, preliminary tax (as such) was not payable in any case where the chargeable person had received an assessment for that tax before the due date for the payment of that preliminary tax. In such a case, the amount of the tax charged in the assessment was payable, instead of any preliminary tax, on the due date for the preliminary tax. This could only happen where the chargeable person had filed the return for the tax concerned before its preliminary tax due date (which would be exceptional). This provision does not apply for the tax year 2013 and subsequent years.

There are two important requirements in relation to the preliminary tax payment namely:

(a) the payment must be made by or on behalf of the chargeable person no later than the due date for the preliminary tax; and

(b) the amount to be paid as preliminary tax must be no less than a minimum amount the rules for the determination of which are contained in TCA 1997, s 959AO.

A chargeable person who fails to satisfy both these requirements – the timing test and the adequacy test – regarding the preliminary tax payment for a tax year may be said 'to fail his (or its) preliminary tax obligation'. Failure to meet the preliminary tax obligation normally results in interest on the tax assessed (after the tax return has been filed) being charged from the due date for the preliminary tax to the actual date(s) of payment.

Due date for preliminary tax

TCA 1997, s 959AO(1) prescribes the date on which the preliminary tax is due and payable (the 'due date') as 31 October in the relevant tax year. In the case of taxpayers filing their 2015 return and paying both their preliminary tax for 2016 and their balance of tax due for 2015 electronically under ROS, the deadline is likely to be extended beyond 31 October 2016 to mid November in line with the practice of previous years (still to be confirmed at the date of writing).

For preliminary tax to be paid on time, it must be paid 'on or before' the relevant due date. In the event that the due date is a Saturday, Sunday or public holiday, it is advisable to make the payment on the immediately preceding working day, although in practice the Revenue Commissioners usually accept a payment received on the immediately following working day as being paid on time.

A taxpayer may pay the preliminary tax in respect of his liability to income tax by direct debit (TCA 1997, s 959AP). The debits must consist of equal monthly instalments of the tax, payable in the calendar year in which the due date for the preliminary tax falls, as follows:

(a) as respects the first period of assessment for which the Collector-General is authorised to collect the tax by direct debit, by a minimum of three equal monthly instalments in that year; and

(b) as respects any subsequent period of assessment for which the Collector-General is authorised to collect the tax by direct debit, by a minimum of eight equal monthly instalments in that year.

Under these arrangements, the taxpayer is required to comply with any conditions which the Collector-General may reasonably impose to ensure that the tax will be paid on time. Where a taxpayer may have difficulties in meeting their direct debit obligations, the Collector-General will be given discretion to vary the number of instalments or to allow an increase or decrease in any particular instalment in order to facilitate the taxpayer in meeting their overall preliminary tax obligations.

Minimum preliminary tax required

TCA 1997, s 959AO(3) sets out the minimum amount of income tax which must be paid as preliminary tax for a tax year (by the due date for that tax) if the due date for all of the tax charged in an assessment is not to be backdated to the due date for the preliminary tax (see *Due date where preliminary tax payments not met* in **2.107**).

The minimum preliminary tax payment required for income tax for the tax year 2015 is the lower of:

(a) 90 per cent of the final income tax payable for the current (2015) tax year;

(b) 100 per cent of the final income tax payable for the immediately preceding (2014) tax year; or

(c) in the case only of taxpayers availing of the direct debit facility (see **2.104**), 105 per cent of the final income tax payable for the pre-preceding (2013) tax year.

It should be noted that the minimum preliminary tax payment required is calculated by reference to an individual's 'income tax' liability. Thus although 'tax' includes domicile levy, an individual who is liable to domicile levy does not have to include the amount of domicile levy payable in his preliminary tax payment. As set out at **2.102** above, 'income tax' includes PRSI and universal social charge and therefore, both PRSI and universal social charge must be included in preliminary tax payments.

For all preliminary tax percentage tests, the income tax payable is taken after deducting any credits or other reliefs against tax to which the person chargeable may be entitled for the relevant tax year. However, in applying the test to any of the percentages under (b) above, the calculation of the income tax payable must be made without allowing any Employment and Investment Incentive relief or any film investment relief (TCA 1997, s 959AO(4)(c)). Relevant tax payable in relation to share options exercised after 28 March 2003 is also disregarded for the purposes of these tests: see **10.113**.

A person who becomes a chargeable person for the first time in say tax year 2015 will have no liability to pay preliminary tax for that year, since the income of the previous tax year (2014) will be treated as nil for the purposes of the calculation under (b), leading to a nil liability under the 100 per cent preceding year rule (TCA 1997, s 959AO(4)(a)). A person may become chargeable for the first time either by acquiring new sources of income or by becoming resident in the State in the tax year concerned.

Where the tax liability of the pre-preceding tax year is nil, or is treated as nil because the individual was not a chargeable person in relation to that year, the direct debit facility based on the 105 per cent of the pre-preceding year will not be available (TCA 1997, s 959AO(3)(b)); otherwise, eg a person who became a chargeable person for the first time in 2015 could escape the liability to pay preliminary tax in both 2015 and 2016.

Where a married couple or a couple in a civil partnership are jointly assessed, their combined incomes are assessed upon whichever one of the spouses or partners is the chargeable person in respect of the tax year concerned (see **3.502**). In principle if one spouse (say the wife) or partner was the chargeable person in the current tax year but the other spouse (the husband) or partner was the chargeable person in a previous tax year, then the wife or partner concerned would have nil income in relation to the previous tax year. However, TCA 1997, s 959AO(5) provides effectively that the spouses or partners will be deemed to have elected that the spouse or partner who is the chargeable person for the current tax year was also the chargeable person for the preceding or pre-preceding year as the case may be. TCA 1997, s 959AO(5) also makes similar provision to cover cases where the couple were assessed as single persons (see **3.503**) or separately assessed under joint assessment (see **3.504**) in the preceding or pre-preceding tax year as the case may be.

As a taxpayer's obligation to pay a minimum amount of preliminary tax by 31 October in the year of assessment can be met if he or she pays 100 per cent of their income tax liability for the preceding year; any underpayment for the preceding year which arises because of computational error automatically causes that person to fail to reach this preliminary tax threshold. Prior to the tax year 2013, there was a provision for the non-application of interest and penalties in the circumstances described in **2.107** (tolerances for computational errors in calculating balance of tax in the absence of an assessment being raised) which was also extended to the person's preliminary tax payment for the current year in so far as the amount of preliminary tax paid was based on 100 per cent of the previous year's tax liability. This facility only applied where the shortfall in preliminary tax is made good by 31 December in that year (TCA 1997, s 958(4A)). This facility no longer exists with effect for the tax year 2013 and subsequent tax years.

Where after 31 October in a tax year additional income tax becomes due for the preceding year, or pre-preceding year, and the additional income tax is payable within one month following the amendment of an assessment (see **2.109**) or the determination of an appeal (see **2.203**) the additional income tax payable is not taken into account in determining whether sufficient preliminary tax has been paid (TCA 1997, s 959AO(4)).

Finally, under TCA 1997, s 65(3) where a person changes their accounting date, the previous year must be reviewed on the basis that the new accounting date applied also for that previous year. Where this review results in the profits of the previous year being higher than the profits actually assessed for that year, the extra profits are taxed. The additional tax due, if any, for the preceding year will be payable at the same time as the tax for the current year is due, that is, on or before 31 October in the year following the year the tax return is being made. This obligation to pay the additional tax, if any, arises notwithstanding that the assessment for the year may not have been amended. Provision is also made to ensure that this additional payment of tax is not taken into account in determining the taxpayer's preliminary tax payments for the tax year concerned or for any tax year for which the tax year reviewed formed the basis of the preliminary tax payment (TCA 1997, s 959AO(6)).

Position where preliminary tax paid late

TCA 1997, s 959AN(3) provides that preliminary tax paid (without being subsequently repaid) in respect of a tax year is to be treated as a payment on account of the tax payable by the chargeable person for the chargeable period. Accordingly, the provisions of TCA

1997, s 1080, which charge interest on late payment of tax due and payable for a chargeable period apply to late payment of preliminary tax (see **Example 2.107.4**).

Position where tax overpaid

The amount of tax paid as preliminary tax for any tax year may sometimes exceed the chargeable person's liability to tax for that tax year. In this event, the amount overpaid is repayable to the chargeable person together with interest. Other situations may also arise where tax is overpaid and repayment thereof is subsequently made.

The general legal right to interest on overpaid tax has been the subject of significant case law developments. In *Woolwich Equitable Building Society v IRC* [1992] STC 657 the House of Lords extended the scope of the principle of restitution. It held that tax paid under *ultra vires* regulations was repayable immediately, even though it was not paid under either a mistake of law or under compulsion or duress (although two of the majority law lords indicated that they felt it was relevant that the tax was paid 'under pressure'). It followed that interest accrued in favour of the taxpayer from the date on which the tax was overpaid. The House of Lords left open the applicability of the doctrine to a situation where the Inland Revenue had collected or demanded excessive tax as a result of their misconstruing the tax laws.

Exactly this situation arose in *O'Rourke v Revenue Commissioners* V ITR 321, where the taxpayer had acquiesced in his treatment as a Sch E taxpayer and suffered deduction of PAYE from his remuneration. Following the decision in *O'Coindealbhain v Mooney* (see **10.103**), the taxpayer was reclassified as a Sch D taxpayer and received a repayment of overpaid PAYE. The Supreme Court held that no interest on the repayment was due under (the since repealed) FA 1976, s 30, which applied only if tax was found to be overpaid following the determination of an appeal against an assessment. The Revenue had agreed the repayments without having raised assessments (indeed the Revenue argued that even if they had raised assessments, the assessments would have been made correctly under Sch D, so that there would have been no grounds for appeal in any event). The Supreme Court referred the issue back to the High Court for further consideration.

In the High Court, Keane J took the view that the principle in *Woolwich* applied in any instance where tax had been paid for 'no consideration' (ie where it was not lawfully due) so that the Revenue Commissioners had been unjustly enriched thereby. This reasoning was approved by the Supreme Court in *Harris v Quigley & Anor* VI ITR 839. The learned judge distinguished *Murphy & Murphy v Attorney General* V ITR 613, where the Supreme Court had refused to order repayment of all the tax paid under the system of taxing married couples which had been declared to be unconstitutional. In the latter case:

> the unravelling of every affected taxpayer's accounts would have meant dire fiscal consequences for the State on behalf of all taxpayers.

By way of contrast, in the present case:

> the numbers (involved) are so relatively small as to render the distortion of the State's finances minimal and legitimately outweighed by the injustice to the plaintiff of having his money withheld from him.

The learned judge held that the rate of interest applicable was that provided under the Courts Act 1981, s 22(1) by analogy with the decision in *Texaco (Ireland) v Murphy* IV ITR 91 (see **2.205**) (see also *Bank of Ireland Trust Services v Revenue Commissioners*).

With general effect from 1 November 2003, entitlement to interest on repayments of tax made from that date onwards is governed by TCA 1997, s 865A as inserted by FA 2003, s 17 and given effect by SI 508/2003.

It may be noted that TCA 1997, s 865(6) provides that the Revenue may not pay interest on overpayments of tax otherwise than in accordance with TCA 1997, s 865A, ie the intention is to provide a comprehensive statutory framework which will supersede the rights established by the foregoing case law. The previous position regarding repayments and interest thereon is dealt with in the 2003 edition of this book.

TCA 1997, s 865A provides that all repayments of tax to which it applies (unless offset against other liabilities under TCA 1997, s 960H: see **2.617**) are eligible to attract interest. Where a repayment arises because of a mistaken assumption by Revenue in the application of the Tax Acts, interest will be paid from the date the tax was paid until the repayment is made. In all other cases, including repayments of preliminary tax, interest will be payable from the end of 93 days after the date on which a claim for the repayment becomes a valid claim up to the date on which the repayment is made (a six month period applied to repayments made prior to 2 April 2007) *Tax Briefing 56*.

The Revenue Commissioners have given their views on the interpretation of 'mistaken assumption' on their part in *Tax Briefing 59*, worthwhile quoting at some length:

> Whether or not a repayment of tax arises from a mistaken assumption in the application of the law by Revenue can only be determined by reference to the relevant facts and circumstances surrounding that repayment. Such a repayment can only arise where the overpaid tax was originally paid because of a position adopted or a ruling made by Revenue in a particular case or because of a published interpretation of the law by Revenue and the position, ruling or interpretation was subsequently revised or found, for whatever reason, to be incorrect. The fact that Revenue processed a return or statement that contained a mistaken treatment of some item by the person making the return does not make any repayment subsequently arising from the correction of that mistake a mistaken assumption repayment.
>
> Revenue will, therefore, accept that a mistaken assumption is established where, for instance, repayments arise because:
>
> (a) The High Court or the Supreme Court or the European Court of Justice has found against Revenue's interpretation of the law;
>
> (b) Revenue accepted a ruling of the Circuit Court or of the Appeal Commissioners that they had incorrectly interpreted a particular provision;
>
> (c) Revenue accepted a recommendation of the Ombudsman that they had applied the law incorrectly in a particular case;
>
> (d) Revenue otherwise revised its published interpretation of a particular provision or a position adopted, or ruling made, in a particular case.
>
> Mistaken assumption would not, however, apply where, in a particular case, Revenue, for whatever reason, settled that case and agreed to repay tax without prejudice to its view of the meaning of a particular legal provision underlying the case. Apart from the situations indicated above, it is difficult to be more specific. Essentially, repayments will have to be looked at on a case by case basis to determine whether they arise because of a mistaken assumption in the application of the law by Revenue or whether they arise for some other reason.

A taxpayer is generally treated as making a valid claim when a return or statement for a tax year which he is required to make contains all of the information reasonably required by the Revenue to calculate the repayment, or in the absence of such information whenever it is subsequently supplied by the taxpayer to the Revenue (TCA 1997, s 865(1)(b)(i), (ii)). With effect from 3 February 2005, it is made clear that a valid claim may relate only to a repayment that would arise out of an assessment that was actually made or (if none was made) the assessment that would have been made at the time the statement or return is delivered and on foot of the statement or return. In *Tax Briefing 59,* the Revenue Commissioners set out their approach to these provisions. They state:

> Where a repayment arises as a result of a mistaken view taken by Revenue of the tax treatment of some item, and that item had either been correctly dealt with in the return or statement or correctly excluded from the return or statement, the return or statement should be regarded as a valid claim for the purposes of the time limit for claims.
>
> An example of an item correctly contained in a return or statement giving rise to a repayment, would be where Revenue disallowed a claim to relief claimed in a return and the relief is subsequently found to be due – the return would be regarded as a valid claim, assuming the return contained the information necessary to quantify the relief.
>
> For practical purposes, a return should be regarded as containing all the information that Revenue may reasonably require to determine if and to what extent a repayment is due if either assessing in accordance with the figures contained in the return or amending the assessment made to bring it into line with the figures contained in the return would result in the repayment concerned becoming due.

An exception to the above rules is any adjustment made under the terms of a Double Tax Agreement (A 'correlative adjustment'), when a valid claim will be treated as arising at the point when the amount of the adjustment is agreed in writing by Ireland and the other treaty state.

Furthermore, the requirement in TCA 1997, s 865(3) that the Revenue Commissioners cannot repay overpaid tax in the absence of a valid claim is not to prevent the Commissioners repaying tax deducted under PAYE in a case where they are satisfied that tax has been overpaid. However, this will not apply in the case of a self assessment taxpayer with PAYE income. They will continue to have to make a claim for any overpaid tax. Under this derogation the Revenue may not make a repayment at a time at which a claim for the repayment would not be allowed, that is, after four years from the end of the year to which the repayment relates.

Where a taxpayer submits a full return but the Inspector makes enquiries into one or more matters contained in the return, including requests for backup documentation, it is the date of the submission of the return and not the date on which the taxpayer satisfies the Inspector's enquiries which is the date of the valid claim (see *Tax Briefing 56*, p 9 Example 8).

The rate of interest provided for overpaid tax is currently 0.011 per cent per day or part of a day (approximately four per cent per annum); the rate may be varied by the Minister of Finance by regulations to be laid before the Dáil (TCA 1997, s 865A(3)). The taxpayer is denied any interest on an overpayment of preliminary tax if the interest is less than €10 (TCA 1997, s 865A(4)(a)). Any interest paid to a taxpayer in respect of an overpayment of tax is received gross by him and is not to be brought into account in computing taxable income for any purpose (TCA 1997, s 865A(4)(b)).

In practice, the Collector General normally makes the repayment to the chargeable person of any excess preliminary tax paid, where this occurs, shortly after a self assessment return has been filed including where a self assessment is made by a Revenue officer for the relevant tax year based on the chargeable person's tax return. The amount of the Collector's cheque includes the appropriate amount (if any) of interest. For overpayments of preliminary tax, the refund may be made immediately after an assessment is made, whether this is before or after the specified return date (see **2.105**). As the submission of a full tax return is treated as the making of a valid claim, it would require a delay of 93 days from the date of submission to create any entitlement to interest.

In relation to repayments, a general right to repayment of tax overpaid is provided for with effect from 31 October 2003 by TCA 1997, s 865. The repayment will be made irrespective of whether the tax was overpaid under an assessment or otherwise and irrespective of the presence or absence of any mistake on the part of the taxpayer. Any repayment must be subject to a valid claim and also must normally be made within four years from the end of the tax year to which it relates (TCA 1997, s 865(4)). However, with effect from 25 March 2005, the Revenue Commissioners are empowered to make repayments of PAYE to individuals who are not chargeable persons within the self assessment system (brought in as part of the rollout of ROS to PAYE taxpayers); such repayments remain subject to the standard four-year time limit (TCA 1997, s 865(3A), inserted by FA 2005, s 24).

TCA 1997, s 865 imposes a four-year time limit on all claims for repayments made on or after 1 January 2005, subject to a number of exceptions where tax is repayable as a consequence of events which take place subsequent to the original transaction, namely: TCA 1997, s 100(2) (charge on sale of land with reconveyance: see **12.206**); TCA 1997, s 480A (relief on retirement for certain sportspersons: see **10.101**; **5.8**); TCA 1997, s 482 (relief for expenditure on significant buildings and gardens: see **18.301**); TCA 1997, s 489(5) (seed capital relief: see **18.112**); TCA 1997, s 774(7) (spreading of special employer pension contributions to an approved pension scheme: see **16.108**); TCA 1997, s 776(2) (spreading of special employee contributions to a statutory pension scheme: see **16.113**); TCA 1997, s 804 (adjustments to assessments following completion of administration of an estate: see **15.203**); TCA 1997, s 959AA(2) (amendment of assessments outside normal four-year limit: see **2.106**) (TCA 1997, s 865(4); FA 2008, Sch 6). For the previous position and related transitional measures see the 2006 edition of this book.

Where a claim is made under a provision which stipulates a shorter time limit than four years, the shorter limit will apply (TCA 1997, s 865(5)). There is a right of appeal against any Revenue decision in respect of a repayment claim which is made by reference to s 865 (TCA 1997, s 865(7)).

Example 2.104.1

Ms N Curtain paid preliminary tax €12,800 for 2016 on 30 October 2016 and filed her income tax return for 2016 on 27 October 2017, paying the balance of tax due in accordance with the return of €700. On 30 November 2016, Ms Curtain belatedly realises that she should have claimed a deduction for interest paid on a loan to acquire shares in a trading company, generating a repayment of €2,100 for 2016. She immediately requests Revenue to repair her tax return and to make the repayment arising therefrom. The claim for repayment is made within four years from the end of the tax year (2016) to which it relates and accordingly meets the requirements of TCA 1997, s 865. The Revenue officer issues an appropriately amended assessment on 1 January 2017 and a repayment of €2,100 is made on 6 January 2017. As the repayment is made within 93 days of the valid claim being made (ie within 93 days of 30 November 2016, the date on which the information needed to determine the amount of the repayment was furnished to the Revenue officer), no interest will run thereon in favour of Ms Curtain.

2.105 Tax returns

Forms of tax return

A return must be in the form prescribed by the Revenue Commissioners or in a form used under the authority of the Revenue Commissioners (TCA 1997, s 959I(1)). FA 1999, s 209 inserted TCA 1997, ss 917D–917N dealing with electronic filing of returns. In essence the provisions confirm that the obligation of any person to make a return to which these sections apply shall be treated as fulfilled by that person if it is made electronically, subject to certain conditions (including bearing a digital signature or other type of electronic identification). Only certain electronic transmissions are 'approved transmissions' (TCA 1997, s 917H). TCA 1997, s 917EA enables the Revenue Commissioners to require by regulation certain taxpayers to file certain returns ('specified returns') and pay their tax liabilities electronically. With effect from 1 January 2009 regulations have been issued by Revenue under TCA 1997, s 917EA introducing mandatory electronic filing on a phased basis for the majority of self assessed taxpayers. Under the mandatory e-filing programme taxpayers are required to pay and file online using Revenue's Online Service (ROS). Under Phase 1 of the programme all taxpayers whose tax affairs are dealt with by Large Cases Division were required to pay and file online with effect from 1 January 2009 (SI 341/2008). Under Phase 2 of the programme, e-filing was extended to certain large companies and all public bodies with effect from 1 January 2010 (SI 341/2008). Under Phase 3 of the programme, with effect from 1 June 2011 (SI 223/2011) e-filing was extended to the following categories:

- (a) all companies;
- (b) all trusts;
- (c) all partnerships;
- (d) self employed individuals subject to the limitation on specified reliefs for high income individuals (see **3.111**);
- (e) self employed individuals with Foreign Life Policies, Offshore Funds or other Offshore products (see **Division 17.4**);
- (f) self employed individuals claiming property based incentives (see **Division 18.6**).

Phase 4 of the programme (SI 156/2012) extended mandatory e-filing with effect from 1 June 2012 to all VAT registered persons and also individuals claiming the following reliefs and exemptions:

- (a) retirement annuity contract payments (TCA 1997, s 787);
- (b) PRSA contributions (TCA 1997, s 787C);
- (c) overseas pension plans: migrant member relief (TCA 1997, s 787N);
- (d) retirement relief for sportspersons (TCA 1997, s 480A);
- (e) relief for AVCs (TCA 1997, s 774 and s 776);
- (f) artists exemption (TCA 1997, s 195);
- (g) woodlands exemption (TCA 1997, s 140 and 232);
- (h) patent income exemption (TCA 1997, ss 141 and 234);
- (i) business expansion scheme relief (TCA 1997, s 489);
- (j) seed capital scheme relief (TCA 1997, s 493);
- (k) film relief (TCA 1997, s 481);
- (l) significant buildings/gardens relief (TCA 1997, s 482);

(m) interest relief on loans to acquire shares in a company/partnership (TCA 1997, ss 248, 250 and 253).

Phase 5 of the programme (SI 572/2014) extended mandatory e-filing with effect from 1 January 2015 to all persons who register for income tax on or after 1 January 2015. An individual who registers for income tax is defined as an individual who is required to file a tax return under TCA 1997, s 917EA, ie a 'chargeable person'. Such persons are required to file a tax return for 2015 and subsequent years electronically. Persons who are already a chargeable person on 31 December 2014 are not included in the category of persons required to file a tax return electronically for 2015 unless they are already required to file a return electronically, eg because they are VAT registered or are claiming one of the reliefs or exemptions set out above. If a person is a chargeable person on 31 December 2014 but informs the Revenue that they are not a chargeable person for 2015 or subsequent years and subsequently becomes a chargeable person again, the person is required to file a return electronically when they recommence to be a chargeable person.

Income tax returns which have been designated 'specified returns' by regulations issued under TCA 1997, s 917EA and which must be filed electronically by the above persons are as follows:

(a) annual tax returns required under self assessment (SIs 441/2001, 522/2001 and 636/2006);
(b) return required to be filed by high income individuals under TCA 1997, s 485FB (see **3.111**) (SI 830/2007);
(c) mandatory third party returns required under the specified provisions defined by TCA 1997, s 894 (see **2.602**) (SI 188/2011);
(d) returns of interest paid to EU residents, required by TCA 1997, s 898H and to residual entities in the EU, required by TCA 1997, s 898I, (see **2.604**) (SI 874/2005);
(e) returns of interest paid to intermediaries for residual entities required by TCA 1997, s 898C, (see **2.604**) (SI 874/2005);
(f) employer PAYE return forms P30, P35, P45 and P46 (SI 289/2000 and 112/2001) (see **11.101**);
(g) professional services withholding tax returns (see **2.505**);
(h) a tax return required to be filed by an individual when notified to do so by an Inspector under TCA 1997, s 879(2) (SI 186/2014).

TCA 1997, s 530K (see **2.311**) separately provides that returns of RCT payments by principals shall be made electronically.

A person may apply to the Revenue in writing to be excluded from the requirement to pay and file online on the grounds that the person does not have sufficient access to the internet or, if the person is an individual, that the individual is prevented by reason of age, mental or physical infirmity from paying and/or filing online. If a person is aggrieved by a decision of the Revenue not to exclude the person from online filing, the person may make an appeal to the Appeal Commissioners within 30 days of receipt of the notice from Revenue of their decision not to exclude the person from e-filing.

The time at which a payment which is made electronically is deemed to be made is the later of the due date for the payment and the time at which the Revenue receive authorisation to debit the amount of the payment from the account of the person in the relevant financial institution.

Income tax may be paid to the Revenue Commissioners by credit card, debit card or any other method or methods of payment which is or are approved by Revenue. The Revenue Commissioners are empowered to make regulations relating to these payment methods (TCA 1997, s 960EA). The Taxes Consolidation Act (Section 960EA) (Payment of Tax By Credit Card via Internet) Regulations 2012 (SI 255/2012) provides that a person can make a payment of tax using certain approved credit cards. The type of cards approved under these regulations are VISA and Master Card. Where a payment is made using one of these cards an additional charge equal to 1.1 per cent of the card must be paid. (The charge was reduced to 1.1 per cent from 1.49 per cent from 1 October 2014 (SI 433/2014)).

The right of appeal and the time at which a payment is deemed to be made is contained in the relevant statutory instrument which brought the person within mandatory e-filing.

TCA 1997, s 864A, inserted by FA 2005, s 23, provided enabling powers for the Revenue Commissioners to introduce facilities, including automated facilities, for PAYE taxpayers to make electronic (including telephone) claims for reliefs which are to be used in the operation of the PAYE system or in relation to repayments of tax paid under that system. The particular type of claims that can be made in accordance with the section must be specified by the Revenue Commissioners. In general, these claims will be in respect of all the main personal tax credits and reliefs, including notifications and notices in relation to the taxpayers circumstances eg change in personal circumstances or details and, in the case of married couples or civil partnerships, in relation to their preferred taxation option, ie single treatment, joint assessment or separate assessment. In the case of automated telephone claims, claims will be restricted to low risk tax credits eg age allowance, trade union subscriptions and service charges. PAYE Anytime is an online interactive system which permits PAYE taxpayers to view their tax details, claim tax credits, declare additional information and to request balancing statements; in order to use the system an individual must first register with PAYE Anytime on the Revenue Commissioners' website. TCA 1997, s 894A, inserted by FA 2007, s 9(1)(e) enables the Revenue Commissioners to require third parties to furnish details of expenditure incurred by individuals which may establish their entitlement to a personal relief within TCA 1997, s 458.

Form 11 is the main return of income form for an individual. Form 11E is a simplified version of form 11 which is suitable for self assessment taxpayers whose affairs are very straightforward; individuals who are required to file online via ROS cannot use Form 11E. For individuals whose main source of income relates to employment earnings or pensions, Form 12 is usually appropriate or Form 12S, which is a simplified version of Form 12; (the eForm 12 is the online version which is available for the tax year 2013 onwards;) such individuals who hold foreign bank accounts or interests in offshore funds in offshore states (see **17.407**) or designated foreign life policies are deemed to be chargeable persons and must therefore complete Form 11 online. The fact that the individual has other sources of income such as deposit interest, rents from property and/or earnings, fees, etc from sources other than his main employment does not of itself prevent him using Form 12, provided he is not a chargeable person required to file online. However, if he has foreign source income or distributions from resident companies, he should normally complete Form 11 instead. Further, if in any case where Form 12 has been completed, but the inspector considers the individual's circumstances require it, the inspector may request him to complete the fuller Form 11. Where the individual is married or in a civil partnership and is assessable jointly with his spouse or civil partner, the Form 11 must be used to include both his own income and that of his spouse or partner unless another form is suitable having regard to the circumstances of both spouses or partners.

Form 12A has a more limited application. It is not a return of income as such, but is an application for a certificate of tax credits and social insurance registration. It should be used by an individual who is taking up employment for the first time, or is resuming employment after a break in employment where his last employment ended before the commencement of the current tax year or is taking up employment in the State having just come from another Member State of the European Union.

For persons other than individuals chargeable to income tax (for example, the personal representatives of estates of deceased persons in course of administration, trustees, unincorporated bodies of persons, non-resident companies), the prescribed form is the Form 1.

Contents of tax return

TCA 1997, s 959I provides that, in the case of any person chargeable to income tax for a year of assessment, the tax return for that year must be in the prescribed form and must contain all the matters and particulars as would be required in a return delivered pursuant to a notice given to the chargeable person by the appropriate inspector under TCA 1997, s 877. Further, if the chargeable person is an individual, his tax return for the year must contain all such additional matters and particulars as would be required by a notice given to the chargeable person by the appropriate inspector under TCA 1997, s 879(1)–(4).

TCA 1997, s 877 provides that, for income tax, the particulars to be contained in a return requested from any person under that section are details of that person's income from each and every source as chargeable under the various Schedules of the Income Tax Acts for the tax year to which the return relates. The income included should be the amounts from each source computed in accordance with the rules provided in the Income Tax Acts.

TCA 1997, s 879(2), which applies only to individuals, overlaps with TCA 1997, s 877. It requires the individual's return (in the prescribed form) to give details of:

- (a) all his sources of income for the tax year to which the return relates;
- (b) the amount of his income from each source for that year (computed in accordance with the rules contained in the Income Tax Acts); and
- (c) such further particulars for the purposes of income tax for that year as may be required in the notice or indicated by the return form.

With effect from tax year 2004 onwards, the return requires additional information to be supplied in relation to specified claims for reliefs, allowances, exemptions, deductions and credits subject potentially to the imposition of penalties and the late return surcharge on failure to comply (see further below).

Latest date for return

TCA 1997, s 959I requires every chargeable person for income tax purposes to prepare and file a return for the tax concerned for the relevant year of assessment on or before the specified return date of the tax year. For the tax year 2015 the date is 31 October in the year of assessment following that year; this deadline is likely to be extended beyond 31 October 2016 to mid November in line with the practice of previous years (still to be confirmed at the date of writing) in the case of taxpayers paying their tax and filing returns electronically under the ROS system, as noted above.

This obligation to make the tax return by the specified return date exists whether or not the chargeable person is sent a return form to complete by an inspector of taxes (TCA 1997, s 959I(4)). If no notice to prepare a return is sent to a chargeable person for any tax year, he or it should seek out a return form and complete it and deliver it to the Collector General by the specified return date. For the exception from the obligation to make the tax return provided by TCA 1997, s 959N, see below.

The 'specified return date for the tax year' is the latest date by which the relevant tax return for a tax year must be delivered to the Collector General if the return is to be treated as filed on time. Failure to file a full and true return of all the particulars required for any of the three taxes by the specified return date may make the chargeable person liable to the 5 per cent or 10 per cent late return surcharge based on the amount of the relevant tax (see **2.110**).

Exclusion from tax return obligation

There is an exception to the requirement to make a return. TCA 1997, s 959N empowers a Revenue officer, by a notice in writing to a person (who would otherwise be a chargeable person), to exclude that person from the obligation to make a tax return. The notice may state that the person to whom it is given is not required to make a return for such tax year or periods as may be specified in the notice or until the happening of some event specified in the notice.

This rule of TCA 1997, s 959N is intended to apply to a person who satisfies the Revenue officer that his (or, if a company, its) income, credits and other circumstances are such that he is not likely to have any liability to tax for one or more tax years.

Notices to make returns

Any person who is chargeable to tax for a tax year must prepare and file the appropriate tax return whether or not he receives a notice from Revenue. By virtue of TCA 1997, s 959O(4), TCA 1997, s 1052 ('penalties for failures to make certain returns') is applied to a person who fails to file a return by the specified due date, even though he has not received a notice from Revenue (TCA 1997, s 1054(2)–(4)), which imposes increased penalties in the case of bodies of persons, is also applied – (see **2.701**).

When a chargeable person for income tax completes and files a tax return for a tax year, whether or not he is sent a return notice from Revenue, he is deemed to have been required by a notice under TCA 1997, s 879 to deliver the relevant tax return. The notice is deemed to have been given to the chargeable person on the specified return date for income tax (TCA 1997, s 959O(1)).

For example, assume that Mr B is sent an income tax return to complete for the tax year 2015 and that Ms G, who has become resident in the State from 1 January 2015 and who is a chargeable person for income tax for 2015, is not sent any tax return. Both individuals are obliged by TCA 1997, s 959I to complete and file a tax return form for 2015 no later than 31 October 2016 (the return filing date for the tax year 2015; subject to any extension for ROS taxpayers). TCA 1997, s 1052(1)–(3) may be applied to Mr B or Ms G if either fails to file their tax return for 2015.

Foreign accounts/offshore funds

TCA 1997, s 895 provides that where a resident person opens either directly or indirectly a 'foreign account' (or causes a 'foreign account' to be opened) to hold moneys beneficially owned by him, then he will automatically be deemed to be a chargeable person for the purposes of TCA 1997, s 959I. The return of income which he is thereby obliged to submit must include the following details of the foreign account:

(a) the name and address of the person with whom the account is held;
(b) the date on which the account was opened;
(c) the amount deposited on opening the account; and
(d) the name and address of the intermediary (if any) who provided any services in connection with the opening of the account (TCA 1997, s 895(6)).

A 'foreign account' is defined as an account in which a deposit is held at a location outside the State. A 'deposit' includes a sum of money which does not bear interest and one which is either repayable on demand or at a future time (TCA 1997, s 895(1)).

The section applies to foreign accounts opened on or after 1 June 1992.

TCA 1997, s 895(2) also imposes a requirement to make a return on any intermediary concerned in the opening of the account (see **2.605**) and requires the depositor to supply the intermediary with the information needed to make such a return. TCA 1997, s 895(4) imposes a penalty of €4,000 on default.

TCA 1997, s 896 applies similar provisions to investment in material interests in offshore funds (as defined by TCA 1997, s 743) see **17.4**) or foreign life policies (ie policies provided by a company carrying on all of its business outside Ireland or otherwise by a branch or agency carrying on business outside Ireland). The intermediary must make a return to the inspector of taxes containing in respect of each person for whom the person acts as intermediary, details of the name, address, tax reference number and details of the facilities provided. Where an intermediary fails to make a full and complete return he shall be held liable to a fine of €4,000 in respect of each failure.

Furthermore a person investing in an offshore fund or a foreign life policy must include details of that investment in their return, including the name or address of the fund or policy provider, the cost of the interest acquired or terms of the policy, including the premiums payable thereunder and the name and address of the relevant intermediary (TCA 1997, ss 896(5); 730I; 747C). In the cases of interests in offshore funds or policies based in designated 'offshore states' it is necessary to make full and timely returns of related income in order to avail of beneficial tax treatment (see **17.407**).

Returns of property transfers to non-resident trustees, returns by settlors in relation to non-resident trustees and returns by certain trustees

Provisions relating to these returns are contained in TCA 1997, ss 917A–917C.

TCA 1997, s 917A deals with returns of property transfers to non-resident trustees. Where, on or after 11 February 1999, a person transfers property to the trustees of a settlement otherwise than at arm's length (eg a gift) and the trustees of the settlement are neither resident nor ordinarily resident in the State at the time the property is transferred and the transferor has reasonable knowledge to believe that the trustees are not resident or ordinarily resident in the State, then the transferor is required to make a return within three months from the date of the transfer. The return must identify the settlement and specify the property transferred, the day on which the transfer was made, and the consideration (if any) for the transfer. Failure to comply with this return filing requirement gives rise to a penalty of €4,000. Such penalties may be proceeded for and recovered summarily.

TCA 1997, s 917B deals with returns by settlors in relation to non-resident trustees. Where a settlement is created on or after 11 February 1999, and at the time it is created the trustees are neither resident nor ordinarily resident in the State, or the trustees are resident and ordinarily resident in the State but fall to be regarded as resident outside the State for the purposes of any 'arrangements' (agreements for relief from double taxation), then within three months of the creation of the settlement the settlor must make a return under this section if domiciled in the State and either resident or ordinarily resident in the State. The return must specify the day on which the settlement was created, the name and address of the person making the statement and the names and addresses of the persons who are the trustees immediately after the return is filed. Similar penalties for non-compliance apply as for TCA 1997, s 917A.

TCA 1997, s 917C deals with returns by certain trustees. It applies where either the trustees of a settlement become neither resident nor ordinarily resident in the State on or after 11 February 1999, or where the trustees, while continuing to be resident and ordinarily resident in the State, are treated as resident in another State under a double taxation treaty. Any person who was a trustee of the settlement on or after 11 February 1999 or a date when one of the two events above happens, falling into one of the above categories, must within three months of such time, file a return setting out the day on which the settlement was created, the name and address of each person who is a settlor in relation to the settlement immediately before filing the return, and the names and addresses of the persons who are the trustees immediately before the delivery of the statement. Similar penalty provisions for non-compliance apply as in the case of TCA 1997, ss 917A–917B.

'Full and true' return

An important requirement is that the tax return by a chargeable person for a tax year should contain a full and true disclosure of all material facts necessary for the making of an assessment for the tax concerned for the relevant tax year. The phrase 'a full and true return' is used in this book, where appropriate, to refer to any tax return giving such a full and true disclosure of all the material facts for the relevant assessment.

Clearly, a tax return must, if it is to be 'full and true', disclose all items of income, in respect of which the person making the return is chargeable to tax for the relevant tax year. In principle, the return should correctly state the amount of each item of income to be taxed. Further, to the extent that any deductions, allowances or reliefs are claimed for the relevant tax year, full and correct details must be given of the facts in relation to these deductions, allowances or reliefs.

The importance of making a full and true return for each tax year cannot be over-emphasised. Failure to do so has, or is likely to have, as is mentioned elsewhere, adverse consequences on the chargeable person who makes a return which is less than a full and true one in the sense stated above. For example, the following points are noted briefly here:

(a) unless and until a full and true return has been filed by (or on behalf) of a chargeable person, the four-year time limit to the period in which an assessment or an amended assessment can be made on that person does not start to run (TCA 1997, s 959AA(1), see **2.108**);

(b) failure to file a full and true return may result in interest being charged on any additional tax becoming payable when an assessment is subsequently amended (see **2.109**);

(c) failure to file a full and true return prevented a taxpayer from availing of the tolerance for computational errors when paying the balance of tax in the absence of an assessment which existed prior to the tax year 2013 (see **2.107**);

(d) failure to file a full and true return (on or before the return filing date) may result in the late return surcharge being imposed if the failure is fraudulent or negligent or the failure is realised but not rectified in good time (see **2.110, 2.701**); and

(e) other penalties may be imposed if an incorrect return is made negligently or fraudulently (see **2.110, 2.701**).

'Expression of doubt'

A chargeable person (or the professional adviser completing that person's tax return) may not be sure if a particular fact is, or is not, material to the making of the assessment for a relevant tax year. Alternatively, the chargeable person may be uncertain as to the proper tax law or treatment of a particular point or matter. He may not, therefore, know whether or not it is necessary to refer to the fact or to bring the matter into account in completing the return. Clearly it may be desirable to resolve any doubts sooner rather than later. Revenue has set out guidelines for practitioners on making enquiries to Revenue offices.

TCA 1997, s 959P provides that where a chargeable person is in doubt as to the correct application of the law to any matter contained in a return which could give rise to a tax liability for that person or could impact on the person's liability to tax or entitlement to an allowance, deduction, relief or tax credit, the chargeable person should complete the return to the best of their belief as to the law applicable to the matter in doubt. In addition the chargeable person is required to include a 'letter of expression of doubt' with the return and submit supporting documentation to the appropriate inspector. In any case in which a chargeable person takes these steps in relation to any matter disclosed in the tax return, he (or the company) is treated as if a full and true disclosure were made regarding that matter. Consequently, the adverse consequences of failing to make a full and true return are avoided. The additional tax arising from the issue of a Revenue assessment to reflect the correct application of the law to the matter is payable within one month of the date of the issue of the amended assessment.

The concept of a 'letter of expression of doubt' was introduced into the legislation with effect for tax returns filed for the tax year 2013 and subsequent years when TCA 1997, s 955(4) was substituted by TCA 1997, s 959P. TCA 1997, s 955(4) provided for situations where a chargeable person was in doubt not only in relation to the application of law to any matter but also where doubt arose as to the 'tax treatment' of any matter. There is no provision for doubt as to the tax treatment of any matter in TCA 1997, s 959P. In addition, under TCA 1997, s 955(4) where a chargeable person was in doubt it was sufficient to draw the inspector's attention to the matter in the return by specifying the doubt. No additional supporting information had to be provided to Revenue at the time of filing the return.

A 'letter of expression of doubt' is defined in TCA 1997, s 959P as a communication by written or electronic means which:

(a) sets out the full facts and circumstances of the matter;

(b) specifies the doubt, the basis of the doubt and the law giving rise to the doubt;

(c) identifies the amount of tax in doubt;

(d) lists or identifies the supporting documentation which is being submitted to the appropriate inspector;

(e) is clearly identified as a letter of expression doubt.

Where the relevant return has been submitted electronically the supporting documentation to be submitted to the appropriate inspector must also be submitted electronically. The electronic means by which such information is to be submitted is to be specified by Revenue. At the time of writing such means had not yet been specified by Revenue.

There is an exception to the 'expression of doubt' rule. TCA 1997, s 959P(6) states that where a Revenue officer does not accept that the expression of doubt is genuine the chargeable person is treated as not making a full and true disclosure with regard to the matter in question. TCA 1997, s 959P(6) provides that an expression of doubt shall not be accepted as genuine in particular where:

(a) having regard to any guidelines published by the Revenue on the application of the law in similar circumstances and having regard to the supporting documentation provided in connection with the matter, the officer is of the opinion that the matter is sufficiently free from doubt; or

(b) the officer is of the opinion that the chargeable person was acting with a view to tax evasion or avoidance. (This presumably means that the taxpayer must have been employing the expression of doubt mechanism itself as a means of avoiding or evading tax, although the point is not beyond doubt.)

The legislation pre-2013 did not provide that an expression of doubt would not be accepted as genuine if having regard to guidelines published by Revenue on the application of the law in similar circumstances the officer is of the opinion that the matter is sufficiently free from doubt. Under the legislation from 2013 onwards the circumstances in which a taxpayer may express genuine doubt have been narrowed considerably. Firstly, there is no longer any provision whereby doubt can be expressed on the tax treatment of any item. This could arise where Revenue applies a concessional tax treatment of a particular item but the taxpayer is in doubt as to whether the concession would apply in his particular circumstances. Secondly, a genuine expression of doubt cannot be made where a taxpayer has a genuine doubt about the application of the law to any particular matter but the taxpayer's interpretation of the law is at variance with Revenue's interpretation as set out in any guidelines. In addition, the legislation would appear to be seeking to elevate Revenue guidelines to something more than just Revenue's interpretation of the legislation in question.

Where a Revenue officer does not accept that an expression of doubt is genuine he must notify the chargeable person and any additional tax due as a result of the amendment of an assessment is due on the same day as the tax contained in the assessment before it was amended was due. Thus if the assessment which is amended is the self assessment made by the chargeable person the additional tax due will be due either on the return filing date or the preliminary tax due date depending on whether the chargeable person is deemed to have underpaid preliminary tax as a result of the additional tax becoming payable.

If the chargeable person is not satisfied with a Revenue officer's decision on the genuineness of the doubt he has the right to appeal to the Appeal Commissioners on this issue.

There is no time limit in the legislation within which Revenue must give an opinion on the genuineness of an expression of doubt. Revenue have indicated that it is their policy to deal with expressions of doubt as they are raised, even if the matter in doubt does not lead to immediate tax consequences (eg the amount of a loss available for carry forward).

They have also stated in a precedent in respect of repayment cases that, in general, pending the examination of an expression of doubt, the Revenue should either amend the assessment in line with their view of the disputed item or make the repayment based on the assessment made in line with the return; however, in their view, they would have good reason to withhold repayment where the taxpayer has provided insufficient information to quantify the effect of the expression of doubt.

Partnership returns

The requirement of TCA 1997, s 880(2) for the precedent acting partner of a partnership, on receipt of a notice from the inspector, to make a return of partnership income and information relating to chargeable gains is dealt with in **4.508**. TCA 1997, s 959M deems the precedent partner of any partnership to be a chargeable person for purposes of the self assessment legislation. He is required to deliver the partnership return for each relevant year of assessment no later than the specified return date for that year (for example, 31 October 2016 for the return of the partnership income for 2015), whether or not he receives a notice from the inspector to do so.

Late return surcharge and penalties

The rules relating to the late return surcharge and to the associated penalties are dealt with in detail in **2.110**.

Amendment of return

TCA 1997, s 959V provides that a chargeable person may amend a return and a self assessment by giving notice in writing to Revenue within four years of the end of the tax year to which the return relates. With effect from 18 December 2013 (the date of the passing of Finance (No 2) Act 2013, a return and self assessment may only be amended under TCA 1997, s 959V where the amendment:

(a) arises from an allowance, credit, deduction or relief due;
(b) is necessary to correct an error or mistake; or
(c) is necessary to comply with any other provision of the Acts.

The notice to Revenue of the amendment must specify whether the amendment arises from (a), (b) or (c) above. Also, from 18 December 2013 a claim for a repayment of tax under TCA 1997, s 865 (see **2.111**), which arose due to an error or mistake in a return, will not be a valid claim unless the return and, in the case of returns for the year 2013 and subsequent years, the self assessment is amended to correct the error or mistake.

Where the original return was filed by electronic means the notice must also be made by electronic means (these electronic means are to be specified by Revenue). Notice to amend a return and a self assessment cannot be made where Revenue has started making enquiries under TCA 1997, s 959Z (see **2.108**), or for tax returns relating to tax years before 2013, under TCA 1997, s 956, in relation to the return or self assessment or where an audit or investigation has commenced relating to the tax affairs of the person to whom the return or self assessment relates for the chargeable period in question. It is accordingly possible for a chargeable person to amend a return for one tax year even though Revenue has started making enquiries or an audit or investigation has commenced with regard to another tax year. Where a person amends a return and does not also amend the self assessment in the return he is liable to a penalty of €100 (TCA 1997, s 959X(2)).

When TCA 1997, s 959V was enacted it was initially thought that the intention was to put on a statutory footing the concept of self correction included in Revenue's Code of Practice for Revenue Audits, although under the Code of Practice self correction was only permitted up to a period of 12 months from the due date for the filing of the return. Under the Code of Practice where a taxpayer self corrects a tax return no penalties are applied, however statutory interest on the underpayment is still due. Revenue has however confirmed that self correction without any penalty only applies if the correction is made within 12 months. A penalty may apply to any amendment of a return in accordance with TCA 1997, s 959V where the return is amended outside the 12-month time limit set out in the Code of Practice where the amendment results in an underpayment of tax.

2.106 Assessment of tax

As set out at **2.101** above, a new Pt 41A (Assessing Rules Including Rules for Self Assessment) replaced Pt 39 (Assessments) and Pt 41 (Self Assessment) with effect for the tax year 2013 and subsequent years. Part 41A reproduces many of the provisions of Pt 39 and Pt 41, however Pt 41A also provides for the move to a full self assessment system by providing for assessments to be made by chargeable persons. For tax years prior to the tax year 2013 only Revenue could make an assessment. While a chargeable person was still obliged to pay his tax liability regardless of whether or not an assessment was issued by Revenue, in order to provide the mechanism for finalising the liability of an individual, Revenue issued an assessment for each chargeable person following the filing of a return. With effect for returns filed for the tax year 2013 and subsequent years chargeable persons are required to make their own assessment. Prior to 2013 assessments were only issued by Revenue. With effect for 2013 and subsequent tax years there are two types of assessments, 'Revenue assessments' and 'self assessments'. A 'Revenue assessment' is any assessment other than a self assessment (TCA 1997, s 959C(1)). A 'self assessment' is an assessment which is required to be included in a chargeable person's return (TCA 1997, s 959R(1)).

An assessment details:

(a) the amount of the income, profits or gains arising to the person;
(b) the amount of tax chargeable on the person for the period;
(c) the amount of tax payable by the person for the period;
(d) the balance of tax payable.

The amount of tax chargeable on the person for the period is the amount of tax chargeable after taking into account any allowances, deductions or reliefs and any increase in the individual's taxable income due to the limitation on specified reliefs for high income individuals (TCA 1997, s 959A(1)) (see **3.111**). The amount of tax payable by the person is the amount of tax chargeable on the person after deduction of any tax credits.

An assessment should be in respect of one chargeable period only and should include all tax charged on the person for that chargeable period, ie an assessment for an individual for 2015 should include the individual's liability to income tax, capital gains tax, PRSI, universal social charge and domicile levy. Where a surcharge for the late filing, or deemed late filing, of a return arises (see **2.110**) this must also be included in the assessment.

Amounts due in respect of income tax, PRSI, domicile levy and universal social charge must be shown separately on a self assessment (TCA 1997, s 959R(4)). Where the assessment includes a surcharge for the late filing of a return this must also be shown separately on a self assessment.

There is no requirement that the assessment should analyse the income arising under the various Schedules/Cases, give a breakdown of the amount of the allowances, deductions or reliefs arising, to show how the tax chargeable, the tax payable or the balance of tax has been calculated. An assessment is not however the same as a notice of assessment and these details must be included on a notice of assessment (see below).

Revenue are required to keep a record of all Revenue assessments made and self assessments made by Revenue (TCA 1997, s 959D(1)). This record may be kept in electronic format.

Self assessments

TCA 1997, ss 959R–959X contain the rules regarding self assessments. A self assessment is an assessment made by the chargeable person (TCA 1997, s 959A). TCA 1997, s 959R provides that every chargeable person must include a self assessment in the person's self assessment return. The details to be included in a self assessment are as set out above for assessments. A self assessment should be made by reference to the details included in the chargeable person's return. A penalty of €250 applies to a chargeable person who does not include a self assessment in the chargeable person's return.

Where a return is filed online using ROS and the self assessment included in a return is based on such 'indicative tax calculation' as may be provided by ROS and the chargeable person pays tax in accordance with that calculation then in the event that the ROS tax calculation is incorrect any additional tax due is deemed to be due and payable no later than one month from the date of amendment of the self assessment and interest, penalties and late filing surcharge will not apply. In order to prove that ROS was relied on the chargeable person must retain a copy of the ROS tax calculation to be provided to Revenue if requested (TCA 1997, s 959R).

An individual is not required to include a self assessment in a self assessment return where a paper return is filed, as opposed to a return filed online, on or before 31 August in the year following the year to which the tax return relates (TCA 1997, s 959S). In such cases a Revenue officer will make the self assessment on behalf of the taxpayer and the €250 penalty is not applied to the chargeable person. In the case of a married couple or civil partners who are separately assessed, a Revenue officer cannot make a self assessment on behalf of the taxpayer until the taxpayer's spouse/civil partner has also filed a return (TCA 1997, s 959S(4)). A Revenue officer can also make a self assessment where a return is filed without the inclusion of a self assessment (TCA 1997, s 959U(1)). Where a Revenue officer makes a self assessment where a self assessment is not included in the return filed, the assessment is deemed to be a self assessment rather than a Revenue assessment. The distinction is important as an appeal cannot be made against a self assessment (see **2.2**). A self assessment made by a Revenue officer must be made by reference to the details included in the chargeable person's return (TCA 1997, s 959W). Where a Revenue officer makes a self assessment a notice of assessment must be issued to the chargeable person. Where a person files a return for a chargeable person acting on the chargeable person's authority, the self assessment made by the person is deemed to have been made by the chargeable person (TCA 1997, s 959T).

As set out under **2.105** above, a chargeable person may amend a self assessment return. The notice given to Revenue amending the return must also amend the original self assessment (TCA 1997, s 959V). If the original self assessment is not amended a penalty of €100 applies (TCA 1997, s 959X).

Revenue assessments

A 'Revenue assessment' is any assessment other than a self assessment (TCA 1997, s 959C(1)). TCA 1997, s 959Y provides that a Revenue officer may at any time, make a Revenue assessment. However, where a chargeable person has delivered a return for a chargeable period and has made in the return a full and true disclosure of all material facts necessary for the making of an assessment for the chargeable period a Revenue assessment cannot be raised after the end of four years commencing at the end of the chargeable period in which the return is delivered (TCA 1997, s 959AA).

The critical date appears to be that on which the Revenue officer makes or amends the assessment, as opposed to the date on which the notice of the assessment is served on the taxpayer (*Honig v Sarsfield* [1986] STC 246).

TCA 1997, s 959AC provides that where a person chargeable to tax does not deliver a tax return, the Revenue officer may make an assessment on that person for such an amount of tax which, to the best of the officer's judgement, ought to be charged for the relevant year of assessment. The Revenue officer may also make an assessment if not satisfied with any tax return filed, having regard to any information received in that regard (including information received from a member of the Garda Síochána), or where the Revenue officer has reasonable grounds for believing that a return does not contain a full and true disclosure of all material facts. There is no definition of 'reasonable grounds' and Revenue Guidance notes do not give any guidance on the term. The term 'reasonable grounds' is also used in TCA 1997, s 959AD where it is provided that a Revenue officer may make a Revenue assessment outside the four-year limit where the officer has 'reasonable grounds' for believing that any form of fraud or neglect has been committed. The Revenue Guidance Notes on TCA 1997, s 959AD say that an assessment may be raised outside the four-year time limit where Revenue 'suspect' fraud or neglect. It has been suggested on this basis that Revenue may be equating having 'reasonable grounds' with having a 'suspicion' (for a commentary on this and case law dealing with the definition of 'reasonable grounds' see the article by Furlong, 'The New Self-Assessment Regime: Plus Ca Change …? 1 January 2013' (2013) Irish Tax Review). Where the Revenue officer enters details of an assessment in an electronic format and a notice of assessment issues in the name of another Revenue officer the officer whose name appears on the notice is deemed to have made the assessment and to have made it to the best of his judgement (TCA 1997, s 959D).

The grounds on which the Revenue officer may be dissatisfied with a return are not stated, but it is suggested here that the Revenue officer of taxes should have some reasonable cause before he can apply TCA 1997, s 959AC to make an assessment based otherwise than on the data in the tax return. However, the Revenue officer has the right to query any fact in a return or to make other enquiries to see if there is any reason to be dissatisfied with the return (TCA 1997, s 959Z). The Revenue officer's right to make enquiries is discussed further in connection with the amendment of assessments (see **2.108**), but it is to be noted here that the Revenue officer is entitled to make such enquiries before making any assessment.

TCA 1997, s 870 provides that an assessment will not be rendered void or voidable 'for want of form' nor will it be affected by reason of a 'mistake, defect or omission therein' if the assessment is 'in substance and in effect in conformity with or according to the intent and meaning of the Act and if the person or property charged or intended to be charged thereby ... is designated therein according to common intent and understanding'. TCA 1997, s 870 states that in particular an assessment will not be impeached by a mistake concerning the name or surname of the taxpayer, the description of any profits or property, or the amount of the tax charged. For cases where the UK equivalent provisions were applied, see *Fleming v London Produce* 44 TC 582; *Hoare Trustees v Gardner* [1978] STC 89, and contrast *Baylis v Gregory* [1987] STC 297.

The section does not apply where the assessment is exactly as the Revenue officer intended, even if based on an erroneous view of the law or facts (*Bath & West Counties Property Trust Ltd v Thomas* [1978] STC 30). However, the discretionary power of the court under TCA 1997, s 941 extends to making an order that a corrected assessment should be raised (see *IRC v McGuckian* [1994] STC 888, in which the Northern Ireland Court of Appeal held that, where an inspector had raised an assessment under the incorrect charging provisions as a result of the withholding of material information by the taxpayer, the court could make an order of this kind). TCA 1997, s 959F provides that any person who is assessed more than once in the same year 'for the same cause' and 'on the same amount' may apply to the Revenue Commissioners to have the double assessment vacated. TCA 1997, s 959F provides that where the Revenue Commissioners are satisfied that there has been a double assessment, they shall order the excess assessment to be vacated. TCA 1997, s 959F provides any overpayment is to be offset against any other tax liabilities of the person in accordance with TCA 1997, s 960H or repaid. No offset or repayment will be made outside the 4-year time limits provided by TCA 1997, s 865B (offset) and s 865 (repayment). TCA 1997, s 959F is a mechanical provision, primarily designed to give relief in cases of administrative errors. In *Bye v Coren* [1986] STC 393, the Court of Appeal upheld the practice of making alternative assessments of the same receipt; the court indicated that where it happened that both assessments had become final and conclusive, relief would be available under the equivalent to TCA 1997, s 959F.

Assessment under rules of self assessment

Before examining the detailed rules, the following summary of the more important principles applying for any relevant tax year is given:

(a) a chargeable person is required to include a self assessment in the chargeable person's return (TCA 1997, s 959R) unless the person files a paper return before 31 August in the year following the year to which the tax return relates (TCA 1997, s 959S). In such cases a Revenue officer will make the self assessment on behalf of the taxpayer. The self assessment should be made by reference to the details contained in the chargeable person's return (TCA 1997, s 959W(2) and (3));

(b) if no tax return is filed by the chargeable person by the relevant return filing date (see **2.105**), if a Revenue officer is not satisfied with any return filed or a Revenue officer has reasonable grounds for believing a return is not a full and true return, a Revenue officer is entitled to make an assessment (see Assessment when no return or inadequate return below) (TCA 1997, s 959AC);

(c) a Revenue officer is not entitled to make any assessment for a tax year before the relevant return filing date for that tax year, unless the chargeable person has filed his (or, if a company, its) tax return for that year (TCA 1997, s 959AE(2)); F(TA)A 2015, s 39 (SI 110/2016 appointed 21 March 2016 as the day on which the Finance (Tax Appeals) Act 2015, came into operation), inserts TCA 1997, s 959AE(5), which makes clear that an assessment may not be amended unless it is so authorised by the Acts.

(d) the amount of tax charged by the assessment for the year (after deducting any preliminary tax already paid) should be paid on or before the due date for the tax in the assessment, ie by 31 October following the end of the tax year concerned, irrespective of whether the assessment has been raised at that point (see **2.107**), except to the extent that a valid appeal is made against any tax assessed which exceeds the tax payable based on the facts disclosed in the relevant tax return (see **2.202**); and

(e) a Revenue officer is entitled to amend an assessment (or a previously amended assessment) if he finds that the assessment (or amended assessment) does not charge the correct amount of tax but no assessment (or an amendment to an assessment) can, in principle, be made more than four years after the end of the tax year in which a 'full and true' return was filed by the chargeable person but an assessment may be made at any time without time limit if no return is made for that year or if any return made is not a 'full and true' one (although the four-year time limit may be activated from the end of a later tax year in which the previous default is fully rectified). (see *Time limit for assessment or amendment of assessment* in **2.108**).

Example 2.106.1

Ms S Longfield filed her income tax return manually for 2016 on 17 June 2017 (well in advance of the specified return date). Mr T Deepwell files his return for 2016 on 31 October 2017 (the specified return date – he does not file under ROS). Both individuals had paid the appropriate amounts of preliminary tax for 2016 before 31 October 2016 (due date for that preliminary tax).

A Revenue officer is entitled to make a 2016 income tax assessment on Ms Longfield at any time after 17 June 2017 (due to her early filing of her return). However, assuming a balance of tax due under the assessment after crediting the preliminary tax paid, this balance is not payable by Ms Longfield until 31 October 2017 (the due date for the balance of the tax assessed when the appropriate amount of the preliminary tax was paid in time, see Due Date for tax charged in assessment in **2.107**).

In the case of Mr Deepwell, TCA 1997, s 959AE(2) prevents a Revenue officer making any assessment on him for 2016 before 31 October 2017 (the specified return date) since Mr Deepwell's return is only filed on that date.

Notice of assessment

Where a Revenue officer makes an assessment the office must give a notice of assessment to the chargeable person (TCA 1997, s 959E(1)). In addition to the details required to be included in an assessment set out above, a notice of assessment issued by a Revenue officer should include the name of the Revenue officer and the address of the Revenue office, the time allowed for giving notice of appeal and, where the assessment includes more than one type of tax (eg income tax, PRSI and USC), must identify separately the liability to the different taxes. A notice of assessment 'may' also give the following details:

(a) details of the income assessed under the various Schedules;
(b) legislative references;
(c) the amount of each allowance, deduction, relief or tax credit to which the person is entitled;
(d) how the tax chargeable has been calculated;

(e) how the tax payable has been calculated; and

(f) how the balance of tax payable/repayable has been calculated.

TCA 1997, s 959E(6) says that the above additional details 'may' be given. The circumstances in which these details may or may not be given are not yet clear at the time of writing.

Where an assessment is issued because a person has failed to deliver a return, because a Revenue officer is not satisfied with the sufficiency of the return or because a Revenue officer has reasonable grounds for believing that a return is not a full and true return TCA 1997, s 959AC provides that it is not necessary to include any particulars in the notice of assessment other than the amount of tax payable.

Appeals against assessments

For a full discussion of the circumstances in which appeals may be made and for the procedure in dealing with such appeals, see **Division 2.2**.

2.107 Payment of tax charged in assessment

As set out at **2.106** above, a chargeable person is required to include a self assessment in the chargeable person's return (unless the chargeable person files a paper return early in which case a Revenue officer will make a self assessment). A Revenue officer can also make a self assessment where a self assessment has not been included in a self assessment return. A Revenue officer can also make an assessment where a return has not been filed, the Revenue officer is not satisfied with the sufficiency of the return or has reasonable grounds for believing the return is not a full and true return. The payment of a chargeable person's tax liability does not depend on the making of an assessment either by the chargeable person or by a Revenue officer. Except in the case of the amendment of an assessment following the submission of a 'full and true' return (see **2.109**) and if certain conditions are satisfied following the determination of an appeal (see **2.203**), the payment of a chargeable person's tax liability is to be made regardless of whether an assessment is made or not.

Example 2.107.1

Mr Jack Lochrant files his income tax return manually for 2016 on 20 August 2017. He had made a preliminary tax payment of €14,000 on 31 October 2016, equal to 100 per cent of his liability for the tax year 2015.

Based on the income, deductions and reliefs disclosed in Mr Lochrant's tax return for 2016, a Revenue officer makes a self assessment for Mr Lochrant on 18 October 2017. The result of the assessment (details of income, deductions, etc not given here) is assumed to be as follows:

	€
Tax payable 2016	19,120
Less: credits against tax	2,530
Net tax payable	16,590
Less: preliminary tax paid	14,000
Balance of income tax due by Mr Lochrant	2,590

The due date for the payment of the €2,590 income tax balance is 31 October 2017 under the 'Pay and File' regime, as discussed at **2.103**.

Example 2.107.2

Ms Clare Whelan files her income tax return manually for 2016 on 1 October 2017. She does not include a self assessment in her return. She had made a preliminary tax payment of €5,200 on 25 October 2016 equal to 100% of her 2015 tax liability. She makes no further payment of tax in respect of 2016.

Based on the details disclosed in her return, a Revenue officer makes a self assessment on 18 December 2017. The result of the assessment is as follows:

	€
Tax payable	8,635
Less: credits against tax	(2,600)
Net tax payable	6,035
Less: preliminary tax paid	(5,200)
Balance of income tax due by Ms Whelan	835

The due date for the payment of the €835 income tax balance is 31 October 2017 under the 'Pay and File' regime, as discussed at **2.103** and Ms Whelan will be charged interest on the underpayment from 31 October 2017 although the self assessment did not issue until 18 December 2017. Ms Whelan will also be liable to a penalty of €250 for not including a self assessment in her return.

Interest on late payment of tax and status of interest on tax

FA 2005, s 145 substituted a new TCA 1997, s 1080 (together with a number of consequential amendments) with effect from 25 March 2005 (the date on which FA 2005 was signed into law) to provide a comprehensive scheme for the treatment of interest on late payment of tax. Prior to the passing of FA 2005, TCA 1997, s 1080 (as substituted by FA 2002, s 129) provided for interest on underpaid tax to be computed on a daily basis at the rate of 0.0322 per cent for each day (equivalent to an annual rate of 11.75 per cent). FA 2002, s 129 provided that this rate was to apply from 1 September 2002, irrespective of whether the underpaid tax was payable before, on or after that date. In the writer's view, this provision merely fixed the effective date for TCA 1997, s 1080 and did not displace the rules for the calculation of interest in force prior to that date; in other words, the pre-FA 2002 regime should always have been used to calculate interest up to 31 August 2002. This point has been the subject of dispute between the Revenue Commissioners and the Institute of Taxation arising in the context of qualifying disclosures of offshore-related tax defaults (see *e-briefs 31, 33*).

TCA 1997, s 1080(2)(a) now provides in effect that any income tax charged by any assessment on a chargeable person (as defined by TCA 1997, s 959A) for a tax year up to 2004 and any income tax due and payable by a chargeable person for tax years from 2005 onwards will carry interest from the date when the tax becomes due and payable up to the date of payment. The rate of interest is set at 0.0219 per cent per day (equivalent to around 8.00 per cent pa) from 1 July 2009.

Where tax was outstanding over periods where different interest rates applied, there is provision for interest to be calculated on the outstanding tax at the rates applicable to each period on a strict time basis (TCA 1997, s 1080(3)). This is designed to eliminate any future disputes regarding the rate of interest applicable prior to 1 September 2002 (see above).

The rates of interest for the periods covered by TCA 1997, s 1080 are as follows:

From 6 April 1963 to 31 July 1971:	0.0164%
From 1 August 1971 to 30 April 1975:	0.0246%
From 1 May 1975 to 31 July 1978:	0.0492%
From 1 August 1978 to 31 March 1998:	0.041%
From 1 April 1998 to 31 March 2005:	0.0322%
From 1 April 2005 to 30 June 2009	0.0273%
From 1 July 2009 to date:	0.0219%

It may be noted that a rate of 0.0274 per cent per day (equivalent to around 10 per cent pa) applies from 1 July 2009 to late payments of non-assessed income tax collected in a fiduciary capacity such as PAYE (see **Division 11**), Deposit Interest Retention Tax (see **2.4**), Relevant Contracts Tax (see **2.3**) and Professional Services Withholding Tax (see **2.5**) as well as exit taxes levied in relation to certain financial products (see **8.4**).

Interest payable on tax is not allowed as a deduction in computing the amount of any income, profits or other gains which are chargeable to income tax, capital gains tax or any other tax. The person paying the interest, must pay it without deducting any tax (TCA 1997, s 1080(3)(a)).

Further, all provisions of every enactment and of the rules of court, so far as they relate to the collection or recovery of tax, apply equally to interest payable on tax as if the interest were a part of the tax. In addition, the Bankruptcy Act 1988, s 81 and Companies Act 1963, ss 98, 285 (which provide priority in bankruptcy or liquidation respectively for prescribed tax debts) apply in this way: see TCA 1997, s 1080(4).

Interest charged under TCA 1997, s 1080 is to be regarded as a debt due to the Minister of Finance payable to the Revenue Commissioners (TCA 1997, s 1080(3)(b)); in proceedings to recover that debt a certificate signed by an officer of the Revenue Commissioners stating that the interest is due by the person concerned will be evidence thereof unless the contrary is proven and any such certificate may be tendered in evidence without proof and shall be deemed to have been duly signed by a Revenue official unless the contrary is proven (TCA 1997, s 1080(5)).

Reliefs given by way of discharge or repayment

Where tax is discharged (ie so that there is no longer an obligation to pay it) by way of an income tax relief, then there will be a consequent refund of any interest charged on late payment of the corresponding tax. The refund will be calculated as the amount necessary to reduce the net interest charged on the taxpayer to the amount which he would have charged on him if the tax discharged him had never been payable in the first instance (TCA 1997, s 1081(1)(a)) as substituted by FA 2005, s 145 preserving the substance of the substituted version).

Where tax is paid and relief from that tax is given by way of repayment any interest charged on late payment may be treated in the same way as if the tax had been discharged in relation to any assessment for the same tax year. However, the relief will not apply to any assessment raised after the repayment has been made. The relief may also not be applied to more than one assessment unless it has eliminated all of the tax due in relation to the other assessments in respect of which the relief has been claimed

(TCA 1997, s 1081(1)(b), as substituted by FA 2005, s 145 preserving the substance of the substituted version).

The provisions of TCA 1997, s 1081 are disapplied in relation to claims for relief under the Employment and Investment Incentive (TCA 1997, s 501(8)).

Due date for tax charged in assessment

Normal due date

As set out at **2.107** above, the payment of a chargeable person's tax liability does not depend on the making of an assessment either by the chargeable person or by a Revenue officer. TCA 1997, s 959AO(2) provides that income tax payable by a chargeable person for a tax year is due and payable on or before the due date for filing the self assessment return for that year (subject to the requirement to make a preliminary tax payment). The due date for payment of tax remains the same whether or not an assessment is made on the chargeable person on or before the due date for filing a return.

In most cases, tax charged by an assessment (either a self assessment or a Revenue assessment) refers to the balance of the income tax after deducting the preliminary tax (if any) previously paid in respect of the tax concerned. Of course, if no preliminary tax was paid, the entire amount of tax charged (after any credits) is payable and, in relation to any such case, any reference in the following discussion to the 'balance of the tax' should be read as referring to the entire amount of tax charged (after any credits).

The due date for the payment of the balance of the tax assessed is important since it is from this due date that interest begins to run against the chargeable person on the tax in question if and to the extent that the tax is not paid by the due date (see the preceding subsection).

The due date for tax charged by an assessment for all years of assessment is 31 October falling in the next year of assessment, irrespective of whether an assessment has been made before or after that date; in other words there is an absolute requirement to pay any balance of tax outstanding for a tax year by 31 October following that year, subject to any extension for ROS taxpayers (TCA 1997, s 959AO(2)).

As the return filing deadline and the due date for the payment of tax coincide, taxpayers are required to pay the tax due by 31 October, subject to any extension for ROS taxpayers, notwithstanding that an assessment to tax has not been made by Revenue or the tax payer by that date. This would arise where a taxpayer files their tax return without the inclusion of a self assessment too late to enable Revenue to make an assessment to tax by 31 October. In such circumstances, as already noted, taxpayers are obliged to 'self-assess' the net tax payable and pay the tax due by 31 October.

Prior to the tax year 2013, where a chargeable person had filed his return by the specified return date (but had not received an assessment by that date), the chargeable person did not suffer interest or penalties on an underpayment of tax by the 31 October deadline if certain conditions were satisfied. The conditions, as set out in TCA 1997, s 958(3A), were as follows:

(a) the return must contain a full and true disclosure of all material facts necessary for the making of a correct assessment;

(b) the underpaid amount must be paid by 31 December in the following year of assessment (ie within two months of the 31 October payment deadline); and

(c) the computational error made by the taxpayer must not be in excess of five per cent of their actual tax liability for the year, subject to a maximum error of €3,175. If five per cent of the taxpayer's actual liability for a year is less than

€635 then an error of up to €635 may still be made and the relief will still apply. Where the relief applies, the taxpayer will not be liable to interest or penalties provided he or she pays the shortfall on or before the following 31 December (TCA 1997, s 958(3A)).

Example 2.107.3

Dr Dre files his income tax return (which was a full and true return) manually for 2016 on 30 October 2017 together with a balancing payment of €2,700 for tax year 2016. He had made a preliminary tax payment of €12,800 on 28 October 2016.

Based on the details disclosed in his return, the inspector makes the income tax assessment on 10 December 2017. The result of the assessment is as follows, showing an underpayment of tax due to computational errors made by Dr Dre:

		€
Tax payable		16,200
Less: preliminary tax paid	(12,800)	
Less: balancing payment	(2,700)	(15,500)
Tax underpaid		700

The underpayment of €700 was less than five per cent of the liability of €16,200 and below €3,175. Accordingly, if the sum of €700 was paid by 31 December 2017 the underpayment did not attract any interest charges.

Due date where preliminary tax requirements are not met

For the purposes of computing interest on underpayments of tax, TCA 1997, s 959AO(3) applies, instead of TCA 1997, s 959AO(2) to determine the due date for the income tax charged by an assessment in any of the following cases:

(a) if the chargeable person failed to make any payment of preliminary tax for the relevant tax year (except in the case of a person who was not a chargeable person for the previous tax year);

(b) if the chargeable person's payment of preliminary tax was not made on or before the due date for the preliminary tax; or

(c) if the preliminary tax paid turns out to be less than the minimum amount required under the 90 per cent test or under the percentage test relating to the preceding or pre-preceding years (if appropriate) (see **2.104**).

In any of these cases, TCA 1997, s 959AO(3) deems the income tax payable for the tax year to have been due and payable on the due date for the payment of the preliminary tax. In other words, the due date for the tax charged in the assessment is backdated to the preliminary tax due date so that interest on the tax is charged from the preliminary tax date until the actual date(s) of payment.

The effect in terms of interest of this backdating of the due date for the tax in the assessment is potentially severe, since the preliminary tax due date occurs on 31 October during the year for which the tax is chargeable (ie 31 October 2015 for 2015). The due date is otherwise 31 October following the specified return date (ie 31 October 2016), ie 12 months later.

Example 2.107.4

Take the case of Mr Jack Lochrant from **Example 2.107.1**, but assume that his €14,000 payment of preliminary tax for income tax in respect of the tax year 2015 was made on 28

November 2016 (and not on 31 October 2016). As noted in that example, the Revenue officer's self assessment for 2016 income tax, made on 18 October 2017, results as follows:

	€
Income tax payable 2016	16,590
Less: amount paid as preliminary tax	14,000
Balance payable as now assessed	2,590

Although the €14,000 preliminary tax met the minimum required (being equal to 100 per cent of the liability for 2016), the fact that it was not paid until after the 31 October 2016 due date for the preliminary tax means that Mr Lochrant has not fully met his preliminary tax obligation for income tax. The rule in TCA 1997, s 959AO(3) therefore applies to backdate the due date for the €2,590 balance specified in the assessment to the due date for the preliminary tax, ie to 31 October 2016.

Assume that Mr Lochrant pays the €2,590 balance on 21 October 2017. Although this falls before the due date for payment of the balance, interest is payable for the period from 31 October 2016 to 21 October 2017, calculated as follows:

	€
€2,590 x 0.0219% x 356 days	201.93

In addition, interest will run on late payment of the preliminary tax as follows:

	€
€14,000 x 0.0219% x 28 days	85.85

2.108 Amendment of assessment

TCA 1997, s 959Y(1) provides that a Revenue officer may, at any time (except where the four-year time limit applies, see below), amend a Revenue assessment or a self assessment to income tax already made on or by a chargeable person. This applies even if all the tax in the assessment (before the amendment) has been paid, whether any tax repayment has been made to the chargeable person and whether or not the assessment has been previously amended on one or more occasions. The Revenue officer is required to give the taxpayer notice of the assessment as amended (TCA 1997, s 959E as applied to amended assessments by TCA 1997, s 959H).

In amending an assessment a Revenue officer may accept in whole or in part any statement or other particulars contained in a self assessment return and may assess any income or allow any deductions, relief or credit. Where income is omitted from or not properly reflected in an assessment a Revenue officer may amend that assessment.

In short, self assessment works on the basis that there is the one assessment (referred to herein as 'the original assessment') on each chargeable person for the relevant tax for each tax year which may be the self assessment made by the taxpayer or by Revenue and that, if necessary, the original assessment may be amended (and the assessment as so amended may be further amended as often as is necessary), whereas under the previous method of assessing tax there could be a first assessment and then one or more additional assessments.

An amendment to an assessment made under TCA 1997, s 959Y may be made to include or correct any income omitted from or included as incorrect amounts in the original assessment, to disallow any incorrect deduction or allowance or to make any other correction necessary to arrive at the proper amount of tax chargeable. An amendment may also be made to reduce the tax chargeable if this is appropriate.

Normally, an amendment to an assessment arises because the chargeable person has not given a full and proper statement (or an incorrect statement) of his (or the company's) income in the relevant tax return and the inspector only becomes aware of this after the tax return has been filed. However, a Revenue officer's right to amend the assessment is not restricted to such cases. TCA 1997, s 959Y permits the Revenue officer to make any amendment which he considers necessary to ensure that the tax stated in the assessment is equal to the tax correctly payable by the chargeable person.

Time limit for assessment or amendment of assessment

TCA 1997, s 959AA places a four-year time limit on a Revenue officer's right to make an assessment or to amend an assessment on any chargeable person for any relevant tax year, but goes on to make a number of important exceptions (see 'Amendments permitted after normal time limit' below). The four-year limit takes effect from 1 January 2005. In effect, therefore, all assessments in relation to tax year 2005 will be subject to a four-year limit and all references thereafter will accordingly refer to that limit. The four-year limit commences at the end of the tax year in which the return is delivered.

A 'full and true' tax return for any tax year is a return which contains a full and true disclosure of all material facts necessary for the making of an assessment for the tax year for which the return is made.

If the taxpayer fails to file any tax return for a tax year, or if it turns out that the tax return submitted does not contain the required full and true disclosure of all the material facts, there is no time limit at all (TCA 1997, s 959AC). However, where the original return has not met this condition, the chargeable person may rectify the position by submitting a revised return and, if this gives the necessary full and true disclosure, no assessment or amendment to an assessment for the relevant tax year can be made later than four years after the end of the tax year in which the revised return is filed.

Under self assessment, even an accidental (and uncorrected) omission or incorrect statement of any material fact from or in the relevant tax return may enable an assessment to be made or amended after the end of the time limit.

Example 2.108.1

Mr A Broadbeam filed his tax return manually for the year 2016 on 30 October 2017 (just before the return filing date). This return contained a full and true disclosure of all his income, deductions and all other material facts necessary for the making of an assessment on him for 2016.

Mr Slim filed his 2016 tax return manually on 1 September 2017. However, through an oversight, Mr Slim omitted to disclose income from certain shares amounting to €3,100. On 25 July 2018, Mr Slim realises that he made a mistake in the 2016 return. On 6 August 2018 he files an amended return.

Applying the appropriate four-year time limit separately for each case, the latest dates by which the income tax assessments for 2016, or any amendment to either assessment, can be made are determined as follows:

Mr Broadbeam: Income tax assessment 2016:

Date when full and true return filed: 30 October 2017;

Tax year in which same filed: 2017;

Latest date for assessment or amendment thereto: 31 December 2021.

Mr Slim: Income tax assessment 2016:

Date when full and true return filed: 6 August 2018;

Tax year in which same filed: 2018;

Latest date for assessment or amendment thereto: 31 December 2022.

Amendments permitted after normal time limit

TCA 1997, s 959AA lists circumstances in which an amendment may be made to an assessment at any time, whether before or after the end of the four-year limit following the tax year in which a full and true return was given. An assessment for any relevant tax year may be amended at any time:

(a) if the relevant tax return for that tax year does not contain a full and true disclosure of all material facts necessary for the making the assessment to the tax concerned (see above);

(b) if an amendment is necessary to give effect to a determination of an appeal against an assessment (see **2.204**) or an appeal against a determination by Revenue under TCA 1997, s 949; F(TA)A 2015, s 39 amends this provision to make clear that an assessment can be amended to give effect to a determination of an appeal by the Appeal Commissioners or a settlement made by the parties in advance of the determination of an appeal.

(c) to take account of any fact or matter arising due to an event occurring after the return is submitted;

(d) to correct a calculation error; or

(e) to correct a mistake of fact whereby the assessment does not properly reflect the facts disclosed by the chargeable person.

With effect from 31 January 2008, any repayment arising from an amendment is not subject to the normal four-year time limit imposed by TCA 1997, s 865(4); (TCA 1997, s 959AA).

Other exceptions to time limit

TCA 1997, s 959AA(3) also provides that the time limit does not apply to limit the making of any assessment or additional assessment within TCA 1997, s 804 in respect of income arising in the course of the administration of a deceased person's estate (see **15.204–15.206**).

Any necessary assessment (usually on a beneficiary of the estate) for any tax year may be made up to three years after the end of the period of the administration. This permits an assessment (or an amendment of one) to be made after the end of the normal four-year period. However, if the said three-year period ends before the end of the four-year period of TCA 1997, s 959AA for a relevant year of assessment, the assessment or amendment may be made up to the end of the normal four-year period.

The four-year time limit is also varied by the rules of TCA 1997, s 1048 which deal with assessments on the personal representative of a deceased person in respect of the deceased's pre-death income. This is dealt with in **15.104**. The four-year time limit also does not apply in respect of assessments under TCA 1997, s 811, s 811A, s 811C or s 811D, the general anti-avoidance provisions (see **17.302**).

TCA 1997, s 959AD provides that an assessment may be amended at any time where a Revenue officer has reasonable grounds for believing that any form of fraud or neglect has been committed by a person in relation to tax due for a chargeable period. There is no definition of 'reasonable grounds'. Revenue Guidance Notes on TCA 1997, s 959AD say that an assessment may be raised outside the four-year time limit where Revenue 'suspect' fraud or neglect. It has been suggested on this basis that Revenue may be equating having 'reasonable grounds' with having a 'suspicion' (for a commentary on this and case law dealing with the definition of 'reasonable grounds' see the article by Furlong, 'The New Self-Assessment Regime: Plus Ca Change …?' 1 January 2013 (2013) Irish Tax Review).

Appeals in relation to time limit

TCA 1997, s 959AF entitles a chargeable person, if aggrieved by an assessment (or an amendment to an assessment) because he considers that the Revenue officer should be debarred by the four-year time limit from making that assessment or amendment, to appeal to the Appeal Commissioners on that ground. This is a special form of appeal against an assessment and is to be distinguished from the type of appeal on other grounds discussed in **2.202**.

An appeal under TCA 1997, s 959AF is likely to occur in a case where the assessment or amendment is made by a Revenue officer after the end of the appropriate four-year period because he considers that the chargeable person did not make a full and true disclosure of all the material facts relevant to the assessment in question. The chargeable person may dispute this. If so, he may require the Appeal Commissioners to decide the matter.

If the Appeal Commissioners rule in favour of the chargeable person on this appeal, the assessment or the assessment as amended is void and ineffective. In the case of an appeal against an amendment made after the end of the four-year period to an earlier assessment, if the chargeable person's successful appeal on the time limit point is the only point in dispute, the assessment as it stood before the disputed amendment will stand (if not under appeal for other reasons). If the Appeal Commissioners decide in favour of the Revenue officer, the assessment or the amended assessment stands good (if not under appeal for other reasons).

A chargeable person may be dissatisfied with the determination of the Appeal Commissioners of an appeal made on the grounds that the assessment (or amendment of an assessment) was made after the end of the four-year period. If so, the chargeable person may use the rule of TCA 1997, s 942(1) which applies to any appeal against an assessment – to require the point to be reheard by the Circuit Court judge.

F(TA)A 2015, s 39 (SI 110/2016 appointed 21 March 2016 as the day on which the Finance (Tax Appeals) Act 2015, came into operation) substitutes TCA 1997, s 959AF as it relocates the general right of appeal against assessments from TCA 1997, s 933(1)(a) into TCA 1997, s 959AF. It clarifies that an appeal against a Revenue officer's right to make or amend an assessment because of certain statutory restrictions on doing so is not a separate appeal to an appeal against the assessment itself. It also inserts a provision in relation to when assessments are to be regarded as final and conclusive. The former provisions of this section are relocated to TCA 1997, Pt 40A as they now have more general application than solely to Pt 41A assessments.

Revenue's right to make enquiries and amend assessments

TCA 1997, s 959Z permits a Revenue officer to make such enquiries or to take any other action which he thinks necessary, within the powers given to him by the Tax Acts, to check the figures, statements and other particulars given in the chargeable person's tax return. This applies whether or not the Revenue officer has previously accepted all or some of the particulars stated in the return. For the extensive range of powers given to

Revenue to make enquiries, inspect books and records, enter business premises, obtain information from banks and other persons, etc, see **Division 2.6**.

If as a result of these enquiries, etc the Revenue officer ascertains that the return is not accurate or complete in any respect, or if he is not satisfied that it is accurate or complete, he may make such amendment to a previous assessment as he considers necessary. Alternatively, if no assessment has yet been made, the Revenue officer may make the assessment to reflect his own estimate of the correct position.

The Revenue officer's right to make enquiries or to take any other actions to check up on the particulars in a chargeable person's tax return for any relevant tax year is subject to the same four-year time limit with effect from 1 January 2005 as applies to the making of an assessment (see above). No enquiries or other actions may be made after the end of the four years unless a Revenue officer is not satisfied with the sufficiency of the return, has reasonable grounds for believing, at the time he makes these enquiries that the return is not a full and true return or is inaccurate due to being completed in a fraudulent or negligent manner.

TCA 1997, s 959Z(5) entitles any chargeable person, who believes that any enquiries or other actions taken by an Revenue officer are debarred by the four-year time limit, to appeal to the Appeal Commissioners against the Revenue officer's action. The chargeable person makes this appeal by giving the Revenue officer notice in writing that he (or the company) considers that the four-year time limit applies. This notice must be given within 30 days from the date on which the Revenue officer makes the enquiry or takes the action. Then, pending the determination of this appeal, the Revenue officer's enquiry or action is suspended as is any action required of the chargeable person by the Revenue officer. The Appeal Commissioners' decision on this issue is directed only to the question as to whether or not the Revenue officer has reasonable grounds for believing that the return is not a full and true return or that any inaccuracy (or alleged inaccuracy) in the chargeable person's return for the relevant tax year is due to fraud or negligence. The Appeal Commissioners are not required to determine whether the return is a full and true return or whether there is actually any fraud or negligence, but only whether there are any reasonable grounds for the belief that this is the case. If the Appeal Commissioners decide the matter in favour of the chargeable person, the Revenue officer cannot continue the enquiry or action the subject of the appeal. If the decision is in favour of the Revenue officer, the enquiry or action may proceed. F(TA)A 2015, s 39 (SI 110/2016 appointed 21 March 2016 as the day on which the Finance (Tax Appeals) Act 2015, came into operation) deletes the provisions relating to an appeal against the right of a Revenue officer to make enquiries as they are effectively relocated to TCA 1997, s 959J.

TCA 1997, s 959Z(9) provides that nothing in the section affects the operation of the general anti-avoidance provisions TCA 1997, ss 811, 811A, 811C or 811D.

2.109 Payment of tax charged in amended assessment

When an assessment is amended, the result of the amendment may be that additional tax, (compared with that payable under the assessment before it was amended) becomes payable by the chargeable person. Alternatively, the effect of the amendment may be to reduce the tax previously charged by the assessment before the amendment so that a repayment is due to the chargeable person (assuming that the tax previously charged was paid).

TCA 1997, s 959AU provides the rules for fixing the due date of any additional tax chargeable as the result of an amendment of an assessment (other than an amendment made to reflect the result of the determination of an appeal, for which see **2.203**). The additional tax may be payable as the result of the first amendment to the original assessment or it may result from a second, third, etc amendment to a previously amended assessment. In stating these rules, it is simpler to deal first with the due date for additional tax resulting from the first amendment to an assessment, and then to deal separately with that in a second, third, etc amendment.

Additional tax on first amendment

In the case of a first amendment to the original assessment for any relevant tax year, TCA 1997, s 959AU provides that the due date (for interest purposes) for the additional tax resulting from the amendment is either:

(a) the date one month after the date of the amendment, but only in any case where the chargeable person has filed a 'full and true' return for the relevant tax before the date of the original assessment; or

(b) the same day as the due date for the tax charged by the original assessment, in any other case.

In other words, the due date (from which interest on any additional tax resulting from the amendment is charged) is backdated to the due date for the tax charged by the original assessment either if no tax return was filed before the date on which the original assessment was made or if the relevant tax return filed before that date was not a 'full and true' return. For the purposes of the above rules, a 'full and true' return is one containing a full and true disclosure of all material facts necessary for the making of the assessment (see **2.108**).

Rule (a), if it applies, is clearly more favourable to the chargeable person. For this rule to apply to make the date one month after the date of the amendment as the due date for the additional tax, the full and true return may be given to the inspector at any time before the original assessment is made. It is not essential (for this purpose) that the return be filed before the specified return date. Even though filing the return after that date gives rise to the late return surcharge (see **2.110**), late filing does not prevent rule (a) applying provided that the 'full and true' return is filed before the inspector makes the original assessment. (This rule, contained in TCA 1997, s 959AU, was previously contained in TCA 1997, s 958(8), and was written before the requirement for a chargeable person to include a self assessment in a self assessment return. A Revenue officer may amend a self assessment. In such cases strictly the requirement that the original assessment, ie the self assessment, must have issued after a full and true return has been filed is not complied with as the self assessment is made at the same time the return is filed. As this would appear to be a technicality it is assumed the rule whereby tax due on the amendment of an assessment is due within one month will also apply to the amendment of a self assessment contained in a full and true self assessment return.)

Rule (b), where it applies, requires reference to be made to the discussion of 'Due date for tax charged in assessment' in **2.107**. As indicated there, the due date for the tax in the original assessment depends on whether or not the chargeable person had properly discharged his (or, if a company, its) preliminary tax obligation for the relevant tax year (ie whether or not he/it had paid, on or before the due date for the preliminary tax, the required minimum amount of preliminary tax).

In summary, putting the rules of TCA 1997, s 959AU together with the rules for the due date for the original tax assessed, the due date for any additional income tax resulting from the first amendment to the original assessment and the cases in which each possible date apply are as set out in the following table:

When it applies	*Due date of additional tax*
If full and true return filed before original assessment or with a self assessment which is subsequently amended	One month after date of amendment
If full and true return not filed before original assessment, but preliminary tax requirements were met	Normal due date – ie 31 October following end of tax year (subject to any extension for ROS taxpayers).
In any other case	Due date for payment of preliminary tax – ie 31 October falling in tax year (subject to any extension for ROS taxpayers).

In other words, the most favourable due date (the latest of the above possible dates) is secured if:

(1) the taxpayer had made a tax return giving a full and true disclosure of all the material facts necessary for the making of the original assessment; and

(2) this return was filed before the original assessment was in fact made.

If both these conditions are satisfied, it is not necessary to look at the question of whether or not the preliminary tax obligation was satisfied.

However, if no return for the tax concerned is filed before the date of the original assessment or if any return so filed is not a full and true one, it then becomes necessary to ask, firstly, whether the chargeable person had made an adequate payment of preliminary tax and, secondly, whether that payment was made no later than the preliminary tax due date. Unless the answer to both these questions in this situation is 'yes', then interest will be charged on any additional tax in the amended assessment from the due date for the preliminary tax (ie 31 October falling in the tax year concerned) up to the date on which the additional tax is paid.

In deciding on whether or not the return filed before the original assessment was one giving the necessary full and true disclosure, the Revenue officer has the benefit of hindsight. If he initially accepts the return as a full and true one, but subsequently – at any time – finds out that it was not, the due date for the additional tax ceases to be one month after the date of the amendment, but is backdated, so that interest is then chargeable from the due tax for the tax charged in the original assessment (to be determined by reference to the preliminary tax test).

The circumstances in which a tax return is one which gives a full and true disclosure of all material facts necessary for the making of the relevant assessment are discussed under 'Full and true' return' in **2.105**. Further, as noted in that chapter under 'Expression of doubt' where, in making a return which is in all other respects a full and true return, the chargeable person expresses a genuine doubt on any matter in the return, that return is deemed by TCA 1997, s 959P to be a 'full and true' return.

Example 2.109.1

Ms P Polliander, a widowed person, is assessable for 2016 on her total income consisting of rental income, deposit interest and dividends from Irish and UK companies. She does not file under ROS.

The following are the main facts relevant to her tax payments, tax return and assessments for the year 2016:

	€
(1) Preliminary tax paid on 31 October 2016 (100% of the income tax payable for 2014 was €10,500, but the 90% test was used as the 2016 liability was then estimated to be €8,000)	7,500
(2) Tax return for 2015 filed on 15 August 2017 (in good time before the 31 October 2016 specified return date). A self assessment was not included in the return.	
(3) On 17 October 2017, Ms Polliander pays the balance of 2016 tax (€8,150 – €7,500)	650
(4) On 20 December 2017, a Revenue officer makes a self assessment based on data in return showing tax payable for 2016 of €8,150	8,150
(5) On 11 May 2018, the Revenue officer amends assessment (agreed) to show net tax payable for 2016	9,480
(6) On 27 July 2018, Ms Polliander pays additional 2016 tax (€9,480 – €8,150)	1,330

When Ms Polliander filed the 2016 return, she availed of the 'expression of doubt' procedure now contained in TCA 1997, s 959P and advised in the letter accompanying the return that she was in doubt as to whether a certain expense item was correctly deductible in computing the amount of her rental income. She indicated that the income shown in the return was computed on the assumption that the item was deductible.

The Revenue officer's original assessment for tax of €8,150 is made without going into the question of the expenses in doubt. On the basis of that figure, the €7,500 preliminary tax payment made on 31 October 2016 works out as 92 per cent (more than 90 per cent) so that the preliminary tax test has been met.

The amendment made on 11 May 2018 of the 2016 assessment, which gives rise to the additional tax of €1,330, is assumed to result from the Revenue officer deciding to disallow as non-deductible the expenses the subject of the expression of doubt. The Revenue officer does not find any other matter incorrect or omitted from the return and he accepts that the expression of doubt was a genuine one. In consequence, the return is deemed to be a 'full and true' one.

Since the original assessment for 2016 was made after Ms Polliander had filed a 'full and true' return for that year, the due date for the additional tax of €1,330 due as the result of the amended assessment is 10 June 2018, ie one month after the date of the amendment (11 May 2018). However, as Ms Polliander has not paid the €1,330 until 27 July 2018, she must pay 47 days interest (based on the current rate laid down by TCA 1997, s 1080), namely:

€1,330 x 0.0219% x 47 days =	€13.69

The €7,500 preliminary tax paid now turns out to be only 79 per cent (less than 90 per cent) of the €9,480 income tax finally due for 2016, and is less than 100 per cent of the €10,500 payable for the preceding year. Accordingly, the due date for the tax on the original 2015 assessment now strictly becomes 31 October 2016 (the due date for preliminary tax).

Interest has therefore to be charged on the €650 balance of 2016 tax (€8,150 – €7,500) specified in the original assessment in respect of the 352 days from 31 October 2015 to the date of its payment 17 October 2017 as follows:

€650 x 0.0219% x 352 days	€50.11

Example 2.109.2

Take the facts of **Example 2.109.1**, except assume that Ms Polliander did not include an expression of doubt in her self assessment return. The absence of this extra disclosure is agreed to have been material to the assessment so that the condition of a full and true return for 2016 before the date of the original assessment (20 December 2017) is not met.

In view of this, the due date for the additional tax of €1,330 in the amendment ceases to be one month after the date of the amendment (11 May 2018), but becomes the same date as the due date for the tax in the original assessment. The latter due date depends on whether or not the payment of €7,500 preliminary tax for 2016 made on 31 October 2016 (in time) meets the adequacy test.

Since the €7,500 preliminary tax paid now turns out to be only 79 per cent (less than 90 per cent) of the €9,480 income tax finally payable for 2016 (and is less than 100 per cent of the €10,500 payable for the preceding year), Ms Polliander again fails to pass the adequacy test for the preliminary tax. This has the following consequences:

(a) the due date for the tax charged in the 2016 original assessment becomes 31 October 2016 (the due date for the preliminary tax for 2016);

(b) the due date for the tax for the €1,330 additional tax resulting from the amendment to the original assessment also becomes 31 October 2016;

(c) interest is now charged on the €1,330 additional tax from 31 October 2016 to the date of its payment, 27 July 2018:

€1,330 x 0.0219% x 635 days	€184.96

(d) interest has to be charged on the €650 balance of 2015 tax (€8,150 – €7,500) specified in the original assessment in respect of the 352 days from 31 October 2016 (revised date for balance of tax specified) to the date of its payment, on 17 October 2017 as follows:

€650 x 0.0219% x 352 days	€50.11

Additional tax on second and subsequent amendment

In the case of a second or later amendment to the original assessment for any relevant tax year, TCA 1997, s 959AU(2) provides that the due date (for interest purposes) for any additional tax becoming payable as the result of the amendment in question is either:

(a) the date one month after the date of the second or later amendment (the 'current' amendment), but only in any case where the chargeable person has filed a 'full and true' return for the relevant tax before the date of the amendment immediately preceding the current amendment; or

(b) the same day as the due date for the tax charged by the assessment before the current amendment if the 'full and true' return was not filed before the date of the preceding amendment.

In other words, the due date for any additional tax in a second, etc amendment is decided in a similar manner to that for the additional tax in the first amendment, but with the difference that the most favourable due date (one month after date of the second, etc amendment) depends on whether or not a full and true tax return has been made before the most recent previous amendment (for example, before the second amendment where the additional tax arises in a third amendment). Otherwise, TCA 1997, s 959AU(1) provides that the due date for the additional tax in the second, etc amendment is the same day as the due date for the tax in the most recent previous amendment.

The effect of these rules for a second amendment of the original assessment is to fix the due date for the additional tax in the second amendment as follows:

When it applies	*Due date of additional tax*
If a full and true return filed before first amendment	One month after date of 2nd amendment
If full and true return not filed before 1st amendment, but preliminary tax requirements were met	Normal due date-31 October following the end of the tax year (subject to any extension for ROS taxpayers).
In any other case	Due date for payment of preliminary tax-31 October falling in tax year (subject to any extension for ROS taxpayers).

For any additional tax as the result of a third amendment, the due date is determined under the above table by substituting '3rd' for '2nd' in the 'due date' column and by substituting '2nd' for '1st' in each place in the 'when it applies' column (and with corresponding substitutions for a later amendment).

These rules emphasise the importance of making a tax return for each year giving a full and true disclosure of all the material facts relevant to the assessment for the year of the return. In addition, the importance of making an adequate preliminary tax payment no later than the relevant 31 October is again stressed.

Should a taxpayer realise that through a mistake or otherwise the tax return he submitted has not given the required full and true disclosure, he should remedy the position at the earliest possible date by submitting an amended return together with an amended self assessment. Any tax due as a result of the amended self assessment will then be due within one month of the date of the amended self assessment. In addition any further amendments of the self assessment by Revenue will also qualify for the later due date for payment of any additional tax.

Example 2.109.3

Take the case again of **Example 2.109.2** in which Ms P Polliander's 2016 return contained an understatement of her rental income due to an incorrect deduction of certain non-deductible expenses (and where no expression of doubt was given on the point). Other points relevant to this example are restated here, as follows:

(a) Preliminary tax 2016 paid on time €7,500;

(b) Tax charged in original assessment (dated 20 December 2017) €8,150;

(c) Due date for balance of tax (€650) in original assessment: 31 October 2016 (same date as preliminary tax due date);

(d) Additional tax charged by first amendment (dated 11 May 2017) €1,330 (bringing total tax chargeable for 2016 up to €9,480);

(e) Due date for additional tax (€1,330) in first amendment: 31 October 2016.

Now assume that, at the end of April 2018, Ms Polliander realises that she had omitted to include in her tax return for 2016 some interest on an Irish government stock (which was therefore omitted from the Revenue officer's original assessment). Ms Polliander immediately writes to the Revenue officer on 4 May 2018 informing him of the omission and giving full details of the previously unreturned income.

Since the Revenue officer has already taken most of the steps to issue the first amended assessment, he goes ahead with its issue on 11 May 2018 without including the additional government stock interest returned by Ms Polliander's letter of 4 May 2018. However, the

Revenue officer accepts that the details in that letter together with the other information given in the earlier tax return now represents a return for the year giving a full and true disclosure of all relevant facts for the 2016 assessment. He also accepts that the surcharge for late submission of returns does not apply on the basis that Ms Polliander is liable to a penalty for carelessly filing an incorrect return (see **2.110**).

On 18 July 2018, the Revenue officer amends the 2016 assessment and issues an amended assessment showing additional income tax and levies payable arrived at as follows:

	€	€
Net amount payable (total now assessable)		9,990
Less:		
Preliminary tax paid 31/10/2016	7,500	
Balance of tax on original assessment paid 17/10/2017	650	
Additional tax on 1st amendment paid 27/6/2018	1,330	9,480
Additional tax now payable		510

Since Ms Polliander made the 'full and true' return, by the letter of 4 May 2018 remedying the earlier omission before the date of the first amendment (11 May 2018), the due date for the additional tax of €510 due to the second amendment is one month after the date of the second amendment, ie 17 August 2018.

Assuming that Ms Polliander pays the €510 on or before 17 August 2018, no interest is chargeable on this amount.

Example 2.109.4

Take the circumstances of **Examples 2.109.2** and **2.109.3**, but assume that Ms Polliander did not advise the Revenue officer of the omitted Irish government stock interest until 1 December 2017. The Revenue officer issues his amendment of the assessment (the second amendment) on 15 December 2018 again showing additional tax of €510 payable.

Since Ms Polliander has not made a full and true tax return for 2016 before the previous amendment (the first amendment) of the assessment, the due date of one month after the date of the second amended assessment does not apply. Instead, the due date for the €510 additional tax is the same due date as that for the tax charged in the first amended assessment (ie the amended assessment of 11 May 2018).

As shown in **Example 2.109.2**, the due date for the tax in the first amended assessment was backdated to 31 October 2016 (due date for the preliminary tax) because of not meeting fully the preliminary tax obligation. This means that the due date for the €510 now payable as the result of the second amendment is also 31 October 2016.

Assuming that Ms Polliander pays the €510 on 22 December 2018, she is charged interest from 31 October 2016 as follows:

€510 x 0.0219% x 783 days	€87.45

2.110 Surcharge and other penalties for late returns

TCA 1997, s 1084 imposes an automatic 'late return surcharge' if a tax return is filed late, or no return is filed, in respect of a tax year, ie it is not delivered to the Collector General no later than the specified return date for the relevant tax year for the tax in question, ie 31 October following the end of the relevant tax year.

With effect for returns delivered on or after the date of passing of FA 2014, 23 December 2014, a surcharge will apply if an incorrect return is deliberately filed in accordance with TCA 1997, s 1077E(2) or carelessly filed in accordance with TCA 1997, s 1077E(5) on or before the due date for filing the return unless the return is corrected by the return filing due date (TCA 1997, s 1084(1)(b)(i)). A return is deemed to be deliberately filed incorrectly in accordance with TCA 1997, s 1077E(2) where:

(a) a person delivers an incorrect return or statement which contains a deliberate understatement of income, profits or gains or a deliberately false or overstated claim in connection with any allowance, relief or credit;

(b) a person makes any incorrect return, statement or declaration in connection with any claim for any allowance, deduction, relief or credit and does so deliberately; or

(c) a person submits any incorrect accounts which contain a deliberate understatement of income, profits or gains or a deliberate overstatement of any claim in connection with any allowance, deduction, relief or credit.

A return is deemed to be carelessly filed incorrectly in accordance with TCA 1997, s 1077E(5) where the person carries out the acts set out in (a) to (c) above however the person does so 'carelessly' rather than 'deliberately'. 'Carelessly' is defined in TCA 1997, s 1077E(3) as 'failure to take reasonable care'.

A surcharge is not however payable where a person deliberately or carelessly delivers an incorrect return and does not correct the return before the due date for filing the return where the person is liable to a tax geared penalty for the failure under TCA 1997, s 1077E and pays this penalty. Prior to the change to TCA 1997, s 1084 made by FA 2014, s 94 set out above, TCA 1997, s 1084(1)(b)(i) provided that a surcharge was payable if an incomplete or incorrect return was filed negligently or fraudulently unless the errors and/or omissions were corrected by the specified return date.

If an incorrect return is filed by the specified return date but it is not done so deliberately or carelessly, the surcharge is imposed unless the errors in the return are corrected without unreasonable delay, TCA 1997, s 1084(1)(b)(ii). Prior to FA 2014 TCA 1997, s 1084(1)(b)(ii) provided that the surcharge would be imposed where an incorrect return was filed by the specified return date but it was not done so fraudulently or negligently provided the errors in the return were corrected without unreasonable delay. For returns delivered on or after the date of passing of FA 2014, 23 December 2014, the test is whether the incorrect return was filed 'deliberately or carelessly' rather than 'fraudulently or negligently' bringing the test for the behaviour which determines whether a surcharge applies into line with the test used in TCA 1997, s 1077E for determining whether tax geared penalties apply (see **2.704**).

If a person is required to file a return electronically (see **2.105**) and files in paper form before the specified return date the person is deemed to have filed a late return, and the surcharge is applied, unless an electronic return is filed before the specified return date. The amount of the late return surcharge depends on when the return is submitted. TCA 1997, s 1084(2) provides that the surcharge is to be equal to:

(a) five per cent of the amount of tax, subject to a maximum surcharge of €12,695 where the return of income is delivered before the expiry of two months after the specified date; or

(b) ten per cent of the amount of tax, subject to a maximum surcharge of €63,495 where the return of income is not delivered within two months after the specified date.

With effect from tax year 2004 onwards, the annual tax return requires additional information to be supplied in relation to specified claims for reliefs, allowances, exemptions, deductions and credits. Where a taxpayer fails to supply this information, he will be treated as if he had failed to deliver the return by the specified return date but did so within two months, ie a 5 per cent surcharge applies (but without prejudice to incurring the higher surcharge if justified on other grounds). This provision will not apply unless after the submission of the return the default had come to the taxpayer's notice or had been brought to his attention and the taxpayer had failed to remedy matters without unreasonable delay (TCA 1997, s 1084(1)(b)(ib) inserted by FA 2004, s 86).

TCA 1997, s 1084(4) also provides for a relaxation of the surcharge provisions for an individual commencing to carry on a trade or profession. The relaxation applies where:

(a) an individual commences business in a tax year (say 2014); and
(b) neither he nor his spouse or civil partner (if joint assessment under TCA 1997, s 1017 or s 1031C applies) was also carrying on another business in that year which had commenced in an earlier tax year.

The specified return date for surcharge purposes becomes the specified return date which would normally apply for the following tax year (ie for 2015 return, 31 October 2017, instead of 31 October 2016) (TCA 1997, s 1084(4)). If the individual was a chargeable person in 2014, the requirement to pay preliminary tax for 2015 by 31 October 2015 will remain unaffected.

For the purpose of the surcharge, the relevant amount of tax to which the 5 per cent or 10 per cent surcharge is applied is the amount of the tax concerned which would, if no surcharge were added, be contained in an assessment to tax made on the chargeable person for the relevant tax year, but reduced by the aggregate of such of the following items as apply in that tax year:

(a) any tax deducted from any income charged in the assessment which the chargeable person is entitled to set off against the tax contained in the assessment (but not including any such tax to the extent that it is repayable, or has been repaid, to the chargeable person); and
(b) any other amounts or reliefs which are set off in the assessment against the tax charged by the assessment.

In other words, the amount of tax on which the 5 per cent or 10 per cent surcharge is levied is the chargeable person's 'net' liability to tax, ie the total amount of the tax charged in the assessment (the 'gross liability') as reduced by the 'deductions from tax' specifically mentioned in (a) and (b) above. In arriving at the gross liability to the relevant tax, all income which ought to be included in the tax return – whether or not actually included in the return – must be brought into the computation of the total income on which the gross liability is computed (after any personal allowances and any other deductions from income are taken off).

In the case of an individual liable to the surcharge for the late filing (or the non-filing) of his income tax return, the gross liability includes not only the individual's gross liability to income tax, but also USC and self-employment PRSI contributions. The late return surcharge is calculated without giving any allowance for any preliminary tax which may have been paid.

The deductions under (a) in arriving at the net liability subject to the surcharge are limited to any Irish tax which has been deducted under any of the provisions in the Tax Acts which require or permit the person making certain payments to withhold the tax. Further, only tax suffered on items of income, etc which are included in the income, etc chargeable to tax by the assessment are deductible.

Examples of deductions under (a) are income tax deducted from Sch E emoluments from an employment under PAYE if the emoluments are included in the assessment, income tax suffered at source from annual payments received and Irish income tax deducted from Sch C income (see **2.309**) or from foreign dividends paid through a bank or other paying agent in the State (see **2.310**).

An important exception to the deduction of tax suffered under PAYE is laid down by TCA 1997, s 1084(3) which effectively requires a company director as defined by TCA 1997, s 116, other than one who is not regarded as a chargeable person (whether by statute or by Revenue concession under SP-IT/1/93: see **2.102**) to be surcharged on his tax payable (before any such deduction) if late in filing his tax return. This exception also applies in the case of a couple jointly assessed to tax under TCA 1997, s 1017 or s 1031C where the spouse or civil partner of the chargeable spouse or partner is such a director.

An example of a deduction under (b) is the actual amount of any professional services withholding tax which is set off against the income tax assessment (whichever applies) for the relevant tax year under TCA 1997, s 526 (see **2.506**). No deduction for this withholding tax is granted to the extent that a refund thereof is obtained under the interim refund procedure of TCA 1997, s 527.

Assessment of surcharge

In any case where the relevant tax return is not filed by the specified date, TCA 1997, s 1084(2)(a) normally requires the amount of the relevant tax contained in any assessment after that date to be increased by the amount of the surcharge. The self assessment included in a self assessment return filed after the specified return date should include the surcharge due (TCA 1997, s 959V). If a surcharge is not so included in an assessment all the rules of the Tax Acts applicable to the collection and recovery of tax, as well as those relating to the payment of interest on unpaid tax, are thereafter applied as if the tax charged in the assessment were an amount equal to the actual tax as increased by the surcharge.

In other words, the amount payable as income tax for the relevant tax year becomes a total amount of tax equal to the aggregate of the actual tax payable and the 5 per cent or 10 per cent surcharge. Interest is payable on this new 'total tax' figure from the appropriate due date for the tax charged by the assessment to the date on which the appropriate payment is made (except to the extent tax has already been paid).

The surcharge is not deemed to be included in an assessment where the surcharge relates to failure to supply additional information re reliefs, credits, etc under TCA 1997, s 1084(1)(b)(ib) above; in this case, the relevant surcharge must be included in the assessment and the normal rights of appeal, etc will accordingly apply.

If the chargeable person had made the necessary minimum payment of preliminary tax on or before the due date for the preliminary tax, the due date for the tax as now increased by the surcharge remains 31 October following the end of the tax year (see **2.107**) and no interest is chargeable if the balance of tax and the surcharge is paid before that date. In evaluating the 90 per cent test for the minimum preliminary tax payable, the surcharge must be included in the tax payable. Similarly, if the preceding year preliminary test is used (see **2.104**) and if there was a late return surcharge in the previous tax year, the preceding year percentage must be applied to the previous year's tax as increased by the surcharge for that year (similar considerations apply to the pre-preceding year test where appropriate).

In any case where the relevant tax return was not filed on time and where additional tax becomes payable as the result of one or more amendments to the original assessment, the additional tax in each amended assessment must also be increased by 5 per cent or 10 per cent as a further amount of surcharge. Again, interest becomes payable on the additional tax and the surcharge thereon from the appropriate due date for the additional tax to the date of payment. For the due dates of the additional tax (and surcharge) in the amended assessment, see **2.109**.

Incorrect returns

A person may deliver a return of income to the Collector-General before the relevant specified date, but this return may be incorrect in one or more respects. If the incorrect return is made deliberately or carelessly, the person is treated as if he had failed to make a return of income before the specified date unless any error in the return is remedied no later than the specified date for that return (TCA 1997, s 1084(1)(b)(i)), or the person pays a tax geared penalty under TCA 1997, s 1077E. Unless the error is remedied by the return filing date, or the person pays a tax geared penalty under TCA 1997, s 1077E, the late return surcharge becomes payable.

The delivery of an incorrect return by the specified date not made either deliberately or carelessly does not, as such, operate to impose the surcharge in respect of the tax on any income, profits or chargeable gains due to be included in the return. However, should it come to the notice of the person who delivered the return that it is incorrect in any respect, he is required to remedy the error (or errors) without unreasonable delay (TCA 1997, s 1084(1)(b)(ii)). Unless he does so, the return is treated as if it were a late return and the surcharge may be imposed.

In the event that a return of income has been made by the specified date for the return and a Revenue officer is not satisfied with any statement of the profits or gains from any trade or profession carried on by the person making the return, the officer may serve notice on that person under TCA 1997, s 900(2) requiring him to do certain things (including sending copies of accounts, making books and records available for inspection, etc) within a time specified in the notice. If the person fails to comply with this notice and does not do what is required by it no later than the return filing date for the return of income, that return is treated as if it were not delivered by the specified date so that the surcharge becomes payable (TCA 1997, s 1084(1)(b)(iii)).

Other returns subject to late return surcharge

Apart from the normal returns of income (generally the individual's Form 11), the late return surcharge is imposed on any chargeable person who fails to deliver by the specified return date any of the following returns:

(a) the return of partnership income, etc under TCA 1997, s 880, due by the precedent acting partner;
(b) the return of rental income, etc chargeable under Sch D Case IV and/or V due by a lessor under TCA 1997, s 888(2)(a) (or any such return due under TCA 1997, s 888(2)(d) from any agent managing premises from which rent accrues);
(c) the return under TCA 1997, s 878 by any person acting on behalf of an incapacitated person or any non-resident person;
(d) a return required from a spouse or partner under TCA 1997, s 881 or from one of the spouses or partners assessable separately under TCA 1997, s 1023 (see **3.504**).

It is to be noted that TCA 1997, s 1084, which imposes the surcharge, charges it only on the chargeable person required to make the specified return (for example, the precedent acting partner) and not on any other person who could be charged to tax as a result of any income or other information in the return (for example, the other partners in the firm). However, if a chargeable person becomes liable to the 5 per cent or 10 per cent surcharge for failure to file one of these other returns on time, the surcharge is imposed on all the chargeable person's tax (net of deductions from tax) and not just the tax affected by one of these other returns.

For example, if a person chargeable to income tax for a tax year is the precedent acting partner in a partnership, he must ensure that both his own tax return and the partnership's tax return for the tax year are delivered to the appropriate inspector no later than the specified return date. Failure to meet the filing deadline for either return will result in the precedent acting partner being liable to the 5 per cent or 10 per cent surcharge on his own tax liability for the tax year. It does not result in any other partner being liable to the surcharge, but the other partner must ensure that his own tax return is filed on time.

Similarly, if the chargeable person is a lessor or the agent managing of rented premises required to make a return of rental income, etc under TCA 1997, s 888, that person must ensure that the said return and his (or, if a company, its) own tax return for the relevant tax year are both filed no later than the specified return date for the relevant tax year or accounting period. Otherwise, the 5 per cent or 10 per cent surcharge is imposed on the chargeable person's own tax liability for the tax year or accounting period.

The rules discussed under 'Incorrect returns' above apply in the same way to these other returns as they do to the main returns of income. For example, an incorrect partnership return made deliberately or carelessly by the precedent acting partner is not regarded as a return made by the specified return date unless the omissions from or errors in the return are remedied no later than the specified return date.

Failure to file a local property tax return or to pay local property tax

Finance (Local Property Tax) Act 2012, s 38 as amended by Finance (Local Property Tax) (Amendment) Act 2013 provides that where a chargeable person who is liable to pay local property tax (LPT):

(a) does not file an LPT return; or

(b) does not pay LPT due or enter into an arrangement with Revenue for the payment of LPT,

on or before the specified return date under TCA 1997, s 959I for filing an income tax return, the person will be treated as if he had failed to deliver a return under TCA 1997, s 959I by the specified return date but did so within two months, ie a 5 per cent surcharge applies. Where a person files a return under TCA 1997, s 959I before the specified return date but after the LPT filing date and has not at that time paid LPT due or entered into an arrangement for its payment, the specified return date is deemed to be the date the return under TCA 1997, s 959I is filed.

If the person files his LPT return and pays the LPT due after the due date for filing a return under TCA 1997, s 959I the surcharge is capped at the amount of the LPT due. The surcharge is not capped at the amount of the LPT due where the person did not file a return under TCA 1997, s 959I by the due date.

A surcharge will arise for each year so long as the LPT return remains unfiled and/or LPT is not paid. Thus a chargeable person who did not file an LPT return for 2015 will be subject to a late return surcharge for 2015 and for subsequent years until the LPT return is filed.

Penalties

In addition to the late return surcharge, a penalty of €3,000 may be levied under TCA 1997, s 1052(1)–(3) if a chargeable person fails to deliver the relevant tax return for a tax year by the specified return date under TCA 1997, s 959I or, with effect from tax year 2004 onwards, relates to failure to supply additional information re reliefs, credits, etc under TCA 1997, s 1084(1)(b)(ib) in circumstances where a liability to the surcharge is incurred (see above). TCA 1997, s 1052(2) increases the penalty to €4,000 where the failure continues after the end of the year of assessment following that in which a notice to deliver a return is given. TCA 1997, s 959O provides that a person is deemed to have been given notice to file a return on the due date for the filing of the return. Therefore if the return has not been delivered before 31 December in the tax year following that in which the specified return date occurs the penalty is increased to €4,000. The failure to submit the income tax return is a 'column 1 offence' under TCA 1997, Sch 29.

In practice no action to enforce a penalty under TCA 1997, s 1052 is likely if the relevant tax return is filed within a reasonable time after the specified return date. While the late return surcharge is applied automatically if the return is late, the penalties for late returns are only imposed if the Revenue Commissioners take specific action and obtain a court judgment to enforce a penalty.

Penalties may also be imposed under TCA 1997, s 1077E(1) on any chargeable person who deliberately or carelessly makes an incorrect return, ie one which omits any income, or which claims improper deductions, reliefs, etc to which the chargeable person is not entitled. However, an incorrect return made accidentally but not carelessly does not give rise to a penalty, although it may result in the late return surcharge in certain circumstances (see 'Incorrect returns' above).

Example 2.110.1

Mr KK Koala, who is chargeable to income tax for 2016, does not file his tax return for the year 2016 (specified return date 31 October 2017) until 25 March 2018. His tax liability for 2016 is assessed by a Revenue officer on 18 April 2018 in the following amount:

	€
Income tax payable	6,500
10% surcharge thereon	650
	7,150

In addition to the late return surcharge, the Revenue Commissioners are entitled to take proceedings to recover a penalty of €4,000 under TCA 1997, s 1052(2) for failure to file the 2015 tax return on or before 31 December 2017 (last day of tax year following that in which 2015 return filing date occurred). If Mr Koala had filed the return on or before 31 December 2016, the penalty would only have been €3,000 under TCA 1997, s 1052(1).

A penalty of €3,000 may be imposed on the precedent partner of a partnership who fails to deliver the appropriate partnership return on or before the specified return date for the relevant tax year as required by TCA 1997, s 880. If the failure to file the partnership return continues beyond 31 December in the income tax year following that in which the specified return date occurs, the penalty is increased to €4,000.

For further discussion of penalties for not filing tax returns, filing an incorrect return deliberately or carelessly, etc, see **2.701**.

2.111 Relief for error or mistake in tax return

TCA 1997, s 930 entitled any person, if he had paid income tax charged by an assessment for any year to apply to the Revenue Commissioners for relief if he considered that the assessment was excessive due to some error or mistake in the return or statement made by him for the purposes of the assessment; the relief under TCA 1997, s 930 did not apply to tax deducted at source. This application had to be made in writing no later than six years after the end of the tax year in which the relevant assessment was made (not necessarily the tax year for which the income was assessable).

However, FA 2003, s 17/SI 508/2003 provided that s 930 ceased to have effect from 1 January 2005, ie no claims for relief may be made on or after that date. Instead, there is a statutory right of repayment under TCA 1997, s 865(2) where a person overpays tax, for whatever reason including as a result of an error or mistake in a return made by the person for the purposes of an assessment to tax. The right to repayment of tax applies whether the tax was paid directly or by way of deduction at source. This is generally subject to the making of a valid claim, although there is an exception to this for PAYE workers: see **2.104**: 'Position Where Tax Overpaid'.

Interest will run on the overpaid tax commencing 93 days after the day on which the valid claim is made (a six month period applied to repayments made prior to 2 April 2007) (TCA 1997, s 865A(2)).

A valid claim is deemed to be made where:

(a) a statement or return which the taxpayer is required to provide contains all the information which Revenue may reasonably require to enable them to determine if and to what extent a repayment of tax is due;

(b) if a statement or return is not required or is required but does not contain the necessary information, when the necessary information is provided;

(c) where an adjustment of profits is required under the terms of a Double Taxation Agreement (a 'correlative adjustment' TCA 1997, s 865(1)) when the amount of the adjustment is agreed between the authorities of both states.

From 18 December 2013 a claim for a repayment of tax under TCA 1997, s 865 which arose due to an error or mistake in a return will not be a valid claim unless the return and, in the case of returns for the year 2013 and subsequent years, the self assessment is amended to correct the error or mistake. An error or mistake claim is important under the self assessment rules, which prevent an appeal against a self assessment or against any assessment to the extent that it is based on the figures and statements in the taxpayer's return. If the person assessed finds that such an assessment is excessive due to his own mistake in overstating some income or in underclaiming a deduction, his only remedy appears to be a claim under TCA 1997, s 865(2), for relief for his error or mistake.

The phrase 'error or mistake' which is used in TCA 1997, s 865, is not defined, but would seem apt to cover such matters as omissions, book-keeping errors and arithmetical errors in a set of accounts, as well as mistakes concerning the correct tax treatment of transactions (see Stopforth: Error or Mistake Relief [1989] BTR 181, which discusses both this and a number of other points raised below).

In *Heastie v Veitch & Co* 18 TC 305, a deduction for the annual value of business premises had been made in the partnership accounts instead of a deduction for the amount of rent actually payable (to the senior partner). The taxpayers succeeded in their claim for relief in respect of the under-deduction of rent.

In *Radio Pictures v IRC* 22 TC 106, the taxpayer's accounts were based on a misunderstanding of the legal effects of a licence agreement into which it had entered. The taxpayers succeeded in their claim for relief and were consequently taxed by reference to the corrected accounts.

In *Carrimore Four Wheelers Ltd v IRC* 28 TC 422, it was held that where the taxpayer had deliberately adopted a treatment which was not strictly correct in law, with the knowledge and consent of the inspector of taxes, it was not entitled to claim the relief. The Court of Appeal held that the Appeal Commissioners' finding of fact on this point was not subject to review (see below).

It is to be noted that the error or mistake must be one occurring in a tax return or other statement (for example, extracts from the accounts of a trade included in the return) by reference to which the assessment was made (see R *v Special Commissioner ex parte Tracy* [1996] STC 34). No relief under the section may be claimed for excessive tax charged under an assessment which has been made by a Revenue officer under TCA 1997, s 959AC in the absence of any tax return or other relevant statement by the taxpayer (see **2.105**).

Under TCA 1997, s 930 (but not TCA 1997, s 865(2)), no relief could be claimed in respect of an error or mistake with regard to the basis on which the taxpayer's liability ought to have been computed where the return or statement was in fact made in accordance with the practice generally prevailing at the time it was made.

In *Rose Smith & Co v IRC* 17 TC 586, the Appeal Commissioners held that a particular method of calculating hire purchase interest, which had been adopted by the taxpayer, was the 'practice generally prevailing at the time'. The Appeal Commissioners relied on evidence by a senior Revenue official who provided a copy of internal revenue instructions to inspectors on the matter. The Appeal Commissioners' finding was upheld as one of fact by the courts. In *Arranmore Investments Co Ltd v IRC* [1973] STC 195, evidence was also produced that taxpayers had generally accepted liability in accordance with the relevant internal Revenue instructions.

The Revenue Commissioners issue a number of Statements of Practice and also clarify their views on various issues in their *Tax Briefings*. These would seem to provide *prima facie* evidence of 'generally prevailing practice'. Significantly, the Revenue Commissioners are now obliged to furnish details of their practices under the Freedom of Information Act 1997, s 16 (see **2.206**).

Where a person is aggrieved by a decision of the Revenue regarding a claim under TCA 1997, s 865, the taxpayer is entitled to make an appeal to the Appeal Commissioners in accordance with TCA 1997, s 949 as if the decision were a determination regarding the taxpayer's entitlement to an allowance, deduction, repayment or relief.

A claim for a repayment under TCA 1997, s 865 must be made within four years after the end of the chargeable period to which the claim relates. However, if a right to repayment arises under another provision and that provision provides for a shorter time limit for repayment the shorter time limit applies.

An interesting question arises as to whether an excess payment of tax, as a result of an error or mistake by the taxpayer, is capable of giving rise to a right of recovery under the principle of restitution, as extended by the decision in *O'Rourke v Revenue Commissioners* V ITR 321. It is arguable that even if this were the position in theory, the specific provisions of TCA 1997, s 930 may preclude the operation of the common law in this area (see Virgo 'The Law of Taxation is not an Island' [1994] BTR, at p 464).

Similar questions may arise in the context of TCA 1997, s 865(2) eg – whether a claim could be made after the four-year time limit relying on common law principles.

Even though a repayment may have been made under TCA 1997, s 865 this does not prevent the Revenue Commissioners from examining a claim, from making or amending an assessment or from making a determination that a refund of tax is due from a person (TCA 1997, s 960Q) after the repayment has been made (TCA 1997, s 865(9)).

2.2 Appeals against Assessments and Judicial Review

2.201 Appeals: general

Every appeal against an assessment is strictly an appeal to the Appeal Commissioners, but this does not necessarily mean that the case will actually be heard by them. In many cases, it is possible for the person who has appealed against an assessment to agree his correct tax liability with the inspector either by correspondence or by a personal interview or, if he has not already done so, by submitting any tax return or other outstanding information that the inspector may require. When this happens, the assessment may stand good, if this is agreed between the taxpayer and the inspector, or may be amended in a particular manner or may be discharged or cancelled by the inspector to give effect to what is agreed. The taxpayer may also avail if appropriate of the Revenue Commissioners' Complaint and Review Procedures (see Revenue leaflet CS4 revised December 2012). Where the subject matter of a review is a legal or technical issue, the taxpayer should submit an analysis of what he or she considers is the proper interpretation. The analysis should be supported, as appropriate, by reference to the legislation and case law. If there is a difference of opinion between a Revenue officer and the taxpayer on a point of law, the reviewers will intervene only where they consider that the Revenue opinion is clearly incorrect. Once a taxpayer has been notified of the time and date for the hearing of an appeal by the Appeal Commissioners, the review procedure will cease to be available in relation to the matter which is the subject of the appeal. The posting of a notice of appeal by registered post where such document should in the ordinary course of post arrive within the 30-day period will satisfy the requirement to give notice within 30 days (*Criminal Assets Bureau v PMcS* VI ITR 421).

PRSI and the Universal Social Charge

SWCA 2005, s 23(4) requires self-employed contributions payable in respect of 'reckonable income' (ie contributions which are not collected under the PAYE system: see **3.403**) to be assessed and charged in the same way as income tax; all of the provisions of the Income Tax Acts (including those relating to appeals) are to apply accordingly. SWCA 2005, s 23(3) applies the provisions relating to the estimation, collection and recovery of PAYE income tax, and also those provisions relating to appeals, to self-employed contributions payable in respect of 'reckonable emoluments' (see **3.403**). SWCA 2005, s 17(4) has similar effect to SWCA 2005, s 20(3) in relation to employment contributions collected under the PAYE system. TCA 1997, s 531AAA applies the provisions relation to the making of returns, the making of assessments, the making of enquiries and appeals to the Universal Social Charge.

It may be noted that, by virtue of SWCA 2005, s 300, a number of issues in relation to PRSI liabilities are to be decided by a 'deciding officer'. These include questions:

(a) as to whether an employment is or was an insurable employment or insurable (occupational injuries) employment;

(b) as to whether a person is or was employed in an insurable employment or insurable (occupational injuries) employment;

(c) as to what rate of employment contribution is or was payable by an employer in respect of an employed contributor;

(d) as to who is or was the employer of an employed contributor;

(e) as to whether an employment is or was an insurable self-employment;

(f) as to whether a person is or was in insurable self-employment; or

(g) as to what rate of self-employment contribution is or was payable by a self-employed contributor.

There is a right of appeal against a decision of a deciding officer to an appeals officer (SWCA 2005, s 311(1)). The appeals officer may decide the question at issue as if it was being decided for the first time (SWCA 2005, s 311(3)). A deciding officer may revise any decision made by a deciding officer (including himself) *inter alia* in the light of new evidence or by reason of a mistake having been made in relation to the law or facts of the case, or due to a change of circumstances (SWCA 2005, s 301(1)). Furthermore, a deciding officer may revise any decision of an appeals officer where there has been a relevant change of circumstances (SWCA 2005, s 301(1)). A right of appeal also lies against a revised decision to an appeals officer (SWCA 2005, s 301(1)). An appeals officer may revise the decision of an appeals officer (including himself) in the light of new evidence or changing circumstances. The Chief Appeals Officer may also revise any decision of an appeals officer by reason of a mistake having been made in relation to the law or facts of the case. There is a right of appeal against the decision of an appeals officer or a revised decision of the Chief Appeals Officer on a point of law to the High Court (SWCA 2005, s 327).

2.202 Procedural requirements

An appeal against an assessment under the self assessment regime may only be made to the extent that the assessment differs in some respect from the details of income, deductions from income, allowances, reliefs and any other relevant facts stated in the taxpayer's tax return for the relevant year in question. Secondly, no appeal can be made until a tax return has been made for the relevant year and the taxpayer has paid the tax due in accordance with the income, etc details in that return (TCA 1997, s 959AH). Thirdly, the notice of appeal must state 'the grounds in detail' for each point of appeal (TCA 1997, s 959AJ). F(TA)A 2015, s 39 replaces TCA 1997, s 959AJ in its entirety. The grounds for appeal requirement is outlined in TCA 1997, s 949I and TCA 1992, s 959AJ will look to appeals against time limits for Revenue making enquiries and taking certain actions. The discussion which follows, which relates only to appeals against assessments under the self assessment regime, covers these points in detail. It should be read in the context of the rules for the assessment of income tax, amendments of assessments, payments of tax and interest on tax for these years dealt with in **Division 2**.

No appeal to the extent that facts agreed

A person cannot appeal against a self assessment whether or not the self assessment is made by the taxpayer or by a Revenue officer where a return is filed but does not include a self assessment (TCA 1997, s 959AG). A self assessment made by a chargeable person must be made in accordance with the details contained in the person's self assessment return (TCA 1997, s 959W(1). A self assessment made by a Revenue officer must also be made in accordance with the particulars contained in the chargeable person's return (TCA 1997, s 959W(3). In effect therefore an appeal cannot be made against an assessment which is in accordance with the details included in a chargeable person's return. An appeal can however be made against a self assessment which has been amended by a Revenue officer (TCA 1997, s 959AK). F(TA)A 2015, s 39 (SI 110/2016 appointed 21 March 2016 as the day on which the Finance (Tax Appeals) Act 2015, came into operation) amends TCA 1997, s 959AK such that that where an appeal against a preliminary matter that is not an assessment is determined that no further right of appeal exists in relation to an assessment made solely to give effect to the determination, unless a party has grounds other than grounds that relate to that preliminary matter. The explanatory memorandum which accompanied the bill referred to this amendment as being done 'to clarify' the position.

In addition, no appeal can be made against an assessment to the extent that it is based only on any amounts of income, etc which the taxpayer (or a person acting on his behalf) has agreed with a Revenue officer before the assessment is made or which have been determined by a Revenue officer based on the details included in the return filed by the person (TCA 1997, s 959AI), and note, in this respect, *R v Inspector of Taxes ex parte Bass Holdings* 1993 STC 122).

Consequently, if all the income, deductions, allowances and reliefs specified in an assessment are exactly in accordance with the data in the taxpayer's return (or have been agreed with a Revenue officer), there is no right at all to an appeal. The assessment is immediately final and conclusive and the tax charged by it therefore becomes payable on the appropriate due date.

If a Revenue officer is not satisfied with all the data in the tax return for the relevant year (or if no return has been made) and he makes an assessment under TCA 1997, s 959AC, the person assessed may appeal against the assessment. Any such appeal may, however, only be made if the conditions mentioned below are met. Further, the appeal must be limited to disputing any amount of income, deduction, allowance or relief specified in the assessment to the extent that it differs from the corresponding amount in the tax return or agreed with the inspector. The income tax payable in the assessment, to the extent that it results from the undisputed amount of income, etc remains payable on the due date(s) notwithstanding the appeal.

In other words, the chargeable person is bound by the income, etc figures and other statements given in his tax return and he is debarred from appealing that the tax in an assessment should be less than the liability based on those figures and statements. For the taxpayer's right to claim a repayment under TCA 1997, s 865, if the assessment on him is excessive due to an error or mistake in his tax return.

Appeal against amended assessment

TCA 1997, s 959AK entitles a chargeable person to appeal against an assessment amended by a Revenue officer (except in the case of an amendment made to reflect the result of the determination of an appeal), but subject to the following restrictions:

(a) no appeal may be made against the amount of any item of income or profits, deduction or relief specified in the amended assessment which does not differ from the amount of the said item stated in the chargeable person's return for the relevant tax (TCA 1997, s 959AK); and

(b) no appeal may be made against any item of income, profits, deduction or relief specified in the amended assessment which has been agreed with the inspector before the amendment to the assessment was made (TCA 1997, s 959AI).

Subject to these restrictions, the chargeable person may appeal against any additions to, deletions from, or alterations in the assessment as a result of the amendment. For example, a right of appeal exists against any new income assessed, any deductions or reliefs disallowed or any increase in the amount of any income assessed. However, the chargeable person has no further right to appeal against matters other than such additions to, deductions from or alterations in the assessment than he would have had if the assessment had not been amended (TCA 1997, s 959AK). F(TA)A 2015, s 39 (SI 110/2016 appointed 21 March 2016 as the day on which the Finance (Tax Appeals) Act 2015, came into operation) amends TCA 1997, s 959AK such that that where an appeal against a preliminary matter that is not an assessment is determined that no further right of appeal exists in relation to an assessment made solely to give effect to the determination, unless a party has grounds other than grounds that relate to that preliminary matter. The explanatory memorandum which accompanied the bill referred to this amendment as being done 'to clarify' the position.

Before any appeal can be made against any amended assessment for a relevant tax year, the chargeable person must have filed his tax return for that period and must have paid an amount of tax at least equal to the tax which would be payable if the amended assessment were made based only on the data in the chargeable person's tax return (TCA 1997, s 959AH as applied to amended assessments by TCA 1997, s 959AH(4)).

Conditions before appeal may be made

TCA 1997, s 959AH imposes two conditions which must both be satisfied before any appeal against an assessment can be made under the self assessment system. Since no appeal exists before the conditions are met, any tax charged by the assessment remains due and payable from the appropriate due date so that interest on the tax assessed accrues from that date on any unpaid tax.

The first condition is that the person assessed must, if he has not already done so, file a return for the relevant year. The second condition is that the person assessed must pay, to the extent that he has not previously done so, an amount of income tax (and PRSI and Universal Social Charge) at least equal to the tax payable by reference to the self assessment included in the return or where no self assessment has been included the amount of tax which would be payable if an assessment were to be made by reference to the details included in the return (TCA 1997, s 959AH(1)). A self assessment must include any surcharge for the late filing of a return which is payable (TCA 1997, s 959R). The amount of tax payable before an appeal can be made must therefore include any surcharge payable. In the discussion which follows, this pre-appeal minimum tax payment is referred to as the 'pre-appeal tax payment'.

Further, if any interest has become due and payable on or before the date on which the pre-appeal tax payment is fully paid (the 'pre-appeal tax payment date'), then an amount of interest must also be paid before the appeal against the assessment can be made. In addition, any tax collection costs sustained by the taxpayer in relation to the tax in question must be paid up before the appeal can be made (TCA 1997, s 959AH(3)).

The amount of interest to be paid before the taxpayer can appeal against the assessment is calculated at the appropriate rate on any part of the pre-appeal tax payment which has not been paid on or before its appropriate due date. The interest is that running from the due date of the tax in question to the date on which the tax is paid (whether on the pre-appeal payment date or earlier). For these purposes, the Revenue will calculate any interest on the basis that the figure for the taxpayer's final liability will be in accordance with his own computation. Thus, for example, if the preliminary tax requirements are not met because the preliminary tax was less than 90 per cent of this figure (and assuming that the 100 per cent or 105 per cent tests (if appropriate are also not met) the due date for both preliminary tax and the balance of the tax due (based on the taxpayer's return) will be 31 October in the relevant tax year.

Period within which appeal must be made

No appeal against an assessment under the self assessment system can be made before the earliest date by which both the tax return for that year has been made and the tax based on that return (including any interest and costs related thereto) has been fully paid. There is an overriding 30-day limit within which an appeal must be made by reference to the date of assessment.

Example 2.202.1

Mr CD Trodgers who is not a ROS taxpayer, made a payment of preliminary tax of €9,000 for 2016 on 11 November 2016 (ie late, after 31 October 2016), so that interest is chargeable from 31 October 2016, both on the late paid preliminary tax and the balance of tax which would otherwise have been payable by 31 October 2017.

Mr Trodgers duly sends the Collector-General his tax return for 2016 on 16 September 2017 (ie in good time before the 31 October 2017 return filing date) including a self assessment made in accordance with the details included in his return showing tax payable for 2016 of €12,440 but fails to pay the balance of tax based on his return by that date.

A Revenue officer has received information which suggests that Mr Trodgers may have omitted certain rental income from his return. The officer therefore decides to make a Revenue assessment including an estimated amount of rental income. The officer recomputes and assesses the tax payable as €14,837. The officer's assessment for 2016 of the €14,837 tax is made on 19 December 2017. Mr Trodgers accepts that he did not include some rental income and his accountant argues with the officer that the taxable income should be increased by this amount only and that the tax payable should be increased only to €12,910. However, the officer is not satisfied that this correctly states the position and he refuses to amend the assessment from €14,837.

Mr Trodgers wishes to appeal against the assessment. Before he can do so, he must have paid tax at least equal to the tax which would be payable if the assessment had been made only by reference to the data in his tax return. The amount of tax to be paid is determined as follows:

	€
Tax based on 2016 return	12,440

Less:	
2016 tax already paid (11/11/2016) (preliminary tax)	(9,000)
Balance of tax due before appeal (subject to interest)	3,440

To the extent that interest is payable by Mr Trodgers in relation to the €12,440 based on the return, this interest must also be paid. Assume that Mr Trodgers pays the balance of €3,440 on 26 December 2017 plus the interest due to that date, but that no tax enforcement costs have arisen.

Mr Trodgers' payment on 26 December 2017 to allow him to make a valid appeal against the officer's assessment is determined as follows:

	€
Interest on late preliminary tax:	
€9,000 x 0.0219% x 11 days[1]	22
Interest on balance of tax (based on return):	
€3,440 x 0.0219% x 422 days[2]	317
Balance of 2015 tax based on return	3,440
Total payment required before appeal	3,779

Having made this required payment on 26 December 2017, Mr Trodgers must therefore give his notice of appeal against the officer's assessment of 19 December 2017 no later than by 18 January 2018 (ie within 30 days from the making of the assessment).

Notes:

1. The interest on the late preliminary tax is due on a daily basis at 0.0219 per cent per day from 31 October 2015 to the 11 November 2016 date of payment.
2. Since the preliminary tax obligation was not properly met, the interest on the balance of the tax is backdated to the due date for the preliminary tax (31 October 2016) so that it is chargeable for the 421 days from 31 October 2016 to 26 December 2017 (the pre-appeal tax payment date).

Appeals against time limits for making enquiries

F(TA)A 2015, s 39 replaced TCA 1997, s 959AJ in its entirety. It notes that where a chargeable person is aggrieved by an enquiry made or an action taken by a Revenue officer under TCA 1997, s 959Z for a chargeable period, after the expiry of the four years from the end of the chargeable period in which the return was delivered on the grounds that the chargeable person considers that the Revenue officer is precluded from making the enquiry or taking the action and an assessment has not been made or amended, as the case may be in respect of the chargeable period on foot of the officer's enquiry or action then the chargeable person may appeal to the Appeal Commissioners, in accordance with TCA 1997, s 949I, within the period of 30 days after the date on which the officer makes that enquiry or takes that action.

2.203 Payment of tax on determination of appeal

Prior to his appeal against an assessment under the self assessment regime, the person assessed will – as one of the pre-conditions for the appeal – have made a payment (or payments) of tax for the relevant year at least equal to the income tax (including PRSI and Universal Social Charge) payable by reference to the income, etc figures given in his tax return for the year. When an appeal against an assessment is determined, whether by agreement between the person assessed and a Revenue officer, or by a decision of the

Appeal Commissioners, any additional tax resulting from the determination of the appeal must be paid.

TCA 1997, s 959AV fixes the due date (and, in consequence, the date from which interest runs) for the additional tax (if any) payable as the result of any determination of an appeal against an assessment under the self assessment system. Although the additional tax is not enforceable until after the appeal has been determined, the due date may be earlier than the date of the determination of the appeal. In the case of appeals determined prior to 2 April 2007, it was provided that the additional tax (and any interest) had to be paid even when due on a decision of the Appeal Commissioners which was to be the subject of a rehearing of the Circuit Court judge or the subject of an appeal on a point of law to the High Court or Supreme Court. F(TA)A 2015 removed the ability to appeal to the Circuit Court.

However, the courts held that the Revenue were not entitled to have their cake and eat it in *Harris v Quigley & Anor* VI ITR 839, where the taxpayer had claimed trading losses against his Sch E income. The Revenue Commissioners denied the claim but the Appeal Commissioners held that it was in fact valid, giving rise to a potential repayment of PAYE in excess of €9,000,000. The Revenue Commissioners required a case to be stated for the High Court and refused to make the repayment on the basis that TCA 1997, s 933(4) provided that the determination of the Appeal Commissioners was not final and conclusive in these circumstances. The Supreme Court had regard *inter alia* to the provisions regulating the rights of repayments of overpaid tax in the case of decisions by the Circuit Court and beyond, as well as the requirement on the taxpayer to pay tax found to be underpaid by the Appeal Commissioners under TCA 1997, s 941(9) where a case stated had been required. Accordingly, the court held that full effect should be given to TCA 1997, s 934(6) which provides that an assessment as determined by the Appeal commissioners is to be treated as an assessment against which no appeal had been given, In the absence of any statutory mechanism for repayment in this situation, the taxpayer was entitled to rely on his common law rights of restitution. (see *Woolwich BS v IRC* [1992] STC 657; *Murphy & Murphy v Attorney General* V ITR 613 and *O'Rourke v Revenue Commissioners*, discussed at **2.203**).

Geoghegan J observed:

> In this case although the determination of the Appeal Commissioner was not final and conclusive within the meaning of the Tax Acts, it was a lawful determination which then had to be put into effect by the inspector. The retention of the excessive tax as found by the Appeal Commissioner was unlawful and was tantamount to an unjust enrichment of the Revenue Commissioners at least for the period between the determination of the Appeal Commissioner and the ultimate determination of the case stated.

After the substitution of TCA 1997, s 934(6) by FA 2007, s 20(1), equity between Revenue and taxpayer had been enshrined statutorily and, it is now provided that no tax will be payable or repayable following a determination by the Appeal Commissioners if the decision is subject to a rehearing by the Circuit Court or an appeal on a point of law to the High Court (see however under 'Payment notices' in **2.618** below where tax may become payable following a determination by the Appeal Commissioners where a payment notice is issued by Revenue). Further, for appeals made after the 'commencement day' (21 March 2016) TCA 1997, s 949AM(1) requires Revenue to give effect to the determination of the Appeal Commissioners unless it has been appealed to the High Court in accordance with TCA 1997, ss 949AP and 949AQ.

Payment of additional tax on determination of appeal

TCA 1997, s 959AV provides that any additional tax which becomes payable on the determination of the appeal against an assessment or an amended assessment under the self assessment regime is deemed to be due and payable either:

(a) on the same due date as the due date for the tax charged by the assessment which was the subject of the appeal (if the two conditions mentioned below are not met) ('rule (a)'); or

(b) no later than one month from the date on which the appeal is determined (if the two conditions mentioned below are satisfied) ('rule (b)').

In practice prior to 1 January 2013 when there was no requirement to include a self assessment in a self assessment return, appeals were more often met as appeals against amended assessments than against an original assessment. This is because of the normal practice of Revenue was to issue an original assessment based on the data in the tax returns of the chargeable persons and then, if found necessary following a later examination of the returns, to make amendments of the original assessments to charge any further tax due. With effect from 1 January 2013 chargeable persons are required to include a self assessment in their self assessment return and an assessment will not be issued by Revenue as a matter of routine following the submission of a return. A Revenue assessment will only generally be issued if necessary following a subsequent examination of the return.

The due date of the additional tax resulting from the determination of the appeal against an assessment or an amended assessment is fixed by 'rule (b)' as the last day of the one month after the date of that determination if, and only if, both the following conditions are met:

(a) the tax paid prior to the appeal (as required by TCA 1997, s 959AH) turns out to be at least 90 per cent of the tax found to be payable as the result of the determination of the appeal; and

(b) the tax charged by the assessment is due and payable under TCA 1997, s 959AO(2), s 959AQ, s 959AR(3) or s 959AS(3) (and not under TCA 1997, s 959AO(3)).

The first condition looks only at the total tax actually paid prior to the appeal and the total tax payable for the year assessed as recomputed to reflect the consequences of the determination of the appeal (the 'final tax'). This condition is not met if the pre-appeal tax paid (including the amounts paid in respect of the self-employment PRSI contribution, Universal Social Charge and surcharge for late filing of a return) is found to be less than 90 per cent of the final tax (including PRSI, Universal Social Charge and surcharge) as determined as the result of the appeal. Prior to 1 January 2013 TCA 1997, s 958(9), which contained the rules for payment of tax on determination of an appeal now contained in TCA 1997, s 959AV, in referring to tax paid before the determination of the appeal, referred to the tax payable in accordance with TCA 1997, s 957(2)(a)(II) (the equivalent of TCA 1997, s 959AH). Thus in comparing tax paid before the determination of the appeal the figure for tax was inclusive of interest and collection costs, but the final tax figure was exclusive of interest and costs. TCA 1997, s 959AV does not make any specific reference to tax payable in accordance with TCA 1997, s 959AH and in s 959AH it is only for the purpose of s 959AH(1) that tax is deemed to include collection costs and interest. From 1 January 2013 onwards in determining whether tax paid before the appeal is at least 90 per cent of the tax payable on the determination of the appeal the tax paid before the appeal does not include interest and collection costs.

The second condition is only met if the chargeable person has properly discharged his preliminary tax obligation for the year assessed. This requires that his preliminary tax payment was, firstly, made no later than 31 October in the tax year concerned (as extended for ROS taxpayers) and, secondly, was an amount no less than the required minimum payment. Where the appeal is against an amendment to an amended assessment, the Revenue accept that condition (b) is still met where part of the tax charged was due in accordance with TCA 1997, s 959AU(2) and not TCA 1997, s 959AO(2) (see **2.109**).

If both conditions (a) and (b) are met, no interest is chargeable on any additional tax resulting from the determination of the appeal provided that this tax is paid no later than the due date one month after the date of that determination. Failure to pay by that date gives rise to interest on the additional tax, but only for the period running from one month after the date of the determination of the appeal to the date on which the additional tax is paid.

Example 2.203.1

Mr Blake Blades, a married man assessed jointly with his spouse, carries on a trade as a jewellery retailer and has profits assessable for 2016. He also has rental income assessable under Sch D Case V for 2016 and his wife has Sch F dividends and interest on Irish government stocks chargeable under Sch D Case III. As a VAT registered person Mr Blades is required to pay and file online using ROS.

The following other facts relevant to Mr and Mrs Blade's tax, assessable on him for 2016 are given:

(a) Mr Blades paid €7,500 online as preliminary tax for 2016 on 31 October 2016 (on time). His tax payable for the preceding year 2014 was €7,500, ie he paid 100% of the preceding year for 2016;

(b) On 12 August 2017, he files his 2016 tax return (including extracts from his business accounts for the year ended 30 June 2016) giving full particulars of his and his wife's income etc and including a self assessment for the year prepared in accordance with the details included in his return showing tax payable of €8,100 for 2016. This is well before the return filing date of 31 October 2017;

(c) In filing the return he includes a letter of expression of doubt, as provided by the rule now contained in TCA 1997, s 959P (see **2.105**), as to whether he has correctly deducted certain expenses in arriving at his Sch D Case I taxable profits disclosed in the return. He also sends in supporting documentation regarding the matter in doubt to Revenue;

(d) The balance of tax payable for 2016 is €600 after deducting the €7,500 paid as preliminary tax;

(e) Since the preliminary tax was paid on time and as the amount paid meets the 100 per cent prior-year test, the due date for the tax contained in the self assessment is on or before 31 October 2017. Note that Mr Blades would ultimately be found to have failed the 90 per cent test, since his preliminary tax payment of €7,500 is only 83.4 per cent of €8,990, the tax determined on appeal (see below);

(f) Mr Blades pays the €600 balance of tax on 12 October 2017 before the 31 October 2017 due date so that no interest arises;

(g) On 8 December 2017, following a 'desk audit' of the 2016 return in which a Revenue officer forms the opinion that the expenses in doubt (see (b) above) should not have been deducted, the officer amends the original self assessment to charge an additional amount of tax which works out at €2,150;

(h) On 23 December 2017, Mr Blades appeals against the amended assessment on the grounds that the expenses in doubt are correctly deductible and that, in consequence, the additional €2,150 should not be charged.

On 12 March 2018, the matter is argued before the Appeal Commissioners who decide on that day that part only of the expenses the subject of the appeal are properly allowable and that the remainder must be disallowed. The result of this decision is that the assessment must be amended to change the 2016 tax payable to €8,990. The additional tax payable is determined as follows:

	€	€
Total tax payable as result of appeal		8,990
Less:		
Preliminary tax paid 31/10/2016	7,500	
Balance of tax in assessment paid 12/10/2017	600	8,100
Additional tax as result of appeal		890

Since the tax of €8,100 paid before the appeal hearing is 90.1 per cent (not less than 90 per cent) of the €8,990 found to be payable as the result of the appeal, and as the tax charged in the assessment was payable under TCA 1997, s 959AO(2), the additional €890 is fixed by TCA 1997, s 959AV(2) as due and payable no later than one month after the determination of the appeal on 12 March 2018, ie the due date is 12 April 2018.

In fact, Mr Blades does not pay the additional €890 until 2 May 2018. Interest is therefore payable on the additional tax, but only from the 12 April due date to the 2 May payment date, as follows:

	€
€890 x 0.0219% x 20 days	3.89

If the tax paid prior to the appeal turns out to be less than 90 per cent of the tax found to be payable as the result of the determination of the appeal, or if the tax charged by the original assessment before any amendment was payable under TCA 1997, s 959AO(3) (ie where the preliminary tax payment was late or insufficient), 'rule (a)' is used instead of rule (b). In any such rule (a) case, TCA 1997, s 959AV(1) provides that any additional tax payable on the determination of the appeal is deemed to be due and payable on the same date as the due date for the tax charged by the assessment the subject of the appeal.

In any such case, the due date for the tax charged by the assessment, and therefore the due date for the additional tax differs depending on whether the assessment which was the subject of the appeal is the original assessment (before any amendment) or an amended assessment.

If the assessment is the original assessment, the due date for the additional tax resulting from the determination of the appeal becomes, as is explained under 'Tax charged in assessment', either:

(a) 31 October following the end of the tax year (ie 31 October 2017 for tax in respect of 2016); or

(b) the same due date as that for the preliminary tax for the year assessed (if the taxpayer had failed to discharge his preliminary tax obligation properly, ie by not making the required minimum payment no later than the due date for the preliminary tax (ie 31 October 2016 or as extended for ROS taxpayers for tax in respect of 2016)).

On the other hand, if the assessment is an amended assessment, the due date for the additional tax resulting from the determination of the appeal becomes the same date as the due date determined under TCA 1997, s 959AU(2) for any additional tax payable as the result of the amendment. As indicated under 'Tax payable on amendment of assessment' in **2.109**, this due date is, dependent on the circumstances, the relevant one of the following:

(a) one month after the date of the amendment to the assessment (if the original assessment was one made after the taxpayer had filed a 'full and true' return. It is assumed this will also include the situation where a self assessment which was included with a 'full and true' return is amended see **2.109** above);
(b) 31 October following the end of the tax year (where a full and true return was not filed before or with the original assessment made by a Revenue officer or the chargeable person, but where the taxpayer had paid a sufficient amount of preliminary tax no later than its due date); or
(c) 31 October in the year assessed, ie the same day as the due date for the payment of the preliminary tax (if neither (1) nor (2) applies).

Example 2.203.2

Take the facts of Mr Blades' case from **Example 2.203.1**, but assume that the decision of the Appeal Commissioners on 12 March 2018 on the Revenue officer's amendment of 8 December 2017 was to the effect that the 2016 tax payable becomes €9,120 (and not the €8,990 assumed in that example). Additional tax of €1,020 (€9,120 less €8,100) becomes payable.

Although the tax charged by the original assessment was payable under TCA 1997, s 959AO(2) it now turns out that the total of €8,100 tax paid before the appeal is only 88.8 per cent (less than 90 per cent) of the €9,120 tax payable as the result of the appeal. Consequently, TCA 1997, s 959AV(1) applies to determine the due date for the additional tax of €1,020 becoming payable on the determination of the appeal.

Since the assessment appealed against was the assessment as amended (rather than the original assessment), the first question to ask is whether the original assessment was one made after or when Mr Blades had filed a full and true return. Although the Sch D Case I income included in the return has turned out to be understated due to the incorrect deduction for some disallowable expenses, the return is deemed by TCA 1997, s 959P(5) to have been a full and true one due to the taxpayer's 'expression of doubt' as to the correctness of the deduction (see **2.105**).

Since the return, so deemed to be a full and true one, was filed on 12 August 2017 and included a self assessment (the original assessment) the due date for the additional tax of €1,020 becomes one month following the date on which the officer made the amendment which is the subject of the appeal, ie the due date is fixed as 8 January 2018.

As in **Example 2.203.1**, Mr Blades pays the additional tax (now €1,020) on 2 May 2018. Interest is now payable for 114 days from 8 January 2017 to 2 May 2018, as follows:

	€
€1,020 x 0.0219% x 114	25.47

Example 2.203.3

Take the facts of **Example 2.203.2**, ie where the €8,100 paid as preliminary tax for 2016 is less than 90 per cent of the €9,120 found to be payable by Mr Blades on the determination of the appeal, but assume that the Revenue officer rejects the expression of doubt given by Mr Blades on the grounds it was not genuine and that he was acting with a view to tax avoidance. Mr Blades does not appeal on this point.

In view of this rejection of the expression of doubt (see **2.105**), Mr Blades is deemed not to have made a full and true return when, on 12 August 2017, he filed the income tax return for 2016 understating his Sch D Case I income. In consequence, the day one month after the date of the 8 January 2018 amendment of the assessment cannot be the due date for the additional €1,020 becoming payable on the determination of the appeal.

The next question is whether, on the facts in this example, Mr Blades has properly discharged his preliminary tax obligation for 2016. As he has done so, the due date for the additional tax of €1,020 will be 31 October 2017. Interest is now payable for 182 days from 1 November 2017 to 2 May 2018, as follows:

	€
€1,020 x 0.0219% x 182	40.66

Overpayments of tax

Where the tax found to be payable on the determination of an appeal turns out to be less than the tax paid by the taxpayer before the appeal is heard, this will normally be attributable to an excess payment of preliminary tax, given the requirement that the taxpayer must pay at least the tax based on his return (the pre-appeal tax) before the appeal will be admitted. However, it is in theory possible that the Appeal Commissioners could determine that the actual liability of the taxpayer is lower than that based on the figures in the return.

In a case where a repayment arises following the determination of an appeal it is not clear whether TCA 1997, s 865(1)(b) is truly in point (even assuming a full return was made) since presumably the information in the return was by definition not sufficient on its own to enable the Revenue to determine to what an extent a repayment was due to the taxpayer (see **2.104**); however, as TCA 1997, s 865A is expressly applied in the context of repayments of tax following a decision by the superior courts (see **2.205**) it would seem that interest will run on overpayments in line with the normal rules.

Finally, it is to be noted that the rules of TCA 1997, ss 941(9), 942(6)(b) which provide for interest payable to or receivable by taxpayers on additional tax or overpayments of tax due to decisions of the Circuit Court judge or of the High Court or Supreme Court remain applicable for tax for all years of assessment (see **2.205**).

2.204 Decision of Appeal Commissioners

There is a certain ambiguity about the role of the Appeal Commissioners. Some of the earlier UK cases characterised their function as that of 'valuers', with responsibility for determining the correct amount of the taxpayer's liability 'in the interests of the country at large'. In The *State v Smidic* I ITR 577 two passages were cited with approval in the High Court. Firstly, there were Lord Justice Green's observations in *IRC v Sneath* 17 TC 149, where he said:

> The estimating authorities, even when the appeal is made to them, are not acting as Judges deciding litigation between the subject and the Crown. They are merely in the position of valuers whose proceedings are regulated by statute to enable them to make an estimate of the income of the taxpayer for the particular year in question.

Secondly, there were Lord Wright's observations in *Elmhurst v IRC* 21 TC 381, where he said:

> I may note here at once that in making the assessment and in dealing with the appeals, the Commissioners are exercising statutory authority and a statutory duty which they are bound to carry out. They are not in the position of judges deciding an issue between two particular parties. Their obligation is wider than that. It is to exercise their judgment on such material as comes before them and to obtain any material which they think is necessary and which they ought to have on that material to make an assessment or the estimate which the law requires them to make. They are not deciding a case *inter partes*, they are assessing or estimating the amount on which, in the interests of the country at large, the taxpayer ought to be taxed.

(See also *Ranaweera v Ramachandran* [1970] WLR 500). The idea that the Appeal Commissioners' function is merely to declare the taxpayer's liability on the basis of the facts before them also underpins the court's reasoning in the *State (Calcul International & Solatrex International) v Appeal Commissioners* III ITR 577, discussed in **1.409**).

In *Wicker v Fraser* [1982] STC 505 it was held, however, that the role of the Appeal Commissioners was not inquisitorial as such, ie their responsibility was not to undertake a full and fresh investigation of the facts in the same manner as the inspector of taxes, but rather to determine the correct tax liability in the light of the evidence brought before them. Thus, for example, they will not err in law by failing to consider points of law or logic not placed before them. This would imply that the Appeal Commissioners' rights of issuing precepts and summoning witnesses should be exercised primarily in order to clarify or fill in gaps in the evidence brought before them (as well as, if they think fit, enabling the Revenue to obtain evidence on their own behalf not otherwise obtainable).

In *Glaxo Group v IRC* [1996] STC 191, it was held that an inspector of taxes was entitled to argue for an increase in the assessment which he had raised; this was notwithstanding that any UK equivalent of TCA 1997, s 934(1)(c) entitles the inspector only to produce evidence and give reasons 'in support of the assessment'. The court was heavily influenced in its decision by the fact that the Appeal Commissioners have the power to increase an assessment. It was inferred from the fact that the Revenue were the only party with an interest in increasing an assessment that they must therefore have been granted the ability to argue in favour of such an increase. The correctness of the decision is nevertheless open to doubt since the words 'in support of the assessment' do not lend themselves easily to the court's interpretation (see *Carr* [1996] ITR 142). It might be argued that the Appeal Commissioner's ability to increase an assessment simply reflects their right to draw their own inferences from the material before them, rather than giving a mandate to the Revenue to 'argue up' the assessment (note the comments of Lord Diplock in *Re Vandervell's Trusts* 46 TC 341.

The ability of the Appeal Commissioners to take an independent line on the evidence before them implies that they could in fact reduce an assessment on grounds not included in the taxpayer's notice of appeal, and which he therefore is normally debarred from raising at the appeal (see Carr, 'The Role of the Appeal Commissioners' [1994] IJOT 1, where Carr also argues that the Appeal Commissioner's role in strictness is fully inquisitorial). In general, however, where the Appeal Commissioners reduce assessments this will relate to the quantum of income in cases where the taxpayer's records are alleged to be unreliable or inaccurate.

In accordance with the general law in civil cases, the burden of proof falls on 'he who asserts', ie it generally falls on the taxpayer-appellant, who asserts that the assessment is excessive (see for example, *Bolands Ltd v Revenue Commissioners* I ITR 34; *MacEachern v Carr* [1996] STC 282; *Menolly Homes v The Appeal Commissioners and The Revenue Commissioners* [2010] IEHC 49). This onus may (perhaps) be justified on the basis that only the taxpayer has access to the full facts relating to his personal tax situation. Of course, where the taxpayer does produce evidence in favour of his contentions, it will then fall upon the Revenue to produce counter-evidence to support their contentions. It is often said that in such case the 'evidential burden' shifts to the Revenue; however, the burden of proof still remains with the taxpayer. Thus, the Revenue will succeed, not only if they can rebut the taxpayer's evidence on the balance of probabilities, but also if they can merely leave the issue in doubt (*Brady v Group Lotus Car Companies* [1987] STC 635). It seems however that an inference of fact which involves fraud or criminal conduct may impose a higher than usual evidential burden on the Revenue (see *Les Croupiers Casino Club v Pattinson* [1985] STC 738 and note also the non-tax case *O'Laoire v The Medical Council* 1997 SC).

The onus of proof also lies with the taxpayer who asserts his claim to a right to a relief or allowance by way of appeal. For further discussion of these issues, see Giblin: 'Rules of Evidence and Procedure of Tax Appeals' [1995] ITR 1289, and Clohessy: Appeal Commissioner Hearings IOT Seminar 24 October 1995).

The doctrine of *res judicata* does not apply to the Appeal Commissioners on the basis that their determination relates only to the year of assessment in question. Thus, their decision on a particular issue, in determining an assessment for year one does not bind them to reach the same decision on the identical issue in year two (see *IRC v Sneath* 17 TC 149; In *R (on the application of Carvill) v IRC* [2003] EWHC 1852 (Admin); *Bourke v Lyster* II ITR 374 and the rating case of *Kildare CC v Keogh* [1976] IR 330). However, in *Barnett v Brabyn* [1996] STC 716, it was confirmed that nevertheless:

> a previous determination of a question may be a cogent factor on a subsequent determination of the same question.

It follows also that the Appeal Commissioners can only rule on the assessment before them and not on the implications of a transaction for assessments in other tax years (*Bourke v Lyster* II ITR 374; note also *Tod v South Essex Motors* [1988] STC 392 and *MacNiven (Inspector of Taxes) v Westmoreland Investments Ltd* [1997] STC 1103).

The right available to either the taxpayer or the inspector to require the Appeal Commissioners to state and sign a case for the opinion of the High Court is only available where either party is dissatisfied with the determination of the Commissioners on the grounds that it is incorrect on a point of law. The distinction between an issue of law and an issue of fact is not clearcut, as acknowledged by Kenny J in *Mara v Hummingbird* II ITR 667, when he observed:

> The line between questions of law and those of fact can rarely be drawn firmly so as to separate one from the other.
>
> A case stated consists in part of findings on questions of primary fact, eg with what intention did the taxpayers purchase the premises? These findings on primary facts should not be set aside by the courts unless there was no evidence whatever to support them. The Commissioners then goes on in the case stated to give his conclusions or inferences from these primary facts. These are mixed questions of fact and law and the courts should approach these in a different way. If they are based on the interpretation of documents, the court should reverse them if they are incorrect for it is in a good position to determine the meaning of documents as is the Commissioner. If the conclusions from the primary facts are one which no reasonable Commissioner could draw, the court should set aside his findings on the ground that he must be assumed to have misdirected himself as to the law or made a

> mistake in reasoning. Finally, if his conclusions show that he has adopted a wrong view of the law they should be set aside. If, however, they are not based on a mistaken view of the law or a wrong interpretation of documents, they should not be set aside unless the inferences which he made from the primary facts were ones that no reasonable Commissioner could draw.

Kenny J, went on to approve the observations of Lord Radcliffe to similar effect in *Edwards v Bairstow* 36 TC 207.

The relationship between the evidence heard by the Appeal Commissioners and the inferences which they draw from that evidence may be subdivided broadly into three main categories. Firstly, the Appeal Commissioners may infer a particular fact or facts from the evidence before them (ie findings of primary fact). They may proceed to infer further, purely factual, conclusions from these primary facts, typically in a case where the taxpayer's underlying records are alleged to be unreliable or inaccurate. As indicated by Kenny J, such findings can only be overturned as raising a point of law if they are such that no reasonable body of Appeal Commissioners could have arrived at them.

Thus for example, in *Billows v Robinson* [1990] STC 162, it was established that a taxpayer's disclosed income was insufficient to meet his living expenses. The court held that in the absence of evidence to the contrary, the Appeal Commissioners were entitled to infer that the shortfall represented undisclosed emoluments. In the absence of reliable records, the Appeal Commissioners estimated the taxpayer's income on the basis of figures for 1972, extrapolating these into subsequent years in line with the retail price index. It was held that:

> it was impossible to say that the estimate they arrived at was outside the range of that which a reasonable body of commissioners properly instructed could have arrived at.

The Appeal Commissioners decision was upheld by the Court of Appeal [1991] STC 127 as one disclosing no question of law (see also eg *Buckley v Edwards* [1982] STC 135).

The second category of inferential relationship (described as one of 'mixed fact and law' by Kenny J) often arises where the Appeal Commissioners are required to apply a 'vague' legal or tax concept to a particular set of facts as found by them. A vague concept is one where in some (possibly many) instances there may be no definite answer as to whether or not a term or expression applies to a given set of facts. The classic example is the concept of 'trade' (see **4.102**). The range of activities which display at least some of the features of trading is practically infinite, and each case which falls to be considered is potentially unique. Accordingly, the inference of the Appeal Commissioners that a particular transaction is of a trading nature will generally be treated as a secondary inference of fact, unless the finding is one that is wholly unreasonable (as indeed was the position in *Edwards v Bairstow* itself) when it will be categorised as an error of law. Another example of the second category of inference is the distinction between items which are, or are not, plant (see **6.202**). In *IRC v Scottish & Newcastle Breweries* [1982] STC 296, Lord Lowry said:

> The law does not supply a definition of plant or prescribe a detailed or exhaustive set of rules for application to any particular set of circumstances and there are cases which, on the facts found, are capable of decision either way … A decision in such a case is a decision of fact and degree …

In effect, the decision as to whether or not a set of facts falls within, or outside a vague concept, is in reality a decision as to whether those facts fall more within the concept than outside it. As Jacob J expressed it in *Vodafone v Shaw* [1995] STC 353, in the context of the capital/income distinction:

> One of the troubles with all the tests propounded by the courts is that they are necessarily imprecise. Given that any expenditure has got to be put in a box labelled 'revenue' or 'capital' there is an obvious difficulty in forcing many kinds of expenditure having some of the characteristics of both into one box or another.

Other examples of this second category of inference include: the distinction between contracts of services and contracts for services (see **10.103**) unless, it seems, all of the terms of the contract are in writing (see below); the distinction between a benefit received as an employee, as opposed to as an investor (see *Tyrer v Smart* [1979] STC 34); the question whether a payment on retirement arises from the taxpayer's employment (see *Mulvey v Coffey* I ITR 618, at **16.107**); and the distinction between domiciled and non-domiciled status (see **1.505**).

The decision of the Appeal Commissioners in this category of case may also involve preliminary findings of law. Thus, as pointed out by Kenny J, if they demonstrate that they have misunderstood the legal meaning of the term or expression in question before applying it to the facts, their decision will be appealable accordingly on a point of law (see eg *Proes v Revenue Commissioners* V ITR 481).

The third category is where the Appeal Commissioners' finding is regarded as purely one of law. This may be because, for example, (as noted by Kenny J in the passage cited above) the issue requires the interpretation of legal documents. Thus, it seems that where all the terms of a contract of service are contained in writing, only the written documentation may normally be considered (see *O'Coindealbhain v Mooney* IV ITR 45, but compare *Henry Denny & Sons v Minister for Social Welfare* V ITR 238) and, accordingly, in such a case, the issue seems to be one of law (*Davies v Presbyterian Church of Wales* [1986] IRLR 194). More commonly, however, this category applies where the courts in effect simply treat the issue as one in which they reserve the right to intervene. Thus, despite the fact that the capital/revenue distinction is inherently 'vague' (and does not seem to raise any profound technical issues which might justify it being reserved to the judiciary as an issue of law); in *Beauchamp v FW Woolworth* [1989] STC 510, the House of Lords held that the distinction between capital and revenue expenditure under Sch D Cases I and II was one of law. In *Brosnan v Mutual Enterprises Ltd* Murphy J stated the issue was essentially one of fact; his conclusion was subsequently upheld by the Supreme Court V ITR 138.

While it may therefore be said that the Irish and the UK courts apply the same principles in distinguishing between issues of fact and issues of law, it of course does not follow that they will always reach the same conclusions as regards the application of those principles. In *Smith v Abbot* [1994] STC 237 the House of Lords held that the cost of newspapers purchased by journalists in order to brief themselves in advance of getting the day's new agenda was not incurred 'in the performance of their duties' and that this was an issue of law rather than that of fact. Apart from the actual correctness of the decision (see the critique at **10.302**), it is doubtful whether this should have been viewed as an issue of law. The circumstances in which employees may undertake work-related activities prior to arriving at their offices are infinitely various; it seems wrong to say that the question of whether or not such activities are an integral part of their duties can be decided without reference to the specific facts concerned.

The decision as to whether an issue should be classed as one of fact or law is in effect itself an issue of law. If the court decides that the issue in dispute is purely one of fact then, as indicated above, it will uphold the determination of the Appeal Commissioners.

The taxpayer cannot require a case stated in respect of any intermediate ruling or decision which does not constitute the actual determination of the appeal (*State v Smidic* I ITR 577).

The Appeal Commissioners' determination of the appeal against an assessment should fix the total amount of tax which becomes payable under the assessment as a result of their decision on the point or points which are the subject of dispute.

Prior to making the appeal heard by the Appeal Commissioners, the taxpayer will, as one of the pre-conditions for the appeal, have paid tax at least equal to the amount due for the relevant tax year as calculated by reference to the income, deductions from income, etc disclosed in his tax return. In *Bairead v Carr* IV ITR 505, Lynch J, in the Supreme Court, indicated that this provision could not be abused in order to impoverish the taxpayer and thus prevent his obtaining the necessary legal assistance to present his appeal in court (as one would expect, there was no suggestion that the Revenue Commissioners had in fact attempted to act in such a manner).

2.205 Appeals to High Court and Supreme Court

An appeal from the decision of the Appeal Commissioners, or from that of the Circuit Court judge on a rehearing, may be taken to the High Court on a point of law by either the taxpayer or the inspector. The Court of Session case of *Murray Group Holdings Ltd & Ors v Revenue and Customs Commissioners* [2016] STC 468 dealt with what the issue of 'a point of law' and outline how such matters arise in the first instance. Lord Drummond Young noted at para 42 *et seq* of his decision as follows:

> 'Although the concept of appeal on a point of law might seem simple, it has given rise to considerable controversy; indeed in the well-known case of *Edwards (Inspector of Taxes) v Bairstow* [1955] 3 All ER 48, [1956] AC 14, an appeal was taken to the House of Lords to adjudicate upon differences of approach that had developed between the Scottish and English courts. We are of opinion that an appeal on a point of law covers four different categories of case.
>
> The first of these categories is appeals on the general law: the content of its rules. In tax appeals these are largely statutory, but the interpretation of a particular statutory provision may be a matter of general law, and tax law also includes a number of general non-statutory rules, such as the redirection principle and the Ramsay principle, both of which are relevant to this case.
>
> The second category comprises appeals on the application of the law to the facts as found by the First-tier Tribunal. This is in our opinion a clear example of an appeal on a point of law: it is the application of the general rules to particular factual situations that defines the frontiers of a legal rule and thus its practical scope. Furthermore, it is the application of the general rules to particular facts that brings about the development of those rules to meet new situations. For these reasons we consider that an appeal on the application of the general law to a particular factual situation must be regarded as being on a point of law. This is illustrated by the facts of *Edwards (Inspector of Taxes) v Bairstow* [1955] 3 All ER 48, [1956] AC 14. There the House of Lords, reversing the decisions of the General Commissioners and lower courts, held that a transaction involving the acquisition of spinning plant, dividing it into lots and selling those lots at a profit was an adventure in the nature of trade. In holding otherwise, the Commissioners and the lower courts had misdirected themselves as to the meaning and proper application of the expression

> 'adventure in the nature of trade' found in the relevant taxing statute, the Income Tax Act 1918: see *Lord Radcliffe* [1955] 3 All ER 48 at 57–58, [1956] AC 14 at 36–37....
>
> The third category of appeal on a point of law is where the tribunal has made a finding 'for which there is no evidence or which is inconsistent with the evidence and contradictory of it': *IRC v Fraser* 1942 SC 493 at 497–498, 24 TC 498 at 501, per Lord President Normand.
>
> This runs into a fourth category, comprising cases where the First-tier Tribunal has made a fundamental error in its approach to the case: for example, by asking the wrong question, or by taking account of manifestly irrelevant considerations, or by arriving at a decision that no reasonable tax tribunal could properly reach. In such cases we conceive that the Court of Session and the Upper Tribunal have power to interfere with the decision of the First-tier Tribunal as disclosing an error on a point of law: *Edwards (Inspector of Taxes) v Bairstow* [1955] 3 All ER 48 at 57, [1956] AC 14 at 36, per Lord Radcliffe....
>
> In practice the main difficulties that arise in determining whether an appeal raises a point of law occur when legal rules are applied to particular factual situations.'

Where the Appeal Commissioners have been requested to state a case for the opinion of the High Court, the Commissioners are required to draw up the case setting forth the facts and the decision given.

2.206 Judicial review; Revenue rulings

In broad terms, judicial review is a process whereby a decision (or an act or omission) by a public body, tribunal or inferior court can be challenged before the courts. If the applicant is successful, the court may issue an appropriate order. The orders which are potentially relevant in the tax context are those of:

(a) certiorari, quashing the relevant decision, etc;

(b) mandamus, directing a body or tribunal to carry out one of its lawful duties; and

(c) prohibition, preventing a body or tribunal from exercising its powers, permanently or only allowing it to do so subject to meeting prescribed conditions.

In addition, the High Court may issue a declaration, setting out the legal position of the parties (Chancery (Ireland) Act 1867; RSC Ord 84, r 18(2)). A declaration is not legally binding, but in practice will always be respected by the public body, tribunal, etc which is a party to the proceedings. An injunction may also be granted by the High Court preventing a course of action on the part of the public body, etc. An appeal against a decision of the High Court may be made to the Supreme Court.

Judicial review is a supervisory function and as such the court is concerned with how a decision is reached and not with the correctness of the decision as such. The whole area of judicial review is an extremely complex and rapidly evolving area of the law (readers are referred to the lengthy discussion in Hogan and Gwynn Morgan, *Administrative Law in Ireland* (4th edn, Round Hall, 2010). However, it may be said, in broad terms, that judicial review may lie where, *inter alia*:

(a) a body, etc has exceeded its statutory powers (so that it has acted *ultra vires*);

(b) a discretion has been exercised or decision made by a body, etc after taking into account irrelevant matters, or after disregarding relevant matters;

(c) a discretion has been exercised or a decision made by a body, etc, which no reasonable body could have arrived at (this would include a course of action which was arbitrary, or unduly burdensome and oppressive);

(d) a body has failed to fulfil a legitimate expectation which it has raised; or

(e) a tribunal or court has erred in law so that it has exceeded its jurisdiction or the error is on the face of the record: see K Costello Documentary Error as a Ground of Judicial Review in Irish Law (1993–1995) IR Jur 148 (usually only relevant where there is no statutory right of appeal on points of law – see below).

The taxpayer may in the first instance avail if appropriate of Revenue Commissioners' Complaint and Review Procedures (see Revenue leaflet CS4 revised December 2012), where it is stated that one of the criterion which will be applied when conducting a review will be to evaluate if the Revenue official applied Revenue powers fairly.

In *Kennedy v Hearne* III ITR 590, the Revenue Commissioners erroneously served an estimate of PAYE under TCA 1997, s 989(2), (3) on a person who had in fact remitted PAYE for the period concerned. Finlay CJ in the Supreme Court commented:

> The section must be construed as vesting in the Revenue Commissioner the power to issue a notice to the sheriff only in cases where an actual default of a levied tax has occurred. Where, as happened in this case, they issued such a notice where the default had not continued up to the time that the notice was issued, what they did was a nullity.

It seems however that an inspector who raises an assessment on a mistaken view of the law, or who applies the law incorrectly to the facts, may still be acting *intra vires*. Thus, in *IRC v Aiken* [1990] STC 497, Fox LJ observed that the making of an assessment is different from determining, an ultimate liability to tax, saying:

> … an inspector can do no more than form a view and the fair and proper administration of the tax machinery in no way requires that any decision he makes should be condemned as *ultra vires* if, in the end, it is proved that he is wrong.

In *Harley Developments Inc v CIR* [1996] STC 440, the Privy Council held that an assessment would be *ultra vires* only if it was so gravely flawed as to amount to a nullity. In the instant case, there was a 'respectable' argument in support of the assessment and accordingly judicial review could not lie.

In *The State (FIC Ltd) v O'Ceallaigh* III ITR 124, the taxpayer obtained an order of mandamus directing the inspector of taxes to issue a capital gains tax clearance certificate under TCA 1997, s 980. Barrington J held that the inspector had exceeded his powers in making a wide-ranging investigation into a suspected tax avoidance scheme and that he was bound to issue the clearance certificate once it had been established that the taxpayer owned the relevant asset (see also *The State (Melbarian Enterprises Ltd) v The Revenue Commissioners* III ITR 290, discussed at **1.407** and *Taxback Ltd v Revenue Commissioners* V ITR 412, a VAT case).

In *Warnock v Revenue Commissioners* III ITR 356 the Revenue served a notice under TCA 1997, s 808 (see **17.212**) requiring the plaintiffs to furnish particulars of a wide range of transactions which any of their individual clients had entered into in relation to ten 'tax haven' jurisdictions. The court held that the Revenue were not acting *ultra vires* in seeking details of transactions undertaken prior to the enactment of TCA 1997, s 808 (see **1.405**). The court also rejected an argument that the information required did not exceed that which was necessary for the purposes of TCA 1997, s 806 (rather disturbingly the court justified this conclusion on the basis that the powers in TCA 1997, s 808 were cast deliberately widely to enable the Revenue to detect tax evasion, whereas TCA 1997, s 806 is in fact concerned exclusively with tax avoidance). The court also held that, on the facts of the case 'the notice would not have involved any excessive amount of time or energy on the part of [the plaintiff] or their staff'. (Compare *R v*

O'Kane & Clarke [1996] STC 1249, where some emphasis was placed on the concept of 'proportionality', which has also influenced the Irish courts in the context of constitutional interpretation – see **1.405**).

The principle of 'legitimate expectation' (see eg *Webb v Ireland* [1988] ILRM 565; *Duggan v An Taoiseach* [1989] ILRM 710 and *Carbery Milk Products v Minister for Agriculture* IV ITR 492), provides another basis for potential judicial review proceedings. The principle was explained in the UK context by Bingham LJ, in *R v IRC ex parte MFK Underwriting Agencies* [1989] STC 873 as follows:

> If a public authority so conducts itself as to create a legitimate expectation that a certain course will be followed, it would often be unfair if the authority were permitted to follow a different course, to the detriment of one who entertained the expectation, particularly if he acted on it. If in private law a body would be in breach of contract in so acting or estopped from so acting a public authority should generally be in no better position. The doctrine of legitimate expectation is rooted in fairness.

In cases where the taxpayer is seeking to assert a substantive right (eg in the tax context, a claim for exemption or relief), the Irish courts have perhaps tended to emphasise the parallels with the common law doctrine of 'estoppel', whereas the UK courts have tended to emphasise that it is the issue of fairness which is central (see *R v IRC ex parte Unilever* [1994] STC 841, [1996] STC 681 below).

In *Wiley v IRC* IV ITR 170, the taxpayer had on two previous occasions successfully claimed a substantial refund of vehicle excise duty under an Order made in 1979. The terms of the Order (based on FA 1968, s 43(1)) required the taxpayer to be 'wholly or almost wholly without the use of each leg'. In fact, the taxpayer clearly did not meet this requirement. The Revenue Commissioners subsequently decided to request medical evidence before granting refunds and in the light of this evidence, rejected the taxpayer's third claim. The taxpayer applied for an order of certiorari quashing the Revenue's decision, on the basis that it was contrary to his legitimate expectation that he would continue to be granted refunds. A majority of the judges in the Supreme Court held that, because the taxpayer knew or ought to have known, that he was clearly ineligible for a repayment, any expectations which he might have held were illegitimate. In the Supreme Court, Finlay CJ (Hederman J concurring) also rejected the taxpayer's application on the additional grounds that it would be *ultra vires* for the Revenue Commissioners to make refunds of taxes to those who were not entitled to them. *Wiley* was followed in the High Court decision in *Fortune v Revenue Commissioners* HC 2009, where it was held that the taxpayer could not claim a legitimate expectation that the Revenue Commissioners would not exercise their power to re-open a claim for Film Investment Relief 'at any time' in respect of a claim made ten years previously under FA 1987, s 35. The taxpayer had been advised that, the relief could be withdrawn at any stage and he had failed to establish that there had been such an inordinate and inexcusable delay on the part of the Revenue in withdrawing the relief that the balance of justice lay in favour of halting the assessment by the Revenue.

Notwithstanding the views of Finlay CJ in *Wiley*, it seems clear that the Revenue Commissioners have at the very least a discretion on foot of their 'care and management' function to waive liabilities which it would be uneconomic for them to seek to collect (see *R v IRC ex parte Federation of Self-Employed* [1985], cited approvingly by O'Flaherty J in *Wiley*). It remains debatable whether the far reaching concessions available to so-called 'bogus non-resident account holders' set out in the

Revenue Statement of Practice of 2/5/2001 fall within the ambit of the 'care and management' function.

Similarly, there should generally be no objection to the relaxation of procedural requirements by the Revenue Commissioners in the interests of the smoother (or fairer) operation of the tax system. In *Bairead v MacDonald* IV ITR 475, Barron J observed:

> In allowing the defendant to make [late] returns … the Revenue was following a practice which had the effect of mitigating the harshness involved in seeking to recover tax on foot of estimates which … may well be considerably above the real liability had proper returns been made. In certain circumstances, this can amount to a promissory estoppel that proper returns will be considered.

In *Al Fayed & Ors v Advocate-General for Scotland* [2002] STC 910, the Inland Revenue entered into an arrangement with three taxpayers, all of whom were not domiciled in the UK and had no intention of becoming domiciled there. As such, they were liable on the remittance basis in respect of overseas income and capital gains accruing to them. Under the arrangement, which applied for a five-year period in advance, the taxpayers agreed to pay a fixed sum of tax each year, without actually having to do a computation strictly in accordance with law. Thereafter, they could remit as much or as little of their income and gains as they pleased, without further tax consequences. The court was required to consider whether the arrangement was a legitimate exercise of the Revenue's powers of management over taxation. The court said in relation to the Revenue's powers of management:

> This exercise involves *inter alia* the making of judgments as to the best deployment of their resources in maximising the collection of tax that is known to be due, and the making of judgments as to the extent of the information that the respondents can reasonably hope to obtain in their investigation of the affairs of taxpayers or potential taxpayers. The making of back duty settlements is an every day example of the exercise of the Inland Revenue's discretion as to care and management. The essence of all such settlements and agreements is the element of compromise. They involve a decision by the Revenue to settle for less than the tax which may be due, or which it knows to be due. In looking at the terms on which such agreements are concluded it is not for the court to substitute its own judgement for that of the Inland Revenue. The decision to enter into such an agreement will therefore not be invalidated by the court merely because it appears to the court to have been unwise from the Revenue's point of view. Provided that the decision is made in good faith in pursuance of the proper care and management purposes, and expressly for 'good management' reasons, it will be *intra vires*.

The Revenue argued that the agreement had been entered into under the threat that if it was not accepted by them, the taxpayers would arrange matters so that they were not taxable at all, either by ceasing residence or by appropriate management of their cash remittances. The court held that nevertheless the agreement was *ultra vires*. The Revenue did not have power to enter into agreements for the payment of money to them by an individual on the basis that he could so organise his affairs so as not to incur any liability to UK tax. The making of a forward tax agreement of this kind, where the Revenue renounced their right and duty to investigate the true financial and other circumstances of taxpayers during the period of the agreement was not a proper exercise of the Revenue's duties of care and management. The effect of the agreement was that the taxpayers became a privileged group which was not so much taxed by law as untaxed by concession. Furthermore, the agreement had failed to take account of the possibility that the taxpayers might acquire a domicile of choice in the UK. Since the agreement had been illegal, the taxpayers could not have any legitimate expectation that the Revenue would continue to abide by it.

In *Keogh v Criminal Assets Bureau* VI ITR 635, the Supreme Court held that an undertaking in the Taxpayer's Charter of Rights that the Revenue Commissioners would provide accurate and timely information about taxpayers' entitlements and obligations under Revenue Law was binding and that failure to meet this undertaking by omitting to inform the taxpayer of his statutory rights of appeal entitled the taxpayer to be restored to the same position as if the undertaking had in fact been met. In the event, an appeal which the taxpayer was not in fact entitled to have made was treated as valid. The court observed that the Revenue Commissioners as a public authority were bound to observe fair procedures; while some of the undertakings in the Charter were merely 'aspirational' in character and so could not give rise to any legitimate expectations on the part of taxpayers, in the present case the taxpayer had a right to information on the provisions of the 'notoriously opaque and difficult' tax code. The Taxpayer's Charter has since been replaced by the 'Revenue Customer Service Charter' which contains a similar undertaking. The relevant information on the appeal procedures is now included in Notices of Assessment.

In *R (on the application of Carvill) v IRC* [2003] EWHC 1852 (Admin) it was held that where VAT was paid following a Commissioner's dismissal of the taxpayer's appeal, and a different Commissioner later allowed his appeal with regard to a similar issue but for different years of assessment, the Revenue's decision not to repay the VAT was lawful. The court held that the Revenue was not required to choose which decision should be regarded as correct in the context of the statutory rules which provided for separate determination in respect of separate tax years. It was therefore entitled to depart from its normal practice in such a case as long as it gave the taxpayer a fair hearing and did not arrive at an irrational decision.

In *R v IRC ex parte Unilever* [1994] STC 841, the Inland Revenue had through an oversight accepted out-of-time loss relief claims from the taxpayer over a number of years. The Court of Appeal held that the Revenue's conduct, since it consisted merely of silence and inaction, could not give rise to an estoppel. Further, the Revenue could not be held to have made a representation to the taxpayer unless they had done so knowingly and deliberately.

The status of the Revenue Commissioners' Statements of Practice and that of Revenue rulings and clearances is open to question. In *Pandion Haliaetus & Ors v The Revenue Commissioners* III ITR 670, the parties to a complex tax-planning scheme obtained rulings from an inspector regarding the tax treatment of certain elements of the scheme, but without disclosing the entirety of the scheme to him. One of the parties sought an order of certiorari quashing a subsequent assessment on him which was contrary to one of the rulings thus obtained. Blaney J, refusing the application, held that on the facts the Revenue Commissioners could not be said to have committed themselves to take a particular view of the tax treatment of the Scheme as a whole. Blaney J's conclusion is consistent with the conclusion of the House of Lords in *R v IRC ex parte Matrix Securities Ltd* [1993] STC 774, where it was held that, in order to hold the Revenue to a ruling the taxpayer 'must have put all his cards upwards on the table'. The House of Lords interpreted this requirement extremely strictly, suggesting *inter alia* that the taxpayer must draw the Revenue's attention to all of the potentially contentious issues raised by the proposed transaction.

However, even if the taxpayer makes what the courts accept as a satisfactory disclosure to the Revenue, it remains unclear in the light of *Wiley* whether the Revenue can be bound by a ruling which they subsequently conclude was incorrect in law (see eg *McCormick* [1993] IJOT 70). The UK case law suggests that even, though an advance ruling may subsequently prove to be incorrect (or arguably incorrect), adherence to the ruling by the Revenue does not necessarily represent a breach of their statutory obligations (and thus may in fact be intra vires). This follows because such rulings are conductive to the better operation of the tax system, and may in fact increase the ultimate tax yield (and, thus, can be argued to form part of the Revenue's 'care and management' function). Further, the making of rulings (taken in the round) does not reflect a policy designed to forgive tax liabilities. The position can be distinguished from that in *Wiley* where the taxpayer had argued that the Revenue Commissioners should be compelled to deliberately flout the statutory regulations concerned.

It may be noted that the Revenue Commissioners stated in the 'Taxpayers Charter' that one of their objectives is to collect taxes in a manner 'which … encourages voluntary compliance with Revenue law and deters evasion and avoidance'. In the 'Revenue Customer Service Charter' which has taken its place it is stated that 'Revenue will administer the tax and duty regimes in ways that will minimise as far as possible compliance costs'. Guidelines on opinions/confirmations relating to cases dealt with by Revenue's Large Cases Division (LCD) are contained in Tax and Duty Manual Part 37-00-40 (formerly Tax Briefing 4 of 2014). Guidelines relating to requests for opinions/confirmations submitted for non-LCD cases through the Revenue Technical Service (RTS) are available on the Revenue website at RTS Guidelines. An opinion/confirmation will only be provided by Revenue where the issues are complex, information is not readily available or there is genuine uncertainty in relation to the applicable tax rules as set down in the legislation. An opinion/confirmation will provide Revenue's view of the application of tax law to a particular transaction or situation and will assist the taxpayer in filing a tax return as required under law.

Taking LCD Guidance firstly, Tax and Duty Manual Part 37-00-40 notes that with the exception of the cases looking at new foreign direct investment, tax treaty issues and advance clearance that is required under legislation/practice all requests for opinions/confirmations from taxpayers/agents are dealt with in the appropriate Revenue District in LCD. Requests for opinions/confirmations on complex issues to do with the interpretation of double tax treaties should be addressed to Tax Treaties Branch, International Tax Division, Dublin Castle, Dublin 2. Requests for an opinion/confirmation must be submitted directly to the Case Manager in the Revenue District in LCD who is responsible for the taxpayer in question. Applications made in any other way could result in delays for which Revenue will not accept responsibility. The aforementioned manual notes that any opinion/confirmation in relation to a proposed transaction or business activity is appropriate only where the circumstances are complex, or unusual, or information is not readily available, or there is genuine uncertainty in relation to the interpretation or application of the relevant tax/duty rules.

Requests for an opinion/confirmation in advance of a transaction taking place will only be accepted by Case Managers where:

(a) the issues are complex, unusual or uncertain and the taxpayer/agent requires clarification of the tax/duty treatment of the proposed transaction or business activity,

(b) clarification of the issue is not already in the public domain,

(c) the request is specific to a particular named taxpayer and relates to an actual proposed (rather than hypothetical) transaction, and

(d) all the relevant information and facts have been provided to enable an opinion/confirmation to be given.

Generally, requests will not be accepted where the matter is straightforward and the taxpayer/agent is simply looking for a letter of comfort from Revenue of a position or issue which can be readily established from existing published information and is not in doubt. Opinions/Confirmations will not be given where the Case Manager is of the view that the proposed transaction is part of a scheme or arrangement the purpose of which or one of the purposes of which is the avoidance of tax/duty. This also applies if Revenue is of the view that the transaction in respect of which an opinion/confirmation is sought is to facilitate the avoidance of tax/duty by a third party.

The purpose of providing opinions/confirmations is to provide clarity and certainty in relation to the applicable tax/duty rules so that a taxpayer can file a correct tax return and comply fully with its tax/duty obligations. While opinions/confirmations are not binding on Revenue, and it is open to Revenue officials to review the position when a transaction has been completed and all the facts are known, generally Revenue will follow an opinion/confirmation once it can be shown that:

(a) all relevant information was disclosed either at the time the application was made or following a request from Revenue for further clarification, and
(b) the transaction as actually implemented did not diverge or deviate from that which was outlined in the information provided in relation to the request for the opinion/confirmation.

For non-LCD cases requests for opinions/confirmations must be submitted through the Revenue Technical Service (RTS). The RTS operates within the four Revenue regions and handles complex technical issues on which practitioners and business taxpayers may need clarity. The relevant guidance which is available from the Revenue website notes that this service, however, should not be used as a first point of contact by either practitioners or businesses. Revenue expects that practitioners and business taxpayers will have researched and analysed the issue themselves in the first place. Where the answer remains unclear they should then seek the assistance of this service. Complex technical queries are to be submitted in writing via 'MyEnquiries' to the Queries Management Officer (QMO) for the relevant local Revenue office or region.

Further the RTS guidance notes that it is extremely important that practitioners and business taxpayers ensure that the query that they are submitting is appropriate to the Revenue Technical Service. The QMO will only accept a query where the following criteria apply:

(a) It has been submitted via MyEnquiries (correspondence and replies are to be sent through the secure facility only)
(b) It is case specific and gives the taxpayer's PPSN (or tax reference number) and name
(c) It is complex and technical
(d) It is not a hypothetical question
(e) The answer is not already in the public domain
(f) The issue is not subject to a current compliance intervention (eg issue under audit, etc).
(g) The practitioner has:
    (i) provided a full explanation of the query;
    (ii) done her/his own research and analysis and set this out in the query;

(iii) made reference to and quoted from relevant legislation and case law to support his or her analysis; and

(iv) provided his or her own interpretation and summary of the issue.

(h) The practitioner is not seeking an advance opinion, unless there is a well established policy of providing advance opinions on such matters, ie:

(i) a company restructuring;

(ii) an inward investment issue.

Submission of a query to the Technical Service is evidently a double-edged sword; while it may in some cases obtain reassurance on the tax treatment of a contentious matter it is also likely to entail the taxpayer disclosing his hand to a fuller extent than would otherwise be the case and it also results in highlighting the transaction. The procedure will clearly be devalued if the service is seen to demonstrate anti-taxpayer bias in its pronouncements.

In general, the Revenue Technical Service will not offer an opinion in advance of a transaction. Where, exceptionally, it is prepared to offer such an opinion, eg in relation to complex issues arising on corporate restructurings or new inward investment projects where clarity is required on whether a particular activity constitutes the 'carrying on of a trade', detailed disclosure requirements will apply, as set out in the relevant guidelines published on the Revenue Commissioners' website. The Revenue Commissioners guidelines expressly state that their opinions are not legally binding and it is open to Revenue officials to review the position when a transaction is complete and all the facts are known. They stress that it is important to disclose the full facts and circumstances surrounding the transaction. It is considered that in the light of the foregoing case law, an opinion will be binding where full disclosure of all the relevant facts has been made.

The Irish Revenue Commissioners issued e-Briefs nos 79 and 89 of 2016 confirming the five-year duration of Revenue opinions/confirmations. As a result they had commenced contacting taxpayers with older opinions to review same. Revenue issued e-Brief no 8/2017 that brings about a form of 'self-assessment' procedure which notes as follows:

'It is Revenue policy that all opinions/confirmations issued by Revenue are subject to a maximum validity period of 5 years, or such shorter period as may have been specified by Revenue when providing the opinion/confirmation. A taxpayer or tax practitioner who wishes to continue to rely on an opinion issued before 1 January 2012 for any transaction, or the whole or part of any period, after 1 January 2017, must:'

(a) supply evidence of the opinion/confirmation, being a copy of a written communication which originated from Revenue, and

(b) lodge a full application for the renewal or extension of the opinion/confirmation with the Revenue District dealing with the taxpayer's affairs by 30 June 2017.

Renewal and extension applications must comply with the requirements contained within the various Revenue guidelines on Revenue opinions.

Where such application has been made by 30 June 2017 then the Revenue District dealing with the taxpayer's affairs will provide an early acknowledgement of the receipt of each application for the renewal or extension of the opinion. In addition, that will confirm where certain terms are met, the opinion will continue to have effect until Revenue has following a review of the application, provided a written response. This response will either accept, accept with amendments or reject the renewal or extension application.

Once evidence of the opinion has been provided and a renewal or extension application has been made by 30 June 2017, provided there has not been a material change in the facts and circumstances on which the opinion is based or it had not otherwise ceased to have effect, then the opinion will continue to apply until such time as Revenue has reviewed the application for its renewal or extension. Where, on reviewing an opinion as a result of the above application and Revenue gives written notice of the withdrawal or amendment of the opinion concerned then this notice will be stated to apply to transactions and chargeable periods to the extent that they are subsequent to the notice. E-Brief no 8 of 2017 notes that Revenue will complete reviews of applications and respond to taxpayers or their tax agents on a timely basis. Following the 30 June 2017 deadline for renewal or extension applications, an estimated response date will be provided by Revenue.

Where an application for the renewal or extension of an opinion is not made by the required date of 30 June 2017 then the opinion, which had not already ceased to have effect, cannot be relied on by the taxpayer from 1 January 2017.

In accordance with EU and OECD initiatives on exchange of information on 'Tax Rulings', any opinion provided by Revenue, including a renewal or extension of an existing opinion, may be subject to disclosure to other tax authorities.

The status of Extra Statutory Concessions is more debatable. The UK courts have now apparently accepted that such concessions may fall within the Revenue's 'care and management' function and that their application is accordingly amenable to judicial review (*R v IRC ex parte Fulford-Dobson* [1987] STC 344). However, in *R v IRC ex parte Wilkinson* [2005] UKHL 30, Lord Hoffman that the Inland Revenue's management powers did not extend to granting an allowance which was in terms restricted to widows to widowers as this was would have been 'on grounds not of pragmatism in the collection of tax but of general equity between men and women'.

The Revenue Commissioners are subject to the provisions of the Freedom of Information Act 2014 (signed on 14 October 2014) (FIA 2014) (which replaced the Freedom of Information Act 1997 (as amended by the Freedom of Information (Amendment) Act 2003), both now repealed by the Freedom of Information Act 2014) (see **1.205**).

FIA 2014, s 8(2) (which comes into effect 12 months after FIA 2014 has been enacted, ie 14 October 2015 unless it is commenced earlier by the Minister for Public Expenditure and Reform) requires that bodies subject to FIA 2014 (FOI bodies), which include the Revenue Commissioners, should as part of a 'publication scheme' publish details of the rules, procedures, practices, guidelines and interpretations used by them, as well as any precedents kept by them, for the purposes of, inter alia, decisions, determinations or recommendations made by them in relation to rights, privileges, benefits, obligations, or penalties to which members of the public may be subject under fiscal legislation. This information is included by Revenue Commissioners on their website www.revenue.ie. FIA 2014, s 8(3) requires a publication scheme to be published not later than six months after the commencement of FIA 2014, s 8 or where under FIA 2014, s 8(7) the Minister for Public Expenditure and Reform has made or revised the model publications schemes to be used then no later than six months after such making or revision. FIA 2014, s 8(4) requires FOI bodies to review and revise the material published under a 'publication scheme' on at least an annual basis or where a model publication scheme has been revised, no later than six months after notice of the revision has been published in Iris Oifigiúil.

FIA 1997, s 16(3), which was repealed by FIA 2014, provided that where the relevant information was not published or was published in an incomplete or inaccurate form, the body was required to ensure that a person was not subjected to any prejudice (other than a penalty imposed by a court) by reason of the application of a rule or requirement which the taxpayer could lawfully have avoided if they had been aware of that rule or requirement. Thus a taxpayer who had been prejudiced by an omission or inaccuracy may have been able to seek redress. The Revenue Commissioners had a defence against such a claim where they showed that all reasonable steps were taken by them to bring the rule or requirement to the notice of the taxpayer (FIA 1997, s 16(4) repealed by FIA 2014). There is no equivalent of FIA 1997, s 16(3) and (4) in FIA 2014.

In the *Wiley* case, O'Flaherty J in the Supreme Court further held that the principle of legitimate expectation could not be invoked to require the Revenue Commissioners to notify persons in advance of its intention to alter guidelines or regulations, in accordance with its statutory discretion to make such alterations. This reflects the well established principle that a public body cannot fetter the future exercise of its statutory powers and discretions. The same principle could be argued to apply to published statements of practice, and indeed, even the granting of advance rulings on an individual basis (see *Eden* [1994] British Tax Review 254). The UK courts have largely resolved the tension between this principle and the doctrine of legitimate expectation by rooting the doctrine in the overriding criterion of 'fairness' (as illustrated in the passage from the *MFK Underwriting* case quoted above). Notwithstanding the dicta of O'Flaherty J, it is likely that the UK case law would be influential in Ireland. The taxpayer in *Wiley* was in a very weak position, arguing as he was against the right of the Revenue Commissioners to clamp down without warning on blatant fiscal abuses.

The emphasis of the UK courts on the public law concept of fairness is illustrated by the decision in *R v IRC ex parte Unilever* [1994] STC 841 where, as noted above, it was held that the taxpayer did not have a legitimate expectation that the Revenue would waive a procedural requirement, thus exposing it potentially to a substantial tax liability. However, the court noted that the doctrine of legitimate expectation was merely an aspect of the duty of the Inland Revenue to act fairly (or, more accurately, not to act in a way that was 'outrageously unfair'). On the facts of this case, where the abrupt enforcement of a procedural requirement (where the Revenue had not been prejudiced under the informal arrangements which had operated over many years) would have resulted in a tax windfall for the Revenue, the court held that it would be an abuse of the Revenue's powers not to exercise their 'care and management' discretion in factor of the taxpayer. The court was however at pains to stress the exceptional circumstances involved.

In *Burke and Son v Revenue Commissioners* V ITR 418 the taxpayer was found to have incorrectly operated a VAT retail scheme over a number of years. The court upheld the Revenue's assessments of the underpayments of VAT which arose as a result, distinguishing the *Unilever* case on two grounds (interestingly, the court thereby implicitly accepted that the general approach of the UK courts in *Unilever* was not contrary to Irish legal principle). Firstly, the Revenue were unaware that the VAT returns had been improperly made, while in the *Unilever* case the Revenue had deliberately exercised their discretion in favour of the taxpayer. In fact (as noted above) the Revenue's actions in *Unilever* were due to an oversight; the real distinction seems to be that in *Unilever* the Revenue had acted consistently in a manner which the taxpayer reasonably came to rely on.

Secondly, the taxpayer was liable for the VAT assessed, whereas in the *Unilever* case the taxpayer would otherwise have forfeited the benefit of tax losses to which it was entitled. It followed that to strike down the Revenue assessments would be to unjustly enrich the taxpayer. It seems unhelpful to introduce the concept of 'unjust enrichment' in this context; the key point appears to be that there was no unfairness involved in the Revenue collecting what was always rightfully due to them.

In *Dunnes Stores v Revenue Commissioners* [2011] IEHC 469, the High Court held that the Revenue Commissioners had not acted unfairly by refusing to furnish the appellant company with the details of their calculation of the Plastic Bag Levy. While the Revenue were entitled to withhold this information under the relevant regulations, This may seem prima facie highly unreasonable. However, the court took the view that in light of the correspondence exchanged between the parties and the fact that all the relevant information was within the possession of the appellant, there was no breach of fair procedures. It does not seem to follow that the appellant was necessarily aware of the interpretation placed on that information by Revenue and in principle it seems unsatisfactory that a liability should be imposed without a clear indication of the basis on which it was calculated.

In the *Haliaetus* case, Blaney J also took the view that the Revenue Commissioners could not be bound by the ruling of an inspector of taxes since he was not an agent of the Revenue Commissioners; it is unlikely that this analysis would now be upheld (see *Maher* [1992] ITR 76).

In the *Haliaetus* case (see above), the Revenue Commissioners had refused to make a repayment of tax to one of the parties to the scheme, on the basis that the scheme was a fiscal nullity (*McGrath v McDermott*, discussed at **1.407**, subsequently established that the doctrine of fiscal nullity did not apply in Ireland). Blaney J held that, because the inspector had previously determined that the repayment was due, the taxpayer had no right of appeal. Accordingly he granted a declaration in favour of the taxpayer, since there was no other means open to it to enforce the repayment (see also *WLD Worldwide Leather Diffusion Ltd v Revenue Commissioners* V ITR 61).

It is in theory open to the courts to grant judicial review where an assessment discloses an error of law (see above and see *R v IRC ex parte Caglar* [1995] STC 741). However, in general, the courts will not grant judicial review where there is an alternative means of redress available. In tax cases this means that taxpayers will normally be required to use the standard appeal procedures where these are available. However, the courts reserve the discretion to grant judicial review even where there is a right of appeal, if justice is best served by so doing (see *The State (Glover) v McCarthy* [1981] ILRM 47 and note *Faulkner v Minister for Industry & Commerce* SC [1996]).

It may be noted that the UK courts have tended to decline judicial review in favour of the 'case stated' procedure, wherever the latter is practicable (see eg *R v IRC ex parte Warburg* [1994] STC 518). It may be that the Irish courts would be more willing to grant judicial review in 'borderline' cases. It may be noted that in *Kennedy v Hearne* III ITR 590 (see above) the Supreme Court held that the erroneous PAYE estimate made in that case would be set aside as a nullity, even though the taxpayer had failed to exercise his right of appeal under the then equivalent of TCA 1997, s 989(3)(a). In *Deighan v Hearne* III ITR 533, the Supreme Court held that the process of raising assessments was constitutional, noting:

> the right of the taxpayer to appeal against the assessment and (the taxpayer's) right', if an assessment were made *ultra vires* the powers vested in the inspector, or upon the basis of an arbitrary or capricious premise to challenge that by way of judicial review …

(Compare the comments of the Privy Council in *Harley Developments Inc v CIR* [1996] STC 440, which suggests that, even where an assessment is *ultra vires*, the appeal mechanism may be the appropriate avenue; see also *IRC v Wilkinson* [1992] STC 454).

In *Criminal Assets Bureau v Hunt* VI ITR 559, [2003] IR 168, Keane CJ observed that the elaborate appeal procedures laid down in the Tax Acts were intended to 'provide an exclusive machinery for the ascertainment of a taxpayer's liability'. This approach was followed in *John Paul Construction v Minister of Environment, Heritage and Local Government* [2006] 197JR where the court, refused to allow a third party to seek judicial review when they would have no standing to do so on the matter being raised under the statutory appeal mechanism.

It may be noted that judicial review is also the means by which a taxpayer may challenge the constitutionality of a tax provision (see **1.409**). One important limitation on the availability of the judicial review process is that the applicant must have *locus standi*. Thus, in *Madigan v Attorney General* III ITR 127 (discussed in **1.409**), the court refused to entertain any objections against the residential property tax which were not relevant to the actual circumstances of the plaintiffs.

Tax paid under assessments which are void on the basis of unconstitutionality (or indeed on other grounds, such as the fact that they are based on *ultra vires* regulations) may be repayable under the principle of restitution, but this is subject to a range of considerations (see *Woolwich BS v IRC* [1992] STC 657; *Murphy & Murphy v Attorney General* V ITR 613 and *O'Rourke v Revenue Commissioners*, discussed at **2.203**).

2.207 Finance (Tax Appeals) Act 2015 (F(TA)A 2015)

The Finance (Tax Appeals) Act 2015 was signed into law on 25 December 2015 (SI 110/2016 appointed 21 March 2016 as the day on which the Finance (Tax Appeals) Act 2015, comes into operation). This text deals only with appeal provisions under this Act and therefore the reader is referred to earlier editions of this text for matters relating to the procedures which predated this Act. For completeness, this text retains the discussions below regarding the transition between the 'old' and 'new' tax appeal provisions. Revenue *eBrief No 21/16* notes that one of the more important measures to strengthen the independence of the Tax Appeals Commission (TAC) will be the requirement for appeals to be submitted directly to the TAC instead of through Revenue. It continues that '... Until the Act was commenced, all of the old appeal procedures continued to apply'.

F(TA)A 2015 is a standalone Act although s 34 et seq make amendments to the TCA 1997, in addition to SDCA 1999, CATCA 2003, VATCA 2010, LPTA 2012 and the Customs Act 2015. F(TA)A 2015, ss 1–33 deal with the following provisions:

Sections	Provisions
1–2	Commencement and interpretation
3–21	Tax Appeals Commission
22–33	Transitional provisions
34	New part 40A insertion into the TCA (the new appeals process)

F(TA)A 2015 is to apply to these Acts when commenced:

'Taxation Acts' means—

(a) the Tax Acts (within the meaning of section 1 of the Act of 1997),

(b) the Capital Gains Tax Acts (within the meaning of section 1 of the Act of 1997),

(c) Parts 18A to 18D of the Act of 1997,

(d) the Stamp Duties Consolidation Act 1999, and the enactments amending or extending that Act,

(e) the Capital Acquisitions Tax Consolidation Act 2003, and the enactments amending or extending that Act,

(f) the Value-Added Tax Consolidation Act 2010, and the enactments amending or extending that Act,

(g) the statutes relating to the duties of excise and to the management of those duties,

(h) the Customs Act 2015 and the enactments amending or extending that Act,

(i) the Finance (Local Property Tax) Act 2012, and the enactments amending or extending that Act,

and any instrument made thereunder and any instrument that is made under any other enactment and which relates to tax (including in respect of stamp duties and of duties relating to customs and excise).

Consequential amendments to the TCA 1997

The following is an extract from the explanatory memorandum that accompanied the F(TA)A 2015 as initiated. This is important in that the amendments made to the TCA 1997 as a result of the aforementioned Act were not limited to including, eg a reference to the new Pt 40A that the F(TA)A 2015 inserted into the TCA 1997 or the deletion of a possible appeal to the Circuit Court.

> While the appeal process itself in terms of the involvement of the Appeal Commissioners is self-contained in the provisions in the new Part 40A (being inserted in the TCA 1997 by section 34 of this Bill), other provisions that are relevant to appeals are spread throughout the various taxation Acts. A consequence of the changes being made to the appeal process is the need to make a large number of consequential amendments to provisions relating to appeals in the TCA 1997 …. The most common amendment is that necessitated by the fact that, under the reformed system, a taxpayer will have to appeal directly to the Appeal Commissioners and not via Revenue as currently happens. Another type of amendment will clarify and make more explicit a right of appeal that is currently only implicitly stated in the various tax and duty Acts. A valid appeal under the revised appeal process will require a specific right of appeal to be given in the relevant taxation Act. Various cross-references that are no longer relevant are being removed; for example, references to Part 40 of the TCA 1997 which is being phased out and replaced with the new Part 40A. Part 40A is concerned solely with the appeal procedures themselves (from the making and acceptance of an appeal, the adjudication and determination procedures and concluding with appeals to the Courts). As a result, other provisions contained in Part 40 relating to income tax appeals are re-located to Part 41A TCA 1997. Within Part 41A itself, the appeal-related provisions are now contained in Chapter 6. The opportunity is being taken to rectify anomalies and inconsistencies that currently exist and to standardise as far as possible the appeal provisions for the various taxes and duties. One example of such standardisation relates to the number of days allowed for the making of an appeal; 30 days is the usual time limit but this is not standard across all of the taxes and duties. Another example is the alignment of the grounds for an appeal against different types of Revenue assessments; for example, the requirement to have submitted an outstanding return to Revenue before an appeal can be made.

One of the consequential changes that is brought about throughout the TCA 1997 is a deletion of references to the required satisfaction of an inspector or Appeal Commissioner in certain matters. For example, F(TA)A 2015, s 35(7) amended TCA 1997, s 189A which looks at special trusts for permanently incapacitated individuals by removing the requirement the trust is established by deed 'in respect of which it is shown to the satisfaction of the inspector or, on appeal, to the Appeal Commissioners, that …' it was established, inter alia, for the benefit of a permanently incapacitated individual. The element in quotation marks has been deleted by the F(TA)A 2015, s 35(7) and thereby makes the qualifying provisions of that section objective and seeks to remove an element of subjectivity from the section. This has little to do with the appeals process in itself but nonetheless is something that the Oireachtas saw necessary to include in the F(TA)A 2015 process.

Tax Appeals Commission

The Finance (Tax Appeals) Act 2015 notes that a Tax Appeals Commission was to be established which is referred to throughout the Acts as the Commission. F(TA)A 2015, s 3 notes that the Commission was to be a body corporate with 'perpetual succession' and shall have the power to sue, and may be sued, in its corporate name. F(TA)A 2015, s 3(5) notes that judicial notice shall be taken of the seal of the Commission and any document purporting to be an instrument made by, and to be sealed with the seal of, the Commission shall, unless the contrary is shown, be received in evidence and be deemed to be such instrument without further proof. F(TA)A 2015, s 4 notes that the Commission is to consist of so much 'and so many members as the Minister determines and appoints' and each member is to be known as 'an Appeal Commissioner'. A temporary Commissioner can be appointed but will not be regarded as a member of the Commission. F(TA)A 2015, s 5 notes that the Commission's functions are to be carried out by the Appeal Commissioners themselves. F(TA)A 2015, s 6 outlines the functions of the Commissioners and they may perform such functions as are assigned to them by the Act and by the Taxation Acts which have been defined above. It is interesting to note that the functions of the Commissioners are outlined as below but this is without prejudice to the generality of sub-s (1) and that subsection allows the Commissioners to perform such duties as are assigned to them under the Appeals Act and the Taxation Acts.

The functions in relation to the Taxation Acts comprise:

(a) deciding whether or not to accept an appeal,
(b) deciding whether to declare, under TCA 1997, s 949N(3), that a refusal to accept an appeal is final,
(c) deciding on the appropriate procedure to be adopted in relation to an adjudication of an appeal,
(d) giving directions to the parties to an appeal,
(e) fixing dates, times and places for the hearings of appeals,
(f) hearing an appeal where the Commissioners have decided that a hearing is the appropriate method of adjudicating on the appeal,
(g) determining appeals,
(h) providing written determinations,
(i) publishing determinations,
(j) stating and signing cases stated for the opinion of the High Court,
(k) establishing and maintaining efficient and effective systems and procedures so as to secure the processing, adjudication and determination of appeals in a timely and effective manner, and
(l) doing 'all such other things as they consider conducive to the resolution of disputes between appellants and the Revenue Commissioners' and the establishment of the correct liability to tax of appellants.

The section notes that the Commissioners shall perform their functions in a manner that has regard to the need for proceedings before the Commissioners to be accessible and fair and 'to be conducted as expeditiously as possible'. That said, it is also noted that the Commissioners may adopt rules of procedures with respect to any of their functions and shall publish any rules so adopted. Any provision of the Tax Acts that confers a function on the Commissioners is to be read as conferring the function to be performed by any one of the Commissioners.

A Commissioner is to be appointed by the Minister from among persons in respect of whom a recommendation has been made. The Minister is to request the Public Appointment Service to assess and select suitable candidates for appointment as a Commissioner in accordance with the relevant provisions of the 2004 Act, being the Public Service Management (Recruitment and Appointments) Act 2004. It is then that such recommendations are made to the Minister for appointment. The Minister can outline the requirements that he or she considers to be the requirements that must be complied with by a candidate for appointment as an Appeal Commissioner but it is without prejudice to the generality of the above the requirements that may be specified by the Minister including:

(a) The minimum period of practical experience, or type of practical experience, required of the candidate;
(b) The academic or professional qualifications to be possessed;
(c) Subject to the Employment Equality Act 1998 the health and age of a candidate.

The Minister can appoint a pre-existing Commissioner who can be appointed for a second term but F(TA)A 2015, s 8(8) notes that a person shall not be appointed as a Commissioner for more than two consecutive terms. However, if the person was already a pre-existing Commissioner and that person's first term of office expires by passage of time, when both those two conditions are met, then where the person is not re-appointed as a Commissioner the Minister is to lay a statement before Dáil Éireann giving the reasoning behind not re-appointing that Commissioner. It is possible that the Minister may from time to time appoint a judge of the Circuit Court to perform the functions of a Commissioner where the Commissioners are precluded from performing the function as they may be recused. This form of 'recusal' occurs where a Commissioner is interested in the Commissioner's own right or in the right of any other person in any matter under appeal to the extent that the Commissioner considers that they will be unable to act impartially in the adjudication and determination of the matter and in that instance the Commissioner shall not take any part in the adjudication and the determination. Where that Circuit Court judge is appointed they will be regarded as a 'temporary Commissioner'. In addition, a temporary Commissioner can be appointed to perform the function of an Appeal Commissioner where in the opinion of the Minister circumstances, other than those of recusal discussed above, require such an appointment to be made. The appointment of a judge of the Circuit Court as a temporary Commissioner shall not be made without the approval of the President of the Circuit Court. It is necessary to note that the appointment of a temporary Commissioner shall specify the period for which the appointment is to remain in force and the functions to be performed by the person as a temporary Commissioner. It is necessary to note that the following provisions of the Act do not apply to a temporary Commissioner:

(a) s 8 – Appointment of Commissioners;
(b) s 12 – Declaration of an Appointment;
(c) s 13 – Term of Office;

(d) s 14 – Terms and Conditions of a Commissioners Appointment; and

(e) s 15(2) to (6) – sub-s (1) of that section applies which requires a Commissioner to retire at retirement age.

As noted earlier, a temporary Commissioner is not to be regarded as a member of the Commission, however, notwithstanding that point where the function of a Commissioner falls to be performed by a temporary Commissioner references in the Act to a Commissioner are to be read as including a temporary Commissioner.

F(TA)A 2015, s 10 points out that 'subject to this act' the Commission and its members shall be independent in the performance of their functions. Every person who is appointed as Commissioner is to make a particular declaration and that declaration is contained in F(TA)A 2015, Sch 1. However, this is not to apply in a case where a Commissioner is re-appointed, as outlined above. The declaration is required to be made before a Peace Commissioner. The appointment of a person as a Commissioner is on a full-time basis and as noted earlier the term cannot exceed a period of seven years and the second term cannot exceed that period also. However, the Act notes that notwithstanding this, a period of office shall be such as will result in the Commissioner retiring at retirement age being complied with. The terms and conditions of the Appeal Commissioner's appointment shall be determined by the Minister after consultation with the Minister for Public Expenditure and Reform and the remuneration shall be such as that Minister may from time to time determine. A Commissioner does have certain restrictions in that he or she is not permitted to hold any other office or employment in respect of which 'emoluments are payable or carry on any trade, profession or business'. A person who is re-appointed after the establishment of the Appeal Commission, their term of appointment shall not be different from those which were in place immediately before the establishment day.

F(TA)A 2015, s 15 notes the provisions relating to pension arrangements for Commissioners and requires a Commissioner to retire when they reach retirement age. However, it is noted that a scheme made under these provisions shall not provide for the granting of pensions, etc to or in respect of a person where the single public service pension scheme applies to that person. The Minister has significant power in this regard in that he or she, with the consent of the Minister for Public Expenditure and Reform, may at any time make out and carry out in accordance with its terms a scheme amending or revoking a scheme under this section. However, a scheme under the superannuation provisions shall be laid before each House of the Oireachtas as soon as may be after it is made.

Although the terms of a Commissioner's appointment are for seven years in the first term and seven years in the second term a Commissioner may resign by written notice to the Minister stating his or her intention to do so and such notice takes effect from a date three months after the date of the notice. A Minister can also remove a Commissioner from office from this behaviour, although the Act does not specify what is meant by 'misbehaviour'. In addition, the Minister may at any time remove a Commissioner from office where the Minister considers that:

(a) the Commissioner has become incapable through ill-health of performing their functions as an Appeal Commissioner;

(b) the Commissioner's removal is necessary or expedient for the effective performance by the Commission of its functions; and

(c) a conflict of interest with regard to the performance by the Commission of its function arises on the part of the Commissioner of such significance that the Minister should cease to hold office.

However, where the Minister removes a Commissioner from office he is to lay a statement before Dáil Éireann giving the reason for the removal. There are some points of interest above in that neither 'misbehaviour' nor reasons 'necessary or expedient for the effective performance by the Commission of its functions' are defined. One can speculate in relation to a conflict of interest but the meaning of 'such significance that the Minister should cease to hold office' is of note. The question arises as to how one determines the distinction between significant and insignificant conflicts of interest.

The provisions regarding a disqualification of a Commissioner add to the above in that a Commissioner shall cease to hold office on:

(a) being adjudicated bankrupt;
(b) making a composition or arrangement with creditors;
(c) being convicted, on indictment, of an offence; or
(d) ceasing to be ordinarily resident in the State.

The question regarding being 'ordinarily resident' is of some note in that no definition of ordinary residence is contained in the Act. It is of interest that TCA 1997, s 820 defines ordinary residence but does so for the purposes of 'the Acts' which in that instance refers to the Tax Acts, the Capital Gains Tax Acts, and the CAT Acts and any Acts amending or extending that Act and any incidents made thereunder. That section was not amended by the F(TA)A 2015 to add the aforementioned Acts to the definition of 'the Acts' in TCA 1997, s 818 for the purposes of the 'ordinarily resident' definition in TCA 1997, s 820. Presumably as F(TA)A 2015 is a tax Act in its nature then a court may have regard to the definition ordinarily resident in TCA 1997, s 820 for some guidance as to its meaning but of course the matter cannot be regarded as being beyond doubt.

Where a Commissioner is nominated as a member of Seanad Éireann, nominated to stand as a candidate for election as a member of either House of the Oireachtas or to the European Parliament, is regarded as having been elected to the European Parliament to fill a vacancy, or is or becomes a member of a local authority then he or she shall thereupon cease to hold office. A person who is for the time being, entitled under the standing orders of either House of the Oireachtas to sit therein or who is a member of the European Parliament shall while they are so entitled or if such a member be disqualified from becoming a Commissioner.

The Commissioners shall on or before 31 March each year, prepare a report in relation to the performance of their functions in the preceding year and submit the report to the Minister. The Minister is to lay the reports before each House of the Oireachtas and 'as soon as practicable after that is done the Commissioners shall publish a report on the Internet'. The reference to 'as soon as practicable' is of note.

The report is to contain such information of a statistical nature in relation to the notification of appeals, refusals to accept appeals and the adjudication on, and the hearing and determination of, appeals. However, the wording in the provision relating to the report is intriguing in that it says 'where the inclusion of the following information is required… by the Minister, which requirement the Minister has power to make or… by virtue of other enactment' apart from 'the provision' then the above information is to be included. This would seem to be permissive in its nature. That said, F(TA)A 2015, s 21 notes that the Commissioners may, from time to time, prepare and submit to the Minister such other reports in relation to their activities as they consider appropriate. The reference to 'other reports' is also of note in that it gives rise to the question as to what other information can be disseminated to the Minister given that it will be seen that determinations must be published which was not the case previously. Indeed, the Minister may require the Commissioners, by direction in writing, to prepare and submit to them a report in relation to any particular matter relating to the activities of the Commissioners as the Minister considers appropriate. However, the requests and information to be supplied by the Commissioners is not unfettered in that the provision is not to operate to require the Commissioners to include information in the reports that 'in their opinion, would prejudice the performance by the Commissioners of their functions'.

Transitional provisions

F(TA)A 2015, s 34 above includes a new Pt 40A into TCA 1997 comprising ss 949A to 949AV and F(TA)A 2015, s 23 makes it clear that Pt 40 shall not apply to an appeal 'made on or after' the commencement date with s 22(3) explaining the 'commencement date' to be the date that F(TA)A 2015, s 34 (which inserts Pt 40A) becomes operational. It was necessary to specify s 34 here because although enacted on 25 December 2015 the Act did not become effective according to F(TA)A 2015, s 1(2) until the Minister specifies by order and the Minister can commence different parts or provisions of the Act separately. (SI 110/2016 appointed 21 March 2016 as the day on which the Finance (Tax Appeals) Act 2015, came into operation).

The question arises as to when an appeal is 'made' so that one can determine the extent of the application of transitional provisions. F(TA)A 2015, s 22(1) and (2) explain as follows:

> (1) For the purposes of this Part an appeal shall be regarded as having been made when an appellant has sent a notice of appeal to the Revenue Commissioners or the Appeal Commissioners, as the case may be, in accordance with the relevant provision of the Taxation Acts.
>
> (2) For the avoidance of doubt, for the purposes of this Part an appeal shall be regarded as having been made when an appellant has sent a notice of appeal in the circumstances specified in section 933(7) of the Act of 1997.

Subsection (1) clarifies that a reference to an appeal having been made is to be interpreted as a notice of appeal having been sent either to Revenue (old appeal process) or to the Appeal Commissioners (new appeal process). Subsection (2) clarifies that a reference to an appeal having been made is to encompass a late appeal made under the old appeal process.

F(TA)A 2015, s 24 is an introductory section stating that the provisions governing the manner in which 'existing appeals' (ie appeals made before the new appeal process comes into operation) are to be dealt with under the new appeal process are contained in a number of sections (ie ss 25 to 31). These sections deal with the following provisions:

> 25. Application of section 933(1) of Act of 1997 to existing appeal
>
> 26. Application of section 933(7) of Act of 1997 to existing appeal
>
> 27. Existing appeals: transition from procedures under Part 40 to those under Part 40A
>
> 28. Appeal Commissioners vacating office before hearing or determination of appeal completed

29. Cases stated – particular instances of steps remaining to be taken
30. Supplemental provisions in relation to section 29
31. Transmission of existing appeals to Appeal Commissioners
32. Transitional provision in relation to records
33. References to Appeal Commissioners in other enactments

These will be dealt with in turn below.

Section 25. Application of section 933(1) of Act of 1997 to existing appeal

It is to be recalled that 'existing appeals' refer to appeals made before the new appeal process comes into operation. TCA 1997, s 933(1)(a), which is contained under the old appeal rules in Pt 40, notes that a person aggrieved by any assessment to income tax or corporation tax made on that person shall be entitled to appeal to the Appeal Commissioners on giving, within 30 days after the date of the notice of assessment, notice in writing to the inspector or other officer. It can be seen that notice of appeal must be given to Revenue in that instance. It will be seen that the new appeals process requires the appeal to be made to the Appeal Commissioners. Under s 933(1)(b) where the inspector or other officer is of the opinion that the person who has given the notice of appeal is not entitled to make such an appeal, the inspector or other officer shall refuse the application and notify the person in writing accordingly, specifying the grounds for such refusal. Under s 933(1)(c) a person who has had an application under para (a) refused by the inspector is entitled to appeal against such refusal by notice in writing to the Appeal Commissioners within 15 days of the date of issue by the inspector or other officer of the notice of refusal. Under TCA 1997, s 933(1)(d) on receipt of an application under para (c), the Appeal Commissioners shall request the inspector or other officer to furnish them with a copy of the notice issued to the person under para (b) and, on receipt of the copy of the notice, they shall as soon as possible—

(i) refuse the application for an appeal by giving notice in writing to the applicant specifying the grounds for their refusal,

(ii) allow the application for an appeal and give notice in writing accordingly to both the applicant and the inspector or other officer, or

(iii) notify in writing both the applicant and the inspector or other officer that they have decided to arrange a hearing at such time and place specified in the notice to enable them determine whether or not to allow the application for an appeal.

F(TA)A 2015, s 25 contains provisions relating to the making of an appeal to Revenue and Revenue's refusal to accept the appeal under the old appeal process. Special transitional arrangements are required because this type of situation (ie appeal refused by Revenue and refusal appealed to the Appeal Commissioners) does not arise under the new appeal process.

F(TA)A 2015, s 25(2) deals with the situation where an appeal has been made to Revenue and has been refused by Revenue before, or is refused a short time after, the new appeal process comes into operation. Paragraphs (a) and (b) provide for the situation where the refusal of the appeal has not itself been appealed and the period within which this must happen has not yet expired. The old provisions governing the manner in which such an appeal is dealt with are applied insofar as an appellant is permitted to appeal the refusal to the Appeal Commissioners until this period expires (ie up to 15 days after the date of the refusal) and, where they do so, until the Appeal Commissioners have decided to accept or refuse the appeal.

F(TA)A 2015, s 25(3) deals with the situation where Revenue has refused to accept an appeal and the refusal has been appealed to the Appeal Commissioners before the new appeal process comes into operation. The old provisions governing the manner in which such an appeal is dealt with are applied until the Appeal Commissioners have decided to accept or to refuse the appeal.

F(TA)A 2015, s 25(4) looks at the position where an appeal has been accepted either by Revenue when it was made or by the Appeal Commissioners following an appeal against Revenue's refusal of the appeal. In both of these situations, the appeal is treated as having been accepted by the Appeal Commissioners under the new appeal process. This treatment brings such an appeal within F(TA)A 2015, s 27(2) and the arrangements for the transition of the appeal to the new appeal process.

Section 26. Application of section 933(7) of Act of 1997 to existing appeal

F(TA)A 2015, s 26 outlines provisions relating to the making of a late appeal and Revenue's refusal to accept that appeal. The explanatory memorandum which accompanied the bill as initiated noted that 'special transitional arrangements are required because this type of situation (ie late appeal refused by Revenue and refusal appealed to the Appeal Commissioners) does not arise under the new appeal process'. Under the new rules the appeal is not made to Revenue but the Appeal Commissioners in the first instance. Subsection (1) makes it clear that references in this section to s 933 are references to TCA 1997, s 933.

Subsection (2) deals with the situation where a late appeal has been made to Revenue and has been refused before or after the new appeal process comes into operation and where the refusal of the appeal has not itself been appealed and the period within which this must happen has not yet expired. The old provisions governing the manner in which such an appeal is dealt with apply insofar as the appellant is permitted to appeal the refusal to the Appeal Commissioners until this period expires (ie up to 15 days after the date of the refusal). Where the appellant appeals the refusal of its appeal within the 15-day requirement then the new rules in accordance with TCA 1997, s 949O relating to the manner in which the Appeal Commissioners deal with late appeals apply.

Subsection (3) deals with the situation where Revenue has refused to accept a late appeal and the refusal has been appealed to the Appeal Commissioners before the new rules comes into effect. Where the Appeal Commissioners have not made their decision about whether or not to accept a late appeal, their decision is to be made in accordance with the new rules in TCA 1997, s 949O relating to the manner in which the Appeal Commissioners deal with late appeals apply.

Subsection (4) looks at the position where a late appeal has been accepted either by Revenue when it was made or by the Appeal Commissioners following an appeal against Revenue's refusal of the appeal. There the appeal is treated as having been accepted by the Appeal Commissioners under the new appeal process. The subsection says that in such a situation that F(TA)A 2015, s 27(2) applies, being the arrangements for the transition of the appeal to the new appeal process. That said this is without prejudice to TCA 1997, s 949N(1)(b) and (c). These latter subsections allow the Appeal Commissioners to refuse to accept an appeal where they become aware, having previously formed the view that an appeal was a valid appeal, that it is not a valid appeal, or are satisfied that an appeal is without substance or foundation.

Section 27. Existing appeals: transition from procedures under Part 40 to those under Part 40A

F(TA)A 2015, s 27 contains provisions relating to the manner in which appeals that have been made under the old appeal process are to transition to the new appeal process.

F(TA)A 2015, s 27(1) outlines the 'steps' as referred to in s 27. It includes steps taken by all persons involved in the appeal process (ie appellant, Revenue, Appeal Commissioners and a court) and the hearing of an appeal by the Appeal Commissioners. The explanatory memorandum which accompanied the bill as initiated noted that '"Steps" essentially means the various stages of the appeal process: for example, the making of an appeal, the acceptance/refusal of an appeal, the holding of a hearing and the determination of an appeal'. Section 27(1) allows for the treatment of the situations dealt with by s 25(2) and (3) whereby certain appeals do not transition to the next stage of the appeal process in accordance with the new provisions but, instead, continue to be dealt with in accordance with the next stage of the old appeal process because, according to the explanatory memorandum there is no analogous stage in the new appeal process. These provisions have been discussed above. The relevance of the reference to 'analogous' provisions can be seen in F(TA)A 2015, s 27(2).

On a related note to the above the decision in *O'Brien v Revenue* [2016] IEHC 2 was given in January 2016. The taxpayer had his appeal on the four-year look back rule in TCA 1997, s 956 dismissed by the Appeal Commissioners. After the decision, he notified Revenue in writing that he wished to state a case to the High Court under TCA 1997, s 941 and gave notification of an intention to appeal to the Circuit Court as provided for in TCA 1997, s 942. Both notices were given within the respective prescribed periods. The High Court noted that 'It is common case that it is a standard practice to initiate both procedures, and that the taxpayer must make an election at some stage as to which remedy he or she intends to pursue. However, the Act does not stipulate how or when the election is to be made, or how or to whom it should be communicated'. There were various discussions between Revenue's solicitors and the taxpayer's solicitors over a period of time.

The High court noted at para 62 that the TCA 1997 does not say so expressly but '...permits a dissatisfied taxpayer to serve the prescribed notification for both a case stated and an appeal by way of rehearing in the Circuit Court. Although the Act does not expressly say so, it seems equally clear that the procedures cannot be run in parallel. The reason for this, in my view, is jurisdictional. Two courts cannot be seised of the same issue at the same time'. In the end the taxpayer has to decide which appeal mechanism is to be chosen. The court notes at para 67 that the requirement to make a choice does not involve any improper restriction on the Constitutional right of access to the courts but 'That right must always be exercised in accordance with any relevant rules, including rules about jurisdiction and any relevant limitation periods. All that is required here is for an appellant to make a choice as to the preferred appellate process, and to then comply with the rules relating to that process'. Paras 70 to 72 of the decision noted as follows:

> ...The choice, in my view, becomes binding when an action is taken which is incompatible with the adoption of the alternative procedure. I do not accept, therefore, the argument that the choice remains open up to the point when a hearing date is fixed... As far as the case stated procedure is concerned, I do not think that the crucial point is reached when the case stated is drafted, agreed or signed. All of these stages can be completed without any step

being taken to transmit it to the High Court, in which case the jurisdiction of that court is not invoked and there is no issue of incompatibility with the Circuit Court process.

The reference by the court to a 'step being taken to transmit it to the High Court' is of note in that F(TA)A 2015, s 27 makes reference to that concept and the High Court speaks of stages happening before a 'step' is taken to transmit it to the High Court. Indeed it will be seen that F(TA)A 2015, s 29 deals with cases stated for the High Court and outlines the position where inter alia 'any of the steps in the stating and signing of a case for the opinion of the High Court on the determination of the Appeal Commissioners remain' outstanding at the commencement date. So it would appear that the High Court's reference to 'step' should not be relied upon for an interpretation of the transitional provisions in F(TA)A 2015.

F(TA)A 2015, s 27(2) outlines the 'general rule' in relation to transitional arrangements for an existing appeal (an appeal 'made' before the commencement date of the new Pt 40A) from the old appeal process to the new appeal process when the new process comes into operation. Various clarifications and exceptions to this general rule are contained in sub-s (3) to (5). The 'general rule' is that an existing appeal that was subject to the provisions of TCA 1997, Pt 40 shall, instead, become subject to the provisions of the new Pt 40A of TCA 1997 and be dealt with under the remaining 'analogous' steps of the new appeal process. So the remaining 'steps' fall into the new process.

F(TA)A 2015, s 27(3) makes clear (ie 'notwithstanding subsection 2') that certain provisions in the new appeals process apply to an existing appeal irrespective of the point reached in appeal process. These are provisions in Chs 1 and 3 of the inserted Pt 40A of TCA 1997 and include matters such as the delegation of functions, the use of electronic means, the giving of directions, the settlement of appeals by agreement, the staying of proceedings together with pre-hearing proceedings, case management conference and interestingly under TCA 1997, s 949U the adjudication without a hearing.

F(TA)A 2015, s 27(4) contains the exceptions to the aforementioned 'general rule' in sub-s (2) in relation to existing appeals, ie the old rules continue to apply in certain instances. These exceptions are where under an existing appeal:

(a) a hearing has commenced but is not completed before the commencement date,
(b) a hearing is completed but a determination has not been made before the commencement date, or
(b) a determination has been made but the 10-day period within which the appellant may give a notice requesting a rehearing of the appeal by a Circuit Court judge has not expired before the commencement date.

In the above circumstances, the explanatory memorandum notes that 'an appellant may continue to avail of a rehearing of his or her appeal by a Circuit Court Judge under the old appeal process'. Section 27(4) notes that in the above position TCA 1997, ss 942 and 943 continue to apply to the appeal. Section 942 deals with appeals to the Circuit Court and s 943 deals with extensions to s 941. The notes for guidance to the TCA 1997 explain that the provisions of s 941 concerning the stating of a case by the Appeal Commissioners for the opinion of the High Court apply also to a determination given by a judge of the Circuit Court. It is to be remembered that F(TA)A 2015, s 27(4) is written as notwithstanding sub-s 2 or notwithstanding the 'general rule'.

Taking all of the above into account it is clear that the above exceptions apply only where a hearing has at least commenced and absent same then the Circuit Court appeal possibility is no longer relevant. That said F(TA)A 2015, s 27(5) states that 'for the avoidance of doubt' where a hearing in respect of an appeal has not commenced when the new appeal process comes into operation, and appellant is not entitled to a rehearing of its appeal by a Circuit Court judge under the old appeal process, ie TCA 1997, s 942 does not apply to the appeal. Unlike F(TA)A 2015, s 27(4) there is no mention of TCA 1997, s 943 as that section merely extends the provisions of stating a case for the opinion of the High Court by the Appeal Commissioners to a Circuit Court judge then a reference to TCA 1997, s 943 would appear unnecessary.

The following may be of assistance for the purposes of determining whether an appeal for rehearing to the Circuit Court can apply.

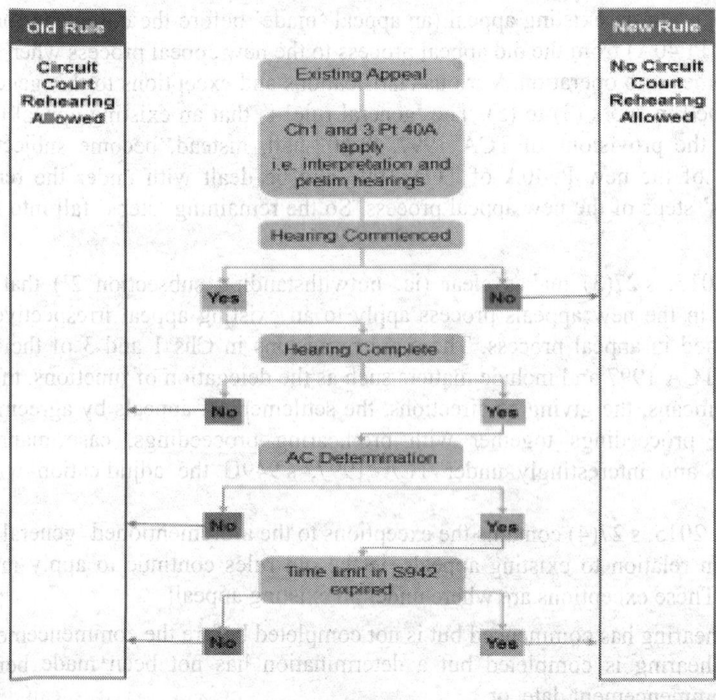

28. Appeal Commissioners vacating office before hearing or determination of appeal completed

F(TA)A 2015, s 28 contains provisions relating to the arrangements that apply where an Appeal Commissioner ceases to serve as an Appeal Commissioner (eg due to retirement, or in accordance with F(TA)A 2015, ss 13 and 8 an Appeal Commissioner can serve two terms for a maximum period of seven years in each term) where the appeal process is not completed in respect of an appeal. F(TA)A 2015, s 28 sets out two points in time in relation to the date on which the new appeal process comes into operation, and in relation to which the Appeal Commissioner involved in the appeal proceedings has ceased to serve as an Appeal Commissioner being:

(a) a hearing has commenced but is not completed, or
(b) a hearing is completed but a determination has not been made.

In such circumstances, the appeal must be reheard as if a previous hearing had not taken place or, instead, may be adjudicated on and determined without a hearing by another Appeal Commissioner. The adjudication without a hearing is subject to TCA 1997, s 949U(3) which says that the Appeal Commissioners 'shall' adjudicate by hearing where a party requests a hearing by notifying the Appeal Commissioners within 21 days of the Appeal Commissioner's notification of their intention to adjudicate without a hearing.

Thereafter, the next 'analogous' step of the new appeal process applies to the appeal.

Section 29. Cases stated – particular instances of steps remaining to be taken

F(TA)A 2015, s 29(1) notes that ss 29 and 30 'supplement' the provisions of s 27(2) which contains the 'general rule' regarding transitional arrangements; ie The '*general rule*' in s 27(2) is that an existing appeal that was subject to the provisions of Pt 40 of TCA 1997 shall, instead, become subject to the provisions of the new Pt 40A of TCA 1997 and be dealt with under the remaining 'analogous' steps of the new appeal process. So the remaining 'analogous steps' fall into the new process.

F(TA)A 2015, s 29(2) applies the 'general rule' to existing appeals in relation to which (a) a 'case stated' for the opinion of the High Court has not been completed and signed when the new appeal process comes into operation and (b) the Appeal Commissioner who heard the appeal vacated his or her office. These are cumulative conditions in the subsection and in such a situation, the appeal may continue under the new appeal process and the 'case stated' may be completed and signed by another Appeal Commissioner.

Subsection (3) provides for sub-s (4)'s application in circumstances where a case stated has not been completed 'irrespective' of whether or not this is caused by the Appeal Commissioner who heard the appeal ceasing to hold office.

Where sub-s (4) applies by reference to the enabling provisions and conditions in sub-s (3) then it requires the Appeal Commissioners, to request the parties to state whether they wish the Appeal Commissioners to rehear the appeal or to proceed with the completion of the case stated for the opinion of the High Court. There would appear to be no question of both options being available to the taxpayer as was the case for rehearing in the Circuit Court and a case stated to the High Court as was the case in the *O'Brien* decision of the High Court discussed earlier. It requires the parties to respond within a timeframe specified in the notice so the Appeal Commissioners can determine the appropriate time and no guidance is contained in the subsection for either party. Presumably, this timeframe would allow the parties sufficient time to cogitate and decide on the matter.

Subsection (5) requires the Appeal Commissioners, where both parties so elect, to either rehear the appeal or proceed to complete the case stated for the High Court. It should be noted that this provision is subject to s 30 which will be discussed below. This requires both parties to elect and where they do not then sub-s (6) applies.

Subsection (6) provides for a situation where both parties do not state within the permitted period that they wish the Appeal Commissioners to rehear the appeal or to complete and sign the case stated for the opinion of the High Court. Where this happens, the Appeal Commissioners are required to complete and sign the case stated. This subsection is subject to sub-s (7).

Subsection (7), as with sub-s (6), provides for a situation where both parties do not state within the permitted period that they wish the Appeal Commissioners to rehear the appeal or to complete and sign the case stated. Where this happens, the Appeal Commissioners are to complete and sign the case stated, but must first comply with s 30.

Subsections (8) and (9) look at the circumstances where a case stated is sent to the High Court that has been completed by a different Appeal Commissioner because the Appeal Commissioner who heard the appeal had ceased to hold office. Subsection (9) gives the High Court discretion not to deal with a 'case stated' that has been completed and signed by an Appeal Commissioner other than the Appeal Commissioner whose determination is being appealed where the High Court is of the opinion that to do so would not be 'consistent with the due administration of justice'. In arriving at such an opinion is to have regard to (a) the particular issues arising in the case stated, or (b) the likelihood of there being exercised by it the powers under TCA 1997, s 949AR(1)(b) or (2) in relation to the case stated. On (b) these situations comprise the High Court remitting the matter to the Appeal Commissioners with its opinion on the matter and sending the case stated back to the Appeal Commissioners for amendment.

Section 30. Supplemental provisions in relation to section 29

F(TA)A 2015, s 30 contains supplementary provisions to those in F(TA)A 2015, s 29 relating to the position where a 'case stated' for an appeal to the High Court has not been completed and signed when the new appeal process comes into operation.

Subsection (2) notes that where a 'case stated' has not been completed and signed when the new appeal process comes into operation because the Appeal Commissioners 'had recourse to the practice' of permitting parties to agree the terms of a draft 'case stated' with each other and they have not done so then the Appeal Commissioners must serve a notice on the parties 'to endeavour to agree' the draft and submit it to them within a period specified in the notice. The legislation does not specify a duration in that regard. The notice is to outline the consequences of not complying with this requirement, ie that the Appeal Commissioners must themselves complete the 'case stated' 'as soon as practicable'.

Subsection (3) points out that a notice under sub-s (2) cannot be issued before a notice under F(TA)A 2015, s 29(4) (ie where the Appeal Commissioners request the parties to state whether they wish the Appeal Commissioners to rehear the appeal or to proceed with the completion of the case stated for the opinion of the High Court) and where both parties have stated after a F(TA)A 2015, s 29(4) notice has been served that they wish the Appeal Commissioners to rehear the appeal.

Subsection (4) notes that where the terms of a draft 'case stated', as agreed between the parties, are not submitted to the Appeal Commissioners within the permitted time specified in the notice in sub-s (2) then the Appeal Commissioners are to complete and sign the 'case stated'. Subsection (5) notes that where the terms of a draft case stated have been agreed between the parties and submitted to the Appeal Commissioners, whether within the time frame specified in the notice as required by sub-s (2) or without the parties having been required to do so by the service of a notice then the Appeal Commissioners are to use this draft, whether modified by them or not, to complete the 'case stated'. The language used in this section is unusual in that the limb of the section outlining the Appeal Commissioners where the conditions for its application are met reads 'the Appeal Commissioners shall, using the whole or part of those terms as they determine for the following purpose (or the whole or part of them with such modifications as they determine and make to them for the following purpose), complete the case stated and sign it'. It would appear the 'following purpose' is to complete the case stated.

Section 31. Transmission of existing appeals to Appeal Commissioners

Section 31 outlines how Revenue is required deal with an existing appeal by, eg settling the appeal by agreement with the appellant or transmitting it to the Appeal Commissioners for adjudication and determination under the new appeal process.

Under the 'old rules' the appeal was to be made to the Revenue Commissioners who, on accepting same, would transmit the Appeal to the Appeal Commissioners. Under the 'new rules' the appeal is made directly to the Appeal Commissioners. Subsection (1) requires Revenue to transfer existing appeals that have been accepted by it to the Appeal Commissioners as soon as practicable after the new appeal process comes into operation. This is subject to sub-s (2) and (6) below.

Subsection (2) requires Revenue, before transmitting an existing appeal to the Appeal Commissioners, to ascertain if the appellant wishes to settle the appeal by agreement in accordance with TCA 1997, s 949V or to have the appeal transmitted to the Appeal Commissioners. Revenue 'may' put a time limit on when an appellant must indicate how it 'wishes' in this regard.

Subsection (3) allows the appellant, as noted in the explanatory memorandum accompanying the bill as initiated 'without having been contacted by Revenue about how it wishes to proceed', to apply to the Appeal Commissioners for a direction requiring Revenue to transmit its appeal to the Appeal Commissioners. This is not to say that Revenue has not acted in accordance with sub-s (2) but rather the appellant can act before Revenue has acted.

Subsection (4) notes that if, for whatever reason, the Revenue Commissioners are unable to effect the notification of an appellant required under sub-s (2), ie to ascertain if the appellant wishes to settle the appeal by agreement in accordance with TCA 1997, s 949V or to have the appeal transmitted to the Appeal Commissioners, then they shall, subject to sub-s (6), transmit the appeal to the Appeal Commissioners.

Subsection (5) notes that where the appellant indicates to Revenue that it wishes to settle its appeal by agreement but where that agreement is not reached then Revenue must transmit the appeal to the Appeal Commissioners.

Subsection (6) notes that notwithstanding the above the Revenue Commissioners shall not be required to transmit an appeal to the Appeal Commissioners if they form the view, having reviewed the matter being appealed, that the action, decision or determination that gave rise to the appeal should not be upheld, and where such a view is formed—

(a) that view shall be reduced to writing, and
(b) all steps as are appropriate in consequence of the formation of that view shall be taken by them.

Section 32. Transitional provision in relation to records and Section 33. References to Appeal Commissioners in other enactments

These are technical provisions which note as follows: Each record held by the Appeal Commissioners appointed in accordance with TCA 1997, s 850, being a record held by them immediately before the establishment day, shall, and on and from that day, be taken to be held by the Commission.

References to Appeal Commissioners (however expressed) in any Act passed before the establishment day, or in any instrument made before that day under an Act, shall be read as references to Appeal Commissioners appointed under this Act, unless the context otherwise requires.

TCA 1997, Part 40A

F(TA)A 2015, s 34 inserted a new Pt 40A into TCA 1997. (SI 110/2016 appointed 21 March 2016 as the day on which the Finance (Tax Appeals) Act 2015, came into operation). The discussion relevant to the 'old' Pt 40 remains within this text for completeness. Much of that discussion is relevant for Pt 40A with some notable exceptions being the inability to appeal to the Circuit Court for a rehearing of the decision of Appeal Commissioners, the possibility of pre-hearing conferences and of the hearing of the Appeal Commissioners' decisions in public. The provisions of Pt 40A apply to all appeals as 'the Acts' in that Part is defined to include tax heads from income tax to local property tax. The entitlement to appeal will be contained in the various Acts as defined with an 'appealable matter' being defined as 'any matter in respect of which an appeal is authorised by the Acts'. TCA 1997, Pt 40A is divided into the following chapters:

1. Interpretation and general;
2. Making and acceptance of appeals;
3. Pre-hearing proceedings;
4. Hearings;
5. Determinations;
6. Appealing determinations of the Appeal Commissioners;
7. Penalties and sanctions.

Chapter 1 – interpretation and general

TCA 1997, s 949A contains a number of definitions which apply for the purposes of Pt 40A as follows:

'Acts' means—

(a) the Tax Acts,

(b) the Capital Gains Tax Acts,

(c) Parts 18A to 18D,

(d) the Stamp Duties Consolidation Act 1999, and the enactments amending or extending that Act,

(e) the Capital Acquisitions Tax Consolidation Act 2003, and the enactments amending or extending that Act,

(f) the Value-Added Tax Consolidation Act 2010, and the enactments amending or extending that Act,

(g) the statutes relating to the duties of excise and to the management of those duties,

(h) the Customs Act 2015 and the enactments amending or extending that Act,

(i) the Finance (Local Property Tax) Act 2012 and the enactments amending or extending that Act, and any instrument made thereunder and any instrument that is made under any other enactment and which relates to tax;

'appealable matter' means any matter in respect of which an appeal is authorised by the Acts;

'Appeal Commissioner' has the same meaning as it has in the Finance (Tax Appeals) Act 2015;

'assessment' means an assessment to tax made under the Acts or an estimate of tax made under section 989(2) or 990(1);

'determination' means a decision made by the Appeal Commissioners, following the completion of their adjudication of a matter under appeal, in disposing of the appeal;

'late appeal' means an appeal that is made after the end of the period specified by the Acts for the making of the appeal;

'party' means either the appellant in the appeal or the Revenue Commissioners;

'proceedings' includes—

(a) all of the proceedings involved in the conduct of an appeal from the making of the appeal, and

(b) if the following step occurs, the sending of a completed and signed case stated to the party requesting the case stated;

'Revenue officer' means an officer of the Revenue Commissioners;

'statement of case' shall be construed in accordance with section 949Q(1);

'tax' means any income tax, corporation tax, capital gains tax, value- added tax, excise duty, customs duty, stamp duty, gift tax, inheritance tax, local property tax or any other levy or charge that is placed under the care and management of the Revenue Commissioners.'

TCA 1997, s 949B allows any functions authorised by Pt 40A to be done by the Revenue Commissioners to be delegated to any one or more officers who act under their authority. TCA 1997, s 949C allows acts or functions required to be done by the Appeal Commissioners or Revenue Commissioners to be done by electronic means. TCA 1997, s 949D outlines the provisions relating to the manner in which a person may act as an agent for an appellant in relation to the conduct of an appeal and the agent must be notified to the Appeal Commissioners together with the agent's name, address and any other information that the Appeal Commissioners may require. The appellant can change its mind and the agent's authority can be revoked and such revocation must be made known to the Appeal Commissioners.

Directions

TCA 1997, s 949E allows the Appeal Commissioners to give directions, whether on their own initiative or by request of one of the parties to the appeal regarding the conduct of an appeal and such direction can amend or set aside previous directions. Among the directions that an Appeal Commissioner can give are the following as set out in TCA 1997, s 949E(2):

(a) requiring a party to provide, to the Appeal Commissioners or to another party, documents, statements, accounts, returns, computations, explanations, particulars, records, certificates, declarations, schedules and such other items or information as they consider relevant to the adjudication of the matter under appeal,

(b) consolidating or hearing together 2 or more appeals raising common or related issues,

(c) staying proceedings,

(d) holding a preliminary hearing,

(e) adjourning a hearing, and

(f) extending the time within which a direction must be complied with.

It is noted that a direction can be given by the Appeal Commissioner orally but the terms of the direction are to be put in writing 'as soon as practicable thereafter' unless the Appeal Commissioners deem it unnecessary.

A party who asserts that a direction ought not to have been given by the Appeal Commissioners or should be amended must apply to the Appeal Commissioners for a direction setting aside or suspending its operation or, as appropriate, amending it. That application must be made not later than 14 days after the date on which the party was notified. Where the direction given is one requiring compliance with its terms it must specify a date by which these terms are to be complied with and where a direction requires the provision of such items or information then it may specify the format in which those items are to be provided. A party to whom a direction is given must comply with it and it will be seen that TCA 1997, s 949AV(1) notes that the Appeal Commissioners may dismiss an appeal where a party has failed to comply with such a direction.

Joining additional parties to the appeal

TCA 1997, s 949F allows the Appeal Commissioners, on application, to make persons other than the appellant in the particular appeal a party to the appeal proceedings. This treatment applies in specified circumstances where a Revenue decision may affect the tax liability of persons other than the person who is the subject of the decision: ie the apportionment of an item between one or more persons, the treatment of certain lease premia under s 100A and the use of a vehicle in a car pooling arrangement under s 121(7). A party affected by the particular Revenue decision may apply to the Appeal Commissioners for such treatment. The provisions relating to the giving of directions by the Appeal Commissioners discussed above apply to a person who is joined as a party to appeal proceedings.

Withdrawal and dismissal of appeals and flexible proceedings

TCA 1997, s 949G outlines provisions relating to the withdrawal or dismissal of appeals before their being determined by the Appeal Commissioners. The party withdrawing an appeal must notify the Appeal Commissioners, who are then required to notify the other party of the withdrawal. TCA 1997, s 949G deems an appeal to be treated as if it has been dismissed in certain instances:

- settlement of the appeal by agreement between the parties;
- the Appeal Commissioners' refusal to accept an appeal on the basis it was not a valid appeal or that it was without substance or foundation; and
- where an appeal 'is treated' as withdrawn due to an appellant's failure to attend a hearing under TCA 1997, s 949AA(2).

Where an appeal is settled by agreement, withdrawn or dismissed then the Appeal Commissioners are not to make a determination and the matter under appeal is treated as if it had not been appealed. The above reference to 'substance and foundation' is curious given one could be forgiven for regarding one as a synonym of the other but such approach is not unusual in that TCA 1997, ss 811 and 811C refer to an abuse or misuse of a relief to which the Irish Supreme Court referred as having similar meanings.

TCA 1997, s 949H requires the Appeal Commissioners to endeavour to conduct proceedings in as informal and flexible manner as possible, to facilitate the settlement of appeals by agreement between the parties and to avoid undue delay in dealing with appeals. The conducting of appeals without undue delay is not unfettered in that this must allow for proper consideration of a matter under appeal.

Chapter 2 – Making and acceptance of appeals

TCA 1997, s 949I requires an appellant to make an appeal by way of a written notice to the Appeal Commissioners. In the past TCA 1997, s 933 required such an application to be made to the Revenue Commissioners and now it is the Appeal Commissioners to decide whether the appeal is valid. The notice of appeal must specify:

(a) The appellant's name and address and agent, if relevant;

(b) The relevant tax reference number;

(c) The appealable matter in respect of which the appeal is being made;

(d) The detailed grounds for the appeal;

(e) A statement whether any conditions necessary for the making of an appeal have been satisfied;

(f) A statement, in the case of a late appeal, outlining why the appeal was not made on time. It is of note that the section does not outline the timeline by which such appeal has to be made in that previously TCA 1997, s 933(1) required that an appeal be made within 30 days after the date of the notice of assessment. These timelines are contained in the consequential amendments to other statutes provisions of the F(TA)A 2015 and is now reflected in the relevant sections of the TCA 1997 and other Acts to which Pt 40A applies. For example, it will be seen that TCA 1997, s 959AF now requires that a person aggrieved by an assessment or amended assessment may appeal same to the Appeal Commissioners 'in accordance with section 949I, within the period of 30 days after the date of the notice of assessment';

(g) A copy of the notification by Revenue to the appellant of the appealable matter (for example, a notice of assessment) is to be appended to a notice of appeal.

Critically an appellant will not be able to rely on any grounds of appeal that were not stated in a notice of appeal unless the Appeal Commissioners are satisfied that the 'ground could not have been reasonably stated in the notice'. Similar requirements regarding Revenue's ground for assessment are not mentioned in the section in that it only speaks of a 'notice of appeal'.

TCA 1997, s 949J notes that an appeal will be a 'valid appeal' if it is made in relation to an appealable matter being 'any matter in respect of which an appeal is authorised by the Acts' and where any conditions that must be satisfied before an appeal is made have been satisfied, eg the submission of a tax return etc. The section notes that an appeal being accepted by the Appeal Commissioners shall be construed as their determining that, for the time being (on the facts and information then available to them) the appeal is a valid appeal and there are no grounds for their regarding the appeal as being without foundation as a basis for not proceeding and that they should proceed to deal with the appeal. This determination can be reversed if facts and information become available to the Appeal Commissioners at a later point.

TCA 1997, s 949K requires the Appeal Commissioners to send a copy of each notice of appeal, and any item that was appended to the notice, to the Revenue Commissioners 'as soon as practicable after they have received them'. TCA 1997, s 949L allows the Revenue Commissioners the possibility of objecting to the appeal where they consider that the appeal is not valid or where the requirements for a late appeal in TCA 1997, s 949O have not been complied with. Such objection has to be notified by the Appeal Commissioners to the appellant. The Revenue Commissioners are required to send a notice of objection to the Appeal Commissioners within 30 days after it receives the

Appeal Commissioners' notification of an appeal if the Appeal Commissioners are required to have regard to its objection.

The Appeal Commissioners are required to accept an appeal at the end of the 30-day period above for the notification of a Revenue objection to the acceptance of an appeal where they have no reason to believe that the appeal is not a valid appeal. However, this acceptance may change later where the Appeal Commissioners form the view that the appeal is not a valid appeal.

The Appeal Commissioners are required to refuse to accept an appeal under TCA 1997, s 949N(1) where they:

(a) are satisfied that an appeal is not a valid appeal;
(b) become aware, having previously formed the view that an appeal was a valid appeal, that it is not a valid appeal; or
(c) are satisfied that an appeal is without substance or foundation.

When this happens the Appeal Commissioners shall notify the parties in writing accordingly stating the reason for the refusal and their decision on such declaration is final and conclusive. The Appeal Commissioners' staff have the authority to refuse to accept appeals. The explanatory memorandum accompanying the F(TA)A 2015 as initiated notes that such staff refusals 'are subject to a "final and conclusive" declaration by the Appeal Commissioners'. A reason for such caveat is that F(TA)A 2015, s 5(2) allows certain functions of the Appeal Commissioners to be delegated to any one or more of the Commission's staff acting under its authority, however the following functions may not be so delegated:

(a) deciding whether to declare, under TCA 1997, s 949N(3) that a refusal to accept an appeal is final;
(b) hearing an appeal where the Commissioners have decided that a hearing is the appropriate method of adjudicating on the appeal;
(c) determining appeals;
(d) stating and signing cases stated for the opinion of the High Court.

For late appeals, TCA 1997, s 949O notes that the Appeal Commissioners (under the previous rules in Pt 40 this would have been the Revenue Commissioners) may accept a late appeal where it is made within a period of 12 months after the date allowed by the relevant taxation provision for making the appeal (it will be recalled that Pt 40A applies in respect of a number of taxes as defined and so the reference to the provisions at issue is generic such that it can be applied to the taxes as defined). The Appeal Commissioners are required to be satisfied that the reason the appellant could not make the appeal on time was because of absence, illness or some other reasonable cause and that the appeal was made without delay after the particular reason had ceased to apply. Where there is such reasonable cause the Inspector is obliged to allow a reasonable period for the late appeal to be made (*Criminal Assets Bureau v PMcS* VI ITR 421). In *Criminal Assets Bureau v D(K)* VI ITR 445, the High Court held that 'other reasonable cause' should be interpreted *ejusdem generis* with 'absence or sickness' and that incarceration was capable of being regarded as similar in nature to absence or sickness.

The 12-month period for the acceptance of a late appeal can be extended where the same reasons for the inability to make a timely appeal apply and where some additional conditions are satisfied. These conditions include that the appellant is required to submit any outstanding tax returns, with sufficient information to enable the Appeal Commissioners to determine the appeal, and to pay whatever tax has been charged by a disputed assessment, including any interest due on the late payment of the assessed tax.

TCA 1997, s 949O(4) allows the Appeal Commissioners to make whatever enquiries they consider necessary, including holding a preliminary hearing, for the purpose of deciding whether or not to accept a late appeal. The provisions of TCA 1997, s 949N relating to the refusal to accept an appeal that is not a valid appeal also apply to the acceptance of a late appeal. TCA 1997, s 949P prevents the Appeal Commissioners from accepting a late appeal in relation to disputed tax that is subject to court or sheriff proceedings until the particular enforcement action has concluded and prevents the repayment of any legal or sheriff fees paid by an appellant where a late appeal is accepted after the conclusion of the particular enforcement action.

Chapter 3 – Pre-hearing proceedings

TCA 1997, s 949Q applies where an appeal has been accepted and allows the Appeal Commissioners to direct that a party provide specified information (referred to as a 'statement of case'). TCA 1997, s 949Q(2) contains a list of information that a party may be directed to provide to the Appeal Commissioners. Although not outlined in the section it is noted in the explanatory memorandum which accompanies the related bill as initiated that the information in the list will be used to assist the Appeal Commissioners in deciding on the appropriate way to conduct the proceedings. It is important to note that this list in sub-s (2) is 'without prejudice to the generality' of the direction that can be given by the Appeal Commissioners and is written as 'includes' the information outlined below which is indicative of a non-exhaustive list such that the Appeal Commissioners can add to it as they see fit which is confirmed in any event by (j) below:

(a) the statutory provisions being relied upon in relation to the matter under appeal;

(b) an outline of the relevant facts;

(c) the relevant case law;

(d) a list of, and copies of, any written material that a party intends to rely on or produce in the proceedings;

(e) brief particulars in relation to any witnesses who might be called upon to provide evidence in the proceedings;

(f) a party's estimation of the likely duration of a hearing;

(g) whether there is assent, on the part of the party, to the Appeal Commissioners determining the appeal without a hearing;

(h) whether a party wishes a hearing or a specified part of a hearing to be held in camera;

(i) whether a party considers that a matter under appeal is one that could be settled by way of an agreement with the other party; and

(j) such other information as the Appeal Commissioners consider necessary to enable them to schedule a hearing.

TCA 1997, s 949R requires a party who sends information ('statement of case') to the Appeal Commissioners to also send it to the other party, together with a copy of the relevant direction, and to notify the Appeal

Commissioners when they have done so. This presumably may replace the Form AH1 process that existed pursuant to the application of TCA 1997, Pt 40. It is noteworthy that TCA 1997, s 949K requires the Appeal Commissioners to send a copy of each notice of appeal, and any item that was appended to the notice, to the Revenue Commissioners 'as soon as practicable after they have received them' but the case stated is to be sent by the required party to the appeal.

TCA 1997, s 949S allows the Appeal Commissioners to direct the parties to provide an outline of the arguments that will be made at the hearing and additional information to a statement of case and to send a copy of this information to the other party. This is the type of information that would be required before a hearing and a direction may impose a 14-day time limit before the date of a hearing for the provision of the information. The Appeal Commissioners can give such a direction to one of the parties only where they consider there are substantial grounds for same otherwise such a direction may be given to both parties.

TCA 1997, s 949T deals with the holding of a 'case management conference' or what has been referred to as 'preliminary hearings' in the explanatory memorandum which accompanied the F(TA)A 2015 when initiated. The use of 'preliminary hearing' is not had in TCA 1997, s 949T but rather a 'case management conference'. TCA 1997, s 949E outlines directions which can be made by the Appeal Commissioners and sub-ss (2)(d) and (3)(b) make references to a 'preliminary hearing' and it is curious that the expression 'preliminary hearing' is not used in TCA 1997, s 949T. The preliminary hearing or case management conference is a concept which did not exist prior to the enactment of Pt 40A. The accompanying explanatory memorandum notes that while the purpose of such hearings will generally be to progress matters to the stage of a full hearing, the Appeal Commissioners may determine the matter under appeal at (or following) a preliminary hearing but this can only happen with the consent of the parties. Interestingly TCA 1997, s 949T(3) allows the Appeal Commissioners to permit a party to participate in a preliminary hearing by means of a 'suitable telecommunications link' instead of in person.

TCA 1997, s 949U(1) allows the Appeal Commissioners not to hold a hearing to adjudicate on a matter under appeal and, instead, to adjudicate the matter on the basis of the statement of a case or other written material from a party or discussions with a party or 'any other means they consider appropriate'. The latter option is initially curious in that it is difficult to determine what other method may be appropriate but TCA 1997, s 949AN(1) notes the situation where the matter can be resolved by reference to a previous determination made by the Appeal Commissioners. The Appeal Commissioners must notify the parties of their intention to adjudicate on a matter under appeal without holding a hearing. This option is not unfettered in that the Appeal Commissioners must hold a hearing where they receive a written request from a party to this effect within 21 days after the notification of the Appeal Commissioners' intention not to hold a hearing. However, such a request for a hearing can be overruled by the Appeal Commissioners under TCA 1997, s 949AN(3), which is written as notwithstanding TCA 1997, s 949U, where inter alia the matter can be resolved by reference to a previous determination made by the Appeal Commissioners. Therefore, the doctrine of judicial precedent applies; the question then arises as to whether the Appeal Commissioners can have regard to any decisions of the Appeal Commissioners prior to the setting up of the Appeals Commission in that many of their decisions may not yet be in the public domain. F(TA)A 2015, s 2 defines an Appeal Commissioner as being a member of the Tax Appeals Commission which is set up by order of the Minister. It would appear that the reference to Appeal Commissioner in TCA 1997, s 949N would have to be read in that context given that F(TA)A 2015, s 35(1) amends the definition of Appeal Commissioner to have the same meaning as in F(TA)A 2015, s 2 and that definition applies for the purposes of the Tax Acts.

TCA 1997, s 949V provides for the settlement of an appeal by way of agreement between the parties and defines 'agreement' for the purpose of this section as an agreement by way of settlement of the matter under appeal. It treats an appeal as having been withdrawn where the parties come to an agreement with each other before a hearing is held. If the agreement was not in writing when it was made, then it must be confirmed in writing from either of the parties to the other. A period of 21 days is given allowing either party to the written agreement to repudiate or withdraw from the agreement. The explanatory memorandum to F(TA) 2015 refers to this period as being allowed for reflection on the agreement and a possible repudiation of the agreement. Revenue is required to give effect to an agreement (eg by amending an assessment to reflect the tax which has been the subject of the agreement between the parties) and to notify the Appeal Commissioners accordingly. In *Tod v South Essex Motors* [1988] STC 392, it was held that an agreement could be corrected by the parties outside the 21-day limit. In *R v Inspector of Taxes ex parte Bass Holdings* [1993] STC 122 it was held on the facts that the court could rectify an agreement where it contained an arithmetical error and thus did not correctly express the true intentions of the parties. Both decisions relied on the fact that the UK equivalent of TCA 1997, s 933(3) was subject to the ordinary law of contract. It may be noted in this context that the inspector has in any event wide powers to amend assessments under TCA 1997, s 959Y.

In *Schuldenfrei v Hilton* [1998] STC 404, it was held that the term 'agreement' in the present context meant a binding contract or something close to it. It followed that the rules governing the formation of a contract would nearly always be conclusive in deciding whether an agreement had been reached. In particular, it is necessary that acceptance of a relevant offer is communicated to the offeror and is not merely left to be inferred by inaction on the part of the offeree. TCA 1997, s 949W allows the Appeal Commissioners to stay proceedings in an appeal at any stage of the proceedings for a variety of reasons where they wish to provide an opportunity for the parties to settle the matter under appeal by agreement, to give a party additional time to prepare for a hearing or to allow a determination to be made in a separate appeal that raises issues common to both appeals or that are otherwise related. The Appeal Commissioners are required to give a direction where they want to stay proceedings and to specify a date by which the proceedings are to be resumed.

Chapter 4 – hearings

TCA 1997, s 949X requires the Appeal Commissioners to arrange hearings and to notify the parties in writing of the location and time for their hearing and allows the Appeal Commissioners to adjourn a hearing for such period they consider appropriate. TCA 1997, s 949Y contains the general position for hearings in that all hearings are to be held in public. The Appeal Commissioners can hold a hearing (or part of a hearing) in camera where they consider that it is necessary in the interests of public order or national security, to avoid serious harm to the public interest to maintain the confidentiality of sensitive information, to protect a person's right to respect for their private and family life and in the interests of justice. That said the Appeal Commissioners are required to hold an *in camera* hearing where an appellant requests a direction that the appeal be so heard or has stated that request as part of the statement of case. The section gives an appellant 14 days after being notified of a hearing to submit a request for an *in camera* hearing.

The general rule for public hearings is a significant shift from the position pertaining before the enactment of TCA 1997, Pt 40A and therefore taxpayers should be cognisant of the timings of election for an in camera hearing. The Revenue Commissioners Appeal manual notes that 'Although the tax legislation is silent on the matter, tax and duty appeals hearings before the Appeal Commissioners are held *in camera*. A possible reason for this is the content of the form of the Declaration made by an Appeal Commissioner under TCA 1997, Sch 27. In addition, appeals to the Circuit Court are heard *in camera* [TCA 1997, s 942(9)] so it would seem illogical not to have appeals before the Appeal Commissioners heard *in camera*'. It is of note that such appeal to the Circuit Court has been removed as part of F(TA)A 2015 but the reader is directed to the transitional rules between Pts 40 and 40A to determine if such an appeal option may still be available depending the timing of the steps of the appeal already taken.

TCA 1997, s 949Z allows the Appeal Commissioners to exclude certain persons from a hearing or part of a hearing. These include disruptive persons, those who might hinder the giving of evidence freely by another person, and those aged under 18 years. Interestingly persons 'whose attendance at the hearing would defeat the purpose of that hearing' may be excluded. The Appeal Commissioners may exclude a witness from a hearing until that witness is required to give evidence. The Appeal Commissioners may give a direction as to 'the means' to be used to exclude a person from a hearing.

TCA 1997, s 949AA requires an appellant to attend a hearing unless the Appeal Commissioners excuse them from attendance and treats an appeal as if it has been withdrawn where an appellant, or their agent, fails to attend a hearing, unless the Appeal Commissioners are satisfied that the reason for the non-attendance was due to absence, illness or another reasonable cause and that the application was made as soon as possible thereafter. A Revenue officer 'may' attend the entire hearing and the determination of the appeal and can give evidence or reasons in support of the matter under appeal but this is not obligatory. A Revenue officer can give evidence or reasons in support of a determination that an appealed assessment should be increased (see the discussion of *Glaxo Group v IRC*). Third parties made a party to an appeal because the outcome of the appeal is likely to affect their tax liability in addition to that of the appellant may attend certain aspects of a hearing, or part of a hearing. TCA 1997, s 949AB requires the Appeal Commissioners to hear a barrister, solicitor, accountant or member of the Irish Taxation Institute who represents a party. In *Cassell v Crutchfield* [1995] STC 663, it was held that the equivalent UK provision was subject to an implied condition that an accountant must be a member of his professional body at the time of the hearing. However the Appeal Commissioners 'may' hear a person who represents a party even though they are not a barrister, solicitor, accountant or member of the Irish Taxation Institute. TCA 1997, s 949AC notes that the Appeal Commissioners 'may' allow oral or written evidence and to adopt a more informal approach to that of a court in relation to the giving of evidence in that they may admit evidence wither or not that evidence would be admissible in an Irish court. They 'may' also exclude certain evidence where it was not given within the directed timeframe or in a manner which did not comply with that direction or where they considered it 'unfair' to admit the evidence. It is of note that the determination of what is and what is not fair in that instance is at the discretion of the Appeal Commissioners. Because a company has a separate legal personality (see **1.107**) a director is not entitled as such to appear on its behalf (see *Battle v Irish Art Promotion Centre* [1968] IR 252, where an individual who was a major shareholder and managing director of a company was not permitted to represent that company in court). It may be that the court would exercise its discretion to allow a major shareholder to appear on behalf of a company in an appropriate case (see Courtney, *The Law of Companies* (4th edn, Bloomsbury Professional, 2016) at para 6.076).

Under TCA 1997, s 949AD the Appeal Commissioners may require a person giving evidence to swear an oath in relation to the evidence and when administering an oath, they must inform the person swearing the oath of the consequences of giving false evidence and that is the same punishment as that applicable to persons convicted of perjury.

The Appeal Commissioners may summon a person for examination where they consider that the person can give evidence relating to the matter under appeal. The summoned person must be given at least 21 days' notice before a hearing date and must be informed of their entitlement to object to the summons or to have its terms varied or set aside. The person must also be informed of the consequences of failure to comply with the summons being liable to a penalty of €3,000 (see TCA 1997, s 949AU). The Appeal Commissioners may limit the number of witnesses whose evidence a party may put forward. The Appeal Commissioners may, at the conclusion of a hearing, make the determination referred orally but such determination shall be reduced to writing thereafter with TCA 1997, s 949AJ applying (see below). In *Johnson v Walden* [1994] STC 124, it was held that, notwithstanding the oath of secrecy (contained in the UK equivalent to F(TA)A 2015, Sch1), the Appeal Commissioners were entitled to deal with two appeals by different taxpayers simultaneously where it was appropriate and expedient to do so, despite the objections of the respective taxpayers concerned. In fact, the financial affairs of the taxpayer were so intermingled that it would have been impracticable to deal with them separately (it would also seem that, on the particular facts of this case, confidentiality was not a real issue). The decision was upheld by the Court of Appeal ([1996] STC 382), who emphasised that no prejudice had been suffered by the taxpayers as a result of their appeals being heard together.

Although it seems that the Appeal Commissioner are not to be viewed as performing a judicial function, nevertheless it is clear that they must exercise their functions in a judicial manner, ie consistently with the requirements of natural justice. In this connection, the UK courts have frequently considered whether or not the Appeal Commissioners have acted properly in refusing to grant adjournments (see eg *Banin v McKinlay* [1985] STC 144, and contrast *Packe v Johnson* [1996] STC 1; note also *R v Brentford Revenue Commissioners* [1986] STC 65, and *Aspinall v Greenwood* [1988] STC 609, where it was accepted that if a material witness was unable to attend the hearing for reasons beyond his control, an adjournment should be granted, unless it would cause injustice to the other party to the appeal). The Appeal Commissioners are now required to act where possible in a manner consistent with the European Convention on Human Rights (see **1.411**). In *Griffin v AC and CAB* VI ITR 371, it was held that the requirement on the Appeal Commissioners to act judicially meant that they were obliged to consider whether allowing an appeal to proceed would breach the taxpayer's constitutional rights to a fair trial or against self-incrimination. This followed from the presumption that all proceedings and adjudications carried out under statutory authority should be conducted in accordance with the principles of constitutional justice.

In the *State (Calcul International & Solatrex International) v The Appeal Commissioners & The Revenue Commissioners* III ITR 577), a judicial review case (see **2.206**), the Revenue Commissioners had alleged that the plaintiffs had defrauded them of various sums of tax. Barron J held that the fact that the Revenue had elected for High Court proceedings did not prevent them from having the tax liabilities which were the subject of those proceedings determined through the normal appeal procedures.

Chapter 5 – determinations

TCA 1997, s 949AG requires the Appeal Commissioners, when adjudicating and determining an appeal, to have regard to the same matters that Revenue may or were required to take account under the Acts (as defined) of in relation to the matter under appeal. TCA 1997, s 949AH requires the Appeal Commissioners to determine a matter under appeal by examining an appellant or by hearing other evidence given orally or in writing and whether or not the evidence would be admissible in an Irish Court. The Appeal Commissioners have discretion to determine an appeal to the best of their judgment in circumstances where a party or another person fails to comply with their direction to provide the type of information and documentation rather than dismissing the appeal under TCA 1997, s 949AV which is within their prerogative.

TCA 1997, s 949AJ requires the Appeal Commissioners to make a determination 'as soon as practicable after completion of their adjudication' on a matter under appeal. An odd number of Appeal Commissioners is required and where the adjudication of the appeal is by three or more Appeal Commissioners, then that determination is to be the majority determination. The Appeal Commissioners must notify their written determination to the parties within 21 days after the date on which the determination is made and advise as to the time within which, and the manner in which, any right of appeal against the determination may be exercised.

The determination is to comprise:

(a) the determination itself;
(b) the material facts as found by the Appeal Commissioners;
(c) the reasons for the determination;
(d) the name of the appellant; and
(e) the date of the determination.

TCA 1997, s 949AK allows the Appeal Commissioners to determine that the relevant assessment is to be reduced, to be increased, or to be left unchanged. The Appeal Commissioners may limit their determination to increasing or reducing the amount to be assessed as chargeable to tax. Where on appeal against an assessment which is outside the 4-year time limit prescribed in the sections referred to in TCA 1997, s 959AF (ie TCA 1997, ss 959AA, 959AC, 959AB or 949AD) the Appeal Commissioners determine that the Revenue officer was bound by this time limit, the assessment or the amendment of the assessment is rendered void and the 'the Acts' apply as if the assessment or the amendment had not been made. The reference to 'the Act' here is a reference to those as defined in TCA 1997, s 959A which comprise the direct taxes together with the Domicile levy and the Universal Social Charge. The difference between TCA 1997, ss 959AF and 949AK is that the latter determines the effect of such a determination by the Appeal Commissioners. Likewise, where the Appeal Commissioners determine that the Revenue officer was not bound by this time limit then the assessment or the amendment of the assessment shall stand but such a determination does not preclude the assessment, or the amended assessment, being revised as a result of another appeal made on grounds other than a breach of the 4-year time limit.

TCA 1997, s 949AL contains provisions relating to determinations made in relation to matters other than assessments to tax made by Revenue. In respect of a Revenue decision, determination or other matter, the Appeal Commissioners are required to determine either that the matter be varied, even if a variation is to the disadvantage of an appellant, or stand. The explanatory memorandum accompanying the F(TA)A 2015 explains that 'Subsection (2) provides for parameters on the Appeal Commissioners' determinations in relation to whether a Revenue officer was precluded from making an enquiry or taking an action outside of the permitted 4-year time limit for doing so. The Appeal Commissioners are required to determine either that the officer was so precluded or was not so precluded'. The subsection speaks of 'making the enquiry or taking the action, as the case may be, referred to in section 959AJ'. The reference to that latter section is initially curious in that it is directed towards actions of the taxpayer and provides that where a person makes an appeal, the person must specify the exact grounds of the appeal and the amounts or matters being appealed. It states that when a person is appealing against an assessment, they must specify each amount in the assessment or amended assessment which they wish to appeal, and the exact grounds for such an appeal and that if such does not contain this information then the notice, in so far as it relates to a specific item, shall be invalid and the appeal deemed not to have been brought. That said, F(TA)A 2015, s 39, replaces TCA 1997, s 959AJ in its entirety. The grounds for appeal requirement is outlined in TCA 1997, s 949I and TCA 1997, s 959AJ will look to appeals against time limits for making Revenue making enquiries and taking certain actions.

TCA 1997, s 959AJ, substituted by F(TA)A 2015, notes that where a chargeable person is aggrieved by an enquiry made or an action taken by a Revenue officer under TCA 1997, s 959Z for a chargeable period, after the expiry of the four years from the end of the chargeable period in which the return was delivered on the grounds that the chargeable person considers that the Revenue officer is precluded from making the enquiry or taking the action and an assessment has not been made or amended, as the case may be in respect of the chargeable period on foot of the officer's enquiry or action then the chargeable person may appeal to the Appeal Commissioners, in accordance with TCA 1997, s 949I, within the period of 30 days after the date on which the officer makes that enquiry or takes that action.

TCA 1997, s 949AM requires Revenue to give effect to the Appeal Commissioners' determinations, unless a determination is appealed to the High Court on a point of law.

TCA 1997, s 949AN allows the Appeal Commissioners to have regard to a previous determination in determining a subsequent appeal that raises issues that are common to both appeals or that are related to the previous appeal and can determine the subsequent appeal without holding a hearing where they consider it appropriate to do so. The Appeal Commissioners must give the parties a copy of the relevant previous determination (suitably adjusted so that the appellant is not identified where the hearing was not held in public) which gives them 21 days from the date of the request to allow them argue that such approach would not be appropriate to look to the previous decision as a basis for determining the appeal under review.

TCA 1997, s 949AO looks at the publication of Appeal Commissioners' determinations and requires the Appeal Commissioners to publish a report of a determination on the internet within a period of 90 days after they notify the parties of the determination. The published report should contain:

(a) a copy of the determination which according to TCA 1997, s 959AJ comprises:
  (i) the determination,
  (ii) a statement of the Appeal Commissioners' material findings of fact,
  (iii) a statement of the reasons for the determination,
  (iv) the name of the appellant, and
  (v) the date on which the determination was made,
(b) the date it was notified to the parties;
(c) whether it was appealed to the High Court; and

(d) any other information that the Appeal Commissioners consider to be relevant to that appeal.

TCA 1997, s 949AO(3) looks to determinations involving issues that are common to more than one appeal or that are related to other appeals and in such instance a single report can be prepared. Where a hearing was held *in camera*, the Appeal Commissioners can satisfy their publication obligations by publishing a report containing a single determination together with a statement of the number of appeals to which the determination applies. Where a hearing was held in public, they must publish the names of all of the appellants to whom the determination applies. The Appeal Commissioners are required to publish a report in a way that conceals the identity of a person whose affairs were treated as confidential in the conduct of an appeal or where the hearing of the appeal was not held in public.

Chapter 6: Appealing determinations of the Appeal Commissioners

TCA 1997, s 949AP allows a party who is dissatisfied with an Appeal Commissioner's determination for a right of appeal to the High Court on a point of law and it can do so by notice in writing requiring the Appeal Commissioners to state a case ('case stated') for the High Court. The aforementioned notice to the Appeal Commissioners requesting a 'case stated' must:

(a) state how the determination is to have erred in relation to a point of law;
(b) be sent to the Appeal Commissioners within a period of 21 days after the Appeal Commissioners have sent their determination to the parties; and
(c) be sent by the party requesting the 'case stated' to the other party when it is being sent to the Appeal Commissioners.

It is of note that the section does not apply in relation to an appealable matter where a provision of the Acts provides that the determination of the Appeal Commissioners in relation to that matter shall be final and conclusive. TCA 1997, s 949AQ notes that the 'case stated' for the High Court must contain:

(i) the Appeal Commissioners' material findings of fact,
(ii) an outline of the arguments made by the parties,
(iii) the case law relied on by the parties,
(iv) the Appeal Commissioners' determination and the reason for the determination, and
(v) the point of law as set out in the notice sent to the Appeal Commissioners on which the opinion of the High Court is sought.

Critically, the party requesting the 'case stated' cannot state an additional or an alternative point of law to that already stated once the 21-day period within which the 'case stated' must be requested has passed. The Appeal Commissioners must draft a 'case stated' and are required to send a draft of that 'case stated' to the parties and to allow them 14 days to submit written representations on that draft which they must consider but they are not required to amend the case stated on that basis. A party making representations on a 'case stated' must send a copy of same to the other party when they send them to the Appeal Commissioners. There is a 3-month time limit, starting when a notice requesting a 'case stated' is sent to the Appeal Commissioners, for the completion, signing of the 'case stated' and sending it to the parties. It is the party who has requested a 'case stated' (not the Appeal Commissioners) that is to send the completed and signed 'case stated' to the High Court within 14 days of it being sent to them by the Appeal Commissioner. The High Court may not decline to hear such an appeal if the above mentioned 3-month and 14-day deadlines for compilation of a case stated and sending it to the High Court are not met where it determines that 'that, in all the circumstances of the matter, it would not be in the interests of justice to so decline to hear and determine that question'.

TCA 1997, s 949AR requires the High Court to hear and determine any question of law that is referred to it by way of a 'case stated'. It may reverse, affirm or amend the Appeal Commissioners' determination, remit the matter to the Appeal Commissioners with its opinion on the determination or make any other order in relation to the matter and costs that it thinks fit. The High Court can refer a 'case stated' back to the Appeal Commissioners for it to be amended and following the required amendment, the High Court must determine the matter. An appeal from a High Court decision can be made to the Court of Appeal. TCA 1997, s 949AT requires Revenue to give effect to determinations of the Appeal Commissioners that have been reversed, affirmed or amended by the High Court or the Court of Appeal or the Supreme Court.

Chapter 7: Penalties and Sanctions

TCA 1997, s 949AU imposes a €3,000 penalty on a person who fails to comply with a summons to attend other than a person who is an employee or agent of an appellant or who is otherwise confidentially employed in the appellant's affairs. TCA 1997, s 949AV gives the Appeal Commissioners the power to dismiss an appeal where an appellant has failed to comply with their direction to provide the type of information and documentation described earlier. However, before dismissing an appeal, the Appeal Commissioners must give a party—

- (a) written notice of their intention to do so,
- (b) a statement of the reasons and considerations on which their intention is based, and
- (c) an opportunity for the party to—
  - (i) provide an explanation as to why the party does not agree with the Appeal Commissioners' proposed course of action, or
  - (ii) comply with the direction to the Appeal Commissioners' satisfaction.

The Appeal Commissioners are required to consider any objection to their proposed dismissal of an appeal but having done so, they may, nevertheless, proceed to dismiss the appeal. Their decision to dismiss the appeal is stated to be final and conclusive and, therefore, cannot be further appealed.

2.3 Collection of Tax at Source

2.301 Outline of collection at source procedure

The system of collection of tax at source is an important feature of income tax procedure. In order to assist the collection of tax and to prevent its avoidance, certain types of income are charged to tax at the point where the income emerges from its source, ie at the point of payment. The following types of payment are subject to collection of tax at source:

(a) annuities and other annual payments, patent royalties and certain rents, royalties and similar payments in respect of certain mines, quarries, etc;

(b) yearly interest paid by any person to another person located outside the State and yearly interest paid by companies (other than banking companies) to any person wherever located (see **2.306**);

(c) payments made to persons located outside the State in respect of:

   (i) any rent for any lands, tenements or hereditaments in the State when paid, whether in the State or elsewhere, directly to a person whose usual place of abode is outside the State (TCA 1997, s 1041),

   (ii) any capital sum paid to a person not resident in the State for the purchase from him of patent rights under an Irish patent (see **8.304**), and

   (iii) any capital sum paid to a person not resident in the State for the purchase from him of scheduled mineral assets;

(d) interest paid or credited on relevant deposits with banks, building societies and certain other financial institutions (see **2.401**);

(e) payments made by any banker or other person in the State of public revenue or foreign public revenue dividends chargeable under Sch C (see **2.309**);

(f) payments obtained by any banker or other person in the State for a resident person of any interest, dividends or other annual payments of any non-resident company, society, association, etc (see **2.310**);

(g) payments of any salaries, wages, directors' fees, etc chargeable to tax under Sch E when made by an employer (see **Divisions 11**);

(h) payments made in the performance of any construction contract to certain subcontractors (see **2.311**);

(i) payments made by government departments, public sector bodies, etc for fees in respect of professional services (see **2.501**); and

(j) dividends paid by Irish resident companies (see **9.102**).

In general, the procedure for collection of tax discussed here involves the assessment by inspectors of taxes of the persons making the payments in question at the standard rate of income tax on the gross amount paid. The person so assessed is not the person who ultimately enjoys the income, but the person making the payment.

2.302 Annual payments and royalties

TCA 1997, s 237 may be read, omitting certain parts of it in this extract, as follows:

> Where any annuity or any other annual payment apart from yearly interest of money (whether payable within or outside the State … or whether payable half-yearly or at any shorter or more distant periods) is payable wholly out of profits or gains brought into charge to income tax … the whole of those profits or gains shall be assessed and charged with income tax on the person liable to the interest, annuity, or annual payment … and the person liable to make such payment, whether out of the profits or gains charged with income tax or out of any annual payment liable to deduction … shall be entitled, on making such payment, to deduct and retain thereout a sum representing the amount of the income tax thereon at the standard rate for the year in which the amount payable becomes due.

TCA 1997, s 237(2) reads:

> Where any royalty, or other sum, is paid in respect of the user of a patent, wholly out of profits or gains brought into charge to income tax, the person paying the royalty or sum shall be entitled, on making the payment, to deduct and retain thereout a sum representing the amount of tax thereon at the standard rate of income tax for the year in which the amount payable becomes due.

The types of payment covered by TCA 1997, s 237 may be referred to as 'charges on income', which expression, and the way in which charges on income affect the liability to income tax are discussed in more detail in the context of the taxation of individuals in **3.103**. The categories of individuals to whom effective transfers of income can be made by way of annual payments is severely restricted (see **15.405**). Furthermore, TCA 1997, s 242 generally prevents a deduction for annual payments made in return for the receipt of consideration which is not liable to income tax (see below).

The deduction of tax from these TCA 1997, s 237 payments is not confined to individuals. The section applies to any person chargeable to income tax, who makes any of the payments covered wholly out of profits or gains on which he is chargeable to income tax. Where any person chargeable to income tax makes any of these types of payment other than wholly out of profits or gains charged to income tax, deduction of tax at source still applies, but under the rules of TCA 1997, s 238 (see **2.304**).

Annuities and other annual payments

It is not every payment made annually that is an annual payment subject to the rules for deduction of tax at source. The meaning of an 'annual payment' subject to the deduction of income tax at source has been the subject of judicial interpretation in various tax cases over the years. While extracts from judgments from these cases may include references to yearly interest, they should now be read on the basis that interest is no longer an annual payment in the context of TCA 1997, s 237. Extracts from two judgments may be useful here.

Scrutton LJ, in *Earl Howe v IRC* 7 TC 289, stated:

> It is not all payments made every year from which income tax can be deducted. For instance, if a man agrees to pay a motor garage £500 a year for five years for the hire and upkeep of a car, no one suggests that the person paying can deduct income tax from each yearly payment. So if he contracted with a butcher for an annual sum to supply all his meat for a

> year, the annual instalment would not be subject to tax as a whole in the hands of the payee, but only that part of it which was profits.

Accordingly, in *Howe*, it was held that premiums paid on a life insurance policy could not qualify as annual payments (see also *British Commonwealth International Newsfilm Agency Ltd v Mahony* 40 TC 550 – annual subventions to trading company held to be part of its trading income and thus not pure income profit).

Greene MR in *Re Hanbury* 38 TC 588 stated:

> There are two classes of annual payments which fall to be considered for income tax purposes. There is, first of all, that class of annual payment which the Acts regard and treat as being pure income profit of the recipient undiminished by any deduction. Payments of interest, payments of annuities … are payments which are regarded as part of the income of the recipient, and the payer is entitled in estimating his total income to treat those payments as payments which go out of his income altogether. The class of annual payment which falls within that category is quite a limited one. In the other class there stand a number of payments, nonetheless annual, the very quality and nature of which make it impossible to treat them as part of the pure income profit of the recipient, the proper way of treating them being to treat them as an element to be taken into account in discovering what the profits of the recipient are.

These quotations emphasise the essential point that only payments which are 'pure income profit' in the hands of the recipient can qualify as annual payments from which income tax can be deducted at source. In general, pure income profit arises to the recipient if he is not required to incur some expense or to provide goods or services or to give some other consideration in return for the annual payment. This requirement flows logically from the philosophy behind the statutory precursors to TCA 1997, s 237. These were designed to have the liability of the recipient discharged by the payer, who would withhold and retain the tax from the annual payment in question. This mechanism could only be workable if the amount from which tax was withheld by the payer was identical to the amount on which the recipient would otherwise have been liable. Gratuitous payments under deeds of covenant are examples of annual payments constituting pure income profit to the recipient.

In *IRC v National Book League* 37 TC 455, a payment to a charitable organisation, which was in effect a subscription for club facilities, was held not to constitute an annual payment (compare *IRC v London (City of) as Epping Forest Conservators* 34 TC 293; *IRC v Whitworth Park Coal Co Ltd* 38 TC 531).

In *IRC v Duke of Westminster* 19 TC 490, it was held that annual payments under a deed of covenant remained pure income profit, even if there was a counter-agreement that the employee would forego an equivalent amount of his wages. The justification for this decision lay in the fact that the employee was legally entitled to receive the payments whether or not he continued to be in the covenantor's employment.

The *Westminster* case was distinguished (without any clear reasons being given for so doing) in *Essex CC v Ellam* [1989] STC 317. In that case, the taxpayer was the parent of a handicapped child who entered into a deed of covenant in favour of his local County Council. The covenant was executed on the basis that the Council would set off the amount of the payment against the contribution due from him in respect of special schooling for his child. Hoffman J at first instance observed:

> I do not think that there is any need to look for whether the Council was carrying on a trade or whether there are sufficient analogies with other cases. One simply asks, as Lord Donovan put it in *Campbell & Anor v IRC* [see below] whether the payment is 'a taxable

> receipt in the hands of the recipient without any deduction for expenses or the like'. That requires one to assume that the Council is hypothetically a taxpayer, and it seems to me quite untenable to suggest that these payments would, if the Council had been a taxpayer, have been taxable in gross in its hands without any regard to the amount which it had paid out [for the special schooling]. The result is that, in my judgement, the payments were not 'pure profit income'; and were therefore not annual payments …

The court disregarded the theoretical possibility that the Council could have enforced payment under the covenant, even if a contribution were no longer to be required from the taxpayer at some future time.

It is also necessary that the payment should be of an income and not of a capital nature, that it should be made under some binding legal obligation as distinct from being a mere voluntary payment and that it must at least have the capability of recurring as implied by the description 'annual'. A payment made under a deed of covenant counts as being made under a binding legal obligation. The fact that a payment is to be made weekly does not prevent its being annual provided that the weekly payments may continue beyond the year.

The discharge of a capital sum by instalments is not an 'annual payment' within the meaning of TCA 1997, ss 237, 238 (*IRC v Mallaby-Deeley* 23 TC 153): in *Campbell v IRC* 45 TC 427 a series of covenanted sums paid to trustees who were obliged to acquire a capital asset out of those sums were held to be capital in nature.

Payments made in return for the acquisition of a capital asset may however be income in nature, where they are regarded as constituting a stream of income payments rather than instalments of a capital sum received as the price of the asset. Thus, in *Delage v Nugget Polish Co* [1905] LT 682 it was held that payments received in return for granting rights to a secret process were income in nature. The payments in this case were based on a percentage of the payer's gross receipts over a period of 40 years (see also *IRC v Hogarth* 23 TC 491, but contrast *Ramsay v IRC* [1981] STC 174). However, unless the disposal of the asset in question gives rises to an income tax liability in the hands of the disponer the anti-avoidance rules of TCA 1997, s 242 will now generally require the payment to be made gross (see below).

It is also essential that the recipient of the annual payment receives it as his income. Thus, in the *Campbell* case noted above, it was also held that, because the trustees were obliged to apply the annual payments in a prescribed manner those payments did not constitute their 'income' for tax purposes. This reasoning could also be used to justify the outcome in the *Essex* case, since for the years in question, the Council were bound to apply the annual payments for a predetermined purpose (compare *Nightingale v Price* [1996] STC (SCD) 116).

Where the circumstances permit it, payments made annually containing both a capital and an income element may be broken down into their respective parts, with the income element being subject, where appropriate, to the deduction at source rules (*Vestey v IRC* 40 TC 112 discussed in **1.408**).

The meaning of the term 'annuity' is considered at **8.101**.

Patent royalties

TCA 1997, s 237 applies to 'any royalty or other sum paid in respect of the user of a patent', ie irrespective of whether or not the royalty, etc may be an annual payment under general principles. It is open to question whether or not in some cases a patent royalty may be an annual payment within TCA 1997, s 237 or 238. In *Rank Xerox v Lane* [1978] STC 449 it was said in the Court of Appeal:

> Where the position of the payee is such that his absolute entitlement to receive the payments is wholly independent of any outgoings or expenses to which he may be liable we can see no reason in principle why the payments should not be 'pure profit income' and therefore an 'annual payment'.

In the House of Lords [1979] STC 740 Lord Russell indicated that he agreed with this view, but the other Law Lords declined to comment on this issue.

Where the royalties are paid to a person who receives them in the course of his trade then they will clearly not be annual payments since they will not be 'pure income profit' in the hands of the recipient. Other types of royalty, for example, copyright royalties, are not covered by TCA 1997, s 237.

There is no express requirement that payments within TCA 1997, s 237 should be chargeable to income tax (ie under Sch D). However, it is clear from the statutory scheme that this must be the case in so far as TCA 1997, s 237 is concerned and indeed the equivalent wording in TCA 1997, s 238 expressly refers to sums 'charged with tax under Sch D'. So far as TCA 1997, s 237 (dealing with patent royalties) is concerned, it seems inconceivable in any event that, in the absence of a clear direction to the contrary, the withholding mechanism could apply to income outside the scope of Irish taxation. This would be inconsistent with the generally accepted territorial limits of Irish tax law (see **1.501**); note also the comments of the court in *IRC v Longmans Green & Co* 17 TC 272.

It is more arguable whether or not TCA 1997, s 237 applies to foreign source income received by an Irish resident (taxable on worldwide income) and thus strictly chargeable under Sch D (albeit as a foreign possession).

For the section to apply, it is necessary that the sum paid be in the nature of income. Sums paid by reference to the degree of usage of the patent will almost invariably be of an income nature, whether paid as recurring royalties or as a lump sum. In *Constantinesco v Rex* 11 TC 730, an award of a lump sum made by the Royal Commission on Awards to Inventors for the use of a patent for a number of years previously was held to be paid in respect of the user of the patent, although paid in one amount.

In the case of *IRC v British Salmson Aero Engines Ltd* 22 TC 29, a lump sum payment of £25,000 payable in three instalments on and following the signing of an agreement for an exclusive licence to use a patent was held to be of a capital nature not subject to the deduction at source rules, but these rules did apply to a further payment by way of royalty of £2,500 for each of the ten years after the signing of the agreement. In *IRC v Rustproof Window Co* 29 TC 243 a lump sum payable under similar arrangements was held to be of an income nature (in this case the license was not exclusive and was subject to a quantitative limit). Where the licensee does not obtain clearly defined rights over the patent in question (such as, for example, exclusive use of the patented invention within a stated territory), then it is likely that any lump sum paid to the patentor will be of an income nature.

Agreements may provide for payments described as royalties as consideration for the use of secret processes, blueprints, designs, drawings, etc not protected by patents or for know-how, technical advice and assistance or for the use of trademarks. Such payments are not covered by the rules for deduction at source unless and to the extent that the rights to use the secret processes, trade marks, etc are incidental to the rights protected by a patent (*Paterson Engineering v Duff* 25 TC 43). Certain capital sums paid to non-residents are also subject to the TCA 1997, s 238 procedure (see **2.304**).

As in the case of TCA 1997, s 237, it is again arguable whether or not TCA 1997, s 238 applies to foreign source income received by an Irish resident (taxable on worldwide income) and thus strictly chargeable under Sch D (albeit as a foreign possession under Case III). Certainly, where a non-resident pays foreign royalties to an Irish resident it appears to be accepted in practice that TCA 1997, s 238 is not at issue (see **Division 8**).

Mining, etc rents

TCA 1997, s 104 requires certain mining, etc rents and royalties to be treated for the purpose of TCA 1997, ss 237 and 238 as if they were royalties paid in respect of the user of a patent so as to be subject to the deduction of tax at source procedure under TCA 1997, s 237 or, where appropriate, under TCA 1997, s 238. The payments in question are any rents, tolls, duties, royalties or annual or periodical payments in the nature of rent, when payable in respect of any premises or easements used, occupied or enjoyed in connection with any of the concerns the profits or gains arising from which are chargeable to tax under Sch D Case I(b).

Sch D Case I(b) charges to tax profits or gains arising out of any lands, tenements and hereditaments in the case of certain types of concern – principally mines, quarries, ironworks, gasworks and other concerns of a similar nature which derive their profits out of lands, etc, listed in the Case. The deduction at source rules do not, however, apply where the rent or other payment is rendered to the person entitled to it by the supply of produce of the concern in question.

2.303 Operation of TCA 1997, s 237

The way in which TCA 1997, s 237 operates to collect tax at source is different in several respects from the operation of TCA 1997, s 238. First, the person making a payment covered by TCA 1997, s 237 is not obliged to deduct income tax, but is entitled to do so. Secondly, the tax which he may deduct is taken at the standard rate on the date the amount payable becomes due, whereas any tax deductible under TCA 1997, s 238(1) is computed at the standard rate in force on the date payment is actually made.

Although not obliged to deduct income tax, any person making a payment covered by TCA 1997, s 237 should not fail to do so, since his entitlement to deduct and retain income tax is his only means of obtaining relief from tax at the standard rate on the payment. If the payer is an individual, the gross amount of the payment is deducted in arriving at his total income but the procedure where income tax at the standard rate is added to his income tax payable has the effect of making him pay income tax at that rate on the payment. If he has not made the tax deduction and retained the tax, he must bear the cost of it himself.

The exercise of the payer's right to withhold and retain income tax from a payment covered by TCA 1997, s 237 does not, except for certain payments under foreign contracts (see **2.307**), give the person entitled to the payment any right to the balance of it. TCA 1997, s 237 provides that the recipient must allow the deduction so that the person making it is discharged of his full obligation to the recipient when he pays him the net after tax amount.

It is important that the person making a payment under TCA 1997, s 237 should deduct income tax at the time of making the payment. If he fails to do so then, he cannot recover the tax from subsequent payments. TCA 1997, s 1087(2) provides a statutory exception where a payment is made in a tax year before the passing of a Finance Act increasing the standard rate of tax. In this event, the payer may make up the shortfall when deducting tax from the next payment made after the passing of the Act; if there are no later payments, the tax under-deducted may be recovered as a debt from the payee. Payments voluntarily made gross under a mistake of law do not generally entitle the payer to recover the tax later (*Warren v Warren* [1895] 72 LT 628). The right to recover an under-deduction is not lost if the failure to deduct was due to a mistake of fact (*Turvey v Dentons* (1923) Ltd [1952] 2 All ER 1025). Where an annual payment is made by instalments then it is possible to recover the tax under-deducted against subsequent instalments of the same payment. This applies even if the instalments are paid in arrears (*Taylor v Taylor* [1937] 3 All ER 571). In some cases, personal representatives may be entitled to recover the tax under-deducted (see *Re Musgrave Machell v Parry* [1926] 2 Ch 417).

The treatment of TCA 1997, s 237 payments in relation to the tax position of an individual payer is referred to under the heading 'charges on income' in **3.103**. An example of the treatment affecting persons other than an individual taxable in his own right may now be useful.

'Payment' for these purposes was said by Lord Wright MR in *Rhokana Corporation v IRC* 21 TC 552, to include 'everything which is in a commercial sense a 'payment' upon the making of which the statutory deduction may be made. Thus, it includes payment by cheque, by transfer of … any … marketable security or by the making of credit entries in books of account'. In the *Rhokana* case it was held that payments in foreign currency fell within the deduction procedures (see also *Butler v Butler* [1961] 1 All ER 810, where payment by way of set off against an amount due to the payer was held to fall within the deduction procedures). As regards the making of accounting entries, see the discussion on this issue in the context of interest payments in **2.306**.

Example 2.303.1

Mrs R Rattler and Quality Bank Ltd, are the joint trustees of a settlement. The trustees' only income assessable for the year 2016 is interest on Irish government loans. On 5 June 2016 the trustees pay an annuity of €2,000 to Mr A Polarbare. The taxable position of the trustees for the year 2016 is as follows:

	€
Income chargeable under Sch D Case III	10,000
Income tax payable:	
€10,000 at 20%	2,000

Although the annuity is the income of Mr Polarbare, the trustees are assessed on their full income for the year of €10,000 without any deduction for the annuity paid out of that income. TCA 1997, s 237 entitles the trustees to deduct and retain income tax of €400 (€2,000 at 20 per cent) and only pay the net amount of €1,600 to Mr Polarbare. The trustees' net tax outlay is therefore €1,600, ie income tax paid to the Collector General of €2,000 less the €400 deducted from the annuity and retained by them.

The trustees' net outlay of €1,600 is the equivalent of income tax at 20 per cent on a net income of €8,000, ie the government loan interest of €10,000 as reduced by the gross annuity of €2,000 payable in that year.

Anti-avoidance measure

TCA 1997, s 242 contains an anti-avoidance measure which excludes certain annuities or other annual payments from the rules of TCA 1997, s 237. This measure applies – with certain exceptions – to any annuity or other annual payment made under a liability incurred for any consideration which is not brought fully into account in computing the taxable income of the person making the payment. The measure is designed to counter the so called 'reverse annuity' scheme under which a person enters into an agreement to make annual payments to another person (usually a finance company) in consideration for a tax free lump sum paid by the other person.

In any case to which TCA 1997, s 242 applies, the payment must be made without deducting any income tax (ie it must be paid gross) and it cannot be treated as a charge against the income of the person making the payment. In other words, the person paying the annuity or making the annual payment ceases to get any form of tax relief for the payment.

The rules of TCA 1997, s 242 are dealt with more fully in **17.305**, where the exceptions are set out.

Example 2.303.2

Take the facts of **Example 2.303.1**, but assume that the trustees are paying the €2,000 annuity to Mr Polarbare in consideration of a lump sum of €10,000 previously paid by him to them. None of the exceptions mentioned in **17.305** applies to the annuity payments.

TCA 1997, s 242 requires the trustees to pay the annuity of €2,000 gross to Mr Polarbare. The trustees' net tax outlay is now €2,000 (ie the income tax paid to the Collector-General without any retention of tax in respect of the annuity).

2.304 Operation of TCA 1997, s 238

TCA 1997, s 238 applies directly to the same types of payment as TCA 1997, s 237, although as noted in **2.303**, s 238(2) explicitly refers to annual payments, etc 'charged with tax under Sch D'. However, TCA 1997, s 238(2) applies only where the payments are not made wholly out of profits or gains 'brought into charge' to income tax. This means that TCA 1997, s 238(2) applies, in the case of any person chargeable to income tax, to payments of the types described in **2.302** if, and to the extent that, the total of such payments made by that person in a given tax year exceeds his income chargeable to income tax for that year. The section applies also to these types of payments made by a company chargeable to corporation tax (since such a company's income is not charged to income tax at all) (see **2.305**). In addition, TCA 1997, s 238 is applied to capital payments made to non-residents in respect of the purchase of Irish patent rights which are charged to tax under Sch D Case IV (see **8.304**). A similar regime applies to capital sums paid to non-residents in respect of scheduled mineral assets.

TCA 1997, s 238(3) requires any person, making any payment to which the section applies, and which is not payable or not wholly payable out of profits or gains brought into charge to income tax, to deduct income tax at the standard rate in force at the time of the payment. The payer is legally bound to deduct the tax, and not just entitled to do so. It is to be noted that this rule applies also where the payment is partially, but not wholly, covered by the payer's income. It seems that, in contrast to TCA 1997, s 237, under-deductions of tax are not recoverable against subsequent instalments of an annual payment (*Tenbry Investments Ltd v Peugeot Motor Co Ltd* [1992] STC 791).

The person making any payment covered by the section is required by TCA 1997, s 238(3) to deliver 'forthwith' to the Revenue Commissioners an account of the payment and of the income tax deducted by him in making it. The TCA 1997, s 238 mechanism applies at the point of payment. In *Rye v Eyre* 19 TC 164, it was held that where a firm of solicitors remitted a payment on the instructions of their clients they were the persons 'by or through whom' that payment had been made. Accordingly, they were the persons liable to account for income tax under provisions analogous to the use of TCA 1997, s 238. In the House of Lords it was suggested that the words 'by whom' were most apt to refer to a principal and the words 'through whom' to an agent.

In *Howells v IRC* 22 TC 501, the taxpayer was a solicitor who had lent money to his client. The taxpayer subsequently received the proceeds of sales made by his client, in his capacity as his client's solicitor. The taxpayer deducted the amount of interest due to him from the sale proceeds before remitting these to his client. The court held that the taxpayer was the person (in his capacity as solicitor) 'by or through whom' the payment of interest had been made to himself (in his capacity as lender). Accordingly, the taxpayer was liable to account for tax under the equivalent to TCA 1997, s 238 (which at that time also covered annual interest).

The inspector of taxes receiving this account is then required to assess the payment on the payer so that the Collector General may issue a demand for the tax due. In practice, individuals and other persons chargeable to income tax normally inform the inspector of TCA 1997, s 238 payments by including particulars in their annual income tax returns.

An assessment made under this rule is generally referred to as a 's 238 assessment'. If the inspector is not satisfied with the account given or if the payer fails to deliver the required account, the inspector is empowered to make an assessment estimating the tax payable to the best of his judgment. The taxpayer has the same rights of appeal against a s 238 assessment as he has against other income tax assessments. The other provisions of the Income Tax Acts relating to the collection and recovery of income tax, to the rehearing of appeals and to cases to be stated for the opinion of the High Court apply also where tax is charged under TCA 1997, s 238.

TCA 1997, s 1087(1) provides that where a payment is made in a tax year before the passing of a Finance Act increasing the standard rate of tax any tax under-deducted in consequence may be recovered from the payee by an assessment under Sch D Case IV; the agent entrusted with the payment must if so required supply the Revenue Commissioners with the names and addresses of the payees and the amounts of the payments.

When the annual payments, etc are made partially, but not wholly, out of income charged to income tax, TCA 1997, s 238 applies rather than TCA 1997, s 237, but in this case the s 238 assessment is only made on the excess of the total annual payments for the year over the chargeable income.

Where TCA 1997, s 237 applies the payer remains liable to tax on an account of his income equal to the annual payment, but his liability in this respect is limited to tax at the standard rate (TCA 1997, s 59). This amount is not included in his total income, so that the gross amount of the annual payment is regarded as a deduction in computing that total income.

TCA 1997, s 959B, which provides that certain persons will not be regarded as a 'chargeable person' for the purpose of the 'self assessment' system for the collection of income tax, provides that a person is not a 'chargeable person' if he is chargeable to tax by reason only of TCA 1997, s 238 (or TCA 1997, s 239). In any such case, the self assessment rules (see **Division 2**) do not apply to that person so that his liability to make a payment of preliminary tax and to make a tax return on or before the specified return date are not applicable. Instead the taxpayer's obligation to make a return is that under

TCA 1997, s 238 and he need not pay over the tax until an assessment is received from the inspector under TCA 1997, s 238.

However, the emphasis given to the word 'only' should be noted. If a person has any tax liability[1] at all for a tax year (other than only on income taxed under PAYE) before considering any tax for which he is entitled by TCA 1997, s 237 or required by TCA 1997, s 238 to deduct from annual payments made by him, then he is a chargeable person for the year in question. He is therefore required to make the normal income tax return by the specified return date (including particulars of all payments within TCA 1997, s 237 or TCA 1997, s 238) if the late return surcharge under TCA 1997, s 1086 (see **2.110**) is to be avoided. If this surcharge applies, the tax subject to it includes any tax for which the chargeable person is liable to account under TCA 1997, s 238.

Notes

1. (If a person has any liability for the self-employed PRSI contribution or universal social charge payable by direct assessment, ie otherwise than by deduction under the PAYE system, then he is a chargeable person for the year concerned even if he has no income tax liability other than under TCA 1997, s 238).

2.305 Profits brought into charge to tax'

These words refer to income chargeable to income tax, and not to any other tax (see definition of 'tax' in TCA 1997, ss 2(1), 3(1)). In addition to payments made by companies chargeable to corporation tax, it follows that annual payments, etc made out of income exempted from income tax or paid by charities or other bodies exempted from income tax cannot be treated as made out of chargeable income and must always fall under TCA 1997, s 238, rather than under TCA 1997, s 237.

In other cases, the question is normally determined by comparing the aggregate of all the relevant annual payments, etc falling due for payment in a tax year with the total of the payer's income as actually chargeable to tax for that year. If the total of the chargeable income is equal to or exceeds the aggregate of the annual payments, etc, then the payments are considered to be made wholly out of profits charged to tax so that the TCA 1997, s 237 procedure applies. For the purpose of this comparison, the income chargeable to tax is the sum of the assessments under the various Schedules plus any income received by the taxpayer which has itself suffered income tax at source, but reduced by any deductions (other than the annual payments, etc) which are made in arriving at his total income for the year.

It has been held that the profits or gains brought into charge to tax are those profits that are assessable for the year and on which tax is payable (*Allchin v Corporation of South Shields* 25 TC 445). For example, a trading loss brought forward from a previous year and set off against Sch D Case I profits of the year of assessment was held to be deductible in arriving at the chargeable income available to cover the annual payments made in the year (*Trinidad Petroleum Development Co Ltd v IRC* 21 TC 1). It is irrelevant whether payment is made out of cash resources representing income or capital (*Postlethwaite v IRC* 41 TC 224).

Annual payments, etc made out of capital are not made wholly out of profits or gains charged to tax and are therefore always covered by TCA 1997, s 238 and not by TCA 1997, s 237. Normally, where a taxpayer has both capital and income funds, the annual payments, etc are presumed to be paid first out of income brought into charge to tax and only, if and to the extent that the income is insufficient, are they regarded as paid out of capital. However, in certain circumstances a taxpayer may by some specific action appropriate the payments to capital so that he effectively denies himself the possibility of claiming that the payments were made out of profits or gains brought into charge to income tax.

This question has been discussed in several English cases relevant to the time when companies were chargeable to income tax. Lord Hanworth MR, in *Central London Railway Co Ltd v IRC* 20 TC 102 stated:

> … in the ordinary course where there is a mixed fund but where there is an abundance of funds brought into charge, the ordinary appropriation should be deemed to take place, namely, that the subject has paid the money which he has paid out of the available fund which has been already brought into charge and that he is entitled, therefore, to retain the tax from the sum which he has paid …

Lord Hanworth described this principle as the 'rule of the road'. But he went on to decide that, on the facts of the case before him, the company had for good reasons, in order to leave a larger sum available for the distribution of dividends, in fact charged the payments in question to capital. Since the company had done this, he concluded that the payments could not then be treated as paid out of chargeable income.

In *Chancery Lane Safe Deposit & Offices Co Ltd v IRC* 43 TC 83, Lord Morris of Borth-y-Gest in approving the decision in the *Central London Railway Co Ltd* case, stated:

> If a company makes and adheres to a decision that a payment should be made out of capital and orders all its affairs on that basis, it would seem strange if it could assert that the payment should be deemed to be one payable out of profits or gains … If a payment is attributed to capital, the practical result follows that the sum available or carried forward as available for distribution by way of dividends is increased … It would seem to be incongruous, however, if a company having decided … to charge a payment to capital and having regulated its proceedings on that basis, could say that the payment was not to be deemed to be charged to capital.

(Note also to similar effect *Fitzleet Estates v Cherry* [1977] STC 397).

It may be noted that both these cases involved annual payments that were charged to capital in the accounts of the companies concerned at a time when company profits in the UK were charged to income tax, so that there was a question of which of the UK sections comparable to the Irish TCA 1997, ss 237 and 238 was to apply.

This particular issue is no longer relevant to any company whose profits are chargeable to corporation tax. In practice, the question of appropriating payments to capital is not likely to be relevant to the taxation of individuals who are presumed as a 'rule of the road' to make annual payments, etc first out of chargeable income to the extent of that income.

The appropriation of annual payments to capital could be relevant in the case of a settlement where there are one or more beneficiaries entitled to the income and one or more others entitled to the capital. While normally any annuity or annual payment made by the trustees is regarded as coming first out of the income, if the trustees in the exercise of a power permitting them to do so, specifically appropriate the annual payment out of capital, it is possible that the inspector of taxes could seek to assess the trustees under TCA 1997, s 238.

Example 2.305.1

> Take the facts of **Example 2.303.1**, but assume that the trustees pay the annuity of €2,000 to Mr Polarbare out of capital in 2016, thus leaving all the income available for distribution to another beneficiary, Ms Redtiger, who is entitled to any residue of income.

In this event, not only are the trustees assessed under Sch D Case III for 2016 on the full assessable income of €10,000 without any deduction for the annuity, but a TCA 1997, s 238 assessment could be made on them to charge the tax of €400 which they should have deducted from the annuity paid otherwise than out of chargeable income (ie out of capital).

2.306 Deduction of tax from interest paid

As a general rule, TCA 1997, s 246(2) requires a person paying yearly interest charged with tax under Sch D to deduct income tax and to account for it under the TCA 1997, s 238 procedure in the case of:

(a) interest paid by any person (including a company) to another person whose usual place of abode is outside the State; and

(b) interest paid by a company to any person irrespective of the situation of the recipient's place of abode.

In any such case where TCA 1997, s 246(2) requires income tax to be deducted from a yearly interest payment, the payer is required to account to the Revenue Commissioners for the tax under the assessment and collection procedure provided for in TCA 1997, s 238 (and not under the TCA 1997, s 237 procedure). The question of whether or not the interest paid exceeds the profits charged to income tax is not relevant. The yearly interest paid does not reduce the payer's income as a charge on income (unlike the other annual payments within TCA 1997, s 237).

It should be noted that a person other than a company is not entitled or required to deduct income tax on paying yearly interest to a person whose usual place of abode is within the State. On the other hand, if the recipient's usual place of abode is abroad, tax is normally deductible irrespective of whether the payer is an individual, a company or any other person, but with certain exceptions. The meaning of the term 'usual place of abode' is discussed in **2.308**. The requirement for a company to deduct income tax does not apply when the yearly interest is paid by it in a fiduciary or representative capacity, for example, as a trustee of a settlement, to a person whose usual place of abode is within the State.

TCA 1997, s 246(2) does not apply to require the deduction of income tax from the payment of interest that is not yearly interest, nor from any yearly interest that is not chargeable under Sch D (the definition of 'interest' is considered in **8.101**; the question of when interest is or is not chargeable under Sch D is discussed at **2.307**). It is necessary, therefore, to distinguish 'short' interest from yearly interest. Interest payable in respect of a short loan is not yearly interest. Short loans are 'loans made for a period short of one year, loans which are not intended to be continued, and are not continued, for a longer period' (*Goslings & Sharpe v Blake* 2 TC 450). The real intention of the parties is critical so that interest on a mortgage loan, albeit technically repayable on demand, was held to be yearly in *Corinthian Securities Ltd v Cato* 46 TC 93: see also *Minsham Properties v Price* [1990] STC 718. Other leading cases include *IRC v Hay STC 636 and Jefford v Gee* [1970] 2 QB 130).

If an interest bearing loan is made for a period which is capable of extending for a year or longer, even if in fact it does not last that long, the interest is almost certain to be treated as yearly interest. For example, if Mr A Beta lends €10,000 to a company for an indefinite period or for, say, 18 months, any interest payable by the company on the loan is yearly interest even if the company subsequently decides to repay the loan after 11 months (or even after one month); the company must deduct income tax unless any of the exceptions mentioned below apply. On the other hand, if the loan had been given for a specific period of, say, 11 months and 20 days, the interest would normally be short interest, payable without any tax deduction. A payment of interest can include the crediting of the amount due in the accounts of the borrower (see *IRC v Doncaster* 8 TC 623). However, where interest is merely accrued and added to the amount due, this will not constitute payment, irrespective of the entries made in the books of the lender (*IRC v Paton* 21 TC 626) and/or the borrower (*Minsham Properties v Price* [1990] STC 718). Interest which is merely capitalised is not regarded as paid until and unless the amount due is actually discharged (*IRC v Oswald* 26 TC 435). In *Cross v London and Provincial Trust Ltd* 21 TC 705, it was held that, where a debtor company issued bonds in discharge of its liability to pay interest, this did not constitute payment, which would only arise when the bonds were redeemed by the issuer. This decision created opportunities for tax avoidance, since the sale of the bonds by the holders did not give rise to a taxable receipt. The decision in *Cross* has been overriden by TCA 1997, s 51 in respect of bonds, stocks, shares, securities and certificates of indebtedness issued by any State or public body, or by any body corporate.

TCA 1997, s 246(3) contains a number of exceptions to the general rule of s (2). Income tax is not deductible from any of the following types of interest payment:

(a) interest paid in the State on a loan or advance from a bank carrying on a *bona fide* banking business in the State (see *Hafton Properties Ltd v McHugh* [1987] STC 16);

(b) interest paid by such a bank in the ordinary course of such businesses (for example, to its depositors);[1]

(c) interest paid by companies to a company which carries on a trade of lending money but who are not licensed banks and interest paid by the latter to Irish resident group companies;

(d) interest paid to a person whose usual place of abode is outside the State by a specified collective investment undertaking within TCA 1997, s 734;

(e) interest paid by a company authorised by the Revenue Commissioners to pay without deduction of tax, for example, when paid to a non-resident person exempted from Irish tax on the interest under a double taxation agreement;

(f) interest on any securities in respect of which the Minister for Finance has given a direction under, Taxes Consolidation Act 1997, s 36 (Government and other public securities);

(g) certain interest paid by Industrial and Provident Societies;

(h) certain interest paid to directors and directors' associates of close companies;

(i) interest paid in the State to an investment undertaking (within the meaning of s 739B);

(j) interest paid to or by the National Asset Management Agency (NAMA);

(k) interest paid to the National Treasury Management Agency (NTMA), the State acting through the NTMA or a fund investment vehicle (within the meaning of NTMA (Amendment) Act 2014, s 37) of which the Minister for Finance is sole beneficial owner (from 22 December 2014);

(l) interest paid in the State to an exempt approved pension scheme (within the meaning of TCA 1997, s 774);

(m) interest paid in the State to a qualifying company (within the meaning of TCA 1997, s 110);

(n) the Strategic Banking Corporation of Ireland or a subsidiary wholly owned by it or a subsidiary wholly owned by any such subsidiary (from 28 July 2014);

(o) interest paid by a qualifying company (again, within the meaning of TCA 1997, s 110) to a person resident in a relevant territory (see meaning of 'relevant territory' set out in (p) below), except where the payee is a company operating in the State through a branch or agency; or

(p) interest, other than interest referred to above, paid by a company or a collective investment undertaking in the ordinary course of a trade or business carried on by that person to a company which is resident for the purposes of tax a 'relevant territory' (ie an EU Member State or a country with which Ireland has a tax treaty or with which Ireland has signed a tax treaty which has yet come into force) and (with effect for loan agreements executed on or after 3 April 2010) where such territory imposes tax generally on the receipt of interest from companies resident outside that territory. Alternatively, no withholding tax is required if the interest is exempt under a double tax treaty or would be so exempt if arrangements entered into with the relevant territory had already entered into force. Neither exception applies where the interest is paid in connection with a trade or business carried on by the recipient in Ireland through a branch or agency.

Notes

1. (While a bank is not required to withhold tax under the above provisions, it may be required to withhold tax under the DIRT provisions).

Parts (l) and (m) above were added by FA 2003, s 48(2) and provided exemption from withholding tax on interest payments to a Special Purpose Vehicle company (SPV) under securitisation transactions (in conjunction with the newly drafted TCA 1997, s 110) in the State and interest payments made by an SPV where the interest is paid to an EU resident or a resident of a State with which Ireland has a double taxation agreement.

TCA 1997, s 246 does not require or entitle a company paying interest that is treated as a distribution by TCA 1997, s 130 to deduct income tax whether the recipient's place of abode is within or outside the State. This type of interest payment is chargeable to tax under Sch F and not under Sch D so that TCA 1997, s 246 does not apply to it at all.

It should also be noted that TCA 1997, s 246 does not apply to interest paid under the European Communities (Late Payment in Commercial Transactions) Regulations 2002 (SI 388/2002) (See **Division 3.2**).

Quoted bearer eurobonds

TCA 1997, s 64 provides another exception to the general rule of TCA 1997, s 246(2). It provides that the requirement of the latter subsection for the person paying yearly interest charged under Sch D to deduct income tax is not to apply to interest paid on any quoted Eurobond (as defined below) in either of two excepted cases. The excepted cases are:

(a) where the person by or through whom the interest payment is made is not in the State; or

(b) where the interest payment is made by or through a person in the State and either:

(i) the quoted Eurobond is held in a recognised clearing system (as defined below), or

(ii) the beneficial owner of the quoted Eurobond (being beneficially entitled to the interest) is a person not resident in the State who has made the 'non-resident's' declaration mentioned in TCA 1997, s 64 (see below).

A 'quoted Eurobond' is defined as a security which:

(a) is issued by a company (which may be either a resident or a non-resident one);
(b) is quoted on a recognised stock exchange;
(c) carries a right to interest.

Prior to 2 February 2006, there was a further requirement that (c) the bond had to be in bearer form.

A 'recognised clearing system' is defined as any system for clearing quoted Eurobonds or relevant foreign securities which is for the time being designed for the purpose of this section by order of the Revenue Commissioners as a recognised clearing system.

'Relevant foreign securities', as mentioned in the definition of a recognised clearing system, are either of:

(I) any stocks, funds, shares or securities of any company or other body of persons not resident in the State (within TCA 1997, Pt 4, see also **2.310**); or

(II) any securities which give rise to foreign public revenue dividends within TCA 1997, s 32 (dividends payable outside the State out of the public revenue of any foreign state, see also **2.309**).

In the case of interest paid on a quoted Eurobond paid by or through a person in the State (the payer) to a non-resident beneficial owner (ie a case within (b)(ii) above), the person in the State by or through whom the payment is made is required to make a return of the payment to the appropriate inspector of taxes. This statement must state the payer's name and address and must describe the payment. It must be delivered to the inspector within 12 months after the payment was made. However, should the inspector request an account of the payment at any earlier date, the payer must give that account to the inspector on demand (TCA 1997, s 64(3)).

TCA 1997, s 64(2)(b)(ii) requires the non-resident beneficial owner entitled to the Eurobond interest (where paid by or through a person in the State) to make a formal declaration of non-residence if he is not to suffer tax by deduction under TCA 1997, s 246. This declaration, which must be in the form prescribed by the Revenue Commissioners and must be signed by the beneficial owner, is required to give the following particulars:

(a) a declaration that, at the time it is made, he is not resident in the State;

(b) his name and the address of his principal place of residence and the name of the country in which he is resident at the time the declaration is made;

(c) an undertaking that, if he should later become resident in the State, he will notify the bank or other person by or through whom the Eurobond interest is paid; and

(d) such other information as the Revenue Commissioners in their prescribed form may require (TCA 1997, s 64(7)).

For the obligation imposed by TCA 1997, s 64 on an Irish collecting agent to withhold and account for tax on Eurobond interest (except where the beneficial owner is a non-resident), see **2.310**.

2.307 Payments to non-residents

Westminster Bank Executor & Trustee Co (CI Ltd) v National Bank of Greece SA 46 TC 491 confirms the principle that an annual payment made by an Irish resident, but which represents a foreign source, and is received by a non-resident falls outside the scope of TCA 1997, ss 237 and 238. This is because such a payment is outside the scope of Irish taxation, and therefore is not chargeable under Sch D (note the discussion of s 237 at **2.301**). In theory, this principle may need to be modified where the recipient is not resident but is ordinarily resident and thus may be liable under Sch D on such payments (see **13.504**). As noted at **2.302** and **2.303**, it is not clear whether s 237 and s 238 apply to foreign source payments, even if they are liable to Irish tax by virtue of the residence (or ordinary residence) status of the recipient.

The rule which generally applies for the purpose of resolving conflict of law issues is that 'choses in action' are situate in the country where they are properly recoverable and can be enforced. In the case of a debt, the rights of recovery and enforcement will normally be where the debtor resides. Thus, in *Alloway v Phillips* [1980] STC 490, the right to receive a lump sum from a newspaper in London under a contract for services rendered outside the UK was held to represent a UK source (taxable under the UK equivalent of Sch D Case IV).

It may be noted that the concept of 'residence' for conflict of laws purposes does not necessarily coincide with that for tax purposes. Thus, for example, a company is regarded as resident for the former purposes where it is incorporated and/or where it does business. If the company is resident in two or more places, the place in which the primary obligation must be performed is decisive (see eg *Kwok Chi Leung Karl v Commissioners of Estate Duty* [1988] STC 728, a Privy Council case).

In *IRC v Broome's Exors* 19 TC 667, the executors of an individual who had resided in Kenya and the UK assumed liability for a loan entered into by the deceased in Kenya and which was secured on non-UK assets. The loan was enforceable in Kenya, and also the UK (once the executors had assumed liability). It was held that interest on the loan arose from a UK source: the executors were resident there and the debt was paid out of UK sources.

In the *National Bank of Greece* case, the relevant territorial factors in respect of a mortgage bearer bond (which it appears was not under seal) were held to be as follows:

(a) the obligation was undertaken by a principal debtor, which was a foreign corporation;
(b) the obligation was guaranteed by another foreign corporation with no place of business in the UK;
(c) the obligation was secured by lands and public revenues in Greece; and
(d) funds for payments by the principal debtor or interest to residents outside Greece would have been provided either by a remittance from Greece or funds remitted by debtors from abroad (even though a cheque might be drawn in London).

In the *National Bank of Greece* case, the debtor had defaulted and a successor to the guarantor which in fact carried on business in the UK paid the interest; the guarantee was enforceable under UK law. Lord Hailsham, giving the main judgment in the House of Lords in that case, commented:

> … the bond itself is a foreign document, and the obligation to pay principal and interest to which the bond gives rise were obligations whose source is to be found in this document.

Lord Hailsham's conclusion suggests that it was the original nature of the obligation in these circumstances which was decisive, since the payments were made under that same obligation, notwithstanding the change in the identity of the payer. The decision in *Broome's Executors* may perhaps be distinguishable on the basis that there was a right of action there against the personal representatives per se. The decision in *National Bank of Greece* may also suggest that, at least in the case of a debt which is not under seal (see below), factors apart from the residence of the debtor may be significant, perhaps in particular the location of land on which the debt is secured.

For conflict of laws purposes, a debt under seal ('specialty debt') is located where the deed is located, a factor not enumerated in the decision in the *National Bank* case, presumably because not relevant there. In *Murtagh v Rusk* VI ITR 817, the High Court distinguished the decision in *National Bank of Greece* on effectively just these grounds in respect of interest payable on bearer loan notes issued under seal by a UK resident company. The loan notes were executed in the UK and were subject to UK law; the interest arising thereon was payable out of UK funds into and was subject to deduction of UK tax at source. However, they were not registered on any register of the company and were physically held in the Isle of Man.

Mr Justice TC Smyth, upholding the decision of the Appeal Commissioners that the loan notes did not represent a UK source, observed:

> In the Conflict of Laws (Dicey and Morris) 12th ed 1993 Vol 2 under the title Law of Property – nature and situs of Property – Specialties, the learned authors observe:
>
> For taxation purposes, a debt due on a deed or other specialty is situate in the country where the deed itself is situate from time to time and not in a country where the debtor resides.
>
> Notwithstanding the want of attraction that as a matter of law, serious consequences may flow from a peripatetic source of income, in the case of a specialty, the situs of the specialty debt must be taken into consideration. The fact that these decisions may appear remarkably dated in their approach and that its analysis may be out of place in Ireland is not for me, in my judgment, to adjust. This is a matter for the legislature. That is matter for judicial restraint. It is not a matter where legal fashion or jurisprudential contemporary thinking must necessarily or can necessarily be brought to adjust taxation arrangements.

In *Hafton Properties Ltd v McHugh* [1987] STC 16 the Special Commissioner had stated that his conclusion that a mortgage secured on United States property, with a United States mortgagor, was a non-UK source was 'fortified' by the location of the deed in the United States.

For the statutory position in respect of quoted Eurobonds (see **2.306**).

The question as to whether or not the source of an annual payment (ie other than interest) is foreign again seems to depend primarily on where the right to the payment can be enforced. In *Forbes v Dundon* II ITR 491 Kenny J in the High Court, considered the cases of *Chamney v Lewis* 17 TC 318, where the taxpayer was a UK resident entitled to an annuity under a deed of separation executed in India, and *IRC v Anderstrom* 13 TC 482, where the taxpayer was a UK resident entitled to alimony under a Swedish court order (discussed at **13.108**). In both cases, the taxpayers were held to be in receipt of income from a foreign possession.

On the basis of these cases, Kenny J concluded that:

> … a legal right to which a person resident in this country is entitled and which is situate outside Ireland and which may be enforced by legal proceedings in a country outside Ireland is either 'a security' or 'a possession' for the purpose of Income Tax Acts and income which comes from such a right is either 'income arising from securities in a place out of Ireland' or 'income arising from possessions in a place out of Ireland'.

The learned judge accordingly concluded that the UK State Retirement Pension was a foreign source, since the taxpayer:

> has a legal right by proceedings before the minister or the tribunal established under the Act to payment of the retirement pension and that the High Court in England has power to review the decisions of the minister or of the tribunals.

In both the *Chamney* and *Anderstrom* cases the payer was resident outside the UK. However, it is the character of the obligation and not the location of the payer which seems to be decisive. Thus, in *Bingham v IRC* 36 TC 254, the taxpayer was a UK resident who made annual payments under a foreign court order to a non-resident. It was held that the court order was a foreign source and the payment, being received by a non-resident, was accordingly outside the scope of UK taxation.

In *Stokes v Bennett* 34 TC 557, the taxpayer was entitled to receive annual payments under a UK court order, payable by a non-UK resident. The court held that the payer was liable to account for tax under the equivalent to TCA 1997, s 238 (as a non-resident with no UK income he had no income liable to tax). In other words, it was accepted that a UK court order was a UK source, irrespective of the residence of the payer.

In the case of *Keiner v Keiner* 34 TC 346, it was held that UK income tax could not be validly deducted from annual payments made by a UK resident to a non-resident under an obligation created by a contract governed by the law of the State of New Jersey, USA. The case arose from a deed executed under New Jersey law under which the plaintiff undertook to make certain payments to his former wife. It was decided that English law entitling or requiring him to deduct income tax (under the UK equivalents to TCA 1997, ss 237, 238) could not override his former wife's right – under the deed – to receive the full amount of the payments without any tax deduction.

The fact that the recipient of an annual payment in a case covered by the *Keiner v Keiner* rule can claim to be paid gross does not necessarily mean that the person making the payment is relieved from his responsibilities to account for the tax to the Revenue if TCA 1997, s 238 applies. That section would clearly apply if the source of the income is in the State. As discussed above, it is possible (although not beyond argument) that it also applies even in the case of a foreign source where the recipient is resident in the State (ie so that tax is chargeable under Sch D). Although this particular issue was left open decided in *Keiner v Keiner*, it would seem that the facts were similar to those in *Bingham v IRC*, so that the equivalent of TCA 1997, ss 237, 238 were in fact not in point.

However, while the source is usually situated in the country the law of which applies to the contract, there may be exceptions (for example, payments out of the Irish estate of a deceased person even though the contract under which the payments were made was executed abroad – as in *IRC v Broome's Executors* (assuming that this was a correct decision). Except for any such cases, there is unlikely to be any conflict between the *Keiner v Keiner* principle (preventing the payer of the annual payment from deducting tax) and the rules of TCA 1997, s 238 (requiring him to deduct tax on any such annual payments chargeable to tax under Sch D).

It may be noted also that, similarly, where the obligation in question is subject to Irish law, the payer will not have the right to deduct any overseas taxes (*India & General Investment Trust v Borax* [1920] 1 KB 539). Exceptionally, a foreign agreement or instrument may expressly allow for deduction of Irish tax or vice versa.

As discussed at **2.302**, it seems that TCA 1997, s 237, s 238 should apply only where royalties paid to a non-resident are within the ambit of Irish taxation. In line with the principles set out above, it would seem that a foreign patent as such is a non-Irish source, and thus royalties in relation to such a patent if paid to a non-resident should normally fall outside the scope of TCA 1997, s 238. However, note should be taken of the somewhat puzzling decision in *International Combustion v IRC* 16 TC 532 where it was held that the source of royalties paid under a UK patent in respect of its use by a licensee in its manufacturing trade was the UK trade itself. It may be noted that a European patent, in so far as it designates the State, grants the same rights and remedies under Irish law as an Irish patent; see Patents Act 1992, s 119(1)(a).

The position where the patent royalties form part of the trading receipts of a non-resident licensor also raises some difficulty. It is arguable that where a non-resident receives royalties in respect of a foreign patent held by his Irish branch, that such royalties, since they form part of his Sch D profits, are within the ambit of Irish taxation (so that TCA 1997, s 237, s 238 should apply). In practice, it may be that an Inspector would take the straightforward view that TCA 1997, s 237, s 238 apply only to royalties, etc, paid under Irish patents. It is arguable however that, where a non-resident receives royalties in respect of an Irish patent which it holds as part of its foreign trade, such royalties may fall outside the ambit of Irish taxation. This is on the basis that the royalties are merely elements in the profits of a trade exercised outside Ireland by a non-resident (and thus outside the scope of Irish taxation): see *Carson v Cheyney's Executors* 38 TC 240, and note the discussion at **8.207**).

2.308 Other payments covered by TCA 1997, s 238

The Income Tax Acts have extended the deduction at source and the assessment and collection procedure set up in TCA 1997, s 238 to cover certain other types of payment. These are the payments to persons located outside the State listed in item (c) in **2.301**. It may be noted that the deduction applies to rents for lands, etc in the State when paid to a person whose usual place of abode is outside the State whereas the deductions from the other two types of payment apply if the recipient is not resident for tax purposes. In many cases, there is no difference, but in certain cases a person with his usual place of abode in another country may be also a resident in the State (see below).

The object of these rules is to prevent the person whose usual place of abode is outside the State from avoiding liability to tax on certain Irish source income. In each case, the tax must be deducted from the gross amount of the payment made to the foreign located person without any allowance for any expenses he may have to bear connected with the income. However, the recipient may claim a repayment of any tax suffered in excess of his net assessable income from the source in question after deducting any allowable expenses, but in order to do so he must make an income tax return of all his income from Irish sources. If the recipient does so, he is given a repayment if the tax deducted at source exceeds his liability to tax on all his income from sources within the State (see also **13.601** and **13.609**).

The phrase 'usual place of abode' has not been subject to judicial interpretation in the tax context, and it would be dangerous to rely on interpretations arrived at in different statutory contexts. In the case of an individual, it probably denotes his main home. It is therefore possible that an individual whose main place of abode is abroad is nevertheless resident in the State for a particular year of assessment. In the case of a company, it is arguable that its usual place of abode is where it is resident, applying Irish tax law principles (see **1.504**). It may be that an inspector would nevertheless accept that payments made to the Irish branch of a non-resident company need not be subject to TCA 1997, s 238 treatment.

2.309 Schedule C: public revenue dividends

TCA 1997, s 17(1) provides for income tax to be charged under Sch C, as a form of collection of tax at source, from interest, annuities, dividends or shares of annuities payable in the State out of any public revenue. Public revenue for this purpose includes the public revenue of the Irish Government or of any foreign government as well as the revenue of any public authority or institution in the State or in any country outside the State.

Public revenue payments, therefore, include dividends on UK government stocks and Irish tax may therefore be deducted by a bank in respect of interest on such stocks even though UK tax may already have been deducted. Double taxation relief in such cases may be claimed (see **Division 14**).

Sch C also charges interest, dividends, etc payable outside the State out of any foreign public revenue when collected by any banker or dealer in coupons in the State. In *Essex Petroleum Co v MOD* [1989] STC 805, it was held that interest payable on damages received from a government department fell outside Sch C. Harman J expressed the (obiter) view that only interest arising on securities was in fact caught.

With effect from 25 March 2005, no charge arises in a case where a banker clears a cheque or arranges for the clearance of a cheque representing a dividend payment but does not act as a collection agent for the recipient (TCA 1997, s 17(3)).

The persons assessed

Assessments under Sch C are made on the persons entrusted with the payment of the relevant public revenue dividends, interest, etc. These persons pay the tax at the standard rate on the amount of the dividends on behalf of the persons entitled to them and pay over to those persons the net amounts after deducting the tax (TCA 1997, s 33).

The following persons are assessable under Sch C:

(a) any person or body of persons entrusted with the payment in the State of any public revenue dividends;

(b) any bank or other person in the State who obtains payment for a person in the State of any foreign public revenue dividends;

(c) any bank in the State which sells or otherwise realises coupons for any foreign public revenue dividends; and

(d) any dealer of coupons in the State who purchases coupons for any foreign public revenue dividends other than from a banker or from another dealer in coupons.

The machinery for the assessment, charge and payment of tax under Sch C is set out in full in TCA 1997, Sch 2. In general, any person assessable under Sch C is required to keep an account of the dividends, interest, coupons, etc entrusted to him for payment, whether out of the public revenue of the State or of any foreign government. These persons are required to deduct the income tax and pay it over to the Revenue

Commissioners on assessment. The Revenue Commissioners have the power to relieve the person so entrusted from these obligations (TCA 1997, Sch 2 para 24).

TCA 1997, s 1087(1) provides that where a payment is made in a tax year before the passing of a Finance Act increasing the standard rate of tax any tax under-deducted in consequence may be recovered from the payee by an assessment under Sch D Case IV; the agent entrusted with the payment must if so required supply the Revenue Commissioners with the names and addresses of the payees and the amounts of the payments.

Exemptions

Interest on certain government securities is paid without deduction of tax under specific statutory provisions. The Minister for Finance has power to direct that a security issued under his authority shall be issued on the basis that any interest is to be paid without deduction of tax (TCA 1997, s 36). Such securities may be issued on terms that neither the capital or interest in respect thereof will be liable to tax where the beneficial owner is not resident in the State (TCA 1997, s 43).

In addition to interest from government stocks, interest on securities issued by the following bodies is paid without deduction of tax:

(a) Dublin Airport Authority (issued after 1 July 1964) (TCA 1997, s 37);

(b) the Electricity Supply Board and Córas Iompair Éireann (issued after 12 July 1954) (TCA 1997, s 37);

(c) Bord Na Móna (issued after 17 July 1957) (TCA 1997, s 37);

(d) Radio Telefís Éireann (issued after 23 May 1989) (TCA 1997, s 37);

(e) Bord Gáis Éireann (issued after 27 May 1992) (TCA 1997, s 37);

(f) local authorities under the Local Government Act 1946, s 87 (issued after 12 July 1955) (TCA 1997, Sch 32 para 1);

(g) any body corporate where the payment of interest and the repayment of principal is guaranteed by a Minister of State under statutory authority (TCA 1997, s 38);

(h) the European Community, the European Coal and Steel Community, the European Atomic Energy Community or the European Investment Bank in respect of securities issued in the State (TCA 1997, s 39);

(i) Securities of the International Bank for Reconstruction and Development (TCA 1997, s 40); and

(j) Profit of Certain Securities issued by a body designated under the Securitisation Mortgages Act 1995 (TCA 1997, s 41);

(k) a company established pursuant to the Gas Regulation Act 2013, s 5 (issued on or after 23 October 2014);

(l) Irish Water (issued on or after 24 October 2013) (TCA 1997, s 37).

Securities issued by these bodies are deemed by the relevant sections to be issued under the authority of the Minister for Finance and are thereby brought within the treatment applied to government securities under TCA 1997, s 36. The fact that income tax is not deductible on the payment of the interest does not mean that the interest is not liable to tax. The interest is normally taxable under Sch D Case III on the recipient (TCA 1997, s 36(2)). However securities issued by the above bodies may be issued on condition that neither the capital nor the interest shall be liable to tax if the security is beneficially owned by a person who is not resident in the State (TCA 1997, s 49(2), Sch 32 para 1(2)). The terms of issue may also provide that the interest on such securities will not be liable to tax if the beneficial owner is domiciled but not resident in the State. Prior to 4 February 2010, such securities could be owned by an individual who was resident but not ordinarily resident in the State and the interest would not have been liable to tax.

Treatment of recipient

The recipient of dividends, etc on which the paying agent has paid tax under Sch C receives them net. He is required to bring the gross amount into his total income, but is entitled to credit the tax suffered by deduction against his total tax liability (TCA 1997, s 59). If the recipient's taxable income is low enough, he can reclaim the excess of the tax deducted over his final liability. Where dividends, etc payable out of any public revenue of the State or out of any public revenue of Great Britain or Northern Ireland are received without deduction of any tax under Sch C, for example, due to one of the exemptions, the recipient may be taxed under the appropriate case of Sch D (TCA 1997, s 54).

A person who establishes to the satisfaction of the Revenue Commissioners that he is not resident in the State is not chargeable to tax in respect of the dividends of any securities of any foreign territory that may be payable in the State. The non-resident person is entitled to relief from any such tax either by way of allowance or repayment on making an appropriate claim to the Revenue Commissioners. The claimant has the right, if aggrieved by a decision of the Revenue Commissioners on the question of his residence, to have his claim for relief heard by the Appeal Commissioners on giving notice in writing to the Revenue Commissioners within two months of being notified of the decision (TCA 1997, s 35). F(TA)A 2015, s 35(2) amended this provision by saying that a person aggrieved by a decision of the Revenue Commissioners on any question as to the residence of that person may appeal the decision to the Appeal Commissioners within the period of two months after the date of the notice of the decision.

2.310 Foreign dividends collected by Irish banks, etc

TCA 1997, Pt 4 (ss 60–63) requires income tax to be collected at source by any bank or any other person in the State in receipt of any interest, dividends and similar payments payable on the stocks, funds, shares or securities of any company or other body of persons not resident in the State. The rules of TCA 1997, Pt 4 require any such bank or other person in the State to deduct income tax in respect of any such foreign dividends, interest, etc that it (company assumed) pays over to or collects on behalf of other persons (TCA 1997, s 60). In practice, however, the procedure of assessing the bank, etc in respect of such foreign dividends is not applied to dividends, etc from UK companies.

TCA 1997, s 61 provides that, if any dividends, interest, etc, to which these provisions apply are entrusted to any person in the State (normally a bank) for payment to any persons in the State, the person so entrusted (the 'paying agent') is assessed to income tax under Sch D on the net amount of the foreign dividends in question. The same assessment and collection machinery that applies under Sch C (see **2.309**) is used – ie the paying agent is required to keep an account of the foreign dividends entrusted to him for payment, to deduct income tax and to pay over that tax to the Revenue Commissioners on assessment. The Revenue Commissioners have the power to relieve the person so entrusted from these obligations (TCA 1997, Sch 2 para 24).

The procedure applies also where a bank or any other person in the State, by means of coupons or otherwise, obtains payment of any foreign dividends outside the State. If the bank or other person sells or otherwise realises coupons for any relevant dividends on behalf of another person, he is required to deduct tax from the proceeds of the realisation and is assessable under Sch D on those proceeds. If a dealer in coupons purchases coupons for any dividends, otherwise than from a bank or from another dealer in coupons, the dealer is similarly chargeable under Sch D on the purchase price (TCA 1997, s 62(1)). With effect from 25 March 2005, no charge arises in a case where a banker clears a cheque or arranges for the clearance of a cheque representing a dividend payment but does not act as a collection agent for the recipient (TCA 1997, s 62(2)).

The paying agent is required to deduct income tax (and is assessable under Sch D) at the standard rate from the foreign dividends. In the event of a change in the standard rate of income tax, the standard rate in force on the date on which the paying agent cashes the dividend is applied.

As mentioned above, this does not apply to UK dividends from which no Irish tax need be withheld by any paying agent.

Treatment of recipient

The recipient of a foreign dividend which has been subject to this taxation at source in the hands of the paying agent should include in his income tax return for the year of receipt the gross amount of the dividend (in euro). It should be included with his other items of taxed income (see **3.103**) and the amount of the foreign tax suffered as well as the Irish tax withheld by the bank should be noted in the return. The recipient is entitled to credit the Irish tax deducted by the paying agent against his tax liability for the relevant tax year. This credit for the Irish tax suffered is in addition to any credit for foreign tax to which the recipient may be entitled under a double taxation agreement (see **14.310**).

Normally, dividends (and interest) from foreign sources are taxable as income within Sch D Case III so as to be charged to income tax on the recipient in the tax year in which they are received (see **8.102**).

However, a person is not chargeable to Irish income tax on the foreign dividends if he satisfies the Revenue Commissioners that:

(a) he owns the foreign stocks, shares, etc on which the dividends are paid;
(b) that he is entitled to the income arising from them; and
(c) that he is not resident in the State.

When such a non-resident person satisfies the Revenue Commissioners on these three points, they may relieve him from any liability to Irish tax either by way of allowance or repayment. Should the Revenue Commissioners refuse to grant the claim for relief on the grounds of the claimant's residence, he may apply – within two months of the date of being notified of their decision – to have his claim heard and determined by the Appeal Commissioners (with the normal rights for a rehearing by the Circuit Court judge or for a case stated for the opinion of the High Court on a point of law). F(TA)A 2015, s 4 amends this ability in that a person aggrieved by a decision of the Revenue Commissioners on any question as to the residence of that person may appeal the decision to the Appeal Commissioners within the period of two months after the date of the notice of the decision; this amendment was subject to Ministerial Order (SI 110/2016 appointed 21 March 2016 as the day on which the Finance (Tax Appeals) Act 2015, came into operation).

Where the Revenue Commissioners are satisfied that the recipient of the foreign dividends is entitled to the exemption from Irish tax due to his non-residence, they may authorise the paying agent not to deduct income tax under the rules of TCA 1997, Pt 4 unless and until they subsequently advise the paying agent otherwise.

Quoted eurobonds

TCA 1997, s 64 requires Irish tax to be withheld at the standard rate from interest on any quoted Eurobond where such interest is collected by a bank in the State on behalf of any person who is resident in the State in either of the following cases:

(a) where the payment of the interest on the quoted Eurobond was not made by or entrusted to a bank or other person in the State; or

(b) where the quoted Eurobond in respect of which the interest was paid is held in a recognised clearing system.

TCA 1997, s 64 achieves this result by applying TCA 1997, ss 62, 63 and Sch 2 (in so far as it relates to the said s 62) to interest on quoted Eurobonds as they would apply to foreign dividends, etc within TCA 1997, Pt 4 discussed above. In so applying TCA 1997, s 62 for Eurobond interest, the modifications shown in (a) and (b) immediately above are imported into that section.

In applying TCA 1997, s 63 for Eurobond interest, that section has to be read as excluding the withholding of tax where the Eurobond interest is payable in the State and the beneficial holder of the quoted Eurobond(s) is (i) not resident in the State and (ii) has made the 'non-resident's' declaration required by TCA 1997, s 64.

For the definitions of 'quoted Eurobond' and 'recognised clearing system' and for particulars of the 'non-resident's' declaration, see **2.306**.

2.311 Payments to subcontractors under relevant contracts

The law is stated below as it applies from 1 January 2012. Significant changes to the operation of the scheme were introduced by FA 2011, s 20 and FA 2012, s 21 and these were brought into effect by way of ministerial order with effect from 1 January 2012. The statutory provisions are supplemented by the Income Tax and Corporation Tax (Relevant Contracts Tax) Regulations 2012 (SI 576/2012) ('the Regulations', hereafter). The law as it applied up to 31 December 2011 is covered in previous editions of this text. All references to the use of electronic communications includes communication by means of electrical, digital, magnetic, optical, electromagnetic, biometric means of transmission of data and other related forms of data transmission technology (TCA 1997, s 917EA(1), as applied by TCA 1997, s 530(1)).

TCA 1997, s 530A applies the provisions of the scheme to every principal contractor as defined who enters into a relevant contract. TCA 1997, s 530(1) provides that a 'relevant contract' is a contract (other than a contract of employment or a contract carried out under the auspices of NAMA) under which a person ('the sub-contractor') is liable to another person ('the principal') either:

(a) to carry out relevant operations;

(b) to be answerable for the carrying out of such operations by others; or

(c) to furnish his own labour or the labour of others, in the carrying out of such operations.

The rules apply to relevant operations which are carried out in the State or with effect from 1 January 2016 within a 'designated area', regardless of whether or not one or more of the following circumstances apply in respect of the operations:

(a) either or both the principal and the subcontractor concerned is not, or are not, resident in the State for the tax year in which the operations are carried out;

(b) either or both the principal and the subcontractor concerned is not or are not (or are not deemed to be), carrying on a trade in the State in respect of the operations through a branch or agency or otherwise, in respect of which either the principal or subcontractor is liable to income tax or corporation tax;

(c) either or both the principal and the subcontractor concerned is not, or are not, (or are not deemed to be,) carrying on a business in the State in respect of the operations through a permanent establishment under the terms of a double tax agreement;

(d) the relevant contract concerned is not subject to Irish law; or

(e) payment in respect of the operations is made outside the State (TCA 1997, s 530(4)).

Reference is made above to a 'designated area' and its definition was inserted into TCA 1997, s 530(1) with effect from 1 January 2016 with it having the meaning assigned to it by TCA 1997, s 13(1) which reads 'an area designated by order under section 2 of the Continental Shelf Act, 1968 which refers to any rights of the State outside territorial waters over the sea bed and subsoil for the purpose of exploring such sea bed and subsoil and exploiting their natural resources'. The section outlines the orders that may be designated by the Government. Therefore, the geographical scope of the Relevant Contracts Tax has been extended.

Revenue Manual 18.2.1 – Relevant Contracts Tax was amended to take account of the above change and notes 'For years up to and including 2015, RCT only applied where the relevant operations were performed in the State, the State is taken to include the territory of Ireland and its territorial waters. For these years RCT did not apply where relevant operations were carried on outside of the State's 12-mile territorial waters. Therefore, relevant operations carried out in designated areas of the Continental Shelf in the years up to and including 2015 were not subject to RCT. However, contracts are sometimes performed partly in the State and or in designated areas of the Continental Shelf and partly outside of these locations. Where the performance abroad is merely incidental to the performance in the State and or designated areas of the Continental Shelf, RCT should be regarded as applying to the full contract. In all other cases, RCT need only be applied to the part of the contract that is performed in the State and or in designated areas of the Continental Shelf. Where there is a single price for the entire contract, payments may be apportioned on a basis agreed in advance with the Inspector of Taxes'.

Where a contract is otherwise performed partly within and partly outside Ireland, the Relevant Contract rules will apply only to the operations carried on within Ireland. Where apportionments are required, as in the case of single price contracts, these can be agreed in advance with the Revenue.

TCA 1997, s 531(6)(b) empowers the Revenue Commissioners to make regulations requiring the parties about to enter into a contract to make a declaration in a specified form, to the effect that, having regard to guidelines published by the Revenue Commissioners regarding distinctions between contracts of employment and 'relevant contracts', they are both satisfied that in their opinion, the contract which they propose to enter into is not a contract of employment (see SI 71/2000). The definition of 'relevant contracts' makes clear that employment agencies who provide labour in the industries in question are within the scope of the tax.

Principal

The term 'principal' includes the person who commissioned a main contractor to carry out relevant operations, as well as a main contractor who subcontracts another contractor to carry out part or all of the operations to be completed under a relevant contract. However, TCA 1997, s 530A limits the application of the scheme to principals falling under any of the following headings:

(a) a person who is himself a contractor under another relevant contract (for example, one under which he subcontracts the work or part of it to another contractor);

(b) (i) a person carrying on a business which includes the erection of buildings or the development of land as defined by TCA 1997, s 639(1): see **12.303**, or the manufacture, treatment or extraction of materials for use in construction operations (there is an exclusion for a person whose construction operations are confined to the erection of buildings for the use or occupation of himself or his employees (TCA 1997, s 530A(2)); in practice, the Revenue also regard a person carrying on a business who arranges to have a building constructed for the sole intention of letting the building to come within the exclusion in TCA 1997, s 530A(2): *Tax Briefing 26*;

(ii) carrying on a business of meat processing operations in an establishment approved and inspected in accordance with the relevant European Commission regulations;

(iii) carrying on a business that includes the processing (including the cutting and preserving) of wood from thinned or felled trees in sawmills or other like premises or the supply of thinned or felled trees in such processing.

(c) a person who is connected with a company carrying on such a business as is mentioned in (b); exceptions apply to:

(i) a company where the payments relate to construction operations in relation to land or buildings for the use or occupation of itself or its employees and that company does not itself carry on a business of construction operations, and

(ii) an individual meeting the conditions under (i),

but only if the company to which he is connected does not carry out construction operations (TCA 1997, s 530A(2));

(d) a local authority, a public utility society within the Housing Act 1966, s 2, or a body referred to in the Housing Act 1966, ss 12(2)(a), 19 or 45;

(e) a Minister of the Government;

(f) a board established by or under statute, or, any board or body established by or under royal charter and funded wholly or mainly out of moneys provided by the Oireachtas;

(g) a gas, water, electricity, hydraulic power, dock, canal or railway undertaking; or

(h) a person who carries out the installation, alteration or repair in or on any building or structure of systems of telecommunications.

It is to be noted that a private individual who contracts with, say, a builder to carry out construction operations for him (for example, to extend his residence) is not a principal to which RCT applies, even though the individual is within the term 'principal' (unless he is connected to a company under (c) above). The same consideration applies to any individual, company or other person – other than one within any of headings (d) to (h) – who is the principal in a relevant contact for, say, the erection of new offices for his trade or profession. Similarly, a farmer who is not himself carrying on forestry operations would not be a principal when paying a person who has contracted with him to plant trees on his land (*Tax Briefing 29*). An individual connected to a company which carries on construction activities would not qualify for the exception set out in (c)(i) above. Nor would the exception in (c)(i) apply to companies connected to a company carrying on a business set out in (b) above where the work is carried out on a let property. In *Tax Briefing 71* Revenue state that the obligation to operate RCT will not apply in relation to a let property where the property is let:

(a) by a person connected with a company in the meat processing or forestry building; and
(b) by companies (ie not individuals) connected with companies carrying on construction and land development.

where the work carried out is minor repair or improvement work and the total value of contracts awarded per property in any tax year in respect of such repairs or improvements does not exceed €20,000 including VAT.

Tax Briefing 71 also states that individuals with a controlling interest in a construction company and also individuals carrying on a business which includes the erection of houses will not be required to operate RCT in respect of minor repairs or improvements carried out in a private capacity on their own home or on private lettings or on other incidental private work (eg the erection of a memorial monument). In this context 'minor' again means where the total cost is less than €20,000 including VAT.

Revenue *eBrief No 38/13* provides that RCT will not apply to a person where the person is only brought within the scheme because the person is connected to a company which carries on a business specified in (b) above outside the State and which is not carrying on a trade in the State through a branch or agency.

'Relevant operations' are defined as construction operations, forestry operations or meat processing operations as the case may be (TCA 1997, s 530(1)). These elements are defined in turn as follows:

'Construction operations' are defined as follows:

(a) the construction, alteration, repair, extension, demolition or dismantling of buildings or structures;
(b) the construction, alteration, repair, extension, or demolition of any works forming or to form part of land, including walls, roadworks, power lines, telecommunication apparatus aircraft runways, docks and harbours, railways, inland waterways, pipelines, reservoirs, water mains, wells, sewers, industrial plant and installations for the purpose of land drainage;
(c) the installation, alteration or repair in any building or structure of systems of heating, lighting, air conditioning, soundproofing, ventilation, power supply, drainage, sanitation, water supply, burglar or fire protection. (In *eBrief No 46/14* Revenue stated that they consider the installation of water meters to be a construction operation whether the installation takes place as a stand-alone operation or as part of the installation of a water supply);
(ca) the installation, alteration or repair in or on any building or structure of systems of telecommunications;
(d) the external cleaning of buildings (other than cleaning of any part of a building in the course of normal maintenance) or the internal cleaning of buildings and structures so far as it is carried out in the course of their construction, alteration, extension, repair or restoration;
(e) operations which form an integral part of, or are preparatory to, or are for rendering complete, such operations as are described above, including site

clearance, earth moving, excavation, tunnelling and boring, laying of foundations, erection of scaffolding, site restoration, landscaping, and the provision of roadways and other access works;

(f) operations which form an integral part of or are preparatory to or are for rendering complete the drilling for extraction of minerals, or natural gas or the exploration or exploitation of natural resources; and

(g) the haulage for hire of materials, machinery or plant for use whether used or not in any of the aforesaid construction operations; the meaning of 'haulage for hire' was examined in *O'Grady v Laragan Quarries Ltd* IV ITR 269, discussed at **1.407**. In *eBrief No 46/14* Revenue confirm that the hire of machinery with an operator is considered to be a relevant construction operation whereas the hire of machinery without an operator does not come within the scope of RCT.

'Forestry operations' are defined as any of the following:

(a) thinning, lopping or felling of trees in woods, forests or other plantations;

(b) the planting of trees in woods, forests or other plantations;

(c) the maintenance of woods, forests and plantations and the preparation of land, including woods or forests which have been harvested, for planting;

(d) the haulage or removal of thinned, lopped or felled trees;

(e) the processing (including cutting or preserving) of wood from thinned, lopped or felled trees in sawmills or other like premises; and

(f) the haulage for hire of materials, machinery or plant for use (whether used or not) in any of the above operations.

'Meat processing operations' are defined as operations of any of the following descriptions:

(a) the slaughter of cattle, sheep, pigs, domestic fowl, turkeys, guinea-fowl, ducks or geese;

(b) the catching of domestic fowl, turkeys, guinea-fowl, ducks or geese;

(c) the division (including cutting or boning) sorting, packaging (including vacuum packaging), rewrapping or branding of, or the application of any other similar process to, the carcasses or any part of the carcasses (including meat) of slaughtered cattle, sheep, pigs, domestic fowl, turkeys, guinea-fowl, ducks or geese;

(d) the application of methods of preservation (including cold storage) to the carcasses or any part of the carcasses (including meat) of slaughtered cattle, sheep, pigs, domestic fowl, turkeys, guinea-fowl, ducks or geese;

(e) the loading or unloading of the carcasses or part of the carcasses (including meat) of slaughtered cattle, sheep, pigs, domestic fowl, turkeys, guinea-fowl, ducks or geese at any establishment where any of the operations referred to in paragraphs (a), (c) and (d) are carried on;

(f) the haulage of the carcasses or any part of the carcasses (including meat) of slaughtered cattle, sheep, pigs, domestic fowl, turkeys, guinea-fowl, ducks or geese from any establishment where any of the operations referred to in paragraphs (a), (c) and (d) are carried on;

(fa) the rendering of the carcasses or any part of the carcasses of slaughtered cattle, sheep, pigs, domestic fowl, turkeys, guinea-fowl, ducks or geese;

(g) the cleaning down of any establishment where any of the operations referred to in paragraphs (a), (c) and (d) are carried on;

(h) the grading, sexing and transport of day-old chicks of domestic fowl, turkeys, guineafowl, ducks or geese; and

(i) the haulage for hire of cattle, sheep, pigs, domestic fowl, turkeys, guinea-fowl, ducks or geese or of any of the materials, machinery or plant for use, whether used or not, in any of the operations referred to in paragraphs (a) to (h).

Notification of Contracts and Register of Principals

TCA 1997, s 530B(1) provides that upon entering into a relevant contract, a principal within the scheme must provide the Revenue Commissioners with

(a) information in relation to:

 (i) the identity of the subcontractor,

 (ii) the estimated contract value,

 (iii) the estimated contract duration including the estimated start date and estimated end date,

 (iv) the location or locations at which relevant operations under the contract are to take place,

 (v) whether or not the contract is a labour only contract; and

(b) a declaration stating that the principal is satisfied, if that is the Case, having regard to guidelines published by the Revenue Commissioners as to the distinction between contracts of employment and relevant contracts, that the named subcontractor is not performing the contract or any part of it as an employee of the principal.

TCA 1997, s 530B(1A) provides that the principal must firstly satisfy themselves as to the identity of the subcontractor and must obtain and then retain copies and details of relevant documentary evidence thereof.

Where a relevant contract was entered into prior to 1 January 2012, a principal to whom section TCA 1997, s 530A applies must provide the information and declaration referred to above if a payment is outstanding under that contract, or under that contract as amended, at that date.

The information and declaration required is to be provided electronically, and the relevant provisions of TCA 1997, Pt 38, Ch 6 (see **2.105**) are to apply. The Revenue Commissioners are empowered to make regulations for the purposes of this provision, providing for:

(a) specification of the manner by which principals will communicate electronically with the Revenue Commissioners. Regulation 4(1) of the Regulations provides that communications made by a principal are to be provided using the Revenue Commissioners electronic RCT (eRCT) system;

(b) in the case of a labour-only contract, the submission of additional information in relation to the contract. Regulation 4(3) provides that where a principal does not indicate that he is satisfied that the contract is not a labour-only contract the eRCT system may require additional information to be provided. In practice the eRCT system will require the principal to answer questions which are designed to ascertain whether the subcontractor should be treated as an employee rather than a self employed contractor; for example the principal is required to say whether the subcontractor will supply materials, provide any plant or engage other people;

(c) the issue and the manner of an acknowledgement by the Revenue Commissioners following the notification (regulation 4(4));

(d) notification to a subcontractor by the Revenue Commissioners of details of a contract, including changes to the terms of a contract, in respect of which a principal has notified the Revenue Commissioners under these provisions that the subcontractor is a party (regulation 4(5));
(e) notification to the Revenue Commissioners by a principal of changes to the terms of a contract which has been notified under these provisions (regulation 4(5));
(f) notification by a principal to a subcontractor where the Revenue Commissioners are unable to verify the identity of the subcontractor by reference to the name and tax reference number supplied to the Revenue Commissioners by the principal under these notification procedures. (regulation 4(2) requires the principal to inform the subcontractor in writing within seven days or before making a relevant payment to the subcontractor, whichever is earlier; and
(e) any other related matters (see regulation 4).

Every principal to whom s 530B applies must register as a principal with the Revenue Commissioners, unless he is already registered and the Revenue Commissioners are obliged to keep and maintain a register of principals for the purposes of these provisions.

TCA 1997, s 530J(3) provides that the Revenue Commissioners are required to make regulations for the purposes of this provision, and such regulations may provide for:

(a) keeping and maintaining the register;
(b) registration and time for registration;
(c) the particulars to be submitted to the Revenue Commissioners for the purposes of registering a person as a principal;
(d) notification of change in relevant details;
(e) notification of cessation as a principal;
(f) cancellation of registration;
(g) the use of electronic means in connection with the registration process; and
(h) any other related matters.

Regulation 3 of the Regulations deals with registration. It provides that a principal is required to register before providing the information required by TCA 1997, s 530B(1) and must provide the particulars required by the Revenue Commissioners. A principal is required to notify Revenue when they cease to be a principal and Revenue are required to notify a principal when they intend to cancel their registration as a principal. Such cancellation takes effect from 21 days of the date of the notification unless within that period the person satisfies Revenue that they are still a principal.

Notification of relevant payments and Deduction Authorisation Procedures

A relevant payment is any payment made by a principal within the scheme under a relevant contract. TCA 1997, s 530C provides that immediately before a principal makes a relevant payment to a subcontractor, the principal must notify the Revenue Commissioners of his intention to make such a payment and of the amount of that payment. The notice must be given by electronic means and the relevant provisions of TCA 1997, Pt 38, Ch 6 (see **2.105**) are to apply. The Revenue Commissioners are to make regulations for the purposes of this provision providing for:

(a) specification of the manner by which principals shall communicate electronically with the Revenue Commissioners;
(b) the details to be supplied by a principal in relation to a payment;

(c) specification of the circumstances in which and the means by which a principal may cancel a notification;
(d) specification the circumstances in which a notification is deemed not to have been given;
(e) notification to a subcontractor where a payment notification is cancelled; and
(f) any other related matters (see regulation 5).

Regulation 5 of the Regulations deals with the notification of relevant payments by a principal. A payment notification must be made using the Revenue Commissioners eRCT system. The payment notification must include details of:

(a) the identity of the subcontractor, including name and tax reference number;
(b) identification of the contract to which the payment relates; and
(c) such other information as may be required by the eRCT system.

Where a principal has entered into more than one relevant contract with a subcontractor the principal can identify the particular contract to which the payment relates or associate the payment with any current contract for the subcontractor. If a principal makes a single payment which relates to more than one contract the principal can give separate notifications identifying part of the payment with the contract to which it relates or alternatively can give a single notification and associate it with any current contract. If a principal anticipates that a payment will not be made before the end of the return period in which the payment notification is given, he is required to cancel the notification using the eRCT system. Revenue are then required to notify the subcontractor of the cancellation of the payment notification by the principal. Revenue *e-brief 85/2015* notes as follows regarding the eRCT Site Identifier Number 'From December 2015, there will be a new mandatory field in the Contract Notification process in the eRCT system. The new field is for a "Revenue Site Identifier Number" (SIN). Each contract will require a SIN when the Contract Notification process is being completed. The SIN is a system-generated identifying number which is applied to the location or locations where relevant operations are due to take place under a particular contract. Upon the introduction of the new field, where a Principal contractor is updating the eRCT system with details of a new contract at a new location for the first time, the system will automatically provide a "Revenue Site Identifier Number" when they enter the location of the relevant operation. When identifying the location of relevant operations, Principals will be required to enter both the Site/Project Name and the Address. The SIN will also be provided on the Contract Notification that issues to the Sub-contractor. Once the system has generated the SIN, the Principal or Sub-contractor should only enter the SIN instead of the location, for any further updates they make to the eRCT system in respect of the same location. Further guidance regarding the use and functionality of the SIN will be provided in the coming months.'

Where a principal has issued the requisite notification to the Revenue Commissioners of his intention to make a relevant payment, the Revenue Commissioners must issue a deduction authorisation electronically to the principal in respect of that relevant payment TCA 1997, s 530D(1). The deduction authorisation must:

(a) specify the rate of tax to be deducted from the payment, including, as appropriate, zero; and
(b) authorise the principal concerned to deduct a specified sum of tax or no tax from the relevant payment.

At the end of each return period, the Revenue Commissioners must issue a deduction summary electronically to each registered principal in respect of that return period. TCA

1997, s 530(1) defines a return period as the period of one or more income tax months for which the principal is obliged to account for subcontractor's tax, or where no such period is specified, an income tax month.

TCA 1997, s 530(1) defines a deduction summary as a statement (adjusted as appropriate in accordance with the Regulations) issued by the Revenue Commissioners to a registered principal setting out, in summary form:

(a) details in respect of each relevant payment notified by that principal which is, in accordance with the Regulations subject of a valid deduction authorisation at the time of issue of the deduction summary; and
(b) the aggregate amount of tax that is, based on the details referred to (a), payable by the principal in respect of the return period, and
(c) a statement to the effect that no such relevant payments were notified, where that is the case.

TCA 1997, s 530D(5) empowers the Revenue Commissioners to make regulations dealing with deduction authorisations and deduction summaries. Regulation 6 of the Regulations deals with deduction authorisations. Deduction authorisations are provided through the eRCT system and are valid until the earliest of the following:

(a) until the payment is made;
(b) until the due date for the filing of the return in which the authorisation is issued;
(c) until the filing of such a return; or
(d) until the cancellation of the related payment notification.

A deduction authorisation is valid only in respect of the subcontractor named on it and the relevant payment to which it relates. Regulation 7 of the Regulations deals with deduction summaries. A deduction summary is issued through the eRCT system at the end of the return period and gives details of the payment notifications made by the principal during the return period.

A principal to whom a deduction authorisation is issued must deduct tax from the relevant payment concerned only in accordance with the terms of the deduction authorisation. The rate of tax will be 0 per cent, 20 per cent or 35 per cent depending on the determination by the Revenue Commissioners (see below); in the case of a partnership it will be the highest rate that would apply to any of the partners following such a determination (TCA 1997, s 530E(1)(d)).

With effect from 1 January 2015 a principal within the scheme who makes a relevant payment to a subcontractor otherwise than in accordance with a deduction authorisation issued (eg where a payment is made without having notified Revenue or where a payment is made and tax is not deducted at the rate set out in the deduction authorisation) is liable to a penalty of a percentage of the relevant payment made. The percentage penalty payable depends on the status of the subcontractor as follows:

(a) where the subcontractor is not known to Revenue (ie Revenue have not determined under TCA 1997, s 530I the rate of tax that should apply to the subcontractor), 35 per cent of the amount of the relevant payment;
(b) where the subcontractor is one to which tax at 35 per cent would normally be required to be deducted, 20 per cent of the relevant payment;
(c) where the subcontractor is a standard rated subcontractor, 10 per cent of the relevant payment; and
(d) where the subcontractor is a zero-rated subcontractor, 3 per cent of the relevant payment (TCA 1997, s 530F(2)).

In addition with effect from 1 January 2015 the principal is required to submit an 'unreported payment notification' to Revenue, ie a notification that a payment was made otherwise than in accordance with a deduction authorisation.

The Revenue Commissioners are empowered to make regulations specifying the manner in which a payment authorisation is to be provided and the details to be supplied (TCA 1997, s 530F(3)). Regulation 9 of the Regulations was amended by SI 5/2015 to provide that an unreported payment notification provided by a principal to Revenue should contain details of the name and tax number of the subcontractor, the contract to which the payment relates and the date and amount of the payment made.

(Prior to 1 January 2015 the principal was required to make a tax payment of 35 per cent of the relevant payment to Revenue in all cases where a payment was made otherwise than in accordance with a deduction authorisation and in addition was liable to a penalty of €5,000 or an amount equal to 35 per cent of the payment made, whichever was the lesser. However, where the principal submitted details of the relevant payment in a return for the relevant return period and, if appropriate, provided the Revenue Commissioners with whatever details they required in relation to the relevant contract in respect of which the relevant payment was made, the Revenue Commissioners would establish the amount of tax that would have been due from the principal in respect of that payment had the rate of tax been the rate of tax last notified by the Revenue Commissioners to the subcontractor concerned and, the principal was liable to pay that amount of tax instead. The amount of the penalty noted above remained payable.).

Where a principal deducts tax from a relevant payment, the principal must:

(a) provide the subcontractor with a copy of the deduction authorisation related to that payment; or
(b) arrange for the following details from the deduction authorisation to be given to the subcontractor by written or electronic means:
   (i) the name and tax reference number of the principal,
   (ii) the name and tax reference number of the subcontractor,
   (iii) the gross amount of the payment, including the amount of tax deducted,
   (iv) the amount of tax deducted,
   (v) the rate at which tax was deducted,
   (vi) the date of the payment, and
   (vii) the unique reference number issued by the Revenue Commissioners on the deduction authorisation.

The amount of tax which the principal is liable to deduct from relevant payments is due and payable in respect of the relevant return period in which the liability to deduct arises. Where, due to a persistent technology systems failure, a principal is unable to give notification to the Revenue Commissioners and has no option but to make a relevant payment without complying with the foregoing provisions, a liability to a penalty for making a payment otherwise than in accordance with a deduction authorisation set out above will not apply in relation to that payment if the principal:

(a) deducts tax from that payment at the rate last notified to the principal in respect of the subcontractor concerned, or if there was no such notification, deducts tax at a rate of 35 per cent from that payment;
(b) immediately upon rectification of the technology systems failure notifies the Revenue Commissioners, in accordance with any appropriate regulations that the payment has been made;

(c) provides all details in relation to the payment that the Revenue Commissioners may require; and

(d) pays the tax deducted in accordance with (a) to the Revenue Commissioners on or before the due date for the making of a return. for the period within which the principal notifies the Revenue Commissioners of the technology systems failure (TCA 1997, s 530F(7)).

Where a principal complies with these requirements, then:

(a) the principal will be deemed to have deducted tax from a relevant payment in accordance with the terms of a valid deduction authorisation; and

(b) the payment shall be deemed to have been made in the return period in which the principal notifies the Revenue Commissioners of the technology systems failure (TCA 1997, s 530F(8)).

A principal must, on request, provide the Revenue Commissioners with information in relation to the circumstances and details of a persistent technology systems failure. (TCA 1997, s 530F(9)). For these purposes, a 'technology systems failure' means circumstances in which the electronic system put in place by the Revenue Commissioners for the efficient operation of these provisions is not functioning or is not functioning properly at any particular time such that a person is unable to comply with an obligation under these provisions or the Regulations, or circumstances where a person concerned is unable to use the electronic system at any particular time because of a general or partial systems failure of an internet service provider or of an electricity service provider, occurring in the general locality of the person's place of business, (TCA 1997, s 530(1)).

Zero-rated and standard-rated subcontractors

Zero-rated subcontractors

In order to completely avoid the tax deduction from payments made to him by principal contractors, TCA 1997, s 530G provides that a subcontractor must satisfy the Revenue Commissioners on a number of matters, set out in TCA 1997, s 530G(1). The object of the conditions which the subcontractor must satisfy for this purpose is to ensure, so far as is possible, that only subcontractors who can be relied upon to comply with their obligations with regard to the keeping of proper records, paying of tax, interest and penalties on time, etc are allowed to receive payments gross from their principal contractors. The Revenue Commissioners must be satisfied that:

(a) the person is or is about to become a subcontractor engaged in the business of carrying out relevant operations;

(b) the business is carried on from a fixed place of business in a permanent building and will have the necessary equipment stock and other facilities as are required for the purposes of the business;

(c) the business records are and will be kept properly and accurately in accordance with TCA 1997, s 886, (see **2.606**) and that all other records customary for such a business will be kept properly and accurately; and

(d) the person, has throughout the previous three years complied with all the obligations imposed by the Tax Acts, the Capital Gains Tax Acts or the Value Added Tax Acts, in relation to the payment or remittance of the taxes, interest and penalties due under the above Acts, the delivery of returns, and requests to supply to a Revenue officer accounts of, or other information about, any business carried on by that person.

A person who was resident outside the State at any time during the previous three years will have to satisfy the Revenue Commissioners that he has complied with their tax obligations corresponding to (c) and (d) above in his state of residence during that period.

The obligations under (c) and (d) must also be satisfied by any partnership in which the person is or was a partner and any company of which he is or was a proprietary director or is or was a proprietary employee. In a case where the person is a partnership, each partner; and in a case where the person is a company, each director of the company and any person who is either the beneficial owner of, or able, directly or indirectly, to control more than 15 per cent of the ordinary share capital of the company, must have similarly complied. The benefit of zero-rating will also be denied to any person whom the Revenue Commissioners consider for good reason is unlikely to comply with his obligations under (c) and (d) (TCA 1997, s 530G(2)).

TCA 1997, s 530G apparently treats a partnership per se as the subcontractor, ie as a person in its own right for these purposes. Presumably any changes in the composition of the partnership are to be ignored so that what are in law successive and distinct partnerships will be regarded as the same 'person' (compare TCA 1997, s 643(16)). It is not made explicit at what point in time it is necessary to establish the identity of the individual partners but it would seem logical that it should be the partners in membership at the date of application.

There does not seem to be any requirement that in the case of a partnership the tax compliance history of other partnerships or companies in which the individual partners are interested should be taken into account. The reference to a 'beneficial owner' of share capital is presumably designed to ensure that nominee shareholdings are attributed to the real owner, although it would also seem to exclude trustee shareholdings.

The significance of the reference to 'control' of share capital is not entirely clear': see the discussion at **2.615**. TCA 1997, s 2(1) defines the term 'ordinary share capital' for the purposes of the Tax Acts as all the issued share capital of a company excluding only shares which are entitled to a fixed rate dividend only.

A person has a 'proprietary' interest in a company if he is the beneficial owner of, or is directly or indirectly able to 'control', more than 15 per cent of that company's ordinary share capital (see again the discussion of the meaning of 'control' at **2.615**) (TCA 1997, s 530(1)). For these purposes, ordinary share capital thus owned or controlled by a spouse or by a minor child (see TCA 1997, s 6) of a director or employee is to be treated as owned or controlled by him and by no other person. Furthermore, the same treatment applies to shares owned or controlled by trustees of a trust for the benefit of persons which include the director or employee or his spouse or minor child) (TCA 1997, s 530(3)) The legislation leaves unclear the position where a spouse or minor child is also an employee/director. For example, if a husband and wife each hold 10 per cent of the ordinary share capital of a company of which both are directors, which one is the proprietary director?

A 'director' is defined as a member of a board of directors or similar body which manages the affairs of a body corporate or where the body corporate is managed by a single director or similar person, that person or a member of a body corporate whose affairs are managed by the members themselves. Significantly, it also includes any person who is or has been a director. A person who is a *de facto* or shadow director but not a member of the board of directors, etc a company does not seem to be covered by the definition. An 'employee' is defined as including any person taking part in the management of the affairs of the body corporate other than a director; it also includes a person who has been or is to be an employee. (presumably in the latter case this implies that there is a contract in place although employment has yet to commence) (TCA 1997, s 530(1)).

The inclusion of these additional rules regarding the good 'tax behaviour' of such persons connected with the applicant may well restrict the cases where zero-rating is available. It may be questionable whether or not, some, at least, of these requirements satisfy the constitutional text of 'proportionality' (see **1.409**).

So-called 'look through' provisions apply, broadly equivalent to those under the tax clearance certificate regime. These provisions are avowedly aimed at tackling the use of 'phoenix companies'. They apply where relevant operations which are either similar to those being carried out by the subcontractor, or which are similar to operations which are to be carried out by the subcontractor, were previously, or are currently being, carried out by another person which is either:

(a) a company connected with the subcontractor, or would have been such a company, but for the fact that the company has been wound up or has been dissolved without being wound up;

(b) a company, and the subcontractor is a partnership in which a partner, or two or more of the partners together, were able directly or indirectly, and either alone or with connected persons, to control more than 15 per cent of the ordinary share capital of that company; or

(c) a partnership, and the subcontractor is a company in which in a partner, or two or more of the partners in the partnership together, were able directly or indirectly, and either alone or with connected persons to control more than 15 per cent of the ordinary share capital of that company.

For these purposes a person is connected with another person within the definition laid down by TCA 1997, s 10 (see **12.304**).

The references in (b) and (c) to more than one partner being a 'shareholder', if taken at face value, seem to imply that it is only partners who hold shares (presumably in the company concerned) who count for these purposes. This seems odd, given that past, as well as present, control and, indirect as well as direct, control, of share capital is treated as relevant.

It may be noted that for the purposes of (b) and (c) it is not merely the control exercised by the partner(s) which must be taken into account when applying the 15 per cent test, but control exercised by them together with any person or persons connected with them, as defined by TCA 1997, s 10. It may also be noted that control exercised by such connected persons on their own (ie where the partners themselves have or had no such control) does not seem to be material for these purposes. The definition of 'control' is again unclear: see the discussion at **2.615**. TCA 1997, s 2(1) defines the term 'ordinary share capital' for the purposes of the Tax Acts as all the issued share capital of a company excluding only shares which are entitled to a fixed rate dividend only.

If any of these circumstances apply, then, zero-rating will not generally be permitted unless that other person is in compliance with its obligations under (c) and (d) above. It is difficult to see how a company which has been wound up or otherwise dissolved can be said to be 'person' at all or how it can be meaningfully be said to be tax compliant.

There is provision for the Revenue Commissioners to disregard failure to meet any of the requirements outlined above (TCA 1997, s 530G(3)).

Standard-rated subcontractors

In order to qualify for the standard-rated tax deduction from payments made to him by principal contractors, TCA 1997, s 530H provides that a subcontractor must satisfy the Revenue Commissioners on a number of matters. set out in TCA 1997, s 530H(1).

The Revenue Commissioners must be satisfied that:

(a) the person is or is about to become a subcontractor engaged in the business of carrying out relevant operations;

(b) the business is carried on from a fixed place of business in a permanent building and will have the necessary equipment, stock and other facilities as are required for the purposes of the business;

(c) the business records are and will be kept properly and accurately in accordance with TCA 1997, s 886, (see **2.606**) and that all other records customary for such a business will be kept properly and accurately;

(d) the person, has throughout the previous three years *substantially* complied with all the obligations imposed by the Tax Acts, the Capital Gains Tax Acts or the Value Added Tax Acts; and

(e) the person does not qualify for the zero rate.

A person who was resident outside the State at any time during the previous three years will have to satisfy the Revenue Commissioners that during that period he has complied with similar obligations to (c) in his state of residence and has *substantially* complied with their tax obligations corresponding to (d) above in his state of residence. The person must also have provided to the Revenue Commissioners whatever information the Revenue Commissioners is required by them in order to register that person.

The obligations under (c), (d) and (e) must also be satisfied by any partnership in which the person is or was a partner and the Revenue commissioners must be satisfied that it will continue to do so, and where the person is a partnership, each partner, must have similarly complied. The benefit of standard-rating will also be denied to any person whom the Revenue Commissioners form the opinion that the tax withheld will be insufficient to discharge the person's income tax liability for the tax year concerned (TCA 1997, s 530H(3)).

The Revenue Commissioners are empowered to make regulations identifying matters in relation to condition (d), including:

(a) the payment or remittance of tax, interest and penalties;

(b) the delivery of returns;

(c) the supply on request of accounts or other information to a Revenue officer; and

(d) the extent to which non-compliance is being addressed (TCA 1997, s 530H(2)).

Returns and payment of RCT deducted

A principal is required to make a return to the Collector-General on or before the due date of all relevant payments made during the return period (TCA 1997, s 530***K***(***1***) and pay any RCT deducted during the return period. The due date for the filing of a return and the payment of RCT electronically is 23 days after the end of the return period (TCA 1997, s 531(3AA)). If the return is not filed and/or the payment is not made electronically the due date for filing the return and payment of the RCT due is 14 days after the end of the return period (TCA 1997, s 531(3A)). If the return is filed or the payment is made later than day 23 the due date for filing the return and paying the RCT due is deemed to be day 14 after the end of the return period (TCA 1997, s 531(3AA)). The Revenue Commissioners must specify the period of the return in a notice in writing to the principal (TCA 1997, s 530(1)). The return period is normally one month. However businesses with annual RCT payments of less than €28,800 can file RCT returns and make payments on a three monthly basis (see *eBrief No 96/14*).

TCA 1997, s 530K(5) empowers the Revenue Commissioners to make regulations dealing with deduction returns by principals. Regulations 8 and 9 of the Regulations deal with returns by principals and adjustments to principal's RCT liabilities

The deduction summary issued by Revenue under TCA 1997, s 53OD(3) is deemed to be the return filed by the principal (TCA 1997, s 53OK(2)). In practice therefore where the deduction summary contains all relevant payments made by the principal during the return period the principal is deemed to have filed a return by the due date. The principal should ensure that the deduction summary accurately reflects the relevant payments made by the principal during the return period. If the deduction summary accurately reflects the relevant payments made during the return period all the principal has to do is arrange for payment of the liability. If the deduction summary does not reflect all the payments made or includes payments not made the principal should amend the deduction summary (regulation 8). If the return is not amended by the due date a €100 surcharge is payable by the principal (TCA 1997, s 53OM(2)).

TCA 1997, s 530M provides that a principal may file a return after the due date or amend a return after a return has been filed or deemed to have been filed under TCA 1997, s 53OK(2). However in such circumstances a surcharge of €100 is payable. A return may not however be amended in relation to a payment in respect of which a deduction authorisation has been issued or after an audit or investigation into the principal's tax affairs has commenced.

Rights of appeal

The usual rights of appeal against the determination of the relevant rate of withholding tax are granted under TCA 1997, s 530I. This provides that any person who is aggrieved by a determination within 30 days of the date of notification thereof may appeal to the Appeal Commissioners. Pending the determination of an appeal the Revenue Commissioners may issue a valid deduction authorisation which is binding on the principal. With effect from 30 March 2012, the Revenue Commissioners are not obliged to make a determination until 30 days have elapsed since a previous determination, if an appeal against a determination is waiting to be heard or 30 days have elapsed since the determination of such an appeal (TCA 1997, s 530I(4)).

Credit for RCT deducted

Any RCT deducted in a basis period will be treated as a payment on account of income tax for the tax year for which it is the basis period (TCA 1997, s 530P(1)). RCT deductions will be available for offset against other tax liabilities of a subcontractor (TCA 1997, s 530P(2)). Any deductions which are not required to meet the income tax liability of a subcontractor, or are not required to meet his other tax liabilities will be available for refund, subject to the provisions of TCA 1997, s 865 (TCA 1997, s 530P(4), (5)). No amount of RCT deductions shall be treated as a payment on account, set off or refunded more than once; and no amount of RCT deductions set off or refunded shall be treated as a payment on account (TCA 1997, s 530P(6)).

TCA 1997, s 530R deems a relevant contract to exist between the principal contractors and each member of a gang. The relevant contract tax regulations apply as if payments to which an individual gang member is entitled were made to that gang member, even though the payment is actually made to some other person (ie generally the 'gangmaster') and credit is allocated accordingly for RCT deductions. In *Tax Briefing 22*, the Revenue Commissioners state that:

> In general gangs consist of labour-only subcontractors. However, the term gang is not confined to such subcontractors. Where a payment covers work done by a number of subcontractors the principal contractor should consider whether the payment is being made to a gang. Unless the principal contractor is satisfied that the subcontractor to whom the payment is being made carries on an established business in the course of which he employs subcontractors, it is advisable to treat the payment as made to a gang.

In computing profits or gains for the purposes of Sch D, a payment received under deduction of RCT from will be included at the amount actually received plus the RCT deduction (TCA 1997, s 530O).

Administrative and miscellaneous provisions

A principal, prior to notifying the Revenue Commissioners of a payment, is required to obtain from the subcontractor a statement setting out details of the work giving rise to the payment and the cost of the work. It requires a subcontractor to keep and maintain records of all relevant payments and to supply a principal with all such information and particulars as are necessary for the principal to comply with the RCT provisions. Provision is made for the making of regulations governing the creation, keeping and retention of records by principals and subcontractors (TCA 1997, s 530S). Regulation 11 of the Regulations provides that principals are required to keep records of the information and declarations to be provided to Revenue on entering into a relevant contract, details of the payments notified to Revenue, registration details, details which must be included in returns and details of relevant payments made. These records and all other records required to be maintained under must be kept for a period of six years after the completion of the transaction to which they relate. If a person fails to deliver a return as required, all records must be kept for a period of six years after the return has been delivered. Principals and subcontractors are obliged to produce RCT records for inspection to a Revenue officer on request (TCA 1997, s 530T). A Revenue official may give certain evidence by certificate in proceedings for the recovery of a penalty under TCA 1997, ss 1052, 1054 or 1077E in connection with RCT and the penalty procedures of TCA 1997, Pt 47 are extended to a penalty under section TCA 1997, s 530F in relation to RCT (TCA 1997, s 530U). There are also various provisions in relation to the making of regulations, the authority of another person to act on behalf of a principal, obligations following the death of a principal, the authority of Revenue Officials to carry out functions under the RCT provisions and the application of RCT to payments to a liquidator and/or receiver (TCA 1997, s 530V).

2.4 Deposit Interest Retention Tax

2.401 Principles of the tax

TCA 1997, Pt 8 Ch 4 & Ch 5 (ss 256–267F) provides for the levying of a retention or withholding tax for certain interest paid or credited on deposits held with banks, building societies and certain other financial institutions. The financial institutions concerned (referred to as 'relevant deposit takers') are required to deduct the 'appropriate tax' from every payment of 'relevant interest' made on every 'relevant deposit' (TCA 1997, s 257(1)). For this purpose, any amount credited as interest in respect of a relevant deposit is treated as the payment of interest so that references in the legislation to interest paid are to be taken as meaning interest paid or credited (TCA 1997, s 256(2)).

The tax which relevant deposit takers must deduct (and pay over to the Collector General) is an income tax called the 'deposit interest retention tax' (often referred to as 'DIRT'). The retention tax is a final tax with no further liability to the higher rate of income tax.

Some key definitions are set out below.

Relevant deposit takers

The relevant deposit takers required to implement the retention tax, when paying or crediting interest on a relevant deposit, are the following:

(a) a person who is a holder of a licence granted under s 9 or an authorisation granted under s 9A of the Central Bank Act 1971, or a person who holds a licence or other similar authorisation under the law of an EEA state, other than the state, which corresponds to a licence granted under the said s 9;

(b) a building society within the Building Societies Acts 1989 or a society established in accordance with the law of any other Member State of the European Union which corresponds to that Act;

(c) a trustee savings bank within the Trustee Savings Banks Acts 1863–1979;

(d) a credit union registered under the Credit Union Act 1997, including a society deemed to be so registered under s 5(3) of that Act (with effect from 1 January 2002);

(e) a specified intermediary (ie a person appointed by the National Treasury Management Agency) in relation only to a specified deposit (ie a 'specified deposit' is one of a class designated by the Minister for Finance such as for example a National Solidarity Bond or State Savings Account as offered by the National Treasury Management Agency); and

(f) the Post Office Savings Bank.

Relevant deposits

For the retention tax to apply, the deposit in respect of which the interest is paid or credited must be a relevant deposit. TCA 1997, s 256(1) provides the definition of a 'relevant deposit'. The effect of this definition is that any deposit held by a relevant deposit taker is a relevant deposit unless it is specifically excepted. The definition of a 'deposit' is any sum of money paid to a relevant deposit taker repayable in whole or part on demand or on an agreed basis; with effect from 6 April 2001 the definition is extended to include deposits where the amount to be repaid may to any extent be linked to changes in a stock exchange index or any other financial index (typically a 'tracker bond').

The deposits which are not relevant deposits (so that interest thereon is paid or credited gross) are the following:

(a) a deposit made by, and the interest on which is beneficially owned by:
   (i) any relevant deposit taker,
   (ii) the National Treasury Management Agency,
   (iia) a fund investment vehicle (within the meaning of the National Treasury Management Agency (Amendment) Act 2014, s 37) of which the Minister for Finance is the sole beneficial owner (from 22 December 2014),
   (iii) the State when acting through the National Treasury Management Agency,
   (iiia) the National Pensions Reserve Fund Commission, (the National Treasury Management Agency (Amendment) Act 2014 provides that (iiia) shall be deleted on the issue of a Ministerial Order which has not yet issued),
   (iiib) the State acting through the National Pensions Reserve Fund Commission, (the National Treasury Management Agency (Amendment) Act 2014 provides that (iiib) shall be deleted on the issue of a Ministerial Order which has not yet issued),
   (iiic) the National Development Finance Agency (from 6 February 2003), (the National Treasury Management Agency (Amendment) Act 2014 provides that (iiic) shall be deleted on the issue of a Ministerial Order which has not yet issued),
   (iiid) the National Asset Management Agency (NAMA),
   (iiie) the State acting through NAMA,
   (iiif) the Strategic Banking Corporation of Ireland or a subsidiary wholly owned by it or a subsidiary wholly owned by any such subsidiary (from 28 July 2014),
   (iiig) the Minister for Social Protection in respect of accounts held under s 9 of the Social Welfare Consolidation Act 2005,
   (iv) the Central Bank of Ireland,
   (v) the Investors Compensation Company Limited (with effect from 10 September 1998),
   (vi) Icarom plc;

(b) a deposit which is a debt on a security issued by the relevant deposit taker and is listed on a stock exchange;

(c) a deposit which, in the case of relevant deposit taker resident in the State for corporation tax, is held at a branch situated outside the State;

(d) a deposit which, in the case of relevant deposit taker not resident in the State for corporation tax, is held otherwise than by a branch situated in the State;

(e) a deposit denominated in a foreign currency made by an individual before 1 June 1991 (see also below), or a person other than an individual, before 1 January 1993;

(f) a deposit:
   (i) which is made on or after 1 January 1993 by, and the interest on which is beneficially owned by, a company chargeable to corporation tax or a pension scheme, and

- (ii) where the company or pension scheme has provided the deposit taker with its PPS number or Revenue reference number;

(g) a deposit in respect of which:
- (i) no person resident in the State is beneficially entitled to any interest, and
- (ii) the non-resident's declaration prescribed by TCA 1997, s 263 has been made to the relevant deposit taker (see **2.402**);

(h)
- (i) the interest on which is exempt from income due to the charity's exemption conferred by TCA 1997, s 207(1)(b) (see **18.203**), and
- (ii) in respect of which the beneficial owner of the interest has provided the deposit taker with the reference number assigned to that person by the Revenue Commissioners in recognition of that person's entitlement to exemption from tax under TCA 1997, s 207 and known as the charity (CHY) number;

(i) a deposit in respect of which:
- (i) the individual beneficially entitled to the interest, or the individual's spouse or civil partner is age 65 or over,
- (ii) the individual's total income for that year does not exceed the amount in order to qualify the individual for exemption from income tax under TCA 1997, s 188(2) (€36,000 for married persons and civil partners and €18,000 for single persons for 2015), and
- (iii) a declaration in writing has been made to the deposit taker, in the form prescribed by Revenue, which gives details of the deposit holder, including PPS number, confirms (i) and (ii) above and declares that if the deposit holder no longer satisfies the above conditions this will be notified to the deposit holder;

(j) a deposit in respect of which:
- (i) the individual beneficially entitled to the interest, or the individual's spouse or civil partner is permanently incapacitated and the individual would otherwise have been entitled to a repayment of tax (eg because the interest is exempt or due to the overall level of income and tax credits), or
- (ii) the person who is entitled to the interest is the trustee of a special trust for permanently incapacitated individuals entitled to exemptions from tax on certain income and gains under TCA 1997, s 189A(2) and who would otherwise be entitled to repayment of DIRT tax (eg because the interest is exempt, or due to the overall level of income and tax credits), and
- (iii) a declaration, in the form prescribed by Revenue, similar to the declaration at (i)(iii) above has been made to the Revenue Commissioners, and
- (iv) the Revenue Commissioners have issued a notification to the deposit taker identifying the account and confirming that DIRT need not be deducted from interest, and
- (v) the individual beneficially entitled to the interest is not otherwise an individual referred to at (i) above, ie 65 or over and otherwise entitled to exemption;

(k) a deposit which is made by a Personal Retirement Savings Account (PRSA) provider and which is held for the purposes of a PRSA where the PRSA provider has provided the deposit taker with its Revenue reference number.

With regard to item (e) above, prior to 1 June 1991 all deposits in foreign currencies were excepted deposits excluded from the retention tax. This complete exception was removed to include as a relevant deposit any foreign currency deposit made on or after 1 June 1991 by any individual (other than a non-resident individual who has made the non-resident's declaration). However, there is one exclusion from item (e). If immediately prior to 1 June 1991 an individual held a deposit denominated in a particular foreign currency (for example, sterling) with a particular deposit taker, then a new deposit made by that individual in the same foreign currency (for example, sterling) on or after 1 June 1991 with the same deposit taker is not a relevant deposit, so that the interest on it continues to be paid without any retention tax. This exclusion does not appear to place any limit to the amount of the new foreign currency deposit which may be made with the same deposit taker, nor does it appear to require the deposit held immediately prior to 1 June 1991 to be withdrawn. However, the exception does not apply to foreign currency deposits made on or after 1 January 1993 (TCA 1997, s 256(1): definition of 'relevant deposit', para (e)).

Relevant interest

The term 'relevant interest' is used to denote the interest to which the retention tax must be applied. It is defined as interest paid in respect of a relevant deposit, subject to the special provisions in TCA 1997, ss 261A, 267C dealing with special term and special term share accounts.

The word 'interest' is itself separately defined as interest of money whether yearly or otherwise, including any amount paid in consideration of the making of a deposit, even if not described as interest; it also includes any dividend or other distribution in respect of shares in a building society. Where the amount to be repaid in relation to a deposit may to any extent be linked to changes in a stock exchange index or any other financial index (typically a 'tracker bond'), any excess of the amount so repaid over the amount of the deposit will be treated as interest from 6 April 2001 onwards.

Appropriate tax

The legislation refers to the tax to be deducted from payments of relevant interest as the 'appropriate tax'. The rate of appropriate tax is as follows:

Year of assessment	*Rate of tax*
2017	39%
2018	37%
2019	35%
2020 and subsequent years	33%

Deduction of tax

TCA 1997, s 257 requires every bank, building society and other relevant deposit taker to deduct the appropriate tax from the gross amount of the interest paid or credited on every relevant deposit which it holds. The amount actually paid or credited is therefore the net interest after retention tax. The person to whom the interest is paid is obliged to accept the deduction of the tax and the bank or other relevant deposit taker is fully discharged from its obligation to the depositor for the gross amount of the interest. For the subsequent tax treatment of the depositor who has suffered this retention tax, see **8.204**.

2.402 Non-residents and the retention tax

In principle, it is intended to exempt persons who are not resident in the State from the deposit interest retention tax. A deposit in which no person resident in the State has any beneficial interest is not a relevant deposit, so that the interest paid or credited on it must be paid without the deduction of the retention tax, provided that the person to whom the interest is payable makes the declaration mentioned in TCA 1997, s 263. This follows from the definition of 'relevant deposit' provided in TCA 1997, s 256. It may be noted that the non-resident person is not exempted as such in respect of such interest.

If a person not resident in the State (the non-resident person) is to avoid the deduction of the retention tax from his interest on a deposit with a relevant deposit taker, it is essential that the non-resident's declaration is made to the relevant deposit taker. It is not sufficient simply to advise the bank or other deposit taker of his non-residence status by a letter or in any other manner short of the proper declaration. Even if the deposit taker knows that the depositor is a non-resident person, the deposit remains a relevant deposit and the retention tax must be applied to any interest which is paid or credited before the non-resident's declaration is received.

TCA 1997, s 263 provides that the non-resident's declaration is a declaration that, at the time it is made, the person who is beneficially entitled to the interest on the deposit to which it applies is not resident in the State. If two or more persons are beneficially entitled to the interest on a deposit, the declaration must be to the effect that all of the persons beneficially entitled are not resident in the State. For example, if in the case of a deposit account held beneficially by four persons, three of the joint holders are resident abroad and the fourth is resident in the State, the declaration cannot be made and the deposit taker must deduct the tax from all the interest paid or credited on the account.

The declaration must be made in writing to the relevant deposit taker in the form prescribed by the Revenue Commissioners. It must be made by the person to whom the interest on the deposit is payable and must be signed by him. The person required to make the declaration is always the person to whom the interest is payable (the declarer), whether or not he is the person beneficially entitled to the interest. The declarer may be a resident person in any case where he has no beneficial entitlement to the interest and the beneficial interest is held only by a person or persons not resident in the State.

An example of a case in which the non-resident's declaration should be made by a resident person is where the interest is payable to a resident trustee of a settlement the income of which is beneficially due to a non-resident person or persons. If there are two or more beneficiaries entitled to the income of the settlement, the non-resident's declaration may only be made if all the beneficiaries are non-residents. In the case of a discretionary settlement where the income of the settlement is only payable to the non-resident beneficiaries if and when the trustee exercises a discretion to distribute income, the beneficiaries are not regarded as being beneficially entitled to the income and the resident trustee cannot make the declaration (so that the retention tax has to be deducted).

The declaration must state, as respects the person beneficially entitled, his name, the address of his principal place of residence and the country in which he is resident at the time the declaration is made. If there are two or more beneficial owners, these particulars must be given for each of them. In addition, it must contain an undertaking by the declarer that, if the person or any of the persons covered by the declaration should become resident in the State, the declarer will notify the relevant deposit taker accordingly.

A non-resident's declaration may be made by or on behalf of any non-resident person, whether an individual, company, foreign pension scheme, etc, provided that the test of foreign residence is met. For example, a non-resident company holding a deposit with a relevant deposit taker is entitled to make the non-resident's declaration and avoid suffering the retention tax, notwithstanding that its deposit is held by, or is otherwise connected with, a trade or business carried on by it through a branch in the State.

Retention and inspection of declarations

TCA 1997, s 263 requires every relevant deposit taker to retain each non-resident's declaration made to it for the longer of:

(a) the period of six years ending after the date that declaration was made; or

(b) the period of three years ending after the date on which the deposit the subject of that declaration is repaid or, if it should happen, three years after the date on which the deposit becomes a relevant deposit.

In other words, in every case the non-resident's declaration in respect of a given deposit must be retained for a minimum period of six years from the date of the declaration. Then, in any case where the deposit is held by the deposit taker for more than three years after the date of the declaration, the period for which the declaration must be retained is extended to the date three years after the date on which the deposit is repaid (or becomes a relevant deposit).

Example 2.402.1

Mr Jacques Mitterois, who is resident only in France, makes a deposit with a bank in Dublin on 16 September 2009. The bank sends him a non-resident's declaration which he completes and is received back by the bank on 23 September 2009.

Assume that the deposit is repaid to Mr Mitterois on 19 January 2010. The bank must retain the declaration made by Mr Mitterois until 22 September 2015. This is the end of the period of six years after the date the declaration was given to the bank (and not the date the deposit was made). The period of three years after the deposit is repaid ends on the earlier date of 18 January 2013 and is not therefore relevant.

Example 2.402.2

Take the facts of **Example 2.402.1**, but assume that Mr Mitterois retains the deposit with the Dublin bank until 10 October 2013 when it is repaid to him. He remains resident only in France throughout this period.

In this case, the bank is required to retain the declaration made by Mr Mitterois until 9 October 2016. This is the date three years after the date of the deposit repayment and applies because it is later than the date six years after the date the declaration was made (23 September 2009).

A deposit of a person not resident in the State at the time the deposit was made becomes a relevant deposit (subject to the retention tax) if the non-resident should subsequently become resident. Should this happen more than three years after the date the non-resident's declaration was made, the period for retaining the declaration is extended to the end of the three years following the change of residence.

Example 2.402.3

The trustees of an Irish trust made a deposit in a building society in Cork on 18 October 2010. Mr Hans Schmidt, who is resident only in Germany, has a life interest in the entire trust fund (so that he is the only person beneficially entitled to the interest on the deposit). The trustees made the non-resident's declaration to the building society on 18 October 2010.

The deposit is not therefore a relevant deposit and the interest becomes payable without the deduction of any retention tax.

On 1 February 2015, Mr Schmidt moves from Germany to live in Ireland and thereby becomes resident in the State. The trustees, meeting their undertaking in the non-resident's declaration to do so, immediately notify the building society that Mr Schmidt has become resident. The trustees' deposit, which has been kept with the building society since 2010, becomes a relevant deposit on 1 February 2015 (since the non-residence condition for its exemption from retention tax no longer applies). In this case, the building society is required to retain the declaration made by the trustees until 31 January 2018. This is the date three years after the date the deposit becomes a relevant deposit and applies because it is later than the date six years after the declaration was made (18 October 2010). The date on which the relevant deposit is repaid is not relevant in this case.

Every relevant deposit taker is required, on receiving a notice in writing from an inspector of taxes, to make available to the inspector all non-residents' declarations made to it. The inspector is entitled to examine, take extracts from or copies of any such declarations made available to him. The deposit taker must provide the inspector with all the declarations required within the time limit specified in the inspector's notice.

TCA 1997, s 891A requires that every relevant person, ie a company or a collective investment undertaking, who pays relevant interest (interest payments by companies and to non-residents) without deduction of tax to submit a return detailing the name, address and country of residence of the recipient and the amount of payment. The penalty provisions of TCA 1997, ss 1052 and 1054 apply to non-returns or late returns of this information. The specified return date is dependent on the chargeable period. Where the chargeable period is a tax year the return must be submitted by the following 31 October.

2.5 Professional Services Withholding Tax

2.501 Principles of professional services withholding tax

TCA 1997, Pt 18 Ch 1 (ss 520–529) provides for the deduction of tax at source from certain fees for professional services. This tax may be referred to as 'the professional services withholding tax', hereafter PSWT.

The 'accountable bodies' listed in **2.502** below are required to withhold the tax at the standard rate from all payments for professional services. The persons providing those services are entitled to set off the PSWT suffered against their income tax liabilities. In certain circumstances, a limited interim refund may be obtained at an earlier date (with a consequential reduction in the later set off).

Deduction of tax

TCA 1997, s 523 requires any 'accountable person' to deduct the 'appropriate tax' from any 'relevant payment' made to a 'specified person'. The specified person to whom the payment is made is required to allow the deduction and to accept the residue of the payment (the net payment) as fully discharging the accountable person's liability to him for the gross amount payable.

Specified person

A 'specified person' is defined, in relation to a relevant payment, as the person to whom that payment is made (TCA 1997, s 520) and with effect from 27 March 2013 (the date of passing of Finance Act 2013) means in the case of a partnership providing a professional service, every person who is a partner in the partnership. The specified person is normally the person who has provided the professional services in respect of which the payment is made. The specified person may be an individual, any person in a partnership, a company or any other person or entity.

The specified person may be a non-resident person who provides professional services to an accountable person (or who receives a relevant payment from an accountable person for professional services provided by someone else). For the circumstances in which a non-resident may receive a refund of professional services tax, see Refunds to non-residents in **2.506**.

Appropriate tax

The 'appropriate tax', which has to be deducted by any accountable person when making any relevant payment, is defined as a sum representing income tax at the standard rate in force at the time of the payment calculated on the amount of the relevant payment (exclusive of any value-added tax which may be included in the payment) (TCA 1997, s 520(1)).

Relevant payments

A 'relevant payment' is defined by TCA 1997, s 520(1) as a payment made by:

(a) an accountable person in respect of professional services whether or not such services are provided for the accountable person making the payment; or
(b) an authorised insurer to a practitioner in the discharge of a claim in respect of relevant medical expenses under a contract of insurance.

There are however exclusions for the following:

(a) payments of Sch E emoluments subject to deduction of tax under the PAYE procedure (see **11.101**);
(b) payments by principals to subcontractors to which the relevant contracts tax deduction scheme applies, TCA 1997, s 530A (see **2.311**);
(c) a payment made to reimburse a relevant payment by one accountable person to another;
(d) (with effect from 25 March 2005) payments by an accountable person to another accountable person whose income is either exempt from Corporation Tax or is disregarded for the purposes of the Tax Acts; and
(e) (with effect from 25 March 2005) payments to a body granted exemption under TCA 1997, s 207 (charitable bodies).

The exclusion from the definition of 'relevant payment' of payments subject to the deduction of tax under TCA 1997, s 530A, applies whether or not any tax is in fact deducted under that section. In other words, even where the zero rate of RCT applies the accountable person paying it does not deduct the PSWT.

The point that all payments by accountable persons in respect of professional services are relevant payments whether or not the accountable person is the person to whom the services are rendered should be emphasised. For example, the Legal Aid Board may make payments to solicitors and barristers for work representing persons entitled to legal aid. Although these services may be rendered to the persons represented and not to the Legal Aid Board, the Board as an accountable person must deduct the professional services tax in making payments to the solicitor or barrister for their services.

In practice, the Revenue apply an exception to the point emphasised in the last paragraph in the case where the employees of an accountable person are, as part of the conditions of their employment, entitled to have their bills for medical treatment paid by the accountable person. In such a case, the Guidance Notes issued by the Revenue Commissioners state that the payment by the accountable person is to be made without the deduction of the tax. In effect, this removes such payments from the definition of 'relevant payment'. The notes go on to indicate that this exception does not apply where the payment for the employees' medical treatment is made under a contractual arrangement between the accountable person and the medical practitioner whereby the latter provides medical treatment free to the employees; such payments must be paid less the tax.

The European Communities (Late Payment in Commercial Transactions) Regulations 2012 (SI 580/2012) as amended by European Communities (Late Payment in Commercial Transactions) (Amendment) Regulations 2013 (SI 74/2013) provides that it is an implied term of any commercial contract that interest is payable where debts are paid late. PSWT should not be deducted from interest payable in respect of payment which is for a professional service. The European Communities (Late Payment in Commercial Transactions) Regulations 2012 replaced the European Communities (Late

Payment in Commercial Transactions) Regulations 2002. *Tax Briefing 52* sets out the tax treatment of such interest.

Professional services defined

TCA 1997, s 520(1) provides that, for the purposes of the professional services tax, the term 'professional services' includes:

(a) services of a medical, dental, pharmaceutical, optical, aural or veterinary nature;

(b) services of an architectural, engineering, quantity surveying or surveying nature, and related services;

(c) services of accountancy, auditing or finance and services of financial, economic, marketing, advertising or other consultancies;

(d) services of a solicitor or barrister and other legal services; and

(e) geological services.

This definition is very wide. By indicating that all the types of services listed in it are included as professional services, it brings within the scope of the tax all the services listed (when rendered to accountable persons), whether or not they would otherwise be regarded as 'professional services' under the normal meaning of the term. Further, any other types of services which can be regarded as professional services in the normal sense are covered even if not specifically mentioned in the definition. Any services which are not professional services in the normal sense and which are not specifically mentioned in the definition are outside the scope of the tax.

The question of what is a 'profession' in the normal meaning of the term is discussed in **4.105**. In deciding whether or not the PSWT is to be deducted from a particular payment to a person who has provided services, the accountable person should refer first to the list of activities mentioned in the TCA 1997, s 520 definition. If the service provided is one within the listed activities, the accountable person should deduct the tax when paying for them. If the service is not one of those listed, the further question must be asked as to whether the service is nevertheless one carried out as part of the activities of a profession in the normal sense. If so, the tax must be deducted.

One example of services caught within the definition of TCA 1997, s 520, although held not to be professional services in another context, is those of advertising agents. In *MacGiolla Mhaith v Cronin & Associates Ltd* III ITR 211, it was held that, for the purposes of the additional 15 per cent corporation tax surcharge on the undistributed income of a person carrying on a profession through a company (see TCA 1997, s 441), the business of an advertising agency did not consist of or include the provision of professional services. However, the services rendered by such a business are considered to be the services of an advertising consultancy within item (c) of the professional services definition of TCA 1997, s 520.

The Revenue Commissioners have issued leaflet IT61 entitled 'A Revenue Guide to Professional Services Withholding Tax (PSWT) for Accountable Persons and Specified Persons' (reissued August 2008 as an updated version of, and replacing, previous statements and Revenue Guidance). This leaflet is referred to in this division as the 'Revenue Guide'. Appendix 4 to this guide sets out Revenue opinions on whether certain activities are regarded as coming within the definition of professional services.

The Revenue Guide indicates that the Revenue regard the provision of independent advice on the installation, development (including the development of a web site) or running of computer systems or on the running of computer systems, as well as other computer consultancy work, as a professional service subject to the tax. This is presumably on the grounds that it is a 'financial or economic or other consultancy' within item (c) of the definition.

On the other hand, the Revenue do not consider the sale of computer hardware and software packages, including software packages developed by the seller, to be a professional service. Any element of service in analysing the work to be computerised and then in developing or programming the software to handle the work, or in providing training or back-up services, is not a professional service provided that it is included in the cost of the software or hardware sold and is not charged to the customer separately.

The question of whether a computer bureau service is a professional service subject to the tax is not addressed in the appendix. It appears that there may be a Revenue view that it is within the definition, but it is suggested that the provision of a computer bureau service in the normal sense (for example, the processing of an accountable person's payroll and PAYE deductions) is not any form of financial, economic or other consultancy nor is it a professional service in the normal sense of a profession. It seems to be the performance of a purely electronic function with no element of consultancy involved.

The earlier version of the Revenue Guide indicated that fees, commissions and charges in respect of banking transactions were considered to be payments in respect of a service of finance within item (c) of the professional services definition but that the Revenue do not regard the normal bank charge debited to a customer's bank account for the ordinary servicing of that account as a relevant payment so that no tax is to be deducted from the amount debited to the account of an accountable person. The revised Revenue Guide does not refer to fees, commissions and charges on banking transactions. However, there is no evidence to suggest that Revenue's opinion on this matter has changed. Neither version of the notes refer to interest charged on a bank account, but it seems clear that interest is paid for the use of money and not for a professional service.

Debt collecting is a service of finance and is strictly a professional service, but the Revenue Guide state that where, instead of receiving a payment from the accountable person getting this service, a percentage of the amount collected is withheld by the debt collector, it would be impractical to apply the withholding tax. In such cases, the tax need not be applied, but the tax would be deductible if a fee was charged separately for collecting debts of an accountable person.

Among the types of services which the Revenue Guide state are not regarded as professional services are:

(a) teaching, training or lecturing services other than training services provided on behalf of An Foras Áiseanna Saothair (FÁS);
(b) services of employment agencies (but the services of providing advice on recruitment would probably be a professional service as a form of economic or other consultancy);
(c) translation (including services of an interpreter) and proof reading services;
(d) services of stenographers;
(e) setting and assessing oral, aural or written exams;
(f) contract cleaning services;
(g) maintenance and repair work (including maintenance of computer hardware or software); and
(h) archaeological work where the payments are in respect of archaeological digs or excavations. Where however the archaeological digs or excavations form part of

an overall professional service the full amount of the payment is subject to PSWT.

The Revenue Guide also makes it clear that dental technicians are regarded as skilled crafts persons who manufacture dentures, dental braces and other prosthetic appliances and that the supply by them of such appliances to accountable persons is not a professional service. Similarly, the supply of artificial limbs and surgical and medical appliances, including any incidental charges for fitting by the supplier, is not treated as a professional service but, if a separate fee is charged for fitting, this is treated as a payment for a service of a medical nature within item (a) of the 'professional services' definition.

Treatment of expenses

A person rendering professional services may incur expenses or outlay in the course of providing those services. Since the definition of 'relevant payment' includes all payments 'in respect of' professional services, the general principle is that the accountable person must deduct the appropriate tax not only from the fee charged by the specified person, but also from any expenses or outlay incurred by the specified person and included in the bill for which the payment is made. For example, if a firm of auditors incurs travelling and hotel expenses in connection with the audit of an accountable person, the tax must be deducted when the accountable person reimburses the firm for those expenses; this applies whether the expenses are included in the fee account or are charged separately.

The Revenue have, however, indicated that no tax need be withheld when an accountable person makes a payment in respect of specific outlay when all the following conditions are met:

(a) the outlay is for goods or services provided as part of the service being performed;
(b) the amount of the payment has been specifically negotiated with the accountable person or, alternatively, is a sum on a scale which is generally accepted as operating within the trade or profession concerned;
(c) the amount is payable as a separate item of charge distinct from any fee or other payment due in respect of the service provided; and
(d) the amount represents actual cost or actual outlay only and does not include any element of profit or earnings of the specified person.

In particular the Revenue Guide confirms that PSWT should not be deducted from stamp duty, Land Registry fees, deed of registration fees, Company Office fees and court fees.

The Revenue Guide contains several paragraphs dealing with certain expenses incurred in connection with the advertising services. It is normal practice for advertising agencies to place advertisements in newspapers, other publications, radio and television acting as agent for the newspaper or other medium concerned. In such cases, the advertising agent is effectively selling space or time in the media on a commission or handling charge and is usually reimbursed for the actual payment to the media plus a commission or handling charge for this service. The Guide indicates that no tax should be deducted by an accountable person paying the advertising agent for the media costs. However, the tax should be deducted from the agent's commission or handling charge.

On the other hand, if the advertising agency provides consultancy services in designing an advertisement or in conducting an advertising campaign for an accountable person and if the space or time in the media is provided as part of this service, the total amount paid for the full service is a payment for professional services. The accountable person must withhold the tax from the total bill.

An advertising agency may pay for various other services used in the course of an advertising campaign for an accountable person. Photographers, models, commercial artists, graphic art designers, freelance writers, printers, etc may be engaged by the advertising agency as part of their service. Again, when the costs of the services of such persons are billed to the accountable person as part of the agency's total bill, the tax must be deducted when the bill is paid. However, the Revenue do not regard the services of the photographers, models, etc as professional services in themselves. If, for example, a commercial artist renders services directly to an accountable person, this is not a professional service and no tax is deductible from the payment for the work.

Costs of legal actions

The Revenue Guide sets out the following rules to be applied in relation to professional costs incurred in connection with legal actions:

(a) where, under a ruling of a court, tribunal or similar body, another party's costs are awarded against an accountable person, no professional services tax should be deducted when the accountable person pays the other party's costs, even if the accountable person makes the payment to the person who provided the professional services;

(b) the tax should, however, be deducted when the accountable person pays his own costs;

(c) the rules in (a) and (b) apply in the same way where amounts are paid by the accountable person in an out of court settlement if the legal action was one in respect of which an order for costs could have been made by the court, tribunal, etc before which it was to be heard; and

(d) in all other cases, the tax must be deducted by an accountable person when paying legal costs, whether he is paying his own costs or those of another party.

2.502 Accountable persons

TCA 1997, s 521(1) provides that the term 'accountable person' means a person specified in TCA 1997, Sch 13. TCA 1997, s 521(2) then states that, where any of the accountable persons specified in TCA 1997, Sch 13 is a body corporate the following will also be an accountable person required to apply the professional services tax when paying fees for professional services:

(a) any subsidiary of that body corporate which is resident in the State. For the definition of 'subsidiary' for this purpose, see below;

(b) with effect from 1 January 2014, a company resident in the State, of which more than one accountable person are members, if the accountable person:

   (i) is a member of the first company and controls the composition of its board of directors,

   (ii) holds more than half in nominal value of its equity share capital, or

   (iii) holds more than half in nominal value of its shares carrying voting rights (other than voting rights which arise only in specified circumstances)

This means that where an accountable person is a body corporate its subsidiaries are also accountable persons and body corporate which are under the control of more than one accountable person are also accountable persons.

In determining whether a company is a subsidiary company of any of the accountable persons specified in TCA 1997, Sch 13 the definition of 'subsidiary' used in Companies Act 1963, s 155 is used (TCA 1997, s 521(2)). This definition provides that a company (the first company) is a subsidiary of another company (the parent company) if, but only if:

(a) the parent company:
   (i) is a member of the first company and controls the composition of its board of directors,
   (ii) holds more than half in nominal value of its equity share capital, or
   (iii) holds more than half in nominal value of its shares carrying voting rights (other than voting rights which arise only in specified circumstances); or
(b) the first company is a subsidiary of any third company which is the parent company's subsidiary (CA 1963, s 155(1)).

For the purpose of this definition, 'company' includes any body corporate and 'equity share capital' means, in relation to a company, its issued share capital excluding any part thereof which, neither as respects dividends nor as respects capital carries any right to participate beyond a specified amount in a distribution (CA 1963, s 155(5)). In applying the above definition, it is also necessary to have regard to CA 1963, s 155(2), (3) and (4) which supplement the definition provided in sub-s (1).

TCA 1997, s 521 empowers the Minister for Finance to add other persons or classes of persons to the list of accountable persons. Any additions to the list may be made by Regulations (if not added by a Finance Act). A draft of any proposed Regulation must be laid before Dáil Éireann and the Regulation is then made after a resolution approving of the draft has been passed by Dáil Éireann. Any new accountable person is required to deduct the appropriate tax from all relevant payments made by him on or after (but not before) a date specified in the particular Regulation.

2.503 Medical insurance payments

The following definitions are provided by TCA 1997, s 520(1) for the application of the PSWT to insurance reimbursements for relevant medical expenses:

'authorised insurer'

Any person lawfully carrying on in the State a business of insuring against medical, surgical or nursing expenses (including hospital maintenance) resulting from sickness or accidents (TCA 1997, s 470 definition applied).

'practitioner'

Any person registered in the register established under the Medical Practitioners Act 1927, s 2(1), or who is temporarily registered under the Medical Practitioners Act 1955, s 3 or who is registered under the Dentists Act 1928, s 23 (TCA 1997, s 469 definition applied).

'relevant medical expenses'

Expenses incurred in respect of professional services provided by a practitioner, being expenses which are or may become the subject of a claim for reimbursement in whole or in part under a contract of insurance, but excluding any expenses that:

(a) are reimbursable under the so called 'out-patients scheme', or

(b) are incurred in respect of professional services provided by a practitioner outside the State.

The out-patients expenses exclusion applies, so that no tax is deductible from the payments to the practitioner, if the terms of the contract of insurance permit the reimbursement only (i) after the end of a stated period of 12 months and (ii) to the extent the total out-patients expenses incurred in that stated period exceeds a stated amount.

'contract of insurance'

A contract which provides insurance specifically, whether in conjunction with other benefits or not, for the reimbursement or discharge, in whole or in part, of actual medical, surgical or nursing expenses (including the cost of maintenance at a hospital, nursing home or sanatorium) resulting from sickness of or accident to an individual who has made the contract (or his spouse, child or other dependant) (definition of TCA 1997, s 470(1) applied).

'member'

Any person named in the relevant contract of insurance and who has been accepted for insurance by the authorised insurer (ie the subscriber, his spouse, child or other dependant).

'subscriber'

The person (other than the authorised insurer) who is a party to the contract and in whose name the relevant policy of insurance is registered.

In order to ensure that all reimbursements of relevant medical expenses made by an authorised insurer are subjected to the deduction of the professional services tax, TCA 1997, s 522 compels the authorised insurer to discharge any claim for the reimbursement of relevant medical expenses by paying the practitioner (and not the subscriber) or with effect from 1 January 2014, to the employer of the practitioner where the practitioner provides the services while acting as an employee rather than as a self employed practitioner). Otherwise, a reimbursement to the subscriber (who has paid the practitioner) would escape as the payment to the subscriber would be a payment in respect of his insurance contract (and not in respect of professional services).

Consequently, when a subscriber has incurred relevant medical expenses in respect of which he has a claim under a contract of insurance, he should not normally pay the practitioner for the part of those expenses covered by his insurance policy. A claim should be made to the authorised insurer as soon as possible leaving it to the insurer to pay the practitioner (less the professional services tax). This does not apply to doctors', etc fees and other amounts reimbursable under the 'out-patients scheme'; since these are not relevant medical expenses, they may be paid direct to the practitioner and included in a subsequent claim to the authorised insurer (to the extent in excess of the stated amount).

The professional services tax does not apply to the part (if any) of the fees, etc payable by the patient to the practitioner in excess of the reimbursement due under the contract of insurance. This excess should be paid by the patient directly to the practitioner.

If, in any case, the subscriber or a member (the patient) does in fact pay any relevant medical expenses covered by the contract of insurance directly to the practitioner, then the practitioner is required to make the appropriate repayment to the subscriber or the member. The amount to be repaid by the practitioner is the excess of:

(a) the aggregate of:
   (i) the amount of the subscriber's/member's payment to the practitioner (less any part of it for medical expenses not covered by the insurance), and
   (ii) the amount of the payment in respect of professional services (the relevant payment) made by the authorised insurer to the practitioner;

over

(b) the amount of the relevant medical expenses covered by the contract of insurance (TCA 1997, s 523(2)).

TCA 1997, s 523(3) authorises the Minister of Finance to make regulations, if he considers it necessary, to give full effect to the provisions which impose the professional services tax on medical insurance payments by authorised insurers.

2.504 Accountable persons with foreign activities

An accountable person may incur professional costs outside the State in connection with a branch, representative office or other activities outside the State. The professional services tax legislation does not contain any explicit territorial limitation as to the scope of the tax. Therefore, on a strict application of the legislation, an accountable person is required to deduct the tax when making payments in respect of professional services to persons outside the State, notwithstanding that the services may be provided fully abroad by foreign persons in relation to a foreign branch or to other activities carried on outside the State by the accountable person.

Clearly, this position is not unreasonable when the foreign professional services are provided in connection with the accountable person's activities in the State. However, it does create problems for the accountable person seeking to obtain foreign professional advice in connection with its foreign activities. If the services are being provided under a foreign contract, the rule of TCA 1997, s 523 obliging a specified person to allow the tax not to be deducted could not normally be enforced against the recipient (see *Keiner v Keiner*, discussed at **2.307**).

The Revenue Guide provides that an accountable person which is an Irish resident company with a foreign branch can make payments for foreign professional services without deducting the tax provided that three conditions are met – namely, that the payment is made abroad by the branch, that the professional services are being provided abroad and that the payee is resident abroad.

For the circumstances in which the Revenue consider that a non-resident person may be given a refund of the withholding tax deducted, see **2.506**.

2.505 Procedural matters

TCA 1997, s 524(1) requires each specified person to furnish certain particulars to each accountable person to whom he (or if a company or partnership, it) renders professional services. If the specified person is either resident in the State or is a non-resident person having a permanent establishment or fixed base in the State, the specified person, or in the case of a partnership the precedent partner, must advise the accountable person of his PPS number (or, if a company or partnership, its tax number). The specified person/ precedent partner must also give his/its value-added tax registration number if the professional services are subject to that tax. If a specified person is a non-resident person without any permanent establishment or fixed base in the State, he or it is required to advise the accountable person of his or its country of residence and his or its tax reference in that country.

For this purpose 'precedent partner' is defined in TCA 1997, s 1007, ie the person first named in the partnership agreement or if the first named person is not an acting partner the precedent acting partner or if there is no agreement the person named singly or with more precedence over the other partners.

Once the specified person or precedent partner has provided the accountable person with the required particulars, the accountable person must give the specified person or precedent partner a tax deduction form (Form F45/1) with each relevant payment. The form must state the following particulars:

(a) the name and address of the specified person or partnership;
(b) that person or partnership's tax reference number;
(c) the amount of the relevant payment;
(d) the amount of the tax deducted from that payment; and
(e) the date of the payment (TCA 1997, s 524(2)).

An accountable person can ask the specified person or precedent partner to provide evidence to support the validity of the tax number supplied. They may also request Revenue to confirm that the tax number is in fact the tax number of the specified person or partnership concerned.

It is important for the specified person to keep all the tax deduction forms received from each accountable person to whom professional services are rendered. The specified person may be asked to submit the forms to the inspector of taxes in claiming the set off under TCA 1997, s 526 for the tax deducted against his/its income tax or in claiming an interim refund under TCA 1997, s 527 (see **2.506**).

Returns by accountable person

TCA 1997, s 525(1) requires each accountable person to make a return to the Collector-General for each income tax month (ending on the fifth day of each calendar month and if in relation to a period prior to 6 December 2001, the period beginning on 6 December 2001 and finishing on 31 December 2001, and thereafter, a calendar month (TCA 1997, s 520(1)). This return is required within 14 days (previously 10 days FA 2001, Sch 2) after the end of each income tax month and must be accompanied by a remittance of all amounts of appropriate tax which the accountable person is liable to deduct from all the relevant payments made in the month in question.

The return must be in the form prescribed by the Revenue Commissioners and must include a declaration by the accountable person that the return is correct and complete. It must state the names of all specified persons or partnerships to whom the accountable person has made relevant payments in the month in question and the total of the tax deducted from such payments in the relevant income tax month.

The Revenue Commissioners require every accountable person to make this return every month whether or not any payments for professional services are made in the month. If no such payments are made in a month, a 'nil' return is required. The question arises as to whether 'nil' returns are required every month by a dormant (ie totally inactive) subsidiary of a semi-State company. It appears that the Revenue's position is that monthly returns are required even in such cases.

Partnerships

Prior to the Finance Act 2013 there were no specific references in the legislation dealing with PSWT and partnerships. It was accepted however that a specified person could include a partnership. TCA 1997, s 528 provided that where a Form F45 referred to two or more persons any necessary apportionment could be made for the purpose of giving a credit or interim refund. In practice in the case of partnerships PSWT was allocated in accordance with the partnership profit sharing ratio for the period to which the relevant payment related.

Finance Act 2013 introduced TCA 1997, s 529A with effect from 27 March 2013. TCA 1997, s 529A provides:

(a) That where a professional service is provided by a partnership an accountable person may make a relevant payment in the name of the partnership.

(b) Where a partnership receives a relevant payment the relevant payment is deemed to have been made to each partner in the partnership in the same ratio as profits are shared between the partners for the relevant period. Also the PSWT withheld from any relevant payment is to be allocated between the partners in accordance with the partnership profit sharing ratio.

(c) Where (b) applies the precedent partner is required to issue a statement, which may be in written or electronic format, to each partner giving details of the apportionment of relevant payments and PSWT among the partners and provide a copy of the F45 given to the precedent partner by the accountable person.

In addition the existing legislation was amended to include references to partnerships or the precedent partner, where appropriate, with effect also from 27 March 2013.

2.506 Relief for withholding tax

PSWT is a sum 'representing income tax' (TCA 1997, s 520(1): definition of 'appropriate tax') and therefore in principle credit is due for it against the tax liability of the person who has suffered it.

TCA 1997, s 526 provides that a specified person, who is chargeable to income tax for a given year of assessment, may claim a set off – against his income tax liability for that year – of the appropriate tax which is referable to his basis period for that year. No set off is, however, given for any appropriate tax referable to that credit period which has been repaid in an interim refund claim for the tax year in question. If the appropriate tax (as reduced by any amount repaid as an interim refund) exceeds the specified person's income tax liability for the year, the excess is refunded to him.

A taxpayer who has suffered PSWT in a given tax year can offset it against his preliminary tax payment for that year by submitting the relevant forms F45 as part payment. Where PSWT has been withheld from a relevant payment made to a partnership the precedent partner is required to issue a statement to each partner giving details of the apportionment of relevant payments and PSWT among the partners and provide a copy of the F45 given to the precedent partner by the accountable person. This statement can be used by a partner in support of a claim for credit or an interim refund.

The first step in determining the amount of the appropriate tax to be set off against the income tax liability for a given year of assessment is to identify the basis period for that year. The 'basis period for a year of assessment' is defined, subject to two provisos (see below), as the period on the profits or gains of which income tax for that year falls to be finally computed under the rules of Sch D Cases I & II (TCA 1997, s 520(1)). The basis period for any tax year is normally the 12-month period of account ending in the same tax year.

Once the relevant basis period has been established, it is the 'appropriate tax' referable to that basis period (net of any interim refunds) which is the appropriate tax to be set off against the taxpayer's income tax liability for the said year of assessment. The appropriate tax referable to a basis period for a year of assessment is defined as the appropriate tax deducted from all relevant payments which are taken into account in computing the specified person's profits or gains for that basis period (TCA 1997, s 520(1)). If the specified person accounts for his trade receipts on an earnings basis, which will almost always be the case (see **5.502**), ie if he includes as trade receipts in each period for which accounts are prepared, all professional fees billed in that period (whether or not paid before the end of the period), the appropriate tax for which the set off may be claimed in respect of that period will include the tax deducted from any relevant payments included in the debtors in the relevant balance sheet. If the specified person accounts for his fees on a cash basis (which in fact rarely applies – see **5.502**), only the tax suffered on the relevant payments received in the credit period can be the subject of a set off claim in respect of that period.

Example 2.506.1

Messrs Plaice, Black and Hall are in practice as solicitors for a number of years. The firm's accounts are prepared on an earnings basis, ie all professional fees are brought into the accounts on the dates the bills are sent out to the clients. The fees include relevant payments received less appropriate tax from four accountable persons, the Legal Aid Board, a harbour authority and the HSE.

The relevant payments from these accountable persons brought into the firm's accounts for the period of account to 30 June 2017 (exclusive of value added tax and before the deduction of appropriate tax) are as follows:

	€
Received in the year	8,400
Billed in the year, but included in debtors at 30/6/2017	5,300
	13,700
Less:	
Billed in previous year and included in debtors at 1/7/2016	1,900
Net trading receipts (from accountable persons)	11,800

The €11,800 relevant payments included in the firm's profits for the year to 30 June 2017 are received when the standard rate of income tax is 20 per cent and therefore the appropriate tax (professional services tax) for the year to 30 June 2017 is (€11,800 x 20% = €2,360).

The year to 30 June 2017 is the basis period for the assessment of the partners' Sch D Case II profits for 2017. Therefore, the credit for each partner's share of the €2,360 appropriate tax on the €11,800 professional fees included in arriving at the Sch D Case II profits is given against each person's share as assessable for 2017.

Assume that no interim refund was claimed for any of the appropriate tax referable to the year ended 30 June 2017, and assume that the profit sharing ratio at all relevant times is 50:30:20, the partners are each entitled to set off against their respective income tax liabilities for 2017 the following amounts:

Mr Plaice:	€
50% x €2,360[3]	1,180

Mr Black:	
30% x €2,360[3]	708
Mr Hall:	
20% x €2,360[3]	472
	2,360

Notes

1. In arriving at the appropriate tax referable to the year ending 30 June 2017, it is assumed that all the fees of €5,300 accrued at 30 June 2017 were in fact received subsequently and that the appropriate tax was deducted.
2. The appropriate tax deducted from the €1,900 fees accrued at 30 June 2016 (and received after that date) is eligible for set off against the partners' income tax liabilities for 2016 (since those fees were brought into account in arriving at the firm's profits for the year ended 30 June 2016, basis period for 2016).
3. In *Tax Briefing 22*, the Revenue Commissioners state that, in exceptional circumstances they are prepared to consider requests by partners to allocate credit for PSWT on a basis other than their profit sharing ratios. An example of a situation where the Revenue might grant such a request is if the partner is entitled to a refund of PSWT, while another owes a significant amount of tax. In practice, an inspector will usually agree to allocate withholding tax in the ratio agreed by the partners so long as this is not changed on a regular basis. This Briefing was published before the requirement to allocate PSWT to partners in the partners' profit sharing ratio was included in the legislation by FA 2013 (TCA 1997, s 529A(2)). Revenue have indicated that this practice may still be applied for post Finance Act 2013 changes (see Revenue Income Tax, Capital Gains Tax and Corporation Tax Manual Part 18.1.4 Professional Services Withholding Tax (PSWT) – General Instructions)

The TCA 1997, s 520(1) definition of the 'basis period for a year of assessment' quoted above is subject to two provisos. Firstly, if any period falls into the basis periods for two years of assessment (ie where two basis periods overlap wholly or partly), the period common to both basis periods (the overlapping period) is deemed to fall only into the basis period for the second of the two years of assessment. The issue of overlapping basis periods usually occurs in the first and second years of a new trade or profession (see **4.205**) or in certain cases of changes of accounting date (see **4.204**).

Secondly, if there is an interval of time or 'gap' between the end of the basis period for one year of assessment and the start of the basis period for the next year of assessment, then the interval is deemed to be part of the basis period for the second (later) year of assessment. This 'gap' rule may apply on a cessation of trade where, dependent on the circumstances, there is likely to be an interval either between the penultimate and final years or between the pre-penultimate and penultimate years, or, again, in certain cases of change of accounting date.

Example 2.506.2

Bloggs & Co (Mr J Bloggs, sole proprietor) commences business as financial consultants on 1 October 2016. The first accounts are made up for the 12 months to 30 September 2017 and subsequent accounts annually to 30 September. The Sch D Cases I & II rules of commencement (see **4.205**) are applied so that Mr Bloggs is chargeable to income tax for the first two tax years of his new business as follows:

2016 (1st year of assessment):

Basis period: period 1 October 2016 to 31 December 2016.

2017 (2nd year of assessment):

Basis period: period 1 October *2017* to 30 September *2017*.

Bloggs & Co provide financial consulting services to a number of clients including two accountable persons within TCA 1997, s 521. The professional fees (relevant payments) from these two clients included as trading receipts in computing the Sch D Case II profits of Bloggs & Co for the 12 months period to 30 September 2017 and the professional fees suffered thereon are as follows:

	Relevant payments	*Appropriate tax*
Fees actually received in period	€	€
Between 1 October 2016 and 31 December 2016 (tax at 20%)	16,800	3,360
Between 1 January 2017 and 30 September 2017 (tax at 20%)	12,100	2,420
Fees billed and unpaid at 30 September 2017 (tax at 20%)	4,400	880
	33,300	6,660

The period 1 October 2016 to 31 December 2016 forms the Sch D Case II basis period for the tax year 2016 but it also forms part of the basis period for the year 2017. For the purposes of granting credit, it is therefore deemed to fall only in the basis period for 2017 (the later of the two years). Therefore all the €6,660 tax suffered in respect of the 12 months ended 30 September 2017 is 'referable to' the basis period for the tax year 2016 and may be offset against Mr Blogg's tax liability for that tax year. However, Mr Bloggs may still be entitled to an interim refund for 2017: see below.

Interim refunds

TCA 1997, s 527(1) provides that a specified person, who is chargeable to income tax for a given year of assessment, may claim an interim refund in respect of the appropriate tax referable to the basis period for that year. With effect from 27 March 2013 an interim refund may only be claimed in respect of any PSWT remaining after the PSWT has been offset against any other outstanding tax liabilities in accordance with TCA 1997, s 960H. Under s 960H the Collector General is entitled to offset any repayment of tax, plus interest, due to a taxpayer against any outstanding tax liabilities of the person. No such interim refund will, however, be made in any case (except where the basis period is the period in which the specified person's trade or profession is set up and commenced) unless the inspector is satisfied that the following requirements are met:

(a) the taxable profits (or loss) of the specified person's basis period for the previous tax year have been finalised. (TCA 1997, s 527(2) actually says the profits for the preceding year must have been 'finally determined' for tax purposes. In a self assessment context when a return is filed generally no assessment will be issued by Revenue and there is no agreement of an assessment. Only if a Revenue assessment is issued and appealed against will an assessment be finally determined. In practice a taxpayer is regarded as complying with TCA 1997, s 527(2)(a) where the taxpayer has filed a return for the previous year and there are no outstanding issues relating to that return);

(b) the specified person's income tax liability for the previous tax year has been paid (up to 27 March 2013 this also included tax paid by set off of the previous year's appropriate tax or otherwise); and

(c) the specified person has furnished to the inspector, for each relevant payment included in the claim, the tax deduction form supplied by the accountable person for that payment (TCA 1997, s 527(2)) or in the case of a partner in a partnership, the statement which the precedent partner is required to give to the partner (see **2.505**).

The basis period for a year of assessment is always a period ending in the year in question. If a specified person liable to income tax wishes to claim an interim refund in respect of the appropriate tax referable to his basis period for such a year (for example, for the 12 months period of account ending 30 June 2015 as the basis period for the tax year 2015), he must have first agreed with the inspector the taxable profits (or loss) of the basis period for the previous tax year (ie the 12-month period of account ending 30 June 2014 as the basis period for the year 2014) and he must have fully paid the tax[1] liability for the previous tax year (ie 2014). He must also supply the relevant tax deduction form(s) F45/1 for the appropriate tax which is the subject of the claim.

The amount of the interim refund which must be made to a specified person, if the inspector is satisfied that these requirements are complied with, may be expressed as the result of the formula:

$$A - B - C$$

where:

A = the appropriate tax borne on all the relevant payments included in the claim (and supported by tax deduction forms);

B = the specified person's tax[2] liability for the previous year of assessment; and

C = the sum of any tax due and payable by the person including any tax estimated to be due and payable. For this purpose 'tax' is as defined for the purpose of s 960H by TCA 1997, s 960A and thus includes, as well as income tax and corporation tax, VAT, CAT, CGT, stamp duty and excise duty. As the collection, recovery and offset provisions which apply to income tax also apply to self employed PRSI by virtue of the SWCA 2005, tax also includes self employed PRSI.

Notes

1. The previous year's tax to be paid before any interim refund is made includes, in addition to income tax, the specified person's liability for any self-employed PRSI contribution and universal social charge due by assessment for the previous year.
2. 'Tax' again includes any self-employed PRSI contribution and universal social charge due by assessment.

No interim refund at all is given (except in respect of the first year of a new trade or profession or in cases of hardship – see below) if the specified person's income tax liability for the previous year ('B') equals or exceeds the appropriate tax for the basis period for the year of the claim ('A'). It is to be noted that the references above to the tax liability for the previous year of assessment is to the specified person's total tax liability, and not merely to his tax liability attributable to the profits of the trade or profession performing the professional services. If the specified person has significant income from other sources for the previous year, this increases his total tax liability for that year and thereby reduces the possibility of any interim refund.

TCA 1997, s 527 provides special rules for the interim refund if the basis period for a given year of assessment is the period in which the trade or profession of the specified person has been set up and commenced. For example, if a specified person commences his profession on 1 September 2014 and makes up his first accounts for the year to 31 August 2015, the basis period for the first tax year of the profession is the period 1 September 2014 to 31 December 2014 (the actual period of the trade in the first tax year

– see **4.205**). In this case, the specified person's claim for an interim refund in respect of the appropriate tax referable to this first basis period is determined under these special rules, and the requirements of TCA 1997, s 527 relating to the preceding years returns and payment of the previous year's income tax liability are not applied.

Instead, the amount available to be offset against any other outstanding tax liabilities before an interim refund can be made is an amount equal to the lesser of:

(a) the amount of the appropriate tax deducted from all relevant payments received in the first basis period (but only to the extent that the appropriate tax is supported by the tax deduction forms, or if a partner in a partnership the statement provided by the precedent partner, submitted to the inspector); and

(b) an amount determined by the formula:

$$\frac{E \times A \times C}{B \times P} \times \text{standard of income tax (\%)}$$

where:

A = the estimated total of the relevant payments to be taken into account as income in computing the taxable profits of the first basis period;

B = the estimated total sum of all amounts taken into account as income in computing the said profits;

C = the estimated number of months (or fractions of months) in the period in respect of which the claim for the interim refund is made;

E = the estimated amount of the expenses laid out wholly and exclusively in the first basis period for the purposes of the trade or profession; and

P = the estimated number of months (or fractions of months) comprised in the first basis period.

In applying the above formula, the inspector is required to make the necessary estimates to the best of his knowledge and belief in accordance with the information available to him.

Refunds where hardship

TCA 1997, s 527 empowers the Revenue Commissioners to waive (in whole or in part) any of the conditions for making an interim refund, but only in cases of hardship. If a specified person, whether chargeable to income tax or corporation tax, claims and proves the presence of a particular hardship, the Revenue Commissioners may authorise the making of a refund of appropriate tax (or an additional refund if one has previously been made). The amount of this refund (or additional refund) is to be such amount as the Commissioners consider to be just and reasonable. The Revenue have indicated in some detail the criteria they will apply in establishing hardship and the basis for calculating the amount of any refund due in SP-IT/3/90.

Refunds to non-residents

The discussion under this heading is intended to cover all types of non-resident persons, individuals, companies and any other form of person.

The fact that the person providing the professional services to an accountable person is not resident in the State or does not carry on business in the State apparently does not alter the requirement for the accountable person to deduct the appropriate tax in accordance with the rules outlined above. The legislation refers only to refunds being potentially available to specified persons who are either within the charge to corporation tax or to income tax (TCA 1997, s 526(1); (2)). Clearly, a tax which was creditable only in the case of those persons within the scope of Irish taxation could well be in breach of EU law in the appropriate circumstances (see **1.410**). The Revenue Commissioners accept that payments 'made abroad' for services rendered abroad to the branch of an Irish resident company by a person with no taxable business presence in the State fall outside the scope of PSWT. Further, a non-resident person who has suffered the appropriate tax may be entitled to obtain a refund of the tax on completing the necessary formalities. The position regarding any such refund varies dependent on whether or not the non-resident resides in a country with which there is a double taxation agreement and on whether he (or, if a company, it) has a place of business in the State.

The Revenue Commissioners accept that a non-resident person, who is resident in a 'tax treaty country' (ie a country which has a double taxation agreement with the State) and who does not carry on business in the State through a permanent establishment therein (see **14.201**), is entitled in all cases to be refunded the full amount of the appropriate tax suffered.

The claim must be supported by the originals of the tax deduction forms (forms F45/1) duly stamped and signed by the accountable persons which deducted the tax. It is also necessary for the non-resident to submit with the claim a letter from the Tax Authorities in his/its own country confirming that he/it is resident in that country for tax purposes there. It should also be stated whether or not the claimant is engaged in trade or business in the State and, if so, should give particulars of that business (its nature, where carried out, tax reference number, etc). If the non-resident is a company, it should indicate the address of its registered office if that is different from the address on the claim form.

In the case of a non-resident who is not resident in a tax treaty country, the Revenue Commissioners are only prepared to refund the appropriate tax if the work in rendering the professional services has been carried on outside the State. For example, if a marketing consultant from Guatemala (not a tax treaty country) came to the State to advise an accountable person on market conditions in that country, it appears that no refund of the tax deducted by the accountable person would be granted as the work was done in the State (note the discussion at **13.602**).

A non-resident, whether an individual, company or other person, may carry on a trade or profession in the State. This is not necessarily a bar to a claim for the non-resident's refund of professional services tax, whether or not the person is resident in a tax treaty country. If the services, the subject of the tax are not rendered as part of or in the course of the Irish trade or profession, the refund should be granted on the same conditions as above. However, if the services are rendered in the course of the Irish trade or profession, it is probable that the Revenue would refuse the non-resident's refund but would allow the appropriate tax suffered to be set off against his Irish income tax or corporation tax liability in the same way as a resident specified person.

Another point about the non-resident's refund is that the Revenue Commissioners will only repay in Euro, even in the case of appropriate tax suffered on the payment of professional fees made in a foreign currency under a foreign contract. In such a case, the amount to be refunded is the euro equivalent of the tax deducted in the foreign currency translated into euro at the exchange rate prevailing on the date the fees were paid by the accountable person.

Overall limitation

TCA 1997, s 529 makes it clear that no amount of appropriate tax can be set off or refunded more than once. It also states that any amount of appropriate tax refunded under TCA 1997, s 527 is not available for a claim for set off against tax liability.

2.6 Third Party Returns and Revenue Powers

2.601 Introduction

The proper assessment and collection of income tax requires chargeable persons to furnish returns of income and to provide such other particulars as the Tax Acts may require to be provided. The rules relating to the obligation of each chargeable person to complete and file an income tax return under the self assessment rules and the matters to be included therein have been dealt with in **2.105**. The inspector may also require a statement of affairs from the taxpayer in order to verify the return, as discussed in **2.609**.

In addition to their obligations to file returns of their own income, persons carrying on businesses and certain other activities, or who undertake certain transactions, are required to make 'information returns' or 'third party' returns to the Revenue of certain payments made to others, of income received on behalf of others and of certain other particulars. The main third party returns and principles common to each are described in **2.602**. These third party returns are then explained in more detail in **2.603–2.605**; the Revenue's powers to obtain information from financial institutions are discussed in **2.610**.

Apart from the right to obtain information from the persons obliged to complete and file third party returns, the Revenue Commissioners have also considerable powers to enter and inspect business premises, require the production of books, documents etc, and require information from third parties, where considered necessary, in following up persons suspected of giving incorrect tax returns or other forms of tax evasion. These powers are described in **2.606–2.608**.

The Revenue's ability to collect unpaid tax is enhanced by the special provisions concerning the attachment of debts (described in **2.612**), and their priority in situations of bankruptcy (described in **2.613**). The limitations which apply to the enforcement of foreign tax liabilities are described in **2.614**. Additional weapons in the Revenue's armoury against tax evasion include the requirement on certain taxpayers to quote their tax reference number (see **2.611**) and the system of tax clearance certificates (see **2.615**). The increasing integration of tax investigations and criminal investigations is described briefly in **2.616**.

2.602 Third party returns: general

The Tax Acts contain many provisions authorising the Revenue Commissioners to seek information from persons resident in or doing business in the State regarding matters relevant to the administration and collection of income tax, corporation tax, and capital gains tax.

In general, these provisions are worded in terms of authorising an inspector of taxes to issue notices to persons within the relevant section requiring the person to whom the particular notice is sent to complete and deliver to the inspector a return giving the information requested by the notice. The return must be made within the time limit specified in the notice. Failure to comply may result in the imposition of penalties.

However, TCA 1997, s 894 makes it compulsory for the relevant persons to make the returns required under a number of 'specified provisions' in respect of every tax year (if a person chargeable to income tax), whether or not a notice is sent by an inspector. This section provides that:

> every relevant person shall, as respects a relevant chargeable period (tax year, or accounting period in the case of a company), prepare and deliver to the appropriate inspector, on or before the specified return date for the chargeable period, a return of all such matters and particulars as would be required to be contained in a return delivered pursuant to a notice given to the relevant person by the appropriate inspector, under any of the specified provisions, for the relevant chargeable period.

The Revenue Commissioners stated however in SP IT/1/92 that where the accounts of a trade or business are normally made up to a date other than 31 December, the return may be made by reference to the accounting date falling in the year of assessment. This is subject to ensuring, that on an ongoing basis, no periods are omitted from the returns.

The fact that it is now mandatory for a relevant person to make the appropriate information return under one or more of the specified provisions as applies to him does not alter the power of the inspector to give the relevant person a notice to complete a return under any of the specified provisions. Further, the obligation of a relevant person to prepare and deliver a return under the mandatory return rules is not removed by the fact that an inspector may give him a notice under any of the specified provisions (TCA 1997, s 894(6)).

In addition, there are mandatory reporting requirements incorporated into the following provisions:

(a) TCA 1997, s 894A (returns in relation to personal reliefs –see **3.104**);

(b) TCA 1997, s 895 (returns in relation to foreign accounts – see **2.605**);

(c) TCA 1997, s 896 (returns of material interests in offshore funds – see **2.605**); and

(d) TCA 1997, s 896A (returns in relation to settlements with non-resident settlors and trustees – see **2.605**).

'Specified provisions'

TCA 1997, s 894(1) defines the 'specified provisions' under which information returns are now required on a mandatory annual basis as the following sections:

(a) TCA 1997, s 889 (return of fees, commissions and other payments by a person carrying on a trade – see **2.603**);

(b) TCA 1997, s 891 (return by a bank or other financial institution of interest paid or credited without deduction of tax – see **2.604**);

(c) TCA 1997, s 890 (return by a person in receipt of income of others – see **2.605**);
(d) TCA 1997, s 888(2)(d) (return by an agent who manages premises or is in receipt of rent or other payments arising from premises – see **12.109**);
(e) TCA 1997, s 888(2)(e) (return by government departments, the Health Service Executive, local authorities or similar statutory bodies of rental payments or rental subsidies – see **12.109**);
(f) TCA 1997, s 892 (return by a nominee holder of securities – see **2.605**);
(g) TCA 1997, s 891A (return of interest paid to non-residents – see **2.605**).

Prior to 18 December 2013 (the date of the passing of Finance (No 2) Act 2013) the 'specified provisions' also included TCA 1997, s 891B (returns of certain payments made by certain persons – see **2.605**), TCA 1997, s 891C (returns of certain information by investment undertakings – see **2.605**) and TCA 1997, s 891D (returns of payment transactions by payment settlers – see **2.605**).

The mandatory returns required under these specified provisions are referred to as 'third party returns'.

These returns may be subject to Revenue Audit to verify their accuracy under all of the specified provisions (TCA 1997, s 899).

Mandatory third party returns due to be filed on or after 1 June 2011 are required to be filed electronically using Revenue's ROS system (SI 188/2011).

'Relevant person'

TCA 1997, s 894(2), in para (a), defines 'relevant person' as any person who:

(a) has information of a kind;
(b) makes a payment of a kind;
(c) pays or credits interest of a kind; or
(d) is in receipt of money or value of profits or gains of a kind, referred to in a specified provision.

This definition is subject to certain qualifications set out in TCA 1997, s 894(2). Subparagraph (b) provides that, if one of the specified provisions itself excludes a person from having to make a return under the provision in question, then that person is not a relevant person (and is not required to make a third party return under the provision in question). Paragraph (c) contains qualifications specific to persons who may be relevant persons to make returns under TCA 1997, s 892 and are dealt with separately when that provision is discussed in **2.605**.

Paragraph (e) of TCA 1997, s 894(2) adds a limitation to the effects of paras (b) or (c). It provides that, if the effect of any of those three paragraphs is to exclude a person from being a relevant person required to make a third party return under one of the specified provisions, it is not to mean that the person is excluded from having to make the third party return under any of the other specific provisions (if that person falls within that other provision).

For example, an individual carrying on a trade is not required to make a return under TCA 1997, s 889(10) for any particular tax year if he does not make in that year any payments of the kind covered by that section totalling more than €6,000 to any person. Although excluded by para (b) from being a relevant person for the purposes of a return under TCA 1997, s 889 for, say 2015, this does not prevent that person from being a relevant person required to make a return under TCA 1997, s 890 if, in 2015, he is in receipt of income of another person.

Notes

1. Although TCA 1997, s 889(7) only excludes payments up to €635, the Revenue Commissioners have increased this to €6,000 with effect for returns due in 2006 and subsequent years (see *Tax Briefing 62*).

The definition of a relevant person appears to be very wide where it refers to information of a kind, a payment of a kind, the receipt of money or value or of profits of a kind, or the paying or crediting of interest of a kind mentioned in a specified provision. However, it should be noted that the wording of TCA 1997, s 894(3) (the main operating clause) links the relevant person to the wording of the particular specified provision under which the third party return by that person is required. The relevant person required to make a return under a particular specified provision is, therefore, limited to a person covered by that provision and the information which the relevant person is required to give in the return is limited to details of the payments made by him (or it), or the interest paid or credited by him/it (dependent on which of the specified provisions is involved).

'Specified return date'

This is defined by TCA 1997, s 894(1) as 31 October in the year of assessment following the tax year. For example, a third party return of a person chargeable to income tax required for the tax year 2015 must be delivered to the inspector no later than 31 October 2016. This specified return date therefore coincides with the latest date by which the person in question must file his income tax return for the relevant tax year. Where the chargeable period is an accounting period of a company, the return is due on the last day of the period of nine months commencing on the day immediately following the end of the accounting period.

Exclusions by inspector

TCA 1997, s 894(4) gives the inspector power to exclude a person from the requirements to make any of the third party returns so that the excluded person ceases to have the obligation to make a return under the specified provision referred to in the notice. Any such exclusion must be by way of a notice in writing. The notice may exclude the person from the obligation to make the return under a particular specified provision for a particular chargeable period or periods stated in the notice. Alternatively, the exclusion may be stated as applying until such later chargeable period or until the happening of such event as is specified in the exclusion notice.

TCA 1997, s 894(5) allows the inspector, if he thinks it appropriate, to notify any relevant person that the return under any specified provision may be restricted to a particular type or category of information, payment or receipt. If a person has been notified under this power, a return made on that restricted basis will satisfy that person's obligation for the relevant return.

Penalties

TCA 1997, s 894(7) applies the provisions of TCA 1997, s 1052, to enable the Revenue to proceed for penalties if a relevant person fails to deliver any return required by any of the specified provisions. These penalty provisions are to be applied in the same way as they apply for the failure to deliver a return referred to in TCA 1997, s 1052. The failure to deliver the information return required by any of the specified provisions is treated as a 'column 2 offence' within TCA 1997, Sch 29. In consequence, the penalty is €3,000.

TCA 1997, s 1052(2) increases the basic penalty to €4,000 if the offence continues beyond the end of the tax year in which the notice to make a return was served by the inspector, but this does not seem relevant in the present context: (see **2.701**). TCA 1997, s 894(7) similarly applies TCA 1997, s 1054 where a body of person fails to deliver a specified return.

For a failure to deliver the return required under TCA 1997, s 889(10), within the time limit specified in a notice served on the taxpayer, the penalty is €3,000 (see **2.603**). TCA 1997, s 889(10) provides that all penalties levied under s 889(10) are to be proceeded for and recovered summarily in the same manner as in summary proceedings relating to excise duties. This is not to prejudice the right of the Revenue to recover the penalties under any other available methods.

Inspector's right to make enquiries

TCA 1997, s 899(2) authorises an inspector to make such enquiries or take such action, within his powers, as he considers necessary to be satisfied as to the accuracy or otherwise of any return, list, statement or particulars contained in a return delivered under a specified provision. The powers of the inspector within which such enquiries may be made generally include any powers given under any other provisions of the Tax Acts. With effect from 28 March 2003, the power to make such enquiries, etc given by this section also extends to the third party return made under TCA 1997, s 891 (return of interest paid or credited) and returns made by intermediaries in relation to those they assist in setting up foreign bank accounts or in purchasing certain foreign investment products under TCA 1997, ss 895, 896 respectively.

The third party return rules in detail

The rules relating to the requirement to make third party returns are discussed in more detail in **2.603–2.605**.

2.603 Returns by persons carrying on trade, business, etc

Probably the most significant and most widely applicable third party return is the return of payments for services required by TCA 1997, s 889(2) from every person carrying on a trade or business and from every body of persons (including government departments and bodies established by statute) carrying on any activity not constituting a trade or business.

TCA 1997, s 889(2) (as applied by (TCA 1997, s 894(3)) requires every person carrying on a trade or business to make a return for each relevant chargeable period of the payments made by him (or, if a company, it) which fall into any of the following categories:

- (a) payments made in the course of that trade or business for services rendered in connection with the trade or business by persons ordinarily resident in the State who are not employed in the trade or business;
- (b) payments for services rendered in connection with the formation, acquisition, development or disposal of the trade or business by persons ordinarily resident in the State who are not employed in the trade or business; and
- (c) periodical or lump sum payments made to persons ordinarily resident in the State in respect of any copyright.

The first provision clearly applies to every individual, partnership, company or other person (including a body of persons) carrying on a trade, profession or other form of business. The term 'business' is wider than a 'trade'; it clearly includes a profession and may include an activity such as the holding of investments particularly if undertaken by a company so that, if payments are made in the course of such a business for services rendered by another person in connection with that business, the return must give details of those payments (as well as of any payments falling under categories (b) and (c) of TCA 1997, s 889(2)).

TCA 1997, s 889(2) (as applied by TCA 1997, s 894) requires every body of persons carrying on any activity not constituting a trade or business to make a return for each relevant chargeable period of the payments made by it which fall into any of the following categories:

(a) payments made in the course of that trade or business for services rendered in connection with the activity by persons ordinarily resident in the State who are not employed by the body of persons in question; and

(b) periodical or lump sum payments made to persons ordinarily resident in the State in respect of any copyright.

This second provision brings into the return requirements of the section every body of persons, whether incorporated or unincorporated, which carries on any form of activity whatsoever (if the body of persons is not already within the section due to carrying on a trade or business). This means that bodies of persons such as charities and trade unions must make a return for each chargeable period in which they pay for services rendered to them for the purposes of or in connection with their activities.

Also, TCA 1997, s 889(3) deems a Minister of the Government and anybody established by or under statute to be a body of persons for the purposes of the section. This means that every government department, local authority, public board or State agency (for example, the Industrial Development Authority) must make the return of the relevant payments made by it in each chargeable period (presumably for each income tax year ending 31 December).

Payments to be returned

The range of payments which the relevant person must include in the TCA 1997, s 889(2) return is very wide indeed. As the section is worded, particulars of all payments for all types of services supplied by ordinarily resident persons (other than employees) in connection with the relevant person's trade, business or activity must be included, except that TCA 1997, s 889(7) excludes certain payments. Apart from the payments excluded by either the legislated or the administrative exceptions, every payment for services rendered to the trade, business or activity must be included in the return every year.

TCA 1997, s 889(1) makes it clear that payments in the nature of commission of any kind made in the course of the trade, business or other activity are regarded as payments for services to be included in the return. Similarly, any payment in respect of expenses incurred in connection with services rendered to the trade, business or activity is to be treated as a payment for the services and therefore included in the return. TCA 1997, s 889(1) also requires any valuable consideration (other than money paid) given for services rendered to be treated in the same way as a payment of money.

The Revenue Commissioners' Statement of Practice (SP IT/1/92) provides a list of services covered by the mandatory return requirements. The items listed are services of accountancy, advertising agency, architecture, bookkeeping, cleaning, commission agency, courier, dentistry, electrical, entertainment, haulage, journalism, legal, medical, plumbing, printing, secretarial, security, veterinary, etc. The Statement, however, adds that this is not an exhaustive list. In fact, as TCA 1997, s 889(1) is worded, there is no limit at all to the type of services covered other than the specific exclusions mentioned in sub-s (7). Therefore, payments for any type of service, if rendered in connection with the trade, business or activity must be included in the return unless excluded either by sub-s (7) or by the Statement of Practice.

Persons who are required to file self assessment returns electronically (see **2.105**) are also required to file a s 889(2) return electronically.

Payments on behalf of other persons

TCA 1997, s 889(6) extends the application of TCA 1997, s 889 to require the person carrying on the trade, profession or other activity to include in the third party return details of any payments made in the course of the trade, profession or activity on behalf of any other person. Sub-s (6) needs to be read in the context of the wording of sub-s (1) or (2), whichever is applicable. For example, in the case of the return of the person carrying on the trade or business, payments within category (a) of sub-s (1) made on behalf of other persons are only required to be included in the return if they are made for services rendered in connection with the trade or business of the person making the return. The Revenue Commissioners have confirmed that TCA 1997, s 889(6) covers payments made by solicitors to third parties out of client accounts; however, the Revenue will respect client confidentiality and will not for example seek information about the client on whose behalf payment was made or about the circumstances surrounding the payment (*Tax Briefing 29*).

Excluded payments

TCA 1997, s 889(7) provides that the return by the person carrying on the trade, business or activity is not required to include:

(a) particulars of any payment from which income tax is deductible; or

(b) particulars of payments made to any one person where the aggregate of the payments to that person does not exceed €6,000 in the relevant chargeable period.

Notes

TCA 1997, s 889(7) actually excludes payments up to €635. This amount was increased to €3,809 in Statement of Practice SP/IT/1/92 but was increased to €6,000 for returns due in the year 2006 and subsequent years (see *Tax Briefing 62*).

The most obvious example of payments from which tax is deductible are fees for professional services paid by accountable persons required to deduct tax under the professional services tax. In determining whether or not the payments to any one person exceeds €6,000, it is necessary to add all the amounts paid in the relevant tax year or accounting period to that person both for services rendered and for expenses incurred by that person in connection with the services rendered by him. Although not stated in either TCA 1997, s 889(7), Revenue's leaflet IT16 the Revenue Statement of Practice SP/IT/1/92, it seems that the €6,000 threshold should be taken as a VAT-inclusive figure, since the full payment is actually made for the service notwithstanding that the recipient must account for an element thereof of VAT (compare, in a different context, *Glenrothes Development Corp v IRC* [1994] STC 74).

In addition to the legislated exclusions of TCA 1997, s 889(7) mentioned above, the Revenue Commissioners' Statement of Practice of January 1992 and leaflet IT16 provides that is not necessary to include in the return particulars of:

(a) payments for services where the value of any goods provided as part of the service exceeds two-thirds of the total charge (for example, the service of installing a new item of equipment the value of which meets this two-thirds condition); and
(b) payments for public utility services (for example, electricity, gas, water, refuse collection, telephone, etc).

TCA 1997, s 889(7)(c) provides that the return need not give particulars of any payment which was made in a tax year ending more than three years before the service of the notice requiring the person concerned to make a return under the section. This does not appear, however, to be relevant to the mandatory return being completed in respect of a relevant chargeable period (tax year) as the result of TCA 1997, s 894 where the taxpayer is only required to detail the relevant payments made in the relevant chargeable period.

Particulars to be returned

TCA 1997, s 889(5) states that the third party return under the section must give the following particulars in respect of each payment required to be included in the return:

(a) the name of the person to whom the payment is made;
(b) the tax reference number of each such person;
(c) the amount of the payment;
(d) particulars as to the services or rights in respect of which the payment was made;
(e) the period over which the services was rendered; and
(f) the business name and the business or home address of the person to whom the payment was made.

2.604 Returns of interest paid or credited by banks, etc

TCA 1997, s 891 (as applied by (TCA 1997, s 894) requires every bank, building society or other person who, in the ordinary course of its trade or business, pays or credits interest without the deduction of income tax, to make a return of the interest so paid or credited. This return must be made by the person carrying on such a trade or business for each relevant chargeable period no later than the specified return date for the period in question, whether or not the person receives any notice from an inspector to make a return. For the definitions of 'relevant chargeable period' and 'specified return date', see **2.602**.

Particulars to be returned

The return for any relevant chargeable period made by a bank, building society or other relevant person who is required to make a return within TCA 1997, s 891 must include the following particulars:

(a) the name and address of every person to whom the relevant person paid or credited interest without deducting income tax in that chargeable period (but see Other exclusions below);
(b) the amount of the interest so paid or credited to each such person; and

(c) the tax reference number of any company or pension scheme which has received interest without deduction of DIRT (see below).

The circumstances in which banks, building societies and other 'relevant deposit takers' are required to deduct the deposit interest retention tax (income tax) when paying or crediting interest are described in **Division 2.4**. As indicated there, the retention tax has to be deducted from interest paid or credited in respect of the deposits held with the relevant bank, etc by individuals, personal representatives, trustees, companies, pension schemes, trade unions and most other bodies of persons (corporate and unincorporated). However, with effect from an 'operative date' (1 January 1993), companies chargeable to corporation tax and pension schemes are entitled to receive deposit interest free of the retention tax, provided that they provide the company tax number or pension scheme Revenue reference number to the deposit taker.

Particulars of the interest paid or credited to the large number of persons who receive interest less the deposit interest retention tax are not required in the TCA 1997, s 891 return. The return must, however, include the required particulars in relation to the companies and pension schemes which receive the interest gross on or after 1 January 1993. If a company or pension scheme has suffers the retention tax on any deposit interest, then that deposit interest should not be included in the return.

The requirement to include the tax reference number of any company or pension scheme which receives interest gross is imposed by TCA 1997, s 265. There is no requirement to give the tax reference number of other persons receiving interest gross for other reasons (for example, a charity which may not have a tax number anyway).

Other exclusions

TCA 1997, s 891(2) excludes from the return any person to whom the interest paid or credited in the relevant chargeable period does not exceed €65. However the Revenue's Statement of Practice on Third Party Returns (SP IT/1/92) increases this *de minimis* exclusion by indicating that only payments (or amounts credited) in excess of €635 to any person need be returned.

In addition, the return under TCA 1997, s 891 is not required to include the following:

(a) interest paid or credited to a person who has made the non-resident's declaration provided for in TCA 1997, s 263 (see **2.402**);

(b) interest paid or credited to a charity who has provided the deposit taker with the charity's Revenue (CHY) reference number in order to receive interest gross (TCA 1997, s 266 (see **2.403**)); or

(c) interest and dividends paid by credit unions to their members after 6 April 1998 other than interest paid to incapacitated individuals and individuals aged 65 and over who are exempt from DIRT (see **2.401**). (TCA 1997, s 891(1A) inserted by FA 1998, s 131(1)(b), which also defines a credit union as a society registered as such under the Credit Union Act 1997, or deemed to be registered as such under s 5(3) of that Act); previously interest paid by a credit union was excluded, other than interest paid to any member in excess of €635.

European Savings Directive

Background

This part of the text is retained for completeness purposes. It should be noted that FA 2015, s 73 inserted TCA 1997, s 898S to provide for the repeal of the Directive legislated for in TCA 1997, Pt 38 Ch 3A with effect from 1 January 2016 however, TCA 1997, ss 898L, 898M and 898O continue to apply. This cessation applies to interest paid to or secured on behalf of a person on or after the 1 January 2016 where the person is (a) resident in another Member State, or (b) resident in a third country or a dependent or associated territory of a Member State which is a reportable jurisdiction within the meaning of Section VIII of the OECD Standard for the Automatic Exchange of Financial Account Information as defined in TCA 1997, s 891F. Notwithstanding the repeal of the Directive, the obligations of paying agents in relation to information collected prior to the date of the repeal should continue be met. Revenue guidance on the section notes 'Liechtenstein and San Marino are adopters of the OECD Standard from 1 January 2016 and therefore Chapter 3A will no longer apply in respect of payments made to residents of these jurisdictions with effect from that date. As Andorra, Monaco and Switzerland are not adopters of the OECD Standard until 2017, relevant interest payments will not fall to be reported in respect of these jurisdictions under section 891F from 1 January 2016 and therefore the provisions of Chapter 3A will continue to apply. Similarly, the dependent and associated territories have all committed to exchanging information under the OECD Standard as and from 2016 or 2017'. The following text must be read with the above in mind.

With effect from 1 July 2005, the European Savings Directive Council Directive 2003/48/EC (as amended) is incorporated into Irish law (TCA 1997, Pt 38 Ch 3A), supplemented by regulations (SI 317/2005). Under the terms of the legislation, all *paying agents* carrying on business in Ireland will be required to collect and report prescribed information in respect of all payments of *interest* made or secured by them in the course of their business which are paid for the immediate benefit of individuals resident in a relevant territory who are the *beneficial owners* of such interest (TCA 1997, s 898H). In addition, reporting requirements apply to any person carrying on business in Ireland who makes or secures an interest payment in the course of their business for a *residual entity* resident in a relevant territory (TCA 1997, s 898I). The relevant territories are the 28 EU Member States or certain dependent and associated territories of the UK and the Netherlands on and from that date. The territories concerned are Anguilla, Aruba, the British Virgin Islands, the Cayman Islands, Gibraltar, Guernsey, the Isle of Man, Jersey, Montserrat, the Netherlands Antilles and the Turks and Caicos Islands. In addition, a series of related agreements between the EU and Andorra, Liechtenstein, Monaco, San Marino and Switzerland also came into effect on 1 July 2005 under which there will be *inter alia* the exchange of information between EU Member States and these countries on request in the case of tax fraud.

Definitions

The term 'interest' is defined widely, and includes the following (without being comprehensive):

(a) interest paid in respect of any interest bearing accounts, such as bank accounts, building society accounts (including share accounts), credit union accounts (including share accounts), post office accounts, national instalment savings accounts, savings certificates and special savings products;

(b) interest paid in respect of corporate and Government bonds and debentures and similar negotiable instruments, including strips of securities;

(c) accrued or capitalised interest realised at the sale, refund or redemption of a security, unit of a security or a strip of a security; accrued or capitalised interest due in respect of loans which are not evidenced by the issue of a formal security;

(d) the accrued interest element of the price when securities are sold before redemption – for example, an interest payment will be considered to arise when a new creditor purchases a security from an individual and the price includes an amount of accrued interest (whether or not this is separately identified in the amount paid);

(e) the profit realised on the redemption of zero-coupon bonds and other discounted securities, or 'strips' of securities; the profit made on the redemption of any other security sold at a discount (eg Government stocks or bonds and commercial paper) or which is redeemed for a premium; and

(f) income deriving from interest payments distributed directly or indirectly by certain UCITS (TCA 1997, s 898E).

The definition excludes amounts paid by way of penalty charges for the late payment of interest (as defined). References to interest being paid include interest being credited, and the amount of interest is always to be taken gross of any withholding taxes. It is not necessary that the interest should be Irish source interest.

The term 'paying agent' comprises:

(a) A person carrying on business in Ireland, who (or which) in the course of its business or profession, makes interest payments to, or secures interest payments for, the *immediate* benefit of individuals; and

(b) A *residual entity* which receives or secures *deemed interest* payments (see further below) (TCA 1997, s 898D(1)).

The term 'paying agent' under (a) includes the following (without being comprehensive):

(i) a bank, building society or credit union;

(ii) An Post, The Prize Bonds Company Limited;

(iii) certain UCITS;

(iv) an individual paying, a receiving or collecting agent such as a stockbroker, solicitor or accountant (acting in a professional capacity);

(v) a registrar under contract to a company to discharge the obligations of paying interest on the company's bonds;

(vi) any other outsource company that makes the payment of interest on behalf of a debtor to another person;

(vii) a nominee or custodian who holds assets on behalf of another person; and

(viii) Government departments, the Central Bank and statutory bodies where they make an interest payment.

The term 'beneficial owner' refers to an individual who is entitled to the interest which is being paid. The recipient of the interest is to be considered the beneficial owner in all circumstances unless he/she can conclusively prove the contrary. If there is any doubt whatever the individual recipient is to be treated as the beneficial owner (TCA 1997, s 898C(6)). Where interest is secured for an individual, ie received by a third party (eg a nominee) who is charged with collecting the interest on behalf of the individual, the individual will be regarded as the beneficial owner.

An individual will however *not* be treated as a beneficial owner if he/she receives interest:

(i) as a paying agent;

(ii) on behalf of company or other legal person, a person within the charge to corporation tax or a similar tax imposed in another Member State or a UCITS or a residual entity that has elected to be treated as a UCITS;

(iii) on behalf of another individual whose identity (ie name and address) has been disclosed to the paying agent; or

(iv) on behalf of a *residual entity* (TCA 1997, s 898C(2)).

A 'residual entity' is defined as a person (although the term 'entity' as used in the Directive seems preferable) or undertaking established in Ireland which receives or secures an interest payment on behalf of a beneficial owner but which is not:

(i) a legal person in its own right within the charge to corporation tax or a similar tax imposed in another relevant territory; or

(ii) a UCITS or a residual entity that has elected to be treated in the same manner as a UCITS for the purposes of the legislation (TCA 1997, s 898D(2)).

In practice, the term covers any grouping of individuals that does not come within the exclusions listed above and could include such entities as trusts, (including approved pension funds and registered charities) pooled or co-mingled funds, partnerships and investment clubs, assuming no election to be treated as if it were a UCITS.

Reporting obligations

There are two forms of reportable payments:

(a) interest payments made by a paying agent for the immediate benefit of beneficial owners resident in a relevant territory; and

(b) interest payments made by a person carrying on business in Ireland to, or secured for, residual entities established in a relevant territory.

As noted above, a paying agent must make or secure an interest payment for the *immediate* benefit of an individual who is the *beneficial owner* of the interest. This means that, if the payment is made through an intermediary or a number of intermediaries the paying agent will be the last person who makes or secures that interest payment. Where two competing organisations have significant claims to the role of paying agent, they may mutually agree which is to be the paying agent and this will be acceptable to the Revenue Commissioners. A bank, etc is not a paying agent as respects amounts of interest it merely credits to its clients' accounts (eg the issuer of a security paying interest to a designed account held at a bank, etc will not mean that the bank is a paying agent in relation to the account holder in respect of the payment by the issuer).

Paying agents will be required to report *inter alia* their own details, together with the details of the beneficial owner of the interest, including their national tax reference number for new customers on or after 1 January 2004, and of the account number and amount of interest. Interest payments made to a deceased person before their date of death are reportable in the name of the deceased provided that she/he was the beneficial owner. Interest paid during the period of administration of the estate is reportable in the name of the executor/personal representative. Interest payments made from the date of assignment are reportable in the name of the beneficiary (TCA 1997, s 898H).

Where a person makes an interest payment to a residual entity established in a relevant territory, that person must report their own details, together with their name, address and tax reference number, the name and address of the residual entity and the amount of the interest payment (TCA 1997, s 898I).

Residual entities that receive or secure interest payments on behalf of individual beneficial owners resident in a relevant territory are treated as if they had paid an equivalent amount of deemed interest on the date of receipt and, as noted above, for these purposes are regarded as paying agents (TCA 1997, s 898E(6)). A residual entity must therefore report the amount of interest that it receives or secures on behalf of the beneficial owner, not the amount (if any) that it subsequently pays out. Residual entities must also report their own name and address and the names and addresses of the individuals entitled to the interest payment. In addition, the type of interest payment received and the amount of each individual's entitlement must again be reported.

Whether payments to trusts established outside the State are reportable under the legislation will depend on the status of the trust under the law of the jurisdiction concerned.

The Revenue Guidelines set out the following rules:

(a) if the trustee is an individual resident in a relevant territory and is himself the beneficial owner, then the payment is reportable;

(b) if the payment is made to a corporate trustee, it is not reportable; and

(c) if there is a lack of certainty (where eg an individual trustee is not the beneficial owner), the trust should be treated as a residual entity and any payments reported.

As outlined in the background paragraph above, it should be noted that FA 2015, s 73 inserted TCA 1997, s 898S to provide for the repeal of the Directive legislated for in TCA 1997, Pt 38, Ch 3A with effect from 1 January 2016 however, TCA 1997, ss 898L, 898M and 898O continue to apply. This cessation applies to interest paid to or secured on behalf of a person on or after the 1 January 2016 where the person is (a) resident in another Member State, or (b) resident in a third country or a dependent or associated territory of a Member State which is a reportable jurisdiction within the meaning of Section VIII of the OECD Standard for the Automatic Exchange of Financial Account Information as defined in TCA 1997, s 891F. Notwithstanding the repeal of the Directive, the obligations of paying agents in relation to information collected prior to the date of the repeal should continue be met.

Time limits for submitting information to Revenue

Paying agents will be required to make annual reports of interest to Revenue. The legislation concerning the reporting of interest payments applies as respects interest payments made on or after 1 July 2005. The reports must be submitted to Revenue by 31 March in the year following the year in which interest payments are made. As outlined in the background paragraph above, it should be noted that FA 2015, s 73 inserted TCA 1997, s 898S to provide for the repeal of the Directive legislated for in TCA 1997, Pt 38, Ch 3A with effect from 1 January 2016 however, TCA 1997, ss 898L, 898M and 898O continue to apply. This cessation applies to interest paid to or secured on behalf of a person on or after the 1 January 2016 where the person is (a) resident in another Member State, or (b) resident in a third country or a dependent or associated territory of a Member State which is a reportable jurisdiction within the meaning of Section VIII of the OECD Standard for the Automatic Exchange of Financial Account Information as defined in TCA 1997, s 891F. Notwithstanding the repeal of the Directive, the obligations of paying agents in relation to information collected prior to the date of the repeal should continue be met.

Client identification issues

For the purposes of the legislation, the country of residence is the country where the individual has their permanent address. For contractual relations that started on or after 1 January 2004 or in the case of a transaction which takes place on or after that date in the absence of contractual relations, the legislation requires that a paying agent should, in the first instance, establish an individual's residence on the basis of the address in the passport or official identity card presented by the individual. This applies to all clients in order to ascertain whether or not interest payable to them is in fact reportable. If the address is not recorded on the passport or official identity card, it may be established using any other documentary proof of identity presented by the individual which is acceptable for the purposes of the money laundering rules.

Individuals may present paying agents with a passport or official identity card issued by an EU Member State and declare themselves to be resident in a third country (that is, a country or territory that is not a member of the EU or another relevant territory). In such cases, the paying agent should establish the country of residence by requiring the production of a tax residence certificate issued by the competent authority in the relevant third country. If such proof cannot be produced, the individual should be regarded as resident in the country that issued the passport or official identity card. Where a paying agent has reason to believe that the individual's country of residence is other than that given by reference to their address as shown in the passport or official identity card or, if no address is shown, the paying agent should establish the country of residence of the beneficial owner by reference to any other documentary proof of identity which is acceptable for money laundering purposes.

Different rules apply in cases where contractual relationships commenced prior to 1 January 2004; the Revenue Guidance Notes set these out together with their criteria for establishing the date on which contractual relationships are to be regarded as commencing.

Withholding taxes

Austria, Belgium or Luxembourg and certain other states under the arrangements made with third countries are entitled to withhold tax from interest payments falling within the scope of Directive as an alternative to following the normal exchange of information rules. TCA 1997, s 898M provides that, where such tax is withheld from an interest payment made to Irish residents, they will get a credit against their Irish tax liabilities. If the individual is exempt from tax or has a liability less than the amount deducted, a refund of the appropriate amount will be given. However, the credit will be denied where the individual has already obtained relief for the tax deducted from another state and the individual was resident in that state at the time he obtained the relief for the tax deducted. As outlined in the background paragraph above, it should be noted that FA 2015, s 73 inserted TCA 1997, s 898S to provide for the repeal of the Directive legislated for in TCA 1997, Pt 38 Ch 3A with effect from 1 January 2016 however, TCA 1997, ss 898L, 898M and 898O continue to apply. This cessation applies to interest paid to or secured on behalf of a person on or after the 1 January 2016 where the person is (a) resident in another Member State, or (b) resident in a third country or a dependent or associated territory of a Member State which is a reportable jurisdiction within the meaning of Section VIII of the OECD Standard for the Automatic Exchange of Financial Account Information as defined in TCA 1997, s 891F. Notwithstanding the repeal of the Directive, the obligations of paying agents in relation to information collected prior to the date of the repeal should continue be met.

Administration

TCA 1997, s 898N provides for the audit, by the Revenue Commissioners, of the procedures put in place by paying agents to comply with their obligations under the legislation. This covers issues such as requiring the paying agents to produce records of the relevant transactions. The penalty provisions of TCA 1997, s 898O, which provide for a penalty of €19,045 for failure to deliver a return or making an incorrect or incomplete return and a daily fine of €2,535 for each day on which the failure continues, apply to the returns under this section. In addition a person who does not comply with the requirements of a Revenue Officer in relation to the section or the regulations or with any requirement of the regulations is liable to a penalty of €1,265.

The EU Savings Directive was amended in March 2014 to close perceived loopholes in the original Directive which were being exploited. In particular because the Directive only applied to interest payments to individuals resident in the EU, paying agents will now be required to look through certain entities and apply the Directive where the beneficial owner of the entity is an EU resident. In addition the scope of the Directive is being broadened to include other types of income which are similar to interest, to include the return from certain types of life insurance contracts and to bring within the directive income from a broader range of collective undertakings. Member States are required to amend domestic legislation to take account of the changes by January 2016. The amended Directive has not yet been incorporated into Irish legislation.

As outlined in the background paragraph above, it should be noted that FA 2015, s 73 inserted TCA 1997, s 898S to provide for the repeal of the Directive legislated for in TCA 1997, Pt 38 Ch 3A with effect from 1 January 2016 however, TCA 1997, ss 898L, 898M and 898O continue to apply. This cessation applies to interest paid to or secured on behalf of a person on or after the 1 January 2016 where the person is (a) resident in another Member State, or (b) resident in a third country or a dependent or associated territory of a Member State which is a reportable jurisdiction within the meaning of Section VIII of the OECD Standard for the Automatic Exchange of Financial Account Information as defined in TCA 1997, s 891F. Notwithstanding the repeal of the Directive, the obligations of paying agents in relation to information collected prior to the date of the repeal should continue be met.

2.605 Other information returns

Persons in receipt of income of others

TCA 1997, s 890 (as applied by TCA 1997, s 894(3)) requires every person who receives money or value or profits or gains on behalf of another person to make a return for each chargeable period giving details of:

(a) the amount received;

(b) the names and addresses of the persons on whose behalf such money or value was received; and

(c) whether such person is married, in a civil partnership, a minor, a non-resident, or incapacitated.

It is compulsory for such persons to return this information to the Revenue where the aggregate payments to any one person in a 12-month period exceeds €6,000, whether or not the person in receipt of the income is given a notice to make the return. *Tax Briefing 62* provides the €6,000 exclusion thresholds as an administrative measure, thereby increasing the €635 threshold which would otherwise apply if TCA 1997, s 890 were applied strictly. The statement also permits the exclusion of income subject to Irish withholding tax, and dividends and other distributions assessable under Sch F. Furthermore, no return will be required from a person who is chargeable to tax on behalf of the beneficial owner of the income (eg a trustee – see the discussion at **15.302**).

In *Fawcett v Special Commissioners & Lancaster Farmers' Action Mart* [1997] STC 163, the taxpayer traded as an auctioneer of livestock. The Inland Revenue served the taxpayer with notices under the UK equivalent of TCA 1997, s 890. The taxpayer argued that the sums it received did not fall within the term 'money or value' since this referred to pure income receipts, as opposed to trading income. The taxpayer further argued that the equivalent of TCA 1997, s 890 did not in fact apply to it since it received only gross amounts and not the net 'profits or gains' of its clients. Both arguments were rejected. The Court of Appeal held that the two expressions 'money or value' and 'profits and gains' were not mutually exclusive; further TCA 1997, s 890 covered all receipts 'in the nature of profit' even though the recipient was not aware of any or all of the expenses or other deductions which could be claimed against those receipts (following *Lord Advocate v Gibb* 5 TC 194).

The taxpayer in the *Lancaster Farmers' Auction Mart* case also argued that it was often unaware whether or not its clients were trading and thus, could not be sure whether or not the receipts passing through its hands were in the nature of taxable income. The court held that the taxpayer could rely on the UK equivalent of TCA 1997, s 1068 which provides *inter alia* that 'where a person has reasonable excuse for not doing anything required to be done, he shall be deemed not to have failed to do it unless the excuse ceased and after the excuse ceased he shall be deemed not to have failed to do it if he did it without reasonable delay after the excuse had ceased'. Thus, if the taxpayer had reason to believe that a transaction was not in the nature of trade it would have been outside the scope of the equivalent of TCA 1997, s 890 (unless it had received information to the contrary at which time it would be obliged to make a supplementary return). The court also stressed that any attempt by the Inland Revenue to act oppressively (perhaps for example, by requiring the taxpayer to make detailed enquiries concerning the trading status of all their clients) would be subject to judicial review (see **2.206**). The scope of the UK equivalent of TCA 1997, s 890 has also been considered in *Attorney General v National Provincial Bank of England* [1924] AC 262.

Leaflet IT16 and the Revenue Statement of Practice SP IT/1/92 states that in broad terms the persons likely to be involved in making returns under the section are accountants, auctioneers, bank trustees, debt collectors, loss adjusters, solicitors, stockbrokers and financial/business advisors (ie who handle client funds). SP IT/1/92 adds that members of the public who are in receipt of occasional amounts on behalf of third parties need not make returns unless, exceptionally, they are requested to do so.

Rental payments and subsidies

TCA 1997, s 888(2)(d) requires any agent who manages premises or is in receipt of rent or other payments from premises in the State or, with effect from 1 January 2008, wherever situated, to deliver a return containing:

- (a) the full address of the premises;
- (b) the local property tax number of each such premises that is a residential property;
- (c) the name and address of the person to whom the premises belongs;
- (d) the tax reference number of every such person;
- (e) the amount of rent or other receipts arising from each premises; and

(f) any other information relating to the premises as may be requested by the inspector of taxes.

Points (b) and (d) above were added by FA 2015 but subject to Ministerial Order; it also requires a person referred to above who manages any premises or is in receipt of rent or other payments arising from any premises shall request from every person to whom such premises belongs—

(i) the person's tax reference number, or
(ii) where the person does not have a tax reference number, confirmation to that effect.

TCA 1997, s 888 requires that any Minister of the Government (ie Government department), the Health Service Executive, or any local authority or other board or authority, or other similar bodies, established under statute which makes a payment in the nature of rent or rental subsidy must also furnish a return providing the above details.

TCA 1997, s 888(2)(e) requires similar details, together with the tax reference number of the landlord concerned (ie PPS number or Revenue reference number on any tax return or assessment) to be returned by any government department, the Health Service Executive, local authority or by any other board in authority or by a similar statutory body, in respect of payments made by them which are either in the nature of rent, or for the purposes of rent or rent subsidy, in relation to any premises.

TCA 1997, s 888(2)(a), (b) and (c) which fall outside the mandatory return regime of (TCA 1997, s 894) empowers the inspector to issue a notice requiring:

(a) any lessor (past or present) of premises to give details of the provisions of the relevant lease and the terms on which it was granted, including payments received by him in respect thereof;
(b) any lessee or occupier (past or present) of the premises to give details of the terms relating to the relevant lease or occupation and to provide any written documents containing those terms; and
(c) any lessee (past or present) of premises to give details of any consideration given in return for the grant to him of the lease.

TCA 1997, s 888(3)(b), inserted by FA 2007, s 123, provides that the relevant public body must request the tax reference number (ie PPS number or Revenue reference number on any tax return or assessment) of the landlord prior to payment of any rent or rent subsidy or otherwise confirmation from the landlord that he does not possess a tax reference number. The landlord must comply with the body's request prior to the making of the payment concerned; where the landlord fails to supply the information and as a result the details cannot be furnished to the Revenue Commissioners, the relevant body must state that fact to the Revenue commissioners.

Nominee holders of securities

TCA 1997, s 892 (as applied by TCA 1997, s 894(3)) requires any person who is registered as the owner of any securities, if sent a notice by an inspector to do so (but see below), to state whether or not he (or, if a company, it) is the beneficial owner of the securities. Then, if the person served with the notice is not the beneficial owner of the securities or of any of them, that person is required to furnish – in respect of each person on whose behalf the securities are registered in his/its name – the following particulars:

(a) the name and address of the beneficial owner;

(b) the nominal value of the securities so registered and, if the securities consist of shares in a company, the number and class of such shares; and

(c) the date on which each security was so registered in the name of the nominee holder on behalf of the beneficial owner.

'Securities', for the purpose of this section, are defined as including shares, stocks, debentures and debenture stock of a company and also any promissory note or other instrument evidencing indebtedness issued to a loan creditor of a company. 'Company' means any body corporate which is a 'company' as defined in TCA 1997, s 4(1). 'Loan creditor' has the meaning given to the term by TCA 1997, s 433. Securities also include any stock, debenture, debenture stock, certificate of charge, or other security, issued with the approval of the Minister for Finance, as well as the securities of any foreign government.

TCA 1997, s 894(3), as applied to TCA 1997, s 892, requires a mandatory return each year from every person who is registered as the holder of any securities otherwise than as the beneficial owner giving the particulars listed at (a) to (c) above in respect of every beneficial owner for which the registered holder is acting as the nominee. This is the Return by Nominee Holders. It must include the required particulars in respect of all securities so held (ie otherwise than as beneficial owner) at any time during the period covered by the return (see **2.602**).

Although TCA 1997, s 892 enables the inspector to give a notice under the section to any person registered as the owner of securities, whether or not the beneficial owner, the mandatory return requirement of TCA 1997, s 894(3) only applies to a person who is not the beneficial owner. TCA 1997, s 894(2)(c) provides that a beneficial owner is not a 'relevant person' so far as the Return by Nominee Holders is concerned.

Further, the Return by Nominee Holders is not required where details have already been supplied under another provision of the Tax Acts or where the nominee shareholder only holds the subscriber shares in a shelf company which has not traded or held any assets. An example of details supplied under another provision is where the details of the beneficial owners have been given in a return by trustees of a profit sharing scheme approved by the Revenue Commissioners (see **Division 11**).

Returns of interest paid to non-residents

TCA 1997, s 891A requires every relevant person, as defined, (a person paying interest without deduction of tax being a company or a collective investment undertaking) to submit a return detailing the name, address and country of residence of the recipient and the amount of the payment. The specified return date for the chargeable period is the same as in s 894(1) ie where the chargeable period is a year of assessment, 31 October in the year of assessment following that year, and where the chargeable period is an accounting period of a company, the last day of the period of nine months commencing on the date immediately following the end of the accounting period. The penalty provisions contained in TCA 1997, ss 1052 and 1054, apply to the late submission of returns and to the failure to submit returns.

Returns of interest and other returns on investments paid to Irish residents

TCA 1997, s 891B, inserted by FA 2006, s 125, is an enabling provision designed to permit the Revenue Commissioners to make regulations with the consent of the Minister of Finance under TCA 1997, s 891B(5) requiring certain '*relevant persons*' to make annual returns in relation to '*relevant payments*' made to their customers, including their names and addresses and other details (including the PPS numbers of individuals and tax reference or VAT registration number of companies). The 'Return of Payments (Banks, Building Societies, Credit Unions and Savings Banks) Regulations 2008' (referred to below as 'the Regulations') were issued on 6 May 2008 (SI 136/2008) and amended with effect from 3 July 2009 by the 'Return of Payments (Banks, Building Societies, Credit Unions and Savings Banks) (Amendment) Regulations (SI 254/2009). Guidance notes on the Regulations, 'Guidance Notes for Financial Institutions' (referred to below as 'the Guidance Notes'), were published on 9 July 2009.

The relevant persons concerned are:

(a) any assurance company;
(b) any financial institution; or
(c) any Minister of the Government, any body established by or under statute, or any other body which undertakes he disbursement of public funds.

For these purposes:

'Assurance company' means:

(a) an assurance company within the meaning of Insurance Act 1936, s 3; or
(b) a person that holds an authorisation within the meaning of the European Communities (Life Assurance) Framework.

'Financial institution' means:

(a) a person who holds or has held a licence under s 9 or an authorisation granted under s 9A of the Central Bank Act 1971, or a person who holds or has held a licence or other similar authorisation under the law of an EEA state, other than the state, which corresponds to a licence granted under the said s 9;
(b) an agent appointed by the National Treasury Management Agency (NTMA) to carry out certain functions of the NTMA in relation to State savings products (ie savings products such as Post Office Savings Bond accounts and prize bonds offered by the Minister for Finance through the NTMA);
(c) a person referred to in the Central Bank Act 1971, s 7(4); or
(d) a credit institution (within the meaning of the European Communities (Licensing and Supervision of Credit Institutions) Regulations, 1992 (SI 395/1992)) which has been authorised by the Central Bank of Ireland to carry on business of a credit institution in accordance with the provisions of the supervisory enactments (within the meaning of those Regulations) (TCA 1997, s 891B(1)).

A *'relevant payment'* means:

(a) in the case of an assurance company or a financial institution is:
    (i) any payment of interest or in the nature of interest,
    (ii) any payment in respect of any investment, or
    (iii) any other similar payment,

    which are of a kind or kinds specified or defined in regulations which is made or credited by or through the entity specified in the relevant regulations;
(b) in the case of any other person specified in regulations, any payment of a kind or kinds specified or defined in those regulations which are made or credited by or through that person (TCA 1997, s 891B(1)).

The Regulations provide that for the tax year 2008 and subsequent years a 'relevant payment' means any payment of interest made by a bank, building society, savings bank or credit union, other than an excepted payment, and includes interest which is paid less frequently than annually in respect of which financial institutions are required to account for DIRT on an annual basis as the interest accrues in accordance with TCA 1997, s 260(2) (such interest is however included in a return when it is paid and not when it is accrued – see para 3.6 of the Guidance Notes). An 'excepted payment' is a payment listed in Sch 2 of the Regulations and includes payments made to, or in respect of, the following:

(a) account holders where the payor holds a non-resident declaration made by the account holder for DIRT purposes (see **2.402**);

(b) a non-resident bank;

(c) a building society which is not resident in the State and which is resident in another EU country;

(d) a non-resident company which is quoted on a stock exchange outside the State;

(e) a body listed in Appendix III para 11.2 of 'Deposit Interest Retention Tax Guidance Notes for Deposit Takers' being certain building societies outside the EU, Regulated Mutual Funds, Life Offices, Lloyds Syndicates, Local Authorities and Regulated Finance Companies, provided the body is not resident in the State and the investment is for a period of less than three months;

(f) certificates of deposit or commercial paper which qualify for interest to be paid without deduction of DIRT under TCA 1997, s 246A;

(g) Medium Term Notes which qualify for interest to be paid without deduction of DIRT where the conditions set out in Appendix III para 11.1 'Deposit Interest Retention Tax Guidance Notes for Deposit Takers' are satisfied;

(h) another resident bank, building society, credit union or the Post Office Savings Bank;

(i) the National Treasury Management Agency;

(j) the Central Bank of Ireland;

(k) the Investment Compensation Company of Ireland;

(l) the National Pensions Reserve Fund Commission;

(m) a debt on a security listed on a stock exchange which was issued by a bank;

(n) investments held by a 'specified person' (see below) outside the State.

Payments under (a) to (e) and (h) to (l) will only be regarded as excepted payments where the financial institution is satisfied that the person to whom the payment is made is beneficially entitled to the payment (regulation 1). In addition the person making the payment must be able to identify from its electronic records that the payment falls within Sch 2 of the Regulations.

Regulation 5 of the Regulations provide that every 'specified person' shall make a return of 'relevant payments' made in the tax year in question. Regulation 3 and schedule 1 of the Regulations provide that a 'specified person' shall be 'financial institution', as defined in TCA 1997, s 891B(1) (see above), which is a bank, building society, credit union or savings bank. Returns for the tax year 2008 and subsequent years must be made on or before 31 March of the tax year following the year in respect of which the return is being made (regulation 6). Only payments in excess of €635 made in respect of an account or investment during the tax year must be included in a return (regulation 4). In the case of joint accounts/investments the €635 threshold applies to the total payments on the account and not to each party's share of the account.

Regulation 5(2) provides that the following details must be included in a return:

(a) the name, address of registered office and tax reference number of the person making the return;

(b) for the payee, the name, if an individual their address and date of birth (if on record) and if a company the address of the registered office;

(c) in the case of accounts opened, or investments made, on or after 1 January 2009 the payee's tax reference number, CHY number (if relevant) or if there is neither of these numbers this must be stated. For accounts opened, or investments made, prior to 1 January 2009 the tax reference number is only required where the payee is a company;

(d) the following details regarding the account/investment:
   (i) the account number or information capable of identifying the investment,
   (ii) the amount of the relevant payment,
   (iii) where DIRT had been deducted, the amount of DIRT deducted;

(e) where the specified person makes a payment to a person which it knows is not the beneficial owner of the payment this must be stated in the return;

(f) in the case of joint accounts, each person's entitlement to the payment must be provided if known. If each person's entitlement is not known the full payment must be attributed to each holder. The return must state that the account is a joint account and the number of account holders;

(g) in the case of partnerships only the partnership details need to be included (para 3.8 of the Guidance Notes).

Regulation 7 provides that the financial institution must, for all accounts opened or investments made on or after 1 January 2009, make all reasonable efforts to obtain a customer's tax reference number. Any application form should require the customer to include their tax reference number on the form and the financial institution is required to verify the tax reference number. Examples of documentation which may be used to verify the tax reference number are given in the Guidance Notes and include various tax documents such as P60, P45, P21. The financial institution must keep a copy of any document used to verify a tax reference number for a period of five years after the relationship between the financial institution and the customer has ended. Where the customer fails to provide a tax reference number or verifying documents the financial institution's obligations are regarded as being fulfilled if this fact is noted in the return or alternatively if the financial institution makes a suspicious transaction report in accordance with the Criminal Justice Act 1994, s 57 provided the surrounding circumstances indicate that such a report is warranted. There are no penalties where a customer fails to provide a tax reference number or verifying documentation. The Guidance Notes confirm that only Irish tax reference numbers are required (para 4.2).

Any amount credited, or set off against any other amount, in respect of a relevant payment shall be treated as a relevant payment (ie 'netting off' is not permitted); where tax is deducted at source, the gross amount of any relevant payment must be reported where relevant (TCA 1997, s 891B(2)).

Payments made for, or by reference to, periods prior to 1 January 2005 are excluded (TCA 1997, s 891B(3)), as are any payments included or liable to be included in a return under TCA 1997, s 891A (see: *Returns of Interest to Non-Residents*) or TCA 1997, Pt 38, Ch 3A (see: **2.604** – EU Savings Directive) (TCA 1997, s 891B(8)). Where a return is made of a relevant payment, this will remove the requirement to make a return of the same payment under TCA 1997, s 891: (see **2.604**) (TCA 1997, s 891B(9)). The

Post Office Savings Bank Act 1861, s 4 which restricts the disclosure of information relating to deposits does not apply to the disclosure of information required in a return under this section (TCA 1997, s 891B(10) inserted by FA 2008, s 133). There are provisions for Revenue Audits and the penalty provisions of TCA 1997, s 898O, which provide for a penalty of €19,045 for failure to deliver a return or making an incorrect or incomplete return and a daily fine of €2,535 for each day on which the failure continues, apply to failures on the part of a relevant person to deliver returns or to make correct and complete returns, as well as a penalty of €1,265 for any person who fails to comply with the regulations or with the requirements of a Revenue officer in the exercise of his powers under the section or the regulations (TCA 1997, s 891B(6), (7)).

Up to 1 January 2012, collective funds were also included within the ambit of TCA 1997, s 891B. Finance Act 2012 removed collective funds from TCA 1997, s 891B and introduced a new TCA 1997, s 891C instead (see below).

Returns of certain information by investment undertakings

TCA 1997, s 891C, inserted by FA 2012, s 121, is an enabling provision designed to permit the Revenue Commissioners to make regulations with the consent of the Minister of Finance under TCA 1997, s 891C(3) requiring certain 'investment undertakings' to make annual information returns in relation to the units of the investment undertaking, including details of the values of the units and the tax reference numbers of the unit holders. The 'Return of Values (Investment Undertakings) Regulations 2013 (referred to below as 'the Regulations') were issued on 12 July 2013' (SI 245/2013) and guidance notes on the Regulations, 'Guidance Notes for Investment Undertakings' (referred to below as 'the Guidance Notes'), was published in August 2013.

The Regulations provide that for the tax year 2012 and subsequent years every investment undertaking shall deliver to the Revenue officer designated for the purpose of the regulations a return of the value of the investment made by a unit holder. The value of the investment to be provided is the value at 31 December in the tax year or the date of first redemption in the tax year if earlier. The return shall include the following details:

(a) the name, address and tax reference number of the investment undertaking;
(b) the name, address and date of birth of the unit holder;
(c) in the case of investments made on or after 1 January 2014 the tax reference number of the unit holder must also be provided;
(d) The following details regarding the investment:
    (i) the investment number associated with the investment or, if there is none, information capable of identifying the investment, and
    (ii) the value of the units held.

A return must be filed no later than 30 September for the tax year 2012 and for subsequent years no later than 31 March in the tax year following the year for which the return is made (regulation 4)

Regulation 5 of the Regulations provides that as respect investments made on or after 1 January 2014 an investment undertaking shall make 'reasonable efforts' to obtain the tax reference of the unit holder from the unit holder. The Guidance Notes give some guidance on what are regarded as 'reasonable efforts' by providing that the application forms for opening new investments should provide for the tax reference number and that documentation should be sought from the unit holder to verify the tax reference number. Examples of documentation which may be used to verify the tax reference number are also given in the Guidance Notes and include various tax documents such as P60, P45, P21. There are no penalties where a unit holder does not provide a tax reference number and where one is not provided this does not prevent the unit holder from opening an account. The Guidance Notes also confirm that only Irish tax reference numbers are required.

An investment undertaking is as defined by TCA 1997, s 739B(1) but does not include a common contractual fund within the meaning of TCA 1997, s 739I or an investment limited partnership within the meaning of TCA 1997, s 739J (s 739J provides that an investment limited partnership is an investment limited partnership within the meaning of the Investment Limited Partnership Act 1994).

TCA 1997, s 739B(1) defines an 'investment undertaking' as meaning:

(a) a unit trust scheme (other than a unit trust mentioned in TCA 1997, s 731(5)(a) or a special investment scheme) which is or is deemed to be an authorised unit trust scheme within the meaning of the Unit Trusts Act 1990;

(b) any other undertaking which is an undertaking for collective investment in transferable securities;

(c) any authorised investment company within the meaning of Pt XIII of the Companies Act 1990 which has been designated as an investment company which may raise capital by promoting the sale of its shares to the public or each of the shareholders of which is a collective investor;

(ca) an authorised ICAV (within the meaning of the Irish Collective Asset-management Vehicles Act 2015) – inserted into TCA 1997 by s 185 of the former act.

Any information that is included or liable to be included in a return (TCA 1997, Pt 38, Ch 3A see: **2.604** – *EU Savings Directive*) (TCA 1997, s 891B(8)) does not have to be included in a return under this section.

The penalty provisions of TCA 1997, s 898O, which provide for a penalty of €19,045 for failure to deliver a return or making an incorrect or incomplete return and a daily fine of €2,535 for each day on which the failure continues, apply to the returns under this section. In addition a penalty of €1,265 applies for non-compliance with a requirement of the regulations or non-compliance with the requirements of a Revenue officer in the exercise of powers under the section or the regulations.

Returns of payment transactions by payment settlers

TCA 1997, s 891D, inserted by FA 2012, s 122, is an enabling provision designed to permit the Revenue Commissioners to make regulations under TCA 1997, s 891D(2) requiring certain 'payment settlement entities' to make annual electronic returns in relation to 'reportable payment transactions' and other information which may be specified in the regulations including details of the tax reference numbers of the merchants. It is understood that the section was introduced as Revenue were concerned that some businesses may be under-declaring receipts processed via credit cards. The Return of Payment Transactions by Payment Settlers (Merchant Acquirers) Regulations 2012 (referred to below as 'the Regulations') were issued in August 2012 (SI 324/2012).

A 'payment settlement entity' means:

(a) in the case of a payment card transactions the merchant acquirer (ie the person who has the contractual obligation to make payment to merchants in settlement of payment card transactions); and

(b) in the case of transactions settled through an electronic network, the electronic settlement organisation.

'Reportable payment transactions' means any payment card transaction (ie any transaction in which a payment card is accepted as payment) and any electronic network transaction (ie any transaction which is settled through an electronic payment network). A payment card is any type of card which can be used by the holder to make a payment to a merchant.

The Regulations provide that every merchant acquirer who makes a payment to a merchant in settlement of payment card transactions in the year 2010 or a subsequent year is obliged to file a return with Revenue of all payment card transactions by the merchant acquirer in the year in question. Regulation 4 provides that the return must include the following details:

(a) the name, address and tax reference number of the merchant acquirer;
(b) the following details regarding the merchant:
  (i) name, trading name, address, email address, website address and reference number used by the merchant acquirer,
  (ii) name and telephone number of designated contact person between merchant and merchant acquirer,
  (iii) unique reference code assigned to merchant to identify the principal nature of the merchant's business,
  (iv) when payment transactions commenced or ceased,
  (v) number of terminals provided to the merchant acquirer subject to lease or rental agreement,
  (vi) bank account number of merchant and national sort code,
  (vii) the tax reference number of the merchant;
(c) the amount of each payment card transaction and the fees associated with each transaction or alternatively the aggregate monthly amounts.

Regulation 5 provides that the return must be made no later than 30 April 2013 for the years 2010, 2011 and 2012 and no later than 30 April following the year end for subsequent years.

Regulation 5 provides that the merchant acquirer shall request the tax reference of the merchant from the merchant. Unlike the Return of Values (Investment Undertakings) Regulations 2013 (see above) there is no requirement that the merchant acquirer should verify the tax reference number of the merchant.

The penalty provisions of TCA 1997, s 898O, which provide for a penalty of €19,045 for failure to deliver a return or making an incorrect or incomplete return and a daily fine of €2,535 for each day on which the failure continues, apply to the returns under this section. In addition a penalty of €3,000 applies for non-compliance with a requirement of the regulations or non-compliance with the requirements of a Revenue officer in the exercise of powers under the section or the regulations.

Returns of accounts held by US persons in Irish financial institutions

The Foreign Account Tax Compliance Act (FATCA) is a US legislative provision. Under these provisions non-US financial institutions are required to identify US investors and account holders and report details of their income and assets to the Inland Revenue Service (IRS). Under FATCA a 30 per cent withholding tax must be applied to payments made to any non-US financial institutions that have not entered into an agreement with the IRS to report information on US account holders. In December 2012 an Intergovernmental Agreement (IGA) on FATCA was signed between Ireland and the US. Under the terms of this agreement, Irish financial institutions are required to provide details of financial assets held by US persons to the Irish Revenue, and US financial institutions are required to report details of financial assets held by Irish persons to the IRS on an annual basis. The Irish Revenue and the IRS will then exchange the information on an annual basis. Financial institutions which comply with the registration and reporting requirements of the Irish legislation which implements the IGA will be deemed to be compliant with FATCA and won't suffer the 30 per cent penalty withholding tax.

The IGA was incorporated into Irish law by the issue of 'The Agreement to Improve Tax Compliance and Provide for Reporting and Exchange of Information Concerning Tax Matters (United States of America) Order 2013' in February 2013, which was included in TCA 1997, Sch 24A, Pt 3 by Finance Act 2013. (TCA 1997, s 826(1B) provides that Orders issued by the Government in which they declare that arrangements made with other governments to exchange information to prevent and detect tax evasion should have the force of law, then the order has the force of law from the date it is inserted into TCA 1997, Sch 24A, Pt 3.) The text of the Agreement is included in a schedule to the Order. References to the Agreement contained in the Order are referred to below as 'the Agreement'. TCA 1997, s 891E, inserted by FA 2013, s 32, with effect from 1 January 2013 is an enabling provision designed to permit the Revenue Commissioners to make regulations to implement the IGA on FATCA. TCA 1997, s 891E(4) provides that the Revenue Commissioners, with the consent of the Minister for Finance, may make regulations requiring financial institutions to register, make returns giving information on accounts held, managed or administered by the financial institution (including tax reference numbers of customers) and give details of payments to non-participating financial institutions. The Financial Accounts Reporting (United States of America) Regulations 2014 (referred to below as 'the Regulations') were issued in June 2014 (SI 292/2014) and come into effect from 1 July 2014 and in October 2014 Revenue published Guidance Notes on the Implementation of FATCA in Ireland (referred to below as 'the Guidance Notes').

Revenue e-brief 60/2015 which comments on the above regulations and guidance notes explains as follows 'While Relevant Holding Company and Relevant Treasury Company have been included in the list of Financial Institution categories as outlined in Reg 3 of the FATCA Regulations and Ch 2 of the Guidance Notes, this is not consistent with the Ireland/United States Inter Governmental Agreement (IGA) which defines a Financial Institution as 'a Custodial Institution, a Depository Institution, an Investment Entity or a Specified Insurance Company'. Accordingly, a Holding Company or Treasury Company will only be considered a Financial Institution if it meets the definition of the four Financial Institution categories specified in the definition above. Where a Holding Company or Treasury Company does not fall into one of the above-mentioned categories of Financial Institution it will be classed as a Non-Financial Foreign Entity (NFFE), and will fall into the category of "active" or "passive" in accordance with the criteria set out in Appendix 2 of the Guidance Notes. However, where a Holding Company or Treasury Company of a financial group no longer meets the definition of Financial Institution and had previously identified itself as a Relevant Holding Company or Relevant Treasury Company and completed its FATCA registration as the lead Financial Institution of an Expanded Affiliated Group (EAG), Revenue will allow the entity to continue to treat itself as the lead Financial Institution for reporting purposes. While the entity may act as the lead Financial Institution for filing purposes, it will still not fall within the definition of Financial Institution and so will have no Irish reporting obligations in its own right. While updated Regulations and Guidance Notes will issue to reflect these changes, as a transitional arrangement the position as outlined in this notice can be applied.'

Reporting financial institutions must register with the IRS before 31 December 2014 or within 30 days of becoming a reporting financial institution if the institution was not a reporting financial institution on 31 December 2014 (reg 5). Once registered, a financial institution will be issued a Global Intermediary Identification Number (GIIN) and will be included on a published list available on the IRS website. On or after 1 January 2015 a financial institution can use their GIIN as evidence of their compliance with FATCA.

A 'reporting financial institution' is one of the following persons carrying on business in the State:

(a) a custodial institution (ie one that holds as a substantial portion (>20 per cent of its income) of its business, financial assets for the account of others;
(b) a depository institution (ie an institution that accepts deposits);
(c) an investment entity (ie an institution trading in money market instruments/foreign exchange/securities, portfolio management or otherwise investing, administering or managing funds or money on behalf of others);
(d) certain insurance companies;
(e) certain holding companies (eg a holding company whose business consists of wholly or mainly of holding shares in any of the above companies); or
(f) a relevant treasury company (company that exists wholly or mainly for the purpose of carrying on qualifying activities (making deposits/providing financing refinancing, investing in securities) on behalf of a financial group or investment entity to which it is related).

The definition of 'reporting financial institution' is contained in reg 3 of the Regulations however the various definitions, ie custodial institution, depository institution etc, are contained within the Agreement. As can be seen from the above the definition of a reporting financial institution is quite wide and will cover not only banks but custodians, investment funds and fund managers and certain insurance companies. More detailed guidance on what is regarded as a reporting financial institution is contained in the Guidance Notes.

'Deemed compliant' financial institutions are excluded from the definition of 'reporting financial institutions'. Part II of Annex II of the Agreement provides that this includes charitable organisations that qualify for exemption under TCA 1997, s 848A and Sch 26A, sporting bodies that qualify for exemption under TCA 1997, s 235, financial institutions with a local client base only (ie those with no place of business outside Ireland, 98 per cent of whose accounts by value are held by EU residents and which do not solicit account holders outside Ireland) and certain collective investment vehicles. Under US Regulations other categories of financial institutions are regarded as deemed compliant. Further details on institutions regarded as deemed compliant may be found in the Guidance Notes.

In addition Government organisations (including NAMA and the NTMA), the Central Bank, EU bodies such as the European Investment Bank, and retirement funds are excluded from the definition of reporting financial institutions and are not required to register with the IRS or to file returns under the Irish legislation.

Reporting financial institutions are required to file a return of US reportable accounts to Revenue on or before 30 June following the end of the tax year (regulation 8). 2014 is the first year for which a return is required so the first returns due under FATCA must be returned on or before 30 June 2015. A 'US reportable account' means a financial account held in a reporting financial institution by one or more 'specified US persons' or by a non-US entity with one or more controlling persons that are 'specified US persons' (Article 1(dd) of the Agreement). A 'financial account' is an account held in a financial institution and includes not only deposit accounts but also certain equity or debt interests in an investment entity (Article 1(s) of the Agreement). A 'US person' is a US citizen or US resident individual, a partnership or corporation organised in the US or under US law, trusts which are governed by US law or where one or more US persons control all substantial decisions regarding the trust. A 'specified US person' are all US persons but excluding quoted companies, certain US tax exempt entities, retirement plans, banks, real estate investment trusts (REITS), regulated investment companies (RICs), US common trust funds and certain exempt trusts (Article 1(ff) and (gg) of the Agreement).

A financial institution does not have to report on holders of depository (ie cash) accounts with a balance not exceeding $50,000 or insurance contracts with a cash value not exceeding $250,000 (reg 6). Details which a financial institution must include in a return include:

(a) the name, address and GIIN of the financial institution;
(b) the name, address and US tax number of the account holder;
(c) the account number and balance at the end of the year or at the date closed if closed in the year;
(d) in the case of a custodial account details of the gross interest, dividends and other income arising from the assets held in the account and also the proceeds from the disposal of property where the financial institution acted as agent, custodian, broker or nominee;
(e) in the case of a depository account, gross interest paid or credited to the account.

The details at (a) to (c) above must be provided in returns for 2014. Returns for 2015 and 2016 must include all details apart from proceeds from the disposal of property where the financial institution acted as agent, custodian, broker or nominee and returns for 2017 and subsequent years must include all details above (regulation 8). A nil return must be filed where a reporting financial institution has no reportable accounts in the tax year (regulation 9).

A reporting financial institution is also required to carry out due diligence procedures to identify US reportable accounts which exist at 30 June 2014. The procedures to be carried out are set out in Annex I of the Agreement and involve electronic or manual reviews to identify indicators that the accounts may be held by a US person. Due diligence does not have to be carried out on depository accounts with balances not exceeding $50,000 and insurance contracts with a cash value not exceeding $250,000. For accounts opened on or after 1 July 2014 financial institutions are required to put in place procedures to determine if the holder is a US person and to obtain the US tax number of the account holder. The US tax numbers of the holders of all reportable accounts held on 1 July 2014 must be obtained by 1 January 2017 (reg 11).

The penalty provisions of TCA 1997, s 898O, which provide for a penalty of €19,045 for failure to deliver a return or making an incorrect or incomplete return and a daily fine of €2,535 for each day on which the failure continues, apply to the returns under this section. In addition a penalty of €1,265 applies to any persons for non-compliance with a requirement of the regulations or non-compliance with the requirements of a Revenue officer in the exercise of powers under the section or the regulations. The Post Office Savings Bank Act 1861, s 4 which restricts the disclosure of information relating to deposits does not apply to the disclosure of information required in a return under this section (TCA 1997, s 891E(9)).

The Common Reporting Standard

In February 2014 the Standard for Automatic Exchange of Information, Common Reporting Standard ***was*** published by the OECD ('the Standard'). There are two components to the Standard:

(a) The Model Competent Authority Agreement (Model CAA); and
(b) The Common Reporting and Due Diligence Standard (CRS).

The Model CAA is a standard agreement which can be entered into between the governments of two jurisdictions. Under the agreement the authorities of each jurisdiction agree to automatically provide on an annual basis information to the authorities of the other jurisdiction regarding financial accounts held by residents of the other jurisdiction in financial institutions in the reporting jurisdiction. The CRS is contained in an annex to the Model CAA and sets out the rules regarding the financial information to be reported, The financial institutions required to report and the information which must be reported. In essence the CRS is very similar to the Intergovernmental Agreement entered into between Ireland and the US to implement FATCA without the provision of a penal withholding tax regime in the absence of non-compliance. Double Taxation Treaties entered into by Ireland generally provide that the parties to the Treaty may exchange information as is necessary for the carrying out of the provisions of the Treaty. In addition the Convention on Mutual Administrative Assistance in Tax Matters which was signed by the Irish Government in 2011 and incorporated into Irish law in 2013 (TCA 1997, s 826(1c) and Sch 24A, Pt 4), provides that parties to the Convention may, by mutual agreement, automatically exchange information covered by the Convention. These mechanisms may be used by the Irish Government to implement the Model CAA without the necessity to introduce further domestic legislation. The CRS however required domestic legislation to be incorporated into Irish legislation. TCA 1997, s 891F, inserted by FA 2014, s 28, with effect from 1 January 2015 is an enabling provision designed to permit the Revenue Commissioners to make regulations to incorporate the CRS into Irish legislation. TCA 1997, s 891F(3) provides that the Revenue Commissioners, with the consent of the Minister for Finance, may make regulations dealing with the returns to be made by reporting financial institutions on reportable accounts held by the institution. TCA 1997, s 891F(4) provides that the regulations should in addition set out when a return is required to be filed, the manner in which it is to be filed and the information to be provided and also the measures to be taken by financial institutions to identify reportable accounts.

The penalty provisions of TCA 1997, s 898O, which provide for a penalty of €19,045 for failure to deliver a return or making an incorrect or incomplete return and a daily fine of €2,535 for each day on which the failure continues, apply to the returns under this section. In addition a person who does not comply with the requirements of a Revenue Officer in relation to the section or the regulations or with any requirement of the regulations is liable to a penalty of €1,265.

Mandatory automatic exchange of information in the field of taxation

TCA 1997, s 891G (inserted by FA 2015, s 74) provides for the collection and reporting of certain information in respect of financial accounts held by any person who is regarded by virtue of the laws of a jurisdiction other than the State as resident in that jurisdiction for the purposes of tax. This is due to the amendment of the Council Directive 2011/16/EU brought about in December 2014 by Council Directive 2014/107/EU or the Directive on Administrative Co-operation (commonly referred to as 'DAC 2'). This requires EU countries to exchange information in connection with financial accounts. Revenue guidance on this new section notes that 'International best practice in this area is set out in the OECD's Common Reporting Standard and this Directive essentially imports this Standard into EU law. The exchange of data is provided for by Ireland's ratification on the Convention on Mutual Administrative Assistance in Taxation which is given legislative effect by section 826 of the TCA.'

The section notes that one has to leave the legislation behind and look to the actual directive for the meanings of the following terms '"account holder", "financial account", "high value account", "lower value account", "reportable account", "reporting financial institution", and "TIN" have the meanings respectively given to them by Section VIII of Annex I to the Directive and "change in circumstances" shall be construed in accordance with Annex II to the Directive'.

The Revenue Commissioners can make regulations with respect to the return by a reporting financial institution of information on reportable accounts held, managed or administered by that reporting financial institution. In addition, the regulations may include provisions—

(a) determining the date by which a return required to be made under the regulations shall be made to the Revenue Commissioners,

(b) prescribing the manner in which returns are to be made,

(c) specifying the information to be reported in a return by the reporting financial institution, to the Revenue Commissioners, in relation to reportable accounts and, where different information is to be reported for different years, specifying the information to be reported for each of those years,

(d) specifying—

 (i) the currency in which the reporting financial institution is required to report, and

 (ii) the rules for conversion of amounts, denominated in another currency, into the currency, referred to in subparagraph (i), for the purposes of a return under the regulations,

(e) requiring reporting financial institutions to identify reportable accounts,

(f) specifying the records and documents that must be examined or obtained by the reporting financial institution to enable the institution to identify reportable accounts,

(g) specifying the records and documents used to identify reportable accounts that must be retained by the reporting financial institution,

(h) specifying additional requirements in relation to the examination of high value accounts and lower value accounts,

(i) setting out the circumstances in which a reporting financial institution is required to aggregate financial accounts held by the same individual or entity for the purposes of identifying reportable accounts as high value accounts or lower value accounts,

(j) specifying the actions to be taken by a reporting financial institution where there is a change in circumstances with respect to the account holder of a financial account,

(k) setting out the conditions under which a reporting financial institution may appoint a third party as its agent to carry out the duties and obligations imposed on it by the regulations,

(l) setting out the circumstances in which a reporting financial institution may make a nil return,

(m) imposing an obligation on—

(i) a reporting financial institution to obtain a TIN from any person—

(I) with whom the institution enters into a contractual relationship, or

(II) for whom the institution undertakes any transaction, on or after a date specified in the regulations, which shall not be earlier than the commencement of the regulations (and such persons are in this paragraph referred to as 'customers') for the purposes of including that number in a return under the regulations, and

(ii) customers to provide a reporting financial institution with their TIN on request by the reporting financial institution where, on or after a date specified in the regulations—

(I) such customers enter into a contractual relationship with the reporting financial institution, or

(II) the reporting financial institution undertakes any transaction for such customers, being respectively—

(A) a relationship which results in the opening, operation, administration or management of a financial account, or

(B) a transaction which arises in relation to a financial account,

(n) defining 'books' and 'records' for the purposes of the regulations,

(o) in relation to any of the matters specified in the preceding paragraphs, determining the manner of keeping records and setting the period for the retention of records so kept,

(p) enabling the authorisation of Revenue officers, for the purpose of such officers—

(i) requiring—

(I) the production of books, records or other documents,

(II) the provision of information, explanations and particulars, and

(III) persons to give all such assistance as may reasonably be required and as is specified in the regulations, in relation to financial accounts within such time as may be specified in the regulations, and

(ii) making extracts from or copies of books, records or other documents or requiring that copies of such books, records and documents be made available, and

(q) specifying such supplemental and incidental matters as appear to the Revenue Commissioners to be necessary—

(i) to enable persons to fulfil their obligations under the regulations, or

(ii) for the general administration and implementation of the regulations, including—

(I) delegating to a Revenue officer the authority to perform any acts and discharge any functions authorised by this section or the regulations to be performed or discharged by the Revenue Commissioners, and

(II) the authorisation by the Revenue Commissioners of Revenue officers to exercise any powers, to perform any acts or to discharge any functions conferred by this section or by the regulations.

A Revenue officer authorised under the regulations may enter any premises or place of business of a financial institution for the purposes of (a) determining whether information (i) included in a return was correct, or (ii) not included in a return was correctly not included, or (b) examining the procedures put in place by the financial institution for the purposes of complying with its obligations under the regulations.

Such regulations were published in Iris Oifigiúil on 5 January 2016 and are contained in SI No 609 of 2015. Regulation 3 thereof notes that a reporting financial institution shall, with respect to the calendar year 2016 and each subsequent calendar year, make and deliver to the Revenue Commissioners on, or before, the return date:

(a) a return in respect of all reportable accounts maintained by the reporting financial institution in that year; or

(b) where it has no reportable accounts in a calendar year, a return which states that it had no such accounts in that year.

That return shall, with respect to each reportable account, include:

(a) in the case of each reportable person that is an account holder of the account and that is an individual:
- (i) the name,
- (ii) address,
- (iii) Member State of residence,
- (iv) TIN, and
- (v) date and place of birth, of that individual;

(b) in the case of each reportable person that is an account holder of the account and that is an entity:
- (i) the name,
- (ii) address,
- (iii) Member State of residence, and
- (iv) TIN;

of that entity, and where that account holder has been identified, pursuant to reg 6 (which outlines certain due diligence procedures), as having one or more controlling persons that is a reportable person then additional information is required such as the date and place of birth of each such reportable person;

(c) the account number or, in the absence of an account number, the functional equivalent;

(d) the name and identifying number, if any, of the reporting financial institution;

(e) the account balance or value, including, in the case of a cash value insurance contract or annuity contract, the cash value or surrender value, as of the end of the relevant calendar year or, if the account was closed during that year, the date of closure of the account;

(f) where the account is a custodial account:
   (i) the total gross amount of interest, the total gross amount of dividends, and the total gross amount of other income generated with respect to the assets held in the account, in each case paid or credited to the account, or with respect to the account, during the relevant calendar year, and
   (ii) the total gross proceeds from the sale or redemption of financial assets paid or credited to the account during the calendar year with respect to which the reporting financial institution acted as a custodian, broker, nominee, or otherwise as an agent for the account holder;

(g) where the account is a depository account, the total gross amount of interest paid or credited to the account during the calendar year;

(h) where the account is a reportable account, other than a custodial account or a depository account, the total gross amount paid or credited to the account holder with respect to the account during the calendar year with respect to which the reporting financial institution is the obligor or debtor, including the aggregate amount of any redemption payments made to the account holder during that year;

(i) the currency in which each amount is denominated.

Certain exceptions to the above are also included in reg 3. Regulations 4 to 7 outline activities of the reporting financial institutions and regs 8 and 9 outline certain Revenue powers to include requiring the furnishing of information to Revenue.

Returns in relation to foreign accounts and offshore funds

TCA 1997, s 895 imposes disclosure requirements on a person whose business includes the provision of services in the State in connection with the opening of foreign accounts (an intermediary), and who provides such services in his/its chargeable period (year of assessment or accounting period as appropriate). A 'foreign account' is defined as an account in which a deposit is held at a location outside the State. A 'deposit' includes a sum of money which does not bear interest and one which is either repayable on demand or at a future time. The section also imposes a requirement to make a return on the individual depositor (see **2.105**).

The intermediary must make a return on or before the specified return date for the tax year (eg 31 October 2016 for the tax year 2015) of all residents for whom he/it has acted in the opening of a foreign account in the period concerned. The return must specify:

(a) the full name and permanent address of the resident;
(b) the resident's tax reference number;
(c) the full name and address of the relevant person with whom the foreign account was opened;
(d) the date on which the foreign account was opened; and
(e) the amount of the deposit made in opening the foreign account.

A resident who uses the services of an intermediary is required to supply the specified details to the intermediary who must take all reasonable care (including, where necessary, calling for documentary evidence) to confirm that the specified details are correct. An intermediary who fails to make a return, or who omits details of any relevant resident in the return, or who fails to take reasonable care that the details supplied by a resident are correct, is liable in respect of each default to a penalty of €4,000.

Returns in relation to certain offshore products

TCA 1997, s 896 applies similar provisions to investments in offshore products. It provides that any intermediary shall as respects a 'chargeable period' prepare and deliver to the 'appropriate inspector', on or before the 'specified return date for the tax year' a return specifying in respect of every person in respect of whom that intermediary has acted in the chargeable period as an intermediary:

(a) the full name and permanent address of the person;
(b) the person's tax reference number;
(c) a description of the relevant facilities provided, including a description of the offshore product concerned and the name and address of the person who provided the offshore product; and
(d) details of all payments made (directly or indirectly) by or to the person in respect of the offshore product.

This obligation is provided for by TCA 1997, s 896(2).

An 'appropriate inspector' with regard to an intermediary means:

(a) the inspector who has last given notice of writing to the intermediary that he/she is the inspector to which the intermediary is required to deliver a return;
(b) if no inspector has given such notice in writing, the inspector to whom the intermediary normally delivers returns; or
(c) where there is no such inspector, the inspector of returns.

The 'specified return date for the chargeable period' is as defined at TCA 1997, s 895(1) (ie 31 October in the year following the tax year).

TCA 1997, s 896(3) provides penalties where an intermediary fails to make a return for a chargeable period in the manner described above, to include in such a return details to which an intermediary provides 'relevant facilities' in the chargeable period or to take reasonable care to confirm the details listed at (a) to (d) above which have been furnished by a person to whom the intermediary has provided relevant facilities in the chargeable period. The penalty may be imposed for each failure and makes the intermediary liable to a fine of €4,000. TCA 1997, s 896(1) defines 'relevant facilities' as:

(a) the marketing in the State of 'offshore products';
(b) the acting in the State as an intermediary in relation to the acquisitions or disposal, in whole or in part, of offshore products by or on behalf of persons who are resident or ordinarily resident in the State; or
(c) the provision in the State of facilities for the making of payments from an offshore product to persons who are entitled to the offshore product, whether on the disposal, in whole or in part of the offshore product or otherwise.

An offshore product is defined by the same subsection as 'a material interest in an offshore fund' or 'a foreign life policy'. In this context, 'material interest' is to be construed in connection with TCA 1997, s 743(2), ie an interest is a material interest if it could be reasonably expected that at some time during the period of seven years beginning at the time of the acquisition the person would be able to realise the value of the interest.

Penalty provisions apply to individuals who fail to furnish the details referred to at (a) to (d) above to an intermediary who has provided the person with relevant facilities or a person who knowingly and wilfully furnished incorrect information of that kind. Again this is subject to a penalty of €4,000. A person investing in an offshore fund or life policy must include details of the following particulars in their tax return for each chargeable period:

(a) the name and address of the offshore fund or the person who commenced the life policy;

(b) a description, including the cost to the person, of the material interest acquired or a description of the terms of the life policy, including premiums payable; and

(c) the name and address of the person through whom the offshore fund was acquired.

In *Tax Briefing 23*, the Revenue Commissioners state:

> It should be noted that the definition of intermediary is very wide. It is not necessary that the intermediary be involved in the opening of a foreign account. All that is required is that the intermediary acts in connection with the transaction. Nor is the section confined to recognised providers of financial services. Any person who in the ordinary course of a trade carried on in the State provides a service as an intermediary is obliged to make a return. For example, auctioneers and accountants who provide an investment service as an ancillary to their core business would be considered to be intermediaries for the purposes of the legislation.

Returns in relation to settlements and trustees

TCA 1997, s 896A was introduced by F(No 2)A 2008. It provides that where any person in the course of a trade or profession carried on by that person and involved with the making of a settlement, knows or has reason to believe that at the time of the making of the settlement:

(a) the settlor was resident or ordinarily resident in the State; and

(b) the trustees of the settlement were not resident in the State;

The professional advisor is obliged to deliver a statement to Revenue with the following information:

(i) the name and address of the settlor;

(ii) the names and addresses of the persons who are the trustees of the settlement; and

(iii) the date on which the settlement was made or created.

(TCA 1997, s 896A(2)).

The professional advisor must provide the information within four months of the making of the settlement if the settlement is made on or after 24 December 2008 or, before 24 June 2009 if the settlement is made within five years prior to 24 December 2008 (TCA 1997, s 896A(3)).

Trustees of a settlement are regarded as non resident unless the general administration of the settlement is ordinarily carried out in Ireland and the trustees or a majority of each class of trustees are resident in Ireland (TCA 1997, s 896A(4)).

Revenue has the power to require any person to furnish information to them if they believe that person possesses information relating to a settlement (TCA 1997, s 896A(5)).

Provision of Information by National Asset Management Agency

The National Asset Management Agency Act 2009, s 204(2) (as substituted by FA 2010, s 154) provides that the National Asset Management Agency (NAMA):

(a) shall make available to the Revenue Commissioners details of each eligible bank asset;
(b) where the Revenue Commissioners require any information or documents, relating to any eligible bank asset or such other matters as may be necessary for the purposes of the performance of their duties;

then they may require NAMA to provide such information as is in the possession or control of NAMA or of which it has knowledge, and such documents as are in the possession or control of NAMA or to make such documents available for inspection.

The Revenue Commissioners may, for the purposes of the performance of their functions under TCA 1997, Pt 42 ('Collection and Recovery of Tax') and any regulations made under that Part, seek from NAMA information in relation to a named relevant person. A 'bank asset' includes:

(a) a credit facility;
(b) any security relating to a credit facility;
(c) every other right arising directly or indirectly in connection with a credit facility;
(d) every other asset owned by an institution participating in NAMA; and
(e) an interest in any of the foregoing assets.

A 'relevant person' means a debtor, associated debtor, guarantor, surety or chargor and includes a connected person (within the meaning of TCA 1997, s 10) in relation to a debtor, associated debtor, guarantor, surety or charger.

Returns in relation to certain awards of shares

See **10.113**.

2.606 Power to inspect books and accounts

TCA 1997, s 886 requires that any person carrying on, either directly or as agent or otherwise on behalf of some other person, any trade, profession or other activity taxable under Sch D or who is otherwise chargeable under Sch F is required to keep such records as are necessary to enable true returns of income to be made. The records must be kept in a timely manner and must be consistent from one year to the next. TCA 1997, s 886(1) states that the records to be kept include a proper record of all monies received and expended in the course of a trade, profession or other activity, with details of the matters in respect of which the receipts or expenditure occurred. They also include records of all sales and purchases of goods and services involved in the business or other activity and of the assets and liabilities thereof (as well as all acquisitions and disposals of assets within the scope of capital gains tax). The person must also retain all linking documents which are involved in the preparation of accounts (TCA 1997, s 886(4)). 'Linking documents' are defined by TCA 1997, s 886(1) as documents which are 'drawn up in the making of accounts and which show details of the calculations linking the records of the accounts'. TCA 1997, s 886(2) requires a taxpayer who produces accounts to retain or to cause to be retained on his behalf linking documents. It is not possible therefore for a taxpayer to disclaim responsibility for furnishing linking records on the basis that they are held by his accountants as auditors' working papers (see *Quigley v Burke*, discussed below).

Records are defined widely as including 'accounts, books of accounts and any other data maintained manually or by an electronic, photographic or other process'. TCA 1997, s 948 provides *inter alia* that records which are required to be retained for tax purposes may be kept in computerised form subject to the agreement of the Revenue Commissioners to such conditions as they may impose.

The records to be kept must be retained for at least six years after the completion of the transactions to which they relate, unless the inspector notifies the person required to keep them that they need not be retained or unless the records have been disposed of on the liquidation of a company in accordance with Companies Act 1963, s 305(1) (TCA 1997, s 886(4)). The time limit is extended where a person fails to submit their tax return prior to the specified return date (see **2.105**), in which case it becomes six years after the year of assessment in which a return is made of the transactions, etc in question. With effect from 23 December 2014, the date of passing of FA 2014, where a transaction is the subject of a Revenue inquiry or investigation or any claim or proceedings under the TCA 1997 the linking documents and records must be maintained until the inquiry or investigation has been completed, any appeal to the Appeal Commissioners has become final and conclusive, any proceedings in relation to any inquiry or investigation are finished and the time limit for instituting further appeal or proceedings has expired. Also with effect from 23 December 2014 the executor or administrator of an estate is required to retain the linking documents and records of the deceased for the relevant time period.

With effect from 21 December 2015, the date of passing of FA 2015 where a person ceases to be a person to whom sub-s (2)(a)(i), (ii) or (iii) applies, that person (or such other person on that person's behalf) required to keep the linking documents and records shall keep or retain the linking documents and records notwithstanding that a period of five years has elapsed from the date of such cessation. The person mentioned in sub-s (2) above every person who:

- (i) on that person's own behalf or on behalf of any other person, carries on or exercises any trade, profession or other activity the profits or gains of which are chargeable under Sch D;
- (ii) is chargeable to tax under Sch D or F in respect of any other source of income; or
- (iii) is chargeable to capital gains tax in respect of chargeable gains.

While the Revenue Commissioners do not normally seek to inspect records kept by any person who gives a full return of income, the Revenue Commissioners have very full powers to inspect books and to enter business premises. This power in the past has been most frequently exercised in carrying out value added tax and/or PAYE inspections, but is now extended to include the general tax audit and is of particular use to the Revenue Commissioners in combating tax evasion.

When a person has failed to make any return when requested to do so by an inspector or if he (or, if a company, it) makes an unsatisfactory return of his/its profits from any trade or profession, an inspector or other authorised officer of the Revenue Commissioners may serve notice on the taxpayer:

(a) to deliver to the inspector or another authorised officer copies of the accounts (including balance sheets) relating to the trade or profession including, where the accounts have been audited, a copy of the auditor's certificate; and
(b) to make available for inspection all books, accounts and documents in the taxpayer's power and possession as specified in the notice and which contain information as to the transactions of the trade or profession (TCA 1997, s 900(2)).

The inspector or other authorised officer is permitted to take copies of or extracts from any books, accounts or documents made available for his inspection under this section (TCA 1997, s 900(6)).

In *Quigley v Burke* V ITR 265, it was held that an accountant engaged by a taxpayer to submit his accounts and other documents in support of a tax appeal was acting as the taxpayer's agent. Accordingly, the taxpayer, as a principal, could require the accountant to hand him over all documents executed in the course of the latter's engagement. It followed that a nominal ledger prepared by the accountant as part of his workings were 'within the possession or power' of the taxpayer.

An accountant acting as an auditor acts as a principal, so that documents prepared solely for the purposes of the audit belong to him. However, in the case of a statutory audit, schedules and workings prepared so that the client can comply with its statutory obligations would belong to the client. The latter analysis would also generally hold true in any other situation where records required by law to be maintained (including linking documents under TCA 1997, s 886) are prepared by an accountant in the course of an assignment. The Revenue Commissioners expect that all business records, including linking documents, should be available at the commencement of a Revenue Audit (*Tax Briefing 22*).

A person who fails to maintain or keep any of the records or documents required under TCA 1997, s 886 for a year of assessment will be subject to a penalty of €3,000, but the penalty will not apply where no liability to tax arises for that year (TCA 1997, s 886(5)).

With effect from 25 March 2005, TCA 1997, s 886A, as inserted by FA 2005, s 25, provides that where an individual wishes to make a claim for any allowance, deduction or relief in respect of income tax for any year, the individual is to keep and preserve all such records as are requisite to make a correct and complete claim (TCA 1997, s 886A(1)).

The records which a taxpayer is required to keep and preserve are to be retained for the longer of six years from the end of the tax year to which the claim relates or the period ending on the date when any enquiry made into the claim or any amendment of the claim (see below) is completed (TCA 1997, s 886A(2)).

Failure to keep and preserve records as required by the section incurs a penalty of €1,520 (TCA 1997, s 886A(3)). However, the penalty will not apply if the taxpayer produces other evidence to confirm the information reasonably required by the Inspector and which would have been proven by the records if they had been retained (TCA 1997, s 886A(4)).

An inspector may enquire into a claim for relief, or an amendment of such a claim, on giving due notice within a four-year period from the end of the tax year in which the claim, or an amendment of a claim made by the taxpayer, is made (TCA 1997, s 886A(5)). Where an Inspector gives notice of intention to enquire into such a claim or amendment to a claim, the Inspector may, at that or any later time, require the taxpayer to produce:

(a) any documentation in the taxpayer's possession or power that may reasonably be required to determine whether the claim or amendment is correct and if so, the extent to which they are correct; and
(b) any accounts or particulars as may be reasonably required for the purpose.

The notice from the Inspector must be in writing and must set a deadline of not less than 30 days to produce the material required (TCA 1997, s 886A(6)). The taxpayer may submit photographic or facsimile copies of the material unless the Inspector notifies him that he requires the originals (TCA 1997, s 886A(7)). Copies or extracts may be made by the Revenue officer of any documents produced him under the terms of the section (TCA 1997, s 886A(8)).

2.607 Power to enter business premises

TCA 1997, s 905(2) empowers an inspector or other authorised officer of the Revenue Commissioners, to enter, at any reasonable time, any business premises or other place where any trade or profession is carried on or where anything is done in connection with the trade or profession or any premises or place where the inspector or authorised officer has reason to believe such an activity is carried on. The inspector or authorised officer making the entry may do any of the following:

(a) require any person on the premises (other than a customer) to produce any books, records, accounts or other relevant documents;
(b) examine any such books, records, etc and take copies of or extracts from them;
(c) remove and retain any such books, records, etc for a reasonable period for examination;
(d) examine any property listed in any balance sheet, stock sheets or other statements;
(e) require the taxpayer or any of his/its employees to give all reasonable assistance;
(f) initiate a search for records and property the inspector or authorised officer considers have not been produced; and
(g) where the business/trade has a computerised system of accounts the same powers of inspection apply.

An application can be made to a judge of the District Court for the issue of a search warrant in relation to any premises. If the judge is satisfied on information given on oath that there are reasonable grounds for suspecting that there has been a failure to comply with the tax legislation, which in turn is seriously prejudicial to the proper assessment or collection of tax and that records containing information material to the assessment and collection are likely to be kept off the premises concerned, then the judge may issue a search warrant (TCA 1997, s 905(2A)). The warrant is effective for one month from the date of issue and must only authorise the authorised officer and such other persons as he considers necessary to enter (forcibly if necessary) and search the premises etc, examine what is found there, inspect any records found there and, if there are reasonable grounds for suspecting any records so found are material to the assessment or collection of tax or may be required for the purposes of legal proceedings initiated by the Revenue

Commissioners (as opposed to criminal proceedings), remove such records and retain them for so long as reasonably required.

An important limitation set out in TCA 1997, s 905(2)(c) to the requirement to produce documents applies in the case of a person carrying on a profession, for example, a solicitor, accountant, etc. A person carrying on a profession is not required to disclose:

(a) information to which a claim to legal professional privilege could be maintained in legal proceedings;
(b) information of a confidential medical nature; or
(c) professional advice of a confidential nature given to a client (other than advice given as part of a dishonest, fraudulent or criminal purpose).

The inspector or other authorised officer may not enter a private residence, without the consent of the taxpayer or a warrant from a judge of the District Court issued under TCA 1997, s 905(2A) above (TCA 1997, s 905(2)). Any person who wilfully obstructs or delays the authorised tax officer in the exercise of these powers can be fined €4,000.

It should be stated that this power to enter a business premises is in practice only likely to be used if the Revenue Commissioners suspect the taxpayer of tax evasion or other improper conduct related to the administration of taxes, but legally there is no such limitation to the application of the section. Similar powers are also provided under TCA 1997, s 904 in respect of payments to certain sub-contractors: (see **2.311)** and under TCA 1997, s 903 in relation to the operation of the PAYE system (with effect from 25 March 2005, in the case of premises or part of a premises occupied wholly and exclusively as a private residence only with the consent of the occupier or on foot of a warrant issued by a District Court judge).

A Revenue official entering premises under TCA 1997, s 903–905 may be accompanied by a Garda officer with powers of arrest where there is interference or obstruction to him in the performance of his duties.

TCA 1997, s 908C introduced a power which enables Revenue to obtain a search warrant from a District Court judge to search any premises together with any persons who are on the premises and anything on the premises. The judge must be satisfied by the information given on oath by an authorised officer that there are reasonable grounds for suspecting that an offence under the Acts (as extensively defined by TCA 1997, s 1078(1): see **2.703**) is being, or is about to be, committed and that material which is likely to be of value to the investigation of the offence or evidence of the commission of the offence or relating to the offence is to be found on those premises TCA 1997, s 908C(2). On issue of a warrant, the Revenue officers may within one month from the date of its issue, enter (forcibly, if necessary) and search the premises; they may also search any person on the premises (on a same-sex basis, unless the person consents otherwise) and require any person on the premises both to give details of his name, address and occupation and to produce material in his custody or possession when requested and also to explain the value and relevance of items found on the premise, including books, documents and records. They may also seize and retain any such material, including computers storing such material, found on the premises or take copies thereof and take any necessary steps to preserve them and prevent them being interfered with TCA 1997, s 908C(3). The Revenue officers are also empowered to operate computers which are on the premises or which can be lawfully accessed from the premises and to require any person on the premises who appears to be the person authorised to facilitate access to the information held by such computers to give them any necessary passwords or otherwise enable a Revenue officer to access the information in visible and legible form and to take hard copies thereof (TCA 1997, s 908C(4)). Any person who obstructs, misleads a Revenue official or fails to provide the details described above is liable to a fine not exceeding €5,000 or imprisonment for a term not exceeding six months or to both the fine and the imprisonment TCA 1997, s 908C(6). The section provides that An Garda Síochána may accompany the Revenue officers and may arrest without warrant any person who obstructs the search, or any person whom they suspect with reasonable cause, of doing so. TCA 1997, s 908C(7).

TCA 1997, s 908D enables Revenue to obtain an order from a District Court judge for a person to produce material if the judge is satisfied by information given on oath by an authorised officer that there are reasonable grounds of suspecting that an offence (as defined for TCA 1997, s 908D), is being, has been or is about to be committed and that material (as defined for TCA 1997, s 908D), which is likely to be of value to the investigation of the offence or which constitutes evidence of the offence is in the possession or control of a person specified in the application. The judge can order that the person produce the material to the authorised officer or give the authorised officer access to it either immediately or within a stated period TCA 1997, s 908D(2). A Revenue officer or any person to whom the warrant relates may apply to a District Court judge to vary or discharge the order TCA 1997, s 908D(7). The Revenue officers may retain any material, or take copies thereof and retain those copies for use as evidence in any criminal proceedings TCA 1997, s 908D(5). The information collected on foot of a warrant will generally be admissible in criminal proceedings as evidence of any fact where direct oral evidence thereof would have been admissible, subject to compliance with relevant provisions of the Criminal Evidence Act 1992. However, there are exceptions for information subject to legal privilege, where the information was supplied by a person who would not be a compellable witness at the instance of the prosecution or where it was compiled for the purposes of or in anticipation of an investigation, enquiry, civil or criminal proceedings or proceedings of a disciplinary nature (TCA 1997, s 908C(6)).

The only documents which may be excluded under this section from the scope of the order are those documents which are subject to legal privilege but otherwise the order will take effect irrespective of any other obligations to secrecy or restrictions on disclosure TCA 1997, s 908D(4). This means that tax advisers generally may be subject to an order under the section. Any person who without reasonable excuse fails or refuses to comply with an order under this section is liable to a fine not exceeding €5,000 or imprisonment for a term not exceeding six months or to both the fine and the imprisonment.

A member of the Gardaí carrying out a search under a warrant issued under the Criminal Justice Act 1994, s 64 (as amended by the Disclosure of Certain Information for Taxation and Other Purposes Act 1996, s 4) may be accompanied by such other persons as he thinks necessary, ie including Revenue officials if appropriate.

TCA 1997, s 912B provides that a Revenue Official may question suspects in Garda custody who have been arrested in respect of certain Revenue offences. The offences fall within the meaning of Criminal Law Act 1997, s 2 (ie offences which may be punished by imprisonment for a term of five years or by a more severe penalty). For income tax purposes the section is limited to offences relating to Relevant Contracts Tax: see **2.311**.

TCA 1997, s 908E provides with effect from 31 March 2012 that a Revenue officer for the purposes of an investigation into a relevant offence (as itemised in TCA 1997, s 908E(1)) may apply to the District Court for an order: (a) to require a person to make particular documents, or documents of a particular type available to him; and/or (b) to require a person to provide particular information either by answering questions and/or making a statement (TCA 1997, s 908E(2)).

A District Court judge may make an order if satisfied by information given on oath by the Revenue officer that:

(a) there are reasonable grounds for suspecting that the person has possession or control of the documents;
(b) there are reasonable grounds for believing that the documents are relevant to the investigation;
(c) there are reasonable grounds for suspecting that the documents, or some of them, may constitute evidence of, or in relation to, the relevant offence; and
(d) there are reasonable grounds for believing that the documents should be produced or made accessible, having regard to the benefit to the investigation and any other relevant circumstances.

The judge may order the person to produce the documents, or to identify and categorise certain documents in such manner as the judge orders and to produce the documents so categorised, or to give access to the documents by the Revenue officer either immediately or within such time as the order may prescribe (TCA 1997, s 908E(3)).

A District Court judge may also make an order if satisfied by information given on oath by the Revenue officer that:

(a) there are reasonable grounds for suspecting that the person has information which he has failed or refused to provide without a reasonable excuse;
(b) there are reasonable grounds for believing the documents are relevant to the investigation;
(c) there are reasonable grounds for suspecting the information (or part thereof) may constitute evidence of or relating to or in relation to the relevant offence; and
(d) there are reasonable grounds for believing the information should be provided, having regard to the benefit to the investigation and any other relevant circumstances. The judge may order the person to provide the requisite information by answering questions together with a declaration of truth of those answers and/or making a statement either immediately or within such time as the order may prescribe (TCA 1997, s 908E(4)).

Information that a person may be required to give is limited to information which the person acquired in the ordinary course of business (TCA 1997, s 908E(5)). Where a person appears to the judge to be entitled to allow entry to a place where documents are located, that person may be required to allow a Revenue officer to enter such the place to obtain access to the documents (TCA 1997, s 908E(6)).

Where documents are not in a legible form, the order will take effect so as to:

(a) require the provision of passwords;
(b) require the documents to be provided in a form that is legible and comprehensible; and
(c) require the provision of documents in a form in which they can be removed, and are or can be made legible and comprehensible (TCA 1997, s 908E(7)).

An order providing for the production or taking away of a document:

(a) thereby empowers the Revenue officer to make a copy and take the copy away;

(b) does not grant a right of production over, or access to, documents that are subject to legal professional privilege;

(c) will have effect notwithstanding any other provisions in relation to secrecy or disclosure of information, whether statutory or otherwise (TCA 1997, s 908E(8)). Where, in relation to any document, legal professional privilege is asserted by a person subject to an order under TCA 1997, s 908E, procedures are provided by TCA 1997, s 908F to allow for a determination of whether privilege arises.

A person may request retention of a document while the authorised officer takes or retains a copy of it. The Revenue officer may accede to the request where he is satisfied that the person requires it for their business and undertakes, in writing, to keep it and furnish it to the Revenue officer when required in connection with any criminal proceedings (TCA 1997, s 908E(9)).

If the person fails to deliver up the document when required, a copy of the document may be admitted in evidence.

Any document taken away by an authorised officer may be retained by use as evidence in a criminal prosecution (TCA 1997, s 908E(10)).

Any information provided by a person following an order shall not be admissible in evidence in any proceedings brought against that person for an offence. This does not apply where the offence relate to non-compliance with the order, where the person deliberately gives incorrect information or the person refuses to deliver up a document in respect of which he had given a written undertaking to produce when required. (TCA 1997, s 908E(11)).

In relation to any documents, the person may be ordered to furnish a statement confirming the authenticity of the documents and, in the case of non-legible documents, to provide details of the system or manner in which the documents were reproduced. This may be required at the time the documents are produced or at a later time, as may be specified by order (TCA 1997, s 908E(12)). The production of any documents shall be without prejudice to any lien that the person may hold over the documents (TCA 1997, s 908E(13)).

A District Court Judge may, following an application by the person concerned, vary or discharge an order (TCA 1997, s 908E (14)). Where a person requests the return of a document and the authorised officer does not accede to the request, the person may apply to the District Court for the return of the document and the Judge may make an order concerning the return of the document subject to such condition as he may direct (TCA 1997, s 908E(15)). A person who refuses to comply with an order under this section will be guilty of an offence and liable to a fine, imprisonment or both (TCA 1997, s 908E(16)). A person who deliberately provides false or incorrect information will be guilty of an offence and liable to a fine, imprisonment or both (TCA 1997, s 908E(17)). A person who, following the giving of a written undertaking to furnish a document to an authorised officer when required in connection with a criminal proceeding, fails to deliver up the document will be guilty of an offence and liable to a fine, imprisonment or both (TCA 1997, s 908E(18)).

An application for an order shall be made to the District Court in the area where:

(a) the documents are located;

(b) the person from whom the documents or information is sought lives or carries on a profession, business or occupation; or

(c) in the case of a company, the registered office is located, or it carries on a business (TCA 1997, s 908E(19)).

TCA 1997, s 908E will not affect the operation of any other provision under which a court may order the production of documents in relation to the investigation of an offence (TCA 1997, s 908E(20)).

2.608 Power to obtain information from other persons

TCA 1997, s 902(2) empowers an inspector of taxes, who is enquiring into the tax liability of any person ('the taxpayer') to seek from a third party books, records or other documents relevant to the tax of the enquiry. An authorised officer (or an officer of the Revenue Commissioners) may serve a notice in writing on a third party to provide certain information and to deliver to or make available for inspection certain information in a given period (of not less than 30 days). FA 2015, s 75 inserted a definition of 'taxpayer' into TCA 1997, s 902 with effect from 21 December 2015, the date of passing of FA 2015, as follows: 'taxpayer' includes any person whose identity is not known to the authorised officer and includes a group or class of persons whose individual identities are not so known to the authorised officer. This expands the Revenue's ability to source information in relation to particular groups where the taxpayer can be identified subsequently.

Before an inspector can use his power to obtain information from persons other than the taxpayer, he is required to first give the taxpayer notice in writing that he is not satisfied with the statement delivered by him. A notice shall not however be served under sub-s (2) unless the authorised officer concerned has reasonable grounds to believe that the person is likely to have information relevant to the establishment of a liability in relation to the taxpayer. Sub-s (4) provides that the persons who may be treated as a taxpayer for the purposes of TCA 1997, s 902 include a company which has been dissolved and an individual who has died. A notice served by an authorised officer under this section shall name the taxpayer in relation to whose liability is being required. Any notice served under sub-s (2) will be copied and provided to the taxpayer concerned.

TCA 1997, s 902(6) requires when the Revenue officer serves the notice on the third party then where the identity of the taxpayer is known to the authorised officer, a copy of the notice must be given to the taxpayer at the time or as soon as is practicable thereafter. In other cases where the identity of the taxpayer is not known to the officer, a copy of the notice must be given to the taxpayer as soon as is practicable after their identity becomes known to the officer.

Where the person on whom notice has been served has delivered any books, records or other documents and such are retained by the authorised officer, that person will be entitled, subject to reasonable conditions, to inspect same and obtain copies of same. Similarly, the authorised officer is permitted to take extracts from or copies of any of the information or documents provided.

Sub-section (9) deals with persons carrying on a profession on whom notice is served to furnish certain information etc. A person carrying on a profession is not required to disclose:

(a) information to which a claim to legal professional privilege could be maintained in legal proceedings;

(b) information of a confidential medical nature; or

(c) professional advice of a confidential nature given to a client (other than advice given as part of a dishonest, fraudulent or criminal purpose).

Sub-section (10) provides that if any of the information, etc is provided electronically or automatically, it is not provided in a legible form or capable of being reproduced legibly, the person on whom notice is served is to assist the authorised officer accordingly.

Any person who fails or refuses to comply with a notice served on them under TCA 1997, s 902(2) or to afford the assistance referred to above will be liable to a penalty of €4,000. Nothing in TCA 1997, s 1078 however shall be construed as applying to such a failure or refusal.

TCA 1997, s 902A gives power to an authorised officer to apply to a judge of the High Court for an order requiring the third party to:

(a) deliver or make available books, records, documents, etc which are in the power, possession or ability to procure of the third party which are, (or in the reasonable opinion of the officer) may be, relevant to the tax liability of a person (even if deceased) including a group or class of persons; and
(b) produce to the officer such information, explanations or particulars as the officer may reasonably require and which are relevant to such liability.

FA 2015, s 75 inserted a new sub-s (2A) which states that in making an application an authorised officer may request the judge to provide that any order made under sub-s (4) shall be subject to a condition that, save for the purposes of complying with the order, the existence of or any details of the order shall not be disclosed (whether directly or indirectly) to any person. Any hearing of an application and of any appeal in relation thereto must be held *in camera* (TCA 1997, s 902A(7)).

However, before making any such applications (whether or not it includes a request under sub-s (2A) discussed above), the authorised officer must have the consent in writing of a Revenue Commissioner and must be satisfied that:

(a) there are reasonable grounds for suspecting that the person or class of persons may have failed or may fail to comply with any provisions of the Tax Acts;
(b) any such failure is likely to have led or is likely to lead to serious prejudice to the proper assessment collection of tax (in a case where a group or class of persons this need not apply to all the members of the class or group);
(ba) that, in a case where the application includes a request made under sub-s (2A) discussed above there are reasonable grounds for suspecting that a disclosure, referred to in sub-s (2A) would lead to serious prejudice to the proper assessment or collection of tax, and
(c) the information likely to be obtained on foot of the order is relevant to the proper assessment and collection of tax.

If the order is granted by the judge, the third party must provide all reasonable assistance to the officer including explaining the institution's information storage and retrieval procedures.

TCA 1997, s 902B inserted by FA 2005, s 140 with effect from 25 March 2005 provides that a Revenue Commissioner may direct a duly authorised officer of the Revenue Commissioners to investigate a class or classes of policies issued by a life assurance company (as defined by Insurance Act 1936, s 3) and the policyholders thereof (TCA 1997, s 902B(2)). A Revenue Commissioner can only issue such a direction if he forms the opinion that there are circumstances that suggest that a class or classes of policies may have been issued by the life assurance company concerned to policyholders some of whom have paid one or more premiums on those policies out of income or gains which were not included as they ought to have been in the appropriate returns. The Revenue Commissioner may take into consideration information regarding policies issued by other life assurance companies and the holders of such policies (TCA 1997, s 902B(2)). An authorised officer may for these purposes enter any office or place of business of the life assurance company at all reasonable times in order to inspect the records (in effect all documentation whether stored electronically or not in relation to policies other than medical records) in respect of a sample of policies and the policyholders to whom they were issued (TCA 1997, s 902B(4)). Any information obtained from an inspection, under TCA 1997, s 902B, of the records of a life assurance company can only be used to enable an application to be made to a judge of the High Court under TCA 1997, s 902A (TCA 1997, s 902B(7)).

TCA 1997, s 960R with effect from 31 March 2012, enables the Collector-General or a nominated Revenue officer to issue a notice requiring a statement of affairs to be delivered within 30 days of the giving of the notice (prior to 18 December 2013, the date of passing of Finance (No 2) Act 2013, the statement had to be returned within a period of time specified in the notice) from persons who are not engaging with the Collector-General's Office in relation to their tax affairs. A statement of affairs can also be sought from the spouse or civil partner of an individual where joint assessment under TCA 1997, s 1017 or s 1031C applies. The statement of affairs must contain details of all assets and liabilities of the persons concerned, including a full description, their location on the date specified in the notice, the date and cost (as defined) of their acquisition, details of any related insurance policies and, with effect from 18 December 2013, their market value and details of any charges or encumbrances on the assets. Prior to 18 December 2013 details of any acquisitions other than by way of arm's length also had to be provided.. The property of minor children and minor children of a civil partner must be included in the statement of affairs where those assets have previously been disposed of by that person, whether to the minor child or not, or where the assets were acquired for the minor child with funds provided directly or indirectly by the individual concerned. With effect from 18 December 2013 the statement of affairs must also include details of the person's income and outgoings in respect of such period or periods specified in the notice and in addition must contain any information requested by the Collector-General in respect of each liability, item of income or outgoings. Trustees may be asked to provide a statement of affairs in respect of the assets and liabilities of a trust and also, with effect from 18 December 2013, the income and outgoings of the Trust. The person completing the statement of affairs must also sign it and include a statutory declaration that the statement is correct to the best of that person's knowledge and belief. Prior to 18 December 2013 it was not a requirement that the declaration made should be a statutory declaration however the Collector-General or Revenue office could require that the declaration be made on oath. Revenue *eBrief No 100/15* outlines further guidance in connection with the above.

2.609 Return of property

TCA 1997, s 909(2) empowers an inspector of taxes, to verify a return of income made by any person, to require that person to make a statement of affairs, thereby enabling the inspector to examine the taxpayer's return in considerably more depth. This statement of affairs must be requested by a notice in writing (referred to here as a 's 909 notice') to be given by the inspector to the person who made the return of income. If that person is an individual treated by TCA 1997, s 1015(2) or s 1031A as living with his spouse or civil partner for the tax year to which the return of income relates, the inspector may also give a s 909 notice to the spouse or civil partner requiring a return of the entire spouse's or civil partner's property.

Any individual to whom a s 909 notice is given must, within the time limit specified in the notice (which cannot be less than 30 days), make a return in the prescribed form of all the property to which he is beneficially entitled as on a date that is specified in the notice. In addition, the individual must also include in the return any property of a minor child of theirs to which either of two conditions apply, namely that property which at any time prior to its acquisition by the minor child was disposed of by the individual concerned, or that property the consideration for the acquisition of which by the minor child was provided directly or indirectly by the individual. A 'minor child' is one under age 18 at the date specified in the return, but only if that child was unmarried at that date. With effect from 25 March 1999 any statement of affairs required under this section must also include details of insurance policies taken out in respect of any of the person's assets.

A s 909 notice may be sent by the inspector to a person chargeable to income tax in a representative capacity on behalf of another person (for example, as the trustee of an incapacitated person). In such a case, the person so chargeable is required to make the return in respect of all the relevant property to which that other person is beneficially entitled. For this purpose, the property to be returned by the person acting in the representative capacity is limited to (a) property giving rise to income in respect of which he is chargeable to income tax in that capacity and (b) any other property in relation to which he performs functions or duties in that capacity.

A s 909 notice may also be sent to a person (including a company) who is chargeable to income tax as a trustee of a trust in respect of which the return of income fails to satisfy the inspector. In this case, the return must include all the property comprised in the trust at the date specified in the notice.

It is to be noted that TCA 1997, s 909 leaves it entirely to the inspector of taxes to decide whether or not any given return of income warrants action to require the person concerned to complete a statement of affairs.

Property

For the purpose of the rules relating to the return of property, a person's 'property' is defined as including all interests and rights of any description and, without limiting the generality of the term, includes:

(a) in the case of a limited interest (for example, a life interest in the estate of a deceased person), the property in which the limited interest subsists;

(b) an interest in expectancy;

(c) an interest or share in a partnership, joint tenancy or estate of a deceased person;

(d) stock or shares in a company in the course of liquidation;

(e) an annuity; and

(f) property comprised in a settlement which the person concerned is empowered to revoke (TCA 1997, s 909(1)).

2.610 Information from financial institutions

TCA 1997, s 906A empowers a duly authorised officer of the Revenue Commissioners to serve a written notice on a financial institution licensed or authorised, etc by the Central Bank or similarly authorised under the law of an EEA State, requiring it:

(a) to make available for inspection books, records or documents (as widely defined) which are within its power, possession or which it is able to procure and which contain, or which in the reasonable opinion of the officer, may contain information relevant to a tax liability of a named taxpayer (including if relevant a deceased individual); and

(b) to furnish information, explanations and particulars as the officer may reasonably require and which are relevant to such a liability.

FA 2015, s 75 inserts a definition of 'taxpayer' into TCA 1997, s 906A with effect from 21 December 2015, the date of passing of FA 2015, as follows: 'taxpayer' includes any person whose identity is not known to the authorised officer and includes a group or class of persons whose individual identities are not so known to the authorised officer. This expands the Revenue's ability to source information in relation to particular groups where the taxpayer can be identified subsequently. The officer must obtain the consent of a Revenue Commissioner and must have reasonable grounds for believing that that the financial institution has relevant information before he can serve the notice. He must issue a copy of the notice to the taxpayer. The institution must provide all reasonable assistance to the officer, including explaining its information storage and retrieval procedures. If the Institution fails to meet any of its obligations under the section is liable to a penalty of €19,045 and a daily fine of €2,535 thereafter.

TCA 1997, s 908(2) empowers a duly authorised officer of the Revenue Commissioners to apply, in certain circumstances, for a High Court order to require a bank or other financial institution to furnish certain information relevant to a person's tax liability (including a group or class of persons and a person who is claiming DIRT exemption on the basis of non-residence in the State). FA 2015, s 75 inserted a new sub-s (2A) which states that in making an application an authorised officer may request the judge to provide that any order made shall be subject to a condition that, save for the purposes of complying with the order, the existence of or any details of the order shall not be disclosed (whether directly or indirectly) to any person. In *Walsh v National Irish Bank* [2007] IEHC 325, the court refused to grant an order in relation to bank accounts held by the Isle of Man branch of an Irish incorporated company. This was on the basis that the branch had to be treated for these purposes as a separate entity subject to Isle of Man laws and regulations and outside the jurisdiction of the Irish courts. There was nothing in TCA 1997, s 908 to demonstrate any intention by the legislature to extend the application of the section outside the territorial limits of the State. The court indicated that even if s 908 did apply in these circumstances it would exercise its discretion to decline the order as there was evidence that it would strongly be objected to by the Manx Courts and would thus be contrary to the principle of comity of courts. The Revenue however appealed this decision to the Supreme Court where the court rejected the bank's contention that the Isle of Man branch should be regarded as a separate entity not governed by the Irish regulatory regime. The Supreme Court looked at the proper approach to be taken where a potential conflict arises between the disclosure obligation in this jurisdiction and the obligation of confidentiality in another jurisdiction and concluded that the correct approach was to issue the disclosure order and to include in the terms of the order measures to allow the court in the other jurisdiction an opportunity to consider whether compliance with the order would breach the law in the other jurisdiction. The Supreme Court accordingly provided that an order under TCA 1997, s 908 should be made but that the making of the order should be deferred for 12 weeks to allow an application to be made by the bank to the Manx courts. The court also provided that in the event that the Manx courts concluded that the disclosure would be in breach of Isle of Man law the bank may return to the Supreme Court where the matter will be considered again (*Walsh v National Irish Bank* [2013] IESC 2).

In *McL v D* [2009] IEHC 184, it was held that there was no requirement on the Revenue Commissioners to exhaust their less invasive powers before invoking TCA 1997, s 908.

An authorised officer shall not make an application under TCA 1997, s 908(3) without the written consent of a Revenue Commissioner, and without being satisfied that:

(a) there are reasonable grounds for suspecting that the taxpayer, or, where the taxpayer is a group or class of persons, all or any one of those persons, may have failed or fail to comply with any provision of the Acts;

(b) any such failure is likely to have led or to lead to 'serious prejudice to the proper assessment or collection of tax' arising; and

(c) the information which is likely to be contained in the books, records, etc or the information, explanations and particulars to which the application relates, is relevant to the proper assessment or collection of the tax in question. The authorised officer may also make an application to the judge for an order in respect of connected parties to the taxpayer;

The persons who may be treated as a taxpayer for the purposes of this section include a company which has been dissolved, and an individual who has died. Every hearing of an application for an order under this section and of any appeal in connection with that application is required to be held *in camera*.

Subsection (8) provides that the authorised officer can also apply for an order of the court to freeze the assets of a person in the custody of the financial institution. It is noteworthy that a copy of any affidavit and an application for an order under this section are to be made available to the taxpayer, or the taxpayer's solicitor or to the financial institution or the financial institution's solicitor, and if the judge is satisfied on the hearing of the application that there are reasonable grounds in the public interest that such copy of an affidavit, etc should not include the name or address of the authorised officer, then such copy, or copies, etc shall not include the name or address of the authorised officer. Furthermore, similar provisions apply to keep the authorised officer's name out of Court and to only cross examine *in camera* in the grounds of public interest.

TCA 1997, s 908A gives power to a duly authorised officer to apply to the Circuit Court or the District Court for an order authorising the officer to inspect and take copies of bank records and associated documents for the purpose of investigating a revenue offence. An order can only be made by a judge if he or she is satisfied that based on information given on oath that there are reasonable grounds for suspecting that an offence which would result in 'serious prejudice to the proper assessment or collection of tax' is being, has been or is about to be committed and that there is material in the position of the financial institution which is likely to be of substantial value in the investigation of that offence. An authorised officer must have a written consent of a Revenue Commissioner before applying for an order under this section. FA 2000 provides this section with a wider definition of 'financial institution' (extends this definition to include a credit institution) and 'documentation' for the purposes of that section. TCA 1997, ss 904A, 904B, 904C and 904D were introduced by FA 2000, s 68. TCA 1997, ss 904A, 904C and 904D grant a power of inspection to the Revenue Commissioners in respect of relevant deposit takers (TCA 1997, s 904A), assurance companies (TCA 1997, s 904C) and investment undertakings (s 904D).

Various penalties ranging from €1,260 (for employers) to €19,045 (the institutions themselves) are applicable for non-compliance with the requirements of an authorised officer. Furthermore, a further penalty of €2,535 may be levied on such institutions for each day on which such a failure to comply with the requirements of an authorised officer of the Revenue Commissioners continues. TCA 1997, s 904B legislates for the Revenue Commissioners to make a report to the Committee of Public Accounts. FA 2001, s 22 introduced similar powers of inspection relating to authorised insurers (TCA 1997, s 904E), qualifying lenders (TCA 1997, s 904F), qualifying insurers (TCA 1997, s 904G) and qualifying savings managers (TCA 1997, s 904H); FA 2002, s 132(c) introduced similar powers of inspection relating to dividend withholding tax (see **Division 9**) (TCA 1997, s 904I); FA 2003, s 159 introduced similar powers of inspection relating to PSWT (see **2.5**) with effect from 28 March 2003 (TCA 1997, s 904J) Similar penalties for non-compliance also apply.

TCA 1997, s 908B (inserted by FA 2004, s 88) enables the Revenue Commissioners to apply to the High Court to seek an order requiring a financial institution to supply documents and information in relation to the tax liabilities of a taxpayer or group of taxpayers (including cases where the identities of the taxpayer(s) are not known to the Revenue Commissioners) held by a non-resident entity over which it has control (as defined by TCA 1997, s 432). The court must be satisfied that there are reasonable grounds for suspecting that the taxpayer(s) concerned have failed to comply with their tax obligations and that the amount of the liabilities related to that failure is such as to lead to serious prejudice to the proper collection or assessment of tax.

TCA 1997, s 907 deals with applications to the Appeal Commissioners. The section conveys power on a duly authorised officer to apply to the Appeal Commissioners for consent to issue a notice to a financial institution requiring it to make available for inspection certain information relating to a person's tax liability, including a group or class of persons, including a person or persons whose identity is not known and the person who is claiming exemption from DIRT on the basis of non-residence in the State. Written consent is however required from a Revenue Commissioner before an authorised officer can make such an application. The officer must be satisfied:

(a) that there are reasonable grounds for suspecting that the taxpayer(s) may have failed or may fail to comply with any provision of the Taxes Acts;

(b) that any such failure is likely to have led or to lead to serious prejudice to the proper assessment or collection of tax; and

(c) that the information:

  (i) which is likely to be contained in the books, records or other documents, or

  (ii) which is likely to arise from the information, explanations and particulars, to which the application relates,

  is relevant to the proper assessment or collection of tax.

The authorised officer may also make application to the Appeal Commissioners for consent to serve a notice on a financial institution in relation to books, records or other documents and information, and to furnish explanations and particulars relating to a person who is connected with the taxpayer. Where the Appeal Commissioners determine that in all the circumstances there are reasonable grounds for making the application, they may give their consent to the authorised officer serving a notice on the third party, requiring the financial institution to make available for inspection by the authorised officer, such books, records or other documents, and to furnish the authorised officer with such information, explanations and particulars, as may, with the Appeal Commissioners' consent, be specified in the notice.

The persons who may be treated as a taxpayer for these purposes include a company which has been dissolved and an individual who has died. Where the Appeal Commissioners have given their consent, the authorised officer shall, as soon as practicable, but not later than 14 days from the time that such consent was made, serve a notice on the financial institution concerned and stating that:

(a) such consent has been given; and
(b) the third party should, within a period of 30 days;

comply with the requirements as specified in the notice.

An application by an authorised officer under this section is to be heard by the Appeal Commissioners with any necessary modifications as if it were an appeal against an assessment to income tax; however, the determination by the Appeal Commissioners will be final and conclusive.

As part of its compliance with a notice under TCA 1997, s 907, the institution must afford the authorised officer reasonable assistance as defined. The authorised officer is entitled to make extracts or copies from the relevant books or documentation. An institution which fails to comply with a notice by an authorised officer will be liable to a penalty of €19,045 and, if the failure continues after the expiry of the 30 day period specified above, a further penalty of €2,535 for each day on which the failure so continues.

TCA 1997, s 907A provides, with effect from 3 April 2010, that virtually identical powers shall apply in relation to a third party whose identity has been furnished to an authorised officer in compliance with a notice issued under TCA 1997, s 907 or a court order made under TCA 1997, s 908. However, TCA 1997, s 907A will not require any person to disclose:

(a) information with respect to which a claim to legal professional privilege could be maintained in legal proceedings;
(b) information of a confidential medical nature; or
(c) professional advice of a confidential nature given to a client (other than advice given as part of a dishonest, fraudulent or criminal purpose);

the latter exception would clearly cover tax advisers in appropriate circumstances.

TCA 1997, ss 904E, 904F, 904G allow the Revenue Commissioners to audit claims for repayment of tax by medical insurers, mortgage lenders and insurers respectively. TCA 1997, s 904H gives the Revenue power to audit banks in relation to Special Savings Incentive Accounts ('qualifying savings manager') as defined in TCA 1997, s 848B. Under the tax relief at source arrangements, tax is deducted at source when making premium payments to medical insurers, to insurers in respect of long term care, and also when paying mortgage interest to mortgage lenders (tax is deducted at the standard rate). The insurers and the lenders will, in turn, claim repayment of equivalent amounts from the Revenue Commissioners.

In order to ensure that the legislation is being complied with, Revenue now have powers similar to those contained at TCA 1997, s 904A, to check procedures relating to the vouching of claims by mortgage lenders, medical insurers and insurers for repayment of tax and to examine, on a sample basis, underlying records to ensure that the procedures are observed and that the claims from individuals are valid.

Revenue are also empowered to audit returns and examine procedures in connection with the special savings incentive scheme to ensure that the provisions governing various aspects of that scheme were being operated in a proper manner.

TCA 1997, ss 904E, 904F, 904G and 904H also provide for certain penalties that will be imposed should the requirements of authorised officers of the Revenue not be complied with. These may be summarised as follows:

TCA 1997, s 904E:

(a) where an employee of an authorised insurer does not comply with the requirements of the authorised officer in the exercise or performance of his duties, he will be liable to a penalty of €1,265;

(b) where an authorised insurer fails to comply with the requirements of the authorised officer in the exercise of performance of his duties, that authorised insurer shall be liable to a penalty of €19,045, and if that failure continues, a further €2,535 for each day on which the failure continues.

TCA 1997, s 904F:

(a) where an employee of a qualifying lender does not comply with the requirements of the authorised officer in the exercise or performance of his duties, he will be liable to a penalty of €1,265;

(b) where a qualifying lender fails to comply with the requirements of the authorised officer in the exercise of performance of his duties, that qualifying lender shall be liable to a penalty of €19,045, and if that failure continues, a further €2,535 for each day on which the failure continues.

TCA 1997, s 904G:

(a) where an employee of a qualifying insurer does not comply with the requirements of the authorised officer in the exercise or performance of his duties, he will be liable to a penalty of €1,265;

(b) where an qualifying insurer fails to comply with the requirements of the authorised officer in the exercise of performance of his duties, that qualifying insurer shall be liable to a penalty of €19,045, and if that failure continues, a further €2,535 for each day on which the failure continues.

TCA 1997, s 904H:

(a) where an employee of a qualifying savings manager does not comply with the requirements of the authorised officer in the exercise or performance of his duties, he will be liable to a penalty of €1,265;

(b) where a qualifying savings manager fails to comply with the requirements of the authorised officer in the exercise of performance of his duties, that qualifying savings manager shall be liable to a penalty of €19,045, and if that failure continues, a further €2,535 for each day on which the failure continues.

'Power to obtain information from ministers of the government'

TCA 1997, s 910 provides that for the purposes of the assessment, collection, etc of tax, the Revenue Commissioners may request any Minister of the Government or any body established under statute by notice in writing, to provide them with such information in relation to payments for any purposes made by them, either on their own behalf or on behalf of other persons as may be specified in the notice. With effect from 2 April 2007, the Revenue Commissioners may require such information to be submitted in an electronic format.

2.611 Quotation of tax reference number

Under TCA 1997, s 885(2) every sole trader (or the precedent partner in the case of a partnership) carrying on a 'business' (as defined) must ensure that his tax reference number (or one of his tax reference numbers, if not two or more) is stated on all of his business documents. The term 'precedent partner' is not defined; presumably it is intended that the definition in TCA 1997, s 1007(1), should apply – see **4.508**).

Business documents comprise invoices, credit notes, debit notes, receipts, accounts, statements of account, vouchers or estimates relating to amounts of €7 or more issued in the course of the business. A 'business' for these purposes means either:

(a) a profession; or
(b) a trade or a part of a trade consisting of the supplies of services, including any such supply which incorporates goods in the course of that supply (TCA 1997, s 885(1)).

The term 'supply' is stated to bear the same meaning as in the VAT Acts. The scope of 'services' for VAT purposes is very wide, but the word 'services' in TCA 1997, s 885(1) is not specifically deemed to carry this extended meaning.

A person's 'tax reference number' means any of the following:

(a) the personal public service number (PPSN) stated on any certificate of tax credits and standard rate cut off point issued to that person by an inspector, not being a certificate issued to an employer in respect of an employee;
(b) the reference number stated on any tax return or notice of assessment issued to that person; or
(c) the VAT registration number of that person (TCA 1997, s 885(1)).

Where a person does not have a tax reference number, he must state his full name and address on his return.

2.612 Attachment of debts

TCA 1997, s 1002 gives the Revenue Commissioners the power to require certain persons owing money to, or holding financial assets of, any taxpayer who has defaulted in paying tax, interest on unpaid tax or penalties, to pay over those assets towards the discharge of the taxpayer's debts to the Revenue. This applies whether the tax (including any interest or penalties in relation thereto) is income tax, corporation tax, income levy, parking levy, domicile levy, universal social charge, capital gains tax, value-added tax, custom or excise duties, local property tax or any other tax, duty, levy or charge which, in accordance with any provision of the relevant Acts is placed under the care and management of the Revenue Commissioners. The relevant Acts are defined in sub-s (1) and include the Customs Acts, the statutes relating to the duties of excise, the Tax Acts, TCA 1997, Pts 18A (Income Levy), 18B (Parking Levy), 18C (Domicile Levy) and 18D (Universal Social Charge), the Capital Gains Tax Acts, VAT Acts, Capital Acquisitions Tax Consolidation Act 2003, Stamp Duties Consolidation Act 1999, The Finance (Local Property Tax) Act 2012 and subsequent enactments amending or extending those Acts. As the SWCA 2005 extends all the provisions regarding the collection of income tax to PRSI, the power of attachment also applies to PRSI liabilities.

The section refers to taxpayers who have failed to pay any relevant tax (and/or interest or penalties related to that tax) within the proper time for the discharge of their obligations for the tax, etc. It gives the Revenue a power of attachment to require the payment to the Collector-General of debts due to the defaulting taxpayer by any 'relevant person'. A 'taxpayer', for the purpose of the section, is defined as any person who is liable to pay, remit or account for tax under the relevant Acts to the Revenue Commissioners. A 'relevant person' is defined, in relation to the defaulting taxpayer, as a person of whom the Revenue Commissioners have reason to believe that the person may, at the time he or it (if a company) receives a notice of attachment, have a debt due to the taxpayer.

TCA 1997, s 1002(2) entitles the Revenue Commissioners to serve a notice in writing ('the notice of attachment') on any person who is a relevant person in relation to a particular defaulting taxpayer. This notice of attachment must state:

(a) the taxpayer's name and address;
(b) the aggregate amount of the taxes, interest on unpaid taxes and penalties in respect of which the taxpayer is in default at the time the notice of attachment is given to the relevant person;
(c) a direction to the relevant person to deliver to the Revenue Commissioners, within seven days after the notice of attachment is received by the relevant person, a return in writing specifying the amount(s) of any debt(s) due by the relevant person to the taxpayer (see further below); and
(d) a direction to the relevant person to pay to the Revenue Commissioners an amount equal to the lower of the aggregate amount of the taxes, interest and penalties mentioned in (b) or the amount of the debt due by the relevant person to the taxpayer (as specified by the relevant person in his return under (c)).

With effect from 18 December 2013 (the date of the passing of Finance (No 2) Act 2013) a notice of attachment may be given electronically.

The 'debt' due by a relevant person to a taxpayer named in the notice of attachment received by the relevant person is defined as the amount or aggregate amount of any money which, at the date of receipt of the notice of attachment, is due by the relevant person to the named taxpayer. This applies whether the amount (or aggregate amount) is due to the taxpayer by the relevant person on his/its own account, or as an agent or as a trustee. It applies whether or not the taxpayer has yet applied to the relevant person for the payment of the debt or, in the case of money on deposit with the relevant person, for the withdrawal of all or part of the money.

If the relevant person is a financial institution, any amount or aggregate amount of money, including interest thereon, which the relevant person holds on deposit to the credit of the taxpayer is regarded as a debt due by the relevant person to the taxpayer. Accounts held in joint names are deemed to benefit each name equally. Consequently, the notice of attachment extends to the amount of the deposit and any accrued interest thereon so that the financial institution is required to pay over the deposit to the Revenue Commissioners. However, as with other debts, the notice of attachment does not extend to the part of the deposit and interest which exceeds the aggregate of the taxes, etc specified in the notice of attachment.

A 'financial institution' is defined as any holder of a banking licence issued under Central Bank Act 1971, s 9 or similarly authorised under the law of another EEA Member State, or any person referred to in s 7(4) of that Act. The term includes any branch of such a financial institution that records deposits in its books as liabilities of the branch. For the types of financial institution within this definition, see the list in **2.610** (where the same definition is applied in TCA 1997, s 907–908 in relation to the Revenue Commissioners' power to obtain information from financial institutions).

Any person who receives a notice of attachment from the Revenue Commissioners must reply (within the 10-day period) stating whether or not he (or, if a company, it) has any debt due to the named taxpayer and, if so, the relevant person must specify the amount of such debt. It is the time of receipt of the notice which counts. Should the relevant person have paid back a debt (or allowed the taxpayer to withdraw a deposit) before the notice is received, the amount so repaid (or withdrawn) is outside the scope of the notice. If the relevant person's debt to the taxpayer at the time in question is less than the aggregate amount of the taxes, interest on unpaid taxes and penalties stated in the notice of attachment, the relevant person is only required to specify the lesser amount in the reply. The relevant person has no obligation to pay over to the Revenue Commissioners any excess of the debt to the taxpayer over the aggregate of the taxes, etc in default.

TCA 1997, s 1002(3) restricts the circumstances in which tax, interest on unpaid tax or any penalty may be subject to, or included in, a notice of attachment. First, no such tax, etc is to be entered in a notice of attachment unless the taxpayer's default has continued for at least 14 days (reduced from one month by FA 2001, s 238). For this purpose, it appears that – in the case of a liability to pay a tax (for example, income tax) – the default commences the day after the date on which the tax in question is due and payable. The fact that no interest may be charged on any tax which is paid after the due date does not, it seems, prevent a notice of attachment being issued immediately after the default has continued for at least 14 days.

In practice, it seems most unlikely that the Revenue Commissioners will issue notices of attachment within 14 days of the tax due date – certainly not in the case of taxpayers who generally comply with their obligations but who may slip occasionally as to the timing of their tax payments. On the other hand, if a taxpayer is already in default with his/its tax, etc payments for previous years and a new liability crystallises for the latest year, it might be reasonable for the Revenue Commissioners to include the latest year's liability immediately after the 14 days due date has past.

Secondly, no tax, interest on unpaid tax or penalty in respect of which a taxpayer is in default can be included in a notice of attachment unless the Revenue Commissioners have previously given the taxpayer a notice in writing which specifies the amount of the tax, interest or penalty in question and which states that, if the amount is not paid, it may be included in a notice of attachment, to be recovered from a relevant person. This 'warning' notice must be given to the taxpayer at least seven days before the date on which the relevant person receives the notice of attachment (TCA 1997, s 1002(3)(b)).

Exclusions

In any case where the whole or a part of a debt (or alleged debt) due by a relevant person to a taxpayer is in dispute, the amount in dispute is to be ignored by the relevant person in making his return to the Revenue Commissioners (and is not required to be paid over to them). Up to 6 February 2011, the date of the passing of Finance Act 2011, any money due by a relevant person to the taxpayer as emoluments under a contract of service was not to be included in the relevant person's return and was not subject to the notice of attachment. From 6 February 2011 a notice of attachment may be issued in respect of emoluments. 'Emoluments' for this purpose is defined as anything assessable to income tax under Sch E. It does not therefore include any remuneration of a foreign office or employment taxable under Sch D Case III (see **13.104**). Where a notice of attachment is issued in respect of emoluments the notice may provide that the amount in default may be paid by the relevant person over a period of time specified in the notice.

Additional debts

A debt due by a relevant person to a taxpayer may, at the date of receipt of a notice of attachment, be less than the taxes, etc in default so that there remains an outstanding balance of such tax, etc after the relevant person has complied with the notice and paid over the amount of debt to the Revenue Commissioners (or there may be no debt outstanding when the notice is received). If, in this case, an additional debt (or a new debt) becomes due by the relevant person to the taxpayer within a stated 'relevant period', TCA 1997, s 1002(4) requires the relevant person to pay over the amount of the additional debt to the Revenue Commissioners (but only to the extent of the balance of the taxes, etc specified in the notice as being in default).

The 'relevant period', in relation to a particular notice of attachment sent to a relevant person, is the period beginning on the date of receipt of the notice and ending (normally) on the date on which that person completes the payment to the Revenue Commissioners of the amount of the taxes, etc in default as specified in the notice of attachment. This applies to require the relevant person to pay over the specified amount out of the original debt (as at the date of receipt of the notice) and any additional debt becoming due to the taxpayer during this relevant period. In other words, once a relevant person has received a notice of attachment in relation to a particular taxpayer, that notice continues to be effective to require the relevant person to keep on making payments to the Revenue Commissioners out of any existing and additional debts becoming due by him/it to that taxpayer until the Revenue Commissioners have obtained their full payment.

There are only two exceptions to this rule. First, the relevant period ends (and the relevant person's obligation to pay over debts or additional debts ceases) on the date he/it receives a notice of revocation of the notice of attachment. Secondly, if either the relevant person or the taxpayer becomes bankrupt or, alternatively, if either person (being a company) commences to be wound up, the relevant period ends on the date of the bankruptcy or on the date of the winding up. The date of a bankruptcy is the date on which the person concerned is declared bankrupt. The relevant date for the commencement of the winding up of the company which ends the relevant period is the 'relevant date' as defined for that purpose in Companies Act 1963 (see definition given above).

TCA 1997, s 1002(6) prohibits a relevant person (in relation to a particular taxpayer) from making any disbursements out of a debt due by him/it to that taxpayer at any time during the relevant period unless, and to the extent that, any such disbursement:

(a) will not reduce the debt and/or additional debts so due by him/it to less than the amount of the taxes, etc specified in the notice of attachment, or
(b) is made pursuant to an order of a court.

Revocation of notice

TCA 1997, s 1002(10) allows the Revenue Commissioners to revoke at any time a notice of attachment previously given to a relevant person in respect of a taxpayer. This notice of revocation has to be given in writing to the relevant person. However with effect from 18 December 2013 (the date of the passing of Finance (No 2) Act 2013) a notice of revocation may be given electronically. If a taxpayer pays up to the Revenue

Commissioners the full amount of tax, etc specified in the notice of attachment, that notice must then be revoked forthwith by the Revenue Commissioners.

If a relevant person has paid the Revenue Commissioners any amount out of a debt or an additional debt due by the relevant person to the taxpayer, but if the Commissioners have been paid by the taxpayer the amount of tax, etc specified in the notice of attachment, the amount paid to them by the relevant person must be refunded forthwith by the Commissioners to the taxpayer.

Penalties, etc

TCA 1997, s 1002(7) applies the provisions of TCA 1997, ss 1052, 1054 to enable the Revenue to proceed for penalties against any relevant person who fails to deliver any return required by a notice of attachment within the 10-day time limit specified in the notice (or if the relevant person fails to deliver a further return if required under TCA 1997, s 1002(4) in relation to additional debts). Any such failure by the relevant person is treated as a 'column 1 offence' within TCA 1997, Sch 29 (see **2.701**).

For the purpose of these penalty rules, an official of the Revenue Commissioners may give a certificate that, having examined the relevant records, it appears from them that, during a specified period, a specified return was not received from a relevant person. Unless the contrary is proved, this certificate so signed is to be evidence that the relevant person did not deliver the required return during the period specified in the certificate.

TCA 1997, s 1002(5) treats the making by a relevant person of an incorrect return under this section, if made either fraudulently or negligently, as a 'revenue offence' within TCA 1997, s 1078. In addition to any other penalties to which he may be subject, he thereby becomes liable to any of the penalties listed in TCA 1997, s 1078 – (see **2.703**).

Miscellaneous

When the Revenue Commissioners sends either a notice of attachment or a notice of revocation to a relevant person, a copy of that notice must be given to the taxpayer concerned at the same time (TCA 1997, s 1002(11)).

The Revenue Commissioners are required to notify the taxpayer concerned of any amounts paid to them by a relevant person in relation to that taxpayer (TCA 1997, s 1002(12)). Where the relevant person pays over to the Revenue Commissioners the whole or part of the amount of his debt to a taxpayer, the latter is required to treat the relevant person as discharged of this amount of the debt as if it had been paid directly by the relevant person to him (TCA 1997, s 1002(13)).

The Revenue Commissioners may issue two or more notices of attachment to two or more debtors of the defaulting taxpayer at the same time.

For the Revenue Commissioners' power of inspection of returns made in accordance with TCA 1997, s 1002, see TCA 1997, s 904K.

In *Orange v Revenue Commissioners* V ITR 70, Geoghegan J held that while he did not envisage that the provisions of s 1002 could be regarded as unconstitutional per se, there could be circumstances where the actual application of the section might represent an unconstitutional exercise of the Revenue Commissioner's powers.

2.613 Priority of tax in bankruptcy

In order to ascertain the extent to which tax liabilities have to be paid in priority to other debts in the case of an insolvent taxpayer, it is necessary to look principally outside the

Tax Acts. The Bankruptcy Act 1988 covers a bankrupt individual, an arranging debtor or a person dying insolvent.

The Bankruptcy Act 1988, s 81 as amended by the Personal Insolvency Act 2012, s 156 includes certain taxes in the payments which have to be paid in priority to all other debts in the distribution of the property of either:

(a) a bankrupt;
(b) an arranging debtor; or
(c) a person dying insolvent.

In the case of a bankrupt, the preferential debts in respect of taxes are stated to be:

> all property or income tax assessed on the bankrupt up to 31 December next before the date of the order or adjudication, not exceeding in the whole one year's assessment (sub-s (1)(a))

TCA 1997, s 960P (see below) provides that the amount referred to in the Bankruptcy Act 1988, s 81(1)(a) is deemed to include capital gains tax and local property tax. TCA 1997, s 994 also provides priority for unpaid PAYE and interest thereon, while TCA 1997, s 531(1), (3)–(6), (8)–(9) gives a similar preference to deductions under the relevant contract rules (see **2.311**).

SWCA 1993, s 16(3) grants similar preferential status to unpaid social insurance employer contributions (see also Health Contributions Act 1979, s 15). SWCA 1993, s 16(3) grants 'super preferential' status to unpaid social insurance employee employment contributions, which are treated in effect as being held on trust (and are thus unavailable even to preferential creditors). Super-preferential status was denied to sums which should have been, but were not in fact, deducted from employees' wages in *Re Coombe Importers Ltd (In Liquidation)* VI ITR 1.

For an arranging debtor or a person dying insolvent, the same rules apply, except that the preferential debts include the assessed taxes (not exceeding one year's assessment) up to 5 April next before the filing of the petition of arrangement (the arranging debtor) or the date of the death (the person dying insolvent). In *Gowers v Walker* 15 TC 165, it was held that the words 'up to the 5th day of April' mean 'in respect of the period up to the 5th day of April'. Consequently, the fact that no assessment is actually made until after the 5 April (or 31 December for the year of assessment 2001 *et seq*) in question does not prejudice the Revenue's preferential position in relation to assessed taxes. The appropriate assessment may be made at a later date, but clearly should be made in time for the Revenue's preferential claim to be submitted in the relevant bankruptcy, liquidation or receivership.

In another UK case, *Re Pratt: ex parte IRC v Phillips* 31 TC 506, it was held that the priority of the Crown is not limited to taxes assessed in respect of the last fiscal year preceding a bankruptcy, but that the Crown is entitled to select any fiscal year before the date of the bankruptcy and to claim priority for unpaid taxes in respect of that year.

In a later UK case, *IRC v Liquidator of Purvis Industries Ltd* 38 TC 155, where there were different taxes outstanding in a liquidation (income tax, profits tax and excess profits tax), it was held that as all the taxes were independent and separate taxes, the Crown was entitled to select any fiscal year (for which tax was outstanding) for its priority claim in relation to each of the taxes. It did not have to claim the same fiscal year in each case, but could select the year most advantageous to it for each separate tax.

In the Irish case, *Attorney General v Irish Steel Ltd & Vincent Crowley* 2 ITC 402, the Supreme Court held, in the case of a receivership where there were amounts unpaid in respect of more than one type of assessed tax, that the Minister for Finance was entitled to preferential payments for the amount of each different tax (not exceeding in each case one year's assessment). It was also held that the different types of taxes for which the Minister claimed priority did not have to be taxes assessed for the one and the same year. Clearly, the approach of the courts has been similar in these matters in both Ireland and the UK.

TCA 1997, s 960P provides that the priority attaching to the taxes to which Bankruptcy Act 1988, s 81 also applies to, arrears of PAYE owed by an employer, arrears of relevant contracts (ie subcontractors) tax (see **2.311**) and regulations made under that Chapter and arrears of tax due under PAYE estimates made under TCA 1997, s 989 or s 990 for the 12-month period ending before the date on which the order for adjudication of the person as a bankrupt was made, the petition of the arrangement of the person as a debtor was filed or the person died insolvent. The employer's liability for a period of twelve months includes all tax which the employer is obliged to deduct under the PAYE system from emoluments paid to employees during that period, reduced by any repayments which the employer is required to make under the PAYE system in that period, together with any interest payable.

2.614 Enforcement of foreign tax liabilities

Ireland follows the well established principle of international law, whereby one state will not enforce directly or indirectly the Revenue laws of a foreign country. This principle is now subject to the European Communities (Mutual Assistance) Regulations 2002 (SI 462/2002) implementing Council Directive 201/44/EC which provides *inter alia* for the Collector-General to collect payments of income taxes arising within the European Union together with associated interest and administrative penalties. The Regulations provide that the Revenue Commissioners must process claims on the same basis as domestic liabilities. There are exceptions for penalties which relate to offences which would be regarded as criminal in nature if committed in the State and for cases where the tax, etc concerned is under appeal in the home state; in addition, all recovery measures should have been exhausted in the home state. In addition, following the High Court decision in *Re Cedarlease* [2005] IEHC 67, the current law is that tax authorities based in the European Union may avail of the Insolvency Regulations (EC 1346/2000) to petition for the winding up of an Irish registered company. Of course, where the relevant regulations do not have effect, general principles will continue to apply.

In *Buchanan v McVeigh* [1954] IR 89, a UK resident company was assessed retrospectively to UK taxation. The taxpayer, who was the controlling shareholder of the company, had sold off the assets of the company and removed the proceeds to Ireland. The Inland Revenue instigated proceedings for the winding up of the company. Apart from the liquidator's fees and expenses, the funds held in Ireland would have been applied solely in paying off the company's tax liabilities.

Kingsmill J observed:

> It is not a question whether the plaintiff is a foreign state or the representative of a foreign state or its revenue authority. In every case, the substance of the claim must be scrutinised and if it then appears that it is really a suit brought for the purpose of collecting the debts of a foreign revenue it will be rejected.

Interestingly, Maguire CJ in the Supreme Court observed:

> I agree that if the payment of a revenue claim was only incidental and had there been other claims to be met, it would be difficult for our courts to refuse to lend assistance to bring assets of the company under the control of the liquidator.

In *Rossano v Manufacturers' Life Insurance Co* [1963] 2 QB 352, the court refused to allow a debtor who had been served with a garnishee order by an overseas revenue authority to rely on the order as a defence against paying its creditor; to do otherwise would have been to enforce an overseas tax liability, albeit indirectly.

In *Re Gibbons* [1960] IR 60, the High Court refused an application to have Irish assets realised under bankruptcy proceedings initiated by the Revenue authorities. A more expansive approach appears in the Australian case of *Re Ayres* [1981] FHR 235, where it was held that an overseas assignee in bankruptcy could bring proceedings in Australia, despite the fact that over half of the bankrupt's debts were due to his home revenue authority.

The decision in *Buchanan* was also followed in *Governor & Co of the Bank of Ireland v Meenaghan & Ors* V ITR 44. In the latter case, Costello J appears to have accepted (obiter) the principle that foreign revenue laws could be recognised in Irish courts albeit not enforced by them. Thus, trustees or executors of an estate would be entitled to be indemnified out of trust/estate assets in respect of sums which they were personally liable to pay in respect of foreign revenue liabilities (see *Re Lord Cable* [1976] 3 All ER 417. For a fuller discussion of the jurisprudence in this area see Baker,. 'The transnational enforcement of tax liabilities' [1993] British Tax Review 313.

In *Byrne v Conroy* [1995] HC it was held that payments of monetary compensation amounts (MCAs) due under the UK Agricultural Levies Regulations did not constitute taxes. As a result, the defendant, who was alleged to have fraudulently evaded such payments in the UK, was not entitled to the protection of the Extradition Act 1965, s 50 (as amended by the Extradition (Amendment) Act 1994) which applies *inter alia* to 'an offence ... in connection with taxes, duties or exchange controls' (subject to certain exceptions, not relevant in the present case).

Kelly J followed *Buchanan v McVeigh* saying:

> In seeking to ascertain whether the offence charged is a revenue offence or not I must look to its true nature.

The learned Judge concluded on the basis of earlier cases decided by the ECJ that the object of the agricultural levy was not to raise revenue, whereas this was the main object of a tax. Furthermore, MCAs could take the form of either levies or refunds which was not a normal characteristic of a tax.

2.615 Tax clearance certificates

A number of activities can only be carried on legally in the State subject to the issue of an appropriate licence. TCA 1997, s 1094 amends the provisions regulating the grant of various licences and renders it mandatory for a person applying for such a licence to obtain a tax clearance certificate. An up-to-date list of the licences concerned as well as various state-based schemes for which a tax clearance certificate is required may be found on the Revenue Commissioners' website. Provisions which govern the granting of a tax clearance certificate are contained in TCA 1997, s 1094. TCA 1997, s 1094 provides that the person who will be the 'beneficial holder' of the licence must apply to the Collector-General for the certificate; the application must be made in the form prescribed by the Revenue Commissioners or in such other manner as the Revenue Commissioners may allow, if less than one year (TCA 1997, s 1094(5)). The 'beneficial holder' is defined by TCA 1997, s 1094(1) as the person who conducts the activities under the licence (ie not a nominee) or an individual authorised or nominated under the Auctioneers and House Agents Act 1947, s 58(4) and s 9(1) respectively.

TCA 1997, s 1094(2) provides that the Collector-General must issue the certificate if the applicant (and other 'associated' persons, as defined – see below) have complied with all of their obligations under the following Acts:

(a) the Tax Acts;
(b) the Capital Gains Tax Acts;
(c) the Value-Added Tax Acts and any instruments made thereunder;
(d) from 2010, the Customs Acts and the statutes relating to excise duties and the management thereof including any statutory instruments, made thereunder (TCA 1997, s 1094(1));
(e) from 2011, Pts 18A (Income Levy), 18B (Parking Levy), 18C (Domicile Levy) and 18D (Universal Social Charge) of the TCA 1997;
(f) from 13 March 2013 the Finance (Local Property Tax) Act 2012;
(g) from 2013, the statutes relating to stamp duty and the management of that duty;
(h) from 2013, the Capital Acquisitions Tax Consolidation Act 2003 and the enactments amending or extending that Act;

For these purposes, compliance denotes:

(a) the payment or remittance of taxes, interest and penalties, due under the Acts; and
(b) the delivery of returns (by implication those due under the Acts) (TCA 1997, s 1094(2)).

It may not only be the 'beneficial holder' who must establish full compliance under the relevant Acts. TCA 1997, s 1094(2) provides that the compliance requirement also extends to certain 'associated persons' in relation to the beneficial holder, namely:

(a) A partnership 'of which he is or was a partner' although this applies only 'in respect of the period of his membership'.
(b) Where the beneficial holder is a company, each person who either beneficially owns, or who is able to control either directly or indirectly more than 50 per cent of the ordinary share capital of that company. The reference to a 'beneficial owner' is presumably designed to ensure that nominee shareholdings are attributed to the real owner, although it would also seem to exclude trustee shareholdings. The significance of the reference to 'control' of share capital is not entirely clear.

    In *Associated Properties Ltd v Revenue Commissioners* II ITR 175, a corporation profits tax (CPT) case, one of the points at issue was whether an individual who held 21 per cent of company A, which in turn owned 96 per cent of company B, was thereby able to 'control (directly or indirectly) more than five per cent of the ordinary shares of B. The Supreme Court held that this was not the case. Maguire CJ said 'control' was not to be equated with a financial interest. Black J took the view that the reference to 'control' in the specific context of the CPT legislation meant the ability to dispose of the shares in question 'either by owning them or by being able to compel and direct their disposition by their legal owner'.

    Up to 5 April 1997, it would seem that the term 'ordinary share capital' bore its general meaning, ie as shares which do not have preferential rights attached to them (see Keane, *Company Law* (5th edn, Bloomsbury Professional, 2016) but see now TCA 1997, s 2(1) which defines the term for the purposes of the

Tax Acts as all the issued share capital of a company excluding only shares which are entitled to a fixed rate dividend only.

It is notable that there is no provision for aggregating the shareholdings or rights of connected persons for the purposes of applying the 50 per cent test.

(c) Where the beneficial holder is a partnership, each partner, ie in respect of their personal as well as their partnership compliance obligations.

It appears therefore by inference in this context that:

(a) a partnership is to be regarded as a 'person' (note the discussion at **1.302**); and
(b) presumably any changes in the composition of the partnership are to be ignored so that what are in law successive and distinct partnerships will be regarded as the same 'person' (compare TCA 1997, s 643).

It is not made explicit at what point in time it is necessary to establish the identity of the individual partners but it would seem logical that it should be the partners in membership at the date of application.

Where within one year prior to the due commencement date of a licence, the licence has been held at any time by a beneficial holder (hereafter 'the previous licensee') who is 'linked' (as defined – see below) to the applicant, then a tax clearance certificate will not be issued unless the previous licensee has also complied with its obligations under the Acts. However, the obligations in question are restricted to those which relate to the previous licensee's activities under the licence (TCA 1997, s 1094(3)). This requirement did not apply where the transfer took effect prior to 24 April 1992, or where the contract or sale of the licensed premises was signed prior to that date (TCA 1997, s 1094(4)).

The 'linkages' between the previous licensee and the applicant can be one of three types (TCA 1997, s 1094(3)):

(a) the previous licensee is a company connected to the applicant within the meaning of TCA 1997 see (**18.102**); for these purposes the winding up or dissolution of the previous licensee is disregarded;
(b) the previous licensee is a company, and the applicant is a partnership in which:
    (i) a partner is or was able, or
    (ii) where more than one partner is a shareholder those partners together are or were directly or indirectly able to control, more than 50 per cent of the ordinary share capital of the company;
(c) the previous licensee is a partnership, and the applicant is a company in which:
    (i) a partner is or was able, or
    (ii) where more than one partner is a shareholder, those partners together are or were able to control, directly or indirectly, more than 50 per cent of the ordinary share capital of the company.

The references in (b)(ii) and (c)(ii) to more than one partner being a 'shareholder', if taken at face value, seem to imply that it is only partners who hold shares (presumably in the company concerned) who count for these purposes. This seems odd, given that past as well as present control and, indirect as well as direct control of share capital is treated as relevant.

It may be noted that for the purposes of (b) and (c) it is not merely the control exercised by the partner(s) which must be taken into account when applying the 50 per cent test, but control exercised by them together with any person or persons connected with them, as defined by TCA 1997, s 10. It may also be noted that control exercised by such connected persons on their own (ie where the partners themselves have or had no such control) does not seem to be material for these purposes.

Where the Collector-General refuses an application for a clearance certificate, the refusal must be notified in writing to the applicant as soon as is practicable (TCA 1997, s 1094(6)). The applicant may appeal against the refusal within 30 days (strictly the 30 days seems to run from the date of refusal as opposed to the date on which the notification is issued or received). The appeal must be notified in writing to the Collector General and cannot be used to raise issues concerning any amounts of tax or interest due under any of the relevant tax Acts (TCA 1997, s 1094(7)(a)). The notice of appeal will only be valid if it:

(a) specifies the matters in dispute and also the declared grounds of appeal in respect of each such matter; and

(b) any amounts due under the relevant Acts and which are not under dispute is duly paid or remitted (there is no requirement that any outstanding returns should be delivered).

The Appeal Commissioners will hear an appeal as if it were an appeal against an assessment to income tax, subject to the usual rules which apply thereto, including the rights of rehearing before the Circuit Court and appeals on points of law to the Higher Courts (see **Division 2**). However, there is a direction that the Appeal Commissioners must have regard to all the matters required to be considered by the Collector-General (ie under (TCA 1997, s 1094)) and not just the matters under appeal; this direction is not expressly made in respect of the Circuit Court judge (but note TCA 1997, s 942(2)). F(TA)A 2015, s 40, which is subject to Ministerial Order, replaces TCA 1997, s 1094(7) in its entirety to take account of the new appeal procedures therein (see **2.207** for further detail).

An application may be made online by an Irish resident for a tax clearance certificate to be issued under TCA 1997, s 1094 and the certificate may be issued in electronic format and, with the agreement of the applicant, be published in a secure electronic medium online and be accessed by persons authorised by the applicant to do so (TCA 1997, s 1094(8) as inserted by FA 2002, s 127(a)(iii) with effect from 25 March 2002). A tax clearance certificate is valid for the period specified in the certificate (TCA 1997, s 1094(9)).

Following the decision in *DPP v Cronin* HC [1995], F(1909–10)A 1910, s 49(1A) (inserted by FA 1992, s 152 as amended by FA 1995, s 115) now provides valuable protection in all cases where a liquor licence is applied for within four months prior to the commencement date thereof. In such a case, F(1909–10)A 1910, s 49(1A)(a) provides that an existing licence may remain in force after its expiry date, where:

(a) either:

  (i) the Collector General has not yet issued, but without having refused to issue, a clearance certificate (hereafter referred to in this text as a situation where there is a 'late determination'),

  (ii) the Collector General has refused to issue the certificate, but an appeal against the refusal has been made and accepted under TCA 1997, s 1094(7); and

(b) the licence could otherwise have been issued, if a tax clearance certificate had been issued.

The extension of the licence continues until either:

(a) the Collector General makes a 'late determination' to issue the certificate;

(b) seven days after the Collector General makes a 'late determination' to refuse the certificate, unless there is an appeal against the refusal when (c) below applies; or

(c) where there is an appeal against a refusal, seven days after the final determination of that appeal (F (1909–10) A 1910, s 49(1A)(c)).

Where the taxpayer is applying for the initial grant of a licence, a temporary licence is granted instead of the extension given to an existing licence holder, subject to the identical time limits. In both cases, the taxpayer must pay over the duty which would have been payable on the grant of the relevant licence. Where the Collector General makes a 'late determination' to issue the clearance certificate, or an appeal against a refusal is upheld, then, at that point in time, the extended or temporary licence (as the case may be) will expire. The original duty paid in respect of the extended or temporary licence will be set off against the duty payable in respect of the new licence issued on foot of the certificate. Where a certificate is refused without appeal or an appeal is finally determined against the taxpayer, a due proportion of the original duty will be refunded (F (1909–10) A 1910, s 49(1A)(d)).

Cassidy takes the view that the tax clearance certificate procedure is likely to be upheld as constitutional, even though it may lead to potential loss of the taxpayer's livelihood (*The Licensing Acts 1833–1995*, at 28.2). However, there must be some doubt as to the 'proportionality' of at least some of these provisions (see **1.409**), given, for example, that in some cases a person's livelihood could be lost because of the fiscal defaults of third parties over which he has no control.

FA 1999 introduced certain anti-avoidance measures in relation to tax clearance. If a licence was transferred to the applicant for a tax clearance certificate within the previous 12 months there are now certain additional persons who must also be tax cleared. This was initially provided for in TCA 1997, s 1094(3). TCA 1997, s 1094(3A) extends this provision to cover the renewal of liquor licences which had lapsed within the previous five years when they had been beneficially held by a person other than the current applicant.

Sector contracts

A condition of obtaining a Public Sector Contract of a value of €10,000 or more (inclusive of VAT within any 12-month period, is that the contractor is required to produce a general tax clearance certificate. This is stated in the Department of Finance Circular 43/2006. In the case of contractors to which the RCT regime applies (see **2.311**) as an alternative such contractors who qualify to receive payments net of RCT at 0 per cent or 20 per cent may produce a Subcontractor's Notification of Determination issued under TCA 1997, s 530I showing the rate determined by Revenue to demonstrate their satisfactory compliance tax record. The notification must have been issued by Revenue within the previous 30 days. Prior to 1 January 2012 contractors could as an alternative to a general tax clearance certificate provide a valid C2 certificate. There is an exemption for bodies registered with the Revenue Commissioners as charities who quote their CHY number. TCA 1997, s 1095 establishes a system of granting general tax clearance certificates very similar to that applicable to licences under TCA 1997, s 1094. It applies to every application by a person to the Collector General for a tax clearance certificate other than an application for such a certificate made:

(a) in relation to a licence;

(b) pursuant to the requirements of:
  (i) TCA 1997, s 847A (as inserted by FA 2002),
  (ii) the Standards in Public Office Act 2001, or
  (iii) Criminal Justice (Legal Aid) (Tax Clearance Certificate) Regulations 1999 regulation 6 (SI 135/1999).

Where a clearance certificate is required, TCA 1997, s 1095 provides that the Collector General will issue the certificate if the applicant and other 'associated persons' – as defined for the purposes of TCA 1997, s 1094(2) (see above) have complied with their tax compliance obligations. Again these obligations seem identical to those laid down by TCA 1997, s 1094(2), although there are some slight differences in wording between the two sections.

TCA 1997, s 1095(5) provides that the compliance requirements are extended to any person 'linked' to the applicant, as defined in similar terms to TCA 1997, s 1094(3), who at any time previously carried on the business activity to which the application relates (hereafter referred to for simplicity as the 'previous contractor'). This includes a case where such activity was carried on as part of another activity. However, the compliance obligations in question are restricted to those attributable to the business activities to which the application relates. It may be noted that where the previous contractor had carried on the applicant's business activity as part of a larger business activity, it will be impracticable to ascertain what proportion of the tax obligations which relate to the larger activity are attributable to the applicant's activity. The legislation does not appear to address the situation where only part of the applicant's business activity was previously carried on by a 'linked person'. There may also be theoretical difficulties in distinguishing between the situation where a business or part thereof has been transferred as opposed to a mere transfer of assets.

The 'previous contractor' rules did not apply where the transfer of a business was effected prior to 9 May 1995 or a contract for the transfer was made prior to that date (oddly there was no explicit reference to the transfer of a part of a business).

TCA 1997, s 1095(6) applies TCA 1997, s 1094(5) to (9) (application and appeal procedures and electronic format) with all necessary modifications. It seems however that if it proves necessary to appeal the refusal to grant a certificate, the delay involved could lead to the loss of a contract.

An application may be made online by an Irish resident for a tax clearance certificate to be issued under TCA 1997, s 1094 and the certificate may be issued in electronic format and, with the agreement of the applicant, be published in a secure electronic medium online and be accessed by persons authorised by the applicant to do so (TCA 1997, s 1094(8). The position is the same for a tax clearance certificate issued under TCA 1997, s 1095 (TCA 1997, s 1095(6)). A tax clearance certificate is valid for the period specified in the certificate (TCA 1997, s 1094(9) as applied to s 1095 by s 1095(6))

FA 2014, s 95 makes a number of changes to TCA 1997, s 1094 which will only come into operation on the issue of an order by the Minister for Finance. When the order is issued and TCA 1997, s 1094 amended, tax clearance certificates will no longer be valid for a specific period, instead a certificate will be valid until it is rescinded by the Collector-General. The Collector-General will from time to time review the compliance obligations of the person and rescind the certificate if it is found that the person is no longer compliant. In addition it is provided that applications for a tax clearance certificate must be made online and when the application is made the applicant will be allocated a unique number known as a 'tax clearance access number' which they must provide, together with their tax reference number, to any person wishing to verify the validity of the tax clearance certificate. The clearance certificate will also be issued electronically.

Grants, subsidies and similar payments

A system of general tax clearance procedures also applies in the case of grants, subsidies and similar types of payment (a 'relevant payment') paid by government departments or public authorities of a value of €10,000 or more within any 12-months period. The basis for these procedures is Department of Finance Circular 44/2006. Exclusions from the procedures apply *inter alia* to social welfare and analogous payments, sums paid under the Criminal Injuries Compensation Tribunal or the Redundancy and Employers Insolvency Fund.

It may be noted that in the case of educational grants, these procedures apply in relation to the applicant's parent(s) or guardian(s) if their financial circumstances are a factor in determining eligibility. These procedures were held to be contrary to EU law in the case of certain EU grants paid to farmers. It may be noted that there is no right of appeal against a refusal to issue a clearance certificate. However, a certificate will only be refused where there are tax liabilities outstanding. In the case of tax which is under appeal, the Revenue may in certain circumstances issue a temporary clearance certificate, pending the outcome of the appeal hearing.

Streamlining of procedures

With effect from August 1997, once a person holds a tax clearance certificate in respect of a contract, a licence or the Criminal Justice Legal Aid Panel every year, a new tax clearance certificate will be issued to the person provided the person has been tax compliant for the three years following the issue of the original clearance certificate. In year five a standard letter is issued to the person one month prior to the expiry date of the current clearance certificate requesting the person to apply for a new tax clearance certificate. In addition, the system was amended so that the certificate will suffice 'as far as possible' for all tax clearance purposes (*Tax Briefing 27*) (see however note above on provisions contained in FA 2014, which will come into operation on the issue of an order by the Minister for Finance, whereby tax clearance certificates will be valid until rescinded by the Collector-General).

The Revenue Commissioners provide a facility via the Revenue website www.revenue.ie to confirm whether a person holds a tax clearance certificate. As a result it is not necessary for a person to produce the original certificate. In order to determine if a person holds a tax clearance certificate using the online facility it is necessary to have the tax clearance certificate number and the customer number which are quoted on the tax clearance certificate. These details can be provided by the person to the authorities to avoid having to produce the original certificate.

2.616 Criminal investigations

The Criminal Assets Bureau Act 1996 provides for enhanced co-operation between the Revenue Commissioners, the Garda Síochána and the Department of Social Welfare. The Bureau, which is staffed by officials from all three bodies, has as its stated objectives:

(a) the identification of criminal assets or suspected criminal assets;

(b) the taking of appropriate steps under the law to deprive the holders of such assets of their use or benefit; and

(c) the doing of preparatory work in relation to any appropriate proceedings.

The Bureau draws on the existing powers of the officials who are seconded to it, and uses those powers to take all necessary actions under the various appropriate statutes to apply the law to the proceeds of criminal activity or suspected criminal activity, and the assets of such activities. The Bureau also investigates and determines claims in respect of social welfare benefits by persons engaged or suspected to have engaged in such activities. The Act permits the Minister for Justice, in consultation with the Minister of Finance, to confer by order additional functions on the Bureau or the Bureau officers. Such orders must be laid before each House of the Oireachtas.

In *McL v D* [2009] IEHC 184, the court held that where the Bureau had uncovered information in the course of an investigation, it could not lawfully pass on that information to the Revenue Commissioners in relation to a person other than the person under investigation. Consequently information in relation to a tax adviser which had been obtained in a raid by the Bureau on the premises of one of the adviser's clients had to be excluded in considering an application under TCA 1997, s 908 brought against the adviser.

It may be noted also that the Disclosure of Certain Information for Taxation and Other Purposes Act 1996 (DCIA 1996) *inter alia* extends the scope of the Criminal Justice Act 1994 (CJA 1994) s 32 (part of the anti-money laundering provisions) which regulates the retention of documents and other materials used to identify customers and other persons by designated bodies. DCIA 1996, s 2 adds a new CJA 1994, s 32(10)(a) which enables the Minister to exempt future designated bodies from their full range of obligations under the CJA 1994 (thus increasing legislative flexibility in this regard). DCIA 1996, s 3 adds a new CJA 1994, s 57(1)(a) to enable information reported under ss 31 or 32 of that Act (on money-laundering) to be used in an investigation into any offence (ie including tax evasion).

The activities of the CAB in the area of taxation has already spawned a considerable body of case law, much of which is referred to elsewhere as appropriate in this text, particularly in the context of assessing and appealing against tax liabilities. In *Griffin v AC and CAB* VI ITR 371, the court provided guidance on the potential admissibility of evidence provided before the Appeal Commissioners in concurrent criminal proceedings (see Gallagher: *Griffin v AC and CAB* VI ITR 371).

Tax advisers, auditors and accountants *inter alia* became subject to the Money Laundering Reporting Regime with effect from 15 September 2003, (SI 242/2003 giving effect to EU Directive 2001/97/EC). The regime requires these professionals to operate client identification procedures and to provide a money laundering report to both the Gardaí and the Revenue Commissioners if they have suspicions that a client holds money or possessions arising from an indictable criminal offence (or an offence committed abroad which would be indictable in Ireland). There is an exemption for advice given by a tax adviser where work is being undertaken in relation to potential or actual judicial proceedings. Counsel opinion exists which treats hearings or potential hearings before the Appeal Commissioners as 'judicial proceedings'. There is also a prohibition on 'tipping off' clients, ie a client must not be alerted to the fact that the adviser intends to report or already has reported their suspicions.

2.617 Powers of collection, right of offset and power to demand security

Tax due and payable under the Income Tax Acts is due and payable to the Revenue Commissioners and is a debt due to Minister for Finance for the benefit of the Central Fund (TCA 1997, s 960D).

The Collector-General is obliged to demand payment of outstanding tax and to collect such tax. A demand may be issued by electronic means to a person who is required to file a return electronically (TCA 1997, s 960E(2A)). The Collector-General may give a receipt in respect of any tax paid, but is not obliged to do so (TCA 1997, s 960E). Income Tax may be paid to the Revenue Commissioners by credit card, debit card or any other method or methods of payment which is or are approved by them. The Revenue Commissioners are empowered to make regulations relating to these payment methods (TCA 1997, s 960EA) (. The provisions for recovery of taxes through the courts or by the Sheriff or County Registrar and the order of priority for taxes on the winding-up of companies or on bankruptcy are set out in TCA 1997, Pt 42, Ch 1C.

TCA 1997, s 960H provides that the Collector-General may set claims for repayment of any tax or duty against any outstanding liabilities including estimated in respect of any tax or duty or withhold repayments until such time as outstanding returns are submitted. This provision is designed to facilitate the generalised use of consolidated billing. The order of offset of repayments against liabilities is laid out in the Taxes (Offset of Repayments) Regulations 2002 (SI 471/2002).

TCA 1997, s 960G provides discretion on the part of the Revenue Commissioners or Collector-General to offset payments against liabilities to taxes where the taxpayer has failed to give clear instructions.

TCA 1997, s 960S, inserted by FA 2012, s 126(1) with effect from 30 March 2012, requires a person in business to give a security to the Collector-General in relation to fiduciary taxes where the Collector-General forms a view that such security is necessary to protect the Exchequer. It shall be an offence for a person, who is required to provide a security, to engage in business without providing the security. A person who is dissatisfied with a requirement to provide a security has a right of appeal to the Appeal Commissioners against such requirement but the prohibition against carrying on business will continue in force until the appeal is determined. Revenue produced guidance in October 2015 through *eBriefs 99 and 101* and includes details, inter alia as to what types of security are acceptable to Revenue.

2.618 Disclosure of certain tax avoidance transactions

Background

TCA 1997, Pt 33, Ch 3, as inserted by FA 2010, s 149, places mandatory disclosure obligations on promoters of certain tax-avoidance schemes, which fall within certain 'specified descriptions' (ie classes of transactions), often referred to as 'hallmarks' set out in the legislation. The hallmarks specified in the legislation include transactions where a person might wish to keep the arrangements confidential from a competitor or the Revenue Commissioners, transactions for which a premium fee could reasonably be obtained, transactions which consist of standardised tax-saving products and transactions which give rise to six other types of tax advantages. The promoter (generally a tax adviser or a bank) is required to furnish prescribed details of the scheme to the Revenue Commissioners shortly after they are first marketed or made available for use. Alternatively, where the promoter is based offshore or claims legal professional privilege, or the user has entered into a transaction not involving a promoter (ie an 'in-house scheme'), the onus falls on the user instead to provide the necessary information. With effect for transactions commenced after 23 October 2014, Revenue are required to assign a transaction number to each transaction disclosed and notify the promoter or other person who has made the disclosure. The promoter is obliged to give the transaction number to anyone to whom the promoter has provided the scheme and to anyone marketing the scheme for the promoter. Any person who seeks to obtain a tax advantage from a disclosed scheme is regarded as a 'chargeable person' (see **2.102**) for self assessment purposes and is required to include the transaction number for the transaction in his tax return. If a person marketing a scheme for a promoter is not provided with a transaction number for a scheme by the promoter the marketer must disclose details of the promoter and the scheme to Revenue. There will be no presumption or inference that a transaction disclosed under the rules is necessarily a tax avoidance transaction within the General Anti-Avoidance Rule. The Revenue Commissioners will have the power to make enquiries where they have reasonable grounds to believe that there has been a default in making a required disclosure. They may also seek determinations from the Appeal Commissioners entitling them to seek further information or documentation as appropriate. When the legislation was originally enacted it provided that the time periods within which a disclosure had to be made, the information to be provided, and the manner in which it is to be provided, along with further details of the classes of transaction that are intended to fall within the disclosure regime, would be set out in regulations. The Mandatory Disclosure of Certain Transactions Regulations 2011 (SI 7/2011) were drafted and came into effect on 17 January 2011. Revenue 'Guidance Notes on Mandatory Disclosure Regime' (hereinafter referred to as the '2011 Guidance Notes') were also published in January 2011. With effect for transactions entered into after 23 October 2014, most of what was contained in the regulations was incorporated into the legislation. The Mandatory Disclosure of Certain Transactions (Amendment) Regulations 2015 (SI 28/2015) were issued and apply to transactions commenced after 23 October 2014, deleted the regulations which, with effect for transactions commenced after 23 October 2014, were incorporated into TCA 1997, Pt 33, Ch 3. Arising from the changes to the legislation and regulations by FA 2014 Revenue issued 'Draft Guidance Notes on Mandatory Disclosure Regime' in November 2014 (hereinafter referred to as the 'Draft Guidance Notes'). Final guidance notes were issued in January 2015.

The objectives behind the regime as set out in the Guidance Notes are:

(i) to obtain early information about certain tax schemes and how they work;

(ii) to obtain information about who has availed of them; and

(iii) to close down such schemes that are viewed as aggressive by amending legislation or using existing anti-avoidance provisions.

The consequences of disclosure, as set out in the Guidance Notes, are as follows:

(a) if the Government and the Oireachtas decide that a particular scheme is aggressive and should be closed down, this may be done by way of an immediate media statement or by way of amendment in the next Finance Bill;

(b) as regards individual users of a disclosed scheme, Revenue may seek to nullify the tax consequences by using the general anti-avoidance provisions of TCA 1997, s 811C or specific anti-avoidance provisions.

Disclosable Transaction

The core concept underpinning the legislation is that of a 'disclosable transaction', which is defined as:

(a) any transaction; or
(b) any proposal for any transaction, which:
    (i) falls within any description specified by TCA 1997, s 817DA, or before FA 2014 by regulation, (a 'specified description') which enables, or might be expected to enable any person to obtain a tax advantage, and
    (ii) is such that the main benefit, or one of the main benefits, which might be expected to arise from the transaction or the proposal is the obtaining of that tax advantage.

This applies whether the transaction or the proposal for the transaction relates to a particular person or to any person who may seek to take advantage of it, ie both to tailor-made or 'off the peg' schemes (TCA 1997, s 817D(1)).

As set out at (b)(i) above, in order for a transaction to be regarded as a disclosable transaction it must fall within a 'specified description'. TCA 1997, s 817DA sets out types of transactions which are regarded as transactions of a 'specified description', often referred to in practice as 'hallmarks'. These nine types of transactions, or hallmarks, are as follows:

(1) Confidentiality (TCA 1997, s 817DA(2))

A transaction will fall within this description if it might reasonably be expected that a promoter or person would wish to keep the way in which the transaction, or any part of the transaction, gives rise to the tax advantage:

(i) Confidential from the Revenue Commissioners for one of the following reasons (TCA 1997, s 817DA(2)(a)):
    (I) to facilitate repeated or continued use of the same or substantially the same, transaction in the future;
    (II) in order to prevent the Revenue Commissioners using the information relating to the transaction to enquire into any return;
    (III) in order to prevent the Revenue Commissioners using the information to withhold a refund or repayment claimed separately to any return;
(ii) Confidential from any other promoter in order to maintain competitive advantage (TCA 1997, s 817DA(2)(b)).

Prior to FA 2014 and the amendment of the Regulations the hallmarks were set out in the Regulations. The confidentiality hallmark was contained in regs 7 and 8. Regulation 7 dealt with transactions where there was a promoter and reg 8 where there was no promoter. Under both regulations the test for confidentiality against the Revenue was a subjective test in that the question posed was whether the particular person implementing the scheme or the particular promoter of the scheme would wish to keep the scheme confidential from the Revenue. On the other hand under reg 7 the test for confidentiality against other promoters was an objective test in that the question posed was whether 'any' promoter might reasonably be expected to wish to keep the scheme confidential from any other promoter. In all cases post-FA 2014 (which applies to transactions commenced after 23 October 2014) the test for confidentiality is an objective one whether the test is against the Revenue

Commissioners or any other promoter. It should be noted however that although the confidentiality test against Revenue under the regulations, before their amendment, was a subjective one TCA 1997, s 817D(2), before amendment by FA 2014, provided that for a transaction to fall within a class of a 'specified description' in addition to coming within one of the hallmarks set out in the regulations it also had to fall within a category of transaction set out in TCA 1997, s 817D(2)(c) (before amendment) ie:

(i) a transaction where a promoter or person would, or might reasonably be expected to, wish to keep the transaction or any element of the transaction (including the way in which the transaction is structured) confidential from the Revenue Commissioners or any other class of person specified by regulation;

(ii) a transaction in relation to which a promoter, whether directly or indirectly, obtains from or charges to, or might reasonably be expected to obtain from or charge to, a person implementing, or considering implementing, such transaction, fees that are to a significant extent attributable to, or to any extent contingent upon, the obtaining of a tax advantage;

(iii) a transaction which involves standardised or mainly standardised documentation, the form of which is largely determined by the promoter and which requires the person implementing the transaction to enter into a specific transaction, or series of transactions, which are standardised, or substantially standardised, in form;

(iv) a transaction, or any element of such transaction (including the way in which the transaction is structured), which gives rise to a tax advantage of a class or classes specified by regulation (TCA 1997, s 817D(2)(c)). Regulation 6 of the Regulations, before they were amended in 2014, provided that the class of tax advantage referred to here were those achieved by transactions falling within the following hallmarks:

(I) loss schemes – individuals,

(II) loss schemes – companies,

(III) employment schemes,

(IV) income into capital schemes,

(V) income into gift schemes.

Because a transaction always had to fall within one of the categories (i) to (iv) above, a transaction which a particular promoter might wish to keep confidential from Revenue might come within the subjective confidentiality test set out in the regulations still had to pass the objective confidentiality test set out in TCA 1997, s 817D(2)(c)(i) in order to be a disclosable transaction by virtue of coming within the confidentiality hallmark.

The Guidance Notes point out that Revenue will not assume that a promoter wanted to keep a scheme confidential from Revenue because the scheme was not disclosed to Revenue. Where Revenue come across a scheme which has not be disclosed in determining whether or not the scheme should have been disclosed the Guidance Notes say factors to be taken into account in determining whether the scheme should have been disclosed include:

(i) how innovative and aggressive the scheme is,

(ii) whether the potential clients were required by the promoter to keep the scheme confidential,

(iii) how cooperative the promoter was when requests for information regarding the scheme were made.

The Guidance Notes also provide that schemes which promoters already know Revenue is aware of do not come within the confidentiality hallmark. This however does not mean schemes which have been brought to the attention of Revenue through discussions with particular Revenue officials, Large Cases Division or Revenue Legislation Services. This is a departure from the advice set out in the 2011 Guidance Notes where it specifically stated that Revenue could be assumed to be aware of a scheme where full details of the scheme had been made known to specialised areas within Revenue such as Large Cases Division or Revenue Legislation Services. The Guidance Notes now say it can only be assumed Revenue knows of a particular scheme if this is evidenced in published technical guidance notes or was the subject of decided Irish case law. Under the 2011 Guidance Notes it could be assumed Revenue knew of a scheme if it was the subject of 'case law' and not just 'Irish law'.

(2) Premium fees (TCA 1997, s 817DA(3))

A transaction will fall within this hallmark where it might reasonably be expected that the transaction is such that the promoter would be able to charge a premium fee to a person implementing such transaction. A premium fee is a fee which is to a significant extent attributable to the tax advantage or which is to any extent contingent on the tax advantage being secured. The Guidance Notes state that fees which are calculated purely on the basis of time and materials, fees which are higher because of the size of the transaction involved or the skill, reputation or location of the adviser or the urgency with which the advice is sought are not to be considered premium fees. It should be noted that it is not a requirement that a premium fee was actually charged but just that it might be 'reasonably expected' that such a fee could be charged. Whether or not such a fee could be charged is to be determined without taking into account the fact that the transaction may have to be disclosed to Revenue.

Prior to FA 2014 and the amendment of the Regulations this hallmark was set out in Regulation 9 of the Regulations.

(3) Standardised tax products (TCA 1997, s 817DA(4))

A transaction will fall within this hallmark if the transaction is a 'standardised tax product'. A transaction is a 'standardised tax product' if the promoter makes, or intends to make, the transaction available for implementation by more than one person and the transaction:

(i) has standardised or substantially standardised documentation:

(I) the purpose of which is to enable the user of the scheme to implement the scheme and

(II) the form of which is determined by the promoter and not tailored to any material extent to reflect the circumstances of user of the scheme

(ii) requires the user of the scheme to enter into a specific series of standardised, or largely standardised transactions.

The Guidance Notes point out that the fact that tax professionals use precedent documents that enable the same or similar type tax solutions to be used by more than one client does not mean that a transaction will automatically fall within this description and that it will be a 'matter of scale and decree' as to whether they would be regarded as 'standardised tax products'.

The Schedule to the Regulations sets out the types of transactions which will not be regarded as a standardised tax products as follows:

(i) an approved profit sharing scheme under TCA 1997, Sch 11, Pt 2;
(ii) an approved employee share ownership trust under TCA 1997, Sch 12, para 2;
(iii) an approved savings related share option scheme under TCA 1997, Sch 12A, para 2;
(iv) a certified contractual savings scheme under TCA 1997, Sch 12B;
(v) an approved share option scheme under TCA 1997, Sch 12C, para 2;
(vi) an approved salary sacrifice arrangement under TCA 1997, s 118B;
(vii) an approved retirement benefits scheme under TCA 1997, Pt 30, Ch 1;
(viii) an approved retirement annuity scheme under TCA 1997, s 784;
(ix) a PRSA contract under TCA 1997, s 787A;
(x) a qualifying overseas pension plan under TCA 1997, Pt 30, Ch 2B;
(xi) a transaction qualifying for film relief under TCA 1997, s 481;
(xii) a transaction qualifying for investment in renewable energy generation under TCA 1997, s 486B;
(xiii) a transaction involving exemption for profits or gains arising from the occupation of woodlands under TCA 1997, s 232;
(xiv) a transaction qualifying for exemption from CGT on proceeds from the sale of woodlands under TCA 1997, s 564;
(xv) a transaction qualifying for relief for investment in corporate trades under TCA 1997, Pt 16;
(xvi) a transaction qualifying for the tax treatment of certain venture fund managers under TCA 1997, s 541C;
(xvii) a transaction qualifying for repayment of tax for relevant employees on not remitted under TCA 1997, s 825B;
(xviii) a transaction with trustees of trustees of a special trust for permanently incapacitated individuals, within the meaning of TCA 1997, s 189A;
(xix) a transaction with trustees of a trust where the trust is of a type listed in the Capital Acquisitions Tax Consolidation Act 2003, s 17 (ie charitable trusts, superannuation or unit trusts, trusts for persons incapable of managing their affairs and trust for the upkeep of heritage houses and gardens);
(xx) a transaction with the trustees of a trust used to hold plant or machinery for finance and lease transactions where the beneficiary under the trust arrangement is treated as the beneficial owner of those assets for the purposes of corporation tax and the transaction relates to the holding, disposing, financing, leasing of, or the dealing in, those assets;
(xxi) a transaction with the trustees of a trust used to hold assets which are securitised by a company to which the provisions of TCA 1997, s 110 apply, where the beneficiary under the trust arrangement being that company, is treated as the beneficial owner of those assets for the purposes of corporation tax and the transaction relates to the holding of those assets;

(xxii) a transaction with the trustees of a trust used to hold debt issued by a company to which the provisions of TCA 1997, s 110 apply, where the beneficiary under the trust arrangement is treated as the beneficial owner of the debt for the purposes of the Principal Act or any other enactment relating to tax and the transaction relates to the holding of that debt;

(xxiii) a transaction with the trustees of a trust used to hold the share capital of a company to which the provisions TCA 1997, s 110 apply, where the trust is established for charitable purposes and the transaction relates to the holding of that share capital;

(xxiv) a trust that is an investment undertaking within the meaning of TCA 1997, s 739B or 731(5)(a)(i), or a special investment scheme within the meaning of TCA 1997, s 737, or any similar investment undertaking which is regulated in another Member State or a territory with the government of which arrangements having the force of law by virtue of TCA 1997, s 836(1) have been made;

(xxv) a transaction with trustees of a trust in respect of securities to which the provisions of TCA 1997, s 128D apply.

Categories (xviii) and (xix) were inserted into the schedule by the Draft Mandatory Disclosure of Certain Transactions (Amendment) Regulations 2014, which are to apply to transactions commenced after 23 October 2014, to take account of the new discretionary trust hallmark inserted by FA 2014 (see below).

As can be seen from the above the above transactions are generally ones in respect of which some form of Revenue approval is otherwise required. However TCA 1997, s 817DA(4)(c) provides that the fact that such transactions shall not be standardised products is without prejudice to TCA 1997, s 817DA(2) or (3), the confidentiality and premium fees hallmarks. Thus the fact that a transaction falls within one of those included in the Schedule to the Regulations does not mean that it can never be regarded as a disclosable transaction. If a transaction falls within either the confidentiality hallmark (TCA 1997, s 817DA(2)) or the premium fees hallmark (TCA 1997, s 817DA(3)) the transaction is disclosable even if it comes within a class of transaction listed in the Schedule to the Regulations. The 2011 Guidance Notes stated that if a promoter were to combine any of the transactions listed in the Schedule with other reliefs, allowances or abatements provided for under tax legislation in a way which gives a result not intended by the legislature and which the promoter might wish to keep confidential or to charge a premium fee the transaction would be disclosable under headings (1) or (2) above.

Prior to FA 2014 and the amendment of the Regulations this hallmark was set out in Regulation 10 of the Regulations.

(4) Loss schemes – individuals (TCA 1997, s 817DA(5))

A transaction falls within this hallmark where the promoter expects more than one individual to implement the same or substantially the same transaction and the transaction is such that an informed observer would reasonably conclude that the main outcome that could be expected for individuals participating in the transaction is the provision of losses which the individuals expect to be able to use to reduce their liability to income tax or CGT. The Guidance Notes give an example of where this would be the case where the tax relief expected by a participant in a scheme would be greater than his at risk investment. The Guidance Notes also state that an 'informed observer' is someone who is independent and has knowledge of tax legislation such as an Appeal Commissioner and that an informed observer would not have to be a tax practitioner.

This transaction heading is aimed at promoters only and according to the Guidance Notes is intended to bring within the disclosure regime various loss creation schemes typically used by wealthy individuals. The Guidance Notes state that it is not intended to capture investments in genuine business start-ups where losses are expected or the use of genuine trading losses against other income.

Prior to FA 2014 and the amendment of the Regulations in 2014 this hallmark was set out in reg 11 of the Regulations.

(5) Loss schemes – companies (TCA 1997, s 817DA(6))

A transaction comes within this description where one of the parties to the transaction is a company that has or expects to have unrelieved losses at the end of an accounting period and having examined the transaction an informed observer could reasonably conclude that a main benefit of the transaction is that either the company is able to use the losses or else the company transfers the losses to another party who would be expected to use the losses.

'Unrelieved losses at the end of an accounting period' means trading losses in respect of which relief could not have been given, apart from the transaction, for that or a previous accounting period (TCA 1997, s 817DA(6)(b)).

Prior to FA 2014 and the amendment of the Regulations in 2014 this hallmark was set out in reg 12 of the Regulations.

(6) Employment schemes (TCA 1997, s 817DA(7))

A transaction falls within this hallmark where a tax advantage is obtained, or might be expected to be obtained, by virtue of the transaction, or part of a transaction, and the tax advantage is obtained by way of a reduction in or deferment of the employer or employee's, or any other person by reason of the employee's employment, liability to tax. For the purpose of TCA 1997, Pt 33, Ch 3 'tax' means any tax, duty, levy or charge which is placed under the care and management of the Revenue Commissioners (TCA 1997, s 817D(1)) and therefore includes USC (see **2.101**).

A transaction will not come within this description where it is a transaction of a kind specified in the Schedule to the Regulations (see under (3) above) (TCA 1997, s 817DA(7)(c)). However this is without prejudice to TCA 1997, s 817DA(2) or (3), the confidentiality and premium fees hallmarks. Thus the fact that a transaction falls within one of transactions listed in the Schedule does not mean that it can never be regarded as a disclosable transaction. If a transaction falls within either the confidentiality hallmark (TCA 1997, s 817DA(2)) or the premium fees hallmark (TCA 1997, s 817DA(3)) the transaction is disclosable even if it comes within a class of transaction listed in the Schedule to the Regulations.

The Guidance Notes state that it is not intended that transactions that rely solely on routine tax planning using statutory exemptions and reliefs for bona fide purposes, such as approved Share Ownership Trusts or pension schemes, would come within this description. Although Revenue provide examples of what *they* consider routine day-to-day tax advice and routine use of statutory exemptions and reliefs (see below), they do not provide a general definition of the term. The legislation does not refer at all to 'routine tax planning'.

Prior to FA 2014 and the amendment of the Regulations in 2014 this hallmark was set out in reg 13 of the Regulations.

(7) Income into capital schemes (TCA 1997, s 817DA(8))

A transaction falls within this hallmark where as a consequence of the transaction a person will incur a lesser or nil liability to income tax and will acquire an asset the disposal of which is within the charge to CGT. The latter also includes gains exempt or relieved from CGT. Thus schemes which convert income into capital receipts come within this description.

Again the Guidance Notes state that is not intended to target ordinary tax planning (see below).

A transaction will not come within this description where it is a transaction of a kind specified in the Schedule to the Regulations (see under (3) above) (TCA 1997, s 817DA(8)(c)). However, this is without prejudice to TCA 1997, s 817DA(2) or (3), the confidentiality and premium fees hallmarks. Thus the fact that a transaction falls within one of transactions listed in the Schedule does not mean that it can never be regarded as a disclosable transaction. If a transaction falls within either the confidentiality hallmark (TCA 1997, s 817DA(2)) or the premium fees hallmark (TCA 1997, s 817DA(3)) the transaction is disclosable even if it comes within a class of transaction listed in the Schedule to the Regulations.

Prior to FA 2014 and the amendment of the Regulations in 2014 this hallmark was set out in reg 14 of the Regulations.

(8) Income into gift schemes (TCA 1997, s 817DA(9))

A transaction falls within this hallmark where as a consequence of the transaction a person will incur a lesser or nil liability to income tax and be deemed to take a gift. Thus schemes which convert income into gifts come within this description.

Prior to FA 2014 and the amendment of the Regulations in 2014 this hallmark was set out in reg 15 of the Regulations.

(9) Schemes involving discretionary trusts (TCA 1997, s 817DA(10))

A transaction falls within this hallmark where a party to the transaction is a trustee of a discretionary trust. This hallmark was not included in the original Regulations.

A transaction will not come within this description where is a transaction of a kind specified in the Schedule to the Regulations (see under (3) above) (TCA 1997, s 817DA(10)(b)). However this is without prejudice to TCA 1997, s 817DA(2) or (3), the confidentiality and premium fees hallmarks. Thus the fact that a transaction falls within one of transactions listed in the Schedule does not mean that it can never be regarded as a disclosable transaction. If a transaction falls within either the confidentiality hallmark (TCA 1997, s 817DA(2)) or the premium fees hallmark (TCA 1997, s 817DA(3)) the transaction is disclosable even if it comes within a class of transaction listed in the Schedule to the Regulations.

Ordinary tax planning

At the start of the Guidance Notes, it is stated that the Mandatory Disclosure rules do not impact on 'ordinary day to day tax advice between a tax adviser and a client that involves, for example, the use of schemes that rely on ordinary tax planning using standard statutory exemptions and reliefs in a routine fashion for bona fide purposes as intended by the legislature'. It should be noted that the 2011 Guidance Notes stated that the rules did not impact on 'ordinary day to day tax advice between a tax adviser and a client' OR 'on the use of schemes that rely on ordinary tax planning using standard statutory exemptions and reliefs in a routine fashion for bona fide purposes as intended by the legislature'. Thus ordinary tax advice which is not disclosable is now limited to advice on the use of schemes. However in practical terms it is difficult to see what difference the restriction in the definition of ordinary tax planning will make and it is noted that the examples of what are regarded by Revenue as routine day to day tax advice and routine use of statutory exemptions and reliefs has not changed. The Guidance Notes set out in Appendix 1 examples of what Revenue would consider as ordinary day to day advice and the routine use of statutory exemptions and reliefs for bona fide purposes. These examples are as follows:

(a) In the context of stamp duty:
- advising on intra group reliefs and reconstruction reliefs;
- advising on young trained farmer relief;
- advising on various rates of duty and requirements for certificates in order to qualify for appropriate rates.

(b) In the context of corporation tax:
- advising on the impact of close company legislation;
- advising on requirements for CGT treatment to apply on a buyback;
- advising on tax consequences of reconstructions undertaken for bona fide commercial reasons;
- advising on requirements to be met to qualify for capital allowances on intangible assets.

(c) In the context of CAT:
- advising on the making of prior gifts to meet the farmer test.
- advising on arrangements of assets within groups to ensure excepted assets not in shares of companies being gifted;
- advising employees who take up residence in the State in relation to avoiding a double charge to tax on gifts or inheritances on estates accumulated prior to their coming to Ireland;
- advising on the creation of a will trust where that trust is established under the laws of a Member State of the European Communities and the trustees are resident in such a jurisdiction;
- advising on the use of a trust to ensure that reliefs and exemptions that would have been available had the person lived, do not cease to be available on death due to time limits, for example using a trust to ensure availability of the dwelling house exemption under CATCA 2003, s 86.

(d) In the context of CGT:
- advising on share buyback so as to qualify for CGT treatment and retirement relief.

(e) In the context of VAT:
- advice in relation to the operation of relief on transfer of a business;

- advice on VAT implications of property transactions;
- advice on VAT groups;
- advice on VAT deductible;
- advice in preparation of a Revenue audit.

(f) In the context of employee share schemes:
- advising on the structure of share based schemes to come within approved profit sharing schemes, savings related share option schemes and employee share ownership trusts.

(g) In the context of income tax:
- advising on reliefs available on the termination of an employment;
- advising on the use of BES schemes/Film relief;
- advising on the use of AVC for the purpose of maximising tax relief and pension benefits;
- advising on the implications of using joint or single assessment;
- advising on the taxation implications of marital breakdown;
- advising on how losses can be used in a self employment situation.

There is no reference in TCA 1997, Pt 33, Ch 3 or in the Regulations to 'ordinary' or 'routine' tax planning and this should be borne in mind in seeking to rely on this exclusion when determining whether or not a transaction in question is a disclosable transaction. (For a useful commentary on the meaning of 'ordinary' or 'routine' tax planning see Fennell 'The Irish Mandatory Disclosure Regime – One Year On' (2011) Irish Tax Review.)

A tax advantage is defined as:

(a) relief or increased relief from, or a reduction, avoidance or deferral of, any assessment, charge or liability to tax, including any potential or prospective assessment, charge or liability;

(b) a refund or repayment of, or a payment of, an amount of tax, or an increase in an amount of tax refundable, repayable or otherwise payable to a person, including any potential or prospective amount so refundable, repayable or payable, or an advancement of any refund or repayment of, or payment of an amount of tax to a person; or

(c) the avoidance of any obligation to deduct or account for tax, arising out of or by reason of a transaction, including a transaction where another transaction would not have been undertaken or arranged to achieve the results, or any part of the results, achieved or intended to be achieved by the transaction (TCA 1997, s 817D(1)).

This definition of 'tax advantage is wider than the already extensive definition in TCA 1997, s 811C, the General Anti-Avoidance Rule (see the discussion at **17.302**). Notably, TCA 1997, s 811C does not refer to 'relief or increased relief from' within (a), the mere advancement of a refund etc within (b), nor does it refer to the avoidance of withholding tax referred to in (c). Furthermore there are no exclusions such as apply under TCA 1997, s 811C(2)(b), nor are the Revenue Commissioners constrained by the factors which they are obliged to consider under TCA 1997, s 811C(2)(a). This of course reflects the fact that these provisions are not charging provisions but are effectively information-gathering powers. The term 'tax' covers any tax, duty or levy or charge under the care and management of the Revenue Commissioners. The definition of 'transaction' follows that of TCA 1997, s 811C(1) as:

(a) any transaction, action, course of action, course of conduct, scheme, plan or proposal;
(b) any agreement, arrangement, understanding, promise or undertaking, whether express or implied and whether or not enforceable or intended to be enforceable by legal proceedings; and
(c) any series or combination of the circumstances referred to in paras (a) and (b), whether entered into or arranged by one person or by two or more persons:
   (i) whether acting in concert or not,
   (ii) whether or not entered into or arranged wholly or partly outside the State, or
   (iii) whether or not entered into or arranged as part of a larger transaction or in conjunction with any other transaction or transactions.

TCA 1997, Pt 33, Ch 2 however also covers a mere proposal for any transaction (as defined above).

The definition of 'disclosable transaction' is effectively narrowed however by the requirement that a transaction should fall within a class of a 'specified description' as set out in TCA 1997, s 817DA.

Promoters

For these purposes, a 'promoter' is defined as a person who in the course of a *relevant business* is:

(a) to any extent responsible for the design of the disclosable transaction;
(b) has specified information relating to the disclosable transaction and makes a marketing contact in relation to the disclosable transaction ('specified information' is defined by TCA 1997, s 817D(2) and is set out below under 'Duty to Disclose');
(c) makes the disclosable transaction available for implementation by other persons. The Guidance Notes state that a scheme is regarded as being made available for implementation by others when the promoter communicates a fully formed proposal to a client in sufficient detail that he could be expected to understand the expected tax advantages and decide whether or not to avail of the scheme. The Notes also confirm that a person who acts solely as a marketer (ie an introducer or intermediary) between the scheme designer and potential clients would not be regarded as making a disclosable transaction available to others and would not therefore be a promoter under this test; or
(d) is to any extent responsible for the organisation or management of the disclosable transaction. The Guidance Notes confirm that this would include for example an accountancy firm that actively manages a scheme bringing together clients and promoters and organising the transfer and completion of scheme documentation.

The Regulations provide that the following persons will not be treated as a promoter:

(a) The person carrying on the relevant business is a company which on the relevant date provides tax services only to other group companies (regulation 28);

(b) Persons who are employees of a promoter of the transaction in question or, where there is no promoter, the employer is a person who is required to make the disclosure (regulation 29);

(c) The person is responsible to any extent for the design but does not provide tax advice (regulation 30(b)). The Guidance Notes state that this would cover situations such as where a promoter consults a law firm, that operates a business which includes tax advice, in relation to company law aspects of a scheme. Provided the law firm does not provide tax advice it will not be regarded as a promoter.

(d) The person is not responsible for the design of all elements of the transaction and could not be reasonably expected to have sufficient information to know if the transaction is disclosable or to comply with the disclosure requirements (regulation 30(c)).

Regulation 30(a) was deleted by the Mandatory Disclosure of Certain Transactions (Amendment) Regulations 2014 which came into operation on 23 December 2014 and applies to transactions commencing after 23 October 2014. Regulation 30(a) provided that a person would not be regarded as a promoter if the person provided tax advice but was not responsible for the design of the disclosable transaction. The 2011 Guidance Notes stated that this would cover situations where the tax advice provided was benign and did not contribute towards the design of the tax advantage element of the scheme. The intention was that persons who were not involved in contributing tax advice on the tax advantage element of the transaction would not be regarded as promoters, however it has been suggested that in practice the exclusion was broad enough to cover situations where a person marketed an existing scheme which they had not designed. Now that this exclusion has been removed such persons will be regarded as promoters. A 'relevant business' is any trade, profession, vocation or business which:

(a) includes the provision to other persons of services relating to taxation; or

(b) is carried on by a bank (within the meaning of Stamp Duties Consolidation Act 1999, s 124(1)(a)).

For the purposes of this definition:

(i) anything done by a company is to be taken to be done in the course of a relevant business if it is done for the purposes of a relevant business referred to in (b) which is carried on by another company, where both companies are members of the same group (as defined by TCA 1997, s 616 if in that section on the assumption that references to residence in a relevant Member State were omitted and that references to '75 per cent subsidiaries' were references to '51 per cent subsidiaries') (TCA 1997, s 817D(1)).

A 'marketing contact' means the communication by a person of the general nature of a disclosable transaction to another person with a view to that person or any other person considering whether:

(a) to ask for further details of the transaction; or

(b) to seek to have the transaction made available for implementation (TCA 1997, s 817D(1)).

Duty to disclose

A promoter (as defined above) must within five working days after the 'specified date' provide the Revenue Commissioners with 'specified information' relating to any disclosable transaction (TCA 1997, s 817E).

Any person who enters into any transaction forming part of any disclosable transaction in relation to which a promoter is outside the State must within five working days after the 'specified date' provide the Revenue Commissioners with 'specified information' relating to the disclosable transaction (TCA 1997, s 817F).

Where a person enters into a transaction forming part of any disclosable transaction in relation to which there is no promoter, the person must within thirty working days after the 'specified date' provide the Revenue Commissioners with 'specified information' relating to the disclosable transaction (TCA 1997, s 817G).

In the case of a person other than a promoter the 'specified date' is the date the person first enters into any transaction which forms part of the disclosable transaction and in the case of a promoter the 'specified date' is the 'relevant date' (TCA 1997, s 817D(1)).

The 'relevant date' is earliest of the following dates:

(a) the date on which the promoter has specified information relating to the disclosable transaction and first makes a marketing contact (as defined above) in relation to the disclosable transaction. The Guidance Notes and Draft Guidance Notes elaborate on this saying that this date happens where the scheme in question has been substantially designed and the person describes the general nature of the scheme to another person with a view to that person considering whether to get further details on the scheme or have it made available to them for implementation;

(b) the date on which the promoter makes the disclosable transaction available for implementation by any other person; or

(c) the date on which the promoter first becomes aware of any transaction which is or forms part of the disclosable transaction having been implemented (TCA 1997, s 817D(1)).

Where a person obtains or seeks to obtain a tax advantage from a disclosable transaction which commenced after 23 October 2014 and the person had not been given a transaction number (see below under 'Transaction numbers') for the transaction, if the person does not otherwise have an obligation to make a disclosure to Revenue under TCA 1997, ss 817F, 817G or 817H (ie the transaction has a promoter in the State), the person is required to provide 'specified information' to Revenue, by the specified return date for the chargeable period, within the meaning assigned to it by s 959A being a year of assessment (TCA 1997, s 817HA(4)). There is no time specified in the legislation within which the 'specified information must be provided'. In addition the person must without 'unreasonable delay' provide Revenue with sufficient information which Revenue might reasonably require in order to decide if an application should be made under TCA 1997, s 817O(3) to the courts for a determination that a penalty should apply to the promoter (see also below under 'Revenue powers of enquiry, information powers and penalties'). The 'specified information' which must be provided is set out in (TCA 1997, s 817D(2)) and should include the following:

(a) such information as might reasonably be expected to enable the manner in which the disclosable transaction operates, or is intended to operate, to be understood by a Revenue officer;

(b) full references to the provisions in TCA 1997, Pt 33, Ch 3 and the Regulations by virtue of which the transaction is considered to be a disclosable transaction;
(c) a summary of the disclosable transaction and the name by which it is known
(d) full references to provisions of the Acts which are considered to be relevant to the treatment of the disclosable transaction for tax purposes;
(e) full details of the transaction explaining each element of the transaction, how the tax advantage is expected to be obtained and explaining how each provision of the Acts referred to in (d) applies;
(f) the name, address, telephone number and tax reference number of the person providing the specified information and where the person making the disclosure is required to make the disclosure because the promoter is outside the State, the name address and telephone number of the promoter.

Prior to FA 2014 and the amendment of the Regulations in 2014 the 'specified information' to be provided was set out in reg 16 of the Regulations and the period within which the information was to be provided, in regs 18, 19 and 20.

Where a person is marketing a scheme which it would be reasonable to consider is a disclosable transaction TCA 1997, s 817L(4) provides that if the person has not been given a transaction number by the promoter (see below under 'Transaction numbers') the person must provide Revenue with the following information:

(a) the name and address of the promoter;
(b) details of the transaction;
(c) all materials used to make a marketing contact (as defined – see above under 'Promoters').

This information must be provided within 30 working days from making the first marketing contact. A marketer is only required to disclose in this context where the transaction in question commenced after 23 October 2014. TCA 1997, s 817L(4)(b) provides that where a marketer provides information to Revenue in this manner it shall be wholly without prejudice as to whether or not the transaction is a disclosable transaction.

The above information must be included in form MD1, in the case of promoters, MD6 in the case of marketers and MD2 for other persons.

A promoter is not required to disclose any information which would be protected by legal professional privilege in any proceedings. The Guidance Notes however point out that merely asserting that legal professional privilege applies is not sufficient and if it transpires that such a claim cannot be maintained the legal professional may be liable to penalties for failure to disclose. Where legal professional privilege has been asserted by the promoter any person who enters into any transaction which is or forms part of any disclosable transaction within five working days following the date of entry into the transaction must provide the Revenue Commissioners 'specified information' (see above under 'Duty to disclose') relating to the disclosable transaction. The promoter must advise each person to whom he has made the disclosable transaction available for implementation of their obligation to disclose. He must also inform the Revenue Commissioners that he has availed of professional privilege not to disclose within five working days following the 'specified date' (ie the date of entry into the transaction. See above under 'Duty to disclose') (TCA 1997, s 817H).

Transaction numbers

TCA 1997, s 817HB(1) provides that where a scheme is disclosed to Revenue under TCA 1997, s 817E, 187F, 817G, 817H or 817L, Revenue must within 90 days either assign a unique transaction number to the scheme or notify the promoter or person who entered into the scheme that the transaction is not a disclosable transaction. It should be noted that if a marketer discloses a scheme to Revenue (see above under 'Duty to disclose') there is no requirement in the section for Revenue to notify the marketer of the transaction number or that the scheme is not a disclosable transaction, if that is the case. Revenue is only required to notify the promoter or the person who entered into the disclosable transaction. Where Revenue request additional information in connection with a transaction (see below) the 90-day period commences from the day after the day on which Revenue receive the additional information requested. TCA 1997, s 817HB only applies to transactions commencing after 23 October 2014. For disclosable transactions entered into before 24 October 2014 there was no requirement for Revenue to notify the person making the disclosure whether the transaction was considered to be a disclosable transaction or not.

If the disclosure is made by a promoter, the promoter must give the transaction number to any person to whom the promoter has made the scheme available for implementation and to any person marketing the scheme on behalf of the promoter within five working days of receiving the number or after making the scheme available to the person, whichever date is earlier (TCA 1997, s 817E(b)).

Any person who obtains or seeks to obtain a tax advantage from a disclosable transaction is deemed to be a chargeable person (see **2.102**) (TCA 1997, s 817HA(1)) and must include the transaction number for the transaction in their return for the period in which the person entered into a transaction which forms part of the disclosable transaction and for the year in which they seek to obtain or actually obtain a tax advantage from the disclosable transaction. It is not clear from the legislation whether a person is only deemed to be a chargeable person for the year in which they enter into a disclosable transaction only or thereafter. A person who enters into a transaction which is or forms part of a disclosable transaction is required to give the transaction number to any other person who obtains or seeks to obtain a tax advantage from the same disclosable transaction. The fact that a promoter is also required to give the transaction number to each person to whom the promoter has made the scheme available for implementation does not remove the obligation from each person entering into the transaction to give everyone else entering into the same transaction the transaction number. In the Draft Guidance Notes Revenue give the example of an employer who puts in place an executive remuneration scheme which is a disclosable transaction and points out that in such a case the employer must provide each executive who seeks to obtain a tax advantage from the scheme with the transaction number. As set out above (under 'Duty to disclose') if a person obtains or seeks to obtain a tax advantage from a disclosable transaction and was not provided with a transaction number they must disclose details of the transaction to Revenue. Provided the person discloses details of the scheme to Revenue they are deemed to have satisfied their obligation to include a transaction number in their return.

Where a person is marketing a scheme which it would be reasonable to consider is a disclosable transaction but the marketer has not been provided with a transaction number by the promoter, as set out under 'Duty to disclose' above, the marketer is required to provide details of the promoter and the scheme to Revenue (TCA 1997, s 817E(b)).

Revenue are only required to assign a transaction number to disclosable transactions which commence after 23 October 2014. A promoter may have disclosed a transaction to Revenue before 24 October 2014 and would not have been assigned a transaction number. Promoters are required to provide a transaction number for transactions commenced after 23 October 2013 and persons who enter into a disclosable transaction after that date need a transaction number to include on their return. If a scheme was disclosed to Revenue before 24 October 2014 but a transaction relating to the scheme is commenced after 23 October 2014 a transaction number will not have been allocated to the scheme and will be required for the scheme. The Guidance Notes provide that in such cases to avoid compliant promoters having to re-disclose their schemes to acquire a transaction number the promoter may use the reference number assigned to the transaction by the Mandatory Disclosure Unit when the scheme was originally disclosed.

Schemes which promoters know Revenue are aware of do not come within the confidentiality hallmark (see above under 'Disclosable transactions', 'Confidentiality' heading). In the 2011 Guidance Notes it stated that it could be assumed that Revenue were aware of a scheme where full details of the scheme had been known to specialised areas within Revenue such as Large Cases Division or Revenue Legislation Services. In addition it stated that a scheme could be assumed to be known to Revenue if this was evidenced in published technical guidance notes or was the subject of decided Irish case law. In the Guidance Notes Revenue now say that it cannot be assumed that a scheme is known to Revenue where it has been brought to the attention of Revenue through discussions with particular Revenue officials, Large Cases Division or Revenue Legislation Services. In addition now only schemes evidenced in 'Irish case law' and not 'case law' in general can be assumed to be known to Revenue. Because of the change in guidance in this area the Draft Guidance notes point out that a scheme may not have been disclosed to Revenue based on the original guidance provided as to what schemes it can be assumed to be known to Revenue but under the new guidance it is necessary now for the scheme to be disclosed and for the promoter to obtain a transaction number.

Revenue powers of enquiry, information powers and penalties

Where the Revenue Commissioners have reasonable grounds for believing that:

(a) a person is the promoter of a transaction which may be a disclosable transaction; or

(b) a person has entered into a transaction where there is no promoter and which may form part of a disclosable transaction,

they may issue a notice specifying that transaction and requiring that person provide a 'Statement of Reasons' setting out:

(i) whether, in that person's opinion, the transaction is a disclosable transaction; and

(ii) if not, the reasons for that opinion.

The Statement of Reasons must demonstrate, by reference to the legislation and regulations why the person holds the opinion that the transaction is not a disclosable transaction and, in particular, if the person asserts that the transaction does not fall within any specified description, the statement shall provide sufficient information to enable the Revenue Commissioners to affirm the assertion. It will not be sufficient for the person to state that they have received an opinion given by a barrister, solicitor, qualified accountant or a member of the Irish Taxation Institute to the effect that the transaction is not a disclosable transaction. The person shall comply with the notice within the period of time specified in the notice, not being less than 21 days from the date of the notice, or such longer period as the Revenue Commissioners may agree (TCA 1997, s 817I).

Where a person has provided the Revenue Commissioners with information in purported compliance with their duty to disclose (see above) and the Revenue Commissioners have reasonable grounds for believing that that person has not provided all of the specified information, they may serve a notice requiring that person to provide the omitted information. Where a person has provided the Revenue Commissioners with information in compliance with their duty to report, the Revenue Commissioners may serve a notice requiring that person to provide such other information about, or documents relating to, the disclosable transaction, as they may reasonably require in support of or in explanation of that specified information. That person shall comply with the notice within the period of time specified in the notice, not being less than 21 days from the date of the notice, or such longer period as the Revenue Commissioners may agree (TCA 1997, s 817K).

Where the Revenue Commissioners have reason to believe that a person is a marketer in relation to a transaction which may be a disclosable transaction, they may serve a notice specifying the transaction and requiring the person to provide the Revenue Commissioners with the name, address and, if known, the tax reference number of each person who has provided that person with any information in relation to the transaction (TCA 1997, s 817K). The marketer must comply with the notice within the period of time specified in the notice, not being less than 21 days from the date of the notice or such longer period as the Revenue Commissioners may agree. A 'marketer' means any person who is not a promoter but who has made a marketing contact (as defined above) in relation to a disclosable transaction (TCA 1997, s 817D(1)).

A promoter must, in relation to each disclosable transaction in respect of which specified information has been provided by that promoter provide to the Revenue Commissioners within 30 days beginning on the day after the day on which:

(a) the promoter first makes the transaction available to a person for implementation; or

(b) the promoter first becomes aware of any transaction which is or forms part of the disclosable transation having been implemented, where this date is the "relevant date" within the meaning set out in TCA 1997, s 817D – see above under Duty to Disclose;

a 'client list', namely the name, addresses and, where known, the tax reference number of each person to whom that person has made the disclosable transaction available for implementation (TCA 1997, s 817M(1)). A client's name does not have to be included in a client list where the promoter is satisfied at the time of providing the list that the person has not entered into any transaction forming part of the disclosable transaction (TCA 1997, s 817M(2)). The client list should be submitted using form MD4. After the first client list has been submitted subsequent client lists must be submitted on a quarterly basis (TCA 1997, s 817M(1)(b)). Quarter means a period of three months on 31 March, 30 June, 30 September and 31 December (TCA 1997, s 817D(1)). A client list does not have to be filed for any quarter during which the promoter has not made the disclosable transaction available to any person for implementation. It is not necessary to include in a client list any client which was included in a previous list (TCA 1997, s 817M(3)). (Prior to FA 2014 and the amendment of the Regulations in 2014 the time period within which client lists had to be provided to Revenue was set out in reg 24.)

A person who fails to comply with his duty to disclose (see above) will be subject to a penalty of an amount not exceeding €500 for each day commencing with the first day of the specified period (the relevant day) and ending on the day on which an application is made to a relevant court to determine the amount of the penalty plus a further fixed penalty of €500 for each day on which the failure continues thereafter, A person who fails to comply with any other reporting obligation will be subject to a fixed penalty of an amount not exceeding €4,000 up to the date on which an application is made to a relevant court to determine the amount of the penalty plus a further fixed penalty of €100 for each day on which the failure continues thereafter. A 'relevant court' means the District Court, the Circuit Court or the High Court, as appropriate, by reference to the jurisdictional limits for civil matters laid down in the Courts of Justice Act 1924, as amended, and the Courts (Supplemental Provisions) Act 1961, as amended. A copy of the application must be sent to the person affected. In determining the amount of a penalty, the relevant court shall have regard:

(a) in the case of a person who is a promoter, to the amount of any fees received, or likely to have been received, by the person in connection with the disclosable transaction; and

(b) in any other case, to the amount of any tax advantage gained, or sought to be gained, by the person from the disclosable transaction.

A person who is required to include a transaction number of their return, because they have obtained or sought to obtain a tax advantage from a disclosable transaction (TCA 1997, s 817HA(3)), is liable to a penalty not exceeding €5,000 if they do not include a transaction number on their return (TCA 1997, s 817O(1)(c)). A penalty will not apply where the person was not required to make a disclosure, the person was not provided with a transaction number and the person provides Revenue with details of the scheme and any other information required by Revenue in order to determine if a penalty should apply to a promoter (TCA 1997, s 817HA(4)).

TCA 1997, s 1077C, but not s 1077B applies for the purposes of these penalties (TCA 1997, s 817O). Prior to FA 2014 TCA 1997, s 1077D, which deals with penalties agreed with an individual but not paid before the death of the individual (see **2.701**) did not apply to penalties imposed under TCA 1997, s 817O. With effect for transactions commenced after 23 October 2014 TCA 1997, s 1077D applies to penalties imposed under TCA 1997, s 817O.

The Revenue Commissioners may make a written application to the Appeal Commissioners for a determination in relation to any of the above information powers, requiring information and/or documents in support of a Statement of Reasons (see above) or in relation to a disclosable transaction. They may also apply for a determination that they are entitled to treat a transaction as a disclosable transaction or that it is in fact a disclosable transaction. In the former case, the Appeal Commissioners will order that the transaction should be treated as disclosable only if they are satisfied that the Revenue Commissioners have taken all *reasonable steps* to establish whether the transaction is a disclosable transaction and have *reasonable grounds* for believing that the transaction may be disclosable.

For these purposes reasonable steps may (but need not) include the making of a pre-disclosure enquiry or the making of a prior application to the Appeal Commissioners in respect of information and/or documents in respect of a Statement of Reasons, or where they have had reasonable grounds for believing that the original disclosure was incomplete. Reasonable grounds for believing that a transaction may be disclosable may include:

(i) the fact that the transaction falls within a description specified by regulation;

(ii) an attempt by the promoter to avoid or delay providing information or documents about the transaction on foot of either a pre-disclosure enquiry or a determination of the Appeal Commissioners in relation to a Statement of Reason;

(iii) the failure of the promoter to comply with either a pre-disclosure enquiry or a determination of the Appeal Commissioners in relation to a Statement of Reasons in relation to a different transaction.

An application under these provisions will, with any necessary modifications, be heard by as if it were an appeal against an assessment to income tax. Prior to FA 2014 TCA 1997, s 817P(5) specifically provided that on application, the Appeal Commissioners must permit any barrister or solicitor to plead before them on behalf of the Revenue Commissioners or the other party either orally or in writing and must hear:

(i) any qualified accountant, being any person who has been admitted a member; or

(ii) any person who has been admitted as a member of the Irish Taxation Institute.

They may also permit any other person representing the Revenue Commissioners or the other party to plead before them where they are satisfied that such permission should be given. This provision has been deleted by FA 2014 however because TCA 1997, s 817P(4) provides that an application for an appeal under the section is to be heard by the Appeal Commissioners as if it were an assessment to income tax the provisions regarding the conduct of an appeal against an assessment to income tax will apply. F(TA)A 2015, s 38 removes the reference to the income tax assessment and refers the reader to TCA 1997, s 949I. TCA 1997, s 934, which deals with procedure on appeals provides that the Appeal Commissioners must permit a barrister or solicitor to plead before them, to hear any qualified accountant or member of the Irish Taxation Institute and to give permission to any other person to plead before them so the deletion of the original provisions of TCA 1997, s 817P(5) has no effect.

Where the Appeal Commissioners make a determination in favour of Revenue that information or those documents must be provided to Revenue within the period of five days beginning on the day after the date of the determination (TCA 1997, s 817P(5), inserted by FA 2014 with effect for transactions commenced after 23 October 2014).

Payment notices

With effect from the date of passing of FA 2014, 23 December 2014, TCA 1997, ss 817S and 817T were inserted in TCA 1997, Pt 33 Ch 4. Normally no tax will be payable or repayable following a determination by the Appeal Commissioners if the decision is subject to a rehearing by the Circuit Court or an appeal on a point of law to the High Court (see **2.202**). F(TA)A 2015, s 38, which was subject to Ministerial Order (SI 110/2016 appointed 21 March 2016 as the day on which the Finance (Tax Appeals) Act 2015, came into operation), removes the possibility of a rehearing at the Circuit

Court. However, TCA 1997, s 817S provides that in cases where a taxpayer has entered into:

(a) a tax avoidance transaction within the meaning of TCA 1997, s 811C (see **17.302.2**),
(b) a disclosable transaction, or
(c) a transaction to which the following anti-avoidance provisions (set out in TCA 1997, Sch 33) apply:
    (i) TCA 1997, s 381B – Restriction of loss relief – passive trades (see **4.414**)
    (ii) TCA 1997, s 381C – Restriction of loss relief – anti-avoidance (see **4.415**)
    (iii) TCA 1997, s 546A – Restrictions on allowable losses
    (iv) TCA 1997, s 590 – Attribution to participators of chargeable gains accruing to non-resident company
    (v) TCA 1997, s 806 – Charge to income tax on transfer of assets abroad
    (vi) TCA 1997, s 807A – Liability of non-transferors
    (vii) TCA 1997, s 811B – Tax treatment of loans from employee benefit schemes
    (viii) TCA 1997, s 812 – Taxation of income deemed to arise from transfers of right to receive interest from securities
    (ix) TCA 1997, s 813 – Taxation of transactions associated with loans or credit
    (x) TCA 1997, s 814 – Taxation of income deemed to arise from transactions in certificates of deposit and assignable deposits
    (xi) TCA 1997, s 815 – Taxation of income deemed to arise on certain sales of securities
    (xii) TCA 1997, s 816 – Taxation of shares issued in place of cash dividends
    (xiii) TCA 1997, s 817 – Schemes to avoid liability to tax under Schedule F
    (xiv) TCA 1997, s 817A – Restriction of relief for payments of interest
    (xv) TCA 1997, s 817B – Treatment of interest in certain circumstances
    (xvi) TCA 1997, s 817C – Restriction on deductibility of certain interest

Revenue may issue a payment notice to the taxpayer requiring immediate payment of tax when a determination is made by the Appeal Commissioners.

TCA 1997, s 817S applies where a person enters into a tax avoidance transaction, a disclosable transaction or a transaction to which one of the specific anti-avoidance provisions referred to above applies and Revenue makes or amends an assessment the effect of which is to deny or withdraw the tax advantage arising from the transaction. Where the taxpayer lodges an appeal against the assessment and the Appeal Commissioners make a determination that the assessment is either to stand or that the assessment is to be reduced by an amount which is less than the amount by which it would be reduced if the full tax advantage was withdrawn, Revenue may issue a payment notice requiring 'immediate' payment of the amount of tax specified in the notice. The amount of tax in the notice will be the lower of:

(a) the amount of tax charged by the assessment as a result of the withdrawal of the tax advantage in question; or
(b) the tax that would be payable if there was no request for a rehearing before the Circuit Court or an appeal to the High Court.

The amount of tax stated in a payment notice must be paid even if there has been a request for a rehearing before the Circuit Court or an appeal to the High Court.

TCA 1997, s 817T(3) allows Revenue to issue a payment notice to other taxpayers who have entered into transactions which are the same, or substantially similar to, transactions to which TCA 1997, s 817S(2) apply, ie which have been the subject of an Appeal Commissioners' determination in respect of which Revenue have issued a payment notice to another taxpayer, whether or not that taxpayer has lodged an appeal against any assessment raised.

A transaction, called the 'second transaction', is deemed to be the same or substantially the same as another transaction, called the 'first transaction', where:

(a) Revenue has issued a payment notice on foot of a determination by the Appeal Commissioners under TCA 1997, s 817S and in Revenue's opinion the following applies:
   (i) the provisions of the Acts or the principles and reasoning given by the Appeal Commissioners in arriving at their determination on the first transaction apply equally to the facts of the second transaction,
   (ii) if an assessment was made or amended by Revenue to deny or withdraw the tax advantage from the second transaction and an appeal was lodged against this assessment, the outcome of such an appeal would be that the assessment would not be reduced by the full amount of the tax advantage;
(b) both transactions have the same transaction number under TCA 1997, s 817HB;
(c) the transaction is one in respect of which the promoter has asserted legal professional privilege and two or more transactions would have been assigned the same transaction number if the promoter had been required to make a disclosure instead of the person who entered into the transaction; or
(d) a scheme was not disclosed to Revenue but if it had been disclosed the two transactions would have been assigned the same transaction number.

A payment notice issued under TCA 1997, s 817T(3) should state the following:

(i) the amount of tax assessed taking account of the Appeal Commissioners' determination in relation to the first transaction;
(ii) the transaction number assigned to the scheme;
(iii) the reason why the transaction entered into by the recipient of the notice is the same or substantially the same as the transaction which was the subject of the Appeal Commissioners' determination; and
(iv) attach a copy of the Appeal Commissioners' determination in relation to the first transaction.

A recipient of a notice under TCA 1997, s 817T(3) may submit a notice in writing within 30 days to Revenue requesting a review of the payment notice. The request should set out reasons why the recipient does not consider that the transaction is the same or substantially the same as the transaction in respect of which another person has received a notice under TCA 1997, s 817S(3). Revenue are required to consider the review notice and either confirm or withdraw the payment notice. A person is entitled to appeal a decision of Revenue to confirm the payment notice to the Appeal Commissioners by notice in writing within 30 days (TCA 1997, s 817T(5)). The notice of appeal should set out the grounds for the appeal and attach a copy of Revenue's determination. If more than one person has made an appeal to the Appeal Commissioners in relation to the same scheme the Appeal Commissioners may hear all the appeals together. In addition the Appeal Commissioners can give their decision without having a hearing (TCA 1997, s 817T(7)). There is no provision for appeal against a decision of the Appeal Commissioners. The legislation does not provide for a deferral of the payment of tax under a payment notice where a request for a review is made.

If an assessment subsequently becomes final and conclusive, ie following a determination by a higher court, and tax is repayable to the person interest is payable by Revenue in accordance with TCA 1997, s 865A as if a valid claim to repayment had been made 93 days before the payment was made to Revenue (TCA 1997, s 817S(6)). The general 4-year time limit for making a claim for a repayment of tax does not apply for the purpose of TCA 1997, ss 817S and 817T.

The provisions regarding the collection of tax by the Collector General under TCA 1997, s 960E apply to tax contained in a payment notice as if the payment notice were a demand for tax (TCA 1997, s 817S(7)).

Interaction with s 811C

Where a promoter provides the Revenue Commissioners with specified information relating to a disclosable transaction and the client list (see above) in respect of that disclosable transaction, the provision of such information shall, as respects any person included on the client list who implements the transaction, be wholly without prejudice as to the correctness or otherwise of any opinion which might be formed by the Revenue Commissioners that the disclosable transaction concerned was a tax avoidance transaction within the meaning of TCA 1997, s 811C (TCA 1997, s 817N(1)) (see the discussion at **17.302**). Similarly, where a person, other than a promoter, provides the Revenue Commissioners with specified information relating to a disclosable transaction, that person shall be treated as making that information available wholly without prejudice as to the correctness or otherwise of any opinion which might be formed by the Revenue Commissioners that the disclosable transaction concerned was a tax avoidance transaction within the meaning of TCA 1997, s 811C (TCA 1997, s 817N(2)). (Before FA 2014 TCA 1997, ss 817N(1) and 817N(2) did not explicitly refer to the definition of 'tax avoidance transaction' as set out then in TCA 1997, s 811. The reference to TCA 1997, s 811C was only inserted by FA 2014 although before this it was understood that the reference to a 'tax avoidance transaction' was clearly meant to be a reference to that term as it applied for TCA 1997, s 811). Where a person provides the Revenue Commissioners with specified information relating to a disclosable transaction, the provision of that information shall not be regarded as being, or being equivalent to, the delivery of a protective notification by that person in relation to the transaction for the purposes of TCA 1997, s 811A or s 811D. Nothing in the legislation is to be construed as preventing the Revenue Commissioners from:

(a) making any enquiry; or
(b) taking any action at any time, in connection with TCA 1997, s 811, s 811A, s 811C or s 811D (TCA 1997, s 817N(4)).

Where a person enters into a tax avoidance transaction within the meaning of TCA 1997, s 811C or a transaction to which the anti-avoidance provisions set out in TCA 1997, Sch 33 apply (listed out above under 'Payment notices'), a 30 per cent surcharge applies where the person seeks to obtain the benefit of the relevant tax advantage either by filing a return, declaration, statement or account or makes any claim. This surcharge may be avoided if a protective notification is filed or the surcharge reduced if a qualifying avoidance disclosure is made (TCA 1997, s 811D). The benefits of making a protective notification do not apply in circumstances where the promoter of a transaction has not complied with the requirement to make a disclosure or has not provided the person who enters into the transaction in question with a transaction number unless the person who has entered into the transaction gives details of the scheme to Revenue. In particular a notification does not qualify as a 'protective notification' if it is made in respect of a disclosable transaction in the following circumstances:

(a) the transaction was disclosable by the promoter and not by the person who entered into the transaction (it is not a transaction which comes within TCA 1997, s 817F, transactions where there is no promoter, TCA 1997, s 817G transactions where the promoter is outside the State and TCA 1997, s 817H transactions where the promoter has asserted legal professional privilege);

(b) by the due date for the filing of the person's tax return, the transaction was not assigned a transaction number or the person was not provided with a transaction number by the promoter;

(c) the person in whose name the protective notification or qualifying avoidance disclosure was made provides a Revenue officer with the specified information ('specified information' is defined by TCA 1997, s 817D(2) and is set out above under 'Duty to disclose'); and

(d) the person in whose name the protective notification or qualifying avoidance disclosure was made provides a Revenue officer without unreasonable delay any other information the officer may require in order to decide if an application should be made under TCA 1997, s 817O(3)(a) to the courts for a determination that a penalty should apply to the promoter (see above under 'Revenue powers of enquiry, information powers and penalties').

In addition where the circumstances set out above apply and a qualifying avoidance disclosure is made the amount by which the surcharge is reduced is less than it would be if those circumstances did not apply. Protective notifications and qualifying avoidance disclosures are dealt with in more detail in **17.302**.

Operative dates

Finance Act 2010, s 149(2) provides that these provisions apply:

In the case of a promoter:

(a) any disclosable transaction in respect of which the relevant date falls on or after 17 January 2011, ie transactions which are first designed, marketed and available for implementation on or after 17 January 2011; and

(b) any disclosable transaction in respect of which the relevant date falls on or after 17 January 2011 (where the relevant date is determined on the basis of whichever of the three dates in the definition of 'relevant date' is the earliest of such date falling on or after 17 January 2011), ie schemes which have been designed and marketed before 17 January 2011 but which are made available for implementation on or after 17 January 2011.

In the case of persons who are required to make a disclosure but who are not promoters the provisions apply where the whole of the transaction is undertaken on or after 17 January 2011. If any part of the transaction is undertaken prior to 17 January 2011 there is no requirement to disclose.

2.7 Penalties and Back Duty Settlements

2.701 Penalties and interest

The Income Tax Acts contain a number of sections providing for penalties to be imposed on persons who fail to make returns or statements or to provide information or do other acts when lawfully requested by an inspector or other authorised officer of the Revenue Commissioners. In particular, penalties are liable to be imposed for incorrect returns, statements, etc when made fraudulently or negligently. TCA 1997, Sch 29 lists under three columns the offences for which the penalties imposed by TCA 1997, ss 1052, 1054 and 1077E may be levied. These offences are referenced to the relevant sections in the Tax Acts which do not impose their own penalties, but which rely on the general penalty rules of the above sections.

TCA 1997, s 1053 applied penalties for fraudulently or negligently making an incorrect return or for failing to file a return, in respect of acts or omissions arising before 24 December 2008, the date of passing of Finance (No 2) Act 2008. TCA 1997, s 1077E applies in respect of acts or omissions on or after 24 December 2008 (see below).

Depending on the column number in TCA 1997, Sch 29 under which the relevant offence is listed, the penalties imposed by these sections differ in some respects. For ease of cross-reference, it is proposed to use the term 'column 1 offence' in referring to any omission, act, etc which may lead to the imposition of a penalty under TCA 1997, ss 1052, 1054 and 1077E at the rate specified for any act, omission, etc listed in column 1. The terms 'column 2 offence' and 'column 3 offence' are used in a corresponding sense.

The column 1 offences relate mainly to non-compliance with requirements to make the various returns of income, etc referred to in the sections listed there. Column 2 offences concern non-compliance with notices given by Inspectors of taxes requiring persons to make information returns and to provide particulars regarding various matter. Column 3 offences concern failures to do certain acts, furnish certain particulars, etc which are not dependent on the person first receiving a notice from an inspector.

Penalties are imposed by TCA 1997, ss 1052, 1077E and Sch 29 for failure to make returns of income or for making incorrect returns under the following main headings:

(a) a return of income required from an individual under TCA 1997, s 879 or TCA 1997, s 959I (see **2.110**);
(b) a return of income made on behalf of an incapacitated or non-resident person by another person under TCA 1997, s 878;
(c) a self assessment return required under TCA 1997, Pt 41A, Ch 3;
(d) a separate return of income made by a husband or wife for the purposes of separate assessment under TCA 1997, s 1023 (see **3.504**);
(e) a return under TCA 1997, s 897(2)(b) of motor cars made available to employees or directors by reason of their employment or directorship;
(f) a return required under TCA 1997, s 473 (rent allowance);
(g) various returns under TCA 1997, s 1002 (attachment of debts): (see **2.612**);

(h) certain returns under WCTIPA 1993;
(i) returns required under TCA 1997, s 477 (relief for service charges, (see **3.320**);
(j) various returns required under the relevant contract provisions (see **2.311**);
(k) delivery of a return under TCA 1997, s 531AF (domicile levy); and
(l) a number of returns listed in TCA 1997, Sch 29, columns 2 and 3.

There are also other sections spread throughout the Tax Acts providing for penalties in relation to other matters.

Without listing all the penalties provided for, some of the more important ones as applicable for income tax may be noted as follows:

(a) For failure to make a return of income when requested to do so under TCA 1997, s 877 or s 879, a penalty of €3,000 applies, which is increased to €4,000 if the return is still not submitted before the end of the tax year following the year of assessment in which the notice to make the return was given by an inspector of taxes (TCA 1997, s 1052(1)). The penalties for a secretary in relation to a body of persons are €1,000 increasing to €2,000 if the return is still not submitted before the end of the tax year following the year of assessment in which the notice was given. Where the secretary acted fraudulently or negligently a penalty of between €1,500 and €3,000 applies (TCA 1997, s 1054(2)). The failure to make a return of income under s 877 in the case of a person who proves he is not chargeable to tax is reduced to €5 (TCA 1997, s 1052(3) applying TCA 1997, s 877(5)(b)).

(b) TCA 1997, s 959O(4) applies the provisions of TCA 1997, ss 1052, 1054 to the mandatory return of income under the self assessment regime under TCA 1997, s 959I. An individual who makes the mandatory return will be deemed to have been required to have done so on foot of a notice from the Inspector under TCA 1997, s 879 issued on the specified return date for the relevant year of assessment (TCA 1997, s 959I(3)).

(c) A penalty of €3,000 applies to failure to make returns within TCA 1997, Sch 29 columns 1 and 2 (€2,000 in the case of a body of persons). The increased penalties for seriously delayed returns apply to all other 'column 1' returns as they do for returns of income.

(d) Where a person makes any false statement or false representation with reference to tax or for the purpose of claiming any allowance, reduction or repayment of tax, the court may impose a fine up to a maximum figure based on the tax evaded, and at its discretion may also impose a prison sentence again up to a maximum period by reference to the tax evaded or both (TCA 1997, s 1056(2)). The greatest possible sanction under these provisions would be a fine of twice the tax evaded and a prison sentence of eight years on conviction on indictment, where the tax evaded was equal to or in excess of €126,970. The full schedule of sanctions is set out in TCA 1997, s 1056(3). The provisions of TCA 1997, s 1078(4) and (6)–(8) inclusive apply also for the purposes of TCA 1997, s 1056 (see **2.703**).

(e) The tax 'evaded' is defined for these purposes as the difference between the tax payable for a year of assessment and the tax which would have been payable if the fraudulent return, etc had not been made or full disclosure of income had been made, as the case may be (TCA 1997, s 1056(1)). Where the tax payable is reduced (eg as a result of loss relief) after the penalty has been imposed, it appears that it is to be assumed that there will be a retrospective mitigation of the penalty under TCA 1997, s 1065 (see below): (*Khan v First East Brixton*

General Commissioners [1986] STC 331; see also TCA 1997, s 1062). Penalties imposed under (a) and (b) were held to be non-criminal in nature in *McLoughlin & Tuite v Revenue Commissioners* III ITR 387 (compare *DPP v Boyle* IV ITR 395).

The penalties imposed for failure to make other information returns or other declarations or statements or to furnish any particulars, to produce any document or make anything available for inspection, etc, in relation to returns, etc listed in column 3 of TCA 1997, Sch 29, is now €3,000. (TCA 1997, s 1052(1)(b)). Where the failure continues after the end of the year of assessment following that during which the notice was given the penalty rises to €4,000 (TCA 1997, s 1052(2)). Note that by virtue of TCA 1997, s 894 the submission of many returns is mandatory: (see **2.602**). Where the person is a body of persons the secretary is liable to a separate penalty of €1,000 and if the failure continues after the year of assessment following that in which the notice is given the secretary is liable to a separate penalty of €2,000. In a case of deliberate behaviour for a body of persons the secretary is liable to a separate penalty of between €1,500 and €3,000.

The following was introduced by F(No 2)A 2008, Sch 5, Pt 1 (TCA 1997, s 1077B): Where:

(a) in the absence of any agreement between a person and a Revenue officer that the person is liable to a penalty under the Acts; or

(b) following the failure by a person to pay a penalty the person has agreed a liability.

If a Revenue officer is of the opinion that the person is liable to a penalty, then the officer shall give notice in writing to the person and the notice shall identify the relevant provisions of the TCA 1997, the circumstances in which the person is liable to a penalty, and the amount of the penalty to which the person is liable and other relevant details (TCA 1997, s 1077B(1)).

The Revenue officer can amend an opinion that a person is liable to a penalty at any time (TCA 1997, s 1077B(2)). Where a person to whom the notice issued does not within 30 days of the date of the notice agree in writing with the opinion and make a payment to Revenue of the amount of the penalty specified in the notice, then the Revenue officer may make an application to a relevant court for the court to determine whether the person is liable to the penalty (TCA 1997, s 1077B(3)). The Revenue officer is required to issue to the person a copy of any application to a relevant court (TCA 1997, s 1077B(4)). A 'relevant court' is defined as the District Court, the Circuit Court or the High Court as appropriate by reference to jurisdictional limits for civil matters laid down on the Courts of Justice Act 1924, as amended, and the Courts (Supplemental Provisions) Act 1961 as amended.

Where a relevant court has made a determination that a person is liable to a penalty, that court shall also make an order to the recovery of that penalty, and that penalty may be collected and recovered in the same manner as an amount of tax (TCA 1997, s 1077C(1)). Where a person is liable to a penalty, that penalty is due and payable from the date it had been agreed in writing that the person is liable to the penalty or Revenue had agreed to accept a settlement for tax, interest and penalties, or the relevant court had determined that the person is liable to the penalty.

Revenue set out in guidelines published in April 2009 that nothing in the legislative changes introduced by F(No 2)A 2008 prevents Revenue and taxpayers from agreeing liabilities and penalties without recourse to the courts.

F(No 2)A 2008, Sch 5, Pt 1 introduced legislation (TCA 1997, s 1077D) in relation to penalties in the case of a deceased person. Where before an individual's death:

(a) that individual had agreed in writing that he or she was liable to a penalty under the Acts;
(b) that individual had agreed in writing with an opinion or amended opinion of Revenue that he or she was liable to a penalty under the Acts;
(c) Revenue had agreed or undertaken to accept a settlement from the individual; or
(d) a court had determined that the individual was liable to a penalty under the Acts;

Then the penalty shall be due and any proceedings for the recovery of the penalty which had been or could have been instituted against the individual may be continued or instituted against their executor, administrator or estate and any penalty awarded in proceedings shall be a debt due from and payable out of their estate (TCA 1997, s 1077D(1)).

Proceedings may not be instituted by Revenue as set out above against the executor or administrator of a person at a time when by virtue of TCA 1997, s 1048(2) that executor or administrator is not assessable and chargeable under that section in respect of tax on profits or gains which accrued to the person before their death (TCA 1997, s 1077D(2)).

A penalty of €4,000 may be imposed on any person who assists or induces another in making any incorrect return, account, statement or declaration known to be incorrect (TCA 1997, s 1055). Further, it is possible for any person who knowingly aids, assists or induces another person to make a fraudulent return or statement or to avoid tax unlawfully by failing to disclose his full income is exposed to the same level of penalties as a person who makes a false statement or representation (see (c) above) (TCA 1997, s 1056(2)(b)). Where the conviction is on indictment, the sentence may be up to eight years depending on the amount of tax evaded. In all cases, the court may impose a fine up to a maximum figure based on the amount of tax evaded, and at its discretion, a prison sentence (TCA 1997, s 1056(3)).

TCA 1997, s 1065 authorises the Revenue Commissioners, at their discretion, to mitigate any penalty, and prior to 18 December 2013 (the date of the passing of Finance (No 2) Act 2013) any fine, or stay or compound any proceedings for the recovery of a fine or penalty and may also, after the judgment of the court, further mitigate a penalty, and prior to 18 December 2013 any fine, up to a maximum of 50 per cent. The Revenue's approach to the imposition of penalties is discussed more fully at **2.704**. However, no mitigation is permitted in the case of an individual who failed to take advantage of the 1993 Tax Amnesty or who made a false declaration thereunder (TCA 1997, s 1065(2)(b)). Prior to 18 December 2013 the Revenue Commissioners could also order any person imprisoned for any offence to be discharged before the term of any imprisonment has expired and in addition the Minister of Finance could also mitigate a fine or penalty after judgment, again up to a maximum of 50 per cent. These powers were abolished by Finance (No 2) Act 2013, s 78.

Other penalties include:

(a) €4,000: graduated penalty system for late filing of the employer's end of year P35 return. There is an initial penalty of €1,000 which increases over a four-month period to €4,000 for employers who file late returns (TCA 1997, s 987(1A));
(b) €4,000: non-compliance with PAYE regulations (TCA 1997, s 987(1));

(c) €3,000: the separate penalty on the secretary of a company for non-compliance with the PAYE regulations (TCA 1997, s 987(2));

(d) €3,000: failure to comply with a notice to furnish an inspector with information for payments related to business, etc transactions (TCA 1997, s 889(8));

(e) €3,000: failure to appear before Appeal Commissioners when duly summoned or failure to answer any lawful question in respect of matters under consideration at an appeal hearing (TCA 1997, s 939(3));

(f) €3,000: failure of a trader, etc to observe the requirements to keep proper records (the penalty does not apply if there is no tax liability for the year of assessment covered) (TCA 1997, s 886(5));

(g) €4,000: wilfully obstructing or delaying an authorised Revenue officer in the exercise of his power to inspect documents and records or not complying with any requirement of an authorised officer (TCA 1997, s 905(3)); and

(h) €4,000: failure to comply with a request to supply an authorised officer with information related to business transactions with a person whose affairs are under enquiry (TCA 1997, s 902(11)).

Recovery of penalties

The fact that a person may be liable to a penalty under any of the provisions of the Tax Acts does not mean that he is automatically chargeable to the penalty. In the absence of the agreement of the taxpayer that a penalty is payable, for any penalty to become payable, the Revenue Commissioners must instigate the appropriate proceedings in the courts to recover the penalty provided for in the appropriate section as a debt due to the Minister for Finance (TCA 1997, s 1077B). The penalty only becomes payable after a judgment for the penalty has been given by the court having the jurisdiction to deal with the matter.

TCA 1997, s 960D provides that tax due and payable to the Revenue Commissioners shall be treated as a debt due to the Minister for Finance. For this purpose TCA 1997, s 960A provides that 'tax' includes income tax, local property tax and any other levy or charge which is placed under the care and management of the Revenue Commissioners which would include universal social charge and domicile levy (see **2.102**). 'Tax' is also deemed to include:

(a) any interest, surcharge or penalty in connection with tax;

(b) any clawback of a relief or exemption relating to tax; and

(c) any tax to be withheld from payments or income.

TCA 1997, s 960I provides that any tax due and payable may be sued for and recovered by the Collector General in any court of competent jurisdiction.

TCA 1997, s 1063 entitles the Revenue Commissioners (or a duly authorised officer subject to TCA 1997, s 1060 or s 1077D) to commence proceedings for the recovery of any fine or penalty at any time within the six years after the date on which the fine or penalty was incurred. The different time limit for the commencement of proceedings to recover penalties from personal representatives in respect of acts, omissions, etc of a deceased person has already been indicated. It is necessary for the proceedings to be brought in the name of an officer (of the Revenue Commissioners), the Attorney General or the Director of Public Prosecutions.

2.702 Interest on tax where fraud or neglect for tax years prior to 2005

For tax years up to and including 2004, TCA 1997, s 1082 (as amended by FA 2005, s 145) imposes a special rule charging interest at a penal rate of two per cent per month (or part of a month) on income tax due on any assessment in respect of tax years made to recover tax previously under-assessed as a result of the fraud or neglect of a person. The rule applied equally to assessments within and outside the self assessment system.

An assessment made to recover an undercharge of tax due to fraud or neglect is normally made one or more years after the tax year affected. Interest on tax charged by such an assessment runs not from the date of the assessment but from the original due date or dates that would have applied to that tax if it had been charged in an assessment made in the relevant year before the applicable due date or dates in that year. The interest runs up to the date of payment. For example, if an inspector made an assessment under this rule on 16 May 2006 to recover tax undercharged for the tax year 1997–98, interest becomes payable from the due date(s) for 1997–98 up to the date the tax is paid.

If an inspector makes an assessment under this rule, he is required to give notice to the person assessed that the tax carries interest from the due date in the original year assessed. The person assessed is entitled to appeal within 30 days on the ground that interest should not be charged under this rule. This appeal is to the Appeal Commissioners with the right to a subsequent rehearing by the Circuit Court judge and, should there be any point of law involved, to the High Court, etc. If, on the appeal, it is determined that interest should not be charged under this rule, then interest becomes chargeable on the tax understated at the normal (non-penal) rate under the normal interest rule of TCA 1997, s 1080(1) (TCA 1997, s 1082(5)). There is no provision for the mitigation of interest under TCA 1997, s 1082.

2.703 Revenue offences

TCA 1997, s 1078(2) sets out a number of 'revenue offences' for which persons found guilty may be made liable for substantial penalties (including possible imprisonment). The penalties for these revenue offences are in addition and without prejudice to any of the other penalties which may apply under the Tax Acts (see **2.701**).

Any person, whether an individual, company or other body corporate, unincorporated body of persons, personal representative, trustee, etc, is guilty of a revenue offence if that person commits any of the acts or omissions enumerated in TCA 1997, s 1078(2). For the purposes of the section, 'tax' means any tax, duty, levy or charge under the care and management of the Revenue Commissioners and the term 'the Acts' means the Customs Acts, the statutes relating to the duties of excise, the Tax Acts, Pts 18A (Income Levy), 18B (Parking Levy), 18C (Domicile Levy) and 18D (Universal Social Charge), the Capital Gains Tax Acts, VAT Acts, Capital Acquisitions Tax Consolidation Act 2003, Stamp Duties Consolidation Act 1999, Part VI of the Finance Act 1983 (Residential Property Tax), the Finance (Local Property Tax) Act 2012 and subsequent enactments amending or extending those Acts.

It is not proposed to list here all the revenue offences, which can be read in TCA 1997, s 1078, but the main thrust of the offences legislated against is that a revenue offence is committed if a person knowingly and/or wilfully delivers any incorrect return, statement or accounts, etc, or wilfully furnishes any incorrect information in connection with any tax. He also commits a revenue offence if he knowingly aids, abets or assists another person to make knowingly or wilfully any incorrect return, statement or accounts, etc in connection with any tax. He commits an offence if he fails without 'reasonable excuse' to comply with any provision of the Acts relating to the furnishing of any return, certificate or any statement, or with regard to the keeping or retention of books, accounts or other documents for the purposes of any tax, and destroys, defaces or conceals any documents or records (written or electronic) from an authorised officer. The term 'reasonable excuse' came into being after the passing of FA 2002, s 133(b) with effect from 25 March 2002 and replaced the term 'knowingly and wilfully' insofar as that term had previously applied to TCA 1997, s 1078(2)(g). With effect from 2 April 2007, a revenue offence is also committed where a person with intention to deceive either purports to be a Revenue official, or makes any statement or makes any statement which would lead a person to believe that he is a Revenue official.

With effect from 6 February 2011, a revenue offence is committed where a person: (a) knowingly or wilfully possesses or uses, for the purpose of evading tax, a computer programme or electronic component which modifies, corrects, deletes, cancels, conceals or otherwise alters any record stored or preserved by means of any electronic device without preserving the original data and its subsequent modification, correction, cancellation, concealment or alteration; or (b) provides or makes available, for the purpose of evading tax, a computer programme or electronic component which modifies, corrects, deletes, cancels, conceals or otherwise alters any record stored or preserved by means of any electronic device without preserving the original data and its subsequent modification, correction, cancellation, concealment or alteration (TCA 1997, s 1078(2)(ba); (bb)).

With effect for acts carried out from 25 March 2005, TCA 1997, s 1078(1A), as inserted by FA 2005, s 142, sets out a new wide-ranging set of revenue offences, namely where a person:

(a) is knowingly concerned in the *fraudulent evasion* of tax by himself or any other person;
(b) is knowingly concerned in, or is *reckless* as to whether or not he is concerned in *facilitating* either the *fraudulent evasion* of tax by another person or the commission of a Revenue Offence by another person under TCA 1997, s 1078(2) (other than under paragraph (b) which is concerned with aiding or abetting or inducing another person to make false returns or statements); or
(c) is knowingly concerned in the *fraudulent evasion* or attempted *fraudulent evasion* of any prohibition or restriction on importation for the time being in force, or the removal of any goods from the State, in contravention of the Acts (TCA 1997, s 1078(1A)(c)).

For these purposes 'fraudulent evasion' is defined as:

(a) evading (or attempting to evade) any payment of tax or deduction of tax required to be made or suffered by the person concerned; or
(b) claiming or obtaining (or attempting to claim or obtain) any relief or exemption from any payment or repayment of tax to which the person concerned was not entitled;

but only where in order to do so, the person concerned deceives, omits, conceals or uses any other dishonest means, including:

(a) providing false, incomplete or misleading information to the Revenue Commissioners or any other persons; and

(b) failing to provide information to the Revenue Commissioners or any other persons (TCA 1997, s 1078(1A)(a)).

A person is to be regarded as 'reckless' for these purposes if he disregards a substantial risk that he is concerned in facilitating the fraudulent evasion of tax or the commission of a Revenue Offence; a 'substantial risk' is a risk of such a nature and degree that having regard to all the circumstances and extent of information available to the individual concerned, the disregarding of that risk involves culpability of a high degree (TCA 1997, s 1078(1A)(b)).

In *DPP v Michael Collins* (discussed in Duggan, *Disclosure to Revenue and the privilege against self-incrimination*) ITR, March 2008, p 79, the Circuit Court judge followed *The State v Treanor* [1942] 2 IR 193 in holding that generally a confession made under the influence of a promise or threat held out by a person in authority and which was calculated to induce a confession and did in fact influence the accused to make a confession was inadmissible in criminal proceedings, including those brought under the Tax Acts. The right against self-incrimination is also entrenched in the European Convention on Human Rights: see **1.412**. TCA 1997, s 1067 however provides that statements shall not be inadmissible in criminal proceedings by reason only of the fact that the Revenue commissioners have drawn attention to the fact that they may accept pecuniary settlements and also that although no categoric undertaking may be given to that effect, it is the practice of the Revenue Commissioners to be influenced by a full confession of any fraud or default in favour of accepting such a settlement. The constitutional validity of this provision appears open to question.

'Facilitating' is defined for these purposes as aiding, abetting, assisting, inciting or inducing fraudulent evasion of tax, etc (TCA 1997, s 1078(1A)(a)).

Where a person has been convicted of certain Revenue Offences, a court may order the person to comply with certain provisions of the tax legislation eg the submission of a tax return (TCA 1997, s 1078(3A)). In *R v IRC ex parte Chisholm* [1981] STC 253, the word 'wilfully' was held to mean 'intentionally' or 'deliberately' in the context of failure to deduct PAYE.

In *O'Callaghan v Clifford & Ors* IV ITR 478 the Supreme Court held that, although guilt of a Revenue offence could be established by a certificate signed by a Revenue official in the absence of evidence of the contrary (see TCA 1997, s 1052(4)), it was necessary to take into account that the burden of proof in a criminal case was higher than that in a civil case. Accordingly, where the certificate in question did not expressly state either:

(a) that the offence had been committed 'knowingly and wilfully'; or

(b) that the return in question had been 'duly given' to (as opposed to 'served on') the taxpayer,

it had been an abuse of due process to deny an adjournment to the taxpayer in the lower court despite his initial non-appearance before that court. The lower court was therefore not entitled in the circumstances to infer that the *mens rea* necessary for the commission of a Revenue offence (ie that it had been committed 'knowingly or wilfully') existed. Hunt takes the view that in view of the high standard of proof required in criminal cases, admissions on the part of the taxpayer by way of voluntary disclosure may be highly prejudicial: see 'The taxman cometh: penalties and the criminal law' 1998 ITR 288, which also explains the significance of the Judge's Rules in the context of voluntary disclosure (note also TCA 1997, s 106(7)). The taxpayer's rights under the European Human Rights Convention are also highly material in this context: (see **1.412**).

In *Lennon v Clifford* [1996] SC, a judicial review case, the Supreme Court upheld the decision of the High Court to refuse to quash a conviction under TCA 1997, s 1078 by the District Court judge on the grounds of insufficiency of evidence.

With effect from 28 March 2003, TCA 1997, s 1078A, made it an offence to falsify, conceal, destroy or otherwise dispose of material which a person knows or suspects is or would be relevant to the investigation of a revenue offence.

With effect from 28 March 2003, TCA 1997, s 1078B created certain rebuttable presumptions as to the origin of certain documents and their contents in a civil or criminal prosecution by the Revenue Commissioners.

With effect from 28 March 2003, TCA 1997, s 1078C the judge, in a trial of an indictable revenue offence, may order that copies of certain documents be supplied to members of the jury in order to assist them in their understanding of the case being heard. Such documents can include not only documents submitted in evidence and transcripts of the proceedings, but also an affidavit of an expert summarising transactions undertaken by the accused or others. However, any such expert must also be summoned by the prosecution to attend the trial and may be required to give evidence.

Penalties for the offences

TCA 1997, s 1078(3) makes a person guilty of any revenue offence liable for the following penalties:

(a) on summary conviction to a fine not exceeding €5,000 (€3,000 for offences committed prior to 13 March 2008) or, at the discretion of the court, to imprisonment for a term not exceeding 12 months, or to both the fine and the imprisonment; or

(b) on conviction on indictment, to a fine not exceeding €126,970 or, at the discretion of the court, to imprisonment for a term not exceeding five years, or to both the fine and the imprisonment.

Where a revenue offence is committed by a body corporate and the offence is shown to have been committed with the consent or connivance of an officer of the body corporate, that officer is also deemed to be guilty of a revenue offence and may be proceeded against for a penalty under these provisions. The person must have been an officer at the time the offence was committed by the body corporate. He may have been a director, manager, secretary or other officer of the body corporate, or a member of the committee of management or other controlling authority of the body corporate. TCA 1997, s 1078(5) is amended with effect from 25 March 2005 in order to extend the attribution of a corporate offence to cover cases where the Revenue Offence is attributable to the recklessness (as defined above) of the directors or of those other persons (TCA 1997, s 1078(5)).

Proceedings may be brought by the Revenue Commissioners against any person within 10 years of the date of the commission of the revenue offence. If a penalty is incurred for a revenue offence, the proceedings to recover the penalty may be brought at any time within 10 years of the date the penalty was incurred, ie from the date of conviction for the offence (TCA 1997, s 1078(7)).

In *R v IRC ex parte Mead* [1992] STC 482, the Inland Revenue's policy of selective prosecution in cases of tax evasion was held not to be *ultra vires*.

Duty to report certain Revenue offences

TCA 1997, s 1079 imposes an obligation on certain professional advisers to companies to report certain offences (being relevant offences) on the part of the company. The obligation is imposed on 'relevant persons'. These are:

(a) the auditor of a company, an industrial provident society or a friendly society; or

(b) any person who, with a view to reward, assists or advises the company in the preparation or delivery of any information, declaration, return, records, accounts or other documents which he knows will be or is likely to be used for any purpose of tax. This does not include employees.

This section obliges a relevant person having regard to information obtained in the course of examining the accounts of the company or while assisting or advising the company in the preparation or delivery of any information, declaration, return, records, accounts or other documents for the purposes of tax becomes aware that the company has committed or is in the course of committing one or more relevant offences.

A list of relevant offences is set out in the section as follows:

(a) knowingly or wilfully delivering any incorrect return, settlement or accounts or knowingly or wilfully furnishing or causing to be furnished any incorrect information in connection with any tax;

(b) knowingly or wilfully claiming or obtaining relief or exemption from, or repayment of any tax, being a relief, exemption or repayment to which there is no entitlement;

(c) knowingly or wilfully issuing or producing an incorrect invoice, receipt, instrument or other document in connection with tax;

(d) knowingly or wilfully failing to comply with any provisions of the Acts requiring the furnishing of a return of income, profits or gains, or sources of income, profits of gains for the purpose of any tax;

Provided that an offence under this paragraph committed by a company shall not be a relevant offence if the company has made a return of income, profits or gains to the Revenue Commissioners in respect of any accounting period falling wholly or partly into the period of three years immediately preceding the accounting period in respect of which the offence was committed.

In this context 'tax' means tax, duty, levy or charge which is included under the care and management of the Revenue Commissioners.

Where the relevant person in the course of the work outlined above becomes aware that the company has committed or is in the course of committing one or more relevant offences then if the offence(s) are material the relevant person must communicate particulars of the offence(s) in writing to the company without undue delay and requesting the company to:

(a) take action as is necessary for the purposes of rectifying the matter; or

(b) notify an appropriate officer of the Revenue Commissioners of the offence or offences not later than six months after the time of the communication.

If it is not established to the relevant person's satisfaction that the necessary action has been taken or notification made to the Revenue Commissioners as the case may be, then the relevant person shall cease to act as auditor to the company or in the case of assistance or advice cease to assist or advise the company. The section also provides that the relevant person shall not act, assist or advise the company:

(a) for a period of three years from the time at which the particulars of the offence were communicated to the company; or
(b) until it is established to the relevant person's satisfaction that the necessary action has been taken or notification made to the Revenue,

whichever is the earlier.

This shall not prevent a person from assisting or advising a company in preparation or conducting legal proceedings, either civil or criminal, which are extant or pending at a time which is six months after the time of the communication to the company.

Where an auditor ceases to act under these provisions he must:

(a) deliver a written notice of resignation to the company; and
(b) within fourteen days after the delivery of the notice of resignation send a copy of that notice to the appropriate officer.

This is not a requirement for advisers. It is not necessary for the auditor to send the Revenue Commissioners a copy of the original communication to the company regarding the offence.

The offences to be reported are those committed by the company in respect of:

(a) corporation tax, for any accounting period beginning after 30 June 1995;
(b) income tax or capital gains tax for the year of assessment 1995–96 onwards;
(c) VAT, PAYE and PRSI for taxable periods beginning after 30 June 1995;
(d) capital acquisitions tax for gifts or inheritances taken on or after 30 June 1995;
(e) stamp duty for instruments executed on or after 30 June 1995; and
(f) any other taxes payable on or after 30 June 1995 (including from 2013 local property tax).

If the relevant person fails to cease to act for the company, to issue notices of resignation or issues an incorrect communication in relation to an offence this will give rise to the following penalties:

(a) €1,265 on summary conviction (which may be mitigated by not more than 75 per cent); and
(b) on conviction of an indictment the penalty is a fine not exceeding €6,345 and at the discretion of the court a term of imprisonment not exceeding two years or both the fine and the imprisonment.

It is possible for proceedings in respect of this section to be taken within six years from the time when the relevant person was required to communicate particulars of the offence to the company. It also states that where a relevant person takes any action required by this section, it shall not be regarded as breaching professional duty and no liability or action shall lie against the person in any court for so doing.

For a critical analysis of these provisions see Bohan, 'FA 1995, s 172', Seminar, ICAI 14/6/1995.

2.704 Back duty settlements

The non-disclosure or incomplete disclosure of taxable income can assume various degrees of seriousness ranging from minor adjustments arising in the course of a routine Revenue Audit (where it is likely that no penalties would be imposed) to systematic and deliberate tax evasion (where the full armoury of sanctions at the Revenue's disposal, including criminal prosecution, may be applied). Where a full-blown back duty investigation has been opened, the Revenue Commissioners will investigate all aspects of the business and personal affairs of the taxpayer concerned, so far as they may be connected in any way with his financial position. It is important that the taxpayer should make a full and complete disclosure of all matters relevant to his tax position and not only those related to the point that gave rise to the investigation in the first place.

Audits of tax returns

Even where the inspector has no immediate reason to be dissatisfied with the chargeable person's return for any tax, it is quite possible that the return may be reviewed by the inspector at a later date and subjected to a more detailed examination sometimes referred to as a 'desk audit'. This examination may lead to questions being raised by the inspector with the chargeable person or with that person's tax adviser and, if the inspector is not satisfied with the answers, the case may be subjected to a full Revenue or 'field' audit, which will be carried out on the taxpayer's business premises.

Alternatively, the inspector may decide to subject a chargeable person to a full audit even where he has no immediate questions to raise. When a full audit is undertaken by an inspector, it is likely that all or a number of aspects of the chargeable person's tax and financial affairs may be examined until the inspector is satisfied that the chargeable person's tax liability is fully and correctly ascertained. It is a part of the scheme of self assessment that a certain number of Revenue audits are undertaken on a random basis as an 'incentive' to chargeable persons to file true and correct returns in the first place. As set out in the Revenue Commissioners 'Customers Services Charter', the Revenue Commissioners' Complaint and Review Procedures (see Revenue leaflet CS4 revised December 2012), the taxpayer can make a complaint regarding the conduct of an audit and obtain a review either at local level by the relevant District Inspector or Regional Director or otherwise by the principal officer in charge of reviews acting either alone or in conjunction with an external reviewer. Once a taxpayer has been notified of the time and date for the hearing of an appeal by the Appeal Commissioners, the review procedure will cease to be available in relation to the matter which is the subject of the appeal.

The Revenue Commissioners have issued a helpful booklet, 'Starting in Business'. In this it is stated that there are three main methods of selecting cases for audit as follows:

(a) computerised case selection;
(b) knowledge of industry practices affecting tax risk; and
(c) proactive system of intelligence gathering.

In addition Revenue initiate projects aimed at tackling tax evasion in specific industries. In such cases compliance levels in particular trades or professions are examined.

Only a small percentage of cases for audit are selected on a random basis (c five per cent of cases). The majority of cases selected for audit are based on risk factors. The cases are selected with the aid of software rolled out to all Revenue districts in 2006 – Review Evaluation Analysis Profile (REAP). This system focuses on the figures in a taxpayer's returns and accounts together with a taxpayer's history of dealings with Revenue, their compliance pattern and their lifestyle information across a number of years. REAP works in such a way that a profile is built up on each taxpayer. When the profile is run against a set of rules a score is assigned for each rule. The score allocated to each profile indicates a risk measurement or the likely success of that taxpayer's affairs being audited. In essence it identifies taxpayers most likely to be non compliant and assists Revenue in their decision of whether to audit a taxpayer. Revenue have stated that the bulk of REAP driven audits will be from the top 20 per cent of risk cases.

In some cases, the Revenue select particular trades or professions as the basis for an intensive screening exercise. The REAP system is also used as a means of gathering intelligence on a specific sector to identify where audit resources should be targeted eg sectoral projects such as the National Construction Sector Project.

F(No 2)A 2008, Sch 5, Pt 1 placed the 'Code of Practice for Revenue Auditors' which was introduced in November 1998 and updated in September 2002 and October 2014 on a legislative footing. Revenue issued guidelines in April 2009 explaining the effect of the changes on the 'Code of Practice for Revenue Auditors (2002)'. They envisage that the majority of audits will continue to be settled by negotiation of monetary settlement.

A number of definitions were introduced by F(No 2)A 2008 (TCA 1997, s 1077E):

> 'carelessly' means failure to take reasonable care.

A 'prompted qualifying disclosure' means a qualifying disclosure that has been made to Revenue in the period between the date on which the person is notified of the date on which a tax investigation or inquiry will start and the date that the investigation or inquiry starts.

A 'qualifying disclosure' means:

(a) for a situation involving deliberate default, a disclosure that Revenue are satisfied is a disclosure of complete information in relation to, and full particulars of all matters that gives rise to that penalty, and full particulars of all matters occasioning any liability to tax or duty that gives rise to a penalty;

(b) for a person acting carelessly but not involving deliberate default, a disclosure that Revenue are satisfied is a disclosure of complete information in relation to all matters that give rise to the penalty for the relevant period.

The disclosure must be made in writing to Revenue signed by or on behalf of the person and accompanied by:

(i) a declaration made in writing that to the best of that person's knowledge, information and belief all matters contained in the disclosure are correct; and

(ii) a payment of either or both of the tax payable in respect of the disclosure and interest on the late payment of that tax.

An 'unprompted qualifying disclosure' means a qualifying disclosure furnished to Revenue:

(a) before an investigation or inquiry had been started by them; or

(b) where the person is notified by Revenue on which an investigation or inquiry will start, before that notification.

A person is liable to a penalty where:

(a) that person delivers an incorrect return or statement which contains a deliberate understatement of income, profits or gains or a deliberately false or overstated claim in connection with any allowance, relief or credit;

(b) that person makes any incorrect return, statement or declaration in connection with any claim for any allowance, deduction, relief or credit and does so deliberately; or

(c) that person submits any incorrect accounts which contain a deliberate understatement of income, profits or gains or a deliberate overstatement of any claim in connection with any allowance, deduction, relief or credit.

(TCA 1997, s 1077E(2)).

A person is also liable to a penalty where that person deliberately fails to comply with a requirement to deliver a return or statement specified in the Tax Acts (TCA 1997, s 1077E(3)).

With effect from 21 December 2015, the date of passing of FA 2015 the wording of the penalty legislation depends on whether TCA 1997, s 1077E(2) or (3) applies. Where it is the former then the TCA 1997, s 1077E(11) states that the penalty is to be the difference between the amount of tax payable 'or could have been claimed' on the incorrect return and the amount payable 'or refundable' on the basis of a correct return. Where it is the former then references to claims and refunds are not present in the legislation.

Penalties are mitigated where the person liable to the penalty cooperated fully with any investigation or inquiry undertaken by Revenue. Penalty is mitigated as follows:

Category of tax default	*Net tax-geared penalty*	*Net penalty after mitigation where there is:*		
		Co-operation only	Co-operation including prompted qualifying disclosure	Co-operation including unprompted qualifying disclosure
Deliberate behaviour	100%	75%	50%	10%
Careless behaviour with significant consequences*	40%	30%	20%	5%
Careless behaviour without significant consequences**	20%	15%	10%	3%

* Where the difference between tax paid and tax that should have been paid exceeds 15 per cent.

** Where the difference between tax paid and tax that should have been paid does not exceed 15 per cent.

Where a person furnishes, gives, produces or makes any incorrect return, declaration etc, that person is liable to:

(a) a penalty of €3,000 where that person has acted carelessly; or

(b) a penalty of €5,000 where that person has acted deliberately (TCA 1997, s 1077E(8)).

Where any incorrect return, declaration etc is submitted neither deliberately nor carelessly and it comes to that person's notice that it is incorrect, then unless the error is remedied without unreasonable delay, the incorrect return, declaration etc shall be treated as having been deliberately made or submitted by that person (TCA 1997, s 1078E(9)).

Subject to TCA 1997, s 1077D proceedings for the recovery of any penalty shall not be out of time because they are commenced after six years after the date on which the penalty was incurred.

Where a second qualifying disclosure is made by a person within five years of that person's first qualifying disclosure the person does not benefit from the penalty mitigation outlined above. Instead as regards the second disclosure penalties are mitigated as follows: (TCA 1997, s 1077E(13))

Category of tax default	*Net tax-geared penalty*	*Net penalty after mitigation where there is:*		
		Co-operation only	Co-operation including prompted qualifying disclosure	Co-operation including unprompted qualifying disclosure
Deliberate behaviour	100%	75%	75%	55%
Careless behaviour with significant consequences	40%	30%	30%	20%

Where a third qualifying disclosure is made by a person within five years of the second qualifying disclosure having been made then penalties will not be reduced (TCA 1997, s 1077E(14)).

A disclosure is not a qualifying disclosure where:

(a) before the disclosure is made a Revenue official had started an investigation into any matter contained in the disclosure and had contacted the taxpayer about the matter; or

(b) matters contained in the disclosure have become known or are about to become known to Revenue through their own investigations or are within the scope of a public enquiry or the taxpayer is about to be linked publicly to the matters.

(TCA 1997, s 1077E(15)).

In the case of 'technical adjustments', ie where a taxpayer ultimately concedes on an argument of interpretation, the Revenue will seek penalties unless they are satisfied that the taxpayer has taken due care and that his position was reasonable. In deciding what is reasonable, the Revenue will look at the complexity of the law involved, the amount of legal and precedent material and the tax implications of the decision taken; clearly, the taxpayer who makes a genuine expression of doubt (see below) should normally be protected in this kind of case.

The benefits of a qualifying disclosure include mitigation of penalties in line with the table above, a guarantee of immunity from criminal prosecution and non-publication of details of the tax default in the public media. However, the Revenue will audit all prompted disclosures and a sample of unprompted disclosures. If as a result it is found that there are additional underpayments of tax over and above those initially disclosed, the benefits noted above will not be withdrawn where the additional amounts are not significant (an issue of judgement on which there is no firm guidance). If on the other hand, the disclosure is significantly incomplete, all of the above benefits will be withdrawn and the Revenue may consider instituting criminal proceedings. Against this, the Revenue will also consider cases for criminal proceedings where in their view a voluntary disclosure should have been made but this was not done. This puts the defaulting taxpayer selected for audit in an invidious position (albeit one primarily of his own making): he may be damned if he does not disclose and he may be damned if he does disclose (but fails to do so fully). It is arguable that the threat of criminal prosecution in this context acts as an inducement to self-incrimination contrary to the European Human Rights Convention: see **1.412**.

The Revenue Commissioners have made use of a self-review process in designated sectors, including the software industry, the licensed trade, the motor trade, estate and letting agency sector, auctioneering businesses and coffee shops. Under this procedure, the Revenue Commissioners write to businesses within a designated sector, inviting them to review their returns on a voluntary basis, paying attention to highlighted issues which have resulted in additional taxes being paid as a result of audits of similar businesses. The letter asks taxpayers who discover non-compliance to make a comprehensive voluntary disclosure together with payment of outstanding tax, interest and penalties within 60 days from the date of the letter. A number of the self-review settlements will be subsequently audited for accuracy.

In general the Revenue Commissioners will not initiate court proceedings for the recovery of fines or penalties, and will instead agree to accept a sum in settlement of the underpaid tax, interest thereon and the related fines or penalties (as mitigated). In *IRC v Nuttall* [1990] STC 194 the Court of Appeal held that the Inland Revenue were entitled to enter into back duty settlements without the necessity of first raising assessments. This was regarded as a longstanding practice which was a legitimate exercise of their 'care and management' function (see also *Cockerline & Co v IRC* 16 TC 1). The court also held that the Revenue were entitled to decide how much information they could reasonably expect to obtain in regard to a taxpayer's affairs and to make an assessment on that basis as to the tax payable (see *R v IRC ex parte Federation of Self-Employed* [1985] STC 260, discussed at **2.206**). This was distinguishable from the hypothetical situation where the Revenue agreed to take a lower sum of tax than that which was due and payable on the information before them (which would be *ultra vires*: see **2.206**).

The effect of a settlement is that when the taxpayer accepts the offer made by the Revenue authorities, a contract between them comes into being. It was held accordingly in *IRC v Woollen* [1992] STC 944 that, since the Revenue's rights under the settlement were purely contractual, the sums due to them had lost their identity as tax. It followed that the Revenue did not rank as a preferential creditor in respect of those sums (see **2.613**). It also follows however that the taxpayer is not entitled to seek an adjustment of the agreed payment under the 'error or mistake' provisions (see **2.111**).

A number of factors will be considered before a case is prosecuted. These include the likely expense of a trial, the need for deterrence (both personal and general) in relation to particular offences, the level of co-operation and disclosure of the taxpayer and the apparent seriousness of the case in comparison with post prosecution cases and other cases under consideration. For Revenue comments on the development of their prosecution policy see *Tax Briefing 36* and *43*.

Offshore matters

TCA 1997, s 1077E(15A) was inserted by FA 2016, s 56. This applies across the tax heads and applies from 1 May 2017. This section effectively withdraws, from 1 May 2017, the penalty mitigation arrangements, currently available to tax defaulters who make a qualifying disclosure to Revenue, in two situations being:

(a) where the disclosure relates directly or indirectly to 'offshore matters' and

(b) where the disclosure relates to any other tax default in circumstances where the person has, before the date of the disclosure, certain 'offshore matters' that are known or become known to Revenue and which are matters occasioning a liability to tax that gives rise to a penalty.

Under (b) if the penalty to which the 'offshore matters' give rise to does not exceed the lower level of penalty that applies where the default was careless in nature rather than deliberate, did not have significant tax consequence and the person co-operated fully with any Revenue investigation, the disclosure will not be affected.

Various definitions are brought about by TCA 1997, s 1077E(15A) including

> 'offshore matters' means any one or more of the following—
>
> (i) a relevant account held or situated,
>
> (ii) relevant income or gains arising from a source or accruing, as the case may be,
>
> (iii) relevant property situated, or
>
> (iv) any income, gains, accounts or assets, other than those referred to in (i) to (iii), arising from a source, accruing, held or situated, as the case may be,
>
> in a country or territory other than the State;
>
> 'relevant account' means an account reportable under the standard or, as the case may be, under the Directive, or an account of a kind reportable under the standard or, as the case may be, under the Directive;
>
> 'relevant income or gains' means income or gains reportable under the standard or, as the case may be, under the Directive, or income or gains of a kind reportable under the standard or, as the case may be, under the Directive;
>
> 'relevant property' means property reportable under the Directive, or property of a kind reportable under the Directive;
>
> 'Directive' means Council Directive 2011/16/EU16 on administrative cooperation in the field of taxation as amended by Council Directive 2014/107/EU of 9 December 2014 as regards mandatory automatic exchange of information in the field of taxation;
>
> 'the standard' has the same meaning as in section 891F(2).

That definition is as follows: 'the standard' means the Standard for Automatic Exchange of Financial Account Information approved on 15 July 2014 by the Council of the Organisation for Economic Cooperation and Development;

As can be seen from the above, the definition of 'offshore matters' is linked to the OECD standard for automatic exchange of financial account information in tax matters and to EU Directives relating to administrative cooperation and mandatory exchange of information in the field of taxation, but essentially covers any income, gains, accounts or assets, accruing, arising, situated or located outside of the State.

2.705 Publication of names of tax defaulters

TCA 1997, s 1086(2), (3) requires the Revenue Commissioners to compile and publish a list of the names, addresses and occupations (or descriptions) of all 'tax defaulters' (as defined: see below). This requirement overrules any obligation to secrecy imposed by the Tax Acts and the Official Secrets Act 1963 (see **1.204**) (TCA 1997, s 1086(3)). The list must be compiled for a 'relevant period'. A relevant period is the six months to 30 June 1997 and each successive three-month period. The list must be published in Iris Oifigiúil within three months of the end of the relevant period in question. There is no requirement for the lists to be published in the Revenue Commissioners' annual report, but the Revenue has the freedom to have the list published in any manner which they consider appropriate (TCA 1997, s 1086(3)). 'Tax' means any tax, duty, levy or charge under the care and management of the Revenue Commissioners. Similarly, any reference in the section to 'the Acts' is to be read as referring to any of the Acts under which those taxes are chargeable or otherwise levied. The term is also to be taken as referring to any instruments (for example, statutory regulations) made under the Acts (TCA 1997, s 1086(1)).

The section operates in respect of both tax and tax geared penalties for fraud or neglect and fixed penalties for non-filing of returns.

Following publication of lists of defaulters in *Iris Oifigiúil*, the Revenue Commissioners may publish or reproduce the lists in any other manner or format they consider to be appropriate. The Revenue Commissioners permanently display the name, address and occupation of any taxpayer who has been subject to a fine in court or Revenue penalties (with or without a court appearance) on the Revenue website.

A 'tax defaulter' – ie a person whose name, etc is required to be included in the published list in any year – is any person falling under any of the following headings (TCA 1997, s 1086(2)):

(a) a person upon whom a fine or other penalty was imposed by a court under any of the Acts (see below for the definition) during that year;

(b) a person upon whom a fine or other penalty was imposed by a court during that year in respect of an act or omission by the person in relation to tax (see below for the definition);

(c) a person in whose case the Revenue Commissioners refrained from initiating proceedings for the recovery of any such fine or penalty, but agreed instead to accept a *specified sum* of money in settlement of any claim by the Revenue Commissioners for any specified liability of the person concerned to any tax, interest thereon and any fine or other monetary penalty in respect of such tax; or

(d) a person in whose case the Revenue Commissioners, having initiated proceedings for the recovery of any fine or penalty, and whether or not a fine or penalty has been imposed by a court, but agreed instead to accept a *specified sum* of money in settlement of any claims by the Revenue Commissioners for any specified liability of the person concerned to any tax, interest thereon (except where such interest arises on Customs and Excise duties), and any fine or other monetary penalty in respect of such tax.

TCA 1997, s 1086 was amended by F(No 2)A 2008, Sch 5, Pt 2. Where Revenue accept or undertake to accept a settlement then they shall be deemed to have done so pursuant to an agreement made with the person and the agreement shall be deemed to have been made in the relevant period. This inclusion was made to ensure publication in a case where a 'tax defaulter' may pay the full settlement terms but argue that the payment is made without an agreement actually being reached with Revenue (note *McGarry v Revenue Commissioners* [2009] IEHC 427) (TCA 1997, s 1086(2A)).

A person is not however regarded as a tax defaulter under (c) or (d) above (subject to the amendments brought about by FA 2016, see below), and is not included in the published list, where the person made a qualifying disclosure before Revenue had commenced any investigation or inquiry, where the amount of the settlement (ie the amount of the tax, interest and penalty) does not exceed €33,000 or where the amount of the penalty included in the settlement does not exceed 15 per cent of the tax included in the settlement (TCA 1997, s 1086(4)). The €33,000 limit was increased from €30,000 by SI 643/2010 and applies to tax liabilities arising on or after 1 January 2010. With effect from 25 December 2016, being the date of passing of FA 2016, the monetary limit was increased where the total amount of tax, interest and penalties comprised in the settlement sum (or comprised in that part of the settlement sum relating to 'relevant matters', ie matters giving rise to a tax default not included in a qualifying disclosure), does not exceed the 'relevant amount' referred to in sub-s (4A)(a) (currently €35,000) then this is the new publication limit. TCA 1997, s 1086(4A)(b) was amended such that the Minister may, from time to time, by order provide, an amount in lieu of the relevant amount, or where an order has been made previously under this paragraph, in lieu of the amount specified in the last order so made. The latter option was taken in 2010 by reference to the aforementioned SI 643/2010.

Every person on whom a fine or penalty was actually imposed by a court under any of the Acts or on whom a fine or penalty was otherwise imposed in relation to tax (for example, on a criminal prosecution under the Criminal Justice Acts) must be included in the list, including cases where the taxpayer has paid a settlement in full. However, F(No 2)A 2008, Sch 5, Pt 2 set out that publication on the 'tax defaulter' list does not occur where the amount of a penalty determined by a court does not exceed 15 per cent of the outstanding tax, the aggregate of the tax, interest and penalty determined by a court does not exceed €30,000 or there has been a qualifying disclosure (TCA 1997, s 1086(4B)). However, with effect from 6 February 2011, where a person fails to pay the specified sum referred to in paragraphs (c) or (d) above, or where following a Revenue audit or investigation, the liability is determined by the Appeal Commissioners or a tax-geared penalty is determined by the courts, the amounts concerned may be published in all cases (TCA 1997, s 1086(2B)).

FA 2016 inserted TCA 1997, s 1086(2C) and (2D) for instances where Revenue enters into a settlement agreement with a taxpayer, or accepts a sum from a taxpayer which is the full amount of their claim, ie the full amount of the taxpayer's liability for tax, interest and penalties, without entering into a settlement agreement in circumstances where the settlement sum or the full amount of the claim, as the case may be, comprises of a liability to which a qualifying disclosure relates and a liability in respect of 'relevant matters' (ie matters giving rise to a tax default not included in the qualifying disclosure). In those instances, then notwithstanding that TCA 1997, s 1086(4)(a) would exclude that person from inclusion in the defaulters list on foot of the making of a qualifying disclosure, the taxpayer will nonetheless be included in the list in respect of the relevant matters assuming the publication criteria are met in respect of those matters.

The list of the tax defaulters must include, in respect of each person named in it, such particulars as the Revenue Commissioners think fit. These particulars may indicate the matter occasioning the fine or penalty or, if appropriate, particulars of the liability to which the person was subject. The amount of any interest, fine or other monetary penalty to which the person was liable or which was imposed on him by a court, may also be given (TCA 1997, s 1086(5)). The Revenue Commissioners may include a summary description of the default in both court and settlement cases.

Where a taxpayer requires the issue to be reviewed under the Revenue Commissioner's internal review procedures (see Revenue leaflet CS4 revised December 2012) an application for review must be made before the terms of settlement are finally agreed.

Division 3 Taxation of Individuals

3.1 Assessment

3.101 Introduction

Every individual who is a *chargeable person* for a year of assessment is assessable to income tax for that year under the self-assessment procedure applied by TCA 1997, Pt 41A and described in **Division 2**. In principle, an individual is a 'chargeable person' for a given year of assessment if he has any income chargeable to income tax for the year in question. For the exceptions to this principle, see the fuller discussion in **2.102** of when a person is, or is not, a chargeable person.

In the case of a married couple or civil partners living together and assessable jointly under TCA 1997, s 1017 or s 1031C for a tax year, only the spouse or nominated civil partner on whom the assessment is to be made is the chargeable person for that tax year (see *Gilligan v Criminal Assets Bureau* V ITR 424). With effect from 25 December 2016, being the date of passing of Finance Act 2016, a husband or wife who is not assessed under joint election can elect to be so assessed. This permits either spouse to file an online return for the previous year of assessment. However, the election will not apply where the husband or wife is a chargeable person and required to submit a return; this applies similarly for civil partners.

The joint assessment may be made on husband or wife in the circumstances provided in TCA 1997, s 1019 (see **3.502**). In any case where the joint assessment is to be made on the wife, she becomes the chargeable person required to make the return, pay the tax, etc. In the case where this joint assessment would alternate from year to year, the preliminary tax requirements for the assessable person will be based on the *couple's* liability for the relevant year.

In the case of a married couple assessed as single persons for a tax year, whether because they have elected to be so assessed (see **3.502**) or because joint assessment is not available (for example, due to their not living together or in the first year of marriage), each spouse is a chargeable person if chargeable to tax in his own right for the year in question. A married couple who have separated will also generally be treated as chargeable persons each in their own right.

The same considerations apply *mutatis mutandis* to civil partners following the enactment of Finance (No 3) Act 2011.

An individual may not be chargeable to income tax, but may be liable to the Universal Social Charge or the self-employed PRSI contribution for a tax year. As indicated under

'*Tax*' in **2.102**, self-employed PRSI [to the extent payable in respect of 'reckonable income' (any income other than Sch E income)] is to be treated for all the rules of self-assessment as if income tax charged by assessment. TCA 1997, s 531AT provides that any liability to the Universal Social Charge for a tax year in respect of an individual who is not a chargeable person for income tax purposes shall nevertheless be assessed, charged and paid in all respects, as if it were an amount of income tax, but without regard to TCA 1997, s 1017 (joint assessment of married couples).

In the rest of this division any reference to 'income tax' should, unless the context requires otherwise, be read as 'income tax' including the Universal Social Charge and self-employed PRSI. Similarly, the word 'tax' should be read accordingly.

The principles, involved in complying with the individuals' obligations under self-assessment have already been discussed in **Division 2**.

Division 3 deals with the main aspects of the taxation of individuals, principally in respect of their incomes. The main tax concerned is income tax, but self-employed PRSI and the Universal Social Charge are also covered (see **3.109**).

Division 3.1 describes the various steps to be taken to compute the amount of income tax payable on an individual's income including the ascertainment of total income and taxable income, the calculation of the income tax payable, the addition of the Universal Social Charge and the self-employed PRSI contribution (where applicable) as well the special rules applicable to certain high income individuals.

Division 3.2 is concerned with the various rules under which an individual is entitled to claim relief in respect of interest paid on borrowed money and the numerous restrictions now contained in the legislation which have the effect of significantly limiting the relief against income tax for interest paid (other than for the purposes of a trade or profession).

Division 3.3 outlines various personal allowances and reliefs given to individuals by deduction from their total incomes in arriving at taxable income or by way of tax credit against tax chargeable and details the conditions to qualify for these credits and reliefs. It also explains the small incomes exemption under which individuals with total incomes below certain levels, dependent on marital status and age, are not charged to income tax, as well as the marginal relief given if an individual's total income only exceeds the exemption limit by a relatively small amount.

Division 3.4 explains, the self-employed PRSI contribution, Universal Social Charge and Domicile Levy charged on the income of certain individuals.

Division 3.5 explains the principles which apply to the taxation of married couples, including the elections for single assessment and separate assessment, the treatment of separated spouses, the year of marriage and the year of separation or death.

Division 3.6 gives a number of illustrations of how an individual's income tax is calculated in a number of special cases (for example, widowed persons, the year of marriage, treatment of separated spouses, etc).

3.102 Total income and taxable income

Computation of tax payable: overview

The main stages in arriving at the tax payable for the relevant tax year may be summarised as follows:

(a) the ascertainment of the individual's '*total income*' for the year (the total of his aggregate income from all sources as computed under the rules of the relevant Schedules and Cases (see below), but as reduced by those deductions from income which the Income Tax Acts require to be deducted in computing total income: see **3.103**);

(b) the determination of the individual's '*taxable income*' for the year (his total income from (a) as reduced by any allowances or reliefs which the Acts require to be deducted from total income in arriving at taxable income: see **3.104** and also **3.111** in relation to the restriction of specified reliefs for certain 'high income' individuals);

(c) the computation of the '*income tax chargeable*' (TCA 1997, s 3(1)) (excluding the Universal Social Charge and self-employed PRSI) on the taxable income from (b) (see **3.105**);

(d) the setting off against the income tax chargeable from (c) those personal or general credits and reliefs which are available for set off only to the extent of the income tax chargeable (ie reliefs by way of tax credits such as personal and employee (PAYE) credits (see **3.106**) to arrive at the income tax payable for the year (TCA 1997, s 3(1));

(e) the setting off of those other credits which cannot give rise to a repayment (see **3.107**);

(f) the addition of the income tax deducted from charges on income to arrive at the *total income tax payable for the year* (see **3.108**);

(g) the computation of the Universal Social Charge and self-employed PRSI on reckonable income, the setting off any unused double tax relief against the Universal Social Charge, and the aggregation of the resulting amount with the total income tax payable from (f) (see **3.109**); and

(h) the deduction from the total income tax, Universal Social Charge and self-employed PRSI, of the 'full credits' (ie tax actually paid by the taxpayer and fully offsettable against his liability under (g)) to arrive at the *net tax payable* for the tax year or, if those credits and reliefs exceed the total income tax, Universal Social Charge, and PRSI, to arrive at the repayment of tax, ie *net tax repayable* due to the individual (see **3.110**).

In the case of an individual assessable jointly with his spouse or civil partner under TCA 1997, s 1017/s 1031C the spouse's or civil partner's income from all sources and total income are calculated separately and the spouse's or civil partner's total income is merged with the total income of the individual assessable to give a single total income figure at the end of (a) so that a single taxable income figure emerges from (b). The Universal Social Charge and self-employed PRSI are computed separately for each spouse or civil partner and the aggregate of their joint amounts due are added at (f).

'Total income' is defined as the taxpayer's total income from all sources as estimated in accordance with the provisions of the Act (TCA 1997, s 3(1)). The determination of an individual's total income for a year of assessment is made by aggregating his income from every source, as calculated and assessable for that year under the rules of the respective Schedules and Cases, and by subtracting the deductions and allowances which the Income Tax Acts require to be deducted in arriving at total income.

'Taxable income' is the term used in the Income Tax Acts to refer to the amount of the income on which an individual is chargeable to income tax for each year of assessment. It is arrived at by deducting from his total income the allowances and reliefs to which he is entitled and which the Acts prescribe are to be given after total income has been ascertained (TCA 1997, s 458(1)).

The correct determination of total income is important as certain allowances and reliefs are expressed as being subject to limitations related to the taxpayer's total income. It is, therefore, important to distinguish between those deductions and allowances which are to be made before total income is determined and the allowances and other reliefs made as deductions from total income in arriving at taxable income.

The income to be included in an individual's income from all sources (and his total income) is normally only the income to which he is beneficially entitled. He is not required to include any income received in a fiduciary or representative capacity, for example, as trustee of a settlement or as the executor of a deceased person. In certain circumstances an individual may, however, be required to include income received by minors or by the trustees of a settlement where he was the settlor (as widely defined) (see **Division 15**).

An individual's total income excludes any types of income which are exempted from income tax by any specific provision of the Tax Acts. A discussion of exempted income is given in **1.306**.

Income received under deduction of tax at source includes any income in respect of which the payer was entitled or required to deduct income tax under TCA 1997, s 237 and s 238 (see **2.302–2.305**). Taxed income also includes income paid or received through a banker or other person in the State entrusted with its collection or payment and assessable on that person under Sch C (see **2.309**) or Sch D (see **2.310**). Although usually referred to in the notice of assessment as 'taxed income', income under this heading is deemed for the purposes of assessing the individual's total income to be income chargeable under Sch D Case IV (TCA 1997, s 15). For the treatment of income received by the taxpayer as a beneficiary of a settlement or beneficiary of the estate of a deceased person paid out of income assessable in the first instance on the trustees or the personal representatives, see **15.305**.

Certain deposit interest from banks, building societies, credit unions, and the Post Office Savings Bank, is received by resident individuals net after the deduction of retention tax. The gross amount of all such taxed deposit interest (other than interest on special savings accounts) is deemed to be Sch D Case IV income for inclusion in the computation of the individual's total income for the tax year in which it is received: see **8.204** (TCA 1997, s 261).

Example 3.102.1

Mr Adam Tollgate is married and assessable jointly with his wife for the tax year 2016. He is in practice as a partner of a firm of solicitors (AT & Co), but has various other sources of income. His wife, Zeta, is an artist of repute and has been determined by the Revenue Commissioners as having painted works generally recognised as having artistic merit so that these and similar works qualify for the 'artists' exemption provided by TCA 1997, s 195 (see **5.701**). She also has certain other income.

Mr Tollgate will file his tax return for the tax year 2016 prior to 31 October 2017 giving full details of his and his wife's income and the other data required in the form 11, including the particulars of his wife's artistic earnings. Based on the income contained in that return as assumed below, the aggregate income from all sources of the couple should be made up as follows:

Mr Tollgate	€	€
Sch D Case II:		
Share of taxable profits of AT & Co (year to 30 June 2016)[1]	67,000	
Sch D Case III:		
Interest from government securities	1,916	

Dividends from UK companies[2]	1,200	
Sch D Case IV		
Gross taxed deposit interest (retention tax €574)	1,400	71,516
Zeta Tollgate		
Sch D Case II (profession as artist)[3]:		
Profits from sale of paintings €13,480 (exempted)	excluded	
Profits from sale of sculptures (not exempted)	600	
Sch D Case IV		
Taxed deposit interest (retention tax €1,025)	2,500	
Sch D Case V		
Net rental income	5,500	
Sch E		
Employee's salary and benefits (Orlando Holyers Ltd) (PAYE deducted €4,951)[4]	16,100	
Sch F		
Distributions from Irish companies (including dividend withholding tax deducted of €1,560)[5]	7,800	
Aggregate of income from all sources		32,500
		104,016

Notes:

1. Mr Tollgate's share of the firm's taxable profits (before capital allowances) for its accounting year ending in the tax year 2016 is treated as his income for that period.
2. The UK dividends included are the dividends actually received.
3. All the paintings sold by Zeta in her accounts year ended 31 December 2016 are similar to her painting works generally accepted by the Revenue Commissioners as having artistic merit. However, her sculptures have not as yet been so accepted. In consequence, TCA 1997, s 195 applies to exempt the profits attributable to her paintings, but the profits attributable to her sculptures are taxed normally. Zeta's exempt income remains liable to self-employed PRSI (see **3.402**), which would be payable directly to the Department of Social, Community and Family Affairs, via the special collection system. Note that Revenue issued a new *eBrief 56/13* on New Guidelines for the Artists Exemption on 23 December 2013.
4. It is assumed that no tax credits or standard rate tax band were claimed against Zeta's PAYE income other than the Employee Tax Credit and that income tax was applied at 40 per cent from the full €16,100, including benefits-in-kind. It is also assumed that Zeta's allowable employment expenses (see below) were not taken account for PAYE purposes. Her position is assumed to be an insurable employment so that the employed person's PRSI contribution was also deducted under the PAYE procedure. The Universal Social Charge on her relevant emoluments of €16,100 will also be collected under the PAYE system.
5. All the distributions from Irish companies received by Zeta this year are subject to dividend withholding tax at a rate of 20 per cent.

3.103 Deductions in arriving at total income

The deductions given in arriving at an individual's total income fall under two headings. First, there are the deductions which are 'specific' to particular classes of income, and which may normally be set off only against the income of the class to which they relate, so that the amount of the deduction in any tax year cannot exceed the income for the year of the class in question. For some of these items there is the possibility of carrying forward any excess to be set off against the income of the same class in the next tax year.

Secondly, there are the 'general' deductions which are set off against the aggregate of an individual's income from all sources. Before these general deductions are made, the income from each source included is reduced by any deduction which is specific to that source. Included in the general deductions are those annual payments paid under deduction of tax referred to as 'charges on income' (see below).

Deductions specific to particular types of income

The deductions and allowances which are specific to particular classes of income include the following:

(a) capital allowances available against income assessable under the appropriate Case of Sch D (see **Division 6**);

(b) losses carried forward under Sch D Cases I and II (see **4.402**);

(c) terminal losses carried back under Sch D Cases I and II (see **4.409**);

(d) losses carried forward under Sch D Case IV (see **8.205**) and Sch D Case V (see **12.107**);

(e) losses in a foreign trade or profession carried forward for set off against future profits of that trade assessable under Sch D Case III (and any terminal losses carried back);

(f) premiums under approved retirement annuity contracts or schemes (see **16.206**);

(g) contributions to exempt approved and statutory pension schemes (see **16.108**);

(h) contributions to PRSAs (see **16.3**);

(i) expenses of an office or employment (see **10.301**); and

(j) capital allowances available against income assessable under Sch E (see **10.305**).

Example 3.103.1

Continue with the case of Adam and Zeta Tollgate from **Example 3.102.1**. For the tax year 2016, they are entitled to the following deductions in arriving at total income:

Deductions against particular types of income:	€
Capital allowances 2016 (Adam):	
Share of AT & Co's capital allowances as adjusted (Sch D Case II)	2,440
Share of AT & Co's tax loss for Y/E 30/6/2015 c/f for set off in 2016[1]	1,720
Retirement annuity premiums (Adam)	5,200
Expenses re employment (Zeta)[2]	260
Capital allowances 2016:	
On commercial buildings in an urban renewal area (Zeta the lessor)[3]	6,100
Charges on income:	
Annual payments under deeds of covenant	
paid by Adam to incapacitated nephew (gross)	1,000
paid by Zeta to her mother (aged 80) (gross)	300

Dealing first with the deductions against specific income, the set off of these items reduces the types of income affected as follows:

		€
Sch D Case II (Adam)		
Share of profits		67,000
Less:		
Capital allowances	2,440	
Share of loss forward from prior year	1,720	(4,160)
		62,840
Less:		
Retirement annuity premiums[4]		(5,200)
Net income from source		57,640
Sch E (Zeta)		
Employee's earnings and benefits-in-kind subject to PAYE		16,100
		16,100
Less:		
Expenses re employment		(260)
Net income from source		15,840
Sch D Case V (Zeta):		
Net rents before capital allowances		5,500
Less:		
Capital allowances (limited to income) [5]		(5,500)
Net income from source		Nil

Notes:

1. Adam's firm had incurred a tax loss in the year ended 30 June 2015 (the 2015 loss) due to paying out a claim against the firm in excess of its professional indemnity cover. It is assumed that Adam had not obtained relief for his share of this loss in 2015, but that the €1,720 was carried forward to 2016 (see **4.4**).

2. The expenses of €260 were incurred by Zeta wholly, exclusively and necessarily for her employment with Orlando Holyers Ltd so as to be deductible under Sch E (see **10.302**).

3. Zeta had invested as a part owner and lessor in a qualifying premises in one of the Town Renewal designated areas and qualifies for the €6,100 capital allowances (see **Division 19** of the 2009 edition of this book).

4. The premiums of €5,200 paid as approved retirement annuity premiums are deductible under TCA 1997, s 787. The amount deductible may not exceed 15 per cent of the 'net relevant earnings' of €62,840, ie €9,426; no restriction applies in this case. The relevant percentage would be higher if Adam was aged 30 or over (see **16.206**). It may be noted that no deductions from aggregate income (income from all sources) will need to be set off against Adam's net relevant earnings (see **16.208**).

5. The deduction at this point for the €6,100 capital allowances on the buildings in the town renewal area designated area cannot exceed Zeta's €5,500 net Sch D Case V rental income, but see **Example 3.103.2** for the deduction of the remaining €600 from the income from all sources.

Deductions from income from all sources

The 'general' deductions, ie those which are set off against the aggregate of an individual's income from all sources, include the following:

(a) qualifying annuities, other annual payments, etc paid by an individual out of his income charged to tax and from which he has deducted income tax under the rules of TCA 1997, s 237 (see *Charges on Income*);
(b) interest paid on certain loans to acquire shares in or to lend to certain companies or an interest in a partnership (see **3.206–3.210**);
(c) Sch D Case I and Case II losses where claimed under TCA 1997, s 381 (see **4.405**);
(d) excess capital allowances of a trade or profession where claimed under TCA 1997, s 392 as an additional Sch D Case I or Case II loss for set off under TCA 1997, s 381 (see **4.405**);
(e) excess capital allowances of a lessor of industrial buildings or buildings treated as industrial where claimed under TCA 1997, s 305(1)(b);
(f) excess capital allowances of a lessor of machinery or plant where assessable under Sch D Case IV, if claimed under the proviso of TCA 1997, s 305(1)(b) (but this deduction is now generally only available in exceptional cases – see '*Non-trading Lessors*' in **6.305**);
(g) losses or excess capital allowances in a foreign trade or profession assessable under Sch D Case III, if claimed under TCA 1997, s 381;
(h) net rental income from leasing farm land in the State (subject to a maximum deduction) when derived by an individual over 40 (or incapacitated) under TCA 1997, s 664;
(i) qualifying expenditure by an owner on certain buildings of significant scientific, historical, etc interest treated as a trading loss under TCA 1997, s 381 within TCA 1997, s 482 up to 2011 at the latest (see **18.301**);
(j) gifts to approved bodies up to 31 December 2012 (TCA 1997, s 848A) or approved sports bodies (TCA 1997, s 847A) made by chargeable persons under the self-assessment system (see **18.304**; **18.305**);
(k) maintenance payments made by a party to a marriage following a dissolution, annulment or separation within TCA 1997, s 1025 (see **3.507**);
(l) excess capital allowances claimed under TCA 1997, s 305(1)(b) by a lessor of certain qualifying premises in designated tax incentive areas (see **Division 19** of the 2009 edition of this book); and
(m) gifts for public purposes under TCA 1997, s 483 (see **18.302**).

The order of priority between these various deductions can be important, because, for example, in some cases, any excess over the amount of income from all sources can be carried forward to future years. A loss claim under TCA 1997, s 381 (see (c), (d) and (g) above) which is matched to particular sources of income in arriving at total income (see **4.404**) is deducted before taking charges and other deductions from total income into account (*Navan Carpets Ltd v O'Culacháin* III ITR 403). Where there is no prescribed order of priority, it seems that the taxpayer may have the right to choose the order most favourable to him (note the comments of Park J in *Major v Brooke* [1998] STC at p 398).

As noted in **3.102**, annual payments are generally set off against income after all other deductions. However, the provisions granting relief for farm leasing income and for maintenance payments (see (h) and (k) above) apply TCA 1997, s 459(1), which gives priority to charges over these deductions.

Charges on income

Charges deductible in computing total income are those types of payment, ie annuities, other annual payments, patent royalties and certain mining, rents, etc from which the person making the payment is entitled to withhold and retain income tax at the standard rate and which are made wholly out of the profits and gains on which he is charged to income tax (TCA 1997, s 237) (see **2.302**).

The categories of individuals to whom effective transfers of income can be made by way of covenanted annual payments are extremely limited (TCA 1997, s 439) (see **15.404**). In addition, TCA 1997, s 242 generally prevents a deduction for annual payments made in return for the receipt of consideration which is not itself liable to income tax (TCA 1997, s 439) (see **17.305**).

Any references in this chapter to the deduction of charges on income are to be taken as a reference only to annuities, annual payments, etc which are deductible as valid transfers of income in arriving at the payer's total income. The amount deducted in arriving at total income in respect of any annuity or other annual payment is the gross amount payable before tax is deducted.

The tax which the person paying any such annuities or annual payments is entitled to deduct under TCA 1997, s 237 is said to be 'income tax which he is entitled to charge against' the payee. Since the payee receives the annuity or annual payment as taxed income (and is able to credit the tax deducted against the payee's own tax), the payer is required to add the tax which he has deducted in his tax computation.

The foregoing discussion relates to those annual payments, etc made out of income brought into charge to income tax. As indicated in **2.305**, the phrase 'brought into charge to tax' indicates the taxpayer's income as assessed to tax and on which tax is payable. In the case of an individual, the normal approach is to compute first his taxable income – ie his total income (after deducting charges on income) less his allowances and reliefs deductible in computing taxable income – and, then, to take separately the total charges on income and to calculate the tax on them at the standard rate.

Example 3.103.2

Continue with the case of Adam and Zeta Tollgate from **Examples 3.102.1** and **3.103.1**. Now that the deductions against particular types of income have been dealt with, the respective total incomes of each spouse can be computed. Each spouse's total income is determined separately before the two total incomes are merged:

	Adam	*Zeta*
Sch D Case II (solicitor):	€	€
Net income from source (**Example 3.103.1**)	57,640	
Sch D Case II (artist):		
Profits from sale of sculptures (not exempted)		600
Sch D Case III		
Interest from government securities	1,916	
Dividends from UK companies	1,200	
Sch D Case IV		
Taxed deposit interest (retention tax €574 and €1,025 respectively)	1,400	2,500

Sch D Case V		
Net income from source (**Example 3.103.1**)		Nil
Sch E		
Net income from source		15,840
Sch F		
Distributions from Irish companies (dividend withholding tax €1,560)	-	7,800
	62,156	26,740
Less:		
Deductions from income from all sources:		
Excess Sch D Case V capital allowances [1]		600
Annual payments (charges on income) [2]:		
paid by Adam to incapacitated nephew	1,000	
paid by Zeta to elderly mother	-	300
Total deductions	1,000	900
Total incomes	61,156	25,840

Since Adam and Zeta Tollgate have 'elected' to be assessed jointly under TCA 1997, s 1017 (as no election for single person assessment has been made), their respective total incomes are 'merged' for the rest of the computation of the tax payable for 2015. Since the joint assessment is being made on Adam, Zeta's total income is now deemed to be part of Adam's total income.

The joint total income for the rest of the computation is therefore determined as follows:

	€
Adam's total income	61,156
Zeta's total income	25,840
Total statutory income (joint)	86,996

Notes:

1. Zeta claims under TCA 1997, s 305(1)(b), to deduct the amount by which the capital allowances for 2016 (€6,100) on her leased town renewals area commercial buildings exceeds her Sch D Case V net rents (€5,500) in the computation of her total income for 2016 (see **Division 19** of the 2009 edition of this book).

2. Each of the two annual payments is payable under a seven-year deed of covenant. Payments to an incapacitated child (other than a minor child of the settlor) are fully allowable. Payments to a non-incapacitated elderly person are also allowable, but subject to a limit of five per cent of total income (which clearly does not apply here) (see **15.405**).

3.104 Allowances and reliefs: deductions in calculating taxable income

After the individual's total income (including, if joint assessment applies, his spouse's or civil partner's total income) has been determined for any tax year, the next stage in the income tax computation is to deduct from total income all the allowances and reliefs to which the individual (and, where relevant, his spouse or civil partner) is entitled to a deduction from total income in arriving at his *taxable* income for the year.

Some general points may be made here which are common to all the above allowances and reliefs. Firstly, TCA 1997, s 458(1) generally makes it a condition for the granting of these allowances and reliefs, that the individual submits a claim for the allowances or relief and makes a tax return in the prescribed form of his total income for the year for which the allowance or relief is claimed. However with effect from 25 March 2005 this requirement does not apply (unless the Revenue Commissioners otherwise direct) where a claim relates to the operation of the PAYE system or to repayments of PAYE to an individual who is not a chargeable person under the self-assessment system (TCA 1997, s 458(1A) inserted by FA 2005, s 24) (see also TCA 1997, s 459(3), (4), (5) and Sch 28 para 8 as applied by TCA 1997, s 458(2)). Further, with effect from 1 January 2008, the Revenue Commissioners may grant reliefs on the basis of information available to them (whether under TCA 1997, s 894A or otherwise) if they consider it appropriate to do so without the submission of a claim by the taxpayer (TCA 1997, s 459(6) inserted by FA 2007, s 9(1)). TCA 1997, s 894A (inserted by FA 2007, s 9(1)(e)) allows the Revenue Commissioners to request details from third parties of expenditure defrayed by individuals relating to their entitlement to reliefs under TCA 1997, s 458; the information must normally be provided in electronic form and include the PPS number of the individual and where necessary the third party is entitled to request that information from the individual.

Secondly, TCA 1997, s 459(1) applies, where relevant, to limit the deduction for those allowances or reliefs so that the amount thereof in any tax year does not exceed the total income of an individual net of charges. This makes clear that charges must be deducted in priority to personal allowances and reliefs.

Thirdly, TCA 1997, s 459(2) states that any of these allowances or reliefs may be given either by discharge or deduction of the income tax assessment on the individual entitled to them, or by repayment of any excess tax that may have been paid (due to the allowance or relief not being given in relation to any earlier tax payment). In practice, the allowances or reliefs are normally given as a deduction in the inspector's assessment, but should any allowance or reliefs not have been given in the assessment, the individual can obtain the benefit of the allowance as a repayment. There are only a small number of personal allowances which are granted by way of deduction from total income. These allowances are as follows:

(a) long-term unemployed allowances (TCA 1997, s 472A, see **3.321**); and
(b) seafarers' allowance (TCA 1997, s 472B, see **3.312**).

The types of expenditure for which relief is given as a deduction from total income in arriving at taxable income (for the tax year 2015) are the following:

(a) donations to certain sports bodies paid by self-assessed individuals (TCA 1997, s 847A: see **18.304**; **18.305**);
(b) permanent health benefit contributions (TCA 1997, s 471, see **3.317**);
(c) housekeeper allowance (employed person taking care of incapacitated individual) (TCA 1997, s 467, see **3.309**);
(d) subscriptions for qualifying shares in a company qualifying under Employment and Investment Incentive (TCA 1997, s 489, see **18.107**);
(e) expenditure incurred on the construction or refurbishment of a qualifying premises for use as the sole or main residence of the individual in a designated area (TCA 1997, s 372AR); and
(f) qualifying nursing home fees within TCA 1997, s 469 (see **3.315**).

Example 3.104.1

Continue with the case of Adam and Zeta Tollgate from the end of **Example 3.103.2** where their joint total income for the tax year 2016 is shown as €86,996. The next step is to deduct their personal allowances and reliefs to determine the taxable income for the tax year 2016. The following allowances are claimed in the tax return for the tax year 2016:

Employment and Investment Incentive[1]:		€
Amount subscribed for eligible shares in the tax year 2016		9,334
Total of personal allowances and reliefs	9,334 x 30/40 =	7,000

Adam's taxable income (including Zeta's income) for the tax year 2016 is now calculated as follows:

	€
Total income (joint) (**Example 3.103.2**)	86,996
Less:	
Personal allowances and reliefs (as above)	(7,000)
Taxable income	79,996

Notes:

1. On 22 July 2016, Adam subscribed €9,334 for eligible shares (qualifying ordinary shares) in High Quality Products Ltd, a company which has met all the conditions for the Employment and Investment Incentive (see **Division 18**). The shares were issued to him on 3 December 2015.

3.105 Computation of income tax chargeable on taxable income

When the individual's taxable income has been ascertained for the relevant tax year, the computation of his tax payable or, if appropriate, repayable is made. The steps in this part of the computation, and the order in which they are taken, may be summarised as follows:

Calculate income tax:

1. At standard rate on taxable income not exceeding standard rate band.
2. At 41 per cent on the gross amount of any deposit interest subject to DIRT.
3. At higher rate on taxable income in excess of standard rate band.

Equals

Income tax chargeable on taxable income.

Rates of income tax for individuals

TCA 1997, s 15 provides that individual's taxable income is to be charged to income tax at the rates specified in one of two tables set out at the end of the section. For 2015 there are two rates, the '*standard rate*' and the '*higher rate*'. The standard rate is 20 per cent and the higher rate is 40 per cent.

There are four 'tax rate tables' – one to be applied where the person assessed for the relevant tax year is a single or widowed person without qualifying children, one to be applied where the person is a single or widowed person with qualifying children (ie a single person child carer), one where the person is a married person assessable jointly with his spouse under TCA 1997, s 1017 or in a civil partnership and assessable jointly under TCA 1997, s 1031C and where the couple have one income, and one where both individuals have separate incomes. The single person's table is used for married persons assessable as single persons, as well as for single and widowed persons. A 'qualifying child' is a child in respect of which the taxpayer qualifies for a tax credit under TCA 1997, s 462B (see **3.304**).

The table giving the rates of income tax chargeable on the taxable income of individuals for the tax year 2015 is as follows:

	Taxable income	*Rate*
Single/widowed: no dependent children	First €33,800	20%
	Remainder	40%
Single/widowed: dependent children	First €37,800	20%
	Remainder	40%
Married couple: one income	First €42,800	20%
	Remainder	40%
Married couple: two incomes	Maximum €67,600*	20%
	Remainder	40%

*Not to exceed the sum of €42,800 plus the amount of total income of the spouse or civil partner with the lower total income.

Income tax chargeable on taxable income

The 'income tax chargeable on taxable income' for the relevant tax year is calculated by applying the standard rate for that year of income tax to the individual's taxable income so far as it does not exceed the relevant standard rate band (single person's, single person child carer or married person's, as appropriate) and then, if the taxable income exceeds the relevant standard rate band, by applying the higher rate of income tax for the year to the amount by which the taxable income exceeds the standard rate band.

In making these calculations, in a case where the individual's taxable income for a tax year includes deposit interest (other than in relation to a special savings account) received in the year subject to retention tax at 41 per cent, such income is charged at the same rate as the retention rate.

Example 3.105.1

Continue from the end of **Example 3.104.1** where the taxable income (joint) of Adam and Zeta Tollgate to be assessed on Adam for the year 2016 was worked out as €79,996. It is noted that this taxable income included €3,900 of deposit interest (subject to 41 per cent rate retention tax) – Adam's €1,400 and Zeta's €2,500 (see **Example 3.103.2**).

The computation of income tax chargeable on taxable income is as follows:

	€
€66,140* x 20%	13,228
€3,900 x 41% (deposit interest)	1,599
€9,956 x 40%	3,982
Income tax chargeable on taxable income	18,809

* €42,800 plus the total income of the spouse with the lower total income equals €(42,800 + 23,340 (25,840–2,500)) = €66,140.

3.106 Allowances and reliefs: tax credits

All personal allowances other than those discussed at **3.104** above, as well as certain reliefs in respect of expenditure incurred by the taxpayer, are given in the form of tax credits. The legislation distinguishes between 'personal tax credits' and 'general tax credits' (TCA 1997, s 3(1)). However, in reality, there is no difference in the treatment of the two types of credits.

Again, TCA 1997, s 458(1) makes it a general condition for these tax credits that the individual makes a claim for them and submits a return of his total income in the prescribed form for the relevant tax year; however with effect from 25 March 2005 this requirement does not apply (unless the Revenue Commissioners otherwise direct) where a claim relates to the operation of the PAYE system or to repayments of PAYE to an individual who is not a chargeable person under the self-assessment system. In addition, TCA 1997, s 458(2) provides that the tax credit cannot be used to cover standard rate tax due in respect of any annual payments which reduce the total income of the taxpayer. Further, the amount of the tax credit cannot exceed the amount of the individual's liability to income tax. In other words, the tax credit is non-refundable and also may not be offset against any liability to self-employed PRSI or the Universal Social Charge.

'Personal credits'

The personal tax credits available for the tax year 2017 are set out below (section references to TCA 1997, unless otherwise indicated):

Credit	€
Married and assessed jointly (s 461(a))	3,300
Single person (s 461(c))	1,650
Widowed person bereaved in tax year (s 461(a))	3,300
Widowed person – additional tax credit (s 461A)	540
Single person child carer (s 462B) (formerly the one parent family (s 462)	1,650
Additional tax credit for widowed parent (s 463):	
1st year after year in which bereaved	3,600
2nd year after year in which bereaved	3,150
3rd year after year in which bereaved	2,700
4th year after year in which bereaved	2,250
5th year after year in which bereaved	1,800
Age: married joint (s 464)	490
Age: single/widowed	245
Blind person (s 468)	1,650
Blind person (s 468) – both spouses or civil partners blind	3,300
Employee (PAYE) (s 472)	1,650
Dependent relative (s 466)	70
Incapacitated child (s 465)	3,300
Home carer (s 466A)	1,100
Earned income credit (s 472AB)	up to 950
Fisher tax credit (s 472BA)	1,270

The circumstances in which these personal credits are given are discussed separately in **Division 3.3**.

'General tax credits'

The categories of expenditure which qualify for general tax credits are as follows:

(a) fees paid for third-level education, approved college and training courses, etc (TCA 1997, s 473A);
(b) rent paid for qualifying residential premises (TCA 1997, s 473): see **3.313**;
(c) training course fees (TCA 1997, s 476) see **3.319**; and
(d) service charges up to 2011 (TCA 1997, s 477) see **3.320**;
(e) medical insurance (TCA 1997, s 470) see **3.314**;
(f) health expenses (TCA 1997, s 469) see **3.315**;
(g) blind persons – trained guide dog see **3.316**;
(h) long term care policies (TCA 1997, s 470A) see **3.323**;
(i) age-related credit for health insurance premiums (TCA 1997, s 470B) see **3.324**.

The same requirements are imposed by TCA 1997, s 458 as apply in the case of personal tax credits.

Example 3.106.1

Continue with the case of Adam and Zeta Tollgate from the end of **Example 3.105.1**. Personal and general tax credits are granted as follows for 2016:

Income tax chargeable	18,809
Less:	€
Basic Personal (Married)	3,300
Employee (PAYE)	1,650
Earned income tax credit	670*
	(5,620)
Income Tax payable	13,189

This assumes (as is clearly the case here) that the tax liability of the couple (assessable on Adam) will exceed €5,620.

*Maximum of €550 + €600 (Zeta Sch D Case II) at 20%

Credits fall into two categories. As noted above, both 'personal tax credits' and 'general tax credits' are generally only allowed if and to the extent that there is income tax chargeable on taxable income (ie *before* adding on the tax deducted from charges on income and *before* allowing any credits or reliefs against tax). These reliefs can do no more than reduce the income tax chargeable on taxable income (they cannot give rise to a repayment of income tax and cannot offset the Universal Social Charge or self-employed PRSI: see **3.104**).

3.107 Other non-repayable credits

Credits which may be set off *only* against income tax payable also include the following:

(a) the deposit interest retention tax suffered on deposit interest received from 'relevant deposit takers' (see **8.204**) (except where the individual or his spouse or civil partner is either over 65 or incapacitated entitled to a full credit, see below); and
(b) marginal relief for small incomes (see **3.322**).

In the case of credits for foreign tax (see **14.301**), the credit cannot exceed the income tax attributable to the *particular foreign income*. All the other credits mentioned above may be set off against the total income tax chargeable on taxable income. None of these credits may be offset against tax on charges or the Universal Social Charge or self-employed PRSI, with the exception of credit for foreign taxes in the case of Universal Social Charge charged on the relevant foreign income.

3.108 Tax on charges

The deduction in arriving at an individual's total income in respect of annuities or annual payments treated as 'charges on income' and how the person making such payments is entitled to withhold income tax at the standard rate (and always should do so) have been explained in **3.102**. Although these annual payments are excluded from the payer's total income and, therefore, from his taxable income, TCA 1997, s 237 requires the person making the payments to be charged to income tax as if the payments in question were not deducted.

In order to bring these payments back into charge to tax (so that the Revenue recover the tax deducted when the payments were made), the amount of income tax chargeable on the taxable income is increased by an amount equal to income tax at the standard rate (TCA 1997, s 16(2)) on the total of the charges on income which were deducted in arriving at the paying individual's total income. In the case of a married couple or civil partners assessed jointly, the income tax added in the computation is tax at the standard rate on the total of charges on income paid by both spouses or civil partners.

However, before the income tax deducted from charges on income is added in the computation, it is necessary first to deduct from the income tax chargeable on taxable income any of those credits and reliefs which are given only against income tax. In other words, the credits/reliefs against income tax are not allowed to produce a negative income tax figure before adding the tax on the charges on income.

The credits and reliefs given only against income tax are to be distinguished from those other types of credits for income tax already paid which are available to set off against all the tax payable and which, if they exceed that tax, give rise to a repayment of tax. Both types of credits have therefore to be discussed before illustrating how the tax on charges is brought into the computation.

Example 3.108.1

Continue with the case of Adam and Zeta Tollgate from the point reached at the end of **Example 3.106.1** where the income tax on the chargeable income was calculated for the period 2016. Two further steps may now be taken based on explanation already given, as follows:

	€	€
Income tax payable (see **3.106**)		13,189
Tax on deposit interest[1] (see **3.105**)		
€1,400 x 41% (Adam)	574	
€2,500 x 41% (Zeta)	1,025	(1,599)
		11,590
Add:		
Income tax on charges on income[2]		
€1,300 x 20%		260
Total income tax chargeable		11,850

Notes:

1. Although the retention tax on the deposit interest is income tax suffered, as neither Adam nor Zeta is over 65 or incapacitated, this credit is not permitted to give rise to any repayment (see **8.204**). It is therefore a credit against income tax deductible at this point.
2. The charges on income paid under the deduction of income tax are the annual payments under deeds of covenant (€1,000 gross paid by Adam to his nephew and the €300 gross paid by Zeta to her mother, see **Example 3.103.2**).

3.109 Computation of Self-Employed PRSI and Universal Social Charge payable under self-assessment

The computation of the tax finally payable by an individual for the relevant tax year or, where appropriate, the amount of any repayment due to the individual next requires the addition to the total income tax chargeable the amounts of the individual's (and, if the individual is assessable under TCA 1997, s 1017 or s 1031C his spouse's or partner's) liabilities to the Universal Social Charge and the self-employed PRSI contribution (see below) due under the Self-Assessment system to arrive at the *total income tax, Universal Social Charge and self-employed PRSI.*

The circumstances in which an individual is liable to the Universal Social Charge and the self-employed PRSI contribution are described in **3.101**. As indicated there, all Sch E emoluments are excluded from the income on which the Universal Social Charge and the self-employed PRSI (Class S) are charged by assessment (as distinct from being deducted under the PAYE system).

Example 3.109.1

Continuing with the case of Adam and Zeta Tollgate from the end of **Example 3.108.1**. It is now necessary to deal with the self-employed PRSI contribution and Universal Social Charge). The following are the relevant facts in the tax year 2016 as given in the earlier examples:

(a) Adam carries on a profession and has income assessable under Sch D Case II, is under 66 and has income in excess of €5,000. He is therefore liable to the self-employed PRSI contribution on his Case II income and his investment income. He is also liable to the Universal Social Charge as his aggregate income exceeds €12,012 *(see below).*

(b) Zeta has income from her profession as an artist, is under 66 and has income (*disregarding* the artist's exemption for this purpose) in excess of €5,000. She is therefore liable to the self-employed PRSI contribution on her reckonable income including her full artist's earnings. She is also liable to the Universal Social Charge as her aggregate income exceeds €12,012 *(see below).*

The liabilities of Adam and Zeta to the various levies are determined, using the income figures set out in earlier examples, as follows:

Self-employed PRSI contributions

The reckonable incomes on which the self-employed PRSI contributions are charged for 2016 are determined as follows:

	Adam	*Zeta*
	€	€
Aggregate of income from all sources (See **Example 3.102.1**)	71,516	32,500

	Adam	Zeta
Less:		
Capital allowances	(2,440)	(6,100)
Retirement Annuity Premiums	(5,200)	
Schedule E Emoluments		(16,100)
Add:		
Exempted artist's income (Zeta)	-	13,480
Reckonable Income	69,076	23,780

The amounts payable are therefore as follows:

	Adam	Zeta
	€	€
Self-employed PRSI @ 4%	2,763	951

Universal Social Charge

The relevant incomes on which the Universal Social Charge is charged for 2016 are determined as follows:

	Adam	Zeta
	€	€
Aggregate of income from all sources[1] (See **Example 3.102.1**)	71,516	32,500
Less:		
Capital allowances	(2,440)	
Case II Loss carried forward	(1,720)	
Deposit Interest subject to DIRT	(1,400)	(2,500)
Add:		
Exempted artist's income (Zeta)[2]	-	13,480
	-	
	65,956	43,480
Less:		
Income from Sch E emoluments included above (Zeta)	-	(16,100)
Relevant income for Universal Social Charge	65,956	27,380

The amounts payable are therefore as follows:

	Adam	Zeta
Adam	€	€
€12,012 @ 1%	120	
€ 6,656 @ 3%	199	
€47,288 @ 7%	2,600	
€ 65,956		
Zeta		
€2,568 @ 3% (€18,668 lower bands – €16,100 Sch E income)		77
€24,812 @ 5.5%		1,365
€27,380		
	2,919	1,442

Notes:

1. No deduction has been given for retirement annuity premiums, enhanced capital allowances or annual payments. The Universal Social Charge in respect of Zeta's relevant emoluments will be collected under the PAYE system.
2. Since Zeta's Sch D Case II income attributable to her paintings having cultural and artistic merit was excluded from her income from all sources for income tax, but is subject to the Universal Social Charge, it has to be added back here.

3.110 Full credits: final computation of net tax payable or repayable

'Full credits' represent income tax which the taxpayer has already paid (for example, under PAYE or as dividend withholding tax). These full credits may be set off against income tax, the Universal Social Charge and self-employed PRSI and, if the total of these credits exceeds the aggregate of the net tax payable, the individual is repaid the excess credits.

The credits for tax paid (or suffered at source) (the full credits) which are set off against income tax, the Universal Social Charge and self-employed PRSI and which, if the total of the full credits exceeds the total tax as payable (as reduced by the reliefs against income tax payable), give rise to a repayment of the excess, include the following:

(a) income tax deducted at source on taxed income (other than deposit interest subject to retention tax);

(b) income tax on Sch E emoluments from offices and employments deducted by the employer under PAYE;

(c) the dividend withholding tax deducted on Sch F distributions;

(d) in the case of individuals over 65 or who are incapacitated (but not for other individuals), the retention tax suffered on deposit interest from 'relevant deposit takers' (see **8.204**);

(e) the professional services withholding tax suffered on certain professional fees received in the course of a profession (or in some cases, a trade) (see **2.5**); and

(f) Irish tax deducted by the paying bank on encashment of foreign dividends (see **2.310**).

However, in any case where the individual assessed has failed to file a complete tax return on or before the return filing date for the tax year involved, the net tax payable is increased by the late return surcharge (see **2.110**).

Assuming that the individual assessed has paid preliminary tax as required by TCA 1997, s 959AN (see **2.104**), the amount so paid is deducted from the net tax payable as increased by any surcharge (or added to any net tax repayable) so as to give the 'balance of tax' due by the individual (or, if relevant, any balance of tax repayable to him).

Example 3.110.1

Continuing with the case of Adam and Zeta Tollgate from the end of **Example 3.109.1**. Apart from the information given in previous examples, it is noted that the firm AT & Co suffers professional services withholding tax on certain of its fees (see **2.501**). Adam's share of the firm's professional services tax borne in respect of the firm's year ended 30 June 2016 was €920, which is the amount available as a credit for 2016.

The final steps in the computation of tax payable for 2016 are as follows:

	€	€
Total income tax payable: See **Example 3.108.1**		11,850

Add:			
Self-employed PRSI contribution:			
Adam		2,763	
Zeta		951	3,714
Universal Social Charge:			
Adam		2,919	
Zeta		1,442	4,361
			19,920
Less:			
Full credits deductible:			
Withholding tax on professional fees (Adam)		920	
Withholding tax on Sch F income (Zeta)		1,560	
PAYE on salary (Zeta)		4,951	(7,431)
Net tax payable for 2015			12,494

The total computation for 2016 for the Tollgates now looks like this:

		Adam	*Zeta*	*Total*
		€	€	€
Sch D Case II (solicitor) Y/E 30/06/2016	67,000			
Less: Capital Allowances	(2,440)			
Loss B/F	(1,720)			
	62,840			
Less: RA Premiums	(5,200)	57,640		
Sch D Case II (artist):				
Exempt paintings	[13,480]		Nil	
Profits from sale of sculptures (not exempted)			600	
Sch D Case III				
Interest from government securities		1,916		
Dividends from UK companies		1,200		
Sch D Case IV		Nil		
Taxed deposit interest		1,400	2,500	
Sch D Case V	5,500			
Less: Capital allowances	5,500		Nil	
Sch E	16,100			
Less: Employment expenses	260		15,840	
Sch F				
Distributions from Irish companies (dividend withholding tax €1,560)		-	7,800	
		62,156	26,740	
Less:				
Deductions from income from all sources:				
Excess Sch D Case V capital allowances			600	

Annual payments (charges on income)			
paid by Adam to incapacitated nephew	1,000		
paid by Zeta to elderly mother	-	300	
Total deductions	1,000	900	
Total income	61,156	25,840	86,996
Less: Personal allowances (EII relief)			7,000
Taxable income			79,996
Income tax chargeable:			
€66,140 x 20%		13,228	
€ 3,900 x 41%		1,599	
€ 9,956 x 40%		3,982	
			18,809
Less: Non-repayable tax credits			
Personal tax credit (married)		3,300	
Employee tax credit		1,650	
Earned income credit		670	
			5,620
Income tax payable			13,189
Less: Tax on deposit interest			
Adam		574	
Zeta		1,025	(1,599)
			11,590
Add: Income Tax on charges on income			260
Total income tax payable			11,850
Add:			
Self-employed PRSI contribution:			
Adam		2,763	
Zeta		951	3,714
Universal Social Charge			
Adam		2,919	
Zeta		1,442	4,361
			19,925
Less:			
Full credits deductible:			
Withholding tax on professional fees (Adam)		920	
Withholding tax on Sch F income (Zeta)		1,560	
PAYE on salary (Zeta)		4,951	(7,431)
Net tax payable for 2015			12,494

It may be noted that the limitation on specified reliefs for high income individuals will not apply to Adam and Zeta (see **3.111**).

3.111 High Earners Restriction (HER) – Limitation on specified reliefs for high income individuals

With effect from the tax year 2007, TCA 1997, Pt 15, Ch 2A, together with Sch 25B and Sch 25C inserted by FA 2006, s 17 and as extensively amended and supplemented by FA 2007, s 18 and amended by FA 2010, s 23, FA 2012, s 16 and F(No 2)A 2013, s 16 and s 28, provide for a potential limitation on the effectiveness of various *specified* tax reliefs claimed by an individual (but *not* a trust or other body liable to income tax) whose '*adjusted income*' (ie his taxable income computed after adding back all those reliefs) is in excess of €125,000. The amount of the specified reliefs will be effectively limited to the greater of €80,000 and 20 per cent of the adjusted income. Any excess of the reliefs over this amount will be deemed to be an additional amount of income chargeable under Sch D Case IV liable at the appropriate rates of tax; however the excess will not be included in total income and will (naturally) be excluded from any of the calculations used in arriving at the amount to be finally taxed under Sch D Case IV (ensuring beyond doubt that no circularity of definition arises) (TCA 1997, s 485G(3)(a)).

The normal provisions relating to assessment, collection and recovery (including interest on late payment of tax) apply to the tax so charged (TCA 1997, s 485G(3)(b)); these provisions will apply, equally together with the right of the Revenue officer to make estimates to the best of his judgement, where no assessment would otherwise have been made in the absence of TCA 1997, Pt 15, Ch 2A (TCA 1997, s 485G(3)(c)).

Where the provisions apply, their effect is to ensure that the individual's minimum effective tax rate in respect of his adjusted income is in the order of 30 per cent. These provisions disregard 'ring-fenced income', ie deposit interest subject to DIRT (see **8.204**), qualifying foreign deposit account interest, income and gains in respect of foreign policies (other than personal portfolio policies) issued from an offshore state which have been correctly returned in accordance with TCA 1997, s 730J(1)(a)(i) clauses (I); (II)(B) or s 730K(1)(b) or income and gains in respect of offshore funds issued from an offshore state which have been correctly returned to tax in accordance with TCA 1997, s 747D(a)(i) or 747E(1)(b) (see **17.407**).

Any unused specified reliefs ('excess relief') will be carried forward against the total income of future tax years, earliest years first, but will be subject to the TCA 1997, Pt 15, Ch 2A restriction in those years. The carry forward of excess relief is given after all other reliefs have been claimed, and excess relief for earlier tax years is given in priority over excess relief arising in later years (TCA 1997, s 485F). Provision is made to ensure that the tax payer cannot find any arguments that part of the adjustment relates to exempt income and thus cannot be taxed or that he is not a chargeable person where all his income would be otherwise exempt (TCA 1997, s 485G(3). The provisions of TCA 1997, Pt 15, Ch 2A will not prevent a claim for repayment of DIRT under TCA 1997, s 267(3) (see **8.204**) (TCA 1997, s 485G(1)). See **6.108** for a discussion on the restriction of unused capital allowances forward and the guillotine of capital allowances. As discussed in **6.108** capital allowances claimed but restricted because of the HER are not subject to the guillotine.

The specified reliefs are set out in TCA 1997, Sch 25B and include:

(a) the exemptions applicable to patent royalties (applied for income received prior to 24 November 2010) (see **8.305**), stallion fees (exemption applied to 31 July 2008) (see **7.305**), greyhound stud fees (exemption applied to 31 July 2008) (see **7.307**), occupation of commercial woodlands (see **7.401**, **7.402**) (as respects profits or gains arising before 1 January 2016), corporate distributions from related income under those categories; distributions out of certain mining operations and qualifying earnings of writers, composers and artists (see **5.701**);

(b) reliefs for investments in qualifying films (applies for investments made up to 31 December 2014) and Employment and Investment Incentive companies except in respect of investments for the three-year period from 16 October 2013. (see **18.1**);

(c) deductions for donations to approved bodies up to 31 December 2012 and certain sports bodies, expenditure on significant buildings, etc (see **18.3**);

(d) relief for interest paid on qualifying loans to invest in companies or partnerships (see **3.2**);

(e) capital allowances under the various tax incentive schemes (see **Division 18**) as well as accelerated allowances in respect of hotels, holiday cottages, nursing homes, convalescent homes, qualifying hospitals, sports injury clinics, mental health care centres, qualifying residential units and childcare facilities; and

(f) rental or trading losses created by claims for allowances under (e) or double rent relief (see **Division 18)** will also be treated as specified reliefs.

There are provisions to ensure that any restriction of reliefs under TCA 1997, Pt 15, Ch 2A will not affect the calculation of industrial buildings allowances (or exceptionally wear and tear allowances on plant and machinery) but a proportionate measure of relief is provided where a balancing charge arises in respect of buildings and structures where the related allowances have been restricted. In the first instance, for the purposes of the rules governing capital allowances, the amount of any specified relief used by an individual will be determined without regard to the recalculation of taxable income under TCA 1997, s 485E (TCA 1997, s 485G)(2)(a)(i)); nor will the application of TCA 1997, Pt 15, Ch 2A affect the amount of any specified relief which is available for carry forward to future tax years (TCA 1997, s 485G)(2)(a)(iv)). The calculation of the tax written down value ('amount unallowed') of plant and machinery under TCA 1997, s 292 in the case of a specified relief is not to take account of the operation of TCA 1997, Pt 15, Ch 2A for any tax year, ie the unallowed amount will reflect the allowances claimed irrespective of any subsequent recalculation of taxable income (TCA 1997, s 485G(2)(a)(ii)).

The application of TCA 1997, Pt 15, Ch 2A to a specified relief for any tax year is not to affect the determination of a balancing charge or balancing allowance on disposal etc of a building or structure (as computed in accordance with TCA 1997, s 274, including buildings etc located in tax incentive areas (see **Division 19** of the 2009 edition of this book) to which s 274 is applied) (TCA 1997, s 485G(2)(a)(iii)). However, the amount of any such balancing charge will be reduced by an amount calculated as shown below (hereafter 'the s 485 reduction') (TCA 1997, s 485G(2)(a)(iii)). Where the s 485 reduction applies, the sum of: (I) the amount of the individual's excess relief for the year in which the balancing charge arises plus (II) the amount of any excess relief carried forward to that year and not deducted for that year will be reduced by the amount of the s 485 reduction, ie the benefit of the reduced balancing charge will be effectively offset against the amount of excess relief available for carry forward to future years (TCA 1997, s 485G(2)(a)(iii)). The amount of the s 485 reduction is equal to the lesser of:

(I) the amount of the individual's excess relief carried forward to the year in which the balancing charge arises and which is not deducted or not fully deducted for that year, before taking account any reduction of the balancing charge above; and

(II) an amount equal to the sum of the amounts determined in the formula immediately below for each tax year for which:

(a) TCA 1997, s 485E (recalculation of taxable income) applied to the individual, *and*

(b) an allowance was made to the individual for the building or structure in respect of which the balancing charge arises.

The formula is as follows:

A x (E/S)

Where:

A is the amount of the allowance made to the individual for a year;

E is the amount of the individual's excess relief for that year; and

S is the individual's aggregate of the specified reliefs for that year.

In effect therefore, the balancing charge will be reduced by the aggregate of the amounts by which the capital allowances claimed on the building etc have been restricted in prior years (based on the proportion of excess relief to total specified reliefs in each year); however, the reduction cannot exceed the amount of excess relief carried forward to the year in question and still unused.

With effect for balancing charges arising on or after 1 January 2012 under TCA 1997, s 274 on the disposal etc of a building, any unused capital allowances carried forward from prior years by virtue of either TCA 1997, s 304 or s 306 which are reduced to reduce the amount of the balancing charge will not be treated as specified reliefs and will be disregarded in computing the adjusted income for the tax year concerned.

A guillotine on the ability to claim certain unused capital allowances was introduced under TCA 1997, s 409G (see **6.108**) and this will prohibit an individual from carrying forward unused capital allowances beyond 31 December 2014 where the tax life of the building has expired.

F(No 2)A 2013, s 16 amends Sch 25B in relation to Investments made under the Employment and Investment Incentive (EII) scheme so that they will not be subject to the restriction where the shares are subscribed for in the period 16 October 2013 to 31 December 2016. This three-year break is in order to stimulate investment in small to medium businesses (see Revenue *eBrief 75/14*).

In addition capital allowances claimed by non-active traders (passive investor) in a leasing trade in respect of plant and machinery used in manufacturing trades will be subject to the high earners restriction with effect from 1 January 2014.

The TCA 1997, Pt 15, Ch 2A restriction will not impact on such items as normal claims for expenses or wear and tear allowances on plant and machinery in relation to business or rental activities nor on any losses arising therefrom. Routine claims for health expenses (see **3.315**) and entitlements to personal tax credits will not be affected. Claims for double tax relief will also not be restricted.

TCA 1997, s 485C(3) sets out the detailed provisions regarding the order of set-off for the purposes of TCA 1997, Pt 15, Ch 2A, where there are both specified and non-specified reliefs being claimed, as follows:

(a) where it is expressly provided that certain ('primary' hereafter) capital allowances must be offset in priority to other ('secondary' hereafter) capital allowances, the order of set off will be as follows:

- primary/non-specified,

- primary/specified,
- secondary/non-specified,
- secondary/specified;

(b) rental expenses specifically mentioned in TCA 1997, s 97 will be offset in priority to specified reliefs which are also given effect by way of a deduction under that section;

(c) non-specified reliefs granted as deductions from total income will be offset in priority to specified reliefs so granted;

(d) loss relief which is not attributable to a specified relief will be offset in priority to loss relief attributable to a specified relief;

(e) double rent relief under TCA 1997, ss 324, 333, 345, 354 or Sch 32 para 13 (see **Division 19** of the 2009 edition of this book).

Accordingly, non-specified reliefs will generally be applied in priority to specified reliefs; thus where there are surplus reliefs to be carried forward these will generally be attributed to specified reliefs in priority to non-specified reliefs, which will usually be favourable to the taxpayer. See **6.110** for a discussion on the order of set-off of capital allowances forward.

The author's interpretation of the effect of TCA 1997, s 485C(3) is that the benefit of unrestricted loss relief can be denied where there is also a claim for specified property reliefs. Revenue's operation manual 15.02a.06 notes at para 4.5 as follows: 'Each category of relief or deduction must be looked at separately. Within each category, non-specified reliefs must be used before specified reliefs. No comparison should be made between categories of relief. Section 485C(3) does not provide that non-specified reliefs in general should be used before specified reliefs. Indeed, given that some reliefs are given in charging income, others in assessing income and others as deductions from, or in computing, total income, it would create an absurdity to attempt to do otherwise. Section 485C(3) is very specific in only providing for priority within each individual category of relief or deduction.'

If we take the example of an individual who has Case V income of €1m, Specified Case V Capital allowances of €600,000 and unrestricted Case I trading losses of €1m. Firstly the computation must be prepared in the normal manner without reference to the TCA 1997, Pt 15, Ch 2A. Assuming a sideways offset for Case I losses this would give the following:

	€
Case I	0
Case V	1,000,000
Case V Capital Allowances	(600,000)
S 381 Relief	(400,000)
Taxable Income	0

The effect of the HER would be to limit the claim for Case V capital allowances to €120,000 leaving adjusted taxable income of €480,000. In other words it is not possible to claim additional TCA 1997, s 381 relief to reduce taxable income to zero. However it is understood that Revenue have in the past allowed a claim to TCA 1997, s 381 relief in priority to a claim for specified Case V capital allowances so that the taxable income is zero and there is no adjustment to taxable income under the HER.

The first step in applying the test is to compute the amount of the '*Adjusted Income*' using the statutory formula:

$$A = (T + S) - R,$$

Where:

T is the amount of the individual's taxable income for the tax year determined on the basis that:

(a) TCA 1997, Pt 15, Ch 2A itself does not apply (except for any 'excess relief' brought forward from prior tax years under TCA 1997, s 485F, ie taxable income is computed net of excess reliefs carried forward and any specified reliefs for the year), and

(b) where the individual is a married person who is not taxed as a single person under TCA 1997, s 1016 (see **3.503**), he is subject to the special rules set out in TCA 1997, s 485FA which disapply the aggregation of total income normally applicable to jointly assessed couples (see *Married Persons* below);

S is the aggregate of the amount of the specified reliefs used to reduce taxable income or to exempt otherwise taxable income for the tax year (TCA 1997, s 485E); and

R is the amount of the individual's ring-fenced income if any, for the tax year.

The 'Income Threshold Amount' must also be ascertained, namely:

(a) €125,000; or

(b) in a case where the individual's income for the tax year includes ring-fenced income and 'A' is less than €400,000, the amount determined by the formula:

$$€125,000 \times A/(B),$$

where B = T+ S (TCA 1997, s 485C(1)).

TCA 1997, Pt 15, Ch 2A will only apply if: (i) A (Adjusted Income) is at least equal to the income threshold amount, *and* S is at least equal to the 'Relief Threshold Amount', ie €80,000; ignoring ring-fenced income such as deposit interest subject to DIRT, this means that the provisions cannot bite where either adjusted income is less than €125,000 *or* the aggregate specified reliefs are less than €80,000. Furthermore, the provisions will not apply unless 20 per cent of A is at least equal to S. Thus, it is possible to reduce 'A', ie adjusted income (income before taking into account any specified reliefs), by up to 20 per cent without incurring any adjustment to taxable income under TCA 1997, Pt 15, Ch 2A (TCA 1997, s 485D).

In all other cases, taxable income must be recalculated in accordance with the formula:

$$T + (S - Y)$$

where:

T is as defined above but with the added assumption that TCA 1997, s 485FA does not apply;

S is as defined above;

Y is the greater of:

(i) the relief threshold amount (€80,000), and

(ii) 20 per cent of A (the adjusted income) respectively,

for the relevant tax year.

With effect for claims in any tax return delivered on or after 31 January 2008, TCA 1997, s 485G(4), as inserted by FA 2008, s 23, provides that the calculation of reliefs, deductions, credits or tax reductions which are dependent on the amount of total income, taxable income, tax payable or tax chargeable as the case may be, should be made prior to the recalculation of taxable income in accordance with the formula above. An example of this may be where double tax relief is restricted by reference to the Irish effective rate (see **14.306**) based on the taxpayer's total income before recalculation of his total income under the formula above. However, as a result of F(No 2)A 2013, s 28, the calculation of the Irish effective tax rate can now be computed by including the high earners restriction as taxable income, so as to increase the Irish effective rate and thereby increasing the foreign tax credit available. The amount of credits or tax reductions thus calculated will then be offset against the tax chargeable on the income as recalculated. The calculation of tax chargeable on the recalculated income is not to be affected by this provision. (see Revenue *eBrief 75/14*) (**Division 14**).

Another example of this would be that the calculation of R&D relief under TCA 1997, s 472D (see **10.115**) should be carried out before the high earners' restriction is applied but the benefit of the allowable amount of the R&D credit (as calculated before applying the restriction) should be given against the tax chargeable following application of the restriction. (see Revenue *eBrief 32/14* dated 1 May 2014.)

It is also provided that TCA 1997, s 188 (Age Income Exemption: see **3.322**) will not apply where TCA 1997, Pt 15, Ch 2A is in point. Thus, eg, a single taxpayer aged 65 or over who reduces his total income by means of specified reliefs to an amount below €20,000 cannot claim exemption under TCA 1997, s 188 if as a defence against the recalculation of his total income under the formula above.

Example 3.111.1

Mr Hugh Networth is a single person. Based on the income, deductions, tax credits, etc detailed below, his income tax computation for the tax year 2016 is as follows prior to the application of TCA 1997, Pt 15, Ch 2A:

			Specified reliefs	*Ring fenced income*
Sch D Case 1:	€	€	€	€
Profits of trade	580,900			
Less capital allowances (€12,200 on plant) €319,400 specified capital allowances	(331,600)		319,400	
	249,300			
Less retirement annuity premium	(40,000)	209,300		
Sch D Case IV:				
Deposit interest (retention tax €5,084)		12,400		12,400
Sch D Case III – foreign dividends (subject to 10% overseas withholding tax (€3,470)		34,700		
Total Income		256,40		
Personal reliefs:				
Permanent Health Insurance		(760)		
Taxable income		255,640		
Specified reliefs/ring-fenced income			319,400	12,400

Calculate income tax	
€33,800 at 20%	6,760
€12,400 at 41% (deposit interest)	5,084
€209,440 at 40%	83,776
Income tax chargeable on taxable income	95,620
Less:	
Single personal tax credit	(1,650)
Earned income credit	(550)
Income tax payable	93,420
Deposit interest retention tax	(5,084)
Double Tax Relief	(3,470)
Net income tax on taxable income	84,866

Applying the formula:

A= (T+S) – R

where:

T = €255,640;
S = €319,400;
R = €12,400.

A (Adjusted Income) = €(255,640 + 319,400) – €12,400 = €562,640. This exceeds the income threshold amount of €125,000. The amount of the specified reliefs (S), €319,400, exceeds the relief threshold amount, ie €80,000. Finally, the specified reliefs (S) €319,400, exceed 20 per cent of A = €121,528 Therefore TCA 1997, Pt 15, Ch 2A applies.

Applying the formula:

T + (S – Y)

where:

T = €255,640;
S = €319,400;
Y = €564,640 x 20%= €112,528 > €80, 000 = €112,528.

Taxable income as recalculated= €255,640 + (€319,400 – 112,528) = €462,512

Mr Networth's final income tax liability for the year must now be computed on the basis of the taxable income as recalculated:

Taxable income per TCA 1997, Pt 15, Ch 2A	462,512
Calculate income tax	
€ 33,800 at 20%	6,760
€ 12,400 at 41% (deposit interest)	5,084
€416,312 at 40%	166,525
Income tax chargeable on taxable income	178,369
Less:	
Single personal tax credit	(1,650)
Earned income credit	(550)

Income tax payable	176,119
Deposit interest retention tax	(5,084)
Double tax relief	(3,470)
Net income tax on taxable income	167,615

The effective rate of income tax payable on adjusted income (A) is €167,615/€562,640 = 30%.

The excess relief (the amount by which the taxable income for the year has been increased under TCA 1997, Pt 15, Ch 2A), ie €(462,512 – 255,640) = €206,872 will be carried forward against total income for 2016 after all other reliefs have been claimed for that year.

Note

The Universal Social Charge property relief surcharge will apply in these circumstances: ie €319,400 x 5% = €15,970 of an additional liability. See **3.404** for consideration of the amount that is liable to the USC property relief surcharge.

Example 3.111.2

Fergal Murphy has Schedule E income of €166,000 and deposit income of €4,000. He has an Irish rental portfolio and because of interest relief the aggregate of surpluses and deficiencies on each property give a net deficiency for the year. He has excess specified reliefs forward under TCA 1997, s 485F of €150,000 because of the HER. In addition he has specified reliefs for the year of €20,000.

	€	€	
Schedule D Case IV		4,000	R
Schedule D Case V		0	
Schedule E		166,000	
		170,000	
TCA 1997, s 485F Forward	150,000		
Unrestricted Specified IBA	20,000	170,000	S
Taxable Income		0	T
Higher Earners Restriction			
Specified Reliefs	170,000		
Ring Fenced Income	4,000		
Adjusted Income (T+S) – R			
Adjusted Income	166,000		
Income Threshold Amount (Note)	122,058		
20% of Adjusted Income	33,200		
Relief Threshold Amount	80,000		Y
Taxable Income T + (S-Y)		90,000	
Revised Taxable Income		90,000	

Note

Income threshold is €125,000 x €166,000/€170,000.

Married persons and civil partnerships

Where TCA 1997, Pt 15, Ch 2A applies to an individual who is married or in a civil partnership and the couple have made:

(a) an election under TCA 1997, s 1018 or s 1031D (including a deemed election under that section) to be assessed jointly to tax in accordance with TCA 1997, s 1017 or s 1031C (husband or nominated civil partner as chargeable person) or with the result that TCA 1997, s 1019 applies (wife as chargeable person); or

(b) an application under TCA 1997, s 1023 or s 1031H for separate assessment, then those provisions are modified. The net effect is that the taxable income rather than the total income of each spouse or civil partner is calculated on the basis that each is a single person and the amounts are then aggregated and assessed on the chargeable spouse or civil partner. The normal entitlement to married tax bands and tax credits is preserved. The purpose of this provision is to apply the TCA 1997, Pt 15, Ch 2A, restriction separately by reference to the adjusted income of each spouse or civil partner. Clearly, if each spouse or civil partner has specified reliefs of less than €80,000 in the tax year, no restriction will apply even though their combined reliefs may exceed €80,000.

Example 3.111.3

Facts as in **3.111.1** except that Mr Networth is married. Mr and Mrs Networth are jointly assessed under TCA 1997, s 1017. In 2015, his wife has self-employed earnings of €480,000 before claiming specified allowances of €30,000 in respect of a building used for her business and she also claims relief under a significant buildings investment of €30,000. She has no other taxable income or outgoings.

Mrs Networth has claimed specified allowances totalling less than the threshold amount of €80,000 and thus falls outside TCA 1997, Pt 15, Ch 2A.

	€	€
Mrs Networth		
Sch D Case 1 (net of capital allowances): €(480,000–30,000) =	450,000	
Less: Significant Buildings	30,000	
Taxable Income – Mrs Networth		420,000
Taxable income – Mr Networth as above		462,512
		882,512
Calculate income tax		
€67,600 at 20%		13,520
€12,400 at 41% (deposit interest)		5,084
€838,512 at 40%		321,005
€918,512		339,609
Income tax chargeable on taxable income		
Less:		
Married personal tax credit		(3,300)
Earned income credit		(1,100)
Income tax payable		335,209
Deposit interest retention tax		(5,084)
Double tax relief		(3,470)
Net income tax on taxable income		326,655

Finance Act 2014, Sch 3, para 1(b) made a technical amendment (to Part 1 of the Table to TCA 1997, s 458) which effectively means that the excess relief carried forward under TCA 1997, s 485F by a spouse to the extent that the benefit from the relief exceeds the tax liability of the spouse to which the relief relates may be used to reduce the income tax liability of the other spouse.

In the author's view the legislation previously did not allow such an offset in a year in which the HER applies and this appears to be an unintended effect of the legislation to date. The author understands that concessionally Revenue allowed the offset of excess reliefs carried forward by one spouse against the income of the other spouse in circumstances where the high income individuals restriction applies to either spouse in the tax year. Under the amended legislation the author understands that the offset of the excess reliefs against the income of the spouse will only apply where the income of the individual to whom the reliefs apply is less than the excess reliefs carried forward.

Example 3.111.4

	€
Income of spouse 1	500,000
Income of spouse 2	100,000
Excess reliefs c/f spouse 1	800,000

Here the income of spouse 2 will be reduced to nil by €100,000 of the excess reliefs carried forward by spouse 1. The relief claimed by spouse 2 will not be restricted as the income of spouse 2 is less than €125,000. Spouse 1 will have relief restricted to €100,000.

Example 3.111.5

Income of spouse 1	500,000
Income of spouse 2	100,000
Excess reliefs c/f spouse 1	400,000

In this instance while the relief claimable by spouse 1 is restricted to €100,000 the excess €300,000 may not be offset against the income of spouse 2 because the excess reliefs of spouse 1 do not exceed the income of spouse 1.

Revenue Operational Manual 15.02A.07 when discussing this matter and the ROS implications notes that 'Where an individual enters an amount for excess relief carried forward onto the Form 11 as deductible from his or her total income, our assessing engine treats that as deductible from the total income of both spouses/civil partners. Our assessing engine will transfer any amount unused from the spouse/civil partner who was subject to the HIER to his or her spouse/civil partner'. Before FA 2014 Revenue and indeed some practitioners took the view that 'excess relief' (as defined by TCA 1997, s 485C) carried forward by an individual could be deducted from the income of the individual and of their spouse even though the excess relief relates to reliefs which were claimed by the individual only. TCA 1997, s 485F(1) provides that where TCA 1997, s 485E applies to an individual, the excess relief shall be carried forward to the next tax year and the individual shall, in computing their taxable income before the application of TCA 1997, s 485E in that next tax year, be entitled to a deduction from their total income of an amount equal to the amount of the excess relief. In the case of a jointly assessed couple the interpretation being taken by some was that because, for example in the case of a jointly assessed couple where the husband is the assessable person, TCA 1997, s 1017(1)(a) provides that the wife's total income is deemed to be the husband's total income, this means that 'total income' in TCA 1997, s 485F(1), and in TCA 1997, s 485F(2), in the case of a jointly assessed couple includes both the income of the husband and the income of the wife and accordingly excess relief carried forward under TCA 1997, s 485F may be offset against the income of the husband and of the wife. The relief ultimately allowed to each would however be subject to the application of TCA 1997, s 485E to each.

TCA 1997, s 485FA(ii), which applies where TCA 1997, Pt 15, Ch 2A applies to an individual or their spouse or civil partner and the couple are jointly assessed then TCA 1997, s 1017(1) (TCA 1997, s 1031C(1)) is applied as if para (a) were substituted by the para (a) set out. The substituted paragraph is the same as the original paragraph (a) except the words 'taxable income' are substituted for 'total income'. This means that, for example in the case of a jointly assessed married couple, instead of a wife's 'total income' being deemed to be her husband's, her 'taxable income' is deemed to be her husband's. Therefore when TCA 1997, s 485F(1) and (2) provide that excess relief may be deducted from the 'total income' of an individual, where TCA 1997, Pt 15, Ch 2A applies to the individual 'total income' does not include his wife's total income. Pre-FA 2014 in the author's view the Revenue's position was not technically correct and the legislation did not allow excess reliefs carried forward in respect of one spouse (or civil partner) to be offset against the income of the other spouse (or civil partner).

The position would be different if say TCA 1997, Pt 15, Ch 2A does not apply to a jointly assessed individual for a particular year because for example the individual's income is less than €125,000. In such a case as TCA 1997, Pt 15, Ch 2A would not apply to the individual for that year there is no deemed amendment of TCA 1997, s 1017 so that the individual's 'total income' would include his wife's 'total income' and excess reliefs carried forward could be offset against the individual's total income and that of his wife.

Part 1 of the Table to TCA 1997, s 485(2) sets out the deductions which may be made in arriving at an individual's total income. Because TCA 1997, s 485FA, provides in effect that in the case of a jointly assessed couple the income of the assessable individual is deemed to include only the 'taxable income' rather than the 'total income' of the non-assessable individual, this could result in amounts which would normally be deductible against the total income of both individuals being only deductible against one spouse. To ensure that reliefs which are normally deductible against the income of either spouse (or civil partner) where a couple are jointly assessed, TCA 1997, s 485FA(vi) provides that where the benefit flowing from deductions specified in the provisions referred to in Part 1 of the Table to TCA 1997, s 458 exceed the income tax chargeable on an individual the excess shall be applied in reducing the income of the spouse or civil partner. In effect this means that although a married couple's, or civil partners', taxable income must be separately calculated for the purpose of TCA 1997, Pt 15, Ch 2A, where the reliefs which one individual is entitled to offset against their total income exceeds their total income the excess can be offset against the income of their spouse or civil partner. FA 2014, s 97 and Sch 3 Pt 1(b), amended TCA 1997, s 458 by including TCA 1997, s 485F (carry forward of excess relief) in Pt 1 of the Table to TCA 1997, s 458. FA 2014, s 97 contains what are described as technical amendments. In the author's view the change is more than a technical amendment but we understand this is confirmation of existing Revenue practice (although previously unpublished).

Generally taking account of the amendment of TCA 1997, s 1017, for the purpose of applying TCA 1997, Pt 15, Ch 2A, while the intention is that where individuals are jointly assessed that their taxable income should be recalculated separately under TCA

1997, s 485E, looking closely at the legislation it is not clear that this is what the legislation states.

Looking at TCA 1997, s 485E, it provides that the individual's taxable income shall be T + (S–Y), instead of being the amount which it would have been had TCA 1997, Pt 15, Ch 2A not applied. However 'T' in the formula is the amount of the individual's taxable income determined on the basis that TCA 1997, Pt 15, Ch 2A 'other than TCA 1997, ss 485F and 485FA' does not apply ie TCA 1997, s 485F and TCA 1997, s 485FA apply. However TCA 1997, s 485FA, in amending TCA 1997, s 1017(1)(a) provides that the spouse's taxable income is deemed to include the other spouse's taxable income. 'Y' in the formula is 'adjusted income' which is defined in TCA 1997, s 485C as being the individual's 'taxable income' determined on the basis that TCA 1997, ss 485F and 485FA applies which again would mean the spouse's income is also included.

TCA 1997, s 485FA was introduced so that the income of jointly assessed individuals would be calculated separately and the High Income Individual's Restriction would apply separately to each and so our reading of the legislation set out above would not achieve this result.

The Revenue are likely to disagree with this interpretation in that TCA 1997, Pt 15, Ch 2A applies on an individual basis and the reference to *individual* is used throughout the chapter such as in T, S and R in the formula for adjusted income in TCA 1997, s 485C. Similarly terms such as ring fenced income, income threshold amount and relief threshold are all defined in relation to an individual.

Self-employed PRSI and Universal Social Charge

In *e-brief 57/2007*, the Revenue Commissioners state that the Department of Social and Family Affairs and the Department of Health and Children have confirmed that neither the recalculation of taxable income nor the carry forward of excess reliefs from prior years under TCA 1997, Pt 15, Ch 2A will affect liability to PRSI. This follows because these adjustments only affect the quantum of taxable income for tax purposes and not total income as measured for the purposes of that levy. The same logic appears applicable to the Universal Social Charge, bearing in mind that a number of exemptions, deductions and reliefs are excluded in calculating aggregate income for its purposes.

Specified reliefs carried forward from 2006

In some cases, reliefs may be available for carry forward from 2006 in relation to capital allowances or loss reliefs under TCA 1997, ss 304, 305, 382 or 384 which will be regarded as attributable in whole or part to specified reliefs. In these circumstances, TCA 1997, Sch 25C provides a means for determining the proportion of the reliefs which are to be regarded as relating to specified reliefs for tax year 2007 and thus potentially exposed to restriction under TCA 1997, Pt 15, Ch 2A in 2007.

The formula which generally applies is:

$$RF \times (SR/TR)$$

In the context of TCA 1997, s 304 (unused capital allowances carried forward in relation to trade or profession):

RF is the amount of the relief carried forward from 2006;

SR is the aggregate of capital allowances which are specified reliefs granted in taxing the individual's trade or profession for the tax year 2006 and each of the three preceding tax years, excluding allowances brought forward from prior years under TCA 1997, s 304(4).

TR is the aggregate of capital allowances granted in taxing the individual's trade or profession for the tax year 2006 and each of the three preceding tax years,

excluding allowances brought forward from prior years under TCA 1997, s 304(4).

This formula therefore attributes capital allowances carried forward which are attributable to specified reliefs on basis of the proportion of capital allowances which are specified reliefs to total capital allowances over the four years ending in 2006.

In the context of TCA 1997, s 382 (losses carried forward carried forward in relation to trade or profession):

RF is the amount of the relief carried forward from 2006;

SR is the sum of (DR + SA).

Where:

DR is the aggregate of the amounts of the further deductions the individual was entitled to by way of double rent relief (under any of TCA 1997, ss 324, 333, 345, 354 and Sch 32 para 13) for the trade or profession for the tax year 2006 and the three preceding tax years, but the amount for each year is not to exceed (L – CA), where:

L is the amount of the loss for that year for which the individual was entitled to make a claim under TCA 1997, s 381 (loss against total income) for that trade or profession; and

CA is the amount of any claim made in that year by the individual for that trade or profession by virtue of the provisions of TCA 1997, Pt 12, Ch 2 (trading losses augmented by capital allowances); and

SA is the aggregate of the amounts of the capital allowances granted for specified reliefs in taxing the trade or profession of the individual for the tax year 2006 and each of the three preceding tax years excluding allowances brought forward from prior years under TCA 1997, s 304(4) and only including capital allowances, subject to a claim under TCA 1997, Pt 12, Ch 2 (trading losses augmented by capital allowances). This part of the formula is designed to isolate the element of losses carried forward referable to double rent relief and to capital allowances which are specified reliefs.

TR is the sum of (TL + TA), where:

TL is the aggregate of the amounts of losses eligible for relief under TCA 1997, s 381 for that trade or profession for the tax year 2006 and each of the three preceding tax years less the amount of any claim made in any of those years by the individual for that trade or profession by virtue of the provisions of TCA 1997, Pt 12, Ch 2 (trading losses augmented by capital allowances); and

TA is the aggregate of the amounts of the capital allowances granted in taxing the trade or profession of the individual for the tax year 2006 and each of the three preceding tax years excluding allowances brought forward from prior years under TCA 1997, s 304(4) and only including capital allowances, subject to a claim under TCA 1997, Pt 12, Ch 2 (trading losses augmented by capital allowances).

This part of the formula is designed to reflect the total of trading losses and capital allowances augmenting those losses for the four years ending in 2006.

This formula therefore attributes losses carried forward which are attributable to specified reliefs on basis of the proportion of:

(a) double rent relief claims and capital allowances augmenting trading losses which are specified reliefs to;

(b) total trading losses as augmented by capital allowances over the four years ending in 2006.

In the context of TCA 1997, s 305 (capital allowances carried forward in relation to Irish rental income taxed under Sch D Case V):

RF is the amount of the relief carried forward from 2006;

SR is the aggregate of capital allowances which are specified reliefs granted in taxing the individual's schedule D Case V income for the tax year 2006 and each of the three preceding tax years;

TR is the aggregate of capital allowances granted in taxing the individual's trade or profession for the tax year 2006 and each of the three preceding tax years.

This formula therefore attributes capital allowances carried forward which are attributable to specified reliefs on basis of the proportion of capital allowances which are specified reliefs to total capital allowances over the four years ending in 2006.

In the context of TCA 1997, s 384 (losses carried forward in relation to Irish rental income taxable under Sch D Case V):

RF is the amount of the relief carried forward from 2006.

SR is the aggregate of deductions available under TCA 1997, ss 372AP, 372AU (relief for lessors of qualifying houses in designated tax incentive areas) for the tax year 2006 and each of the three preceding tax years.

TR is the aggregate of deductions granted in calculating Sch D Case V income (including under ss 372AP, 372AU) for the tax year 2006 and each of the three preceding tax years.

This formula therefore attributes rental losses carried forward which are attributable to specified reliefs on basis of the proportion specified reliefs to Sch D Case V deductions over the four years ending in 2006.

In all cases there was a right to seek a different apportionment basis under TCA 1997, Sch 25C para 5. The taxpayer could have applied by notice in writing to the Revenue Commissioners for the amount calculated under the relevant formula to be replaced by an amount determined by reference to such longer or shorter continuous period before the tax year 2006, but always including that tax year, that in the opinion of the individual gives a more just and reasonable result. Following the application, the Revenue Commissioners must issue a determination in writing to the individual either accepting the amount or amounts on the basis proposed by the individual, or setting out an amount which is just and reasonable determined by reference to some other time period, or confirming the amount determined under the formula. If the individual was not satisfied with the determination of the Revenue Commissioners, he may by notice in writing given to the Revenue Commissioners within 30 days of the receipt of the determination appeal to the Appeal Commissioners. The Appeal Commissioners shall hear and determine the appeal as if it were an appeal against an assessment to income tax and all the normal provisions relating to such appeals will apply. F(TA)A 2015, s 41, which was subject to Ministerial Order (SI 110/2016 appointed 21 March 2016 as the day on which the Finance (Tax Appeals) Act 2015, came into operation), removes the reference to a rehearing at the Circuit Court and makes amendments for the provisions in that Act, see **2.207**.

Neither the Revenue Commissioners nor the Appeal Commissioners may have any regard to an application or appeal that:

(a) requires specified reliefs to have been given effect to before reliefs that are not specified reliefs, unless a provision of the Tax Acts authorises such priority, or
(b) requires that an amount be determined otherwise than is provided for by TCA 1997, Sch 25C.

Any amount which displaces the original amount determined by the Revenue Commissioners is to be treated thereafter as if it had been determined under the general provisions of TCA 1997, Sch 25C.

Requirements to provide estimates and other information

TCA 1997, s 485FB provides for additional reporting requirements in relation to TCA 1997, Pt 15, Ch 2A. Where TCA 1997, Pt 15, Ch 2A applies to an individual for a tax year that individual will always be regarded as a chargeable person for the purposes of the self-assessment system (see **2.102**) (TCA 1997, s 485FB(2)). He will be required to file by the specified return date, along with his tax return (as required under TCA 1997, Pt 41A, Ch 3) a full and true statement in a prescribed form (including statements delivered electronically or photographically) detailing for that tax year:

(a) the aggregate amount of the specified reliefs;
(b) the determination of those amounts;
(c) the estimates set out below; and
(d) such further particulars as may be required by the prescribed form (TCA 1997, s 485FB(3)).

Where TCA 1997, Pt 15, Ch 2A applies to both a husband and a wife or civil partners who are not singly assessed under TCA 1997, s 1016, s 1031B, then separate statements will be required from each on the same prescribed form, referred to as a 'combined statement' (TCA 1997, s 485FB(5)).

The provisions of TCA 1997, s 951(9) (no requirement to file prior to specified return date); TCA 1997, s 959I) (Revenue powers to certify a person as chargeable: see **2.102**) and TCA 1997, s 1052 (penalties for failure to make returns: see **2.701**) are applied.

The required estimates consist of the following (to be made to the best of the individual's knowledge and belief):

(a) the individual's taxable income determined as if TCA 1997, Pt 15, Ch 2A (other than TCA 1997, s 485F: carry forward of excess reliefs) did not apply;
(b) the individual's taxable income determined in accordance with TCA 1997, s 485E (recalculation of taxable income); and
(c) the amount of tax that should be assessed on the individual as a consequence of the application TCA 1997, Pt 15, Ch 2A (TCA 1997, s 485FB(4)).

A Revenue officer may make such enquiries or take such actions within their powers as he considers necessary for the purposes of determining the accuracy or otherwise of any details, particulars or estimates contained in a statement. He may also make similar enquiries in order to determine whether or not an individual who has not provided a statement is in fact an individual to whom TCA 1997, Pt 15, Ch 2A applies, In this latter case, he may require the individual by notice in writing to furnish in writing within such time, not being less than 14 days, details of each provision for which the individual is claiming tax relief for a tax year together with the amount of each separate claim and the particulars of each separate claim under that provision. However this provision will only apply to an individual who has made a return under TCA 1997, s 959I for a tax year and whose income, including income exempt from tax, from all sources and disregarding all deductions, allowances and other tax reliefs is equal to or greater than the threshold amount (TCA 1997, s 485FB(6)).

3.2 Interest Paid

3.201 Interest relief: general

The Income Tax Acts contain a number of different rules which enable a person who has paid interest on certain loans to obtain relief in respect of that interest in arriving at his final income tax liability.

The rules under which relief for interest paid may be obtained are summarised as follows:

Relief by way of deduction

(a) Against income from particular sources:

- (i) interest on money borrowed for a trade or profession deductible under the ordinary rules of Sch D Cases I and II (see **5.315**);
- (ii) interest paid on money borrowed for the purchase, improvement or repair of premises situated in the State if and to the extent deductible under the rules of Sch D Case V (see **12.104**); and
- (iii) interest paid on money borrowed for the purchase, improvement or repair of premises situated outside the State if and to the extent deductible from the rental and related income taxable under Sch D Case III (see **13.202**).

(b) Against total income:

- (i) interest on loans to acquire shares and other interests in companies where deductible under TCA 1997, s 248 (see **3.206–3.207**); and
- (ii) interest on loans to acquire certain interests in partnerships where deductible under TCA 1997, s 253 (see **3.208**), subject to restrictions (see **3.203**).

Relief by way of tax relief at source or tax credit

Relief at the appropriate percentage applies to interest on certain qualifying home loans under TCA 1997, s 244. This division deals firstly with the circumstances in which the relief may be claimed, the limits to the relief and the additional relief which may be available for interest on certain bridging loans (see **3.202–3.204**). The relief is only available for interest on qualifying loans in connection with a 'qualifying residence' as defined. For the full definition of a 'qualifying loan' and a 'qualifying residence', see **3.202**. The restrictions affecting mortgage interest relief are discussed in detail in **3.203**. The interaction of the 'preferential loan' rules and the relief for home loan interest is dealt with in **3.205**.

TCA 1997, s 244A introduced a system with effect from 1 January 2002 whereby tax relief on most loans qualifying for relief under TCA 1997, s 244 is granted at source. The loan repayment deducted by the lender from the bank account of the borrower is net of tax relief at rates varying between 15 per cent and 30 per cent (prior to 2009, always at the standard rate of tax on the qualifying interest).

The legislation is supported by regulations (SI 558/2001) which govern the actual operation of the scheme. The regulations are quite broad and allow the Revenue Commissioners and individual lending institutions to agree certain administrative measures to ensure smooth operation of the scheme. FA 2009, s 4 inserted TCA 1997, s 244A(7) which permits the Revenue Commissioners to require a lending institution to furnish such information as it requires in order to determine the amount of relief due in relation to qualifying loans and to administer the provisions of the section properly. The information so provided may not be used for any other purpose. However, the rules for computing the amount of interest which will qualify for relief at source are based on the general rules set out in TCA 1997, s 244.

TCA 1997, s 244A(1)(b) effectively provides that relief in respect of qualifying mortgage interest on a qualifying mortgage loan will be granted at source and in *no other manner*. The reference to the fact that relief will not be available in any other manner places the onus on the borrower to ensure that Revenue are aware that the individual has a qualifying mortgage loan.

Relief continues to be given by way of tax credit in respect of bridging loan interest under TCA 1997, s 245 (see **3.204**) and interest on loans to acquire private residences in the UK as well as loans which are not secured on the property in question (typically loans to finance improvements or refurbishments of the property in question). The relief on such qualifying home loans is given as a 'general tax credit', ie purely by way of a reduction of tax chargeable (see **3.102**) calculated by applying the appropriate percentage to the amount of interest eligible for relief ('relievable interest'). As is normally the case, the tax credit is limited to the amount which would reduce the income tax chargeable to nil, ie no repayment of the income tax credit is possible, which brings such interest relief generally within the rules applicable to personal reliefs, discussed in **3.301**).

The rate of the credit varies according to the status of the borrower (see below). The relief has been abolished for loans taken out after 1 January 2013 except under certain conditions outlined below. The maximum qualifying interest in respect of all eligible loans is the lower of the interest actually paid and the following thresholds:

	€
First time buyers: First 7 years of loan	
jointly assessed couple	20,000
widowed person	20,000
single person	10,000
First time buyers: 8th year of loan onwards	
jointly assessed couple	6,000
widowed person	6,000
single person	3,000
Non-First time Buyers:	
jointly assessed couple	6,000
widowed person	6,000
single person	3,000

The 'appropriate percentage' varies as between 'first time buyers' (see **3.203**) and non-first time buyers. The latter are only entitled to an appropriate percentage of 15 per cent, whereas first time buyers who took out their loans between 2004 and 2008 qualify for an appropriate percentage of 30 per cent; first-time buyers who took out their loans between 2009 and 2012 qualify for an appropriate percentage of 25 per cent for the first two tax years in which they qualify as such; the percentage is reduced to 22.5 per cent in the following three tax years and falls to 20 per cent in the following two years and 15 per cent thereafter. By virtue of TCA 1997, s 244(1A)(b), as inserted by FA 2010, s 7, no relief will be available in respect of home loans from 2018 onwards nor in respect of loans taken out from 2013 onwards except under certain circumstances provided for in FA 2013, s 9.

There is one exception to the rule that qualifying mortgage interest is allowable only by way of tax relief at source or by way of tax credit; in calculating eligibility for the 'small income' exemption or marginal relief, the interest is allowable as a deduction in calculating total income (TCA 1997, s 244(2)(c)) (see **3.322**).

New loans

Finance Act 2013 extended mortgage interest relief to certain new loans taken out on or after 1 January 2012 and on or before 31 December 2013. Mortgage interest relief applies to interest on such loans where:

(a) the loan was taken out in 2012 to acquire land on which a qualifying residential premises is constructed; or

(b) the loan was taken out in 2012 or 2013 to construct a qualifying residential premises on land acquired in 2012 which was funded by a loan taken out in 2012; or

(c) the loan was used partly in 2012 and partly in 2013 in the repair, development or improvement of a qualifying residential premises and there was a written loan agreement in 2012.

In all cases planning permission must have been granted on or before 31 December 2012 for the construction, repair, development or improvement of the residential premises.

3.202 Interest on qualifying residence loans

The rules which define the interest eligible for relief under TCA 1997, s 244, and the manner in which the relief is given, are discussed in this section. Once the interest eligible for relief by way of tax relief at source or tax credit in any tax year has been determined, it is necessary to consider the restrictions on the amount of interest (or the aggregate amount) for which relief can actually be given. These restrictions are dealt with in **3.203**.

TCA 1997, s 244 provides relief on interest, irrespective of whether or where the lender is located and whether or not the interest is taxable in the lender's hands.

TCA 1997, s 244(1) provides that relief thereunder may be claimed only in respect of interest paid by an *individual* on a 'qualifying loan' obtained in respect of a 'qualifying residence' (see definitions below). This rule is subject to the exception given by TCA 1997, s 244(6) for interest payable on a qualifying loan by the personal representatives of a deceased person or by the trustees of a will settlement (see **15.107**). An individual who is not resident in the State is not entitled to relief under s 244, subject to the provisions of TCA 1997, s 1032 (see **13.610**).

Qualifying loan

TCA 1997, s 244(1) defines a qualifying loan, in relation to an individual, as:

> A loan or loans which without having been used for any other purpose, is used by the individual solely for the purpose of defraying money employed in the purchase, repair, development or improvement of a qualifying residence or in paying off another loan or loans used for such purpose.

A loan is defined as 'any loan or advance or any other arrangement whatever by virtue of which interest is paid or payable'; thus, overdrafts are not excluded.

In other words, there are three conditions to be met before a loan (or a number of loans together) can be treated as a qualifying loan. Firstly, the loan (as defined) must be used solely for one of these stated purposes. Secondly, the loan proceeds must not be applied, even temporarily, for another purpose before being used for any qualifying purpose. Thirdly, the application of the loan proceeds must be in connection with a qualifying residence.

One point to be noted is that, although the relief given by TCA 1997, s 244 may be referred to as 'mortgage interest' relief, it is not one of the conditions of a qualifying loan that it must be secured by a mortgage or in any other way. While the great majority of loans for which relief is claimed under TCA 1997, s 244 are in fact mortgage loans, any loan meeting all three conditions mentioned above is a qualifying loan whether or not secured.

The qualifying loan is in many cases one to finance the purchase of a new residence, which may be the individual's first residence of his own or, equally, may be a residence to replace his existing residence. Alternatively, it may be a loan to help the individual extend, repair or alter the qualifying residence. Further, since the definition of residential premises includes the garden or other land used and occupied with the residence (see under 'qualifying residence' below), a loan obtained to finance the development or improvement of the garden, etc may be a qualifying loan, as would a loan to help purchase an additional plot of ground immediately adjoining his garden, provided that the additional ground is to be added to the land occupied with the residence.

In March 1986, the Revenue Commissioners issued a leaflet entitled *Tax Relief for Interest on Personal Borrowing*. This states that:

> As a general rule any expenditure on a sole or main residence (but no expenditure on furniture, curtains, drapes, floor coverings and removable fittings) will be accepted as being in respect of its repair, development or improvement. Typical examples of qualifying expenditure would be expenditure incurred on extensions, conversions, painting and decorating, re-wiring, installation of central heating, installation of replacement windows, treatment of damp, treatment of wood worm and similar services, installation of fitted kitchens and general repair work. The inspector of taxes will give advice on whether or not any proposed expenditure would qualify for tax relief purposes.

The definition of a 'qualifying loan' includes the requirement that the proceeds of the loan obtained from the lender must be used solely for one of the permitted purposes (purchase, repair, etc) in connection with the qualifying residence. If the proceeds of a loan should be used partly – even if mainly – for such a purpose, but are also applied – even if to a relatively minor extent – in purchasing (say) furniture for the residence, this sole purpose test is not strictly satisfied. In such a case, the inspector of taxes would be entitled to deny the individual any relief by reference to TCA 1997, s 244 in respect of the interest payable on the full loan, but in practice the Revenue Commissioners will allow the appropriate percentage of a loan which has not been used solely for a qualifying purpose or which arises as the result of the consolidation of a number of loans where one or more of the pre-existing loans had been raised for a qualifying purpose. The Revenue Commissioners have expressed the view that where a qualifying residence is used partly for commercial or professional purposes then a proportionate part of the loan should be treated as non-qualifying. However, the mere use of an individual's home for business purposes would not seem to render it any less his main residence. The position will be different where part of a premises is dedicated for use as a shop or an office, but in some cases the borderline may be difficult to draw.

Qualifying residence

TCA 1997, s 244(1) (amended FA 2014, s 7) provides that a 'qualifying residence', in relation to an individual, means:

> a residential premises situated in an EEA state, which is used as the sole or main residence of (a) the individual, or (b) a former or separated spouse of his, or (c) a former or separated civil partner, or (d) a person who in relation to the individual is a dependent relative and is, where the residential premises is provided by the individual, provided rent free and without any other consideration.

The following definitions have been added under FA 2014;

'EEA Agreement' means the Agreement on the European Economic Area signed at Oporto on 2 May 2992, as adjusted by all subsequent amendments to that Agreement;

'EEA State' means a state (including the State) which is a contracting party to the EEA Agreement'.

As noted above, an individual may have loans on up to three qualifying residences. Where the loan is in relation to a residence of a dependant relative, the person paying the interest must be entitled to the dependant relative tax credit in respect of that dependant relative. The overall limit of interest relief as described at **3.203** applies regardless of the number of qualifying residences; in other words, each residence does not have a separate limit.

Normally, a house or other residential premises is only a qualifying residence at the time when it is used as the sole or main residence of the individual claiming interest relief in respect of the loan for the purchase, repair, etc of the premises in question. For the circumstances in which TCA 1997, s 244(6) treats an individual's former sole or main residence as continuing to be a qualifying residence for a 12-month period after a new sole or main residence is acquired, see **3.204**.

The Revenue leaflet noted above states that:

> In general, the sole or main residence of an individual is the residence which is his home for the greater part of the time (for example, a holiday home would not be regarded as a sole or main residence). However, duration of occupation is not the sole test and if an individual uses two different residences on a regular basis the advice of the inspector of taxes should be sought as to which would be regarded as the sole or main residence for tax relief purposes. It is not necessary that a residence be owned by an individual for it to be his sole or main residence.

In *Frost v Feltham* [1981] STC 115, the taxpayer was obliged to live in accommodation attached to the public house which he managed. However, he also spent time each month with his wife at a house some distance away, which was fully furnished and equipped as his private residence. Nourse J upheld the Appeal Commissioners' finding of fact that the latter house was the taxpayer's sole or main residence. The Revenue leaflet also indicates that special treatment may be granted to individuals with job related accommodation (as well as to cases involving residences under construction and purchases of residences in anticipation of marriage).

Anti-avoidance rule

TCA 1997, s 244(4) contains an anti-avoidance rule designed to prevent certain arrangements which might otherwise be employed to create a qualifying loan in non-arm's length transactions involving a residential premises. TCA 1997, s 244(4) provides that a loan is not to be regarded as a qualifying loan in relation to an individual if it is used to defray money applied by the individual:

(a) to purchase a residential premises or any interest therein from his spouse [no reference to civil partner in the legislation];

(b) to purchase a residential premises or any interest therein if, at any time after 25 March 1982, that premises or interest had been previously disposed of by the purchaser or by his spouse, or if any interest in the premises reversionary to the interest now purchased was so disposed of after that date; or

(c) to purchase, repair, develop or improve a residential premises in the case where:

   (i) the recipient of the money for the purchase, repair, etc is connected with the individual, and

   (ii) it appears that the price paid for the purchase or the work done is substantially in excess of its proper value.

In applying para (c) above, a person is regarded as connected with the individual who paid the interest if any of the 'connected person' rules of TCA 1997, s 10 treat him as being so connected (see **12.304**). In applying paras (a) and (b), the reference to a spouse does not include the wife or husband of the purchaser who is separated from him under an order of a court of competent jurisdiction or who is separated in such circumstances that the separation is likely to be permanent (on which note discussion at **3.501**). This means, for example, that a loan to an individual to enable him to purchase a qualifying residence from his separated spouse is a qualifying loan (provided that the purchase price is not substantially in excess of the market value).

3.203 Restrictions on mortgage interest relief

Once it is established that an individual has paid interest on a qualifying loan to purchase, extend, alter, improve, etc a qualifying residence, it is then necessary to apply the restrictions described in **3.201** to determine the amount of relievable interest by reference to which relief is given.

In the case of persons making their first claim under TCA 1997, s 244, the maximum amount which may be claimed is increased as follows:

> The lesser of the amount of interest paid during the year of assessment or €20,000 in the case of persons who are jointly assessed or widowed persons; In all other cases, the lesser of the amount of interest paid during the year of assessment or €10,000.

While an individual who makes their first claim under TCA 1997, s 244 is often described as a 'first time buyer' this term may be misleading. The relief is in fact available to an individual for the first seven years during which they are eligible to make a claim under TCA 1997, s 244 or its predecessor provisions in respect of one or more loans. Prior to the enactment of Finance Act 2003, s 9, the qualifying period for which interest relief could be claimed, was five years. Although the following extract from *Tax*

Briefing 15 refers to a five-year period, it would seem reasonable that Revenue practice on this matter would also apply to the new provisions and as such, where the term 'five years' is referred to below, this should be read in the context of the new provision as 'seven years'. Revenue had not issued any further statements on the matter since the publication of the FA 2003. In *Tax Briefing 15*, the Revenue Commissioners confirmed that:

> Where, within the first five years, a person buys a 'qualifying residence', sells it and buys another qualifying residence he will qualify as a first-time buyer in relation to the second qualifying residence, ie in respect of the remainder of the five-year period, which commenced on taking out the loan for the first qualifying residence.

Similarly, an individual who had previously lived in a residence acquired by inheritance and who then sells it, will be able to claim relief based on the increased limits for the first seven years of a loan to acquire a new residence (assuming that this is his first home loan). The Revenue have also confirmed that:

> the 'five-year' period refers to the first five years in which interest is paid on a qualifying residence. In cases where a gap of (say) two years occurs between the first residence being sold and the second residence being acquired, these two years are not counted in the five-year period, so that in such cases interest paid in years six and seven qualify for relief.

Married couples and civil partners

TCA 1997, s 244(1)(b) now expressly provides for the situation where the spouse or civil partner of an individual who is a chargeable person jointly assessed under TCA 1997, s 1017 or s 1031C pays interest on a home loan. The subsection provides that the individual will be deemed to have made any payment of '*qualifying interest*' made by the spouse or civil partner, if that payment would have been eligible for relief assuming the spouse or civil partner had been assessed as a single person under TCA 1997, s 1016. Given that '*qualifying interest*' is in fact defined as interest paid by the individual who is claiming the benefit of the tax credit there is an element of circularity in this provision. However, the intention is clearly to ensure that interest paid on a qualifying loan (or loans) by the spouse or civil partner of a chargeable person is treated as paid by him.

TCA 1997, s 244(3)(b) addresses the situation where:

(a) a married couple are jointly assessed under TCA 1997, s 1017 or s 1031C; and

(b) one of the spouses or civil partners qualified as a first-time buyer but the other did not.

The legislation is quite complex but, in essence, each spouse or civil partner is deemed to have paid half of the interest, regardless of the amount paid by each spouse or civil partner. The spouse or civil partner who has already claimed relief in an earlier year(s) is restricted to the lower limit for a single individual while the other spouse or civil partner is entitled to the higher limit. For example, if the couple pay interest of €12,000, each spouse or civil partner is deemed to have paid €6,000; this means that the limit for the non-first-time buyer is €3,000 and for the other spouse or civil partner is €9,000; thus, the interest deemed paid by the other spouse or civil partner of €6,000 is all allowed and the aggregate allowed for the couple is €9,000.

It is thought that in practice an inspector may interpret these provisions so as to reduce interest relief only in cases where one or both spouses do not qualify as 'first time buyers'. It has been assumed that this is the treatment which would be applied for the purposes of all the examples in this book.

Other points

The fact that an individual may occasionally have qualifying loans in respect of two residences at the same time (for example, a loan to purchase, improve, etc his own main residence and a separate loan in relation to his separated spouse's or civil partner's residence) does not alter the maximum deduction he may obtain for the interest payable on those loans. If both qualifying loans are taken out and the interest is payable by only one of two separated spouses or civil partners, and if the two spouses or civil partners are assessed separately, it is to be noted that the aggregate interest eligible for deduction is restricted so as not to exceed the single person's overall limit of €3,000 on an annualised basis, or €10,000 in the case of a first time buyer. However, if each spouse or civil partner pays part of the interest, each has a separate €3,000 or €10,000 limit applied to the interest paid by him or her.

3.204 Bridging loan relief

The first thing to note about bridging loan relief is that the term 'bridging loan' may be quite misleading and TCA 1997, s 245 has a much wider application than the rubric to the section, 'Relief for certain bridging loans', would suggest. The term 'bridging loan', as generally understood, refers to a situation where a person has purchased a property which is to be part-funded by the sale of another property but the sale of the other property has not yet been finalised and additional borrowings are required until the sale proceeds of the old property are received.

TCA 1997, s 245 does cover such a scenario but it also covers a much more common scenario. In simple terms, the more common scenario is where an individual sells his sole or main residence and purchases another sole or main residence with the aid of a loan, relief for the interest on the new loan for the first 12 months is available separately from 'normal' mortgage interest relief. This separate relief may, in many instances, give aggregate interest relief in excess of the normal limits for TCA 1997, s 244. In this scenario, there is no requirement that the old property be still owned by the individual when the new property is acquired. Before analysing the relief in detail, two simple examples will be given to aid understanding of the two possible scenarios.

Example 3.204.1

Mr A purchased a new home on 1 July 2011 for €250,000. He funded the purchase with savings of €50,000 and a loan of €200,000. On 31 December 2011 he sold his old home, which had been on the market for a considerable time, for €150,000. On 1 January 2012 Mr A repaid the mortgage of €70,000 on the old home and used the remaining €80,000 of the sales proceeds to reduce the borrowings on the new home.

In the tax year 2011, Mr A will have paid interest on his old home for the full year and he will be entitled to 'normal' interest relief for the entire year, subject of course to the normal limits. In the tax year 2011, Mr A will also be entitled to relief for the new loan from 1 July 2011 to 31 December 2011, being six months out of the first 12 months of the new loan. Again, the relief in respect of the new loan cannot exceed the 'normal' TCA 1997, s 244 limits, but this is a separate limit to the limit for the old home. However, in this case, the 'normal' limit is time-apportioned as the period of the new loan is only six months.

The only loan in existence for the tax year 2012 is the loan on the new house (now reduced to €130,000). From 1 January 2012 to 30 June 2012, the new loan is treated as a 'bridging loan' subject to the TCA 1997, s 245 limit, which in this case will be the normal limit again time-apportioned. From 1 July 2012 onwards, the new loan is treated as a normal mortgage subject to the normal TCA 1997, s 244 limits. There is no time-apportionment of the limits for the normal mortgage.

Example 3.204.2

Mr B purchased a new home on 1 October 2011 for €250,000 having sold his old home on 30 June 2011 for €150,000. On 30 June 2011 Mr B repaid his mortgage of €50,000 on his old home and he used the remaining €100,000 to part fund the purchase of his new home. On 1 October 2011 Mr B took out a mortgage of €150,000 on his new home.

In the tax year 2011, Mr B will have paid interest on his old home up to 30 June. He will be entitled to relief on this interest under the normal mortgage interest relief rules. The new loan taken out on 1 October 2011 is treated as a 'bridging loan' for the first 12 months. Therefore, from 1 October to 31 December 2011, the limits relevant to TCA 1997, s 245 apply – these are the normal TCA 1997, s 244 limits but time-apportioned for three months.

In the tax year 2012, the 'bridging loan' will continue for another nine months until 30 September and time apportioned relief is available under TCA 1997, s 245. From 1 October 2012 the new loan is treated as a normal mortgage and for the remaining three months of 2012 normal mortgage interest relief is available.

We return now to a more detailed analysis of TCA 1997, s 245. For the provisions of the section to apply it is necessary that the individual claiming the relief dispose of his only or main residence and acquire another residence for use as his only or main residence. While it would be relatively uncommon today, a 'first-time buyer' may require a loan commonly referred to as a 'bridging loan' where there is likely to be a delay in finalising a mortgage on the property. As this individual will not have disposed of a sole or main residence, relief under TCA 1997, s 245 will not be available; however, relief under TCA 1997, s 244 should be available as the temporary loan would be regarded as a 'qualifying loan' within the meaning of TCA 1997, s 244(1)(a).

TCA 1997, s 245(1)(b) states that the proceeds of the loan must be used to defray in whole or in part the cost of the acquisition of the new property or the cost of the disposal of the old property or both. It is not totally clear what the cost of disposal of the old property means as generally a new loan would be used for the acquisition of the new property. Perhaps, the section envisages a situation whereby a mortgage on an old property would have to be cleared before the lender would advance a new mortgage. The borrower may be able to raise a separate loan to clear the old mortgage and this new loan would appear to qualify for relief under TCA 1997, s 245.

Interest paid in respect of the new loan for the first 12 months of the loan qualifies for relief under TCA 1997, s 244 as if no other interest was paid in respect of that period. In effect, what this means is that both a normal TCA 1997, s 244 deduction is available, if 'relievable interest' is paid in the relevant tax year and the special relief afforded by TCA 1997, s 245 is also available. The 12-month period will nearly always form part of two tax years. The legislation does not stipulate how the TCA 1997, s 245 relief is to be granted over the two years in the context of the limits imposed under TCA 1997, s 244. However, an Appeals Commissioners decision determined that the normal TCA 1997, s 244 limits should be time-apportioned as between the two tax years covered by the 12-month period.

The reason that interest on two loans may qualify for relief, at the same time is that TCA 1997, s 244(5) allows an 'old' residence to continue to be regarded as a sole or main residence (in addition to a new sole or main residence) for a period of 12 months after the date of acquisition of the new residence provided that the individual shows to the satisfaction of the inspector that he has taken and continues to take all reasonable steps necessary to dispose of the old residence.

It should be noted above that bridging loan relief is only available in respect of a change in the individual's own residence and does not apply to a change in the residence of a former or separated spouse nor to a change in the residence of a dependent relative (qualifying residences for the normal interest relief). In the case of a married couple living together, the bridging loan may be one taken out, and on which the interest is paid, by either spouse or it may be one taken jointly. Should the couple living together be assessed separately, the relief is given to the spouse paying the interest, but is divided between them if each contributes to the interest.

For bridging loan relief to apply, the proceeds of the loan – whether the original bridging loan or any subsequent loan to replace it (or pay interest on it) – must not be used for any other purpose before it is applied to meet the cost of the acquisition of the new residence or the disposal of the old one or, in the case of a subsequent loan, to repay the original bridging loan (or interest on it).

Example 3.204.3

Using the scenario set out in **Example 3.204.1**, assume that interest rates of five per cent and six per cent applied to the new loan and the old loan respectively, that Mr A is married and jointly assessed and that he has claimed mortgage interest relief for more than seven years. The interest payable by Mr A on the two loans is computed below.

	2011	*2012*
	€	€
Old loan		
Year ended 31/12/2011: €70,000 x 6% x 12 months	4,200	
New loan		
1/7/2011 to 31/12/2011: €200,000 x 5% x 6 months	5,000	
1/1/2012 to 30/6/2012: €130,000 x 5% x 6 months		3,250
1/7/2012 to 31/12/2012: €130,000 x 5% x 6 months		3,250

For the tax year 2011, Mr A paid a total of €9,200 in interest. The normal mortgage interest is €4,200 and since this is below the limit of €6,000 for tax year 2011, it is all allowed. The 'bridging loan' interest paid was €5,000. As the bridging loan was in existence for half of the tax year, the limit of €6,000 is halved to €3,000. As the bridging loan interest payable in 2011 was greater than €3,000, an amount of €3,000 is allowed. Therefore, the total interest allowed for the tax year 2011 is €7,200.

For the tax year 2012 Mr A paid a total of €6,500 in interest. For the first six months of the tax year, the loan is deemed to be a bridging loan and thereafter it is treated as a normal mortgage loan. The annualised limit for the bridging loan is €3,000 being the limit of €6,000 pro-rated for six months. The amount allowed is €3,000. The mortgage interest paid of €3,250 is less than the limit of €6,000 and is therefore all allowed. The total relievable interest for 2011 is €6,250.

3.205 Preferential and other loans from employer

TCA 1997, s 122(2) charges an individual to income tax for any tax year in which he has a 'preferential' loan from his employer (or from any person connected with his employer) or from his spouse's or civil partner's employer (or from a person connected with the spouse's or civil partner's employer). The tax is charged on the amount of the 'interest benefit' derived in the year from the preferential loan. A preferential loan is a loan on which the interest (if any) charged in the year is less than interest at the 'specified rate'. For the tax year 2015, the specified rate is 4.0 per cent for loans which are qualifying loans within the meaning of TCA 1997, s 244(1)(a), irrespective of whether or not they actually attract relief, and 13.5 per cent in any other case. TCA 1997, s 122(3) charges an individual to income tax on any amount of interest which is released or written off on any loan from his employer (or spouse's or civil partner's employer), whether or not the loan is a preferential one. Further, it charges tax on any amount of principal which is written off any such employer loan, whether or not preferential. The circumstances in which interest is charged to income tax by TCA 1997, s 122(2), (3) are explained more fully in **10.211**.

TCA 1997, s 122(4) entitles an individual charged to tax under TCA 1997, s 122(2) on his interest benefit from the preferential loan to claim relief under TCA 1997, s 244 (see **3.202**). Similarly, this subsection entitles an individual charged to tax under TCA 1997, s 122(3) on the amount of any interest released or written off any 'qualifying loan' from his employer (or spouse's or civil partner's employer) to claim relief under TCA 1997, s 244. No relief is, however, available for any amount of loan principal written off or released.

TCA 1997, s 122(4) operates by treating the individual as if he had actually paid an amount of interest equal to the amount of the preferential loan interest benefit on which he is charged to tax or equal to the amount of the interest written off or released from any employer loan and charged to tax under TCA 1997, s 122(4). Consequently, if the loan involved is a qualifying loan, the amount of interest deemed to have been paid is eligible for relief under TCA 1997, s 244.

The amount of interest which TCA 1997, s 122(4) deems to have been paid in any tax year on any qualifying employer loan is added to the interest actually paid in the same year on that loan and on any other qualifying loan(s). Relief under TCA 1997, s 244 is given for the resulting aggregate of interest deemed paid and actually paid. Only the one overall limit applies to this aggregate interest paid.

Example 3.205.1

George Johnson, a married man, receives an interest-only loan of €120,000 from his employer (which is not a financial institution) on 1 January 2012 to assist in the purchase of his new home. George has Sch E earnings for 2012 (before taking the benefit of the preferential loan into account) of €93,000. The rate of interest on the loan is 1.5 per cent. There were no other borrowings in relation to the property. George does not qualify as a 'first time buyer'. The overall tax implications of the loan are as follows:

	€	€ *Tax payable/ (relief)*
Benefit in kind:		
€120,000 x 3.5% (5.0 – 1.5) =	4,200[1] x 41% =	1,722
Relief under TCA 1997, s 244:		
Interest actually paid:		
€120,000 x 1.5% =	1,800	
Notional interest treated as benefit	4,200	
Total	6,600	
Relief (maximum)	6,000 x 15% =	(900)

Notes

1. The benefit will also attract liability to the USC and Employer's PRSI.
2. The specified rate was 5 per cent in 2012 (4 per cent in 2015).

3.206 Loans to acquire certain shares, etc (abolished from 2014 onwards)

TCA 1997, s 248 generally entitles an individual to a deduction in arriving at his total income for interest paid on a loan *made on or before 7 December 2010*, the moneys from which are applied for certain types of investment in:

(a) an unquoted trading company or a qualifying holding company of such companies; or

(b) (for loans made prior to 8 December 2005) a Sch D Case V rental company or a qualifying holding company of such companies.

FA 2011, s 11 restricted the deduction available under TCA 1997, s 248 so that the relief has been tapering out since 2011. Only 75 per cent of the deduction was available for interest paid in 2011, 50 per cent of the interest paid in 2012, 25 per cent of the interest paid in 2013. No relief at all is available in respect of interest paid in 2014 and subsequent years of assessment.

Restrictions also applied to interest accrued on a loan before 1 January 2002 where the proceeds of the loan were used to finance residential property (see under *Restriction of Relief; Residential Letting Investment* below). It seems that the term 'loan' in its ordinary sense is wide enough to include an overdraft (*Lawson v Brooks* [1992] STC). For the purposes of TCA 1997, s 248 (and for the related TCA 1997, s 250) (and for the related TCA 1997, s 253, see **3.208**), an unquoted company is any company which is not a 'quoted company' as defined in TCA 1997, s 252(1) (see *Loans for Investment in Quoted Companies* below).

In any case where all the necessary conditions for relief under TCA 1997, s 248 are met, a set percentage of the amount of the interest paid on the qualifying loan is deducted in arriving at the total income of the individual who pays the interest. The percentage for 2011 was 75 per cent falling to 50 per cent in 2012 and 25 per cent in 2013. The relief has been abolished from 2014 onwards.

There are no requirements that the interest should be paid by an Irish resident or should otherwise be charged under Sch D. In practice the Revenue Commissioners will allow relief on a duly apportioned amount of interest on a loan which is used only partially for qualifying purposes (a Revenue Precedent refers to a situation where a loan was used partly to acquire a private residence and partly to make a qualifying loan to a company under TCA 1997, s 248). However, this relief will be subject to the restrictions applicable to high income individuals discussed at **3.111** from tax year 2007 onwards.

TCA 1997, s 248 provides relief for interest paid on any loan to defray monies which are applied for any one or more of the following purposes:

(a) to acquire any part of the ordinary share capital of a trading company, or, in the case only of loans made prior to 8 December 2005 or certain replacement loans, of a company whose income is derived wholly or mainly from rents, etc (from premises, etc in the State) chargeable to tax under Sch D Case V; (but see *Residential Rental Investments* below);

(b) to acquire any part of the ordinary share capital of a company the business of which consists wholly or mainly of holding stocks, shares or securities in one or more trading companies, or, in the case only of loans made prior to 8 December

2005 or certain replacement loans, property rental companies (a 'qualifying holding company');

(c) to lend money to any of these types of company to be used wholly and exclusively for its trade or business or for the trade or business of a connected company; and/or

(d) to repay another loan qualifying for the interest relief under (a), (b) or (c) above.

The reference to a 'trading company' is in fact to a company 'which exists wholly or mainly for the purpose of carrying on a trade or trades'. In Lord v Tustain *[1993] STC 755* the taxpayers subscribed for shares in a 'shell company' formed to acquire the trade of another company in the course of a management buyout. Vinelott J held that interest on loans taken out to finance the cost of those shares qualified for relief, saying:

> In my judgment, if a loan is made and shares are subscribed for to enable a company to acquire a trade at a time when the company is a shell it can fairly be said that the company exists for the purpose of carrying on that trade. The acquisition of the trade may then be said to be the means through which the purpose is achieved. The Crown's contention involves treating the acquisition of the trade as an end in itself, ignoring the underlying intention to carry on the trade. It is possible to imagine a case in which a trade is acquired not for the purpose of carrying it on but to hold it as an investment and sell it at a profit. But that is not the case.
>
> The Revenue Commissioners have issued a precedent to the effect that where individuals borrowed money which was applied in acquiring an interest in a trading company, they could no longer claim relief under s 248 TCA 1997 when the company subsequently ceased to trade and another precedent to contrary effect. It is by no means clear that the first-mentioned precedent is the correct interpretation.

There is no requirement that the company be Irish resident or that the trade should be carried on in the State. In strictness, a holding company which holds its shares in trading or rental companies indirectly through an intermediate holding company will not qualify under (b), but in practice the Revenue may be prepared to grant a concession on this point. The Revenue Commissioners have not indicated their practice in determining whether or not the 'wholly or mainly' criterion is justified. However, they have indicated their views on the interpretation of the same criterion in CATCA 2003, s 93 (definition of relevant business property for the purposes of Capital Acquisitions Tax).

There is an exception to the relief for 'replacement' loans under (a) (TCA 1997, s 248(1A) inserted by FA 2006, s 9). A 'new' loan used to pay off an 'old' pre-8 December 2005 loan in relation to a property rental company (or a qualifying holding company of such companies) will not be eligible for relief unless the new loan does not exceed the balance outstanding on the old loan *and* the term of the new loan does not exceed the term of the old loan. The first requirement seems superfluous since any borrowing in excess of the old loan would not be applied in paying off the old loan and thus could not attract relief in any event. The second requirement does not prevent the term of the old loan being extended; it would not appear that such a variation should not give rise to a 'new 'loan. These rules do not apply to a second 'new' loan which replaces the first 'new' loan.

Apart from the requirement that the loan be applied for one of these qualifying investments, all the following further conditions must be satisfied before relief under TCA 1997, s 248 is given in respect of any interest paid on the loan:

(a) the individual must have a material interest in the company or in a connected company at the time the interest is paid*; and

(b) during the period from the application of the loan proceeds for the qualifying purpose until the interest is paid, the individual must have worked for the greater part of his time in the actual management or conduct of the business of the company or of a connected company*; and

(c) the individual must show that, in the period from the application of the loan to the date that interest is paid, he has not recovered any capital from the company or from a connected company (except that money recovered which is fully used by the individual to repay any part of the loan on which he is claiming the interest relief does not disqualify the individual from the relief (TCA 1997, s 248(2)).

* (But see **3.207** for alternative conditions which allow relief under TCA 1997, s 248 as extended by TCA 1997, s 250 when conditions (a) and (b) are not met.)

For condition (a), an individual is treated as having a material interest in a company if he beneficially owns, or has the ability to control, directly or by any indirect means including holding through a connected company or companies, more than five per cent of the ordinary share capital of the company. The ordinary share capital of a company is all its share capital, irrespective of the name by which that capital is called, other than any share capital giving the holders the right to a dividend at a fixed rate but with no other right to share in the profits of the company (TCA 1997, s 2(1)).

The requirement to have at least five per cent of the ordinary share capital of the company must be met at the date the interest is paid rather than at the time the loan is applied in making the qualifying investment. It would, for example, be possible for an individual to obtain relief under the section on interest paid on, say, 10 August 2013 on a loan applied on 15 June 2005 to acquire say a three per cent holding of ordinary shares in an unquoted trading company if between 15 June 2005 and 10 August 2013 he individual has built his holding of ordinary shares up to five per cent or more.

For an individual to satisfy conditions (a) and (b) through having a material interest in and working for a company connected with the company in which the investment is made, the connected company must also be either a trading company, a property rental company (relevant only for loans made prior to 8 December 2005 and certain replacement loans) or a qualifying holding company (TCA 1997, s 248(1)(b)). In determining whether one company is connected with another company, the connected person rules set out in TCA 1997, s 10 must be applied (TCA 1997, s 10(2)) (see **12.304**). In considering the question of the control of a company for the connected person rules, the word 'control' is given the meaning it has in TCA 1997, s 432.

The meaning of 'control' in TCA 1997, s 432 is also the one to be used in determining whether an individual controls more than five per cent of the ordinary share capital of any relevant company (TCA 1997, s 247(1)). This control may be held by the individual either directly in the company or indirectly through a holding in another company controlling the relevant company. The other company through which indirect control is exercised need not necessarily be a trading company, property rental company (relevant only for loans made prior to 8 December 2005 and certain replacement loans) or qualifying holding company. For example, if an individual held a 5.1 per cent in the controlling share capital of G Ltd (not a property rental or qualifying holding company) which itself owns 100 per cent of the share capital of H Ltd, a qualifying holding company he would still satisfy the material interest test.

For the position when the third condition for relief under TCA 1997, s 248 is not met, see the discussion of the recovery of capital rules in **3.209**. For the alternative conditions (instead of conditions (a) and (b)) which may allow an individual interest relief under TCA 1997, s 248 as applied by TCA 1997, s 250, see **3.207**.

Example 3.206.1

Mr Reilly has, since January 2005, worked whole time in the management of Rackrent Ltd (a commercial property rental company) which is a subsidiary of Myre Holdings Ltd, a quoted company whose business consists of the holding of shares and securities of three trading companies and two property rental companies.

On 1 April 2005, Mr Reilly obtained a loan of €60,000 from his bank which he applied the same day in purchasing from the executors of a deceased shareholder four per cent of the ordinary shares in Fastbuck Ltd, an unquoted trading company in which Myre Holdings Ltd holds 60 per cent of the ordinary shares. On 9 March 2012, Mr Reilly inherits a further two per cent of the ordinary shares of Fastbuck Ltd so that he now holds six per cent of that company (a material interest).

On 31 December 2012, Mr Reilly pays interest of €6,600 to the bank in respect of the year ended on that date. Mr Reilly meets all the conditions for relief under TCA 1997, s 248, namely:

(a) he has worked whole time in the management of Rackrent Ltd (a company connected with Fastbuck Ltd due to their common parent company) between 1 April 2005 (date loan applied) and 31 December 2012 (date he paid the interest);

(b) he holds a material interest in Fastbuck Ltd on 31 December 2012 (date interest paid);

(c) he has not recovered any capital from Fastbuck Ltd (nor from any company connected with it) between 1 April 2005 (date loan applied) and 31 December 2012 (date interest paid); and

(d) although the group parent company (Myre Holdings Ltd) is a quoted company, the company whose shares have been acquired with the loan is an unquoted company.

TCA 1997, s 248 therefore entitles Mr Reilly to deduct 50 per cent of the €6,600 interest paid on 31 December 2012 (ie €3,300) in arriving at his total income for 2012. If Mr Reilly were to take out an additional loan to acquire additional shares in Fastbuck Ltd on or after 8 December 2005, he would no longer satisfy the conditions of TCA 1997, s 248 since Rackrent Ltd, being a property rental company, would no longer rank as a 'connected company.'

Loans for investment in quoted companies

TCA 1997, s 252 provides that no relief is to be given under TCA 1997, s 248 for interest paid on any loan applied after 29 January 1992 to acquire shares in or to lend to a quoted company (or applied after that date to repay any such loan).

TCA 1997, s 252(1) defines 'quoted company' as meaning any company whose shares, or any class whose shares, are (a) listed in the official list of any stock exchange or (b) whose shares are quoted on an unlisted securities market of any other exchange (this would cover companies quoted on the Developing Companies Market of the Irish Stock Exchange).

In the case of a loan applied for a qualifying investment in a company which, at the time of that application, was not a quoted company, but which subsequently becomes a quoted company, the normal TCA 1997, s 250 rules continue to apply as if the company was not a quoted company for the remainder of the tax year in which the company first becomes a quoted company and also for the next tax year. In the next tax year, relief is calculated by reference to 70 per cent of the interest paid and in the next tax year by reference to 30 per cent of the interest actually paid but no relief will be available thereafter.

For 2013 only 25 per cent of the relief so calculated may be claimed, with no relief being granted on or after 2014. Any such loan must have been taken out on or before 7 December 2010.

Example 3.206.2

Mr McGovern took out a loan to purchase ordinary shares in an unquoted trading company and purchased the shares on 16 June 1998 with the money thus borrowed. The company became a quoted company on 1 May 2010. Assuming Mr McGovern satisfies all other conditions for relief, his entitlement to relief for the interest on the loan paid in the under mentioned tax years is as follows:

2011	75%
2012	50% x 70%
2013	25% x 40%
Thereafter	0%

Restrictions of relief: tax incentive companies

TCA 1997, s 251 provides that no relief at all is given under TCA 1997, s 248 for interest on a loan applied in acquiring any ordinary shares issued on or after 20 April 1990 if a claim for relief under TCA 1997, Pt 16 (Employment and Investment Incentive Scheme previously BES relief/Seed Capital Scheme – see **18.1**) is made in respect of the amount subscribed for those shares.

It is to be noted that any interest paid on a loan applied to acquire shares issued before 20 April 1990 in a BES company continued to be deductible under TCA 1997, s 248 until the relief was abolished, if the conditions were met, notwithstanding that BES relief was obtained for the subscription for the shares.

TCA 1997, s 251 similarly provides that no relief at all is given under TCA 1997, s 248 for interest on a loan applied in acquiring any ordinary shares issued on or after 6 May 1993 if a claim for relief under TCA 1997, s 481 (relief for investment in films) is made in respect of the amount subscribed for those shares. Since only shares issued on or after 6 May 1993 can be qualifying shares to give an individual (as distinct from a company) any film investment relief under TCA 1997, s 481, no 'double relief' arises for loans to acquire film shares issued before 6 May 1993.

Anti-avoidance: general

TCA 1997, s 248(3) provides that no relief at all is to be given under the section for interest on a loan applied on or after 24 April 1992 unless the loan is applied:

(a) for *bona fide* commercial purposes; and

(b) not as part of a scheme or arrangement the main purpose or one of the purposes of which is the avoidance of tax (see the discussion of the similar anti-avoidance clause in the USC rules at **18.111**, and note the conclusions of the Special Commissioners, on similar wording, in MacNiven (Inspector of Taxes) v Westmoreland Investments Ltd *[1997] STC (SCD) 61* (not considered by the High Court in [1997] STC 1103)).

The provisions of TCA 1997, s 817A (discussed at **3.210**) should also be noted.

Anti-avoidance: companies acquiring buildings eligible for capital allowances

A potential restriction applies in relation to relief for interest paid on or after 19 March 2003 by an individual on a loan otherwise eligible under TCA 1997, s 248 (an 'eligible loan') to the extent that all or part of the moneys provided by the individual is used by the investee company after 1 January 2003 directly or indirectly in any of the following ways:

(a) in acquiring (whether or not by the company itself) the relevant interest in respect of any capital expenditure incurred (or deemed to be incurred) on the construction or refurbishment of a specified building; or
(b) in replacing money in acquiring such an interest; or
(c) in paying off a loan used in acquiring such an interest.

The restriction also applies to eligible loans used to replace eligible loans, where all or part of the moneys used by the earlier loan (or a loan which it had replaced, and so on) fall within the description above.

A restriction also applies in respect of interest paid on or after 20 February 2004 to the extent that an eligible loan was applied on or after 20 February 2004 in acquiring any part of the ordinary share capital of a company at least 75 per cent of the income of which consists of Sch D Case V income in respect of one or more specified buildings. This may be a problematic issue where eg a company owns a portfolio of properties some of which are 'specified' and some of which are not, and where one or more of its properties generates a net deficit, in so far as there is no guidance as to how to match losses against profits from different properties.

The amount of a loan used to provide moneys for any of the purposes above which give rise to potentially restricted relief is termed the 'specified amount' (TCA 1997, s 250A(1)).

The term 'relevant interest' bears its meaning for industrial buildings allowances purposes: see **6.403**.

The term 'specified building' refers to one which meets three conditions:

Firstly, it must be a building or structure or part of a building or structure:

(a) which is, or is to be, an industrial building within TCA 1997, s 268 and in respect of the actual or deemed capital expenditure thereon an industrial buildings allowance under TCA 1997, Pt 9, Ch 1 has been, or is to be made to a company (see **6.401**);
(b) in respect of the actual or deemed capital expenditure thereon an allowance under TCA 1997, Pt 10 (see **Division 19** of the 2009 edition of this book re industrial and commercial buildings in tax incentive areas) or under TCA 1997, s 843 (buildings used for Third Level Educational purposes see **6.503**) or under TCA 1997, s 843A (*Childcare Premises*: see **6.401**) has been, or is to be, made to a company.

Secondly, the company mentioned in the first condition (ie which has, or is to, receive capital allowances in respect of the building or structure, etc), the 'first company', (not a term used in the legislation) must be entitled to the relevant interest in respect of the capital expenditure or residue thereof (see **6.403**) on which the allowances were based, at some time on or after 1 January 2003.

Thirdly, another company (the 'second company') (not a term used in the legislation) must be entitled to an allowance under TCA 1997, Pt 9 Ch 1 in respect of the capital expenditure (or residue thereof) for which the first company had claimed allowances;

this must arise subsequent to the time at which the relevant interest was held by the first company. It is irrelevant whether or not other persons had held the relevant interest (or the part of it in question) at some point in the interim. It may be noted that allowances granted to the tax incentive buildings, etc noted above which would not otherwise qualify under TCA 1997, s 268 receive allowances under TCA 1997, Pt 9 Ch 1 on the basis of the statutory fiction that they do so qualify (TCA 1997, s 250A(1)).

In very broad terms therefore, a specified building is one which qualifies for industrial buildings allowance and where on or after 1 January 2003 the relevant interest is acquired by a company having been previously owned by another company.

TCA 1997, s 250A(2) restricts the amount of interest qualifying for relief attributable to the 'specified amount' to a maximum amount equal to the individual's 'return from the company' in relation to the specified amount. This latter maximum figure is based on the gross dividends received so attributable where the individual had applied the eligible loan to acquire shares in the company concerned or the gross interest received which is so attributable where he had applied the eligible loan to on-lend moneys to the company. The restriction can if necessary be traced through a chain of one or more loans replacing an eligible loan (TCA 1997, s 250A(3)). Where interest has to be attributed to a specified amount in relation to either interest paid on an eligible loan by the individual investor or interest received from a loan made by the individual to a company and which was financed by an eligible loan, an apportionment will be made in the same ratio as the specified amount bears to the amount of the eligible loan (TCA 1997, s 250A(4)).

3.207 Alternative conditions for share loans

The discussion which follows in this chapter of the application of TCA 1997, s 250 ('s 250') to modify TCA 1997, s 248 ('s 248') should be read in the context that the modifications in s 250 only apply in those cases in which the conditions for the operation of s 248 on its own are not fully met. In particular, the extension of s 248 relief provided by s 250 is intended primarily for the individual who does not have the necessary 'material interest', but who is an employee or director in a relevant company.

Section 250 extends the circumstances in which an individual is entitled to relief under s 248 for interest on any loan applied for any of the types of investment qualifying for the purposes of the latter section. Section 250 permits an individual who does not satisfy either or both of the first two conditions in s 248 to obtain the relief under s 248 provided that certain alternative tests are satisfied. It must be noted that the restrictions of relief that apply in the case of certain tax incentive companies and certain rental residential companies are not modified or overruled by TCA 1997, s 250.

In other words, an individual who does not own or control more than five per cent of the company concerned or of a connected company, or who has not worked for the greater part of his time in the management, etc of the company or a connected company between the application of the loan and the payment of the interest, should look at the alternative tests of TCA 1997, s 250.

The alternative conditions provided by TCA 1997, s 250 for interest relief under TCA 1997, s 248 vary depending on the type of company in which the proceeds of the qualifying loan are invested (the 'investee company'). The following types of company are to be distinguished:

(a) a trading company or (relevant only for loans made prior to 8 December 2005 and certain replacement loans: see **3.206**) a Sch D Case V property rental company which is a private company;

(b) a trading company or (relevant only for loans made prior to 8 December 2005 and certain replacement loans: see **3.206**) a Sch D Case V property rental company which is a public company;

(c) a qualifying holding company of trading companies or (relevant only for loans made prior to 8 December 2005 and certain replacement loans: see **3.206**) a qualifying holding company of property rental companies which is a private company; and

(d) a holding company of trading companies or (relevant only for loans made prior to 8 December 2005 and certain replacement loans: see **3.206**) a qualifying holding company of property rental companies which is not a private company.

The definitions of trading company, Sch D Case V property rental company and qualifying holding company are those provided by TCA 1997, s 248.

Apart from the different conditions to qualify for TCA 1997, s 248 relief in these cases, another difference is that there is a limit to the amount of interest for which the relief is given if the investee company is a public company under (b) or (d).

Before dealing separately with each of these four classes of investee company, the following definition common to all the provisions of TCA 1997, s 250 are given:

A 'full-time employee' or 'full-time director', in relation to a company, is an employee or director of the company who is required to devote substantially the whole of his time to the service of the company.

A 'part-time employee' and 'part-time director', in relation to a company, is an employee or director of the company not required to devote substantially the whole of his time to the service of the company.

In *Palmer v Maloney* [1999] STC 890 (a CGT case 425): the court held that in the context of the UK equivalent of TCA 1997, s 598, the term 'substantially the whole of his time' meant the whole of the director's or employee's time as a full-time worker; it followed that an individual who worked a normal full-time number of hours would qualify as full-time, irrespective of the amount of time devoted to other employments or activities.

'Private company' is given the same meaning as in Companies Act 1963, s 33, ie a company which, by its articles, restricts the right to transfer its shares, limits the number of its members to 50 (other than present or former employees) and prohibits any invitation to the public to subscribes for its shares or debentures.

'Public company', although not specifically defined, also has its Companies Act 1963 meaning, ie any company which is not a private company within that Act.

This relief is subject to the restrictions applicable to high income individuals discussed at **3.111** from tax year 2007 onwards.

(a) Private trading or property rental company

In the case of a loan applied to acquire ordinary shares in, or lend to, a trading company or (relevant only for loans made prior to 8 December 2005 and certain replacement loans: see **3.206**) to a property rental company, which is in either case a private company, TCA 1997, s 250(2)(a)(i) allows relief under TCA 1997, s 248 to be given to an individual for the interest on the loan provided that he is, for the relevant period, either a full time or a part time employee or director in the particular company. If the individual meets this condition, it does not matter that he does not have a material interest in the company. In fact, there is no requirement for him to hold any shares in the company (although he may do so) and the relief is given for the full amount of the interest.

The relevant period during which the individual must be an employee or director (whether full time or part time) is the period, taken as a whole, from the date the loan proceeds were applied to acquire the shares until the date the particular interest is paid. It is possible that this condition could be met for one interest payment, but not for the next due to the individual ceasing to be an employee or director before the next payment is made. Should this happen, the later interest payment would not qualify for relief.

The rule of TCA 1997, s 250(2)(a)(i) is likely to be particularly relevant in the case of a family company to enable relatives involved in the business only as a part time employee or director, but who would not otherwise qualify due to not having a material interest in the shares, to obtain full interest relief on borrowings applied to invest in its share capital or in lending to the company.

Example 3.207.1

Mr Paul Rominger was a full time employee of Kimmage Ltd, a trading company for a number of years before being made a director of the company on 1 May 2012. Since he is now over 60, he ceases from that date to be required to devote substantially the whole of his time to the service of the company (although he does work for the company for three days each week). Kimmage Ltd is a private company as defined in Companies Act 1963, s 33.

On 1 February 2010, Mr Rominger obtained a loan of €50,000 from his bank which he applied on 5 February 2010 as to €36,000 to purchase a three per cent holding of ordinary shares in Kimmage Ltd and as to €10,000 by way of loan to the company to be used wholly and exclusively for the purposes of its business. Mr Rominger does not hold any other shares in the company at any relevant time so that his holding is not a material interest (being less than five per cent of the ordinary shares).

During the year ending 31 December 2012 (on 31 May 2012), Mr Rominger pays interest of €5,200 on the loan. The following points are noted in relation to his claim for relief in respect of this interest in 2012:

(a) He does not have a material interest in Kimmage Ltd (or in any connected company) which means that he is not entitled to relief directly under TCA 1997, s 248 (so that he has to look to TCA 1997, s 250 to see what (if any) relief is available).

(b) During the relevant period from the application of the loan (5 February 2010) to the date the €5,200 interest is paid (31 May 2012), he was a full time employee for the period to 1 May 2012 but was only a part time director for the rest of the period. He must therefore be regarded only as a part time director or employee for the relevant period in relation to the €5,200 interest payment.

(c) Since Kimmage Ltd is a private company, the fact that Mr Rominger is a part time director or employee for the relevant period is sufficient to allow him full relief under TCA 1997, s 248 (as that section is extended by TCA 1997, s 250).

Mr Rominger is as a result of these points entitled to deduct 50 per cent of the €5,200 interest paid in 2012 (ie €2,600) in computing his total income for that year.

(b) Public trading or property rental company

In the case of a loan applied to acquire ordinary shares in, or to lend to, a trading company or (relevant only for loans made prior to 8 December 2005 and certain replacement loans: see **3.206**) to a property rental company which in either case is not a private company, TCA 1997, s 250(3) allows relief to be given for the interest only if the individual paying it is a full time director or employee in the particular company for the relevant period (being a part time director or employee is not sufficient). Again, it is not a condition for relief when provided through TCA 1997, s 250 for the full time director or full time employee to have a material interest or indeed to have any shares in the company.

In the case where the investee company is not a private company, the relief under TCA 1997, s 248 (as applied by TCA 1997, s 250) given to the full time director or employee for any tax year is limited to €3,050 or, if lower, to the amount of interest paid in the year.

The cases in which any TCA 1997, s 248 relief is given through TCA 1997, s 250 for interest on a loan applied to invest in a public trading or property rental company are significantly reduced by TCA 1997, s 252. As indicated in **3.206**, the latter section denies any TCA 1997, s 248 relief at all where a loan is applied after 28 January 1992 to invest in (or lend to) any quoted company and phases out TCA 1997, s 248 relief for interest on a loan applied before 29 January 1992. However, not every public company is a quoted company as defined in TCA 1997, s 252. Therefore, the restricted TCA 1997, s 248 relief (maximum deduction €3,050) continues to apply after 28 January 1992 in the case of a loan to invest in a public company which is not a quoted company.

Example 3.207.2

Ms W Decent has been a full time director of Liners Ltd, a trading company, for a number of years. In 1995, she borrowed €45,000 and applied it to invest in ordinary shares in that company acquiring a 3.5 per cent holding (her only shares). On 10 September 1997, she obtained a new loan of €29,000 which she applied immediately to repay the then outstanding balance of the 1995 loan.

During the year ending 31 December 2013 (on 16 May 2013), Ms W Decent pays interest of €3,190 on the September 1997 loan. The following points are noted in relation to her claim for relief for 2013 in respect of this interest:

(a) Liners Ltd is a public company in that it is not a private company as defined in Companies Act 1963, s 33. It is not however a quoted company as defined in TCA 1997, s 252 since it does not have any class of shares listed in the official list of any stock exchange or dealt in on any of the other markets mentioned in the definition in TCA 1997, s 252 (see **3.206**).

(b) Since Ms Decent does not have a material interest in Liners Ltd (or in any connected company), she can only obtain TCA 1997, s 248 relief in respect of the loan interest paid if TCA 1997, s 250 applies.

(c) Since she has been a full time employee in the company between 10 September 1997 (date the current loan applied to repay the former qualifying loan) and 16 May 2013 (date interest paid), she is entitled to claim the TCA 1997, s 248 relief through TCA 1997, s 250.

(d) Since Liners Ltd is not a quoted company, the rules of TCA 1997, s 252 are not relevant to deny the TCA 1997, s 248 relief. However, since Liners Ltd is a public company, TCA 1997, s 250(3) applies so that the TCA 1997, s 248 relief for 2013 is only given for the first €3,050 of the interest paid.

Ms Decent is therefore entitled to deduct 25 per cent of the interest paid of €3,050 (ie €763) in arriving at her total income for 2013.

(c) Private qualifying holding company

In the case of a loan applied to acquire ordinary shares in, or to lend to either (i) a qualifying holding company of trading companies, or (ii) (relevant only for loans made prior to 8 December 2005 and certain replacement loans: see **3.206**) to a qualifying holding company of property rental companies which in each case is a private company,

TCA 1997, s 250(2)(a)(ii) allows TCA 1997, s 248 relief to be given to an individual for the interest on the loan provided that he is, for the relevant period, a full time director or full time employee either of that qualifying holding company or of a trading or (relevant only for loans made prior to 8 December 2005 and certain replacement loans: see **3.206**) property rental company (including a public company) which is connected with it. If this condition is met, TCA 1997, s 248 relief is given for the full amount of the interest paid. For interest relief under TCA 1997, s 248 in respect of the loan applied to invest in a private qualifying holding company, being a part time director or employee is not sufficient.

For example, an individual who is a full time employee in a trading company is entitled to interest relief under TCA 1997, s 248 (as extended by TCA 1997, s 250) on a loan applied to lend to a qualifying private holding company that owns 51 per cent of the ordinary share capital of the trading company.

Example 3.207.3

Mr R Smith is a full time employee of Kelly Trading Ltd (a public company) which is a 51 per cent subsidiary of Kelly Enterprises Ltd, a private company whose business consists solely in holding shares and securities of a number of trading companies (including Kelly Trading Ltd). Mr Smith does not hold a material interest in any of the companies in the group.

On 1 April 2008, Mr Smith borrows €100,000 from his bank which he invests in an unsecured loan stock of Kelly Enterprises Ltd (a loan to the company) which is used wholly and exclusively for the business purposes of that company and its connected companies. He pays €9,500 interest on this loan on 31 December 2013.

Since Mr Smith is a full time director of a trading company connected with Kelly Enterprises Ltd and since the holding company is a private company, TCA 1997, s 250(2)(a)(ii) as restricted by TCA 1997, s 248(7) allows him to deduct 25 per cent of the interest paid of €9,500 (ie €2,375) in arriving at his total income for 2013.

(d) Public holding company

In the case of a loan applied to acquire ordinary shares in, or to lend to, a holding company resident in the State which is not a private company, TCA 1997, s 250(1)(a) (as applied by TCA 1997, s 250(5)(e), (f)) allows TCA 1997, s 248 relief to be given to an individual for the interest on the loan provided that he is, for the relevant period, a full time director or full time employee of either the holding company or of any other company which is a 90 per cent subsidiary of the holding company.

For the purpose of relief under this provision, a company is only regarded as a holding company if its business consists wholly or mainly in the holding of shares or securities of trading companies which are its 90 per cent subsidiaries (definition of 'holding company' in TCA 1997, s 411 applied by TCA 1997, s 250(1)). A '90 per cent subsidiary' of the public company is a company of which not less than 90 per cent of the ordinary share capital is directly owned by the public company.

It is to be noted that this definition of a public holding company is more restrictive than that of a qualifying holding company for the relief in the case of a private company (see (c) above). The TCA 1997, s 411 definition requires that the public company's holdings must be wholly or mainly in companies at least 90 per cent controlled by it whereas the private holding company's investments need not necessarily be in controlled companies. Further, the TCA 1997, s 411 definition does not refer to holdings in property rental companies at all.

Finally, if the public holding company is a quoted company as defined in TCA 1997, s 252 (see above), the rules of that section deny any TCA 1997, s 248 relief at all if the loan is one applied on or after 29 January 1992 and, for interest on loans applied before that date, phase out the relief in the same way as explained under Loans for investments in quoted companies in **3.206**. If the public holding company is not a quoted company (as is possible), the relief continues to be available to the extent just mentioned (maximum €3,050 deductible).

When the conditions for the relief are met for a loan to a public holding company, the TCA 1997, s 248 relief given to the full time employee or director through TCA 1997, s 250 is restricted by TCA 1997, s 250(3) to an amount of interest not exceeding €3,050 for the relevant tax year (or to the actual interest paid in the year, if less).

Anti-avoidance rule

No TCA 1997, s 248 relief can be obtained under the TCA 1997, s 250 rules if the company in which the loan proceeds are invested, or any person connected with that company, has during the period between the investment and the payment of the interest made any loans or advanced any money to the individual or to an individual connected with him. However, a loan made or money advanced in the ordinary course of a business that includes the lending of money (for example, by a banker) does not cause this disqualification to apply provided the loan was made on normal commercial terms (TCA 1997, s 250(2)(b)).

For the purpose of this anti-avoidance rule in TCA 1997, s 250(2)(b), a person is connected with the company in which the loan proceeds are invested if he would be so connected by applying the connected person rules of TCA 1997, s 10 (TCA 1997, s 250(5)). Further, TCA 1997, s 250(5)(b) also treats a person as being connected with the investee company if that company makes any loans or advances any money to that person (other than a loan or advance made in the ordinary course of a business which includes the lending of money). This prevents the company in which the loan proceeds are invested from advancing money to an otherwise unconnected person to be lent back to the individual seeking to benefit from the rules of TCA 1997, s 250.

3.208 Loans to invest in partnerships

An individual is generally entitled to relief under TCA 1997, s 253 for interest paid on a loan the proceeds of which are applied in making a qualifying investment in a partnership in which he is an active partner. The relief is given by deducting the interest paid on the qualifying loan in arriving at the borrower's total income. There is no upper limit to the amount of interest deductible under TCA 1997, s 253 if the conditions for this relief are met. There are however restrictions imposed on the availability of this relief in respect of limited or non-active partners under TCA 1997, s 1013.

Relief is given for interest on a loan applied to meet the cost of money invested in any of the following ways:

- (a) purchasing a share in a partnership; or
- (b) contributing money to a partnership on capital or current account or by way of loan, premium or otherwise, provided that the money is used wholly and exclusively for the purposes of a trade or profession carried on by the partnership; or
- (c) paying off another loan the interest on which would have qualified for relief under the section (TCA 1997, s 253(1)).

Two further conditions must be satisfied by the individual claiming relief before interest is deductible under TCA 1997, s 253, namely:

(d) he must have acted personally as a partner in the conduct of the trade or profession carried on by the partnership throughout the period from the application of the loan to the date of payment of the interest for which relief is sought; and

(e) he must be able to show that he has not recovered any capital from the partnership during this period other than an amount applied towards the repayment of the loan qualifying for the relief (TCA 1997, s 253(2)).

The recovery of capital from the partnership not used to repay the loan does not result in a complete loss of TCA 1997, s 253 relief if the amount involved is less than the amount of the loan, but it reduces the interest on which relief is given. The circumstances in which there is a recovery of capital and the effect it has on the interest relief are dealt with in **3.209**.

The individual claiming relief must be an active partner although there is no requirement as to how much time he devotes to the partnership business. The relief is therefore not normally available to a 'sleeping' partner nor to a limited partner who, by definition, is not permitted to take an active part in a partnership business. Further, if a partner who has made a qualifying investment in the firm retires as a partner, he ceases to be entitled to this relief in respect of any interest paid by him after the date of retirement even if the full investment in the firm is not withdrawn until a later date.

There is a third condition for relief under TCA 1997, s 253. No interest deduction is given under the section if the loan is not obtained in connection with the relevant investment in the partnership either at the time of, or within a reasonable time of, the application of the loan proceeds. Further, no relief is available if the loan proceeds are applied for some other purpose before being invested in the partnership (TCA 1997, s 253(6)). In other words, a loan made for some other purpose, whether or not it is first applied for that purpose, does not qualify, while a loan even if obtained to make the qualifying investment must not be used first for any other purpose.

TCA 1997, s 1013 limits the extent to which a limited partner (as widely defined in the section) may claim an unrestricted deduction under TCA 1997, s 253 for interest paid on a loan applied to invest in the partnership in which he is a limited partner. The circumstances in which this restriction applies and the manner in which it is implemented are discussed in **4.512**.

Finance (No 2) Act 1998, s 2 introduced TCA 1997, s 248A which applied a further restriction on interest relief which would otherwise be available under TCA 1997, s 253 and TCA 1997, s 248. However, this restriction has generally been lifted for interest accruing on or after 1 January 2002 but was reinstated with respect to interest accruing from 6 February 2003 in relation to purchases of rented residential premises from a spouse or civil partner of the investor claiming the relief (TCA 1997, s 248A(4); there is an exception in the case of separated and divorced spouses or civil partners (TCA 1997, s 248A(5))). The effect of the restriction is to deny relief in so far as the loan made to the company concerned is used either wholly or partly or directly or indirectly for the purposes of purchasing, improving or repairing a rented residential premises or to pay off a loan incurred for such purposes (TCA 1997, s 248A(2)); the restriction applies only to the extent that the premises is a rented residential premises in the tax year.

A 'residential premises' is defined as 'a building or part of a building used or suitable for use as a dwelling, together with any out-office, yard, garden or other land appurtenant to, or usually enjoyed with, that building or part of a building'; a 'rented residential premises' is a residential premises in respect of which a person is entitled to a rent or receipt from any easement (ie any right, privilege or benefit in, over, or derived from the premises)' TCA 1997, s 96(1).

The practical operation of this provision may be problematic where eg several properties are financed from a variety of funding sources.

Tax relief for acquiring an interest in a partnership

With effect for loans taken out from 15 October 2013, F(No 2)A 2013, s 3 provides that relief will no longer be available for interest on a loan taken out by individuals to acquire a share in or lend to a partnership other than certain farming partnerships.

With regard to existing loans, relief for interest is being phased out and will no longer be available after 2016. In the next four years the relief will be at a reduced level as follows:

Tax Year	Level of Relief
2013	100%
2014	75%
2015	50%
2016	25%
2017	0%

Where an existing loan is refinanced then the relief can continue provided the amount of the new loan does not exceed the balance on the existing loan and the term of the new loan does not exceed the balance of the term of the existing loan. (See also Revenue *eBrief 23/14* issued 24 March 2014.)

3.209 Recovery of capital

The entitlement of an individual to claim relief for interest paid under the rules of TCA 1997, s 248 and s 253, have been discussed in **3.207–3.208**. TCA 1997, s 249 adds further rules dealing with repayments and/or other returns of capital connected with loans qualifying for the interest relief under TCA 1997, s 248. TCA 1997, s 253(4) contain similar rules relating to repayments and returns of capital affecting loans to acquire interests in partnerships for which relief has been claimed under TCA 1997, s 253.

The relief under both sections, including relief under TCA 1997, s 248 as extended by TCA 1997, s 250, is not affected if all capital subsequently recovered in connection with a qualifying investment is applied to reduce the loan qualifying for relief. By reducing the loan outstanding, subsequent interest payments relievable under the sections are correspondingly lower. However in the absence of any provision to prevent it, it would be tempting for a borrower to use capital recoveries to reduce other borrowings not qualifying for an unlimited interest deduction while continuing to claim relief under TCA 1997, s 248 or 253 for the interest on the full amount of the original qualifying loan.

When any capital recovered from the company in which the investment was made, or from any company connected with that company, is not applied in repaying or reducing the outstanding loan balance, the interest otherwise eligible for relief under TCA 1997, s 248 in respect of any period after the capital recovery is reduced (TCA 1997, s 249). Similarly, if any capital recovered from a partnership is not applied in repaying the outstanding loan qualifying for TCA 1997, s 253 relief, the amount of interest deductible under that section for any subsequent period is reduced (TCA 1997, s 253(4)).

The calculation of the reduction in the interest eligible for relief is the same in each case. The calculation must be made separately for each year of assessment commencing with that in which the capital recovery is obtained and continuing so long as there is any claim for relief for interest on the loan in question. The amount of interest otherwise eligible for relief under the relevant section is first determined. It is then reduced in the proportion which is the amount of capital recovered but not used in reducing the loan to the amount of the whole loan.

For the purposes of restricting relief under TCA 1997, s 248, a borrower is treated as having recovered an amount of capital from a company:

(a) if he receives consideration of that amount or value for the sale of any part of his ordinary share capital in that company or in a connected company;
(b) if he receives a repayment of any part of the ordinary share capital in the company or in a connected company;
(c) if the company or a connected company repays a loan or advance from him; or
(d) if he receives any consideration for the assignment of a debt due to him from the company or a connected company.

Further, if he sells or assigns ordinary share capital or a debt otherwise than in a bargain made at arm's length, the sale or assignment, and therefore the amount of capital recovered, is deemed to be for a consideration equal to the market value of the asset disposed of (TCA 1997, s 249(2)).

In applying these rules, one company is connected with another if the connected person rules of TCA 1997, s 10 apply and if it is either a trading company, a property rental company or a qualifying holding company.

Example 3.209.1

Mr CK borrows €10,000 on 1 May 2010 which he invests as to €8,000 in additional ordinary shares in a trading company in which he is a full time employee and already holds over five per cent of its ordinary share capital. He lends the balance of €2,000 to the company at the same time.

On 1 November 2010 he makes an arm's length sale of ordinary shares for €6,000 of which he applies €4,000 in reducing the May 2010 loan, but uses the balance for other purposes. On 1 December 2010 he assigns the debt due from the company to his nephew for a consideration of €1,000 when the market value of the debt is still €2,000; on the same date he is repaid €1,500 of a loan made earlier to a property rental company, a subsidiary of the trading company; neither sum is applied in reducing the May 2010 loan.

Assuming Mr CK pays a constant rate of interest of 13 per cent pa on the loan of €10,000, the total interest payable by him for 2010 is made up as follows:

	€
€10,000 x 13% x 6/12 to 1/11/2010	650
€6,000 x 13% x 2/12 to 31/12/2010	130
	780

The recovery of capital rules apply to the €2,000 of the 1 November 2010 share sale proceeds not applied in reducing the May 2010 loan; the rules apply also the value of the debt assigned to the nephew and to the loan repayment from the connected company.

Consequently, the €780 interest otherwise eligible for relief under TCA 1997, s 248 is reduced to €699 by an amount of €81 calculated as follows:

	€
Capital recovered 1/11/2010 and not used in loan repayment:	
€2,000 x 13% x 2/12 to 31/12/2010	43
Value of debt assigned and not used in loan repayment:	
€2,000 x 13%x 1/12 to 31/12/2010	22
Loan repayment from connected company:	
€1,500 x 13% x 1/12 to 31/12/2010	16
	81

An individual is treated as having recovered an amount of capital from a partnership if he receives a consideration of that amount or value for the sale of any part of his interest in the partnership, or if the partnership returns any amount of capital to him or repays any money advanced by him, or if he receives a consideration of that amount or value for assigning any debt due to him by the partnership. Further, if any such sale or assignment is made in a non-arm's length bargain, it is deemed to be made for an amount equal to the market value of the asset disposed of (TCA 1997, s 253(4), (5)). There is no requirement that the capital recovered should be identified with the original capital invested and which was the subject of the relevant borrowing.

In a partnership, movements on partners' capital and current accounts may be flexible. It may not always be easy in practice to pinpoint when, and to what extent, a partner is receiving a return of capital from the firm. Partnership drawings are frequently made of varying amounts at different times during the firm's accounting period and it may not always be clear whether such drawings are of capital or on account of the partners' expected shares of partnership profits. To the extent that a partner's drawings are in respect of or on account of his profit shares, there is no question of a recovery of capital (unless they turn out to be in excess of the profit shares as ultimately ascertained). In the note of arrangement between the Chief Inspector of Taxes and the CAB issued by the latter on 26 November 1987, the Revenue Commissioners stated their practice as follows:

> In deciding whether there is a recovery of capital, any undrawn profits at the end of an accounting period will not be regarded as forming part of the capital of the partnership unless they remain undrawn for a period of more than two years from the end of the accounting period.

In fact, there seems to be no basis for assuming that profits undrawn for two years or longer have been invested as capital in the partnership, in the absence of a partnership agreement to this effect.

A better, and arguably often the only, practical approach may be to compare the firm's balance sheet at the end of its latest period of account with that at the end of the period in which the investment qualifying for relief was made. If the sum of the capital and loan accounts in the latest balance sheet standing to the credit of the partner claiming the relief has fallen below the sum of the corresponding amounts in the earlier balance sheet, this may suggest that an appropriate part of the individual's interest deduction should be disallowed unless it can be shown that the capital withdrawn from the firm was applied in reducing the relevant loan. Any increase (or decrease) in the partners' account balances due to the revaluation of partnership assets should be excluded (since this does not represent a monetary transaction). Other adjustments may also be necessary depending on the facts (eg where a current account has become overdrawn).

3.210 General restriction on interest relief

TCA 1997, s 817A provides that interest paid on or after 29 February 2000 will not qualify for tax relief under TCA 1997, Pt 8 if a scheme has been effected or arrangements have been made such that the sole or main benefit which might be expected to accrue from the transaction under which the interest is paid is the obtaining of a reduction in tax liability by means of interest relief. TCA 1997, s 817A potentially impacts on relief for interest on qualifying residence loans, loans to invest in qualifying companies and loans to invest in partnerships. The wording of this provision is similar to that of TCA 1997, s 312(2)(a)(ii) and the comments thereon at **6.105** should be noted accordingly.

There is a strong argument that TCA 1997, s 817A should not apply to a *bona fide* loan arrangement entailing substantive commercial benefits notwithstanding there are also tax benefits.

The wording of TCA 1997, s 817A is almost identical to the equivalent legislation in the UK, contained in ITCA 1988, s 787. At the time of the introduction of the UK section the Minister gave undertakings that the section would not be used for genuine commercial transactions structured in a tax efficient manner and that the section was introduced to catch out and out tax avoidance transactions. The section has been invoked by the UK Inland Revenue in the case of *MacNiven (Inspector of Taxes) v Westmoreland Investments Ltd* [1997] STC 1103. Westmoreland Investments Limited ('WIL') was owned by the trustees of an exempt approved superannuation scheme to whom it owed substantial sums of money and as a result had a huge accrued interest liability. It was decided by the scheme's trustees that the best course of action was for the company to be wound down. Accordingly they refinanced WIL allowing it to pay off its existing debts to the scheme, together with the accrued interest. The net effect was to leave the scheme in the same financial position (since in broad terms it had merely lent money to have the same amount repaid to it). The trustees argued that the company had actually paid the accrued interest and it was therefore deductible as a charge. The Inland Revenue refused relief and argued *inter alia* that the provisions of ITCA 1988, s 787 applied (equivalent to TCA 1997, s 817A). Lord Hoffman in delivering the leading judgment in the House of Lords rejected the Revenue's argument, stating:

> In my opinion it is plain that the 'transaction under which the interest is paid' is the original loan and not the arrangements which enabled WIL to pay it.

In *Lancaster v IRC* [2000] STC (SCD) 138, a partner in a firm of chartered accountants transferred part of his property, which consisted of part of the partnership capital, to his wife and thereafter replaced the capital with a loan from his wife. With regard to the interest paid to his wife of the loan, the Special Commissioners held that ITCA 1988, s 787 applied and disallowed the interest deduction claimed. They were satisfied that the scheme was effected and arrangements had been made so that the sole benefit that accrued was a reduction in a tax liability.

3.3 Personal Allowances and Reliefs

3.301 Introduction

As discussed at **3.106**, personal allowances may be granted either as tax credits or, rarely, as deductions from total income in arriving at taxable income; similar considerations apply in the case of reliefs for particular types of expenditure incurred by an individual.

The present division deals with most of the allowances and reliefs governed by TCA 1997, s 458. The relief for qualifying home loan interest under TCA 1997, s 244 is dealt with in **3.202–3.204**. Other reliefs for particular expenditure given as deductions from total income falling within the scope of TCA 1997, s 458 but which are dealt with elsewhere in this book comprise the following: Employment and Investment Incentive (see **18.1**); film investment relief (abolished for 2015 and subsequent tax years) (see **18.4**); expenditure on construction/refurbishment of owner occupied residences in urban renewal, seaside resort areas, etc (see **Division 19** in the 2010 and earlier editions of this text).

A resident individual is entitled to the full amount of the allowances or reliefs, to which his circumstances entitle him. A non-resident individual subject to income tax on income arising in the State may be able to claim a proportion (or all) of the allowances or reliefs specified in TCA 1997, s 458 if he meets the conditions of TCA 1997, s 1032(2), (3) or qualifies for personal allowances under the terms of a double taxation agreement (see **13.610**).

The total exemption from income tax for individuals whose total income do not exceed certain specified amounts (and the related marginal relief) are also discussed in this division (see **3.322**).

The same considerations as apply to married couples apply *mutatis mutandis* to civil partners following the enactment of F(No 3)A 2011.

3.302 Basic personal tax credits

Married persons' or civil partners' basic personal tax credit

The married persons' or civil partners' basic personal tax credit for the tax year 2015 is set at €3,300.

The credit applies in four separate circumstances:

(a) the taxable person is a married person or civil partner, living with their spouse or civil partner, and that taxable person is assessed to income tax under joint assessment;

(b) the taxable person is assessed to income tax under joint assessment by virtue of TCA 1997, s 1026 or s 1031K in the case of separated persons (see **3.508**) or divorced persons (see **3.509**);

(c) the taxable person is a married person or civil partner who is separated but that person wholly or mainly maintains the other spouse or civil partner and does not get a tax deduction for maintenance payments. This would apply generally in circumstances where informal maintenance arrangements are in place and the second spouse or civil partner has little income in their own right. It should be noted that the option for separated spouses or civil partners to elect for joint assessment noted at (b) above is not available unless there is a legally enforceable maintenance agreement in place.

    It should be noted that the second spouse or civil partner is entitled to the single person's basic personal tax credit of €1,650, notwithstanding the fact that the other spouse or civil partner may be entitled to the €3,300 credit. From a practical perspective, the inspector would have regard to the level of the second spouse's or civil partner's income in ascertaining if the other spouse or civil partner was wholly or mainly maintaining the second spouse or civil partner; and

(d) the taxable person is a person whose spouse or civil partner died during the tax year. However, this credit is not available where the surviving spouse or civil partner is entitled to the married persons' credit at (a) above. Therefore, the individuals to whom this credit applies are bereaved spouses or civil partners who were the non-assessable spouse or civil partner in a joint assessment scenario or bereaved spouses or civil partners who were assessed under single assessment.

Single person's basic personal tax credit

The single person's basic personal tax credit for the tax year 2015 is set at €1,650. The credit applies in three separate circumstances:

(a) the taxable person is a single person;

(b) the taxable person is a married person who is assessed under joint assessment but who has opted for separate assessment under TCA 1997, s 1023 (see **3.504**); and

(c) the taxable person is a married person who is assessed as a single person. This could either be a married person or civil partner living with their spouse or civil partner who has elected to be taxed as a single person under TCA 1997, s 1018(4) or a separated person who has not elected for joint assessment.

Widowed person/surviving civil partner tax credit (in year of bereavement)

TCA 1997, s 461A grants a tax credit of €540 to a widowed person or surviving civil partner in any year in which that person is not entitled to the married persons' basic personal tax credit of €3,300 (year of death of spouse or civil partner) or the single person child carer credit. If the widowed person or surviving civil partner remarries, the widowed person tax credit is retained unless that person opts for joint assessment.

3.303 Blind person's tax credit

TCA 1997, s 468 provides an additional personal tax credit of €1,650 – the blind person's tax credit – for the tax year 2015 to an individual who proves that he was a blind person for the whole or any part of that year. Further, if an individual (whether the husband or his wife) on whom a joint assessment under TCA 1997, s 468 is made proves that his spouse or civil partner is a blind person for the whole or any part of the tax year, the person assessed is given the blind person's tax credit.

In the event that, in the case of a joint assessment, both spouses or civil partners are blind in any part (or all) of the tax year 2015, the tax credit is €3,300. For spouses or civil partners assessed as single persons, the single blind person's credit is given to the spouse or civil partner who is blind person or, if both are blind, each gets the tax credit for a single blind person.

A 'blind person' is defined as one whose central visual acuity does not exceed 6/60 in the better eye with correcting lenses, or whose central visual acuity exceeds 6/60 in the better eye or in both eyes but is accompanied by a limitation in the fields of vision that is such that the widest diameter of the visual field subtends an angle no greater than 20 degrees.

A blind person may also claim the cost of a guide dog as a medical expense: see **3.316**.

3.304 Single person child carer credit (formerly the one-parent family credit)

TCA 1997, s 462B (inserted by F(No 2)A 2013, s 7) introduced the single person child carer credit to replace the one-parent family credit from 1 January 2014 onwards. (see also *Revenue leaflet IT74* issued January 2015.)

While the value of the new single person child carer credit is unchanged at €1,650, the availability of the credit to an individual operates differently from the one-parent family credit.

The 'primary claimant', is entitled to the credit in respect of a qualifying child, being an individual who

(i) is not married, cohabiting or in a civil partnership

(ii) is not jointly assessed or receiving the widowed person/surviving civil partner basic personal tax credit.

(iii) has a qualifying child residing with him/her for the whole or the greater part of the year. (Revenue guidelines say more than six months of the year)

If the primary claimant does not wish to claim the credit they can give it up to another person who has a significant role in caring for the child, the 'secondary claimant'. The criteria of the secondary claimant is as per (i) and (ii) above and the secondary claimant has a qualifying child residing with him/her for at least 100 days a year.

TCA 1997, s 462B defines a 'qualifying child' as–

(i) who is born in the tax year, or
(ii) who is under 18 years of age at the start of the tax year, or
(iii) who is over 18 years of age at the start of the tax year but in receipt of full-time instruction (in an education establishment). For example taking a full-time degree course in a university.
(iv) who is over 18 years of age at the start of the tax year but is permanently incapacitated and was incapacitated before the age of 21 years or, if incapacitated after the age of 21, it occurred while in receipt of full-time instruction.

The child must be the individual's own child or a child who is in the custody of the individual and who is maintained by the individual at their own expense. Custody refers to having day-to-day responsibility for the upbringing of the child and for their charge and care. This is distinct from the concept of guardianship where the person may not have regular contact with the child but may have the power to make significant decisions in relation to the child.

Revenue will allocate the credit automatically to the persons who are in receipt of the Child Benefit and who claimed the one-parent family credit in 2013. However a primary claimant who has not been allocated the new credit can do so by completing a form SPCCC1. Where a primary claimant wishes to relinquish the credit to the secondary claimant they can also do so by completing the relevant section on the SPCCC1 form. The secondary claimant should complete the form SPCCC2 in order to claim the tax credit where they are aware the primary claimant is willing to give up the credit.

Only one person can claim one credit in respect of a qualifying child or children.

The credit cannot be apportioned between the primary and secondary claimant. The person in receipt of Child Benefit is the determining factor as to who is the primary claimant.

TCA 1997, s 6 defines a child for the purposes of the Tax Acts and includes a stepchild, an adopted child and a child born to parents who are not married.

One-parent family credit (up to 2013, replaced from 2014 by the single person child carer credit)

TCA 1997, s 462 (substituted by TCA 1997, s 462B from 2014) provides for an additional personal tax credit – the one-parent family tax credit of €1,650 which is granted to an individual where the following conditions are met in relation to the tax year 2013:

(a) the individual is not entitled for that year to the married persons' basic personal tax credit of €3,300 (see **3.302**);
(b) the individual is not a husband living with his wife or a wife living with her husband in that year (ie where single person assessment has been elected for, although joint assessment could be obtained);

(c) the individual is not a man living with a woman as man and wife in that year or vice versa; and
(d) the individual proves that he has a 'qualifying child' (see definition below) residing with him for the whole or any part of that year.

In other words, the credit given by TCA 1997, s 462 is intended as an additional credit for a single parent meeting conditions (a), (b) and (c) to assist him in providing for the qualifying child or children living with him. The single parent may be an unmarried person, a deserted spouse, a separated or divorced spouse, a separated civil partner, a widowed person or surviving civil partner. The additional widowed person tax credit (see **3.302**) is not available where there is an entitlement to the one-parent family tax credit.

Qualifying child

The credit may be claimed by the single parent for a tax year provided that at least one 'qualifying child' resides with him for at least a part of that tax year. Only one credit is given irrespective of the number of qualifying children living with the single parent in the relevant year (TCA 1997, s 462(3)). However, it is possible that a separated couple could both claim the full credit in respect of the same child if the child resided with each parent for part of the relevant year.

The concept of residence in this context almost certainly implies at the least a degree of settled presence or continuity of occupation sufficient to say that the child has his home with the claimant, although this does not mean that it was necessarily his only home at any given time. In practice, where a child stays in total for three months or longer during any tax year in the home of the claimant, the Revenue Commissioners are likely to accept that this constitutes residence for the purposes of TCA 1997, ss 462.

TCA 1997, s 462(1)(a) defines a 'qualifying child' as a child:

(a) who is born in the tax year for which the one-parent family tax credit is claimed;
(b) who is under the age of 18 years at the commencement of the year; or
(c) who, if over the age of 18 years at the commencement of the tax year, either:
    (i) is receiving full time instruction at any university, college, school or other educational establishment, or
    (ii) is permanently incapacitated by mental or physical infirmity from maintaining himself and became permanently incapacitated either before his 21st birthday or, if after that birthday, while he was receiving such full time instruction; and
(d) who is either:
    (i) a child of the individual, or
    (ii) if not a child of the individual, is in the custody of the individual and is maintained by the individual at the individual's own expense for the whole or a part of the tax year concerned.

In applying condition (c)(i), full time instruction at an educational establishment includes undergoing training with any employer for any trade or profession, but only in the case of a child required to devote the whole of his time to the training for a period of not less than two years. In any such case, the employer may be required by the inspector to provide details of the nature of the training to support the claim for the allowance.

The term 'child' is defined for the purposes of the Income Tax Acts to include a stepchild, an adopted child of whom an adoption order under the Adoption Acts is in force (or who is the subject of a foreign adoption order deemed to be a valid order under the Adoption Acts), as well as an illegitimate child (TCA 1997, s 6).

3.305 Widowed parent or surviving civil partner tax credit

TCA 1997, s 463 provides an additional tax credit for a widowed parent or surviving civil partner for each of the five tax years immediately following the tax year in which the spouse or civil partner has died (but not for the year of the death itself).

The amount of the credit is as follows for the tax year 2016:

	€
First year after year of death	3,600
Second year after year of death	3,150
Third year after year of death	2,700
Fourth year after year of death	2,250
Fifth year after year of death	1,800

An individual is entitled to claim the tax credit for each of the five tax years after the year of bereavement provided that, in relation to each year for which the credit is claimed, the following conditions are met:

(a) the individual has at least one 'qualifying child' residing with him for the whole or part of the year;

(b) the individual has not remarried before the commencement of the year; and

(c) the individual is not living together as man and wife with another person in the year.

The three conditions are applied separately for each of the five years so that if all the conditions are met in some of the years, but not in the others or other, the tax credit is given for only the years in which all the conditions are met. For example, a widower might live as man and wife with another woman in the fourth of the five years only. In this case, he is entitled to the tax credit for the first year, second year, third year and the fifth year, but not to any tax credit for the fourth year.

A qualifying child is defined in the same manner as for the purposes of the single person child carer credit of TCA 1997, s 462B (see **3.304**). The widowed parent's child allowance is given even if the qualifying child has a substantial income. Only one qualifying child living with the widowed person is necessary and there is only the one credit available regardless of the number of qualifying children. (See *Revenue leaflet IT40* updated October 2014.)

While remarriage during one of the five years does not prevent the credit being given for that year due to the inclusion of 'commencement' in condition (b), it would appear that living together with another person for part only of one of the relevant years means that no credit for that year can be claimed.

3.306 Age credit

TCA 1997, s 464 provides an additional personal tax credit – the 'age tax credit' – for a tax year to an individual who proves that he is over 65 or reaches that age before the end of the tax year. Further, for an individual living together with his spouse or civil partner and assessed to tax jointly under TCA 1997, s 1017 or s 1031C for a tax year, the age tax credit is given if either spouse or civil partner is over 65 or reaches that age before the end of the year. It should be noted that a reference to spouses or civil partners assessed under joint assessment is deemed to include spouses or civil partners assessed separately (TCA 1997, s 1015(3)(b)); therefore, where one spouse or civil partner satisfies the age requirement, both spouses or civil partners qualify for the credit.

Where the qualifying person is assessed jointly, the amount of the age credit is €490 for the tax year 2015. Where the qualifying person is assessed as a single person, the amount of the credit is €245 for the tax year 2016.

Example 3.306.1

John Alsace, who is 57 on 29 August 2016, lives with his wife, Brigid, who reaches her 65th birthday on 3 June 2016. John and Brigid have elected that the joint assessment for 2016 is to be made on Brigid (see *Joint Assessment on Wife* in **3.502**).

Although John is well under 65, in the joint assessment for 2016 made on Brigid an age tax credit of €490 is given (provided that Brigid claims it when making the joint return). It is sufficient that she became 65 in the tax year.

Example 3.306.2

Same facts as in **Example 3.306.1**, except assume that Brigid had elected to be assessed as a single person in 2016 and has not withdrawn that election so that single person assessment applies to John and Brigid for 2016.

Brigid is entitled to an age tax credit of €245 in arriving at her tax payable for 2016 since she has reached 65 by 31 December 2016. John is not entitled to any age tax credit.

3.307 Incapacitated child credit

TCA 1997, s 465 provides for the tax year 2016 a tax credit of €3,300 – the incapacitated child tax credit – for each incapacitated child of the individual claiming the tax credit or, subject to certain conditions, for any other incapacitated child of whom he has the custody and maintains at his own expense. In the case of an individual assessed jointly with his spouse or civil partner, the tax credit is given to the chargeable person, ie the spouse or civil partner on whom the joint assessment is made (see **3.502**). There is no express provision governing the case where the spouse or civil partner of the chargeable person would be entitled to make the claim but the chargeable person would not be so entitled (unusual in these circumstances). In practice the Revenue would not take this point; it may be noted that TCA 1997, s 1024(2)(a)(xi) envisages an apportionment of relief between the spouses or civil partners by reference to expenditure borne by each for the purposes of separate assessment where TCA 1997, s 465(3) applies: see below.

No dependent relative tax credit (see **3.308**) may be claimed for any child for whom the incapacitated child tax credit is given in any relevant year.

Conditions for tax credit

The term 'child' follows the general definition laid out at **3.304** above.

An incapacitated child, who is not a child (as defined) of the individual is deemed a qualifying child if the claimant proves that for the relevant year of assessment:

(a) the claimant has the custody of, and maintains at his own expense, the incapacitated child; and

(b) neither the claimant nor any other person is entitled to a credit in respect of the same child under TCA 1997, s 465(1) or under any other relevant provision (for example, the allowance given to a single parent), unless any other individual entitled to such a deduction has relinquished his claim to it (TCA 1997, s 465(3)).

The incapacitated child tax credit is given for a tax year in respect of a child if, at any time in that year, the child is either:

(a) under the age of 18 years (age raised from 16 to 18 by FA 1999) and permanently incapacitated by reason of mental or physical infirmity (but see qualification below); or

(b) if over the age of 18 years (age raised from 16 to 18 by FA 1999) at the commencement of the year:

   (i) permanently incapacitated by mental or physical infirmity from maintaining himself, and

   (ii) had become so permanently incapacitated before the age of 21 years or, if after the age of 21 years, had become incapacitated at a time when he was in receipt of full-time instruction at any university, college, school or other educational establishment (TCA 1997, s 465(1)).

A child under the age of 18 years only qualifies for the incapacitated child allowance only if his mental or physical state is such that there would be a reasonable expectation that, if he were over the age of 18 years, he would be incapacitated from maintaining himself.

The reference in (b)(ii) to a child being in receipt of full-time instruction at an educational establishment includes a case where the child was undergoing full-time training by an employer for any trade or profession in circumstances where the child was required to devote the whole of his time to the training for a period of not less than two years. Consequently, a child who became permanently incapacitated when he was undergoing such training is a qualifying child for the allowance although becoming incapacitated when over 21. In any such case, the employer in question may be required to give the inspector information about the nature of the training that was involved (TCA 1997, s 465(4)).

Two or more claimants

It is possible that two or more individuals may be entitled to claim an incapacitated child tax credit in respect of the same child. The most obvious example is for a child of a married couple who are assessed as single persons for the tax year for which an allowance is to be claimed, whether by an election under TCA 1997, s 1018(4) or because they are separated.

In any case where two or more individuals would otherwise be able to claim the tax credit for the same child, TCA 1997, s 465(6) deals with the position. First, it provides that only one tax credit for that child can be given. It then goes on to state that, if the child is maintained by one parent only, that parent alone is entitled to claim the tax credit, but that, if both parents share in the maintenance, each parent is entitled to the part of the tax credit that is proportionate to the amount expended by him on the child's maintenance.

If either parent contributes towards the maintenance in a manner which allows any part of the cost to be deducted from that parent's total income, for example, by a payment under deed of covenant to an incapacitated child over 18, that part of the contribution is deemed not to be part of that parent's contribution towards the cost of maintaining the child. It must therefore not be counted in any apportionment of the incapacitated child credit between the claimants involved. It may be noted that TCA 1997, s 1025(4) prevents any deduction for payments of maintenance made directly or indirectly for the benefit of a child of the payer, including for these purposes a child in respect of whom the payer was at any time prior to the making of the maintenance arrangements entitled to the Incapacitated Child Tax Credit (TCA 1997, s 1025(1)).

The constitutionality of the predecessor to TCA 1997, s 465 was upheld in *MhicMhathuna v Ireland* [1995] ILRM 69, discussed at **1.409**.

3.308 Dependent relative tax credit

TCA 1997, s 466 entitles an individual to claim the dependent relative tax credit of €70 for the tax year 2016 if in that year he maintains at his own expense:

(a) a relative of the individual or of the individual's spouse or civil partner, which relative is incapacitated by old age or infirmity from maintaining himself; or
(b) the widowed mother (or the widowed father) of the individual or of his spouse or civil partner (whether or not the parent is incapacitated); or
(c) a son or daughter of the individual or of the individual's civil partner who resides with him and on whose services the individual, by reason of his own old age or infirmity, is compelled to depend.

It should be noted that there is no statutory definition of 'relative' for the purposes of TCA 1997, s 466. The term must therefore be interpreted very broadly.

However, no credit is available if the relative's total income for the tax year of claim exceeds 'the specified amount'. The 'specified amount' is defined as the aggregate of the payments to which any person is entitled in that year in respect of an old age (contributory) pension at the maximum rate under the Social Welfare Acts on certain stated assumptions. In effect, the specified amount is the single person's old age (contributory) pension which would be payable in respect of the relevant tax year to an individual without dependants who is over the age of 80 years, living alone, and is ordinarily resident on an island.

In the case of a married couple assessed as single persons, the tax credit is given to the spouse or civil partner who maintains the dependent relative, irrespective of the spouse or civil partner to which the dependent relative is related. It is not essential for a married couple or civil partners assessed as single persons to be living together for one spouse or civil partner to be given the allowance for maintaining the dependent relative of the other. In the case of a married couple or civil partners who are jointly assessed there is no provision deeming expense borne by the spouse or civil partner of the chargeable person to have been borne by the partner. In practice the Revenue do not take the point and it may be noted that TCA 1997, s 1024(2)(a)(iii) envisages an apportionment of relief by reference to the actual expenditure incurred by each spouse or civil partner for the purposes of separate assessment.

If two or more persons jointly maintain a dependent relative, for example, two brothers maintain their incapacitated father, the dependent relative tax credit is apportioned between them by reference to their proportionate contributions towards the relative's maintenance. Apart from the case where the dependent relative tax credit is claimed for a son or daughter on whose services an incapacitated taxpayer depends, there is no requirement that the relative maintained should reside with the person claiming the tax credit.

An individual who maintains two or more dependent relatives is entitled to a separate dependent relative tax credit for each such relative, provided that the conditions for the tax credit are met in each case. For each dependent relative, the tax credit is subject to the specified amount restriction applied separately by reference to each relative's total income.

While the amount of the credit is relatively small, entitlement to the credit is a pre-requisite for entitlement to mortgage interest relief on the purchase, repair, development or improvement of a principal residence of a dependent relative (see **3.202**).

3.309 Employed person taking care of incapacitated individual

TCA 1997, s 467 provides an allowance – the 'housekeeper' allowance – for an individual where, either he or his spouse or civil partner (if they are jointly assessed under TCA 1997, s 1017 or s 1031C) employs another person (including a person whose services are provided by or through an agency) to take care either of him/herself or a relative. The individual or the relative as the case may be, must be totally incapacitated by physical or mental infirmity throughout the tax year (TCA 1997, s 467(2)). Relief will be granted in the first year where an individual becomes totally incapacitated notwithstanding the strict requirement that the individual should be incapacitated 'throughout' the year; this reflects previous Revenue administrative practice TCA 1997, s 467(2A)). A relative for these purposes is to include a relation by marriage or a person in respect of whom the individual is, or was, the legal guardian TCA 1997, s 467(1)).

It is not a requirement as such for obtaining the relief, the individual employing such a person is likely to have to register for, and account for, PAYE, if that person is his employee (see **11.103**).

The amount of the housekeeper allowance is €75,000 for the tax year 2015, or, if lower, the actual amount expended in the relevant tax year by the individual or his spouse or civil partner in employing the employed person. It may be noted that TCA 1997, s 1024(2)(a)(iv) provides for an apportionment of the relief by reference to the costs actually borne by each spouse or civil partner for the purposes of separate assessment. (See also Revenue *eBrief 14/15* issued 29 January 2015.)

The relief cannot exceed the €75,000 limit for any one incapacitated individual but there is no limit to the number of individuals by whom it may be claimed (TCA 1997, s 467(2)). Where two or more individuals are entitled to claim a deduction in respect of the same incapacitated individual in a tax year, the aggregate of the deductions claimed by them may not exceed €75,000, and the relief will be allocated between them in proportion to the amounts incurred by them in employing the carer (TCA 1997, s 467(3)).

The allowance is granted as a deduction from total income in arriving at taxable income. The amount of the allowance will be calculated as the lower of (i) the actual cost incurred and (ii) €75,000 scaled down by reference to the proportion of the year for which the individual was incapacitated (eg this becomes €75,000 x 6/12 = €37,500 for 2015 where the individual became incapacitated on 1 July 2015). Where the person is an incapacitated child of the claimant or a dependant relative of the claimant, the incapacitated child credit and the dependant relative credit respectively cannot be claimed under TCA 1997, s 465; 466: see **3.307**; **3.308** (TCA 1997, s 467(4)).

3.310 Employee tax credit

TCA 1997, s 472 provides a tax credit – the 'employee tax credit' – to an individual who has emoluments subject to deduction of income tax under the PAYE procedure (except for any 'excluded' emoluments: see below). For the exception where the credit is now given for certain emoluments taxable under Sch D, see *Foreign Emoluments* below.

TCA 1997, s 126(2) provides that the widow's contributory pension (now replaced by the survivor's contributory pension), orphan's contributory pension, retirement pension, and old age contributory pension are deemed to be emoluments to which the PAYE system applies. In addition, TCA 1997, s 126(2A) (introduced by FA 2013, s 8) provides that maternity benefit, adoptive benefit and health and safety benefit payable from 1 July 2013 are subject to PAYE (but not PRSI or USC). Thus, although in practice all social welfare payments are made gross, the benefits in question are still eligible for the employee tax credit.

The amount of the employee tax credit for 2015 is the lower of €1,650 or the amount of the qualifying emoluments multiplied by the standard rate of tax for the year (20 per cent).

In the case of married persons or persons in civil partnerships, a separate tax credit up to €1,650 is available for each spouse or civil partner, but only up to the extent of each spouse's or civil partner's separate emoluments. If the spouses or civil partners are assessed jointly under TCA 1997, s 1017 or s 1031C, the assessable person is given – any tax credit attributable to the Sch E emoluments of the other spouse or civil partner.

In *Tax Briefing 21*, the Revenue Commissioners state that the employee tax credit has been extended to social security pensions received by Irish residents from EU Member States, notwithstanding the absence of any PAYE-type deduction.

TCA 1997, s 126(3) also deems disability benefit, unemployment benefit (to the extent taxable) occupational injury benefit, and pay-related benefit as emoluments to which the PAYE system applies. The arrangements for dealing with these benefits under the PAYE system are described in **11.101**.

Excluded emoluments

TCA 1997, s 472(1)(a)(i) and (ii), provide that the Sch E emoluments in respect of which an employee credit may be given are to exclude:

(a) any emoluments paid, directly or indirectly, by a body corporate to a proprietary director of the body corporate or to the spouse or child of such a proprietary director;

(b) any emoluments paid, directly or indirectly, by any person connected with a body corporate to a proprietary director of the body corporate or to the spouse or child of such a proprietary director; and

(c) any emoluments paid, directly or indirectly, by an individual (or by a partnership of which the individual is a partner) to the spouse, civil partner or child or child of the civil partner of the individual (but see *Exceptions to Exclusions* below).

For the purpose of (a), a proprietary director of a body corporate is one who is the beneficial owner of, or able to control, more than 15 per cent of the ordinary share capital of the company. For the purpose of (b), the persons who may be connected with a body corporate and the circumstances in which they may be so connected are determined in accordance with the rules in TCA 1997, s 10.

'Child' bears the general meaning described at **3.304** above.

There is no upper age limit so that any son or daughter (stepson, adopted daughter, etc) of a proprietary director is not eligible to claim the employee tax credit in respect of emoluments from the parent's company, business or firm, unless within the exceptions mentioned below.

Where an individual has both excluded emoluments and other emoluments, that individual is entitled to the employee credit to the extent of the other emoluments.

Exceptions to exclusions

TCA 1997, s 472(2) enables an individual, who is a child of a proprietary director, to obtain the employee (PAYE) tax credit, in respect of Sch E emoluments received from a company or other body corporate of which his parent is a proprietary director, but only if the conditions mentioned below are met. Similarly, it allows a child employed by his parent, or by a partnership of which the parent is a partner, to qualify for the tax credit in respect of emoluments from the employment by the parent or the partnership. The conditions to be met for such an individual to qualify for the employee tax credit are as follows:

(a) either:
   (i) the individual must be a 'specified employed contributor' (as defined – see below), or
   (ii) the employer paying the emoluments to the individual – whether the body corporate, the individual's parent or the parent's firm – must have applied the proper PAYE procedure when paying the emoluments; and
(b) the conditions of the office or employment in respect of which the emoluments are paid must require the individual to devote, throughout the tax year for which the tax credit is claimed, substantially the whole of his time to the duties of the office or employment;
(c) the individual must in fact devote substantially the whole of his time to the duties of the office or employment throughout the tax year for which the tax credit is claimed;
(d) the individual must not be a proprietary director of the company paying the emoluments or of any connected company; and
(e) the emoluments paid to the individual from the relevant employment must be €4,572 or more in the tax year of claim.

A 'specified employed contributor' is defined as a person who is an employed contributor for the purposes of the Social Welfare Consolidation Act 2005, but excluding:

(a) a person who is an employed contributor only by virtue of s 9(1)(b) of that Act (ie as a person in insurable (occupational injuries) employment as defined by s 50 of the Act); or
(b) a person to whom Articles 81, 83 or 83 of the Social Welfare (Consolidated Contributions and Insurability) Regulations 1996 (SI 312/1996) applies.

The intention of these conditions is to ensure that the tax credit is only given if the employment is a genuine one. It is also to be noted that the benefit of the credit is to be given by repayment. This means that the credit cannot be assumed until after the end of the year of claim when it can be established whether conditions (b) and (c) have been satisfied.

It is to be noted that the exception to the exclusions for the emoluments paid to the proprietary director, etc is only applicable to a child of the proprietary director, etc. It does not extend to the spouse or civil partner of the proprietary director, etc, nor does it extend to the proprietary director himself.

Foreign emoluments

TCA 1997, s 472(3) extends the PAYE tax credit to the emoluments of an office or employment held or exercised outside the State, but only if all the following conditions are met:

(a) the emoluments of the foreign office or employment are chargeable to tax in the foreign country in which they arise;

(b) the emoluments are subject in that country to a system of tax deduction similar to the Irish PAYE system;

(c) the emoluments are chargeable to Irish income tax on the full amount thereof under Sch D (ie as foreign income chargeable under Case III of that Schedule and are not taxable on the remittance basis); and

(d) the emoluments would, if the office or employment were one held or exercised in the State and the person was resident in the State, be emoluments qualifying for the employee (PAYE) tax credit.

3.311 Home carer's credit

TCA 1997, s 466A provides a tax credit to married couples who are jointly assessed where one spouse or civil partner works in the family home (referred to as the carer spouse), caring for a qualifying person or persons. The maximum tax credit is €1,100 for the tax year 2017.

The following conditions must be satisfied to qualify for the credit:

(a) the claimant must be married or in a civil partnership and assessed to income tax under joint assessment;

(b) one or more qualifying persons being:

  (i) a child in respect of whom child benefit under Social Welfare Consolidation Act 2005 has been received by the claimant or the spouse or civil partner of the claimant during the year,

  (ii) an individual aged 65 years or over, or

  (iii) an individual who is permanently incapacitated by reason of mental or physical infirmity;

normally resides with the claimant and is cared for by the carer spouse or civil partner.

Where the qualifying person is an aged or incapacitated individual, the individual will regarded as normally residing with the claimant if they live within 2 kilometres of each other. The Revenue Commissioners have indicated that individuals on short-term assignments to Ireland who remain within their home country's social security system will be regarded as meeting condition (b)(i) if they receive a comparable benefit in their home state (*Tax Briefing 51*).

TCA 1997, s 466A(6) provides that the credit will be reduced by 50 per cent of the income of the carer spouse or civil partner in excess of €7,200. In calculating the carer's income, no account should be taken of any Carer's Allowance from the Department of Social, Community and Family Affairs.

Under TCA 1997, s 466A(7), the provisions of TCA 1997, s 466A(6) may be disregarded where all of the other relevant qualifying conditions are satisfied and a home carer's tax credit had been obtained in the previous tax year. The credit thus granted cannot exceed the amount of the home carer credit claimed in the previous year.

The Revenue have expressed the view in Leaflet IT 66 that TCA 1997, s 466A(7) only takes effect if the taxpayer would not be entitled to any home carer's credit in the tax year. The contrary view is the taxpayer can elect to substitute a higher amount of tax credit based on the previous tax year for a lower amount of tax credit otherwise available in the current tax year. The area of ambiguity effectively centres on the scenario where the income of the carer spouse or civil partner in the current year is greater than €5,080 but is less than €6,880. The Revenue view may be preferable since s 466A(7) states that 'notwithstanding [s 476A(6)] a tax credit may be granted …', implying that a credit would not otherwise be granted. However, the point remains open to doubt.

Carer credit or wider band

It will be recalled from **3.105** that the standard rate band of a married couple jointly assessed can be increased from the basic €42,800 by the amount of the 'specified income' of the lower earning spouse or civil partner up to a maximum increase of €24,800 (thereby, giving a total of €67,600, see **3.105**). A couple jointly assessed must choose between the home carer credit and the widening of the standard rate band.

3.312 Seafarer's allowance

TCA 1997, s 472B provides an allowance for certain seafarers holding a 'qualifying employment'. The amount of the allowance for the tax year 2015 is €6,350. The allowance cannot exceed the amount of emoluments from the qualifying employment. The allowance is given by way of a deduction from total income in arriving at taxable income. FA 2016 brought about a fisher tax credit which is discussed at para **3.330** and it is necessary to note that it cannot be claimed where a seafarer allowance is claimed.

The allowance is available only to a qualifying individual ie one holding a qualifying employment and who has entered into articles of agreement with the master of the ship in question (TCA 1997, s 472B(1)). The qualifying individual must be resident in the State (TCA 1997, s 472B(4)). A qualifying employment is one where:

(a) the emoluments therefrom are chargeable to tax under either Sch E or Sch D, unless the remittance basis applies (see **13.401**) or the income from the employment is subject to TCA 1997, s 822 (split year residence rule; see **13.503**); it is highly arguable that this exclusion only applies to the extent that the income is exempted under TCA 1997, s 822 (see the discussion of this same issue and of the relevant Revenue practice in the context of TCA 1997, s 823 at **10.306**; 'Applicable Income');

(b) the duties thereof are performed wholly on board a seagoing ship on an international voyage (ie a voyage beginning or ending in a port outside the State); duties which are incidental to duties are those treated as if they too were performed on board a ship, by virtue of TCA 1997, s 472B(6). A 'seagoing ship' is a ship (other than a fishing vessel) which is:
   (i) registered in a EU Member State, and
   (ii) used solely for a trade of carrying passengers or cargo for reward (TCA 1997, s 472B(1)). For these purposes a port outside the State will include a mobile or fixed rig, platform or installation of any kind in any maritime area including Irish waters. (TCA 1997, s 472B(2)(b)).

The following are excluded from the definition of a qualifying employment:

(i) An employment where the emoluments are paid out of State revenues;

(ii) An employment with any statutory board, authority or other similar body established in the State (TCA 1997, s 472B(3)(a)).

The qualifying individual will be entitled to the deduction if he satisfies an authorised officer of the Revenue Commissioners that he was absent for at least 161 days in the tax year for the purposes of performing the duties of the qualifying employment. It is not necessary that he should be actively performing the duties for each day of the period concerned: (TCA 1997, s 472(4)).

An individual is treated as absent from the State if he is absent at the end of the day in question (TCA 1997, s 472 B(2)(a)).

The Minister of Finance may vary the period of absence by order, following consultation with the Minister for Marine and Natural Resources (TCA 1997, s 472B(4)). An individual who claims the deduction will not be entitled to also claim the 'foreign earnings deduction' (see **10.306**) (TCA 1997, s 472B(5)) or the restriction in income tax under TCA 1997, s 825A (TCA 1997, s 825A(5)): see **13.501**. In the case of a married couple or civil partnership the allowance is potentially a deduction in respect of both spouses or civil partners, irrespective of whether or not they are jointly assessed under TCA 1997, s 1018 or s 1031D. While the legislation does not expressly entitle the chargeable person to make a claim in respect of his spouse or civil partner in the case of a jointly assessed couple, the Revenue do not take this point in practice (note also TCA 1997, s 1024(2)(a)(viii)) which envisages that relief will be allocated by reference to the relevant emoluments of each spouse or civil partner for the purposes of separate assessment.

3.313 Credit for rent paid

TCA 1997, s 473, as amended by FA 2011, s 14, entitles an individual to claim a tax credit if he pays rent (qualifying rent) for any residential premises which, during the period for which the rent is paid, was his only or main residence. The legislation does not actually mention the term 'tax credit' but, in substance the 'allowance' granted is a tax credit.

In the case of a married person or civil partners assessed jointly, the credit is also given in respect of qualifying rent paid by their spouse or civil partner.

The relief will only apply to the individuals who were paying qualifying rent on 7 December 2010 and is being phased out entirely by 2017.

Definitions

'Residential premises' are defined as a building or part of a building used or suitable for use as a dwelling held under a tenancy. The term also includes land which the occupier of the building or part of a building has for his own occupation and enjoyment with the building as its garden or grounds of an ornamental nature. The following tenancies are excluded so that any rent payable for them does not qualify:

(a) a tenancy held for a definite period of 50 years or more apart from any statutory extension;

(b) a tenancy where the rent is payable to a Minister of the Government, the Commissioners of Public Works in Ireland or a housing authority for the purposes of the Housing Act 1966; or

(c) a tenancy where part of the rent paid is or may be treated as part of the consideration for the creation of a further interest in the residential premises or in any other property.

The condition that the residential premises must be the only or main residence of the payer has to be met during the period in respect of which the rent payment is made. The fact that the premises may have ceased to be the payer's only or main residence in or before the tax year of the claim does not prevent the credit being given where the main residence condition was met during the rental period in the preceding calendar year. If that condition was satisfied for only a part of a rental period, then only the rent payable in respect of that part of the rental period qualifies for the rent credit (to be given in the following tax year).

The Revenue Commissioners have accepted that there is no requirement that the premises should be located in the State.

'Rent', to qualify for the credit, is defined as including any periodical payment in the nature of rent made in return for a special possession of residential premises, or for the use, occupation or enjoyment of such premises. However, the definition goes on to deny any credit for so much of any rent or other payment (which would otherwise be allowable) as:

(a) is paid to defray the cost of maintenance of or repairs to residential premises for which the tenant would normally be responsible;
(b) relates to the provision of goods or services (for example, cleaning services);
(c) relates to any right other than the bare right to use, occupy and enjoy the residential premises; or
(d) is the subject of a right of reimbursement or a subsidy from any source (unless such reimbursement or subsidy cannot be obtained).

The credit is calculated by applying the standard rate of income tax to the lower of the 'relevant limit' and the actual rent paid in the tax year.

The 'relevant limit' for the tax year 2015 is one of the following:

(a) €1,200 if the individual is entitled to a married person's credit under TCA 1997, s 461(a) or if the claimant is a widowed person (€2,400 if aged 55 or over);
(b) €600, in any other case (for example, single person, separated spouse, married spouse or civil partner electing to be assessed as single person, etc (€1,200 if aged 55 or over).

The 55 years of age condition is satisfied if the person who pays the rent becomes 55 at any time in the tax year for which the rent credit is claimed (eg if he only becomes 55 on 31 December 2015, the condition is met for a 2015 claim). These limits are set to progressively reduce up to 2017 with no rent relief available for the tax year 2018 and onwards.

A claim for the rent credit must be accompanied by a completed form RENT1 which can be obtained on application to the inspector. This form, which contains certain information required by TCA 1997, s 473(6), must also be accompanied by a receipt or acknowledgement of each payment of rent in respect of which the credit is claimed. The person entitled to the rent is required, on being so requested by the tenant who is (or may be) entitled to the credit, to furnish him with the necessary receipt or acknowledgment within seven days from the date of the request.

The Income Tax (Rent Relief) Regulations (made under powers granted by ITA 1967, s 142A(7)) now TCA 1997, s 473(9) require the person claiming relief to provide particulars of any contributions made by third parties towards the rent paid by him. The Regulations also oblige a person in receipt of rents who is required under a notice issued by an inspector to provide particulars of his name, address and tax reference number, as well as details of rents received by him, and of the persons paying such rents, if so required by a notice issued by the inspector. In addition, he must (if relevant) disclose details of any person on whose behalf he received the rents, or any person with whom he jointly received such rents.

3.314 Medical insurance

TCA 1997, s 470 provides for tax relief at source in respect of eligible payments under a qualifying contract for medical insurance and, with effect from 25 March 2004, under a qualifying contract exclusively for dental insurance.

For policies entered into or renewed on or after 16 October 2013, relief is only available on the first €1,000 of a premium for an adult and the first €500 of a premium for a child. In instances where a qualifying student is charged a full adult premium the adult ceiling for the relief will apply (F(No 2)A 2013, s 8) (see Revenue *eBrief 47/14* issued June 2014). For relevant contracts entered into or renewed after 1 May 2015 a child is defined for these purposes meaning an individual under the age of 21 years in respect of whom the payment under a relevant contract has been reduced in accordance with the Health Insurance Act 1994, s 7(5)(a)(ii) or (b)(i)(I); this reduces the relevant age from 23 years but removes the requirement that the individual was in full time education.

So for example if a premium was renewed from 1 November 2013, an individual would get tax relief on 10/12ths of the actual premium paid on their behalf and then 2/12ths of the new limits apply which are €1,000 per adult and €500 per child covered by the policy. (See also *Revenue leaflet IT5* updated October 2014.)

For any such payment to qualify for the relief, it must satisfy the following conditions:

(a) it must be paid to an 'authorised insurer', defined as:

  (i) an undertaking entered on the Registrar of Health Benefits Undertakings established under the Health Insurance Act 1994, s 14, which is a person lawfully carrying on in the State the business of providing insurance against the expenses of illness or those resulting from accidents; a list of undertakings entered on the Register to date is included in *Tax Briefing 30*),

  (ii) an insurer authorised by the EU where the contract was entered into while the individual was not resident in the State but was resident in another EU state (the relevant EU directives are 72/239/EEC, 88/357/EEC and 92/49/EEC),

  (iii) with effect from 25 March 2004, any undertaking authorised under EC non-life insurance regulations (SI 359/1994; SI 115/1976; SI 142/1991),

  (iv) with effect from 25 March 2004, any undertaking lawfully carrying on the business of providing dental insurance for other than routine dental expenses (defined as in the case of the relief for medical expenses under TCA 1997, s 469: see **3.315**) and which is authorised in accordance with article 6 of EU directive 72/239/EEC;

(b) made under a 'relevant contract' which provides specifically for the reimbursement or discharge, in whole or in part of actual health expenses as defined in TCA 1997, s 469 (relief for health expenses: see **3.315**) or dental expenses other than routine dental expenses, defined as in the case of the relief for medical expenses under TCA 1997, s 469: see **3.315**) (TCA 1997, s 470(1) as substituted by FA 2004, s 11).

The contract of insurance may cover other benefits in conjunction with the qualifying benefits mentioned in (b). However, if it does, so much of the premium paid as is attributable to those non-qualifying benefits must be excluded from the amount which is eligible for relief. Apart from this exclusion, the full amount of the premium paid is relievable. There is no upper limit to the amount relievable. Qualifying premiums will be reduced by a sum equal to the amount of the premiums eligible for relief multiplied by the standard rate of income tax (TCA 1997, s 470(3)). This means individuals whose liability to income tax is less than the amount of the tax relieved at source will be at an advantage compared to a tax credit regime.

In the majority of cases, employees will contribute to health or dental insurance policies via their payroll. In some cases, this expense will also be discharged on their behalf by their employer as a perquisite. Employees will then be charged to tax on the resultant benefit-in-kind on the gross value of the premium with a credit (based on the relievable amount multiplied by the standard rate of income tax) granted via the PAYE system or on submission of a tax return (TCA 1997, s 112A).

For the age-related tax credit which afforded an additional tax credit on certain medical insurance premiums, see **3.324**. Where this was granted, the relievable amount was reduced by the amount of the credit so granted. The age-related tax credit no longer applies in respect of policies entered into or renewed with effect from 1 January 2013.

3.315 Health expenses

TCA 1997, s 469, as amended by FA 2011, s 6 and F(No 2)A 2013, s 9 entitles an individual to claim a credit for 2015 in respect of qualifying health expenses actually paid by him in a tax year. The credit is calculated by applying the standard rate of income tax to the amount paid in the tax year. In the case of eligible nursing home fees, the amount paid is to be claimed instead as a deduction from total income. No relief is available for any such expenses recoverable under the relevant contract of insurance, from any public or local authority or by way of compensation or otherwise. The Revenue Commissioners have indicated that it is their general policy to process claims for relief under TCA 1997, s 469 on the basis that the taxpayer will lodge any claims for recovery with the medical insurance company, health board, etc (1997 ITR 90).

In the case of a married couple or civil partners jointly assessed for a tax year in the name of one of the spouses or civil partners (the chargeable person), any payments for qualifying health expenses made by the spouse or civil partner of the chargeable person are deemed to have been made by the chargeable person so as to qualify for the relief as if paid by that person.

'Health expenses', for the purpose of the relief, is defined as meaning expenses in respect of the provision of health care, being expenses representing the cost of:

- (a) the services of a practitioner;
- (b) diagnostic procedures carried out on the advice of a practitioner;
- (c) maintenance or treatment necessarily incurred in connection with services under (a) or procedures under (b);
- (d) drugs or medicines supplied on the prescription of a practitioner;
- (e) the supply, maintenance or repair of any medical, surgical, dental or nursing appliance used on the advice of a practitioner;
- (f) physiotherapy or similar treatment prescribed by a practitioner;
- (g) orthoptic or similar treatment prescribed by a practitioner;
- (h) transport by ambulance; or
- (i) as respects a person who for the year of assessment:
  - (a) is under the age of 18 years, or
  - (b) if over the age of 18 years, at the commencement of the year of assessment is receiving full-time instruction at any university, college, school or other educational establishment,

Either or both:

(i) Educational psychological assessment carried out by an educational psychologist and

(ii) Speech and language therapy carried out by a speech and language therapist.

The Minister of Finance in consultation with the Minister for Health and children and any other appropriately qualified persons, bodies or institutions as the ministers may decide may make an order that any expense or class of expense listed above should cease to be eligible for relief on the grounds of public policy.

Only health expenses incurred in the provision of health care are eligible for relief. 'Health care' is defined as meaning prevention, diagnosis, alleviation or treatment of an ailment, injury, infirmity, defect or disability and includes care received by a woman in respect of a pregnancy as well as routine maternity care. It does not, however, include routine ophthalmic treatment, routine dental treatment or cosmetic surgery or similar procedures unless these are necessary to ameliorate a physical deformity arising from or directly related to a congenital abnormality, personal injury or disfiguring disease. (see also *Routine Treatments Excluded* below). The Revenue Commissioners accept that treatment, etc of mental, as well as physical, ailments will qualify as health care. Revenue practice in relation to kidney patients and the parents/guardian of child oncology patients and children with permanent disabilities is set out in *Tax Briefing 55*. 'Practitioner' is defined as any registered medical doctor or dentist or, where the health care is provided in another country, any person entitled under the laws of that country to practice medicine or dentistry there.

The type of expense which may, in appropriate circumstances, qualify for health expenses relief, but which is not always thought of as doing so, is the expense of maintenance paid for elderly and infirm persons in certain homes for the elderly. For relief for such maintenance expenses to be obtained under TCA 1997, s 469 it is necessary that the home in question provides 24 hour nursing care on-site. If the home does do so, and if the person in respect of whom the maintenance, etc is provided avails of those nursing services by reason of his age and/or state of health, then the expenses of maintenance (including the sums paid for the elderly person's maintenance in the home) should qualify for relief by way of a deduction from total income. When the relief is first claimed in respect of the expenses in relation to the elderly person, the inspector may request a medical certificate to the effect that the individual in question has need of the nursing services.

In *Tax Briefing 17*, the Revenue Commissioners state that in so far as health expenses are defrayed directly or indirectly out of the elderly person's personal income, such expenses may not be claimed. In this connection they will adopt as a rule of thumb that where the elderly person is maintained full time in a nursing home or hospital a deduction of 60 per cent of the dependant relative's old age pension, or similar income, should be set off against the associated health expenses. The Revenue will accept a lower (or nil) percentage where this justified by detailed evidence of the facts. The Revenue states that they will not seek to apply this restriction in the case of 'one-off' treatments, such as a serious operation.

In *Tax Briefing 68*, the Revenue Commissioners indicate that relief under TCA 1997, s 469 may be available for constant nursing care by fully qualified nurses where there is a medical certificate showing the nature of the patient's illness and confirming such care is required; various record-keeping requirements are imposed.

With effect from 2011, contributions made in relation to nursing home fees under the 'Fair Deal' scheme (within Nursing Homes Support Scheme Act 2009, s 3(1)) will qualify for relief, but Financial Support as defined by the Act will not do so.

Routine treatments excluded

It has been indicated above that heath expenses relief is not available for routine dental treatment or routine ophthalmic treatment.

'Routine ophthalmic treatment' is defined as sight testing and advice as to the use of spectacles or contact lenses and the provision and repairing of spectacles or contact lenses. Any other health expenses for opthalmic care qualify for the relief.

'Routine dental treatment' is defined as the extraction, scaling and filling of teeth and the provision and repairing of artificial teeth or dentures. No relief can be obtained for the cost of such items.

Lists of the main dental treatments which in the view of the Revenue Commissioners do, and do not, qualify for health expenses relief are included in *Tax Briefing 6* and *37*.

Amount of claim

There is no upper limit to the amount of qualifying health expenses (the 'amount of the relief'). Relief is given for the tax year in which the expenses are actually defrayed or paid out. However, where qualifying expenses are paid out after the end of a tax year, but relate to health care received in that year, the individual may elect to have the appropriate relief for the expenses of that health care granted for that year (and not for the later year in which he actually pays the expenses). If this election is made, any reliefs for health expenses for subsequent years must also be taken on the same basis, ie by reference to the tax year in which the health care was actually provided (TCA 1997, s 469(5)).

In the case of qualifying expenses paid out of the estate of a deceased person by his personal representatives, the expenses are deemed to have been paid by the deceased person immediately before his death. Such expenses therefore, attract relief in the tax year in which the death occurred (in taxing the income to the date of death). However, the personal representatives, in making a claim for expenses not previously claimed by the deceased, may elect under TCA 1997, s 469(5) to have the relief given in the tax year(s) in which the health care was provided.

It may be desirable to make this election if the death has occurred early in a tax year, but where there were heavy medical expenses accrued but unpaid in the previous year. If the election is not made by the personal representatives, the income in the part of the year to the date of death may not be sufficient to allow relief for all the expenses deemed paid immediately before the death.

The relief for unreimbursed health expenses is only given if the individual concerned completes form MED1 and returns it to the inspector together with the receipts and other necessary vouchers in respect of all items of expense for which relief is claimed. This form is issued on request by the inspector of taxes. It may be submitted with the individual's income tax return or, alternatively, may be returned separately.

3.316 Blind persons – trained guide dog

Where a blind person maintains a trained guide dog registered with the Irish Guide Dogs for the Blind, a maximum sum of €825 may be claimed as a tax credit for the tax year 2015. The credit can be claimed by way of an amendment to an individual's Tax Credit Certificate or by making a claim in their income tax return after the end of the tax year.

Claimants will not be requested to vouch such claims, but an initial claim should be supported by a letter from the Irish Guide Dogs for the Blind confirming that the claimant is a registered owner of a guide dog. This letter should be retained by the claimant for a period of six years.

3.317 Permanent health benefit contributions

TCA 1997, s 471 entitles an individual to claim a deduction from his total income for contributions made by him to a *bona fide* permanent health benefit scheme (see also Revenue *eBrief 13/15* issued 29 January 2015).

The amount of the deduction in the tax year 2015 is the lower of:

(a) the amount of the contribution, or the aggregate of the contributions if more than one, made in that year to the *bona fide* permanent health benefit scheme; or

(b) an amount equal to 10 per cent of the individual's total income for that year.

In the case of a couple assessed jointly under TCA 1997, s 1017 or s 1031C, the upper limit to the deduction is 10 per cent of their joint total incomes. Although TCA 1997, s 471(2) only states that the deduction is not to exceed 10 per cent of the total income of the individual who makes the contribution to the health scheme, TCA 1997, s 1017 and s 1031C provides that, for the purposes of the Income Tax Acts, the total income of the chargeable spouse or civil partner is deemed to include the total income of the other spouse or civil partner. There is no express provision deeming contributions made by the spouse of the chargeable spouse to have been made by the chargeable spouse, but it is thought that the Revenue Commissioners would not take this point in practice. It may be noted that TCA 1997, s 1024 and s 1031I envisage an apportionment of relief between the spouses or civil partners by reference to expenditure borne by each for the purposes of separate assessment.

An individual is also entitled to claim the deduction in respect of any contributions made by an employer on his behalf to a permanent health benefit scheme, but only for such contributions as are chargeable to tax on the individual under the Sch E benefit in kind rules as a perquisite of his office or employment as an employee or director (see **10.203**). In fact, any such permanent health benefit contributions by an employer on behalf of an employee or director are almost invariably treated as taxable income of the individual in question. It is to be noted that, while the full amount of the contribution made by the employer should be included in the individual's total income, the individual's deduction under TCA 1997, s 471 remains limited to 10 per cent of total income (including the taxable benefit).

For the purpose of this relief, a 'permanent health benefit scheme' is defined under TCA 1997, s 125 as any scheme, contract, policy or other arrangement approved by the Revenue Commissioners which provides for periodic payments to an individual in the event of loss or diminution of income in consequence of ill health. For the contribution to qualify for relief, it must be a premium or other periodic payment made to the scheme to provide the specified benefits and the contribution must bear a reasonable relationship to the benefits secured by it.

TCA 1997, s 125(2) provides that a policy of permanent health insurance, sickness or other similar insurance issued in respect of an insurance made after 5 April 1986 automatically qualifies as a permanent health benefit scheme provided that it is issued in a standard form which has been approved by the Revenue Commissioners.

A permanent health, sickness, etc insurance policy may also qualify the contributor automatically for relief if it varies from the standard form in no other respect than by making such alterations that are approved by the Revenue Commissioners as being compatible with a permanent health benefit scheme in the standard form. In approving a standard form of health benefit scheme, the Revenue Commissioners are authorised to disregard any provision in a policy which appears to them to be insignificant.

This now enables insurance companies providing permanent health benefit cover to do so by way of policies drawn up in the standard form, or in an approved variation of that form, so that the person taking out any such policy is assured from the beginning that his contributions will qualify for the relief. However, it remains necessary to have any other form of permanent health benefit scheme specifically approved by the Commissioners (or by an inspector acting on their behalf).

Any benefits payable under the terms of an approved permanent health benefit scheme are deemed by TCA 1997, s 125(3)(a) to be profits or gains arising or accruing from an employment. This even applies if the member of the scheme is a self-employed individual. PAYE must be applied by the operator of the scheme to the payments under the scheme. However, by way of concession, a self-employed individual may apply to his inspector of taxes on form PH(5) for authorisation to treat the payments as part of his trading/professional receipts. If this authorisation is granted, the inspector will inform the operator of the scheme that PAYE should not be applied and that the operator should make an annual return to the inspector of the amounts paid under the scheme.

Employers may deduct qualifying contributions from the employee's gross pay and the tax relief will be given automatically under the PAYE system. In effect, the contribution reduces gross pay for tax and PRSI purposes in the same way as pension contributions (TCA 1997, s 986(1)(g)).

3.318 Relief for college fees

TCA 1997, s 473A, as amended by F(No 2)A 2013, s 14 provides a relief for by way of tax credit in respect of qualifying tuition fees paid to approved colleges for approved part-time or full-time courses. The credit is equal to the amount of the qualifying fees net of a 'disregard' amount, multiplied by the standard rate of income tax for the tax year concerned. The maximum disregard amount for full-time courses from 2015 is €3,000 and for part-time courses is €1,500.

In the case of undergraduate courses, the course must be of at least two academic years' duration and the college must be based in the European Union. The college must be either a publicly funded college or a duly accredited private college. For post-graduate courses, the course must last at least one year but no more than four years and must be based in a public college or a duly accredited private college; in the case of post-graduate courses, there is no requirement that the college be based in the European Union.

The Minister for Education and Science, in consultation with the Minister for Finance, determines the level of fees qualifying for relief.

In certain cases, the Minister for Science and Education must approve colleges and/or courses. The colleges that require approval are:

(a) a private college in Ireland; and
(b) a distance education college based elsewhere in the European Union.

The courses that require approval are:

(a) undergraduate courses in a private college in Ireland;

(b) distance education undergraduate courses in colleges based elsewhere in the European Union; and
(c) postgraduate courses in private colleges in Ireland.

The Minister for Education and Science will supply a list of approved courses and the level of qualifying fees to the Revenue Commissioners by 1 July each year.

This relief is granted to the person who pays the fees who may not be the person undertaking the course. A payment made by the spouse or civil partner of an individual who is assessed under TCA 1997, s 1017 or s 1031C (joint assessment) is deemed to have been made by that individual (TCA 1997, s 473A(3)). Where relief is obtained under TCA 1997, s 473A, the person paying the fees is not permitted to claim relief on them under any other provisions.

Where all or part of the fee is refunded by means of a grant or scholarship by an approved college then relief will not be available on that part of the fee.

Where relief has been claimed in respect of fees partly or fully refunded then the individual must notify Revenue within 21 days of receipt of the refund. Penalties apply where this notification is not made to Revenue or is made incorrectly.

3.319 Relief for training course fees

TCA 1997, s 476 provides relief by way of credit in respect of 'qualifying fees' ie tuition fees paid in respect of an 'approved course (TCA 1997, s 476(2)). The credit is equal to the amount of the qualifying fees multiplied by the standard rate of income tax for the tax year concerned. An 'approved course' is a course of study or training, other than a post-graduate course, provided by an 'approved course provider' which:

(a) is confined to:
  (i) such aspects of information technology, or
  (ii) such foreign languages (ie excluding English and Irish),

  as are approved by the Minister for Enterprise, Trade and Employment, with the consent of the Minister for Finance, for the purposes of the section;
(b) is of less than two years duration;
(c) results in the awarding of a certificate of competence; and
(d) having regard to a code of standards which, from time to time, may, with the consent of the Minister for Finance, be agreed between An Foras and the Minister for Enterprise, Trade and Employment in relation to:
  (i) the quality and standard of training to be provided on the approved course, and
  (ii) the methods and facilities to be used by the course provider in delivering the course and in assessing competence,

  is approved by An Foras for the purposes of the section (TCA 1997, s 476(1)).

An 'approved course provider' is a person providing approved courses who:

(a) operates in accordance with a code of standards which from time to time may, with the consent of the Minister for Finance, be agreed between An Foras and the Minister for Enterprise, Trade and Employment; and
(b) is approved by An Foras for the purposes of the section (TCA 1997, s 476(1)).

A 'certificate of competence' is a certificate awarded in accordance with the standards set out in the code of standards referred to in paragraph (d) of the definition of 'approved course' and certifying that a minimum level of competence has been achieved by the individual to whom the certificate is awarded: TCA 1997, s 476(1).

The relief may be claimed by an individual who has paid qualifying fees which amount to at least €315; no relief is available to the extent that the fees exceed €1,270 (TCA 1997, s 476(1)). The individual must have paid the fees on his behalf or on behalf of a 'dependant', ie a spouse or civil partner or child of the individual or a child of a civil partner of the individual or a person or a person in respect of whom the individual is (or was) the legal guardian. The individual undergoing the training must have been awarded a 'certificate of competence' in respect of the course concerned. Where an individual is the 'chargeable person' by virtue of TCA 1997, s 1017 or s 1031C (joint assessment) any payment by that individual's spouse or civil partner will be deemed to have been made by that individual.

3.320 Relief for service charges (abolished from 2011)

TCA 1997, s 477 (as substituted by FA 2006, s 8) provides for a tax credit in respect of the 'specified amount' of service charges incurred up to the financial year 2011, and paid in full and on time in respect of:

(a) a supply of water for domestic purposes by either a local authority or a group water scheme (TCA 1997, s 477(1), (4));
(b) domestic refuse collection or disposal facilities provided by either a local authority or a private contractor which has duly notified the relevant local authority and provided it with all information required by it (TCA 1997, s 477(1), (4)); and
(c) domestic sewage disposal facilities provided by a local authority (TCA 1997, s 477(1)).

The 'specified amount' is the lower of €400 or full amount of the service charge paid in the previous calendar year. However if an amount in excess of €400 was paid by way of a fixed charge for 2005, that will be the 'specified amount' for the year of assessment 2006. The credit is calculated as the specified amount multiplied by the standard rate of income tax for the particular tax year (TCA 1997, s 477(1), (2)).

The credit is granted to the person liable for the service charges though he may disclaim it in favour of another individual person who resides full-time in the premises and who pays the charges on behalf of the claimant (TCA 1997, s 477(3)(b)).

A payment by the spouse of an individual who is assessed under TCA 1997, s 1017 (joint assessment) is deemed to have been made by that individual (TCA 1997, s 477(3)(a)).

The claimant when requested by the Revenue Commissioners must indicate the name of the local authority or other service provider and whether the charges consist of either or both fixed and non-fixed charges (TCA 1997, s 477(6)).

Any deduction under TCA 1997, s 477(7) is to be in substitution for and not in addition to any other deduction to which the individual might be entitled in respect of the same payment under the Income Tax Acts (TCA 1997, s 477(7)). No relief is available in respect of service charges paid in the year 2011 and in respect of subsequent years.

3.321 Relief for the long-term unemployed

TCA 1997, s 472A provides incentives for both employers and employees in relation to the hiring of long-term unemployed individuals. The tax implications for employers are discussed at **5.308**. Finance Act 2013, s 7 provides for this relief to be discontinued upon the making of a ministerial order (SI 227/2013) and ceased to have effect for such employments commencing on or after 1 July 2013. This relief has been effectively replaced by the Start Your Own Business Relief (see **3.327**) introduced by Finance (No 2) Act 2013, s 6.

The relief provided that where a 'qualifying individual' took up a 'qualifying employment' he was entitled to a series of deductions from his total income for a maximum of three years of assessment, commencing with the year a qualifying employment was first taken up (or the following year if the taxpayer so elects) (TCA 1997, s 472A(2)). The relief ceased if the individual did not remain in the 'qualifying employment' for the three years of assessment (subject to the special rules which apply where the employee has taken up a second qualifying employment in the three-year period: see below).

A 'qualifying individual' was defined as an individual who commenced a 'qualifying employment' and who:

(a) had been continuously unemployed throughout the 12 months prior to commencement is either entitled to credited contributions within SWCA 2005, s 33 throughout that period, or was in receipt of unemployment assistance, unemployment benefit or the one-parent family payment;
(b) belongs to a special category approved by the Minister for Social, Community and Family Affairs with the consent of the Minister for Finance; and
(c) was not previously a qualifying individual (TCA 1997, s 472A(1)(a)).

The period of unemployment required under the first limit of condition (a) above will include any period spent on specified FÁS schemes if the individual was in receipt of unemployment assistance or unemployment benefit. Furthermore, any payments received under such a scheme shall be deemed to be an 'unemployment payment' if the individual was in receipt of such a payment immediately prior to entering the course or scheme (TCA 1997, s 472A(1)(b)). An unemployment payment is defined as either unemployment benefit or unemployment assistance. An individual in this position is thereby enabled to meet the second limit of condition (b) above.

The term 'qualifying employment' means an employment which:

(a) is for a minimum period of 30 hours per week; and
(b) is capable of lasting at least 12 months.

The term does not include an employment from which the previous holder was previously unfairly dismissed, or one in which more than 75 per cent of the emoluments consist of commission. Further, the employer must not have reduced his level of staff in the previous 26 weeks. The emoluments of the employment must be chargeable under Sch E and must not include employments excluded for the purposes of the PAYE credit (ie by virtue of TCA 1997, s 472(1), (2), (see **3.310**) TCA 1997, s 472A(1)(a). The deductions from total income will not be available in respect of an employment where either the individual or the employer is benefiting under an employment scheme (TCA 1997, s 472(5)(a)). An employment scheme means any programme or scheme funded wholly or mainly and directly or indirectly by the State or by any statutory board or any public or local authority (TCA 1997, s 472(1)(a)). The various employment schemes participation in which may be treated as periods of unemployment for the purposes of the deductions are however excluded from the definition (TCA 1997, s 472A(5)(b)).

The amounts of the deductions from total income are as follows:

Personal deduction	€
First year of claim	3,810

Second year of claim	2,540
Third year of claim	1,270
Additional deduction for each qualifying child	
First year of claim	1,270
Second year of claim	850
Third year of claim	425

The total amount of the deductions cannot exceed the amount of emoluments from the qualifying employment in the tax year. (TCA 1997, s 472A(2) (subject to the individual taking up a second qualifying employment in the three-year period, see below)).

The additional child deduction is due for each qualifying child resident with the claimant for the whole or part of a year of assessment. The definition of a qualifying child is the same definition as that used for the purposes of the single parent child carer credit (formerly the one-parent family credit) (see **3.304**). Where a child is maintained by one or more individuals who are eligible for the deduction, the deduction will be allocated between them in the same ratio as each contributes to the maintenance of the child (but excluding any payments which are deductible for income tax purposes) or in any other ratio which they jointly notify to the inspector of taxes. Where the child is maintained solely by one individual then only that individual is entitled to claim the deduction in full (TCA 1997, s 472A(3)(c)). It is also provided that only one deduction of €1,270, €850 and €425 will be granted in respect of each qualifying child. (TCA 1997, s 472A(3)(b)).

Thus, if a qualifying child resides with two individuals A and B (who could be a married couple – see below), in 2010 and 2011 and A commences a qualifying employment in 2010 while B commences a qualifying employment in 2011 the position seems to be as follows:

2010: A is entitled to the 'year one' deduction of €1,270.

2011: A is entitled to the 'year two' deduction of €850; B is not entitled to his 'year one' deduction of €1,270 (since it has already been claimed in respect of the same child) nor can he claim his share of the 'year two' deduction as he is only on year one of his employment.

2012: A is entitled to the deduction of €425; B is again not entitled to any current deduction.

Where the qualifying employment ceases within the three-year period the individual may also claim the benefit of the deductions by reference to the amount of the emoluments of a second qualifying employment taken up within the three-year period. This facility does not permit the individual to claim more than one set of deductions in any year of assessment. There is no provision for offsetting the deductions against a third or subsequent qualifying employment taken up within the three-year period (TCA 1997, s 472A(4)).

A claim for relief is to be made in such form as the Revenue Commissioners may prescribe and must contain any information or statements as the Revenue Commissioners may reasonably require (TCA 1997, s 472A(6)). In the case of a married couple/civil partners, the allowances are potentially available in respect of both spouses irrespective of whether or not they are jointly assessed under TCA 1997, s 1018, s 1031D; it must be borne in mind however that only one child deduction is available per qualifying child (see the discussion on this point, above). In fact, that legislation does not expressly entitle the chargeable person to make a claim in respect of his spouse or civil partner in the case of a jointly assessed couple. The Revenue do not however take this point in practice, note also TCA 1997, ss 1024(2)(a)(viii) and 1031I(2)(a)(viii) which envisage that the allowances will be allocated by reference to the relevant emoluments of each spouse or civil partner for the purposes of separate assessment.

3.322 Age income exemption

The TCA 1997, s 188 complete exemption from income tax for a year of assessment for which an individual's *total* (as opposed to *taxable*) income does not exceed a specified amount where either he or his spouse/civil partner (if he is jointly assessed and thus entitled to the married person's tax credit: see below) are 65 or over at any time in the tax year. The condition for this exemption is that the person claiming it should make an income tax return for the year on one of the prescribed forms (see **3.102**). The definition of 'total income' differs from that which normally applies as it includes income arising outside the State which is not chargeable to tax (TCA 1997, s 188(1)); this ensures *inter alia* that a non-resident with a modest amount of Irish source income does not escape or reduce his liability, and may also deny the benefit of the exemption/marginal relief to individuals eligible for the remittance basis (see **13.401**).

The specified amounts of total income, below which no income tax is payable for 2015 are as follows:

	€
Married* and aged 65 or over	36,000
Single/widowed and aged 65 or over	18,000

* The higher specified amounts available to married persons/jointly assessed civil partners are only available to those jointly assessed (including separate assessment) and to individuals entitled to the married persons' basic personal tax credit of €3,300 under the provisions of TCA 1997, s 461(a)(ii), ie a married person or civil partner who proves that their spouse/civil partner is not living with him or her but is wholly or mainly maintained by him or her for the year of assessment and no tax-deductible maintenance payments are made.

The specified amounts noted above may be increased where the chargeable person has qualifying children (see below) and by the gross amount of any 'relevant' interest included in total income, ie interest subject to deposit interest retention tax (TCA 1997, s 261(c)(i)(I)).

Qualifying children

TCA 1997, s 188(2A) entitles an individual, who has a qualifying child or children living at any time during the tax year for which either of the above income exemptions is claimed to have his specified amount increased for each such qualifying child. For example, a child born on 31 December 2015 (the last day of tax year) allows the increased exemption level for 2015 to be increased.

The amounts by which the specified amount is increased for each qualifying child are as follows:

Increase per qualifying child	€
First child	575
Second child	575
Third and each subsequent child	830

A 'qualifying child' for the purposes of the general income exemptions is given the same meaning as in TCA 1997, s 462B (re the single person child carer credit, see **3.304**).

TCA 1997, s 187(3) deals with the scenario where two (or more) individuals would otherwise be entitled to claim the qualifying child increased specified amount in respect of the same child, the following rules are applied:

(a) only one increased specified amount is to be given in respect of each qualifying child;
(b) if any child is maintained by one individual only, that individual only is entitled to claim the increase for that child;
(c) if the child is maintained by more than one individual, the increase for that child is apportioned between the two individuals in the ratio of the maintenance expenditure (in proportion to the total maintenance for the year) incurred by each individual; and
(d) any payment which one of the individuals makes for or towards the maintenance of the child which that individual is entitled to deduct in computing his total income for tax purposes is not to be counted as payment for or towards the maintenance of the child.

Example 3.322.1

Seán MacDomnaill is jointly assessable for 2016 under TCA 1997, s 1017 with his wife, Máire. Seán and Máire have two qualifying children; Máire reached 65 years of age during the tax year 2016. Their respective total incomes for 2016 are made up as follows:

	Seán	*Máire*
	€	€
Director's emoluments	35,850	
Interest on Government stock	290	290
Net rental income (Máire)		200
Deposit interest	-	64
Total incomes	36,140	554
Joint total income:		
€36,140 + €554		36,694

The specified amount for 2015 is made up as follows:

	€
Married	36,000
First 2 qualifying children:	1,150
Deposit interest (only that subject to DIRT at 41%)	64
Specified amount	37,214

Since Seán and Máire's joint total income (€36,694) does not exceed the specified amount (€37,214), their income is exempt from income tax for 2016 (but Seán is required to file his tax return in the normal way and must claim the exemption).

Marginal relief

TCA 1997, s 188(5) entitles an individual who (or whose spouse) is 65 or over, to claim 'marginal relief' for any tax year where his total income for that year exceeds his specified amount, but does not exceed a sum equal to twice that specified amount (but see *Effect of Deposit Interest on Marginal Relief* below).

In the case of a person assessed to tax jointly under TCA 1997, s 1017 or s 1031C in respect of the couple's total income, marginal relief is given by reference to the joint total income. All references below to total income should be interpreted accordingly.

The effect of marginal relief is to limit the income tax payable for a tax year in respect of the individual's total income to 40 per cent of the excess of total income over the specified amount.

Example 3.322.2

Mr K Antler's, total income for 2016 is €33,000 (including a Sch E pension of €14,000 from which PAYE of €1,500 was deducted) and his wife's total income for that year is €5,100 made up of €3,000 from rents and gross Sch F income of €2,100. The couple are not in receipt of deposit interest. The couple are jointly assessed and Mr Antler is the assessable person.

Mr Antler is 67 and the couple have one dependent child, Robert aged 16. Mr Antler's specified amount for 2015 is therefore €36,575 (€36,000 plus €575 for first, and only, qualifying child). Since the specified amount is less than the total income of €38,100, the age income exemption does not apply.

The calculation of the income tax payable for 2016 (before considering marginal relief) is as follows:

	€
Taxable income	38,100
Income tax payable x 20% (before credits):	7,620
Age tax credit	(490)
Married persons tax credit	(3,300)
PAYE credit	(1,650)
	2,180

Since Mr Antler's total income (joint) of €38,100 does not exceed €73,150 (twice the specified amount of €36,575), he is entitled to claim marginal relief under TCA 1997, s 188(5). This limits his income tax payable to the amount calculated as follows:

	€
Total income (joint)	38,100
Less:	
Specified amount	(36,575)
Excess over specified amount	1,525
Maximum income tax payable x 40%:	610

The final calculation of income tax payable for 2015 is now made as follows:

	€
Income tax payable (before marginal relief)	2,180
Less: Marginal relief	(1,570)
Income tax payable (maximum as above)	610
Dividend withholding tax	(420)
PAYE deducted	(1,500)
Refund due	(1,310)

Where a deduction from income tax payable is made for marginal relief under TCA 1997, s 188 in the case of a husband and wife or civil partners assessable jointly, but who have applied for separate assessment, under TCA 1997, ss 1024(2)(b) and 1031I(2)(b) (see **3.504**), the deduction for marginal relief is apportioned between the spouses in the ratio of the income tax payable by each before deducting the marginal relief.

It is to be noted that the effect of marginal relief, where it applies, is normally to reduce the income tax payable figure before any credits against income tax are deducted. On the other hand, neither the small income exemption nor the marginal relief is to operate to prevent recovery by the Revenue Commissioners from the taxpayer of any income tax he is entitled to charge against another person TCA 1997, s 459(1) and (2) as applied by TCA 1997, s 188(6)).

Example 3.322.3

Mr KT Garters, a married man aged 77 assessed jointly with his wife (age 53), has total income (including his wife's income) for 2016 of €9,850, which figure has been arrived at after deducting a gross amount of €800 paid to his incapacitated mother under a deed of covenant from which he withheld income tax of €160.

Were it not for the covenanted payment to his mother, Mr Garters would have been fully exempted from income tax for 2016 as his total income for the year (€10,650) is lower than the TCA 1997, s 188 specified amount of €36,000. However, he does have a liability to account for the tax withheld from the covenanted payment. His 2016 income tax is computed as follows:

	€
Total income before deducting charge	10,650
Less:	
Specified amount (€36,000) restricted to the amount of total income in order to retain in charge to tax annual payments from which income tax withheld	9,850
Amount on which tax payable	800
Income tax payable:	
€800 x 20%	160

Effect of deposit interest on marginal relief

TCA 1997, s 261 adds two further rules affecting marginal relief in any case where the individual claiming the relief (or his spouse or civil partner if assessed jointly) has interest from a relevant deposit subject to the deposit interest retention tax at the standard rate (see **2.401, 8.204**).

Firstly, in any such case, an individual is permitted to claim marginal relief (to the extent to which it may apply) for any tax year in which his total income does not exceed the aggregate of:

(a) twice his specified amount (before being increased by the deposit interest, including any such interest received by his spouse or civil partner, if assessable jointly); plus

(b) the amount of deposit interest subject to standard rate retention tax received in the tax year (including any such interest received by his spouse or civil partner, if assessable jointly).

Secondly, the income tax payable in respect of total income against which marginal relief may be granted is the net income tax payable after giving credit for the retention tax deducted from the deposit interest.

Example 3.322.4

Mr R Catchers, a single person age 65, carries on a business as a sole trader. He has no dependent children. His total income for 2016 is made up as follows:

	€
Sch D Case I:	
Taxable profits less capital allowances	30,900
Less:	
Trading loss carried forward from 2016	(9,300)
	21,600
Sch D Case IV deposit interest:	5,000
Total income	26,600

Mr Catchers's specified amount for 2016 is €23,000 (ie the standard single person's specified amount of €18,000 increased by the deposit interest of €5,000). Since this specified amount is less than his total income of €26,600, the income exemption does not apply.

His only personal tax credits are his basic personal tax credit and he is entitled to a deduction in respect of €175 permanent health benefit contributions (see **3.317**). The calculation of the income tax payable for 2016 (before considering marginal relief) is as follows:

	€
Total income	26,600
Less:	
PHI contribution	(125)
Taxable income	26,475
Income tax payable (before credits): €21,475 x 20% =	4,295
Dirt Interest € 5,000 x 41%=	2,050
Less:	7,345
Personal tax credit	(1,650)
Earned income credit	(550)
Credit for DIRT on deposit interest:	(2,050)
Income tax payable	2,095

Marginal relief may apply, as his total income does not exceed €41,000 being twice the specified amount as defined by TCA 1997, s 261(c)(ii)(II) (even though the specified amount is deemed to include relevant interest, in computing the amount 'twice the specified amount' relevant interest is only included once).

	€
Total income	26,600
Less:	
Specified amount	23,000
Excess over specified amount	3,600
Maximum income tax payable: €3,600 x 40% =	1,440

Since the maximum income tax payable (after marginal relief), ie €1,440, is lower than the €2,645 income tax payable by Mr Catchers on his taxable income after giving the credit for the retention tax suffered on his deposit interest as required by TCA 1997, s 261(c)(iii), marginal relief will again apply in this case. The interaction of the incomes exemption and claims for repayments of Deposit Interest Retention Tax is discussed at **8.204**.

3.323 Long-term care policies (abolished from 2010)

TCA 1997, s 470A contained provision for tax relief to be available at source up to 31 December 2009 (at the standard rate of tax) for premiums paid on qualifying insurance policies designated to cover in whole or in part the future care needs of individuals who were unable to perform at least two activities of daily living or who suffered from severe cognitive impairment.

TCA 1997, s 470A(1) defined the activities which were required for daily living as washing, dressing, feeding, toilet, mobility and transferring (ie the ability to move from a bed to an upright chair or a wheelchair, or vice versa).

Qualifying policies had to provide for the discharge or reimbursement of expenses of long-term care services for a relevant individual and had to be approved by the Revenue Commissioners.

The relief applied where an individual paid a premium on a qualifying policy in respect of a qualifying individual. A 'qualifying individual' in relation to an individual was that individual, the spouse or child of the individual or a relative of the individual or of the spouse of the individual. The term 'relative' was not defined, but was deemed to include a relation by marriage and a person in respect of whom he is or was the legal guardian.

The policy generally had to be renewable, not connected with any other policy, not be capable of surrender for cash, and provide a termination lump sum or any other cash payments other than periodic payments designed to cover eligible expenses. The claimant had to furnish the insurer with a declaration *inter alia* stating that he was resident in the State and that he would undertake to satisfy the insurer of any change to his residence status (TCA 1997, s 470A(6)).

3.324 Age-related credit for health insurance premiums

TCA 1997, s 470B, inserted by the Health Insurance (Miscellaneous Provisions) Act 2009, s 22, and as most recently amended by FA 2012, s 6 and supplemented by the associated regulations (SI 343/2009) provides for an Age-Related Credit for Health Insurance Premiums ('age-related tax credit') in respect of medical insurance premiums paid to an *authorised insurer* under a qualifying contract which provides for the making of in-patient indemnity payments (as defined by Health Insurance Act 1994, s 2(1)). The contract must have been renewed or entered into between 1 January 2009 and 31 December 2012. The cover must relate exclusively to insured persons (ie the individual, his spouse or civil partner, their children or their dependants) aged 60 years or over on the date the contract was renewed or entered into, as appropriate. The payment must qualify for relief under TCA 1997, s 470(2) (see **3.314**). An 'authorised insurer' has the same meaning as in (a)(i) and (ii) of the definition applicable for medical insurance premiums in **3.314**, but with the exclusion of restricted membership schemes as defined by the Health Insurance Act 1994, s 2(1).

The contract must not be either: (a) a contract of insurance which falls within Health Insurance Act 1994, s 2(1) para (d) of the definition of 'health insurance contract'; or

(b) a contract of insurance relating solely to charges for public hospital in-patient services made under the Health (In-Patient Charges) Regulations (SI 116/1987).

In general, age-related tax credit is only available for the tax years 2009, 2010, 2011 and 2012. However, in the case of medical insurance premiums payable under contracts of insurance renewed or entered into before 31 December 2012, where the premium is payable in instalments and some of those instalments are payable in 2013, age-related tax credit may be given in the year of assessment 2013. The total amount of tax credits granted for 2012 and 2013 cannot exceed the amount of the tax credits which would have been granted had the premiums not spilled over into 2013. The 'age related tax credit' for health insurance premiums has been replaced with 'risk equalisation credits' with respect to the year of assessment 2013 and subsequent years.

The age-related tax credit will be given at source by authorised insurers. The 'relievable amount', is the amount of the payment which refers to the reimbursement or discharge for the reimbursement or discharge, of actual health expenses (within the meaning of TCA 1997, s 469 (see **3.315**). The payment may be made by the assessable individual or, if the individual is a married person or in a civil partnership jointly assessed to tax in accordance with TCA 1997, s 1017 or s 1031C, the individual's spouse or civil partner. The tax credits for contracts entered into or renewed on or after 1 January 2012 are calculated as follows: Age 60–65: €600; Age 65–69: €975; Age 70–75: €1,400; Age 75–79: €2,025; Age 80–85: €2,400; 85 and over: €2,700. The relief may be allocated pro rata against instalments of an annual premium. The relief may be allocated pro rata against instalments of an annual premium. The amount of age-related tax credit is given as a deduction from the relievable amount but together with any relief under TCA 1997, s 470 (see **3.314**) cannot exceed the amount of the payment made to an authorised insurer under a in respect of the insured person for the relevant tax year. The usual limitation on tax credits (ie that they may not exceed the income tax liability for the year) applies.

Where, for any tax year, an employer provides a benefit to an employee in the form of a payment to an authorised insurer under a qualifying contract, and the aggregate of age-related credit and any relief under TCA 1997, s 470 exceeds the tax payable on the benefit, the excess may not be credited against the liability on any other income for that tax year.

3.325 Expenditure to improve energy efficiency of residential premises

TCA 1997, s 477A, as inserted by FA 2011, s 13, provided (from a date to be established by ministerial order) for a credit for expenditure on 'qualifying work' on a 'qualifying residence'. However, it never became effective as the ministerial order was never granted. The section was repealed by F(No 2)A 2013, s 5.

3.326 Home Renovation Incentive (HRI)

TCA 1997, s 477B, inserted by F(No 2)A 2013, s 5, provides for tax relief for home owners who carry out repair, renovation or improvement work on their principal private residence. The HRI provides a tax credit of 13.5 per cent of qualifying expenditure on residential premises situated in Ireland. (See Revenue *eBrief 29/14* dated 24 April 2014.)

The section was amended by Finance Act 2014, s 13 and as a result the tax relief is also available to landlords. (see Revenue *eBrief 19/15* dated 2 February 2015). It was further extended by Finance Act 2016, s 8 such that it is available to tenants of properties owned by housing authorities.

'Qualifying expenditure' for an individual is expenditure incurred by them on qualifying work carried out by a qualifying contractor on a qualifying residence.

'Qualifying work' is any work of repair, renovation or improvement to which the rate of tax specified in VATCA 2010, s 46(1)(c) applies, and which is carried out on a qualifying residence.

Examples of work that qualifies are painting, rewiring, tiling, fitted kitchens, extensions, garages, landscaping, plastering, plumbing, bathroom upgrades, window replacement, attic conversions, driveways and septic tank repair/replacement, wardrobes, central heating systems.

Examples of work that do not qualify are carpets, furniture, white goods such as fridges/cookers and services such as architects' fees (VAT rate 23 per cent).

'Qualifying residence' in relation to an individual is a residential premises situated in Ireland which they own and

(a) occupy as their only or main residence; or
(b) which was previously occupied as a residence before it was acquired by the individual for occupation by them as their only or main residence on completion of the qualifying work and which is indeed occupied by them on completion of the work; or
(c) is occupied by a tenant under a tenancy for which registration is required with the Private Residential Tenancies Bord (PRTB) (and have been complied with); or
(d) which is intended by the individual to be occupied by a tenant under a tenancy for which registration is required with the PRTB (and such registration has been complied with) and which is occupied by a tenant within six months of completion of the qualifying work.

As discussed earlier, this definition was added to by Finance Act 2016, s 8 such that a qualifying residence 'in respect of an individual' includes that covered by a new paragraph being:

> (e) which is owned by a housing authority and for which the housing authority is charging rent pursuant to section 58 of the Housing Act 1966 for the tenancy or occupation thereof by the individual and where the housing authority has given its prior written consent to the individual to qualifying work being carried out on the residential premises.

On point (e) above, a 'housing authority' is defined as having the same meaning as it has in the Housing (Miscellaneous Provisions) Act 1992. Section 23 of that Act outlines what is meant by a housing authority and has different meanings depending on the involved, eg for certain county health districts it would mean the council of the county in which such county health district is situate, for 'a county borough' it would mean the corporation of such county borough.

'Qualifying contractor' is a contractor who satisfies the conditions set out in TCA 1997, s 530G (0 per cent subcontractor) and TCA 1997, s 530H (20 per cent subcontractor) para **2.311**.

The contractor must be VAT registered and tax compliant to carry our HRI work.

There is a minimum spend of €4,405 excluding VAT which must be incurred, ie tax credit €595 (€4,405 x 13.5 per cent)

There is a capped total spend of €30,000, ie tax credit €4,050 (€30,000 x 13.5 per cent).

If there is a grant or insurance claim used for the expenditure, then the qualifying expenditure will be reduced by the amount of the grant or insurance claim.

The scheme runs from 25 October 2013 to 31 December 2018 for qualifying residences (a) or (b) detailed above. The scheme will run from 15 October 2014 to 31 December 2018 for qualifying residences (c) or (d) above. It runs from 1 January 2017 to 31 December 2018 in the case of a qualifying residence under (e) above. Where, during the period from 25 October 2013 to 31 December 2013, qualifying work is carried out on a qualifying residence to which paragraph (a) or (b) of the definition of 'qualifying residence' and where payments in respect of such work are made during that period, any such payments shall be deemed to have been made in the year of assessment 2014. Where, during the period from 15 October 2014 to 31 December 2014, qualifying work is carried out on a qualifying residence to which paragraph (c) or (d) of the definition of 'qualifying residence' refers, and where payments in respect of such work are made during that period, any such payments shall be deemed to have been made in the year of assessment 2015. Where qualifying work, for which planning permission is required, is carried out during the period from 1 January 2019 to 31 March 2019, then provided such permission is granted on or before 31 December 2018, that work shall be deemed to be carried out in the year of assessment 2018.

It is important to note that where a property is converted into more than one rental unit, each rental unit would be deemed a qualifying residence for the purposes of the relief provided the tenancy for each rental unit is registered separately with the PRTB. If a rental property is in six units prior to qualifying work being carried out, but following the carrying out of such work is converted into four rental units, the Incentive will be available in respect of each of the four final units and not each of the initial six units.

The relief is granted over the two years following the year in which payments for the work are made. So the first year for the HRI tax credit will be 2015. If the total tax credit available is €1,000 based on qualifying expenditure of €7,407 made in 2014, a tax credit of €500 is available in 2015 and 2016.

Individuals must comply with Local Property Tax requirements on all residential properties for which they are the liable person, both filing of tax returns and payment of the tax due, in order to avail of the HRI tax credit.

Revenue have stated that the system is to be administered using a new HRI electronic online system from April 2014. The contractor will be required to enter details of the work onto this system once it becomes available. If work is completed before April 2014 then the individual should ensure that the contractor enters the details of the work done on the electronic system in April 2014 otherwise they will not be able to claim the credit. The individual needs to provide the contractor with their Local Property Tax Property ID in order to use the online system. (Not Personal Public Services Number PPSN or Local Property Tax PIN).

Example 3.326.1

Jake paid a VAT registered and tax compliant;

plasterer €3,000 before VAT for plastering work in his home;

painter €4,500 before VAT for internal paint work on his home;

The tax credit is €7,500 x 13.5.% = €1,013.

Example 3.326.2

Ryan paid a VAT registered and tax compliant builder €50,000 before VAT for an extension to his house.

The tax credit is €30,000 x 13.5% = €4,050 (maximum tax credit available).

3.327 Start Your Own Business (SYOB)

A new relief for the long term unemployed was introduced with effect from 1 July 2013 under Finance (No 2) Act 2013, s 6 and is contained in TCA 1997, s 472AA.

The relief takes the form of an income tax exemption. Where a qualifying individual has been unemployed for at least 12 months prior to establishing a new business they can avail of an income tax exemption on the business profits up to a maximum of €40,000 per annum for the first two years. The relief applies to new businesses, ie a trade or profession, set up in the period 25 October 2013 to 31 December 2018. (See also Revenue *eBrief 03/14*.)

Qualifying individual

You may qualify for this relief if:

You have been unemployed for 12 months or more, and

during that period you were in receipt of any of the following:

(a) crediting contributions;
(b) jobseekers allowance;
(c) jobseekers benefit;
(d) one-parent family payment;
(e) partial capacity payment.

Any period spent on certain training courses and schemes can be treated as part of the period of unemployment. Examples of training courses and schemes would include FÁS training courses, Community Employment Schemes, Job Initiative and Back to Education Schemes.

Example 3.327.1

Mary was in receipt of jobseekers benefit for nine months. She then commenced employment but after three months of working the job didn't work out and she is now back in receipt of jobseekers allowance for the last five months. Can she avail of the relief upon setting up a new business?

Yes. The first 9 months' unemployment is linked to the five months giving her a total of 14 months. This only applies in the case where the two unemployment periods are separated by less than 12 months.

Example 3.327.2

Jack is unemployed for the past 13 months and signs on at his local Social Welfare office but does not receive any payments, benefits or allowances due to means testing. Can he avail of the relief upon setting up a new business?

Yes. He is in receipt of crediting contributions in respect of his 13 months' unemployment.

Example 3.327.3

Bernard is working a three-day week and in receipt of job seekers allowance for the other three days a week, for the past two years. Can he avail of the relief upon setting up a new business?

Yes. Social Welfare view is that he is unemployed. He is in receipt of jobseekers allowance for 312 days (3 days a week for 104 weeks) or equivalent to 12 months' unemployment.

'The relief'

The SYOB relief only applies to income tax. USC and PRSI will apply normally to any profits earned in the new business.

The relief does not require pre-approval from the Department of Social Welfare. The relief is claimed when completing your income tax return form each year.

The amount which can be set off against the profits of the new business assessed under Schedule D Case I or II is 'an amount equal to the lesser of:

A x B/C OR €40,000 x B/12

Where:

A is the profit or gains of the new business which would but for this section be charged to tax in the year of assessment

B is the number of months or fractions of months within the year of assessment which fall within the qualifying period and

C is the number of months or fractions of months in the basis period for the year of assessment.

'Qualifying period' means a period of 24 months beginning on the date the qualifying individual commenced a new business.'

How the relief operates is probably best illustrated using an example:

Example 3.327.4

Dale starts a new business on 1 January 2015 and prepares his accounts to the calendar year ended 31 December 2015. His profits are €25,000. For the year ended 31 December 2016 his profits are €50,000. For the year ended 31 December 2017 his profits are €45,000.

Year 1 The full €25,000 is tax free. Business commenced on 1 January and the cap is €40,000. PRSI and USC apply at the relevant rates to the €25,000.

Year 2 The first €40,000 are not subject to income tax with the balance €10,000 as taxable profits. PRSI and USC apply at the relevant rates to the €50,000.

Year 3 Establish the 24 months relief left available;

Year 1 – claimed 12 months

Year 2 – claimed 12 months

Full 24 months already claimed therefore no relief available in Year 3. The full €45,000 is taxable.

Example 3.327.5

Madison starts a new business on 1 March 2015. She has profits in the first 10 months of €40,000 up to 31 December 2015. Her profits for the year ended 31 December 2016 are €50,000 and for the year ended 31 December 2017 are €45,000.

Year 1 The tax free cap is 10/12 x €40,000 = €33,333 (1 March to 31 December) Income tax is payable on the balance of €6,667. PRSI and USC apply at the relevant rates to the €40,000.

Year 2 The first €40,000 are not subject to income tax with the balance €10,000 as taxable profits. PRSI and USC apply at the relevant rates to the €50,000.

Year 3 Establish the 24 months relief left available:

Year 1 – claimed 10 months

Year 2 – claimed 12 months

Year 3 – 2 months available to claim

So the tax free cap is 2/12 x €40,000 = €6,667

The actual profits for 2 months are 2/12 x €45,000 = €7,500.

Therefore, the first €6,667 are not subject to income tax with the balance €38,333 as taxable profits. PRSI and USC apply at the relevant rates to the €45,000.

The total SYOB relief claimed is:

Year 1	€33,333
Year 2	€40,000
Year 3	€6,667
Total	€80,000

TCA 1997, s 472AA(6) provides that where a person commences two or more new businesses the total deduction shall not exceed €40,000 for a year of assessment (F(No 2)A 2013, s 6(6)).

3.328 Compensation for certain living kidney donors

A new relief was introduced in the Finance Act 2014, s 6, to ensure any compensation received by a living kidney donor for the donation of a kidney for transplantation under certain conditions will be exempt from income tax.

This section provides that, with effect from 1 January 2015, compensation for donation of a kidney for transplantation payable to a living donor under conditions defined by the Minister for Health shall be exempt from income tax and shall not be reckoned in computing income for the purposes of the Income Tax Acts. The statutory basis under which the Minister for Health may define conditions under which compensation may be granted is contained in the European Union (Quality and Safety of Human Organs Intended for Transplantation) Regulations 2012 (SI 325/2012), reg 21(2).

The compensation payable relates to necessary expenses of travel and accommodation actually incurred and also loss of income, subject to such conditions as specified by the Minister for Health.

3.329 Earned income tax credit

TCA 1997, s 472AB provides a tax credit to the self-employed and proprietary directors. It applies for the 2016 year of assessment and subsequent years. The credit applies in respect of 'qualifying earned income' which is defined as earned income but does not include emoluments within the meaning of TCA 1997, s 472. Earned income is defined in TCA 1997, s 3(3) for the purposes of the Income Tax Acts:

'earned income', in relation to an individual, means—

(i) any income arising in respect of any remuneration from any office or employment of profit held by the individual, or in respect of any pension, superannuation or other allowance, deferred pay, or compensation for loss of office, given in respect of the past services of the individual or of the individual's husband, civil partner, parent or parent's civil partner in any office or employment of profit, or given to the individual in respect of the past services of any deceased person, whether or not the individual or the individual's husband, civil partner, parent or parent's civil partner shall have contributed to such pension, superannuation allowance or deferred pay,

(ii) any income from any property which is attached to or forms part of the emoluments of any office or employment of profit held by the individual, and

(iii) any income charged under Schedule D and immediately derived by the individual from the carrying on or exercise by the individual of his or her trade or profession, either as an individual or, in the case of a partnership, as a partner personally acting in the partnership.

The above can be summarised as including Sch E and Sch D income. This is supplemented on a without prejudice basis unless otherwise expressly provided by TCA 1997, s 3(2)(b) to include:

(a) any annuity made payable to an individual under the terms of an annuity contract or trust scheme for the time being approved by the Revenue Commissioners for the purposes of Ch 2 of Pt 30 to the extent to which such annuity is payable in return for any amount on which relief is given under s 787, and

(b) any payment or other sum which is or is deemed to be income chargeable to tax under Sch E for any purpose of the Income Tax Acts.

It is submitted that an express provision is not provided by TCA 1997, s 472AB such that the above can be included in the definition of earned income. That said, emoluments within the meaning of TCA 1997, s 472 are excluded from the definition of 'qualifying earned income' for the purposes of the Earned Income Tax Credit. That is defined as:

'emoluments' means emoluments to which Chapter 4 of Part 42 applies or is applied, but does not include—

(i) emoluments paid directly or indirectly by a body corporate (or by any person who would be regarded as connected with the body corporate) to a proprietary director of the body corporate or to the spouse, civil partner, child or child of the civil partner of such a proprietary director, and

(ii) emoluments paid directly or indirectly by an individual (or by a partnership in which the individual is a partner) to the spouse, civil partner, child or child of the civil partner of the individual;

A proprietary director is defined in that section as a director of a company who is either the beneficial owner of, or able, either directly or through the medium of other companies or by any other indirect means, to control, more than 15 per cent of the ordinary share capital of the company. The reference above to emoluments within the meaning of Ch 4 of Pt 42 is a reference to the relevant definition for PAYE purposes which means anything assessable to income tax under Sch E, and references to payments of emoluments include references to payments on account of emoluments. It can be seen from the above that 's 472 emoluments' are to be excluded from the definition of earned income for the purposes of the 'qualifying earned income' definition such that eg proprietary director emoluments are an exclusion from the 's 472 emoluments' exclusion and therefore should qualify for the 'qualifying earned income credit'. This is reasonable given that such directors were excluded from the benefit of the PAYE allowance.

Subject to limits discussed below where for 2017 and subsequent years of assessment, where a taxpayer's total income for the year consists in whole or in part of qualifying earned income (including, where the claimant is a married person or a civil partner jointly assessed any qualifying earned income of the taxpayer's spouse or civil partner deemed to be income of the taxpayer) the taxpayer shall be entitled to the earned income tax credit of—

(a) where the qualifying earned income (but not including, where the taxpayer is a married person or a civil partner so assessed, the qualifying earned income, if any, of the claimant's spouse or civil partner, as the case may be) arises to the taxpayer, the lesser of an amount equal to the appropriate percentage of the qualifying earned income and €950; and

(b) where, in a case where the taxpayer is a married person or a civil partner so assessed, the qualifying earned income arises to the taxpayer's spouse or civil partner, as the case may be, the lesser of an amount equal to the appropriate percentage of the qualifying earned income and €950.

The 'qualifying percentage' referred to above is a percentage equal to the standard rate of tax for that year of assessments. The limits referred to above are as outlined in TCA 1997, s 472AB as follows.

> Where the claimant is entitled to—
>
> (a) employee tax credit in accordance with subsection (4)(a) of section 472 and earned income tax credit under paragraph (a) of subsection (2), the aggregate of those tax credits shall not exceed €1,650, and
>
> (b) employee tax credit in accordance with subsection (4)(b) of section 472 and earned income tax credit under paragraph (b) of subsection (2), the aggregate of those tax credits shall not exceed €1,650.

Therefore if either person is entitled to the employee tax credit then the maximum credit of employee and earned income tax credits cannot exceed €1,650. This section is written similarly to s 472 which comprises the employee tax credit which is reasonable given its raison d'etre to give a similar tax credit to persons other than employees.

Revenue Manual 15.1.44 Earned Income Tax Credit notes that the tax credit is based on an individual's income. Where joint assessment applies, a separate tax credit may be due in respect of each spouse's individual income.

3.330 Fisher tax credit

TCA 1997, s 472BA brings about a credit for certain 'fishers' for the 2017 and subsequent years of assessment. Where for a year of assessment an individual to whom this section applies has spent not less than 80 days at sea actively engaged in seafishing, he or she is entitled to a tax credit (to be known as the 'fisher tax credit') of €1,270. It is important to note that where for a year of assessment an individual makes a claim under this section, relief will not be given under TCA 1997, s 472B for that year of assessment so there can be no double counting in that instance. It applies to an individual resident in the State:

> (a) the profits or gains of whom in relation to their trade as a fisher are charged to tax under Schedule D, or
>
> (b) the emoluments of whom in relation to their employment as a fisher are charged to tax under Schedule E.

The following definitions apply for the purposes of the section.

> 'aquaculture animal' means an aquatic animal at all its life stages, including eggs, sperm and gametes, reared in a farm or mollusc farming area, including an aquatic animal from the wild intended for a farm or mollusc farming area;

'day at sea' means a cumulative period of 8 hours within any 24 hour period during which the fisher undertakes fishing voyages;

'fisher' means any person engaging in fishing on board a fishing vessel;

'fishing vessel' means a vessel which is—

(a) registered on the European Community Fishing Fleet Register in accordance with Commission Regulation (EC) No. 26/2004 of 30 December 2003, and

(b) is used solely for the purposes of sea-fishing, but does not include a vessel that is engaged in fishing or dredging solely for scientific, research or training purposes;

'fishing voyage' means a fishing trip commencing with a departure from a port for the purpose of fishing, and ending with the first return to a port thereafter upon the conclusion of the trip, but a return due to distress only shall not be deemed to be a return if it is followed by a resumption of the trip;

'sea-fish' means fish of any kind found in the sea, whether fresh or in other condition, including crustaceans and molluscs, but does not include salmon, fresh water eels or aquaculture animals;

'sea-fishing' means fishing for or taking sea-fish.

It can be seen from the above that the tracking of times 'at sea' is important for the purposes of this relief. Revenue eBrief No 05/17 refers to a new Tax and Duty Manual, Part 15-01-45 which notes that 'the credit may be offset against an individual's total income, ie income from fishing and other sources. The type of fishing that is covered is fishing for any kind of fish found in the sea, including crustaceans and molluscs, but does not include salmon, fresh water eels or aquaculture animals'.

3.331 "Help to buy" scheme

Background

Finance Act 2016 enacted the above scheme and brought about a new TCA 1997, s 477C into law. The purpose of this provision is to provide a refund of income tax to first time buyers who buy or acquire a newly constructed residential property or a self-build property. It allows a refund of income tax up to a maximum of 5 per cent of the purchase subject to certain limits. No application or claim can be made for this relief after 31 December 2019.

Definitions

'appropriate payment' shall be construed in accordance with subsection (4);

'appropriate tax' has the meaning assigned to it by TCA 1997, s 256;

This is effectively Deposit Interest Retention Tax (DIRT).

'approved valuation', in relation to a self-build qualifying residence, means the valuation of the residence that, at the time the qualifying loan is entered into, is approved by the qualifying lender as being the valuation of the residence;

'first-time purchaser' means an individual who, at the time of a claim under subsection (3) has not, either individually or jointly with any other person, previously purchased or previously built, directly or indirectly, on his or her own behalf a dwelling;

The reference above to 'directly or indirectly' is of some note. Further the reference to 'dwelling' is undefined for the purposes of the section. It is noteworthy that the legislature chose to use such term instead of 'dwelling-house' which is used in TCA

1997, s 604 which deals with principal private residence relief for capital gains tax purposes and similarly for capital acquisitions tax purposes in respect of the exemption relating to same. However, in the latter instance CATCA 2003, s 86 defines a 'dwelling house' as certain structures capable of use 'as a dwelling'. For example in the case of *Matkins v Elson* [1977 STC 46] it was held that a caravan on bricks which had water, electricity, phone and so on was a principal private residence for the UK equivalent of TCA 1997, s 604. That may be but it will be seen below that 'qualifying residence' for the purposes of this relief must include a new 'building' and it is at least arguable that such structure may not constitute one for the purposes of this relief.

> 'income tax payable' has the meaning assigned to it by TCA 1997, s 3;

This is defined in TCA 1997, s 3 'in relation to an individual for a year of assessment, means the chargeable tax less the aggregate of the personal tax credits and general tax credits'.

> 'loan' means any loan or advance, or any other arrangement whatever, by virtue of which interest is paid or payable;

It can be seen that this is prima facie a wide definition. For 'interest' to exist then there must, inter alia, be a sum of money by reference to which the payment is calculated and the sum of money must be due to the person entitled to the payment (eg see *Bennett v Ogston* [15 TC 374], *re Euro Hotel Belgravia Ltd* [15 TC 293]).

'loan-to-value ratio' means the amount of the qualifying loan as a proportion of the purchase value of the qualifying residence or the self-build qualifying residence; TCA 1997, s 477C(11) notes that the loan-to-value ratio in respect of a claim under this section shall not be less than 70 per cent.

> 'PPS number', in relation to an individual, means the individual's personal public service number within the meaning of section 262 of the Social Welfare Consolidation Act 2005;
>
> 'purchase value' means—
>
> (a) in the case of a qualifying residence, the price paid for the qualifying residence, being a price that is not less than its market value, or
>
> (b) in the case of a self-build qualifying residence, the approved valuation;
>
> 'qualifying contractor' has the meaning assigned to it by subsection (2);

Such a contractor means a person who applies to the Revenue Commissioners for registration as a qualifying contractor (pursuant to arrangements for such registration that are put in place by the Revenue Commissioners) and in respect of whom the Revenue Commissioners are satisfied is entitled to be so registered and who—

(i) complies with the obligations referred to in section 530G or 530H (being the Relevant Contractors Tax requirements regarding zero and standard rate contractors respectively), or

(ii) in the case of a contractor who is not a subcontractor to whom the Relevant Contractors Tax requirements applies, complies with the obligations referred to in (i) above other than the obligations referred to in paragraphs (a) and (b) of subsection (1) of section 530G or 530H. The respective paragraphs (a) and (b) refer to a person as follows:

(a) is or is about to become a subcontractor engaged in the business of carrying out relevant operations,

(b) carries on or will carry on business from a fixed place established in a permanent building and has or will have such equipment, stock and other facilities as in the opinion of the Revenue Commissioners are required for the purposes of the business.

In addition the contractor must have been issued with a tax clearance certificate and provides to the Revenue Commissioners—

(i) details of qualifying residences which the contractor offers, or proposes to offer, for sale within the qualifying period,

(ii) details of any planning permission under the Planning and Development Acts 2000 to 2015 in respect of the qualifying residences referred to in subparagraph (i),

(iii) details of the freehold or leasehold estate or interest in the land on which the qualifying residences referred to in subparagraph (i) are constructed or to be constructed, and

(iv) any other relevant information that may be required by the Revenue Commissioners for the purposes of registration of a person as a qualifying contractor.

'qualifying lender' has the meaning assigned to it by section 244A(3);

The following are qualifying lenders under the abovementioned section:

The following bodies shall be qualifying lenders—

(a) a bank holding a licence under section 9 or an authorization granted under section 9A of the Central Bank Act 1971;

(b) a building society incorporated or deemed to be incorporated under the Building Societies Act, 1989;

(c) a trustee savings bank within the meaning of the Trustee Savings Banks Act, 1989;

(d) ACC Bank plc;

(e) a local authority;

(f) a body which—

(i) (I) holds a licence or similar authorisation, corresponding to a licence granted under section 9 of the Central Bank Act 1971, or

(II) has been incorporated in a manner corresponding to that referred to in paragraph (b),

under the law of an EEA state, other than the State,

and

(ii) provides qualifying mortgage loans (as defined in that section);

and

(g) a body which applies to the Revenue Commissioners for registration as a qualifying lender and in respect of which the Revenue Commissioners, having regard to the activities and objects of the body, are satisfied is entitled to be so registered.

'qualifying loan', means a loan, which—

(a) is used by the first-time purchaser wholly and exclusively for the purpose of defraying money employed in—

(i) the purchase of a qualifying residence, or

(ii) the provision of a self-build qualifying residence (including, in a case where such acquisition is required for its construction, the acquisition of land on which the residence is constructed),

(b) is entered into solely between a first-time purchaser and a qualifying lender (but this does not exclude a loan to which a guarantor is a party), and

(c) is secured by the mortgage of a freehold or leasehold estate or interest in, or a charge on, a qualifying residence or a self-build qualifying residence;

'qualifying period' means the period commencing on 19 July 2016 and ending on 31 December 2019;

'qualifying residence' means—

(a) a new building which was not, at any time, used, or suitable for use, as a dwelling, or

(b) a building which was not, at any time, in whole or in part, used, or suitable for use, as a dwelling and which has been converted for use as a dwelling,

and—

(i) which is occupied as the sole or main residence of a first-time purchaser,

(ii) in respect of which the construction work is subject to the rate of tax specified in section 46(1)(c) of the Value-Added Tax Consolidation Act 2010, and

(iii) where the purchase value is not greater than—

(I) where in the period commencing on 19 July 2016 and ending on 31 December 2016, a contract referred to in subsection (3)(a) is entered into between a claimant and a qualifying contractor or the first tranche of a qualifying loan referred to in subsection (3)(b) is drawn down by a claimant, €600,000, or

(II) in all other cases, €500,000;

A contract referred to in sub-s 3(a) is one entered into a contract with a qualifying contractor for the purchase by that individual of a qualifying residence, that is not a self-build qualifying residence. A loan referred to in sub-s 3(b) is a qualifying loan in respect of that individual's self-build qualifying residence.

'relevant tax year' means a year of assessment, within the 4 tax years immediately preceding the year in which an application is made under this section, in respect of which a claim for an appropriate payment, or part of such appropriate payment, is made by an individual;

'Revenue officer' means an officer of the Revenue Commissioners;

'self-build qualifying residence' means a qualifying residence which is built, directly or indirectly, by a first-time purchaser on his or her own behalf;

'tax reference number' means in the case of an individual, the individual's PPS number or in the case of a company, the reference number stated on any return of income form or notice of assessment issued to that company by the Revenue Commissioners;

'tax year' means a year of assessment within the meaning of the Tax Acts;

'VAT registration number', in relation to a person, means the registration number assigned to the person under section 65 of the Value-Added Tax Consolidation Act 2010.

The relief

Claim

TCA 1997, s 477C(3) notes that where an individual has, in the qualifying period (being the period commencing on 19 July 2016 and 31 December 2019), either—

(a) entered into a contract with a qualifying contractor for the purchase by that individual of a qualifying residence, that is not a self-build qualifying residence, or

(b) drawn down the first tranche of a qualifying loan in respect of that individual's self-build qualifying residence, that individual may make a claim for an 'appropriate payment'.

That 'appropriate payment' in accordance with TCA 1997, s 477C(5) shall not be greater than the lesser of:

(i) the amount of €20,000,

(ii) the amount of income tax payable and paid by the claimant in respect of the 4 tax years immediately preceding the year in which an application is made, or

(iii) the amount equal to 5% of the purchase value of the qualifying residence or self-build qualifying residence, as the case may be.

It can be seen from the above that a 'claim' is necessary, this is referred to here as a 'sub-s (3) claim'.

TCA 1997, s 477C(5)(b) and (c) clarifies that for the purpose of (ii) above income tax paid is to include any amount of 'appropriate tax' which has, in accordance with TCA 1997, s 257 (effectively DIRT) and TCA 1997, s 267AA (which deals with the taxation of dividends on regular share accounts), been deducted from payments of relevant interest made to the claimant in the 4 tax years immediately preceding the year in which an application is made. Such clarification is caveated by the fact that the 'appropriate tax' deducted is to be reduced by any appropriate tax repaid to the claimant taxpayer under TCA 1997, s 266A, being repayments of appropriate tax to first time buyers). Further notwithstanding the joint assessment of married couples (TCA 1997, s 1017) and that of civil partners (TCA 1997, s 1031C) the amount of income tax paid by a taxpayer claimant for (ii) above is to be determined by the formula:

$$\frac{A \times C}{B}$$

where—

A is the amount of the total income (if any) of the claimant for the tax year,

B is the sum of the amount of the total income (if any) of the claimant and the amount of the total income (if any) of the claimant's spouse or civil partner, and

C is the amount of income tax paid for the tax year.

The above formula therefore allocates the tax paid to the claimant in respect of his or her income. The reference in 'C' above does not specify a taxpayer but it must be inferred from the wording of TCA 1997, ss 1017 and 1031C that it be the tax payable by the couple concerned. An 'appropriate payment' is made on a FIFO basis in that it will comprise a refund of income tax paid by the claimant for refund of income tax paid by the claimant in respect of the earliest relevant tax year and followed by each succeeding relevant tax year, and thereafter as a refund of the amount of appropriate tax paid by the claimant in respect of the earliest relevant tax year and followed by each succeeding relevant tax year.

Making of appropriate payment

Period commencing 19 July 2016 to 31 December 2016

TCA 1997, s 477C(16)(a)(i) notes that 'Subject to the provisions of this section' where

(a) a contract entered into a contract with a qualifying contractor for the purchase by that individual of a qualifying residence that is not a self-build qualifying residence, entered into by the claimant and qualifying contractor, or

(b) the first tranche of a qualifying loan in respect of that individual's self-build qualifying residence is drawn down by the claimant,

the appropriate payment will be made by the Revenue Commissioners to the claimant's bank account. A different position is taken for later periods.

Period commencing 1 January 2017 to 31 December 2019

TCA 1997, s 477C(16)(a)(ii) and (iii) deal with such period. These provisions note that 'Subject to the provisions of this section'.

Where a contract entered into a contract with a qualifying contractor for the purchase by that individual of a qualifying residence that is not a self-build qualifying residence, entered into by the claimant and qualifying contractor then in that instance the payment will be made to the qualifying contractor's bank account. In this instance here the appropriate payment is made in respect of a claimant to a qualifying contractor then the contractor is required to treat the appropriate payment as a credit against the purchase price of the qualifying residence.

Where the first tranche of a qualifying loan in respect of that individual's self-build qualifying residence is drawn down by the claimant then in that instance the payment will be made to the claimant's qualifying loan bank account. In this instance, the claimant is required to consent to the appropriate payment being paid by the Revenue Commissioners to the qualifying contractor.

Application

In accordance with TCA 1997, s 477C(6)(a) prior to submitting a 'sub-s (3) claim' for the relief, an individual shall make an application to the Revenue Commissioners (referred to here as a 'sub-s (6) application') which shall include—

(i) an indication that he or she intends to make a claim under this section,

(ii) his or her name and PPS number, and

(iii) confirmation by the individual, where such is the case, that the conditions specified below have been met.

The conditions referred to in above are that—

(I) he or she is a first-time purchaser,

(II) where the individual is a chargeable person within the meaning of Part 41A or, as appropriate, Part 41 for a tax year within the 4 tax years immediately preceding the year in which the application is made, he or she has complied with the requirements of that Part or, as appropriate, those Parts and has paid the amount of income tax payable and of universal social charge which he or she is liable to pay, in respect of each such tax year,

(III) where the individual is not a chargeable person within the meaning of Part 41A or, as appropriate, Part 41 for a relevant tax year, he or she has made a return of income, in such form as the Revenue Commissioners may require, and has paid the amount of income tax payable and of universal social charge which he or she is liable to pay, in respect of each such relevant tax year, and

(IV) in the case of an individual to which subparagraph (ii) refers, he or she has been issued with a tax clearance certificate which has not been rescinded.

(V) Where section 1017 or 1031C applied in respect of a tax year, the individual who must meet the conditions referred to in subparagraphs (ii) and (iii) of paragraph (b) shall be the person assessed to tax under joint assessment or the nominated civil partner.

A taxpayer can elect to be treated as having made his or her 'sub-s (6) application' above by 31 December 2016 where:-

(a) (i) in the period commencing on 19 July 2016 and ending on 31 December 2016, a contract with a qualifying contractor for the purchase by that individual of a qualifying residence, that is not a self-build qualifying residence is entered into between the applicant and a qualifying contractor or, as appropriate, the first tranche of a qualifying loan in respect of that individual's self-build qualifying residence is drawn down by the applicant, provided the application is made on or before 31 March 2017, or

(ii) in the tax year 2016 where, in the period commencing on 1 January 2017 and ending on 31 March 2017, a contract with a qualifying contractor for the purchase by that individual of a qualifying residence, that is not a self-build qualifying residence is entered into between the applicant and a qualifying contractor or, as appropriate, the first tranche of a qualifying loan in respect of that individual's self-build qualifying residence is drawn down by the applicant, provided the application is made on or before 31 May 2017.

Where such an election is made, the sub-s (6) application shall be deemed to have been made in the tax year 2016 and the corresponding sub-s (3) claim, where it is made in the tax year 2017, shall be deemed to have been made in the tax year 2016. Further, notwithstanding the obligation on an individual under para (a)(i) above, to, as appropriate, make a sub-s (6) application on or before 31 March 2017, where such an individual makes such an application in 2018 or 2019, the application shall be deemed to have been made in the tax year 2017, and the corresponding sub-s (3) claim shall be deemed to have been made in the tax year 2017. It can be seen that the effect of the above is to 'push' the sub-s (6) application and sub-s (3) claim into the same tax year. The rationale for same can be seen when one looks to TCA 1997, s 477C(8) which deals with when a sub-s (6) application ceases to be a valid claim.

A sub-s (6) application made in any tax year shall cease to be valid on the earlier of the following events:

(i) failure by the applicant to satisfy the conditions specified above;

(ii) on the rescission of the applicant's tax clearance certificate; or

(iii) on the falling of 31 December in the tax year in which the application is made.

However where a sub-s (6) application is made in the period commencing on 1 October and ending on 31 December in any of the tax years 2017, 2018 or 2019 the 'first mentioned period'), and the sub-s (3) claim is made in the period commencing on 1 January and ending on 31 March of the following year, the applicant shall be deemed to have made his or her claim in the first-mentioned period. No claim may be made on foot of an application which ceases to be valid.

Where a sub-s (6) application is made and more than one individual is a party to the application, each such individual is required to—

(a) confirm that he or she is a first-time purchaser,

(b) satisfy the conditions specified above,

(c) consent to provide to the other parties his or her name, address and PPS number, and

(d) agree with each of the other parties as to the allocation between them of the amount of the appropriate payment and notify the Revenue Commissioners of such allocation.

Information requirements of parties concerned

On making a sub-s (3) claim the information requirements of the taxpayer differ depending on whether the qualifying residence is, or is not a self build.

Other than a self build

On making a sub-s (3) claim the claimant is required to provide to the Revenue Commissioners:

(I) his or her name and PPS number,

(II) the address of the qualifying residence,

(III) the purchase value of the qualifying residence,

(IV) details of the qualifying lender,

(V) confirmation that a qualifying loan has been entered into,

(VI) the qualifying loan application number or reference number used by the qualifying lender,

(VII) the amount of the qualifying loan,

(VIII) evidence of the qualifying loan entered into,

(IX) evidence of the contract entered into with a qualifying contractor,

(X) the amount of deposit payable by the claimant to the qualifying contractor,

(XI) the amount, if any, of deposit paid by the claimant to the qualifying contractor,

(XII) confirmation that, on its completion, the qualifying residence will be occupied by the claimant as his or her only or main residence, and

(XIII) in the case of a claimant where in the period commencing on 19 July 2016 and ending on 31 December 2016, a contract with a qualifying contractor for the purchase by that individual of a qualifying residence, that is not a self-build qualifying residence is entered into between the claimant and a qualifying contractor then details of the claimant's bank account to which the appropriate payment shall, subject to the qualifying contractor having satisfied the requirements below, be made.

Critically, a claimant is required to satisfy himself or herself that the contractor is a qualifying contractor so the taxpayer bears the burden of proof in that instance.

Following the making of a claim as described above then the qualifying contractor is required to provide to the Revenue Commissioners—

(a) the contractor's name,

(b) the contractor's tax reference number and VAT registration number,

(c) the name of the claimant,

(d) the address of the qualifying residence,

(e) the purchase value of the qualifying residence,

(f) the amount of deposit payable by the claimant to the qualifying contractor,

(g) the amount, if any, of deposit paid by the claimant to the qualifying contractor, and

(h) in the case of a contract to which in the period commencing on 1 January 2017 and ending on 31 December 2019, a contract with a qualifying contractor for the purchase by that individual of a qualifying residence, that is not a self-build qualifying residence is entered into between the claimant and a qualifying contractor, details of the qualifying contractor's bank account.

A self build

On making a sub-s (3) claim in the case of a self-build qualifying residence, the claimant is required to provide to the Revenue Commissioners—

(a) his or her name and PPS number,

(b) the address of the self-build qualifying residence,

(c) the purchase value of the self-build qualifying residence,

(d) details of the qualifying lender,

(e) confirmation that a qualifying loan has been entered into,

(f) the amount of the qualifying loan,

(g) confirmation that, on its completion, the self-build qualifying residence will be occupied by the claimant as his or her only or main residence, and

(h) details of the qualifying loan bank account to which the appropriate payment shall, subject to a solicitor, acting on behalf of the claimant, having satisfied the below requirements, be made.

Following the making of a claim above, a solicitor, acting on behalf of the claimant, is required to provide to the Revenue Commissioners—

(a) the name of the claimant,

(b) the address of the self-build qualifying residence,

(c) evidence of the qualifying loan entered into between the claimant and the qualifying lender,

(d) evidence of the drawdown of the first tranche of the qualifying loan, and

(e) confirmation of the purchase value of the self-build qualifying residence.

Clawback of relief

On its completion, a qualifying residence or a self-build qualifying residence is required to be occupied by the claimant as his or her only or main residence. A clawback occurs where the residence is not used for the stated purpose within differing timeframes discussed below. Where an appropriate payment is made as a result of a claim and the qualifying residence or self-build qualifying residence ceases to be occupied—

(I) by the claimant, or

(II) where more than one individual is a party to the claim, by all of those individuals,

within five years from occupation of the residence, the claimant shall notify the Revenue Commissioners and pay to the Revenue Commissioners an amount equal to the amount of the appropriate payment, or the lesser percentage there specified of the amount of the appropriate payment. Determining the amount of a lesser payment is arrived at as outlined below being clawbacks between 100 per cent and 20 per cent of the appropriate payment. It is to be noted that this clawback depends on the year 'within' which the cessation of occupation occurs. Where the residence ceases to be occupied as above—

Within the first year from occupation

The claimant shall, within three months from the residence ceasing to be so occupied, pay to the Revenue Commissioners an amount equal to the 100 per cent of the appropriate payment;

Within the second year from occupation

The claimant shall, within three months from the residence ceasing to be so occupied, pay to the Revenue Commissioners an amount equal to 80 per cent of the appropriate payment;

Within the third year from occupation

The claimant shall, within three months from the residence ceasing to be so occupied, pay to the Revenue Commissioners an amount equal to 60 per cent of the amount of the appropriate payment;

Within the fourth year from occupation

The claimant shall, within three months from the residence ceasing to be so occupied, pay to the Revenue Commissioners an amount equal to 40 per cent of the amount of the appropriate payment; or

Within the fifth year from occupation

The claimant shall, within three months from the residence ceasing to be so occupied, pay to the Revenue Commissioners an amount equal to 20 per cent of the amount of the appropriate payment.

TCA 1997, s 477C(18)(a) takes the above matters further and notes that where arising from a claim, an appropriate payment is made to, or in respect of, a claimant, and any condition that imposes a qualification, as respects the claimant, in relation to the making of an appropriate payment is not satisfied by the claimant then the claimant is required to, within 3 months from the date on which the appropriate payment is made, pay to the Revenue Commissioners an amount equal to the amount of the appropriate payment, or part of such an amount, as appropriate. The 'conditions' mentioned above include:

In connection with as self-build qualifying residence TCA 1997, s 477C(18)(b) notes that where, arising from a claim, an appropriate payment is made to an individual, the individual shall pay to the Revenue Commissioners an amount equal to the amount of the appropriate payment—

(I) where the self-build qualifying residence is not completed within two years from the date on which the appropriate payment was made by the Revenue Commissioners, or

(II) if within that two-year period, there are, in the opinion of the Revenue Commissioners, reasonable grounds to believe that the self-build qualifying residence will not be completed within that period.

The above payments to the Revenue Commissioners are require to be made within three months from the end of the two-year period referred to in (I) or, as appropriate, within three months from the Revenue Commissioners issuing notice to the individual to the effect that they had formed an opinion in accordance with (II) above. Para (II) is intriguing in that it would seem that Revenue could form the belief at any point during that two-year timeframe.

Further TCA 1997, s 477C(18)(c) notes that where arising from a claim other than for a *self-build qualifying residence* as outlined above, an appropriate payment is made directly to an individual (who is not a qualifying contractor) then the individual is required to pay to the Revenue Commissioners an amount equal to the amount of the appropriate payment—

(I) if the qualifying residence is not subsequently purchased by the individual within two years from the date on which the appropriate payment was made by the Revenue Commissioners, or

(II) if within that two-year period, there are, in the opinion of the Revenue Commissioners, reasonable grounds to believe that the purchase of the qualifying residence by the individual will not be completed within that period.

The above payments to the Revenue Commissioners shall be made within three months from the end of the two-year period referred to in para (I) or, as appropriate, within three months from the Revenue Commissioners issuing notice to the individual to the effect that they had formed an opinion in accordance with para (II).

Similarly TCA 1997, s 477C(18)(d) where, arising from a claim, an appropriate payment claimed by an individual is made to a qualifying contractor (being one made in the period 1 January 2017 to 31 December 2019 as discussed earlier), and—

(I) the qualifying residence is not subsequently purchased by the individual within two years from the date of the making of the appropriate payment by the Revenue Commissioners, or

(II) if within that two-year period, there are, in the opinion of the Revenue Commissioners, reasonable grounds to believe that the purchase of the qualifying residence by the individual will not be completed within that period,

then the qualifying contractor is required to pay to the Revenue Commissioners an amount equal to the amount of the appropriate payment. Such payment is required to be made within three months from the end of the two-year period referred to in para (I) or, as appropriate, within three months from the Revenue Commissioners issuing notice to the qualifying contractor to the effect that they had formed an opinion in accordance with para (II).

It can be seen that there are many instances above to Revenue forming an opinion within a two-year period of non-completion etc. Revenue issued a FAQ document which notes that 'There will be some flexibility around the two-year period where Revenue are satisfied that the qualifying residence is substantially complete at the end of the two year period or is likely to be completed within a reasonable period of time thereafter'. TCA 1997, s 477C(18)(e) notes that an individual may notify the Revenue Commissioners where he or she has reasonable grounds to believe that the purchase of the qualifying residence by the individual will not be completed within the two-year period referred to in that paragraph.

Where the Revenue Commissioners are satisfied that a qualifying residence or self-build qualifying residence is substantially complete at the end of the two-year period referred to above, and is likely to be completed thereafter within a period of time that, in the opinion of the Revenue Commissioners, is a reasonable one (and such opinion shall be communicated to the person concerned), the aforementioned two-year period shall be extended by that reasonable period.

Administration

Where more than one individual is a party to a claim and a liability arises under the clawback provisions then each party to the claim shall be liable jointly and severally. Where a person who is liable to pay to the Revenue Commissioners an appropriate payment, or part thereof, fails to pay that amount, then an assessment or amended assessment can be made on such persons but this can be appealed within the period of 30 days after the date of the notice of assessment or amended assessment. Such assessed tax shall be deemed to be tax due and payable in respect of the tax year in which the person is liable to pay the amount involved to the Revenue Commissioners. The amount due shall carry interest as determined in accordance with s 1080. Any clawback liability arising unpaid by a qualifying contractor shall be and remain a charge on the freehold or leasehold estate or interest in the land on which the qualifying residence was to be constructed but only where the contractor retains such estate or interest in the land and is not subject to the time limits under the Statute of Limitations 1957, s 36. A person aggrieved by a decision by the Revenue Commissioners to refuse a claim for HTB may appeal to the Appeal Commissioners within a period of 30 days of the notice of the decision.

TCA 1997, s 1021 will not apply to a Help to buy refund under this section such that, eg for a jointly assessed couple, an appropriate payment claimed solely by one of them will not be split between them.

3.4 Self-Employed PRSI, Universal Social Charge and Domicile Levy

3.401 The health contribution and income levy

In addition to income tax, individuals were liable, prior to 2011, to pay the health contribution and the income levy on their income from all sources as adjusted for the purpose of those levies respectively. Both these levies are dealt with comprehensively in the 2010 edition of this book. The Universal Social Charge has replaced the health contribution and the income levy.

3.402 Social insurance for the self-employed

The Social Welfare Consolidation Act 2005 ('SWCA 2005') as amended by subsequent legislation, provides for the payment of social insurance contributions to fund the payment of social welfare benefits to contributors.

The Social Welfare Acts require not only 'employed contributors' in 'insurable employments' but also 'self-employed contributors' to pay 'self-employment contributions' by way of social insurance on income other than from insurable employments. These self-employed contributors are now covered for contributory old age, widows' and orphans' pensions, but not for short term benefits such as unemployment and disability benefits.

In this book, the term 'self-employed PRSI contributions' is generally used to refer to 'self-employment contributions' rather than the latter term itself.

The discussion in this chapter is limited to the liability of the individuals liable to make self-employed PRSI contributions (self-employment contributions) and the manner in which such contributions are collected. The treatment of employed contributors in insurable employments is dealt with in **Division 11** under the heading 'pay-related social insurance.

The same considerations as relate to married couples will apply *mutatis mutandis* to civil partners following the enactment of Finance (No 3) Act 2011.

Legislation and regulations

The main legislation governing self-employed PRSI contributions is contained in SWCA 2005, ss 20 to 23 and Sch 1, Pt 3 (which lists persons who are specifically excluded from being self-employed contributors), but with certain definitions and other points elsewhere in that Act, as amended by subsequent Social Welfare Acts (SWAs).

In addition, the rules in the SWCA 2005 ('Principal Act') for self-employed PRSI contributions are supplemented by provisions in the Social Welfare (Consolidated Contributions and Insurability) Regulations 1996 ('SW Regs') (SI 312/1996) – as amended to date.

Persons liable

Self-employed PRSI contributions are payable by self-employed contributors. A 'self-employed' contributor is defined as any person (other than an 'excepted self-employed contributor' – see below) who:

(a) is over the age of 16 years; and
(b) is under the age of 66 years (pensionable age); and
(c) has reckonable income or reckonable emoluments (see definitions below),

whether or not he is also an employed contributor in an insurable employment (SWCA 2005, ss 2(1), 20).

In the case of married couples, the question of whether a spouse is a self-employed contributor liable to pay these contributions has to be decided separately by reference to the circumstances of each spouse. The fact that, in the case of a couple assessed to income tax jointly under TCA 1997, s 1017, the contributions on the reckonable income of each spouse are charged together in the one tax assessment does not affect the question of whether each spouse is a self-employed contributor and, if so, on how much income.

Income chargeable

Every self-employed contributor is liable to pay self-employed PRSI contributions for each contribution year based on his reckonable income and reckonable emoluments for that year. Since the method by which self-employed PRSI contributions are paid differs dependent on whether charged on reckonable income or reckonable emoluments (see **3.403**), the terms need to be separately defined, as follows:

(a) Reckonable income

An individual's 'reckonable income' for a contribution year is defined as:

> the aggregate of his income from all sources for the year as estimated in accordance with the provisions of the Income Tax Acts, but excluding:
>
> (a) reckonable earnings (see below);
> (b) reckonable emoluments (see below);
> (c) such other income as regulations prescribe is to be excluded;
>
> but without regard to:
>
> (i) the writers, composers, artists, etc exemption of TCA 1997, s 195 (see **3.102**);
> (ii) the stallion fees exemption of TCA 1997, s 231 (see **7.305**);
> (iii) the woodlands exemption of TCA 1997, s 232 (see **7.4**);
> (iv) exemption for provision of certain childcare services TCA 1997, s 216C;
> (v) the income tax rules of TCA 1997, s 1017 regarding the joint assessment of husband and wife (see **3.502**);
>
> but after deducting:
>
> any capital allowances (as referred to in TCA 1997, s 2) to which the self-employed contributor is entitled for the year to the extent that such allowances are deducted from or set off against the income included in reckonable income for the year (SWCA 2005, s 2(1)).

The definition would seem to include income taxed under Sch D Case IV charged as a result of restricting specified reliefs on certain high income individuals: see **3.111**.

From 2011 relief is no longer extended to pension contributions of any description. The requirement to disregard the income tax exemptions mentioned in (i), (ii) and (iii) in determining reckonable income means that any income under these headings is chargeable to self-employed PRSI contributions although exempted from income tax. An individual in receipt of exempt income will apparently need to register as a self-employed contributor in respect of such income.

Balancing charges, while assessed to tax in the same manner as trading profits, are not 'income' as such (see *IRC v Wood Bros* 38 TC 275). The legislation itself recognises that capital allowances would not be a deduction in computing income in the absence of a specific provision to this effect.

Interest from deposit accounts which is subject to DIRT, other than interest on Special Savings Accounts (which is excluded from the computation of total income and is therefore effectively exempt: see **8.204**) is potentially subject to self-employed PRSI. Any gains which may be taxable in respect of Special Savings Incentive accounts are taxed in the hands of the qualifying fund manager and do not form part of the deposit holder's total income so that there can be no liability thereon in respect of self-employed PRSI.

Income deemed to arise on the disposal of interests in offshore funds or foreign life policies based in designated 'offshore states' is not liable to Self-Employed PRSI (see **17.407**). Similar considerations apply to profits and gains in respect of Irish collective investment undertakings and Irish life policies (see **8.401**).

The requirement under (iv) to ignore the income tax joint assessment rules in the case of married persons means that the self-employed PRSI contributions for a husband and his wife must be determined separately for each, whether the spouses are charged to income tax jointly or as single persons.

'Reckonable earnings', which are excluded from reckonable income (and from reckonable emoluments) so as not to be charged to the self-employed PRSI contributions, are all earnings derived from an insurable employment or an insurable (occupational injuries) employment (SWCA 2005, s 2(1)) (these are potentially liable to employed PRSI contributions – see **11.202**).

An 'insurable employment' is basically any employment exercised in the State under any contract of service or apprenticeship by a person over age 16 and under age 66 (but excluding certain employments listed in SWCA 2005, Sch 1, Pt 2). An 'insurable (occupational injuries) employment' is similarly defined, but with the exception that it includes an employment exercised in the State by a person under age 16 or by a person over age 66. For a detailed discussion of the distinction between insurable and non-insurable employments, see **11.202**.

(b) Reckonable emoluments

'Reckonable emoluments', for the purposes of self-employed PRSI contributions, are defined as:

> emoluments chargeable to income tax under Sch E and subject to PAYE under TCA 1997, Pt 42, Ch 4 (see **11.101**, **11.102**), but excluding:
>
> (a) reckonable earnings (see above);
>
> (b) such other income as regulations prescribe is to be excluded;
>
> disregarding (from 2011 onwards) allowable contributions referred to in Income Tax (Employments) (Consolidated) 2001 Regulations, Regs 41 and 42, as are deducted on payment of emoluments (ie qualifying permanent health

contributions (see **3.317**), any contribution paid by the individual under an exempt approved pension scheme or a statutory scheme under a PRSA or qualifying premiums under an approved retirement annuity contract) and the pension levy imposed on the earnings of public servants.

The 'prescribed exclusions' are listed in SW Regs, reg 27 which states that the following items shall not be reckonable emoluments for the purpose of self-employment PRSI:

(a) any payments received by way of pension;

(b) any emoluments (within the meaning of TCA 1997) received in respect of any of the following offices:

  (i) offices of either House of the Oireachtas,

  (ii) membership of the European Parliament,

  (iii) offices of any court in the State, and

  (iv) public offices under the State with income not exceeding €5,200 pa;

(c) any payments under any scheme, contract, policy or other arrangement approved by the Revenue Commissioners under TCA 1997, s 125(3) (periodic payments under approved permanent health insurance policies, etc);

(d) any payment, whether or not in pursuance of any legal obligation, made directly or indirectly in connection with or in consequence of the termination of an office or employment (for example, a redundancy payment, 'golden handshake', etc payment);

(e) any income arising under certain provisions in the Health Acts by way of benefit or maintenance allowance;

(f) any social welfare payments received by way of allowance, assistance, benefit or supplement under the Social Welfare Acts (including disability benefit, maternity allowance, unemployment benefit, occupational injuries benefit, pay-related benefit, retirement pension, survivor's contributory benefit, deserted wife's benefit);

(g) any sums received in respect of attendance at a training course provided or approved by An Foras Áiseanna Saothair (FÁS);

(h) any sums received in respect of participation in either the Alternance or the Enterprise Allowance Schemes administered by FÁS; and

(i) any sums received in respect of employment under either the Teamwork or Social Employment Schemes administered by FÁS.

It is to be noted that reckonable income and reckonable emoluments liable to self-employed PRSI contributions between them include various types of income which go beyond what may be considered income from self-employment in the normal understanding of 'self-employment'. For example, a director of a company or companies in receipt of directors' fees is normally liable to self-employed PRSI contributions in respect of those fees (as reckonable emoluments). Also, an individual who has investment income such as dividends, interest and rents is normally liable to self-employed PRSI contributions in respect of that investment income (as reckonable income), unless he is an employed contributor or is in receipt of a pension and has no Sch D Case I or II income (see *Excepted Persons* below). From 1 January 2013 the Social Welfare and Pensions (Miscellaneous Provisions) Act 2013, extended the 4 per cent PRSI liability to certain modified rate employees (classes B, C and D) who also have Sch D Case I or II income.

From 1 January 2014, (The Social Welfare and Pensions (Miscellaneous Provisions) Act 2013) unearned income of certain employed contributors and occupational pensioners will become liable to PRSI at 4 per cent. This will apply where all of the following conditions are satisfied:

(a) the individual is either an employed person or an occupational pensioner (whether the pension income arises from the individual's own previous employment or that of a spouse or civil partner); and
(b) the individual is aged 16 years or over, but under the age of 66; and
(c) the individual has unearned income, ie income other than income from a trade, profession or partnership (eg investment income or rental income); and
(d) that 'unearned income' is the individual's only additional income aside from their employment or pension income; and
(e) the individual is a 'chargeable person', as defined in TCA 1997, s 959A.

Revenue Tax Briefing 62 contains some information on the definition of 'chargeable person' and states that: '[a]n individual who is in receipt of income chargeable to tax under the PAYE system but who is also in receipt of income from other non-PAYE sources will not be regarded as a 'chargeable person' if the total gross income from all non-PAYE sources is less than €50,000 and the net assessable income is less than €3,174 and the income is coded against PAYE tax credits'.

Examples

The following examples illustrate how this change will apply in the relevant circumstances:

1. An employee who also has gross rental income of less than€50,000 and net assessable rental income of €2,500 currently pays tax on this income through the PAYE system, by having their tax credits reduced. In practice, this person is not a chargeable person and their net rental income will not become subject to PRSI.

2. An employee who also has net rental/interest income of €3,300 is a chargeable person and is therefore required to file a tax return. This person's net rental/interest income will be subject to 4% PRSI from 1 January 2014.

Excepted persons (from 1 January 2014 subject to whether the person is a chargeable person as discussed above)

SWCA 2005, Sch 1, Pt 3 specifies that the following persons are excepted persons, ie are not self-employed contributors and are not, therefore, liable to pay the self-employed PRSI contributions for any contribution year in which they meet the terms of the relevant exception:

(a) a prescribed relative (see below) of a self-employed contributor who participates in the business of the self-employed contributor (other than as a partner) and performs the same or ancillary tasks (ie who helps out in the business as an employee or otherwise);
(b) a person in receipt of unemployment assistance by reason of SWCA 1993, s 141;
(c) a person in receipt of the pre-retirement allowance by reason of SWCA 2005, s 149;
(d) a person the aggregate of whose reckonable income, reckonable emoluments and reckonable earnings (before deducting capital allowances or pension scheme contributions) is less than a prescribed amount (at present €5,000);

(e) an employed contributor whose reckonable income for the relevant year does not include any reckonable emoluments or income from a trade, profession or vocation taxable under Sch D Case I or II;

(f) a person in receipt of a pension from a previous employment (which could be the employment of a deceased spouse) whose reckonable income for the relevant year does not include reckonable emoluments or any income from a trade, profession or vocation taxable under Sch D Case I or II;

(g) a person employed in the public service whose social insurance contributions (under regulations made under SWCA 2005, s 11) are to cover only a widow's contributory pension, deserted wife's benefit or orphan's contributory allowance; and

(h) a person who is not resident or ordinarily resident in the State for income tax purposes and whose reckonable income for the relevant year does not include any income from a trade, profession or vocation taxable under Sch D Case I or II.

The relatives of a self-employed contributor who are 'prescribed relatives' for (a) above are:

father, mother, grandfather, grandmother, stepfather, stepmother, son, daughter, grandson, granddaughter, stepson, stepdaughter, brother, sister, half brother or half sister (SW Regs, reg 93).

Up to 31 December 2013 a 'prescribed relative' included 'husband or wife' but this was removed under Social Welfare and Pensions Act 2014, s 19 (SI 347/2014).

A prescribed relative is only an excepted person in relation to his income from the self-employed contributor's business. If the relative is also self-employed in his own right or has any other reckonable income or reckonable emoluments, he is not an excepted person under (a) above and must pay the self-employed PRSI contributions (unless covered by any of the other exceptions).

Exceptions (d) and (e) are noteworthy. If an individual is employed in an insurable employment so as to be an employed contributor, it does not matter how much investment income (or reckonable emoluments) he may have. He will not be a self-employed contributor for any year for which he does not have any reckonable emoluments or any Sch D Case I or II income.

Example 3.402.1

Mr Edwards receives a pension of €9,000 from a previous employment in 2016. He also receives rental income of €12,000 in the year. Mr Edwards is an excepted self-employed contributor. If Mr Edwards carried out consulting activities which generated a net taxable profit of €500 in 2016, he would cease to be an excepted self-employed contributor. He would be liable to pay self-employed PRSI contributions of €12,500 x 4% = €500 for 2016 (see below).

Exception (g) would be relevant, eg to a non-resident and non-ordinarily resident individual who receives director's fees from an Irish incorporated company or dividends from an Irish resident company and who does not receive any Irish trading or professional income. It may be noted that TCA 1997, s 153 removes the charge to income tax in relation to dividends received by an individual who is not resident or ordinarily resident in the State and who is resident in an EU Member State or a tax treaty state but does not in terms exclude such dividends from the total income of the individual or otherwise exempt them.

Rates of self-employed PRSI contributions

SWCA 2005, s 18(1)(a) and (c) prescribe the amounts of self-employed PRSI contributions to be paid on reckonable income and reckonable emoluments of the contribution year 2016. These amounts are determined by applying the contribution rate of 4 per cent to the self-employed contributor's reckonable income and reckonable emoluments for 2016. The rates of self-employed PRSI contribution, the PRSI income ceiling and the minimum contribution for the year 2016 are as follows:

Rate of contribution	*Income ceiling*	*Minimum contribution*
	€	€
4%	None	500

Minimum contribution

The minimum contribution for each contribution year for the normal case is the fixed sum shown in the table above. However, if the individual is informed that he is not required to file a tax return for the year in question, the minimum becomes €310. If the application of the 4 per cent rate to a self-employed contributor's reckonable income and reckonable emoluments for a year results in a total of less than this fixed amount, the contributor's liability for the year is that fixed amount.

The minimum contribution is €9.62 per week (or €500 per annum) for each week of insurable self-employment in either of the following cases:

(a) where the person concerned has become a self-employed contributor in a contribution year after being an employed contributor in the same year; or

(b) where the person has been a self-employed contributor prior to becoming an employed contributor in the same year.

'Insurable self-employment' is defined as self-employment of such a nature that a person engaged therein would be a self-employed contributor (SWCA 2005, s 2(1)). Consequently, a week of insurable self-employment is a week in which the individual concerned is within the definition of a self-employed contributor.

Example 3.402.2

Mr V Weekes has been an employed contributor in an insurable employment for some years. He leaves this employment on 7 February 2016. On 1 March 2016, he commences to carry on a trade as a greengrocer so as to start insurable self-employment. His taxable profits (after deducting his capital allowances) for his first year's trading ending 28 February 2016 are only €6,000 so that his reckonable income from his trade for 2016 is €5,000 (10/12ths of €6,000, see **4.205**). He has no other reckonable income or reckonable emoluments for 2016.

Mr Weekes has 44 weeks of insurable self-employment in 2016 from 1 March 2016 to 31 December 2016. Since he was an employed contributor in the same year before starting insurable self-employment, SW Reg 25 applies to determine the minimum self-employed PRSI contribution.

Mr Weekes' liability for the self-employed PRSI contribution for 2016 is determined as follows:

	€
Percentage calculation:	
Reckonable income 2016: €5,000 x 4%	200
Or	

Minimum contribution:	
€9.62 x 44 weeks	423
Self-employed PRSI contribution for 2016 (higher amount)	423

It is to be noted that the minimum contribution remains at the fixed €500 (ie no reduction by reference to the number of weeks of insurable self-employment) in the case where an individual becomes a self-employed contributor for the first time not having previously been an employed contributor (SW Reg 21). Similarly, if a self-employed contributor ceases insurable self-employment in a contribution year and does not become an employed contributor in the same year, the minimum contribution remains the fixed amount (SW Reg 22).

Example 3.402.3

Facts as in **3.402.2**, except that Mr Weekes was not in insurable employment up to 7 February 2016.

	€
Percentage calculation:	
Reckonable income 2016: €5,000 x 4%	200
Or	
Minimum contribution:	
	500
Self-employed PRSI contribution for 2016 (higher amount)	500

In a case falling within either SW Regs 121 or 22, even if the actual period of self-employment in the year is significantly less than the full year, the individual is deemed to have paid self-employment contributions for 52 weeks in the year (whether he pays the minimum contribution or a higher amount resulting from the application of the appropriate percentage to his reckonable income/emoluments).

3.403 Collection of self-employment contributions

Two different procedures exist for the collection of self-employed PRSI contributions dependent on whether these contributions are payable on reckonable income or reckonable emoluments. First, SWCA 2005, s 23(4) requires self-employed PRSI contributions in respect of reckonable income to be paid directly to the Collector General under the same rules as apply for the collection of income tax chargeable by assessment. In effect, the self-employed contributor is required to 'self-assess' his liability.

SWCA 2005, s 23(4) then provides for the Minister for Social Welfare making regulations to deal with the manner and time for the payment/collection of the contributions on reckonable emoluments (and for the fixed amount payable by the individual notified by the inspector of taxes that he need not file an income tax return). SW Regs Pt 1 requires the self-employed PRSI contributions on reckonable emoluments to be collected by the employer or company paying such emoluments to the self-employed contributor. In effect, the PAYE/PRSI system of collection is employed for reckonable emoluments.

Furthermore under SWCA 2005, s 23(4) the provisions of TCA 1997, Pt 42, Ch 4 and TCA 1997, s 1086 (with regard to the collection and recovery of income tax or the inspection of records for the purposes of appeals and the publication of names) in relation to the self employment contributions, with regard to reckonable emoluments, which the Collector General is obliged to collect, as if such contributions were an amount of income tax remittable to the Collector General under the Income Tax (Employments) (Consolidated) Regulations 2001 (SI 559/2001).

Contributions on reckonable emoluments

Self-employed PRSI contributions on an individual's reckonable emoluments are collected through the PAYE system. The SW Regs require an employer, on paying any reckonable emoluments to a self-employed contributor, to deduct the amount of self-employed PRSI contributions due by that contributor in respect of those emoluments.

If the employer cannot ascertain exactly the amount so due at the time the emoluments are paid, the employer is required to deduct the amount which he, or if a company, it reasonably believes to be due. In the absence of other information, the employer should make the deduction for the self-employed PRSI contributions at the 4 per cent rate for the year on all payments of reckonable emoluments. An employer who has paid reckonable emoluments is required to remit to the Collector all self-employed PRSI contributions deducted from those payments. This remittance must be made by the employer within nine days after the end of the income tax month during which the emoluments are paid. For example, the contributions deducted by an employer during the month ended 30 November 2015 must be remitted to the Collector before the close of business on 14 December 2015/23 December if paying and filing on ROS. In fact, the remittance by employers of self-employed PRSI contributions on reckonable income is integrated into the system of PAYE/PRSI remittances (see **11.201**).

If the employer fails to remit the self-employed PRSI contributions deducted in any month before the 14th/23rd day of the calendar month in which the contribution month ends, simple interest is chargeable thereon from the 14th day of the month until the actual date of payment. The rate of interest for periods from 1 July 2009 to the date of payment is 0.0274 per cent. The Collector is responsible for collecting any interest due and is required to pay all interest collected on late contributions into the Social Insurance Fund.

An employer is required to give to any self-employed contributor, who ceases to hold an insurable self-employment with that employer (ie a position from which reckonable emoluments arise), a certificate showing in respect of that self-employment:

(a) the total of self-employed PRSI contributions which the employer was liable to remit to the Collector for the contribution year up to and including the date of cessation of that insurable self-employment;

(b) the number of contribution weeks in the year in which the contributor was in insurable self-employment up to and including the date of cessation;

(c) the date of commencement of the insurable self-employment (where it occurred during the same year as the cessation); and

(d) the total reckonable emoluments in the contribution year up to and including the date of cessation.

This certificate is to be in the form approved by the Revenue Commissioners. It is the equivalent of the form P45 required under the PAYE regulations where an employee leaves any employment. An employer is required to furnish the Collector with a return in respect of each year listing all the self-employed contributors to whom the employer paid reckonable emoluments during the year. The return is required to state, in respect of each such self-employed contributor, the following details:

(a) the total self-employed PRSI contributions payable by the contributor in respect of reckonable emoluments in the year;
(b) the number of contribution weeks in the year in which the contributor was in insurable self-employment with the employer making the return;
(c) the dates of commencement and cessation of insurable self-employment with the employer (if either occurs in the year); and
(d) the total reckonable emoluments paid to the self-employed contributor in the year.

In addition, the employer is required to furnish the Collector with a statement, declaration and certificate, in a form approved by the Revenue Commissioners, showing the total self-employed PRSI contributions which the employer was liable to remit in the contribution year in respect of every self-employed contributor (on reckonable emoluments paid to each contributor). Both the return and the statement, etc must be submitted to the Collector within 46 days after the end of the contribution year.

An employer who ceases to be an employer during a contribution year is required to make the same return and the statement, etc in respect of that year within 25 days after the day on which the person ceases to be an employer. An employer is required to give, to each self-employed contributor to whom the employer has paid reckonable emoluments in the contribution year, a certificate stating:

(a) the total self-employed PRSI contributions deducted in the year from the reckonable emoluments of the contributor;
(b) the total self-employed PRSI contributions which the employer was liable to remit to the Collector for the year;
(c) the number of contribution weeks in the year in which the contributor was in insurable self-employment;
(d) the date of commencement of the insurable self-employment (if it occurred during the year); and
(e) the total reckonable emoluments paid by the employer in the year.

This certificate is to be in the form approved by the Revenue Commissioners. It is in fact equivalent to the form P60 required under the PAYE regulations. It must be given to each self-employed contributor within nine days after the end of the contribution year.

Contributions on reckonable income

SWCA 2005, s 23(4) requires self-employed PRSI contributions in respect of reckonable income (but not reckonable emoluments) to be paid by the self-employed contributor direct to the Collector in the same way as income tax which is chargeable by assessment. It provides that the self-employment contributions payable for a contribution year on reckonable income are to be assessed, charged and paid in all respects as if they were an amount of income tax contained in a computation of, or assessment to, income tax made by, or on, the self-employed contributor for the year of assessment which coincides with the contribution year.

The self-employed PRSI contributions payable on reckonable income for a given contribution year/period (eg year ending 31 December 2015) and the income tax payable by the same person for the same income tax year (for example, year 2015) may be stated in one sum (referred to as the 'aggregated sum'). All the provisions of the Income Tax

Acts (except those relating to allowances, deductions and reliefs) are applicable to this aggregated sum as if it were a single sum of income tax.

This inclusion of self-employed PRSI contributions on reckonable income in this single aggregated sum applies for each relevant year whether or not the person concerned has in fact any income tax liability for the year. In other words, even if the income tax payable for the year is nil, the aggregated single sum of 'income tax' is assessable and collectible exactly in the same way as any income tax liability would be assessable and collectible.

Further, in the case of a married couple who are assessed to income tax jointly under TCA 1997, s 1017 (see **3.502**), SWCA 2005, s 23(5) requires any self-employed PRSI contributions payable by the wife on her reckonable income to be charged, collected and recovered as if they were contributions payable by her husband. In other words, the wife's self-employment contributions on her reckonable income are assessable on her husband in the joint assessment and his preliminary tax payment, due on 31 October in the contribution year, must include both his own and his wife's self-employment contributions on their respective reckonable incomes. If the joint assessment is made on the wife, the same applies in reverse for the husband's self-employed PRSI contributions.

This requirement to include both husband's and wife's self-employed PRSI contributions on reckonable income in the joint assessment does not alter the rules for the separate calculation of each spouse's liability for the contributions by reference to his own reckonable income. However, if either spouse is excluded from the definition of a self-employed contributor (eg if he is over the age of 66 or if he is an employed contributor without any Sch D Case I or II income), no self-employed PRSI contributions have to be included for that spouse.

The effect of these provisions is that a person who is a self-employed contributor with reckonable income must pay the self-employed PRSI contributions on that income each year at the same time as he pays his income tax liability for the year. If the self-employed contributor is a married person assessed jointly under TCA 1997, s 1017, the payment to the Collector must also include the spouse's liability (if any) for self-employed PRSI contributions on reckonable income. The person does not, however, pay to the Collector any self-employed PRSI contributions on his own or the spouse's reckonable emoluments since those contributions are collected by the employer paying the reckonable emoluments (see above).

The self-assessment system of income tax contained in TCA 1997, Pt 41A is, therefore, applied for each relevant tax year/contribution year to collect, charge and assess the aggregate of an individual's liabilities for the year to:

(a) total income tax chargeable on all his taxable income (see **3.106**);
(b) self-employed PRSI contributions on reckonable income (see above);
(c) Universal Social Charge on relevant income (see **3.404**); and
(d) after deducting full credits (eg *Dividend Withholding Tax*, tax suffered at source (see **3.110**)).

3.404 The Universal Social Charge

The Universal Social Charge is imposed with effect from 2011 onwards by TCA 1997, Pt 18D, inserted by FA 2011, s 3, as supplemented by the Universal Social Charge Regulations 2011 (as amended for 2017 and subsequent years of assessment by the Universal Social Charge (Amendment) Regulations 2016, SI 654/2016), as enabled by

TCA 1997, s 531AAB, on the *aggregate income* of an individual. 'Aggregate income', means the aggregate of the individual's *relevant emoluments* and *relevant income* in the relevant tax year (TCA 1997, s 531AL).

Revenue manuals relating to the Universal Social Charge have been consolidated into one single manual (see Revenue *eBrief 74/2014*).

Relevant emoluments

'Relevant emoluments' are emoluments to which TCA 1997, Pt 42, Ch 4 (the PAYE system) applies or is applied, other than:

(i) Payments made under the Social Welfare Acts and other payments of a similar character but which are made by:
  (a) the Health Service Executive;
  (b) the Department of Community, Equality and Gaeltacht Affairs;
  (c) the Department of Enterprise, Trade and Innovation;
  (d) the Department of Education and Skills;
  (e) the Department of Agriculture, Fisheries and Food;
  (f) An Foras Áiseanna Saothair, in respect of schemes mentioned in clauses (I), (II) and (III) of TCA 1997, s 472A(1)(b)(i)); or
  (g) any other state or territory; and

(ii) excluded emoluments, ie those gifted to the Minister for Finance under (TCA 1997, s 483);

(iii) reimbursed expenses which are excluded from PAYE under Reg (10)(3) of the Income Tax (Employments) (Consolidated) Regulations 2001 ('the PAYE regulations');

(iv) termination payments which are exempt from income tax, under TCA 1997, s 201 and Sch 3, by virtue of the basic exemption, the increased exemption and the Standard Capital Superannuation Benefit (SCSB);

(v) payments made under TCA 1997, s 782A(3) by an administrator of up to 30 per cent of the value of an AVC to an individual before retirement.

(vi) emoluments in the nature of a contribution by an employer to a PRSA (within the meaning of Ch 2A of Pt 30).

However, there is no deduction to be allowed in respect of permanent health contributions, qualifying pension contributions or pension levy contributions qualifying for the 'net pay' regime under Regs and 41 and 42 of the PAYE regulations nor for the specified amount deducted in computing earnings under TCA 1997, s 825C (the Special Assignee Relief Programme).

The Universal Social Charge is chargeable on the excess of termination payments over the statutory exemptions provided for under TCA 1997, s 201, including any additional relief or deduction for the increased exemption and the SCSB under TCA 1997, Sch 3, Pt 2 (TCA 1997, s 531AM(1)). It will also apply to the excess over €575,000 of any lump sums taken by way of commutation of a pension of annuity from an approved pension fund and treated as emoluments subject to PAYE by virtue of TCA 1997, s 790AA. From 2013 (FA 2013, s 2) *(Revenue eBrief 25/2013)* very limited access to certain AVC and PRSA schemes has been introduced by way of an option to take up to 30 per cent of the fund pre-retirement. Universal Social Charge will not apply in these circumstances though strictly speaking under the definitions of 'relevant income' and 'relevant emoluments' such income should be liable to the USC. See **Division 16** for more on this.

There is also an express exemption for employment earnings of an individual resident in a double tax treaty jurisdiction where such earnings have been the subject of a PAYE exclusion order under TCA 1997, s 984(1) (see **11.101**). In addition, the Revenue have updated their manual on the USC in respect of a non resident individual who exercises the duties of their employment wholly outside Ireland to state that such income will not be liable to the USC where it is not liable to Irish income tax. However directors' fees paid to a non-resident director from an Irish company will be liable to USC, unless the director obtains relief under the terms of a double taxation agreement in which case, the relevant income will not be subject to the USC. Revenue FAQs have also been updated to advise that an Irish resident but non domiciled individual is liable to USC on the individual's Irish income and on any foreign income which is remitted into the State.

Revenue *eBrief 52/14* clarifies that a USC liability arises where payment of arrears or bonuses is made to an individual who as a consequence of the split year treatment is deemed not to be resident at the time the payment is made.

There is an extension of the definition of relevant emoluments to include the initial market value of shares appropriated to an employee under an approved profit sharing scheme except where such shares were held by an approved Employee Share Ownership Trust prior to 1 January 2011 (see **11.401** and **11.503**) as well as both the value of the right to acquire shares under an approved SAYE scheme (see **11.601**) and any notional gain accruing on the exercise of such a right under TCA 1997, s 128, but net of the amount already charged to the Universal Social Charge on acquisition of the right (see **10.113**). Where the Universal Social Charge has been charged on the initial market value of shares when they are appropriated to an approved profit sharing scheme (see **11.4**) it is not subsequently charged on the locked-in value of those shares (within the meaning of TCA 1997, s 512(1)) in the event of an early disposal of the shares or on the amount or value of a capital receipt (within the meaning of TCA 1997, s 513(1)) where a capital receipt is subsequently received before the end of the required holding period for the shares.

Relevant income

'Relevant Income' is income from all sources, as computed under the Income Tax Acts, without regard to any amount deductible from total income or deductible in computing total income; this definition serves to exclude in the first instance claims for losses and capital allowances as well as pension, retirement annuity contract contributions and PRSA contributions. However, exceptions are provided for trading losses brought forward from prior years under TCA 1997, s 382 as well as capital allowances granted under TCA 1997, ss 284, 272(3)(a), (b), (c)(iii), (da), (db), (e) or (g), 658(2) or 659(3) (viz allowances for plant and machinery, non-enhanced ('standard') allowances for industrial buildings, allowances for farm buildings and allowances for farm pollution control structures respectively) which are set off against the profits of a trade or profession of that tax year, including any such allowances brought forward from prior years under TCA 1997, s 304(4). Allowances granted to non-active partners as defined by TCA 1997, s 409A are not eligible for this exception. Any claims under TCA 1997, s 381 continue to be disregarded.

The deemed rental income which arises on the clawback of 'Section 23' relief under TCA 1997, s 372AP(7) will be disregarded for Universal Social Charge purposes if the individual received or was entitled to claim the relief on or after 1 January 2012.

As and from tax year 2013 under FA 2013, s 2, the Universal Social Charge will apply to any balancing charge arising as a result of a disposal of plant and machinery, industrial buildings and farm buildings if USC relief was availed of when the allowances were originally claimed. The intention is that the USC relief availed of when claiming the capital allowances is clawed-back on a future disposal.

The definition excludes relevant emoluments (although these of course remain taxable, albeit under the PAYE system), social welfare payments and similar type payments, excluded emoluments and all other emoluments expressly excluded from the definition of relevant emoluments (see above). There are exclusions also for gains, income or payments within TCA 1997, Pt 8, Ch 4 (relevant interest within the DIRT regime) Ch 5 (certain dividends paid by Credit Unions and Ch 7 certain interest received from EU deposit Takers; Pt 26, Ch 5 (income and gains from Irish life assurance policies) and Ch 6 (Income and gains from approved foreign life assurance policies); Pt 27, Ch 1A (income and gains from certain investment undertakings); Ch 4 (income and gains from certain approved foreign investment undertakings);

The definition of 'relevant income' is then extended, so that the exemptions under the following provisions are disregarded: TCA 1997, ss 140, 141, 142, 143 (various distributions out of exempt profits), 195 (exemption for artist's earnings), 231, 232, 233, 234 (exemptions for certain income from woodlands, as well as those which no longer apply to certain greyhound and stallion fees, and certain patent royalties) and 664 (exemption for certain income from leasing of farmland) were never enacted; further, the following deductions are to be disregarded:

(I) in respect of double rent allowance under TCA 1997, ss 324(2), 333(2), 345(3) or 354(3);

(II) under TCA 1997, s 372AP, in computing the amount of a surplus or deficiency in respect of rent from any premises;

(III) under TCA 1997, s 372AU, in computing the amount of a surplus or deficiency in respect of rent from any premises;

(IV) under TCA 1997, s 847A, in respect of donations to certain sports bodies, or

(V) under TCA 1997, s 848A, in respect of donations to approved bodies, which applied to 31 December 2012;

However, there is a deduction for any maintenance payment to which TCA 1997, s 1025 applies, unless TCA 1997, s 1026 applies in respect of such payment (ie where there is an election for joint assessment (TCA 1997, s 531B(1)). No deduction however is available in respect of the amount paid under a deed of covenant where the recipient of the funds is not liable to income tax on the income. In circumstances where the recipient is liable to income tax and the USC on the receipt of funds under a deed of covenant, such as an individual aged 65 or over, or a permanently incapacitated individual, the disponer is entitled to a deduction for this amount for USC purposes.

Where section TCA 1997, s 825A (dealing with certain cross-border employments: see **13.501**) applies in respect of an individual for a tax year, there is an exemption for an amount equal to the difference between the individual's total income for the tax year had s 825A not applied for that year, and the amount of total income which if charged to income tax for the year would have given an amount of income tax payable equal to that which would be payable by virtue of the operation of that section. In effect the tax saved under s 825A is grossed up to find the equivalent amount of taxable income and that amount is exempted from the charge. Thus, the exemption may well apply only to part of the cross-border earnings concerned. In addition, it makes it more likely that a claim under s 825A will be favourable, since the alternative (claiming by way of credit for double tax relief) will not generate an equivalent exemption.

A non-resident individual who has income within the charge to tax under TCA 1997, s 127B (dealing with tax treatment of flight crew in international traffic) will be liable to USC on such income subject to the normal USC thresholds. It should be noted that when the threshold is exceeded then the individual's entire income is liable to USC.

Exemptions

The following income tax exemptions carry through by default for Universal Social Charge purposes:

TCA 1997, s	*Title*
42	Interest on savings certificates
118	Specified exemptions from charge on Benefits-in-Kind
153	Distributions to certain non-residents
189	Payments in respect of personal injuries
189A	Special trust for permanently incapacitated
190	Haemophilia Trust
191	Hepatitis C
192	Thalidomide
192A	Exemption in respect of certain payments under employment law
192B	Foster Care Payments
193	Income from Scholarships
194	Child benefit
194A	Early Childcare Supplement
194B	Back to work family dividend
195A	Exemption in respect of certain expense payments
196	Expenses of members of Judiciary
196A	State Employees: Foreign Service Allowance
196B	Employee of certain agencies: foreign service allowances
197	Bonus or interest paid under instalment savings schemes
198	Certain interest not to be chargeable
199	Interest on certain securities
200	Certain foreign pensions
201	Basic and increased exemptions in respect of tax under 123 (Redundancy) SCSB
203	Payments in respect of Redundancy
204	Military & other pensions, gratuities and allowances
205	Veterans of war of independence

205A	Magdalen Laundry Payments
216A	Rent a Room relief
216B	Scrim na bhFoghlaimeoirí Gaeilge
216C	Childcare service relief
782A	Pre-retirement access to AVCs

Exemption from the Universal Social Charge also applies where an individual's aggregate income for the year of assessment does not exceed €13,000 for 2016 and subsequent years of assessment. Universal Social Charge is charged on annual aggregate income at the following rates for 2017: (see earlier editions for rates of prior years)

(a) Relevant Emoluments

	Rate of charge (aged under 70 or aged 70 and over with income over €60,000)	*Rate of Charge (aged 70 and over or with income of less than €60,000 or aged under 70 with income of less than €60,000 and holding a full medical card)*
First €12,012	0.5	0.5
Next €6,760	2.5	2.5
Sum €18,772		
Next €51,272	5	2.5
Excess	8	n/a

(b) Relevant Income

	Rate of charge (aged under 70 or aged 70 and over with income over €60,000)	*Rate of Charge (aged 70 and over or with income of less than €60,000 or aged under 70 with income of less than €60,000 and holding a full medical card)*
First €12,012	0.5	0.5
Next €6,760	2.5	2.5
Next €51,272	5	2.5
Next €29,956	8	n/a
Excess over €100,000	11	n/a

For these purposes, a person holds a full medical card if by virtue of the Health Act 1970, s 45 or Council Regulation (EEC) No 883/2004 he has full eligibility for services under Pt IV of that Act (ie a Medical Card Holder) (TCA 1997, s 531AN(3)). The Revenue Commissioners have stated that they will only accept that frontier workers resident in other EU Member States and employed in the State automatically qualify for a full Irish medical card for the tax year 2011 (see *e-brief 81/11*). From 1 January 2012 frontier workers will be liable to USC at the 7 per cent rate unless they hold a full Irish medical card. For the purpose of applying these rates, any notional gains arising on or after 1 January 2012 on the exercise of an option chargeable within TCA 1997, s 128(2) will not be counted as relevant income. Similarly, any encashment or deemed encashment amounts in relation to private pensions which are chargeable to income tax under Sch D Case IV by virtue of TCA 1997, s 787TA will not be counted as relevant income for these purposes and furthermore will be charged at a flat rate of 3.5 per cent.

For the purposes of double tax treaty relief, the Universal Social Charge is treated as equivalent to income tax (TCA 1997, Sch 24, Pt 1 para 1(1)).

For the year of assessment 2016 and each subsequent year the inserted TCA 1997, s 531AN(5) deals with the position regarding relevant emoluments that are paid on 31 December (or 30/31 December in a leap year ie a week 53 payment), the rate bands set out in the Table above are to be increased by 1/52 where relevant emoluments consist of weekly pay and 1/26 where the relevant emoluments consist of fortnightly pay. However, where the actual payments of relevant emoluments on those days are less than the abovementioned increases then the increase in the rates bands is restricted to the actual amount of the relevant emoluments. TCA 1997, s 531AN(6) continues on from TCA 1997, s 531AN(5) discussed above and the income figures in sub-s (1) and (3) are also expanded by 1/52 or 1/26, as appropriate – these subsections refer to the income limits of €60,000 and €18,668 respectively. In addition, the exemption threshold in TCA 1997, s 531AM(2) of €13,000 is also expanded by 1/52 or 1/26, as appropriate. However, where the actual payments of relevant emoluments on those days are less than the expansion provided above, the expansion is restricted to the actual amount of the relevant emoluments. Revenue guidance on TCA 1997, s 531AN(7) notes that it is an anti-avoidance provision to prevent pay dates being changed or manipulated with a view to benefiting from the widened rate bands. Subsections (5) and (6) do not apply where the normal pay date in the year, or the previous year, has changed and it would appear to matter not the rationale behind the date change in the first instance.

Administration

The general PAYE provisions apply to the collection and transmission of the Universal Social Charge and there is extensive provision for the rendering of returns and payments by employers in respect of the Universal Social Charge to the Collector-General contained in the Universal Social Charge Regulations 2011 (as amended for 2017 and subsequent years of assessment by the Universal Social Charge (Amendment) Regulations 2016, SI 654/2016). Where an employer makes notional payments to an employee in the form of shares, or an employee realises a gain by exercising an option under a Revenue approved savings-related share option (SAYE) scheme, he is obliged to account for the Universal Social Charge on the value of those shares or the amount of the gain. An employer is entitled to withhold sufficient shares to fund that the Universal Social Charge liability if the employee does not otherwise provide the employer with sufficient means to do so. The employee must allow the employer to withhold sufficient shares to fund the Universal Social Charge liability. Even though the employee has not actually received the shares, he is to be treated as if the value of the shares had been paid by the employer. An employer is only entitled to withhold shares where the employee does not otherwise provide the employer with sufficient means to fund the Universal Social Charge liability (TCA 1997, s 531AO).

In the case of relevant income, the Universal Social Charge will be collected under the self-assessment system as if it were income tax, but disregarding the effect of joint assessment under TCA 1997, s 1017 and s 1031C. The Universal Social Charge will however be assessed on the chargeable spouse or nominated civil partner in the same manner as income tax (TCA 1997, s 531AV). Persons who are not chargeable persons as a result of income tax exemptions which do not apply to the Universal Social Charge will be regarded as chargeable persons for the purposes of the latter; further the self-assessment provisions are extended to any other non-chargeable persons who are liable to the Universal Social Charge. The Universal Social Charge will be collected along with income tax due (if any) as a single sum; however any excess tax credits or reliefs may not be offset against any liability to Universal Social Charge (TCA 1997, ss 531AS; 531AT).

The Universal Social Charge is brought within the definition of 'relevant tax' in section TCA 1997, s 128B (see **10.113**). The formula used in section TCA 1997, s 128B(2) to render the relevant tax chargeable at the higher rate of income tax in force in a particular tax year is adapted to charge the Universal Social Charge at its highest rate, unless the individual satisfies the Revenue Commissioners that he will actually be chargeable at a lower rate of the Universal Social Charge.

Various income tax provisions governing the making of returns and the making of enquiries, the making of assessments, appeals, collection and recovery of unpaid tax, interest and penalties are extended to the Universal Social Charge under TCA 1997, s 531AAA.

Excess bank remuneration charge

This supplement to the Universal Social Charge is imposed at a swingeing rate of 45 per cent, but will only apply to employees of specified institutions, principally those covered by the Irish Bank Guarantee Scheme. It applies to employees who are Irish tax resident, or who exercised the duties of the employment wholly or partly in the State in the tax year concerned, in relation to relevant remuneration in excess of €20,000 received in any tax year. Relevant remuneration is defined in broad terms as any element of remuneration, over and above regular pay, which varies by reference to performance of all or part of the institution's business or the individual's contribution or personal performance in relation to all or part of that business. The provisions also apply where the business concerned is that of a person connected to the institution. Relevant remuneration will be regarded as received in a year where there is a contractual obligation to pay, or where it is paid without any such obligation arising in that year. The value of the relevant remuneration will be ascertained by reference to TCA 1997, s 548, without regard to any conditions or restrictions which might attach to it (TCA 1997, s 531AAD).

The Revenue Commissioners may delegate acts and functions that are required to be carried out by them to Revenue officers or, if appropriate, they may allow such acts or functions to be performed or discharged through electronic means (TCA 1997, s 531AAF).

Property surcharge for tax years 2012 onwards

A property relief surcharge is applied by TCA 1997, s 531AAE at a rate of 5 per cent over and above the rate which would otherwise apply to the amount of a *specified individual's* aggregate income (for Universal Social Charge purposes) against which any *specified property relief or reliefs* have been used in that year. A 'specified individual' is one whose aggregate income, as calculated for the payment of USC, for the year is €100,000 or more. A 'specified property relief' is:

(a) any area-based capital allowance or any specified capital allowance; or

(b) any eligible expenditure, to which TCA 1997, s 372AP applies, ie reference to what is commonly known as 'Section 23'-type relief (See **Division 19** of the 2009 edition of this text) and includes such relief as it is carried forward in the form of losses from earlier years.

An 'area-based capital allowance' is a reference to any of the accelerated capital allowances provided for under any of the designated area or urban or rural renewal schemes. It also includes all of the older schemes, which have formally ended or have been replaced in more recent times (See **Division 19** of the 2009 edition of this text) and include allowances carried forward from earlier years.

A 'specified capital allowance' is any specified relief, being a writing down allowance under TCA 1997, s 272 or s 273, a balancing allowance under TCA 1997, s 274, or any of the other property-based accelerated capital allowances, and includes any unused amount of such allowances carried forward from an earlier period.

A 'specified relief' means any relief arising under any of the provisions set out in' TCA 1997, Sch 25B, column (2) ie as defined for the purposes of the high earners restriction (see **3.111**).

The provisions of TCA 1997, s 485C(3) and Sch 25C (ie as applicable for the purposes of the high earners restriction (see **3.111**), are applied to any amounts carried forward from 2011 into the tax year 2012 or to any subsequent tax years. Specified reliefs to be used in any particular tax year are segregated into those which are specified property reliefs and those which are not. For these purposes, specified property reliefs are treated as being used in priority to other specified reliefs.

If the property relief surcharge is due to be paid by a specified individual in respect of the tax year 2012, then the calculation of preliminary tax under TCA 1997, s 958 must be computed as if the property surcharge had applied in 2011.

Interaction with the High Earners Restriction

In the author's view the surcharge is payable on the specified property reliefs claimed after any restriction for specified reliefs are imposed for high income individuals. This is because the legislation refers to specified property reliefs to which *full effect has been given for that tax year*. If you are entitled to claim €200,000 of specified reliefs but after the restriction for high income individuals the specified reliefs for that year are reduced to €80,000 it is difficult to see how you have received the full effect of €200,000 of capital allowances in that year. It could be that the individual would never receive the benefit of the restricted property reliefs in future years, eg lack of income or death. At the time of writing we understand the Revenue disagree with this interpretation and are of the view that the surcharge is payable on the gross claim, ie €200,000 (*TaxFax 26 July 2013 from Irish Tax Institute*). The Revenue view is that the issue turns on whether 'full effect' has been given to a relief in a case where the restriction on specified reliefs for a higher income individual applies. Their view is that the choice of words is deliberate and it was also used in TCA 1997, s 304 and in Sch 25B. Revenue's view is that full effect has been given to a property relief if there is sufficient income to absorb the claim. On the other hand, the Minister for Finance in his Dáil Speech, at the opening of the Second Stage to the Finance Bill 2012 said:

> Section 3 introduces an additional amount of Universal Social Charge (USC) to be paid by investors in Section 23 and accelerated capital allowances schemes with gross incomes over €100,000. This property relief surcharge, which is effective from 1 January 2012, will apply at a rate of 5 per cent on the amount of income sheltered by property reliefs in a given year.

The examples below are prepared on the basis that the 5 per cent surcharge is payable on the gross claim.

Example 3.404.1

Specified reliefs available in the tax year are €150,000 made up of specified property relief €110,000 and EII relief €40,000.

The surcharge will be €5,500 (€110,000 @ 5%)

Assuming the specified reliefs are restricted to €80,000 because of the high earners restriction therefore the restricted relief carried forward is €70,000 (which includes some restricted property relief) then no further surcharge is payable in the following year on this.

Example 3.404.2

An individual has aggregate income for USC purposes of €200,000 and has €220,000 of specified property relief in 2015.

The surcharge will be €10,000 (€200,000 @ 5%) which is the specified relief used in 2015, even where the individual has only been able to use €80,000 of reliefs due to the imposition of the high earners restriction.

Assuming the specified reliefs are restricted to €80,000 which is the maximum relief available under the high earners restriction, the restricted reliefs to be carried forward will be €140,000 (€20,000 specified property relief and €120,000 restricted reliefs carried forward)

In the following tax year the property relief surcharge will only be payable on the €20,000 specified property relief carried forward.

3.405 The Domicile Levy

From 2010 onwards, the levy (set at a fixed amount of €200,000: TCA 1997, s 531AB) applies to *relevant individuals* (TCA 1997, Pt 18C, inserted by FA 2010, s 150). These are individuals who meet the following conditions:

(i) they are Irish domiciled and also (for 2011 only) Irish citizens;

(ii) they own *Irish property* with a *market value* (ignoring debts and encumbrances) in excess of €5 million on 31 December in the relevant tax year (the *valuation date*);

(iii) they enjoy annual *worldwide income* of over €1 million;

(iv) they have a final liability to income tax of less than €200,000 in that year (TCA 1997, s 531AA(1)).

The individual's residence or ordinary residence status is not a factor, and while the legislation is clearly aimed primarily at affluent expatriates, it also applies to Irish resident individuals. A 'final liability to income tax' is defined as one against which no appeal has been made or where the time within which an appeal could have been made has expired. The implications where the Revenue Commissioners exercise their powers to raise or amend an assessment under TCA 1997, s 952 or the taxpayer claims a repayment of tax under the 'error or mistake' provisions of TCA 1997, s 865 are left unexplored (TCA 1997, s 531AA(1)).

Irish property

'Irish property' is defined in the first instance as all property, including rights and interests of every description, situated in the State and to which the individual is beneficially entitled in possession on the valuation date. This wide definition of property could encompass choses-in-action such as eg, rights to compensation or even a right to pursue a legal action may fall within its scope (see eg Zim v Proctor *[1985] STC 90*, although this was decided in the specific context of the Capital Gains Tax charging provisions). The term 'entitled in possession' is not defined, but generally denotes an immediate right to the enjoyment of property. In the absence of any extended statutory definition, it should be borne in mind that interests or rights arising in respect of foreign death estates, foreign trusts or foreign partnerships may not themselves represent Irish property under general law, notwithstanding that the relevant entities hold Irish property (TCA 1997, s 531AA(1)).

There are significant exclusions from the definition in respect of: (a) shares in a company which exists wholly or mainly for the purpose of carrying on a trade or trades; or (b) shares in a holding company which derive the greater part of their value from its subsidiaries which wholly or mainly carry on a trade or trades. The terms 'holding company' and 'subsidiary' bear the same meanings as in Companies Act 1963, s 155. There is an anomaly here in that direct minority shareholdings in trading companies will qualify for the exclusion, but shares in a company which itself holds minority shareholdings in trading companies, will not normally do so. It is also notable that interests in unincorporated Irish business activities do not benefit from any exclusion (TCA 1997, s 531AA(2)).

World-wide income

'World-wide income' is defined as the individual's total income, as computed in accordance with the Tax Acts, but on the assumption that he is resident and ordinarily resident in the State in the relevant tax year, irrespective of his actual residence status. Thus, an individual resident and ordinarily resident outside the State would have to include all of his non-Irish income for these purposes, including in some cases income accumulated in offshore structures falling within TCA 1997, s 806 or s 807A (see **17.2**). This would not appear to include any income exempted under a relevant Double Tax Treaty since TCA 1997, s 826 merely enables the provisions of a Treaty to take effect as if they were enacted by the Oireachtas but does not per se grant any exemption or relief. Additionally, any amounts which would normally be deductible in computing total income must also be ignored for these purposes. Exceptionally, a deduction may be claimed for any alimony or maintenance payments to an ex-spouse or civil partner within TCA 1997, s 1025, s 1031J, unless TCA 1997, s 1026, s 1031K (joint assessment of separated spouses/civil partners) applies. This relief is purportedly extended to similar payments which attract the same tax treatment, a provision of some obscurity. Finally, no deduction is given for double rent allowances under any of the old Urban Renewal, Seaside Resort schemes etc, certain capital allowances in relation to residential premises, or for donations to approved bodies (charities etc, which was available as an income tax deduction up to 31 December 2012) or to approved sports bodies within TCA 1997, ss 848A; 847A (TCA 1997, s 531AA(1)).

Market value

'Market value' in relation to property is defined as the price which such property would fetch if sold on the open market on the valuation date, in such manner and subject to such conditions as might reasonably be calculated to obtain for the vendor the best price for the property. This definition goes back to the days of Estate Duty and has been the subject of a considerable body of case law (see eg *IRC v Crossman* [1937] AC 26; *Lynall v IRC* [1972] AC 680; *Duke of Buccleuch v IRC* [1967] 1 AC 506; *IRC v Gray* [1994] STC 360). Thus, it is well-established that pre-emption rights attaching to shares must be disregarded for the purposes of postulating an open-market sale but that they must then be taken into account in the actual valuation of the shares (TCA 1997, s 531AA(1)).

In estimating the market value of any property, no deduction can be made for any debts or encumbrances. However, this does not apply to assets held by a company or other legal entity. Accordingly, an individual might, for example, own shares in an investment company which owns Irish assets of €5 million but also has liabilities of €5 million. On a simple analysis, those shares would have a nil market value for levy purposes. If the individual held the same assets and liabilities in his own name, the market value of his Irish property for levy purposes would be €5 million (TCA 1997, s 531AA(5)).

Anti-avoidance measures

Shares in non-Irish incorporated companies, even if they own Irish incorporated subsidiaries or other Irish assets, do not constitute Irish property under the general definition cited above. The legislation attempts to counter strategies exploiting this factor by creating a special rule for shares in a non-Irish company which would be a close company (as defined by TCA 1997, s 430 for corporation tax purposes, TCA 1997, s 531AA(1))) if it were incorporated in the State.

Where the whole or the greater part of the market value of the shares in such a company is attributable, directly or indirectly, to property located in the State, then those shares will be deemed to constitute Irish property. This provision is oddly worded, since close company status is dependent on residence status and not on the state of incorporation as such. Thus, eg a non-Irish company resident in a Double Tax Treaty Country would continue to be non-resident (and therefore not a close company), even on the assumption that it was incorporated in the State. This provision does not affect the valuation of the shares, so that, as discussed above, the value of shares in an investment company would continue to be based on net asset value. The provision has no application to entities other than companies (TCA 1997, s 531AA(4)).

The legislation also tries to forestall the individual 'hiving off' assets in order to fall below the €5 million threshold. Accordingly, an individual will be deemed to be beneficially entitled in possession to any Irish property which he has transferred to his spouse, civil partner or to a minor child or a minor child of a civil partner (ie a child who has not attained the age of 18 years and is not and has not been married) other than a maintenance arrangement within TCA 1997, s 1025. This treatment will also extend to assets which the individual has disposed of transferred to a discretionary trust or a foundation. These provisions will however only apply if the transfer in question was for a consideration which was less than market value and it occurred on or after 18 February 2010 (TCA 1997, s 531AA(3)).

The reference to market value seems peculiar, and will hardly inhibit many obvious planning measures. Thus eg assume Mr Magmond, who is resident in Jersey, has Irish property valued at €9 million. He sells half those assets for €4.5 million on 6 May 2010 to his wife (who is also resident in Jersey and who owns no other Irish property) leaving the consideration outstanding as an unsecured simple debt. He now owns Irish property valued at €4.5 million and a debt of €4.5 million which under general law would normally be located in Jersey. A point to watch however is, the artificial definition of 'market value' means that this value may be in excess of a commercial arm's length price. Thus if in the previous hypothetical the commercial value of the assets sold by Mr Magmond to his wife were €4.5 million, but the 'market value' as defined for levy purposes was €4.75 million, the entire transfer would be disregarded. This anti-avoidance measure only catch transfers of Irish property and not transfers of wealth generally. Thus, eg if Mr Magmond were to transfer €5 million from his Jersey bank account to a discretionary trust which then invested that amount in Irish assets, he would not be treated as being beneficially entitled to those assets.

A 'discretionary trust' is broadly defined as any disposition (see below) which results in property being held subject to a trust or power to apply all or part of the income or capital at the discretion of the trustees or any other person, notwithstanding that there may be a power to accumulate all or any part of the income. A 'disposition' is stated to include any covenant, agreement or arrangement whether effected with or without writing. Given that the identity of the settlor of the trust is irrelevant, this latter definition seems to serve little useful purpose. A 'foundation' is defined as any legal entity, wherever established, irrespective of: (a) how that entity is described in the place of establishment; or (b) the name by which that entity is called in the place of establishment. This definition is wide enough to catch not only the versatile entities commonly referred to as foundations or anstalts, but it could equally apply to companies (which does not seem to have been what was actually intended) (TCA 1997, s 531AA(1)).

Transfers etc to a discretionary trust or foundation will be disregarded where it is shown to the satisfaction of the Revenue Commissioners that they have been created exclusively either: (a) for charitable purposes, as defined under Irish law; or (b) for the benefit of one or more named individuals who because of age, improvidence, or physical, mental or legal incapacity, are unable to manage their own affairs (TCA 1997, s 531AA(3)).

Administration

Domicile levy is under the care and management of the Revenue Commissioners and TCA 1997, Pt 37: Administration applies to the levy as it applies to income tax. References to the Revenue Commissioners are to be construed as including references to any of their officers (TCA 1997, s 531AA(6)). A relevant individual is required to submit a return in the prescribed format for each tax year on or before the following 31 October, together with the payment of the levy. The amount of the domicile levy (ie €200,000) is payable annually where the conditions are met. A credit is allowed against the domicile levy for any income tax paid in the year. Revenue Commissioners have stated *(Domicile Levy – information leaflet)* that a credit for any USC paid is not available against the domicile levy. The author would point out that the legislation is not that clear-cut but on balance would agree that it would appear not to allow a credit for USC paid. While the USC is deemed to be an 'amount of income tax due and payable', that does not mean that it is an amount of income tax which can be credited against the domicile levy in determining the amount of levy payable.

The return must be signed by the relevant individual, and include a declaration by him that the return is correct to the best of his knowledge, information and belief (TCA 1997, s 531AF as amended by Finance Act 2014, s 85(a)). *E-brief 50/12* provides for an extension to the filing deadline for the domicile levy return to the ROS filing date. This extension will only apply to individuals who pay and file using the Revenue Online Service in respect of their income tax return for the relevant tax year. Payment of the levy is required to be made by Electronic Fund Transfer as there is no provision on ROS for the payment of the levy. In addition the domicile levy return Form DL1 is required to be sent directly to the Large Cases Division. Where a return is not delivered to the

Revenue Commissioners on time or they are dissatisfied with a return, they may make an assessment or an amending assessment upon an individual whom they have reason to believe is chargeable to the levy. The Revenue Commissioners may withdraw such an assessment and make an assessment of the amount of domicile levy payable on the basis of a return which, in their opinion, represents reasonable compliance with their requirements and which is delivered to them within 30 days after the date of the assessment. As the levy is at a fixed rate, presumably the only options which are in fact open to the Revenue Commissioners appear to be to let the levy stand or reduce it to zero. Where the Revenue Commissioners have reason to believe that an individual is chargeable to domicile levy for any year they may by notice in writing request an individual to deliver, with 30 days of the date of the notice, a full and true return together with payment of the domicile levy and all such particulars as the Revenue may require (Finance Act 2014, s 85).

TCA 1997, s 959Z; (Inspector's right to make enquiries and amend assessments (see **2.106**) will apply, with any necessary modifications, for the purposes of the levy as it does for income tax, and the Revenue Commissioners shall have all such powers as an inspector would have under TCA 1997, s 959Z in relation to making enquiries or taking such actions as he considers necessary to satisfy himself or herself as to the accuracy or otherwise of any statement or particular contained in a return delivered for the purposes of income tax (TCA 1997, s 531AI). F(TA)A 2015, s 39, which was subject to Ministerial Order (SI 110/2016 appointed 21 March 2016 as the day on which the Finance (Tax Appeals) Act 2015, came into operation), deletes the provisions relating to an appeal against the right of a Revenue officer to make enquiries as they are effectively relocated to TCA 1997, s 959J.

The provisions of TCA 1997, Pt 40, Ch 1: Appeals against Assessments (see **2.2**), Pt 47, Ch 1: Penalties (see **2.7**), TCA 1997, s 1080: Interest on Overdue Tax (see **2.107**), Pt 47, Ch 4: Revenue Offences (see **2.703**) will apply to the levy as they apply to income tax. The collection and recovery procedures under TCA 1997, Pt 42, Ch 1A, Ch 1B and Ch 5 are also extended to the levy (TCA 1997, ss 531AJ, 531AK).

If the Revenue Commissioners are not satisfied with the market value of property estimated in a return, or if they consider it necessary to do so, they may estimate the value of that property and, where the market value as so estimated by the Revenue Commissioners exceeds the market value estimated in the return, any charge to tax will be made by reference to the market value estimated by the Revenue Commissioners and not by reference to the market value estimated in the return. The market value of any property for these purposes will be ascertained by the Revenue Commissioners in such manner and by such means as they think fit and they may authorise a suitably qualified person to inspect any property and report to them the value of such property for the purposes of the levy and the person having custody or possession of that property must permit the person so authorised to inspect it at such reasonable times as the Revenue Commissioners consider necessary. The Revenue Commissioners must bear the costs of any such valuation (TCA 1997, s 531AD).

Where an individual is aggrieved by a decision of the Revenue Commissioners as to the market value of any real property, the individual may appeal against the decision in the manner prescribed by the Finance (1909–10) Act 1910, s 3, and the provisions as to appeals under that section shall apply accordingly with any necessary modifications (TCA 1997, s 531AE).

A relevant individual's liability to income tax for a tax year will be credited against the amount of domicile levy chargeable for that year, but only to the extent that such income tax has been paid at the same time as, or before, the domicile levy for that year is paid (31 October following the end of the relevant tax year) (TCA 1997, s 531AC). As noted above an extension to the ROS filing date for the domicile levy return has been provided to those who file their income tax returns on ROS. Given that the credit for income tax only applied where the income tax was paid at the same time as, or before the domicile levy was paid, this provided some issues in 2011 for individuals who filed on ROS but did not have final details as to their income tax liability until the ROS filing deadline. *E-brief 50/12* has also clarified Revenue's view that no credit is available for the USC payable against the domicile levy. *E-brief 72/14* reiterates Revenue's position that there is no credit allowed against the domicile levy by using the income levy, universal social charge, pay related social insurance or health levy.

Advance clearances

On an application to the Revenue Commissioners by an individual who is considering the making of a significant investment (not defined) in the State, they may (but are not obliged to) give an opinion to the individual as to whether or not the individual would be likely to be regarded as a 'relevant individual' in the tax year in which the application is made. How much comfort is to be derived from such a non-committal procedure is debatable.

3.5 Taxation of Married Couples

3.501 Taxation of married persons: general

In the *Murphy* case the then prevailing system of taxing married couples was held to be unconstitutional – see **1.409**. The present rules enable a married couple living together to elect to be assessed jointly on their combined total incomes, even where one spouse has no income. In any case in which this election for joint assessment is made, the couple are generally given the benefit of double the personal tax credits available to single persons. In addition 'single-income' couples are entitled to an enhanced standard rate band of €42,800 for the tax year 2015 (compared to €33,800 for a single person); this is further increased in the case of 'two income' spouses by the lower of €24,800 and the amount of total income attributable to the spouse with the lower income. The enhanced standard rate band and the home carer tax credit (see **3.311**) are mutually exclusive but an individual may opt for whichever is the more beneficial.

For the special considerations that apply in the context of the restriction of specified reliefs in relation to certain high income individuals see **3.111**.

The same considerations as relate to married couples will apply *mutatis mutandis* to civil partners following the enactment of Finance (No 3) Act 2011. (See Revenue's frequently asked questions on 'Taxation and Civil Partnerships' updated May 2014.)

The Revenue manuals for married couples have been consolidated as of September 2014 – see Revenue *eBrief 76/14* which covers material in relation to the income taxation of married, separated and divorced persons. It includes taxation in year of marriage, basis of assessment for married couples, non-residence of one or both spouses, taxation in year of death and taxation of maintenance payments.

FA 2015 amended TCA 1997, s 2 to take account of the Marriage Act 2015 and SI No 504/2015 noted that 16 November 2015 is appointed as the day on which the Marriage Act 2015 came into operation. It also deleted s 1019(6) and instead brought about a new TCA 1997, s 2(3B) which reads any reference, howsoever expressed, to an individual or a claimant, (a) being a man, a married man or a husband, to be construed as including, as necessary, a reference to a woman, a married woman or a wife, and (b) being a woman, a married woman or a wife to be construed as including, as necessary, a reference to a man, a married man or a husband. The above means that where a marriage comprises a same sex couple then the Taxes Acts should recognise such arrangements.

Husband and wife living together

TCA 1997, s 1015(2) provides that a husband and wife are treated for income tax purposes as living together unless either:

(a) they are separated under an order of a court of competent jurisdiction or by deed of separation; or

(b) they are in fact separated in such circumstances that the separation is likely to be permanent.

In other words, if a couple are married, it is automatically assumed that they are living together unless there is a definite separation. Exception (a) is clear. As regards exception (b), it is arguable that separation implies physical separation, combined with an intention not to live together. Thus, in *Ua Clothasaigh v McCartan* II ITR 75, it was held that where there was a lengthy period of separation but clearly no intention on the part of either spouse to break up the matrimonial home, the couple were still 'living together'. Presumably, one can infer from the *McCartan* case (even though decided in the context of different statutory wording) that a couple which is thus capable of being regarded as still 'living together' are not within exception (b).

The question as to whether the separation is likely to be permanent will again depend primarily on the intention of the parties. If either one of the parties intends to end the marriage, this should be sufficient. In *Ward-Stemp v Griffin* [1988] STC 47, a wife left her husband and shortly thereafter filed for divorce. It was held that exception (b) was satisfied from the date of her leaving. An estranged couple sharing the same house, but living as separate households, were held to fall within the UK equivalent of exception (b) in *Holmes v Mitchell* [1991] STC 25. The declaration by one party that he intended to sue for divorce was accepted as evidence that the separation was likely to be permanent (note also the Irish Family Law case *McA (M) v X McA* (1988) HC.

In the absence of clear-cut evidence of the intentions of the parties, the inspector may argue that a couple who have been living apart for a period in excess of one year fall within exception (b). However, it is axiomatic that each case must be decided by reference to its own particular facts.

A divorce obtained in a jurisdiction outside Ireland will be recognised in Ireland if either spouse was domiciled in the relevant jurisdiction at the time when divorce proceedings were commenced. However, a number of individuals resident in Ireland have 'remarried', following a divorce which would not be recognised under Irish law. In practice, the Revenue Commissioners have normally treated the remarriage as valid for income tax purposes, so long as it has not been legally contested. In these circumstances, the Revenue will not however apply the provisions of TCA 1997, s 1025 (see **3.507**) to any maintenance agreements with a former spouse. It seems that a decree of nullity should be treated in the same manner as a divorce for tax purposes, ie the parties should be treated as married up to the date of annulment. This is notwithstanding the fact that for legal purposes the marriage is treated as void *ab initio* (*Dodsworth v Dale* 20 TC 283).

It may be noted that individuals making alimony and similar payments following a valid foreign divorce may now be eligible for the election for joint assessment under TCA 1997, s 1026 (see **3.508**). Similar treatment now applies in the case of Irish divorces under the Family Law (Divorce) Act 1996 (see **3.509**).

Assuming that it is accepted that a husband and wife are living together in a tax year, there are three alternatives open to the couple as to the manner in which they are assessed to income tax for any tax year (except for the tax year in which their marriage takes place), namely:

(a) to be assessed jointly under TCA 1997, s 1017, in which case one assessment only is made on either the husband or wife in respect of their joint incomes and the spouse assessed is the chargeable person responsible for paying all the tax (see **3.502**); or

(b) to be taxed as if they were single persons, in which case each spouse is assessed on his taxable income as if he were a single person and without any reference to the other spouse's income (see **3.503**); or

(c) although electing to be assessed jointly as in (1), the couple may apply under TCA 1997, s 1023 to have the tax payable in the joint assessment under TCA 1997, s 1017 subdivided between them in separate assessments (see **3.504**).

The reference in (1) to the joint assessment being made on either husband or wife is the current rule which applies if the assessment is for the tax year 1994–95 or any subsequent year. For the tax year 1993–94 and earlier years, a joint assessment had to be made on the husband. For the rules for determining whether the assessment for 1994–95 or later is made on the husband or the wife, see *Joint Assessment on the Wife* in **3.502**.

3.502 Married persons: joint assessment

A husband and wife, if living together in a tax year, are entitled to choose whether they wish to be charged to income tax jointly in the one assessment or to be assessed as single persons. The principles of joint assessment and the circumstances in which it applies are discussed in this chapter. The effect of single person assessment is dealt with in **3.503**.

When joint assessment applies

For the tax year in which the marriage takes place (the 'year of marriage'), the option for joint assessment is not available and each spouse must be assessed as a single person TCA 1997, s 1020(2). However, a special 'year of marriage relief' may apply.

For each subsequent tax year, the question of whether a husband and wife (living together) are to be assessed jointly or as single persons is determined under the following rules:

(a) the husband and wife may, at any time during any year of assessment, elect to be assessed jointly for that year under the rules of TCA 1997, s 1017 by jointly giving the inspector notice in writing to that effect (TCA 1997, s 1018(1));

(b) if the husband and wife have not made that election for a tax year (or for any prior year), they are deemed to have made an election for joint assessment for that year (and are assessed jointly) unless either husband or wife gives the inspector notice in writing – before the end of that tax year – that he or she wishes to be assessed to income tax as a single person (TCA 1997, s 1018(4));

(c) where an election for joint assessment for any tax year has been made under TCA 1997, s 1018(1), or has been deemed by TCA 1997, s 1018(4) to have been made, the husband and wife are assessed jointly for that tax year and for each subsequent year in which they are living together (TCA 1997, s 1018(2)), unless and until either husband or wife gives the inspector notice in writing to withdraw the notice for joint assessment;

(d) where either husband or wife – before the end of a tax year – gives the inspector a notice in writing that he or she wishes to be assessed as a single person for that year or a notice that he wishes to withdraw a previous notice, then each spouse is assessed as a single person for that tax year and for each subsequent year (TCA 1997, s 1018(3)), unless and until any subsequent notice for joint assessment is given;

(e) if either spouse gives the inspector notice in writing of their wish to be assessed as a single person for a tax year, both spouses are assessed as single persons under TCA 1997, s 1016; for that tax year and every subsequent tax year (unless and until both spouses make the election mentioned in (a) for joint assessment in any subsequent year or until the spouse who made the single person election withdraws it); and

(f) in the event that husband and wife cease to live together in any tax year (ie if they separate before 31 December in a tax year), joint assessment ceases to be available and they must be assessed as single persons from the date of the separation onwards (unless they come to live together again).

In the case of a newly married couple, the first tax year for which they may be assessed jointly is the year following the year in which they are married. If neither spouse takes any action (other than to advise the inspector that they are married), the couple automatically become assessable jointly for the first year after the year of marriage under rule (b) above. In practice, joint assessment is the norm for most married couples living together, but as indicated it is not compulsory and can be ended by either spouse at any time by giving the appropriate notice.

Any notice for single person tax assessment must be made no later than the last day of the tax year for which it is to apply. Similarly, a notice to the inspector withdrawing a previous year's single person election must, to be valid, be made not later than the last day of the tax year for which joint assessment is required.

For the treatment in the year of marriage when a special relief may be available, see **3.505**. For the position in the tax year in which either spouse dies, see **3.506**. For the treatment in the event of separation, dissolution of marriage, etc, see **3.507–3.509**.

Example 3.502.1

John and Betty, who are both aged 28, are married on 5 May 2014. For the tax year 2014 (year of marriage), they are assessed as single persons, but are eligible to claim 'year of marriage' relief under TCA 1997, s 1020 if the facts of their income, etc for 2014 justify the relief (see **3.505**). The first tax year in which joint assessment may apply to John and Betty is 2015.

Neither John nor Betty takes any steps during 2015 regarding their type of assessment for that year. TCA 1997, s 1018(4) therefore applies and they are deemed to have elected for joint assessment under TCA 1997, s 1017 for 2015.

If John and Betty continue to live together, and if neither spouse notifies the inspector of an election to the contrary in any tax year, they will automatically continue to be assessed jointly for 2016 and subsequent years.

Example 3.502.2

Take the facts of **Example 3.502.1**, but assume that on 22 December 2015 (ie before the end of the tax year 2015) Betty (against John's wishes) writes to the inspector notifying him that she wishes to be assessed as a single person under TCA 1997, s 1016 for the tax year 2015.

Even if John should write to the inspector stating that he wishes joint assessment to apply, the inspector must assess John and Betty as single persons for 2015. The inspector must also assess them as single persons for 2016, etc unless and until Betty writes to the inspector again withdrawing her notice for single person assessment (or if she joins with John in a notice requiring joint assessment for a subsequent year).

Effect of election for joint assessment

The principle of joint assessment is that only one assessment is made on the joint total income of the married couple (ie on the aggregate of their respective total incomes) but that the assessment is made on the husband who is the chargeable person responsible for making the tax return and for paying the tax (TCA 1997, s 1017).

TCA 1997, s 1019 permits and, in certain circumstances, requires the joint assessment (where it applies) to be made on the wife rather than on the husband. In any such case, it is the wife who becomes the chargeable person responsible for making the tax return and for paying the tax. However, for ease of explanation, the discussion herein of the principles of joint assessment assumes that the assessment is being made on the husband. The circumstances in which the wife is the person assessed are outlined separately at the end of this chapter.

When joint assessment is applicable for any tax year, TCA 1997, s 1017(1)(a) provides that the wife's total income (if any) – once it has been established (see below) – must be treated for all purposes of the Income Tax Acts as if it were the husband's income in addition to his own total income (if any). The husband is, therefore, assessed and charged to tax in respect of both his own and his wife's total income.

TCA 1997, s 1017(1)(a) provides that the amount of any income of the wife that is to be charged to tax (in the joint assessment on her husband) must be computed separately without regard to the fact that her total income (when determined) is then aggregated to become part of her husband's total income. It follows that the husband's total income is also to be determined separately before the aggregation of the total incomes of both spouses. This means that both the computational rules and the basis of assessment rules of the various Schedules and Cases must be applied separately to each spouse to arrive at his income from its various sources.

An individual's 'total income' is the aggregate of his income from all sources as reduced by certain allowances (eg capital allowances) and deductions which the Income Tax Acts provide are to be deducted in arriving at that total income. In determining the total income of each spouse, the general principle is that each spouse's deductions in arriving at total income are deductible only from his income from all sources.

This general principle normally applies to those deductions and allowances available against particular types of income (for example, capital allowances of a trade, self-employed retirement annuity premiums, etc). Any such deductions may normally only reduce the relevant income of the spouse in question and, if that income is not sufficient to absorb the full deduction, no part of the excess may be deducted in arriving at the other spouse's total income.

However, certain types of deduction which cannot be fully absorbed by the income of the spouse to whom the deduction relates are available to reduce the total income of the other spouse where the relevant section giving the deduction provides for this.

For example, TCA 1997, s 381, which allows an individual a deduction from his income from all sources for a loss incurred in the same tax year in a trade or profession, specifically provides that any part of that loss which cannot be absorbed by the income of the spouse incurring it is then to be treated as reducing the income of the other spouse (where husband and wife are assessed jointly under TCA 1997, s 1017).

Example 3.502.3

John and Betty are assessable jointly on John under TCA 1997, s 1017 for the tax year 2015 (see **Example 3.502.1**). The first part of the computation of their income tax payable for 2015 is to compute their respective total incomes in accordance with the principles discussed in more detail in **Division 3.1**. Based on the data shown below for the year 2015 (some items summarised rather than in full detail), their total incomes are worked out as follows:

	John	*Betty*
	€	€
Profits from profession as surveyor net of capital allowances (John)	19,220	
Profits from trade as hair stylist net of capital allowances (Betty)		14,300
Directors fees (John)	3,000	
Investment income (each)	12,500	4,900
Total of income from all sources	34,720	19,200
Deductions in arriving at total income:		
Retirement annuity premium (single):		
paid by John €4,000		
deduction limited to[1]	(3,333)	
paid by Betty[2]		(1,000)
Deed of covenant (elderly parent)		
paid by John[3]	(500)	
Total deductions	(3,833)	(1,000)
Total income of each spouse	30,887	18,200

TCA 1997, s 1017(4)(c) requires John to be assessed to income tax in respect of both his own total income and Betty's total income. Once the two total incomes have been separately determined, Betty's total income is deemed to be John's income for all the purposes of the Income Tax Acts. John is therefore assessed in respect of a total income (joint) made up as follows:

	€
John's total income	30,887
Betty's total income	18,200
Joint total income (deemed to be all John's)	49,087

Notes:

1. John's deduction for his retirement annuity premium is restricted to €3,333, being 15 per cent (under 30 years of age) of net relevant earnings €22,220, made up of profits net of capital allowances €19,220 plus directors' fees €3,000; (see **16.202**, **16.208**).
2. Betty's retirement annuity premium of €1,000 is well within her limit of €2,145, being 15 per cent (under 30 years of age) of net relevant earnings of €14,300 and is therefore fully deductible.
3. The amount of the covenant is clearly within the five per cent limit (discussed at **15.405**).

Once the joint total income (deemed to be the husband's income) has been established, the various reliefs available to the married couple are then deducted to arrive at taxable income on which the joint income tax liability for the year is computed. In principle, the reliefs which the Income Tax Acts provide are to be given as a deduction from total income are deducted from the joint total income, but it remains necessary to have regard to any rules relating to these allowances and reliefs. Similar consideration applies to personal and general tax credits (see **3.106**).

Thus, for example, should the rules for any type of relief specifically provide that the relief for any expenditure incurred by one spouse is to be limited to the income of that spouse, or to the amount paid out of that income, then the amount of the deduction from the joint total income for that spouse's expenditure is restricted accordingly. However, in the absence of any such specific restriction, the deduction should be given to the extent of the full joint total income. The manner in which each of the various reliefs applies to a couple who are jointly assessed is discussed under the heading for each relief below; see also the relevant chapters for reliefs which are the subject of separate discussion (eg the Employment and Investment Incentive at **18.1**).

Apart from the special election which can be made under TCA 1997, s 1026 for joint assessment by certain separated and divorced spouses (see **3.508** and **3.509**), the rules for joint assessment under TCA 1997, s 1017 only apply for tax years during which husband and wife are living together. Should husband and wife separate in any tax year, they cease to be entitled to be assessed jointly from the date of separation onwards and must be assessed as single persons for the remainder of that year, and for subsequent years so long as the separation continues. Unless joint assessment applies for a given year or part of a year, any provision in the Acts which authorises a relief or credit to be granted to a husband by reference to his wife's income, profits, losses or payments made (for example, her Sch D Case I trading loss under TCA 1997, s 381), has no application (TCA 1997, s 1017(2)). In the case of certain allowances and reliefs the legislation fails in fact to expressly authorise relief to be given by reference to payments made by his wife, although in practice the Revenue Commissioners do not take this point.

With effect from 25 December 2016, being the date of passing of Finance Act 2016, TCA 1997, s 1017(3) and (4), a husband or wife who is not assessed under joint election can elect to be so assessed. This permits either spouse to file an online return for the previous year of assessment. However, the election will not apply where the husband or wife is a chargeable person and required to submit a return.

Joint assessment on wife

TCA 1997, s 1019 entitles a husband and wife who are assessable jointly, to elect that the joint assessment for that tax year be made on the wife instead of the husband. For this election to be valid, it must be made in writing jointly by husband and wife no later than 1 April in the tax year for which it is to apply.

Once this election has been made, the joint assessment for the tax year in question and for each subsequent year is made on the wife unless and until the election is withdrawn by a further notice in writing also made jointly by both spouses. For a withdrawal of the election to have the wife as the assessable spouse to be effective for any tax year, the notice of withdrawal must be given before 1 April in that year (TCA 1997, s 1019(5)). The effect of the notice of withdrawal is that the assessment for this tax year (and subsequent years) reverts to one made on the husband.

The joint assessment on the wife may also, in certain circumstances, be made at the instigation of the inspector. TCA 1997, s 1019(2)(b) requires the inspector to make the joint assessment for a tax year on the wife (rather than the husband) in any case where the following circumstances are present:

(a) the couple have been deemed by the rule in TCA 1997, s 1018(4) to have made an election for joint assessment (because no notice for assessment as single persons has been given before the end of the tax year);

(b) the couple have not made an election under TCA 1997, s 1018(1) to be assessed jointly on the husband; and

(c) the inspector, to the best of his knowledge or belief, considers that the total income of the wife for the year of marriage exceeded the total income of the husband for that year.

This provision is intended to apply for the first year following the year of marriage where the wife is considered by the inspector to have been the higher income earner in the year of marriage. If the inspector does not have the necessary information about their respective incomes in the year of marriage (the 'basis year'), the inspector is required to make the joint assessment on the wife if, in the most recent year before the year of marriage for which the inspector has the information, the total income of the wife exceeded the total income of the husband (TCA 1997, s 1019(2)).

In any case in which the inspector has made the joint assessment for a tax year on the wife under this rule of TCA 1997, s 1019(2)(b), the assessment for each subsequent year is also made on the wife unless and until the husband and wife jointly give notice under TCA 1997, s 1018(1) that they wish the joint assessment to be made on the husband or, alternatively, until either husband or wife gives notice that he wishes to be assessed as a single person (or until they cease to live together) (TCA 1997, s 1018(4)).

The continuation after the first year of the joint assessment on the wife made by the inspector under the rule of TCA 1997, s 1019(2)(b) is not altered by the fact that the total income of the husband may exceed that of the wife in any tax year after the year of marriage. The only year for which the comparison of total incomes is made in applying this rule is the year of marriage or, if necessary, the most recent year prior to the year of marriage. However, as indicated in the previous paragraph, the husband and wife can always opt to change the assessment to one on the husband by giving the appropriate notice.

Example 3.502.4

Anthony and Cleo were married on 14 June 2014. Their total incomes for 2014 are €26,000 for Anthony and €15,000 for Cleo assessable separately on each under the rules for the year of marriage.

The couple wish to be assessed jointly for 2015, the first year for which joint assessment is possible. For there to be joint assessment for 2015 (and subsequent years), they need take no action since TCA 1997, s 1018(4) applies to deem an election for joint assessment to have been made (as no election for single person assessment is made). Since Anthony's income exceeded Cleo's in the year of marriage, this assessment will be made on Anthony if no other action is taken.

However, the couple would prefer to have the joint assessment for 2015 (and subsequent years) to be made on Cleo since she is better at handling financial matters. In order to achieve this, Anthony and Cleo have to give the inspector notice in writing no later than 31 March 2015 (before 1 April in the first year to be affected) requiring the inspector to make the assessment for 2015 on Cleo.

Example 3.502.5

Take the facts of **Example 3.502.4** except assume that Anthony's total income for 2014 (the year of marriage) was €17,000 and Cleo's was €22,000 (facts known to the inspector) and that no election is taken by either spouse in relation to the form of assessment for 2014 so that there must be a joint assessment.

Since, on these facts, all the circumstances required by TCA 1997, s 1019(2)(b) are present (including Cleo's total income exceeding Anthony's for the year of marriage), the inspector is required to make the joint assessment for 2015 on Cleo as the wife (even should Anthony's total income be the greater in 2015).

Anthony and Cleo will continue to be assessed jointly with Cleo as the assessable person for 2015 and subsequent years unless and until the couple jointly gives notice requiring a joint assessment on Anthony (or unless either spouse gives notice requiring assessment as a single person).

In any case where the assessment is to be made on the wife – whether due to an election or a deemed election by the husband and wife or, if required by TCA 1997, s 1019(2)(b), at the instigation of the inspector – then TCA 1997, s 1017 should be read as if the references therein respectively to 'husband' and 'wife' were reversed. Any reference in the Income Tax Acts, howsoever expressed, to an individual or a claimant, (a) being a man, a married man or a husband, shall be construed as including, as necessary, a reference to a woman, a married woman or a wife, and (b) being a woman, a married woman or a wife shall be construed as including, as necessary, a reference to a man, a married man or a husband (TCA 1997, s 2(3B)).

Example 3.502.6

Take the case of John and Betty whose total incomes for 2015 have been determined in the manner set out in **Example 3.502.3**. Assume that they wish Betty to be the chargeable person on whom the joint assessment is to be made for 2015. In order to achieve this, they write to the inspector (letter signed by each) on 31 March 2015 (before 1 April in the year) advising him of their election for the joint assessment to be made on Betty.

The inspector must therefore make the joint assessment for 2015 (and subsequent years) on Betty. For 2015, this assessment is in respect of a joint total income (subject to credits, etc) made up as follows:

	€
Betty's total income	18,200
John's total income	30,887
Total income (deemed to be all Betty's)	49,087

Repayments of tax

TCA 1997, s 1021 deals with the allocation of any repayment of tax due to a husband and wife who are assessed jointly under TCA 1997, s 1017, whether the husband or the wife is the assessable person for the year involved. It applies to any repayment due in respect of the aggregate of the net tax paid or deducted under any of the provisions of the Income Tax Acts on the total incomes of both spouses (or of either spouse).

However, in the case of a jointly assessable couple who have opted for separate assessment under TCA 1997, s 1023, the section does not apply and any repayment in that case is divided under the same principles as any net tax liability is actually divided between the spouses under the rules of TCA 1997, ss 1023, 1024 (see **3.504**).

The general rule is that the amount to be repaid in respect of the joint assessment is allocated between the husband and wife in the proportion to the net amounts of tax paid or deducted in respect of the respective total incomes of husband and wife (TCA 1997, s 1021(2)). In effect, this means that the total amount of the repayment is apportioned between husband and wife in the proportion which each spouse's total income bears to the aggregate of their total incomes.

Example 3.502.7

Arthur and Eve are jointly assessed for 2015 (Eve being the person assessed by inspector under TCA 1997, s 1019(2)(b)) on the undermentioned income as follows:

	Arthur	*Eve*
	€	€
Income from profession (net of capital allowances and losses carried forward)	12,000	
Sch F distributions (including €3,000 dividend withholding tax)	-	15,000
	12,000	15,000
Deductions:		
Retirement annuity premium	(300)	
Total incomes (each spouse)	11,700	15,000
Joint total income (deemed to be Eve's total income)		26,700
Less:		
Employment and Investment Incentive subscription €7,333 x 30/40=		(5,500)
Taxable income (joint)		21,200
Income tax payable (€21,200 x 20%)		4,240
Less:		
Married persons' tax credit		(3,300)
Dividend withholding tax		(3,000)
Net tax repayable		(2,060)

The repayment is apportioned in the ratio of total incomes as follows:

	€
Repayment due to Eve:	
(€2,060) x €15,000/€26,700	(1,157)
Repayment due to Arthur:	
(€2,060) x €11,700/€26,700	(903)
	(2,060)

TCA 1997, s 1021(3) provides an exception to the general rule of allocating the repayment in proportion to the respective total incomes. It entitles the inspector to make the repayment to the husband and wife otherwise than in such proportion if the inspector is satisfied that, by reason of some allowance or relief which is attributable to one spouse only, there would be a greater repayment to that spouse if the rules of TCA 1997, ss 1023, 1024 were applied (ie the rules for the separate assessment of a husband and wife (see **3.504**)).

In any case which falls within TCA 1997, s 1021(3), the inspector may divide the repayment between the spouses in such proportions as he considers just and reasonable. The inspector should make a calculation applying the rules of TCA 1997, ss 1023, 1024 to ascertain whether or not this would give a greater repayment to one spouse (and a lesser one to the other spouse) than the total incomes apportionment. However, if this 'notional' calculation would give a greater repayment, the inspector is not bound to make the repayments in accordance with that calculation. The inspector is left with the discretion as to dividing the total repayment in the amounts which he considers just and reasonable.

Other examples

A comprehensive example is given in **Division 3.1** of the computation of the total income, taxable income, tax payable, credits against tax, etc in cases of a married couple whose assessment is made on the joint incomes of husband and wife under the rules of TCA 1997, s 1017.

Rights of recovery against non-assessable spouse

Where a couple is jointly assessed, the Revenue Commissioners nevertheless retain a power of recovery in relation to income tax in respect of the spouse who is not the assessable spouse under TCA 1997, s 1017. Where all or part of the tax due under joint assessment has not been paid within 28 days of the due date, the Revenue may raise an assessment on the tax on which the non-assessed spouse would have been assessed if an election for separate assessment under TCA 1997, s 1023 had been in force for the relevant year of assessment (TCA 1997, s 1022(1)). The assessment is subject to the normal recovery and appeals procedures (amended by F(TA)A 2015, s 59 which was subject to Ministerial Order, (SI 110/2016 appointed 21 March 2016 as the day on which the Finance (Tax Appeals) Act 2015, came into operation)), to take account of the new provisions therein, as if an election under TCA 1997, s 1023 had actually been made for the year of assessment; the Revenue's information seeking powers are correspondingly preserved (TCA 1997, s 1022(2), (4)). The original assessment in respect of the joint income of the couple made on the 'assessed spouse' is reduced by the amount assessed on the 'non-assessed' spouse, with any repayments being made as necessary (TCA 1997, s 1022(3)). Prior to 10 February 2000 an assessment under TCA 1997, s 1022 could only be made on a husband.

3.503 Assessment as single persons

A husband and wife living together are assessed as single persons for any tax year for which no election for joint assessment is in operation (TCA 1997, s 1016). As a married couple living together is deemed to have elected for joint assessment commencing with the tax year following the year of marriage unless either specifically notifies the inspector in writing to the contrary, single assessment only applies if either spouse takes positive action to require it.

When single person assessment has been claimed for any tax year, or is in force as a result of a previous election which has not been withdrawn, each spouse is taxed entirely separately from the other in exactly the same way as if they were not married. Each spouse computes his total income without any reference to the other spouse's income from its various sources. No account can be taken of any deductions or reliefs available to the other spouse, whether or not that other spouse has sufficient income to absorb those deductions. Each spouse receives a separate single person's basic personal tax credit and any other allowances and reliefs in computing tax payable are similarly dealt with as for two unrelated single persons.

One credit requires to be mentioned separately – the credit given by TCA 1997, s 465 for one or more incapacitated children. This credit is allocated between the spouses depending on how they divide the cost of maintaining the child between them (see **3.307**).

Assessment as single persons is not likely to give any advantage in terms of a lower combined income tax liability for the married couple in a normal case. Joint assessment usually gives a better result unless the taxable income of each spouse is high enough to attract the higher rate of income tax. In such a case, the total income tax liability may sometimes be the same whichever option is taken, but regard should also be had to the deductions of each spouse, the upper limits of which may be better used where the spouses are jointly assessed.

One singly assessed spouse may sometimes have a tax loss or excess capital allowances from a trade or profession which may either be deducted from income from all sources in the same year or carried forward for a future set off against income from the same class. Should the spouse with the loss or excess capital allowances have insufficient other income to absorb them fully in the same tax year, the fact that the excess could be set off against the other spouse's income – should there be joint assessment – should be borne in mind. It might be worth considering whether an election for joint assessment might be beneficial. However, note that such an election must be made before the end of the tax year in which the loss, etc is incurred.

It is possible to elect to be taxed as single persons in one year and then to revert back to a joint assessment the next year, or vice versa, provided that the proper notices are given to the inspector (see **3.502**).

3.504 Claim for separate assessment

A husband and wife may consider it beneficial to be assessed jointly under TCA 1997, s 1017, but may wish to keep their tax affairs separate so that each receives his own assessment and can pay his share of the tax bill separately. This may be achieved by an application for separate assessment under TCA 1997, s 1023.

Separate assessment is not to be confused with the option open to a married couple to be taxed as single persons. When separate assessment is in force for any tax year, income tax is charged and collected on the income of each spouse separately as if they were not married, but with the important proviso that the total personal reliefs allowed in the separate assessments and the total tax payable by both spouses together are to be the same as if they were assessed together in the one joint assessment.

The application to have the TCA 1997, s 1017 joint assessment subdivided into two separate assessments respectively on husband and wife for any tax year must, unless they were separately assessed for the previous tax year, be made within the six months before 1 April in the tax year for which separate assessment is required. The application may be made by either spouse (TCA 1997, s 1023(2)). For example, if separate assessment is required for the first time for the tax year 2015, either husband or wife (or both) must make the application between 1 October 2014 and 31 March 2015.

An application for separate assessment applies not only for the tax year for which it is made but also for each subsequent year unless and until the application is withdrawn by the spouse who originally made it. The withdrawal must be made before 1 April in the tax year for which it is intended to be effective. Once the separate assessment application is withdrawn, it ceases to have effect for all subsequent years but a new application may be made for a later year.

When separate assessment under TCA 1997, s 1023 is in force for any tax year, the respective aggregate incomes from all sources of husband and wife are each determined in the same way as in the case of joint assessment under TCA 1997, s 1017. The same deductions in arriving at their respective total incomes for a joint assessment are made to determine their separate total incomes as would be made in a joint assessment.

Normally any deductions in arriving at total income for payments made or losses incurred are given to the spouse making the deductible payment or incurring the allowable loss. However, if a joint assessment were to be made, a deduction to which one spouse is entitled would be set off against the income of the other spouse due to the spouse entitled not having sufficient income to absorb it (for example, a trading loss within TCA 1997, s 381, see **4.404–4.405**), the unabsorbed part of the deduction is set off against the income of the other spouse in the separate assessment calculation.

In short, the aggregate of the separate total incomes should always equal the joint total income that would have arisen without a claim for separate assessment under TCA 1997, s 1023. After the total incomes of each spouse have been determined, the same personal allowances and other reliefs as would apply in a joint assessment are allocated between the spouses to arrive at their separate taxable incomes. If any such allowance or relief is limited by reference to total income, the amount of the allowance or relief (to be allocated between the spouses) is calculated by reference to the total income figure that would result in a joint assessment.

TCA 1997, s 1024 contains the rules for allocating the personal reliefs, tax credits and tax rate bands for the tax year between husband and wife who have applied for separate assessment. The basis of allocation of the reliefs and tax credits is as follows:

(a) equally between the spouses:
 (i) the basic personal tax credit under TCA 1997, s 461,
 (ii) the incapacitated child credit under TCA 1997, s 465 except for a child within (c)(i) below,
 (iii) blind person's tax credit under TCA 1997, s 468 (it is rather unusual to have this credit shared as it would normally derive from one of the spouses being blind), and
 (iv) the age tax credit under TCA 1997, s 464;

(b) to each spouse according to his qualifying emoluments:
 (i) the employee tax credit under TCA 1997, s 472,
 (ii) relief for the long-term unemployed under TCA 1997, s 472A, and
 (iii) seafarer allowance under TCA 1997, s 472B;

(c) to the husband or to the wife depending on which spouse maintains:
 (i) an incapacitated child, other than a child of the couple, maintained at the expense of one spouse for whom an incapacitated child credit under TCA 1997, s 465(4)) is given, and
 (ii) a dependent relative for whom a dependent relative tax credit is given under TCA 1997, s 466;

(d) to the husband or to the wife according to which makes the payment giving rise to relief under:
 (i) TCA 1997, s 473 for rent for residential premises, and
 (ii) TCA 1997, s 470 for medical insurance*;

 (*relief for medical insurance is granted at source; however, if paid by an employer, the gross premium is treated as a benefit in kind and the employee/director is entitled to a tax credit.)

(e) in the proportions in which the husband and wife bore the expenditure giving rise to relief for health expenses under TCA 1997, s 469; (the use of the word 'bore' here is to take account of the fact that certain amounts of expenditure on health expenses may be covered by insurance or by otherwise);

(f) in the proportions in which husband and wife respectively incurred the expenditure giving rise to the relief:
   (i) under TCA 1997, s 476, in respect of fees for training courses,
   (ii) relief for contributions to permanent health benefit schemes under TCA 1997, s 471, where relief not given at source,
   (iii) relief for subscription of new shares issued to employees under TCA 1997, s 479 no longer available for 2011 onwards (see **Division 11**),
   (iv) under TCA 1997, s 372AR, in respect of qualifying expenditure on owner-occupied residences in certain designated areas (see **Division 19.1** of the 2009 edition of this book),
   (v) under TCA 1997, Sch 32 para 20, in respect of qualifying expenditure on certain historic and other significant buildings in designated areas (see **Division 19** of the 2009 edition of this book),
   (vi) under TCA 1997, s 473A, in respect of fees paid to certain approved colleges and universities,
   (vii) under TCA 1997, s 244, in respect of mortgage interest, where relief is not given at source;

(g) in the proportions in which husband and wife respectively have subscribed for eligible shares/qualifying for relief under TCA 1997, Pt 16 in respect of eligible shares in companies qualifying under the Employment and Investment Incentive and seed capital scheme (see **Division 18.1**);

(h) in the proportions in which husband and wife respectively have made a relevant investment in a qualifying film production and distribution company for which relief is given under TCA 1997, s 481 (relief no longer available for individuals from 2015) (see **18.401**);

(i) in the proportions in which husband and wife respectively bear the cost of employing a person to take care of an incapacitated person under TCA 1997, s 467;

(j) in the proportion in which husband and wife respectively made a relevant donation for which relief is given under TCA 1997, s 848A. Relief for charitable donations is no longer available to an individual from 1 January 2013 (see **Division 18.2**).

In addition, TCA 1997, s 664(3) (exemption of certain income from leasing of farmland) provides that the deduction(s) from total income granted in relation to that income is to be allocated as if the couple were not married.

Each spouse is initially allocated the single person's standard rate band of €33,800. Where the income of the spouse with the lower income is less than the amount of the standard rate band, the shortfall may be transferred to the other spouse (TCA 1997, s 1024(4)). However, the shortfall thus transferred cannot increase the other spouse's standard rate band above €42,800. This provision reflects the fact that a jointly assessed couple are entitled to an increase in the married couples standard rate band of €42,800 equal to the lower of €24,800 and the income of the spouse with the lower income. Where one spouse has unused allowances or credits due to an insufficiency of income, the surplus allowances or credits are transferred to the other spouse.

The fact that separate assessment is in operation does not necessarily mean that each spouse must complete a separate income tax return, although this may well be the more satisfactory arrangement in practice. The return(s) of the respective total incomes of the husband and the wife and the appropriate claim(s) for allowances may be made by either spouse. However, if the inspector of taxes is not satisfied with any such return made by one of the spouses, he may require a return to be made as well by the other spouse (TCA 1997, s 1023(5)).

Example 3.605.1 shows how the foregoing principles are applied where separate assessment has been claimed under TCA 1997, s 1023. It shows that, in certain circumstances, where there are credits against income tax payable, the result may be a net balance of tax payable by one spouse and a net refund repayable to the other.

3.505 Married persons: year of marriage

TCA 1997, s 1020(2) provides that, the rules of TCA 1997, s 1018 permitting an election for joint assessment under TCA 1997, s 1017 do not apply to a husband and wife in the tax year in which their marriage takes place (the year of marriage). Both husband and wife continue, therefore, to be taxed as single persons for the year of marriage. However, the income tax payable by each may be subject to a special year of marriage relief provided by TCA 1997, s 1020(3).

The year of marriage relief may be claimed if the aggregate of the income tax payable and paid for the year of marriage by both spouses (as single persons) exceeds the income tax that would be payable if they had been assessed jointly under TCA 1997, s 1017 in respect of their joint total incomes (on the assumption that they had been married to each other for the whole year of marriage).

The year of marriage relief is given by repayment of tax. Any claim for this relief must be made in writing to the inspector after the end of the year of marriage and must be made by both husband and wife (TCA 1997, s 1020(5)). The amount repayable is allocated between husband and wife in proportion to their respective total incomes for the year of marriage (TCA 1997, s 1020(4)).

The amount of the income tax repayable is computed by a formula provided in TCA 1997, s 1020(3). For ease of explanation, the formula provided in the Act may, without changing its effect, be changed to the following:

$$(A-B) \times N/12$$

where

A = the aggregate of the income tax payable for the year of assessment by both spouses (as single persons);

B = the income tax which would be payable for the year of marriage in respect of their joint total incomes if a joint assessment under TCA 1997, s 1017 were to be permitted (the notional joint income tax payable); and

N = the number of calendar months between the date of the marriage and the end of the year of marriage (a part of a month is treated as a whole month).

TCA 1997, s 1020(6) provides that all the provisions of the Income Tax Acts related to the deductions for personal allowances, etc are to apply also for the purpose of the year of marriage relief. This means that each spouse should claim the relief in their respective income tax returns (TCA 1997, s 458). Also, the amount of the repayment must not reduce the aggregate income tax payable separately by husband and wife to less than the aggregate of the income tax deducted by them from charges on income (TCA 1997, s 459).

In applying the above formula to determine the amount (if any) of the repayment, the income tax payable by each spouse included in A and the notional joint income tax payable in B may be taken as the 'net income tax on taxable income', ie as the 'income tax chargeable on taxable income' as reduced by the 'non-repayable credits', but before adding on the 'income tax on charges on income' (see **3.1** for the explanation of stages in computing an individual's tax liability). This is because the result of 'A – B' is not altered by PRSI, Universal Social Charge or the credits fully deductible (which will be the same in both A and B).

For an example of the application of TCA 1997, s 1020 and of the claim for the year of marriage relief, see **3.606**.

3.506 Married persons: year of death

The death of either spouse in a year of assessment (the year of death) usually affects the taxation position of both spouses. For the deceased spouse, the death results in an automatic cessation of all his sources of income. This principle applies whether it is the husband or the wife who has died and irrespective of whether they have been assessed jointly under TCA 1997, s 1017 or as single persons prior to the death. There are, however, various differences in the tax position dependent on whether the couple were assessed jointly or as single persons prior to the death of one spouse.

Death of spouse assessed as single person

In the case where the spouse who has died has been taxed as a single person up to his death, either because of an election under TCA 1997, s 1016(1) or because the spouses were not living together, it is generally only the deceased spouse whose tax computations may have to be adjusted. Clearly, his tax for the year in which the death occurs has to be calculated on the basis that only income arising in that year up to the date of death is included.

The computation of the tax payable by the surviving spouse for the year of death may also be affected notwithstanding the single person assessments for the period to the date of the death. For example, the surviving spouse may inherit income-bearing assets in which case he may receive additional income from the deceased's estate in the remainder of the year to include in his return for the whole year. The surviving spouse will always be entitled to the married person's basic personal tax credit of €3,300 in the year of death regardless of the method of assessment (TCA 1997, s 461).

If the incapacitated child credit is being claimed for any child and the deceased spouse had maintained the child up to his death, the credit for the year of death has to be apportioned on a time basis. (This is not a strict interpretation of TCA 1997, s 465(6). That subsection effectively states that only one incapacitated tax credit shall be allowed for each tax year in respect of each child. It deals with the situation where two or more individuals jointly maintain a child; the credit is apportioned by reference to the proportionate amount expended on the maintenance of the child. As the concept of joint maintenance implies contemporaneous maintenance, that method of apportionment is not specifically stipulated. As there is no specific method of apportionment stipulated, it is considered that a time basis would be the most equitable). The foregoing treatment would also apply to the dependant relative tax credit.

In the event that husband and wife (who have been living together) were being assessed as single persons prior to the death, but could have elected for joint assessment (if they had chosen to do so), consideration should be given to whether there is any overall tax saving to be made by reversing the previous decision and to elect for joint assessment for the year of death. Any election under TCA 1997, s 1018(1) to revert to joint assessment for the year of death would have to be made before the end of that year (and would have to be made jointly by the surviving spouse and the personal representatives of the deceased spouse).

Joint assessment: death of assessable person

In the following analysis and commentary, it is assumed that the husband is the assessable person. Where the wife is the assessable person (TCA 1997, s 1019), the material should be interpreted accordingly.

There are no provisions in the Income Tax Acts which deal explicitly with the assessment of a jointly assessed married couple in the year of death. However, an analysis of the wording of TCA 1997, s 1017 yields the relevant treatment. Sub-s (1)(a) states that the husband shall be assessed to income tax on his wife's total income for any part of the year during which she is living with him and that that her total income (for the part of the year during which she is living with him) shall be deemed to be his income. Therefore, by implication, the total income of the wife for any part of the year that she is not living with her husband is assessable on her in her own right. This is confirmed by sub-s (1)(b) which effectively states that sub-s (1)(a) shall not affect the question as to whether there is any income of the wife chargeable to tax for any year of assessment. TCA 1997, s 1015(3), an interpretation section, states that references to the income of a wife include references to any sum which apart from this Chapter (ie Ch 1 of Pt 44) would be included in her total income; therefore, the reference in sub-s (1)(b) to the income of the wife is to be construed as the amount of the income of the wife arising during the period when she is not living with her husband.

The treatment in the year of death of the husband, as the assessable person, is as follows:

(a) The joint assessment to the date of death is made on the husband (usually in the names of his personal representatives) in respect of his and his wife's total incomes as calculated up to the date of his death;

(b) Amounts available as deductions against total income up to date of death such as eligible nursing home fees, the Employment and Investment Incentive, etc are set against the total computed at (a) to yield taxable income;

(c) The taxable income (per (b)) is taxed at the normal married person's tax rates and bands for the tax year, with no adjustment to the tax bands for the fact that the income relates to a period of less than a year;

(d) The treatment of tax credits, where applicable, is as follows:

   (i) A basic personal tax credit of €3,300 is available against the tax computed at (c) regardless of when husband dies in the tax year,

   (ii) The husband is entitled to the employee tax credit both for himself and his wife, based on their respective Sch E emoluments up to the date of the death of the husband,

   (iii) The husband is entitled to the age credit of €490 if either he was aged 65 or over at the date of his death or if his wife is aged 65 or over before the end of the tax year. It would appear that if the wife reaches 65 years of age in the tax year of death of the husband but after the date of his death that the credit is available,

   (iv) to the extent relevant, any other credits on the appropriate basis for the year in question; and

(e) the total income of the widow for the remaining part of the year (ie from the date of death to the following 31 December) is assessed on her and taxed at the single person's tax rates for the year;

(f) The tax credits available to the wife, in the year of death, are dealt with as follows:

   (i) a full basic personal tax credit of €3,300 is available (TCA 1997, s 461(b)),

   (ii) if the widow has qualifying earnings in the part of the year after the death, the employee tax credit (given re pensions, also) notwithstanding that her husband may have already been entitled to a full employee tax credit in respect of her earnings up to the date of his death,

   (iii) the age credit of €245 if she is 65 years or older at the end of the tax year,

   (iv) to the extent appropriate, any other tax credits to which she may be entitled based on her personal circumstances.

It is to be noted that both the joint assessment on the deceased husband (pre-death position) and the single person's assessment on the widow (post-death) are, broadly speaking, each made on the basis that they are assessments on separate persons for the tax year as a whole. This has the result that many of the personal tax credits, etc normally given on an annual basis are duplicated. This favourable treatment only applies for the year of death.

Clearly, any deductions or tax credits which are given in respect of actual expenditure incurred by either husband or wife are only allowed once, either in the joint assessment for the pre-death period or in the surviving spouse's assessment for the post-death period, depending on the part of the year in which the expenditure falls.

For example, if the wife had made a subscription for eligible shares qualifying for the Employment and Investment Incentive and if the date of issue of those shares (the relevant date for the Employment and Investment Incentive) was the day before the date of her husband's death, then the deduction would be made in arriving at the taxable income for the joint assessment for the period to the date of death.

Example 3.607.1 shows how some of the foregoing matters are dealt with where the husband dies in a year for which joint assessment applies to the date of death (where the husband was the spouse the subject of the joint assessment before his death).

Joint assessment: death of non-assessable person

Again, it is assumed that the husband is the assessable person. The tax treatment of the husband for the year of the death is as follows straightforward. The normal joint assessment rules apply but, obviously, the total income of the wife to be included in the joint total income will only be her income up to the date of death.

Clearly, there are significant advantages to be gained if the deceased spouse is the assessable spouse. While tax planning may appear a little inappropriate where the non-assessable spouse is terminally ill, significant tax savings may be available if the couple jointly elect for the ill spouse to be the assessable person. Unfortunately, this must be done before 1 April in the tax year (TCA 1997, s 1019(2)).

Residential property – 's 23/43' clawbacks

Where the owner of a residential property which has qualified for relief under TCA 1997, s 372AP (see **Division 19** of the 2009 edition of this book) dies within ten years of first letting the property, a clawback of the relief arises. The clawback is equal in amount to the deductions obtained in respect of the property and takes the form of a deemed rental receipt, arising immediately prior to the date of death.

Where such a property passes on death to the taxpayer's spouse, the surviving spouse is entitled to a deduction for the year in which the property passes. Where the couple were jointly assessed, and the surviving spouse was the assessable spouse in the tax year of death, then he can generally set off the deduction against the clawback for that year. As a result, there should be no tax liability in respect of the transfer of property.

However, where the couple were singly assessed, or were jointly assessed, but the deceased spouse was the assessable spouse for the tax year of death, then a liability would normally arise in respect of the transfer. This follows because the clawback in both instances will be included in the total income assessed on the deceased spouse, while the deduction will accrue to the surviving spouse. However, the Revenue Commissioners will operate a concession in such instances, as set out in *Tax Briefing 23*.

The Revenue Commissioners are prepared to allow a set-off of the deduction due to the surviving spouse against the amount assessable on the deceased spouse in the year of death in respect of the property. The maximum set-off will be equivalent to the amount of the rent deemed to have been received by the deceased in accordance with TCA 1997, s 372AP(7).

A formal undertaking will have to be given by the surviving spouse to the effect that if, within the 10-year period from the date the property was first let, any event occurs which gives rise to a clawback, the amount of the clawback on the surviving spouse will be the full amount of the deduction allowed in relation to the property, including any amount of such relief set off against the income of the deceased spouse from whom the property was transferred.

The Revenue Commissioners are also prepared to apply the new practice where a property passes to a spouse as a result of a maintenance agreement (as defined in TCA 1997, s 1025) or in circumstances where a property is transferred from the sole name of one spouse into the joint names of both spouses. The Revenue add that the new practice will not apply to the transfer of a property which is part of a scheme or arrangement one of the main purposes of which is the avoidance of tax.

Discontinuance of trade on death

Where the deceased spouse was carrying on a trade or profession then the date of death normally marks a discontinuance of that trade, resulting in the relevant basis of assessment rules applying. This treatment may be concessionally relaxed where the trade is taken over by the surviving spouse: see **4.207**.

3.507 Separation: maintenance agreements

The entitlement of married persons to choose between joint assessment (with the possible further right to elect to divide the amount payable on the joint assessment between the spouses under the separate assessment rules of TCA 1997, s 1023) and single person assessment depends, as already indicated, on their being treated as living together for the relevant tax year. In the event that they are separated under an order of a court of competent jurisdiction or by deed of separation, or if they in fact separated in such circumstances that the separation is likely to be permanent, different rules have to be considered. If the separation occurs in the course of a tax year, the rules relating to separated spouses come into effect immediately and affect the tax assessments for that year, as well as those for subsequent years.

A married couple treated as separated for either of the reasons mentioned in the last paragraph are, subject to the possible exception of joint assessment within TCA 1997, s 1026 (see **3.508**), taxed as two entirely single persons. Each separated spouse is responsible for making his own income tax return. Each computes his own total income entirely separately from that of the other and claims his own personal allowances and other reliefs in arriving at taxable income and is responsible for dealing with his own tax assessments, appeals and payments of tax. However, two matters require further consideration – the question of maintenance payments and the treatment of the tax credits for any incapacitated children.

These matters are discussed here in **3.507** on the basis that the election under TCA 1997, s 1026 for joint assessment is not applicable or is not made.

Maintenance payments

Two types of maintenance payments need to be distinguished – one which is paid under a 'maintenance arrangement' involving payments under a legally enforceable obligation, and the other the making of maintenance payments under an informal arrangement not involving a legal obligation.

TCA 1997, s 1025 deals with payments made, directly or indirectly, by either party to a marriage pursuant to a maintenance arrangement relating to the marriage ('maintenance payments', see below). The payments, to be within the section, must be for the benefit of either:

(a) the other party to the marriage; or
(b) a child (or children) of either party; and

must also meet three further conditions – namely the payments must:

(i) be made at a time when the wife is not living with the husband;
(ii) be legally enforceable; and
(iii) be annual or periodical.

A 'maintenance arrangement' is defined as an order of a court, rule of court, deed of separation, trust, covenant, agreement, or any other act, giving rise to a legally enforceable obligation and made in consideration or in consequence of either:

(a) the dissolution or annulment of a marriage (on which, see **3.509**); or
(b) any such separation of the parties to the marriage that results in their being treated as separated for the purposes of the income tax rules relating to marriage.

Legally enforceable maintenance payments within TCA 1997, s 1025 exist in the case of separated spouses not only if the payments are provided for by a court order or by a legal deed of separation, but also if one spouse has executed a covenant or entered into some other form of legal commitment to make annual or periodical payments to the other.

In this section legally enforceable payments under TCA 1997, s 1025 are termed 'maintenance payments', and any other payments are referred to as 'voluntary payments'.

Payments made under a maintenance arrangement concluded before 9 June 1983 are not maintenance payments subject to the rule of TCA 1997, s 1025, unless and until either (a) the maintenance arrangement is replaced by another maintenance arrangement after 8 June 1983, or (b) both parties to the marriage, by notice in writing to the inspector, jointly elect that TCA 1997, s 1025 apply to the payments. If neither of these two events occurs, the payments made under the pre-9 June 1983 maintenance arrangement continue to be treated for tax purposes under the old rules (see below).

All maintenance payments that are within TCA 1997, s 1025 are treated in the same way irrespective of whether the relevant maintenance arrangement has been executed in the State or in any foreign country. The Appeal Commissioners decision [06TCAD2016] dealt with a taxpayer who was required to make maintenance payments in a single lump sum maintenance payment of €38,000. This was to be paid by means of two instalments, the first within six weeks of the date of the court order and the second within six months of the date of the order. The Appeal Commissioners noted that the taxpayer 'was not required to pay the two instalments on dates determined by reference to the passage of years or other set periods; the fact that one instalment was ordered to be paid in one calendar year and the second instalment was to be paid in the following calendar year does not mean that the instalments were annual payments. Equally, the fact that the two instalments were to be paid on two separate dates does not render them periodical within the ordinary and natural meaning of that word.'

Effect of TCA 1997, s 1025

The treatment of maintenance payments differs depending on whether the payments are made for the benefit of the other party to the marriage or for the benefit of a child (or children) of the spouse making the payments. TCA 1997, s 1025(2)(c) defines when a maintenance payment is to be treated as made for the benefit of a party to the marriage and when for a child of the payer. Broadly for the payment to be treated as for the benefit of such a child, it is necessary that the maintenance arrangement specifically contain two provisions.

First, the maintenance arrangement should direct that the payments specified be made either (a) for the use and benefit of the child of the person making the payment, or (b) for the maintenance, support, education or other benefit of such a child, or (c) in trust for such a child. Secondly, the arrangement must specify either the amount, or the method of calculating the amount, of the payments. Any other payments made directly or indirectly under a maintenance arrangement relating to the marriage are deemed to be made to the other party to the marriage (except in the case of any other payments specified in amount from which neither the other party to the marriage nor any child of the payer derives any benefit).

A child includes a stepchild or adopted child and an illegitimate child (TCA 1997, s 6) and also includes any child in respect of whom the payer was entitled to an incapacitated child credit under TCA 1997, s 465 at any time prior to the making of the maintenance arrangement (TCA 1997, s 1025(1)).

Maintenance payments to the other party

TCA 1997, s 1025(3) provides that the maintenance payments made directly or indirectly for the benefit of the other party to the marriage are to be deducted in computing the payer's total income for the tax year in which the payments are made where the individual makes the appropriate claim to the inspector (TCA 1997, s 1025(3)(c)). The deduction for such maintenance payments in any tax year must not, however, reduce the individual's total income to less than the amount necessary to retain in charge to tax any annual payments made by him from which he is entitled to deduct income tax. There is no express requirement that the payer be resident in the State (see the comments in the following paragraphs).

The other party to the marriage is required to include in her (or, if the payments are made by the wife or former wife, his) income each year the full amount of the maintenance payments received in that year for her (or his) benefit. The payments are treated as income chargeable to tax under Sch D Case IV and, therefore, become part of her (or his) income from all sources in respect of which she (or he) is assessable as a single person. Although the payments may be made annually, they are excluded from the rules for deduction of income tax at source. The payments are, therefore, made and received gross.

It should be noted that payments of maintenance may be made to cover expenditure incurred by the recipient which will generate tax deductions or tax credits in their hands. Thus, eg one spouse could pay interest on a home loan in respect of a house occupied by the other spouse and could potentially claim relief by reference to TCA 1997, s 244, subject to the limits of relief for interest on all of the first spouse's qualifying loans; alternatively the first spouse might pay an increased amount of maintenance to cover the other spouse's interest payments. If the spouses are subject to single assessment, this will mean that the first spouse will obtain a deduction for their maintenance payments in full while the other spouse will be taxed on the receipt of the maintenance payments but can claim relief for their home loan interest within the appropriate limits.

The principle of territoriality (see **1.405**) probably implies that payments made by an Irish resident under a foreign deed to a non-resident should fall outside the scope of Irish taxation. It is unclear whether the deductibility of payments under TCA 1997, s 1025 should depend on the recipient being chargeable under Sch D Case IV on general principles but in practice a deduction would be granted to the Irish resident payer in these circumstances. A payment under an Irish deed made by an Irish resident to a non-resident would appear to be clearly taxable in the hands of the non-resident; however, this is subject to possible exemption under the terms of a relevant double tax treaty (see in particular **14.217**).

In the case of a non-resident, it is arguable that he may only claim a deduction if the recipient is in fact taxable under TCA 1997, s 1025, typically on the grounds of Irish residence.

Example 3.608.1 deals with a case of maintenance payments within TCA 1997, s 1025, covering the main points made above.

Maintenance payments to children

TCA 1997, s 1025(4) takes a completely different approach to maintenance payments made directly or indirectly for the benefit of any child (as defined above) of the taxpayer. The payments, although they are made annually, are paid without the deduction of income tax. The payments are not taxable in the hands of the child, and are not deductible from the total income of the parent.

Revenue *ebrief 21/13* refers to the tax treatment of maintenance payments to children by civil partners and notes that the Revenue manual has been updated in this regard.

Treatment of incapacitated child tax credit

In the case of separated spouses, the income tax credit for any qualifying incapacitated child is given by TCA 1997, s 465 to the spouse who actually maintains the child. If both spouses contribute to the maintenance of the child, the credit for that child is apportioned between them in the ratio of their respective expenditures on maintaining the child in the relevant tax year (TCA 1997, s 465(6)). For this purpose any maintenance payments for the benefit of a child of the payer are treated as the expenditure of the payer (TCA 1997, s 1025(4)). On the other hand, any expenditure on maintaining the child made by the other party to the marriage out of maintenance payments received for her (or his) own benefit is treated as expenditure by that other party.

Voluntary payments

If husband and wife separate without entering into a legally enforceable agreement for payment of maintenance, then no deduction is given for any payments which one spouse may make to maintain the other spouse or any children. The spouse or child in receipt of such voluntary payments for maintenance is not regarded as receiving any taxable income as a result of the payment. However, payments made by one separated spouse under a deed of covenant to the other spouse do not come within this category of 'voluntary' payments, even if the covenant is executed in an informal separation. Since the deed of covenant is legally enforceable, it is a maintenance arrangement within TCA 1997, s 1025 (see above).

Where one of two separated spouses makes voluntary payments for the maintenance of the other, the spouse making the payments is entitled to claim the married persons' basic personal tax credit of €3,300 (double the single person's basic personal tax credit which would otherwise available to him as a separated spouse), but only if he can show that the other spouse is wholly or mainly maintained by him and that he is not entitled to deduct any sums in respect of maintenance paid to his spouse. The Revenue interpret 'mainly' as implying that the maintenance payments must exceed the other income of the recipient spouse. These conditions must be met for each tax year for which the €3,300 basic personal tax credit is claimed (TCA 1997, s 461(a)(ii)). The granting of the married person's allowance in this case does not alter the fact that each separated spouse is taxed on his separate income as a single person; there is no question of applying the married person's tax rate bands.

Maintenance and cohabitants

Following the enactment of the Finance (No 3) Bill 2001 as a consequence of the Civil Partnership and Certain Rights and Obligations of Cohabitants Act 2010 a relief is available for maintenance payments between cohabiting couples in certain circumstances.

On the break up of a cohabiting arrangement, a person who has been in such a relationship for a period of five years or more ('qualified cohabitant') or for a reduced period of two years where they are the parents of dependent children, can now apply to the court for a maintenance order. These include annual or periodic payments.

Payments that are made for the benefit of a former cohabitant should meet the following criteria:

(a) the payments should be made without deduction of tax;
(b) the cohabitant who makes the payments is entitled to tax deduction from their own income in respect of the maintenance payments made to the other cohabitant;
(c) the receiving cohabitant is taxable on the payment under Case IV Sch D; and
(d) both cohabitants continue to be taxed as single persons.

If the only income a person receives is maintenance payments under a legally enforceable agreement then they will need to register as a self-employed individual. If the person in receipt of the maintenance payments is an employee then it may be possible to have the tax collected by adjusting tax credits and standard rate cut offs band. There is no tax relief for maintenance payments made in respect of dependent children.

(See *Revenue leaflet IT2* issued June 2014.)

(See also Revenue frequently asked questions on 'Taxation and the Redress Scheme for Cohabiting Couples' dated September 2012.)

Pre-9 June 1983 maintenance arrangements

The rules of TCA 1997, s 1025 regarding the treatment of maintenance payments do not apply to payments under a maintenance arrangement made before 9 June 1983 if no step has been taken on or after that date to bring the rules of TCA 1997, s 1025 into operation (see above). If no post-8 June 1983 joint election has been made to have TCA 1997, s 1025 apply or, alternatively, if the earlier maintenance arrangement has not been replaced or suitably varied, the previous rules relating to maintenance arrangements continue to apply.

The rules which apply to those arrangements are as follows:

(a) the maintenance payments to a separated spouse under a legally executed deed or under a separation agreement approved by the court or made by a rule of court are treated as annual payments from which tax is deductible at source by the payer (and are treated as taxed income in the hands of the recipient);
(b) maintenance payments under a judgment or order of an Irish court are payable in full, but are not deductible from the income of the payer and are not treated as income of the recipient;
(c) in the case of payments made so that the legal recipient is a child (or where the payments are made to the other parent or another person in trust absolutely for the child), no deduction is given to the payer and the payments are not treated as taxable income of the child;
(d) if the payments for the benefit of a child are made to the other spouse in circumstances other than those in (c), ie so that the other spouse may voluntarily apply the payments to maintain the child, then the payments are dealt with as annual payments in the same way as under (a) above; and
(e) maintenance payments under orders of foreign courts are dealt with as annual payments in the same way as under (a) above (however, note the discussions of *Keiner v Keiner* and *Bingham v IRC* at **2.307**).

Separation during tax year

The tax treatment of married couple's in the tax year of separation is very similar to that which applies in the year of death of one of the spouses (see **3.506**). Clearly, if the couple have elected to be treated assessed under TCA 1997, s 1016 as single persons, the separation has no direct impact on the assessment of either spouse. Where the couple are assessed jointly up to the date of separation, the treatment is exactly as outlined at **3.506** for the year of death except, obviously, that both spouses are alive after the separation. The reason that the rules are basically the same is that there are no specific provisions relating to year of death or to year of separation and the general assessment rules are applied (for a discussion of these general rules as they apply to year of death, see **3.506**).

The commentary that follows assumes that the husband is the assessable person. Where the wife is the assessable person (TCA 1997, s 1019), the material should be interpreted accordingly. By way of brief recapitulation, the rules that apply to the husband in the year of separation are exactly the same as the scenario where the wife, as non-assessable person dies, in a tax year. The husband, as assessable person, is taxed in the year of separation on his entire income for the year of separation plus his wife's total income up to the date of separation. He is entitled to the full 'married' tax credits such as the basic personal tax credit, the age credit, the employee credit, etc and the married tax bands.

The rules that apply to the wife, as non-assessable person, in the year of separation are very similar to the rules that apply to the year of death where the assessable person dies. She is taxed as a single person on her income for the remainder of the year of separation with no time-apportionment of credits. The single person's tax band is applied, again with no adjustment for the 'short' tax year. Unlike the year of death scenario, however, she will obtain the €1,650 single basic personal tax credit, as the €3,300 basic personal tax credit available to the wife in the year of death under TCA 1997, s 461(b), only applies where the spouse dies in the tax year.

The one-parent family credit is not available to either spouse in the year of separation. In the case of the husband, it is not available under TCA 1997, s 462(1)(b), while in the case of the wife, the credit is denied by TCA 1997, s 462(2). The wider standard rate band for one-parent families is not available to either spouse in the year of separation as neither spouse is entitled to the one-parent family credit for that year.

3.508 Separated spouses: election for joint assessment

TCA 1997, s 1026 entitles a separated husband and wife to make an election under TCA 1997, s 1018(1) to be assessed jointly in accordance with the rules of TCA 1997, s 1017, but only where:

(a) both spouses are resident in the State;

(b) legally enforceable maintenance payments within TCA 1997, s 1025 are made by either party to the marriage in the tax year for which this joint assessment election is to apply; and

(c) the election is made in writing to the inspector jointly by both spouses before the end of the tax year for which it is to apply (except if the separated spouses have made the election for a previous tax year and if neither spouse has withdrawn that election).

This separated spouses' joint assessment election under TCA 1997, s 1026 is not permitted if the only payments being made between the spouses are voluntary payments for maintenance, ie payments made otherwise than under a legally enforceable maintenance arrangement. Further, the election may not be made if the payments are being made under a pre-9 June 1983 maintenance arrangement which has not been brought within TCA 1997, s 1025. However, the latter difficulty may be overcome simply by a joint election by the separated spouses that the arrangement become one to which TCA 1997, s 1025 applies.

If either spouse ceases to be resident in the State for any tax year, an election under TCA 1997, s 1026 ceases to apply in that year. A new election may be made for a subsequent tax year if both spouses are resident in that year.

For any tax year in which an election under TCA 1997, s 1026 is in force, the separated spouses are taxed jointly under the rules of TCA 1997, s 1017, but on the basis that separate assessment within TCA 1997, s 1023 has been applied for. The effect is to charge tax at the married person's tax rate bands as if in a normal joint assessment, but with all the deductions, credits and other reliefs being allocated between the separated spouses in the manner described in **3.504**.

One other consequence of the election is that the maintenance payments made by one party to the marriage for the benefit of the other party are ignored in computing the respective total incomes of the separated spouses. In other words, the deduction that would otherwise be given by TCA 1997, s 1025 for the maintenance payments in arriving at the total income of the spouse making them is not given, while the payments received are not included in the total income of the other spouse.

Apart from the benefit which may result from the married person's double rate bands and the married person's basic personal tax credit, the joint assessment election may allow a greater relief for qualifying home loan interest if interest in excess of the single person's limits is paid by one of the separated spouses only (granted now generally by way of relief at source: see **3.201**) or doubled relief by way of credit for rent paid (see **3.313**) or doubled age credit by reference to the age of one party only (see **3.306**). Also, a trading loss incurred by one spouse in excess of his income from other sources could be set off against the other spouse's income applying TCA 1997, s 381 (which could not be done if they are taxed as single persons). In some cases, it may be beneficial to claim the home carer's tax credit (see **3.311**) which is only available where joint assessment is in force. There is also the consideration that where joint assessment applies, certain deductions and credits may be claimed by one party for expenditure incurred for the benefit of the other; these include health expenses (see **3.315**), college fees (see **3.318**), training course fees (see **3.319**), relief for medical insurance (see **3.314**) which is now given at source; donations to certain sports bodies (see **18.305**). Further, in some cases the allowability of certain payments may be calculated as a percentage of the combined total incomes of a jointly assessed eg permanent health benefit contributions: see **3.317**, or certain covenanted annual payments: see **15.404**); in addition, the disregard of maintenance payments under joint assessment may result in an increase in net relevant earnings for pension contribution purposes which could result in enhanced relief (see **16.208**; **16.303**).

The single person child carer credit (formerly the one-parent family tax credit) should be considered in determining if joint assessment should be elected for.

The election for joint assessment may also have implications for the Universal Social Charge and self-employed PRSI contributions (see **3.4**). Where single assessment applies, the spouse paying maintenance may be entitled to deduct his payments in computing the PRSI or the Universal Social Charge; the spouse receiving the payments may be liable to PRSI, or the Universal Social Charge in respect thereof. Where joint assessment applies, the maintenance payments are ignored for PRSI and Universal Social Charge purposes.

If the separated spouses agree, it is possible to vary from year to year their decision between joint assessment (under the separate assessment rules) and assessment as single persons, depending on the relative advantages each year. Any decision to vary the previous year's treatment must, however, be notified to the inspector in writing before the end of the tax year for which the new decision is to apply.

A new decision for joint assessment under TCA 1997, s 1026 must always be made by both of the separated spouses, but any decision to revert back to assessment as single persons may be made by either spouse. Since each spouse pays his own tax whichever form of assessment is chosen, a decision which results in a reduction of the aggregate tax may sometimes leave one of the spouses paying more tax than if that decision had not been made. For agreement to be reached in such a case, this may require a voluntary cash adjustment between them.

Example 3.608.1 shows the effect of an election for joint assessment by separated spouses within TCA 1997, s 1026. By taking the same facts as those used in **Example 3.608.1**, the results of the joint assessment as compared with those under separated spouses' single assessments under TCA 1997, s 1025 can be seen. However, it is to be stressed that on different facts, the comparative results would not be the same and the merit of one course against the other could be different.

3.509 Divorced couples

A couple who have divorced must each be assessed as single persons unless and until either remarries, after which the normal considerations will apply to that individual and his new spouse.

As noted in **3.507**, maintenance payments deductible under TCA 1997, s 1025 may be made in relation, not only to a separation, but also to the dissolution or annulment of a marriage. Thus, a divorced person may claim relief subject to the same conditions and considerations as apply to a separated person. There is nothing to prevent a divorced person who remarries from continuing to claim relief. Where an individual is the chargeable person in relation to a married couple jointly assessed under TCA 1997, s 1023, any payments eligible for relief under TCA 1997, s 1025 which is made by that person's spouse reduce the latter's total income. This will in turn result in a reduction of the combined total income of both spouses in respect of which the chargeable person is assessable.

The Family Law Act 1995, s 49 extended the election for joint assessment to cover the case where:

(a) a couple have been validly divorced in an overseas jurisdiction;
(b) both spouses are resident in the State in the tax year;
(c) neither spouse has remarried; and
(d) a payment has been made in the year which falls within TCA 1997, s 1025.

TCA 1997, s 1026(3) also extends the election for joint assessment where a couple have been divorced under the Family Law (Divorce) Act 1996, s 5.

3.510 Increased rate band for jointly assessable individuals with dual income

TCA 1997, s 15 provides that in the case of jointly assessed couples, where both spouses are in receipt of income, the standard rate band of €42,800 for the tax year can be increased by the lesser of €24,800 or the total income (net of any deductions attributable to the particular sources of income comprised in such total income) of the individual or their spouse whichever is the lesser (referred to as the 'specified income'). The definition of total income above implies that payments such as allowable payments under deeds of covenant (see **15.404**) which are offset against total income as such and not particular items of income can be disregarded for these purposes.

The increased standard rate tax band and the home carer's allowance (see **3.311**) are mutually exclusive but a person may opt for whichever is the more beneficial.

If a jointly assessed couple are entitled to the home carer tax credit (see **3.311**) and the carer spouse has income, the couple must choose between the home carer credit and the increased standard rate band available to dual income couples (see **3.105**). If no action is taken, the couple are entitled to the home carer tax credit. If the couple wish to have the benefit of the wider standard rate tax band, the assessable person must elect by notice in writing to the inspector to have the benefit of the wider band rather than the home carer tax credit.

Whether the home carer tax credit or the increased standard rate band would be more beneficial will be determined by the facts of each individual case but the following general guidelines should be taken into account:

(a) Where the joint income of the couple is less than €42,800, claiming the home carer credit will always yield lower tax as none of the income of the couple would suffer income tax at the higher rate in any event.

(b) Where the joint income of the couple is greater than €42,800, a 'cost-benefit' analysis must be carried out. The 'benefit' is the value of the home carer tax credit and the 'cost' is the increased income tax payable by virtue of not having the wider standard rate band. The 'benefit' will normally be €810 unless a reduced home carer tax credit is available due to the income of the carer spouse being greater than €5,080. The 'cost' will be 20 per cent of the amount of income of the carer spouse taxable at the higher rate of 40 per cent.

3.6 Tax Computation: 2017

3.601 Introduction

The various steps in the computation of the net tax payable in the case of an individual chargeable to tax by assessment in respect of his income (and, where the assessment is under TCA 1997, s 1017, in respect also of his spouse's income) have been explained in detail and illustrated by examples in the previous chapters of this Division. In the main, the examples have set out to show the computation of the tax payable for the tax year 2017.

In this chapter, a number of other examples are set out to illustrate the single person's tax computation, the joint person's tax computation where separate assessment is elected (see **3.504**), computations for married persons in the year of marriage, including civil partnership in year of registration of civil partnership (see **3.505**), where one spouse dies (see **3.506**), as well as some other special cases. These examples are all in respect of the tax year 2016 the special rules applicable to the restriction of specified reliefs in the case of certain high income individuals is dealt with in **3.111**.

3.602 Single person assessment

This is relevant for an unmarried individual (including a widow or widower) as well as for a married man or woman who elects to be assessed as a single person. It also applies to charge both a husband and a wife not living together (except where they are entitled by TCA 1997, s 1026 to elect for joint assessment and in fact do so). While there may be some differences in the personal credits between these cases, they all have in common the facts that the individual assessed is charged in respect of his own total income only and that the single person's tax rate table is applied to his taxable income.

Example 3.602.1 deals with the taxation of an unmarried individual. Since it is the first main illustration of an individual's personal income tax computation, all the main steps from the determination of total income through the calculation of the income tax chargeable in respect of that total income, down to the deductions given by relief against the tax payable and by credits against tax, are covered.

Example 3.602.1

Mr Reginald Royce is a single person. Based on the income, deductions, tax credits, etc detailed below, his income tax computation for the tax year 2017 is as follows:

	€	€
Assessable under Schedules, etc:		
Sch D Case 1:		
Profits of trade	30,900	
Less capital allowances[1]	(1,680)	

	29,220	
Less retirement annuity premium[2]	(2,300)	26,920
Sch D Case IV:		
Deposit interest (retention tax €451)		1,100
Other taxed income (tax suffered €360)		1,800
Sch F dividends (dividend withholding tax €472)		2,360
Sch E:		
Controlling director of family company (PAYE deducted €1,390)	12,012	
Less Allowable expenses[3]	2,192)	9,820
Income from all sources		42,000
Deductions in computing total income:		
Charges on income (annual payment)[4]		(600)
Total income		41,400
Personal reliefs:		
Medical expenses-re nursing home	(360)	(360)
Taxable income		41,040
Calculate income tax		
(single person's tax rate table)		
€33,800 at 20%		6,760
€ 1,100 at 41% (deposit interest)[5]		451
€6,140 at 40%		2,456
€41,040		
Income tax chargeable on taxable income		9,667
Less:		
Non-repayable tax credits/DIRT[6]:		
Single personal tax credit		(1,650)
Earned income credit		(550)
Deposit interest retention tax		(451)
Net income tax on taxable income		7,016
Add:		
Income tax on charges on income[4]		
€600 x 20%		120
Total income tax payable		
		7,136
Add:		
Self-employed PRSI contribution[7]:		
€32,180 x 4%		1,287
Universal Social charge[8]		
€6,656 x 3%	199	

€26,724 x 5.5%	1,469	1,668	2,955
€33,380			
Total tax and (before full credits)			
			10,091
Less:			
Full credits:			
Tax on taxed income		(360)	
Dividend withholding tax		(472)	
PAYE on Sch E income		(1,390)	(2,222)
			7,869

Notes:

1. The capital allowances related to the trade are specifically deductible from the Sch D Case I income (see **4.301**).
2. The retirement annuity premium is deductible from 'net relevant earnings' (in this case, the net trading income after capital allowances; the directors' salaries (net of expenses) would also be included if the directorship was non-pensionable – see **16.208**).
3. The expenses of employment are incurred personally by Mr Royce specifically deductible from the Sch E income from the office or employment in question (see **10.301**).
4. The charges on income are deductible from the income from all sources without distinguishing between the items making up that aggregate income; the tax which Mr Royce should have withheld on making the annual payment is now collected by adding the €120 to the income tax chargeable.
5. Only tax at the appropriate rate of 41% is charged on deposit interest received less retention tax.
6. As a controlling director, Mr Royce will not be entitled to the employee tax credit.
7. The reckonable income for self-employed PRSI is determined as follows:

	€
Income from all sources	42,000
Less: Sch E emoluments (at amount included therein, ie net of expenses)	(9,820)
Reckonable income to be assessed directly:	32,180

The gross Sch E emoluments of €12,012 will be subject to the universal social charge and PRSI under the PAYE system.

8. The relevant income for the purposes of the Universal Social Charge on relevant income is determined as follows:

	€
Income from all sources	42,000
Add: Schedule E expenses-included in relevant emoluments	2,192
Less: Relevant Emoluments	(12,012)
Less: Interest subject to DIRT	(1,100)
Add: Retirement Annuity Contributions	2,300
Relevant income to be assessed directly:	33,380

The gross Sch E emoluments of €12,012 will be subject to employee's PRSI and to the Universal Social Charge on relevant emoluments under the PAYE system. The first €12,012, liable at 1%, is assumed to be dealt with under the PAYE system.

3.603 Widowed person's assessment

Example 3.603.1 takes the case of a widower (his wife died over a year ago and he has not remarried). He is assumed to have incurred a Sch D Case I trading loss for which he claims relief under TCA 1997, s 381. He also has significant Irish company dividends.

This example illustrates the widowed parent's additional tax credit given, if the conditions for it are met (see **3.305**), in the five tax years after the tax year in which his spouse has died. This example will apply equally to a surviving civil partner.

Example 3.603.1

Mr B Riverson, a widower aged 54 with two children, a daughter aged 15 and a son (permanently incapacitated by mental illness and unable to maintain himself) aged 23. Mr Riverson's wife died on 26 March 2015. Based on the income, deductions, allowances, tax credits, etc detailed below, his income tax computation for the tax year 2017 is as follows:

Sch D Case I		€	€
Profits of trade (year to 31/12/2017)[1]			Nil
Sch F income:			
Irish company distributions			37,900
Sch D Case V:			
Net rental income (year ended 31 December 2017)			9,020
Sch D Case IV:			
Debenture interest (tax deducted €956)			4,780
Income from all sources			51,700
Less:			
Deductions from income:			
TCA 1997, s 381 loss (trade):		(9,880)	(9,880)
Taxable income			41,820
Income tax chargeable on taxable income			
€37,800 x 20%			7,560
€ 4,020 x 40%			1,608
€41,820			9,168
Less:			
Non-repayable tax credits:			
Personal tax credit (widow)		1,650	
Single Person Child Carer tax credit		1,650	
Widowed parent with children tax credit[2]		3,150	
Total credit			(6,450)
Income Tax payable			2,718
Self-employed PRSI contribution[3]			
€51,700 x 4%		2,068	
Universal Social Charge[4]			
€12,012 x 1%	120		
€6,656 x 3%	199		

€33,032 x 5.5%	1,816	2,135	4,203
€51,700			6,921
Less:			
Full credits:			
Dividend withholding tax			(7,580)
Tax deducted from debenture interest			(956)
Net tax repayable 2016[4]			(1,615)

Notes:

1. The TCA 1997, s 381 claim is for the actual loss incurred in the accounting year ending in the current year of assessment (see **4.401**).
2. Because his wife died within the tax year 2015, the first year in which Mr Riverson becomes entitled to the widowed parent's child allowance in 2016. He is entitled to the tax credit because he has at least one qualifying child living with him. For 2017 as the second tax year after his wife's death, the tax credit is €3150 (see **3.305**).
3. The reckonable income in this example is the same for the self-employed PRSI contribution, and is the same as the relevant income for the purposes of the Universal Social Charge
4. Since the full credits exceed the total income tax and self employed PRSI and the Universal Social Charge, the excess is repayable to Mr Riverson.

3.604 Married person's joint assessment

The example of Adam and Zeta Tollgate in **3.110** illustrates the computation of the net tax payable in the case of a married couple assessed jointly under TCA 1997, s 1017. The case of a joint assessment divided between two spouses where an election is made under TCA 1997, s 1023 is a separate matter, discussed below.

3.605 Joint assessment: election for separate assessments

Example 3.605.1 below shows the computation of the net tax payable in the case of a married couple who, although taxed jointly, have made an election under TCA 1997, s 1023 to have the joint assessment split up between them in accordance with the rules explained in **3.504**. As indicated there, separate assessment is distinguished from assessment as single persons in that all the allowances, deductions, credits, reliefs, etc are – unlike single person assessment – the same in total as for a joint assessment made on one of the spouses under TCA 1997, s 1017. This example will also be relevant for civil partners in a registered civil partnership who elect under s 1031H to be separately assessed.

Example 3.605.1

Mr and Mrs Henry and Flo Mann, a married couple living together, are assessable jointly for the tax year 2017. On March 2016 (just before the 1 April deadline for the 2017 year of assessment), Mrs Mann applies to the inspector under TCA 1997, s 1023 to have their joint income tax liability assessed separately.

Henry pays the expenses of maintaining an elderly aunt who has no income. Flo makes gross annual covenanted payments to her elderly mother of €500.

Applying the rules of TCA 1997, ss 1023, 1024, as explained in **3.504**, and working on the above data and the other figures for income, deductions, etc assumed below, the net tax payable for 2017 by each spouse on their respective separate assessments is computed as follows:

	Henry	Flo
Husband's income:	€	€
Sch D Case II profits (as solicitor) net of normal plant/machinery capital allowances (€1,800)	46,000	
Sch D Case III income	2,000	
Sch E: director's fee (PAYE €210)	500	
Sch F income (dividend withholding tax €652)	3,258	
Deposit interest (retention tax €410)	1,000	
Wife's income		
Sch E salary (PAYE €3,000)		10,100
Sch D Case V rental income		400
Sch F income (dividend withholding tax €129)		647
Other taxed income (tax deducted €360)	-	1,800
Income from all sources (= A)	52,758	12,947
Deductions in computing total income		
Charges on income:		
Payment to elderly mother (by Flo)	-	(500)[1]
Total deductions (= B)		(500)
Total income (A – B) = Total Income (as divided)	52,758	12,447

Income tax chargeable on taxable income:

Henry	Flo		Henry	Flo
€33,800	€12,447	at 20%	6,760	2,489
€500[3]		at 20%	100	
€9,000[4]		at 20%	1,800	
€1,000		at 41%	410	
€8,458	-	at 40%	3,383	-
€52,758	€12,447		12,453	2,489

	Henry	Flo
Less:		
Non-refundable tax credits		
Personal tax credit[6]	(1,650)	(1,650)
Dependent relative tax credit	(70)[2]	
Employee PAYE tax credit[7]	(100)	(1,650)
Earned income credit	550	
Excess tax credit transferred[8]	(811)	811
Retention tax on deposit interest	(410)	nil
	(3,591)	(2,489)
Tax Payable	8,862	Nil
Add:		
Income tax on charges on income:		
€500 x 20% (Flo)	-	100

Total income tax payable		8,862	100
Add:			
Self-employed PRSI contribution			
€52,258 x 4% (Henry)[9]		2,090	
€2,847 x 4% (Flo)			14
Universal Social Charge[10]			
Henry:			
€(12,012–500) = €11,512 x 1%	115		
€6,656 x3%	199		
€32,590 x 5.5%	1,792	2,106	
€51,258			
Flo: €1,912 (12,012–10,100) x 1.5%			28
€935 x3.5%			32
Total income tax, SE PRSI and Universal Social Charge		13,058	274
Less:			
Credits deductible:			
PAYE deducted		(210)	(3,000)
Dividend withholding tax		(652)	(129)
Tax on other taxed income		-	(360)
		(862)	(3,489)
Net tax payable/(repayable) 2017		12,196	(3,215)

Further comment:

The effect of separate assessment of husband and wife or civil partners is to allocate the net tax payable (or repayable) which would result from the one joint assessment between husband and wife or civil partners if no election for separate assessment were made. In this case, the working out of the one joint assessment would give a single figure for net tax (inclusive of self employed PRSI and the Universal Social Charge) payable of €8,981 (ie Henry's net tax payable of €12,196 less Flo's net tax repayable of (€3,215).

Notes:

1. Flo's annual payment of €500 is not restricted as it is less than five per cent of the joint total incomes of the couple (and in this case less than five per cent of her total income) (see **15.404**; **15.405**).
2. Since the husband maintains the dependent relative, he is given the full allowance.
3. In order to ensure that the total tax payable under separate assessment is identical to the liability under a straightforward joint assessment, it is necessary to adjust for the fact that the standard rate band of the higher-income spouse or civil partner will be extended by reference to the total income of the lower income spouse or civil partner before deducting annual payments: see **3.510**. TCA 1997, ss 1024, 1031I, 1032, do not expressly deal with how such an adjustment should be made and the method used here represents the author's view of the most logical procedure in such a case.
4. The single person's standard rate band is allocated initially to each spouse. Flo (the lower income spouse) has income which falls short of her standard rate band by €(33,800–12,347) = €21,453. This amount is transferred to Henry, but it cannot increase his standard rate band to an amount in excess of €42,800.

5. The €1,000 deposit interest (standard rate deducted) received by Henry is taxed at 41%.
6. The married person's tax credit is allocated equally between husband and wife.
7. The PAYE credits are allocated to the respective spouses to set against the income(s) from the employments to which the allowances relate. Henry's credit is limited to €500 @ 20% = €100.
8. The excess credit is transferred against the liability of the other spouse or civil partner under TCA 1997, ss 1024(4), 1031I(4).
9. Henry's reckonable income for PRSI is his income from all sources €52,758. Of this, €500 relating to directors fees will be collected under the PAYE system leaving a net of €52,258 to be assessed directly. Flo is a chargeable person in 2016 so PRSI at 4% applies to her unearned income.
10. Henry's and Flo's relevant income for the purposes of the Universal Social Charge is determined as follows:

	Henry	*Flo*
	€	€
Income from all sources	52,758	12,947
Less: Sch E emoluments	(500)	
		(10,100)
Less: Interest subject to DIRT	(1,000)	
Relevant Income	51,258	2,847

Henry's Sch E emoluments of €500 and Flo's Sch E emoluments of €10,100 will be subject to the Universal Social Charge under the PAYE system.

3.606 Year of marriage or registration of civil partnership

The rules of TCA 1997, s 1020 and s 1031E under which a married couple or civil partners remain assessable as single persons for the whole of the year of marriage or registration of civil partnership, but may claim the year of marriage or year of registration relief determined by a reference to a notional joint assessment, have been explained in **3.505**. **Examples 3.606.1** and **3.606.2** below show the effect of these rules. It is to be noted that the assessments on the husband and wife or civil partners are direct single person assessments and are not to be confused with the separate assessments under the joint income rules shown in **Example 3.605.1**. There is no question of the transfer of any unused allowances, tax rate bands, etc from one spouse or civil partner to the other in the year of marriage or registration.

Example 3.606.1

Paul and Roberta are married on 24 July 2017. Based on their respective incomes, personal tax credits, etc assumed below, their respective income tax liabilities as single persons before credits against tax (and before any year of marriage relief) for 2017 are computed as follows:

	Paul	*Roberta*
	€	€
Paul's income:		
Sch D Case II profits (net of normal plant and machinery capital allowances €923)	37,377	
Sch D Case III income	3,035	

Roberta's income:				
Sch E (salary as secretary) (PAYE €1,300)			-	10,200
Income tax from all sources = total income			40,412	10,200
Total incomes (as single persons)				
Taxable incomes (as single persons)			40,412	10,200

Income tax:					
(single person's table)				€	€
P	R				
33,800	10,200	at 20%		6,760	2,040
6,612	-	at 40%		2,645	-
40,412	10,200			-	-
Income tax chargeable on taxable income				9,405	2,040
Less:					
Non-repayable credits					
Personal tax credit				(1,650)	(1,650)
Earned Income credit				(550)	
Employee PAYE tax credit				-	(1,650)
Net income tax on taxable income				7,205	Nil
Add: SE PRSI €40,412 @ 4%				1,616	
Universal Social Charge					
€12,012 x 1%			120		
€6,656 x 3%			199		
€21,744 x 5.5%			1,195	1,514	
Less: PAYE				10,335	(1,300)

In the absence of any year of marriage relief (see next example), Paul's final tax payable for 2017 is €10,335 and Roberta's is a repayment of €1,300. For 2017 and later years they are entitled to be assessed jointly unless they elect to continue single person assessments.

Example 3.606.2

Continue from **Example 3.606.1** with the case of Paul and Roberta who were married during the tax year 2017 (the year of marriage). Assume that Paul and Roberta each claim the year of marriage relief of TCA 1997, s 1020(3) when filing their respective single person tax returns for 2017.

In order to evaluate this claim, the income tax which would be payable for 2017 if a joint assessment under TCA 1997, s 1017 were to be made for the year of marriage (the notional joint income tax payable for 2017) is calculated as follows:

	€
Incomes from all sources (as above):	
Paul	40,412
Roberta	10,200
Joint Income (notional)	50,612

Income tax:	
(married person's table)	
€50,612 x 20%	10,122
Income tax chargeable on taxable income	10,122
Less:	
Married persons tax credit	(3,300)
Earned income credit	(550)
Employee PAYE tax credit	(1,650)
	(5,500)
Income tax payable on notional joint taxable income	4,622
Add: SE PRSI and Universal Social Charge as above 1,616 + 1,514	3,130
	7,752
Less: PAYE as above	(1,300)
Net income tax payable (notional) (= B)	6,452

The question as to whether there is year of marriage relief due under TCA 1997, s 1020(3) and, if so, how much is now determined as follows:

Net income tax on taxable incomes:	€
Paul (from **Example 3.606.1**)	10,335
Roberta (same)	(1,300)
aggregate as single persons (= A)	9,035
Excess of single persons' tax/over notional joint tax:	
(€9,035 – €6,452) (ie A – B) =	2,583
Number of months from 24/7/2016 to 31/12/2016 (=n)	
5 months + 8 days (taken as 6 months)	
Year of marriage relief:	
€2,583 x 6 months/12 months	1,292

Division of year of marriage relief

The relief of €1,292 must be allocated between Paul and Roberta in proportion to the income tax payable by each as single persons on their respective total incomes. Based on their respective liabilities shown above (before credit for PAYE suffered at source) and the aggregate net income tax on taxable incomes, the relief is subdivided as follows:

Paul:	€
€1,292 x €10,335 /€10,335	1,292
Roberta:	
N/a	0
	1,292

3.607 Married persons and civil partners: year of death

The rules for assessing a married couple or civil partners taxed jointly to the date of death and for taxing the surviving spouse or surviving nominated civil partner for the rest of the year have been explained in **3.506. Example 3.607.1** below shows the effect of some of the main rules where it is the assessable spouse or nominated civil partner who dies. To avoid undue repetition, the same detail is not given as in previous illustrations and the tax computations are only taken down to the point of arriving at the total income tax chargeable/taxable income.

Example 3.607.1

Mr and Mrs S Soap were assessed jointly for 2017, with Mr Soap being the assessable spouse, and no election to withdraw the joint assessment basis for 2017 is made before Mr Soap dies on 10 September 2017. Subject to paying his debts, etc he leaves his entire estate absolutely to Mrs Soap (who is aged 37). She therefore succeeds to his investment income and also becomes entitled to a widow's pension from her late husband's employer's pension scheme. The couple had no children.

Mr Soap has paid interest of €3,330 between 1 January 2017 and 10 September 2017 on a first-time qualifying loan taken out in June 2008 to purchase the family residence. Mrs Soap assumes responsibility for the loan on her husband's death and pays interest of €1,000 between his death and 31 December 2017. Mr Soap paid €300 (gross) under a qualifying deed of covenant on 15 June 2017.

Based on the income, deductions, etc detailed below, the respective assessments for 2017 for the two parts of the year before and after Mr Soap's death, are computed as follows:

(1) Period to date of death (10/9/2017)

		€	€
Joint assessment 2016 (on Mr Soap's executors):		€	€
Husband's income:			
Sch E salary:			
actual to 10/9/2017		46,400	
Sch D Case III income			
actual to 10/9/2017		4,300	50,700
Wife's income:			
Sch D Case 1 €35,570 x 254/365[1] =		24,753	
Sch D Case III income			
actual to 10/9/2017		2,040	
Sch F income			
actual to 10/9/2017		1,070	27,863
			78,563
Income from all sources			
Deductions in computing total income (to 10/9/2017):			
Deed of Covenant			(300)
Total income (joint)			78,263
Personal reliefs:			
Health expenses-nursing home (Mr Soap ill before death)		(1,264)	
Investment in EEI Company	4,133 x 30/40 =	(3,100)	(4,364)
Taxable income			73,899
Income tax chargeable on			
taxable income			
(married person's table)			
€(42,800 + 24,800 max) =	67,600 x 20%	13,520	
	6,299 x 40% =	2,520	16,040
	73,899		

Less:		
Non-repayable credits		
Married persons' basic personal tax credit	(3,300)	
Earned income credit	(550)	
Employee PAYE tax credit	(1,650)	(5,500)
Income tax payable [2]		10,540
(2) Post-death period (from 11/9/2017):		
Single person assessment 2016 on Mrs Soap		
Her own income		
Sch D Case 1 €35,570 x 111/365 =	10,817	
Sch D Case III income:		
from 11/9/2017	740	
Sch F income:		
from 11/9/2016	6,300	
Sch E pension:		
from 11/9/2017	2,200	
Income from husband's estate:		
Sch D Case III income	2,100	
Income from all sources = Total income =		22,157
Income tax chargeable on taxable income:		
(single person's table)		
€22,157 x 20%		4,431
Less:		
Non-repayable credits		
Personal tax credit		
Basic Personal tax credit – year of bereavement[3]	(3,300)[5]	
Earned income credit	(550)	
Employee PAYE tax credit €2,200 x 20%=	(440)	(4,290)
Income tax payable [4]		141

Notes:

1. Mrs Soap, who has been trading for many years made taxable trading profits of €35,570 in the period of account ended 30 June 2017. These form the basis of the computation of assessable profits for 2017 and require to be apportioned on a daily basis between the pre-death and post-death period (TCA 1997, s 107(2)).

2. The computation for the pre-death period would be continued by the addition of the tax deducted from charges on income paid in this period (€300 x 20% = €60 in this case) and PRSI and the Universal Social Charge for both spouses on the income in this period and, finally, by the deduction of any full credits (only Sch F tax credits of €214 in this case) to arrive at the net tax payable by Mr Soap's executors. These details are not given here. His employed PRSI contributions and the Universal Social Charge in respect of his Sch E earnings will have been collected under the PAYE system. He will have a liability to PRSI and the Universal Social Charge on

his investment income. Mrs Soap's income will be liable to the Universal Social Charge as her aggregate income for 2017 *taken as a whole* exceeds the relevant exemption thresholds. Mrs Soap's income will also be liable for self-employed PRSI contributions for 2017.

3. As Mrs Soap, the surviving spouse, was the non-assessable spouse, she is entitled to the doubled basic personal tax credit: see **3.302**.

4. The computation for the post-death period for the assessment on Mrs Soap would be continued by the addition of the tax deducted from charges on income paid in this period (none in this case) and any self employed PRSI and the Universal Social Charge on her income (including the income from Mr Soap's estate) in this period. Mrs Soap's income will be liable to the Universal Social Charge as her aggregate income for 2017 taken as a whole exceeds the relevant exemption threshold. The final step is the deduction of the full credits to arrive at her net tax payable. (Sch F tax credit €1,260)

5. Since the €3,330 interest paid by Mr Soap in the part of the year before his death is less than the married person's maximum allowable amount of €20,000 (no apportionment required), the amount eligible for relief at source is €3,330. Mrs Soap is entitled to a separate widowed person's maximum allowable amount of €10,000 (not apportioned) for the home loan interest relief in the post-death period. Since the €1,000 interest paid by her is less than that limit, the amount eligible for relief at source in the post-death period is €1,000.

3.608 Separated spouses or civil partners etc maintenance arrangements

The rules relating to the taxation of the parties to a marriage or civil partnership who are separated by court order, or in circumstances likely to be permanent, are explained in **3.507**. **Example 3.608.1** below deals with the case of such separated spouses or civil partners where legally enforceable maintenance payments are being made by one of the parties (the husband) both to the other party and for the benefit of children of the marriage or civil partnership. It deals with the treatment under TCA 1997, ss 1025, 1031J on the assumption that no election for the separated spouses or civil partners joint assessment is made under TCA 1997, ss 1026, 1031K.

Example 3.608.1

Mr and Mrs R Fight (who are both aged 33) separated on 25 March 2016 and entered into a legally enforceable maintenance arrangement under which Mr Fight agrees to pay each year the following maintenance payments:

(a) €3,000 to be paid to Mrs Fight in trust for the benefit of the children (out of which she is to pay school fees and related expenses), and

(b) €8,600 for the benefit of Mrs Fight.

The children reside solely with Mrs Fight.

Assuming no election for joint assessment is made, Mr and Mrs Fight are assessed to tax for 2017 as separate single persons under the rules of TCA 1997, s 1026 (and Mr Fight pays all the maintenance payments without deducting any income tax). Based on the income, deductions and tax credits detailed below, their respective tax liabilities are computed as follows:

	Husband	*Wife*
	€	€
Sch D Case I	59,000	

Less: retirement annuity premiums	(11,200)[1]	
	47,800	
Sch D Case V	5,600	
Sch E – Pension		8,000
Deposit Interest credited February 2017 (Gross – DIRT €511)		1,246
Add:		
Sch D Case IV (wife):		
Maintenance payments received for her benefit	-	8,600
Incomes from all sources	53,400	17,846
Deductions in computing total incomes:		
Maintenance payments for benefit of wife[2]	(8,600)	
Annual payment €1,000 to her mother aged 66 (wife)	-	(849)[3]
Total incomes = taxable incomes =	44,800	16,997
Income tax chargeable on taxable incomes		
Single person's tables		
€33,800 x 20% (husband)	6,760	
€11,000 x 40% =	4,400	
€44,800		
€ 15,751 x 20% (wife)		3,150
€ 1,246 x 41% (DIRT interest – wife)		511
€ 16,997	11,160	3,661
Less:		
Non-repayable credits:		
Single persons tax credit	(1,650)	(1,650)
Earned income credit	(550)	
Employee PAYE tax credit[4]	-	(1600)
Single person child carer credit[5]		(1,650)
Retention tax on deposit interest (wife's)	-	(511)
	8,960	Nil
Add:		
Income tax on charges on income (wife)		
€849 at 20%	-	170
Total income tax payable [6]	8,960	170

Notes:

1. In fact, Mr Fight paid retirement annuity premiums in the year totalling €12,000, but the limit to the deduction of 20 per cent of net relevant earnings (see **16.206**) applies. The deductible maintenance payments of €8,600 after being offset against Sch D Case V income of €5,600 leaves an amount of €3,000 which reduces the net relevant earnings to €56,000, thereby permitting a maximum deduction of 20 per cent of €56,000 = €11,200 since Mr Fight is aged 33 – see **16.206**).

2. Only the maintenance payments for the benefit of the other party to the marriage are deducted by the person paying them. The maintenance payments for the benefit of the children (€3,000) remain part of the payer's income.

3. Restricted under TCA 1997, s 792(2) to five per cent of total income of the disponer, ie 5/105 x €17,846=€849: see **15.405**.

4. Mrs Fight is in receipt of a pension, taxable under Sch E. (€8,000 x 20% = €1,600). The PAYE credit is restricted to the pension payable of €8,000 at the standard rate of tax.

5. As a separated spouse with the children residing with her, Mrs Fight is entitled to the single person child carer credit. (see **3.304**).

6. The details of the rest of the separate computations for each spouse (adding self employed PRSI and the Universal Social Charge on income and deduction of any full credits to arrive at the net tax payable by each separated spouse) is not given here.

3.609 Separated spouses or civil partners: joint assessment election

The circumstances in which separated spouses or civil partners may elect under TCA 1997, ss 1026, 1031K to be taxed jointly under the rules of TCA 1997, ss 1017, 1031C (but separately assessed under TCA 1997, ss 1023, 1031H) have been explained in **3.508**. These circumstances are present in the case of Mr and Mrs R Fight covered in **Example 3.608.1**. **Example 3.609.1** shows the computations required assuming that Mr and Mrs Fight decide to make the election under TCA 1997, ss 1026, 1031K to be taxed jointly (but assessed separately).

Example 3.609.1

Take the facts of **Example 3.608.1**, but assume that Mr and Mrs Fight decide to make the joint election permitted by TCA 1997, s 1026 to be taxed jointly (but with separate assessment) for 2017 and they notify the inspector in writing of this on 23 September 2016 (before the end of 2016 as is required).

Among the differences to be noted in the computation on this election is the fact that there is no additional single parent credit for Mrs Fight (often a material factor against making the TCA 1997, s 1026 election). The joint assessment rules of TCA 1997, s 1017, as applied in separate assessment under TCA 1997, s 1023 (see **Example 3.605.1** above), result in assessments for 2017 respectively on each separated spouse as follows:

		Husband	*Wife*
		€	€
Sch D Case 1[1]		59,000	
Less: retirement annuity[2]		(11,800)	
Sch E		47,200	8,000
Deposit Interest			1,246
Sch D Case V		5,600	
Deductions in computing total income:			
Annual payment to her mother		-	(1,000)[3]
Total incomes (separate)	61,046	52,800	8,246
Income tax chargeable on taxable income			
(single rate)[4]			
€ 7,000[4] x 20%			1,400
€ 1,246[4] x 41%			511
€ 8,246			

€33,800 x 20%	6,760	
€1,000[4] x 20%	200	
€9,000[4] x 20%=	1,800	
€9,000 x 40%=	3,600	
€52,800	12,360	1,911
Less:		
Non-repayable credits:		
Married persons basic tax credit[5]	(1,650)	(1,650)
Earned income credit	(550)	
Employee PAYE tax credit		(1,600)
Transfer of surplus allowances	(1,339)	1,339
Retention tax on deposit interest (wife's)[6]	(511)	Nil
Add:		
Tax on charges on income (wife)		
€1,000 x 20% [7]	-	200
Total income tax payable	8,310	200

Comments on effect of the election:

In this case, the extra retirement annuity relief, additional relief for Mrs Fight's annual payment, the ability to absorb Mrs Fight's otherwise wasted tax credits and DIRT and the saving of higher rate tax with joint assessment outweigh the loss of the extra single parent allowance with single person assessments and the higher-rate tax relief for the maintenance payments foregone by Mr Fight. In fact, the single parent allowance was purely academic, given that the non-repayable single person and employee tax credits attributable to Mrs Fight together exceeded the tax chargeable on her.

1. With joint assessment under the TCA 1997, s 1026 election, Mrs Fight's income is taken excluding the payment received under the maintenance agreement and Mr Fight does not get any deduction for the payment.
2. Since Mr Fight's net relevant earnings of €50,000 are not reduced by any deduction for the maintenance payments in a joint assessment, total retirement annuity premiums of €11,800 are allowable (being 20 per cent of €59,000)
3. No restriction applies in respect of the annual payment under TCA 1997, s 792(2), as combined total income is €61,046.
4. A significant factor with the joint assessment election is that the full married person's standard rate band up to €42,800 (€67,600 if both spouses have separate incomes and the second spouse's income is at least €24,800) of taxable income is potentially available. In this case, the standard rate band will be €42,800 + €8,246 = €51,046. In order to ensure that the total tax payable under separate assessment is identical to the liability under a straightforward joint assessment, it is necessary to adjust for the fact that the standard rate band of the higher-income spouse will be extended by reference to the total income of the lower income spouse *before* deducting annual payments: see **3.510**. TCA 1997, ss 1032, 1024 do not expressly deal with how such an adjustment should be made and the method used here represents the author's view of the most logical procedure in such a case. The single person's standard rate band is allocated initially to each spouse. Mrs Fight (the lower income spouse) has income which falls short of her standard rate band by € (33,800 – 7,000) = €26,800. This amount is transferred to Mr Fight, but it cannot increase his standard rate band to an amount in excess of €42,800.

5. For the principles for allocating the personal allowances, etc in separate assessment under TCA 1997, s 1024, see **3.504**. Note that there is no single person child carer credit available.
6. Although the retention tax suffered by Mrs Fight would normally be a relief against her income tax chargeable, since she is not liable to tax in this case, the unused relief for her retention tax is available to deduct from the income tax chargeable on the husband (separate assessment rules).
7. Since the wife has retained the tax on the annual payments, she must pay it over in the separate assessments.
8. The decision to opt for joint assessment will also have implications for the self-employed PRSI and the Universal Social Charge. Mr Fight will not now be able to claim a deduction for the maintenance payments in computing the self employed PRSI and the Universal Social Charge.

Division 4 Trades and Professions: Basis of Assessment

4.1 Introduction

4.101 Introduction

Income tax is charged under Sch D on the profits accruing from any trade (Case I) or any profession (Case II) exercised in the State, whether they accrue to a resident or a non-resident person (TCA 1997, s 18(1)(a)). The criteria for determining whether or not the activities of a non-resident amount to a trade or profession carried on within the State are discussed in **13.602**; the special rules applicable to individuals who are not resident but who are ordinarily resident in the State are also discussed in **13.504**. In addition, TCA 1997, s 18(1)(a)(iv) charges tax on the profits of a non-resident person from the sale of any goods, wares or merchandise manufactured or partly manufactured by that person in the State.

TCA 1997, s 18(1)(a)(ii) brings into charge the annual profits and gains of any trade or profession accruing to a resident person, whether or not such trade or profession is carried on in the State. Foreign trades or professions, ie those which are exercised wholly outside the State, are taxed under Sch D Case III. However, the profits therefrom are in practice calculated by applying the computational rules of Sch D Cases I and II (unless the remittance basis applies: see **13.401**). The criteria for determining whether a trade or profession is foreign in nature are discussed in **13.103**.

TCA 1997, s 18(2) expressly charges tax under Sch D Case I on certain activities representing the commercial exploitation of land or rights over land (albeit in most cases such activities would fall within Sch D Case I in any event). In particular, the subsection applies to the profits attributable to any of the following concerns:

(a) quarries of stone, slate, limestone or chalk or quarries or pits of sand, gravel or clay;
(b) mines of coal, tin, lead, copper, pyrites, iron and other mines; and
(c) ironworks, gasworks, salt springs or works, alum mines or works, waterworks, streams of water, canals, inland navigations, docks, drains or levels, fishings, rights of markets and fairs, tolls, railways and other ways, bridges, ferries and other concerns of like nature having profits from or arising out of any lands, tenements or hereditaments.

The meaning of the term 'mine' above was considered in *Rogers v Longsdon* 43 TC 231 and the expression 'like concern' in this context was subject to interpretation in *Russell v Scott* 30 TC 394.

By virtue of TCA 1997, s 56, the person assessable on the profits is the body of persons carrying on the relevant concern or the agents or other officers who either have the management or direction of the concern or who receive the profits therefrom. TCA 1997, s 56 also contains references to companies of adventurers carrying on mines but these references appear to be obsolete despite having survived the consolidation process.

The taxation of trades and professions is probably the largest single topic dealt with in this book. It is appropriate, therefore, to break the subject up into several parts. This Part deals with the basis of assessment to income tax of the profits of a trade or profession, ie with the rules under which the taxable profits of the taxpayer's business are allocated to the years of assessment for which they are charged to tax (**Division 4.2**). It covers also the allocation to years of assessment of capital allowances given in respect of capital expenditure in providing certain assets for use in the trade or profession (**Division 4.3**), the ways in which relief may be claimed for trading losses (**Division 4.4**) and the rules for taxing trades or professions carried on by partnerships (**Division 4.5**). It also gives a commentary on what constitutes respectively a trade and a profession (**Division 4.1**).

The computational rules of Sch D Cases I and II regarding the manner of calculating the annual profits and gains chargeable to income tax are dealt with in detail in **Division 5**. These computational rules are, subject only to a few modifications, applicable also to the calculation of the profits of a company chargeable to corporation tax under Sch D Cases I and II. The discussion in this chapter, however, regarding the basis of assessment rules, the treatment of capital allowances and the reliefs available for losses is relevant only to individuals and other non-corporate persons chargeable to income tax.

The taxation of income from farming activities in the State, are automatically treated as the carrying on of a trade (whether or not they would otherwise be so) and are thus taxable under Sch D Case I. However, farming is subject to a number of special rules, which are discussed separately in **Division 7**. Similarly, a number of special factors apply in the case of a trade of dealing in or developing land and are given more detailed treatment in **Division 12** as part of the discussion of the taxation of income from immovable property.

4.102 Trades

The word 'trade' is defined as including 'every trade, manufacture, adventure or concern in the nature of trade' (TCA 1997, s 3). This definition extends the meaning of 'trade' to include 'adventures in the nature of the trade', but sheds no light on the meaning of the term itself. In *Ransom v Higgs* [1974] STC 539 Lord Wilberforce stated:

> Trade involves, normally, the exchange of goods, or of services, for reward, not of all services, since some qualify as a profession, or employment or vocation, but there must be something which the trade offers to provide by way of business. Trade moreover, presupposes a customer (to this too, there may be exceptions, but such is the norm), or, as it may be expressed, trade must be bilateral – you must trade with someone. The mutuality cases are based in part at least upon this principle.

In the same case, Lord Reid observed:

> Leaving aside obsolete or rare usage [trade] is sometimes used to denote any mercantile operation but is commonly used to denote operations of a commercial character by which the trader provides to customers for reward some kind of goods or services.

Agency arrangements

In *Ransom v Higgs*, it was decided that an individual who procured other persons to carry out a complex scheme, designed to realise a profit could not be said to be personally trading (see also: *Williams v Davies* 26 TC 371 where two individuals, who had for many years been concerned in land development, each bought parcels of land and gave them to their respective wives. A few days later, acting on their husband's advice, the wives sold the land to a land development company in which the two husbands owned all the shares. It was held on the facts that the wives were not carrying on a trade).

If however, those other persons had been simply carrying out those transactions on his behalf ie as his agents, then the position would have been different; in that case, the transactions would have been treated as those of the individual himself and the profit would have attributable to him as a trader. While the particular type of scheme in *Ransom v Higgs* has been countered by specific anti-avoidance rules in the context of transactions in land (see **12.310**), the general principle remains valid.

A distinction may also be drawn between:

(a) an individual who merely owns a trade (or a share in a trade) which is carried on wholly by agents on his behalf; and

(b) an individual who carries on a trade, through his agents, but where he exercises 'control and management' over the activities of the trade.

This distinction may be particularly important in two situations:

(a) Where an individual is resident in Ireland, a trade owned by him or her but which is carried on wholly by his agents overseas will be a 'foreign possession' assessable under Sch D Case III (*Exors & Trustees of AC Ferguson v Donovan* I ITR 183). However, even passive management and control exercised in Ireland will mean that the trade is carried on here and will be assessable under Sch D Case I (*Ogilvie v Kitton* 5 TC 338, discussed at **13.103**).

(b) Where an individual owns a trade which is carried on wholly by his agents, then the profits will not be relevant earnings for the purpose of retirement annuity relief since they are not 'derived' from the carrying on of this trade (see **16.202**); similarly, the life tenant of a trust the trustee of which carries on a trade, (although he is absolutely entitled to the trading profits) does not 'carry on' the trade in question (*Fry v Shiels Trustees* 6 TC 583).

Mutual trading

As indicated by Lord Wilberforce in the extract cited above, 'mutual trading' activities do not amount to a trade for tax purposes: just as an individual cannot trade with himself/herself, a group of individuals cannot trade with itself. The most important example of this principle in the income tax context is a members' club. Thus, the surplus of the members' subscriptions over club expenses incurred is not a trading profit – the same conclusion applies to contributions made by members in exchange for goods and services provided by the club where the surplus forms part of the club funds (eg a members-only bar) – see also *NALGO v Watkins* 18 TC 499.

However, where goods and services are provided for a consideration to non-members, any surplus arising will be taxable (see eg *Carlisle & Silloth Golf Club v Smith* 6 TC 198 where green fees charged by a golf club to non-members were held to constitute taxable income).

While the mutuality principle can extend to cases where the group incorporates itself as a distinct legal entity, a company which trades only with its shareholders is not per se engaged in mutual trading (*English v Scottish Joint Co-Op Society v Assam Agricultural* ITC [1948] AC 405).

In *Westbourne Supporters of Glentoran v Brennan* 1995 STC (SCD) 137, an unincorporated members' club had two classes of members: only members of one of the classes were entitled to vote and to serve on the club's management committee. The

Special Commissioner observed that equality of voting rights was not a prerequisite of mutuality, although in some cases it might reflect a real difference between voting and non-voting members which would negate the existence of mutuality. Given the facts of the instant case, he held that there was in fact no such difference and that the 'mutuality' principle applied accordingly.

Trading or taxing?

The sometimes fine distinction between levies imposed by state-sponsored bodies which are in the nature of taxes as opposed to charges for services rendered have been the subject of three leading Irish cases: *Exported Live Stock (Insurance) Board v Carroll* II ITR 211; *Moville DBC v Ua Clothasaigh* II ITR 154 and in *Racing Board v O'Culacháin* IV ITR 73. In the *O'Culacháin* case, Murphy J in the Supreme Court said with reference to *Forth Conservancy Board v IRC* 16 TC 103:

> … rates as such imposed by a rating authority are not liable to tax whereas … dues and tolls collected from persons who were enjoying the services in respect of which the tolls and dues were imposed were taxable as constituting a trade or something analogous to a trade even though the service was a public service which was monopolistic in character and provided in accordance with express statutory requirements … I see no basis on which the fruits of pure taxation, whether local or national, could be taxed as constituting something analogous to a trading activity. (Indeed the ultimate absurdity would be the imposition on the Revenue Commissioners of tax on the tax raised by them annually or even any surplus which remained after expenditure in any year). On the other hand there is no reason why a public body should be exempt from taxation on moneys received by them for services which they provide whatever the reason for providing those services or on whatever basis the cost may be calculated or imposed.

Income from property rights

Trading must also be distinguished from the mere exploitation of property rights. In *Fry v Salisbury House Estate* 15 TC 266 (followed in *Pairceir v EM* II ITR 596), a company let out offices and also provided ancillary services such as cleaning and caretaking. It was held that the profit on the provision of services was taxable under Sch D Case I while the rental element was the subject of a separate assessment (under the then UK equivalent of Sch D Case V). (It may be noted that where consideration for services is reserved as additional rent under a lease, then there should be no question of a separate Sch D Case I assessment: see TCA 1997, s 96(1)).

In *Webb v Conelee Properties Ltd* [1982] STC 913, the taxpayer was engaged in the business of acquiring properties, finding licensees to occupy them and generally managing the properties. The court held that the 'mere management' of land was not an activity that was capable of giving rise to the existence of a trade and the degree or amount of that activity made no difference so long as it was only of a managerial nature.

In *Sywell Aerodrome v Croft* 24 TC 126, Lord Greene, MR said:

> … I cannot see on what principle the profit which the person in question makes from granting temporary licenses to park motor cars on … land can be said not to be covered by the [Sch D Case V] assessment … if, on the other hand, more is done than the mere granting of licences, for example, if the cars are washed or repairs effected, the profits realised by those activities will clearly fall outside [Sch D Case V]. If the grant of one licence is merely an exercise of such rights I cannot see that the grant of half-a-dozen licences bears a different character.

In broad terms, the provision of the temporary use of land as part of a 'package' of services, is likely to count as an element of a larger trading activity and thus need not be separately taxed under Sch D Case V (eg the trade of hotel keeping). The issue is, however, ultimately one of 'fact and degree'.

The letting or leasing of assets other than land is more likely to be regarded as a trade. In *Griffiths v Jackson* [1983] STC 184, Vinelott J said:

> It is a peculiar feature of United Kingdom tax law that the activity of letting furnished flats or rooms, while it may be a business and, in this case, a demanding and time-consuming business, is not a trade … the business may, as in this case, occupy much of the taxpayer's free time or even be one which requires his whole time and attention. The taxpayer may put as much or more work into his business as, for instance, someone whose business consists in arranging licences to fix vending machines on the property of others and who daily or at less frequent intervals collects the proceeds and replenishes the machines. It is not too easy to see why in the modern world a business consisting of the exploitation of the right of property in land should be treated differently from a business consisting of the exploitation of other assets. However, the principle is now too deeply embedded in the law to be altered except by legislation.

In *Noddy Subsidiary Rights v IRC* 43 TC 458, the taxpayer was a company formed to exploit the copyright of a fictional character. Pennycuick J observed:

> It seems to me that where a person owns a property and grants licences under it, those activities may or may not, according to the particular circumstances, amount to a trade … It seems to me that, where you have this position, that a person owns an asset of any kind, whether physical or not, and grants licences under it, the activities which he carried on in connection with the grant of those licenses may amount to a trade and then Case I of Sch D applies. On the other hand, at the other end of the scale, the activities may amount to the mere holding of an investment, so that the receipt of income is in the nature of pure income profit and then [Case III] of Sch D applies. There may be intermediate cases in which Case IV of Sch D might apply.

In the *Noddy* case, the taxpayer company, which actively engaged in promotional work and granted a number of short-term licences, was in fact held to be trading. Clearly, in this context, relevant indicators of trade will include the frequency of transactions, the degree of activity and organisation involved (eg in seeking out customers, negotiating agreements, etc) the presence of elements of risk and speculation and the prospect of earning profits through sound management or the exercise of judgement in the marketplace, etc.

Employing these kinds of criteria, the letting of plant by way of operating leases should normally constitute a trading activity, particularly if there is a reasonable frequency of transactions involved. Even where the various indicators noted above are not present to any pronounced degree, the courts may still uphold a finding of fact by the Appeal Commissioners (or Circuit Court, as appropriate) that the transactions under review constitute trading: see eg the discussion of the *Daly* case (below) and the discussion of *Edwards v Bairstow* at **2.204**.

The letting of plant under pure finance leases may arguably raise different considerations, since the lessor is usually in effect providing a secured loan, and neither he (nor his agents, if relevant) would normally be involved in the acquisition, management or disposal of the leased assets. However, the grant of finance leases by a financial concern must logically form part of its trading activities; it is understood that the Revenue Commissioners accept in practice that such is the case. For a statutory attempt to define a 'finance lease', albeit in a different context, see TCA 1997, s 345, discussed at **19.204** in the 2009 edition of this book.

Where a non-profit making organisation exploits its image and reputation systematically in order to raise funds (eg through sponsorship agreements, etc) it will be a matter of fact as to whether that amounts to a trade (see eg *BOA v Winter* [1995] STC (SCD) 28).

In *Degorce v Revenue and Customs Commissioners* [2015] UKUT 447 (TCC) the taxpayer entered into a tax avoidance scheme involving the acquisition and subsequent assignment of film rights and claimed a trading loss thereon. The First Tier Tribunal held there was no repetition in the activity to argue that transactions were a trade; the question whether a person was carrying on a trade was essentially a question of fact, although there was some guidance in law as to what the meaning of that term was. The Upper Tribunal held that this finding to be acceptable because the key was whether the taxpayer had merely acquired an income stream as opposed to having carried out a trade.

Tax-based transactions

An activity does not lose its trading character merely because it would not have been undertaken in the absence of tax considerations, or because it has been structured in such a way as to maximise available tax benefits. In other words, tax is one of a number of factors which a trader may take into account in making commercial decisions without prejudicing his tax status as a trader. However, a transaction which is wholly driven by, or overwhelmingly dominated by, tax considerations, may be treated as non-trading in nature; such transactions will almost invariably lack any real elements of commercial risk or any real prospects of profit being earned through the exercise of sound management and/or of judgement in the marketplace.

In *Lupton v FA & AB Ltd* 47 TC 580 it was said by Megarry J (in a passage cited with approval by O'Hanlon J in *MacCarthaigh v Daly* III ITR 253):

> If at the end of the day a transaction, viewed as a whole, appears to be merely, or substantially, a trading transaction then despite the presence of fiscal elements or fiscal motives a trading transaction it remains. If, on the other hand, the transaction as a whole appears not to be a trading transaction but an artificial device remote from trade to secure a tax advantage, then the presence of trading elements in it will not secure its classification as a trading transaction.

In the same case, Lord Morris said:

> It is manifest that some transactions may be so affected or inspired by fiscal considerations that the shape and character of the transaction is no longer that of a trading transaction. The result will be not that a trading transaction with unusual features is revealed but that there is an arrangement or scheme which cannot fairly be regarded as being a transaction [in the nature of trade].

In *Ensign Tankers v Stokes* [1989] STC 705, Millet J, at first instance, commented on this last passage as follows:

> In my judgment this is the true significance of a fiscal motive. Fiscal considerations naturally affect the taxpayer's evaluation of the financial risks and rewards of any proposed venture, and are often the decisive factor in persuading him to enter into it. First-year allowances, enterprise zones, government grants and the like operate as financial inducements to businessmen to engage in commercial activities which would be financially unattractive or unacceptably speculative without them. Such motivations, even if paramount, do not alter the character of the activities in question. But while a fiscal motive, even an

> overriding fiscal motive, is irrelevant in itself, it becomes highly relevant if it affects, not just the shape or structure of the transaction, but its commerciality so that, in Lord Morris's words, 'the shape and character of the transaction is no longer that of a trading *transaction*'. But nothing less will do.

In the *Lupton* case, the taxpayer was a dealer in shares. The taxpayer purchased shares in O, on the basis that the vendor of the shares and the taxpayer would share equally in any tax repayments obtained in respect of those shares by the taxpayer. O consequently paid a large dividend, reducing the value of its shares and, thus (it was hoped) creating a trading loss in the hands of the taxpayer. Under the UK tax rules at that time, the taxpayer was entitled to set off a trading loss against the dividend and reclaim the income tax which was deducted at source therefrom. In the event, the House of Lords held that the transaction concerned did not comprise share dealings but was merely 'a device to secure a fiscal advantage'. A similar decision was reached in *Thompson v Gurneville Securities* 47 TC 633, where a small fixed profit margin (less than 25 per cent of the hoped for tax repayment) was granted to the 'dividend stripper' (note also *Sugarwhite v Budd* [1988] STC 533, and compare *Newstead v Frost* [1980] STC 123, discussed under Motive below, where a partnership designed to exploit a loophole in the tax system was nevertheless held to be trading).

In *MacCarthaigh v Daly* III ITR 253, the taxpayer was one of seven individuals who formed a limited partnership together with a hotel company. Five of the seven members were directors of the company. The company lent funds to the partnership at an undisclosed rate of interest. These funds were used to acquire plant and equipment which was then leased to the company under a five-year agreement at a rent of 10 per cent pa. It was conceded that an important reason behind these arrangements was the achievement of tax benefits (ie free depreciation claims in respect of the leased assets) for the participants. The Appeal Commissioners nevertheless found that the arrangements constituted a trade carried on in partnership.

In the High Court O'Hanlon J rejected the Revenue Commissioners' contention that the partnership was a 'colourable' tax-saving device. He said:

> The annual rent of 10 per cent of the cost price of the plant was not a very handsome return for a letting of goods and chattels of a perishable character, but neither was it a derisory figure or one which, of necessity, was bound to leave the lessors in a loss-making position. The scheme was not of such an extreme character as to convince me that it should be regarded as having no commercial reality and I think it may fairly be regarded as a trading transaction which qualifies for the tax relief claimed by the taxpayer.

In fact, since the arrangements had the legal effect which they professed, there was no question of their being 'colourable' (ie a sham (see **1.407**)). The critical issue was whether or not the arrangements (viewed objectively) had been so influenced by fiscal considerations as to remove them from the sphere of trading.

In *Reed v Nova Securities* [1985] STC 724, the taxpayer company which traded in shares and securities, acquired bank debts and shares from its parent company. It would have been highly beneficial from a tax perspective for the taxpayer if these assets were to have been treated as trading stock in its hands. The House of Lords upheld a finding of fact that the bank debts, being capable of onward disposal at a profit, represented trading stock. However, the House overturned a similar finding of fact in respect of the shares, on the basis that they were worthless and unrealisable and thus could not have been acquired in the course of the taxpayer's trade. The acquisition of property which had no resale value and was thus inherently incapable of producing a profit could not form part of a trading transaction. Adopting the terms employed by O'Hanlon J in *MacCarthaigh v Daly*, the transaction lacked 'all commercial reality'.

In *Reed v Nova*, Lord Templeman suggested that trading stock must be acquired with 'a view to resale at a profit'. This suggestion is difficult to reconcile with the principle that a trading transaction need not presuppose an actual profit motive on the part of the trader (although it usually will do so: see below). Furthermore, as Kerr LJ pointed out in *GMAC v IRC* [1987] STC 122:

> Assets may be acquired as trading stock with a view to reselling them at a loss as 'loss leaders' or without any certainty of profit in order to promote the sale of other assets or other trading activities.

The rationale underlying the arrangements in the *Daly* case also operates in a somewhat more sophisticated type of case. This arises where a trader brings third parties into a venture, but in such a way as to:

(a) limit their share of risk; and
(b) gear the tax benefits of the venture (typically capital allowance claims) in their favour.

The attraction of such an arrangement to the trader is that it allows him or her to offer a reduced financial return to the third parties concerned. The question then arises as to whether the participation of those third parties in the venture is in the characters of investors or as co-traders.

This kind of arrangement was the subject of a High Court case in *Airspace Investments Ltd v Moore* V ITR 3. The facts of that case, subject to some simplification, are as follows. The taxpayer company entered into a series of arrangements with RTÉ designed to exploit the overseas rights to a film made by RTÉ. The taxpayer company effectively acquired their rights for £910,000, of which £613,000 was provided by way of interest free loan by RTÉ. The taxpayer granted a licence to RTÉ to exploit these rights, in return for a share of the gross income generated as a result of such exploitation. The gross income was to be distributed equally between the taxpayer and RTÉ after the first £180,000 had been used to defray RTÉ's distribution and marketing expenses. The taxpayer only became liable to repay its loan to RTÉ if and when it had received £300,000 under the licence agreement. If any of the loan remained unpaid after approximately six and a half years, RTÉ was entitled to appropriate the master tapes of the film. Such appropriation was to be deemed to constitute full repayment of the loan (ie RTÉ could not proceed against any other of the taxpayer's assets: a so-called 'non recourse' loan). Where the taxpayer received less than £300,000 under the licence agreement, an option agreement allowed it to sell the tape to a subsidiary of RTÉ for £860,000 (ie at a small loss).

It is clear that in economic terms the taxpayer had entered into an arrangement in which it had limited prospect of profit, but also incurred restricted risk. In return for a net outlay of £217,000 (£910,000 – £693,000) it would receive the benefit of capital allowances on expenditure of £910,000. However, there was sufficient commerciality in the arrangement for the Circuit Court judge to find that the taxpayer was engaged in trading and for that decision to be upheld as a finding of fact by Lynch J in the High Court.

The decision in the UK case of *Ensign Tankers v Stokes* [1992] STC 226, which concerned a scheme with similar objectives to that in the *Airspace* case, is discussed fully in the context of TCA 1997, s 811, at **17.302**. In the former case, the House of Lords applied the so-called doctrine of 'fiscal nullity' in order to disregard for tax purposes the part of the taxpayer's investment funded by way of non-recourse finance (together with the supporting income sharing arrangements). The court held that once the transaction had been 'stripped' of its tax avoidance elements, what remained was unambiguously a trading activity. This type of analysis is of course unacceptable in Ireland under general tax law principles, and was firmly rejected by Lynch J in the *Airspace* case. Nevertheless, it is notable that the House of Lords in the *Ensign Tankers* case reasserted the general principle that a trading activity does not lose its character as such, simply because there is an ulterior fiscal motive (note also *Newstead v Frost* [1980] STC 123, discussed under Motive below). The views of the Court of Appeal which placed great significance on the 'paramount objective' of the transaction were rejected (the same court had adopted a similar analysis in *Overseas Containers (Finance) Ltd v Stoker* [1989] STC 364 discussed below, and see also *Kirkham v Williams* [1991] STC 342). It will remain the case, however, that where the facts are such that it is not clear on which side of the borderline a transaction falls, the presence of a fiscal, as opposed to a profit-making, motive, may be a critical indicator against the existence of a trade (note *Jenkinson v Freedland* 39 TC 636, discussed under Supplementary Work below).

It will be appreciated however that the general anti-avoidance provisions of TCA 1997, s 811, s 811C and other more specific anti-avoidance provisions must now be borne in mind whenever arrangements designed primarily to obtain tax benefits are undertaken.

Dealing or investment

The majority of the cases concerned with the classification of an activity as either trading or non-trading involve the acquisition and disposal of assets that arise in respect of 'isolated' transactions, (ie a single transaction or a series of transactions, which lack the continuity, scale and organisational infrastructure of a full-blown trade, but which may nevertheless qualify as an 'adventure or concern in the nature of trade'). Typically, the contrast is between a capital profit made on the disposal of an investment (or an asset simply held for personal use) as opposed to a trading profit made as the result of a 'deal'.

The distinction was expressed in *Californian Copper Syndicate v Harris* 5 TC 159, when it was said:

> It is quite a well settled principle in dealing with questions of assessment of income tax, that where the owner of an ordinary investment chooses to realise it, and obtains a greater price for it than he originally acquired it at, the enhanced price is not profit in the sense of Sch D … assessable to income tax. But it is equally well established that enhanced values obtained from realisation or conversion of securities may be so assessable, where what is done is not merely a realisation or change of investment, but an act done in what is truly the carrying on, or carrying out, of a business. The simplest case is that of a person or association of persons buying and selling lands or securities speculatively, in order to make gains, dealing in such investments as a business, and thereby seeking to make profits.
>
> What is the line which separates the two classes of cases may be difficult to define, and each case must be considered according to its facts; the question to be determined being – is the sum of gain that has been made a mere enhancement of value by realising a security, or is it a gain made in an operation of business in carrying out a scheme for profit making?

The Royal Commission on the Taxation of Profits and Income which reported in the UK in June 1955 claimed to identify a number of 'badges of trade', ie factors which were likely to have a greater or less significance when deciding whether or not a transaction was in the nature of trade. It should be appreciated that these badges were formulated in the context of the acquisition and disposal of assets. They are of limited applicability to situations involving the exploitation of property rights (see above) or the provision of professional services. In fact, 'isolated' services are taxed, if at all, under Sch D Case IV (see eg *Ryall v Hoare* discussed at **8.201**).

The badges were identified by the Royal Commission as follows:

(i) The subject-matter of the realisation

Whilst almost any form of property can be acquired to be dealt in, those forms of property, such as commodities or manufactured articles which are normally the subject of trading, are only very exceptionally the subject of investment. Again, property which does not yield to its owner an income or personal enjoyment merely by virtue of its ownership is more likely to have been acquired with the object of a deal than property that does.

(ii) The length of period of ownership

Generally speaking, property meant to be dealt in is realised within a short time after acquisition. But there are many exceptions from this as a universal rule.

- The frequency or number of similar transactions by the same person
- If realisations of the same sort of property occur in succession over a period of years or there are several such realisations at about the same date a presumption arises that there has been a dealing in respect of each.

(iii) Supplementary work on or in connection with the property realised

If the property is worked upon in any way during the ownership so as to bring it into a more marketable condition, or if any special exertions are made to find or attract purchasers, such as the opening of an office or large-scale advertising, there is some evidence of dealing. For when there is an organised effort to obtain profit there is a source of taxable income. But if nothing at all is done, the suggestion tends the other way.

(iv) The circumstances that were responsible for the realisation

There may be some explanation, such as a sudden emergency or opportunity calling for ready money that negatives the idea that any plan of dealing prompted the original purchase.

(v) Motive

There are cases in which the purpose of the transaction and sale is clearly discernible. Motive is never irrelevant in any of these cases. What is desirable is that it should be realised clearly that it can be inferred from surrounding circumstances in the absence of direct evidence of the seller's intentions, and even, if necessary, in the face of his own evidence.

Each of these factors, together with some additional factors not mentioned by the Royal Commission, are discussed in turn below. It is essential to appreciate that the 'whole picture' must be taken into account, so that the weight to be given to the various factors may vary according to circumstances. Furthermore, it is important to recognise that any given factor may be present to a greater or less degree, and that the absence (or presence) of any single factor is unlikely to be conclusive in its own right.

In an early case, *Erichsen v Last* 4 TC 422, Cotton LJ stated:

> I do not think here is any principle of law which lays down what carrying on of trade is. There are a multitude of incidents which together make the carrying on of a trade, but I know of no one distinguishing incident which makes one practice a carrying on of trade and

another practice not carrying on of trade. If I may use the expression, it is a compound fact made up of a variety of incidents.

This is an example par excellence therefore of the situation where a decision of fact (by the Appeal Commissioner or Circuit Court judge as appropriate) will not be overturned by the courts unless it is wholly unreasonable or where the appropriate tribunal of fact has proceeded on a misunderstanding of the law (see *Edwards v Bairstow*, discussed at **2.204**).

The case of *Akhtar Ali v HMRC* [2016] UKFTT 008 was a First Tier Tribunal decision in the UK which dealt with a pharmacist who also bought and sold shares over a period from a room above the shop. The First Tier Tribunal noted that that 'the courts are wary of awarding "trading" status to an individual speculating in shares'. The Court of Appeal noted in *Eclipse Film Partners No 35 LLP v Revenue and Customs Commissioners* [2015] STC 1429 at para 112 of its decision 'Whether or not a particular activity is a trade, within the meaning of the tax legislation, depends on the evaluation of the activity by the tribunal of fact. These propositions can be broken down into the following components. It is a matter of law whether some particular factual characteristic is capable of being an indication of trading activity. It is a matter of law whether a particular activity is capable of constituting a trade. Whether or not the particular activity in question constitutes a trade depends upon an evaluation of all the facts relating to it against the background of the applicable legal principles. To that extent the conclusion is one of fact, or, more accurately, it is an inference of fact from the primary facts found by the fact-finding tribunal'.

Ali bought a pharmacy before he graduated from university and he ran it as a successful business for nearly 30 years. He described his share activities in the period from 1995 to 2002 as 'investing' in shares, as he would buy shares and hold them for a few months. His early losses gradually turned to profits. In 2000, he made around £200,000. During this period, he started to 'trade options', using one of the strategies he had learned. He described himself as gradually building up expertise in buying and selling shares. He said he was looking for a use for the profits of his successful pharmacy business. He told the First Tier Tribunal that he wanted to take up trading shares in a professional matter, as a second business in addition to his pharmacy business. He said that between 2000 and 2005 his activities moved from 'investing' to 'trading' in shares. He started buying large amounts of shares and writing call options against them. He said he realised he needed to devote himself full time to this activity. He said that in and around 2005 he decided to become a 'day trader' by buying and selling shares whose prices were moving rapidly on the market. He had access to 'live' prices through a software system called 'Synergy'. He said he undertook this activity on a commercial basis, to make a profit. At this stage, he did not enter into derivatives such as call options to hedge his positions; rather he bought and sold shares within short time periods. He began employing locums at his pharmacy to free up his time for 'day trading' which he carried on in an upstairs office in the same building as the pharmacy. The total transactions in the periods were as follows:

Year of assessment	*Yearly*	*Weekly (average)*	*Daily (average)*
2006–07	980	21	4
2007–08	950	21	4
2008–09	1,370	30	6
2009–10	1,825	40	8
2011–12	775	17	3

It was also noted that Ali spent 4–5 hours a day trading and 10 hours a week on research. It can be seen from the above that his activity decreased substantially in the final year mentioned above and the reason being 'The appellant said that his "day trading" activity decreased in 2011–12 because it was becoming evident that HMRC did not agree with his tax position and he needed to liquidate his positions to pay tax "on account" … In correspondence with HMRC (letter of 18 October 2013), the appellant stated that he ceased his share activity altogether in 2013'. In this instance, the tax treatment dictated the behaviour of the taxpayer. He funded his activity through his own money which was principally generated by his pharmacy business and he had a short term credit line of about €200k with Natwest. His business plan was a succinct unwritten 'buy and sell fast moving stocks to make a profit' and he saw his share activities as part of a longer term plan over 15 years where the losses he incurred did not cause him to cease the activity because he felt he was getting better at it and that the activity would turn profitable. Regard was had to *Lewis Emanuel & Son, Ltd v White* (1965) 42 TC 369, where the taxpayer company started to buy and sell stock exchange securities in addition to its other activities as a fruit and vegetable importer. Additional staff were engaged and separate books of account were opened. The taxpayer sought to use losses which it contended were incurred in carrying on a separate trade of dealing in securities. The High Court held that the company did carry on the separate trade of dealing in securities. The judge put considerable weight on the fact that the taxpayer in the case was a company rather than an individual, and made it clear that he was not expressing any view one way or the other as to the position of an individual who carries out comparable transactions. In *Lewis Emanuel*, Pennycuick J noted '[Counsel for the Crown] does not contend that the Company acquired the Stock Exchange securities by way of investment. He contends that the Commissioners could legitimately answer the question, "If it is not trade, what is it?", by finding that, in carrying out these transactions, the Company was speculating on the Stock Exchange. The word 'speculation' is not, I think, as a matter of language, an accurate antithesis either to the word 'trade' or to the word 'investment': either a trade or an investment may be speculative. On the other hand, it is certainly true, at any rate in the case of an individual, that he may carry out a whole range of financial activities which do not amount to a trade but which could equally not be described as an investment, even upon a short-term basis. Those activities include betting and gambling in the narrow sense. They also include, it seems to me, all sorts of Stock Exchange transactions. For want of a better phrase, I will describe this class of activities as gambling transactions: see *Graham v Green*, for an analysis of these transactions in relation to an individual who made a living from betting. It seems to me, however, that in general it is much more difficult to bring the activities of a company within this class of gambling transactions. An individual may do as he pleases: a corporation must act within the limitations of its memorandum of association.'

Regard was had in *Ali* to Rowlatt J's decision in the abovementioned *Graham*. There the taxpayer '… was in the habit of betting on horses at starting prices. He did it on a large and sustained scale and he did it with such shrewdness that he made an income out of it and it is found that substantially it was his means of living'. The judge held that this was not profits or gains assessable to income tax but rather winnings from gambling. He said 'A bet is merely an irrational agreement that one person should pay another person something on the happening of an event. A agrees to pay B something if C's horse runs quicker than D's or if a coin comes one side up rather than the other side up. There is no relevance at all between the event and the acquisition of property. The event does not really produce it at all. It rests, as I say, on a mere irrational agreement … then there is no doubt that if you set on foot an organised seeking after emoluments which are not in themselves profits, you may create, by way of a trade or an adventure or a vocation, a subject matter which does bear fruit in the shape of profits or gains …' There is a clear distinction here between irrationality on the one side and organisation on the other. In the end the judge held that the taxpayer in *Graham* was addicted to betting and one could not say that his 'vocation is betting'; it was clear that the judge did not want the exchequer being a party to his gambling.

The First Tier Tribunal in *Ali* held that the taxpayer there was not 'impelled by addiction or habit' while noting that his activities had at least the possibility of gambling, ie there was a high degree of risk, he persevered with the activities even though generating losses, he was self-taught, he operated informally in the room above the shop and he was self-funded so could do as he pleased. These were first blush arguments which the First Tier Tribunal countered by reference to the fact that the informality of his operations did not contradict other decisions on this activity which demonstrated that the 'physical accoutrements' required by a dealer in securities were minimal; the self-taught argument could be applied to many self-made business entrepreneurs and trades can indeed be self-funded. The key point for the First Tier Tribunal was the taxpayer's business plan 'unsophisticated as it was … dislodging the 'prima facie presumption' that individuals engaging in this kind of speculation in shares, are not trading. For the same reasons, we find that the appellant did indeed have a deliberate and organised scheme of profit-making. We conclude that, on the facts as we have found them, the appellant was carrying on a trade in undertaking his share activities during the tax years in question'. A key point here came down to the organised manner in which the activity was carried out.

One of the requirements of the statute at issue was that the trade be commercial, which arguably at least, is implicit with the badges of trade in the first instance. The First Tier Tribunal referred back to the absence of complexity surrounding the taxpayer's activities noting 'It may have been an unsophisticated endeavour, but it does not seem to us "uncommercial": transactions took place at market prices and a business plan was pursued with sufficient application. We do not consider that the circumstances of the appellant …– that he was "self-taught", arguably over-confident of his own abilities, and undertook considerable risk – caused his trade to be "uncommercial", … these are indicia of the risk-taking entrepreneur, not of "uncommercial" activity … The appellant in our view answers to Robert Walker J's description of a "serious trader … seriously interested in profit". His lack of success in the trade seems to us attributable not to insufficient application – like the amateur or dilettante mentioned by the judge – but rather (with the benefit of hindsight) at least in part to one of three "shortcomings" mentioned by the judge as irrelevant to the question of "commerciality" – namely, a shortcoming in "skill".'

The abovementioned reference to Walker J was to his dicta in *Wannell v Rothwell* [1996] STC 450. That case dealt with a taxpayer who gave up his employment as a commodities trader and began dealing, on his own account, from his home. He bought and sold shares and commodity futures, buying and selling within a short time and financing his purchases with a combination of borrowing and taking advantage of deferred settlement arrangements. He had no clients of his own and used only very basic equipment. He sustained losses on his commodity dealings which were refused by the Inland Revenue. The number of transaction in that case comprised between 11 and 19 in each year which differs substantially from that of *Ali*. On appeal to the High Court,

Walker J dismissed the taxpayer's appeal as he was not satisfied that the decision of the Special Commissioner was wrong in law, as the taxpayer had admitted '...in cross examination that his activities might have been casual and lacking in self-discipline but not that he was a gambler'. In particular Walker J noted that his inclination would have been to remit the case back to the Special Commissioner for additional findings in that it '... would have been useful to know what exactly the admission of casualness or lack of self-discipline amounted to in this context, and what other activities (if any) the Appellant was undertaking at the time. But both sides urge me not to take that course, and so I must do my best to decide the appeal on the materials before me as best I can ... even if I have difficulty (as I do) in fully understanding the Deputy Special Commissioner's views ... but in the end I am not satisfied that the final decision was wrong in law ...' So it appears the judge could have construed the matter differently with further evidence.

The badges of trade: the cases

The subject matter of the realisation

In *IRC v Fraser* 24 TC 498, a taxpayer who bought and sold a large quantity of whiskey, was held to be trading. Lord Normand delivered the following highly significant comments:

> The individual who enters into a purchase of an article or commodity may have in view the resale of it at a profit, and yet it may be that, that is not the only purpose for which he purchased the article or commodity, nor the only purpose to which he might turn it if favourable opportunity of sale does not occur. In some of the cases the purchase of a picture has been given as an illustration. An amateur may purchase a picture with a view to its resale at a profit and yet he may recognise at the time or afterwards that the possession of the picture will give him aesthetic enjoyment if he is unable to realise it at a profit. A man may purchase stocks and shares with a view to selling them at an early date at a profit but, if he does so, he is purchasing something which is itself an investment, a potential source of revenue to him while he holds it. A man may purchase land with a view to realising it at a profit but it may also yield him an income while he continues to hold it. If he continues to hold it, there may also be a certain pride of possession. But the purchaser of a large quantity of a commodity like whisky, greatly in excess of what could be used by himself, his family and friends, a commodity which yields no pride of possession, which cannot be turned to account except by a process of realisation. I can scarcely consider to be other than an adventurer in a transaction in the nature of trade.

While commodities such as whiskey and toilet rolls, when sold on a large scale, are clearly the subject matter of 'dealing', the position of land and securities is, as noted by Lord Normand, more ambiguous. In *IRC v Reinhold* 34 TC 389 Lord Carmont observed:

> If however, the subject of the transaction is normally used for investment – land, houses, stocks and shares – the inference is not so readily to be drawn from an admitted intention in regard to a single transaction to sell on the arrival of a suitable preselected time or circumstance and does not warrant the same definite conclusion as regards trading or even that the transaction is in the nature of trade.

In *Spa Estates v O'hArgain* 1975 HC (discussed further in **12.305**), Kenny J said:

> The assessment in this case is on profits made from property dealing and one transaction, a purchase and a sale, cannot in my opinion be evidence of dealing. The fact that property is

> purchased with a view to resale does not of itself establish that the transaction is an adventure in the nature of trade (*IRC v Reinhold* 34 TC 389, *Taylor v Good* 49 TC 277).

Land which is ripe for development or which bears significant 'hope' value is probably more likely to be regarded as being in the nature of a 'commodity'. Conversely, land with a high amenity value to the purchaser may be more likely to be seen as being held for personal use. As usual, all of the surrounding facts will require consideration.

Other things being equal, shares and securities are less likely to be treated as the subject matter of trading than land for reasons set out by Nourse J in *Cooper v Clark* [1982] STC 335, as follows:

> Marketable securities, being income-yielding assets usually capable of appreciating in value, are *prima facie* purchased and sold by way of investment and not by way of trade.

Length of ownership

An investment is held with a view to enjoying capital appreciation, normally over a reasonable time-scale. Trading stock is held, not for its own sake but in order to be realised at the most opportune moment. A short period of ownership may therefore be indicative of trading. However, it must be borne in mind that 'short' is a relative term eg land, even if held as trading stock, will often take some time to realise and may even be let out to tenants in the meanwhile (see eg *IRC v Toll Property Co* 34 TC 13). Where a building contractor constructed a property, the fact that he occupied it for a short period did not rule out an intention to acquire it for the purposes of his trade (*Kirby v Hughes* [1993] STC 77).

The significance of a short period of ownership may also be diluted where the taxpayer disposes of the asset as a result of unexpected events (see below). In *Turner v Last* 42 TC 517, Cross J commented as follows:

> A man may buy something, whether it be land or a chattel for his own use and enjoyment with no idea of a quick resale, and then quite unexpectedly he may receive an offer to buy which is too tempting to refuse. That is a perfectly possible state of facts: but the fact that there was a quick resale naturally leads one to scrutinise the evidence that it was not envisaged from the first very carefully.

At the extremes, a taxpayer who contracts to sell land before he has completed his purchase of it will almost certainly be engaged in 'dealing' (*Eames v Stepnell* 43 TC 678, see also *Iswera v IRC*, discussed below). Buckley J observed in the former case:

> The purchase of property which is on the verge of being sold can [not] be properly regarded as an investment, for one element at least of investment must be that the acquirer of the investment intends to hold it, at any rate for some time, with a view to obtaining either some benefit in the meantime or obtaining some profit, but not an immediate profit by resale [emphasis added].

In *Edwards v Bairstow & Harrison* 36 TC 207 two taxpayers bought and sold a second-hand spinning plant. They had made arrangements for its resale before they purchased it, and sold it in five separate lots within a period of eight months. The House of Lords held that the only true and reasonable conclusion to be drawn from the facts was that the taxpayers were trading.

The frequency of transactions

The repetition of a particular type of transaction raises a presumption that a 'course of dealing' is taking place. A classic instance of this presumption proving decisive may be found in *Pickford v Quirke* 13 TC 251. In that case, the taxpayer agreed to form a syndicate together with a number of other individuals, in order to acquire and then liquidate a mill-owning company. Following the successful conclusion of this transaction, the taxpayer was approached by a number of other individuals with proposals for similar transactions. In the event, he agreed to form a further three syndicates (not all consisting of the same individuals) each of which made a profit on their respective liquidations. It was held that the taxpayer's participation in all of these transactions amounted to trading, even though each transaction was not in itself an adventure in the nature of trade (so that the other members of the various syndicates were not liable in respect of their shares of the profits).

A similar result was reached in *Smith Barry v Cordy* 28 TC 250 where a taxpayer who systematically purchased endowment polices and held them to maturity was said to be trading. However, this was a rather passive undertaking and is hard to distinguish from an organised programme of investment. The decision has been doubted in the House of Lords (see *Ransom v Higgs* [1974] STC 539), and may be contrasted with that in *Marson v Morton* [1986] STC 463 (discussed below).

In *Leach v Pogson* 40 TC 585, the taxpayer set up a driving school and subsequently disposed of it. Within the following four years he had carried out twenty-nine similar transactions. The taxpayer claimed that the initial driving school was disposed of in order to enable him to raise money to buy subsequent driving schools which he could then dispose of at a profit. Ungoed, Thomas J, said:

> … the Commissioners were clearly entitled to take into consideration the subsequent 29 transactions to throw light upon the nature of the original transaction of sale … and to come to the conclusion that, at the time the appellant sold … he had intended to embark … and was in fact embarking … upon a course of trade consisting of selling schools of motoring.

Supplementary work

A full-blown trade will require the management and organisation of its constituent activities. While the absence of organisational infrastructure is certainly not sufficient to establish non-trading status, its presence is likely to be a significant indicator of trading status. Thus, in *Martin v Lowry* 11 TC 297, a taxpayer who rented offices and hired employees in order to sell off a large stock of surplus linen to various customers was held to be trading. Clearly, the subject matter of the transaction also marked it as a dealing in a commodity (see above).

The carrying out of substantial work to an asset with a view to its subsequent disposal will almost invariably be regarded as an adventure in the nature of a trade, even though it may be an isolated transaction. Thus, in *IRC v Livingston* 11 TC 538, three individuals who had acquired a cargo vessel, converted it into a steam drifter and then sold it off at a profit, were held to be trading. Lord Clyde observed:

> If the venture was one consisting simply in an isolated purchase of some article against an expected rise in price and a subsequent sale it might be impossible to say that the venture was 'in the nature of trade' because the only trade in the nature of which it could participate would be the trade of a dealer in such articles and a single transaction falls as far short of constituting a dealer's trade as the appearance of a single swallow does of making a summer. The trade of a dealer necessarily consists of a course of dealing, either actually engaged in or at any rate contemplated and intended to continue. But this principle is difficult to apply to ventures of a more complex character such as that with which the present case is concerned. I think the test, which must be used to determine whether a venture such as we are now considering is, or is not, 'in the nature of trade' is whether the operations involved

> in it are of the same kind and carried on in the same way as those which are characteristic of ordinary trading in the line of business in which the venture was made. If they are, I do not see why the venture should not be regarded as 'in the nature of trade' merely because it was a single venture which took only three months to complete.

Some qualifications need to be added to Lord Clyde's statement of principle. Firstly, it is clear that a single transaction of purchase and sale (ie without any supplementary work being undertaken) may be an adventure in the nature of trade. However, in practice, this usually only applies where the asset concerned is capable of being regarded as a commodity, as in the case of land (see above). Secondly, Lord Sands in the same case underlined the distinction between the nature of the operations in *IRC v Livingston* and work merely designed to enhance the saleability of a 'capital' asset, stating:

> [T]he subject of purchase and sale may be so treated in the interval as to bring the transaction within the category of carrying on a trade. I do not think that putting the article in question in a suitable condition for a favourable sale would necessarily have this effect, as, for example, having a picture cleaned, or a ship's boilers cleaned and the hull repainted. But I am disposed to think that it would introduce the element of carrying on a trade if the purchaser were … to carry through a manufacturing process which changed the character of the article. An illustration might be the purchasing of a quantity of pig iron and having it manufactured into steel, or of gold-bearing ore and having the gold extracted by milling the ore.

In *Hudson's Bay Co Ltd v Stevens* 5 TC 424, Farwell LJ observed:

> Again a landowner may lay out part of his estate with roads and sewers and sell it in lots for building, but he does this as owner, not as a land speculator. It would be different if a landowner … entered into the business of buying and developing and selling land; but the case of the owner, whether of land, or pictures, or jewels, selling his own land, etc, although he may have expended money on them in getting them up for sale, is entirely different; he sells as owner not as trader.

The principle set out in the *Hudson's Bay* case was extended to the situation where a company was formed by various persons in order to realise their interests in a block of land in the most favourable manner (*Rand v Alberni Land Co* 7 TC 629, but note also *Alabama Coal, Iron Land & Colonization Co v Mylam* 11 TC 232; this principle was also discussed in *Pilkington v Randall* (see below)).

Finally, and perhaps most importantly of all, it always remains to be seen whether or not it was intended that the asset, once converted, should be held as an investment. This will not usually be an issue if the taxpayer has merely converted raw materials into stocks of a marketable commodity which are clearly destined for resale (see eg *Cape Brandy Syndicate v IRC* 12 TC 358, where the blending and sale of brandy was held to be trading).

By way of contrast, in *Mara v Hummingbird* II ITR 667, a property which was in the course of redevelopment with a view to holding it as an investment was sold following receipt of a very attractive offer. The Supreme Court upheld the Appeal Commissioner's finding of fact that the acquisition, part development and sale of the property was not an adventure in the nature of trade. Clearly, the special circumstances which prompted the ultimate sale helped to confirm the original intention to hold the land as an investment (see below). The decision is discussed more fully in the context of TCA 1997, s 640 (see **12.305**).

In *Jenkinson v Freedland* 39 TC 636, the taxpayer restored two stills, using a chemical process devised by himself, and sold them to a company which he controlled.

The transaction was held not to be trading on the basis that the whole purpose behind it was not to resell the assets for profit but rather to enable the company to obtain enhanced capital allowances. The decision might be regarded as generous, since viewed objectively, the transactions in question looked typical of a trading adventure, irrespective of the motive behind them.

Finally, it may be noted that it is possible in principle even for a builder to hold some properties which he has built as trading assets and other properties as investments, (see *West v Phillips* 38 TC 203; *Bradshaw v Blunden* 36 TC 397, both cases where a builder was held to have ceased trading and to have appropriated the properties to investment purposes; but note the special rules which apply to dealing in land, discussed at **12.307**: *Trading Stock*).

Circumstances responsible for realisation

A 'deal' presupposes an acquisition for the purpose of resale. Accordingly, the fact that an asset is sold as a result of an unexpected turn of events may support a contention that the asset was not acquired purely for resale. Examples of such events include a particularly favourable offer to buy (see *Mara v Hummingbird* and also *Beautiland v IRC* [1991] STC 467) or financial pressures (see *West v Phillips*). The fact of an unanticipated sale will not generally be relevant if the asset was being held for resale, in any event (ie there is merely an accelerated disposal of trading stock). However, in *Spa Estates v O'hArgain* (discussed more fully in **12.305**) it was held that an intending land developer which sold off its land before it had commenced any development activities was not engaged in an 'adventure' in the nature of trade.

Motive

The factors outlined above may be regarded as objective criteria which are used to infer the purpose of the taxpayer's transactions. There may also be available what the Royal Commissions terms 'direct' evidence of the 'subjective' purposes of the taxpayer ie whether or not there was an actual profit motive behind the transaction(s) in question. This would include the taxpayer's own account of what was in his mind, as well as evidence based on correspondence and conversations relating to the transaction.

Indeed there would seem to be no limits regarding the admissibility of extrinsic evidence in this regard (see **1.408**). The accounting treatment of a transaction (where this is relevant) will also be persuasive, but not conclusive, evidence of intention. In *Shadford v Fairweather* 43 TC 291, Buckley J commented:

> The way in which the company keeps its accounts must, I think, be admissible evidence to show what, in the view of the company's directors and auditors at that time, was the intention or view of the company; but it is only evidence in that way, which must be weighed against the other evidence available to the tribunal that has to decide the nature of the transaction .... For however, genuinely the accounts may have been framed by those responsible for them, and however carefully they may have been studied by those responsible for auditing them, the other evidence may show that in fact they do not truly indicate the nature of the relevant operations.

Again, as the Royal Commissioners indicated, evidence of his purposes or motive given by the taxpayer clearly needs to be evaluated carefully. It will be necessary to evaluate such evidence in the light of the objective indicators discussed above. On occasions, it may indeed be discounted altogether (see, eg *Gray & Gillet v Tiley* 26 TC 80).

In *Iswera v IRC* 44 ATC 157, a Privy Council case, Lord Reid analysed the role of 'motive' in an influential speech. In the *Iswera* case, the taxpayer wished to live near to the school at which her daughters attended. She had offered to buy part of a large site near the school, but the owner was only prepared to sell the site as a whole. Accordingly, the taxpayer agreed to buy the entire site. She then divided and resold the greater part of it to a number of sub-purchasers, retaining the balance for her own use. The Privy Council upheld the conclusion of fact that this was a trading transaction. Lord Reid commented as follows:

> Before their Lordships, counsel for the appellant came near to submitting that, if it is a purpose of the taxpayer to acquire something for his own use and enjoyment, that is sufficient to show that the steps which he takes in order to acquire it cannot be an adventure in the nature of trade. In their Lordships' judgement that is going much too far. If, in order to get what he wants, the taxpayer has to embark on an adventure which has all the characteristics of trading, his purpose or object alone cannot prevail over what he in fact does. But if his acts are equivocal, his purpose or object may be a very material factor when weighing the total effect of all the circumstances.
>
> In the present case, not only has it been held that the appellant's dominant motive was to make a profit, but her actions are suggestive of trading as regards the greater part of the site which she bought. She had to and did make arrangements for its sub-division and immediate sale to the nine sub-purchasers before she could carry out her contract with the vendor of the site.

Lord Reid seems to be suggesting here that consideration of the taxpayer's subjective purposes should be suspended until all the objective evidence has been weighed up. It is only if the transaction appears 'equivocal' at that stage, that his actual purposes be brought into account as a potentially decisive factor. This distinction is often not observed in the cases themselves. Thus, in general the courts will consider all of the evidence in the round, looking at what the taxpayer actually did and also his subjective purposes in doing what he did. However, where the transactions in question are clearly commercial in nature, the fact that the trader did not necessarily have the subjective purpose of making a profit will not prevent a finding of trading (*IRC v Incorporated Law Council of Law Reporting* 3 TC 105 and note also *Clarke v BTPS Trustees* [1998] STC 1075); contrast the position where a venture or transaction is conducted in such a wholly uncommercial manner that as a consequence it is inherently incapable of making a profit (see *Religious Tract & Book Society of Scotland v Forbes* 3 TC 415 and note also the discussion of *Reed v Nova Securities* [1985] STC 724 under Tax-Based Transactions above).

It is suggested that the key point in the *Iswera* case was that, taking all of the evidence into account, the taxpayer was engaged in trading. The fact that her decision to acquire land for resale was made for an ulterior motive (ie in order to acquire a particular plot of land) was not relevant to the issue of whether or not she had traded in the first place. Similarly, in *British Legion, Peterhead Branch v IRC* 35 TC 509 it was held that the running of dances constituted a trade, even though the proceeds were to be applied for benevolent purposes. The court contrasted the position where a benevolent or charitable organisation used some of the trappings of trade as a means of attracting donations but these were not related to the provision of goods or services eg hawking flags, occasional sales of work, etc (see also *Exported Live Stock (Insurance) Board v Carroll* II ITR 211).

A further parallel may be drawn with the House of Lords decision in *Newstead v Frost* [1980] STC 123. In that case, the taxpayer, a television personality, entered into a partnership with an overseas company which exploited his skills. The practical effect of this was to divert the taxpayer's earnings to the partnership. The partnership was managed and controlled outside the UK with the result (under the UK tax rules at that time) that the taxpayer was not liable to income tax on his (95 per cent) share of the partnership's earnings so long as they were not remitted to the UK. The House of Lords held that the partnership was trading with a view to profit. The fact that both this particular activity and the structure of the overseas partnership were undertaken for ulterior purposes of a purely fiscal nature did not detract from the fact that the activity itself was clearly commercial in nature and constituted a trade for tax purposes.

The *Frost* case was distinguished in *Overseas Containers (Finance) Ltd v Stoker* [1989] STC 364, where a ship operating company formed a subsidiary (the taxpayer). The taxpayer company borrowed foreign currency and on-lent equivalent sterling funds to the parent company, on a number of occasions. The taxpayer received a mark-up on the interest which it charged to its parent company. Subsequently, sterling was devalued with the result that the taxpayer incurred a significant loss. The Court of Appeal held that the loan transaction did not constitute trading; consequently, the loss was not eligible for group relief against the trading profits of the parent company. It was clear that the ulterior purpose which lay behind the formation of the taxpayer company and the transactions which it consequently undertook was to generate allowable revenue losses (if the parent company had incurred the foreign currency borrowings directly, the exchange losses would have been indisputably capital in nature).

The Court of Appeal held that looking at the position of the group as a whole, the transactions lacked any commercial objective and were solely motivated by fiscal considerations. However, the assumption of currency risks in return for an appropriate interest differential would seem in fact to be an inherently commercial activity. It is suggested that this is a matter which can only be properly judged in the context of treating the taxpayer as a distinct legal entity (see **1.407**), ie it is not permissible to 'set off' the gains and losses of the group as a whole, in order to assess the commerciality of the activities of a single company. If, looked at objectively and in isolation, the taxpayer was trading, the existence of an ulterior fiscal motive (assuming that the motives of the group and the motives of the taxpayer were the same, which is an issue of fact) should not have been a material consideration.

However, where a purchase and resale is carried out by a 'conduit company' in the furtherance of a tax avoidance scheme, the transaction may be so uncommercial in nature that in objective terms it does not constitute trading; even if it can be viewed as equivocal in nature, the transaction will probably require the presence of a profit motive if it is to be regarded as trading in nature, which is unlikely to be present in these circumstances (see *Sugarwhite v Budd* [1988] STC 533, and note also *N Ltd v IOT* (1996) STC (SCD) 346).

Where an asset is acquired by gift or inheritance and subsequently resold the motive to resell at a profit will generally be absent at the time of acquisition (*see McClelland v FCT* [1971] All ER 969, a Privy Council case). However, it is possible for an asset acquired by gift or inheritance to be appropriated by a taxpayer for the purposes of an existing trade, or as the initial trading stock of a new trade. In *Pilkington v Randall* 42 TC 662, the taxpayer and his sister inherited joint interests in land. The taxpayer bought out his sister's interest and then made roads, constructed drains and installed services on the land. He subsequently sold the land for a substantial profit. The Court of Appeal upheld the Appeal Commissioners' finding of fact that these transactions amounted to an adventure in the nature of trade.

Salmon LJ commented:

> I do not read the decision of this court in *Hudson's Bay Co v Stevens* or the decision of Rowlatt J in *Rand v Alberni Land Co Ltd*, as laying down a proposition of law to the effect that, whenever a property owner develops his land by making roads and laying sewers and selling plots, he can never be carrying on a trade. This would be opening the door very wide to modern property developers. I think the highest it can be put is that usually in such circumstances the property owner is not carrying on a trade, but whether in the particular case he is or is not doing so much depends on the facts of the particular case. It is essentially a question of fact and degree … I agree that this case is very close to the borderline, and I am by no means certain that if I had been sitting as a Commissioner and had had to draw inferences of fact, I should have come to the same conclusions as the Commissioners … I think one of the circumstances which is in favour of the Commissioners … view is that the Appellant, when he bought out his sister's share, did so, as the Commissioners have found, with the intention of making a profit out of the whole of the land by reselling it after development. Although the intention with which the land was acquired is by no means an absolute criterion, it is a factor, when there is doubt, which can be thrown into the balance, as is laid down by Lord Reid in *Iswera v Commissioner of Inland Revenue*. It is further to be observed that, at the time the Appellant acquired his sister's share, the whole of the land, as it was, was worth something between £24,000 and £25,000. The Appellant spent as much again on developing the land with a view to reselling portions of it at a profit. Again I do not think this is by any means conclusive, and the Commissioners might well have come to a different conclusion. But on the facts here is seems to me quite impossible to say that, because they decided as they did, they must have been misdirecting themselves in law, and equally impossible to say that no reasonable man could have reached the same conclusion.

It may be seen that even where the approach set out by Lord Reid in *Iswera* is invoked, it has limited practical effect, since the vast majority of cases before the court will be equivocal (ie doubtful) to at least some extent: accordingly, it will usually be necessary to throw the actual purposes of the taxpayer into the equation.

Similarly, an asset acquired as an investment will normally retain that character unless there is a clear intention subsequently on the part of the taxpayer to appropriate it for trading purposes. In *Simmons v IRC* [1980] STC 350 Lord Wilberforce observed:

> Trading requires an intention to trade; normally the question to be asked is whether this intention existed at the time of the acquisition of the asset. Was it acquired with the intention of disposing of it at a profit, or was it acquired as a permanent investment? … Intentions may be changed. What was first an investment may be put into trading stock, and, I suppose, vice versa. If findings of this kind are to be made precision is required, since a shift of an asset from one category to another will involve changes in the company's accounts, and possibly liability to tax (see *Sharkey v Wernher* [see below]). What I think is not possible is for an asset to be both trading stock and permanent investment at the same time, nor for it to possess an indeterminate status, neither trading stock nor permanent asset. It must be one or the other, even though, and this seems to me legitimate and intelligible, the company, in whatever character it acquires the asset, may reserve an intention to change its character. To do so would, in fact, amount to little more than making explicit what is necessarily implicit in all commercial operations, namely that situations are open to review.

In the *Simmons* case, the taxpayer company which disposed of investment properties as a result of unfavourable market conditions and subsequently went into liquidation was accordingly held not to be trading.

The same principle was applied in *Taylor v Good* [1974] STC 148, 49 TC 277, where the taxpayer purchased a property on impulse, without any clear idea as to what he would do with it. Having decided against residing in it, he obtained planning permission for further development and subsequently resold it at a profit. Megarry J, at first instance, held in effect that the property had been appropriated to an adventure in the nature of trade once the taxpayer had decided not to occupy the property personally. This analysis received short shrift in the Court of Appeal. Russell LJ observed:

> If, of course, you find a trade in the purchase and sale of land, it may not be difficult to find that properties originally owned (for example) by inheritance, or bought for investment only, have been brought into the stock-in-trade of that trade … but where, as here, there is no question at all of absorption into a trade of dealing in land or lands previously acquired with no thought of dealing, in my judgement there is no ground at all for holding that activities such as those in the present case, designed only to enhance the value of the land in the market, are to be taken as pointing to, still less as establishing, an adventure in the nature of trade.

The decision in *Taylor v Good* may be contrasted with that in *Mitchell Bros v Tomlinson* 37 TC 224. In that case, the taxpayers had acquired a number of houses as an investment fund for their old age. Subsequently, they changed their policy and began to buy and sell houses; the houses which they sold included houses originally acquired as part of their investment fund. The court upheld the Appeal Commissioners' finding of fact that all the sales arose in the course of trading. An Irish case, *O'hArgain v B Ltd* III ITR 9, where the court held that land originally held as an investment had been appropriated to trading stock for the purposes of development is discussed further below. In *Richfield International Land and Investment Co v IRC* [1989] STC 820, a Privy Council case, it was held that a company which had initially acquired a number of properties as investments had subsequently appropriated them as trading stock, although it had not undertaken any development activities nor did it otherwise engage in buying or selling properties. The decision is probably explained by the fact that the taxpayer had acquiesced in the taxation of the profits on the first two disposals as income although it can hardly be justified in principle on these grounds.

In ascertaining the motives of a company, the objectives of its promoters in forming it may be relevant. However, this will probably be true only to the extent that the persons actually controlling the affairs of the company continue to adhere to those objectives. In general, the courts will look primarily to the persons who exercise managerial control over the company in order to ascertain its motives. The key decision makers will normally be the board of directors, but this of course will not be the case if, for example, the board merely acts as a 'rubber stamp' for a controlling shareholder (cf the discussion of corporate residence at **1.504**).

In *O'hArgain v B Ltd*, a company (B Ltd) had engaged in land development activities but also owned farmland which had been let out on conacre for some time; it was held on the facts by the Appeal Commissioners that the farmland had been acquired solely for farming purposes. The farmland was subsequently rezoned for development. In response to an enquiry by the Revenue as to whether the company had ceased its development activities, the company's accountant indicated that all available sites had been sold but that it was possible that the farmland might also be developed, albeit this was not in current contemplation. A and B were shareholder/directors of B Ltd. The court held that, because A was an architect (and thus familiar with the development possibilities), an inference arose that the company had definitely formed the intention to exploit the land for development and thus appropriate it to its (existing) trade of development once it had been rezoned. While the actual inference itself may seem somewhat strong, the imputation to B Ltd of its shareholder/directors' intentions concerning it was clearly unobjectionable in principle.

In *Mara v Hummingbird* II ITR 667, Kenny J commented as follows on the significance of a company's objects as stated in its Memorandum of Association:

> Counsel for the Inspector relied strongly on the objects of the taxpayers stated in the memorandum of association. The fourth object gives the taxpayers power to buy, hold, sell, invest in, develop and deal with real and personal property of all kinds. In the days when companies were incorporated with very limited objects as a protection for shareholders, this argument had some force in deciding whether a purchase and sale of land was an adventure in the nature of trade. But today all companies are formed with numerous objects (the taxpayers who have paid up share capital of £2 have twenty nine) and the fourth object would, I think, be found in the objects clause of about 98 per cent of the companies incorporated since about 1940. The argument that a transaction is within the powers of the company is one to which little weight should be attached today when the question is whether the transaction is an adventure in the nature of trade or not.

Notwithstanding Kenny J's comments, it is possible that a company may have a relatively narrowly-framed objects clause. In such a case the terms of the objects clause will not be conclusive, but there will be a natural presumption that the directors have acted *intra vires*.

Mixed motives

An interesting issue arises where the taxpayer is acting out of 'mixed motives' ie where an asset is acquired for two distinct, but concurrent, purposes. In *Iswera v IRC* (cited above) Lord Reid indicated that it is the dominant motivation which is relevant. It may be recalled that the view taken above is that *Iswera* was in fact a case where there was an exclusively trading purpose, but the trading was carried out in order to finance an ulterior, non-trading objective.

In *Kirkham v Williams* [1991] STC 342 the taxpayer acquired a large site, primarily in order to provide premises for his business. On one analysis of the facts, he also intended to develop and sell the site if:

(a) he could obtain planning permission to do so; and
(b) he was in a position to relocate his business premises.

Per Nourse J, because the latter intention was so 'severely circumscribed', and 'its implementation indefinite in point of time' it was not possible as a matter of law to say that the site had been acquired as trading stock. Ralph Gibson J (dissenting) took the view that this intention was sufficiently concrete to be taken into account (and, to similar effect, see Lloyd J who found in favour of the taxpayer on a different analysis of the underlying facts). It is striking that both Ralph Gibson J and Nourse J, agreed that a sufficiently precise intention to develop and sell the site would have marked the transaction as an adventure in the nature of trade, even though that intention was subsidiary to the main intention of acquiring a fixed asset. This approach was influenced by that adopted by the Court of Appeal in the *Ensign Tankers* case, and subsequently rejected by the House of Lords. Adoption of this approach could have led to the bizarre conclusion that the site in *Kirkham v Williams* was regarded at one and the same time as a capital asset in one trade and as trading stock in another (compare Lord Wilberforce's observations in *Simmons v IRC* quoted above).

Other factors

Other factors, not expressly dealt with by the Royal Commission, but which may also act as indicators of a trading intention include the following:

The background of the taxpayer

If the taxpayer undertakes a transaction which has a close affinity to a trade which he carries on, this increases the likelihood that it will be regarded as being of a trading nature. In *Benyon & Co v Ogg* 7 TC 125, the taxpayer, which acted as an agent for the purchase of wagons, was held to be trading when it bought and sold some wagons on its own account.

In *Harvey v Caulcott* 33 TC 159 a builder sold shops which he had previously let out and a house which he had built as a residence for one of his employees. Donovan J observed:

> Such a case as the present is always coloured by the fact that the man is a builder. That no doubt puts a peculiar onus on him to show that the profit from the sale of some property is profit from an investment or profit from something which is not trading stock.

However, as usual, the weight to be given to this factor must be evaluated in the light of all of the surrounding circumstances. In *Guinness & Mahon v Browne* III ITR 373, the Supreme Court rejected the proposition that 'any profit made by a bank on the realisation of an investment (ie securities) is part of the bank's taxable profits'. In that case, the taxpayer was a merchant bank which had acquired a property investment company as a subsidiary. The acquisition was by way of long term investment and lay outside the normal course of the taxpayer's trading activities. The subsidiary unexpectedly sold its property (the subsidiary was in fact the taxpayer in *Mara v Hummingbird* discussed above) and was, as a result, subsequently liquidated. The gain on the consequent realisation of the subsidiary was held not to constitute a trading profit (a similar outcome was reached on a different set of facts in *Waylee Investment Ltd v CIR* [1990] STC 780, a Privy Council case).

The financing arrangements for the transaction

The use of borrowings to acquire an asset where the taxpayer cannot meet the repayments out of his income indicates an intention to realise the asset from the outset (see eg see *Johnson v Heath* 46 TC 463). In *Wisdom v Chamberlain* 45 TC 92 the taxpayer financed the purchase of a silver bullion by loans with a high rate of interest, subsequently selling the bullion for a handsome profit. The Court of Appeal held that this was an adventure in the nature of trade, placing some emphasis on the fact that the silver had not been acquired in substitution for the taxpayer's existing investments.

Where the financing arrangements are such that retention of the asset yields a negative cash flow, this may indicate that the asset is not being held as an investment (this was the position in the *Wisdom* case). In *Cooke v Haddock* 39 TC 64, this factor was one of a number of indicators taken into account by the court. Pennycuick J commented also on the land in question:

> The land was ripe for building subject to the necessary licenses being obtained; the land was unsuitable for occupation by the appellant or for retention as an income producing investment by the appellant; the appellant obtained planning permission for development of the estate (although this was to safeguard himself against the threat of compulsory purchase and not with a view to developing the estate himself); the appellant sold parts of the land

piecemeal and the appellant has been concerned in companies and a partnership firm engaged in dealings in land.

In *Marson v Morton* [1986] STC 463, Sir Nicholas Browne-Wilkinson suggested that non-income producing assets should be viewed more flexibly, saying:

> … in my judgment it (the fact that income is produced) plainly is a relevant factor. But in my judgment in 1986, it is not any longer self-evident that unless land is producing income it cannot be an investment. The legal principle of course cannot change with the passage of time: but life does. Since the arrival of inflation and high rates of tax on income new approaches to investment have emerged putting the emphasis in investment on the making of capital profit at the expense of income yield. For example the purchase of short-dated stocks giving a capital yield on redemption but no income has become commonplace. Similarly, split-level investment trusts have been invested which produce capital profits on one type of share and income on another. Again, institutions now purchase works of art by way of investment … those are plainly not trading deals; yet no income is produced from them. I can see no reason why land should be any different and the mere fact that land is not income-producing should not be decisive or even virtually decisive on the question whether it was bought as an investment.

The use of temporary finance to fund the acquisition of an asset may be an indicator of an intention to resell from the outset, but not, for example, if it is merely bridging in nature, and long term finance is being arranged.

Incorporation

There is a tendency to regard a company as more likely than an individual to be trading in comparable circumstances. This reflects the fact that companies are normally formed to carry on business for the benefit of their shareholders, so that they will generally be either traders or investors. In the case of an individual the non-trading options are greater: thus, for example, he may be merely carrying on an activity for his personal enjoyment or interest. The contrasting decisions in *Salt v Chamberlain* 53 TC 143 and *Lewis Emmanuel and Son Ltd v White* 42 TC 369 illustrate this point.

Substance over form

The trading versus non-trading distinction usually centres on the issue of the taxpayer's intentions: this is primarily a matter of substance than one of legal form, (of course, the legal rights and obligations of the parties to the transactions in question must still be ascertained in order to understand the commercial implications of the taxpayer's activities). In *Lim Foo Yong v CG* [1986] STC 255, the Privy Council took the view that the sale and leaseback of a property was indicative of an intention to retain the asset. Furthermore, where the sale and leaseback was accompanied by an option to repurchase the property at the same price, this was equivalent in economic terms to raising finance by way of a mortgage loan. Accordingly, to describe the resulting surplus as a profit was said to be a 'misuse of language'.

4.103 Illegal trading activities

It has been held in the Irish courts that the profits from a trade or business that is wholly illegal cannot be assessed to tax as resulting from a trade or an adventure in the nature of trade. In the Supreme Court in *Hayes v Duggan* I ITR 195, Fitzgibbon J distinguished between cases in which it appeared from investigation into the accounts of a lawful business that part of the profits may have been derived from illegal methods of conducting it and, on the other hand, cases such as the one before him where the entire transaction or trade is an illegal one. In the former instance, the profits were taxable, but in the latter they were not. The Revenue had attempted unsuccessfully to tax the profits of the trade of promoter of lotteries, an activity which was regarded as illegal and a criminal act under the law.

In fact, the *Hayes v Duggan* decision was rejected in the subsequent UK case of *Mann v Nash* 16 TC 523 where it was held that once transactions were considered trading, the fact that the trade was illegal could not prevent assessment and that in consequence the profits from providing illegal automatic machines were taxed.

The *Hayes v Duggan* decision was, however, followed in the later Irish case of *Collins v Mulvey* 31 TC 151, which also involved the business of setting up automatic slot machines for public use in various places. The machines were of a type the results from which depended on chance and not on skill and, in consequence, the placing out of the machines constituted a criminal offence under the law and the business was wholly illegal. The High Court held that the case was indistinguishable from *Hayes v Duggan* and that, as a result, the profits could not be taxed. This was one instance where the Irish courts took a different view on similar law to their UK counterparts (for a fuller discussion: see *Dockley (T)* [1994] IJOT 12). A trade which is not illegal, but is contrary to public policy, may fall outside the scope of the principle in *Hayes v Duggan* (see *IRC v Aiken* [1990] STC 497).

The rules contained in TCA 1997, s 58 were brought in to enable the profits of any trade consisting or involving illegal activities to be assessed to tax under Sch D Case IV (not Case I). The rules of that section – which go wider than taxing only illegal trading profits – are dealt with in **8.213**.

4.104 Realisation of assets

A liquidator of a company may realise assets formerly held as trading stock without being regarded as trading. In *IRC v Old Bushmills Distillery Co Ltd* 12 TC 1148, the selling off of whiskey stocks over a period after the liquidator had ceased to trade was held to be the only practical way of realising the asset and was not trading. Similarly, in *Wilson Box (Foreign Rights) Ltd v Brice* 20 TC 736 a company formed to exploit various patent rights was wound up; it was held that the sale of these rights in the course of the winding-up did not constitute trading. However, in *Baker v Cook* 21 TC 339 a liquidator who held the benefit of contracts for distributing films was held to be trading through the agency of two specially formed companies which carried out the contracts on his behalf.

Personal representatives, like liquidators, are under a duty to realise the assets under their control to best advantage.

In *N Cohan's Executors v IRC* 12 TC 602, executors were held not to be trading when they completed the purchase of a contract to buy a ship entered into by the taxpayer before his death and when they resold the ship to a shipping company. The court considered they were doing no more than realising an asset to the best advantage or alternatively, in preventing a loss to the estate.

In *IRC v Donaldson's Trustees* 41 TC 161, the Court of Session upheld a decision of the Special Commissioners that the deceased's will trustees did not carry on a trade of farming, but that they had only disposed of a pedigree herd and the farm at the earliest possible moment. In this case, the farmer had died in March 1955 and in implementing a decision to comply with the deceased's wishes to sell the herd, the trustees accepted advice in April 1955 from a firm of cattle auctioneers to sell the heifers and heifer calves in September 1955 and the young bulls in February 1956. Although extra nurse cows for the bull calves had to be bought as well as extra cattle to keep down the grass, and although rotation ploughing took place in February 1956, these steps were considered to be necessary for the best realisation of the assets and did not constitute trading.

Conversely in *Patillo's Trustees v IRC* 36 TC 87, the personal representative of a cattle dealer not only sold off the deceased's existing stock but also bought and sold additional cattle in the course of winding up the estate. Although their motive in doing so was to use up existing foodstuffs the court upheld the Appeal Commissioners finding of fact that they were trading (see also *Weisberg's Exors v IRC* 17 TC 696).

In *Wood v Black's Executors* 33 TC 172, the will directed that the deceased's businesses of trawler owner, fish merchant, coldstore proprietor, coal merchant and estate developer be wound up within three years after his death. He died in June 1942 and the businesses and their assets were disposed of at various dates up to December 1943. The General Commissioners concluded that the businesses were only carried on for the purposes of winding them up and that this did not constitute trading. The court held that this was the wrong conclusion on the facts and that, except in the case of the estate development business, the personal representatives had carried on a trade.

An interesting issue arises as to whether the executor of a deceased partner is merely realising the deceased's share of the partnership assets (as in *Marshall's Exors, etc v Joly* 20 TC 256) or is carrying on the trade with the surviving partners (as in *Newbarns Syndicate v Hay* 22 TC 461). Again, this will be an issue of fact and degree although, all other things being equal, there will as usual be a presumption in favour of realisation.

Finally, it may be noted that special rules apply to disposals by a liquidator of land previously held as trading stock: see **12.306**.

4.105 Professions

A person carrying on a profession is taxed under Sch D Case II on the annual profits or gains derived from his business. There is not in fact a major distinction between a person carrying on a profession and one who trades. In nearly all respects the tax treatment under Sch D Case II is the same as that under Sch D Case I, but there are a few places where the distinction may be relevant. In some instances a person carrying on a profession may be entitled to calculate the taxable profits of his business on a 'cash' or 'conventional' basis of accounting instead of on the normal 'earnings' basis which must be applied to trades and most professions (see **5.502**). Further, a company carrying on a profession is subject to an additional charge to corporation tax on certain undistributed income that does not apply to a company carrying on a trade (TCA 1997, s 441).

The question of what is a profession came up in a number of English cases connected with excess profits duty and excess profits tax which applied during the 1939–45 World War period. In one of these cases, *IRC v Maxse* 12 TC 41, Scrutton LJ gave a good description:

> … a 'profession' in the present use of language involves the idea of an occupation requiring either purely intellectual skill, or any manual skill controlled, as in painting and sculpture or surgery, by the intellectual skill of the operator, as distinguished from an occupation which is substantially the production or sale or arrangements for the production or sale of commodities. The line of demarcation may vary from time to time. The word 'profession' used to be confined to the three learned professions, the Church, Medicine, and Law. It has now, I think, a wider meaning.

These older cases decided *inter alia* that the following exercised professions: an optician (*Carr v IRC* [1944] 2 All ER 163); a headmaster (*IRC v North & Ingram* [1918] 2 KB 705); a journalist (*IRC v Maxse* 12 TC 41), an actress (*Davies v Braithwaite* 18 TC 198) and a barrister (*Sheldon v Croom-Johnson* 16 TC 740). The following were *inter alia* held not to exercise professions: a photographer (*Cecil v IRC* 36 TLR 164), a stockbroker (*Barker & Sons v IRC* [1919] 2 KB 222), an insurance broker (*Durant v IRC* 12 TC 245). In addition, in two cases decided on their specific facts, it was held that the following did not exercise professions: a tax agent (*Currie v IRC* 12 TC 245) and a firm of chartered secretaries (*Burt & Co v IRC* [1919] 2 KB 650). In a later case concerning the surcharge under TCA 1997, s 441, *MacGiolla Mhaith v Cronin & Associates Ltd* III ITR 211, it was held that an advertising agency did not carry on a profession. The Revenue Commissioners have indicated that they regard estate agents and quantity surveyors as carrying on professions.

The concept of a profession embraces also that of a vocation and it is in fact difficult to separate the two. It is, however, only persons carrying on a profession or vocation on their own account, as distinct from a professionally qualified person who may provide his services as an employee of another person, that are taxed under Sch D Case II. The distinction between the person carrying on an independent profession and one taxable as an employee under Sch E may materially affect the tax treatment of the person concerned. In general, the rules for deducting expenses in calculating taxable income are more liberal under Sch D Case II than under Sch E, while the income of an employee is subject to PAYE, which does not apply to the earnings of a profession.

Other persons when carrying on business or similar income earning-activities on their own account who are generally accepted by Revenue as carrying on professions include artists, architects, accountants, chartered surveyors, engineers, actuaries, solicitors, dramatists, musicians, sculptors, quantity surveyors, estate agents, insurance brokers, taxation consultants, doctors, dentists, teachers, etc.

4.2 Trading Profits

4.201 Introduction

Income tax is charged under Sch D Case I (trade) or Case II (profession) for each year of assessment on the annual profits or gains of a trade or profession carried on by an individual or other person (except a company or other body corporate). There are four stages in arriving at the amount to be charged for each year of assessment during which the trade or profession continues:

(a) the determination of the taxable profit (or loss) of each period of account of the trade or profession;
(b) the allocation of the taxable profit (or loss) of the various periods of account to years of assessment;
(c) the computation for each year of assessment of the appropriate capital allowances in respect of qualifying capital expenditure incurred for the trade or profession; and
(d) the deduction from the taxable profit assessable for each year of assessment of the capital allowances appropriate to that year.

The annual profits and gains of a trade or profession chargeable to income tax under Sch D Cases I and II are determined, in the first instance, for each period for which the taxpayer makes up the accounts of his business, ie for each 'period of account'. When these taxable profits have been determined for each relevant period of account, it is then necessary to allocate them to the year or years of assessment in which they are to be taxed. Assessments to income tax under Sch D Cases I and II are made on the taxable profits of 'basis periods' which generally, but not always, coincide with the taxpayer's periods of account.

Under the current year basis, the normal basis period for the assessment for a tax year (eg 2015) is the 12-month period of account ending in the same tax year (for example, the 12-month period of account ending 30 September 2015). There are exceptions to the normal current year basis period rule for the first two tax years of a trade or profession, for the year in which a trade or profession is permanently discontinued, for cases where there are periods of account of less than or more than 12 months ending in a tax year, or where there is no period of account ending in a tax year. The basis period rules for the current year basis are covered more fully in **4.203** to **4.208**.

The computation of the taxable profits (or losses) of a trade or profession starts with the profit (or loss) disclosed in the taxpayer's accounts for each period of account. In most cases, various adjustments to the accounting profit are required when the income tax computation rules differ from the accounting treatment adopted. The taxable profit (or tax loss) resulting from the Sch D Case I or Case II computation, after all necessary adjustments have been made, is often referred to as the 'adjusted tax profit' (or 'adjusted tax loss'). The terms 'taxable profits' or 'tax loss' are, however, also used in this book to denote respectively an adjusted tax profit or adjusted tax loss.

The profits and gains taxable under Sch D Cases I and II are confined to those of an income or revenue nature. Capital gains and any other profits of a capital nature are excluded and, if they were included as receipts in arriving at the accounting profit, must be deducted in the tax computation. Conversely, no deduction is in general given for capital expenditure in calculating the taxable profit or loss nor for any amortisation or depreciation of capital assets and, to the extent that any such items have been deducted in the taxpayer's accounts, the necessary adjustments must be made in the tax computation. The format of the Sch D Case I (or Case II) computation of the taxable profits (or loss) is illustrated in **4.202**.

While no deduction is allowed for capital expenditure or for its amortisation in arriving at the adjusted tax profit or loss chargeable to income tax, relief is given separately by way of 'capital allowances' in respect of capital expenditure incurred in providing certain types of capital assets for use in the trade or profession. The scheme of capital allowances, discussed in detail in **Division 6**, is intended to enable the relevant capital expenditure to be written off over the period of use of the assets in the business.

Separate computations are required of the adjusted tax profit or loss on the one hand and of the capital allowances on the other. In the case of an individual or other person chargeable to income tax, the adjusted tax profit or loss for each period of account, that is allocated by the basis period rules to years of assessment, is taken from the Sch D Case I or II computation before taking capital allowances into account. Any reference in this book to a taxable profit or tax loss of a trade or profession is, in any income tax application, a reference to the adjusted tax profit or loss before capital allowances. The manner of granting capital allowances in assessing the profits of a trade or profession to income tax is dealt with in **Division 4.3**.

The rules for calculating the taxable profits or tax losses of a trade or profession under Sch D Cases I and II are for all practical purposes identical. Unless expressly indicated to the contrary any such reference is to be taken as applying equally to the taxing of a profession under Sch D Case II.

4.202 The Sch D Case I computation

The Sch D Case I or Case II taxable profit for a period of account is arrived at by making various 'add backs' and 'deductions' to adjust the pre-tax accounting profit shown by the taxpayer's financial accounts to comply with the rules for computing profits chargeable under Sch D Case I and generally to reflect the proper income tax principles. It may also be necessary on occasions to make adjustments if the accounting profits are not ascertained in accordance with normal principles of commercial accounting. If any items that should be treated as trading receipts under income tax law have not been included in the profit and loss account, the appropriate amounts must be added in the tax computation. Similarly, if any deductible expenses have been charged directly to reserves or dealt with otherwise than in the profit and loss account the appropriate deduction should be made in the tax computation.

The Taxes Consolidation Act 1997 contains a number of rules related to the calculation of the taxable profits of a trade and, where relevant, these rules must be applied irrespective of the accounting treatment adopted by the person carrying on the trade. There is a considerable volume of case law regarding the interpretation of the statutory phrase 'the annual profits or gains arising or accruing from the trade'. The statutory rules and case law and their practical effect on the computation of the taxable profits of a trade are discussed in **Division 5**.

The form of the Sch D Case I computation which converts the taxpayer's pre-tax accounting profit or loss into an adjusted tax profit or loss (before capital allowances) is set out below. Clearly, not all the adjustments illustrated in the table will apply in every case and other types of adjustment not mentioned may be needed from time to time. The references to items charged or credited in the accounts are to expenses or receipts debited or credited in the profit and loss account before the pre-tax accounting balance used as the starting figure in the tax computation is struck. In many cases, items such as capital expenditure, appropriations of profit, capital profits, etc may not have been put through the profit and loss account so that no adjustment may be necessary.

Sch D Case I computation:

Mr Alpha Beta: accounts year ended 30 June 2015:

	Ref
Pre-tax profit (or loss) per accounts	
Add backs:	
Disallowable expenses charged in accounts	
not wholly and exclusively for trade purposes	**5.305/5.306**
Capital expenditure	**5.307**
Depreciation of fixed assets	**5.307**
Losses on sales of fixed assets	**5.307**
Other capital losses	**5.307**
Losses not connected with trade	**5.303/5.304**
Business entertainment expenses	**5.313**
Losses recoverable by insurance	**5.301**
Annual payments, royalties, etc payable less income tax deductible at source	**5.316**
Increase in general bad debt provisions during the year	**5.314**
Interest paid on overdue tax	**5.315**
Expenses deductible from income taxed under other Cases or Schedules[1]	
Other disallowable debits in accounts	
Provisions for losses not realised	**5.302**
Appropriations of profits and/or transfers to reserves[2]	
Trading receipts not credited in accounts[3]	
Profits realised this year accrued and disallowed in previous year(s)[4]	
Deductions:	
Income taxed under other Cases or Schedules[5]	
Items credited in accounts but not trading receipts chargeable under Sch D Case I or II	

Annual payments, royalties, etc received less income tax deducted at source	
Profits on sales of fixed assets	**5.202/5.203**
Other receipts or profits of a capital nature	**5.202/5.209**
Interest received on tax overpaid	**5.210**
Decreases in general bad debt provisions (previously added back) during the year	**5.314**
Trading profits accrued in accounts but not yet realised[4]	
Any allowable expenses for year not charged in the accounts	
Deductions under special statutory rules or Revenue concessions	**5.308**
Sch D Case I profit (or loss) before stock relief	
Less:	
Stock relief deduction (if relevant)	**7.106/7.107**
(farming trades only)[6]	
Final Sch D Case I profit (or loss) for year (before capital allowances)	

Notes:

1. Any expenses deductible in computing income taxable otherwise than under Sch D Case I (or Case II), including the appropriate proportion of any expenses incurred partly for the trade and partly for the other purpose, must be disallowed.
2. Any appropriations of profits (including the cash drawings of a sole trader or the partners in a firm) charged in the accounts must be added back (but normally they would be debited in any event against capital or current account).
3. Any items properly regarded as receipts of the trade (see **5.202**) which are credited directly to reserves, without first being brought into the profit and loss account, must be added back.
4. The trader's accounting practice may involve his accruing unrealised trading profits in one year, the proceeds of which are realised in a later year. If the inspector accepts that the accrual in the first year is not to be included in the Sch D Case I computation for that year, the corresponding add back must be made in the year the profit is realised.
5. Any income or receipts credited in the accounts in respect of items taxable under other Cases or Schedules are excluded from the Sch D Case I or Case II computation, as is any taxed income received so credited.
6. Except for the trade of farming, no stock relief deduction is now available in any Sch D Case I computation.

The calculation of a tax loss is made in exactly the same way as that of a taxable profit. An accounting profit may well be converted into a taxable loss by the adjustment required in particular cases, and vice versa. Throughout this work, in referring to the adjustments to the pre-tax profit (or loss) shown in the accounts, the term 'add back' is used to indicate an adjustment against the taxpayer, ie one which increases the taxable profit or decreases a tax loss. Conversely, the term 'deduction' is used to denote an adjustment in favour of the taxpayer, ie one which decreases the taxable profit or increases a tax loss. In practice, care is required to be taken to ensure that add backs are subtracted when the starting figure in the computation is an accounting loss and to ensure that the deductions are added in any case where the starting figure is a loss.

4.203 Basis period rules

The Sch D Cases I and II basis period rules for the current year basis are contained in TCA 1997, ss 65–69. The basis period rules as they apply up to and including the transitional year 2001 are discussed in the 2002 edition of this book.

The current basis period rules are discussed under the following headings:

(a) a continuing business (see **4.204**);
(b) the commencement of a new business (see **4.205**);
(c) the discontinuance of trade (see **4.206**);
(d) the discontinuance of trade on death (see **4.207**); and
(e) change of ownership of trade (see **4.208**).

General

TCA 1997, s 65(1) provides that tax under Sch D Case I and Case II is to be charged on the full amount of the profits or gains of the year of assessment (the 'general rule'). In the absence of any other rule, this would mean that the taxable profits earned in each calendar year would be the basis of the assessment to income tax for the year of assessment ending on that 31 December. However, this statement is modified by the rules of TCA 1997, s 65(2), (3), by certain other rules in TCA 1997, ss 66, 67, 68 (commencements and cessations) and by TCA 1997, s 69 (successions to trades). These various sections provide the basis period rules for the current year basis of assessment which are discussed in detail below.

Before dealing with these basis period rules, it should be noted that the basis period for a year of assessment may not coincide with the period for which the taxpayer makes up his accounts (the period of account). If the relevant basis period rule for any tax year requires the taxable profits (or tax loss) to be taken as those of a period not coinciding with a period of account, any taxable profits (or tax loss) of a period of account which overlaps the beginning and/or the end of the basis period for the tax year concerned are apportioned on a time basis in determining the taxable profits (or tax loss) of the basis period.

Any apportionments necessary to arrive at the taxable profits or tax loss of the relevant basis period are made in months and fractions of months (TCA 1997, s 107). In practice, apportionments in months and decimals of months are acceptable.

4.204 Continuing business

Normal case

It is simplest to deal first with what may be referred to as the 'normal case'. For any trade or profession (the 'business'), the normal case of a continuing business is one where:

(a) it is customary to make up accounts for the business;
(b) accounts are made up for the period of a year (12 months) to a date within the relevant year of assessment;
(c) there is no other period of account ending in the same tax year; and

(d) the year of assessment is not one to which any of the rules of commencement (see **4.205**), cessation (see **4.206**) or change of ownership (see **4.208**) are applicable.

In this normal case of a continuing business, the basis period for any year of assessment is the 12-month period of account ending in that year. In any such case, the rule of TCA 1997, s 65(2)(a) modifies the general rule of TCA 1997, s 65(1) (see **4.203**) and requires the taxable profits of that 12-month period of account to be taken as the profits or gains of the year of assessment (before capital allowances). This normal basis period for a year of assessment may, however, be changed if the basis period for the next year of assessment is determined under any of the 'change of accounting date' rules discussed below.

Example 4.204.1

Mr A Corn, who commenced to trade in 2007, makes up accounts annually to 30 June. His taxable profits (before capital allowances) for the three years to 30 June 2016 are as follows:

	€
Y/E 30/06/2014	13,500
Y/E 30/06/2015	3,500
Y/E 30/06/2016	23,400

This is a normal continuing business case. Mr Corn's basis periods for the tax years 2013 to 2015, and the taxable profits (before capital allowances) assessable under Sch D Case I for each year are as follows:

	€
2014:	
12-month period of account to 30/6/2014	13,500
2015:	
12-month period of account to 30/6/2015	3,500
2016:	
12-month period of account to 30/6/2016	23,400

Notes:

1. It is assumed that Mr Corn continues to make up accounts to 30 June in succeeding years. For the circumstances in which his assessment could be varied if he made a change in his accounting date in 2016, see Change of Accounting Date Rules below.

Change of accounting date rules

TCA 1997, s 65(2)(b) and (c) contains other rules for determining the basis period for any year of assessment where, although it is customary to make up accounts, any of the following circumstances exist:

(a) there is more than one period of account ending on dates within that year of assessment; or

(b) the only period of account ending in that year is shorter or longer than one year; or

(c) there is no period of account made up to a date within that year.

These other rules are referred to herein as the 'change of accounting date' rules.

Where any of these change of accounting date rules apply to a year of assessment it is to be noted that it may be necessary to revise the Sch D Case I or Case II assessment for the immediately preceding tax year under the rule of TCA 1997, s 65(3). TCA 1997, s 65(3) requires the taxable profits (before capital allowances) of the basis period otherwise applicable for the previous tax year (the 'original assessment') to be compared with the taxable profits (before capital allowances) of the period ending in the previous tax year (the 'corresponding period') which corresponds to the basis period for the tax year in which the relevant change of accounting date rule applies.

Then, if the taxable profits in the original assessment for the previous year are less than the taxable profits of the corresponding period, the assessment for the previous tax year must be increased to charge an amount of taxable profits equal to the taxable profits of the corresponding period. In this case, the corresponding period becomes the basis period for that year (instead of the original basis period for that year). On the other hand, if the taxable profits in the original assessment equal or exceed the taxable profits of the corresponding period, the original assessment stands and there is no change in the basis period for the previous year.

TCA 1997, s 959AO(6) provides that where it is necessary to make an adjustment to a taxpayer's prior year tax liability by reason of a change in the accounting period any additional tax due is payable through the self assessment system at the same time as the tax for the current year is due (on or before 31 October in the year following the year for which the tax return is made or the relevant extended filing deadline if filing the tax return using the Revenue Online Service ('ROS')).

In any case where there is more than one period of account ending on dates in a year of assessment (ie where circumstance (a) occurs) the rule of TCA 1997, s 65(2)(b) provides that the taxable profits of the period of 12 months ending on the later (or latest, if more than two) of the accounting dates in that year of assessment are to be taken as 'the profits or gains of the year of assessment' as referred to in the general rule of TCA 1997, s 65(1). In other words, the said 12-month period becomes the basis period for the tax year in which there are two or more accounting dates so that the Sch D Case I or Case II assessment for the year is made on the taxable profits attributable to that basis period (except if the rule in TCA 1997, s 65(3) applies, see below).

Example 4.204.2

Take the facts of **Example 4.204.1**, except assume that Mr A Corn decides to change his normal accounting date to 31 December by making up his next accounts for the six months ending 31 December 2016. His taxable profits (before capital allowances) for the six months to 31 December 2016 are assumed to be €3,600.

Since he has now two periods of account ending in 2016, the rule of TCA 1997, s 65(2)(b) requires his basis period for that year to be taken as the 12 months ending on the later accounting date, 31 December 2016 (instead of the 12 months ending 30 June 2016 shown in **Example 4.204.1**). His 2016 taxable profits are now recalculated as follows:

2016:	€
Period 1/1/2016 to 30/6/2016	
6/12ths x €23,400 (12 months to 30/06/2016)	11,700
Period 1/7/2016 to 31/12/2016	
Taxable profits of six-month period of account	3,600
Assessable profits 2016 (subject to capital allowances)	15,300

Mr Corn's assessment for 2016 is therefore changed from the €23,400 shown in **Example 4.204.1** to the €15,300 now calculated.

Further, since this change of accounting date rule has applied for 2016, the original assessment for the previous year 2016 (€3,500 see **Example 4.204.1**) must be revised under the rule of TCA 1997, s 65(3) explained above to charge the higher taxable profits of the 12 months to 31 December 2015 (ie the 'corresponding period' ending in 2015). This results in a revised 2014 assessment of €13,450, calculated as follows:

	€
Period 1/1/2015 to 30/6/2015	
6/12ths x €3,500 (12 months to 30/06/2015)	1,750
Period 1/7/2015 to 31/12/2015	
6/12ths x €23,400 (12 months to 30/06/2016)	11,700
Assessable profits 2015 (subject to capital allowances)	13,450

For any tax year in which circumstance (b) occurs (ie the only period of account ending in the year is shorter or longer than 12 months), the rule of TCA 1997, s 65(2)(b) requires the Sch D Case I or Case II assessment to be made on the taxable profits attributable to the period of 12 months ending on the only accounting date in that year (except if the rule of TCA 1997, s 65(3) applies).

Example 4.204.3

Ms B Black, who has carried on her profession as a tax consultant for many years, has taxable profits (before capital allowances) for periods of account as follows:

	€
12 months to 30/09/2013	45,000
12 months to 30/9/2014	127,500
8 months to 31/5/2015	60,000
15 months to 31/8/2016	150,000

Her taxable profits for each of the tax years 2014 to 2016 before considering whether the rule in s 65(3) is relevant for any year are as follows:

	€	€
2014		
12-month period of account to 30/9/2014		127,500
2015:		
12 months to 31/5/2015 made up:		
Period 1/6/2014 to 30/9/2014		
4/12ths x €127,500 (12 months to 30/9/2014)	42,500	
Period 1/10/2014 to 31/5/2015		
Profits of full 8 months to 31/5/2015	60,000	
		102,500
2016:		
12 months to 31/8/2016 made up:		
12/15ths x €150,000 (15 months to 31/8/2016)		120,000

Since the change of accounting date rules apply in each of 2016 and 2015 it is necessary to consider whether or not any revision is required by the rules of TCA 1997, s 65(3) in the original assessment for either or both of the years 2015 and 2014. It is necessary to apply the rule in TCA 1997, s 65(3) firstly to the later of the two years (2014) since this will determine whether or not the profits in that year are computed under the rules of TCA 1997, s 65(2)(b) or (c), which in turn will determine whether the rule in TCA 1997, s 65(3) applies to the year 2013.

The 12 months ended 31 August 2015 is the 2015 corresponding period to that used for the 2016 assessment. The taxable profits for that corresponding period are computed as follows:

	€
Period 1/9/2014–30/9/2014	
1/12th x €127,500	10,625
Period 1/10/2014–31/5/2015– full period	60,000
Period 1/6/2015–31/8/2015	
3/15ths x €150,000	30,000
Total	100,625

Since the taxable profits of the corresponding period are less than the €102,500 originally chargeable for 2015, the basis period for that year remains the 12 months ending 31 May 2015.

The 12 months ending 31 May 2014 is the 2014 corresponding period to that finally used for the 2015 assessment under TCA 1997, s 65(2)(b). The taxable profits for that corresponding period are computed as follows:

	€
Period 1/6/2013–30/9/2013	
4/12ths x €45,000	15,000
Period 1/10/2013–31/5/2014	
8/12ths x €127,500	85,000
	100,000

Since the taxable profits of the corresponding period (€100,000) are less than the €127,500 originally chargeable for 2014, the basis period for that year remains the 12 months to 30 September 2014.

Notes:

1. Normal case, but subject to the rule in TCA 1997, s 65(3).
2. Only period of account ending in 2015 is one shorter than 12 months. Therefore assessment is on the period of 12 months ending on the only accounting date in the year (and also subject to the rule in TCA 1997, s 65(3)).
3. Only period of account ending in 2016 is one longer than 12 months. Therefore assessment is on the period of 12 months ending on the only accounting date in the year.

For any tax year where circumstance (c) occurs (ie no period of account ending in the year), the rule of TCA 1997, s 65(2)(c) requires the Sch D Case I or Case II assessment for that tax year to be made under the general rule of TCA 1997, s 65(1) (except if the rule of TCA 1997, s 65(3) applies). In other words, the taxable profits of the tax year itself (the year to 31 December) are assessed and the year to 31 December is the basis period.

Mr W White, who has traded for many years, has the following taxable profits (before capital allowances) for periods of account as follows:

	€
12 months to 31/10/2013	21,800
20 months to 30/6/2015	45,000
(next period of accounts: 12 months to 30/6/2016)	

His taxable profits for each of the tax years 2013 to 2015 (before considering if the rule in TCA 1997, s 65(3) is relevant for any year) are as follows:

	€
2013	
12-month period of account to 31/10/2013[1]	21,800
2014:	
12 months to 31/12/2014[2] made up:	27,000
12/20ths x €45,000 (20 months to 30/6/2015)	
2015	
12 months to 30/6/2015[3] made up:	
12/20ths x €45,000 (20 months to 30/6/2015)	27,000

Since the change of accounting date rules apply in each of 2015 and 2014, it is necessary to consider whether or not any revision is required by the rules of TCA 1997, s 65(3) in the original assessment for either or both of the years 2014 and 2013. It is necessary to apply the rule in TCA 1997, s 65(3) firstly to the later of the two years (2014), since this will determine whether or not the profits in that year are computed under the rules of TCA 1997, s 65(2)(b) or (c), which in turn will determine whether the rule in TCA 1997, s 65(3) applies to the year 2013.

The 12 months ended 30 June 2014 is the 2014 corresponding period to that used for the 2015 assessment. The taxable profits for that corresponding period are computed as follows:

	€
Period 1/7/2013–31/10/2013	
4/12ths x €21,800	7,267
Period 1/11/2013 to 30/6/2014	
8/20ths x €45,000	18,000
	25,267

Since the taxable profits of the corresponding period are less than the €27,000 originally chargeable for 2014, the basis period for that year remains the 12 months ending 31 December 2014 and the 2014 assessment stays at €27,000 (subject to capital allowances).

The 12 months ending 31 December 2013 is the 2013 corresponding period to that finally used for the 2014 assessment. The taxable profits for that corresponding period are computed as follows:

	€
Period 1/1/2013–31/10/2013	
10/12ths x €21,800	18,167
Period 1/11/2013 to 31/12/20122013	
2/20ths x €45,000	4,500
	22,667

Since the taxable profits of the corresponding period (€22,667) are greater than the €21,800 originally chargeable for 2013, the basis period for that year is changed to the 12 months to 31 December 2013 and the 2013 assessment is increased to €22,667 (subject to capital allowances).

Notes:

1. Normal case, but subject to the rule in TCA 1997, s 65(3).
2. No period of account ending in 2014. Therefore the assessment is on the taxable profits of the year to 31 December 2014 (and also subject to the rule in TCA 1997, s 65(3)).
3. Only period of account ending in 2015 is one longer than 12 months. Therefore assessment is on the period of 12 months ending on the only accounting date in the year.

Not customary to make up accounts

In the unusual case where it is not customary to make up accounts, the general rule of TCA 1997, s 65(1) applies (without any reference to TCA 1997, s 65(2)) to require the Sch D Case I or Case II assessment to be made on the taxable profits of the year of assessment itself (see **4.203**). The basis period in any such case is therefore the year ending 31 December.

This position might occur in the case of a once off operation or a series of transactions taxable under Sch D Case I due to being regarded as an adventure in the nature of a trade (see **4.102**). It could also occur if a trader simply does not make up accounts so that the inspector has to assess him for each tax year in which he carries on the trade on the actual taxable profits earned in that year.

4.205 Commencement of trade

In many cases the date on which a trade commences will be reasonably clear-cut. However, the issue has been the subject of a number of important cases.

In *Birmingham & District Cattle By-Products Co Ltd v IRC* 12 TC 92, a company was held to commence trading only at the point it began to receive raw materials and to turn out its product. Preparatory activities such as installing plant and machinery and executing supply and sale agreements were held not sufficient to mark the commencement of the trade (see *also Spa Estates v O'hArgain,* discussed further in **12.305**), and compare *Cannop Coal Ltd v IRC* 12 TC 31, decided on a somewhat unusual set of facts).

Where a person who is already trading initiates a new set of activities, it will (as usual) be an issue of fact whether or not those activities represent an extension of his existing activities as opposed to the launch of a new and distinct trade (see *Howden Boiler Armaments Co v Stewart* 9 TC 205; *Cannon Industries Ltd v Edwards* 42 TC 625, *O'Loan v Noone* II ITR 147). In the latter case, a separate computation of taxable profits will be necessary in respect of the new trade, and the commencement rules will apply. The fact that a single set of accounts for two (or more) activities has been prepared does not necessarily mean that a person is carrying on a single trade (*Fullwood Foundry Ltd v IRC* 9 TC 101). Conversely, the initiation or acquisition of new activities may lead to formation of a new trade altogether and the discontinuance of the old trade (see *George Humphries & Co v Cook* 19 TC 121 where the amalgamation of two trades gave rise to a new trade). Similarly, an existing trader may reduce his activities or otherwise alter his course of trading so that his existing trade ceases and a new trade commences (see *Gordon v Blair Ltd v IRC*, discussed at **4.206**).

TCA 1997, s 66(1), (2) contain special rules which are applied to determine the basis period for each of the first two tax years of a new trade or profession (the new business). In addition, TCA 1997, s 66(3) provides a relief in relation to a particular position which may arise in the second year (see below). The commencement rules are as follows:

First tax year

Where a new business commences in a year of assessment from 2001 onwards the Sch D Case I or Case II assessment for the tax year is made on the full amount of taxable profits arising from the date of commencement of the business to the following 31 December.

TCA 1997, s 66(1) provides a possible alternative, in that the inspector is permitted to assess the average taxable profits of such period (not being a period greater than one year) as the case may require. In fact, with the rule of TCA 1997, s 107 permitting the apportionment on a time basis of the profits of any period of account spanning the beginning or end of a year of assessment, the need for any separate one year's average does not appear to arise.

Second tax year

TCA 1997, s 66(2) provides that the Sch D Case I or II assessment for the second year of assessment shall be made as follows:

(a) where there is only one period of account ending on a date falling in the year of assessment and that period is for one year, then the profits for that year are to be assessed;

(b) where (a) does not apply, but there is only one period of account ending on a date falling in the year of assessment and that date falls more than one year after the commencement of the business, then the profits for the year ending on that date are to be assessed;

(c) where (a) does not apply, but there are two or more periods of account ending on dates falling in the year of assessment and the latest of those dates falls more than one year after the commencement of the business, then the profits for the year ending on that date are to be assessed; and

(d) where none of (a), (b) or (c) apply, the profits for the year of assessment itself are to be assessed.

Example 4.205.1

Mr S Smith commences a profession on 1 June 2014. His opening period of accounts and related taxable profits (before capital allowances are as follows):

12 months to 31/05/2015 €90,000

His basis periods and the taxable profits (before capital allowances) assessed for the first two tax years are as follows:

	€
2014 (1st year)[1]	
Actual profits of tax year 1/06/2014 to 31/12/2014	
7/12ths x €90,000	52,500
2015 (2nd year)[2]	
Y/E 31/05/2015	90,000

Notes:

1. In practice, a precise *per diem* apportionment would be required.
2. The period of account to 31/05/2015 ends on a date falling in the tax year, and as this is the only period of account which does so and is for a period of twelve months the taxable profits for the period are assessed.

Example 4.205.2

Ms M Poppins commenced a trade on 1 March 2013. Her opening period of accounts and the related taxable profits (before capital allowances) are as follows (subject to the potential application of TCA 1997, s 65(3) – see 'Third and Subsequent Tax Years' below):

	Taxable profits
	€
5 months to 31/07/2013	6,000
12 months to 31/07/2014	19,200
12 months to 31/07/2015	18,000
3 months to 31/10/2015	7,000

Her basis periods and the taxable profits (before capital allowances) assessed for the first two tax years are as follows:

	Taxable profit
2013 (1st year)[1]	€
(Actual profits of tax year: 1/03/2013 to 31/12/2013)	
Period 1/03/2013–31/07/2013	6,000
Period 1/08/2013–31/12/2013	
5/12 x 19,200 (12 months to 31/07/2014)	8,000
	14,000
2014 (2nd year)[2]	
Period of account ending 31/07/2014	19,200

Note:

1. In practice, a precise *per diem* apportionment would be required.
2. The period of account to 31/07/2014 ends on a date falling in the tax year, and as this is the only period of account which does so and is for a period of 12 months the taxable profits for the period are assessed. This is subject to the potential application of TCA 1997, s 65(3): see **Example 4.205.5** below.

The question of whether there is any 'second year excess' as discussed below is only relevant in providing relief for the third year's assessment (see **Example 4.205.8**). The second year's assessment is never affected by this issue.

Example 4.205.3

Ms J Andrews commences a trade on 1 February 2013. Her opening periods of account and the related taxable profits (before capital allowances) are as follows:

	€
8 Months to 30/09/2013	16,000
6 months to 31/03/2014	43,400
12 months to 31/03/2015	121,800

Her basis periods and the taxable profits (before capital allowances) for the first two tax years are as follows:

	€
2013 (1st year)[1]	
Period 1/02/2013 to 31/12/2013 (actual profits of the tax year)	
Period 1/2/2013–30/09/2013	16,000
Period 1/10/2013 to 31/12/2013	
3/6ths x €43,400 (6 months to 31/03/2014)	21,700
	37,700
2014 (2nd year)[2]	
Profits of 12 months 31/03/2014[2]	
Period 1/04/2013 to 30/09/2013	
6/8ths x €16,000 (8 months to 30/09/2013)	12,000
Period 1/10/2013 to 31/03/2014	43,400
	55,400

Notes:

1. In practice, a precise *per diem* apportionment of taxable profits would be required.
2. The period of account has an end date falling in the tax year, and is the only period of account which does so; furthermore, that end date falls more than one year after the date of the commencement of the trade. Accordingly, the profits for the year to that end date are assessed. This is subject to the potential application of TCA 1997, s 65(3): see **Example 4.205.6** below.
3. The question of whether there is any 'second year excess' as discussed below is only relevant in providing relief for the third year's assessment (see **Example 4.205.9**). The second year's assessment is never affected by this issue.

Example 4.205.4

Mr Van Dyck commenced a profession on 1 August 2012. His opening period of accounts and the related taxable profits (before capital allowances) are as follows:

	Taxable profits
	€
10 months to 31/5/2013	39,000
12 months to 31/5/2014	93,600
12 months to 31/5/2015	48,900

His basis periods and the taxable profits (before capital allowances) assessed for the first two tax years are as follows:

	Taxable profit
2012 (1st year)[1]	€
(Actual profits of tax year: 1/8/2012 to 31/12/2012)	
5/10ths x €39,000 (10 months to 31/5/2013)	19,500
	19,500
2013 (2nd year)[2]	
(Actual profits of tax year)	
Period 1/01/2013–31/05/2013	
5/10ths x €39,000 (10 months to 31/5/2013)	19,500

Period 1/06/2013 to 31/12/2013	
7/12ths x €93,600	54,600
	74,100

Notes:

1. In practice a precise *per diem* apportionment would be required.
2. The period of account to 31 May 2013 ends on a date falling in the tax year, and is the only period of account which does so; however that end date falls less than one year after the date of commencement of the profession. Accordingly, the actual profits for the year of assessment are assessed. This is subject to the potential application of TCA 1997, s 65(3) (see **Example 4.205.7** below).
3. The question of whether there is any 'second year excess' as discussed below cannot arise in this case since the assessment for the second year is already based on the actual profits of that year.

Third and subsequent tax years

In the normal case, where there is only one period of account ending in the third tax year and that is a period of 12 months, the basis period for the third tax year is that 12-month period of account. In any other case, the 'change of accounting date' rules of TCA 1997, s 65(2)(b) and (c) are applied in the manner described in **4.204** to determine the fourth and subsequent years (unless and until the rules of cessation apply on a permanent discontinuation of the trade or profession, see **4.206**). In other words, the basis period rules for a continuing business are applied – ie the general rule of TCA 1997, s 65(1) as modified by TCA 1997, s 65(2)(a) or s 65(2)(b) or (c) (see **4.204**), whichever is appropriate, applies from the third year onwards.

Example 4.205.5

Take the facts of **Example 4.205.2** where Ms Poppin's taxable profits for the first two years have been determined. For the third tax year 2015, there are two periods of accounts made up to dates in that year. Therefore TCA 1997, s 65(2)(b) requires the assessment for the year to be made on the taxable profits for the 12 months ending on the later of these two dates. The basis period for 2015 is therefore the 12 months to 31 October 2015. The taxable profits (before capital allowances) assessable for 2015 are computed as follows:

	€
Period 1/11/2014–31/07/2015	
9 months to 31/07/2015	
9/12ths x €18,000 (12 months to 31/07/2015)	13,500
3 months to 31/10/2015 (full profits)	7,000
	20,500

The 2015 assessment (subject to capital allowances) is therefore made on €20,500 (unless there is any 'second year excess' available for relief: see that subheading below).

Prior to the enactment of FA 2003, s 11 there was some doubt as to whether TCA 1997, s 65(3) took priority over TCA 1997, s 66(2) in computing the profits of the second year of trading (see the discussion in the 2002 edition of this book). With effect from 1 January 2003, the doubt has been removed by providing that TCA 1997, s 65(3) is to apply 'notwithstanding anything to the contrary in s 66(2)'. This means that since the change of accounting date rules apply in 2015 it is necessary to consider whether or not any revision is required by the rules of TCA 1997, s 65(3) in the original assessment for 2014.

The 12 months ended 31 October 2014 is the 2014 corresponding period to that used for the 2015 assessment. The taxable profits for that corresponding period are computed as follows:

Period 1/11/2013– 31/10/2014:	€
Period 1/11/2013 – 31/07/2014	
9/12ths x 19,200 (12 months to 31/07/2014)	14,400
Period 1/08/2013 – 31/10/2014	
3/12ths x €18,000 (12 months to 31/07/2015)	4,500
Total	18,900

Since the taxable profits of the corresponding period are less than the €19,200 originally chargeable for 2014, the basis period for 2014 remains the 12 months ended on 31 July 2014.

Example 4.205.6

Take the facts of **Example 4.205.3** where Ms Andrew's taxable profits for the first two years have been determined.

For the third tax year 2015 there is a 12-month period of account made up to 31 March 2015. Therefore, since there is only one period of account ending in the third tax year and it is a period of 12 months, the basis period is that 12-month period of account. The taxable profits (before capital allowances) assessable for 2015 are as follows:

2015	12 months to 31/3/2015	€121,800

The 2015 assessment (subject to capital allowances) is therefore made on €121,800 (unless there is any 'second year excess' available for relief (see **4.205.9** below)).

Example 4.205.7

Take the facts of **Example 4.205.4** where Mr Van Dyck's taxable profits for the first two years have been determined.

For the third tax year 2015 there is a 12-month period of account made up to 31 May 2015. Therefore, since there is only one period of account ending in the third tax year and it is a period of 12 months, the basis period is that 12-month period of account. The taxable profits (before capital allowances) assessable for 2015 are as follows:

2015	12 months to 31/5/2015	€48,900

The 2015 assessment (subject to capital allowances) is therefore made on €48,900 (unless there is any 'second year excess' available for relief (see **4.205.8** below). As TCA 1997, s 65(2) ('Change of accounting date') has no application, no question arises of applying TCA 1997, s 65(3) to the second year of assessment.

Relief for 'second year excess'

TCA 1997, s 66(3) gives a person chargeable to income tax the right to claim a special relief if the amount of the profits otherwise assessable in respect of the second year of his trade or profession (the 'original taxable profits') exceeds the amount of the taxable profits arising in the second year of assessment ending 31 December (the 'actual taxable profits'). Any such excess of the original taxable profits of the second tax year over the actual taxable profits is referred to herein as the 'second year excess'.

In ascertaining whether or not there is a second year excess, the respective taxable profits are taken before deducting any capital allowances. This rule applies equally in a case where the profits otherwise assessable for the second year have been computed in accordance with TCA 1997, s 65(3).

The taxpayer's relief for the second year excess (if any) is given as a deduction from the amount of the assessment which would otherwise be made for the third year of assessment (before capital allowances). In order to obtain this relief, the taxpayer must specifically claim it when submitting his return of income for the third year of assessment (due no later than the 31 October after the end of the third year or the relevant extended filing date if submitting his return of income using the Revenue Online Service ('ROS'), see **2.103**).

If the amount of the second year excess is greater than the amount of the third tax year's taxable profits (before capital allowances), then the part of the second year excess which cannot be absorbed by the third year's taxable profits is treated as if it were a loss of the trade or profession eligible for relief by carry forward under TCA 1997, s 382. This loss carry forward is then eligible for set off against the profits of the trade or profession assessable for the fourth and later tax years until fully absorbed (see **4.402**).

It is to be noted that the existence of a second year excess does not alter the basis period for either the second or third year of the new business. Where a second year excess arises, it is given merely as a relief to reduce the assessment for the third tax year or, if any part of the second year excess is carried forward, to reduce the assessment for a later tax year.

Example 4.205.8

Take the facts of **Example 4.205.2** where Ms Poppins computes her actual taxable profits for the second year and computes a 'second year excess' as follows:

	€
Period 1 January 2014 – 31 December 2014:	
Period 1/1/2014 – 31/7/2014	
7/12ths x €19,200 (12 months to 31/07/2014)	11,200
Period 1/8/2014 – 31/12/2014	
5/12ths x 18,000 (12 months to 31/07/2015)	7,500
Actual taxable profits 2014	18,700
Compare with original assessment 2014 (as above)	19,200
Second year excess	500

In sending in her tax return for 2014, Ms Poppins makes a claim under TCA 1997, s 66(3) to set the second tax year excess off against her Sch D Case I assessment for 2015. The result is as follows:

	€
Taxable profits 2015 (before capital allowances)	
Basis period (12 months to 31/10/2015)	20,500
Deduct	
Second year excess	500
Reduced assessment 2015 (before capital allowances)	20,000

Example 4.205.9

Take the facts of **Example 4.205.3** where Ms Andrews computes her actual taxable profits for the second year and computes a 'second year excess' as follows:

Period 1 January 2014 – 31 December 2014:	€
Period 1/1/2014 – 31/3/2014	
3/6ths x €43,400 (6 months to 31/03/2014)	21,700
Period 1/4/2014 – 31/12/2014	
9/12ths x 121,800 (12 months to 31/03/2015)	91,350
Actual taxable profits 2014	113,050
Compare with original assessment 2014 (as above)	55,400
Second year excess	Nil

Since there is no second year excess, the third year's assessment remains unchanged.

Capital allowances and trading losses

The manner in which capital allowances and balancing charges are given or made in the opening years of a new business is explained in **4.304**. The effect of losses in the opening years is dealt with in **4.409**.

4.206 Cessation of trade

TCA 1997, s 67(1) provides separate basis period rules for the final tax years of a trade or profession which is permanently discontinued. These may be referred to as the rules of 'cessation'. Before these rules can be applied, it is necessary to establish that there is in fact a permanent discontinuance, as distinct from a temporary cessation of trading, and then to fix the date on which the permanent discontinuance has occurred.

The question of when a trade (or profession) is permanently discontinued is discussed in more detail below. For ease of reference, the word 'cessation' is used herein to denote a permanent discontinuance of a trade or profession.

Final tax year

For the year of assessment in which the cessation occurs, the Sch D Case I or Case II assessment is made on the taxable profits of the period beginning on the first day of the year of assessment (ie 1 January) in that year and ending on the date of cessation (TCA 1997, s 67(1)(a)(i)).

This basis period rule for the final year of assessment applies notwithstanding any other provision in TCA 1997. If, for example, the cessation occurs in the tax year after that in which the trade had commenced (ie in the second year of assessment), the cessation rule applies to tax the profits of the actual period of trading in the final year and overrides the second year commencement rules (see **4.205**).

If the profits of the final tax year have already been assessed on the continuing business basis (normally on the taxable profits of the 12-month period of accounts ending in that year), then the figures must be revised so that the taxpayer is charged to income tax by reference to the actual taxable profits of the final tax year. Any tax overpaid by reference to an assessment or computation of tax made on any other basis must be repaid or, if the tax already assessed and/or paid is too low, the necessary additional assessment must be made to correct the position.

Penultimate tax year

In the case of the cessation of a trade or profession, TCA 1997, s 67(1)(a)(ii) provides a special rule for the assessment of the tax year preceding that in which the cessation occurs. The effect of this rule is to require the Sch D Case I or Case II assessment for the penultimate year to be made on the higher of:

(a) the taxable profits on which the person chargeable would be assessed for the year if he or she had not ceased to trade; or

(b) the taxable profits arising in the penultimate year ending 31 December (the actual taxable profits).

The taxable profits taken in (a) are those determined for the year of assessment in question under the rules for a continuing business (see **4.204**) or, if the penultimate year is also one of the opening years of the business, those arrived at under the rules of commencement (see **4.205**). Therefore, in the normal case of a continuing business which has made up accounts (except, perhaps, the final year) for 12-month periods of account ending on the same date each year, the taxable profits used in (a) are normally those of the 12-month period of account ending in the penultimate tax year.

If the profits of the penultimate year have already been assessed on the figure determined in (a), and if it turns out that the actual taxable profits of the penultimate year are higher, then the inspector is required to make the necessary additional assessment to charge the higher amount of profits. This means that the basis period for the penultimate tax year becomes the 12 months ending on 31 December of that year.

If the taxable profits arrived at in (a) are higher than the actual taxable profits of the penultimate year, there is no change in the basis period for the penultimate year due to the cessation. The assessment continues to be made on the taxable profits of the relevant basis period determined under the other current year basis of assessment rules.

Example 4.206.1

Mr M Maroon, who has traded for many years making up accounts to 31 May, ceases to trade on 31 August 2015. He has the following taxable profits and a tax loss (before capital allowances) for his last three periods of account:

	€
12 months to 31/5/2014	
Taxable profit	16,800
12 months to 31/05/2015	
Taxable profit	24,000
3 months to 31/08/2015	
Tax loss	(3,000)

If he had not ceased to trade, Mr Maroon's Sch D Case I assessments (before capital allowances) for 2014 and 2015 would have been made as follows:

	€
2014:	
Taxable profits (12 months to 31/5/2014)	16,800
2015:	
Taxable profits (12 months to 31/05/2015)	24,000

Following the cessation of trade on 31 August 2015, the assessments (before capital allowances) for these two tax years have to be recomputed as follows:

2014 (penultimate year):	€
Original assessment (as above)	16,800
Possible revised assessment to taxable profits of 12 months to 31/12/2014 (actual year)	
Period 1/1/2014–31/05/2014	
5/12ths x €16,800 (12 months to 31/5/2014)	7,000
Period 1/06/2014 to 31/12/2014	
7/12ths x €24,000 (12 months to 31/05/2015)	14,000
Total	21,000
Final assessment	21,000

(since the actual taxable profits for the year are higher than the original assessment of €16,800)

2015 (final year):	€
Period 1/01/2015 to 31/08/2015:	
Period 1/01/2015 to 31/05/2015	
5/12ths x €24,000 (12 months to 31/05/2015)	10,000
Period 1/06/2015 to 31/08/2015	
Actual tax loss of period	(3,000)
Taxable profits	7,000

The basis period for the final year 2015 is the period from 1 January 2015 to 31 August 2015 (date of cessation) and therefore the profits assessable are €7,000.

Example 4.206.2

Take the facts of **Example 4.206.1**, except assume that Mr Maroon's taxable profits (before capital allowances) for the 12-month period of accounts ending 31 May 2014 were €30,000 (and not €16,800).

On this assumption, his final Sch D Case I assessments (before capital allowances) for 2014 and 2015 are as follows:

2014 (penultimate year):	€
Original assessment (12 months to 31/5/2014)	30,000
Possible revised assessment to taxable profits of 12 months to 31/12/2014	
Period 1/01/2014 to 31/05/2014	
5/12ths x €30,000 (12 months to 31/05/2014)	12,500
Period 1/06/2014 to 31/12/2014	
7/12ths x €24,000 (12 months to 31/05/2015)	14,000[1]
	26,500
Final assessment	30,000[1]

(original assessment not changed since it is higher than actual taxable profits of the penultimate year)

2015 (final year):

Final assessment (same as **Example 4.206.1**)	€7,000

Notes:

1. The basis period for the penultimate year 2014 remains the 12 months ended 31 May 2014.

Example 4.206.3

Mr H Hay, who has traded for many years, makes up accounts to 30 September and ceases to trade on 31 March 2015. He has the following taxable profits (before capital allowances) for the last three periods of account:

			€
Period	Y/E 30/9/2013	Taxable profits	36,000
	Y/E 30/9/2014	Taxable profits	25,000
	6 months to 31/3/2015	Taxable profits	4,000

If he had not ceased to trade, Mr H Hay's Sch D Case I assessments (before capital allowances) for 2013 and 2014 would have been made up as follows:

		€
2013	Taxable profits (12 months to 30/9/2013)	36,000
2014	Taxable profits (12 months to 30/9/2014)	25,000

Following the cessation of trade on 31 March 2015, the assessment (before capital allowances) for 2014 has to be recomputed as follows:

		€
2014	Penultimate year	
	Original assessment (as above)	25,000

Possible revised assessment to taxable profits of 12 months to 31/12/2014 (actual basis)

	€
Period 1/1/2014 to 30/9/2014	
9/12ths x €25,000 (12 months to 30/9/2014)	18,750
Period 1/10/2014 to 31/12/2014	
3/6ths x €4,000	2,000
	20,750

No revision is made since the taxable profits for 2014, €25,000, are higher than the actual profits for the year, €20,750.

Cessation of trade within three years of commencement

A permanent discontinuance of trade may occur in circumstances where there is an overlapping of the cessation rules with those of commencement. Under the current year basis of taxation, this may happen if the trade (or profession) ceases in the third year of assessment of a new business, or earlier. For example, a business which commences on 1 June 2013 (in 2013) and ceases on 31 March 2015 (in 2015) has 2014 as its second year of assessment to be assessed under the commencement rules of s 66(2). However, 2014 is also the penultimate year of assessment so that the cessation rules of s 67(1)(a)(ii) may also apply to it.

In such a case, the assessments for the opening tax years are first determined under the rules of commencement (see **4.205**). Then, the rules of cessation are applied to the final and penultimate tax years and any necessary revision of the assessments are made for those years under those rules. In principle, the rules of cessation (contained in TCA 1997, s 67(1)) apply in priority to the rules of commencement where there is a difference for any year affected by the cessation rules. However, if the cessation occurs in the third tax year of the business, the taxpayer remains entitled to claim a set off for any 'second year excess' (see **4.205**) against the amount assessable for the third (and final) tax year.

Example 4.206.4

Mr C Brady commenced trade on 1 March 2013 and has the following taxable profits (before capital allowances) for his periods of account:

	€
12 months to 28/02/2014	6,000
12 months to 28/02/2015	4,000
10 months to 31/12/2015	8,000

Applying the rules of commencement, Mr Brady's taxable profits for the first three years of assessment are as follows:

	€
2013:	
Period 1/3/2013 to 31/12/2013	
10/12ths x €6,000 (12 months to 28/02/2014	5,000
2014:	
Period of account of one year (12 months to 28/02/2014)	6,000
2015:	
Basis period (12 months to 28/02/2015)	4,000
	15,000

Mr Brady ceases to trade on 31 December 2015. He has to apply the rules of cessation to determine the taxable profits (before capital allowances) for the penultimate (2014) and final tax year (2015) as follows:

	€
2014:	
Original assessment (as above)	6,000
Possible revised assessment to taxable profits of 12 months to 31/12/2014 (actual basis)	
Period 1/1/2014 to 28/02/2014	
2/12ths x €6,000 (12 months to 28/2/2014)	1,000
Period 1/3/2014 to 31/12/2014	
10/12ths x €4,000 (12 months to 28/02/2015)	3,333
	4,333
Final assessment 2014	6,000

(original assessment not changed since it is higher than the actual taxable profits of the penultimate year (€4,333))

2015:

1/1/2015 to 31/12/2015	
Period 1/1/2015 to 28/02/2015	
2/12ths x €4,000 (12 months to 28/02/2015)	667
Period 1/3/2015 to 31/12/2015	
Full taxable profits of period of account	8,000
	8,667

Mr Brady claims relief under TCA 1997, s 66(3) for a 'second year excess' computed as follows:

	€	
Actual taxable profits of 2nd tax year 2014		
Period 1/1/2014 to 31/12/2014	4,333	(as above)
Compare with final assessment for 2014	6,000	(as above)
Therefore, the second year excess is	1,667	

The assessment is finally made for all the tax years as follows:

	€
2013 (first tax year)	
Amount under commencement rules	5,000
2014 (second year and penultimate year)	
Original assessment (not changed by cessation rule)	6,000
2015 (third year and final year)	
Amount under cessation rule	8,667
Less relief for second year excess	(1,667)
Amount fully assessed	7,000

Short-lived businesses

A special rule is contained in TCA 1997, s 68, which provides in effect that the taxpayer may elect that the total amounts of profits assessed of any trade or profession which commences and ceases within three years of assessment should equal the actual profits arising in that period.

Notice in writing must be served on the Inspector where it is proposed to make a claim under TCA 1997, s 68. The notice must be given before the specified return date (within the meaning of TCA 1997, s 959A) for the year in which the trade is discontinued.

The purpose of the section is to grant relief in a situation where the taxable profits for the three year period could in fact exceed the actual profits earned. This could arise in a situation where the profits decrease in year two with the result that the taxable profits for year two will be the profits assessed in accordance with TCA 1997, s 66(2) rather than the actual profits. While it is possible to get relief under s 66(3) for the second year excess, against the taxable profits of subsequent years, it may be that the excess will be greater than the taxable profits and the third (and final) year so that no relief would otherwise be available.

Example 4.206.5

Mr H Casement commences trading on 1 February 2013 and ceases on 30 November 2015 with the taxable profits for the period:

	€
12 months to 31/1/2014	18,000
12 months to 31/1/2015	10,000
10 months to 30/11/2015	2,000

Applying the rules of commencement, Mr Casement's taxable profits for the first three years of assessment are as follows:

	€
2013	
Period 1/2/2013 to 31/12/2013	
11/12ths x €18,000 (12 months to 31/1/2014)	16,500
2014	
Period of account of one year ending on 31/1/2014	18,000

Mr Casement ceases to trade on 30 November 2015. The rules of cessation must be applied to determine the taxable profits (before capital allowances) of the penultimate (2014) and final (2015) tax years as follows:

	€
2014	
Original assessment (as above)	18,000
Possible revised assessment to taxable profits 31/12/2014	
Period 1/1/2014 to 31/1/2014	
1/12ths x €18,000 (12 months to 31/01/2014)	1,500
Period 1/2/2014 to 31/12/2014	
11/12ths x €10,000 (12 months to 31/01/2015)	9,166
Total	10,666
Final assessment	18,000

(Original assessment stands as it is higher than the actual profits of €10,666)

	€
2015	
1/1/2015 to 30/11/2015	
Period 1/1/2015 to 31/1/2015	
1/12th x €10,000	833
Period 1/2/2015 to 30/11/2015 (10 months to 30/11/2015)	2,000
	2,833

Mr Casement claims relief under TCA 1997, s 66(3) for the second year excess as follows:

	€
Assessable profits 2014 (as above)	18,000
Actual profits 2014 (as above)	10,666
	7,334

As the second year excess (€7,334) is greater than the taxable profits of the following year (€2,833) relief for the full amount of the excess cannot be obtained. The assessable profits, but for TCA 1997, s 68, would have been as follows:

	€
2013	16,500
2014	18,000
2015	Nil
	34,500

TCA 1997, s 68 provides that the taxpayer is entitled to have the taxable profits for the penultimate year (2014) reduced to the amount of the actual profits for that year. This would result in all three years being calculated on an actual basis. The taxable profits for all years will be as follows:

	€
2013	16,500
2014	10,666
2015	2,833
Total taxable profits for the period	29,999

Discontinuance of trade

Where all the activities of a trade cease, then clearly there is a discontinuance of a trade. Where only a part of those activities cease, it is a question of fact as to whether what remains can be said to be the same (although diminished) trade or whether it is a new trade. In *Rolls Royce Ltd v Bamford* [1976] STC 162, approximately 20 per cent of the activities of a trade (in terms of sales and labour costs) were transferred to a new company. The court upheld the Appeal Commissioners finding of fact that the transferred activities carried on by the new company represented a new trade and not a continuation of the old trade. The court also expressed the view that if the facts in *George Humphries & Co v Cook* (see **4.208**) had been reversed, the division of the partnership trade in that case into its component parts would have resulted in a discontinuance.

In the *Rolls Royce* case the court was careful to distinguish between the natural decline (or growth) of a trade and a sudden violent contraction (or expansion) of its activities. Thus, it seems that a trade can expand (or reduce) its scale of activities significantly over time without ceasing to be the same trade, whereas a similar expansion or reduction as a result of a single disposal (or acquisition) may give rise to a discontinuance. (As already noted in **4.205**, the acquisition of additional activities may also give rise to a discontinuance.)

In *Boland v Davis* I ITR 86, the taxpayer carried on the trade of millers and bakers. One half of the flour produced in its mills was sold to the public and the other half was used in its bakeries. The taxpayer ceased milling for a period of approximately nine months and bought in the flour it needed for its bakeries over that period. It then resumed its milling activities, although on a lesser scale. The Court upheld the Appeal Commissioners finding of fact that the company's trade had not been discontinued.

In *Gordon v Blair Ltd v IRC* 40 TC 358, a company which had been trading as brewers, ceased its brewing operations and began to sell beer supplied to its own specifications by another brewery. The finding of fact by the Appeal Commissioners that this represented a discontinuance of the old trade and the commencement of a new trade was upheld.

It is also possible that even where there is a major cessation of activities that this relates to a separate trade rather than to a part of a larger trade (see *Boland v Davis* I ITR 86 and *Connelly v Wilbey* [1992] STC 783, where such contentions were rejected on the facts).

Another important distinction which may need to be made is between a permanent and a merely temporary discontinuance. Again this will be an issue of fact and degree (see eg *Ingram v Callaghan* 45 TC 151; *Kirk & Randall Ltd v Dunn* 8 TC 663, *Robroyston Brickworks v IRC* 51 TC 230, *Wild v Madam Tussauds* 17 TC 127). The issue of temporary versus permanent discontinuance was not at issue in *Boland v Davis*, presumably on the basis that the same trade continued throughout the period, despite the cessation of milling activities.

In *Cronin v Lunham* III ITR 363 the taxpayer was a company engaged in slaughtering pigs and manufacturing meat products. The company subsequently ceased its slaughtering and manufacturing activities and acted as a distribution centre for its parent company, selling similar products to the same customers for a period of 16 months. Following the sale of the taxpayer company by its parent company to a new owner, the new owner transferred its existing slaughtering operations to the taxpayer company. There was evidence that the parent company had always intended that the taxpayer should either resume its slaughtering activities or be sold as a going concern. The factory machinery was maintained in working order and an offer to buy the assets of the taxpayer (ie on a break-up basis) was rejected. The workforce had not initially been made redundant, but were told that the factory would be reopened in the future. The court upheld the Circuit Court judge's finding of fact that there had only been a temporary cessation of trade.

Marriott v Lane [1996] STC 704 (a capital gains tax case) contains a useful review of the UK cases in this area. The learned Judge indicated that the intention to resume a trade is a strong indicator of merely temporary discontinuance where the trade is actually resumed at a later date. However, if this intention is not fulfilled and the trade is never, in fact, resumed, then the discontinuance takes effect from the date on which the trade was closed down. It is not clear how far the court's conclusions depended on the specific statutory context, which required the taxpayer to establish his position within reasonably tight time limits.

The date of the permanent discontinuance of a trade or profession is also a matter of fact in each case. In many cases, this date may be fairly obvious from the circumstances. If there is a doubt, it is necessary to have regard to all the circumstances, including the particular nature of the trading activities that were carried on. A manufacturing business may sometimes cease when production stops, the workforce is laid off and no new materials purchased, notwithstanding that sales of already manufactured goods may continue for some time as part of the selling off of the stock in trade. On the other hand, the trade of a retail store might be considered to be continuing so long as its doors remain open to the public in the ordinary way for some time after the business has ceased to buy new goods for resale.

In *O'Kane & Co v IRC* 12 TC 303, the taxpayers, after announcing their decision to retire from business as wine and spirit merchants, issued to their regular customers lists of spirits for sale under the heading 'Retiring from business'. During the same year few sales were made, but in the following year practically all the stock was sold. In part of this period, the taxpayers acquired a certain quantity of spirits under existing contracts, but made no other purchases. The Special Commissioners found that they were still carrying on their trade during the period and that the profits in question were made in the ordinary course of trade. It was held in the House of Lords that there was good evidence on which the Special Commissioners could arrive at these findings of fact and their decision was therefore upheld.

In *Hillerns & Fowler v Murray* 17 TC 77, it was held on the facts that the completion, after the dissolution of a partnership, of existing contracts for the supply of grain by a business of corn and seed merchants was a continuance of trading during the winding up and the profits were therefore taxable. (This does not mean that the completion of existing contracts after an apparent cessation of business is always a continuance of trade; in some circumstances, it may be no more than the realisation of assets after the taxpayer has permanently ceased to trade.)

In *Gloucester Railway Carriage & Wagon Co Ltd v IRC* 12 TC 720, a company was incorporated to manufacture, buy, sell, hire and let on hire wagons. The wagons were manufactured and sold either outright or on hire purchase or let out on hire. Those built for letting out on hire were capitalised in the books at a figure including the manufacturing profit. The value of those wagons was depreciated annually. When the company decided to discontinue its hire business and sell off those wagons at a surplus, it was held that the profit was assessable as the object of the company was to make a profit out of the wagons.

The case of *Keyl v Revenue and Customs Commissioners* [2016] STC 410 was a UK Upper Tier Tribunal decision and dealt with a taxpayer who transferred his trade to a company at the end of the taxpayer's period of account for a particular year of assessment. Judges Sinfield and Raghavan noted as follows 'The question raised by this appeal is whether the discontinuance of a trade at the end of a chargeable period is a discontinuance in the chargeable period. In our view, the answer is Yes ... it is not possible for the trade to end at a point in time between the end of one accounting period and the start of another that falls in neither period. The question is, where a trade ceases at the end of an accounting period, in which period does the trade end? ... In our view, an activity that is discontinued at the end of a period is not discontinued in the next period because it was never 'continued' in it: the trade is discontinued in the period that ends simultaneously with it.'

Sales after date of cessation

The fact that goods held as the stock of trade of a business may be sold after the trade has ceased does not necessarily mean that any profit realised will escape taxation altogether. In arriving at the taxable profit for the period of account ending on the date of cessation, any unsold trading stock at that date must be credited in the accounts at the value determined by applying the rules of TCA 1997, s 89(2), usually at its market value on the date of cessation. In the case of a profession taxed on an earnings basis, the closing work in progress must be valued on the similar rules of TCA 1997, s 90. This closing valuation may result in an element of profit taxable in the final period, but any additional profit realised on a later sale is not taxable as income. It may, however, give rise to a chargeable gain liable to capital gains tax.

The rules for the valuation of trading stock and work in progress on a cessation are dealt with in **5.603** and **5.604**, while rules relating to the taxation under Sch D Case IV of certain post-cessation receipts are covered in **5.605**. Note also the special rule applying to certain disposals of land in the course of winding up at **12.306**.

4.207 Discontinuance on death

A trade or profession carried on during his lifetime by an individual is, in law, treated as being permanently discontinued on the date of his death, whether or not the business is in fact carried on after that date by the deceased person's personal representatives or successors (TCA 1997, s 67(2)). It therefore follows that the income tax assessment for the tax year in which the death occurs is based on the taxable profits of the period from the preceding 1 January to the date of death (final year, TCA 1997, s 67(1)(i)). Also, the penultimate year rule of TCA 1997, s 67(1)(ii) is applied to require the assessment for the immediately preceding year to be reviewed to charge the actual taxable profits of that year to 31 December (but only if that results in a higher assessment than the original assessment for the penultimate year). Any assessment made after the date of death, whether for the penultimate or final year (or any earlier year), is made on the deceased trader's personal representatives (see **15.103**).

In practice, the Revenue will permit a deceased trader's widow, who continues to carry on his trade immediately after his death, to elect (should she wish to do so) to be taxed as if the trade were a continuing business, thereby avoiding the application of the rules of cessation to the assessments on the husband to the date of his death and avoiding the rules of commencement in assessing the widow in respect of the taxable profits from the date of death onwards. Similar treatment is extended to the situation where a widower succeeds to the trade of his deceased spouse and the terms 'widow' and 'husband' in the text should accordingly be read as covering a 'widower' or 'wife'.

A widow is permitted to make this continuing business election only if the interest which she takes in the business on her husband's death is an absolute interest and if she is the sole successor to that interest. Should the widow be left only a life interest or other form of limited interest in the business, the election is not available to her. Should she be left only a share of an absolute interest (eg if the business is bequeathed to her and her son jointly), the election is not available. In either of these cases (or if the widow becoming absolutely entitled to a sole interest decides not to make the widow's election), the cessation rules are applied in the normal way in taxing the deceased husband to the date of death and the commencement rules are used in taxing the widow from the date of death.

In any case where a widow succeeds solely and absolutely to her husband's business on his death and elects to apply the continuing business basis, the Sch D Case I assessment for the tax year in which her husband dies is apportioned between them on a time basis. The taxable profits to be apportioned are those of the basis period for the year of death taken under the ordinary rules for a continuing business (see **4.204**). The apportionment is always made by reference to the number of months and fractions of months in the year of death respectively before and after the date of death (TCA 1997, s 107(2)).

Where the widow's election is made, the capital allowances for the year of death are determined in the ordinary way as for a continuing business (see **4.302**). The total of the capital allowances for that year (after deducting any balancing charges) is then apportioned between the deceased husband and the widow on the same time basis as used for the apportionment of the taxable profits. A similar apportionment is made of any excess of balancing charges over capital allowances should such a position occur.

Example 4.207.1

Mr LMN, who has traded for many years, dies on 30 November 2014, leaving his business to his widow absolutely. She elects to have the continuing business concession applied.

Mr LMN had made up accounts annually to 31 January until 2014 when he decided to change his accounting date to 30 September by making up accounts for the eight months to 30 September 2014. Mrs LMN continues after his death to use the new accounting date. The Sch D Case I profits (before capital allowances) for the relevant periods of account are as follows:

	€
12 months ended 30/01/2014	20,400
8 months to 30/09/2014	16,000
12 months ended 30/09/2015	30,000

The first step is to determine the taxable profits assessable for 2014 (year of death) as if there were no cessation. Since there are two accounting dates in that year, the basis period for the assessment is the 12 months to 30 September 2014, the later of the two dates (TCA 1997, s 65(2)(b)) The taxable profits assessable for 2015 (again on a continuing business basis) are those of the 12-month period of accounts ending 30 September 2015, ie €30,000. The allocation of the taxable profits assessable for 2014 and 2015 is now made as follows:

Taxable profits 2014	€
Period 1/10/2013 – 31/01/2014:	
4/12ths x €20,400 (12 months to 31/01/2014)	6,800
Period 1/02/2014 – 30/09/2014:	
Full taxable profits of 8 months to 30/09/2014	16,000
	22,800

	Mr LMN deceased	*Mrs LMN*
2014 (year of death):	€	€
Period 1/01/2014 – 30/11/2014		
11/12 x €22,800[1]	20,900	
Period 1/12/2014 – 31/12/2014		
1/12 x €22,800[2]		1,900
2015 (year following death):		
All assessed on widow		30,000

Assume that there are capital allowances of €5,600 and balancing charges of €700 for 2014 and capital allowances of €3,000 and no balancing charges for 2015 (continuing business basis in each case, see **4.302**). The final net Sch D Case I income chargeable for 2014 and 2015 is then determined as follows:

	Mr LMN deceased	*Mrs LMN*
	€	€
Taxable profits allocated as above	20,900	1,900
Less:		
Capital allowances less balancing charges to be apportioned €4,900 (€5,600 – €700)		
Period 1/01/2014 – 30/11/2014		
11/12 x €4,900[1]	(4,492)	
Period 1/12/2014 – 31/12/2014		

1/12 x €4,900[2]		(408)
Net Sch D Case I assessments	16,408	1,492

2015:

Taxable profits as above	30,000
Less:	
Capital allowances	
All due to widow	(3,000)
Net Sch D Case I assessment	27,000

Notes:

1. The proportion allocated to the deceased husband is in the ratio which the part of the year ending 31 December 2014 up to the date of his death bears to the full tax year.
2. The proportion allocated to the widow for 2014 is in the ratio which the remainder of the year to 31 December 2014 bears to the full year.
3. Because of the change in accounting date the profits assessable for 2013 may need to be increased in accordance with the rule in s 65(3).

In considering whether or not to seek the concessionary continuing basis assessment, the widow should consider not only the question of whether the application of the cessation rules on her husband's death would cause any revision of the original assessment for the penultimate year, but also how her own position is likely to be affected by the expected trading results in the year or two following his death.

However, unless there is likely to be a material advantage from the combined effect of the application of the rules of cessation and commencement, it is generally likely to be simpler to make the continuing business election. Apart from avoiding revising the husband's capital allowances computations for the penultimate and final tax years to the date of death, the election may leave it unnecessary to make up accounts for the period from the last pre-death accounting date to the date of death.

4.208 Changes in ownership of business

A trade or profession may be sold or otherwise transferred as a going concern by the person who carried it on up to the date of the change. TCA 1997, s 69(1), (2) contain rules which require certain changes in the ownership of a trade or profession to be treated as the permanent discontinuance of the trade or profession and/or the commencement of a new trade or profession. They apply in cases where there is not otherwise a permanent discontinuance and/or a commencement. The rules are now described under two headings as follows:

Individual transferring business

TCA 1997, s 69(1) provides a special rule which is applied in the following circumstances:

(a) where a trade or profession (the business) has up to any given time been carried on by an individual; and

(b) where immediately after that time, the business becomes carried on by any other individual or by a partnership of persons.

Where these circumstances occur, the rule requires that the individual who carried on the business (the 'predecessor') must be taxed for all relevant years of assessment as if the business had been permanently discontinued at the time in question, ie at the time of the change of ownership of the business. The effect is to require the predecessor's Sch D Case I or Case II assessment for the tax year in which the change of ownership occurs to be based on the taxable profits of the period from the preceding 1 January to the date of the change of ownership. Also, the penultimate year rule of TCA 1997, s 67(1)(a)(ii) is applied to require the assessment for the immediately preceding tax year to be reviewed to see whether a higher assessment is needed (see **4.206**). Similarly, the rules for dealing with capital allowances on a cessation must be applied.

TCA 1997, s 69(1) does not deal with the transfer of a business by an individual to a company (except for the case of a transfer to a partnership which includes a company or companies, whether or not it also includes one or more other individuals). It does, however, deal with a transfer of business from an individual (as a sole trader) to a partnership of which the individual is a partner. For example, if an individual sole trader (Mr Orange) takes in a partner (Mr Green) on, say, 12 July 2015 so that the business is carried on from that date by Messrs Orange and Green in partnership, then TCA 1997, s 69(1) deems Mr Orange to have a permanent discontinuance of his sole trade on 12 July 2015.

Individual succeeding to business

TCA 1997, s 69(2) provides a special rule which is applied in the following circumstances:

(a) where, at any given time, an individual (the 'successor') succeeds to a trade or profession (the business); and
(b) where immediately before that time, the business was carried on by any other individual or by a partnership of persons (including a partnership in which the successor was a partner).

Where these circumstances occur, the rule requires that the successor must be taxed for all relevant years of assessment as if he or she had set up and commenced the business at the time at which he succeeded to the business. The effect is to apply the rules of commencement to determine the individual's taxable profits for the tax year in which he or she takes over the business and for the immediately following year. Also, it enables him to claim relief for any 'second year's excess' by set off against the third year's assessment (or to carry any unused excess forward for set off in a later year) (see **4.205**). Similarly, the rules governing treatment of capital allowances on a commencement are applied.

This rule deals only with cases where the successor to the trade or profession is an individual. The succession may, however, be a taking over of a business previously carried on by a partnership of persons (whether the partners are individuals, unincorporated bodies of persons or companies). The rule also applies where the individual succeeds as a sole trader to a business previously carried on by a partnership in which he or she was a partner, for example, on the death or retirement of the other partner in a two partner firm.

Succession to business

Where a person acquires the trade (as opposed to merely the trading assets) of another person, a number of analyses of the underlying facts are possible, including the following:

(a) the first person was not previously trading and carries on the newly acquired trade (so that there is a clear case of succession);
(b) the first person may already carry on a trade but carries on the newly acquired trade as a separate activity (so that there is again a clear case of succession);
(c) the first person may already carry on a trade and merges the newly acquired trade into his existing trade but in a way which constitutes a succession;
(d) the first person was not previously trading but carries on a new trade using merely the assets of the acquired trade (ie so that there is no succession);
(e) the first person may already carry on a trade and uses the acquired trade to extend that trade in a way which does not amount to a succession;
(f) the first person may already carry on a trade, but extends that trade by using merely the assets of the acquired trade (ie so that, again, there is no succession); and
(g) the first person may already carry on a trade and the acquisition of the new trade causes the formation of a new trade altogether (so that a succession does not take place).

If the person acquiring the business or the assets is setting up a trade for the first time, the commencement rules will apply to him in any event and the distinction is not so important. If the acquisition of the new trade causes the previous trade to cease and a new trade to commence (analysis (g)) then the commencement provisions will also apply (this time to all the trading activities). On the other hand, if the business or the assets are being merged with or added to an ongoing business of the acquirer, then the distinction can be quite important in terms of tax payable.

If there is a succession to the business of another, the person succeeding is taxed on a commencement basis on the profits of that business, even if he or she is merging the business acquired with an existing one taxable as a continuing business. Where this happens, the profits of the original business continue to be taxed on the continuing business basis, but the commencement rules are applied separately to the profits of the acquired business. This may result in additional tax to be paid in the first two tax years in which the latter profits are assessed.

The question of whether there is or is not a succession is one of fact. The fact that the goodwill of the business is transferred to the purchaser, is often indicative of a succession (but note *Reynolds & Sons Co Ltd v Ogston* 15 TC 501). A transfer of the assets or some of them, other than goodwill, eg items of plant or a building, is unlikely on its own to be regarded as a succession to a business. It always remains necessary to ask whether the acquired business was in fact continued after the date of change.

While there can be no succession if a trade has ceased completely before the assets comprised in it are transferred to another trader, the issue of cessation will, again, be a matter of fact and degree. Thus, in *Wild v Madam Tussauds* 17 TC 127, a business which closed for 17 months following a serious fire was held not to have ceased (see also the cases discussed at **4.206**).

A succession implies a deliberate transfer of a trade from one party to another. Thus, if a trader on his own initiative manages to attract the business of a trade which has ceased, then he will not be regarded as succeeding to that trade (*Thomson & Balfour v*

Le Page 8 TC 541). It may be that even the direct transfer of a trade which has been making unsustainable losses will be regarded as not constituting a succession, ie on the footing that there is no goodwill remaining (*Wilson & Barlow v Chibbett* 14 TC 407); however, the particular facts of the case must (as always) be considered.

In *Bell v National Provincial Bank of England Ltd* 5 TC 1, a bank with 199 branches in England and Wales purchased the business of another bank which had only one office. A large sum was paid for goodwill, premises, furniture, etc and the manager and staff of the other bank were taken over. The profits earned after the takeover by the one office of the acquired business were merged and formed part of the total profits of the National Provincial Bank without being distinguished in any way. It was however, held that there was a succession to trade by the acquiring bank (this is an example of analysis (c) above).

In *Watson Bros v Lothian* 4 TC 441, it was held that the purchase of a ship from another trader did not constitute a succession to the latter's trade. In this case, the purchaser acquired nothing in the way of goodwill such as a list of customers, or rights over any particular routes. Thus analysis (f) above applied, since there had been the mere acquisition of assets and not the acquisition of a trade.

In *George Humphries & Co v Cook* 19 TC 121, the taxpayer carried on a business of contracting to process films. The taxpayer employed only clerical staff, with the processing work being sub-contracted out to another individual, T. The taxpayer subsequently went into partnership with T, who then carried out the processing work as part of the partnership trade. The court upheld the Appeal Commissioner's finding of fact that the partnership trade was a new trade altogether (and that H's previous trade had been permanently discontinued as a result – ie analysis (g) above (under Irish tax law the creation of a new partnership would mark the commencement of a 'relevant period' (see **4.504**), but the principle at issue remains applicable).

In *Laycock v Freeman Hardy & Willis Ltd* 22 TC 288, the taxpayer carried on a large retail business selling boots and shoes. On 1 April 1935, it acquired all the assets and goodwill of two subsidiary companies on their liquidation. The subsidiaries had previously manufactured boots and shoes and sold all their finished products on a wholesale basis to the company. Thereafter, the taxpayer manufactured the products in the factories previously occupied by the subsidiaries and sold all the finished products through their retail outlets. It was held that the businesses of the subsidiaries had ceased on the date of acquisition, but that the company had not succeeded to those businesses.

In his judgment in the Court of Appeal, Sir Wilfrid Greene MR laid importance on the fact that the businesses of the subsidiaries had been 'manufacturing wholesale concerns' and he posed the question whether the business of manufacturing and disposing of products wholesale was a business which, after the change, was carried on by the respondent company. He took the view that the part of the business which had been essential for the realisation of taxable profit, namely, the selling of goods wholesale, had disappeared so that there was no succession to this business. Sir Wilfrid distinguished this position from that which existed in *Bell v National Provincial Bank*, where the business that had been acquired by National Provincial Bank was a banking business and where that banking business, ie that of the acquired bank, was carried on both before and after the acquisition (ie this case was an example of analysis (e) above).

In *Falmer Jeans v Rodin* [1990] STC 270, Millet J took the view that the decision in the *Laycock* case was unsatisfactory. He noted that the fact that the subsidiaries' trade was described as one of 'manufacturing wholesale' merely indicated the type of customer as opposed to the type of business involved. He said:

> If the business [of the subsidiaries] had been described as … 'manufacturing goods for sale', the result would seemingly have been different.

In *Briton Ferry Steel Co Ltd v Barry* 23 TC 44, a parent company was held to have succeeded to the trades of its subsidiaries which had consisted of converting steel bars provided by the parent company into tinplate and blackplate. The fact that under the new trading conditions, the steel bars were produced by the trader, rather than being 'bought in', was held not to be material. The apportionment of profits between the trade previously carried on by the subsidiaries and the existing trade of the parent company was obviously a matter of difficulty, since the commercial reality was that a single integrated trade was being carried on. The court held (perhaps unsatisfactorily) that the profits of the subsidiaries' former trade should be computed on the assumption that the steel bars were acquired at their production cost.

In the *Falmer Jeans* case, Millet J commented that it was illogical that a change in the means whereby raw materials are acquired would not prevent a succession taking place (as in the *Briton Ferry* case), whereas a change from selling wholesale to selling retail (as in the *Laycock* case) would do so. The distinction between the two cases can perhaps be justified on the grounds that the customers of the trade are more significant than its suppliers, since the 'reputation and connection' of the business (part of its goodwill) are valuable primarily in relation to the former (this however is a very broad generalisation and will not apply in all cases).

In *Maidment v Kibby* [1993] STC 494, the taxpayers who ran a fish and chip shop acquired an existing fish and chip shop in a nearby town as a going concern. The new shop was fully integrated into the existing business; the name of the shop was changed and its operating style was altered; the taxpayers also installed new management and operated centralised buying and accounting systems for both shops. The court refused to overturn the Appeal Commissioners' finding of fact that the taxpayers had expanded their existing trade into the new premises, rather than continuing the business already carried on there (ie this was viewed as an example of analysis (f) above).

It seems clear that the court in *Maidment* would not have overturned a decision of fact to the contrary effect. If the taxpayers had acquired a fish and chip shop and had converted it into a hairdressing salon then self-evidently there could have been no succession. The fact that the taxpayers continued to operate a similar type of trade – in particular a trading operation where, on the facts, there was probably limited scope for variation in trading methods or in developing a different market – meant that the decision was likely to be a borderline one. The fact that the taxpayer had an existing trade was not an essential factor in the decision, although in this instance it helped to substantiate the fact that a new and different trade was now being carried on in the acquired premises.

While in all cases the person transferring the whole of his trade is treated as permanently discontinuing it, the *Freeman Hardy & Willis* case shows that this does not always involve the transferee in being treated as succeeding to the trade. However, it was noted in that case that it was not essential that the old trade should be carried on in exactly the same way as before. It should also be noted that this issue is now of much less significance so far as companies are concerned since the income tax basis period rules no longer have relevance for corporation tax.

The date of change of ownership of a business is a matter of fact to be determined on the exact circumstances of each case. Normally, the date specified in the agreement between the parties for the transfer of the business is taken but if in fact the business was taken over at a different date, this actual date of takeover must be used. It is a question of determining the date when there was a succession '*de facto*' (*Todd v Jones Bros Ltd* 15 TC 396).

The effect of the application of the succession rule is shown in the following example:

Example 4.208.1

Mr D Bend, who has traded for some years in Waterford as a bookseller, acquires on 1 June 2013 a bookselling and publishing business in Dublin, previously carried on by a partnership of which he was a partner. He merges the two businesses and carries on trade as a sole trader from 1 June 2013 through separate branches in Waterford and Dublin.

The taxable profits (before capital allowances) as calculated separately for the two branches for the accounting years ending 30 September 2013 to 2015 are as follows:

	Waterford	*Dublin*
	€	€
12 months to 30/09/2013	23,000	
4 months to 30/09/2013		11,000
12 months to 30/09/2014	25,000	28,000
12 months to 30/09/2015	22,000	9,000

Since Mr Bend, as an individual, has succeeded to the partnership's Dublin business on 1 June 2013, TCA 1997, s 69(2) requires him to be taxed for 2013 and subsequent years as if he had commenced that business on 1 June 2013. At the same time, he remains taxable in respect of his Waterford profits on a continuing business basis.

His taxable profits (before capital allowances) for 2013 to 2015 are determined as follows:

	€	€
2013:		
Waterford branch:		
12 months to 30/09/2013		23,000
Dublin branch (1st year)[1]		
4 months to 30/09/2013	11,000	
3 months to 31/12/2013		
3/12 x €28,000 (12 months to 30/09/2014)	7,000	
		18,000
Total Sch D Case I profits 2013		41,000
2014:		
Waterford branch:		
12 months to 30/09/2014		25,000
Dublin branch (2nd year)		
Period of account of one year ending in tax year		
12 Months to 30/09/2014		28,000
Total Sch D Case I profits 2014		53,000
2015:		
Waterford branch:		
12 months to 30/09/2015		22,000

Dublin branch (3rd year)		
12 months to 30/09/2015	9,000	
Less:		
Relief for second year's excess[3]	(4,750)	
		4,250
Total Sch D Case I profits 2015		26,250

Notes:

1. For the first tax year of the 'new' Dublin business, the assessment is on the actual taxable profits for the period 1 June 2013 (date of 'commencement') to 31 December 2013.
2. For the second tax year of the Dublin business, the assessment is on the first period of 12 months up to the end date of the one year period of account falling in that tax year.
3. The second year's excess for which relief is claimed in the third year of the Dublin business is computed as follows:

	€	€
Taxable profits on normal 2nd year basis (as above)		28,000
Compare		
Actual taxable profits for 2014:		
Period 1/01/2014– 30/09/2014		
9/12ths x €28,000 (12 months to 30/09/2014)	21,000	
Period 1/10/2014– 31/12/2014		
3/12ths x €9,000 (12 months to 30/09/2015)	2,250	
		23,250
Second year excess		4,750

4. The amounts assessable for the three tax years in respect of the new Dublin business as compared with what would have been assessable if the succession rule did not apply may be shown as follows:

	Succession (as assessed)	*No succession (hypothetical)*
	€	€
2013	18,000	11,000
2014	28,000	28,000
2015	4,250	9,000
Total	50,250	48,000

4.3 Relief for Capital Expenditure

4.301 How relief is given

Relief for capital expenditure incurred for the purposes of a trade or profession is given through the scheme of capital allowances discussed in detail in **Division 6**. Capital allowances are given as a substitute for the depreciation or amortisation of the capital expenditure which the taxpayer normally charges in arriving at his accounting profit. However, while all such depreciation or amortisation charged in the accounts must be added back in the Sch D Case I or II computation, capital allowances are only available on those types of capital expenditure specified in the Taxes Consolidation Act 1997.

The capital assets and other forms of capital expenditure on which capital allowances may be claimed are set out in **6.101**.

The most common capital allowances are given in respect of machinery and plant (widely defined to include such items as motor vehicles, office machinery, as well as industrial plant and equipment) but similar considerations apply inter alia to certain expenditure on patents and scientific research (see **6.601**). These allowances may be annual allowances referred to, in the case of machinery or plant, as 'wear and tear' allowances (see **6.203**). In the case of industrial buildings (see definition in **6.401**), there are also annual and initial allowances to be considered; in this case, the annual allowance is referred to as a 'writing down' allowance. The industrial buildings regime has previously been extended to certain buildings located in tax incentive areas (see **Division 19** in the 2010 and earlier editions of this text). However, it is likely that such a capital allowances regime has since expired or is subject to the guillotine provisions as set out in more detail in **Division 6**.

The scheme of capital allowances involves also the concept of balancing allowances and balancing charges which arise on the disposal of assets in respect of which any capital allowances have previously been given. A balancing charge is made, where the sale or other proceeds (eg insurance monies) exceed the tax written down value (usually cost less capital allowances already given) of the asset in question. A balancing allowance is given where the tax written down value exceeds the sale proceeds. In other words, the balancing charge is made where appropriate to 'recapture' any excess capital allowances given during the period of use of the asset in the business and the balancing allowance is given, in the alternative case, where the capital allowances already given have not provided full relief for the net capital expenditure (original cost less sale, etc proceeds).

The relief for capital allowances (including any balancing allowances) and the imposition of any balancing charges are said to be given or made in 'taxing the profits' of the trade. TCA 1997, s 321(4) provides that references to allowances or charges being made in taxing a trade are to be construed as references to charging the profits or gains of the trade to income tax. Effectively, this means that the capital allowances (or balancing charges) for a year of assessment are deducted from (or added to) the taxable profits of the trade as allocated to that year of assessment by the basis period rules described in **4.2**.

The relevant references in relation to the allowances mentioned above are as follows:

(a) plant and machinery: TCA 1997, s 300(1);
(b) industrial buildings: TCA 1997, s 278(1);
(c) patents: TCA 1997, s 761; and
(d) scientific research: TCA 1997, s 765(1).

In all income tax applications, it is important to note that the deduction of the capital allowances, or the addition of any balancing charges, is made after the taxable profits assessable for the tax year have been ascertained and does not have any bearing on the allocation of the taxable profits (before capital allowances or charges) to years of assessment. In other words, the relevant allowances or charges do not form part of the taxable profits although they will reduce or increase as appropriate the amounts assessable under Sch D Case I or II (compare *IRC v Wood Bros* 38 TC 275).

The computation of each type of capital allowance to which the trader is entitled, together with that of any balancing charges, is made by reference to events taking place in, or assets in use at the end of, a basis period. The basis period for capital allowances purposes is usually, but not always, the period for which the accounts of the business are made up. In general, the capital allowance basis period for a year of assessment is the same as the basis period used for allocating the taxable profits of the trade to the same tax year.

The capital allowance basis period rules are discussed in principle in **6.102**. The application of these rules in allocating capital allowances and balancing charges to years of assessment for the purposes of taxing the profits of a trade (or profession) are best dealt with separately for a continuing business, for the opening years of a new business, for the closing years of a trade that ceases and for the position where there is a change of accounting date. First, the general principle of how capital allowances are granted and balancing charges made in taxing the profits of a trade may be illustrated.

Assume that a person carrying on a trade or profession (the business) has computed the taxable profits of the business for the relevant basis period for a given year of assessment and has also ascertained the capital allowances and any balancing charges to be given or made for that year of assessment. He then arrives at his net Sch D Case I or II income for the year of assessment by deducting from the taxable profits the total capital allowances to be given for the year and by adding any balancing charges due to be made for the year.

Example 4.301.1

Mr Thorwoden carries on trade as a manufacturer. His basis period for the tax year 2015 is his accounting year ending 30 September 2015. His taxable profits (before capital allowances) for that year, computed under the rules of Sch D Case I, are €77,610. He is entitled to (and claims) capital allowances for the year 2015 by reference to qualifying expenditure incurred in, and to qualifying assets used in his trade at the end of his accounting year to 30 September 2015.

Similarly, any balancing allowances or balancing charges are given or made for 2015 in respect of any relevant assets disposed of during the year to 30 September 2015.

Mr Thorwoden's net Sch D Case I income (taxable profits less capital allowances) for 2015 (to be included in his total income for that year), assuming the capital allowances and balancing charges set out below, is arrived at as follows:

Taxable profits 2015	€	€
Per computation for Y/E 30 September 2015		77,610

Less:		
Capital allowances 2015		
Plant & machinery		
Wear & tear	14,870	
Balancing allowances	1,060	
Industrial buildings – writing down allowances	1,200	
Patent rights writing down allowances	460	
		17,590
		60,020
Add:		
Balancing charges 2015:		
Plant and machinery		1,480
Net Sch D Case I income 2015		61,500

General points

Some general points should be made before dealing in more detail with the manner in which the different types of capital allowances are given (and balancing charges made) in the different circumstance described in the rest of **4.3**. Two points relate to terms used in the narrative and the third concerns references to certain accelerated capital allowances.

The term 'taxable profits' used in this division refers to the adjusted profits of the trade or profession as computed under the rules of Sch D Case I or Case II before deducting capital allowances or adding balancing charges.

The phrase 'net Sch D Case I (or Case II) income' used in this division refers to the net amount assessable after deducting capital allowances and adding balancing charges to be given or made in taxing the trade.

The normal capital allowances are annual allowances designed to write off the relevant capital expenditure at the same percentage rate each year over the period of use of the relevant asset. Capital expenditure incurred on plant and machinery prior to 1 January 2001 attracts wear and tear allowances at 15 per cent per annum for the first six years the asset is in use with a 10 per cent rate in the seventh year. Wear and tear allowances are available at 20 per cent per annum over a five year period on capital expenditure incurred on machinery or plant in the period from 1 January 2001 to 3 December 2002. A taxpayer can elect to claim wear and tear allowances on the written down value of expenditure incurred prior to 1 January 2001 at a rate of 20 per cent per annum over five years. This election can be made for any basis period ending on or after 1 January 2002. The rate of wear and tear allowances on expenditure incurred on plant after 3 December 2002 is 12.5 per cent per annum over eight years. Special provisions apply under TCA 1997, s 286 to certain taxis and short-term hire cars which attract a writing down allowance of 40 per cent per annum on the reducing balance basis and under TCA 1997, s 284(3A) to certain whitefishing boats. The relevant provisions are discussed in detail in **Division 6**. For a number of years, certain accelerated allowances – initial allowances and increased annual allowances (free depreciation) – were generally available in respect of plant and certain buildings. These are no longer generally available. The extent to which accelerated capital allowances continued to be available in certain cases most notably in certain tax incentive areas after they no longer continued to apply generally is dealt with in **Division 19** of the 2009 edition of this book.

4.302 Continuing business

The determination of the capital allowances and any balancing charges to be given or made in taxing the profits or gains of a trade or profession (the business) for any year of assessment, is made by reference to events taking place in, or to qualifying assets in use for the business at the end of, the basis period for the year in question. This applies whether the trade or profession is a continuing business, one which has recently commenced or one which is subject to the rules of cessation.

In principle, the basis period by reference to which the capital allowances and balancing charges are computed for any year of assessment is the same period as that finally used as the basis period for charging the taxable profits of the business to income tax. There are special rules for dealing with cases where the event giving rise to a capital allowance or balancing charge occurs in a period which falls into the basis periods for more than one tax year, or where that event falls in an interval between the basis period for one tax year and that for the next tax year (the effect of which is discussed at **4.304** and **4.305**).

In the case of a continuing business, the basis period for a tax year is normally the taxpayer's 12-month period of account ending in that year (see normal case in **4.204**). However, if any of the 'change of accounting date' rules apply to require the taxable profits to be charged for a tax year by reference to a different basis period (the revised basis period), then the revised basis period becomes the basis period for capital allowances and balancing charges for that tax year (see Change of accounting date rules in **4.204**).

It is appropriate to deal separately with the different types of capital allowances and balancing charges for the continuing business, as follows:

(a) Machinery or plant

Wear and tear allowances

The wear and tear annual allowance is given by TCA 1997, s 284 for a year of assessment for each item of machinery or plant (the plant) which is in use for the business at the end of the basis period for that year. The allowance is computed at the appropriate wear and tear rate applied to the relevant capital expenditure.

A full year's annual allowance is given for a year of assessment in respect of the capital expenditure in providing additional plant which is acquired at any time during the basis period for that year provided that the plant is brought into use for the business on or before the last day of the basis period (and is in use on that day). However, where the basis period is less than 12 months (typically arising in the year of commencement), the allowance is scaled back in the same proportion as the basis period bears to 12 months (ie if the basis period is only nine months and the normal rate of allowance is 12.5 per cent, the rate will be scaled back to 12.5 per cent x 9/12 = 9.375 per cent (TCA 1997, s 284(2)(b)).

Balancing charges

TCA 1997, s 288 generally requires a balancing allowance or balancing charge (whichever is the case) to be given or made when an item of machinery or plant is sold or otherwise permanently ceases to be used for the trade or profession, but only if a wear and tear, increased wear and tear or initial allowance has previously been given in respect of the relevant capital expenditure. The detailed rules for balancing allowances and charges are explained in **6.207–6.212**.

The balancing allowance or balancing charge is given or made for the year of assessment in the basis period for which the sale or other event triggering the allowance or charge occurs. In broad terms, a balancing allowance is given if the net sale proceeds (or, where relevant, any insurance, salvage or other compensation monies) are less than the tax written down value of the item of plant sold or otherwise permanently ceasing to be used in the business. The amount of the allowance is the excess of the tax written down value of the plant over the net sale or other monies received for the plant. A balancing charge is made if the net sale proceeds exceed the tax written down value of the item of plant sold, etc; the amount of the charge is the excess of the net sale, etc proceeds over the tax written down value of the plant sold, etc.

The tax written down value used in the computation of the balancing allowance or charge is that for the relevant item of plant at the start of the year of assessment for which the allowance or charge is to be given or made. It is the last figure in the previous year's capital allowances computation representing the unrelieved capital expenditure in respect of the item of plant (ie its tax written down value after deducting the previous year's capital allowances from it).

Example 4.302.1

Mr Sacrilege, who has carried on a trade of printing and distributing religious books for many years making up accounts annually to 31 January, purchases a new printing machine for his business for €50,000 on 30 December 2012, at which point it is immediately put into use. On 14 August 2014, Mr Sacrilege sells the printing machine for €36,600 but incurs selling costs of €2,000 so that the net proceeds are €34,600. He has continued to make up accounts to 31 January.

The computation of the balancing allowance or charge (working forward from the tax written down value at 1 January 2015) involves first determining the tax written down value (unrelieved capital expenditure) for the printing machine, as follows:

	Machinery *(12.5% rate)*
	€
Acquisition Cost 30/12/2012	50,000
Capital allowances 2013 (basis period Y/E 31/01/2013)	
€50,000 x 12.5%	(6,250)
Tax WDV at 31/12/2013	43,750
Capital allowances 2014 (basis period Y/E 31/01/2014)	
€50,000 x 12.5%	(6,250)
Tax WDV at 31/12/2014	37,500

The balancing allowance or charge will now be computed for 2015 as follows:

	€
Sale on 14/08/2014 (in Y/E 31/1/2015)–	
(Basis period for 2015)	
Net proceeds	34,600

Less:	
Tax WDV at 31/12/2014	(37,500)
Balancing allowance 2015	(2,900)

Example 4.302.2

Take the facts of **Example 4.302.1**, but assume that the net sale proceeds on 14 August 2014 were €38,750. There is now a balancing charge to be made for 2015 computed as follows:

	€
Sale on 14/08/2014 (in Y/E 31/01/2015)	
(Basis period for 2015)	
Net proceeds	38,750
Less:	
Tax WDV at 31/12/2014	(37,500)
Balancing charge 2015	1,250

(b) Industrial buildings (including tax incentive buildings)

The full definition of an industrial building or structure is given in **6.401**. In addition, the industrial buildings regime is extended to qualifying capital expenditure incurred during a 'qualifying period' in relation to certain buildings or structures ('qualifying premises') which are situated in any of the 'urban renewal designated areas' or certain other tax incentive areas (see **Division 19** of the 2009 edition of this book). Basically, all the rules relating to industrial buildings are applied as if the relevant building were a building in use for a trade carried on in a mill, factory or similar premises. In addition accelerated capital allowances (initial allowance or free depreciation: see **6.405** and **6.407**) were available for both industrial buildings and 'qualifying premises' located in the 'tax incentive' area. Certain multi-storey carparks (see **6.605**) and childcare facilities (see **6.406**) also attract enhanced allowances. The rules governing the industrial buildings writing-down allowances (ie annual allowances) are given in **6.406** and the rules for balancing allowances and balancing charges in **6.409**.

The manner in which the different capital allowances and balancing charges are given or made for industrial buildings in the case of a continuing business may now be explained.

Writing-down allowances

TCA 1997, s 272 entitles a person carrying on a trade to an industrial buildings writing-down allowance for a tax year in respect of capital expenditure on an industrial building or structure if, at the end of the basis period for that year, he holds the 'relevant interest' (see **6.403**) in relation to the capital expenditure. He continues to be entitled for each subsequent tax year where he retains the relevant interest at the end of the basis period for the relevant year. This assumes that the building remains in use for the trade as an industrial building (ie it assumes that the person in question continues to carry on a trade of a type which qualifies the building as an industrial building or, if the building is in a designated urban renewal or other tax incentive area, that he continues to use the building for any type of trade or profession).

For a full explanation of the rules for industrial buildings writing-down allowances, see **6.406**, **6.408** and **6.410**.

Example 4.302.3

Mr Vanbasten carries on a manufacturing business established many years ago. On 17th June 2013 he incurred qualifying expenditure of €755,000 on the construction of a new factory which met the conditions of TCA 1997, s 268(1)(a) and which was immediately brought into use (see **6.401**). Mr Vanbasten makes up his accounts to 30 June each year. He is entitled to writing down allowances for 2013, 2014 and 2015 as set out below.

	€
2013 (basis period 12 months to 30/06/2013)	
Construction expenditure	755,000
Industrial building writing down allowance (IBWDA) for year 2013	
€ 755,000 x 4%	(30,200)
Residue of expenditure 31/12/2013	724,800
2014 (basis period 12 months to 30/06/2014)	
IBWDA for year 2014	
€ 755,000 x 4%	(30,200)
Residue of expenditure 31/12/2014	694,600
2015 (basis period 12 months to 30/06/2015)	
IBWDA for year 2015	
€ 755,000 x 4%	(30,200)
Residue of expenditure 31/12/2015	664,400

Balancing allowances and balancing charges

TCA 1997, s 274 requires a balancing allowance or balancing charge (whichever is the case) to be given or made when the relevant interest in an industrial building is sold, if the industrial building ceases altogether to be used or if it is demolished or destroyed (and in certain other circumstances). The cessation of use of a relevant facility (see **6.409**) may give rise to a balancing charge. However, no such balancing adjustment is allowed or required if the sale or other relevant event occurs after the end of the writing down period in relation to the original construction expenditure. The detailed rules for balancing allowances and charges for industrial buildings are explained in **6.409**. The year of assessment for which any balancing allowance is given or any balancing charge made is the tax year applicable to the basis period during which the sale or other relevant event occurs. The computation of the balancing allowance or charge is, as with the corresponding computation of balancing allowances and charges for machinery or plant (see above), made by comparing the net sale proceeds or, where relevant, any insurance or other compensation monies with the residue of the construction expenditure at the end of the previous year of assessment.

Example 4.302.4

Take the facts of **Example 4.302.3** and assume that on 8 September 2014 Mr Vanbasten's factory referred to in that example is destroyed in a disastrous fire. His business continues through other buildings.

Mr Vanbasten receives insurance proceeds in respect of the buildings destroyed of €600,000 on 15 November 2014 and a final amount of €150,000 on 22 August 2015. He has to compute a balancing allowance or balancing charge for the tax year 2015 (notwithstanding that the second part of the insurance monies is only received in the basis period for the next tax year). This is because the event triggering the allowance or charge is the destruction of the buildings which occurred in the basis period for the 2015 assessment (ie the year ending 30 June 2015).

The balancing allowances or charges for 2015 will be calculated as follows:

	€
Full insurance compensation monies	750,000
Less:	
Tax Residue of expenditure at 31/12/2014	
As above	((694,600))
Excess of insurance monies over	
Residue (=A)	55,400
Total capital allowances previously allowed[1] (= B)	60,400
Balancing charge 2015	
Lower of A and B[1]	55,400

Notes:

1. Since a balancing charge in respect of any capital expenditure cannot exceed the aggregate of the writing down allowances (including any increased writing down allowances) and initial allowances previously granted to the same person, it is useful to set out the computation in the above 'lower of A and B' form.

(c) Patents rights expenditure

TCA 1997, s 755 entitles a person carrying on a trade to a writing down allowance for each tax year in a writing down period in respect of capital expenditure incurred on the purchase of patent rights. This writing down allowance is given for a tax year (eg 2015) if the purchased patent rights are used for the trade at any time in the basis period for the year in question (eg the 12-month period of account ending 31 May 2015).

For a full discussion on the writing down period for patent rights expenditure and the detailed rules for capital allowances on such expenditure see **6.7**.

Example 4.302.5

Mr F Meridien, who trades as a printer, purchases the patent to a new process for use in his printing trade. The life of the patent at the time of purchase is eight years. Mr Meridien makes up accounts annually to 31 August. He incurs a total expenditure of €82,500 on the purchase on 27 May 2015.

The writing down period is the eight years commencing 1 January 2015 since this is the first day of the 2015 tax year and since the capital expenditure is incurred in Mr Meridien's basis period for 2015 (the 12-month period of account to 31 August 2015 which ends in that tax year).

Mr Meridien is entitled to a patent rights writing down allowance for 2015, and for each of the following seven years (assuming that he continues to trade and to use the patent rights for his trade). The amount of this allowance for each such tax year is:

€82,500 x 1/8th	€10,313

4.303 Continuing business: change of accounting date

A change in the date to which accounts are made up for a trade or profession results in a change in the basis period by reference to which capital allowances are given or balancing charges made. In the continuing business this means that the basis period for the tax year in which the new accounting date occurs normally becomes the period of 12 months ending on the new accounting date and, as indicated in **4.204**, it may also result in a revision of the basis period for the immediately preceding tax year.

If the change of accounting date rules change the basis period for any tax year, then the various rules for allocating capital allowances and balancing charges to tax years are applied by reference to the new basis period for the year in question. The effects may be seen in the next two examples.

Example 4.303.1

Ms LA Law carries on a wheel grinding business and has made up annual accounts for a number of years up to 31 March. After the accounts for the year to 31 March 2015, she decides to change the accounting date to 30 September by making up six months accounts to 30 September 2015.

Her Sch D Case I taxable profits (before capital allowances) for the relevant periods of accounts are as follows:

	€
12 months to 31/03/2014	34,000
12 months to 31/03/2015	28,000
6 months to 30/09/2015	18,000

Before considering the capital allowances, it is necessary to determine the basis periods for assessing the taxable profits for 2015 and 2014. Applying the rules of TCA 1997, s 65, these basis periods are determined to be as follows:

(a) 2015 (year of change of date):

basis period: 12-month period to 30 September 2015 (the later of accounting dates in the year); and

(b) 2014 (previous year):

basis period: 12 months to 31 March 2014 (the only accounting date in the year and not changed by the rule of TCA 1997, s 65(3)).[1]

Effect on capital allowances

The details of the machinery and plant acquired by Ms Law in her trade and used throughout her period of ownership which are relevant to the capital allowances for 2015 and 2014 are as follows:

	€
Tax WDV at 1/01/2014:	
Computer system (12.5% rate applies) Cost:	18,192
Tax WDV	4,548
Additions after 1/04/2013	
In 12 months to 31/03/2014:	
New office machinery (acquired 18/04/2013) at cost	8,000
In 12 months to 31/03/2015:	
Office Furniture (acquired 13/08/2014) at cost	5,200
Sales after 1/04/2014:	
In 12 months to 31/03/2015	
Old machine sold (18/07/2014) for	2,500
(Tax WDV at 1/01/2015 €1; original cost €4,000)	

The capital allowances computations for 2014 and 2015 are as follows:

2014	€
(Basis period: 12 months ended 31/03/2014)	
Computer – Tax WDV 1/01/2014	4,548
W&T 2014: €18,192 x 12.5%[2]	(2,274)
Tax WDV 31/12/2014	2,274
New machine (acquired 18/04/2013) at cost	8,000
W&T 2014: €8,000 x 12.5%[3]	(1,000)
Tax WDV 31/12/2014	7,000

2015	
(Basis period: 12 months ended 30/09/2015)	€
Computer – Tax WDV 1/01/2015	2,274
W&T 2015: €18,192 x 12.5%[2]	(2,274)
Tax WDV 31/12/2015	Nil
New machine – Tax WDV 1/01/2015	7,000
W&T 2015: €8,000 x 12.5%[3]	(1,000)
Tax WDV 31/12/2015	6,000
Office furniture (acquired 13/08/2014) at cost	5,200
W&T 2015 5,200 X 12.5%[4]	(650)
Tax WDV 31/12/2015	4,550
Old machine – Tax WDV 1/01/2015[5]	1
Sale proceeds 18/07/2014	2,500
Balancing charge	2,449

Notes:

1. The figures to determine whether or not the 2014 basis period is to be changed to a 12-month period ending in that year to correspond with the 12-month period used as the basis period for 2015 are as follows:

Profits of original basis period for 2014	€
12 months to 31/03/2014	34,000
Profits of 12 months to 30/09/2014	
6 months 1/10/2012 to 31/03/2014	
6/12ths x €34,000 (12 months to 31/03/2014)	17,000
6 months 1/04/2014 to 30/09/2014	
6/12ths x €28,000 (12 months to 31/03/2015)	14,000
	31,000

Since the taxable profits of the 12 months to 30 September 2014 are less than those of the original basis period, there is no change in the basis period for 2014 (which remains the 12 months to 31 March 2014).

2. The existing computer system is in use at the end of the basis periods for 2014 and 2015 and continues to attract a 12.5% per cent W&T allowance.
3. The new machine was in use at the end of the basis period for 2014 and continued to be used at the end of the basis period for 2015 and so qualifies for W&T allowance at a rate of 12.5 per cent for 2014 and 2015.
4. The first basis period at the end of which the office furniture was in use was the period ending 30/09/2015. Accordingly, the first entitlement to a W&T allowance arises in 2015.
5. With regard to the old machine sold for €2,500 on 18 July 2014, there is a balancing charge. Since the sale occurred in the interval between the basis periods for 2014 and 2015, it is deemed to have occurred in the basis period for the later of the two years under TCA 1997, s 306(2)(b)(ii) (see **4.304**). The balancing charge therefore arises in 2015.

The next example shows how the capital allowances may be changed if the taxable profits (before capital allowances) in the corresponding period in the previous year are higher than the taxable profits (before capital allowances) otherwise assessable for the previous year.

Example 4.303.2

Take the facts of **Example 4.303.1**, but assume that Ms Law's taxable profits for the 12-month period of accounts ending 31 March 2015 were €36,000 (and not €28,000)[1].

Applying the rules of TCA 1997, s 65, the basis periods for 2015 and 2014 are determined to be as follows:

(a) 2015 (year of change of date):
basis period: 12-month period to 30 September 2014 (the later of the two accounting dates in the year) (same as **Example 4.303.1**); and

(b) 2014 (previous year):
basis period: 12 months to 30 September 2014 (changed by the rule of TCA 1997, s 65(3) to the period corresponding to the basis period for 2015).[2]

Notes

1. The higher profits in the year to 31 March 2015 result in the following computation of taxable profits for the year to 30 September 2014 (the 12-month period ending in 2014 corresponding to the new basis period for 2015):

	€
Profits of 12 months to 30/09/2014	
6 months to 31/03/2014	
6/12ths x €34,000	17,000
6 months to 30/09/2014	
6/12ths x €36,000	18,000
	35,000

2. Since the taxable profits of the 12 months to 30 September 2014 (€35,000) are greater than the taxable profits of the original basis period for 2014 (€34,000), the final basis period for 2014 now becomes the 12 months to 30 September 2014.

Effect on capital allowances:

There is now no interval between the basis period for 2015 and that for 2014, but there is an interval between the basis period for 2013 (12 months to 31 March 2013) and the new basis period for 2014, ie an interval running from 1 April 2013 to 1 October 2013. As compared with the position shown in **Example 4.303.1**, one consequence is that the sale of the machine on 18 July 2014 now falls in the basis period for 2014, ie the 12 months ended 30 September 2014. Secondly, the first basis period at the end of which the office furniture was in use is the basis period for 2014, ie the period to 30 September 2014. Accordingly, W&T allowances at 12.5 per cent are now available for both 2014 and 2015.

The capital allowances computations for 2014 and 2015 are as follows:

	€
2014	
(Basis period: 12 months ended 30/09/2014)	
Computer – Tax WDV 1/01/2014	4,548
W&T 2014: €18,192 x 12.5%[1]	(2,274)
Tax WDV 31/12/2014	2,274
New machine (acquired 18/04/2013) at cost	8,000
W&T 2014: €8,000 x 12.5%[2]	(1,000)
Tax WDV 31/12/2014	7,000
Office furniture (acquired 13/08/2014) at cost	5,200
W&T 2014 5,200 x 12.5%[3]	(650)
WDV 31/12/2014	4,550
Old machine – Tax WDV 1/01/2014[4]	1
Sale proceeds 18/07/2014	2,500
Balancing charge	2,449
2015	
(Basis period: 12 months ended 30/09/2015)	€
Computer – Tax WDV 1/01/2015	2,274
W&T 2015: €18,192 x 12.5%[1]	(2,274)
Tax WDV 31/12/2015	Nil
New machine – Tax WDV 1/01/2014	7,000
W&T 2015: €8,000 x 12.5%[3]	(1,000)
Tax WDV 31/12/2015	6,000
Office furniture –Tax WDV at 1/01/2015	4,550
W&T 2015 5,200 X 12.5%[3]	(650)
WDV 31/12/2015	3,900

Notes

1. The existing computer system is in use at the end of the basis periods for 2014 and 2015 and continues to attract a 12.5% per cent W&T allowance.
2. The new machine was in use at the end of the basis period for 2014 and continued to be used at the end of the basis period for 2015 and so qualifies for W&Ts at a rate of 12.5 per cent for 2014 and 2015.

3. The first basis period at the end of which the office furniture was in use was the period ending 30 September 2014. Accordingly, it qualifies for W&T allowances at a rate of 12.5 per cent for 2014 and 2015.
4. With regard to the old machine sold for €2,500 on 18 July 2014, there is a balancing charge. Since the sale occurred in the period ended 30 September 2014, the basis period for 2014, the balancing charge therefore arises in 2014.

4.304 Commencement of trade

The treatment of capital allowances is more complicated in the opening years of assessment of a new trade or profession, or where the rules of commencement are applied in the case of a person succeeding to a trade or profession previously carried on by another person. Apart from the possible application of the rules which may substitute market value for the actual cost of assets acquired (see **6.105**), the allocation of capital allowances to years of assessment is affected by the different basis periods applicable in a commencement.

In the case of a trade or profession which is set up and commenced, the basis periods by reference to which the taxable profits are assessed for the first three tax years are:

(a) first tax year: the period from the date of the commencement to the following 31 December in the year of assessment;
(b) second tax year: generally the profits for the 12 months ending on the latest accounting date falling in the tax year, or failing which, the actual profits for the 12 months comprising the tax year itself; and
(c) third tax year: normally the 12-month period of account ending in the third year (but may be a different 12-month period ending in the third year if any of the 'change of accounting date' rules apply) (see **4.205** for a full discussion).

The rules for giving capital allowances in the opening years of a new trade or profession have therefore to be applied by reference to these basis periods. However, the rules relating to overlapping basis periods and intervals between basis periods are also relevant.

It may be useful to deal separately with the different types of capital allowances as applicable on the commencement of business, as follows:

Machinery or plant

Annual allowances

The annual allowance (wear and tear) is given for the first tax year in respect of the relevant capital expenditure if the machinery or plant is put into use for the business on or before the last day of that year and is still in use on that day. Similarly, for the second tax year, the annual allowance is given where the relevant machinery or plant is in use for the business on the last day of the relevant basis period.

The amount of wear and tear allowed in the first tax year is reduced to a proportion of a full year's allowance to reflect the fact that the basis period during which the plant is in use is less than a full year (TCA 1997, s 284(2)(b)). The annual wear and tear allowance given in the first tax year for each item of plant is the proportion of a full year's annual allowance represented by the ratio which the number of months (and fractions of months) of the basis period for the first year of assessment bears to 12 months.

TCA 1997, s 306 contains the definition of 'basis period' for all capital allowance purposes. In the case of the second year of assessment, the relevant rule is contained in

TCA 1997, s 306(2)(b) which states that where two basis periods overlap, the period common to both shall be deemed '... to fall in the first basis period only'. This rule means that for all capital allowance purposes (including wear and tear allowances) the period of overlap between the 'profits' basis periods for the first two years of assessment must be excluded from the 'capital allowance' basis period for the second year of assessment. This will result in reduced wear and tear allowances for the second year of assessment, since the corresponding basis period will be less than 12 months. However, it is not clear whether this reduction of the wear and tear allowances is actually intended. The strict legal position is set out below.

Example 4.304.1

Mr P Poire commenced a trade on 1 May 2013 and makes up his first accounts for the five months to 30 September 2013; he makes up his second set of accounts for the 10 months to 31 July 2014 and subsequent accounts up to 30 September 2015. He acquires the following assets for purposes of the trade (first used for the trade on the dates in brackets):

	Cost
In 5-month period of account to 30/09/2013:	€
General plant (1/05/2013)	4,500
In 10-month period of account to 31/07/2014:	
Fittings (20/01/2014)	3,800
Delivery van (1/06/2014)	12,000
Machinery (18/08/2014)	6,600

Mr Poire's first tax year is 2013, for which the basis period is the period 1 May 2013 to 31 December 2013. Only one item of plant has been acquired and is in use for the trade on 31 December 2013 ie the general plant acquired for €4,500. He obtains a wear and tear allowance for 2013 determined as follows:

	€
Capital expenditure incurred – general plant	4,500
Normal full year's allowance	
€4,500 x 12.5%	563
Basis period as fraction of 12 months	
1/05/2013 to 31/12/2013 = 8 months	
Annual allowance 2013 (as restricted)	
8/12ths x €563	375

Example 4.304.2

Take the facts of **Example 4.304.1** and consider the second tax year (2014). The basis period for 2014 is the 12 months ended 31 July 2014, the end date of the only period of account whose end date falls in 2014 and which falls more than 12 months after the commencement of the trade (see TCA 1997, s 66(2)(b)). It is assumed that based on the profit figures in question the rule in TCA 1997, s 65(3) will not give rise to a revision of the basis period for 2014 as a result of the change of accounting date in 2014 (see **4.205**). Mr Poire's capital allowances for 2014 are computed as follows:

2014	€
General plant	
Tax WDV 1/01/2014 (€4,500 – €375)	4,125

W&T 2014 €4,500 x 12.5% x 7/12[1]	(328)
Tax WDV 31/12/2014	3,797
Delivery van	
Brought into use 1/06/2014	12,000
W&T 2014 €12,000 x 12.5% x 7/12[1]	(875)
Tax WDV 31/12/2014	11,125
Fittings	
Brought into use 20/01/2014	3,800
W&T 2014 €3,800 x 12.5% x 7/12[1]	(277)
Tax WDV 31/12/2014	3,523

Notes:

1. Mr Poire's 'profits' basis period for 2014 runs from 1 August 2013 to 31 July 2014. However, his 'capital allowance' basis period for 2014 only runs from 1 January 2014 to 31 July 2014, ie seven months. Accordingly, in strictness, his wear and tear allowance should be restricted to 7/12ths of that otherwise available.

For the third and subsequent years of assessment, the normal rules for a continuing business apply as explained in **4.302** or, if there is a change of accounting date, as outlined in **4.303**. This means that a full year's annual allowance is given on all items of plant in use at the end of the basis period for the relevant tax year.

In the case of the third year of assessment the rule in TCA 1997, s 306(2)(b)(ii) may also become relevant. This states that 'where there is an interval between the end of the basis period for one year of assessment and the basis period for the next year of assessment ... the interval shall be deemed to be part of the second basis period' (the rule is modified in the case of cessations: see **4.305** below).

For the third tax year, the position is generally straightforward if the accounts in the opening years are made up for successive periods of 12 months running from the date of commencement of trading. In this case, the 'capital allowance' basis period for the third tax year is normally the second 12-month period (since this period falls immediately after the basis period for the second tax year).

In any case where the basis period for the third tax year is not the period of 12 months immediately following the first 12 months of trading, there will be either an overlap of the basis periods for the second and third years or an interval between them. In any such case, the rules of TCA 1997, s 306 for overlapping basis periods and intervals between basis periods must be applied to determine the relevant basis periods.

Example 4.304.3

Continue with Mr P Poire's case from **Examples 4.304.1/4.304.2**. The profits basis period for 2015 (the third tax year) is determined under the normal rules for a continuing business as the 12-month period of account ending 30 September 2015 (the 12-month period of account ending in 2015).

The 'capital allowance' basis period for 2015 includes the period between 1 August 2014 and 30 September 2014 (ie the interval between the end of the 'profits' basis period for 2014 and the commencement of the 'profits' basis period for 2015).

The ordinary annual allowances for 2015 are given on the items of machinery and plant in use for the business on 30 September 2015 (last day of the basis period).

	€
2015	
General plant	
Tax WDV 1/01/2015	3,797
W&T 2015 €4,500 x 12.5%	(562)
Tax WDV 31/12/2015	3,234
Delivery van	
Tax WDV 1/01/2015	11,125
W&T 2015 €12,000 x 12.5%	(1,500)
Tax WDV 31/12/2015	9,625
Fittings	
Tax WDV 1/01/2015	3,523
W&T 2015 €3,800 x 12.5%	(475)
Tax WDV 31/12/2015	3,048
Machinery	
First brought into use 18/08/2014[1]	6,600
W&T 2015 €6,600 x 12.5%	(825)
Tax WDV 31/12/2015	5,775

Notes:

1. The expenditure incurred on additions in the interval period cannot qualify for W&T in 2014 since they were not in use at the end of the capital allowance basis period for that year of assessment (ie 31 July 2014). The additions cannot qualify for a higher rate than 12.5 per cent, even though they have been in use for a basis period in excess of 12 months.

Balancing allowances and charges

The rules for determining the basis periods by reference to which balancing allowances and balancing charges are given or made for the opening tax years of a new business in respect of any relevant disposals (sales, loss by fire, etc) of machinery or plant are again those laid down by TCA 1997, s 306. A short example will illustrate the matter.

Example 4.304.4

Take the facts of Mr Poire's case again as used in **Example 4.304.2** and assume that the item of general plant first used in the business on 1 May 2013 is sold for €4,185 on 23 August 2014. Since the sale occurs in the interval (1 August 2014 to 30 September 2014) between the profits basis period for 2014 (the second tax year) and that for 2015 (the third tax year), the balancing allowance or balancing charge must be given or made for 2015 (the later year).

The computation is as follows:

	€
Original cost of item sold	4,500
Less:	
W&T 2013	(375)

W&T 2014	(328)
Tax WDV at 1/01/2015	3,797
Sale price 23/08/2014	4,185
Balancing charge 2015	388
(excess of sale price over tax WDV)	

Industrial buildings (including urban renewal and other tax incentive buildings)

Balancing allowances, writing down allowances and increased writing down allowances

The ordinary writing down allowances for industrial buildings are given for the first tax year of the new business if the person carrying it on holds the relevant interest in the building at the end of the basis period. It is also necessary that the building on which the expenditure is incurred has gone into use by the end of the basis period. In contrast to the position for the annual allowances on machinery or plant, there is no restriction to the full year's writing down allowance for income tax purposes even though (unless the basis period commences on 1 January) it will be less than a full tax year from the date of commencement.

Increased writing down allowances under TCA 1997, s 273 may similarly be claimed for the first tax year up to the maximum available where the relevant interest is held at the end of that year (on 31 December). This again assumes that the building (or part of the building) on which the qualifying expenditure is incurred has gone into use by the end of the basis period.

The same position applies for the second tax year where the basis period is not the actual tax year itself (see TCA 1997, s 66(2)). In this case, the person carrying on the business, so long as he holds the relevant interest at the end of the basis period, may claim the ordinary writing down allowance (or where available an increased writing down allowance as appropriate) for the second tax year, again without any restriction by reference to the length of the basis period as ascertained under TCA 1997, s 306.

Example 4.304.5

Mr S O'Reilly commences a trade of operating a hotel falling within TCA 1997, s 268(1)(d) (see **6.401**) on 1 April 2013, making up accounts annually to 31 March. Having acquired a 999 year leasehold interest he incurs capital expenditure of €660,000 on qualifying premises in the period 1 February 2012 to 31 March 2013, a further €200,000 on certain improvements to the original building in December 20113 and a further €400,000 on an extension to the premises in February/March 2014.

The basis periods for his first three tax years are as follows:

2013: 1/04/2013 to 31/12/2013

2014: 12 months to 31/03/2014

2015: 12 months to 31/03/2015

The industrial buildings annual allowances for the first three years of the trade are as follows:

	€
2013 (1st year):	
Qualifying capital expenditure incurred	
In February 2012 – March 2013[1]	660,000

In December 2013[1]	200,000
	860,000
Writing down allowance thereon	
4% x €860,000[2]	34,400
2014 (2nd year)	
Qualifying expenditure	
Total to 31/12/2013	860,000
Incurred in February/March 2014[3]	400,000
	1,260,000
Writing down allowance thereon	
4% x €1,260,000[2]	50,400
2015 (3rd year)	
Qualifying expenditure	
Total to 31/03/2014	1,260,000
Incurred between 1/04/2014 and 31/03/2015	None
	1,260,000
Writing down allowance thereon	
4% x €1,260,000[2]	50,400

Notes:

1. The first year's writing down allowance is given in full on all the industrial buildings expenditure incurred up to the end of the basis period for 2013, ie to 31 December 2013 (including the expenditure incurred in the period from February 2012 to March 2013 before trading commenced).
2. The allowance for each year is at the rate of 4 per cent provided in TCA 1997, s 272(3)(c)(iii). It is assumed that Mr O'Reilly continues to hold the relevant interest (the 999-year lease) at the end of the basis period for each tax year.
3. The expenditure qualifying for the second year's allowance includes the additional expenditure incurred in the capital allowance basis period for 2014, ie the part of the profits basis period for the second year not overlapping with the profits basis period for the first year (ie in the period 1 January 2014 to 31 March 2014). It is assumed that the extension on which the €400,000 is incurred is in use for the trade by 31 March 2014.

Balancing allowances and balancing charges

The rules for determining the basis periods by reference to which balancing allowances and balancing charges are given or made for the opening tax years of a new business in respect of any relevant disposals, loss by fire, etc of industrial buildings are exactly the same as for those for the initial allowances on industrial buildings (see above). It is unnecessary to repeat the rules here.

Patent rights expenditure

The full writing down allowance for capital expenditure incurred on the purchase of patent rights is given for each of the opening years of a new trade if the expenditure is incurred at any time before the end of the basis period for the year in question. The first writing down allowance is given for the tax year in the basis period for which the qualifying expenditure is incurred.

The definition of a basis period provided by TCA 1997, s 306 is applied by TCA 1997, s 762. Consequently, if the expenditure is incurred in a period which falls into the basis periods for two tax years (eg the first and second tax years), the first writing down allowance is given for the earlier of these two tax years and a further writing down allowance is given for the second of the two years. If the expenditure is incurred in the interval between the basis periods for two tax years (eg the second and third years in a case where such an interval occurs), the first writing down allowance is given for the later of the two years and no writing down allowance is available for the earlier year.

Example 4.304.6

Mr R Coyote commences to trade on 1 October 2013, making up his first accounts for the 12 months ending 30 September 2014 and his next accounts for the 15 months ending 31 December 2015. He incurs capital expenditure on the purchase of the rights to new patents as follows:

	€
Patent no 1 acquired on 14/09/2013	30,600
Patent no 2 acquired on 20/11/2014	20,400

The basis periods for assessing Mr Coyote's first three tax years are as follows:

2013 (1st year):

Period 1/10/2013 to 31/12/2013

2014 (2nd year):

12 months 1/10/2013 to 30/09/2014[1]

2015 (3rd year):

12 months 1/01/2015–31/12/2015

The capital allowances (writing down allowances of 1/17th of qualifying expenditure) for the first three tax years are computed as follows:

	€
2013:	
Capital expenditure: Patent no 1	30,600
WDA thereon[2]	
1/17th x €30,600	1,800
2014:	
Patent no 1	
1/17th x €30,600	1,800
2015:	
Patent no 1	
1/17th x €30,600	1,800
Patent no 2	
1/17th x €20,400[3]	1,200

Notes:

1. It is assumed that based on the profit figures in question the rule in TCA 1997, s 65(3) will not give rise to a revision of the basis period for 2014 as a result of the change of accounting date in 2015 (see **4.204**).

2. The €30,600 expenditure on patent no 1 incurred before trading commenced is deemed to be incurred on 1 October 2013, ie in the basis period for 2013. Therefore, the first writing down allowance on that expenditure is given for 2013.
3. The €20,400 expenditure on patent no 2 is incurred in the interval between the basis periods for 2014 and 2015 (ie in the period 1 October 2014 and 31 December 2014). Therefore, the first writing down allowance on that expenditure is given for 2015 (the later year).

4.305 Cessation of trade

The capital allowances computation for the last two years of assessment is required to be reviewed when there is a permanent discontinuance of a trade or profession. This also applies where a trade or profession (the business) is treated by TCA 1997, s 69 as if it were permanently discontinued due to a change of ownership (ie a deemed cessation, see **4.208**), but not where there is a change in one or more partners in a partnership that does not result in the termination of the 'relevant period' of the firm (see **4.502**).

The computation of the capital allowances and any balancing charges for the year of assessment in which the cessation occurs (the final year) and for the immediately preceding year (the penultimate year) are made by reference to facts and events in the basis periods for each year. The basis periods used are those as finally determined for assessing the taxable profits of the business in cessation. As explained in **4.206**, the basis period for the final tax year is, in all cases, the period from the 1st January of the final year to the date of cessation. The basis period for the penultimate year is either the actual penultimate year ending 31 December or its 'original basis period', dependent on which gives the higher taxable profits (before capital allowances).

The term 'original basis period' as used herein in relation to the penultimate year refers to the period which if there were no cessation would be the basis period for that year. Normally the original basis period is the 12-month period of account ending in the penultimate year. However if a different basis period results from any of the change of accounting date rules (see **4.204**), or because the penultimate year is also the first or second tax year in a commencement (see **4.205**), it is that basis period which is referred to herein as the original basis period for the penultimate year.

Once the final basis periods for the penultimate and final years of assessment are established, the final computations of the capital allowances and balancing charges for the two years can be made. In principle, the normal rules for capital allowances (and balancing charges) are followed by reference to those basis periods, but it is necessary to apply the rules of TCA 1997, s 306 to purchases, disposals, etc in certain intervals between basis periods.

Two types of cases arise, depending on whether the final basis period for the penultimate year turns out to be its original basis period or the actual penultimate year. In the first type of case, the interval occurs between the last day of the basis period for the penultimate year and the first day of the final year. In the second, the interval falls between the last day of the year preceding the penultimate year (the 'pre-penultimate year') and the first day of the penultimate year.

Machinery or plant

The treatment of capital allowances and balancing charges on a cessation is now discussed separately for the different types of allowances and balancing charges in the two types of case mentioned above. There is in fact one other type of case, this is where the original basis period for the penultimate year is the 12 months ending 31 December of the penultimate year. In this case, the final basis period for the penultimate year is always that 12-month period. It is not proposed to comment further on this third case.

Firstly, TCA 1997, s 306(2)(b)(iii) states that the interval between the basis period for the penultimate year and the final year is deemed to fall into the basis period for the penultimate year (ie the earlier year) and not the later year as is otherwise the case.

The effects of the capital allowances rules as applicable in the closing years where the interval period immediately precedes the profits basis period for the final year are therefore as follows:

(i) The 'capital allowance' basis period for the penultimate year will include the interval period between the end of the 'profits' basis period for the penultimate year and the basis period for the final year. Only expenditure incurred on plant which is in use at the end of that extended basis period can qualify for W&T.

(ii) The annual allowances (if available) are given for the final year on any items of plant in use for the business on the date of cessation.

(iii) For any item of machinery or plant disposed of or otherwise ceasing to be used in the business, the balancing allowance or charge (whichever arises) is given or made as follows:

   (I) for the penultimate year, if the sale or other relevant event occurs in the extended 'capital allowance' basis period for the penultimate year,

   (II) for the final year, if the sale or other relevant event occurs during the actual basis period for the final year and before the date of cessation, and

   (III) for the final year, if the item of plant has continued to be used for the business right up to the cessation of the business.

One further point arises in relation to the annual allowances on machinery or plant for the final tax year of a trade or profession which ceases or which is treated as if permanently discontinued on a change of ownership. In such a case, there is not a full year's wear and tear through use in the business in the final tax year. This requires the ordinary annual allowances for the final tax year on any machinery or plant used right up to the date of the cessation to be restricted to the proportion thereof which the number of months of trading in the final tax year bears to 12 months.

In practice, this restriction of the final year's annual allowances is not always applied on the plant held up to the cessation since any reduction in the final year's annual allowances results in an exactly corresponding increase in the balancing allowances (or decrease in the balancing charges) which are given (or made) for the final year as a result of the cessation. However, for machinery or plant acquired or first used in the final tax year (ie too late to qualify for any capital allowances for the penultimate year), and still in use up to the date of cessation, it is essential to claim the annual allowance for the final year if a balancing allowance is to be claimed on the cessation. This is because strictly a balancing allowance is only given (or a balancing charge made) where at least one annual allowance has previously been obtained (TCA 1997, s 288(1)).

Secondly, the effects of the capital allowances rules as applicable in the closing years where the interval period precedes the basis period for the penultimate year (ie the actual preceding year) are as follows:

(i) The 'capital allowance' basis period for the penultimate year will include the interval period between the end of the 'profits' basis period for the pre-penultimate year and the 'profits' basis period for the penultimate year (TCA

1997, s 306(2)(b)(ii)). Only expenditure incurred on plant which is in use at the end of that extended basis period can qualify for W&T allowances.

(ii) Annual W&T allowances for the final year are given on any items of plant remaining in use for the business on the date of cessation (after adding any additions and deducting the tax written down values of any sales in the final year prior to the cessation).

(iii) For any item of machinery or plant disposed of or otherwise ceasing to be used in the business, the balancing allowance or charge (whichever arises) is given or made as follows:

(I) for the penultimate year, if the sale or other relevant event occurs either in the extended 'capital allowance' basis period for the penultimate year to 31 December,

(II) for the final year, if the sale or other relevant event occurs during the basis period for the final year, and

(III) for the final year, if the item of plant has continued to be used for the business right up to the cessation of the business.

The point mentioned above regarding the restriction of the final year's annual allowance on machinery or plant used right up to the date of cessation also applies where the interval precedes the basis period for the penultimate year.

Example 4.305.1

Jim has been trading since 2000 and makes accounts up to 30 September each year. The trade ceases on 31 May 2015. Adjusted trading profits were as follows:

	€
Period to 30/09/2013	29,000
Period to 30/09/2014	33,000
Period to 31/05/2015	10,000

Details relevant to Jim's capital allowance computations are as follows:

Cost and tax WDVs 31/12/2013	*Cost*	*Tax WDV*
	€	€
Machine A (12.5% rate of W&T)	8,000	4,000
Machine B (12.5% rate of W&T)	24,000	6,000
Additions		
Machine C (1/12/2013)	6,000	

Disposals

Machine A (1/11/2014) sold for €400

Machine B (30/04/2015) sold for €500

Machine C was sold on 1 August 2015 for €5,000

All plant is in use for Jim's trade throughout his period of ownership.

Given that profits were falling in the period 1 October 2014 to 31 May 2015, it was not necessary to revise the assessable profits for the penultimate year, 2014, to the actual basis.

Basis periods for the final three years were therefore as follows:

2015: (1/01/2015 – 31/05/2015) – 5 months

2014: (1/10/2013 – 30/09/2014)

2013: (1/10/2012 – 30/09/2013)

The interval of unassessed profits therefore falls between 1/10/2014 and 31/12/2014. This interval is treated for capital allowance purposes as part of the basis period for the penultimate year (2014). Capital allowances are calculated as follows for 2014 and 2015:

2014	*Machine A*	*Machine B*	*Machine C*
	€	€	€
Tax WDV 1/01/2014	4,000	6,000	-
Addition (1/12/2013)			6,000
Disposal (1/11/2014)	(4,000)	-	-
	-	6,000	6,000
W&T 2014			
€24,000 x 12.5%		(3,000)	
€ 6,000 x 12.5%	-	-	(750)
Tax WDV 31/12/2014	-	3,000	5,250
Capital allowances 2014			
W&T (as above): (€3,000 + €750) =			3,750
Balancing allowance[1]			
Machine A: Tax WDV 1/1/2014	4,000		
Disposal proceeds	(400)		
Balancing allowance			3,600
			7,350
2015			
Tax WDV 1/01/2015		3,000	5,250
Disposal (30/04/2015)		(3,000)	-
		0	5,250
W&T 2015			
€ 6,000 x 12.5% x 5/12[2]		-	(313)
Tax WDV 31/12/2015		-	4,937
Capital allowances 2015			
W&T (as above)			313
Balancing allowance:[3]			
Machine B: Tax WDV 1/01/2015		3,000	
Disposal proceeds		(500)	
Balancing allowance			2,500
			2,813
Balancing charge 2015:[4]			
Machine C: Tax WDV 31/12/2015			4,937
Disposal proceeds			(5,000)
Balancing charge			63

Notes:

1. A balancing allowance/charge has to be computed for 2014 in respect of Machine A, sold in the interval before the commencement of the final year's 'profits' basis

period (since this interval is deemed to fall into the 'capital allowance' basis period for the penultimate year).

2. Because Machine C is still in use at the end of the basis period for 2015, there is an entitlement to W&T in respect of that period. Since there is only a five month basis period for 2015, the W&T allowance on Machine C is restricted accordingly. This is the technically correct method of dealing with the matter.

3. Machine B does not attract a W&T for 2015 as it was sold before the end of the basis period for that year.

4. A balancing adjustment must be made in respect of Machine C on the permanent discontinuance of the trade: see **6.207**; **6.208**.

Example 4.305.2

Facts as in **Example 4.305.1,** except that Jim's adjusted profits for the period to 31 May 2015 were €50,000. Given that profits were rising in that period, the assessable profits for the penultimate year 2014[1] need to be revised to the actual basis. Basis periods for the final three years will therefore be as follows:

2015: (1/01/2015–31/05/2015) – 5 months

2014: (1/01/2014–31/12/2014)

2013: (1/10/2012–30/09/2013)

The interval of unassessed profits therefore falls between 1/10/2013 and 31/12/2013. The interval period for capital allowance purposes is part of the basis period for the penultimate year (2014).

Capital allowances are calculated accordingly as follows for 2014 and 2015:

	Machine A	*Machine B*	*Machine C*
2014	€	€	€
Tax WDV 1/01/2014	4,000	6,000	-
Addition (1/12/2013)[1]			6,000
Disposal (1/11/2014)	(4,000)	-	-
	-	6,000	6,000
W&T 2014			
€24,000 x 12.5%		(3,000)	
€6,000 x 12.5%	-	-	(750)
Tax WDV 31/12/2014	-	3,000	5,250
Capital allowances 2014			
W&T (as above) (€3,000 + €750)			3,750
Balancing allowance[2]			
Machine A: Tax WDV 1/01/2014		4,000	
Disposal proceeds		(400)	3,600
			7,350
2015			
As in **Example 4.305.1**[3]			

Notes:

1. As Machine C is in use at the end of the basis extended 'capital allowance' period for 2014 (and this is the first basis period of use) the W&T is given based on the

original cost. As is normally the case, therefore, W&T (and any increased W&T) is unaffected by the change in basis periods.

2. The disposal of machinery now falls within the 'profits' basis period for 2014 and therefore automatically falls within the 'capital allowance' basis period for that same tax year. There is accordingly no change from the outcome in example **4.305.1**.

3. The tax WDV's at 31 December 2014 are, in fact, identical to that as under the previous basis of assessment.

Industrial buildings (including urban renewal area and other tax incentive premises)

Writing down and increased writing down allowances (free depreciation)

For the final tax year, the writing down allowance is given, if the relevant interest in a qualifying industrial building is still held at the close of business on the date of cessation of the business, (ie at the end of the basis period for the final year). Similarly, an increased writing down allowance may, if available, be claimed for the final year if the same condition is met. These rules apply even in respect of any new industrial buildings expenditure incurred in the final year. In all cases, a full year's allowance is available without restriction by reference to the fact that the basis period will normally be less than a full year.

For the penultimate tax year, the writing down and, if available, the increased writing down allowances are similarly given where the relevant interest in the qualifying building is held on the last day of the basis period for the penultimate year. Again, the basis period for the penultimate year may be either the 'original' basis period (normally, but not always, the period of 12 months for which accounts are made up to an accounting date in the penultimate year) or the actual penultimate year. Again, it is necessary to apply the rules of TCA 1997, s 306(2)(b)(iii) to deal with any interval period between the basis periods for the penultimate and final years or between the pre-penultimate and penultimate years (whichever applies).

In the case where there is an interval between the basis period for the penultimate year and that for the year in which the business is finally discontinued (the 'first case'), the interval is as usual deemed to fall into the basis period for the earlier of the two years (the penultimate year). In the other case, where the interval period falls between the basis periods for the pre-penultimate and penultimate years (the 'second case'), the interval is again deemed to become part of the basis period for the later of the two years (again the penultimate year).

In the first case, the effect is as usual to extend the 'capital allowance' basis period for the penultimate year to the last day of the penultimate year itself (ie 31 December). This permits the writing down allowance and, if available, the increased writing down allowance to be claimed for the penultimate year on any additional qualifying expenditure incurred in the interval period immediately preceding the final year, as well as for qualifying expenditure in the actual basis period for the penultimate year. It is of course necessary that the relevant interest in the building continues to be held at the end of the extended basis period.

In the second case, the 'capital allowance' basis period for the penultimate year is effectively the penultimate year ending 31 December plus the interval period between the end of the basis period for the pre-penultimate year and the penultimate year itself. This again permits the writing down and increased writing down allowances to be claimed for the penultimate year on any additional qualifying expenditure incurred up to the end of the penultimate year (including qualifying expenditure incurred during the interval period preceding the penultimate year). It is of course again necessary that the relevant interest in the building continues to be held at the end of the extended basis period.

Balancing allowances and balancing charges

The rules for determining the basis periods for the closing years of a business for the purpose of balancing allowances or balancing charges on disposals of industrial buildings are the same as those used for the industrial buildings writing down allowances and initial allowances. A balancing allowance or balancing charge must be computed for either the penultimate or final tax year if the relevant interest in an industrial building is sold (or if certain other events happen, see **6.409**) during the basis period for the year in question. Again, if the sale (or other relevant event) occurs in an interval period immediately preceding either the penultimate or final tax year, the balancing allowance or balancing charge is, in effect, always given or made for the penultimate year.

It is to be noted that the permanent discontinuance of the business does not automatically involve a balancing allowance or balancing charge on an industrial building (in contrast to the position for machinery or plant). If the relevant interest in the building remains unsold at the date of cessation, there is generally no such balancing adjustment (except in the case of the cessation of use of a relevant facility which may give rise to a balancing charge) unless and until any of the events set out in TCA 1997, s 274(1) take place (see **6.409**). In certain cases, a balancing charge or allowance may arise where a tax privileged premises ceases to qualify under the relevant legislation.

4.4 Relief for Trading Losses

4.401 Loss relief: introduction

The rules for providing relief for the tax losses and unused capital allowances of a trade or profession outlined in **4.4** are those applicable under the current year basis of assessment.

The Sch D Case I or Case II computation for one or more periods of account may result in an adjusted loss (referred to herein as a 'tax loss'). As with taxable profits, the tax loss is the figure resulting from the computation for the period of account before any capital allowances or balancing charges are taken into account. Capital allowances are then considered separately from tax losses for the purposes of the various forms of relief for losses, etc discussed herein.

If the period of account in which there is a tax loss forms the whole of the basis period for a year of assessment, this results in a 'Nil' Sch D Case I or Case II assessment for that year. A Nil assessment also results if a tax loss in one period of account (or the appropriate proportion of that loss) when taken together with the taxable profits of another period of account (or the appropriate proportion thereof) produces a loss for a basis period made up of two or more periods of account.

Example 4.401.1

Mr P Polymer, who has traded for a number of years, has the following taxable profits and tax losses (before capital allowances) computed under the rules of Sch D Case I for the under mentioned periods of accounts:

	€
12 months ended 31/03/2013	
Taxable profits	6,600
6 months to 30/09/2013	
Tax loss	(8,300)
12 months ended 30/09/2014	
Tax loss	(10,800)
10 months to 31/07/2015	
Taxable profits	32,000
(subsequent accounts made up to 31 July)	

Under the change of accounting date rules for a continuing business (see **4.204**), the basis period for Mr Polymer's Sch D Case I assessment to income tax for 2013 would be, if there were a taxable profit, the year to 30 September 2013 (12 months ending on his latest accounting date in 2013). The computation of the taxable profit or loss for this period requires the results of two periods of account to be used as follows:

	€
Period 1/10/2012 to 31/03/2013	
6/12ths x €6,600	3,300
(12-month period of accounts to 31/03/2013)	
Period 1/04/2013–30/09/2013	
Tax loss of 6-month period of accounts to 30/09/2013	(8,300)
Tax loss in basis period[1]	(5,000)
Sch D Case I assessment 2013	Nil

The basis period for the tax year 2014 is the 12 months to 30 September 2014 (the only accounting date in the year)[2]. Here there is a tax loss in this basis period:

	€
12 months to 30/09/2014	
Tax loss in basis period[3]	(10,800)
Sch D Case I assessment 2014	Nil

The basis period for the tax year 2015 is the 12 months to 31 July 2015 (the only accounting date in 2015). The computation for this 2015 basis period is, subject to the point made in note 4, as follows:

	€
2 months to 30/09/2014	
Tax loss €10,800[4] x 2/12	(1,800)
10 months to 31/07/2015	
Taxable profits of period of accounts	32,000
Taxable profit for basis period	30,200
Sch D Case I assessment 2015	30,200
(subject to capital allowances)	

Notes:

1. Mr Polymer is entitled to claim relief under one or other of the loss reliefs discussed below in respect of the unused loss of €5,000 falling in the year ended 31 December 2013. Note that special considerations would apply in the opening and closing years of a business, discussed below.

2. In view of the application of the change of accounting date rule for 2015, it is necessary to consider whether the basis period for 2013 should be changed to the 12 months to 31 July 2014. However, as there would be a loss in a 12-month period ending 31 July 2014, such a basis period would not result in higher taxable profits for 2014 than the original basis period to 30 September 2014. The original basis period is thus unchanged.

3. Mr Polymer is entitled to claim relief under one or other of the loss reliefs discussed below in respect of the loss of €10,800 falling in the year ended 31 December 2014.

Note that special considerations would apply in the opening and closing years of a business, discussed below.

4. If Mr Polymer were to claim (and obtain) relief under TCA 1997, s 381 for 2014 for the loss of €10,800 (or a part of that loss), the rule of TCA 1997, s 381(5)) would exclude that loss (or the part of it so relieved) from the computation of the taxable profits for 2015 (see Prevention of double relief in **4.404**).

Reliefs for tax losses and unused capital allowances

When a taxpayer incurs a trading loss he may be entitled to obtain relief for that loss in one of several ways depending on the circumstances.

Further, when a taxpayer has a tax loss he also requires relief for any capital allowances (net of any balancing charges) attributable to the tax year for which his Sch D Case I or Case II assessment (before capital allowances) is nil. Alternatively, he may have a taxable profit that is insufficient to absorb all the capital allowances set against it, so that there is the need to obtain relief for these excess capital allowances.

For income tax purposes, there are separate but interrelated rules for giving relief for tax losses and unused capital allowances arising in a trade or profession. These rules discussed below in the context of a trade apply equally to tax losses and unused capital allowances of a profession.

In principle, there are two main forms of relief for tax losses and unused capital allowances available to a person carrying on a trade (or profession). He may carry forward the losses and unused allowances for set off against future taxable profits of the same trade under TCA 1997, s 382 or, alternatively, he may claim a 'current year' set off against his total income from all sources as chargeable to income tax for the same year under TCA 1997, s 381.

Strictly speaking, the taxpayer may only claim a loss arising in the actual tax year and not the basis period for the year (if different) under TCA 1997, s 381. The strict basis is always applied in the opening three tax years of a trade (see **4.404**), the tax year of cessation and the penultimate tax year of cessation (see **4.409**) and any other tax year following a tax year in which the strict basis has been applied. In any other case, the Revenue Commissioners will permit the taxpayer to claim a loss under TCA 1997, s 381 by reference to the basis period of the tax year although it remains open to the taxpayer to claim under the strict basis if he so wishes. The position in relation to losses falling in the short tax year was discussed in **4.405** of the 2002 edition of this book; Revenue practice in this regard has also been clarified in *Tax Briefing 47*. If a trade (or profession) is permanently discontinued, any tax loss and/or unused capital allowances of the last 12 months' trading may be carried back under TCA 1997, s 385 for set off against any unrelieved taxable profits of the trade assessable in any of the three tax years prior to that in which the trade is permanently discontinued.

One general point to note is that, although an adjusted loss in a particular period of account may sometimes be included in determining the quantum of the taxable profit for more than one year of assessment, relief is not given more than once for the same loss whichever form of loss relief claim is made. This point and a preliminary view of the two most common forms of loss relief (the current year set off under TCA 1997, s 381 and the carry forward and set off against later profits under TCA 1997, s 382) are now illustrated in the example which follows:

Example 4.401.2

Take the facts of **Example 4.401.1**. The following are the possible reliefs for the losses shown there:

(1) Loss in 6 months to 30/09/2013 (€8,300):	€
Relieved by reducing 2013 assessment to nil	3,300
Balance eligible for other relief	5,000

Relief for €5,000 either:

(a) section 381 claim to reduce total income for 2013[1] (current year set off in year loss incurred); or

(b) carry forward for set off under TCA 1997, s 382 against Sch D Case I profits in 2014 or if not fully deducted in that year, against such profits in next tax year in which there are such profits in the same trade.[2]

(2) Loss in 12 months to 30 September 2014 (€10,800)

Relief for €10,800 either:

(a) section 381 claim to reduce total income for 2014[3] (current year set off in year loss incurred); or

(b) carry forward for s 382 set off against Sch D Case I profits in 2015 or, if not fully deducted in that year, against such profits in next tax year in which there are such profits in the same trade.

Notes:

1. If total income of same year (2013) is less than amount of loss of €5,000, the set off of the loss in any 's 381' claim made is limited to said total income (before the loss deduction) and the balance of the loss is carried forward for relief under TCA 1997, s 382 in a later year.
2. Since in this example, there are no taxable profits in the basis period for 2014, the first year for which the carry forward relief under 's 382' is available for the 2013 loss is 2015 (and the relief must be set off in that year to the extent of the taxable profits (after capital allowances) for 2015.
3. If total income of same year (2014) is less than the loss of €10,800, the set off in any s 381 claim is limited to the said total income and the balance of the loss is carried forward to set off under TCA 1997, s 382 in a later year.

It is the responsibility of the taxpayer to claim whichever form of available loss relief he requires. However, relief for a current year loss set off against total income is only given if the taxpayer makes a specific claim within two years of the end of the tax year concerned. There is no specific time limit within which a claim for terminal loss relief must be made. However the general four-year time limit within which a claim for a repayment can be made will apply (TCA 1997, s 865).

In light of the fact that a taxpayer's final tax position over a period of years may be materially affected, for better or for worse, by the form of loss relief he claims, a full understanding of the rules involved is important not only to ensure that any necessary time limits for claim are observed, but also to enable him to make the claim most suitable to the circumstances.

The rules for loss relief, including relief for unused capital allowances, are now discussed under the following headings:

(a) the carry forward of trading losses (**4.402**);
(b) the carry forward of unused capital allowances (**4.403**);

(c) the current year set off of trading losses against total income (the s 381 claim) (**4.404**);
(d) the inclusion of capital allowances in a 's 381' claim (**4.405**);
(e) restrictions on s 381 claim (**4.406**);
(f) loss relief for certain charges on income under TCA 1997, s 238 (**4.408**);
(g) some special points regarding trading losses in the opening and closing years of assessment including terminal loss relief (**4.409–4.410**);
(h) restriction of losses from dealing in residential land including restriction of the TCA 1997, s 381 current year set off (**4.411–4.412**); and
(i) FA 2014 anti-avoidance restrictions of TCA 1997, s 381 current year set off of trading losses (**4.413**).

4.402 Carry forward of trading losses

TCA 1997, s 382(1) allows a person, who has sustained a tax loss in a trade or profession to carry forward the loss for set off against the taxable profits of the same trade or profession assessable for any subsequent year of assessment. No such carry forward is available if, and to the extent that, relief for the loss is given under a current year set off claim under TCA 1997, s 381 (see **4.404**) or under any other provision in the Act (eg where part of the loss is apportioned to a basis period and is accordingly utilised in offsetting profits apportioned to the same basis period). For the special rules governing certain losses from dealing in residential development land, see **4.411**.

TCA 1997, s 382(2) requires any tax loss incurred in and carried forward from any year of assessment to be set off as far as possible against the taxable profits assessable for the next year of assessment. For this purpose, the taxable profits for the next year available to cover the loss forward are the taxable profits for that year after deducting the relevant capital allowances (see also **4.403**). If those taxable profits (after capital allowances) are insufficient to absorb fully the tax loss brought forward, the unrelieved balance of that loss is carried forward again to the next year of assessment, and so on indefinitely so long as the trade (or profession) continues until the loss carried forward is fully used up.

If there are any taxable profits for the next year (after deducting the capital allowances for that year and any unused capital allowances brought forward from earlier years), the tax loss brought forward must be set off to the full extent of those profits. It is not possible, for example, to preserve some or all of the loss forward for use in a later year by utilising an individual's personal tax credits or deductions against total income in priority to that loss forward. Should there be a further tax loss sustained in the tax year to which an earlier loss is brought forward, the further tax loss is then carried forward to the succeeding tax year together with the tax loss(es) brought forward from the earlier year(s) (unless a current year set off is claimed for the further loss).

Example 4.402.1

Take the case of Mr P Polymer from **Example 4.401.1**. Assume that he has unrelieved tax losses coming forward from previous years amounting to €13,600.

Assuming that Mr Polymer does not claim a current year set off under TCA 1997, s 381 for the tax losses shown in **Examples 4.401.1** and **4.401.2**, he has the following further losses to be carried forward to later years:

	€
Loss in 6 months to 30/09/2013 (balance)	5,000
Loss in 12 months to 30/09/2014	10,800

Adding these tax losses to the €13,600 cumulative losses forward from previous years results in cumulative tax losses forward of €29,400 at 30 September 2014.

Assume that Mr Polymer's capital allowances (less balancing charges) for the relevant tax years are as follows:

	€
Capital allowances forward from 2012	600
2013	400
2014	200
Capital allowances forward after 2014	1,200
2015 allowances	330

Mr Polymer requires relief for his tax losses by carry forward under TCA 1997, s 382. The first year for which there are any taxable profits to absorb the tax losses (and capital allowances) forward is 2015. As shown at the end of **Example 4.401.1** the taxable profits for 2015 work out at €30,200 after using up €1,800 of the loss in the 12 months account to 30 September 2014.[2]

Relief is now obtained for the losses and capital allowances in 2015 as follows:

	€	€
Taxable profits for basis period (per **Example 4.401.1**)		30,200
Less:		
Capital allowances 2015	330	
Unused capital allowances forward from previous tax years[1]	1,200	
		(1,530)
Net assessment (before loss relief)		28,670
Less:		
Unrelieved losses forward after 2014	29,400	
Less:		
Part of 2014 loss used in basis period for 2015 in arriving at taxable profits for that period[2]	(1,800)	
		(27,600)
Net Sch D Case I assessment 2015 (after TCA 1997, s 382 relief)		1,070

Notes:

1. The €1,200 unused capital allowances at the end of 2014 are carried forward to be treated as if part of the capital allowances for 2015 (see **4.403**) and are relieved in that year.
2. No relief under TCA 1997, s 382 is available for the two months proportion (€1,800) of the €10,800 loss incurred in the year to 30 September 2014 but it is used to reduce the quantum of the taxable profits of the basis period for 2015 (see **Example 4.401.1**).

4.403 Carry forward of capital allowances

TCA 1997, s 304(4) provides that, if capital allowances on machinery or plant or industrial buildings cannot be fully used in the year of assessment to which they relate due to there being insufficient or no taxable profits for that year, any part of the allowances not used is to be carried forward and treated as an addition to the wear and tear allowances for the next year of assessment. If the allowances for the next year, as increased by any amount carried forward from previous years cannot be fully allowed in that year, the unused amount is carried forward to the following year. This carry forward of unused allowances continues indefinitely so long as the trade continues. The provisions of TCA 1997, s 304(4) are extended to scientific research allowances by TCA 1997, s 765(5) and to patent right allowances by TCA 1997, s 762(1).

The right to carry forward capital allowances is only given where the allowances claimed are greater than the taxable profits for the trade chargeable for that year. The allowances claimed for the year must first be deducted from the Sch D Case I (or Case II) profits. The taxpayer does not have the option to defer taking relief for his capital allowances in one year where, for example, the tax payable on his taxable profits is such that it could be fully covered by his tax credits. Once the capital allowances are claimed for a tax year, there is no alternative. This is a different matter from a decision not to claim an accelerated allowance under the free depreciation or initial allowance rules (now generally available only in respect of qualifying premises in tax incentive areas, etc see **Division 19** *et seq* of the 2009 edition of this book); such a decision is a perfectly valid method of deferring capital allowances to a later year since the taxpayer is under no obligation to claim the accelerated allowances.

Since unused capital allowances carried forward must be treated as part of the capital allowances of the next year, they are in effect deducted from the next available taxable profits before losses carried forward. To the extent that there are sufficient taxable profits in the ensuing year, both the capital allowances for that year and those carried forward from previous years must be fully set off against those profits. Any losses carried forward are then set off. In fact, the treatment of capital allowances and losses forward is very similar and there is little practical significance in the distinction between the two for income tax and USC purposes. However for PRSI contributions, while capital allowances are deductible when calculating the liability to PRSI no deduction is available for losses.

Example 4.403.1

Mr A N Iceberg, who has traded for some years, whose basis period for each year of assessment is his accounting period ended on 30 September in the tax year concerned, has the following Sch D Case I profits and losses and capital allowances related to each basis period:

	Sch D Case I profits	*Sch D Case I losses*	*Capital allowances*
	€	€	€
Y/E 30/09/2012	2,000	-	4,000
Y/E 30/09/2013	-	1,000	1,500
Y/E 30/09/2014	2,300	-	1,650
Y/E 30/09/2015	8,200	-	2,200

Assuming Mr Iceberg claims relief for both losses and capital allowances under the carry forward rules, the set off of losses and capital allowances is as follows:

	Set off	*Case I assessment*	*Net Sch D Amounts*
2012:	€	€	€
Sch D Case I profits			
(Y/E 30/09/2012)	2,000		

Capital allowances 2012 (part)	(2,000)		
		Nil	
Capital allowances c/f			
2012 allowances (balance)			2,000
2013:			
Sch D Case I profits			
(Y/E 30/09/2013)		Nil	
Capital allowances c/f			
2013 allowances			1,500
b/f from 2012			2,000
c/f to 2014			3,500
Tax loss c/f			
Y/E 30/09/2013			1,000
2014:			
Sch D Case I profits			
(Y/E 30/09/2014)	2,300		
Capital allowances 2014	(1,650)		
Capital allowances b/f (part)	(650)		
		Nil	
Capital allowances c/f			
b/f from 2013			3,500
used in 2014 (above)			(650)
c/f to 2015			2,850
Tax loss c/f			
As per 2013 (still unused)			1,000
2015:			
Sch D Case I profits			
(Y/E 30/09/2015)	8,200		
Capital allowances 2015	(2,200)		
Capital allowances b/f	(2,850)		
Tax loss b/f	(1,000)		
		2,150	
Capital allowances c/f			
b/f from 2014			2,850
used in 2015			(2,850)
			Nil
Tax loss c/f			
b/f from 2014			1,000
used in 2015			(1,000)
			Nil

4.404 Loss set off against income from all sources

TCA 1997, s 381 permits a person chargeable to income tax to claim relief for a tax loss incurred in a trade or profession carried on by him, whether solely or in partnership, by set off against his income from all sources for the relevant tax year by the amount of the loss. Relief may only be claimed under this section in respect of a tax loss sustained in the tax year for which the claim is made (the 'year of loss'). A claim for loss relief under this section may be referred to as a 's 381 claim' or as a 'current year set off claim'. This set off against income from all sources has the effect of reducing the taxpayer's total income for the year of claim. For the special rules and restrictions governing certain losses from dealing in and developing land and losses incurred in a passive trade, see **4.411, 4.412** and **4.413**.

A current year set off claim entitles the taxpayer to have his income tax liability for the year of loss recalculated by reference to a revised total income resulting from the deduction of the tax loss. To the extent that the recalculation shows an overpayment of tax was made, the taxpayer is entitled to the appropriate repayment, but not to any interest on the amount overpaid. If a valid TCA 1997, s 381 claim is submitted to the inspector before the taxpayer has been fully assessed on all his income for the relevant year, it may in practice be possible to have the final assessment made on the income as reduced by the amount of the loss claim, thus avoiding the taxpayer having to seek a repayment. However, a s 381 claim is strictly one of a repayment of income tax previously assessed.

The amount of the loss set off against other income in a s 381 claim is the tax loss for the tax year (or its basis period) computed under the rules of Sch D Case I or Case II in the same way as any taxable profits would be computed (TCA 1997, s 381(4)). The loss is taken before giving effect to any capital allowances or balancing charges. However, the taxpayer has the option of claiming under TCA 1997, s 392 to have the loss increased by the appropriate capital allowances less any balancing charges (see **4.405**). If this option is not exercised, the s 381 claim is limited to the tax loss.

It may not always be desirable to use TCA 1997, s 392 to increase the tax loss by the capital allowances. Once a s 381 claim is made, the full loss must, to the extent there is sufficient total income, be deducted from that income even if this involves completely offsetting the income so that no benefit is obtained from the taxpayer's personal tax credits or deductions that are available against total income. One way to avoid this result may be to set off the tax loss only, but to carry forward the capital allowances to the next tax year for which there is a taxable profit.

A s 381 claim can be made on the income tax return Form 11. The inspector of taxes is required to determine the claim, but if the taxpayer is not satisfied with the inspector's determination, he may appeal by notice in writing to the inspector within 21 days of being notified of the determination, to have the case heard by the Appeal Commissioners. The usual rights to a rehearing by the Circuit Court judge or to an appeal to the High Court on a point of law apply (TCA 1997, s 381(6), (7)). F(TA)A 2015, s 36(4) amends TCA 1997, s 381(6) and (7) such that the person aggrieved makes the appeal to the Appeal Commissioners within 30 days of the date of the notice of determination but such adjustment is subject to Ministerial Order with appeal possible to the High Court on a point of law. If the taxpayer wishes to include capital allowances in the claim, this must be specified when making the claim.

A taxpayer, who has sustained a tax loss in a year of assessment (or in its basis period), usually has to consider whether it is more advantageous to claim a current year set off for it under TCA 1997, s 381 or to carry the loss forward for relief in a later tax year by set off under TCA 1997, s 382 against subsequent taxable profits of the same trade or profession (see **4.402**).

While a s 381 claim will obtain relief in an earlier tax year, this may be less beneficial if the effect of reducing the total income of the year of claim is to leave some of his personal tax credits and other deductions or reliefs unused. It may be more advantageous to carry forward the loss to reduce the taxable profits (and thereby his total income) assessable for a later year if the result is to save tax at a higher rate in the later year. On the other hand, if after setting off a tax loss against the other income of the same tax year (and after taking the personal tax credits, etc) there would still be income taxable at the higher rates of income tax, the s 381 claim may be the more beneficial.

Example 4.404.1

Mr N Nettles, a single person aged 45 who has traded for a number of years making up accounts to 31 May, has the following tax losses and capital allowances in respect of his two periods of account ending 31 May 2014 and 2015:

	€
12 months to 31 May 2014	
Tax loss	8,340
Capital allowances 2014	1,050
12 months to 31 May 2015	
Tax loss	5,850
Capital allowances 2015	800

These tax losses incurred respectively in the tax year 2014 and 2015 are available for s 381 relief, if Mr Nettles wishes to claim it. Also, the capital allowances 2014 and 2015 may be eligible to increase the relief under s 381 for either or both years if he wishes to make the election under TCA 1997, s 392 (see **4.405**).

Mr Nettles' income from all sources for 2014 and 2015 and deductions therefrom are as follows:

	2014	*2015*
Sch D Case I:	€	€
2014: 12 months to 31/5/2014	Nil	
2015: 12 months to 31/5/2015		Nil
Sch D Case III:		
Interest on government securities	4,000	1,000
Sch D Case V:		
Net rents	8,140	5,570
Sch F:		
Dividends from Irish companies (including Dividend Withholding Tax)	8,820	4,550
	20,960	11,120
Less:		
Annual payment:		
Deed of covenant to incapacitated brother	(2,000)	(2,000)
Total income (before s 381 relief)	18,960	9,120

Mr Nettles claims s 381 relief for 2014 in respect of the tax loss of €8,340, but makes no election to include the capital allowances for 2014. The effect on his total income computation is as follows:

	€
Total income 2014 (before charge and s 381 relief):	
As above	20,960
Less:	
Tax loss incurred in 2014[1]	(8,340)
Charge	(2,000)
Total income 2014 (final)	10,620

If Mr Nettles were to make a s 381 claim for 2015 in respect of his tax loss of €5,850, it would reduce his total income for that year to (€11,120 – €5,850 – €2,000) = €3,270. Tax on this income at 20 per cent would amount to €654 which after deduction of the single personal tax credit of €1,650 would reduce his liability to nil. However, tax on the pre-s 381 claim income of €9,120 at 20 per cent would only amount to €1,824 which net of the single personal tax credit of €1,650 would only leave tax payable of €174. Since he expects to have a much larger total income for 2016 (including an expected taxable profit from his trade in the year to 31 May 2016), he considers it preferable to carry forward the tax loss incurred in 2015.

Mr Nettles therefore carries forward to 2016 the following tax loss and unused capital allowances:

	€	€
Unused capital allowances forward:		
2014 (not elected under TCA 1997, s 392)	1,050	
2015	800	
		1,850
Tax loss forward under TCA 1997, s 382		5,850

Note:

1. The s 381 loss must be offset in priority to the annual payment (*Navan Carpets Ltd v O'Culacháin* III ITR 403).

It may be seen from this example that there must be income from other sources for the tax year in which the loss is sustained in the trade or profession if there is to be a s 381 loss relief claim in respect of that loss. The tax loss sustained in one tax year (the current year) can only be set off against income from other sources arising in the current year.

Prevention of double relief

TCA 1997, s 381(5)(a) provides that, to the extent that relief is obtained in a s 381 claim for a tax loss by reducing the claimant's income for any year of assessment, the amount so relieved cannot be taken into account in computing the amount of taxable profits assessable for any subsequent tax year. Apart from preventing the carry forward of the relieved loss for set off against future profits of the same trade (see **4.402**), this rule may be relevant if, part of the period of accounts in which the loss is incurred has to be included in the basis period for a later tax year.

Section 381 claim: change of accounting date

Example 4.404.2

Take the facts of **Example 4.401.1** where Mr P Polymer (who is a single person aged 52) had the following results for his two periods of account ending 30 September 2014 and 31 July 2015:

	€
12 months to 30/09/2014:	
Tax loss (before capital allowances)	(10,800)
10 months to 31/07/2014	
Taxable profits (before capital allowances)	32,000

Assume that Mr Polymer's total income (before any s 381 loss relief) for 2014 amounts to €8,200. He decides to make a s 381 claim for 2014 in respect of the tax loss of €10,800, but only €8,200 of this loss is needed to reduce his total income for 2014 to nil.

It has been shown in **Example 4.401.1** that Mr Polymer's basis period for his 2015 Sch D Case I assessment is the 12 months ending 31 July 2015. The computation of his taxable profits for that period involves including the results of two months of the year to 30 September 2014 in which the tax loss of €10,800 is incurred. TCA 1997, s 381(5)(a) requires the computation of the assessable profits for 2015 (a later year) to ignore the part (€8,200) of the 2014 loss used in the s 381 claim for 2014.

The computation of the taxable profits (before capital allowances) for the 2015 assessment for the 12 months basis period ending 31 July 2015 is therefore as follows:

	€
2 months to 30/09/2014	
Part of tax loss in 12 months to 30/09/2014	
(€10,800 less €8,200) x 2/12ths	(433)
10 months to 31/07/2015	
Taxable profits of period of accounts to 31/07/2015	32,000
Taxable profits 2015 (subject to capital allowances)	31,567

The unrelieved part of the loss € (10,800 – 8,200 – 433) = €2,166 is carried forward eligible for relief under TCA 1997, s 382 (see **4.402**).

Section 381 claim: commencement of trade

The first few years of a new trade (or profession) may well see tax losses and, assuming that the person carrying on the trade has income from other sources, the ability to claim relief under TCA 1997, s 381 so as to reduce the tax on his other income may be an important factor in the trader's overall financial situation. In the case of a commencement, the tax loss eligible for s 381 relief (the 's 381 loss') for the first three tax years of trading is always the actual tax loss incurred in or apportioned to the tax year. In the first year this will be the period from the date of commencement to 31 December of the first tax year; for the second and third years of trading it will be the loss incurred in or apportioned to the period from 1 January to the following 31 December.

Example 4.404.3

Mr XY commences to trade on 1 March 2013. The results of his first two periods of account are as follows:

	€
12 months to 28/02/2014	
Tax loss	(36,000)
12 months to 28/02/2015	
Taxable profit	6,600

Mr XY has incurred tax losses eligible for relief under s 381 in 2013 and 2014 as follows:

	€
Incurred in 2013:	
10 months to 31/12/2013	
10/12ths x €36,000 (12 months to 28/02/2014)	(30,000)
Incurred in 2014	
2 months to 28/02/2014	
2/12ths x €36,000 (12 months to 28/02/2014)	(6,000)
10 months to 31/12/2014	
10/12ths x € 6,600 (12 months to 28/02/2015)	5,500
	(500)

The strict basis applies for both 2013 and 2014. Mr XY's Sch D Case 1 assessments for the first two years will be based on the accounts ended 28 February 2014 showing a tax loss (ie 2013: assessment on actual basis from 1 March 2013 to 31 December 2013, based on first 10 months of accounts to 28 February 2014; 2014: assessment on full set of 12 month of accounts ending in 28 February 2014). This will result in a nil assessment in both years but without any requirement of use of the opening year's loss against profits in computing those assessments. Assuming that all losses are claimed under TCA 1997, s 381 to the full extent possible, the unused loss of €(36,000 – 30,000 – 500) = € 5,500 will be carried forward under TCA 1997, s 382 against trading profits of 2015 (based on the profits of the accounts year ended 28 February 2015) and if necessary subsequent tax years. Mr XY will have nil taxable profits for 2013 and 2014 based on the above figures.

Example 4.404.4

Mr PQ commences to trade on 1 June 2013. The results of his first three periods of account are as follows:

	€
10 months to 31/03/2014	
Tax loss	(8,000)
8 months to 30/11/2014	
Tax loss	(4,200)
12 months to 30/11/2015	
Taxable profit	1,800

Mr PQ has incurred tax losses eligible for relief under s 381 in 2013 and 2014 as follows:

	2014	*2013*
	€	€
Incurred in 2013:		
7 months to 31/12/2013		
7/10ths x €8,000		(5,600)
Incurred in 2014:		
3 months to 31/03/2014		
3/10ths x €8,000	(2,400)	
8 months to 30/11/2014		
Full period's loss	(4,200)	
1 month to 31/12/2014		
1/12 x € 1,800	150	
	(6,450)	

Mr PQ's Sch D Case I assessments for the first two years will be based on the accounts for the periods ended 31 March 2014 and 30 November 2014, each showing a tax loss (ie 2013: assessment on actual basis from 1 June 2013 – 31 December 2013, based on first seven months of accounts to 31 March 2014; 2014: based on 12 months ending 30 November 2014 being the latest date for which accounts were made up in 2014 more than 12 months following date of commencement). This will result in a nil assessment in both years but without any requirement to use the opening year's loss against profits in computing those assessments. Assuming that all losses are claimed under TCA 1997, s 381 to the full extent possible, the unused losses of € [(8,000 + 4,200) – (5,600+ 6,450)] = €150 will be carried forward under TCA 1997, s 382 against trading profits of 2015 (based on the profits of the accounts year ended 30 November 2015) and if necessary subsequent tax years. Mr XY will have nil taxable profits for 2013 and 2014 based on the above figures.

Example 4.404.5

Ms R Undertree, who has substantial income from rents and dividends, sets up and commences a trade on 1 September 2012. She has the following adjusted Sch D Case I figures for her opening periods of account as follows:

	€
7 months to 31/03/2013	
Tax loss	(15,050)
4 months to 31/7/2013	
Tax loss	(2,700)
9 months to 30/04/2014	
Tax loss	(7,200)
15 months to 31/07/2015	
Taxable profits	21,000

Ms Undertree wishes to claim relief for the tax losses under s 381 to the maximum extent possible, but she decides not to use TCA 1997, s 392 to increase the losses by the amount of available capital allowances (see **4.405**).

2012 and 2013 (first two years)

The tax losses eligible for relief for the first two years of the new trade are determined as follows:

	€
2012:	
Loss in period 1/09/2012 to 31/12/2012[1]	
4/7ths x €15,050 (7 months to 31/03/2013)	(8,600)
2013:	
Loss sustained in 2013[2]	
Loss in 3 months to 31/03/2013	
3/7ths x €15,050 (7 months to 31/03/2013)	(6,450)
Loss in 4 months to 31/07/2013	
Loss for full 4-month period	(2,700)
Loss in 5 months to 31/12/2013	
5/9ths x €7,200 (9 months to 30/04/2014)	(4,000)
	(13,150)

It is assumed that Ms Undertree's total income from other sources is €57,600 for 2012 and €64,220 for 2013 so that full relief is obtained under TCA 1997, s 381 in each year respectively for the 2012 loss of €8,600 (by deduction from the €57,600) and for the 2013 loss of €13,150 (by deduction from the €64,220).

Position for 2014

There is still a loss sustained in part of 2014 (€3,200, ie the other 4/9ths of the loss of €7,200 apportioned to the four months ending 30 April 2013). However, it is now necessary to consider whether there are any taxable profits in the basis period for 2014. Normally the basis period for 2014 would be the 12 months ending 30 April 2014 (the only accounting date in 2014). However, it is to be noted that there is no 12-month period of account ending in the next year (2015) so that the basis period for 2015 is taken as the 12 months to 31 July 2015 (the period of 12 months ending on the only accounting date in the year).

Therefore, the rule of TCA 1997, s 65(3) has to be considered (see **4.204**). Under this rule, the assessment for 2014 will be based on the taxable profits of the 12 months ending 31 July 2014 (the date in 2014 corresponding to the last day of the 2015 basis period) if that results in greater taxable profits than those of the 12 months ending 30 April 2014 (the original basis period for 2014).

In making the computation of the taxable profits (if any) assessable for 2014, it is necessary to leave out of account any tax loss for which s 381 relief has been given for any earlier year (TCA 1997, s 381(5)(a), see Prevention of double relief above). Taking this rule into account, the computation to determine the taxable profits for 2014, applying also the rule of TCA 1997, s 65(3), is as follows:

Higher taxable profits of	€	€
(1) 12 months to 30/04/2014		
Period 1/05/2013 – 31/07/2013		
3/4ths x loss €2,700 (4 months to 31/07/2013)	(2,025)	
Less:		
This amount used in s 381 claim for 2013	2,025	
(re the 3 months to 31/07/2013)		

		Nil
Period 1/08/2013 – 30/04/2014		
Full loss of 9-month period to 30/04/2014	(7,200)	
Less:		
Part thereof used in s 381 claim for 2013		
(re the 5 months to 31/12/2013)	4,000	
		(3,200)
Total loss of this period		(3,200)
Taxable profits of this period (=(1))		Nil
(2) 12 months to 31/07/2014		
Period 1/08/2013 to 30/04/2014		
Full loss of 9 months to 30/04/2014	(7,200)	
Less:		
Part thereof used in s 381 claim for 2013		
(re the 5 months to 31/12/2013)	4,000	
		(3,200)
Period 1/05/2014 – 31/07/2014		
3/15ths x €21,000 (15 months to 31/07/2015)		4,200
Taxable profits of this period (=(2))		1,000
Final taxable profits assessable 2014		
(the higher taxable profits of (1) and (2))		

The result is that there are now taxable profits of €1,000 for 2014 with the final basis period becoming the 12 months ending 31 July 2014. There is no 2014 loss eligible for relief under TCA 1997, s 381 (or for any other loss relief). It is also to be noted that relief for the €3,200 loss attributed to the nine months to 30 April 2014 has been obtained in the 2014 profits computation by reducing the €4,200 taxable profits earned in the last three months of the final basis period (three months to 31 July 2014).

Notes:

1. For the first tax year of the new trade, the actual tax loss sustained in the tax year (which corresponds with its basis period) must be taken.
2. For the second tax year, the actual tax loss sustained in the year to 31 December is taken. Because the latest date to which a period of accounts is made up in the year is less than 12 months, the basis period for the second year is also the actual profits for the year, ie a nil assessment arises.

Section 381 claim: cessation of trade

The tax loss (if any) eligible for s 381 relief in respect of the tax year in which a trade or profession is permanently discontinued is always the loss incurred in that year from 1 January to the date of cessation. The tax loss (if any) eligible for relief under s 381 in the penultimate tax year will be the tax loss incurred in the penultimate year ending 31 December.

The general point to look out for is whether there is a tax loss in any period of account which is not used to offset any taxable profits in arriving at the result of the basis period for any year of assessment. If and to the extent that there is such an unused loss, the next thing is to identify the tax year or tax years in which such loss was actually incurred and to claim s 381 relief for the year or years in question (unless another form of relief is available and is considered to give a better result).

Example 4.404.6

		€
Mr LE Foliage ceases trade on 30 April 2015		
10 months to 30/04/2015:		
Tax loss		(7,580)
12 months to 30/6/2014:		
Taxable profit		3,320
12 months to 30/6/2013:		
Tax loss		(1,890)

Mr Foliage is assessable for 2014 (penultimate year) on the taxable profits of €3,320 earned in the 12 months ending 30 June 2014 (the original basis period for 2014, not revised on the cessation as the actual penultimate year ending 31 December 2014 would not give a higher assessment).

He has tax losses eligible for relief under s 381 for tax years as follows:

	€	€
2015:		
Period 1/01/2015 to 30/04/2015		
4/10ths x €7,580		(3,032)
2014:[1]		
Period 1/07/2014 to 31/12/2014		
6/10ths x €7,580	(4,548)	
Period 1/01/2014 to 30/06/2014		
6/12ths x 3,320	1,660	(2,888)
2013:		
Loss in 12 months to 30/06/2013[2]		(1,890)

Notes:

1. The loss in respect of the penultimate tax year of trading is computed on the strict actual basis.
2. The normal practice for a continuing business is followed here for 2013, ie taking the loss incurred in the basis period for assessing taxable profits (if there were any).

Example 4.404.7

Mr G Grasse ceases trade on 31 July 2015 with the following results in his last three periods of account:

	€
10 months to 31/07/2015:	
Tax loss	(2,600)
12 months to 30/09/2014:	
Tax loss	(4,500)
12 months to 30/09/2013:	
Tax loss	(880)
(taxable profits in previous periods of account)	

Assuming that Mr Grasse claimed (and was allowed) s 381 relief for 2013 on the normal continuing business basis, ie for the loss of €880 incurred in the 12 months ending 30 September 2013, he may now claim s 381 relief for the subsequent losses as follows:

Relief in 2013 (strict basis) in place of previous claim:	€	€
Loss incurred in period 1/1/2013 – 31/12/2013		
Loss incurred in period 1/1/2013 – 30/09/2013		
9/12ths x €880	(660)	
Loss incurred in period 1/10/2013 – 31/12/2013		
3/12ths x €4,500	(1,125)	(1,785)
Relief in 2014 (penultimate year)		
Loss incurred in 12 months to 31/12/2014		
9/12ths x €4,500 (12 months to 30/09/2014)	(3,375)	
3/10ths x €2,600 (10 months to 31/07/2014)	(780)	
		(4,155)
Relief in 2015 (final year)		
Loss incurred from 1/01/2015 to 31/07/2015		
7/10ths x €2,600		(1,820)

Time limit for claim

No claim for loss relief under TCA 1997, s 381 is valid unless it is made no later than two years after the end of the year of assessment to which it refers (TCA 1997, s 381(6)). For example, a claim for the tax year 2015 for a trading loss incurred in a taxpayer's accounting year ended 30 September 2015 must be made no later than 31 December 2017.

Clearly, the earlier a claim is made, the sooner the repayment of tax may be expected; this can be an important factor if a significant sum is to be repaid. On the other hand, it may sometimes be useful to delay making the claim for as long as possible so as to give the taxpayer more time to decide which loss relief claim is likely to give him the best overall result. However, the taxpayer must be careful not to miss the relevant time limit for the claim.

4.405 Capital allowances in a s 381 claim

TCA 1997, s 392 permits a person making a claim for s 381 relief in respect of a tax loss incurred in a year of assessment to elect, should he wish to do so, to increase the tax loss in the claim by the capital allowances for that year of assessment (the 'year of loss'). Alternatively, if he has taxable profits chargeable for a year of assessment which are less than the capital allowances for that year, TCA 1997, s 392 allows him to elect to deduct the capital allowances from the taxable profits to create a loss to be relieved in the s 381 claim (by reducing his total income for the year in question). In either case, the election to use the capital allowances in this way must be made at the time the s 381 claim is lodged (within the time limit referred to in **4.404**).

The rules of TCA 1997, s 392 (and of its supporting sections) are expressed in terms of relief for the capital allowances of trades. However, TCA 1997, s 391(3) extends the application of all the rules of TCA 1997, ss 391–395 also to professions.

TCA 1997, s 395 provides that, if a claim has been made under TCA 1997, s 392(1) to create or increase a loss using capital allowances and if the entitlement to relief for those capital allowances is affected by a subsequent change in the legislation or by a discontinuance of the trade (or profession) or by any other event occurring after the end of the year in question, then the relief is to be taken back and any necessary additional assessment made to correct the position.

Example 4.405.1

Mr A Apple, who has traded for some years, has taxable profits of €10,000 (before capital allowances) for his 12 month period of account ending 30 September 2015 (his basis period for the tax year 2015). There are no unused capital allowances forward from any earlier tax year.

Mr Apple's capital allowances for 2015 are €20,330.

Mr Apple has income from other sources totalling €63,760 for 2015. He wants to minimise his taxable income for the year. He therefore makes a claim for relief under s 381 and uses TCA 1997, s 392 to require that the amount eligible for relief is computed after deducting the relevant capital allowances. TCA 1997, s 392 is applied as follows:

(a) The 'year of the loss' is the tax year 2015;

(b) The year of the loss is the basis year for 2015;

(c) A loss is created by deducting the capital allowances for 2015 as follows:

	€
Taxable profits 2015	10,000
Deduct:	
Capital allowances 2015 (as above)	(20,330)
s 381 loss (with TCA 1997, s 392 election)	(10,330)

Mr Apple's total income for 2015 is therefore recalculated as follows:

	€
Income from all sources	63,760
Deductions in arriving at total income:	
s 381 loss (with TCA 1997, s 392 election)	(10,330)
(assumed no other deductions)	-
Total income (after s 381 relief)	53,430

There are a number of supporting rules which are relevant to any claim to increase or create a s 381 loss where there are balancing charges or unused capital allowances forward from earlier years. The following rules must be used, to the extent relevant, where TCA 1997, s 392 is applied to a s 381 claim made for a particular tax year (the 'year of loss'):

(a) only the capital allowances for the year of loss may be used in the s 381 claim, ie any unused capital allowances carried forward from any earlier year or years are excluded from the claim (TCA 1997, s 391(2)(a));

(b) however, any unused capital allowances carried forward from earlier years are to be applied to reduce the taxable profits before capital allowances (if there are any such profits) in priority to the capital allowances for the year of loss (TCA 1997, s 391(2)(b));

(c) if there are any balancing charges for the year of loss, those balancing charges must be fully offset by the capital allowances of the year of loss before any such capital allowances may be used in the s 381 claim (TCA 1997, s 393(1)); and

(d) however, any such balancing charges are to be offset firstly by any unused capital allowances from earlier years to the extent that those allowances exceed the taxable profits of the year (if there are any such profits) (TCA 1997, s 393(2)).

Example 4.405.2

Take the facts of **Example 4.405.1**, except assume that there are unused capital allowances of €12,380 carried forward from the previous tax year (2014). Although these allowances cannot be included in the s 381 claim for 2015, they are dealt with as follows:

	€
Taxable profits 2015	10,000
Capital allowances forward from 2014 (part)[1]	(10,000)
Taxable profit/tax loss	Nil
Capital allowances forward still unused[2]	2,380

The s 381 claim under the TCA 1997, s 392 election is now made for a loss in 2015 computed as follows:

	€
Taxable profits 2015 (as reduced above)	Nil
Deduct:	
Capital allowances 2014 (as before)	(20,330)
s 381 loss (TCA 1997, s 392 election)[3]	(20,330)

Notes:

1. The capital allowances forward are set off first against the taxable profits of 2015 to the full extent of those profits in priority to the capital allowances for 2015.
2. The capital allowances forward from 2014 not fully used (€12,380 less €10,000) are carried forward to 2016.
3. Although the capital allowances forward from 2014 are not used in the s 381 claim for 2015, the effect of their being set off first against the taxable profits is to increase by €10,000 the loss created by the capital allowances for the year of the claim.

Example 4.405.3

Take Mr Apple's case again, but assume that the facts are now as follows:

	€
Taxable profits 2015 (before capital allowances)	10,000
Capital allowances 2015	20,330
Balancing charges 2015	2,300
Capital allowances forward from 2014	12,380

The required order of set off for the €12,380 capital allowances forward from 2014 is as follows:

	Taxable profits	*Balancing charges*
	€	€
Amounts chargeable 2015	10,000	2,300

Capital allowances forward from 2014:		
First against taxable profits	(10,000)	
Next against balancing charges	-	(2,300)
Balances before TCA 1997, s 392 deduction	Nil	Nil
Capital allowances forward still unused		
€12,380 less €10,000 less €2,300 = €80[1]		

The s 381 claim under the TCA 1997, s 392 election for 2015 is now made for a loss computed as follows:

	€
Taxable profits 2015 (as reduced above)	Nil
Deduct:	
Capital allowances 2015[2]	(20,330)
s 381 loss (TCA 1997, s 392 election)	(20,330)

Notes:

1. The €80 of the capital allowances forward from 2014 is carried forward for use in 2016.
2. Since the 2015 balancing charges have been fully offset by the capital allowances forward, the full amount of the 2015 capital allowances remain available to increase the s 381 loss.

Example 4.405.4

Take the facts in **Example 4.405.3** except assume that the balancing charges for 2015 are €3,750 (and not €2,300).

The set off of the €12,380 capital allowances carried forward from 2014 is now as follows:

	Taxable profits	*Balancing charges*
	€	€
Amounts chargeable 2015	10,000	3,750
Capital allowances forward from 2014:		
First against taxable profits	(10,000)	
Next against balancing charges	-	(2,380)
Balances before TCA 1997, s 392 deduction	Nil	1,370
Capital allowances forward still unused		
€12,380 less €10,000 less €2,380 = €nil[1]		

The s 381 claim under the TCA 1997, s 392 election for 2015 is now made for a loss computed as follows:

	€	€
Taxable profits 2015 (as reduced above)		Nil
Deduct:		
Capital allowances 2015	(20,330)	

Less:		
Balancing charges 2015[2]	1,370	
		(18,960)
s 381 loss (TCA 1997, s 392 election)		(18,960)

Notes:

1. In this case, all the capital allowances forward from 2014 are fully used up against the taxable profits and balancing charges for 2015.
2. The part of balancing charges for 2015 not offset by the capital allowances forward must be fully offset by the capital allowances for 2015 before any part of the latter allowances may be used in the s 381 claim for 2015.

Allocation of capital allowances in case of excess s 381 losses

If the s 381 loss (as increased or created by the TCA 1997, s 392 election) exceeds the income from all sources against which it is set off, the s 381 relief is deemed to have been given first in respect of the tax loss in the trade in priority to the capital allowances (thereby leaving the capital allowances not set off under the claim to be carried forward to the next tax year TCA 1997, s 392(2)).

Example 4.405.5

Ms B Plum has a tax loss of €14,500 in her trade of market gardening for the 12 months ending 30 April 2015 (her basis period for a 2015 assessment, if there were taxable profits). The other relevant facts are:

	€
Capital allowances 2015	4,640
Balancing charges 2015	1,500
Capital allowances forward from 2014	820

Ms Plum claims s 381 relief for 2015 requiring the loss of €14,500 to be increased by capital allowances under TCA 1997, s 392. The first step is to deal with the €820 unused capital allowances carried forward from 2014. Since there are no taxable profits assessable for 2015, the capital allowances forward are set off as follows:

	€
Balancing charges 2015	1,500
Less:	
Capital allowances forward from 2014	(820)
Balancing charges 2015 remaining	680

The amount of the s 381 loss for 2015 is now computed as follows:

	€	€
Tax loss 2015		(14,500)
Capital allowances 2015	(4,640)	
Less:		
Balancing charges 2015 (as reduced above)	680	
		(3,960)
s 381 loss (TCA 1997, s 392)		(18,460)

Assume that Ms Plum's total income for 2015 (before reduction by any s 381 relief) is €16,590. Since full relief for the €18,460 loss cannot be given, TCA 1997, s 392(2) requires relief to be given as follows:

	€
Total income 2015 (before relief)	16,590
Set off s 381 relief:	
Tax loss (before capital allowances)[1]	(14,500)
	2,090
Set off capital allowances included in s 381 claim, but limited to[2]	(2,090)
Total income 2015 (after relief)	Nil

Notes:

1. TCA 1997, s 392(2) requires the relief under s 381 to be given first in respect of the tax loss in priority to the capital allowances where there is insufficient income to absorb both.
2. The capital allowances for which the s 381 relief cannot be given in 2015 due to the rule of TCA 1997, s 392(2) are carried forward to 2016. The amount to be carried forward is:

	€
Capital allowances 2015 (not used to offset balancing charge 2014)	3,960
Less: amount used in s 381 claim	2,090
Capital allowances 2015 forward to 2016	1,870

The €1,870 of capital allowances carried forward may be included with the capital allowances for 2016 for set off against Sch D Case I profits in the ordinary way. Alternatively, if there should be a s 381 claim (increased by capital allowances) for 2016, they are used first to offset balancing charges 2016 thereby enabling a greater use in the s 381 claim for the capital allowances for 2016.

Prevention of double relief

TCA 1997, s 394 prevents double relief for any capital allowances. It provides that to the extent any capital allowances are included in a s 381 claim, those allowances are not available for use in any other way (for example, they cannot be carried forward in a subsequent tax year). If in fact a deduction has been made in any assessment for a subsequent year in respect of any capital allowances which are used in a s 381 claim for an earlier year, then the inspector is authorised to make any necessary additional assessment for the subsequent year to correct the position.

Example 4.405.6

Mr R Aspberry has taxable profits of €5,000 in his trade for his 12-month period of account ending 30 September 2014 (basis period for 2014) and capital allowances for 2014 of €8,000. For 2015 (basis period: 12 months ending 30 September 2015), his taxable profits are €12,500 and he has capital allowances of €4,700.

He does not initially make any claim under TCA 1997, s 381, and the figures for his net Sch D Case 1 assessments for 2014 and 2015 are arrived at as follows:

	2014	*2015*
	€	€
Taxable profits	5,000	12,500

Less:		
Capital allowances	(5,000)	(4,700)
(unused allowances 2014: €3,000)		
Capital allowances forward from 2014	-	(3,000)
Net Sch D Case I assessment	Nil	4,800

On 28 December 2015 ie within two years of the end of 2014, Mr Aspberry makes a s 381 claim for 2014 in which he elects under TCA 1997, s 392 to require the inclusion of the relevant capital allowances in the claim. He has a s 381 loss for set off against his income from other sources for 2014 as follows:

	€
Taxable profits 2014	5,000
Deduct:	
Capital allowances 2014	(8,000)
s 381 loss 2014 (with TCA 1997, s 392)	(3,000)

He receives the appropriate repayment in respect of his 2014 income tax. Since all the 2014 capital allowances are now used in the s 381 claim, they cease to be available for carry forward to 2015 (TCA 1997, s 394).

4.406 Restrictions on s 381 losses

Pre-trading expenditure

Pre-trading expenses which are deductible under TCA 1997, s 82(3) (see **5.306**) are not allowed to create or increase a claim for a loss under TCA 1997, s 381.

Disposals of foreign life policies and offshore funds

The restrictions which apply to a claim under TCA 1997, s 381 against income deemed to arise on the disposal of certain foreign life policies and non-qualifying offshore funds are discussed at **8.4**.

Transactions in securities

The restrictions which apply to a claim under TCA 1997, s 381 for losses in relation to certain dealings in securities are discussed at **17.1**.

Losses attributable to Relevant Planning Permissions

See **12.317**.

Farming losses

The restrictions which apply to a claim under TCA 1997, s 381 for losses in relation to farming trades are discussed at **7.206**.

Limited partnerships

The restrictions which apply to a claim under TCA 1997, s 381 for losses in relation to limited partnerships are discussed at **4.512**.

Leasing trades

The restrictions which apply to a claim under s 381 for capital allowances in relation to leasing trades are discussed at **6.305**.

Expenditure on significant buildings

The restrictions which apply to a claim under TCA 1997, s 482 for notional losses in relation to expenditure on significant buildings are discussed at **18.301**.

Holiday cottages

TCA 1997, s 405 imposes certain restrictions on the use of the industrial buildings writing down allowances and initial allowances given for capital expenditure incurred on the acquisition or construction of a building or structure which is, or is to be, an industrial building by being a holiday cottage (as defined in TCA 1997, s 268(1)). Holiday cottages ceased to qualify as industrial buildings in relation to expenditure incurred on or after 4 December 2002 (subject to transitional provisions): see **6.401**.

The section restricts the use of these capital allowances where the capital expenditure on the holiday cottage or cottages is incurred after 23 April 1992 (except for expenditure incurred between 24 April 1992 and 5 April 1993 to which the transitional rule mentioned below applies). There are no restrictions for capital expenditure on holiday cottages incurred before 24 April 1992 or in relation to purchasers of second-hand cottages after that date who claim allowances by reference to the residue of expenditure incurred before that date.

The effect of the section is that the writing down allowances (including increased writing down allowances) and any initial allowance for capital expenditure incurred after 23 April 1992 on holiday cottages (other than any excepted expenditure) may not be used to create or increase a trading loss to be set off against income from all sources in a claim under TCA 1997, s 381. In other words, in the case of a person chargeable to income tax, the industrial buildings writing down allowance and any initial allowance in respect of capital expenditure on holiday cottages within TCA 1997, s 405 are only available to be set off against the taxpayer's Sch D Case I income or balancing charges, if the holiday cottages are in use for a trade. The allowances may be so set off against the Sch D Case I income, either in the tax year to which they relate or in a subsequent tax year in a carry forward claim.

It is to be noted that TCA 1997, s 405 makes no mention of balancing allowances. Consequently, there is no restriction on the use of any balancing allowance which may arise on the disposal of the holiday cottages (or other event requiring a balancing adjustment) and any such balancing allowances continue to be available for set off against income from all sources.

Capital expenditure incurred on a holiday cottage between 24 April 1992 and 5 April 1993 is excepted from the restrictions imposed by TCA 1997, s 405, so that the facility remains to make all the available uses of the industrial buildings allowances in respect of the excepted expenditure, in either of the following circumstances:

(a) if a binding contract in writing for the construction of the holiday cottage was entered into before 24 April 1992; or

(b) (1) if a binding contract in writing for the purchase or lease of land for the construction of the holiday cottage was entered into before 24 April 1992, and

(2) if an application for planning permission for the construction of the holiday cottage was received by a planning authority before 24 April 1992.

A similar limitation applies with effect from 6 April 1996 to qualifying expenditure on holiday apartments registered under the Tourist Traffic Act 1939 and other self-catering accommodation (including holiday cottages) listed under the Tourist Traffic Act 1957, which are located in designated seaside areas (TCA 1997, s 355(4): see **Division 19** of the 2009 edition of this book).

The TCA 1997, s 405 restrictions on the use of capital allowances do not apply to certain registered holiday cottages which are first registered on or after 6 April 2001, provided that prior to such registration:

(a) the cottage qualified for capital allowances under TCA 1997, s 353, as a listed holiday cottage in one of the 15 designated seaside resort areas; and

(b) those capital allowances were not subject to the provisions of TCA 1997, s 355(4), which ring-fenced capital allowances in respect of listed holiday cottages.

Non-active partner: losses created/increased by industrial buildings allowances

TCA 1997, ss 409A and 409B significantly restrict the ability of a 'non-active' partner to create or increase a trading loss under TCA 1997, s 381 by virtue of a claim under TCA 1997, s 392(1) made by reference to industrial buildings allowances. A non-active partner is defined negatively by implication as one who does not work for the greater part of his time on the day-to-day management or conduct of the partnership trade (TCA 1997, s 409A(1)) (note in this connection *Palmer v Maloney* [1999] STC 890 discussed at **3.207**). These provisions have no application to sole traders.

TCA 1997, s 409A(3) restricts the ability of a non-active partner to create or enhance a loss under TCA 1997, s 381 by virtue of a claim under TCA 1997, s 392(1) in respect of the industrial buildings or structures specified in TCA 1997, s 409A(1). The restrictions apply to expenditure incurred on or after 3 December 1997, subject to the transitional provisions described further below. The specified industrial buildings and structures are those as defined by TCA 1997, s 268 (see **6.401**) as well as any commercial buildings or structures located in tax incentive areas (eg Urban/Rural renewal areas, etc: see **Division 19** of the 2009 edition of this book) which are treated as industrial buildings for capital allowance purposes. The only exceptions are:

(a) buildings and structures falling within TCA 1997, s 268(1)(d), ie those in use for the purposes of the trade of hotel-keeping or which are deemed to be so used (eg registered holiday cottages); hotels and holiday camps are in fact subject to the generally more stringent provisions of TCA 1997, s 409B (see below), while registered holiday cottages are potentially within the ring-fencing provisions of TCA 1997, s 405, described immediately above;

(b) an apartment/self-catering accommodation in a designated seaside resort area, these being potentially within the ring-fencing provisions of TCA 1997, s 355(4), described immediately above (TCA 1997, s 409A(1)).

Where TCA 1997, s 409A applies, the non-active partner's claim for the industrial buildings allowances affected under TCA 1997, s 392(1) is reduced to an amount equal to:

$$A + €31{,}750$$

Where:

A = the amount of the individual's Sch D Case I/II income from his several partnership trade (see **4.503**) before taking into account any claim under TCA 1997, s 392(1) (TCA 1997, s 409A(3)). The effect of the formula is to ensure that a claim for the allowances affected cannot create or increase a loss by any amount in excess of €31,750.

Where an individual is a non-active partner in two or more partnerships, all the several trades in question are treated as a single several trade (TCA 1997, s 409A(4)). Thus, it is not possible to circumvent the €31,750 cap merely by splitting one's activities across a number of partnerships.

TCA 1997, s 409B(3) is even more stringent than TCA 1997, s 409A(3) and in fact completely removes the ability of a non-active partner to create or enhance a loss under TCA 1997, s 381 by virtue of a claim under TCA 1997, s 392(1) in respect of the industrial buildings or structures specified in TCA 1997, s 409B(1). The specified buildings and structures are defined as those which are, or which are deemed to fall within TCA 1997, s 268(1)(d), but excluding registered holiday cottages (potentially within the ring fencing provisions of TCA 1997, s 405, described immediately above). There is however one further exception in favour of hotels of a standard specified in guidelines issued for the purpose (normally three star accommodation and above) and which are located in any of the following counties:

(a) Cavan;
(b) Donegal;
(c) Leitrim;
(d) Mayo;
(e) Monaghan;
(f) Roscommon; and
(g) Sligo.

Hotels located in a qualifying seaside resort area do not qualify for this latter exception (TCA 1997, s 409B(1)(a)).

The following transitional provisions apply equally for the purposes of TCA 1997, ss 409A and 409B:

(i) in the case of construction expenditure, the entire foundations of the building or structure were laid prior to 3 December 1997;

(ii) in the case of refurbishment expenditure, work to the value of at least five per cent of the total cost of refurbishment was carried out prior to 3 December 1997 (TCA 1997, ss 409A(5)(a), 409B(4)(a)).

(a) Expenditure incurred on or after 3 December 1997 will not be subject to the ring fencing rules where:

(i) either an application for all necessary planning permission for the expenditure concerned was made prior to a planning authority prior to 3 December 1997 or the individual concerned can satisfy the Revenue Commissioners that a detailed plan had been prepared for the work and that detailed discussions had taken place in respect of the building concerned with a planning authority prior to 3 December 1997 (this must be supported by an affidavit or statutory declaration from the planning authority); and

(ii) the expenditure incurred on or after 3 December 1997 is incurred under a binding written contract entered into by the individual concerned prior to 3 December 1997 or 1 May 1998 if the obligation was entered into pursuant to negotiations in respect of which preliminary written commitments or agreements had been entered into prior to that date (TCA 1997, ss 409A(5), (6), 409B(4)(5)); where the individual dies before part of the expenditure has been incurred, and another individual who undertakes in writing to take over the obligation, he can avail of the transitional relief on expenditure which he incurs on the building or structure (TCA 1997, ss 409A(7), 409B(6)).

There is one other transitional provision, which is relevant only to TCA 1997, s 409A.

Expenditure incurred on or after 3 December 1997 will not be subject to the ring fencing rules of TCA 1997, s 409A where a project for which the building or structure is to be provided was approved for grant assistance by an industrial development agency within the two years prior to 3 December 1997 (TCA 1997, s 490A(5)(a)(iii)).

Non-active traders participating in specified trades

TCA 1997, s 409D provides that a loss incurred by a 'non-active' trader engaged in a 'specified trade' may only be offset under TCA 1997, s 381 against income from that same trade with effect from 2003 onwards (2002 onwards in the case of trades consisting of or including the generation of electricity) (TCA 1997, s 409D(2)(a)). A similar provision applies to any part of a claim under TCA 1997, s 381 attributable to capital allowances (including balancing allowances) relating to plant and machinery (TCA 1997, s 409D(2)(b), s 409(1)). A loss is stated to include one which is computed taking account of interest laid out or expended by the individual in respect of a loan where the proceeds of the loan were used to incur expenditure on machinery or plant used for the purposes of the specified trade. There is no statutory basis for relief where interest is paid on a loan used for capital purposes. In practice a deduction for such interest is allowed in computing taxable profits (see **5.315**). This provision makes it clear that the deduction for trade interest will only be allowed against income from the trade.

An 'active trader' is defined as an individual who works for the greater part of their time on the day-to-day management or conduct of the specified trade concerned (note in this connection *Palmer v Maloney* [1999] STC 890, discussed at **3.207**). The wording clearly applies to a sole trader but also seems to apply to a partner in a partnership carrying on a specified trade since a partnership trade is regarded as being carried on by each of the partners; this is notwithstanding the statutory fiction of the several trade deemed to be carried on by each partner which is applied for the purpose of assessing each of the individual partners: see **4.503**.

A 'specified trade' is defined as a trade consisting of or including:

(a) the generation of electricity,

(b) trading operations which are petroleum activities (within the meaning of TCA 1997, s 21A),

(c) the development or production of:

(i) films,

(ii) film projects,

(iii) film properties, or

(iv) music properties,

(d) the acquisition of rights to participate in the revenues of:
   (i) film properties, or
   (ii) music properties,

(e) the production of, the distribution of, or the holding of an interest in:
   (i) either or both a film negative and its associated soundtrack, a film tape or a film disc,
   (ii) an audio tape or audio disc, or
   (iii) a film property produced by electronic means or
   (iv) a music property produced by electronic means (for these purposes, 'electronic' includes electrical, digital, magnetic, optical, electro-magnetic, biometric, photonic and any other form of related technology **4.407**).

4.407 Calculation of tax payable where s 381 relief is claimed

When the amount of the s 381 loss (as increased or created by capital allowances, if elected under TCA 1997, s 392) has been determined, the taxpayer's income tax liability for the year of claim is recalculated. A revised total income for the year is computed by deducting from his income from all sources the amount of the s 381 loss, as well as any other deductions given in arriving at total income. Then the deductions from total income in arriving at taxable income are made before the calculation of income tax payable is redone on the new taxable income figure. The revised income tax liability is compared with that previously calculated before s 381 loss relief and any excess tax paid is repaid to him.

For the purposes of the calculation of the revised total income, there are rules giving the order in which the s 381 loss must be set off. In the case of a loss incurred by an individual assessed jointly with his spouse under TCA 1997, s 1017, the amount of a s 381 loss incurred by one spouse is available to reduce the joint total income of both spouses. In this case, TCA 1997, s 381(3) requires the s 381 loss incurred by an individual in a tax year to be set off and treated as reducing the named categories of income, until fully used up, in the following order:

(a) first, against the individual's earned income of the tax year in which the loss is incurred (also the year of claim);
(b) second, against the individual's other income (the unearned income) of that year;
(c) third, against his spouse's earned income of that year; and
(d) fourth, against his spouse's other income of that year.

In the case of loss incurred by an individual assessed as a single person, TCA 1997, s 381(3) requires the amount of a s 381 loss to be set off and treated as reducing the named categories of income in the following order:

(e) first, against the individual's earned income of the tax year in which the loss is incurred (also the year of claim); and
(f) then, against his unearned income of that year (if the loss is not fully set off against the earned income).

'Earned income' is defined by TCA 1997, s 3(2). It includes any income taxable under Sch E or otherwise arising by way of remuneration, pension or compensation in respect of an office or employment, as well as income immediately derived from the carrying on of a trade or profession by a sole trader or by a partner personally acting in the partnership.

Where the loss relates to an activity in respect of which any profits would be regarded as unearned income (eg the several trade of a limited partner), then the order of set off is correspondingly reversed. Thus, in such a case, 'unearned' should be 'substituted' for 'earned' and vice versa in (a) to (d) and (e) to (f) above. For the restriction of losses incurred by limited partners, see **4.512**.

In practice, the main effect of the distinction between earned and unearned income drawn by TCA 1997, s 381(3) applies where the individual claiming the s 381 loss relief is entitled to a deduction in respect of a premium paid under a Retirement Annuity Contract (see **16.208**) or a premium paid to secure a Personal Retirement Savings Account. The effect of TCA 1997, s 381(3) is normally to secure that the s 381 loss reduces firstly the 'net relevant earnings' by reference to which an upper limit is fixed to the deduction allowed for the premium concerned. The interaction of TCA 1997, s 381 loss claims and the relief for retirement annuity premiums under TCA 1997, s 784 is illustrated at **16.208**.

Another consequence may be to affect an individual's Employee Tax Credit (see **3.310**) in respect of any Sch E emoluments he may have. If any part of the s 381 loss reduces such emoluments so that the amount thereof multiplied by the relevant percentage is less than the amount of the Employee Tax Credit, then that credit must be reduced accordingly. This may affect the relevant Employee Tax Credit for a jointly assessed spouse of the person incurring the loss, if the s 381 loss has to be set off against the spouse's earned income consisting of such emoluments. Where that spouse's earned income consists of such emoluments and other sources of income the order of set-off would appear to be at the discretion of the taxpayer (see **1.405**: Presumption re reliefs and allowances).

It is also to be noted that, as compared with the income tax computation before the loss relief, the deduction of the s 381 loss causes a reduction in any other deductions or reliefs which are restricted by reference to a percentage or fraction of total income. For example, the five per cent of total income limit to the deduction for certain covenanted payments (see **15.405**) will be affected. While the s 381 loss may reduce particular categories of income in a particular order of priority it does not appear to constitute a 'deduction attributable to a particular source of income' which may reduce the 'specified income' of a spouse within TCA 1997, s 15(4). Accordingly, a s 381 claim should not result in a restriction in the amount of the standard rate band of income tax otherwise available to a jointly-assessed married couple.

Example 4.407.1

Louis and Antoinette are a married couple who have elected for joint assessment under TCA 1997, s 1017. Antoinette is the chargeable person for 2015. Details of their income and outgoings for 2015 are as follows:

Louis	€
Occupational pension (PAYE suffered €1,070)	17,500
UK Rents (Gross) – €200 UK tax payable	3,000
Trading loss (as hairdresser)	

Accounts to 31/12/2015		(21,800)
Capital allowances 2015		1,400
Antoinette		
Employment income		26,000
(PAYE suffered €1,270)		
Irish dividends (gross)		3,900
Deed of covenant to Amnesty International (gross)		2,200
Tax liability without s 381 claim:		
Sch D Case I (his)		Nil
Sch D Case III (his)		3,000
Sch E (his)		17,500
Sch E (hers)		26,000
Sch F (hers)		3,900
Income from all sources		50,400
Less:		
Annual payment		(2,200)
Total income		48,200
Income tax payable		
48,200 x 20%		9,640
Less: tax credits		
Married personal credit	3,300	
Employee credit; €1,650 x 2 =	3,300	
Medical Expenses Credit	800	
Double tax relief (see **Division 14**)	200	(7,600)
		2,040
Add: income tax on charge €2,200 x 20%		440
		2,480
Less: tax suffered at source		
PAYE (hers)	1,270	
PAYE (his)	1,070	
Dividend withholding tax	780	(3,120)
Tax repayable		(640)

Tax Liability with s 381 Claim:

Louis – earned income	€	€
Sch D Case I	Nil	
Sch E	17,500	
	17,500	
Less: s 381 loss[1]	(17,500)	-
Louis – unearned income		
Sch D Case III	3,000	
Less: s 381 loss[1]	(3,000)	-

Antoinette – earned income		
Sch E	26,000	
Less: s 381 loss[1]	(2,700)	23,300
Antoinette – unearned income		
Sch F		3,900
Income from all sources (after s 381 loss)		27,200
Less: annual payment[2]		(1,295)
Total income		25,905
Tax €25,905 @ 20% =		5,181
Less: credits and reductions		
Married persons credit	3,300	
Medical Expenses Credit	800	
Employee credit (his)[3]	-	
Employee credit (hers)	1,650	
Double tax relief[4]	-	(5,750)
Non–repayable credits: see **3.107**		569
Income tax on charge[2]		
€1,295 x 20%		259
Less: Tax suffered at source – as above		(3,120)
Repayment due		(2,861)

Notes:

1. The s 381 loss claim is computed on the basis that an election is made to increase it under TCA 1997, s 392 as follows:

Tax loss 2015	21,800
Add: 2015 capital allowances	1,400
	23,200

2. The deductible amount of the annual payment is now restricted to €27,200 x 5/105 = €1,295 (see **15.405**). The tax retained is reduced accordingly.
3. The employee allowance cannot exceed the taxable amount of Louis's PAYE emoluments, which have been reduced to nil by the s 381 claims.
4. Because the s 381 claim has reduced the amount of the foreign income to nil, the claim for double tax relief is forfeited.
5. In such circumstances Louis might be advised to carry the loss forward under s 382 instead of making a s 381 (with s 392) claim, to obtain greater benefit from the loss and capital allowances.

4.408 Loss relief for certain charges on income

In calculating the taxable profits (or tax loss) of a trade or profession, no deduction is allowed for annuities, other annual payments (except annual interest) or royalties or other sums paid for the use of a patent. Normally, a taxpayer making such payments is able to compensate himself for the non-deductibility of the payments by deducting and retaining income tax under the rule of TCA 1997, s 237 (see **2.303**). However, to the extent that such payments are made otherwise than out of income brought into charge to income tax, the payer is assessed under TCA 1997, s 238 and liable to pay income tax at the standard rate (see **2.304**).

The effect of the TCA 1997, s 238 assessment on a payment affected, coupled with the disallowance of the payment in the Sch D Case I or Case II computation would, in the absence of any other provision, be to disregard a genuine commercial loss where the payment is made for a trade or profession. In order to avoid this result, relief is available under TCA 1997, s 390(1) which permits relief to be claimed in the case where:

(a) an annuity or other annual payment (except annual interest), or a royalty paid in respect of the use of a patent, is paid wholly and exclusively for the purposes of a trade or profession; and
(b) is assessed to income tax under TCA 1997, s 238.

TCA 1997, s 390 provides relief by treating any payment meeting these conditions as if it were a tax loss of the trade or profession, but only to the extent that it is actually assessed under TCA 1997, s 238. Any payment so treated is referred to herein as a 's 238' loss. It is to be noted that a payment assessed under TCA 1997, s 238 which is not incurred wholly and exclusively for a trade or profession is not eligible for any loss relief under TCA 1997, s 390 (or otherwise).

TCA 1997, s 390 permits the s 238 loss to be used for the purposes of carry forward relief under TCA 1997, s 382 (see **4.402**) or, if the s 238 loss occurs in the final 12 months of trading in the case of a cessation of the trade or profession, for carry back as a terminal loss available for set off under TCA 1997, s 385 against the net Sch D Case I or Case II income of the three tax years prior to the year of assessment in which the cessation occurs (see **4.410**). However, the s 238 loss is not eligible for inclusion in a current year set off against total income in a s 381 claim.

TCA 1997, s 238 is also used as a mechanism to charge income tax on certain types of payment made to non-resident persons or to persons whose usual place of abode is outside the State – eg payments of annual interest or of rents payable in respect of land and buildings situated in the State. A person required to withhold and account for income tax on such payments by TCA 1997, s 238 is not entitled to claim any loss relief under this rule (TCA 1997, s 390(3)).

Example 4.408.1

Mr A Charmer, a married man assessable jointly with his wife, carries on a manufacturing trade for which he has made up accounts annually to 31 December for a number of years. He pays royalties each year in respect of certain patent rights acquired for the purposes of his trade. He deducts income tax at the standard rate from each royalty payment under the rules of TCA 1997, ss 237 and 238.

The royalties debited in the accounts are added back as annual payments in the Sch D Case I computation for each accounting year, but he is entitled to deduct the actual royalties paid in each tax year to 31 December as charges on income in computing his total income. His total income for 2015 (including his wife's income) is as follows:

	€	€
Trading loss per accounts (Y/E 30/09/2015)		(1,340)
Add backs:	€	€
Royalties paid (Y/E 30/09/2015)	2,100	
Other disallowable items	1,910	
		4,010
Adjusted Sch D Case I profits 2015		2,670
Capital allowances 2015		(2,490)
Net Sch D Case I income		180

Income from other sources:		
his income	560	
his wife's	200	
		760
Income from all sources		940
Deductions:		
Charges on income:		
Royalties paid in 2015		
€2,100, but deduction limited to		(940)
Total income 2015		Nil

The royalties paid in the year 2015, to the extent not covered by the income chargeable to tax for that year, are assessable under the rules of TCA 1997, s 238. This assessment made for 2015 requires Mr Charmer to pay tax at 20 per cent on a gross amount of €1,160 (ie the €2,100 royalties paid in the year less the above €940).

On the assumption that these royalties were paid wholly and exclusively for the purposes of his trade, Mr Charmer is entitled under the provisions contained in TCA 1997, s 390 to carry forward this 's 238 loss' of €1,160 to be set off under the provisions of TCA 1997, s 382 against his Sch D Case I assessable profits for 2016 or later years.

4.409 Losses in opening years

It is not unusual for there to be losses in one or more of the opening years of a new trade or profession. Reliefs for any such losses are available under the various forms of loss relief already discussed ie by carry forward for set off under TCA 1997, s 382 against later taxable profits of the same trade or profession or, if the individual carrying on the trade or profession (or his spouse in a joint assessment) has other income for the same tax year as that in which the loss is incurred, by set off against that other income in a claim under TCA 1997, s 381. Also, if the individual has any 's 238 loss' in respect of annuities, royalties, etc paid, he may claim under TCA 1997, s 390 to carry forward this loss for set off against future profits of the trade or profession (see **4.408**).

The different basis periods used for assessing taxable profits in the opening years of assessment of a new business, or of one deemed to have been commenced under the change of ownership rules, have an effect on the determination of tax losses for which relief may arise in the opening years.

It is necessary to distinguish between a loss available for carry forward and a loss of one period of account used in whole or in part to reduce or cancel out the taxable profits of another period of account where both periods fall, at least partly, into the basis period for the same year of assessment. If the period of account in which a tax loss occurs is part of the basis period for more than one year of assessment, the same loss may be used in the calculation of the profits assessable for each relevant tax year. However, if the tax loss of one period of account is used to produce losses in the basis periods for more than one year of assessment, the relief claimed for such losses by carry forward under TCA 1997, s 382, cannot exceed the actual tax loss sustained in the period of account. This principle was confirmed by the decisions in *IRC v Scott Adamson* 17 TC 679 and *Westward Television Ltd v Hart* 45 TC 1.

Example 4.409.1

Mr C Carlton commences trading on 1 October 2013. His Sch D Case I computations for his first two periods of account are as follows:

	€
6 months to 31/03/2014	
Tax loss	(12,000)
12 months to 31/03/2015	
Taxable profits	6,000

His Sch D Case I assessments (subject to capital allowances) for his first two tax years are as follows:

	2013	2014
2013:	€	€
Period 1/10/2013–31/12/20122013		
3/6ths x loss €12,000	(6,000)	
Taxable profits	Nil	
2014: (Actual basis)		
Period 1/01/2014–31/03/2014		
3/6ths x €12,000 (6 months to 31/03/2014)		(6,000)
Period 1/04/2014 to 31/12/2014		
9/12ths x €6,000 (12 months to 31/03/2015)		4,500
Tax loss for period		(1,500)
Taxable profits		Nil

Mr Carlton has therefore nil Sch D Case I assessments for 2013 and 2014. He makes a claim to carry forward his unused losses under s 382 losses for set off against his taxable profits of 2015 and subsequent tax years. The principle in *IRC v Scott Adamson* applies and the amount to be carried forward cannot exceed the actual loss incurred (€12,000). Further the amount carried forward must be restricted to exclude the part of the loss for which relief has been obtained under any other rule.

The correct loss to be carried forward for set off in 2015 *et seq* is determined as follows:

	€
Tax loss actually incurred in 6 months to 31/03/2014	12,000
Less:	
Part of loss already used in reducing the 2014 assessment to nil (as above)	4,500
Tax loss to carry forward to 2015 *et seq*	7,500

For further points relating to losses in the opening years of a new trade or profession, see s 381 claim: commencement of trade in **4.404**.

In determining the extent to which relief has been given for a tax loss incurred in any period of account, it is necessary to look back at the basis period computation for each tax year in which that loss has been included in whole or in part. The question is then asked – what would have been the taxable profits for that basis period if the period of account in which the tax loss occurred had produced neither a profit nor loss (ie a nil profit)? Then, to the extent that any such taxable profits have been reduced by the amount of the tax loss actually brought into the basis period computation, the loss is treated as having been relieved.

Although mentioned here in the context of the opening years of a trade or profession, the same point may also arise in the closing years and, sometimes, where the change of accounting date rules are applied.

4.410 Losses prior to cessation of trade

When a trade or profession is permanently discontinued, the question of relief for losses incurred in one or more of the last few periods of account often arises. Both the current year relief under TCA 1997, s 381 ('s 381 relief') which reduces the taxpayer's total income for the year in which the loss is sustained (see **4.404–4.406**) and the carry forward of losses under s 382 ('carry forward relief') for set off of an earlier year's loss against taxable profits of a later year in the same trade or profession (see **4.402**) are available. However, where there is a cessation, there may well be no later year's taxable profits to absorb earlier losses and the taxpayer may not have sufficient other income against which to offset a current year loss. For the special rules governing certain losses from dealing in residential land, see **4.411**.

A third form of loss relief is available where there is a permanent discontinuance of a trade or profession. This is the 'terminal loss relief' provided by TCA 1997, s 385 which may be claimed by the person ceasing to trade (or by his personal representatives if the cessation has occurred due to his death). Terminal loss relief is available for any tax losses and unrelieved capital allowances attributable to the last 12 months of trading immediately before the date of cessation. If claimed, terminal loss relief is given by carrying back the tax losses and capital allowances eligible for the relief and by setting them off against the net Sch D Case I or Case II income of the trade or profession assessable in one or more of the three years of assessment prior to that in which the cessation occurred.

Determination of losses for closing years

Before a taxpayer considers the alternative forms of relief for losses in the closing years of a trade or profession, the first step is to determine whether there are any taxable profits in the basis periods for either or both of the penultimate and final tax years and, if so, the amount thereof. As explained in **4.206**, the basis period for the final year is the period from 1 January to the date of cessation and that for the penultimate year is either the original basis period for the year or, if it gives greater taxable profits, the actual penultimate year ending 31 December. Then the capital allowances and any balancing charges for each of the penultimate and final years are determined in the manner explained in **4.305**.

Once the step to identify the taxable profits (if any) in the relevant basis periods has been taken, the next step is to ascertain if there is any tax loss in any period of account which has not been fully used to reduce taxable profits in the basis period for any year and, if so, the amount of that loss. If so, relief should be sought for this tax loss under one of the forms of loss relief available. The relief is normally given by reference to the tax year in which the loss is incurred.

If a tax loss is incurred in either or both the penultimate and final years, or if the capital allowances for either or both years exceed any taxable profit, then it is necessary to consider the alternative forms of loss relief available to see which gives the best result. Should there be any unused tax losses and/or capital allowances brought forward from earlier years, these have also to be considered.

It is to be noted that there may sometimes be a tax loss between the end of the basis period for the penultimate year and 31 December of that year. This may occur where that basis period is a period of 12 months ending before the end of the penultimate year. Similarly, in the alternative case where the basis period for the penultimate year is revised to become the actual year to 31 December, there may be a loss in the interval between the end of the basis period for the tax year immediately preceding the penultimate year and 31 December of that 'prepenultimate' year. In either type of case, the appropriate form of loss relief should be available. For further comments on these points, see s 381 claim: cessation of trade in **4.404**.

It is now necessary to explain the rules for claiming terminal loss relief.

Terminal loss relief

TCA 1997, s 385(1) allows a person who has permanently discontinued carrying on his trade or profession to claim to have the amount of any 'terminal loss' set off against his net Sch D Case I or Case II taxable income of the three tax years immediately preceding the tax year in which the cessation occurs. TCA 1997, s 385(2) requires any such terminal loss set off to be made first against the net Sch D Case I or Case II income of the most recent of the three preceding years up to the full amount of that income, then against the said Case I or Case II income of the next most recent year and finally, if necessary, against that of the earliest of the three preceding years.

A terminal loss claim may also be made where a trade has been treated under TCA 1997, s 69 as being permanently discontinued on a change of ownership (see **4.208**), but a person engaged in the trade before and after the change of ownership is not entitled to claim any terminal loss relief in such a case (TCA 1997, s 388(1)(a)). For example, a person whose trade is deemed to cease on his taking in a partner with whom he continues to trade in partnership cannot claim terminal loss relief for any tax loss or unused capital allowances prior to turning his business into a partnership. For the terminal losses of partners, see also **4.507**.

There are two main questions to be considered in relation to relief for terminal losses. The first is to determine the amount of the terminal loss (including any capital allowances) eligible to be carried back for relief under the section. The second concerns the amount of the taxable income from the trade in the three preceding years of assessment against which the terminal loss is to be set off. A third question relates to the order in which the set off is to be made.

Amount of terminal loss

A terminal loss is made up of the following four elements in so far as they arise:

(a) the tax loss sustained in the trade or profession in the year of assessment in which the cessation takes place;
(b) the capital allowances attributable to the trade or profession for that year of assessment;
(c) the loss sustained in the trade or profession in that part of the penultimate year of assessment falling within the 12 months immediately prior to the date of the cessation; and
(d) the appropriate fraction (see below) of the capital allowances for the penultimate year of assessment (TCA 1997, s 386(2)).

The tax losses and capital allowances taken into account are those as finally determined under the normal Sch D Case I and Case II and capital allowances rules applicable to a cessation of trade. The loss incurred in the relevant part of the penultimate tax year is arrived at by making any necessary time apportionment of the adjusted tax losses (or profits) of the period or periods of account falling within the last 12 months of trading. The loss for the final year of assessment is similarly determined. The appropriate fraction of the capital allowances for the penultimate year is one the numerator of which is the number of months between the date one year before the date of cessation and the 31 December of the penultimate year, and of which the denominator is the number '12'.

In addition to the four elements listed above, a terminal loss may include a 's 238' loss to the extent that it falls into the final year of trading or to the extent that it is apportioned to the part of the penultimate year within the last 12 months of trading. For the details of this further relief given by TCA 1997, s 390, see **4.408**.

In ascertaining the four elements of a terminal loss, the following items must be excluded:

(a) any tax losses or capital allowances for which relief is otherwise obtained under any other provision of the TCA 1997, (eg in a s 381 loss claim) (TCA 1997, s 385(2));

(b) any part of a tax loss or capital allowances used to offset a balancing charge; and

(c) any unrelieved capital allowances carried forward from an earlier tax year (TCA 1997, s 386(1)).

Example 4.410.1

Mr EC Dealer, who has traded for many years, sells his business on 20 July 2015 so that his trade is treated as ceasing on that date. He has made up accounts to 28 February for a number of years. His final accounts are made up for the period 1 March 2015 to 20 July 2015.

Mr Dealer's Sch D Case I taxable profits and tax losses for each of his last three periods of account, and capital allowances and balancing charges for the last two tax years of the trade, are as follows:

Period 1/03/2015 to 20/07/2015	€
Tax loss	(6,000)
Capital allowances 2015[1]	(5,000)
Balancing charges 2015[1]	1,800
12 months to 28/02/2015	
Tax loss	(24,000)
12 months to 28/02/2014	
Taxable profit	7,200
Capital allowances 2014[2]	(9,820)
Balancing charges 2014[2]	700

The first step is to set out Mr Dealer's assessable profits (if any), tax losses, capital allowances and balancing charges for the last two tax years of his trade as follows:

	2014	*2015*
	€	€
Sch D Case I assessment:		
Taxable profits[3]	7,200	Nil

Balancing charges	700	1,800
	7,900	1,800
Capital allowances used:		
2014 (part of €9,820)	(7,900)	
2015 (part of €5,000)	-	(1,800)
Net Sch D Case I assessment	Nil	Nil
Unused capital allowances		
2014 (€9,820 less €7,900)	(1,920)	
2015 (€5,000 less €1,800)		(3,200)
Tax loss incurred in 2014 (strict basis applies):		
Period 1/01/2014 to 28/02/2014		
2/12ths x €7,200 (12 months ended 28/02/2014)	1,200	
Period 1/03/2014 to 31/12/2014		
10/12ths (€24,000) (12 months ended 28/02/2015)	(20,000)	
Tax loss incurred in 2015:		
Period 1/01/2015 to 28/02/2015		
2/12ths x €24,000 (12 months ended 28/02/2015)		(4,000)
Period 1/03/2015 to 20/07/2015		
Full period's loss		(6,000)
	(18,800)	(10,000)

Mr Dealer now has to consider the best form of relief to claim for these tax losses sustained in the years 2014 and 2015. Since his other income for each year is not large, a s 381 claim to set the losses of €18,800 and €10,000 against his other income respectively in 2014 and 2015 would give little relief. He therefore decides to claim terminal loss relief.

Computation of terminal loss

The amount of the terminal loss to be carried back under TCA 1997, s 385 is computed as follows:

	€	€
(1) Tax loss in 2015 (final year)		
Loss for period 1 January 2015 to 20 July 2015		
As above		10,000
(2) Capital allowances 2015	5,000	
Less:		
Part thereof to offset balancing charges 2015	1,800	3,200
(3) Part of tax loss in 2014 (penultimate year)[4]		
Loss from 21 July 2014 to 31 December 2014		
5.5/12ths x loss €24,000		11,000
(4) Part of net capital allowances for 2014		
Total allowances for year	9,820	
Less:		
Used to offset taxable profits and balancing charges	7,900	
Balance eligible	1,920	

Appropriate proportion	
5.5/12ths x €1,920[5]	880
Amount of terminal loss available to carry back	25,080

Notes:

1. The capital allowances and balancing charges for 2015 are those as finally calculated for the year having regard to the cessation of trade on 20 July 2015.
2. The capital allowances and balancing charges for 2014 are those as finally calculated for the year after it has been determined that the basis period for the year remains unchanged as the 12 months ending 28 February 2014.
3. The assessment for 2014 continues to be based on the profits of the 12-month period of account ending 28 February 2014. The possible alternative basis period of the actual penultimate year ending 31 December 2014 would not produce a higher taxable profit than €7,200 (in fact it would produce a loss). For 2015, the final year's basis period (1 January 2015 to 20 July 2015) clearly has no taxable profits.
4. Only the part of the loss in 2014 apportioned to the period from 21 July 2014 (12 months before date of cessation) to 31 December 2014 (last day of penultimate year) is included in the terminal loss eligible for relief.
5. The appropriate proportion of capital allowances for the penultimate year included in the terminal loss is the proportion of the full year's allowances (as reduced by the allowances used to offset taxable profits and balancing charges) attributable to the 5.5 months from 21 July 2014 to 31 December 2014.

How terminal loss relief is given

TCA 1997, s 385 provides relief for a terminal loss in a trade or profession by carrying back the amount of that loss and offsetting it against the net Sch D Case I or Case II income from the same trade or profession in one or more of the three tax years immediately prior to the tax year in which the business is permanently discontinued. The terminal loss must be used first against the net Sch D Case I or Case II income of the most recent of the three prior years, then against that of the second most recent year and finally, if necessary, against that of the earliest of the three prior years. No terminal loss relief is available for any part of the loss still unused after the carry back to the earliest year.

When the terminal loss (or a part of it) is set off against the net Sch D Case I or Case II income of one of the three prior tax years, the taxpayer's total income, taxable income and income tax payable for that year are recalculated. The excess of the income tax already paid over the revised income tax payable (after terminal loss relief) is then repayable to the taxpayer. If the set off for the terminal loss is obtained against the relevant Case I or Case II income of more than one of the three prior tax years, the appropriate repayment is calculated for each of the years for which there is such a set off.

TCA 1997, s 387(1) prescribes that the net Sch D Case I or Case II income for each prior year of assessment against which the terminal loss may be set off is calculated as follows:

(a) the Sch D Case I (or Case II) profits as finally assessable for the relevant prior year; less

(b) the total of the capital allowances, including any unused capital allowances brought forward from previous years, deductible in charging the profits of the trade for that year; less

(c) the total deductions, if any, in respect of payments made or losses sustained that fall to be made from the profits of the trade in computing the taxpayer's total income for that year (TCA 1997, s 387(1)).

In arriving at each prior year's taxable income from the trade or profession, any balancing charges that were made in taxing that income should be added to the final Sch D Case I assessable profits for each such year. In making any relevant deductions required under (c) above, any deduction which, under the other rules in the Taxes Consolidation Acts 1997, may be made either from the income of the trade or profession or from any other income, must be deducted so far as possible first from any such other income which the, taxpayer had in the prior year in question (TCA 1997, s 387(1)).

The latter rule enables such items as interest deductible under TCA 1997, s 248 (see **3.2**) and charges on income (see **3.103**) to be deducted first from any non-trading income. On the other hand, deductions for such items as a TCA 1997, s 381 loss (deductible first from earned income), a trading loss carried forward under TCA 1997, s 382 or retirement annuity premiums in respect of earnings from the trade or profession deductible under TCA 1997, s 784 must be deducted first in arriving at the amount of the trading income available to cover the terminal loss.

When a deduction for a payment made (eg an annual payment) reduces the trading income for a relevant prior year of assessment, then, unless the payment in question was made wholly and exclusively for the purposes of the trade or profession, the amount of any unused terminal loss carried back for set off in an earlier tax year must be reduced by the amount of the payment deducted. This does not apply to any such payment which can be fully deducted from non-trading income (TCA 1997, s 387(2)).

Example 4.410.2

Take the facts of **Example 4.410.1** where there is a terminal loss of €25,080 eligible for relief under TCA 1997, s 385 following Mr EC Dealer's cessation of trade on 20 July 2015. Mr Dealer's final taxable profits, capital allowances and balancing charges for the final tax year of the trade and for each of the three prior tax years are as follows:

	Sch D Case I profits	*Balancing charges*	*Capital allowances*
2015:	€	€	€
Period 1/01/2015 to 20/07/2015	Nil	1,800	(5,000)
2014:			
12 months to 28/02/2014	7,200	700	(9,820)
2013:			
12 months to 28/02/2013[1]	11,500	500	(3,000)
2012:			
12 months to 29/02/2012[1]	29,000	Nil	(1,680)

Other relevant facts are:

(a) Mr Dealer obtained relief in 2012 for previously unused capital allowances of €1,420 carried forward from 2011;

(b) In each of the three prior years, Mr Dealer's only other income apart from that from his trade is interest on government securities and UK dividends each taxable under Sch D Case III totalling €3,600 for 2012, €2,700 for 2013 and €5,000 for 2014;

(c) Mr Dealer has deductions in computing his total income of €3,950 in 2012 and €4,000 in 2013 and 2014; and

(d) Mr Dealer is a single person.

The terminal loss of €25,080 is eligible to be set off against Mr Dealer's net Sch D Case I income from the trade in 2014, 2013 and 2012 (the 'three prior years'). In order to determine the net Sch D Case I income for each year, it is necessary to reduce the Sch D Case I income otherwise available for each year by any deductions for payments made or losses sustained which are given in computing his total income for each year (other than any such deductions which can be set off against non-trading income).

Treatment of deductions

The deductions in arriving at total income that may properly be deducted from Mr Dealer's non-trading income, and the 'excess deductions' which must be deducted from trading income, are determined as follows:

	2012	*2013*	*2014*
	€	€	€
Deductions in computing total income	3,950	4,000	4,000
Other income available to cover deductions	(3,600)	(2,700)	(5,000)
Excess – deduct from trading income	350	1,300	Nil

Available profits in prior years

Taking the Sch D Case I profits, the capital allowances and balancing charges for the three prior years, the taxable trading income available for each year to offset the terminal loss carried back is now calculated:

	2012	*2013*	*2014*
	€	€	€
Sch D Case I profits	29,000	11,500	7,200
Balancing charges	Nil	500	700
Capital allowances	(1,680)	(3,000)	(7,900)
	27,320	9,000	Nil
Deductions			
Capital allowances 2012 used			
2012[1]	(1,420)		
Excess deductions[2]	(350)	(1,300)	Nil
Available Sch D Case I income	25,550	7,700	Nil
Set off of terminal loss			

The carry back and set off of the terminal loss of €25,080 may now be dealt with as follows:

(a) The loss is first carried back to 2014 (the latest of the three prior years), but there is no available taxable income from the trade for that year. The full terminal loss must therefore be carried back to 2013.

(b) €7,700 of the terminal loss carried back to 2013 is set off against the available taxable income from the trade for that year (€7,700) thereby reducing it to nil. Since €1,300 of the deductions in 2013 has been used to reduce the available Sch D Case I income for that year, the rule of TCA 1997, s 387(2) requires the balance of the terminal loss available for relief in any earlier year to be reduced by that amount. The balance of the terminal loss for carry back to 2012 is determined as follows:

	€	€
Terminal loss carried back from 2014		25,080
Less:		
Part used in 2013	7,700	
Reduction under TCA 1997, s 387(2) in 2013	1,300	
		(9,000)
Terminal loss carried back to 2012		16,080

(c) This balance of the terminal loss carried back from 2013 is set off against the €25,550 available taxable income from the trade for 2012 as follows:

	€
Available Sch D Case I income 2012	25,550
Less:	
Terminal loss relief [3]	16,080
Revised Sch D Case I income 2012	9,470

(d) The income tax payable for 2014 is not affected by the terminal loss claim, but the income tax payable for 2013 and 2012 must now be recomputed by reference to Mr Dealer's income from all sources now including (instead of the original figures) the following revised Sch D Case I income figures:

	€
2013 (per (b) above)	Nil
2012 (per (c) above)	9,470

He should then receive the appropriate repayments of tax for each year resulting from his terminal loss claim.

Notes:

1. The capital allowances carried forward from an earlier year and used in 2012 must be deducted in arriving at the available taxable income from the trade for 2012.
2. The claim for a terminal loss relief will reduce total income and thus could reduce the deductible amount of any annual payment subject to the five per cent restriction applicable to certain covenants (see **15.405**). In theory this might then require the excess (if any) of the annual payment over other income to be recalculated (and so on) but it is unlikely that this point would be taken in practice.
3. In this case, relief has been obtained for the full amount of the terminal loss (subject to the TCA 1997, s 387(2) restriction). However, assume that the available Sch D Case I income for 2012 was only €13,000. In this event, only €13,000 of the loss carried back would be used in 2012 and, as 2012 is the last of the three prior years, no further carry back of the unused balance of the loss (€3,080) would be possible.

General points

The choice of the best form of loss relief to claim for losses incurred in the closing years of a trade or profession is likely to depend on the extent to which the taxpayer has income from other sources in the relevant tax year(s) against which the loss(es) in the trade or profession may be offset (if a s 381 claim were made). The choice is also dependent on whether the loss is incurred in the final or penultimate year, or perhaps in both. It is not possible to cover all permutations without going into excessive detail.

Therefore, the discussion in the following paragraphs is intended only to give some general pointers.

For a tax loss incurred in the final year of assessment, relief is available in a s 381 claim by set off against the taxpayer's income from all sources in the final year. Alternatively, relief may be claimed as part of a terminal loss for set off against the net Sch D Case I or Case II income in the three tax years prior to that in which the cessation occurs (assuming there is such income available not already offset by any earlier relief for losses or capital allowances). Clearly, no carry forward relief under TCA 1997, s 382 is available for a loss or unused capital allowances in the final year.

For a loss or part thereof falling in the penultimate year, relief may be available by carry forward under TCA 1997, s 382 to set off against the taxable profits of the final year (if there is any excess of those taxable profits over the capital allowances of the final year as increased, where relevant, by any unused capital allowances carried forward from any earlier year). It must be borne in mind that the loss will not be available under s 382 to the extent that it has been offset in computing the profits for the basis period of the penultimate year (see **4.408**) Alternatively, s 381 relief may be claimed (but on the strict basis only: see **4.404**) against the taxpayer's income from all sources for the penultimate year or the appropriate part (see above) of any loss falling in the penultimate year may be included in a terminal loss for set off against the net Sch D Case I or Case II in the three prior years.

If there is a terminal loss, but net Sch D Case I or Case II income in any of the three prior tax years, it may sometimes be more advantageous to claim relief for that loss against such income rather than to make a s 381 claim in either, or both, of the penultimate and final years. The existence of taxable profits from the business in any of the three prior years when added to the taxpayer's income from other sources in those years may result in his having a greater total income (before loss relief) and higher tax rates for each such year than he has in the year in which the loss is incurred. In such a case, a terminal loss claim may result in a greater saving in tax than a s 381 claim.

In some cases, it may not be possible to get relief in a s 381 claim for the whole of the tax loss incurred in the penultimate or final year because the amount of the loss exceeds the taxpayer's total income (including any of his spouse's total income, if a joint assessment) for the penultimate or final year. In this event, a claim may also be made under TCA 1997, s 385 to set off the appropriate amount of the terminal loss against the net Sch D Case I or Case II income of the three prior years. However, in computing the terminal loss eligible for carry back, any loss or capital allowances for which relief is obtained in the s 381 claim must be excluded (TCA 1997, s 385(2)).

Example 4.410.3

Mr PB Byron ceases to trade on 31 March 2015 having incurred a tax loss of €32,000 in his final period of accounts made up for the 12 months to the date of cessation. His Sch D Case I taxable profits, capital allowances and balancing charges figures for his year of cessation (2015) and the three immediately preceding tax years (the three prior years) are summarised as follows:

	€
2015:	
Taxable profits (3 months to 31/03/2015)	Nil
Balancing charges	4,000
Capital allowances	(14.050)

Net Sch D Case I income	Nil
Capital allowances 2015 unused	(10,050)
2014:	
Taxable profits (Y/E 31/03/2014)	6,000
Balancing charges	1,600
Capital allowances	(9,600)
Net Sch D Case I income	Nil
Capital allowances 2014 unused	(2,000)
2013:	
Taxable profits (Y/E 31/03/2013)	34,940
Balancing charges	400
Capital allowances	(13,400)
Net Sch D Case I income	21,940
2012:	
Taxable profits (Y/E 31/03/2012)	12,820
Balancing charges	Nil
Capital allowances	(6,000)
Net Sch D Case I income	6,820

Mr Byron is a single person. His total income, taxable income and income tax payable before claiming any loss relief for the four years are as follows:

	2015	*2014*	*2013*	*2012*
	€	€	€	€
Net Sch D Case I	Nil	Nil	21,940	6,820
Income from other sources	16,150	12,100	26,600	38,200
Taxable Income	16,150	12,100	48,540	45,020
Income tax payable:				
€16,150 x 20%	3,230			
€12,100 x 20%		2,420		
€32,800 x 20%			6,560	
€32,800 x 20%				6,560
€15,740 x 41%			6,453	
€12,220 x 41%				5,010
Income tax chargeable	3,230	2,420	13,013	11,570
Less: Personal tax credits, say	(2,000)	(2,000)	(2,000)	(2,000)
Total income tax chargeable	1,230	420	11,013	9,570

Assume that Mr Byron decides to make first a s 381 claim for his losses (increased by capital allowances under TCA 1997, s 392) in the final and penultimate years and then to claim terminal loss relief for any balances of the losses and capital allowances still unrelieved.

Section 381 relief

The losses eligible for the relief are determined as follows:

		€
2015:		
Loss in period 1/01/2015 to 31/03/2015		
3/12ths x loss €32,000		(8,000)
Capital allowances 2015 (unused part)		(10,050)
s 381 loss 2015		(18,050)
2014:		
Loss in period 1/01/2014 to 31/12/2014[1]		
Period 1/01/2014 to 31/03/2014		
3/12ths x € 6,000 (12 months to 31/03/2014[1])	€1,500	
Period 1/04/2014 to 31/12/2014		
9/12ths x €32,000 (12 months to 31/03/2015)	€(24,000)	(22,500)
Capital allowances 2014 (unused part)		(2,000)
s 381 loss 2014		(24,500)

Mr Byron's income tax repayable for the two years as a result of the s 381 claims is now calculated as follows:

	2015	*2014*
	€	€
Total income (before s 381 relief)		
As before	16,150	12,100
Less:		
s 381 loss 2015 (€18,050) limited to	(16,150)	
s 381 loss 2014 (€24,500) limited to	-	(12,100)
Taxable income	Nil	Nil
Income tax payable:	Nil	Nil
Income tax already paid	(1,230)	(420)
Income tax repayable	(1,230)	(420)

Mr Byron now claims relief under TCA 1997, s 385 for a terminal loss calculated as follows:

	€	€
(a) Tax loss in 2015 (final year)		
Period 1 January 2015 to 31 March 2015		
3/12ths x loss €32,000	8,000	
Less:		
Used in s 381 claim (loss used before capital allowances)[2]	(8,000)	Nil
(b) Capital allowances 2015	14,050	
Less:		
Used to offset balancing charges 2015	(4,000)	

Actually used in s 381 claim 2015[2]	(8,150)	1,900
(c) Part of tax loss in 2014 (penultimate year)		
Loss in period 1 April 2014 to 31 December 2014		
9/12ths x loss €32,000 =	24,000	
Less:		
Actually used in s 381 claim 2014[3]	(12,100)	11,900
(d) Proportion of available capital allowances 2014		
Total capital allowances	9,600	
Less:		
Used to offset balancing charges 2014	(1,600)	
Used to reduce taxable profits 2014 to nil	(6,000)	
Actually used in s 381 claim 2014[3]	Nil	
	2,000	
Appropriate proportion[4]:		
9/12ths x €2,000		1,500
Amount of terminal loss to carry back		15,300

Since Mr Byron's net Sch D Case I income for 2014 is nil, the whole terminal loss of €15,300 must be carried back to 2013 where it can be fully set off. His income tax payable (and the resulting income tax repayable) for 2013 is now calculated as follows:

	€
Net Sch D Case I income (before terminal loss)	21,940
Less:	
Terminal loss carried back	(15,300)
	6,640
Income from other sources	26,600
Taxable income	33,240
Income tax payable	
€32,800 x 20%	6,560
€440 x 41%	180
	6,740
Less:	
Tax credits	(2,000)
	4,740
Income tax already paid	(11,013)
Income tax repayable	(6,273)

Notes:

1. The s 381 loss must be calculated on the strict basis in the penultimate year.
2. TCA 1997, s 392(2) requires the amount of relief obtained under s 381 loss to be attributed first to the tax loss and then to the capital allowances. For 2015, this

means that the full tax loss of €8,000 is used first, then the €8,150 balance of the s 381 deduction of €16,150 is taken from the capital allowances (leaving €1,900 of the 2015 capital allowances available for the terminal loss claim).

3. Similarly, in 2014, all the available s 381 deduction of €12,100 must be attributed to the tax loss (€22,500) for that year so that none of the 2014 capital allowances are used in this year's s 381 claim.

4. The appropriate proportion of the 2014 capital allowances still available is that attributable to the nine months from 1 April 2014 (12 months before date of cessation) to 31 December 2014.

Unused losses and post cessation receipts

A person who has ceased to carry on a trade or profession may sometimes receive sums subsequent to the date of cessation which were not accrued as trading receipts in his final accounts in arriving at his final taxable profit or tax loss to the date of cessation. It is shown in **5.605** that TCA 1997, s 91 charges to tax under Sch D Case IV any such post-cessation receipts which, if they had been received prior to the date of cessation, would have been included in arriving at the taxable profits or tax loss of the trade or profession.

In any case where a Sch D Case IV assessment is made on such post-cessation receipts, any unused tax losses incurred in or any unused capital allowances related to the trade or profession before its cessation are available for set off against that assessment (TCA 1997, s 91(4)). This is an exception to the normal rule that unused tax losses and capital allowances cannot be carried forward for use after the date of cessation of the trade or profession.

4.411 Losses forward from dealing in residential land

Finance Act 2009 abolished the 20 per cent flat rate of income tax for residential development land dealers with effect for the tax year 2009 and subsequent tax years. From 1 January 2009, residential land dealing profits are taxable at the individual's marginal rate of tax. At the same time a new section, TCA 1997, s 644AA, was inserted by FA 2009 which restricted the relief which residential land dealers could claim in respect of current year losses under TCA 1997, s 381 and terminal loss relief under TCA 1997, s 385 in respect of their residential land dealing losses arising in a tax year before 2009 unless such claims had been made to the Revenue prior to 7 April 2009. The effect of these measures was to amend the manner in which these reliefs would be granted. Essentially relief for residential development land dealing losses under TCA 1997, s 381 were instead given in the form of a credit to be granted against (but not to exceed) the taxpayer's income tax liability for the tax year. The tax credit given was 20 per cent of the relevant loss. These new rules were designed to prevent taxpayers getting tax relief at their marginal rate for such losses thus correcting an anomaly in the legislation which historically had allowed residential land dealers to offset their residential land dealing losses against other income taxable at the higher rate by making a TCA 1997, s 381 claim. This tax treatment was perceived to be inequitable given that the same trade, if profitable, would have been taxed on its profits at the lower 20 per cent flat rate of income tax.

Terminal loss relief was also amended in respect of losses attributable to a tax year before 2009, to restrict the carry back of residential development land dealing losses arising in the final year of trading to residential land dealing profits only, unless a claim for the terminal loss relief was made before 7 April 2009.

The above two restrictions no longer have significant relevance given that they were introduced to counter reliefs which could only have been claimed in respect of the 2008 income tax year of assessment and earlier years. Therefore, only a general summary has been provided in relation to the operation of such restrictions. For a more detailed analysis of the relevant legislation, please refer to earlier editions of this book.

However, TCA 1997, s 644AA(8) remains relevant in terms of setting out the tax relief which is available for residential development land dealing losses which are still being carried forward where such losses arose prior to the 2009 year of assessment. For the purposes of this section, a residential development land dealing loss is a 'relevant loss' which has been sustained in a 'specified trade'. A 'specified trade' is a trade or the part of a 'combined trade', the profits or gains of which would have qualified for the 20 per cent flat rate of income tax, ie namely residential development land dealing losses as defined by TCA 1997, s 644A.

A 'combined trade' is defined in TCA 1997, s 644AA as meaning a trade consisting partly of a specified trade and partly of a non-specified trade. It follows that in the context of a combined trade, an individual would need to identify the proportion of the loss which relates to the specified trade in order to apply the rules in relation to carrying forward pre 2009 losses to subsequent years. In a combined trade, it is necessary to apportion the total amount receivable from sales made and services rendered in the course of the trade and of expenses incurred in that trade between the specified trade and the non-specified part of the trade with such apportionment being made in a manner that is just and reasonable (TCA 1997, s 644AA(2)).

To the extent the taxpayer did not make a claim under TCA 1997, s 381 in relation to a relevant loss for a tax year prior to 2009 and instead opted to carry it forward in accordance with TCA 1997, s 382, relief can only be given in relation to this loss in the form of a tax credit (TCA 1997, s 644AA(8)) which is calculated by multiplying the relevant loss by 20/100. This tax credit may only be offset against the tax payable on the profits arising in the combined trade in subsequent tax years. Relief must be given, as far as possible, against the tax payable on the profits arising in the combined trade for the first subsequent tax year and where it cannot be so given against the tax payable for the next tax year and so on.

The tax payable on the profits arising in the combined trade is calculated as follows:

$$B \times \frac{C}{D}$$

Where:

- B is the 'interim amount of tax payable for the tax year';
- C is the adjusted profits from the combined trade for the tax year and
- D is the claimant's adjusted income for the tax year

The 'interim amount of tax payable for the tax year' is the tax borne by the person for the tax year after taking into account any claim for loss relief under TCA 1997, s 381(1) for losses arising in the non-specified part of the trade or for losses arising in another trade. The adjusted profits from the combined trade is the profits from the combined trade after taking account of any allowances, charges, deductions or losses to which the person is entitled in taxing the trade. The claimant's adjusted income is the person's income from all sources after taking into account any allowances, charges, deductions or losses which can be deducted from a specific source but before deducting allowances, charges, deductions or losses which may be deducted in calculating a person's income from all sources.

Example 4.411.1

Mr E Bishop, a single man, is a property developer who has been carrying on a trade of dealing in and developing land for many years. Mr Bishop makes up accounts annually to 31 December. Mr Bishop's Sch D Case I taxable profits for 2015 amount to €200,000. He also had Sch E income of €50,000 from a construction company of which he holds 100% of the share capital and had paid allowable charges of €10,000. At 1 January 2015 Mr Bishop had Sch D Case I losses carried forward of €960,000 of which €900,000 were residential land development losses which arose in 2008. Mr Bishop's income tax liability for 2015, before taking account of relief for residential land development losses is as follows:

	€
Sch D Case I income	200,000
Less:	
Non-residential land losses carried forward	(60,000)
'Adjusted profits from combined trade' **(C)**	140,000
Schedule E income	50,000
'Adjusted Income' **(D)**	190,000
Less charges	(10,000)
Taxable income	180,000
Income tax payable	
€33,800 x 20%	6,760
€147,200 x 40%	58,880
	65,640
Less:	
Tax credits	(1,650)
'Interim Tax Payable' **(B)**	63,990
Credit for 2008 residential land losses (B x C/D) ie €63,990 x (€140,000/€190,000) (Note)	(47,150)
Income Tax Payable	16,840

Note

The tax credit carried forward by Mr Bishop in respect of his 2008 residential development land losses is €180,000 (€900,000 x 20/100). The amount of the credit which he may claim in 2015 is restricted to the income tax of €47,150 attributable to his combined trade (ie B x C/D above). Mr Bishop will have a residential tax credit of €132,850 available to carry forward to 2016 and subsequent years in respect of his 2008 residential development land losses.

4.412 Restriction of loss relief in land dealing or developing trades

A new section, TCA 1997, s 381A was introduced by FA 2013 to disallow a claim for loss relief under TCA 1997, s 381 in certain circumstances.

A detailed analysis of this new provision has been included at **12.316** of this text.

The section only applies to land dealers or developers or those individuals who are deemed to be carrying on a land dealing or development trade by virtue of TCA 1997, s 640(2)(a), individuals which are collectively referred to as carrying on a 'specified trade'.

Where the section applies such individuals may not make a claim under TCA 1997, s 381 to offset any losses incurred in their 'specified trade' (referred to as a 'specified loss') against other income in cases where such losses are derived from either of the following:

1. Interest on borrowed money employed in the purchase or development of land that is held as trading stock, as defined by TCA 1997, s 89, unless the interest has been paid prior to the claim being made.
2. A reduction in the value of land held as trading stock, unless the loss has been realised by way of a disposal of the land (other than to a connected person) prior to the claim being made.

The exception to the above rule is where the individual's income from his specified trade is more than 50 per cent of his 'aggregate income' as defined for the purposes of the Universal Social Charge (contained in TCA 1997, Pt 18D) for the relevant tax year and the two immediately preceding years. In this scenario, the individual will not be restricted from making a TCA 1997, s 381 loss claim even if the loss has been arrived at by claiming a deduction for unpaid interest etc. Although given the current economic climate, it is difficult to imagine many land dealers or property developers coming within this definition.

TCA 1997, s 381A(4) and (5) sets out specific computational rules which need to be taken into account in the application of this section.

Firstly, in determining the amount of any interest which has been paid and which is referable to a 'specified loss' sustained in any particular tax year, the interest is to be treated as having been paid in respect of an earlier tax year in preference to a later tax year.

Secondly, in determining the amount of a 'specified loss' sustained in any particular tax year which relates to a deduction allowed in respect of either interest or a reduction in land value, the following rules should be taken into account:-

(a) the deduction allowed in respect of interest is treated as being deducted after all other deductions, and

(b) the deduction allowed in respect of a reduction in the value of land is treated as being deducted immediately prior to the deduction allowed in respect of interest.

This new section is deemed to take effect in respect of any interest becoming payable or a reduction in land value which occurs on or after 13 February 2013. Therefore any reduction in land values which occurred prior to this date should not be affected by this section although presumably such reductions in land value will need to be reflected in prior year trading accounts or proven by the taxpayer (by way of written independent valuation) to have occurred before 13 February 2013. The amendment of prior year accounts to reflect a reduction in land value will only be of benefit to the taxpayer in the context of making a TCA 1997, s 381 claim if the relevant time limit for making the claim can still be satisfied, ie within two years of the relevant year of assessment affected. The onus of proof will also be on the individual taxpayer to support the basis for amending prior year accounts to reflect a reduction in land value whether this be by way of independent valuation report or otherwise.

Finally, it should be noted that to the extent the above provision applies to an individual, such losses which are disallowed for the purposes of a TCA 1997, s 381 claim, will still be available to carry forward against any future profits arising from the same trade under TCA 1997, s 382.

4.413 Restriction of loss relief – FA 2014 anti-avoidance measures

FA 2014 introduced significant restrictions to the application of the sideways offset loss relief provision as originally set out in TCA 1997, s 381. Two new sections, TCA 1997, ss 381B and 381C have been introduced to restrict or disallow completely a claim for loss relief under TCA 1997, s 381. FA 2013 had previously restricted claims for loss relief in certain circumstances for land dealers and property developers as outlined earlier in **4.412**. However, new sections TCA 1997, ss 381B and 381C will have a much wider-ranging impact for individuals carrying on a trade or profession.

The objective of the new sections is to restrict individuals from using their trading losses to shelter other income in certain circumstances.

4.414 Passive trades

TCA 1997, s 381B deals with individuals who are not considered to actively carry on their respective trades.

Where an individual falls within the scope of this new section as s/he cannot satisfy the active trader test which is elaborated on further below, it will restrict any loss relief to be claimed under TCA 1997, s 381, including any amount of capital allowances which is also treated as a loss (by virtue of TCA 1997, s 392), to the lower of €31,750 or the actual loss sustained. To the extent that the basis period for a year of assessment is shorter than 12 months, then the €31,750 limit must be time-apportioned accordingly.

The active trader test can also simultaneously apply to a number of trades carried out by an individual. The €31,750 limit will be divided between such trades, ie the €31,750 is an absolute limit on the amount of loss relief that can be claimed in any one year.

In order to be regarded as an active trader, an individual must work for the greater part of their time on the day to day management or conduct of the trade or profession during the period in question. According to the legislation, this will entail spending an average of at least ten hours a week personally engaged in the activities of the trade over the course of that period and also that those activities are carried on a commercial basis and in such a way that profits of the trade or profession could reasonably be expected to be made in that period or within a reasonable time afterwards.

It follows that there are two tests that an individual will have to satisfy in order to fall outside the scope of this provision. Firstly, the onus of proof will be on an individual taxpayer to evidence his personal engagement in the trade on a weekly basis over the period in question. It remains to be seen as to how the Revenue may audit or assess the degree of passivity in which a trade is carried out. In order to defend against any future challenge to the validity of a TCA 1997, s 381 loss relief claim, it may be good practice for sole traders to actively maintain a diary documenting their day-to-day activities with regard to their trade. The above test may be problematic for certain seasonal traders to satisfy on the basis that they might only be personally engaged in their trade for specific times of the year. Furthermore, what would happen in a scenario where an individual falls ill during the year and is unable to personally conduct his trade for part of the year? In that regard Revenue *eBrief No 54/16* which issued Revenue manual 12.01.02 notes that 'There may be circumstances in which an individual could temporarily become a non-active trader due to, for example, illness or maternity. The 10 hour a week test is an average test which must be met over the course of a year. So for an on-going trade, an individual must spend, on average 10 hours a week for 52 weeks a year, or 520 hours in total for a year engaged in the trade. This is around 30% of the hours a full time employee would work in a year. Therefore, it is anticipated that it is only in very limited circumstances that an individual, who had been working in a full time trade and who will resume work in that trade in the future, will fail to meet that test for a given year. However, in exceptional or unique circumstances Revenue may determine whether, based on the facts and circumstances of that particular case, the loss relief should be restricted.'

In relation to the second requirement, ie that the trade's activities are carried on, on a commercial basis and in such a way that you could reasonably expect there to be a profit in either the relevant period or within a reasonable time afterwards, this second test may be even more difficult to satisfy. *Revenue eBrief No 54/16* issued Revenue manual 12.01.02 which makes the following points on the trade being carried on on a commercial basis: 'Activities which are not undertaken in a commercial manner with a view to the realisation of profits e.g. reading the newspapers or emails, will not count towards the 10 hour minimum test. There must at least be a realistic prospect that the activity undertaken will result in an enhancement to the trade (for example, an increase in income, a reduction in costs or attracting additional customers or suppliers). Simply carrying out some activity that is related to the trade may not be sufficient. Activities undertaken in start-up trades which generate losses in the initial years while the business is being built up and/or in trades which encounter unexpected market conditions due to circumstances outside their control, (for example economic downturn, increasing interest rates etc.), will not be excluded provided the activities are being conducted in a manner which is conducive to the generation of profits and a reasonable expectation exists that a profit will be turned in the future. However, a trade which is virtually certain to lead to a loss cannot be said to be carried on on a commercial basis and is more likely to be carried on as a hobby.'

It should be noted there is also a restriction on the entitlement to claim loss relief under TCA 1997, s 381 where the particular losses have been incurred in a farming or market gardening context. Presumably this is why farming losses have been specifically excluded from the ambit of this provision as highlighted below. TCA 1997, s 662(2)(a) disallows such a loss relief claim unless it is shown that the farming trade has been carried on, on a commercial basis with a view to the realisation of profits in the trade. TCA 1997, s 662(2)(c) further expands on this to say that for the purposes of this section, the fact that a trade of farming was being carried on at any time so as to afford a reasonable expectation of profit shall be conclusive evidence that it was then being carried on with a view to the realisation of profits. The Revenue Notes for Guidance interpret the above rule as applying to cases where:

> exceptionally, the farmer or market gardener can point to activities which could reasonably be expected to produce a profit but might, nevertheless, find it difficult to maintain that the conditions of TCA 1997, s 662(2)(a) were satisfied at any given time.

There is also a restriction on claiming loss relief in a farming context where losses have been incurred for a consecutive three-year period. However, TCA 1997, s 662(2)(d) disapplies this rule in circumstances where losses have been incurred for three years or more where the farming activities were carried on in such a way, as would have justified a reasonable expectation of profits in the future, if those activities had been carried out by a competent farmer. In accordance with the Revenue Notes for Guidance:

> this provision is designed to meet the genuine case of a farmer who sets out an undertaking realising that losses will be incurred for a substantial initial period but with a justifiable expectation of building up a profitable operation in the long run.

The particular example provided in the Revenue guidance includes a farmer trying to regenerate marginal land over a long period.

It would be prudent for traders to produce and retain business plans which show from the outset that a profit can at the very least be achieved in future years. It would also be appropriate to update such business plans on an ongoing basis and compare to the actual trading results.

This section does not apply to individuals carrying on a farming trade within the meaning of TCA 1997, Pt 23. It also does not apply to a market gardening trade or to an individual who carries on a trade which consists of the underwriting business of a member of Lloyd's. Finally, the section does not apply to a loss which arises as a result of making a significant buildings claim under TCA 1997, s 482(2) or where the loss has arisen as a result of a claim for capital allowances within the meaning of TCA 1997, s 531AAE.

TCA 1997, s 381B is effective for 2015 and subsequent years of assessment. This new provision could affect many individuals who carry on a number of trades, particularly a land dealer who may also be a partner in a number of partnerships. Such partnerships may already be subject to loss restrictions under the limited partnership rules as set out in further detail in **4.512**. It would also impact on a sole trader who may also be a company director. It should be noted that where any part of a trading loss is denied loss relief under TCA 1997, s 381B, it should still be otherwise available to carry forward and offset against future trading profits of the same trade under TCA 1997, s 382.

Example 4.414.1

Mr V Busy operates a hotel as a sole trader and also carries on a land dealing trade in 2017. Separately, Mr V Busy owns a number of investment properties which generate him a net Case V rental profit of €200,000 per annum. The hotel trade incurred a loss of €50,000 before capital allowances during 2015. His land dealing trade also incurred a trading loss of €70,000.

Mr V Busy spends approximately 30 hours a week on average overseeing the running of his hotel. He spends approximately five hours a week carrying out his land dealing trade.

In preparing his income tax return for 2017, a s 381 claim was made in respect of his respective hotel and land dealing trading losses.

	€
Case I Hotel Trade	Nil
Case I Land Dealing Trade	Nil
Case V Rental Income	200,000
	200,000
Less:	
s 381 Hotel Trade Loss[1]	(50,000)
s 381 Land Dealing Trade Loss[2]	(31,750)
Total Income	118,250

Notes:

1 It is assumed for the purposes of this example that Mr V Busy is satisfied that he is an active hotel trader and that the hotel trade is being carried out on a commercial basis fulfilling the criteria set out in TCA 1997, s 381B. Therefore there is no restriction on the s 381 claim made in respect of the hotel loss.

2 Mr V Busy does not spend the requisite average 10 hours a week personally engaged in the running of his land dealing trade. Therefore any claim to be made under s 381 is restricted to €31,750. It is also assumed there are no further loss relief restrictions in respect of this trade as provided for in TCA 1997, s 381A.

Example 4.414.2

Taking the facts of example **4.414.1** above, it is assumed that Mr V Busy falls ill during 2017 and is unable to be personally engaged in the running of his hotel trade and therefore cannot be considered an active trader in respect of this trade for 2017.

In preparing his income tax return for 2017, the following s 381 claim was made.

	€
Case I Hotel Trade	Nil
Case I Land Dealing Trade	Nil
Case V Rental Income	200,000
	200,000
Less:	
s 381 Loss Hotel Trade[1]	(31,750)
s 381 Loss Land Dealing Trade[1]	(0)
Total Income	168,250

Notes:

1 As Mr V Busy may not be in a position without Revenue confirmation to satisfy the active trader test in respect of either of his trades for 2017, the maximum s 381 loss relief claim he can make is €31,750 for the year. The legislation is silent as to how this €31,750 is to be allocated so presumably the tax payer can choose how the loss relief claim can be allocated to the relevant trades. The balance of losses arising may be carried forward to be offset against future profits of the respective trades.

4.415 Anti-avoidance

TCA 1997, s 381C is a similar provision to TCA 1997, s 381B as it also targets non-active traders seeking to claim loss relief under TCA 1997, s 381 (including a loss which has arisen by virtue of an s 392 capital allowances claim). As with TCA 1997, s 381B, an individual will be regarded as carrying on a trade in a non-active capacity during the relevant period for a year of assessment if the individual does not work for the greater part of their time on the day to day management or conduct of the trade or profession during that period. The relevant tests to satisfy in order to fall outside of the above definition are as explained above in **4.414.1**.

However, TCA 1997, s 381C will only apply to non-active traders who have sustained a loss in a trade or profession which has arisen in whole or in part, directly or indirectly, in consequence of or otherwise in connection with relevant tax avoidance arrangements.

Relevant tax avoidance arrangements are defined within the section as meaning arrangements, the main purpose or one of the main purposes of which, is to give rise to a claim under TCA 1997, s 381. Arrangements are further defined as including any agreement, understanding, scheme, transaction or series of transactions (whether or not legally enforceable).

The relevant period for a year of assessment is also defined in this section as meaning the basis period for the year of assessment. However, where the basis period is shorter than six months, specific rules apply. In a case where a trade has been permanently discontinued, the basis period is the period of six months ending on the last day of that basis period. In all other cases, a basis period must be for a minimum period of six months starting on the first day of the basis period. *Revenue eBrief No 54/16* which issued Revenue manual 12.01.02 gives the following examples in connection with the application of TCA 1997, s 381C as follows:

Examples of 6 month period:

John has been trading for many years. He ceased to trade on 31 March 2016. For the 2016 year of assessment, John's basis period is the account profits/losses from 1 January 2016 to 31 March 2016. The period of 6 months is the 6-month period ending on 31 March 2016.

Joan has been trading for a number of years and will continue to trade for the foreseeable future. She changed her year end, and for the 2016 year of assessment, Joan's basis period is her accounts from 1 November 2015 to 31 March 2016. The period of 6 months is the 6-month period starting on 1 November 2015.

Jo commenced her trade on 1 January 2016 and ceased the trade on 31 January 2016. For the 2016 year of assessment, Jo's basis period is her accounts from 1 January 2016 to 31 January 2016. The period of 6 months is the 6-month period ending on 31 January 2016.

Mark prepares 12-month accounts from 1 January 2016 to 31 December 2016. As the basis period for the year of assessment is longer than 6 months, the basis period itself is used.

Examples of 10 hours a week on average:

John must have worked 10 hours a week, on average for a period of six months to cessation. John's final basis period is 3 months. Therefore, this 6-month period covers a longer period than his final basis period. Jo must have worked 10 hours a week, on average, for a period of six months. (10 x 4 x 6 = 240 hours). As she was only trading for one month, she must, in effect, work 240 hours in that one-month period in order to avoid failing this test. Mark must work 10 hours a week, on average, for the 12-month period.

This anti-avoidance section completely denies loss relief for an individual coming within the scope of this section as the individual is deemed not to have sustained a loss in that trade or profession for that year of assessment for the purposes of TCA 1997, s 381. However, the individual should be able to carry forward the trading loss as it is only for the purposes of s 381, that the individual is deemed not to have sustained a trading loss. This section is effective as respects any basis period which commences after 23 October 2014.

Excluded from the scope of this provision are losses which have arisen as a result of either a significant buildings claim under TCA 1997, s 482(2) or any amount in respect of specified capital allowances as defined in TCA 1997, s 531AAE.

It should be noted that the new surcharge which has been introduced by FA 2014 as part of the new general anti-avoidance provisions (New GAAR), (TCA 1997, s 811D) is stated to apply specifically to TCA 1997, ss 381B and 381C. It follows that where a taxpayer submits a tax return or otherwise and seeks to obtain the benefit of a tax advantage and the transaction that gives rise to the tax advantage comes within either TCA 1997, ss 381B or 381C, the taxpayer may be liable to the 30 per cent surcharge under TCA 1997, s 811D. The surcharge will only apply to transactions which commenced on or after 24 October 2014. The surcharge and ways to mitigate the surcharge are discussed further in **17.302**.

Finally, if a taxpayer enters into a transaction to which either TCA 1997, ss 381B or 381C applies, it should be borne in mind that in the event that an assessment is raised by Revenue withdrawing part or all of the tax advantage gained by entering into the transaction any additional tax may be collected by Revenue when any appeal has been heard and determined by the Appeal Commissioners by the issue of a payment notice. This is the case even if the taxpayer has requested a rehearing by the Circuit Court (for periods prior to the application of F(TA)A 2015) or lodged an appeal to the High Court. Furthermore, Revenue can issue a payment notice requesting immediate payment of tax due in such an assessment if a similar transaction has been the subject of an Appeal Commissioners determination which resulted in the issue of a payment notice to another taxpayer (see under Payment notices in **2.618** as part of the new FA 2014 mandatory disclosure rules).

4.5 Partnerships

4.501 General

A trade or profession may be carried on by two or more persons in partnership. A partnership is defined in the Partnership Act 1890, s 1 as 'the relation which subsists between persons carrying on business in common with a view of profit'. The Partnership Act 1890, s 45 defines a business as including 'every trade, occupation or profession'.

The definition of 'business' for the purposes of the Partnership Act is capable of including activities which would not be trades for income tax purposes (see *Three H Aircraft Hire v C & E* [1982] STC 653). Conversely, an activity may still be a trade for tax purposes, although not carried on with a 'view of profit' (see **4.1**). In such a case, the trade would not be a partnership trade (see *McCarthaigh v Daly* III ITR 253, where the court upheld, with some reservations, a finding of fact that a trade of dubious commerciality was a 'business' for the purposes of the Partnership Act). However, a partnership created to make profits, albeit in a form which escapes taxation, is carrying on a business 'with a view of profit' (*Newstead v Frost* [1980] STC 123). A single venture can be the subject of a partnership, although the term 'business' has been taken to imply continuity and/or repetition in other contexts (*Mann v Darcy* [1968] 2 All ER 172).

In practice, most partnerships are between individuals, but a partnership may exist between one or more individuals and one or more companies or between two or more companies. Unless indicated to the contrary at any point, the discussion in **4.5** deals only with partnerships between individuals. The way in which a company carrying on a trade in partnership is charged to corporation tax on its partnership income is outside the scope of this work.

The existence of a partnership is a question of fact. The parties' own description of their arrangements cannot overrule the true legal position (see **1.407**). Thus, in *Alexander Bulloch & Co v IRC* [1976] STC 514, the partners of a firm purported to take on two of the partners' daughters as partners. The daughters drew neither salaries nor shares of profit from the business and in fact continued to receive pocket money as before. Furthermore, they remained at school and carried out only routine shop work in exactly the same way as they had always done. The Court of Session upheld the finding of fact by the Appeal Commissioners that the partners' daughters had not themselves become partners (see also eg *Dickenson v Gross* 11 TC 614 and *IRC v Williamson* 14 TC 355).

Similarly, the taxpayer cannot backdate the commencement of a partnership prior to the date when it actually took legal effect (see *Macken v Revenue Commissioners* [1962] IR 302; *Ayrshire Pullman Motor Services & Ritchie v IRC* 14 TC 754; *Saywell v Pope* [1979] STC 824).

A frequent source of difficulty is the distinction between an employee and a so-called 'salaried partner'. Again, the fact that such a person is held out as a 'partner' cannot overrule the true legal nature of the relationship concerned, which will depend on the particular facts of the case (see *Stekel v Ellice* [1973] 1 All ER 465 and also *O'Kelly v Darragh* [1988] ILRM 304; the latter case underlines the principle set out in the Partnership Act 1890, s 2 that receipt of a share of profit is only *prima facie*, and not conclusive, evidence of partnership status). In *Horner v Hasted* [1995] STC 766, it was held that the taxpayer who was treated for all internal purposes as a partner was in fact an employee of the partnership, a significant (although not the only) factor in reaching this conclusion was that it would have been illegal for the taxpayer to have been a partner.

The distinction between a partner and an employee has also been drawn, in the context of share fishing ventures, in *DPP v McLoughlin* III ITR 467. In that case, it was held that there was a partnership between the skipper of the boat and the fishing crew. Costello J relied principally on the fact that each voyage was a separate venture, that the crew received their remuneration by way of profit-sharing, and that the rate of remuneration was not set by the skipper. These elements outweighed the fact that the crew members were not liable for losses and that the skipper exercised an element of control over the crew (this was held to be inherent anyway in the nature of the particular operations concerned). For a critical analysis of the decision, see Cousins [1994] DULJ 207.

In other cases, the distinction may lie between a person with a mere financial involvement in a business venture as opposed to a partner in the venture (see *Pratt v Strick* 17 TC 459 and contrast *Fenston v Johnstone* 23 TC 29).

The sharing of gross returns does not of itself create a partnership (Partnership Act 1890, s 2(2)). This may enable persons, or indeed separate partnerships, to enter into a venture where eg one party provides capital and the other labour and/or skill, each taking a share of the turnover of the venture, without the venture being considered a partnership.

The law governing limited partners is set out in the Limited Partnership Act 1907. In a limited partnership there must be at least one limited partner and one general partner, whose liability is unlimited. A limited partner is liable only to the extent of his capital contributed which he may not withdraw during the continuance of the partnership. A limited partner cannot take part in the management of the business and has no power to bind the firm, although he may inspect the books of the firm. A limited partnership must be registered as such with the Registrar of Companies. However, the partnership agreement may provide that any losses incurred by the partnership may result in him or her losing his right to undrawn or future profits (see *Reed v Young* [1985] STC 25). As discussed in **4.512**, there are a number of restrictions applicable to loss reliefs claimed by a limited partner. For these purposes, the concept of 'limited partner' is extended beyond the strict Partnership Act definition.

The term 'sleeping partner' does not have a legal meaning, but is generally used to indicate a partner who in practice plays little or no active part in the management of the partnership business. As in the case of a limited partner his profits will not usually rank as 'earned income' for the purposes of retirement annuity relief (see **16.202**) and for the purposes of determining the order of set-off in an TCA 1997, s 381 loss claim (see **4.407**).

The partnership entity, usually called 'the firm', does not have any legal status apart from that of its partners. It does not enter into contracts in the firm name, but in the names of its partners. Although most partnerships prepare annual or other periodic accounts to determine the profits or losses of the firm's trade and a balance sheet showing the assets and liabilities of the firm, the assets usually belong collectively to the persons making up the partnership and the partners are jointly and severally liable for the debts of the firm.

Some variations on the traditional partnership structure may give rise to problematic tax consequences. Thus, for example, a parallel partnership may be formed alongside the main partnership as a means of overcoming the statutory limits on the number of partners (where this applies), or perhaps as a means of allowing unqualified persons partnership status without breaching professional regulations. It will be a question of fact whether the two partnerships are carrying on two separate businesses or whether there is in reality a single partnership business. In the latter case this would result in the partnership being rendered illegal; it seems that this would result in the 'partnership' ceasing to be a partnership for all legal (including tax) purposes (note *American Foreign Insurance Association v Davies* 32 TC 1).

It is also possible for a partner to enter into a 'subpartnership' with one or more third parties, the business of which would be the management of that partner's share in the main partnership. However, it seems that a mere assignment of a partnership share may not be effective to alienate the assignor's partnership profits for tax purposes: *Hadlee v CIR* [1993] STC 294. The *Hadlee* decision was based on the premise that an assignment of a partnership share does not normally involve a transfer of property (but note *Lindley and Banks on Partnerships* 6th edn, at 1973). The *Hadlee* decision also relied on the established principle in New Zealand tax law that income from personal exertions cannot be alienated. It is an open question whether such a principle applies for Irish tax purposes (see *Parker v Chapman* 13 TC 677, a Sch E case, at first instance). The *Hadlee* decision is naturally of no relevance where the assignee becomes a partner in his own right (although this will usually require the consent of the other partners).

The Tax Acts set out to tax the partners in a partnership rather than the firm itself, although as part of the tax mechanism the firm – through its 'precedent partner' – is required to make annual returns of the partnership income and chargeable gains. In principle, each partner is taxed separately on his share of the firm's trading and other income and of any chargeable gains realised on the disposal of assets held as partnership property. The firm's Sch D Case I or Case II income from the trade or profession is first ascertained under the ordinary computational rules of those Cases before being allocated between the partners. Similarly, capital allowances and balancing charges are first calculated for the firm before allocation.

TCA 1997, ss 1007 to 1012 contain the rules for allocating between the partners the taxable profits, tax losses, capital allowances and balancing charges arising from the firm's trade or profession. These rules are discussed in this Division in the context of a trade, but apply equally to professions. For the anti-avoidance rules which apply to partnerships where a trader brings one or more of his children into partnership, see **15.409**.

Finally, it may be noted that a European Economic Interest Grouping (a European entity established by EC Council Regulation 2137/85 and given effect in Ireland by the

European Economic Interest Grouping Regulations 1989), is treated as a partnership for the purposes of income tax, capital gains tax and corporation tax (TCA 1997, s 1014).

4.502 The partnership trade

TCA 1997, s 1007(1) defines 'partnership trade' as a trade which is carried on by two or more persons in partnership. Since TCA 1997, s 1007(3) applies, with any necessary modifications, the provisions in TCA 1997, Pt 43 to professions in the same way as they apply to trades, the term applies equally to the business of a profession carried on by two or more persons in partnership. Consequently, any reference here to a partnership trade taxable under Sch D Case I is to be taken as applying in the same way to a profession carried on in partnership chargeable under Sch D Case II.

An important concept in the taxing of partnerships is that of 'the relevant period'. In effect, the relevant period is the entire period during which a particular partnership trade is regarded as continuing irrespective of changes which may take place in the partners. However, as indicated in the next paragraph, certain changes in the persons carrying on the trade result in the termination of the relevant period and in the cessation of the partnership trade in question.

The relevant period of a partnership trade is deemed to begin on the date on which the trade is first carried on by two or more persons in partnership. This may be either (a) when the trade itself is first set up and operated from the beginning by a partnership of persons, or (b) when a person carrying on a trade on his own takes in one or more partners, or (c) when there is a complete change in the partners carrying on the trade. The relevant period is treated as terminating either (a) on the date when the trade itself is permanently discontinued, or (b) when it ceases to be carried on by at least two persons in partnership, or (c) when there is a complete change in the partners carrying on the trade (TCA 1997, s 1007(1)).

Example 4.502.1

A and B commence a practice in partnership as chartered surveyors on 1 January 1995 under the firm name 'Survey & Co'. The firm of Survey & Co continues in practice as chartered surveyors while the following changes in partners take place in the meantime:

(a) 23 March 2005 – B dies and A continues the practice on his own account until;

(b) 1 January 2006 – A takes C into partnership;

(c) 1 January 2008 – D and E are admitted as additional partners;

(d) 30 June 2010 – A retires owing to ill health;

(e) 15 May 2015 – C, D and E sell the business to a new partnership of N and M who continue practising as Survey & Co.

There are three different relevant periods for the business of Survey & Co, as follows:

(a) The first relevant period begins on 1 January 1995 when the partnership trade (the profession) is first set up by A and B; this relevant period ends on 23 March 2005 when there ceases to be a partnership on B's death.

(b) The second relevant period begins on 1 January 2006 on the admission of C as a partner; this relevant period ends on 15 May 2015 on the complete change of partners on the sale of the business to N and M, but it is not affected by the admission of D and E nor by the retirement of A.

(c) The third relevant period begins on 15 May 2015 on the succession of N and M to the partnership trade carried on immediately prior to that date by C, D and E (as there was no partner common to the firm both before and after 15 May 2015).

The relevant period of a partnership comes to an end when the trade ceases, notwithstanding that the relationship of the partners between themselves may continue. If, for example, N and M in the above example cease to trade as chartered surveyors on 1 October 2015 and start a new trade as partners as property dealers, there is a cessation of one trade and a commencement of a new one under general income tax principles. Even though the new property dealing trade is carried on under the same partnership agreement as to the sharing of profits, etc, a new relevant period for the property dealing trade commences on 1 October 2015 and the relevant period for the chartered surveyor business ends on the same day.

It is to be noted that the death of a partner does not cause the partnership trade to cease if the business is carried on after the death by two or more persons who were partners of the deceased person. Whether the trade continues is a question of fact. Even if the partnership deed provides for the partnership to be dissolved on the death of a partner, if the surviving partners (two or more) in fact continue to trade as partners without any interruption of business, the partnership trade and its relevant period continues for tax purposes.

In *IRC v Lebus' Executors* 27 TC 136, the taxpayer was the widow of a deceased partner. She was entitled under the will to be paid a share of the partnership profits. It was held that, unlike a partner (who was assessable on his share of profits as they arose) the taxpayer was assessable only in respect of income received by her (or on her behalf by her husband's executors). This decision followed that of *Dewar v IRC*, discussed at **15.202**.

4.503 How partners are taxed

TCA 1997, s 1008(1) provides that each partner in a partnership is to be taxed on his share of the taxable profits from the partnership trade as if that share arose from a separate trade (referred to as his 'several trade') carried on by him. Similarly, if there is a tax loss in the partnership trade for any period in which he is a partner, he is entitled to claim any available loss relief for his share of that tax loss as if it were a loss of his several trade (see **4.507**). He is entitled also to his share of the capital allowances attributable to the partnership trade and is liable to tax on his share of the firm's balancing charges (if any) for each year of assessment in which he is a partner (see **4.505**).

Computation of firm's taxable profits

The first step in taxing the several trades of the different partners in respect of their shares of the firm's trading profits is to determine the full amount of the firm's taxable profit or tax loss for each period for which the partnership makes up accounts. TCA 1997, s 1008(3) requires the full amount of the firm's taxable profit or tax loss for any relevant period of account to be determined as if the trade had commenced at the beginning of the 'relevant period' (see **4.502**) and as if it has been continued at all times in the relevant period by the one person.

This has the effect that, notwithstanding that some partners may cease to be involved in the trade and others may commence as new partners, the firm's taxable profits (or tax losses) are calculated on this same basis so long as the firm's relevant period lasts. This means that the rules relating to the calculation of taxable profits respectively on a commencement and on a cessation of trade (see **5.601–5.604**) apply only at the beginning and end of the firm's relevant period.

For example, on the commencement of the relevant period (eg when a sole trader takes in a partner), no deduction is available in computing the new firm's taxable profits for any expenses incurred prior to the date of the new partner's admission unless they fall within TCA 1997, s 82 (see **5.601**). However, thereafter changes in the partners not involving the end of the relevant period do not result in any application of this rule regarding the non-deductibility of pre-trading expenses.

In the event that the relevant period should come to an end (eg by the death of a partner in a two partner firm), the firm's taxable profits or tax loss for the firm's last period of account must be computed on the basis of a permanent discontinuance of trade. In other words, any computational rules relating to a permanent discontinuance of trade must be applied. For example, the rules of TCA 1997, s 89 regarding the valuation of the closing stock in trade on a cessation of trade (see **5.603**) must be applied. The rules relating to the computation of taxable profits on a cessation have no relevance in computing taxable profits or tax losses (either of the firm or of any partner) on the occasion of a partner leaving the firm where there is no termination of the relevant period.

In calculating the firm's taxable profit or tax loss to be allocated to the several trades of the partners, all the normal Sch D Case I and Case II computational rules are applied and any income not assessable as income of the trade or profession is excluded as are any expenses relating to such other income. Each partner's share of income assessable under other Schs or other Cases of Sch D is separately charged on the partner concerned (see **4.508**). It may be noted that because the partnership is not a separate entity distinct from the persons who made it up, any payment for the personal benefit of a partner are appropriations of profit (see **4.504**) and thus can never be deductible expenses (see *McKinlay v Arthur Young McClelland Moores & Co* [1986] STC 491). However payments made to a partner in a different capacity (eg rent paid to a partner as a landlord of the premises used by the partnership) are deductible, subject to the normal rules: *Heastie v Veitch & Co* 18 TC 305 (see **5.306**: Appropriations and applications of profit).

A partnership expense which it is agreed should be borne by some, but not all of the partners is deductible in computing the profits of the partnership trade: *Bolton v Halpern & Woolf* [1981] STC 14. However, it should be noted that the allocation of the expense between the partners will normally form part of the profit sharing arrangements of the partnership.

Allocation of firm's profits to several trades

Once the partnership's Sch D Case I or Case II profit or loss has been calculated for a period of account, the second step is to allocate that taxable profit or tax loss between the persons who were partners during that period. TCA 1997, s 1008(2) requires this allocation to be made in the proportions in which the partners share the accounting profits or losses in accordance with the partnership agreement. If, as may happen in some partnerships from time to time, the partners agree to vary the terms of their agreement as to profit-sharing and in fact divide the accounting profit or loss in different proportions for a particular period the allocation of the taxable profit or tax loss is made in the same proportions as those used in which the accounting profit or loss of the period is actually divided.

Example 4.503.1

A, B and C trade as partners under an agreement providing for the sharing of profits and losses 50:30:20. The profits for the firm's accounting year ended 31 August 2014 are divided in these ratios. In the following accounting period for the nine months ended 31 May 2015 A is away owing to illness for most of the period and C works unusually long hours to help out with A's work. Consequently, it is agreed verbally that the profit sharing for that period only would be 40:30:30.

The accounting profits for the two periods of account are respectively €231,000 and €228,000; the adjusted Sch D Case I profits (after add backs for depreciation and certain other items) are respectively €244,000 and €236,300. The accounting and adjusted tax profits for the two accounting periods are allocated as follows:

	Total	*A*	*B*	*C*
y/e 31/08/2014:		€	€	€
Profits per accounts	231,000	115,500	69,300	46,200
Adjusted Sch D Case I profits (before capital allowances)	244,000	122,000	73,200	48,800
		(50%)	(30%)	(20%)
Period to 31/5/2015:				
Profit per accounts	228,000	91,200	68,400	68,400
Adjusted Sch D Case I profits (before capital allowances)	236,300	94,520	70,890	70,890
		(40%)	(30%)	(30%)

Taxing of the several trades

The third step is to deal separately with each partner to whom a share of the firm's taxable profits of each period of account is allocated. The share allocated to each partner for any period of account of the firm is treated as if it were a taxable profit arising in his several trade in the same period. The income basis period rules (as distinct from the profit computational rules) are then applied separately to the share of the firm's taxable profits allocated to each partner's several trade to determine the amount of his taxable profit for the purpose of his Sch D Case I or II assessment for each tax year in which he is a partner.

The income tax basis period rules are applied separately to each partner on the assumption that his several trade commenced on the date on which he became a partner, whether by admission as a new partner in an existing firm during a continuing relevant period or by being one of the partners when this relevant period commenced. Each partner's several trade is thereafter treated as continuing until either he ceases to be a partner or the firm's relevant period comes to an end (TCA 1997, s 1008(1)).

It follows that the rules of commencement (see **4.205**) are applied to each new partner's several trade starting from the date on which that several trade commences (with the right to carry forward any 'second year excess' to reduce the third year's taxable profit). From then onwards, he is assessed on a continuing business basis unless and until his several trade ceases. In the normal case, this means that he is assessed each tax year from the third year onwards on his share of the firm's taxable profits for the firm's 12-month period of account ending in the tax year in question.

When a partner retires, dies or otherwise ceases to be a partner in the firm, his several trade ceases and he is assessed to income tax under the basis period rules applicable on the permanent discontinuance of a trade (see **4.206**). These basis period rules are applied on the assumption that the partner's several trade ceases on the date on which he ceases to be a partner. In other words, he is taxed for the year of assessment in which he ceases to be a partner on his share of the firm's taxable profits for the period from 1

January (the first day) of that year to the date of his cessation; and his assessment for the immediately preceding tax year is made on the higher of his share of the actual taxable profits in that preceding year (to 31 December) or the amount otherwise assessable on him if his several trade had not ceased.

The legal fiction that each partner may have a trade of his own commencing and, in due course, ceasing on dates different from those of other partners enables the commencement, continuing and cessation basis period rules to be applied separately to each partner as appropriate to his case. For example, a partner who joins an existing partnership (which makes accounts up to 30 June each year) on 1 November 2014 is assessed for his first tax year on his share of the firm's taxable profits apportioned to the period 1 November 2014 to 31 December 2014 and he is assessed for the second year on his share of the firm's profits apportioned to the period 1 January 2015 to 31 December 2015 (the actual basis applies in the second year of his several trade as there is no accounting date ending at least 12 months from the commencement of his several trade). Then, should he have a 'second year excess' (see **4.205**) in his several trade, he is entitled by TCA 1997, s 66(3) to have it set off against the taxable profits of his several trade for his third tax year. Similarly, when a partner leaves a continuing firm, the assessment for the penultimate year of his several trade may be adjusted to the actual basis without affecting the basis of the assessments of the continuing partners; again, the assessment for the final year of his several trade will always be on the actual basis without affecting the basis of assessment for the continuing partners.

In short, once the adjusted Sch D Case I (or Case II) profit or loss of the partnership for each relevant period of account has been agreed with the inspector and allocated between the partners, each partner is on his own and may deal separately with the inspector. For the treatment of partnership losses, see **4.507**, and for that of the firm's capital allowances and balancing charges, see **4.506**.

Example 4.503.2

Mr Crock and Mr Odd have traded in partnership since 1 January 1991 when the relevant period of the firm began. Up to 31 March 2013 they share profits and losses equally. On 1 April 2013, they admit Mr Dile as a new partner giving him a 20 per cent share and continuing to share equally between themselves. Accounts are normally prepared to 30 September in each year, but in view of the admission of Mr Dile, two separate six monthly accounts are made up to 31 March 2013 and 30 September 2013 respectively.

The adjusted Sch D Case I profits and their allocation between the partners for the three years ending 30 September 2015:

	Total	*Crock*	*Odd*	*Dile*
	€	€	€	€
6 months to 31/03/2013	30,000	15,000	15,000	-
6 months to 30/09/2013	20,000	8,000	8,000	4,000
12 months to 30/09/2014	52,000	20,800	20,800	10,400
12 months to 30/09/2015	5,000	2,000	2,000	1,000

Mr Crock and Mr Odd are each separately assessed on a continuing business basis on the taxable profits allocated to their respective several trades for the tax years 2013 to 2015 as follows:

	Crock	*Odd*
2013:	€	€
Basis period: 12 months to 30/09/2013[1]	23,000	23,000

2014:		
Basis period: 12 months to 30/09/2014	20,800	20,800
2015:		
Basis period: 12 months to 30/09/2015	2,000	2,000

Mr Dile's several trade is separately assessed under the rules of commencement in respect of his share of the firm's taxable profits as follows:

	€
2013 (1st year):	
Period 1/04/2013 to 31/12/2013	
6 months to 30/09/2013	4,000
3 months to 31/12/2013	
3/12ths x €10,400	2,600
	6,600
2014 (2nd year):	
12 months to 30/09/2014	10,400
2015 (3rd year):	
12 months to 30/09/2015	1,000

However, Mr Dile then calculates his several trade taxable profits for his second tax year in the partnership on the 'actual' (ie year to 31 December) basis as follows:

	€
Period 1/01/2014 to 30/09/2014	
9/12ths x €10,400	7,800
Period 1/10/2014 to 31/12/2014	
3/12ths x €1,000	250
	8,050

Since the actual second year taxable profits of €8,050 are lower than the €10,400 assessed for 2014 Mr Dile has a 'second year excess' of €2,350. He therefore claims relief under TCA 1997, s 66(3) as follows:

	€
Reduce 2015 assessment:	
Amount assessable (as above)	1,000
Less:	
Set off of 2nd year excess (part used)	1,000
Amount finally assessable	Nil
Carry forward to 2016 (as 'loss')[2]:	
Part of 2nd year excess unused in 2015	
€2,350 – €1,000	1,350

Notes:

1. Although the firm has two accounting dates in the year 2013, there is no change in the normal accounting date (30 September) other than the extra period of account to

deal with Mr Dile's admission. The basis period for assessing the continuing partners remains the 12 months ending 30 September 2013.

2. The part of the second year's excess which exceeds the taxable profits otherwise assessable for the third year is treated as if a loss eligible for carry forward for set off under TCA 1997, s 382 against Mr Dile's future profits of his several trade (see **4.205**).

Change of accounting dates rules

The firm's periods of account are, in effect, also the periods of account of the partner's several trade. It follows that the rules of TCA 1997, s 65 dealing with periods of account of less than or more than 12 months, two periods of account ending in the same tax year, etc (the 'change of accounting date' rules) are applied in taxing the several trade of the partner in a corresponding way to that explained in **4.204** for a sole trader.

Example 4.503.3

Smith and Jones have traded in partnership as greengrocers for a number of years making up their firm's accounts annually to 31 March. After the accounts for the 12 months to 31 March 2015, they then decide to change the firm's accounting date to the end of November by making up accounts for the eight months to 30 November 2015. They had shared profits in a 40 (Smith): 60 (Jones) ratio up to 31 March 2014, but then agreed to share in a 50:50 ratio effective from 1 April 2014.

The firm's Sch D Case I profits (before capital allowances) for the three periods of account to 30 November 2015 are determined to be as follows:

	€
12 months to 31/03/2014	225,000
12 months to 31/03/2015	240,000
8 months to 30/11/2015	222,000

These taxable profits are allocated on the different profit-sharing ratios as follows:

	Smith	*Jones*
	€	€
12 months to 31/03/2014 (40:60)	90,000	135,000
12 months to 31/03/2015 (50:50)	120,000	120,000
8 months to 30/11/2015 (50:50)	111,000	111,000

For the tax year 2015, each partner's several trade is treated as having two periods of account ending in the year. Therefore, applying the rule of TCA 1997, s 65(1)(b) each partner's Sch D Case I assessment for 2015 is made on his several trade's taxable profits for the 12 months ending 30/11/2015 (ie the 12 months ending on the later of the two accounting dates in 2015) (see **4.204**).

The Sch D Case I assessment for 2015 for each partner based on the 12 months ending 30/11/2015 is determined as follows:

	Smith	*Jones*
Period 1/12/2014 to 31/03/2015:	€	€
Smith: €120,000 x 4/12	40,000	
Jones: €120,000 x 4/12		40,000
Period 1/04/2015 to 30/11/2015:		
Smith: his share for full 8-month period	111,000	

Jones: his share for full 8-month period	-	111,000
Profits assessable	151,000	151,000

Due to the change of accounting date in 2015, it is necessary to review the previous year's assessment (ie the 2014 assessment) for each partner's several trade on a comparable basis period to that finally used for 2015. As indicated in **4.204**, it is necessary to compare for each several trade the original assessment based on the 12 months ending 31 March 2014 with the taxable profits of each several trade based on the 12 months ending 30 November 2014 (the period corresponding to that used for 2015).

This review results as follows:

	Smith	*Jones*
Original assessments for 2014:	€	€
Shares for 12 months to 31/03/2014	90,000	135,000
Profits for 12 months to 30/11/2014		
Period 1/12/2013 to 31/03/2014		
Smith: €90,000 x 4/12	30,000	
Jones: €135,000 x 4/12		45,000
Period 1/04/2014 to 30/11/2014		
Smith: €120,000 x 8/12	80,000	
Jones: €120,000 x 8/12	-	80,000
	110,000	125,000

The rule of TCA 1997, s 65(2) now applies to require Smith's Sch D Case I assessment for 2014 in respect of his several trade to be revised to tax profits of €110,000 since his taxable profits of the 'corresponding period' are higher than the profits in the original assessment. However, in the case of Jones, the original assessment is higher than the taxable profits of the corresponding period so that his 2014 assessment remains unchanged at €135,000.

Partnership successions

Where two partnerships (say A and B) are merged to form a new partnership (say C), which contains at least one member from each of the previous partnerships, there are a number of possible analyses (depending on the underlying facts). These include the following:

(a) C continues to carry on A's trade and B's trade as separate entities (presumably a relatively unusual occurrence). Under this analysis, each of A's and B's (now C's) relevant periods continue (in strictness, the two trades will usually be viewed in law as being carried on by two partnerships (say C1 and C2), even though these are composed of the same persons);

(b) C carries on A's and B's trades in merged form, but in such a manner that, nonetheless, both trades continue in existence. This analysis assumes that the decision in *Bell v National Provincial Bank* 5 TC 1 (discussed at **4.208**) on the issue of succession to a trade is equally relevant in this context. It is thought that this assumption is both correct in law and unlikely to be challenged by the Revenue in practice. Under this analysis, each of A's and B's (now C's) relevant periods will again continue, so that the discontinuance provisions will not apply to A and B. C's merged trade should in practice be treated as a single trade for tax purposes as soon as it is practicable to do so;

(c) C continues to carry on A's trade, following its absorption of B's trade on the merger. This could arise where eg A's trade is dominant, or where only B's assets, rather than its trade, is taken over. Under this analysis, B's relevant period will end on the merger (thus triggering off the discontinuance provisions for B) while A's (now C's) relevant period continues. In this case, it would in fact make no difference whether or not any member of the B partnership was included in the C partnership. Naturally, the same logic applies in reverse if it is B's trade which absorbs A's trade; and

(d) C carries on a new trade altogether, following the amalgamation of A's trade and B's trade. In this case both A's and B's relevant periods end on the merger (triggering off the discontinuance provisions for A and B). C's trade will be subject to the commencement provisions. It would again in fact make no difference whether or not any member of the A or B partnerships was included in the C partnership.

Conversely where, a partnership (C) demerges, giving rise, say, to two new partnerships (A and B), possible analyses include the following:

(a) C (normally, in strict law, say C1 and C2) was carrying on two distinct trades, which are now carried on by A and B respectively. In this case, C's relevant periods (now A's and B's relevant periods) continue;

(b) A continues to carry on C's trade, while the remaining activities taken over by B represent a new trade. In this case, A's (now C's) relevant period continues, while B commences a new relevant period following the demerger. In this case, it would in fact make no difference whether or not any member of the B partnership was included in the C partnership. Naturally the same logic applies in reverse, if it is B which continues to carry on C's trade; and

(c) A and B each carry on new trades following the demerger: in this case C's relevant period ends and A and B begin their respective relevant periods following the demerger. Clearly, it is not possible to argue that A and B are both carrying on the trade previously carried on by C. It would in fact make no difference whether or not any member of the A or B partnership was included in the C partnership.

In practice, the Revenue Commissioners may be prepared to adopt a reasonably flexible approach to partnership mergers and demergers. The position where two merging firms have different accounting year ends and/or accounting policies (eg in respect of stock valuation) is likely to require negotiation between the taxpayer and the inspector.

4.504 Appropriations of profit

The terms of a partnership agreement may provide for the payment of salaries to one or more partners before dividing the balance of profits or losses shown by the accounts. The agreement may provide for interest to be paid or credited to partners on their respective capital or current account balances or may require a partner to pay interest if his capital or current account is overdrawn. In determining the firm's Sch D Case I profits or losses for each period of account, both salaries to partners and interest on partners' accounts are treated as appropriations of profits and must be added back with any other disallowable expenses. The allocation of the adjusted profit or loss between the partners must then take any such salaries or interest on capital into account in the manner shown in the next example. If a partner pays in (or is charged) interest on an overdrawn current or capital account, this is not included as a trading receipt, but regarded as a reduction in his profit share.

A partner may rent or hire to the partnership for a separate consideration assets which he owns personally. In this case, the rent or hire charge will be deductible as a trading expense in arriving at the firm's taxable profits if it meets the 'wholly and exclusively' test discussed in **5.310** (*Heastie v Veitch & Co* 18 TC 305): see **5.306** *Appropriations and application of profits*. On the other hand, a partner may contribute a personally owned asset for use in the partnership trade as part of his total capital contribution to the firm. If there is nothing in the partnership arrangements giving that partner a specific rent or other consideration for the use of the asset, then the contributing partner's reward is simply reflected in his share of the firm's profits.

Example 4.504.1

Hatos, Sotrop and Marais are trading as partners. Their profit and loss account for the year ended 28 February 2015 is summarised as follows:

	€	€
Gross profit		395,000
Administration, selling and other expenses	142,200	
Rent to Marais for offices owned by him	13,000	
Depreciation on fixed assets	1,800	
		(157,000)
Interest on capital:		
Hatos	2,400	
Sotrop	1,700	
Marais	600	
		(4,700)
Partner's salary:		
Sotrop		(13,000)
Net profit		220,300
Divided between:		
Hatos (40%)	88,120	
Sotrop (35%)	77,105	
Marais (25%)	55,075	
		220,300

The Sch D Case I profit of the firm for the year ended 28 February 2015 is computed as follows:

	€	€
Net profit per accounts		220,300
Add back:		
Depreciation	1,800	
Other disallowable items (included in administration expenses), say	1,300	
		3,100
		223,400

Appropriations of profits:		
Partner's salary (Sotrop)	13,000	
Interest on capital (all partners)	4,700	
		17,700
Adjusted Sch D Case I profit (firm)		241,100

The €241,100 adjusted Sch D Case I profit of the firm is now allocated between the partners as follows:

(a) the €4,700 interest on capital is allocated in the way actually received by the three partners;

(b) the salary of €13,000 paid to Sotrop is allocated to him; and finally

(c) the balance of €223,400 is divided between the three partners in the 40:35:25 ratio in which they shared the accounting profits in the period of account.

The final result is as follows:

	Total	*Hatos*	*Sotrop*	*Marais*
	€	€	€	€
Interest on capital	4,700	2,400	1,700	600
Partners salary	13,000	-	13,000	-
Balance of adjusted profit	223,400	89,360	78,190	55,850
	241,100	91,760	92,890	56,450

Assuming that all partners are assessable on the continuing business basis in respect of their respective several trades. Sch D Case I assessments are made on each partner for 2015 (same basis period for each: 12 months to 28 February 2015) on taxable profits as follows:

	€
Hatos	91,760
Sotrop	92,890
Marais	56,450

In addition, Marais is assessable under Sch D Case V on his €13,000 rent received less any expenses paid by him deductible under the rules of that Case (see **12.102**, **12.105**). It has been assumed that the rent of €13,000 is fully deductible as an expense in computing the taxable profits of the partnership trade.

4.505 Partnership capital allowances

Each partner is allocated a share of the firm's capital allowances and balancing charges for each year of assessment or part of a year in which he is a partner. The share of the allowances and of any balancing charges allocated to a partner is then granted to or charged on him in taxing the profits of his several trade for each tax year in the same way as capital allowances and balancing charges are given to or made on a sole trader.

Before any capital allowances for a year of assessment can be allocated between the partners, the precedent partner is required to make a claim for the capital allowances applicable to the firm as a whole (referred to as a 'joint allowance') for that year (TCA 1997, s 1010(2)). This claim for a joint allowance should be made in the annual return of the partnership income, etc required by TCA 1997, s 880 and TCA 1997, s 959M. Delivery of return by precedent partner (see **4.508**); this claim is deemed to be a proper claim by each partner for his share of the firm's allowances for the relevant year (TCA

1997, s 1010(9)). The joint allowance is in fact the total of all the firm's capital allowances on the different types of qualifying expenditure incurred for the partnership trade. Similarly, the total of all the firm's balancing charges for a year of assessment is referred to as a 'joint charge' (TCA 1997, s 1010(3)).

The capital allowances and balancing charges of the firm for each year of assessment are calculated under the ordinary rules for each type of allowance or charge, but on the assumption of a continuing partnership trade that commenced at the beginning of the relevant period and continues so long as the relevant period continues, notwithstanding changes in partners that do not result in the termination of the relevant period.

In other words, it is necessary to allocate the firm's capital allowances and charges to years of assessment by reference to events in, or assets in use for, the partnership trade at the end of the same basis period that would apply if the partnership trade were carried on by the same person throughout the entire relevant period. The basis periods used in assessing the profits of the several trades of the different partners have no relevance either in calculating the joint allowances and charges or in allocating them between the partners (TCA 1997, s 1010(2); s 313(2)).

Example 4.505.1

The relevant period of a partnership began on 1 January 1995 when A took B into partnership in his builders' providers business. On 1 October 2005, C is admitted as an additional partner. A retires on 31 March 2015, and on 1 July 2015 D and E become partners. The firm of B, C, D and E continues to carry on the partnership trade.

The firm prepares accounts annually to 30 September. In the year ended 30 September 2015, the firm sells machinery on 31 December 2014 incurring a balancing charge of € 4,700. New machinery is purchased on 30 November 2014 on which a wear and tear allowance of €5,300 is claimed. In addition, the firm claims a wear and tear allowance of €960 on motor vehicles in use at 30 September 2015. There are no other items qualifying for capital allowances.

The firm's capital allowances and balancing charges are allocated to years of assessment on the assumption of a trade commenced on 1 January 1995 and still continuing.[1] If such a trade were carried on by a single person, the year ended 30 September 2015 would form the basis period for assessing his profits for the tax year 2015. Consequently, the firm has the following joint allowance and joint charge for that year:

Joint allowance 2015:	€
New machinery – W & T allowance	5,300
Motor vehicles – W & T allowance	960
	6,260
Joint charge 2015:	
Machine sold 31/12/2014	4,700

In submitting the firm's tax return for the tax year 2015 which he is required to send to the Collector General (due no later than 31 October 2016 or the relevant extended filing deadline if filing online using ROS) (see **4.508**), the precedent partner (Mr B) is required to give details of these joint allowances and joint charges and to show the breakdown of the total joint allowances (€6,260) and total joint charges (€4,700) for the year 2015 between the partners.[2]

Notes:

1. Since B and C are partners before and after A's retirement the original relevant period is not interrupted so that the continuing business treatment applies for the

purposes of the firm's capital allowances. This would not have been the case if C had not become a partner before A's retirement.

2. For the rules to allocate the 2015 joint allowance of €6,260 and 2015 joint charge of €4,700 between A (re period 1/01/2015 to 31/03/2015), B and C (each re full year to 31/12/2015) and D and E (re period 1/07/2015 to 31/12/2015), see **4.506**.

Example 4.505.2

F, who has traded for some years on his own, takes G and H into partnership with him on 1 November 2014. The new firm makes up its first set of accounts from 1 November 2014 to 31 October 2015. The partnership takes over his office machinery which has a tax written down value of €500 at 31 October 2014, but which has a market value at that date of €2,800. A balancing charge of €2,300 is made on F for 2014 and the market value of €2,800 is taken as the opening written down value of the office machinery for capital allowance purposes in the new partnership (TCA 1997, s 300(1) – see below and **6.106**). An additional machine is purchased secondhand on 1 October 2015 for €810.

In this case, the relevant period of the new partnership commences on 1 November 2014 so that the capital allowances of the firm are calculated under the same commencement rules that would apply to a trade set up on that date by a sole trader. The 2014 balancing charge made on F is relevant only to him. The capital allowances of the partnership (joint allowances) for the first two tax years (to be allocated between F, G and H) are calculated as follows:

Machinery taken over from F:	€
Market value 1/11/2014 (deemed cost)	2,800
W & T allowance 2014	
€2,800 x 12.5% x 2/12[1]	(58)
Tax WDV 31/12/2014	2,742
Additions 1/10/2015	810
W & T allowance 2015	
€2,800 x 12.5% x 10/12[2]	292
€810 x 12.5% x 10/12[2]	84
	(376)

Notes:

1. Since the relevant period of the firm only commenced on 1 November 2014, the rules for calculating wear & tear allowances in the opening years of a new trade (see **4.304**) are applicable. Since the basis period is only for two months in the year of commencement (ie from 1 November 2014 to 31 December 2014), only 2/12ths of a full year's wear and tear allowance are given in 2014 (see **4.304**).
2. For the same reason, the wear and tear allowance for 2015 is restricted by reference to the capital allowance basis period of 1 January 2015 to 31 October 2015, ie 10 months (see **4.304**).
3. The firm's joint allowances of €58 and €376 respectively for 2014 and 2015 are allocated between F, G and H for the purposes of the assessments on their respective several trades (see **4.506**).

Plant and machinery belonging to one or more partners, but which is not partnership property, may be used for the firm's trade. If the owner hires or leases the plant to the partnership for a separate consideration, the owner is entitled to the capital allowances personally and is taxable under Sch D Case IV on his leasing income. On the other hand, if the partner owning the plant does not receive any consideration that is treated as a deductible expense in computing the firm's taxable profits, then the capital allowances on the plant are included in the joint allowance and allocated between the partners in exactly the same way as if the plant were partnership property (TCA 1997, s 293(2)).

The rules of TCA 1997, s 403 (which restrict the right of a lessor of machinery or plant to set off excess capital allowances in respect of the leased machinery, etc against his income from all sources (see **6.305**)) will apply in most situations and will be relevant to the decision as to whether the partner owning the plant should lease it to the partnership for a separate consideration or should simply provide it as part of his capital contribution without receiving a separate consideration. If he takes the former course, he is entitled to all the capital allowances on the plant, but if the capital allowances exceed the leasing income received from the partnership, he may be prevented by the rules of TCA 1997, s 403 from setting off the excess capital allowances against his other income. If he takes the second course, he only obtains his share of the firm's capital allowances on the plant, but any part of that share of those allowances which exceeds his share of the firm's Sch D Case I or II profits is eligible for set off against his other income in a claim under TCA 1997, s 381 (see **4.405**) subject to the limited partnership rules (see **4.512**).

Example 4.505.3

R and S have traded in partnership for several years. In the firm's accounting year ended 30 September 2015, R purchases new machinery costing €24,000 in his own name on 1 May 2015 and retains ownership personally, but contributes the plant immediately on its acquisition for use in the partnership trade. There is no hire or leasing agreement. R and S share profits and losses equally.

A wear and tear allowance is claimed on this plant and is given as a joint allowance for the tax year 2015. Assuming R and S continue to be the only partners and continue to share equally in 2015, the joint allowance of €3,000 (€24,000 x 12.5 per cent) is divided equally between them. The fact that R incurs all the expenditure does not entitle him to any greater share of the capital allowances.

The transfer of ownership of machinery or plant from one or more of the partners in a firm to one or more other partners, whether by sale or by gift, does not give rise to either a balancing allowance or a balancing charge, provided that:

(a) the machinery or plant is not the subject of a letting or hire agreement between the partner(s) owning it and the firm; and

(b) the relevant plant is used in the partnership trade both before and after the transfer (TCA 1997, s 293(3)).

In *IRC v Francis West & Ors* 31 TC 402, the taxpayer sold his share in a boat which represented the entire capital of a partnership engaged in a share-fishing venture. The Inland Revenue argued that the sale gave rise to a balancing charge (based on comparing the sale proceeds with the proportion of the tax written down value of the boat attributable to the taxpayer). The court held that no balancing charge arose, since the sale of a share or interest in plant could not be equated to the sale of plant itself. The decision in the *West* case has been overridden by TCA 1997, s 320(3), which ensures that the provisions of TCA 1997, Pt 9 (which cover balancing allowances and charges) apply to a share or interest in plant as they do to plant itself. For these purposes, a share or interest in plant is deemed to be in use for the purposes of a trade for so long as the plant itself is so used. However TCA 1997, s 293(3) will remove any potential charge where the disposal is to a fellow partner and the plant continues to be used in the trade.

The legislation does not expressly deal with the position regarding capital allowances where there is joint ownership of plant, but where there is no underlying partnership relationship. Where plant is acquired jointly by two or more persons in such circumstances then they should be entitled between them to the same allowances as a person acquiring it on his own would be (since the singular 'person' imports the plural 'persons': Interpretation Act 2005, s 18(a)). The sale of an interest in plant in these circumstances seems to fall within TCA 1997, s 320(3) for the purposes of computing a balancing charge or allowance.

While neither the introduction of new partners nor the retirement of a partner in a continuing partnership has any effect on the calculation of the firm's capital allowances or balancing charges, the rules dealing with capital allowances on the succession to a trade discussed in **6.106** have to be considered, if relevant, at the beginning and the end of the firm's relevant period. The rule in TCA 1997, s 313(1), illustrated in **6.106** by reference to a former sole trader taking in a partner, applies to require the transfer of assets subject to capital allowances to be made at market value on the commencement of the new partnership unless there is an actual sale of the assets. While the parties may be able to substitute the tax written down value for the market value under TCA 1997, s 289(6) (see **6.206**), it is unlikely in an arm's length agreement that the parties will make this election as the effect would normally be to give one of them a tax advantage at the expense of the other.

TCA 1997, s 313(1) is also applied at the end of a firm's relevant period to treat assets subject to capital allowances as being disposed of at market value where there is a succession to the partnership trade and where the assets are not sold but continue to be used in the trade by the successors (TCA 1997, s 1010(4)). Consequently, the old firm's capital allowances and/or balancing charges for the year of assessment in which the succession takes place must include the appropriate balancing allowances and balancing charges on such assets based on a deemed sale at market value. Again, in the case of plant and machinery, the partners ceasing the trade and the persons succeeding to it may have the option under TCA 1997, s 289(6) to substitute tax written down values for market values.

4.506 Allocation of firm's capital allowances and charges

The joint allowance and the joint charge (if any), as determined for a year of assessment for the firm as a whole, are allocated between the persons who are partners in the firm for the whole or part of that year of assessment. The allocation is made in the ratios in which those partners share in the firm's profits during the year of assessment, and not in relation to their shares in the basis period for that year. The ratios used are those in which the residue of profits are shared after any salary, interest on capital or other similar entitlement of any partner is deducted (TCA 1997, s 1010(7)).

If a new partner is admitted or an existing partner retires at a date during a particular year of assessment, or if the profit sharing ratios change in the middle of a tax year, the joint allowance and joint charge for that year are each apportioned on a time basis between the parts of the year falling respectively before and after the date of the change. The part of the joint allowance (or joint charge) apportioned to the part of the year before the change in partners and/or the change in the profit-sharing ratio is then allocated between the partners in the ratios in which they share profits and losses in the pre-change period. Similarly, the amount of the joint allowance (or joint charge) apportioned to the part of the year after the change is allocated in the profit-sharing ratio in which the partners share profits and losses after the change.

Example 4.506.1

John and Roger have traded as partners for some years sharing profits in the ratio 60:40, making up accounts each year to 30 June. On 1 April 2014 Maria is admitted as a partner entitled to a salary of €30,000 per annum and to a 15 per cent share in the residue of profits after charging that salary; it is agreed that John's and Roger's shares in the residue of profits after the salary are to be 45 per cent and 40 per cent from the date of Maria's admission.

Maria's admission does not affect the firm's relevant period. Consequently, the capital allowances and balancing charges of the firm continue to be calculated by reference to basis periods ending on 30 June. The joint allowances (net of joint balancing charges) for the years 2013 to 2015 are as follows:

	€
2013 (basis Y/E 30/06/2013)	60,000
2014 (basis Y/E 30//06/2014)	80,000
2015 (basis Y/E 30/06/2015)	36,000

The capital allowances are allocated as follows:

	Total	*John*	*Roger*	*Maria*
2013:	€	€	€	€
Allocated in ratio 60:40	60,000	36,000	24,000	-
2014 (€80,000):				
Proportion in 1/01/2014 to 31/03/2014				
€80,000 x 3/12[1]	20,000			
Allocated in ratio 60:40		12,000	8,000	-
proportion in period 01/04/2014 to 31/12/2014				
€80,000 x 9/12[2]	60,000			
Allocated in ratio 45:40:15[3]	-	27,000	24,000	9,000
	80,000	39,000	32,000	9,000
2015:				
Allocated in ratio 45:40:15[4]	36,000	16,200	14,400	5,400

Notes:

1. This is the proportion of the 2014 allowances attributed to that part of the year of assessment in which John and Roger only were partners. This part of the year's allowances is allocated in their profit sharing ratio for that part of the tax year.
2. This is the proportion of the 2014 allowances for the part of the year when Maria was a partner (ie from 1 April 2014 onwards).
3. It is allocated in the ratios in which John, Roger and Maria shared profits in the period commencing 1 April 2014.
4. It is assumed that there is no further change in the profit sharing ratio between John, Roger and Maria prior to 1 January 2015.

Example 4.506.2

Take the facts of the previous example, but assume that the profit sharing ratio for the accounting year ended 30 June 2015 is changed to 25:50:25. Apart from its effect on the allocation of the firm's joint allowance and/or joint charge for the tax year 2015, this change means that the 2015 joint allowance of €36,000 previously divided as to €16,200 (John), €14,400 (Roger) and €5,400 (Maria) must be reallocated as follows:

	Total	*John*	*Roger*	*Maria*
2015:	€	€	€	€
Period 01/01/2015 to 30/06/2015				
€36,000 x 6/12	18,000			
Allocated 45:40:15[1]		8,100	7,200	2,700
Period 01/07/2015 to 31/12/2015				
€36,000 x 6/12	18,000			
Allocated 25:50:25[2]	-	4,500	9,000	4,500
	36,000	12,600	16,200	7,200

Notes:

1. The proportion of the 2015 capital allowances (basis period year to 30/06/2015) attributable to the part of the tax year up to 30/06/2015 is allocated in the profit sharing ratios used in the accounts to that date.
2. The part of the 2015 capital allowances attributable to the period subsequent to 30/06/2015 is allocated in the profit sharing ratios applying from 01/07/2015 onwards, (ie that in the firm's accounting year to 30 June 2016).

Set off of partners' capital allowances

Each partner's share of the firm's joint allowance for a year of assessment is set off against his share of the firm's taxable profits which have been allocated to his several trade for that year of assessment (see **4.503**). His share of the firm's joint charge is treated as if it were an additional trading receipt of his several trade.

In practice, it is usual to set off a partner's share of the joint charge for a year of assessment first against his share of the joint allowance for that year and then to allow him relief in any of the normal ways for the excess of the share of his joint allowance over the share of his joint charge. If his share of the joint charge for a year exceeds the share of the joint allowance, the excess, ie the net joint charge, is added to the partner's share of the firm's taxable profits for the year or, if relevant, is used to reduce his share of any tax loss of the firm.

If a partner's share of a net joint allowance for a year of assessment exceeds the taxable profits of his several trade for that year, he may elect under TCA 1997, s 392 to use the net joint allowance in a claim under TCA 1997, s 381 to reduce his total income (subject to the application of the limited partnership rules (see **4.512**)). If and to the extent that a partner's net joint allowance either cannot be fully set off against his share of taxable profits for a year of assessment or is not used in an election under TCA 1997, s 392, it is available for carry forward to any subsequent year of assessment in which the partnership trade is continued. However, the unused allowance is carried forward not as one attributable to the several trade of the partner concerned, but as a joint allowance to be reallocated between all partners in the next year of assessment.

This is because of the rule of TCA 1997, s 1010(8) which provides that the aggregate of all partnership capital allowances brought forward from a previous year is deemed to be a joint allowance for the next year of assessment. This deemed joint allowance is then required to be allocated under the rule of TCA 1997, s 1010(7) among all the partners in accordance with the profit sharing ratios applicable for that next year (and not in the ratios applying in the year in which the unused allowances first arose). In effect, it is added to the actual joint allowance for the next year, except that when allocated in that year the deemed joint allowance may only be used to offset the partners' Sch D Case I or Case II profits (ie no part of it may be used in any claim under TCA 1997, s 381).

Example 4.506.3

Seamus, Maeve and Tadhg trade as partners making up accounts each year to 31 December. For the year to 31 December 2014 they share profits and losses in the ratio 50:30:20. For the year ending 31 December 2015, they share in the ratio 40:35:25. The taxable profits and capital allowances for the two years are as follows:

	Year ending 31/12/2014	*Year ending 31/12/2015*
	€	€
Taxable profits		
Y/E 31/12/2014	12,000	
Y/E 31/12/2015		36,000
Capital allowances:		
2014 (based on 2014 accounts)	22,000	
2015 (based on 2015 accounts)		18,000

The firm's taxable profits for the year ending 31 December 2014 and the 2014 capital allowances are dealt with as follows:

	Seamus	*Maeve*	*Tadhg*
	€	€	€
Taxable profits assessable 2014:			
Allocated 50:30:20	6,000	3,600	2,400
Deduct:			
Capital allowances 2014			
Allocated 50:30:20	(11,000)	(6,600)	(4,400)
Net Sch D Case I income	Nil	Nil	Nil
Unused capital allowances:			
Seamus €11,000 – €6,000	5,000		
Maeve €6,600 – €3,600		3,000	
Tadhg €4,400 – €2,400	-	-	2,000

It is assumed that these excess capital allowances are all carried forward (ie not used by any partner to increase any loss of his several trade in a claim under TCA 1997, s 381).

TCA 1997, s 1010(8) requires the aggregate of the unused 2014 capital allowances carried forward to 2015 (ie a total of €10,000) to be treated as a joint allowance for 2015 and apportioned between all the partners in accordance with the allocation rule of TCA 1997, s 1010(7) – ie apportioned in the 2015 profit-sharing ratios (and not in the 2014 ratios).

This results in the €10,000 capital allowances carried forward being allocated for relief in 2014 in accordance with the rule of TCA 1997, s 1010(7) as follows:

	Seamus	*Maeve*	*Tadhg*
	€	€	€
Seamus:			
€10,000 x 40/100	4,000		
Maeve:			
€10,000 x 35/100		3,500	
Tadhg:			
€10,000 x 25/100	-	-	2,500

The final position for each partner's several trade for 2015 is now determined as follows:

	Seamus	*Maeve*	*Tadhg*
	€	€	€
Taxable profits assessable 2015:			
Allocated 40:35:25	14,400	12,600	9,000
Deduct:			
Capital allowances 2015 (€18,000):			
Allocated 40:35:25	(7,200)	(6,300)	(4,500)
Deemed joint allowance for 2015			
Allocated as above	(4,000)	(3,500)	(2,500)
Net Sch D Case I income	3,200	2,800	2,000

Comment

The allocation of the €22,000 capital allowances actually arising for the firm in 2014 as between the partners may be summarised as follows:

	Seamus	*Maeve*	*Tadhg*
	€	€	€
First allocation in 2014:			
Amount deductible from taxable			
Profits if sufficient profits	11,000	6,600	4,400
Allowances as finally used:			
Against taxable profits 2014	6,000	3,600	2,400
Used as deemed joint allowance for 2015	4,000	3,500	2,500
	10,000	7,100	4,900

It may be seen that the partner reducing his share of profits in 2015, Seamus, has 'lost' capital allowances of €1,000, while Maeve and Tadhg have 'gained' €500 each, as compared with the position if there has been sufficient taxable profits in 2014 to absorb all the capital allowances in that year.

Relief for hardship

In certain circumstances, the allocation of the firm's joint allowance or joint charge in accordance with the rule of TCA 1997, s 1010(7) may give rise to an inequity as regards one or more of the partners. This may sometimes occur where this rule is applied to allocated unused capital allowances of partners brought forward from an earlier year and deemed by TCA 1997, s 1010(8) to be a joint allowance for the later year. For instance, **Example 4.506.3** has shown that, where there is a change in the profit sharing ratios, a partner reducing his share of profits in the year to which unused capital allowances are carried forward may end up receiving a lower amount of capital allowances in the later year where there is a deemed joint allowance under TCA 1997, s 1010(8) than he would have received if his share of taxable profits in the earlier year had been high enough to absorb fully his share of the joint allowance for that year.

TCA 1997, s 1010(7)(c) may allow relief to be obtained for such an inequity. It provides that, if all the partners give notice in writing to the Revenue Commissioners claiming that hardship is caused to one or more partners as the result of the method of allocating the firm's joint allowance or joint charge, the Commissioners may give such relief as they consider just if satisfied that hardship has been caused. This relief may take the form of such new apportionment of the joint allowance or joint charge as the Commissioners think fit. In this case, such additional assessments or repayments of tax are to be made as is necessary to reflect the new apportionment.

The notice under TCA 1997, s 1010(7)(c) must, if it is to be valid, be given within 24 months after the end of the tax year in respect of which the allocation claimed to cause hardship is made. All the partners affected by the allocation of the joint allowance or joint charge for that year must sign the notice. If any partner affected has died, his personal representatives must sign the notice in his place. It is to be noted that the Revenue Commissioners are required, before granting any relief, to be satisfied that hardship is actually caused to at least one partner by the allocation in question. 'Hardship' appears to involve something more than a mere inequity and it may be difficult to determine in what cases hardship in fact occurs.

4.507 Partnership losses

The tax loss of a partnership trade is calculated in the same way and is allocated between the partners in the same manner as are the firm's taxable profits. To the extent that a partner shares in the tax loss of the partnership for any period of account, that share is treated as a trading loss of his several trade sustained in the period in question and he has the same alternative forms of loss relief claims open to him as does a sole trader (see **4.4**). The loss of a partner's several trade in relation to a given year of assessment may, therefore, be carried forward and set off under TCA 1997, s 382 against the taxable profits of his several trade assessable for a subsequent year of assessment so long as he continues to be a partner. Alternatively, he may claim a current year set off under TCA 1997, s 381 for a loss against his income from all sources for the same year of assessment (subject to the limited partnership rules (see **4.512**) and also the new anti-avoidance rules brought in by Finance Act 2014, TCA 1997, ss 381B and 381C (see **Division 4.4**). Each partner is entitled to make his own decision as to the form of the loss relief claim of his several trade irrespective of the decision of any other partner.

TCA 1997, s 383(2) also makes provisions for a partner to claim his share of any Sch D Case IV losses incurred by the partnership.

Example 4.507.1

Mr T Tiger and Mr L Lion, who trade in partnership, sharing profits and losses in the ratio 50:50 after charging interest on capital and partners' salaries, have the following Sch D Case I computation for their financial year ending 31 December 2015:

		€	€
Net loss per accounts			(80,000)
Add back:			
Partners' salaries			
	Tiger	25,000	
	Lion	35,000	
			60,000
Interest on capital			
	Tiger	2,200	
	Lion	600	
			2,800
Other items			700
Adjusted loss			(16,500)

The adjusted loss is allocated between Messrs Tiger and Lion as follows:

	Total	*Tiger*	*Lion*
	€	€	€
Partners' salaries[1]	60,000	25,000	35,000
Interest on capital[1]	2,800	2,200	600
Balance of loss			
Allocated 50:50	(79,300)	(39,650)	(39,650)
	(16,500)	(12,450)	(4,050)

Mr T Tiger has, therefore, a Sch D Case I loss of €12,450 for his several trade for the year ending 31 December 2015. His wife, with whom he is assessed jointly under TCA 1997, s 1017, has substantial income in her own right and they decide to set off this loss against their joint total incomes assessable for 2015 by making a claim under TCA 1997, s 381 (see **4.404–4.406**).

Mr L Lion has a Sch D Case I loss of €4,050 for his several trade for the year ended 31 December 2015. Since his taxable income for 2015 is negligible, he decides not to make any current year set off against total income under TCA 1997, s 381 for the year. Instead, he carries forward the loss for set off against an expected future profit in his several trade in the next year.

To the extent that Mr Tiger and Mr Lion share in the firm's capital allowances for 2015 (basis period year ended 31 December 2015), they may each decide separately whether to include their respective shares in a claim under TCA 1997, s 381 (see **4.405**) or carry the unused allowances forward to a later year (see **4.403**).

Note:

1. Although each partner has a salary and interest on capital due to him, there is no Sch D Case I assessment on either partner for 2015 since these items are no more than elements in their respective shares of the firm's adjusted loss.

In certain cases, the result of charging interest on partners' capital and/or partners' salaries in arriving at the final profit or loss (to be divided in the profit/loss sharing ratios), may be to leave one partner with an accounting profit (after his interest on capital and/or salary is credited to him) while another partner may have an accounting loss (perhaps because he has no interest or salary or significantly smaller interest or salary). Before the tax treatment of such a case is discussed, it may be useful to illustrate the effect of the accounting treatment.

Example 4.507.2

Fox, Bear and Wolf trade in partnership and their partnership deed provides as follows:

(a) Wolf, who has just been admitted into the partnership, is to be paid a salary of €20,000 (to be charged in arriving at the final profit or loss to be divided in the ratios in (c) below);

(b) there is to be no interest on capital; and

(c) the partnership profit or loss (after charging Wolf's salary) is to be divided:
50% – Fox,
40% – Bear, and
10% – Wolf.

The accounts for the firm's 12-month period of account ending 30 September 2015 show a net loss of €4,000 before charging Wolf's salary. The final accounting loss to be divided between the partners is then determined as follows:

	€
Loss before salary	4,000
Add: partner's salary (Wolf)	20,000
Final accounting loss	24,000

The accounting loss (the actual loss) is shared between the partners in the 50:40:10 ratio provided in the deed. The result is that the actual amounts to be credited or debited to the partners' capital accounts are arrived at as follows:

	Fox	*Bear*	*Wolf*
	€	€	€
Partner's salary (Wolf)			20,000
Accounting loss			
Fox €24,000 x 50%	(12,000)		
Bear €24,000 x 40%		(9,600)	
Wolf €24,000 x 10%	-	-	(2,400)
Final share (losses)	(12,000)	(9,600)	17,600

In other words, Wolf is left with an actual profit (including his salary) of €17,600 while Fox sustains an actual loss of €12,000 and Bear sustains an actual loss of €9,600 – ie between them there is an actual net loss of €4,000.

The tax treatment of the partners in the type of case illustrated in **Example 4.507.2** is governed by paragraph (a) of TCA 1997, s 1008(2). This paragraph deals with profits and losses in one long sentence. Its meaning can more easily be seen by outlining its main effects separately for profits and losses.

In its application to profits, paragraph (a) of TCA 1997, s 1008(2) provides that, for any year or period within the partnership's relevant period, the amount of the profits or gains (the taxable profit) arising to any partner from his several trade shall be his due proportion of the full amount of the profits or gains (the adjusted Sch D Case I or Case II profit, ie the taxable profit) of the partnership trade. For this purpose, a partner's due proportion of the taxable profit of the partnership is the amount which would fall to his share on an apportionment of the firm's taxable profit made in accordance with the terms of the partnership agreement as to the sharing of profits and losses.

In its application to losses, paragraph (a) provides that, for any year or period within the relevant period, the amount of the loss (the tax loss) sustained by any partner to be attributed to his several trade shall be his due proportion of the full amount of the loss (the tax loss) incurred in the partnership trade. For this purpose, a partner's due proportion of the tax loss of the partnership is the amount which would fall to his share on an apportionment of the firm's tax loss made in accordance with the terms of the partnership agreement as to the sharing of profits and losses.

It is to be noted that these rules provide only for the apportionment of a partnership profit where there is an adjusted Sch D Case I or Case II profit (after adding back any partners' salaries or interest on capital) or, as a straight alternative, only for the apportionment of a partnership loss where there is an adjusted loss (after any add back for salaries or interest). They do not allow for a result which leaves any partner with a tax loss in his several trade where the partnership has an adjusted profit or which gives any partner a taxable profit if the partnership has an adjusted loss. The effect of these rules is considered in the next two examples.

Example 4.507.3

Take the facts of **Example 4.507.2** which shows the actual sharing of the partnership accounting loss resulting in one partner (Wolf) having an accounting profit (including his partnership salary) and which leaves the other two partners with accounting losses.

For simplicity, it is assumed that there are no adjustments to the accounting loss other than the disallowance of the partner's salary. The Sch D Case I computation is therefore:

	€
Final loss per accounts	24,000
Deduct (disallow);	
Salary to Wolf	20,000
Adjusted Sch D Case I loss	4,000

The required allocation of this tax loss of €4,000 between the partners is made in the following manner:

	Total	*Fox*	*Bear*	*Wolf*
	€	€	€	€
Partner's salary	20,000			20,000
Balance of loss				
Allocated 50:40:10	(24,000)	(12,000)	(9,600)	(2,400)
Provisional allocation of				
Firm's tax loss	(4,000)	(12,000)	(9,600)	17,600

Since there is an overall tax loss, the view generally applied for tax purposes is that no partner can have a taxable profit and also that the aggregate of tax losses allocated to the partners' several trades cannot exceed the adjusted Sch D Case I loss of €4,000. TCA 1997, s 1008(2)(a) requires this tax loss of €4,000 to be allocated between the several trades of the partners in accordance with the terms of the partnership agreement regarding the sharing of profits and losses.

In fact, there is a major difficulty in the circumstances of this example (and of other cases like it) where the partnership agreement does not make any provision for the sharing of a tax loss of €4,000, but provides in effect for the sharing of the loss of €24,000 resulting from the charging of Wolf's salary (with the salary being credited separately to Wolf). How is this difficulty to be dealt with?

The solution generally put forward is that, where there is an overall tax loss but where a partner has a taxable profit provisionally allocated to him as the result of crediting his partner's salary (or interest on capital) to him, that partner's provisional taxable profit must be used to reduce the tax losses of the other partners proportionally to their profit sharing ratios between themselves. The former partner's final result is a nil taxable profit and a nil tax loss.

Applying this solution to the facts in this example results as follows:

(1) Wolf has to have a nil taxable profit and a nil tax loss; and

(2) the taxable profit provisionally attributed to Wolf must be reallocated between Fox and Bear in the following way:

	Fox	*Bear*	*Wolf*
	€	€	€
Tax loss as provisionally allocated	(12,000)	(9,600)	17,600
Reallocate Wolf's profit:			
Fox:			
€17,600 x 12,000/21,600	9,778		
Bear:			
€17,600 x 9,600/21,600		7,822	
Wolf:			
Profit reallocated	-	-	(17,600)
Tax losses of several trades	(2,222)	(1,778)	(Nil)

Comment:

The application of the above solution is far from satisfactory, although it does appear to follow the wording of TCA 1997, s 1008(2)(a) which only permits the final adjusted tax loss (the full amount of that loss) to be apportioned between the partners. It may be seen from the following summary that the tax result (see above) is very different from that actually occurring when the firm's actual loss is shared between the partners in accordance with the terms of the deed (see **Example 4.507.2**):

	Actual result		*Tax result*	
	Profit	*Loss*	*Profit*	*Loss*
	€	€	€	€
Fox	Nil	(12,000)	Nil	(2,222)
Bear: (loss)	Nil	(9,600)	Nil	(1,778)
Wolf: profit/(loss)	17,600	Nil	Nil	Nil

Can this tax result really be the correct final answer? If so, it appears that the tax law needs to be revised to enable the tax result to get much closer to the actual sharing between the partners in this type of case!

Example 4.507.4

Continue with the case of Fox, Bear and Wolf and move to the next accounting year. The partnership's accounts for the year ending 30 September 2016 show a net profit of €15,000 before charging Wolf's salary (still €20,000). There is therefore a final accounting loss to be divided between the partners determined as follows:

	€
Profit before salary	15,000
Less: partner's salary (Wolf)	20,000
Final accounting loss	(5,000)

The accounting loss (the actual loss) is shared between the partners in the 50:40:10 ratio provided in the deed. The result is that the actual amounts to be credited or debited to the partners' capital accounts are arrived at as follows:

	Fox	*Bear*	*Wolf*
	€	€	€
Partner's salary (Wolf)			20,000
Accounting loss			
Fox €5,000 x 50%	(2,500)		
Bear €5,000 x 40%		(2,000)	
Wolf €5,000 x 10%			(500)
Final share (losses to be debited)	(2,500)	(2,000)	
Final share (profit to be credited)			19,500

The firm's Sch D Case I tax computation is now made as follows:

	€
Final loss per accounts	(5,000)
Deduct (disallow);	
Salary to Wolf	20,000
Adjusted Sch D Case I profit	15,000

This taxable profit of €15,000 is provisionally allocated between the partners as follows:

	Total	*Fox*	*Bear*	*Wolf*
	€	€	€	€
Partner's salary	20,000			20,000
Balance: (loss)				
Allocated 50: 40: 10	(5,000)	(2,500)	(2,000)	(500)
Provisional allocation	15,000	(2,500)	(2,000)	19,500

Since there is an overall partnership taxable profit, the application of TCA 1997, s 1008(2)(a) appears to prevent any partner having a tax loss and this requires the tax losses provisionally allocated to Fox and Bear to be deducted from Wolf's provisional taxable profit with the following results:

(a) Fox and Bear are left with nil losses and nil taxable profits; and

(b) Wolf's final taxable profit is €15,000 (€19,500 less the €4,500 provisional tax losses of Fox and Bear).

Partner's terminal loss

A person whose several trade is treated as ceasing on his retirement as a partner in a partnership is entitled to make a terminal loss claim in respect of his share of the firm's loss in the 12-month period immediately prior to the date of his cessation, including his share of the firm's capital allowances for the tax year in which he ceases to be a partner and for the appropriate proportion of his share of the capital allowances for the previous tax year. The amount of the terminal loss of his several trade is calculated using the principles outlined in **4.410**. The amount of this terminal loss may be carried back for relief against the profits of his several trade as assessable on him for the three tax years prior to that in which he ceased to be a partner.

A terminal loss claim may also be made by each partner of a firm the relevant period of which terminates either on the cessation of the entire trade or on a complete change in the partners. However, if the same trade continues to be carried on by one of the partners on his own, the person continuing to be engaged in the trade is not entitled to claim relief under TCA 1997, s 385 for any terminal loss at the end of the firm's relevant period (TCA 1997, s 388). Although his several trade as a partner is deemed to be permanently discontinued, he is not treated as having a cessation for the purposes of terminal loss relief (but remains entitled to the other forms of loss relief for any loss in his several trade).

Should the person continuing the trade on his own in such a case subsequently cease to carry on the trade himself/herself, he is entitled to claim terminal loss relief for any terminal loss of the trade as a sole trader in the 12 months prior to this 'final' cessation date. Normally, the relief is only available for the terminal loss relative to the 'new' trade as a sole trader and the set off of the loss carried back is confined to previous assessable profits of his sole trade (within the three-year period).

However, if he has been continuously engaged in carrying on the same trade between the first cessation (that of the partnership) and his own final cessation and if the first cessation occurred within the 12 months before his final cessation, then the following consequences ensue:

(a) the first cessation is ignored (so that his terminal loss may, as well as his sole trader's loss and capital allowances, include his share of any tax loss of the former partnership in the 12 months prior to the date of his final cessation and also his share of the partnership's capital allowances attributable to the same 12-month period); and

(b) the net Sch D Case I assessable profits of the three prior tax years against which his terminal loss may be set off include any assessable profits of his several trade prior to the first cessation (if assessable for any of the three tax years prior to that in which the final cessation occurs) (TCA 1997, s 388).

Example 4.507.5

Reid, Tomelty and Gazzerini have traded as sports goods retailers in partnership for a number of years. Reid and Tomelty retire on 30 April 2014, but Gazzerini continues the business as a sole trader until 28 February 2015 when he dies. The firm has taxable profits for all accounting years up to the year ended 30 April 2013, but incurred a tax loss of €18,200 for the year ended 30 April 2014. Gazzerini incurred a tax loss of €5,300 in the period from 1 May 2014 to 28 February 2015. Capital allowances are ignored in this example.

Assume the following Sch D Case I taxable profits are assessable in respect of each individual's several trade for the tax years 2011 to 2015:

	Reid	*Tomelty*	*Gazzerini*
2011:	€	€	€
Taxable profits			
(12 months to 30/04/2011)[1]	2,000	2,000	3,000
2012:			
Taxable profits			
(12 months to 30/04/2012)[2]	1,100	1,100	1,650
2013:			
Taxable profits			
(12 months to 30/04/2013)[2]	4,000	4,000	6,000
Partnership tax loss:			
12 months to 30/04/2014	(5,200)	(5,200)	(7,800)
Sole trade (Gazzerini) – tax loss:			
Period 01/05/2014 to 28/02/2015			(5,300)

Following the termination of the firm's relevant period on 30 April 2014, Reid and Tomelty are each entitled to a terminal loss claim for the tax loss incurred in the last 12 months of their respective several trades which ceased on that date. However, although Gazzerini's several trade (as a partner) is also deemed to cease on 30 April 2014, he is not entitled to any terminal loss relief in respect of that cessation since he continued to carry on the same trade (albeit as a sole trader).

Reid and Tomelty each claim terminal loss relief to carry back their losses of €5,200 incurred in the last 12 months of their respective several trades for set off against their Sch D Case I taxable profits for the three tax years prior to 2014 and obtain full relief as follows (same for each):

	€
Against 2013 (first)	4,000
Against 2012 (second)	1,100
Against 2011 (third)	100
	5,200

There is deemed to be a permanent discontinuance of his trade on Gazzerini's death on 28 February 2015. Through his executors, he is entitled to claim terminal loss relief for the tax losses incurred by him in the trade in the 12 months ending on the date. Since the previous discontinuance of his trade (that of his several trade on 30 April 2014) occurred less than 12 months before 28 February 2015, that discontinuance is ignored so that he can include his share of the partnership loss within the 12 months prior to 28 February 2015.

Gazzerini's terminal loss eligible for relief is therefore computed:

	€
Period 01/03/2014 to 30/04/2014:	
€7,800 (his share 12 months to 30/04/2014) x 2/12[1]	(1,300)
Period 01/05/2014–28/02/2015:	
Full amount of tax loss for 10 months	(5,300)
His terminal loss	(6,600)

This terminal loss may be carried back for set off against the taxable profits for the three tax years prior to 2015 (the tax year of his 'final' cessation).[2] He claims this terminal loss relief and it is given in full as follows:

	€
Against 2014 (first):	
Period 01/01/2014 to 30/04/2014 as partner	
Taxable profits of several trade	Nil
Period 01/05/2014 to 31/12/2014	
Taxable profits as sole trader	Nil
Against 2013 (second)	
Taxable profits of several trade	6,000
Against 2012 (third)	600
Taxable profits of several trade	6,600

Notes:

1. In Gazzerini's case, only two months of the 12-month period of account ending 30 April 2014 comes into his last 12 months of trading so that only the proportion of the tax loss of that period attributable to those two months is eligible for inclusion in his terminal loss (see **4.410**).
2. Also, in his case, the fact that his cessation occurs in 2015 (as compared with 2014 for Reid and Tomelty), means that his three prior years run from 2014 to 2012 (as compared with 2013 to 2011 for Reid and Tomelty).

4.508 Partnership returns

The 'precedent partner' in a partnership is the person responsible each year for the partnership return of income (and chargeable gains, if any). The precedent partner is normally the senior acting partner if there is such a person. If not, he is the first named partner in the partnership agreement or, if there is no such agreement, the person listed first on the firm's notepaper would normally be regarded as the precedent partner. The precedent partner must, however, be a person resident in the State. If no partner is so resident, then the inspector may serve the appropriate notice on any resident agent, manager or factor of the firm requiring him to make the partnership return (TCA 1997, s 1034).

TCA 1997, s 880 provides that the precedent partner of every partnership, when required to do so by a notice from the inspector in relation to a stated year of assessment (eg 2015) (the 'year of the return'), must give a return in the prescribed form of:

(a) all the sources of income of the partnership for the year of the return;
(b) the amount of income from each source for the year of the return; and
(c) such further particulars required for income tax purposes for the year of the return as may be indicated by the notice or in the prescribed form (eg partnership charges on income).

Further, the partnership return of income is required to include details of any chargeable capital gains realised in the year of the return by the partnership (as distinct from any personal chargeable gains of individual partners) as well as details of chargeable assets acquired by the partnership in that year (TCA 1997, s 913(7)).

With effect from 2013 onwards, TCA 1997, s 959M deems the precedent partner of any partnership to be a chargeable person for purposes of the self-assessment legislation. He is therefore required to deliver to the Collector General the prescribed partnership return of income form for each year of assessment before the latest date for the return (see below), whether or not the firm is sent a notice or a return form. With effect from 1 June 2011 returns for partnerships must be filed electronically (see **2.105**). The amount of income from each source to be included in the partnership return for any tax year is to be the income assessable for that year as computed in accordance with the computational rules provided in the Income Tax Acts for the type of income in question. In the case of a partnership trade (or profession), the income to be included in the return for any year is the Sch D Case I (or Case II) adjusted profits (or loss) for the firm's period of account ending in the year in question. However, if the firm has two or more periods of account ending in any tax year, the partnership return must state the Sch D Case I (or Case II) adjusted profits (or loss) for each period of account so ending (TCA 1997, s 880(3)). For partnership income from other sources, the amount of income to be returned is that computed under the relevant Sch or Case for the year ending 31 December.

The completion of the partnership tax return does not excuse the individual partners from including in their respective returns of income their shares of the partnership's income from its various sources and their shares of the firm's capital allowances, balancing charges, charges on income and gains from the sale of partnership assets. Each partner must make his own tax return in the normal way which must include the appropriate details of his share of the firm's taxable profits, capital allowances/charges, charges on income and chargeable capital gains (see **2.105**).

Latest date for partnership return

The partnership return for any tax year must be delivered to the Collector General no later than the 31st day of October in the next tax year (the latest return date). For example, the firm's return for the year 2015 (income, etc for the year to 31 December 2015) must be submitted no later than 31 October 2016. The Revenue may allow for an extension to the return filing date to the ROS online return date in a particular year. If the precedent partner fails to make the partnership's return of income for any tax year by the latest return date for that year, he is liable to the late return surcharge (see **2.110**) on any partnership income (or capital gains) in respect of which he is chargeable in his capacity as precedent partner.

A late submission of the partnership's return of income does not render individual partners (or the precedent partner) liable to the late return surcharge in respect of their own shares of partnership income. However, each partner (including the precedent partner) must make his personal return of income before the specified latest return date if he is to avoid the surcharge on his personal tax liability based on his own income including his share of the firm's income.

Determination of profits

TCA 1997, s 1012 provides that the determination of the profits of the partnership trade is to be made by the inspector. TCA 1997, s 1010(6)(a) makes similar provision for joint allowances and joint charges; TCA 1997, s 1010(6)(b) further permits the Inspector to revise a determination of joint allowances or joint charges where he becomes aware of facts or events which in his opinion render that determination incorrect.

TCA 1997, s 1012(1) provides that notice of a determination should be delivered in writing to the precedent partner and that the provisions relating to appeals, etc shall apply to the determination as if it were an assessment; this was amended by F(TA)A 2015, s 39, which was subject to Ministerial Order (SI 110/2016 appointed 21 March

2016 as the day on which the Finance (Tax Appeals) Act 2015, came into operation), to take account of the new appeal provisions brought about therein. TCA 1997, s 1012(1) may seem to indicate that it is the partnership as such which must appeal. However, in *Re Sutherland & Partners Appeal* [1994] STC 387, the Court of Appeal held that any person who was the subject of a joint assessment was entitled to appeal against that assessment, either alone or jointly with others. In the instant case, the court accordingly permitted a partner to bring an appeal against the wishes of the rest of his partners. While the partners in the *Sutherland* case were jointly liable in respect of the tax payable on partnership profits, the principle seems to be equally applicable to TCA 1997, s 1012(1).

Where a determination of the partnership profits or of the partnership joint capital allowances/balancing charges has become final and conclusive, the correctness of such a determination may not be challenged by a partner in the course of any appeal relating to an assessment in respect of his several trade or of a claim under TCA 1997, s 381 (TCA 1997, s 1012 (2)). Where the subject of the appeal concerns an apportionment of the partnership profits to a partner's several trade or an apportionment of partnership capital allowances/balancing charges to a partner, any other partners whose tax liability might be affected by the outcome of the appeal have a right to attend the appeal or make written representations to the Appeal commissioners (TCA 1997, s 1012(3)).

4.509 Unexhausted profits

In *Franklin v IRC* 15 TC 444, following the death of a partner, there was disagreement for several years as to whether his son should be admitted as a partner; what would have been the son's share of profit was accumulated in a reserve and not apportioned between the remaining partners. When it was eventually decided that the son should not be admitted, it was held that in each of the intervening years the other partners had no entitlement to the amounts accumulated, and that those amounts could not be assessed on the individual partners.

If, for any reason, the allocation between the partners of the profits of the trade for any period of account does not exhaust or fully use up the profits for a period ending *prior to 1 January 2007,* then the inspector of taxes was historically required to make an assessment under Sch D Case IV on the precedent partner in respect of the unexhausted profits. This assessment charged the unexhausted profits to income tax at the standard rate only, since the precedent partner was not charged in his personal capacity (see **1.305**). If and when the unexhausted profits were subsequently allocated to one or more partners, their shares were paid out net of income tax (TCA 1997, s 1008(4)). An individual partner receiving such a subsequent allocation was required to include the grossed up amount in his total income in the year of receipt, but was entitled to deduct the income tax paid in arriving at his final income tax liability for the year.

The Revenue Commissioners had issued a precedent expressing the view that TCA 1997, s 1008(4) did not apply where the partners merely failed to allocate the full amount of profits between them but remained collectively entitled to all of the profits. However, the subsection referred to the 'shares to which the partners are entitled' failing to exhaust the partnership profits; further, there did not seem to be any mechanism for apportioning unallocated profits to the several trade of the partners.

With effect for any period falling on or after 1 January 2007, TCA 1997, s 1008(2)(a)(ii) (as inserted by FA 2007, s 30, which also deleted existing TCA 1997, s 1008(4)) provides that where the aggregate of the amounts attributed to the partners in relation to their several trades by reference to their profit-sharing ratios is less than the full amount of the partnership's profits for that period, then the shortfall must be apportioned between the partners. The apportionment must be in the ratio which has been agreed for these purposes by the partners if such exists. Failing any such agreement, the profits must be apportioned in the general profit-sharing ratio already applied to attribute profits to each partner's several trade; where no amount of profits were taken as arising to any individual partner, then the apportionment must be made in equal shares.

4.510 Other income and charges on income

The rules for first determining the partnership profits and then allocating them to the several trades of the partners apply only to the Sch D Case I or II profits from the partnership trade. If the firm derives income from other sources, eg dividends, interest, rents, etc, such income is simply divided between the partners in the proportions in which they are entitled to it in the accounting year or period of account in which it is received. Each partner takes his share and brings it into his own income tax return for the appropriate year of assessment as if it were his own income from the source in question. Similarly, any expenses borne by the partnership in relation to such income, eg costs of repairs and maintenance of a rented property, are similarly divided between the partners and each claims any relief available in respect of his share of any expenses that may be deductible in computing income under the relevant Sch or Case.

If the firm makes any 'annual payments' in any period of account, each partner is treated as if he had personally paid the proportion that he has actually borne in that period (TCA 1997, s 1008(1)(b)). 'Annual payment' for this purpose is limited to those types of payment from which income tax would be deductible under TCA 1997, s 237 if paid out of profits or gains brought into charge to tax. In other words, it applies to patent royalties, annuities or other annual payments (excluding annual interest), and to certain mining, etc rents and royalties (see **2.302**). It does not apply to those other types of payment brought under the deduction of tax at source rule of TCA 1997, s 238 by those other provisions in the Act designed to prevent avoidance of tax by non-residents, etc (see **2.307**).

Example 4.510.1

Messrs Able, Baker, Carlos and Doggett carry on the profession of chartered accountants in partnership, making up accounts for the firm to 30 June in each year. Apart from its Sch D Case II income from the partnership trade, the partnerships only other income is deposit interest (received less retention tax) from short term investment of surplus cash. The partners jointly pay an annuity under a deed of covenant to a former partner who is now permanently incapacitated (payable quarterly on 3 January, 3 April, 3 July and 3 October each year).

For the year to 30 June 2014, the partners have agreed to share the profits, losses and charges on income in the ratios 30 (Able): 30 (Baker): 20 (Carlos): 20 (Doggett). From 1 July 2014 onwards, it is agreed that the sharing ratios are to be changed to 30 (Able): 25 (Baker): 25 (Carlos): 20 (Doggett). The partnership's income and charges on income for its two accounting years ending 30 June 2014 and 30 June 2015 are analysed as follows:

	Year ended 30/6/2014	*Year ended 30/6/2015*
	€	€
Net trading profits for year	120,000	145,000

Deposit interest (gross before retention tax):		
Period 1/07/2013 to 31/12/2013	12,000	
Period 1/01/2014 to 30/6/2014	8,000	
Period 1/07/2014 to 31/12/2014		10,000
Period 1/01/2015 to 30/06/2015	-	5,000
	140,000	160,000
Firm's annual payments (the annuities):		
Period 1/07/2013 to 31/12/2013	(7,500)	
Period 1/01/2014 to 30/6/2014	(2,500)	
Period 1/07/2014 to 31/12/2014		(7,500)
Period 01/01/2015 to 30/6/2015	-	(2,500)
Total net income divisible between partners	130,000	150,000
Sharing of net income in agreed ratios:		
Y/E 30/6/2014		
Able (30%)	39,000	
Baker (30%)	39,000	
Carlos (20%)	26,000	
Doggett (20%)	26,000	
Y/E 30/06/2015		
Able (30%)		45,000
Baker (25%)		37,500
Carlos (25%)		37,500
Doggett (20%)	-	30,000
	130,000	150,000

The partnership's Sch D Case II computation and capital allowances for the tax year 2014 (basis period: year to 30 June 2014) are as follows:

	€	€
Net trading profit for year		120,000
Add:		
Depreciation on fixed assets	19,900	
Entertainment expenses	2,100	
		22,000
Adjusted Sch D Case II profits		142,000
Capital allowances 2014 (same basis period)		36,000

Take the case of Baker to illustrate the allocation between the partners of the various items for the tax year 2014. He must include in his tax return for 2014 the following amounts in respect of the various items:

	€	€
Adjusted Sch D Case II profits:		
Firm's Y/E 30/06/2014		
€142,000 x 30% (his share)[1]		42,600

Capital allowances 2014:		
Period 01/01/2014 to 30/6/2014		
€36,000 x 6/12 x 30% (his share)[2]	5,400	
Period 1/07/2014 to 31/12/2014		
€36,000 x 6/12 x 25% (his share)[2]	4,500	
Total for year (his share)		9,900
Deposit interest:		
Period 1/01/2014 to 30/6/2014		
€8,000 x 30% (his share)[3]	2,400	
Period 1/07/2014 to 31/12/2014		
€10,000 x 25% (his share)[3]	2,500	
Total for year (his share)		4,900
Charges on income:		
Period 01/01/2014 to 30/6/2014		
€2,500 x 30% (his share)[4]	750	
Period 1/07/2014 to 31/12/2014		
€7,500 x 25% (his share)[4]	1,875	
Total for year (his share)		2,625

Notes

1. Baker has been a partner for a number of years. The basis period for 2014 of his several trade is the firm's 12-month period of account to 30 June 2014.
2. Baker's appropriate share of the firm's 2014 capital allowances is determined by reference to his profit sharing ratio in the actual tax year ending 31 December 2014, notwithstanding that the partnership's capital allowances are computed by reference to the facts in the firm's period of account ending 30 June 2014 (see **4.506**).
3. Baker's deposit interest for 2014 is his share of the firm's deposit interest actually received in the year to 31 December 2014. This involves applying his different sharing ratios to the interest received respectively prior to and after 1 July 2014.
4. Baker's share of the firm's charges on income is his share of the firm's joint charges actually paid in the year to 31 December 2014. His different sharing ratios are applied to the sums under the covenant paid respectively prior to and after 1 July 2014.

4.511 Partnerships involving companies

In practice, most partnerships are made up of individuals who are chargeable to income tax in respect of their shares of the firm's taxable profits. A partnership may, however, consist of one or more individuals liable to income tax and one or more companies chargeable to corporation tax or, alternatively, a partnership may exist with two or more companies as the partners.

In any case where a company is, becomes or ceases to be a partner, TCA 1997, Pt 4, Ch 3 applies, in the same way as for individual partners, to determine the corporate partner's share in the firm's taxable profits (or tax loss) and in allocating to the corporate partner its share of the firm's capital allowances and/or balancing charges. The allocation of any other income or charges on income of the partnership between the individual partner(s) and the corporate partner(s) similarly follows the principles explained in **4.510**. However, once the allocation of taxable profits, capital allowances, balancing charges, other income and charges on income has been made, it is necessary to look at the Tax Acts to see how the corporate partner is to be charged to corporation tax in respect of its share of these items.

The rules for charging the corporate partner to corporation tax in respect of its share of the firm's taxable profits, capital allowances, etc are contained in TCA 1997, s 1009. This section applies only to the taxation of the corporate partner or partners. It does not apply to any individual or any other non-corporate partner liable to income tax who continues to be dealt with under the Income Tax Acts in the manner explained in **4.502–4.509**. It does not affect the concept of the 'partnership trade' which continues without regard to changes in particular partners, whether individuals or companies, until the trade ceases to be carried on by at least two persons in partnership, or until there is a complete change in all the partners or until the trade itself is permanently discontinued (see **4.502**).

4.512 Limited partnerships: restriction of reliefs

TCA 1997, s 1013 is primarily an anti-avoidance measure designed to counteract schemes under which partnership arrangements could be manipulated to create inflated tax losses otherwise available to a limited partner.

The definition of 'limited partner' contained in TCA 1997, s 1013(1) includes more than a limited partner in its legal sense and essentially deems certain partners 'limited partners' for the purposes of the legislation. TCA 1997, s 1013(1) provides that a 'limited partner' is defined in relation to a trade, as:

(a) a person who is carrying on the trade as a limited partner in a limited partnership registered under the Limited Partnerships Act 1907; or

(b) a person who is carrying on the trade as a general partner in a partnership who:
   (i) is not entitled to take part in the management of the trade, and
   (ii) is entitled to have his liabilities, or his liabilities beyond a certain limit, for debts or obligations incurred for the purposes of the trade discharged or reimbursed by some other person,

(c) a person carrying on the trade jointly with others in circumstances where under the law of any foreign country:
   (i) he is not entitled to take part in the management of the trade, but
   (ii) he is not liable beyond a certain limit for debts or obligations incurred for the purposes of the trade,

(d) a person who carries on the trade as a general partner in a partnership otherwise than as an active partner,

(e) A person who carries on the trade as a partner in a partnership registered under the law of a foreign territory, other than as an active partner, or

(f) A person who carries on the trade jointly with others under any agreement, scheme or arrangement which is governed by the law of any territory outside the State, otherwise than as a person who works for the greater part of their time on the day-to-day management or conduct of the trade.

In *Quigley v Harris* HC 2008, the High Court held that a taxpayer who was a partner in a partnership governed by foreign law under which he was entitled to participate in the management of the partnership but whose liability for the partnership debts was limited, and who was not an active partner as defined, did not fall within limb (d) because he was accordingly not a 'general partner'. However limb (e) would now cover his situation.

An 'active partner' is defined as a partner who works for the greater part of his time on the day-to-day management or conduct of the partnership trade (TCA 1997, s 1031(1): see *Palmer v Maloney* [1999] STC 890, discussed at **3.207**).

A limited partner under the Limited Partnerships Act 1907 is, by the definition contained in that Act, not entitled to take part in the management of the firm and has his liability for the debts of the firm limited to his capital contribution to it. A partner who is not legally a limited partner is, however, also brought within the definition of a limited partner subject to the restrictions of TCA 1997, s 1013 if, under the terms of the actual partnership arrangements, he is not permitted to take part in the management of the trade and has his normal joint and several liability for the debts of the firm limited in the manner stated in (b)(ii) above. Any person, whether an individual, company or any other person, may be a limited partner within the above definition, but it is to be noted that the restrictions actually imposed by TCA 1997, s 1013 only deal with individuals and companies.

For contributions by a partner to the trade of the partnership TCA 1997, s 1013(4)(b) treats two categories of general partners as limited partners. These are as follows:

(a) where there is an agreement, arrangement, scheme or understanding that requires the partner to withdraw from the partnership before he is entitled to recover the full amount of his contribution to the partnership; or

(b) where by virtue of any agreement, arrangement scheme or understanding, a creditor of the partnership has no, or limited, recourse to the partner's assets for the purpose of recovering his debt.

The meaning of the terms 'agreement, etc' are discussed in the context of TCA 1997, s 811 at **17.3**.

TCA 1997, s 1013(2) deals with the case of an individual who is a limited partner in or deemed to be such in relation to any trade. It firstly restricts the extent to which such an individual may have any of the 'specified reliefs' mentioned below set off against or deducted from any of his income other than his share of the profits or gains of the trade in question. Secondly, it restricts the amount of such reliefs which can be claimed to the amount of the individual's contribution to the partnership trade.

The specified reliefs subject to this restriction in the case of a limited partner who is an individual are:

(a) any loss sustained by him by reason of his participation in the trade which is normally available under TCA 1997, s 381 (ie a 's 381' claim) for set off against his income from all sources (see **4.404**);

(b) any capital allowances given in taxing the profits of the trade to which he is entitled by reason of his participation in the trade and which are included in such a 's 381' claim by virtue of TCA 1997, s 392 (see **4.405**);

(c) any capital allowances given by way of discharge or repayment of tax to which he is entitled by reason of his participation in the trade and which, to the extent that they exceed the income of the class to which they relate, are normally available under TCA 1997, s 305 for set off against his income from all other sources (see **6.107**); and

(d) any interest paid by him by reason of his participation in the trade which, by virtue of TCA 1997, s 253 (interest on a loan to acquire an interest in a partnership, etc), is normally available for set off against his income from all sources (see **3.208** for information in respect of this relief and in particular the restrictions which have been imposed by F(No 2)A 2013); in most but not all cases such relief will not be available in any event because of the requirement that the individual should be 'personally acting' in the partnership trade.

One example of capital allowances given by way of discharge or repayment of tax under (c) above which may be relevant occurs if the limited partner leases to the partnership for a separate consideration machinery or plant belonging to him (instead of including it as part of his contribution to the firm without a separate consideration). It has been noted in **4.505** that, in such a case, the partner leasing the plant to the firm is chargeable to tax under Sch D Case IV on the leasing income derived from the firm and is entitled to all the capital allowances on the plant in question for deduction primarily against the plant leasing income. Any claim which the limited partner may then make under TCA 1997, s 305 in respect of any excess of his capital allowances for the leased plant over his leasing income from the plant is a specified relief subject to the restrictions of TCA 1997, s 1013.

Taking this example a stage further, a limited partner may allow his machinery or plant to be used by the partnership as part of his capital contribution without a separate lease consideration. In this case, his profit share taxable under Sch D Case I in effect includes an element attributable to this contribution and he is entitled to his proportionate share of the firm's capital allowances on the machinery or plant contributed. His share of these capital allowances given in taxing his share of the taxable profits of the trade is also a specified relief subject to the restrictions of TCA 1997, s 1013 under (b) above.

As noted already, TCA 1997, s 1013 also applies to restrict the deduction of specified reliefs so that it cannot exceed:

(a) the individual's contribution to the trade (as defined below) as at the end of the relevant tax year; as reduced by

(b) the aggregate amount of deductions in respect of any of the specified reliefs obtained in all previous tax years.

It is to be noted that any reliefs previously obtained under any of the specified provisions in respect of any earlier tax year must be brought into account in determining the 'aggregate amount' deducted from the individual's contribution at (b) above. If the individual has obtained substantial benefits from the specified reliefs in earlier years of assessment without making at least an equivalent contribution to the trade, the effect may be to deny him the benefit of the specified reliefs for a number of years ahead if his contribution to the trade is not increased sufficiently.

An individual's contribution to a trade at any time is defined as the aggregate of:

(a) all amounts contributed by him to the trade as capital;

(b) the amount of the profits or gains of the trade to which he is entitled (ie his share of the partnership's profits) for all years of assessment to date; as reduced by

(c) all amounts in respect of capital contributed which he has, directly or indirectly, drawn out or received back either from the partnership or from any person connected with the partnership; and

(d) the amount of any drawings of or on account of his share of the partnership profits which he has received in money or money's worth (TCA 1997, s 1013(3)).

In determining the aggregate of the individual's contributions to the trade under (a) above, no account is to be taken of any expenditure which he has incurred on behalf of the partnership trade, or in providing facilities for the partnership trade, which he is entitled to receive back (at any time when he continues to be a limited partner) or which he is entitled to require another person to reimburse to him.

For the purposes of (c) above, an individual is treated as having received back an amount of capital contributed to the partnership if and to the extent that:

(a) he receives consideration of that amount or value for the sale of his interest or any part of his interest in the partnership; or

(b) the partnership or any person connected with the partnership repays that amount of a loan or an advance from him; or

(c) he receives that amount of value for assigning any debt due to him from the partnership or from any person connected with the partnership (TCA 1997, s 1013(3)).

For the purpose of these rules, the connected persons rules of TCA 1997, s 10 are applied to determine whether any person (an individual, company or any other person) is to be treated as connected with a partnership. In fact, those connected person rules do not use the phrase 'a person connected with a partnership'. Given that a partnership is not a separate entity as such, but merely consists of the individual partners who make it up, it is arguable that only a person who is connected to all the partners could be regarded as being connected to 'the partnership'. It is unclear whether a person who is a partner (whether general or limited) in the partnership can him/herself be connected with the partnership. If this is possible, then it would appear that any husband, wife, civil partner, brother, sister, ancestor or lineal descendant of any partner would be connected with the partnership since he or she is regarded as connected with every other partner in the firm making up the partnership.

The limited partner is entitled to carry forward his share of the partnership's Sch D Case I tax loss and any unused capital allowances relating to the partnership trade for set off against his share of partnership trading profits in any subsequent tax year under TCA 1997, ss 382 and 304 (see **4.402** and **4.403**). Consequently, if any claim to set off any such loss or capital allowances against his other income is restricted by TCA 1997, s 1013(2), the balance of any such loss or capital allowances disallowed in the claim under TCA 1997, s 381 is carried forward for set off against subsequent Sch D Case I profits. Such losses and capital allowances to be carried forward are not subject to the restriction under TCA 1997, s 1013(2) and are not limited to the partner's contribution to the trade. Similarly, any unused capital allowances given by discharge or repayment of tax against income of a specified class (eg a non-trading lessor's income from the leasing of machinery or plant) remain eligible for carry forward and set off under TCA 1997, s 305 against future income of the same class (see **6.107**).

On the other hand, TCA 1997, s 253 does not permit any carry forward for future use of any interest paid on a loan to make a qualifying partnership investment if that interest cannot be fully set off against the limited partner's other income for the year in which the interest is paid. Therefore, if the limited partner has both losses and/or capital allowances related to the partnership trade and interest eligible for relief under TCA 1997, s 253, it may be to his advantage to claim relief under that section for the interest paid before he claims either of the other specified reliefs. This assumes that his contribution to the trade is at least sufficient to enable some relief to be obtained under the specified provisions.

The provisions of TCA 1997, s 1013(2C)(b)(i) provide that restrictions shall not apply to individuals who are limited partners only by virtue of being non-active partners where:

(a) the partnership trade is wholly the leasing of machinery or plant to a company as defined in TCA 1997, s 486B (Relief for investment in renewal energy generation) and the expenditure was incurred under an obligation before 1 March 2001;

(b) the partnership is entitled to capital allowances in respect of expenditure incurred on sea fishing boats registered in the register of fishing boats and certified by Bord Iascaigh Mhara pursuant to TCA 1997, s 284(3A) (White Fish Fishing Boats Trade) in respect of:

   (i) the relief for interest paid by the limited partner where the interest is paid on a loan taken out before 4 September 2000;

   (ii) the limited partner's share of the partnership's capital allowances, for capital expenditure incurred before 4 September 2000; and

   (iii) the limited partner's share of any partnership trading losses sustained prior to the tax year 2002;

   (iv) the limited partner's share of any partnership trading losses sustained for a tax year from 2002 onwards to the extent that it is attributable to capital allowances made under TCA 1997, s 284(3A) (ie as a result of a TCA 1997, s 392 claim in relation to a s 381 loss relief claim: see **4.405**).

(c) the partnership qualifies for a double rent deduction in calculating the profits or gains of the partnership for the period, except for double rent deductions provided for in TCA 1997, s 354(3) (ie seaside resort areas) for so long as the partnership is entitled to the deduction provided that:

   (i) the individual became a partner before 29 February 2000;

   (ii) the individual made a contribution to the partnership before 29 February 2000; and

   (iii) the qualifying lease is granted or acquired by the partnership before 29 February 2000.

   (This means that where the partnership is entitled to a double rent deduction (apart from under TCA 1997, s 354(3)) the restrictions will not apply so long as the partnership is entitled to claim the double rent deduction or if earlier where the lessee and lessor become connected);

(d) where the partnership qualifies for a double rent allowance, in calculating the profits or gains of the partnership in seaside resort areas, as provided for in TCA 1997, s 354(3) up to 31 December 2004.

However, once the transitional measures set out above have expired and no longer apply, the interest, losses and capital allowances of the limited partner are restricted as provided for in TCA 1997, s 1013(2).

TCA 1997, s 1013(2C)(b)(ii) provides for certain exclusions from the ring fencing and anti-avoidance provisions outlined in TCA 1997, s 1013(2), for limited partners (as defined in TCA 1997, s 1013(1)(d)) for interest on borrowings, losses and capital allowances which are attributable to excepted expenditure. These exclusions can be contrasted to the transitional measures as their availability is not subject to any time limit.

TCA 1997, s 1013(2C)(a) defines 'excepted expenditure' as the following:

(a) expenditure to which the provisions of TCA 1997, s 409A apply restricting the amount of excess capital allowances which can be offset against an individual's total income to a maximum of €31,750;

(b) expenditure incurred on or after 3 December 1997 on hotels wholly in any of the counties of Cavan, Donegal, Leitrim, Mayo, Monaghan, Roscommon, Sligo, save such hotels in those counties which are situated in designated seaside resort areas within TCA 1997, Pt 10, Ch 4 and provided such hotels meet the specified standards and guidelines issued by the Minister for Tourism, Sport and Recreation;

(c) expenditure incurred by the partnership covered by the transitional measures excluded from TCA 1997, ss 409A and 409B.

Division 5 Trades and Professions: Calculation of Profits

5.1 Profits Taxable

5.101 General principles

In general, the taxable profits (or losses) of a trade are calculated in the same way as they are arrived at for accounting purposes, but on the assumption that proper and generally accepted accounting principles have been applied. There are, however, a number of tax law principles which must be adhered to and which override any conflicting accounting principle. The relationship between tax law and commercial accounting principles is examined at **5.102**.

In most cases, it is quite clear what are the trading receipts both for accounting and tax purposes. From time to time, unusual transactions may occur giving rise to receipts, and the question of whether such items should properly be included in computing the taxable profit (and if so, for what period) may require further consideration. It is also necessary that the profit or receipt has been earned or received by the trader concerned on revenue account and not on capital account. A number of these issues have been before the courts; the leading cases and the principles established by them are discussed in **5.2**.

With regard to expenses, for these to be deductible in arriving at the taxable profit, the tax law requires that they have been incurred wholly and exclusively for the purposes of the trade and also that they not be of a capital nature. There are also some special rules that disallow certain types of expenses, eg business entertainment expenses, even if incurred wholly and exclusively for the trade and of a revenue nature.

The rules for distinguishing between those expenses that are deductible for tax purposes, whether or not treated as expenses in arriving at the accounting profit (as well as the rules for determining the period in which such expenses relate) are covered in **5.3**. Apart from the important questions that arise in determining whether certain expenses are of a revenue or a capital nature (**5.307**) and the concept of expenses incurred 'wholly and exclusively' for the trade (**5.305**), particular reference should be made to certain deductions that might not otherwise be allowable but that are permitted by special provisions in the Tax Acts (**5.308**). A number of expense items which commonly have to be considered in the computation of the taxable profits of a trade are then dealt with in **5.308**.

The requirement to bring trading stock and work in progress into account and the rules for valuing them for tax purposes are discussed in **5.4**. A number of special rules affecting the calculation of taxable profits on the commencement or on the cessation of a trade are referred to in **5.6**, as are the provisions for taxing certain receipts after a trade has been permanently discontinued.

All the general rules governing the computation of the profits of a trade taxable under Sch D Case I are applicable also to the profits of a profession taxable under Sch D Case II. Further, since trading losses for tax purposes are calculated in the same way as taxable profits, references in this Division to matters to be taken into account in calculating taxable profits may be applied in a corresponding way to the calculation of a trading loss for which tax relief may be available.

In the case of a profession, the principle that taxable profits are measured on an earnings basis may not always apply. The circumstances in which a person carrying on a profession may use a 'cash' or 'conventional' basis of accounting, and the manner in which this is implemented, are discussed in **5.502**. The special exemption for the earnings of certain writers, composers, artists and sculptors is described at **5.7**.

It is worth noting at this point the decision in *Sharkey v Wernher* 36 TC 275, in which it was held that where trading stock was withdrawn from the trade (in that case, appropriated to personal use), the figure to be credited in the accounts was the market value of the trading stock at the time of withdrawal. At first sight, this conflicts with the principle set out by Palles CB, in *Dublin Corporation v McAdam* 2 TC 387, where he said in the context of 'mutual trading':

> No man in my opinion can trade with himself: he cannot in my opinion make in what is its true sense of meaning, taxable profit by dealing with himself.

Lord Radcliffe, who delivered the majority speech in the House of Lords in *Sharkey*, argued that the dictum of Palles CB should in fact be confined to cases of mutual trading, but without providing any convincing reasons why:

(a) such an important principle should be limited in this fashion; and
(b) normal accounting practice should be overridden (see **5.102** below).

Lord Radcliffe proceeded to prefer market value to cost as the basis for adjustment on the grounds that to do so was 'fairer' and 'better economics'. It may be thought that such speculative policy considerations might have been better excluded from the deliberations of the court.

The principle in *Sharkey v Wernher* was applied in *Petrotim Securities v Ayres* 41 TC 389. In the latter case, the taxpayer (a share-dealing company), sold shares worth £835,000 to an associated company for £205,000. Lord Denning in the court of Appeal commented as follows:

> It seems to me that, when there is a sale at a gross under-value by one associated company to another, the Commissioners are entitled to find that it is not a transaction made in the course of trade. Whoever would suppose that any trader in his right senses would enter into transactions of this kind, that he would sell at a gross under-value were it not that he had in mind some benefit out of making a loss? … Such a transaction is so outside the ordinary course of business of any trader that the Commissioners were entitled to find that it was not done in the course of trade … The case of *Sharkey v Wernher*, … is not confined to cases where a person is a 'self-supplier'. It applies to any case where a trader may, for no reason, choose to give things away or throw them into the sea. So when he puts securities through his books at a derisory price, the figures are to be regarded as struck out for tax purposes; and in their place you must put in the market realisable value at the time.

Lord Denning suggested that the purchasing company should probably also be treated as acquiring the shares at market value, since the transaction was not carried out in the ordinary course of its trade.

In *McCarthaigh v Daly* III ITR 253 (discussed at **4.102** below), O'Hanlon J accepted the correctness of the decisions in *Wernher* and *Petrotim*. However, he did not consider that the transaction in the *Daly* case was:

> so obviously devoid of commercial characteristics as to bring it within the scope of the *Petrotim* decision.

In fact, it would seem that the decision in *Petrotim* was not wholly in point. The Revenue Commissioners were not arguing in *Daly* that the level of leasing rentals charged by the taxpayers was so low that a market value figure should be substituted. The decision in *Petrotim* is not a judicial general anti-avoidance rule designed to prevent the artificial manufacture of trading losses, (although it may have this effect in many cases). As O'Hanlon J acknowledged, the line of reasoning in *Lupton Ltd v FA & AB* 47 TC 580 seems to have been more relevant to the Revenue Commissioners' argument (ie that the transaction in *Daly* was wholly uncommercial, and so could not constitute a trading activity in the first instance).

In *Belville Holdings v Cronin* III ITR 340, the taxpayer was a holding company which also carried on the trade of managing and financing its subsidiaries. The taxpayer recharged only a part of its operating expenses to the subsidiaries and claimed the resulting deficiency as a trading loss. The taxpayer sought to set off this purported loss against dividends received by its subsidiaries under what are now TCA 1997, s 396 and TCA 1997, s 157 (deleted from TCA 1997, s 157 in 2003). The Appeal Commissioner, following the decision in *Petrotim*, held that the taxpayer should be deemed to have rendered its management services to the subsidiaries at market value. For these purposes, he estimated market value as equivalent to 10 per cent of the income of the subsidiaries.

In the High Court, Carroll J said:

> In my opinion, the Appeal Commissioner was correct to apply the principles enunciated in the *Petrotim* case. Although that case concerned goods, services are also a marketable commodity and therefore the principle is the same. The Appeal Commissioner was entitled to find that the situation was similar and accordingly that the transaction was so outside the ordinary course of business of any trader that it was not done in the course of trade.

The learned judge also held however that the market value fixed by the Appeal Commissioners was not based on any evidence. She said:

> I do not wish to say that the appropriate figure should be the cost price to the parent company, or that there must be a notional profit-cost built in, or that no discount at all may be allowed to an associated company, or that the market value must be the price chargeable by a third party. All I would say is that in my opinion the accounts must be adjusted by the inclusion of some figure which brings the transaction within the realm of being a *bona fide* transaction in the ordinary course of business. It will be for the Appeal Commissioners to decide on evidence adduced before him what is the appropriate figure in any given case to be included as the market value.

Unfortunately, the learned judge omitted to refer the issue of valuation back to the Appeal Commissioner under the discretion available to her under TCA 1997, s 941(6) and an order was made simply stating (in effect) that the Appeal Commissioners decision was wrong in law. The Supreme Court held that this order must stand and that a subsequent variation to the order, purporting to remit the issue of valuation back to the Appeal Commissioners, was invalid.

It is open to question whether Carroll J was correct in applying the decision in *Petrotim* to a case involving the provision of services (see *Mason v Innes* 44 TC 326). As already discussed, it is also open to debate whether a cost or market value basis should apply where disposals outside the course of trade are concerned. The arguments against the use of market value in a 'self-supply' situation obviously carry less force in a situation involving a disposal between two legally distinct entities. As appears in the passage cited above, Carroll J, to some extent kept her options open by suggesting that 'cost' might itself be the current measure of 'market value'. It is suggested that this would be an exceptional outcome. (In practice, the Revenue Commissioners do apply a cost basis where 'self-supplies' are involved; thus, for example the accounts of a trader who withdraws trading stock for 'own use' should already include an adjustment at cost price, and no further adjustment would need to be made for tax purposes).

The issue also arises whether the taxpayer in *Belville* was in fact carrying on a trade, given that it systematically and deliberately failed to charge its 'customers' adequate fees. Against this, it may be said that the taxpayer was nevertheless acting commercially, in a broad sense. This is on the footing that the taxpayer, by undercharging its 'customers', thereby enabled them to pay it higher dividends (even though these were received in the taxpayer's capacity as a holding company). The counter argument is that all this proves is that the taxpayer decided *not* to trade in order to gain a counteracting advantage as an investor. For a critique of the decision in *Belville*, see J McAvoy 'Transfer Pricing: The Law and Practice in Ireland' [1993] IJOT 21.

Finally in this connection, it should be noted that it seems that the principle in *Wernher* and *Petrotim* can only be invoked where the price which is struck represents a 'gross undervalue'. In other situations, general principles dictate that the Revenue Commissioners cannot rewrite genuine bargains made by taxpayers, even if the price agreed appears to deviate markedly from market values (see *Craddock v Zevo Finance Co Ltd* 27 TC 267; *Jacgilden (Western Hall) v Castle* 45 TC 685, discussed at **5.602**).

The distinction made in tax law between an application of income and the alienation of income holds equally true in the context of trading receipts: (see *O'Coindealbhain v Gannon*, discussed at **1.403**) and trading profits generally (see: *Mersey Docks and Harbour Board v Lucas* 2 TC 25).

5.102 Importance of commercial accounting principles

As a preliminary point, it should be noted that in the case of a company adopting International Financial Reporting Standards, a special statutory regime introduced by TCA 1997, s 76A (inserted by FA 2005, s 48) (see *e-Brief 32/06*) applies. Discussion of these provisions belongs properly to a work on Corporation Tax and readers are referred to Feeney, *Taxation of Companies* for the relevant analysis.

The relationship between accounting profits and taxable profits has been considered in two important Irish cases, *Cronin v Cork and County Property Co Ltd* III ITR 198 and *Carroll Industries plc v O'Culacháin* IV ITR 135, heard by the Supreme Court and High Court respectively.

In the *Cork & County* property case, the Supreme Court approved two passages from leading UK judgments. The first of these was delivered by Lord Clyde in *Whimster & Co v IRC* 12 TC 813, in which he said:

> In computing the balance of profits and gains for the purposes of income tax, two general and fundamental commonplaces have always to be kept in mind. In the first place, the profits of any particular year or accounting period must be taken to consist of the difference between the receipts from the trade or business during such year or accounting period and the expenditure laid out to earn those receipts. In the second place, the account of profit and loss to be made up for the purpose of ascertaining that difference must be framed consistently with the ordinary principles of commercial accounting, so far as applicable and in conformity with the rules of the Income Tax Act … For example, the ordinary principles of commercial accounting require that in the profit and loss account of a merchant's or manufacturer's business the values of the stock-in-trade at the beginning and at the end of the period covered by the account should be entered at cost or market price, whichever is the lower; although there is nothing about this in the taxing statues.

The second of these passages was delivered by Pennycuick VC in *Odeon Associated Theatres v Jones* 48 TC 257:

> The effect of the principles laid down in *Usher's Wiltshire Breweries Ltd v Bruce* and other cases, including those in which the expression 'ordinary principles of commercial accountancy' is used is this first one must ascertain the profits of the trade in accordance with ordinary principles of commercial accountancy. That, of course, involves bringing in as items of expenditure such items as would be treated as proper items of expenditure in a revenue account made up in accordance with the ordinary principles of commercial accountancy. Secondly, one must adjust this account by reference to the express prohibitions contained in the relevant stature, those being now contained in (TCA 1997, s 81(2)) [ITA 1967, s 61]. That is to say, an item of expenditure, even if it would be allowed as a deduction in accordance with the ordinary principles of commercial accountancy, must be struck out if it falls within any of those statutory prohibitions.

In the *Carroll* case, Carroll J also cited Pennycuick VC's explanation in the *Odeon* case of what he meant by 'the ordinary principles of commercial accountancy' as follows:

> I ought to say a few words by way of explanation of the time-honoured expression 'ordinary principles of commercial accountancy'. The concern of the court in this connection is to ascertain the true profit of the taxpayer. That and nothing else, apart from express statutory adjustments, is the subject of taxation in respect of a trade. In so ascertaining the true profit of a trade the court applies the correct principles of the prevailing system of commercial accountancy. I use the word 'correct' deliberately. In order to ascertain what are the correct principles it has recourse to the evidence of accountants. That evidence is conclusive on the practice of accountants in the sense of the principles on which accountants act in practice. That is a question of pure fact, but the court itself has to make a final decision as to whether that practice corresponds to the correct principles of commercial accountancy. No doubt in the vast proportion of cases the court will agree with the accountants, but it will not necessarily do so. Again, there may be a divergence of view between the accountants, or there may be alternative principles, none of which can be said to be incorrect, or, of course, there may be no accountancy evidence at all. The cases illustrate these various points. At the end of the day the court must determine what is the correct principle of commercial accountancy to be applied. Having done so, it will ascertain the true profit of the trade according to that principle, and the true profit so ascertained is the subject of taxation. The expression 'ordinary principles of commercial accountancy' is, as I understand it, employed to denote what is involved in this composite process.

In the *Carroll* case, Carroll J took the view that Lord Clyde's approach in *Whimster* was preferable to that of Pennycuick VC in the *Odeon* case. She commented:

> I do not think that the 'prevailing' system is the correct test. Time and again the courts have held that no one system should be applied. If there is a system of commercial accounting which is appropriate to the company involved and which correctly ascertains the full profits for tax purposes being the receipts during the year and the expenditure laid out to earn those receipts, then it is possible that that system may be accepted. But, conversely if there is a system of commercial accounting which is appropriate to the company involved but which does not correctly ascertain the full profits for tax purposes then that system cannot be used for the computation of tax.

The learned judge accordingly rejected Current Cost Accounting (CCA) as an acceptable method for computing profits for tax purposes, saying:

> In my view, the correct approach in this case is that there is a basic premise that profit is to be taken as described in *Whimster* case as the difference between receipts from the trade or business during the accounting period and the expenditure laid out to earn those receipts.

> The essence of CCA is as follows …
>
> The charge against income in arriving at profit for stocks consumed and fixed assets used is based on current replacement costs and not on out-of-date and irrelevant historical costs. Similarly the balance sheet shows up-to-date values in place of historical costs.
>
> It is clear therefore that regardless of whether CCA is a prevailing system or a system which is appropriate for the corporate purposes of appellants, it does not show the expenditure laid out to earn receipts during the accounting period.

It may be noted that it was highly unlikely that CCA could have been properly regarded at the time as a 'prevailing accounting system' in any case, (see the judgment to this effect in the Privy Council case of *Lowe & Ors v IRC* [1983] STC 816). It is suggested that Carroll J was justified in preferring the dictum of Lord Clyde, because this makes clear that the accounting treatment must be 'in conformity with the rules of the Income Tax Act' as opposed to being merely subject to adjustment 'by reference to the express prohibitions contained in the relevant statute'. Pennycuick VC's formulation (if taken at face value) gives inadequate weight to those cases in which the courts have decided that the ordinary principles of commercial accounting are unacceptable for tax purposes.

Thus, in *Minister of National Revenue v Anaconda American Brass Ltd* [1956] AC 85, the LIFO system of stock valuation was rejected for tax purposes. Viscount Simonds asserted that the LIFO system was not in accordance with the physical facts, adding:

> there is no room for theories as to flow of costs, nor is it legitimate to regard the closing inventory as an unabsorbed residue of cost rather than a concrete stock of metals …

In *Willingale v International Commercial Bank Ltd* [1978] STC 75, a majority in the House of Lords held that it was not acceptable to accrue for discount receivable on a bill of exchange, on the basis that profits could only be taxed when they were realised (see **5.201**). In *Gallagher v Jones* [1993] STC 537 Lord Nolan suggested that this decision reflected the statutory requirement that tax should be charged 'on the full account of the profits or gains of the year – no more and no less'. The anticipation of unrealised losses, although commercially prudent, was similarly held not to be a permissible deduction for tax purposes (in *IRC v Collins* 12 TC 773). However, this decision was overruled in *Herbert Smith (a firm) v Honour* [1999] STC 173 (discussed further in **5.302**); it is open to question whether this decision would be followed by the Irish courts. As discussed further below, the tax rules for the recognition of expenses and receipts have also evolved independently of developments in financial reporting although the UK courts have recently sought to bring about greater convergence between accounting and tax treatments (*Herbert Smith (a firm) v Honour* representing a rather strong manifestation of this tendency).

In addition, the Inland Revenue issued a press release on 20 July 1999 entitled 'Tax Provisions Move Closer to Accounting Practice' confirming that the Inland Revenue was not proceeding with their appeal on the decision of *Herbert Smith (a firm) v Honour*, and clarified the position on the tax deductibility of provisions and the treatment of FRS12 on provisions. The following extract summaries their approach:

> Although Herbert Smith was about rent provisions, we accept that the case establishes generally that there is no longer a tax rule which denies provisions for 'anticipated' losses or expenses. This means in particular that accurate provisions for foreseen losses on long term contracts (for example, in the construction industry) made in accordance with the correct accounting practice will be tax deductible … FRS12 sets out a new code of accounting rules which applies to most provisions for periods ending after 22 March 1999. We now accept

> that provisions correctly made under FRS12 are tax deductible except where there remains specific tax rules to the contrary.

The press release also stated that in light of the Inland Revenue's decision not to pursue the appeals in view of the decisions, 'the tax treatment of provisions moves substantially closer to UK generally accepted accounting practice' (see *Tax Briefing 41*, which includes details of the Revenue's views on prior year adjustments arising as a result of the implementation of FRS 12).

The press release clarified the UK position and confirmed the Inland Revenue's tendency to follow accountancy principles. To date, the Irish courts have held that accountancy principles are helpful in deciding an issue but not necessarily the deciding factor. However, it appears that the Revenue Commissioners now in fact intend to follow UK practice in this area (see *Tax Briefing 41*, which includes details of the Revenue's views on prior year adjustments arising as a result of the implementation of FRS 12): see the further discussion at **5.302**.

In *Gallagher v Jones* Sir Thomas Bingham asserted that judges would only overrule a generally accepted accounting treatment if 'it was shown to be inconsistent with the true facts or was otherwise inapt to determine the true profits or losses of the business'. It is suggested that Carroll J's decision in the *Carroll* case was clearly correct and is amply justified on the basis that the CCA system of accounting was based on theory rather than facts, and disclosed a notional, rather than a 'true' profit.

In the *Gallagher* case the taxpayer had entered into a lease under which the rental charges were heavily 'frontloaded'. Total rentals of £49,000 were payable in the primary period of the lease (lasting two years) while a rental of £5 pa was chargeable in the secondary period (lasting 21 years). The taxpayer argued that he could claim the 'frontloaded' primary period rentals in full in the year in which they were incurred. This argument was based on the decision in *Vallambrosa Rubber Co v Farmer* 5 TC 529, where the taxpayer had incurred costs on tending young rubber trees which were not due to become productive for several years. The court rejected the proposition that the expense could not be claimed in the year in which it was incurred, merely because it could not be related to income earned during that year. In effect, this decision recognised the established accounting convention whereby overheads are generally matched on a 'periodic' or time-basis (ie by reference to the period of time to which they relate) and not on an earnings basis (ie by reference to the period in which the associated revenues arise).

It may be noted in this regard that the Lord Clyde's reference in the passage quoted above to 'receipts … and the expenditure laid out to earn *those receipts*' cannot be taken too literally. Thus, in *BSC Footwear Ltd v Ridgway* 47 TC 495 Lord Reid observed:

> It is commonplace that a trader's profit for tax purposes must be determined by framing a profit and loss account in which there is set against his gross receipts all relevant expenditure. It has often been said that you set against the receipts all expenditure incurred in earning these receipts. But that is not quite accurate. If you manure the field in year 1 in order to reap the harvest in year two, no one now doubts that the cost of the manure is a proper charge against the receipts in year one although that cost produces no return until the next year. There are no statutory rules about this, and it is well settled that the ordinary principles of commercial accounting must be used except in so far as any specific statutory provision requires otherwise. The question is what is fair to the taxpayer and fair to the Revenue.

The taxpayer in *Gallagher* claimed that the decision in *Vallambrosa* overruled the principles of ordinary commercial accounting. However, in the *Gallagher* case the taxpayer had conceded that the treatment which he had adopted involved a *mismatching* of expenditure, which offended against the basic principles of accountancy. The *Vallambrosa* case in contrast was one where the courts had upheld an accounting treatment based on the matching principle for tax purposes, and did not reflect any wider judge-made principle.

In the *Gallagher* case, the Inland Revenue proceeded to argue that the taxpayer's accounts should be rewritten in line with the correct principles of accountancy. They contended that the relevant rules were those laid down by SSAP 21. No argument was put to the court in favour of any alternative treatment, such as the spreading of the 'frontloaded' payments over the life of the lease (this was in fact the adjustment which the inspector had originally sought to make). The court held that SSAP 21 was valid for tax purposes, even though it applied a 'substance over form' approach by capitalising the leased asset on the balance sheet and charging notional depreciation and interest costs to the profit and loss account.

While the court in *Gallagher* cited *Southern Railways of Peru v Owen* 37 TC 602 (discussed at **5.302**) as a precedent for the adoption of SSAP 21 for tax purposes, as Freedman points out:

> There was no suggestion [in *Southern Railway*] that the [provisions for obligations which might or might not mature] should be treated as transactions of a different kind altogether and their legal nature completely ignored ([1993] BTR 434).

It is suggested that the Irish courts, having rejected the legitimacy of a 'substance over form' approach in tax matters generally, (see *McGrath v McDermott* (discussed at **1.407**)) would be unlikely to admit it through the 'back door' of an accounting standard. The Revenue Commissioners do not seek in practice to apply SSAP 21 treatment (see **5.310**). As discussed at **5.302** the Revenue Commissioners have intimated that they will follow FRS12 (regarding provisions).

It is true that the computation of trading profits is not based on a strict legal analysis: the 'matching principle' which eg allocates expenses legally *incurred* in one period to a different period for accounting purposes is an obvious example. However, the application of the matching basis is a very different proposition from accounting for a legal transaction as if a *different* legal transaction had taken place.

The manner in which the Irish courts would deal with 'frontloaded' leasing payments can only be a matter of speculation. If the taxpayer could not establish that the charging of such payments on an 'incurred' basis was consistent with correct accounting principles, then it seems the court would have to apply the correct principles, so long as these were consistent with tax law. As discussed above, it seems unlikely that the principles contained in SSAP 21 would be regarded as acceptable. A viable alternative might be to spread the frontloaded payments over the life of the lease, ie in line with the 'matching' principle (see the discussion at **5.310** below).

Of course, as Carroll J's judgment in the *Carroll* case makes clear, the court would reserve the right to strike down the accounting treatment, even in a situation where the taxpayer might be able to show that charging frontloaded payments *was* consistent with accepted accounting principles. The court might exercise this right if it took the view that the 'incurred' basis did not reflect the 'true profits' in the particular circumstances of the case, although this would seem to be unlikely. The wider tax implications of arrangements such as those undertaken in *Gallagher* are considered below at **5.310**.

The significance of accounting evidence in other areas such as the distinction between capital and revenue expenditure is debatable. In the latter case, the courts have refined a series of artificial tests to assist in making this capital/revenue distinction which have no counterpart in financial reporting theory. Thus, while judges do occasionally refer to the accounting treatment of an item as influential, this is likely only to be so in borderline cases. Lord Denning commented as follows in *Heather v PE Consulting Group*:

> The courts have always been assisted greatly by the evidence of accountants. This practice should be given due weight; but the courts have never regarded themselves as being bound by it. It would be wrong to do so. The question of what is capital and what is revenue is a question of law for the courts. They are not to be deflected from their true course by the evidence of accountants, however eminent.

For example, therefore, payments made to enhance or secure goodwill may well not appear on the trader's balance sheet as an asset (as pointed out by Lord Greene MR in *Associated Portland Cement Manufacturers v Kerr* 27 TC 103; see also SSAP 22), but will clearly be capital in nature. The UK courts have underlined the legal nature of the tests concerned by declining to treat appeals on the issue as raising an issue of fact (see *Beauchamp v Woolworth* below, and contrast *Brosnan v Cork Communications* IV ITR 349).

In deciding whether an asset qualified as trading stock, the accounting treatment has been held to be strong evidence of the 'commercial reality' of the situation (*Fraser v London Sportscar Centre* [1985] STC 6881, followed by the Supreme Court in *Murnaghan Bros v O'Maoldomnhaigh* IV ITR 304).

It should be stressed that the potential for conflicts between tax law and accounting practice is likely to grow, as the latter progressively places more emphasis on the measurement of economic performance rather than on objective and verifiable records of stewardship. Carroll J's analysis in the *Carroll* case may be viewed as the court's expression of its concern that long established principles of tax law should not be eroded by developments in financial reporting.

It may be also noted (as stated by Pennycuick J above) that the courts reserve the right to determine the correct principles of commercial accountancy as an issue of fact. This will depend primarily on the evidence of accountants, although the growth of detailed formal accounting standards will clearly be an important source of objective evidence in this regard. In *Symons v Weeks* [1983] STC 195. Warner J made the following observation:

> Pennycuick VC … envisaged the possibility of a court deciding that a prevailing system of commercial accountancy did not correspond to the correct principles of commercial accountancy. It is however to be observed that no case was cited to me, nor do I know of any, where a court has in fact done that.

The courts will naturally also reserve the right to reject accounting treatments which are flawed as a result of a misunderstanding of the legal nature of the underlying transaction (see *Merchant (Peter) Ltd v Stedeford* 30 TC 496).

It may be noted that in the *Gallagher* case Sir Thomas Bingham also implied that the courts can arbitrate where there is a *choice* of acceptable accounting treatments, even if the treatment adopted by the taxpayer does not conflict with tax law (see also *Britannia Airway* discussed below, where the Appeal Commissioners' finding in this respect was upheld as an issue of fact). This view does not seem to be consistent with the decision in *Ostime v Duple Motor Bodies Ltd* 39 TC 537 (see **5.401**), where the Revenue were not allowed to substitute their choice out of acceptable methods of stock calculation for that adopted by the taxpayer.

Finally, it would seem that the taxpayer cannot seek to be taxed on the basis of an accounting method or policy which he has not actually adopted in his accounts unless of course the method used in the accounts offends against tax law, as in the *International Commercial Bank Ltd* case (discussed above): see *Imperial Fire Insurance Co v Wilson* 1 TC 71.

5.2 Trading Receipts

5.201 When are receipts taxable?

In cases involving the supply of goods and services, a receipt cannot be recognised for tax purposes until all the conditions and obligations necessary to become entitled to earn that receipt have been fulfilled. In *JP Hall & Co Ltd v IRC* 12 TC 382, the profit on the sale of goods was held to be properly included in the accounts for the years in which goods were delivered, and not in previous years, when the contracts had been originally executed. Atkin LJ commented that any other course 'would be quite contrary to commercial procedure' (see also *Sturge (J & E) v Hessell* [1975] STC 573). In other words, the primary focus is placed on what the courts regard as the time of *realisation* (ie when entitlement to the relevant receipt arises), as opposed to the period over which the profit accrues (see also Freedman, 'Profits and Prophets' [1987] BTR 61).

The principle was also applied in *Johnson v Try* 27 TC 127 to compensation received by a land dealer for a refusal of planning permission in respect of one of its properties. The court held that the sum arose only when there was a final award or final agreement, since the refusal could have been cancelled at any time up to that point (see also *Eckel v Board of Inland Revenue* [1989] STC 305).

As already noted, this same principle was applied by the House of Lords in *Willingale v ICB* [1977] STC 183, where the court held that no profit could be recognised in respect of a bill of exchange held by a bank until it had been realised ie when the bill had either matured, or been disposed of. In the Court of Appeal, Ormrod LJ observed:

> In the case of work or services, the value of the work must be brought into the accounts for the year in which the work is done or the services rendered, but, presumably, only if the taxpayer has completed the work, or done enough under the contract to entitle him in law to receive payment at some future time. If this reasoning is correct, the profit is realised when the taxpayer becomes legally entitled to payment either immediately or at some future date …

In the House of Lords, Lord Salmon said that a profit may not be taxed until it has been 'ascertained and earned', commented as follows:

> The solution to the problem depends in my opinion on the true nature of what the bank is doing when it discounts or purchases a bill. In my view it is acquiring an asset and so long as it continues to hold that asset, it does not and cannot, realise any profit or loss in respect of it. If the bank takes credit for any 'accrued discount' while it is still holding the bill, it is therefore anticipating a profit that has not yet been realised.

In the *Willingale* case, the taxpayer was allowed to override the treatment which it had adopted in its accounts (where it had accrued the interest over the economic life of the bill). The taxpayer's auditor stated that the realisation basis would have been acceptable for accounting purposes if accompanied by an explanation why a departure from the general accounting practice of the clearing banks was justified in the circumstances of this case. However, it seems that the decision does not depend on the fact that the 'realisation' basis was also acceptable for accounting purposes (although this was the view of the decision apparently taken by the court in the *Gallagher* case).

It may be noted that under Generally Accepted Accounting Principles, which are in a state of continuous evolution, it is now generally the case for accounting purposes:

> where the substance of a contract for services is that the seller's contractual obligations are performed gradually over time, revenue should be recognised as contract activity progresses to reflect the seller's partial performance of its contractual obligations. The amount of revenue should reflect the accrual of the right to consideration as contract activity progresses by reference to the value of work performed.

Further:

> the amount of revenue will reflect the fair value of the services provided as a proportion of the total fair value of the contract, which will reflect the time spent and skills and expertise that have been provided (UTIF Abstract 40, issued on 10 March 2005).

Whether this statement of principle with its emphasis on commercial substance and which is in contradiction of the 'realisation' principle would have been accepted on general principles by the Irish courts may perhaps be questioned (see **5.102**). However, the legislature has sought to pre-empt such issues by the enactment of TCA 1997, s 95A (inserted by FA 2006, s 56(1)). This section assumes that the recognition of additional income in these circumstances will give rise to uplift in the opening balance sheet figure for work-in-progress in the year of the change of policy (which is then charged to tax); accordingly the section is discussed in full at **5.404**.

Matters become more complicated where there is a right to a receipt at a future date, but the amount thereof is unascertainable at the time at which the accounts are prepared (eg a commission depending on future events). In *IRC v Gardner Mountain & D'Ambrumenil*, Viscount Simon analysed the correct treatment of such situations as follows:

> … services completely rendered or goods supplied, which are not to be paid for till a subsequent year, cannot generally be dealt with by treating the taxpayer's outlay as pure loss in the year in which it was incurred and bringing in the remuneration as pure profit in the subsequent year in which it is paid or due to be paid. In making an assessment … the net result of the transactions setting expenses on the one side and a figure for remuneration on the other side, ought to appear … in the same year's profit and loss account and that year will be the year when the service was rendered or the goods delivered … This may involve … an estimate of what the future remuneration will amount to … [but this provisional estimate] could be corrected when the precise figure was known, by additional assessment …

In *Isaac Holden & Sons v IRC* 12 TC 768, a sum reflecting a retrospective price increase was 'related back' to the accounting year for which it was made. Although the taxpayer had no enforceable legal right to the sum in question in that year, the sum was treated by the court as comparable to a trade debt. Similarly, in *IRC v Newcastle Breweries* 12 TC 927, compensation for assets confiscated under wartime regulations was related back to the date of confiscation (see also *Severne v Dadswell* 35 TC 649; *Ensign Shipping Co v IRC* 12 TC 116).

Where a sum due under a trading agreement was calculated by reference to a shortfall in the taxpayer's turnover over the period of the agreement, that sum was held to arise at the end of the period concerned. This was on the basis that it was not possible to allocate such a sum to goods or services previously supplied: *Rownson, Drew & Clydesdale v IRC* 16 TC 545, 595.

In the case of authors it has been held that the only practicable method of accounting for their royalty income is on a receipts basis (see *Carson v Cheyney's Exors* 38 TC 240). An advance against royalties which was recoupable only against future royalties was held to be a taxable receipt in *Taylor v Dawson 22 TC 189*.

The principle of 'relating back' a receipt to the year of account in which the right to be paid arose was not, however, applied in *John Cronk & Sons v Harrison* 20 TC 712. In the *Cronk* case, the taxpayer was entitled to receive a trading debt by instalments, payment of which was dependent on the debtor receiving corresponding sums from third parties. The court held that the debt had to be brought into the tax computation at its market value and not at face value. If the market value was not ascertainable, then the instalments were to be brought into the tax computations for future years on a receipts basis. A similar analysis was applied in *Absalom v Talbot* 26 TC 166.

In the *Gardner Mountain* case, Viscount Simon and Lord Porter said that the decisions in *Cronk* and *Absalom* should be confined to their facts. It may be, however, that the latter two cases can be distinguished on the basis that they were concerned with rights to ascertained amounts which were subject to future uncertainty, as opposed to rights to unascertained future amounts.

The treatment by the UK courts of payments received in advance seems to represent a qualification of the principles established in the cases cited above. In *Sun Insurance Co v Clark* 6 TC 59, the taxpayer received insurance premiums during its accounting year, but the risks covered by the premiums extended beyond the end of that year. The House of Lords held that the taxpayer was entitled to carry forward an agreed proportion of these premiums as a reserve for unearned premiums. It was not made entirely clear whether this reserve was a provision for the contingent liabilities attached to the unexpired risks, as opposed to a *deferral* of income, although both Lords Haldane and Atkinson opted for the latter analysis, which indeed seems to be the better view.

It might appear, in the light of decisions such as that in *JP Hall & Co*, that the receipt of the premiums in the *Sun Insurance* case should only have been recognised when they were fully earned ie when all the conditions and obligations undertaken in order to become entitled to them had been fulfilled (in other words, at the end of the period of risk cover). However, the UK courts have seemingly taken the view that the physical receipt of money or money's worth in the year of account should be taken into account, on the basis that there has been a potential or actual realisation of profit. In the case of advance receipts, an *earnings* basis should then be applied ie to determine what amount should be excluded as being attributable to later years. Accordingly, in the case of a trader who receives a payment in advance of the supply of goods or services, the receipt should normally only be recognised in the period in which the relevant supply takes place.

In *Tapmaze Ltd v Melluish (Inspector of Taxes)* [2000] STC 189, Hart J held that advance payments made to a company whose business consisted of the hiring of motor vehicles and related to periods after the sale of the company to a third party were part of the company's profits in the accounting period in which the business is sold. The Share

Purchase Agreement for the company's sale provided for the benefit of the pre-payments to be kept by the Vendors. It was held that the profits arose since the pre-payments accrued from the company's trade in the first instance and not from the Share Purchase Agreement.

A rather troublesome decision in this context was reached in *Elson v Price's Tailors* 40 TC 671, where the court held that 'non-reclaimable' deposits received from customers by the taxpayer should be treated as taxable at the time they were received. Following *Jay's The Jewellers Ltd v IRC* 29 TC 374, the court held that the deposits belonged to the taxpayer when they were received, subject only in limited circumstances to a contingent right of repayment (the court suggested that a provision for the contingent liability to make repayments might therefore be appropriate). It is open to argument that the recognition of the receipts in the *Price's Tailors* case should have been deferred, ie on the *earnings* basis. It may be noted however, that the court did not consider the *Sun Insurance* case, and that no evidence of relevant accounting practice was advanced, so that the decision may have been *per incuriam*. On the other hand, it may be argued that this case *can* be distinguished, on the basis that the receipts in question belonged to the taxpayer even if no supply of goods ever actually took place.

In the *Sun Insurance* case, the House of Lords held that there was no fixed rule of law governing the time when receipts (or expenses) should be brought into account. The appropriate basis for allocating advance receipts to periods of account would therefore seem to be primarily a matter of 'ordinary accounting practice' (see also *Symons v Weeks* at **5.403** and note the approach of the Special Commissioners in *Robertson v IRC* [1977] STC (SCD) 282). As discussed above, the Irish courts may however be unwilling to give effect to any accounting standards which apply the doctrine of 'substance over form'.

The treatment of trading receipts which do not refer to the supply of goods or services, etc by the taxpayer also deserves discussion. In general, the principle of 'relating back' has not been applied in such cases. The decision in *Rownson, Drew & Clydesdale v IRC* 16 TC 545 was followed in *Corr v Larkin* II ITR 164, when a sum payable under a loss of profits policy was held to arise at the end of the policy period since it was only at that time that the sum concerned could be determined. In *Gray v Lord Penrhyn* 21 TC 252, a sum paid to make good trading losses caused by the negligence of a firm of auditors was treated as arising in the year in which liability was agreed (and the compensation paid) and not the years in respect of which the losses arose. Similarly, in practice, a rebate received at the end of a leasing agreement is not related back (see *Revenue Leaflet IT 52*). In *Smart v Lincolnshire Sugar Ltd* 20 TC 643 it was held that a government subsidy to assist a company in meeting its current trading obligations should be taxed in the year of receipt. The grants in the *Lincolnshire Sugar* case were repayable in certain circumstances and again the court suggested that a provision for the contingent liability to repay them could be made in the accounts, if the position was still open at the date that they were finalised.

5.202 Income and capital receipts distinguished

Only receipts of an income (revenue) nature arising from, or in the course of, a trade are included in computing the taxable profits of that trade. Receipts from the disposal of capital assets or otherwise arising on capital account must be excluded.

The question of whether a particular receipt is received in the course of the trade or not, and whether a particular receipt is of an income as opposed to of a capital nature, have been considered by the courts in a number of cases over the years. The cases considered by the courts have been classed under a number of convenient headings and are discussed accordingly at **5.203** to **5.210** below.

It may be noted that where a trading receipt takes the form of an asset rather than of money, it seems that the market value of that asset must be taken into account and not the price fixed under the relevant transaction (if different): *Gold Coast Selection Trust Ltd v Humphrey* 30 TC 209; see also *Murphy v Australian Machinery & Investment Co Ltd* 30 TC 244.

Where the sale of a capital asset is combined with a distinct and separable trading agreement, receipts from the latter remain taxable in the normal manner. It will be a matter of construing the particular contractual arrangements in order to determine their true legal effect (*Orchard Wine and Spirit Co v Loynes* 33 TC 97; *Lamport & Holt Line v Langwell* 38 TC 193).

5.203 Circulating v fixed capital

The realisation of any element of circulating (or 'working') capital should normally give rise to a taxable profit or allowable loss. Thus, profits on the disposal of trading stock, work-in-progress or raw materials should be reflected in the computation of taxable profits. In *George Thompson & Co v IRC* 12 TC 1091, a shipping company which used coal fuel in its ships lost the use of a number of its ships. The court held that the receipt of consideration in return for transferring its rights under coal supply contracts (which it no longer needed for trading purposes) was taxable under Sch D Case I, (note also *Diamond v Campbell-Jones* [1961] Ch 22, where damages received by a land developer for the failure of a contract to purchase land were held to be taxable.)

The distinction between circulating and fixed capital in the context of foreign exchange transactions is dealt with in **13.303**.

In *Wain v Cameron* [1995] STC 555, it was held that the sale of property rights created in the course of a profession were taxable professional receipts. Accordingly, profits on the sale by an author of his manuscripts and working papers were assessable under Sch D Case II.

Conversely, the realisation of any element of fixed capital (including goodwill) will give rise to capital receipts. Thus, in *British Borneo Petroleum Syndicate v Cropper* 45 TC 201, a sum received in exchange for the surrender of a royalty agreement was held to be on capital account. However, sums received in return for the *use* or *enjoyment* of capital assets will be in the nature of income receipts.

In some cases the distinction between fixed and circulating capital can become rather blurred. In *Snell v Rosser Thomas & Co* 44 TC 343, a developer had to buy land surplus to his requirements in order to obtain the particular property which he wanted. He subsequently sold off the surplus land when the opportunity arose. The transaction was held to be equivalent to a disposal of trading stock and was therefore taxable (compare *Stott v Hoddinott* 7 TC 85, where an architect acquired shares in a company as a condition of that company providing him with work; a subsequent loss on the disposal of the shares was held to be capital in nature).

5.204 Agency agreements

Sums received in consideration for, or as compensation for the termination of, agency and other agreements, may fall on either side of the revenue/capital divide, depending on the specific facts. In *London & Thames Haven Oil Wharves Ltd v Attwooll* 43 TC 491, Lord Diplock, stating the general principle to be applied in this area, said:

> I start by formulating what I believe, to be the relevant rule. Where, pursuant to a legal right, a trader receives from another person compensation for the trader's failure to receive a sum of money which, if it had been received, would have been credited to the account of profits (if any) arising in any year from the trade carried on by him at the time when the compensation was so received, the compensation is to be treated for income tax purposes in the same way as that sum of money would have been treated if it had been received instead of the compensation.

Thus in *Deeny v Gooda Walker* [1996] STC 299, compensation received by a Lloyds name from his agents in respect of trading losses caused by their negligence was held to be a trading receipt.

In *Van den Berghs Ltd v Clark* 19 TC 390 it was held that damages paid for the breach of a joint venture agreement related to a capital asset. This was on the footing that the contract 'related to the whole structure of the [taxpayer's] profit making apparatus'. Conversely, in *Kellsall Parsons & Co v IRC* 21 TC 708, compensation for the loss of an agency agreement, which did not result in the substantial stultification of the taxpayer's business, was held to be in the nature of income; in other words it was characterised as a payment made in lieu of lost profits rather than as compensation for the sterilisation of the underlying source of those profits. Emphasis was placed in this case on the fact that the contract had only one year to run.

The courts have generally been reluctant to apply the reasoning in the *Van De Bergh's* case, unless the agency agreement in question represents, more or less, the entire framework of the trade (see eg *Wiseburgh v Domville* 36 TC 527 (approved in *Hickey & Co v Roches Stores* [1980] ILRM 107), where an agency agreement which contributed 60 per cent of the trader's profits was held not to be a capital asset, and also, to similar effect, *Fleming v Bellow Machine Co* 42 TC 308).

Payments made for the mere variation of an agreement, even one which forms the core of the profit making structure of the trade, will normally be of a revenue nature (see *Sabine v Lockers Ltd* 38 TC 120). Similarly, as indicated by Lord Macmillan in the passage cited above, compensation for a cancelled sale agreement will generally relate to profits foregone and not to the loss of the profit-making structure of the trade (see *Shore Brothers v IRC* 12 TC 955; *Shove v Dura* 23 TC 779). Exceptionally, in *Barr Crombie v IRC* 26 TC 405, the taxpayer was held to be non-taxable in respect of compensation received on the loss of its only customer. Lord Normand said:

> In the present case virtually the whole assets of the appellant company consisted in this agreement. When the agreement was surrendered or abandoned, practically nothing remained of the company's business. It was forced to reduce its staff and to transfer into other premises, and it really started a new trading life. Its trading existence as practised up to that time had ceased with the liquidation of the [customer].

The type of reasoning in the *Van den Bergh's* decision has been extended in *Higgs v Olivier* 33 TC 136 to cover the case where an actor received a lump sum for entering into a restrictive covenant, under which he agreed to work for nobody other than the payer for an 18-month period. The taxpayer did not undertake to carry out any work for the payer, nor was the payer obliged to provide him with any work over the relevant period. The Appeal Commissioners held that the lump sum was a capital receipt because it accrued to the taxpayer, 'for refraining from carrying on his vocation'. The Court of Appeal upheld this finding as one of fact, while noting that payments for limited and partial covenants would be more likely to be on revenue account. In *IRC v Biggar* [1982] STC 677, Lord Cameron described the case as one where the taxpayer's capital was his acting capacity, and where the consideration which he received was for the temporary and partial sterilisation of his principle asset, ie his professional skill. It is very unlikely that restrictions which are ephemeral in nature or which are undertaken in the normal course of a trade or profession would fall within the scope of *Higgs v Oliver*. In *Bush Beach & Gent v Road* 22 TC 519, damages for the cancellation of a contract by a supplier were held to relate to loss of profits, notwithstanding the fact that it was a term of the contract that the supplier would not deal with the taxpayer's competitors. This term was held merely to constitute an ordinary incident of such trading contracts (note also *Vaughan v Parnell & Zeitlin* 23 TC 505).

5.205 Intellectual property

A series of cases concerning disposals of 'know how' (including secret processes, blueprints, specialised technical knowledge, etc) illustrate the fine distinction between the part-disposal of a capital asset and the exploitation of that asset to generate revenue. The position is generally straightforward where the consideration is clearly of an income nature (eg recurrent royalties or license fees). It is mainly in other cases, where lump sum payments are involved, that the difficulties arise. Here the main test in determining whether the receipts are taxable was stated by Bankes LJ in *British Dyestuffs Corporation (Blackley) Ltd v IRC* 12 TC 586 as follows:

> … is the transaction in substance a parting by the company with part of its property for a purchase price, or is it a method of trading by which it acquires this particular sum of money as part of the profits and gains of that trade?

In *Evans Medical Supplies v Moriarty* 37 TC 540, the taxpayer, which produced medical supplies, agreed to provide the government of an overseas state with all of the know-how needed to produce such supplies (thereby cutting itself out of one of its existing markets). The House of Lords held that the lump sum consideration received by the taxpayer for entering into this agreement was capital in nature, on the basis that 'the taxpayer's foreign operations will become progressively less important, or in other words, … the company had parted with an asset which was the *source* or one of the *sources* of its profits … the [taxpayer] has parted with its property for a purchase price' (emphasis added).

In *Handley Page v Butterworth* 19 TC 328, the taxpayer parted with his secret processes and all of his technical knowledge in return for a lump sum. The lump sum was held to be capital since the taxpayer had in effect given up the entire basis of his trading activities.

In *Jeffrey v Rolls-Royce Ltd* 40 TC 443, the company manufactured aero engines and engaged in metallurgical research and the development of engineering techniques as a result of which it had acquired a fund of know-how. Between 1946 and 1953 it entered into a number of agreements with governments and companies in countries to which the export of its aero engines was not possible, for the supply of know-how and information necessary to enable the other party to manufacture the engines. It was held that the payments for know-how arose as part of the recurring profit-making operations of the taxpayer and were therefore trading receipts on revenue account. It was indicated there was nothing to indicate that the capital assets of the company were in any way diminished by entering into these agreements. The receipts from these agreements arose from another way of deriving profits from the use of the technical know-how, experience and ability.

The *Rolls Royce* case was distinguished in *Wolf Electric Tools Ltd v Wilson* 45 TC 326. The taxpayer company manufactured electric power tools in which it had an extensive export trade. In 1950 its sole agency in India was taken over by R Ltd, an Indian company, which bought tools from the company on a principal to principal basis. In 1954 when the company's exports to India represented over 10 per cent of its total exports, R Ltd informed the company that, because of the Indian government's policy of encouraging the setting up of local factories for making tools, the whole market would be lost unless it undertook to manufacture tools in India. The company supplied drawings, designs, technical knowledge and other know-how to a new company set up in India to manufacture the tools there. In exchange the company was issued with shares in the new company. At the same time it agreed with the new company not to sell in India and Nepal the types of tools to be manufactured by the new company.

It was held that the transaction was of a wholly capital nature, the effect of which was for the taxpayer to receive a new capital asset, ie the shares in the foreign company, in exchange for what it had previously possessed, ie its connection or goodwill in India (see *also English Electric Co v Musker* 41 TC 550).

In *John & E Sturge Ltd v Hessel* [1975] STC 573, information was given as to secret processes in return for lump sum payments. The object of the transaction had been to invest the proceeds in a company set up to exploit the secret processes, thus, it was claimed, enlarging the trader's profit earning base. The disclosure of the information was not incidental to any disposal of any branch of the trader's business or of any capital asset. It was held accordingly that the proceeds were trading receipts to be taxed as part of the profits or gains of the trade.

In *Thompsons (Carron) Ltd v IRC* [1976] STC 317, the taxpayer company, faced with a dwindling market for its exports to Belgium due to tariffs, transferred know-how, plans, etc to a Belgian company in consideration for shares in the latter. It was held that the value of the shares received should be treated as a trading receipt since the taxpayer company had parted neither with its know-how nor with its goodwill, but had retained both for exploitation through its partnership in the Belgian company. The *Wolf Electric Tools Ltd* case was distinguished as in that case the company effectively gave up its business in India as part of the consideration for the shares in the new Indian company. The loss of the taxpayer's pre-existing connection or goodwill in India was considered to be the crucial factor in the latter case.

The references above to know-how relate to information, secret processes, methods, etc not protected by a patent. The rights available to a person under a patent owned by him or licensed from someone else constitute a capital asset and any sums received for the outright sale of patent rights should not be included as a trading receipt in computing his profits taxable under Sch D Case I. However, the net profit from the sale of patent rights is normally taxed as income under Sch D Case IV (see **8.302**).

In some cases, the provision of 'know-how' may be merely incidental to the grant of a patent, and receipts will be taxed under the regime appropriate thereto.

5.206 Insurance and compensation proceeds

The treatment of insurance proceeds, like that of other compensation monies that may be received by a trader, follows the principles already discussed. If received for the loss of, or damage to, a capital asset, the monies recovered under a policy of insurance are received on capital account and should not be treated as trading receipts. If received in compensation for loss of profits or to make good, in whole or in part, some receipts which, due to the risks insured against, did not materialise and which, if they had been received, would have been taxable as Revenue receipts of the trade, the insurance proceeds are themselves similarly taxable. In *London & Thames Haven Oil Wharves Ltd v Attwooll* 43 TC 491, the taxpayer operated a jetty which was damaged by the negligence of a third party. The taxpayer received compensation both for the physical damage to the jetty (accepted as being capital in nature) and also for the loss of profits incurred while the jetty was being repaired (held to be revenue in nature).

In *Corr v Larkin* II ITR 164, a sum recovered under a policy providing indemnity for loss of profits and increased working costs sustained through the interruption of normal business following a fire was held to be taxable as a trading receipt. In *Corr v Larkin*, it was also accepted that the accountants' fees in preparing the loss of profits claim were deductible expenses. Damages representing loss of profits in respect of a breach of contract were treated as taxable in *Hickey & Co v Roches Stores* [1980] ILRM 107.

The full amount recovered under an insurance policy in respect of trading stock destroyed by fire was held to be a trading receipt which must be credited in computing taxable profits (*Green v Gliksten & Son* 14 TC 364). To the extent that insurance monies are received to compensate for damage to fixed assets, eg premises, plant, machinery, etc caused by the fire, they are treated as received on capital account.

A taxpayer may insure against loss to his business that may result from the loss, through death or disablement, of the services of employees or, in the case of a company, of directors. He may also take out insurance to meet any compensation that may be payable to employees in excess of that provided under the statutory workers' compensation scheme. In *Murphy v Thomas E Gray & Co Ltd* 23 TC 225, insurance proceeds covering compensation payable to the company in respect of accidents to certain members of its staff were held to be trading receipts. In *IRC v Williams' Executors* 26 TC 23, it was held that £15,000 payable under an assurance policy against the death or disablement of a director of a private company was a revenue receipt of the company.

The person covered by a death or disability policy need not necessarily be an employee of the taxpayer. In *Keir & Cawder Ltd v IRC* 38 TC 23, a construction company insured a partner in a firm of consulting engineers whose advice and involvement was considered essential in connection with certain public works contracts sought and obtained abroad. The consultant was killed in an air accident. It was held that the object of the assurance was to compensate the company for loss of profits resulting from the loss of the consultant's services and was taxable. The company's argument that the assurance was against the loss of goodwill built up by its association with the consultant was rejected.

In general, the Revenue Commissioners will seek to tax receipts maturing under so-called 'keyman' policies only where a deduction for the relevant premiums has been granted for tax purposes. However, the Revenue have indicated that this will not be their invariable practice. In particular, they take the view that if the policy was intended to insure against loss of profits, they will seek to tax part or all of the policy proceeds, notwithstanding any 'technical contrivances' designed to render the premiums non-deductible. Furthermore, mere failure to seek a deduction for the payment of premiums will not protect the taxpayer against potential liability on receipt of the policy proceeds.

In *Glenboig Fireclay Co v IRC* 12 TC 427, the taxpayer received compensation for being prevented from working its fireclay fields. The argument that the payment was made in lieu of profits was rejected, notwithstanding the fact that the fields had an expected useful life of less than three years. Lord Buckmaster said:

> In truth the sum of money is the sum paid to prevent the [taxpayer] obtaining the full benefit of the capital value of [the fields]. It appears to me to make no difference whether it be regarded as the sale of the asset out and out or whether it is treated merely as a means of preventing the acquisition of the profit which would otherwise be granted. In either case, the capital asset of the company has to that extent been sterilised and destroyed.

The learned judge added:

> It is now well settled that the compensation payable in such circumstances is the profit that would have been obtained were [the fields] … in fact worked. But there is no relation between the measure that is used for the purposes of calculating a particular result and the quality of the figure that is arrived at by means of the application of that text.

(See also *McClure v Petre* [1988] STC 749, a rental income case, discussed at **12.102**, and also *Robinson v Dolan* at **5.208**).

The decision in *Glenboig* has been applied in the Irish case of *Arthur Guinness & Co v IRC* I ITR 1. In that case, the taxpayer was a business which owned a large stock of barley held as raw material for the manufacture of stout. These stocks were requisitioned by the Government under wartime regulations and compensation was subsequently paid to the taxpayer. The Court of Appeal held that the transaction was not in the course of trade and that the stock represented a capital asset. However, it would seem that raw materials are properly regarded as trading stock and in any event (as pointed out by Pimm J in his dissenting judgment) form part of the circulating capital of the trade. The decision is difficult to reconcile with general principles, and was disapproved in the UK case of *IRC v Newcastle Breweries* 12 TC 927.

Following general principles, the consideration for disposal of a capital asset may nevertheless take the form of a series of income payments (see, eg *Beveridge v Ellam* [1996] STC (SCD) 77). In some cases, an award of damages may also include an identifiable element of interest (see *Riches v Westminster Bank Ltd* 28 TC 159, discussed at **8.101**).

Where an asset is acquired by way of compulsory purchase, the sum received in respect of that asset may include an element reflecting, *inter alia* loss of profits incurred by the owner of the asset. It is arguable that, although this sum is a single amount under general law (see *IRC v Glasgow & Southern Railway* (1887) 12 AC 315 and *Horn v Sunderland* [1941] 2 KB 26), nevertheless an apportionment between capital and income elements is permissible for income tax purposes. In *Stoke-on-Trent City Council v Wood Mitchell & Co Ltd* [1979] STC 197, the Court of Appeal relied on a provision of the UK Capital Gains Tax Act (for which there is no equivalent in the Irish legislation) to justify just such an apportionment. However, it is difficult to see how a provision of the Capital Gains Tax Act could impose an income tax charge if one did not exist previously (the logic of the Capital Gains Tax legislation is rather to bring into charge only amounts which are not already liable to income tax).

In *Lang v Rice* [1984] STC 172, the taxpayer's premises were destroyed by a bomb. Under the terms of the relevant statute, he was entitled to receive *inter alia* distinct and separable amounts of compensation:

(a) in order to restore his premises; and
(b) to make good his loss of profits due to the loss of his premises.

It was held that amount (b) was liable to income tax under general principles.

Compensation for profits foregone

Compensation paid in respect of revenue expenditure incurred by a trader will itself be revenue in nature. Thus, in *Alliance & Dublin Consumers Gas Co v McWilliams* I ITR 207, compensation for the loss of use of ships and also for their running costs while detained by the UK customs authorities were held to be on revenue account (see also *Ensign Shipping Co v IRC* 12 TC 116 and *Burmah Steamship Co v IRC* 16 TC 67).

By way of contrast, in *Crabb v Blue Star Line* 39 TC 402, compensation received by a ship operator under an insurance policy for a delay in the building of a ship was held to relate to the acquisition of a capital asset and was therefore itself on capital account. The court reasoned that the compensation was paid not in respect of the loss of profits caused by the delay, but to defray the price paid for the ships, which had been computed on the basis of a timely delivery date.

In *Donald Fisher (Ealing) Ltd v Spencer* [1982] STC 423, the taxpayer recovered damages from their agent, because he had failed to serve the necessary notice under the terms of their lease to prevent the rent thereunder being increased to an excessive level. The taxpayer argued that the compensation related to a diminution in the value of its lease and was therefore capital in nature. This argument relied on the decision in *Tucker v Granada Motorway Services Ltd*, discussed at **5.307** below (where a payment to obtain a reduced rent under a business lease was held to be capital expenditure). The court held that in the present case there had been no alteration in the terms or conditions of the lease. Instead the agent had simply failed to implement properly the taxpayer's rights as established by those terms and conditions. Accordingly, the compensation related to the excess rent paid by the taxpayer and was of a revenue nature. Walton J commented:

> If compensation is received which is in substance payable in respect of either the non-receipt of what ought to have been received or the extra expense which would not have been incurred if all had gone properly it seems to me that the principle is exactly the same.

(See also *Gray v Lord Penrhyn* 21 TC 252 where compensation for defalcations caused by the negligence of an auditor was held to be taxable trading income). It should be borne in mind that the extent to which a compensation payment is not liable to income tax, a liability to capital gains tax may arise (see *Lang v Rice* [1984] STC 172; *Pennine Raceway v Kirkless MC* [1989] STC 122).

In *Murray v ICI Ltd* 44 TC 175, the taxpayer (ICI) granted exclusive patent licenses in respect of one of its products in return for royalties (which were admittedly taxable). In addition, it entered into a 'keep out' covenant in return for a lump sum, whereby it agreed not to manufacture or sell the product in any of the territories affected. It was held that the lump sum was capital in nature, being received in return for agreeing to the imposition of a substantial restriction of the taxpayer's trading activities (see also *Margerson v Tyresoles Ltd* 25 TC 59 and compare *Higgs v Olivier* at **5.204**).

By way of contrast, in *Thompson v Magnesium Electron Ltd* 26 TC 1, the taxpayer was a producer of magnesium which proposed to manufacture its own requirement of chlorine. The cost of so doing would have been significantly reduced by sales of caustic soda (a by-product of manufacturing chlorine). ICI, which manufactured chlorine, subsequently entered into two concurrent 10-year agreements with the taxpayer whereby:

(a) the taxpayer was to buy all of its chlorine from ICI at an agreed price; and
(b) the taxpayer was not to manufacture chlorine or caustic soda, and ICI agreed to pay the taxpayer an agreed sum for every ton of caustic soda which the taxpayer would otherwise have produced (based on its consumption of chlorine).

The Court of Appeal found that, on the facts, agreement (a) and (b) constituted a single composite agreement. On this basis, the court proceeded to hold that the sums received by the taxpayer under (b) were paid as part of the consideration of obtaining a firm contract for the supply of chlorine; accordingly they were to be treated as trading receipts. The Court of Appeal's analysis seems to give insufficient weight to the fact that the immediate consideration for the sums in question was the restrictive covenant. However, the decision can be justified on the basis that the restriction was not sufficiently substantial to rank as a capital transaction. Alternatively it could be said that the sums in question were received in the form of rebates on purchases of trading stock and thus acquired an income character (see also *Orchard Wine and Spirit Co v Loynes* 33 TC 97, where the receipt of commission on future sales as consideration for the sale of a secret formula, a trademark and goodwill was held to be on revenue account).

Where a court awards damages based on profits foregone, but the damages are not themselves taxable, it will take into account the tax status of that income. If the income would have been subject to tax, then the damages will be based on the after-tax amount of such income (*British Transport Commission v Gourley* [1956] AC 188 (discussed at **10.409**)). This rule does not apply where the damages are themselves taxable (*Parsons v BNM Laboratories* [1964] 1 QB 95, followed in *Hickey & Co v Roches Stores* [1980] ILRM 107). In the latter case, the court in effect assumes that the tax payable on the damages equates to the tax that would have been payable on the profits foregone. This reflects the court's pragmatic refusal to become unnecessarily involved in detailed tax calculations, although this approach clearly results in a rather rough form of justice (see also *John v James* [1986] STC 352, where the court in effect assumed that the damages would be taxable in a complex case while it was unclear whether or not this would in fact turn out to be the position). A sum based on profits foregone may be capital in nature (as eg in *Van den Berghs Ltd v Clark* and see *McGhie & Sons v BTC* [1963] 1 QB 125), but if it is liable to capital gains tax then the rule in *Gourley* will still not apply (*Pennine Raceway v Kirkless* MC [1989] STC 122).

In *Deeny v Gooda Walker* [1996] STC 299 the taxpayers were awarded damages in respect of lost profits (see **5.204**). As both the damages and the profits fell within Sch D Case II, the level of damages did not take into account the impact of tax. The court held, however, that when calculating interest on the damages, it was permissible to take tax effects into account. This followed (broadly) because interest was designed to compensate for a delay in the receipt of (*after tax*) cash receipts. In the instant case, a 'broad brush' approach was applied on a group-wide basis, with the consent of the plaintiffs (see also *Tate & Lyle v GLC* [1983] 2 AC 809, where the calculation involved was straightforward).

In *Stoke-on-Trent City Council v Wood Mitchell & Co Ltd* [1979] STC 197, it was unclear whether or not a sum of damages was liable to tax (and the Inland Revenue were not prepared to give an undertaking as to whether or not they would in fact seek to tax it, in contrast to the position in *West Suffolk CC v W Rought* 3 All ER 216). The court held that in such a case the benefit of the doubt should go to the defendant and the damages should be paid without any reduction in respect of tax (note also *Patrick Sullivan v Southern Health Board* [1997] 3 IR 123); however, in *The Scouts Association Trust Corporation v Secretary of State for the Environment* [2005] NPC 106, the UK Court of Appeal held that it was the responsibility of the Tribunal fixing the compensation to arrive at a view on the tax position which was merely one of a number of uncertain and contingent factors to be taken into account by it.

5.207 Grants and subsidies

The identification of subsidies and grants as income or capital will normally depend on their purpose. If the purpose of the relevant payment is to relieve the company of the burden of trading expenses, to supplement its trading receipts or to make good trading losses then the payment will be revenue in nature. Thus, in *Jacob International v O'Cléirigh* III ITR 165, training grants received from the IDA were held by the Supreme Court to be revenue in nature. Hederman J said:

> From the viewpoint of the company, the object of qualifying for the grant was to aid its new industrial venture in Ireland by making subventions towards the relief of the wages and salaries bill in the training of new employees in that industrial undertaking.
>
> In my opinion, money paid and received in those circumstances does not qualify for inclusion in the company's accounts as capital. It passed to the company as payment of the wages and salaries bill and as an incentive to encourage the engagement of new employees. On receipt of the money, the company's capital position was unaffected in any direct way, whereas its outgoing, and, therefore, its trading or profit or loss position, was palpably and directly affected by the amounts received under the training grant. I find no essential difference between the accountancy status of those payments and that of any other trading revenue. They merely reduced the figure to be entered up in the annual accounts under the category of disbursements for wages and salaries.

(See to similar effect, *Smart v Lincolnshire Sugar* 20 TC 643, where repayments to defray the cost of manufacturing sugar were held to be on revenue account, and *British Commonwealth International Newsfilm Agency Ltd v Mahony* 40 TC 550, where covenanted payments made to cover a trader's annual trading losses were held to be trading receipts).

In *Seaham Harbour Dock Co v Crook* 16 TC 333, a payment made to enable the taxpayer to carry out capital works was held to be itself capital (this was notwithstanding that it was calculated on the basis of the interest costs of the project). By way of contrast, in *Burman v Thorn Domestic Appliances* [1982] STC 407, a grant specifically designed to relieve the taxpayer's interest costs in respect of a capital project was held to be taxable (on similar logic to that applied in the *Jacob International* case).

Where the immediate purpose of a grant is indeterminate (ie it is not clearly earmarked for revenue or capital purposes) the UK courts have held that it should be treated as a revenue receipt (see eg *Poulter v Gay John Processes* [1985] STC 174 and *Ryan v Crabtree Denims Ltd* [1987] STC 402, where Hoffman J suggested that receipt of a very large sum might however still qualify as capital). It may be that the Irish courts would take a more conservative approach on the basis that the benefit of any doubt should go to the taxpayer (see **1.406**).

In *White v G & M Davies* [1979] STC 415, a dairy farmer was entitled under EC Council regulations to a grant if he changed from dairy to beef cattle. To benefit from the grant he had to undertake to give up selling or supplying milk or milk products for a period of four years, while maintaining his livestock numbers throughout the period. Under the regulation, the grant was to be 'fixed at such level that may be considered as compensation for temporary loss of income from the marketing of the products in question'. On entering into the scheme, the farmer ceased to sell any milk or milk products and shortly afterwards received the first instalment of the grant. The taxpayer contended that the sum was not taxable as a profit of the trade, being a capital sum in consideration for his ceasing to engage in the trade of dairy farming and ceasing to sell milk products. It was held that the grant was paid, not in return for the cancellation of the whole structure of his profit making apparatus, nor for the sterilisation of assets used in his trade, but as compensation for a temporary loss of income from the marketing of the products in question. The grant was a payment designed to make good the loss of income which, if it had been received, would have been taxable, and was therefore itself taxable as income. The argument that the money did not arise from the trade of farming was also rejected as the undertaking given was considered a positive obligation to conduct the farming trade in a particular way distinguishing the case of *Higgs v Olivier* above (see also *IRC v Biggar* [1982] STC 677 where a grant received by a farmer to convert from milk producing to meat producing was held to relate to the loss of profits arising during the process of transition, but contrast the Circuit Court decision reported in [1990] *ITR* 45). The treatment of Mulder compensation payments in the hands of farmers is discussed at **7.103**. The Revenue accept that grants received by doctors under the drug target scheme are capital to the extent that they are applied in acquiring capital items: see *Tax Briefing 30*.

A 'reverse premium' (ie a financial inducement to a tenant to enter into a lease) will be capital in nature if it relates to the lease itself (see *CIR v Wattie* [1998] STC 1160), but will be revenue in nature if eg it relates to the rent paid under the lease or is designed to relieve other revenue expenditure associated with the lease. The issue may also arise as to whether the rent payable under the lease was incurred partly to obtain the benefit of the reverse premium (see **12.204**). In all cases, the precise purpose of the grant, subsidy, etc received by the taxpayer must be ascertained, taking into account not only the relevant documentation but also all the relevant surrounding circumstances.

A number of employment grants and recruitment subsidies which would be taxable under Sch D Cases I or II on general principles are the subject of specific statutory exemptions as follows:

(a) employment grants made under s 10(5)(a) of the Údarás na Gaeltachta Act, 1979 under the schemes known as 'Deontais Fhostaíochta ó Údarás na Gaeltachta do Thionscnaimh Sheirbhíse Idir-Náisiúnta' and 'Deontais Fhostaíochta ó Údarás na Gaeltachta do Thionscail Bheaga Dhéantúsaíochta' (TCA 1997, s 223);

(b) employment grants made under s 21(5)(a) of the Industrial Development Act 1986 under the scheme known as 'Scheme Governing the Making of Employment Grants to Small Industrial Undertakings' (TCA 1997, s 223);

(c) employment grants made under s 10(5)(a) of the Údarás na Gaeltachta Act, 1979 under the schemes known as 'Deontais Fhostaíochta ó Údarás na Gaeltachta do Ghnóthais Mhóra/Mheánmháide Thionsclaíochta' (TCA 1997, s 224);

(d) employment grants made under s 21(5)(a) of the Industrial Development Act 1986 under the scheme known as 'Scheme Governing the Making of Employment Grants to Medium/Large Industrial Undertakings' (TCA 1997, s 224);

(e) employment grants made under s 3 or 4 of the Shannon Free Airport Development Company Limited (Amendment) Act 1970 Employment grants made under s 21(5)(a) of the Industrial Development Act 1986 under the scheme known as 'Scheme Governing the Making of Employment Grants to Small Industrial Undertakings' (TCA 1997, s 225);

(f) employment grants made under s 25 of the Industrial Development Act 1986 (TCA 1997, s 225);

(g) employment grants made under s 12 of the Industrial Development Act 1993 (TCA 1997, s 225);
(h) under TCA 1997, s 226 employment grants or recruitment subsidies made to an employer under:
  (i) the Back to Work Allowance Scheme,
  (ii) any scheme established by the Minister for Enterprise, Trade and Employment for the purposes of promoting the employment of individuals who have been unemployed for more than three years,
  (iii) any operating agreement between Minister for Enterprise, Trade and Employment and a County Enterprise Board,
  (iv) the Employment Support Scheme administered by the National Rehabilitation Board,
  (v) the Wage Subsidy Scheme administered by the Department of Social Protection,
  (vi) the European Union Leader II Community Initiative 1994 to 1999 administered by the Minister for Agriculture and Food,
  (vii) the European Operational Programme for Local Urban and Rural Development administered by Area Development Management Limited,
  (viii) the Special European Union Programme for Peace and Reconciliation in Northern Ireland and the Border Counties of Ireland,
  (ix) the Joint Northern Ireland/Ireland INTERREG Programme 1994 to 1999 approved by the European Commission,
  (x) any initiative of the International Fund for Ireland,
  (xi) the JobsPlus scheme administered by the Department of Social Protection.

Grants made towards the cost of acquiring a capital asset while not taxable as such will normally reduce the cost of the relevant asset for capital allowance purposes: see **6.103**.

5.208 Voluntary payments

The position regarding voluntary payments is broadly comparable to the position prevailing under Sch E (see **10.107**). The fact the trader has no legal right to receive a particular sum does not mean that the sum is therefore outside the scope of Sch D Case I/Case II. The key issue is whether or not the trader receives the sum by virtue of being, or in his capacity, as a trader or whether he receives it for purely personal, compassionate or other non-trading reasons. The Sch E case law sometimes expresses this issue as the difference between the '*causa causans*' and the '*causa sine qua non*' of a payment (see **10.106**).

The importance in cases concerning voluntary payments of looking at the particular facts of each, and the principle that it is the nature of the payment in the hands of the recipient which counts, were noted by Buckley LJ in *Murray v Goodhews* [1978] STC 207:

> In my opinion, a perusal of these authorities leads to the conclusion that every case of a voluntary payment … must be considered on its own facts to ascertain the nature of the receipt in the recipient's hands. All relevant circumstances must be taken into account.

In *Goodhews'* case, the taxpayer was the tenant of a number of tied public houses owned by a brewery company. The brewery company terminated a number of tenancy agreements and, although under no legal obligation to do so, made voluntary lump sum payments to the taxpayer over a two-year period. The taxpayer was assessed on these payments on the basis that they represented compensation for loss of profits due to the termination of the tenancies. It was held on the facts of the case that the sums were not trading receipts arising from his trade. There had been no negotiation on the amounts, there was no connection with the profits earned by the taxpayer nor were the payments linked with any future trading relationship between him and the brewery company.

In *Walker v Carnaby Harrower Barham and Pykett* 46 TC 501, an *ex gratia* payment made to a firm of accountants by a client who had decided not to reappoint them as auditors was held not to constitute trading income. Again, the mere fact that no such payment would have been made if the taxpayer had not previously acted as auditors was held to be insufficient to give rise to a taxable receipt: in other words the profession was regarded as the *causa sine qua non,* but not the *causa causans* of the payment. Pennycuick J stated:

> It seems to me that a gift of that kind made by a former client cannot reasonably be treated as a receipt of a business which consists in rendering professional services. It does not seem to me that ordinary commercial principles require the bringing into account of this sort of voluntary payment, not made as the consideration for any services rendered by the firm, but by way of recognition of past services or by way of consolation for the termination of a contract …

A similar result occurred in *Simpson v John Reynolds & Co (Insurances) Ltd* [1975] STC 271, where a wholly unexpected and unsolicited gift, made in recognition of past services to a client over a long period of years, and after the business connection had ceased, was held not to be a receipt of the trade.

In *McGowan v Brown & Cousins* [1977] STC 342, the owner of a building estate voluntarily paid £2,500 to a firm of estate agents as compensation for the loss of the opportunity to secure profitable business acting as agents on sales of developed lots. The agents had previously accepted uneconomic fees in the hope of gaining the more profitable agency work to come. It was held that the £2,500 was a profit of the trade of estate agents. It was held that in determining whether a voluntary payment is taxable in the hands of the recipient, the material question was not who made the payment, but why the payment had accrued to the recipient.

In *Rolfe v Nagel* [1982] STC 53, the taxpayer was a diamond broker who had done unpaid work for a client who subsequently transferred his custom to a rival broker, H. The taxpayer felt aggrieved and pressed H for compensation and eventually received a payment from him. The Court of Appeal held that the immediate purpose of the payment was to compensate the taxpayer for work done or profits foregone, and was accordingly a revenue receipt. The fact that the ultimate purpose of the payer in making the payment was to preserve good trading relationships did not affect the nature of the receipt.

A payment which is made in order as to induce or to facilitate the future provision of services will be taxable as income from the trade or profession. Thus, in *IRC v Falkirk Ice Rink* [1985] STC 434, an *ex gratia* payment made to the operators of an ice rink by some of its customers in order to supplement its income, was held to be trading income, notwithstanding its non-contractual nature.

In *Robinson v Dolan* I ITR 927, the taxpayer was a British subject who was well known as a loyalist prior to the creation of the Irish Free State. This led to his business being boycotted and his goods looted, with the result that the business was practically ruined. The British Government paid him an *ex gratia* sum under a scheme designed to compensate for hardship and loss suffered by its supporters. The High Court held that the sum was not taxable. Hanna J commented:

> The main argument put forward by the Commissioners was founded upon the fact that [the taxpayers] claim was calculated upon a trading loss and that he got it as a trader. … I think there are two answers to this – first, his being a trader is not the *causa causans* of his compensation. It is merely the *causa sine qua non*; and secondly, the compensation is primarily for special hardship suffered as a loyalist, and the claimant merely proves his hardship by giving evidence of his trade loss. The amount claimed was based upon his incapacity or inability to make a profit out of his business.

5.209 Exclusivity payments

A further group of tax cases concerns receipts under agreements between garage proprietors and petrol marketing companies where, in return for certain amounts payable by the petrol company, the garage proprietor undertook to buy only the particular company's brand of petrol. These are very much borderline cases. In general, these types of agreement provided for the sums payable by the petrol company to be applied by the garage proprietor in a particular way. On general principles, a lump sum which is paid in respect of a substantial restriction on the taxpayer's activities should normally be capital. However, if the payments in such a case are made in an income form, then these should nevertheless be taxable. In practice, the results of the cases have tended to vary depending on the particular application of the payments required by the agreement in question.

In *Evans v Wheatley* 38 TC 216, the proprietor agreed to accept a reimbursement from the company up to a certain limit of sums expended on sales promotion and advertising. Apart from committing him exclusively to buy from the petrol company, the agreement placed restrictions upon the proprietor's right to dispose of the business. He contended that, since he did not in fact incur any expenses upon sales promotion or advertising, the sums received were on capital account in respect of the restrictive covenant in the agreement and should not be taxable as income. This was rejected by the court and the receipts were held to be taxable on revenue account.

In *IRC v Coia* 38 TC 334, the proprietor agreed to take all his requirements of motor fuels exclusively from the company for 10 years. In return he received contributions from the company towards the cost of purchasing additional ground and building extensions to his garage and workshop. It was held that the sums were in the nature of capital receipts, being the reimbursement of capital expenditure incurred and paid in consideration for accepting a restriction in his future trading rights. In coming to this decision, the Scottish Court of Session relied on two matters. First, it relied on the nature of the payments themselves and on the agreement which contemplated they would be used to effect improvements in the business premises. Secondly, it relied upon the agreement tying the proprietor to a particular type of petrol, considering that the effect of this was to reduce the goodwill of the garage business.

The *Coia* decision was followed in *McLaren v Needham* 39 TC 37 where the agreement provided that the petrol company make a payment to cover three items: (a) the redecoration of the proprietor's petrol station in the company's standard colours; (b) the cost of advertising; and (c) such other items as might mutually be agreed. In fact, the sum paid to the proprietor was applied by him to items of a capital character, including a new canopy at the service station. It was held that the payments were to be treated as capital in the hands of the proprietor as having been in effect made under the third heading.

The payments by the petrol company were also held to be capital receipts in *Walker W Saunders Ltd v Dixon* 40 TC 329 where, although there was some initial similarity with the facts in *Evans v Wheatley*, the sums paid by the petrol company were in fact applied in structural alterations to the proprietor's site. Although these type of payments do not necessarily become capital just because of what the recipient does with them, the use of the money was linked in this case to a supplemental agreement. On the facts of the case, including evidence of the surrounding circumstances, it was considered that the payments contemplated by that agreement included capital items and that the payments in question were in fact applied largely on capital account.

In the case of *Tanfield v Carr* [1999] STC (SCD) 213 a lump sum payment by a petrol company pursuant to an agreement that the garage proprietor would not sell any fuels other than the petrol company's for the period of the agreement, was held to be revenue in nature. The agreement did not specifically provide how the funds were to be used. The garage proprietor claimed that it was a capital receipt. In reaching their decision that the payment was revenue in nature, the Appeal Commissioners examined the business carried on by the taxpayer and held the restrictions being placed on the taxpayer by the petrol company only affected a small part of the taxpayer's business. The taxpayer was also involved in the sale of tow brackets and the forecourt turnover only represented 30 per cent of the total turnover.

In some cases, exclusivity payments may be structured as an 'abatable loan', ie the loan is written off over the life of the agreement. It would appear that only the amount written off in each accounting year should be treated as a receipt (it will then be necessary to classify it as capital or revenue in nature). The benefit of any favourable interest terms granted in connection with the loan is unlikely to be taxable, since this will not usually represent money or money's worth.

5.210 Interest income as a trading receipt

A person may receive interest income in the course of his trading activities. In most cases, any such interest receivable is not taxed under Sch D Case I or II and, if credited in the accounts, should be deducted in the computation of the taxable trading profits and should be taxable separately under Sch D Case III. In certain trades (eg banking) interest may be received as a trading receipt and, if so, it may be assessed under Sch D Case I (although the inspector may elect to tax it instead under Sch D Case III – see below).

In *Bank Line Ltd v IRC* 49 TC 307, a company owned and operated a fleet of ships. It financed the replacement of ships from its own funds. Sums surplus to immediate business needs were set aside in a reserve fund and invested to be available for replacement of ships in the future. The company claimed the investment income should be included as trading receipts in arriving at its trading income available for set off against trading losses from earlier years. It was held that the interest and dividends in question could not be regarded as trading receipts because they arose from a fund that was not actively employed and risked in the company's current trading. The case was distinguished from that of *Liverpool & London Globe Insurance Co v Bennett* 6 TC 327. The latter case involved an English company carrying on business in Great Britain and abroad. Interest from funds invested abroad was assessed by the inspector and were held by the House of Lords to be properly included as trading receipts under Sch D Case I. The funds invested abroad were considered to be an essential part of the conduct of the fire insurance business of the company in each year in which the funds were at risk in respect of their current policies. Its business of insurance included providing and keeping funds ready to meet its obligations as insurer for claims under its policies as and when they arose. The funds were clearly held, risked and employed in the business of insurance.

In *Owen v Sassoon* 32 TC 101, interest received by a Lloyd's underwriter on securities deposited with the Society of Lloyd's as security against his default on his obligations was held to arise as a trading receipt of his business as underwriter and could be taxed under Sch D Case I. The securities were regarded as being employed and risked in the business. The treatment of Lloyd's underwriters is dealt with at **13.506**.

In *Northend v White and Leonard* [1975] STC 317, interest received by a solicitor on general deposit account was held not to be 'immediately derived' from his profession (see the discussion at **16.202**, where the relevant test is more narrowly phrased).

In *Nuclear Electric plc v Bradley* [1996] STC 405, the taxpayer company had taken over the business of supplying nuclear energy from the public sector. This entailed assuming liability for significant future costs relating, *inter alia* to the decommissioning of reactors and the disposal of radioactive waste. The taxpayer accordingly set aside funds to meet these liabilities and claimed that the interest arising on investment of those funds should be treated as trading income.

The House of Lords rejected this contention. It was held that the making of investments was neither an integral, nor indeed any part of the taxpayer's business; furthermore, the investments were in no sense employed in the business of producing electricity. On a wider front, the House indicated that there was a spectrum at each end of which it was clear either that investment income was not on trading account (as in the taxpayer's case) or that it was on trading account (as in the use, for example, of a bank or insurance company). Between these two extremes there could be cases where the position was unclear. The House left open the possibility that income on short-term investments to meet current liabilities might qualify as trading income.

In the main, therefore, it is banks, insurance companies and other financial institutions that earn interest income taxable under Sch D Case I (see to this effect the views of the Revenue Commissioners in *Tax Briefing 44*). The fact that such interest income may be taxed under Sch D Case I as a trading receipt does not necessarily mean that the Revenue must tax it under that Case. There is a general rule of income tax law that income that may be taxed under more than one Case of Sch D may be taxed under the Case the Revenue selects. In practice, with banks and other persons carrying on banking business, the Sch D Case I basis is almost invariably used. With other types of business, even where it might be argued that the interest arose from funds employed and risked in the business, the Revenue generally assesses interest income under Sch D Case III.

The Revenue Commissioners have stated that in practice interest received under the terms of the Prompt Payments Act 1997 may be treated as a trading receipt for tax purposes at the discretion of the taxpayer (*Tax Briefing 31*); similar treatment will apply to interest and compensation paid under SI 580/2012, The European Communities (Late Payment in Commercial Transactions) Regulations 2012 which replaced SI 388/2002 implementing the European Directive on Late Payment in Commercial Transactions (*Tax Briefing 52*).

5.211 Transfer pricing

A transfer pricing regime based on the OECD Guidelines was introduced with effect for tax years from 1 January 2011. It applies to both domestic and international trading (but not financing) transactions carried out between associated entities. The regime does not apply to contracts or terms and conditions agreed before 1 July 2010. The provisions do not apply to micro, small or medium-sized enterprises, broadly as defined by European Commission Recommendation 2003/361/EC of 6 May 2003 (TCA 1997, Pt 35A, as inserted by FA 2010, s 42).

5.3 Deductions

5.301 What expenses are deductible?

The Taxes Acts do not lay down how the taxable profits (or losses) of a trade should be computed. TCA 1997, s 65(1) simply states that '… tax shall be charged under Case I or Case II of Sch D on the full amount of the profits and gains … of the year of assessment'. TCA 1997, s 81(2) provides that in computing such profits or gains, sums falling within prescribed categories will *not* be permissible deductions.

TCA 1997, s 81(2)) therefore does not specify what items can be deducted, but simply prescribes certain expenses which *cannot* be deducted in computing profits – these are dealt with comprehensively in this division. It may be noted that the basic scheme of TCA 1997, s 81(2) has been supplemented by a number of subsequent provisions. In some cases, these provisions consist of additional prohibitions against expenses which are not caught by TCA 1997, s 81(2) (TCA 1997, s 840, which disallows entertaining expenses: see **5.313**). In other cases, these provisions consist of a relaxation of the prohibitions set out in TCA 1997, s 81(2) (eg TCA 1997, s 86, which grants an allowance for the costs of registering trademarks (see **5.308**)).

It is essential that the expenditure is actually borne by the trader. Thus, in *Rutter v Charles Sharpe & Co Ltd* [1979] STC 711 the taxpayer established a trust which was to apply income in favour of the taxpayer's employees. The taxpayer had the right to wind up the trust at any time and recover its payments. The payments were held to be non-deductible since they gave rise to a corresponding asset (the right of recovery), in the same way as a loan. Conversely, in *Bolton v Halpern & Woolf* [1981] STC 14, a partnership had agreed that any loss arising on a guarantee should be borne by only one of the partners, H. H died, and the loss subsequently crystallised. The Inland Revenue argued that the loss was not deductible, since the partners at the time the loss was incurred were entitled to recover the loss against H's personal representatives. The Inland Revenue relied specifically on the UK equivalent of TCA 1997, s 81(2)(k) which denies relief for 'any sum recoverable under an insurance or contract of indemnity'. The

Court of Appeal rejected this contention, holding in effect that the *allocation* of profits and losses between partners (including partners who subsequently retired) could not affect the deductibility of expenses wholly and exclusively incurred for the purposes of the partnership trade.

Where the taxpayer subsequently becomes entitled to a rebate of an expense incurred, this should be treated as a trading receipt. The Revenue Commissioners have emphasised this point in connection with rebates of lease payments (see *Tax Leaflet IT 52*), and it is understood that they have issued similar warnings in connection with rebates in respect of insurance premiums (see [1996] *ITR* 47). Grants and other contributions towards expenditure (other than by way of insurance or indemnity contracts) should normally be treated as trading receipts as opposed to being 'netted off' against the relevant expenditure (see *O'Cléirigh v Jacobs International* III ITR 165).

TCA 1997, s 81(2) prohibits the deduction, unless specifically permitted by some other provision in the Tax Acts, of any of the following items of expenditure, losses, etc:

(a) any expenses not being money, wholly and exclusively laid out or expended for the purposes of the trade or profession;

(b) any expenses of maintenance of the trader or his family, or any sums spent for any other domestic or private purposes;

(c) the rent of any dwelling house or domestic offices, except for such part thereof as is used for the trade or profession;

(d) any sum expended for repairs of premises or for items used for the purposes of a trade or profession in excess of the sum actually expended;

(e) any loss not connected with or arising out of the trade or profession;

(f) any capital withdrawn from, or any sum employed or intended to be employed as capital in the trade or profession;

(g) any capital employed in improvements of premises occupied for the purposes of the trade or profession;

(h) any interest which might have been made if any such sums as aforesaid had been laid out as interest;

(i) any provision for, or write off of, debts, except for any debts proved to the satisfaction of the inspector to be bad debts and except for provisions for specific doubtful debts estimated to be bad;

(j) any average loss beyond the actual amount of loss after adjustment;

(k) any sum recoverable under an insurance or contract of indemnity;

(l) any annuity, or other annual payment (other than interest) payable out of the profits or gains of the trade; and

(m) any royalty or other sum paid in respect of the user of a patent.

(n) any amount paid or payable under an agreement or understanding whereby a person is obliged to make a payment to a connected person resident outside the State for an adjustment made to the profits of the connected person where relief may be given under the terms of a double tax treaty. This exclusion was inserted by Finance (No 2) Act 2008. It is understood that claims were being made for a deduction for payments made in compensation for transfer pricing adjustments made in other jurisdictions and this measure was introduced so that persons will have to engage with Revenue to determine if relief for such payments can be claimed.

The reference in (a) above to expenses being *money* expended for the purposes of the trade may be taken literally to imply that payments in kind should not be deductible under the tax rules. This may be too narrow a reading of the wording; certainly in practice, it is accepted that expenses represented by accruals and unpaid creditors are fully allowable in principle, notwithstanding that no moneys may have passed at the time at which the relevant accounts were drawn up.

TCA 1997, s 81(2) also provides that in the case of expenditure on the repair of premises, or on the supply, repair or alterations of any implements, utensils or articles employed for the purposes of the trade or profession, the amount deductible must not exceed the sum actually expended on those items so employed. Since the whole question of repairs to premises, machinery, etc and their distinction from improvements, alterations, etc has proved over the years to be one of the more potentially contentious tax issues, this matter is discussed in more detail in **5.309**.

5.302 When are expenses deductible?

In the same way that tax law requires that profits must be realised, it also generally requires that expenses must be incurred before they can be deducted. Thus, no deduction can be made simply because the time has arrived when it would be prudent or desirable to incur such expense, but without any actual expense having actually been incurred (see *Naval Colliery Co Ltd v IRC* 12 TC 1017; *Collins & Sons v IRC* 12 TC 773 and note *Meat Traders Ltd v Cushing* [1997] STC (SCD) 245). In *Spencer v IRC* 32 TC 111, the expense of meeting claims for workmen's compensation was held to be deductible only at the point in time when the claims were conceded or, if disputed, at the time the dispute was determined. In *Merchant (Peter) Ltd v Stedeford* 30 TC 496 it was held that a liability to replace broken crockery at the end of a fixed-term contract could only be recognised once the contract had been completed.

As noted at **5.201**, in *Sun Insurance Co v Clark* 6 TC 59 it was stated that there was no fixed rule of law governing the time when receipts or expenses should be brought into account. Thus, while a liability should not normally be recognised until it is incurred, it is not contrary to tax law to allocate the corresponding expense to the future periods to which it relates by reference to the 'matching principle', normally on a periodic or time basis (see the *Gallagher* case, discussed at **5.102** and **5.310**).

If an overhead is incurred and fully consumed in the period of account, it will normally be treated as an expense of that period, even if it may lead to benefits in future years. This approach is exemplified in the *Vallambrosa* case, where the yearly cost of tending rubber plants was held to be deductible, even though the plants would not become productive for several years.

In *Albion Rovers FC v IRC* 33 TC 331, the taxpayers were obliged to pay their players (who were under 15-month contracts) for a period of six-months when no matches were being played (the 'close season'). The taxpayers accordingly claimed the cost of paying their players for that part of the close season which fell *after* the end of their accounts year. In a sense, this case is the mirror image of *Vallambrosa*, in that the taxpayers were seeking to *bring forward* expenditure into the year of account where the benefit would be received. However, subject to rare exceptions, wages will clearly be a time-related cost and will be matched to the period of which they are incurred.

As Lord Reid pointed out in the *Albion* case, it would also normally be impracticable in any event to allocate wages to the periods in which the benefits from paying them are enjoyed. This can be seen most clearly in the case of payroll costs incurred in the areas of marketing or research and development. The same argument applies to many other recurring expenses, such as repairs, where the benefit of restoring an asset to working order will often be enjoyed over several periods of account (see also *Worsley Breweries v IRC* 17 TC 349, where the expenses of revising previous sets of accounts were held to be deductible in the year in which they were incurred, and not in the years to which the accounts related).

In the *Albion* case, Lord Reid also made clear that it is the date on which an expense is incurred as opposed to the date on which it becomes *payable* which is critical. He said:

> I think that ultimately it was conceded that a sum which became payable during the year but was not actually paid until later might be a proper deduction, but even so I think that the proposition is too narrow. For example, if a transaction is completed during the year but the contract provides for postponement of payment of the whole or part of the price until a later date, it may well be that the whole price is a good deduction during the current year, although not payable until after the end of that year.

The observations above must be qualified in respect of contingent liabilities. In *Southern Railways of Peru Ltd v Owen* 37 TC 602 Lord Radcliffe commented as follows:

> I think that, for liabilities as for debts, their proper treatment in annual statements of profit depends not upon the legal form but upon the trader's answers to two separate questions. The first is: Have I adequately stated my profits for the year if I do not include some figure in respect of these obligations? The second is: do the circumstances of the case, which include the techniques of established accounting practice, make it possible to supply a figure reliable enough for the purpose?

In the *Southern Railway* case, the taxpayer had claimed the cost of a provision for its liability to pay *ex gratia* sums to employees on their leaving its employment. The sums increased in proportion to the employees' length of service but in certain circumstances ceased to be payable altogether. The House of Lords held that on the facts, the provision which had been made was *not* deductible, since it had not been calculated on sound actuarial principles. Lord Radcliffe observed:

> I am bound to say that … the charges for retirement benefits which the Appellant has claimed to make were well on the wrong side of what was permissible. When account is taken of all the circumstances I should have thought that the sums charged were a very long way from affording a scientific appraisement of the additional burden arising in respect of the year's services, and were, therefore, in the nature of a rough reserve against the future rather than a measured provision.

By way of contrast, provision made in similar circumstances was held to be allowable in *IRC v Titaghur Jute Factory* [1978] STC 166. In that case, the taxpayer company became liable to pay gratuities to certain of its employees on their leaving their employment. The amount of the gratuity was to be calculated by reference to each employee's salary and length of service at the date of leaving. Faced with this liability, the company decided to make provision annually to meet the liability rather than to charge the actual liability in the company's accounts for the year in which the payment was made. The total accrued liability to pay the gratuity in respect of its employees in an accounting year, taking into account the service of the employees in prior years as required by the statute, was held to be an allowable deduction.

In *Johnston v Britannia Airways* [1994] STC 763, a provision for the future overhaul costs of aeroplane engines was allowed in the case of an airline operator. The prohibition in the UK equivalent to TCA 1997, s 81(2)(d), which apparently permits a deduction only for sums *actually expended* on repairs, was not applicable, since (it seems) the process of overhauling entails the servicing, rather than the repairing, of assets (and note the decision of the UK Special Commissioners in *Jenners Princes Street Edinburgh* [1998] STC (SCD) 196 discussed at **5.309**).

In *Herbert Smith (a firm) v Honour* [1999] STC 173, it was held that the taxpayer was entitled to a deduction for a provision of future rental payments in respect of business premises which had become surplus to requirements; the UK Revenue had argued that the rental payments could only be deducted as they were actually incurred. The court took the view that under generally accepted accounting principles, the prudence concept required that in certain cases losses should be anticipated. The earlier decision to contrary effect in *Collins & Sons v IRC* 12 TC 773 was distinguished on the basis that the provision there was not justified by reference to generally accepted accounting principles.

It is difficult to reconcile the court's analysis in the *Southern Railway* case, and the actual decisions in the *Titaghur* and *Britannia* cases, with the decisions in the *Spencer* and *Merchant* cases. Certainly, the principle that the taxpayer may in some cases claim expenditure in advance of actually legally incurring it differs from the approach generally adopted in respect of trading receipts (see **5.201**). It may be noted that Lord Radcliffe's analysis in the *Southern Railway* case relied in part on the decision in *Harrison & Cronk & Sons* 20 TC 612, which was a rather special case (see **5.201**). Furthermore, Lord Radcliffe took the view that the reserve in *Sun Insurance Co v Clark* 6 TC 59 was in the nature of a contingent liability, whereas the better view seems to be that it represented a deferral of income (see **5.201**). Nevertheless, the analysis in the *Southern Railway* case is generally accepted in Ireland as correct. On this basis, the decisions in the *Merchant* and *Spencer* cases may be regarded as of doubtful authority.

The UK Inland Revenue have since confirmed that they accept the change of law as a result of the decision in *Herbert Smith (a firm) v Honour* and that since the introduction of FRS12 in relation to provisions (introduced with effect for accounting periods ending on or after 23 March 1999) that a provision will be tax deductible once it has been made in accordance with FRS12 except if it relates to capital or is specifically disallowed by the taxes legislation. In broad terms, FRS 12 prescribes that a provision should be recognised only where a business has incurred a present obligation as a result of past events and where that obligation will probably result in a financial outlay for the business which can be reliably estimated. The obligation concerned may be legally binding or may be constructive in the sense that the business has by its past actions created a valid expectation that it will honour the obligation. The provision in *Johnston v Britannia Airways* which related to a future obligation would not appear to meet the relatively stringent criteria of FRS 12; it would appear that under those criteria no provision could be recognised until a contract to undertake the servicing work had been executed with a third party. In contrast, an obligation to maintain assets under the terms of an operating lease would fall within the terms of FRS 12.

The Revenue Commissioners have indicated that they intend to follow the Inland Revenue's approach in *Tax Briefing 41*. The Revenue have also issued a precedent stating that they accept there is no statutory rule preventing a deduction for a provision for a loss in respect of legal proceedings. It remains open to question whether the Irish Courts would accept that a provision for a probable loss would give rise to a deductible expense but the position is unlikely to be challenged by taxpayers.

Where a liability can only be estimated at the time the accounts are prepared, it seems that the true figure may be substituted when this is known (*Bernhard v Gahan* 13 TC 723). In practice, the Revenue Commissioners will not normally seek to reopen *bona fide* accounting estimates. Furthermore, the principle can hardly apply to contingent liabilities which are, by their very nature, estimates.

Where a mistake has been made in the accounts, it seems that any correction should be made in the light of all the facts known at the time correction is made. Thus in *Simpson v Jones* 44 TC 599, a liability of £28,000 had been omitted from the accounts. In the meanwhile, the creditor had released £25,000 of the liability. It was held that the liability should be included in the accounts, but in the sum of £3,000 only.

The position is different where a liability is correctly stated in the accounts, but is then subsequently released. In *British Mexican Petroleum Co Ltd v Jackson* 16 TC 570 a trader who was in financial difficulty obtained a release from a liability to one of its creditors. It was held that this did not justify reopening the accounts for the year in which the liability was incurred. Furthermore, on the facts, the release did not constitute a trading receipt (the most plausible reason given being that it was equivalent to an additional contribution of capital see *Dispensing Canada Ltd v The Queen* 97 DTC 5463). However, by virtue of TCA 1997, s 87(1) a person carrying on a trade or profession who has incurred a liability, either for an item of purchases or for a trading expense which has been deducted in computing his taxable profits for any period of account, and that liability is subsequently released in whole or in part during the continuance of his business, then the amount of release must be included as a trading receipt in the period in which the release is affected.

Example 5.302.1

Messrs East and West purchase goods for resale in their trade from North Ltd at a cost of €8,000, which they debit as purchases in their accounts for the year end 31 December 2016. They pay €6,300 of their liability by 30 November 2017, at which date North Ltd agrees to write off the balance of the debt due to it. East and West are required to include €1,700 of the liability that was released as a trading receipt in arriving at their Sch D Case I profit for the year ended 31 December 2017.

The principle in the *British Mexican* case seems to have been followed in a decision of the Appeal Commissioners on 7 April 1997 (see *Taxfax,* 11 April 1997). The Appeal Commissioners held that VAT which ceased to be due and payable as a result of a switch from the cash receipts basis to the invoice basis did not constitute a trading receipt. Under FRS 12, more stringent criteria apply before accounting provisions may be properly charged against profits. As a consequence it would have been necessary in some cases to write back existing provisions. In *Tax Briefing 41*, the Revenue express the view that such a write back will give rise to a taxable profit where the original provision had been a deductible expense. It is arguable that a mere accounting adjustment of this nature, which does not impugn the correctness of previous accounting profits, is a non-taxable item.

Employee benefit schemes

Contributions to Employee Benefit Schemes will often be deductible under general principles (see *Heather v PE Consulting Group* 48 TC 293 at **5.307**). However, by virtue of TCA 1997, s 81A, inserted by FA 2005, s 17 and amended by FA 2008, s 25, with effect for contributions made on or after 31 January 2008, even those contributions which would be deductible on general principles will only be deductible under Sch D Case I or Case II if they are paid or payable to an Employee Benefit Scheme where *qualifying benefits* or *qualifying expenses* (see below) are paid out of the contributions in the same chargeable period or within nine months from the end of that chargeable period. The previous rules, which took effect for chargeable periods commencing 2 February 2005, are dealt with in the 2007 edition of this book.

For the purposes of these rules, an '*Employee Benefit Scheme*' is defined as a trust, scheme or other arrangement for the benefit of persons who are employees (including office holders, such as directors, as appropriate) of the person making contributions to the scheme (TCA 1997, s 81A(1)(a); (b)(iii)). The definition apparently does not cover schemes designed to benefit relatives of employees.

The rules do not apply to amounts which are deductible in respect of consideration for goods or services provided in the course of a trade or profession or in relation to an approved pension scheme within TCA 1997, Pt 17, an Approved Profit Sharing scheme or Employee Share Ownership Scheme within TCA 1997, Pt 30, or an accident benefit scheme (defined within TCA 1997, s 81A(1)(a) as an employee benefit scheme under which benefits may be provided only by reason of a person's disablement, or death, caused by an accident occurring during the person's service as an employee of the employer) (TCA 1997, s 81A(7)).

An *employee benefit contribution* is treated as being made if, as a result of any act or omission:

(I) any assets are held or may be used under an employee benefit scheme; or
(II) there is an increase in the total value of assets that are so held or may be so used (or a reduction of liabilities under an employee benefit scheme) (TCA 1997, s 81A(1)(b)).

This wording is designed to ensure that not only transfers by the employer to third parties such as trusts but the allocation of assets to a scheme by a declaration of trust on its part in relation to some of its existing assets also fall within the scope of the section.

A deduction in respect of any employee benefit contributions will be available in the first instance only to the extent that either:

(a) *qualifying benefits* are provided out of the contributions; or
(b) *qualifying expenses* are paid out of the contributions;

during the tax year in question, or within nine-months from the end of the year (TCA 1997, s 81A(3)(a)).

For these purposes *qualifying benefits* are provided where there is a payment of money or a transfer of assets, otherwise than by way of a loan, *and* either:

(a) the recipient is chargeable to income tax in respect of the provision of such benefits, or would be so chargeable, if he was resident, ordinarily resident and domiciled in the State; or
(b) a person other than the recipient is chargeable to income tax in respect of the provision of such benefits or would be so chargeable, if he was resident, ordinarily resident and domiciled in the State (TCA 1997, s 81A(1)(b)).

The above definition assumes that somebody apart from the recipient may be taxable on the benefit. This seems designed to cover eg benefits provided to a relative of an employee, which may be taxed on the employee under TCA 1997, s 116(2) (see **10.203**). However, as noted above, the section only seems to cover trusts, etc for the benefits of employees and not their relatives, etc. The wording ensures that the provision of a benefit to an employee who falls outside the scope of Irish taxation (eg as a result of being non-resident and carrying out all of his duties outside the State: see **13.607**) may still be a qualifying benefit.

For these purposes, '*qualifying expenses*' are all expenses incurred by the scheme manager in the operation of the scheme which would have been deductible if they had been incurred by the employer, but excluding the cost of providing any benefits to employees (ie the term is defined so as to avoid any potential double counting). A 'scheme manager' is a person who administers an employee benefit scheme or any person to whom an employer pays money or transfers an asset and such person is entitled or required under the scheme to retain or use the money or assets for, or in connection with, the provision of benefits to employees of the employer (TCA 1997, s 81A(1)(a)).

The primary provision states that a deduction is only allowed in respect of employer contributions to the extent that qualifying benefits or qualifying expenses are provided or paid in the same tax year or within nine-months from the end of that year (TCA 1997, s 81A(3)(a)). For these purposes qualifying benefits and expenses are matched against previous employer contributions (to the extent not already so matched under the primary provision). For these purposes, any payments made or received by the scheme manager other than employer contributions, qualifying benefits or qualifying expenses are disregarded, which is probably a statement of the obvious (TCA 1997, s 81A(3)(b)). The calculation of taxable profits may be adjusted retrospectively as necessary where benefits are provided or expenses paid within the nine-month period of grace (TCA 1997, s 81A(6)(b)).

The secondary provision states that where some or all of an amount of employer contributions is disallowed because there is an insufficiency of matching payments of qualifying payments and/or qualifying expenses made within nine-months from the end of the relevant tax year, those contributions may be allowed to the extent that qualifying benefits (but not qualifying expenses) are paid in a subsequent tax year (TCA 1997, s 81A(4)(a)). The contributions will be allowed in that tax year only to the extent that they have not already been taken into account under the primary provisions of TCA 1997, s 81A(3)(a) or already under the secondary provisions themselves (TCA 1997, s 81A(4)(b)(i)). Again, for these purposes, any payments made or received by the scheme manager other than employer contributions, qualifying benefits or qualifying expenses are disregarded (TCA 1997, s 81A(4)(b)(ii)).

Where a qualifying benefit is provided in the form of an asset rather than cash, rules apply in order to attach a monetary value to the benefit. Where the asset was acquired by the scheme manager it will generally be the amount paid by the trustees. However, if it was acquired by the scheme manager from the employer, it will be the total sum of the amount (if any) expended on the asset by the trustees plus the amount in respect of which the employer could have claimed a deduction from his profits under general principles in relation to the transfer of the asset to the trustees. Where the asset consists of new shares in a company connected (as defined by TCA 1997, s 10) with the employer or of rights in respect of such shares, issued by the connected company, the benefit will be the market value of those shares or rights at the time of transfer (TCA 1997, s 81A(5)(a), (b)). However, if the employee is chargeable to tax by reference to a lower valuation of the asset in question, the deduction available under Sch D Case I or II will be restricted by reference to the amount of that valuation (TCA 1997, s 81A(5)(c)). This latter proviso will by definition have no effect in a case where an employee is not chargeable to tax.

5.303 Expense or loss?

TCA 1997, s 81(2)(a) prohibits any deductions for 'any disbursement or expenses not being money wholly and exclusively laid out or expended for the purposes of the trade or profession'. TCA 1997, s 81(2)(e) prohibits any deduction for 'any loss not connected with or arising out of the trade or profession'. The distinction between 'expenses' and 'losses' was explained by Finlay J in *Allen v Farquharson Bros & Co* 17 TC 59 as follows:

> It is conceivable that there may be cases in which a thing might be either within (a) or within (e), but, nonetheless, I do think that there is a distinction to be drawn between the two: (a) relates to disbursements; that means something or other which the trader pays out; I think some sort of volition is indicated. He chooses to pay out some disbursement; it is an expense; it is something which comes out of his pocket. A loss is something different. That is not a thing which he expends or disburses. That is a thing which, so to speak, comes upon him *ab extra*.

Logically, it would seem that a distinction should be drawn between expenses, which are made in order to implement a trading purpose, and a loss which falls upon the trader, and is connected to his trade, but without his seeking purposefully to bring it about. It is very difficult to see how a *loss* incurred by the trader could ever satisfy TCA 1997, s 81(2)(a), as by definition, the loss will not normally reflect any underlying purpose or intention. In *McKnight v Sheppard* [1997] STC 846, the suggestion was made that, at least in some cases, the tests under TCA 1997, s 81(2)(a) and s 81(2)(e) were equivalent, but it seems preferable to keep them conceptually distinct.

In practice, the courts have by no means constantly adhered to the distinction between expenses and losses. In *Strong & Co of Romsey Ltd v Woodifield* 5 TC 215, the taxpayer was an innkeeper who claimed a deduction for damages paid to a guest who was injured when a chimney fell on him. The accident was attributable to the negligence of the taxpayer's employees. Lord Davey took the view that the term 'loss' in the equivalent to TCA 1997, s 81(2)(e) referred only to a loss in respect of a trading or speculative venture. He accordingly based his judgment on the equivalent of TCA 1997, s 81(2)(a), saying, in an oft-cited passage:

> I think that the payment of these damages was not money expended 'for the purpose of the trade'. These words appear to me to mean for the purpose of enabling a person to carry on and earn profits in the trade, etc. I think the disbursements permitted as such are made for that purpose. It is not enough that the disbursement is made in the course of, or arises out of, or is connected with, the trade, or is made out of the profits of the trade. It must be made for the purpose of earning the profits.

It is suggested that Finlay J's comments above are to be preferred to the views of Lord Davey, in so far as the deductibility of *losses* incurred by a trader should be determined only under TCA 1997, s 81(2)(e). Accordingly such losses will be allowable if they are connected with or arise out of the trade, etc even though they are involuntary (so that it cannot be said that the trader had any 'purpose' in incurring them, with reference to TCA 1997, s 81(2)(a)). This principle would seem to cover such matters as not only awards of damages but, also for example, losses due to defalcations by shop assistants or customers (but not defalcations which arise outside the course of trading operations, as when a director misappropriates company funds: *Bamford v ATA Advertising Ltd* 48 TC 359).

In *McKnight v Sheppard* [1996] STC 627, [1997] STC 846; [1999] STC 669, the taxpayer, a stockbroker, incurred legal expenses in defending himself against disciplinary charges brought by the UK Stock Exchange. These charges could have led to his expulsion or suspension from the Stock Exchange. In the event, his appeal succeeded in part and he was fined, rather than suspended, in respect of professional misconduct. Lightman J, at first instance, took the view that legal expenses incurred by the taxpayer in defending himself against disciplinary charges should be regarded as an integral part of the loss he incurred in respect of the fines imposed on him in relation to those charges. This may seem logical, as payments made to avoid or to reduce a loss should presumably take their character from the loss itself. However, the expenses were incurred not merely to avoid or mitigate the fines, but to protect the taxpayer from suspension or expulsion, which could have led to the destruction of his profession (see *Morgan v Tate & Lyle Ltd* 35 TC 367, discussed at **5.304**). It followed that so long as the taxpayer did not pay the legal expenses partly in order to preserve his *personal* reputation that they were incurred wholly and exclusively for the purposes of his profession (per the House of Lords).

Lightman J had also taken the view that the fines fell not only within TCA 1997, s 81(2)(e), but also TCA 1997, s 81(2)(a), since they were made 'knowingly and deliberately', (albeit unwillingly). However, simply because the taxpayer deliberately *paid* his fine (as he was obliged to do) does not mean that he deliberately *incurred* it: accordingly, only TCA 1997, s 81(2)(a) should have applied to the fines (arguably resulting in their disallowance: see **5.306**: *Legal and professional fees, damages and penalties*).

In the *Strong & Co of Romsey Ltd* case, Lord Loreburn, delivering the majority judgment, held that the claim was not deductible by reference to the then UK equivalent of TCA 1997, s 81(2)(e). He said:

> In my opinion, however, it does not follow that if a loss is in any sense connected with the trade, it must always be allowed as a deduction; for it may be only remotely connected with the trade, or it may be connected with something else quite as much as or even more than with the trade. I think only such losses can be deducted as are connected with in the sense that they are really incidental to the trade itself. They cannot be deducted if they are mainly incidental to some other vocation or fall on the trader *in some character other than that of trader* … In the present case I think that the loss sustained by the appellants was not really incidental to their trade as innkeepers, and fell upon them in their character not of traders, but of householders [emphasis added].

The scope of this dictum is considered full further below. Although Lord Loreburn's words in *Strong & Co* were delivered in the context of the UK equivalent to TCA 1997, s 81(2)(e), they have nevertheless sometimes been invoked in the context of the UK equivalent to TCA 1997, s 81(2)(a). However, in practice, Lord Loreburn's focus on the 'character' of the taxpayer in which he incurs expenditure has often been found unhelpful. Thus, for example, in *Smiths Potato Estates Ltd v Bolland* 30 TC 267, the taxpayer had claimed a deduction for the legal costs of a successful appeal against a charge to Excess Profits Tax (a tax which was supplementary to the existing UK equivalent of corporation tax). In the Court of Appeal, Lord Greene MR laid particular emphasis on the fact that the relevant costs had been incurred by the taxpayer *in its character* as a taxpayer and not *in its character* a trader (see also the approach of the same judge in *Rushden Hill Co Ltd v Keene* 30 TC 298).

However, the ratio of the House of Lords in rejecting the taxpayer's claim was somewhat different, and is well encapsulated in the following comment by Lord Simonds:

> … neither the cost of ascertaining taxable profit nor the cost of disputing it with the Revenue authorities is money spent to enable the trader to earn profit in his trade. What profit he has earned, he has earned before ever the voice of the tax-gatherer is heard. He would have earned no more and no less if there was no such thing as income tax. His profit is no more affected by the eligibility of tax than is a man's temperature altered by the purchase of a thermometer, even though he starts by haggling about the price of it.

In other words, the *application or appropriation of profits after* they have been earned is not part of the cost of actually earning them (see **5.306**, under this subheading).

In *Smith v Lion Brewery Ltd* 5 TC 568, the taxpayer was a brewery company which claimed the cost of a special levy imposed on its tied licensed premises. The Inland Revenue had argued that the levy was paid by the taxpayer not in its capacity as brewers, but in its capacity as landowners. In the House of Lords, Lord Atkinson said:

> Again, it is urged that the landlord pays his contribution as landlord … because of his proprietary interest in the premises and not as trader, since he would be equally liable to it whether he traded or not. That, no doubt, is so but in the present case the Company have become landlords and thus liable to pay the charge, for the purpose solely and exclusively of setting up the tied house system of trading.

A similar decision was reached in *Usher's Wiltshire Breweries Ltd v Bruce* 6 TC 399 where the cost of rates, insurance and premises were allowed in respect of brewery premises even though in strictness the tenant was responsible for these outlays.

In *Harrods (Buenos Aires) Ltd v Taylor-Gooby* 41 TC 450, the taxpayer operated a business in Argentina, where it was subject to a flat rate annual tax based on the amount of its capital, irrespective of the level of profits which it earned. The Court of Appeal allowed the cost of the Argentinian tax. Diplock LJ said:

> In order to engage lawfully in its trading activities in the Argentine at all, whether or not it made a profit by doing so, it had to pay the tax.
>
> Why, then is it not deductible? … You can always find some label other than 'trader' to describe the capacity in which a trader makes any disbursement for the purposes of his trade. He pays rent for his business premises in the capacity of 'tenant', rates in the capacity of 'occupier', wages in the capacity of 'employer', the price of goods in the capacity of 'buyer'. But if he has become tenant or occupier of those particular premises, employer of those particular servants or buyer of those particular goods solely for the purposes of his trade, the money which he has expended in any of the capacities so labelled is a deductible expense in computing the profits of his trade.

It is suggested accordingly that Lord Loreburn's concept of expenditure incurred 'in the character' of either trader or non-trader is of dubious usefulness. Indeed, the correctness of the actual decision in *Strong & Co* may itself be open to question. The distinction drawn between the taxpayer as trader (ie innkeeper) and as a householder (ie as a mere occupier of his inn) seems somewhat unreal, given that the premises were occupied and used for business purposes. It is worthy of note that Lord Loreburn accepted that losses sustained by a railway company in compensating passengers for an accident *would* be allowable. It is difficult to see the logic behind the purported distinction between this situation and the facts in *Strong & Co*. Nevertheless, it should be noted that in *Fitzgerald v IRC* I ITR 91, Murnaghan J took the *obiter* view that a sum paid by a trader under a repairing covenant was paid in his capacity as lessee, since he would have been legally obliged to pay it even if he had not been trading. With respect, this view seems mistaken, since the obligation to repair was an inherent element of a tenancy agreement undertaken solely for business purposes.

5.304 The purposes of the trade

Even within the context of TCA 1997, s 81(2)(a), Lord Davey's dictum cited at **5.303** may be criticised for being too restrictive, since it suggests that there must be a clear 'cause and effect' relationship between the expense incurred and the trading profits earned. In *Morgan v Tate & Lyle Ltd* 35 TC 367, the House of Lords held that expenditure incurred by a taxpayer in order to protect its trade from the threat of nationalisation was allowable. Lord Reid said:

> Lord Davey used the two expressions 'for the purpose of enabling a person to carry on and earn profits' and 'for the purpose of earning the profits' in close juxtaposition and he cannot have intended them to mean different things. He obviously intended the former to be the more accurate phrase because that is what he said he thought the words of the Rule meant. I doubt whether in any case the shorter phrase was intended to be an accurate definition, and I am satisfied that 'purposes of the trade' has a wider meaning than purposes directly related to the earning of profits. Defending or preserving a profit-earning asset of the business is within the purposes of the trade and that must apply equally to a single asset or a collection of assets.

In the Court of Appeal, Jennings LJ had taken the view, similarly, that payments to protect a trader from losses, or from being deprived of the means of carrying on the trade, were just as deductible as payments made for the direct purpose of earning profits.

In *Vallambrosa Rubber Co v Farmer* 5 TC 529 Viscount Cave commented as follows:

> … a sum of money expended, not of necessity and with a view to a direct and immediate benefit to the trade, but voluntarily and on the grounds of commercial expediency, and in order indirectly to facilitate the carrying on of the business, may yet be expended wholly and exclusively for the purposes of the trade.

Viscount Cave's *dictum*, which demonstrates greater flexibility than that of Lord Davey, also has the merit of more closely reflecting the wording of TCA 1997, s 81(2)(a), which makes no mention of 'profits' as such.

In determining the purpose of the expenditure, the subjective intentions of the taxpayer will often be conclusive (but not invariably – see the discussion of *Mallalieu v Drummond* below). This follows from the fact that a fundamental characteristic of trading is the making of commercial decisions and the exercise of personal judgment. There is no requirement that allowable expenditure should be *necessarily* incurred (compare the Sch E expenses rule: **10.302**), or even that it should be wisely incurred. This does not mean that the taxpayer's own account of his intentions will automatically be accepted at face value. The Appeal Commissioners (or, if appropriate, the Circuit Court judge) are the primary tribunals of fact; accordingly, they are entitled to draw inferences about the taxpayer's purposes from the evidence of all of the surrounding circumstances.

In *Garforth v Tankard Carpets* [1980] STC 251, the taxpayer company had an associated company with which it had a close trading relationship. The directors of the taxpayer company (who were also directors of the associated company) decided that the taxpayer should give guarantees in respect of liabilities incurred by its associated companies; the company subsequently had to pay money under the guarantee. It was held on the evidence that the decision to undertake the guarantee was not made solely for the purposes of the taxpayer company, and the expenditure incurred as a result was accordingly disallowable (see the 'dual purpose' rule, below). Walton J observed:

> It must in the nature of things be extremely difficult for the directors of two associated companies in the position of the taxpayer company and [the associated company] to be certain in whose best interests, or, rather, in whose exclusive interests, any step which they take is being taken. Obviously, there is nobody but themselves to say what was in their own minds; and obviously, again, it must require a superhuman effort of mind (of which extremely few persons, if any, are capable) to rule out entirely from consideration the possibility of benefit to one's other company when concentrating on the exclusive requirements of just one of them. In my judgment, commissioners should be extremely slow in coming to any conclusion that the act was done solely for the benefit of the trade of one of the companies concerned, and should in general do so only where there are wholly separate findings of primary fact not depending on the say so of the directors concerned.

(See also *Vodafone v Shaw* discussed under *Transactions with related parties* at **5.306** below). In *McKinlay v Arthur Young McClelland Moores & Co* [1989] STC 898, the House of Lords (reversing the Court of Appeal) held that a partnership, however large in size, could not be treated as a separate entity from the individuals who made up the partnership. As a result, expenditure which was sanctioned by an executive committee of the partnership but which was incurred for the personal purposes of an individual partner, was not allowable.

It would appear that the *immediate* purpose of the relevant expenditure must always be considered. Thus, in the *Smith Potato's Estates* case (above), the *direct* purpose of the expenditure was to reduce the tax burden on the company. The fact that the *ultimate* purpose of the taxpayer was to generate additional funds for use in its trade could not transform the expense into a deductible item.

An interesting issue arises where a taxpayer chooses to buy trading stock from a related third party rather than from an alternative supplier. It is suggested that the expense involved should be deductible, since the taxpayer's purpose in carrying out *the particular transaction* is to benefit his trade. The fact that the trader may have a personal purpose in carrying out that transaction *with a particular third party* should not be material. In other words, a transaction which would have been carried out, even if the related third party was not involved, does not reflect a non-trading dimension. The position is potentially different where, for example, the price paid to the related party appears unduly generous. In this case, it seems that *part* of the price may not be regarded as incurred paid 'wholly and exclusively' (see the discussion of 'apportionment' in the following section, and also the observations of Lord Cross in *Kilmorie (Aldridge) v Dickinson* [1974] STC 539).

Finally, where a trader enters into an obligation to make a series of future payments, it would appear that it is the purpose behind undertaking the obligation *at the time* which is critical, even if circumstances change thereafter. Thus, for example in *IRC v Falkirk Iron Co* 17 TC 625 the taxpayer was allowed the cost of its rent under an on-going lease, even though the premises in question had become surplus to trading requirements: see also *Hyett v Leonard* 2 TC 346; *Westmoreland Investments v MacNiven* [1975] STC (SCD) 69 and *CIR v Cosmotron Manufacturing Ltd* [1997] STC 1134, discussed at **5.306**: *Expenses of cessation and commencement*. It is arguable that the position may be different where the trader could free himself from an existing obligation but elects not to do so for non-trading reasons or where the asset concerned is transferred subsequently to a non-trading use (and see also the discussion of interest expense in relation to TCA 1997, s 81(2)(e) at **5.315**); see also *Wharf Properties v CIR* [1997] STC 351).

It should be noted that lump sum payments made to cancel a lease would normally be disallowable, as capital in nature (see **5.307–5.308**). Logically, a payment made to discharge an obligation to pay expenses which would not themselves be 'wholly and exclusively' incurred, cannot be deductible (see *Alexander Howard & Co Ltd v Bentley* 30 TC 334).

5.305 The 'wholly and exclusively' test: general principles

The courts have held that expenditure which is incurred for both business and non-business purposes is not allowable. The source of this strict approach is the word 'exclusively'. The prohibition on 'duality' of *purpose* does not extend to 'duality' of *effect*. Thus, even if the expenditure results in a personal benefit to the trader, this does not necessarily mean that such expenditure must be disallowed. Lord MacDermott CJ, in the Sch E case of *Elwood v Utitz* 42 TC 482, *observed*:

> In their ordinary significance, these adverbs ('wholly and exclusively') seem to me to demand some consideration of the purposes or objects which the particular individual or individuals concerned had in mind. Expenditure may be 'wholly and exclusively' incurred for one intended purpose, although it also produces or brings about some other incidental result or effect. In the nature of things it must often be impossible to incur a necessary expenditure for a necessary purpose without causing or reaping some side-effect which may be unwanted as it is unavoidable. Travelling which is entirely necessary … may provide the traveller with appreciable personal benefits of a social, cultural or health-giving nature, but so far as I am aware it has never been suggested that the expenses of such travelling cannot be deducted for that reason.

Similarly, the fact that a third party may also benefit from the expenditure does not necessarily cause it to be disallowed. In the case of *Usher's Wiltshire Brewery Ltd v Bruce* 6 TC 399 the question was whether the brewery was entitled to deduct from the profits of the brewing expenses incurred in connection with its tied houses, although in strictness these were liabilities of third parties, namely, the publicans who carried on their business in the various tied houses. Lord Sumner in that case stated:

> Where the whole and exclusive purpose of the expenditure is the purpose of the expender's trade, and the object which the expenditure serves is the same, the mere fact that to some extent the expenditure enures to a third party's benefit, say that of the publican, or that the brewer incidentally obtains some advantage, say in his character of landlord, cannot in law defeat the effect of the finding as to the whole and exclusive purpose.

In *Calders v IRC* 26 TC 213, the taxpayer took over an onerous purchase contract from a third party which would otherwise have been unable to survive financially. It was held that because the taxpayer's purpose behind so doing was to preserve price stability in its market place (and thus maintain its own profitability) the loss on taking over the contract was allowable. In the same case the court also held that sums paid to discharge the liabilities of a company, the shares in which were security for a trade debt, were allowable. The expense involved was regarded as equivalent to the cost of collecting a trade debt.

However, where the payment benefits a party connected to the taxpayer, it may be difficult to demonstrate that there is not duality of purpose (see *Kealy v O'Mara* I ITR 642, and also the discussion in **5.306**: *Transactions with related parties*).

The distinction between duality of *purpose* and duality of *effect* is most clearly expressed in the leading Sch D case of *Bentleys, Stokes & Lawless v Beeson* 33 TC 491, where the taxpayers were a firm of solicitors who entertained their clients to lunches during which business matters were discussed. The Court of Appeal held that there was no evidence upon which the Appeal Commissioners could have reasonably concluded that the expenditure on entertainment was not exclusively incurred in the promotion of the taxpayer's professional activities.

The comments of Romer LJ in the Court of Appeal are of special interest, in particular the following passage:

> The sole question is whether the expenditure in question was 'exclusively' laid out for business purposes, that is: What was the motive or object in the mind of the two individuals responsible for the activities in question? It is well established that the question is one of fact and again, therefore the problem seems simple enough. The difficulty, however, arises as we think, from the nature of the activity in question. Entertaining involves inevitably the characteristic of hospitality. Giving to charity or subscribing to a staff pension fund involved inevitably the object of benefaction. But the question in all such cases is: was the entertaining, the charitable subscription, undertaken solely for the purposes of business, that is, solely with the object of promoting the business of its profit-earning capacity? It is, as we have said, a question of fact. And it is quite clear that the purpose must be the sole purpose. The paragraph says so in clear terms. If the activity be undertaken with the object both of promoting business and also with some other purpose, for example, with the object of indulging an independent wish of entertaining a friend or stranger or of supporting a charitable or benevolent object, then the paragraph is not satisfied though in the mind of the actor the business motive may predominate. For the statute so prescribes. Per contra, if in truth the sole object is business promotion, the expenditure is not disqualified because the nature of the activity necessarily involves some other result, or the attainment or furtherance of some other objective, since the latter result or objective is necessarily inherent in the act.

A clearcut application of the rule in *Bentleys'* case can be found in *Bowden v Russell & Russell* 42 TC 301 where a solicitor visited Northern America; he admitted that this was both in order to attend some conferences and to have a holiday at the same time. Pennycuick J overturned the Commissioners' finding that expenses of the visit were deductible, stating:

> ... this statement by the (taxpayer) represents an unequivocal admission by him that the expenses of the American visit were incurred for a dual purpose.

He added that:

> ... so far as I can see Mr Taylor's admission on this point accords with the realities of the matter. It is clear from the facts found in this case that this was, at any rate in part, a holiday trip ...

In practice, the inspector would probably be prepared to grant a concessional apportionment in this kind of case.

Bowden v Russell & Russell is traditionally contrasted with *Edwards v Warmsley Henshall & Co* 44 TC 431, where the taxpayer was a partner in a firm of Chartered Accountants who travelled to the United States to attend a conference and also (it appears) spent some time holidaying there. The activity of travelling was found to have been undertaken solely in order to attend the conference and, accordingly, took its colour from the latter, which was clearly a 'business only activity', any expenditure referable to his holiday activities was of course disallowable. In *Interfish Ltd v Revenue and Customs Commissioners* ((2015 STC 55) a company, whose main business was in the fishing industry, made payments of about £1.2m to Plymouth Albion rugby club which was in severe financial difficulties. The company claimed many benefits as a result of its association with the rugby club including the promotion of the Interfish main brands on hoardings at the club grounds and on the players' shirts. In addition it was claimed that involvement with the club facilitated the building of business relationships including access to local bank managers to facilitate accessing funds for expansion. It was argued that although the payments had a dual purpose, ie improving the financial position of the club and also improving the financial position of Interfish, the objective of improving the financial position of the club was only an intermediate or incidental, albeit necessary, purpose on the road to the ultimate purpose, ie the improvement of the financial position of Interfish. It was held that the purpose of providing financial assistance to the rugby club could not be regarded as an incidental purpose to a main purpose of improving the financial position of Interfish. Because there were two purposes in making the payments in question they were not made wholly and exclusively for the purpose of the trade of Interfish and were not deductible.

The UK courts have however tempered the subjective approach in the *Bentley* case. They have taken the view that expenditure which is purely personal in nature inevitably possesses a non-trading purpose, even though the *amount* of the expenditure may be greater than it otherwise would be as a result of the taxpayer's trading activities. This effectively introduces an objective element into the expenses rule.

Thus, in *Caillebotte v Quinn* [1975] STC 265 the taxpayer was a self-employed carpenter who claimed the additional cost of his lunches when working away from home. In the case stated it is noted that:

> … the taxpayer stated that his main reason for consuming lunch on working days was to sustain him in his work, and in the winter to keep warm. He did not regard lunch as a personal habit …

As Templeman J pointed out:

> A Sch D taxpayer, like every other taxpayer, must eat in order to live; he does not eat in order to work. Counsel for the Crown, submits – and I accept – that in these circumstances no part of the cost of the taxpayer's lunch was exclusively … expended for the purposes of his trade as a carpenter … the Commissioners appear to have derived some assistance from the fact, which they found, that the taxpayer's appetite at work exceeded his appetite at home, and from the taxpayer's evidence, which they accepted, that he did not regard lunch as a personal habit. In this court, counsel for the taxpayer disclaimed any such assistance.

Caillebotte was followed in the recent case of *Watkis v Ashford, Sparkes & Harward* [1985] STC 451 where the taxpayers claimed *inter alia* the cost of 'working lunches'. Nourse J concluded that:

> the lunches … took the place of meals which would have been consumed in any event, but even if that is not so … the taxpayers need food and drink irrespective of whether they were engaged in a business activity or not.

In *Mallalieu v Drummond* [1983] STC 665, the taxpayer was a practising lady barrister who bought black clothing for her court appearances, in conformity with the Bar Council's guidance notes on dress. Her personal preference was for more colourful garments, and she already owned a sufficient number of these to meet her needs without having to resort to court clothes. She claimed the cost of replacing and laundering her court clothes.

Lord Brightman, in the House of Lords, said:

> Of course the taxpayer thought only of the requirements of her profession when she first bought (as a capital expense) her wardrobe of subdued clothing and, no doubt as and when she replaced items or sent them to the launderers or the cleaners she would, if asked, have

> repeated that she was maintaining her wardrobe because of those requirements. It is the natural way that anyone incurring such expenditure would think and speak. But she needed clothes to travel to work and clothes to wear at work and I think it is inescapable that one object, was the provision of the clothing that she needed as a human being. I reject the notion that the object of a taxpayer is inevitably limited to the particular conscious motive in mind at the moment of expenditure. Of course the motive of which the taxpayer is conscious is of vital significance but it is not inevitably the only object which the commissioners are entitled to find to exist. In my opinion the commissioners were not only entitled to reach the conclusion that the taxpayer's object was both to serve the purposes of her profession and also to serve her personal purposes, but I myself would have found it impossible to reach any other conclusion.

Vinelott J in the course of his judgment at first instance in *McKinlay v Arthur Young McClelland Moores & Co* [1986] STC 491 observed:

> I do not think that Lord Brightman intended to ascribe … an unconscious motive. As I understand it, the ground of the decision in the House of Lords, in *Mallalieu* was that the expenditure by (the taxpayer) plainly served a private purpose … although the purpose which presented itself to her mind was that of meeting the requirements of her profession. In cases where expenditure plainly serves two purposes an inquiry into the state of mind of the taxpayer is unnecessary and may be misleading.

A particularly vivid illustration of the 'duality principle' can be found in *Murgatroyd v Evans-Jackson* (1966) 43 TC 581. There, the taxpayer was a commission agent who had to enter a nursing home as a result of an accident. The taxpayer could have obtained his treatment free of charge under the National Health Service, but declined this opportunity since it would have been impossible for him to conduct his business under those conditions. He used his room in the nursing home to meet staff and clients while he was there, and claimed 60 per cent of the home's charges as a business expense. Plowman J held that the fact that the claim was for only 60 per cent of the expense was an admission of a dual purpose so that no part of the claim could be allowed. The fact that 60 per cent of the expenses was claimed by the taxpayer seems in fact to have been an irrelevance, based purely on a previous *ad hoc* arrangement with the Revenue. However, Plowman J also made it clear that he would have turned down the taxpayer's claim even if he had claimed *all* the expense, because:

> it would offend common sense … to say that one of his motives or purposes in going into the nursing home was not to receive treatment for (his) injury.

The decision in the *Murgatroyd* case is consistent with the principle expressed in *Mallalieu*. Objectively speaking, expenditure on medical treatment will always have a personal purpose. The fact that such expenditure may be *greater* as a result of trading considerations cannot save the day for the taxpayer, because of this duality of purpose. In the *Murgatroyd* case, it so happened that the expenditure was greater to the extent of 100 per cent as a result of trading considerations; however, this factor would not override the principle involved.

The principle that expenditure which is personal in nature is always regarded as possessing a 'dual purpose' only extends to expenditure which is of an 'everyday' kind, which is liable to be incurred by *any* individual, whether a trader or not. Expenditure which reflects the specific needs of the trade will not be disallowable, even though it also serves the personal needs of the trader. Thus in *Caillebotte*, Templeman J remarked:

> The cost of tea consumed by an actor at the Mad Hatter's Tea party is different, for in that case the quenching of a thirst is incidental to the playing of the part. The cost of protective

> clothing worn in the course of carrying on a trade will be deductible, because warmth and decency are incidental in the protection necessary to the carrying on of the trade.

Similarly, in the *Bentley Stokes* case, the consumption of food by the taxpayer was incidental to the provision of business hospitality.

In the *Mallalieu* case, Lord Brightman observed:

> In the case of the nurse, I am disposed to think, without inviting your Lordships to decide, that the material and design of the uniform may be dictated by the practical requirements of the art of nursing and the maintenance of hygiene. There may be other cases where it is essential that the self-employed person should provide himself with and maintain a particular design of clothing in order to obtain any engagements at all in the business that he conducts. An example is the self-employed waiter, who needs to wear 'tails'. In his case the 'tails' are an essential part of the equipment of his trade, and it clearly would be open to the commissioners to allow the expense of their upkeep on the basis that the money was spent exclusively to serve the purposes of the business.

It is important to appreciate that the 'duality' principle only applies where an item of expense serves two (or more) purposes at the same time. Thus, the taxpayer in *Caillebotte v Quinn* who ate his lunch at a distant location could not say 'I am incurring expenses on *one part* of this meal exclusively for trading purposes and the *other part* of this meal for personal purposes'.

The position is different where a single item of expense relates to business and non-business usage, which can be separated on a time, space or *per capita* basis. In *Bentley Stokes & Lawless*, Romer LJ said:

> The words … 'wholly and exclusively laid out or expended for the purpose of the trade or profession appear straight-forward enough'. It is conceded that the first adverb 'wholly' is in reference to the quantum of money expended.

This might be taken to imply that the word 'wholly' imports a quantum test, and prohibits a deduction unless the entire amount of a given expenditure is exclusively incurred for business purposes, ie preventing apportionment being made. However, there is, it seems, no recorded instance of the courts ever relying on such a construction and the word 'wholly' in fact seems to be virtually redundant.

Thus, in *Caillebotte v Quinn*, Templeman J said:

> Counsel pointed out that in *Horton v Young* 47 TC 60 the taxpayer appears to have been allowed a proportion of the most of a study used partly for business and partly or leisure. But is it possible to apportion the use and cost of [a study] … on a time basis and to allow the expense of the room during the hours in which it is used exclusively for business purposes, in the same way as it is possible to calculate the business expenses of a car which is sometimes used for business purposes exclusively and sometimes for pleasure.

Similarly, Lord MacDermott CJ (again speaking *obiter*) in *Elwood v Utitz*:

> The expenditure entailed in providing (a private residence) will not be wholly and exclusively incurred. But if the total expenditure can be severed or apportioned so that a part thereof can be fairly associated solely to the accommodation and services (of a study) … that part may be allowed.

Interestingly, both Templeman J and Lord MacDermott CJ appeared to accept that, not only the variable costs of heating and lighting a study, but *also* the fixed costs of both private rent and rates (the latter not currently an issue in Ireland) would be eligible for apportionment (see below).

It appears that apportionment may also be permissible in other, exceptional circumstances. In *Copeman v Flood* 24 TC 53 remuneration of an arguably excessive amount was paid to the directors of a family company. Lawrence J held that the full amount of the remuneration was *not necessarily* incurred 'wholly and exclusively', etc, and referred the case back to the Appeal Commissioners to determine what proportion thereof fell within the then UK equivalent of TCA 1997, s 81(2)(a) (in fact it appears that the Appeal Commissioners proceeded to allow the remuneration in full). Presumably, Lawrence J took the view that the expenditure in *Flood* was potentially incurred on two distinct counts:

(a) the provision of the director's services (deductible); and
(b) the distribution of profits to shareholders (non-deductible).

The payment of remuneration might appear to be simply an expense serving two purposes at the same time. However, in the context of the Sch D expenses rule the substance of a payment and not merely its legal form, can be legitimately taken into account. Accordingly, what was a payment of remuneration in law, could be split into its component parts, adopting a 'commercial' perspective.

The approach of Lawrence J in *Copeman v Flood* is given further support by an *obiter dictum* of Lord Reid in the case of *Kilmorie (Aldridge) v Dickinson* [1974] STC 539, where a grossly excessive sum was paid for trading stock on foot of an elaborate tax-avoidance scheme. He said:

> But what happens if even without the non-trading purpose the trader would have spent part of the sum for the purposes of his trade? On one view [TCA 1997, s 81(2)] is so unreasonable that it forbids deduction even of that part which would in any case have been expended for trading purposes. It seems to me that the section could well be read as meaning that, if it can be shown that a part of the expenditure was in fact wholly and exclusively for trading purposes, then that part is a proper deduction.

Again, the payment in question referred to two distinct matters: (a) the purchase of trading stock and, (b) a transfer of value to advance the scheme.

5.306 The 'wholly and exclusively' test: particular expenses

Subscriptions and donations

Subscriptions to trade-related journals, etc, and other sources of information are clearly allowable on general principles. Subscriptions to organisations which exist to promote the interests of a particular category of traders should also normally qualify. Thus, in *Guest Keen and Nettleford v Fowler* 5 TC 511, payments to a trade association which fixed prices on behalf of a particular industry (conduct most unlikely to be legal today) were held to be deductible.

Strictly, a subscription or levy paid to a trade association is only a deductible expense for the payer if, and to the extent that, the trade association applies the contributions for a purpose which would permit the deduction if incurred directly by the contributing business. In *Lochgelly Iron & Coal Ltd v Crawford* 6 TC 267, a colliery company paid annual levies to an association of coal owners. It was held that only the part of the levies applied by the association for qualifying purposes could be deducted by the colliery company.

In practice, a trade association may sign an agreement with the Revenue Commissioners to pay tax on the excess of its receipts over allowable expenses; where an association signs such an agreement, the whole of the subscriptions or levies paid by its members are treated as deductible expenses in the members' accounts. In the absence of such an agreement, the Revenue could not charge tax on a trade association on profits arising from services provided to members (see **4.102**: *Mutual trading*). Each inspector of taxes has a list of the associations which have entered into such agreements. Unless a particular association is on that list, the inspector is likely to resist the deduction of the contribution. However, if it can be established that the association uses the contributions solely for purposes justifying a deduction if the money were applied directly by the member, the deduction should be allowed. In practice, subscriptions to trade associations in the UK which have entered into agreements with the UK Inland Revenue are allowed in calculating profits taxable under Sch D Case I in the State. A fuller account of Revenue practice is set out in *Tax Briefing 29*.

The *Lochgelly Iron* case also illustrates that subscriptions made for the general social good, even if related to the trade in question, are not allowable on general principles. Thus, in that case, contributions by a mining company to a Government research project on the explosive properties of coal dust were held to be disallowable. A special regime in fact applies to payments made to further scientific research (as defined) – see **5.308**.

The cost of subscriptions to political parties or associations or of disseminating politically-orientated materials may be allowable if these are simply a means to achieving a trading end. If this is the case, the fact that a particular political party or grouping, etc, may benefit from the expenditure is merely an 'unavoidable side-effect' and not part of the purposes of the expenditure (see the discussion at **5.305**). However, the UK courts have tended to take an objective approach in this area. In *Boarland v Kramat Pular Ltd* 35 TC 1, the taxpayer company incurred expenses in circulating a pamphlet expressing strong and wide-ranging anti-Government sentiments. The taxpayer argued that it honestly believed that it was in the company's economic interests that people should be influenced against what it saw as the anti-business philosophy of the Government of the day. Dankwerts J held that it was a question of law as to whether or not the expenses in question were *capable* of being 'wholly and exclusively' for the purposes of the trade. The learned judge held that, given the overtly party political nature of the pamphlet, the expenses of producing it were not so capable (even accepting for the sake of argument, that it might have been partly directed to the benefit of the trade).

Similarly, in *Joseph L Thompson & Sons Ltd v Chamberlain* 40 TC 657, the cost of subscriptions to the 'economic league', a free enterprise organisation dedicated to the advancement of conservative views, was disallowed. This was despite the fact that the taxpayer had made the subscription in order to encourage the league to direct its attention to the position of its particular industry. The court held that because the taxpayer's subscription went into the league's general funds and was used to further all of the taxpayers 'admittedly wide aims and objects' it could not have been 'wholly and exclusively' expended for the purposes of its trade.

The logic of these cases indicates that straightforward donations to political parties should not be allowable on principle (see also TCA 1997, s 840 which prohibits a deduction for gifts, discussed at **5.313**). Indeed, it would seem that only very specific and targeted contributions could qualify (as in *Morgan v Tate & Lyle Ltd* 35 TC 367, where payments to a propaganda organisation were earmarked for an anti-nationalisation campaign in response to the imminent threat of nationalisation of the taxpayer's trade).

The deductibility of charitable donations is also likely to be debatable, since there is a natural presumption that they are inspired by philanthropy rather than by commercial considerations. Payments to local charities or to churches directly connected with the trader's customers may be justified on the basis of maintaining goodwill. In other cases, a donation by way of sponsorship may be justifiable as a form of advertising (see below). In *Bourne & Hollingsworth Ltd v Ogden* 14 TC 349 regular annual subscriptions, but not two substantial special subscriptions, to a local hospital were allowed. In practice, subscriptions to hospitals at which employees of the business are regularly or frequently treated may be allowed.

Sponsorship expenses may be justifiable if they are designed to produce benefits in the shape of favourable publicity for the trader. It will of course be primarily the function of the Appeal Commissioners (or Circuit Court judge as appropriate) to decide as an issue of fact whether or not the intentions of the trader were solely directed to the furtherance of the interests of his trade. The taxpayer may face a difficult task in this respect if the expected trade-related benefits of the sponsorship are small in relation to the amount expended. In practice, the Revenue will challenge the deductibility of sponsorship payments unless the trader is receiving a reasonable return in terms of publicity.

Sponsorship of activities in which the trader takes an active personal interest is likely to be the subject of particularly close scrutiny (see *Executive Network v O'Connor* [1996] STC (SCD) 29). In *Morley v Lawford* 14 TC 229, the taxpayer agreed to subsidise losses incurred by the British Empire Exhibition, as this increased his opportunity of being awarded a contract to do work for the exhibition. The sums paid by the taxpayer in respect of his share of the losses were held to be allowable (notwithstanding that, in the event, he was not awarded the contract, since the test is one of *purpose*).

Contributions to trusts established to enable employees to acquire shareholdings in the taxpayer company will be allowable if the only purpose behind them is to motivate or otherwise to encourage the trader's workforce (*Heather v PE Consulting Group* 48 TC 293). The fact that such a trust is set up in a tax-efficient manner will not prejudice the deductibility of the expense incurred (*E Bott Ltd v Price* [1987] STC 100). The potential significance of the capital/revenue distinction also needs to be borne in mind (see **5.307** below); see also *Profit Sharing Schemes* at **Division 11**.

Medical expenses

As discussed above, medical expenses will generally be regarded as incurred, in part at least, for personal purposes. The decision in *Murgatroyd v Evans-Jackson* (1966) 43 TC 581 has already been discussed above. In *Norman v Golder* 25 TC 293 the taxpayer was a self-employed shorthand writer who suffered a severe illness. The Court of Appeal rejected his claim for his related medical costs. Lord Greene MR said:

> True it is that if you do not get yourself well and so incur expenses to doctors you cannot carry on your trade or profession … But expenses of that kind … are laid out in part for the advantage of the taxpayer as a living human being.

The learned judge also took the view that such expenses also fell under the then equivalent of TCA 1997, s 81(2)(b).

While the expense of restoring the general health of the trader will invariably be disallowed, it may be that some medical costs could be allowable in nature. In *Prince v Mapp* 46 TC 169, Pennycuick J commented as follows:

> It is quite easy to think of instances in which someone carrying on a trade or profession incurs some injury which is trivial in itself and in respect of which he would never otherwise

expend money on medical care but which happens to be of vital importance for the purpose of that particular trade or profession. In such a case, I am prepared to assume in favour of the taxpayer here that it would be possible for a taxpayer to incur expense which was wholly and exclusively for the purpose of his trade or profession.

Legal and professional fees, damages and penalties

In general, the deductibility (or otherwise) of legal and professional costs is determined by the nature of the event or transaction to which they relate. At its simplest, this means that costs associated with the acquisition (or disposal) of a capital asset (or liability) will themselves be capital in nature. Such costs, if attributable to the provision of acquisition of plant or machinery or qualifying buildings, may constitute eligible expenditure for capital allowance purposes (see **Division 6**).

Where a trader commits a *civil* wrong (eg a breach of contract, an act of negligence, etc) then any resultant legal damages (and associated legal fees) which he incurs will presumably represent a 'loss', within TCA 1997, s 81(2)(e) rather than an 'expense or disbursement' within TCA 1997, s 81(2)(a): see the discussion at **5.303**. It follows, therefore, that if the wrong is committed in the course of carrying on the trade the associated loss should be deductible.

Applying this logic, libel damages and associated legal fees incurred by a newspaper or product liability costs incurred by a manufacturer should normally be deductible, as should damages for wrongful dismissal of an unsatisfactory employee. In an Australian case *Herald and Weekly Times Ltd v Federal Comr of Taxation* (1932), referred to in the UK Upper Tribunal case of McLaren Racing Ltd which dealt with the deductibility of a penalty (see below), the costs incurred by a newspaper in contesting claims by persons defamed in the newspaper and the damages paid for defamation were held to be laid out or expended wholly and exclusively for the production of assessable income. It was concluded that the inclusion in the newspaper of matters alleged to be defamatory was 'a regular and almost unavoidable incident of publishing it, so that the claims directly flow from acts done for no other purpose than earning revenue, acts forming the essence of the business'. In the judgment the case was distinguished from the *Strong* case because of the degree of connection between the cause of the liability for the damages and the business carried on. Furthermore the damages were compensatory in nature rather than punitive.

In *Golder v Great Boulder Proprietary Gold Mines* 33 TC 75, the taxpayer settled a claim for damages relating to the conduct of its trade, which, if it had succeeded would have gravely damaged its reputation. Significantly, the taxpayer would have suffered serious financial loss if the claim had gone to court, *regardless* of the outcome. The court held that a sum paid to avoid a greater loss must have been incurred 'wholly and exclusively' for the purposes of the trade. While the actual decision seems correct, the court's reasoning seems dubious; the fact that the payment reduced a potential loss was not sufficient. If the potential loss was not itself deductible, then any sum paid to avoid it would have been equally non-deductible. The real point seems to have been that the loss in this case arose in the course of the carrying on of the trade and therefore was not prohibited by the equivalent of TCA 1997, s 81(2)(e) (although, in fact, the court stated that if the damages had actually been paid, the issue of deductibility would have been an open one).

In *Fairrie v Hall* 28 TC 200, the taxpayer maliciously libelled a competitor in order to undermine his influence in the market place. The court held that he was not entitled to a deduction for the cost of the resultant damages awarded against him. The loss he suffered was only 'remotely' connected with his trade and did not arise therefrom. A similar line was taken by the courts in *IRC v Alexander Von Glehn & Co* 12 TC 232 (see also *IRC v Warnes & Co* 12 TC 227). The taxpayer had incurred a fine for exporting goods during wartime which he had failed to ensure would not be passed on to enemy jurisdictions. Lord Sterndale stressed the difference between a 'commercial loss' and a penalty for a breach of the law in carrying out one's trade. The loss was not allowable, since the taxpayer could have chosen to trade lawfully. A UK Upper Tribunal case, *McLaren Racing Ltd v Revenue and Customs Commissioners* (2014) STC 2417 dealt with the deductibility of a penalty imposed on a motor racing organisation. McLaren, a well known Formula One racing team, designed, manufactured and raced Formula One cars at grand prix events. In 2006 an employee of the Ferrari Formula One team passed detailed plans and information regarding Ferrari cars to an employee of McLaren. The World Motor Sport Council concluded that McLaren had obtained a sporting advantage because of having this information and a substantial penalty was levied on McLaren. It was held the penalty was not deductible because the activities which were carried out, ie in essence 'cheating', which gave rise to the penalty were not carried out in the course of McLaren's trade. The judgment distinguished between normal or acceptable activities carried on in the course of a trade and abnormal or unacceptable activities. It was concluded that although in this case it was a normal part of the trade that employees would endeavour to obtain information about competitors' cars, deliberately flouting the rules of a body governing the trade and doing something which is not an unavoidable consequence of carrying on the trade is not an activity carried on in the course of trade. The decision in the *Glehn* case was probably influenced in part by the courts' reluctance to subsidise State-imposed penalties out of State Revenues (this was made explicit in the House of Lords' decision in *McKnight v Sheppard* [1999] STC 669, where fines imposed by a professional body for gross misconduct were held to be disallowable); however the McLaren case rejected the notion that in order for a penalty to be non-deductible its deduction would have to be contrary to a serious public interest which suggests that it is not necessary for a penalty to be imposed by the State or a body sponsored by the State in order for it to be non-deductible. If indeed the real justification for disallowing such expenses is that the penalty was imposed by the State, or a state sponsored body, it is arguable that the Irish courts might reach a different conclusion, given their reluctance to read in broad policy considerations into tax statute: see **1.401**. The Revenue Commissioners have issued a precedent stating that payment of protection moneys is not deductible, although it is unclear as to why this should be so as a matter of principle.

However, with effect for basis periods for the tax year 2008 onwards, TCA 1997, s 83A, inserted by FA 2008, s 41, provides expressly that no deduction will be available for payments, the making of which constitutes a criminal offence or which, if made outside the State, would have constituted a criminal offence if made within the State.

In *Hammond Engineering Co v IRC* [1975] STC 334, it was held that costs incurred by a company in defending an action of reinstatement by a former director might be incurred 'wholly and exclusively' if the sole reason behind them was to protect the interests of the trade.

In other cases, legal costs may be deliberately incurred, for example, in defending the trader's title to his assets or in preserving the value of such assets, so that it is TCA 1997, s 81(2)(a) which would seem to be in point. In *Scammell & Nephew Ltd v Rowles* 22 TC 479, the costs incurred by a company to enable the compromise of an action affecting its trading position, including a payment to a director in a position to block the compromise, were held to be deductible. The effect of the compromise was to enable the company to collect payment of a substantial trading debt which might otherwise not have been recoverable. The same principle covers sums paid to preserve the fixed assets of the business, including goodwill (see *Southern Borax Consolidated Ltd v IRC* 23 TC 597 and *Cooke v Quick Shoe Repair Service* 30 TC 460).

In *Strachan v The Queen* [1983] STC 195 legal fees paid by a company which had been incurred by its sole shareholder (who was also an employee of the company) in defending title to the premises owned by him and being the premises where the company operated its business was held to be a payment by the company in the ordinary course of business and was not a taxable benefit in the shareholder's hands. The court held that the primary purpose of paying the legal fees was a business motive in protecting the asset which was crucial to the operation of the company's trade.

In *Davis v X Ltd* II ITR 45, a contention that legal expenditure on defending the taxpayer's title to a building incurred 'in his character' as a land owner was rejected (contrast *Fitzgerald v IRC* discussed at **5.303**). Conversely, in *Connelly v Wilbey* [1992] STC 783, legal costs incurred in connection with a partnership dispute (which ended in a dissolution) were held not to have been incurred 'wholly and exclusively': sums incurred to protect a partner's personal ownership interest in the trade were not incurred with a view to the earning of profits in that trade.

In *Morgan v Tate & Lyle Ltd* 35 TC 367, the taxpayer successfully claimed the costs of a campaign to prevent the confiscation of its entire trade under a proposed programme of nationalisation. While the costs in question were not legal in nature, the principle established by the case is clearly wide enough to embrace such costs. The House of Lords only reached this conclusion by a 3–2 majority. The majority rejected a Revenue argument that the expenditure was incurred by the taxpayer in its capacity as 'owner' of the trade, as opposed to its capacity as trader. Lord Reid commented:

> I do not see how a person can be the owner of the trade unless he is also the trader or how he can be the trader unless he is the owner of the trade.

This is a further example of the limited usefulness of Lord Loreburn's concept of the 'character' in which expenditure is incurred.

The decision in the *Tate & Lyle* case may be contrasted with *Knight v Parry* [1973] STC 56, where a solicitor was disallowed the costs of defending himself against charges of professional misconduct; this was on the grounds, *inter alia*, that his purpose was to protect himself from being debarred by the Law Society. The distinction between this case and the *Tate & Lyle* case may appear fine: it would seem that, in the former case, the taxpayer was incurring expense in order to preserve his personal right to carry on trading in general. A similar logic was applied in *Spofforth & Prince v Golder* 26 TC 310 where costs incurred by a chartered accountant and his partners in defending him against a charge of fraud were disallowed (compare *McKnight v Sheppard* discussed above).

Legal costs which have been held to be deductible include the costs of altering a corporate constitution in order to remove restrictions which prevented the trader operating at optimum efficiency (*IRC v Carron Co* 45 TC 18: see also the discussion of the same case at **5.307** below). The fact that the taxpayer also availed of the opportunity to make some convenient amendments of a non-trading nature did not mean that there was 'duality' of purpose. The Revenue Commissioners take the view that the costs associated with a company buying back its own shares are not incurred 'wholly and exclusively' for the purposes of the trade, even if the buyback is made for the benefit of the trade (*Taxfax* 14 February 1997); this proposition is open to doubt.

As noted at **5.303**, *Smith's Potato Estates Ltd v Bolland* established that the costs of tax appeals, including legal and accountancy fees, are not allowable in principle. In practice, the inspector will normally allow accountancy fees incurred in the normal process of preparing tax computations and agreeing liabilities.

In *Bamford v ATA Advertising Ltd* 48 TC 359, the taxpayer company claimed the cost of PAYE tax which it had failed to deduct from salary paid to a director. The court held that the payment of a third party's tax liability was not incurred for the purposes of the trade. In fact, the real source of the loss was not the payment of PAYE as such but the failure to recover this tax from the director. This loss was equivalent to a bad debt incurred in respect of a non-trading transaction, which would be a disallowable loss (see eg *Roebank Printing Co v IRC* 13 TC 864, and the discussion at **5.314**).

The Revenue Commissioners take the view that PAYE accounted for under a settlement (eg following a Revenue audit) is equally disallowable. However, it appears that, in practice, the Revenue will grant a deduction where the outstanding PAYE is calculated on the basis of grossing up the relevant remuneration, (ie so that can it be regarded as an element of the expense of remuneration in the normal way): see [1993] ITR 421. The Appeal Commissioners have held that no deduction was available for a sum paid under a settlement agreed on the basis of treating the amounts paid to employees as gross amounts from which PAYE should have been deducted; this is consistent with the decision in *Bamford*.

Travelling and subsistence expenses

The cost of journeys between the taxpayer's home and the place where he carries on his trade is not generally allowable. This is because at least one of his purposes in making such journeys is 'not to enable a man to do his work but to live away from it' (per Romer LJ in *Newsom v Robertson* 33 TC 152). In other words, because the expenditure is inherently personal in nature, it follows that, objectively speaking, the taxpayer must possess a non-trading purpose (see the discussion of the *Mallalieu* case, above). The fact that the taxpayer takes work home with him on a regular basis will, at best, establish an *additional*, 'trading' purpose: thus, the expenditure will still fail under the principle of duality.

An exception to this principle arises where the trader's home also serves as his base (or, possibly, *one* of his bases – see however *Samadian v Revenue Commissioners* (2014 UKUT 13 (TCC) below). In *Horton v Young* 35 TC 452, the taxpayer was a self-employed bricklayer who worked at various sites at a distance from his home, for periods of up to three weeks at a time. He claimed the cost of travelling between his home and the sites. The taxpayer kept his tools and books of account at his home; all his engagements were negotiated at his home, and it was the place where his only client knew that he was always to be found. The Inland Revenue argued that the taxpayer's base at any one time was the particular site at which he was working, and that his travelling was therefore of the 'home to workplace' variety. The Court of Appeal upheld the taxpayer's claim on the grounds that the taxpayer's home was *also* his base. Given that the taxpayer had nowhere else which could be called a base, and that one might reasonably expect a trader to have something in the nature of a headquarters, this seems a sensible conclusion The position under Sch E in similar circumstances may be stricter – see **10.302**.

Horton v Young was distinguished in *Jackman v Powell* [2004] STC 645. In that case, the taxpayer was a milkman who rented his float under a franchise arrangement from a dairy and used to distribute milk bought from the dairy on a designated round which was some distance from his home. The taxpayer spent approximately eight hours per week at his home attending to general administration and bookkeeping matters and occasionally received telephone orders from customers there. The High Court refused his claim for the cost of travelling between his home and the milk round (via the dairy). The court held that it was wrong to assume that every business necessarily had a fixed location and that in the present case the base was the milk round itself; travel between the taxpayer's home and his base of operations was therefore private in nature. The decision seems harsh, given that the management of the business was carried on in the taxpayer's home notwithstanding that the trading activities were carried on elsewhere.

It is, however, not sufficient for the trader to show that he is travelling between his base and a client's location, or travelling between two bases (eg where he has offices located in different areas). The journey must always be for business purposes; thus, eg the taxpayer in *Horton v Young* would not have been allowed the cost of journeys to return home during the day-time simply because he preferred to dine there. In the UK Upper Tribunal case of *Samadian v Revenue and Customs Commissioners* (2014 UKUT 13 (TCC)) a consultant geriatrician was held to have three places of business, one of which was his home from where he carried out a private practice. However, the cost of travel between his home and his other two places of business was held not to be incurred wholly and exclusively in carrying on his trade. It was held that the journeys between his home and his other places of business inevitably had a dual purpose, ie journeys to his home were made not only because he had a place of business there but also because he lived there; journeys from his home to his other places of business were made partly in order to carry out his business at the other location and also for the purpose of enabling him to maintain a home at a location of his choosing.

In addition, it seems that a 'base' must be something in the nature of a fixed establishment or a 'seat of business'. In other words, it is not enough that it is a place where the taxpayer finds it generally convenient to do some of his work. Thus, eg the fact that the taxpayer in *Newsom v Robertson* took work home (and was in fact allowed a small deduction for his 'study' expenses) did not convert his home into a 'base'. Romer LJ observed:

> Is the position altered, then, by the fact, as found by the Commissioners, that [the taxpayer] worked in his house at Whipsnade as well as his chambers in Lincoln's Inn? I am clearly of opinion that it is not. It seems to me impossible to say that this element assimilates the case to that of a man who possesses two separate places of business, and for, the furtherance and in the course of his business activities, has to travel from one to another.

In *Sargent v Barnes* [1978] STC 322, the taxpayer was a dental surgeon who maintained a laboratory in which dentures were manufactured and repaired by a self-employed technician. The laboratory lay between his home and his surgery. Each morning, on his way from his home to the surgery, the taxpayer collected completed dentures spending ten minutes at the laboratory; on his return journey home in the evening, the taxpayer left in dentures for repair, sometimes spending up to one hour there, giving instructions, etc. Oliver J, rejecting the taxpayer's claim for the costs of his journey between the laboratory and surgery, said:

> What the court is concerned with is not simply why he took a particular route (although that may be of the highest relevance in considering the deductibility of any additional expense

caused by a deviation) but why the taxpayer incurred the expense of the petrol, oil, and wear and tear and depreciation in relation to this particular journey.

In my judgment, the facts found, in the stated case leave no room for doubt that the answer to that question must be that it was incurred, if not exclusively then at least in part, for the purpose of enabling the taxpayer to get from his private residence to the surgery where his profession was carried on. The fact that it served the purpose also of enabling him to stop at an intermediate point to carry out there an activity exclusively referable to the business cannot, as I think, convert a dual purpose into a single purpose …

In the instant case, on the facts found it would in my judgment be absurd to say that the taxpayer was in any relevant sense carrying on his practice as a dentist at [the laboratory]. He had established a facility [there] and he was merely utilising his journey between his residence and the base of operations where the practice was carried on to avail himself of this facility: that is to say, to visit this intermediate point, … the journey did not thus assume a different purpose once the intermediate point was passed, or cease to be a journey for the purpose of getting to or from the place where the taxpayer chose to live.

On general principles, a trader whose trade involves travelling (eg a self-employed salesman) should be entitled to the costs of his travel (see eg the judgment of Brightman J at first instance in *Horton v Young*). It should not generally matter in this case whether the trader starts his travelling from his home or his base (ie assuming that his home does not in any event double up as his base). However, if the taxpayer's home is located outside his general area of operations, an apportionment of the travelling costs would probably be justified (ie to exclude expenditure attributable to the element of travelling between home and his area of operations).

Subsistence costs should normally be allowed if they represent an integral component of either the costs of travelling or of 'staying away' temporarily from home on business purposes. Thus, eg in *Edwards v Warmsley Henshall & Co* 44 TC 431, the taxpayer was allowed the costs of travelling to an overseas conference of six days duration. In *Watkis v Ashford, Sparkes & Harward* [1985] STC 451, the taxpayers were a firm of solicitors who held a weekend conference for partners and their wives. Nourse, J at first instance, upheld the taxpayer's claim for the proportion of hotel accommodation and meals expenses attributable to the partners themselves (see also *Elwood v Utitz*, a Sch E case, discussed at **10.302**); however, in the same case, the cost of 'working lunches' was disallowed (see *Caillebotte v Quinn* discussed above).

In practice, the Revenue Commissioners will accept claims for reasonable subsistence expenses incurred by traders whose work involves travelling (eg a self-employed lorry driver) or occasional business trips away from home (see *Tax Briefing 31*).

Revenue *eBrief* No 104/15 discusses travel and subsistence expenses for sole traders and brings about two operational manuals for travel [01.10.01] and food and accommodation expenses [04.6.17] and discusses the deductibility of both on the basis of the wholly and exclusively test. On travel the following 'principles' on deductibility are established:

- There is no requirement that the expense is necessarily incurred, for the purpose of the trade or otherwise. The necessity is irrelevant once the expense is incurred in furtherance of the trade.
- One must look at the purpose of the expense (whether stated or subconscious) and not just its effects.

- As a general rule, travel between home and work, even if some work is carried on at home, always carries the purpose of getting home – it facilitates living away from work. The duality of purpose renders the expense non-deductible.
- So-called 'itinerant' traders are an exception to the general rule that travel between home and work is incurred by the decision to live away from work. Home, for such traders, is the only place new customers can contact them, where they store their tools etc. Therefore, they go home to look for new work. In these instances, getting home is an effect and not a purpose of the journey.
- It is not necessary to determine where a trade is carried on, or to establish a 'base of operations'. Travel between a home office and a main 'base of operation' will not necessarily be deductible. One must look solely to the statutory test, the main focus of which is the purpose for which the expenditure was incurred
- There is a distinction between 'travelling in the course of a business and travelling to get to the place where the business is carried on'.

The above are referenced to case-law in connection with the above. A similar set of 'principles' is arrived at from the perspective of the deductibility of food and accommodation expenses as follows:

- One must look at the purpose of the expense (whether stated or subconscious) and not just its effects.
- Humans eat to live, they do not eat to work. Therefore expenditure incurred on food in the course of a trade or profession will nearly always have a duality of purpose in that the person has the ordinary physical human need of eating. Where additional expenditure is incurred on food because the taxpayer must eat away from home, that expenditure still has a duality of purpose meaning it is not an allowable expense.
- Hotel accommodation incurred on a business trip – where there is no personal motive in the trip – is an allowable deduction.
- Where a hotel bill for a business trip includes reasonable amounts for both overnight accommodation and food then these two amounts should not be disaggregated. If the accommodation is allowable then so too is the food.

Household and property expenses

A proportion of the taxpayer's household expenses may be allowable if he uses his home partly for business purposes. It is not necessary that his home should also be his base. The only issues are whether:

(a) the taxpayer has chosen to carry out some of his work at home; and
(b) has incurred additional expense as a consequence.

As noted above, there should be no difficulty in principle with the apportionment of running costs such as heat and light, insurance and telephone call charges, etc. The treatment of fixed costs may be more problematic. As noted above, there is some *obiter* support for the proposition that a proportion of rent and domestic rates (if reintroduced) should be allowable in the case of a home study.

In this connection, it may be noted that TCA 1997, s 81(2)(c) prohibits a deduction *inter alia* for 'the rent … of any dwelling house … except such part thereof as is used for the purposes of the trade …'. TCA 1997, s 81(2)(c) also imposes a maximum allowable cap of 2/3rds of the rent payable, unless the Inspector is of the opinion that in the circumstances some greater sum ought to be deducted. It may well be appropriate that the proportion of running costs such as light and heat repairs, etc, should be disallowed on a different basis to that adopted in respect of rent, depending on the specific circumstances concerned.

TCA 1997, s 81(2)(c) appears to confirm that apportionment is permissible where this can be carried out on a spatial basis (typically covering the situation where the trader lives 'over the shop'). This still leaves open the situation where the taxpayer uses a room or rooms in his home partly for personal purposes and partly for business purposes. It is then impossible to split the rental cost on a spatial basis; splitting the cost on a *time* basis also seems illogical, since the rental cost, is fixed and does not vary with the amount of business usage. In *Lucas v Cattell* 48 TC 353, a Sch E case (but one concerned with the interpretation of the phrase 'wholly and exclusively'), the taxpayer had installed a telephone for business purposes but also made substantial private use thereof. Brightman J disallowed the entire cost of the rental, holding that no apportionment was possible.

In practice, however, it is likely that an inspector would agree to a reasonable apportionment of fixed household costs. Nevertheless if (as seems likely), this treatment is purely concessional, it will not be open to the taxpayers to appeal against the inspector's conclusions.

It may be noted that the cost of *moving* house will be viewed as inevitably reflecting the personal purposes of the trader. This remains the case, even if the trader is relocating only in order to be closer to his place of work, as in *McKinlay v Arthur Young McClelland Moores & Co* [1989] STC 898. In that case, Lord Oliver observed:

> The question in each case is what was the object to be served by the disbursement or expense? As was pointed out by Lord Brightman in *Mallallieu's* case, this cannot be answered simply by evidence of what the payer says that he intended to achieve. Some results are so inevitably and inextricably involved in particular activities they cannot but be said to be a purpose of the activity. Miss Mallallieu's restrained and sober garb inevitably served and cannot but have been intended to serve the purpose of preserving warmth and decency and her purpose in buying cannot but have been, in part at least, to serve that purpose whether she consciously throughout about it or not. So here the payment of estate agents' fees, conveyancing costs and so on, and the provision of carpets and curtains cannot but have been intended to serve the purpose of establishing a comfortable private home for the partner concerned even though his motive in establishing a home in that particular place was to assist him in furthering the partnership interests. Nobody could say with any colour of conviction that in purchasing new curtains he or his wife was acting on partnership business.

Similarly, in *Mason v Tyson* [1980] STC 294 the taxpayer failed in his claim for the costs of maintaining a flat above his place of work, even though this facility enabled him to work longer hours than would otherwise have been the case.

It is also the case that part (b) of TCA 1997, s 81(2) explicitly disallows any expenses of 'maintenance of the parties or their families or any sums expended for any other domestic or private purposes distinct from the purposes of [the] trade or profession'. In practice, however it is difficult to envisage expenditure prohibited by para (b), which would not also fall foul of para (a).

Any deduction for rent or associated expenses incurred in relation to the provision of residential accommodation for *employees* of the trader does not require to be restricted if it can be established that the accommodation is provided wholly and exclusively for the purposes of the trade.

As noted above, rent payable under a lease entered into for business purposes will be allowable even if the premises subsequently become surplus to requirements (*IRC v*

Falkirk Iron Co 17 TC 625; see also *Hyett v Leonard* 2 TC 346, where the taxpayer closed down a branch and sublet the branch premises, the shortfall being allowed as a deductible expense).

In *Allied Newspapers Ltd v Hindsley* 21 TC 422, the taxpayer rented a site in order to secure continuing access to its own premises. Although the taxpayer occupied only a small part of the site, the costs of renting it were held to be deductible.

Transactions with related parties

(a) Associated companies

Where a taxpayer company in a corporate group incurs an expense on behalf of another company in the same group, it will often be difficult for the taxpayer company to establish that the expense was incurred solely in the interests of its trade (see the discussion of *Garforth v Tankard Carpets Ltd* at **5.304**). It will of course be insufficient for the taxpayer company to show that it will derive a benefit indirectly as the parent of the other company, since this benefit does not relate to its own trading activities. On the other hand, it will be easier to demonstrate that a payment made on behalf of a group company which has ceased to trade is activated solely in the interests of the taxpayer's trade (see *Sycamore & Maple v Fir* [1997] STC (SCD) 1).

In *Watney Combe Reid & Co Ltd v Pike* [1982] STC 733, the taxpayer, a brewery company, was denied a deduction for payments made to convert tied tenancies into managed tenancies. The court held that the purpose behind the payment was to provide additional business for the taxpayer's subsidiaries, which operated the managed tenancies.

In *Marshall Richards Machine Co Ltd v Jewitt* 36 TC 511, a company undertook to pay a minimum annual contribution towards the expenses of a subsidiary which acted as its agent overseas. The court held that on the facts the immediate purpose of the payment was to advance the trade of the subsidiary (although there was also an ulterior purpose, ie to benefit the UK company by maintaining an overseas presence). Accordingly, the payment was disallowed.

In *Odham's Press Ltd v Cooke* 23 TC 233, a parent company did work for a subsidiary and charged full trade prices. During one year the subsidiary made a loss and the parent company wrote off an equal amount of the debt due to it from the subsidiary. The amount written off was disallowed. Although the company may have had a trading purpose in writing off the debt, namely that it would continue to receive orders in the future from the subsidiary, it was held on the facts that this was not the only purpose for which the payment was made. A second purpose was to enable the *subsidiary* to continue in business; the expense could therefore not be said to have been incurred wholly and exclusively for the purpose of earning the *parent* company's own profits or gains.

In *Milnes v J Beam* 50 TC 575, the taxpayer, (a UK company) entered into a guarantee on behalf of an Irish company which sold its products on the Irish market. The Irish company also sold products other than those manufactured by the taxpayer. It was held that on the facts the guarantee could not have been incurred wholly and exclusively for the purposes of the taxpayer's trade. Accordingly, the loss which subsequently arose in respect of the guarantee was non-deductible.

In *Vodafone v Shaw* [1995] STC 353, [1997] STC 734, the activities of a mobile telephone network operation were split between three companies in order to meet regulatory requirements. The taxpayer company, which was the parent of the group, paid a large sum in order to terminate an onerous technical service agreement which it had entered into with a third party. It was contemplated that the subsidiaries would reimburse the parent for the proportion of the fees paid under the agreement which related to their activities. The Appeal Commissioners found that the directors of the taxpayer company regarded the group as 'one functioning trading entity' in relationship to the service agreement. The High Court held that it was inevitable that the purpose behind making the termination payment was to benefit the combined trading activities of the whole group, and that the payment was not deductible. The Court of Appeal held that the payment *was* deductible because the object behind it was to relieve the parent and the parent alone of the liability to the third party. The fact that it would no longer be necessary for the other group companies to contribute towards the parent's obligations under the technical agreement was held to be a consequence, and not a purpose, of the transaction. This rather legalistic analysis may arguably have been generous to the taxpayer.

In *Robinson v Scott Bader & Co* [1981] STC 436, the taxpayer was a company which had seconded an employee to work for a French subsidiary in order to rescue it from its financial difficulties. The court upheld the Appeal Commissioners' finding that the payment by the taxpayer of the seconded employee's salary was deductible. This was on the basis that the sole purpose of the secondment was to protect the taxpayer's own commercial interests in France. It should however be pointed out that the facts of the case were highly unusual and it would be unwise to rely too heavily on the decision as a precedent.

Complex considerations arise where a company makes purchases of goods or services, but there are arrangements in existence whereby the benefit of rebates or discounts in respect of such purchases are diverted to another group member. If these arrangements are legally binding then it seems clear that an appropriate part of the cost of those purchases is not incurred 'wholly and exclusively'. It would also seem that even if the arrangements are only based on an 'understanding', rather than a binding agreement, similar results should follow. This is because it is the *purpose* behind the purchases which counts, which is a matter of commercial reality or 'substance', rather than of legal form (see **1.407**). Support for this analysis can be found in Lord Wilberforce's dissenting speech in the Privy Council case of *Europa Oil (NZ) v IRC (NZ)* [1976] 1 All ER 503 (the majority held that the New Zealand business expenses rule, which is worded in a significantly different way to TCA 1997, s 81(2)(a), was to be applied in a purely legalistic fashion).

The kind of case just mentioned can be distinguished from one where a trader simply acquires goods or services on 'arms-length' terms from an entity in which it has a financial interest. All other things being equal, the purpose behind acquiring such goods or services will be solely to benefit the taxpayer's trade; the decision by the trader to carry out the transaction with a *particular* third party, thus benefiting its financial investment, arguably does not detract from this argument (see **5.304** above). In *Clifford v Son & Puttick* 14 TC 184, a mutual trading organisation (see **4.102**: *Mutual trading*) sold goods at a profit to one of its members and credited the surplus to the member's share of the mutual fund. This share of profit was not capable of being attributed to the trader, since it could not be drawn down by him. The Inland Revenue did not seek to argue that the price paid for the goods (which was in line with market values) was not incurred 'wholly and exclusively' for the purposes of the taxpayer's trade (following the decision in *Thomas v R Evans* 11 TC 790).

The treatment of bad debts in the group context is considered further in **5.314**.

(b) Family members

There is always a likely possibility that payments to members of the taxpayer's family may not have been incurred wholly and exclusively for the purposes of the trade. Following *Copeman v Flood* above (see also *Earlspring Properties v Guest* [1993] STC 472) it would seem that it is only the element of remuneration paid to a family member which is not incurred for trading purposes that should be disallowed. This will be a question of fact.

In *Dollar v Lyon* [1981] STC 333, the taxpayer was a farmer who made payments to his four children (aged 8 to 14) for their help on the farm. The court upheld the Appeal Commissioner's finding of fact that the payments to the three youngest children were paid as pocket money and not (as the taxpayer claimed) as wages. The Appeal Commissioners were entitled to take into account that the employment of the three youngest children would have been illegal on account of their ages.

The Appeal Commissioner decision [13TACD2016] looked at the case where a taxpayer claimed deductions in respect of wages in the sums of €18,200 for the tax year of assessment 2012 and €39,125 for 2013 in relation to Miss X, his sister, who he submitted was his employee during the relevant tax years of assessment. The Commissioner allowed a lower amount of wages noting 'The deficiency in records and documentation in proof of payment of Miss X's wages, in particular, the absence of weekly time sheets and payslips, prove disadvantageous for the Appellant in terms of the deduction claimed, in circumstances where he bears the burden of proof'.

Cost-sharing agreements

Cost-sharing agreements are typically (but not exclusively) found in the context of research and development expenditure incurred within a multinational group. The company which carries on a trade in the State will be required to bear a due proportion of such expenditure, commonly calculated by reference to its share of worldwide sales of products to which the expenditure relates. On the basis that the correct legal analysis is that the relevant expenditure is in fact jointly incurred, such expenditure should be analysed into its separate components; the normal rules for determining deductibility should then be applied to each component element of the expenditure. Where the apportionment between the various companies is skewed for non-commercial reasons (eg to save tax on a group-wide basis), this may infringe the 'wholly and exclusively' test. It is however generally unlikely that a multinational would seek to load costs on to its Irish subsidiaries.

Expenses of cessation and commencement

The expenses of closing down a trade are not deductible on general principles. This is simply because such expenses are by definition not designed to earn future profits or otherwise to enable or to facilitate, the *carrying on* of the trade. In *Godden v A Wilson's Stores (Holdings) Ltd* 40 TC 161 it was held that a payment in lieu of notice made to an employee in the course of closing down a trade was not deductible. In *O'Keeffe v Southport Printers* [1989] STC 443, payments made to employees in lieu of notice in order to bring forward the date of cessation of the taxpayer's trade were, however, held to be deductible. This was on the basis of the finding of fact of the Appeal Commissioners that the sole purpose of the payments was to avoid disruption of the trade up to the date of cessation.

In *CIR v Cosmotron Manufacturing Ltd* [1997] STC 1134, a Privy Council case, the taxpayer ceased business under the relevant employment legislation, and thereupon became liable to make severance payments to his employees. The court distinguished *Godden v Wilson's Stores* and held that such payments were deductible, since the original obligation to make them was incurred as a necessary condition of securing and retaining the services of the employees. The cessation of the taxpayer's trade was regarded as merely the event which caused this contingent obligation to crystallise. The decision looks dubious on its own facts, since it is hard to see how an obligation imposed by statute could have been incurred purposefully by the taxpayer. The decision, even if correct, would seem to have no relevance to *ex gratia* or additional termination payments made on the cessation of a trade, the nature of which presumably would have to be evaluated at the time when they are incurred.

The principle behind the decision in *Cosmotron* seems easier to justify in the context of payments to which employees are entitled under their contracts of service. However, it might even be argued in this case that it is the purposes behind the decision of the employer to *trigger off* the entitlement which should be the determining factor. In other words, if the taxpayer decides to cease trading, and thus to make his employees redundant, the purpose behind the payments which he becomes obliged to pay as a consequence, is that of ceasing to trade. Interestingly in *Mairs v Haughey*, a Sch E case discussed at **10.111**, the court held in effect that the loss of the employee's job was the direct cause of the termination payment received by him. The special treatment afforded to statutory redundancy payments is dealt with in **10.401**.

Where the trade is being transferred to a third party so that it is deemed to have been discontinued in the hands of the current trader, then expenses incurred on foot of the transfer may be disallowed in the same way as if there had been an actual cessation (see *Bidwell v Gardner* 39 TC 31, disapproving the decision in *IRC v Patrick Thompson Ltd* 37 TC 145, and see also *CD v O'Sullivan* II ITR 140).

Pre-trading expenses are similarly disallowable on general principles simply because at the time they are expended, the taxpayer is not a trader. TCA 1997, s 82(2) now provides statutory relief to a trader for certain pre-trading expenditure incurred for the purposes of a trade or profession set up or commenced by him on or after 22 January 1997. The expenditure must have been incurred no more than three years prior to commencement and must be such that it would have been allowable if it had been incurred after the commencement of the trade, etc. TCA 1997, s 390(2)(b) extends the relief to annual payments incurred wholly and exclusively for the purposes of the trade or profession within the three-year period if these were subject to assessment under TCA 1997, s 238(1) (see **2.304**). Expenditure relieved under TCA 1997, s 82(2) is treated as incurred at the date of commencement, but it is not allowed to create or increase a loss relief claim under TCA 1997, s 381. Annual payments relieved under TCA 1997, s 390(2)(b) are treated as falling within TCA 1997, s 382 (see **4.408**). The date on which expenditure is regarded as being 'incurred' is not spelt out by the legislation. Applying its normal usage, this would appear to be the date on which the legal obligation to make payment first arises (and not the date when payment falls due, if different). It may be noted that TCA 1997, s 82 does not provide relief for pre-trading expenses incurred by any person other than those actually commencing the trade. This could be particularly relevant in the case of pre-incorporation expenses.

The categories of expenditure which are likely to qualify would include the rent and running costs of business premises, payments of wages to employees engaged in activities preliminary to trading, accountancy fees, etc. Expenditure which is capital in nature, or is subject to a specific statutory disallowance, (eg entertaining expenses) will of course not be eligible for relief. The position regarding expenditure on feasibility studies is less clear in theory, since it could be argued that it is not incurred for the purposes of the trade but rather in order to determine whether or not to establish a trade in the first place. However, in *Tax Briefing 27*, the Revenue Commissioners indicate that they regard such expenditure, as well as the costs of preparing business plans, as deductible.

Where relief is obtained for expenditure by virtue of TCA 1997, s 82, no other allowance or deduction in respect of that expenditure is permitted (TCA 1997, s 82(4)). The availability of capital allowances for pre-commencement trading is discussed at **6.502**.

The Revenue Commissioners will concessionally allow interest paid on sums borrowed to fund capital projects to be set off against interest received on such sums where they are placed on deposit during the pre-trading period (*Tax Briefing 11*).

Appropriations and applications of profit

Appropriations are payment made out of profits, but *after* the profits have been earned or ascertained. Self-evident examples are a sole trader's drawings, salary and interest on capital paid to a partner, and dividends paid by a company. Payments made for the personal benefit of a partner are treated as appropriations in the usual way (see *McKinlay v Arthur Young* discussed above), but payments to the partner in return for services rendered, or goods supplied by him (other than as a partner) are deductible. Thus, in *Heastie v Veitch & Co* 18 TC 305, the cost of rental payments under a lease granted by an individual to a partnership of which he was a member was held to be allowable. The Revenue Commissioners have expressed the view that rent payable to *all* of the partners is not a deductible expense following *Rye v Rye* [1962] AC 496 where it was held that a lease to oneself is void, (but note *Ingram v IRC* [1999] STC 37 where it was held that a lease to a nominee is effective). The Appeal Commissioners have upheld the deductibility of rent paid to partners who owned a premise's in a different proportion to their profit shares in the partnership 7 AC 2000.

Payments to a person who is held out as a partner but who is in reality an employee (see *Stekel v Ellice* [1973] 1 WLR 191) will however be deductible to the same extent as payments to employees in general.

Payments to directors (or other employees) will not generally be rendered disallowable simply because they are expressed as a percentage of profits. However, where the directors are also shareholders, it is a matter of fact whether payments to them are in the nature of distributions of profits (see eg *Overy v Ashford Dunn & Co Ltd* 17 TC 497).

In *Union Cold Storage Co Ltd v Adamson* 16 TC 293, the taxpayer paid a rent which was subject to a downward adjustment if its profits fell below an agreed threshold. The court held that this factor did not convert the rent into a form of distribution. In *British Sugar Manufacturers Ltd v Harris* 21 TC 528, a payment for technical and financial services rendered to a business was held to be deductible as an expense, notwithstanding that the amount of the payment was calculated as a percentage of net profits. The payment was not an appropriation of profits, since the profits of the business were only arrived at after making the deduction.

Taxes levied on profits only arise when the profits have already been ascertained. Consequently, they represent a mere application of profits, as do any costs associated with disputing the correct amount of taxation due (see the discussion of *Smith Potato*

Estates Ltd v Bolland at **5.303** and see also *IRC v Dowdall O'Mahoney Ltd* 33 TC 259). The position is different where the tax in question is not levied on profits eg rates in respect of the occupation of business premises (see also *Harrods (Buenos Aires) Ltd v Taylor-Goodby*, discussed at **5.303**). Where such a tax is one which is imposed on specific transactions, then the deductibility (or otherwise) of that tax will follow the treatment of the underlying transaction.

One of the most significant taxes imposed on business is VAT. Expenditure will be computed net of recoverable VAT (in keeping with normal accounting practice); correspondingly, any irrecoverable VAT will form part of the expenditure to which it relates. Thus, eg if a VAT-exempt trader incurs irrecoverable VAT on the acquisition of new equipment, the VAT element will be disallowable as capital (it may however enhance the qualifying cost for the purposes of capital allowances (see **6.104**)). Conversely, irrecoverable VAT on the costs of heating the premises will be fully deductible.

Transfers to and from reserves, and the making of general provisions against future expenditure or losses are again merely applications of profits. In *Revenue Commissioners v Latchford & Sons Tralee* I ITR 240, the taxpayers had contracted to buy goods, the market value of which had subsequently fallen below the contract price. The High Court rejected a claim for the shortfall as a deductible expense, and held that no claim could be entertained for an 'apprehended and future loss not suffered during the accounting period'. The key point was that until the goods in question were actually sold, no loss (or profit) could actually arise. The importance of the 'realisation principle' is discussed at **5.201**. Exceptionally, trading stock may normally be valued at the lower of cost or net realisable value (see **5.401**).

Payments to terminate onerous obligations

Payments made in order to dispense with the services of an unsatisfactory employee will usually be allowable under general principles. In *Mitchell v BW Noble Ltd* 11 TC 372 Rowlatt J observed:

> I think that in the ordinary case a payment to get rid of a servant when it is not expedient to keep him in the interests of the trade would be a deductible expense. I leave out of consideration … special cases as when a servant is dismissed on the ground of a purely personal quarrel although his staying would not affect the trade at all … [A trader] has to employ a staff that will prove satisfactory to the customers of the trade, and he has also to cease from employing an inefficient staff and a staff that does not get on with the customers of the trade; and if he has to pay for that cessation, it seems to me that there is no reason why that should not be an expense incurred for the purposes of the trade.

However, payments made under the terms of a larger bargain may fail to qualify as a deductible expense. The tribunal of fact will, as usual, look at all the surrounding circumstances in order to ascertain the true intentions behind the payment. In *James Snook & Co v Blasdale* 33 TC 244, the shares of the taxpayer company were sold, but under the terms of the sale agreement, the purchasers of the shares were obliged to procure the taxpayer to pay compensation for loss of office to its existing directors and auditor (who themselves were bound to resign under the terms of the sale agreement). While the retirement of the existing directors was genuinely considered to be advantageous to the trade of the company, the payments made to obtain their retirement formed part of the bargain with a third party (ie the purchasers) in order to satisfy their commercial requirements. Accordingly, there was a 'duality of purpose' to the payments, which meant that they had to be disallowed in full. Donovan J, at first instance, observed:

> The mere circumstances that compensation to retiring directors is paid on a change of shareholding control does not of itself involve the consequence that such compensation can never be a deductible trading expense. So much is common ground. But it is essential in such cases that the company should prove to the Commissioner's satisfaction that it considered the question of payment wholly untrammelled by the terms of the bargain its shareholders had struck with those who were to buy their shares and came to a decision to pay solely in the interests of its trade.

Donovan J's observations formed the basis of the decision in *George J Smith & Co Ltd v Furlong* 45 TC 384 where two directors of the taxpayer company had agreed to sell their shares and also to resign their offices. The court took the view that the decision of the two directors to vote themselves payments for loss of office:

> is hardly likely to have been made because they thought the interests of the company required them to be made.

(See also *Peters & Co v Smith* 41 TC 264). In practice, an inspector is also likely to scrutinise closely any ex gratia payments made to proprietary directors on termination of their offices/employments.

Redundancy and analogous payments to ex-employees will normally be allowable (as will payments under pay restructuring agreements which attract Sch E exemptions under TCA 1997, s 202). The position of such payments in the context of a closure of business is considered separately under *Expenses of commencement and cessation*, above.

Payments made to terminate other types of onerous obligations will normally be deductible if the obligation itself is of the required trading nature. Thus, in *Anglo-Persian Oil Co Ltd v Dale* 16 TC 253, a payment to terminate an agency agreement which had become unprofitable was held to be allowable. The critical issue arising in respect of such payments tends to be whether or not they are capital in nature (see **5.307**).

Insurance costs

The expense of insuring assets – whether fixed assets, or assets which form part of the 'circulating capital' of the trade – is deductible. This is on the basis that such expense is incurred in order to preserve the profit-making structure of the trade, enabling any assets which are damaged or destroyed to be restored or replaced respectively.

The cost of insuring against potential expenses or losses is also generally allowable. In *Thomas v R Evans & Co Ltd* 11 TC 790, the cost of insuring against workmen's compensation claims was held to be allowable, since it served to mitigate a potential future expense. By way of contrast, in *Thomas Merthyr Colliery Co Ltd v Davis* 18 TC 519, subscriptions paid into a fund which provided indemnity against losses due to industrial action were disallowed. It was held that the subscriptions were paid not for the purposes of the trade, but 'to protect the trader against the absence of trade.'

The decision in the *Merthyr Colliery* case seems harsh. If the cost of insuring against potential losses and expenses is allowable, it is difficult to see why the cost of insuring against potential shortfalls of income (even if associated with a temporary cessation of trading) should not be equally allowable. This is particularly so given the decision in the *Tate & Lyle* case at **5.304**, where the costs of protecting the trader from the loss of his entire trade were allowed. This decision should therefore probably be regarded with considerable caution. In practice, premiums paid under loss of profits policies are likely to be accepted as deductible.

The Revenue Commissioners' practice concerning 'keyman' insurance policies has been clarified in *Tax Briefing 11*. The Revenue will treat premiums under such policies as deductible where the following conditions are met:

(a) the life covered must be that of an employee/director, and that must be the sole relationship with the employer;
(b) the life covered must not control more than 15 per cent of the ordinary capital of the company;
(c) the policy must be for a fixed term with no surrender value or endowment/investment content and must be payable only to the employer;
(d) the policy must relate to loss of profits only and not cover damage to goodwill or other capital loss and it must not cover repayment of loans on the death of an employee; and
(e) the policy must not be for a period exceeding five years and must not have a surrender value. Periods beyond five years will however be accepted in some cases.

Conditions (c) to (e) are concerned primarily with the issue as to whether the premiums refer to a capital investment. It is not clear however, why a policy designed to cover *damage* to goodwill should be regarded as disallowable in this regard (see the discussion below). The taxpayer is of course free to argue that on the facts a premium under a policy which falls outside the Revenue guidelines is nevertheless deductible under general principles. It is unlikely, however, that the taxpayer could succeed in such a claim where the policy had an investment element, as well as providing risk cover.

For the treatment of premiums under stop-loss policies, etc in the case of Lloyd's Underwriters see **13.506**. Premiums on a policy to cover potential loss of tax benefits are not deductible for obvious reasons; (conversely receipts under the policy are not taxable: see *Tax Briefing 11*).

5.307 Capital or revenue expenditure?

It is not sufficient that an item of expense has been incurred wholly and exclusively for the purposes of the trade. In order to secure the deduction of the expense, it is also necessary that it should not be of a capital nature. The prohibition of any deduction in respect of capital expenditure has probably been the subject of more tax cases than any other matter. The prohibition applies not only to the capital expenditure when incurred, but also to any losses of capital or losses on the disposal of fixed assets; it also requires any depreciation or amortisation of fixed assets that was charged in the accounts to be added back.

Where a proportion of the depreciation charged for the year is added to the value of closing stock (as eg in the distilling industry) it follows that only the net amount of depreciation actually debited in the profit and loss account should be added back *IOT v Mars UK Ltd* [2007] UKHL 15.

By definition capital expenditure should not be allowable in computing the *income* of a trade or profession. TCA 1997, s 81(2)(f) specifically prohibits a deduction in respect of 'any capital withdrawn from, or any sum employed or intended to be employed as capital in [a] trade or profession'. This wording seems to add nothing to the basic principle involved. In *Beauchamp v FW Woolworth plc* [1988] STC 714, the Court of Appeal held that an exchange loss incurred in connection with a capital liability did not fall within the UK equivalent of TCA 1997, s 81(2)(f). It would appear that TCA 1997, s 1088(2) which prohibits 'any deduction on account of the diminution of capital employed in any trade or profession', again adds nothing to general principles.

In *Ounsworth v Vickers* 6 TC 671, Rowlatt J took the view that the distinction between revenue and capital expenditure was between expenditure to meet a continuous demand and expenditure made once and for all. This rather simplistic approach may be useful in straightforward situations (eg in drawing the distinction between ongoing repairs and the cost of rebuilding premises: see *Fitzgerald v IRC* I ITR 91, where Rowlatt J's observations were in fact cited). Rowlatt J's approach was also applied in a situation where a 'once off' lump sum was paid to discharge a future stream of revenue expenditure (see *Hancock v General Reversionary & Investment Co* 7 TC 358 discussed below). However, a major limitation of this approach is that it does not address the nature of the means by which the 'continuous demand' of the trade is met. Thus, eg the payment of a premium to obtain a lease in one sense meets the continuous demand on the business for the right to occupy premises. Further, not all 'once and for all' payments are necessarily capital (see eg *Smith v Incorporated Council for Law Reporting* 6 TC 647, where an *ex gratia* lump sum paid to a retiring employee was held to be deductible).

In *Mallett v Staveley Coal & Iron Co* [1928] 13 TC 772, Lord Hanworth, MR said:

> It has been said that you may look to see whether or not you are dealing with a recurrent item, an item which would appear year by year in the profit and loss account, and if you are dealing with such an item, then even though you are making an out-and-out expenditure to redeem it you are still dealing with something which belongs to the profit and loss account. For my part, I do not believe that those tests, although they may be of some help in certain cases, are either fundamental, exact, or accurate. I think one has to keep clear in one's mind that in dealing with any business there are two kinds of capital, one the fixed capital which is laid out in the fixed plant, whereby the opportunity of making profits or gains is secured, and the other the circulating capital, which is turned over and over in the course of the business which is carried on.

The distinction between fixed and circulating capital is useful in many situations. It also emphasises that an asset may be 'fixed' by the very nature of the role it plays in the trade, even though it may be relatively short-lived in nature (in *Hinton v Madden and Ireland* 38 TC 391, various instruments with average lives of two years were held to be capital, albeit attracting allowances as plant); in *Abbot v Albion Greyhounds* 26 TC 390, greyhounds with a racing life of two years at most were held to be fixed assets in a trade of running greyhound races (it is arguable that they should have qualified as plant: see **6.202**). In *Henriksen v Grafton Hotel Ltd* 24 TC 353, a levy imposed on the grant of a publican's license, which confirmed the taxpayer's very right to trade and which attached to his premises, was held to be capital in nature, even though the license ran for only three years (note also *Dhendra v Richardson* [1997] STC (SCD) 265). It would seem most unlikely however that a payment which produces benefits spanning less than a year could ever be capital in nature (see eg *Tax Commissioner v Nchanga Consolidated Copper Mines Ltd*, considered below). The Revenue Commissioners have issued a precedent stating that they regard trade-related registration fees and licence renewal fees as being deductible in principle.

Lord Hanworth's approach has since been refined; this was necessary in order to classify expenditure on various intangibles which did not fall neatly within the 'fixed capital *v* circulating capital' dichotomy. An example of this kind of intangible was the cost of establishing a pension fund in *British Insulated & Helsby Cables Ltd v Atherton* 10 TC 155. In that case, Viscount Cave said:

> But when an expenditure is made, not only once and for all, but with a view to bringing into existence an asset or an advantage for the enduring benefit of a trade, I think that there is very good reason (in the absence of special circumstances leading to an opposite conclusion) for treating such an expenditure as properly attributable not to revenue but to capital.

The significance of Viscount Cave's words have been authoritatively clarified by Rowlatt J in *Anglo-Persian Oil Ltd v Dale* 16 TC 253, when he said:

> ... when an expenditure is made, not only once and for all, but with a view to bringing into existence an asset or advantage for the enduring benefit of a trade, then it is capital ... What Lord Cave is quite clearly speaking of is a benefit which endures, in the way that fixed capital endures; not a benefit that endures in the sense that for a good number of years it relieves you of a revenue payment. It means a thing which endures in the way that fixed capital endures. It is not always an actual asset but it endures in the way that getting rid of a lease or getting rid of onerous capital assets ... endures.

The implication of these observations is that benefits which are purely ephemeral, or which consist merely of improvements to trading methods or trading relationships, endure only in the ways that circulating capital endures. In *Tucker v Granada Motorway Services* [1979] STC 383, Lord Wilberforce observed:

> I think that the key to the present case is to be found in those cases which have sought to identify an asset. In them it seems reasonably logical to start with the assumption that money spent on the acquisition of the asset should be regarded as capital expenditure. Extensions from this are, first, to regard money spent on getting rid of a disadvantageous asset as capital expenditure, and, secondly, certainly to regard money spent on improving the asset, or making it more advantageous, as capital expenditure.

He added:

> ... the disposition of a source of liability may be equivalent to the acquisition of a source of profit – an extension perhaps of, but not an exception to, the principle that in some sense or other, an asset of a capital nature, tangible or intangible, positive or negative, must be shown to be acquired.

In *Tax Commissioners v Nchanga Consolidated Copper Mines Ltd* [1964] 1 All ER 200, Lord Radcliffe expressed the basis for the distinction in slightly wider terms, contrasting the cost of:

> creating, acquiring or enlarging the permanent (which does not mean perpetual) structure of which the income is to be the produce and the fruit with a cost of earning that income itself or performing the income earning operations.

This test has the virtue of covering expenditure which refers to the general framework of the trade (including fundamental contractual relationships), which might be difficult to conceive of as giving rise to an asset as such.

In *Regent Oil Co v Strick* 43 TC 1, Lord Reid cautioned against rigid reliance on any particular verbal formulae, saying:

> ... no one test or principle or rule of thumb is paramount. The question is ultimately a question of law for the court, but it is a question which must be answered in light of all the circumstances which it is reasonable to take into account, and the weight which must be given to a particular circumstance in a particular case must depend rather on common sense than on strict application of any single legal principle.

It appears that the distinction between capital and revenue must be made on the basis of commercial substance. According to Lord Pearce in *BP Australia v Commissioners of Taxation* [1966] AC 224, the distinction:

> depends on what the expenditure is calculated to effect from a practical point of view rather than upon the juristic classification of the legal rights, if any, secured employed or exhausted in the process.

Nevertheless, it will be important to carry out a correct legal analysis of the transaction, since any right or obligation created by the transaction may be a significant factor in ascertaining its commercial effect. Thus, for example a payment for a petrol tie which would otherwise be revenue in nature will usually become a capital item if it is built into the terms of a lease (see *Regent Oil v Strick*, discussed below). Similarly a payment of rent will generally be a revenue expense, whereas a premium, even if paid in instalments, will be capital (see *O'Sullivan v P* II ITR 464, which illustrates the fineness of this distinction).

It also appears that the revenue/capital distinction is objective in nature: ie one must look at *what* was actually done, rather than *why* the taxpayer did it (see *Lawson v Johnson Mathey plc* [1992] STC 466). As Rowlatt J pointed out in *Anglo-Persian Oil Ltd v Dale* 16 TL 253, the cost of a:

> fixed asset is capital even though one purpose behind acquiring it is to reduce revenue expenditure.

The dividing line between capital and revenue is often therefore a matter of overall impression. The problem is that there is an infinite variety of possible sets of facts but each set of facts must nevertheless be assigned to a simplistic 'black or white' category, ie revenue or capital. Exactly the same problem arises in the context of the distinctions between employment and self-employment (see **10.103**) and trading and non-trading (see **4.102**). As Jacob J expressed the matter in *Vodafone v Shaw* [1995] STC 353:

> One of the troubles with all the tests propounded by the courts is that they are necessarily imprecise. Given that any expenditure has got to be put in a box labelled 'revenue' or 'capital', there is an obvious difficulty in forcing many kinds of expenditure having some of the characteristics of both into one box or the other. Counsel on both sides used the expression 'capital feel' or 'revenue feel' about items under discussion. Even though it is a question of law there is a measure of gut reaction about the decision.

A number of cases have been set out below illustrating how the capital/revenue has been applied in practice by the courts. The cases have been grouped in a manner designed to illustrate how transactions which appear to bear a 'family resemblance' may nevertheless fall on different sides of the capital/revenue borderline.

In *McGarry v Limerick Gas Co* I ITR 375, the costs of promoting a bill in the Oireachtas to empower a gas undertaking to compensate employees dismissed as a result of improved efficiency, were held to be revenue in nature. The enactment of the bill did not give rise to any 'capital asset', and its effect was to allow the taxpayer to modernise its ongoing trading operations. Contrastingly, in *Moore v Hare* 6 TC 572, the costs of promoting two bills to empower the taxpayer to construct a railway line were disallowed. It was irrelevant that the bills were ultimately abandoned: it sufficed that the outcome which the expenditure was designed to bring about was itself capital in nature.

In *IRC v Carron Co* 45 TC 18, the costs of amending the terms of a company's charter, in order that it could trade more efficiently were held to be revenue in nature. Contrastingly in *Whitehead v Tubbs (Elastic) Ltd* [1984] STC 1, the costs of obtaining the release of certain onerous obligations contained in a loan agreement were held to be capital in nature. This was because they related to the alteration of a capital liability (similarly a payment to extinguish a capital liability was held to be non-deductible in *Countess Warwick Steamship v Ogg* 9 TC 652). In *Texas Land & Mortgage Co v Hallam* 3 TC 285, the expenses of issuing debentures and raising capital generally were held to be capital.

In *Kealy v O'Mara* I ITR 642, three companies were amalgamated under a common holding company in order to enhance their profitability. The High Court held that the costs of forming the new holding company were capital. Maguire P observed:

> We must consider the effect of the expenditure apart from the object in view. Did its use produce profits in the way in which circulating capital does or did it bring into being something permanent of enduring? The transformation which has taken place involves the [taxpayer] company, alters its structure and destroys its independence. Something enduring has come into being which will affect the future working of all the companies concerned.

Similarly, in *Watney Combe Reid & Co Ltd v Pike* [1982] STC 733, costs associated with a corporate restructuring under which a brewery company bought out individual tenants in order to transfer the tenancies to its subsidiary companies, were held to be capital. These last two cases may be distinguished from *IRC v Carron Co* on the basis that the expenses in the latter case concerned the internal constitution of the taxpayer company, as opposed to its capital structure. Consequently no identifiable 'asset' was brought into being, nor could it be said that the structure of the trade had been altered.

In *Cooke v Quick Shoe Repair Service* 30 TC 460, the taxpayer acquired a trade on terms which required the vendor to discharge all the liabilities to suppliers and employees. When the vendor subsequently defaulted, the taxpayer discharged these liabilities in order to protect the goodwill of the trade. It was held that the cost of so doing was a revenue expense (see also *Sycamore & Maple v Fir* [1997] STC (SCD) 1). Contrastingly, in *Casey v AB Ltd* II ITR 500, the taxpayer was a company which had acquired a trade, agreeing to take over all of the existing assets and liabilities. The High Court held that the legal costs of settling the amount due in respect of one of the liabilities were capital. In effect, these costs related to the ascertainment of part of the consideration payable by the taxpayer for the trade. In the *Quick Shoe Repairs Service* case the payments were *ex gratia* sums, the effect of which was to preserve ongoing trading relationships.

In *Commissioner of Inland Revenue v New Zealand Forest Research Institute Ltd* (NZFRI) [2000] STC 522 the payment by the purchaser of certain of the vendor's liabilities as part of the purchase consideration was held to be a capital payment irrespective of the fact that if the payments had been made by the vendor that they would have been regarded as revenue expenses. The taxpayer company agreed to purchase the business and assets of the vendor, whereby part of the purchase consideration was the assumption of certain liabilities of the vendor, including certain of the vendor's contractual obligations to its employees. It was held that since the payments related to the acquisition of a capital asset, that they constituted a capital expense.

In *Ogden v Medway Cinemas* 18 TC 691, an annual payment for the goodwill of a cinema business was held to be a revenue expense. The company had acquired an underlease of the cinema premises at an annual rent and had, at the same time for the same period, acquired the goodwill of the business carried on in the premises, with an option to purchase the headlease and goodwill outright for £3,500. In *Walker v Joint Credit Card Co* [1982] STC 427, the taxpayer, a credit card operator, paid a competitor a lump sum to cease trading permanently. The sum was held to be capital in nature, since it had the effect of enabling the taxpayer to become the sole licensee of an international network, as well as protecting the taxpayer's goodwill permanently from the risks of competition from an aggressive rival (see also *United Steel Companies Ltd v Cullington (No 1)* 23 TC 71). The *Joint Credit Card Co* case differs from the *Medway Cinemas* case in so far as the former involved an outright acquisition of a 'capital' advantage; it also differs from the *Quick Shoe Repair Service* case, in that the latter case did not entail any enhancement or addition to the trader's goodwill.

In *Associated Portland Cement Manufacturers v Kerr* 27 TC 103, a payment to an employee in return for a worldwide restrictive covenant effective for the employee's lifetime was held to be capital on similar reasoning to that applied in the *Walker* case. The effect of that particular decision has now been largely reversed by statute (see **5.308**: *Restrictive Covenants*). In *Commissioner of Taxes v Nchanga Consolidated Mines* [1964] AC 468, the taxpayer, a copper-producing company, paid a lump sum to a competitor to suspend its trading for 12-months. The Privy Council held that because the rights obtained were exhausted within 12-months, the lump sum was revenue expenditure. It is not possible to state precisely how long rights of this kind must endure before they cross the borderline and become capital.

In *Pyrah v Annis* 37 TC 163, the costs of a failed application to upgrade a public carrier's licence was treated as capital, (this case again illustrates that expenditure designed to achieve a capital outcome remains capital in nature, even if that outcome is not in fact achieved). Clearly, a licence may well form part of the 'profit making structure' of the trade if it confers the right to trade (or to expand one's trade); see also *Henriksen v Grafton Hotel Ltd* 24 TC 353, noted above. On the other hand, the cost of renewing an annual licence (ie preserving an existing capital asset) was allowed in *Usher's Wiltshire Breweries Ltd v Bruce* 6 TC 399. The Revenue Commissioners have issued a precedent stating that they regard trade-related registration fees and licence renewal fees as being deductible in principle.

The costs of acquiring new premises are clearly capital, as are associated costs such as the laying of roads (see *Pitt v Castle Hill Warehousing Co Ltd* [1974] STC 420 where the taxpayer gave up its right to use a road in exchange for the right to build a new road); the installation of drainage (*Bean v Doncaster Amalgamated Collieries* 27 TC 296); the costs of deepening a channel to enable a shipbuilder to launch his ships, even though the channel was not on the taxpayers property (*Ounsworth v Vickers* 6 TC 671); the cost of rebuilding premises which had been destroyed, even though this was under a tenants repairing covenant (*Fitzgerald v IRC* I ITR 91).

As already noted, the economic cost represented by the wasting or wearing away of capital (ie depreciation or amortisation) is equally capital in nature. This remains the position, even though the asset is consumed in the process of production, as in the case of a mine: *Coltness Iron Co v Black* 1 TC 311. The position is rectified to some extent by the availability of capital allowances (see **Division 6**).

In *Rolfe v Wimpey Waste Management* [1989] STC 454, the taxpayer was a waste disposal company which had acquired various landfill sites. The sites were typically held for 7 to 11 years and were in use for waste-tipping purposes for four years on average. The Court of Appeal held that the costs of these sites were capital, rejecting an argument that what the taxpayer had acquired in reality was 'airspace'. Given the length of time for which the sites were held, the court also held that they were clearly capital assets (see *IRC v Adam* 14 TC 34, where the right to deposit slag on land for eight years was held to be capital). On the other hand, costs associated with the on-going occupation or use of premises (eg rent and rates, which are recurrent in nature are clearly allowable: see eg *Wildbore v Luker* 33 TC 46). Payments of a sum to acquire an interest in a capital asset by instalments remain capital in nature (see *IRC v Land Securities Trust Ltd* 45 TC 495).

The costs of moving to new premises (whether or not this involves relocating from existing premises) are also capital in nature (see *Granite Supply Assoc v Kitton* 5 TC 168, followed in *Fitzgerald v IRC* I ITR 91; see also *Smith v Westinghouse Brake Co Ltd* 2 TC 357). In practice, the Revenue Commissioners are generally prepared to allow the expenses of moving trading stock in the case of a continuing trade. Disallowed expenses which relate to moving plant and machinery should be added to the cost of the relevant assets for capital allowance purposes (see **6.202**).

The costs of acquiring or improving a fixed asset may be contrasted with the costs of protecting and preserving it. In *Southern v Borax Consolidated* 23 TC 597, legal costs incurred to protect the taxpayer's title to land and buildings abroad, which were used for the purposes of its business, were held to be deductible. The Crown had contended that the expenditure was capital, having been incurred to preserve the capital assets of the company. Rejecting this argument, Lawrence LJ stated:

> ... in my opinion the principle which is to be deduced from the cases is that where a sum of money is laid out for the acquisition or the improvement of a fixed capital asset, it is attributable to capital, but that if no alteration is made in the fixed capital asset by the payment, then it is properly attributable to revenue, being in substance a matter of the maintenance of the capital structure or the capital assets of the company.

(See also *Morgan v Tate & Lyle Ltd* 35 TC 367, where the cost of preserving the entire trade from the threat of nationalisation was held to be revenue in nature).

Similarly, in *Davis v X Ltd* II ITR 45, the taxpayer was a manufacturing company which had built a new factory. A number of householders subsequently claimed compensation on the basis that the factory infringed their rights to light and air. The taxpayer's lawyers advised that these claims were unsustainable, but that it would nevertheless be financially expedient to settle them. The Supreme Court held that the compensation payments to the householders and associated legal costs were allowable. Murnaghan J observed:

> ... this was not a capital payment ... for, if the action had gone to trial and the company had won, it would have been established that no asset had been created, no enduring benefit would have ensued, but only a declaration that the company was within its rights in building the factory.

The position would have been different if the householders claim had been valid (or tenable); in this latter case, the compensation would have been made in effect to 'buy out' their rights and would have been an element of the capital cost of creating the new factory. This latter analysis was adopted by Judge Sheridan in *Insulation Products Ltd v IOT* [1984] ILRM 610, where the costs of settling a claim for nuisance in respect of a premise's used for manufacturing were held to be capital. In *Hibernian Insurance Co v MacUimis* V ITR 495, [2000] ILRM 196, Carroll J held that costs incurred by an investment company in evaluating potential future investments were capital in nature. The learned judge took the view that the costs in question were so closely linked to the transaction of purchase that they could be regarded as part of the costs of purchase. This decision was affirmed in the Supreme Court. In fact it does not seem to have been necessary to characterise the costs in question in this way; the fact that they were intimately related to the process of acquiring fixed assets would have been sufficient to establish their disallowable nature. Thus, it is clear, that the non-allowability of such costs would not be affected by the fact that the taxpayer decided not to proceed with a particular purchase (compare the arguably generous decision in *Holdings Ltd v IRC* [1997] STC (SCD) 144).

In *Bradbury v United Glass Bottle Manufacturers Ltd* 38 TC 369, a trader made a payment to the national coal board in return for their agreeing not to mine coal in the proximity of the trader's factory, which was otherwise in danger of subsiding; the payment was held to be capital since it had the effect of enhancing a capital asset (which was now free of the threat of subsidence).

In *EEC Quarries v Watkis* [1975] STC 578, the taxpayer was a company whose trading operations included the extraction of stone and gravel. It was held that the costs of obtaining planning permission for such extraction in respect of land which it owned were capital (ie it entailed the enhancement of an existing capital asset). Similarly, the cost of sinking a mine shaft in order to enable trading by way of extraction to take place is capital in nature (*Bonner v Basset Mines* 6 TC 146).

By way of contrast, in *Milverton Quarries v Revenue Commissioners* II ITR 382, the taxpayer company worked a limestone quarry. It needed to ensure that the topsoil was removed before blasting in order to maintain the purity of the limestone. Maguire J, delivering the judgment of the Supreme Court, observed:

> … The expense of removal of the top soil is a recurrent expenditure becoming necessary from time to time as the rock face is blasted out and removed for processing. No capital asset is created. There is no once and for all operation. The conditions of this business seem to be more akin to what is called surface coal mining. There is no shaft. A shaft however deep may be necessary as an initial capital expenditure to get down to the coal or the mineral which it is sought to remove from the earth. It may have to be extended. But in any event it is intended as a lasting benefit which may endure for the life of the mine. Essentially the purpose of the company's business was to convert the raw material, limestone, into a marketable product, limestone flour.

In *Dolan v AB Co Ltd* II ITR 575, the taxpayer was a petrol marketing company which paid lump sums and reimbursed certain costs to retailers in order to induce them to enter into exclusive or 'solus' agreements. The lump sums were calculated by reference to estimated gallonage over the life of the relevant agreements. 75 per cent of the agreements were for periods of five years or less; 22 per cent were for periods of between 8 and 10 years, and the remaining 3 per cent were for periods of between 11 and 20 years. The majority in the Supreme Court held that the lump sums paid in respect of all the agreements were revenue items. Budd J, delivering the majority judgment, relied heavily on the decision in *Bolam v Regent Oil Co Ltd* 37 TC 56 (as approved by the Privy Council in *BP Australia v Commissioners of Taxation* [1966] AC 224), where sums paid to obtain exclusivity agreements for periods up to six years were held to be revenue in nature. Budd J cited the following factors as influential in his reasoning:

(a) The expenditure was made in acquiring 'floating [ie circulating] capital'; the lump sum payments were made:

> with a view to acquiring a market, the returns from which will be turned over in the course of trade and the process commences almost immediately.

In effect, the expenditure was similar to a lump sum paid in lieu of granting rebates in order to secure custom. The learned judge did however concede that if a case arose where there was a heavy preponderance of long-term agreements then:

> It could well be demonstrated that something more than circulating capital was being used to make the payment … and the amounts expended could not be met out of the returns of income save over a very lengthy period and hence … a capital expenditure was involved.

The logic here indicates that a payment, which is otherwise revenue in nature, can lose that revenue quality because it relates to a sufficiently lengthy period.

(b) The outlay was recurrent in so far as the ties had to be continuously renewed. Accordingly, it was not incurred on a 'once and for all' basis. The true significance of this factor is perhaps doubtful. Fixed assets may equally require regular replacement: the issue should probably have been the recurrence (or otherwise) of *each tie*, looked at separately.

(c) The exclusivity agreements did not involve an alteration in 'the profit-making structure of the business', since they were merely another method of obtaining sales. There was no reason for treating the agreements for periods in excess of 10 years any differently, since the method of trading did not differ in those cases.

(d) The proper accounting treatment was in line with the taxpayer's contentions and was a 'factor weighing heavily in favour of the [taxpayers] unless and until it is shown that the deductions may fall under some prohibition contained in the Income Tax Acts' (but see the discussion at **5.102**).

In *Strick v Regent Oil* 43 TC 1, the taxpayer was again a petrol marketing company. On this occasion, the lump sum for the exclusivity agreement was paid to the retailer as a premium for the grant of a lease of his business premises; the premises were subsequently leased back to the retailer, who covenanted to sell only the taxpayer's products under the terms of the sublease. The House of Lords held *inter alia* that the payment of premiums were capital in nature, since the taxpayer had thereby acquired an interest in land. The interest in land was not merely technical in nature, since from a business perspective, it enabled the taxpayer to grant a sublease with a valuable covenant in its favour.

Lord Reid suggested that the cost of leases for less than two to three years might be revenue in nature. It is unlikely however that the cost of a straightforward lease of business premises for a period of this length could be other than capital, given that it relates to what is unequivocally a fixed asset. In *Owen & Gadson v Brock* 32 TC 206, a property acquired to provide temporary accommodation for an employee and which was sold after 18-months, was held by the High Court to be a capital asset although in this case, the court did take the view that the taxpayer's intentions were such that the asset might have been held indefinitely.

The Law Lords also indicated in the *Regent Oil* case that sums paid for agreements for periods of 20 years or longer had the 'once and for all' quality of capital expenditure; this view is not consistent with the more liberal approach adopted by the Supreme Court in *Dolan v AB*. The treatment of the receipt of the lump sums in the hands of the retailers is discussed at **5.209**. It may be noted however, that there is no necessary correlation between the tax treatments of the payer and the recipient.

Payments to discharge onerous obligations will normally be revenue in nature if the obligation does not represent an element of a capital asset or of a capital liability. Thus, in *Mitchell v Noble* 11 TC 372, a sum paid to an unsatisfactory director in consideration for her retirement was accepted to be a revenue expense; (in effect, it discharged all future obligations to make payments of salary to the individual concerned).

In *Anglo-Persian Oil Co Ltd v Dale* 16 TC 253, a lump sum payment to terminate an agency agreement, made because the commission due under it had become disproportionately costly, was treated as a revenue item. Lawrence LJ stated that the termination of the agreement 'merely effected a change in the company's business methods and internal organisation' (compare the similar analysis in *IRC v Carron* discussed above). However, it is possible that an agency agreement may be so central as to form part of the 'profit making' structure of the trade: see *Van den Berghs v Clarke* discussed at **5.204**.

In *Vodafone v Shaw* [1997] STC 734, the taxpayer had entered into an agreement with a third party under which the latter agreed to supply initial know-how together with technical support and training services in return for a fee equivalent to 10 per cent of the taxpayer's profits. The agreement subsequently became uneconomic and the taxpayer paid the third party a lump sum in order to terminate it. The Court of Appeal held that the lump sum was revenue in nature on two grounds. Firstly, at the date of termination (the critical date) the contract did not relate to the whole structure of the appellant's profit-making apparatus (ie as in *Anglo-Persian Oil Co v Dale*). Secondly, the agreement did not relate to the acquisition of a capital asset. Millet LJ observed:

> High technology, particularly in modern times, is quickly obsolete. Expenditure to acquire *future* know-how is paid to obtain a service; it is not made to acquire an enduring asset, but a commodity which is turned over or exploited in the course of trade at a comparatively early date (emphasis added).

(See also *Croydon Hotel and Leisure Co v Bowen* [1996] STC (SCD) 466 where the Special Commissioners also took into account the position of the recipient of the payment, which should have been irrelevant; however, this does not seem to detract from the correctness of the actual decision.)

Contrastingly, in *Tucker v Granada Motorway Services* [1979] STC 393, the taxpayer held a lease under which part of its rent varied according to its turnover. The court held that a lump sum paid to reduce this variable element, which had become excessive, was capital, ie it was an enhancement of the lease, which was a capital asset, even though ultimately the result of the expenditure was to reduce the revenue outgoings of the trader (see also *Mallett v Staveley Coal & Iron Co* [1928] 13 TC 772, and *IRC v Wm Short & Sons* 38 TC 341). Limited reliefs will usually be available under TCA 1997, s 102 for payments of this nature (see **5.308** *Premiums for leases, etc*).

An onerous obligation which would normally be revenue in nature will however be capital if it is assumed as part of the cost of acquiring the trade. Accordingly, the cost of terminating the obligation will also be capital (see *Casey v AB Ltd* discussed above).

Logically, a sum paid in order to commute, or to be freed from, an ongoing revenue expense, should be revenue in nature, unless this entails the creation of an enduring asset. Thus, in *Hancock v General Reversionary & Investment Co* 7 TC 358, the cost of purchasing an annuity for the benefit of a retired employee was held to be a revenue expense (ie it displaced the need to make future pension payments; see also *Green v Cravens Railway Carriage & Wagon Co* 32 TC 859). In *Heather v PE Consulting Group* 48 TC 293, payments made under a covenant to trustees of a discretionary trust established to buy shares on behalf of the trader's employees were held to be deductible.

In *Jeffs v Ringtons Ltd* [1985] STC 809, contributions to a trust fund set up in order to supplement the pensions of certain employees were again held to be revenue in nature. Conversely, in *British Insulated & Helsby Cables Ltd v Atherton* 10 TC 155, a 3–2 majority in the House of Lords held that a single lump sum paid to establish a pension fund was capital, although subsequent contributions were held to be on revenue account. The basis of the distinction is difficult to discern, since the effect of *all* the contributions, initial or otherwise, was to fund future pension payments. In *Jeffs v Ringtons Ltd* [1985] STC 809 Scott J sought to distinguish the *PE Consulting* case from the *Atherton* case on the basis that, in the former case, the fund was uncertain as to amount and duration, and could be wound up at short notice. This does not appear to be altogether convincing. In the *PE Consulting* case, the court distinguished *Atherton* on the basis that the benefits provided to employees in the former case were discretionary in nature. However, it seems that the *legal* costs of establishing a fund designed to form a permanent vehicle for the investment of funds for the benefit of employees would be capital in nature. The treatment of approved superannuation schemes is dealt with at **16.102**.

The distinction between payments for the ongoing supply of technical assistance or information (revenue) and acquisition of enduring intellectual property rights (capital) can also give rise to difficulties. In *S Ltd v O'Sullivan* II ITR 602, the taxpayers, decided to expand one of their manufacturing activities. In order to achieve this, they entered into a contract for 10 years with a UK firm, W, which had specialised knowledge of the relevant production methods. Under the contract W agreed *inter alia* that it would:

(a) make available to J over the life of the agreement all necessary technical information;
(b) allow S to take copies of all relevant patterns, designs and property belonging to W and to grant S an exclusive license under any patents taken out by W over the life of the agreement; and
(c) not disclose any relevant information or techniques to any other traders in Ireland (or Northern Ireland).

In return, S was obliged to pay W what was described as a 'capital sum' of £15,000 in a number of instalments. Kenny J in the High Court held that the capital sum was exactly that. The factors which influenced his conclusion included:

(a) the length of the agreement;
(b) the fact that the taxpayer acquired a knowledge base which was used to produce income;
(c) the fact that the agreement was associated with the development of an important branch of the business, so that its 'profit-making structure' was thereby altered;
(d) the fact that the payment itself did not vary with turnover or profits (ie so that it could not have been argued to have been in the nature of a service charge or commission); and
(e) the exclusivity of the rights acquired.

In *Vodafone v Shaw* [1997] STC 734, Millet LJ (see above) contrasted the arrangements in that case with those in the *O'Sullivan* case, in which he said there were three significant features:

> Firstly, the payments were expressed to be instalments of capital; secondly they were payable for present as well as future know-how; and thirdly the taxpayer company obtained the benefit of an agreement by the other party that it would not disclose the information to any other person carrying on business in Ireland.

In some cases, a statutory deduction is granted in respect of capital expenditure on know-how (see **5.308**).

A Circuit Court judge has held that the cost of course fees in order to obtain an additional qualification are capital in nature (depending on the relevance of the qualification to the taxpayer's trade, such expenses may also be open to challenge under the 'wholly and exclusively' test). The cost of courses merely to update the expertise of the trader or his employees should however be revenue in nature.

In unusual cases, expenditure which relates to a transaction in respect of a capital asset may not itself be capital in nature. In *Lawson v Johnson Mathey plc* [1992] STC 466, the taxpayer company owned a banking subsidiary, J which had become insolvent. If J had been allowed to go into liquidation, the resulting loss of confidence in the taxpayer company would have led to the collapse of its trade. The Bank of England also wished to avoid the failure of J and agreed in effect to acquire J and to support it thereafter. However, the taxpayer company was firstly required to inject a payment of £50 million on a non-refundable basis into J. The House of Lords held the this payment was on revenue account, since it was not paid to dispose of an onerous asset (ie the shares in J) but as part of the price for rescuing J. (It may be noted that the payment was 'wholly and exclusively' for the purpose of the taxpayer's trade: although the payment benefited J, this was only an incidental side effect, particularly since the taxpayer was giving up any future financial interest in J in any event).

In *Walker v Cater Securities* [1974] STC 390, the taxpayer was a company which held shares in its main customer, X. A third party held an option over the shares enabling him to buy them at market value. The taxpayer subsequently paid a lump sum to the third party in exchange for his surrendering the option. This was done to eliminate the possibility of the third party exercising his option and then using his shareholding influence to cause X to stop doing business with the taxpayer. The court held that the payment was a revenue expense, being made to retain a key customer. It was significant that the surrender of the option did not enhance the value of the shares held by the taxpayer, so that there was no enhancement of a capital asset involved. Contrastingly in *Bolton v International Drilling Co* [1983] STC 70, a payment for the release of an option which was necessary to secure ownership of the asset in question was held to be capital (the expenditure was however eligible for capital allowances as part of the cost of providing the asset for the purposes of the trade).

The cost of purchasing an asset from which trading stock will ultimately be extracted or produced will be capital. Thus in *IRC v Pilcher* 31 TC 314, the cost of acquiring a cherry orchard, including the current year's maturing crop, was held to be capital. The cost of acquiring stock as a distinct and separate item from the other assets of a business will however be deductible on general principles.

The cost of circulating capital other than trading stock (eg debtors) acquired on taking over a business will generally be capital in nature. This includes the cost of taking over uncompleted contracts (even though subsequently carried out at a profit) as in *City of London Contract Corporation v Styles* 2 TC 239. In *John Smith & Son v Moore* 12 TC 266, the benefit of short-term purchase contracts taken over as part of the acquisition of an entire business, was held to be a capital item. The benefit of accumulated know-how is likely to attract similar treatment if acquired on the takeover of a business; no statutory deduction is available in this case: see **5.308**.

Losses associated with liabilities of a capital nature will themselves be capital in nature. In *Beauchamp v FW Woolworth* [1989] STC 510, the taxpayer company borrowed Swiss Francs for a five-year period. When the loan was redeemed the taxpayer incurred a large exchange loss due to the fall in value of the sterling.

Lord Templeman, following *Farmer v Scottish North American Cross Ltd* 5 TC 693, held that:

> The basic principle in regard to loans in that if they are a means of fluctuating and temporary accommodation they are to be regarded as revenue transactions and not accretions to capital.

In the House of Lords, Lord Templeman took the view that a five-year loan could never qualify as a fluctuating and temporary accommodation. He distinguished *Regent Oil v Strick* where Lord Reid had held that the cost of securing six-year long petrol 'ties' could qualify as a revenue expense, on the basis that such ties were 'an ordinary incident of marketing'. He also held that the use to which the borrowed money was put was of relevance only in doubtful cases (see also the discussion of *Wharf Properties v CIR*, at **5.315**.)

The *Beauchamp* decision may be contrasted with that of the High Court, subsequently upheld by the Supreme Court, in *Brosnan v Mutual Enterprises Ltd* V ITR 138. In that case, the taxpayer borrowed £250,000 from a bank in order to acquire business premises. The loan, which was secured on the premises was due to be repaid on a reducing basis over five years, although legally repayable on demand. Over the period of repayment the loan was switched into various foreign currencies with a view to minimising interest costs. These switches resulted in the taxpayer incurring exchange losses. In the High Court, Murphy J upheld the finding of Appeal Commissioners that the losses were revenue in nature as a finding of fact, ie following the principle set out in *Edwards v Bairstow* (see **2.204**). This approach was endorsed by the Supreme Court, in contrast to the decision of the House of Lords in the *Woolworth* case, where the capital/revenue distinction was held to be one of law. The Supreme Court rejected Lord Templeman's contention that a five-year loan could never be 'fluctuating and temporary', (so that it could not be said that no reasonable tribunal of fact could conclude that a loss in respect of such a loan was revenue in nature).

5.308 Deductions permitted by statute, concessions etc

The Tax Acts contain a number of provisions permitting the deduction of certain items of expense which might otherwise be disallowable through failing to satisfy either or both of the wholly and exclusively and the revenue expenditure tests. Deductions are specifically permitted under the Acts for certain expenses under the headings and in the circumstances noted below.

Contributions to pension schemes

TCA 1997, s 774 grants a deduction for contributions paid by an employer to provide pensions and related benefits for his employees (including the directors of a company), but only if the contributions are paid to an exempt approved pension scheme. TCA 1997, s 84 permits the deduction of expenses paid in connection with the setting up or alteration of a pension or superannuation scheme, provided that it is a scheme approved by the Revenue Commissioners under TCA 1997, s 772. The expenses incurred, which may include professional fees, are deductible in arriving at the taxable profits for the period of account in which they are paid. It may be noted that accrued contributions or expenses are not allowable.

TCA 1997, s 787J grants a deduction for contributions actually paid under PRSA contracts (see **16.3**) for employees but excludes a deduction for any other expenses incurred in relation to such contributions; a deduction is only allowed in respect of employees who work in a business the profits of which are liable to Irish tax.

Unless the scheme is an exempt approved one, the deductibility of the employer's contributions will be subject to general principles (see the discussion of *British Insulated & Helsby Cables v Atherton* at **5.307** and *Hancock v General Reversionary & Investment Co* 7 TC 358 at **5.307**; note also *Dracup v Dakin* 37 TC 377). The conditions for the approval by the Revenue Commissioners of a pension scheme, the circumstances in which a scheme is an exempt approved scheme and the manner of allowing contributions, including those that are not ordinary annual contributions, are dealt with in **Division 16**.

Patents and trade marks

Any fees paid or expenses incurred in obtaining, for the purposes of a trade, the grant of a patent or an extension of the term of a patent are deductible as an expense of the trade TCA 1997, s 758. This deduction refers to the legal, patent agent or other fees or expenses incurred in carrying out the formalities for the granting or extension of the patent rights, whether in the State or in any other country, but it does not refer to the capital cost of acquiring patent rights.

Any fees paid or expenses incurred in obtaining, for the purposes of a trade, the registration of a trade mark or the renewal of the registration of a trade mark are deductible as expenses of the trade TCA 1997, s 86.

Payments for know-how

A trader may incur expenditure on acquiring for use in his business technical or other information coming under the general description of know-how. In the ordinary way, if the expenditure is not of a capital nature it is fully deductible, but capital expenditure would not be allowed (see the *O'Sullivan* case discussed at **5.307**). TCA 1997, s 768 provides that subject to certain exceptions a trader may deduct as a trading expense any expenditure including capital expenditure in acquiring know-how for use in his trade, if it would not otherwise be deductible.

Apart from permitting the deduction of capital expenditure on know-how, TCA 1997, s 768 allows qualifying expenditure incurred before the commencement of trading to be deducted as an expense in the period of account in which the trade is set up and commenced, provided the know-how is in fact used in the trade (TCA 1997, s 768(2)).

'Know-how' is defined for the purpose of the section as:

> industrial information and techniques likely to assist in the manufacture or processing of goods or materials, or in the carrying out of any agricultural, forestry, fishing, mining or other extractive operations (TCA 1997, s 768(1)).

The adjective 'industrial' presumably applies to both the terms 'information' and 'techniques'. There is considerable Irish case law on the meaning of the term 'manufacturing', with respect to the 10 per cent rate of Corporation Tax, which may arguably be of relevance in the present context (see **6.401**). It would seem clear that know-how in relation to the marketing and distribution of a product does not qualify under this definition.

There are two exceptions. Firstly, no deduction is given for capital expenditure where a person (the 'acquirer') acquires the whole or part of a trade together with know-how used therein or, with effect for the tax year 2008 onwards, where the acquirer acquires the whole or part of a trade and a person connected to him (as defined by TCA 1997, s 10) (the 'associate') acquires the know-how used in such trade (TCA 1997, s 768(3)). This provision is designed to prevent connected parties splitting the purchase of the trade and the know-how between them. However, with effect from 2009 onwards, a deduction will be available to the associate against the profits of any trade carried on by the associate in which such know-how is put to use, unless at any time that trade or a part of that trade is transferred to the acquirer. Where the deduction creates or increases a trading loss, that element of the loss will be carried forward as treated as expenditure incurred on know-how in computing the relevant trading profits of subsequent tax years. In addition, from 2009 onwards, no deduction will be available either as an expense or annual charge in relation to royalties or any payments made for the use of the know-how to the associate by the acquirer or any person connected to the acquirer (again, as defined by TCA 1997, s 10) (the 'associate'). Provision is made for the claw-back of relief subsequently found not to be due by way of assessment under Sch D Case IV, which may be raised at any time TCA 1997, s 768(6).

Secondly, no deduction is given where:

(a) the buyer is a body of persons over whom the seller has control;
(b) the seller is a body of persons over whom the buyer has control; or
(c) both the seller and the buyer are bodies of persons over both of which some other person has control (TCA 1997, s 768 (4)).

For this purpose, a body of persons may be either a company or a partnership, as distinct from an individual, but the person having control in any of these cases could be either an individual or a company. In applying this second exception, a person is regarded as having control of a body of persons if he has control over its affairs, within the definition of 'control' given in (TCA 1997, s 312(1) (see **6.105**)).

Further, with effect for basis periods for the tax year 2008 onwards, the amount of any deduction will be limited to the amount which has been incurred wholly and exclusively on the acquisition of know-how for *bona fide* commercial purposes and was not incurred as part of a scheme or arrangement the main purpose or one of the main purposes of which is the avoidance of tax (TCA 1997, s 768(3A)).

Arguably only artificial schemes will be caught by this provision: see the discussion of similar wording in TCA 1997, s 502 at **18.111**. The term '*bona fide*' normally means no more than genuine. The 'wholly and exclusively' test may perhaps be liable to be invoked where the know-how is acquired as part of a wider transaction where allocation of the consideration is loaded towards the potentially tax-deductible know-how.

With effect for basis periods for the tax year 2008 onwards, the Revenue Commissioners may consult with any expert who in their opinion can assist them in ascertaining the extent to which expenditure is incurred by a taxpayer on know-how. They are entitled to disclose details of the claim to the expert notwithstanding any statutory obligations of secrecy or confidentiality but must firstly disclose to the taxpayer the identity of the expert and the information which they intend to disclose. Where that person shows to the satisfaction of the Revenue Commissioners (or on appeal, to the Appeal Commissioners) that such disclosure could prejudice the taxpayer's trade, no such disclosure will be made (TCA 1997, s 768(5)). F(TA)A 2015, s 38(7), which was subject to Ministerial Order (SI 110/2016 appointed 21 March, 2016, as the day on which the Finance (Tax Appeals) Act 2015, comes into operation), amends the above to note that before disclosing information to any expert the Revenue Commissioners shall give notice in writing to the person of:

(i) their intention to disclose information to the expert;

(ii) the information that they intend to disclose; and

(iii) the identity of the expert whom they intend to consult and shall give the person a period of 30 days after the date of the notice to show to their satisfaction that disclosure of such information to that expert could prejudice the person's trade. Where, on the expiry of the above period it is not shown to the satisfaction of the Revenue Commissioners that disclosure of such information to that expert could prejudice the person's trade, they may disclose the information where they:

(I) give the person notice in writing of their decision to so disclose; and

(II) allow that person a period of 30 days after the date of the notice to appeal their decision to the Appeal Commissioners before disclosing the information.

A person aggrieved by an above decision may appeal the decision to the Appeal Commissioners, in accordance with s 949I, within the period of 30 days after the date of the notice of that decision.

It is arguable that capital expenditure on know-how which fails to qualify under TCA 1997, s 768 may attract capital allowances under TCA 1997, s 291 as software, if it is stored or transmitted in electronic form (see **6.202**: *Intellectual Property*).

Expenditure on scientific research

A person carrying on a trade (but not one carrying on a profession) is entitled to deduct the full amount of any non-capital expenditure on scientific research, whether or not the scientific research is related to his trade. He is also entitled to deduct any sums paid to:

(a) a body carrying on scientific research that is approved for this purpose by the Minister for Finance; or

(b) an Irish university in order to enable the body or university in question to undertake scientific research, whether or not that research relates to the payer's trade (TCA 1997, s 764).

Scientific research is defined as meaning 'any activities in the fields of natural or applied science for the extension of knowledge'. TCA 1997, s 764 also provides a 100 per cent deduction for capital expenditure on scientific research, but as this is effectively given under the capital allowance rules the circumstances and manner in which the deduction is given are discussed in **6.601**.

Redundancy payments

Any lump sum redundancy payment under the Redundancy Payments Act 1967 paid by an employer to a redundant employee who had been employed in his trade or profession is deductible as an expense in calculating the taxable profits, even if it would not otherwise be deductible (TCA 1997, s 109(2)). In fact, redundancy payments would probably be deductible under the ordinary wholly and exclusively rule in any case where an existing business is continuing, but this section ensures that the statutory redundancy payments are deductible even if the trade ceases (note also *CIR v Cosmotron Manufacturing Ltd* [1997] STC 1134, discussed in **5.306**: *Expenses of cessation and commencement)*. TCA 1997, s 109(2) is, however, only applicable to the extent of the employer's statutory obligations. If, as frequently happens, he makes larger redundancy payments, the extra amounts are only deductible if they meet the wholly and exclusively test; this test is unlikely to be met where additional payments are made in connection with the cessation of a trade.

Where the amount of the statutory redundancy payments borne by the employer is *deductible* under TCA 1997, s 109(2) any rebate from the State under the Redundancy Payments Act 1967 has to be brought into account as a trading *receipt*. If the statutory lump sum payment is made by the employer after his trade or profession has ceased, the net amount borne by him is deductible as if it were a payment made on the last day of trading.

Premiums for leases etc

TCA 1997, s 102(2) permits deductions in calculating the taxable profits of a trade or profession in respect of certain premiums (and deemed premiums) paid for the granting of a lease of premises that are occupied for the purposes of a trade or profession. The lease premiums which qualify for this treatment are those in respect of which the person granting the lease is chargeable to tax under Sch D Case V by reason of TCA 1997, s 98(1)–(5) inclusive (see **12.201**). The deductions given under Sch D Cases I and II effectively allow the lease premiums paid to be spread over the duration of the lease.

It is not essential that the person carrying on the trade be the original lessee to whom the lease was granted and by whom the premium was paid. A person who acquires an existing lease granted earlier subject to a premium chargeable under TCA 1997, s 98 is entitled to the deduction if he uses the premises for his trade within the original lease period.

TCA 1997, s 102(2) also gives the person occupying premises for his trade or profession a similar type of deduction where an assignor of a lease granted at an undervalue was taxed under TCA 1997, s 99 or where the person carrying on the trade or profession holds the relevant interest in land which gave rise to a tax charge under TCA 1997, s 100. The deductions which may be taken in a Sch D Case I or II computation in respect of these lease premiums and other amounts are explained and illustrated in **12.208** immediately following the discussion of TCA 1997, ss 98–100.

In view of the possibility of a deduction under TCA 1997, s 102, a person taking over an existing lease by purchase or otherwise should seek to ascertain whether any person had previously been assessed under Sch D Case V by reason of either TCA 1997, s 98 or TCA 1997, s 99 in respect of a premium or on a gain from assigning a lease granted at an undervalue. If a trader acquires an interest in land which is subject to the right of an earlier vendor to a reconveyance or a leaseback in respect of which the vendor was chargeable under TCA 1997, s 100 (see **12.206**), he should be aware of this fact as it should have been disclosed to him. In any of these cases, the trader needs to ascertain the further particulars to determine the deductions to which he becomes entitled.

Short-term leases

The costs of renewal of an existing lease of less than 50 years' duration are concessionally treated as a revenue item.

Double rent deductions

For qualifying premises sited in certain tax incentive areas, an additional rent deduction was given during a 10-year period if the qualifying premise's was occupied for the purposes of a trade or profession under a qualifying lease. The additional deduction given in computing the Sch D Case I or II profits for any relevant period of account was an amount equal to the normal deduction on account of rent to which the lessee was entitled for that period. The availability of this 'double rent' allowance, the conditions which must be complied with and in particular its future availability in light of the EU

Commission's position on the matter, were dealt with in **Division 19** of the 2009 edition of this book.

Restrictive covenants

Under general principles, payments made in return for restrictive covenants (ie covenants not to compete) are likely to be capital expenditure, unless short-term in nature (*Associated Portland Cement Manufacturers v Kerr* 27 TC 103). However, TCA 1997, s 127(2) provides that a payment for consideration given to an individual who holds, has held or is about to hold an employment or office, in respect of an undertaking to restrict his conduct or activities will be charged as earnings of his employment, if not already liable to tax. TCA 1997, s 127(4) provides that notwithstanding TCA 1997, s 81(2), any sum or consideration charged to tax by virtue of TCA 1997, s 127(2)–(5) may be deducted in computing the payer's taxable profits for the period in which it is paid. It may be noted that no deduction is available under these provisions if the payment is made to an individual other than an employee or director.

Pre-trading expenses

See Expenses of Cessation and Commencement at **5.306**.

Relief for taking on long-term unemployed

TCA 1997, s 88A provides for a double deduction in respect of deductible emoluments paid to a 'qualifying individual' in respect of a 'qualifying employment' (both these terms are as defined for the purposes of TCA 1997, s 472A, which provides an additional personal relief for the individual concerned: see **3.321** (TCA 1997, s 88A(1)). The benefit of the double deduction extends to employer's PRSI contributions incurred in relation to those emoluments. The benefit of the deduction is only available for emoluments which relate to the qualifying period ie the period of 36 months from the date of commencement of the employment (TCA 1997, s 88A(2)(b)(i)); expenditure incurred after the end of the qualifying period could still qualify if it related to that period. The double deduction is also denied if either the employer or the qualifying individual has benefited under any employment scheme, whether statutory or otherwise (TCA 1997, s 88A(2)(b)(ii)). An employment scheme is as widely defined by TCA 1997, s 472A, but excludes the various programmes (eg the Community Employment scheme) which do not prejudice the long-term unemployment status of a qualifying individual under TCA 1997, s 472A(1)(b)(i): see **3.321**. The section ceases to have effect for employments which commence on or after 1 July 2013 (TCA 1997, s 88A(3) and SI 229/2013). The double deduction will continue to be available for qualifying employments which commenced before 1 July 2013. TCA 1997, ss 88A and 472A are both reliefs provided under the Revenue Job Assist Scheme. A new scheme, called 'JobsPlus', to encourage employment of the long term unemployed was introduced to replace the Revenue Job Assist Scheme. Under the JobsPlus scheme monthly cash payments are made to employers who recruit long-term unemployed individuals. Cash payments under the JobsPlus scheme are exempt from income tax (see **5.207**).

5.309 Repairs, renewals etc

Expenditure on repairs to premises occupied for the purposes of the trade, or to other fixed assets such as machinery, motor vehicles, etc employed in a trade are deductible. Only the actual sums *expended* can be deducted (TCA 1997, s 81(2)(d)) so that, for example, a contingent liability in respect of repairs should not be allowable but note the contrary decision of the UK Special Commissioners in *Jenners Princes Street Edinburgh* [1998] STC (SCD) 196; this decision has been accepted by the UK Inland Revenue, although this is in the context of a growing trend in the UK to assimilate tax and accounting treatments: see **5.102**.

Where any repairs to premises or the repair, replacement or renewal of any machinery, equipment, implements, etc involves improvements or alterations of a capital nature, the expenditure must be disallowed if it has been charged in arriving at the accounting profit. In the case of premises, the distinction between what is a repair on the one hand and what is a disallowable renewal, improvement or alteration of the premises on the other is sometimes difficult to draw.

The question of whether the works carried out represent an improvement have been considered in a number of cases. In *Lawrie v IRC* 34 TC 20, a factory roof which had fallen into disrepair was not merely replaced, but the building was also heightened and lengthened in the course of the construction works. The fact that the building's functions were enhanced as a result of these works inevitably meant that the work was one of improvement. In *Wilson v Emerson* 39 TC 260, the work involved replacement of a roof as well as the removal of gable walls and a floor. However, the work was carried out so as to create an extra floor and overall enhanced floor space. Danckwerts J upheld the Appeal Commissioners' finding of fact that these were works of improvement.

In *Conn v Robins* 45 TC 266, substantial works were carried out on an old building necessitating the use of modern materials (including the replacement of wooden lintels by steel joists and the replacement of oak floors by concrete). Buckley LJ commented as follows:

> In the course of carrying out these works certain structural alterations were made as one would expect with an extensive repair of a building over 400 years old, when repairs were being carried out at a time when building techniques have completely altered … but the fact of these alterations does not seem to me to be a good ground for proceeding upon the basis that the work produced something new.

It appears that the issue of improvement should be tested by reference to the *original* condition of the premises in the hands of the trader. If this were not the case, then every repair would be an improvement, since the effect thereof would be to enhance the premises by comparison with its unrepaired condition (see the discussion of the *Law Shipping* case below).

The distinction between a 'repair' and a 'renewal' was put in the course of a judgment by Buckley LJ in *Lurcott v Wakely and Wheeler* [1911] 1 KB 905, as follows:

> Repair is restoration by renewal or replacement of subsidiary parts of the whole. Renewal, as distinguished from repair, is reconstruction of the entirety, meaning by the entirety not necessarily the whole but substantially the whole subject matter under discussion … The question of repair is in every case one of degree and the test is whether the act to be done is one which in substance is the renewal or replacement of defective parts or the renewal or replacement of substantially the whole.

This principle has been applied in a number of tax cases. In *O'Grady v Bullcroft Main Collieries Ltd* 17 TC 93, a colliery company built a new factory chimney close to an existing chimney; the chimney stood apart from the other surface buildings in the colliery. The new chimney was much larger and taller than the old one and it cost double what it would have cost to replace the old chimney with one of similar dimensions.

Rowlatt J decided the cost was disallowable as capital expenditure on the grounds that it was incurred on replacing the entirety, ie the whole chimney.

By contrast, in *Samuel Jones & Co (Devondale) Ltd v IRC* 32 TC 513, expenditure on a new factory chimney erected beside, and in replacement of, an old chimney which had fallen into disrepair, was held to be deductible. In this case, the new chimney was of the same dimensions as the old one. The replacement was held to be a repair and the chimney was considered to be only a portion of the entirety, ie of the whole unit which was the factory of which the chimney was only part. While it may be difficult to see why the chimney in the *Bullcroft* case was not considered to be part of the factory there (even taking into account its physical separateness), the key to the decision in the *Jones* case may be seen in the words of Lord Carmont (at page 519):

> Rowlatt J, it is true, found that he could regard the chimney in the *O'Grady* case as being the unit or the entirety as he called it. In the present case I am clearly of opinion that the unit to be considered is the factory and the chimney cannot be taken in isolation. There was no improvement in the factory, on the findings of the case, by the erection of the new chimney in place of the old.

In *Lawrie v IRC* 34 TC 20 and *Wilson v Emerson* 39 TC 260 it was accepted that where the roof of a building was replaced, the building was the entirety. In *Conn v Robins* 45 TC 266, a building had fallen into substantial disrepair. Expenditure was incurred inter alia on the replacement of the existing roof, replacement of some floors, rebuilding of internal walls and inserting steel joists for load-bearing purposes, replacing flooring and the replacement of a shop front. The taxpayer argued that the work consisted of the repair or replacement of subsidiary parts of an entirety ie the building itself. Buckley J upheld the Appeal Commissioners' finding of fact that the work constituted repairs. As noted above, the fact that modern building techniques and materials had to be used (so that the building was not restored to its identical original state) did not prejudice this finding.

In the Irish case of *Vale v Martin Mahony & Brothers Ltd* II ITR 32, a company running a mill was required by the Public Health Authority to replace old primitive sanitation with up to date water closets. Expenditure of £4,000 was incurred in bringing water from the mains to the mill premises, in constructing the necessary drains and sewers and erecting new buildings on the mill premises to house the water closets. The Supreme Court rejected the finding of the Circuit Court judge that the payment was not capital because it did not increase the earning capacity or otherwise benefit the taxpayer's trade. The fallacy behind the Circuit Court judge's reasoning was his conclusion that the replacement of a fixed asset by another fixed asset is not capital because the total stock of fixed assets is not increased as a result. As Murnaghan J observed:

> Here the company have … provided new buildings with new lavatory accommodation … unless that fact can be displaced or offset by evidence that the work done constituted a renewal amounting to repairs it must … be treated as capital.

Geoghegan J regarded the expenditure as being simply incurred on an improvement to the existing premises, taken as a whole.

A different result occurred in *Hodgins v Plunder & Pollak (Ireland) Ltd* II ITR 267. In that case, a leather manufacturing company used a weighbridge next to which was a small building which housed part of the weighbridge machinery and which provided workshop and storeroom accommodation. The building was seriously damaged by a storm and had to be demolished. A new building, designed for the sole purpose of housing the weighbridge machinery, was erected on a part of the site. This new building was smaller than the old one and was admitted not to be an improvement. The Supreme Court upheld the decision of the Appeal Commissioners and allowed the cost of demolition and replacement of the weighbridge house as a sum expended in respect of repairs.

Kingsmill Moore J observed:

> The profit earning entity is the whole of the premises taken together and the replacement of a unit, even if such a unit be a separate building must be viewed in relation to the profit earning entity.
>
> If the question whether a rebuilding is or is not a repair is a question of degree then it appears to me to be a question of fact, and unless it can be shown that the Commissioner has erred in the application of such legal principle or had not evidence before him on which to form his determination, his findings should not be disturbed … The Commissioner, in the Case Stated, has found that the weighhouse, though physically separate from the main factory buildings, yet formed part of them and that the buildings as a whole and not the weighhouse, must be regarded as the entirely. He regarded the reconstruction as repairs to a small part of the entire factory. I cannot see that he has in any way misconceived the law and in so far as his findings are findings of fact they are binding on me.

In *Phillips v Whieldon Sanitary Potteries Ltd* 33 TC 213, the taxpayer's factory stood by a canal protected by an old brick and earth embankment. The embankment subsided, allowing water to seep into buildings already affected by subsidence. The old embankment was removed, and an iron and concrete barrier was constructed in its place. Donovan J observed:

> There is no one line of approach to the problem which is exclusively correct. In some cases it will be right to regard the premises (ie the entirety) as the entire factory, and in other cases some part of the factory. Whichever alternative is the right one to adopt will depend upon the facts of the particular case.

In regarding the work in this case as being on capital account, the learned judge placed great weight on the extent of the work, the permanency of the new barrier, and the enduring nature of the benefit conferred. While the work alone did not represent an improvement to the factory premises taken as a whole, the size and importance of the work indicated that the barrier was the 'entirety'. Thus, the work done was effectively to be regarded as the *replacement* of a distinct capital asset (ie the barrier).

In *Brown v Burnley FC Ltd* [1980] STC 424, an old stand at the taxpayer's premises, a football stadium, had become unsafe. The old stand was demolished and a new one of a similar capacity, (but housing in addition a directors' suite, office accommodation and a social club), was erected in its place. The club contended that this work represented a repair to the club's premises. The court held that on the facts the Appeal Commissioners were not entitled to regard the whole ground as the 'entity'. According to Vinelott J:

> the premises consisted of a number of distinct structures (including the stand) each serving a distinct function; furthermore, no part of the ground except the pitch was necessary to carry out the central activities of the taxpayer.

This analysis would seem to differ from the more expansive approach taken by the Supreme Court in the *Plunder & Pollak* case. Indeed, Vinelott J took the view that the decision of the Special Commissioners laid too much stress on the latter decision.

In *Wynne-Jones v Bedale Auction Ltd* [1977] STC 50 the cost of replacing a cattle ring in a cattle-mart was held to be capital. Foster J took the view that the ring was the 'nerve centre' of the mart and that the rest of the mart was only ancillary to the ring.

In *O'Grady v Roscommon Race Committee* IV ITR 425, expenditure was incurred on extensive alterations to a racecourse stand, as follows:

(a) the walls of the stand were replaced with new cavity walls, including glazing at the sides; the old walls had been described as 'saturated, wet and crumbling';
(b) the entire roof was replaced by a new roof which incorporated new guttering and drainage; the new roof extended beyond the level of the old roof both at the front and the rear; and
(c) the steps on the lower terrace were made shorter and wider; this alteration extended the terrace frontwards, and increased overall standing capacity by 40 per cent.

In the High Court, Carroll J reached the following conclusions:

(a) the work undertaken on the external walls (item (a)), with the exception of the glazing, was deductible as repairs; and
(b) the new roof (item (b)), the extension to the lower terracing (item (c)) and the glazing (the remaining element of item (a)) were capital improvements; (the learned judge's conclusion that these items qualified as plant was upheld by the Supreme Court: see **6.202**).

The basis for the learned judge's conclusion on point (i) was as follows:

(a) the alterations to the wall were restorations of subsidiary parts of an entirety, and did not amount to the reconstruction of substantially the whole of the stand; and
(b) the restoration of the walls was a repair, and was not in the nature of an extension or improvement to the old walls.

The decision appears to be generous to the taxpayer, given that the work involved seems to have incorporated a significant element of improvement.

In *Auckland Gas Company v CIR* [2000] STC 527, expenditure was incurred on the insertion of polyethylene pipes into existing old leaking cast iron pipes. In deciding whether the costs were revenue or capital in nature the Privy Council considered the nature and scale of the work carried out and whether the character of the object had changed. They said that it was really a matter of degree in each case whether an item should be considered a revenue or capital item. It was held that the insertion of the polyethylene pipes were an improvement over the old system and that the expenditure was capital in nature.

This decision may be compared with that in *Transco Plc v Dyall (Inspector of Taxes)* [2002] STC (SCD) 199 (Sp Comm) where it was decided that a gas supplier's expenditure on polyethylene inserted into pipes otherwise at risk of fracture was revenue in nature. The process did not enhance the capacity or longevity of the pipeline system and it only affected 1 per cent of the total system each year.

No relief is available in respect of 'notional' repairs. Thus, in *Curtin v M & Co Ltd* II ITR 360, a company had carried on trade in premises which were about 300 years old and which were in very bad repair. The company was advised that it was not feasible to put these premises into a proper state of repair. In these circumstances, the premises were demolished except for the rear wall and part of the side wall and replaced by a modern two storey shop with display windows added. The company contended that it was entitled to analyse the work done and attribute to 'repairs' such items of the reconstruction as related to items in the old building in need of replacement. The company's architect apportioned 75 per cent of the total cost as representing repairs, for which a deduction was claimed. It was held on the facts of the case that the whole cost was laid out on the reconstruction and improvement of the premises and that it was not possible to allocate the expenditure between repairs and capital so that the total cost was disallowed (see also, to similar effect, *Lawrie v IRC* 34 TC 20 where, as noted above, a dilapidated factory roof was not merely replaced but the building was also heightened and lengthened in the course of the construction works). However, on the facts, it may be possible to analyse building works into discrete and separate elements consisting of *actual* repairs and *actual* improvements (*Conn v Robins* 45 TC 266).

Another important aspect of the distinction between 'repair' and 'renewal' made by Buckley LJ in *Lurcott v Wakely and Wheeler* is the dividing line between reconstruction and repair. As Buckley LJ pointed out, reconstruction may be not only of the entirety but of 'substantially the whole subject matter' thereof. In *Conn v Robins* 45 TC 266, the substantial works entailed there were not regarded as works of reconstruction. *Conn v Robins* was distinguished in *Palace (Derry) v IRC* [1997] SpC where the interior of a building was completely gutted, with virtually all of the internal floors, walls and timbers being replaced. The Special Commissioner took the view that the interior of a building 'is normally what a building is all about' (a proposition which may be open to question).

The question of the allowability of expenditure on repairs incurred on assets shortly after their acquisition has been the subject of several cases. In *Law Shipping Co v IRC* 12 TC 621 a ship was bought second hand at a date when the periodical Lloyd's survey was overdue. The survey was deferred pending the completion of a voyage under the new owner. On its completion six-months later the survey was made and substantial expenditure incurred on repairs. The cost of the repairs attributable to the period prior to the acquisition by the company was held to be of a capital nature and disallowable. It was considered that, had the survey been carried out and the repairs completed before the sale was made, the ship would have commanded a higher price which the purchaser would have incurred in full as capital.

In *Odeon Associated Theatres Ltd v Jones* 48 TC 257, it was held that expenditure on the repair of assets, including repairs accumulated before the use of the assets in the claimant's business, was deductible provided that it was treated as a revenue payment on correct accounting principles. This decision contrasts with the *Law Shipping* case. In the *Odeon* case, the company had acquired a number of cinemas and incurred expenditure on repairs, but the properties had been owned previously by other companies in the same group. If the expenditure had been incurred by the vendor companies it would have been allowed and on the facts of the case it was considered the price was not materially affected by the state of repair.

Where a lease was taken of premises which had been unoccupied for 18 years and which were in a bad state of repair, the cost of the accumulated repairs incurred by the lessee under a term of the lease was held to be capital; in effect the execution of the repairs formed part of the consideration for the grant of the lease (*Jackson v Laskers Home Furnishers Ltd* 37 TC 69).

A final issue in this context is whether or not expenditure which constitutes 'repairs' may be capital under general principles of tax law. In *Phillips v Whieldon Sanitary* 33 TC 213, the judge held that the works in that case were of such size and importance relative to the factory as a whole that even if the barrier there had not been the entirety, the expenditure concerned would still have been capital in nature. In *Conn v Robins*, the decision in *Whieldon Sanitary* was drawn to the attention of Buckley J. However, the learned judge simply observed that the effect of the work in question was not to produce something new but rather to repair something which had previously existed.

Accordingly, there was 'no ground for regarding this expenditure as capital expenditure'. The learned judge indicated that he would only have been prepared to find that repairs were not of a revenue nature if there were 'special circumstances' eg if the expenditure has been associated with the acquisition of the premises (ie as in the *Law Shipping Co* case). It is submitted that the approach of Buckley J is to be preferred to that of Donovan J in *Whieldon Sanitary*.

In *Palace (Derry Ltd) v IRC* [1997] SpC (unreported), the Special Commissioner suggested that the quantum of the expenditure incurred might itself be grounds for treating it as capital; the case law as a whole provides little authority for this approach. In *Law Shipping v IRC* (discussed above) the court appears to have accepted that repair expenditure of £51,328 incurred in relation to a ship (which was sold for £97,000 in its unrepaired state) would have been deductible if incurred by the original owner. The Special Commissioner in *Palace (Derry)* also suggested that it was relevant that the premises were unusable in their pre-repair condition, but this again seems to be incorrect. Again, it may be noted that the ship in *Law Shipping* could have been unusable in the hands of the original owner but this was not considered to be relevant in that case. In *Conn v Robins* (see above) the relevant expenditure was incurred expressly in order that the premises could continue to be used.

Where renewals or replacement of plant and machinery are concerned, difficulties normally arise as the expenditure is usually capitalised as part of normal accounting practice and capital allowances are claimed. In the case of loose tools and miscellaneous items of equipment which are of relatively small value and which tend to wear out and need replacement frequently, it may be more practical and is generally acceptable to Revenue to deal with them on a renewals or replacement basis. The initial expenditure on such items in the case of a new trade would, however, be disallowed as capital expenditure as would subsequent expenditure on such items incurred in increasing their number as part of an expansion of activity in the business.

Where the renewals or replacement basis is claimed, no capital allowances are given on the initial capital expenditure, but the full renewal cost is allowed as an expense deduction when the items are replaced. Any sale or other disposal proceeds realised for the assets being replaced are deducted from the cost of the replacements and only the net outlay on the new items is deductible.

Example 5.309.1

A business setting up in 2015 purchases a stock of loose tools at a cost of €800. Additional tools are purchased in 2016 for €400. In 2017 one half of the stock of tools is sold as scrap for €150 and twice as many new tools are purchased for €1,100. The 2015 and 2016 expenditures of €800 and €400 respectively were charged in the trader's profit and loss account and have been added back in the relevant tax computations. The treatment of the 2017 sales and purchases is as follows:

	€
New tools purchased cost (debited in accounts)	1,100
Of which one-half are considered additional to the previous stock so that the add back of the total cost charged to P & L account is	550
And of which the balance are replacements so that the amount deductible in arriving at the taxable profits is	
Balance of cost of new tools:	550
Less: scrap value of sales	150
Allow as net replacement cost	400

5.310 Leasing and rental charges etc

There are various ways in which a person can obtain plant, machinery, equipment, motor vehicles, etc for use in his business other than by a straight purchase. He may lease or hire an asset from another person who has incurred the capital expenditure and retains ownership. He may acquire an asset by hire purchase, ie under an agreement which entitles him to become the owner at the end of the period of hire when he has paid the hire purchase instalments provided for in the agreement. He may also buy assets on a credit sale agreement under which the purchase price is paid by instalments with interest. The tax treatment of hire purchase and credit sale agreements is dealt with in **5.311**.

When assets are leased, the full lease rental or hire charge is generally deductible in calculating taxable profits, except that the amount deductible may be restricted in the case of leased motor cars (see **5.312**). The Revenue Commissioners issued a statement in July 1981 relating to certain practices which had been used in the context of vehicle leasing to give the person carrying on the trade a higher deduction for tax purposes than would otherwise apply in a normal commercial lease. In some cases, the statement covers arrangements. While this statement has been made specifically in relation to vehicle leasing, it appears that its principles are capable of being applied to similar arrangements designed to give undue tax advantages from leasing other types of asset. The Revenue Commissioners' statement, in so far as it is relevant to the present discussion, is as follows:

> Revenue policy on vehicle leasing:
>
> (a) Vehicle leases usually run for a specified number of years, and the rentals payable take into account an estimate of the market value of the vehicle at the end of the lease. Under contracts of this kind the vehicle is normally sold on the open market at the end of the lease and any excess or shortfall of the sale proceeds over or below the anticipated residual value on which the rentals were based leads to an adjustment of the rental payments. The tax effects of such leases normally raise no problems. By the end of the lease the lessor has been allowed tax relief for the actual depreciation he has borne, taking into account the net proceeds of the sale of the vehicle. The lessee qualifies for relief on the net rentals he has paid, taking into account any rebate he receives, or any shortfall he has to pay, on the disposal of the vehicle.
>
> (b) The leases with which this statement is specifically concerned involve some variations from the traditional provisions of vehicle leases described at (a) above. Rentals may be calculated by reference to a residual value which is lower than the expected open market value of the vehicle at the end of the lease. The vehicle, on the termination of a primary leasing period, is either then re-leased back to the lessee at very much reduced rental rates or disposed of for less than market value to a nominee of the lessee who acquires the vehicle for less than full and adequate consideration. In some cases the residual value of the vehicle used in calculating the rentals may be purely nominal or may be a conservative estimate of the market value. The lease itself may, in certain cases, provide for the sale of the vehicle to a nominee of the lessee, or the vehicle may pass through several hands before reaching the person connected with the lessee.
>
> (c) Taxation provisions not normally relevant to the leases described at (a) above may need to be considered in connection with leases of the kind referred to at (b) above. The lessee's rental payments may be disallowed, in whole or in part … as not being

made wholly and exclusively for the purposes of the business or as being in part capital expenditure.

(d) Inspectors of taxes will carefully examine leasing arrangements which are of the kind referred to at (b) above and will make such adjustments in assessments as may be considered necessary. Where a taxpayer cannot reach agreement with the inspector of taxes about his liability, the usual right of appeal will be available.

Where payments are significantly 'frontloaded' in order to secure accelerated deductibility, the decision in *Stephenson v Payne, Stone, Fraser & Co* 44 TC 507 may be relevant. In that case, the taxpayer was a professional partnership which formed a service company controlled by the partners. In the first year of this arrangement, the taxpayer claimed the full cost of the service charge paid to the company, which resulted in a substantial profit for the company. However, there was an understanding in existence that the service charges for later years were to be adjusted downwards, so as to ensure that the company only made a nominal profit over the long term. Pennycuick J held that the taxpayer could only deduct that part of the service charge which related to the year of account; the treatment of the whole amount of the service charge as an expense in the year was a '*misattribution manifestly contrary to the ordinary principles of commercial accounting*'.

However, the decision in the *Payne, Stone & Fraser* case may be explicable on the narrow grounds that the taxpayer had made an excess payment which was recoverable in future periods and this fact was not correctly reflected in the accounting treatment adopted.

Where it is a question of a lease contract explicitly allocating periodic charges in an uneven manner (eg loading them more heavily in the earlier periods) then the position is potentially more complex. It seems most unlikely that, other than in extreme cases, it could be argued that the allocation was misleading as a matter of law. This means that it ought to be necessary to show that the allocation violates the 'matching principle' and is thus contrary to correct accounting practice (the point conceded in the *Gallagher* case (considered at **5.102** above). Failing this, as discussed at **5.102**, it is most debatable whether the Revenue Commissioners could succeed in imposing an 'SSAP 21' treatment on the taxpayer. In any event, the Revenue Commissioners have indicated in *Tax Briefing 20* that they do not believe that SSAP 21 is valid for tax purposes.

The Revenue Commissioners' actual practice (subject to certain transitional provisions discussed below) is stated in their leaflet *IT 52*. While Revenue practice may go further than the law permits, it is most important to be aware of the position in practice. The Revenue state in *IT 52* that 'all lease payments including upfront payments are spread evenly over the expected period of the lease in the period during which it is expected that the asset will be leased'. Depending on the terms of the lease, this could include the secondary period of the lease; however, the Revenue state that they will generally accept that lease payments may be spread over the primary period where this is standard for the type of the asset in question and it is not clear at the outset that the asset will be leased beyond that period. For these purposes, the primary period should not be less than three years.

'Up front payments' which are potentially subject to spreading treatment include:

(a) lump sum initial payments;

(b) the trade-in value of an asset previously owned by the trader; and

(c) rebates of lease rentals in respect of an asset previously leased by the trader.

Where a number of rental payments have to be paid in advance then these will not be subject to 'spreading' where these do not relate to a period in excess of three-months and all other payments under the lease are spread evenly over the period of the lease. In the case of a seasonal trader, the Revenue Commissioners accept that the lease payments may be spread evenly over the tax years corresponding to the seasons to which the lease period relates. The following example is given:

Example 5.310.1

An agricultural contractor who makes up accounts to 31 December annually takes out a three-year lease on a combine harvester in August 2017. Under the lease, one annual lease payment is to be made in August of each year of the lease (to correspond with the harvesting season). A deduction for the August 2017 lease payment may be taken in the accounts year ended 31 December 2017 which forms the basis period for the tax year 2017.

IT 52 also deals with rebates of rentals on the termination of a lease. The rebate is taxable when received, irrespective of whether it is paid directly in cash or whether it is set off against the purchase of the asset by the lessee (ie under the LADCO procedures: see **6.301**), or is used as equivalent to a trade-in under a new lease. In the last situation the amount will be subject to spreading treatment in the manner discussed above in relation to the new lease. The Revenue Commissioners provide the following examples of their approach.

Example 5.310.2

At the termination of a lease in the basis period for 2017, the market value of the leased asset is €10,000. The lessee opts to purchase the asset. The finance company refunds the market value of €10,000 to the lessee (less a small transaction cost) by way of credit against the cost of the asset. The lessee is chargeable on the €10,000 for 2017 and may claim capital allowances on the asset for that and subsequent years.

Example 5.310.3

Assume the asset in **Example 5.310.2** is used as a trade-in against a further leased asset with an expected lease period of four years. The rebate of €10,000 is taxable in 2017 and the up-front payment is spread over four years ie the lessee claims €2,500 per annum for 2017 to 2020.

Where the amount of lease rentals are restricted under the rules pertaining to private motor vehicles (see **5.312**), any rebate will be taxed in the same proportion as the lease rentals were treated as allowable under those rules.

Leaflet *IT 52* does not deal with the position regarding early settlements ie where the lessee makes a payment to terminate a lease before the end of the primary period. Where the payment is made simply in order to discharge future rental obligations it seems that it should be regarded as revenue in nature; however, if the payment is in the nature of a penalty for early release from the leasing contract then it seems that it should be regarded as capital in nature (in accordance with *Tucker v Granada Motorway Services* [1979] STC 393; see *Kerrane* 1997, Irish Tax Reports 147). In *Tax Briefing 24* the Revenue Commissioners indicate that where the asset is acquired on an early termination, but this is as a result of a genuine change of intentions on the part of the lessor and lessee, the lease will not be reclassified as a hire purchase agreement (**5.311** below).

Similar considerations to those raised by the Revenue Commissioners' Statement on vehicle leasing may also need to be taken into account where a property is sold and then leased back by the original vendor. In *IRC v Land Securities Investments Trust Ltd* 45

TC 495 the taxpayer held leasehold interests in various properties in which it subsequently purchased the superior interests. The consideration for the purchase was in the form of rent charges payable over a fixed period. The House of Lords held that, although the taxpayer had no longer to pay rent as a leaseholder in respect of the properties, it had avoided this expense by acquiring capital assets (ie the superior interests in the properties); accordingly, the rent charges, being the price paid for those assets, were disallowable in full.

The *Land Securities* decision was followed by the UK Special Commissioners in *Austin Reed v IRC* (unreported). In that case, the taxpayer was a lessee which was paying a below-market rent. The taxpayer surrendered its lease for a capital sum, having agreed to enter subsequently into a new lease of the same property at a market rent. The Special Commissioners held that the increased element of rent under the new lease was consideration for the capital sum received. It is also arguable that the rentals in this case were not 'wholly and exclusively' incurred, ie that one of the purposes behind entering the new lease was to secure a profit on a non-trading transaction (ie the initial sale of the premises). In practice, it is thought unlikely that the Revenue Commissioners would seek to challenge rentals payable under sale and leaseback arrangements which were not in excess of the market rate.

Where the actual rent payable for the period of account on a straightforward lease agreement has been debited in arriving at the accounting profit, no adjustment is required in the tax computation (other than the restriction of the deduction for motor cars). However, particularly in the case of companies, compliance with SSAP 21 may require the taxpayer to capitalise leased assets and to charge to the profit and loss account the annual depreciation on the notional asset plus the 'interest' element in the lease rentals, rather than the rentals themselves.

Where leased assets are capitalised in this way, the tax computation must contain adjustments, as follows:

(a) *add back*:
- (i) depreciation on leased assets charged in the accounts,
- (ii) lease interest charged in accounts,
- (iii) loss (if any) compared with net book value of any leased assets sold in the period if charged in accounts;

(b) *deduct*:
- (i) actual lease rentals payable in period of account (subject to the discussion above), and
- (ii) profit (if any) on any leased assets sold in period if credited in accounts.

In *Gallagher v Jones* [1993] STC 537, the UK Court of Appeal held that SSAP 21 should be followed in respect of a finance lease, and that the treatment laid down there overrode the accounting treatment adopted by the taxpayer. As discussed above, the Revenue Commissioners apparently do not follow this decision, and it seems most unlikely that the Irish courts would endorse it in any event.

5.311 Assets acquired by hire purchase

In practice, if normal commercial principles are applied in preparing the trader's accounts, the cash price of an asset which is the subject of a hire purchase agreement will have been capitalised and an appropriate part of the instalments payable representing the interest element will have been charged in each relevant profit and loss account. Where this happens, the interest actually charged in the accounts, as calculated on any appropriate basis, is normally allowed. The interest element in the hire purchase instalments is deductible in calculating the taxable profits of each relevant period of account either:

(a) on the basis of spreading the total instalments payable evenly over the full hire period provided for in the agreement; or
(b) on the basis of an actual calculation of the interest based on the original cash price and having regard to the capital element in previous instalments paid.

Assets acquired on credit sale by instalments are treated similarly. The Revenue Commissioners state in *Tax Briefing 25* that any arrangement whereby the lessee can acquire the relevant asset will be treated as a hire purchase transaction (see also **5.311** *Purchase of leased car*).

The above treatment of hire purchase instalments received judicial approval in *Darngavil Coal Co Ltd v Francis* 7 TC 1. Payments to a wagon company under a hire purchase agreement were held to be allowable in so far as the annual payments represented consideration for the hire of the wagons (the 'interest') as distinct from payments representing the purchase price. It may be noted that in this case, the agreement contained an option to purchase the asset at a nominal price. Where the option price is more than nominal then it seems that in strictness the disallowance for the capital element of the hire purchase payments should be adjusted accordingly. The treatment of hire purchase agreements for capital allowance purposes is discussed at **6.203**.

5.312 Restriction of motor expenses deduction

In the absence of any other provision to the contrary, the expenses incurred in running motor cars used by the proprietor of a business, by the partners of a partnership or by their employees (and directors of a company) would be fully deductible in computing the taxable profits of the trade, provided that they satisfied the wholly and exclusively test. The same would apply to the rents payable for leased cars provided for use for the purposes of the trade.

TCA 1997, s 377 applies a restriction on the deduction for the lease rent or other hiring cost of any private motor car, the retail price of which (when the car was made) exceeds the 'specified amount' (as defined below) for expenditure incurred upon hiring a vehicle up to 30 June 2008. This restriction is complementary to the rules of TCA 1997, s 374 which provide that capital allowances in respect of capital expenditure in purchasing a private motor car are given only up to the same limit (see **6.212**). With effect for expenditure incurred on hiring a vehicle from 1 July 2008 onwards, the adjustments are set by reference to the specified amount and the retail price at the time the vehicle was first made, but also by reference to the carbon dioxide emissions level of the vehicle concerned: see **6.212** for a fuller explanation of the criteria involved (TCA 1997, s 380M).

The reference to the retail price at the time a vehicle was 'first made' indicates that the retail price of the leased vehicle at the time it was new should be taken, whether or not the car was new at the time the lease was entered into. In practice, the retail price of a leased car is usually taken for these purposes as being 90 per cent of its list price (for a retail sale), as published by the main distributor in the country for the type of car in question (based on the 10 per cent discount normally available where a new car is purchased for cash).

The 'specified amount' for purposes of TCA 1997, s 377 and TCA 1997, s 380M respectively has been set at €24,000 (previously €23,000) as amended by FA 2007, s 21, where the relevant expenditure was incurred in a basis period which ends on or after 1 January 2007.

The restriction of the leasing cost deduction only applies in the case of private motor cars which are within the definition of 'motor vehicles' provided by TCA 1997, s 373(1). This is the same definition as that used for the restriction of capital allowances in **6.212**, and limits the motor vehicles to which both the leasing cost and capital allowance restrictions apply as mechanically propelled road vehicles constructed or adapted for the carriage of passengers, but excluding any vehicles of a type not commonly used as a private vehicle and unsuitable to be used as such.

Expenditure on hiring vehicles from 1 July 2008

TCA 1997, s 380M adjusts the allowable deduction for the lease rent or other cost of hiring (other than hire purchase) in respect of any private motor car, the retail price of which (when new) exceeds the specified amount and also in certain cases by reference to its carbon dioxide emissions level. The deduction in respect of the lease rent (or hire charge) payable for each leased car is adjusted as follows:

(a) where the emissions level does not exceed 155 g/km, adjusted either upwards or downwards in the same proportion as the specified amount bears to the retail price of the car at the time it was made;

(b) where the emissions level exceeds 155 g/km but not 190 g/km, reduced by 50 per cent if the retail price when the car was made was less than or equal to the specified amount or, otherwise reduced in the same proportion as 50 per cent of the specified amount bears to that retail price;

(c) where the emissions level exceeds 190 g/km, adjusted downwards to nil.

It does not seem, despite the language of the provision, that the adjustment under (b) will always result in a reduction (eg where the cost of the car when new is less than 50 per cent of the specified amount, though in practice this seems rather improbable).

Example 5.312.1

May Dockray who makes up accounts to 31 March each year leases a salesman's car for three years from 1 October 2016 for an annual lease rent of €5,400. The retail price of the car when new is €30,000. The carbon dioxide emissions of the car is 140 g/km. May's Sch D Case I computation for the 12 months to 31 March 2017 is as follows:

Lease rent charged in accounts:	€
€5,400 x 6/12 (period 1/10/2016 to 31/03/2017)	2,700
Allowable proportion of lease rent:	
€2,700 x 24,000/30,000	2,160
Add back in computation	
€2,700 – €2,160	540

Example 5.312.2

Facts as in **Example 5.312.1**, except that the price of the car when new was €18,000. May's Sch D Case I computation for the 12 months to 31 March 2017 is now as follows:

Lease rent charged in accounts:	€
€5,400 x 6/12 (period 1/10/2016 to 31/03/2017)	2,700

Allowable proportion of lease rent:	
€2,700 x 24,000/18,000	3,600
Additional deduction in computation	
€3,600 – €2,700	900

Example 5.312.3

Catherine Bailey who makes up accounts to 31 December each year, leases a salesman's car for three years from 1 July 2017 for an annual lease rent of €5,400. The retail price of the car when new in July 2017 is €30,000. The carbon dioxide emissions of the car is 180 g/km. Catherine's Sch D Case I computation for the 12 months to 31 December 2017 is as follows:

	€
Lease rent charged in accounts:	
€5,400 x 6/12 (period 1/07/2017 to 31/12/2017)	2,700
Allowable proportion of lease rent:	
€2,700 x (24,000 x 50%)/30,000	1,080
Add back in computation	
€2,700 – €1,080	1,620

Where the trader receives a rebate of his rental payments on the termination of the lease, the rebate will only be subject to tax in the same proportion as the rental payments were treated as deductible under TCA 1997, s 377: see *Revenue Leaflet IT 52*, and the discussion at **5.310**.

The leasing restriction does not apply in respect of a vehicle provided or hired wholly or mainly for the purpose of hire to members of the public, or for the purpose of the carriage of members of the public in the ordinary course of a trade carried on by a person using the vehicle for either of these purposes (TCA 1997, s 380(1)). The exception applies, for example, to taxi cabs or hire cars used wholly or mainly for a taxi or hire car business. It applies also to a person carrying on a business of leasing cars to the public generally, but only in respect of cars so leased; any cars provided for the use of the proprietor of the business, its directors (if a company) and/or its employees remain subject to the restrictions.

Purchase of leased car

TCA 1997, s 380O provides a special rule which applies in any case where a person has first leased or hired (other than by hire purchase) a motor car on or after 1 July 2008 and then subsequently becomes the owner of the car. The aggregate of the payments for the hire and subsequent acquisition of the vehicle (A) are treated as capital expenditure on the provision of the vehicle up to the amount of the retail price of the vehicle when new (B); any hire payments will then be proportionately reduced so that the total hire payments are equal to the excess (if any) of the aggregate sums paid over the retail price (ie A–B). The exception for public hire vehicles which applies to the leasing restriction (see immediately above) applies equally to s 380O (TCA 1997, s 380P(1)). Further, the rule does not apply to a vehicle provided by a manufacturer of vehicles of the type in question, or of parts or accessories for such vehicles, if he shows that it was provided solely for the purpose of testing such vehicles or parts or accessories for such vehicles (TCA 1997, s 380P(2)). The second exception is a very narrow one. The vehicle must be provided by the manufacturer solely for testing purposes and not for use for any other purpose. Further, if at any time within five years from the date the vehicle was first provided, it is used to any substantial extent for any other purpose, then the original exception is retrospectively withdrawn and any necessary additional assessments may be made to recapture any excessive expense deductions and/or capital allowances given on an unrestricted basis while the vehicle was being used solely for the prescribed purposes.

Where TCA 1997, s 380O applies, it requires the initial tax treatment as a leased car to be revised at the time the original lessor acquires ownership of the car, but with retrospective effect to the date the original leasing began. In this revised treatment, capital allowances are granted on a notional capital cost (deemed to have been incurred on the date the leasing began) per the formula above, ie equal to the lower of:

(a) the retail price of the car when new; and

(b) a sum equal to the capital payment made by the lessee to acquire ownership of the car plus the actual lease rents paid during the period of the leasing.

The calculation of the capital allowances on this notional capital cost is made subject to the capital allowances restriction of TCA 1997, s 374 (see **6.212**). For this purpose, the capital cost is deemed to have been incurred when the hiring began (ie the commencement of the lease).

Next, the excess (if any) of the aggregate of the capital payment and the actual lease rents over the retail price of the car (when made) is treated as if it had been the lease rent paid over the full period for which the car was actually leased. In other words, this notional lease rent is treated as a deductible expense, but restricted by TCA 1997, s 380O in the proportion provided by s 380M above. The actual lease rents previously charged (as restricted by TCA 1997, s 377) are now disallowed.

Example 5.312.4

Platini and Zico, a partnership carrying on business as leather merchants, lease a second hand car for the firm's general manager for four years from 1 January 2014. The retail price of the car when it was new was €26,000. Assume that on 1 July 2015, the firm buys the car from the leasing company for a capital payment of €18,000. The lease rents payable at the rate of €8,000 per annum totalled € 12,000 for the full 18-months' leasing period to 30 June 2015. The carbon dioxide emissions of the car is 180 g/km.

The rule now contained in TCA 1997, s 380O requires the firm's Sch D Case I computations for each of its periods of account spanning the leasing period to be revised. Assuming the firm has been making up its accounts annually to 31 March, this requires the years to 31 March 2014 (assessable 2014), 31 March 2015 (2015) and 31 March 2016 (2016) to be revised on the following basis:

Capital allowances: The computations have to be revised to give capital allowances for each accounting period for which the car continues to be used for the trade (none previously). The capital allowances, commencing with those based on the year ended 31 March 2014, are based on a notional capital cost as at 1 January 2014 (date leasing began) determined as follows:

The lower of	€	€
(a) retail price of car when new		26,000
and		
(b) capital payment to acquire ownership	18,000	
Add: rents paid during leasing period	12,000	
		30,000
Notional capital cost at 1/01/2014		26,000

Although the notional capital cost is €26,000, the rule in TCA 1997, s 380L only permits capital allowances to be claimed on €24,000 x 50% = €12,000; the notional capital cost of €26,000 should be noted as it will be relevant in due course for the calculation of any balancing allowance or balancing charge when the car is ultimately sold (see **6.212**).

Lease rents: Instead of the lease rentals (as restricted by TCA 1997, s 380M) previously deductible, which have to be added back retrospectively, the partners are now entitled – in addition to the capital allowances, to a deduction (to be spread over the 18-month period to 30 June 2015) calculated as follows:

	€
Capital payment to acquire ownership	18,000
Rents paid in period to 30/06/2015	12,000
	30,000
Less:	
Notional capital cost	26,000
Notional rent for 18 months to 30/06/2015	4,000
Restrict this notional rent	
€4,000 x 12,000/26,000=	1,846
Allow in relevant accounting periods:	
Y/E 31/03/2014: €1,846 x 3/18	308
Y/E 31/03/2015: €1,846 x 12/18	1230
Y/E 31/03/2016: €1,846 x 3/18	308
	1846

Cars on hire purchase

In the case of a motor car acquired by hire purchase, the position is generally straightforward if the trader goes through with the agreement by paying all the instalments and duly becomes the owner of the car. Capital allowances are given from the beginning, subject to the relevant limits (see **6.203**). The interest element in the hire purchase instalment under normal principles will be fully deductible as a trading expense (see **5.311**).

On the other hand, where a person has first leased or hired (other than by hire purchase) a motor car on or after 1 July 2008, and he pays some of the instalments but does not complete the agreement so that he never becomes the owner, TCA 1997, s 380N treats all the instalments and any other amounts paid by him under the agreement as if they had been lease rents. In other words, the capital allowances are withdrawn retrospectively and the Sch D Case I computations are amended by allowing as a deduction the actual hire purchase instalments paid (restricted as appropriate under s 380M, see above) as if each instalment (capital and interest elements) had been a least rent under a leasing agreement. The deduction previously allowed for the hire purchase interest is added back in the revised Sch D Case I computation for each period of account affected.

5.313 Business entertainment expenses

TCA 1997, s 840(2) requires the disallowance of all expenses incurred in providing business entertainment in arriving at the taxable profits of any trade or profession. It also prohibits the deduction of any such business entertainment expenses that might otherwise be deductible by an employee or director from his salary, etc assessable under Sch E (see **10.304**), or by an investment company in a management expenses claim.

'Business entertainment' is defined in TCA 1997, s 840(1) as:

> entertainment (including the provision of accommodation, food and drink or any other form of hospitality in any circumstances whatsoever) provided directly or indirectly ... in connection with a trade ...

The complete disallowance of business entertainment expenses applies whether the entertainment is provided by (a) the person(s) carrying on the trade ('the proprietor'), or (b) by any member of the proprietor's staff, or (c) by any other person performing any service for the proprietor if the entertainment is provided in the course of, or is incidental to, the performance of that service. Entertainment provided by any such person in connection with any business profession or employment is similarly within the definition (TCA 1997, s 840(1)). A member of the proprietor's staff includes any person employed by the proprietor and, if the proprietor is a company, any director of that company or any other person employed in its management (TCA 1997, s 840(1)).

In addition, any expenses incurred by or on behalf of the trader in providing gifts to his customers or other business or other connections are treated as business entertainment expenses and disallowed (TCA 1997, s 840(5)). It would appear, for example, that the cost to a trader of making Christmas gifts to his customers, even if considered important to maintain their goodwill and business connection, must also be added back in the tax computation. On the other hand, the handing out of free samples of the products in which the taxpayer deals to customers or potential customers should not require any add back in the computation, if done as part of sales promotion normal in the type of trade concerned. The Revenue Commissioners have issued a precedent accepting that 'free gifts' offered to purchasers of goods as part of a sales promotion are in effect part of the consideration provided by the seller of the goods; accordingly the cost of providing those 'gifts' is not disallowable under TCA 1997, s 840.

In practice, the Revenue will not normally seek to disallow small gifts to local charities or other *bona fide* benevolent organisations where such gifts would be deductible under the 'wholly and exclusively' criterion.

Hospitality provided on a contractually reciprocal basis was held not to constitute entertainment in *Celtic FC v C&E* [1983] STC 470. (Compare *BMW (GB) Ltd v C & E* [1997] STC 824.)

Expenses incurred in providing entertainment, accommodation, food, etc for *bona fide* members of the proprietor's staff are specifically excluded from the business entertainment expenses that are disallowable and, in consequence, are deductible under the ordinary Sch D Case I rules, except where incurred incidentally to providing business entertainment for customers or other persons (TCA 1997, s 840(1)). In other words, the expenses of a canteen or similar facility provided primarily for the proprietor's staff are allowable, but any expenses incurred in providing hospitality to members of the staff taking part in the business entertainment of other persons must be added back. For example, the cost of a company's annual staff dinner should be allowed provided that this function is not held incidentally to providing hospitality for outside persons. The fact that there might be a small number of outside guests at a function held primarily for the staff (and directors) is not thought likely to alter this conclusion.

TCA 1997, s 840(6) contains a further rule dealing with the case where a person performing any service for the proprietor provides business entertainment incidental to the performance of that service. It deems a part of any payment made by the proprietor to the person performing the service for him to have been incurred in providing business entertainment. This part of the payment, taken as being equal to the cost of the business entertainment involved, must be disallowed in the proprietor's tax computation in the same way as if the business entertainment had been provided by him. The cost of the business entertainment to be added back in this case is to be determined by the inspector according to the best of his knowledge and judgment, but an appeal may be made to the Appeal Commissioners, or to the Circuit Court for a rehearing, if the proprietor is dissatisfied with the determination of the inspector on the matter. F(TA)A 2015, s 39, which was subject to Ministerial Order (SI 110/2016 appointed 21 March 2016 as the day on which the Finance (Tax Appeals) Act 2015, came into operation), removes the reference in TCA 1997, s 840(6) for an appeal to the Appeal Commissioners or a rehearing at the Circuit Court.

5.314 Bad debts

TCA 1997, s 81(2)(i) prevents a deduction for debts except to the extent that they are shown to the satisfaction of the inspector to be bad; further, provisions made in the accounts against specific debts considered to be doubtful may be allowable, but only to the extent it is estimated that the debts are likely to prove irrecoverable. If a debtor is bankrupt or insolvent, the debt should be estimated at such an amount as may reasonably be expected to be recovered on or during the settlement of the debtor's affairs; only the difference between the debt in the books and the expected recovery is allowable as a bad or doubtful debt. No deduction may be taken for a provision against doubtful debts generally and, if such a general provision has been charged in the accounts, it must be added back in the tax computations. However, the Revenue Commissioners will accept that a deduction of a proportion of longstanding small debts based on previous experience is equivalent to a specific provision (*Statement of Practice IT/2/92*).

In *Curtis v Oldfield* 9 TC 319, Rowlatt J stated that the equivalent of TCA 1997, s 81(2) applied only to treating debts which would appear as such in a balance sheet. Furthermore, it must be borne in mind that losses not connected with the trade, etc are, in any event non-deductible by virtue of TCA 1997, s 81(2)(e). In addition, losses on debts which are in the nature of investments will be disallowable as being capital in nature. The better view seems to be that the 'wholly and exclusively' test under TCA 1997, s 81(2)(a) will not apply to losses which are incurred involuntarily (see the discussion at **5.303**); where a debt is *deliberately* written off in order to subsidise a subsidiary (as in *Odham's Press Ltd v Cooke* 23 TC 233, 237), the 'wholly and exclusively' test will clearly also be relevant.

A trading debt is allowed to be written off as bad in the period it proves to be irrecoverable – see the obiter dicta to this effect in *Absalom v Talbot* 26 TC 166. Debts previously written off as bad must, to the extent recovered in a subsequent period of account, be credited as trading receipts in the period or periods in which recovered (*Bristow v William Dickinson & Co Ltd* 27 TC 157). Similarly, a specific provision for doubtful debts allowed in one period must be credited as a trading receipt if and to the extent that the debtor's circumstances change and a recovery is received or expected in a later period. If normal accounting practice is followed, these items should be debited or credited in arriving at the net bad debts charge or credit in the profit and loss account so that no adjustment will be required for them in the tax computation. On the other hand, if the whole or a part of a general provision previously added back is reversed by a credit in the profit and loss account, the amount of this credit should be deducted in the tax computation.

Example 5.314.1

Smith, Jones & Co, a trading partnership making up accounts each year ended 31 December, had no specific or general provisions for bad or doubtful debts in its accounts up to 31 December 2014, but had the following entries in its bad debts account for the two accounting years to 31 December 2015 and 2016:

	Year ended 31/12/2015	*Year ended 31/12/2016*
	€	€
Debts written off as bad (not previously provided for)	1,580	425
Provisions created for doubtful debts:		
Specific – Mrs S	260	
Mrs J	380	
BC Limited		1,680
AD & Co		820
General provision	3,000	-
	5,220	2,925
Less:		
Bad debts previously written off now recovered	190	375
Cancellation of provisions no longer required		
Specific – Mrs J (she won sweep)		380
General provision reduced (as now considered excessive)	-	1,000
Net charge in P & L a/c	5,030	1,170

The only items where the tax treatment differs from that used in the above account and the adjustments required in the tax computations to deal with them, are as follows:

	Year ended 31/12/2015	*Year ended 31/12/2016*
Add back:	€	€
General provision created not allowable for tax purposes	3,000	
Deduct:		
Reduction in general provision credited in P & L a/c but not chargeable to tax		1,000

In *Curtis v J & G Oldfield Ltd* 9 TC 319, a managing director of a company in sole control of the business passed through the books payments and receipts relating not to the business, but to his own private affairs. After his death, a debt of £14,000 was discovered, but could not be collected from his estate and was written off as bad. It was held that this was not a loss arising out of trading activities and was therefore not deductible.

In *English Crown Spelter Co Ltd v Baker* 5 TC 327, it was held that advances made by the taxpayer to another company to ensure continuity of supplies from the latter were not incurred in the course of the taxpayer's trade and were not, therefore, allowable (see also to similar effect *James Waldie & Sons v IRC* 12 TC 113). By contrast, in *Reids Brewery Company Ltd v Male* 3 TC 279, bad debts resulting from loans made by a brewery company to its customers were held on the facts of that case to be deductible since the provision of the loans were considered to be a branch or adjunct of their brewery business.

In the case of a guarantee, it will however, normally be the purpose in giving the guarantee which is critical. The analysis of payments made under guarantees seems to fall into two stages. Firstly, it is necessary to ask what was the purpose of entering into the guarantee: if this was wholly or partly for non-trading purposes, then it would appear that any loss in relation thereto would be disallowed under TCA 1997, s 81(2)(a) (see *Garforth v Tankard Carpets* [1980] STC 251, at **5.304** and *Milnes v J Beam* 50 TC 575 at **5.306**). In *Jennings v Barfield* 40 TC 35, a loss incurred by a firm of solicitors on meeting a guarantee given on a client's overdraft was held to be allowable. The court accepted that it was common practice for solicitors to give guarantees in the course of a transaction in which they acted professionally. Thus, even if the issue of the allowability of a loss is determined at the time when it arises, it would seem that the test under TCA 1997, s 81(2)(e) would be met. The second stage of the analysis reflects the fact that payment of a guarantee in the true sense gives rise to a right of recovery (see *Garforth v Tankard Carpets* [1980] STC 251 and contrast *Morley v Lawford* 14 TC 229). The issue will therefore arise whether the loss is on the capital or revenue account. Where a guarantee is given as part of the trading activities of the taxpayer it will usually follow that the debt is in the nature of circulating capital in the trade, so that any loss incurred thereon is revenue in nature.

Where the making of loans or incurring of debts is considered to be part of the trading activities of the taxpayer, it will usually also follow that they are not capital in nature, and vice versa (see **5.307**). In *Lunt v Wellesley* 27 TC 78, the taxpayer made a loan to a film company in order that it could make a film out of one of his scripts, thus showcasing his talents. The company became insolvent and the resultant loss in respect of the loan (as well as associated guarantees) was held to be deductible. The court held that the sole *purpose* behind the loan and guarantees was to advance the taxpayer's professional activities and that it was not in the nature of fixed capital.

Where a trader supplies goods and services on credit to a related party (typically a company in the same group) and the resultant debt become bad or doubtful, it does not automatically follow that this loss is deductible. Thus, for example, if the credit terms granted to the third party are excessively liberal, Revenue could argue that the debt (or at least some part of it) was in effect a loan designed to finance the activities of the third party and thus not on trading account. If this is the case, it would also be open to Revenue to argue that the loss related to a capital transaction.

In *Sycamore & Maple v Fir* [1997] STC (SCD) 1, a parent company continued to supply goods to a subsidiary which was in financial difficulties. The Special Commissioner held that the bad debts incurred as a consequence were commercial in nature, since the parent had good reason to believe that the subsidiary was in a position to become profitable so that it would be capable of paying its debts. The Special Commissioner also had to consider the implications of the fact that the taxpayer had applied payments by the subsidiary towards the repayment of an inter-company loan in preference to repayment of the trading debts due to the taxpayer. This factor should only have been relevant if the bad debts had to qualify under the 'wholly and exclusively' test, (which arguably does not appear to be the case generally for bad debts, as discussed above). In the event, the Special Commissioner held that, even if the 'wholly and exclusively' test did apply, it *was* satisfied on the particular facts of the present case.

A surplus arising from the subsequent recovery in full of a debt taken over at a reduced valuation on a change of ownership of a continuing business was held to be analogous to a profit on the sale of a capital asset; it was not, therefore, taxable as a profit accruing in the course of trade (*Reynolds & Gibson v Crompton* 33 TC 288). A person succeeding to or acquiring a trade previously carried on by another person is not permitted a deduction in respect of any loss occurring subsequently on debts taken over at the time of the succession or acquisition (nor is he taxable in respect of any bad debts recovered subsequently (*CD v O'Sullivan* II ITR 140)). These considerations should not apply where a succession is disregarded for tax purposes (as in the case of most changes in the composition of a partnership see **4.503**) (see also **5.608** for the possible application of TCA 1997, s 92).

In *Calders v IRC* 26 TC 213 the taxpayer agreed that the shareholder of a company which owed it money should be substituted as a debtor. The court rejected an argument that the old debt should be treated as discharged by the acquisition of the new debt (so that the latter should be treated as an investment). Accordingly, the loss arising when the new debt became bad was allowable. The decision may be somewhat generous to the taxpayer, since the new debt was not incurred on trading account.

5.315 Interest payable

Interest payable and money borrowed for use in a trade is in principle fully deductible as an expense in calculating the profits of the trade, subject to the anti-avoidance rule contained in TCA 1997, s 817C, discussed below. This principle applies whether the interest is short interest or yearly interest (see **2.306** for the distinction between these two types of interest). This deduction stems from the general principle that expenses incurred wholly and exclusively for the purposes of a trade are allowed unless prohibited by any statutory exception. It is applicable for both income tax and corporation tax purposes and is not affected by those other provisions in the Acts which restrict or prohibit the allowance of interest as a deduction from non-trading income (see **Division 3**). The deduction applies equally for interest on money borrowed wholly and exclusively for use in a profession. On general principles, interest on loans incurred in whole or part for the purpose of the trades of other group companies will normally fall foul of the 'wholly and exclusively' criterion (*Commercial Union Assurance Co v Shaw* [1998] STC 386).

There are, however, several exceptions to be considered. TCA 1997, s 81(2)(h) disallows 'any interest which might have been made' if any sums employed as capital in the trade or profession 'had been laid out at interest'. The wording of this disallowance is difficult to interpret precisely. It may have the effect of preventing a deduction for a notional interest charge which a trader might seek to make in his accounts for the equivalent of the interest that should be returned on the capital employed in the business.

In *European Investment Trust Co Ltd v Jackson* 18 TC 1, the finding of the Appeal Commissioners that interest paid by a company on a loan from its American parent company was not deductible because the loan was money employed or intended to be employed as capital in the trade, was upheld. This was a surprising conclusion since interest for the use of money would seem to be of an inherently revenue nature (in the same way, for example as rent for the use of premises). In *Beauchamp v FW Woolworth plc* [1988] STC 714, Nourse J in the Court of Appeal, took the view that the decision in the *European Investment Trust* case was in fact incorrect, noting also that the point had been conceded in that case by the taxpayer without argument. The House of Lords did not comment further on this aspect of the case.

However, in *Wharf Properties v CIR* [1997] STC 351, the Privy Council held that interest on capital borrowings was itself capital in nature, relying on a dictum of Upjohn J in *Chancery Lane Safe Deposit & Offices Co Ltd v IRC* 43 TC 83, that 'the cost of hiring money to rebuild a house is just as much a capital cost as the cost of hiring labour to do the rebuilding'. This analysis implies that the capital or revenue nature of the borrowings is determined by the use to which those borrowings are put in the relevant period of account. However, this proposition is inconsistent with previous authority which indicates that it is the degree of permanence of the borrowings themselves which is critical (see the final two paragraphs of **5.307**). In *Wharf Properties*, the Privy Council sought to distinguish the earlier cases on the somewhat puzzling basis that these were concerned with the question as to whether or not particular borrowings represented a capital or revenue *receipt*.

The Revenue Commissioners have issued a precedent stating their view that notwithstanding the actual decision in *Brosnan v Mutual Enterprises Ltd* V ITR 138 (discussed at **5.307**) there are dicta in the High Court indicating that the judge would have attached significance to the fact that the borrowings in question were incurred to acquire a capital asset. The weight to be attached to such dicta is questionable. The decision in *Wharf Properties* necessarily implies that the deductibility or otherwise of interest could alter over time; it is not clear how in practice the borrowed funds would be traced and matched against specific assets of the business (see also the discussion of the *Ringmahon* case below).

Following the *European Investment Trust* decision, the corresponding UK legislation was amended to negate its apparent effect, but there has been no corresponding amendment in Irish income tax law. In practice, however, the Irish Revenue Commissioners do not usually seek in any normal case to disallow interest actually paid on money borrowed for use wholly and exclusively in the trade or profession, even if the borrowed money is used as capital. The Revenue Commissioners take the view that interest payable on borrowings to fund a company's purchase of its own shares is not incurred wholly and exclusively for the purposes of the trade (*Taxfax* 14 February 1997) (see however discussion of *Ringmahon* case below).

An interesting question is at what point the 'wholly and exclusively' test under TCA 1997, s 81(2)(e) should be applied. In *MacNiven v Westmoreland* [1977] STC 1103, the UK Special Commissioners applied the decision in *Hyett v Leonard* 2 TC 346 (see also *IRC v Falkirk Iron Co* 17 TC 625, discussed at **5.304**) and held that interest on a loan originally borrowed for the purposes of a business was deductible by reference to those purposes (even though the taxpayer company was insolvent at the time of payment). They added:

> We do not take the view that one has to look into the taxpayer's mind when he pays arrears of rent or accrued interest and ask the question what was the object of paying that rent or that interest since the object of taking a lease at rent or a loan at interest has long been identified.

The point was not considered when it came before the High Court [1997] STC 1103. As discussed above, in *Wharf Properties*, it was held in effect that the nature of a loan must be considered by reference to use to which the borrowed funds were put in the relevant period of account. As noted above, the decision in that case seems questionable in so far as the capital or revenue nature of borrowings is concerned. However, it does appear to be the position in Ireland in so far as the application of the 'wholly and exclusively' test is concerned.

The authority for this is *Sean MacAonghusa (IOT) v Ringmahon Company* [2001] ITR 117 where, the Supreme Court upheld the High Court decision of Budd J that interest on a loan taken out to redeem the preference share capital of the Ringmahon company was deductible in calculating the company's profits. Ringmahon Company raised a loan in order to redeem its preference shares. The company claimed a deduction for the interest paid on the loan. The Revenue argued that a deduction should not be allowed since the interest paid was not wholly and exclusively for the purposes of the trade since the loan was obtained for share restructuring rather than for the trade of the company. However, the company argued that they were entitled to redeem the preference share capital of the company where the shareholders required capital and that once the company had redeemed the share capital, that it required a certain level of funding to continue carrying on the business. They argued that these monies were used wholly and exclusively for the purposes of the trade and that as such an interest deduction should be allowed.

Geoghegan J upheld the High Court and Circuit Court decisions that the interest on the loan was deductible since the funds were used to finance the trade and that it was necessary to consider how the funds were used at the time when the interest deduction was being paid in order to determine whether they were wholly and exclusively for the purpose of a trade. It is therefore necessary to consider how the borrowings are used in each accounting period to decide if the interest is deductible.

Allocating specific borrowings to particular activities or assets is a problematic exercise given the fluidity and fundability of a business's sources and applications of finance. A pragmatic approach may be to compare the value of borrowings with the value of assets (including net working capital) used in the relevant trade (disregarding any asset revaluations); interest on the borrowings would be disallowed to the extent (if any) that the borrowings exceeded that of the trading assets. The Revenue have issued a precedent stating that they would seek to disallow interest on borrowings to the extent that these are used to finance a negative balance on the trader's capital account.

In *Tax Briefing 25*, the Revenue Commissioners indicated that they are prepared to treat payments for interest caps as part of the interest cost of a loan.

Anti-avoidance

One further rule that may, in certain circumstances, be relevant to the question as to whether interest payable may be deducted as an expense of the trade is that contained in TCA 1997, s 254. The various rules that severely restrict the deduction of non-trading interest from a taxpayer's total income from all sources have been discussed in detail in **Division 3**. TCA 1997, s 254 is by way of being an anti-avoidance rule designed to prevent a sole trader, the partners of firms carrying on trades or professions or the shareholders of a company, themselves unable to get full interest relief on non-trading borrowings, from using capital withdrawn from the business for their own private purposes, while the business borrows other funds to obtain a trade expense deduction for the resulting interest.

TCA 1997, s 254 operates by disallowing the deduction of interest payable on money borrowed to replace capital that was employed in the business but which the proprietor has withdrawn for other non-business use. It provides that the interest on such new borrowings is not to be regarded as wholly and exclusively incurred for the purposes of the trade, profession or other business. It applies where the capital replaced was withdrawn at any time within five years before the date of the new borrowings. In the case of *Sean MacAonghusa (Inspector of Taxes) v Ringmahon Company* (see above), it would appear that the Revenue Commissioners accepted on the facts of that case that the section was not appropriate as the borrowings did not *replace* capital formerly employed in the trade, although this must be an arguable proposition.

The section is not intended to prevent the proprietors from withdrawing their profits from the business by way of drawings or, in the case of companies, by dividends or other distributions of profits (compare the discussion at **3.209**).

In the case of an individual or other non-corporate trader, interest paid by him to any connected person could be disallowed to the extent that it is at an excessive rate, ie on the ground that this excessive element is not incurred wholly and exclusively for the purpose of earning the profits.

TCA 1997, s 817C (inserted by FA 2003, s 44) also operates to defer or deny relief in certain circumstances where timing differences could otherwise be potentially exploited by taxpayers. The section applies as respects tax years from 2003 onwards.

TCA 1997, s 817C is expressed to apply where:

(a) interest is payable by a trader (directly or indirectly) to a person who is connected with the trader;

(b) if the interest had actually been paid it would have been chargeable under Sch D;

(c) the interest would otherwise have been allowable in computing the trader's profits; and

(d) (i) in a case where the connected person is chargeable to tax in respect of the interest, the interest does not fall to be taken into account in computing that person's trading income, or

(ii) in a case where the connected person is not so chargeable, the interest would not fall to be taken into account in computing that person's trading income if he were resident in the State.

Section 817C is therefore aimed at the situation where the interest would be taxable under Sch D Case III had it been actually paid to the lender; the Sch D Case III charge will only arise if the payment is actually made (see **8.102**) while the trader would be entitled to claim a deduction for the accrued interest in the absence of these provisions under the normal principles of accounting. The section will clearly not apply to a case where a trader pays non-Irish source interest to a person who is neither resident or ordinarily resident in the State; as discussed in **2.307** it is debatable however whether interest paid by an Irish resident is ever capable of constituting a non-Irish source.

The general definition of a 'connected person' set out in TCA 1997, s 10 applies (for a full discussion see **12.304**).

There is an exception where interest is paid to a connected person which is a company resident outside the State and is not under the control (directly or indirectly) of a person or persons who are resident in the State (TCA 1997, s 817C(2A)). For these purposes, the term 'control' is construed in accordance with the very wide close company provisions of TCA 1997, s 432(2)–(6) (see the discussion of these provisions in **12.304**) (TCA 1997, s 817C(2A)(a)); the scope of the phrase 'direct or indirect' is unclear but will presumably extend to control exercised through subsidiary companies. In addition, a company is not to be treated as under the control (direct or indirect) of a person or persons if that person or those persons are in turn under the control of another person or persons (TCA 1997, s 817C(2A)(b)). It is not clear if this provision applies where some but not all of the persons controlling a company are controlled in turn by other persons.

The reference to payments being made 'directly or indirectly' appears to envisage the use of conduit entities. In addition, TCA 1997, s 817C(4) attempts to deal expressly with such rerouting devices. This subsection provides that interest will be deemed to be payable by one person ('A') to a person connected with A ('B') where there are arrangements made by *any* person under which:

(a) interest is payable by A to a person not connected with A; and

(b) interest is payable to B by a person not connected with B.

It is not necessary that the person receiving the interest within (i) should be the same as the person paying the interest in (ii). Where the amount of the interest payable under (i) is different to the amount payable under (ii), the subsection does not make clear which amount should be treated as being payable by A. Logic might suggest that the lower amount of interest should be taken but that this should be done on a cumulative basis over the life of the arrangements.

Where the section applies, the interest payable by the trader on the relevant loan or other indebtedness in a basis period will only be allowed up to an amount calculated as (A–B), where:

A is the aggregate of amounts of interest in respect of the loan, etc which are chargeable to tax as income of the connected person (or *would* be so chargeable but for the provisions of TCA 1997, s 198 or the provisions of a double tax agreement) for basis periods up and including the current basis period concerned; and

B is the aggregate of the amounts of interest in respect of the loan, etc which have been allowed as deductions in computing trading income or have otherwise been relieved for tax purposes for basis periods excluding the current basis period concerned. Necessarily, B does not include interest payable for the current basis period, as it is the purpose of the formula to ascertain how much of that interest will be allowed (TCA 1997, s 817C(3)).

Again, it may be noted that interest which is not chargeable by virtue of a Double Tax Agreement does not seem to fall within the scope of the section in the first instance; the formula may however be relevant in a case where interest had been protected from the charge under Sch D in previous basis periods but this is no longer the case. Similarly, interest relievable other than in computing trading income is not within the section, but the formula may be relevant in a case where trading interest had been relieved under different provisions in previous basis periods (although this seems rather unlikely).

While as noted above TCA 1997, s 817C takes effect from tax year 2003 onwards, the effect of the section could be retrospective since the formula appears to apply to interest in respect of the same loan for all basis periods up to the end of the current basis period. This presumably would not apply if the parties were to negotiate a genuinely new loan in the current basis period.

Interest which is disallowed on foot of the section is treated as if it had been payable in the following basis period and so on for the purposes of the formula above (TCA 1997, s 817C(4)).

Interest on tax

No interest paid on any overdue tax, whether a tax on income, capital gains or on expenditure is deductible in computing profits under Sch D Case I or II. Correspondingly, no interest received on overpaid tax is included as a trading receipt.

5.316 Annual payments, royalties etc

Certain types of payment, although incurred wholly and exclusively for the trade and not being of a capital nature, are not deductible in calculating the taxable profits of the trade. These are the payments subject to the deduction of tax at source rules referred to in **2.302**, namely:

(a) annuities and other annual payments (but excluding annual interest) 'payable out of the profits or gains';
(b) royalties or other sums paid for the use of patents; and
(c) mining, etc rents and similar payments made by mining, quarrying and similar concerns.

The disallowance of the abovementioned annuities, annual payments and patent royalties is provided for by TCA 1997, s 81(2)(l), (m), and that of the mining, etc rents by TCA 1997, s 104(2)(a)(ii) which requires them to be treated as if they were patent royalties. Instead of the deduction of these types of payment in arriving at the taxable profits of his trade, the person making them, if chargeable to income tax, obtains relief for them by withholding and retaining income tax under the TCA 1997, s 237 procedure (see **2.303**), provided that they are paid out of 'the amount of the profits or gains to be charged to tax under case I or II' which is a reference to the first sentence in TCA 1997, s 81(2). To the extent the trader is required to pay over the income tax deducted at source to the Revenue under TCA 1997, s 238 (see **2.304**), loss relief may be available in the manner explained in **4.4**.

Revenue's published guidance differs on this matter and is not beyond doubt because it is arguable that taxable Case I or II profits must have already been calculated and the annual payment referred to in para (l) must come 'out of' such profits. This conclusion receives further weight when TCA 1997, s 81(2)(l) is compared with that of TCA 1997, s 81(2)(m) and reads '… in computing the amount of the profits or gains to be charged to tax under Case I or II of Schedule D, no sum shall be deducted in respect of—… (m) any royalty or other sum paid in respect of the user of a patent;'. It can be seen from that no reference is made in TCA 1997, s 81(2)(m) to the profits from which the sum is to be paid. The legislature saw it necessary to pinpoint particular profits from which the annual payment in TCA 1997, s 81(2)(l) were paid in ensuring its non-deductibility.

This issue came before the UK courts in *Moss' Empires Ltd v Commissioners of Inland Revenue* [1937] 21 TC 264 and the question in that case was whether payments made were annual payments charged with tax under Sch D within the then equivalent of TCA 1997, s 238. The company had claimed a deduction for the annual payments on the basis of the amounts concerned being wholly and exclusively incurred for the purposes of the trade and the House of Lords explained:

> …the Appellants, in computing the amount of their profits and gains for tax purposes, were permitted to deduct the sum paid under the agreement as being a disbursement or expense wholly and exclusively laid out or expended for the purposes of their trade. Consequently, the payments were not payable out 'of profits or gains brought into charge…'.

A patent royalty, annuity or other annual payment may sometimes be paid gross to a non-resident person entitled to the benefit of a double taxation agreement and who obtains the specific approval of the Revenue Commissioners to be paid without the deduction of income tax (see **14.205**). In this case, he is allowed to deduct the gross payment in arriving at the taxable profits of the trade. However, if the trader is a person chargeable to income tax by reference to a year of assessment, the gross payments actually charged in the period of the accounts are added back and the deduction is given instead in each tax year for the payments actually made in that year, rather than in the accounting period that is the basis period for that year.

5.317 Relief on retirement for certain sportspersons

TCA 1997, s 480A provides that sportspersons specified in TCA 1997, Sch 23A may on retirement claim deductions from their total income for 10 years based on their earnings from the sport concerned. The sportspersons concerned are athletes, badminton players, boxers, cricketers (with effect from 2012 onwards), cyclists, footballers, golfers, jockeys, motor racing drivers, rugby players, squash players, swimmers and tennis players.

Where the individual retires on or after 1 January 2014 he can claim the deduction from income arising in any ten of the fifteen tax years before retirement (including the year of retirement). Individuals who retired before 1 January 2014 could claim the deduction from income arising in any 10 years from 1990/91 onwards, including the year of retirement. The deduction is computed for any given tax year as 40 per cent of the gross receipts included in the profits of the basis period of that year which arose wholly or exclusively ie deriving directly from the actual carrying on of his profession, such as match or performance fees, prize moneys and appearance moneys paid as a direct consequence of participating in the sport concerned but not other earnings such as sponsorship fees, advertising or promotional income, media fees, or fees for personal interviews or appearances, magazine articles, the use of the sportsperson's image or name for promotional or endorsement purposes etc (TCA 1997, s 480A(6)).

Example 5.317.1

Pat Golden is a professional rugby player who retired from rugby in 2015. Of the fifteen years (2001 to 2015 inclusive) before he retired, the 10 years in which his salary from playing rugby were highest were the years 2009–2013 and 2003–2007 and so Pat's claim for relief under TCA 1997, s 480A will be made for those years. Pat's taxable income for 2013 was as follows:

	€
Salary	250,000
Employment expenses	(5,000)
Net Schedule E Income	245,000
Case IV: Sponsorship income	10,000
Total/Taxable Income	255,000

Pat will be entitled to claim a deduction of €100,000 (40% of €250,000) from his taxable income for 2013 which will give rise to a refund of €41,000 (€100,000 at 41%). Similar relief will be claimed and tax refunds due for the years 2009–2012 and 2003–2007.

Because USC is calculated on income without regard to any amount deductible in calculating total income (TCA 1997, s 531AM(1)(b) (see **3.404**)), the individual remains liable to USC on his income before the relief is given. PRSI also continues to be payable because it is charged on income before deductions (see **3.402** and **11.2**).

An individual can only claim the relief where he is resident in the State, an EEA state (ie EU Member States plus Iceland, Liechtenstein and Norway) or an EFTA state (ie Iceland, Liechtenstein, Norway and Switzerland) in the retirement year. Individuals who retired prior to 1 January 2014 had to be resident in the State in the year of retirement in order to claim the relief. In addition, for individuals who retired before 1 January 2014 the deduction could only be claimed for tax years in which the individual was resident in the State. This is no longer a requirement for individuals who retire on or after 1 January 2014. Such individuals must only be resident in the State, an EEA or EFTA state in the retirement year. The retirement year is the year in which the individual proves to the satisfaction of the Revenue Commissioners that he has ceased permanently to be engaged in carrying on his sporting profession or occupation. When the individual ceases permanently is a matter of a fact to be determined by examining the circumstances in each particular case. In order to be entitled to claim the relief the individual must cease to carry on the sport as a profession or as an employee, the fact that the individual continues to participate in the sport in question as an amateur would not preclude him from claiming the relief. Furthermore, the relief is only available to an individual who complied with the Income Tax Acts. In the author's view this potentially gives the Revenue Commissioners discretion to disallow a claim where the individual making the claim has at some point not been income tax compliant.

Where the individual is required to file a return for the year in which the individual retires, the relief must be claimed in the return for the year in which the sportsperson retires. An individual who qualifies for relief under TCA 1997, s 480A is required to file a return electronically under ROS (see **2.105**) however the online Form 11 does not cater for relief claimed in respect of years prior to the current year and any claim included in the Form 11 is treated as a claim in respect of income for the current year. In practice therefore an individual must claim relief under TCA 1997, s 480A by writing separately to Revenue. If an individual is not required to file a return for the year in which the individual retires, TCA 1997, s 480A(7) provides that he can submit a claim for the relief to the Revenue Commissioners. The claim must be made within four years from the end of the retirement year (TCA 1997, s 480A(3)). The normal four-year time limit on claiming repayments under TCA 1997, s 865 will not apply (TCA 1997, s 480A(4)).

The relief cannot create or augment a loss under Sch D Case II; this seems to follow in any event from the fact that the relief is granted as a deduction from total income (TCA 1997, s 480A(8)(c)). The relief will not affect the calculation of the sportsperson's net relevant earnings as defined for the purposes of TCA 1997, ss 787 and 787B (level of allowable contributions for the purposes of retirement annuity contracts, occupational pension schemes and personal retirement savings accounts): see **16.2** (TCA 1997, s 480A(9)); the reference to TCA 1997, s 787B applies for 2017 and subsequent years of assessment. The relief will be given by way of repayment of tax subject only to any right of offset under TCA 1997, s 960H (see **2.617**) but will not carry interest. (TCA 1997, s 480A(8)). Provision is made to withdraw the relief by way of a Sch D Case IV assessment at any time for the tax years in respect of which the relief was originally given if the person subsequently recommences to be engaged in that sport, though this does not prevent a subsequent claim for the relief if and when the sportsperson finally does retire at a later time (TCA 1997, s 480A(10)).

5.4 Stock in Trade and WIP

5.401 Valuation of trading stock

The term 'trading stock' when used in the context of the calculation of profits taxable is not defined as such. However, the definition contained in TCA 1997, s 89(1) (dealing with the valuation of trading stock on the discontinuance of a trade) is accepted as generally applicable. Thus, trading stock is generally taken to include the stock of all goods or property of any description, whether real or personal, which are sold in the ordinary course of a trade (or will be so sold in their completed form), as well as materials used in the manufacture, assembly, preparation or construction of such goods or property. The term, therefore, is taken to include raw materials, partially processed goods, work in progress, goods in an immature state which are normally held until they mature before sales, finished goods, etc.

Nevertheless, the definition contained in TCA 1997, s 89(1) may, in some unusual cases arguably be wider than the ordinary sense of the term 'trading stock' (see *GMAC v IRC* [1987] STC 122). It appears that on general principles trading stock need not necessarily be in the ownership of the trader. The question of what should be included as trading stock appears to be primarily an issue of correct accounting principles rather than legal niceties (see *Fraser v London Sportscar Centre* [1983] STC 75; *Murnaghan Bros v O'Maoldomnhaigh* IV ITR 304). This does not mean that the correct legal position is not relevant, merely that it is not conclusive per se. An accounting treatment based on an erroneous appreciation of the true legal position may well, therefore, lead to an incorrect application of accounting principles (see *Merchant (Peter) Ltd v Stedeford* 30 TC 496).

Where goods are transferred subject to reservation of title, (so that ownership thereof remains with the 'vendor' until the goods are sold on by the 'purchaser'), the generally accepted accounting practice is to treat the goods as sold to the 'purchaser' at the date of transfer in both the accounts of the 'vendor' and 'purchaser'. This assumes that there is no intention that the 'vendor' will exercise his ownership rights other than in the event of the insolvency of the customer (see Miscellaneous Technical Statement M09 Accounting for goods sold subject to reservation of title issued November 1976). The Revenue Commissioners have indicated that they will accept the above accounting treatment if it is adopted consistently by 'vendor' and 'purchaser'. It seems in fact that if the purchaser adopts correct accounting principles, then the Revenue must accept the position in the accounts irrespective of the vendor's accounting treatment (although it would remain open to the Revenue to seek to adjust the vendor's profits, if appropriate).

Trading stock may also exist in the form of work in progress in certain professional businesses, eg those of accountants, solicitors, etc (see TCA 1997, s 90).

The items comprising the trading stock of any particular business depend on the nature of that business and of the goods and services provided in the course of the trade. For example, the trading stock of a person carrying on a trade of dealing in or developing land comprises the land and buildings acquired for the purposes of sale or development in the course of that business, but in most other businesses land and buildings are fixed assets and not trading stock. In some businesses, goods of the same category may be either trading stock or fixed assets depending on the use to which they are put (note the discussion in *MacGiolla Riagh v G Ltd* II ITR 315). For example, a business which sells computers is likely to use a certain number of these computers as office equipment in the business, although most of the machines will be held as trading stock for resale. In such a case, accurate accounting is desirable to distinguish the two categories.

The valuation of trading stock for tax purposes is primarily a matter of accounting practice. Following *Ostime v Duple Motor Bodies Ltd* 39 TC 537, the Revenue Commissioners are not entitled to insist on the use of any particular method of valuation, but the taxpayer must value his stock on a consistent basis in successive periods of account and under a method which conforms to generally accepted accounting principles as applied in his particular trade or industry. Moreover, certain stock valuation methods, eg 'LIFO' and 'base stock', have been held to conflict with income tax principles and are not normally acceptable for tax purposes (see below).

The basic principle is that trading stock in hand at the end of the period of account (the opening stock of the next period) is to be valued at the lower of cost to the trader and net realisable value. The phrase 'the lower of cost or market value' has been used in various tax cases, but modern accounting practice has for most applications defined 'market value' more precisely as net realisable value. This latter phrase is taken to mean the amount estimated to be realised on a sale less the estimated costs which must necessarily be incurred to effect the sale. The cost of replacing the items in question is not strictly acceptable as market value, except to the extent that replacement cost may on occasions be the best or the only measure of realisable value.

The 'lower of cost or market value' rule is an exception to the general principle that losses must be realised before they are recognised for tax purposes. In *Whimster & Co v IRC* 12 TC 813 Lord President Clyde said:

> For example, the ordinary principles of commercial accounting require that in the profit and loss account of a merchant's or manufacturer's business the values of the stock in trade at the beginning and at the end of the period covered by the account should be entered at cost or market price, whichever is the lower, although there is nothing about this in the taxing statutes.

The rule only applies to stock in hand and not eg to a forward contract to acquire stock (*Collins & Sons v IRC* 12 TC 773) or to stock-in-transit (*Green & Co (Cork) Ltd v IRC* I ITR 130).

AB Ltd v MacGiolla Riagh II ITR 419 has apparently established that the lower of cost or market value rule does not extend to the trading stock of a dealer in investments. Teevan J noted that the taxpayer did not produce any evidence that the application of the rule was in accordance with ordinary accounting practice in respect of finance and investment companies. Further, a number of earlier cases implied that only realised losses in respect of shares and securities were recognisable for tax purposes. The learned judge concluded that the non-application of the rule was justified on the basis that investments which are in hand can still produce income for their owner.

In practice, not all accounts adopt fully the best accounting practice and some may fall considerably short of it. In such cases, particularly the latter, the attitude of the inspector of taxes is likely to depend on whether he considers the trader in question is preparing proper and complete accounts and whether the stock valuation method used results in a reasonable approximation to the cost or if lower, market value of the stock, and whether it is being consistently applied. If it is, Revenue is likely to accept the accounts, but if Revenue has any reason to suspect that any stock is being omitted or undervalued they are likely to enquire more deeply into the matter.

In arriving at the 'cost' value of trading stock, most normal accounting methods are accepted for tax purposes, including 'FIFO' (first in first out), standard cost and average cost. However, in *Patrick v Broadstone Mills Ltd* 35 TC 44, the base stock method, although accepted in the industry in question as proper accounting, was held to be unacceptable for tax purposes since, when changes in stock levels or rises in prices took place, the method involved an understatement of profits. It was held that the items of stock should be taken into account at both beginning and end of the accounting period at their actual cost or market price, whichever was lower. Base stock was found not to relate to the actual cost of the goods in hand on these dates.

In *IRC v Cock, Russell & Co Ltd* 29 TC 387, it was held to be proper accounting practice, not varied by any statutory rule, to value some items of stock at cost (when lower than market value) and to value other items at market value (where this was lower). The attempt by the UK Inland Revenue to impose a 'global' value, ie the lower of total cost or total market value of all items, was rejected.

In *BSC Footwear Ltd v Ridgway* 47 TC 495, the company carried on business as shoe retailers, buying most of its stock wholesale. Stock in trade had been valued for a number of years at the lower of cost and an estimated replacement value taken as being the notional purchase price which would yield the requisite gross profit at the expected selling price. It was held that, in the case of a retail trade, market value meant the value realisable in the retail market and that the notional replacement value could not be justified.

The importance of normal accounting principles was again emphasised in *Ostime v Duple Motor Bodies Ltd* 39 TC 537. In this case a company carrying on a trade of building motor bodies had for many years used the direct cost method of valuing work in progress, ie by including only the cost of direct materials and labour. The UK Revenue made assessments on the basis that the on cost method, ie involving the addition of a proportion of factory and office expenses, should be substituted. The Appeal Commissioners had found that the accountancy profession at that time was satisfied that either the direct or on cost method would produce a true figure of profit. In view of this finding, and as the direct cost method had been applied consistently over the years, the House of Lords held there was no reason to require the company to change its method of valuation. It may be noted that SSAP 9 now requires *inter alia* that production overheads should be included in stock valuations.

Where the value of trading stock includes depreciation in accordance with SSAP 9, the UK Inland Revenue take the view that nevertheless the full amount of depreciation charged in the accounts should be disallowed (and not merely that amount net of depreciation included in the valuation of trading stock). It is submitted that it is the correct approach since one must distinguish between the depreciation charged in the accounts (disallowable) and the valuation basis for trading stock (where commercial principles apply subject to any conflict with tax law).

5.402 Changes in stock valuation

Changes in stock valuation may occur either because the trader changes the basis of valuing his stock or because the Revenue determines that the taxpayer's stock has not been properly valued. In an Indian case, *Bombay Commissioner of Income Tax v Ahmedabad New Cotton Mills Co Ltd* 46 TLR 68, it was held by the Privy Council that, where both opening and closing stocks are undervalued, the real profits of the year cannot be ascertained by raising only the valuation of the closing stock and not taking into account a similar undervaluation of the opening stock. The principle is that it is the profit of the year (or other period of account) that is to be measured and that cannot be done properly without adjusting both opening and closing stock so that they are valued on the same basis.

While it is to be expected that whatever basis is used by a particular business for valuing its trading stock will be applied every year in the same manner, it does happen in practice that a business may decide one year, usually for some good reason, to change the basis of valuation previously used. In the period of account in which the new basis is first applied to the closing stock, it is necessary, for tax purposes at least, to adjust the opening stock to the new basis to provide a proper measure of the profit of the period. The result may be that the opening stock value taken into the year's accounts may be higher or lower than that given to the same stock at the close of the previous year. How is the profit or loss resulting from the difference between these two figures dealt with? Is it necessary to adjust the closing stock value in the previous accounts to the same basis?

The Revenue Commissioners generally distinguish between 'valid' and 'non-valid' bases of valuation. A valid basis is one which is acceptable for tax purposes, ie is consistent with ordinary accounting practice, does not violate any tax principles and has been implemented currently. A non-valid basis is one which is either non-acceptable in itself or which would be valid except that it has not been implemented correctly. Where a taxpayer moves from a non-valid to a valid basis then the Revenue will follow the *Ahmedabad* decision. The Revenue will review the liabilities of previous years, but provided that there has been no fraud, wilful default or neglect, the excess liability will normally be restricted to the amount of the uplift of the opening stock valuation for the period in which the valid basis is first adopted (see Feeney: *Valuation of Stocks and Work in Progress* [1993] ITR 637).

A taxpayer may also switch from one valid basis to a different valid basis, eg in order to reflect changed trading conditions, or to adopt a policy consistent with other members in a corporate group, etc. The Revenue have indicated (in their Memorandum published with SSAP 9 in May 1975) that in such cases the valuations of stock adopted for previous periods would not normally be reopened. However, it should be noted that this treatment is not consistent with the decision in *Pearce v Woodall-Duckham Ltd* [1978] STC 372. There, a company carrying out design and construction work on long term contracts, decided to include for the first time in its closing work-in-progress valuation for the year 1969 an estimate of the profit attributable to the proportion of the work done. The adjustment of the opening valuation for the year to the new basis threw up a profit of £580,000 in excess of the closing valuation for 1968. It was held that the £580,000 was a trading profit to be taxed in 1969. This was said to be a genuine economic writing up of the work in progress and it was not a profit that could be attributed to earlier years. TCA 1997, s 95A (inserted by FA 2006, s 56), provides with effect from tax year 2006 onwards that any uplift in the opening valuation of work-in-progress will be charged under Sch D Case I or II as appropriate, generally in the year in which the change is effected (ie reflecting the decision in *Pearce v Woodall-Duckham Ltd*): this provision is discussed fully at **5.404**.

Example 5.402.1

A manufacturing business has valued its work in progress on the basis of direct cost for a number of years up to 31 December 2016. In preparing its accounts for the year ended 31

December 2017, it decides to change to the on cost method. Its preliminary trading account for that year appears as:

	€	€
Sales		120,000
Cost of sales:		
Purchases	30,000	
Opening stock (1/1/2017) (including work in progress at direct cost)	16,000	
	46,000	
Closing stock (31/12/2017) (including work in progress at on cost)	(25,000)	
		(21,000)
Wages and other direct costs		(42,000)
Gross profit		57,000

Assume that a revaluation of the work-in-progress included in the opening stock on the cost basis results in its values being increased to €19,500 (an increase of €3,500). The correct accounting would be to substitute this new value in the trading account, thus increasing the cost of sales to €24,500 and decreasing the gross profit by €3,500 to €53,500. The €3,500 profit thrown up on the revaluation of the opening stock would normally be included in the prior year adjustments, thus increasing reserves by €3,500.

Assuming Revenue is satisfied that the original direct cost valuation basis was an acceptable method of stock valuation, then prior to 2006, he would not have included the revaluation profit of €3,500 in the taxable profit. However, TCA 1997, s 95A now provides that the revaluation profit should be charged to tax under Sch D Case I for the basis period for tax year 2017.

Example 5.402.2

Assume another manufacturing business, whose trading account shows the same figures as those in **Example 5.402.1**. Assume that the closing stock has been valued on the correct basis, but it is discovered that in previous years there were improper understatements in the stock valuations and that the proper valuation of the 2016 closing stock, and therefore the 2017 opening stock, is €19,500.

In this case, the extra profit of €3,500 on the revaluation of the opening stock is likely to be assessable as additional income either for the year ended 31 December 2016 or by spreading it over several previous years if the understatement of profits has built up over more than one year.

5.403 Work in progress: long-term contracts

Accounting principles permit the inclusion of a profit element in the valuation of work-in-progress on long-term contracts, the work on which is spread over more than one period of account. This treatment is consistent with the principle (discussed at **5.201**) that the receipt of advance payments may result in partial recognition of the profit to be made in respect of the relevant transaction. In *Symons v Weeks* [1983] STC 195, Warner J held, in fact, that this treatment was designed to prevent profit being anticipated. This was because it excluded the receipt of the stage payments altogether, and only incorporated a conservative proportion of the predicted final profit on the contract in the work in progress valuation.

As Warner J pointed out, there is no fixed rule for allocating receipts (or expenses) to periods of account. However, this is true only subject to conformity with the basic principles of income recognition set out at **5.201**. Thus, it seems that an upward valuation of work in progress which exceeded the amount of stage payments actually received could represent a breach of the realisation principle. Warner J also took the view that once an allocation of this kind had been made in accordance with correct accounting practice there was no scope for revising it in the light of later events.

It is arguable that in some cases the treatment of long-term contracts may strictly be over-generous to the taxpayer. This is because a long-term contract may be 'divisible' ie full entitlement to the interim payments arises, irrespective of whether or not the entire contract is completed. On this analysis, the taxpayer would have fulfilled all the obligations necessary to earn the interim payment, so that *all* of the profit up to that point would be realised. The decisions in *JP Hall & Co* and *IRC v Gardner Mountain & D'Ambrumenil* (see **5.201**) were not cited to Warner J in the *Symons* case.

The position for the year in which the taxpayer first includes a profit element in his work in progress and thus moves from one value basis to another has been considered in **5.402**. A reduction in the value of work-in-progress to reflect the anticipated unprofitability of a long-term contract was always regarded as acceptable for tax purposes under the 'lower of cost or net realisable value' principle. Where an anticipated loss exceeded the value of work in progress the Revenue previously argued that the corresponding provision was not deductible for tax purposes. However, in *Tax Briefing 41* they have indicated that they will accept such provisions in relation to accounting periods on or after 23 March 1999, in light of FRS 12 (see also the discussion of the Revenue approach to FRS12 in **5.302**).

5.404 Work in progress: professions

It is correct practice for persons carrying on certain professions to bring in work in progress figures into their accounts. A firm of accountants, for example, may carry out an audit or other assignment spreading over a number of months or sometimes longer. To the extent that professional staff spend time on work in one period of account that is billed in a subsequent period, normal accounting on an earnings basis required the *cost* of the accrued time on unbilled work to be credited in the accounts as work in progress at the end of the period, with a corresponding deduction as the opening work in progress of the next period. However, by virtue of UTIF Abstract 40 (including associated guidance notes) issued on 10 March 2005, it is now provided that:

> where the substance of a contract for services is that the seller's contractual obligations are performed gradually over time, revenue should be recognised as contract activity progresses to reflect the seller's partial performance of its contractual obligations. The amount of revenue should reflect the accrual of the right to consideration as contract activity progresses by reference to the value of work performed.

Further, 'the amount of revenue will reflect the fair value of the services provided as a proportion of the total fair value of the contract, which will reflect the time spent and skills and expertise that have been provided'. TCA 1997, s 95A(2) (inserted by FA 2006, s 56) effectively brings into charge any upward revaluation of work-in-progress arising on a change of accounting basis from tax year 2006 onwards. Specifically, it provides that where the revalued figure for opening work in progress following the change of accounting basis (the 'relevant amount'), is allowed as a debit in computing profits for a chargeable period (the 'relevant period'), then if the relevant amount exceeds the counterbalancing credit for closing work in progress in the previous chargeable period, tax will be charged under Sch D Case I or II on the excess (TCA 1997, s 95A(1), (2)). The definition of 'chargeable period' is that provided by TCA 1997, s 321(2) (see **6.102**) so that for 2006 the reference is apparently to the basis period for 2006; this could be problematic in cases where the basis period includes more than one period of account. One would have expected the legislation to deal initially in terms of periods of account.

Where the work in progress relates to a partnership, any excess will be treated as a profits or gains of the partnership trade or profession (TCA 1997, s 95A(3)). The provisions do not apply to a situation where TCA 1997, s 94(3) is in point (change from conventional to earnings basis: see **5.502**: *Work in Progress on Change of Basis in Accounting*).

The legislature has assumed that the recognition of additional income under Abstract 40 will give rise to a corresponding increase in the balance sheet figures for work in progress and has accordingly provided a form of deferral relief in these circumstances. Where the charging provisions would otherwise apply to a relevant period ending in the period of two years beginning on 22 June 2005 *and* the change arises *only* as a consequence of the application of Abstract 40, then for persons other than companies, the following spreading relief applies:

(a) one-fifth only of the excess is chargeable for the relevant period; and
(b) a further one-fifth of the excess is chargeable for each succeeding chargeable period until the whole amount of the excess has been accounted for.

The relief is mandatory and not at the election of the taxpayer.

Where the trade or profession is permanently discontinued, then any untaxed balance of the excess amount will be chargeable in the chargeable period of discontinuance (TCA 1997, s 95A(4)). The retirement of a partner would be treated as the discontinuance of his notional separate trade under TCA 1997, s 1008(1), thus triggering off this provision in relation to his share of the excess amount.

Prior to the issuance of Abstract 40 only the *cost* of the employees' time on professional work, ie on work for which a fee would be charged to the client, required to be brought into the work in progress valuation. The time of the proprietor or of partners in a firm was not part of the cost borne by them and could legitimately have been excluded. Work in progress may normally be excluded in the case of a person carrying on a profession who uses a 'conventional' basis of accounting which is acceptable to the Revenue Commissioners (see **5.502**).

Example 5.404.1

George Johnson is a sole trader providing accountancy services. He makes accounts up to 31 March each year. In his accounts ended 31 March 2005, closing work in progress was valued at €18,500, based purely on the cost of his employees' time incurred on unbilled work. For the accounts ended 31 March 2006, Abstract 40 applies. Accordingly, opening work in progress is revalued at €32,000 to reflect the fair value thereof at 1 April 2005, and closing work in progress at €44,000. The accounts for the year ended 31 March 2006 show the following:

	€	€
Sales		340,000
Less:		
Opening Work in Progress (revalued)	(32,000)	

Add:		
Closing work in progress	44,000	12,000
		352,000
Less: Deductible expenses		(67,000)
Tax-adjusted Sch D Case I profits		285,000

The uplift in valuation of work in progress (the excess) of €(32,000 – 18,500) = €13,500 is liable to tax. However only 1/5 of the excess is subject to tax under Sch D Case II for 2006, ie €2,700, in addition to the profits of €285,000 as computed above. In the normal run of events, an additional sum of €2,700 would be taxed for tax years 2007, 2008, 2009 and 2010. If George ceased his profession in 2008, then an additional sum of €13,500 – €(2,700 x 2) = €8,100 would be taxed in that year.

5.5 Other Matters

5.501 Exchange gains and losses

An exchange gain or loss normally arises in one of two ways. A person carrying on a trade or profession may purchase goods or pay expenses to a supplier, etc to be paid for in a foreign currency at a date other than that on which the purchase or expense is first recorded in the books. Alternatively, goods may be sold to a customer payable at a different date in a foreign currency. If the rate of exchange for the foreign currency is different from that when the transaction was first booked, an exchange gain or loss arises on the settlement. Secondly, exchange gains or losses are likely to arise when liabilities or monetary assets denominated in foreign currencies are translated into Euro at the end of the period of account, normally at the exchange rate prevailing at the balance sheet date.

In preparing the tax computations, it is necessary to analyse the exchange gains or losses credited or debited in arriving at the accounting profit to determine how far the credits are properly included as trading receipts for tax purposes and how far the debits are allowable deductions as expenses. Since both the accounting (for exchange gains and losses) and the tax treatment is a rather specialised subject, it is discussed separately in **13.302–13.307** as part of the treatment of foreign aspects of taxation.

5.502 The conventional basis of accounting

The normal basis of calculating the taxable profits that arise or accrue in the period of account irrespective of the date of payment by the customer is referred to as the 'earnings' basis. There has been, however, a long established practice under which the Revenue Commissioners were willing to accept for tax purposes the accounts of a person carrying on a profession prepared on what is referred to as a 'conventional' basis of accounting. A conventional basis is any basis other than a full earnings basis, including a pure cash basis.

Following SP–IT/2/92, the Revenue Commissioners clarified (and tightened) their practice in this context. The statement of practice reiterates the Revenue view that the only legally correct basis is the 'earnings basis', defined by TCA 1997, s 91(5)(a) as that under which 'all credits and liabilities accruing during that period as a consequence of the carrying on of the trade or profession are brought into account in computing those profits or gains for tax purposes, and not otherwise'. In fact this view seems over-rigid. Thus, for example, in *Absalom v Talbot* 26 TC 166 (discussed at **5.201**) the House of Lords accepted that debts due by instalments, but which were not capable of being valued actuarially, should be brought into account on a cash receipts basis. More significantly, in the case of royalties received by writers and other artists normally the only practicable (and thus, it would seem, the correct) accounting treatment is a cash receipts basis (see eg *Stainers Exors v Purchase* 32 TC 367 and *Walker v O'Connor* [1996] STC (SCD) 218). The Revenue Commissioners also take the view that work in progress should be accounted for where ordinary accounting principles would require this to be done. Accounting for the time costs of staff in respect of unbilled work as work in progress would seem to fulfil the requirements of the basic principle of matching (see **5.102** above).

The Revenue Commissioners state in SP–IT/2/92 that they will now only permit the use of an *acceptable* conventional basis in the case of professions. An 'acceptable' conventional basis is one where all of the following conditions are met:

(a) there will be no material difference between the amount of profits computed on the conventional basis and the amount that would have been arrived at on a full earnings basis;

(b) bills for services rendered or work done are issued at regular and frequent intervals; and

(c) the accounts include a note containing precise details of the basis used.

The Revenue state that an 'acceptable' conventional basis should also *usually* include debtors and creditors. Work in progress need only be included where its exclusion would materially affect the profit figure. Provisions for specific doubtful debts made in accordance with accepted accountancy principles are allowable for tax purposes. As noted at **5.314**, a provision consisting of a proportion of long standing small debts will rank a specific provision for tax purposes, provided the amount can be justified by reference to previous experience. In effect, therefore, the Statement of Practice is designed to permit professionals to exclude work in progress from their accounts, if the above conditions are satisfied.

However, the Revenue state that they will not permit even an acceptable conventional basis to be adopted in the first three years of trading, including both the first three years of the 'relevant period' of a professional partnership (see **4.502**), and any case where an individual who succeeds to a profession is treated as commencing to carry it on (see **4.502**). After the end of the three-year commencement period, a professional firm may then switch from an earnings basis to an 'acceptable' conventional basis. This means that there will be a credit for closing work-in-progress in the accounts for the third year but no corresponding debit for opening work-in-progress in the following set of accounts (since these will be prepared on a conventional basis), leading to potential double taxation.

Barristers are outside the scope of the new statement of practice and may operate on a pure cash basis from the year of commencement onwards. The reason for this concession is stated to lie in the fact that barristers are unable to sue for their fees.

In order for any conventional basis to be accepted for tax purposes, it is necessary that the accounts of the business be actually prepared in that form. There can be no question of producing a tax computation on a cash or similar basis where the accounts are prepared on an earnings or other type of conventional basis. This reflects the principle that a taxpayer is generally bound by the treatment adopted in his accounts. Further, once a business has used an earnings basis, it cannot subsequently change to a conventional basis (other than in the situation where a professional switches after the first three years of business).

The normal rules regarding the type of items to be included as trading receipts and the non-deductibility of expenses are applied irrespective of the basis of accounting used. Capital allowances may be claimed in the ordinary way in respect of expenditure on qualifying assets, eg office equipment, motor vehicles, etc.

Change in basis of accounting

Following the *Statement of Practice IT/2/92* it will generally be the case that in the Revenue's view only barristers will be entitled to use the pure cash receipts basis. However, given that the statement says only that taxpayer's using the conventional basis will *usually* be required to include debtors and creditors, it is possible that there will also still be other taxpayers on a cash receipts basis.

A taxpayer who has used a cash receipts basis may wish to switch to a conventional basis incorporating debtors or to a full earning basis. It is also presumably possible that the Revenue Commissioners may require such a switch if there is a change in the conduct of the taxpayer's business which means that he no longer meets the requirements of the Statement of Practice.

Such a change may have the result that trading receipts accruing in one period of account but received in the next might not, in the absence of any rule to the contrary, come into the taxpayer's taxable profits in either period. This could occur, for example, if he changes from a pure cash basis in one year to a fees furnished basis in the next, with the result that fees furnished but unpaid at the end of the first year are not entered as a trading receipt in the accounts for either year.

TCA 1997, s 94 deals with this situation. It charges to tax under Sch D Case IV all trading receipts accruing to a trade or profession in any period before the change of basis of accounting, but received after the change, to the extent that they are not otherwise taken into account in computing taxable profits (or losses). It may be noted that this rule applies to a trade as well as to a profession. It recognises that in practice the conventional basis of accounting was sometimes applied to trades (although as the Statement of Practice makes clear the Revenue Commissioners no longer intend to continue this practice) despite the fact that its use should in the view of the Revenue strictly be confined to professions.

The Sch D Case IV assessment on trading receipts accruing before, but received after, the change of accounting basis is normally made in the year of assessment in which the amounts in question are received. However, the person assessed (or, if relevant, his personal representatives) may elect by notice in writing to the inspector to be assessed as if any relevant amounts were received on the last day of the last period for which the old basis of accounting was used; this only applies to amounts received within four years (reduced from 10 years for 2013 and subsequent years of assessment FA 2013, s 92 and Sch 1, Pt 2(a)) of that day (TCA 1997, s 95(3)). In the case of a person born before 6 April 1919 the amount assessed may be reduced in the same manner as the net amount assessable under TCA 1997, s 91 on post-cessation receipts if two further conditions are met. These two conditions, and the manner in which this reduction in the amount assessable is made, are the same as those explained and illustrated in **5.607** for an assessment on post-cessation receipts of a person born before 6 April 1919.

Example 5.502.1

Messrs Boru and Camelot have made up their accounts for their architects' business on a cash basis up to and including their financial year ended 31 March 2016 (ie Revenue have agreed that they need not include debtors, which in practice would be somewhat unusual). For their financial year ended 31 March 2017, they change over to the normal 'conventional' basis (ie including debtors) but they continue to exclude work in progress from their accounts. The relevant figures for each of the two years are:

	Year ended 31/3/2016	Year ended 31/3/2017
	€	€
Opening debtors for fees:		
1/4/2015	27,000	
1/4/2016		34,000
Fees furnished in year	137,000	163,000
	164,000	197,000
Fee accounts paid in year (cash receipts)	130,000	156,000
Closing debtors for fees:		
31/3/2016	34,000	
31/3/2017	-	41,000
	164,000	197,000
Deductible business expenses for year	86,000	107,000

The financial accounts are made up on the cash basis for the first year and on the normal conventional basis for the second year, as follows:

	31/3/2016	31/3/2017
	€	€
Cash receipts for fees in year	130,000	
Fees furnished in year		163,000
Less:		
Deductible expenses for year	86,000	107,000
Taxable profits (Sch D Case 11)	44,000	56,000

The change to the normal conventional basis of accounting for the year ended 31 March 2017 (ie effective from 1 April 2016 onwards) has had the effect that the closing debtors of €34,000 at 31 March 2016 (representing fees furnished in the year ended that date) has not been included as a trading receipt in the accounts of that year (only cash received in the year included). Further, it has not been included as a trading receipt in the accounts of the year ended 31 March 2017 (only fees furnished in that year included).

Assume that €28,500 of the debtors at 31 March 2016 is received in the tax year 2016 and that a further balance of €2,500 is received in May 2017, but that remaining €3,000 has to be written off as a bad debt. The rule in TCA 1997, s 94 applies and each partner is assessed on his share (assumed one half each) of these amounts which, due to the change in basis of accounting, have so far been omitted from the trading receipts charged to tax, as follows:

	Boru	Camelot
Sch D Case IV assessments (additional income):	€	€
2015: receipts in year (€28,500)	14,250	14,250
2016: receipts in year (€2,500)	1,250	1,250
	15,500	15,500

Either Boru or Camelot may, if he wishes, elect under TCA 1997, s 95(3) to have his separate Sch D Case IV assessment made instead on additional income of €15,500 for the tax year 2016 (ie as if the total of €31,000 actually received after 31 March 2015 had been received on that date).

Work in progress on change in basis of accounting

TCA 1997, s 94(3) imposes a charge to tax under Sch D Case IV where a change in the basis of accounting from a conventional basis to the earnings basis, or a change from one conventional basis to another, results in the bringing in of work in progress to the accounts of a profession for the first time or involves a change in the basis of valuing work in progress. In such a case, the normal accounting rules for dealing with trading stock on a change in basis of accounting require the opening work in progress to be revalued (and debited in the accounts) on the same basis as that used for the closing work in progress. In the absence of any provision to the contrary, this debit (or increased debit) – assuming there was no work in progress included previously or work in progress valued on a lower basis – would cause an element of profit to fall out of account.

TCA 1997, s 94(3) provides that, where these circumstances arise, tax is charged under Sch D Case IV on an amount equal to the debit (or the increase in the debit compared with that on the old basis) for the opening work in progress for the period of accounts in which the change in basis of accounting is made. If and to the extent that there was in fact any counterbalancing credit brought into account in computing the Sch D Case II taxable profits (or losses) for the last period of accounts for which the old basis was used (or for any earlier period) then the amount chargeable under TCA 1997, s 94(3) is reduced accordingly. The Sch D Case IV assessment is made for the tax year in which the change in the method of accounting for work in progress occurs. The provisions of TCA 1997, s 95A (see **5.404**) do not apply in these circumstances.

Example 5.502.2

Mr C H Art, in practice on his own account as a chartered accountant, has made up his accounts up to and including the year ended 30 September 2016 on a conventional basis bringing in as trading receipts the fees furnished in the period of accounts, but not including any work in progress. For his accounting year ending 30 September 2017, he changes over to a full earnings basis. His accounts for that year including work in progress properly valued at 30 September 2017 at €26,900, but before debiting any opening work in progress figure as for 1 October 2016, show an accounting profit of €39,600. There are disallowable expenses charged in those accounts totalling €1,110, but no other items requiring adjustment in the tax computation apart from dealing with work in progress.

Mr Art's first step is to adjust his accounts for the year ended 30 September 2017 by debiting an opening work in progress figure valued on a basis corresponding to that used at 30 September 2017. The Sch D Case II profits of his profession for the year ended 30 September 2017 (assessable 2017) now result as follows:

	€
Trading profits per unadjusted accounts	39,600
Less:	
Debit in accounts opening work in progress valued at say	19,500
Profits per accounts as adjusted	20,100
Add back:	
Disallowable expenses	1,110
Sch D Case II profits assessable 2016	
(before capital allowances)	21,210

Since there was no closing work in progress (nor any opening figure) included in the previous accounting year, ie that ended 30 September 2016, the above adjustment has resulted in the reduction of the Sch D Case II profits for the year ended 30 September 2017 by €19,500 without any counterbalancing credit for the previous accounting year (or any earlier year). Since the previous fees furnished basis of accounting was an accepted and proper conventional basis for a profession, there is no reason to make any adjustment in the Sch D Case II computation for any year prior to that ended 30 September 2016 (see **5.404**).

The rule in TCA 1997, s 94(3) therefore requires Mr Art to be assessed under Sch D Case IV on the sum of €19,500. The Sch D Case IV assessment is made for the tax year 2016, ie the tax year in which the change in basis of accounting occurred with the revaluation of the opening work in progress on 1 October 2016.

5.6 Commencements, Cessations and Post-cessation Receipts

5.601 Calculation of profits on commencement

The calculation of the taxable profits of the first period of account in which a trade is set up and commenced is affected by a few additional rules. These rules also apply to the extent relevant to the commencement of a profession.

A person setting up a new trade may incur expenses before he is ready to start trading. For example, a company setting up a new manufacturing business may incur significant expenses on wages, salaries, interest on loans, rents, rates, etc in acquiring fixed assets, getting its factory organised, recruiting and training staff and workers and so on before it can start trading. Even though these expenses are essential, and may be properly treated under normal accounting principles on revenue account, they are not allowable under general principles as an expense in calculating the taxable profits of the trade if incurred before trading commenced. However, by virtue of TCA 1997, s 82(2)) most pre-trading expenses incurred within three years of commencement may be relieved in relation to trades or professions commenced on or after 22 January 1997 (see **5.306**: *Expenses of Cessation and Commencement*).

It is necessary in each case to ascertain the date on which trading commences to determine when expenses become deductible in calculating taxable profits under general principles (bearing in mind that expenses allowable only by virtue of TCA 1997, s 82(2) are not permitted to create or increase loss claims under TCA 1997, s 381). This date will also be relevant in applying the Sch D Case I/II commencement provisions (see **4.205**). Where the business is a manufacturing one, the date of commencement is normally when the trader first starts a proper manufacturing process with the intention of producing goods for resale at the end of it. The mere purchase of raw materials prior to starting manufacture or the test running of machinery are by themselves not sufficient to be regarded as commencing trading (see *Birmingham & District Cattle By-Products Co Ltd v IRC* 12 TC 92; see also *Spa Estates v O'hArgain* discussed at **12.305** and compare *Cannop Coal Ltd v IRC* 12 TC 31, decided on somewhat unusual facts). On the other hand, a trade can commence before the first sale is made. In the case of a wholesale or retail business, the trade is normally regarded as commencing when the doors are first open for business or when the trader first seeks customers for his goods or services. It may in appropriate cases be possible to establish that trade has commenced when goods are first purchased with the intention of reselling them in the course of trading. Each case depends on its own facts.

When a person succeeds to an existing trade previously carried on by another person (and this is treated as a commencement by him for tax purposes (see TCA 1997, s 69, discussed at **4.208**)), there is not normally any question of pre-trading expenses. The expenses incurred before the succession are deductible under ordinary rules in calculating the profits of the person ceasing to carry on the trade, while those expenses incurred after the succession are normally deductible by the successor. However, if outstanding debtors are taken over with the business, the person succeeding is not (in principle) entitled to deduct any bad debts arising subsequently on any balances taken over but he may be able to claim a deduction under TCA 1997, s 92: see **5.608**. Expenditure on repairs to capital assets taken over from the previous trader may in some cases be disallowable as capital in nature (see **5.309**).

Where pre-trading staff recruitment and training expenses are not deductible as expenses of the trade, TCA 1997, s 769 permits such expenses to be written off over a three year-period as capital allowances, but only where the expenditure is incurred for a trade consisting of the production for sale of manufactured goods. See further the discussion at **6.502**.

5.602 Trading stock on commencement

The opening valuation to be attributed to trading stock acquired on the commencement of a business is straightforward where the goods are purchased for cash or on credit in the normal way. In practice, this may not always be the case. Trading stock may be acquired for a consideration other than cash, for example, in exchange for the issue of its own shares by a company, or the trading stock may be acquired as part of a larger consideration for the purchase of a business or of a group of assets. In such cases, the trader is entitled to debit in his accounts an opening stock figure in respect of the cost to him of acquiring the trading stock items.

In *Craddock v Zevo Finance Co Ltd* 27 TC 267, a new investment dealing company took over as trading stock, on the reconstruction of another company, the investments dealt in at their original cost to the other company of £1,030,000 and at the same time assumed responsibility for that company's liabilities of £410,000. In exchange, the new company issued its own shares to a nominal value of £620,000. The investments acquired had a market price at the time of approximately £363,000. It was held that the company was entitled to debit the investments as trading stock at their cost to it of £1,030,000, ie the £620,000 share capital issued plus the liabilities taken over of £410,000.

The *Zevo Finance* case also illustrates that, under general principles the Revenue Commissioners are not normally entitled to overrule a price genuinely agreed between vendor and purchaser. This is subject to the putative principle in *Sharkey v Wernher* (see **5.101**) under which market value may be substituted for the sale price in a wholly uncommercial transaction (the same principle potentially applies where a non-trading asset is appropriated to stock or stock is received by way of gift; but in the latter case, note the special rules for certain farmers, discussed at **7.206**; in practice the Revenue Commissioners do not apply the *Wernher* principle to appropriations of trading stock). It should also be borne in mind that where an excessive price is paid, the 'wholly and exclusively' rule may be relevant (particularly where the vendor and the purchaser are associated with each other). Special rules also apply in the case of certain transfers of land between connected persons.

The *Zevo Finance* case further indicates that the Revenue Commissioners will normally be bound to accept that where shares are issued in order to discharge payment of a genuinely agreed price, it is that price and not the market value of the shares (if different) which should be regarded as the purchase consideration (see also *Stanton v Drayton Commercial Investments Co* [1981] STC 585, a capital gains tax case). It was significant in the *Zevo Finance* case that it would have been illegal for the company to have issued shares at a discount (in *Murphy v Australian Machinery & Investment Co* 30 TC 244 the court overrode what it regarded as a purely fictitious and inflated valuation agreed by the parties, ie it was treated as a 'sham'). It may be noted that a vendor who disposes of trading stock in exchange for shares is apparently required to account for those shares at market value (*Consolidated Gold Coast Selection Trust Ltd v Humphrey* 30 TC 20).

In *Osborne v Steel Barrel Co Ltd* 24 TC 293, a company acquired trading stock as part of the total assets taken over from the receiver of another company. In exchange for all the assets acquired, the company gave £10,500 in cash and issued £29,997 of its own £1 shares fully paid up. There was no provision in the agreement allocating the total consideration between particular assets. It was held that the proper opening figure for the trading stock acquired was a proportionate part of £40,497, ie £10,500 plus the £29,997 par value of the share capital issued.

Where trading stock is acquired with other assets and the total consideration is allocated between the different types of asset in the agreement between the parties, this allocation should normally be followed for tax purposes and the amount debited in the trading account for the stock accepted.

5.603 Trading stock on cessation

TCA 1997, s 89 and s 656(2) provides rules for valuing unsold trading stock at the date on which a trade has been discontinued. They apply also where a trade carried on by an individual is treated as if permanently discontinued under TCA 1997, s 69 on the succession by someone else to the trade (see **4.208**) and also where a company ceases to carry on a trade or to be chargeable to corporation tax on its profits. They do not apply to a trade carried on by a single individual that ceases on his death, but do apply to a partnership trade carried on by two individuals ceasing to be carried on in partnership by reason of the death of one of them.

Prior to 6 December 2000 TCA 1997, s 89(2)(a) required the closing trading stock at the date the trade was discontinued was to be valued at the price for which it was sold, or at the value of any other consideration given for its transfer, if and to the extent that:

(a) the trading stock is sold, or is transferred for valuable consideration, to a person who carries on or intends to carry on a trade in the State; and

(b) the stock is acquired by that person as trading stock or for a purpose such as would enable the cost to that person of acquiring the stock to be deducted as an expense in computing the taxable profits of his actual or intended trade.

FA 2001, s 42 (amended TCA 1997, s 89) introduced new rules on the valuation of trading stock at the discontinuance of a trade on or after 6 December 2000 where the parties are connected and where paragraphs (a) and (b) above apply. For the purposes of TCA 1997, s 89, two persons are regarded as connected with each other if:

(a) they are connected with each other within the meaning of s 10;

(b) one of them is a partnership and the other has a right to a share in the partnership;

(c) one of them is a body corporate and the other has control over that body;

(d) both of them are partnerships and some other person has a right to a share in each of them; or

(e) both of them are bodies corporate or one of them is a partnership and the other is a body corporate and, in either case, some other person has control over both of them.

When the parties are connected, TCA 1997, s 89(3)(b) provides that the trading stock is to be valued at its market value, being the value which would be received on an arm's length sale to a third party. TCA 1997, s 89(4) provides that if the market value exceeds both the actual transfer price and the book value of the stock that the connected parties can elect for the stock to be transferred at the higher of the two amounts.

These rules would apply either if the person acquiring the stock is succeeding to the trade of the person disposing of the stock, or if the stock is being acquired for use as trading stock in an entirely separate trade. It would seem that this express statutory rule should override the principle in *Sharkey v Wernher*, assuming that the latter holds good in Ireland (see **5.101**). In fact, a disposal of trading stock following the discontinuance of a trade may not itself be a trading transaction, in which case the *Wernher* decision would seem to have no relevance (note also *Moore v MacKenzie* 48 TC 196) It is understood that the Revenue Commissioners apparently take a contrary view on this issue.

For any other case not covered by the rule in para (a) (apart from a cessation on the death of an individual), TCA 1997, s 89(2)(b) requires the value of the closing trading stock to be taken as being the amount it would have realised if sold in the open market at the date on which the person in question ceased to trade. This market value rule would apply, for example, if the trading stock of the person ceasing to trade is acquired as a fixed asset for use in the trade of another person, since it does not thereby result in that other person's being able to deduct his cost of acquisition as an expense in computing his taxable profits. Market value at the date of discontinuance would also be taken if the closing trading stock is not sold or transferred, but is retained by the person ceasing to trade for personal or other non-trading purposes. Special rules may apply to farmers (TCA 1997, s 656 and see **7.206**).

These two rules are applied to the entire trading stock of the business remaining unsold at the date of the cessation of trade. For this purpose, TCA 1997, s 89(1) defines 'trading stock' as:

(a) … property of any description, whether real or personal, which is either:

(i) property such as is sold in the ordinary course of the trade in relation to which the expression is used or would be so sold if it were mature or if its manufacture, preparation or construction were complete, or

(ii) materials such as are used in the manufacture, preparation or construction of property such as is sold in the ordinary course of that trade.

(b) (i) … 'trading stock', in relation to a trade, includes any services, article or material which, if the trade were a profession, would be treated as work in progress of the profession for the purposes of s 90 …

and the sale or transfer of trading stock shall be constructed accordingly (for an analysis of the applicability of TCA 1997, s 89(2)) to hire purchase debts, see *Lions Ltd v Gosford Furnishing* 40 TC 256). Further, TCA 1997, s 90(1) requires, in the case of a trade that ceases, the closing trading stock value to include the value of any services, article or material which would, if the trade were a profession, be treated as work in progress. For example, if a person ceases to carry on the trade of motor car repairs and servicing, his stock of spare parts, etc held for the purpose of that trade must be included in his closing trading stock even though those items may not strictly speaking have been held for resale.

Closing stock on death

As indicated above, the closing stock valuation rules of TCA 1997, s 89 do not apply to the trade of a single individual that is treated as discontinued by reason of his death. Irrespective of whether or not the trade of a deceased person is carried on by anyone else after his death, the accounts of the business for the last period up to the date of death should be credited with the closing trading stock on that date valued in the ordinary way, ie at the lower of cost or market value. In the case of the death of a sole trader, it is completely irrelevant that the trading stock may have a net realisable value substantially in excess of its cost value included in the final accounts of the deceased person, at least so far as the computation of his Sch D Case I profits for the last period to the date of his death is concerned.

When the trade of a deceased person is carried on by his personal representatives or by his heirs, the normal closing stock value at the date of death becomes the opening stock value for the new trade deemed to be commenced on that date by the person(s) succeeding to it under the deceased's will or intestacy. However, should the personal representatives or the heirs, having first decided to continue the trade, subsequently decide to sell the trade or to cease to carry it on, then the rules of TCA 1997, s 89 apply to the valuation of the trading stock at the date of their ceasing to trade. On the other hand, if the personal representatives or heirs do not carry on the trade after the date of death, but set out to realise the assets of the trade, then any profits on the realisation after the death of the deceased person's closing stock are not taxable as trading receipts under Sch D Case I, nor are any losses eligible for loss relief.

5.604 Work in progress: cessation of profession

TCA 1997, s 90 contains rules for valuing work in progress at the date on which a person who has carried on a profession ceases to do so. These rules apply also where a profession is deemed by TCA 1997, s 69 to cease in the case of a succession to a person's profession by another person or by a partnership. The rules apply also when there is a succession to a profession carried on by a partnership at the end of the firm's relevant period (see **4.502**). TCA 1997, s 90 is only relevant, however, if it has been the practice to prepare accounts of the profession on a basis that brings in work in progress. It does not apply if accounts have been prepared in previous periods on a conventional basis of accounting which omits any form of work in progress valuation. Further, as with the rules of TCA 1997, s 89 for valuing the closing stock on a cessation of trade, TCA 1997, s 90 does not apply if the cessation occurs by reason of the death of an individual who was carrying on the profession on his own account without any partners.

TCA 1997, s 90(4) defines 'work in progress' for these rules as any services performed in the ordinary course of the profession, the performance of which was wholly or partly completed at the time of the discontinuance of the profession and for which it would be reasonable to expect that a charge would have been made on completion of the services if the profession had not been discontinued. Work in progress also includes any article produced, and any such material as is used, in the performance of any such services, for example, the drawings and plans of a proposed factory produced by an architect.

The work in progress valuation rules on a cessation parallel those in TCA 1997, s 89 for the trading stock of a trade. They provide that:

(a) if the work in progress is transferred to another person who carries on or intends to carry on, a profession in the State for which the cost of the work may be deducted as an expense in computing his taxable profits, the closing work in progress valuation for the person ceasing the profession is taken as the actual amount paid or the value of any other consideration given to him for the work in progress; and

(b) in any other case, the closing value of the work in progress is taken as being equal to the consideration that would be paid for the sale or transfer of the work in progress in a transaction between parties dealing at arm's length.

TCA 1997, s 90(2) adds a further rule in connection with the work in progress of a profession that has no parallel in TCA 1997, s 89 for the closing stock of a trade. It provides that the person who carried on the profession immediately before the cessation may elect to exclude from the computation of his Sch D Case II taxable profits (or losses) the excess (if any) of his closing work in progress as valued under TCA 1997, s 90 over the actual cost of the work to the date of cessation. If this election is made, then the amount by which the total consideration received by the person ceasing the profession exceeds the actual cost of the work is taxable under Sch D Case IV as if it were a post-cessation receipt (see **5.605**).

Since post-cessation receipts are normally taxable under TCA 1997, s 91 in the tax year in which they are received, this election could be advantageous if the rules of TCA 1997, s 90 would otherwise include a material profit element in the closing work in progress valuation, and if there is a delay in receiving payment in full for the work in progress. This might occur, for example, where the work in progress is sold for a consideration which is to vary depending on the amount that the purchaser can ultimately realise for it. It might also be useful if the person ceasing the profession expects to take some time after the date of cessation before he can collect all that is owing to him by his clients for work done (but not billed) at the date of the cessation.

Any election under TCA 1997, s 90(2) for Sch D Case IV treatment must be made by notice in writing sent to the inspector no later than 24 months after the date the cessation of the profession occurred. If the person in question dies after the date of cessation without having made the election, it may still be made by his personal representatives within the same 24-month period.

5.605 Post-cessation receipts

In *Carson v Cheyney's Executors* 38 TC 240, an author had been assessed during his lifetime under Sch D Case II on his royalties (net of expenses) on a receipts basis. It was accepted that the receipts basis was the only practical way of computing his profits. The Inland Revenue sought to assess his executors on royalties received after his death under Sch D Case III or Case VI (equivalent to Irish Case IV). The Inland Revenue conceded that during the taxpayer's lifetime the royalties could have been assessed only under Sch D Case II (since they did not represent 'pure income profit': see **2.302**). The House of Lords rejected the proposition that they could be assessed under a different heading after the taxpayer's death; in other words, the royalties retained their character as professional income. The decision in *Cheyney's Executors* followed that of *Purchase v Stainer's*

Executors 32 TC 367, where a similar analysis had been applied to shares in the profits of films received by the executors of a film actor and producer. In that case Lord Simonds LC observed:

> How else could these sums be in the hands of [the taxpayer] or his executor other than as the remuneration for his professional activities, the reward for services rendered by him during his life and unpaid for at his death.

Lord Simonds rejected the idea that the royalty contracts could be regarded as 'income bearing assets' in their own right; Lord Asquith said in this regard:

> The contracts in this case enjoy … no … independent vitality … The contracts were mere incidental machinery regulating the measure of the services to be rendered by him on the one hand and on the other that of the payments to be made by his employers: they were not the source but the instrument of payment.

In *Cheyney's Executors* and *Stainer's Executors*, the courts declined to follow *Bennett v Ogston* 15 TC 374, where Rowlatt J held that interest on debts held by a moneylender arising after his death was assessable on his executors. Although some doubt has been cast on the correctness of the decision in *Bennett*, the latter case may perhaps be distinguished on the grounds that the income there related to the use of money *after* the taxpayer's death. Furthermore, (unlike the position in *Cheyney's Executors* and *Stainer's Executors*) it would have been open to the Inland Revenue to assess interest receipts as such under Sch D Case III during his lifetime.

The effect of the decisions in *Cheyney's Executors* and *Stainer's Executors* was that the sums received by the executors in those cases could not be subjected to income tax. This followed because the receipts in question arose after the cessation of the taxpayer's trade (and so could not be assessed as professional earnings upon him) but they were not income in the hands of the executors (since the source was the taxpayer's profession, as opposed to a source held by them). As a consequence, legislation was enacted to prevent receipts of this kind and analogous profits from escaping the tax net.

TCA 1997, s 91 charges to tax under Sch D Case IV certain sums received after the discontinuance of a trade or profession which, if they had been received before the date of cessation, would have been included as trading receipts in arriving at the taxable profit or loss under Sch D Case I or II. It is, however, important to note that the section does not apply to the proceeds of the realisation of trading stock properly included in the closing stock valuation at the date of cessation, nor to any receipts from realising the closing work in progress of a profession that was included as such in the accounts at the date of cessation and valued on a full earnings basis of accounting, ie at cost or, if lower, market value.

In other words, TCA 1997, s 91 is designed primarily to prevent sums arising as trading receipts of a trade or profession from escaping taxation where a conventional, as distinct from the earnings, basis of accounting has been used. It does not set out to charge to tax any post-cessation profits which may be made on selling off the closing trading stock in the course of closing down a business and realising its assets provided that the earnings basis was used and properly applied. In general, the closing trading stock and work in progress valuation rules previously discussed should ensure that on an earnings basis of accounting the proper value of the trading stock is brought into account when the cessation occurs.

TCA 1997, s 91 does not apply to sums received on capital account or to sums not arising out of a trade or profession. In addition, the following other post-cessation receipts are specifically excluded from the tax charge under Sch D Case IV:

(a) sums received by or on behalf of a person not resident in the State representing income arising directly or indirectly from a foreign source;
(b) a lump sum paid to the personal representatives of the author of literary, dramatic, musical or artistic work for the assignment by them of the copyright in the work; and
(c) sums receivable by an individual from a work of artistic merit exempt from income tax under TCA 1997, s 195 (see **Division 5**).

TCA 1997, s 91(5)(a) provides that accounts are to be treated as having been prepared on an earnings basis if, but only if, all the credits due for trading receipts and all the liabilities in respect of trading expenses accruing during any relevant period of account have been included in computing the taxable profits (or loss) of the period in question. Where this condition is not strictly met in any particular period of account, the accounts for that period are treated as prepared on the 'conventional basis' (TCA 1997, s 91(5)(b)).

Even if accounts have been prepared on a full earnings basis, the taxation definition of the term means that, should it turn out that some trading receipts earned in the period of trading were not in fact credited in any account before the cessation, then – to the extent that they are received at any later time – they become assessable as post-cessation receipts, under Sch D Case IV. On the other hand, if credit has been taken during the period of trading by way of accrual or otherwise for amounts received after the cessation, those amounts are not taxable again as post-cessation receipts, even if a 'conventional basis' of accounting has been used.

If any bad debts (or any provisions for bad debts) were written off and allowed for tax purposes for any period of account prior to the cessation, then any amount recovered after the cessation in respect of any such debt (or any provision found to be excessive) is taxable as a post-cessation receipt (TCA 1997, s 91(5)(c)).

The Sch D Case IV assessment is normally made on the actual amounts received, after subtracting any deductions to which the person assessed may be entitled (see **5.607**) in the year of assessment or, in the case of a company, in the accounting period, in which the sums are received. Post-cessation receipts do not necessarily have to be received by the person who had formerly carried on the trade or profession. If paid to the personal representatives of a deceased trader or to the beneficiaries of his estate, they are taxable on the recipient. *Shop Direct Group v HMRC* [2016] UKSC came before the House of Lords in the UK and dealt with the issue of post cessation receipts received by a member of a corporate group who was not the company carrying on the original trade. Although a corporation tax case it is relevant for income tax purposes given the subject matter. The facts were that over many years companies within the Littlewoods corporate group paid HMRC substantial sums as VAT on an incorrect understanding of the law. HMRC later repaid the sums, which had been incorrectly paid, to a nominated member of the corporate group together with interest on those sums. The question was whether a repayment of overpaid VAT of £124m was liable to corporation tax in the hands of the Shop Direct Group ('SDG') under the UK equivalent of TCA 1997, s 91. The House of Lords held that such payment was taxable accordingly.

Further, if the person entitled to the receipts sells or otherwise transfers for value his right to them, the sale price or, if the transfer was not made in an arm's length transaction, the market value of that right, is treated as the amount taxable under (TCA 1997, s 95(1)).

Instead of being assessed in the year of receipt, the former trader or his personal representatives may elect by notice in writing to the inspector to be assessed on any chargeable post-cessation receipts as if the amount in question had been received on the date the trade ceased. This election must be made within 24 months of the end of the year of assessment or, in the case of a company, within 24 months of the end of the accounting period in which the amount is received (TCA 1997, s 95(3)). It appears that this election to bring forward Sch D Case IV assessment could be made for some post-cessation receipts and not for others. In considering whether to make the election for any receipts, the taxpayer should compare his taxable income and the tax rates applying respectively in the year of the cessation and in the year of the receipts. The election may only be made if the tax year (or accounting period) in which the sum is received begins no later than four years (reduced from 10 years for 2014 and subsequent years of assessment FA 2013, s 92 and Sch 1 Pt 2(a)) after the date of cessation.

In any case where a taxpayer makes this election under TCA 1997, s 95(3), the inspector of taxes is authorised to make any necessary additional assessment for the earlier year. If the taxpayer had previously claimed deductions under TCA 1997, s 91(4) for losses, capital allowances or expenses against previous assessments on post-cessation receipts (see **5.607**), he is not entitled to any further deduction from the new assessment.

5.606 Liabilities released after cessation

If before the cessation the person carrying on the trade or profession has incurred a liability for the purchase of goods for the business or for any expense which was deducted in computing the taxable profits for any period during which trading continued, then if after the cessation of the trade or profession that liability is released, the amount released is taxable as a post-cessation receipt under Sch D Case IV (TCA 1997, s 87(2)). This rule applies whether the earnings or conventional basis of accounting was used, but would clearly not be relevant if a pure cash basis involving the deduction only of expenses actually paid was employed up to the date of cessation (normally applicable now only in the case of barristers).

Example 5.606.1

Mr RS, a solicitor, ceased his profession on his retirement on 30 September 2015. He had made up his accounts on an acceptable conventional basis, excluding work-in-progress. His closing balance sheet at 30 September 2015 was:

	€	€
Capital account:		
Including 2015 profit less 2015 drawings		7,200
Represented by:		
Debtors for fees	6,000	
Office machinery	4,500	
		10,500
Creditors – expenses charged	1,800	
Office machinery	1,500	

	(3,300)
	7,200

After he had ceased to do any more professional work, Mr RS completed the winding up of his professional practice between 1 October 2015 and 30 June 2016. The following matters relevant to his taxation position took place in this period:

		€
(a)	fees of €3,900 furnished in October/November 2015 for work-in-progress before the cessation on 30/09/2015 – amounts received for the year to that date;	3,380
(b)	cash collected from former clients between October 2015 and June 2016 in respect of fees billed and included in trading receipts to 30/09/2015 (bad debts written off €480)	5,520
(c)	payment re collection of debtors 01/10/2015 – 30/04/2016 paid April 2016;	90
(d)	a creditor for office stationery accrued as trading expense in accounts to 30/09/2015 released Mr RS from his liability to pay an outstanding debt of €175.	

The Sch D Case IV assessment to be made on Mr RS is worked out as follows:

	€	€
Post-cessation receipts (TCA 1997, s 91):		
Fees billed Oct/Nov 2015 (to the extent actually paid)		3,380
Liability released after cessation (TCA 1997, s 87(2)):		
Stationer's bill		175
		3,555
Less:		
Expenses, etc deductible (see **5.607**):		
Debt collectors fees	90	
Debts for fees furnished in 2015 found to be Irrecoverable (€6,000 – €5,520)	480	
		570
Assessable under Sch D Case IV		2,985

Assuming none of the fees billed in Oct/Nov 2015 were received until after 31 December 2015, and that the stationer only released the liability of €175 in February 2016, the Sch D Case IV assessment is made on the sum of €2,985 for the tax year 2016, ie the year of the receipts, etc. Mr RS has the option of electing under TCA 1997, s 95(3) to have this assessment made on him instead for 2015, ie for the tax year in which his cessation occurred.

TCA 1997, s 87B (inserted by FA 2013, s 18 – see **12.318**) provides that where a debt incurred by an individual in respect of borrowings taken out to purchase or develop land held as trading stock of a trade of dealing in or developing land, is released the amount released is treated as a receipt of the trade arising in the year in which the release is effected. (For the date on which a release is treated as being effected see **12.318.**) Where the trade has been discontinued in a tax year before the release is effected the amount released is treated as a post-cessation receipt assessable under TCA 1997, s 91 (TCA 1997, s 87B(3)). The amount of the debt released will therefore be taxable under Sch D Case IV in the year the release is effected subject to the right of the individual to elect under TCA 1997, s 95(3), where the release is effected within four years of the discontinuance of the trade, to be taxed on the amount released in the year of cessation of the trade. TCA 1997, s 87B came into operation in respect of debts released on or after 13 February 2013.

5.607 Deductions from post-cessation receipts

TCA 1997, s 91(4) allows certain deductions to be made from the amount assessable under Sch D Case IV on post-cessation receipts or from any assessment in respect of a released liability. Deductions are available for:

(a) any unrelieved tax loss incurred in the trade or profession before the cessation which would have been available for carry forward for set off against future profits if the business had continued;
(b) any expense or debit which would have been eligible for deduction if the business had continued; and
(c) any capital allowances to which the taxpayer was entitled in respect of his trade or profession but for which relief had not been given to him either in taxing the profits of the trade or profession or in any other manner.

Example 5.607.1

Mr D P Undersea ceased to carry on his trade due to ill health on 31 December 2013. Based on Mr Undersea's Sch D Case I computations for his final period of account ended 31 December 2013, prepared on the normal earnings basis of accounting, Mr Undersea's 2013 income tax position was as follows:

	€
Sch D Case I: profits of trade	Nil
income from other sources	2,400
	2,400
Less:	
TCA 1997, s 381 claim for trading loss to 31/12/2013	
(part only)	2,400
Total income 2013	Nil

Mr Undersea dies on 15 February 2015. In the course of administering his estate, his executors find that certain old trading debts written off as bad in Mr Undersea's accounts for the year ended 31 December 2013 are in fact recoverable. Owing to his ill health, Mr Undersea had not taken sufficiently strong action to enforce their recovery. His executors take the necessary steps and recover a total of €4,750 of these debts between 1 April 2015 and 31 December 2015. This sum of €4,750 is a post-cessation receipt assessable under Sch D Case IV TCA 1997, s 91(5).

The Sch D Case IV assessable on the executors for the tax year 2015 will be made as follows:

	€	€
Post-cessation receipts (collected in 2015)		4,750
Less:		
Deductions under TCA 1997, s 91(4) assumed to be:		
Sch D Case I loss to 31/12/2013	3,100	
Less: part claimed in 2013	2,400	
	700	

Unused capital allowances 2013	1,200	
Sch D Case I losses		
c/f under TCA 1997, s 382	940	
Unused capital allowances 2012	1,640	
		4,480
Sch D Case IV assessment 2015		270

5.608 Receipts after change of ownership

TCA 1997, s 92 applies the post-cessation rules to any case where, as a result of a change in the persons engaged in carrying on a trade or profession, the business is treated for tax purposes as if it had been permanently discontinued and a new business set up and commenced (see **4.208**). In such a case, TCA 1997, s 92 applies TCA 1997, s 91 to charge tax under Sch D Case IV on the person treated as ceasing to carry on the trade or profession on any receipts attributable to that business that accrued before, but which were received by him after, the date of the change of ownership. In determining the extent to which the person treated as ceasing the business is taxable under Sch D Case IV, the other rules of TCA 1997, ss 91, 95 already discussed are applied. For example, if the person in question had any unused capital allowances or losses carried forward after the date of the change of ownership, he is entitled to apply TCA 1997, s 91(4) to deduct those items from his post-change of ownership receipts.

The arrangements between the parties concerned in the change of ownership of the trade or profession may be such that the persons carrying on the business after the change of ownership may be entitled to all trading receipts that accrued before, but which were not paid until after, the change. If the right to receive such sums is in fact transferred to the persons succeeding to the business, the person(s) who had previously carried it on are not to be taxable under these rules. Instead, any such sums received by the successors to the business are to be treated as their trading receipts to be brought into the Sch D Case I or II computation for the period of account in which they are received.

TCA 1997, s 92(3) provides one further rule that may apply for the benefit of the person succeeding to the business. If that person takes the assignment of debts which had previously been credited for tax purposes in the accounts of the person treated as ceasing the business, then if any of these debts turn out to be irrecoverable, the person succeeding to the business is entitled to deduct the resulting bad debts in his tax computation. This deduction is given to the successor in the period of account in which the debts are proved to be irrecoverable; however, the amount deductible must be reduced to the extent that any deduction for any of the debts in question had been given in any accounts of the previous proprietor before the change of ownership.

Example 5.608.1

Mr H Mountain sells his business to Mr L Valley on 30 September 2014 and assigns to him trade debts shown in his books of €6,750, but against which he had previously claimed a tax deduction for specific bad debt provisions of €1,140. After trading for 12 months and after making all reasonable efforts to collect these debts, €2,300 of the total of €6,750 turns out to be irrecoverable. Only €450 of the €2,300 had been included in the previous bad debts provision.

Mr Valley is entitled to the following deduction in calculating his taxable profits for the year ending 30 September 2015:

	€
Irrecoverable debts	2,300
Less:	
Amount previously allowed to Mr Mountain	450
Allowable deduction	1,850

5.7 Writers, Composers and Artists ('Artists Exemption')

5.701 Writers, composers and artists

TCA 1997, s 195 provides an exemption from income tax for income received from the production of certain original and creative works. The maximum amount of income which can be exempted is capped at €40,000 from 2011 to 2014 (inclusive) and at €50,000 for 2015 and subsequent years. The exemption will also be potentially subject to the restrictions applicable to high income individuals discussed at **3.111**. For tax years prior to 2015, the relief could only be claimed by a resident individual, or ordinarily resident domiciled individual, but only if he was not resident in any other country as well. For 2015 and subsequent years the relief can be claimed by an individual who is resident in one or more Member States of the EU or in an EEA state (ie EU Member States plus Iceland, Liechtenstein and Norway), or ordinarily resident and domiciled in such a state, provided the individual is not also resident outside the EU/EEA. The question as to whether an individual is resident in another jurisdiction can only be decided by reference to Irish law. However, the rules of TCA 1997, s 819 *et seq* are expressed as applying only for the purposes of determining whether an individual is resident *in the State*. There is accordingly a strong argument that in strictness the issue of overseas residence for TCA 1997, s 195 purposes should be resolved on the general principles noted at **1.503**. However in practice the Revenue take the view that the issue of whether or not an individual is resident in another state has to be decided by reference to the tax laws of that state. In applying this principle the Revenue will take account of any double tax treaty between the state in question and Ireland. If the individual is treated as a resident of Ireland for treaty purposes by reference to a 'tie breaker' article in the relevant treaty (see **14.105**), the Revenue will regard the individual as not being resident in the other state (*Tax Briefing* 56).

The individual need not be resident in the EU/EEA if he is ordinarily resident and domiciled in the EU/EEA and is not resident elsewhere. This provision has the effect that an individual who would otherwise be taxable (ie as an individual who is ordinarily resident but not resident in the State) by virtue of TCA 1997, s 821 (see **1.502**) may still be able to claim the benefit of TCA 1997, s 195.

The exemption is given for the profits from the publication, production or sale of an *original and creative* work (or works) falling under one of five categories, namely:

(a) a book or other writing;

(b) a play;

(c) a musical composition;

(d) a painting or other like picture; or

(e) a sculpture.

The exemption may, therefore, be claimed by a writer, a dramatist or playwright, a musical composer, a painter or a sculptor who produces an original or creative work. For any exemption to be granted, it is also necessary that the work is adjudged to have cultural or artistic merit.

In the case of *Gormley v EMI Records* [1998] ILRM 124, the court considered whether an item was 'original' in the context of a claim to copyright. Although this is not a case interpreting the taxes legislation it may be useful in the context of interpreting the word 'original' contained in TCA 1997, s 195.

The exemption, if granted, applies only to those profits which would otherwise fall to be taxed on the individual under Sch D Case II as the profits of his profession or vocation. It is only the profits from the writing, composition or execution of the work that are exempted. For example, an individual who derives profits both from the composition of music and also from performing it may be exempted from tax on the former, but remains taxable normally on any earnings he may derive as a performer. The Revenue Commissioners accept that mechanical royalties paid in respect of studio work involved in producing a piece of music may amount to 'composition' for these purposes (*Tax Briefing 42*). Royalties or similar income earned by an individual from the performance of his work *by other persons* are eligible for the exemption.

Two types of claim for exemption are distinguished – one which is made in respect of *a particular work* and the other which relates to the claimant's work generally. For the exemption to be granted for a particular work, it is essential that the Revenue Commissioners make a determination that the work in question has *cultural or artistic merit*. It is also necessary that the work is determined to be original and creative.

For the exemption to be given for an individual's *works generally*, the Commissioners must determine that the individual has already written, composed or executed an original and creative work (or works) generally recognised as having *cultural or artistic* merit. In either type of case, the Commissioners are – if they consider it necessary – empowered to consult with any person or body of persons who may be of assistance to them in reaching a proper conclusion (TCA 1997, s 195(2)(a)(ii)).

For any claim under TCA 1997, s 195 made to them for a determination under the section, the Revenue Commissioners must have regard to certain Guidelines to be drawn up by An Comhairle Ealaíon (the Arts Council) and the Minister for Arts, Culture and the Gaeltacht. This requirement is discussed in more detail under *Guidelines* below.

With effect from 2012, the Revenue Commissioners are statutorily entitled to publish the name of any individual who has been the subject of a determination including the title or category of the work of that individual (TCA 1997, s 195(16)).

Claim for particular work

A claim for exemption in respect of a particular work can only be made after the publication, production or sale, whichever is the case, of that work. If the work is a book, other writing, play or musical composition, the Revenue Commissioners may request to be furnished with three copies of it. If it is a painting, other picture or a sculpture, they may request the individual to provide, or to arrange for the provision of, such facilities as they consider necessary to make their determination as to whether the work has the necessary cultural or artistic merit. If the painting, picture or sculpture is owned or in the possession of another person, the individual may be requested to secure any necessary permissions or consents from that person (TCA 1997, s 195(4)(b)). In practice, a non-resident writer, etc who is proposing to move to Ireland can obtain a provisional ruling in advance from the Revenue Commissioners. This requires the individual to complete an official form and submit this with samples of his work and supporting evidence as appropriate. It appears that there is a lead time of up to six-months before a ruling will be given. Further details of the relevant procedures are described in *Haccius* [1996] ITR 263 and see also *Tax Briefing 42*.

Claims for works generally

An individual who has already written, composed or executed works generally recognised as having cultural or artistic merit, may claim exemption from the Revenue

Commissioners. In such a case, the Commissioners require to be satisfied that the existing work or works of the individual in question are in fact generally recognised as having the necessary qualities. Where this claim is made, the individual may be required to furnish to the Commissioners such information, books, documents or other evidence as may appear necessary to them (TCA 1997, s 195(4)(a)).

Effect of granting claim

When a claim for exemption in respect of a particular work has been made by an individual, and has been granted by the Revenue Commissioners, TCA 1997, s 195(3)(a) provides that the profits or gains arising to the individual from the publication, production or sale of that work are to be disregarded for all purposes of the Income Tax Acts, up to a maximum amount of €40,000 for 2011 to 2014 and €50,000 for 2015 and subsequent years. The exempt profits are excluded from the individual's income assessable under Sch D Case II and form no part of his total income subject to the restrictions applicable to high income individuals discussed at **3.111.** The income exempt is however liable to universal social charge (TCA 1997, s 531AM) and PRSI (Social Welfare Consolidation Act 2005, s 2(1)).

Further, any profits or gains from the publication, production or sale of any other work(s) of the individual that is in the same category as the work which the Commissioners have determined as having cultural or artistic merit are similarly exempted fully from income tax. However, for a work by the same individual in the same category as the work or works previously determined to have such merit, and which is first published, produced or sold after 2 May 1994, the exemption is only given if the work complies with the Guidelines mentioned below (TCA 1997, s 195(13)).

Similarly, where the Commissioners have made a determination that previous works of an individual are generally recognised as having cultural or artistic merit, any profits or gains from the publication, production or sale either of those existing works, or of any other work(s) of the individual in the same category as those works, are entirely exempted from income tax. The profits covered by this exemption include any current royalties or other income derived from previous works in the exempted category or categories.

In both types of case, no exemption from income tax may be granted under TCA 1997, s 195 which has effect for any tax year prior to that in which the individual concerned makes his claim for exemption (TCA 1997, s 195(3)(b)). In other words, the claim (if accepted) only exempts income arising in the tax year in which the claim is made and, if relevant, income arising in subsequent years. It is to be noted that the claim for the Revenue's determination must be made during the current tax year if the exemption is to be obtained for that year. It is too late to wait for the time the individual files his tax return for the year after the year end.

Where an individual receives advance royalties which are attributable to the subsequent publication of a book or other writing, a claim must be lodged with Revenue in the tax year in which the royalties are received if the royalties are to be exempt. Confirmation from the publisher that the book will be published must accompany the claim.

Where a claim is received in the tax year in which the advance is received, but where a determination has not been granted, any tax liability arising on the advance must be paid. If a determination is subsequently granted, the inspector of taxes will review the taxpayer's liability and make any appropriate refund if tax has been overpaid. Advance royalties paid before the year of claim will not be granted exemption (*Tax Briefing 42*).

An individual, who has income exempted under these rules, may also have other earnings from his profession as writer, dramatist, etc that are not of the same category as the exempted work(s), so that those other earnings are not exempted. For example, an individual carrying on a profession of musical composer and performer may have trading receipts and incur expenses in connection with both activities. In order to break down the total profits in any period of account or tax year between taxable and exempted income, the Revenue Commissioners (or the inspector) are authorised to make any necessary apportionments of receipts and expenses (TCA 1997, s 195(6)).

The Revenue Commissioners accept in principle that 'mechanical royalties', ie royalties paid in respect of the studio work leading to the final recording of a CD/tape can qualify for artists exemption as a musical composition, albeit – there might have to be apportionment of the recording royalty between the composition and recording elements in order to ensure that artists exemption was not granted in respect of any income derived from performance (see *Tax Briefing 42*).

Appeals

TCA 1997, s 195(6) provides for an appeals procedure which may be invoked if the Revenue Commissioners, within the period of six-months *commencing* with the date on which the individual's claim is first made (the 'relevant period'), fail to make a determination in relation to a claim made by an individual that a particular work of his or his works generally (whichever is the subject of the claim) has or have cultural or artistic merit. The Commissioners' failure to determine may be either failure to make any decision at all or a failure to decide in the claimant's favour.

TCA 1997, s 195(6) entitles the claimant to appeal to the Appeal Commissioners where the Commissioners fail to make their determination within the said six-months' period provided that, in addition to making his claim in the proper manner, the individual has given the Revenue Commissioners all the information, evidence, etc duly requested by them within TCA 1997, s 19(4), (5). Then, the individual may appeal to the Appeal Commissioners, on whichever of the following grounds, is applicable, that:

(a) the work or works is or are generally recognised as having cultural or artistic merit; *or*

(b) the particular work has cultural or artistic merit.

The appeal must be made by notice in writing sent to the Revenue Commissioners (not the Appeal Commissioners). The notice must be given to the Revenue Commissioners no later than 30 days after the end of the relevant period. However, F(TA)A 2015, s 35(7)(b) requires the taxpayer appeal to the Appeal Commissioners (not Revenue) within the abovementioned 30 days, however such change was subject to Ministerial Order (SI 110/2016 appointed 21 March 2016 as the day on which the Finance (Tax Appeals) Act 2015, came into operation).

In view of this time limit on the making of an appeal, it is important that any individual making a claim (or his tax adviser) should carefully note the date on which he submitted his claim and, it is suggested, enter the date six-months ahead by which he should expect to have the Revenue's decision on the matter. Then, if the individual has not had a determination of the claim (or an unfavourable decision has been given), he is ready to make the appeal in time.

On an appeal being duly made, the Appeal Commissioners are required to hear and determine the appeal as if it were an appeal against an income tax assessment. All the rules applicable to such an appeal (see **2.204**&&) are applicable, but with certain further points set out in TCA 1997, s 195(8). The rules relating to the rehearing on an appeal by the Circuit Court judge and those regarding the statement of a case for the opinion of the High Court on a point of law (see **2.205**) are also applicable (TCA 1997, s 195(7)).

On the hearing of the appeal, the Appeal Commissioners are required to hear any evidence on the matter submitted to them by or on behalf of the individual concerned and the Revenue Commissioners. They may consult with any person or body of persons whose views on the work or works they consider to be necessary. After such hearing, the Appeal Commissioners may, if they so conclude, make a determination that the claim for the exemption succeeds (they may of course determine that it does not) (TCA 1997, s 195(8)).

On a determination by the Appeal Commissioners that the claimant has written, composed or executed

(a) a work or works generally recognised as having cultural or artistic merit; or
(b) a particular work which has cultural or artistic merit;

whichever is the case, then the individual is given the appropriate exemption (see *Effect of granting exemption* above) (TCA 1997, s 195(8)(a)).

In making their determination, the Appeal Commissioners are required to have regard to the Guidelines mentioned immediately below.

It is important to note that F(TA)A 2015, s 35(7)(b) deletes TCA 1997, s 195(7), (8)(b) and (9) but such deletions were subject to Ministerial Order (SI 110/2016 appointed 21 March 2016 as the day on which the Finance (Tax Appeals) Act 2015, came into operation).

Guidelines

TCA 1997, s 195(12) requires An Comhairle Ealaíon and the Minister for Arts, Culture and the Gaeltacht to draw up guidelines for determining, for the purposes of TCA 1997, s 195, whether a work by a writer, playwright, composer, painter or sculptor is an original and creative work and whether it has, or is generally recognised as having, cultural or artistic merit.

The section authorises the guidelines to include:

(a) specific criteria by reference to which the questions (i) whether works are original and creative and (ii) whether they have, or are generally recognised as having, cultural or artistic merit, are to be determined; and
(b) specification of kinds of works that are not original and creative or that are not generally recognised as having cultural or artistic merit.

The Guidelines are to be mandatorily applied. TCA 1997, s 195(13)(a) provides that – in the case of any claim to the Revenue Commissioners made after 2 May 1994 for a determination under TCA 1997, s 195 – the Revenue Commissioners must not make a determination that any work is original and creative, or that it has or is generally recognised as having artistic or cultural merit, unless it complies with the Guidelines for the time being in force.

Similarly, TCA 1997, s 195(13)(b) requires the Appeal Commissioners and, on a rehearing, the Circuit Court judge, to apply the Guidelines in making their decision on an appeal against a determination of the Revenue Commissioners on either or both of these questions. It then goes on to make the same rule for the High Court should there be a case stated to the High Court for a decision on any point of law in relation to either question. The Circuit Court rehearing is to be removed by F(TA)A 2015, s 35(7)(b)(v) but such removal was subject to Ministerial Order (SI 110/2016 appointed 21 March 2016 as the day on which the Finance (Tax Appeals) Act 2015, came into operation).

Guidelines were first issued in 1995 and revised in 2013. The revised Guidelines are mainly intended to remove some restrictions on the conditions to be satisfied in order for non-fiction works (in particular autobiographies, biographies and works relating to archives) to qualify as 'original and creative'. (For a useful commentary on anomalies in the original Guidelines see Kennedy 'Interpretation of the Artists' Exemption Guidelines' (2011) Irish Tax Review. In addition the revised Guidelines broaden the definition of the type of sculpture which may qualify (see below). For commentary on the position before the issue of the revised Guidelines see previous editions of this book.

The revised Guidelines (hereinafter referred to as the 'Guidelines') provide definitions of the terms 'original and creative', 'cultural merit' and 'artistic merit'.

A work is considered under the Guidelines as having 'cultural merit':

> if by reason of its quality of form and/or content it enhances to a significant degree one or more aspects of national or international culture.

A work is considered to have 'artistic merit':

> only if its quality of form and/or content enhances to a significant degree the canon of work in the relevant category.

In the Guidelines a work is regarded as 'original and creative' 'only if it is a unique work of creative quality brought into existence by the exercise of its creator's imagination'.

However, a book or other writing which is non-fiction will only qualify as 'original and creative' and having 'cultural' or 'artistic' merit if it comes within one of (a) to (d) below:

(a) In the opinion of the Revenue Commissioners, having consulted with the Arts Council, the work falls within one of the following categories:
  - (i) arts criticism;
  - (ii) arts history;
  - (iii) arts subject work, being a work the subject matter of which is, or is a combination or, visual arts, theatre, literature, music, dance, opera, film, circus or architecture;
  - (iv) artists' diaries;
  - (v) belles-lettres essays;
  - (vi) literary translation;
  - (vii) literary criticism;
  - (viii) literary history;
  - (ix) literary diaries.

(b) In the opinion of the Revenue Commissioners the work is:
  - (i) a biography; or
  - (ii) an autobiography.

(c) In the opinion of the Revenue Commissioners, following consultation with the Heritage Council, the work is related to a function or functions of the Heritage Council as described in the Heritage Act 1995.

(d) In the opinion of the Revenue Commissioners the work relates to archives which are more than 30 years old relating to Ireland or Irish people and is based on research from such archives.

In addition in order for a non-fiction work to qualify the work should:

(a) incorporate the author's unique insight into the subject matter,
(b) be regarded as a pioneering work and
(c) make a significant contribution to the subject matter by casting a new light on it or by changing the generally accepted understanding of it.

The Guidelines also provide that the following types of work falling within the categories laid down by TCA 1997, s 195 will not be regarded as 'original and creative' and as not having 'cultural' or 'artistic' merit:

(a) *book or other writing* –
    (i) published primarily for, or which is or will be used primarily by, students pursuing a course of study, or
    (ii) published primarily for, or which is or will be used primarily by persons engaged in any trade, business, profession, vocation or branch of learning as an aid therein (overriding the decision in *Revenue Commissioners v O'Loinsigh* [1994] ITR 199),
(b) *work of journalism* – any work of journalism published in a newspaper, journal, magazine or similar medium or published on the internet or on any other similar medium (confirming the decision in *Healy v Breathnach* III ITR 496). The original Guidelines specifically provided that a book consisting of a series of articles by the same author connected to a common theme and therefore capable of existing independently in its own right was not excluded. The fact that such works are no longer specifically mentioned as not excluded should not mean that they cannot qualify for the exemption. Provided such works can be regarded as 'original and creative' and having 'cultural' or 'artistic' merit they can qualify in the same manner as other works;
(c) *advertising* – any writing, visual or musical work, or other like work, created for advertising or publicity purposes;
(d) *musical composition* – arrangements, adaptations and versions of musical compositions or other like work which is not of such musical significance as to amount to an original composition. In the original Guidelines only compositions by a *bona fide* composer who was also actively engaged in musical composition would be considered;
(e) *drawings/paintings* – types or kinds of photographs, drawings or paintings which are mainly of record, or which primarily serve a utilitarian function, or which are created primarily for advertising, publicity, information, decorative or similar purposes. The original Guidelines excepted from this exclusion a set or sets of photographs or drawings that are collectively created for an artistic purpose. Again the fact that such works are no longer specifically mentioned as not being excluded from this category should not mean that they cannot qualify for the exemption. Provided such works can be regarded as 'original and creative' and having 'cultural' or 'artistic' merit they should be able to qualify in the same manner as other works;
(f) *a sculpture* – types or kinds of works of sculpture which primarily serve a utilitarian function. In the original Guidelines objects produced by processes other than by hand and objects produced by hand by persons other than those actively engaged as bona fide artists in the field of the visual arts were also specifically a type of sculpture which could not be regarded as being 'original

and creative'. Thus the type of sculpture and the persons creating such sculptures has been broadened considerably under the revised Guidelines.

Division 6 Capital Allowances

6.1 Principles and Definitions

6.101 Introduction

A person may incur capital expenditure on acquiring capital assets or in providing other enduring benefits of a capital nature to be used in the course of a trade, profession, office, employment or other income generating activity. In general, no deduction for the capital expenditure is given in arriving at the taxable income from the activity in question, but the Income Tax Acts provide relief for certain types of capital expenditure by way of a scheme of capital allowances.

In broad terms, capital allowances are given as a deduction against income from the relevant activity, writing off the taxpayer's capital expenditure on assets qualifying for the allowances over the period of their use in the income earning activity. In some cases, if the allowances exceed the relevant income, the excess may be offset against other income of the taxpayer, or may enhance or create losses which can be offset in this manner. When an asset on which capital allowances have been given is sold or otherwise ceases to be used for the purposes of the relevant activity, a balancing allowance or balancing charge is normally made to ensure that the total capital allowances given over the period of use for the activity do not exceed or fall short of the taxpayer's net capital outlay (after taking into account any sale proceeds or other residual value) on the asset concerned. A balancing charge is, in effect, a negative allowance.

This chapter outlines the types of capital expenditure qualifying for capital allowances and the circumstances in which the allowances are given and how they are calculated. A number of principles and definitions common to the calculation of capital allowances for most, if not all, types of qualifying expenditure are first discussed here in **6.1**. Capital allowances on plant and machinery are covered as regards their general application in **6.2**, while the additional rules as to the granting of capital allowances on leased plant and machinery are dealt with in **6.3**. The capital allowances allowable for industrial buildings and structures are discussed generally in **6.4** and in the context of taxing rental income under Sch D Case V in **6.5**.

Capital allowances for capital expenditure on scientific research, dredging expenditure and certain other miscellaneous items are discussed in **6.6**. The capital allowances available on expenditure incurred on the purchase of patent rights are dealt with in **6.7**. Other types of capital allowances are covered in the context of other topics, as follows:

(a) Farm buildings and certain other farm works (see **7.202**);
(b) Mining exploration and development (see **12.4**); and

(c) Buildings and structures in various tax incentive areas (see **Division 19** in the 2009 edition of this book).

6.102 Fundamentals

The legislation dealing with capital allowances is framed so as to apply to both income tax and corporation tax. For income tax purposes, capital allowances are given and balancing charges made for years of assessment; there are also rules for allocating allowances and charges to years of assessment by reference to expenditure incurred or events taking place in or at the end of the relevant basis periods.

TCA 1997, s 321(2) defines certain phrases used in the legislation which have dual meanings to be applied respectively for income tax and corporation tax applications. These phrases and their meanings for income tax purposes are:

(a) 'chargeable period' means a year of assessment;

(b) 'chargeable period or its basis period' means the basis period for a year of assessment;

(c) 'chargeable period related to expenditure' means the year of assessment in the basis period for which, the expenditure is incurred; and

(d) 'chargeable period related to a sale (or other event)' means the year of assessment in the basis period for which, the sale or other event takes place.

Example 6.102.1

Mr JR Haggle has carried on a trade for several years. He makes up accounts annually to 30 April. On 19 September 2015 (in his accounts year ending 30 April 2016), he incurs capital expenditure of €8,000 on the purchase of a personal computer and software for use in his trade.

The 12 months ending 30 April 2016 is the basis period for Mr Haggle's trade for the year of assessment 2015, the capital expenditure of €8,000 is incurred in this basis period. The tax year 2016 is, therefore, the chargeable period related to the expenditure of €8,000.

Writing down allowance

Certain capital allowances (eg those in respect of the purchase of patent rights) are expressed as being made to write down certain capital expenditure during a writing-down period of a specified length, usually of a certain number of years. Such a writing down allowance is given at a flat rate so as to write-off the expenditure evenly over the specified writing down period (unless any initial or other accelerated allowances are also involved) (TCA 1997, s 321(5)). Normally, this gives annual allowances of equal amounts until the expenditure is completely written off, but if any writing down allowance applies for a chargeable period of less than one year, the allowance for that period is proportionally reduced (this position is not usually relevant for income tax purposes since the chargeable period is the year of assessment). Similarly, if part of a chargeable period for which the writing down allowance is claimed falls outside the writing down period, a proportionate reduction is also made.

An allowance on account of wear and tear of machinery or plant, or a writing down allowance on other expenditure, may be expressed as a fraction or as a percentage of the expenditure or of some other sum. In such a case, if the relevant allowance is being claimed for a chargeable period of less than one year, then the rate of the allowance, ie the fraction or the percentage, is proportionately reduced (TCA 1997, s 321(7)). This provision is again not normally relevant for income tax purposes as the chargeable period is the year of assessment. By virtue of TCA 1997, s 284(2)(b), the wear and tear allowance in respect of plant and machinery is reduced proportionately where the basis period for income tax purposes is less than a year.

Basis periods

Capital allowances and balancing charges are given to or made on individuals and other persons chargeable to income tax for years of assessment, but by reference to the basis periods for those years of assessment. In general, the basis period for capital allowance purposes for a particular year of assessment is the same period as that used under the relevant schedule or case in arriving at the taxable income for the year of assessment, but there are certain rules for dealing with overlapping income tax basis periods and with cases where events related to capital allowances occur in a period not falling in any income tax basis period. These rules are dealt with in detail at **4.3**.

6.103 Capital expenditure

All capital allowances are, in principle, based on the capital expenditure incurred by the taxpayer concerned on the qualifying assets, etc. The term 'capital expenditure' would naturally exclude any expenditure that is deductible in computing the taxable income of any trade, profession, office or employment carried on by the person incurring the expenditure (this is made explicit by TCA 1997, s 316(1)(a)). Similarly, any expenses deductible in computing rental income taxable under Sch D Case V do not rank as capital expenditure. The nature of the capital expenditure qualifying for capital allowances is considered separately in dealing with the different types of qualifying assets, but there are certain general rules which may conveniently be discussed briefly here.

Multiple purchases

Where two or more assets are purchased in the one transaction, whether on the purchase of a business or otherwise, there must be a just apportionment of the total consideration to arrive at the acquisition cost of each asset on which capital allowances may be claimed. For this purpose, all the assets or other property that are acquired in one bargain are deemed to have been purchased together so that the total price paid must be apportioned in a just manner, even if the parties have allocated separate prices to the different items (TCA 1997, s 311(1)). This rule is designed to override the principle that a *bona fide* allocation of consideration cannot normally be overridden by the tax authorities, unless it is unsustainable as a matter of law. In practice, if the parties to the transaction agree separate prices for different assets, the inspector of taxes may accept this allocation if he considers it reasonable, but this rule entitles him to reject the parties' allocation of the total consideration if he does not consider it just and proper.

By virtue of TCA 1997, s 314(1) there is a right of appeal against an apportionment made by an inspector under TCA 1997, s 311(1) in the same manner as if it were an assessment; this right of appeal exists only where the liability of two or more persons will be affected by the apportionment; all such persons are entitled to appeal and to be heard by the Appeal Commissioners. In *Fitton v Gilders and Heaton* 36 TC 233, the taxpayer amended a draft agreement to sell the assets of his trade. The court held that the Appeal Commissioners were not entitled to rely on the draft agreement as evidence of the true intentions of the parties; however they were entitled under the equivalent of TCA 1997, s 311(1) to override the allocation of consideration in the final agreement.

Exchange of assets

Where any asset is acquired not for cash, but in consideration for the exchange of any other property, then the capital expenditure incurred on its acquisition is deemed for capital allowance purposes to be an amount equal to the value of the property given in exchange for the asset, with any necessary apportionment between different assets if the exchange involves more than one asset (TCA 1997, s 311(3)). However, the transfer of an industrial building to a person in trust on behalf of creditors under a Debt Settlement Arrangement or the Personal Insolvency Act is not treated as an exchange of property (TCA 1997, s 311(3A)).

TCA 1997, s 314(1) grants a right of appeal against a determination of market value by the inspector as if it were an assessment; the right of appeal exists only where the liability of two or more persons will be affected by the apportionment; all such persons are entitled to appeal and to be heard by the Appeal Commissioners or to make written representations to them.

Grants

TCA 1997, s 317(2) provides that capital allowances are to be calculated on a net of grant basis where the expenditure on the asset was met directly or indirectly by the State or by *any* other person except the person incurring the expenditure. The treatment of capital grants in relation to machinery and plant is dealt with more fully in **6.208**.

Effect of VAT

A person incurring capital expenditure on a qualifying asset is normally invoiced not only with the actual cost of purchase, but also with VAT charged on the price in the transaction. Alternatively, he may have to pay VAT at the point of importation of any machinery or plant, etc acquired from a non EU supplier. Normally a person carrying on a trade or a profession is himself a taxable person for VAT and is entitled to a credit for any VAT invoiced which may be offset against VAT due on his business supplies or fully or partly repaid, as appropriate. However, a person carrying on a trade or profession the sales from which are exempt from VAT is not entitled to any such credit for the VAT on his business inputs; correspondingly, a trader who is partially exempt may only be entitled to credit for a proportion of his input VAT. Further, the VAT paid on the purchase of private motor cars is not, in most cases, eligible for credit.

TCA 1997, s 319(1) provides that any VAT for which the person incurring capital expenditure is entitled to credit must be excluded from the cost of acquiring any machinery or plant or from any other expenditure eligible for capital allowances. On the other hand, if no credit or refund in respect of the VAT payable on the purchase is available, then the capital expenditure on which the capital allowances are based is taken as inclusive of the VAT borne. For example, the VAT payable by a manufacturer of carpets on the purchase of private motor cars for his salesmen is included in the cost of the cars for capital allowance purposes, but a company purchasing cars for hiring to the public in its car hire business must exclude the VAT payable as it is entitled to a credit for the VAT. In cases where TCA 1997, s 319(1) does not apply, it is arguable that the amount of expenditure incurred includes recoverable VAT. The argument is that it is the very fact of incurring the expenditure which generates a right of recovery. Furthermore, it might be said that if this were not the case, TCA 1997, s 319(1) would be superfluous.

Acquisitions at market value

There are various rules that, in particular circumstances, deem the capital expenditure on which the capital allowances are based to be the market value of the asset concerned at the date it is acquired for use in the trade, profession, etc. In some of these cases, there may be an option to use instead of the market value the tax written down value of the asset that has been acquired from another person who was previously entitled to the capital allowances on that asset. The main rules to be considered under this heading, with appropriate cross references to where they are dealt with, are as follows:

(a) non-arm's length transactions (all assets) – **6.105**;

(b) transfers on certain successions to trade (all assets) – **6.106**; and

(c) assets acquired by way of gift or at less than market price from a donor or vendor who was himself subject to a balancing allowance or balancing charge on his disposal (machinery or plant) – **6.206**.

Financing arrangements

The fact that an asset is financed by a non-recourse loan (ie a loan where the lender has no recourse against the property of the borrower, other than the asset itself and any income generated therefrom) does not mean that the relevant expenditure has not been incurred on the asset. In *Ensign Tankers (Leasing) Ltd v Stokes* [1989] STC 705, the taxpayers financed 75 per cent of the cost of investing in an item of plant by means of an (effectively) interest-free, non-recourse loan. The obligation to repay the loan ranked equally with the taxpayers' right to recover their 25 per cent balance of the investment (which was funded out of their own resources). The House of Lords held that the 75 per cent element of the expenditure had not been 'incurred' and thus could not attract capital allowances.

Although Lord Templeman used language in his judgment which suggests that no borrowing (and thus no corresponding expenditure) had taken place as a matter of general law, it seems clear that the decision in the *Ensign* case depends for its justification on the doctrine of 'fiscal nullity' first established in *Ramsay v IRC*. As discussed at **17.302**, this doctrine was historically rejected in Ireland but TCA 1997, s 811 (since replaced by TCA 1997, s 811C for transactions entered into on or after 24 October 2014) and the Supreme Court decision in *Revenue Commissioners v O'Flynn Construction Ltd* [2011] IESC 47 has significantly changed this approach. In an earlier High Court case in 1994 *Airspace Investments Ltd v Moore* V ITR 3, an interest free, non-recourse loan (with repayment only being due when profits generated by the asset in question exceeded a prescribed limit) was upheld as valid in law. Accordingly, the corresponding expenditure on plant qualified for capital allowances. The *O'Flynn* decision and the provisions of TCA 1997, s 811C must be borne in mind where there is a tax avoidance element of any arrangements undertaken (see **Division 17.3**).

In *Stokes v Costain* [1984] STC 204, it was held that land development expenditure financed by a loan which was discharged on the satisfactory completion of the development agreement had been 'incurred' by the developer; further it could not be said to have been met directly or indirectly by a third party.

In *Van Arkadie v Sterling Coated Metals* [1983] STC 95, the taxpayer was obliged to pay for an item of plant by instalments denominated in a foreign currency. The relevant capital allowances were granted by reference to the date on which expenditure became payable. It was held that the additional sterling cost of paying the instalments (caused by subsequent depreciation in the value of sterling) was allowable. In effect, the case decided that the sterling value of the instalments at the time when they fell due for payment was the correct measure of expenditure. The position would have been different if the taxpayer had borrowed foreign currency in order to purchase the asset outright and had then incurred an additional sterling cost in repaying those borrowings. In this case, the principle in *Ben-Odeco* would have denied a claim for capital allowances in relation to that cost. In the *Van Arkadie* case, the taxpayer had entered into a tripartite arrangement with the vendor of the plant and a bank, under which it was obliged to pay the same instalments originally due to the vendor to the bank under the terms of a 'credit contract'. It was held that the relevant expenditure on plant was incurred when the instalments fell due in accordance with the original contract, even though the relationship between the taxpayer and the bank was possibly one of borrower and lender.

In *Barclays Mercantile Business Finance Ltd v Mawson* [2004] UKHL 51, the House of Lords upheld the decision of the Court of Appeal that Barclays Mercantile Business Finance was entitled to writing down allowances for capital expenditure incurred on plant purchased under a sale and lease back arrangement which was entered into wholly and exclusively for the purposes of its trade of finance leasing. In the Court of Appeal Park J said that the right to the writing down allowance is based on the purpose of the lessor's expenditure not the benefit of the finance to the lessee.

6.104 Sale, insurance, salvage or compensation

An important feature of the scheme of capital allowances is the requirement to calculate a balancing allowance or a balancing charge when an asset on which capital allowances have been granted is sold or ceases in certain other circumstances to be used in the trade, profession, etc. In the case of either machinery or plant or industrial buildings, the calculation of the balancing allowance or charge is made by comparing the 'sale, insurance or compensation monies' with the tax written down value of the asset concerned. The manner of arriving at the tax written down value is dealt with separately for machinery or plant (see **6.203**) and for industrial buildings (see **6.409**).

The phrase 'sale, insurance or compensation monies' is defined by TCA 1997, s 318 as follows:

(a) if the event is the sale of any property, the phrase refers to the net proceeds of the sale;

(b) if the event is the grant of a right to use or otherwise deal with computer software (that software being plant or machinery for the purposes of TCA 1997, s 291), the consideration received in money or money's worth for the grant of that right;

(c) if the event is the demolition or destruction of any property, it refers to:

  (i) the net amount received for any residual value of the property, plus

  (ii) any insurance monies received in respect of the demolition or destruction, plus

  (iii) any other capital sums received as compensation;

(d) if the event is the permanent loss of any machinery or plant (other than due to its demolition or destruction), it refers to:

  (i) any insurance monies received in respect of the loss, plus

  (ii) any other capital sums received in compensation;

(e) if the event is that of an industrial building or structure ceasing altogether to be used, it refers to any capital sums received as compensation of any description in respect of that event, and

(f) if the event is a building ceasing to be a relevant facility, it refers to the residue of the expenditure immediately before that event and the allowances made in respect of the capital expenditure incurred on the building. Relevant facility includes certain health care facilities and childcare facilities first used or first used after refurbishment on or after 1 January 2006.

The references to the '*net* sales proceeds' and the '*net* amount received' indicate that any expenses directly incurred in the disposal of the asset concerned may be deducted in arriving at the sale, insurance, salvage or compensation monies. Examples of such deductible expenses are the expenses of advertising the sale, commissions paid to auctioneers, etc, salvage payments or other realisation expenses to the extent borne by the vendor.

In applying these rules, any sum or amount received which is treated as a receipt in computing the taxable income of any trade, profession, office or employment carried on or held by the person receiving the payment is not a capital sum and must, therefore, be excluded from the sale, etc monies (TCA 1997, s 316(1)(b)). The same applies to any sum or amount which would be treated as a trading receipt or otherwise in computing taxable income, but which may not in fact be brought into account due to there being a loss. It may also be noted that sale, insurance, salvage or compensation monies may also arise due to the sale of part of an asset or due to the demolition of any such part, eg where part only of an industrial building is destroyed by a fire or an explosion.

TCA 1997, s 320(4) defines the time of a 'sale' for virtually all capital allowance purposes as the time of completion or the time when possession is given, if earlier.

Multiple sales

See the discussion of *Multiple purchases* in **6.103**.

Exchange of assets

See the discussion of *Exchange of assets* in **6.103**.

Effect of VAT

TCA 1997, s 319(2) provides that the amount of the VAT chargeable on the sale must be excluded completely from the sale monies brought into the computation of any balancing allowance or charge. Similarly, should there be any VAT chargeable in respect of any other insurance, salvage or compensation monies that VAT must also be excluded, (see also the discussion at **6.103**: *Effect of VAT*).

Sales at market value

There are various rules which, in particular circumstances, require the market value of the asset to be brought into the computation of the balancing allowance or charge instead of any actual sale, etc monies that may be received. In some of these cases, there may be an option to use instead of the market value the tax written down value of the asset to the seller immediately before the sale. The main rules to be considered under this heading, with appropriate cross references, are as follows:

(a) non-arm's length transactions (all assets) – **6.105**;

(b) transfers of assets on certain successions to trade (all assets) – **6.106**;

(c) machinery or plant disposed of by gift or by a sale at less than market value – **6.206**; and

(d) machinery or plant ceasing to be used for trade, but continuing to belong to trader, and/or machinery or plant remaining unsold on cessation of trade – **6.206**.

6.105 Non-arm's length transactions

TCA 1997, s 312 contains certain special rules, referred to herein as the 'non-arm's length transactions rules', which must be considered in either of two sets of circumstances. The rules, where they apply, normally require the relevant capital allowances or balancing charges to be based on the open market value of the asset at the time of the sale (and purchase), but there may be an option to use the tax written down value instead.

The two sets of circumstances and the rules applicable in each are now discussed under separate headings referred to respectively as 'transactions in common control cases' and 'transactions to obtain capital allowances'.

Transactions in common control cases

TCA 1997, s 312(2) applies the non-arm's length transactions rules to be used, to the extent relevant, in relation to the sale of any asset subject to capital allowances in any of the following cases:

(a) where the buyer is a body of persons over whom the seller has control; or

(b) where the seller is a body of persons over whom the buyer has control; or

(c) where both the buyer and seller are bodies of persons and some other person has control over both of them.

For the rules to apply in these common control cases, one or both of the parties to the transaction must be a body of persons. A 'body of persons' is defined by TCA 1997, s 2(1), as including a company or any other body corporate, while TCA 1997, s 312(2)(b) extends the definition to cover a partnership (which would normally not otherwise be within the definition – see **1.302**). The term does not include trustees, who, in any event, would not be under the control of a third party by virtue of their fiduciary role. The rules also apply where the seller in case (a), the buyer in case (b) or the person controlling both the buyer and seller in case (c) is an individual or any other person who is not a body of persons (eg a trustee of a settlement).

TCA 1997, s 312(1) prescribes the circumstances in which, for the purpose of the other rules of the section, a person is to be regarded as controlling a partnership or a company or other body corporate. Any person, whether an individual or a company, is regarded as having control over a partnership if he has the right to a share of more than 50 per cent of the partnership assets or of more than 50 per cent of its income. In the case of a company (or other body corporate) any person is regarded as having control over it if he has the power to secure that the affairs of the company be conducted in accordance with his wishes; this power may be exercisable by means of the holding of a sufficient number of shares or holding sufficient voting power in the company, or by virtue of any powers conferred by the articles of association or other document regulating its affairs; (see the discussion at **12.304**).

Examples of transactions between a buyer and a seller in common control cases are:

(a) sale of office equipment by a sole trader to a company incorporated to take over his business and in which he has a controlling shareholding;

(b) sale of motor cars by a sole trader to a partnership in which he is entitled to 60 per cent of the profits;
(c) sale of patent rights by a partnership to a retiring partner entitled to 51 per cent of the firm's assets who leaves the partnership to commence his own sole trade; and
(d) sale of a commercial building in the Dublin Custom House Docks Area by a company (A Ltd) to another company (B Ltd) where Mr X and Mr Y between them hold more than 50 per cent of the voting share capital in both companies.

In any case where there is a common control relationship between the buyer and the seller, TCA 1997, s 312(3) provides that the open market price (and not the actual price if different) should be used for all purposes of capital allowances and balancing charges relevant to both buyer and seller. Subject to possible variation under the rules of TCA 1997, s 312(4)–(5) (see below), this means that the consequences are as follows:

(a) the open market price is deemed to be the buyer's acquisition cost on which any subsequent capital allowances to which he may be entitled are based; and
(b) the open market price is deemed to be the seller's sale price by reference to which any balancing allowance or balancing charge is computed in respect of the sale.

Example 6.105.1

Mr BB is in partnership with Mr CC as B and C & Co, under a partnership agreement which entitles Mr BB to a 51 per cent share in the profits and losses of the firm. Mr BB is therefore regarded as having control of the partnership for the purposes of TCA 1997, s 312.

Mr BB also holds 51 per cent of the 1,000 voting shares in a company, G Ltd, but holds none of the other issued share capital in that company (10,000 non-voting shares). Although these non-voting shares rank *pari passu* in all other respects with the voting shares so that BB's entitlement to share in dividends, assets on winding up, etc in G Ltd is relatively small, he is regarded as having control of G Ltd as he can use his voting share majority to secure that the affairs of the company are conducted in accordance with his wishes.

G Ltd acquired certain items of machinery several years ago at a cost of €21,000. On 12 June 2016, it sells these machines to the firm of B and C & Co, for €3,400 and €1,900 respectively. The tax written down values and the open market prices to that date are as follows:

	Machines	
	No 1	*No 2*
	€	€
Tax WDV	4,000	Nil
Open market prices	7,000	2,800

Since both G Ltd and B and C & Co are regarded as bodies of persons, and as each is under the control of the same person, ie Mr BB, G Ltd's balancing charges on the sales must be computed as follows:

	Machines	
	No 1	*No 2*
	€	€
Open market prices	7,000	2,800
Less:		
Tax WDV	4,000	Nil
Balancing charges	3,000	2,800

Assuming B and C & Co use the machines for the purposes of the firm's trade, the firm's capital allowances are based on the open market price of €7,000 and €2,800 respectively (and not on the actual prices of €3,400 and €1,900).

TCA 1997, s 312(4) provides one exception to the requirement to use the open market value in a transaction between two persons in a common control relationship. It applies in any such transaction where, on the sale of machinery or plant (but not other assets), the open market price at the time of the sale is greater than the amount which would be taken – for the purpose of calculating a balancing charge on the seller – as the seller's original capital expenditure in providing the plant for the trade, profession, etc. In any such case, the rule of TCA 1997, s 312(3) is applied on the assumption that the plant had been sold by the seller for an amount equal to the capital expenditure incurred by the vendor in providing the plant.

In the normal case where this rule applies, it deems the seller to have sold the plant (and the buyer to have bought) the plant for a consideration equal to the actual capital expenditure incurred earlier by the seller at the time of his original acquisition of the plant. However, the rather involved wording used in TCA 1997, s 312(4)(a)(ii) to describe the amount to be substituted for the open market price (where it is less than the open market price) is necessary because, in certain circumstances, the seller's capital allowances during his period of ownership of the machinery or plant may have been based on a starting amount other than his actual capital expenditure incurred in acquiring the machinery or plant. For example, the seller may have acquired the plant in an earlier transaction itself within TCA 1997, s 312, so that his deemed acquisition cost for capital allowances may have been the open market value at the date of that earlier acquisition.

The rule of TCA 1997, s 312(4)(a) does not apply in the case of new machinery or plant sold in the ordinary course of the business of the seller where that business consists in whole or in part of the manufacture or supply of machinery or plant of the type in question (TCA 1997, s 312(4)(b)). In such a case, assuming the seller and purchaser are under common control within the section, the sale is deemed by TCA 1997, s 312(3) to take place at the open market price whether or not that price exceeds the cost to the seller.

TCA 1997, s 312(5) allows the buyer and the seller in a common control case to make a joint election to substitute the seller's tax written down value of the asset sold for the open market price otherwise required by TCA 1997, s 312(3) provided that:

(a) the tax written down value is lower than the open market price; and

(b) the transaction is not one to which TCA 1997, s 312(2)(a)(ii) applies (ie it is not a transaction the sole or main benefit of which is to obtain a capital allowance – see below).

The right to elect under TCA 1997, s 312(5) to substitute a lower tax written down value does not apply, however, if one (or both) of the parties to the sale is (or are) not resident in the State at the time of the sale, unless at that time the non-resident party (or both non-resident parties) is (or are) entitled to or subject to any capital allowances or any balancing charges in consequence of the sale (TCA 1997, s 312(6)). For example, if a resident company sells used machinery on which it has obtained capital allowances to its non-resident parent company, no election may be made under TCA 1997, s 312(5) to substitute a lower tax written down value, unless the non-resident parent is entitled to capital allowances on the machinery acquired. The parent company is only likely to have a claim for capital allowances if it uses the machinery for the purposes of a trade it carries on itself in the State.

For the purposes of the rule permitting an election under TCA 1997, s 312(5), the meaning of the 'tax written down value' varies depending on the nature of the assets involved, as follows:

(a) for industrial buildings, the residue of the capital expenditure on their construction as it stands immediately before the sale (see **6.409**); and

(b) for machinery or plant, the amount of the expenditure on its provision still unallowed immediately before the sale (see **6.205**) (TCA 1997, s 312(5)(b)).

Any election under TCA 1997, s 312(5) to substitute a lower tax written down value must be made in writing to the inspector by both the buyer and the seller. Neither the buyer nor the seller can make the election on his own. The section does not prescribe any time limit within which the notice must be given, but in practice under the self-assessment system of income tax or corporation tax, it is recommended that the notice should be given at the time the parties submit their income tax or corporation tax returns.

Example 6.105.2

Ms HRR has traded on her own account for several years as a ladies costumier. On 1 October 2016 she sells her business and all its assets to a company, RR & SS Limited, incorporated on 21 August 2016, in which she has taken a 95 per cent shareholding and in which a Mr TT holds the remaining five per cent.

The assets sold to the company with market values and tax written down values at 1 October 2016 are as follows:

	Market values	*Tax written down values*
	€	€
Machinery and plant (sold to company for €4,500)	6,000	2,000
Motor vehicle (sold to company for €5,000)	5,500	4,800

Since the seller (Ms HRR) controls the buyer (RR & SS Limited), TCA 1997, s 312(3) requires Ms HRR's closing capital allowances computations and the company's opening capital allowances computations to be made by reference to the above market value figures, thus imposing balancing charges on Ms HRR on the respective excesses of market values over tax written down values (€4,000 and €700). Ms HRR had previously acquired the plant for €15,000 and the vehicle for €7,000 so that the rule in TCA 1997, s 312(4)(a) is not relevant.

However, Ms HRR and the company elect under the rule in TCA 1997, s 312(5) to substitute tax written down values for the market values so that the company's opening capital allowances are based on deemed purchase price of €2,000 for the machinery and plant and €4,800 for the motor vehicle. Ms HRR's closing computations for her sole trade are as follows:

	Motor vehicles	*Machinery and plant*
	€	€
Deemed sales prices (= tax WDVs)	2,000	4,800
Less:		
Tax written down values	2,000	4,800
Balancing allowance/charge	Nil	Nil

Transactions to obtain capital allowances

TCA 1997, s 312(2)(a)(ii) applies the non-arm's length transactions rules to the sale of any asset subject to capital allowances where it appears with respect to the sale, or with respect to transactions of which that sale is one, that the sole or main benefit which might otherwise have been expected to accrue to the parties, or to one of them, was the obtaining of capital allowances. In *Barclays Mercantile Industrial v Melluish* [1990] STC 314, it was held that this is intended as an anti-avoidance provision aimed at artificial transactions designed wholly or mainly to create tax allowances (see the discussion at **18.111**).

The application of this rule of TCA 1997, s 312(2)(a)(ii) is not limited to cases where there is a common control connection between the buyer and the seller, nor is it a condition for its application that one of the parties must be a body of persons. One or both of the persons involved may be an individual, partnership, body corporate or unincorporated body of persons, personal representatives of a deceased person, trustees of settlement, etc.

In any case to which the rule is relevant, the rules of sub-ss (2) and (3) apply in exactly the same way as for a transaction in a common control case (see above). In other words, where the actual price for the sale of the asset is greater or lower than the open market price, the open market price must be substituted for the actual price in computing the seller's balancing allowance or balancing charge and as the basis for the subsequent capital allowances of the buyer.

However, in any case brought within the section by TCA 1997, s 312(2)(a)(ii), the buyer and the seller do not have any option to elect to substitute a lower tax written down value as the price for capital allowances. Therefore, the open market price at the time of the sale must be used in all these cases, except that the rule in TCA 1997, s 312(4)(a) does apply, in the same way as mentioned above, in the case of machinery or plant, to prevent an open market price being used which exceeds the seller's previous acquisition or deemed acquisition cost.

6.106 Effect of certain successions to trade

TCA 1997, s 313(1) requires the price which an asset qualifying for capital allowances would fetch if sold in the open market (the open market price) to be used for capital allowances purposes in any case where all of the following circumstances occur:

(a) a person succeeds to a trade or profession which until the time of that succession was carried on by another person;

(b) the trade or profession is required by any of the provisions of TCA 1997, s 69 to be treated as discontinued;

(c) the asset was in use for the purposes of the trade treated as discontinued immediately before the succession takes place; and

(d) the asset, without being sold, is used for the new trade or profession immediately after the succession takes place.

TCA 1997, s 69 applies to treat a trade or profession as being discontinued where the person carrying on the trade or profession immediately before the succession is an individual person (referred to as 'the predecessor') and where the person succeeding to the trade or profession ('the successor') is either an individual person or a partnership of persons (which partnership may include the predecessor). Therefore, the open market rule of TCA 1997, s 313(1) is relevant in these types of succession provided that the conditions in (c) and (d) are also met. TCA 1997, s 69 does not apply to treat a trade or profession as discontinued where the successor to the individual person's trade is a company, nor does it apply where one company succeeds to the trade of another company; therefore, TCA 1997, s 313(1) does not apply in these types of succession.

TCA 1997, s 313(1) is also required by TCA 1997, s 1010(4) to be used where an asset subject to capital allowances is taken over, without being sold, by a person or by a new partnership of persons succeeding to a trade or profession which, immediately before the succession, was carried on by a partnership of persons. This type of case occurs when the succession occurs on the termination of the 'relevant period' of the partnership trade or profession concerned (see **4.502**), but only if the asset is used for the discontinued trade or profession immediately before the succession and is used for the trade or profession of the successor immediately after the succession. The application of TCA 1997, s 313(1) is also discussed in **4.505** in the context of partnership capital allowances generally.

It is to be noted that TCA 1997, s 313(1) is not relevant where there is simply a change in one or more partners, but not in all the partners, so that there is no termination of the partnership's 'relevant period' (see **4.502**). So long as there is no permanent discontinuance of a partnership trade or profession, all capital allowances for the partnership as a whole are computed without regard to changes in individual partners (not involving a complete change in all the partners) as if the same persons had been carrying on a partnership trade throughout the relevant period (TCA 1997, s 313(2)).

Although TCA 1997, s 313(1) is not relevant where a company takes over the trade of an individual, it should be pointed out that the rules of TCA 1997, s 312 need to be considered in the case where the individual transfers his trade by incorporating it into a company. In such a case, if the individual controls the company at the time he sells the assets carrying capital allowances, TCA 1997, s 312(2)(a)(i) applies to require an open market value transfer price for capital allowances purposes. However, the individual and the company may together elect under TCA 1997, s 312(5) to substitute the tax written down value as the transfer price, if it is so desired (see **6.105**).

In any case to which it applies, TCA 1997, s 313(1) requires the relevant machinery or plant, industrial buildings, urban renewal area buildings, patent rights or other asset subject to capital allowances to be treated as if it were sold by the predecessor to the successor for a net consideration equal to the open market price of the asset on the date of the succession. This means that the open market price is used as the net proceeds of sale in the computation of the balancing allowance or balancing charge to be given to or made on the predecessor. It also means that the successor bases his subsequent capital allowances on the open market price at the date of the succession.

Example 6.106.1

Mr GF has carried on a trade on his own account for a number of years. On 1 July 2015, he takes Mr TS into partnership and he contributes certain existing items of plant to the partnership as part of his capital contribution (ie there is no sale). The partnership makes up its first accounts for the year ending 30 June 2016.

The plant in question with the figures for Mr GF's original cost, tax written down values at 1 July 2015 (after his last wear and tear allowances as a sole trader) and open market values at 1 July 2015 is as follows:

	Cost	*Market price (1/7/2015)*	*Tax WDV (1/7/2015)*
	€	€	€
Machine No 1	6,200	3,800	4,154

Machine No 2	4,800	4,400	3,675
Machine No 3	10,200	7,000	Nil

These machines had been used by Mr GF in the trade immediately prior to the succession of the partnership (including Mr GF) to his sole trade and the machines continue to be used in the partnership trade from the succession onwards. Mr GF is deemed by TCA 1997, s 69 to have discontinued his trade on 1 July 2015 and TCA 1997, s 313(1) requires his balancing allowances and/or charges to be computed as if had sold the machines for the open market prices shown above, as follows:

	Machines		
	No 1	*No 2*	*No 3*
	€	€	€
Net sales proceeds (TCA 1997, s 313(1))	3,800	4,400	7,000
Less:			
Tax WDV	4,154	3,675	Nil
Balancing (allowance)/charge	(354)	725	7,000

The partnership of GF, TS and Co is deemed by TCA 1997, s 313(1) to have purchased the plant at the open market prices at 1 July 2014 so that the subsequent capital allowances of the partnership are computed accordingly.

The capital allowances computation for the new partnership of GF, TS and Co for 2015 and 2016 is as follows:

	No 1	*No 2*	*No 3*
Deemed acquisition cost – TCA 1997, s 313(1):	€	€	€
Open market prices 1/7/2015	3,800	4,400	7,000
Wear and tear allowance 2015:			
€3,800 x 12.5% x 6/12ths[1]	238	-	-
€4,400 x 12.5% x 6/12ths[1]	-	275	-
€7,000 x 12.5% x 6/12ths[1]	-	-	437
Tax WDV at 31/12/2015	3,562	4,125	6,563
Wear and tear allowance 2016:			
€3,800 x 12.5%	475	-	-
€4,400 x 12.5%	-	550	-
€7,000 x 12.5%	-	-	875
Tax WDV at 31/12/2016	3,087	3,575	5,688

Notes:

1. Since this is the first year of the new partnership trade, the first year's (2015) wear and tear allowance is restricted to a 6/12ths proportion of a full year's allowance to reflect the fact that the basis period for 2015 is a six-month period from 1 July 2015 to 31 December 2015 (see **4.304**).

The rule of TCA 1997, s 313(1), which treats the assets passing to the new trade or profession without being sold as if they were sold for the open market value, is expressed as being for the purposes of TCA 1997, Pt 9. Since TCA 1997, s 312 (which applies to an asset which is sold) is within Part 9, this means that a case within TCA 1997, s 313 may be brought within TCA 1997, s 312 also if the conditions for the application of the latter section are met (ie if either the predecessor or successor is a partnership of persons and if there is a common control connection between predecessor and successor). The significance of this is that the predecessor and successor in such a case have the option of using TCA 1997, s 312(5) to elect to substitute the predecessor's tax written down value for the open market price (see **6.105**).

Example 6.106.2

Take the facts of **Example 6.106.1** and assume that Mr GF has a 55 per cent share in the profits of the new partnership of GF, TS and Co. He is thereby deemed by TCA 1997, s 312(1) to control the partnership and as the machinery taken over by the partnership is deemed by TCA 1997, s 313(1) to have been sold by Mr GF (the predecessor and the 'seller') to the partnership (the successor and the 'buyer'), the transaction is within TCA 1997, s 312 as well as within s 313.

If Mr GF and the firm of GF, TS and Co agree, both parties may serve a notice under the rule in TCA 1997, s 312(5) on the inspector electing to use Mr GF's tax written down values at 1 July 2015 as the basis for the capital allowances computations for both parties (instead of the open market prices at 1 July 2015), but only for any relevant asset for which the tax written down value is lower than the open market value.

If this election is made, the computations shown in Example **6.106.1** would be revised as follows:

	No 1	*No 2*	*No 3*
	€	€	€
Mr GF (predecessor):			
Net sales proceeds (open market price)	3,800	4,400	7,000
Tax WDV	4,154	3,675	Nil
Deemed sales proceeds:			
Lower of 2 figures above	3,800	3,675	Nil
Less:			
Tax WDV	4,154	3,675	Nil
Balancing (allowance)/charge[1]	(354)	Nil	Nil
GF, TS and Co:			
Deemed acquisition costs – TCA 1997, s 313(1)			
Lower of 2 figures above	3,800	3,675	Nil
Wear and tear allowance 2015			
€3,800 x 12.5% x 6/12ths[2]	238	-	-
€3,675 x 12.5% x 6/12ths[2]	-	230	-
€ Nil x 12.5% x 6/12ths[2]	-	-	Nil
Tax WDV 31/12/2015	3,562	3,445	Nil
Wear and tear allowance 2016			
€3,800 x 12.5%	475	-	-
€3,675 x 12.5%	-	460	-
€Nil x 12.5%	-	-	Nil
Tax WDV 31/12/2016	3,087	2,985	Nil

Notes:

1. Compared with the result in **Example 6.106.1**, the balancing charges levied on Mr GF are reduced from €7,725 to nil.
2. Compared with the result in **Example 6.106.1**, the total wear and tear allowances for 2014 for the new partnership are reduced from €950 to €468 (a loss of €482) and there will be further lost annual allowances for the partners in succeeding years.

The new partner has to bear 45 per cent of the higher tax resulting in the succeeding years, and Mr GF has to bear 55 per cent.

In the case of machinery or plant, TCA 1997, s 295 permits a person who succeeds to a trade as a beneficiary under a will or on the intestacy of a deceased person to elect to vary the open market price which TCA 1997, s 313(1) otherwise requires to be assumed as the transfer price on a succession. TCA 1997, s 313 applies where a person succeeds to a trade carried on by another person and by virtue of TCA 1997, s 69 the trade is treated as discontinued. It could be argued that death is a discontinuance by virtue of TCA 1997, s 67 and not s 69 and that s 313 does not apply in a death situation however in practice this point is not taken by Revenue. The beneficiary may, if he wishes, elect by notice in writing to the inspector to have the capital allowances of both the predecessor (normally the deceased person) and the successor (the beneficiary himself) computed on an assumed transfer price equal to the lower of:

(a) the tax written down value of the plant in question immediately prior to the succession as computed for the purposes of a balancing allowance or charge (this value technically referred to as 'the amount of the capital expenditure still unallowed' – see **6.207**); and

(b) the open market price of the plant at the date of the succession.

This election can only be made for machinery or plant which was used by the deceased person for the trade immediately before his death and which, after his death, is used by the beneficiary in the trade to which he has succeeded. If this election is made, usually to avoid a balancing charge on an item of plant which has a tax written down value lower than its market value, then the following consequences ensue:

(a) no balancing charge is made on the predecessor (or his personal representatives) in respect of any plant that is the subject of the election (but a balancing allowance is given if the open market price is lower than the amount of the expenditure still unallowed);

(b) the successor's subsequent wear and tear allowances are based on an assumed cost equal to the lower of the two above values; and

(c) the beneficiary as the successor must compute any balancing charge to which he may be subject on a subsequent sale, etc by reference to the deceased person's earlier cost of acquisition as reduced by both the deceased's and the successor's capital allowances over the entire period of ownership by both of them.

Example 6.106.3

Take the facts of **Example 6.106.1**, but assume that Mr GF dies on 1 July 2015 and that Mr TS succeeds to the trade under Mr GF's will (without any partnership). Since Mr TS is also the sole beneficiary of the estate and wishes to save the tax otherwise payable by the executors on the net balancing charges of €7,371 on Mr GF's trade at the date of death, he makes the election under TCA 1997, s 295 with the following consequences:

Mr GF deceased's balancing allowances/charges for 2015 are now computed as follows:

	No 1	*No 2*	*No 3*
Deemed net sale proceeds (TCA 1997, s 295)	€	€	€
Machine 1 – open market price	3,800		
Machine 2 – tax WDV (lower)		3,675	
Machine 3 – tax WDV (lower)			Nil

Less:			
Tax WDV	4,154	3,675	Nil
Balancing allowance (and no balancing charges)	(354)	Nil	Nil

Mr TS's capital allowances for 2015 onwards are based on deemed acquisition costs respectively of €3,800, €3,675 and €nil, but if he subsequently disposes of either machine No 2 or machine No 3, the computation of any balancing charge that may result must take into account Mr GF's original costs of €4,800 and €10,200 respectively and the capital allowances obtained on these machines by Mr GF up to the date of his death (see **6.205** for limits on balancing charges).

6.107 Manner of granting capital allowances and making charges

The Taxes Consolidation Act 1997 provide for the capital allowances in respect of machinery or plant, industrial buildings, patent rights, scientific research, farm buildings and works, dredging expenditure, etc to be given in one of three ways, namely:

(a) in taxing the trade, profession, office or employment carried on, held or exercised by the person entitled to the allowance;

(b) in charging the income of the person entitled under Sch D Case V/Sch D Case III; or

(c) by way of discharge or repayment of tax.

Capital allowances are given in taxing a trade if the qualifying capital expenditure was incurred for the purposes of a trade by the person carrying it on and if, at the relevant time, the assets in question (eg machinery, industrial buildings, patent rights, scientific research expenditure, etc) were held or used for the trade. The way in which the trader's capital allowances are given in charging the profits of his trade is explained in more detail in the context of a person chargeable to income tax in **4.3**. Any balancing charges on assets used for the purposes of a trade are made in taxing the profits of that trade.

The effect of giving capital allowances in taxing the profits of a trade is to require those allowances for each year of assessment (income tax) to be deducted from the taxable income of the trade for that year or period. Similarly, capital allowances on qualifying assets used for a profession, office or employment are given in a corresponding manner in taxing the income therefrom, while any balancing charges in respect of those assets are made in taxing the profession, office or employment. In effect, any balancing charges are added to the taxable income of the trade, etc under the schedule or case in question for the relevant year of assessment.

Capital allowances are given in charging income under Sch D Case V in the case of a lessor entitled to the writing down allowances and any balancing allowances in respect of industrial buildings situated in the State. Any balancing charges on such a lessor are made in charging his income under Sch D Case V. The same principles apply for the corresponding capital allowances and balancing charges when given to or made on such a lessor of other buildings or structures in the State to which the industrial buildings allowances are applied, eg non-industrial buildings in designated urban renewal areas or multi-storey car parks (see **6.605**).

Capital allowances are given by discharge or repayment in the case of any wear and tear or writing down allowances or balancing allowances in respect of any machinery or plant, industrial buildings, urban renewal buildings, etc which produces income taxable under Sch D Case IV. Where a balancing charge arises in respect of any such asset, it is chargeable under Sch D Case IV.

Capital allowances given in this way include the capital allowances given to a lessor for machinery or plant leased other than as part of a trade of leasing machinery or plant (see **6.3**), the capital allowances for patent rights (see **6.7**) and the industrial buildings allowances given to a lessor deriving income from industrial buildings which is taxed under Case IV of Sch D (very few cases).

The granting of capital allowances by discharge or repayment of tax is not really any different from giving the allowances as a deduction in assessing the profits of a trade under Sch D Case I or in charging rental income under Sch D Case V. In theory, the allowances are given by discharging the whole or a part of the relevant Sch D Case IV assessment or, if the tax has already been paid without giving relief for the capital allowances, by repaying the tax overpaid.

In practice, relief for the allowances given by discharge or repayment can normally be obtained before the tax is assessed if the person entitled to them gives the necessary details in his tax return. Further, in calculating the amount of a preliminary tax payment, the allowances given by way of discharge or repayment may be deducted from the Sch D Case IV income, but any balancing charges must be added.

Set off of allowances against income of relevant class

In all cases, the capital allowances for any year of assessment must first be deducted from or set off against the income of the relevant class for that year or period, whether the allowances are given in taxing a trade, profession, etc, in charging income under Sch D Case V or by discharge or repayment of tax. In the event that the relevant income is insufficient in any year of assessment to absorb fully the capital allowances deductible, the rules for providing for the excess capital allowances differ depending on which method of granting allowances is involved. The manner of dealing with excess capital allowances due to be granted in taxing a trade, profession, etc has already been discussed in **4.3** and **4.4**.

TCA 1997, s 305(1) provides that any capital allowances given by discharge or repayment of tax or in charging income under Sch D Case V, and which are available against, or available primarily against, a specified class of income are to be deducted from income of that class for the relevant year of assessment to the maximum extent possible, ie up to the full amount of that income for the year if the allowances are high enough. To the extent that those capital allowances cannot be fully relieved by deduction from the income of the class in question, the unrelieved allowances are available for carry forward for deduction from income of the same class for the next year of assessment, and so on for subsequent years until fully relieved. Capital allowances deductible from one class of income cannot be deducted from any other class of income, unless the election provided for in TCA 1997, s 305(1)(b) is available (see below) and is actually made.

Election for set off against other income

The way in which capital allowances may be used to augment or create a trading loss for set off against income from all sources in a claim under TCA 1997, s 381 has been fully explained in **4.405** in the context of a trade or profession. It is to be noted that the capital allowances to be used to augment or create the loss in this type of claim are the full amount of the capital allowances for the tax year for which the claim is made as reduced by any part of those allowances required to offset a balancing charge for the same tax year.

TCA 1997, s 305(1)(b) permits an election to be made within 24 months of the end of a year of assessment by the taxpayer in respect of any excess capital allowances available by discharge or repayment of tax or in charging income under Sch D, Case V. This election may be made only in respect of any excess capital allowances of a kind that are available *primarily* against income of a specified class. If this election is made in respect of any eligible excess capital allowances for the year of assessment in question, the amount of the excess is deducted from the taxpayer's income from all sources for that year. The taxpayer is then entitled to be repaid any excess income tax he may have already paid for that year, or to have any tax still due reduced. TCA 1997, s 305(1)(b) also sets out the order of offset where there are allowances carried forward from prior years as well as current year allowances; in this case, the allowances brought forward are set off against the income of the specified class before the current year's allowances are set off. In effect, this helps to maximise the amount of current year's allowances that can be set against other income.

For capital allowances given by discharge or repayment or in taxing income under Sch D Case V, it is to be noted that only certain allowances are stated in their particular rules as being 'available primarily against' a specified class of income. Other capital allowances are stated to be 'available against' a particular class of income. The taxpayer is not entitled to elect under TCA 1997, s 305(1)(b) (or under any other rule) to use capital allowances which are not 'available primarily against' to offset or reduce income from a source or sources other than the relevant specified class of income. Therefore, any excess 'available against' allowances can only be carried forward for set off against the specified income in a later year of assessment.

Restrictions on set off against other income

The ability of a taxpayer to elect under TCA 1997, s 381 or TCA 1997, s 305(1)(b) to create or increase an allowable loss or to set off against other income excess capital allowances available primarily against a specified class of income has been curtailed by a number of provisions in recent years. These provisions are frequently referred to as 'ring fence' rules in that they usually put a kind of fence around the capital allowances affected, so that they can only be used to reduce the income of the class to which they relate either in the year in which they arise or, by carry forward, in a later year. The effect of these ring-fencing rules are discussed at **6.305** and **6.509**.

6.108 Restrictions on carry forward of unused capital allowances

Finance Act 2012 introduced a guillotine on the ability to claim unused capital allowances on specified capital allowances and area based capital allowances to the *relevant tax year* and any subsequent tax year. TCA 1997, s 409G provides that the amount of any specified capital allowances or area based capital allowances that are available to carry forward for income tax purposes against trading income or rental income to a relevant tax year shall, subject to certain exceptions, be zero. The *relevant tax year* is the later of 2015 or the year after the tax life of the building has expired. Therefore the earliest date that these provisions will take effect will be 2015. For example if the tax life of a building ceased in 2012, any unused capital allowances in relation to that building are available for carry forward to 2013 and 2014, however there is no carry forward after 2014. If the tax life of a building ceases in 2017, the capital allowances will be available until 2017. However there will be no carry forward of unused capital allowances to 2018 and subsequent years. The tax life of a building begins on the date the building is first used for any purpose and ends a number of years later, depending on the trade category and the date of the expenditure (see **6.409**).

TCA 1997, s 409F contains a number of definitions used in TCA 1997, s 409G. It prescribes what constitutes a specified capital allowance and an area based capital allowance. A summary of the type of allowances falling within these definitions are as follows:

Specified capital allowance

A specified capital allowance is a specified relief that is a writing down allowance, an accelerated writing down allowance or a balancing allowance, including allowances carried forward under TCA 1997, Pt 9. The type of capital allowances considered to be specified reliefs are set out in column 2 of TCA 1997, Sch 25B for the purposes of TCA 1997, s 485C and include the following:

- Hotel including registered holiday camps, holiday cottages, caravan parks and guest houses (excluding writing down allowances granted at 4 per cent per annum);
- Qualifying convalescent home;
- Qualifying nursing home and qualifying residential units deemed to be in use as a nursing home for the purposes of capital allowances;
- Qualifying hospital;
- Qualifying sports injury clinic;
- Qualifying mental health centre;
- Qualifying specialist palliative care;
- Certain aircraft facilities;
- A balancing allowance claimed under TCA 1997, s 274 which is a specified relief as set out in column (2) of TCA 1997, Sch 25B;
- Certain accelerated writing down allowances in accordance with TCA 1997, s 273;
- Capital allowances for holiday camps and tourism facilities under the Mid Shannon Corridor Scheme (TCA 1997, ss 372AX and 372AY);
- Childcare facilities (TCA 1997, s 843A);
- Third level facilities (TCA 1997, s 843);
- Capital allowances brought forward under any of the above in either a trading context or a rental context. If the capital allowances forward originated pre 2007, the amount of capital allowances determined in accordance with TCA 1997, Sch 25 para 1 which is referable to specified reliefs.

Area based capital allowances

- Commercial premises in the Customs House Docks Area (TCA 1997, s 323);
- Industrial Buildings in Temple Bar (TCA 1997, s 331);
- Commercial Buildings in Temple Bar (TCA 1997, s 332);
- Buildings in a Designated Area or a Designated Street (TCA 1997, s 341);
- Commercial Buildings in a Designated Area or a Designated Street (TCA 1997, s 342);
- Qualifying Buildings in an Enterprise Area (TCA 1997, s 343);
- Multi-Storey Car Parks (TCA 1997, s 344);
- Industrial Buildings in Resort Areas (TCA 1997, s 352);
- Commercial Premises in Resort Areas (TCA 1997, s 353);
- Industrial Buildings in Qualifying Areas (TCA 1997, s 372C);

- Commercial Premises in Qualifying Areas (TCA 1997, s 372D);
- Industrial Buildings in Rural Areas (TCA 1997, s 372M);
- Commercial Buildings in Rural Areas (TCA 1997, s 372N);
- Park and Ride Facilities (TCA 1997, s 372V);
- Commercial Buildings in Park and Ride Facilities (TCA 1997, s 372W);
- Industrial and Commercial Building in Designated Towns (TCA 1997, ss 372AC, 372AD, 372AAC or 372AAD);
- Conversion or refurbishment of commercial buildings in specified regeneration areas (TCA 1997, s 372AAC);
- Urban Renewal Scheme, 1986 – Capital allowances in relation to certain commercial premises in designated areas other than the Custom House Docks Area (TCA 1997, Sch 32 para 11).

As can be seen the above list does not include s 23 type reliefs including student accommodation. Therefore there is no restriction on the carry forward of such reliefs.

Specifically excluded from the restrictions are allowances made in taxing the trade of an individual who is an active trader or an active partner. An active trader and an active partner are defined as an individual who works for the greater part of their time in the day-to-day management or conduct of that trade or partnership (TCA 1997, ss 409A and 409D).

Generally a balancing charge or allowance will not arise after the tax life of a building has ended. However in certain restricted circumstances a balancing charge may arise on a disposal of a building after its tax life has ceased. An example would be in the case of a childcare facility where the capital allowances are available over seven years but in order to avoid a balancing event the relevant interest in the building must be retained for 15 years. There is provision that where a balancing charge arises in such circumstances that any capital allowances forward restricted under this section are unlocked to set against the balancing charge

It is important for the purposes of limiting the future application of TCA 1997, s 409G that where there are excess capital allowances for any year of assessment that area based capital allowances and specified capital allowances are claimed in priority to other allowances. This would assist in minimising the restrictions imposed.

TCA 1997, s 409G does not impact on capital allowances which have previously been claimed but restricted under the high earners restriction. This is because when the specified reliefs are finally used they are not capital allowances forward under TCA 1997, Pt 9.

Example 6.108.1

Mr Black has rental losses forward of €100,000 at 1 January 2016. These losses arise from deficiencies of expenses over income as computed under TCA 1997, s 97. He also has capital allowances carried forward to 2015 of €125,000 in respect of plant and capital allowances forward of €500,000 in respect of industrial buildings allowances from a specified property. In 2016 his rental surplus is €300,000, his claim for plant capital allowances is €50,000 and capital allowances from the specified property are €75,000. The tax life of the specified property ceases on 31 October 2016.

2016 Income Tax Computation

	€
Rental surplus	300,000
Unspecified capital allowances forward[1]	(125,000)

	175,000
Specified capital allowances forward	(175,000)
Total income	0
Deductions	0
Taxable income	0
Recalculated taxable income[2]	95,000
Carried Forward to 2017	
High earners restriction[2]	95,000
Unspecified capital allowances	50,000
Rental losses	100,000

(1) TCA 1997, s 485C(3) provides that capital allowances which are not in respect of a specified property are given relief in priority to capital allowances from a specified property. Consequently, €400,000 of specified property capital allowances are lost.

(2)

High earners restriction calculation		€
Specified reliefs	S	175,000
Ring fenced income	R	0
Taxable income	T	0
Adjusted income	(T+S)-R=	175,000
Income threshold amount		125,000
20% adjusted income		35,000
Relief threshold amount	Y	80,000
Recalculated taxable income = 0+ (175,000–80,000)	= 0+ (175,000–80,000)	95,000

6.109 Order of set off for capital allowances forward

It is interesting that TCA 1997, s 485C(3)(a) provides that 'where, in relation to any tax year and the capital allowances to be given effect to in that year, any provision of the Tax Acts requires allowances (in this paragraph referred to as the 'first-mentioned allowances') for one period to be given effect to, or to be deemed to be given effect to, in priority to allowances for another period (in this paragraph referred to as the 'second-mentioned' allowances) then:

(i) As respects the first-mentioned allowances, effect shall be given, or to be deemed to be given, as the case may be, for an allowance which is not a specified relief in priority to any such allowance which is a specified relief and in priority to the second-mentioned allowances and

(ii) As respects the second-mentioned allowances, effect shall be given, or be deemed to be given, as the case may be, for an allowance which is not a specified relief in priority to any such allowance which is a specified relief.

As can be seen from the first sentence above, TCA 1997, s 485C(3) only comes into effect where in relation to a particular tax year the Tax Acts require allowances for one period to be given effect to or be deemed to be given effect to in priority to allowances for another period. In the author's opinion the only situation where the Tax Acts requires allowances for one period to be given effect to in priority to allowances for another period is in a case where an individual has Case V capital allowances carried forward and current year Case V capital allowances in excess of Case V income plus allowances forward. In the case of an individual who has no current year capital allowances and only has Case V capital allowances carried forward, there is no question of the Tax Acts requiring allowances for one period to be given in priority to another. For this reason it would seem that TCA 1997, s 485C(3)(a) would not apply to such an individual and accordingly that there is nothing in the legislation which would require such an individual to claim relief for unspecified capital allowances carried forward in priority to specified capital allowances carried forward. In such circumstances therefore it would be up to the individual taxpayer to claim relief for capital allowances carried forward in whichever way is most beneficial to him.

This could lead to decisions by individuals in preparing their tax returns as to which capital allowances to claim in order to minimise a tax payment because of the High Earners Restriction (HER) but preserving entitlement to specified capital allowances subject to the guillotine rules.

If we assume in 2014 Mr X has €800,000 of Case V Rental income, no current year capital allowances but capital allowances forward of €1m. The €1m comprises of €800,000 specified capital allowances and €200,000 non specified capital allowances. We will also assume that the tax life of the building on which the specified capital allowances have been claimed expired in 2013. Mr X can claim €800,000 capital allowances forward which reduces his taxable income to zero. However the HER applies and there will be a restriction on the quantum of capital allowances on which relief can be claimed in that year. The quantum will depend on the split of the €800,000 claimed between specified and non-specified. If Mr X claims the full €800,000 from specified capital allowances after adjusting for the HER only 20 per cent or €160,000 will be available in 2014 and the balance of €640,000 will be carried forward to future years under s 485F. There will be no restriction on the €640,000 under the guillotine provisions. Alternatively Mr X could claim €200,000 of non-specified capital allowances and €600,000 of specified capital allowances in 2014. After adjusting for the HER €120,000 or 20 per cent of the specified reliefs would be available in 2014. This leaves €480,000 in charge to tax compared to €640,000 in the previous scenario. However although €480,000 of allowances are available for carry forward under s 485F €200,000 of allowances are lost under the guillotine provisions.

It should be noted that Revenue's operational manual 15.02a.06 notes:

> Section 485C(3) does not alter the priority in which capital allowances are given but does provide that where another provision requires that carried forward allowances are used in priority to current year allowances (E.g. s.305(1)(b)(i) or s.391(2)(b)) then non-specified capital allowances carried forward (e.g. industrial buildings allowance on a factory) are deemed to be used in priority to specified capital allowances (e.g. industrial buildings allowance on a nursing home).
>
> So in general terms (Refer to paragraph 3.1 and 3.3 on two instances where there is no order of offset between carried forward and current year allowances contained within the Tax Acts.), the order of priority for these allowances for the purposes of the Tax Acts is:
>
> (i) Carried forward non-specified capital allowances
>
> (ii) Carried forward specified capital allowances
>
> (iii) Current year non-specified capital allowances
>
> (iv) Current year specified capital allowances.

The reference above to paragraphs 3.1.and 3.3 are to those in the manual which look at rental and trading capital allowances.

6.110 Claims for capital allowances

For a person chargeable to income tax, the general principle is that he should include his claim for capital allowances in the annual statement which he is required to make of his income, ie his annual income tax return. TCA 1997, s 304(2) states this requirement for allowances that are given in taxing the profits or gains of any description.

6.2 Machinery or Plant

6.201 Capital allowances available

Capital allowances are given in respect of capital expenditure on 'machinery or plant' provided for use in a trade, profession, office or employment carried on or exercised by the person incurring the expenditure. Capital allowances may also be claimed, if certain conditions are met, by a person incurring capital expenditure on machinery or plant that is leased for use by someone else (see **6.301**); in certain circumstances, a lessee of plant may obtain the allowances (see **6.303**).

The types of allowance that are given in respect of machinery or plant are:

(a) A wear and tear allowance is given in respect of capital expenditure incurred on machinery or plant for each year of assessment in which certain conditions are satisfied (see **6.203**).

(b) A balancing allowance is given on the sale of, or on the occurrence of certain other events relating to, machinery or plant after its use in the trade, profession, office or employment in the case where the taxpayer's net capital outlay (after taking into account the sales or similar proceeds) has not been fully relieved by capital allowances by the date of the sale or other relevant event. Alternatively to a balancing allowance, if capital allowances have been obtained over the period of use in excess of the net capital outlay (after sales proceeds, etc), a balancing charge is made on the taxpayer to 'recapture' the excess allowances (see **6.207**).

(c) A scientific research allowance under TCA 1997, s 765 is given where a person carrying on a trade incurs capital expenditure on machinery or plant as part of expenditure on scientific research (see **6.601**).

Increased wear and tear allowances (free depreciation) and initial allowances were available in respect of plant provided for a trade or profession before 1 April 1992. In certain circumstances these allowances were also available where the plant was provided on or after 1 April 1992. A full account of these allowances and the relevant exceptions is provided in the 1997/98 edition of this book.

TCA 1997, s 840(3) provides that no capital allowances are to be given in respect of any asset that is used or is provided for use, wholly or partly for the purpose of providing business entertainment, but this applies only to the extent that the asset is used for this purpose. When any machinery or plant, or any other relevant asset subject to capital allowances, is used wholly for business entertainment purposes, no capital allowances at all are granted. If the machinery or plant, etc is used partly for business entertainment and partly for other purposes of the trade, then the normal capital allowances are calculated, but are restricted to allow only a proportion that reflects the extent of their use for those other purposes. For example, if an item of plant is used as to 40 per cent for business entertainment and as to 60 per cent for other purposes of the trade, only 60 per cent of the capital allowances that would normally apply can be granted.

6.202 What constitutes machinery or plant?

There is no definition of the term 'machinery or plant' in the Taxes Acts. The scope of the term 'machinery' does not usually give rise to difficulties (for two Irish cases in a non-tax context see *Irish Refining v Commissioner of Valuation* [1995] SC and *Coakley & Co/Arkady Feed Co v Commissioner of Valuation* 1996 2 ILRM 90). In any event, the term 'plant' is wide enough to include both machinery and many other items which would not qualify as machinery.

The scope of the term 'plant' has been the subject of considerable judicial interpretation in the context of tax law. The result is that the term has acquired a somewhat specialised meaning for tax purposes. In *Cole Brothers v Phillips* [1982] STC 307, Oliver LJ, in the Court of Appeal commented: 'It is now beyond doubt that 'plant' is used in an artificial and largely judge-made sense'. In *Attwood v Andruff Car Wash* [1996] STC 110, Carnwath J observed:

> … the concept has lost touch with any ordinary dictionary meaning of the word, embracing such diverse subject matter as a horse and cart, a swimming pool and barrister's books and it is necessary to refer to a large body of precedents before deciding whether or not a particular item qualifies as 'plant'.

In *Gaffney v Inspector of Taxes*, the Circuit Court held that a business suit was plant [1989] ITR 481 (although allowances in respect of expenditure thereon will now be denied by s 284(1): see **6.203**: *Conditions for wear and tear allowances*). In *Abbot v Albion Greyhounds* 26 TC 390 the *obiter* view was expressed that, while expenditure on greyhounds owned by a taxpayer carrying on a trade of running greyhound races was capital, the greyhounds did not qualify as 'plant'; however, it would seem highly arguable that the greyhounds were as much apparatus used in the conduct of the taxpayer's trade as the horse in *Yarmouth v France*.

The decision remains primarily one of fact, so that the courts will not overturn a finding by the Appeal Commissioners (or Circuit Court judge as appropriate), unless it is wholly unreasonable or based on a misunderstanding of the proper legal tests which should be applied (see *Edwards v Bairstow*, discussed at **2.204**).

The traditional starting point in attempting to lay down the scope of the word 'plant' is that of Lord Lindley in *Yarmouth v France* [1887] 19 QBD 647 (a non-tax case where a horse was held to fall within the term), when he said:

> There is no definition of 'plant' in the Act but, in its ordinary sense, it includes whatever apparatus is used by a businessman for carrying on his business – not his stock in trade which he buys or makes for sale; but all goods and chattels, fixed or moveable, live or dead, which he keeps for permanent employment in his business.

Of course, expenditure on ephemeral items may be on revenue account and thus will not relate to plant. In *Hinton v Madden and Ireland* 38 TC 391, large numbers of knives and lasts, with lives ranging from one to five years, and which were inserted into heavy complicated machinery used in manufacturing, were held to be plant. This case concerned a claim for an investment allowance and the Crown had contended that the expenditure was on revenue account. The fact that the average life of the items was only three years did not prevent them from being capital items in the circumstances of the case. This decision may be contrasted with that in *Rose v Campbell* 44 TC 500, where expenditure on wallpaper patterns with a life of less than two years was held to be on revenue account.

Plant or premises?

The courts have built on Lord Lindley's definition by drawing a distinction between the 'premises' *within* which the trade is carried on, and the 'plant' *with* which the trade is carried on. The role of 'premises' is to provide shelter, security and the general framework for the trade, typically housing employees, customers, etc and the persons and chattels (goods, equipment, etc) used in the trade. On the other hand, plant is something which is itself used in the conduct of the trade.

A number of UK cases demonstrate that even moveable assets which serve merely to house personnel and/or equipment, etc do not rank as plant. In *St John's School v Ward* [1975] STC 7, moveable, prefabricated buildings used by a school as a laboratory and a gymnasium were held not to constitute plant. The structures were merely the means of sheltering pupils and equipment. Similarly in *Thomas v Reynolds* [1988] STC 135, an inflatable cover for a tennis court was held not to be plant.

In *Benson v Yard Arm Club* [1979] STC 266, a hulk used as a floating restaurant was regarded as a structure in which the business was carried on rather than apparatus employed in the carrying on of the trade; it was irrelevant that the appearance and location of the restaurant was attractive to patrons. Buckley LJ observed that such features were equally true of a restaurant at the top of the Post Office Tower:

> they may serve to attract customers but they play no part in the conduct of the business. A characteristic of plant appears to me to be that it is an adjunct to the carrying on of a business and *not the essential site or core of the business* itself [emphasis added].

In *Shove v Lingfield Park 1991 Ltd* [2003] STC 1002 it was held that an all-weather race track functioned as part of the premises of the company's business of organising and promoting horse races. Although the all-weather race track was separately identifiable from other parts of the premises, both visually and in the way in which it was constructed and maintained, it did not lose its character as part of the premises.

Plant as well as premises?

'Premises' and 'plant' are *not* mutually exclusive concepts – in unusual instances an asset may function as *both*, in which case it will qualify as plant. Some examples illustrating this point are given below. These demonstrate the point that immovable structures, although they serve the purpose of housing equipment, may also constitute apparatus used in the trade.

In *IRC v Barclay Curle & Co Ltd* 45 TC 221, the cost of excavating and concreting a dry dock was allowed as capital expenditure on plant. Taken together with the hydraulic equipment and dock gate incorporated in it, the dock formed an indivisible unit which qualified as a plant; it had the trading function of getting large vessels into position to allow work on them to begin. Lord Guest observed:

> It is said that the dry dock is like a factory building in which the trade is carried on. The factory is itself a building in which trade can be carried on. But the excavation and concrete

work is useless for any trade purpose unless used in conjunction with the rest of the equipment.

In *Schofield v R & H Hall* [1975] STC 353, grain silos were also held to be plant. The silos in question consisted broadly of large concrete structures into which were built concrete bins and a small structure containing plant and machinery, consisting of gantries, conveyor belts, mobile chutes, etc. The silos were held to play a part in the distributive processes of reception, distribution and discharge of grain. Although the silos were used to store grain, they were more than mere premises: they were 'specially constructed for the purpose of rendering more efficient the process of unloading and distribution'. The court cited Lord Guest in *Margrett v Lowestoft Water & Gas Co Ltd* 19 TC 488 where he said of the function of a water tower:

> It was the harnessing of the natural element of gravity to perform a trade function.

In *O'Srianáin v Lakeview* Ltd III ITR 219, the High Court upheld a finding of fact that a deep pit poultry house together with the equipment within it constituted plant used in the trade of egg production. The structure contained tiered stacks of cages (which held the hens) underneath which was a deep concrete pit to collect the hens' droppings. The structure was specially designed to provide thermostatically controlled heating and light, and fans were located within it to provide ventilation to take away harmful fumes. It was found that the walls, roof and floor of the house all played an essential role in maintaining and controlling the required environment. Murphy J commented as follows:

> If the findings of fact had concluded at [this] point perhaps the proper inference would be that the building in question merely provided a suitable and hygienic setting within which the taxpayer or his employees carried on their work but … [there] is to be found the further finding in the following terms: … the entire design is so made up as to create the most conducive and efficient environment in which hens will lay eggs and without this design the hens would not lay as many eggs.
>
> It follows that the environment is designed for the benefit of the hens (and not the humans) and for the purpose of increasing the egg production which is in fact the business carried on by the taxpayer.

Accordingly, the learned judge declined to reverse the finding of fact by the Circuit Court judge, on the principle laid down by *Edwards v Bairstow* (see **2.204**).

In *Wangaretta Woolen Mills Ltd v FCT* 1 ATR 329 (an Australian capital allowances case), the taxpayer carried on a business of dyeing and spinning worsted yarn which it then sold on to knitting mills. The dyeing was carried out in a specialised dye house built by the company to prevent problems with ventilation, condensation, corrosion and drainage. The machinery used in the actual dyeing process was embedded in the walls of the dye house. The dye house was designed in a certain way and had a ventilation and drainage system built into it, so as to overcome the problems which would arise if the process was carried out in a standard factory building.

It was held, following *IRC v Barclay Curle*, that the dye house was in the nature of a tool in the trade and played a part in the manufacturing process (see also *Broken Hill Pty Co Ltd v FCT* (1952) 85 CLR 423, cited with approval in the *O'Srianáin* case).

In *Cooke v Beach Station Caravans Ltd* [1974] STC 402, the entire cost of excavating and installing a swimming pool was allowed to the owners of a caravan park. *IRC v Barclay Curle* 45 TC 221 was followed on the basis that the pool performed the function of giving buoyancy and enjoyment to the persons using the pool. It was held that the shell of the pool could not be divorced realistically from the chlorination, heating and filtering equipment affixed to it and which together with it formed an integrated whole, providing clean, warm water safe for swimmers. In his judgment, Megarry J also noted that:

> Nobody could suggest that the principal function [of the pool] was merely to protect the occupants from the elements.

He also commented:

> The pools are part of the means whereby trade is carried on and *not merely the place at which it is carried on* [emphasis added].

By way of contrast, in *Gray v Seymours Garden Centre* [1995] STC 706, the taxpayers, who operated a garden centre, had claimed that a specialised glasshouse constituted plant. The glasshouse had a roof which could be used to control ventilation, but had no integrated heating. The glasshouse protected plants from the elements and created an environment in which they could grow securely. The internal layout of the glasshouse allowed customers free passage between the benches on which the plants were displayed. The court rejected the taxpayer's claim, saying that at best the glasshouse could be categorised as a 'purpose built structure'. This case may, perhaps, be distinguished from the *O'Srianáin* case, on the basis that in the former case the structure merely protected the taxpayer's existing stock-in-trade, while in the latter it played a part in the process of egg production. The poultry house as designed would have been useless without the cages (and vice versa), so that it was perhaps not unreasonable to regard the poultry house and the cages within it as an indivisible unit.

Vinelott J, at first instance in the *Seymour* case, also expressed the view that a glasshouse with internal temperature and humidity controls, as well as automatic ventilation, shade screens and other equipment could be considered to rank as 'apparatus used in the trade' and therefore rank as plant (see also *Wimpy v Warland* [1988] STC 149, where a finding of fact by the Appeal Commissioners that the cost of a plant-room itself qualified as plant, was not challenged by the Inland Revenue). In *Carr v Sayer* [1992] STC 396, purpose-built quarantine kennels were also held not be plant, because they simply provided shelter for the animals. However, it appears that a Circuit Court judge has held that a slatted unit cow-house does constitute plant (see [1997] ITR 133).

In *Attwood v Andruff Car Wash* [1997] STC 1167, a car wash hall was held to be merely a building which housed machinery. The wash hall also contained a lobby, WC, pump room, an inspection area and a store (factors which clearly weakened the taxpayer's case). However, the court also held that even if it had been permissible to look only at the part of the building through which the cars passed, that part would not have qualified either. The court took the view that, although purpose-built, that part of the wash hall functioned as the premises, providing shelter and retaining noise and heat. Interestingly, the court also doubted the correctness of the decision in *O'Srianáin v Lakeview* and it certainly seems that the UK courts have adopted a more stringent approach than their Irish counterparts in this area of tax law (see also *Bradley v London Electricity plc* [1996] STC 1054).

In *Dixon v Fitch's Garage [1975] STC 480,* it was held that a canopy constructed over the pumps of a petrol filling station to provide shelter while the commercial process of delivering fuel was carried on was not plant. Brightman J, ruled that, as the canopy did not help to supply the petrol, but only made the motorist and staff more comfortable, it did not qualify as plant. This approach seems unduly narrow, since an asset can play a part in the conduct of the trade without being directly involved at the point of sale. Indeed, recent UK and Irish cases seem to recognise that the bringing in of custom *in itself* represents an important trading function (see *Leeds Permanent Building Society v Proctor*, discussed below).

In *O'Culacháin v McMullan Bros* [1995] ITR 173, the Supreme Court upheld a finding of fact by the Circuit Court judge that a canopy of this kind constituted plant. The learned judge had found *inter alia* that the canopy provided: '… an attractive setting for the sale of the [taxpayer's] product'. He added:

> They advertise and promote the [taxpayer's] products, they create an overall impression of efficiency and of financial solidarity and most important of all they attract customers.

The Supreme Court distinguished the *Dixon* case on the basis that the canopy there had been held to do no more than provide shelter and light.

The potential difficulty in reconciling the *McMullan* case with the UK authorities is that if the canopy was premises (an issue on which there was no finding of fact) then it was attracting customers *in its role as premises*. As Buckley LJ noted in the *Yard Arm* case (above) the appearance and location of the floating restaurant made it a more attractive premises, but this did not convert it into an apparatus of the taxpayer's trade. In the *Scottish and Newcastle* case, Lord Lowry carefully distinguished (in the context of a hotel) between a 'beautiful or unusual or historic building, attractive views, gardens, shrubbery's and waterfalls' on the one hand, and 'ornaments, the equipment used by the staff and the glasses, china, cutlery, table linen, and the tables and chairs used by the customers', on the other. Both categories of items could be used, he said, for 'the creation of the right atmosphere' but the former category is excluded as plant under the 'premises' test.

This issue was not addressed by the court in the *McMullan* case, who simply noted that premises and plant are not mutually exclusive concepts. A possible distinction may lie in the fact that the canopy was a structure distinct from the principal place of business and thus did not form part of that premises as such. Using the formulation cited in the *Yard Arm* case above, it was an 'adjunct to, rather than the essential site or core of the business'. It may be added that, like the swimming pool in the *Beach Stations Caravans* case, it could also be said that the *primary* function of the structure was not to provide shelter.

This general analysis seems to gain support from the decision in *O'Grady v Roscommon Race Committee* IV ITR 425, which distinguished *Brown v Burnley FC Ltd* [1980] STC 424. In the latter case, it was held that a concrete stand at a football ground which incorporated seating was not itself plant (although the seating did qualify as such). Vinelott J held that the stadium, including the stand was the place *within* which the football matches took place before the spectators. In *The Roscommon Race Committee* case, the Supreme Court held that improvements to a racecourse stand (but excluding work on two bars) qualified as expenditure on plant. The Circuit Court judge had found that the stand, as well as providing shelter, raised patrons to a higher level to view the races, and helped to create an atmosphere of excitement during the race, due to the close proximity of the patrons to each other.

O'Flaherty J, in the Supreme Court, commented as follows:

> It is clear that the business of the respondents could be conducted without the stand. I think the stand is more than simply a constituent part of the setting in which the business is carried on; rather it carries on an active function. It can properly be said to be part of the apparatus used for the carrying on of the business of the respondents.
>
> The Burnley stadium stand is in a different category. In fact, it provided seating accommodation for patrons. The patrons paid to get in, sit down and watch the matches. At

> Roscommon races, in contrast, the patrons in general will spend only a small part of the duration of the races in the stand. There are substantial periods of time between one race and another. I have no doubt that the races constitute a very important social occasion as well as everything else. The spectators will circulate, meet friends, express opinions on the prospects of the courses, place bets, go to the bars and so forth. When a race is about to start they will tend to congregate in the stand to get a good view and, in general, avail of it in the manner which has also been described by the learned Circuit Court judge. The stand is truly not the place of business of the respondents but rather an attractive addition to their actual business which is that of promoting and organising horse races.

Thus, it may be that a structure or building which does not form part of the *main* business premises can qualify as plant if it can be shown to play a part in the conduct of the trade by way of the general attraction of custom and/or the promotion of the 'brand image' of the trade, etc. The fact that it also functions as premises, in the sense that it may provide shelter, etc, will not be fatal since (as discussed above) plant and premises are not mutually exclusive; however, the case law so far suggests that in this kind of case the *primary* function of the building or structure should be that of plant.

The case of *Anchor International v Inland Revenue* [2003] UKSC SPC00354 was concerned with whether capital expenditure incurred by Anchor International in relation to the construction of artificial five-a-side football pitches was plant. The expenditure covered investigation work, excavation, filling and draining, the artificial turf itself and its installation. Special Commissioner Avery Jones said that 'one can regard the pitch or the carpet as both the setting and the means by which the business is carried on. The dual nature is no different from the dry dock in Barclay Curle, the swimming pool at the caravan site in *Cooke v Beach Station Caravans Ltd* … and the murals in *IRC v Scottish and Newcastle Breweries Ltd* …. Here the trade is the provision of synthetic football pitches, which generates 70 per cent of the turnover, and so in one sense the trade is the provision of setting, but in another sense the pitch and the carpet are the plant with which the trade is carried on … The fact that there are cases where plant serves both purposes shows that once the plant is used in the trade it does not matter that it is also the setting'. It was held that the carpet which was not a fixed structure and was used for the purpose of generating profits was plant.

Part of premises or separate asset?

It will be important to establish whether an asset which is attached to premises forms part of those premises, or whether it ranks as a distinct, self-contained asset. In the former case, expenditure on the asset will be treated as relating to the premises itself and therefore cannot qualify as plant (other than in the rare instances when the premises is *also* plant – see above). In *IRC v Scottish & Newcastle Breweries* [1982] STC 296, Lord Lowry acknowledged that an asset which is annexed to a building so that legally it becomes part of the building and the land on which it stands (see the discussion of 'fixtures' at **6.203**: *Fixtures*), does *not* necessarily form part of the premises for capital allowance purposes. Thus, in the *IRC v Scottish & Newcastle Breweries* case, a finding by the Appeal Commissioners that a fixed metal sculpture attached to a hotel was not part of the premises was upheld (albeit with some reluctance).

The court held that the relevant considerations in deciding whether an item formed part of premises included the following:

(a) whether the item appeared visually to retain a separate identity;
(b) the degree of permanence with which it was attached;
(c) the incompleteness of the structure without the item; and

(d) the extent to which it was intended to be permanent or was likely to be replaced in the short term.

Certainly, in practice, the Revenue Commissioners generally accept that items such as central heating, lifts, elevators, security and fire alarm systems, heating, ventilation, and sprinkler systems, internal communication systems and shelving do qualify as plant.

In the *Scottish and Newcastle* case Lord Lowry differentiated between items attached to the premises such as removable murals in panel form, and items which formed part of the premises such as murals painted on to the walls. He said:

> … the mural paintings … when executed or applied, are part of the walls and not plant, whereas the 'murals', being apparatus, are plant. The fact that two things perform the same function or role is not the point. One thing functions as part of the premises, the other as part of the plant.

In *Wimpy International Ltd v Warland* [1989] STC 273, the Court of Appeal upheld findings of fact by the Appeal Commissioners in relation to a restaurant premises that items including the following were not part of the premises: external fascia boards; wall panels; mirrors; fixed internal dividing screens; units of decorative brickwork fixed to walls by steel ties; colourful ceiling rails and built-in storage units and dispensers. Conversely, the court also upheld findings that the following did form part of the premises: artex (a decorative finish used to coat walls); floor tiles and other fixed floor-coverings; wall tiles; shopfronts; suspended ceilings; raised floors and stairways. It would seem correct that firedoors and the cost of fireproofing should have been regarded similarly.

In the *Wimpy* case, the Inland Revenue did not contest the eligibility of various items of soft furnishings, such as carpets and curtains as plant. This is consistent with the normal practice of the Revenue Commissioners. It was also accepted in *Wimpy* that light fittings were not an integral part of the premises (for a discussion of when expenditure thereon can qualify as plant, see below).

In *Jarrold v Good* 40 TC 681, the taxpayer used moveable partitioning to adjust the floor space in its office premises between various departments in order to meet changing business requirements. The court held that the partitioning provided flexibility of accommodation commercially required by the taxpayer; accordingly, they upheld the finding of the Appeal Commissioners that it constituted plant. The Appeal Commissioners did not regard the partitioning in the *Good* case as a temporary wall, in which case it *would* have formed part of the premises. Since the premises in this case could not themselves have been regarded as plant, this would have meant that the relevant expenditure would have failed to qualify (see also *Hunt v Henry Quick Ltd* [1992] STC 633 where moveable mezzanine storage platforms installed in a warehouse were held to be plant).

Assets supplementary/complementary to premises

Where an asset is designed simply to adorn or embellish the business premises then, it will not normally qualify as plant. This is because such an asset is not usually playing a part in the conduct of the trade. It is often said that it merely forms part of the setting. However, where as in the case of a hotel or restaurant the trade includes, the *provision* of a setting (or 'ambience'), such assets will qualify as plant. Thus, in the *IRC v Scottish & Newcastle Breweries* case, the House of Lords held that fixed metal sculptures, mural panels, decorative items such as plaques, tapestries and brassware, all ranked as plant. Whilst such items formed part of the setting, the creation of a pleasing atmosphere was a specific function of the hotel trade, and this function was fulfilled by the items in question.

The importance of considering matters in the context of the particular circumstances was emphasised by Lord Cameron in the Court of Session when he said:

> Further, the question is a practical one and the answer is … conditioned not only by reference to the nature of a trade but to the particular operations and methods of the taxpayer in the pursuance of his particular business. There can, in my opinion, be no standard pattern of permissible plant in respect of each industry, trade or profession covered by the Act. The problem to be solved in light of the general principle accepted by the courts since *Yarmouth v France* is one to be solved with reference to the particular circumstances of the case under review. I see no reason in principle, why, in the case of a taxpayer engaged in this service industry, he should not be entitled to claim that what has been provided to embellish the surroundings provided by him in his premises should be held to be as much 'plant' of his business as the beds or chairs or carpets with which he had furnished his bedrooms or lounges.

Similarly, in the *Wimpy* case, all those items which were not regarded as forming part of the premises (see above) were held to qualify as plant.

The *Scottish & Newcastle* case was distinguished in *Dunnes Stores (Oakville) Ltd v Cronin* IV ITR 68, where it was decided that a supermarket which supplied grocery and draperies was not in the business of supplying ambience. Accordingly, it was held that a demountable suspended ceiling, albeit of an attractive design, did not qualify as plant. It is notable that the court did not address the question of whether or not the ceiling formed part of the business premises, although the Circuit Court judge had concluded that this was in fact the case (see the similar conclusion in *Hampton v Forte Autogrill* [1980] STC 80 as discussed by Lord Lowry in the *Scottish & Newcastle* case). In the *Wimpy* case, the question of whether or not suspended ceilings formed part of the premises was treated as an issue of fact, depending on the particular circumstances of the case.

If the court in the *Dunnes Stores* case had simply accepted the Circuit Court judge's conclusion, this would have led to an automatic rejection of the taxpayer's claim. It is only if the ceiling did *not* form part of the premises that it was necessary to move on to the next question, and decide whether the asset performed a function in carrying on the activities of the trade, even though it also formed part of the general setting. Following the *McMullan* case, taxpayers in a similar position should succeed in answering this question affirmatively if they can show, for example, that the ceilings in question are used to establish a 'brand image', or otherwise act as a marketing tool.

An asset will not qualify as plant if it is simply a standard attachment merely needed to complete the bare premises. Thus in *J Lyons & Co Ltd v Attorney-General* [1944] Ch 281, (a non-tax case) it was held that standard lighting equipment in a restaurant was not plant. Uthwatt J, commented:

> But the presence of lamps in this building is not dictated by the particular trade there carried on, or by the fact that it is for trade purposes that the building is used. Lamps are required to enable the building to be used where natural light is insufficient. The actual lamps themselves, so far as the evidence goes, present no special features either in construction, purpose or position and, being supplied with electricity from public suppliers, they form no part of an electric lighting plant in or on the hereditament.

In other words, the lamps, although not part of the premises, were part of the general setting. Although the business of a restaurant includes the provision of ambience, the lamps, because they were not different in quantity or quality to those appropriate for any use of the building did not qualify as plant.

In the *Wimpy* case, light fittings designed to produce a high quality of light, in order to create an atmosphere of brightness and efficiency in a restaurant were held to be plant. Hoffman J, at first instance, commented:

> if the provision of such lighting is a necessary feature of the setting for the trade of preparing and serving meals the light fittings must be apparatus used in that trade.

This observation needs to be slightly qualified: it should suffice to show that the taxpayers installed a special level of lighting in order to promote his trading activities, not that it was *necessary* for him to do so.

In *Cole Bros v Phillips* [1982] STC 307, the taxpayers incurred expenditure on electrical installations in a large department store. The installation included:

(a) transformers and switch gear to reduce the voltage to a viable level, needed due to the size of the store;
(b) specially designed lighting fittings and associated cabling; and
(c) electrical wiring to a number of specific items such as fire alarms, heating and ventilation systems, sprinkler systems, lifts, elevators, the internal telephone system, etc.

As already noted, the items falling under (c) are themselves plant and the Inland Revenue did not contest that the wiring relating to those particular items also qualified as plant. Item (a) was also held to constitute plant, (ie in effect because the requirement for such equipment was due to the abnormally high energy requirements imposed by this particular trading operation), but the finding of the General Commissioners that items within (b) did not qualify (apart from special window lighting designed to showcase goods) was upheld by the House of Lords as an issue of fact. The fact that the lighting was specially designed was immaterial once it was held that it simply fulfilled the function of providing general illumination in the normal way.

The taxpayer's primary argument in the *Cole* case was that the electrical installation should be viewed as an entirety. A finding to this effect would have enabled all of the expenditure on the installation to be claimed as plant, since viewed as a whole, the installation comprised more than a standard feature of an otherwise incomplete premises. While this argument was rejected by the General Commissioners, the court made clear that this was a finding of *fact* which could just as easily have gone the other way.

In the *Wimpy* case, it was held that cold water tanks and piping which reflected a considerable greater capacity than would normally have been the case qualified as plant. In other words, the abnormal capacity of the tanks was dictated by the specific demands of the trade.

In *Leeds Permanent Building Society v Proctor* [1982] STC 821, it was held that moveable decorative screens, incorporating the taxpayer's name and crest and displayed in its various branch offices, were plant. It was held that the screens played a part in the carrying on of the trade by attracting the attention of passers-by and thus bringing in business. They were thus 'part of the shop furniture with which the trade of the [taxpayer] is carried on'.

Ancillary expenditure as plant

In general capital allowances are granted in respect of capital expenditure incurred '*on the provision* of machinery or plant', as opposed to merely 'on the acquisition' thereof.

It follows from this that the costs of installing plant and machinery should also qualify. In the *Barclay Curle* case, Lord Reid stated that the necessary costs of altering business premises in order to enable the installation of plant were equally allowable. In *Ben-Odeco v Powlson* [1978] STC 360 Lord Wilberforce and Lord Russell took the view that transportation costs also qualified. Where the item of plant is itself a structure, the costs of excavation, laying foundations, etc, will again be allowable (as in the Barclay Curle case).

In *Bolton v International Drilling Co [1983] STC 70* expenditure on obtaining the release of an option over an item of plant was held to qualify as expenditure on plant (the expenditure had been disallowed as being capital in nature – see **5.307**). However, in the *Ben-Odeco* case, interest on a loan to acquire plant was held to be too indirectly related to the acquisition of the plant in order to qualify as expenditure incurred on its provision. Such interest can however normally be claimed as a deductible expense (see **5.315**).

In the *Wimpy* case, the Inland Revenue did not contest the finding of the Appeal Commissioners that the proportion of engineers', architects' and planning fees, attributable to the installation of plant qualified as the cost of providing plant.

Intellectual property

In *Breathnach v McCann* III ITR 113 it was held that a barrister's collection of law books constituted 'plant', being chattels kept for use in the carrying on of his profession. This is an example of how far removed from ordinary usage the tax sense of the word has now become.

Whether expenditure on intellectual property rights *as such* can qualify as relating to plant is more doubtful (see *McVeigh v Sanderson* 45 TC 273, where wallpaper designs were held to be ineligible, although the cost of printing blocks incorporating and reflecting the value of those designs *did* qualify as plant). This decision raised doubts as to the correct treatment of expenditure on computer software. Firstly, there was the intangible nature of the asset involved (while often stored in physical form, eg, on a tape or disk, it has become more common for software to be downloaded directly). Secondly, what was acquired was normally a licence to use the software rather than outright ownership thereof, so that it was doubtful whether the software 'belonged' to the taxpayer. In some cases, the nature of the payment for the rights obtained would mark the expense as a deductible revenue item (eg on-going licence fees) or the ephemeral nature of the rights would mark the expenditure as revenue in nature (eg temporary licensing arrangements: see the discussion at **5.307**).

The position was resolved by TCA 1997, s 291, which provides for the granting of capital allowances in respect of expenditure incurred by a person carrying on a trade or profession, on the purchase of computer software or on the right to use or otherwise deal with computer software. The term 'software' is not defined; it seems that its ordinary meaning is capable of encompassing not only programmes but also data stored or transmitted in electronic form. This would include the rights to duplicate or further develop computer programs. The capital expenditure is regarded as expenditure on plant and machinery provided that it is acquired for the purposes of the trade or profession.

TCA 1997, s 288(1)(d) also provides for balancing allowances and charges where the right to use or otherwise deal with computer software is granted to another person for a capital sum. This is in addition to the usual events giving rise to a balancing allowance or charge.

The Revenue Commissioners accept that the original master negative of a film (including soundtrack) qualifies as plant (note *Airspace Investments Ltd v Moore* V ITR 3). Revenue practice in relation to capital allowances for video tapes in the case of a video rental business is set out in *Tax Briefing 14*.

In *Barclays Mercantile v Melluish* [1990] STC 314, Vinelott J held that in the case of a film, the item of plant was the physical asset concerned ie the master copy and not the intellectual property rights per se, such as copyright, which rendered that asset more valuable. It appears that any apportionment of value between plant and intellectual property rights in these circumstances should normally be loaded significantly towards the former (see eg *Monroe and Nock on Stamp Duty* at 3–03).

Parts of plant

TCA 1997, s 320(2) provides that any reference to machinery or plant is to include a reference to a *part* of any machinery or plant. In practice expenditure on parts of a machine will often either constitute revenue repair expenditure, or a capital renewal or improvement eligible to be included in the cost of the original asset under (TCA 1997, s 284(2)(a)(i)). For the treatment of shares in plant and machinery see **4.505**.

6.203 Wear and tear allowances

TCA 1997, s 284(1) entitles a person carrying on a trade to an annual allowance, normally referred to as the 'wear and tear' allowance, where he has incurred capital expenditure in providing machinery or plant for the purposes of the trade. A person carrying on a profession is similarly entitled to this wear and tear allowance in respect of machinery or plant provided for the purposes of his profession, as is a person incurring such expenditure on machinery or plant provided for the purposes of an office or employment held or exercised by him (TCA 1997, s 301). The allowance is based on the actual cost of the machinery or plant, as defined to include any capital expenditure on renewal, improvement or reinstatement (TCA 1997, s 284(2)).

TCA 1997, s 298(1) entitles a person who is the lessor of machinery or plant to the same annual allowance as a person carrying on a trade, provided that he bears the burden of the wear and tear; it may be that a trading lessor can base his claim under TCA 1997, s 284(1), (see **6.301**). TCA 1997, s 299(1) grants the annual allowance to a person carrying on a trade who is the lessee of machinery or plant on terms which place the burden of wear and tear directly on him (and not on the lessor) (see **6.303**). TCA 1997, s 301 extends the annual allowance to a lessor or lessee (whichever bears the burden of wear and tear) of machinery or plant used for a profession, office or employment.

The discussion which follows in relation to the wear and tear (or annual) allowance refers only to a person entitled to the allowance for machinery or plant provided for the purposes of a trade or profession. Similar principles apply where the machinery or plant is provided for use for the purposes of an office or employment by the person holding or exercising that office or employment (see also **10.305**).

Date expenditure incurred

TCA 1997, s 316(2) provides that, expenditure is deemed to be incurred for the purposes of the TCA 1997, s 284 when it becomes payable. Thus, it is the time at which payment falls due and not the time at which the legal obligation to make the payment arises which is critical.

Conditions for wear and tear allowance

A person carrying on a trade or profession in a year of assessment is entitled to a wear and tear allowance for that year in respect of any item of machinery or plant (the 'plant') if the conditions for the allowance are met.

The conditions to be met so that the allowance may be given to the person carrying on the trade or profession for any year of assessment are the following:

(a) that person has incurred capital expenditure in providing the plant for the purposes of the trade or profession;

(b) the plant was in use for those purposes at the end of the basis period for that year;

(c) the plant continued to belong to that person at the end of the basis period for that year;

(d) the plant, while it is being used for the purposes of the trade or profession, is wholly and exclusively so used (TCA 1997, s 284(1)); and

(e) the claim for the allowance is included in the annual statement which that person is required to make of the profits or gains of his trade or profession (TCA 1997, s 304(2)).

Condition (b) requires that the asset actually be in use at the end of the year of assessment and not merely available for use and/or waiting to be used (*Schapira v Kirby 46 TC 320*). Condition (d) was brought in following *Gaffney v Inspector of Taxes*, a case decided by the Circuit Court judge where it was held that an accountant's suit qualified for capital allowances as 'plant' (reported in [1989] ITR 481). The fact that the accountant wore the suit in order to be properly dressed for his employment at the same time as he wore it to satisfy his own personal need to be clothed did not disqualify the suit because, prior to the amendment, there was no requirement that it had to be wholly and exclusively used for his profession. The intention of condition (d) is to prevent any wear and tear allowance being given for an item of plant where the business use and non-business use occur simultaneously. The use of the word 'while' permits an item of plant to be used partly for business purposes and partly for non-business purposes without disqualifying it from wear and tear provided that the business and non-business uses occur at different times (even if in the same day). For example, a motor car may be used for business journeys and non-business journeys and wear and tear allowances will continue to be given.

It is generally accepted that where there is a mixture of business and non-business use of machinery or plant, capital allowances in respect thereof must be restricted to the business proportion of total use. There is however no express statutory provision to this effect. TCA 1997, s 284(1) does require that the expenditure on the asset in question must be 'for the purposes of the trade', which might perhaps be taken to imply that an apportionment is possible; however, TCA 1997, s 284(2)(ad) stipulates simply that the allowance is to be a percentage of 'the actual cost', etc of the asset in question. It has been assumed in the text that the private use restriction applied in practice is justified in law (in some cases the provisions applying prior to 1996–97 could be argued to provide a legal basis for the restriction).

Hire purchase transactions

The rationale for the current tax treatment of hire purchase transaction is open to debate. It seems that the Revenue Commissioners rely on the decision in *Darngavil v Francis* (see **5.311**) as authority for regarding hire rentals as a mixture of instalments of the purchase price of the asset and financing charges. However, until the hire purchase agreement is completed, no wear and tear allowances are strictly due to the hiree since, until that time, the relevant asset does not belong to him. In practice, the Revenue do not generally take this point and have allowed the trader to compute wear and tear allowances by reference to the full cash price of the asset at the commencement of the agreement. The difference between the total rental payments under the agreement and the cash price is treated as a revenue expense, written off over the life of the agreement (see **5.311**). Because wear and tear allowances are based on the 'actual cost' of the asset as opposed to the amount of expenditure incurred on the asset at the end of the relevant basis period (see TCA 1997, s 284(2)(ad)), this ensures that there can be no argument that the allowances should be restricted by reference to the latter amount. The fact that TCA 1997, s 284 grants allowances by reference to 'actual cost' could however in theory also allow the Revenue Commissioners to argue on this analysis that the capital sums for which a claim can be made should equate with the capital element in the lease rentals (as ascertained in accordance with the principle established in *Darngavil v Francis*). This might differ from the cash price of the asset, particularly where the option price represents more than a nominal amount. However, it seems that the Revenue would not usually take this point.

An alternative analysis is that (subject to the terms of the actual agreement) the hiree is entitled to the allowances under TCA 1997, s 299(1) as the person who bears the burden of wear and tear (see **6.304**). In this case, the lessee is deemed to have incurred the capital expenditure on the provision of the relevant asset. Thus, it seems that where the lessor has paid (or is due to pay) for the asset, then the lessee should be entitled in law to allowances in respect of the full cost of the asset. There is some support for the argument that TCA 1997, s 299(1) can cover hire purchase agreements, since TCA 1997, s 299(2) restricts the operation of the 'free depreciation' provisions relating to plant and machinery expressly to situations where the lessee 'shall or may become the owner of the plant, etc on the performance of the contract'.

Fixtures

The requirement of 'belonging' or 'ownership' may raise difficulties if items of plant within a building (or the surrounding land) are regarded as 'fixtures' in law. In broad terms, a fixture is any object which is placed on land and/or buildings in order to improve them on a permanent basis. In general, the more firmly annexed to the premises the item in question, and the greater the difficulty and damage caused in removing it, the more likely it is to be a fixture. Thus, for example, in *Maye v Revenue Commissioners* (a value added tax case) III ITR 332, a television aerial was held to be a fixture because of the degree of annexation to the building and the fact that it was designed to enhance the use of the building as a dwelling.

In many cases, fixtures will become a part of the land and buildings in law, so that ownership of the fixtures lies with the owner of the land. In *Stokes v Costain Property Investments Ltd* [1984] STC 204, a tenant installed plant which became landlord's fixtures. The result was that the landlord could not claim any capital allowances (as lessor) because it had not incurred any expenditure on providing the plant, while the tenant could not claim any capital allowances because the plant did not belong to it.

In *Melluish v BMI* [1995] STC 964, the taxpayer had leased equipment to local authorities. The equipment became fixtures on property owned by the local authorities in question. The agreement between the taxpayer and the local authorities provided that the equipment should be returned on the termination of the lease or on certain specified breaches of the term of the lease. The agreement also expressly provided that the equipment should continue to be movable property owned by the lessor. The House of Lords held that the fixtures were owned by the local authorities as owners of the land. The contingent rights of the taxpayer to remove the equipment at a future date did not mean that the local authorities ceased to own the equipment while it was attached to their land. Further, the terms agreed between the parties could not affect the correct legal analysis of what had actually happened: in other words the parties could not change the true legal nature of a fixture by 'labelling' it as movable property (see **1.407**). The House of Lords concluded that plant 'belongs to a person, if he is in law or equity, the absolute owner of it'. From this, it followed that the taxpayer was not entitled to capital allowances (for the treatment of lessors of plant see **6.301**) (see also *JC Decaux v Frances [1996] STC (SCD) 281*).

It may be noted that in the case of certain trading and agricultural fixtures, a tenant has a right to sever the fixtures (generally only during the period of the tenancy): see, in particular, Deasy's Act, s 17. The fact that the landlord retains title to such fixtures until, and if, the tenant exercises his right to sever them suggests that they belong to the landlord until, and unless, that right is exercised.

Amount of wear and tear allowance

As mentioned above the wear and tear allowance is based on the actual cost of the plant. There are certain exceptions where the taxpayer is deemed to have purchased the plant for a price equal to its open market value at the time of purchase or, in certain circumstances, for a price equal to its tax written down value in the hands of the person from whom he acquired it (see **6.103**, **6.105** and **6.106**). In any such case, the wear and tear allowance is calculated by reference to the deemed purchase price and not by reference to the actual cost of the purchase.

In certain cases the taxpayer may receive, or be due to receive, a capital grant towards his capital expenditure in providing an item of plant. In such a case, the general rule is that the wear and tear allowances are based on the actual cost of the asset in question, including any capital expenditure in the nature of renewal, improvement or reinstatement of that asset after deducting any grants or other subsidies obtained in respect thereof (TCA 1997, s 317(3)). For a fuller discussion of grants, see **6.208**.

Plant and machinery

The amount of wear and tear allowances available in respect of plant varies depending on the date that the capital expenditure is incurred. Where expenditure is incurred after 3 December 2002 on the provision of plant the amount of wear and tear allowances is 12.5 per cent of the actual cost (TCA 1997, s 284(2)(ad)). The effect of this provision is that the capital expenditure is written off as wear and tear allowances over eight years. For a discussion of the regime prior to 3 December 2002, the reader is referred to the 2009 edition of this book.

There are three qualifications to these rules in relation to wear and tear allowance. Firstly, TCA 1997, s 284(4) limits the amount of the wear and tear allowance which may be given for any year of assessment so that it cannot exceed the actual cost of the machinery or plant to the person claiming the allowance as reduced by the aggregate of all wear and tear allowances and any initial allowance (if relevant) given for previous chargeable periods in respect of the same capital expenditure. Actual cost, for this purpose, again includes any expenditure of a capital nature on the machinery or plant by way of renewal, improvement or reinstatement (ie as well as the cost of acquisition). In certain cases, the person carrying on the trade or profession may not actually receive a wear and tear allowance for one or more years of assessment in respect of an item of plant, or he may receive less than the normal wear and tear allowance for one or more periods. In any such case, TCA 1997, s 284(4) has to be applied as if a normal wear and tear allowance had been given for each year (TCA 1997, s 287(2)). This point is explained in more detail in **6.204**.

Example 6.203.1

Mr R Bluebeard has carried on a trade as a retailer of groceries for some years. He makes up annual accounts to 30 September so that his basis period for each tax year is his 12-month period of account ending in that tax year. On 4 April 2016 (in accounts year ending 30 September 2016, basis period for the tax year 2015), he purchased a new refrigeration cabinet for use in the trade at a cost of €22,000 and incurs further capital expenditure of €3,000 in transporting and installing it.[1]

His wear and tear allowances on the cabinet for the tax years 2016 and 2017, and the tax written down value at the end of each year is as follows:

Qualifying capital expenditure:	€
Cost of purchase	22,000
Transport and installation costs	3,000
Total expenditure	25,000
Wear and tear allowance 2016	
12.5% x 25,000	3,125
Tax WDV 31/12/2016	21,875
Wear and tear allowance 2017[3,4]	
12.5% x 25,000	3,125
Tax WDV 31/12/2017	18,750

Notes:

1. It is assumed that the refrigeration cabinet is used wholly and exclusively for the purposes of Mr Bluebeard's trade while it is being used for his trade. Were he to use it partially for storing his personal goods *at the same time*, he would lose the entitlement to the wear and tear allowance.
2. It is assumed that the cabinet is in use for the trade at 30 September 2016 (end of basis period for tax year 2015) as a condition for getting the allowance for 2015.
3. It is similarly assumed that the cabinet is in use for the trade at 30 September 2017 (end of basis period for tax year 2016) as a condition for getting the allowance for 2016.
4. Assuming that the cabinet continues to be used in Mr Bluebeard's trade, he will get wear and tear allowances of €3,125 for each of the next six tax years (2017 to 2022).

The second qualification is contained in TCA 1997, s 284(2)(b), which, for a person chargeable to income tax, requires the amount of the wear and tear allowance for a year of assessment to be proportionately reduced in any case where the basis period for that year is less than one year in length. The amount of the allowance in such a case is arrived at by taking the amount of the capital allowance and multiplying it by the length of the relevant basis period (in months and any fraction of a month) and dividing by 12. The resulting amount must not exceed the balance of the capital expenditure as reduced by previous wear and tear allowances and, if relevant, any previous initial allowance.

Examples of the effect of this provision are given for persons chargeable to income tax in connection with the commencement or cessation of a trade or profession respectively in **4.304** and **4.305**.

The third qualification is that contained in TCA 1997, s 283(6) which provides that, if an initial allowance is obtained for any year of assessment in respect of the capital expenditure incurred on an item of machinery or plant, then no wear and tear allowance is given for the capital expenditure on that item for the same year. TCA 1997, s 283(6) also prevents the increased wear and tear (or free depreciation) allowance (see **6.204**) being claimed on the capital expenditure for any chargeable period subsequent to that for which the initial allowance is given. As mentioned at **6.201** free depreciation and initial allowances are unlikely to be of any continuing relevance for income tax purposes.

In certain cases a wear and tear allowance under TCA 1997, s 284 is deemed to be granted. Where an individual avails of the rent a room relief under TCA 1997, s 216B or the relief in respect of the provision of certain childcare services under TCA 1997, s 216C any allowance which would be due on a claim being made is deemed to have been granted.

Registered sea fishing boats

TCA 1997, s 284(3A) provided for enhanced rates of allowances in relation to a registered sea fishing boat the expenditure on which is certified by Bord Iascaigh Mhara as being incurred for the purposes of fleet renewal in the polyvalent and beam trawl segments of the fishing fleet. The enhanced rates were in respect of capital expenditure incurred in the six years prior to 3 September 2004. For expenditure incurred up to 24 March 2004 the allowances were 50 per cent of the actual cost for the first basis period in which the normal conditions of ownership and use are met. The remainder of the allowances were available at 15 per cent (10 per cent in the final year) of the actual cost net of the allowance granted in the first basis period. The allowances for expenditure incurred on or after 24 March 2004 were available at 50 per cent in the first year and 20 per cent per annum of the actual cost net of the allowance granted in the first basis period for the following five years. As usual, the allowances were restricted *pro rata* where the basis period is less than 12 months.

FA 2008, s 30 inserted TCA 1997, s 288(6A) relating to the decommissioning of fishing vessels. Where a payment is made under the scheme for compensation in respect of the decommissioning of fishing vessels (in accordance with Council Regulation (EU) No 508/2014 of the European Parliament and of the Council of 15 May 2014 and a balancing charge is to be levied on the person on account of the receipt of the payment then the balancing charge can be spread over five years commencing in the year in which the compensation is paid (TCA 1997, s 288(6A), (1)). The provision came into effect from 17 April 2008 (SI 104/2008). The reference to Council Regulation (EU) No 508/2014 of the European Parliament and of the Council of 15 May 2014 was inserted into TCA 1997, s 288(6A) by FA 2016, s 19 and that substitution is due to take effect by Ministerial Order.

Taxis and cars for short term hire

TCA 1997, s 286(2) provides that the actual rate of the wear and tear allowance for taxis and cars used for short term hire to the public is to be 40 per cent on a reducing balance basis. The increased rate of 40 per cent applies to the annual wear and tear allowances in respect of the capital expenditure on any cars used for a qualifying purpose. The increased rate is only available for capital allowances given in taxing a trade which consists of, or includes the carrying on, of qualifying purposes. It is not therefore available to a lessor who leases the car to the person carrying on the trade.

A car is used for 'qualifying purposes' if it is used, in the ordinary course of a trade, for the purposes of:

(a) short term hire (as defined below) to members of the public; or
(b) the carriage of members of the public in a car which is a licensed public hire vehicle fitted with a taximeter (ie a proper licensed taxi).

For any car to be regarded as used by a person for qualifying purposes so as to attract the 40 per cent wear and tear rate, a minimum of 75 per cent of its total use must be for qualifying purposes. This 'qualifying use' test is made by reference to the periods of time in which the car is used or is available for use. In determining whether the test is met, the periods of time during which the car is actually used for a qualifying purpose is measured as a percentage of the total periods of time when the car is either used or is available for use for any purpose. Any period in which the car is off the road for repairs, servicing, etc may be disregarded. The mileage covered in use for a qualifying purpose or for any other purpose is not relevant.

The test must be made separately for each year of assessment to determine whether the 40 per cent rate or 12.5 per cent rate is to be given for that year of assessment. The test to determine the rate of allowance for a given year of assessment (eg 2015) is made by reference to the use of the car in the basis period for that year (eg a 12-month period of account ended 30 June 2015).

There is an exception to the 75 per cent qualifying use rule. This occurs – and the use test is deemed to be satisfied – for any basis period, if:

(a) the car is in use in that basis period for qualifying purposes for not less than 50 per cent of the total time in use or available for use; and
(b) the 75 per cent use test is met for either the immediately preceding or immediately succeeding basis period.

'Short-term hire' is defined, in relation to any car, as the hire of a car under a hire-drive agreement for a continuous period not exceeding eight weeks (a period of short term hire). A hire-drive agreement is given the same meaning as in Road Traffic Act 1961, s 3.

For the qualifying use test to be met by any car used for short term hire 75 per cent or more of the total use of the car during the relevant basis period must be used under hire-drive agreements for periods of short term hire. Any period for which the car is hired for a continuous period exceeding eight weeks or any period for which it is in use for any other purpose is counted as a period of non-qualifying use.

For the purpose of the qualifying use test, if one period of hire of a car to a person (the hirer) by another person (the car hire trader) is followed within seven days by a further period of hire to the same hirer by the same car hire trader, the two periods of hire are aggregated. If the aggregated period exceeds eight weeks, neither of the two periods counts as a period of short term hire. In applying this aggregation rule, the hire of a car (whether or not the same car) within seven days to a person connected with the hirer is treated as hire by the same car hire trader to the same hirer. The standard definition of 'connected person' applies: see **12.304**.

TCA 1997, s 286A provides wear and tear allowances for capital expenditure incurred by an individual carrying on a qualifying trade on the acquisition of a taxi licence on or before 21 November 2000 (date of taxi deregulation). A qualifying trade consists of the carriage of members of the public for reward in a vehicle in respect of which a licence has been granted, but excluding any trade which consists of the letting of a vehicle. The capital expenditure is deemed to be incurred on 21 November 1997 or if later the date of commencement of the trade. The capital expenditure could have been written off over five years or a rate of 20 per cent per annum. The section was deemed to have come into operation from 6 April 1997.

6.204 Notional wear and tear allowances

TCA 1997, s 287 has to be considered in any case where, for any year of assessment during which any item of machinery or plant has been used by a person (whether or not for the trade or profession), either no wear and tear allowance or an allowance less than the normal wear and tear allowance is actually given to that person. It is assumed that 'during' the year means 'at some time in, or throughout the year' and not simply 'throughout the year'. In any such case TCA 1997, s 287 requires that, for the purposes of TCA 1997, s 284(3), (4), a normal wear and tear allowance shall be deemed to have been given to the person in question. It appears that TCA 1997, s 287 does not apply where the asset has not been used by the person in question (including, arguably situations where the asset has been used by *another* person) at some time in a particular year of assessment. It is also somewhat odd that TCA 1997, s 287 refers to usage in the year of assessment rather than to the basis period for the year of assessment.

In effect, TCA 1997, s 287(2) requires – in applying the rules of these subsections – a 'notional wear and tear allowance', ie one which reduces the tax written down value but which provides no tax relief, to be taken into account for each relevant year of assessment in addition to the actual wear and tear allowance (if any) given for that year. The amount of the notional allowance is an amount equal to the excess of the normal wear and tear allowance for the relevant year of assessment over the amount of the wear and tear allowance (if any) actually given for that year.

For the purpose of TCA 1997, s 287, the normal wear and tear allowance for a year of assessment is defined as the wear and tear allowance (excluding any free depreciation element) which would have been made for that year if all of the following conditions had been fulfilled in relation to that year:

(a) the trade (or profession, etc) had been carried on by the person in question ever since the date he acquired the plant;

(b) the full amount of the profits or gains from the trade had been chargeable to tax since that date;

(c) the plant had been used by him solely for the purposes of the trade ever since that date;

(d) a proper claim had been duly made by him for a wear and tear allowance in respect of the plant for every relevant year of assessment; and

(e) there was no question that any sums payable to him, directly or indirectly, were in respect of or took account of the wear and tear of the plant (TCA 1997, s 287(3)).

In short, the normal wear and tear allowance for any year of assessment is determined on the assumption that a full wear and tear allowance had actually been obtained for each relevant year of assessment since the taxpayer had acquired the plant, whether or not that had actually occurred. The various circumstances in which a taxpayer may not receive a normal wear and tear allowance for a chargeable period are indicated in the above list of assumptions on which the normal wear and tear allowance has to be determined in applying TCA 1997, s 287.

For example, a person chargeable to income tax may purchase an item of plant for use in his trade, but may use it for purposes outside his trade during a part or all of the basis period for a tax year. Assume that this happens for five months in the 12-month period of account ending 28 February 2015 (the basis period for the 2015 tax year). In that case, the wear and tear allowance actually given to him for 2014 would in practice be restricted to a 7/12ths proportion of the normal wear and tear allowance; the correctness of this treatment is considered in **6.203**: *Conditions for wear and tear allowance*. It must be also borne in mind that where the asset is not in use at the end of the basis period, no wear and tear allowance may be claimed for the related year of assessment (TCA 1997, s 284(1)).

TCA 1997, s 287(2) is only relevant in applying TCA 1997, s 284(4) which, in effect, limits the total amount of wear and tear allowances available to the actual cost of the asset, net of any initial allowance (rarely relevant now).

The fact that TCA 1997, s 287(2) may require a notional allowance to be deducted for one year of assessment does not therefore affect the amount of the actual wear and tear allowance for the next chargeable period except where TCA 1997, s 284(4) comes into play. The calculation of the wear and tear allowance for each succeeding year of assessment – before applying any reduction thereof on account of use outside the trade, etc – continues to be made as 12.5 per cent of the actual cost of the plant.

TCA 1997, s 284(4), in any case where TCA 1997, s 287 applies to an item of plant, provides (in effect) that no wear and tear allowance shall be made for a basis period if any such allowance, when added to the actual and notional wear and tear allowances and any actual initial allowance made to a taxpayer for that plant for any year of assessment, will make the aggregate amount of the allowances exceed the actual cost of the plant to that taxpayer.

In practice, the best way of working out the effect of TCA 1997, s 287 in relation to TCA 1997, s 284(4) is to deal with the notional allowance, if relevant for any year of assessment, in arriving at a tax written down value at the end of that year of assessment notwithstanding that for plant, the tax written down value may not be needed until the year of assessment in which the aggregate of the actual and notional allowances would exceed the actual cost of the plant.

Example 6.204.1

On 14 April 2016, Mr B Haren purchases a new item of office machinery at a cost of €10,000 for his profession as financial and tax consultant. This machine is first used on 30 April 2016 during his basis period for 2016, the 12-month period of account ending 30 June 2016.

During his period of account ending 30 June 2017 (basis period for 2017), Mr Haren lends this item of machinery to a charity for 10 months commencing 1 July 2015 so that his actual wear and tear allowance for 2017 is reduced to a 2/12ths proportion. For all subsequent basis period, he uses the machine solely for his profession.

The capital cost is written down for tax purposes as follows:

	€	€
Actual cost (item first used 30/4/2016)		10,000
Wear and tear allowance (actual) 2016:		
€10,000 x 12.5%		1,250
Tax WDV 31/12/2016		8,750

Wear and tear allowance (actual)[1] 2017:		
€10,000 x 12.5% x 2/12ths	208	
Notional wear and tear allowance 2017:		
€1,250 – €208	1,042	1,250
Tax WDV 31/12/2017		7,500
Wear and tear allowances (actual) for later years:[2]		
2018 €10,000 x 12.5%	1,250	
2019	1,250	
2020	1,250	
2021	1,250	
2022	1,250	
2023[3]	1,250	
		7,500
Tax WDV 31/12/2023		Nil

Notes:

1. Since the wear and tear allowance actually given for 2016 (€208) is less than the normal 12.5 per cent straight line allowance for that year (€1,250), TCA 1997, s 287 requires an amount equal to the normal allowance to be deducted for 2016 (for the purpose of determining when the capital expenditure has been fully allowed so that, when this happens, no further wear and tear allowances can arise). This means a notional allowance equal to the excess of the normal allowance over the actual allowance is deducted in arriving at the tax written down value.
2. The wear and tear allowances for 2018 to 2023 assume that the machine continues to belong to Mr Haren and to be in use for the profession at the end of each basis period.
3. Since the capital expenditure will be fully allowed by actual or notional allowances when the 2023 wear and tear allowance is given, no further allowance is available for 2024 or later.

6.205 Balancing allowances and balancing charges

TCA 1997, s 288(1) requires a balancing allowance or a balancing charge to be given to or made on a person carrying on a trade if any of the following events occur in relation to any item of machinery or plant (the plant) for which any wear and tear allowance, free depreciation or initial allowance has previously been obtained by that person:

(a) the plant is sold or some other event occurs whereby the plant ceases to belong to the person carrying on the trade;

(b) the plant permanently ceases to be used for the trade, but continues to belong to the trader;

(c) there is a permanent discontinuance of the trade where the plant has not previously ceased to belong to the trader;

(d) in the case of plant and machinery consisting of computer software or the right to use/deal with computer software, the grant of a right to another person to use or deal with the whole or part of that software where the consideration is a capital sum; and

(e) the trade is treated as being permanently discontinued by reason of the change of ownership rules or by any other provision in the Act (see TCA 1997, s 320(5)).

TCA 1997, s 301(1) extends the requirement to give a balancing allowance or to make a balancing charge, and the other rules relating to such an allowance or charge, to any case in which the corresponding event occurs after any of the capital allowances on machinery or plant have previously been obtained by a person for the purposes of his profession, office or employment. Similarly, TCA 1997, s 298(2) applies the rules relating to balancing allowances and balancing charges in corresponding circumstances to a lessor of machinery or plant let on such terms that the burden of wear and tear falls directly on him (see **6.301**). In the explanations which follow, the matter is dealt with in the context of a person carrying on a trade.

For ease of explanation, any of the foregoing events which require a balancing allowance to be given to, or a balancing charge made on, the person carrying on the trade may from time to time be referred to in the discussion which follows as a 'balancing event'. Similarly, the term 'balancing adjustment' may be used to indicate either a balancing allowance or a balancing charge, whichever applies.

The purpose of this balancing adjustment is to equate the total capital allowances given in respect of the plant over its entire period of use for the trade with the trader's net capital outlay (after crediting the sale proceeds or any other residual value required by the Acts to be taken into account). The balancing allowance or charge is given to or made on the person carrying on the trade for the chargeable period related to the sale or other balancing event that requires the computation of the balancing adjustment.

For example, if a person chargeable to income tax sells an item of plant in his basis period for the tax year 2015 (say, the 12-month period of accounts to 30 June 2015), any resulting balancing allowance is given as an additional capital allowance for 2015, a balancing charge is taxable as if it were *additional income* from the trade assessable for 2015.

The calculation of the balancing adjustment for each item of plant concerned is made by comparing the 'sale, insurance, salvage or compensation monies' (see **6.104**) with the 'amount still unallowed' of the capital expenditure on the provision of the plant for the trade. The form of the computation may be broadly summarised as follows:

Capital expenditure amount still unallowed

less

sale, insurance, salvage or compensation monies

equals

balancing allowance (if positive)

or

balancing charge (if negative).

In a straightforward case, the amount still unallowed is the same as the tax written down value of the item of plant concerned at the commencement of the chargeable period related to the sale or other balancing adjustment event, ie it is the original capital expenditure in providing the plant for the trade less the sum of the wear and tear, free depreciation and initial allowances previously obtained. Assuming a sale in a normal commercial transaction, the net sale proceeds are compared with this tax written down value. If the net sale proceeds are less than the tax written down value, there is a balancing allowance; if the net sale proceeds exceed the tax written down value, there is a balancing charge.

A balancing charge will not be made where the sale, insurance, salvage or compensation proceeds in respect of machinery or plant is less than €2,000. It should be noted that this provision does not apply in the case of disposals of machinery or plant to a connected person. There is no restriction on claiming a balancing allowance where the compensation proceeds is less than €2,000.

Before dealing with less straightforward cases, a simple example may be useful to illustrate these principles. A balancing adjustment has to be calculated separately for each item of plant ceasing to be used in the trade during a particular basis period. All the balancing allowances for the same basis period are aggregated, as are the balancing charges. Any excess of balancing allowances over balancing charges are then treated as additional capital allowances for the relevant income tax year; any excess of balancing charges over balancing allowances is assessed, in effect, as additional income from the trade.

Example 6.205.1

Mr RM, who has carried on a road haulage business for a number of years, sells one of the lorries used in his trade for €16,000, as well as a computer for €600, in his accounting year ended 31 July 2016 (the basis period for his 2016 Sch D Case I assessment). A second lorry is stolen during the same year and Mr RM is paid €4,500 by his insurance company in full settlement of his loss claim. Assuming the tax written down values stated below after capital allowances were given for 2016, the balancing adjustment computations for these items are as follows:

		Lorry	
	No 1	*No 2*	*Computer*
	€	€	€
Tax WDV at 1/1/2016	13,000	5,000	200
Less:			
Sale/insurance proceeds in basis period	16,000	4,500	600
Balancing allowance 2016	–	500	–
Balancing charges 2016	3,000	–	N/A

There are therefore net balancing charges for 2016 of €2,500, ie balancing charge of €3,000 less the balancing allowance of €500. A balancing charge does not arise in relation to the sale of the computer as the sale proceeds is less than €2,000.

Meaning of 'amount still unallowed'

TCA 1997, s 292 defines the amount still unallowed of any expenditure incurred on the provision of machinery or plant as being the amount of that expenditure less the sum of the following allowances previously made in respect of the expenditure:

(a) any initial allowance made to the person who incurred it;
(b) all wear and tear allowances (including any free depreciation allowances);
(c) any wear and tear allowances made or deemed to have been made (by TCA 1997, s 296 or s 287) (see **6.207**);
(d) any scientific research allowance (see **6.601**); and
(e) any previous balancing allowances (see **6.210**).

For the purposes of determining the amount still unallowed, any part of the expenditure on providing the plant that is met directly or indirectly by the State or by *any* person on or after 6 May 1993 is disregarded. The rule does not apply to certain machinery or plant used by a company in a food processing trade (TCA 1997, s 317(4)(a)). In other words, *any* relevant capital grant or subsidies received from 6 May 1993 onwards from any agency (eg Enterprise Ireland), any statutory board, public authority or from any other third party must normally be deducted from the 'gross' capital cost of the plant. The effect of capital grants on the computation of balancing allowances, etc is discussed further in **6.208**. No further comment is required for the deductions from the net capital expenditure under items (a) and (b) above, nor for the deduction of the scientific research allowance (which has limited application in practice).

Limit to balancing charge

TCA 1997, s 288(4)(b) provides that the amount of any balancing charge in respect of any item of plant is not to exceed the aggregate of the capital allowances previously given to the person who incurred the expenditure and in whose trade the plant has been used. In applying this limit, only capital allowances actually given to the person who has carried on the trade are taken into account. Any wear and tear allowances deemed to have been made (item (c) above) are ignored. This is quite logical as the object of the balancing charge is to recapture only the excess (if any) of the aggregate capital allowances actually given over the taxpayer's net capital outlay (after crediting the sales proceeds or other residual value).

Example 6.205.2

Makepeace, a trader making up accounts each year ended 31 December, purchased an item of plant at a cost of €10,400 on 10 July 2015. No capital grants or any subsidies of any sort are received. He received normal wear and tear allowance for 2014 at a rate of 12.5 per cent. He sells the plant for €11,600 on 15 February 2016, but incurs realisation costs on €480 in advertising that the plant was for sale.

The computation of the balancing adjustment on this sale is as follows:

		Plant
	€	€
Capital expenditure (10/7/2015)		10,400
Wear and tear allowance 2015		(1,300)
		9,100
Gross sale proceeds (Y/E 31/12/2016)	11,600	
Less: expenses of realisation	(480)	
Surplus on sale		(11,120)
Balancing charge 2016:		(2,020)
Limited to allowances obtained		(1,300)

This rule that the amount of the balancing charge cannot exceed the aggregate of the capital allowances actually given to the person disposing of the plant is subject to certain exceptions. These involve cases in which an election has previously been made – where permitted by certain other provisions – for the person now disposing of the plant to have his capital allowances from the time of his acquisition based on the amount still unallowed of the capital expenditure of the person from whom he acquired the plant. In any of these cases, the upper limit to the balancing charge is – in effect – the aggregate of the capital allowances actually obtained by both the current vendor and by the previous owner of the plant.

The cases in which the normal TCA 1997, s 288(4)(b) limit to the balancing charge is varied in this way after an election to use a previous vendor's amount still unallowed are:

(a) where the current vendor had acquired the plant for use in his trade (or profession) by way of gift or at less than market value from the previous owner (see **6.206**);
(b) where an election was made under TCA 1997, s 312(5) in respect of a transfer of plant between persons under common control (see **6.105**); and
(c) where the current vendor succeeded to his trade as a beneficiary under the will or on an intestacy of a deceased person and has made an election under TCA 1997, s 295 (see **6.106**).

Example 6.205.3

Jim Sterling makes up accounts annually to 30 June, purchased a new item of plant for his trade on 13 February 2016, falling in the basis period ended 30 June 2016, ie tax year 2016, at a cost of €25,000.

Jim uses the plant in his trade until 24 May 2017, falling in the basis period ended 30 June 2017, ie tax year 2017 when he sells the plant for €8,000 to a partnership in respect of which he is the controlling partner. The open market value of the plant on 24 May 2017 is €24,000. The partnership makes up accounts annually to 31 December.

Since Jim (the seller) and the partnership (the buyer) are connected persons within TCA 1997, s 10, TCA 1997, s 312 is applied to determine the transaction price for purposes of capital allowances for both parties to the transaction (see **6.105**). Jim's tax written down value for the plant (amount still unallowed) at the time of the transfer to the partnership is arrived at as follows:

	€
Cost of plant (13/2/2016)	25,000
Capital allowances obtained:	
Wear and tear allowances – 2016	
€25,000 x 12.5%	3,125
Tax WDV at 31 December 2016	21,875

TCA 1997, s 312(2) requires the transaction price to be taken as the €24,000 market value on 24 May 2017, instead of the actual price of €8,000, but TCA 1997, s 312(5) entitles the two parties to the transaction to elect to substitute a price equal to the seller's tax written down value of €21,875 since it is lower than the market price of €24,000. The two parties to the transaction jointly make this election. The immediate consequences are as follows:

(a) since the transaction price elected (€21,875) equals Jim's amount still unallowed, he gets no balancing allowance and is not subject to any balancing charge in respect of his sale; and

(b) The partnership's capital expenditure incurred in providing the plant for its trade is deemed to be €21,875.

The partnership uses the plant in his trade from 24 May 2017 until it sells it for a net €22,000 on 11 September 2018 during the basis period ending 31/12/2018, ie the tax year 2018. The partnership's capital allowances computations in respect of this item of plant for the two tax years to 31 December 2018 are as follows:

	€
Deemed cost of acquisition (per TCA 1997, s 312(5) election)	21,875
Wear and tear allowance 2014 €21,875 x 12.5%	2,734
Tax WDV 31.12.2017	19,141

The balancing adjustment computation in respect of the sale of the plant on 11 September 2018 is as follows:

	€
Amount still unallowed (Tax WDV 31/12/2017)	19,141
Sale proceeds	22,000
Excess of proceeds over amount unallowed (A)	2,859
Limit on balancing charge (B):	
€3,125 + €2,734	5,859
Amount of balancing charge (on the partnership) for 2018	
Lower of (A) and (B)	2,859

Notes:

Due to the election made by the two parties to the transaction under TCA 1997, s 312(5), the limit to the balancing charge on the partnership is the aggregate of the capital allowances obtained by both parties.

TCA 1997, s 288(3A) outlines the method of calculating a balancing adjustment where the capital sum received is for the grant of a right to use or otherwise deal with computer software. It is necessary to apportion the tax written down value between the value of the interest granted and the value of the interest retained. TCA 1997, s 288(3A)(a) directs that the amount of the full remaining tax written down value to be taken into account in the balancing adjustment calculation is the amount arrived at by applying the formula:

$$\text{WDV} \times \frac{\text{Consideration Received}}{\text{Consideration Received} + \text{Market Value of Interest Retained}}$$

Example 6.205.4

Microsurf has developed and claimed capital allowances on computer software which now has a tax written down value of €100,000. The original qualifying cost was €160,000. Microsurf grants a licence to Softfun for a capital sum of €90,000 but retains a proprietary interest in the software. The value of this proprietary interest is €170,000.

In calculating the balancing adjustments on receipt of the capital sum for the grant of the licence, the amount of the tax written down value that may be deducted from the capital sum is:

$$100{,}000 \times \frac{90{,}000}{90{,}000 + 170{,}000} = 34{,}615$$

Consequently, a balancing charge of €55,385 arises (ie consideration €90,000 less allowable tax written down value €34,615). However, the amount of this balancing charge may be restricted (see **Example 6.205.5**).

In calculating the amount of any balancing charge, the normal rule applies viz the amount of any balancing charge cannot exceed the amount of capital allowances granted. TCA 1997, s 288(4)(c) maintains this rule in the case of computer software where an apportionment of tax written down value has occurred as described above. TCA 1997, s 288(4)(c) directs that the capital allowances granted on the computer software cost (ie €60,000 in **Example 6.205.5**) are to be apportioned between the element of the software retained and the element of the software granted in return for the capital sum. The apportionment of the allowances attributed to the grant of the right in the software is made by reference to the formula:

$$\text{Capital allowance} \times \frac{\text{Consideration received}}{\text{Consideration received} + \text{Market value of interest retained}}$$

Example 6.205.5

In **Example 6.205.4**, the consideration received was €90,000 and the market value of the interest retained by Microsurf in the computer software was €170,000. Therefore, the allowances granted to Microsurf to date which are attributable to the grant of the software in return for the consideration of €90,000 are:

$$60{,}000 \times \frac{90{,}000}{90{,}000 \times 170{,}000} = 20{,}769$$

As the amount of the allowances granted to date in respect of the element of the software over which Microsurf has granted a licence to Softfun is only €20,769, the balancing charge calculated in **Example 6.205.4** must therefore be restricted to €20,769.

In view of the fact that only part of the tax written down value has been attributed to the grant of the right to use or otherwise deal in the software that resulted in the receipt of the capital sum, and an interest in the software has been retained by the original owner, that person's tax written down value in the software must be adjusted in the period immediately following the receipt of the capital sum. TCA 1997, s 288(3A)(b) directs that the revised tax written down value remaining will be reduced by the amount treated as deductible in the balancing adjustment calculation.

Example 6.205.6

Details are the same as in **Example 6.205.4**. In calculating Microsurf's entitlement to capital allowances following the grant of the licence to Softfun, the previous tax written down value (€100,000) is reduced by the tax written down value deducted against the consideration received from Softfun. Therefore, Microsurf's tax written down value on the interest retained in the software is €65,385 (ie €100,000 less €34,615).

6.206 Balancing adjustments: cessation of trade, gifts etc

The event giving rise to a balancing allowance or charge is not always a sale or other form of disposal for which sale, insurance, salvage or compensation monies are actually received. It is necessary, therefore, to have some other figure with which the amount of the capital expenditure still unallowed can be compared to determine the balancing allowance or charge. In such cases the general rule is that the event in question is treated as if it were a sale of the plant at its open market value at the date on which the event giving rise to the balancing adjustment occurs. There are also other rules which require the market value of the plant to be used in certain circumstances even though there may be a sale or other disposal of the plant other than at such value.

Cessation of trade

When there is a permanent discontinuance of a trade including a deemed discontinuance (TCA 1997, s 320(5)), any plant remaining unsold at the date of discontinuance has to be valued in one of two ways for the balancing adjustment computation. First, if at or about the time the trade ceases, the plant is sold for no less than its open market price, then the amount of the net proceeds of that sale is taken as the sales, insurance, salvage or compensation monies for the computation. Similarly, should the plant be destroyed or should it be permanently lost at or about the time of the cessation of trade, then any insurance or other compensation monies actually received in respect of the plant, plus the net proceeds (if any) for the remains of the property, is taken as the sales, insurance, etc monies (TCA 1997, s 289(2)).

The effect of the rule in TCA 1997, s 289(2) is generally to enable the actual net sale proceeds to be used in the case where the plant is sold off within a reasonable time after the cessation of trade as part of the normal process of realising the assets. There is no specific time limit within which the sales must be made for the rule to apply. If it is evident that reasonable attempts are being made to realise the plant as soon as possible after the cessation of the trade, the net proceeds ultimately realised are likely to be accepted for the balancing adjustment computation even if it takes up to, say, six months or a year to complete the realisation.

Secondly, if after the permanent discontinuance of the trade the plant continues to belong to the person who had carried on the trade, then – unless the case is one falling within the first rule – the open market price of the plant at the date of the cessation of trade is taken as being the sale, insurance, etc monies for the balancing adjustment computation (TCA 1997, s 289(3)(a)(i)). In practice it may be difficult to estimate what is the open market price of many types of second-hand plant, unless there is an active second-hand market for them (as there is in the case of motor cars).

Gifts and sales at less than market price

In the event of any gift of plant, whether during the continuance of the trade or on its cessation, the balancing adjustment computation is made as if the plant had been sold at its open market price at the date of the gift; similarly, the open market price is deemed to be the sales consideration if the plant is sold at less than its open market price at the date of the sale (TCA 1997, s 289(3)(a)(ii)). This open market price rule is not used for a sale of plant to which the non-arm's length transaction rules of TCA 1997, s 312 apply. The latter section, which is relevant to sales of plant between persons under common control (at least one of whom must be a body of persons), has its own market price rule applicable whether the sale is at less than or more than that price (see **6.105**). By contrast, TCA 1997, s 289 does not substitute the open market price for an actual sale consideration that is higher than the open market price.

The open market price rule of TCA 1997, s 289(3) does not apply where plant is given away or sold at less than its market price to an employee or to a director in circumstances where the recipient is chargeable to income tax under the Sch E benefit in kind rules (see **Division 10**). In this event, the actual sale proceeds (if any) and not the open market price are used in calculating the employer's balancing allowance or charge (TCA 1997, s 289(4)). To the extent that the price (if any) paid by the employee or director falls short of the open market price, it is to be expected that he will be assessed to income tax on the difference under Sch E.

In some cases, the person receiving plant that is given away or sold at less than market price may be taking it with a view to using it for the purposes of a trade carried on by him (or for a profession, office, employment or leasing activity). In this event, the recipient of the plant is deemed to have purchased it at its open market price at the date of the gift or sale so that his subsequent wear and tear allowances and, when the time comes, his balancing allowance or balancing charge, is computed by reference to that price, except if the election permitted by TCA 1997, s 289(6) is made (TCA 1997, s 289(5)).

TCA 1997, s 289(6) permits the person giving away or selling the plant at less than market value and the person receiving it for use in his own trade (or profession, etc) to make an election to substitute for the open market price the amount of the former's expenditure on providing the plant that is still unallowed immediately before the gift or sale, but only if it is lower than the open market price. With effect from 6 February 2003 this election may only be made in a case where the person giving away or selling the plant is connected with the recipient. Furthermore with effect from 6 February 2003 an election cannot be made if the donor or vendor is not a company and the recipient or purchaser is a company. This anti avoidance provision prevents a balancing charge arising to a person being passed to a company and taxed at the corporate tax rate of 12.5 per cent as opposed to the person's marginal rate of tax. (See however **6.105** for circumstances in which an individual may elect under TCA 1997, s 312 for assets to transfer at tax written down value to a company which the individual controls.)

An election under TCA 1997, s 289(6) must be made jointly by the vendor (or donor) and the purchaser (or donee) in writing to the inspector. The following consequences arise where the parties elect for the transfer to take place at the amount still unallowed:

(a) the balancing adjustment computation of the vendor (or donor) uses the amount still unallowed as the sale consideration so that there is no balancing allowance or balancing charge; and

(b) the purchaser (or donee) bases his subsequent wear and tear allowances, and if relevant, any later balancing allowance, on a deemed acquisition cost equal to the vendor's amount still unallowed; but

(c) if in the event of a later sale or other balancing adjustment event affecting the purchaser (or donee) there is a balancing charge, the upper limit to that charge is the aggregate of the capital allowances on the plant that were actually made to both the vendor and the purchaser during the successive periods of use in their respective trades.

It is to be noted that the election under TCA 1997, s 289(6) requires the amount still unallowed as defined by (TCA 1997, s 292) (see **6.205**) to be used and not, if different, the tax written down value as computed for wear and tear purposes (see **6.203**).

Example 6.206.1

LB purchases a lorry at a cost of €35,000 on 5 January 2014 in his basis period for 2014 (year ended 30/4/2014). He uses it fully in his trade for that basis period. For the full year ended 30 April 2015, Mr LB lends the lorry to his son who has been carrying on a trade of his own for several years making up accounts annually to 31 December.

On 1 May 2015, in his basis period for 2016 (year ended 30/4/2016). Mr LB sells the lorry to his son for use in the latter's trade for a consideration of €15,000. The open market price of the lorry at 1 May 2015 is agreed as being €28,000. Unless the TCA 1997, s 289(6) election is made, TCA 1997, s 289(3) requires the open market price of €28,000, as the actual sale price is lower, to be used by both Mr LB and his son in their respective capital allowance computations, as follows:

	€
Mr LB	
Amount still unallowed:	
Cost price (Y/E 30/4/2014)	35,000
Wear and tear allowance obtained 2014	
€35,000 x 12.5%	(4,375)
	30,625

Notional wear and tear allowance 2015	
€35,000 x 12.5%	(4,375)
Amount still unallowed 31/12/2015	26,250
Deemed sale price	
Open market price at 1/5/2015	(28,000)
Balancing charge 2016	(1,750)
Mr LB junior (son)	
Cost of acquisition (1/5/2015):	
Open market price at 1/5/2015	28,000
Wear and tear allowance 2015 (basis period: Y/E 31/12/2015)	
28,000 x 12.5%	(3,500)
Tax WDV 31/12/2015	24,500

If Mr LB junior subsequently sells the lorry, his balancing adjustment computation will be made by reference to the capital expenditure amount of €28,000 as written down by his capital allowances for 2015 and any later years.

Take the facts of **Example 6.206.1**, but assume that Mr LB and Mr LB junior (being connected persons) elect jointly under TCA 1997, s 289(6) to substitute Mr LB's amount still unallowed (€26,250) immediately before the sale for the open market price. The consequences of this election are that no balancing charge will arise on Mr LB and Mr LB Jnr will be treated as though he had purchased the lorry for €26,250. Assume that Mr LB junior sells the lorry on 5 June 2015 (in his basis period for 2016) for €27,000, the respective capital allowance computations will now look like follows:

Mr LB	€
Amount still unallowed as per **Example 6.206.1**	26,250
Deemed sales price equal to amount still unallowed	(26,250)
Balancing adjustment 2016	Nil
Mr LB Junior	€
Amount still unallowed	26,250
Sales proceeds	(27,000)
Surplus on sale	(750)
Balancing charge limited to:	
Wear and tear allowances (actual only) – Mr LB (before sale to son)	4,375
Balancing charge 2016 (Mr LB junior)	(750)

Notes:

The balancing charge may be reduced on the basis that it is just and reasonable to do so (see **6.211**).

6.207 Balancing adjustments: notional allowances

For the purposes of the balancing adjustment computation being made for a year of assessment on the sale of an item of plant, TCA 1997, s 296(1) deems a wear and tear allowance to have been made for such one or more *previous* years of assessment in which certain circumstances existed. This deemed wear and tear allowance may be referred to as a 'notional allowance' in that it does not confer any tax relief, but reduces the amount still unallowed to be used in the computation of the balancing allowance or balancing charge on the sale. The provisions of the section also apply, in the same circumstances, in the case of a balancing event other than a sale.

The circumstances in which the capital expenditure must be written down by this notional allowance are set out in TCA 1997, s 296(2). The notional allowance must be made for each previous year of assessment in which the plant belonged to the taxpayer who incurred the expenditure on the plant, if any of the following circumstances existed in that year of assessment:

(a) the plant was not used by the taxpayer for the purposes of his trade or profession during the year of assessment;
(b) the trade or profession was not carried on by him during the year of assessment; or
(c) the trade or profession was carried on in such circumstances during the year of assessment that the full amount of the profits was not liable to be charged to tax.

If any of circumstances (a), (b) or (c) exist in the *basis period* for any year of assessment, the taxpayer will not usually obtain a normal wear and tear allowance for that year of assessment (subject in the case of (a), to the points discussed in **6.203**: *Conditions for wear and tear allowance*). The requirement to deduct the notional allowance when calculating the balancing adjustment is to ensure that the expenditure is written down to the same extent as if the plant had been used for the trade or profession throughout each year of assessment and as if the profits of the trade or profession had been fully subject to tax.

The notional allowance to be written off for any year of assessment to which TCA 1997, s 296 applies is the excess of the 'normal' wear and tear allowance for the relevant year of assessment over the wear and tear allowance (if any) actually given for that year. For this purpose, the 'normal' wear and tear allowance for any year of assessment is defined as the wear and tear allowance which would have been given to the taxpayer for that year of assessment if all of the following conditions were met (whether or not they had in fact been met) in that year and for every previous year of assessment during which the plant belonged to him:

(a) the trade had been carried on by the person in question ever since the date on which he acquired the plant now the subject of the balancing adjustment computation;
(b) he had carried on the trade since that date in circumstances under which his profits were fully chargeable to tax;
(c) the plant had been used by him solely for the purposes of the trade ever since that date (note the comments in **6.203**: *Conditions for wear and tear allowance)*; and
(d) he had made a proper claim for a wear and tear allowances in respect of the plant for every relevant chargeable period.

In most cases, the notional allowances to be deducted in arriving at the amount of the capital expenditure still unallowed for the balancing adjustment computation will be the same as those required in corresponding circumstances for the wear and tear computations for the chargeable periods over the period of use (see **6.206**).

TCA 1997, s 296(5) provides that nothing in the section is to affect the rule in TCA 1997, s 288(4), which limits any balancing charge so that it can never exceed the aggregate of the capital allowances actually received in respect of the plant sold, etc during the period of its use in the trade. In other words, in any case where the balancing adjustment computation shows a surplus of the sale, insurance, salvage or other compensation monies over the amount still unallowed (after all actual and notional allowances have been deducted), then that surplus must be compared with the total of the actual allowances obtained (ie excluding the notional allowances). The balancing charge must therefore be restricted to recapture only the actual allowances.

Example 6.207.1

Mr H Hurricane has carried on a trade as a farmer for several years making up accounts annually to 31 December. He purchases a new cultivator (at a capital cost of €50,000) which he puts into use in the farming trade on 22 March 2014 (in his basis period for 2014).

On 1 January 2015, Mr Hurricane lends the cultivator to the local rugby football club which is carrying out a ground reclamation scheme for new pitches. The machine is returned to Mr Hurricane on 30 September 2015 when he uses it again in his farming trade. He sells the machine for €48,000 on 10 January 2016.

The balancing adjustment computation for the sale in the basis period for 2016 (year ended 31 December 2016) is as follows:

		€
Cost of machine (Y/E 31/12/2014)		50,000
Deduct:		
Actual wear and tear allowance 2014		
€50,000 x 12.5%		6,250
Tax WDV 31/12/2014		43,750
Deduct:		
Actual wear and tear allowance 2015		
€50,000 x 12.5% x 3/12		1,562
Notional wear and tear allowance 2015		
€50,000 x 12.5% x 9/12[1]		4,688
Tax WDV 31/12/2015		37,500
Sale proceeds (10/1/2016)		48,000
Surplus on sale		10,500
But balancing charge cannot exceed actual allowances obtained, being:		
Wear and tear 2014 (actual)	6,250	
Wear and tear 2015 (actual)	1,562	7,812
Therefore, balancing charge 2016		7,812

Notes:

1. TCA 1997, s 296 requires such an amount of wear and tear allowance to be deducted as would have been deducted had the machine been used solely for the purpose of the trade since acquisition.

   In fact, the balancing charge of €7,812 may be reduced on the basis that it is just and reasonable to do so (see **6.211**).

TCA 1997, s 297 also requires the deduction of a notional allowance in arriving at the amount unallowed in respect of the cost of machinery or plant for the purposes of a balancing adjustment computation in another type of case. This notional allowance must be deducted in any case where both of the following conditions are fulfilled:

(a) any sums have been paid, or are to be payable, to the person concerned by way of subsidy towards, or which take account of, the wear and tear of the plant due to its use for the purposes of the trade; and
(b) the sums in question received do not fall to be taken into account as the income of the person concerned or in computing the profits of the trade (or profession, employment, etc) carried on or exercised by him.

In any such case, the amount of the expenditure unallowed immediately before the sale (or other balancing adjustment event) is reduced by a notional allowance equal to the total of the sums received by the vendor towards the wear and tear of the plant (less any part of those sums taken into account as income). The effect of any such adjustment is to decrease a balancing allowance or to create or increase a balancing charge. The amount of any such balancing charge may not, however, exceed the aggregate of the capital allowances actually obtained by the vendor during his period of use of the plant.

6.208 Treatment of capital grants

In *Cyril Lord Carpets v Schofield* 42 TC 637, it was held that where capital expenditure which had already been incurred, was subsequently reimbursed by means of a grant, it had been 'met directly or indirectly' by the payer of the grant (see also **6.103**: *Financing Arrangements*).

General rule: net expenditure treatment

The general rule under TCA 1997, s 317(3) is that all the capital allowances for machinery or plant are calculated by reference to the capital expenditure incurred in providing the plant for the trade as reduced by the amount of that expenditure which is met directly or indirectly by the State, or *by any other party*.

Example 6.208.1

Roger Lodger acquired an item of plant for €55,000. It had a tax written down value of €6,250 at the time of sale. In order to illustrate the point in relation to grants, it is assumed that a grant of €5,000 was received at the time of acquisition. Capital allowances claimed were based on the cost after deduction of the grant received ie €50,000. The plant was sold for €10,000.

Since the capital allowances on this plant have been based on the net cost of €50,000 no adjustment is required to the balancing adjustment computation. The computation is as follows:

	€
Tax WDV	6,250
Compare with net sale proceeds	10,000
Balancing charge	3,750

6.209 Rollover of balancing charges on replacement

TCA 1997, s 290 entitles a person who incurs a balancing charge on the sale of any machinery or plant to make a 'rollover' election if he replaces the plant sold. The same election may also be made if a balancing charge occurs as the result of the giving away of the plant or of its withdrawal from use in the trade, etc, but again only if the plant is replaced. There is no special definition of what constitutes a replacement and the question is interpreted fairly broadly. The replacement plant, which may be new or second-hand, need not be identical with that replaced, but should normally perform a broadly similar function. In practice, there is generally little difficulty in determining when there is a replacement.

The rollover election must be made by notice in writing to the inspector. There is no specific time limit for making the election. It is not essential that the plant be replaced in the same basis period (income tax) as that in which the sale, etc occurs. The election may be made even if the replacement plant is provided a number of months later in a different basis period.

The effect of the rollover election varies depending on whether the capital expenditure on providing the replacement plant is greater or less than the amount of the balancing charge. If the net capital expenditure on the replacement plant exceeds the balancing charge that would otherwise be made, no balancing charge at all is made; this may be referred to as a 'complete' rollover. If the balancing charge exceeds the net capital expenditure on replacement, then the balancing charge actually made is reduced to the amount of the excess; this may be called a 'partial' rollover. For the effect of a rollover election in the case of private motor vehicles costing more than a 'relevant capital limit' (which varies dependent on the date the vehicle was acquired) see **6.212**. From 1 July 2008 a rollover election in the case of private motor vehicles needs to be adjusted in line with the applicable carbon emissions level – see **6.212**.

In the case of a complete rollover, the amount of the balancing charge that would otherwise have been made is deducted from the cost of the replacement plant on which any subsequent wear and tear allowances are calculated. Further, when a balancing adjustment has to be made in respect of a later sale, etc of the replacement plant, the amount still unallowed of the expenditure on that plant prior to that sale has to be reduced by an amount equal to the balancing charge rolled over on the previous sale. This deduction is referred to as a 'deemed initial allowance'.

In the event of a partial rollover of a balancing charge on the sale, etc of any plant, no wear and tear allowance or balancing allowance may be claimed in respect of the cost of the replacement plant. Further, on the occasion of a subsequent balancing adjustment event affecting the replacement plant, the amount of the expenditure still unallowed is reduced by a deemed initial allowance of an amount equal to the capital expenditure on the replacement plant net of any government, etc grants. This always has the effect of producing a nil amount still unallowed for the balancing adjustment computation.

In the event that the replacement plant is itself replaced at a later date, any new balancing charge may be the subject of a new rollover election against the cost of the new plant. This may be continued indefinitely so long as there is replacement, if the taxpayer wishes. It should not, however, be taken that a rollover election is always to be preferred to a balancing charge. If, for example, a balancing charge arises for a year of assessment in which the taxpayer's total income is low or, perhaps, in respect of which he has a trading loss, it may be preferable to accept the balancing charge in that year so as to be able to claim higher capital allowances on the replacement plant in later years when his total income is greater.

Example 6.209.1

Arthur, a trader making up accounts annually to 31 December, sold an item of plant for €16,000 on 15 May 2016. A balancing charge of €10,000 arises on the sale.

Arthur purchases a new item of plant on 10 October 2016, which is used to replace the item sold in May 2016, at a purchase cost (including installation costs) of €25,000. In order to illustrate the point in relation to grants, it is assumed that a grant of €6,000 is obtained from Enterprise Ireland.

Since the net after grant cost of the replacement plant (€19,000) exceeds the balancing charge of €10,000 due to be made for the basis period ending 31 December 2016, Arthur is entitled to make an election under TCA 1997, s 290 to effect a complete rollover of the balancing charge.

If Arthur makes this election, the consequences are as follows:

(a) no balancing charge is made for the accounting period ending 31 December 2016 (the charge of €10,000 is 'rolled over');

(b) Arthur's capital allowances for that basis period (and subsequent accounting periods) in respect of the plant acquired in October 2016 are limited to capital expenditure reduced as follows:

	€
Cost of new plant (net of grant)	19,000
Less:	
Amount of balancing charge rolled over	10,000
Available for new capital allowances	9,000

(c) Since the new plant is in use for the trade on 31 December 2016, Arthur is entitled to a wear and tear allowance for 2015. The wear and tear allowance for the year of assessment is computed as follows:

	€
€9,000 x 12.5%	1,125

(d) When the new plant is eventually sold (or becomes the subject of any other balancing event), the balancing allowance or charge is to be based on a tax written down value based on the net after grant cost of €19,000 reduced by the aggregate of the following:

	€
Deemed initial allowance (= amount rolled over)	10,000
Wear and tear allowances: 2016	1,125
Those for subsequent years of assessment ending prior to date of sale, say sale in 2019 €1,125 x 2 =	2,250
	13,375

6.210 Successive balancing adjustments

A person may in certain circumstances be subject to more than one balancing adjustment at different times in respect of the same item of machinery or plant. Successive balancing adjustments could occur, for example, if any item of plant ceases permanently to be used in a trade but continues to belong to the trader (the first event) and, if on a later date, either the plant is subsequently sold or given away while the trade continues or the trade is permanently discontinued (the second event). Successive balancing adjustments would also be required if the plant is first withdrawn from one trade and then used by the same person in another trade and subsequently becomes subject to a balancing allowance or balancing charge on, say, a later sale in respect of the second trade.

TCA 1997, s 288(5)(b) provides that the computation of the balancing adjustment on the plant for the second event is to take account of the balancing allowance or balancing charge previously given or made in respect of the first event. The second computation is made by applying the ordinary rules to the taxpayer's original capital expenditure, grants (if any) received and the total capital allowances made or deemed to have been made to him over the entire period of his ownership. Any balancing allowance given in respect of the first event should be deducted in arriving at the amount of the expenditure still unallowed at the time of the second event, whereas any balancing charge made on the first event should be taken as increasing the amount still unallowed.

6.211 Plant used partly for non-trading purposes

An item of plant may have been used only partially in the trade and may be used for other purposes as well. Where this occurs, then it has been generally accepted that there should be a restriction of part of the capital allowances that would otherwise be given during the period of use (but note the discussion in **6.203**: *Conditions for wear and tear allowance*). However, for the purposes of calculating the balancing charge it is assumed that full wear and tear allowances were received although the amount of the charge cannot exceed allowances actually granted (see **6.207**). In such a case, for the purposes of the balancing adjustment computation when the plant is sold (or on any other balancing adjustment event), TCA 1997, s 294 requires regard to be had to all the relevant circumstances and, in particular, to the extent of the use of the plant for the non-trade purposes. The balancing allowance or charge is then given or made on such an amount as may be just and reasonable.

Example 6.211.1

Mr Thor Friday purchases a second-hand lorry on 1 April 2014 for €25,000 for use in his trade for which he has made up accounts annually to 30 September for a number of years. During his period of accounts to 30 September 2014 Mr Friday lends the lorry to his son for use outside the trade for three months, and during the year ended 30 September 2015 he lends it to him for four months. The lorry is sold on 15 October 2015 in the basis period ended 30 September 2016 (ie basis period for 2016) for €22,000. Mr Friday's wear and tear allowances for the relevant chargeable periods are made as follows:

	Disallow for non-business use	*Total allowances granted*
	€	€
2014 (Basis period: Y/E 30/9/2014):		
Cost of lorry	25,000	
Wear and tear allowance – actual	2,344	2,344
Non-trade use (3/12ths) – notional	781	
Tax WDV 31/12/2014	21,875	
2014 (Basis period: Y/E 30/9/2015):		
Wear and tear allowance – actual	2,083	2,083
Non-trade use (4/12ths) – notional	1,042	
Tax WDV 31/12/2015	18,750	4,427

Clearly a balancing charge of €3,250 arises prior to any s 294 adjustment, since the net sale proceeds of €22,000 exceed the tax written down value of €18,750 (amount still unallowed). The following is suggested as a suitable method of arriving at the just and reasonable balancing charge required by TCA 1997, s 294 having regard to the non-trade use:

(a) Ascertain the net capital outlay after crediting the sale proceeds: cost €25,000 less sale proceeds €22,000, ie a net €3,000.

(b) Deduct from this net €3,000 the appropriate part of the net capital outlay attributable to the non-trade use (seven months) over the full period of ownership (18.5 months) of the lorry, as follows:

	€
Net capital outlay	3,000
Less:	
Non-trade proportion	
$3{,}000 \times \frac{7}{18.5}$	1,135
Net capital outlay for trade use	1,865

(c) The balancing charge to be made (2016) may now be calculated as follows:

	€
Net capital outlay for trade use	1,865
Actual capital allowances given	4,427
Balancing charge 2016	2,562

6.212 Restriction of capital allowances on private cars

FA 2008, s 31(1) inserted TCA 1997, Pt 11C. These provisions linked the availability of capital allowances and leasing expenses to the carbon emissions level of cars. They came into effect from 1 July 2008 and do not apply to short term hire (taxi) vehicles or vehicles acquired for testing.

The normal principle that capital allowances are given in respect of the full capital cost incurred in providing machinery or plant for the use in a trade, profession, office or employment was, for many years, subject to the 'private motor vehicles' restriction in the case of such vehicles costing more than an amount specified in TCA 1997, s 373(2) (TCA 1997, s 374) ie the 'specified amount'.

If the capital expenditure incurred (or, deemed to be incurred) in providing a private motor vehicle for the trade exceeded the relevant capital limit existing at the time the expenditure was incurred, then all the capital allowances over the entire period of use of that motor vehicle in the trade, etc were based on an amount equal to that capital limit. The fact that the capital limit might be subsequently increased for expenditure incurred at a later date did not alter the limit for the vehicles provided before that date and subject to a lower capital limit.

For motor vehicles the restriction of TCA 1997, s 374 in fact applied for wear and tear allowances under TCA 1997, s 284, and for any balancing allowance or balancing charge under TCA 1997, s 288.

The capital allowances restriction of TCA 1997, s 374 applied to all private motor vehicles within the definition provided by TCA 1997, s 373(1), namely mechanically propelled road vehicles constructed or adapted for the carriage of passengers, other than vehicles of a type not commonly used as a private vehicle and unsuitable to be so used.

In *Tapper v Eyre* 43 TC 720, it was held that a mini-van used solely for business purposes was nevertheless a vehicle commonly used as a private vehicle (see, to similar effect *Laing v IRC* 44 TC 682). A different conclusion was reached in *Roberts v Granada TV Rental* 46 TC 295, where Megarry J commented on the definition as follows:

> 'Private' means 'domestic, pleasure or social purposes'. 'Suitable' seems to me to bear the meaning of 'fitted for, adapted or appropriate', and 'unsuitable' the opposite meaning.

> There was ample evidence before the Commissioners to support a finding of unsuitability, and I cannot see that this is displaced or destroyed by the statistical evidence, even when read in the way which is most favourable to the Crown … 'Commonly' I take to mean 'usually' or 'ordinarily' or 'generally', though not necessarily in the sense of constituting a majority … I must not be taken as accepting that the percentage approach is necessarily right. If only fifty vehicles of a particular type had been imported into this country and forty-five of them were used as private vehicles, I think it at least possible that it could be said of the other five that 'they are of a type not commonly used as private vehicles'. One swallow does not make a summer, nor it may be said, does the use of a mere forty-five vehicles for a particular purpose amount to a common use for that purpose.

In the *Roberts* case, Megarry J also took the view that even if a majority of vehicles were registered for private use, this did not mean that they were necessarily *suitable* for such use; the factual evidence in this case rebutted any such inference.

In *S & U Stores v Gordon* [1970] 1 WLR 889 a similar decision was reached to that in the *Roberts* case. Megarry J, who also heard this case, emphasised that the test was one of suitability and not usability; he commented:

> True, the vans are not unusable as private vehicles, but the evidence … shows that those who had bought these vans for private use soon provided extra seats in them for passengers … this seems to me to amount to evidence of some weight as to the unsuitability of the type in its natural state for use as private vehicles. A vehicle of a type unsuitable for use for a purpose may, of course, be suitable for adaptation so as to make it into a type suitable for that use; but the test is suitability (or unsuitability) of the type for use, not for adaptation.

In *Bourne v Auto School of Motoring (Norwich)* 42 TC 217, it was held that a family car fitted with dual controls (which could have been removed within two hours) were of a type not commonly used on a private vehicle and unsuitable to be so used.

In *Gurney v Richards* [1989] STC 682, it was held that a saloon car fitted with a flashing light for use by a fireman was not commonly used as a private vehicle and was unsuitable for such use. The court relied on the fact that it would be illegal for anyone other than a member of the emergency services to drive a vehicle adapted in this way. It was irrelevant that the *taxpayer* could make private use of the vehicle.

It may be noted that the question of whether or not a motor vehicle falls within TCA 1997, s 373(1) is an issue of fact, so that a decision of the Appeal Commissioners (or Circuit Court judge, as appropriate) will be overturned only if it is wholly unreasonable: see **2.204**.

The capital allowances restrictions under TCA 1997, s 374(1) did not apply to any vehicle which is provided, or as the case may be, hired, wholly or mainly for the purpose of hire to, or for the carriage of, members of the public in the ordinary course of trade (TCA 1997, s 380(1)). A car used in the course of a trade of providing driving instruction was held not to be subject to a contract of hire in *Frazer v Trebilcock* 42 TC 217.

It follows from the definition of TCA 1997, s 373(1) that there was no restriction in the capital allowances for lorries and other genuine commercial vehicles which are not constructed or adapted for the carriage of passengers, nor for vehicles provided or leased wholly or mainly for the purpose of hire to members of the public or for the purpose of the carriage of members of the public (eg buses).

The capital limit for capital allowances on private motor vehicles corresponded to the 'specified amount' which, in the case of a leased or hired car, was applied under TCA 1997, s 377 to reduce the deduction for the lease rents or other costs of hiring. In other words, the effect of the legislation was to provide corresponding restrictions whether the private motor vehicles are provided for the trade or profession of the taxpayer by purchase or by leasing. Also, a corresponding restriction applied to any deduction against profits for the cost of replacing private motor vehicles where a taxpayer uses the renewals basis (see **5.309, 5.312**).

Specified amount

For capital expenditure on a private motor vehicle, TCA 1997, s 374 provided that the maximum capital cost eligible for capital allowances was the relevant capital limit. TCA 1997, s 380K(4) provides that a specified amount of €24,000 applies where expenditure is incurred in a basis period that ends on or after 1 January 2007.

Since it is the capital limit in force at the time the capital expenditure is incurred which normally governs the capital allowances (and any balancing allowance or charge on the disposal, etc) over the entire period of use in the trade, etc, it is also necessary to detail the various capital limits which have applied for expenditure on private motor vehicles incurred at various dates prior to a basis period ending on or after 1 January 2007, as follows:

Date relevant expenditure incurred	*Relevant capital limit*
	€
Expenditure incurred in a basis period ending on or after 1 January 2002 and before 1 January 2006.	22,000.00
Expenditure incurred in a basis period ending on or after 1 January 2006 and before 1 January 2007	23,000.00

Notes

It appears clear that expenditure should be regarded as being incurred for these purposes when it falls due and payable; TCA 1997, s 373(3) requires that TCA 1997, ss 373–374 should be construed as one with TCA 1997, Pt 9, which includes the definition of 'incurred' in TCA 1997, s 316(2).

Wear and tear allowances

The wear and tear allowances for motor vehicles used in a trade, profession, office or employment were calculated under the ordinary rules for calculating capital allowances except that the allowances are based only on the first €24,000 (in the case of expenditure incurred in a basis period ending on or after 1 January 2007) of the capital expenditure incurred in providing the car. For any car costing less than the relevant capital limit, the full wear and tear allowances are given on the actual capital expenditure incurred. The previous limits were relevant where it was necessary to use the original cost of the car for more up to date purposes (eg in the balancing allowance or charge computation).

With effect for vehicles provided on or after 1 July 2008, the above system is modified so that the wear and tear allowances for motor vehicles used in a trade, profession or employment are set with reference to both the specified amount and the applicable vehicle category (see table below):

(a) for vehicles in Category A, B or C the actual cost of the vehicle used to calculate wear and tear allowances is taken to be equal to the specified amount (ie €24,000) (TCA 1997, s 380L(3)(a));

(b) for vehicles in Category D or E the actual cost of the vehicle used to calculate wear and tear allowances is taken to be, where the retail price when the vehicle was made is less than or equal to the specified amount (€24,000) 50 per cent of that price and where the retail price is greater than the specified amount 50 per cent of the specified amount (€24,000) (TCA 1997, s 380L(3)(b));

(c) for vehicles in Category F or G the actual cost of the vehicle used to calculate wear and tear allowances is taken to be nil (TCA 1997, s 380L(3)(c)).

CO_2 emissions means the level of carbon dioxide emissions for a vehicle measured in accordance with the provisions of Council Directive 80/1268/EEC of 16 December 1980 (as amended) and listed in Annex VIII of Council Directive 70/156/EEC of 6 February 1970 (as amended) and contained in the relevant EC type approval certificate or EC certificate of conformity or any other appropriate documentation. The following table sets out the vehicle categories and their reference to CO_2 emissions confirmed by reference to the relevant EC type certificate or EC certificate of conformity (TCA 1997, s 380K(2)).

CO2 Emissions (CO2 g/km)	Vehicle Category
0g/km up to and including 120g/km	A
More than 120g/km up to and including 140g/km	B
More than 140g/km up to and including 155g/km	C
More than 155g/km up to and including 170g/km	D
More than 170g/km up to and including 190g/km	E
More than 190g/km up to and including 225g/km	F
More than 225g/km	G

Where the Revenue are not satisfied with CO_2 emissions relating to a vehicle by reference to any document other than the two types of certificate listed above or where no document is provided, the vehicle shall be treated as a Category G vehicle (TCA 1997, s 380K(3)).

Balancing allowances and balancing charges

In the case of a vehicle where the related expenditure was incurred in a basis period ending on or after 1 July 2008, any balancing allowance or balancing charge is adjusted with reference to the vehicle category:

(a) for vehicles in Category A, B or C the sale, insurance, salvage or compensation proceeds are increased or reduced in the proportion which the specified amount bears to the actual amount of expenditure;

(b) for vehicles in Category D or E where the retail price when the vehicle was made was less than or equal to the specified amount (€24,000), the sale, insurance, salvage or compensation proceeds are reduced by 50 per cent and where expenditure incurred was greater than the specified amount the balancing charge or allowance is reduced in the applicable proportion;

(c) for vehicles in Category F or G the sale, insurance, salvage or compensation proceeds are deemed to be nil (TCA 1997, s 380L(3)).

Example 6.212.1

On 1 August 2015 Boylan purchases a new car for his own use in his profession as an auctioneer. The purchase price is €45,000. The car is fully used in the business until it is sold for €25,000 on 31 July 2018. Boylan makes up the accounts of his business annually to

31 December. His capital allowances computations for the relevant years are as follows depending on which of the three categories the vehicle falls under:

Vehicle Category	*Class A, B or C*	*Class D or E*	*Class F or G*
	12.5%	*12.5%*	*12.5%*
	€	€	€
Capital expenditure (Y/E 31/12/2015)	45,000	45,000	45,000
Cost allowable for capital allowances	24,000	12,000	0
Less: Wear and tear allowances:			
2015	3,000	1,500	0
2016	3,000	1,500	0
2017	3,000	1,500	0
Tax WDV at 31/12/2017	15,000	7,500	0
$25{,}000 \times \frac{24{,}000}{45{,}000}$			
$25{,}000 \times \frac{12{,}000}{45{,}000}$			
$25{,}000 \times \frac{0}{45{,}000}$	13,333	6,667	
Balancing allowance/(charge) 2018	1,667	833	

Acquisition at market value or written down value etc

Certain rules require the open market price (or another person's tax written down value) to be substituted for the trader's actual acquisition cost. These have been discussed in relation to machinery and plant generally at **6.105**, **6.106** and **6.208**.

The types of acquisition of private motor cars requiring this adjustment to be made are:

(a) where the car is acquired in a transaction covered by TCA 1997, s 312, ie one solely or mainly to obtain capital allowances or one between persons under common control one of whom must be a body of persons in circumstances where TCA 1997, s 289(5) or s 289(6) is applied (see **6.105**);

(b) where the prior owner gave or sold the car at less than its market value to the person acquiring it for use in his trade in circumstances where TCA 1997, s 312 is applied (see **6.105**); or

(c) where the car is acquired, without being purchased, by a person succeeding to a trade previously carried on by the prior owner in circumstances where TCA 1997, s 313(1) is applied (see **6.106**).

In the case of a vehicle where the initial expenditure was incurred in a basis period ending on or after 1 July 2008, and where any of these special rules would otherwise require the new owner to base his capital allowances on the open market price at the date of acquisition, or the amount of the transferor's unallowed expenditure on the vehicle, as the case may be, then the open market price of the vehicle or the amount of expenditure originally incurred by the transferor, as the case may be, is deemed to be the following:

(a) for vehicles in Category A, B or C, the specified amount;

(b) for vehicles in Category D or E where the retail price was less than or equal to the specified amount, 50 per cent of such expenditure, and where expenditure incurred was greater than the specified amount 50 per cent of the specified amount;

(c) for vehicles in Category F or G, nil.

In any subsequent sale etc by the new owner, he is deemed to have incurred the expenditure incurred by the original owner for the purposes of computing any subsequent balancing allowance or charge on a disposal by him and so on (TCA 1997, s 380L(5)).

Example 6.212.2

Mr LA, who makes accounts up to 31 July, purchased a new motor car for his profession costing €35,000 in August 2010, ie in the basis period ending 31/07/2011, assessable in tax year 2011. In May 2014, ie in the basis period ending 31/07/2014, assessable in tax year 2014, he sold the car to a connected person, Cow Partnership for €6,000 when its market value was €14,000. Cow Partnership's accounts are also made up to 31 July. Mr LA had obtained wear and tear allowances at the rate of 12.5 per cent based on 50 per cent of the specified amount, ie €12,000, resulting in a tax written down value at 31 December 2013 of €7,500. Since the parties are connected, TCA 1997, s 312 applies to the sale between them in May 2014. Assuming no election is made under TCA 1997, s 312(5) to substitute a lower tax written down value, Cow Partnership is required to bring the car into its capital allowance computations at €12,000.

Assume now that Cow Partnership uses the car for its trade for the remainder of the year ended 31 July 2014 and for the year ended 31 July 2015, but that during the year ended 31 July 2016 the car is damaged in an accident and is sold for €1,000. The company only had third party insurance so that no insurance or any other compensation for the loss is received. Cow Partnership's capital allowances are determined as follows:

	€
Deemed acquisition cost qualifying for allowances:	
As above (50% of the specified amount)	12,000
Wear and tear allowance – 2014 & 2015: 2 x 12,000 x 12.5%=	(3,000)
WDV 31/12/2015	9,000
Sale: €1,000 x (€12,000/€35,000)=	343
Balancing allowance – 31/07/2016	8,657

The right given by TCA 1997, s 290 to a person replacing any machinery or plant to elect to rollover any balancing charge arising on the sale of the replaced plant has been discussed in **6.209**. In the event that a taxpayer is replacing a motor car affected by the rules of TCA 1997, s 380L, the rollover rules are applied as if the capital expenditure incurred by the person replacing the car was restricted to the specified amount as adjusted by reference to the relevant carbon emissions limit (assuming the replacement cost exceeded that limit) (TCA 1997, s 380L(6)).

Example 6.212.3

On 19 May 2013 in his accounting year ending 31 July 2013 (basis period for tax year 2013), Mr HC acquires a new car costing €30,000 and with CO_2 emissions of 125 g/km for use in his trade.[1] The specified amount of €24,000 applied. On 25 February 2015 (in his accounting year ending 31 July 2015, basis period for 2015), he trades in the car for €25,000 and replaces it with a new 'Class A' car costing €35,000.[2]

Mr HC's capital allowances in respect of these cars for the tax years 2013 to 2014 are as follows:

	€
Cost of first car (19/5/2013)	30,000
Cost allowed for capital allowances	24,000
Wear and tear allowance 2013	(3,000)
Wear and tear allowance 2014	(3,000)
Tax WDV 31/12/2014	18,000
Sale proceeds €25,000 x (€24,000/€30,000)=	(20,000)
Balancing charge 2015 (if no rollover election)	(2,000)

Owing to a particularly good trading year ended 31 July 2015 Mr HC's total income for 2015 is already such as to make him taxable at a higher rate of income tax than usual. He decides to elect under TCA 1997, s 290 to roll over this balancing charge of €2,000, thus avoiding any further increase in his total income for that year. Since the expenditure (€35,000) on the replacement car (as limited to €24,000) exceeds the amount of the balancing charge, there is a complete rollover.

Mr NC's capital allowances for 2015 on the replacement car are determined as follows:

	€
Cost of car (25/2/2015): €35,000 limited to	24,000
Less:	
Balancing charge rolled over	2,000
Net expenditure for capital allowances	22,000
Wear and tear allowance 2015 €22,000 x 12.5%	(2,750)
Tax WDV 31/12/2015	19,250

Notes:

1. Since the car is purchased in a basis period that will end on or after 1 July 2008 and it qualifies as 'class B', the relevant capital limit is €24,000 – TCA 1997, s 373(2)(p); TCA 1997, s 380L(3).
2. Since the replacement car is purchased in a basis period that will end on or after 1 July 2008 and it qualifies as 'class A', the relevant capital limit is €24,000 – TCA 1997, s 373(2)(p); TCA 1997, s 380L(3).

6.3 Leased Machinery or Plant

6.301 Capital allowances for lessors

A person who owns any machinery or plant is entitled to claim wear and tear allowances if he leases it to another person and if 'the burden of the wear and tear' in respect of the plant falls directly on the lessor (TCA 1997, s 298(1)). Similarly, a lessor who has obtained capital allowances on any plant is entitled to a balancing allowance, or is subject to a balancing charge, when the plant is disposed of or ceases to be leased by him (TCA 1997, s 298(2)). The question of when the lessor is regarded as bearing the burden of the wear and tear is discussed in **6.304**.

The relevant legislation is worded in terms of permitting the lessor who bears the burden of wear and tear in respect of any plant to claim wear and tear allowances *as if* during the period of the letting, the plant were in use for the purposes of a trade carried on by him. It might be thought that this wording implies that use for the purposes of leasing does not qualify as use for the purposes of a wear and tear allowance, ie that only *physical* use in the course of a trade can so qualify, so that even a trading lessor must rely on TCA 1997, s 298(1) in order to claim the allowance. However, in practice, the Revenue Commissioners accept that wear and tear allowances may be claimed by a trading lessor under TCA 1997, s 284(1) ie on the basis that the relevant asset is in use for the purpose of a trade of leasing. It may be observed that it is difficult to see how the functional test (used in determining whether or not an asset qualifies as plant: see **6.202**) could ever be failed in the case of a leased asset, if TCA 1997, s 284(1) is in fact applicable. In *Barclays Mercantile Business Finance Ltd v Mawson* [2004] UKHL 51, the House of Lords held that Barclays Mercantile Business Finance was entitled to writing down allowances under the UK equivalent of TCA 1997, s 284(1) for capital expenditure incurred on plant purchased under a sale and lease back arrangement which was entered into wholly and exclusively for the purposes of its trade of finance leasing.

Even if it is accepted that TCA 1997, s 284(1) applies to a trading lessor, TCA 1997, s 299(1) should remain potentially relevant. Thus, if a trading lessor leases an asset to a lessee under a finance lease who bears the burden of wear and tear, it is the lessee who will be able to claim the allowances by virtue of TCA 1997, s 299(1) subject to certain conditions being satisfied (see **6.303**).

TCA 1997, s 298(1) does of course make clear that it is not essential for the lessor of any plant to be carrying on a trade of leasing machinery or plant for him to obtain the capital allowances. If he in fact does carry on a trade consisting of or including the leasing of plant, he is entitled to the capital allowances and is subject to any balancing charges in the ordinary way in taxing the profits of that trade under Sch D Case I (or under Sch D Case III if the leasing trade is carried on wholly abroad – see **13.103**) This applies not only to a specialist machinery/plant leasing trade (including vehicle leasing), but also to banks and similar financial institutions that include plant leasing as part of their trades. It is also possible for individuals and other persons to carry on leasing activities in circumstances giving rise to the conclusion that they are doing so in the course of trade. It is a question of fact in each case whether or not a person leasing plant is doing so as a trade (see **4.102**).

When a person leases out machinery or plant otherwise than in the course of a trade, the income derived from the leasing is generally taxable under Sch D Case IV. However, where the plant and machinery are fixtures in a building (and thus constitute part of the building in law: see *Stokes v Costain* [1984] STC 204, discussed at **6.203**, under *Fixtures*) the income attributable to them should normally in strictness be chargeable under Sch D Case V. In practice, the Revenue accept that where a 'composite payment' made under a lease refers both to a building and to plant, the entire payment is chargeable under Sch D Case V (irrespective of whether or not the plant qualifies as a fixture): *Tax Briefing 42*.

If there is a significant interest deduction against the rental income under TCA 1997, s 97, the benefit of capital allowances is unlikely to be significant. Although with falling interest rates and the restriction on specified reliefs for high income individuals, the availability of plant and machinery capital allowances is more important

In *MacSaga Investment Co Ltd v Lupton* 44 TC 659, it was held that the expression plant and machinery applied only to assets used in a trade. As noted above, it seems to be accepted that a trading lessor is regarded as using the relevant plant in his leasing trade. It seems to follow that, in the case of a non-trading lessor, it is necessary that the plant should be in use in a trade (profession/employment or office) of the lessee. This is the view of the Revenue Commissioners (note in this respect, the treatment of plant in multi-tenanted buildings: see *Tax Briefing 42*). The remarks that follow concern the treatment of such a non-trading lessor who must, if he wishes to obtain the capital allowances to which he is entitled on the leased plant, make a claim to the inspector within 24 months of the end of each relevant chargeable period (TCA 1997, s 298(1)). The requirement for a claim to be made within this 24 month time limit applies to a lessor of plant taxable under Sch D Case IV on the letting income. It contrasts with the treatment of the trading lessor who, if a person chargeable to income tax, is not subject to a specific time limit for claiming the capital allowances.

Wear and tear allowances and any balancing allowances are given to the non-trading lessor by way of discharge or repayment of tax and are available primarily against his income from the letting of machinery or plant (TCA 1997, s 300(2)), ie as assessable normally under Sch D Case IV. Any balancing charges made on such a lessor are made under Sch D Case IV (TCA 1997, s 300(3)). This means that the lessor's capital allowances for a given year of assessment (income tax) must first be deducted from the plant leasing income assessable for that year to the extent that the income equals or exceeds the capital allowances claimed.

Where plant is leased with a commercial building in return for a composite payment treated as fully taxable under Sch D Case V (see above), the plant leasing element of the Sch D Case V income should in strictness be separately identified for the purposes of TCA 1997, s 305(1)(a). In practice, the Revenue will allow the taxpayer to offset capital allowances on such plant primarily against the total Case V income from the building and the plant (*Tax Briefing 42*). The Revenue view is that TCA 1997, s 300(2) provides that the allowances available under TCA 1997, s 298 are available primarily against income from the letting of the plant and any excess can be relieved by means of discharge or repayment of tax. As excess capital allowances on plant leasing are restricted, the capital allowances are available against the plant letting income only. In order to avoid unnecessary apportionments the Revenue will allow the capital allowances against the rental income from that building. Some practitioners are of the view that the capital allowances are available against all Case V income, due to the single source concept. The same restriction does not apply to capital allowances on residential property as TCA 1997, s 300(4) specifically provides that capital allowances which are available under TCA 1997, s 284(6) are available against Case V income.

The quantum of expenditure attributable to plant depends on the extent of the fit out. For example a warehouse would have less plant than a modern office building. It should be remembered that a balancing charge (or balancing allowance) would arise on a sale of the building. A Revenue Precedent states that a professional valuation should be sought to identify the plant element.

It should be noted that expenditure on plant and machinery regarded as integral to a building which itself qualifies for capital allowances may be treated as forming part of the expenditure on that building: (see **6.404**); accordingly, the present discussion will not be relevant in those circumstances.

The allocation of the capital allowances or balancing charges of a lessor chargeable to income tax to years of assessment is much simpler where the allowances or charges are given or made under Sch D Case IV than under Sch D Case I. The Sch D Case IV basis period for each year of assessment is always the tax year itself, since the measure of the income taxable under that Case is in all cases the actual income arising in the tax year. It follows that a wear and tear allowance is given for a particular year of assessment if the plant in question was leased at the end of the year, ie on 31 December.

The Revenue Statement on vehicle leasing issued in July 1981, while in practice is likely to be of most relevance to vehicle leases, is potentially relevant to all leased assets. The Statement is directed at leases where at the completion of the primary leasing period the leased asset is transferred to the lessee or a connected person at a substantial undervalue, or is re-leased at a nominal rental. The Revenue state their position as follows in regard to the lessor in such circumstances:

So far as the lessor is concerned, it may be appropriate to regard the *transaction as a sale of stock in trade* rather than the lease of an asset qualifying for capital allowances. If capital allowances are given, the provisions of TCA 1997, s 289(2) may require the open market value of the vehicle to be brought into the taxation computation at the end of the lease rather than the sale proceeds. In certain circumstances the right of the lessor to claim wear and tear allowances may be in doubt, having regard to TCA 1997, s 298(1), on the ground that the burden of the wear and tear did not fall directly on the lessor.

For a discussion of the Revenue-approved procedures for the purchase of a leased asset by the lessee at the end of the primary leasing period (entailing a sale by the lessor of the asset at market value to the Leased Asset Disposal Company (LADCO)) see Revenue Staff Instruction (4.6.4) in the context of finance leasing and companies. Supplementary Revenue guidance has also since been provided in *Revenue SOP IT 52 (2004)* setting out the tax treatment of finance leases for lessees.

6.302 Relief for lessor's unused capital allowances

In the absence of any overriding statutory restrictions, a person chargeable to income tax who leased machinery or plant in the course of a trade of leasing would automatically be entitled to relief for any excess capital allowances in respect of the leased plant in one of two ways. If the capital allowances for the leased plant for any year of assessment exceeded the Sch D Case I income from the trade for that year, the excess could either be carried forward for set off against the leasing trade income for the next tax year (and for succeeding years) in the same way as for other types of trade (see **4.403**). Alternatively, the excess capital allowances for any tax year could be included in a claim under TCA 1997, s 381 for set off against the taxpayer's income from all sources for the same year in the manner described in **4.405**. In other words, the normal rules for capital allowances in respect of any trade would apply. However, as set out in detail in **6.305** the ability to claim sideways offset for excess capital allowances on leased plant is significantly restricted. The most recent restrictions have been the curtailment of sideways offset for non-active traders in TCA 1997, ss 381B and 381C (see **4.413**).

Similarly, a non-trading lessor of plant taxable under Sch D Case IV (or Case V), who could not fully set off the capital allowances claimed against his plant leasing income for any tax year, would be able to obtain relief for the excess capital allowances by carrying them forward and adding them to the corresponding capital allowances on leased plant for the next tax year and, if necessary, for succeeding tax years, and set off against the plant leasing income for the year to which it was carried forward (TCA 1997, s 305(1)(a)). An election could also have been made to have any capital allowances (other than an initial allowance) in excess of the Sch D Case IV plant leasing income for any tax year set off against the taxpayer's income from all sources for the same year (TCA 1997, s 305(1)(b)). **6.305** sets out the restrictions on the ability to claim sideways offset for excess capital allowances. If it is possible to make such a claim, in determining the excess capital allowances for any year available for set off under this election, any capital allowances carried forward from any previous year would have to be excluded. The election would have to be made by notice in writing to the inspector no later than 24 months after the end of the tax year to which it relates. Any capital allowances for the year which could not be absorbed by the taxpayer's other income for the same year would remain eligible for carry forward for set off against future plant leasing income taxable under Sch D Case IV.

The non-trading lessor's right to carry forward unused wear and tear allowances or balancing allowances claimed in respect of the leased plant generally remains an automatic one not requiring a specific claim within any time limit. Any capital allowances carried forward under this rule (and added to the corresponding leased plant allowances for the next tax year) must be set off against the next available Sch D Case IV (or Case V) leasing income. To the extent that the leasing income for the next chargeable period is insufficient to absorb the amount brought forward, the unused balance is carried forward without time limit to successive chargeable periods until fully absorbed by subsequent Sch D Case IV leasing income.

However, TCA 1997, s 403 severely limits the circumstances in which any taxpayer may use excess capital allowances on leased plant in a claim for set off against his income from all sources. Corresponding rules apply whether the plant is leased in the course of a trade of leasing or by a person chargeable to tax under Sch D Case IV (or Case V) in respect of plant leasing income.

The current rules apply, subject to certain exceptions, to prevent any person who leases machinery or plant in the course of *any* trade from setting off capital allowances on the leased plant (other than certain excepted capital allowances) against any trading or other income not derived from the leasing of plant. The current rules are discussed in detail in **6.305**.

The current rules generally apply also to prevent a non-trading lessor of machinery or plant from using an election under TCA 1997, s 305(1)(b) from setting off his capital allowances (other than certain excepted allowances) on plant provided for leasing against any income other than plant leasing income. However, the non-trading lessor remains entitled to include any excepted capital allowances in a claim for set off against his income from all sources. Again, the current rules are dealt with more fully in **6.305**.

Both the trading and the non-trading lessor remain generally entitled to carry forward, for use in the next and, if necessary, subsequent chargeable period(s), any capital allowances on leased plant to the extent that the allowances cannot be fully used against the plant leasing income for the chargeable period to which they relate. The right to carry forward any unused allowances in respect of the leased plant is an automatic one and does not require a specific claim within any time limit (TCA 1997, s 305(1)(a)).

The manner in which a trading lessor chargeable to income tax utilises his leased plant capital allowances brought forward is the same as that for any other capital allowances of a trade (see **4.403**), but with the restriction that the leased plant capital allowances brought forward (other than any excepted capital allowances) can only be set off against the leasing trade income for the next tax year (and, if necessary, later years). Any excepted capital allowances brought forward may be set off against *any* income of the trade for the next year (and later years).

In the case of the non-trading lessor chargeable to income tax, any capital allowances brought forward are added to the corresponding leased plant allowances for the next tax year and must be set off against the next available Sch D Case IV (or Case V) leasing income (note the treatment of income from leasing plant with a building described above). To the extent that the leasing income for the next tax year is insufficient to absorb the amount brought forward, the unused balance is carried forward without time limit to successive tax years until fully absorbed by subsequent Sch D Case IV leasing income. Where both wear and tear allowances under TCA 1997, s 298 and industrial building allowances (see **6.402**) are available in respect of the same premises, the taxpayer may choose the order of setoff against the rental income arising from the premises (a point accepted by the Revenue: see *Tax Briefing 42*); it will normally be preferable to offset 'ringfenced' allowances first.

TCA 1997, s 300(4) provides that capital allowances claimed by virtue of TCA 1997, s 284(6) (allowances available on plant, fixtures, etc in a let residential property) are to be made in charging the person's income under Sch D Case V, rather than being treated as arising under a separate Case I or Case IV source. The excess wear and tear allowances over rental income may not be offset against other income (TCA 1997, s 406). Any unutilised allowances may be carried forward to a succeeding year of assessment will be available for set off only against the person's Case V income in that subsequent year.

TCA 1997, s 404 places further restrictions on the set-off of capital allowances on certain leases of plant and machinery with a value in excess of €63,500 (where the lease was entered into on or after 23 December 1993). The section restricts the set-off of the capital allowances in that they can only be set-off against income from that particular lease, as distinct from income from all other leases, which applied previously.

The section is aimed at so-called 'balloon' leases of plant and machinery where there is fluctuation in the repayments so that most of the repayments are not made until the end of the primary period of the lease. The section provides for the restriction on the set off of the capital allowances. The rules are relaxed in certain circumstances including in the case of agricultural machinery to allow for seasonal factors which may influence the repayments.

6.303 Capital allowances for lessees

In certain circumstances, a lessee who takes a lease of plant for use in his own trade, but who does not incur the capital expenditure, may receive capital allowances. With effect from 3 April 2010, such a lessee is entitled, instead of the lessor, to claim a wear and tear allowance on the relevant capital expenditure incurred by the lessor if, but only if, the following conditions are met, namely:

(a) the machinery or plant is let under a finance lease (within the meaning of TCA 1997, s 76D, in broad terms a lease that transfers substantially all the risks and rewards of ownership of the relevant asset to the lessee) to a person carrying on a trade;

(b) the terms of the lease bind that person to maintain the machinery or plant and deliver it over in good condition at the end of the lease; and

(c) the burden of the wear and tear of the plant will in fact fall directly on that person (TCA 1997, s 299(1).

Further, the lessor and lessee must jointly elect for this treatment to apply, unless the lessor is not within the charge to Irish tax, in which case the lessee must elect. The election must be made in the form prescribed by the Revenue Commissioners on or before the specified return date for the tax year concerned (ie by 31 October 2015, for 2014) (TCA 1997, s 299(1), as substituted by FA 2010, s 36).

Where this treatment applies, the capital expenditure on the provision of the machinery or plant is deemed to have been incurred only by the lessee and the machinery or plant is deemed to belong to him and to no other person (TCA 1997, s 299(1)). A deduction in computing the lessee's trading profits will only be granted for the element of lease payments which would be deducted in a profit and loss account in accordance with generally accepted accounting practice for that period (in effect the deemed interest element). The amount treated as capital expenditure on plant and machinery may not exceed the excess of the total amount of the lease payments over the total amounts deductible in computing trading profits (TCA 1997, s 299(3)(c)).

For the previous provisions governing the availability of capital allowances for lessees, please see the 2009 edition of this book.

Wear and tear allowances are given if the same conditions are met in the case of a lessee who uses the plant in his profession, office or employment (TCA 1997, s 301(1)).

6.304 Who bears the burden of wear and tear?

It is important to determine whether the lessor or the lessee bears the burden of wear and tear in any case where capital allowances are to be claimed on leased plant. The capital allowances on any item of plant cannot be obtained by both lessor and lessee. As discussed at **6.303**, the lessee can only claim the allowances under TCA 1997, s 299(1) if he in fact does directly bear the wear and tear and if he is bound to hand over the plant in good condition at the end of the lease.

The exact meaning of the phrase 'the burden of wear and tear' in this context gives rise to some difficulty and it may not always be clear which party bears it. In *Lupton v Cadogan Gardens Developments Ltd* 47 TC 1, a hotel premises containing lifts, boilers and other machinery and plant was leased by a company for 90 years. The lease contained covenants by the lessees to maintain the premises, including the plant, and keep them in good and substantial repair and to deliver them up so maintained and repaired at the end of the lease, and as often as necessary to replace worn out plant with other items of similar quality. It was accepted that all the items of plant were likely to require replacing once or more during the full term of the lease. Both lessors and lessees claimed the capital allowances.

It was held in the Court of Appeal that the burden of wear and tear fell on the lessees. The lease was still in its earlier years and there was no doubt that the plant in question would have worn out and disappeared before the end of the lease and would, under its terms, require to be replaced by the lessees at their expense. The fact that the lessees would be allowed to deduct the whole cost of replacing the lifts, etc in calculating their trading profits was not considered to affect the issue.

The phrase was also subject to judicial comment in *MacSaga Investment Co Ltd v Lupton* 44 TC 659 where the company had contended that the words meant something quite different from a mere obligation to maintain and keep the plant in good repair. They claimed the words meant depreciation in value in so far as it could not be made good by proper and adequate expenditure on maintenance and repair. Lord Denning MR considered that wear and tear meant depreciation and that the burden fell on the company, but Salmon LJ took the view that the burden of the wear and tear fell on the tenant who covenanted to maintain the plant and deliver it over in good condition at the end of the lease.

Since the requirement that the burden of wear and tear must 'in fact' fall directly on the lessee was introduced in response to the decision in *Union Cold Storage Co Ltd v Simpson* 22 TC 547 (where the taxpayers had assumed the obligation to maintain the plant in good repair but in practice failed to do so), Salmon LJ's analysis may be preferable. The Court of Appeal adopted the same analysis in *Lupton v Cadogan Gardens* 47 TC 1, although the views expressed there were strictly *obiter*. However, in *McCarthaigh v Daly* III ITR 253, O'Hanlon J construed the phrase 'wear and tear' in this context as denoting depreciation, ie as:

> that sort of wearing out of articles due to use which is not capable of being avoided by ordinary processes of maintenance and repair and which will eventually necessitate a replacement or abandonment of the plant and machinery.

In view of the doubt that may arise as to where the burden of wear and tear lies, a lessor of plant should take care with the wording of the lease agreement if he wishes to make sure of getting the capital allowances. This is particularly the case if the agreement contains a clause, as a number of leases do, requiring the lessee to maintain the plant in good repair. In such a case, it is usual to add the words 'fair wear and tear excepted' at the end of such a clause. A lessor is normally regarded as satisfying the wear and tear test if the obligation to replace the plant falls on him or, if it is intended that the plant will simply wear out during the lease and not need replacing, if he is the person who actually bears the capital loss as the plant wears out. The fact that the lease agreement may require the lessee to keep the plant insured during the period of the letting does not, of itself, put the onus of replacement on the lessee.

As noted above, the fact that the lease agreement contains a covenant by the lessee to maintain the plant and deliver it over in good condition at the end of the lease may not be sufficient to give the lessee the capital allowances. He must also be able to show that the burden of wear and tear actually does or will fall on him. A provision in the lease to the effect that the lessee is obliged to contribute to a sinking fund for the replacement of fixed assets would normally indicate that the burden of wear and tear falls on the lessee.

6.305 Lessor's capital allowances restricted

TCA 1997, s 403 provides that, subject to certain exceptions, the capital allowances given to a lessor of machinery or plant can only be used to reduce or offset the income arising from the letting of plant, whether that income is taxable under Sch D Case I as the profits of a trade of leasing, or under Sch D Case IV if no trade is involved, or under Sch D Case III if the leasing activity is carried on outside the State. To the extent that the capital allowances on leased plant create or increase a trading loss for which relief may be claimed under any of the loss relief rules in the Tax Acts, the relevant part of that loss is only available to reduce or offset any income from plant leasing, but not any other income or profits.

TCA 1997, s 403 does not prevent the lessor from claiming the full capital allowances to which he is entitled under the ordinary rules, but it restricts the use of what (in the case of a trade of leasing) it terms 'the specified capital allowances' to offsetting only the income from the trade of leasing. It does not affect the carry forward of any unused capital allowances (or a loss created or increased by specified capital allowances) which remain eligible to be deducted from future income from the trade of leasing. Any capital allowances ('the excepted capital allowances') which are not specified capital allowances continue to be available for set off against non-leasing income (if the lessor is entitled to any such other relief, eg under a TCA 1997, s 381 loss claim – see below).

In applying the rules of TCA 1997, s 403 as outlined in this subdivision, the letting of any item of machinery or plant on hire is regarded as the leasing of machinery or plant. The letting on charter of a ship or aircraft which has been provided for such letting is similarly treated as the leasing of machinery or plant. These provisions are intended to remove any doubt as to whether such lettings would otherwise be considered to be such leasing (TCA 1997, s 403(1)(b)). The treatment of certain qualifying ships is dealt with in **6.306**.

'Trading lessors'

A trade of leasing is defined as either (a) a trade consisting wholly of the leasing of machinery or plant, or (b) any part of any other trade (eg banking) where any leasing of machinery or plant is carried on in the course of that trade. If a person leases any machinery or plant in the course of a trade which does not consist wholly of such leasing, TCA 1997, s 403(2) requires that trade to be treated for all the purposes of the Tax Acts – except only in applying any of the rules of those Acts to the commencement or the cessation of a trade – as if it were two separate trades.

This separate trade rule means that the Sch D Case I trading income or loss of the whole trade has to be broken down as between the profit or loss of the 'separate trade' of leasing and the profit or loss of the other trading activities. The capital allowances for the plant provided for the separate trade of leasing (other than any excepted capital allowances) are then restricted to offsetting only the leasing profits. In breaking down the total profit or loss between the two trades, the appropriate apportionments must be made of any receipts or expenses not directly related only to either the leasing or non-leasing activities.

Special rules apply to the chartering of qualifying ships (as defined): see **6.306**.

Another type of trade affected is the trade of leasing films, whether for showing in cinemas, on television or otherwise. In such a trade, it is the film itself which is treated as the machinery or plant on which capital allowances are given by reference to the cost of making the film (if leased by the film making company) or its cost of purchase (if acquired for leasing by another person (see **6.202**: *Intellectual Property*). TCA 1997, s 403 excepts certain films from its restrictions (see below).

'The specified capital allowances'

These are defined by TCA 1997, s 403(1) as the capital allowances in respect of:

(a) expenditure incurred on machinery or plant provided after 24 January 1984 for leasing in the course of a trade of leasing; or

(b) the diminished value of such machinery or plant by reason of wear and tear,

but excluding the excepted capital allowances.

In other words, TCA 1997, s 403 starts with the premise that all capital allowances, if given in respect of machinery or plant (provided after 24 January 1984) for leasing in the course of a trade of leasing, are specified capital allowances *unless* one of the exceptions applies.

The excepted capital allowances

The excepted capital allowances (which may be the subject of a claim for set off against the lessor's non-leasing income), leaving aside a number of rather remote transitional provisions dealt with in the 1997/98 edition of this book, refer to the following assets:

(a) Machinery or plant (other than a film) the expenditure on which is incurred under an obligation entered into between the lessor and the lessee after 12 May 1986 (or after 31 August 1986, if pursuant to negotiations in progress before 13 May 1986), but only if the following conditions are all met:

  (i) the terms of the lease include an undertaking by the lessee that the machinery, etc will be used only for the purposes of a 'specified trade' (see below) for a period of at least three years from the date the machinery, etc is first brought into use by the lessee. TCA 1997, s 403(9)(b), also requires the lessee to undertake that any asset provided for leasing on or after 4 March 1998 will not be used for the purposes of a third party's trade (ie preventing onward leasing),

  (ii) the machinery, etc is in fact used for the specified trade for that three-year period, and

  (iii) the machinery, etc is provided for leasing to a lessee who is not connected with the lessor;

(b) a film provided for leasing which is a film made wholly or partly in the State, but only if the cost of making the film is met directly or indirectly, wholly or partly, by the Irish Film Board under the authority given to it by the Irish Film Board Act 1980, s 6 or 7 (TCA 1997, s 403(7));

(c) a registered sea fishing boat within TCA 1997, s 284(3A) provided for leasing and in respect of which the lessor incurred capital expenditure in the two years commencing on 4 September 1998. For a corporate lessor the allowances comprise excepted allowances if the expenditure was incurred in the six years commencing on 4 September 1998 (TCA 1997, s 403(5A)).

Apart from grant-aided films made wholly or partly in the State, the main test for excepted capital allowances status has been changed by TCA 1997, s 403 to one related to the nature of the trade carried on by the lessee as compared with one dependent on the lessor's expenditure being grant aided. Expenditure which has been the subject of an initial allowance or free depreciation allowance (now rarely relevant) is disqualified (TCA 1997, s 403(8)).

As noted in **6.302** additional restrictions apply to so-called 'balloon' leases with effect from 23 December 1993. In addition, the provisions of TCA 1997, s 1013 (Limited Partnerships) may in certain circumstances be relevant: see **4.512**.

The specified trades

TCA 1997, s 403(9) details the classes of trade which entitle the lessor to the 'excepted capital allowances' treatment in respect of his capital allowances on the leased machinery, etc. It provides that, in order that the conditions as to the specified trade for which the leased machinery, etc is used may be satisfied, the trade carried on by the lessee must, throughout the relevant three-year period, consist wholly or mainly of either:

(a) the manufacture of goods; or

(b) any other activity which would, if the lessee were to claim manufacturing relief under Pt 14, be regarded as the manufacture of goods; or

(c) Shannon exempted trading operations (no longer relevant).

It is to be noted that some of these activities only became eligible for the 10 per cent rate of corporation tax with effect from various dates in the year 1987. One important exception: a qualifying shipping trade – although entitled to the 10 per cent rate of corporation tax with effect from 1 January 1987 – is specifically excluded and is not a specified trade for the purposes of TCA 1997, s 403 (TCA 1997, s 407(6)). The lessor of a ship or any other machinery or plant leased to a person carrying on a qualifying shipping trade does not, therefore, have any excepted capital allowances.

For the lessee's trade to consist wholly or mainly of any particular activity (eg ship repairs carried out in the State regarded by TCA 1997, s 443 as the manufacture of goods), not less than 75 per cent of the total amount receivable by the lessee from all sales rendered in the course of the trade in the relevant three-year period must be from sales made or services rendered in the course of that particular activity (TCA 1997, s 403(9)(ii)).

The connected person rules of TCA 1997, s 10 (see **12.304**) are applied to determine whether or not the lessee is connected with the lessor if the lessor is an individual or other person whose profits or gains are chargeable to income tax.

In any case where it appears to the Revenue Commissioners (or, on appeal, to the Appeal Commissioners) that the lessee's undertakings to use the leased plant only for his specified trade for the whole of the three-year period has not been fulfilled, then any relief obtained by the lessor in any claim to offset excess capital allowances in respect of the plant in question against any non-leasing income must be retrospectively withdrawn. Any necessary assessments may be made on the lessor for this purpose.

Trading lessors

Any person carrying on a trade of leasing machinery or plant should subdivide his capital allowances computations into two parts – one dealing with plant attracting the specified capital allowances and the other with plant the capital allowances on which are not subject to the TCA 1997, s 403 restrictions. In dealing with the matter further in this book, the two classes of capital allowances affecting the lessor of plant are referred to respectively as 'specified capital allowances' and 'other capital allowances'; the latter comprise both the excepted capital allowances on plant provided for leasing and the capital allowances on any other plant used for the trade other than for leasing (eg office equipment).

A person chargeable to income tax is entitled to claim under TCA 1997, s 381 to set off a trading loss against his income from all sources for the same year of assessment and, if he so requires, to include capital allowances in respect of plant used in his trade in arriving at the loss available for this set off (see **4.405**). In the case of a trade of leasing, TCA 1997, s 403(3)(a) provides that – to the extent that the trading loss is created or increased by any specified capital allowances – the amount of the loss available for set off against other income must be restricted. The amount of the loss set off is limited so as not to exceed any taxable profits from the trade of leasing included in the trader's income from all sources for the year of the claim. Since the leasing trade is generating a TCA 1997, s 381 loss claim, there will in fact normally be nil assessable profits under the current year basis of assessment.

Any specified capital allowances which have to be excluded from the TCA 1997, s 381 loss claim remain available for carry forward for set off against any trading profits of the leasing trade chargeable for any subsequent year of assessment (see **4.403**). Similarly, the restrictions of TCA 1997, s 403 do not alter the taxpayer's right to carry back the specified capital allowances in a TCA 1997, s 385 terminal loss claim for set off against earlier profits of the leasing trade on a cessation of trade (see **4.410**).

There is no corresponding restriction affecting capital allowances that are not specified capital allowances. Any such other capital allowances remain fully available for inclusion in the TCA 1997, s 381 claim; they may be applied to reduce the taxpayer's income from all sources without having to distinguish that income as between leasing trade income and other income. Further, the restrictions of TCA 1997, s 403 have no effect on the set off against other income of the adjusted Sch D Case I loss (before capital allowances).

When a TCA 1997, s 381 loss claim is affected by TCA 1997, s 403, the person making the claim is entitled to specify the extent to which any reduction of income occurring as the result of the claim is to be referred to:

(a) the actual loss (if any) sustained in the trade of leasing; or
(b) the specified capital allowances; or
(c) any other capital allowances (TCA 1997, s 403(3)(b)(ii)).

This right to specify how the set off of the TCA 1997, s 381 loss that includes capital allowances is to be made is stated to be without prejudice to the general principle that specified capital allowances can only be used to reduce profits from the trade of leasing. It does, however, enable the taxpayer to have any actual loss from the leasing trade and any other capital allowances deducted first from the non-leasing income. Finance Act 2014 introduced TCA 1997, ss 381B and 381C which reduces sideways offset for non-active traders. For a discussion on these two sections see **4.413**.

Example 6.305.1

Mr PX carries on a full time trade consisting wholly of the leasing of machinery and plant for which he has specified capital allowances and other capital allowances. For his 12-month period of the accounts ended 30 April 2015, he has a loss in his leasing trade eligible for TCA 1997, s 381 relief for 2015, including capital allowances claimed under TCA 1997, s 392, made up as follows:

	€
Actual Sch D Case I Loss	5,000
Capital allowances 2015:	
Specified capital allowances	6,420

	€
Other capital allowances	4,190
Total TCA 1997, s 381 Loss	15,610

Mr PX claims under TCA 1997, s 381 to set off this loss, so far as permitted, against his total income for 2015 which is as follows:

	€
Sch D Case I (leasing) Profits	Nil
Sch E Income	12,400
Total Income (before claim)	12,400

Mr PX specifies (as he is entitled to do) that the actual Schedule D Case I loss sustained (ie before capital allowances) and the other capital allowances are to be treated as reducing his non-leasing income. Mr PX's total income for 2015 now works out as follows:

	€	€
Sch E Income		12,400
Less:		
TCA 1997, s 381 claim:		
Actual Case I loss	5,000	
Other capital allowances	4,190	
		(9,190)
Total Income 2015		3,210

Notes:

1. Specified capital allowances of €6,420 are available for carry forward for set off against future profits from the trade of leasing.

TCA 1997, s 403(3)(b)(i) contains a further rule which is relevant if there are any balancing charges for the same tax year as that in which there are capital allowances to be included in the TCA 1997, s 381 loss claim. In any such case, TCA 1997, s 393 imposes a limitation which restricts the capital allowances in the loss claim to those allowances not required to offset the balancing charges. In applying the rules of TCA 1997, s 403, this limitation must be referred, so far as possible, to the specified capital allowances in priority to any other capital allowances.

Example 6.305.2

Take the facts of **Example 6.305.1**, but assume that there are balancing charges of €2,500 for the tax year 2015 as well as the same capital allowances as were included in the previous example.

The 2015 capital allowances for inclusion in the (TCA 1997, s 381) loss claim are determined as follows:

	€
Specified capital allowances	6,420
Other capital allowances	4,190
	10,610
Less:	
Balancing charges	(2,500)
Capital allowances for loss claim	8,110

TCA 1997, s 403(3)(b)(i) requires the balancing charges of €2,500 to be attributed first (and, in this case, fully) to the specified capital allowances of €6,420, thereby reducing them to €3,920 and leaving the other capital allowances intact. Mr PX's total income for 2015 now works out as follows:

	€	€
Income other than from trade of leasing:		
As per example **6.305.1**		12,400
Less:		
TCA 1997, s 381 claim:		
Actual Sch D Case I loss	5,000	
Other capital allowances	4,190	
		(9,190)
Total income 2015		3,210

Notes:

1. In this case, the balance of the specified capital allowances of (€6,420 – €2,500) = €3,920 are available for carry forward against future profits from the trade of leasing.

Non-trading lessors

The right of a person chargeable to income tax to elect under TCA 1997, s 305(1)(b) to set off against his total income any excess capital allowances in respect of plant leased in circumstances in which the leasing income is taxable under Sch D Case IV (or, strictly, in the case of certain fixtures, Sch D Case V) has been discussed in **6.302**. TCA 1997, s 403(5) provides that the capital allowances set off against total income in any such election must exclude capital allowances in respect of expenditure incurred on the provision of the leased machinery or plant, but with certain very limited exceptions. In the same way as with the trading lessor, all the capital allowances for the leased plant (including the excepted capital allowances) are available for set off against the leasing income for the tax year to which they apply or, if not fully used against that income, for carry forward to be set off against the leasing income in the next or any subsequent tax year. Only the excepted capital allowances are available for inclusion for set off against total income in the TCA 1997, s 305(1)(b) election. In fact, again leaving aside rather remote transitional provisions dealt with in the 1997/98 edition of this book, the only excepted capital allowances available for non-trading lessors refer to:

(a) a film provided for leasing which is a film made wholly or partly in the State, but only if the cost of making the film is met directly or indirectly, wholly or partly, by the Irish Film Board under the authority given to it by the Irish Film Board Act 1980, s 6 or 7 (TCA 1997, s 403(6), (7));

(b) with effect from 4 September 1998, a registered sea-fishing boat within TCA 1997, and s 284(3A): see **6.203**, if the expenditure is incurred within two years from that day (TCA 1997, s 403(5A)(b)(i)).

The provisions of TCA 1997, s 404 ('balloon leasing') noted above again apply with effect from 23 December 1993. In addition, the provisions of TCA 1997, s 1013 (Limited Partnerships) may in certain circumstances be relevant: see **4.512**.

TCA 1997, s 409D restricts the offset of capital allowances that are given in taxing a specified trade to the income from that trade in a case where the trade is not carried on by an active trader. An active trader is one who works for the greater part of his time in the day-to-day management or conduct of the trade. The specified trades comprise electricity generation, the film and music industries and oil and gas exploration. TCA 1997, s 409D(2)(b) provides that the restriction applies to an allowance that is made by discharge or repayment of tax to which the individual is entitled by reason of carrying on the specified trade.

6.306 Qualifying shipping trades: special rules

TCA 1997, s 407(4) contains rules to 'ring fence' capital allowances for qualifying ships so that they are not available to reduce or offset any income or profits chargeable to income tax other than the trading income of a qualifying shipping trade or certain ship chartering income. The section applies to restrict the use of the 'specified capital allowances' (see below) which, it provides, shall be allowed only:

(a) in computing the income from a qualifying shipping trade; or
(b) in computing or charging to tax any income from the letting on charter of the qualifying ship to which the specified capital allowances refer (this does not include any letting on charter which is a qualifying shipping activity already covered in (a)).

It is then provided, to emphasise the point, that the specified capital allowances shall not be allowed in computing any other income or profits or in taxing any other trade or in charging any other income. The use of the specified capital allowances envisaged in (a) is the deduction of the allowances as an expense in computing the Sch D Case I income of a qualifying shipping trade carried on by a company chargeable to corporation tax. Since a person chargeable to income tax cannot carry on a qualifying shipping trade, this provision has no relevance to income tax.

It is, however, possible for an individual, unincorporated body of persons or other person liable to income tax to own a ship which may be let on charter as a qualifying ship. In any such case, rule (b) above applies to allow the specified capital allowances to be used only to reduce or offset the income from such chartering, but for no other purpose. It is to be noted that rule (b) restricts the use of the specified capital allowances in respect of a particular qualifying ship to the income from the chartering of that ship.

The 'specified capital allowances', which are subject to the restrictions of TCA 1997, s 407(4) are defined as capital allowances in respect of:

(a) expenditure incurred by any person in the relevant period in providing a qualifying ship for use in, or intended to be used in, a qualifying shipping trade; or
(b) the diminished value by reason of wear and tear during the relevant period of a qualifying ship in use for the purposes of a qualifying shipping trade (TCA 1997, s 407(1)).

The 'relevant period' is the period from 1 January 1987 to 31 December 2010. A qualifying shipping trade is a trade or part of a trade carried on by a company consisting of the carrying on of qualifying shipping activities. The 'wet leasing' of a qualifying ship, ie where the ship is operated by, and its crew remain under the direction and control, of the company entitled to the 10 per cent rate of corporation tax is also a qualifying shipping activity.

The terms 'qualifying ship', 'qualifying shipping trade' and 'qualifying shipping activities' are defined by TCA 1997, s 407(1).

The definition of the specified capital allowances confines the allowance subject to the ring fence restriction to the capital allowances in respect of a qualifying ship. The restrictions do not apply to limit the uses otherwise available for capital allowances on other ships

Another effect of TCA 1997, s 407(4) is to deny any relief at all for specified capital allowances to any person who owns a qualifying ship and leases it for use in a qualifying shipping trade, unless the leasing is by way of letting on charter. For a leased ship which is not a qualifying ship, or which is a qualifying ship not being used in a qualifying shipping activity, this section does not apply, but the lessor is subject to the not dissimilar restrictions of TCA 1997, s 403 (see **6.305**).

TCA 1997, s 407(4)(c) also requires that the letting on charter of a qualifying ship should be treated as a separate trade of leasing for the purposes of TCA 1997, s 403 (see **6.305**). However, this additional restriction does not apply in relation to expenditure incurred in the construction or acquisition of a qualifying ship under a contract concluded on or after 1 July 1996 where:

(a) the terms of the charter letting comply with TCA 1997, s 404(1)(b)(i), I and II (ie the letting is not a 'balloon lease': see **6.302**); and
(b) the Minister for the Marine issues a certificate certifying that he is satisfied *inter alia* that the ship will enhance the lessee's fleet, has the potential to create jobs and other socio-economic benefits in Ireland, and meets current environmental and safety standards; the Minister must issue the certificate with the consent of the Minister for Finance on the basis of a business plan and any other information supplied by the lessee, and only if he is satisfied that the lease is for *bona fide* commercial purposes and not part of a tax avoidance scheme.

The Revenue Commissioners apparently take the view that where these conditions are met, the capital allowances in relation to the ship may be set off against all of the taxpayer's leasing income. However, this view is difficult to reconcile with the wording of TCA 1997, s 407(4)(a), which, as noted above, prohibits any offset of such allowances against income other than that from the chartering of the qualifying ship.

6.4 Industrial Buildings and Structures

6.401 What buildings qualify?

Capital allowances are given in respect of capital expenditure incurred on the construction of a building or structure occupied for the purposes of a trade as an industrial building or structure. An 'industrial building or structure' (referred to here as an 'industrial building') is defined by TCA 1997, s 268(1) as a building or structure in use for the purpose of any of the following types of activity:

(a) a trade carried on in either (i) a mill, factory or other similar premises, or (ii) a laboratory the sole or main function of which is the analysis of minerals (including oil and natural gas) in connection with the exploration for, or the extraction of, such minerals;

(b) a dock undertaking;

(c) growing fruit, vegetables or other produce in the course of a trade of market gardening;

(d) the trade of hotel-keeping (extended to registered guest houses, registered holiday hostels, registered caravan and camping sites and registered holiday cottages, as defined);

(e) the intensive production of cattle, sheep, pigs, poultry or eggs in the course of a trade other than the trade of farming (as defined by TCA 1997, s 654: see **7.101**);

(f) a trade consisting of the operation or management of an airport where the structure is an airport runway or apron meeting certain conditions;

(g) a trade consisting of the operation or management of a registered nursing home;

(h) a trade consisting of the operation or management of an airport where the structure does not fall within (f) above;

(i) a trade which consists of the operation or management of a convalescent home for the provision of medical and nursing care for persons recovering from treatment in a hospital, where the convalescent home meets certain conditions;

(j) a trade which consists of the operation or management of a qualifying hospital;

(k) a trade which consists of the operation or management of a qualifying sports injuries clinic;

(l) a trade which consists of the operation of management of a qualifying mental health centre; and

(m) (subject to ministerial order) a trade which consists of the operation or management of a qualifying specialist palliative care unit;

(n) (subject to ministerial order) a trade which consists of the maintenance, repair or overhaul of passenger aircraft or cargo aircraft for hire or reward or the dismantling of such aircraft for the purposes of salvaging or recycling of the parts or materials in regionally assisted areas that comply with EU guidelines.

In addition, certain buildings and structures are rendered eligible for the same allowances as if they were industrial buildings within TCA 1997, s 268. The most notable examples are buildings within certain 'tax incentive' areas, such as urban or renewal areas, enterprise areas, etc. These buildings and structures are dealt with fully in **Division 19** in the 2009 edition of this book. The treatment of certain multi-storey car parks is outlined at **6.605** and third-level education buildings are dealt with in **6.503**. In addition certain childcare facilities are treated as if they were industrial buildings (TCA 1997, s 843A): see below.

For the restriction of losses created or increased by industrial building allowances, see **4.406, 4.413** and **6.509.**

The term 'structure' clearly bears a wider meaning than that of 'building'. In *IRC v Smyth* [1914] 2 KB 423 (a case not concerned with industrial buildings allowances), Scrutton J observed:

> I think a structure is something artificially erected, constructed, put together, of a certain degree of size and permanence, which is still maintained as an artificial erection, or which, though not so maintained, has not become indistinguishable in bounds from the natural earth surrounding. What degree of size and permanence will do is a question of fact in every case.

The UK Inland Revenue have accepted that the term 'structure' encompasses walls, bridges, drains, roads, culverts and tunnels. It is thought that the Revenue Commissioners are likely to follow this approach.

In principle, the capital allowances for industrial buildings are only given in respect of buildings or structures that are in use, or are to be used, in one of these qualifying categories of trade. However, the types of buildings, etc for which the allowances are available have been extended by various provisions to include also:

(a) Any harbour, wharf, pier or jetty or other works in or at which vessels can ship or unship merchandise or passengers (treated by TCA 1997, s 268(2) as a dock for a dock undertaking).

(b) Any building or structure provided by the person carrying on any of the qualifying categories of trade or undertaking, if provided for the recreation or welfare of workers employed in the trade or undertaking in question, if used for that purpose (treated by TCA 1997, s 268(1) as an industrial building in use for the trade in question).

(c) Any building or structure in use as a qualifying residential unit (treated by TCA 1997, s 268(3B) as a building in use for a trade which consists of the operation or management of a nursing home) up to 30 April 2010 (see **6.406**).

TCA 1997, s 268(6) provides that where only *part* of a trade is carried on in a factory, mill, etc, then buildings in use for the purposes for *that* part of the trade will qualify as industrial buildings. The point at which it is possible to say that some of the activities of trade are sufficiently independent so as to represent a separate 'part' of that trade will depend on the facts of each case. However, a common-sense approach will presumably prevail (as illustrated in *Patrick Monaghan (Drogheda) v O'Connell* (below), albeit not decided directly on this issue). In *Bestway (Holdings) v Luff* [1998] STC 357, it was held that a part of a trade must constitute a significant, separate and identifiable activity.

Where part of a building is used for non-qualifying purposes, then that part is excluded from relief, subject to the 10 per cent exception noted further below. In *Saxone Lilley & Skinner (Holdings) Ltd v IRC* 44 TC 122, it was held that a building *all* of which was used *concurrently* for both qualifying and non-qualifying purposes was eligible for industrial building allowances. The court rejected the argument that the requirement for a building to be in use for the purposes of a qualifying trade meant that it had to be 'wholly or mainly' in use for those purposes (although it also held that small or intermittent use for qualifying purposes was not sufficient).

The words 'mill' and 'factory' must be construed in their ordinary and natural sense. In *Ellerker v Union Cold Storage* 22 TC 195 these words were defined as follows:

> What then do the words 'factory' and 'mill' mean according to the common understanding of mankind? I take it that a factory is a building used for the purpose of manufacture of goods equipped with machinery and that the word is generally understood in that sense. It is a building where goods are made. The meaning of the word 'mill' is also, I think, plain enough. A mill is a building where goods are subjected to treatment or processing of some sort and machinery is used for that purpose.

Factories

It is thought that in determining what constitutes 'manufacturing', the case law on the meaning of this term in the context of the repealed 10 per cent rate of corporation tax and the stock relief provisions will be relevant (for activities held to be manufacturing see eg *McCann Ltd v O'Culacháin* III ITR 304; *Irish Agricultural Machinery v O'Culacháin* III ITR 611; *Cronin v Strand Dairy* III ITR 441; *O'Laochda v Johnson & Johnson* IV ITR 361; *Kelly v Cobb Straffan* IV ITR 526 and note also the rating case of *Coakley & Co/Arkady Feed Co v Commissioner of Valuation* 1996 2 ILRM 90; the unappealed decision of the Appeal Commissioners in *IOT v Highway Markings* [1993] ITR 587 and *O'Culacháin v O'Connor* (unreported). For activities held not to be manufacturing see *O'Culacháin v Hunter Advertising* IV ITR 35; *Brosnan v Leeside Nursing* V ITR 21).

The general principles emerging from these cases may be summarised broadly as follows. Firstly, there is the issue as to whether the final product which emerges from whatever process or processes is/are applied is/are not a commercially different product to the raw material, components or other goods which went into the process at the beginning. Secondly, if the final product is such a commercially different product, then does it or does it not owe this difference to the process to which it has been subjected by the taxpayer? Thirdly, is the process applied, a process which an ordinary individual (assuming that he is properly informed on the issues involved) would consider to be one of manufacture? Thus in *Irish Agricultural Machinery v O'Culacháin* III ITR 611, it was held by the Supreme Court that the business of assembling and selling agricultural machinery qualified as a manufacturing process. Griffin J observed:

> In my view what was said in *McCausland v Ministry of Commerce* [1956] NI 36 by the learned Lord Chief Justice can be applied to the present case. The end product produced by the company (the completed machines) are a marketable commodity and commercially are something quite different from the component parts from which they have been assembled. The completed machines are, when completed, much more than an aggregation of the individual component parts and have a utility, a quality and a worth which are due to and cannot be dissociated from the process carried out in the company's premises.

Conversely, in *O'Culacháin v Hunter Advertising* IV ITR 35 it was held in the High Court by Murphy J that the production for sale of advertising materials such as TV videos, master negatives and posters was not the manufacture of goods. It was contended on behalf of the company that it sold a tangible physical product constituting manufactured goods and that these goods were created by it. The blank or unexposed celluloid film (the raw material) was of minimum value whereas the exposed and edited film sold to the customer was of substantial value. On behalf of the inspector, it was contended that no manufacturing process was applied by the company to the blank film or, alternatively, if the filming of the particular sequences shown on the videos, etc amounted to a manufacturing process, the work which was actually carried out by the company, ie that of selecting and engaging actors, the creation of the concept and the writing of the script and organisation of the programme generally, were separate from any such manufacturing process.

In his judgment, Murphy J referred to the principles applied above. Applying those principles, the finished product in this case was an exposed and edited film, in contrast with the raw material which was the original blank celluloid film. However, he said that it was difficult to see how the enhanced value due to the activity of the company was conferred on the film by any manufacturing process. He considered that the visual recording of images on the blank film was not a manufacturing process applied by the company.

The Appeal Commissioners have held that the processing of ore overground in the course of mining operations constituted manufacturing.

A number of activities established as manufacturing by these cases were excluded from the benefit of the 10 per cent corporation tax rate by subsequent legislation (see TCA 1997, s 443). This does not affect the question as to whether such activities constitute manufacturing for the purposes of industrial building allowances. Conversely, a number of activities which do not constitute manufacturing in its ordinary meaning are deemed to be so for the purposes of the 10 per cent rate; a building or structure housing these activities should not usually qualify as an industrial building.

The Revenue Commissioners have stated that in general it can be taken that industrial buildings allowances will be available in respect of a building where the duplication of software is carried out subject to the normal legislative conditions. However, where a building is being used for software development which qualified for manufacturing relief under TCA 1997, s 443(10), the matter would need to be considered on a case-by-case basis, which would involve a close examination of the nature of the trade being carried on. The Revenue's interpretation of the word 'factory' in the context of industrial buildings allowance does in fact take recent technological advances into account.

When deciding whether or not a trade is carried on in a factory, a flexible approach should apparently be taken. In *Blinson v West Midlands Gas Board* 33 TC 315 (a case dealing with an earlier version of the legislation in the UK) it was said:

> I would not agree that when one is dealing with a work consisting of a number of buildings the right approach to the problem is to consider each individual building separately and to ask whether it has the required characteristics, wholly regardless of the part it plays in the entire manufacturing process. I think that that part should be taken into full consideration and one should then ask whether in the light of the result it is proper to include the building among those premises which, taken together, constitute a factory. Confining myself for the moment to the word 'factory', I think a building may be fairly said to be among the premises which together warrant the description if what goes on in the buildings is one of the chains of operations which are designed at the end to yield the manufactured article. Take for

> example a factory making fireworks or similar things … the gunpowder would be stored in one building, other explosives in another. These will be drawn upon by the person who does the mixing, and taken to a separate building, where he will make the mixture according to a prescribed formula. The mixture will then go into another building where girls will fill cylindrical cardboard containers with it, plug the container and add a fuse. In another building the labels will go on. No one can segregate a particular building out of these and say: 'that is a factory and that alone'. In each of these buildings something is done, being part of the several operations designed to produce fireworks – even if it is only to store and hand out the raw materials … and each building can properly be included in the group of buildings collectively called the factory. Indeed, it is difficult to see how any one of them could be left out.

(See also *Sinclair v Cadbury Bros* 18 TC 157.)

A broad approach to the question of what constitutes a factory was followed in *O'Conaill v Waterford Glass* III ITR 65, where a factory complex, including a building designed as an administrative centre, the main part of which played a key role in the manufacturing operations, was held to constitute a single industrial unit. However, buildings or part of buildings in use for 'non-industrial' purposes may be expressly excluded from relief (see below). It would certainly seem that warehouses used to store finished goods as they come off the production line should normally be classed as part of the factory premises. If this is the case, then such a warehouse, being itself part of a factory, must necessarily be in use for a trade carried on in a factory.

It is not, however, essential that a qualifying building or structure should itself form part of the factory, so long as it is in use for 'the purposes of' a trade which is carried on there. Thus, it is generally accepted that warehouses used to store raw materials or finished goods will qualify as industrial buildings, even if not part of the factory premises. Similarly, if manufacturing operations are regulated and controlled by sophisticated computer facilities, the building housing those facilities should still qualify, even if that building is at a remote location. Accordingly, the findings in the *Waterford Glass* case that the building there formed part of a single industrial complex does not seem to have been essential to the conclusion that it qualified for industrial building allowance. It should have qualified simply by being regarded as being in use for the purposes of the factory trade.

Mills

In *Ellerker v Union Cold Storage* 22 TC 195, cold stores for meat storage were found on the facts to be premises similar to mills since they were equipped with machinery for the purpose of subjecting the meat and other commodities to an artificial temperature (see also *IRC v Leith Harbour and Dock Commons* 24 TC 118, where grain elevators were also held to be similar to mills). It would seem, however, that the structures in the *Ellerker* and *Leith* cases would, in any event, qualify as plant (see *IRC v Barclay Curle* discussed at **6.202** above).

In *Viboplant Ltd v Holland* [1982] STC 164, it was held that a building used for the servicing and repair of plant was not 'a factory or … other similar premises' since it was not used to make goods. The building could not have qualified as a 'mill … or other similar premises' because in the words of Dillon J:

> The essence of the treatment which is provided in these buildings is that it is individual for the particular defects or needs of a particular piece of plant: each item is treated individually. By contrast, in my view 'process' connotes a substantial measure of uniformity of treatment or system of treatments. I note that a dictionary definition of process is: 'a continuous and

> regular action or succession of actions, taking place or carried on in a definite manner; a continuous (natural or artificial) operation or series of operations'.

However, in *Girobank plc v Clarke* [1996] STC 540, Lindsay J observed:

> I see mills as premises at which, chiefly by way of the use of machinery, one or more processes which require the use of that machinery are applied substantially to alter the physical nature of the materials to which they are applied and with a view to that alteration making that material more suitable for, or to add to its value for, commercial use as merchandise or wares.

It followed that a building which housed high speed machinery for processing documents was not a 'premises similar to a mill', even though the documents were subject to a uniform and systematic process.

Dock undertakings

In *Patrick Monahan (Drogheda) Ltd v O'Connell* III ITR 661 it was held that the term 'undertaking' denotes 'the business or enterprise undertaken by a [trader]' (following *Baytrust Holdings Ltd v IRC* [1971] 1 WLR 133). In the *Monahan* case, the taxpayer carried on a business of shipping agent, stevedore, customs clearance agent and coal importers, which was accepted to comprise a 'dock undertaking'. The taxpayer claimed industrial buildings allowance in respect of three transit sheds which were used to store goods under bond while they were being cleared by customs. The provision of temporary storage allowed the taxpayer's clients to turn around their ships more rapidly.

The inspector argued that the taxpayer's business of 'dock undertaking' ceased once the goods had been disembarked, or alternatively at the point when they were stored in the transit sheds. Murphy J rejected this argument, holding that the taxpayer was not carrying on the business of storekeeper and warehouseman, and that the retention of goods in the sheds was 'merely ancillary' to his business of dock undertaking. Accordingly the transit sheds qualified as industrial buildings.

Market gardening

A trade of market gardening is taken as being one within the definition or the term given in TCA 1997, s 654, ie a trade carried out on land in the State that is occupied as a nursery or garden for the sale of produce (except land used for the growing of hops). For some further remarks on what constitutes 'market gardening', see **7.102**. The most obvious type of market gardening buildings are greenhouses and similar buildings used for the intensive cultivation of fruit, vegetables, flowers etc.

Laboratories for mineral analysis

The definition of industrial building is extended to include any building or structure in use for a trade carried on in a laboratory the sole or main function of which is the analysis of minerals in connection with the exploration for, or the extraction of, such minerals. The term 'mineral' is expressed as including oil and natural gas, but clearly covers also any other types of minerals, eg zinc, coal, gold, etc.

The requirement that the laboratory for mineral analysis be used in connection with the exploration for or the extraction of minerals does not necessarily require that the person claiming the allowances be the person carrying out the exploration/extraction activity. A person carrying on the trade of providing a mineral analysis service for other persons carrying on the mineral exploration or extraction activity is also entitled to claim the allowances.

Hotels

The term 'hotel' and the cognate expression 'trade of hotel-keeping' are not defined. In its ordinary sense, a hotel connotes a premises which provides accommodation and also usually meals and other services for travellers. It may also be that a characteristic of a hotel is its obligation to receive all comers in the absence of reasonable grounds for refusal (see the Hotel Proprietors Act 1963, s 3(1)). In a 1987 case, a Circuit Court judge held that the term 'hotel' had to be construed in the light of modern conditions, under which such an establishment might offer a wide range of ancillary services and facilities, including bars and discotheques. In that particular case, an establishment where the non-accommodation space exceeded the accommodation space by a ratio of ten to one was held to qualify as a hotel.

A building in use for a trade of hotel keeping will not be treated as an industrial building if any part of the construction or refurbishment expenditure, incurred on or after 20 March 2001, is met by grant or other assistance provided by or through the State or any of its agencies. This provision found in TCA 1997, s 268(11) was inserted in order to comply with the European Commission rules on State Aid.

TCA 1997, s 268(12) provides that a building in use for the purpose of a trade of hotel-keeping will not be treated as an industrial building, as respects capital expenditure incurred on work which commenced after 5 April 2001 and which would have qualified for a writing down allowance in excess of four per cent (ie capital expenditure incurred before 4 December 2002 or falling within the transitional arrangements set out in **6.406**), unless the National Tourism Development Authority certifies that:

(a) it has received a declaration from the person who incurred the capital expenditure as to whether the applicant falls within the definition of a small or medium sized enterprise or a micro, small or medium sized enterprise as set out by the EU Commission;

(b) The expenditure is an 'initial investment' as defined in the 'Guidelines on National Regional Aid' prepared by the European Commission;

(c) In the case of expenditure incurred on or after 1 January 2003 approval of the potential capital allowances involved has been received by the Minister for Finance (or other nominated person) from the Commission in any case where the hotel is part of a project which is subject to the notification requirements of the 'Multisectoral framework on regional aid for large investment projects' prepared by the European Commission and dated either 7 April 1998 or 19 March 2002 (in such cases if and when approval is received, capital allowances will apply from the date the hotel was first used following construction or refurbishment, subject to any ceiling set on permissible expenditure by the Commission: TCA 1997, s 268(12A), as inserted by F(No 2)A 2008, s 22); and

(d) The person who incurs the capital expenditure has undertaken to furnish to a Government Minister or nominated body the information that is required to comply with the reporting requirements of the Commission Regulation (EC) no 70/2001, the 'Multisectoral framework on regional aid for large investment projects', 'the community guidelines on State aid for rescuing and restructuring firms in difficulty', the 'Community guidelines on State aid for rescuing and restructuring firms in difficulty' or any other EC Regulation or Directive under the EC Treaty governing State aid in specific sectors.

In *McGarry v Harding Properties Ltd* VI ITR 699 the High Court upheld the decision of the Circuit Court that a building which was not in fact a hotel, but which was in use for the trade of hotel-keeping, was a building in respect of which capital allowances could be claimed. Justice Laffoy said that when the expression 'trade of hotel keeping' is considered in its immediate context, in line with the scheme and purpose of the particular statutory pattern of the whole, it was reasonable to infer that the legislature did not intend that the allowance should be confined to a building in use for the purpose of a trade of hotel-keeping which was registered with Bord Fáilte. Following that decision the legislation was amended to provide that a building or structure actually in use for the purposes of the trade of hotel-keeping (but not one deemed to be so used) will not be regarded as an industrial building or structure, as respects capital expenditure incurred on or after 3 February 2005 on its construction or refurbishment, unless it is registered in the register of hotels kept under the Tourist Traffic Acts. This provision does not apply where the transitional arrangements set out in TCA 1997, s 268(15) apply.

The transitional rules provide that the registration requirements do not apply as respects capital expenditure incurred on or before 31 July 2006 on the construction or refurbishment of a building or structure where:

(a) A planning application (not being an application for outline planning permission), in so far as planning permission is required, in respect of the building is made in accordance with the Planning and Development Regulations 2001 to 2004, an acknowledgement of the application which confirms that it was received by 31 December 2004 is issued by the planning authority and the application is not an invalid application; or

(b) A planning application (not being an application for outline planning permission), in so far as planning permission was required, in respect of the building was made in accordance with the Local Government (Planning and Development) Regulations 1994, an acknowledgement of the application which confirms that it was received by 10 March 2002 was issued by the planning authority and the application was not an invalid application; or

(c) Where the construction or refurbishment work on the building represented by the expenditure is an exempted development for the purpose of the Planning and Development Act 2000, s 4 or Pt 2 of the Planning and Development Regulations 2001 and the following conditions are satisfied by 31 December 2004:

   (i) a detailed plan in relation to the development work is prepared,

   (ii) a binding contract in writing, under which the expenditure on the development is incurred is in existence, and

   (iii) work to the value of five per cent of the development costs is carried out; or

(d) A valid application for a certificate is made under the Dublin Docklands Development Authority Act 1997, s 25(7)(a)(ii) and the Authority issues an acknowledgement of the application which confirms that it was received by 31 December 2004.

TCA 1997, s 409 prevents any allowance being given in respect of a '*hotel investment*' made by a '*hotel partnership*' where a '*room ownership scheme*' exists in connection with such an investment. TCA 1997, s 409 applies to any hotel investment in relation to which capital expenditure is incurred on or after 26 March 1997.

'*Hotel investment*' is defined as capital expenditure on the construction of, or the acquisition of a relevant interest, in a building or structure within TCA 1997, s 268(1)(d), but disregarding the extension of that subsection by TCA 1997, s 409(3) to a holiday camp or a holiday cottage registered with Bord Fáilte. A '*Hotel Partnership*' is defined as including any syndicate, group or pool of persons, whether or not a partnership, through, or by means of which, a hotel investment is made. A *room ownership scheme* exists if, at the time a hotel investment is made by a hotel partnership, there exists any agreement, arrangement, undertaking, or promise (whether expressed or implied and whether or not enforceable or intended to be enforceable by legal proceedings), under or by virtue of which any *member* of that hotel partnership, or a person connected with such a member (as defined by TCA 1997, s 10: see **12.304**) may:

(a) acquire *on preferential terms* an interest in; or
(b) retain for use other than for the purposes of the trade of hotel-keeping,

any room or rooms in, or any particular part of, the building or structure which is the subject of the hotel investment.

A '*member*' of a hotel partnership includes every person who participates in that partnership or who has contributed capital directly or indirectly to that partnership. '*Preferential terms*' means terms under which an interest is acquired for consideration which at the time of acquisition is, or may be, other than its market value as defined by TCA 1997, s 548 ie the price which it might be reasonably expected to fetch on a sale in the open market. A hotel investment made by one or more than one member of a hotel partnership will be deemed to be made by the hotel partnership; this provision is designed to deal with changes in the composition of the partnership, etc.

There is a transitional exemption where before 26 March 1997:

(a) a binding contract in writing was entered into for the construction of, or the acquisition of a relevant interest in, the building or structure which is the subject of the investment; or
(b) an application for planning permission for the construction of the building or structure was received by a planning authority (TCA 1997, s 409(5)).

Holiday accommodation

The following may also be treated as a building in use for the trade of hotel-keeping:

(a) Any building or structure in use as a holiday camp registered in the register of holiday camps kept under the Tourist Traffic Acts 1939 to 2003 (TCA 1997, s 268(3)).
(b) Any building or structure which is in use as a guest house or a holiday hostel that is registered in the appropriate register kept under the Tourist Traffic Acts 1939 to 2003. This provision applies to expenditure incurred after 2 February 2005 on the construction or refurbishment of registered guest houses and holiday hostels (TCA 1997, s 268(2C)).
(c) Any building or structure in use as a caravan site or camping site which is registered in the appropriate register kept under the Tourist Traffic Acts 1939 to 2003 (treated as a building or structure in use for the purposes of the trade of hotel keeping). The provision applies to expenditure incurred on or after 1 January 2008 on the construction or refurbishment of caravan sites and camping sites (TCA 1997, s 268(2D)).
(d) Any building or structure in use as a holiday cottage if registered in any register of holiday cottages established by Bord Fáilte Éireann. This provision no longer

applies where the construction expenditure on a holiday cottage is incurred after 3 December 2002. However, transitional arrangements provide that a holiday cottage will continue to be regarded as a building in use for a trade of hotel keeping, in respect of capital expenditure incurred on construction or refurbishment up until 31 July 2006 if:

(i) a planning application (not being an application for outline planning permission), in so far as planning permission is required, in respect of the holiday cottage is made in accordance with the Planning and Development Regulations 2001 to 2002, an acknowledgement of the application which confirms that it was received by 31 December 2004 is issued by the planning authority and the application is not an invalid application,

(ii) a planning application (not being an application for outline planning permission), in so far as planning permission was required, in respect of the holiday cottage was made in accordance with the Local Government (Planning and Development) Regulations 1994, an acknowledgement of the application which confirms that it was received by 10 March 2002 was issued by the planning authority and the application was not an invalid application, or

(iii) where the construction or refurbishment work on the holiday cottage is an exempted development for the purpose of the Planning and Development Act 2000, s 4 or the Planning and Development Regulations 2001, Pt 2 and the following conditions are satisfied by 31 December 2004:

(I) a detailed plan in relation to the development work is prepared,

(II) a binding contract in writing, under which the expenditure on the development is incurred is in existence, and

(III) work to the value of five per cent of the development costs is carried out.

FA 2006, s 27 provided for the extension of the transitional period from 31 July 2006 to 31 December 2006. A further extension to 31 July 2008 applied where:

(a) The extension to 31 December 2006 applies by virtue of the conditions set out above under (a), (b) or (c) being satisfied.

(b) The person who is constructing or refurbishing the holiday cottage has carried out work to the value of not less than 15 per cent of the actual cost by 31 December 2006. This condition will not be treated as satisfied unless the relevant local authority certifies in writing by 30 March 2007 that it is satisfied that work to the value of not less than 15 per cent of the actual costs was carried out by 31 December 2006, the actual amount of expenditure incurred on the construction or refurbishment by 31 December 2006 and the projected balance of the capital expenditure which is to be incurred on the construction of the building. The application for the certificate must be made by 31 January 2007.

(c) The person who is constructing the holiday cottage or where the holiday cottage is sold the person claiming the relief can show that condition (ii) is satisfied. Where the building is sold by the person who constructed or refurbished it then the vendor should provide the purchaser with a copy of the certificate from the relevant local authority for the purpose of enabling the purchaser to claim allowances.

(d) A binding contract under which the expenditure on the construction or refurbishment of the holiday cottage is incurred is in existence by 31 July 2006.

(e) Such other conditions required to ensure compliance with the laws of the EC as may be specified in regulations are satisfied.

Where the expenditure is incurred on or after 1 January 2007 the amount of capital expenditure which is to be treated as incurred for the purpose of making allowances cannot exceed the amount certified by the relevant local authority in relation to that building. The amount of expenditure that will qualify for relief where the expenditure is incurred on or after 1 January 2007 will be reduced. If the expenditure is incurred in the calendar year 2007 the reduction will be to 75 per cent of the actual expenditure incurred in that period. If the expenditure is incurred in the period from 1 January 2008 to 31 July 2008 the expenditure that will qualify for allowances will be reduced to 50 per cent. The restriction of the expenditure by reference to the amount certified by the local authority applies in priority to the 75 per cent/50 per cent reduction in the amount of the expenditure on which capital allowances may be claimed. Where the expenditure incurred in the period from 1 January 2007 to 31 July 2008 exceeds the amount certified by the relevant local authority then the reduction will be made from the actual expenditure incurred in the period from 1 January 2008 to 31 July 2008 in priority to the expenditure incurred in the calendar year 2007. This order of restriction maximises the relief because a higher proportion (75 per cent) of expenditure incurred in 2007 qualifies for relief compared to the later period (TCA 1997, s 268(3)).

Nursing homes and qualifying residential units

TCA 1997, s 268(1)(g), as amended by FA 2009, provided that a building or structure in use for the purposes of a trade which consists of the operation or management of a nursing home as defined by the Health (Nursing Homes) Act 1990 and which is registered under s 4 of that Act will be treated as an industrial building or structure in relation to capital expenditure incurred on construction or refurbishment of such a building or structure on or after 3 December 1997 and prior to 31 December 2009, subject to the transitional provisions immediately following. Firstly, the cut-off date would be extended to 30 June 2010 where the construction or refurbishment work was exempted development for the purposes of the Planning and Development Act 2000 by virtue of s 4 of that Act or by virtue of Pt 2 of the Planning and Development Regulations 2001 (SI 600/2001) and not less than 30 per cent of the total construction or refurbishment costs had been incurred on or before 31 December 2009. Secondly, the cut-off date was extended to 30 June 2011 where a planning application (not being an application for outline permission within the meaning of the Planning and Development Act 2000, s 36), in so far as planning permission was required, in respect of the construction or refurbishment work concerned was made in accordance with the Planning and Development Regulations 2001 (SI 600/2001) and an acknowledgement of the application, which confirms that the application was received on or before 31 December 2009, was issued by the planning authority in accordance with art 26(2) of those Regulations *and* the application was not an invalid application in respect of which a notice was issued by the planning authority in accordance with art 26(5) of those Regulations of 2001 (TCA 1997, s 17).

For the purposes of these cut-off provisions, capital expenditure will only be regarded as having been incurred within any given period to the extent that is properly attributable to work on construction or refurbishment of the relevant building or structure actually carried out in that period (TCA 1997, s 316(2B)).

TCA 1997, s 268(3B) provides that the building in use as a qualifying residential unit will be treated as though it were a building in use for a trade of operating or managing a nursing home within TCA 1997, s 268(1)(g). Capital expenditure incurred on the construction or refurbishment of a qualifying residential unit in the period commencing on 25 March 2002 and ending on 30 April 2010 will also qualify for capital allowances in the same way as an industrial building (TCA 1997, s 268(3B); a substituted version being inserted with effect for capital expenditure incurred on or after 1 May 2007 under a contract or agreement entered into from that date, by FA 2007, s 28). No part of the expenditure may be met directly or indirectly by grant assistance or any other assistance from the State or a State agency (TCA 1997, s 268(3C)).

With effect for expenditure incurred on or after 1 May 2007 under a contract or agreement entered into on or after that date, a number of administrative requirements must be satisfied. Firstly, the following information must be provided to the Health Service Executive by the person entitled to the relevant interest for onward transmission to the Minister for Health and Children and the Minister for Finance:

(i) the amount of the capital expenditure actually incurred on the construction or refurbishment of the house;
(ii) the number and nature of the investors that are investing in the house;
(iii) the amount to be invested by each investor; and
(iv) the nature of the structures which are being put in place to facilitate the investment in the house,

together with such additional information as may be specified by the Minister for Finance, in consultation with the Minister for Health and Children.

Secondly, the Health Service Executive, in consultation with the Minister for Health and Children, must give a certificate in writing after the house is first leased or, where capital expenditure is incurred on the refurbishment of a house, first leased subsequent to the incurring of that expenditure, stating that it is satisfied that:

(i) the house and the development in which it is comprised complies with the conditions for the tax relief (see below) has been provided to the Health Safety Executive; and
(ii) all the information required as set out above has in fact been provided to the Health Safety Executive.

Thirdly, an annual report in writing must be provided by the person entitled to the relevant interest to the Health Service Executive, for onward transmission to the Minister for Health and Children and the Minister for Finance, which:

(i) confirms whether the house and the development in which it is comprised continue to comply with all the conditions for tax relief; and
(ii) provides details of the level of occupation of the house for the previous year including the age of and, as the case may be, the nature of the infirmity of the occupants (TCA 1997, s 268(3E)).

A qualifying residential unit is a house that is constructed on the site of or on a site adjacent to the site of a registered nursing home. Where the construction expenditure was incurred before 4 February 2004 each qualifying residential unit had to be either a single storey house or a house comprised in a two storey building. As regards expenditure incurred on or after 4 February 2004, the residential unit can be comprised in larger building of one or more storeys where a fire safety certificate in respect of the building is required under Part III of the Building Control Regulations 1997 and before the construction works commence, the certificate is issued by the building control authority. A two storey house itself cannot qualify since it is neither comprised in a building of one or more storeys nor is a fire certificate required under the relevant provisions. With effect for expenditure incurred on or after 1 May 2007 under a contract or agreement entered into on or after that date, a number of administrative requirements must be satisfied, a house is defined as any building or part of a building used or suitable as use for a dwelling and any out office, yard, garden or other land appurtenant to or usually enjoyed with that building or part of a building.

The qualifying units must be designed and constructed to meet the needs of people with disabilities, and in particular to meet the needs of people who are confined to wheelchairs. Each qualifying unit must consist of one or two bedrooms, a kitchen, a living room, bath or shower facilities, toilet facilities and a nurse call system linked to the nursing home.

Where the construction expenditure was incurred prior to 4 February 2004 the residential unit had to be part of a development of at least 20 units. As regards expenditure incurred on or after 4 February 2004 the number of units required in order for the scheme of allowances to apply has been reduced from 20 to 10. The development must include a day-care centre. The units must be operated or managed by the registered nursing home and an on-site caretaker must be provided. Revenue have issued guidance on the requirement for the units to be operated and managed by the nursing home in *Tax Briefing 59*. The registered nursing home must provide back-up medical care to the occupants of the units when required. At least 20 per cent of the houses in the development must be available for renting to persons who are eligible for a rent subsidy from a Health Board. The rent charged in such cases must be at a discount of at least 10 per cent as compared with the fee charged to a person who is not in receipt of a rent subsidy. The unit must be leased to a person or persons who has or have been certified by a registered medical practitioner as requiring the accommodation by reason of old age or infirmity. With effect for expenditure incurred on or after 1 May 2007 under a contract or agreement entered into on or after that date, the unit may be leased to such a person together with their spouse or civil partner. However, for expenditure incurred from that date, the following conditions will also apply:

(i) neither the tenant or if, relevant the tenant's spouse or civil partner, may be connected with the lessor (within the meaning of TCA 1997, s 10); and

(ii) the tenant (and spouse if relevant) must have been selected for occupation by the registered nursing home (TCA 1997, s 268(3A)).

With effect from 1 January 2006 the residential units can also be let to the registered nursing home provided that the home subsequently leases the units to the infirm, etc persons and the units are used for no other purpose. The 75 per cent and 50 per cent expenditure restrictions apply to the residential units similar to hotels and sports clinics.

Convalescent homes

TCA 1997, s 268(1)(i) provided that a building or structure in use for the purposes of a trade consisting of the operation or management of a convalescent home for the provision of medical and nursing care to people recovering from treatment in a hospital, that provides treatment for acutely ill patients, will be treated as an industrial building in relation to capital expenditure incurred on the construction or refurbishment of such a building or structure on or after 2 December 1998 and prior to 31 December 2009, subject to the transitional provisions immediately following. Firstly, the cut-off date was extended to 30 June 2010 where the construction or refurbishment work is exempted development for the purposes of the Planning and Development Act 2000 by virtue of s 4 of that Act or by virtue of Pt 2 of the Planning and Development Regulations 2001 (SI 600/2001) and not less than 30 per cent of the total construction or refurbishment costs had been incurred on or before 31 December 2009. Secondly, the cut-off date was extended to 30 June 2011 where a planning application (not being an application for outline permission within the meaning of the Planning and Development Act 2000, s 36), in so far as planning permission was required, in respect of the construction or refurbishment work concerned was made in accordance with the Planning and Development Regulations 2001 (SI 600/2001) and an acknowledgement of the application, which confirms that the application was received on or before 31 December 2009, was issued by the planning authority in accordance with art 26(2) of those Regulations and the application was not an invalid application in respect of which a notice was issued by the planning authority in accordance with art 26(5) of those Regulations of 2001 (TCA 1997, s 17).

For the purposes of these cut-off provisions, capital expenditure will only be regarded as having been incurred within any given period to the extent that is properly attributable to work on construction or refurbishment of the relevant building or structure actually carried out in that period (TCA 1997, s 316(2B)).

The local Health Board must be satisfied that the home satisfies the requirements of the Health (Nursing Homes) Act 1990, ss 4 and 6, and any regulations made under s 6 of that Act as if it were a nursing home within the meaning of s 2 of that Act.

Hospitals

TCA 1997, s 268(1)(j) as amended by FA 2009 provides that a building or structure in use for the purposes of a trade that consists of the operation or management of a qualifying hospital will be treated as an industrial building or structure in respect of capital expenditure incurred on construction or refurbishment of such a building or structure on or after 15 May 2002 and prior to 31 December 2009, subject to the transitional provisions immediately following. Firstly, the cut-off date was extended to 30 June 2010 where the construction or refurbishment work is exempted development for the purposes of the Planning and Development Act 2000 by virtue of s 4 of that Act or by virtue of Pt 2 of the Planning and Development Regulations 2001 (SI 600/2001) and not less than 30 per cent of the total construction or refurbishment costs had been incurred on or before 31 December 2009. Secondly, the cut-off date was extended to 31 December 2013 where a planning application (not being an application for outline permission within the meaning of the Planning and Development Act 2000, s 36), in so far as planning permission is required, in respect of the construction or refurbishment work concerned was made in accordance with the Planning and Development Regulations 2001 (SI 600/2001) and an acknowledgement of the application, which confirms that the application was received on or before 31 December 2009, was issued by the planning authority in accordance with art 26(2) of those Regulations and the application is not an invalid application in respect of which a notice was issued by the planning authority in accordance with art 26(5) of those Regulations of 2001 (TCA 1997, s 17).

For the purposes of these cut-off provisions, capital expenditure will only be regarded as having been incurred within any given period to the extent that is properly attributable to work on construction or refurbishment of the relevant building or structure actually carried out in that period (TCA 1997, s 316(2B)).

Qualifying hospital is a hospital which satisfies the following:

(a) is a private hospital (with the meaning of Health Insurance Act 1994 (Minimum Benefits) Regulations 1996 (SI 83/1996);

(b) has the capacity to provide and normally provides medical and surgical services all year round;

(c) has the capacity to provide:

   (i) out-patient services and overnight accommodation of at least 70 in-patient beds, or

   (ii) say-case and out-patient medical and surgical services and accommodation for such services of not less than 40 beds,

   the alternative (more lenient) capacity requirement set out under (ii) above applies with regard to capital expenditure incurred on the construction of a qualifying hospital on or after 28 March 2003;

(d) contains at least one operating theatre and on-site diagnostic and therapeutic facilities;

(e) has facilities to provide at least five of the following range of services:

   (i) accident and emergency,

   (ii) cardiology and vascular,

   (iii) eye, ear, nose and throat,

   (iv) gastroenterology,

   (v) geriatrics,

   (vi) haematology,

   (vii) maternity,

   (viii) medical,

   (ix) neurology,

   (x) oncology,

   (xi) orthopaedic,

   (xii) respiratory,

   (xiii) rheumatology paediatric,

   (xiv) mental health services,

   the range of services is extended to include mental health services where the capital expenditure is incurred on or after 1 January 2006;

(f) undertakes to the local health board that at least 20 per cent of its annual capacity will be available for the treatment of persons who have been waiting for in-patient or out-patient hospital services as public patients – the fee charged for these services will be at a discount of at least 10 per cent as compared with the fee charged to the private patients for similar services;

(g) provides information to the Health Service Executive on the amount of the capital expenditure actually incurred on the construction of the building, the number and nature of the investors that are investing in the building, the amount to be invested by each investor, the nature of the structures which are being put in place to facilitate the investment and any other information required to evaluate the costs and benefits arising from the operation of the tax relief – this information must be provided where the hospital is first used on or after 1 February 2007 or is first used subsequent to incurring refurbishment expenditure on or after 1 February 2007; and

(h) receives an annual certificate from the Health Service Executive in consultation with the Minister for Health and Children and with the consent of the Minister for Finance stating that the hospital complies with the necessary conditions:
   (i) the annual certificate must be provided for a period of 10 years from the date of first use of the hospital where the hospital was first used before 1 February 2007,
   (ii) here the hospital is first used or is first used subsequent to incurring refurbishment expenditure on or after 1 February 2007 then the annual certificate of compliance with the conditions must be provided for a period of 15 years from the date of first use or date of first use subsequent to incurring the refurbishment expenditure.

The qualifying hospital includes any rooms used exclusively for the assessment or treatment of patients but excludes any part of the hospital which comprises consultant's rooms or offices.

There are restrictions on the availability of allowances in respect of expenditure on private hospitals if excluded categories of person hold the relevant interest in relation to the capital expenditure on the hospital. These excluded persons are a company, the trustees of a trust, an individual involved in the operation or management of the hospital as an employee or director, etc, or a property developer developers (or a person connected to the developer, with effect from 1 January 2008) where the property developer or a connected person incurred the capital expenditure on the construction of the hospital. Where the capital expenditure is incurred on or after 1 May 2004 the restriction operates so that the hospital is not an industrial building as regards a capital allowance claim by an excluded person. Accordingly if the relevant interest is held by a group of investors the relief will be denied only to the excluded persons in the group. As regards expenditure incurred prior to 1 May 2004 the hospital is not an industrial building if the relevant interest is held by an excluded person with the result that the relief is denied to all of the members in the group if any of them fall into an excluded category (TCA 1997, s 268(1A)).

Sports injuries clinics

TCA 1997, s 268(1)(k) provides that a building or structure in use for the purposes of a trade which consists of the operation or management of a qualifying sports injuries clinic will be treated as an industrial building in relation to expenditure incurred up to 31 December 2006 (subject to transitional provisions: see below). A qualifying sports injuries clinic is a medical clinic:

(a) which does not provide health care services to a person pursuant to his entitlements under Health Act 1970, Pt IV, Ch II;
(b) in which the main business carried on is the diagnosis, alleviation and treatment of sports injuries;
(c) which has in patient accommodation of at least 20 beds;
(d) which contains at least one operating theatre and related diagnostic and therapeutic facilities;
(e) undertakes to the local health board that at least 20 per cent of its annual capacity will be available for the treatment of persons who have been waiting for day-patient, in-patient or out-patient hospital services as public patients. The fee charged for these services will be at a discount of at least 10 per cent as compared to the fee charged to private patients; and

(f) in respect of which the Heath Service Executive, in consultation with the Minister for Health and Children and with the consent of the Minister for Finance, gives an annual certificate for a period of 10 years from the date of first use stating that the conditions outlined above are satisfied.

A qualifying sports injuries clinic includes any part of the clinic which consists of rooms used exclusively for the assessment or treatment of patients but excludes consultant's rooms and offices.

As regards expenditure incurred prior to 1 May 2004 TCA 1997, s 268(1B) provides that a sports injuries clinic will not be treated as an industrial building if the relevant interest in relation to the construction expenditure is held by a company, the trustees of a trust, an individual involved in the operation or management of the sports injuries clinic as an employee or director, etc or a property developer where the property developer or a connected person incurred the capital expenditure on the sports injuries clinic. Where the expenditure is incurred on or after 1 May 2004 the sports injuries clinic will not be regarded as an industrial building insofar as an excluded person makes a claim for any allowance. Where a member of a group of investors falls into any of the excluded categories relief will be denied to that person only and not to the other members of the group.

FA 2006, s 28 provides that the relief for capital expenditure incurred on qualifying sports injuries clinics will apply only up to 31 December 2006. Capital expenditure incurred up until 31 July 2008 will qualify for relief provided:

(a) the person who is constructing or refurbishing the clinic has carried out work to the value of not less than 15 per cent of the actual construction or refurbishment costs of the clinic by 31 December 2006; and

(b) the person carrying out the work or where the clinic is sold the person claiming the deduction can show that the condition at (i) is satisfied.

As regards expenditure incurred in the period from 1 January 2007 to 31 July 2008, only reduced relief will be available. 75 per cent of the expenditure incurred in the calendar year 2007 and 50 per cent of the expenditure incurred in the period from 1 January 2008 to 31 July 2008 will qualify for relief.

Qualifying mental health centres

TCA 1997, s 268(1)(l) as amended by FA 2009 provided that a building or structure in use for the purposes of a trade of the operation or management of a qualifying mental health centre will be treated as an industrial building or structure in respect of capital expenditure incurred on construction or refurbishment of such a building or structure on or after 23 January 2007 and prior to 31 December 2009 subject to the transitional provisions immediately following. Firstly, the cut-off date was extended to 30 June 2010 where the construction or refurbishment work was exempted development for the purposes of the Planning and Development Act 2000 by virtue of s 4 of that Act or by virtue of Part 2 of the Planning and Development Regulations 2001 (SI 600/2001) and not less than 30 per cent of the total construction or refurbishment costs had been incurred on or before 31 December 2009. Secondly, the cut-off date was extended to 30 June 2011 where a planning application (not being an application for outline permission within the meaning of the Planning and Development Act 2000, s 36), in so far as planning permission was required, in respect of the construction or refurbishment work concerned was made in accordance with the Planning and Development Regulations 2001 (SI 600/2001) and an acknowledgement of the application, which confirms that the application was received on or before 31 December 2009, was issued by the planning authority in accordance with art 26(2) of those Regulations and the application was not an invalid application in respect of which a notice was issued by the planning authority in accordance with art 26(5) of those Regulations of 2001 (TCA 1997, s 17). For the purposes of these cut-off provisions, capital expenditure will only be regarded as having been incurred within any given period to the extent that is properly attributable to work on construction or refurbishment of the relevant building or structure actually carried out in that period (TCA 1997, s 316(2B)).

A qualifying mental health centre is an approved centre for the purpose of the Mental Health Act 2001, s 62. It must have a minimum of 20 in-patient beds. Details of the amount of expenditure incurred on the on the construction of the centre, the number and nature of investors, the amount invested by each investor, and the nature of the structures that are being put in place to facilitate the investment together with other information required to evaluate the costs and benefits of the operation of the tax relief must be provided to the Health Service Executive. The centre must make 20 per cent of its annual capacity available for the treatment of public patients and the fees for these services will not be more than 90 per cent of the amount that would be charged to private patients. In order to qualify for relief the mental health centre will need an annual certificate from the Health Service Executive for a period of 15 years from the date of first use of the building stating that it is satisfied that the centre complies with the conditions of the relief.

Certain persons are excluded from claiming relief in respect of expenditure incurred on a centre. These include a company, the trustees of a trust, an individual involved in the operation or management of the centre as an employee or director, etc or a property developer (or a person connected to the developer, with effect from 1 January 2008) where the property developer or a connected person incurred the capital expenditure on the centre.

Qualifying specialist palliative care units

Subject to ministerial order FA 2008, s 26(1) extends TCA 1997, s 268(1) to provide that a building is in use for the purposes of a trade which consists of the operation or management of a qualifying specialist palliative care unit will be an industrial building.

Palliative care means the active total care of patients who suffer from illnesses or diseases which are active, progressive and advanced in nature and which are no longer curable by means of the administration of existing or medical treatments.

TCA 1997, s 268(2BA) provides that a qualifying specialist palliative care unit means a building or structure:

(a) which is a hospital, hospice or similar facility which has palliative care as its main activity;

(b) which is approved by the Health Service Executive with the consent of the Minister for Health and Children as being in accordance with national development plans or national needs assessments for palliative care facilities;

(c) which has the capacity to provide day-patient and out-patient palliative care services and palliative care accommodation on an overnight basis of not less than 8 inpatient beds;

(d) in respect of which data is provided to the Health Service Executive in relation to the total amount of the capital expenditure actually incurred on construction or refurbishment of the unit, the amount if any of that expenditure met by way of grant or other financial assistance, the number and nature of the investors, the amount to be invested by each investor, the nature of the structures being put in place to facilitate the investment in the unit together with such other information as may be specified by the Minister of Finance;

(e) in respect of which 20 per cent of its annual capacity is made available for the treatment of public patients and the fees for these services will not be more than 90 per cent of the amount that would be charged to private patients; and

(f) in respect of which the Health Service Executive gives an annual certificate in writing during the period of 15 years of the date of first use (or first use after incurring refurbishment expenditure) that it is satisfied that the unit complies with the conditions from (a) to (e).

A qualifying specialist palliative care unit includes the parts of the unit which consists of rooms used exclusively for the assessment, treatment or care of patients. It does not include any part of the unit which consists of consultants' rooms or offices. Nor does it include any part of the unit in which a majority of the persons being maintained are being treated for acute illnesses (TCA 1997, s 268(2BB)).

Certain persons are excluded from claiming relief in respect of expenditure incurred on a centre. These include a company, the trustees of a trust, an individual involved in the operation or management of the centre as an employee or director, etc, a property developer or a person connected with the property developer where the property developer or a connected person incurred the capital expenditure on the centre.

Childcare facilities

TCA 1997, s 843A, as most recently amended by FA 2010, s 26, provides for capital allowances on certain childcare facilities as if they qualified as industrial buildings. The measure applies to construction, refurbishment or conversion expenditure incurred on or after 2 December 1998 on a building in use for the purposes of providing a pre-school service, or a pre-school service and a day-care or other service to cater for children other than pre-school children. Where the building is used to provide a pre-school service, it must be shown that the requirements of Regulation 10 or 11(1), as appropriate, of the Child Care (Pre-School Services) (No 2) Regulations 2006 (SI 604/2006) have been complied with. The terms 'pre-school child' and 'pre-school service' have the meaning assigned to them by the Child Care Act 1991, s 49. The allowances are available in respect of qualifying expenditure incurred on or after 1 December 1999 up to 30 September 2010 (TCA 1997, s 843A(3A)). However, the cut-off date was extended to 31 March 2011 where the construction or refurbishment work is exempted development for the purposes of the Planning and Development Act 2000, s 4 or the Planning and Development Regulations 2001 Pt 2 and not less than 30 per cent of the total construction or refurbishment costs has been incurred on or before 30 September 2010. Secondly, the cut-off date was extended to 31 March 2012 where a planning application (not being an application for outline permission within the Planning and Development Act 2000, s 36, in so far as planning permission is required, in respect of the construction or refurbishment work concerned was made in accordance with the Planning and Development Regulations 2001 and an acknowledgement of the application, which confirms that the application was received on or before 30 September 2010, was issued by the planning authority in accordance with Art 26(2) of those Regulations and the application is not an invalid application in respect of which a notice was issued by the planning authority in accordance with art 26(5) of those Regulations) (TCA 1997, s 843(6)). For the purposes of these cut-off provisions, capital expenditure will only be regarded as having been incurred within any given period to the extent that is properly attributable to work on construction or refurbishment of the relevant building or structure actually carried out in that period (TCA 1997, s 843(7)).

A building in use as a childcare facility is a relevant facility (TCA 1997, s 274(2A)(vi)). Where capital allowances have been claimed on a childcare facility which is first used on or after 1 January 2006 the cessation of use of the building as a childcare facility is an event which may give rise to a balancing adjustment (see **6.409**).

This relief is subject to the limitations on specified reliefs for higher income individuals discussed at **3.111**.

Aviation facilities

FA 2013 introduced, subject to a Ministerial Order due to EU State Aid concerns, capital allowances for expenditure incurred on aviation facilities. Instead of such a Ministerial Order, FA 2015, s 27 commenced those provisions as coming into operation on 13 October 2015. Certain further amendments were made by FA 2015, s 27 to comply with EU State Aid *de minimis* guidelines with effect from 1 January 2016. FA 2013 inserted TCA 1997, s 268(1)(n) which includes capital expenditure on the construction of a building or structure in use for the purposes of a trade consisting of:

(i) the maintenance, repair or overhaul of aircraft used to carry passengers or cargo for hire or reward; or

(ii) the dismantling of aircraft of the kind referred to above for the purposes of the salvaging or recycling of parts or materials

as an industrial building for capital allowances purposes.

With effect from 1 January 2016, and subject to TCA 1997, s 268(5C) (see below), TCA 1997, s 268(5A) states that expenditure incurred by a person on the construction of an industrial building or structure (within the meaning of the above mentioned TCA 1997, s 268(1)(n)) shall be treated as 'specified capital expenditure' for the purposes of this Part—

(a) only to the extent that the aggregate of such expenditure does not exceed—
  (i) €5,000,000, where the person concerned is a company, and
  (ii) €1,250,000, where the person concerned is an individual,

  and

(b) where the following information has been provided to the Revenue Commissioners before the first claim for a writing-down allowance is made, in accordance with s 272, by the person:
  (i) the name, address and tax reference number of the person making the claim;
  (ii) the address of the building or structure in respect of which the expenditure was incurred or deemed to have been incurred;
  (iii) details of the aggregate of the amount of such expenditure which has been incurred or deemed to have been incurred by the person making the claim.

The reference above to 'specified capital expenditure' is important in that it determines the rate of allowance available to the expenditure on aviation facilities. Where the capital expenditure is regarded as 'specified capital expenditure' in that TCA 1997, ss 272 and 274 were amended by FA 2015, s 27 to allow for a seven-year write off period (15 per cent in the first six years and the balance in year seven for 'specified capital expenditure' with the 4 per cent writing down allowances and 25-year life applying for other expenditure. It should be noted that the accelerated allowances mentioned above and indeed the definition outlined of aviation facilities in TCA 1997, s 268(1)(n) apply as respects (i) specified capital expenditure incurred in the period commencing on the date of the coming into operation of s 31 of the Finance Act 2013 and ending on the fifth anniversary of that date (ie the period of five years from 13 October 2015), and (ii) capital expenditure other than specified capital expenditure incurred on or after the date of the coming into operation of s 31 of the Finance Act 2013 (13 October 2015). The original provisions were subject to Ministerial Order but instead of such a Ministerial Order, FA 2015, s 27 commenced those provisions as coming into operation on 13 October 2015.

TCA 1997, s 272(4)(k) notes that the tax life of such specified capital expenditure (during which allowances may be transferred to a purchaser) of the above aviation facilities is: (i) seven years from the time the building or structure was first used; or (ii) where capital expenditure on the refurbishment of the building or structure is incurred, seven years from the time it was first used subsequent to the incurring of that expenditure. In addition, TCA 1997, s 274(1)(b)(x) notes that no balancing allowance or charge may be made by reason of an event occurring more than seven years after the building or structure was first used or, where capital expenditure on the refurbishment of the building or structure is incurred, seven years after it was first used subsequent to incurring that expenditure.

The Revenue Commissioners can furnish to persons such information as is referred to in para (b) above where they are satisfied that doing so is necessary to ensure compliance with the provisions of TCA 1997, Pt 9 (ie capital allowances purposes) and any European Commission guidelines, regulations or other reporting requirements that may be relevant. The section does not expand further on the other reporting requirements but Revenue guidance notes that this essentially means that Revenue may disclose this information to officials of the European Commission, who are responsible for monitoring and supervising the *de minimis* Guidelines.

A new sub-s (5C) was brought about by FA 2015, s 27 and came into operation on 1 January 2016 stating that where capital expenditure has been incurred, or deemed to have been incurred, on the construction of an industrial building of structure to which TCA 1997, s 268(1)(n) applies (aviation facilities) by two or more persons (individuals or companies, or both) the amount of such expenditure which is to be treated as specified capital expenditure for the purposes of TCA 1997, Pt 9 (ie capital allowances purposes) shall, if necessary and notwithstanding TCA 1997, s 279, be reduced such that the amount determined by the formula:

$$(A \times 50 \text{ per cent}) + (B \times 12\tfrac{1}{2} \text{ per cent})$$

does not exceed €625,000, where:

A is the aggregate of all 'such specified capital expenditure' which has been incurred, or deemed to have been incurred, by the individual or individuals concerned, and

B is the aggregate of all 'such specified capital expenditure' which has been incurred, or deemed to have been incurred, by the company or companies concerned.

The reference to 'such specified capital expenditure' would presumably be a reference to the earlier mentioned 'an industrial building of structure' which would mean that a structure by structure approach is to be taken. The above is written from the perspective of the amount of 'specified capital expenditure' on the structure rather than the taxpayer concerned. Revenue guidance on the section notes that the amount of capital expenditure that will qualify as specified capital expenditure where a number of individuals or companies or both invest in a project will be determined by the above mentioned formula. The specified capital expenditure must not exceed an amount that will give rise to tax relief greater than €625,000. This is the maximum amount of relief from corporation tax that is allowable given that a cap of €5m of qualifying expenditure incurred over seven years applies to a company. The formula reflects that individuals are taxed at a higher rate than companies. Revenue will not prescribe how the specified capital expenditure is actually apportioned between the individual or the company but rather imposes a cap on the maximum amount of relief that can be claimed over seven years, ie €625,000. It is of note that the above subsection requires the specified capital expenditure for capital allowances purposes to be reduced 'if necessary' such that the amount determined by the formula does not exceed €625,000 without specifying tax relief reductions in the subsection.

The above reference to TCA 1997, s 279 is of note. TCA 1997, s 271 provides that the industrial buildings initial allowance is given to the person who incurs the capital expenditure on the construction of the building or structure which is to be used for a qualifying trade. TCA 1997, ss 272, 274 provide respectively for annual allowances and balancing allowances (or charges) on the same construction expenditure to be given to the person owning the relevant interest which the person who incurred the construction expenditure had at the time it was incurred. TCA 1997, s 277 contains rules relating to the writing off of the construction expenditure. TCA 1997, s 279 adapts these rules to deal with the case where the relevant interest in any building or structure is sold after expenditure has been incurred on the construction of the building, but before the building is first used for any purpose. This may occur where the construction expenditure is incurred by a speculative builder or other person carrying on a trade of constructing buildings for sale. It may also arise where a person constructs a building expecting to use it for his own trade or for leasing, but who for any reason sells his relevant interest before the building is used for any purpose. The section also applies if the relevant interest is sold when the building is only partly constructed, eg when a speculative builder goes out of business. It also applies where the building is bought within one year after it is first used, or within two years after it is first used for sales of a relevant interest occurring on or after 14 October 2008, but only if no other person has claimed any industrial building allowance for that building. In any case where it applies, TCA 1997, s 279 requires any industrial buildings initial, writing down and balancing allowances (or balancing charges) to be based on a deemed cost of construction instead of the actual expenditure on construction incurred by the person selling the relevant interest.

TCA 1997, s 268(11A), which comes into operation on 1 January 2016, restricts grant aided expenditure. It notes that capital expenditure which has been incurred on the construction of an industrial building (within the meaning of sub-s (1)(n)) (ie aviation facilities) shall not be treated as specified capital expenditure where any part of that expenditure has been or is to be met, directly or indirectly, by grant assistance or any other assistance which is granted by or through the State, any board established by statute, any public or local authority or any other agency of the State.

TCA 1997, s 268(1F) notes that where the relevant interest in relation to the capital expenditure incurred on the construction of the building or structure in use for the above purposes is held by a property developer (within the meaning of TCA 1997, s 843A) or a person who is connected with the property developer, in the case where either of such persons incurred the capital expenditure on the construction of that building or structure, or such expenditure was incurred by any other person (ie, who does not hold the relevant interest) connected with the property developer, that building or structure will not, as regards a claim for any industrial building allowance by any such person, be regarded as specified capital expenditure irrespective of whether that relevant interest is held by the person in a sole capacity or jointly or in partnership with another person or persons.

In addition, this relief qualifies for the application of the high earner restriction – see **3.111**.

Runways and airport buildings

Annual allowances at 4 per cent are available on capital expenditure incurred on a building in use for the purposes of a trade of the operation and management of an airport including runways and runway aprons. The capital allowances are available at 4 per cent per annum and the tax life (ie writing down period; see **6.409**) is 25 years. The period after which no balancing charge or allowance will be made on a disposal is also 25 years. There is no cut-off date for the expiry of the capital expenditure.

Industrial buildings abroad

By virtue of TCA 1997, s 268(5) expenditure incurred on a building or structure situated outside the State on or after 23 April 1996 no longer generally qualifies for industrial buildings allowances, subject to transitional relief. TCA 1997, s 268(5) states that expenditure on acquiring a relevant interest in, or on constructing a building or structure situated outside the State, is not to be treated as expenditure on a qualifying building, etc, *unless*:

(a) the person who incurs the expenditure:
   (i) entered into a written option agreement or a written contract to acquire the site on or before 23 April 1996, and
   (ii) entered into a contract for the construction of the building on or before 1 July 1996, and
   (iii) the construction of the building commenced on or before 1 July 1996 and was completed before 30 September 1998; and
(b) the building is used for the purposes of a trade, the profits or gains from which are taxable in the State.

In the author's view the significance of the reference to 'expenditure incurred on the acquisition of the relevant interest' is unclear. Claims are normally made by reference to the construction expenditure incurred on the building (see TCA 1997, s 272(3), but note TCA 1997, s 279); more significantly, the exception in TCA 1997, s 268 is applied by reference to the person who entered into the construction contract concerned. Accordingly, TCA 1997, s 268(5) does not generally appear to prevent a purchaser of a relevant interest claiming allowances by reference to TCA 1997, s 272(3) where the person(s) who originally incurred the construction expenditure complied with the requirements noted above.

Excluded buildings

Certain types of building are specifically excluded and do not qualify for industrial buildings allowances, even though they may be in use for the purposes of a qualifying trade or undertaking (see *Sarsfield v Dixons* [1998] STC 938). Thus, no allowances can be claimed for any building or structure in use as:

(a) a dwelling house (except for the holiday cottages or the qualifying residential units mentioned earlier);
(b) a retail shop;
(c) a showroom; or
(d) an office,

or in use as part of, or for any purpose ancillary to that of, a dwelling house, retail shop, showroom or office (TCA 1997, s 268(7)(b)). It was held in *Sarsfield v Dixons* [1998] STC 938 that the disallowance applies to any building which is ancillary to a dwelling house, etc irrespective of whether the dwelling house, etc is owned by the taxpayer and irrespective of whether the dwelling house would itself have qualified as an industrial building in the absence of TCA 1997, s 268(7)(b).

A 'dwelling house' need not be the private residence of an individual (see the rating case of *Kerry County Council v Kerins* [1996] 3 IR 493); indeed, if this were not the case, the express exclusion for holiday cottages would be redundant. A retail shop includes any premises of a similar character where retail trade or business, including repair work, is carried on (TCA 1997, s 268(7)(a)).

This particular definition of 'retail shop' has been considered in a number of UK rating cases. In *Turpin v Middlesborough Assessment Committee* [1931] AC 451 it was held that the phrase 'of a similar character' was not limited to the physical character of the premises:

> It must be a building to which the public can resort for the purpose of having particular wants supplied and services rendered therein.

In *Dolton Bournes & Dolton Ltd v Osmond* [1955] 1 WLR 621, it was held accordingly that premises to which only trade customers (and not the general public) had access was not a retail shop. The approach in the rating cases was upheld by the Court of Session in *Kilmarnock Equitable Co-Op v IRC* 42 TC 675 (concerning the UK provisions equivalent to TCA 1997, s 268(7)).

In *O'Connaill v Waterford Glass* III ITR 65, it was held that a showroom which was used merely for display purposes (ie which was not used for retailing activities) was nevertheless disqualified. In *Bestway (Holdings) v Luff* [1997] STC (SCD) 87, it was held that the fact that a 'cash and carry' premises incorporated some displays of goods was not sufficient to make it a showroom.

The meaning of an office was considered in the Scottish case of *IRC v Lambhill Ironworks Ltd* 31 TC 393. In that case, the part of a building containing the drawing office of a company carrying on business as structural steel engineers was held to be an industrial building or structure, and was not disqualified on the grounds of being an office. The Court of Session held that the office in question was clearly in use 'for the purposes of a trade … carried on in a factory'. If it had failed this general test, then it would of course not have been eligible for an allowance in the first place. The court then rejected the argument that the office was nevertheless excluded by the equivalent provision to TCA 1997, s 268(7)(b).

The court held that:

> An office must be something which clearly has not got anything of an industrial character or is not directly ancillary to the industrial operations conducted in the rest of the works.

In this case, it was found that the purpose of the drawing office related directly to the manufacturing operations of the taxpayer. The fact that a small proportion of work carried out in the office was for general administrative purposes was regarded as immaterial. The test of whether a building (or part thereof) is used 'as an office', etc under TCA 1997, s 268(7)(b) accordingly seems to depend on its predominant purpose or use; this test is stricter than that employed in deciding whether or not a building is being used 'for the purposes' of a qualifying trade (see eg the *Saxone* case above). In *Girobank plc v Clarke* [1998] STC 182, it was held that an office was a place where the management or administration of an enterprise is carried on.

The *Lambhill* case was followed in *O'Connaill v Waterford Glass* III ITR 65. That case concerned a building described as an 'administrative centre', which was constructed apart from the main factory premises. The principal part of the centre housed a computer, but it also included a canteen, a showroom and general administrative facilities. The computer was used to produce various reports and schedules which were essential to the manufacturing operations of the taxpayer, and was also used to a minor extent for general administrative purposes. McWilliam J, in the High Court, upheld the finding by the Circuit Court judge that the administrative centre qualified as an industrial building, but excluded those parts of the building which consisted of the showroom and administrative facilities.

McWilliam J's conclusions are consistent with the logic underlying the *Saxone* and *Lambhill* cases. Firstly, the main part of the building (ie excluding the showroom and administrative facilities) was clearly used for the purposes of a qualifying trade and thus qualified for allowances under TCA 1997, s 268(1); secondly, that part of the building was used predominantly for industrial (as opposed to administrative) purposes and therefore did not fall to be excluded under TCA 1997, s 268(7)(b).

It seems that in deciding whether or not a building or structure is in use for a purpose which is ancillary to a retail shop, etc, the specific objectives of the taxpayer are a relevant consideration (see *Kilmarnock Equitable Co-Op v IRC* 42 TC 675). In *Sarsfield v Dixons* [1998] STC 938, it was held that a building was used for the purposes of a retail shop if its usage was confined to furthering the purposes of the retail shop, ie subservient and subordinate to retail selling; furthermore, the retail shop need not be owned by the trader. In the instant case, goods were being held in a warehouse by a manufacturer exclusively for delivery to a retailer which was a member of the same corporate group; it was held that the warehouse accordingly could not qualify as an industrial building. The Court of Appeal rejected the view of Lightman J at first instance that the 'retail shops' in question must be of a kind which would fall to be classed as industrial buildings, but for the application of the UK equivalent of the TCA 1997, s 268(7); this conclusion seems preferable.

Where part of a building or structure qualifies as an industrial building, but another part does not, the whole of the building still qualifies if the cost of construction of the non-qualifying part does not exceed 10 per cent of the total capital expenditure incurred on the construction of the whole building (TCA 1997, s 268(8)). This rule can apply either because the part of the building is not in use for the purposes of a qualifying trade or because it is in use for such purposes but would fall to be excluded under TCA 1997, s 268(7) (*Sarsfield v Dixons* [1997] STC 283). For example, if a factory building including offices and showrooms costs €1 million to construct, the full amount of the expenditure qualifies for industrial buildings allowances if the cost of the offices, showrooms and any other non-qualifying part included in the building is not more than €100,000. If, however, the cost of the non-qualifying parts is €100,500, the industrial buildings allowances are only given on the remaining €899,500 of the €1 million expenditure.

As noted above, in *O'Connaill v Waterford Glass*, it was held that an administrative centre which was housed in a building at a distance from the main factory premises should nevertheless be regarded as an integral part of the entire factory complex. The case is not, however, an authority for saying that a factory cannot consist of separate buildings and structures (notwithstanding a passing reference to TCA 1997, s 268(7) by the learned judge).

This issue arose in *Abbott Laboratories v Carmody* 44 TC 569 in which a factory manufacturing pharmaceutical products was erected in four different blocks, one of which was an administrative block. There were properly made up roads connecting the various blocks. All were served by a common heating system involving physical connection by pipes. The administrative block, with which the case was concerned, was physically connected to the pharmaceutical block by a covered passageway. The Special Commissioners held that the provisions of the Act were not intended to apply to an extensive factory site to enable it to be treated as one unit for capital allowances. The High Court disagreed and sent back the case to the Commissioners to reconsider it on the footing that the layout of the buildings was not in law incapable of being a single industrial building or structure. The Commissioners then ruled that the administrative block still must be regarded as a separate entity since it was not sufficiently physically integrated with the other structural units within the complex (accordingly it was not eligible for the allowance, although the cost thereof was less than 10 per cent of the factory premises taken as a whole).

TCA 1997, s 270(3) makes clear that where expenditure is incurred on an industrial building or structure which either:

(a) forms part of a building;
(b) is one of a number of buildings in a single development; or
(c) forms part of a building which is one of a number of buildings in a single development;

then any necessary apportionment shall be made in order to determine the expenditure which relates to the construction of the industrial building or structure.

Capital expenditure on the construction of part of a building qualifies for the industrial buildings allowance if the whole building or the part on which the expenditure is incurred is an industrial building within the definition of TCA 1997, s 268(1). References in the Tax Acts to a building or structure are taken to include references to a part of a building or structure, except where the reference is one to the whole of the building (TCA 1997, s 320(2)). This permits capital expenditure on altering or extending an existing building to qualify for the industrial buildings allowance on its own. It also means that expenditure incurred at different times on the same building is treated separately for purposes of the allowance and has its own separate 'writing down' life (see **6.402**).

6.402 General scheme of industrial buildings allowances

There are two types of industrial building allowances available – the industrial buildings (initial) allowance ('IBA'), only rarely applicable now (see **6.405**) and the industrial buildings writing down (or annual) allowance ('IBAA') (see **6.406**). In addition, increased writing down allowances (free depreciation) may in rare cases be claimed for qualifying expenditure on certain industrial buildings (see **6.407**). The rate of these allowances varies with the trade category into which the building falls.

The industrial buildings initial allowance may be claimed by the person incurring the qualifying expenditure on the construction of the building or structure in the circumstances outlined in **6.405**. The person who incurred the expenditure on the building is also entitled to annual writing down allowances, and to claim any increased allowances that may be available, if he continues to hold the 'relevant interest' in relation to that expenditure. A person who acquires the 'relevant interest' may also be entitled to annual writing down allowances so long as he continues to hold that interest. The writing down allowances are given to a person chargeable to income tax for each relevant year of assessment if he holds the relevant interest in relation to the expenditure at the end of the basis period for that year.

The 'relevant interest' is defined as the particular interest (eg freehold, leasehold, etc) which the person who incurred the expenditure held in the building or structure in question at the time he incurred the expenditure (see **6.403**).

The tax life (ie writing down life; see **6.409**) of the construction expenditure on any building begins on the date the building is first used for any purpose and ends a number of years later, depending on the trade category and the date of the expenditure; generally no balancing allowances or charges will arise as a result of events occurring after the end of the tax life of a building however for certain types of industrial buildings (eg registered nursing homes, qualifying private hospitals) a balancing charge or allowance may arise after the tax life has ended (see **6.409**). The rate of writing down allowance is generally computed differently in the case of a person who purchases the relevant interest in an industrial building (see **6.410**).

Special rules apply where a building is purchased unused or within the year of its first use, where it has not been the subject of a claim for any industrial buildings allowances (see **6.408**).

The calculation of any balancing allowance or charge on a sale, etc of an industrial building the expenditure on which has been incurred at different dates is set out in **6.412**.

Since the definition of an industrial building depends on the use to which the building or structure is being put at any relevant time, there are rules for dealing with cases where a building that has qualified for initial and/or writing down allowances ceases to be used as an industrial building (but disregarding periods of temporary disuse: see **6.411**).

The treatment of capital allowances (including balancing charges) for lessors of industrial buildings is outlined in **6.5**.

6.403 Meaning of 'relevant interest'

A person incurring capital expenditure on a building may hold the freehold interest in the land on which the building is constructed or, alternatively, he may hold some form of leasehold interest in the land. He may have the leasehold interest that has been created directly out of the freehold (the head lease) or he may be entitled to an inferior lease or sublease granted out of a superior leasehold interest which may, or may not, be the head lease. He may be the person who occupies the land (including any buildings on the land) or he may hold his particular interest subject to a lease or sublease granted to someone else who either occupies the land or holds that sublease subject to an inferior sublease. In short, it is possible for the land to be occupied by the freeholder or there may be a chain of leases and subleases between the freeholder and the person occupying the land.

The entitlement to the industrial buildings writing down allowances and balancing allowances, and the liability to any balancing charge, in respect of any capital expenditure always follows the person holding the relevant interest in relation to that expenditure, whether or not that relevant interest has changed hands since the expenditure was incurred. It should be noted that the term, while it refers to a particular interest in the building (and land), is expressed as being 'in relation to' expenditure on the building.

TCA 1997, s 269(1) defines the 'relevant interest', in relation to any particular expenditure incurred on the construction of a building or structure, as the interest in that building or structure to which the person who incurred the expenditure was entitled when he incurred it. This definition applies whether or not the building is being constructed for use in a type of trade or undertaking qualifying for industrial buildings allowances. Even if a building is used for other purposes for some years after its construction, the person holding the relevant interest in relation to any qualifying construction expenditure is entitled to the industrial buildings writing down allowances in any later year (so long as there is a balance of unclaimed expenditure) if the building is subsequently used for a qualifying trade or undertaking.

Example 6.403.1

In 2012, C incurs capital expenditure of €340,000 in constructing a building on land in which the various interests at the time the expenditure was incurred were held as follows:

Holder of interest;

Type of interest:

A	freehold, subject to;
B	999-years lease (head lease), subject to;
C	99-year sublease.

The relevant interest in relation to the €340,000 expenditure is the 99-year sublease held by C since 1998. Should C sell or otherwise assign this 99-year sublease to D, in say, 2015, then D becomes the holder of the relevant interest and is entitled to the industrial buildings writing down allowances from that year onwards if the building is used for a qualifying trade or undertaking.

TCA 1997, s 269(2), (3) adds the following rules to supplement the main definition of the relevant interest:

(a) the relevant interest in relation to any expenditure does not cease to be the relevant interest where a lease or other inferior interest is created out of it;

(b) if a person is entitled to two or more interests in a building or structure at the time he incurs the construction expenditure, the relevant interest is the interest that is reversionary on all the other interests; and

(c) where the relevant interest is a leasehold interest, and if it is extinguished either (1) by being surrendered or (2) by the acquisition by the person entitled to the relevant interest of the interest which is reversionary on that interest, then the interest into which that leasehold interest merges thereupon becomes the relevant interest.

Example 6.403.2

Take the facts of **Example 6.403.1** and assume that, after C's assignment to D of the 99-year sublease, D creates a further sublease for 35 years to E so that D's 99-year lease becomes subject to this 35-year sublease. E uses the building as a factory in his manufacturing trade, but as it needs modification for this purpose, E incurs further capital expenditure in 2015 of €120,000 on alterations and improvements to the building.

The creation of the 35-year sublease to E does not cause D's 99-year lease to cease to be the relevant interest in relation to the 2012 expenditure of €340,000 so that D continues to be entitled to the writing down allowances in respect of that expenditure (so long as he holds the 99-year lease). These allowances are given against Sch D, Case V income from the sublease to E (see **6.5**).

The relevant interest in relation to the €120,000 expenditure incurred in 2015 is the 35-year sublease that was held by E at the time he incurred that expenditure. He is therefore the person entitled to the industrial buildings allowances on €120,000 (but not on the €340,000) so long as he retains this interest in the land and buildings, assuming the buildings continue to be used for a qualifying purpose.

Example 6.403.3

Take the fact of **Example 6.403.2**, but assume that it is B to whom the 35-year sublease is granted by D in 2015. Assume that it is B who incurs the capital expenditure of €120,000 in altering the building for use in her manufacturing trade. The interests in the building are now held as follows:

A	freehold, subject to;
B	999-year head lease, subject to;
D	99-year sublease, subject to;
B	35-year sublease.

Since B holds both the 999-year head lease and the 35-year sublease when she incurs the expenditure of €120,000 in 2015, the relevant interest in relation to that expenditure is the 999-year head lease, ie the interest that is reversionary on (superior to) the interests below it in the chain. This does not affect the relevant interest in relation to the 2012 expenditure of €340,000 so that D as the holder of the 99-year sublease remains the person entitled to the writing down allowances on this expenditure so long as B (or any subsequent holder of the 35-year sublease) continues to use the building for a qualifying purpose.

Example 6.403.4

Take the facts of **Example 6.403.3**, and assume that in 2015 D surrenders his 99-year sublease to B for a suitable consideration and that it and the 35-year sublease are both extinguished by being merged into B's 999-year head lease.

B is now the person holding the relevant interest in relation to the 2012 expenditure of €340,000 which had previously attached to the 99-year sublease. He therefore becomes entitled to the writing down allowances on this expenditure as well as to the allowances on the 2015 expenditure of €120,000 provided that the building continues to be used for a qualifying purpose.

Special rules for leasehold interests

A person holding a leasehold interest in land (and buildings) may have incurred capital expenditure in constructing a building on the land (or in extending an existing building); alternatively, he may have purchased or otherwise acquired a leasehold interest that is the relevant interest in relation to such capital expenditure. In either event, such a person is entitled to the writing down allowances so long as he retains that interest and the buildings are in use for a qualifying trade or undertaking. If this leasehold interest comes to an end when the building is an industrial building, a balancing allowance or charge has to be computed by comparing the residue of the expenditure related to the leasehold interest with any sale, insurance, salvage or compensation monies (see **6.409**).

TCA 1997, s 281 contains three special rules relating to the termination of a leasehold interest which may vary the writing down allowances and/or balancing allowances or charges in respect of the capital expenditure attaching to a leasehold interest. These rules are:

(a) if a lessee of a building remains in possession after the termination of the lease, with the consent of the lessor but without the granting of a new lease to him, the original lease is deemed to continue so long as the lessee actually remains in possession. Consequently, the lessee continues to be entitled to the writing down allowances on any qualifying expenditure incurred by him, or by any previous holder of the leasehold interest; further, no question of a balancing allowance or charge arises so long as the lessee continues to remain in possession with the consent of the lessor;

(b) where, on the termination of a lease, a new lease is granted to the lessee either due to his being entitled by statute to a new lease or on the exercise of an option available to him under the terms of the first lease, then the second lease is treated as if it were a continuation of the first lease. In other words, no question of a balancing allowance or charge arises and the lessee continues to be entitled to the writing down allowances; and

(c) where, on the termination of a lease, the lessor pays any sum to the lessee in respect of a building or structure comprised in the lease, the lease is treated as if it had come to an end by reason of its surrender in consideration of the payment received. This means that the sum paid to the lessee on the termination of the lease must be brought into account in the sale, etc monies used in the computation of any balancing allowance or charge in respect of any capital expenditure attaching to the leasehold interest. This might arise, for example, if the lessee agrees for a consideration to surrender his leasehold interest before its proper termination date or where he receives some payment from the lessor at the end of a lease period, perhaps in consideration for not exercising a legal right or an available option for a renewal or the granting of a new lease.

6.404 Qualifying expenditure

The industrial buildings initial, writing down and balancing allowances are all given by reference to the capital expenditure incurred on the construction of an industrial building (as defined – see **6.401**). In order to qualify for the allowances, the expenditure must be on the construction of the building; any expenditure incurred on the acquisition of, or of rights in or over, any land is specifically excluded and does not qualify (TCA 1997, s 270(2)(a)). However, it is accepted that the cost of work done on the site by way of levelling, cutting or otherwise preparing the land as a proper preliminary to erecting the building is part of the cost of construction of the building. TCA 1997, s 270(2) expressly includes expenditure on refurbishment of a building or structure as construction expenditure. 'Refurbishment' is defined as 'any work of construction, reconstruction, repair or renewal, including the provision of water, sewerage or heating facilities carried out in the course of repair or restoration or maintenance in the nature of repair or restoration, of the building or structure'. For a discussion of the circumstances in which repairs will be regarded as being capital in nature see **5.309**. No allowances may be claimed in respect of any expenditure, including repairs, which is deductible in computing income under Sch D Case I and II (TCA 1997, s 316(1)). It may be noted that refurbishment expenditure on certain buildings and structures in Urban/Rural Renewal

Areas, etc may qualify for accelerated allowances (see **Division 19** of the 2009 edition of this book).

Other types of expenditure which must be excluded from the industrial buildings allowance computation are expenditure on the provision of machinery or plant, or on any asset treated as machinery or plant, and any expenditure on which a scientific research or a mine development allowance may be claimed (TCA 1997, s 270(2)(b), (c)). Notwithstanding this, an Inspector will be prepared to regard certain fixtures which form an integral part of the premises as qualifying for industrial buildings allowances (see *Tax Briefing 42*). This may favour the taxpayer where the building is eligible for accelerated allowances (relevant mainly now to buildings and structures located in the tax incentive areas such as the Urban/Rural renewal areas, etc: see **Division 19** in the 2009 edition of this book) or where the ring fencing provisions of TCA 1997, s 403(5) would otherwise apply. This concession covers items of the type that are necessary for the basic functioning of the building regardless of the trade carried on there. Expenditure on lifts, heating systems, air-conditioning systems, electricity/gas distribution services, water and water services, alarm and security systems, fire fighting/prevention systems and wiring associated with, or ancillary to, any of the above would qualify for the concession. On the other hand, any capital expenditure incurred on preparing, cutting, tunnelling or levelling land in preparing that land to be a site for the installation of machinery or plant is automatically treated as expenditure on a building or structure (TCA 1997, s 268(4)). In light of the provisions introduced by FA 2006, s 28 in relation to the phasing out of capital allowances for certain industrial and commercial buildings, Revenue have stated that taxpayers may elect to treat expenditure on the provision of integral plant and machinery that is incurred by 31 December 2006 as expenditure qualifying for industrial buildings allowances, while a taxpayer may elect to treat expenditure incurred after that date as expenditure on the provision of plant and machinery *(see Tax Briefing 68)*.

The capital expenditure incurred on certain industrial buildings is restricted where it is incurred at any time in the period from 1 January 2007 to 31 July 2008. The restriction of the expenditure applies to hotels, holiday cottages and sports injuries clinics. The expenditure treated as incurred for the purpose of making allowances or charges is reduced to 75 per cent of the actual expenditure incurred in the calendar year 2007 or 50 per cent of the expenditure incurred in the period from 1 January 2008 to 31 July 2008. The restriction of the expenditure on the relevant industrial buildings is dealt with further at **6.406** below. For the purpose of determining whether and to what extent expenditure is incurred by a specified date (say 31 December 2006, 31 December 2007 or 31 July 2008) only such an amount of that expenditure as is properly attributable to work on the construction of the building actually carried out by the specified date will be treated as incurred by that date. In the case of qualifying residential units, expenditure is reduced to 75 per cent of actual incurred from 23 March 2007 to 31 December 2007 and 50 per cent thereafter, but subject in all cases to a cap of 50 per cent of actual expenditure incurred on or after 1 May 2007 under a contract or agreement entered into on or after 1 May 2007, a number of administrative requirements must be satisfied.

The capital expenditure on which all industrial buildings allowances are computed excludes any part of the expenditure that has been, or is to be, met directly or indirectly by the State, by any board established by statute or by any public or local authority or since 6 May 1993, by any party other than the actual taxpayer in question (TCA 1997, s 317(2)).

6.405 Initial allowances

In general, the initial allowance discussed below has ceased to be available for capital expenditure on industrial buildings or structures within TCA 1997, s 268 incurred after 31 March 1992. The phasing out and removal of the initial allowance is subject to a number of exceptions, dealt with fully in the 1997/98 edition of this book. More recently, the initial allowance rules remain relevant in the case of many of the buildings and structures located in the various 'tax incentive' areas (Urban/Rural renewal areas, etc), albeit subject to some variations, discussed in **Division 19** of the 2009 edition of this book.

A 100 per cent initial allowance (TCA 1997, s 271) had been made available by TCA 1997, s 843A(3A) in respect of expenditure incurred on or after 1 December 1999 up to 30 September 2010 (subject to transitional provisions: see above) in relation to approved childcare facilities. A lessor claim may claim the allowance, typically for the period in which the property is first let. However, due to constraints imposed by the EU, no capital allowances will be available under TCA 1997, s 843(3A) where the claimant is a property developer or (with effect from 1 January 2008) a person who is connected with the property developer and that property developer or a connected person incurred the qualifying expenditure on the qualifying premises on or after 1 December 1999.

TCA 1997, s 271 provides for an industrial buildings allowance to be given to a person who incurs capital expenditure on the construction of a building or structure (the building) if the required conditions are met. The conditions are:

(a) The building is to be an industrial building for use in a trade or undertaking carried on either:

 (i) by the person incurring the expenditure, or

 (ii) by a qualifying lessee (TCA 1997, s 271(2)); and

(b) The building is in fact an industrial building, ie one used in a qualifying trade, when it first comes to be used (TCA 1997, s 271(6)).

Apart from the case of a person purchasing a new building before it has been used for any purpose (see **6.408**), no initial allowance may be claimed by any person who does not himself incur the expenditure on the construction of the building. However, a person incurring capital expenditure on the refurbishment of an existing building (as defined by TCA 1997, s 270(1): see above) is entitled to the initial allowance on that expenditure if the two conditions are met in relation to that expenditure at the time it is incurred. It is important that the building not be used for a non-qualifying purpose, even if on a temporary basis only, before being used for the purposes for a qualifying trade, as this will disqualify the expenditure from entitlement to the initial allowance.

As is the case for capital allowances generally, expenditure is treated as being incurred when the amount in question becomes payable (TCA 1997, s 316(2)); however, any expenditure incurred by a person about to carry on a trade is treated as being incurred on the first day of trading (TCA 1997, s 316(3)).

Apart from the case where an industrial building is first used in his own trade by the person incurring the expenditure, the initial allowance may also be claimed by a lessor incurring qualifying expenditure if the building is first occupied by a qualifying lessee for the purposes of a qualifying trade carried on by that lessee. The treatment of leased buildings is discussed at **6.5**.

6.406 Writing-down allowances

The industrial buildings writing down or annual allowance is given to a person chargeable to income tax for each year of assessment who holds the relevant interest in the building or structure at the end of the basis period for that year of assessment, provided that at the end of that period the building or structure is an industrial building (TCA 1997, s 272(2)). This generally requires that it is in use for the purposes of a qualifying trade or undertaking or having been in such use is then subject to a period of temporary disuse (see below). The writing down allowance follows the relevant interest in the building and may therefore be claimed by a taxpayer who has acquired the relevant interest either directly from the person who incurred the expenditure originally, or from any intermediate purchaser, as well as by the person who incurred the expenditure if he continues to hold the relevant interest.

No writing down allowance is available after the qualifying capital expenditure has been fully written off by previous initial allowances and/or writing down allowances (TCA 1997, s 272(6)). Further, if the building has ceased – other than temporarily – to be used as an industrial building, no writing down allowances can be claimed, but should it be used again for a qualifying trade, the right to claim the annual allowances is resumed ie provided that there is an unclaimed balance or 'residue' of expenditure.

A building which ceases temporarily to be used and which, immediately before the period of temporary disuse, was an industrial building, is deemed to continue to be an industrial building while in temporary disuse (TCA 1997, s 280(1)). The writing down allowances therefore continue during this period. There is no precise definition of what constitutes 'temporary' in this context, but it is thought that a period of temporary disuse could extend for several years if on the facts there is a reasonable likelihood that the premises will be used again. It would seem sufficient that the premises will be used again for *any* purpose, 'industrial' or otherwise. HMRC unlike the Irish Revenue have issued guidelines on what they consider to be a period of temporary disuse. For the UK equivalent of TCA 1997, s 280 HMRC state that a building is in temporary disuse if it is capable of being used for something and this does not necessarily mean for a qualifying trade. If it is not capable of use at all it is not temporarily disused. HMRC also take the view that there is a period of temporary disuse only where the building is used again. If the building is subsequently demolished without being used again it is not a period of temporary disuse. The point is caveated in cases where, in a recession, it subsequently becomes clear that the building must be sold for redevelopment. In other words, you look at the intention at the end of each basis period.

In some cases, the person who originally incurred the capital expenditure on the construction of a building may not have been able to claim any industrial buildings allowance because the conditions for that allowance were not met at the time. This does not prevent a claim for writing down allowances by the person holding the relevant interest in relation to that expenditure if the conditions for writing down allowances are met at a later date. In the case of a building which was not used in a qualifying trade originally, but which later comes to be used for such a trade, the industrial buildings allowance may be claimed by the person holding the relevant interest in relation to any construction expenditure incurred on or after the earliest qualifying date for the trade in question.

The rates of writing down allowance for each of the main qualifying categories, the corresponding writing down lives (tax life) and the expiry dates for qualifying expenditure, where relevant, are set out below, together with the associated period in which a balancing adjustment can be made, as explained in **6.409**:

	Rate	*Balancing Adjustment Period* (s 274*(1)(b)*)	*Tax Life* (s 272*(4)*)	*Expiry Date for Expenditure*
Mill, factory or similar premises	4%	25 years	25 years	
Dock undertaking	4%	25 years	25 years	
Laboratory for mineral analysis	4%	25 years	25 years	
Market gardening etc	10%	10 years	10 years	
Intensive production of cattle etc	10%	10 years	10 years	
Holiday cottages	10%	10 years	10 years	31 July 2008
Hotels and holiday camps to 3/12/2002*	15% – 6 years 10% – 7th year	7 years	7 years	
4/12/2002 onwards	4%	25 years	25 years	
Guest houses and holiday hostels	4%	25 years	25 years	
Caravan sites and camping sites	4%	25 years	25 years	
Registered nursing homes	15% – 6 years	10 years	7 years	30 June 2011
	10% – 7th year	(15 years from 1/02/2007)	(15 years from 1/02/2007)	
Qualifying sports injuries clinics	15% – 6 years 10% – 7th year	10 years	7 years	31 July 2008
Qualifying residential units	15% – 6 years	10 years	7 years	30 April 2010
	10% – 7th year	(15 years from 1/02/2007)	(15 years from 1/02/2007)	
		(20 years from 1/05/2007)	(20 years from 1/05/2007)	
Qualifying private hospitals	15% – 6 years	10 years	7 years	31 December 2013
	10% – 7th year	(15 years from 1/02/2007)	(15 years from 1/02/2007)	
Certified convalescent homes	15% – 6 years	10 years	7 years	30 June 2011
	10% – 7th year	(15 years from 1/02/2007)	(15 years from 1/02/2007)	

	Rate	*Balancing Adjustment Period (s 274(1)(b))*	*Tax Life (s 272(4))*	*Expiry Date for Expenditure*
Qualifying mental health centres	15% – 6 years 10% – 7th year	15 years	15 years	30 June 2011
Qualifying palliative care units	15% – 6 years 10% – 7th year	15 years	15 years	
Approved childcare facilities	15% – 6 years 10% – 7th year	10 years (15 years from 1/02/2007)	7 years (15 years from 1/02/2007)	31 March 2012
Airport Runways & Buildings Management of an Airport	4%	25 years	25 years	
Aviation Facilities	15% – 6 years 10% – 7th year	7 years	7 years	5 years from commencement order

* Subject to detailed transitional provisions as described in the text.

Irrespective of the date on which expenditure was incurred, if a hotel, which has been the subject of at least one writing down allowance, is converted for use into a registered nursing home, writing down allowances will continue to be available as if the building were still a hotel (TCA 1997, s 272(7)).

Accelerated capital allowances are also available in respect of qualifying capital expenditure on childcare facilities. 100 per cent free depreciation (TCA 1997, s 273) has been made available by TCA 1997, s 843A(3A) in respect of expenditure incurred on or after 1 December 1999 up to 30 September 2010 (subject to transitional provisions: see above). An owner-occupier/operator may claim up to 100 per cent free depreciation in any single year. However, due to constraints imposed by the EU, no enhanced capital allowances will be available under TCA 1997, s 843A(3) where the claimant is a property developer or (with effect from 1 January 2008) a person who is connected with the property developer and that property developer or a connected person incurred the qualifying expenditure on the qualifying premises on or after 1 December 1999.

The rates of writing down allowances are based on a chargeable period of 12 months. Since the income tax chargeable period is always the relevant year of assessment, whether or not the taxpayer is carrying on the qualifying trade (or is a qualifying lessor) for the whole of that year, the full year's writing down allowance is given if the conditions for the allowance are met at the end of the relevant basis period. The entitlement to the full year's allowance is not altered even in the case where the rules of commencement or cessation apply to tax less than a full year's trading profits.

The writing down allowances on certain industrial buildings are subject to the restrictions applicable to high income individuals discussed at **3.111**.

Transitional measures re reduced writing down allowances – hotels

The writing down allowance in respect of capital expenditure incurred after 3 December 2002 on the construction or refurbishment of a building in use for a trade of hotel keeping will qualify for writing down allowances at a reduced rate of four per cent per annum unless the transitional provisions set out in TCA 1997, s 272(8) apply. Under the transitional arrangements writing down allowances at 15 per cent will be available in respect of capital expenditure incurred on the construction or refurbishment of hotels up until 31 July 2006 if:

(a) A planning application (not being an application for outline planning permission), in so far as planning permission was required, in respect of the building was made in accordance with the Planning and Development Regulations 2001 to 2002, an acknowledgement of the application which confirms that it was received by 31 December 2004 was issued by the planning authority and the application is not an invalid application;
(b) A planning application (not being an application for outline planning permission), in so far as planning permission was required, in respect of the building was made in accordance with the Local Government (Planning and Development) Regulations 1994, an acknowledgement of the application which confirms that it was received by 10 March 2002 was issued by the planning authority and the application was not an invalid application;
(c) Where the construction or refurbishment work on the building represented by the expenditure was an exempted development for the purpose of the Planning and Development Act 2000, s 4 or Pt 2 of the Planning and Development Regulations 2001 and the following conditions were satisfied by 31 December 2004:
    (i) a detailed plan in relation to the development work was prepared,
    (ii) a binding contract in writing, under which the expenditure on the development was incurred is in existence, and
    (iii) work to the value of five per cent of the development costs was carried out; or
(d) A valid application for a certificate was made under the Dublin Docklands Development Authority Act 1997, s 25(7)(a)(ii) and the Authority issued an acknowledgement of the application which confirms that it was received by 31 December 2004.

FA 2006, s 27 provided for the extension of the transitional period from 31 July 2006 to 31 December 2006. There is also provision for a further extension to 31 July 2008 where:

(a) The extension to 31 December 2006 applied by virtue of the conditions set out at (a), (b), (c) or (d) above being satisfied.
(b) The person who constructed or refurbished the hotel has carried out work to the value of not less than 15 per cent of the actual cost by 31 December 2006. This condition will not be treated as satisfied unless the relevant local authority certified in writing by 30 March 2007 that it was satisfied that work to the value of not less than 15 per cent of the actual costs were carried out by 31 December 2006, the actual amount of expenditure incurred on the construction or refurbishment by that date and the projected balance of the capital expenditure which was to be incurred on the construction of the building. The application for the certificate must have been made by 31 January 2007.
(c) The person who constructed the hotel or where the building is sold the person claiming the relief can show that condition (ii) is satisfied. Where the building is sold by the person who constructed or refurbished it then the vendor should

provide the purchaser with a copy of the certificate from the relevant local authority for the purpose of enabling the purchaser to claim allowances.

(d) A binding contract under which the expenditure on the construction or refurbishment of the hotel is incurred is in existence by 31 July 2006.

(e) Such other conditions required to ensure compliance with the laws of the EC as may be specified in regulations are satisfied.

The capital expenditure incurred on the construction or refurbishment of a hotel in the period to 31 December 2006 will qualify for capital allowances at the higher rate of 15 per cent per annum for six years and 10 per cent in the final year. The amount of expenditure incurred in the period from 1 January 2007 to 31 July 2008 for the purpose of making allowances and charges cannot exceed the amount certified by the relevant local authority. The amount of expenditure incurred after 31 December 2006 which is to be treated as incurred for the purpose of making allowances and charges is further restricted. If the expenditure was incurred in the calendar year 2007 the reduction will be to 75 per cent of amount that would otherwise qualify for relief. If the expenditure was incurred in the period from 1 January 2008 to 31 July 2008 the expenditure that qualifies for allowances is reduced to 50 per cent. The restriction of the expenditure by reference to the amount certified by the local authority applies in priority to the 75 per cent/50 per cent reduction in the amount of the expenditure on which increased capital allowances may be claimed. Where the expenditure incurred in the period from 1 January 2007 to 31 July 2008 exceeds the amount certified by the relevant local authority then the reduction will be made from the actual expenditure incurred in the period from 1 January 2008 to 31 July 2008 in priority to the expenditure incurred in the calendar year 2007.

6.407 Increased writing-down allowances ('free depreciation')

In general, the right to claim the increased writing down allowance (free depreciation) discussed herein ceased to be available for industrial buildings or structures where the capital expenditure was incurred after 31 March 1992. There are a number of transitional exceptions to the general rule, discussed fully in the 1997/98 edition of this book.

6.408 Buildings purchased unused

TCA 1997, s 271 provides that the industrial buildings initial allowance is given to the person who incurs the capital expenditure on the *construction* of the building or structure which is to be used for a qualifying trade. TCA 1997, ss 272, 274 provide respectively for annual allowances and balancing allowances (or charges) on the same construction expenditure to be given to the person owning the relevant interest which the person who incurred the construction expenditure had at the time it was incurred. TCA 1997, s 277 contains rules relating to the writing off of the construction expenditure.

TCA 1997, s 279, as most recently amended by F(No 2)A 2008, s 19, adapts these rules to deal with the case where the relevant interest in any building (or structure) is sold after expenditure has been incurred on the construction of the building, but before the building is first used for *any* purpose. This position may occur where the construction expenditure is incurred by a speculative builder or other person carrying on a trade of constructing buildings for sale. It may also arise where a person constructs a building expecting to use it for his own trade or for leasing, but who for any reason sells his relevant interest before the building is used for any purpose. The section also applies if the relevant interest is sold when the building is only partly constructed, eg when a speculative builder goes out of business. It also applies where the building is bought within one year after it is first used, or within two years after it is first used for sales of a relevant interest occurring on or after 14 October 2008, but only if no other person has claimed any industrial building allowance for that building.

In any case where it applies, TCA 1997, s 279 requires any industrial buildings initial, writing down and balancing allowances (or balancing charges) to be based on a deemed cost of construction instead of the actual expenditure on construction incurred by the person selling the relevant interest. It achieves this by applying the rules of TCA 1997, ss 271, 272, 274 and 277 on the following assumptions:

(a) The person who purchased the relevant interest in the unused building (or, if there is more than one sale of the relevant interest before the first use of the building, the latest purchaser before the building is used) is deemed to be the person who incurred the construction expenditure;

(b) The person in question is treated as if he had incurred expenditure on the construction of the building of an amount determined in one of two ways (instead of the actual expenditure on the construction); and

(c) The construction expenditure is deemed to have been incurred on the date on which the purchase price becomes payable (and not when the construction actually took place).

The construction expenditure deemed to have been incurred by the purchaser depends on whether the actual expenditure before the sale was incurred either by a person carrying on a trade which consists, wholly or partly, in the construction of buildings with a view to their sale eg a builder, or by a person not carrying on such a trade. The different rules for determining the deemed cost of construction, by reference to which all subsequent industrial buildings allowances are given, are discussed separately below for buildings constructed in the course of a building trade and for buildings erected by persons other than builders, property developers, etc.

In strictness TCA 1997, s 279 cannot apply where the person incurring the expenditure transfers less than the full relevant interest. Thus, where a developer who owns the freehold interest in an industrial building grants a 999-year lease at a peppercorn rent to a taxpayer, the taxpayer does not meet the terms of TCA 1997, s 279. An inspector may be prepared to disregard the strict legal position, although he will require the developer to formally disclaim any entitlement to allowances in relation to the property.

Construction by builder

Where the construction expenditure has been incurred by a builder and the relevant interest has been sold by him in the course of his trade to the purchaser and the building is unused (or is sold on or after 14 October 2008 and within two years (previously one year) of its first being used) and has not been the subject of a claim for any industrial buildings allowances, the purchaser is deemed to have incurred capital expenditure on the construction of the building of an amount equal to the net price paid by him to the builder for the relevant interest in the building. The actual construction cost to the builder then ceases to have any relevance for all purposes of industrial buildings allowances and balancing charges. In other words, any initial allowances, writing down allowances or subsequent balancing adjustments are based on the builder's sale price including his profit (if any), but excluding any stamp duty, legal or other costs of acquisition.

Example 6.408.1

Mahon, a builder, erected a building on a site in which he had inherited the freehold interest. The building, suitable for use either as a factory or a warehouse, costs him €200,000 to erect. The construction was completed on 30 April 2014.

Mahon sold his freehold interest (the relevant interest) for a net €250,000 to Bloom on 25 May 2014 and the full consideration was payable on that date. The building was not used at all until the purchaser acquired possession for his qualifying trade. This trade commenced on 1 July 2014 and his first period of account was the 12 months to 30 June 2015.

The consequences were as follows:

(a) Mahon was not entitled to any industrial buildings allowances in respect of his construction expenditure of €200,000;

(b) Bloom was treated as the person who incurred the construction expenditure, but for industrial buildings allowances purposes the construction expenditure is deemed to be the €250,000 net price paid to the builder (and the actual construction expenditure incurred by Mahon is disregarded completely);

(c) The 'construction expenditure' of €250,000 was treated by the rule in TCA 1997, s 279 as having been incurred on 25 May 2014, the date on which Bloom's purchase price was payable (and not on the actual dates of construction);

(d) Bloom was entitled, to claim a writing down allowance for the period to 30 June 2015:

	€
Writing Down Allowance €250,000 x 4%	10,000

(e) No adjustment is made to the net price paid to the builder in respect of the land element as Mahon did not actually incur any expenditure thereon (see *Treatment of land cost* below).

Where there is more than one sale of the relevant interest in a building constructed by a builder before the building is first used (or within a period of two years after it commences to be used or one year for sales prior to 14 October 2008), the last purchaser is deemed to have incurred, on the date when his purchase price becomes payable, construction expenditure equal to the lower of (a) the purchase price that was paid on the sale by the builder and (b) the net price paid by the last purchaser. In other words, the price paid to the builder (including his profit) remains the figure by reference to which the industrial buildings allowances are given, unless the last purchaser actually pays a lower price when he acquires the relevant interest.

Example 6.408.2

Take the facts of **Example 6.408.1**, but assume that Mahon sold the freehold interest in the building to MacCarthy on 15 May 2014 for a net price of €240,000. MacCarthy had intended to lease the building to Bloom, but the latter then offered to purchase the freehold interest for €270,000. MacCarthy accepted this offer and the building was sold to Bloom for this price, payable on 25 June 2014.

The consequences are as follows:

(a) neither Mahon nor MacCarthy is entitled to any industrial buildings allowances;

(b) Bloom is deemed to have incurred capital expenditure on the construction of the building on 25 June 2014 and is entitled to industrial buildings allowances on deemed expenditure of €240,000, ie on Mahon's sale price, as this is lower than the €270,000 paid on the last sale before the first use of the building.

Construction by non-builder

Where the construction expenditure has been incurred by a person not carrying on a building trade, the person purchasing the relevant interest in the building from him is deemed to have incurred construction expenditure equal to the lower of the actual construction expenditure incurred before the sale of the relevant interest and the net price paid by the purchaser for the relevant interest. If there is more than one sale of the relevant interest before the first use of the building (or within two years of first use), the actual cost of construction is again taken, unless the net price paid on the last sale before the building is used is lower than the actual construction cost.

Example 6.408.3

Conlon, who has a wholesaling and warehousing trade, owns a freehold site, and employs a building contractor to construct a new building for use in his trade. The building is completed in March 2014 at a construction cost to Conlon of €310,000. However, before the building can be used, Conlon goes out of business. On 5 September 2014, he sells the freehold interest to MacCarthy for €280,000 payable on 15 October 2014. On 20 December 2014, MacCarthy grants a 35-year lease in the building (still unused) to O'Brien who immediately starts to use the building for his qualifying trade.

The consequences of these transactions are as follows:

(a) MacCarthy, as the purchaser of the freehold interest (the relevant interest) in the building, is deemed to have incurred construction expenditure of €280,000 (ie its purchase price, as this is lower than Conlon's actual cost of construction);

(b) MacCarthy (as lessor) is entitled to the writing down allowance on this 'construction' cost of €280,000, deemed to have been incurred by him on 15 October 2014; and

(c) So long as the building continues to be used for a qualifying trade, MacCarthy (or any subsequent holder of the freehold interest) is entitled to an annual writing down allowances of four per cent until the deemed construction expenditure of €280,000 is fully written off.

Treatment of land cost, etc

The normal rule is that the land acquisition cost or the cost of acquiring the relevant interest in the land must be excluded in arriving at the expenditure qualifying for industrial buildings allowance (see **6.404**).

TCA 1997, s 279 ensures the that allowances on an industrial building which is purchased unused is computed by reference to the net price paid as restricted by the land element cost, and indeed other non-allowable elements within TCA 1997, s 270(2). The 'net price' thus restricted is computed according to the formula:

$$B \times \frac{C}{C + D}$$

Where

B = the amount paid for the relevant interest;

C = the amount of the expenditure actually incurred on the construction of the building or structure;

D = the amount of expenditure actually incurred which is disqualified under TCA 1997, s 270(2) (ie expenditure on land, or plant and machinery, or expenditure which qualifies for allowances under TCA 1997, s 670 (mining development) or 765(1) (scientific research)).

The Revenue Commissioners point out in *Tax Briefing Issue 65* that they regard the amount under 'B' as consisting exclusively of the cost of the premises, disregarding legal and stamp duty costs, house contents and the price of any benefits such as membership of sports or leisure clubs etc.

Example 6.408.4

In January 2012, O'Brien, a builder, purchases a derelict site for €350,000. At a cost of €2,000,000 he builds a hotel on the site during the period February 2012 to December 2012. As a result of cash flow difficulties, the hotel is only fitted-out and ready for use on 1 March 2014.

It has always been O'Brien's intention, as a speculative builder, to sell the hotel upon completion, but the proposed purchaser withdraws from the deal.

On 15 October 2014, O'Brien, under pressure from his bank appoints himself as hotel manager and recruits six staff to operate the hotel until a buyer is found. O'Brien does not claim any allowances (and indeed would not be entitled to do so, since the building is trading stock in his hands). On 16 January 2015, the hotel is sold at arm's length for €3,500,000 to Jack Lord, and Jack Lord immediately commenced to trade from the building.

Jack Lord prepares his accounts for the period ended 31 December 2015. The 'net price paid' by Jack Lord is computed as follows:

$$3{,}500{,}000 \times \frac{2{,}000{,}000}{1{,}000{,}000 - 350{,}000} \qquad €2{,}978{,}723$$

The industrial building annual allowance for 2015 is €2,978,723 x 4% = €119,149.

Notes:

1. Because Jack bought the building within two years of its first being used, and since no other person including O'Brien has claimed an industrial building allowance in relation to the building, TCA 1997, s 279 applies.

As outlined at **6.404** where capital expenditure on the construction of hotels, holiday cottages, qualifying residential units or sports injuries clinics is incurred in the period from 1 January 2007 to 31 July 2008 the expenditure that will qualify for allowances will be reduced; a reduction of 75 per cent or 50 per cent will also apply from 1 January 2007 to expenditure on qualifying residential units. The net price paid formula is adjusted to deal with the fact that only 75 or 50 per cent of the capital expenditure as the case may be will qualify for relief. The adjusted Net Price Paid formula is:

$$B \times \frac{C}{D + E}$$

Where:

B = the amount paid for the relevant interest;

C = the amount of the expenditure actually incurred on the construction of the building or structure as reduced under the transitional provisions (this reduction could be due to the fact that the actual expenditure cannot exceed the amount certified by the relevant local authority and/or the reduction to 75 per cent/50 per cent as appropriate);

D = the amount of expenditure actually incurred on the construction of the building;

E= the amount of expenditure actually incurred which is disqualified under TCA 1997, s 270(2) (ie expenditure on land, or plant and machinery, or expenditure which qualifies for allowances under TCA 1997, s 670 (mining development) or 765(1) (scientific research)).

6.409 Balancing allowances and balancing charges

TCA 1997, s 274(1) requires a balancing adjustment to be made – either a balancing allowance or a balancing charge, whichever is appropriate – where:

(a) capital expenditure has been incurred on the construction of a building or structure;

(b) any industrial buildings allowance (initial or writing-down) has been made for any one or more chargeable periods; and

(c) any of the following events (balancing events) occur;

  (i) the relevant interest in the building is sold,

  (ii) the relevant interest, if it is a leasehold interest, comes to an end (otherwise than as the result of the acquisition by the person entitled to the leasehold interest of the immediately superior interest),

  (iii) the building is demolished or destroyed or otherwise ceases altogether to be used, or

  (iv) consideration, other than rent or an amount treated, or (if received on or after 26 March 1997) partly treated, as rent under TCA 1997, s 98 is received by the person entitled to the relevant interest in respect of an interest which is subject to the relevant interest.

In addition, TCA 1997, s 311(3) treats as a sale for these purposes an exchange of the relevant interest (for some other asset or consideration) or, if the relevant interest is a leasehold interest, the surrender thereof for valuable consideration. In either of these cases, the value of the consideration given by the other party for the exchange or surrender is taken as being the net sale proceeds for the balancing adjustment computation. In addition, the general rule of TCA 1997, s 313(1) applies, whereby a building or structure was used in a trade immediately before and immediately after a succession to that trade covered by TCA 1997, s 69. In this last case, the relevant interest is treated as if it were sold to the successor to the trade for a consideration equal to its open market price at the date of the succession.

For any of the foregoing balancing events occurring before 6 April 1990, a balancing adjustment was only required if the event occurred at a time when the building or structure was an industrial building (ie when it was in use for one of the qualifying industrial trades, but disregarding any period of temporary disuse). This condition was unsatisfactory because it enabled the person owning the relevant interest to avoid a balancing charge (more likely than a balancing allowance) by changing the building from an industrial to a non-industrial use for a period, even a short one, before disposing of the relevant interest. This is not a condition for any balancing event occurring after 5 April 1990.

In so far as (c)(iii) is concerned, the latter element of this condition does not apply if the building continues to be used, albeit for a non-qualifying purpose. The phrase 'ceases altogether to be used' seems to denote a permanent state of affairs, ie where on the facts there is no reasonable likelihood of the building being used again (for any purpose). TCA 1997, s 280(1) states that where a building or structure falls 'temporarily out of use', it shall not be deemed to have ceased altogether to be used.

As noted above, where a building ceases to be used for a qualifying 'industrial purpose' and is used for other purposes instead, no balancing adjustment arises at that time. However, if any of the events which trigger off a balancing adjustment subsequently occurs within the period set out in TCA 1997, s 274(1)(b) relevant to the building in question, a balancing adjustment will take place at that time instead (TCA 1997, s 274(1)). However there are a number of exceptions to this. Firstly, where a holiday cottage falling within TCA 1997, s 268(1)(d) ceases to be registered and a balancing event would not otherwise arise, the building is deemed to have been sold for an amount equal to the expenditure on its construction (TCA 1997, s 274(6)); there is provision for entitlement to allowances to be regained where the building becomes registered again in the same ownership (TCA 1997, s 274(7)). Secondly, the cessation of use of buildings in use for certain purposes (referred to as relevant facilities) is treated as an event that gives rise to a balancing charge. A relevant facility includes buildings in use as a registered nursing home, a qualifying residential unit, a convalescent home, a qualifying hospital, a qualifying mental health centre, a qualifying specialist palliative care unit or certain childcare facilities. Where an allowance is made in respect of expenditure incurred on a relevant facility and it ceases to be a relevant facility then a balancing charge is made on the person entitled to the relevant interest. The provision applies where the building is first used or first used after refurbishment on or after 1 January 2006. The balancing charge can be avoided if within a period of six months of the building ceasing to be one type of relevant facility it is put into use as another type of relevant facility.

The balancing event described at (c)(iv) needs a further explanation. It was originally added primarily as an anti-avoidance measure and was expressed to apply to consideration 'other than rent or an amount treated as rent' under TCA 1997, s 98. It was intended to deal with the case where the owner of the relevant interest in the industrial building created a new interest in the building which was marginally inferior to the relevant interest and, in consideration for this, received any sum which was not taxable as income (or brought into account in computing taxable income). However, where a premium was received for the grant of a 'short' lease (ie one running for less than 50 years) only *part* thereof would normally be treated as rent under TCA 1997, s 98 so that the balance would fall within TCA 1997, s 274(1). The present wording ensures that most premiums for 'short' leases received on or after 26 March 1997 are excluded from the scope of TCA 1997, s 274(1), (ie since *part* of the amount of the premium received will usually be taxed as rent under TCA 1997, s 98). One effect of this amendment is to prevent the artificial generation of balancing allowances. This rule is illustrated in **Example 6.409.2** below. However, it transpired that there was still scope for generating balancing allowances by arranging for the receipt of sums no part of which were taxed as rental income; accordingly, TCA 1997, s 274(3) provides that the receipt of such sums on or after 5 March 2001 cannot give rise to a balancing allowance.

TCA 1997, s 274(2) provides that the receipt of such consideration is not a balancing event described at (c)(iv) where the relevant interest is in a building or structure in use for the purposes of a trade of hotel-keeping and a binding contract for the provision of the building or structure was entered into after 27 January 1988 and before 1 June 1988.

A balancing allowance on certain industrial buildings may be subject to the high earners restrictions discussed at **3.111**.

Writing down life and tax life

Generally no balancing allowance or balancing charge will arise on a sale (or other event) occurring after the end of the writing down life of the expenditure in question. The writing down life of a building commences on the date of first use of the building and expires at the end of the period of time set out in TCA 1997, s 272(4) which varies depending on the type of industrial building. The writing down life of a building is the length of time by reference to which it would normally be expected that the qualifying construction expenditure would be fully written off, assuming that only normal writing down allowances were claimed in respect thereof.

The period in which a balancing event can occur on traditional industrial buildings or structures is set out in TCA 1997, s 274(1)(b) and usually equates to the writing down life of the building or structure. This can be seen by looking at the writing down life of buildings that have traditionally qualified as industrial buildings, ie factories, buildings in use for the intensive production of livestock, buildings in use for a trade of market gardening and hotels. The period during which a balancing charge can occur on buildings in use for trades which have more recently qualified as industrial buildings generally extend beyond their writing down life. The trend of extending the balancing event period of industrial buildings beyond their writing down life was evident in a number of FA 2006 provisions which extended the balancing event period of certain industrial buildings which were first used (or first used subsequent to incurring refurbishment expenditure) on or after 1 February 2007 to 15 years from the date of first use, and also to 20 years in the case of qualifying residential units. The industrial buildings in question are a qualifying private hospital, a registered nursing home, a certified convalescent home, a qualifying sports injuries clinic and an approved childcare facility.

TCA 1997, s 409F introduced the concept of a tax life of a building. This concept was introduced for the purposes of determining the end of the tax life of specified capital allowances where capital allowances cannot be carried forward. See **6.107** and the table at **6.406**. For the purpose of s 409F the tax life of a building is set out in TCA 1997, s 272(4) and may not be the same period in which a balancing event can take place as set out in TCA 1997, s 274(1)(b).

TCA 1997, s 276 provides that for the purposes of calculating balancing charges or balancing allowances on refurbishment expenditure, the writing down period for the expenditure runs from the date on which the relevant expenditure was incurred. Where there is a sale, etc of the building before that writing down period expires, 'just and reasonable' apportionments will be carried out (see **6.412**).

The death of an individual who holds the relevant interest in an industrial building does not give rise to a balancing allowance or charge. This is because death is not an event included in TCA 1997, s 274(1). This is confirmed in a Revenue precedent with the question being asked '*is the death of an individual a balancing event for the purposes of the section. Decision No*'. Unlike plant capital allowances, there is no requirement for a claimant to have incurred capital expenditure. All that is required is that the claimant holds the relevant interest at the end of the basis period (TCA 1997, s 272(2)). In other words the successor steps in to the shoes of the deceased and claims the capital allowances at the same rate as the deceased. However, if another individual or a partnership of persons should succeed to the deceased person's trade, and if the buildings were used as industrial buildings immediately prior to the succession and continue to be used for the trade after the succession, then the appropriate balancing adjustment must be made on the person holding the relevant interest at the time immediately before the succession (see **6.106**). The balancing allowance or charge is calculated by reference to an assumed sale consideration equal to the open market price of the relevant interest at that time. Where the person succeeding to the trade does so as a specific or residuary legatee under the deceased's will, the date of the succession is the date of death and the balancing adjustment is, therefore, made in assessing the deceased's income to the date of death.

Similarly, if the relevant interest in an industrial building is sold by the deceased person's personal representatives in realising his estate, the personal representatives are entitled to the appropriate balancing allowance or are subject to a balancing charge, calculated by reference to the proceeds of the sale. In this event, it is the date of sale that is the relevant date so that any balancing allowance or balancing charge is given to or made on the personal representatives in taxing them for the relevant year of assessment in the administration period (see **15.106**); the deceased person's assessments to the date of death are not affected.

Any balancing allowance is given to, or any balancing charge is made on, the person entitled to the relevant interest in the building immediately before it is sold (or before any other relevant event). The balancing adjustment is made for the chargeable period related to the sale or other event. For example, if a person liable to income tax sells the relevant interest in an industrial building during his 12-month period of account ended 31 December 2007 and any balancing allowance or balancing charge resulting from that sale is given or made for the year 2007.

A gift of a building is not a balancing event nor is the transfer of the building by way of distribution in specie by a liquidator.

Where an industrial building is inherited from an individual and the building had not been in use for the purpose of a trade by the deceased TCA 1997, s 313 does not apply. As death in itself is not a balancing event no balancing charge is made on the deceased. The successor steps into the shoes of the deceased and is entitled to claim annual allowances at the same rate as the deceased.

Computation of balancing adjustment

The calculation of the balancing allowance or balancing charge is made by comparing the 'sale, insurance, salvage or compensation monies' or consideration (if any) with the 'residue of the expenditure' immediately before the sale or other relevant event (TCA 1997, s 274(3), (4)). The form of the computation may be summarised as follows:

Residue of expenditure,

Less

Sale, insurance, salvage or compensation monies,

Equals

Balancing allowance, (if positive),

Or

Balancing charge (if negative),

But subject to the restriction that the amount of any balancing charge cannot exceed the aggregate of the industrial buildings allowances actually made previously to the person concerned in respect of the capital expenditure in question. In other words, the balancing charge can recapture as additional income the full amount of all initial, writing down and free depreciation allowances previously given, if the sale, etc monies are high enough (TCA 1997, s 274(8)).

The meaning of the phrase 'sale, insurance, salvage or compensation monies', as defined in by TCA 1997, s 318, has been explained in **6.104**. As indicated there, in the normal case of the sale of an industrial building (other than one affected by any special rule), it is the net proceeds of the sale that are taken. In the case of the cessation in use of a relevant facility the phrase means the aggregate of the residue of expenditure immediately before the event and the allowances made in respect of the building. For the special rules which require the open market price of the relevant interest in the building to be used instead, see **6.105** (non-arm's length transactions).

The sale of the relevant interest in a building may involve the sale of an asset the capital expenditure on which only partly qualified for industrial buildings allowances. For example, no such allowances could have been given on the cost of acquiring the land on which subsequent expenditure in constructing the buildings was incurred. Similarly, construction expenditure incurred before 30 September 1956 (or a later starting date for certain of the qualifying trade categories) was not eligible for the allowances. In any such case, the sale proceeds or any other sale, insurance, etc monies must be apportioned on a 'just' basis to exclude from the balancing adjustment computation any part attributable to assets representing expenditure for which no industrial buildings allowances could be claimed (TCA 1997, s 282(2)): see **6.412**.

TCA 1997, s 277 provides the rules for determining the 'residue of expenditure' in respect of any capital expenditure incurred on the construction of any building or structure. In the more usual case where there is a sale of, or other balancing adjustment event affecting, an industrial building which has not been the subject of any previous sale or other relevant event, the residue of the expenditure is determined as follows:

The qualifying expenditure on the building (as reduced by any government, etc grants),

Less

Any initial allowances previously obtained,

Less

All writing down allowances previously obtained (including any increased allowances claimed),

Less

Any notional allowances required to be deducted (see **6.411**).

TCA 1997, s 277(7) requires any balancing allowances arising as a result of a receipt within TCA 1997, s 274(1)(a)(iv) (receipt of consideration not treated as rent or partly as rent) to be deducted from the residue (as noted above, no such allowances will arise on or after 5 March 2001). This rule (which does not contain any provision for adjustment of the residue by reference to balancing charges arising in these circumstances) requires the deduction from the residue to be made at the time of the receipt, or 26 March 1997, if later.

The times at which the various allowances are regarded as being written off are laid down in TCA 1997, s 277, as follows:

(a) any initial allowance is written off at the time when the building (or the relevant part of the building) is first used;

(b) the writing down allowance (including any increased allowances) for each year of assessment is written off at the end of its basis period;

(c) if the balancing adjustment event also occurs on the last day of the basis period, the writing down allowance for the year of assessment is deducted first before the balancing adjustment is calculated; and

(d) any notional allowance required to be deducted in respect of a period of non-qualifying use is written off at the particular time when it is necessary to determine the residue of the expenditure.

Example 6.409.1

Danny Mulvenna constructed a factory building in 2012 at a capital cost of €400,000 on a site in which he held a 999-year lease when the factory was built. Danny makes up his accounts to 31 December each year. His residue of expenditure at 31 December 2014 is as follows:

	€
Capital expenditure on construction	400,000
Less:	
Capital allowances to date:	
Annual allowance (2012) €400,0000 x 4%	16,000
Annual allowance (2013) €400,000 x 4%	16,000
Annual allowance (2014) €400,000 x 4%	16,000
Residue of expenditure 31/12/2014	352,000

On 15 June 2015, Danny creates a 99-year sub-lease of the factory building in favour of George Johnson, a trader for a premium of €385,000 and an annual rent of €1. Since this premium is not treated as rent by TCA 1997, s 98 (lease for more than 50 years – see **12.202**), TCA 1997, s 274(1)(a)(iv) applies and a balancing adjustment computation must be made resulting in a balancing charge on Danny, computed as follows:

	€
Residue of expenditure at 31/12/2014	352,000
Less:	
Amount received for grant of inferior interest	385,000
Balancing charge y/e 31/12/2015	33,000

Notes:

Danny continues to hold the relevant interest and therefore continues to be entitled to claim writing down allowances by reference to his construction expenditure. The final writing down allowances thus claimed may not exceed the 'residue' of the expenditure, which is to be computed without any adjustment for the balancing charge.

Example 6.409.2

Assume the same facts as in **Example 6.409.1**, except that Danny creates a 49-year sub-lease for a premium of €300,000 and an annual rent of €1.

TCA 1997, s 274(1)(a)(iv) does not apply as part of the premium will be treated as rent under TCA 1997, s 98.

Anti-avoidance: balancing allowances

TCA 1997, s 275 contains rules to prevent the avoidance of tax by a person (the 'relevant person') obtaining a balancing allowance through certain types of arrangement involving the sale of the relevant interest in an industrial building where that interest is subject to an inferior interest. An 'inferior interest' is defined as any interest in or right over the building or structure in question, whether granted by the relevant person or by someone else.

TCA 1997, s 275 applies if the following three conditions are met:

(a) the relevant interest in a building or structure is sold subject to an inferior interest; *and*

(b) as a result of the sale an industrial buildings balancing allowance would were it not for TCA 1997, s 275, be made to or for the benefit of the relevant person (the person entitled to the relevant interest immediately before the sale); and

(c) *either:*

  (i) any two (or all three) of the relevant person, the purchaser of the relevant interest and the grantee of the inferior interest are 'connected persons' (as defined by TCA 1997, s 10 – see **12.304**), *or*

  (ii) it appears with respect to the sale or the grant of the inferior interest, or with respect to transactions including the sale or grant, that the sole or main benefit expected to accrue to the parties or any of them was the obtaining of an industrial buildings writing down or balancing allowance.

In any case where all three conditions are met, TCA 1997, s 275(3) requires the net sales proceeds for the computation of any balancing allowance (but not a balancing charge) in respect of the sale of the relevant interest in the building to be taken as either:

(a) the actual net proceeds of sale plus an amount equal to any premium receivable by the relevant person for the grant of the inferior interest (in the case where a proper commercial rent is payable by the grantee of the inferior interest); or

(b) the amount of any premium receivable by the relevant person for the granting of the inferior lease, plus an amount equal to what the sales proceeds would have been if a proper commercial rent (having regard to any premium actually payable) had been payable on an open market sale of the relevant interest (in the case where a proper commercial rent was not in fact payable).

This 'notional' net sales proceeds figure is, however, not to exceed the amount necessary to reduce the balancing allowance that would otherwise be made to nil. It cannot create a balancing charge in a case where no balancing charge would result in the absence of these rules. If in any case the result of TCA 1997, s 275 is to reduce or cancel entirely the normal balancing allowance in respect of any capital expenditure, the normal balancing allowance must still be deducted in arriving at the residue of that expenditure immediately after the sale (TCA 1997, s 275(4)).

In applying rules (a) and (b) in arriving at the notional sales proceeds used, the term 'premium' is defined as including any capital consideration except so much of any sum corresponding to any rent falling to be computed by reference to that sum under (TCA 1997, s 98) (see **12.201**). In effect, this means that any premium or other sum payable in respect of the granting of a lease, to the extent that it is taxable as rent by TCA 1997, s 98, is not to be treated as a premium in applying the above rules of (TCA 1997, s 275(1)). However, any part of the premium that is not so taxable under the rules of TCA 1997, s 98 must be taken into account in arriving at the above net sales proceeds.

6.410 Capital allowances after sale of building

Any person who purchases the relevant interest in a building or structure the capital expenditure on the construction of which is eligible for an allowance under TCA 1997, s 272 is entitled to the industrial buildings writing down allowances if the building is used by him (or by a lessee) in one of the qualifying trade categories. It does not matter that the building may not have been used immediately previously for a qualifying industrial purpose, nor even if there had never been any such use previously. It is the type of use to which the building is put at any relevant time following the new owner's acquisition of the relevant interest that counts in determining whether or not he is given any writing down allowance for any year of assessment. However, the approach to the computation of the writing down allowances after the purchase varies depending on whether or not any industrial buildings allowances had been previously granted in respect of the building and, if so, whether or not the building was an industrial building at the time the relevant interest was sold.

Sale of building on which industrial buildings allowances were granted

A balancing adjustment arises in any case where the building which has been sold has been the subject of industrial building allowances, even if it is not an industrial building at the time of sale (TCA 1997, s 274(1)). When the relevant interest in such a building is sold, the residue of the expenditure immediately before the sale is treated as being reduced by any balancing allowance given to, or increased by any balancing charge made on, the vendor (TCA 1997, s 277(5), (6)).

Where the building is an industrial building at the time of sale, the purchaser of the relevant interest is then entitled, so long as the building continues to be an industrial building, to writing down allowances based on the residue of the expenditure, as adjusted (TCA 1997, s 272(4)); where the amount of the residue exceeds the purchase cost of the building, the latter amount is treated as the residue of expenditure (TCA 1997, s 272(5)). It should be noted again that where a building which was last used for a qualifying 'industrial' purpose has been in temporary disuse up to the date of sale, it continues to be regarded as an industrial building (TCA 1997, s 280(1)). Only a sale of the full relevant interest will be sufficient; thus in *Woods v RM Mallen* 45 TC 619, the grant of a sub-lease by a headlessor for a period of three days less than the headlease did not entitle the sub-lessee to any writing down allowances in relation to expenditure incurred by the headlessor. At the extremes, the same principle would apply to a 999-year lease granted at a peppercorn rent by the owner of the freehold interest in the land (notwithstanding that this would be treated as a balancing event for the owner: see TCA 1997, s 274(1)(a)(iv), discussed above).

In these circumstances, the rate of writing down allowance after the sale is, however, changed. The statutory formula requires that for income tax purposes the expenditure should be written off for a year of assessment in the ratio which the length of the year of assessment bears to the unexpired 'writing down life' of the building in question (although the ratio is not permitted to exceed 100 per cent). The 'writing down' life is defined in **6.409** above (see *Writing Down Life and Tax Life*). It is seemingly implicit in the formula that no claim can be made under TCA 1997, s 272 where the writing down life has expired prior to the sale in question. The new rate is that necessary to write off the residue of the expenditure on a straight line basis evenly over the rest of the writing down life of the expenditure (TCA 1997, s 272(4)). For example, if a building with a 25-year writing down life commencing from its first use on 1 July 1992 is sold, while an industrial building, on 1 July 2007, the subsequent writing down allowances are made at the rate of one tenth of the adjusted residue of the expenditure for each 12-month chargeable period between 1 July 2007 and 30 June 2017. As regards refurbishment expenditure TCA 1997, s 276 provides that the writing down life runs from the date that such expenditure was incurred.

In the event of any subsequent sale of the relevant interest in the building while it is an industrial building during the writing down life, the residue of the expenditure must again be decreased or increased, as appropriate, by the balancing allowance or charge on that sale and a new rate of writing down allowance struck for the balance of the writing down life remaining at the time of that sale. The writing down life of the construction expenditure on a building never changes irrespective of the number of times the relevant interest may change hands. Further, even if the original owner of the relevant interest has obtained capital allowances totalling 100 per cent of the construction expenditure before selling it, the adjustment of the residue of the expenditure by the amount of a balancing charge made on the seller has the effect of reinstating capital expenditure for purposes of writing down allowances after the sale.

Example 6.410.1

Paul Rowlandson, a hotelier, making up accounts annually to 31 May, incurred qualifying capital expenditure of €500,000 up to August 2006 in constructing a new hotel on land, the freehold interest in which he had acquired previously for €80,000. Following delays the building was first used in his trade on 1 April 2010. The expenditure qualified for 15% writing down allowances under the relevant transitional provisions: see **6.406**.

Paul used the building in his trade from 1 April 2010 until, on 30 June 2011 he sold the entire freehold interest (the relevant interest) for €522,000 to Bill Anderson, another hotelier. The respective positions of the two taxpayers as a result of the sale are as follows:

Paul Rowlandson:

Paul had obtained the following capital allowances in respect of the qualifying construction expenditure of €500,000 as follows:

	€
Basis period to 31 May 2010 (when first brought into use)	
Annual allowance 2010 €500,000 x 15%	75,000
Annual allowance 2011 €500,000 x 15%	75,000

Paul's balancing charge computation for 2012 (basis period ending 31 May 2012) is as follows:

	€	€
Cost of construction		500,000
Less:		
Total industrial buildings allowances (as above)		150,000
Residue of expenditure (prior to sale)		350,000
Sales proceeds (30/6/2011)	522,000	
Less:		
Proportion allocated to land cost, say		
€522,000 x (80,000/500,000+80,000)=	72,000	
		450,000
Surplus on sale allocated to buildings		100,000
Less than the €150,000 allowances obtained so Balancing charge		100,000

Bill Anderson:

Bill, already trading as a hotelier, makes up his accounts annually to 30 June. Bill puts the newly acquired hotel into use in his trade on 1 July 2011. Bill is entitled to claim the industrial buildings writing down allowance for 2012 (basis period ended 30 June 2012) and for each subsequent year of assessment so long as the building is in use for the hotel trade.

Bill's writing down allowance computed for each 12-month basis period during which the hotel remains an industrial building is determined as follows:

	€
Residue of expenditure (prior to sale by Paul)	350,000

Add:

Balancing charge made on Paul	100,000
Residue of expenditure (after sale)	450,000
Length of remainder of writing down life:	
30 June 2011 to 31 March 2017	
ie 5 years 9 months (5.75 years)	
IBAA for each 12-month period:	
€450,000 x (1/5.75)=	78,260

Where the relevant interest which is sold relates to a building in respect of which industrial buildings allowances were granted, but at a time when the building is *not* an industrial building (again ignoring any periods of temporary disuse which follow on immediately from a period of qualifying use), different considerations apply. A balancing adjustment is made on the vendor in the usual way (TCA 1997, s 274(1)). It is again necessary to recalculate the residue by reference to any balancing adjustments on the sale. However, this calculation is only relevant in so far as the purchaser of the building cannot subsequently claim writing down allowances in excess of the amount of the residue following the sale (TCA 1997, s 272(6)). The writing down allowance to which the purchaser is entitled is the normal rate referable to the category of use (eg four per cent pa for a mill or factory), applied to the original construction expenditure incurred. The result seems to be that, exceptionally, writing down allowances may be claimed after the expiry of the writing down life of the building.

Sale of building on which no industrial buildings allowances were granted

If a building not previously put to an 'industrial' use should subsequently start to be used for the purposes of a qualifying industrial trade by a person holding the relevant interest in relation to the *original construction* expenditure, that person becomes entitled to claim the industrial buildings writing down allowances under the ordinary rules.

There is normally no change in this position where the building has been purchased prior to its first use for industrial purposes since the rule of TCA 1997, s 272(4) (discussed above) only applies where there is a sale at a time when the building is an industrial building.

In effect, this means that the new owner now carrying on a qualifying trade for the first time is given the writing down allowances at the standard rate (four per cent for factories, mills, etc) on the original cost of construction incurred by the previous owner. However, where the building is purchased unused (or within two years of first use in the case of a sale on or after 14 October 2008 (previously, within one year) if it has not been the subject of a claim for any industrial building allowances), the special provisions of TCA 1997, s 279 may apply (see **6.408**). Subject to this, the rate of the new owner's writing down allowances is determined for the particular qualifying trade category by the date(s) on which the original construction expenditure was incurred (or deemed to have been incurred). The writing down life of the building similarly remains fixed for the relevant trade category by reference to the date of its first use for any purpose by the previous owner (or by any earlier owner). If and when the new owner sells the relevant interest in the building during its writing down life then, for the purposes of calculating any balancing charge/allowance, the residue of the expenditure is determined as the original construction expenditure less all previous industrial buildings allowances given to the current vendor and to any previous owner while it was an industrial building, and less the appropriate notional allowances (see **6.411**) for all periods of non-industrial use since the building was first used for any purpose by any owner of the relevant interest. Any balancing charge cannot exceed the total amount of writing down allowances granted to the new owner TCA 1997, s 274(8)).

Example 6.410.2

A speculative builder constructs a building on a freehold site owned by him. The building is completed at a cost to the builder of €300,000 on 31 July 2013. He sells the freehold interest in the building for €350,000 on 1 September 2013 to Moore, a person carrying on a distribution (non-qualifying) trade who puts the building into use for that trade on 1 October 2013.

On 1 October 2014, after using the building only for the distribution trade, Moore sells the freehold interest for €500,000 to Humbert Ltd, which immediately puts the building into use in its manufacturing (qualifying) trade. The consequences of these transactions are as follows:

(a) Moore is deemed to have incurred on 1 September 2013 construction expenditure on the building of €350,000 (the net price paid to the builder – see **6.408**), but is not entitled to claim any writing down allowance on the building due to its non-qualifying use;

(b) On putting the building to use in a qualifying trade, Humbert Ltd becomes entitled to writing down allowances from 1 October 2014, but based on Moore's deemed construction expenditure of €350,000;

(c) Assuming a continued qualifying use from 1 October 2014, an annual allowance of €14,000 (4% x €350,000) is available to write off the residue of expenditure of €336,000 (€350,000 less €14,000 notional allowances (see note (d)), ie up to 30 September 2038 (25 years from the date of first use of the building); and

(d) If there should be a further sale of the relevant interest before 1 October 2038, the notional allowances to be written off the expenditure of €350,000 include the year of non-qualifying use up to 1 October 2014, namely:

€350,000 x 4% x 1 year = €14,000 (see **6.411**)

Disposal of industrial building other than by way of sale

Where the relevant interest in an industrial building is disposed of other than by way of sale so that no balancing adjustment arises (eg by way of gift or on the liquidation of a company) the person acquiring the interest (the 'acquiror') will be entitled to the writing down allowances at the relevant rate on the original cost of construction incurred by the previous owner under TCA 1997, s 272(2), assuming he puts the building to a qualifying use. The total writing down allowances which he claims as usual cannot exceed the residue of the expenditure TCA 1997, s 272(6)). On a subsequent sale, a balancing adjustment will be computed in the usual manner but a balancing charge cannot exceed the total amount of writing down allowances granted to the acquirer (TCA 1997, s 274(8)).

6.411 Deduction of notional allowances

TCA 1997, s 277(4) requires a notional writing down allowance, ie one that does not confer any tax relief, to be deducted in arriving at the residue of the expenditure if, for any period or periods after the date on which the building is first used after the construction expenditure has been incurred, the building is not in use for the purposes of a qualifying trade or undertaking. However, it must be recalled that where a building which was in use for a qualifying 'industrial' purpose is immediately following such use, subject to a period of temporary disuse, it continues to be regarded as an industrial building during that period of such disuse (TCA 1997, s 280). Accordingly, *actual* writing down allowances will be granted during the period of such disuse. Notional allowances must be written off the expenditure at any time thereafter that it is necessary to determine the residue. A writing down allowance cannot be granted if it would exceed the residue of expenditure (TCA 1997, s 272(6)). Accordingly, the effect of TCA 1997, s 277(4) may be to deny writing down allowances otherwise available.

Example 6.411.1

Georgina who makes accounts up to 31 December each year is a long established trader on 1 June 2010 she acquires an industrial building for €500,000 (excluding site costs) which qualifies for the 15% writing down allowance. The premises are immediately put into use in her trade up to 31 March 2011 after which it is used solely for non-trading purposes. On 1 August 2012 Georgina decides to reconvert the use of the premises to that of an industrial building. Georgina's entitlement to writing down allowances are as follows:

	€
Basis period ended 31 December 2010	
Writing down allowance 2010	75,000
Basis period ended 31 December 2011	
Writing down allowance 2011	Nil[1]
Basis period ended 31 December 2012	
Writing down allowance 2012	75,000[2]

The residue of expenditure at 31/12/2012 is computed as follows:

	€	€
Cost		500,000
Less: actual writing down allowances	150,000	
Less: notional writing down allowances	99,750 [3]	249,750
Residue		250,250

Assuming that Georgina continues to use the building in her trade, she will be entitled to an allowance of €75,000 in 2013, 2014 and 2015 and an allowance equal to the balance of the residue, ie €25,250, in 2016.

Notes:

1. The building is not an industrial building at the end of the basis period, so that a writing down allowance is not available.
2. The building is once more an industrial building at the end of the 2012 basis period so that an actual writing down allowance may be claimed.
3. The period of non-industrial use is calculated as follows:
   01/04/2011 to 31/07/2012: 1.33 years
   The notional writing down allowances therefore amount to
   €500,000 x 1.33 x 15% — €99,750

It is the residue as reduced by both actual and notional writing down allowances which must be taken into account at the time of a sale of the relevant interest in the building, or on the occurrence of one of the other events that requires a balancing allowance or charge to be computed.

The amount of the notional allowances to be taken into account at any such time is determined by adding up the lengths of all periods of time during which the building was not used for the purposes of a qualifying trade or undertaking, and, then computing the notional writing down allowance at the appropriate rate for the aggregate time of the non-industrial use. If there has been no sale (or other balancing adjustment event) between the date of first use as an industrial building and the balancing adjustment event, the rate of the notional allowance is the normal writing down allowance rate for the trade category concerned appropriate to the date of the expenditure. Alternatively, if the building was previously sold while an industrial building, any notional allowance required for a period subsequent to such previous sale is made at the same annual rate as that determined under (TCA 1997, s 272(4)) (see **6.410**).

The rules for determining the amount of a notional writing down allowance do not fit well with the rules determining entitlement to an *actual* writing down allowance. The former rules relate to the period of non industrial use while the latter relate to the position at the end of a basis period. Thus, if a building was in use say for non-qualifying purposes for the first few months of a particular 12-month basis period but was in use for a qualifying purpose at the end of that basis period it seems that an actual writing down allowance *and* a notional writing down allowance should in strictness arise in respect of that period.

When a balancing allowance or charge has to be made on the sale of a building while it is an industrial building, but where there has been any period of non-industrial use since the first use of the building (or since any prior sale as an industrial building), TCA 1997, s 274(5)(b) requires that the balancing allowance or charge to be reduced to allow for the fact that writing down allowances were not available for the period of non-industrial use. Where this position arises, the balancing allowance or charge that would otherwise apply is first computed by comparing the residue of the expenditure (after actual and notional allowances) with the sale, etc monies. This 'provisional' allowance or charge is then adjusted to arrive at the final balancing allowance or charge, as follows:

$$\text{Final Allowance Charge} = \frac{\text{Industrial Use Provisional Allowance Charge}}{\text{Relevant Period}}$$

(but balancing charge must not exceed actual allowances granted).

For this calculation, it is necessary to determine the lengths of the relevant period and the industrial use period, defined respectively as follows:

'Relevant period'

The period beginning when the building was first used for any purpose (whether industrial or non-industrial) and ending on whichever of the following days is appropriate, namely:

(a) If the event giving rise to the balancing allowance or charge occurs on the last day of the basis period for any year of assessment, then that day is the last day of the relevant period; or

(b) If the event occurs other than on the last day of a basis period for any year of assessment, then the last day of the immediately preceding basis period is taken as the last day of the relevant period;

'Industrial use period'

A period of time equal in length to the aggregate of the length of all the basis periods for which an industrial buildings writing down allowance was given (but excluding the whole or any part of any basis period that does not fall within the relevant period).

Several qualifications are required. Firstly, if there was any previous sale of the building when it was an industrial building, the relevant period in relation to the current sale is treated as beginning on the day immediately following the date of that prior sale (and not on the date of first use of the building). Secondly, it may happen that no writing down allowance will be given in respect of a basis period within the writing down life of the building due not to its being used for a non-qualifying trade, but due to the fact that the construction expenditure has previously been written down to nil. In any such case, that basis period remains part of the industrial use period.

If there was a previous sale when the building was not an industrial building (ie disregarding any period of temporary disuse following a period of industrial use), the beginning of the purchaser's *relevant* period is the date of first use for any purpose by the current vendor. In such a case, the industrial use period is limited to the industrial use period of the current vendor.

Example 6.411.2

The same facts as in **Example 6.411.1**, but assume now that Georgina sells the building while still in use in her trade on 1 September 2012 for €600,000 (excluding site value). The balancing adjustment (clearly a balancing charge in this instance) is computed as follows:

		€
Cost		500,000
Less: actual writing down allowances €75,000	75,000	
Notional writing down allowances (as in **6.411.1**)	99,750	174,750
Residue		325,250
Sale proceeds 01/09/2012		600,000
Provisional balancing charge		274,750
Relevant period:		
01/06/2010 (date of first use) to 31/12/2011 (1.58 years)		
Industrial use period (falling within relevant period):		
01/06/2010 to 31/12/2010 (.58 years)		
Balancing charge 2012: Basis period ended 31/12/2012		
€274,750 x .58/1.58		100,857

The balancing charge is however restricted to the IBAA's granted ie €75,000.

Henrietta takes over the residue of expenditure, computed as follows:

	€
Original residue as above	325,250
Add: balancing charge	75,000
Residue	400,250

Assuming that Henrietta continues to use the building for qualifying purposes, she will be entitled to writing down allowances, calculated to write off the residue over the unexpired portion of the writing down life of the asset in the usual way (see **6.410**).

Notes:

The relevant period ends on the same date as the basis period which precedes the basis period in which the event giving rise to the balancing adjustment takes place (the only exception to this rule – not applicable here – arises if the event takes place on the final day of a basis period)

6.412 Sale of building constructed at different dates

An industrial building may have been constructed in more than one basis period so that the construction expenditure may be at different stages in its writing down life or, alternatively, some of the expenditure may have been incurred before the commencement date for industrial buildings allowances in the trade concerned. If such a building is sold as one unit while still an industrial building, it may be necessary to apportion the sales consideration for the whole building between the parts of the building representing the different expenditures so as to exclude from the balancing adjustment computation the appropriate proportion of the sale proceeds attributable to any construction expenditure not subject to a balancing allowance or charge.

The requirement of TCA 1997, s 282(2) to apportion the sales consideration on a 'just' basis where part of the expenditure did not qualify for industrial buildings allowances has been discussed in the context of the land cost element in **6.408**. This subsection is also applicable if part of the expenditure had been incurred before industrial buildings allowances were available for the particular trade category, but where a balancing adjustment falls to be made in respect of later construction expenditure which did qualify. The question of what is a just apportionment of the sale proceeds must depend on the facts of the particular case.

For example, if a factory building had been constructed as one unit over a period that fell partially before and partially after 30 September 1956 so that only the expenditure after that date qualified for industrial buildings allowances, the apportionment of the proceeds of a sale in, say, 1985 might appropriately be made by reference to the respective pre and post-30 September 1956 construction costs. On the other hand, a different basis of apportionment might be required on the sale of a factory building constructed originally in 1953 (no capital allowances), but which had been extended by qualifying expenditure in, say, 1975.

Example 6.412.1

Dunk constructed a sports injury clinic between January 2002 and December 2003 for use in his trade of operating and managing clinics. The total capital expenditure involved was incurred as follows:

	€
Cost of freehold land (acquired September 2000)	30,000
Expenditure on construction:	
Incurred between 1/1/2002 and 14/05/2002	150,000
Incurred between 15/05/2002 and 31/12/2002	100,000
	280,000

The clinic was put into use in Dunk's trade on 1 January 2003. Dunk makes up accounts annually to 31 March. Prior to the sale of the freehold interest in the sports injury clinic (including the land) on 27 January 2012 (falling within the 10 year balancing event period) for a consideration of €900,000, Dunk obtained industrial buildings writing down allowances on the post-14/05/2002 construction expenditure (€100,000) totalling €100,000 for the relevant chargeable periods up to and including his 12-month accounting period ended 31 March 2009 (the basis period for 2009). He obtained no allowances on the earlier expenditure so that the part of the building attributable to the expenditure of €150,000 is not subject to any balancing allowance or charge on the sale.

Assuming that the inspector and he agree to make any necessary apportionments on the basis of the pre and post 14/05/2002 expenditures, the balancing adjustment computation in respect of the part of the building attributable to the latter expenditure is as follows:

	€	€
Cost of construction (post 14/05/2002)		100,000
Less:		
Actual capital allowances obtained to 2011		100,000
Residue of expenditure at 31/12/2011		Nil
Sales proceeds (whole building, including land)	900,000	
Less:		
Proportion allocated to land[1]	96,430	
Brought forward	803,570	
Less:		
Proportion allocated to non-qualifying		
Construction expenditure[2]	482,140	
		321,430
Surplus on sale of part of building		321,430
Balancing charge 2012		321,430
Charge limited to actual allowances obtained		100,000

Notes:

1. The proportion of the sales proceeds allocated to the land element is calculated:

$$900{,}000 \times \frac{\text{land cost } 30{,}000}{\text{total cost } 280{,}000}$$ €96,430

2. The proportion of the balance of the sale proceeds allocated to the non-qualifying construction expenditure is calculated:

$$803{,}570 \times \frac{150{,}000}{250{,}000}$$ €482,140

3. While the balancing charge finally made cannot exceed the actual industrial allowances obtained, the possibility of Dunk's being liable to tax on a capital gain should be considered.

While no question of any balancing allowance or charge has to be considered if there is a sale or other relevant event after the end of the writing down life of all the construction expenditure on an industrial building, an apportionment of the sale, etc monies is required if one part of the construction expenditure (including refurbishment expenditure) has reached the end of its writing down life, but another part has not.

Example 6.412.2

Lindeman Ltd constructs a hotel building at a cost of €340,000 which was first put into use in its hotel trade on 1 January 1997. The company constructs an extension to the hotel at a further cost of €150,000 in its 12-month accounting period ended 31 December 2005. The expenditure was eligible for the 15% rate of writing down allowance under the relevant transitional provisions. The extension was first used for the trade on 1 July 2005. The entire hotel building was destroyed by fire on 5 November 2009 and, in due course, insurance proceeds of €250,000 are received in full settlement of the company's insurance claim (the hotel was underinsured).

Since the writing down life of the original expenditure of €340,000 had expired on 31 December 2003 (seven years after the original building was first used), the balancing adjustment computation has to be confined to the extension expenditure of €150,000. How are the insurance monies to be apportioned?

Lindeman Ltd is professionally advised that the entire building (including the extension) would have cost €800,000 (excluding land costs) if it had been fully constructed in 2005 when the extension was added. A balancing adjustment computation might therefore be prepared as follows:

	€	€
Cost of construction (extension only)		150,000
Less:		
Industrial buildings allowances obtained:		
Annual –2005, 2006, 2007 and 2008 (15% hotel rate)	90,000	
Residue of expenditure		60,000
Insurance proceeds (re 2009 fire) – proportion		
Attributable to 2005 expenditure:		
$250{,}000 \times \frac{150{,}000}{300{,}000} =$		46,875
Balancing allowance (extension only)		13,125

6.5 Leased Industrial Buildings

6.501 Introduction

Any person with rental income from an industrial building or structure is entitled to the same capital allowances as a person using an industrial building for a trade, provided that individual meets the conditions under which the various allowances are available to a lessor. One exception is that a lessor was not entitled to claim an increased writing down allowance (free depreciation) given by TCA 1997, s 273 (see **6.407**). The circumstances in which the lessor may claim the industrial buildings allowances (and is subject to balancing charges), and the manner in which the allowances are granted and the charges made are now discussed. Since rental income is assessable in respect of the rents arising in the current year of assessment (see **12.103**), allowances and charges are calculated by reference to events arising in, or at the end of, the relevant year of assessment.

The definition of an 'industrial building or structure' has been explained in **6.401** – ie a building or structure in use for the purposes of certain specified types of trade (eg manufacturing, market gardening, hotel-keeping, etc). The lessor's entitlement to capital allowances against Sch D Case V income is limited to capital expenditure on industrial buildings that are at the relevant time, in use by the lessee for one of the types of qualifying trade. The writing down allowance may, however, continue to be claimed during a period of temporary disuse immediately following use in a qualifying trade (see **6.503**). Balancing allowances or charges will arise, irrespective of the use to which the building is put at the time of disposal etc.

In general, it may be taken that the principles regarding the application of capital allowances and the various definitions, etc explained in **6.110** are all of similar relevance in the context of the lessor's industrial buildings allowances and charges.

In this context, it may be useful to state here that a non-resident company with Sch D Case V rental income from leasing an industrial building in the State is normally chargeable to income tax (and not corporation tax) so that it is given industrial buildings allowances by reference to years of assessment. A non-resident company with Sch D Case V income from an industrial building held in the course of, or as part of the property of, a trade carried on through a branch or agency in the State is, however, given the industrial buildings allowances by reference to corporation tax accounting periods.

The treatment of industrial buildings allowances in this Division is confined to dealing with points relevant specifically to the taxing of the lessor of the industrial building. It does not purport to cover all aspects of the subject most of which has already been dealt with in **6.4** in the context of industrial buildings allowances generally. The reader's attention is directed particularly to the discussion in **6.403** of the meaning of the term 'relevant interest' in relation to a building or structure, ie the type of interest (eg freehold, 35-year lease, 10-year sublease, etc) held in the building or structure by the person who incurred the capital expenditure at the time he incurred it. The particular lessor claiming industrial buildings allowances (other than the initial allowance) need not necessarily have incurred the capital expenditure to be entitled to the allowances, but he must hold the relevant interest in relation to the capital expenditure at the relevant time (see **6.503**, **6.504**).

The industrial buildings allowances to which the lessor may be entitled provided that he meets the necessary conditions for each are summarised as follows:

(a) an initial allowance in respect of qualifying capital expenditure (see **6.405**) incurred by the lessor himself, if the conditions set out in **6.502** are met;

(b) the writing down (or annual) allowance in respect of qualifying capital expenditure, whether or not incurred by the lessor himself, if he holds the relevant interest in relation to that expenditure at the relevant time (see **6.503**); and

(c) a balancing allowance in respect of unallowed qualifying expenditure (if any) on the sale of (and certain other events) the relevant interest (see **6.504**).

As discussed in **6.4**, the rates of writing down allowances vary depending on the trade category of the industrial buildings concerned and the date on which the qualifying capital expenditure was incurred.

The manner in which a lessor may utilise his allowances are discussed at **6.505** and the restrictions which apply in relation to claims for offset of excess allowances is discussed at **6.509**. The interactions between claims for loss and allowances by a lessor are discussed at **6.506**. The issues raised by lessors whose income is liable under Sch D Case IV or Sch D Case III are discussed at **6.507** and **6.508** respectively.

6.502 Initial allowance

With a few exceptions (see **6.405**), the initial allowance was abolished in respect of expenditure incurred in respect of industrial buildings on or after 31 March 1992. However, the allowance has been restored, subject to some modifications, in respect of industrial buildings located in urban/rural renewal areas, etc (see **Division 19** in the 2009 edition of this book). The discussion here which in most cases will be of academic interest is confined to buildings outside such areas.

The industrial buildings initial allowance is given to the lessor of an industrial building or structure (the building), who has incurred capital expenditure on its construction, if the following conditions are met:

(a) the building is occupied by a qualifying lessee for the purposes of a trade carried on by that lessee;

(b) the building is occupied by the qualifying lessee as an industrial building at the time of the commencement of his tenancy; and

(c) the building, or the part of the building, on which the capital expenditure has been incurred has not been used for any purpose before the qualifying tenancy commences (TCA 1997, s 271(2)).

The lessor's entitlement to claim the initial allowance (strictly called the 'industrial buildings allowance' or 'IBA') may, therefore, be seen to depend primarily on the type of trade carried on by the qualifying lessee at the time his lease or tenancy commences to run (assuming this is after the lessor constructed the building). In the case of capital expenditure incurred by the lessor on extending or altering an existing building already occupied by a qualifying lessee, it is the type of trade carried on by the lessee at the time the expenditure is incurred that is relevant. If at the relevant time, the lessee's trade (for which he occupies the building) is eg a manufacturing or similar trade, or a trade of hotel-keeping, the lessor may claim the industrial buildings allowance.

For this purpose, a qualifying lessee is defined in TCA 1997, s 271(2)(b) as a lessee occupying the industrial building either:

(a) under a lease to which the relevant interest in the building is reversionary (a 'relevant lease'); or

(b) under a lease to which such a relevant lease mentioned in (a) is reversionary, but only if the relevant lease is a lease granted to the Industrial Development Authority (IDA), the Shannon Free Airport Company Limited (SFADCO) or Údarás na Gaeltachta (UnaG).

For a lessor to obtain the industrial buildings initial allowance in respect of any qualifying construction expenditure, the lease held by the person who carries on the particular qualifying trade (eg manufacturing, market gardening) must be one of either of the above types of qualifying lease. It is also important to emphasise that no initial allowance is given to a lessor unless the lessee in fact uses the building for the purposes of a qualifying trade from the commencement of his tenancy (or if later, from the date on which the building is first used for any purpose after its construction). In the event that the building is first used, even if only temporarily, by a person other than a qualifying lessee before its use by him, the lessor is not entitled to the initial allowance. These rules may be modified in the case of qualifying premises in the urban renewal areas, etc (see **Division 19** in the 2009 edition of this book).

The question of when a particular lease is a lease to which the relevant interest is reversionary gives rise to some difficulty. This question has to be considered in relation to the particular lessor who is seeking to obtain the initial allowance for the construction expenditure incurred by him (or, if he has purchased the building before its first use for any purpose, for the expenditure deemed to have been incurred – see **6.408**). Clearly, if the lessor's interest in the building at the time he incurred the expenditure was, say, the freehold interest, and if the lessee carrying on the qualifying trade holds the head lease (or only lease) granted out of the freehold, the lessee's interest is the lease to which the relevant interest (in this case, the freehold) is reversionary. The same applies if the person incurring the expenditure is the person holding the head lease and the lessee carrying on the qualifying trade has a sublease granted directly out of the head lease.

However, what is the position where the person incurring the capital expenditure (the superior lessor) holds his interest in the building (the relevant interest in relation to that expenditure) subject to a lease granted to another person (the main lessee) and the main lessee holds his interest subject to a sublease held by the person carrying on the qualifying trade (the sublessee)? Although it may be argued that the superior lessor's interest is reversionary on both the inferior leasehold interests, it would appear that the legislation may have been intended to deny the superior lessor the initial allowance in this case, unless the main lessee is either the IDA, SFADCO or UnaG. If this is the right interpretation, it would be on the basis that it is only the main lessee's interest (and not that of the sublessee) that is the lease to which the superior lessor's relevant interest is reversionary.

It is understood that the Revenue Commissioners apply the legislation in accordance with the interpretation just given. Consequently, to be sure of being entitled to the industrial buildings allowances, an intending lessor incurring construction expenditure should do one of two things. He may grant the lease directly to the person carrying on the qualifying trade (or who is about to do so). Alternatively, he may grant a lease directly to the IDA, SFADCO or UnaG on the understanding that the body in question will grant a sublease directly to the qualifying trader.

The initial allowance is given to a person carrying on a trade for the chargeable period related to the expenditure. For a person chargeable to income tax, the allowance is therefore given for the year of assessment in the basis period for which the trader has incurred the expenditure.

It is not essential for the qualifying lease to exist at the time the expenditure is incurred. The person incurring the expenditure may claim the initial allowance if he subsequently grants a qualifying lease, but only where the building is not used for any purpose between the date of the expenditure and the commencement of the qualifying tenancy. Further, even if the building is leased for a qualifying purpose, but when the building first comes to be used it is not in fact used as an industrial building, the lessor loses his entitlement to the initial allowance; if any allowance has already been granted, it must be withdrawn and any necessary additional assessments made (TCA 1997, s 271(6)).

The initial allowance is given to a lessor for the 'appropriate chargeable period' (TCA 1997, s 271(2)). The appropriate chargeable period is defined, in relation to the person who incurred the expenditure (the lessor), as *the later of*:

(a) the year of assessment in whose basis period the expenditure is incurred; or
(b) the year of assessment in whose basis period the relevant tenancy commenced (TCA 1997, s 271(1)).

In the case where the lessee carrying on the qualifying trade occupies the building under a lease from one of the State's industrial development companies within TCA 1997, s 271 (see above), the relevant tenancy is the tenancy which the industrial development company in question holds under its lease from the lessor so that it is the date on which that tenancy commences which is used in (b) above. In the case where the said lessee occupies the building under a lease directly from the lessor (ie under the lease to which the relevant interest in the building is reversionary), then the lessee's tenancy under that lease is the relevant tenancy.

Exceptionally, the lessor may be entitled to claim the industrial buildings allowance although he did not incur the expenditure on the actual construction of the building under the rules of TCA 1997, s 279: (see **6.408**).

The rate of initial allowance for a lessor of an industrial building is the same as that available to the person carrying on a trade. For a building used in a trade carried on in a mill, factory or similar premises, an initial allowance equal to 50 per cent of the qualifying expenditure is given (generally confined to expenditure incurred before 1 April 1992).

6.503 Writing-down allowances

The industrial buildings writing down allowance is given to the lessor of a building for each year of assessment (income tax) if, at the end of his basis period for that year, the following conditions are met:

(a) the building is an industrial building or structure, ie one in use for a qualifying trade; and

(b) the interest in the building to which the lessor is entitled is the relevant interest in relation to the capital expenditure in respect of which the allowance is claimed (TCA 1997, s 272(2)).

It is not necessary for the expenditure to have been eligible for an initial allowance when it was incurred, nor does it matter whether the person who incurred the expenditure did so at the time in the capacity of trader, lessor or otherwise. Once the lessor is entitled to the relevant interest related to the construction expenditure at the end of a particular basis period he is entitled to the writing down allowance for that period, if the building is occupied at that time by *any* lessee carrying on a qualifying trade.

For the purpose of the writing down allowance, it is clear that the relevant interest held by the lessor in the building does not have to be the interest immediately superior to the leasehold interest held by the person for the time being occupying the building for the qualifying trade. This contrasts with the Revenue Commissioners' interpretation of the rule governing the lessor's entitlement to the initial allowance (see **6.502**). For example, assume that Mr A holding the freehold interest had constructed a building in 2007 at a cost of €500,000, had granted a lease to B Ltd, which in turn had granted a sublease to C Ltd. If this building is in use as a factory for C Ltd's manufacturing trade on 31 December 2009 then Mr A is entitled to claim the four per cent writing down allowance for 2009. Since the freehold interest is the relevant interest in relation to the €500,000 expenditure, the fact that Mr A now derives his rent from the sublessor (B Ltd) does not prevent his getting the annual allowance.

A lessor holding the relevant interest in a building which ceases temporarily to be an industrial building, either because the lessee ceases to carry on a qualifying trade or because the lease comes to an end, remains entitled to the writing down allowance during a period of temporary disuse *immediately* following use as an industrial building (TCA 1997, s 280). Even if the eventual new use is not as an industrial building, the lessor continues to be entitled to the writing down allowance if he holds the relevant interest at the end of the relevant basis period while the temporary disuse continues. However, if a new non-qualifying use begins, he ceases to be able to claim the writing down allowance (unless and until the building is used again for a qualifying trade).

The rate of writing down allowance given to a lessor is the same as that to which a person carrying on a trade would be entitled, ie dependent on the type of qualifying trade being carried on by the lessee and on the date on which the qualifying expenditure was incurred (see **6.406**). For example, if the expenditure is incurred in the qualifying period on a building in use for a trade which consists of the operation or management of a sports injuries clinic, the writing down allowance is 15 per cent for each relevant year of assessment.

As a general rule the allowance is based on the actual construction expenditure incurred. There are a number of exceptions. Firstly the rules of TCA 1997, s 279 for buildings purchased unused may apply (see **6.408**). Secondly, if the relevant interest in a building changes hands, the allowance may be based on the residue of the expenditure (as adjusted) at that time. In these circumstances, if the building was an industrial building at the time of changing hands, the lessor's subsequent writing down allowances are at the rate to write off the residue of the expenditure evenly over the rest of the writing down life of the relevant construction expenditure (see **6.410**). Thirdly, in the case of expenditure incurred on certain industrial buildings in the calendar year 2007 and in the period from 1 January 2008 to 31 July 2008 the expenditure will be subject to respective reductions to 75 per cent and 50 per cent of the actual capital expenditure incurred in those periods. The industrial buildings in question are hotels, holiday cottages, sports injuries clinics and qualifying residential units associated with registered nursing homes.

Capital expenditure after 31 March 1989

TCA 1997, s 271(5) denies any lessor of an industrial building an annual allowance for the same year of assessment (income tax) or accounting period (corporation tax) as that for which he is given an initial allowance in respect of the same expenditure. This applies where the capital expenditure in question is incurred after 31 March 1989. For qualifying expenditure incurred on or before that date, the previous rules allowed the lessor both an initial allowance and the ordinary annual allowance for the relevant year of assessment or accounting period.

Buildings used for third-level educational purposes

TCA 1997, s 843 provided capital allowances in respect of qualifying expenditure incurred in the qualifying period on the construction of qualifying premises to be leased to an approved institution. The capital allowances were available in respect of expenditure incurred between 1 July 1997 and 31 July 2008, subject to meeting transitional rules.

Qualifying expenditure is capital expenditure on the construction of a qualifying premises, or the provision of machinery or plant. For the capital allowances to be given for expenditure or machinery or plant, the plant must be part of the qualifying premises for example, a lift. It is therefore the intention that the plant would not be moveable plant in relation to the building.

A qualifying premises is defined as a premises which is not an industrial building under TCA 1997, s 268, and

(a) is in use for the purposes of third-level education or associated sporting or leisure facilities provided by an approved institution; and
(b) is let to an approved institution.

Any part of a building or structure in use as or as part of a dwelling house is excluded from the definition of qualifying premises.

An approved institution means any of the following:

(a) an institution of higher education under the Higher Education Authority Act 1971, s 1;
(b) an institution in the Republic of Ireland which receives public funding and provides courses to which a scheme approved by the Minister for Education, under the Local Authorities (Higher Education Grants) Acts 1968 to 1992 applies; or
(c) a body in receipt of public funding in respect of the provision of third-level health and social services education or training which is approved by the Minister for Health and Children for the purposes of TCA 1997, s 843.

The qualifying period for scheme commenced on 1 July 1997 and was due to expire on 31 July 2006. FA 2006, s 34 provides for the extension in the qualifying period from 31 July 2006 to 31 December 2006. There is also a further extension in the qualifying period to 31 July 2008 where the person who is constructing the qualifying premises has carried out work to the value of not less than 15 per cent of the actual construction costs by 31 December 2006 and that person or the person who is claiming the allowances can show that the condition is satisfied. The extension of the qualifying period from 31 July

2006 to 31 December 2006 and the further extension to 31 July 2008 came into operation by Ministerial Order SI 332/2006. Capital expenditure incurred on the construction of a qualifying building will be treated as having been incurred in the qualifying period to the extent that the expenditure is attributable to work on the construction of the building actually carried out during the qualifying period.

In order for the structure to qualify for capital allowances it is necessary that before the commencement of construction of the premises, the Minister for Finance certifies that:

(a) the approved institution has raised money, none of which is met by the State, which is not less than 50 per cent of the qualifying expenditure to be incurred on the qualifying premises; and

(b) the money raised by the approved institution is used solely for the following purposes:

   (i) to pay interest on money borrowed for the purpose of funding the construction of the qualifying premises,

   (ii) to pay any rent on the qualifying premises during such times as the qualifying premises is the subject of a letting, and

   (iii) to purchase the qualifying premises following the termination of the letting.

The Minister for Finance may not issue such a certificate unless the application for certification was made by 1 January 2005.

TCA 1997, s 843(2) provides that, subject to modifications, all of the rules of the Tax Acts (other than TCA 1997, s 317(2)) regarding allowances in respect of capital expenditure on an industrial building apply as if the qualifying premises were an industrial building and as if the activity carried on in that premises were a trade. Where the expenditure on the qualifying premises is incurred in the period from 1 January 2006 to 31 July 2008 then the amount of qualifying expenditure which is to be treated as incurred for the purpose of making allowances and charges is reduced. If the expenditure is incurred in the calendar year 2007 the reduction will be to 75 per cent of the amount which would otherwise be treated as expenditure incurred on the construction of the building. There is a 50 per cent reduction for expenditure incurred in the period from 1 January 2008 to 31 July 2008.

The allowances are available at 15 per cent of the capital expenditure in each of the first six years and 10 per cent in year seven. The legislation provides that no balancing charge will arise more than seven years after the qualifying premises is first used so the period within which a balancing charge or allowance can arise matches the tax life of the building.

With effect from 6 April 1999, the obligations of the Minister for Finance and the Minister for Education and Science in regard to approval/certification functions may be delegated to An tÚdarás as the Ministers see fit. This is apparently intended to cater for the administration of projects funded by the Research and Development Fund, established in 1998, which may qualify under TCA 1997, s 843.

The intention of TCA 1997, s 843 is to allow the approved institution enter into a financial arrangement with a sponsoring authority (ie a bank) whereby it incurs the capital expenditure on the qualifying premises and obtains the capital allowances on leasing the premises to the approved institution. This would allow the institution to pay a lower rent in respect of the premises.

This relief is subject to the high earners restriction (HER) discussed at **3.111**.

6.504 Balancing allowances and balancing charges

A lessor who has obtained any writing down allowance (or initial allowance) in respect of any capital expenditure on a building or structure, whether in his capacity as lessor or previously as the person carrying on a qualifying trade, is entitled to a balancing allowance, or is subject to a balancing charge, under the circumstances described at **6.409**.

The balancing allowance or balancing charge, computed under the same rules as apply on the occurrence of any of the above events where the relevant interest is held by a person carrying on a trade, is given to or made on the lessor (see **6.409**).

Again, the lessor is not entitled to any balancing allowance, nor is he subject to any balancing charge, if the sale, demolition, termination, etc of the relevant interest in the building occurs after the end of the balancing charge period of the expenditure in question as set out in TCA 1997, s 274(1)(b).

A sale or other disposal by the lessee of his leasehold interest in an industrial building does not itself require any balancing adjustment to be made for the lessor. If the assignee of that leasehold interest (the new lessee) does not continue to use the building as an industrial building, this results in a cessation of the lessor's writing down allowances, but except in the case of a relevant facility it does not trigger any balancing adjustment. In the case of buildings other than a relevant facility it is only if the building ceases entirely to be used for any purpose that the balancing adjustment is made.

A relevant facility is a building which is in use as a registered nursing home, a qualifying residential unit, a certified convalescent home, a qualifying hospital, a qualifying mental health centre or certain childcare facilities. Where an allowance has been made in respect of a relevant facility and the building ceases to be a relevant facility then the cessation of use is treated as an event that gives rise to a balancing charge. The balancing charge is made on the person who was entitled to the relevant interest in the building immediately before the event. The balancing charge can be avoided if within six months of the building ceasing to be one type of relevant facility it is put into use as another type of relevant facility. For example if a building ceases to be a relevant facility by virtue of ceasing to be used for the purpose of the operation of a registered nursing home the balancing charge could be avoided if within a period of six months of the cessation the building was put into use as a certified convalescent home. The balancing charge on a building ceasing to be a relevant facility applies where a building is first used on or after 1 January 2006 or where the building is first used after incurring refurbishment expenditure on or after that date.

The calculation of balancing allowances and charges in respect of an industrial building, ie as the difference between the sale, insurance, salvage or compensation monies and the residue of the expenditure immediately before the sale or other relevant event, has been fully explained in **6.409** and no further illustrations are considered necessary here.

6.505 Manner of granting allowances to lessors

The lessor's capital allowances on industrial buildings (initial, writing down and balancing allowances) are given, and balancing charges made, in charging his income under Sch D Case V (TCA 1997, s 278(1)). The allowances are available primarily against the lessor's income taxable under Sch D Case V or against any balancing charges under that Case (TCA 1997, s 278(6)). In practice, a lessor's balancing charges for a given chargeable period are usually deducted first from his Sch D Case V capital allowances (including any balancing allowances) for the same period, but any excess of balancing charges over allowances is assessable under Sch D Case V as if it were additional rental income for the period.

The industrial buildings allowances are deducted from the total of the lessor's Sch D Case V income for the relevant chargeable period, ie from the excess of the aggregate of his rent surpluses over deficiencies as assessable to tax for that period (see **12.106**). The fact that part of the total Sch D Case V income is made up of surpluses (less any deficiencies) mainly from rents from premises other than industrial buildings does not restrict the deduction of the industrial buildings allowances. These allowances are given if there is an overall net surplus in the Sch D Case V computation, even if there is a net deficiency on the rents from the industrial buildings.

TCA 1997, s 305(1)(a) as applied to industrial buildings allowances by TCA 1997, s 278(6) requires the lessor's capital allowances for a given year of assessment to be deducted firstly from his Sch D Case V income (including any balancing charges) assessable for that year. If the Sch D Case V income for the year is less than the capital allowances, the excess allowances are carried forward to the next year of assessment (unless and to the extent that they are used in a claim against the lessor's other income see below). Any excess allowances carried forward must be set off against the Sch D Case V income chargeable for the next year to the full extent of that income. If the allowances carried forward cannot be fully absorbed by the next year's income, any unused balance of allowances is carried forward to the year after, and so on without time limit until they are fully used up. The right to claim the deduction for capital allowances against all Case V income under TCA 1997, s 305(1)(a) is subject to a restriction where an industrial building is transferred from a company to an individual under TCA 1997, s 409E (see **6.509**).

The lessor has a possible alternative way open to him of using any excess Sch D Case V capital allowances for any given year of assessment, instead of carrying them forward to the next year. TCA 1997, s 305(1)(b) entitles him to claim to have any such excess industrial buildings allowances (initial, writing down or balancing) set off against his other income from all sources assessable for the *same* year of assessment. Unused industrial buildings, etc allowances carried forward from a previous tax year are not eligible for inclusion in this claim. If the claim is made, the full amount of the excess allowances must be deducted from the taxpayer's other income to the extent that it is sufficient to absorb the set off. Where the lessor is jointly assessable with his spouse under TCA 1997, s 1017 the industrial building allowances in excess of his other income can be set off against his spouse's income for that year of assessment. To the extent that the income is insufficient to cover the excess allowances, the unabsorbed balance is carried forward for set off against the lessor's Sch D Case V income (but not any other income) assessable in the next tax year and, if necessary, for set off against Sch D Case V income in later years. The right to claim the offset under TCA 1997, s 305(1)(b) is however subject to various restrictions, discussed at **6.509**.

Any claim under TCA 1997, s 305(1)(b) must be made by notice in writing to the inspector no later than 24 months after the end of the tax year for which the claim arises.

It is important to note that the lessor chargeable to income tax must, if he wishes to obtain the industrial buildings initial allowance, make a specific claim for it in his annual income tax return or other statement in which he declares the profits and gains from his Sch D Case V sources; the claim must be accompanied by a certificate signed by him giving the necessary particulars establishing his entitlement to the allowance

(TCA 1997, s 304(2)). A similar claim must be made by him for any writing down allowance or balancing allowance to which he is entitled.

Example 6.505.1

Mr T O'Mato constructed glasshouses costing €500,000 between June and December 2014 and leased them to Tomatose Ltd for use in its trade of market gardening under a 10-year lease commencing on 1 January 2015. The rent payable by the tenant company, which is responsible for all outgoings in respect of the leased premises is €35,000 per annum. In addition, the company paid a premium of €50,000 for the granting of the lease.

Mr O'Mato has also Sch D Case V income from other lettings, one of which is the lease of a building (constructed many years ago and the tax life has expired) currently in use by the lessee as a warehouse for a manufacturing trade. On 1 March 2015, Mr O'Mato pays a building contractor €100,000 as the agreed contract price for constructing an extension to this warehouse which becomes immediately available to the lessee. Mr O'Mato pays interest on various loans used to help finance his costs of construction and/or purchasing his leased properties (interest deductible as expense under TCA 1997, s 97).

His Sch D Case V computation for 2015 is summarised as follows:

	Glasshouses	*Warehouse*	*Other lettings*
	€	€	€
Y/E 31 December 2015:			
Rents receivable	35,000	20,000	5,000
Premium on lease	41,000		
	76,000		
Expenses, etc:			
Interest on loans	30,000	6,000	1,300
Other allowable expenses	15,000	4,700	1,900
	45,000	10,700	3,200
Surplus for year	31,000	9,300	1,800

Mr O'Mato claims the industrial building writing down allowance for the market gardening buildings (10 per cent pa) and the additional expenditure on the manufacturing trade warehouse (4 per cent pa)

The industrial buildings allowances for the tax year 2015 are dealt with as follows in the Sch D Case V computations:

	2015
	€
Surpluses for year:	
Glasshouses	31,000
Warehouse	9,300
Other lettings	1,800
Total Sch D Case V income	42,100
Industrial buildings allowances:	
Glasshouses – IBA (10% of €500,000)	50,000
Warehouse – WDA (4% of €100,000)	4,000
	54,000
Net Sch D Case V income (after capital allowances)	Nil
Excess Case V capital allowances	11,900

Notes:

1. The amount taxable under TCA 1997, s 98 as additional rent in respect of the premium of €50,000 payable on 1 January 2015 on the granting of the 10-year lease to the glasshouses is:

   €50,000 x (51 – 10)/50 = €41,000

2. For the relief available for the excess capital allowances of €11,900 in 2015, see **Example 6.505.2**. below.

Example 6.505.2

Take the facts of **Example 6.505.1**. Assume that Mr T O'Mato is assessable jointly with his wife and that their joint total income for 2015 is made up as follows:

	€	€
Sch D Case II (self)		86,000
Sch E (wife's salary)		19,400
Other sources (joint)		6,800
Net Sch D Case V (as per Example **6.505.1**)		Nil
		112,200
Less:		
Qualifying Interest on loan to invest in a partnership	3,300	
Covenant to elderly dependent relative	1,300	
		4,600
Total income (before TCA 1997, s 305(1)(b) claim)		107,600

Mr O'Mato is entitled under TCA 1997, s 305(1)(b) to claim to have the excess capital allowances for 2015 set off against his total income for the same tax year, with the following results:

	€
Income from all sources 2015 (as above):	112,200
Less:	
Interest	(3,300)
Excess capital allowances (TCA 1997, s 305(1)(b))	(11,900)
Covenant[1]	(1,300)
Revised total income 2015	95,700

Notes:

1. The annual payment is not restricted. The maximum deductible amount is €4,619 ((€112,200 – €3,300 – €11,900) = €97,000 x 5/105) which is less than the covenanted payment (see **15.405**).

6.506 Schedule D Case V losses and industrial buildings allowances

A Sch D Case V rental loss, ie the aggregate of the rent deficiencies over the rent surpluses, is calculated for any year of assessment before bringing in any relevant capital allowances in respect of leased industrial buildings. The reliefs for Sch D Case V rental losses are discussed in **12.106** in the context of lessors not having any Sch D Case V industrial buildings allowances. It is now necessary to consider the order in which capital allowances and losses are set off in any case where both occur.

TCA 1997, s 278(1) provides that capital allowances on leased industrial buildings are given in charging the person's income under Case V income. TCA 1997, s 305(1)(a), as discussed above, provides for unused allowances to be carried forward against Schedule D Case V income of future years. TCA 1997, s 384 provides that the excess of any deficiencies over any surpluses must be carried forward and set off so far as possible against the profits or gains assessable under Sch D Case V for any subsequent periods. Case V losses can only be set off to the extent of the profits or gains assessed for that year. The better view has always been that capital allowances have to be deducted in arriving at the assessable Case V profit it follows that capital allowances are deducted in priority to Case V losses brought forward from previous tax years. This interpretation has been confirmed statutorily from 2011 onwards by TCA 1997, s 384(4) inserted by FA 2010, s 15. Although both the unused capital allowances carried forward to the next year and the actual capital allowances for that year must both be deducted from the lessor's Sch D Case V income for that year, it may be useful to repeat here the point made in **6.505** that the allowances carried forward to a later year must be excluded from any claim against other income under TCA 1997, s 305(1)(b) in respect of that year. TCA 1997, s 305(1)(b) makes it clear that prior year allowances are to be offset against rental income in priority to the current year allowance thereby maximising the quantum of the excess allowances available to offset against total income. However, the ability to make a claim to sideways offset may be significantly restricted (see **6.509**).

In applying the foregoing rules, any balancing charge made on the lessor of industrial buildings is, strictly, treated as additional income assessable under Sch D Case V as it may be separately assessed (TCA 1997, s 304(5)). In practice, it is usual to simply deduct any balancing charges for any year of assessment from the total capital allowances for that year and to work in terms of the net capital allowances (ie as reduced by balancing charges). However, if the balancing charges exceed the total allowances for any year, then the excess charges must be added to the other Sch D Case V income for the year.

6.507 Schedule D Case IV lessors

Where the person entitled to an industrial buildings writing down allowance, balancing allowance or initial allowance in respect of any premises is a lessor chargeable to tax otherwise than under Sch D Case V, the allowance is given by way of discharge or repayment of tax (TCA 1997, s 278(2), (3), (4)). In fact, except in the case of rental or other income from the leasing of premises situated outside the State which is taxable under Sch D Case III as the income from a foreign possession (see **13.108**), any income from the leasing of premises not within Sch D Case V is chargeable to tax under Sch D Case IV (although there are very few such instances). Where such an instance occurs, any industrial buildings allowances in respect of the premises are available primarily against income chargeable under Sch D Case IV and/or any balancing charge within that case (TCA 1997, s 278(6)). Where the income from the building is chargeable under Sch D Case IV, any balancing charge will be made under the same case (TCA 1997, s 278(5)).

All the rules of TCA 1997, s 305(1), as discussed above in relation to Sch D Case V lessors, are applicable in a corresponding way to any instances where any of the industrial buildings allowances are available primarily against income or balancing charges chargeable under Sch D Case IV. In this connection it is to be noted that the available income is all income chargeable under that Case, which includes many types of miscellaneous income (see **8.201**, **8.202**). Any Sch D Case IV industrial buildings allowances are available to be set off against the total of the income taxable within that Case (and not only against the income from premises).

To the extent that any industrial buildings allowances within Sch D Case IV for any year of assessment exceeds the total income and any balancing charges taxable under that Case, the taxpayer has the same alternatives as for Sch D Case V industrial buildings allowances – namely, to carry forward the excess for set off against the Sch D Case IV income of succeeding years or to set off against other income of the same year. The ability to make a claim to sideways offset may be significantly restricted (see **6.509**).

6.508 Foreign leased industrial buildings

A resident person in receipt of rents from immovable property situated outside the State is taxable on the net income under Sch D Case III (and not under Sch D Case V).

As discussed at **6.401**, by virtue of TCA 1997, s 268(5) expenditure incurred on a building situated outside the State after 22 April 1996 will not qualify for industrial buildings allowance, subject to transitional provisions.

Although the entitlement to industrial buildings allowances in respect of overseas buildings falling outside the prohibition of TCA 1997, s 268(5) is clearly within the legislation, there appears to be a problem in determining how such allowances are to be granted. The legislation is silent on the matter where the relevant leased buildings give rise to foreign source rental income taxable under Sch D Case III. It seems that the lessor should be permitted to set off the industrial buildings allowances in respect of his foreign situated buildings against the rental income that is taxable under Sch D Case III. There is then a further question to consider: namely, if a taxpayer's industrial building allowances for foreign situated buildings exceed his net rental income chargeable under Sch D Case III for the relevant chargeable period, is he entitled to have the excess capital allowances set off against his income from all sources for that period?

It is understood that the Revenue were prepared to accept claims for industrial buildings allowances by a lessor of foreign situated buildings which, applying the normal tests for entitlement to the allowances, met the conditions required in the legislation. The Revenue were also prepared to accept that an election may be made under TCA 1997, s 305(1)(b) to set off any excess industrial buildings allowances on foreign situated buildings in arriving at the taxpayer's total income (and to grant the corresponding treatment to a company under the relevant corporation tax rules).

6.509 Restrictions on offsets against Sch D Case V income and total income

Property investment schemes ('unitisation')

TCA 1997, s 408 imposes restrictions in respect of certain unitised property investment schemes. A 'property investment scheme' is defined as:

> any scheme or arrangement, made for the purpose, or having the effect, of providing facilities, whether promoted by way of public advertisement or otherwise, for the public or a section of the public to share, either directly or indirectly and whether as beneficiaries under a trust or by any other means, in income or gains arising or deriving from the acquisition, holding or disposal of, or of an interest in, a building or structure or a part thereof.

The meaning of the term 'public' has proven elusive in other statutory contexts (see eg *Nash v Lynde* [1929] AC 158, a company law case).

Where there is a property investment scheme as defined, other than an 'excepted scheme' (see below) any person holding an interest in, or deriving from, any buildings or structures pursuant to such a scheme may only claim his share of industrial building allowances against his rental income. In other words, TCA 1997, s 305(1)(b) (permitting excess rental capital allowances to be offset against total income) does not apply to these industrial building allowances. However, the section does not apply where a claim is made under say TCA 1997, s 381 to create or increase a loss. Such a claim might arise where eg a number of professionals purchase a building used by them for the purpose of their professions.

The restriction applies to all allowances under TCA 1997, ss 271, 272 and thus covers schemes involving 'normal' industrial buildings, as well as qualifying premises within the various 'tax incentive' areas such as urban renewal schemes, etc (see **Division 19** in the 2009 edition of this book), which apply TCA 1997, ss 271, 272 for their own purposes. The restriction does not apply to balancing allowances under TCA 1997, s 274.

There is an exception to this restriction where, in the opinion of the Revenue Commissioners, the manner in which the investors share in the income or gains from the building or buildings and the number of persons who so share, are in accordance with a practice commonly prevailing in the State during the five years ending on 29 January 1991. A taxpayer aggrieved by the decision of the Revenue Commissioners on this point has a right of appeal to the Appeal Commissioners (with the usual provisions for a hearing by the Circuit Court judge and for a case stated to the High Court on a point of law). F(TA)A 2015, s 36(4)(c) amends TCA 1997, s 408 to say that a person aggrieved by a decision made by the Revenue Commissioners may appeal the decision to the Appeal Commissioners with the possibility of a High Court appeal on a point of law.

It appears that this exception is intended to apply to cases where a relatively small number of investors are involved, each entitled to a proportionately large share of the income, capital gains and capital allowances arising. In the Dáil debate on the section, it was indicated that a property investment spread between, for example, four investors would be within the exception (in some cases up to thirteen investors, particularly if the project is reasonably sizeable, may be acceptable to the Revenue Commissioners, although this will depend on whether the investors have family, social or business ties in common (as opposed say to being brought together for the specific purposes of the investment by an intermediary)).

Holiday cottages

Capital expenditure incurred from 1 August 2008 (subject to meeting transitional relief requirements) on holiday cottages no longer qualifies for industrial buildings allowances. TCA 1997, s 405 did impose certain restrictions on the use of the industrial buildings writing down allowances and initial allowances given for capital expenditure incurred on the acquisition or construction of a building or structure which is, or is to be, an industrial building by virtue of being a registered holiday cottage (within TCA 1997, s 268(3)).

TCA 1997, s 405(3) provides that the restriction does not apply to a holiday cottage which is comprised in a premises first registered after 5 April 2001 in a register of approved holiday cottages established by Bord Fáilte under Pt III of the Tourist Traffic Act 1939, provided that prior to registration;

(a) the building was a qualifying premises under TCA 1997, s 353 (seaside resorts) by virtue of being in use for the purpose of the operation of a tourism accommodation facility under the Tourist Traffic Act 1957, s 9; and

(b) the capital allowances were not subject to the ring-fencing provisions in TCA 1997, s 355(4) (seaside resorts) by virtue of the transitional measures in s 355(5).

The effect of TCA 1997, s 405 applying is that the writing down allowances and any initial allowance for capital expenditure incurred after 23 April 1992 on holiday cottages (other than any excepted expenditure) may *not* be used for set off against the taxpayer's income other than Sch D Case V income in an election under TCA 1997, s 305(1)(b).

In other words, in the case of a person chargeable to income tax, the industrial buildings writing down allowance and any initial allowance in respect of capital expenditure on holiday cottages within TCA 1997, s 405 are only available to be set off against all of his Sch D Case V income or balancing charges (if he is entitled to the allowances as a lessor of the holiday cottages). The allowances may be so set off against the Sch D Case V income either in the tax year to which they relate or in a subsequent tax year in a carry forward claim.

General restrictions on offset against total income

TCA 1997, ss 409A and 409B impose significant restrictions on the ability of a lessor of an industrial building to offset industrial buildings allowances of any kind against his total income under TCA 1997, s 305(1)(b). These restrictions mirror those which apply to claims for such allowances by non-active partners under TCA 1997, s 391(1) to create or enhance TCA 1997, s 381 losses (see **4.406**). The restrictions apply to expenditure incurred on or after 3 December 1997, subject to the transitional provisions described further below. The specified industrial buildings and structures are those as defined by TCA 1997, s 268 (see **6.401**) as well as any commercial buildings or structures located in tax incentive areas (eg Urban/Rural renewal areas, etc: see **Division 19** in the 2009 edition of this book) which are treated as industrial buildings for capital allowance purposes. The only exceptions are:

(a) buildings and structures falling within TCA 1997, s 268(1)(d), ie those in use for the purposes of the trade of hotel-keeping or which are deemed to be so used (eg registered holiday cottages); hotels and holiday camps are in fact subject to the generally more stringent provisions of TCA 1997, s 409B (see below), while registered holiday cottages are potentially within the ring-fencing provisions of TCA 1997, s 405, described immediately above; and

(b) an apartment/self-catering accommodation in a designated seaside resort area, these being potentially within the ring-fencing provisions of TCA 1997, s 355(4), described immediately above (TCA 1997, s 409A(1)).

Where TCA 1997, s 409A applies, the lessor's claim for the industrial buildings allowances affected under TCA 1997, s 305(1)(b) is effectively capped at €31,750 (TCA 1997, s 409A(2)).

TCA 1997, s 409B(3) is even more stringent than TCA 1997, s 409A(3) and in fact completely removes the ability of a lessor to make a claim under TCA 1997, s 305(1)(b) in respect of the industrial buildings or structures specified in TCA 1997, s 409B(1) (TCA 1997, s 409B(2)). The specified buildings and structures are defined as those which are, or which are deemed to fall within TCA 1997, s 268(1)(d), but excluding registered holiday cottages (potentially within the ring-fencing provisions of TCA 1997, s 405), described immediately above. Hotels, holiday camps, etc generally fall within these provisions (TCA 1997, s 409B(1)(b)). There is however one further exception in favour of hotels of a standard specified in guidelines issued for the purpose (normally three star accommodation and above) and which are located in any of the following counties:

Cavan
Donegal
Leitrim
Mayo
Monaghan
Roscommon
Sligo

Hotels located in a qualifying seaside resort area do not qualify for this latter exception (TCA 1997, s 409B(1)(a)).

Transitional provisions

The following transitional provisions apply equally for the purposes of TCA 1997, ss 409A and 409B. The restrictions on the allowances will not apply to expenditure incurred on or after 3 December 1997 where:

(a) (i) in the case of construction expenditure, the entire foundations of the building or structure were laid prior to 3 December 1997,

(ii) in the case of refurbishment expenditure, work to the value of at least five per cent of the total cost of refurbishment was carried out prior to 3 December 1997 (TCA 1997, s 409A(5)(a); TCA 1997, s 409B(4)(a));

(b) expenditure incurred on or after 3 December 1997 will not be subject to the ring-fencing rules where *either*:

(i) an application for all necessary planning permission for the expenditure concerned was made to a planning authority prior to 3 December 1997, *or*

(ii) the individual concerned can satisfy the Revenue Commissioners that a detailed plan had been prepared for the work and that detailed discussions had taken place in respect of the building concerned with a planning authority prior to 3 December 1997 (this must be supported by an affidavit or statutory declaration from the planning authority), and

(iii) the expenditure incurred on or after 3 December 1997 is incurred under a binding written contract entered into *by the individual concerned* prior to 3 December 1997 or 1 May 1998 if the obligation was entered into pursuant to negotiations in respect of which preliminary written commitments or agreements had been entered into prior to 3 December 1997 (TCA 1997, ss 409A(5), (6); 409B(4), (5)); where the individual dies before part of the expenditure has been incurred, and another individual who undertakes in writing to take over the obligation, he can avail of the transitional relief on expenditure which he incurs on the building or structure (TCA 1997, s 409A(7); TCA 1997, s 409B(6)).

Restrictions on offset against total income and rental income

TCA 1997, s 409E restricts the deduction for capital allowances against Case V income and the offset of excess allowances against other income where a specified building is transferred from a company to an individual. This is an anti avoidance provision designed to prevent the effective transfer of industrial building allowances from companies (liable to corporation tax at 12.5 per cent/25 per cent) to individuals, who in the absence of this provision, would be entitled to allowances that would shelter income taxable at the individual's marginal rate. A specified building means:

(a) a building, or part of a building, which is or is to be an industrial building by reason of its use or deemed use for a purpose specified in TCA 1997, s 268(1) and in relation to which an allowance has or is to be made to a company; or

(b) any other building, or part thereof, in relation to which an allowance has or is to be made to a company under Pt 10 (Urban/Rural Renewal relief, etc), TCA 1997, s 843 (buildings used for third-level education) or TCA 1997, s 843A (buildings used for childcare purposes).

The section applies where:

(a) a company is entitled to the relevant interest in the capital expenditure incurred or deemed to be incurred on the construction or refurbishment of a specified building;

(b) an individual subsequently acquires the relevant interest or any part thereof, whether or not any other person or persons had in the intervening period become entitled to the relevant interest; and

(c) the individual is entitled to deduct capital allowances in respect the capital expenditure on the industrial building or the residue of that expenditure in charging income under Case V.

The allowances made to an individual in respect of the capital expenditure on the building concerned may not exceed the rent net of allowable expenses from that building for the year of assessment. The allowances will be made in charging the net rental income from the specified building for the year of assessment and will be available only in charging that rent. TCA 1997, s 305(1)(c) provides that the capital allowances in excess of the net rental income from the building may be carried forward and offset against the net rental income from the building for the next and subsequent years of assessment.

6.6 Miscellaneous Capital Allowances

6.601 Scientific research allowances

A person carrying on a trade, who incurs capital expenditure on scientific research, is entitled to a capital allowance of 100 per cent of the expenditure. The allowance is made in taxing the profits of his trade for the year of assessment (income tax) or accounting period (corporation tax) in which the expenditure is incurred and with effect from 1 January 2016 any asset representing such capital expenditure on scientific research is in use for the purposes of scientific research at the end of the chargeable period. It should also be noted that the allowance only applies to trades and not to professions or to persons carrying on other income earning activities (TCA 1997, s 765(1)).

'Scientific research' is defined as meaning any activities in the fields of natural or applied science for the extension of knowledge whether or not related to the taxpayer's own trade. The scientific research allowance does not, however, apply to any expenditure incurred on the acquisition of rights in, or arising out of, scientific research. For example, scientific research may lead to an invention which is patented; the allowance is not given for purchasing or acquiring rights in a patent. The definition of scientific research excludes exploring for specified materials, petroleum exploration and extraction activities. TCA 1997, s 763 contains the definitions of these terms.

In *Texaco (Ireland) Ltd v Murphy* IV ITR 91, it was held in the High Court that exploring for oil constituted 'scientific research'. The subsequent drilling for oil was however a commercial operation and not carried out for the extension of knowledge (even though there was a spin-off of knowledge gained in the course of such drilling). An argument that the scope of the term 'scientific research' nevertheless had to be restricted by reference to other relieving sections was rejected by the Supreme Court (see **1.402**). The actual decision of the High Court has been overruled in the context of oil exploration (see TCA 1997, s 763(3)), but the general approach underlying the decision may still be persuasive.

A trader who incurs capital expenditure on scientific research before he sets up and commences his trade is entitled to the allowance for the year of assessment (income tax) in which his trade does commence, but in this instance only where the research is related to his trade. In *Tax Briefing 18*, the Revenue Commissioners express the view that while pre-trading expenditure is not *necessarily* capital in nature, generally it will rank as such since it arises in the course of creating an enduring benefit for the purposes of the trade. This analysis is questionable since, in strictness, the 'enduring benefit' must be one which is analogous to a fixed asset if it is to represent capital expenditure (see **5.307**). If the expenditure is revenue in nature then the provisions of TCA 1997, s 82 will be in point (see **5.306**). No allowance is given for capital expenditure on scientific research incurred before the commencement of a trade if the research is not related to the trade.

The capital expenditure on which the scientific research allowance is given may be incurred on the purchase or production of an asset to be used in the trade for the research in question. In *Tax Briefing 18*, the Revenue Commissioners confirm that expenditure on plant, equipment and laboratories will qualify for the allowance. If any such asset ceases for any reason to be used for the research relating to the trade of the person who incurred the expenditure, then the trader must include as a trading receipt in his Sch D Case I computation the lower of (a) the value of the asset at the time it ceases to be used for the scientific research and (b) the scientific research allowance previously granted for the expenditure on the asset (TCA 1997, s 765(3)).

Capital expenditure on scientific research that is met directly or indirectly out of monies provided by the State, or by any person other than the person claiming the scientific research allowance, must be excluded and cannot be the subject of any allowance (TCA 1997, s 763(5)). Further, the same expenditure cannot give rise to an allowance in relation to more than one trade (TCA 1997, s 763(6)). Where the expenditure is represented wholly or partly by assets, then no wear and tear or other form of capital allowance can be obtained for the expenditure, except for a possible wear and tear allowance after any such asset ceases to be used for scientific research (TCA 1997, s 765(4)).

When the scientific research expenditure was in respect of an asset that is machinery or plant, then if the asset ceases to be used for the research, but is used for other purposes in the trade of the person who incurred the expenditure, a wear and tear allowance may be claimed under the ordinary rules. The capital cost of the plant on which this wear and tear allowance is based becomes the actual cost of the plant as reduced by the net scientific research allowance previously obtained in respect of this plant. In other words, the reduction from the actual capital cost equals the scientific research allowance made originally less the amount credited as a trading receipt at the time the plant ceased to be used for the research (TCA 1997, s 765(3)).

Example 6.601.1

TEC, trading as a manufacturer, incurred capital expenditure of €20,000 on scientific research in its accounting year ended 31 December 2014. The expenditure included €8,000 on items of plant to be used wholly for the research. Capital grants of 15 per cent were received towards the cost of the expenditure.

On 15 February 2015, an item of plant which had cost €3,000 (before the grant) was withdrawn from the scientific research use and transferred to normal production; the value of this item of plant was agreed at €2,200 on 15 February 2015. The consequences of the foregoing are as follows:

	€	€
Accounting period ended 31/12/2014:		
Scientific research allowance		
€20,000 – grant of €3,000, ie €17,000 x 100 per cent		17,000
Accounting period ended 31/12/2015		
Include as trading receipt for machine withdrawn from scientific research use:		
Lower of: Value of asset 15/2/2015,	€2,200	
Or		
Scientific research allowance on plant (€3,000 – grant €450),	€2,550	(2,200)

TEC is entitled to claim wear and tear allowances on the machine withdrawn from scientific research use with effect from its accounting period to 31 December 2015 on a deemed capital cost of €2,650. In calculating the tax written down value of the asset it will be reduced by notional wear and tear allowances as follows:

	€	€
Actual cost (before grant)		3,000
Less: Scientific research allowance in 2014	2,550	
Add allowance withdrawn as trading receipt 2015	(2,200)	
		(350)
Deemed cost in 2014		2,650
Less: Notional wear and tear allowances (see **6.204**)		
2014– €2,650 x 12.5%	331	331
Tax WDV 15/2/2015		2,319
Wear and tear allowance 2015 €2,650 x 12.5%		331

6.602 Pre-commencement training

A person who is about to carry on a trade in the production for sale of manufactured goods is entitled to writing down allowances for expenditure incurred before the date of commencement of trade on the recruitment and training of workers or staff for employment in the trade. In practice, most manufacturing activities will be undertaken by companies, in order to avail of the 12.5 per cent corporation tax rate. These staff training writing down allowances are only available for expenditure which, if it had been incurred after the commencement of trade, would have been deductible as an expense under the rules of Sch D Case I. In other words, the expenditure must have been incurred wholly and exclusively for the purposes of the intended trade (TCA 1997, s 769).

It is a further condition that the expenditure on the recruitment and training must have been in respect of persons all or a majority of whom are Irish citizens (a requirement that is unlikely to be consistent with EU law), but there is no requirement that the trainees should have been resident in the State before their recruitment. Any expenditure that is met directly or indirectly by the State, by any board established by statute or by any public or local authority, or by any person other than the taxpayer (since 6 May 1993), must be excluded and is not eligible for the writing down allowances.

These allowances are regarded as capital allowances and the rules applicable to capital allowances generally apply to them. The writing down allowances are given for a writing down period of three years beginning on the date the trade actually commences. Expenditure is treated as being incurred on the date on which the sum in question becomes payable; consequently, if this date is on or after the first day of trading, the expenses are deductible in the ordinary way in the Sch D Case I computation and the writing down allowances do not apply.

TCA 1997, s 769 has been largely superseded by TCA 1997, s 82 which grants relief for certain pre-trading expenditure (see **5.306**: *Expenses of cessation and commencement*).

Example 6.602.1

Messrs Green and Yellow agree to set up a business of manufacturing coloured pencils and incur expenditure of €7,400 on the recruitment and training of workers between 1 July 2012 and 31 December 2012. Their partnership trade is accepted as commencing on 1 January

2013. Between that date and 31 March 2013, a further €2,500 is spent on recruitment and training of additional workers. All the workers are Irish citizens.

The later expenditure of €2,500 is deductible as a trade expense in the firm's Sch D Case I computation for its first period of accounts, the year ended 31 December 2013. The writing down allowances given in respect of the pre-commencement training, etc expenditure of €7,400 are given as follows:

	€
2013 €7,400 x 12/36	2,467
2014 €7,400 x 12/36	2,467
2015 €7,400 x 12/36	2,467

6.603 Dredging expenditure allowances

A person carrying on a qualifying trade, who incurs capital expenditure on dredging, may be entitled to capital allowances in respect of the expenditure. A qualifying trade for these allowances, given by TCA 1997, ss 302, 303, is one which either (a) consists of the maintenance or improvement of the navigation of a harbour, estuary or waterway, or (b) is any of those types of trade or undertaking mentioned in TCA 1997, s 268(1) entitled to industrial buildings allowances (see **6.401**). 'Dredging' is limited to things done in the interests of navigation, but this includes the removal of anything forming part of or projecting from the bed of the sea or of any inland water; the allowances are also available for capital expenditure on the widening of an inland waterway in the interests of navigation under the same rules as apply to dredging (TCA 1997, s 302(1)).

The capital allowances for dredging expenditure are given to a person carrying on a trade falling under category (a) above if the expenditure is incurred for the purposes of that trade. In the case of trades falling under category (b), the dredging allowances may only be claimed if the capital expenditure on dredging is for the benefit of vessels coming to, leaving or using any dock or other premises occupied by the taxpayer for the purposes of his trade. This implies that the trader in the second category must occupy a dock, warehouse or other premises directly adjoining a harbour, estuary, canal or inland waterway. The allowances could be claimed, for example, by a dock undertaking or by a manufacturer who has premises situated beside the sea or waterway that has been dredged.

A person who would qualify for the dredging allowances if he incurred the relevant capital expenditure himself is entitled to the allowances on any capital sum contributed by him to dredging expenditure incurred by another person. If the other person is also entitled to the allowances, he can only claim them on his capital expenditure as reduced by the amount of capital sums contributed by other persons towards the dredging expenditure (TCA 1997, s 303(7)). No dredging expenditure allowance can be claimed if an industrial buildings initial allowance or an industrial buildings writing down allowance may be claimed for the expenditure (TCA 1997, s 303(8)). The dredging allowance may, however, be claimed where qualifying dredging expenditure is incurred before the relevant trade is commenced but with a view to the carrying on of the trade (TCA 1997, s 303(6)).

When capital expenditure on dredging is incurred partly for the purposes of a qualifying trade and partly for other purposes, the expenditure is to be apportioned in a manner that is just and fair between the qualifying trade and the other purposes. In the case where part only of a trade or undertaking is a qualifying trade, the part which qualifies and the other part are to be treated as if separate trades (TCA 1997, ss 302(1), 303(5)).

The capital allowances given for qualifying dredging expenditure are:

(a) an initial allowance equal to 10 per cent of the expenditure;
(b) writing down allowances during a writing down period of 50 years; and
(c) a balance allowance given on the permanent discontinuance of the trade (TCA 1997, s 303(2)).

For a person chargeable to income tax in respect of a trade already commenced, the allowances begin with the year of assessment in the basis period for which the expenditure is incurred (TCA 1997, s 302(2)).

The person who incurred the relevant capital expenditure is entitled to a balancing allowance on the permanent discontinuance of his trade if the expenditure in question has not already been fully written down by the initial allowances and writing down allowances given for previous chargeable periods plus that for the chargeable period in which the trade or undertaking ceases.

The balancing allowance is of an amount equal to the residue of the expenditure for which no other capital allowances have been obtained (TCA 1997, s 303(2)). A trade is not, however, treated as being discontinued, so that no balancing allowance arises, where there is a change in the persons carrying on the trade (TCA 1997, s 303(3)).

The dredging capital allowances are not given to a taxpayer on any capital expenditure to the extent that it has been met directly or indirectly by the State, by any board established by statute or by any public or local authority or by any person other than the taxpayer in question (TCA 1997, s 317(2)).

6.604 Trade effluents expenditure

A person carrying on a trade or about to commence a trade is entitled to capital allowances in respect of capital sums contributed by him to a local authority towards the capital expenditure incurred by the authority after 14 February 2001 on the provision of an asset for the purposes of an approved trade effluents scheme or for the supply water under an agreement in writing between the authority and the person. An approved scheme is a scheme undertaken by a local authority with the approval of the Minister for the Environment for the treatment of trade effluents. Trade effluents are liquid or other matter discharged into public sewers from premises occupied for the purposes of a trade.

The trader is entitled to claim the same capital allowances as would have been made if the capital contribution were expenditure incurred by him on the provision of a similar asset for his trade and that asset was in use for the purpose of the trade. Depending on the nature of the asset, the trader is entitled to a wear and tear allowance or, alternatively, industrial buildings writing down allowances for buildings, on the amount of his capital contribution (TCA 1997, s 310(2)).

A trade effluent scheme may be provided by a local authority to deal with the trade effluents to be discharged from a particular trader's factory premises or the scheme may service a number of such premises, eg in an industrial estate. Each trader involved is entitled to the allowance on his particular contributions to assets provided by the local authority for the scheme.

Where a trader has made a capital contribution towards expenditure incurred by the local authority on an asset for the purpose of the supply of water or an approved scheme, and if he should subsequently transfer the whole of his trade, then the person taking over the trade is entitled to any wear and tear or industrial buildings writing down allowances after the transfer as the transferor would have had if he continued the trade. If only part of the trade is transferred, this provision applies only to so much of the allowances as is properly referable to the part of the trade transferred.

Example 6.604.1

Roger, who is about to commence a trade, makes a capital contribution of €15,000 to Dublin City Council on 1 January 2016 to meet the costs of an approved trade effluents scheme. The expenditure is allocated as to €6,000 towards the cost of buildings to be used for the scheme and the balance of €9,000 for new machinery and plant.

Roger is entitled to the following capital allowances for his first period of account, the year ended 31 December 2016.

	€
Industrial building allowance:	
€6,000 x 4%	240
Machinery and plant:	
€9,000 x 12.5% wear and tear allowance	1,125

6.605 Multi-storey car parks

TCA 1997, s 344 provided a scheme of capital allowances for capital expenditure on qualifying multi-storey car parks, effectively extending the reliefs available to car parks in areas designated under the 1994 Urban Renewal (see **Division 19.2** in the 2009 edition of this book) to car parks outside those areas. The provisions of the Tax Acts were to apply as if such car parks were an industrial building falling within TCA 1997, s 268(1)(a) (mill, factory, etc), subject however to certain modifications noted below. The scheme applied to capital expenditure attributable to construction or refurbishment works carried out in the 'qualifying period', irrespective of when the expenditure was incurred or deemed to have been incurred (TCA 1997, s 344(7)). The qualifying period was the period commencing on 1 July 1995 and ending on 30 June 1998; this was originally subject to an extension to 30 June 1999 where the local authority certified in writing that by 30 September 1998 that not less than 15 per cent of the total cost of the car park and the site thereof was incurred prior to 1 July 1998. However, the 30 June 1999 deadline was prolonged to 30 September 1999 following an announcement to this effect by the Minister for Finance on 24 June 1999 – this was not a new extension with new conditions but an amendment to the original extension. A further new extension was introduced originally to 31 December 2000 where the local authority issued a certificate by 30 September 1999 stating that at least 15 per cent of the total cost of the car park and site thereof was incurred prior to 30 June 1999. This extension was further extended on a number of occasions and the conditions in order to qualify for the extension were amended. With effect from 1 January 2004 the qualifying period extended to 31 July 2006 provided that the relevant local authority certified in writing by 31 December 2003 that 15 per cent of the cost of the car park and the site thereof was incurred by 30 September 2003. FA 2006, s 29 provided for the extension of the qualifying period from 31 July 2006 to 31 December 2006. The 31 December 2006 deadline was further extended to 31 July 2008 where the relevant local authority issued the certificate referred to above by 31 December 2003, work to the value of not less than 15 per cent of the actual construction costs was incurred by 31 December 2006 and the person who was constructing the car park or the person who was claiming the relief could prove that the last mentioned condition was satisfied. The extensions came into operation by way of Ministerial Order SI 2006/324. The extensions beyond 30 September 1999 did not apply to car parks in the county boroughs of either Dublin City or Cork.

Where the capital expenditure on the construction or refurbishment of a multi-storey car park was incurred in the period from 1 January 2006 to 31 July 2008 the amount of expenditure to be treated as incurred for the purpose of making allowances or charges was reduced. In the case of expenditure incurred in the calendar year 2007 the reduction will was 75 per cent of the amount which would otherwise have been treated as incurred in the period. If the expenditure was incurred in the period from 1 January 2008 to 31 July 2008 the reduction was 50 per cent of the amount that would otherwise have qualified.

A 'multi-storey car park' is defined as a building or structure consisting of two or more storeys wholly in use to provide for members of the public generally parking space for mechanically propelled vehicles. The car park must not make any preference for any particular class of person and the parking facility must be provided upon payment of an appropriate charge (TCA 1997, s 344(1)). A 'qualifying' multi-storey car park is one in respect of which the 'Relevant Local Authority' has certified that the car park has been developed in accordance with criteria laid down by the Minister for the Environment. In this context, the 'Relevant Local Authority' is the corporation of a county or other borough or the urban district council in whose area the car park is situated or in the cases of the administrative counties of Dun Laoghaire/Rathdown, Fingal and Dublin, the council of the county.

Both new construction expenditure and refurbishment expenditure may qualify for the capital allowances. However, where the expenditure is refurbishment expenditure, the amount incurred must equal at least 20 per cent of the site exclusive pre-refurbishment market value of the property; otherwise none of the refurbishment expenditure actually incurred qualified for capital allowances under TCA 1997, s 344.

The person incurring the qualifying expenditure may have claimed either the industrial building initial allowance or, if he is a car park operator, free depreciation. The rate of allowances available is set in the first instance at 50 per cent initial allowance and at up to 100 per cent free depreciation and 4 per cent annual allowance (TCA 1997, s 344(4)). Where allowances have been claimed under any other provision in respect of the same expenditure no allowances may be claimed. (TCA 1997, s 344(8)). These reliefs are potentiality subject to the limitations on specified reliefs for high income individuals discussed at **3.111**.

TCA 1997, s 344(6)(a) restricted the allowances which were actually granted to one-half of the amount which would otherwise be available. In effect, this means that the effective rate of allowances was 25 per cent initial allowance, 50 per cent free depreciation and two per cent annual allowance. The maximum allowances which may have been claimed cannot, in the aggregate, exceed 50 per cent of the amount of qualifying expenditure. Thus, a person claiming the full amount of free depreciation available to him as an owner operator will have received allowances on 50 per cent of the expenditure incurred; a lessor will have received initial allowances of 25 per cent of the expenditure incurred and annual allowances thereafter of two per cent per annum until the aggregate amount claimed totals 50 per cent of the expenditure incurred. The operation of TCA 1997, s 344(6)(a) was curtailed by TCA 1997, s 344(6A) to cases in respect of expenditure incurred after 31 July 1998 where a qualifying lease had been granted for double rent relief purposes; in that instance the allowances were restricted to one half.

The industrial buildings rule relating to the making of balancing allowances or charges as applicable as discussed in **6.4** with two exceptions. First, in cases where the allowances granted were subject to the one-half restriction, whatever balancing allowance or charge is calculated is reduced to one-half of the amount so calculated, just as the amount of capital allowances granted was reduced by one-half from the amount otherwise due (TCA 1997, s 344(6)(b)). The amount of any balancing charge is subject to the normal overall limit as set out in TCA 1997, s 274, ie the balancing charge cannot exceed the aggregate of the allowances actually granted. Second, no balancing charge can arise if the event which would otherwise give rise to the charge occurs more than 13 years after the car park was first used or, in a case where TCA 1997, s 276 (allowances for refurbishment expenditure) applies, more than 13 years after the expenditure was incurred (TCA 1997, s 344(5)). It is important to note, however, that while a balancing charge cannot arise after this time, a balancing allowance may still arise at any time up to 25 years after first use or the date on which the expenditure was incurred. This is because TCA 1997, s 344(5) does not amend TCA 1997, s 274(1)(b)(i) which sets out the period during which a balancing charge or allowance may arise on the disposal of a building which is an industrial building within the meaning of paragraph (a) or (b) of TCA 1997, s 268(1). By the same token, a purchaser of the car park after year 13 may qualify for capital allowances if, under the normal rules used in calculating the residue before sale as discussed in **6.410**, a residue before sale exists by reason of the qualifying expenditure not having been entirely written down prior to the end of year 13. Whatever allowances the new owner would be entitled to under the normal rules of TCA 1997, s 272(4) may be reduced by one-half by virtue of the operation of TCA 1997, s 344(6)(a) if the original owner's allowances were subject to the one-half restriction.

Example 6.605.1

Derek built and opened a new car park in his period of account ended 31 December 2005 at a cost of €2,500,000. Derek claimed only the basic annual allowances in the 13 years up to 31 December 2017. In January 2018 Derek sells the car park to Stephen for €1,000,000.

The balancing allowance due to Derek and the allowances due to Stephen are calculated as follows:

	€
Qualifying cost	2,500,000
Allowances claimed by Derek	1,300,000
Residue before sale	1,200,000
Sale price	1,000,000
Balancing allowance	200,000

The balancing allowance due to Derek will be €200,000.

Stephen will be entitled to allowances based on his purchase price over the remainder of the car park's writing down life, ie €1,000,000/12 years = €83,333 pa for 12 years.

The aggregate allowances claimed by both Derek and Stephen over the car park's 25 year writing down life (including the balancing allowance given to Derek) will be €2,500,000.

A double rent allowance was available for a maximum period of 10 years against trading or commercial income of the lessee in respect of rent payable on the lease of the car park where the lease was entered into in the 'qualifying period' (TCA 1997, s 345(1)(a)(v) and s 345(1A)) or within one year from the end of the 'qualifying period'. The 'qualifying period' for a lease of a multi-storey car park ended on 31 July 1997 or 30 September 1998 if the extension to 30 September 1999 applied in relation to the construction or refurbishment of the car park. The normal restrictions and anti-avoidance rules apply in relation to the double rent deduction as in the case of the FA 1994 Urban Renewal Scheme (see **19.204** of the 2009 edition of this book).

The FA 2012 restrictions on carry forward of unused capital allowances (discussed at **6.107**) apply to this scheme.

6.606 Toll roads and bridges

A description of the relevant provisions is contained in the 1997/98 edition of this book.

6.607 Reliefs for removal and relocation of certain facilities in Urban Docklands

F(No 2)A 2008, s 21 introduced a new scheme to grant allowances for capital expenditure and accelerated capital allowances in relation to removal costs of industrial facilities which house potentially dangerous activities and which may consequently impede the regeneration of urban docklands. The scheme was to take effect subject to the making of a Ministerial Order. However the Ministerial Order never issued so this text is reproduced for academic interest. The legislation is contained in TCA 1997, Pt 11D.

Relocation allowance

A person carrying on a *relevant trade* (the *operator*) may claim an allowance (referred to as a 'relocation allowance') for *relocation expenditure* incurred up to January 2014 in relation to that trade (TCA 1997, s 380R(1)). The allowance is to be made in taxing the trade (TCA 1997, s 380R(2)) in the same way as capital allowances generally; the provisions of (TCA 1997, Pt 9, Ch 4 are to apply to this allowance as for capital allowances generally (**See 6.1**). Where the relief is given in relation to relocation expenditure, then no relief is to be given in respect of that expenditure under any other provision of the Taxes Acts (TCA 1997, s 380W(3)).

A 'relevant trade' means a trade of operating an *establishment* or *installation*. An '*establishment*' means the whole area under the operator's control where *dangerous substances* are present in one or more *installations,* including common or related infrastructure or activities; an '*installation*' means a unit within an establishment in which *dangerous substances* are produced, used, handled or stored, and includes:

(a) equipment, structures, pipe work, machinery and tools;
(b) docks and unloading quays serving the installation; and
(c) jetties, warehouses or similar structures, whether floating or not, which are necessary for the operation of the installation.

A '*Dangerous Substance*' in turn bears the meaning assigned to it by the European Communities (Control of Major Accident Hazards Involving Dangerous Substances) Regulations 2000 (SI 476/2000), reg 3 (TCA 1997, s 380Q(1)).

The '*relocation expenditure*' which potentially attracts the allowance is defined as *relevant expenses* incurred by the operator based in an establishment situated within an *urban dockland area* in relocating that trade to an establishment in a new location.

'*Relevant expenses*' means *capital* expenditure (ie only expenditure which is not deductible in computing the profits of a trade carried on by the person incurring the expenditure: (TCA 1997, s 380W(2)) incurred in connection with the removal of an *old installation* (ie an installation located in an urban dockland area which, by agreement with the relevant *local authority*, the operator relocates to facilitate the regeneration of that area) and the setting up of a replacement installation, including the cost of acquiring such land as is necessary for the operation of the *new* (ie replacement) *installation*.

A '*local authority*' means:

(a) in the case of a city, the city council; and
(b) in the case of a county, the county council, being a city council or a county council, as the case may be, for the purposes of the Local Government Act 2001 (TCA 1997, s 380Q(1)).

However there must be excluded any expenditure relating to:

(a) any building or structure on that land, other than a building or structure which is demolished in the course of the set-up;
(b) the construction of any building or structure; or
(c) machinery or plant'.

An '*urban dockland area*' is a dockland area which is the subject of either a local area plan adopted by the relevant local authority under the Planning and Development Acts 2000 to 2006 or a planning scheme approved by the Minister for the Environment, Heritage and Local Government under the Dublin Docklands Development Authority Act 1997, s 25 and comprises an area designated by that Minister, with the approval of the Minister for Finance, to be regenerated for the purposes set out in the local area plan or planning scheme (TCA 1997, s 380Q(1)).

There are restrictions on the amount of the allowance which can be claimed.

Where the operator owns or owned the area of land (including any interest in such land) of which the old installation is a unit ('*the establishment land*') and the whole of that land or interest therein has not been disposed of at the end of the basis period, then the following provisions apply:

(a) no amount incurred in the basis period in respect of the cost of acquiring land may be included as relevant expenses unless the aggregate of the expenditure incurred in acquiring land necessary for the operation of the new installation in that and previous basis period exceeds the market value of the establishment land at the date relevant expenses were first incurred. For these purposes '*market value*' means the price that the whole or part of the establishment land as appropriate might reasonably be expected to fetch on a sale in the open market if the old installation were removed;
(b) for the first basis period in which the aggregate of the expenditure incurred in acquiring land necessary for the operation of the new installation exceeds the market value mentioned in paragraph, the amount to be included is the excess (TCA 1997, s 380R(3)).

Where the operator is entitled to a relocation allowance for establishment land for a basis period, which is, or is subsequent to the first basis period at or before the end of which the whole of that land is disposed of, then, the following provisions shall apply:

(a) no expenditure incurred in the basis period in respect of the cost of acquiring land may be included as relevant expenses unless the aggregate of the expenditure incurred on acquiring land necessary for the operation of the new installation in that and previous basis periods exceeds the total consideration received on the disposal of the establishment land reduced by any *enhancement expenditure* in relation to that establishment land incurred by that person at a time after all the old installations have been removed from that land; and
(b) the amount of expenditure which is included in relevant expenditure in respect of the cost of acquisition of land is not to exceed that excess (TCA 1997,

s 380R(4)). '*Enhancement expenditure*' means the amount of any capital expenditure wholly and exclusively incurred on establishment land for the purpose of enhancing the value of the land, being expenditure reflected in the state or nature of the land at the time of the disposal but does not include expenditure for which a relocation allowance relief may be claimed under these provisions.

Where, in a basis period, an operator who has had a relocation allowance granted for previous basis periods, disposes of the whole or part of the establishment land and as a consequence the whole of the establishment land of at the end of the period, then the following provisions apply:

(a) if the aggregate of all consideration received on disposals of all establishment land reduced by any enhancement expenditure in relation to that establishment land incurred by the operator at a time after all the old installations have been removed from that land is:

  (i) less than the market value mentioned above, then a relocation allowance shall be made in respect of the difference, in addition to a relocation allowance (if any) which may be due in respect of expenditure incurred in that basis period,

  (ii) greater than the market value mentioned above,

  then the difference shall, subject to (b) below be treated as a trading receipt of the operator's trade; and

(b) the amount treated as a trading receipt of the trade by (a)(ii) above shall not exceed the aggregate of relocation allowances in respect of establishment land allowed in previous basis periods (TCA 1997, s 380R(5)).

Where an operator does not dispose of the whole of the establishment land within a period of two years beginning on the date on which the operator ceases to use the old installation for the purposes of his trade, then the operator shall be deemed to have disposed of the establishment land on the last day of the basis period in which that period ends for a consideration equal to the aggregate of all of the consideration (if any) received in respect of parts of establishment land which have been disposed of and the market value of the whole or part of such land which the operator owns at that date reduced by any enhancement expenditure in relation to that establishment land incurred by the operator at a time after all the old installations have been removed from that land (TCA 1997, s 380R(6)).

Where land is appropriated as trading stock, TCA 1997, s 596(1) shall apply for the purposes of these provisions as it applies for the purposes of the Capital Gains Tax Acts (TCA 1997, s 380R(7)).

Where the relevant trade ceases before all establishment land in relation to that trade is disposed of, then the remaining land shall be deemed for the purposes of this section, to have been disposed of on the date of cessation of the trade for its market value at that date (TCA 1997, s 380R(8)).

Where the whole or part of the establishment land is owned by a person connected with the person claiming the relocation allowance relief, then that whole or part of the land, as the case may be, shall be treated as being owned by the person claiming relief and these provisions will apply as if all actions of the connected person in relation to the whole or part were the actions of the person claiming relief (TCA 1997, s 380R(9)).

Additional relocation allowance

Where an operator incurs qualifying relocation expenditure, there shall in addition to any relocation allowance made in respect of such expenditure, be made to him for the same basis period, an additional relocation allowance equal to 50 per cent of the expenditure, again in taxing his trade (TCA 1997, s 380S(1)).

Where, in a basis period, an amount is treated as a trading receipt of a trade under TCA 1997, s 380R(5)(b) above, an additional amount equal to 50 per cent of that amount shall also be treated as a trading receipt of the trade for that basis period (TCA 1997, s 380S(2)).

Enhanced capital allowances: plant and machinery and industrial buildings

Where, for any basis period, an operator incurs expenditure ('*qualifying expenditure*') on a new installation which relates to the provision of new machinery or new plant (other than vehicles suitable for the conveyance by road of persons or goods or the haulage by road of other vehicles) provided for use in the relevant trade, then the following provisions shall apply:

(a) that person may claim that the wear and tear allowance to be made under TCA 1997, s 284 to the person in respect of that expenditure is to be granted at a rate of 100 per cent as opposed to the standard 12.5 per cent pa; and

(b) there shall be made to the operator for the basis period related to the expenditure an additional allowance equal to 50 per cent of the qualifying expenditure in taxing the relevant trade (TCA 1997, s 380T(1)).

This additional allowance is to be disregarded in computing the availability of capital allowances in respect of the qualifying expenditure (ie all of the expenditure is still claimable under the normal provisions) (TCA 1997, s 380T(2)).

Where an operator incurs expenditure ('*qualifying expenditure*') on a new installation which relates to capital expenditure on the construction of a new building or structure which is to be an industrial building or structure to be occupied for the purposes of the relevant trade, then TCA 1997, s 271 is to apply as if it provided for an initial allowance of 100 per cent in the basis period of expenditure (TCA 1997, s 380U).

However a potential restriction applies. Where qualifying expenditure is incurred as part of the provision of an *improved installation,* then the amount qualifying for relief must be reduced by the amount thereof representing improvement, namely such proportion of the qualifying expenditure in relation to the new machinery or new plant or in relation to the construction of a new building or structure, as the case may be, as appears to the Inspector (or on appeal, the Appeal Commissioners) to be just and reasonable as representing costs relating to providing increased capacity or improved efficiency or productivity. An *improved installation* is one where its capacity is greater or it has improved efficiency or productivity beyond normal modernisation or upgrading than the old installation which it replaced (TCA 1997, s 380V).

Further where enhanced capital allowances have been granted and the machinery or plant or building or structure as relevant is sold by that person without having been used by the operator for the purposes of a relevant trade or within two years from the day the relevant asset was first used, then the enhanced allowance shall be withdrawn and all such additional assessments and adjustments of assessments shall be made as may be necessary for or in consequence of the withdrawal of the allowance (TCA 1997, s 380V).

General prohibitions on relief

No relief will be granted for expenditure under any of the above provisions:

(a) where any part of such expenditure has been or is to be met, directly or indirectly, by grant assistance or any other assistance which is granted by or through the State, any board established by statute, any public or local authority or any other agency of the State; or

(b) where the potential allowances in relation to that expenditure do not comply with:

  (i) the requirements of the Guidelines on National Regional Aid for 2007–2013 prepared by the Commission of the European Communities and issued on 4 March 2006,

  (ii) the National Regional Aid Map for Ireland for the period 1 January 2007 to 31 December 2013 which was approved by the Commission of the European Communities on 24 October 2006, and

  (iii) the requirements of the Community Guidelines on State Aid for Environmental Protection prepared by the Commission of the European Communities and issued on 1 April 2008;

(c) where the person who is entitled to the allowances in relation to that expenditure is subject to an outstanding recovery order following a previous decision of the Commission of the European Communities declaring aid in favour of that person to be illegal and incompatible with the common market; or

(d) where the person who is entitled to the allowances is a person in difficulty under the Community Guidelines on State Aid for Rescuing and Restructuring Firms in Difficulty (TCA 1997, s 380V).

6.7 Capital Allowances For Patent Rights

6.701 Allowances for expenditure on the purchase of patent rights

TCA 1997, s 755 entitles any person who incurs capital expenditure on the purchase of patent rights, whether by purchasing a patent outright or by acquiring a licence (or sublicence) in respect of a patent, to a writing down allowance in respect of that expenditure. In the case of any purchaser of patent rights where the consideration given by the purchaser consists both of a capital payment and an undertaking to pay a royalty, only the capital payment qualifies for the writing down allowance.

The writing down allowance is given for each chargeable period during a defined writing down period or, if it is shorter, to the length of the period for which the rights have been acquired. This writing down period commences with the chargeable period related to the capital expenditure on the purchase of the patent rights (see **6.102**). If, for example, a person chargeable to income tax incurs capital expenditure on patent rights for use in his trade in his 12-month period of account ended 30 June 2015 and if this is the basis period for his Sch D Case I assessment for the tax year 2015, then the writing down period for that expenditure commences on 1 January 2015.

The length of the writing down period is whichever of the following periods that is appropriate:

(a) 17 years (the 16 years' previously normal life of a patent plus one year), unless the patent rights are acquired for a specified period or unless they begin at least one complete year after the commencement of the patent; or

(b) in the case of patent rights purchased for a specified period of less than 17 years, the number of years comprised in that period; or

(c) where the rights purchased begin one complete year or more after the commencement of the patent (and where not purchased for a specified period of less than 17 years), 17 years as reduced by the number of complete years between the commencement of the patent and the date on which the rights purchased begin. If 17 complete years have elapsed the writing down period is one year (TCA 1997, s 755(2)).

The length of the writing down period determines the rate of the writing down allowance. For patent rights purchased at the commencement of a patent (or within one year of it), the writing down allowance is one-seventeenth of the expenditure for each relevant tax year except if the rights are acquired for a specified period of less than 17 years. For patent rights acquired for such a shorter specified period, or where the rights purchased begin more than one complete year after the commencement of the patent, the rate of the writing down allowance is adjusted by reference to the number of years in the writing down period.

'The commencement of the patent' is defined, in relation to any patent, as the date as from which the patent rights become effective (TCA 1997, s 754(1)). This commencement date is the date of the patent, ie the date on which the complete specification was filed (see **8.301**), irrespective of the date on which the patent was actually granted. At first sight, it may appear curious why, if the normal life of a patent was previously 16 years from the date of the patent, the maximum writing down period is 17 years. It seems that this may be due to the fact that the first application for the patent may be made up to one year before the complete specification is lodged, thus giving up to 17 years between the original application and the end of the normal life of the patent.

Example 6.701.1

Mr S Tapnet, an Irish resident individual, purchased the following patent rights in the tax year ended 31 December 2016:

	Capital expenditure
	€
Irish patent of Irish invention (date of patent 1/1/2012 – purchased 1/3/2016)	10,000
Licence to exploit (including sublicensing) Irish patent of foreign invention for 10 years to 30/6/2023 (date of patent 1/7/2013 – purchased 1/7/2016)	7,000
German patent of French invention (date of patent 1/3/2011, but Mr Tapnet's rights to use patent begin on date of purchase 1/3/2016)	22,000

Since Mr Tapnet does not use these patent rights in any trade or profession, the capital (writing down) allowances on this capital expenditure are given by discharge or repayment of income tax and are available against his income from patents (TCA 1997, s 761(2)). The writing down periods for the various patent rights purchased in the year to 31 December 2015 are as follows:

Irish patent to Irish invention: 17 years from 2016	
Writing down allowance 2016 1/17 x €10,000	588
Licence to Irish patent of foreign invention: 7 years from 2016 to 2023 (specified period for which rights acquired, ie from date of purchase 1/7/2016 to 30/6/2023)	
Writing down allowance 2016 1/7 x €7,000	1,000
German patent of French invention: 12 years from 2016 (17 years less the 5 complete years between 1/3/2011 and 1/3/2016)	
Writing down allowance 2015 1/12 x €22,000	1,833

Notes:

1. Since Mr Tapnet's rights under the German patent did not commence until 1/3/2016 (date of purchase), ie just over five years after the commencement of the patent (1/3/2011), the writing down period has to be reduced to 12 years.
2. Each writing down allowance commences with the first day of the relevant year of assessment, even if the patent rights are not purchased until near the end of that tax year.

In certain circumstances, the capital allowances on patent rights expenditure must be based on the open market value of the patent rights acquired rather than on the actual capital expenditure incurred. TCA 1997, Pt 9, Ch 4 applies in the same way to capital expenditure on patent rights as it does for other assets qualifying for capital allowances (see **6.105**). For example, if there is a purchase and sale of patent rights between two bodies of persons (eg companies) under common control, at other than an open market price, TCA 1997, s 312(2) requires both purchaser and seller to be treated as if the transaction were at market value. For a purchase of patent rights in a common control case, an election may be made under TCA 1997, s 312(5) to use the seller's tax written down value of the patent rights sold instead of their market value, but only if the Irish residence, etc rule of TCA 1997, s 312(6) is met by both parties.

Similarly, TCA 1997, s 313(1) may deem there to be a purchase of patent rights at open market value if they are acquired, without being purchased, by the successor to a trade or profession that is taken over within the rules of TCA 1997, s 69 (see **6.106**).

6.702 Balancing allowances and balancing charges

TCA 1997, s 756 provides for balancing allowances and balancing charges in respect of patent rights in a similar way to those in respect of other assets qualifying for capital allowances, but with certain differences. In the case of machinery or plant or of an industrial building, once it is sold the seller no longer has an interest in it, but with patent rights it is quite possible for the owner to make a sale of part of his rights while retaining other rights in the same patent. For example, the owner of a patent may grant a non-exclusive licence to another person for a capital payment and/or a royalty, while retaining for himself the continued use and benefit of the patent subject only to non-infringement of the rights granted to the licensee. There are therefore rules dealing with the sale of part of a person's rights under a patent.

The question of a balancing allowance or a balancing charge only arises, whether there is a partial or a total sale of patent rights, if the person making the sale had previously incurred capital expenditure on their acquisition (or was deemed to have incurred such expenditure under the market value rules of TCA 1997, Pt 9, Ch 4 – see **6.701**). If he had simply acquired the rights in consideration for the payment of a royalty, then even if the consideration for his sale consists of or includes a capital sum, no balancing allowance or charge arises, but a liability to tax may arise under TCA 1997, s 757 if the consideration includes a capital sum (see **8.303**).

Sale of whole of patent rights

The net proceeds of sale (so far as they consist of capital sums) are compared with the amount of the capital expenditure remaining unallowed, ie with the tax written down value of the patent rights in question. If the net proceeds of sale are less than the tax written down value, a balancing allowance is given to the seller of an amount equal to the excess of the tax written down value over the net proceeds of sale. Conversely, if the net proceeds of sale exceed the tax written down value, a balancing charge is made on the seller of an amount equal to the excess sale proceeds (but subject to the limit of TCA 1997, s 756(6) mentioned below).

The balancing allowance is given or the balancing charge made, whichever is the case, for the chargeable period related to the sale of the patent rights. The tax written down value used in the computation is the amount of the capital expenditure previously incurred on the acquisition of the patent rights as reduced by the total of the writing down allowances given in respect of that expenditure for previous chargeable periods and the net proceeds of any previous sale(s) of any part of the rights acquired by that expenditure (TCA 1997, s 756(5)).

A person's patent rights may come to an end otherwise than by a sale. If he owns a patent or has been licensed to use it for the remainder of its term, his patent rights automatically lapse at the end of the life of the patent (normally 20 years after the date of the patent or 10 in the case of a short-term patent). If he has been licensed to use the patent for a specified period, he ceases to have any rights under that patent at the end of that period. In any such case where a person's patent rights come to an end without being subsequently revived, he is entitled to a balancing allowance equal to the tax written down value of those rights immediately before they came to an end.

Example 6.702.1

Mr T Panset purchased all the rights to a new invention for a capital sum of €10,200 on 27 February 2007 after a patent application had been filed with a complete specification of the invention on 1 October 2006 The patent was in due course granted with retrospective effect from 1 October 2006 and its term ran for the 16 years to 30 September 2022 tax year 2022. He also took out patents to the invention in a number of other countries.

Mr Panset has derived an income from these patent rights since 27 February 2007 by way of royalties under various licensing arrangements none of which involved him receiving any capital sums (nor selling the whole of his rights under the patents). He first obtained the patent rights writing down allowance in respect of the capital expenditure of €10,200 for the tax year 2007 since the capital expenditure was incurred in the year 2007.

The capital allowances for the tax years from 2007 onwards are as follows:

	€
Capital expenditure (27 February 2007)	10,200
Writing down allowances:	
2007–2022: €10,200 x 1/17 x 16	
	(9,600)
Tax WDV 31/12/2022 –	600
2022:	
Balancing allowance	600

Notes:

1. Since the patent rights were purchased less than one year after the date of the patent (1/10/2006), the writing down period was 17 years.
2. The balancing allowance is equal to the tax written down value of the patent rights immediately before they terminated on 30 September 2022.

Sale of part of patent rights

Where a person sells only part of his rights under a patent, the net proceeds of sale (so far as consisting of capital sums) are deducted from the tax written down value of those patent rights immediately before the sale. The tax written down value is the original capital expenditure on the purchase of the rights under the patent in question as reduced by all writing down allowances previously given and, if relevant, by the net proceeds of any earlier sales of part of those patent rights. If the net proceeds of sale exceed the tax written down value, a balancing charge is made on the amount of the excess (subject to the balancing charge limit); also, no further writing down allowance may be claimed in respect of the unsold rights (TCA 1997, s 756(1), (3)).

Where the net proceeds of a sale of part (but not all) of the rights under a patent are less than the tax written down value, there is no balancing allowance or charge, but the net proceeds are deducted from the tax written down value and a new writing down allowance is calculated to write off this reduced written down value over the remainder of the original writing down period. The new writing down allowance, which is given for the chargeable period related to the sale and for subsequent chargeable periods, is computed as follows:

$$\text{Writing down allowance (12 months)} \times \frac{\text{Tax written down value (as reduced)}}{n}$$

where

n = the number of complete years of the writing down period remaining at the beginning of the chargeable period related to the sale (TCA 1997, s 756(4)).

If a person chargeable to income tax under Sch D Case I had previously purchased the patent rights used in his trade for, say, a specified ten year period in his accounting year ended 31 December 2008 (the basis period for 2008), the original writing down period would have been the ten years from 1 January 2008 to 31 December 2018. If that person sells part of those patent rights, and if the sale is made in his Sch D Case I basis period for the tax year 2012 (say his period of account for the 12 months ended 31 December 2012), then the writing down allowance for 2012 and subsequent years is calculated by reference to the number of complete years comprised in the period from 1 January 2012 to the end of the original writing down period. Since there are seven complete years remaining of this period between 1 January 2012 and 31 December 2018, the new writing down allowance is one seventh of the tax written down value (as reduced by the net proceeds of sale); this allowance is first given for the tax year 2012. In *Green v Brace* 39 TC 281, it was not contended that a sum received as damages in respect of an aborted sale of patent rights fall within the UK equivalent of TCA 1997, s 756(1).

Limit to balancing charge

The amount on which a balancing charge is made in respect of any capital expenditure on patent rights, whether as a result of a sale of the whole or a part of those rights is limited so as not to exceed the total writing down allowances previously made in respect of that expenditure (TCA 1997, s 756(6)). If a previous balancing charge has been made in respect of an earlier sale of part of the rights under the same patent, the balancing charge on the sale of the remainder of those rights (or a further partial sale) is not to exceed the total writing down allowances as reduced by the previous balancing charge.

6.8 Allowances for Certain Energy-efficient Equipment

6.801 Background

TCA 1997, s 285A was first brought about by FA 2008 and it applied to companies only. FA 2016 extended this relief for the first time to individuals. It allows accelerated capital allowances to be claimed on certain energy efficient equipment acquired for the purposes of a trade carried on by the taxpayer. This relief is due to expire on 31 December 2017. The relief does not apply where the energy-efficient equipment is leased, let or hired to any person.

6.802 Definitions

'energy-efficient equipment' means equipment, named on and complying with the criteria stated on the specified list, provided for the purposes of a trade and which at the time it is so provided is unused and not second-hand;

'relevant period' means the period commencing on the date on which the first order is made (SI No 397/2008 was signed by the Minister for Finance in 2008) under sub-s (4) and ending on 31 December 2017; however, this applies for individuals from 1 January 2017.

'the specified list' means the list of energy-efficient equipment which—

(a) complies with the conditions below, and
(b) is maintained for the purposes of this section by Sustainable Energy Ireland — The Sustainable Energy Authority of Ireland;

The conditions mentioned above comprise: the specified list shall contain only such equipment that—

(a) is in a *class of technology* specified in the Table in TCA 1997, Sch 4A (hereinafter 'the Table' and copied below) and
(b) is of a *description* for that *class of technology* specified the Table.

The Minister for Communications, Energy and Natural Resources, after consultation with and the approval of the Minister for Finance outlines ministerial orders making the specified list stating the energy efficiency criteria to be met for, and naming the eligible products in, each class of technology specified the Table, and may by order amend same.

Table

Class of Technology	Description	Minimum Amount
Column 1	Column 2	Column 3
Motors and Drives	Electric motors and drives designed to achieve high levels of energy efficiency and that meet specified efficiency criteria.	€1,000
Lighting	Lighting equipment and systems designed to achieve high levels of energy efficiency and that meet specified efficiency criteria.	€3,000

Class of Technology	Description	Minimum Amount
Column 1	Column 2	Column 3
Building Energy Management Systems	Building energy management systems designed to achieve high levels of energy efficiency and that meet specified efficiency criteria.	€5,000
Information and Communications Technology (ICT)	ICT equipment and systems designed to achieve high levels of energy efficiency and that meet specified efficiency criteria.	€1,000
Heating and Electricity Provision	Heating and electricity provision equipment and systems designed to achieve high levels of energy efficiency and that meet specified efficiency criteria.	€1,000
Process and Heating, Ventilation and Air-conditioning (HVAC) Control Systems	Process and heating, ventilation and air-conditioning (HVAC) equipment and systems designed to achieve high levels of energy efficiency and that meet specified efficiency criteria.	€1,000
Electric and Alternative Fuel Vehicles	Electric and alternative fuel vehicles and equipment designed to achieve high levels of energy efficiency and that meet specified efficiency criteria.	€1,000
Refrigeration and Cooling Systems	Refrigerating and cooling equipment and systems designed to achieve high levels of energy efficiency and that meet specified efficiency criteria.	€1,000
Electro-mechanical Systems	Electro-mechanical equipment and systems designed to achieve high levels of energy efficiency and that meet specified efficiency criteria.	€1,000
Catering and Hospitality Equipment	Catering and hospitality equipment and systems designed to achieve high levels of energy efficiency and that meet specified efficiency criteria.	€1,000

6.803 Allowances available

The relief does not apply where the energy-efficient equipment is leased, let or hired to any person. Nor does it apply in respect of expenditure incurred in a chargeable period on the provision of energy-efficient equipment in relation to a class of technology where the amount of that expenditure is less than the minimum amount specified in column (3) of the Table in relation to that class of technology.

The relief applies to capital expenditure incurred by a person on the provision of energy-efficient equipment and that equipment would not, apart from the relief, be treated as machinery or plant, then that equipment shall be treated as machinery or plant for the purposes of TCA 1997, Pt 9, Chs 2 and 4. Therefore TCA 1997, s 285A imports statutory fiction such that capital allowances can be claimed on such energy efficient equipment. However, the rate of capital allowances to be applied is determined in accordance with TCA 1997, s 285A rather than that specified in TCA 1997, s 284. TCA 1997, s 285A(2) notes that where for any chargeable period a wear and tear allowance is to be made under TCA 1997, s 284 to a person who has incurred capital expenditure on the provision of energy-efficient equipment for the purposes of a trade carried on by that person, TCA 1997, s 284(2) shall apply as if the reference in TCA 1997, s 284(2)(ad) of that section to 12.5 per cent were a reference to 100 per cent. So the allowance is an accelerated one.

Notwithstanding TCA 1997, Pt 11C (which deals with emissions-based limits on capital allowances and expenses for certain road vehicles), where an allowance is increased under TCA 1997, s 285A in respect of expenditure incurred in a chargeable period on the provision of any vehicle (being a vehicle to which sub-s (1) of TCA 1997, s 380K relates) in relation to the class of technology described in column (1) of the Table as 'Electric and Alternative Fuel Vehicles', then TCA 1997, s 285A(2) shall apply as if the reference in paragraph (ad) of s 284(2) to the actual cost were a reference to the lower of the actual cost of the vehicle or the specified amount referred to in TCA 1997, s 380K(4), ie €24,000.

The relief in TCA 1997, s 285A(2) does not apply where an allowance in respect of expenditure incurred on the provision of a vehicle referred to above is made under TCA 1997, s 284(2) as applied by TCA 1997, s 380L which looks at emission based limits for certain cars. It is interesting to note that TCA 1997, s 380K(1), which is within TCA 1997, Pt 11C states that 'Subject to section 380P(1), this Part and not Part 11 shall apply to a vehicle which is a mechanically propelled road vehicle constructed or adapted for the carriage of passengers, other than a vehicle of a type not commonly used as a private vehicle and unsuitable to be so used, but this Part shall not apply where an allowance for a vehicle is increased under section 285A'.

Division 7 Farming and Other Income from Land

7.1 Farming under Sch D Case I

7.101 Taxation of profits from farming

This Division is primarily concerned with the taxation of income from farming but deals also with the subject of commercial woodlands. The taxation of income from the ownership and occupation of land in the State has always been the subject of special rules. These rules have been changed from time to time over the years and some discussion of their development is necessary as a background to the taxation of income from farming and from other uses of land.

The present position is that farming is taxable as a trade under Sch D Case I, but with some special rules particular to farming. On the other hand, any profits derived from the occupation of woodlands in the State that are managed on a commercial basis with a view to the realisation of profits are exempted from both income tax and corporation tax. Market gardening, which is distinguished from farming, is also taxable under Sch D Case I, but is not affected by the special rules (eg stock relief) relating to farming. Profits earned from other uses of land that is managed on a commercial basis with a view to the realisation of profits, eg mink farming or the commercial production of turf, are taxable as the profits of a trade under Sch D Case I without any special rules.

Income from land may also be received in the form of rents for leasing the land (and any buildings on it) or as receipts from easements over the land (eg from granting grazing, shooting, fishing, etc rights). These are dealt with as income taxable under Sch D Case V in **Part 12**, as is the subject of profits from dealing in or developing land taxable as a trade under Sch D Case I. The taxation of mining and other forms of extraction of natural resources from land is a specialised subject and is referred to in **Division 12.4**.

The development of the taxation of income from farming and woodlands leading up to the present position may be divided into two main phases. First, up to 6 April 1969 tax was charged in respect of the *ownership* of land under Sch A and in respect of the *occupation* of land under Sch B. In each case, the assessment was based on a notional annual value of the land determined many years earlier, which did not change from year to year.

Secondly, so far as farming was concerned, there was the period from 6 April 1969 to 5 April 1974 when profits or gains from farming land in the State were exempted from income tax, but, in the case of a company, were chargeable to the former corporation profits tax. So far as commercial woodlands in the State are concerned, the present exemption from income tax discussed in **Division 7** has applied since 6 April 1969.

TCA 1997, s 655(1) provides that all farming in the State shall be treated as the carrying on of a trade or, as the case may be, of part of a trade so that the profits or gains shall be charged to tax under Sch D Case I but with certain special provisions applicable to farming which do not apply to other types of trades. In many cases, farming activities would constitute trading activities in their own right (note the decision of the Appeal Commissioners in *Knockhall Piggeries v Kerrane* III ITR 319), but such activities will also fall within the special rules.

For the purposes of certain special rules available to an individual farmer, the term 'full time farmer' has been used to denote any individual carrying on farming who, for the relevant tax year, is not a 'part time farmer' within the meaning of TCA 1997, s 657(1). In brief, an individual isa full time farmer for any tax year in which neither he, nor his spouse or civil partner, is carrying on any trade or profession other than farming or is a director or employee of any company in which he controls more than 25 per cent of the ordinary share capital. Finance Act 2014 has relaxed these conditions in relation to another trade which relates to on-farm diversification. For illustrations of this definition, see **Examples 7.109.1** to **7.109.3** in relation to income averaging in **7.109**.

For details of other special rules which were intended to ease in the introduction of farming taxation, please see earlier editions of this book.

While, in general, all the Sch D Case I computational rules and the treatment of capital allowances, balancing charges, losses, etc that apply to other trades are equally applicable to farming, there are certain provisions and certain practices which have particular relevance to the taxing of the 'trade' of farming. The special treatment available to individual full-time farmers, ie the right to elect to average farming profits over a five-year period with effect from the year of assessment 2015 (previously over a three-year period), is dealt with in **7.109** and **7.110**.

7.102 The charge to tax: general principles

TCA 1997, s 655 is the section which charges the profits from farming to tax. TCA 1997, s 655(1) treats all farming in the State as the carrying on of a trade or, if appropriate, as part of a trade and charges the profits or gains of that trade to tax under Sch D Case I. All farmers irrespective of whether an individual or other person, are fully taxable each year on their farming profits as calculated under the Sch D Case I computational rules. In the case of persons chargeable to income tax, the assessments are based on the adjusted profits of the relevant basis period as determined by TCA 1997, Pt 4 Ch 3. TCA 1997, s 654 defines 'farming' as: farming farm land, that is, land in the State wholly or mainly occupied for the purposes of husbandry, other than market garden land. There is no definition in the Tax Acts of the word 'husbandry' upon which the definition of farming depends. The word must, therefore, be given its normal English meaning. Husbandry (and, therefore, farming) may perhaps best be described as the working of land with the object of extracting the produce of the land; it includes the growing and harvesting of crops, the breeding and/or rearing on the land of animals, cattle, horses, sheep, goats, deer, llamas, pigs, poultry, etc and the sale of animal produce (milk, butter, wool etc). The Revenue Commissioners have issued a precedent to the effect that they have accepted a Circuit Court decision that bee-keeping constitutes husbandry.

Husbandry is limited to those activities which have traditionally been accepted as the farming of land. Certain other profits derived from land or the use of land, such as commercial turf production or mink farming, are not regarded as farming and are taxable as the profits of an ordinary trade without reference to any of the special rules that apply to farming. In *Knockhall Piggeries v Kerrane* III ITR 319 it was held that modern developments should not be excluded from the definition and that a large scale intensive piggery operation constituted 'husbandry'. The court also held that the taxpayers:

> in using the land for the purposes of rearing and fattening pigs and generally looking after their health and welfare were farming the lands.

The activity of market gardening, which might otherwise be regarded as husbandry, is also taxable under the ordinary Sch D Case I rules due to the specific exclusion of market garden land from farm land in the definition quoted above. 'Market gardening' is defined by reference to 'market garden land', ie land in the State occupied as a nursery or garden for the sale of its produce (TCA 1997, s 654). Market gardening produce may be either vegetables, fruit or flowers (excluding hops), the growing of which would not normally be regarded as farming, but if such produce is grown on farm land (rather than in a nursery or garden) as part of a person's main activity as a farmer, it may be treated as farming rather than as market gardening.

The distinction between farming and market gardening has been the subject of several tax cases, mainly relevant to the question as to whether the profits were covered by the old (pre-FA 1969) Sch B assessment on the annual value of the land occupied (if farming) or were taxable under Sch D Case I (if market gardening). While in many instances, a market garden may be an enclosed piece of ground devoted to the cultivation of flowers, fruit or vegetables, the fact that a defined area used as gardens is not enclosed or fenced round does not necessarily prevent it being a market garden. Each particular case must be decided on its own facts.

In *Bomford v Osborne* 23 TC 642, it was stated that the main test whether lands were occupied as 'gardens' was whether the defined area had some degree of fixity and local continuance and was subject to that kind and intensity of treatment which was characteristic of horticulture. It is possible to split a single holding into two parts of which one part could be a market garden and the other a farm, but only if the part occupied as gardens for the sale of the produce is distinct and separate from the other part. However, in that case it was also stated (by Lord Maugham) that a mixed farm involving separate activities is normally a single assessable unit and strong reasons must exist to justify dividing it for tax purposes.

In *Cross v Emery* 31 TC 194, the taxpayer occupied 7.3 acres of land of which 3.5 acres were admitted to be market garden land. The remainder of the land was a fruit orchard. The General Commissioners had held that the taxpayer carried on the business of a market gardener, to which the growing of fruit was merely ancillary. However, it was held that, on the facts found by the Commissioners, the orchard profits should not have been taxed as market gardening profits but should have been treated as farming profits then taxable under Sch B.

The Revenue take the view that income from conacre lettings falls within Sch D Case V rather than Sch D Case I farming profits (see the discussion at **12.102**).

In practice, an inspector may be willing to treat minor amounts of letting income as part of the overall farming profits rather than insisting on a separate Sch D Case V assessment.

'Occupation' defined

A person is regarded as occupying farm land when he has the use of the land or has the right by virtue of any easement to graze livestock on the land (TCA 1997, s 654). In the normal case, the person farming land may either be the owner of the land, or may be leasing the land from another person, but as this definition implies, being the owner or a lessee is not essential. A person who farms land owned or leased by someone else (eg a spouse) who allows him or her to use it is taxable on any farming profits he may derive from such use.

Cattle and milk dealers

TCA 1997, s 53 provides that where a dealer in cattle or a dealer in or a seller of milk occupies farm land in any case where the land is insufficient for the keep of the cattle brought onto the land, this is treated as the carrying on of a trade the profits of which are chargeable to tax under Sch D Case I (and not the trade of farming). This means that such a cattle or milk dealer is not entitled to the benefit of any of the special rules applicable to farming (eg income averaging). The question of whether the land is sufficient for the keep of the cattle (so that the farming tax rules apply) is a question to be determined on the facts of the particular case.

In *Huxham v Johnson* 11 TC 266, the taxpayer occupied a farm charged to tax under the former Sch B on which he kept a number of cows for milking. The soil was of such a poor quality that he had to expend large sums each year on feeding stuffs. The produce grown on the land represented only about 30 per cent of the food required for the cows. He sold the milk to regular customers in the district and only purchased milk for resale when his own supply was insufficient. He sold his cows when they became dry. On these facts, it was held that the taxpayer was a dealer in milk whose land was insufficient for the keep of the cows using the land. If a similar case occurred now, TCA 1997, s 53 would also apply to exclude the special farming rules.

All farming a single trade

TCA 1997, s 655(2) provides that all farming within the State carried on by any person, whether solely or in partnership, is to be treated as the carrying on of a single trade. This means that any farmer who has more than one farm or who may, perhaps, farm on his own account in one place and may at the same time be a partner in a farming partnership with one or more other persons, must aggregate the results of all these farming activities to determine the farming profits on which he is taxable for any year of assessment or, if a company, for any accounting period. Should the farmer also graze livestock on another person's land under any easement, any profits (or losses) from such grazing are similarly treated as arising from his single trade of farming.

The 'basis period' rules, which determine the period by reference to which the farming profits are taken for the assessment to income tax for each year of assessment, are exactly the same as those for any other trade (see **Division 4**). However, the question of when there is a commencement of farming and when a cessation has to be determined under the single trade rule (which has no application for any non-farming trade).

The most significant effect of the single trade rule is that, in the case of a farmer chargeable to income tax, the Sch D Case I basis period rules of TCA 1997, Pt 4 Ch 3 have to be applied by considering together all his farming activities, irrespective of whether one or more separate trades of farming are involved. Subject to the exception mentioned below, a farmer carrying on either solely or in partnership more than one set of farming activities is not affected by the rules of cessation unless and until he ceases all those activities.

Similarly, a person who has an existing farming activity and who then commences a second (or third, etc) farming activity, even of a completely different type of farming, continues to be assessed on all his farming as an existing trade, ie the rules of commencement are not applied again in relation to the new farming activities.

TCA 1997, s 655(2) contains a proviso to the effect that the single trade rule is not to prejudice or restrict the operation of the TCA 1997, Pt 4 Ch 3 commencement or cessation rules as they apply to the setting up and commencement of a partnership trade of farming or to its permanent discontinuance. Consequently, if there is a commencement or cessation of a partnership trade of farming (as distinct from a mere change in the partners), the TCA 1997, Pt 4 Ch 3 commencement or cessation rules apply in determining the basis periods to be used in assessing each partner for the relevant tax years, irrespective of whether or not any partner has any other farming activities.

It is to be noted that this proviso to TCA 1997, s 655(2) has no relevance and the single trade rule prevails, where a person with other farming activities is admitted to or retires from a continuing farming partnership. For the circumstances in which a partnership trade is regarded as being set up and commenced or as being permanently discontinued, see **4.502**.

Example 7.102.1

Mr A Finch commenced farming on his own account in Co Meath on 1 October 2013. He makes up accounts of his farming trade to 30 September each year. He had not previously carried on any other farming activities in the State so that he was assessed on his farming profits under the Sch D Case I rules of commencement (TCA 1997, s 66) for the first two years and then under the continuing business rule of TCA 1997, s 65(2), as follows:

2013: First three months from 1/10/2013 to 31/12/2013

2014: 12-month period of accounts to 30/9/2014

2015: 12-month period of accounts to 30/9/2015

On 1 May 2014, Mr Finch was admitted as a new partner into an existing farming partnership with Mr B Swallow and Mr C Wren who had been farming in Co Louth since January 2005. Mr Finch continues to run his Co Meath farm separately on his own account. The partnership makes up its accounts to 30 April each year.

In the absence of TCA 1997, s 655(2), the normal basis period rules for a partnership trade would require Mr AF's first assessment on his share of the farming partnership's Sch D Case I profits to be made for 2014 as if he had commenced a separate trade on 1 May 2014, ie he would be assessed for 2014 on his share of the partnership's farming profits for the period 1 May 2014 to 31 December 2014.

Since no question of a commencement (or cessation) of the partnership trade is involved, TCA 1997, s 655(2) applies (without its proviso) so that Mr Finch's share of the farming partnership profits from 1 May 2014 are attributed to his single trade of farming which had commenced on 1 October 2013.

Since Mr Finch's single trade of farming had commenced on 1 October 2013, his farming assessment for the whole of that single trade (including his share of partnership farming profits) for the year 2014 is made on the basis of a continuing business. Assuming that his own farming profits for the year ended 30 September 2014 are €15,000 and his share of the partnership's farming profits for the firm's year ended 30 April 2015 is €10,000, his Sch D Case I assessment for 2014 on farming profits is made up as follows:

	€
Own farming (Co Meath):	
Profits of year to 30/9/2014	15,000
Share of partnership profits (Co Louth):	
Period 1/5/2014 to 30/9/2014 (part of firm's year)	
€10,000 x 5/12ths	4,167
Total profits assessed 2014 (subject to capital allowances)	19,167

Assuming that his own farming profits for the year ended 30 September 2015 are €18,000 and that his share of the partnership's farming profits for the year ended 30 April 2016 is €12,000, his Sch D Case I assessment for 2015 on farming profits is:

	€
Own farming (Co Meath):	
Profits of year to 30/9/2015	18,000
Share of partnership profits (Co Louth):	
Period 1/10/2014 to 30/4/2015 (part of firm's year)	
€10,000 x 7/12ths	5,833
Period 1/05/2015 to 30/9/2015 (part of firm's year)	
€12,000 x 5/12ths	5,000
Total profits assessed 2015 (subject to capital allowances)	28,833

Example 7.102.2

Take the same facts as in **Example 7.102.1**, except assume that the farming partnership between Messrs A Finch, B Swallow and C Wren was for a new partnership trade commencing on 1 May 2014 (Swallow having previously farmed on his own account only, but deciding to take in Finch and Wren as his partners as he wishes to retire on his 70th birthday in 2016).

Since a partnership trade is deemed to be set up and commenced when a person who has traded on his own account takes in one or more partners (see **4.502**), the proviso to TCA 1997, s 655(2) requires the rules of commencement to be applied to determine Mr Finch's assessable profits from the partnership for 2014 and 2015 (the first two tax years of the partnership trade). It similarly applies for the other two partners.

Mr Finch's Sch D Case I farming profits assessment for 2014 (although still treated as arising from a single trade) now have to be calculated as follows:

	€
Own farming (Co Meath):	
Profits of year to 30/9/2014	15,000
Farming partnership (1st year, actual from 1/5/2014 to 31/12/2014) (his share)	
8/12ths x €10,000	6,667
Total profits assessed 2014 (subject to capital allowances)	21,667
Own farming (Co Meath):	
Profits of year to 30/9/2015	18,000
Farming partnership (2nd year, 1st 12 months)	10,000
Total profits assessed 2015 (subject to capital allowances)	28,000

Example 7.102.3

Mr S Oats has been farming on his own land in Co Wicklow for a number of years making up accounts annually to 31 March. He commenced this farming on 1 April 2008. Further developments then occur as follows:

1. Following his father's death he inherits his father's farm in Co Tipperary and commences to farm it on 1 June 2012 (but continues to farm in Co Wicklow at the same time).
2. On 1 October 2013, he takes an 11 months' letting of additional land adjoining his Co Wicklow farm and grazes cattle on it for sale up to 31 August 2014. He does not take this letting again.
3. On 15 December 2013, he sells his Co Wicklow farm and from that date onwards he only farms the land in Co Tipperary.

Mr S Oats is assessable for all relevant years under TCA 1997, s 655(2) on the profits of an assumed single trade of farming (including the profits from the livestock grazed on the lands of which he had the use during the 11 months' letting). Although he ceased to carry on the Co Wicklow farm on 15 December 2013, the rules of cessation are not applied in respect of that farm since he continues farming in Co Tipperary. Similarly, the rules of commencement had no application to the 1 June 2012 commencement of his farming in Co Tipperary.

The relevant farming profits assessments for the years from 2012 to 2015 would be based as follows:

2012:

profits from Co Wicklow farm (year to 31/3/2012)

2013:

profits from Co Wicklow farm (1/04/2012 to 31/3/2013)

profits from Co Tipperary farm (1/6/2012 to 31/3/2013)

2014:

profits from Co Wicklow farm (period 1/4/2013 to 15/12/2013/when sold)

profits from Co Tipperary farm (1/4/2013 to 31/03/2014)

profits from livestock on additional lands under 11 months' letting (01/10/2013 to 31/03/2014).

2015:

profits from Co Tipperary farm (year to 31/03/2015)

profits from livestock on additional lands under 11 months' letting (01/04/2014 to 31/08/2014).

7.103 Computation of farming profits

The computation of a farmer's taxable profits (or tax loss) for any relevant period of account is, in principle, made in exactly the same way as for any trade other than farming. The farmer is required to prepare accounts in the same way as any other trader and to submit them each year to the inspector of taxes together with the necessary supporting data.

All the Sch D Case I computational rules contained in the Income Tax Acts and any relevant court decisions regarding their interpretation are equally applicable to the farmer's Sch D Case I computation. These principles are discussed in **Division 5**.

There are, however, certain statutory as well as practical differences in the taxation of farming profits and in relation to the capital allowances that may be set off against the farmer's Sch D Case I profits. One area requiring separate discussion concerns the practical approach adopted in arriving at the cost of a farmer's trading stock to be used for tax purposes; this is covered in some detail in **7.105**. Next, a person carrying on the trade of farming is entitled to a stock relief deduction in respect of the increase (if any) in the value of his trading stock (see **7.106**). For the capital allowances that are available against farming profits, and for certain special rules regarding farming losses see **7.2**.

The approach to the Sch D Case I computation of the profit or loss from farming for each relevant period of account follows that outlined for trades generally in **4.202**. The pre-tax profit (or loss) shown by the accounts is adjusted by adding back any disallowable items charged in arriving at the pre-tax accounting profit (eg capital expenditure, depreciation, personal and other non-farming expenses) and, to the extent relevant, deductions are made for items credited in the accounts which are chargeable to tax under any other case, capital profits, etc. Any stock relief deduction should be taken at the end of the computation.

Personal consumption of farm produce

It is common, if not invariable, practice for a farmer to take farm produce out of his business for the personal consumption of his family. He may also on occasions give away farm produce to relatives or other personal friends. If the appropriate credit for the farm produce withdrawn for such private use and gifts has not been made in the farm accounts, it is necessary to make an add back in the Sch D Case I tax computation equal to the estimated cost value of the produce concerned. The fact that the produce withdrawn from the business may have a market or net realisable value in excess of its cost value is ignored in practice (see the discussion of *Sharkey v Wernher* at **5.101**).

Disallowance of certain wages

It is not uncommon for a farmer to use some of his farm workers from time to time either in carrying out improvements or other work of a capital nature on the farm or in work not related to the farming activities at all. For example, farm labour may be used for erecting new fences (as distinct from repairing or replacing existing ones), for constructing or extending farm buildings or for such works as land reclamation or new drainage. The farmer may also use a farm employee to do work in his private garden or on non-farm land (eg separate woodlands). To the extent that farm wages have been charged in the accounts for such capital works or non-farm purposes, the appropriate add back must be made in the Sch D Case I tax computation.

To the extent that any such farm wages (and other expenses) are disallowed in the Sch D Case I computation due to their being of a capital nature, the farmer is entitled to claim the appropriate capital allowances available having regard to the nature of the expenditure.

For example, expenditure on the construction of farm buildings (other than farm dwelling houses), land reclamation, drainage, new fencing, etc qualifies for the farm buildings allowance (see **7.202**), while any such capital expenditure in relation to farm machinery (eg on the installation of new milking equipment) attracts the usual wear and tear allowances. It is, of course, a matter of fact in each case whether the work on which the wages are incurred is of a capital nature or whether it is properly deductible as a trading expense. For example, in some cases it may be possible to justify new temporary fencing as a trade expense. Payments of wages to family members which appear excessive may be challenged under the 'wholly and exclusively' rule in the usual way (see eg *Dollar v Lyon* [1981] STC 333).

Payments of superlevy

It would appear that payments of superlevy in respect of milk levy should be deductible as revenue expenditure but that the cost of acquiring additional milk quotas in order to avoid making such payments is capital in nature.

REPS compensation

Payments to farmers for income losses caused by subscribing to the Rural Environment Protection Scheme are taxable as income.

EU installation grants

The Revenue Commissioners have issued a precedent to the effect that these grants should be treated as capital in nature.

Sheep headage and ewe premium payments

The Revenue Commissioners have issued a precedent to the effect that these grants should be treated as revenue in nature.

7.104 Farm records, accounts and tax forms

TCA 1997, s 886 applies, in the same way as to any other person carrying on a trade or profession, to require all farmers to keep such books of account and other records as will enable true returns of their farming profits to be made. The Revenue Commissioners or any of their duly authorised officers have the various powers to inspect the farmer's books, to enter the farming premises, to obtain information from other persons regarding transactions with the farmer, etc, as are mentioned in **Division 2** in relation to any person carrying on a trade or business.

Apart from keeping full and accurate records of all farming receipts and payments, the farmer should make a detailed stocktaking at the end of each period for which he makes up accounts to enable the inspector of taxes to be given the required analysis of the farmer's opening and closing trading stocks, as well as of changes in livestock held during the period (see below).

In principle, every farmer is now required to prepare a set of accounts and to insert in his tax return extracts from these accounts of the farming activities each year and to provide the inspector with such additional information as is necessary to enable the farmer's Sch D Case I profit (or loss) to be determined. Ideally, the farmer's accounts should consist of a full profit and loss account and balance sheet certified by an accountant, although, as with other traders, there is no legal requirement (other than for a company) to give the inspector certified accounts.

Additional information to accompany tax return

In addition to the farm accounts, the farmer may be required to provide the inspector with certain minimum additional information as set out in schedules to his accounts or in covering or explanatory notes in the accounts. This applies whether the farmer is an individual, a person acting in a representative capacity (eg an executor or a trustee), a company, etc. In the case of farming carried on in partnership, the precedent acting partner is required to provide this information for the partnership trade.

The information required is similar to that which historically had to be included in form AG 3 in particular relating to stocks and may be summarised as follows:

A: livestock analysis in numbers (see Table 1 below);

B: livestock analysis with values (see Table 2 below);

C: crops analysis (see Table 3 below);

It also should include analysis of wages paid and analysis of payments made to contractors for ploughing, sowing, harvesting and similar work.

Table 1 Livestock analysis in numbers

The analysis is required in the following form for cattle, horses, sheep, pigs and poultry illustrated here by reference to cattle, horses and sheep:

	Cattle	*Horses*	*Sheep*
	No	*No*	*No*
On hand at beginning of year			
Bought during year			
Born during year			
TOTAL			
To reconcile with:			
Sold during year			
Killed for home use during year			
Died during year			
Given as gifts during year			
On hand at end of year			
TOTAL			

Table 2 Livestock analysis with values

The analysis in the form set out below requires the opening and closing stock values under each subheading to be included at the lower of cost and market value; for further discussion on arriving at these values, see **7.105**. The figures for purchases and sales are for the actual transactions that physically took place during the year, whether the money involved was paid or received in the year or in a different year.

Table 2 Livestock analysis (numbers and values)

Description		*Bought in the year*	*Sold in the year*	*Stock on hand at end of the year*	
		Number value	*Number cost*	*Number price*	*Number value*
		€	€	€	€
CATTLE	Bulls				
	Dairy cows				
	Sucking cows				
	Other cows				
	In-calf heifers				
	Other cattle 1–2 yrs				
	Other cattle + 2 yrs				
HORSES	Stallions				
	Brood mares				

	Foals				
	Others				
SHEEP	Rams				
	Breeding ewes				
	Lambs under 1 yr				
	Others				
PIGS	Boars				
	Sows				
	Bonhams				
	Others				
POULTRY	Hens				
	Turkeys				
	Others				
		TOTAL €	TOTAL €	TOTAL €	TOTAL €

Table 3 Crops analysis

The analysis again requires the opening and trading stock values of crops to be given at the lower of cost or market value (see **7.105**). Purchases and sales are to be included as the actual physical transactions which have taken place, irrespective of the date of payment. The analysis required is:

	Value of opening stock	*Bought in year*	*Sold in year*	*Value of closing stock*
	€	€	€	€
Wheat				
Oats				
Barley				
Potatoes				
Beet				
Fruit & vegetables				
Feed roots, kale, rape, etc				
Hay				
Silage				
Other harvested crops				
Other produce				
Feedstuffs				
	———	———	———	———
	———	———	———	———

7.105 Valuation of farm trading stock

The valuation of a farmer's trading stock at the beginning and end of each period of account is an important element in arriving at the farmer's profits (or loss) for that period. The same principles apply to the valuation of farm trading stock as are used in valuing the trading stocks of other businesses. Livestock, harvested crops and other trading stock must be valued at its 'cost' to the farmer, except for any trading stock which has a market value (ie net realisable value) of less than its cost. In examining any farm accounts submitted, the inspector of taxes requires to be satisfied that the farmer has not only included all items of trading stock, but also that the different items have been correctly valued in accordance with this cost or lower market value principle.

In practice, due to the nature of farming it may be more difficult than for most other trades to put an accurate cost figure on many items of farm stock. In order to deal with this problem, the Revenue has devised a rule of thumb approach which deems the cost of livestock (except horses) bred on the farm or purchased as immature stock to be a certain percentage of their market values as estimated at the year end accounting date.

The same approach is used to arrive at the cost value of harvested crops, but crops still in the ground at the year end date need not be valued and may therefore, be excluded from farm trading stock. Any farmer who has sufficiently accurate costing records to do so may, if he wishes, value trading stock at their actual cost, but in practice the Revenue's rule of thumb approach is widely accepted.

The discussion which follows of the Revenue's practical approach to farm stock valuation is largely taken from certain notes dated 21 May 1980 issued by the Dublin Farming District for the guidance of those preparing farm accounts for taxpayers whose liability to income tax is dealt with in that district, but it is understood that the same approach is taken in other tax districts dealing with farmers' accounts.

These guidance notes indicate also that the Revenue requires each farmer to carry out an accurate stocktaking on each accounting date and to have the stock analysed and recorded under the classifications set out at section E (livestock) and F (crops) of form AG 3 as outlined at **7.014**. Although section E provides spaces for horses (stallions, brood mares, foals, etc), the guidance note states that the percentage of market values do not apply to the valuation of horses. If any horses are included in a farmer's trading stock, it is generally necessary to arrive at actual cost figures. For the method of valuing bloodstock in a stud farm, see **7.302**.

Livestock

A farmer's livestock may be either animals bred by him as part of his farming activities or animals that he has purchased either for fattening and resale or for breeding purposes either immediately or at a future time when fully reared. For stock valuation purposes, it is necessary to distinguish between immature and mature animals. For this purpose, a cow, ewe or sow only becomes mature following the birth of its first calf, lamb or bonham; a bull, ram or boar becomes mature when it goes into service for the first time. All other animals, whether bred on the farm or purchased after birth, are regarded as immature. For example, an in-calf heifer is immature until after the birth of its first calf, while a bullock is always immature.

Strictly, the 'cost' of an immature animal (eg a calf) bred on the farm includes any sire's fee paid by the farmer for the services of the bull (if not his own), the keep of the cow while in calf, the keep of the calf from its birth to the relevant accounting date of the valuation, and any other direct expenses during this period. For an animal purchased while immature, eg a calf acquired for fattening and resale, its cost is its purchase price plus the cost of its keep from the date of purchase to the accounting date and any other direct costs incurred in this period.

Instead of taking such actual cost figures, the Revenue's rule of thumb method is to assume that the cost value of each immature animal at the relevant accounting date is, for the different types of animal, arrived at as follows:

cattle:	60% of its market value (at the accounting date),
sheep:	75% of its market value, and
pigs:	75% of its market value.

This method of valuation must, whenever it is adopted, be applied each year for all immature stock, whether bred on the farm or purchased after birth. If the same immature animal is in stock at two or more accounting dates, its cost value on each occasion automatically varies in accordance with changes in its market value, but the percentage applied to that value always remains the same. Clearly, when cost is determined in this manner, there can never be any question of writing down this cost to a lower market value. In the case of any farm animal killed for personal consumption of the farmer's family, the 'cost' figure to be credited in the farm account should normally be taken as being the same percentage of its market value unless a more accurate cost figure can be established.

Mature animals, ie breeding stock, differ from immature livestock in that their cost value once established remains the same at all subsequent accounting dates until they are either sold or die. However, if the farmer can show that the market value of any animal falls below its cost at any accounting date after that cost was established, then the lower market value is substituted in the trading stock valuation at that accounting date.

Any animal purchased as breeding stock in a mature state, ie after previously giving birth, has a cost value equal to its purchase price. An animal bred by the farmer on his own farm which develops from an immature animal to a mature one, ie on giving birth for the first time, is assumed to acquire a cost value as breeding stock equal to the appropriate percentage of its market value at the first accounting date after it becomes mature. This cost value continues to be used until it is sold or dies. For this purpose the same percentages are used as noted above for immature animals – ie 60 per cent for cattle, 75 per cent for sheep and pigs.

The determination of the market values of livestock at each accounting date is therefore a most important matter in farm accounting. There are no tax rules as to who should estimate the market value of livestock. While it may help the farmer or his tax advisor in agreeing the farm accounts with the inspector if the animals are valued by a professional valuer used to valuing livestock, it is perfectly valid for the farmer to make his own valuations. The farmer may in fact be as well versed as anyone else in his knowledge of market prices and probably knows the quality of his own animals better than anyone else.

Irrespective of who makes the valuation, the inspector is likely to scrutinise carefully the market values placed on the livestock used as part of the formula for determining their cost or, in the case of mature animals, to satisfy himself/herself as to the validity or otherwise of any writing down to a market value below cost. The inspector is likely to have available to him or her various published data regarding livestock prices; if the values placed on any farmer's livestock show material variations from comparable published statistics of livestock prices, the inspector will probably query the stock valuations produced by or on behalf of the farmer. Since the available statistical data tend to relate to average prices, it may in appropriate cases be possible for the farmer questioned to establish that the animals or some of them are below average quality or, perhaps, not all in the best of health.

Crops, fertilisers, etc

The guidance notes adopt a similar approach to arrive at the cost of production of harvested crops remaining unsold at the accounting date. 'Cost' is to be taken as 75 per cent of the market value of the crops in question. Effectively, this assumes that the market value at which it is expected the crops can be sold is such as to give the farmer a 33.3 per cent mark up on the assumed cost figure. Crops for the purpose of the farm trading stock valuations may, according to the guidance notes, exclude home produced hay, silage, feed roots and fodder produced and held for the maintenance of the livestock on the farm. No valuation is therefore required of such home produced items.

The guidance notes also state that crops in the ground, ie still growing, at the accounting date need not be valued, nor feed fertilisers which have been spread but which are still unexhausted. However, any fertiliser that has been purchased, but which has not yet been spread, must be taken into the farm stock valuation at its cost of purchase. Similarly, any hay, silage, feeding stuffs, etc that have been purchased and which remain unconsumed at the accounting date must also be taken into trading stock at their purchase price unless it can be shown that their market value at the accounting date has fallen below that price.

The Revenue have issued a precedent to the effect that they accept that as well as fertilisers, pesticides, purchased feeds and home produced feeds constitute trading stock (and may therefore be taken into account for the purposes of computing stock relief: see **7.106**).

Transfers of stock on discontinuance

In *Tax Briefing 21*, the Revenue Commissioners state their view of the correct valuation of stock which is transferred by a farmer on the discontinuance of his trade to a person who will then carry on the trade. The Revenue state the position as follows: where stock is sold for valuable consideration to a trader, and the trader is entitled to deduct that cost in computing his profits, then the stock should be valued at the sale price or the value of the consideration given (this rule has been substantially modified in the case of sales between connected persons by TCA 1997, s 89(3). See **5.603**). They also state that sales or transfers at gross under-value or over-value do not come within this provision and in such circumstances stock should be valued at market value in the hands of both the transferor and transferee (this seems to be a reference to the principle in *Sharkey v Wernher* (see **5.101**), although it is arguable that in fact this principle is overridden by TCA 1997, s 89.

Where stock is transferred for no consideration, for example, from a parent to a child who is farming or commencing to farm, then the Revenue state that:

(a) the stock should be valued at market value in the parent's accounts (TCA 1997, s 89(2) applies); and

(b) the child, who has in effect received a gift and has appropriated it to trading stock, is entitled to claim a deduction equivalent to the market value of the stock in computing the trading profits (this again follows the principle underlying *Sharkey v Wernher*).

However, TCA 1997, s 656(2) provides that where the trading stock in question is transferred from one farmer to another, they may jointly elect that the stock should be valued at the figure appearing in the transferor's accounts at the date of cessation (ie as opposed to its market value). The stock will be included in the transferee's opening stock valuation at the same figure. The election must be made in writing before the specified return date for the year of assessment in which the stock is transferred (ie 31 October 2016 for tax year 2015).

7.106 Stock relief

Stock relief, which is available only in respect of the computation of farming profits, is a 'temporary' relief in that the legislation has always included a provision that it is not to apply for years of assessment after a specified year. The relief, granted under TCA 1997, s 666 which was originally due to expire in 2012 has been extended to 31 December 2018 in FA 2015.

In the case of a farmer who is a partner in a registered farm partnership, ie a milk production partnership within the meaning of the European Communities (Milk Quota) Regulations 2008 (SI 2008/227) and with effect from 27 March 2013 a farm partnership included on a register of farm partnerships established by regulations made by the Minister for Agriculture, Food and the Marine after consultation with and approval of the Minister of Finance, the relief will apply at an enhanced rate of 50 per cent for accounting periods beginning after 1 January 2012 and ending on or before 31 December 2018. It is expected that other farm enterprise partnerships including tillage, beef and sheep will be able to avail of the relief. The income tax and USC reduced by the additional relief over the standard 25 per cent stock relief has been capped by Finance (No 2) Act 2013 at an amount not exceeding €7,500 in aggregate over three succeeding years of assessment. In respect of a qualifying period commencing on or after 1 January 2014 the relief is capped at €15,000 in aggregate over three succeeding years of assessment. Finance Act 2014, s 20(e).

A special enhanced stock relief for certain young trained farmers under TCA 1997, s 667B is described in **7.107** and a special relief in relation to the compulsory disposal of certain livestock, together with provision for deferring certain related compensation receipts, is described in **7.108**.

General

TCA 1997, s 666(1) entitles a '*person*' who carries on the trade of farming in respect of which he is chargeable to tax under Sch D Case I to a 'stock relief' deduction for any '*accounting period*' in which there is an increase in the value of the trading stock of his farming trade. This amount to be deducted is determined as explained under *Amount of deduction* below. The deduction is allowed by treating the amount so determined as if it were a trading expense in computing the person's Sch D Case I profits from his trade of farming for the accounting period concerned.

If there is a decrease in the trading stock value (or if there is no increase) in any accounting period, there is no 'negative' stock relief for that accounting period.

Partnerships

TCA 1997, s 666(6) states that the provisions of TCA 1997, s 666 are to apply to a farming trade carried on by a partnership as they apply to a trade carried on by a person. Given that the singular includes the plural (unless the context indicates otherwise: Interpretation Act 2005, s 18(a)) and that a partnership in these circumstances, although not a taxable 'person' (singular) certainly consists of taxable 'persons' (plural), it is arguable that this provision was not in any event strictly necessary. The legislation does not prescribe how the stock relief granted in respect of the partnership trade is to be allocated to the 'several' trade of each partner (see **4.503**), a point that is highly relevant where some partners are entitled to a different rate of stock relief to others. Revenue practice in this connection is noted below in the context of the enhanced relief for qualifying young farmers.

'Accounting period' defined

'*Accounting period*' has a special meaning for the purpose of a person's stock relief under TCA 1997, s 666. The term is defined for the purpose of this section in TCA 1997, s 665 as a period of one year ending on the date to which the accounts of the person (not being a company) are usually made up, provided that – where no accounts have been made up or where accounts have been made up for a greater or lesser period than one year – the accounting period for stock relief shall be such period not exceeding one year as the Revenue Commissioners may determine.

In the normal case, the accounting period by reference to which stock relief for a given income tax year is calculated is the farmer's period of accounts for the 12 months ending in that tax year (eg the 12-month period of accounts ending 31 July 2015 is the basis period for stock relief for 2015). If the farmer makes up accounts for a period other than for 12 months, the inspector (on behalf of the Revenue Commissioners) is required to determine the accounting period to be used for stock relief.

'Trade of farming' defined

For a person to qualify for a stock relief deduction for any accounting period, the person's trade during that accounting period must consist of farming as defined by TCA 1997, s 654 (see **7.102**).

Trading stock: definition and valuation

In order to calculate the stock relief deduction for an accounting period, it is necessary to define the trading stock of the farming trade and then to value it at the beginning and end of the accounting period. TCA 1997, s 665 defines 'trading stock' by giving the term the same meaning for stock relief as it has in TCA 1997, s 89, which defines the term as meaning:

(a) property of any description, whether real or personal, which is sold in the ordinary course of the trade, or would be sold if it were mature or if its manufacture, preparation or construction were complete; or
(b) materials that are used in the manufacture, preparation or construction of property of a type that is sold in the ordinary course of the trade.

(Note also the discussion at **5.401**.)

In relation to a trade of farming, this definition clearly includes all livestock, poultry, etc kept on the farm land either for rearing for sale or for producing offspring or farm produce (milk, eggs, etc), all farm produce, crops, etc, as well as all fertilisers, seeds, etc held to be used on the farm itself. These items are not intended to be an all-inclusive list of what may be included in a farmer's trading stock.

The values of the farmer's opening and closing trading stock used to determine the increase (if any) in trading stock value by reference to which the stock relief is calculated are normally taken as being the trading stock figures used in the farmer's accounts. This assumes that the method of valuing the trading stock for the accounts follows normal principles for stock valuations for tax purposes (see **5.401**, **7.105**), but if any adjustments to the accounting figures are required to reflect proper tax principles, the same adjustments need to be made in the opening and closing stock values which are used in calculating stock relief.

In the event that any payments on account have been received by the farmer in respect of a forthcoming sale of any item(s) still included in either the opening or closing trading stock, then the definition of trading stock in TCA 1997, s 665 requires the relevant stock value to be reduced by the amount(s) of the payment(s) on account (see *O'Laoghaire v Avonree Buildings* III ITR 51).

For the special rules of TCA 1997, s 669(5) which may apply to the valuation of the opening stock for the first accounting period in which a person carries on a trade of farming, see *Opening stock of New Business* below.

Amount of deduction

In an accounting period in which thc pcrson carrying on the farming trade has an increase in stock value, the person is entitled to claim a deduction under TCA 1997, s 666(1) of an amount equal to the lower of:

(a) 25 per cent of the increase in the stock value for that accounting period and 50 per cent in the case of a partner in a registered farm partnership for accounting periods ending after 1 January 2012 subject to the aggregate cap over three succeeding years of assessment of income tax and USC of €7,500. For a qualifying period commencing on or after 1 January 2014 the cap is increased to €15,000. This cap was inserted by Finance (No 2) Act 2013 (TCA 1997, s 667C) and increased by Finance Act 2014, and

(b) the Sch D Case I trading profits (before stock relief) of that accounting period (TCA 1997, s 666(3)(d)).

The increase in stock value (if any) for the purpose of stock relief is the excess (if any) of the value of the person's trading stock at the end of the accounting period (the 'closing value') over its value at the beginning of the accounting period (the 'opening value'). If the opening value of the trading stock of any accounting period equals or exceeds its closing value, no stock relief deduction is given for that accounting period.

A farmer's stock relief deduction (so long as the relief continues to be available) is therefore, in principle, a 25 per cent relief, but the deduction for an accounting period is restricted, where necessary, so as not to exceed the farmer's trading profits for the accounting period. For the special 100 per cent relief available to certain 'young trained farmers' for a limited period, see **7.107**.

For the purpose of calculating the amount of the deduction, '*trading profits*' are the adjusted profits as computed according to the ordinary Sch D Case I rules as applicable to farming, and are before deducting capital allowances or adding balancing charges for the current year and before giving any relief for capital allowances or farming losses carried forward or for any terminal loss carried back from another year (TCA 1997, s 665).

Reference is made above to TCA 1997, s 667C which was significantly amended by FA 2015, s 19 and was extended to 31 December 2018. This provision deals with registered farm partnerships which is defined with effect from 1 January 2016 as 'meaning a farm partnership entered on the register' with a register being a register of farm partnerships established and maintained by the Minister for Agriculture, Food and the Marine. A 'register of succession farm partnerships' is to be construed in accordance with TCA 1997, s 667D(1) which is a new provision brought about by FA 2015. The registration process allows the 'primary participant' or precedent partner within the meaning of TCA 1997, s 1007 to apply to the Minister to enter the partnership on the register. To be entered in the register the farm partnership must comply with the following:

(i) the farm partnership shall exist wholly for the purpose of carrying on the trade of farming;

(ii) the farm partnership agreement shall be in writing and shall:

  (I) comply with the Partnership Act 1890;

  (II) include information identifying the partners, the farm land farmed by the partnership, relating to their shares in the partnership and to the operation of the partnership;

  (III) commit the partners to the agreement to a period of operation as a farm partnership of not less than 5 years,

(iii) subject to subsection (1C), the farm partnership shall have at least 2 members and not more than 10 members;

(iv) no member of the farm partnership shall be a non-active partner;

(v) of the members of the farm partnership:

  (I) at least one shall be a person who has been engaged in the trade of farming on farm land owned or leased by that person, consisting of at least 3 hectares of useable farm land, for at least 2 years immediately preceding the date of formation of the partnership, and

  (II) other than the person referred to in clause (I), at least one is a natural person and either satisfies the requirements of clause (I) or:

    (A) has a qualification in agriculture specified in regulations made under subsection (4A) or, if not so specified a qualification determined by Teagasc – the Agriculture and Food Development Authority, to the satisfaction of the Minister, as being equivalent to a qualification so specified, and

    (B) under the terms of the farm partnership, holds an entitlement to at least 20 per cent of the profits of the partnership;

(vi) other than an excluded farm asset, a partner in a farm partnership shall not have an interest in any farm asset outside of the farm partnership at any time during the period of registration of the farm partnership, and for the purposes of this section, farm land owned or leased by a partner but licensed to the farm partnership concerned shall not be treated as the partner having an interest in land outside of the farm partnership;

(vii) any payment arising to a partner in a farm partnership, from the trade of farming for the purposes of the farm partnership agreement is liable to be, and shall be paid by the partner to the farm partnership.

Point (vi) above notes that a partner in a farm partnership can hold certain assets outside the partnership in the form of an 'excluded farm asset'. This is defined in TCA 1997, s 667C(1) as meaning farm land or livestock or machinery used for certain farming activities where that activity is excluded, by the terms of the partnership agreement, from the partnership. The aforementioned activities are outlined in the definition and comprise (a) pig farming; (b) poultry farming; (c) mushroom farming; (d) forestry; (e) bloodstock farming; (f) intensive horticultural cropping; (g) on-farm milk processing, other than milking and storage of milk; (h) generation of fuel or electricity.

TCA 1997, s 667C(1B) requires the Minister to be notified within 21 days of any change to the firm partnership or its activities with failure to do so resulting in the removal of the partnership from the register unless the Minister receives certain satisfactions regarding activity. TCA 1997, s 667C(1C) explains that a farm partnership shall not be eligible to be entered on the register if any partner in that partnership is a director of a company that is also a partner in that farm partnership, or has a shareholding in a company that is also a partner in that farm partnership, or has a shareholding in a company which directly or indirectly has a shareholding in a company which is a partner in that farm partnership. The section does not prescribe a minimum or maximum shareholding in this regard.

TCA 1997, s 667C(1D) notes that the Minister shall only enter a farm partnership on the register where he or she is satisfied that the farm partnership has met the conditions discussed above. Where the Minister is not satisfied that the farm partnership continue to meet the conditions then the Minister shall remove the partnership from the register with effect from the date upon which the partnership ceased to meet those conditions. A farm partnership shall stand suspended from the register where an order has been made under s 9 of the Animal Health and Welfare Act 2013, which relates to an area where any part of the farm land of the partnership is situated, but each partner in a partnership that is so suspended shall continue to be treated as a partner in a registered farm partnership for the purposes of stock deductions.

Example 7.106.1

Séamus O'Keeffe, who has carried on a farming trade for some years making up accounts annually to 31 December, has the following figures from his farming trade relevant to stock relief for the year ended 31 December 2014:

	€
Closing stock (31 December 2014)	100,000
Opening stock (1 January 2014)	85,000
Increase in stock value	15,000
Sch D Case I profits (before stock relief)	12,000

Mr O'Keeffe's period of accounts ended 31 December 2014 forms the basis for his 2014 income tax assessment. His stock relief deduction for that accounting period is calculated:

Stock relief deduction:	€
25% x €15,000	3,750

(which is the final deduction since it does not exceed the €12,000 Case I profits)

Example 7.106.2

Continue with the case of Séamus O'Keeffe. The following figures are relevant for his stock relief claim in respect of the year ended 31 December 2015:

	€
Closing stock	128,000
Opening stock	100,000
Increase in stock value	28,000

Sch D Case I profits (before stock relief)	6,500

Mr O'Keeffe's period of accounts ended 31 December 2015 forms the basis for his 2015 income tax assessment. His stock relief deduction for that accounting period is calculated:

	€
Stock relief deduction:	
25% x €28,000	7,000
But not to exceed farming (Case I) profits	6,500
Therefore deduction restricted to	6,500

How stock relief is given

Stock relief under TCA 1997, s 666 is given for income tax by deducting the amount determined as above as an 'expense' in the computation of the Sch D Case I taxable profits of the farming trade of the accounting period in which the increase in stock value occurs. It follows that the deduction is taken before considering capital allowances, whether of the current year or whether carried forward or carried back from another tax year (but for the effect of stock relief on capital allowances or losses carried forward or carried back, see below).

For the stock relief deduction to be obtained to affect the Sch D Case I assessment on the farming profits for a given tax year, the person assessable must claim the relief in writing on or before the 'specified return date' for that tax year (TCA 1997, s 666(5)). In effect, this means that the stock relief claim relevant for a tax year (eg 2014) must be made no later than 31 October 2015 (see **2.105**). Normally, the claim is made by including the farming profits computation showing the stock relief deduction in the documents submitted with the tax return for the year concerned (but note that return filed after the relevant specified return date would result in the loss of the stock relief unless a stock relief claim was made separately before the return date).

Example 7.106.3

Take the case of Séamus O'Keeffe from **Example 7.106.2**. He duly files his 2014 tax return with the inspector on 12 October 2015 (before the 31 October 2015 due date for the return). He includes with his tax return his farm accounts for the year ended 31 October 2014 with a computation showing a stock relief deduction of €3,750 (the proper amount as computed in the earlier example). He has a balancing charge of €1,500 and is entitled to capital allowances of €5,200 for 2014.

Mr O'Keeffe's assessment for 2014 in respect of his farming profits for the year ended 31 December 2014 is as follows:

	€
Sch D Case I farming profits (before stock relief)	12,000
Less:	
Stock relief deduction (as per **Example 7.106.2**)	3,750
Final Sch D Case I farming profits	8,250
Add:	
Balancing charge 2014	1,500
	9,750
Less:	
Capital allowances 2014	5,200
Net assessment after capital allowances	4,550

In the event that the income tax assessments for more than one tax year are based in whole or in part on the taxable profits of the one accounting period, the stock relief deduction for that accounting period will normally affect each year's tax assessment.

Example 7.106.4

Robert Allicadoo (age 38) commences a trade of farming on 1 July 2014 and makes up accounts annually to 30 June. The accounts for his first period of accounts, the 12 months ended 30 June 2015, produce the following figures:

	€
Closing stock (30 June 2015)	64,000
Opening stock (1 July 2014): Determined by inspector as €36,000 [1]	36,000
Increase in stock value	28,000
Sch D Case I profits (before stock relief)	16,600

Mr Allicadoo's stock relief deduction for his 12-months accounting period ended 30 June 2015 is calculated:

	€
Stock relief deduction:	
25% x €28,000	7,000
(which is the final deduction since it does not exceed the €16,600 Case I profits)	

The final Sch D Case I profits from the farming trade for this accounting period are therefore €9,600, ie the original €16,600 less the €7,000 stock relief deduction. These final farming profits of €9,600 after stock relief are used to determine the Sch D Case I assessable profits (subject to capital allowances) for each tax year for which the 12-months accounting period is used under the rules of commencement of trade, as follows:

	€
Tax year 2014 (1st tax year):	
Period 1/7/2014 to 31/12/2014[2]: €9,600 x 6/12 =	4,800
Tax year 2015 (2nd tax year):	
12-month period of accounts ending in 2015 (Y/E 30/06/2015)[3]	9,600

Notes:

1. Mr Allicadoo did not acquire his opening stock from another person ceasing to trade. Therefore, the inspector was required to determine the opening stock as such figure as is just and reasonable (see *Opening Stock of New Business* below).
2. For the first tax year of the new farming trade, the part of the taxable profits (after stock relief) attributable to the actual period of the trade in the first tax year are taken (see **4.205**).
3. For the second tax year, the taxable profits (after stock relief) for the 12-month period of accounting ending in the second tax year trading are taken (see **4.205**).

Special stock valuation rules

The legislation contains several special rules relating to the valuation of the opening or closing stock for use, in certain circumstances, in determining the amount of the increase in stock value (if any) over the accounting period. These rules are relevant only for the purposes of stock relief and do not affect the normal stock valuations used in computing the accounting profits (and taxable profits before stock relief).

The special rules may be required in the following circumstances:

(a) for the opening trading stock value for the accounting period in which the trade of farming commences (rule of TCA 1997, s 669(5) may apply);

(b) for the opening and/or closing stock values, as appropriate, for an accounting period in which trading stock is acquired or disposed of otherwise than in the normal conduct of the trade in question (rule of TCA 1997, s 669(1)(a) applies); and

(c) for the opening stock in an accounting period in which the basis of valuing the closing stock is not the same as that used for the opening stock valuation (rule of TCA 1997, s 669(1)(b) applies).

(a) Opening stock of new business

When a person commences to carry on a farming trade, the opening stock at the start of the first accounting period is often very low or perhaps there is no opening stock. In order to provide a reasonable measure of stock relief for the first accounting period, TCA 1997, s 669(5) requires stock relief to be calculated as if the farmer had a trading stock at the beginning of the accounting period of such value as the inspector of taxes considers reasonable and just; the reference to inspector of taxes was removed by F(TA)A 2015, s 37(8) but such adjustment was subject to Ministerial Order (SI 110/2016 appointed 21 March 2016 as the day on which the Finance (Tax Appeals) Act 2015, came into operation). This rule applies where, immediately before the beginning of an accounting period for which a stock relief deduction is claimed, the trade was not being carried on by the person claiming the relief.

This rule is therefore always relevant for a person starting a new farming trade, but may also be relevant for a person succeeding to an existing farming trade previously carried on by another person. For the circumstances in which there is an exception to this rule in the case of a person starting the trade who takes over trading stock from the person previously carrying on the trade, see below.

When the inspector is required to make a valuation under the rule, the 'reasonable and just' valuation of the opening stock is relevant only for the purposes of determining the increase in stock value (if any) for the stock relief computation. No adjustment is made to the opening trading stock value which is used in arriving at the trading profits (and taxable profits) of the accounting period.

In making the 'reasonable and just' valuation, the inspector is required (see above note regarding the F(TA)A 2015 amendment) to have regard to all the relevant circumstances of the case. In particular, the inspector is required to take account of movements during the accounting period in the costs of items of a kind included in the farmer's trading stock during the period, and of changes during the period in the volume of the trade carried on. On any appeal against the decision of the inspector, the Appeal Commissioners are similarly directed to have regard to all the relevant circumstances.

While no other directions are given to the inspector as to how he should make this notional opening trading stock valuation, the particular circumstances mentioned in the section do suggest a line of approach which can best be explained by the example which follows.

Example 7.106.5

Mr Mulligan commences to trade as a farmer on 1 July 2014 with a trading stock of €1,000. At the close of his first accounting period, the year ended 30 June 2015, trading stock is valued at €80,000. Prices for the type of farm products included in stock at 30 June 2015 are approximately 12 per cent higher than those a year earlier. By the end of the first year, Mr Mulligan's farm sales are running at an average of €30,000 a month compared with €10,000 per month between July and September 2014.

In seeking to arrive at a reasonable and just opening stock value, the inspector might approach the matter on the following lines:

	€
Closing stock value	80,000
Allowing for price changes between the beginning and end of the period would reduce this to a comparable opening value:	
€80,000 x 100/112, ie to	71,429
Adjust monthly sales at year end to equate sales price with those in opening months (say 15% higher):	
€30,000 x 100/115, ie	26,087
Adjust €71,429 to allow for lower sales levels in opening months:	
$71{,}429 \times \frac{10{,}000 \text{ (per month)}}{26{,}087 \text{ (per month)}}$	27,381

Assuming Mr Mulligan accepts without appeal the inspector's figure of €27,381 as a reasonable estimate of the opening stock value for the purpose, the increase in stock value by reference to which his stock relief deduction for the accounting period is calculated:

	€
Closing stock value	80,000
Less:	
Opening stock value (per the inspector's working)	27,381
Increase in stock value for AP	52,619

There is an exception to the general rule in TCA 1997, s 669(5). The inspector is not required (or permitted) to make the 'reasonable and just' estimate of the opening stock value, if:

(i) the person commencing to carry on the trade of farming has acquired the initial trading stock on a sale or transfer from another person on that other person's ceasing to carry on the trade; and

(ii) the stock acquired from the other person is, or is included in, the opening trading stock as valued at the beginning of his first accounting period.

When this exception arises, the opening stock value for the new farmer's stock relief computation for the accounting period in which he commences to carry on the farming trade is determined under the ordinary rules. This means that the opening stock value will be taken as the amount of the consideration paid for the stock by the new farmer or, if no consideration was given, the market value at the date of transfer would be used (subject to the right to elect for the stock to be transferred at 'book value' under TCA 1997, s 89(2) – see **7.105**).

(b) Abnormal transactions

TCA 1997, s 669(1)(a) requires the inspector or the Appeal Commissioners on appeal to determine the opening and/or closing trading stock of an accounting period as having such value as he considers to be reasonable and just in all the circumstances in any case where a farmer has acquired or disposed of trading stock other than in the normal course of the farming trade. The reference to Inspector or Appeal Commissioners above has been removed by F(TA)A 2015, s 37(8) but such adjustment was subject to Ministerial Order (SI 110/2016 appointed 21 March 2016 as the day on which the Finance (Tax Appeals) Act 2015, came into operation).

This rule is intended as an anti-avoidance provision directed against artificial changes in the level of a farmer's trading stock which might otherwise be contrived to inflate the amount of the stock relief deduction. An inspector of taxes could invoke this rule if, for example, the farmer claiming stock relief has abnormally increased his closing trading stock value for an accounting period by a special large purchase of, say, livestock, from a related person just before the relevant date and then resells the same goods to the same person or another related person shortly afterwards.

Before granting a stock relief claim, the inspector of taxes may well ask the taxpayer whether the trading stock includes any items acquired other than in the course of normal trading (eg from a connected person) and if so, to give particulars of the value of such stock. The rule is not, however, directed against the case where the farm trading stocks may be built up towards the end of an accounting period in the normal course of the trade.

(c) Change in basis of stock valuation

TCA 1997, s 669(1)(b) deals with the case where the farmer makes any change in the basis of valuing the farm trading stock so that the basis on which the closing stock of an accounting period is valued is different from the basis which was used to value opening stock (which was the closing stock of the previous accounting period). In any such case, para (b) requires the opening stock to be revalued on the same basis as used for the closing stock.

'Reference periods'

The farmer's stock relief deduction to be allowed in the assessment for a given tax year is, in the normal case, calculated by reference to the excess (if any) of the closing stock value over the opening stock value in the farmer's 12-month period of accounts ending in that tax year. Except where either the rules of commencement (see **4.205**), the rules of cessation (see **4.206**) or the change of accounting date rules (see **4.204**) apply to fix a different basis period for the Sch D Case I assessment, the accounting period for stock relief purposes will be the same as, or will coincide with, the farmer's period of accounts ending in the relevant tax year.

It is necessary to have rules to deal with the less usual case where the accounting period, as defined for stock relief purposes (see *General* above), does not coincide either with a period for which accounts are made up or with two or more successive periods of accounts. In any such case, TCA 1997, s 669(2) requires the increase in stock value (or any decrease) for the relevant accounting period to be determined by reference to the increase (or decrease) in stock value between the beginning and end of a '*reference period*' (and not as the increase or decrease in stock value in the accounting period).

The rules for ascertaining the reference period to be used are set out in TCA 1997, s 669(2). It may be noted that the rules always result in a reference period which commences on the first day of a period of account, so that the opening stock value of that period of accounts becomes the opening stock value of the reference period. Similarly, the reference period always ends on the last day of a period of account, so that the closing stock value of the period of accounts becomes the closing stock value of the reference period.

The rules to determine the reference period may be expressed as follows:

(a) if the accounting period relevant for the stock relief calculation for a given tax year does not commence on the first day of a period for which accounts are made up, the reference period is taken as beginning on the first day of the period of account which is 'current' (ie still running) at the start of that accounting period;

(b) if the accounting period does not end on the last day of a period for which account are made up, the reference period is taken as ending on the last day of the period of accounts which is current at the end of the accounting period; and

(c) if the accounting period commences on the first day of a period of account, the reference period is taken as commencing on that day; and

(d) if the accounting period ends on the last day of a period of account, the reference period is taken as ending on that day.

The essence of a reference period determined under these rules is that it always begins on the first day of a period of account and always ends on the last day of a period of account. If there is a period of account greater than 12 months, the reference period – but not the accounting period – may, but may not, coincide with the period of account. If there is a period of account of less than 12 months, normally the reference period will run from the first day of one period of account to the last day of the next period of account. In any event, the result is to enable the reference period to have an actual opening stock value and a closing stock value taken from a period or periods of account.

Example 7.106.6

Séamus Smith has been carrying on a farming trade for a number of years making up the accounts annually to 31 December until, in 2015, he decides to change the accounting date to 31 October 2015 (also used for subsequent years). Smith has the following periods of account as a result:

Period from 1/1/2014 to 31/12/2014 (12 months)

Period from 1/1/2015 to 31/10/2015 (10 months)

Due to the change in the accounting date, Smith's only period of accounts ending in 2015 is that for the 10 months ending 31 October 2015, ie a period of less than 12 months. Before considering the stock relief position, the basis period for the 2015 Sch D Case I assessment on Smith's farming profits is fixed under the rule of TCA 1997, s 65(2)(b) (see **4.204**) as being the 12 months ending 31 October 2015 (involving 2/12ths of the trading profits from the period of accounts ending 31 December 2014 plus the profits of the 10 months ending 31 October 2015).

The inspector also determines the 12 months from 1 November 2014 to 31 October 2015 as being the accounting period for stock relief relevant for 2015 (see definition of 'accounting period' under General above). Since this accounting period does not coincide with any period for which accounts are made up, it is necessary to ascertain the reference period for stock relief (if any) to be given in taxing the farming profits of this accounting period.

Since the accounting period does not commence on the first day of any period of accounts, the first day of the reference period is taken as 1 January 2014 (the first day of the period of accounts still current on 1 November 2014, ie on the commencement of the accounting period). On the other hand, the accounting period ends on the same day as the 10-month period of accounts to 31 October 2015. Therefore the reference period ends on 31 October 2015.

The result is a reference period of 22 months from 1 January 2014 to 31 October 2015. For the actual stock relief calculation, see **Example 7.106.8**.

Example 7.106.7

Katie Jones, who has been carrying on a farming trade since 1 December 2008, has been making up her farm accounts annually to 30 November including the period of accounts ending 30 November 2013. She then decides to change her accounting date to end-March making up her next accounts up to 31 March 2015. She therefore has the following periods of account:

Period from 01/12/2012 to 30/11/2013 (12 months)

Period from 01/12/2013 to 31/3/2015 (16 months)

Due to the change in the accounting date, Ms Jones does not have any period of account ending in the tax year 2014. Consequently, the rule of TCA 1997, s 65(2)(c) (see **4.204**) fixes the basis period for the 2014 Sch D Case I assessment on her farming profits as being the 12 months ending 31 December 2014 (involving assessing 12/16ths of the trading profits of the period of account running from 1 December 2013 to 31 March 2015).

It is assumed that the inspector also determines the 12 months from 1 January 2014 to 31 December 2014 as being the accounting period for stock relief. Since this accounting period does not coincide with any period for which account are made up, a reference period must be ascertained for the calculation of stock relief (if any).

Since the 12-months accounting period from 1 January 2014 to 31 December 2014 fixed by the inspector does not commence on the first day of any period of account, the first day of the reference period is taken as 1 December 2013 (the first day of the period of account still current on 1 January 2014). Since the accounting period does not end on the last day of any period of account, the reference period ends on 31 March 2015 (the last day of the period of account still current on 31 December 2014).

The result is a reference period of 16 months from 1 December 2013 to 31 March 2015. For the actual stock relief calculation, see **Example 7.106.9**.

Once the reference period has been determined for the given tax year, the farmer's increase (if any) in stock value for the accounting period relevant to the tax year under review is calculated under TCA 1997, s 669(3) by the following formula:

$$\frac{A(C - D)}{N}$$

Where:

A = the number of months in the *accounting* period;

C = the value of the farmer's trading stock at the end of the *reference* period;

O = the value of the trading stock at the start of the *reference* period; and

N = the number of months in the reference period.

The stock relief deduction for the accounting period is then 25 per cent of the increase in stock value as determined by the formula just given, but the deduction is not to exceed the appropriate fraction of the farming profits of the *reference period.* This means that the stock relief deduction is worked out as the lower of:

(a) 25 per cent of the increase in stock value as determined by the formula; and

(b) the amount resulting from:

$$\frac{A}{N} \times \text{Farming profits of the reference period (before stock relief)}$$

where:

A and N have the same meanings as for the formula given above to determine the amount of the stock increase for the accounting period.

Example 7.106.8

Continue with the case of Séamus Smith from **Example 7.106.6** where, for the purposes of his farming stock relief deduction for the tax year 2015, it has been established that the stock relief position has to be calculated using a reference period running for the 22 months from 1 January 2014 to 31 October 2015 and where the inspector has fixed the 12 months ending 31 October 2015 as the 'accounting period' for stock relief purposes.

Smith's stock valuations and his Sch D Case I farming profits (before stock relief and subject to capital allowances) for the two periods of account comprised in the reference period are as follows:

	€
12 months from 1/1/2014 to 31/12/2014:	
Opening stock value at 1/1/2014	88,000
Closing stock value at 31/12/2014	85,000
Sch D Case I farming profits (before stock relief)	6,450
10 months from 1/1/2015 to 31/10/2015:	
Opening stock value at 1/1/2015	85,000
Closing stock value at 31/10/2015	219,000
Sch D Case I farming profits (before stock relief)	10,360

Smith's farming profits (before stock relief) assessable for 2015 in respect of the 12-months basis period 1 November 2014 to 31 October 2015 are arrived at as follows:

	€
Period 1/11/2014 to 31/12/2014:	
2/12 x €6,450 (Y/E 31/12/2014)	1,075
Period 1/1/2015 to 31/10/2015:	
Profits of the 10 months period	10,360
Farm trade profits before stock relief	11,435

The increase in stock value on which stock relief is to be attributed to the 12-months accounting period ending 31 October 2015 is determined as follows:

	€
Stock value at 31/10/2015 (end of reference period) (= C)	219,000
Stock value at 1/1/2014 (start of reference period) (= O)	88,000
Increase in stock value for reference period1	131,000
Number of months in accounting period (= A):	12
Number of months in reference period (= N):	22
Increase in stock value for accounting period:	
12/22 x €131,000 =	71,455
Provisional stock relief deduction (25%)	17,864

Before the stock relief deduction for the 12-months accounting period ending 31 October 2015 is finally ascertained, the possible application of the trading profits restriction must be considered. Once the reference period rules apply as in this case, it is not the farm trade profits of the accounting period/basis period (€11,435), but the appropriate proportion of the farm trade profits of the two periods of account comprised in the reference period, which is used in applying the restriction.

The upper limit to the stock relief deduction for Séamus Smith is now computed as follows:

Farm trade profits (before stock relief) for reference period:	€
Profits of 12 months to 31 December 2014	6,450
Profits of 10 months to 31 October 2015	10,360
	16,810
Proportion attributed to 12 months AP to 31/10/2015:	
12/22 x €16,810 =	9,169

Since the provisional stock relief deduction of €17,684 exceeds the farm trade profits of €9,169 attributed to the accounting period as above, the stock relief deduction is the lower figure, ie €9,169. Mr Smith's assessment (before capital allowances) for 2015 in respect of his farming profits for the 12-months basis period ending 31 October 2015 is therefore arrived at follows:

	€
Sch D Case I farming profits (before stock relief)	11,435
Less:	
Stock relief deduction (as restricted)	9,169
Final Case I farming profits (subject to capital allowances)	2,266

Example 7.106.9

Continue with the case of Katie Jones from **Example 7.106.7** where, for the purposes of her farming stock relief deduction for the tax year 2014, the following facts were given or established:

Period of accounts:	16 months from 1 December 2013 to 31 March 2015
Basis period for assessment on farming profits:	12 months from 1 January 2014 to 31 December 2014
Accounting period for stock relief:	12 months from 1 January 2014 to 31 December 2014
Reference period for stock relief:	16 months from 1 December 2013 to 31 March 2015

Since the reference period in this case comprises only one period of accounts longer than 12 months, and as the 12-month accounting period falls wholly within this reference period, it is only necessary to consider the opening and closing stocks and the farming profits of this one 16-month period of accounts, but with apportionments. Assume that the following figures are ascertained for the reference period:

	€
Opening stock value (1/12/2013)	52,000
Closing stock value (31/3/2015)	63,000
Sch D Case I Farming profits (before stock relief) for the 16 months ended 31/3/2015	14,600

The stock relief deduction to be given for the 12-months accounting period ending 31 December 2014 is computed as follows:

	€
Stock value at 31/3/2015 (end of reference period) (= C)	63,000
Stock value at 1/12/2013 (start of reference period) (= O)	52,000
Increase in stock value for reference period	11,000
Number of months in accounting period (= A):	12
Number of months in reference period (= N):	16
Increase in stock value for accounting period:	
12/16 x €11,000 =	8,250

The provisional stock relief deduction for the 12-months accounting period ended 31 December 2014 is therefore €2,063 (25 per cent of €8,250), except that the deduction cannot exceed the farm trade profits (before stock relief) to be attributed to this accounting period. The calculation of the farm trade profits (before stock relief) for the accounting period (the upper limit to the deduction) is:

	€
Farm trade profits (before stock relief) for reference period	14,600
Proportion for accounting period:	
12/16 x €14,600 =	10,950

Since the provisional stock relief deduction of €2,063 of the accounting period (and basis period) does not exceed the €10,950 farm trade profits, the stock relief deduction is the full €2,063.

Ms Jones's assessment (before capital allowances) for 2014 in respect of her farming profits for the 12-months basis period ending 31 December 2014 is therefore arrived at follows:

	€
Sch D Case I Farming profits (before stock relief)	
12/16ths x €14,600 (16 months ended 31/3/2015)	10,950
Less:	
Stock relief deduction	2,063
Final Case I Farming profits (subject to capital allowances)	8,887

Effect of cessation of trade, ceasing to be resident

TCA 1997, s 669(4)(a) denies any stock relief deduction at all for any accounting period which ends by virtue of a person:

(a) ceasing to carry on his trade of farming;

(b) ceasing to be resident in the State; or

(c) ceasing to be within the charge to income tax under Sch D Case I.

TCA 1997, s 669(4)(b) extends the effect of TCA 1997, s 669(4)(a) to cover also the case where it is necessary to determine a farmer's increase in stock value for an accounting period by reference to the increase in stock value over a reference period (see '*Reference periods*' above). In any such case, s 669(4)(b) denies the stock relief deduction if the cessation of trade, ceasing to be resident or ceasing to be within the charge under Sch D Case I occurs at the end of any of the accounting periods comprised in the reference period.

Example 7.106.10

Gerald Evans, who has traded as a farmer for a number of years making up his accounts annually to 31 December, dies on 12 February 2015 so that his farm trade is treated as ceasing on that date. His executors make up farm accounts for the period 1 January 2015 to 12 February 2015 (which period is the final accounting period of his trade).

The opening and closing trading stocks and the Sch D Case I profits of the last two accounting periods are as follows:

	€
Accounting period 1/1/2014 to 31/12/2014:	
Opening stock value	59,000
Closing stock value	68,000
Increase in stock value	9,000
Sch D Case I farm profits (before stock relief)	22,600
Accounting period 1/1/2015 to 12/2/2015:	
Opening stock value	68,000
Closing stock value	82,000
Increase in stock value	14,000
Sch D Case I farm profits (before stock relief)	5,400

Since the period of accounts and accounting period from 1 January 2015 to 12 February 2015 has ended due to Evans' ceasing to trade (due to his death which constitutes a discontinuance, see **4.207**) TCA 1997, s 669(4)(a) denies any stock relief for that accounting period so that the Sch D Case I profits (subject to stock relief) are finally determined at €5,400. No benefit arises from the €14,000 increase in stock value.

However, since the previous accounting period of the 12 months ending 31 December 2014 coincides with the period of accounts ending on that date, there is no question of there being any reference period. Consequently, the rule of TCA 1997, s 669(4)(b) is not applicable. It is appropriate therefore to calculate a stock relief deduction for that accounting period and the final Sch D Case I profits, as follows:

	€
Period 1/1/2014 to 31/12/2014	
Increase in stock value	9,000
Stock relief deduction 25% x €9,000	2,250
(final deduction as not exceeding the Case I profits of €22,600)	
Farm profits (before stock relief)	22,600
Less: Stock relief	2,250
Final Sch D Case I Profits	20,350

The Sch D Case I assessment (subject to capital allowances) for 2015 tax year (final year of trade) is then:

	€
Period 1/1/2015 to 12/2/2015:	
Sch D Case I Profits	5,400
Total amount assessable	5,400

Effect on capital allowances forward, losses forward etc

The deduction of stock relief as a trading expense in arriving at the taxable profits (before capital allowances) of the relevant accounting period may have the effect of displacing at least part of the capital allowances for the same year and, if relevant, of capital allowances or losses carried forward or carried back. In some cases, the taxable profits (after stock relief) may be high enough so that full benefit can also be obtained for the capital allowances of the same year and of any capital allowances or losses carried forward or carried back. However, in other cases, this may not be so and it may not be possible to use some or all of the capital allowances and/or losses in question in the same tax year.

TCA 1997, s 666(3) is relevant to the latter cases. It provides that, in any case where a stock relief deduction has been allowed in computing the Sch D Case I farming profits for any accounting period used for a given tax year (the 'year of claim'), then the following consequences ensue:

(a) (i) the person claiming stock relief is not allowed relief under TCA 1997, s 382 to carry forward to any tax year later than the year of claim any loss sustained in his trade before the commencement of the year of claim,

(ii) he is not allowed relief under TCA 1997, s 385 to carry back to any tax year earlier than the year of claim any terminal loss incurred in relation to his ceasing to trade;

(b) if his Sch D Case I trading profits (after stock relief) are insufficient to absorb fully all the capital allowances for the year of claim (including any unused capital allowances carried forward from an earlier year), then any unused capital allowances cannot be carried forward under TCA 1997, s 304(4) for set off in any tax year later than the year of claim; and

(c) no part of any unused capital allowances for the year of claim can be used under TCA 1997, s 392 to increase a TCA 1997, s 381 loss claim for set off against income from all sources.

Example 7.106.11

Patrick Kelly claims a stock relief deduction of €6,150 as a trading expense in computing his farming profits for the 12 months accounting period ending 31 December 2015 used for his Sch D Case I assessment for the tax year 2015. Other relevant figures are:

	€
Farming profits (before stock relief and capital allowances)	7,840
Capital allowances 2015	3,220
Capital allowances forward from 2014	730
Farm losses forward from 2014	4,440

Kelly's Sch D Case I assessment in respect of his farming profits is as follows:

	€
Sch D Case I farming profits (before stock relief)	7,840
Less:	
Stock relief	6,150
Sch D Case I profits (after stock relief)	1,690
Less:	

Capital allowances 2015 (part of €3,220)	1,690
Net Sch D Case I assessment for 2015	Nil

TCA 1997, s 666(3) applies as the result of the stock relief claim with the following consequences:

(1) The unused capital allowances for 2015 of €1,530 (€3,220 less €1,690) cannot be used at all, neither by carry forward to 2016 nor by inclusion in a s 381 loss claim for use in 2015 claim against income from all sources.

(2) The €730 unused capital allowances brought forward from 2014 cannot be used later than 2015. Since there are no taxable profits left for 2015, the benefit of these allowances is lost.

(3) Similarly, the €4,440 losses brought forward from 2014 cannot be used later than 2015. Since there are no taxable profits left for 2015 after allowing part of the capital allowances, the benefit of these losses is also lost.

(4) In summary, there is a nil assessment on farming profits for 2015 and there are no capital allowances or losses to carry forward to 2016. For the position if stock relief were not to be claimed, see **Example 7.106.12**.

In view of the rules of TCA 1997, s 666(3), the farmer should – before claiming stock relief for any accounting period – consider the possible effect on his capital allowances and any losses forward from a previous year. If the farming profits (before stock relief) are large enough to absorb in full the stock relief deduction, all capital allowances of the current year as well as any unused capital allowances and any tax losses forward, there is no problem.

On the other hand, if the Sch D Case I profits (after stock relief) are not sufficient to absorb fully all the capital allowances and any losses forward, the farmer (as in the last Example) should do the sums to work out whether the immediate benefit of the stock relief deduction might not be outweighed by the loss of the future benefit of the unused capital allowances and losses. If the capital allowances and losses carried forward from previous tax years are greater than the adjusted Sch D Case I farming profits (before stock relief) for the current accounting period, stock relief should not normally be claimed.

Example 7.106.12

Take the case of Patrick Kelly from **Example 7.106.11** again, but assume that he considers the possible effect of TCA 1997, s 666(4) before making his claim for stock relief in respect of the accounting period ending 31 December 2015.

He calculates the consequences of not making a stock relief claim in respect of that accounting period. The effect on his Sch D Case I assessment on his farming profits would be as follows:

	€	€
Sch D Case I Farming profits (before stock relief)		7,840
Less:		
Stock relief		Nil
Sch D Case I profits		7,840
Less:		
Capital allowances 2015	3,220	
Capital allowances forward from 2014	730	3,950
		3,890

Less:	
Losses forward from 2014 (part of €4,440)	3,890
Net Sch D Case I assessment for 2015	Nil
Losses available	
Losses forward from 2014	4,440
Less:	
Amount used in 2015 (TCA 1997, s 382)	3,890
Losses forward to 2016	550

In summary, there is again a nil assessment on farming profits for 2015, but without the stock relief claim there are losses of €550 to be carried forward to 2016. This is an improvement on the position if stock relief is claimed. Therefore, Patrick Kelly would be advised not to claim the stock relief in 2015.

7.107 Special stock relief for 'young trained farmers'

TCA 1997, s 667B (superseding TCA 1997, ss 667 and 667A) provides a special 100 per cent stock relief (instead of the normal 25 per cent relief) for limited periods for certain young trained farmers ('*qualifying farmers*', as defined below). For the 100 per cent relief to be given in any eligible tax year, it is of course necessary that there should be an increase in stock value for the basis period for that tax year. Finance Act 2015, s 19(2)(d) extended the relief to 31 December 2018. In addition, Finance Act 2013 made two significant changes to claiming the relief for farmers who first qualify in the year of assessment 2012 or subsequent years. A qualifying farmer must come within the definition of 'small and medium sized enterprises in Art 2 of Commission Regulation (EC) No 1857/2006 of 15 December 2006. All Irish farmers would fall within this definition given that a small or medium size enterprise is one with less than 250 employees. In addition, the cash benefit of claiming the relief at 100 per cent is capped at €40,000 in a single year and €70,000 in aggregate over four years. Again this cap should not affect most young farmers.

'Qualifying farmer' defined

TCA 1997, s 667B defines a 'qualifying farmer' (the 'young trained farmer'), for the purpose of the 100 per cent stock relief, as an *individual* who:

(a) first qualifies in the tax year for grant aid under the Scheme of Installation Aid for Young Farmers operated by the Department of Agriculture and Food under Council Regulation (EEC) no 797/85 of 12 March 1985 (or that Regulation as it may be revised from time to time);

(b) first becomes chargeable to income tax under Sch D Case I in the tax year in respect of the profits from a trade of farming;

(c) is under the age of 35 years at the beginning of the tax year in which he commences the trade of farming (eg if Mr X becomes 35 on 7 April 2013 and commences a farming trade on 1 April 2013, he meets this condition); and

(d) holds one of the qualifications set out in the Table to TCA 1997, s 667B, or an equivalent qualification as duly certified by Teagasc (TCA 1997, s 667B(2), (4) or, as an alternative, meets certain other conditions as to the extent of his training (the 'qualification/training condition' TCA 1997, s 667B(3))).

(e) and where the conditions at (a)-(d) above are first satisfied in the year of assessment 2012 or any subsequent year of assessment, who submits a business plan to Teagasc for the purposes of the relief or submits a plan to Teagasc or the Minister for Agriculture, Food and the Marine for any other purpose. The plan has to be submitted by 31 October in the year following the first year of assessment.

The first three of these conditions are clear as to their meaning and require little elaboration. The intention is to encourage and aid the young trained farmer to build up his farm trade stocks at the time when he commences to trade as a farmer for the first time. Condition (b) refers to the tax year in which the individual's farm trade is commenced.

The circumstances in which the young farmer satisfies the qualification/training condition referred to in (d) are now described in detail. First, it is to be noted that the particular qualification and/or training requirement must have been obtained or met no later than the end of the tax year in which the young farmer has commenced his farming trade. This contrasts with the 35 years of age requirement where an individual becoming 35 during the tax year in which he commences the farming trade does not disqualify him from the 100 per cent relief.

Example 7.107.1

Robert Tankheart, who was awarded a Certificate in Farming by Teagasc in February 2012, commences to trade as a farmer on 1 November 2012. He is 34 years of age on 1 January 2012 (beginning of tax year in which he qualifies) and meets the other conditions to be a 'qualifying farmer'.

He makes up accounts annually to 31 October so that each 12-month period of accounts ending 31 October is an accounting period for stock relief purposes. The basis periods for his Sch D Case I assessments on the profits of his farming trade for the first four tax years from the commencement onwards are:

2012: Period 1/11/2012 to 31/12/2012 (assessed on 2/12ths profits year to 31/10/2013)
2013: Period 1/11/2012 to 31/10/2013 (period of accounts)
2014: Period 1/11/2013 to 31/10/2014 (period of accounts)
2015: onwards: Period of 12 months ending on 31 October in relevant year

Mr Tankheart is entitled to claim the benefit of the 100 per cent stock relief by virtue of TCA 1997, s 667A for each of 2012, 2013, 2014 and 2015, provided that he has an increase in stock value in the accounting period relevant to the tax year in question.

Example 7.107.2

Alice Darwin, who was age 34 on 1 January 2012, holds a Bachelor of Agricultural Science/Animal Science awarded by University College Dublin (a specified qualification). She commences to carry on a trade of farming on 1 October 2012 and makes up accounts annually to 30 September. She meets all the conditions to be a qualifying farmer from 1 January 2012.

Ms Darwin is entitled to claim the 100 per cent stock relief TCA 1997, s 667B to have effect for the Sch D Case I assessments on her farming profits for the tax years 2012 (tax year in which she becomes a qualifying farmer) and for each of the next three years, ie 2013, 2014 and 2015.

Amount of deduction

The 100 per cent stock reduction is given to the qualifying farmer under the normal rules of TCA 1997, ss 665–669. Consequently, the deduction in any accounting period used for any of the eligible tax years is an amount equal to the lower of:

(a) 100 per cent of the increase in the stock value in the accounting period; and

(b) the Sch D Case I profits (before stock relief) of the farming trade for the accounting period.

All the other rules relating to stock relief for a person chargeable to income tax apply in the same way as explained in **7.106**. The only difference for the qualifying farmer is that '100 per cent' is substituted for '25 per cent' as the rate of relief. The cash benefit is limited to €40,000 in a single year of assessment or €70,000 in aggregate over the course of the scheme which is four years where the qualifying farmer first qualifies in the year of assessment 2012 or a subsequent year of assessment.

Example 7.107.3

Take Alice Darwin's case from **Example 7.107.2** where she has become a qualifying farmer in 2012 having commenced to trade on 1 October 2012. She is entitled to claim the 100 per cent stock relief for the tax year 2012 (year of commencement) and for each of the next three tax years 2013 to 2015. However, due to the Sch D Case I rules of commencement, only the first three accounting periods are relevant for the first four tax years for which the 100 per cent stock relief is available.

The relevant stock values and adjusted Sch D Case I profits from farming (before stock relief) for each of her first three accounting periods are given as follows:

		AP to	
	30/09/2013	*30/09/2014*	*30/09/2015*
	€	€	€
Opening stock value[1]	45,000	57,000	56,000
Closing stock value	57,000	56,000	88,000
Increase in stock value in AP	12,000	Decrease	32,000
Farming profits (before stock relief)	13,240	23,890	19,030

Ms Darwin is entitled to claim the 100 per cent stock relief for each of the tax years 2012, 2013, 2014 and 2015, but only if there is a stock increase in the relevant stock relief accounting period. The stock relief deductions are first worked out for each of the three accounting periods, as follows:

		AP to	
	30/09/2013	*30/09/2014*	*30/09/2015*
Lower of:	€	€	€
(a) 100% x increase in stock			
and Value in AP	12,000	Nil	32,000
(b) Farming profits (before stock relief)	13,240	23,890	19,030
Stock relief for AP[3]	12,000	Nil	19,030

The final Sch D Case I profits (after stock relief but before capital allowances) for each of the three accounting periods are now ascertained as follows:

		AP to	
	30/09/2013	*30/09/2014*	*30/09/2015*
	€	€	€
Farm profits (before stock relief)	13,240	23,890	19,030
Less:			
Stock relief	12,000	Nil	19,030
Sch D Case I profits	1,240	23,890	Nil

The assessments in respect of these post-stock relief profits for the four eligible tax years during which the 100 per cent relief is available (to the extent it actually applies in this case) are determined, applying the Sch D Case I rules of commencement, as follows:

	€
2012 (1st tax year of farming):	
Period 1/10/2012 to 31/12/2012 3/12 x €1,240[2]	310
2013 – (2nd tax year)	
Period 1/10/2012 to 30/09/2013 (12-month period of account ending in tax year)[2]	1,240
2014 – (3rd year)	
12-month period of accounts to 30/09/2014[3]	23,890
2015 (4th year)	
12-month period of accounts to 30/09/2015.[4]	Nil

Notes:

1. The opening stock value (€45,000) at the commencement of trading (1 October 2012) used here is the amount assumed to have been fixed by the inspector as being a reasonable and just value in accordance with the rule of TCA 1997, s 669(5) (see *Opening stock of new business* in **7.106**).
2. The benefit of the €12,000 stock relief deduction obtained in the accounting period ending 30 September 2013 may be seen to have affected the assessments for the two years 2012 and 2013. In effect the tax assessments for the two years have been reduced by €15,000 – 3/12ths of €12,000 in 2012 and a full €12,000 in 2013.
3. Due to the decrease in stock value in the accounting period ending 30 September 2014, there is no stock relief benefit at all for 2014 (and there would have been none under the 25 per cent relief either).
4. Since the farming profits (before stock relief) in the accounting period ending 30 September 2015 (2015) are less than the €32,000 stock relief deduction otherwise available, the full 100 per cent deduction has to be restricted to the farming profits (€19,030).

Young trained farmers in partnership

As noted above, the legislation offers little guidance on the application of the stock relief provisions to partnership trades. In *Tax Briefing 21*, the Revenue Commissioners set out their views on the application of those provisions with particular reference to the enhanced relief for young farmers. They state their position as follows:

> Stock relief is a deduction in arriving at the Case I profit. In the case of a partnership the practice has been to deduct the stock relief due in arriving at the partnership profit. This practice will continue where all the partners come within the same stock relief regime.
>
> Where some partners in a partnership are entitled to 100 per cent stock relief while others are entitled to the usual 25 per cent relief, the partnership profit to be allocated in accordance with the profit sharing ratios is the profit before stock relief but after making all other adjustments. To arrive at the assessable profit of each partnership, the stock increase will be allocated in accordance with the profit sharing ratios and stock relief will be allowed accordingly.

The Revenue warn that they will look closely at cases where a partnership may not exist in fact or where profit sharing ratios are not 'factual' and appear to have been altered in order to maximise the benefit of the 100 per cent relief. In fact, where the profit sharing arrangement reflects a genuine, legally binding agreement (and is thus not a 'sham' – see **1.408**), it is difficult to see how it can be displaced for tax purposes (subject possibly to the operation of TCA 1997, s 811 – see **Division 17**).

Finance Act 2014 limited the cash benefit for individuals in farming partnerships to €15,000 in aggregate over three successive years of assessment. This limitation was first introduced in Finance (No 2) Act 2013 where the cash benefit for individuals in farming partnerships was limited to an amount not exceeding €7,500 in aggregate over three successive years of assessment. However, the limit does not apply to young trained farmers in partnership who are still subject to the cash benefit of up to €40,000 in a single year of assessment or €70,000 in aggregate over the course of the scheme which is four years where the qualifying farmer first qualifies in the year of assessment 2012 or a subsequent year of assessment.

7.108 Compulsory disposal of livestock

TCA 1997, s 668 as substantively amended by FA 2002, s 29 entitles a person carrying on a trade of farming in the State to elect to take certain special tax benefits if such person is compulsorily required, under any statute relating to the eradication or control of diseases in livestock, to dispose of livestock, subject to meeting various conditions (see *Revenue Tax Briefing 50*). The pre-FA 2002 regime is covered in earlier editions of this book.

Livestock for these purposes consists of cattle and animals and poultry of a kind specified in Parts I and II of the Diseases of Animals Act 1966, First Sch, forming part of the trading stock of the trade of farming.

In the case of cattle, the election could not generally be claimed prior to 2008 unless the disposal was of *all* the cattle which were included in the farmer's trading stock.

There was however an exception in the case of a compulsory disposal under a disease eradication scheme relating to the eradication or control of brucellosis in livestock. In the case of brucellosis, the farmer was treated as disposing of all his cattle if the disposal was of all eligible cattle for the purpose of the said scheme, together with such other cattle as were required to be disposed of (TCA 1997, s 668(1) as subsequently amended by FA 2008, s 33). In the case of animals and poultry, the election can be claimed where all animals or poultry of the particular kind forming part of that trade of farming are disposed of and where compensation is paid by the Minister for Agriculture, Food and Rural Development in respect of that disposal (TCA 1997, s 668(1)(b)).

For the special benefits of TCA 1997, s 668 to be given to a farmer, the farmer must make an election to avail of the section by giving notice in writing to the inspector no later than the 'specified return date' for the chargeable period in which the compulsory disposal is made (but see exception in next paragraph). For example, if a farmer chargeable to income tax makes a compulsory disposal of his herd in the tax year ending 31 December 2015, the election must be made no later than 31 October 2016 (the specified return date for the tax year 2015).

There are two types of benefit available under TCA 1997, s 668 in respect of any profit realised from the compulsory disposal of cattle. First, there is a deferral of taxable income. Secondly, a special 100 per cent stock relief deduction may be elected for during the same deferral period provided that expenditure is incurred in replacing the animals disposed of.

Deferral of taxable income

TCA 1997, s 668(3) entitles the farmer who has realised a 'profit' (as defined below) from the compulsory disposal to defer recognition of the profit on either of two alternative bases:

(a) by electing to ignore the said profit in arriving at his (or its) Sch D Case I farming profits or loss of the accounting period in which the compulsory disposal is made and, instead, to include four equal instalments of the said profit in the farming profits (or losses) of each of the four immediately succeeding accounting periods. In effect, this is a deferral of the full 'profit' to be spread over the four succeeding accounting periods; or

(b) by electing to include four equal instalments of the said profit in the farming profits (or losses) of the accounting period in which the compulsory disposal is made and in each of the three immediately succeeding accounting periods. In effect, this is a deferral of 3/4 of the full 'profit' to be spread over the three succeeding accounting periods (TCA 1997, s 668(3)).

Example 7.108.1

Mr AB, a farmer making up accounts to 31 December, is required to dispose of his herd of cattle under a disease eradication order. He realises a 'profit' of €34,000 from the compensation received from a compulsory disposal of his herd of cattle in March 2012. He is entitled to elect under TCA 1997, s 668(3) to deal with this profit as follows:

(a) to ignore the full €34,000 in arriving at his adjusted Sch D Case I farming profits or loss for the 12-month accounting period ending 31 December 2012 (period in which the disposal made); and

(b) to include €8,500 of the said 'profit' in computing his adjusted Sch D Case I farming profits or loss for each of the four accounting periods ending respectively on 31 December 2013, 31 December 2014, 31 December 2015 and 31 December 2016 (the four succeeding periods).

Example 7.108.2

Mr AB from **Example 7.108.1** may, instead of the election made in that example, elect to include the €34,000 'profit' from the compulsory disposal in March 2012 as follows:

(a) to include €8,500 in arriving at his adjusted Sch D Case I farming profits or loss for the 12-months accounting period ending 31 December 2012 (period in which the disposal made); and

(b) to include €8,500 in computing his adjusted Sch D Case I farming profits or loss for the accounting periods ending 31 December 2013, 31 December 2014 and 31 December 2015 (the succeeding three periods).

For the rest of this discussion, the accounting periods over which the 'profit' is spread in any particular case is referred to as the *'deferral period*'. As indicated the deferral period may comprise either the accounting periods following that of the compulsory disposal or, if so elected, the accounting period of the compulsory disposal and the immediately following accounting period.

The 'profit' on the compulsory disposal (referred to in TCA 1997, s 668 as the 'excess') – which may be spread over the succeeding accounting periods in the deferral period – is defined as the excess of:

(a) the 'relevant amount' over

(b) the value of the cattle included in the farmer's trading stock on the first day of the accounting period in which the compulsory disposal takes place.

The '*relevant amount*' is in turn defined, for the purposes of TCA 1997, s 668 as the amount of any *income* received as a result, or in consequence, of the compulsory disposal of the cattle. The use of the word 'income' in this definition (rather than 'receipt') implies that the 'relevant amount' is determined after deducting from the compensation received any expenses which may be incurred by the farmer directly for the purposes of the compulsory disposal.

It is to be noted that the exclusion of the 'profit' when arriving at the taxable profits of the accounting period in which the compulsory disposal is made may, in appropriate circumstances, have the effect of creating a Sch D Case I farming loss for that accounting period. The section provides that the 'excess' is to be disregarded as respects the accounting period in which the disposal is made. All the normal loss reliefs (including a set off against other income) are available for any loss resulting from the deferral of the profit on the compulsory disposal.

In making the decision on which accounting periods are to comprise the deferral period over which the 'excess' is to be spread, the farmer (or farming company) should bear in mind the condition for the full enhanced stock relief deduction discussed below, namely that the required amount of expenditure on replacing the animals the subject of the compulsory disposal has to be incurred before the end of the deferral period actually elected. This may make it preferable to elect for the accounting periods immediately succeeding that in which the compulsory disposal is made since this gives a longer period in which to incur the necessary replacement expenditure.

Example 7.108.3

Mr T Evergreen, a farmer, is required to have his entire herd of cattle destroyed during his 12-month period of accounts ending 31 May 2011 due to an outbreak of a cattle disease (not brucellosis). This period of accounts (accounting period for TCA 1997, s 668) is the basis period for the Sch D Case I assessment for 2011 on the farming profits.

Assume that Mr Evergreen is entitled to receive compensation totalling €135,000 under the relevant disease eradication scheme which required the compulsory disposal, but that he incurs expenditure of €9,000 directly in connection with the disposal. The stock value of the herd of cattle at 1 June 2010 is assumed to have been €81,000 (which value excludes all other trading stock). The 'excess' for which the benefit of TCA 1997, s 668(3) is available is calculated:

	€
Compensation for compulsory disposal	135,000
Less:	
Expenses of the disposal	9,000
'Relevant amount' (income from disposal)	126,000
Less:	
Value of cattle at 1 June 2010	81,000
'Excess' from disposal in AP to 31/05/2011	45,000

Mr Evergreen wishes to elect under TCA 1997, s 668(3) to defer this €45,000 'excess' so as to have it spread in equal instalments between the next four accounting periods ending respectively on 31 May 2012, 31 May 2013, 31 May 2014 and 31 May 2015.

Based on the figures given on the first line below for Mr Evergreen's Sch D Case I farming profits/loss (before stock relief), the effect of this election in respect of the 'excess' for each of the five accounting periods affected is as follows:

	AP to				
	31/05/2011	31/05/2012	31/05/2013	31/05/2014	31/05/2015
	€	€	€	€	€
Case I profits/(loss) (before stock relief)	52,360	(3,200)	40,020	38,190	43,400
Less:					
'Excess' deferred by election	(45,000)	-	-		
Add:					
'Excess' treated as income	-	11,250	11,250	11,250	11,250
Revised Case I profits (before stock relief)	7,360	8,050	51,270	49,440	54,650

The foregoing profits (assessable respectively for the income tax years 2011 to 2015) are subject to any stock relief deductions (including any under TCA 1997, s 668(4), see below) and capital allowances. No stock relief will be available in this case for the accounting period ended 31 May 2011 since this is the year of compulsory disposal and the deferral of income does not begin until the following accounting period (see further the discussion of TCA 1997, s 668 below).

Where the trade in question is permanently discontinued, any part of the excess which would otherwise have been included in the computation of the profits of subsequent accounting periods is taxable under Sch D Case IV in the period in which such discontinuance takes place (TCA 1997, s 668(3A)).

Example 7.108.4

Take the facts of **Example 7.108.3** but assume now that Mr Evergreen ceases to trade on 31 March 2014, and made profits of €9,600 in his final accounting period before taking into account the deferral of income under TCA 1997, s 668.

	AP to			
	31/05/2011	31/05/2012	31/05/2013	31/03/2014
	€	€	€	€
Case I profits/(loss) (before stock relief)	52,360	3,200	40,020	9,600
Less:				
'Excess' deferred by election	45,000	-	-	
Add:				
'Excess' treated as income	-	11,250	11,250	11,250
Revised Case I profits (before stock relief)	7,360	8,050	51,270	20,850

An assessment of tax on an amount of €11,250 will be made under Sch D case IV for the year 2014.

Enhanced stock relief

TCA 1997, s 668(4) provides for the second type of benefit following a compulsory disposal due to a disease eradication or control scheme – the enhanced stock relief deduction which may be claimed instead of the normal 25 per cent relief. It entitles the farmer, if he incurs expenditure on replacing the animals which were the subject of the compulsory disposal, to elect to take a stock relief deduction under TCA 1997, s 666 in substitution for any other deduction to which he might otherwise be entitled in each of the four accounting periods which together comprise the deferral period (the period over which the 'excess' from the compulsory disposal is spread, viz either the four accounting periods following the period in which excess arises or that accounting period together with the three following accounting periods).

In order to obtain the maximum deduction under this subsection, it is a condition that the expenditure on replacing the animals is of a total amount at least equal to the 'relevant amount' (the amount of income received by the farmer/farming company as a result, or in consequence, of the compulsory disposal). It is a further condition that this replacement expenditure is incurred no later than the end of the deferral period.

The next part of this discussion assumes that the expenditure on replacing the animals incurred by the end of the deferral period at least equals the relevant amount. For the position where the expenditure on replacing the animals incurred within this time limit is less than the relevant amount, see below.

TCA 1997, s 668(4) provides that the enhanced deduction is to be an amount equal to the instalment of the 'excess' included in the farming profits for each accounting period in which the deferral of income takes effect.

The effect is that, for all of the four accounting periods in the deferral period, the person carrying on the farming trade is entitled to claim a stock relief deduction equal to the deferred income arising in the period. This is not subject to the normal stock relief restriction that the amount of the deduction cannot exceed the Sch D Case I trading profits (before any stock relief) for the accounting period, (see *Amount of deduction* in **7.106**).

Replacement expenditure less than relevant amount

The farmer which has been required to dispose of the animals may not always incur expenditure on replacing or restocking of as much as the relevant amount or, alternatively, he (or it) may not have incurred this amount of expenditure before the end of the deferral period elected. Where either of the circumstances outlined above occur, a 'ceiling' (or upper limit) applies to the amount which may be deducted under TCA 1997, s 668(4) if the restocking expenditure is less than the relevant amount.

Where after the four-year period, for whatever reason, the restocking expenditure is less than the relevant amount, the aggregate stock relief for the four years is reduced to an amount that bears the same proportion to the aggregate stock relief as the expenditure actually incurred in the four-year period bears to the compensation received. This reduction is to take place in so far as it is possible, in the later years.

Example 7.108.5

Take the facts in **Example 7.108.3**, and assume that Mr Evergreen only incurred restocking expenditure of €106,000, ie €20,000 less than the relevant amount of €126,000. The aggregate stock relief which would be granted under TCA 1997, s 668 on the basis of restocking expenditure equal to, or greater than, the relevant amount would be equal to the total amount of the deferred income, ie €45,000. The aggregate stock relief available is therefore reduced to € 45,000 x 106,000/126,000 = €37,857.

	AP to					
	31/05/2011	*31/05/2012*	*31/05/2013*	*31/05/2014*	*31/05/2015*	
Case I profits/(loss) (before stock relief)	€52,360	€(3,200)	€40,020	€38,190	€43,400	
Less:						
'Excess' deferred by election	(45,000)	-	-			
Add:						
'Excess' treated as income	-	11,250	11,250	11,250	11,250	
Revised Case I profits (before stock relief)		8,050	51,270	49,440	54,650	
Stock Relief under s 668		11,250	11,250	11,250	4,107	37,857
	7,360	(3,200)	40,020	38,190	50,543	

Notes:

1 The deduction under TCA 1997, s 666 as provided by TCA 1997, s 668 is not restricted in 2012 notwithstanding that it creates a loss.

2 The restriction on the deduction is applied to the latest years first; in this case all of the shortfall is used to restrict the deduction for 2015.

7.109 Election to average farming profits

TCA 1997, s 657 as amended by Finance Act 2014, s 20 gives an individual carrying on the trade of farming, where certain conditions are met, the right to make an election to be assessed to tax for a tax year based on the average of five years' (previously three years') farming profits ending in that year, instead of under the normal assessment on the farming profits of a 12-month period ending in the tax year. This election is not available to any unincorporated body or any other person who is not an individual.

Where the individual carries on farming as a sole trader and also in partnership the profits from all those sources will be treated as arising in relation to a single trade of farming by virtue of TCA 1997, s 657 and therefore the averaging provisions will generally apply to the profits of the deemed single trade. This subject to meeting the '*Two Prior Years of Normal Assessment*' condition (see below).

TCA 1997, s 657(4) entitles an individual to make an election to be assessed to income tax on his farming profits under the income averaging rules of TCA 1997, s 657(5), *provided that* the conditions described below are satisfied. The section provides that, where an assessment for the relevant year of assessment is made by the inspector on a farmer satisfying the conditions, the farmer may make the election for income averaging by giving notice of election in writing to the inspector within 30 days of the date of the notice of assessment. The inspector is then required to amend the assessment so as to give effect to the election and to tax the individual's farming profits in the manner prescribed in TCA 1997, s 657(5) (see *Effect of election* below).

In practice, however, it is now better under the self-assessment procedure for the individual entitled, to make the election at the same time as filing his tax return for the first tax year for which the election is to take effect, thereby allowing the inspector to give effect to the election in making the income tax assessment based on the tax return.

Once a farmer has made an election for income averaging for a particular year of assessment, income averaging must be applied in taxing his farming profits, not only for that year but also for every subsequent tax year unless and until:

(a) the individual makes a later election under TCA 1997, s 657(7) to opt out of income averaging after at least five years of being taxed under income averaging (see **7.110**);

(b) the individual ceases or, where relevant, his spouse or civil partner ceases to satisfy any of conditions (1) to (4) mentioned under *'Full-time farmer' requirement* below; or

(c) the individual permanently ceases to carry on his trade of farming (see *Effect of cessation* below).

Conditions for election

For an individual to be entitled to make the election for 'income averaging' for a year of assessment, the following conditions must be met:

(a) the individual must have been charged to income tax *in respect of* his farming profits under Sch D Case I in accordance with the provisions of TCA 1997, s 65(1) for each of the two years of assessment immediately preceding that for which the election is made; and

(b) the individual must be a 'full-time farmer' throughout the year of assessment (see below).

'Full-time farmer' requirement

Condition (b) implies that the individual must *not* be any of the following (TCA 1997, s 657(1)):

(a) the individual who, at any time in that year of assessment, carries on any other trade or profession, whether solely or in partnership. Finance Act 2014 relaxed this condition to allow a trade which is ancillary to the trade of farming and which is carried on land used for the trade of farming;

(b) the individual whose spouse or civil partner, at any time in that year of assessment, carries on any other trade or profession, other than an ancillary trade as mentioned above whether solely or in partnership (but see below);

(c) the individual who is, at any time in that year of assessment, a 'proprietary' director (see below) of a company which carries on a trade or profession; and

(d) the individual whose spouse or civil partner is, at any time in that year of assessment, a 'proprietary' director of a company which carries on a trade or profession (but see below).

It is not, however, relevant to consider the position of the individual's spouse or civil partner (conditions (b) and (d)) unless husband and wife or civil partners are treated for income tax purposes as living together. For the circumstances in which a husband and wife are treated as living together for income tax purposes, see *Husband and wife living together* in **3.501**.

If the individual making the election is a single or widowed person, or if the individual and his spouse or civil partner is not living together, conditions (b) and (d) may be ignored. Note that conditions (b) and (d) must both be met where the individual and his spouse or civil partner are living together even though they may have elected for assessment as single persons.

By way of exception to condition (b) (where it is relevant), the individual's spouse or civil partner may, without failing that condition, carry on another trade which consists *solely* of the provision of accommodation in buildings on the farm land occupied by the individual, provided that the provision of such accommodation is ancillary to the farming of that farm land. For the purposes of conditions (c) and (d), a 'proprietary' director is a director who is either the beneficial owner of, or who is able to control, more than 25 per cent of the ordinary capital of the company carrying on the trade or profession. This control of more than 25 per cent of the ordinary capital of such a trading company may be held either directly, through one or more other companies, or by any other means. 'Ordinary share capital' is as defined in TCA 1997, s 2(1) as 'all the issued share capital (by whatever name called) of a company, other than capital the holders of which have a right to a dividend at a fixed rate but have no other right to share in the profits of the company'.

It is to be noted that the conditions for an individual being treated as a 'full-time farmer', so as to be entitled to make the income averaging election for a year of assessment, must be satisfied for the whole of that year. Failure by the individual or, where relevant, his spouse or civil partner, to satisfy any of the conditions for even a few days of the year of assessment is sufficient to prevent the election being made for that year.

However, while the two immediately preceding years of assessment have to be considered in relation to condition (a), the fact that the individual may not have been a 'full-time farmer' in either or both of the two preceding years does not prevent the individual making the election for a tax year if he is a full time farmer for the whole of the tax year for which the election is made.

For example, an individual may not have been a 'full-time farmer' for either 2011 or 2012 due to his wife carrying on a profession as a solicitor in those years. Assuming that all the other conditions for being a 'full time farmer' are met in 2013, should his wife retire from her professional practice before 1 January 2013, he becomes a 'full time farmer' for 2013. In this event, this individual may elect for income averaging for 2013 provided that he has been charged to tax on his farming profits under TCA 1997, s 65(1) for both 2011 and 2012 (ie condition (a) satisfied).

Example 7.109.1

Sarah Smith, who carries on a trade of farming, does not have any other trade or profession, but she is a director of Ten and Twelve Ltd, a company controlled by her father that carries on a retail trade. Sarah holds all the preference share capital in that company and is the beneficial owner of 22.5 per cent of its ordinary share capital.

Since Sarah (who is single) does not carry on any other trade or profession and since, although a director of Ten and Twelve Ltd, she does not beneficially own more than 25 per cent of its ordinary share capital, she is not 'an individual to whom sub-s (1) applies'.

On the assumption that all these facts stay the same for the whole of 2015, Sarah is a 'full-time farmer' for 2015 and is entitled to elect for income averaging for 2015.

Example 7.109.2

Same facts as in **Example 7.109.1**, except that Sarah gets married on 15 February 2015. Her husband, Paul, is an employee (but not a director) of a brewery company. He holds ordinary shares in a number of trading companies, including Three Ton Ltd in which he owns 28 per cent of the ordinary share capital. He is not a director of Three Ton Ltd, but is a director of Shortweight Ltd in which his beneficial holding of ordinary share capital is only 11 per cent thereof.

None of these facts about Paul's occupation, directorships or shareholdings breach any of the conditions relevant to Sarah's 'full-time farmer' status so that she remains entitled to make the election for income averaging for 2015.

Example 7.109.3

Same facts as the previous two examples, except that on 1 April 2015 Sarah's husband Paul joins a firm of accountants and commences to practise as a partner, having left his position with the brewery company.

Since her husband is now carrying on a profession in the tax year 2015 (even though only for a part of that year), Sarah has become 'an individual to whom sub-s (1) applies' and, therefore, is not 'full-time farmer' throughout 2015. She is not therefore entitled to make an election for income averaging for that year.

Four prior years of normal assessment

Condition (a) mentioned earlier has the effect that the election to start income averaging in a given tax year cannot be made unless the individual was charged to income tax in respect of his farming profits under TCA 1997, s 65(1) for the four tax years immediately preceding that for which the election for income averaging is made. Up until 1 January 2015 this had been two years. This means that the four preceding years must have been charged on the normal continuing business basis (see **4.204**).

This rules out an election for income averaging if any of the four preceding years the farmer was charged to tax under the rules of commencement under TCA 1997, s 66 (see **4.205**). In effect, this means that the earliest tax year for which income averaging may be elected after the commencement of a farming trade is the seventh (previously fifth) tax year of farming since assessments under TCA 1997, s 65(1) only start in the third tax year.

Example 7.109.4

Ms L Anders, who has not previously farmed, commences farming on 1 July 2011 and meets the conditions to be treated as a 'full time farmer'. She decides to make up accounts for her farming trade to 30 June in each year. She has taxable profits (before capital allowances) for her first six accounting years as follows:

	€
Y/E 30 June 2012	5,000
Y/E 30 June 2013	9,000
Y/E 30 June 2014	12,000
Y/E 30 June 2015	15,000
Y/E 30 June 2016	20,000
Y/E 30 June 2017	25,000

Applying the normal basis period rules for a commencement in 2011, her taxable profits (before capital allowances) for these opening years are charged as follows:

Rules of commencement	€
2011	
1st year of farming trade – TCA 1997, s 66(1)	
Period from 1 July 2011 to 31 December 2011 (actual) 5,000 x 6/12=	2,500
2012	
2nd year – TCA 1997, s 66(2)	
12-month period of account: Y/E 30 June 2012	5,000
2013	
3rd year – TCA 1997, s 65(1) Y/E 30 June 2013	9,000
2014	
4th year – TCA 1997, s 65(1) Y/E 30 June 2014	12,000
2015	
5th year – TCA 1997, s 65(1) Y/E 30 June 2015	15,000
2016	
6th year – TCA 1997, s 65(1) Y/E 30 June 2016	20,000
2017	
7th year – TCA 1997, s 65(1) Y/E 30 June 2017	25,000

Ms Anders is entitled to make an election for income averaging (if she wishes) for 2017 since her farming profits are charged to income tax under Sch D Case I under TCA 1997, s 65(1) for each of the four immediately preceding tax years (2013–2016).

She is not, however, entitled to make the income averaging election for any earlier tax year since condition (a) was not met before 2017.

It is to be noted that condition (a) requires that tax 'was charged' (rather than 'was chargeable') for the four preceding years. This appears to mean that an individual is not entitled to make an election for income averaging for a tax year if, due to having incurred a tax loss in any of the four preceding tax years, no tax was in fact charged in respect of any profits for any of the four preceding years. However, once the election has been made for any tax year after at least four years of taxable profits under TCA 1997, s 65(1), the fact that a tax loss is incurred in a subsequent year does not prevent income averaging from continuing to apply for that or later years (but see *Effect of losses* below). Similar considerations apply if profits are entirely eliminated by a deduction for stock relief, a point taken in a Revenue Precedent.

On the other hand, if there are taxable profits (before capital allowances) in each of the four preceding tax years, the fact that these taxable profits may be reduced to nil by capital allowances of the year in question, or by capital allowances or by a loss carried forward from a previous tax year, does not appear to prevent the income averaging election being made. This is because the taxable profits are charged to tax, but with the capital allowances or the relief for any loss carried forward being given as a set off in charging those profits to tax. Conversely, if there is a trading loss the fact that there is a balancing charge for the year will not enable the averaging election to be made, a point taken in a Revenue Precedent.

Example 7.109.5

Mr W Boar has been carrying on a farming trade for a number of years being charged to tax based on his farming profits earned in his 12-month periods of accounts ending on 30

November in each tax year – ie without any election for income averaging. He meets the conditions to be a 'full-time' farmer.

Mr Boar's adjusted Sch D Case I profits or loss (before capital allowances) and his capital allowances for recent years are noted as follows:

	Profits/(loss)	*Capital allowances*
	€	€
12 months to 30 November 2011	(1,050)	3,335
12 months to 30 November 2012	2,460	3,005
12 months to 30 November 2013	19,880	2,300
12 months to 30 November 2014	34,600	2,170
12 months to 30 November 2015	35,000	3,000
12 months to 30 November 2016	40,000	3,500

Mr Boar thought that he would like to elect for income averaging for 2015 (normal basis period being the 12 months to 30 November 2015) and requested advice from his tax consultant. However, the latter advised him that he could not make any election for 2015 because he was not charged to tax in respect of farming profits for all of the previous four years due to the loss of €1,050 in the 12 months to 30 November 2011 (basis period for 2011).

Mr Boar is, however, entitled to elect for income averaging for 2016 since:

(1) he was charged to income tax for 2012 in respect of his farming profits of €2,460 earned in the 12 months to 30 November 2012 (even though the capital allowances reduced the assessment to nil), and

(2) he was charged to income tax for 2013–2015 in respect of his farming profits, (ie for all of the four preceding tax years).

Effect of election

When an individual, with conditions (a) and (b) both met, has elected to apply income averaging for the taxation of his farming profits for a given year of assessment (the year of the election), the consequences are as follows:

(a) the assessment under Sch D Case I for the year of the election in respect of the individual's farming profits is made on the average of the taxable profits from farming in the five years ending on the date in the year of the election to which it has been customary to make up accounts (TCA 1997, s 657(5)); and

(b) the assessment for each subsequent year of assessment must also be based on average of the taxable profits from farming in the five years ending on the relevant accounting date in the subsequent year (TCA 1997, s 657(6)).

For example, if an individual has made an election to be assessed under income averaging for the tax year 2016, and if the farming accounts are customarily made up to 30 April, then the 2016 income averaged assessment is made on the one year's average of the taxable profits from farming of the five years ending respectively 30 April 2012, 2013, 2014, 2015 and 2016.

It then follows that the income averaged assessment for the next tax year 2017 must be based on the one year's average of the taxable profits from farming of the five years ending 30 April 2013, 2014, 2015, 2016, and 2017. Should there be a change of accounting date, say in 2017 by having accounts made up to, say, 30 June 2017, the 2017 assessment would be based on the average taxable profits for the five years ended 30 June 2017.

Finance Act 2014 introduced transitional measures for the change from three to five years Where an individual is first charged to tax in relation to income averaging for the year of assessment 2014 then the individual shall be charged to tax in 2015 on the basis of four years of income averaging rather than five as they would not otherwise qualify as they would not be in their fifth year of income averaging.

Similarly transitional measures are incorporated for those farmers who elect to opt out of income averaging in 2015 and 2016. In 2015 a farmer can opt out provided he has been averaging for three years and in 2016 a farmer can opt out provided he has been averaging for four years, TCA 1997, s 657(7A) inserted by Finance Act 2014, s 20(a)(vi).

Taxable profits for averaging

The taxable profits from farming to be averaged, whether the average is being taken for the year of the election or for a subsequent tax year, are the adjusted Sch D Case I profits (or, if relevant, any tax losses), before considering any capital allowances or balancing charges (but after any stock relief adjustment). This involves making a normal Sch D Case I computation for each period of account falling within the period of five years ended on the relevant accounting date. If any period for which accounts are made up falls partly within and partly outside the five-year averaging period, then only the appropriate proportion of the adjusted profits of that period is brought into the averaging calculation.

Where it has not been customary to make up accounts, the five-year look back period will end on 31 December in the year of assessment where no accounts are made up to a date in the year of assessment (TCA 1997, s 657(5)(a)).

Example 7.109.6

Mr A Carrott, a farmer meeting all the conditions, makes an election for income averaging for the tax year 2015. He had previously made up his farming accounts to 30 June, but changed his accounting date to 31 August with a 14-month period of account from 1 July 2013 to 31 August 2014.

Mr Carrott's taxable profits (before capital allowances) for the periods of account relevant to the income averaging calculation for 2015 are as follows:

Accounting period	€
12 months ended 30 June 2012	12,000
12 months ended 30 June 2013	13,000
14 months ended 31 August 2014	8,400
12 months ended 31 August 2015	21,500

Sch D Case I assessments (before capital allowances) for 2011, 2012, 2013, 2014 and 2015 (without income averaging) are:

	€
2011	
On 12 months to 30/6/2011	10,200
2012:	
12 months to 31/6/2012	12,000

2013	
12 months to 31/6/13	13,000
2014	
14 months to 31/8/2014 = €8,400, therefore 12/14 x €8,400	7,200
2015:	
12 months to 31/8/2015	21,500

The income averaging computation, for the amendment of the 2015 assessment, requires the average of the taxable profits for the five years commencing 1 September 2010 and ending 31 August 2015. In view of the change of accounting date, only 10 months of the profits of the 12 months ended 30 June 2011 is taken into the averaging calculation.

The calculation of the income averaged profits to be assessed (before capital allowances) for 2015 is as follows:

	€
Taxable profits of 5 years ended 31/8/2015:	
10 months from 1/9/2010 to 30/6/2011	
12 months to 30/6/12	12,000
12 months to 30/6/13	13,000
14 months from 1/7/2013 to 31/8/2014	8,400
12 months ended 31/8/2015	21,500
Total	63,400
Average for one year:	12,680

The Sch D Case I farming profits assessed for 2015 assessment is therefore reduced from the original (non-averaged) figure of €21,500 to €12,680. As indicated below, capital allowances are dealt with independently of the income averaging rules.

Treatment of capital allowances and charges

TCA 1997, s 657(9) provides that capital allowances and balancing charges are to be dealt with separately without any averaging. The capital allowances to be allowed, and any balancing charges to be included, in the assessment for any tax year are determined in all respects as if the individual remained chargeable in respect of his farming profits in accordance with the provisions of TCA 1997, s 65(1).

In other words, although the income tax assessment for a tax year may be based on the averaged profits of a five-year period ending in that tax year, the basis period by reference to which the capital allowances rules are applied remains the same period of 12 months ended in that tax year which would be the basis period for assessing the profits if income averaging did not apply. When ascertained, the capital allowances for any tax year are given in charging the individual's Sch D Case I farming profits resulting from the averaging calculation for that year; similarly, any balancing charges for the tax year are added to the averaged profits.

Example 7.109.7

Mrs OT Barley has been carrying on a farming trade making up accounts to 31 December. Up to the tax year 2011, she did not meet the conditions for being a 'full time farmer' for income averaging due to her husband carrying on trade as a butcher. He died on 31 December 2010 and his business passed to their two sons. Mrs Barley becomes a 'full time farmer' for 2011 (she does not acquire any interest in the butcher's business).

On 24 August 2017, Mrs Barley makes her tax return for 2016 (including details of her farming profits and related capital allowances) for the year ended 31 December 2016). On 18 September 2017, the inspector assesses her to income tax for 2016 including her farming profits charged under Sch D Case I for the year ended 31 December 2016.

Mrs Barley notes that the farming taxable profits (after stock relief) and her capital allowances for 2016, and those for the previous four tax years, are as follows:

Basis period	*Tax year*	*Taxable profits*	*Capital allowances*
		€	€
	2011	11,420	1,370
Year to 31/12/2012	2012	12,000	1,500
Year to 31/12/2013	2013	13,000	2,000
Year to 31/12/2014	2014	4,500	2,000
Year to 31/12/2015	2015	7,350	2,480
Year to 31/12/2016	2016	29,420	3,600

On receipt of the assessment, Mrs Barley is disturbed about the much higher tax about to be payable for 2016 due to the large increase in profits in the year ended 31 December 2016, she asks her tax consultant for advice. The latter recommends that, having regard to the above figures, Mrs Barley should elect for income averaging under TCA 1997, s 657, but warns her that this will mean that she will be assessed also under income averaging for at least the next four years (2017, 2018, 2019 and 2020).

Mrs Barley writes to the inspector on 16 October 2017 (just within the 30 days after the date of the inspector's assessment) giving notice that she is electing for income averaging for 2016. Instead of the original Sch D Case I assessment for 2016 on taxable profits of €29,420 reduced by capital allowances (net of balancing charges) of €3,600 to an assessment on a net €25,820, the income averaging calculation is made to give an amended Sch D Case I assessment 2016 on a net €9,654, arrived at as follows:

	€
Taxable profits	
Year to 31/12/2012	12,000
Year to 31/12/2013	13,000
Year to 31/12/2014	4,500
Year to 31/12/2015	7,350
Year to 31/12/2016	29,420
Aggregate profits	66,270
One year's average	13,254
Less: Capital allowances 2016	(3,600)
Net Sch D Case I Farming income	9,654

Effect of losses

TCA 1997, s 657(5) (b) provides that, if the result of the Sch D Case I computation (before capital allowances) for any one or more periods of account falling within the five year averaging period is a tax loss or losses, the amount of that loss (or those losses) is to be deducted from the aggregate of the taxable profits of the other periods of account in the averaging period. If the aggregate for the five years after deducting any such loss or losses is a net taxable profit, the one year's average of that profit is the amount assessable for the relevant tax year.

In the event that the aggregate of the taxable profits and the tax loss(es) in the five year averaging period is an aggregate net loss, ie an excess of loss(es) over taxable profits, there is a nil tax assessment for the tax year for which the averaging is made. It is then necessary to consider the question of loss relief in respect of the aggregate net loss.

TCA 1997, s 657(11) deals with the question of loss relief. It provides that the amount of tax loss eligible for loss relief is restricted to an amount equal to one-fifth of the aggregate net loss. Where the year of assessment 2014 was the first year of averaging the restriction is one-fourth. This one-fifth of the aggregate net loss is then treated as if it were a trading loss sustained in the last of the five years of the averaging period. This one fifth of the aggregate net loss may be referred to as the 'averaged loss'.

Relief for the averaged loss attributed to the last of the five years may be claimed under any of the ordinary loss relief rules for a trading loss incurred in that year. It may, for example, be set off in a claim under TCA 1997, s 381 against the individual's income from all sources for that year. Alternatively, it is available for carry forward under TCA 1997, s 382 for set off against the individual's farming income in the next tax year (and later years).

The remaining four fifths of the aggregate net loss are not eligible for any form of loss relief under any of the provisions of the Income Tax Acts. Further, any loss in any of the five years in the averaging period which is aggregated with profits in the averaging calculation does not qualify for any of the loss reliefs.

Example 7.109.8

Mr R Silage, a farmer who first elected for income averaging for 2010 has the following Sch D Case I profits and losses (before capital allowances) in the respective three-year periods relevant for his 2015, 2016 and 2017 income averaging computations:

Year ended	*2015*	*2016*	*2017*
	€	€	€
31/12/2011 – profit	13,000		
31/12/2012 – (loss)	(8,400)	(8,400)	
31/12/2013 – (loss)	(7,900)	(7,900)	(7,900)
31/12/2014 – profit	11,000	11,000	11,000
31/12/2015 loss	(12,000)	(12,000)	(12,000)
31/12/2016 – loss	(9000)	(9,000)	
31/12/2017 – profit			50,000
Aggregate net profit/(loss) for 5 years	(4,300)	(26,300)	32,100
Average profit/(loss)			
1/5 of aggregate	(860)	(5,260)	6,420

Mr Silage's assessments for the three tax years (before capital allowances) are as follows:

	€
2015:	
Sch D Case I – averaged profits/(losses)	Nil
Deemed tax loss for year to 31/12/2015	(860)

2016:	
Sch D Case I – averaged profits/(losses)	Nil
Deemed tax loss for year to 31/12/2016	(5,260)
2017:	
Sch D Case I – averaged profits/(losses)	6,420

Use of averaged losses

In the tax year 2015, Mr Silage had a substantial amount of Sch D Case V income from rented property. He is entitled, if he wishes, to claim under TCA 1997, s 381 (see **4.404**) to set off the €860 averaged loss for 2015 against his income from all sources for that year. He decides to make this claim and thereby obtains full relief for the whole of that averaged loss.

In the tax year 2016, Mr Silage decides not make any claim under TCA 1997, s 381 in respect of the averaged loss of €5,260 attributed to 2016. He is therefore entitled to carry forward the €5,260 averaged loss for 2016 to be set off under TCA 1997, s 382 against his future assessable profits from his farming trade (see **4.402**).

In the tax year 2017, Mr Silage sets off the €5,260 loss brought forward from 2016 against his averaged profits for that year as follows:

	€
Averaged profits for 2017	6,420
Deduct:	
Capital allowances 2017 (say)	(,600)
	5,820
Deduct:	
Averaged loss for 2016 brought forward	(5,260)
Net Sch D Case I assessment 2017	560

Notes:

1. Apart from the loss reliefs available for the averaged losses shown above, no other loss relief may be claimed for any part of the losses of €8,400, €7,900, €12,000 and €9,000 actually incurred respectively in the tax years 2012 2013, 2015 and 2016.

Effect of cessation

TCA 1997, s 657(10) provides that the cessation rules of TCA 1997, s 67 must be applied in the normal way where the individual's trade of farming is permanently discontinued, even though an income averaging election may still be in force. From 2008 onwards, TCA 1997, s 657(10A) was inserted by FA 2008, s 15 and provides that an exception applies where the permanent discontinuation of a trade is attributable to the commencement of a milk production partnership to which European Communities (Milk Quota) (Amendment) Regulations 2002 (SI 97/2002) applies. In this case, the milk production partnership trade shall be treated as a continuation of that other trade for the purposes only of the income-averaging provisions. This was amended in FA 2015, s 19(2)(a) by replacing the reference to 'European Communities (Milk Quota) (Amendment) Regulations 2002 (SI 97/2002)' with a reference to TCA 1997, s 667C.

Consequently, if the individual permanently ceases to carry on any farming activities in the State in a given tax year for the purposes of TCA 1997, s 657, the Sch D Case I cessation rules are applied. The Sch D Case I assessment for the tax year in which the cessation occurs must be based on the actual profits of that year in the period from the first day of the year of assessment to the date of cessation. The profits assessed for the year of the cessation can never be income-averaged profits.

For the tax year preceding the year of the cessation (the penultimate year), TCA 1997, s 67(1)(a)(ii) applies to require the Sch D Case I assessment to be increased, if necessary, to tax the actual taxable profits earned in the penultimate year. However, if the taxable profits which would have been taxable for that year (the original profits) if there had not been a cessation are higher than the actual taxable profits of the penultimate year, then the assessment for the penultimate year remains on the original profits (the income averaged profits).

In other words, where income averaging is in place for the penultimate year, the amount assessable (subject to capital allowances) for the penultimate year is the higher of:

(a) the one year's average of the taxable profits of the five years ending on the relevant accounting date in the penultimate year; and

(b) the actual taxable profits of the penultimate year ending at the last day of the tax year.

Example 7.109.9

Ms H Hedges is a farmer making up accounts to 30 June each year. As the result of an election for income averaging made for the tax year 2011, she was assessed on the income averaging basis from 2011, 2012, 2013, 2014 and 2015 (not necessary to give the details for this example).

Her income averaging calculation of her farming profits (before capital allowances) assessable for 2015 is made on the figures given below, as follows:

Aggregate profits of 5 years ended 30/6/2015:	€
Y/E 30/6/2011	
Taxable profits	12,000
Y/E 30/6/2012	
Tax loss	(2,400)
Y/E 30/6/2013	
Taxable profits	2,000
Y/E 30/6/2014	
Taxable profits	15,000
Y/E 30/6/2015	
Taxable profits	5,500
Net taxable profits for averaging period (5 years)	32,100
Average for one year:	
€32,100 ÷ 5 =	6,420

Based on this computation, Ms Hedges would be assessed for 2015 on farming profits of €6,420, but subject to the deduction in respect of her capital allowances for 2015.

However, Ms Hedges dies on 15 May 2016, thereby causing her farming trade to cease on that date. Apart from requiring a new basis for her assessment for 2016 (year of cessation), her assessment for 2015 (now the penultimate year of the trade) based on income averaging has to be reviewed.

The executors have the final accounts of Ms Hedges' farming trade prepared for the period from 1 July 2015 to 15 May 2016 (a 10.5-month period). The Sch D Case I computation based on those accounts results in taxable profits (before capital allowances) of €3,300.

2016 Final year's assessment

The taxable profits assessable for 2016 are the actual profits earned from 1 January 2016 to 15 May 2016:

	€
4.5 months/10.5 months[1] x €3,300 =	1,414

Income averaging has no application and the normal rule of assessing the final year under TCA 1997, s 67(1) is applied.

2015 Penultimate year's assessment

	€	€
Higher of:		
(1) Taxable profits under income averaging as computed above		6,420
And		
(2) Actual profits for year from 1/1/2015 to 31/12/2015		
Period 1/1/2015 to 30/6/2015		
6/12 months[2] x €5,500 =	2,750	
Period 1/7/2015 to 31/12/2015		
6 months/10.5 months[3] x €3,300 =	1,886	
		4,636

Since the actual taxable profits of the penultimate year 2015 (€4,636) do not exceed the amount calculated originally under income averaging (€6,420), Ms Hedges remains taxable on the original amount calculated under income averaging.

Notes:

1. The final period of account from 1/7/2015 to 15/5/2016 is for 10.5 months (10 months, 15 days), but only 4.5 months (4 months, 15 days) of this period fall into the final tax year 2016.
2. The proportion of the taxable profits of the 12 months ended 30/6/2015 attributed to 2015 is that represented by the 6 months from 1/1/2015 to 30/6/2015.
3. The proportion of the taxable profits of the 10.5-month period ended 15 May 2016 attributed to 2015 is that represented by the 6 months from 1/7/2015 to 31/12/2015.

Where the deceased farmer's spouse or civil partner takes over the entire farming trade, then the Revenue are prepared not to apply the usual cessation and commencement provisions if the surviving spouse or surviving civil partner wishes to avail of this concession. If he does so, then the averaging of profits may also continue without any need for revision (*Tax Briefing 9*).

Individual farming as sole trader and in partnership

Where an individual who is farming as a sole trader commences to trade in a partnership that is itself just commencing, then notwithstanding that the individual is treated as carrying on a single trade of farming, the Sch D Commencement provisions will apply in respect of the partnership profits. Arguably, the fact that the individual is not taxed under TCA 1997, s 65(1) in respect of *some* of his farming profits (ie instead under TCA 1997, s 66, in relation to his partnership profits) would disqualify him from availing of income averaging in relation to *all* of his farming profits, in view of the wording of TCA 1997, s 657(4)(b). However, the Revenue Commissioners have issued a precedent to the effect that in these circumstances income averaging will continue to be granted in relation to the 'sole trade' profits and will be extended to the partnership profits once they have been subject to the rules of TCA 1997, s 65(1) for the requisite two years.

7.110 Opting out of income averaging

Once an individual, meeting the conditions, has made an income averaging election for a year of assessment (eg 2012), he must continue to be taxed under income averaging for that year and at least the next two tax years (eg 2013 and 2014). In fact, subject to certain exceptions, the income averaging continues indefinitely unless and until the individual makes a specific election under TCA 1997, s 657(7) to opt out of income averaging so as to be taxed normally again on the profits of a single year.

TCA 1997, s 657(7) permits an individual to opt out of income averaging if he has been taxed under income averaging for at least five years of assessment (including the year for which the income averaging election was made). Please note transitional rules included in TCA 1997, s 657(7A). In order to opt out of income averaging for a particular year of assessment (the 'opting out year'), the individual who has been assessed under income averaging for the five previous years of assessment must include a claim with his income tax return for that year of assessment of an election to revert to being taxed normally in accordance with the provisions of TCA 1997, s 65(1) on the profits of a single year.

Effect of opting out election

When an individual exercises his right under TCA 1997, s 657(7) to opt out of income averaging for a year of assessment (the opting out year), TCA 1997, s 657(8), as amended by Finance Act 2014, provides that the following consequences ensue:

(a) the individual becomes taxable on his farming profits for the opting out year on the normal single year basis in accordance with TCA 1997, Pt 4 Ch 3 (ie without income averaging);

(b) the individual is also taxable for each subsequent tax year on the normal single year basis; and

(c) the assessments for each of the first four of the five years of assessment immediately preceding the opting out year must be increased, if it is necessary, so that the amount of profits finally assessed for each of the first four of the five preceding years is not less than the income averaged profits assessed for the last of the five preceding years. This look back of six years overrides the normal four-year look back in TCA 1997, s 959AA in relation to revenue assessments.

The references in (c) to the profits assessed and to profits finally assessed are references to taxable profits before deducting any capital allowances and before adding any balancing charges. In the event that the profits already assessed for any or all of the first four of the five years are greater than the income averaged profits of the fifth of the years, the higher figures already assessed remain the final assessable profits. In all opting out cases, the profits assessed for the fifth of the five preceding years remain the income averaged profits of the five years ended on the relevant accounting date in that fifth year.

Example 7.110.1

Mr C Butterman is a farmer making up accounts to 30 September each year who has been taxed under income averaging since 2011. His income averaged profits assessed for the years 2012, 2013, 2014, 2015, 2016 and 2017 and his capital allowances and balancing charges for each of those years have been as follows:

	2012	*2013*	*2014*	*2015*	*2016*	*2017*
	€	€	€	€	€	€
Y/E 30/09/2010	6,900					
Y/E 30/09/2011	9,300	9,300		9,300		
Y/E 30/09/2012	27,300	27,300	27,300	27,300	27,300	
Y/E 30/09/2013		19,200	19,200	19,200	19,200	19,200
Y/E 30/09/2014			7,500	7,500	7,500	7,500
Y/E 30/09/2015				10,000	10,000	10,000
Y/E 30/09/2016					12,000	12,000
Y/E 30/09/2017 Loss						(6,600)
Aggregate net profits for 3 or 5 years	43,500	55,800	54,000	73,300	76,000	42,100
Assessable profits: One year's average	14,500	18,600	18,000	14,660	15,200	8,420
Capital allowances	6,000	3,660	4,800	5,000	5,250	120

Mr Butterman's Sch D Case I computation for the 12 months ended 30 September 2017 results in an adjusted loss of €6,600 in the farming trade and he is entitled to capital allowances for 2017 of €120. If he continues with income averaging, his 2017 assessment (before capital allowances) would be as follows:

2017 Profits of averaging period	€
Y/E 30/09/2013	19,200
Y/E 30/09/2014	7,500
Y/E 30/09/2015	10,000
Y/E 30/09/2016	12,000
Y/E 30/09/2017 (loss)	(6,600)
Aggregate net profits for 5 years	42,100
One year's average (amount assessable)	8,420

Despite the loss of €6,600 in the 2017 tax year he will be assessed on an income averaged profit of €8,420 and will get no immediate relief for any part of the loss. He therefore decides that on filing his tax return for 2017 to elect under TCA 1997, s 657(7) to opt out of income averaging for 2017 and subsequent years. In consequence of this election, his position for 2017 will be as follows:

	€
Sch D Case I	
Profits of year to 30/09/2017	Nil
Tax loss as incurred in year to 31/12/2017	6,600

This loss is set off against his other income for the year in a claim under TCA 1997, s 381.

The further consequence of the opting out election is that the five preceding years (2012–2016) are reviewed to see if any revisions are required to the assessments of the first four of these years. Mr Butterman's averaged profits for 2016 were €15,200 before capital allowances. The effect on 2012–2015 is as follows:

	€
2012:	
Sch D Case I profits (averaged)	14,500
Increase the amount assessed to	15,200
Deduct:	
Capital allowances 2012 (as before)	6,000
Final revised assessment for 2012	9,200
2013:	
Sch D Case I profits (income averaged)	18,600
No change since this exceeds income averaged profits for 2016 (€15,200)	
Deduct:	
Capital allowances 2013 (as before)	3,660
Final assessment for 2013 (as before)	14,940
2014	
Sch D Case I profits (income averaged)	18,000
No change since this exceeds income averaged profits for 2016 (€15,200)	
Deduct:	
Capital allowances 2014 (as before)	4,800
Final assessment for 2014 (as before)	13,200
2015	
Sch D Case I profits (income averaged)	14,660
Final revised assessment for 2015	10,200
Capital allowances 2015 (as before)	5,000
Deduct:	15,200
Increase the amount assessed to	15,200

Effect of ceasing to be 'full-time farmer'

It has been pointed out in **7.109** that only an individual who is a 'full-time farmer' in the year of election is entitled to make an election for income averaging. If the individual who has made the income averaging election ceases to be a 'full-time farmer' in any subsequent tax year, TCA 1997, s 657(7) deems him or her to have made an opting out election for that year. Consequently, the individual concerned immediately ceases to be entitled to average his farming profits, whether or not he has had five previous tax years of income averaging.

Example 7.110.2

Ms Rose Oliver, who makes up accounts of her farm trade to 30 November each year, met all the conditions to be a 'full-time farmer' throughout the tax year 2013 and she elected for income averaging for that year. She continued as a 'full-time farmer' throughout the tax year 2014 so that income averaging was also applicable for that year.

Ms Oliver was married on 21 April 2015 to Peter Twist who is a partner in a firm of architects. Since her husband carries on a profession, the new Mrs Twist has ceased to be a 'full-time farmer' within the definition given in **7.109**.

Consequently, Mrs Twist is deemed by TCA 1997, s 657(7) to have made an election to opt out of income averaging with effect from 2015 (the deemed opting out year). Her farming profits must therefore be taxed again in accordance with TCA 1997, Pt 4 Ch 3 on the normal single year basis for 2015 and subsequent years. (Note previous commentary on transitional arrangements for opt out of averaging in 2015 and 2016 as a result of amendments in Finance Act 2014).

When an individual is deemed to have made an opting out election for the year in which the conditions for full-time farmer status cease to be met, TCA 1997, s 657(8) applies in the same way as for an actual opting out election. In other words, the individual is taxed again on the normal single year basis for the deemed opting out year and subsequent tax years and, in addition, the assessments for each of the first four of the five tax years preceding the deemed opting out year must be increased, where necessary, so that the amount of profits assessed for each of these four years is not less than the income averaged profits assessed for the last of the five preceding years.

In the case of such a deemed (or 'involuntary') opting out election, any or all of the first four of the five tax years preceding the deemed opting out year may or may not be years for which income averaging applied. For example, if an individual elected for income averaging for 2013 but then lost full-time farmer status in 2017 (the deemed opting out year), income averaging will only have applied to four of the five years preceding the deemed opting out year and the first of these five preceding years (2012) will have been taxed without income averaging.

However, whether or not the first four of the five preceding years was an income averaging year, it remains necessary to make any necessary adjustment to ensure that the final amount assessed (before capital allowances) for each of the four years is not less than the income averaged assessment for the last of the five preceding years.

It should be noted that, although the cessation of the farming trade brings income averaging to an end, the opting out rule of TCA 1997, s 657(8) requiring a review and, where necessary, a revision of the assessments for the first four of the five preceding tax years does not apply. However, as already indicated under *Effect of cessation* in **7.109**, the normal rules of TCA 1997, s 67(1) may require an amendment to the profits assessed for the penultimate year of farming and always assess the final year on the actual profits.

Example 7.110.3

Take the facts of **Example 7.109.7** where Mrs OT Barley elected for income averaging for the tax year 2016. Her Sch D Case I assessments on farming profits (before capital allowances) for that year and the four previous tax years may be restated here as follows:

2012:	€
Year to 31/12/2012	12,000
2013:	
Year to 31/12/2013	13,000
2014:	
Year to 31/12/2014	4,500
2015:	
Year to 31/12/2015	7,350
2016:	
Year to 31/12/2016	29,420

2016:	
Income averaged profits 5 years to 31/12/2016	13,254

Assume that Mrs Barley remarries on 2 March 2017 and that her husband is a director of a company carrying on a trade as undertakers and that he is the beneficial owner of 33 per cent (more than 25 per cent) of the ordinary share capital of that company. This breaches one of the conditions for full-time farmer status so that Mrs Barley is deemed to have opted out of income averaging for 2017 (and subsequent years).

Mrs Barley's taxable profits (before capital allowances) for the year ended 31 December 2017 are €35,000. The assessment for 2017 is therefore made on this single year's figure (instead of the income averaged assessment of €17,854 which would have applied if she had not remarried).

In addition, TCA 1997, s 657(8) requires the assessments for the first four of the five tax years preceding 2017 to be reviewed. Since the amounts previously assessed for each of these four years (2012 and 2015) are less than the €13,254 income averaged profits for 2016, the assessments for each of those four years must be increased to €13,254.

The final assessments on farming profits (before capital allowances) for the six years may be summarised as follows:

	€
2017:	
Profits year to 31/12/2017	35,000[1]
2016:	
Income averaged profits	13,254
2015:	
Original assessment €7,350 increased to	13,254
2014:	
Original assessment on €4,500 increased to	13,254
2013:	
Original assessment on €13,000 increased to	13,254
Original assessment on €12,000 increased to	13,254
Aggregate assessed for 6 tax years[2]	101,270

Notes:

1. The income averaged assessment for 2017 would have been:

   €13,000 + 4,500 + 7,350 + 29,420 + 35,000 ÷ 5 = €17,854.

2. The effect of the income averaging has, in this case, been cancelled out by the adjustments to the 2012 and 2017 assessments. This €101,270 aggregate of the six years' assessments compares with the amounts which would have been assessed if no election at all had been made:

	€
Year to 31 December 2012	12,000
Year to 31 December 2013	13,000
Year to 31 December 2014	4,500
Year to 31 December 2015	7,350
Year to 31 December 2016	29,420

Year to 31 December 2017	35,000
	101,270

New election for income averaging (after opting out)

An individual who has been taxed under the income averaging rules, but who has later opted out, may subsequently elect again for income averaging, but only after his farming profits have been assessed under TCA 1997, s 65(1) for at least four tax years before that for which the later election for income averaging is made. Similarly, an individual who was deemed to have opted out due to losing full time farmer status may, if he becomes a full time farmer again, re-elect for income averaging after a minimum of four years taxed on the normal single year basis.

Temporary opt-out

For the 2016 year of assessment and subsequent years, farmers can opt out of income averaging for election to defer the tax due under the income averaging rules and pay tax based on their actual income for that year. The tax deferred must be paid in four equal instalments.

'Deferred tax' is defined in TCA 1997, s 657(1) as the amount of income tax determined by the formula—

$$A - B$$

where—

A is the amount of income tax which would, apart from sub-s (6A), be charged on an individual by virtue of income averaging in respect of a year of assessment, and

B is the amount of income tax which would, apart from this section, be chargeable in accordance with TCA 1997, Ch 3 of Pt 4 (being the income tax basis of assessment under Cases I and II) in respect of a year of assessment;

TCA 1997, s 657(6A), as inserted by FA 2016, s 18, allows the farmer to elect to defer payment of the deferred tax for that year of assessment. Where an individual duly elects in accordance in respect of a year of assessment, the deferred tax in respect of the year of assessment shall be payable in four equal instalments. The first instalment of the four instalments is due and payable on or before the specified return date for the chargeable period of the year of assessment following the year of assessment in which the election is made and the remaining three instalments shall be due and payable respectively on or before each of the following three anniversaries of the date on which the first instalment was due and payable. Critically, an individual is only entitled to make an election in accordance with this subsection in a year of assessment provided an election has not been made in any of the four years of assessment immediately preceding such year of assessment. Further, notwithstanding TCA 1997, s 959AA, there shall be made such assessment or assessments, if any, as may be necessary to secure the payment of any deferred tax which remains due and payable.

7.111 Restructuring aid for sugar beet growers

A farmer who is in receipt of a 'specified payment' may elect that all such payments which would otherwise be taken into account for a particular tax year under Sch D Case I should instead be disregarded for that tax year and be treated as arising in five equal instalments in the tax year concerned and the following four tax years (TCA 1997, s 657B(2), (3)). A 'specified payment' is a payment made to a farmer under the EU temporary scheme for the restructuring of the sugar industry in the Community, operated by the Department of Agriculture and Food under any of Articles 3(6) first indent, Article 6 or Article 7 of Council Regulation (EC) No 320/2006 as amended by Council Regulation EC 1261/2007 (TCA 1997, s 657B(1) as substituted by FA 2008, s 20). A farmer who is availing of income averaging in the tax ycar concerned will be entitled to make the election.

The election for this spreading treatment must be made on or before the tax return filing date eg for 2014, by 31 October 2015; the election is to be in a form prescribed by the Revenue Commissioners (TCA 1997, s 657B(2), (5)). The election may not be altered or varied during the period to which it relates (TCA 1997, s 657B(6)). Where an individual ceases to trade as a farmer, the amount of any relevant payments which would otherwise be treated as arising in any tax years following the tax year of discontinuance will be charged to tax under Sch D Case IV in the tax year of discontinuance (TCA 1997, s 657B(4)).

Example 7.111.1

Svetla Green has carried on a trade of farming in for many years, making accounts up to 31 December. She has not elected for income averaging. In the accounts year ended 31 October 2009, she receives specified payments of €50,000. She makes the election under TCA 1997, s 657B, ultimately with the following results:

	AP to				
	31/10/2009	*31/10/2010*	*31/10/2011*	*31/10/2012*	*31/10/2013*
	€	€	€		
Case I profits/(loss) (before election)	92,500	83,200	75,770	98,300	75.900
Less:					
'Relevant Payments'	(50,000)	-	-		
Add: Instalments	10, 000	10,000	10,000	10,000	10,000
Revised Case I profits	52,500	93,200	85,770	108,300	85,900

Example 7.111.2

Take the facts of **Example 7.111.1** but assume now that Ms Green ceases to trade on 31 March 2010, and made profits of € 19,600 in her final accounting period before taking into account the spreading of income under TCA 1997, s 657B. The results will be as follows:

		AP to
	31/10/2009	*31/3/2010*
	€	€
Case I profits/(loss) (before election)	92,500	19,600
Less:		
'Relevant Payments'	(50,000)	-
Add: Instalments	10,000	10,000
Revised Case I profits	52,500	29,600

In addition, an assessment on the balance of the relevant payments which would otherwise have been included in taxable farming profits in subsequent tax years *viz* €30,000 (€10,000 in 2011, 2012 and 2013) was raised under Sch D Case IV in 2010.

7.112 Succession farm partnerships

TCA 1997, s 667D was enacted by FA 2015, s 19 and is due to come into operation by Ministerial Order. It provides that each partner in that partnership shall be entitled to a tax credit (to be known as the 'succession tax credit') of the lesser amount of—(i) €5,000 per year of assessment divided between the partners in accordance with their profit sharing ratio under their partnership agreement, or (ii) the assessable profits (after deducting any capital allowances related to that trade) of that partner's several trade. This credit is for the year of assessment in which the farm partnership is registered as a succession farm partnership and the four years of assessment immediately following that year of assessment. The purposes of this relief is to encourage succession such that a clawback of the credit applies if the respective assets are not transferred within 10 years of making the application for the register the partnership as a succession farm partnership.

A primary participant (as defined in s 667C(1) for the purposes of TCA 1997, s 667D as meaning the precedent partner within the meaning of TCA 1997, s 1007) in relation to a 'registered farm partnership' (see discussion earlier regarding TCA 1997, s 667C) may apply to the Minister to also enter the registered farm partnership on the register of succession farm partnerships established and maintained under and in accordance with TCA 1997, s 667D and related regulations and shall comply with all requirements relating to the application so specified. So the partnership will appear on both registers as a result. In order to be entered on the register of succession farm partnerships, a registered farm partnership shall comply with all of the following conditions:

(a) subject to sub-ss (3) and (4), the farm partnership shall have at least two members, each of whom shall be a natural person. Subsections (3) and (4) look at owning assets jointly and the involvement of spouses and civil partners as part of the succession farm partnership.

(b) of the members of the farm partnership—
   (i) at least one shall be a person who has been engaged in the trade of farming on farm land owned or leased by that person, consisting of at least three hectares of useable farm land, for at least two years immediately preceding the date of formation of the partnership (the 'farmer'), and
   (ii) of the others, each member shall not yet have reached 40 years of age and has a qualification in agriculture specified in regulations or, if not so specified a qualification determined by Teagasc – the Agriculture and Food Development Authority, to the satisfaction of the Minister, as being equivalent to a qualification so specified, and under the terms of the farm partnership, holds an entitlement to at least 20 per cent of the profits of the partnership; ('successor'),

(c) the business plan of the farm partnership shall have been submitted to, and approved by, the Minister,

(d) subject to sub-s (3)(a), the farmer shall enter an agreement with one or more than one of the successors to transfer or sell at least 80 per cent of the farm assets to which the farm partnership applies, to the successor, or successors, at a time during the period beginning 3 years after and ending 10 years after the date that the application is made under subsection (1), and

(e) the terms of the partnership agreement shall include—

(i) the farm assets of the farm partnership on the day that the application is made as discussed above,

(ii) any conditions to which the transfer or sale will be subject,

(iii) the year in which the proposed transfer may take place, and

(iv) any other terms agreed between the farmer and successor, or successors, including in relation to the farm assets, the conduct of the farming trade or the creation of any rights of residence in dwellings on the farm land.

TCA 1997, s 667D(1) states that it is the precedent partner in a registered farm partnership is to make the application to register the 'registered farm partnership' (as defined in TCA 1997, s 667(1)) as a succession farm partnership. This implies that the partnership be regarded as a 'registered farm partnership' before it can be registered as a 'succession farm partnership'. TCA 1997, s 667D(3) says that where farm assets or an interest in such assets are jointly owned prior to the formation of the succession farm partnership, then no agreement shall be made unless each person who jointly owns or jointly holds an interest in the land concerned, gives full and informed consent to the agreement to the transfer of those assets and joins in the agreement. Further where farm assets or an interest in such assets are jointly *farmed* prior to the formation of the succession farm partnership, whether jointly owned or not, any individual who jointly farmed the lands which are to be transferred under sub-s (2)(d) with the farmer, may become a partner in the partnership notwithstanding that that individual would be a non-active partner. TCA 1997, s 667D(4) states that where the farmer wishes to form a succession farm partnership with both the successor and that successor's spouse or civil partner then that spouse or civil partner may become a partner in the partnership notwithstanding that that individual would be a non-active partner and the agreement may provide for the joint transfer or sale of the farm assets concerned to both a successor and that successor's spouse or civil partner. Looking again at TCA 1997, s 667C(1A) which deals with 'registered farm partnerships', sub-s (1A)(b)(iv) states that no member of the farm partnership shall be a non-active partner. This would seem contra to the ability of a person to be a non-active partner in a succession farm partnership. A non-active partner is defined for the purposes of both TCA 1997, ss 667C and 667D as meaning '(a) in the case of an individual, an individual who, during the accounting period spends not more than an average of at least 10 hours per week personally engaged in the activities of the several trade, or (b) in the case of a company, a company whose officers and employees, during the accounting period between them, spend an average of not more than 10 hours per week personally engaged in the activities of the several trade'.

The Minister shall enter a partnership on the register of succession farm partnerships when satisfied that the conditions outlined above have been met. TCA 1997, s 667D(6)(c) allows a clawback of the tax relief if the farm assets are not transferred in accordance with the agreement then, the farmer shall be deemed to have paid an annual payment, to which TCA 1997, s 238 applies, of €125,000, or such lower amount as would result in the tax due under s 238 equalling the succession tax credit claimed by all partners, in the latest year of assessment in which the transfer could have taken place. TCA 1997, s 238 requires withholding tax at the standard rate of tax to be withheld and paid to Revenue. Such clawback will be assessed on the farmer unless it is shown to the satisfaction of a Revenue officer that the farm assets would have been transferred but the successor was no longer willing to proceed in accordance with the agreement then the clawback arises on the successor. If it is shown to the satisfaction of a Revenue officer that the farm assets were not transferred because of mutual agreement between the farmer and the successor, then each partner shall be deemed to have paid an annual payment in an amount that would result in the tax due pursuant to s 238 equalling the succession tax credit claimed by that partner, in the year of assessment in which the mutual agreement not to transfer the farm assets takes place.

TCA 1997, s 667E allows certain powers to 'authorised officers' for the purposes of TCA 1997, ss 667C and 667E. An authorised officer is appointed by Minister for Agriculture, Food and the Marine and has the power to do any one or more of the following:

(a) at all reasonable times enter, inspect, examine and search any lands or place to which the authorised officer has reasonable grounds for believing that this section applies, including for the purpose of surveying or mapping any land for any purpose under those provisions;

(b) while on the lands or at the place referred to above, may inquire into, search, examine and inspect any records relating to the operation of the farm partnership, registered farm partnership or, as the case may be, succession farm partnership;

(c) inspect and take copies of or extracts from any such records or any electronic information system at that place, including in the case of information in a non-legible form, copies of or extracts from such information in a permanent legible form or require that such copies be provided;

(d) require the person in charge to give the authorised officer such information as the authorised officer may reasonably require for the purposes of any search, examination, investigation, inspection or inquiry under those provisions, including the name and address of the owner or manager of the lands;

(e) require any person whom the authorised officer reasonably believes to be able to give to the authorised officer information relevant to any search, examination, investigation, inspection or inquiry under those provisions to answer such questions as the authorised officer may reasonably require relative to the search, examination, investigation, inspection or inquiry and to sign a declaration of the truth of the answers.

A 'person in charge' referred to above is defined in that section as meaning, in relation to a 'place', any of the following: (a) the owner; (b) the person under whose direction and control the activities at that place are being conducted; (c) the person whom the authorised officer has reasonable grounds for believing is in control of that place; (d) the driver of a vehicle. A 'place' includes a vehicle or any attachment to a vehicle.

The powers referred to above are not unfettered in that an authorised officer shall not enter a dwelling other than with the consent of the occupier, or in accordance with a warrant of the District Court. Finally, where an authorised officer has reasonable grounds for apprehending any serious obstruction in the performance of their functions or otherwise considers it necessary, the officer may be accompanied by other authorised officers or any other person authorised by the Minister when performing any functions conferred on them by or under the relevant statutory provisions.

TCA 1997, ss 667F and 667G look at the appointment of an appeals officer and the carrying on of appeals. In particular TCA 1997, s 667G notes that the Minister is to give notice in writing to the primary participant concerned of his or her decision. The Minister shall give notice in writing to the primary participant concerned of their decision:

(a) to refuse to enter, under s 667C(1D)(a), the farm partnership on the register of farm partnerships (hereinafter 'the register');
(b) to refuse to enter, under s 667D(5)(a), the farm partnership on the register of succession farm partnerships;
(c) to remove, under s 667C(1B)(a), the farm partnership from the register;
(d) not to amend an entry on the register under s 667C(1B)(b);
(e) to refuse to approve the business plan of a farm partnership for the purposes of s 667D(2)(c);
(f) to remove, under s 667C(1D)(b), the farm partnership from the register; or
(g) to remove, under s 667D(5)(b), the farm partnership from the register of succession farm partner.

Similar procedures regarding tax appeals are applied for the purposes of these appeals.

7.2 Farming: Capital Allowances and Losses

7.201 Introduction

Since 1974–75 when farming was first treated as a trade, the same forms of relief for capital expenditure and losses have been available as apply in other trades. A farmer chargeable to tax under Sch D Case I is entitled to claim capital allowances in respect of capital expenditure on machinery or plant incurred for the purpose of his trade of farming. In principle, the rules relating to capital allowances and balancing charges on machinery or plant apply to farming in the same way as to other trades, but there are a few special rules which require separate consideration; these are dealt with in **7.203**. The farmer is also entitled to capital allowances for qualifying expenditure on farm buildings, fences and other farm works, a form of capital allowance relevant only to farming. The allowances for capital expenditure on farm buildings and other farm works, including the enhanced allowances for pollution control expenditure are covered in detail in **7.202**. Capital allowances may also be granted in respect of expenditure incurred on the purchase of a milk quota to persons carrying on the trade of farming. These allowances are covered in detail in **7.204**.

The different forms of relief that may be claimed for losses in trades generally are available in corresponding circumstances for farming losses. The different types of loss relief are discussed in detail in **Division 4**, but the application of the main loss relief rules to a farmer chargeable to income tax is discussed more specifically in **7.205** below. Certain restrictions which may deny loss relief under TCA 1997, s 381 to farmers and market gardeners not carrying on business on a commercial basis are covered in **7.206**.

7.202 Capital allowances: farm buildings and works

TCA 1997, s 658 provides capital allowances for capital expenditure on the construction of farm buildings (other than dwellings) and certain farm works when incurred by any person carrying on the trade of farming the profits of which are charged to tax under Sch D Case (TCA 1997, s 658(1)). It follows that an individual who ceases all farming activities and leases the relevant buildings to another farmer is not eligible to claim the allowances (confirmed by a Revenue Precedent).

The allowance is granted where the person concerned incurs expenditure on the construction of eligible buildings for the purpose of a trade of farming land occupied by that person; the inference is that the expenditure should refer to buildings constructed on the land in question. The allowance is given in taxing the trade concerned (TCA 1997, s 658(2)(a)).

The Revenue have issued a precedent to the effect that allowances are available for a farm building let by an individual to a farming partnership of which he is a partner, but only if the building is let at market value and the rental payment is not in respect of services to the partnership. The justification for these conditions is not clear since the individual will have incurred expenditure on constructing buildings on land which he occupies (albeit jointly with his co-partners) for the purposes of a farming trade.

The capital allowances given under this section, whether on farm buildings or on farm works, are referred to as 'farm buildings allowances'.

Farm buildings allowances are given in respect of capital expenditure incurred on:

(a) the construction of farm buildings (excluding a building or part of a building used as a dwelling);

(b) fences; and

(c) roadways, holding yards, drains or land reclamation or other works (TCA 1997, s 658(2)).

Farm buildings qualifying for the allowance may be cattle sheds, milking parlours, pig houses or any other buildings of any kind used for the purposes of the trade of farming. Apart from fences and the other works specifically mentioned in (b) and (c), any other works of a capital nature on the farm land to improve that land for the purpose of the farmer's farming activities of any kind, or to provide other facilities for the purposes of the farming, attract the farm buildings allowances. For example, capital expenditure on the control of farm pollution qualifies as an 'other work'. Clearly, it is necessary to exclude any capital expenditure on machinery or plant in respect of which other capital allowances are given (eg the milking machinery installed in a milking parlour).

As noted above, for capital expenditure to qualify for farm buildings allowances, it must have been incurred for the purposes of a trade of farming land in the State occupied by the person claiming the allowances (but see *Disposal of farm land: new owner's allowance* below).

Any capital expenditure met directly or indirectly by the State or by any public or local authority grant or otherwise does not qualify for allowances and must be excluded (TCA 1997, s 658(13)).

Any capital expenditure incurred by a person about to carry on farming, but before he commences to farm, is deemed to be incurred on the day on which the farming commences (TCA 1997, s 658(5)). Where any expenditure is incurred partly for the purposes of farming and partly for other (non-farming) purposes, only the part of that expenditure fairly apportioned to the farming purposes qualifies for the allowances (TCA 1997, s 658(11)).

The writing down period

TCA 1997, s 658(2) provides for the granting of farm buildings allowances in respect of the qualifying expenditure over the writing down period of seven years which begins with the 'chargeable period related to the expenditure'.

'Chargeable period', for a farmer chargeable to income tax, means an income tax year of assessment (TCA 1997, s 321(2)).

The 'chargeable period related to any particular farm buildings, etc expenditure' is, in the case of an individual or other person chargeable to income tax, the year of assessment which has as its basis period the period in which the qualifying farm buildings or farm works expenditure is incurred (TCA 1997, s 321(2)(b)): see **6.102**).

For example, if Mr CD's basis period for assessing his farming profits for the tax year 2015 is the 12 months ending 31 May 2015, the chargeable period related to any expenditure incurred in that 12-month period is the tax year 2015. This means that the seven years writing down period for expenditure incurred by Mr CD in the 12 months ending 31 May 2015 commences with the tax year 2015.

For a summary of the main rules for determining the basis periods for income tax under Sch D Case I, see *All farming a single trade* in **7.102**.

Rates of farm buildings allowances

Farm buildings allowances in respect of any qualifying expenditure are, in principle, given at the rate necessary to write off 100 per cent of the expenditure on a straight line basis over the duration of the writing down period.

The farm buildings allowance is given as an annual writing down allowance over a *seven year* writing down period, as follows:

(a) an allowance equal to 15 per cent of the expenditure for each of the first six years of the writing down period; and

(b) an allowance equal to 10 per cent of the expenditure for the seventh and final year of the writing down period (TCA 1997, s 658(2)).

However, for the writing down allowances to be given for all years in the writing down period, the person must carry on his single farming trade for the whole of that period.

For a person chargeable to income tax, since the chargeable period is always the income tax year of assessment, the writing down period for expenditure will consist of seven complete income tax years without any need to apportion the allowances.

Example 7.202.1

Mr S Barness acquired farm land with some farm buildings, but which was not then being farmed, in September 2013. Between 1 October 2014 and 28 February 2015, he incurs the following capital expenditure:

	€
New farm buildings (not dwellings)	21,000
Extensions to existing farm buildings (not dwellings)	14,500
New fences	5,000
Holding yards and a new farm road	7,800
Total expenditure before commencement	48,300

Mr Barness receives certain grants towards the above expenditure. The total of the grants is €4,800 which is paid to him in June 2015. He commences to trade on 1 March 2015 when he purchases some cattle and sheep which are immediately put on the land.

All this expenditure qualifies for farm buildings allowances on the basis that it is deemed to have been incurred on 1 March 2015, the date on which Mr Barness commenced to farm the land, but the amount eligible for allowances has to be taken as follows:

	€
Total expenditure on farm buildings and works as above	48,300
Less:	
Grants towards expenditure	4,800
Net expenditure eligible for allowances	43,500

Under the rules of TCA 1997, s 66 for taxing the opening years of a new trade (including farming), the basis period for Mr Barness' first tax year, 2015, is the period from 1 March 2015 to 31 December 2015 (see **4.205**). During that period, he incurred further expenditure on farm works (but without any grants) which when added to the net pre commencement expenditure gives the following result:

	€
More new fences	2,400
New drains	3,900

Total expenditure 1/3/2015 to 31/12/2015	6,300
Add:	
Net expenditure deemed incurred 1/3/2015	43,500
Total in basis period for 1st tax year	49,800

How allowances are given

In the case of a farmer chargeable to income tax, the farm buildings allowances are said to be given in taxing the profits of his trade of farming (the single farming trade, see **7.102**). As with all capital allowances for trades generally, this means that the farm buildings allowances are set off in the income tax assessment under Sch D Case I by deducting them from the adjusted farming profits charged in the assessment or, where appropriate, as a set off against any balancing charges in respect of sales, etc of farm machinery or plant.

If the total farm buildings allowances (when added to any capital allowances in respect of farm machinery or plant) for any income tax year exceed the Sch D Case I adjusted farming profits, the excess is carried forward along with any unused capital allowances on machinery or plant and treated as capital allowances for the next, and if necessary, succeeding years of assessment (TCA 1997, s 658(6) which applies the carry forward rule of TCA 1997, s 304(4) to farm buildings allowances).

Since the farm buildings allowances have to be given in taxing the profits of the farming trade, it follows that the farmer ceases to be given any allowance for any income tax year after that in which he has ceased to carry on trade as a farmer (even though the writing down period may not have expired). However, as noted earlier, a farmer's trade of farming does not cease until he has ceased to carry on all farming activities in the State.

Claim for farm buildings allowances

TCA 1997, s 658(6) requires a farmer chargeable to income tax, who wishes to claim the farm buildings allowance in respect of any qualifying expenditure, to give notice of his claim for the allowances in submitting to the inspector of taxes his annual statement or return of farming profits (ie with his tax return for the tax year concerned).

In the event that the inspector's decision on the claim for the farm buildings allowance is unfavourable to the farmer, TCA 1997, s 658(7) entitles the farmer to appeal to the Appeal Commissioners against the inspector's decision. Any such appeal must be made within the time limit for an appeal on a matter within TCA 1997, s 949(1). In brief, this means that the appeal must be made within 30 days after notification of the inspector's decision or, if later, within 30 days after the taxpayer has both filed his tax return for the relevant chargeable period and paid his tax based on his tax return.

Although TCA 1997, s 658(7) refers to a 21-day time limit for making an appeal, the rule just quoted referring to the two alternative 30-day periods is substituted by TCA 1997, s 949(1) which applies notwithstanding any other provision.

When a taxpayer appeals against a decision of the inspector (or other authorised officer of the Revenue Commissioners) on the claim for the farm buildings allowance, all the rules of Income Tax Acts relating to the hearing of an appeal against an assessment to income tax are applied. In particular, the rules of TCA 1997, s 933 as discussed in **2.201**, are applied with any necessary modifications. F(TA)A 2015, s 37(8) deletes TCA 1997, s 658(7) and (8) but such deletion was subject to Ministerial Order

(SI 110/2016 appointed 21 March 2016 as the day on which the Finance (Tax Appeals) Act 2015, came into operation).

No Balancing Allowances Nor Balancing Charges

There are no provisions in TCA 1997, s 658 (or elsewhere) permitting or requiring any balancing allowances or balancing charges in respect of capital expenditure on farm buildings or farm works in the event of the sale or other disposal of the relevant farm lands or buildings. Nor is there any balancing allowance or balancing charge in the event of the farmer ceasing to use the land for farming.

Consequently, the farmer who incurred the original qualifying expenditure gets the normal writing down allowance for each chargeable period in the writing down period up to and including the sale, transfer, etc of the land, and there is never any clawback or recapture of the allowances obtained (even where a significant profit is realised on the sale of the land).

Disposal of farm land: new owner's allowances

TCA 1997, s 658(9) provides that, where a farmer sells or otherwise transfers to another person his interest in any farm land on which that farmer had incurred any capital expenditure which qualified for farm buildings allowances, then that other person takes over the entitlement to claim farm buildings allowances on any part of the original expenditure not already written off (on the assumption that the other person farms the land). The farmer who incurred the expenditure is, however, allowed to claim the allowances for the year of assessment in which the transfer of the interest in the land took place.

Should the farmer transfer a part only of his farm land, then any previous expenditure on farm buildings or farm works must be analysed as to whether referable to the part of the land transferred or referable to the part retained (or to both). The new owner is then entitled to farm buildings allowances on the part of the qualifying expenditure properly referable to the land acquired by him or her for the unexpired part of the writing down period. The original owner, if he or she continues to farm the land retained, remains entitled to the allowances on the balance of the expenditure referable to the land retained until the end of the writing down period.

The expenditure in respect of which the new owner is entitled to farm buildings allowances may have been incurred by the original farmer in two or more income tax basis periods. In this case, the new owner acquires different unexpired writing down periods over which the balance of the expenditure may be written off as allowances for the new owner.

The new owner's entitlement to farm buildings allowances by reference to the amount of the qualifying expenditure incurred by the vendor or transferor is totally unaffected by how much or how little is paid for the purchase or transfer of the land. Clearly, if the purchase or transfer occurs after the end of the writing down period in respect of the vendor's (or transferor's) expenditure or, where that expenditure was 100 per cent written off before the end of the writing down period due to free depreciation in one or more earlier years, the vendor (or transferee) is not entitled to any farm buildings allowances in respect of that expenditure.

Example 7.202.2

Mr G Alway has farmed in the State for many years making up accounts to 30 June. He has two separate farms. On 1 February 2012 (ie in the course of the period of accounts ending

30 June 2012, the basis period for 2012) he sells the land (including the farm buildings, etc on that land) of one of these farms to Mrs G Gilryne who continues to farm that land. Mr Alway continues to own and to farm the other farm. Mrs Gilryne, who has also traded as a farmer for many years, made up accounts to 31 March 2013.

This example is concerned only with the farm buildings allowances in respect of previous qualifying expenditure incurred by Mr Alway on farm buildings and farm works on the land that has been sold to Mrs Gilryne. No such capital expenditure had been incurred in respect of such land or buildings for many years up to 30 June 2008 but Mr Alway had incurred the following capital expenditure thereon between 1 July 2008 and 30 June 2009:

	€
Capital improvements to general farm buildings	6,700
Drainage scheme improvements	2,500
Total in year	9,200

The amount still unallowed at 31 December 2012 is as follows:

Expenditure in year to 30 June 2009	9,200
Writing down allowances – 2009, 2010, 2011 & 2012	
€9,200 x 15%= €1,380 x 4 =	5,520
Amount still unallowed at 31.12.2012	3,680

Since Mrs Gilryne farms the land purchased from Mr Alway she is entitled to farm building allowances in respect of the capital expenditure incurred by the vendor in the periods mentioned above, but only for relevant tax years after 2012 (it is irrelevant that she incurs the expenditure in the course of the period of accounts ended 31 March 2012, which is the basis period for 2012, since Mr Alway is entitled to the allowances for that tax year). The allowances available to her are as follows:

		€
Amount still unallowed		3,680
Writing down allowances 2013–2014 inclusive		
€9,200 x 15% x 2 years =	2,760	
Writing down allowance 2015	920	3,680

The Revenue have issued a precedent to the effect that a transfer by an individual of farm buildings to a trust falls within TCA 1997, s 658(9) notwithstanding that the individual is a life tenant of the trust and continues to farm the land.

Pollution control expenditure

TCA 1997, s 659 provides enhanced capital allowances for expenditure on the construction of either a farm building (other than a building or part of a building used as a dwelling) or a structure listed within the Table to TCA 1997, s 659 (see below) in accordance with a farm nutrient management plan ('plan' hereafter). The expenditure must have been incurred between 6 April 1997, and 31 December 2011 (deadline most recently extended by F (No 2) A 2008, s 17) and the building must be occupied in the course of the taxpayer's trade of farming (as defined by TCA 1997, s 655): TCA 1997, s 659(1)(c).

Expenditure will be regarded as being incurred within the relevant period if the work to which it relates was actually carried out during that period. For all other purposes of TCA 1997, s 659 the term 'incurred' would seem to bear its ordinary meaning since no other statutory provisions could seem to govern the meaning thereof in this context (TCA 1997, s 659(13)).

The plan must have been drawn up by an agency or planner approved to draw up such plans by the Department of Agriculture and Food, and must be drawn up in accordance with:

(a) the guidelines in relation to such plans entitled 'Farm Nutrient Management Plan' which were issued by the Department of Agriculture, Food and Forestry on 21 March 1997; or

(b) a plan drawn up under the scheme known as the Rural Environment Protection Scheme (REPS) or the scheme known as the Erne Catchment Nutrient Management Scheme, both of which are administered by the Department of Agriculture and Food (TCA 1997, s 659(1)(b)).

The building or structure under the plan must be certified as being necessary by the appropriate agency or planner for the purpose of securing a reduction in, or the elimination of, any pollution arising from the farming trade (TCA 1997, s 659(1)(c)).

The structures listed within the Table to TCA 1997, s 659 are as follows:

(a) waste storage facilities including slurry tanks;

(b) soiled water tanks;

(c) effluent tanks;

(d) tank fences and covers;

(e) dungsteads and manure pits;

(f) yard drains for storm and soiled water removal;

(g) walled silos, silage bases and silo aprons;

(h) housing for cattle, including drystock accommodation, byres, loose houses, slatted houses, sloped floor houses and kennels, roofed feed or exercise yards where such houses or structures eliminate soiled water; and

(i) housing for sheep and unroofed wintering structures for sheep and sheep dipping tanks.

Subject to the provisions of Article 6 of Council Regulation (EEC) No 2328/91 of 15 July 1991, on improving the efficiency of agricultural structures as amended (see OJ No L218 of 6 August 1991, p 1), writing down allowances will be granted to an individual who has delivered a duly prepared farm nutrient management plan to the Department of Agriculture, Food and Rural Development. The allowances which are to be made in taxing the farming trade are to be granted over a writing down period of eight years where that expenditure is incurred before 6 April 2000 and over seven years where it is incurred on or after 6 April 2000, commencing with the year of assessment in whose basis period the expenditure is incurred (TCA 1997, s 659(2), (4), TCA 1997, s 321).

Where the expenditure was incurred on or after 6 April 1998 and before 6 April 2000, the writing down allowance for the first year of assessment is 50 per cent of the expenditure, up to a maximum of €19,050. If the expenditure was incurred prior to 6 April 1998, the writing down allowance for the first year of assessment is 50 per cent of the expenditure, up to a maximum of €12,700. In either case, the allowance in the following six years is 15 per cent of the balance of the expenditure net of the writing down allowance granted in the first year. For the final (eighth) year of the writing down period the allowance is the remaining 10 per cent of the said balance (TCA 1997, s 659 as amended by FA 1998, s 38).

For qualifying pollution control expenditure incurred on or after 6 April 2000 and up to 31 December 2004 the writing down period is reduced from eight years to seven years. The standard rates of wear and tear were 15 per cent per annum for the first six years and 10 per cent in the final year (TCA 1997, s 659(3A)). For expenditure incurred on or after 1 January 2005, the writing down period is reduced to three years. The standard rates of wear and tear are 33.33 per cent per annum (TCA 1997, s 659(3AA)).

For expenditure incurred on or after 6th April 2000, a farmer has discretion to claim enhanced rates of wear and tear (TCA 1997, s 659(3B); (3BA), as amended by FA 2006, s 19). There are two definitions included in these subsections as follows:

(a) 'residual amount': an amount equal to 50 per cent of the expenditure or €50,000 (€31,750 for tax years prior to 2006) whichever is the lesser; and

(b) 'specified amount': the balance of the expenditure after deducting the residual amount.

As an alternative to claiming the standard rate of wear and tear on the full expenditure, the farmer may elect to claim the standard rates in respect of the specified amount together with the whole or part of the 'residual amount' in any tax year in the writing down period (TCA 1997, s 659(3B)(c); (3BA)(b)). The aggregate allowances claimed in any one year must not exceed the residual amount (TCA 1997, s 659(3B)(d); (3BA)(c)). The election by the farmer must be made in writing before the specified return date applicable to the tax return for that year. An election cannot be altered or varied during the writing down period (TCA 1997, s 659(3C)).

Example 7.202.3

A farmer incurred €122,000 on farm pollution control measures in relation to the 2011 tax year. He elects for the enhanced rates of capital allowances so that the position will be as follows:

		€
Year 2011		
Residual amount	€122,000 x 50% = €60,000, limited to	€50,000
Years 2012–2013		
Annual amount	€(122,000–50,000) = €72,000 x 1/3 = €24,000 x 3 =	€72,000
Total allowances		€122,000

The €50,000 residual amount can be written off over any of the three years 2011–2013, subject to an overall limit of €50,000 on the aggregate amount being claimed in any one year (taking into account the annual amount and the part of the 'residual amount' being claimed).

If it is wished to claim the maximum allowances as early as possible, the farmer would claim them as follows:

2011: Annual amount €24,000 + Residual amount €50,000 = €74,000, limited to €50,000

2012: Annual amount €24,000 + Balance of Residual amount € (50,000 – 26,000) = €48,000

2013: Annual amount €24,000

Any allowance or part thereof which cannot be set off against the trading profits of one year of assessment can be carried forward to the following year of assessment, and so on (TCA 1997, s 304(4) as applied by TCA 1997, s 659(5)).

Where a person entitled to the allowances transfers his interest in the buildings or structures, the transferee takes over his entitlements to the writing down allowances with effect from the year of assessment following the year in which the transfer takes place (TCA 1997, s 659(8)). No question of balancing charges or allowances arises. Where only part of the interest in the buildings, etc is transferred, a due proportion only of the entitlement to the writing down allowances is taken over by the transferee (TCA 1997, s 659(9)).

Where expenditure is incurred partly for a purpose for which a writing down allowance falls to be made and partly for another purpose the writing down allowances will apply to so much only of that expenditure as on a just apportionment ought fairly to be treated as incurred for the first-mentioned purpose (TCA 1997, s 659(10)).

No writing down allowances will be granted if the building or structure has been, or is, granted any of the following in any year of assessment:

(a) industrial buildings initial allowance, (see **6.405**);

(b) industrial buildings writing down allowance, (see **6.406**);

(c) industrial buildings balancing allowance, (see **6.409**);

(d) farm building allowance (see above); and

(e) plant and machinery wear and tear allowance or balancing allowance: see **7.203** (with effect from 1 January 2005);

(TCA 1997, s 659(11) as amended by FA 2005, s 30(h).)

Recoverable VAT is excluded from the amount of the allowable expenditure (TCA 1997, s 319(1)(b)).

Expenditure will not be regarded for any of the purposes of TCA 1997, s 659 as having been incurred by a person in so far as it has been or is to be met directly or indirectly by the State or by any other third party (TCA 1997, s 659(12)). This includes payments under REPS to compensate for identifiable capital expenditure.

A claim for writing down allowances must be made in the annual return of farming profits (TCA 1997, s 659(5)). As with farm buildings allowances, there is a right of appeal against the inspector's determination in relation to a claim; the provisions relating to an appeal against as assessment apply subject to any necessary modifications (TCA 1997, s 659(7)). F(TA)A 2015, s 37(8) deletes TCA 1997, s 659(6) and (7) but such deletion was subject to Ministerial Order (SI 110/2016 appointed 21 March 2016 as the day on which the Finance (Tax Appeals) Act 2015, came into operation).

7.203 Capital allowances: farm machinery and plant

A person carrying on the trade of farming has been entitled to the same capital allowances, and under the same rules, for capital expenditure on machinery or plant as a person carrying on any other type of trade.

Since the subject of capital allowances for machinery or plant is discussed fully in **Division 6** in relation to trades generally, and as the same rules apply for farming trades, it is not necessary to repeat the details here. It may be noted however that the Kilkenny Circuit Court has held that a slatted unit cowhouse is 'plant'.

In certain circumstances, a person carrying on the trade of farming (the farmer) may not actually receive any wear and tear allowance in respect of an item of machinery or plant for one or more chargeable periods during his period of ownership of that plant. For example, the farmer may not use the plant at all for the farming trade in a basis period. Alternatively, the farmer may only use the plant for farming for a part of a basis period so that only part of the normal wear and tear allowance is obtained.

In any such circumstances, the farmer would – in the absence of any other provision – gain a benefit to the extent that a higher amount of capital expenditure would be left 'unallowed' so that he would receive a higher wear and tear allowance in a subsequent chargeable period, or would benefit from a higher balancing allowance or a lower balancing charge when the plant is disposed of. In fact, the legislation contains other provisions to prevent the farmer obtaining such future benefits.

TCA 1997, s 660 applies specifically in the case of a farming trade and requires the writing off of notional or deemed wear and tear allowances for any chargeable period or periods during the farmer's period of ownership for which a normal wear and tear allowance is not obtained due to certain specified circumstances. Also, TCA 1997, s 287 is applicable in similar circumstances in relation to all types of trades (including the trade of farming) – provides for the writing off of notional wear and tear allowances. The same rules also apply to professions under TCA 1997, s 301.

In effect, the provisions of TCA 1997, s 660 and those of TCA 1997, s 287 are broadly similar (although the latter is expressed to apply only where the plant has been used by the trader in the relevant year of assessment: see the discussion at **6.204**) except that the latter is relevant only in relation to later wear and tear allowances and is supported by TCA 1997, s 296 relating to the balancing allowance/balancing charge computation, whereas TCA 1997, s 660 affects both wear and tear allowances and the balancing allowance/balancing charge computation.

The reason for having a separate section specifically applicable to farming only appears to have been to cover the situations where, at one time, certain individuals carrying on the trade of farming were exempted from income tax (up to 1982–83) or where certain individuals could opt to be taxed on a special notional basis (and not on actual farming profits) (up to 1979–80). Were it not for TCA 1997, s 660, such individuals who later became subject to normal taxation on their farming profits would have benefited from higher amounts of capital expenditure 'unallowed' carried forward for use in the period of normal taxation.

Since this is a chapter dealing specifically with farming trades, it deals only with TCA 1997, s 660. For a discussion of notional allowances under TCA 1997, s 287 and TCA 1997, s 296 affecting trades and professions generally, see **6.205** and **6.207** respectively.

Application of TCA 1997, s 660

TCA 1997, s 660 requires a notional wear and tear allowance to be written off the cost of any item of farm machinery or plant belonging to a person for every chargeable period which is a 'chargeable period to be taken into account for the purpose of this section' (ie year of assessment).

The section is applicable, where relevant, for the purpose of determining whether any, and if so what, wear and tear allowance, balancing allowance or balancing charge is to be given or made for a particular year of assessment (income tax) in respect of any item of machinery or plant. In dealing with this question for a particular year of assessment (eg 2014), it is necessary to consider all previous tax years since that in which the farmer now owning it acquired that item of plant, whether or not he was then carrying on his 'single trade' of farming. The first question to be answered in respect of each previous year is whether or not it is a chargeable period to be taken into account for the purpose of TCA 1997, s 660.

TCA 1997, s 660(3) provides that a year of assessment is, in relation to a person, to be taken into account for the purpose of this section if it is a tax year in which the following circumstances existed:

(a) the machinery or plant belonged to the person in question; and

(b) (i) the machinery or plant was not used by that person for the purposes of farming during the tax year,

(ii) farming was not carried on by that person during the tax year,

(iii) farming was carried on by that person during the tax year in circumstances in which that person was not liable to be taxed under Sch D Case I for that year on the full amount of his farming profits (eg due to the small farmers' exemption which applied up to 1982–83), or

(iv) that person was charged to income tax for that tax year in respect of farming profits on the notional basis of assessment under FA 1974, s 21 (which applied up to 1979–80).

All the above mentioned circumstances refer to cases in which either no wear and tear allowance or only a reduced or restricted allowance is given for a tax year. In fact, the circumstance described in (b)(iii) will not be met in any case of machinery or plant acquired subsequent to the tax year 1982–83 and the circumstance mentioned in (b)(iv) cannot occur in any tax year after 1979–80. However, if any old machinery or plant within (b)(iii) or (b)(iv) has continued to be used to the present day, the rules of TCA 1997, s 660 are still relevant until such plant is sold or otherwise becomes the subject of a balancing allowance or balancing charge. The circumstances described in (b)(i) and (ii) are capable of being met for plant acquired either currently or at any time in the past.

In determining the wear and tear allowance, balancing allowance or balancing charge for a given year of assessment, TCA 1997, s 660 provides that, for every previous tax year in which the plant belonged to the farmer and which is a 'relevant tax year', the farmer shall be deemed to have obtained a 'normal wear and tear allowance'. To the extent that the wear and tear allowance (if any) actually obtained in respect of the item of plant for a relevant tax year falls short of the normal wear and tear allowance for that year, a 'notional wear and tear allowance' is deducted from the tax written down value of the plant.

For the purpose of TCA 1997, s 660, a 'normal wear and tear allowance' for a relevant tax year is such wear and tear allowance as would have been made to the farmer for that year if, in relation to *every previous tax year* (which is a chargeable period to be taken into account for the purpose of this section), the following circumstances had applied:

(a) the profits from farming had been chargeable to tax under Sch D Case I;

(b) the profits from farming had been charged to tax according to TCA 1997, Pt 4 Ch 3 (based on the farming profits in the basis period for the year in question), and not on the notional basis under FA 1974, s 21 (only relevant up to 1979–80);

(c) farming had been carried on by the farmer in question ever since the date on which he acquired the plant;

(d) the plant had been used by that farmer solely for the purposes of farming ever since the date on which he acquired the plant; and

(e) a proper claim had been made by that farmer for a wear and tear allowance in respect of the plant for each of the previous tax years.

The reference above to 'such wear and tear allowance' refers to the case where no wear and tear allowance at all was actually obtained for the relevant tax year. The reference to 'such greater wear and tear allowance' refers to the case where a wear and tear allowance was obtained but one which was less than the normal wear and tear allowance.

The way in which TCA 1997, s 660 operates, where relevant, differs for machinery or plant (other than road vehicles) provided for (first used in) the farming trade on or after 1 April 1992 and before 1 January 2001 and from 1 January 2001 and before 4 December 2002, as compared with machinery or plant so provided before that date (or compared with road vehicles whenever provided). This difference is to reflect the fact that the normal wear and tear allowance for machinery or plant (other than road vehicles) provided on or after 1 April 1992 and before 1 January 2001 is the 15 per cent straight line allowance (up to 100 per cent write off) as compared with the former reducing balance method applicable for machinery or plant provided before 1 April 1992 (and for road vehicles whenever provided). In respect of capital expenditure incurred on or after 1 January 2001 and before 4 December 2002, on the provision of machinery or plant and motor vehicles, the wear and tear allowance is equal to 20 per cent of the actual cost. For expenditure incurred on qualifying plant and machinery or motor vehicles after 4 December 2002, the wear and tear allowance is equal to 12.5 per cent of the actual cost. For a fuller description of the relevant provisions, see **6.203**. For examples of the application of TCA 1997, s 660 for machinery and plant acquired before 1 April 1992, see the 1997–98 and earlier editions of this book.

Example 7.203.1

Mr GG Gander, a farmer who makes his accounts up to 30 September each year, purchased a new machine for €6,400 on 25 June 2011 (ie in the course of the period of accounts ended 30 September 2011, the basis period for tax year 2011). He immediately put the machine into use for his farming trade.

During his period of accounts ended 30 September 2012 (basis period for tax year 2012), Mr Gander lends this machine to Mr Drake for the five months ending 2 September 2012. The actual wear and tear allowance for 2012 is therefore reduced to a 7/12ths proportion of the normal allowance (but note the discussion at **6.203**: *Conditions for wear and tear allowances*). The machine was otherwise used only in Mr Gander's farming trade.

This means that 2011 is a year of assessment to which TCA 1997, s 660 applies so that a notional allowance has to be made for that tax year. Although, under the 12.5 per cent straight line scheme, the notional allowance required to be deducted does not affect the amount on which the 2012 wear and tear allowance is calculated, it will become relevant in a later tax year. Therefore, as recommended in **6.204** the notional allowance for 2012 is best written off in arriving at the tax written down value at 31 December 2012.

The capital allowances computations, for this item of plant for the years 2011 to 2014 are:

	€	€
Cost of machine (25/6/2011)		6,400
W & T allowance 2011 €6,400 x 12.5%		800
Tax WDV 31/12//2011		5,600
W & T allowance 2012 (actual): €6,400 x 12.5% x 7/12ths[1]	467	

Notional W & T allowance 2012		
(€6,400 x 12.5%) – (actual €467)[2]	333	800
Tax WDV 31/12/2012		4,800
W & T allowance 2013 (actual)		
€6,400 x 12.5%		800
Tax WDV 31/12/2013		4,000
W & T allowance 2014 (actual)		
€6,400 x 12.5%		800
Tax WDV 31/12/2014		3,200

Notes:

1. The actual wear and tear allowance for 2012 is only given for the seven months in the basis period for that year in which the machine was used in the farming trade.
2. Since the actual wear and tear allowance given for 2012 (€467) is less than the normal straight line allowance (€800), TCA 1997, s 660 requires the deduction of the excess (€333) of the latter over the former to be deducted to affect the wear and tear allowance for the last tax year in which a wear and tear allowance is to be made or, if it comes earlier, to affect the calculation of a balancing allowance or balancing charge.

Example 7.203.2

Take the same facts of Mr GG Gander's case as in **Example 7.203.1**, except assume that the machine in question was sold for €5,160 on 13 June 2015 (in the period of accounts ending 30 September 2015, the basis period for 2015).

TCA 1997, s 660 is applicable for the purpose of the balancing allowance or balancing charge computation. However, as the notional allowance for 2012 the only year for which such an allowance was required) has already been taken off in arriving at the €3,200 tax written down value at 31 December 2014, no further adjustment is required so that the balancing allowance/balancing charge computation is made as follows:

	€
Tax WDV 31/12/2014 after actual and notional allowances	3,200
Sale proceeds	5,160
Balancing charge 2015[1]	1,960

Notes:

1. Since the €1,960 excess of the sale proceeds over the tax written down value (after notional allowance) is less than the actual wear and tear allowances obtained (€800 for 2011, €467 for 2012, €800 for 2013 and €800 for 2043, ie a total of €2,867), there is no restriction to the amount of the balancing charge.

7.204 Capital allowances: milk quotas

Annual allowances for capital expenditure on purchase of milk quota

TCA 1997, ss 669A to 669F grant capital allowances with effect from 6 April 2000 in respect of expenditure incurred on the purchase of a milk quota. TCA 1997, s 669A has been partly amended by FA 2002, s 30. These amendments are discussed below. TCA 1997, s 669E states that the provisions of TCA 1997, Pt 9 Ch 4 are applied to Pt 23, Ch 3. TCA 1997, Pt 9, Ch 4 contains the miscellaneous and general provisions dealing with capital allowances. TCA 1997, s 669D states that the writing down allowances, balancing allowances and balancing charges in respect of a qualifying milk quota are to be made to or on a person in taxing the profits or gains from farming. This applies only if the quota is being used for the farming trade at any time in the chargeable period or its basis period.

Where a person incurs qualifying expenditure on or after 6 April 2000 on the purchase of a qualifying quota, writing down allowances are granted. The writing down allowances are only made to a person in taxing that person's trade of farming. The writing down period is seven years commencing with the beginning of the chargeable period related to the qualifying expenditure. The allowances are time apportioned to each writing down period by reference to the length of the relevant basis period (TCA 1997, s 669B(3)). If a farmer commences to trade on 1 October 2010 and purchases a milk quota on that day, the writing down allowance in 2010 (granted in respect of the basis period 1 October 2010 to 31 December 2010: see **4.205**) will therefore be effectively 3/84ths of the capital expenditure incurred.

A 'qualifying quota' is defined in TCA 1997, s 669A as:

(a) a milk quota purchased by a person on or after 1 April 2000 under a milk quota restructuring scheme (ie a scheme introduced by the Minister for Agriculture, Food and Rural Development under the provisions of Council Regulation (EEC) No 3950 of 28 December 1992 (as amended) Article 8(b)); or

(b) any other milk quota purchased on or after 1 April 2000.

'Milk quota' is defined as:

(a) the quantity of a milk or other milk products which may be supplied by a person carrying on farming, in the course of a trade of farming land occupied by such person to a purchaser (as defined in Council Regulation (EEC) No 3950 of 28 December 1992) in a milk quota year (ie a 12-month period beginning on 1 April and ending on the following 31 March) without that person being liable to pay a levy (as referred to in Council Regulation (EEC) No 3950 of 28 December 1992, as amended); or

(b) the quantity of a milk or other milk products which may be sold or transferred free for direct consumption by a person carrying on farming, in the course of a trade of farming land occupied by such person in a milk quota year (ie a 12-month period beginning on 1 April and ending on the following 31 March) without that person being liable to pay a levy (as referred to in Council Regulation (EEC) No 3950 of 28 December 1992, as amended).

In the definition of 'milk quota' the term 'milk' means the produce of the milking of one or more cows and 'other milk products' includes cream, butter and cheese. The expenditure incurred must be 'qualifying expenditure' and this is also defined in TCA 1997, s 669A.

For a person who purchases a milk quota on or after 1 April 2000 under a milk quota restructuring scheme, the amount of the capital expenditure incurred on the purchase of that quota will be 'qualifying expenditure' for capital allowances purchases. If the milk quota is a qualifying quota purchased by a lessee who entered into a lease agreement with a lessor, the qualifying expenditure up to 31 December 2006 will be the lesser of the capital expenditure incurred on the purchase of that qualifying quota or the capital expenditure which would have been incurred on the purchase had the maximum price set for that milk quota year in which the purchase took place, by the Minister for

Agriculture, Food and Rural Development for the purposes of a milk quota restructuring scheme applied. From 1 January 2007, this definition is amended to reflect the provisions of the Milk Quota Trading System and will apply to the lesser of the capital expenditure incurred on the purchase of that qualifying quota or the amount of the capital expenditure which would have been incurred on the purchase if the price paid were set otherwise than by the Minister for Agriculture and Food for the purposes of a milk quota restructuring scheme in the area in which the land, with which the milk quota is associated, is located (TCA 1997, s 669A(1) as amended by FA 2007, s 25).

Effect of sale of quota

TCA 1997, s 669C deals with the writing down allowance, balancing allowance and balancing charge consequences where certain events occur.

Cessation of writing down allowance

TCA 1997, s 669C(1) states that where a person incurs qualifying expenditure on the purchase of a qualifying quota and, before the end of the writing down period, any of the following events occur:

(a) the person sells the quota or such much of the quota as the person still owns;

(b) the quota comes to an end or ceases altogether to be used;

(c) the person sells part of the quota and the net sale proceeds are not less than the tax written down value of the qualifying expenditure;

no writing down allowance is made to that person for the chargeable period related to the event or any subsequent chargeable period.

Milk quotas are due to be abolished from 1 April 2015.

Continuation of writing down allowance

TCA 1997, s 669C(4) states how the writing down allowance is to be determined where a part disposal arises and no balancing charge occurs (because the sale proceeds are less than the tax written down value). The writing down allowance for that expenditure for the chargeable period related to the sale or any subsequent period shall be calculated by subtracting the net sale proceeds of the sale from the tax written down value of the expenditure at the time of sale and dividing the result by the number of complete years of the writing down period remaining at the beginning of the chargeable period related to the sale.

Balancing allowance

TCA 1997, s 669C(2) provides for a balancing allowance where before the end of the writing down period, any of the following events occurs:

(a) the qualifying quota comes to an end or ceases altogether to be used; and

(b) the person sells all of the quota or so much as the person still owns and the net proceeds of the sale are less than the tax written down value of the qualifying expenditure.

In the case of (a), the balancing allowance is the tax written down value of the qualifying expenditure. In the case of (b), the balancing allowance is an amount equal to the excess of the tax written down value of the qualifying expenditure over the net sale proceeds. In either case, the balancing allowance is given for the chargeable period related to the event giving rise to the balancing allowance. As the milk quota system comes to an end in 2015, there will be a balancing allowance for farmers with quotas which have not been fully written down.

There is no balancing allowance available in respect of a part disposal of a quota. No balancing allowance can be made in respect of any expenditure unless a writing down allowance has been made in respect of that expenditure or could have been made but for the happening of the event giving rise to the balancing allowance (TCA 1997, s 669C(6)(a)).

Balancing charge

A balancing charge will arise if the person sells all or any part of the quota and the net sale proceeds exceed the tax written down value of the qualifying expenditure. The balancing charge will equal the excess of the net sale proceeds over the tax written down value and where the tax written value is nil, it will equal the net sale proceeds (TCA 1997, s 669C(3)). It is made on the person for the chargeable period related to the sale. The total amount on which a balancing charge is made in respect of any expenditure must not exceed the total writing down allowances made in respect of that expenditure, less, if a balancing charge has previously been made in respect of that expenditure, the amount on which the charge was made (TCA 1997, s 669C(6)(b)).

Example 7.204.1

Assume that Gerard McNickle who has been trading as a farmer for many years and makes his accounts up to 31 May each year acquired a qualifying milk quota for €30,000 on 25 June 2009 (in the course of the period of accounts ended 31 May 2010, basis period for 2010). The WDV of the quota at 1 January 2013 will be as follows:

	€
Cost of Quota (25/6/2009)	30,000
W & T allowance 2010	
€30,000 x 12/84=	4,286
Tax WDV 31/12//2010	25,714
W & T allowance 2011:	
€30,000 x 12/84=	4,286
Tax WDV 31/12/2011	21,428
W & T allowance 2012	
€30,000 x 7/84=	4,286
Tax WDV 31/12/2012	17,142

Assume that Mr McNickle sells the quota to Mr Harkin in February 2013 (in the course of the period of account ending 31 May 2013, his basis period for the tax year 2013). Mr Harkin has traded as a farmer for many years and makes his accounts up to 31 January each year; he will therefore commence to claim the writing down allowances by reference to the amount of his expenditure for the basis period commenced 1 February 2013 and ended 31 January 2014, ie tax year 2014 onwards.

The effect on the capital allowance position of Mr McNickle will vary depending on whether he sells the entire quota or just part thereof and also depending on the amount of the sale proceeds ie whether they are less than tax WDV, greater than tax WDV but less than the original cost of the quota or excess in of the original cost. The range of possible outcomes is illustrated in the following table:

Sells all or part of quota	*Sale proceeds*	*Effect on capital allowance position for 2013*	
	€		€
ALL	15,000	Balancing allowance	(17,142–15,000) = 2,142
ALL	25,000	Balancing charge	(25,000–17,142) = 7,858
ALL	35,000	Balancing charge	(35,000–17,142) =17,858 restricted to WDA received (4,286 x 3) = 12,858
PART	15,000	Writing down allowance	2,142/4 = 536*
PART	25,000	Balancing charge	(25,000–17,142) = 7,858
PART	35,000	Balancing charge	(35,000–17,142) =17,858 restricted to WDA received (4,286 x 3) = 12,858

* Writing down allowances of €536 pa will continue to be granted for the three remaining tax years falling within the writing down period, *viz* 2013–2015 inclusive assuming the quota continues to be used in the farming trade and there are no further disposals thereof.

7.205 Relief for farming losses

The entitlement of a person chargeable to income tax to claim under TCA 1997, s 381 to have a trading loss set off against his total income for the same year of assessment in which the loss is incurred and the manner in which the relief is calculated, has been discussed in **4.404**.

A person carrying on the trade of farming who sustains a Sch D Case I farming loss in any tax year is normally entitled to claim under TCA 1997, s 381 to have that loss set off against his total income for the same year in exactly the same way. TCA 1997, s 381 relief is, however, denied where farming is not carried on with a view to the realisation of profits and in certain other circumstances (see **7.206**). Alternatively, the farmer is entitled to carry forward the loss for set off under TCA 1997, s 382 against his farming profits of the next and, if necessary, following years.

The factors governing a farmer's decision on whether to make a TCA 1997, s 381 claim for a farming loss eligible for relief are the same as those discussed in **4.404** for trading losses generally. The farmer also has the option given by TCA 1997, s 392 to require his capital allowances for the relevant tax year to be used to augment or create a farming loss for the purposes of a TCA 1997, s 381 claim (see **4.405**). The claim under TCA 1997, s 381 (and s 392) to set off a farming loss against other income for a given year of assessment must be made no later than two years after the end of that year.

In principle, a farming loss incurred in one tax year may be carried forward under TCA 1997, s 382 for set off against the same person's profits from farming assessable for any subsequent year. Certain farming losses may not, however, be carried forward for future set off in this way. A farming loss sustained by an individual in any year of assessment in which he was not chargeable to tax is not eligible for carry forward under

TCA 1997, s 382 for set off against the individual's farming profits in any later year (TCA 1997, s 661).

The discussion in **4.402** of the manner of implementing relief under TCA 1997, s 382 is, for the most part, equally applicable to farming losses. For example, no carry forward may be made for any part of a farming loss for which relief has been given in a TCA 1997, s 381 claim against total income.

One different point to be noted is that, as all farming in the State carried on by the one person is treated as a single trade, a farming loss sustained in any of that person's farming activities may be carried forward and set off under TCA 1997, s 382 against future profits in any of his farming activities. For example, if an individual farms on his own account and is also a partner in a farming partnership, an overall farming loss in one year due mainly to bad results on his own farm may be set off under TCA 1997, s 382 against an overall farming profit in a later year in which the partnership farm is profitable, even if the individual's own farm is still incurring losses.

When a farmer chargeable to income tax ceases permanently to carry on any farming activities in the State, he is entitled to claim under TCA 1997, s 385 to have any farming loss incurred in the last 12 months prior to the cessation carried back for set off against the farming profits on which he was assessed to income tax for the three tax years preceding that in which the cessation occurs. The manner in which this terminal loss relief is granted, including the relief for any relevant farming capital allowances, is the same as that discussed for trades generally in **4.410**.

A person taxable on his farming profits for any year of assessment must first deduct the farming capital allowances for that year from the assessable profits and any balancing charges. If the adjusted Sch D Case I profits are insufficient to absorb fully the relevant capital allowances, the normal rules relating to the carry forward of the unused capital allowances apply (see **4.403**).

Finally, TCA 1997, s 390 applies to farming as it does to other trades to allow annual payments made wholly and exclusively for the purposes of the trade of farming, but not deductible in computing Sch D Case I profits or losses, to be added to a farming loss carried forward under TCA 1997, s 382 or carried back in a terminal loss claim under TCA 1997, s 385 (see also **4.410**).

7.206 Losses: non-commercial farming and market gardening

TCA 1997, s 662(2)(a) provides – in an income tax case – that no TCA 1997, s 381 relief is to be given for a loss incurred in a trade of either farming or market gardening unless it can be shown that, in the year of assessment in which the loss was incurred, the trade in question was being carried on '*on a commercial basis and with a view to the realisation of profits in the trade*'. In interpreting this rule, if the farming or market gardening has in fact been carried on during the year in question in such a way as to afford a reasonable expectation of profit, this is to be taken as conclusive evidence that the trade was in that year being carried on with a view to the realisation of profits. It seems clear that 'profits' in this context are those ascertained on commercial principles and not profits as adjusted for tax purposes (note *Brown v Richardson* [1997] STC (SCD) 233). The Revenue have indicated that they will take particular note of the level of loan repayments to be met by the farmer when deciding if he is operating on a '*commercial basis*'. In fact, while interest costs should be taken into account in ascertaining profits, the capital element of the loan repayments would not be relevant for this purpose. Further, it is not clear that a farmer whose farming cash flows will not suffice to repay his borrowings is necessarily operating on an uncommercial basis as opposed to merely capitalising his business partly out of his own resources.

This commercial basis test might on occasions be difficult to apply in practice (but note *Wannell v Rothwell* [1996] STC 450); in *Walls v Livesey* [1995] STC (SCD) 12, the UK Special Commissioners held that the expression 'with a view to the realisation of profits' had to be interpreted subjectively (ie the actual intentions of the particular taxpayer are what counts). The test is also supported by a 'three prior years' losses' rule which is capable of more precise interpretation. This supporting rule provides that, without limiting the general application of the main rule, no TCA 1997, s 381 relief is to be given for a farming or market gardening loss incurred in a tax year (the 'year of the loss') if, in all of the three tax years immediately prior to the year of the loss, there was also a farming or market gardening loss (TCA 1997, s 662(2)(b)). The question of whether there is a loss in any tax year is determined by applying the normal Sch D Case I computational rules, ie it is the actual adjusted Sch D Case I loss (if any) for that year after adding back depreciation, etc, but before considering capital allowances or balancing charges, that is taken. Therefore any claim for income averaging is ignored in applying the three-year test.

The main commercial basis test can be applied on its own to prevent TCA 1997, s 381 loss relief for any tax year, even if losses have not been incurred in prior years. The onus is on the taxpayer to satisfy the inspector, if required, that the farming or market gardening is being undertaken on a commercial basis in the year of the loss for which the relief is sought. On the other hand, the three prior years' losses rule only operates to deny TCA 1997, s 381 relief in the fourth, etc successive tax year if there have been losses in the three or more successive prior years. It does not stop the making of a TCA 1997, s 381 claim in respect of the losses of up to three successive years for which the main commercial basis test is met.

TCA 1997, s 662(5) provides that the provisions of TCA 1997, s 662(2) will not deny relief where a trade was commenced in the previous three years and in particular that a trade shall be regarded as discontinued and a new trade set up for these purposes in any circumstances where there is deemed to be a permanent discontinuance for income tax purposes. However, this principle is qualified by TCA 1997, s 662(6) where there has been a change in the persons carrying on the trade by: (a) treating any person who was carrying on the trade before and after the change as carrying on the same trade, and (b) treating any person and a person to whom they are connected as the same person. Thus if a father ceases his trade of farming and his son succeeds to the trade, then for the purposes of TCA 1997, s 662 the son is treated as carrying on the same trade as his father and is if he had been carrying on the trade during the time his father had carried it on.

There are three exceptions to both the main commercial basis test and the three prior years' losses rule. A claim under TCA 1997, s 381 for a farming or market gardening loss incurred in any tax year may still be made, notwithstanding the foregoing rules, if any of the following exceptions apply:

(a) if the farming or market gardening trade forms part of, *and* is ancillary to, a larger trading undertaking (TCA 1997, s 662(2)(e));
(b) if the farming or market gardening trade was set up and commenced within the prior three tax years (TCA 1997, s 662(5)); or
(c) if the person claiming the relief can show that the whole of his farming or market gardening activities – in the tax year immediately following the three

prior tax years – are of such a nature, and carried on in such a way, as would have justified a reasonable expectation of the realisation of profits in the future if they had been undertaken by a competent farmer or market gardener *and* that if such a farmer or market gardener had undertaken those activities at the start of the 'prior period of loss', he could not have reasonably expected those activities to become profitable until after the end of the year following the prior period of loss (TCA 1997, s 662(2)(d)).

The 'prior period of loss' is defined as the three tax years prior to the relevant year or if there was more than three successive tax years of losses prior to the relevant year the period covering all of those tax years.

In relation to exception (a), the Revenue Commissioners have issued a precedent to the effect that 'ancillary' means subservient to and annexed to a larger undertaking, citing *Cross v Emery* 31 TC 194 (examples offered are those of a butcher fattening bullocks for his main business, a manufacturer growing his own raw materials and a chemical or fertiliser manufacturer running a farm in order to test or improve their products). They express the opinion (which is surely correct) that a trade of farming would not be regarded as part of, or ancillary to, a trade of land dealing.

In determining whether exception (c) applies to permit a TCA 1997, s 381 claim, it is also necessary to establish that, if the hypothetical competent farmer or market gardener mentioned had carried on the relevant activities during the 'prior period of loss', that person could not reasonably have expected those activities to have become profitable until at least a year after the end of that prior period of loss. For this purpose, 'the prior period of loss' is either the three tax years preceding the year of the loss or, should it be the longer, the period of all successive tax years in each of which losses were incurred prior to the year of the loss. There is an interesting insight in the recent UK tribunal case *CJ & MA French v HMRC* (TC04053) which examines the reasonable expectation of the realisation of profits by a competent farmer. It held that the farmer was entitled to sideways offset of losses for a period of seven years on the basis he did not anticipate making a profit until year eight.

Example 7.206.1

Mr I Hope commenced farming on 1 October 2011. He prepared his first farm accounts for the three months ended 31 December 20110 and has since then prepared accounts to 31 December in each year. He incurs farming losses for the three months ended 31 December 2011 and for each of the next four years ended 31 December 2012, 2013, 2014 and 2015. He seeks to make TCA 1997, s 381 claims to set off these farming losses against his total income for each of the five tax years 2011 to 2015. To what extent are these claims permitted by TCA 1997, s 662?

Claims for 2011 to 2014:

The inspector of taxes is not satisfied that the trade was being carried on commercially and with a view to the realisation of profits. However, as the farming trade was set up within the last three years prior to each of these three years, exception (b) applies with the following results:

(1) Mr Hope is allowed his TCA 1997, s 381 claim for 2011 and his adjusted loss for the three months' accounts to 31 December 2011 may be set off to reduce his total income for 2011;

(2) He is allowed his claim under the section for 2012 and his adjusted loss for the 12 months' accounts to 31 December 2012 may be set off to reduce his total income for 2012;

(3) He is allowed his claim under the section for 2013 and his adjusted loss for the 12 months' accounts to 31 December 2013 may be set off to reduce his total income for 2013; and

(4) He is allowed his claim under the section for 2014 and his adjusted loss for the 12 months' accounts to 31 December 2014 may be set off to reduce his total income for 2014.

Claim for 2015:

The inspector is now prepared to accept that Mr Hope is farming on a commercial basis and with a view to the realisation of profits. However, Mr Hope is now caught by the supporting rule as he has had farming losses in each of the three previous tax years, 2012, 2013 and 2014. Exception (b) no longer applies, but is it possible that exception (c) may apply so as to allow Mr Hope to claim a set off under TCA 1997, s 381 for his farm loss in the year ended 31 December 2015?

To deal with the latter question, the first step is to establish the 'prior period of loss' in relation to 2015. The prior three tax years consist of 2012, 2013 and 2014. However there were four successive tax years of loss prior to 2015 so the prior period of loss is extended to include 2011.

Exception (c) will therefore apply to allow Mr Hope TCA 1997, s 381 relief for his farming loss for the 12 months ended 31 December 2015 if he can satisfy the inspector that a competent farmer, who had undertaken the same farming activities from 2011 onwards, could not reasonably have expected those activities to become profitable until after 31 December 2015, ie until after the year following the prior period of loss. If this cannot be shown, Mr Hope is not entitled to any relief under TCA 1997, s 381 for his 2015 loss.

The application of the main commercial basis test and the three prior years' losses rule is not, of course, limited to the years following the commencement of farming or market gardening activities. A farmer or market gardener who has traded on a commercial basis for a number of years may cease to do so without actually ceasing trading. Alternatively, he may run into a number of consecutive loss years. If the inspector considers that the taxpayer is not farming on a commercial basis for any such year, the inspector may refuse, subject to the taxpayer's right of appeal, to accept a TCA 1997, s 381 claim for that year, even if there was not a loss in one or more prior years. Alternatively, if there are losses in each of the three prior years, even after one or more previous profitable years, the rule will operate to deny TCA 1997, s 381 relief for the fourth year.

TCA 1997, s 662 only affects a loss claim made under TCA 1997, s 381, but is applied in the same way and subject to the same exceptions, whether the claim is only for the adjusted Sch D Case I loss or is for a loss created or augmented by capital allowances through an election under TCA 1997, s 392.

TCA 1997, s 662 does not operate to restrict or deny loss relief by carry forward under TCA 1997, s 382 or by carry back as a terminal loss under TCA 1997, s 385. For example, a person who has carried on farming unsuccessfully for a number of years remains entitled to carry forward for relief under TCA 1997, s 382 all his Sch D Case I farming losses (other than losses not eligible for carry forward). Should such a farmer, or any market gardener, achieve a farming profit a number of years later, the losses carried forward remain available for deduction provided that there has been no cessation of the farmer's single trade of farming in the meantime.

7.3 Bloodstock

7.301 Introduction

The use of land as a stud farm for the breeding of thoroughbred racehorses, hunters, etc is, and always has been, regarded as husbandry or farming. Consequently, all the principles of TCA 1997, Pt 23 for the taxation of farming profits are equally applicable to the taxing of stud farms as they are to farming generally. In fact, while a number of stud farm operations are run mainly or wholly as such, it is not unusual for an ordinary farmer or farming company to carry on stud farm activities as part of the one trade. Similarly, a specialised stud farmer may also carry on some general farming activities in conjunction with his stud farm business. Irrespective of the mix between stud farming and general farming carried on by any particular person, and whether or not all the activities are being conducted in the same place, TCA 1997, s 655(1) applies to treat all the stud farming and general farming as a single trade (see **7.102**).

The object of a stud farm is usually to breed horses suitable for racing either for sale or, in many instances, for the owner of the stud farm's own racing activities, or for both purposes. Apart from the case of a racehorse trainer (see **7.306**), an individual's racing activities are always treated as 'hobby' or 'recreational' activities outside the scope of the income tax system. Any profits which he may derive from racing are not taxable and, correspondingly, his racing losses (often more likely) are not eligible for any form of tax relief and are not deductible in arriving at his taxable income for any year. Consequently, if a stud farmer also races horses, it is necessary to separate the financial results of his horse breeding (and other farming) activities from those of his racing activity. Any expenses of racing, including those of training his horses, must be excluded from his stud farm accounts, as must any prize monies or other receipts from his racing activity.

A stud farm business may be carried on by an individual, a partnership, a company or by any other person. Racing activities are normally carried on by individuals or, sometimes, by a partnership of individuals. However, should a company own and race horses as well as carrying on the trade of a stud farmer, it would appear that the company's racing activities could in certain circumstances be regarded as part of the one trade of breeding and racing. If this could be established in any particular case, any losses on the racing side of the business could be offset against profits from the breeding, or vice versa. This particular question is not free from doubt, but an argument in favour of this conclusion is that a company can hardly be said to have a hobby or to indulge in recreational activities. On the other hand, for the racing to be accepted as part of the company's overall trade, it would seem that the racing must be closely linked to the breeding activities and organised and managed in the way a trade is normally operated.

Apart from the distinction between breeding and racing, it may be necessary sometimes to distinguish a stud farmer from a dealer in bloodstock. The latter is a person who buys and sells bloodstock with the intention of making a profit, but without using the animals for breeding. While a stud farmer and a dealer in bloodstock are each taxable on their profits under Sch D Case I as traders, the distinction remains important as the dealer in bloodstock is not entitled to benefit from the stock relief and income averaging rules for which a farmer (including a stud farmer) may be eligible.

In general, the adjusted Sch D Case I profits or losses of a stud farm are arrived at in the same way as for other farming profits or losses (see **7.103**). Stock relief is given to a stud farmer under the rules relating to farming (see **7.106**). The farm buildings capital allowances, the rules restricting the extent to which initial allowances or free depreciation may be claimed on farming machinery or plant, and the rules relating to relief for farming losses, are applied to stud farms in the same way as to other farming trades (see **Division 7**).

In considering the taxation treatment of stud farms there are, however, several aspects which require separate discussion. First, the rules for the valuation of a stud farmer's trading stock, ie his mares, foals, yearlings, etc, differ from those used to value an ordinary farmer's livestock. Secondly, if animals bred in the stud are transferred to the stud farmer's own racing (or hunting) activities, it is necessary to consider the values at which they are transferred out of the stud and, if relevant, the values at which animals may be transferred back to the stud for breeding purposes after they have finished racing. Thirdly, there is the treatment of stallions and of income received for the services of stallions.

7.302 Valuation of bloodstock as trading stock

The accounts of stud farms are generally made up annually to 31 December. A stud farmer's trading stock at 31 December in any year normally consists of his brood mares (most of whom are likely to be in foal), his foals, yearlings and, sometimes, two-year olds and three-year olds. Under the Rules of Racing (flat racing) and the National Hunt Rules (steeplechasing), a horse is treated as becoming a year older on 1 January in each year, irrespective of its actual date of birth. Consequently, taking a stud farmer's closing stock included in his balance sheet at, say, 31 December 2015, the foals included are all animals born at any time in the calendar year 2015, the yearlings those born in 2014, the two-year olds in 2013, etc. Any foal born in 2015 becomes a yearling on 1 January 2016 and, if not intended to be retained for the owner's own racing establishment, may well be sold at one of the yearling sales in 2016, thus ceasing to be trading stock before the 31 December 2016 balance sheet date.

In practice, horses intended for the owner's racing activities are generally transferred out of the stud farm and sent for training prior to racing while two-year olds, although animals expected to be steeplechasers, ie under National Hunt rules, are more likely to remain in the stud farm trading stock until after becoming three-year olds. This brief outline of the times at which animals bred on the stud farm cease to be trading stock is only intended to indicate the general position. There may, of course, be two-year olds and three-year olds remaining in stud farm trading stock after the time at which the progeny of the stud are normally sold or transferred to racing.

The valuation of all animals in the closing trading stock at any relevant balance sheet date should be made under the normal rule for valuing trading stock generally, ie each animal should be brought into stock at its 'cost' unless its 'market value' at the balance sheet date is lower, in which case the lower market value figure should be used. Due to the special nature of a stud farm business, it may not be easy to arrive at an accurate figure for the cost of any animal, but the Revenue Commissioners have drawn up a number of principles which are, in general, accepted by stud farmers as providing a reasonable approach to the determination of the cost of the animals within each category. These are now discussed as follows:

Brood mares

The largest element of the trading stock of a stud farmer is normally his stock of brood mares, some of which may have high stock values attaching to them, particularly if purchased for the stud farm from another owner after a successful racing career. Each mare must be brought into trading stock at the lower of her cost or market value. Each mare has her own base cost which, if the mare is in foal at the balance sheet date, must be increased to reflect the cost of producing the foal. For the 'cost' value as trading stock of the mare at any later balance sheet date, the same base cost is taken, but the addition in respect of any foal conceived in the later year is the cost of producing that foal. In short, each mare retains the same base cost until she is sold, dies or otherwise ceases to be stud farm trading stock.

The base cost of any mare purchased from another owner, whether the mare was acquired by the stud farmer first for racing (or hunting) or was purchased directly for the stud, is the actual purchase price paid. The cost of any mare that was originally bred by the stud farmer himself, and which he has continued to own, is her cost of production as previously determined in the stud farm accounts, whether or not the mare has been raced in the meantime. This cost of production should be taken as the 'cost' value of the animal concerned that was credited to the stud farm accounts at the time she was transferred out to racing (see **7.303**). Should the own bred mare not have been raced, but retained throughout as stud farm trading stock, her base cost as a brood mare is her cost of production up to the 1 January in the year she became a three-year old (see below).

For the mare in foal at the balance sheet date, the addition to the base cost of the mare to reflect the cost of producing the foal may be taken as the sum of the following items:

(a) the stud fee (if any) paid for the services of the stallion with which the mare was mated to produce the foal;

(b) the cost of keep of the mare while at stud with the stallion;

(c) the costs of carriage of the mare from the stud farm to where the stallion was standing and of her return to the stud farm;

(d) the costs of keep of the mare at the stud farm from the date of her return from the stallion to the accounting date; and

(e) the cost of insurance of the mare (and the foal) over the period covered by (a) to (d).

In practice, the addition to the mare's base cost in respect of the foal is often taken as the sum of (a) the stud fee (if any) paid for the stallion and (b) the cost of keep of the mare from the time she goes to the stallion to the end of the accounting period (ie items (a), (b) and (d) above). This simpler formula is normally accepted by inspectors of taxes in cases where it is used, although it is understood that the Revenue considers the more detailed costing approach indicated above is technically more correct. Whichever method is used, it should be applied consistently in each successive year.

In *Tax Briefing 25*, the Revenue Commissioners state that, in ascertaining the net realisable value of a brood mare, a number of factors need to be taken into account. These include the mare's own physical appearance, bloodlines and racing history, age, fertility, history in the sales ring or on the racing track of any progeny, etc. While the above criteria must be taken into account in estimating the net realisable value of the mare, the valuation is nonetheless largely a matter of judgment on the part of the person who values the mare. The Revenue will not object in principle to the revaluation of a brood mare which results in a reduction of its value in the accounts to net realisable value, so long as this is justified on the facts. The Revenue point out that the taxpayer may be asked to justify the valuation in the course of a Revenue audit. However, it has been agreed that where the valuation of a thoroughbred brood mare becomes an issue during an audit, the taxpayer may request the inspector to refer the matter to the Technical Services Unit of the Office of the Chief Inspector of Taxes for consideration. The Revenue Commissioners point out that this facility will not affect the taxpayer's right to an independent review as laid down in the *Taxpayer's Charter of Rights* or to any statutory right of appeal to the Appeal Commissioners. This review procedure is only available for thoroughbred mares.

If instead of paying a stud fee for the stallion, the stud farmer purchases a 'nomination' to the stallion from another person entitled to the use of the stallion's services (see **7.305**), the cost of that nomination is taken into the cost of the foal instead of the stud fee. If the stud farmer uses the stallion free of charge, either because he owns the stallion himself or owns a share in him which entitles him to a free service, no addition is made under heading (a) as only actual costs incurred may be brought in. For the cost of keep of the mare, a round sum estimate is usually taken instead of an exact figure, particularly if there are a number of mares involved.

Finally, if the mare has proved barren after being with the stallion, there is of course no addition to be made in respect of a foal in her 'cost' for the next balance sheet stock valuation. In practice, if a mare has been barren for a few years, this may be accepted by the inspector of taxes as a good reason for justifying a market value below cost, especially if the mare was one bought in at a high figure. Otherwise, inspectors of taxes tend to resist the writing down of a mare to a claimed market value below cost so long as the mare continues to be used for breeding purposes. It is of course open to the taxpayer to produce evidence to satisfy the inspector that a lower market value is justified in any particular case.

Mares bought in foal

A stud farmer may purchase a mare that is already in foal. In this case, the purchase price is treated as if it included the advertised stallion fee and the relevant costs of keep of the mare up to the date of purchase. Consequently, her trading stock 'cost' at the end of the year is taken as full purchase price plus the further costs of keep from the date of purchase to the year end. In arriving at the base cost of the mare for all subsequent years, the purchase price is reduced by the advertised stallion fee and the cost of keep to the date of purchase which were treated as included in the purchase price. This deduction of the advertised stud fee is made even if the previous owner did not in fact pay any stud fee or purchase any nomination to the stallion, perhaps because he had the free use of the stallion's services. The advertised stud fee for any stallion is normally published each year by its owner(s).

Foals

The 'cost' of each foal in trading stock at the first year end following its birth is taken as being the sum of its cost of production as included in the stock value of its mother at the previous year end and the cost of keep for the whole of the year to the current balance sheet date. In fact, part of the cost of keep is for the mare before the birth of the foal during the year just ended and the rest is for the keep of the foal itself after its birth. However, as it is normal practice to assume the same per annum cost of keep for a mare as for a foal, only one per annum figure is normally added. Strictly, the cost of insurance of the foal for the year should probably be included also in its stock cost value, but in practice this is not always done.

Yearlings, two-year olds, etc

The 'cost' of each yearling in trading stock is normally the sum of its cost value as a foal at the end of the previous year and a further per annum addition for the cost of its keep in the year just ended (again usually taken at the same figure used for the cost of keep of a mare or foal). Similarly, the cost of a two-year old is the previous year's cost value as a yearling plus a further annual charge for the cost of keep in the year just ended. The concept behind this yearly addition for the cost of keep is that this is a further cost of producing the animal until it becomes mature. Bloodstock are regarded for tax purposes as becoming mature when they become three-year olds. Therefore no cost of keep addition should be made for any time after the year as a two-year old. It is also to be noted that the cost of keep addition only applies so long as the animal continues to be maintained at the stud. It is not, however, relevant for (say) a two-year old after the time it is taken out of stud for training or racing.

7.303 Transfers between stud farm and racing

When the person carrying on the stud farm business transfers animals bred on the stud to his own racing stable or sends them to a trainer prior to racing, the stud farm accounts must be credited with the cost value of each animal concerned at the date of its transfer. Cost for this purpose is the trading stock cost value at the balance sheet date preceding the transfer to racing/training plus, in the case of any animal younger than a three-year old, the cost of its keep from the previous year end to the date of the transfer. For example, if a colt which was in trading stock as a yearling on 31 December 2014 at a cost value of €9,100 (cost as foal at 31 December 2013 of €7,800 plus 2014 keep of €1,300) is transferred to the stud farmer's racing stable on 31 March 2015, the amount to be credited to the stud farm account for the year to 31 December 2015 would be arrived at as follows:

	€
Cost value of yearling at 31/12/2014	9,100
Add:	
Cost of keep 1/1/2015 to 31/3/2015:	
€1,500 per annum (say) x 3/12	375
Transfer price	9,475

When racehorses are transferred back to the stud farm for breeding purposes after their racing careers, the stud farm trading account should then be debited with the *cost* of the animal to its owner, irrespective of its actual market value at the time of the transfer. This is normally relevant only for mares as it is the exception rather than the rule for a stallion to become trading stock of a stud farm (see **7.304**). In the case of a mare that was purchased while still in racing from any other person, it is the cost of this purchase that is taken as the transfer price to be charged to the stud farm account when the animal is brought back to stud. On the other hand, if the animal is one bred originally by the stud farmer himself prior to her transfer to his own racing activity, then on her subsequent transfer back to the stud farm, her original cost value (ie that credited to the stud farm account on the earlier transfer to racing) is the figure to be debited. In this latter case, the fact that the own bred filly may have appreciated many times in value due to a highly successful racing career is irrelevant.

It is interesting to note that, once an animal has been transferred out of the stud to racing/training, any profit on a subsequent sale by the owner is related to the racing activity and is not subject to any income tax (or corporation tax). Correspondingly, no loss on such a sale or on the death of the animal after it leaves the stud is deductible for tax purposes. This applies notwithstanding that the market value of the animal at the time it left the stud may have been substantially in excess of its cost value credited to the stud farm accounts on the transfer out. This practice of crediting transfers from stud farm to racing at cost, and of debiting transfers back at cost, is in contrast to that used in the UK where, as a result of the House of Lords decision in *Sharkey v Wernher* [1953] 36 TC 275, the accounts of a UK stud farm have to be credited or debited, whichever is the case, with the market value of the animals transferred to or from the same person's racing activities. The Irish Revenue has made it clear that it does not seek to apply the *Sharkey v Wernher* decision in this context (but see **5.101**, **5.602**) and that it considers that the proper treatment for Irish tax purposes is to make the transfers at cost.

The principle that these transfers to and from racing are at cost does not apply if the stud farm and the racing establishment are owned by different persons. For example, a racehorse owner may set up a company to carry on the stud farm business, but may race in his own name. In this case, there is normally a sale by the company to the individual shareholder or, perhaps, to the shareholder's spouse, or even to a racing partnership in which one or more of the shareholders are partners. The stud farm accounts should in any such case reflect the actual sale that takes place and, usually, it is to be expected that the sale price in the transaction will be a reasonably commercial one.

7.304 Illustrations of bloodstock valuations

The principles just described for the valuation of bloodstock as trading stock, and for the 'transfer values' on transfers from stud farm to racing and from racing back to stud farm, may be more easily understood if a few examples are given.

Example 7.304.1

Mr A Breeder, who has carried on business as a stud farmer for a number of years, has three mares in foal at his 31 December 2014 balance sheet date – Floss, Moss and Candy. Relevant facts regarding the acquisition of these mares are:

Floss:

Born on the stud farm on 28/2/2009, transferred to Mr Breeder's racing stable as a two-year old (2 YO) on 1/5/2011, raced for several years before being transferred back to stud on 1/4/2014;

Moss:

Purchased for racing by Mr Breeder from another owner on 1/7/2010 for €30,000, raced in 2010 and 2012 and then transferred by Mr Breeder to his stud farm on 1/4/2014;

Candy:

Purchased directly for his stud farm by Mr Breeder on 1/11/2009 for €120,000 and has since remained one of the stud farm's brood mares (although both its 2010 and 2012 matings proved barren).

The trading stock 'base costs' of Moss and Candy are respectively €30,000 and €120,000, ie their costs of purchase. The fact that Moss won several important races after being acquired by Mr Breeder and had an estimated market value of €100,000 when transferred to stud on 1/4/2014 is irrelevant. Floss's base cost as trading stock is her cost of production as an own bred filly up to the date of her transfer to racing (1/5/2011); this is determined as follows based on the figures assumed below:

	€
Sire's fee paid (mare Dentist with stallion Doctor)	2,200
Mare's keep while with stallion and carrying foal:	
Say €800 per annum for 12 months	800
Carriage of mare to and from stallion, insurance, etc	1,800
Cost to date of birth (28/2/2009)	4,800
Keep as foal (1/3/2009 to 31/12/2009) say €800 per annum x 10/12	667
Keep as yearling (year 2010): say €880	880
Keep as 2 Y O (1/1/2011 to 1/5/2011): say €1,000 per annum x 4/12	333
Cost when sent to racing (1/5/2011)	6,680

Since Floss has continued in Mr Breeder's ownership from 1/5/2011 until her transfer back to the stud farm as trading stock on 1/4/2014, her base cost as a stud farm brood mare is her 'cost' up to the date of transfer to racing, ie €6,680.

Example 7.304.2

Take the facts of **Example 7.304.1** and assume that the three mares were each sent to stallions on 1/4/2014 and that after mating they were returned to the stud farm each having received a foal. They were mated as follows:

Floss: with stallion Nurse owned by a Mr B Boru for a stud fee of €3,600;

Moss: with stallion Hospital owned by a syndicate of which Mr Breeder was not a member, nomination to the stallion purchased by him for €2,400;

Candy: with stallion Surgery owned by a syndicate of which Mr Breeder was a member, right to service obtained free of charge.

The trading stock 'cost' values of each mare in foal at 31/12/2014 are determined as follows:

	Floss	*Moss*	*Candy*
	€	€	€
(a) Cost of foal (up to 31/12/2014):			
Sire's fee	3,600		
Cost of stallion nomination		2,400	
Free stallion service			
Mare's keep (1/4/2014 to 31/12/2014):			
say €1,200 per annum x 9/12	900	900	900
Carriage of mares, insurance, etc			
say, with differences due to varying			
values for insurance	2,900	2,600	2,200
	7,400	5,900	3,100
(b) Base cost of mare:			
as per **Example 7.304**.1	6,680	30,000	120,000
Cost of mare in foal	14,080	35,900	123,100

The trading stock values of Floss and Moss are taken as these cost values of €14,080 and €35,900 respectively. However, in view of Candy's previous two barren services, and also having regard to her only being expected to have a few breeding years left, Mr Breeder obtains expert opinion that Candy's market value as a mare in foal at 31/12/2014 is only €45,000. Since this figure is less than its cost as a mare in foal of €123,100, the lower market value of €45,000 is taken into the closing stock valuation. Assuming that the inspector of taxes is satisfied that €45,000 is a valid market value, the Sch D Case I computation must follow this accounting treatment.

Example 7.304.3

Mr A Breeder purchased a mare already in foal for €52,000 on 15 September 2014. The previous owner had mated the mare with his own stallion, Buonaparte, and had not therefore paid any stallion fee. The mare had been put with the stallion on 1 March 2014 and the previous owner had met the cost of the mare's keep from that date to the sale on 15 September 2014. Mr Breeder charges the keep of the mare in foal from 15 September 2014 onwards in his stud farm accounts. The previous owner had advertised the services of Buonaparte for €1,900 for the 2014 mating season.

The mare in foal's 'cost' value for inclusion in Mr Breeder's trading stock at 31 December 2014 is arrived at as follows:

	€
Purchase price paid (15/9/2014)	52,000
Keep of animal (16/9/2014 to 31/12/2014) say 1,200 per annum x 3.5/12	350
Insurance (16/9/2014 to 31/12/2014)	430
Cost as trading stock	52,780

The mare's base cost for future trading stock valuations is arrived at as follows:

	€	€
Purchase price paid (15/9/2014)		52,000
Less:		
Advertised stud fee for Buonaparte	1,900	
Keep (1/3/2014 to 15/9/2014) €1,200 X 7.5/12	750	
		2,650
Base cost of mare (ex foal)		49,350

Example 7.304.4

Take the three mares in **Example 7.304.2** included in Mr Breeder's stud farm trading stock at 31 December 2015. Floss gives birth to a colt and Moss to a filly, each new foal being born towards the end of February 2015. Unfortunately, the mare Candy dies in January 2015 and there is no foal. The trading stock 'cost' values of the two foals at 31 December 2015 are determined as follows:

	Colt *(ex Floss)*	*Filly* *(ex Moss)*
	€	€
Cost of foal (up to 31/12/2014) as per **Example 7.304.2**	7,400	5,900
Keep for whole of 2015 say €1,300 each	1,300	1,300
Cost as trading stock 31/12/15	8,700	7,200

Since the 31 December 2014 closing stock value of €45,000 for Candy with foal (see **Example 7.304.2** above) is also debited as part of the opening stock value at 1 January

2015, the death of the mare results in the reflection of a gross loss of €45,000 in the stud farm accounts for the year 2015.

7.305 Treatment of stallions, stallion fees etc

The stud farmer may own one or more stallions for the service of his mares, or he may send his mares to the stallions of other owners to be serviced for a stud or stallion fee, or he may acquire a share in a syndicate stallion, ie one owned jointly by a number of persons under a syndication agreement. In practice, since thoroughbred racing stallions are very expensive, especially those that have been successful in racing so as to be much sought after for breeding, the syndication route is the approach that is taken in many cases. Further, even where a stallion is owned by a single person, it is more than likely that it will be used to service not only its owner's mares, but also the mares of other owners in consideration for stud fees.

In theory, a stallion owned by a stud farmer, kept on his land and used mainly for the servicing of his own mares might be regarded as trading stock in the same way as the mares used for breeding. In practice, even where a stallion is wholly owned by a stud farmer, it is more than likely that the stallion will be used to a significant extent to service also the mares of other owners. The fact that fees earned for such services were tax exempt up to 31 July 2008 (see below) generally provided a strong reason for using the stallion in this way, particularly as the stud farmer can charge in his accounts (and therefore in his Sch D Case I computation) any stud fees he himself pays for using another person's stallion. Consequently, there were few (if any) cases where stallions were owned and used in such a way as to require them to be treated as trading stock.

The more usual form of stallion syndicate is one where the ownership of the stallion is divided into 40 shares and the members of the syndicate own one or more shares each. The original owner of the stallion, often the person who had previously raced it, may well have retained a number of shares himself, but this is not essential. Depending on the exact terms of the syndication agreement, each share usually entitles its holder to have one of his mares serviced by the stallion each year. Any member of the syndicate not wishing to use this right to the stallion's services in any year is entitled to sell that right (the 'nomination' to another person who would like to mate one of his mares with the stallion in that year).

A stallion owned by a syndicate is usually kept on the land of one of the members, although it may sometimes be kept on the land of another person in consideration for an appropriate charge and the reimbursement of its expenses of keep, etc. The expenses of keep of the stallion, veterinary and other expenses, any rent or other charge paid to the person on whose land it stands, its insurance, etc must be shared by the members of the syndicate in proportion to the number of shares held by each. In practice, there are often one or two additional nominations to the stallion available and the syndicate may itself sell those nominations and use the proceeds to offset the syndicate expenses. However to the extent that there are excess expenses, each member has to pay in his appropriate share of the excess. If the syndicate income for any year should exceed its expenses, the excess income is usually divided among the members in proportion to their shares.

Stallion fees *paid* by a stud farmer, or the cost of purchase of the rights to nominations to stallions, for the purpose of servicing his mares are a deductible expense in his stud farm accounts. As previously mentioned in **7.302**, any stallion fee paid for the servicing of a mare is included in arriving at that mare's trading stock cost value if the mare is in foal at the following year end and, after the foal is born, becomes part of the foal's cost for trading stock purposes. In short, the stallion fee or the cost of purchasing a nomination is in effect carried forward in the trading stock valuation until the progeny is sold or transferred out of the stud to training/racing. Any stallion fee or cost of a nomination paid for a service that turns out to be barren is not included in any trading stock valuation, so that the effect of the deduction for the expense is felt in arriving at the stud farm profit or loss for the year in which the expense is incurred.

While the stud farmer who pays a stallion fee or purchases a nomination to a syndicate stallion deducts the amount paid as a trading expense, the cost of acquiring a share in a stallion is treated as capital expenditure for which no deduction is available under normal Sch D Case I principles. The fact that a stud farmer's object in acquiring a share in a stallion is almost invariably to enable him to have the use of the stallion's services each year does not alter this. Further, it has been held that capital expenditure on the purchase of a stallion does not qualify as expenditure on machinery or plant for which a wear and tear allowance can be claimed. In *Earl of Derby v Aylmer* 6 TC 665, Rowlatt J held that a stallion kept for breeding purposes was a wasting source of production which, although his value might diminish year by year as it grew older, did not diminish in value by reason of wear and tear.

The Revenue is now, however, prepared to allow a special deduction to the stud farmer who uses a free service from a syndicate stallion in which he has acquired a share. The same deduction is also given where he uses his own stallion to service a particular mare or mares in his own stud farm. In either of these cases, the deduction is given in the computation of the stud farm profit (or loss) for the year in which the colt or filly resulting from the particular stallion service is sold. It is not given at all if the mare does not produce a foal as a result of the service or if the foal dies before it is sold, but the death of the mare after giving birth does not prevent the giving of the deduction if the colt or filly survives and is sold while still stud farm trading stock.

The deduction given is of an amount equal to the fee that was being advertised for the services of the particular stallion at the time the mating took place, but is limited (if necessary) so that no loss arises on the sale of the colt or filly. In effect, therefore, the amount deductible is the lower of the advertised stallion fee and the excess of the sale price for the colt or filly over its 'cost' as trading stock at the date of the sale. This means that no deduction is available if the colt or filly is transferred to the stud farmer's racing stable since, in that case, as the transfer price is credited to the accounts at 'cost', any deduction at all would result in a loss.

Example 7.305.1

Take the facts of **Example 7.304.2**. Mr Breeder was entitled to deduct as trading expense, in his stud farm accounts for the year to 31 December 2014, the sire fee of €3,600 paid in that year to have his mare Floss serviced by the stallion Nurse. Similarly, he was entitled to deduct in the same year the €2,400 paid for the nomination to the stallion Hospital used to service his mare Moss. He was not entitled to any expense deduction in 2014 for the cost of purchasing his share in the stallion Surgery, nor for any proportion of that cost.

Assume that the mare Candy had not died (as assumed in **Example 7.304.4**) but had lived to produce a colt born on 1 March 2015. This colt is in due course sold as yearling for €9,000 on 15 September 2016. On the assumption that the stallion fee advertised by the syndicate for the services of Surgery in 2014 was €4,300, the tax treatment of the colt is as follows:

	€
Cost as a foal (up to 31/12/2014) as per **Example 7.304.2**	3,100
Keep as foal to 31/12/2015 say	1,200

Keep as yearling (1/1/2016 to 15/9/2016) say €1,400 per annum x 8.5/12	992
Cost up to date of sale	5,292
Sale as yearling	9,000
Gross profit on sale	3,708

Mr Breeder is given the special deduction in his stud farm Sch D Case I computation for the year to 31 December 2016, as follows:

	€
Advertised stud fee for Surgery in 2014	4,300
but deduction cannot produce loss on sale of colt	
Deduction limited to 'gross profit'	3,708

The stallion fees exemption and the replacement regime

TCA 1997, s 231 exempted from income tax the profits or gains arising to the owner of a stallion from the sale of services of mares by the stallion or to the *part-owner* of a stallion in respect of any profits or gains from either the sale of the stallion's services or the sale of rights (nominations) to his services. The exemption applied only if the stallion was ordinarily kept on land in the State and if the servicing of the mares took place in the State. TCA 1997, s 231(4) as inserted by FA 2006, s 22 terminated the exemption with effect from 31 July 2008. This relief was potentially subject to the restrictions applicable to high income individuals discussed at **3.111**.

The term 'part-owner' would not include a lessee but would seem apt to cover a partner in a partnership owning a stallion (unless the terms of the partnership were such that he had no beneficial interest in the stallion).

In the case of a stallion ordinarily kept on land outside the State, a part-owner (but not a sole owner) was also entitled to the exemption in respect of the profits from the sale of the stallion's services or of rights to those services, but only if:

(a) the part-owner carried on *in the State* a trade consisting of or including bloodstock breeding; and

(b) it is shown to the satisfaction of the inspector or on appeal to the Appeal Commissioners that the part-ownership of the stallion was acquired, and was held primarily, for the purposes of the service of mares owned or partly-owned by the part-owner of the stallion in the course of that trade. The satisfaction requirement mentioned above was removed by F(TA)A 2015, s 35(7) but such amendment was subject to Ministerial Order (SI 110/2016 appointed 21 March 2016 as the day on which the Finance (Tax Appeals) Act 2015, came into operation).

As noted above, the tax exemption for stallion stud fees expired on 31 July 2008. With effect from 1 August 2008, profits arising from stallion stud fees or from the disposal of stallions are subject to taxation. FA 2007, s 26 introduced new sections TCA 1997, s 669G–669K to cater for the new regime and to provide for appropriate transitional measures. The new regime applies to the owners of stallions and also the owners of interests in stallions through a syndicate. Stallion fees and other profits arising to farmers are taxed under the new regime as part of their farming profits under Sch D case I (TCA 1997, s 669H(2)(a)), whereas such income arising to non-farmers is taxed under Sch D Case IV (TCA 1997, s 669H(2)(b)), although still computed under Sch D Case I principles (TCA 1997, s 669I(2)(b)). However, in the case of farmers, stallions do not qualify for stock relief (TCA 1997, s 669K(2)).

The normal expenses for the upkeep of stallions are allowed in computing profits and a deduction by way of revenue expense in respect of the purchase cost of a stallion is provided over four years at 25 per cent per annum. Where the stallion was at stud on 1 August 2008, the first such deduction was granted in the period of account in which that date fell; in all other cases, the first such deduction was granted in the period of account in which the date of acquisition or appropriation fell as appropriate (TCA 1997, s 669I). The cost of stallions purchased after 31 July 2008 is to be taken, for the purposes of the 25 per cent deduction, as their purchase price in the cases of an arm's length transaction between persons who are not connected within the meaning of TCA 1997, s 10 (see the discussion at **12.304**); otherwise, open market value will apply. In cases where stallions were standing at stud prior to 1 August 2008, the cost of the stallion for the purposes of the 25 per cent per annum deduction is their open market value at 1 August 2008; where stallions transfer to stud from racing or training or are bred on farm or held as stock in trade after that date the cost of the stallion for the purposes of the 25 per cent per annum deduction in the open market value on the date of appropriation to stud (TCA 1997, s 669G). The Revenue Commissioners may consult with any person they see fit in order to determine the open market value of a stallion (TCA 1997, s 669K(1)).

On the disposal or death of a stallion, the 'residual value' of the stallion, ie its opening ('initial') value net of any 25 per cent deductions written off as an expense in previous periods of account, will be written off as a revenue expense in the period of disposal; the disposal proceeds (if any) will be taken into account as revenue profits of the same period (TCA 1997, s 669K(1)).

Where the profits from ownership or part ownership of a stallion or stallions are chargeable under Sch D Case IV any losses arising may not be offset against other Sch D Case IV income of that tax year but may only be carried forward for offset against profits from the same activities (TCA 1997, s 669K(3)).

Provision is made also so that the amounts of any additional tax arising as a result of the cap placed on the exemption for stallion fees and dividends from companies with exempt stallion income under TCA 1997, s 485C for 2007 and 2008 (see **3.111**) may be carried forward and credited against the tax liabilities of subsequent years (TCA 1997, s 669J).

Requirement to include profits or gains in annual return

Notwithstanding that the profits or gains arising from stallion activities were deemed to be exempt up to 31 July 2008 by the Income Tax Acts, TCA 1997, s 231(2), (3) as inserted by FA 2004, s 35 introduced a requirement that the full profits or gains arising from such an activity were required to be included in the annual return of income for each period of assessment with effect for the tax year 2004 onwards. Similarly, where losses were incurred, these were also required to be included in the return. Furthermore, the fact that a person would not be a chargeable person for self-assessment purposes (see **2.102**) as a result of their income comprising exempt stallion fees would not have prevented them from being treated as such, so that they would have been obliged to make a return. Any notice issued under TCA 1997, s 951(6) (excluding a taxpayer from having to file a tax return) was also disregarded. The normal rules relating to the keeping of records and the making available of such records for inspection by the Revenue Commissioners also applied.

7.306 Racehorse trainers

A racehorse trainer is regarded by the Revenue as an exception to the principle that the racing of horses is a recreational activity not subject to income tax. A trainer's ownership and racing of horses is normally considered to be part of his trade or profession as a trainer. Apart from training the racehorses of his patrons (racehorse owners), it is not unusual for a trainer to acquire promising animals and to turn them into racehorses and either race them himself with the intention of selling them in due course or of selling them directly to other racehorse owners with whom he is in contact. In effect, he may be dealing in horses, often using his skills as a trainer to improve their racing abilities to enable him to make more profitable sales.

In *Tax Briefing 20*, the Revenue Commissioners state that they take the view that once a trainer has the use of land, or the right by virtue of any easement (as defined by TCA 1997, s 96) to graze livestock on land, then he will be regarded as carrying on the trade of a farmer. As a result the trainer would be entitled to farm buildings allowances and presumably also, stock relief, as appropriate (but note *Wheatley v IRC* [1198] STC (SCD) 60).

The trainer is taxable on any profits he may make on the sale of racehorses acquired by him, whether he sells them immediately, after training them or after training and/or racing them. Any racehorses which the trainer has acquired in the course of his business are treated as trading stock.

In arriving at the Sch D Case I profits on which a trainer is chargeable to income tax, it is necessary to bring in as trading receipts all fees, etc he receives for training the horses of his patrons, the proceeds of all sales of horses owned by him and sold in the course of his trade, any winnings or prize money he may receive from racing his own horses, etc. It is usual for trainers to receive presents from racehorse owners for training winners (often a percentage of the owner's prize money). Clearly any such presents must be included as the receipts of his trade. In calculating his taxable profits, the trainer is entitled to deduct as part of his trading expenses the costs of training his own horses, as well as all other revenue expenses incurred wholly and exclusively for the purpose of his trade or profession (subject to any restrictions applicable to Sch D Case I and II generally, eg business entertainment expenses not deductible).

7.307 Stud greyhound service fees

TCA 1997, s 233 provided an exemption for profits from the sale of qualifying greyhound services in terms which are modelled on those applicable to stallion fees. TCA 1997, s 233 exempted profits or gains arising either to:

(a) the owner or part-owner of a stud greyhound which was ordinarily kept in the State, from the sale of services, or the rights to such services, of greyhound bitches within the State by the stud greyhound; or

(b) the part-owner of a stud greyhound which was ordinarily kept outside the State from the sale of services of greyhound bitches by the stud greyhound or the rights to such services where the part-owner carried on, in the State, a trade which consisted of or included greyhound breeding.

In case (b), it must also have been shown to the satisfaction of the inspector of taxes or on appeal the Appeal Commissioners that the part-ownership of the stud greyhound was acquired and held primarily for the purpose of the service by the stud greyhound of greyhound bitches owned or partly owned by the part-owner of the stud greyhound in the course of that trade. The abovementioned satisfaction requirement was removed by

F(TA)A 2015, s 35(7) however such change was subject to Ministerial Order (SI 110/2016 appointed 21 March 2016 as the day on which the Finance (Tax Appeals) Act 2015, came into operation).

TCA 1997, s 140 provides that dividends paid out of income exempted by virtue of TCA 1997, s 233 would themselves qualify for exemption in the same manner as applies to commercial woodlands and stallion service fees.

TCA 1997, s 233(5) as inserted by FA 2006, s 22 terminated the exemption with effect from 31 July 2008. This relief was potentially subject to the restrictions applicable to high income individuals discussed at **3.111**.

Requirement to include profits or gains in annual return

Notwithstanding that the profits or gains arising from stud greyhound activities were deemed to be exempt up to 31 July 2008 by the Income Tax Acts, TCA 1997, s 233(3), (4) as inserted by FA 2004, s 35 introduced a requirement that the full profits or gains arising from such an activity was required to be included in the annual return of income for each period of assessment with effect for the tax year 2004 onwards. Similarly, where losses were incurred, these were also required to be included in the return. Furthermore, the fact that a person would not be a chargeable person for self-assessment purposes (see **2.102**) as a result of their income comprising exempt greyhound fees would not have prevented them from being treated as such, so that they were obliged to make a return. Any notice issued under TCA 1997, s 951(6) (excluding a taxpayer from having to file a tax return) would also have been disregarded. The normal rules relating to the keeping of records and the making available of such records for inspection by the Revenue Commissioners would also apply.

7.4 Woodlands

7.401 Woodlands inside the State

The operation of woodlands is normally a long-term venture. Usually, it starts with the planting by the owner of suitable land with young trees which take a number of years to grow until they mature and are ready to be cut down so that the 'crop' can be harvested and profits made. The period of growth depends on the nature of the trees. For example, trees grown for the Christmas tree market may be ready to harvest in eight to ten years after planting while, at the other extreme, some trees may be left to grow for 40 or 50 years, or even longer. The operation generally involves a certain amount of maintenance each year in keeping the estate pathways clear, in dealing with storm damage and, usually, in thinning out the trees from time to time.

Except for receipts from the sale of trees or wood resulting from storm damage or thinnings, the normal pattern is for the operator of the woodlands to incur expenses for a number of years with no real income to offset them. It is only a number of years after planting when profits can be earned as the trees grow to maturity and are felled for the sale of the timber.

TCA 1997, s 232 provides that the profits or gains arising from the occupation of woodlands managed on a commercial basis and with a view to the realisation of profits are not to be taken into account for any purpose of the Income Tax Acts. In other words, such profits are completely exempted from income tax and are not included in the occupier's total income, taxable income or otherwise.

For the purposes of this exemption, 'woodlands' means woodlands in the State and 'occupation', in relation to any land, means having the use of it (TCA 1997, s 232(1)). In *Jaggers v Ellis* [1997] STC 1417, Lightman J held that the term 'woodlands' implies the production of timber (so that a plantation of Christmas trees was more in the nature of a nursery rather than woodlands). It is understood however that the Revenue accept that the cultivation of Christmas trees qualifies for the exemption (see ITR November 1997 p 22).

An Irish resident person who derives any profits or gains from woodlands situated outside the State (eg in the UK) is not, therefore, covered by the exemption and is chargeable under Sch D Case III or Case I (see **7.402**) in respect of any such profits if the foreign woodlands are managed on a commercial basis with a view to the realisation of profits. The exemption is only given to the occupier of woodlands managed on a commercial basis, etc. In the majority of cases, the owner of the lands on which the trees are growing is also the occupier of the woodlands and no difficulty arises. However, the definition of 'occupier' given in the previous paragraph makes it clear that a person who may be in a position to make a profit from felling trees and selling the timber, is not entitled to have his profit exempted unless he has the use of the lands in the accepted sense of the word 'use'. Since it is not uncommon practice for an owner of woodlands to grant to another person the right to enter his lands to fell the trees and take away the timber, it may be necessary in such a case to ask the question whether it is the owner of the woodlands or the person felling the trees and actually selling the timber that is entitled to the exemption.

In *Russell v Hird* [1983] STC 541, Mr H agreed in February 1976 to purchase the timber from certain woodlands for £38,345 on certain terms as to the management of the land during the felling, the operations of which were to be completed by 31 January 1979. In March 1976, H entered into an agreement with a Mr M to sell a one half share in the timber to him and to form a syndicate with him to fell, market and sell the timber. H and M insured the timber, constructed two roadways through the woodlands, gave permission to an adjoining occupier to use the roadways, provided equipment and labour for felling the timber and, in accordance with the purchase agreement, made good any damage caused by the felling operations, maintained the gates and ditches and cleared the land for the next planting.

The Inland Revenue contended that a person could not be said to be in occupation of woodlands unless he had the exclusive, or at least the 'paramount', use of them and that H & M, who had only a limited right of entry for the specific purpose of taking a particular crop, should be regarded as being in a subordinate position to the landowner whose occupation was paramount. This argument went on to claim that the granting of rights to take the timber was merely the means by which the landowner realised the fruits of his land.

Warner J held that the question of who was the occupier of particular land at a particular time was a question of fact. In deciding that question, one should look not only at the legal rights of the persons concerned, but also at what was done by each of them on the land. There was no finding by the Commissioners that the landowner did anything on the land while the taxpayers were active there and even if he had walked or shot over the land, as he was entitled to do so provided that he did not interfere with the exercise by the taxpayers of their contractual rights, it was open to the Commissioners on the evidence to find that the taxpayers' occupation was paramount and the landowner's occupation subordinate.

It should be emphasised that the facts in *Russell v Hird* were somewhat unusual and that, should a similar case occur where it is a question of whether persons in a corresponding position to that of H & M would be entitled to the Irish woodlands exemption, it is not certain that the Appeal Commissioners (or the Circuit Court judge) would take the same view on the particular facts and evidence before them. Almost certainly, should a timber merchant or any other person merely be given the right to enter woodlands for the purpose of felling trees and taking away the timber, without being involved in various other acts of an 'occupier' such as H & M performed in *Russell v Hird*, the timber merchant would not be given the woodlands exemption, but would be taxable under Sch D Case I on his profits from selling the timber. In any event, it is the particular facts of each separate case that must be applied to determine who is the occupier of the woodlands.

In *O'Conaill v Z Ltd* II ITR 636, the Supreme Court in construing the phrase 'have the use therefore' upheld the two principles, namely that:

(a) it was necessary to look at the effect of the actual use of the land in question by the taxpayer; and

(b) where there were two concurrent users of the land in question, it was only the predominant use which should be taken into account.

The exemption given by TCA 1997, s 232 is limited to the profits or gains 'from the occupation of' the woodlands. The exemption clearly applies where the profits from the sale of the trees, whether as standing timber or as felled and cut up, are made by a landowner who has planted the trees and managed the woodlands estate. It applies also where the sales are made by a landowner who has acquired by purchase, inheritance or otherwise woodlands previously planted, assuming he continues to occupy and manage them on a commercial basis. No difficulty arises where the occupier realises his profits from trees on his own woodlands even though he may use a sawmill to cut up the felled timber into logs, lengths of planking, etc to make the timber more marketable, but, should the sawmill or other operation involved go beyond that and carry out further processing of the timber before its sale, then he may be subject to tax under Sch D Case I on the profits of a trade.

In short, it may sometimes be necessary to consider whether, and to what extent, the profits from the sale of the timber arise from the occupation of the woodlands or, alternatively, whether a part of the profits are attributable to a separate and distinct operation unconnected with the occupation of the woodlands. Any profit arising from such a separate operation is not covered by the woodlands exemption, but is taxable under Sch D Case I. However, there have been various UK tax cases which suggest that a commercial woodland operation may involve a reasonable amount of work on the felled timber before the question of there being a separate trade arises. Further, if there should be such a separate trade carried on by the person entitled to the woodlands exemption, it is only that part of the total profits realised by the occupier of the woodlands which arises subsequent to what may be regarded as normal exploitation of his woodlands and its crop that is taxable under Sch D Case I.

In *IRC v Williamson Bros* 31 TC 370, a firm carrying on business as timber merchants and sawmillers purchased an estate including 60 acres of woodlands. During the next four years, they cut, removed to their sawmills and sold, about one ninth of the standing timber. The timber was not cut to specified lengths or into planks, but was sent out in a rough state. The Scottish Court of Session held that the profits from the sale of the timber out of the sawmill were attributable to the occupation of the woodlands and not to a separate and distinct operation unconnected with that occupation. In a corresponding case under current Irish tax law, it would follow that the profits would be exempted from tax by TCA 1997, s 232 as being derived from the occupation of commercial woodlands.

In an earlier case, *Christie v Davies* 26 TC 398, the occupier of woodlands set up a sawmill in which the timber from the woodlands was cut up and worked into hurdles, fences, gates, etc some of which were used on his estate and others sold. The sawmill had been set up because it had not been found profitable to sell standing timber alone. The mill was well equipped and included items of plant not usually found in such sawmills. In order to keep the mill fully working, outside timber was bought in and worked up in the same way as the timber from the owner's estate. It was accepted that the profits attributable to the working of the outside timber were not attributable to the occupation of the woodlands (and thus in Ireland would be properly assessable under Sch D Case I), but the taxpayer contended that the profits from the working of the timber from his estate were derived from the occupation of the woodlands.

Wrottesley J held that the working of the sawmill was the ordinary method of rendering the timber marketable so that the profits attributable to the timber from the estate were fully attributable to the occupation of the woodlands and could not be taxed under Sch D Case I. It is to be observed that the work done in the sawmill in Mr Christie's case was more significant than that of simply cutting it up into lengths for sale, but nevertheless the same end result occurred as in the *Williamson Bros* case. However, the decision in *Christie* was criticised in the judgments in the later *Williamson Bros* case.

In view of this doubt cast on the correctness of the *Christie* decision, it is thought that the Revenue Commissioners could, in a corresponding case under current Irish tax law, resist a claim to exemption under TCA 1997, s 232 for the profits attributable to the sale of articles worked up from the timber to the extent that was done in Mr Christie's case. The question to ask seems to be how far can it be said, having regard to the facts in each particular case, that the operations carried out on the timber felled by the occupier of the woodlands are doing no more than making the timber more marketable as timber. At what point in the operations does the timber become part of the stock in trade of a separate trade, ie when does the operation pass beyond normal exploitation of the woodlands crop? It is also to be noted that profits earned by a sawmill or similar operation that are attributable to timber purchased from sources other than the sawmiller's own woodlands are always taxable under Sch D Case I irrespective of the stage at which that timber is acquired.

One further UK case may be usefully mentioned. In *Collins v Fraser* 46 TC 143, the appellant operated a sawmill which converted round timber into planks, then into thin boards, selling some of it in that condition and some in the form of boxes and crates. The Crown contended that the timber became stock in trade in the form of round timber and that the profits attributable to its processing beyond that stage did not arise from the occupation of the woodlands. However, it was held that up to and including the planking stage the appellant had done no more than market his timber, so that the profits to that point were attributable to the occupation of woodlands. On this analysis only, the profits attributable to the conversion into thin boards and into boxes and crates would be taxable under Sch D Case I in Ireland.

Requirement to include profits or gains in annual return

Notwithstanding that the profits or gains arising from the occupation of commercial woodlands are deemed to be exempt by the Income Tax Acts, TCA 1997, s 232(3), (4) as inserted by FA 2004, s 35 introduced a requirement that the full profits or gains arising from such an activity must be included in the annual return of income for each period of assessment with effect for the tax year 2004 onwards. Similarly, where losses are incurred, these must also be included in the return. Furthermore, the fact that a person would not be a chargeable person for self-assessment purposes (see **2.102**) as a result of their income comprising exempt income from the occupation of woodlands will not prevent them from being treated as such, so that they will be obliged to make a return. Any notice issued under TCA 1997, s 959N (excluding a taxpayer from having to file a tax return) will also be disregarded. The normal rules relating to the keeping of records and the making available of such records for inspection by the Revenue Commissioners will also apply.

This relief was subject to the restrictions applicable to high income individuals discussed at **3.111** but has been removed from TCA 1997, Sch 25B as respects profits or gains to which TCA 1997, s 232 applies arising on or after 1 January 2016. Prior to that date Revenue in *eBrief* No 80/15 noted that it had come to Revenue's attention that a number of individuals, who were not carrying on a forestry trade, were incorrectly in Revenue's view 'attempting to use generally accepted accounting principles to spread the exempt income over a number of years. In that way, these individuals are attempting to avoid the application of the restrictions applicable' to high income individuals. Revenue published guidance in Tax and Duty Manual Part 07-03-09 on the calculation of profits from the occupation of woodlands on a commercial basis, for the purposes of determining the amount of the specified relief claimed, as required to apply the restrictions applicable to high income individuals.

7.402 Woodlands outside the State

An Irish resident person may occupy woodlands that are situated outside the State and not, therefore, covered by the exemption of TCA 1997, s 232(2). If he operates those woodlands on a commercial basis, he will be taxable on any such profits under Sch D Case III as income from a foreign possession. It would appear that such foreign woodlands profits are taxable as income from a trade, so that the rules of Sch D Case I are applied in computing those profits. In fact, if the Irish resident is managing the woodlands at least partly from the State, then any assessment on profits should be made under Sch D Case I (see **13.103**).

7.5 Farm Land Leasing Income

7.501 Deduction under TCA 1997, s 664

TCA 1997, s 664(1)(a) entitles a *qualifying lessor* to a deduction in respect of any net rental income from the leasing of farm land under a *qualifying lease* to a *qualifying lessee*. This deduction – which is one given in arriving at the qualifying lessor's total income (and not as a deduction therefrom in calculating taxable income (TCA 1997, s 664(2)) – may be claimed for any tax year if the individual's income from all sources for that year includes any such qualifying farm leasing income. However, the deduction cannot be made in respect of any income covered by retainable charges (TCA 1997, s 459(1)) as applied by TCA 1997, s 664(6)). There is nothing to prevent a non-resident individual from claiming the relief.

The definition of qualifying lessor or qualifying lessors as the case may be was amended by Finance Act 2014, s 20(b) and is now defined simply as an individual who has not, after 30 January 1985, leased the relevant farm land from any person connected with him (unless this lease was made on such terms as would be included in a lease negotiated on a fully arm's length basis). Prior to 1 January 2015 a 'qualifying lessor' *was* defined as an individual who:

(a) is aged 40 years or more (55 years or more for leases entered into prior to 1 January 2004) or who, without reference to age, is permanently incapacitated by mental or physical infirmity so as to be unable to carry on a trade of farming; and

(b) has not, after 30 January 1985, leased the relevant farm land from any person connected with him (unless this lease was made on such terms as would be included in a lease negotiated on a fully arm's length basis).

The reference to the lower age threshold of 40 years of age for eligibility or to persons who are incapacitated has been removed with effect from 1 January 2015. The reference to permanent incapacity in condition (a) has traditionally been interpreted very liberally by the Revenue Commissioners.

The term 'connected' is as defined in TCA 1997, s 10 (see the discussion at **12.304**).

A Revenue precedent indicates that a lease which is initially operated on a verbal basis but is subsequently reduced to writing may be acceptable.

A 'qualifying lessee' is defined as an individual who satisfies two conditions. First, the lessee must not be connected with the qualifying lessor or, if there is more than one qualifying lessor, with any of them. The rules for establishing whether or not persons are connected are those laid down by TCA 1997, s 10. Secondly, the lessee must use the farm land leased from the qualifying lessor for the purposes of a trade of farming which the lessee carries on whether solely or in partnership. From 1 January 2015 a qualifying lessee includes a company provided:

(I) it is not connected with the qualifying lessor or with any of the qualifying lessors;

(II) is not controlled either directly or indirectly by a person who is connected with the qualifying lessor or with any of the qualifying lessors; and

(III) uses any farm land leased from the qualifying lessor or the qualifying lessors for the purposes of a trade of farming which the lessee carries on whether solely or in partnership.

It is to be noted that only an individual qualified as a qualifying lessee prior to 1 January 2015.The exemption is still not available if the farm land is leased to any other person (say to an unincorporated body of persons). Further, it would appear that if the qualifying lessee should die and their personal representatives assume their rights under the lease, the qualifying lessor ceases to be entitled to the exemption unless and until the personal representatives pass on the land to an individual beneficiary of the estate who is a qualifying lessee.

'Farm land' is defined as land in the State wholly or mainly occupied for the purposes of husbandry. It may include farm buildings (other than any building or part of a building used as a dwelling). A farm building is one situated on the land and used for the purposes of farming the land.

A 'qualifying lease' is a lease of farm land which satisfies the following three conditions:

(a) it must be in writing or evidenced in writing;

(b) it must be for a definite term of five years or more; and

(c) it must be made on an arm's length basis between a qualifying lessor and a lessee who, in relation to the qualifying lessor, is a qualifying lessee.

The Revenue Commissioners generally require in relation to condition (b) that the term of the lease should be expressly set out in the lease or memorandum. They will not otherwise accept that condition (b) is notwithstanding that there is provision for renewal of the lease or that there is a possibility that it may in practice last for five years.

With effect from 1 January 2005, TCA 1997, s 664(7) as inserted by FA 2006, s 12 provides that payments received by a lessor in relation to a qualifying lease in consequence of the actual or expected receipt of a sum under the EU Single Payment Scheme attributable to the leased land are to be treated as rent eligible for the exemption. FA 2015, s 19(2)(b) inserted a definition of an 'EU Single Payment Scheme' into TCA 1997, s 664 as follows:

'EU Single Payment Scheme' means the scheme administered by the Minister for Agriculture, Food and the Marine under Regulation (EU) No 1307/2013 of the European Parliament and of the Council of 17 December 2013, amended by Commission Delegated Regulation (EU) No 639/2014 of 11 March 2014, Commission Delegated Regulation (EU) 994/2014 of 13 May 2014, Commission Delegated Regulation (EU) 1001/2014 of 18 July 2014, Commission Delegated Regulation (EU) 1378/2014 of 17 October 2014 and Commission Delegated Regulation (EU) 2015/851 of 27 March 2015.

With effect from 1 January 2016, TCA 1997 s 664(8) provides that a lease which would otherwise be a qualifying lease shall not be so regarded where:

(a) a qualifying lessee of the lease (the 'first mentioned lease'), or a person connected with that qualifying lessee of the first mentioned lease, is a qualifying lessor of another qualifying lease (the 'second mentioned lease') where the qualifying lessee of the first mentioned lease is a qualifying lessor of the second mentioned lease;

(b) a qualifying lessee of the lease (the 'first mentioned lease') is a qualifying lessor of another qualifying lease (the 'second mentioned lease') where that qualifying lessee of the first mentioned lease, or a person connected with that qualifying lessee, is a qualifying lessor of the second mentioned lease; or

(c) the farm land which is the subject of the lease is farmed, in whole or in part, by the qualifying lessor.

This is in essence providing an anti-avoidance provision for the mutual leasing of farmland.

In the event that a qualifying lease relates to both farm land and other property, goods or services, the inspector is required to determine, according to the best of his knowledge and judgment, how much of the net rent (for example, the surplus from the lease) is properly attributable to the lease of the farm land (TCA 1997, s 664(4)(a)). Only so much of that net rent that is attributable to the farm land is eligible for the exemption. In making his determination, the inspector may make such apportionments of rent, expenses and other deductions as he/she considers necessary.

If the qualifying lessor is not satisfied with the inspector's determination of the amount of the net rent surplus attributable to the farm land part of the lease, he may appeal against the determination by notifying the inspector in writing of his appeal within 30 days (TCA 1997, s 949). The amount determined by the inspector to be the net rent properly attributable to the farm land lease may be amended by the Appeal Commissioners or by the Circuit Court on the hearing or rehearing of this appeal (TCA 1997, s 664(4)(b)). TCA 1997, s 664(4)(b) was deleted by F(TA)A 2015, s 37(8) but such deletion was subject to Ministerial Order (SI 110/2016 appointed 21 March 2016 as the day on which the Finance (Tax Appeals) Act 2015, came into operation)

Amount of deduction

The deduction in arriving at the qualifying lessor's total income for any tax year is given by reference to the surplus from the rent arising in the same year from the letting of the farm land which is let under the qualifying lease or leases (but subject to a maximum deduction). The amount of the surplus from any rent under a qualifying lease is determined after deducting therefrom the various expenses, etc permitted by TCA 1997, s 97 (see **12.104**). If the qualifying lessor has two or more qualifying leases, the aggregate of the surpluses from the two or more qualifying leases is eligible for relief (subject to the same maximum deduction).

In the following discussion, the surplus from the qualifying lease or the aggregate of the surpluses from the two or more qualifying leases, whichever is relevant, is referred to as the 'net rental income from the qualifying lease(s)'.

The amount of the deduction for any tax year for each individual qualifying lessor is *the lower of:*

(a) the *specified amount* in relation to the net rental income from the qualifying lease; and

(b) the aggregate of the individual's net rental income chargeable to tax for the year from all his rentals within Sch D Case V (TCA 1997, s 664(2)).

In arriving at the individual's aggregate net rental income for (b) above, all their Sch V rental surpluses and deficiencies are taken together to arrive at the net surplus. Any net deficiency brought forward from a previous year is deducted as are any capital allowances to be given in charging Sch D Case V income. It is the final amount of Sch D Case V income included in the individual's total income (before the deduction under TCA 1997, s 664) which is the figure for (b). Should that figure be nil for the relevant tax year, there is no deduction under the section for that year.

In practice, the first step is to determine the specified amount which, as explained below, may vary depending on the date on which the lease(s) was (were) entered into. If rents are received from two or more qualifying leases in the one tax year, it may be necessary to make separate calculations for each, but only one specified amount can emerge (see **Example 7.501.1** below).

TCA 1997, s 664(1) as amended by Finance Act 2014, s 20(b) provides that for a qualifying lease or qualifying leases made on or after 1 January 2015, the 'specified amount' is defined as the lowest of:

(i) €40,000, if the qualifying lease (s) is (are) for a definite term of fifteen years or more;
(ii) €30,000 if the qualifying lease(s) is (are) for a definite term of ten years or more but is (are) less than fifteen years;
(iii) €22,500, if the qualifying lease(s) is(are) for a definite term of seven years or more but is (are) less than ten years in the case of any other qualifying lease(s); and
(iv) €18,000 in the case of any other qualifying lease (s) (these leases must be for a minimum of five or six years);
(v) if the rent(s) in question is (are) not receivable in respect of a full year's letting, an amount equal to the appropriate proportion of €40,000, €30,000, €22,500 or €18,000, whichever applies (TCA 1997, s 664(1)(a)).

TCA 1997, s 664(1) as amended by FA 2007, s 16 provides that for a qualifying lease or qualifying leases made on or after 1 January 2007, the specified amount is defined as the lowest of:

(i) €20,000, if the qualifying lease (s) is (are) for a definite term of ten years or more;
(ii) €15,000 if the qualifying lease(s) is (are) for a definite term of seven years or more but is (are) less than ten years;
(iii) €12,000, in the case of any other qualifying lease(s) (but which must be for at least five years); and
(iv) if the rent(s) in question is (are) not receivable in respect of a full year's letting, an amount equal to the appropriate proportion of €20,000, €15,000 or €12,000, whichever applies (TCA 1997, s 664(1)(a)).

For qualifying lease(s) made on or after 1 January 2006 but prior to 1 January 2007, the specified amount is defined as the lowest of:

(a) (i) €15,000, if the qualifying lease(s) is (are) for a definite term of seven years or more;
    (ii) €12,000 in the case of any other qualifying lease(s) (but which must be for at least five years);
(b) the surplus or surpluses arising from the rent from the farm land let under the qualifying lease(s); or
(c) if the rent(s) in question is (are) not receivable in respect of a full year's letting, an amount equal to the appropriate proportion of, €15,000 or €12,000, whichever applies (TCA 1997, s 664(1)(a))).

For rent(s) receivable in a tax year under a qualifying lease or leases in respect of lettings for less than a full year, the appropriate proportion is the proportion which the total rent actually *receivable* in the tax year under the qualifying lease(s) bears to the rent which would be receivable for full year's letting(s) under the qualifying lease(s). Note that it is the rent receivable (before deducting any expenses) which is taken and not the net rent after expenses.

For a qualifying lease or leases made between 1 January 2004 and 31 December 2005, the monetary limits above were as follows:

(i) €10,000, if the qualifying lease(s) ran for a definite term of seven years or more;

(ii) €7,500 in the case of any other qualifying lease(s) (but which must be for at least five years).

Lower limits applied in respect of qualifying leases entered into between 6 April 1985 (when the relief commenced) and 31 December 2003.

In any case where there are separate surpluses from qualifying leases made on or after 1 January 2015 and also before 1 January 2015 it is apparently necessary to determine separate specified amounts in relation to the respective surpluses. The separate specified amounts are then added to give the specified amounts in relation to the surpluses from all the qualifying leases. However, where there are qualifying leases entered into on or after 1 January 2015 if the sum of the two or more separate specified amounts exceeds €40,000 (or €30,000, €22,500 or €18,000 as appropriate), the specified amount finally used is restricted to €40,000 (or €30,000, €22,500 or €18,000 as appropriate). Similarly if there were qualifying leases executed before 1 January 2015 but both before and after 1 January 2007, the specified amount finally used would if necessary be restricted to €20,000, €15,000 (or €12,000 as appropriate), etc.

Example 7.501.1

Mr A Farrow, aged 59, derives rent during the year ending 31 December 2015 from qualifying leases of farm land made on 25 July 2006 and 1 May 2014 respectively for eight years and ten years. In addition, he has rents from other leases also assessable under Sch D Case V (several houses including a 's 23' property in an urban renewal area).

Mr Farrow's rents (before deducting expenses, etc) for the year to 31 December 2015 are as follows:

	€
Qualifying leases:	
Lease of 25 July 2006	6,800
Lease of 1 May 2014 (eight months at €1,500 pm)	12,000
Other leases	12,650

Calculation of Sch D Case V income

Before the amount of the deduction under TCA 1997, s 664 can be determined, the surpluses or deficiencies for 2015 on the different rentals need to be calculated. Using the figures for expenses assumed below, these are calculated as follows:

	Qualifying leases		*Other leases*
	25 July 2006	*1 May 2014*	
	€	€	€
Rents	6,800	12,000	12,650
Less:			
Expenses deductible	(705)	(1,070)	16,950
Surpluses	6,095	10,930	

Deficiencies	(4,300)

Mr Farrow's total Sch D Case V income for the year 2015 is then computed as follows:

	€
Sch D Case V income 2015:	
Surplus from lease of 25 July 2006	6,095
Surplus from lease of 1 May 2014	10,930
	17,025
Less:	
Deficiencies from other leases	(4,300)
Net rental income all leases	12,725

Mr Farrow is entitled to a deduction under TCA 1997, s 664 for the tax year 2015 in respect of the surpluses from the two qualifying leases included in his total Sch D Case V income for the year. It is necessary first to compute the specified amount in relation to the surpluses from the qualifying leases. Since one lease is for eight years made after 1 January 2006 but before 1 January 2007, for which there is a €15,000 limit to the specified amount and the other for ten years made after 1 January 2014 at €18,000 pa, for which there is a €20,000 x 8/12 = €13,333 limit (scaled back because the period during which rents were receivable was only eight months), separate calculations are necessary as follows:

	Lease 25/07/2006	*Lease 01/05/2014*
Lowest of:	€	€
(a) Maximum specified amount	15,000	13,333
(b) Amount of surplus from lease	6,095	10,930
'Specified amount' (the lower figure)	6,095	10,930

On its own, the ten-year lease of 1 May 2014 would give a specified amount of €10,930 and, on its own, the eight-year lease of 25 July 2006 would have a specified amount of €6,095, giving a total of €17,025. However, under the rule in TCA 1997, s 664(1)(b), where there are qualifying leases falling either side of 1 January 2007, the specified amount cannot exceed €20,000 (the fact that the 2014 lease runs for less than 12 months in 2014 does not appear to impact on this rule).

In this case, the cap does not take effect.

Mr Farrow's deduction under TCA 1997, s 664 – in computing his total income is now determined as the lower of:

	€
Lower of	
(1) Specified amount (as above)	17,025
or	
(2) Net Sch D Case V income (as above)	12,725
Deduction under TCA 1997, s 664	12,725

Husband and wife or civil partners treated separately

If a husband and wife or civil partners assessable jointly under TCA 1997, s 1017, s 1031C are both qualifying lessors each spouse or civil partner is entitled to a deduction up to the annual maximum (see below) per annum to be determined separately by reference to their respective separate net rents from qualifying leases. In applying the restriction which prevents the deduction from exceeding the total profits chargeable to tax under Sch D Case V for the year in question, each spouse's or civil partner's deduction must not exceed their separate total Sch D Case V profits (without reference to the Sch D Case V profits of the other) (TCA 1997, s 664(3)). Each spouse's or civil partner's deduction is then allowed in arriving at their total income included in the joint assessment.

If the husband and wife or civil partners assessable jointly under TCA 1997, s 1017, s 1031C apply for separate assessment under TCA 1997, s 1023, s 1031H (see **3.504**), each spouse or civil partner gets their own deduction under TCA 1997, s 664 exactly as if they were not married or in a registered civil partnership. Clearly, in the case of husband and wife/civil partners assessable as single persons, or of separated spouses or civil partners, each spouse or civil partner is entitled to their deduction computed by reference to their respective separate circumstances.

Example 7.501.2

Mr Farrow is assessed to tax jointly with his wife, Ann, for 2015. She has recently inherited her father's farm (she was his only daughter).

Ann has from 1 January 2015 rented out the farm land and farm buildings and farm house to her cousin on a five-year lease at a full arm's length rent (such full rent necessary for there to be a qualifying lease) of €16,500 of which €3,500 is attributed by the inspector to the farm dwelling house (which does not qualify as farm land for the deduction).

In the year 2015, Ann pays the fire insurance and certain other deductible expenses which she has agreed to bear in relation to the farm buildings. Excluding the part of these expenses attributable to the farm dwelling house, these expenses amount to €1,240 in total in this year. Ann has no other income from rents within Sch D Case V.

Ann is entitled to a deduction under TCA 1997, s 664 separately from and in addition to her husband's deduction of €12,725 from example **7.501.1**. First her Sch D Case V income is determined as follows:

	€	€
Rent from qualifying lease	13,000	
Less: deductible expenses	(1,240)	11,760
Rent from dwelling house	3,500	
Less: deductible expenses	(680)	2,820
Total Sch D Case V income		14,580

The specified amount is the lower of €18,000 and the net surplus on the qualifying farmland, *viz*, €11,760. Since the total Sch D Case V income for the year is slightly l in excess of the specified amount, the amount of her deduction under TCA 1997, s 664 will be equal to the specified amount. She will be assessed under Sch D Case V on a net amount of (€14, 580–€11,760) = €2,820.

7.6 Income Tax Treatment of Animal Leasing

7.601 General

Revenue published *ebrief 17/15* on 31 January 2015 and inserted a new chapter Part 23.02.08 in the Tax and Duty Manual.

In summary it appears to only apply to a dairy farmer with surplus cattle who can lease them to another farmer. Where the farmer continues to farm, the income from leasing is regarded as income from farming and the farmer will continue to be able to claim stock relief provided there is no agreement to sell the cattle.

The lessee farmer can claim a tax deduction for the lease payments.

Division 8 Schedule D Cases III and IV; Income from Patents; Investment Products

8.1 Schedule D Case III

8.101 The income charged

TCA 1997, s 18(2) charges tax under Sch D Case III on the types of income listed in headings (a) to (f). The requirement to tax any income under Sch D Case III may, however, be varied if some other provision in the Income Tax Acts requires tax to be charged under one of the other Cases of Sch D (TCA 1997, s 18(3)). For example, while interest and discounts are normally chargeable by Sch D Case III, interest and discount income received by a bank in the ordinary course of its trade of banking are included as trading receipts in calculating its profits taxable under Sch D Case I.

Similarly, deposit interest received from banks, buildings societies and certain other deposit takers carrying on business in the State is, in general, taxable under Sch D Case IV and not under Case III (see **8.204**).

Certain types of interest are exempted by statute and reference should be made in this respect to **1.306**.

Interest, annuities and annual payments

Heading (a) of Sch D Case III charges tax on any interest of money, whether yearly or otherwise, or any annuity or other annual payment, whether such payment is payable in or outside the State, or as a personal debt or obligation by virtue of any contract. The meaning of 'annual payment' has already been considered in **2.302**, where it was explained that only payments which are 'pure income profit' (per Lord Greene MR in *Re Hanbury* 38 TC 588) in the hands of the recipient are annual payments in the sense used in the Income Tax Acts. The fact that a payment is receivable half-yearly or at any shorter or longer intervals does not prevent it from being an annual payment chargeable under Sch D Case III, but any rent or other payment taxable under Sch D Case V is specifically excluded.

An annuity has been said to represent the liquidation of a capital sum in return for a right to future income (*Foley v Fletcher & Rose* [1858] H&N 769). Thus each instalment of the annuity is regarded as consisting wholly of income and *not* as including a partial return of capital (there is a statutory exception for certain purchased life annuities: see **16.5**).

In fact, annuities or other annual payments liable to tax under Sch D generally fall under Sch D Case IV, which effectively covers investment income taxed at source (see **8.2**). However, annuities or other annual payments received in return for a non-taxable consideration, and which thereby fall within TCA 1997, s 242 are not subject to tax at source and accordingly remain within Sch D Case III (see below). Similarly, annual interest received from a non-banking company is normally received as taxed income and is, therefore, excluded from assessment under Sch D Case III.

Where it is a term of a sale agreement that the sale consideration should be paid by instalments then it may also be provided that interest will accrue on the unpaid balance of the consideration. Clearly, in such a case the interest if payable by an individual will be paid gross (unless paid to a person whose usual abode is outside the State: see **2.306**) and will be taxable in the normal way under Sch D Case III. Even where an agreement for payment by instalments does not expressly provide for interest to be charged, the courts may be prepared to infer (at least in extreme cases) that in fact such instalments consist partly of instalments of a capital price and partly of interest (*Vestey v IRC* 40 TC 112, discussed at **2.302**). This situation must be distinguished from one where a capital asset is disposed of in return for a series of annual payments which represent pure income. Following TCA 1997, s 242, such annual payments will generally no longer fall within the provisions of TCA 1997, ss 237, 238 and will not be subject to deduction of tax at source. Accordingly, such payments will be fully taxable under Sch D Case III and not Sch D Case IV in the hands of the recipient.

Similar considerations apply to the receipt of annuities. While these are generally in the nature of income, they may in some circumstances, be treated as consisting of a combination of a return of capital and interest, particularly if they are made for a fixed period (*Perrin v Dickson* 14 TC 608). However, as noted above, the test is whether or not the capital consideration for the annuity was given up in return for the annuity. Thus, where a capital sum was paid in return for the right to receive sums equal to a percentage of the profits made by a third party over a fixed period, these sums were wholly in the nature of income. *McCabe v South County Investment* V ITR 107). Annuities in the nature of pure income will again generally fall within TCA 1997, s 242 where they are paid in return for the receipt of a capital sum. As a result they will fall outside the provisions of TCA 1997, ss 237 and 238 and will be taxed under Sch D Case III in the hands of the recipient as untaxed income. Annuities granted in the ordinary course of a business of granting annuities (eg by an insurance company) are however, outside the scope of the section (TCA 1997, s 242(1)(a)(ii)).

Interest of money

The interest of money that is taxable under Sch D Case III is, therefore, restricted to untaxed interest, but includes short interest as well as any yearly interest from which income tax has not been deducted by a company payer.

Interest paid on any 'relevant deposit' with a bank, building society, trustee savings bank, the Post Office Savings Bank and certain other deposit takers is now payable less the deduction of income tax at source (**2.401**). For the normal treatment of deposit interest paid subject to this retention tax, see **8.204**.

In *Re Euro Hotel (Belgravia) Ltd* [1975] STC 682, it was held that in order for a payment to be 'interest of money' two requirements had, normally, to be satisfied, namely (a) there must be a sum by reference to which interest was to be ascertained and (b) that sum of money must be due to the person entitled to the interest. In his judgment in this case, Megarry J quoted some authorities on the meaning of 'interest', including:

> money paid for the use of money lent (the principal), or for forbearance of a debt, according to a fixed ratio (rate per cent) – *Shorter Oxford English Dictionary* (3rd edn);
>
> compensation for a delay in payment – Farwell J in *Bond v Barrow Haematite Steel Co* [1902] 1 Ch 353, a case on company law;
>
> payment by time for the use of money – Rowlatt J in *Bennett v Ogston*;
>
> the essence of interest is that it is a payment which becomes due because the creditor has not had his money at the due date. It may be regarded either as representing the profit he might have made if he had had the use of the money or, conversely, the loss he suffered because he

> had not that use. The general idea is that he is entitled to compensation for the deprivation. – Lord Wright in *Riches v Westminster Bank Ltd*.

The *Euro Hotel* case emphasises that there must be indebtedness for interest to arise. Thus, a contract price may be set which consists of a valuation of the property being sold plus a figure described as interest accruing from the date of valuation to the date of completion. The figure concerned will usually be no more than an ingredient in computing the price and not 'interest in the true sense' (since there is no debt outstanding to the vendor prior to the completion date). It is unlikely that the principle in *Vestey* discussed above would be of relevance other than in exceptional circumstances. Similarly, the element of notional interest in computing a gain arising under a contract for difference is not interest as such and is not liable to income tax (as accepted by the Revenue Commissioners in *e-brief 36/2007*).

Apart from interest on deposits, loans, etc, those and other authorities make it clear that there is interest of money in any case where, on a proper construction of the matter, money is paid by one person (the debtor) to compensate another person (the creditor) for the fact that over a certain period of time the debtor has had the use of money due to the creditor, whether as the result of a deposit or loan or by reason of a delay in the debtor's paying to the creditor a sum of money owed. For example, in *The Norseman* [1957] 2 All ER 660, it was held that interest awarded by the Admiralty Court on damages for collision, and included in the total award of damages, is interest of money.

Similarly, in *Riches v Westminster Bank Ltd* 28 TC 159, it was held that a sum of money awarded as interest, and included in the total sum for which a judgment was given, was interest of money. Lord Simonds said:

> The proposition that interest is awarded as damages or by way of damages … imparts the justification for the award for the rate awarded, but does not affect the quality of interest as such … The [defendant] … must pay interest to [the plaintiff] for the interest he has lost. It might equally be called damages or interest by way of damages.

The position in *Riches v Westminster Bank Ltd* may be distinguishable in a case where an interest factor is built into the calculations when measuring the compensation for the loss of, or damage to, a capital asset (see *Glenboig Fireclay Co v IRC* 12 TC 427). Further in appropriate cases, a settlement between the parties may simply reflect an undifferentiated lump sum (ie in which no element thereof represents interest). The principle in *Vestey v IRC* 40 TC 112, noted above, is again only likely to be of relevance in exceptional circumstances.

In *Bennett v Ogston* 15 TC 374, where a loan was repaid by instalments, it was held that so much of the instalments collected as did not represent repayment of capital were interest of money within Sch D Case III. On the other hand, in the *Euro Hotel* case, payments made because of a delay in performing other obligations, and not for the delay in making a payment of money, were held not to be payments of interest, although calculated at an annual rate per cent by reference to a sum of money (compare *Chevron Petroleum UK Ltd v BP Development* [1981] STC 689, where a sum described as interest charged on a net shortfall under a cost-sharing agreement was held to be interest in law, even though it was not known in advance which of the parties would incur the interest). The fact that interest is rolled up and is not payable until the principle is repaid does not alter it character as interest: *Re Cravens Mortgage* [1907] 2 Ch 448.

There is some judicial support for the proposition that interest paid on foot of a guarantee is interest proper: see Lord Halisham's comments in *Westminster Bank v National Bank of Greece* 40 TC 472 (but note *IRC v Holder* 16 TC 540). If such payments are not interest they will clearly nonetheless be income in the hands of the recipient, possibly being classed as either annual payments or miscellaneous receipts within Sch D Case IV. The issue as to whether or not such payments rank as interest may be of more concern to the payer in view of the withholding tax requirements which may arise as a result (see **2.306**).

Under general principles a payment which is not interest in law cannot be given that character merely by labelling it as such (see *Ridge Securities v IRC* 44 TC 373 discussed at **1.407**).

Discounts

Heading (b) of TCA 1997, s 18(2) Sch D Case III charges all discounts and applies to tax under this Case profits on discount transactions other than those carried out in the course of a trade, which are taxable under Sch D Case I. Discounts normally arise on bills of exchange, promissory notes, Exchequer bills, (UK) Treasury bills and similar instruments. A profit on a discount transaction may be realised either by holding the bill until its maturity or by selling it earlier at a price in excess of that paid for it, although a loss may also occur on such a sale in certain circumstances. In *Brown v National Provident Institution* 8 TC 57, it was held that the whole of the difference between the amount paid for a Treasury bill and the amount received on its sale and maturity was a profit on a discount and was taxable under Sch D Case III.

The nature of discounts was considered in relation to bills of exchange by Stamp LJ in the course of his dissenting judgment in the Court of Appeal in *Willingale v International Commercial Bank Ltd* [1977] STC 183, at page 187, when he said:

> The discounts at which the payment for the bills was made or the premiums at which they were made payable were not calculated by reference to the degree of risk of the bills not being met on maturity. The amount payable at maturity represents the money advanced, plus interest at a commercial rate compounded annually the period during which the bills were to mature. Accordingly, the discount or premium was, as Lord Greene MR put it in *Lomax v Peter Dixon* 25 TC 353, '... the reward and in the normal case (since such bills do not as a rule carry interest) the only reward which the person discounting the bill obtains for his money'. Each bill creates a present obligation to pay a sum of money on a future date.

In the same case, Sir John Pennycuick noted that, while discount has many features in common with interest, it differs in the critical respect that, whereas interest accrues from day-to-day and is usually payable at periodical intervals in each year, nothing accrues or falls due for payment under a discount transaction before maturity of the bill. Although that case concerned a discount taxable under Sch D Case I, the decision of the Court of Appeal (confirmed by the House of Lords) that no profit arises in a discount transaction until it is realised, either on maturity or on a prior sale of the bill, is equally applicable to discounts assessable under Sch D Case III (see *Ditchfield v Sharp* [1983] STC 590).

The use of the words 'all discounts' might suggest that the profit realised on the redemption at par or at premium of a security or loan stock issued at a discount is chargeable to tax under heading (b) of Sch D Case III. In fact, this is not necessarily so. In *Lomax v Peter Dixon & Son Ltd* 25 TC 353, an English company advanced £319,600 to a Finnish company. In 1933, the Finnish company issued £340,000 in notes of £500 at a discount of 6 per cent (£20,400) in respect of the sum owing to the English company. Interest on the notes was payable at 1 per cent above the lowest discount rate of the Bank of Finland during each year. The notes were to be paid off in a certain manner at a premium of 20 per cent if the Finnish company's profits permitted. Between 1933 and

1940, the proper number of notes was duly paid off at a premium. The Court of Appeal held that the discount and premium on the notes were capital payments and therefore not chargeable to income tax.

By contrast, in *Davies v Premier Investment Co Ltd* 27 TC 27, a premium paid by a company on the redemption of six-year registered convertible notes issued at par and carrying no interest was held to be interest of money within Sch D Case III. The fact that there was no commercial rate of interest charged was the important difference compared with *Lomax v Peter Dixon & Son Ltd* so that, on a proper construction of the matter, the premium received by the company was in the nature of interest to compensate the company for being deprived of the use of its money over the six-year period.

Discounts on non-interest bearing government securities are exempt in the hands of non-resident persons (TCA 1997, s 45).

Interest on government securities

Heading (c) of TCA 1997, s 18(2) Sch D Case III charges tax on interest payable out of the public revenue on securities other than interest charged under Sch C; heading (d) charges tax on any securities issued or deemed by TCA 1997, s 36 to be issued under the authority of the Minister for Finance, where such interest is paid without deduction of tax. In effect, this covers all interest on Irish government national loans and on loan stocks and similar securities issued by such bodies as Bord na Móna, Córas Iompair Éireann, etc (see **2.309**).

Interest on the government etc securities taxable under these headings is normally payable half-yearly on dates which vary with the security concerned. While the underlying price of each security may move up or down as the general level of interest rates and other market conditions change, the normal tendency is for the price to harden as interest accrues over each half-year period up to the 'ex div' date. Each security normally goes 'ex div' about five weeks before the date on which the half-yearly interest is payable, ie if the security is sold after this date, it is the vendor and not the purchaser who is entitled to the next interest payment. Conversely, if the security is sold 'cum div', no part of the accrued interest is payable to the vendor although the price he receives for the sale is inflated to reflect the accrued interest element.

Since 1984, the vendor of a security sold 'cum div' may be taxable on the interest element accrued in his sale price and the purchaser would not be assessed under Sch D Case III. TCA 1997, s 815 provides that the vendor may be taxed on the accrued interest element on a 'cum div' sale or transfer under Sch D Case IV, but only where he had held the security for less than two years, see **8.209**.

Security strips

TCA 1997, s 55 sets out the tax regime for 'security strips' with effect from 6 April 1997. A 'strip' of an interest-bearing security arises where the rights to receive each interest payment and the right to receive the ultimate redemption proceeds are traded separately. A security for these purposes includes stocks, bonds and obligations of any government, municipal corporation, company or any other body corporate; it is not necessary that it should be secured on assets of the owner (TCA 1997, s 815(1), as applied by TCA 1997, s 55(1)). It may be noted that TCA 1997, s 48 empowers the Minister of Finance to create strips of Irish Government Securities.

Where a person who owns a unit of security (unit) creates strips of that unit, the creation of those strips is deemed to be a disposal of the unit at market value (as defined by TCA 1997, s 548). This may give rise to Capital Gains Tax consequences.

On the creation of a security strip, each strip is deemed to be acquired for a notional cost, computed as follows:

$$\frac{\text{Market value strip (at date of strip)} \times \text{Opening value of unit}}{\text{Aggregate market value of strips (at date of strip)}}$$

The opening value is the market value of the unit on the date of strip, unless the person creating the strip is *not* a dealer in securities, when it is the lower of that market value or the nominal value of the unit. Where the security does not have a nominal value (as in the case of certain overseas investments) the amount paid for the unit on its issue is taken as the nominal value (TCA 1997, s 55(1)). Where a person who is *not* a dealer in securities acquires a strip of a security which is one to which TCA 1997, s 607 applies (exempt government securities, etc) that person will be deemed to acquire the strip for a notional cost, computed as follows:

The lesser of:

(a) $$\text{Nominal value of the securities (as defined above)} \times \frac{\text{Market value of the strip*}}{\text{Aggregate market value of all strips*}},$$

and

(b) the price actually paid for the strip (TCA 1997, s 55(3)).

* As at the date of the issue of the security.

Having established the acquisition cost of a strip under the above rules, any profit arising on a subsequent disposal (or redemption, if relevant) of a strip is taxed as income under Sch D Case III (Case I in the case of a dealer in securities; there is no relief for losses arising (TCA 1997, s 55(2)(c)). In the case of a person liable to income tax there is also a deemed disposal (and reacquisition) at market value (as defined by TCA 1997, s 548) in respect of strips held at the end of each year of assessment, giving rise in effect to an annual tax on capital growth (TCA 1997, s 55(5)).

In computing the Sch D Case III liability arising under TCA 1997, s 55(5), the aggregate amount of profits, net of losses, arising in respect of deemed disposals for the year of assessment is taken; losses on deemed disposals which could not be netted off in previous tax years may also be deducted (TCA 1997, s 55(6)). Where strips of a unit are reconstituted into a unit, by any person, then all of the strips held by him are deemed to have been disposed by him at market value (as defined by TCA 1997, s 548). He is similarly regarded as having acquired the unit for an amount equal to the aggregate of the market value of all of the strips.

FA 1970, s 54(10) allows existing and future government securities to be the subject of strips. TCA 1997, s 48(5) exempts income arising in relation to such strips held by a non-resident individual.

Foreign source income

Heading (e) of Sch D Case III charges to tax income arising from foreign securities (if not taxed under Sch C); heading (f) charges tax on income from foreign possessions. Between them, headings (e) and (f) tax all forms of income from foreign sources, notwithstanding that such income is of a type which would, if it arose within the State, be taxable under a different Case or Schedule. The only exceptions are income charged under Sch C and income (including benefits) – from an office or employment (which collectively would be of the type that would attract income tax under Sch E), where the income is attributable to duties of that office or employment which have been performed in the State.

The rules for determining when income arises from a foreign source, as distinct from an Irish source, and the meanings of the terms 'foreign securities' and 'foreign possessions' are discussed in detail in **Division 13**; as are certain special rules relating to the computation of the amount of the foreign source income chargeable to tax under Sch D Case III. At this stage, it may however be noted that, although the foreign source income is assessed under Sch D Case III, the main computational rules of the Schedule or Case under which any particular type of income would be chargeable if arising from an Irish source are, for the most part, applied. On the other hand, in applying the Sch D Case III basis of assessment rules (see **8.102** to **8.103**), all foreign income irrespective of its nature is treated as Sch D Case III income (except if received after deduction of Irish income tax by a paying agent, etc).

8.102 Basis of assessment: general

TCA 1997, s 70(2) provides that income tax under Sch D Case III shall be computed on the full amount of profits or gains (ie income) arising within the year of assessment. For example, an individual is assessed for the tax year 2015 on the income arising from all his Sch D Case III sources in the period from 1 January 2015 to 31 December 2015. This rule applies for all income tax purposes including, for example, in assessing the executors or administrators of the estate of a deceased person in respect of the income of the administration period (see **15.105**) or in assessing the trustees of a settlement in respect of trust income (see **15.303**).

TCA 1997, s 70(1) historically required all income or profits chargeable under Sch D Case III to be treated as issuing from a *single source* so that only one assessment is necessary for any tax year to cover all the taxpayer's income within Case III arising during that year, notwithstanding that several different types of income may be involved. Finance Act 2013, s 16 amended this provision to exclude any foreign rental loss from being included in the calculation of a taxpayer's total Case III income. The purpose of this amendment was to eliminate the practice whereby a taxpayer used foreign rental losses to reduce his taxable Case III income. Revenue confirmed at TALC that the amendment does not restrict the availability of claiming a deficiency on one foreign rental property against a surplus arising on another foreign rental property.

There is a line of UK cases which indicate that income is taxable on a receipts basis, unless the Taxes Acts indicate otherwise (see eg *Leigh v IRC* 11 TC 590; *Whitworth Park Coal Co Ltd v IRC* 38 TC 531 and *Parkside Leasing Ltd v Smith* [1985] STC 63 which also decided that payment by cheque does not give rise to the receipt of money until the cheque is honoured). This line of authority has been most recently upheld in *Girvan v Orange Personal Communications Services* [1998] STC 567. However, in practice, deposit and other interest received gross is treated as being taxable by reference to the amount which accrues over the year of assessment. Where DIRT is deductible, so that the interest is taxable under Sch D Case IV, different considerations apply – see **8.204.** Interest received gross from securities, such as loan stock, is generally treated as taxable by reference to the amount falling due in the year of assessment.

A payment of interest to which a taxpayer is entitled will be regarded as being received by him, if and when it 'enures to his benefit'. Thus, in *Dunmore v McGowan* [1978] STC 217, the taxpayer had guaranteed a loan made by a bank to a company. He opened a deposit account in the bank's name, the moneys in which were to be retained by the bank while the taxpayer remained liable under the guarantee. The court held that interest credited to the account was received by the taxpayer for the purposes of the UK equivalent of (repealed) TCA 1997, s 52. It may be seen that even if the interest had ultimately been used to discharge the payer's guarantee this would have been merely an application of the taxpayer's income. In other words the fact that the taxpayer has restricted his rights of disposal over his income did not make it any less his income (see also *IRC v Paterson* 9 TC 163, where it was held that the income of the taxpayer which was charged in favour of her creditors (and used to reduce her debt) remained her income for tax purposes; the decision would have been the same even if the debt had not been hers, as pointed out by Rowlatt J in *Perkins Excrs v IRC* 13 TC 851).

Dunmore v McGowan was followed in *Peracha v Miley* [1979] STC 6 but distinguished in *Macpherson v Bond* [1985] STC 678. In the latter case, the taxpayer lodged moneys in a deposit account charged in favour of a bank as security for the debts of a company; he did not give a guarantee in favour of the bank; the bank was entitled to transfer the balance on the account at any time to discharge the company's debt. The company was eventually wound up and the entire balance of the deposit account was applied in discharging part of its debts. The court held that the taxpayer had neither received, nor was he entitled to, the interest credited to the account. In effect, the bank was only liable to pay interest to the taxpayer if and when a surplus remained on the deposit account after the company's debts has been discharged.

Where income belonging to a third party is used to discharge the debts of a taxpayer (and thus enures to his benefit) it does not thereby become his income (*IRC v Wemyss* 8 TC 557; and note also the decision in *Dormers Building (London) Ltd v C & E*). Further, it would seem that the company in *Macpherson v Bond* would not have been taxable in relation to the interest there, even though the taxpayer in that case was not entitled to it.

In *Aplin v White* [1973] STC 322, it was held that an estate agent who received interest on client account, but who was not beneficially entitled thereto, was nevertheless assessable under Sch D Case III in respect thereof. This follows because the UK equivalent of (repealed) ITA 1967, s 105 charges the person receiving or entitled to the income in question (this also appears to be the basis on which trustees may be assessed in respect of income to which a beneficiary is absolutely entitled, and note also *Way v Underdown (No 2)* [1974] STC 293, discussed in **8.205**).

8.103 Computation of income

TCA 1997, s 70(3) requires the profits or income chargeable under Sch D Case III to be taxed on the full amount of the income arising without any deductions subject to TCA 1997, s 71. There is one type of exception. An individual, who is not domiciled in the State may claim to be taxed on the 'remittance basis' in respect of his income from foreign securities and possessions. This means that, instead of being assessed on the full income arising, such an individual is taxed on the full amount of his remittances into the State from such foreign source income (see **13.403**), but with no deductions.

Sch D Case III income is by its nature generally receivable as pure income profit so by definition no expenses are incurred in earning it. Any expense incurred in acquiring an investment or other source of Sch D Case III income is regarded as capital expenditure so that no deduction may be expected. An investment company whose income often includes Sch D Case III income is allowed to deduct its expenses of management from its total profits for corporation tax purposes, but that is a matter of express statutory provision. There is no corresponding relief for expenses given to an individual or other person chargeable to income tax in managing his investments.

There are no capital allowances or other reliefs for capital expenditure available where Sch D Case III income from sources within the State is concerned. Any loss that may be incurred on the disposal of an investment or other source of Sch D Case III income is a capital loss which is completely disregarded in taxing income under this Case. Relief for any such loss may, however, be available against chargeable capital gains in accordance with the rules of the Capital Gains Tax Acts.

Different considerations arise in connection with certain types of income from foreign sources. These affect those 'profits or gains' of a nature such that there cannot be said to be any profit realised unless expenses, etc incurred for the purpose of making those profits are first taken into account. The most obvious examples are trades and professions exercised wholly abroad so as to be taxable as foreign possessions (see **13.103**) and rental income derived from foreign situated real estate (see **13.108**). The question of the computation of the amount of income from foreign sources that is assessable under Sch D Case III is discussed in **Division 13**. At this stage, it is sufficient to mention that – in practice – the same deductions and allowances are generally made in taxing any particular type of foreign source income that would be given if the particular type of income had arisen from a source within the State.

8.2 Schedule D Case IV

8.201 The income charged

TCA 1997, s 18(2) charges tax under Sch D Case IV on any annual profits or gains not falling under any other Case of Sch D and not charged by any other Schedule. In addition, Sch D Case IV is used for charging to tax a number of other types of gain most of which were not originally considered to be income, but which have been brought into the tax net by special provisions in the Tax Acts. The 'income' that is charged under Sch D Case IV may, therefore, be considered under two main headings, namely (a) income not otherwise charged and (b) gains charged by special provisions.

Sch D Case IV has since the early days of income tax been in the nature of a 'sweeper' intended to tackle and catch as income all annual profits or gains not specifically within any of the other Cases or Schedules. This does not mean that every profit or gain not otherwise chargeable as income must necessarily be taxed under Sch D Case IV. The limitations of the main Sch D Case IV rules now in TCA 1997, s 18(2) are clearly expressed in the following extract from the judgment of Lord Dunedin in the House of Lords in *Leeming v Jones* 15 TC 333:

> Case VI necessarily refers to the words of Sch D, that is to say it must be a case of annual profits and gains … The limitations of the words 'profits and gains' were pointed out by Lord Blackburn long ago in the case of the *Attorney General v Black* 1 TC 52 when he said that profits and gains in Case VI must mean profits and gains '*ejusdem generis*' with the profits and gains specified in the preceding five Cases.

In order for a profit or gain to be taxable under the main Sch D Case IV charging rule of TCA 1997, s 18(2) as distinct from any of the special provisions which may apply different criteria, it must be capable of being regarded as 'annual' and it must be of the nature of income and not of capital. It has become accepted that while the word 'annual' may mean something that recurs every year, that is only one of its meanings and it is not limited to that meaning. In a frequently quoted passage, Rowlatt J in *Ryall v Hoare* 8 TC 521, at page 525, said:

> It is inveterate now that the letting of a furnished house for a few weeks in one year will attract income tax, under this Case, upon the profit made by the letting … Now, recognising that position, it seems to me that 'annual' here can only mean 'in any year', and that the phrase 'annual profits or gains' means profits or gains in any year as the succession of the years comes round.

While the income from the letting of a furnished house is now taxable under Sch D Case V, this reference to a short letting of a furnished house illustrates the point that it is possible for a casual profit or gain realised over a very short period to be 'annual' so as to be taxable under Sch D Case IV. The test is essentially whether the gain is of an income as distinct from a capital nature, ie to be taxable under Sch D Case IV the gain must be of a type analogous to or, using Lord Blackburn's words, '*ejusdem generis*' with the types of profits or gains mentioned in the other Cases of Sch D. The circumstances in which a profit or gain may be taxed under Sch D Case IV can be further explained by reviewing a few of the tax cases on the subject.

In *Leeming v Jones* 15 TC 333, the respondent was one of a syndicate of four who secured an option to purchase a rubber estate; their object was the promotion of a company to whom the estate should be sold at a profit. The General Commissioners had, after the case had been sent back to them by Rowlatt J for the purpose, found as a fact that there was no trade or adventure in the nature of a trade. Basing itself on that finding, the House of Lords held that the profit was not of an income nature, but was a profit arising from an accretion in value of the asset and the realisation of that enhanced value. The gain was not, therefore, taxable under Sch D Case VI (now Sch D Case IV).

Leeming v Jones involved an isolated transaction where property was acquired and resold within two months. The question of whether a profit from an isolated transaction can be taxed under Sch D Case I as being from an adventure in the nature of a trade has been discussed in **4.102**. It appears to be firmly established by case law that a profit on an isolated transaction consisting of the purchase and resale of any property, when not undertaken in the course of a trade, can only be taxed under Sch D Case I if the transaction is an adventure in the nature of a trade. If, as was held as a fact by the Commissioners in *Leeming v Jones* there is no trade or adventure in the nature of the trade, the profit cannot be assessed under Sch D Case IV (then Sch D Case VI). Lawrence LJ, whose reasoning was later approved by Lord Dunedin in the House of Lords, could not see how an isolated transaction consisting of the purchase and resale of property, if it was not an adventure in the nature of a trade, could be a transaction '*ejusdem generis*' with such an adventure.

In his Court of Appeal judgment, he said:

> All the elements which would go to make such a transaction an adventure in the nature of trade would, in my opinion, be required to make it a transaction '*ejusdem generis*' with such an adventure.

It is necessary to distinguish what may be an isolated transaction involving the rendering of services from one of the purchase and resale of an item of property. While the latter cannot be taxed unless falling within Sch D Case I, there have been a number of decisions where a profit from a one off service transaction has been held taxable under Sch D Case VI (Irish Sch D Case IV).

In *Ryall v Hoare* 8 TC 521, a director of a company was held to be taxable under Sch D Case VI on a commission received for personally guaranteeing the company overdraft at the bank, although done once only. Similarly, an isolated commission received by a company director from a syndicate for underwriting shares in a new company being floated was held taxable under Sch D Case IV (*Lyons v Cowcher* 10 TC 438).

It seems that the arrangement to be taxable under Case IV will need to be contractual in nature and relate to the performance of services (*Brocklesby v Merrick* 18 TC 576); thus, an '*ex gratia*' payment in return for an isolated service will almost certainly not be taxable. A fee paid for introducing one party to another and enabling them to carry out a commercial transaction may well not be taxable, even if contractual in nature, as it does not relate to the performance of services. However, if the arrangement is contractual in nature and refers to the performance of services, any sum received thereunder will usually be taxable even if the services in question are not actually required (*Brocklesby v Merrick*). The commission in each case was considered to be within the concept of annual profits or gains or 'something which is in the nature of interest or fruit, as opposed to principal or tree'. Rowlatt J (again in *Ryall v Hoare*) used those words and distinguished such income from:

> the well known case of a casual profit made upon an isolated buying and selling of some article; that is a capital accretion, and unless it is merged with other similar transactions in the carrying on of a trade, and the trade is taxed, no tax is exigible in respect of a transaction of that kind.

Cooper v Stubbs 10 TC 29 was another case where the Commissioners had found as a fact that there was no trade carried on. In this case, two individuals had undertaken on their own account over a period of years a series of speculations by way of buying and selling cotton futures, not with a view to receiving or delivering cotton, but with a view to gaining a profit on the balance. The Commissioners had further held that the dealings were gambling transactions and that the profits were not annual profits assessable under Sch D Case VI. It was held by the Court of Appeal that the finding of the Commissioners that the transactions in question did not constitute the carrying on of a trade was entirely one of fact with which the court could not interfere, but that the profits arising from the transactions were annual profits or gains taxable under Sch D Case VI.

In his judgment in the Court of Appeal, Atkin LJ considered the transactions entered into by Mr Stubbs to be real transactions and not mere bets, although they may have been of a speculative nature. The contracts entered into gave rise to real contractual rights which could be enforced by either party to the contracts. Relating this to the main charging words of Sch D, which refers to annual profits or gains arising from any kind of property whatsoever, these contractual rights were property and the gains derived from them were, in the circumstances of the case, annual profits or gains taxable under Sch D Case VI.

There have been several cases where the question of whether sums paid by publishers or newspapers for stories, etc of public interest to persons not otherwise taxable as writers were taxable under Sch D Case VI. In *Trustees of Earl Haig v CIR* 22 TC 725 the trustees of the late Earl Haig were paid certain sums by a publisher for authorising his war diaries to be used for a biography of the Field Marshal. The biography was written by Mr Duff Cooper who had full use of the material in the diaries (subject to certain restrictions). The diaries remained the property of the trustees. The Special Commissioners had found as a fact that the trustees, in turning the diaries to account, had not carried on any trade or adventure. It was held that the sums received by the trustees were capital payments in return for a partial realisation of an asset and were not assessable under Sch D Case VI.

By contrast, in *Hobbs v Hussey* 24 TC 153, sums paid by *The People* for the serial rights of a once infamous individual, William C Hobbs, for his life story, were held to be taxable under Sch D Case VI. The articles were compiled from the appellant's dictation, but he was not otherwise involved in any literary newspaper work. He contended that the transaction was an isolated sale of property, namely, the copyright in the series of articles, and that the payments received were capital in his hands. It was held that the true nature of the transaction was the performance of services by the appellant, the sale of the copyright in the articles being subsidiary to those services, and that the payments received were annual profits or gains. The case of *Earl Haig's Trustees* was distinguished.

Similarly, in *Housden v Marshall* 38 TC 233, an amount paid to a well known jockey for his reminiscences of his life and experiences on the turf was held to be taxable under Sch D Case VI. The fact that the jockey, Bryan Marshall, performed some services in the matter by making his reminiscences available and by providing photographs etc was held to be sufficient to make the matter one a reward for services. Further, in contrast to the *Earl Haig's Trustees* case, where the war diaries were very valuable and the subject of copyright, nothing similar applied in Mr Marshall's case.

Similar considerations were present in *Alloway v Phillips* [1980] STC 490, but a further interesting point had to be considered as to whether there were profits or gains arising from property in the United Kingdom, as the recipient was a non-resident. The taxpayer was a wife of a Mr Wilson who was convicted and sentenced to imprisonment in the 'great train robbery' case. He escaped from prison to Canada where the taxpayer joined him. While she was in Canada a reporter from an English newspaper visited her there to get information for writing articles about her for publication in the newspaper. Based on a contract which provided, *inter alia*, for the newspaper company to have the sole and exclusive world rights to publish her story, and on covenants by the taxpayer restricting her from providing material relating to the matter to other persons, sums were paid by the newspaper to an intermediary in London for the taxpayer.

It was accepted that the sums were earned in a tax year when the taxpayer was not resident in the United Kingdom. Consequently, for tax to be charged on her under Sch D Case VI, there had to be income from property in the United Kingdom. It was argued that the taxpayer had derived her profits from the services that she had rendered in Canada and that the contract was only machinery for collecting the reward for her services. This argument was rejected and it was held she was taxable on the sums paid by the newspaper company. In his judgment in the Court of Appeal, Lord Denning MR said:

> This case comes under Case VI of Sch D. It seems to be clear that this wife had property in the United Kingdom. She had a chose in action here. She had a right to receive from the News of The World the sum of £39,000. That was situate in England. Dicey and Morris on the Conflict of Laws says: 'Choses in action generally are situate in the country where they are properly recoverable or can be enforced'. It seems to me that she had her chose of action in this country worth an actual gain of £39,000.

The foregoing references to tax cases dealing with assessments under the UK Sch D Case VI illustrates various types of income or gains which would, in corresponding circumstances based on similar facts, be considered taxable now in the State, under Sch D Case IV. Among other types of income which do not fall under any Case or Schedule and which are, therefore, assessable under Sch D Case IV are income from leasing machinery or plant (other than as a trade), copyright royalties (when not received as trading receipts of a profession) and income from patents. The first two of these are discussed respectively in **8.206** and **8.207**; the third is part of a larger topic and is dealt with separately in **Division 8.3**.

8.202 Other gains chargeable under Sch D Case IV

Apart from annual profits or gains taxable under Sch D Case IV because they do not fall under any other Case or Schedule, there are now a number of gains or transactions which are regarded by special provisions in the Acts as being or giving rise to income chargeable to income tax (or corporation tax) under Sch D Case IV. The table below details in summary form the provisions involved with cross references to the places in this work where they are further discussed.

Special provisions charging tax under Sch D Case IV

	Ref
Post-cessation receipts after discontinuance of trade or profession	**5.605**
Certain receipts after change in basis of accounting	**5.502**
Capital sums for sale of patent rights	**8.303–8.304**
Fees etc from stallions accruing to non-farmer from 1 August 2008	**7.305**
Capital sums for sale of scheduled mineral assets	**12.403**
Rent, royalties, etc received from mining, quarrying, etc	**12.401**
Premiums on granting of leases, for varying terms of lease, etc when received by person other than lessor	**12.203**
Refunds of employees' and employers' (non-trading) contributions from approved pension schemes	**16.109**
Excess commutation payments	**16.110**
Chargeable amount in excess of the limit on tax-relieved pension funds	**16.504**
Pension lump sum in excess of the limit on tax-relieved pension funds	**16.504**
Anti-avoidance measures:	
Gains on certificates of deposit and assignable deposits	**8.208**
Shares issued in lieu of dividends	**8.208**
Sale or transfer of right to untaxed interest without sale or transfer of securities	**8.208**
Government securities, etc sold 'cum div'	**8.209**
Transactions associated with loans or credit	**8.210**
Gains from illegal or unknown sources	**8.213**
Transfers of rent	**12.102**
Assignment of lease granted at undervalue	**12.205**
Sale of interest in land with right to reconveyance	**12.206**
Gains of capital nature from land or property deriving value from land	**12.310**
Transfer of assets abroad to avoid tax:	**17.201**
Certain balancing charges (on disposals, etc of):	
Machinery or plant leased otherwise than in course of trade of leasing	**6.301**
Industrial buildings sold while temporarily out of use after cessation of trade	**6.409**
Patent rights where not taxable under Sch D Case I	**8.302**
Recovery of excess reliefs, etc:	
Excess TCA 1997, s 381 loss relief re capital allowances	**4.405**

8.203 Individuals: treatment of taxed income

TCA 1997, s 59 requires specified income received by *an individual* and subject to the deduction of income tax at source to be regarded as income chargeable under Sch D Case IV. This is stated to be for the purpose of charging the individual's total income to income tax at the rate or rates of tax that apply in taxing individuals for the relevant year of assessment. It is primarily a mechanism for charging the individual at the higher rates of tax and seemingly does not convert such taxed income into Sch D Case IV income for other purposes (eg in relation to relief for Sch D Case IV losses). TCA 1997, s 59 does not apply to persons who are not chargeable to income tax as individuals, nor to companies chargeable to corporation tax. Since a person other than an individual (eg the trustee of a settlement or the personal representative of a deceased person) is not liable to income tax at the higher rates, no income tax assessment under any Case or Schedule is needed to tax such a person on income which has already suffered income tax at source at the standard rate.

The income in respect of which an individual is chargeable under Sch D Case IV by reason of TCA 1997, s 59 is specified in the section, as follows:

(a) income from which tax is deductible by reason of the provisions of Sch C (see **2.309**) or of Sch D (foreign dividends, etc – see **2.310**);

(b) income from which tax is deductible by virtue of TCA 1997, s 237 or 238.

Apart from annuities, other annual payments, patent royalties, etc covered directly by TCA 1997, ss 237, 238, an individual is chargeable under Sch D Case IV by TCA 1997, s 59 on any yearly interest received from a company which has deducted income tax in accordance with the rules of TCA 1997, s 246 (see **2.306**). The object of TCA 1997, s 59 is to ensure that the individual's taxed income, which would not otherwise be assessable to income tax, is included to arrive at his proper total income for all purposes of the Taxes Consolidation Act 1997. In order to prevent the individual's being taxed twice, once by deduction and then again when his total income (less allowances, reliefs, deductions, etc) is charged, TCA 1997, s 59(ii) provides that the income tax suffered by deduction is to be credited against the individual's income tax liability.

8.204 Deposit interest subject to retention tax

TCA 1997, Pt 8 Ch 4, as amended by F(No 2)A 2008 and FA 2009, s 9, requires banks, building societies and other 'relevant deposit takers' to deduct, and pay over to the Collector-General, the appropriate tax when paying or crediting 'relevant interest' on 'relevant deposits', as discussed in **2.401**. The charge to tax on interest subject to DIRT is imposed by reference to payments of such interest: TCA 1997, s 261(c)(i) thus, such interest is taxed when credited to the account concerned and not as it accrues (compare the position under Sch D Case III).

The definition of 'appropriate tax' was simplified by F(No 2)A 2013, s 23 to express appropriate tax as a rate which was 41 per cent for 2014. This rate has not changed notwithstanding that the marginal rate of income tax has been reduced to 40 per cent. For 2013 and earlier years the definition was more detailed as follows:

(a) (i) Where the deposit was made prior to 23 March 2000, at a rate of 33 per cent for interest on relevant deposits (other than special savings accounts);

(ii) Where the deposit was made on or after 23 March 2000, at a rate of 33 per cent *unless* the interest is not payable annually or more frequently or the payment interval cannot be determined until the actual date of payment, in which case it is at a rate of 36 per cent (excluding special savings accounts, special term accounts, special term share accounts and special share accounts);

(b) 33 per cent for relevant deposits held in special savings accounts;

(c) 33 per cent for relevant deposits held in special term accounts;

(d) 33 per cent for dividends paid by Credit Unions in relation to special term share accounts and special share accounts.

It should be noted that a number of conditions had to be satisfied before a deposit account qualified as a special savings account. It is not possible to open such an account since 6 April 2001, see 2011 edition of this text.

Relevant deposits other than special savings accounts, special term accounts, special term share accounts and special share accounts.

The following rules apply in relation to the income tax position of the individual in receipt of interest paid or credited on a relevant deposit which is not a special savings account, and is not a special term account, special term share account or special share account. These rules are as follows:

(a) The relevant interest is received net of the retention tax. The appropriate rate of tax has been discussed previously above.

(b) The gross amount of the relevant interest is treated as income chargeable to tax under Sch D Case IV and is included in the computation of the total income of the person entitled to that interest.

(c) The retention tax is treated as falling within TCA 1997, s 59, so that credit is given for that tax in computing the tax payable by the individual.

(d) Where the relevant interest is liable to tax at 41 per cent for 2015 an amount of taxable income equal to the amount of the relevant tax interest will be taxed at 41 per cent. In other words, the retention tax deducted at 41 per cent is the final income tax to be borne by the person entitled to the relevant interest (TCA 1997, s 261(c)(i)(II)).

(e) In general, no repayment of tax is to be made in respect of the retention tax suffered on the relevant interest (but see *Repayments of retention tax* below).

Since the relevant interest continues to be part of the taxpayer's total income for other purposes of the Taxes Consolidation Act 1997, it continues to be assessable to the self-employed PRSI contribution which – in the case of individuals – is chargeable on income from all sources as determined under the Taxes Consolidation Act 1997 (see **3.401–3.403**). Employed PRSI contributors who are chargeable persons are also be subject to PRSI on their relevant interest with effect from 1 January 2014. See **2.102** for the definition of chargeable persons and in particular the exclusion from the definition for PAYE individuals with non PAYE sources which total less than €50,000 gross and net assessable income of less than €3,174. It should also be noted that the other rules which have regard to total income (eg the 5 per cent of total income restriction on the allowability of certain covenants (see **15.405**)) remain applicable. Income that is subject to DIRT is not liable for the Universal Social Charge.

Example 8.204.1

Mrs Freda Handle, a widow, opened an ordinary deposit account with the Watermusic Bank, Waterford on 1 January 2015. The bank credits interest on deposits held with them on 31 March each year and deducts the retention tax at the appropriate rate.

Mrs Handle receives the following annual interest on her deposit credited to her account on 31 March 2015:

Deposit account	€
Interest	1,750
Less: retention tax at 41%	717
Net interest credited	1,033

Mrs Handle's only other income for the year ending 31 December 2015 is a pension of €37,000 (as translated from the sterling amount received) from her late husband's former UK employment. Mrs Handle has personal tax credits of €2,430 but no other allowances or other deductions from income.

Mrs Handle's total income 2015 is computed as follows:

Sch D Case III income:	€
UK pension	37,000
Sch D Case IV:	
Deposit interest gross (Watermusic Bank)	1,750
Total income 2015	38,750

Although the bank interest is included in Mrs Handle's total income, this interest is taxable only at the appropriate rate of tax and remains chargeable to self-employed PRSI (see **3.401–3.403**). It is therefore necessary to compute Mrs Handle's assessable income for 2015 as follows:

	€
Total income (as above)	38,750

Mrs Handle's income tax payable by assessment for 2015 is now calculated as follows:

	€		€
First	33,800	at 20%	6,760
Deposit interest:	1,750	at 41%	717
Balance:	3,200	at 40%	1,280
	38,750		
Income tax payable			8,757
Less: Personal Tax Credits			(2,430)
Income tax payable			6,327
Less: DIRT deducted			(717)
Net income tax payable			5,610

Other persons chargeable to income tax, eg personal representatives, trustees of settlements, unincorporated bodies, etc, are subject to the retention tax on the interest from all relevant deposits held by them. Since no person other than an individual may have a special savings account (see above), these persons do not receive any such interest with retention tax withheld.

The retention tax withheld is accepted as discharging these persons' full liability to income tax on the relevant interest so that no further assessment is required. Only trustees for charitable purposes or of special trusts for permanently incapacitated persons which are exempted from income tax may be entitled to claim a repayment (see below). For the position in relation to the 20 per cent income tax surcharge imposed by TCA 1997, s 805 on the undistributed income of the trustees of discretionary trusts, see **15.309**.

Any interest received from a building society in respect of shares in that society is treated as interest income in the hands of any recipient. For the purposes of the Corporation Tax Acts, it will not be treated as a distribution of the society nor as franked investment income in the hands of any company resident in the State (TCA 1997, s 261(a)). This is to ensure that the deposit interest retention tax rules apply and that the income is taxable under Sch D Case IV and not under Sch F.

Repayments of retention tax; receipt of interest gross

Apart from companies chargeable to corporation tax, the legislation only permits four classes of person to claim any repayment of the retention tax deducted from deposit interest – charities, trustees of special trusts for incapacitated persons within TCA 1997, s 189A (see **1.307**), individuals aged 65 or over and incapacitated persons. However, a non-resident person of any class may, if he has not avoided the tax under the non-resident's declaration procedure, be able to obtain a repayment by invoking the interest clause in any relevant double taxation agreement which entitles him to an exemption or a reduced rate of tax in respect of Irish source interest income (see **14.205**).

In addition:

(i) TCA 1997, s 256(1A) enables an individual aged 65 or over or whose spouse or civil partner is aged 65 or over and whose income does not exceed the age exemption limit set by TCA 1997, s 188(2) for the tax year (see **3.322**) (and who would therefore otherwise be eligible for a repayment of DIRT: see below) to receive interest gross on the making of an appropriate declaration to the appropriate relevant deposit taker;

(ii) TCA 1997, s 256(1B) enables an individual, or whose spouse or civil partner, is permanently incapacitated in the tax year, or the trustees of a special trust for permanently incapacitated individuals falling within TCA 1997, s 189A(2) to receive interest gross if they would otherwise have been entitled to repayment in full of DIRT thereon (see below), on the making of an appropriate declaration to the appropriate relevant deposit taker.

The person making the declaration in the foregoing cases must undertake to notify the Revenue Commissioners if the conditions for receiving interest gross are no longer satisfied. In a case where interest is paid gross by virtue of the foregoing provisions, the amount of income on which the recipient is taxable for the year at the appropriate rate will be increased by the amount of the interest received gross (TCA 1997, s 261B).

TCA 1997, s 267(2) permits a repayment claim to be made by any tax exempted charity that has actually suffered the deduction of tax on its interest from any relevant deposit. For this purpose, a charity is any body of persons or trust established for charitable purposes only or any other person exempted from income tax or corporation tax in respect of the deposit interest by the rules of TCA 1997, s 207(1)(b) (see **18.203**). In practice, most charities should avoid suffering any retention tax by providing the relevant deposit taker with its charity (CHY) number before the interest is paid or credited (see **2.403**).

TCA 1997, s 267(3) allows an individual aged 65 or over, who is not liable or not fully liable to income tax for any year of assessment, to claim a repayment in respect of any retention tax he has suffered in that year. If married or in a civil partnership, he or she may also claim this repayment if his (her) spouse is 65 or over. It is sufficient if either spouse or civil partner has reached the age of 65 at any time in the relevant year, eg by 31 December 2015 for a 2015 claim. An individual's right to a repayment under this rule due to his (her) spouse being 65 or over does not depend on the couple being assessed jointly, nor is it a condition that they should be living together.

The same rule permits an incapacitated person or an individual whose spouse or civil partner is incapacitated to claim a repayment of retention tax, irrespective of age, but again only if he is not fully liable to income tax for the year in question. Before any repayment may be made, the individual making the claim must satisfy the inspector that either he or his spouse or civil partner was permanently incapacitated by reason of mental or physical infirmity from maintaining himself throughout the year or, alternatively, that he or she became so incapacitated from some time during the year. The Revenue Commissioners have confirmed in a precedent that mental infirmity can include depression and ME. Such an individual may where appropriate claim a repayment by virtue of the exemptions conferred by TCA 1997, ss 189(2) (interest on investment of payments from personal injuries), 189A(3) (interest from trusts for permanently incapacitated individuals), 192(2) (interest on investment of payments in respect of thalidomide children): see **1.306**.

In determining whether and, if so, how much retention tax may be repaid to the individual claiming under either the 65 or over or the incapacitated person rules, it is necessary to compute the income tax chargeable in respect of his total income (including the relevant interest) for the tax year in which the interest is paid or credited. He is then given any credits and reliefs against income tax payable to which he is entitled including a credit for the retention tax actually suffered.

For the purposes of the age exemption under TCA 1997, s 188, the specified amount is to be increased by the gross amount of the individual's interest from relevant deposits. The 'specified amount' is the amount of the individual's total income which, if not exceeded, entitles the individual to total exemption from income tax. It is also the amount used to determine any marginal relief under either section where the individual's total income exceeds the specified amount by a relatively small amount. However, this provision does not allow such individuals to create or increase a repayment claim under TCA 1997, s 267(3) in respect of deposit interest retention tax suffered (where the individual's income tax chargeable is less than the retention tax). Correspondingly, the marginal relief is given by comparing the tax charged at 40 per cent on the excess over the marginal relief threshold with the individual's tax liability *before* deducting DIRT (TCA 1997, s 261(c)).

Example 8.204.2

Joe Green who is single and aged 69, receives taxed investment income of €21,475 and Deposit Interest of €600 gross, subject to retention tax at 41 per cent in 2015. Mr Green's tax liability for 2015 should be computed firstly on the normal basis, ie that he is not entitled to a repayment, as set out below.

			€
Taxed income			21,475
Sch D Case IV			600
Total income			22,075
€21,475 x 20% =			4,295
€600 x 41%			246
			4,541
Less:	Personal Tax Credit	1,650	
	Age Tax Credit	245	(1,895)
Income tax payable			2,646
Less: DIRT €600 @ 41% =			(246)
			2,400
Less: marginal relief[1]			(1,010)
			1,390
Less: tax at source on taxed income			
€21,475 @ 20% =			(4,295)
Repayment[2]			(2,905)

Mr Green's tax liability for 2015 should then be computed on the basis that he is entitled to a repayment of DIRT, as set out below.

		€
Total income (as above)		22,075
Income tax payable as above		4,541
Less: Personal Tax Credits (as above)		(1,895)
Income tax payable		2,646
Less: marginal relief[3]		(1016)
		1,630
Less: DIRT	246	
Tax at source on taxed income	4,295	(4,541)
Repayment[4]		(2,911)

The second computation would therefore be applied to Mr Green on the basis that it would be beneficial to claim repayment of DIRT. This contrasts with a similar example in the 2013 edition where it was not beneficial to claim a repayment of DIRT as the DIRT rate in 2013 was 33%.

Notes:

1. The 'specified amount and marginal relief threshold are computed on the basis that no repayment of DIRT arises, ie as €(18,000 + 600) = €18,600 and €(18,000 x 2) + 600 = €36,600 respectively. Marginal relief is therefore available in accordance with TCA 1997, s 188(5), so that Mr Green's tax liability (net of DIRT) cannot exceed €(22,075 – 18, 600) = €3,475 @ 40% = €1,390.

2. This repayment is attributable to tax suffered on the taxed investment income; the DIRT is given as non-refundable credit against income payable.

3. The specified amount and marginal relief thresholds are now computed on the basis that a repayment of DIRT arises, ie, as €18,000 and € (18,000 x 2) = €36,000 respectively. Marginal relief is therefore again available, so that Mr Green's tax liability (before deducting DIRT) cannot exceed € (22, 075 – 18 000) = €4,075 x 40% = €1,630.

4. In this case, the repayment is regarded as partly attributable to DIRT. The Revenue Commissioners apparently do not take the view that this form of computation only applies where a repayment of DIRT would arise irrespective of the availability of the tax credits: see *Tax Briefing 18*.

If the result of this computation is an overpayment of income tax, the full amount overpaid including any retention tax element is repayable. However, no such repayment may be made before the end of the tax year in which the relevant interest is received.

For all other persons, the deduction of retention tax by the relevant deposit taker is final and no repayment claim may be made. Thus, certain persons otherwise exempt from income tax, eg approved pension funds and certain sporting clubs, must bear the tax without any right to repayment.

In the case of a claim for a repayment of retention tax under TCA 1997, s 267(1) in respect of interest received by an individual over 65 (or his spouse or civil partner) or by an incapacitated individual (or his spouse or civil partner), the calculation of the amount repayable must include the gross interest in the individual's total income. For this purpose, there is an exception to the normal rule that interest on a special savings account is ignored in arriving at total income (TCA 1997, s 261 as applied by TCA 1997, s 264(4)).

Interest on special term accounts

A discussion of the relevant regime can be found in the 2011 edition of this text. If reading the 2011 edition you should note that F(No 2)A 2013, s 23 provides that the rules relating to special term account do not apply to accounts opened from 16 October 2013. Also the rules relating to special term accounts existing on that date cease to apply after either three or five years depending on whether it is a special medium term account or a special long term account.

Dividend payments by credit unions

The tax treatment of dividends paid by credit unions as set out in TCA 1997, Pt 8, Ch 5. F(No 2)A 2013 significantly changed the tax treatment of dividends paid by credit unions. Firstly, prior to 2014 dividends on regular share accounts were paid gross and the account holder was liable to income tax at their marginal rate on the dividends under self-assessment. From 2014, 41 per cent DIRT is deducted on any dividend, and as with bank deposits, this is the final income tax liability of the individual. The balance on any credit union account other than the special term accounts (referred to below) is now a relevant deposit as defined under DIRT rules. Secondly, the rules relating to special term share accounts no longer apply for accounts opened from 16 October 2013. DIRT at 41 per cent (from 2014) applies to dividends on all such accounts opened from 16 October 2013. In relation to special term accounts opened before 16 October 2013 the first €480 of dividends received if invested for three years or €635 if invested for five years continues to be exempt. These are annual limits and DIRT (41 per cent from 2014) is deducted on the excess. The exemptions only apply to special term share accounts where:

(a) the special medium term share account has not been opened for three years by 15 October 2013;

(b) the special long term share account has not been opened for five years by 15 October 2013; and

(c) the special long term account which was originally opened as a special medium term account has not been opened for five years.

The rate of DIRT of 41 per cent continues to apply for 2015.

Definitions relating to Special Share Term Accounts

These definitions continue to be relevant for such accounts opened before 16 October 2013.

TCA 1997, s 267A defines the following:

(a) 'special share account' – this is an account in which shares subscribed for by a member are held by a credit union on terms under which the member has agreed with the credit union that the value of the shares held in the account at any time is to be treated as a relevant deposit held by the credit union at that time and the value of any dividend paid on those shares is to be treated as an amount of relevant interest (as defined by TCA 1997, s 256(1)).

A 'share' has the same meaning as in the Credit Union Act 1997, s 2(1) and 'dividend' means a dividend on shares declared by a credit union at an annual general meeting of that credit union;

(b) 'long term share account' is defined as an account opened by a member (being an individual) with a credit union on terms under which the member has agreed that each share subscribed for by the member to be held in the account is to be held in the account for a period of not less than five years;

(c) 'medium term share account' is defined as an account opened by a member (being a individual) with a credit union on terms under which the member has agreed that each share subscribed for by the member to be held in the account is to be held in the account for a period of not less than three years; and

(d) a 'special term account' to have the same meaning as in TCA 1997, s 256(1).

TCA 1997, s 267B states that in respect of the period before 16 October 2013 a person, who is a member or is about to become a member of a credit union may either or both:

(1) make an election in writing to the credit union to open an account which is a special share account; and

(2) where the person is an individual, make an election in writing to the credit union to open either a medium term share account or a long term share account.

Conditions and declarations relating to special term share accounts

TCA 1997, s 267D outlines the conditions to be satisfied by the special term share accounts as follows:

(a) The account must have been opened and designated by the credit union as a medium term share account or long term share account.

(b) The account must not have been denominated in a foreign currency.

(c) The account must not be connected with any other share account or deposit account held by the member or any other person. An account will be connected with another if:

  (i) either account was opened with reference to the other account, or with a view to enabling the other account to be opened on particular terms, or with a view to facilitating the opening of the other account on particular terms and the terms on which either account was opened would have been significantly less favourable to the member if the other account had not been opened, or

  (ii) the terms on which either account is operated are altered or affected in any way because of the existence of the other account.

(d) All shares held in the account must be subject to the same terms.

(e) There must not be any agreement, arrangement or understanding in existence, express or implied, which influences or determines, or could influence or determine, the rate (other than an unspecified and variable rate) of dividend which is paid or payable, in respect of the share or shares held in the account, in or in respect of any period which is more than 12 months.

(f) Dividends paid or payable in respect of the share(s) held in the account must not be directly or indirectly linked to or determined by any change in the price or value of any shares, stocks, debentures or securities listed on a stock exchange or dealt in on an unlisted securities market.

(g) The account must not have been opened by or held in the name of a member who is under 16 years of age.

(h) The account must have been opened by and held in the name of the member beneficially entitled to the dividend payable in respect of the share(s) held in the account.

(i) The account can be held jointly by not more than two individuals.

(j) A member must not simultaneously hold, whether solely or jointly, another special term account. However, where the account is held jointly by individuals who are married to each other or are civil partners of one another, they may simultaneously hold one other such account jointly.

(k) The amount of a subscription or aggregate amount of subscriptions for shares which may be added to an account in any one month must not exceed €635. However, at the time a member opens an account with a credit union, a single subscription for shares consisting of all or part of the savings of the member which are already held by the same credit union, may be transferred to the account. Other than such a transfer, shares at a cost of not more than €7,620 may be added by a member once during the period in which the account is a special term share account.

(l) A share may not be withdrawn from an account held by a member within three years from the date the share was subscribed for in the case of a medium term share account and five years in the case of a long term share account, except on the death of the member or, where the account is held jointly by two members, on the death of one of them.

A transfer of shares from an account by a credit union to reduce a balance outstanding on a loan from the credit union to a member will not be treated as a withdrawal from the account where:

  (i) such shares were pledged as security for the loan at the time the loan was granted,

(ii) a default (of interest or otherwise) in the terms of the repayment of the loan of not less than six months has occurred, and

(iii) the credit union has followed its standard procedures in seeking to recover the loan.

(m) Any disbursement of the surplus funds of a credit union in the form of dividends or rebate of loan interest, which is added to the account will not be treated as a subscription for shares for the purposes of calculating the monthly subscription or satisfying the three or five year test, outlined above.

However, such a dividend or rebate of loan interest may not be withdrawn from the account (unless it is one withdrawal made by a member who is 60 years of age or over on the date of the withdrawal, provided the account was opened when the member was under 60) unless the withdrawal is made within the 12-month period from the date it was added.

A declaration in writing must have been made to the credit union by the member ('declarer') who holds the account. It must be signed by the declarer and made in such form as may be prescribed or authorised by the Revenue Commissioners. It must have contained the full name and address of the declarer and confirm that the following conditions are satisfied in relation to the account:

(1) The account was opened and held in the name of a member who is 16 years of age or over.

(2) The account was opened and held in the name of the member beneficially entitled to the dividend payable in respect of the share(s) held in the account.

(3) The member will not simultaneously hold, whether solely or jointly, another special term account (subject to where an account is held jointly by individuals who are married to each other or are civil partners of each other, they may simultaneously hold one other such account jointly).

The declaration must have contained an undertaking by the declarer that if any of these conditions cease to be satisfied, the declarer will notify the credit union. It must also have contained other information that the Revenue Commissioners may reasonably require.

The declarations must be held by the relevant deposit taker for a certain period and these provisions are outlined in TCA 1997, s 263(2). TCA 1997, s 267E governs provisions relating to returns to be provided by credit unions.

TCA 1997, Pt 8 Ch 5 also provided an extra condition to be satisfied in order for a special term share account to be valid to the effect that a member cannot hold a special term deposit account and a special term share account at the same time.

Taxation of dividends on special share accounts

Where a person opened a special share account, the value of the shares held in the account is treated as an amount of a relevant deposit. The value of any dividend paid on these shares is treated as an amount of relevant interest paid (TCA 1997, s 267B(2)). The provisions of TCA 1997, Pt 8 Ch 4 apply to this relevant interest and the appropriate tax is at a rate of 41 per cent for 2015. TCA 1997, s 267F states that this relevant interest, except for the purposes of a claim to repayment under TCA 1997, s 267(3) (see above) in respect of appropriate tax deducted from this, will not be included in the computation of total income.

Taxation of dividends on special term share accounts

Where a person opened a special term share account, the value of the shares held in the account is treated as an amount of a relevant deposit. Subject to TCA 1997, s 267C, the value of any dividend paid on those shares will be treated as an amount of relevant interest. The provisions of TCA 1997, Pt 8 Ch 4 will apply to this and the appropriate rate of tax is 41 per cent for 2014. This rate of tax also continues for 2015.

TCA 1997, s 267C contains the following provisions in relation to the tax treatment of such dividends:

(1) The value of the dividend paid in a year of assessment on shares held in a medium term share account is treated as relevant interest paid in a year of assessment, only to the extent that such value exceeds €480.

(2) The value of the dividend paid in a year of assessment on shares held in a long term share account is treated as relevant interest paid in a year of assessment, only to the extent that such value exceeds €635.

(3) Where an account is opened as a medium term share account, the member may subsequently make an election in writing to the credit union to have the account converted to a long term share account. Where this election is made, the value of the dividend paid on shares in a year of assessment which commences on or after the date the election is made will be treated as an amount of relevant interest paid for that year of assessment, only to the extent that such value exceeds €635.

(4) An account will cease to be a special term share account if any of the conditions specified in TCA 1997, s 267D(1) cease to be satisfied. Where that occurs, the account will be treated as a special share account from the time the conditions cease to be satisfied. The value of all dividends paid prior to the date on which the conditions cease to be satisfied, will be treated as relevant interest to the extent it has not already been treated as relevant interest and the appropriate tax deducted. From 2014, 41 per cent DIRT is deducted.

Where on the date that the conditions cease to be satisfied, the past dividends have already been withdrawn from the account, the credit union will deduct from the value of the shares in the account on that date, the appropriate tax which would have been deducted from the past dividends, but for the withdrawal. The rate of DIRT to be deducted in these circumstances is 41 per cent for 2015.

TCA 1997, s 267F states that, TCA 1997, s 261 will apply to any dividend paid on shares held in a special term share account which under TCA 1997, s 267B is treated in whole or in part as relevant interest paid on a relevant deposit. The amount of any payment of relevant interest paid in respect of a relevant deposit will not, except for the purposes of a claim to repayment under TCA 1997, s 267(3) (see above) in respect of appropriate tax deducted from such relevant interest, be taken into account in the computation of total income.

Repayment of DIRT to first-time purchasers

Finance Act 2014 introduced a new section s 266A into TCA 1997, Pt 9, Ch 4 to grant DIRT refunds to first-time purchasers on their saving deposits where the relevant individuals are purchasing or building a place of residence for their occupation at any time after 14 October 2014 up to 31 December 2017.

In order to qualify for a refund of DIRT, the individual must be a first-time purchaser which means that they must not have either individually or jointly, directly or indirectly, previously purchased or built on their own behalf a dwelling. The specific wording of the definition of first-time purchaser appears to allow individuals who have previously received a gift or inheritance of a dwelling to still qualify for this relief. However a first-time buyer who purchases a house with a non-first-time buyer will not qualify for this relief.

The DIRT refund granted is limited to DIRT which has been earned on deposit interest within a 48-month period ending either with the date of purchase of the relevant residence or the completion date in the case where the dwelling in question has been constructed. The completion date in the case of a constructed house is considered to be the date on which the new dwelling becomes suitable for immediate occupation as a dwelling. The date of purchase essentially means the date of conveyance or transfer of the dwelling.

The DIRT refund is also restricted to deposit interest which has been earned on a capped amount of savings. In the case where the individual is purchasing their place of residence, the maximum DIRT that can be refunded is DIRT which has been deducted in respect of interest earned on an amount of savings which does not exceed 20 per cent of the purchase price paid for the dwelling. This 20 per cent limit equally applies to cases where a dwelling has been constructed and in this scenario the DIRT refund is restricted to DIRT which has been deducted from interest earned on an amount of savings as does not exceed 20 per cent of the completion value of the dwelling. The completion value is defined in TCA 1997, s 266A, as the price which the unencumbered fee simple of the dwelling might reasonably be expected to fetch on a sale in the open market were that dwelling to be sold on the relevant completion date and subject to such conditions as might reasonably be calculated to obtain for the vendor the best price for the dwelling and with the benefit of any easement necessary to afford the same access to the dwelling as would have existed prior to that sale. It follows that an individual who is availing of the DIRT refund in the case of a constructed dwelling may need to seek a valuation from an independent valuer to establish the amount of DIRT refund he may be entitled to.

Any individuals who wish to obtain a repayment of DIRT must make a claim for this repayment to their relevant inspector of taxes. While any tax incentives to be provided to first-time purchasers is welcomed, it is questionable how valuable this DIRT repayment scheme will really be given the low deposit interest rates currently on offer by Irish banks.

8.205 Basis of assessment and Sch D Case IV losses

The basis on which income chargeable under Sch D Case IV is assessed to income tax is much simpler than that for the other Cases of Sch D. TCA 1997, s 74(1) provides that the Sch D Case IV computation for any tax year shall be made on either the full amount of the profits or gains arising in that year or the average of such a period, not being greater than one year, as the case may require, and as may be directed by the inspector. In practice, income chargeable under Sch D Case IV is almost invariably assessed on the full amount of the annual profits or gains arising in the year of assessment, ie on a current year basis, but the wording of TCA 1997, s 74(1) would appear to permit the inspector to base his assessment on the profits of a 12-month period ending in the tax year. There are no special rules for dealing with the commencement or cessation of Sch D Case IV source income. It seems that the general rule applicable to Case IV income is that it arises when it is received, rather than when it falls due (*Grey v Tiley* 16 TC 414, approved in *Whitworth Park Coal Co Ltd v IRC* 38 TC 531) on the basis that income is taxed on a receipts basis, unless the Taxes Acts indicate to the contrary.

In *Way v Underdown (No 2)* [1974] STC 293, the taxpayer worked as a casual agent of an insurance company, N. He sold policies on behalf of N to M and under a 'friendly' agreement handed over all of his commission on the sale to M. He also sold policies to J Ltd, of which he was a director; J Ltd paid the premiums on the policies to N net of the commission, which would otherwise have been claimed by the taxpayer. No sums were received by the taxpayer in respect of any of these policies. The Inland Revenue assessed the taxpayer on the commissions under the UK equivalent of Sch D Case IV on the basis that he was the person receiving or entitled to them. The court held that even if the commissions had been passed on to M under a binding obligation, the taxpayer would still have been liable thereon as the person 'receiving' the income (however the payments to M would in that case presumably have been deductible as an expense in computing the taxpayer's Case IV profit).

The court held that the legal nature of the transaction with J Ltd was that the taxpayer had foregone his commission. Accordingly he had neither received nor was he entitled to it and was not chargeable thereon. The position of J Ltd was not under consideration. If there had been an implied agreement that J was permitted to pay a reduced premium, then there could clearly have been no income arising in its hands. If instead there had been an implied agreement that J should receive commission instead of the taxpayer, it seems unlikely that it would have represented income in its hands under the UK equivalent of Sch D Case IV, since no services would have been rendered by J Ltd to the insurance company.

Exceptionally, an annual payment subject to voluntary deduction of income tax under TCA 1997, s 237 is income of the year in which it falls due. Accordingly, a payment due in 2014 but not actually paid until 2015 is taxable in respect of 2014 (but does not become taxable until it has actually been paid). An annual payment subject to deduction of income tax under TCA 1997, s 238 is income of the year in which it is paid; (TCA 1997, s 16 as confirmed by the Revenue Commissioners in the context of Deeds of Covenant in *Tax Briefing 18*) (see also *IRC v Crawley* [1987] STC 147 confirming that the principle also applies to a trustee, since he also has a total income *qua trustee*).

In *Morley-Clarke v Jones* [1985] STC 660, a maintenance order in favour of the taxpayer was varied retrospectively in favour of her child. The court held that sums received under the order prior to the amendment variation remained taxable in the hands of the taxpayer. The variation could not change the fact that the sums had been paid under a legal obligation existing at the time of payment. Equally, for the purposes of the equivalent of TCA 1997, s 17 the payments 'fell due' at the time when the original legal obligation to make them arose. The decision in the *Tattersall* case can be distinguished from cases where the legal effect of a transaction has to be ascertained in retrospect, for eg in the case of income attributable to specific legacies (see *IRC v Hawley* 13 TC 327, discussed at **15.202**). It seems to be open to question whether the same principle applies to the rectification of contractual documents (see **1.408**).

Unlike the position in Cases I, II and V of Sch D, there are no specific rules within Sch D Case IV regarding the method of computing the amount of the income taxable under this Case other than the statement that the full amount of the profits or gains arising in the tax year is to be computed. However, as the concept of an annual profit or gain implies an excess of receipts over any expenses incurred in earning those receipts, it may in principle be taken that expenses of a revenue nature incurred directly for that purpose should be deductible. In practice, it is likely that an inspector will apply some form of 'wholly and exclusively incurred' test, although this does not have any statutory basis for Sch D Case IV. Expenditure of a capital nature is clearly not deductible on general principles. Further, no deduction may be claimed in computing any Sch D Case IV income for any business entertainment expenses; the rules of TCA 1997, s 840 discussed in the context of a trade or profession are equally applicable to all Cases of Sch D (see **5.313**).

Relief for losses

If, in any tax year, a person sustains a loss in a transaction of a type which, if it had been profitable, would have been taxable under Sch D Case IV, he may claim under TCA 1997, s 383 to have that loss set off against any other profits or gains on which he is assessed under Sch D Case IV for the same year. If and to the extent that the other Sch D Case IV income for that year is insufficient to absorb the loss, the unused loss is carried forward for set off against Sch D Case IV income in the next or any subsequent tax year. If carried forward, a Sch D Case IV loss must be set off to the maximum extent possible from the first available Sch D Case IV income and so on until fully absorbed. There are no provisions whereby a Sch D Case IV loss may be set off against any other type of income, whether in the same or any other tax year (but see **6.302** re excess capital allowances for leased machinery). Losses in relation to stallions at stud incurred by non-farmers will only be permitted to be carried forward against losses arising in relation to such activities (prior to 1 August 2008 such activities were tax-exempt): see **7.305**.

While taxed income is taken into account under Sch D Case IV in computing an individual's total income for the purposes of charging it to the various rates of income tax (see **8.203**), it seems that this does not convert the taxed income into profits or gains assessed under Sch D Case IV against which TCA 1997, s 383 allows any Sch D Case IV loss to be set off.

8.206 Leasing of machinery or plant

The profits or gains from the leasing of machinery or plant are taxable under Sch D Case IV if the leasing activity is not carried out in the course of a trade of leasing. The question of whether or not a person exercises a trade of leasing has to be determined on the facts in each particular case. Clearly often, if there is a full leasing business, it is taxable under Sch D Case I. Since leasing is in effect another form of providing finance, a bank or other financial concern which leases machinery or plant in conjunction with its other business is usually taxable under Sch D Case I, and not Sch D Case IV, on its leasing profits. However, a manufacturing or other type of business which happens to lease machinery which it does not at the time require for its own trade is not normally regarded as trading in leasing and would probably be taxable under Sch D Case IV, and not under Sch D Case I, on its leasing profits. On the other hand, a manufacturing company which sells and leases the goods it produces is more likely to be taxable under Sch D Case I. In the case of leases of a single big ticket item, for example, an aircraft and where there is significant commercial risk to the lessor it would be difficult to argue that the leasing activity is not carried out in the course of a trading activity. This position would appear to be confirmed by Revenue in their determinations on what constitutes trading for corporation tax purposes where they accept in a number of cases that once-off transactions qualify for the 12.5 per cent rate.

Any person taxable under Sch D Case IV on the leasing of machinery or plant (or indeed any other goods) should compute the taxable profit in a somewhat similar way to the computation that would be made under Sch D Case I if his leasing activity were to be carried on as a trade. The Sch D Case IV leasing profit is normally the excess of the lease rents, etc receivable in the period for which it is to be computed over any expenses of a revenue nature incurred in that period wholly and exclusively in earning the leasing income. For a person chargeable to income tax, the period of computation is normally the income tax year of assessment. In practice, it may well be that most of the expenses of repairs, servicing, etc of the leased machinery will be made the responsibility of the lessee so that the lessor may not have many expenses to deduct. However, if he does incur expenses on repairs, etc he should deduct those in computing the Sch D Case IV leasing profit.

It can be doubtful whether interest (or other financing) costs incurred on borrowing raised to acquire assets for leasing would be deductible. This is because such costs could only be indirectly related to the generation of the leasing income. While such costs may be allowable in the Sch D Case I context, this is because the computation there follows general commercial principles subject only to statutory exclusions and judge-made principles (note, in a different context, *Ockenden v Mackley* [1982] STC 513; *Chetwode v IRC* [1977] STC 64). However in the case of large ticket items it may not be feasible for a lessor to purchase the asset without bank finance. Therefore it could be argued that the interest payable directly relates to the generation of the leasing income as without the bank finance the leasing activity would not be possible.

Clearly, no expenditure of a capital nature can be deducted in the computation and the Sch D Case IV leasing profit (or loss) is arrived at before considering the question of possible capital allowances on any capital expenditure incurred in acquiring, constructing or producing the leased machinery. The capital allowances that are available to a person leasing machinery or plant, provided that the burden of wear and tear falls on him, and the manner in which they are given, have been discussed in **Division 6**.

Should the validly deductible expenses incurred for the purpose of the Sch D Case IV leasing activity exceed the lease rents, etc in any year, perhaps because the lessor incurs substantial repair costs in a year when he cannot fully lease the machinery or plant, this leasing loss may be set off against any other profits or gains from *any* Sch D Case IV activities in the same year. The leasing loss may not, however, be set off against any other income from non-Sch D Case IV sources, but is carried forward for set off against *any* Sch D Case IV income in the next year, and so on (see **8.205**).

8.207 Copyright royalties

In many cases, the recipient of royalties or other receipts arising from a copyright is an author, dramatist, composer, songwriter or some other person who receives them in the course of his profession and is taxed under Sch D Case II after deducting the expenses of earning them. In fact, where such a person carries on a profession, he is taxable not only on royalties, performance fees, etc received, but also on the proceeds of any outright sale or other form of exploitation of the copyright in his works. For example, in *Howson v Monsell* 31 TC 529, an author of historical works was held taxable under Sch D Case II on sums received for the sale of the copyright in the film rights of two books she had written. Even if the sums could otherwise have been considered as of a capital nature, it was held that she had received them in the course of her profession as author and they were, therefore, subject to tax as trading receipts. Similarly, in *Glasson v Rougier* 26 TC 86, a sum paid to an author in commutation of her right to receive royalties under a number of existing agreements with her publishers was held to be taxable under Sch D Case II as a receipt of her profession (see also *Wain v Cameron* [1995] STC 555).

There seems to be no persuasive reason why copyright royalties which do not form part of the receipts of a profession should not constitute annual payments (ie as pure income profit). Thus, in *Carson v Cheyney's Executors* 38 TC 240, a Sch D Case III assessment on copyright royalties was escaped only on the basis that these were (post-cessation) trading receipts (see **5.605**). However, in *Curtis-Brown v Jarvis* 14 TC 644 it was decided at first instance (somewhat hesitantly) that UK copyright royalties received by non-residents were taxable under the UK equivalent of Sch D Case IV and not Sch D Case III (see further below). This enabled the non-residents to claim commissions and incidental expenses incurred by their UK literary agents in collecting the royalties on their behalf. The decision in *Curtis-Brown* was followed in *Lawrence v IRC* 23 TC 333, where the taxpayers were trustees holding the copyrights of a deceased author. In practice, the Revenue Commissioners do follow the decisions in the *Curtis Brown* and *Lawrence* cases. This also means that the payer of such royalties is not concerned with the tax deduction mechanisms of TCA 1997, ss 237, 238 (see **2.303–2.304**). The Revenue Commissioners have issued a precedent stating their view that film royalties will normally constitute pure income profits and will consequently be subject to TCA 1997, ss 237 and 238.

There are accordingly two main sets of circumstances in which copyright royalties may fall under Sch D Case IV rather than Sch D Case II. Firstly, the royalties may be received by the author, dramatist, etc after he has ceased to carry on his profession or they may be received by his personal representatives or the beneficiaries of his estate after his death. In this type of case, the assessment under Sch D Case IV is made in accordance with the rules of TCA 1997, s 91 for taxing 'post cessation' receipts from a trade or profession that has been permanently discontinued (see **5.605**).

Secondly, a person may receive royalties from copyrights in someone else's works which have been assigned to him by purchase, gift, etc. In this case, the income is charged under the general rule of Sch D Case IV. If, as is likely, the royalties are collected by a literary agent or similar person who deducts a commission and any incidental expenses, these expenses should be deducted in arriving at the amount of the royalties taxable, following *Curtis Brown v Jarvis*.

Thirdly, and perhaps more doubtfully, a non-resident author may be taxable in respect of his Irish royalties. In *Curtis Brown v Jarvis*, the literary agents in question were assessed under the UK equivalent of TCA 1997, s 1034 (see **13.603**) on behalf of the non-resident authors whose royalties they had collected. It was held that the assessment was properly made as the copyright royalties arose from property in the UK (publication contracts made there), notwithstanding that the authors did not exercise any trade or profession in the UK. It is arguable that the *Curtis Brown* case was wrongly decided in principle. Following *Cheyney v Carson Executors* 23 TC 333, it would seem arguable that the contracts entered into by the non-residents lacked any 'independent vitality', so that the royalties formed an integral part of their professional receipts and should not have been taxed as royalties (contrast *Alloway v Phillips* [1980] STC 490). Even if an inspector of taxes was to consider assessing a resident literary agent on behalf of a non-resident author in respect of royalties from an Irish copyright contract, relief may be available under a double taxation agreement. If the foreign author is resident in a country which has such an agreement with the State, his Irish copyright royalties should be exempted from Irish tax by the relevant article in the agreement dealing with professional services (see **14.209**) or miscellaneous income (see **14.217**).

The sale for a lump sum of copyright rights by a person other than the author, dramatist, etc who produced the works that are the subject of the copyright does not normally give rise to any taxable income, but is the sale of a capital asset, which may give rise to a chargeable capital gain. TCA 1997, s 91(2)(b) makes it clear that the rules for taxing as income post-cessation receipts from a discontinued trade or profession do not apply to a lump sum paid to the personal representatives of a literary, dramatic, musical or artistic work in consideration for the assignment by them of the copyright in the work. This exemption does not, however, apply if the lump sum paid to the personal representatives arises from an assignment of the copyright made by the author himself before his death. While TCA 1997, s 91(2)(b) does not refer to an assignment of copyright made by a beneficiary of the deceased author's estate, it would seem that this should also be treated as the sale of a capital asset, outside the scope of the post-cessation rules.

In considering the taxation of copyright royalties, it is to be noted that the exemption given by TCA 1997, s 195 to income arising to an individual from works recognised as having artistic or cultural merit (see **5.7**) only applies if the copyright royalties or proceeds of sale of copyright are taxable on that individual either under Sch D Case II or under Sch D Case IV by virtue of the post-cessation rules of TCA 1997, s 91 (see above). Copyright royalties taxable under the general rule of Sch D Case IV, eg on a beneficiary of a deceased author's estate or on a purchaser of the copyright, are not exempted even though continuing to flow from a work which had qualified for the exemption in the hands of the author.

Copyright royalties from a foreign source, eg from a copyright contract with a UK publisher, are assessable as a foreign possession under Sch D Case III (and not Sch D Case IV) if received by a resident person otherwise than as income of the profession of author, dramatist, etc. If the foreign royalties are received in the course of a relevant profession by a resident person, the assessment is made under Sch D Case II unless the profession is carried on wholly abroad (in practice unlikely – see **13.103**), when Sch D Case III would apply.

8.208 Anti-avoidance measures

Sch D Case IV has come to be used as the Case for taxing various gains arising from schemes to avoid tax. A common feature of many such schemes is that they often seek to convert what would otherwise be income into a gain of a capital nature. Measures to deal with three such schemes are now discussed.

Certificates of deposit

Unlike an ordinary bank deposit on which interest is regarded as accruing to the depositor on a day-by-day basis so that he can receive his interest by withdrawing the deposit, interest on certificates of deposit or assignable deposits is normally only payable if and when the maturity date is reached. By selling the certificate or assignable deposit before the maturity date for a capital sum which reflected the accrued interest, the depositor would on general principles succeed in deriving a capital profit not chargeable to income tax.

TCA 1997, s 814 provides that any gain arising from the disposal of a certificate of deposit or an assignable deposit is deemed to be an annual profit or gain chargeable under Sch D Case IV unless it is otherwise taxable as income on the person making that disposal. One example of a person taxable otherwise on such a gain is a banker or other dealer in deposits who is taxable on the gains under Sch D Case I, but for other persons TCA 1997, s 814 charges the tax under Sch D Case IV.

In applying TCA 1997, s 814, a 'certificate of deposit' is defined as:

> a document relating to money in any currency, which has been deposited with the issuer or some other person, being a document which recognises an obligation to pay a stated amount to bearer or to order, with or without interest, and being a document by the delivery of which, with or without endorsement, the right to receive that stated amount, with or without interest is transferable.

An 'assignable deposit' is defined as:

> a deposit of money in any currency, which has been deposited with any person, whether it is to be repaid with or without interest and which at the direction of the depositor may be assigned with or without interest to another person.

Shares issued in lieu of dividends

TCA 1997, s 816 taxes as income under Sch D Case IV the issue of shares in a company resident in the State if the person receiving the shares does so as the result of the exercise of an option to take those shares in lieu of a dividend or other distribution of profits by the company. The income charged is an amount equal to the sum which the person in question would have received if he had taken the distribution in cash.

TCA 1997, s 816(1) defines 'shares' as including stock and any other interest in the company. Consequently, the tax charge applies whether the option is to take shares, stock or any other interest (eg an unsecured loan stock) in the company. The section does not, however, apply to tax a bonus or other issue of shares if the recipient has no option to take a cash distribution instead. A person is regarded as having an option to receive either cash or shares not only when he is required to choose one or the other, but also where he is offered either alternative and given the right to choose the other instead. A person's abandonment of, or failure to exercise, any right to take shares, etc in lieu of a dividend (or vice versa) is treated as if it were the exercise of an option.

In practice, this section has had the result that resident companies are less likely to declare dividends with an option to take shares instead. However, TCA 1997, s 816 applies also in similar circumstances to tax a person resident in the State if he receives shares, stock or any other interest in a non-resident company in lieu of a cash dividend. In this event, the assessment is again made on an amount equal to the cash distribution which could have been taken, but it is made under Sch D Case III (and not under Sch D Case IV). The section deems the receipt of the additional share capital to be income received by the individual but does not deem it to be received in the State; in the case of individuals who are entitled to the remittance basis, it is arguable that liability to tax may not arise in these circumstances notwithstanding that the section states that the notional income 'shall be assessed and charged' under Sch D Case III.

Quoted companies resident in the State are excluded from the above treatment. For these purposes, a quoted company is one quoted on any Stock Exchange or on the Developing Companies Market or the Exploration Securities Market of the Irish Stock Exchange or any similar market or corresponding market of any other stock exchange (TCA 1997, s 816 (1)). However, for shares issued in a quoted company resident in the State in lieu of a cash dividend, the taxpayer is taxable under Sch F on the amount of cash distribution forgone; for the operation of Dividend Withholding Tax where applicable in these circumstances.

Transfer of right to receive interest

TCA 1997, s 812(2) applies to deem the owner of any securities to have received any particular interest payable on those securities if he sells or transfers the right to receive that particular interest, but does not sell or transfer the securities themselves. The section applies irrespective of whether or not the interest would have been otherwise chargeable to tax; thus sale of the right of interest to an exempt individual or body will remain within the scope of these provisions. For the purposes of TCA 1997, s 812, the term 'securities' is taken as including stocks and shares of all descriptions, ie it includes government, local authority, etc loan stocks, shares in companies and any other stocks and shares, whether issued in the State or anywhere else in the world. The term 'interest' as used in this section includes dividends, annuities and shares of annuities, as well as interest on any securities, stocks and shares (TCA 1997, s 812(1)).

In any case where there is such a sale or transfer of any interest, dividends, etc on any securities which are not themselves sold or transferred, the interest, dividends, etc are deemed for all purposes of the Tax Acts to be the income of the owner of the securities, but subject to one exception. This exception occurs where the owner is not the beneficial owner of the securities (eg he may be a trustee of a settlement) and where some other person ('the beneficiary' – eg a life tenant) is beneficially entitled to the income arising from the said securities. In such a case, the interest, dividends, etc the right to which has been sold (without the sale of the securities) are treated as the income of the beneficiary.

The interest, dividends, etc the right to which has been sold or transferred is deemed to be the income of the owner or, if the exception applies, of the beneficiary for the tax year in which the right to receive the particular interest dividends, etc is sold or transferred. This means that the income from the securities may be taxable on the owner of the securities or the beneficiary in a different tax year to that in which the income is actually payable if the sale or transfer of the right to the income is made in a different tax year. For example, if Mr X sold on 31 December 2014 his right to receive the next two half-yearly payments of interest on €10,000, 5.5 per cent Treasury Bond 2017 without selling the security, he is assessable for 2015 on the €,550 interest due to be paid in the year to 31 December 2014.

Prior to 7 March 2006, it was provided that the interest in question could not be deemed to be the income of any other person, so that inter alia the person who purchased the right to the interest could not be taxed when he received it. This meant that if a non-resident sold the right to receive interest to an Irish resident, he could not have been taxed thereon; depending on the facts, the non-resident may not have been taxable in respect of such income either under domestic tax law or by virtue of a double tax agreement (see **Division 14**). This provision was repealed by FA 2006, s 40.

The assessment on the owner of the securities or, where relevant, on the beneficiary, due to TCA 1997, s 812, is made under Sch D Case IV if the securities are of such a character that the interest, dividends, etc payable on them may be paid without the deduction of income tax. Unless the owner or beneficiary shows that the proceeds of any sale or other realisation of the right to receive the interest, have been charged under Sch C or under TCA 1997, Pt 4 Ch 2, the owner or beneficiary is chargeable to tax under Sch D Case IV in respect of that interest, but is entitled to credit for any tax which that interest has borne.

Finance Act 2014 amended TCA 1997, s 812 to exclude certain persons from coming within the scope of this provision. The first exclusion disapplies this provision where the interest would not have been subject to Irish tax had it been received by the owner or the beneficiary at any time in the period commencing with the date of the sale or transfer of the right to receive the interest and ending on the date the interest was paid. The section is also amended to not apply in cases where the owner or the beneficiary is a person who carries on either a trade, profession or business, the profits of which are chargeable to income tax or corporation tax computed in accordance with Case I and Case II provisions and principles. In this scenario, any consideration received for the sale or transfer must be taken into account in computing the profits of the relevant trade, profession or business for income tax or corporation tax purposes in order for the exclusion to apply.

The above new amendment will apply to the sale or transfer of a right to receive particular interest payable where that sale or transfer takes place after 23 October 2014.

8.209 Sales of government securities etc 'cum div' (bond washing)

In the absence of specific counteracting measures, it would be possible for any person, other than one carrying on a trade that included dealing in securities and other investments, to realise gains in a tax free form by acquiring government securities, usually shortly after the last 'ex div' date, and by selling them 'cum div' shortly before the next 'ex div' date. This device, sometimes referred to as 'bond washing', was formerly used particularly in buying and selling short dated securities where material variations in the underlying capital price are unlikely, so that a gain almost invariably arose which approximated to the accrued interest element in the sale price.

TCA 1997, s 815 counters this form of bond washing and has effect for all sales or transfers of securities (to the extent within the section). 'Securities', for this purpose, are defined in TCA 1997, s 815(1) as excluding shares of a company or similar body, but including:

(a) securities issued under the authority of the Minister for Finance;

(b) stocks issued by any local authority or harbour authority;

(c) land bonds issued under the Land Purchase Acts;

(d) debentures, debenture stock, or other forms of security issued by the Electricity Supply Bord, Bord Gáis Éireann, Radio Telefís Éireann, Córas Iompair Éireann, Bord na Móna or Dublin Airport Authority;

(e) securities issued by the Housing Finance Agency under s 10 of the Housing Finance Agency Act, 1981;

(f) securities issued by a body designated under s 4(1) of the Securitisation (Proceeds of Certain Mortgages) Act, 1995;

(g) securities issued in the State, with the approval of the Minister for Finance, by the European Community, the European Coal and Steel Community, the International Bank for Reconstruction and Development, the European Atomic Energy Community or the European Investment Bank;

(h) securities issued by An Post and guaranteed by the Minister for Finance; and

(i) stocks, bonds and obligations of any government, municipal corporation, company or other body corporate, whether creating or evidencing a charge on assets or not.

TCA 1997, s 815(2) charges tax under Sch D Case IV on the owner of a security if he or she sells or transfers the security in a transaction as a result of which interest becomes payable in respect of the security to a person other than that owner. However, this tax charge does not arise, and TCA 1997, s 815 does not apply, in any of the following cases:

(a) where the security has been held by the same owner for a continuous period of at least two years immediately before the later of the date of the contract for the sale or transfer and the date of the payment of the consideration for the sale;

(b) if the owner of the security (before the sale) carries on a trade consisting wholly or partly of dealing in securities chargeable to income tax (or corporation tax) under Sch D Case I;

(c) where the owner is an undertaking for collective investment within the meaning of TCA 1997, s 738 and any gain or loss accruing on the sale or transfer is a chargeable gain or an allowable loss;

(d) if the sale or transfer is one between spouses or civil partners at a time when they are treated for income tax purposes as living together; or

(e) if the security is one the interest on which is treated as a distribution for the purposes of the Corporation Tax Acts (TCA 1997, s 815(3)).

The personal representatives of a deceased person are treated, for exception (a) above, as the same owner as the deceased person, but only while their estate is in the course of administration. Consequently, if a deceased person – who died on 25 July 2014 – had acquired a government security on, say, 25 March 2013, and if his executor sells the security on 27 March 2015 in the course of the administration of the estate, the executor is treated as if owning the security for the whole period from 25 March 2013 to 27 March 2015, ie more than two years. The transaction is therefore covered by exception (a) and TCA 1997, s 815(2) does not apply.

In the case of a sale or transfer between spouses or civil partners living together, exception (d) applies whether they elect to be assessable to income tax jointly or as single persons. They are treated as being the same owner so that, in the case of a subsequent sale or transfer to another person, the two-year period starts to run from the date the security was first acquired by either spouse or civil partner.

TCA 1997, s 815(2) treats the owner, who has sold or transferred any security within the section as if he or she had received an amount of interest accruing on a day-to-day basis over the period from the date the owner acquired the security up to the date of the contract for the sale or transfer or, if it gives a longer period, up to the date of the payment of the consideration for the sale. The said amount of interest for this period is the 'accrued interest'. The rate of interest used in computing this accrued interest is the rate of interest actually payable on the security in question.

The said owner is then charged to income tax (under Sch D Case IV on the amount of the 'accrued interest' as reduced by the amount of the interest (if any) actually received on the security and chargeable to tax during their period of ownership; the legislation only provides for the amount otherwise chargeable under s 815 to be *reduced* by the amount of interest otherwise chargeable, so that it is not possible to create a Sch D Case IV loss under these provisions (a point confirmed in a Revenue Precedent). The interest actually received is also taxable on the owner under the ordinary rules (eg if it is interest on a Government security which is not taxed at source, the actual interest is taxed under Sch D Case III).

The period of ownership over which accrued interest has to be taken into account may all be within one tax year or it may straddle two or three tax years. For example, TCA 1997, s 815 may be relevant to charge tax for a period of ownership running from 25 November 2013 (date of acquisition) to 18 October 2015 (date of sale). If the relevant period over which the interest accrued falls in two or three tax years, assessments under Sch D Case IV are made for each tax year straddled by the period of ownership to the extent appropriate.

Example 8.209.1

On 15 February 2015, Mr James Goldbond purchased €10,000 (nominal) of a government security carrying a 13.5 per cent interest coupon, with interest payable half-yearly on 15 April and 15 October. On 15 April 2015, Mr Goldbond received his half-yearly interest payment of €675, but contracted to sell the entire holding on 31 August 2015 just before the stock went 'ex div'. The consideration for the sale is paid on 11 September 2015.

Mr Goldbond is taxable for 2015 under Sch D Case III in the ordinary way on the €675 interest received on 15 April 2015.

Since his sale of the security has the result that the interest due on 15 October 2015 is receivable by a person other than Mr Goldbond (ie by the purchaser), TCA 1997, s 815(2) applies so that he is assessable under Sch D Case IV for 2015 on an amount computed as follows:

Period of ownership (or accrual):

Date security acquired by vendor – 15 February 2015

Date of contract for sale – 31 August 2015

Date of payment for sale – 11 September 2015 (the later date)

Period of accrual: 15 February 2015 to 11 September 2015

	€
Interest accrued from 15 February 2015 to 11 September 2015	
€10,000 x 13.5% pa x 209 days/365 days =	773
Less:	
Amount of interest on security taxed normally:	
Interest received 15 April 2015	675
Amount taxed under Sch D Case IV	98

Example 8.209.2

Assume that Mr Goldbond had not purchased the €10,000 holding of government stock until 16 March 2015 after it had gone 'ex div' in respect of the 15 April 2015 interest payment. He does not therefore receive any interest at all on the holding prior to its 'cum div' sale on 31 August 2015 (payment received 11 September 2015).

Interest accrued from 16 March 2015 to 11 September 2015	
€10,000 x 13.5% pa x 178 days/365 days	658
Less:	
Amount of interest received taxed normally	Nil
Amount taxed under Sch D Case IV	658

TCA 1997, s 815(2) also charges tax under Sch D Case IV where the owner of a security within the section causes or authorises that security to be sold or transferred (as well as where the owner sells or transfers the security himself/herself).

TCA 1997, s 815(2)(c) contains another anti-avoidance rule. It deals with the case where, under the terms of a sale or transfer, or any associated agreement, arrangement, understanding, promise or undertaking, the owner of the security agrees to buy back or reacquire the security. It also covers the case where the said owner acquires an option, which he or she subsequently exercises, to buy back the security. In any such case, the charge on the said owner is based on the interest deemed to accrue up to the next interest date after the date of the sale or transfer. However, if the owner, having reacquired the securities then resells or retransfers them, the provisions of s 815 will only apply as if interest had accrued from that interest date at the earliest (TCA 1997, s 815(2)(d)). Thus, for example assume that an owner sells securities on 12 September 2015 with a right to reacquire them and is accordingly taxed by reference to interest accrued up to the next interest date of 30 November 2015. If he reacquires those securities on 15 October 2015, he will only be potentially chargeable under s 815 in relation to his second period of ownership by reference to interest accruing from 30 November 2015.

Securities acquired at different times

A person may sell or transfer part only of a holding of a security which he has built up by two or more separate acquisitions at different times. Unless this sale or transfer occurs two years or more after the date of the later or latest acquisition (when TCA 1997, s 815 does not apply at all), the part sold must be matched with the appropriate acquisition. This is necessary to determine whether any part of the amount sold is derived from an acquisition made two years or more before the date of the sale or transfer (so that no charge arises in respect of that part included in the sale or transfer). It is also necessary to determine the start of the period of ownership over which interest is deemed to accrue for the computation of the amount to be charged in respect of the part sold or transferred. TCA 1997, s 815(5)(a) provides that securities of the same class are to be matched on a LIFO basis; for these purposes, securities are treated as being of the same class if they entitle their owners to the same rights against the same person in relation to capital and interest and the same remedies for the enforcement of those rights.

Undertakings for collective investments in transferable securities (UCITS)

TCA 1997, ss 738 and 739 deal with the taxation of UCITS and are set out in **Division 8.4**.

TCA 1997, s 815(3)(c) excludes UCITS and unit trusts from the bond washing provisions of TCA 1997, s 815 where any gain or loss accruing to the owner on the sale or transfer is a chargeable gain or an allowable loss (TCA 1997, s 815(3)(c)).

8.210 Transactions associated with loans

The rules restricting the amount of interest paid that may be deducted from a person's income under TCA 1997, Pt 8, Ch 3 are covered in **Division 3**. In order to prevent these rules from being circumvented, TCA 1997, s 813 charges to tax under Sch D Case IV certain sums arising as the result of transactions connected with loans or the giving of credit. The special rules of TCA 1997, s 813 apply if there is a transaction of one of the kinds specified in the section which is effective either:

(a) with reference to the lending of money or the giving of credit;
(b) to vary the terms on which money is lent or credit is given; or
(c) to enable or facilitate any arrangements concerning the lending of money or the giving of credit.

The transaction may be one between the lender and the borrower (or between the creditor and the debtor) or it may be one involving a person connected with either of them.

TCA 1997, s 813(3) treats a payment as if it were a payment of annual interest although the transaction between the parties may provide that the payment in question is to be an annuity or other annual payment that is chargeable under Sch D but which is not interest. In the absence of this provision, it would be possible for a lender to advance money in consideration for the borrower's contracting to pay him an annuity or other annual payment not covered by the interest restrictions, instead of interest. Any such annuity or annual payment is now deemed to be interest so the payer gets no greater relief for the payment than he would if he had paid interest on the borrowing. This rule has no effect on the deduction in arriving at the payer's total income of any annuity or other annual payment that is not connected with a borrowing or credit transaction covered by TCA 1997, s 813, although the rules of TCA 1997, s 242 must also be borne in mind (see **17.305**).

TCA 1997, s 813(4)–(6) deals with three different types of transaction which would otherwise enable a person to reduce his total income chargeable to tax. These rules can best be explained by assuming that a particular person (Mr A) wishes to obtain the use of €10,000 for a period of 18-months commencing on 1 December 2013. Mr A does not want to pay any interest on the money as it is not being applied for any purpose for which he can deduct the interest from any income. He is unaware of the rules in TCA 1997, s 813 and comes up with three schemes any one of which he thinks will enable him to compensate the 'lender' for the use of the money and to reduce his own total income on which he is taxable. His three 'plans' and the way they are defeated by the TCA 1997, s 813 anti-avoidance rules, are as follows:

Plan 1

Mr A enters into an arrangement with the 'lender' (B Ltd) under which Mr A agrees to sell to B Ltd an income producing asset (say, a holding of an Irish government loan stock) for €10,000. The loan stock carries interest of €1,500 pa payable on 15 May and 15 November each year. At the same time, B Ltd agrees with Mr A to sell back to him the holding of government stock for €10,500 on 1 June 2015. In the absence of TCA 1997, s 813, Mr A would effectively have borrowed €10,000 and would have reduced the income otherwise attributable to him in 2014 by €1,500 and in 2015 by €750, ie by government stock interest payments due on 15 May 2014, 15 November 2014 and 15 May 2015.

TCA 1997, s 813(4) prevents the success of this type of device. Without affecting the liability of B Ltd to tax on the government stock loan interest it receives between 1 December 2013 and 1 June 2015, it charges tax under Sch D Case IV on Mr A for each relevant tax year on an amount equal to the income arising from the income producing assets that are the subject of the transaction until the 'loan' is repaid and the asset reconveyed to Mr A. In other words, Mr A is taxed under Sch D Case IV on a sum of €1,500 in 2014 and on €750 in 2015. The assessment is on the normal Sch D Case IV arising basis.

TCA 1997, s 813(4) would also apply if the 'buy-back' agreement is one under which Mr A is given an option to buy or otherwise acquire either the same assets or any other property from B Ltd, if in fact he duly exercises this option. The buy-back agreement may be made by either the original sale agreement or by any associated or collateral agreement. It does not matter if the arrangement is for a person connected with B Ltd to sell back the same or any other asset to Mr A, nor if it is for the same or any other asset to be sold back to a person connected with Mr A. The original conveyance of the asset may be by simple transfer or gift instead of by an actual sale. In any of these events, Mr A as the 'borrower' is taxable in the same way.

Plan 2

Instead of selling or otherwise transferring his holding of government stock to B Ltd, Mr A agrees in consideration for an advance of €10,000 from the company to assign to B Ltd his right to receive the interest on the government stock so long as the advance remains outstanding. In fact Mr A repays the advance on 1 June 2015, but B Ltd has received the half-yearly interest payments of €750 made on 15 May 2014, 15 November 2014 and 15 May 2015.

Without affecting the liability of B Ltd to tax on the loan stock interest being received in the period when the advance was outstanding, TCA 1997, s 813(5) charges tax under Sch D Case IV on Mr A for each relevant tax year on a sum equal to the loan stock interest assigned to B Ltd. As with Plan 1, Mr A is assessable on €1,500 for 2014 and on €750 for 2015.

TCA 1997, s 813(5) would apply in the same way if the transaction had provided for Mr A's surrendering, waiving or otherwise forgoing the loan stock interest, rather than actually assigning it. If the income assigned, surrendered, waived, etc is income payable subject to the deduction of income tax (eg should it be an annuity to which Mr A is entitled), TCA 1997, s 813(7) makes it clear that the 'borrower' is taxable by TCA 1997, s 813(5) on the gross amount of the income assigned, etc. Again, the assignment, etc of the income could be made by a person connected with Mr A and/or it could be in favour of any person connected with B Ltd. In either event, Mr A as the person who receives the advance of €10,000 is the person taxable on the income assigned.

Plan 3

Instead of borrowing from B Ltd, Mr A is about to purchase an income producing asset, say, the film rights to a novel of which B Ltd holds the copyright. The transaction is completed on 1 December 2013 under a contract whereby Mr A purchases the film rights for €10,000 with B Ltd's agreement to allow the debt to remain outstanding until 1 June 2015 in consideration for Mr A's agreement that the first €1,200 pa of copyright royalties continue to be payable to B Ltd until the purchase price is paid. If in any period the total royalties receivable fall short of €1,200 pa B Ltd is entitled to recoup the arrears due to it out of future royalties.

TCA 1997, s 813(6) applies in this case and requires Mr A to be treated under TCA 1997, s 813(5) in the same way as if he had surrendered a right to income of an amount equal to the royalties forgone under the agreement for the credit in respect of the €10,000 purchase price. This means that he is taxed under Sch D Case IV in each relevant tax year on a sum equal to the royalties forgone in that year. TCA 1997, s 813(7) again provides that it is the gross royalties forgone that are taxable.

Example 8.210.1

Take the facts of Plan 3 and assume that Mr A does not in fact pay up the outstanding purchase price of €10,000 until 1 December 2015. Assume that there were no royalties receivable for the period 1 December 2013 to 31 December 2013, that the royalties due for the year to 31 December 2014 were only €1,000 but that in the period 1 January 2015 to 1 December 2015, royalties of €1,800 are received.

The Sch D Case IV assessments on Mr A due to TCA 1997, s 813(6) for the tax years affected are as follows:

	€
2013:	
Royalties forgone 1/12/2013 to 31/12/2013	Nil

2014:	
Royalties forgone in year to 31/12/2014	1,000
2015:	
Royalties forgone in period 1/01/2015 to 1/12/2015	
€1,200 pa x 334/365	1,098
Deficit for 2014 (1,200 – 1,000) *	200
€1,200 pa x 31/365 (deficit for 2013)*	102
	1,400

* Arrears that would have been recouped in last period if no credit agreement.

In applying the rules of TCA 1997, s 813, the connected person definitions in TCA 1997, s 10 are applied.

Furthermore Revenue can issue a payment notice requesting immediate payment of tax due in such an assessment if a similar transaction has been the subject of an Appeal Commissioners determination which resulted in the issue of a payment notice to another taxpayer (see under Payment notices in **2.618**, Disclosure of tax avoidance transactions).

8.211 Payment notices – anti-avoidance

With effect from the date of passing of FA 2014, TCA 1997, ss 817S and 817T were inserted. Normally no tax will be payable or repayable following a determination by the Appeal Commissioners if the decision is subject to a rehearing by the Circuit Court or an appeal on a point of law to the High Court (see **2.202**). However TCA 1997, s 817S provides that in cases where a taxpayer has entered into a transaction to which either TCA 1997, ss 812, 813, 814, 815 and 816 applies, it should be borne in mind that in the event that an assessment is raised by Revenue withdrawing part of all of the tax advantage gained by entering into the transaction any additional tax may be collected by Revenue when any appeal has been heard and determined by the Appeal Commissioners by the issue of a payment notice. This is the case even if the taxpayer has requested a rehearing by the Circuit Court or lodged an appeal to the High Court.

8.212 Tax avoidance surcharge

A new surcharge has been introduced by FA 2014 as part of the new general anti-avoidance provisions. TCA 1997, s 811D is stated to apply specifically to TCA 1997, ss 812–816 inclusive.

Under this new provision, where a taxpayer submits a tax return or otherwise seeks to obtain the benefit of a tax advantage and the transaction that gives rise to the tax advantage is caught by TCA 1997 ss 812–816 inclusive, the taxpayer may be liable to the 30 per cent surcharge under TCA 1997 s 811D. The surcharge only applies to transactions which commenced on or after 24 October 2014. The surcharge is discussed further in **17.302**.

8.213 Gains from illegal or unknown sources

Prior to FA 1983, the profits or gains from a trade or business that was wholly illegal could not be taxed (see **4.103**). TCA 1997, s 58 now applies to enable an inspector of taxes to assess under Sch D Case IV any profits or gains notwithstanding that at the time the assessment is made either:

(a) the source from which they arose was not known to the inspector;

(b) they were not known to him to have arisen wholly or partly from a lawful source of activity; or

(c) they arose, and were known to him to have arisen, from an unlawful source or activity.

Any profits or gains charged under this section are to be described in the assessment as 'miscellaneous income'. An assessment so made cannot be discharged by the Appeal Commissioners or by any court by reason only of the fact that the income should have been described in some other way.

TCA 1997, s 58 may have retrospective application. The original legislation, FA 1983, s 19(4), provides that the section applies and has effect in respect of assessments to tax made on or after 8 June 1983 (when the Act was passed). FA 1983, s 19(3) indicated that it enabled assessments to be made for income tax, corporation tax or corporation profits tax. The inclusion of the latter tax which, for profits or gains of lawful activities ceased on 5 April 1976, clearly points to the intended retrospective application of TCA 1997, s 58. It is very widely drawn and is an important weapon in the State's armoury to reach, through the tax code, persons suspected of making gains from illegal or criminal activities. Any person assessed to tax under TCA 1997, s 58 is put in the position of having to prove, if he can, that he has not made such gains.

The establishment of the Criminal Assets Bureau should be noted in this respect. The Disclosure of Certain Information for Taxation and Other Purposes Act 1996, s 10 provides that with effect from 30 June 1996 TCA 1997, s 58 also applies to profits brought into charge following an investigation by the Bureau and allows the assessment to be raised solely in the name of the Bureau (although any tax paid must then be transferred to the Revenue Commissioners and full details thereof supplied to the Collector-General). The same Act ensures that the anonymity of Revenue officials seconded to the Bureau is preserved (TCA 1997, s 859). TCA 1997, s 859 also provides that a Revenue official acting on behalf of the Bureau may be accompanied by an officer of the Garda Síochána when exercising his powers or duties on behalf of the Bureau.

8.3 Income from Patents

8.301 Introduction

A patent is the right conferred by letters patent of the exclusive use and benefit of a new invention. An application for an Irish patent in respect of a new invention may be made to the Patents Office either by the first inventor or by an assignee to whom the first inventor has assigned his right to make the application for the patent. The application must be accompanied by a specification giving details of the invention; if this specification is only a provisional one, a complete specification must be filed within 12 months from the date of the application. The date of filing the complete specification is important since this date becomes the date of the patent, even if the letters patent are not actually granted until several years later (as may well happen in practice). The normal term or life of an Irish patent is 20 years from the date of the patent, ie from the date that the complete specification is filed; previously the normal term was 16 years. However, the Patents Act 1992 also provides for a form of Irish short-term patent, with a term of 10 years which is subject to less rigorous scrutiny than a full-term patent.

When granted, an Irish patent confers on the person to whom it is granted (and, if relevant, his executors, administrators and assigns) the sole and exclusive right to exploit the invention commercially in the State either directly himself or indirectly through licensing arrangements. If the grantee of the patent wishes to ensure that the invention cannot be used outside the State by other persons except under a proper licence, he must apply for a patent in every other country in which this protection is sought. Where an application is filed in Ireland, this provides the person with a 12-month 'period of grace' in which to file applications in other jurisdictions. Correspondingly, a person to whom a patent for an invention has been granted under the patent laws of another country may apply to the Irish Patents Office for an Irish patent to prevent the unauthorised use of the invention in the State. It is also possible to obtain patent protection in the EU as a whole by applying directly to the European Patents Office.

The owner of a patent may use the patented invention in his own trade to help him generate trading profits, he may license another person to use the invention or he may make a profit by selling the patent outright so that all his rights under it pass to the purchaser who may exploit it for his own benefit. The current owner of the patent may also use it in his own trade and at the same time license one or more other persons to use it, but generally such licensees are only given the right to exploit the invention in countries in which the owner of the patent does not himself trade. Depending on the terms of his licence, a licensee may be able to sublicence a third party to use the invention in any of the countries for which he himself has the right of user. He may also be able to sell the licence to another person who then assumes fully all the rights which the original licensee possessed under the patent in question.

The Tax Acts set out to tax as income all types of profits or gains derived from a patent and from any rights under a patent, whether received as royalties for the licensing or sublicensing of the right to use the patented invention or as a capital sum for the sale of the patent or for the granting of a licence or any other rights under the patent (but with a deduction for any capital cost of purchase). Apart from royalties which are taxable under normal rules, TCA 1997, Pt 29, Ch 1 (ss 754–762) contains a number of special rules relevant to the taxation of income from patents, including the provision of capital allowances in respect of capital expenditure on the purchase of patent rights and certain other expenses.

The following definitions given in TCA 1997, s 754 are relevant both for the rules relating to capital allowances for patent right expenditure and for the taxation of capital sums received for the sale of patent rights.

Patent rights means the right to do or authorise the doing of anything which but for that right would be an infringement of a patent. It follows that not only does the owner for the time being of a patent have patent rights, but so does any other person who is currently entitled to use the patented invention under a licence or a sublicence. Further, since the filing of a complete specification of an invention in connection with the application for a patent operates to prevent the unauthorised use of the invention, the person who has made this application is treated as having patent rights capable of being sold (see *Green v Brace* 39 TC 281).

Sale of part of patent rights includes the grant of a licence (or a sublicence) in respect of the patent in question. This is relevant in any case where the granting of the licence (or sublicence) is made for a consideration that consists of or includes a capital sum. If the only consideration given by the grantee of the licence (or sublicence) is a royalty or some other non-capital sum for the use of the patent, the royalty is taxable normally and there are no other tax implications for the person granting the licence.

Sale of whole of patent rights includes, in addition to an outright sale, the case where the person entitled to any patent rights grants a licence to another person to exercise those rights to the exclusion of the grantor and of all other persons for the whole of the remainder of the term for which the rights subsist. For example, there is such a sale if Mr A, who owns a patent due to expire on 1 January 2015 entitling him to the exclusive use, etc of an invention in the State grants Mr B an exclusive licence to use the invention in the State up to that date. However, for example if Mr B is only given the exclusive licence up to (say) 1 January 2014, or is given a non-exclusive licence, Mr A is treated as selling part of his patent rights.

Purchase of patent rights includes the acquisition of a licence (or sublicence) in respect of a patent. Consequently, if and to the extent that the grantee of the licence (or sublicence) gives consideration consisting of or including a capital sum, he is treated as having incurred capital expenditure on the purchase of patent rights.

TCA 1997, Pt 9 Ch 4, as applied by TCA 1997, s 762(1), indicates how 'capital sums' and 'capital expenditure' are to be interpreted by stating what sums or expenditure are to be excluded respectively from each. So far as the person receiving a capital sum is concerned, the term does not include either:

(a) any amount or sum which is taken into account as a receipt in computing the profits or gains of any trade, profession, office or employment carried on or held by him; or

(b) any royalty or other sum payable for the user of a patent, or any annuity, other annual payment or any other sum from which income tax is deductible under TCA 1997, s 237 or 238.

However, the requirement of TCA 1997, s 757(2) for income tax to be deducted under TCA 1997, s 238 from a capital sum paid to a non-resident seller of Irish patent rights (see **8.304**) does not change the status of what is otherwise a capital sum.

Correspondingly, references in the legislation to capital expenditure or to any capital sum paid are to be taken as excluding both any expenditure or sum which is deductible in computing the profits or gains of a trade, profession, office or employment and any royalty or similar sum paid for the use of a patent, or any other annual payment, etc, from which income tax is deductible under TCA 1997, s 237 or 238. Capital expenditure incurred in purchasing patent rights must be taken after deducting any part of that expenditure met by grant or otherwise by the State, any statutory board, public or local authority, etc (TCA 1997, s 317(2)). Again, the requirement of TCA 1997, s 757(2) to deduct income tax under TCA 1997, s 238 from a capital sum paid to a non-resident seller does not affect the status of that capital sum.

'Net proceeds of sale' is not expressly defined, but may be taken as the amount of any capital sum(s) received for the sale of any patent rights as reduced by any expenses incurred by the seller directly for the purposes of the sale. Deductible expenses of sale may include the costs of advertising the patent rights for sale, any patent agent's fees in connection with the sale, etc. Any royalty or other payment that is not a capital sum (see above), even if receivable as part of the consideration for the sale of any patent rights, is always excluded in determining the net proceeds of sale.

8.302 How income from patents is taxed

TCA 1997, s 754(1) defines 'income from patents' as meaning (a) any royalty or other sum paid in respect of the user of a patent and (b) any amount on which tax is payable for any chargeable period by virtue of any of the provisions of TCA 1997, Pt 29 Ch 1. In effect, this means that income from patents may be made up of royalty or other income sums (including any income taxable under Sch D Case III in respect of foreign possessions: see **13.108**) as well as:

(a) any capital sum received for the sale of any patent rights to the extent taxable under Sch D Case IV in accordance with the provisions of TCA 1997, s 757 (see **8.303, 8.304**); and
(b) any balancing charge that may arise on the sale of any patent rights which, except if relevant to patent rights used for a trade, is taxable under Sch D Case IV (see 6.7).

In taxing a person's income from patents for any year of assessment in a non-trading context, TCA 1997, Pt 29 Ch 1 provides for 'allowances' for the following:

(a) the capital allowances (including any balancing allowances) for the tax year in respect of capital expenditure on the purchase of patent rights (see **6.7**);
(b) any fees paid or expenses incurred by the taxpayer in the year of assessment in connection with the grant of the patent, or with its maintenance or the obtaining of an extension of the term of the patent (TCA 1997, s 758(2)); and
(c) any expenses incurred in the year of assessment (income tax only) to the extent properly attributable to the devising of the invention that is the subject of the patent, but only if the taxpayer is an individual and is the person who, either alone or in conjunction with any other person, actually devised the invention (TCA 1997, s 758(3)).

Except where given in taxing the profits of a trade, all these allowances are given by way of discharge or repayment of tax and are available against income from patents (TCA 1997, s 761(2)). The total of these allowances for any year of assessment must, therefore, be set off against the taxpayer's income from patents as chargeable to tax for that year of assessment. For this purpose, all the income from patents for the year of assessment is added together, even if assessable under different Cases or if received as taxed income. If the total of the allowances for any year of assessment exceeds the taxpayer's income from patents for that period, then the unused allowances are carried forward for set off against his income from patents in the next year of assessment, and so on without time limit until fully used (TCA 1997, s 305(1)). There is no right to set off any of the unused allowances for any year of assessment against income from any other source.

Capital allowances in respect of capital expenditure on the purchase of patent rights are given, and any relevant balancing charges made, in taxing the trade of the taxpayer concerned if, at any time in the relevant basis period for a year of assessment, the patent rights in question, or any other rights out of which they were granted, were used for the purposes of that trade (TCA 1997, s 761(1)). In such a case, any fees paid or expenses incurred in obtaining, for the purposes of the trade, the grant of a patent or an extension of the term of a patent are allowed as expenses, and not as capital allowances (TCA 1997, s 758(1)).

Example 8.302.1

Jim Bell, an Irish resident individual trading in the State, purchased several years ago the Irish and French patents to a foreign devised invention for use in his trade. He also owns other patents taken out in the State and in a number of foreign countries to inventions not used in his trade, but from which he derives a royalty income from licences to other parties (taxable under Sch D Case III and Sch D Case IV respectively). He claims writing down allowances on the capital expenditure in purchasing all these patent rights (trade and non-trade). He makes up his accounts to 31 December each year. During his 12-month accounting period ended 31 December 2016, he sells the French patents (trade) and also some German patent rights (non-trade), each sale resulting in a balancing charge (see 6.7) and a charge to tax under Sch D Case IV in respect of the capital sums received for the sales (see **8.303**). In the same period, Jim pays fees and certain other expenses in connection with his application for two new patents, one for use in his trade and the other to be licenced outside his trade.

Based on the figures assumed below, Jim's income from patents, patent rights capital allowances, balancing charges and other allowances for the accounting period ended 31 December 2016 are dealt with as follows:

	€	€
(a) In taxing profits of trade under Sch D Case I:		
Balancing charge (additional income):		
Sale of French patent (trade)		1,500
Capital allowances (deduct):		
Writing down allowances (all trade patents)		(5,640)
fees, etc for applications for new patents (trade)		
Deduct as trade expenses		(1,970)
Case I Trading loss carried forward including capital allowances	(6,110)	
(b) Taxable separately as income from patents:		

Royalties received		
Sch D Case III: licences of various foreign patents (non-trade)		8,400
Irish taxed royalties		
Licences of Irish patents (non-trade)		1,200
Capital sums for sales of patent rights		
Sch D Case IV: net amount taxable for year		
Sale of French patent (trade)[1]		900
Sale of German patent rights (non-trade)		
Balancing charge (Sch D Case IV)		800
Sale of German patents rights (non-trade)		2,200
Total (non-trade) income from patents		13,500
Capital, etc allowances for year (non-trade):		
Writing down allowances	3,150	
Fees, etc re applications for new patent (non-trade)	2,370	
		(5,520)
Taxable income from patents (year to 31/12/2016)		7,980

Notes:

1. Although the balancing charge on the sale of the French patent used for the trade is dealt with in the Sch D Case I assessment (TCA 1997, s 761(1)), the 'income' arising from the capital sum for the sale of the rights remains taxable under Sch D Case IV (see **8.303**).

8.303 Capital sums: resident vendor

TCA 1997, s 757(1) charges tax under Sch D Case IV on any resident person who sells any part or all of his rights under a patent for a capital sum, but in computing the amount chargeable, TCA 1997, s 757(4) allows the capital expenditure (if any) in acquiring those patent rights to be deducted from the net sale proceeds. This charge is made under Sch D Case IV even if the patent rights sold had previously been used in the trade of the vendor; also, it arises whether or not any writing down or other capital allowances have been obtained in respect of the patent rights in question. If capital allowances have been obtained in a case where the net proceeds of the sale exceed the original capital expenditure, there is both a balancing charge to write back the earlier capital allowances and the TCA 1997, s 757(1) charge under Sch D Case IV to tax the excess sale proceeds.

The amount chargeable under Sch D Case IV by TCA 1997, s 757(1) is not normally taxed all in the one year, but is spread equally over six years. If the seller of the patent rights is liable to income tax, one sixth of the excess of the net sale proceeds over the amount deductible for the capital expenditure in acquiring those rights is charged under Sch D Case IV for the tax year in which the capital sum is received; a further one sixth of the excess is taxed in each of the next five tax years.

Example 8.303.1

Mr V E Clever devises a new invention and is in due course granted patent rights in the State and certain other countries. After granting licences and receiving royalties for the use of these patents for several years, he sells these patent rights outright for a capital sum of €57,000 on 18 November 2016. Since he did not incur any capital expenditure on purchasing these patents, he has not received any writing down allowances.

Assuming that Mr Clever incurred expenses of €600 in advertising his patent rights for the sale, he is taxable under Sch D Case IV for each of the six tax years 2016 to 2021 on an amount determined as follows:

	€
Capital sum for sale (18/11/2016)	57,000
Less:	
Expenses of advertising sale	(600)
Net proceeds of sale	56,400
Less:	
Capital expenditure on purchase	Nil
Total amount assessable (net gain)	56,400
Sch D Case IV income 2016:	
1/6th of net gain €56,400	9,400
Sch D Case IV income 2017 to 2021	
1/6th of net gain €56,400, ie €9,400 x 5 years	47,000
	56,400

Successive sales

A person may sell the whole or a further part of his rights under a patent after having made one or more previous sales of rights under the same patent. If the consideration received for any such previous sale consisted of or included a capital sum, the amount of the capital expenditure deduction from any capital sum received on the current sale is itself reduced by the capital sum(s) on the earlier sale(s). If any previous capital allowances have not been fully recaptured by the earlier sale(s), a balancing charge must also be computed on the current sale.

Example 8.303.2

On 1 October 2012, Mr R Daft had purchased for €60,000 all the rights to a Dutch patent for a 12-year period (writing-down period commencing in his Sch D Case IV 2012 year of assessment). He obtains writing-down allowances totalling €18,000 for the four years 2012 to 2015 before, on 1 April 2016, he grants a licence to another person to use the Dutch patents (due to expire on 30 September 2024) up to 30 September 2019. He receives a capital sum of €46,000 for this sale of part of his patent rights.

Mr Daft's tax treatment in respect of this sale is as follows:

	€
Capital expenditure (1/10/2012)	60,000
Writing down allowances:	
2012 to 2015	(18,000)
Tax WDV 31/12/2015	42,000
Sale of part of rights (1/04/2016)	46,000
Balancing charge 2016	(4,000)

A gain is not taxable under TCA 1997, s 757 as the proceeds of €46,000 are less than the capital expenditure of €60,000.

Assume that Mr Daft sells his remaining rights under the Dutch patents on 1 February 2017 for a capital sum of €16,400. The total amount on which he now becomes chargeable to tax under the successive sales rule of TCA 1997, s 757, to be spread over the six tax years commencing 2017 is computed as follows:

	€	€
Capital sum for sale (1/2/2017)		16,400
Less:		
Capital expenditure on purchase (1/10/2012)	60,000	
As reduced by capital sum on previous sale (1/4/2016)	(46,000)	
		14,000
Total amount assessable 2017 etc[1]		2,400

Note:

1. In addition, a balancing charge of €14,000 is made for 2017 to recapture the balance of the writing down allowances not covered by the previous balancing charge of €4,000.

Election for single year assessment

Any person chargeable under TCA 1997, s 757(1) in respect of a capital sum received for the sale of the whole or a part of any patent rights is entitled to elect to have the total amount chargeable in the one year, instead of having it spread over six years (TCA 1997, s 757(1)(b)). This election must be made by notice in writing to the inspector no later than 12 months after the end of the tax year in which the capital sum was received. A taxpayer might wish to make this election, for example, if his taxable income in that tax year is lower than normal or if he has a trading loss or Sch D Case V excess capital allowances available for set off against his total income (including the amount assessable under TCA 1997, s 757) for that year or period.

Alternatively, the person taxable may apply, by notice in writing to the inspector within the same time limit, to have the total amount chargeable under TCA 1997, s 757(1) spread over a number of years other than six. Then, if it appears to the Revenue Commissioners that hardship is likely to arise to the taxpayer if he is taxed over the six-year period, they may direct that the taxable amount should be spread over such other number of years as they consider appropriate. In making their decision on this application, the Commissioners are required to have regard to all the circumstances of the case (TCA 1997, s 757(1)(b)).

8.304 Capital sums: non-resident vendor

TCA 1997, s 757(2) charges tax under Sch D Case IV on any person not resident in the State who sells any patent rights for a capital sum, but only if the patent in question is an Irish patent. An 'Irish patent' is defined as a patent granted under the laws of the State (TCA 1997, s 754(1)); the term therefore includes any patent taken out under the consolidated Patents Act 1992, whether the invention protected by the patent was devised in the State or in any foreign country. The definition does not seem to cover a European patent even if this confers rights and remedies identical to those conferred by an Irish patent (ie by virtue of the Patents Act 1992, s 119(1)). The tax charge under this subsection applies whether the non-resident person sells his Irish patent rights outright or grants a licence or sublicence for a capital sum to any other person to use his Irish patent (or any rights he possesses under an Irish patent). The subsection does not of course charge tax on any part of the consideration for the sale that is not a capital sum, eg a royalty.

The method of taxing the non-resident person, whether an individual, a company or any other person, under TCA 1997, s 757(2), is different from that used by TCA 1997, s 757(1) to tax a resident person (see **8.303**). TCA 1997, s 757(2) requires the person paying the capital sum to the non-resident vendor to deduct Irish income tax at the standard rate from the amount of that sum and to account to the Revenue Commissioners under TCA 1997, s 238 for the tax deducted. Income tax must be deducted from the full amount of the capital sum(s) paid by the purchaser without making any allowance for the fact that the vendor may be able to claim a deduction in respect of his capital expenditure on his original acquisition of the Irish patent rights (TCA 1997, s 757(4)(b)).

The non-resident seller, who has received any capital sum(s) from which Irish income tax has been deducted under the foregoing rule, is entitled to elect by notice in writing to the Revenue Commissioners to be taxed in respect of his sale of the Irish patent rights over a six-year period on his 'net gain' on the sale, rather than on the full capital sum(s). The effect of this election is to leave the non-resident person liable to Irish income tax on one sixth of his net gain on the sale in the tax year in which he received the capital sum, and on a further one sixth of that profit for each of the next five tax years. In computing the net gain that is chargeable over these tax years, the same deduction is given in respect of capital expenditure as applies in computing the total amount taxable under TCA 1997, s 757(1) for a resident vendor.

In any case where the non-resident vendor elects under TCA 1997, s 757(2) to be taxed over the six-year period, he obtains the benefit of his election by obtaining a repayment of the excess of the income tax deducted under TCA 1997, s 238 over his final Irish tax liability for each relevant tax year in the six-year spreading period. The election to be taxed over the six-year period does not avoid the requirement of the payer of the capital sum(s) to deduct and account for income tax under the TCA 1997, s 238 procedure.

In the event that the non-resident vendor electing to be taxed over the six-year period is an individual, his Irish income tax liability for each tax year is based on his total income from Irish sources (including the amount assessable under TCA 1997, s 757(2)) and, if this total income is high enough, the higher rates of income tax may be applicable as well as the standard rate. In any event the non-resident vendor making the election is likely to be required to make an Irish income tax return for each of the tax years and no repayment of the excess income tax deducted is made for any tax year until the non-resident person's final Irish tax liability for that year is determined.

Effect of double taxation agreement

One important qualification must be made to the foregoing discussion of the non-resident vendor's liability to Irish income tax. If the vendor is a resident of another country with which the government of Ireland has made a double taxation agreement (see **Division 14**), the terms of that agreement should be examined. The majority of the double taxation agreements made with other countries provide that a resident of the other country in receipt of royalties and other income from patents is to be exempted from Irish income tax or corporation tax in respect of such income. If the non-resident seller is eligible to benefit from such an agreement, he is entitled, on making the appropriate claim, to be repaid all the Irish income tax deducted by the payer of the capital sum(s) for the sale of the Irish patent rights.

'Royalties' are however generally defined for treaty purposes as payments 'for the use of or the right to use … any patent'. The Commentary to the OECD Model Convention Art 12 indicates that payment for the transfer of full (or in some cases, extensive, but less than full) ownership rights will not be payments 'for the use of rights'. Exemption may however still be available under a different article of the relevant treaty, if appropriate.

8.305 Exemption for certain income from patents

TCA 1997, s 234 historically provided an exemption from tax for income from 'qualifying patents' when received by the 'inventor' (see below) of the patented invention. This relief was potentially subject to the restrictions applicable to high income individuals discussed at **3.111**. A full description of the relevant regime is provided in the 2011 edition of this text. The income tax exemption ceased to apply to income from a qualifying patent paid to a person on or after 24 November 2010.

8.306 Spreading of royalty income

A royalty or other sum may be received for the use of a patent that extends over a period of years. Normally any such payment is taxable as taxed income for the year in which it is received or, if it is from a foreign source, it is chargeable under the rules for Sch D Case III. TCA 1997, s 759 entitles the recipient of such a royalty, etc to require his tax liability to be computed as if it had been paid over a number of years, but only in the case of a royalty or similar sum to which TCA 1997, ss 237, 238 apply (see **2.302**).

In effect, therefore, the right to have the royalty income spread over a number of years seems only available to such income from Irish sources that is subject to the rules on deduction of income tax at source. If the period over which the use of the patent has extended is six complete years or more, the taxpayer is entitled to require the inspector to recompute his tax liability for the relevant tax years on the assumption that the royalty was paid in six equal instalments at yearly intervals, the last of which was paid on the date on which the payment was in fact made.

In the event that the royalty or other sum is paid in respect of the use of a patent for two complete years or more, but less than six complete years, then the taxpayer's tax liability may be recomputed as if the royalty had been paid in such a number of equal annual instalments as there are complete years comprised in the period over which the use of the patent extended.

The years over which the royalty is spread are the actual years working backwards from the date on which the particular royalty payment was made. For example, if a single royalty payment of €12,000 was made to an individual on 4 January 2015 in respect of the use of a patent for the five years ended 30 September 2014, the recipient of the royalty may have his tax liabilities recomputed on the assumption that he had received five royalty payments of €2,400 each on 4 January 2015, 4 January 2014, 4 January 2013, 4 January 2012 and 4 January 2011. This would require the individual's income tax liabilities for the tax years 2011 to 2014 inclusive to be recomputed by including royalty income of €2,400 for each year, and by excluding from his income for the year 2015 the actual royalty received of €12,000.

8.4 Investment Products

8.401 Taxation of collective investment undertakings

Collective investment undertakings (CIUs) may take the form *inter alia* of an authorised unit trust (as defined by the Unit Trusts Act 1990) or a UCITS (see TCA 1997, s 738(1)). A UCITS is a collective fund authorised under the European Union UCITS directive, implemented in Ireland by means of SI 78/1989. A UCITS is defined as an undertaking 'the sole object of which is the collective investment in transferable securities of capital raised from the public and which operates on the principle of risk spreading and the units of which are at the request of holders repurchased or redeemed directly or indirectly out of those undertakings' assets'. SI 78/1989 imposes restrictions on the investment and borrowing policy of a UCITS. A UCITS may either be a unit trust or, its corporate equivalents, including a variable capital company (SICAV) or a fixed capital public limited company (SICAF). Once established in Ireland, a UCITS may be marketed throughout the European Union. For a full description of the fund industry in Ireland, see Wall & O'Donnell 'Taxation of Investment Funds (Ireland)': (1997) Cahiers de Droit Fiscal International, Volume LXXXX 11b.

With general effect from 6 April 1994, TCA 1997, s 738 *et seq*, as most recently amended by F(No 2)A 2008, set out the regime for the taxation of CIUs resident in Ireland. Under this regime, the CIU was liable at the standard rate of income tax on both the income and chargeable gains arising each year. The individual investor therefore normally had no further liability on either the income from the fund or capital gains on the disposal thereof.

Offshore (in broad terms, non-resident) funds within TCA 1997, s 743 which are subject to a special tax charge (see **17.4**) and a 'specified collective investment undertaking' within TCA 1997, s 734 did not fall within the general regime.

A 'specified collective investment undertaking' (SCIU) is defined as a collective investment undertaking (as defined by TCA 1997, s 734(1)) the business of which is carried on in the Custom House Docks Area, within the meaning of TCA 1997, s 446 or in Shannon Zone and the units of which (other than those held by the undertaking itself, its qualifying management company, another specified undertaking or an IFSC life assurance company) are held by persons who are not resident in the State (TCA 1997, s 734(1)(a), (c)).

The tax treatment of a SCIU could be summarised as follows:

(a) the income and gains of the SCIU were exempt from Irish tax; and
(b) the SCIU was not required to deduct tax from payments out of its income or gains, nor to account for tax on its undistributed income (TCA 1997, s 734).

These SCIUs were therefore in effect totally tax-transparent.

The taxation system applying to CIUs was changed by FA 2000, s 58, inserting TCA 1997, Pt 27, Ch 1A, in respect of:

(a) a CIU issuing its first units on or after 1 April 2000; or
(b) all SCIUs irrespective of when they were first set up, with effect from 1 April 2000.

Non-IFSC collective undertakings which first issued units before 1 April 2000 therefore continue to be taxed under TCA 1997, s 738, even in relation to issues made after that date. The regime does not apply to CIUs which are 'offshore' (broadly speaking non-resident funds (see **17.4**) (TCA 1997, s 739B(1)).

Under the FA 2000 rules, the funds accumulate on a gross rollup basis and 'appropriate tax' is levied on a chargeable event, in a manner similar to that applicable to life assurance policies under the equivalent FA 2000 regime, discussed in **8.402**. However, with effect from 13 March 2008, the self-assessment system may apply to unit-holders in CIUs where 90 per cent or more of the unitholders (in value) are exempt from appropriate tax, but only in relation to the 8-yearly anniversary charge (see below).

Chargeable events include:

(a) the making of 'relevant' payments, ie on an annual or more frequent basis (otherwise than on the cancellation, redemption or repurchase of a unit to a unit holder);

(b) the making of any other payment to a unit holder (including the cancellation, redemption or repurchase of a unit);

(c) the transfer by a unit holder of their entitlement to a unit in a CIU;

(d) the appropriation or cancellation of units by a CIU in order to meet the payment of 'appropriate tax' (see below) arising under (c) (with effect from 4 February 2004); and

(e) the occurrence of every 8th anniversary of the acquisition of the units, with effect from 31 March 2006 (the 'ending of a relevant period') unless this is otherwise a chargeable event (TCA 1997, s 739B(1)(a), (b), (c), (cc), (ccc); FA 2004, s 29; FA 2006, s 50; FA 2008, s 39).

A chargeable event was also deemed to occur on 31 December 2000 in respect of a CIU which commenced on or after 1 April 2000, or which on 31 March 2000 was located in the IFSC (TCA 1997, s 739B(1)(c)).

However, a chargeable event does not occur on the occasion of an arm's length exchange of units in a sub-fund of an umbrella fund for units in another sub-fund of that umbrella fund, or any arm's length exchange of units in the CIU for units in the same CIU or (as clarified by FA 2005, s 40 with effect from 1 January 2005) a change of investment managers in the case of funds administered by the Courts Service (TCA 1997, s 739B (1)). Transfers between spouses or civil partners, including transfers between former spouses or civil partners in respect of divorce, separation or dissolution proceedings, do not give rise to a chargeable event, but the spouse or former spouse acquiring the units is then treated as acquiring them at the same cost as the transferor (TCA 1997, s 739B(1)).

The amount of the gain which arises on a chargeable event is computed as follows:

(a) on the making of a relevant payment, or any payment arising otherwise than on the cancellation, redemption or repurchase of a unit, the amount of that payment;

(b) on the making of a payment for the cancellation, redemption or repurchase of units, the amount of the payment (disregarding any appropriate tax arising on the chargeable event) less the cost of the units concerned calculated on an average cost basis net of any tax paid on foot of the eight-yearly anniversary charge or, at the election of the CIU in relation to all its unit holders, the amount of the payment less the cost of the units computed on a first-in first-out basis;

(c) on the transfer of units by the unit holder, the value of the units transferred (disregarding any appropriate tax arising on the chargeable event) less the cost of the units concerned, calculated on an average cost basis net of any tax paid on foot of the eight-yearly anniversary charge, or at the election of the CIU in relation to all its unit holders, the value of the units, less the cost of the units computed on a first-in first-out basis;

(d) on the appropriation or cancellation of units for the purpose of paying tax computed in accordance with (c), otherwise than as a consequence of a gain arising on the eight-yearly anniversary charge, the tax attributable to the appropriation or cancellation of those units; and

(e) on the ending of a relevant period on an eight-yearly anniversary, the excess (if any) of the value of the units held by the unit holder on that day less the cost of the units concerned, subject to a right of the CIU to elect irrevocably on behalf of all its unit holders that the units should be valued at the later of 30 June or 31 December prior to the date of the chargeable event concerned rather than the date of that event itself. The election must be made on the first eight-yearly anniversary which arises.

'Averaged cost' where relevant is based on the total costs of all units held in the CIU immediately prior to the chargeable event; no provision is made to cover the situation where the unit holder holds different classes of units in the same CIU.

Note that under (c) it is not the amount actually received by the unit holder, but the value of the units at the date of transfer which is taken into account. Thus, for example a gift of units will trigger off a gain in the same way as a sale. Where a unit was acquired otherwise than by investment by the unit holder, including by way of gift, the cost to the unit holder will be treated as the value of the unit at the date of acquisition.

Under (c) and (d), in cases where the relevant election by the CIU has not been made, and a chargeable event was deemed to arise on 31 December 2000, (see above), the acquisition cost of the units is treated as the greater of the actual cost and the value at 31 December 2000 disregarding any appropriate tax arising on that date (TCA 1997, s 739D(2)–(5A); FA 2004, s 29; FA 2006, s 50).

TCA 1997, s 739D(2A), as inserted by FA 2006, s 50, provides that where there has been an eight-yearly chargeable event which is followed at a later time by a 'new' gain arising on another type of chargeable event (eg the transfer or redemption of the units) the calculation of the 'new' gain will proceed on the basis that the provisions for imposing the eight-yearly charge had not been enacted. However, TCA 1997, s 739E(1A), as inserted by FA 2006, s 50, provides that in this situation, a proportion of the tax ('first tax') paid on the gain arising on the eight-yearly chargeable event may be credited against the tax ('second tax') on the subsequent 'new' gain. The proportion of the first tax is B/C where B is the new gain and C is the gain which would arise if the units had been cancelled at the time of the new gain, ie on the basis of a notional full disposal of the units at that time.

Where the due proportion of the first tax exceeds the second tax, a repayment of the excess must generally be made by the assurance company to the policy holder. However, with effect from 13 March 2008, where no more than 15 per cent of unit-holders in terms of value in a CIU (either an umbrella fund or sub-fund) are liable to appropriate tax (see below), the CIU may elect that the amount of any such excess tax may be repaid directly to the unit holder by the Revenue Commissioners on receipt of a claim by the holder. The CIU must inform the unit holder that the election is being made and supply him with all the information necessary to make his claim, This provision, designed to simplify the administration of funds, will primarily impact on funds with a substantial number of non-resident investors.

Furthermore, it is necessary that the assurance company does not have reasonable grounds to believe that the declaration by the policyholder is false. A chargeable event in respect of a unit holder does not arise to a CIU in the case of certain entities, including pension schemes (see **16.1**), charities (see **18.2**), approved retirement funds and approved minimum retirement funds (see **16.2**) and PRSAs (see **16.3**) which comply with a declaration procedure (TCA 1997, s 739D(6)). The format of the declarations required is set out in (TCA 1997, Sch 2B). TCA 1997, s 739H provides that where, in furtherance of a scheme of reconstruction or amalgamation, a CIU transfers to another CIU all its assets and liabilities in exchange for units (new units) being issued by that other undertaking to unit holders of the first mentioned undertaking, the cancellation of the original units will not give rise to a chargeable event. However the cost of those new units will be taken to be the cost of the original units.

Furthermore, a gain does not arise on the happening of a chargeable event where the unit holder is neither resident nor ordinarily resident in the State (or is an intermediary acting on behalf of such person) and the CIU is in possession of the appropriate declaration to that effect. TCA 1997, s 739D(7), (9). The exemption will only apply if at the time of a chargeable event the life company is not in possession of information suggesting that either the declaration is not materially correct or has ceased to be so or that the individual is resident or ordinarily resident in the State (TCA 1997, s 739D(7)(b)).

Where a gain arises on the happening of a chargeable event, CIUs are generally required to account for tax on that gain, referred to as 'appropriate tax'. Where the chargeable event is:

(a) the making of a regular payment to the unit holder, the rate of tax is 41 per cent (33 per cent for 2013); and
(b) the making of any other payment (including the redemption of units, etc) or the transfer of units or (with effect from 4 February 2004) the appropriation or cancellation of units to pay an amount of appropriate tax the rate of tax or (with effect from 31 March 2006) ending of an eight-yearly relevant period is 41 per cent for 2015 and 2014 (36 per cent for 2013); there is no exemption for payments arising on death (TCA 1997, s 739E(1)).

The CIU is entitled to deduct the appropriate amount of tax from payments to a unit holder or where necessary cancel sufficient units to cover such liability (TCA 1997, s 739D(6)).

However, with effect from 13 March 2008, where no more than 10 per cent of unit holders in terms of value in a CIU (either an umbrella fund or sub-fund) are liable to appropriate tax (see above), the CIU may elect in writing that the requirement to deduct appropriate tax in relation to an eight-yearly anniversary charge should not apply. The CIU must make an annual return setting out details of unit holders and the value of their units and any other prescribed information to the Revenue Commissioners. It must also inform the unit holder that the election is being made. An Irish resident non-exempt unit holder will be deemed to be a chargeable person for the purposes of filing his annual return under TCA 1997, s 959I and will be liable to account for income tax under Sch D Case IV on his notional gain at the relevant rate of 41 per cent for 2015 and 2014 (36 per cent for 2013). The income will be ring-fenced and will not be included as part of his total income. At present, there is no provision for crediting tax payable under the self-assessment system against appropriate tax arising on a subsequent chargeable event. This appears to be an inadvertent omission. This provision, designed to streamline the administration of funds, will primarily impact on funds with a substantial number of non-resident investors.

Where an individual suffers appropriate tax on the receipt of a payment from a CIU, the payment is excluded from the computation of his total income (TCA 1997, s 739G(2)(a)). In a case where appropriate tax does not apply (as where units are held on a recognised clearing system), the units in the CIU are subject to the special offshore fund regime described in **17.407**.

Although a gain arising on a chargeable event does not form part of the policyholder's income, for the purposes of a claim to relief under TCA 1997, ss 189 (Age Exemption Relief), 189A (Trusts for Permanently Incapacitated Individuals) or 192 (Payments in respect of Thalidomide Children), the amount of a payment to a policyholder is deemed to be Case III income received net of appropriate tax (TCA 1997, s 739G(2)(j)).

TCA 1997, s 747G as recently amended by FA 2014, s 30 provides that:

(a) an investment undertaking for collective investment in transferable securities which is authorised in accordance with the European Parliament Directive 2009/65/EC, and

(b) An alternative investment fund which is authorised in accordance with Directive 2011/61/EU,

will not be liable to tax in Ireland by reason only of having a management company or manager authorised under Irish law to operate in accordance with the Directives or is managed in the State through a branch or agency of a manager authorised in an EEA state.

Personal portfolio investment undertakings

With effect for chargeable events arising on or after 20 February 2007, gains made in respect of 'personal portfolio investment undertakings' are subject to a charge of 60 per cent (prior to 2014 the rate was an additional charge of 20 per cent in addition to the normal then exit charge of 36 per cent) (TCA 1997, s 739BA inserted by FA 2007, s 40). If details of the personal portfolio undertaking are not included in the return or if the return is submitted late by the unit holder the rate increases to 80 per cent for 2015 and 2014. For 2013 the rate was the unit holder's marginal rate of income tax plus 33 per cent. The definition of a personal portfolio life policy is extremely complex; in broad terms, it is a policy under which the investor or a person acting on his behalf ('agent') or a person connected with the investor or with his agent, can select or influence the selection of assets which is used to determine some or all of the benefits conferred by the policy. The legislation also aims to cover cases where the right to make or influence a selection is contingent on (a) the exercise of an option or (b) the exercise of its discretion by the undertaking or (c) a right to request a change in the terms of the policy so as to create rights of selection or (d) the right to require the undertaking to appoint an investment advisor in relation to the selection process.

If certain conditions are met, the additional charge will not apply. Firstly, the opportunity to select a particular item of land (including interests in land and unquoted shares deriving all or most of their value from land) or to select any other assets falling within a specified category must be identified clearly and be marketed as being generally available to the public. Secondly, the investment undertaking must deal on an equal basis with all those persons who have an opportunity to make or influence the selection process; furthermore, where the investment undertaking is marketed on the basis that a majority of the assets concerned will consist of land (including interests in land and unquoted shares deriving all or most of their value from land) and the total amount to be invested by the public is predetermined, each investment by an individual investor must not exceed 1 per cent of that total amount.

Example 8.401.1

Damien McKenna, who is Irish tax resident, acquired 5,000 units in the Fifth Trust UCITS (not a personal portfolio investment undertaking) on 17 January 2008 at a cost of € 21,000. He subsequently inherited a further 1,000 units in the same UCITS on 5 July 2009, valued at €9,000. On 6 May 2015, he sold 3,000 units at their value of €33,000. There has been no election made by the Fifth Trust for gains to be calculated on a first-in, first-out basis. The tax consequences of this transaction is as follows:

Damien: Sale 6 May 2015:

	€
Proceeds 3,000 units	33,000
Less: cost – on averaged basis	
€(21,000 + 9,000) x 3,000/6,000=	(15,000)
Gain on chargeable event	18,000
Tax: 18,000 @ 41%	7,380

Example 8.401.2

Facts as in **Example 8.401.1**, except that instead of selling any units, Damien continues to hold them until 17 January 2016 when each unit is valued at €10. The tax consequences of this transaction are as follows:

Damien: eight-yearly chargeable event 17 January 2016: Taxation of life policies

	€
Value of 5,000 units	50,000
Less: Cost	(21,000)
Gain on chargeable event	29,000
Tax: 29,000 @ 41%	11,890

8.402 Taxation of life assurance policies

Pre-FA 2000 regime

Under the system which prevailed prior to FA 2000, gains on the maturity or sale of domestic life assurance policies were generally outside the scope of income tax.

Prior to 6 April 1997, IFSC life companies were not permitted to conduct life assurance business with individuals who resided outside the State (TCA 1997, s 451). FA 1997, s 66 relaxed these requirements, so that policies or annuities could be sold to individuals who resided outside the State at the time the policy, etc was written (prior to this it appears that, in strictness, an individual who became resident at some point in time after the policy was written was required at that time to encash the policy). The policy could not however provide for the granting of any additional rights thereunder or an option to substitute it by another policy, etc at a time when the holder thereof resided in the State.

Where an individual who held an IFSC policy subsequently came to reside in the State, a tax charge arose under TCA 1997, s 710 if the policy matured at a time when (other than on the death or disability of the holder) the individual was resident or ordinarily resident in the State. In effect, the life assurance company had to deduct from the proceeds income tax at the standard rate on the amount by which the market value of the benefits under the policy increased while the policy holder resided in the State; however, the value of premiums paid during the period(s) of residence had to be deducted in the computation of this amount. However, in the case of a retirement benefits policy the withholding tax was calculated by reference only to 75 per cent of this amount. A 'retirement benefits policy' is one whose terms include the condition that the main benefit secured by the policy is the payment of a sum to the holder between the ages of sixty and sixty nine, other than on his death or disability.

The amount which was subjected to withholding tax under this procedure was not to be included in the total income of the policyholder and he was not to be entitled to any credit or repayment for the tax so deducted.

Where the policyholder failed to reside continuously outside the State for a period of six months following the date of issue of the policy, etc the withholding tax was not to apply. Instead, a capital gains tax charge under TCA 1997, s 594 was to be imposed ultimately on the difference between the proceeds of the policy and the amount of premiums paid under the policy (TCA 1997, s 594).

The special taxation system applying to IFSC life policies has been phased out with the introduction of the new taxation system for life assurance policies in general (see below).

IFSC policies falling outside the new system remain taxable under TCA 1997, s 710.

Post-FA 2000 system

TCA 1997, Pt 26, Ch 5 as most recently amended by F(No 2)A 2008, s 27 and FA 2009, s 10, contains the rules which apply to individuals who are resident or ordinarily resident in the State in respect of:

(a) policies issued by an assurance company which commenced carrying on life business on or after 1 April 2000 or non-industrial assurance policies issued by an assurance company on or after 1 January 2001 by an existing assurance company where trading operations at 1 April 2000 did not consist solely of foreign life assurance business within the meaning of TCA 1997, s 451(1) (ie IFSC life assurance companies); and

(b) policies issued on or after 1 January 2001 by an assurance company whose business consisted at 1 April 2000 solely of foreign life assurance business within the meaning of TCA 1997, s 451(1).

For these purposes an 'assurance company' is defined as one which is within the charge to Irish corporation tax (TCA 1997, s 730A(1)); the treatment of foreign policies is noted at the end of this section.

Policies issued prior to the relevant dates remain subject to the previous tax rules as noted above.

Under the current rules the investment income and gains within the life policy will accumulate on a gross rollup basis and 'appropriate tax' is levied on any gain treated as arising on the occurrence of a chargeable event. The tax is payable by the life company which has a right of recovery (by withholding or application of underlying policy assets) against the policyholder (TCA 1997, s 730F). The gain is not treated as income of the policyholder. There is also provision for repayment of appropriate tax to the policyholder in some cases.

There is provision from 1 January 2003 for treating group policies paid under the control of or subject to the order of a Court as consisting of separate policies corresponding to the rights held by the various beneficiaries of the group policy (TCA 1997, s 730B(4)); in such cases, the Court Service will be responsible for operation of the appropriate tax.

A chargeable event occurs prior to 15 February 2001 on:

(a) the maturity of the policy, other than in respect of death or disability, giving rise to benefits under the life policy;
(b) the surrender in whole or in part of the rights conferred by the life policy, other than in respect of any death or disability giving rise to benefits under the life policy;
(c) the assignment in whole or in part, of those rights; and
(d) In the case of a life policy issued by an assurance company which could have made an election under TCA 1997, s 730A(2), but did not so do, a chargeable event shall be deemed to happen on 31 December 2000, where the life policy was commenced before that date – 40 per cent tax applies in this case only.

A chargeable event prior to 15 February 2001 does not occur:

(a) on the assignment of a policy as a security for a debt, or the discharge of a debt secured by the rights concerned; and
(b) where an appropriate declaration is completed by the policy holder confirming that he is not resident or ordinarily resident (TCA 1997, s 730D(2)).

A chargeable event occurs on or after 15 February 2001 on:

(a) the maturity of the life policy (including payments made on death or disability);
(b) the surrender in whole or in part of the rights conferred by the life policy (including where payments are made on death or disability, which payments do not result in the termination of the life policy);
(c) the assignment in whole or in part of those rights;
(d) in the case of a life policy issued by an assurance company which could have made an election under TCA 1997, s 730A(2), but did not so do, a chargeable event shall be deemed to happen on 31 December 2000, where the life policy was commenced before that date – 40 per cent tax applies in this case only; and
(e) the occurrence of every 8th anniversary of the entry into the policy ('ending of the relevant period'): see under *Eight-yearly chargeable event* below.

A chargeable event does not occur on or after 15 February 2001 on:

(a) an assignment by way of security (on a debt, or the discharge of a debt secured by the rights concerned, where the debt is a debt due to a financial institution (including an EU authorised credit institution with effect from 1 January 2003));
(b) an assignment between husband and wife; and
(c) transfers between spouses, including transfers between former spouses in respect of divorce or separation proceedings, do not give rise to a chargeable event, but the spouse or former spouse acquiring the units is then treated as acquiring them at the same cost as the transferor (TCA 1997, s 730C(2)(b)–(e)).

The amount of the gain which arises on a chargeable event is generally computed as follows (disregarding any amount of appropriate tax which may be due (TCA 1997, s 730D(3)):

(a) where the chargeable event is the maturity of the policy, the amount payable to the policyholder less the amount of allowable premiums;
(b) where the chargeable event is the assignment of the whole of the rights of the policy, the value of the rights assigned less the amount of allowable premiums;
(c) where the chargeable event is the surrender of part of the rights conferred by the policy, the proceeds on part surrender, less the amount of allowable premiums multiplied by a factor equal to those proceeds divided by the total value of the policy before the partial surrender; and
(d) where the chargeable event is an assignment of part of the rights conferred by the policy, the value of those rights assigned, less that value multiplied by a factor equal to the amount of allowable premiums divided by the total value of the policy before part assignment (TCA 1997, s 730D(1), (3)).

Under (b) and (d) it is the value of the rights assigned and not the consideration received which is taken into account so that, for example a gift of a policy would give rise to a gain in the same way as a sale.

In all cases, no account is to be taken of the appropriate tax arising in relation to the chargeable event itself.

The amount of allowable premiums under (c) and (d) is the total amount of premiums paid in respect of the policy up to the date of the chargeable event, less the amount of premiums used in calculating a gain on any earlier chargeable event(s). The amount of premiums used in calculating an earlier gain cannot exceed the amount of the proceeds or value arising in respect of the event (this follows since the premiums can only be used at most to eliminate a potential gain and cannot create an allowable loss). Even though a gain does not arise on the occurrence of a chargeable event while the policyholder in question is neither resident nor ordinarily resident in the State at that time, where a later chargeable event occurs, when the policyholder is so resident or ordinarily resident, the earlier chargeable event is taken into account for the purposes of computing the gain on that later chargeable event (TCA 1997, s 730D(4)).

On an assignment of the whole of the rights contained in a life policy, the amount of allowable premiums immediately following the assignment are deemed to be the greater of the value of the policy following the assignment and the amount of allowable premiums immediately before the assignment (TCA 1997, s 730D(4)(c)). This ensures that the assignee can claim the amount of the premiums incurred by the assignor (or the value of the policy on assignment if this is greater) when computing the gain on any subsequent chargeable event in his hands.

On assignment of part of the rights contained in a life policy, the assignee is treated as incurring allowable premiums equal to the value of the rights on assignment at the date of assignment when computing the gain on any subsequent chargeable event in his hands; the assignor is treated as having paid allowable premiums up to the date of assignment of an amount equal to allowable premiums at that date less any amount of such premiums taken into account when computing the gain on the assignment (TCA 1997, s 730D(4)(d)).

In the case of a chargeable event arising on death or disability the benefit received is computed as the excess of the value of the policy before the chargeable event over the value of the policy immediately after the event. The value for these purposes is the surrender value of the policy or, failing a surrender value, the market value of any rights or benefits attaching to the policy. A pure risk policy (ie with no investment element) would not result in a gain on this basis (TCA 1997, s 730C(3)(a), (b)).

The gain arising on the occurrence of a chargeable event is generally subject to appropriate tax at the rate of 41 per cent (36 per cent in 2013) (TCA 1997, s 730F(1)). There is an exemption where the individual policyholder is not resident or ordinary resident and an appropriate declaration to this effect has been made (TCA 1997, ss 730D(2), 730E). Previously the declaration had to be made at or about the date of inception of the policy but that provision was removed by FA 2015, s 23 and applying to any life policy commenced on or after 1 May 2006. However, as respects chargeable events occurring on or prior to 31 December 2015 in relation to policies commenced on or after 1 May 2006, TCA 1997, s 865(4) shall apply as if the reference in that subsection to the making of a claim within four years after the end of the chargeable period to which the claim relates was a reference to the making of a claim within four years after the end of the chargeable period ending on 31 December 2016. This change means that a gain arising on a chargeable event will not be so treated if the declaration was made before the chargeable event occurs. The exemption will only apply if at the time of a chargeable event the life company is not in possession of information suggesting that either the declaration is not materially correct or has ceased to be so or that the individual is resident or ordinarily resident in the State (TCA 1997, s 730D(2)).

Although a gain on a chargeable event does not form part of the policyholder's income, for the purposes of a claim to relief under TCA 1997, ss 189 (Age Exemption Relief), 189A (Trusts for Permanently Incapacitated Individuals) or 192 (Payments in respect of Thalidomide Children) (see **1.306**), the amount of a payment to a policyholder is deemed to be a Case III income received net of appropriate tax (TCA 1997, s 730GA).

Example 8.402.1

Patrick Melmount, who is Irish tax resident took out a life policy (not a personal portfolio policy) with the Irish branch of a UK life assurance company on 1 February 2006. He paid a total amount of premiums of €12,000 up to 30 June 2012 when he assigned the policy to Edward Villa, who is also Irish tax resident, for a sum of €7,000, which was equal to its market value. Edward surrendered part of the rights under the policy in May 2015 for a sum of €16,000. The value of the policy immediately prior to the surrender was €32,000. Edward had paid premiums of €9,000 between July 2012 and May 2015. In December 2015, Edward became entitled to receive €18,000 (gross) on the maturity of the policy. Edward had paid premiums of €6,000 between June 2015 and December 2015. The tax consequences of these transactions under the current rules are as follows:

Patrick: Assignment June 2012:

	€
Value of policy	7,000
Less: Allowable Premiums	12,000
Gain on chargeable event	Nil

As there is a nil gain, no appropriate tax is required to be accounted for.

Edward: Partial surrender of policy in May 2015:

		€
Proceeds of surrender		16,000
Less: Allowable Premiums:	(12,000[1] + 9,000)=21,000 x 16,000/32,000[2] =	10,500
Gain on chargeable event		5,500

The Life Assurance company will withhold appropriate tax of €5,500 x 41% = €2,255 from the surrender proceeds.

Edward: Maturity of policy in December 2015:

		€
Maturity proceeds		18,000
Less: Allowable Premiums	(21,000 – 10,500[3]) + 6000	16,500
Gain on chargeable event		1,500

The Life Assurance company will withhold appropriate tax of € 1,500 x 41% = €615 from the maturity proceeds.

Notes:

1. The amount of allowable premiums following the assignment is the greater of the value of the policy immediately after the assignment and the amount of allowable premiums paid up to the date of the assignment.
2. The allowable premiums are multiplied by a factor equal to the value of the surrender proceeds divided by the value of the policy immediately prior to the assignment.
3. The allowable premiums are the premiums paid to date less the amount used in the calculation of the gain on the previous part surrender.

Personal portfolio life policies

With effect from 26 September 2001, payments made in respect of 'personal portfolio life policies' are subject to an additional charge. From 2014 the applicable rate is 60 per cent. There has not been any change to this rate in 2015. Prior to F(No 2) A 2013, for years 2013 and earlier, the charge was expressed as being 20 per cent in addition to the normal exit charge of 36 per cent (TCA 1997, s 730BA). The definition of a personal portfolio life policy is extremely complex; in broad terms it is a policy under which the policyholder or a person acting on his behalf ('agent') or a person connected with the policyholder or with his agent can select or influence the selection of assets which is used to determine some or all of the benefits conferred by the policy. The definition also covers the case where the selection process relates to an index or to fluctuations in the value of assets or in the value of an index. The legislation also aims to cover cases where the right to make or influence a selection is contingent on (a) the exercise of an option or (b) the exercise of its discretion by the life assurance company or (c) a right to request a change in the terms of the policy so as to create rights of selection or (d) the right to require the life assurance company to appoint an investment advisor in relation to the selection process.

There are exceptions to the additional charge where the only assets which can be selected consist of units in a CIU within TCA 1997, s 739B, assets held within an internal fund of the company, cash or a combination of any of these elements. The right of selection must be widely available to the general public, as evidenced by marketing or promotional material in existence at the date the selection was made. A similar exception applies in the case of policies where the benefits are related to an index or basket of indices. In the case of policies issued on or after 5 December 2001, the exceptions will only apply where the life assurance company deals on an equal basis with all those persons who have an opportunity to make or influence the selection process; furthermore, where a majority of the assets concerned consist of land (including unquoted shares deriving all or most of their value from land) *and* the total amount to be invested by the public is predetermined, each investment by an individual policyholder must not exceed 1 per cent of that total amount.

Eight yearly chargeable event

FA 2005, s 42 as amended by FA 2006, s 48 introduces a series of amendments with effect from 31 March 2006 to provide for a chargeable event to arise on every 8th anniversary of the inception of a life policy.

FA 2006, s 48(1) inserts a new subparagraph TCA 1997, s 730C (1)(a)(iv) to provide that a chargeable event will arise on the ending of each 'relevant period' unless the ending of the period is already a chargeable event (eg where a policy matures on 8 or 16 years, etc from inception). A 'relevant period' is defined as an eight-year period beginning with the inception of the policy, and each subsequent eight-year period beginning when the previous relevant period ends. It had been provided that the eight-year period should be extended to 12 years where the premiums in question were paid at least annually and where the total amount of the premiums did not exceed €3,000 pa, but this relaxation was rescinded by FA 2007, s 43.

TCA 1997, s 730D(3)(da), as inserted by FA 2005, s 42(1) and as amended by FA 2007, s 43 with effect for chargeable events from 2 April 2007, gives the formula for calculating the gain in the case of the eight-yearly chargeable event. This is defined as V – P, where:

V = the value of the rights and other benefits under the policy immediately before the chargeable event; and

P = the value of the premiums paid on the policy immediately before the chargeable event (less any amounts which have already been taken into account in determining a gain on the occurrence of a previous chargeable event, other than an eight-yearly chargeable event).

In applying the formula, no account is to be taken of appropriate tax arising in relation to the chargeable event.

TCA 1997, s 730D(1A) as inserted by FA 2007, s 43(1)(b) in respect of any chargeable event arising on or after 2 April 2007, provides that where there has been an eight-yearly chargeable event which is followed at a later time by a 'new' gain arising on a subsequent chargeable event, then the calculation of the 'new' gain will proceed on the basis that the provisions for imposing the eight-yearly charge had not been enacted. However, TCA 1997, s 730F(1A), as inserted by FA 2007 with effect from 2 April 2007, provides that in this situation, a proportion of the tax ('first tax') paid (and not subsequently repaid) on a gain arising on the eight-yearly chargeable event may be credited against the tax ('second tax') on the subsequent 'new' gain. The proportion of the first tax is B/C where B is the new gain and C is the gain which would arise if the policy had matured at the time of the new gain, ie a notional full disposal of the policy at that time. Where the new gain relates to the surrender or assignment of part of the rights under the policy, then the amount of the first tax must be deducted from the amount of the premiums taken into account in the computation of the gain. In all other cases, the amount of the first tax must be added to the value of the rights or other benefits under the policy immediately prior to the chargeable event concerned, in the computation of the gain. Where the due proportion of the first tax exceeds the second tax, a repayment of the excess must be made by the assurance company to the policy holder. For the position prior to FA 2007, s 43, please see the 2006 edition of this book.

TCA 1997, s 730D(5) as inserted by FA 2005, s 42(1) and amended by FA 2006, s 48 provides that where an assurance company (or a predecessor company) did not hold a declaration of non-residence immediately prior to the inception of a policy taken out before 1 May 2006, the company does not have to discharge appropriate tax in respect of the ending of an eight-year relevant period if:

(i) the permanent address of the policyholder is stated in the policy as being outside the State; and

(ii) the company does not have reasonable grounds to believe that the policyholder is resident in the State.

However, the exemption thus granted will be retrospectively withdrawn if the assurance company does not hold the declaration of non-residence at the time that a subsequent chargeable event (other than the ending of an eight-year relevant period) arises. Thus, if a company issued a policy on 1 March 2007 falling within the eight-yearly chargeable event regime, and the policy gives the holder's address as outside Ireland, no appropriate tax need be accounted for on the ending of the relevant period on 1 March 2015 (assuming that there are no reasonable grounds for believing the holder is Irish tax resident: note that a mere suspicion does not count in this context). However, if the policy matures on 1 March 2016 and at that time the company does not hold the declaration of non-residence, appropriate tax will be due in respect of *both* chargeable events, *viz* the ending of the relevant period and subsequent maturity of the policy.

Example 8.402.2

Rory Devlin, who is Irish tax resident, took out a life policy (not a personal portfolio policy) with an Irish life assurance company on 15 December 2007. Rory paid a total amount of premiums of €35,000 up to 15 December 2015 at which time the policy was valued at €47,500.

Rory paid further premiums of €16,000 up to 15 December 2019, at which point he became entitled to receive €59,000 (gross) on the maturity of the policy. The tax consequences of these transactions under the new rules are as follows:

Rory: eight-yearly chargeable event:

	€
Value of policy 15/12/2015	47,500
Less: Allowable Premiums	35,000
Gain on chargeable event	12,500

The life assurance company will discharge appropriate tax due of (12,500 x 41%) = €5,125 at current rates. The tax will be paid out of the underlying assets attributable to the policy by virtue of TCA 1997, s 730F(3)(a)(ii)(Ia)).

Rory: Maturity of policy:

		€
Maturity of policy 15/12/2019		59,000
Add: First Tax paid		5,125
		64,125
Less: Allowable Premiums to date (€35,000 + €16,000)		(51,000)
Gain on chargeable event		13,125
Tax on chargeable event €13,125, x 41% =	5,381	

Less: credit €5,125 x 59,000/59,000*	(5,125)	
(Refund due)/Additional tax payable		256

*As the chargeable event triggering off the new gain is itself the maturity of the policy, 100 per cent of the amount of the 'first tax' in respect of the eight-yearly chargeable event is creditable against the 'second tax' on the maturity of the policy.

Foreign life assurance policies

Foreign life policies, ie those falling outside the regime described above, are generally subject to the provisions of the Capital Gains Tax code. However, from January 2001, TCA 1997, Pt 26, Ch 6 provides a special regime for the taxation of holders of designated 'foreign life policies' (generally irrespective of the date of issue). A *foreign life policy* is defined as a life policy issued by a branch of an assurance company carrying on business in an 'offshore state' or by an assurance company carrying on business in an offshore state other than through an Irish branch or agency (TCA 1997, s 730H(1)). An offshore state is defined as either a Member State of the EU or the EEA, or an OECD state with which Ireland has a double taxation agreement (TCA 1997, s 730H(1)). The tax treatment of such policies follows closely that applicable to offshore funds based in an offshore state, described fully in **17.407**. A personal portfolio policy is as defined above (TCA 1997, ss 730J; 730K).

The general rule is that any payments received in respect of a foreign life policy will be subject to income tax at the rate of 41 per cent assuming that the payment has not been made in respect of a personal portfolio policy and also that the income represented by the payment has been correctly included in the relevant income tax return. Where the payment relates to a personal portfolio policy, it will be subject to tax at the rate of 60 per cent. A higher rate of 80 per cent will apply if the payment from the personal portfolio policy has not been correctly included in the relevant income tax return. The above rates of income tax apply for both income tax years 2015 and 2014.

Any gain on disposal or part-disposal of the foreign life policy is computed under the Capital Gains Tax rules but without the benefit of indexation and is also subject to income tax under Schedule D Case IV (TCA 1997, s 730H(2)(a) and s 730K(2)). The appropriate rate of tax for 2015 and 2014 is 41 per cent (36 per cent in 2013), or 60 per cent (56 per cent in 2013) in the case of a personal portfolio policy (TCA 1997, s 730K(1)). Prior to 2015, there was no penal rate which applied where a gain arose on the disposal of a personal portfolio life policy which had not been correctly disclosed in the relevant income tax return. However, Finance Act 2014 amended this for 2015 and onwards whereby a higher rate of 80 per cent will apply to gains which arise on a disposal of a personal portfolio life policy if it has not been correctly included in the taxpayer's income tax return. Payments from foreign life policies are not subject to PRSI or the USC.

With effect from 31 March 2006, in relation to policies taken out on or after 1 January 2001, there is a deemed disposal and reacquisition at market value of the policy by the individual on the occurrence of every 8th anniversary of the inception of the policy (the 'ending of the relevant period'). (TCA 1997, ss 730H(1)(ii), 730K(6) inserted by FA 2006, s 49). This provision is designed to create a level playing field with the treatment of Irish policies. For 2015 and 2014 all such gains will be liable to income tax at 41 per cent (36 per cent rate in 2013) or 60 per cent (56 per cent in 2013) in the case of a personal portfolio policy.

Any loss may not generally be used to offset against gains arising in respect of other disposals under the foreign life policy regime (TCA 1997, s 730K(2)). However, where tax is payable on foot of a deemed disposal under TCA 1997, s 730K(6) on an eight-yearly relevant event (see above) and a loss arises on a subsequent actual disposal of the policy, a refund may be claimed so that the total tax payable in respect of the interest is the same as if TCA 1997, s 730K(6) had not been enacted; the normal four-year time limit for claims under TCA 1997, s 865 does not apply (see **2.104**) (TCA 1997, s 730K(3)(b) (inserted by FA 2006, s 49)). This provision is necessary to avoid the inequity of tax being paid on a notional disposal when a monetary loss has been incurred over a longer period of ownership.

8.403 Investment limited partnerships

Finance Act 2013 changed the tax treatment of investment limited partnerships. Previously, investment limited partnerships were taxed under the 'investment undertaking' regime, hence were considered opaque for tax purposes resulting in the unit holders being subject to tax on exit. Following FA 2013, investment limited partnerships will be transparent for tax purposes.

The purpose of the change is to make investment limited partnerships in the State more attractive as a type of investment fund vehicle. This change should also improve Ireland's overall competitiveness in the Alternative Investment Fund industry placing it on an equal footing with other regulated jurisdictions.

Finance Act 2013 inserted a new section TCA 1997, s 739J which defines investment limited partnerships and provides for its tax treatment. The new section applies in respect of an investment limited partnership that has been granted an authorisation under Investment Limited Partnerships Act 1994, s 8 on or after 13 February 2013.

An investment limited partnership is defined for the purposes of the section as an investment limited partnership within the meaning of the Investment Limited Partnerships Act 1994 (TCA 1997, s 739J(1)(a)).

For the purposes of interpreting the section, certain definitions such as 'relevant gains', 'relevant income', 'relevant payment', 'relevant profits', 'unit' and 'unit holders' are applied, with any necessary modifications, to investment limited partnerships as they also apply in the context of investment undertakings. Such definitions are contained in (TCA 1997, Pt 27, Ch 1A).

An investment limited partnership is not chargeable to tax on its relevant profits (TCA 1997, s 739J(2)(a)). Relevant profits (TCA 1997, s 739B(1)) are the relevant income and gains of the investment limited partnership. The relevant income and gains of the investment limited partnership are treated as arising or accruing to each unit holder in proportion to the value of units that each unit holder beneficially owns, ie the investment limited partnership is treated as a fully transparent vehicle for tax purposes.

The new section also provides that any deposit held by an investment limited partnership will not be subject to deposit interest retention tax (TCA 1997, s 739J(4)).

The new section also introduces a reporting requirement and requires every investment limited partnership to deliver a statement in an approved electronic format to the Revenue Commissioners on or before 28 February in the year following the year of assessment. The details that need to be included in the statement are as follows:

(a) the total amount of relevant profits arising to the investment limited partnership in respect of the units in investment limited partnership;

(b) the name and address of each unit holder;

(c) the amount of relevant profits to which each unit holder is entitled; and
(d) any other information which the Revenue Commissioners may require.

A statement must be made even where it is a statement with a nil amount (TCA 1997, s 739J(3)).

8.404 Irish Real Estate Funds (IREFs)

Background

Prior to FA 2016, Irish funds were not generally subject to Irish tax on their profits and withholding tax (save to certain investors' resident in Ireland for tax purposes) was not applied on returns to investors. FA 2016 brought about a new regime for funds holding Irish real estate assets and it will be seen that this is a broad term for the purposes of the legislation – this regime is contained in TCA 1997, Pt 27, Ch 1B. FA 2016 brought about a new term to Irish tax law being the Irish Real Estate Fund (IREF) which is an investment undertaking (other than certain UCITS) where 25 per cent of the value of that undertaking derives from IREF assets (as defined). Such IREFs remain exempt on their profits but must deduct 20 per cent withholding tax in certain distributions to investors. There are certain exceptions to this withholding tax including where the recipient is inter alia, a pension fund, a life company, credit union and a securitisation vehicle to which TCA 1997, s 110 applies. The legislation is complex and serves to establish the profits to which the aforementioned withholding is to apply and from the recipient's perspective it will be a case of ensuring the distribution and withholding tax is correctly stated on his or her tax return with the mechanics behind the calculation of that withholding tax being done by the administrator. It is important to note that an IREF remains a fund but that this new regime applies to funds with certain characteristics and the latter determines the taxability or otherwise of certain transactions.

Commencement

TCA 1997, s 739X outlines the commencement provisions to Pt 27, Ch 1B as inserted by FA 2016, s 23 as follows:

This Chapter shall apply to—

(a) accounting periods commencing on or after 1 January 2017; or
(b) where an investment undertaking's immediately preceding accounting period ended on or after 31 December 2015 and a decision was made after 20 October 2016 to change the accounting period such that paragraph (a) would not apply, that accounting period commencing on or after 20 October 2016.

It can be seen that this refers to 'accounting periods' rather than years of assessment and that is because the chapter is written from the perspective of the IREF as opposed to that of the individual recipient. An 'accounting period' is defined in TCA 1997, s 739K for the purposes of the chapter and that will be discussed under the definitions section of this part.

It can be seen from the above that the commencement date of the legislation is dependent on the intent of the investment undertaking. If the investment undertaking does nothing then the legislation commences in whatever accounting period commences in 2017 but if it decides to change its accounting period then it is the 'changed' accounting period that sees the commencement of that legislation for the respective IREF. Therefore, the commencement provisions are based on fact pattern of the respective IREF.

Definitions

TCA 1997, s 739K outlines the following definitions for the purposes of the chapter:

> 'accounting period' means the period for which an investment undertaking or sub-fund, as the case may be, makes up its accounts and subsections (2) and (3) of section 27 shall have application for the purposes of determining the accounting period of an investment undertaking or sub-fund;

TCA 1997, s 27(2) and (3) outline when an accounting period commences and ends for corporation tax purposes.

> 'accrued IREF profits' means the IREF profits, including any retained IREF profits, that have arisen and accrued to a unit since that unit was acquired by the person who, on the happening of an IREF taxable event, is the unit holder;

The meaning of IREF taxable event will be discussed later in the text but it should be pointed out that although 'IREF profits' is defined there is no definition for 'IREF retained profits' which is used in the above definition and it is presumed that this will have its ordinary meaning being those profits which have not yet been distributed by the respective IREF.

> 'arrangement' includes any agreement, understanding, scheme, course of action, course of conduct, transaction or series of transactions;
>
> 'connected' has the meaning assigned to it in section 10;
>
> 'EEA state' means a state, not being a Member State or the State, which is a contracting party to the Agreement on the European Economic Area signed at Oporto on 2 May 1992 as adjusted by the Protocol signed at Brussels on 17 March 1993;
>
> 'income statement' means the profit and loss account, income statement or equivalent prepared in respect of an investment undertaking or sub-fund, as the case may be, in accordance with international accounting standards or alternatively in accordance with the generally accepted accounting practice specified in the investment undertaking's prospectus;

'International accounting standards' are defined in TCA 1997, s 4 and also comprise International Financial Reporting Standards. '*Generally Accepted Accounting Practice*' or GAAP is also defined in TCA 1997, s 4 as comprising international accounting standards and in any other case Irish GAAP with the latter being defined as GAAP with respect to accounts (Other than International Accounting Standards accounts) of companies incorporated under the laws of the State, beings accounts intended to give a true and fair view. The definitions in TCA 1997, s 4 are stated as applying to the corporation tax acts unless the context otherwise requires and it is submitted that the reference in the above to 'specified in the investment undertaking's prospectus' is one of those times where the context is determined by the prospectus of the investment undertaking. To say otherwise would be to require GAAP to mean IAS or Irish GAAP only.

> 'IREF' means an investment undertaking or, where that investment undertaking is an umbrella scheme, a sub-fund of an investment undertaking—
>
> (a) in which 25% or more of the value of the assets at the end of the immediately preceding accounting period is derived directly or indirectly from IREF assets, or
>
> (b) where paragraph (a) does not apply, it would be reasonable to consider that the main purpose, or one of the main purposes, of the investment undertaking or the sub-

> fund, as the case may be, was to acquire IREF assets or to carry on an IREF business,
>
> other than an investment undertaking within the meaning of paragraph (b) of the definition of 'investment undertaking' in section 739B, and where this Chapter applies to a sub-fund of an umbrella scheme, for the purposes of the calculation, assessment and collection of any tax due under this Chapter, each sub-fund of such umbrella scheme shall be treated as a separate legal person;

This definition is critical for an understanding of the chapter and the definitions in TCA 1997, s 739B apply for the purposes of this chapter also. Therefore, the definition of 'investment undertaking' in that section applies equally here. This is a two limb definition with the first limb being objective and the second being somewhat subjective and applying where the first limb does not apply. Taking limb (a) firstly, this is objective and it should be noted that TCA 1997, s 739K(2) contains the following provision:

> In calculating the portion of the value of assets of an investment undertaking or sub-fund attributable to IREF assets for the purposes of determining whether or not an investment undertaking or sub-fund is an IREF—
>
> (a) account shall not be taken of any arrangement that—
>
> (i) involves a transfer of assets, other than IREF assets, from a person connected with—
>
> (I) the investment undertaking or sub-fund, as the case may be, or
>
> (II) a unit holder in the investment undertaking or sub-fund, and
>
> (ii) the main purpose or one of the main purposes of which is the avoidance of tax under this Chapter,
>
> and
>
> (b) regard shall be had to the gross value of the assets of which the IREF asset is part.

Para (a) above is an anti-avoidance provision which is similar in its nature to that contained in TCA 1997, s 29(1A). That provision seeks to prevent 'cash flooding' of a company such that its shares would no longer derive their value from land and other specified assets for Capital Gains Tax purposes. The provision in TCA 1997, s 739K(2) seeks to prevent 'other asset flooding' of an investment undertaking such that the value of 25 per cent of the assets of an investment undertaking do not derive from IREF assets. The reader is directed to para **17.303** of this text for a discussion of the meaning of 'main purpose or one of the main purposes' tests inherent in tax statute.

If the objective test in para (a) of the IREF definition is failed then an investment undertaking can still be regarded as an IREF where a subjective test is met. This is a 'reasonable to consider' test combined with a 'main or one the main purposes' test in order to determine whether main purpose, or one of the main purposes, of the investment undertaking (or the sub-fund) was to acquire IREF assets or to carry on an IREF business. This is a broad test but one would have to question how broadly this test could be interpreted if 25 per cent of the value of the assets of the undertaking were not IREF assets however the prospectus of the undertaking would be indicative of the corporate strategy behind the asset profile of the undertaking in the first instance. It will be seen that the definition of IREF assets is itself broad in its approach.

> 'IREF assets' means one or more of the following held by an IREF:
>
> (a) relevant assets (within the meaning of section 29(1A));
>
> (b) shares in a REIT (within the meaning of Part 25A);

(c) shares deriving their value or the greater part of their value directly or indirectly from the assets referred to in paragraph (a) or (b), other than shares quoted on a stock exchange except as provided for in paragraph (b) of this definition;

(d) specified mortgages, other than those which—

(i) are issued by a qualifying company as part of a CLO transaction, a CMBS/RMBS transaction or a loan origination business (each within the meaning of section 110), or

(ii) form part of a loan origination business of the IREF, and any necessary amendments to the definition of 'loan origination' shall be made so that it applies to a business carried on by an IREF rather than a qualifying company;

(e) units in an IREF;

TCA 1997, s 29(1A) refers to elsewhere in that section in defining 'relevant assets' as meaning land in the State, minerals in the State or any rights, interests or other assets in relation to mining or minerals or the searching for minerals, exploration or exploitation rights in a designated area (being an area designated by order under the Continental Shelf Act, 1968, s 2). It should be noted that 'land' is defined in the schedule to IA 2005 as including '… tenements, heridaments, houses and buildings, land covered by water and any estate, right or interest in or over land'. Further, *e-brief 43/16* refers to Revenue manual 42.3.1 which notes that 'The Revenue view in regard to loans secured on land in the State is that, in general, such loans are interests in land for the purposes of section 980 and are regarded as securities for the purposes of that section.' TCA 1997, s 980 deals with a withholding tax for Capital Gains Tax on gains arising in the disposals of, inter alia, 'land in the State'. Therefore, it could be presumed that Revenue would take a similar view where an interest in land is referred to in Irish law thereby making this provision quite broad in its application. It should also be noted that such interpretation is not beyond doubt in that it is not shared by all tax practitioners.

'IREF business' means activities involving IREF assets, the profits or gains of which, apart from section 739C, would be chargeable to income tax, corporation tax or capital gains tax, including, but without limitation to the generality of the preceding words, activities which would be regarded as—

(a) dealing in or developing land, or

(b) a property rental business;

This definition is a very broad one with the only apparent limitation on such business being that it would be chargeable to direct taxation absent the application of TCA 1997, s 739C. That section ensures that such profits are not chargeable to tax.

'IREF excluded profits' means—

(a) in relation to a unit holder in respect of which an IREF is not a personal portfolio IREF having regard to the IREF assets concerned (other than those referred in paragraphs (b) to (e) of the definition of 'IREF assets')—

(i) any profits or gains as shown in the income statement of the IREF in relation to the disposal of those assets where—

(I) such asset was held by the IREF, or an investment undertaking of which the IREF is a sub-fund, for a period of at least 5 years from the date on which it was acquired, and

(II) the disposal of such asset would be a disposal of a chargeable asset for the purposes of capital gains tax or corporation tax on chargeable gains and would otherwise form part of relevant profits of the IREF which are not chargeable to tax under section 739C, and

(ii) any unrealised profits or gains as shown in the income statement of the IREF in relation to those assets where the disposal of such asset would be a disposal of a chargeable asset for the purposes of capital gains tax or corporation tax on chargeable gains and would otherwise form part of relevant profits of the IREF which are not chargeable to tax under section 739C,

and where such asset was acquired through a transaction in respect of which relief was availed of under section 615 or 617, excluded profits shall be calculated with reference to the market value of the asset on its acquisition,

(b) in relation to shares, within the meaning of paragraph (c) of the definition of 'IREF assets', any distribution made in relation to those shares, and

(c) in relation to shares, within the meaning of paragraph (b) of the definition of 'IREF assets', any profits or gains other than property income dividends in relation to those shares;

It will be seen that such 'IREF excluded profits' are carved out from the definition of 'IREF profits'. A 'personal portfolio IREF' (ppIREF) is explained in TCA 1997, s 739M as an IREF under the terms of which some or all of the IREF assets or IREF business may be, or was, selected or influenced by certain persons. This will be discussed later in this chapter but for present purposes it should be noted that a ppIREF can be so designated by that definition by reference to any IREF asset rather than '… IREF assets concerned (other than those referred in paragraphs (b) to (e) of the definition of "IREF assets"' being assets in para (a) only, ie relevant assets.

It can be seen from the above that para (a) deals with profits in relation to a unit holder (other than a ppIREF) and paras (b) and (c) apply in relation to certain shares. Para (a) is in turn split between (i) certain realised and (ii) unrealised profits of an IREF being those in relation to relevant assets within IREF assets, ie assets which are relevant assets in themselves and not shares or units in an entity deriving from such assets. The five-year exemption in para (a)(i) must be a capital gains tax event absent the application of TCA 1997, s 739C. The reader will recall that TCA 1997, s 604A allowed an exemption for a proportion of a capital gain where such asset was acquired in the period between 7 December 2011 and 31 December 2014 and was held for a period of 7 years. If a company had acquired such an asset, then it would have been eligible for such exemption however absent such requirement in the definition of 'excluded IREF profits' then such IREFs would have been disadvantaged vis-à-vis such companies. The IREF legislation was brought about by FA 2016, being two years after the date of the acquisition date outlined in TCA 1997, s 604A, therefore, one can see a policy rationale for the five year restriction being brought about for IREFs.

Para (a)(i) deals with the 'realised' element of those profits on 'those assets' with para (a)(ii) looking to the 'unrealised' profits on 'those assets'. It is necessary that the realised and unrealised profits be shown in the 'income statement' of the IREF in order to be considered excluded profits. A definition of 'income statement' is included within TCA 1997, s 739K and is discussed above. It can be seen that para (a)(i) refers to realised profits on 'those assets' and continues to expand that in connection with the five year exemption but para (a)(ii) speaks of unrealised profits or gains shown in the income statement of the IREF in relation to 'those assets' where the disposal of such asset would be a disposal of a chargeable asset for the purposes of capital gains tax or corporation tax on chargeable gains and would otherwise form part of relevant profits of the IREF which are not chargeable to tax under TCA 1997, s 739C. The references to 'those assets' is presumably a reference to IREF assets concerned other than those referred in paragraphs (b) to (e) of the definition of 'IREF assets' in the first limb of the definition. Therefore, realised and unrealised gains on any other IREF assets would not be excluded IREF profits.

The reference to TCA 1997, ss 615 and 617 is important in that both of these sections allow assets to be acquired at their original base cost and not the consideration given (if such is given in the first instance) for such assets for Capital Gains Tax purposes by the respective corporate recipient. TCA 1997, s 615 deals with assets acquired by a company in connection with a reorganisation and TCA 1997, s 617 deals with assets acquired by one company from another company in the first company's group. Taking the latter, if an IREF acquires an asset from a company within the same corporate group as the IREF with a market value of €100m but was acquired by the disposing company for €10m, then the 'latent gain' of €90m should not form part of the excluded profits of the IREF. Given that para (a) in the definition of excluded IREF profits are calculated by reference to the IREF's income statement in the first instance then in many cases the 'excluded profits' will be calculated by reference to market value on their acquisition in any event, ie the statutory fiction applied by TCA 1997, ss 615 and 617 would not form part of that income statement in that instance.

Paragraphs (b) and (c) of the definition of 'excluded profits' refer to (b) any distribution made in relation to shares deriving their value or the greater part of their value directly or indirectly from relevant assets (within the meaning of s 29(1A) as discussed above) or shares in a Pt 25A REIT, other than shares quoted on a stock exchange except as provided for shares in a Pt 25A REIT; and (c) any profits or gains other than '*property income dividends*' in relation to shares in a Pt 25A REIT. In essence therefore, any distribution on non-REIT quoted shares and any profits or gains of a REIT other than REIT 'property income dividends'. The latter is not defined in TCA 1997, s 739K but presumably takes its meaning from that in TCA 1997, s 705A being a dividend paid by a REIT or the principal company or a group REIT from its property income.

> 'IREF profits' means the profits and gains of an IREF business as shown in the income statement of the IREF, any amount of the profits and gains realised on the disposal of an IREF asset (other than those referred to in paragraphs (b) to (e) of the definition of 'IREF assets') not otherwise shown in the income statement and excluding IREF excluded profits;

The starting point here is the income statement and to which one must add 'realised' profits or gains on disposal of 'relevant assets' which are not within the income statement and deduct IREF excluded profits.

> 'IREF taxable amount', in relation to an IREF taxable event and a unit holder, means an amount calculated in accordance with section 739L;
>
> 'IREF taxable event' in respect of a unit holder means—
>
> (a) the making of a relevant payment,
>
> (b) the cancellation, redemption or repurchase of units from a unit holder, including on a liquidation,
>
> (c) any exchange by a unit holder of units in a sub-fund of an investment undertaking for units in another sub-fund of that investment undertaking,
>
> (d) the issuing of units as paid-up, otherwise than by the receipt of new consideration,

(e) an IREF ceasing to be an IREF including on it ceasing to be an investment undertaking or on it ceasing to have 25 per cent of its value derived from IREF assets,

(f) the disposal of a unit by a unit holder, other than in circumstances that would give rise to an IREF taxable event under paragraph (b) or (c), or

(g) the sale or transfer of the right to receive any of the accrued IREF profit without the sale or transfer of the unit to which the accrued IREF profit relates or where the accrued IREF profit in respect of the unit becomes receivable otherwise than by the unit holder;

It can be seen that the taxable event is defined by reference to 'in respect of a unit holder' which is similar to the approach taken by the legislature in connection with the meaning of a 'chargeable event' as defined in TCA 1997, s 739B(1). That said, the definition is wider than that used for the purposes of the investment undertaking legislation. It will be seen that the definition of 'relevant payment' is similarly broader for IREF purposes.

'IREF withholding tax', in relation to an IREF taxable event, means a sum representing income tax at a rate of 20 per cent on the IREF taxable amount;

'purchased IREF profits' means the IREF profits, including any retained IREF profits, which have arisen and accrued to a unit prior to that unit being acquired by the unit holder;

'relevant payment', means a payment including a distribution, whether in cash or non-cash, made to a unit holder by an IREF by reason of the rights conferred to the unit holder as a result of holding a unit or units in the IREF, other than a payment made in respect of the cancellation, redemption or repurchase of a unit;

This definition is similar to that contained in TCA 1997, s 739B(1) however, in that instance the definition of a relevant payment is narrower in that it applies 'where such payments are made annually or at more frequent intervals'. It can be seen from the above that cancellation, redemption or repurchase of a unit does not fall within the definition of a relevant payment but that does not exclude such events from being an IREF taxable event, see para (b) of that definition.

'retained IREF profits' means the portion of the retained profits of the investment undertaking attributable to the IREF profits, and where those profits arose in an accounting period which commenced prior to 1 January 2017 or 20 October 2016, as the case may be, those profits shall be the profits which would be IREF profits if they arose in an accounting period which commenced on or after that date;

It is presumed that such retained profits are to be calculated by reference to the financial statements of the IREF.

'specified person' means a unit holder in respect of which a gain is not treated as arising to an investment undertaking on the happening of a chargeable event under subsection (6) (other than paragraphs (cc), (e), and (kb)), (7), (7A) (as it applies to a declaration made under subsection (6) or (7)), (7B) (as it applies to a declaration made under subsection (7) or (9)), (8), (8A), (8D), (8E), (9) or (9A) of section 739D, but shall not, subject to section 739M, include—

(a) a fund approved under section 774, 784(4) or 785(5), a PRSA within the meaning of section 787A, or a person exempt from income tax under section 790B,

(b) an investment undertaking,

(c) a company carrying on life business (within the meaning of section 706),

(d) a person who is exempt from—
  (i) income tax under Schedule D by virtue of section 207(1)(b), or
  (ii) corporation tax by virtue of section 207(1)(b) as it applies for the purposes of corporation tax under section 76(6),

(e) a credit union,

(f) a scheme, undertaking or company equivalent to those referred to in paragraphs (a) to (c), authorised by a Member State or an EEA state and subject to supervisory and regulatory arrangements at least equivalent to those applied to those schemes, undertakings or companies, as the case may be, in the State, or

(g) a qualifying company, within the meaning of section 110,

where the IREF is in possession of a valid declaration, in accordance with Schedule 2C, immediately before the IREF taxable event;

This is a detailed definition with its key focal point being TCA 1997, s 739D with various exemptions attaching. Reference is made above to valid declarations in accordance with TCA 1997, Sch 2C. The declarations in that schedule comprise the following:

(a) Declaration of pension scheme;
(b) Declaration of PRSA administrator;
(c) Declaration of investment undertaking;
(d) Declaration of company carrying on life business;
(e) Declaration of charity;
(f) Declaration of credit unions;
(g) Declaration of qualifying company.

'TIN' has the meaning assigned to it in section 891F and includes a tax reference number as defined in section 891B;

'umbrella scheme' has the meaning given to it in section 739B.

Calculating the IREF taxable amount and applicable tax

TCA 1997, s 739L explains the IREF taxable amount 'in relation to an IREF taxable event' as being calculated as:

$$A \times \frac{B}{C} - D$$

where—

A is the portion of the IREF taxable event which is attributable to the retained profits of the IREF,
B is the retained IREF profits,
C is the retained profits of the IREF, and
D is the purchased IREF profits not previously distributed by the IREF.

It will be recalled that 'retained IREF profits' as mentioned in 'B' above is defined in TCA 1997, s 739K and outlined earlier in this chapter. This must be distinguished from the expression used in 'C' above which presumably refers to the ordinary meaning of 'retained profits' of an entity; to give it the same meaning as 'retained IREF profits' would bring about a conclusion which would be contrary to the purpose of the section in the first instance. This is important in that same expression is used in the calculation of 'A' above.

If we say for a moment that the IREF has issued a distribution of €1,000, which would be a 'relevant payment' in accordance with the definition of same in TCA 1997, s 739K which gives rise to an 'IREF taxable event' in accordance with its definition in that same section and the retained profits of the IREF comprised, say, €20,000 before the distribution then arguably the full distribution is 'attributable to' the retained profits of the IREF. A typical dictionary definition of 'attributable' is 'belonging to a person, thing, group, etc.; a quality, character, characteristic, or property…' and it is clear that the €1,000 forms part of the €20,000 retained profits so one can see how the €1,000 is attributable to the €20,000 of retained profits. It should be noted that the above 'A' does not make reference to the time at which such retained profits are to be established. One would have to assume that this would be at the time of 'IREF taxable event' and in this instance that would be time of payment of the distribution. To look at such retained profits after the distribution is made would arguably offend the use of the words 'attributable to' in the definition of 'A' above.

If a redemption of a similar amount occurred then presumably that redemption would have to be funded from such retained profits and a similar issue would arise. A disposal (or exchange etc) of a unit by a unit holder is more problematic in that it is difficult to see what portion of that 'IREF taxable event' could be construed as being 'attributable to the retained profits of the IREF'. As above a typical dictionary definition of 'attributable' is 'belonging to a person, thing, group, etc.; a quality, character, characteristic, or property …'. The gain on the disposal of units might be attributable to the undertaking's nature and that of the assets it holds but arguably that gain could not be 'attributable' to the retained profits of the IREF. It will be seen that the application of a withholding tax differs where the IREF taxable event is with (f) and (g) of the definition of an 'IREF taxable event', ie certain disposals of units and transfers of rights to accrued property respectively. Reverting to the distribution example earlier 'A' would then be €1,000 in this formula.

The 'retained IREF profits' as mentioned in 'B' above is defined in TCA 1997, s 739K and continuing the example above would be €20,000 if the entity concerned had no other activities from which it derives profits which would not be regarded as IREF profits. 'C' would also be regarded as €20,000 given the assumptions made and assuming there were no purchased IREF profits then applying the formula would mean that the full distribution of €1,000 would comprise the 'IREF taxable amount'. It will be seen later that in this instance a withholding tax of 20 per cent will apply such that the unit holder receives €800 with €200 being required to be transmitted to Revenue.

Reverting to the 'purchased IREF profits' in 'D' for moment. This is defined earlier as in TCA 1997, s 739K as meaning '… the IREF profits, including any retained IREF profits, which have arisen and accrued to a unit prior to that unit being acquired by the unit holder'. It can be seen that this definition looks to 'a unit' of the IREF and to the current holder of that unit rather than the IREF in total. Looking at the formula again:

$$A \times \frac{B}{C} - D$$

'A' is the amount of the portion of the IREF taxable event. This could be a distribution etc and the ratio ($^B/_C$) applied to this amount is IREF specific, ie a total ratio is applied to a unit holder amount which then can be reduced by profits previously purchased by that unit holder which were not distributed by the IREF. If that is not the case, then the reference to 'D', which is unit holder specific, would appear of little consequence. The effect of this is that the IREF taxable event is limited to those IREF profits which accrued during the current holder's holding period.

TCA 1997, s 739P outlines the rules in calculating the amount of the IREF withholding tax on the happening of an event mentioned in paragraphs (a) to (e) of the definition of IREF taxable event. Where the event relates to paragraphs (f) and (g) of that definition then TCA 1997, s 739T applies.

Looking firstly to TCA 1997, s 739P(1) thereof applies the IREF withholding tax. Subsection (2) deals specifically with the reference to para (d) in the definition of IREF taxable event (being, the issuing of units as paid-up, otherwise than by the receipt of new consideration). It states that in order to satisfy the withholding requirement, then the IREF shall reduce the amount of the additional units to be issued to the specified person by such amount as will secure that the value at that time of the additional units issued to the specified person does not exceed an amount equal to the amount which the person would have received, after deduction of IREF withholding tax, if the person had received the value of the IREF taxable event in cash instead of in the form of additional units in the IREF, ie the effective bonus issue of units will be reduced to an amount to take account of the IREF withholding tax. Similarly, TCA 1997, s 739P(3) looks to the position where the IREF taxable event consists of a non-cash amount (which poses difficulties for withholding tax in the first instance). In that instance sub-s (3) requires that the IREF:

(a) shall be liable to pay to the Collector-General an amount (which shall be treated as if it were a deduction of IREF withholding tax in relation to an IREF taxable event) equal to the IREF withholding tax which would have been required to be deducted from the amount of the IREF taxable amount,
(b) shall be liable to pay that amount in the same manner in all respects as if it were the IREF withholding tax which would have been required to be deducted from the IREF taxable amount, and
(c) shall be entitled to recover a sum equal to that amount from the specified person as a simple contract debt in any court of competent jurisdiction.

The wording in sub-s (3) above is not unlike that used in TCA 1997, s 980(9) which deals with a withholding tax for capital gains tax on gains arising in the disposals of, inter alia, 'land in the State' where the 'consideration for acquiring the asset is of such a kind that the deduction [of withholding tax] cannot be made out of the consideration'. It can be seen that the CGT version is less specific than that of sub-s (3) in that it makes no reference to non-cash consideration but the effect of the two provisions is similar. The permissive, rather than prescriptive, nature of recovering the withholding tax from the specified person is also present in TCA 1997, s 980(9)(c) and must be compared with the prescriptive nature of reducing the number of units to be issued to the specified person where bonus units are issued. The issuing of such units would comprise 'non-cash consideration' but sub-s (3) would be superseded by sub-s (2) given its more specific application to the transaction of what this author has referred to as the issue of 'bonus units'. That said TCA 1997, s 739P(4) allows the IREF withholding tax to be treated as a payment on account of the income tax payable by the unit holder but where sub-s (3) and non-cash consideration has been received by the unit holder then such payment on account will not be allowed until such time as the debt is made good to the IREF, therefore although permissive in nature, the non-payment of the related debt may have additional cash flow consequences for the respective unit holder.

Further, TCA 1997, s 739P(4)(a), notes that where the payment on account equals the income tax payable under TCA 1997, s 739O then that unit holder shall not be regarded as a chargeable person with the self-assessment provisions in Pt 41A 'in respect of an IREF taxable event'. That last limb is important in that that unit holder still be regarded as a chargeable person for the self-assessment provisions for reasons other than an IREF taxable event.

TCA 1997, s 739O deals with assessing the IREF taxable event. The purpose of that section is (1) to determine how that taxable event is to be treated for double tax treaty purposes, (2) to determine the assessable basis of such event (Case V) and (3) to make the 20 per cent tax a final liability in respect of that income. TCA 1997, s 739O(1) defines a 'holder of excessive rights' as meaning 'a person who is beneficially entitled, directly or indirectly, to at least 10% of the units in an IREF'. That definition is used in sub-s (2) which determines how the IREF taxable event is treated for the purposes of affording relief under an arrangement made with the government of a territory outside the State having the force of law under the procedures set out in TCA 1997, s 826(1). In that regard the IREF taxable amount in respect of an IREF taxable event and a unit holder—

(i) who is a holder of excessive rights, is income from immovable property, and
(ii) who is not a holder of excessive rights, shall be treated as a dividend,

Looking at the UK double tax treaty for a moment. Article 7(1) which deals with income from immoveable property notes 'Income from immovable property, including income from agriculture or forestry, may be taxed in the Contracting State in which such property is situated'; art 11(1) which deals with dividend income notes 'Dividends derived from a company which is a resident of a Contracting State by a resident of the other Contracting State may be taxed in that other Contracting State. Such dividends may also be taxed in the Contracting State of which the company paying the dividends is a resident, and according to the laws of that State, but provided the beneficial owner of the dividends is a resident of the other Contracting State the tax so charged shall not exceed:

(a) 5 per cent. of the gross amount of the dividends if the beneficial owner is a company which controls directly or indirectly 10 per cent. or more of the voting power in the company paying the dividends;

(b) in all other cases 15 per cent. of the gross amount of the dividends.

In short, both are 'may be taxed' articles allowing the source country to subject the IREF taxable event to tax albeit the tax applicable in the source country is not restricted for income from immoveable property. In that instance, the same taxable event is treated differently depending on the beneficial entitlement of the unit holder in the units concerned.

TCA 1997, s 739O(2)(b) and (c) ensure that the IREF taxable amount is chargeable under Sch D Case V and no loss, deficit expense or allowance may be set off against it and para (d) ensures that TCA 1997, s 188 (age exemption) and the reductions in Pt 2 of the table to TCA 1997, s 458 cannot apply. All of this serves to ensure that that para (c)'s final liability determination remains intact at 20 per cent.

Finally TCA 1997, s 739P(5) notes that other than as provided for in TCA 1997, s 739Q no repayment of any IREF withholding tax shall be made to any person receiving or entitled to the IREF taxable amount.

TCA 1997, s 739Q deals with the repayment of IREF withholding tax. It defines a 'relevant person' in that section as a specified person, who during an accounting period was subject to withholding tax on an IREF taxable event and would but for TCA 1997, s 739P be entitled to a repayment of tax. It goes on to state that notwithstanding TCA 1997, s 739P(5) and subject to TCA 1997, s 739T repayment of withholding tax in respect of an IREF taxable event shall be made to a relevant person to the extent provided for in double tax treaty and the rate of tax specified in TCA 1997, s 739O(2)(c) shall be the rate applicable pursuant to the treaty (being 20 per cent).

TCA 1997, s 739Q(3) provides that notwithstanding TCA 1997, s 739P(5) (ie no repayment of IREF withholding tax) where a scheme, undertaking or company, as referred to in paragraphs (a) to (c) or (f) of the definition of 'specified person' (see definition of 'specified person' earlier in this chapter but in sum being certain pensions funds, investment undertakings or life assurance companies or similar EU/EEA undertakings), can prove—

(a) that it has indirectly invested in units of an IREF,
(b) that the IREF would not be regarded as a personal portfolio IREF of that scheme, undertaking or company, and
(c) that an amount of withholding tax was operated on an IREF taxable event to which it is indirectly entitled which is not otherwise repayable,

then that scheme, undertaking or company shall be entitled to a refund of withholding tax as if the units concerned were *directly* held and to make a claim to the Revenue Commissioners for repayment of that withholding tax in the form prescribed by the Revenue Commissioners and the rate of tax specified in s 739O(2)(c), being 20 per cent, shall be reduced accordingly.

TCA 1997, s 739Q(4) notes that the return made by the IREF under s 739R shall be deemed to be a return made by the unit holder for the purposes of an assessment to tax for the purposes of TCA 1997, s 865(2). TCA 1997, s 865(2) notes that subject to its own provision, where a person paid, whether directly or by deduction, an amount of tax which is not due from that person or which, but for an error or mistake in a return or statement made by the person for the purposes of an assessment to tax, would not have been due from the person, then the person shall be entitled to repayment. It can be seen that section requires a return to be made by the person seeking a repayment of the tax but TCA 1997, s 739R requires the return to be made by the IREF and not the direct or indirect recipient such that absent TCA 1997, s 739Q(4) a refund would not have been available.

TCA 1997, s 739R deals with the payment and collection of the IREF withholding tax. These provisions relate to the IREF's obligations. An IREF shall for each accounting period make to the Collector-General a return of the IREF withholding tax in connection with an accounting period—

(a) which ends on or before 30 June in a financial year, within 30 days of 31 December of that year, and
(b) which ends between 1 July and 31 December, within 30 days of 30 June of the following year.

The IREF withholding tax which is required to be included in the above return shall be due at the time by which the return is to be made and shall be paid by the IREF to the Collector-General and subsections (3) to (9) of s 739F shall apply to IREF withholding tax, with any required modifications, as they apply to the appropriate tax. The above mentioned return shall contain the following details:

(a) the name and tax reference number of the IREF in respect of which the IREF taxable event occurred;

(b) the name, address, TIN and unit holding of each unit holder in respect of whom the IREF taxable event happened;
(c) the date on which the IREF taxable event occurred;
(d) the amount of the IREF taxable event for each unit holder;
(e) the amount of IREF withholding tax (if any) in relation to the IREF taxable event deducted by the IREF in respect of each unit holder.

TCA 1997, s 739T deals with a withholding tax other than IREF withholding tax. It will be recalled that TCA 1997, s 739P outlines the rules in calculating the amount of the IREF withholding tax on the happening of an event mentioned in paragraphs (a) to (e) of the definition of IREF taxable event. Where the event relates to paragraphs (f) and (g) of that definition, ie certain disposals of units and transfers of rights to accrued property respectively, then TCA 1997, s 739T applies. The section will not apply where the amount or value of any consideration payable in relation to the happening of such an IREF taxable event does not exceed the sum of €500,000; but where the taxable event involves a disposal, sale or transfer by the unit holder in parts—

(i) to the same person, or
(ii) to persons who are acting in concert or who are connected persons,

whether on the same or different occasions, the several disposals, sales or transfers shall, for the purposes of this paragraph, be treated as a single disposal, sale or transfer.

This is not unlike some of the provisions behind TCA 1997, s 980 requiring a withholding tax to be deducted from consideration in connection with certain specified assets for CGT purposes. TCA 1997, s 739T(2) notes that on payment of any consideration in relation to the happening of an IREF taxable event to which the section applies—

(a) the person by or through whom any such payment is made shall deduct from that payment a sum representing an amount of income tax equal to 20 per cent of that payment,
(b) the person to whom the payment is made shall allow such deduction on receipt of the residue of the payment, and
(c) the person making the deduction shall, on proof of payment to the Revenue Commissioners of the amount so deducted, be acquitted and discharged of so much money as is represented by the deduction as if that sum had been actually paid to the person making the disposal.

In that regard it can be seen that the withholding tax may be deducted by a person other than the IREF itself. TCA 1997, s 739R outlines the return and payment obligations of the IREF for IREF withholding tax but this tax is a withholding by the acquirer such that the TCA 1997, s 739T(3) goes on to outline the return and payment requirements of the acquirer 'notwithstanding any other provision of the Tax Acts' as follows:

(a) The person who was required to deduct the withholding tax under TCA 1997, s 739T shall, within 30 days of the date of the IREF taxable event, deliver to the Revenue Commissioners an account of the IREF taxable event and of the amount deducted.
(b) The above account shall contain details of the following:
   (i) the name and tax reference number of the IREF in respect of which the IREF taxable event occurred;
   (ii) the name, address, TIN and unit holding of the unit holder in respect of whom the IREF taxable event occurred;

(iii) the date on which the IREF taxable event occurred;
(iv) the amount of the consideration paid or payable to the unit holder;
(v) the amount of withholding tax deducted under this section.

(c) Income tax which by virtue of this section is payable by a person shall—
(i) be payable by that person in addition to any income tax which by virtue of any other provision of the Tax Acts is payable by that person,
(ii) be due within 30 days of the IREF taxable event, and
(iii) be payable by that person without the making of an assessment.

Where, in relation to any payment of withholding tax referred to above, any person has made default in delivering an account required by TCA 1997, s 739T, or where the Revenue officer is not satisfied with the account, the officer may estimate the amount of the payment to the best of his or her judgment and, notwithstanding TCA 1997, s 18, may assess and charge that person to income tax for the year of assessment in which the payment was made on the amount so estimated at the rate of 20 per cent. The amount of withholding tax deducted in respect of a unit holder in accordance with TCA 1997, s 739T is to be treated as a payment on account of the income tax chargeable on that unit holder on that IREF taxable event for that year of assessment. Repayment of withholding tax deducted in respect of a unit holder in accordance with TCA 1997, s 739T in respect of an IREF taxable event shall be made to a relevant person, within the meaning of TCA 1997, s 739Q, to the extent provided for in the double tax treaty and the rate of tax in TCA 1997, s 739O(2)(c) applies pursuant to the relevant treaty. A claim for repayment of any withholding tax deducted under TCA 1997, s 739T which is in excess of the income tax chargeable on the IREF taxable event under TCA 1997, s 739O shall be made by the unit holder in a return made under the self-assessment provisions.

Anti-avoidance provisions

The effect of making an IREF into a personal portfolio IREF (ppIREF) is that the relevant 'scheme, undertaking or company' will then be a 'specified person' for the purposes of the IREF withholding tax where it may otherwise not have been. Further the definition of 'excluded profits', discussed earlier, contains provisions which apply in relation to a unit holder in respect of which an IREF is not a ppIREF. The concept of a ppIREF is discussed below.

It will be recalled from the definition of '*specified persons*' that certain entities are exempted from its application. The definition of 'specified person' has been discussed earlier but for present purposes it is to be regarded as a certain unit holder in an exempt fund. TCA 1997, s 739M(3) says a 'scheme, undertaking or company' as referred to in paras (a) to (c) or (f) of the specified person definition shall be a 'specified person' in certain instances. It should be noted that the expression 'scheme, undertaking or company' is only used in para (f) of the definition of 'specified person' but is used in para (f) to refer to entities in paras (a) to (c). Therefore the expression 'scheme, undertaking or company' as used in TCA 1997, s 739M(3) is a collective one designed to take account of all entities mentioned in paras (a) to (c) or (f) of the 'specified person' definition. The entities mentioned in paras (a) to (c) or (f) of the 'specified person' definition are exceptions from the application of the 'specified person' definition so TCA 1997, s 739M serves to bring such excluded unit holders back into the meaning of a 'specified person' where certain conditions are met. Those entities mentioned above are as follows:

(a) a fund approved under section 774, 784(4) or 785(5), a PRSA within the meaning of section 787A, or a person exempt from income tax under section 790B,

(b) an investment undertaking,

(c) a company carrying on life business (within the meaning of section 706),

…

(f) a scheme, undertaking or company equivalent to those referred to in paragraphs (a) to (c), authorised by a Member State or an EEA state and subject to supervisory and regulatory arrangements at least equivalent to those applied to those schemes, undertakings or companies, as the case may be, in the State…

The instances where such entities are to be regarded as a 'specified person' are outlined in TCA 1997, s 739M(3)(b) as follows:

(a) subject to TCA 1997, s 739N, the IREF is 'a personal portfolio IREF' in respect of the unit holder, or

(b) (i) that scheme, undertaking or company, as the case may be, would, if it was an IREF and if the holding of the units in the IREF was part of its IREF business, be regarded as a personal portfolio IREF in respect of any of its unit holders, and

(ii) it would be reasonable to consider that the investment in the IREF by the scheme, undertaking or company was part of a scheme or arrangement the main purpose, or one of the main purposes, of which was the avoidance of tax under TCA 1997, Pt 27, Ch1B which deals with IREF taxation.

Para (a) is fact specific or objective test requiring that the entity be a personal portfolio IREF. Such IREF is explained for the purposes of TCA 1997, Pt 27, Ch 1B in TCA 1997, s 739K(1) as follows:

> 'personal portfolio IREF' means an IREF under the terms of which some or all of the IREF assets or IREF business may be, or was, selected or influenced by—
>
> (a) the unit holder,
>
> (b) a person acting on behalf of the unit holder,
>
> (c) a person connected with the unit holder,
>
> (d) a person connected with a person acting on behalf of the unit holder,
>
> (e) the unit holder and a person connected with the unit holder, or
>
> (f) a person acting on behalf of both the unit holder and a person connected with the unit holder.

This is similar, but not identical, language to that used in TCA 1997, s 739BA(2) which looks at Personal Portfolio Investment Undertakings (PPIU). Similarly with the PPIU legislation the above is supplemented by sub-s (2) which reads as follows:

> (2) For the purposes of subsection (1) and without prejudice to the application of that subsection, the terms of an IREF shall be treated as permitting the selection referred to in that subsection where—
>
> (a) the terms of that IREF or any other agreement between any person referred to in that subsection and that IREF—
>
> (i) allow the exercise of an option by any person referred to in that subsection to make the selection referred to in that subsection,
>
> (ii) gives that IREF discretion to offer any person referred to in that subsection the right to make the selection referred to in that subsection, or

(iii) allow any of the persons referred to in that subsection the right to request, subject to the agreement of that IREF, a change in those terms such that the selection referred to in that subsection may be made by any of those persons,

or

(b) the unit holder or any person connected with the unit holder has or had the option of requiring that IREF to appoint an investment advisor (regardless how such a person is described) in relation to the selection of IREF assets or business, or the conduct of the IREF business.

On point (b) above and looking to the Revenue guidance on the PPIU legislation the following point is made 'To counter an attempt to cloak what in substance is the exercise of the power to select by the investor etc. in a form which apparently confers the power of selection to some other unconnected person the terms of the investment undertaking or offshore fund are treated as allowing the selection by the investor etc. in certain specified circumstances whereas a strict analysis of the terms of the fund might not give such a result. These rules also apply where any such agreement, rather than forming part of the terms of the fund, is implemented in some other fashion. The reference to an 'investment advisor (no matter how such a person is described)' is deliberately left undefined so as to allow the term to take on as wide a meaning as possible. The intention is to catch anyone who is given the authority to select or advise on the selection of the assets, which are to determine the fund benefits'. Given the similarity in approach between the two sections one could see Revenue taking a similar view in this instance. The effect of making the existence of a ppIREF is that the entity will be a specified person for the purposes of the IREF withholding tax where it may otherwise not have been.

There is an alternative limb to the objective test discussed above in TCA 1997, s 739M(3)(b). That is a 'main purpose' test and the reader is referred to **17.303** for a discussion of the issues involved in such tests. The main purpose test is contained in TCA 1997, s 739M(3)(b)(ii) however TCA 1997, s 739M(3)(b)(i) brings about a statutory fiction to be complied with. It looks at the 'scheme, undertaking or company' which is itself a unit holder in the IREF and asks the question as to whether it would be a ppIREF if it were an IREF. To do this of course then presumably the 'scheme, undertaking or company' should not already be an IREF. If that is the case and once this IREF fiction has been complied with then the objective questions as to whether the holding of units in an *actual* IREF was part of its IREF business then would that 'deemed IREF' be a ppIREF of its unit holders. Therefore, consider a shareholder in say a life company (being an entity carved out from the definition of 'specified person' in para (c) of that definition) which in turn holds units in an IREF; in that instance the IREF withholding tax should not generally apply as the unit holder in the IREF is a life company. If that life company were an IREF and would be considered a ppIREF in respect of the life company's 'unit holders' then that life company will be regarded as a 'specified person' for the purposes of the IREF withholding tax on IREF taxable events accruing to the actual IREF once the 'main purpose' test has been adhered to. Put another way the life company does not influence the asset selection decisions of the IREF but the 'unit holders' influence the asset selection decisions of the life company then that life company will be regarded as a 'specified person' for the purposes of the IREF withholding tax as pertaining to the *actual* IREF once the 'main purpose' test has been adhered to.

It will be recalled from the above that TCA 1997, s 739M(3) is subject to TCA 1997, s 739N which therefore provides for certain exceptions from the its application. TCA 1997, s 739N(1) notes that where:

(a) an IREF would otherwise be a ppIREF in accordance with TCA 1997, s 739M(3)(a), and
(b) 'the scheme, undertaking or company ... in respect of which it' is a ppIREF would not be a ppIREF under TCA 1997, s 739M(3)(b)(i),

then the IREF shall not be considered to be ppIREF in respect of the unit holder concerned.

Para (a) above refers to TCA 1997, s 739M(3)(a) and one would expect to see a form of condition in that subsection and the condition there is that the IREF under review be a ppIREF 'in respect of the unit holder'. Regard must then be had to conditions elsewhere in that section regarding the meaning of a ppIREF and hence the reference to 'otherwise' in para (a). Further TCA 1997, s 739M(3)(a) is subject to TCA 1997, s 739N so a statutory circularity arises and in order to adhere to the purposes of both sections then presumably the 'subject to' reference must be obviated when revisiting that subsection from TCA 1997, s 739N. It will be seen that the further exceptions provided by TCA 1997, s 739N(2) and (3) also apply where TCA 1997, s 739M(3)(a) is in point and that section is factual in its nature in that the statutory deeming in TCA 1997, s 739M(3)(b) is not in point, ie it asks the question as to whether the IREF 'is' a personal portfolio IREF in respect of the unit holder; it does not use words like 'would be considered' a ppIREF in accordance with the taxes acts or the like.

The reference to 'it' in para (b) above is presumably a reference to the 'IREF' in para (a). Consider a shareholder in say a life company (being an entity which is carved out from the definition of 'specified person' in para (c) of that definition) which in turn holds units in an IREF; in that instance the IREF withholding tax should not generally apply as the unit holder in the IREF is a life company.

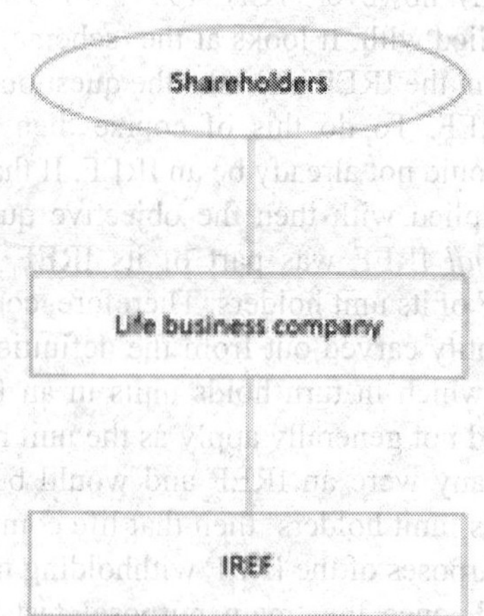

TCA 1997, s 739M(3)(b)(i) applies a statutory fiction such that if that life company were an IREF and it would be considered a ppIREF in respect of the life company's 'unit holders' then that life company will be regarded as a 'specified person' for the purposes of the IREF withholding tax on IREF taxable events accruing to the actual IREF. It is of note that the 'main purpose' test in TCA 1997, s 739M(3)(b)(ii) is not referred to and so it is not required for the test to apply. Put another way if the life company does not influence the asset selection decisions of the IREF but the 'unit holders' influence the asset selection decisions of the life company then that life company will be regarded as a 'specified person' for the purposes of the IREF withholding tax as pertaining to the *actual* IREF once the 'main purpose' test has been adhered to.

TCA 1997, s 739N(2) notes that where an IREF would '*only*' be a ppIREF of a unit holder in accordance with TCA 1997, s 739M(3)(a) because of a scheme of amalgamation to which TCA 1997, s 739D(8C) applied, the IREF shall not be considered to be a personal portfolio IREF in respect of the unit holder concerned. Under TCA 1997, s 739D(8C) a scheme of amalgamation means an arrangement where the unit holders in an unauthorised unit trust exchange their units for units in an investment undertaking. The reference to 'only' in TCA 1997, s 739N(2) is important in that that if the IREF can be considered a ppIREF by virtue of another reason then TCA 1997, s 739N(2) will not be sufficient to save that IREF from such a classification.

TCA 1997, s 739N(3) notes that where an IREF would be a ppIREF of a unit holder in accordance with TCA 1997, s 739M(3)(a) 'solely' because a person connected with the unit holder may select or influence the IREF assets or IREF business where that connected person *cannot*—

(a) be influenced by that unit holder in the exercise of their duties, or
(b) show any preference, or give any consideration, to that unit holder over and above any other unit holder,

then that IREF shall *not* be considered to be a personal portfolio IREF in respect of the unit holder concerned.

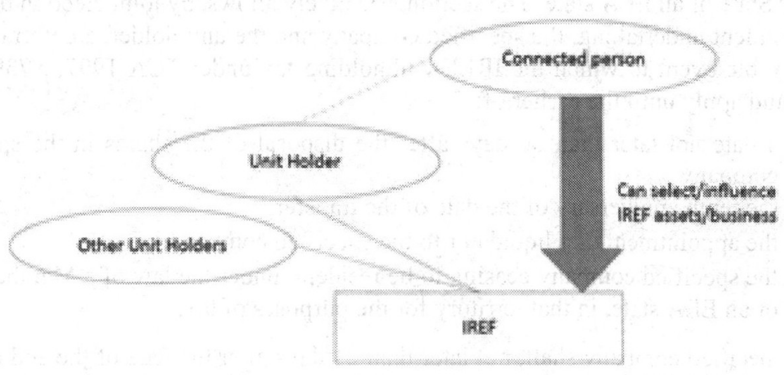

It can be seen that a wide test is to be applied to the person connected with the unit holder in this instance. Limbs (a) and (b) of that test have different 'influencing' directions in that (a) applies where the unit holder 'can' influence the connected person and (b) applies where the connected person can show any preference to the connected unit holder 'above any other' unit holder. It is necessary to note that this is written using permissive language in that it would not appear necessary that the connected person act in such a manner but rather have the ability to act in such a manner in the first instance. Therefore, if the unit holder has no power over the connected person with selection abilities then that relationship is of no consequence to the unit holder in terms of the

IREF such that it would be unreasonable for such unit holder to be penalised because of having that relationship in the first instance.

Retention and examination of documentation

There are documentation retention requirements in relation to declarations etc prescribed in TCA 1997, s 739U. These form the burden of the IREF. An IREF shall keep and retain declarations made to it in accordance with TCA 1997, Sch 2C for a period of six years from the time the unit holder of the units in respect of which the declaration was made ceases to be such a unit holder. The IREF is required on being served by notice in writing from the Revenue Commissioners, to make available to the Revenue Commissioners, within the time specified in the notice—

(a) all declarations, certifications or notifications which have been made or, as the case may be, given to the IREF in accordance with TCA 1997, Sch 2C, or
(b) such class or classes of such declarations, certificates or notifications as may be specified in the notice.

The Revenue Commissioners may examine or take extracts from or copies of any declarations, certificates or notifications made available to the Revenue Commissioners.

Certain IREF reorganisations

There are two specific reorganisations mentioned in TCA 1997, ss 739V and 739W. These are the transfer of IREF business to a company and to a Real Estate Investment Trust (REIT) respectively.

Transfer of the IREF business to a 'specified company'

TCA 1997, s 739V deals with the transfer of the IREF business to a 'specified company' which means a company formed under the laws of, and is registered in, a Member State or an EEA state. The section effectively allows, by joint election between the investment undertaking, the specified company and the unit holder, a deferral of the IREF taxable event to which the IREF withholding tax under TCA 1997, s 739O and 739P could apply until the earlier of:

(a) a date not later than 60 days after the disposal of the shares in the specified company,
(b) the tenth anniversary of the date of the transfer,
(c) the appointment of a liquidator to the specified company, or
(d) the specified company ceasing to be resident, under the law of a Member State or an EEA state, in that territory for the purposes of tax,

and the specified company shall, not later than 21 days after the date of the end of each of the calendar years which follow the year in which the transfer occurs, deliver a statement to the Revenue Commissioners, in the prescribed form, providing such information as may be required.

The conditions for such treatment are outlined in TCA 1997, s 739V(2) and the treatment applies—

(a) where an investment undertaking—
  (i) transfers the whole of its IREF business and its IREF assets, including any assets ancillary to the IREF business, or
  (ii) which carries out activities which would be regarded as dealing in or developing land and other IREF business, transfers the part of its IREF

business and its IREF assets, including any assets ancillary to the IREF business, that relate to dealing in or developing land,

to a specified company which is within the charge to corporation tax in respect of the transferred business and the charge to capital gains tax in respect of any IREF assets the disposal of which would not be within the charge to corporation tax,

(b) (i) where shares in the specified company are issued to the unit holders in the investment undertaking in respect of and in proportion to (or as nearly as may be in proportion to) their unit holdings in the investment undertaking,

(ii) all of the shares issued are ordinary shares with equal rights, and

(iii) the investment undertaking receives no part of the consideration for the transfer referred to in paragraph (a) (otherwise than by the specified company taking over the whole or part of the liabilities of its business),

(c) where upon completion of the transfer referred to in paragraph (a), the investment undertaking has no assets that relate to the transferred business,

(d) where the shares concerned are issued on or before 1 July 2017, and

(e) where the investment undertaking does not carry on any business similar to the transferred business after the date of such transfer referred to in paragraph (a).

It can be seen that all of the above conditions are to apply. Where they apply then TCA 1997, s 739V(3) notes that:

(a) the investment undertaking shall be deemed to have disposed of all assets in use for the purposes of the transferred business for the value at which they are carried in the accounts,

(b) the specified company—

(i) shall be deemed, as if it had been in existence since the commencement of the transferred business by the investment undertaking, in relation to the transferred business up to the date of transfer—

(I) to have carried out all activities, incurred all expenses, acquired all assets, borrowed all monies, and monies borrowed at or about the time of the purchase of premises shall be treated as having been employed in the purchase of those premises, and earned all profits and incurred all losses of the investment undertaking, and

(II) to have made all such claims for any allowances, deductions and reliefs as it would have been entitled to had it carried on the transferred business since its commencement, and shall, after the date of transfer, be subject to tax under the Acts as if it had carried out all transactions carried out by the investment undertaking prior to the transfer, and

(ii) for the purpose of the Capital Gains Tax Acts shall be treated as if any assets included in the transfer were acquired by the specified company on the date of transfer for consideration equal to the value of the assets in the accounts of the investment undertaking,

and

(c) the unit holder shall not be treated as having disposed of the units or as having acquired the shares or any part of them, but the units (taken as a single asset) and the shares (taken as a single asset) shall be treated as the same asset acquired as the units were acquired.

The above is subject to TCA 739V(4) which treats the matter as an IREF taxable event subject to the deferral mechanism discussed earlier.

Transfer of the IREF business to a REIT

TCA 1997, s 739W deals with the above and has similar provisions to these outlined in the previous reorganisation. TCA 1997, s 739V(4) notes that transfer shall constitute an IREF taxable event but the IREF, the unit holder and the qualifying REIT may jointly elect that the tax due under TCA 1997, ss 739O and 739P becomes due and payable on the earlier of—

(a) a date not later than 60 days after the disposal of the shares in the qualifying REIT,
(b) the tenth anniversary of the date of the transfer,
(c) the appointment of a liquidator to the qualifying REIT, or
(d) the company ceasing to be a REIT,

and the qualifying REIT shall, not later than 21 days after the date of the end of each of the calendar years which follow the year in which the transfer occurs, deliver a statement to the Revenue Commissioners, in the prescribed form, providing such information as may be required for the purposes of this subsection. TCA 1997, s 739W(2) notes that the treatment in the section applies:

(a) where notice is given to the Revenue Commissioners specifying a date not later than 31 December 2017 in respect of a company which is to carry on the property rental business previously carried on as part of the IREF property business of an IREF,
(b) where that IREF transfers the whole of its property rental business to the qualifying REIT referred to in paragraph (a),
(c) (i) where ordinary shares in the qualifying REIT are issued to the unit holders in the IREF in respect of and in proportion to (or as nearly as may be in proportion to) their unit holdings in the IREF, and
 (ii) where the IREF receives no part of the consideration for the transfer referred to in paragraph (b) (otherwise than by the qualifying REIT taking over the whole or part of the liabilities of the property rental business transferred),
(d) where the shares concerned are issued on or before 31 December 2017, and
(e) where the IREF does not carry on any business similar to the transferred business after the date of transfer referred to in paragraph (b).

Division 9 Schedule F: Distributions from Companies

9.1 Introduction

9.101 Income chargeable under Sch F

TCA 1997, s 20 charges income tax under Sch F on all dividends and other distributions of every company resident in the State, unless they are specifically excluded from income tax by any other provision in the Tax Acts. In fact, almost all such distributions are within this charge to tax under Sch F when received by or on behalf of any person liable to income tax, but distributions paid out of certain types of income which are exempted from corporation tax were formerly excluded from income tax in some cases by specific provisions in the Tax Acts. TCA 1997, s 816 also brings shares issued by an Irish quoted company in place of cash dividends within the charge to Sch F. Sch F does not apply to the distributions of any non-resident company (which are instead taxable under Sch D Case III).

TCA 1997, s 20 provides that no distribution chargeable under Sch F is to be charged under any other provision of the Income Tax Acts. However, TCA 1997, s 436(3)(b) also provides that benefits provided to the 'participators' of a 'close' company (as defined), or to their 'associates' (again as defined) will *not* be treated as distributions, if they are provided to a person to whom TCA 1997, s 118 (ie the Sch E benefits-in-kind rules: see **10.203**) applies *as a director or employee of the company*. TCA 1997, s 118(1)(b) only applies where the expense of providing a benefit would not otherwise be chargeable to tax. On the face of it, these provisions seem contradictory. The most logical reading, which resolves the apparent contradiction, is that persons to whom TCA 1997, s 118 applies (as being chargeable without reference to TCA 1997, s 436) fall outside the scope of TCA 1997, s 436; as there is consequently no charge under Sch F, tax must be charged under Sch E. This exclusion from chargeability under Sch F does not in strictness apply to holders of a foreign employment charged under Sch D Case III (even though, by virtue of TCA 1997, s 57, they may otherwise be chargeable on an equivalent benefit-in-kind (see **13.105**).

It may be noted that, in strictness, benefits provided to an *associate* of a director or employee within TCA 1997, s 118 (such as a spouse) as opposed to a participator or an associate of a participator who is himself a director or employee are not excluded from liability under Sch F. This is despite the fact that the benefit would in many cases otherwise fall within Sch E, ie by virtue of TCA 1997, s 116(2).

In addition, TCA 1997, s 436(3)(b) excludes from Sch F any expenses incurred in providing retirement and death benefits for a person to whom TCA 1997, s 118 applies or for their spouse, civil partner, children or dependants, children of civil partner (such benefits are equally exempt under TCA 1997, s 118(5)).

The term 'distribution' is defined in some detail in TCA 1997, s 130, as amplified by TCA 1997, ss 131, 132, 135 and, in the case of a close company, by TCA 1997, ss 436–437. Discussion of this topic is complex and is covered in detail in Feeney, *Taxation of Companies 2014* (Bloomsbury Professional, 2014). It is sufficient to note that the term is very widely defined with the intention of bringing within the charge to tax under Sch F not only all dividends paid by any resident company, but also most other distributions of profits in whatever form those distributions may take (except for distributions in respect of a company's share capital on its winding up). The Appeal Commissioner Decision [10TACD2016] dealt with a particular fact pattern involving transfer of rights between shareholdings which was held to be a distribution on the basis that assets were transferred at undervalue to the members of a company. The steps in the transaction comprised as follows:

> Company 'X' was incorporated in 1985. The taxpayer and spouse were the sole shareholders in the company from 1986. Company 'Y' was incorporated in 2004.
>
> 17 January 2006 – Taxpayer and spouse (hereinafter referred to as the taxpayer for convenience) were appointed directors of Company 'Y'.
>
> 30 January 2006 – Company 'X' as controlling member of Company 'Y' tabled a special resolution which was passed by Company 'Y', amending the memo and arts of Company 'Y' whereby:
>
> - The authorised share capital of the company of 1m ordinary shares of €1 each was increased to 3m by the creation of 2m 'A' ordinary shares of €1 each.
> - Company 'Y' allotted 100 ordinary shares of nominal value of €1 each to Company 'X' at a premium – so consideration given was €100 + Premium (P) and given later steps one could assume that P comprised a significant amount.
> - Company 'Y' allotted 94 'A' ordinary shares of nominal value of €1 to the taxpayer at par.
> - Company 'Y' allotted 6 'A' ordinary shares of nominal value of €1 to his spouse at par.
>
> 31 January 2006 – Company 'X' tabled a special resolution proposing to amend the articles of association, which was passed by Company 'Y', whereby the rights attaching to the ordinary shares and the 'A' ordinary shares were altered with the effect that the voting rights, rights to receive the surplus on a winding up and the rights to receive the share premium (the above-mentioned 'P') on a winding up were exchanged between the classes of shares so that the 'A' ordinary shares carried these rights and not the ordinary shares.
>
> 1 February 2006 – special resolution was passed for a voluntary winding up of Company 'Y' and the company was subsequently wound up.

The case turned on TCA 1997, s 130(3)(a) which deals with a transfer of assets at undervalue between a company and its members being regarded as an income distribution in the members' hands. The taxpayer argued that there was no transfer of assets given that the shares remained intact such that nothing was transferred, rather it was the rights in the shares which were exchanged as opposed to being transferred. The Commissioner disagreed and held for Revenue.

TCA 1997, Pt 6, Ch 8A imposes a dividend withholding tax on all 'relevant distributions' made by companies resident in the State on or after 6 April 1999.

A taxpayer is chargeable for each year of assessment on all his Sch F income received in that year. For this purpose, a dividend is treated as paid on the date it became legally due and payable TCA 1997, s 4(5); any other form of distribution is assessable by reference to the date on which it is paid or otherwise executed.

A final dividend is normally due and payable when it is declared (*Re Severn and Wye and Severn Bridge Railway Co* [1896] 1 Ch 559) unless it is expressed as being payable at a future date (*Re Kidner* [1929] 2 Ch 121). In the case of an interim dividend, it is normally due on the date on which it is actually paid (since the directors may resolve to rescind it at any time prior to payment: *Potel v IRC* 46 TC 658). In *Murphy v Borden Co Ltd* III ITR 559, the High Court upheld the decision of the Circuit Court judge on the particular facts that a dividend was paid when a set-off through an inter-company current account was agreed (and not when the accounting entries were made after the year end). It would seem that a waiver of a dividend before the date it is due and payable will be effective for tax purposes, subject possibly to the operation of the settlement anti-avoidance rules (see **Division 15**). See Sims, 'Waiver of Dividends' [1977] British Tax Review 28.

The income charged under Sch F is the amount of the distribution received inclusive of dividend withholding tax. Total income includes the aggregate of the distribution received and the withholding tax on it. However the dividend withholding tax may be set off against the income tax payable for the relevant tax year. In the case of an Irish resident, should the withholding tax exceed the tax payable the excess may be reclaimed from the Collector General. An Irish resident company is exempt from corporation tax in respect of Sch F income (TCA 1997, s 129); however, it may be liable to income tax on such income if it receives it in a fiduciary or representative capacity (eg as a trustee): see TCA 1997, s 26(2).

TCA 1997, s 153 provides that with effect from 6 April 1999, exemption from liability under Sch F will only apply to non-residents who are exempt from dividend withholding tax (see **9.106**). This would mean that, for example a resident of Isle of Man will be liable to Irish income tax in respect of any distributions which they receive. However, the Irish liability is restricted to an amount equal to the dividend withholding tax deducted, ie no liability to the higher rate of tax arises in relation to the distribution.

A person regarded as ordinarily resident in Ireland cannot claim exemption from dividend withholding tax under TCA 1997, s 172D(1). However if such a person is entitled to be regarded as resident of a treaty country under a double taxation treaty, it may be possible to claim treaty relief in respect of Irish dividends under the relevant treaty.

Example 9.101.1

Mr IN Vestor received dividends of €4,320 net from his investment in Irish resident companies in the year ended 31 December 2016, each of which was subject to full dividend withholding tax. The gross amount of the dividends was therefore €5,400.

Mr Vestor is chargeable to income tax under Sch F for the tax year 2016 in respect of these dividends as follows:

	€
Dividends received from resident companies in the year	4,320
Sch F income for the tax year 2016	5,400
Income tax at 40%*	2,160
Less dividend withholding tax	(1,080)

Net Income Tax liability on dividends	1,080
Net Dividend received after income tax	3,240

* Note: assumes that Mr Vester pays income tax at 40% on the full dividend.

9.102 Dividend withholding tax – general outline

With effect from 6 April 1999, a withholding tax equal to the standard rate of tax (currently 20 per cent) applies to dividends (including scrip dividends and non-cash dividends) and other distributions (referred to as relevant distributions) paid by an Irish resident company. Certain shareholders are exempt from the withholding tax, these include:

(a) certain amateur and athletic sports bodies (from 6 April 2000);
(b) charities;
(c) pension funds;
(d) certain collective investment undertakings;
(e) certain employee share ownership trusts;
(f) certain residents of the EU Member States or tax treaty countries; and
(g) distributions made to designated brokers for the benefit of a holder of a special portfolio investment account.

Distributions made to Irish resident companies and certain non-resident companies are also exempt and further commentary on this aspect may be in found in *Taxation of Companies* by Michael Feeney.

Distributions paid out of exempt profits which are not taxable in the hands of the recipients are exempt from the withholding tax.

It is necessary to declare one's entitlement to exemption from dividend withholding tax and documentary evidence is required in appropriate cases. The legislation provides that the obligation to withhold tax on relevant distributions falls on the paying company or on the authorised withholding agent acting for the company. That agent is entitled to receive distributions from the company without deduction of withholding tax and is obliged to apply withholding tax on payment of amounts representing those distributions on the same basis as if the distributions had been made directly by the company.

Relevant distributions may be made by a company or a withholding agent directly to the beneficial owners of those distributions, or indirectly to such owners through one or more qualifying intermediaries.

Where a distribution is to be made by a company or an authorised withholding agent directly to an exempt person, that person is obliged to provide evidence of entitlement to the exemption to the company or the agent. Where the distribution is made through a qualifying intermediary, evidence of entitlement to exemption must be furnished to the intermediary whereupon the intermediary will notify the company of the amount of the distribution to be received on behalf of exempt persons.

Where a distribution is to be made to an exempt person through a series of qualifying intermediaries, evidence of entitlement to exemption must be given to the qualifying intermediary from whom that person will finally receive payment. The intermediary will in that event convey to the intermediary next before in the series the amount to be received on behalf of exempt persons. The intermediary next before will then convey details of the amount of the distribution to be received by it, which will ultimately be passed on to exempt persons, to the company or, where there is another intermediary involved, to that intermediary. This process is repeated through any number of qualifying intermediaries. If any intermediary in the series is not a qualifying intermediary, withholding tax must be applied where the distribution is paid by that intermediary.

Qualifying intermediaries and qualifying withholding agents must be authorised by the Revenue Commissioners with whom they must enter into formal agreements for that purpose; the maximum period of this agreement is six years. Further details are set out at **9.107** and **9.108**. Qualifying withholding agents must be resident in the State or be carrying on a trade in the State through a branch or agency.

Qualifying intermediaries may be resident outside Ireland in a Member State of the EU or in a tax treaty country but in that event must enter into an agreement with the Revenue Commissioners with a view to protecting the Exchequer. A person may not be an authorised withholding agent or a qualifying intermediary unless the person is, or is a subsidiary of, a licensed bank, a member of a recognised stock exchange in a Member State of the EU or in a tax treaty country or is otherwise considered by the Revenue Commissioners to be suitable to be such an agent or intermediary. Special arrangements are made for intermediaries being depositary banks which receive distributions on behalf of the holders of American depositary receipts. American depositary receipt is defined in TCA 1997, s 172A(1) (See **9.103**).

Tax withheld from a relevant distribution must be paid to the Collector General by the 14th of the month following the month in which the distribution is made. A return of all distributions must be made by companies, or withholding agents, and by qualifying intermediaries, indicating details of recipients, payments made and the amount of withholding tax deducted.

9.103 Definitions

TCA 1997, s 172A contains a number of important definitions relating to the legislation dealing with dividend withholding tax as provided for in Ch 8A. Some of the more important definitions are dealt with below.

TCA 1997, s 172A(1)(a) defines dividend withholding tax in relation to a relevant distribution as a sum representing income tax on the amount of the relevant distribution at the standard rate in force at the time the relevant distribution is made (currently 20 per cent). A relevant distribution is defined as:

(i) a distribution within the meaning of Sch F paragraph 1 in TCA 1997, s 20(1), other than such a distribution made to

- (I) a Minister of the Government in their capacity as such a Minister
- (II) the National Pensions Reserve Fund [Commission]
- (III) a Commission investment vehicle (within the meaning given by section 2 of the National Pensions Reserve Fund Act 2000 (as amended by section 2 of the Investment of the National Pensions Reserve Fund and Miscellaneous Provisions Act 2009)),]
- (IV) the National Asset Management Agency, or a company referred to in section 616(1)(g), and

(ii) any amount assessable and chargeable to tax under Case IV of Sch D by virtue of TCA 1997, s 816 (taxation of shares issued in place of cash dividends).

As regards (i) above, TCA 1997, s 20(1) refers in turn to TCA 1997, Pt 6, Ch 2 and ss 436, 436A, 437, 816(2)(b) and 817. Part 6, Ch 2 (ss 130–135) contains the basic legislation dealing with the meaning of 'distribution' and is dealt with fully in **9.104**. TCA 1997, ss 436, 436A and 437 deal respectively with distributions made by close companies by way of expenses for participators, certain settlements made by close companies and interest paid to directors.

The operation of the dividend withholding tax is to a significant extent governed by the roles of the authorised withholding agent and the qualifying intermediary and these terms are defined in TCA 1997, ss 172G and 172E.

An 'intermediary' means a person who carries on a trade consisting of or including:

(a) the receipt of relevant distributions from a company or companies resident in the State, or

(b) the receipt of amounts or other assets representing such distributions from another intermediary or intermediaries.

A 'non-liable person' in relation to a relevant distribution means the person beneficially entitled to the relevant distribution, being an excluded person or a qualifying non-resident person. The key terms 'excluded person' and 'qualifying non-resident person' are defined in TCA 1997, ss 172C and 172D(3) respectively and are dealt with below in **9.105** and **9.106**.

A 'relevant territory' means a Member State of the European Communities other than Ireland, or a territory (not being such a Member State) with the government of which arrangements having the force of law by virtue of TCA 1997, s 826 have been made (ie with which Ireland has concluded a tax treaty).

'American depositary receipt' has the same meaning as in FA 1992, s 207. It is an instrument:

(a) which acknowledges:

  (i) that a depositary or a nominee acting on his behalf holds stocks or marketable securities which are dealt in and quoted on a recognised stock exchange, and

  (ii) that the holder of the instrument has rights in or in relation to such stocks or marketable securities including the right to receive such stocks or marketable securities from the depositary or his nominee; and

(b) which:

  (i) is dealt in and quoted on a recognised stock exchange which is situated in the US, or

  (ii) represents stocks or marketable securities which are so dealt in and quoted.

A 'collective investment undertaking' means a collective investment undertaking within the meaning of TCA 1997, s 734 or an undertaking for collective investment within the meaning of TCA 1997, s 738 or an investment undertaking within the meaning of s 739B or a common contractual fund within the meaning of s 739I, not being an offshore fund within the meaning of s 743.

'Pension scheme' means an exempt approved scheme within the meaning of TCA 1997, s 774 or a retirement annuity contract or a trust scheme to which TCA 1997, s 784 or s 785 applies.

A 'special portfolio investment account' and a 'designated broker' are defined as for TCA 1997, s 838.

A 'qualifying employee share ownership trust' means an employee share ownership trust which the Revenue Commissioners have approved of as a qualifying employee share ownership trust in accordance with TCA 1997, Sch 12 and where such approval has not been withdrawn.

An 'approved body of persons' means a body established for and existing for the sole purposes of promoting athletic or amateur games or sports, and is eligible for exemption under TCA 1997, s 235.

'Approved minimum retirement fund' has the same meaning as in TCA 1997, s 784C.

'Approved retirement fund' and 'qualifying fund manager' have the same meanings as in TCA 1997, s 784A.

The persons making and receiving relevant distributions are respectively referred to as the 'relevant persons' and the 'specified person'. A 'relevant person' in relation to a relevant distribution means:

(a) where the relevant distribution is made by a company directly to the person beneficially entitled to it, that company; and
(b) where the relevant distribution is not made by the company directly to the person beneficially entitled to it but is made to that person through one or more qualifying intermediaries, the qualifying intermediary from whom the distribution, or an amount or other asset representing the distribution, is receivable by the person beneficially entitled to the distribution.

The 'specified person' in relation to a relevant distribution means the person to whom the distribution is made, whether or not that person is beneficially entitled to the distribution.

The amount of a relevant distribution is an amount equal to:

(a) where the relevant distribution consists of a payment in cash, the amount of the payment;
(b) where the relevant distribution consists of an amount which is treated under TCA 1997, s 816 (taxation of shares issued in place of cash dividends) as a distribution made by a company, the amount so treated;
(c) where the relevant distribution consists of an amount which is assessable and chargeable to tax under Case IV of Sch D by virtue of TCA 1997, s 816 (taxation of shares issued in place of cash dividends), the amount so assessable or chargeable; and
(d) where the relevant distribution consist of a non-cash distribution, other than a distribution referred to in (b) or (c), an amount equal to the value of the distribution (TCA 1997, s 172A(2)).

Tax in relation to a relevant territory means any tax imposed in that territory which corresponds to income tax or corporation tax in the State.

References to the making of a relevant distribution by a company, to a relevant distribution to be made by a company, or to the receipt of a relevant distribution from a company do not include, respectively, references to the making of a relevant distribution by a collective investment undertaking, to a relevant distribution to be made by a collective investment undertaking, or to the receipt of a relevant distribution from a collective investment undertaking (TCA 1997, s 172A(1)(b)).

9.104 Dividend withholding tax

A withholding tax equal to the standard rate of tax (currently 20 per cent) applies to dividends and other relevant distributions paid by Irish resident companies. TCA 1997, s 172B(1) provides that where, a company resident in the State makes a relevant distribution to a specified person:

(a) the company is required to deduct dividend withholding tax in relation to the relevant distribution out of the amount of that relevant distribution;

(b) the specified person must allow such deduction on receipt of the residue (ie the balance after the withholding tax) of the relevant distribution; and

(c) the company is to be acquitted and discharged of so much money as is represented by the deduction as if that amount of money had actually been paid to the specified person.

TCA 1997, s 172B(7) provides that dividend withholding tax will not apply to a relevant distribution made by a resident company where the distribution is:

(i) a distribution made out of exempt profits within the meaning of TCA 1997, s 140 (occupation of certain woodlands),

(ii) a distribution made out of exempted income within the meaning of TCA 1997, s 142 (distributions out of profits of certain mines), or

(iii) a distribution made out of disregarded income within the meaning of TCA 1997, s 141 (patents) and to which subsection (3)(a) of that section applies.

TCA 1997, s 172B(2) deals with the situation in which a relevant distribution is made by a company by way of giving additional share capital in the company (scrip dividends). In short, the company is required to reduce the amount of additional share capital it issues by an amount equal to the amount of the dividend withholding tax.

Where an Irish resident company makes a relevant distribution to a specified person and the distribution consists of an amount referred to in TCA 1997, s 172A(2)(b) or (c) (see amount of a relevant distribution, (b) and (c), in **9.103** above), the dividend withholding requirement of TCA 1997, s 172B(1) is not to apply but, instead:

(a) the company is required to reduce the amount of the additional share capital to be issued to the specified person by such amount as will secure that the value at that time of the additional share capital issued to the specified person does not exceed an amount equal to the amount which the person would have received, after deduction of dividend withholding tax, if the person had received the distribution in cash instead of in the form of additional share capital of the company;

(b) the specified person must allow such reduction on receipt of the additional share capital;

(c) the company is to be acquitted and discharged of so much money as is represented by the reduction in the value of the additional share capital as if that amount of money had actually been paid to the specified person;

(d) the company becomes liable to pay to the Collector General an amount (treated as a deduction of dividend withholding tax in relation to the relevant distribution) equal to the dividend withholding tax that would otherwise have been deductible from the relevant distribution; and

(e) the company becomes liable to pay that amount in the same manner in all respects as if it were the dividend withholding tax which would otherwise have been deductible from the relevant distribution.

Example 9.104.1

Eire plc, a quoted company, pays a dividend to its ordinary shareholders on 10 October 2016. The shareholders are given the option to elect to acquire 1 new ordinary share for every €5 of dividend. Mr Murphy, an Irish resident individual, who is otherwise entitled to a cash dividend of €700, elects instead to take the additional shares. If DWT did not apply, Mr Murphy would receive 140 new ordinary shares.

Mr Murphy would be taxed under Sch F on the full €700. The number of additional shares to be issued to him is to be reduced from 140 shares to the number of shares which have a value calculated as follows:

	€
Amount of dividend if taken in cash	700
Less:	
DWT on cash foregone	
€700 x 20%	(140)
Reduced value of new shares to be issued	560

Assuming Eire plc's shares at 10 October 2016 (date of scrip dividend) is still €5 per share, the reduced number of shares to be issued to Mr Murphy is:

560 ÷ 5	112 shares

Although only receiving 112 shares valued at €500, Mr Murphy is still charged under Sch F for 2016 on the full €700 as if he had received cash. He would however be given a credit for DWT of €140 against his income tax chargeable.

TCA 1997, s 172B(3) is concerned with cases in which a relevant distribution is made by a company in non-cash form, other than a relevant distribution in the form of a scrip dividend (see above).

Where, an Irish resident company makes a relevant distribution to a specified person and the distribution consists of a non-cash distribution, not being a relevant distribution to which TCA 1997, s 172B(3) applies, the dividend withholding requirement of TCA 1997, s 172B(1) is not to apply but, instead:

(a) the company becomes liable to pay to the Collector General an amount (treated as a deduction of dividend withholding tax in relation to the relevant distribution) equal to the dividend withholding tax that would otherwise have been deductible from the relevant distribution;

(b) the company becomes liable to pay that amount in the same manner in all respects as if it were the dividend withholding tax which would otherwise have been deductible from the relevant distribution; and

(c) the company will be entitled to recover a sum equal to that amount from the specified person as a simple contract debt in any court of competent jurisdiction.

It will not always be possible to know with certainty whether or not a relevant distribution being made by a company is one to which the dividend withholding provisions of TCA 1997, Pt 6, Ch 8A apply. For example, it will sometimes be difficult to know with certainty whether or not a particular shareholder is an excluded person or a qualifying non-resident person. TCA 1997, s 172D(4) accordingly permits a company which has satisfied itself that a relevant distribution to be made by it to a specified person is one to which the withholding provisions do not apply to treat it as such until such time as it has information to the effect that the distribution is or may be a relevant distribution to which the withholding provisions apply.

9.105 Excluded persons

Distributions made to approved (sporting) bodies, pension schemes, qualifying employee share ownership trusts, collective investment undertakings, charities and to designated brokers who receive distributions on behalf of investors in special portfolio investment accounts (from 6 April 2000) are exempt from the dividend withholding tax, subject to the recipient in each case making a declaration regarding entitlement to exemption. The definitions of these terms are covered in **9.103**.

TCA 1997, s 172C(1) provides that dividend withholding tax is not to apply where an Irish resident company makes a relevant distribution to an excluded person. Excluded persons in relation to a relevant distribution include:

(a) a pension scheme which has made a declaration to the relevant person in relation to the relevant distribution in accordance with TCA 1997, Sch 2A para 4;
(b) a qualifying employee share ownership trust (ESOT) which has made a declaration to the relevant person in relation to the relevant distribution in accordance with TCA 1997, Sch 2A para 5;
(c) a collective investment undertaking which has made a declaration to the relevant person in relation to the relevant distribution in accordance with TCA 1997, Sch 2A para 6;
(d) a charity which has made a declaration to the relevant person in relation to the relevant distribution in accordance with TCA 1997, Sch 2A para 7;
(e) an approved body of persons which has made a declaration to the relevant person in relation to the relevant distribution in accordance with TCA 1997, Sch 2A para 7A;
(f) a designated broker who has made a declaration to the relevant person in relation to the relevant distribution in accordance with TCA 1997, Sch 2A para 7B;
(g) approved retirement funds (ARF's) or approved minimum retirement funds which have made a declaration to the relevant person in relation to the relevant distribution in accordance with TCA 1997, Sch 2A para 4A;
(h) permanently incapacitated individuals who are exempt from income tax in respect of income arising from the investment of compensation payments made by the court or under an out of court settlement, in respect of a personal injury claim;
(i) trustees of 'qualifying trusts' which are defined as trusts which raise funds by public subscription on behalf of individuals who are permanently incapacitated from maintaining themselves and who are exempt from income tax in respect of income arising from the investment of trust funds;
(j) permanently incapacitated individuals who are exempt from income tax in respect of payments from trust funds as set out in (i) together with any income arising from investment of such payments;
(k) thalidomide victims who are exempt from income tax in respect of income arising from the investments of compensation payments made by the Minister for Health and Children or the 'thalidomide victims foundation' – for the purposes of the above exemption, the collective investment undertaking, or a designated broker who receives a relevant distribution shall be treated as being beneficially entitled to the relevant distribution;
(l) with effect from 3 February 2005, a PRSA administrator (as defined by TCA 1997, s 787A) who is receiving relevant distributions as income arising in respect of PRSA assets (again as defined by TCA 1997, s 787A) and who has made the appropriate declaration; and

(m) with effect from 3 February 2005, an exempt Unit Trust to which TCA 1997, s 731(5)(a) applies which is receiving relevant distributions in relation to units in that trust (TCA 1997, s 172C(2)).

9.106 Exemption for certain non-residents

Relevant distributions made to certain non-residents are exempt from dividend withholding tax, being relevant distributions made to residents of foreign countries with which Ireland has a tax treaty (tax treaty countries), residents of EU Member States (other than Ireland), and certain companies not resident in the State (not dealt with in this work). In each case, an appropriate declaration must be made and evidence of entitlement to exemption provided.

TCA 1997, s 172D(2) provides that dividend withholding tax is not to apply where a company resident in the State makes a relevant distribution to a qualifying non-resident person. A qualifying non-resident person in relation to a relevant distribution includes a person beneficially entitled to the relevant distribution and who is:

(a) a person, other than a company, who:
  (i) is neither resident nor ordinarily resident in the State;
  (ii) is, by virtue of the law of a relevant territory, resident for the purposes of tax in a tax treaty country or in another EU Member state; and
  (iii) has made a declaration (see below) to the relevant person in relation to the relevant distribution in accordance with TCA 1997, Sch 2A para 8 and in relation to which declaration the certificate (see below) referred to in TCA 1997, Sch 2A para 8(f) is a current certificate at the time the relevant distribution is made.

It should be noted that the above provisions only govern a non-resident's entitlement to exemption from dividend withholding tax, but their entitlement to exemption for Irish income tax is governed by TCA 1997, s 153.

The certificate referred to in TCA 1997, Sch 2A para 8(f) (non-resident other than a company) is a certificate given by the tax authority of the relevant territory in which the person is, by virtue of the law of that territory, resident for the purposes of tax certifying that the person is so resident in that territory.

A certificate may be a current certificate if, at the time of the relevant distribution, it is one made no later than 31 December in the fifth calendar year following the calendar year in which the certificate was issued.

The declaration to be made by a non-resident person in accordance with TCA 1997, Sch 2A para 8 is a declaration in writing to the relevant person in relation to relevant distributions which:

(a) is made by the person ('the declarer') beneficially entitled to the relevant distributions in respect of which the declaration is made;
(b) is signed by the declarer;
(c) is made in such form as may be prescribed or authorised by the Revenue Commissioners;
(d) declares that, at the time the declaration is made, the person beneficially entitled to the relevant distribution is a person which is a qualifying non-resident person;
(e) contains the names and address of that person;

(f) is accompanied by a certificate given by the tax authority of the relevant territory in which the person is by virtue of the law of that territory, resident for the purposes of tax certifying that the person is non-resident in that territory;

(g) in the case where the relevant distributions are to be received by a trust, is accompanied by:

  (i) a certificate signed by the trustee or trustees of the trust which shall show the name and address of:

    (I) the settlor or settlors in relation to the trust, and

    (II) the beneficiary or beneficiaries in relation to the trust,

  and

  (ii) a certificate from the Revenue Commissioners certifying that the certificate referred to in clause (i) has been furnished to the Revenue Commissioners and that they are satisfied that that certificate is true and correct;

(h) contains an undertaking by the declarer that, if the person mentioned in (d) ceases to be a qualifying non-resident person, the declarer will, by notice in writing, advise the relevant person in relation to the relevant distribution accordingly; and

(i) contains such other information as the Revenue Commissioners may reasonably require for the purposes of dividend withholding tax.

Finance Act 2013 provided for the introduction of Real Estate Investment Trusts with effect from 1 January 2013. Distributions made by REITs are known as 'property rental dividends' and are subject to withholding tax at 20 per cent regardless of whether they are paid to non-residents. Therefore, if a double taxation agreement provides for a lower rate of withholding tax, it may be necessary for the non-resident to apply for a refund. The relevant form is available on the Revenue website and is called Dividend Witholding Tax Refund Claim Form REIT.

9.107 Authorised withholding agent

The obligation to deduct withholding tax on relevant distributions falls on the paying company or on the authorised withholding agent acting for the company. That agent generally receives distributions from the company for the benefit of the person beneficially entitled to them without deduction of withholding tax (TCA 1997, s 172G(1)) and is obliged to apply withholding tax on payment of amounts representing those distributions on the same basis as if the distributions had been made directly by the company. In effect, an authorised withholding agent will step into the shoes of the company making the distribution, and will assume its responsibility.

An authorised withholding agent in relation to relevant distributions to be made by an Irish resident company is an intermediary who:

(a) is resident in the State or, if not so resident, is, by virtue of the law of a relevant territory, resident for the purposes of tax in that territory, and carries on through a branch or agency in the State a trade consisting of or including the receipt of relevant distributions from an Irish resident company or companies on behalf of other persons;

(b) has entered into an authorised withholding agent agreement (see below) with the Revenue Commissioners; and

(c) has been authorised by the Revenue Commissioners, by way of notice in writing, to be an authorised withholding agent in relation to relevant distributions to be made to the person by Irish resident companies for the benefit of other persons who are beneficially entitled to the relevant distributions, which authorisation has not been revoked under TCA 1997, s 172G(6) (TCA 1997, s 172G(2)).

The Revenue Commissioners may not authorise an intermediary to be an authorised withholding agent unless the intermediary is:

(a) a company which holds a licence granted under s 9 or an authorisation granted under s 9A of the Central Bank Act 1971, or a person who holds a licence or other similar authorisation under the law of any relevant territory or of an EEA state which corresponds to the said s 9;

(b) a person who is wholly owned by a company or person referred to in (a);

(c) a member of the Irish Stock Exchange Limited or of a recognised stock exchange in a relevant territory; or

(d) a person suitable, in the opinion of the Revenue Commissioners, to be an authorised withholding agent for the purposes of TCA 1997, Pt 6, Ch 8A (TCA 1997, s 172G(4)).

Authorised withholding agent agreement

An authorised withholding agent agreement is an agreement entered into between the Revenue Commissioners and an intermediary under the terms of which the intermediary undertakes:

(a) to accept any declarations and notifications made or given to the intermediary in accordance with TCA 1997, Pt 6, Ch 8A (Dividend withholding tax) and Sch 2A and to retain such declarations and notifications for a period of the longer of six years, or a period which, in relation to the relevant distributions in respect of which the declaration or notification is made or as the case may be, given, ends not earlier than three years after the date on which the intermediary has ceased to receive relevant distributions on behalf of the person who made the declaration or as the case may be give the notification of the intermediary;

(b) on being requested by notice in writing by the Revenue Commissioners to make available within the time specified in the notice:

  (i) all declarations, certificates or notifications referred to in paragraph (a) which have been made or given to the intermediary, or

  (ii) such class or classes of such declarations, certificates or notifications as may be specified in the notice;

(c) to inform the Revenue Commissioners if the intermediary has reasonable grounds to believe that any such declaration or notification made or given by any person was not, or may not have been, a true and correct declaration or notification at the time of the making of the declaration or the giving of the notification;

(d) to inform the Revenue Commissioners if the intermediary has at any time reasonable grounds to believe that any such declaration made by any person would not, or might not, be a true and correct declaration if made at that time;

(e) to operate the provision of TCA 1997, s 172H (obligations of authorised withholding agent in relation to relevant distributions – see below) in a correct and efficient manner;

(f) to provide to the Collector General the return referred to in TCA 1997, s 172K(1) (see **9.111** below) and to pay to the Collector General any dividend withholding tax required to be included in such a return, within the time specified in that section;

(g) to provide the Revenue Commissioners not later than three months after the end of the first year of the operation of the agreement by the intermediary, a report on the intermediary's compliance with the agreement in that year. This report should be signed by:

(i) the auditor of the company, if the intermediary is a company, or

(ii) if the intermediary was a company, a person who would be qualified to be appointed as the auditor of the company,

this requirement to provide the above report will also apply on notice in writing to the intermediary by the Revenue Commissioners, within a time specified in the notice in respect of the period specified in the notice; and

(h) to allow for the verification by the Revenue Commissioners of the intermediary's compliance with the agreement and the provisions of TCA 1997, Pt 6, Ch 8A in any other manner considered necessary by the Commissioners.

TCA 1997, s 172G(3A) provides that the agreement should be extended so that the Revenue Commissioners may examine or take extracts or copies from any declarations, certificates or notifications which are made available to the Commissioners under TCA 1997, s 172G(3)(b).

TCA 1997, s 172G was also extended to provide that the authorisation to an intermediary to act as an authorised withholding agent shall cease on the day before the seventh anniversary of the date from which the authorisation applied, but this shall not prevent the intermediary and the Revenue Commissioners agreeing to renew the agreement in accordance with TCA 1997, s 172G(3) or to enter into further such agreements.

List of authorised withholding agents

A list of authorised withholding agents is required to be maintained by the Revenue Commissioners. Notwithstanding any obligations as to secrecy or other restriction on disclosure, the Commissioners may make available to any person the name and address of any such authorised withholding agent (TCA 1997, s 172G(5)). If the Commissioners are satisfied at any time that an authorised withholding agent has failed to comply with the authorised withholding agent agreement or the provisions of TCA 1997, Pt 6, Ch 8A, or is otherwise unsuitable to be an authorised withholding agent, they may, by notice in writing served by registered post on the agent, revoke the authorisation with effect from such date as may be specified in the notice (TCA 1997, s 172G(6)). Notice of the revocation is to be published in *Iris Oifigiúil*.

Obligations of authorised withholding agent

TCA 1997, s 172H imposes certain obligations on authorised withholding agents in relation to relevant distributions. Where an authorised withholding agent is to receive, on behalf of other persons, any relevant distributions to be made by an Irish resident company, it must notify that company by notice in writing that it is an authorised withholding agent in relation to those distributions. An authorised withholding agent essentially steps into the shoes of the company making the relevant distribution. Where the agent receives, on behalf of another person, a relevant distribution from an Irish resident company, and gives that distribution, or any amount or other asset representing that distribution, to that other person, the dividend withholding tax as provided for in TCA 1997, Pt 6, Ch 8A is to operate with any necessary modifications as if:

(a) the authorised withholding agent were the company making the distribution; and

(b) the giving by the authorised withholding agent of the relevant distribution, or another amount or other asset representing that distribution, to that other person were the making of the relevant distribution by the authorised withholding agent to that other person at the time the relevant distribution was made by the company to the authorised withholding agent,

so that, except where otherwise provided, TCA 1997, s 172B (dividend withholding tax on relevant distributions) is to apply in relation to that relevant distribution and the authorised withholding agent will be obliged to pay and account for the dividend withholding tax, if any, due in relation to the relevant distribution (TCA 1997, s 172H(2)).

Where at any time an Irish resident company makes a relevant distribution to a person and the relevant distribution would otherwise be treated as being made to an authorised withholding agent for the benefit of another person, the distribution is to be treated as not being made to the authorised withholding agent for the purpose unless, at or before that time, the authorised withholding agent has notified the company in accordance with TCA 1997, s 172H(1) (see above) that it is an authorised withholding agent in relation to the relevant distribution. In the absence of such notification, TCA 1997, s 172B will accordingly apply in relation to the relevant distribution (TCA 1997, s 172H(3)).

9.108 Qualifying intermediary

Relevant distributions may be made by a company or a withholding agent directly to the beneficial owners of those distributions, or indirectly to such owners through one or more qualifying intermediaries.

Where a distribution is to be made by a company or an authorised withholding agent directly to an exempt person, that person is obliged to provide evidence of entitlement to the exemption to the company or the agent. Where the distribution is made through a qualifying intermediary, evidence of entitlement to exemption must be furnished to the intermediary whereupon the intermediary will notify the company of the amount of the distribution to be received on behalf of exempt persons.

Withholding tax not to apply

TCA 1997, s 172E(1) provides that, subject to TCA 1997, s 172F(6), dividend withholding tax is not to apply where a company resident in the State makes a relevant distribution through one or more than one qualifying intermediary for the benefit of a person beneficially entitled to that distribution who is a non-liable person in relation to the distribution.

Qualifying intermediary

A person is a qualifying intermediary in relation to relevant distributions to be made to the person by a company resident in the State, and in relation to amounts or other assets representing such distributions to be paid or given to the person by another qualifying intermediary, if the person is an intermediary who:

(a) is resident in the State or who, by virtue of the law of a relevant territory, is resident for the purposes of tax in the relevant territory;

(b) has entered into a qualifying intermediary agreement (see below) with the Revenue Commissioners; and

(c) has been authorised by the Revenue Commissioners, by way of notice in writing, to be a qualifying intermediary in relation to relevant distributions to be made to the person by Irish resident companies, and in relation to amounts or other assets representing such distributions to be paid or given to the person by another qualifying intermediary, for the benefit of other persons who are beneficially entitled to the relevant distributions, which authorisation has not been revoked under TCA 1997, s 172E(6) (TCA 1997, s 172E(2)).

The Revenue Commissioners may not authorise an intermediary to be a qualifying intermediary unless the intermediary is:

(a) a company which holds a licence granted under s 9 or an authorisation granted under s 9A of the Central Bank Act 1971, or a person who holds a licence or other similar authorisation under the law of any relevant territory or of an EEA state which corresponds to the said s 9;

(b) a person who is wholly owned by a company or person referred to in (a);

(c) a member firm of the Irish Stock Exchange Limited or of a recognised stock exchange in a relevant territory; or

(d) a person suitable, in the opinion of the Revenue Commissioners, to be a qualifying intermediary for the purposes of TCA 1997, Pt 6, Ch 8A (TCA 1997, s 172E(4)).

American depositary receipts

The dividend withholding tax legislation makes special arrangements for Irish companies using American depositary receipts (ADRs) through American depositary banks. ADRs are dollar denominated negotiable instruments which enable US investors to trade in non-US securities. They are traded on the principal US stock exchanges (New York, AMEX, NASDAQ) and afford non-US companies easy access to the US capital markets. Many quoted companies and some emerging new companies in Ireland have raised substantial amounts of capital in the US through the use of ADRs.

To secure the payment of a dividend free of withholding tax, it is generally necessary to arrange for a series of certifications from the individual shareholder through all relevant intermediaries up to the company paying the dividend. Thus, only genuine residents of tax treaty countries will be able to benefit from the exemption from dividend withholding tax. The scale of US investment in Irish companies through the use of ADRs, however, is such that the burden of certification necessary to secure exemption from the withholding tax would be unduly onerous. Accordingly, American depositary banks in receipt of dividends from Irish banks for transmission to US based holders of ADRs are facilitated through a less burdensome certification procedure.

An American depositary bank may receive and pass on Irish dividends without deduction of withholding tax where the bank's ADR register shows that the direct beneficial owner of the dividends has a US address on that register, even though this is not supported by a certificate of US tax residence. If there is a further intermediary, for example a mutual fund, between the bank and the beneficial owner, dividends may also be paid gross where the bank receives confirmation from the intermediary to the effect that the owner's address in the intermediary's records is in the US, again without being supported by a certificate of tax residence in the US.

Qualifying intermediary agreement

A qualifying intermediary agreement is an agreement entered into between the Revenue Commissioners and an intermediary under the terms of which the intermediary undertakes:

(a) to accept and to retain for the longer of six years, or a period no later than three years after the date on which the intermediary has received relevant distributions on behalf of the person who made the declaration or as the case may be, give the notification to the intermediary, all declarations and notifications which are made or as the case may be, given to the intermediary in accordance with TCA 1997, Pt 6, Ch 8A and Sch 2A;

(b) on being requested to do so by notice in writing given to the intermediary by the Revenue Commissioners, to make available to the Commissioners, within the time specified in the notice:

  (i) all declarations, certificates or notifications referred to in paragraph (a) which have been made or given to the intermediary, or

  (ii) such class or classes of such declarations, certificates or notifications as may be specified in the notice given to the intermediary;

(c) to inform the Revenue Commissioners if the intermediary has reasonable grounds to believe that any such declaration or notification made or given by any person was not, or may not have been, a true and correct declaration or notification at the time of the making of the declaration or the giving of the notification;

(d) to inform the Revenue Commissioners if the intermediary has at any time reasonable grounds to believe that any such declaration made by any person would not, or might not, be a true and correct declaration if made at that time;

(e) to operate the provisions of TCA 1997, s 172F (see *Obligations of qualifying intermediary* below) in a correct and efficient manner and provide to the Revenue Commissioners the return referred to in TCA 1997, s 172F(7) within the time specified in TCA 1997, s 172F(8) (see *Returns by qualifying intermediaries* below);

(f) to provide to the Revenue Commissioners, not later than three months after the first year of operation of the agreement by the intermediary, a report on the intermediary's compliance with the agreement in that year, this report should be signed by:

  (i) the auditor of the company, if the intermediary is a company, or

  (ii) a person who would be qualified to be appointed as the auditor if the intermediary was a company,

  following the submission of the above report, the intermediary shall be obliged on receipt of notice in writing from the Revenue Commissioners, to provide them with a similar report within the time specified in the notice for the period as specified in the notice;

(g) if required by the Revenue Commissioners, to give a bond or guarantee to the Commissioners sufficient to indemnify them against any loss arising by virtue of the fraud or negligence of the intermediary in relation to the operation by the intermediary of the agreement and the provisions of TCA 1997, Pt 6, Ch 8A;

(h) where the intermediary is a depositary bank holding shares in trust for, or on behalf of, the holders of American depositary receipts:
   (i) if authorised to do so by the Revenue Commissioners, to operate the provisions of TCA 1997, s 172F(3)(d) (obligations of qualifying intermediary, being a depositary bank: persons to be included in Exempt Fund – see *Exempt fund* below), and
   (ii) to comply with any conditions in relation to such operation as may be specified in the agreement,

   and

(i) to allow for the verification by the Revenue Commissioners of the intermediary's compliance with the agreement and the provisions of TCA 1997, Pt 6, Ch 8A in any other manner considered necessary by the Commissioners (TCA 1997, s 172E(3)).

The Revenue Commissioners may examine or take extracts from or copies of any declarations, certificates or notifications made available to them under (b) above.

List of qualifying intermediaries

A list of qualifying intermediaries is to be maintained by the Revenue Commissioners. Notwithstanding any obligation as to secrecy or other restriction on disclosure, the Commissioners may make available to any person the name and address of any such qualifying intermediary (TCA 1997, s 172E(5)). If the Commissioners are satisfied at any time that a qualifying intermediary has failed to comply with the qualifying intermediary agreement or the provisions of TCA 1997, Pt 6, Ch 8A, or is otherwise unsuitable to be a qualifying intermediary, they may, by notice in writing served by registered post on the intermediary, revoke the authorisation with effect from such date as may be specified in the notice (TCA 1997, s 172E(6)). Notice of the revocation is to be published in *Iris Oifigiúil* (TCA 1997, s 172E(7)).

FA 2000 further amended TCA 1997, s 172E to provide that authorisation under this section to act as a qualifying intermediary for the purposes of TCA 1997, Pt 6, Ch 8A shall cease following the seventh of the date from which the authorisation applied, this cessation shall not prevent:

(a) the intermediary and the Revenue Commissioners from agreeing to renew the agreement or to enter into further such agreements, and
(b) a further authorisation by the Revenue Commissioners to the intermediary as a qualifying intermediary under TCA 1997, Pt 6, Ch 8A.

Obligations of qualifying intermediary

TCA 1997, s 172F sets out the obligations of a qualifying intermediary. A qualifying intermediary is required to maintain a record of two categories of shareholders, an Exempt Fund and a Liable Fund. The Exempt Fund will contain details of non-liable persons or other intermediaries who will receive amounts from the first intermediary on behalf of non-liable persons. Non-liable persons may be included in this fund only if the first intermediary receives declarations and evidence of exemption from the non-liable persons or from another intermediary to whom payments will be made on behalf of non-liable persons. The Liable Fund will contain details of all other shareholders. The first intermediary will notify the company making the distribution of the Exempt and Liable Funds and the company will then apply withholding tax to the distributions relating to the Liable Fund. The qualifying intermediary is obliged to make a return to the Revenue

Commissioners of all amounts received by it as well as details of persons to whom it makes payments, distinguishing which persons are non-liable.

TCA 1997, s 172F(1) provides that a qualifying intermediary which is to receive on behalf of another person:

(a) any relevant distributions to be made by any company resident in the State; or
(b) from another qualifying intermediary amounts or other assets (referred to here as 'payments') representing such distributions,

is to create and maintain, in relation to such distributions and payments, two separate and distinct categories to be known respectively as the 'Exempt Fund' and the 'Liable Fund', and is to notify that company or that other qualifying intermediary by notice in writing whether the relevant distributions or the payments representing such distributions to be made to it are to be received by it for the benefit of a person included in the Exempt Fund or a person included in the Liable Fund.

Exempt fund

A qualifying intermediary is required, subject to TCA 1997, s 172F(3), (5) (see below), to include in its Exempt Fund, in relation to relevant distributions to be made to it by an Irish resident company and payments representing such distribution to be made to it by another qualifying intermediary, only those persons on whose behalf it is to receive such distributions or payments, being:

(a) persons beneficially entitled to such distributions or payments who are non-liable persons in relation to such distributions; and
(b) any further qualifying intermediary to whom such distributions or payments (or amounts or other assets representing such distributions or payments) are to be given by the qualifying intermediary for the benefit of persons included in that further qualifying intermediary's Exempt Fund (TCA 1997, s 172F(2)).

A qualifying intermediary may not include a person mentioned in (a) above in its Exempt Fund unless it has received from that person:

(a) a declaration made by the person in accordance with TCA 1997, s 172C(2) (excluded persons – see **9.105** above); or
(b) a declaration made by the person in accordance with TCA 1997, s 172D(3) (qualifying non-resident persons – see **9.106** above) in relation to which:
   (i) the certificate referred to in TCA 1997, Sch 2A para 8(f) is a current certificate (see above), or
   (ii) the certificates referred to in TCA 1997, Sch 2A para 9(f), (g) are current certificates

   at the time the relevant distributions are made (TCA 1997, s 172F(3)(a)).

A qualifying intermediary may not include a further qualifying intermediary, referred to in (b) above, in its Exempt Fund unless it has received from that further qualifying intermediary a notification in writing in accordance with TCA 1997, s 172(1) (see above) to the effect that the:

(a) relevant distribution made by the Irish resident company or, as the case may be;
(b) the payments representing such distributions;

which are to be given by the qualifying intermediary to that further qualifying intermediary are to be received by that further qualifying intermediary for the benefit of a person included in that further qualifying intermediary's Exempt Fund (TCA 1997, s 172F(3)(b)).

Notwithstanding TCA 1997, s 172F(3)(a) and (b), a qualifying intermediary, being a depositary bank holding shares in trust for, or on behalf of, the holders of American depositary receipts, is required, if provided for in the qualifying intermediary agreement and subject to any conditions specified in that agreement, to operate the provisions of TCA 1997, s 172F(3)(d) as set out below (TCA 1997, s 172F(3)(c)).

The qualifying intermediary, in the circumstances referred to in TCA 1997, s 172F(3)(d), is required to include in its Exempt Fund:

(a) any person on whose behalf it is to receive any relevant distribution to be made by a company resident in the State, or on whose behalf it is to receive from another qualifying intermediary payments representing such distributions, being a person who is beneficially entitled to such distributions or payments, who is the holder of an American depositary receipt and whose address on the qualifying intermediary's register of depositary receipts is located in the United States of America; and

(b) any specified intermediary (see below) to which such distributions or payments (or amounts or other assets representing such distributions or payments) are to be given by the qualifying intermediary and are to be received by that specified intermediary for the benefit of:

   (i) persons who are beneficially entitled to such distributions or payments, who are the holders of American depositary receipts, whose address on that specified intermediary's register of depositary receipts is located in the United States of America, and who in accordance with TCA 1997, s 172F(3)(e)(iii)(I) (see below in relation to definition of 'specified intermediary') are to be included in that specified intermediary's Exempt Fund, or

   (ii) any further specified intermediary to which such distributions or payments (or amounts or other assets representing such distributions or payments) are to be given by the first-mentioned specified intermediary and are to be received by that further specified intermediary for the benefit of persons who in accordance with TCA 1997, s 172F(3)(e)(iii)(I) or (II) (see below in relation to the definition of 'specified intermediary') are to be included in that further specified intermediary's Exempt Fund (TCA 1997, s 172F(3)(d)).

For the purposes of TCA 1997, s 172F(3)(d), an intermediary is a specified intermediary if it:

(a) is not a qualifying intermediary but is a person referred to in TCA 1997, s 172E(4)(a), (b), (d) or (d) (see (a)–(d) under Qualifying intermediary above) who is operating as an intermediary in an establishment situated in the United States of America;

(b) creates and maintains, in relation to such distributions or payments (or amounts or other assets representing such distributions or payments) to be received by it on behalf of the persons from a qualifying intermediary or another specified intermediary, an Exempt Fund and Liable Fund in accordance with TCA 1997, s 172F(1), (5) but subject to (c) and (d) below, as if it were a qualifying intermediary;

(c) includes in its Exempt Fund in relation to such distributions or payments (or amounts or other assets representing such distributions or payments), only:

  (i) those persons who are beneficially entitled to such distributions or payments, being persons who are the holders of American depositary receipts and whose address on its register of depositary receipts is located in the US, and

  (ii) any further specified intermediary to which such distributions or payments (or amounts or other assets representing such distributions or payments) are to be made by the intermediary and are to be received by that further specified intermediary for the benefit of persons who are to be included in that further specified intermediary's Exempt Fund;

(d) includes in its Liable Fund in relation to such distributions or payments (or amounts or other assets representing such distributions or payments), all other persons (being persons who are holders of American depositary receipts) on whose behalf such distributions or payments (or amounts or other assets representing such distributions or payments) are to be received by it from a qualifying intermediary or a further specified intermediary, other than those persons included in its Exempt Fund;

(e) notifies in writing or in electronic format, in accordance with TCA 1997, s 172F(1) (see above), the qualifying intermediary or, as the case may be, the further specified intermediary from who it is to receive, on behalf of other persons, such distributions or payments (or amounts or other assets representing such distributions or payments), whether such distributions or payments (or amounts or other assets representing such distributions or payments) are to be so received by it for the benefit of persons included in its Exempt Fund or persons included in its Liable Fund;

(f) notifies the qualifying intermediary or, as the case may be, the further specified intermediary, by way of notice in writing or in electronic format, at the time it gives such distributions or payments (or amounts or other assets representing such distributions or payments) to other persons, the name and address of each such person; and

(g) agrees that the information given in accordance with (f) to the qualifying intermediary or, as the case may be, the further specified intermediary is to be returned to the Revenue Commissioners in accordance with TCA 1997, s 172F(7A)(f) (see below under *Returns by qualifying intermediaries*) (TCA 1997, s 172F(3)(e)).

FA 2000 amended TCA 1997, s 172F(3) to provide that where the Revenue are satisfied that the specified intermediary has failed to comply with TCA 1997, s 172F(7A) (see returns by qualifying intermediaries), the Commissioners may by notice in writing notify the intermediary that it shall cease to be treated as a specified intermediary from the date as may be specified in the notice, and notwithstanding any obligation as to secrecy or other restriction upon disclosure of information the Revenue Commissioners may make available to any qualifying intermediary or specified intermediary a copy of such notice.

TCA 1997, s 172F(3)(h) provides that where the Revenue are satisfied that the intermediary has provided the information required under TCA 1997, s 172F(7A) and will in future comply with that subsection if and requested to do so, may give the intermediary notice of the revocation of the notice issued above. In such a case, the

Revenue will also forward a copy of this notice of the revocation to all persons who received a copy of the original notice.

Where, by virtue of TCA 1997, s 172F(3)(a)–(e) (see above), any person, being a person who would not otherwise be a non-liable person in relation to the distributions or payments (or amounts or other assets representing such distributions or payments) to be received on that person's behalf by a qualifying intermediary or a specified intermediary, included in the Exempt Fund of the qualifying intermediary or, as the case may be, of the specified intermediary, that person is to be treated as a non-liable person in relation to such distributions (TCA 1997, s 172F(3)(f)).

A qualifying intermediary is required to update its Exempt Fund in relation to relevant distributions to be made to it by an Irish resident company and payments representing such distributions to be made to it by another qualifying intermediary, as often as may be necessary to ensure that the provision of TCA 1997, s 172E(1) (*Withholding tax not to apply* – see above) and 172F(2), (3) are complied with, and to notify the company or, as the case may be, that other qualifying intermediary, by way of notice in writing, of all such updates (TCA 1997, s 172F(5)).

Liable fund

A qualifying intermediary is required, subject to TCA 1997, s 172F(5) (see below), to include in its Liable Fund, in relation to relevant distributions to be made to it by an Irish resident company and payments representing such distributions to be made to it by another qualifying intermediary, all persons on whose behalf it is to receive such distributions or payments, other than those persons included in its Exempt Fund in relation to such distributions and payments (TCA 1997, s 172F(4)).

A qualifying intermediary is required to update its Liable Fund in relation to relevant distributions to be made to it by an Irish resident company and payments representing such distributions to be made to it by another qualifying intermediary, as often as may be necessary to ensure that the provision of TCA 1997, s 172E(1) (*Withholding tax not to apply* – see above) and s 172F(4) are complied with, and to notify the company or, as the case may be, that other qualifying intermediary, by way of notice in writing, of all such updated (TCA 1997, s 172E(5)).

In addition, as was seen above, a specified intermediary is required to include in its Liable Fund in relation to such distributions or payments (or amounts or other assets representing such distributions or payments) to be received by it on behalf of other persons from a qualifying intermediary or another specified intermediary, all other persons (being persons who are holders of American depositary receipts) on whose behalf such distributions or payments (or amounts or other assets representing such distributions or payments) are to be received by it from a qualifying intermediary or a further specified intermediary, other than those persons included in its Exempt Fund (TCA 1997, s 172D(3)(e)(iv)).

A company must deduct dividend withholding tax from a relevant distribution where it has not been notified by a qualifying intermediary as to the inclusion in the Exempt Fund of the person beneficially entitled to the distribution. Where at any time an Irish resident company makes a relevant distribution to a qualifying intermediary and the distribution would otherwise be treated as being made to the qualifying intermediary for the benefit of a person beneficially entitled to it who is a non-liable person in relation to it, the distribution is to be treated as if it were not made to the qualifying intermediary for the benefit of that person unless, at or before that time, the qualifying intermediary has notified the company in accordance with TCA 1997, s 172F(1) or (5), as the case may be, that the distribution is to be received by the qualifying intermediary for the benefit of a person included in the qualifying intermediary's Exempt Fund in relation to relevant distributions to be made to the qualifying intermediary by the company. Otherwise, dividend withholding tax is to apply to the distribution in accordance with TCA 1997, s 172B (TCA 1997, s 172F(6)).

Returns by qualifying intermediaries

A qualifying intermediary shall, on being requested to do so by notice in writing from the Revenue Commissioners under TCA 1997, s 172F(7) make a return within the time specified in the notice (which shall not be less than 30 days), in respect of the years of assessment specified in the notice showing:

(a) the name and address of:
   (i) each Irish resident company from which they receive on behalf of another person, a relevant distribution in the year of assessment to which the return refers,
   (ii) each other person from whom they, on behalf of another person, receive an amount or other asset representing a relevant distribution, in the year of assessment to which the return refers;

(b) the amount of each relevant distribution;

(c) the name and address of each person to whom a relevant distribution, or an amount or other asset representing a relevant distribution has been given by the qualifying intermediary; and

(d) the name and address of each person referred in (c) above who has made a declaration under TCA 1997, s 172C, ie an exempt person on the grounds that the beneficial owner is a company, a pension scheme, a ESOP trust, a collective investment, or finally a person entitled to exemption from income tax under Sch F under TCA 1997, s 207(6) or under TCA 1997, s 172D, ie certain non-residents.

TCA 1997, s 172F(7A) sets out procedures in respect of what a specified intermediary should provide to a qualifying intermediary who has received a notice under TCA 1997, s 172F(7A).

On receipt of a notice under TCA 1997, s 172F(7A) the qualifying intermediary shall immediately request the specified intermediary to notify them or the Revenue Commissioners of the name and address of each person to whom the specified intermediary gave such a distribution and of the amount of each such distribution.

The specified intermediary is required to provide the above details within 21 days of the receipt of the notice to the qualifying intermediary, or at its discretion can provide the information directly to the Revenue Commissioners.

If the specified intermediary provides the above information to the qualifying intermediary, the qualifying intermediary should include the information in his return. If the information is being provided directly to the Revenue Commissioners, the qualifying intermediary should indicate this fact in his return.

The section also provides that if the specified intermediary in turn passed the relevant distribution onto another specified intermediary they in turn should request the information from that specified intermediary and in effect take the place of the qualifying intermediary, etc.

9.109 Statement to be given to recipients of relevant distributions

TCA 1997, s 172I, as amended by FA 2010, s 33(1)(c), provides for the giving of a statement to a shareholder by a company making relevant distributions, or, where applicable, by an authorised withholding agent, setting out details of the distributions and the tax withheld. The requirement may be satisfied by including details on the relevant dividend counterfoil. For distributions made on or after 3 April 2010, the details may be provided instead by means of electronic communication.

Every person ('the payer') who makes, or who (being an authorised withholding agent) is treated as making, a relevant distribution must, at the time the relevant distribution is made or, in the case of an authorised withholding agent, at the time of the giving by the agent of the relevant distribution, or an amount or other asset representing that distribution, to another person, give the recipient of the relevant distribution or, as the case may be, that other person, a statement in writing showing:

(a) the name and address of the payer and, if the payer is not the company making the relevant distribution, the name and address of that company;
(b) the name and address of the person to whom the relevant distribution is made;
(c) the date the relevant distribution is made;
(d) the amount of the relevant distribution; and
(e) the amount of the dividend withholding tax, if any, deducted in relation to the relevant distribution (TCA 1997, s 172I(1)).

The requirements of TCA 1997, s 172I(1) may be satisfied by the inclusion of the particulars listed above in a statement in writing made in relation to the distribution in accordance with TCA 1997, s 152(1).

With effect from 1 February 2007, an 'electronic dividend voucher' may be issued to an intermediary, bearing an electronic number, a unique code that identifies the recipient and a unique International Securities Identification Number (ISIN) and including details of the date and amount of the relevant distribution and the amount of dividend withholding tax deducted. The intermediary must have consented to receiving the electronic voucher and the Revenue Commissioners must have agreed to accept it for tax purposes (TCA 1997, s 172I(1A) inserted by FA 2007, s 38(1)).

Where a person fails to comply with any of the provisions of TCA 1997, s 172I(1), TCA 1997, s 152(2) is to apply as it applies where a company fails to comply with any of the provisions of TCA 1997, s 152(1) (TCA 1997, s 172I(3)).

9.110 Credits or repayments – dividend withholding tax

Dividend withholding tax deducted in a year of assessment may be set off against a shareholder's tax liability for that year. Where the withholding tax exceeds that liability, the excess may be repaid. A non-liable person who has been charged withholding tax will be entitled to a refund of the tax withheld.

Where a person is within the charge to income tax in relation to a year of assessment and has borne dividend withholding tax in relation to a relevant distribution to which he is beneficially entitled and which is referable to that year, he may claim to have that dividend withholding tax set against income tax chargeable for that year. Where the withholding tax exceeds the income tax, a claim may be made to have the excess refunded (TCA 1997, s 172J(1)).

Where a person is not within the charge to income tax in relation to a year of assessment and has borne dividend withholding tax in relation to a relevant distribution to which he is beneficially entitled and which is referable to that year, he may claim to have that dividend withholding tax refunded (TCA 1997, s 172J(2)).

Where a person has borne dividend withholding tax in a tax year in relation to a relevant distribution to which that person is beneficially entitled and the person:

(a) is a non-liable person in relation to the relevant distribution; and

(b) would have been a non-liable person in relation to the relevant distribution if the requirement for the person to make the appropriate declaration referred to in TCA 1997, Sch 2A had not been necessary;

a claim may be made to have the amount of the dividend withholding tax refunded to that person; the wording of this subsection has been clarified with effect from 1 February 2007 to ensure that the general four-year time limit for repayments applies: (see **2.104**) (TCA 1997, s 172J(3)).

Relevant distributions include distributions which are exempt from taxation by reason by being paid out of exempt profits, for example, distributions out of income from commercial woodlands. Accordingly, dividend withholding tax may be deductible from these distributions although they are exempt from taxation. The recipient of such a distribution may then make a claim for a refund of the tax deducted.

A person making a claim for a credit or a refund is required to furnish, in respect of each amount of dividend withholding tax to which the claim relates, the statement in writing given to that person in accordance with TCA 1997, s 172I(1) by the person who made, or who (being an authorised withholding agent) was treated as making, the relevant distribution in relation to which the dividend withholding tax was deducted (TCA 1997, s 172I(4)).

The Revenue Commissioners may not authorise the setting-off of dividend withholding tax against income tax chargeable on a person for a year of assessment, or make a refund of dividend withholding tax to a person, unless they receive such evidence as they consider necessary that the person is entitled to that setting-off or refund (TCA 1997, s 172I(5)).

9.111 Returns, payment and collection of dividend withholding tax

TCA 1997, s 172K provides for the making of returns and payment of tax withheld in respect of relevant distributions to the Revenue Commissioners by the company making the distribution (or by the authorised withholding agent if appropriate). Any tax withheld from a distribution made in a calendar month must be paid to the Revenue Commissioners by the 14th of the following month. A return must be furnished to the Commissioners at the same time showing the name and address of each recipient, the amount paid to each and whether tax was withheld.

A person ('the accountable person'), being a company resident in the State which makes, or an authorised withholding agent treated under TCA 1997, s 172H as making, any relevant distribution to specified persons in any month must, within 14 days of the end of that month, make a return to the Collector General containing details of:

(a) the name and tax reference number of the company which actually made the relevant distribution;

(b) if different from the company which actually made the relevant distributions, the name of the accountable person, being an authorised withholding agent, in relation to those distributions;

(c) the name and address of each person to whom a relevant distribution was made or, as the case may be, was treated as being made by the accountable person in the month to which the return refers;
(d) the date on which the relevant distribution was made to that person;
(e) the amount of the relevant distribution made to that person;
(f) the amount of the dividend withholding tax, if any, in relation to the relevant distribution deducted by the accountable person or, as the case may be, the amount (if any) to be paid to the Collector General by the accountable person in relation to that distribution as if it were a deduction of dividend withholding tax;
(g) the aggregate of the amounts referred to in (f) in relation to all relevant distribution made or treated under TCA 1997, s 172H (see *Obligations of authorised withholding agent* in **9.107**) as being made by the accountable person to specified persons in the month to which the return relates (TCA 1997, s 172K(1)); and
(h) in the case of TCA 1997, s 172B not applying to a relevant distribution by virtue of the operations of sub-s (7) of that section, whether the relevant distribution is a distribution within paras (a), (b) or (c) of that subsection.

Dividend withholding tax which is required to be included in a return is due at the time by which the return is to be made and is payable by the accountable person to the Collector General. The tax so due is payable without the making of an assessment. Dividend withholding tax which has become due may, however, be assessed on the accountable person (whether or not paid at the time the assessment is made) if that tax or any part of it is not paid on or before the due date (TCA 1997, s 172K(2)).

Where it appears to the inspector of taxes that any amount of dividend withholding tax in relation to a relevant distribution which ought to have been, but has not been, included in a return, or where the inspector is dissatisfied with any such return, he may make an assessment on the accountable person in relation to the relevant distribution to the best of his judgement. Any amount of dividend withholding tax due by reason of such an assessment is to be treated for the purposes of interest on unpaid tax as having been payable at the time when it would have been payable if a correct return had been made (TCA 1997, s 172K(3)).

Where any item has been incorrectly included in a return as a relevant distribution in relation to which dividend withholding tax is to be deducted, the inspector may make such assessments, adjustments or set-offs as may in his judgement be required to secure that the resulting liabilities to tax, including interest on unpaid tax, whether of the accountable person in relation to the relevant distribution or any other person, are so far as is possible the same as they would have been if the item had not been so included (TCA 1997, s 172K(4)).

Any dividend withholding tax assessed on an accountable person will be due within one month after the issue of the notice of assessment (unless the tax is due earlier under TCA 1997, s 172K(2)), subject to any appeal against the assessment. No such appeal may affect the date when any amount is due under TCA 1997, s 172K(2) (TCA 1997, s 172K(5)).

The provisions of the Income Tax Acts relating to:

(a) assessments to income tax;
(b) appeals against such assessments (including the rehearing of appeals and the statement of a case for the opinion of the High Court); and

(c) the collection and recovery of income tax;

are, in so far as they are applicable, to apply to the assessment, collection and recovery of dividend withholding tax (TCA 1997, s 172K(6)(a)).

Any amount of dividend withholding tax payable without the making of an assessment carries interest at 0.0274 per cent for each day or part of a day from the date when the amount becomes due and payable until payment (TCA 1997, s 172K(6)(b))

The provisions of TCA 1997, s 1080(3)–(5) are to apply in relation to interest payable under TCA 1997, s 172K(6)(b) as they apply to interest payable under TCA 1997, s 1080 (TCA 1997, s 172K(6)(c)). In its application to any dividend withholding tax charged by assessment, TCA 1997, s 1080 is to apply as if TCA 1997, s 1080(2)(b) were deleted (TCA 1997, s 172K(6)(d)). That paragraph provides that interest on unpaid tax is to run on any tax charged by an assessment to income tax notwithstanding any appeal against the assessment, from the date it would run if there had been no assessment.

Subject to TCA 1997, s 172K(8), every return by an accountable person is to be made in an electronic format approved by the Revenue Commissioners and must be accompanied by a declaration made by the accountable person, on a form prescribed or authorised for that purpose by the Commissioners, to the effect that the return is correct and complete (TCA 1997, s 172K(7)).

Where, however, the Revenue Commissioners are satisfied that an accountable person does not have the facilities to make a return in electronic format as required above, the return is to be made in writing in a form prescribed or authorised by the Commissioners and must be accompanied by a declaration made by the accountable person, on a form prescribed or authorised for that purpose by the Commissioners, to the effect that the return is correct and complete (TCA 1997, s 172K(8)). F(TA)A 2015, s 35(6) inserts a right of appeal against an assessment under TCA 1997, s 172K and such insertion was subject to Ministerial Order at the time of writing (SI 110/2016 appointed 21 March 2016 as the day on which the Finance (Tax Appeals) Act 2015, came into operation).

Stapled stock agreements

Under TCA 1997, s 172L, a resident company is required to make a return to the Revenue Commissioners within 14 days of the end of a calendar month where any of its shareholders elect, under a right given in a 'stapled stock arrangement', to receive distributions from a non-resident company instead of from the resident company. The return of the resident company is to include details of the relevant distributions by the non-resident company. No DWT is deductible in such circumstances. The purpose of this provision is to ensure the Revenue will have full information of distributions made by resident companies and also of linked distributions under stapled stock agreements.

TCA 1997, s 172LA provides statutory backing to the administrative arrangement for dealing with dividend withholding tax in the case of market claims. The legislation is aimed at the position where dividends are incorrectly paid to a person due to delays in updating the share registers. The section imposes an obligation on a broker which is defined as a member of the Irish Stock Exchange or other recognised stock exchange in another territory or a qualifying intermediary or an authorised withholding agent to deduct dividend withholding tax in all such cases where dividend withholding tax was not deducted from the original made. The section also obliges the broker or intermediary to pay over all amounts deducted and extends all reporting requirements under this Chapter to dividend withholding tax.

9.112 Delegation of powers of Revenue Commissioners

The Revenue Commissioners may delegate the operation of the dividend withholding tax to any of their officers. TCA 1997, s 172M provides that the Revenue Commissioners may nominate any of their officers to perform any acts and discharge any functions authorised by TCA 1997, Pt 6, Ch 8A or Sch 2A to be performed or discharged by the Revenue Commissioners.

TCA 1997, s 1078 which deals with Revenue offences has been extended to add to the list of Revenue offences the following omissions:

(a) failure by a resident company to deduct DWT when required;
(b) failure by a resident company to issue a reduced number of shares in accordance with the DWT provisions relating to scrip dividends contained in TCA 1997, s 172B(2);
(c) failure by a resident company to account for DWT to the Collector-General by the 14th day of the month following that in which relevant distributions were made;
(d) failure by a resident company to pay to the Collector-General (within the same time limit) an amount of DWT equal to tax at the standard rate on the value of any scrip dividends liable to tax;
(e) failure by a resident company to pay to the Collector-General (within the same time limit) the appropriate amount of DWT at the standard rate on the value of any non-cash distribution; and
(f) failure by an authorised withholding agent to carry out any of the actions in (a) to (e) where the agent makes a relevant distribution on behalf of a resident company.

TCA 1997, Sch 29 has been extended. The list of actions, omissions, etc for which penalties may be imposed under TCA 1997, s 1052, 1053 or 1054 now includes the following:

(a) the failure by a resident company or an authorised withholding agent to make a return of relevant distributions; and
(b) the failure by a resident company to make a return of relevant distributions made by any non-resident company under a stapled stock agreement.

9.113 Distributions out of tax exempt income

Where a distribution is made out of exempt profits to a second company, the distribution is treated as if it were exempt profits of the second company (TCA 1997, s 140(3)(a)). Distributions are matched firstly against the income of the accounting period to which they relate and next against the most recently accumulated income (TCA 1997, s 140(7)). The position in relation to distributions out of patent income is more complex and is discussed below. Where a distribution is exempt from income tax, no dividend withholding tax will apply thereto with effect from 6 April 2000 up to the abolition of the exemption on 24 November 2010. These reliefs were potentially subject to the restrictions applicable to high income individuals discussed at **3.111**.

Exempt patent distributions

The exemption for dividends paid out of disregarded income (broadly speaking, exempt patent income or distributions made out of such income) no longer applies to distributions made on or after 24 November 2010. A full discussion of the exemption is contained in the 2010 edition of this work.

Division 10 Schedule E: Income from Offices and Employments

10.1 Principles of Schedule E

10.101 Income chargeable

TCA 1997, s 112 charges tax under Sch E on every person having or exercising anoffice or employment of profit mentioned in that Schedule and on any person to whom any annuity, pension or stipend chargeable under that Schedule is payable. The tax is charged on 'all salaries, fees, wages, perquisites or profits whatsoever therefrom', ie on all profits or gains arising from the office, employment, pension, etc. In determining the income on which a person is taxable under this main charging section of Sch E, two principal questions have to be answered. First, does the person have or exercise an office or employment of profit chargeable under Sch E or is he entitled to any pension, annuity, etc covered by Sch E? Secondly, what income in the form of salaries, fees, wages, perquisites or other profits does he derive from the office, employment, pension, etc?

While it might appear at first sight that the answers to these questions should be straightforward, in fact the questions have given rise to a considerable volume of litigation over the years and the provisions in the statute have been materially amplified by case law. Before going on to discuss these questions in more detail, some other general points should first be made. The term 'emoluments' is used to describe anything assessable to income tax under Sch E. Apart from the emoluments of an office, employment or pension that are charged to tax directly by TCA 1997, s 112, the Income Tax Acts contain other provisions which charge income tax under Sch E on the following:

(a) certain expenses, expense allowances and benefits in kind in connection with an office or employment (see **Division 10.3**);
(b) certain payments made in connection with the termination of an office or employment or a change in its functions or emoluments (see **Division 10.4**);
(c) certain payments by an employer to provide pension or other retirement benefits for an employee otherwise than through an approved or statutory retirement benefit scheme (see **16.104**);

(d) certain receipts before the normal release date in connection with an approved profit sharing scheme (see **11.408–11.409**);

(e) gains realised on the exercise, assignment or release of share options or other rights to acquire assets when obtained by reason of an office or employment (see **10.113**); and

(f) any sickness, etc benefit payable under an approved permanent health benefit scheme (see **10.112**).

Income chargeable to tax under Sch E includes pensions, annuities (other than annuities taxable under Sch C) and similar payments payable out of the public revenue of the State (TCA 1997, s 19(1)) – Sch E, para 2). Apart from pensions, etc payable by the State to persons who had previously held offices or employments in the government service, this brings within the ambit of Sch E all long term pensions and similar benefits payable under the Social Welfare Acts. In addition, short-term disability benefit, injury benefit and unemployment and pay-related benefit (subject to certain exceptions) are taxable under Sch E. With effect from 1 July 2013, maternity benefit, adoptive benefit and health and safety benefit are taxable under Sch E.

Income which would or might otherwise be chargeable to tax under the general provisions of Sch E, but which is exempted from income tax by specific provisions in the Income Tax Acts, includes:

(a) redundancy payments made under the Redundancy Payments Act 1967, s 46;

(b) specified compensation payments received under employment legislation (see **10.111**);

(c) provision of retraining courses as part of a redundancy package; subject to various conditions (see **10.407**):

(d) wound and disability pensions under the Army Pensions Acts, military gratuities and demobilisation pay, etc; and

(e) emoluments payable by a foreign state to members of its diplomatic or consular service acting in the State and the emoluments of certain administrative, technical, etc staff of a foreign diplomatic or consular mission in the State (see **1.308**).

Tax is not charged under Sch E in respect of a foreign office, employment or pension the income from which is taxable under Sch D Case III. For the rules which distinguish a foreign office, employment or pension from one in the State, see **Division 13**. It should be noted that earnings from a foreign employment to the extent that they are attributable to the performance of Irish duties are chargeable under Sch E (TCA 1997, s 18(2)(f)), albeit subject to a restricted version of the remittance basis in certain cases: see **10.115.**

With effect from 2011 onwards, income arising to any individual, whether resident in the State or not, from any employment exercised aboard an aircraft operated in international traffic by an enterprise that has its place of effective management in the State, is to be charged under Schedule E. For these purposes, 'international traffic' does not include purely domestic flights in another State (TCA 1997, s 127B).

TCA 1997, s 480A provides for relief from income tax for certain earnings of sports persons listed in TCA 1997, Sch 23A. For an illustration of how this section is applied, see **10.307**.

In addition, the vast majority of taxable emoluments, whether or not received in the form of cash, fall within the scope of the PAYE system: see **11.1**.

10.102 Basis of assessment

By virtue of TCA 1997, s 112, tax under Sch E is imposed on every person having or exercising an office or employment in respect of all salaries, fees, wages, perquisites, or profits ... for the year of assessment. This effectively means that all Sch E income (including any employment income not subject to PAYE which is an exceptional occurrence) (see **11.102**) is taxable on the current year basis. Emoluments are to be taxed on an earnings rather than a receipts basis as considered in *MacKeown v Roe* I ITR 214; see also *Heasman v Jordan* 35 TC 518 and *Board of IR v Suite*, a Privy Council case, [1986] STC 292. Given that the vast majority of taxable emoluments are subject to PAYE and that PAYE operates generally on a payments basis, a receipts basis of assessment would probably be more logical.

In practice, the Revenue may agree to assess directors on the basis of the remuneration credited to them in the accounts for the year falling in the relevant year of assessment (not normally appropriate in the first year of the directorship). The Revenue Commissioners will not apply this concession where it would lead to a 'tax advantage', ie where there is a material difference between the statutory basis and the concessionary basis which is favourable to the taxpayer (see *Tax Briefing 50*).

10.103 The meaning of an office or employment

The first prerequisite for tax to be charged under Sch E is that there be an office or employment in the State. Apart from pensions and similar payments dealt with separately (see **10.112**) and certain foreign source employments (see **13.104**), no tax can be assessed or otherwise levied under Sch E unless the person whom it is sought to tax holds or exercises such an office or employment. Sch E refers to offices and employments in two ways. Paragraph 2 brings within the Schedule 'every public office or employment of profit' (TCA 1997, s 19(1)). This was the original Sch E and it was only after the decision in the *Great Western Railway Co* case mentioned below that Sch E was extended by the addition of paragraph 2 to include also other offices and employments in the State which had, prior to the FA 1922, been taxable under Sch D.

There is no statutory definition of 'office', nor of the term 'employment'. TCA 1997, s 19(2) gives a list of public offices and employments of profit within the State the income of which is taxable under Sch E. Such public offices, etc mentioned there include, *inter alia*, offices of either House of the Oireachtas, offices belonging to any court in the State, public offices under the State, offices of the Defence Forces, offices under any ecclesiastical body, company, public institution, public corporation, local authority, etc.

Offices

In practice, there is now no distinction made between public offices of the type listed in TCA 1997, s 19(2) and other offices. An early and often quoted definition of 'office' is that given in 1920 by Rowlatt J, and approved by Lord Atkinson in the House of Lords, in *Great Western Railway v Bater* 8 TC 231 as:

> an office or employment which was a subsisting, permanent, substantive position, which had an existence independent of the person who filled it, which went on and was filled in succession by successive holders.

In that case, the position of a clerk in the Great Western Railway Co was held not to be a public office or employment of profit as it did not fit within those words. Rowlatt J's words have been repeated in numerous other cases since. In *McMillan v Guest* 24 TC

190, Lord Atkin in the House of Lords considered the sentence to be 'a generally sufficient statement' of the meaning of the term 'office', although not necessarily a complete definition; he held that there was no doubt that the director of a company holds an office such as that covered by the words quoted.

The meaning of 'office' was considered again more recently in *Edwards v Clinch* by both the Court of Appeal [1980] STC 438 and by the House of Lords [1981] STC 617. In that case, Mr Clinch was one of a panel of persons whom the UK Secretary of State for the Environment from time to time invited to conduct independent public local inquiries. He was appointed separately for each inquiry and was remunerated by daily fees according to the length of the inquiry, but received no retainer or salary. He was a civil engineer by profession. The Crown claimed that each appointment to hold an inquiry was an 'office' and assessed him to tax under Sch E in respect of the total fees received for conducting the inquiries. Mr Clinch contended that this appointment to hold a public local inquiry was not an 'office' since the holding of each inquiry was an *ad hoc* appointment of indeterminate length which he was free to accept or refuse.

In considering the case, Buckley LJ in the Court of Appeal gave a useful review of the legislative history of Sch E and of previous cases in which the meaning of 'office' was considered. He indicated that, having regard to legislative changes, there was a need to guard against treating as authoritative earlier decisions which were reached for reasons which may no longer be appropriate. Lord Wilberforce in the House of Lords also considered it open to the courts now to consider whether the ingredients of the Rowlatt definition in the *Great Western Railway* case were still appropriate in all respects. Buckley LJ's judgment included the following passage:

> Before considering the authorities which bear on this question, I may perhaps be allowed to say in what sense, unguided by authority and without attempting to formulate a precise definition, I should be inclined to understand the word office as used in Sch E. An office in this context is, in my opinion, a post which can be recognised as existing, whether it be occupied for the time being or vacant, and which if occupied, does not owe its existence in any way to the identity of the incumbent or his appointment to the post … It also follows, in my view, that the office must have a sufficient degree of continuance to admit of its being held by successive incumbents; it need not be capable of permanent or prolonged or indefinite existence, but it cannot be limited to the tenure of one man, for if it were so it would lack that independent existence which to my mind the word 'office' imports.

The Court of Appeal unanimously held in favour of the taxpayer. The House of Lords later confirmed by a three-two majority that Mr Clinch did not hold an office within the meaning of the word as used in Sch E and that, in consequence, he could not be assessed under that Schedule. This decision was arrived at on the facts of the case that each local inquiry appointment was personal to the taxpayer and lacked the characteristic of independent existence and continuance which is still regarded as one of the essential characteristics of an 'office'.

In the course of his judgment, Lord Wilberforce also questioned the word 'permanent' in the earlier Rowlatt judgment in the *Great Western Railway* case. He said:

> For myself I would accept that a rigid requirement of permanence is no longer appropriate nor is vouched by any decided case and continuity need not be regarded as an absolute qualification. But still, if any meaning is to be given to 'office' in this legislation, as distinguished from 'employment' or 'profession' or 'trade' or 'vocation' (these are the various words used in order to tax people on their earnings), the word must involve a degree of continuance (not necessarily continuity) and of independent existence. It must connote a post to which a person can be appointed … Thus Buckley L J accepted that to constitute an

> office a post need not be capable of permanent or prolonged or indefinite existence, a development of the law with which I agree.

It is therefore probably the case that the term 'office' has by now acquired a specific meaning for tax purposes. However, it is worth nothing that the scope of the term has also been expounded in a non-tax context by Kenny J in *Glover v BLN Ltd* [1973] IR 388, where he stated:

> [an office] is created by Act of the National parliament, charter, statutory regulation, articles of association of a company or of a body corporate formed under the authority of a statute, deed of trust, grant or by prescription.

Note also the discussion in Ward, 'What can it matter? Why should it matter?' [1989] British Tax Review 281.

In *McMenamin v Diggles* [1991] STC 419 the head clerkship of a barrister's chambers was held on the facts not to constitute an office. While the clerkship carried a title to which other individuals might succeed, it was in fact simply a contract agreed between the parties for their convenience at the particular time; in the words of Scott LJ, it was a 'job description' rather than an office.

By contrast, in *Mitchell and Eden v Ross* 40 TC 11, it was held that a taxpayer appointed as a part time consultant with a regional hospital board held an office assessable under Sch E. In that case, Lord Evershed MR placed reliance on the terms of the National Health Service Act 1946 which required the Minister to appoint consultants and on the fact that the taxpayer's appointment was made by the regional hospital board under powers delegated to it under the Act by the Minister. An important consequence of this conclusion was that the taxpayer had to claim his expenses by reference to the relatively strict Sch E expenses rule (see **Division 10.2**), rather than under the rules appropriate to Sch D.

Similarly, in *IRC v Brander & Cruickshank* 46 TC 574, the House of Lords held that a Scottish firm of advocates who also acted as secretaries and registrars to a number of companies were assessable in respect of the profits derived from those engagements under Sch E by reason of the fact that they represented offices within the meaning of Sch E. In that case, a sum received by the firm as compensation for the loss of positions as registrars to two companies was exempted from tax under Sch E, whereas if it had been received as a receipt of the taxpayers' profession, it would have been taxable under Sch D.

The decision in the *Brander & Cruickshank* case would, if applied strictly, result in the taxation of firms of accountants, solicitors, etc who act as secretaries or registrars of client companies under Sch E on the resulting fees separately from their other profits taxable under Sch D Case II. In practice, however, the Revenue Commissioners generally accept that such fees earned by the firm or its partners should be treated as trading receipts in arriving at the firm's Sch D Case II profits, provided that the fees are in fact credited in the firm's accounts in arriving at the profits that are divided between the partners.

In SP-IT/1/04 (Revised April 2011), the Revenue Commissioners express the view that members of committees or boards created by statute will invariably be thereby appointed to statutory offices. in the light of their experience to date, they express the further view that members of non-statutory committees or boards [eg members of what are known as '*ad-hoc*' committees or boards] are either office holders and/or employees. Factors that influence Revenue's view include:

(a) the content of the documents relating to the appointment of the members to the committee/board indicating the existence of an office or employment;
(b) many committees/boards and members of such committees/boards have the use of departmental or other state body facilities including support staff;
(c) committee/board members are generally appointed as individuals and cannot sub contract the work assigned to them;
(d) the mode of remuneration; and
(e) committee/board members are not generally exposed to personal financial risk in carrying out their work and many are reimbursed for expenses on the same basis as for civil servants.

Employments

In the great majority of cases, it is perfectly clear whether or not a person has or exercises an employment for the purposes of Sch E. The question of whether an employee/employer relationship or some other type of relationship exists between two parties may, however, cause a problem from time to time. Generally, this difficulty arises in cases where it is unclear whether a person is providing services as an employed person so as to be taxable under Sch E in respect of the resulting emoluments or is acting in a self-employed capacity so as to be chargeable under Sch D on the profits of a trade or profession. The meaning of 'employment', as used in Sch E, may best be explained by examining the distinction between a person who is an employee and one who is self-employed.

The basic distinction between a person who is acting as an employee and one who is acting as a self-employed person is that the former provides his services under a contract of service while the latter renders his under a contract for services. The difference between these two types of contract was considered by Pennycuick VC in the case of *Fall v Hitchen* 49 TC 433. He drew attention to the use of the expression 'contract of service' in the UK National Insurance Act 1965 which distinguished between employed persons:

> that is to say, persons gainfully occupied in employment … being employment under a contract of service, and self-employed persons, that is to say, persons gainfully occupied in employment … who are not employed persons.

He then referred to the words of Cooke J in *Market Investigations v Minister of Social Security* [1969] 2 QB 173:

> … the fundamental test to be applied is this: 'Is the person who has engaged himself to perform these services performing them as a person in business on his own account?' If the answer to that question is 'yes', then the contract is a contract for services. If the answer is 'no', then the contract is a contract of service.

Pennycuick VC then observed that:

> The expressions 'contract of service' and 'contract for services' are of general application, and, unless one finds in the context some limitation upon the meaning of the words, those words must bear the same meaning in any other context as they do under the National Insurance Act.

In this case, Mr Hitchen was a professional dancer. He was engaged by Sadler's Wells Trust Ltd under a standard form of contract to work for a minimum period of rehearsals plus 22 weeks, and thereafter until the contract was determined by 14 days' notice on either side. He was required to work full time during specified hours for a regular salary. During the engagement he was not to perform elsewhere without the consent of the management, such consent not to be unreasonably withheld. With one exception, the management was required to provide, and entitled to retain, the property and costumes used by him on the stage. The management encouraged him to carry on outside work on days on which he was not required to work for them. It was held on these facts that Mr Hitchen had acted under a contract of service and that, in consequence, his remuneration from Sadler's Wells Trust Ltd was taxable under Sch E and not under Sch D.

Pennycuick VC distinguished Mr Hitchen's case from that of *Davies v Braithwaite* 18 TC 198. In that case, Miss Braithwaite was a professional actress who had entered into separate contracts for each play, film, radio appearance, etc for which she was engaged. Rowlatt J had held that on the particular facts of the case these were not employments or 'posts' (his own expression) taxable under Sch E, but they were only engagements or incidents in the conduct of her professional career. Pennycuick noted that in her case Miss Braithwaite had not held any post and that none of her particular engagements could be treated as a post. He then went on to observe:

> The learned Judge (Rowlatt) nowhere says that, if an actor enters into a contract in such terms as to amount to what he calls a post, then that actor is not chargeable under Sch D, but under Sch E. On the contrary it is implicit in the whole of his judgment, it seems to me, that if a professional person, whether an actor or anyone else enters into a contract involving what the learned Judge calls a post, then that person will be chargeable in respect of the income arising from the post under Sch E notwithstanding that he is at the same time carrying on his profession, the income of which will be chargeable under Sch D.

This last reference to the possibility that a person carrying on a profession (which could also apply to a trade) is not thereby prevented from being taxed under Sch E on any income from a separate employment is worth noting. Rowlatt J made a similar point in *Braithwaite* when he noted that a musician who holds an office or employment under a permanent engagement can at the same time follow his profession privately, eg by giving music lessons. It is also worth noting Pennycuick VC's linking of contracts of service for income tax purposes with the National Insurance Act. A similar connection can be made with the Social Welfare Consolidation Act 2005 in the State. Section 12 in defining 'employed contributors' for purposes of social welfare contributions, etc includes (with certain exceptions) persons employed in 'any of the employments specified in Pt I of Schedule I'; that Schedule refers to:

> Employment in the State under a contract of service or apprenticeship, written or oral, whether expressed or implied …

In this respect, therefore, Pennycuick VC effectively rejected Rowlatt J's concept of a 'post' in favour of the idea that an 'employment' equated to a 'contract of service'. In *Davies v Braithwaite* Rowlatt J had reasoned that:

> … when you get into Sch E you are beginning to use the word employment with a different value and you use it as something more or less analogous to an office and conveniently amenable to the scheme of taxation which is applied to offices … I thought of the expression 'posts'.

Indeed, it seems that some of the contracts which Rowlatt J regarded as 'posts' in the *Braithwaite* case were in fact contracts of service.

It is clear that Rowlatt J's concept of a 'post' was influenced by the existence of ITA 1918, Sch E Rule 2, which stated that:

> every assessment shall be made for one year … without any new assessment, notwithstanding any change in the holder of any office or employment.

This rule was, however, specifically framed to deal with 'public offices and employments' (within what is now TCA 1997, s 19(1)) and not the general run of employments which were later brought under Sch E (within what is now repealed). In any event, the rule has long disappeared from the Irish legislation and it would seem correct that 'employment' should now be understood in its generally accepted legal sense.

In *Fall v Hitchen* Pennycuick VC commented:

> I do not think most people today would use the word 'post' which does not seem very apt to cover the countless instances of employment in the sense of a contract of service.

(See also *Graham v White* 48 TC 163 and the discussion in *Ward* [1992] ITR 151.)

There seems no reason to doubt therefore that the term 'contract of service' has the same meaning in the State, as Pennycuick VC considered it has in the UK, for both Sch E income tax purposes and for the liability to social welfare contributions. It should, however be noted that the Social Welfare Consolidation Act 2005 does list in Sch 1 Pt II certain employments which are excepted and do not give rise to compulsory contributions (see **11.202**). The fact that an employment is a non-insurable one for social welfare purposes does not prevent the employee from being liable to income tax under Sch E if his emoluments are derived from a contract of service.

In *McDermott v Loy* (July 1982) HC (reported as *McDermott v BC* III ITR 43), a similar line of reasoning was followed to that in *Fall v Hitchen*. It was held that the Appeal Commissioners were on the facts of the case, entitled to reach the conclusion that the respondent, an insurance agent who had purchased his own collection book and who was not subject to any restrictions on his activities, was in business on his own account so as to be allowed the deduction for various expenses under the rules of Sch D Cases I and II. In his concluding remarks, Mr Justice Barron indicated it was a relevant consideration that certain of these expenses would have had to be disallowed were he to decide the case differently. This latter observation appears highly dubious. As stated by Pennycuick J, in the passage cited above, the definition of an employment for tax purposes follows the definition for general legal purposes. Logically, therefore, the general legal analysis of any given contract cannot vary with the tax consequences for the individual concerned. Furthermore, the tax treatment is not conclusive for other purposes. In *Re Sunday Tribune Ltd* [1984] IR 505 (a company law case) Carroll J held that, although certain journalists had been treated as self-employed for tax purposes, the court was obliged to look at the realities of the situation (see also the *Henry Denny* case below).

One of the most influential exposition of the principles to be applied in this area is to found in the judgment of McKenna J in *Ready Mixed Concrete (SE) Ltd v Minister of Pensions and National Insurance* (1968) 2 QB 497. The learned judge observed:

> I must now consider what is meant by a contract of service. A contract of service exists if these three conditions are fulfilled.
>
> (a) The servant agrees that, in consideration of a wage or other remuneration, he will provide his own work and skill in the performance of some service for his master.

(b) He agrees, expressly or impliedly, that in the performance of that service he will be subject to the other's control in a sufficient degree to make that other master.

(c) The other provisions of the contract are consistent with its being a contract of service.

I need say little about (a) and (b). As to (a), there must be a wage or other remuneration. Otherwise there will be no consideration, and without consideration no contract of any kind. The servant must be obliged to provide his own work and skill. Freedom to do a job either by one's own hands or by another's is inconsistent with a contract of service, though a limited or occasional power of delegation may not be …

As to (b) control includes the power of deciding the thing to be done, the way in which it shall be done, the means to be employed in doing it, the time when and the place where it shall be done. All these aspects of control must be considered in deciding whether the right exists in a sufficient degree to make one party the master and the other his servant. The right need not be unrestricted. 'What matters is lawful authority to command so far as there is scope for it. And there must always be some room for it, if only in incidental or collateral matters' – *Zuijs v Wirth Bros Proprietary* [1955] 93 CLR 561, 571.

Each of the three conditions was regarded by the learned judge as necessary, but not sufficient. It will be clear that while condition (a) is reasonably clear-cut, conditions (b) and (c) are framed in such a fashion as to beg the very question which they are supposed to resolve.

So far as condition (b) is concerned, it would appear that in practice the more extensive the degree of control, the more likely is a finding that a contract of service exists. On the other hand, while some degree of control is probably necessary, this may, in some circumstances be confined to 'incidental' or 'collateral' matters. This is likely to be the case when the employer cannot realistically control 'how' the taxpayer performs his duties. In *Horner v Hasted* [1995] STC 766, it was held that the taxpayer, who was treated as a partner for virtually all the internal purposes of the firm for which he worked was nevertheless an employee. Lightman J commented as follows:

The lack of 'control' or the relationship of boss and underling, or master and servant … certainly is not a universal litmus test and its importance (and indeed relevance) must depend in particular on the role to be played by the 'employee' in the 'employer's' business.

For example, the position of managing director of a company, or a qualified professional such as a surgeon or consultant engaged by a health trust, will be very different from that of a manual worker. The avoidance of any subordination of the taxpayer to the partners was a legitimate special term of his contract of employment appropriate to the role he was to perform.

The learned judge also noted that it would have been illegal for the taxpayer to have been a partner and that the taxpayer's employer consistently treated him as an employee for PAYE and pension scheme purposes.

The observations of Cooke J in *Market Investigations v Minister of Social Security* [1969] 2 QB 173 are particularly illuminating in this connection. The learned judge commented as follows:

I think it is fair to say that there was at one time a school of thought according to which the extent and degree of the control which B is entitled to exercise over A in the performance of the work would be a decisive factor. However, it has for long been apparent that an analysis of the extent and degree of such control is not in itself decisive.

Thus, in *Collins v Hertfordshire County Council* [1947] KB 598, it had been suggested that the distinguishing feature of a contract of service is that the master cannot only order or require what is to be done but also how it shall be done. The inadequacy of this test was pointed out by Somervell LJ in *Cassidy v Minister of Health* [1951] 2 KB 343, 352, where he referred to the case of a certified master of a ship. The master may be employed by the owners under what is clearly a contract of service, and yet the owners have no power to tell him how to navigate his ship. As Lord Parker CJ pointed out in *Morren v Swinton and Pendlebury Borough Council* [1965] 1 WLR 576, 582, when one is dealing with a professional man, or a man of some particular skill and experience, there can be no question of an employer telling him how to do the work; therefore the absence of control and direction in that sense can be of little, if any, use as a test.

Cases such as *Morren's case* [1965] 1 WLR 576 illustrate how a contract of service may exist even though the control does not extend to prescribing how the work shall be done. On the other hand, there may be exceptional cases when a person who engages another to do work may reserve to himself full control over how the work is to be done, but nevertheless the contract is not a contract of service. A good example is *Queensland Stations Proprietary Ltd v Federal Commissioner of Taxation* [1945] 70 CLR 539, where Dixon J said at p 552:

> In considering the facts it is a mistake to treat as decisive a reservation of control over the manner in which [work] ... is performed. For instance, in the present case the circumstance that the [worker] agrees to obey and carry out all lawful instructions cannot outweigh the countervailing considerations which are found in the employment by servants of his own, the provision of horses, equipment, plant, rations and a remuneration at a rate per head delivered.

Condition (c) is particularly open-ended; it is sometimes described as an 'enterprise test', in that it focuses on the typical characteristics of an 'entrepreneur', ie a person who is in business on his own account. Per Cooke J in *Market Investigations*:

> factors which may be of importance are such matters as whether the man performing the services provides his own equipment, whether he hires his own helpers, what degree of financial risk he takes, what degree of responsibility for investment and management he has, and whether or how far he has an opportunity of profiting from sound management in the performance of his task.

Similarly, in *Graham v Minister for Industry and Commerce* [1933] IR 156, Kennedy CJ observed of the categories of 'contract of service' and 'contract for services':

> No exhaustive definition of either category has yet been settled and established either by statute or judicial decision and there is a zone of uncertainty. A commonly accepted test is that of control. Is the alleged 'employed person' ... subject to be controlled by the employer in executing the work, eg as to the order and manner in which he carries out the work in detail? ... The most usual test, is far from sufficient as a single test ... There are other and equally important tests: eg is the engaged person engaged to execute the whole of a given piece or work? Can the engagement be terminated before completion of the piece of work without cause assigned, only for misconduct or for malperformance of the work? Is the agreed remuneration on a wage basis or on a percentage or other commercial profit basis? Are the necessary materials to be provided by the engaged person on his own account and, if necessary, his own credit? Are such other workmen (if any) as have been taken into employment upon the work by the engaged person so employed by him as agent for the principal or are they his own employees paid by and subject to him?

In *Argent v Minister of Social Security* [1968] 1 WLR 1749 it was also observed that an individual who undertakes a short-term engagement is more likely to be self-employed particularly if he enjoys the right to work for others.

An approach which is related to the 'enterprise test', but with a different emphasis, is associated with Lord Denning. This asks whether or not the individual is 'part and parcel' of the relevant organisation (the so-called 'integration' test). This test has been often criticised and can sometimes look rather unconvincing in the more flexible labour markets of the today, when there is increased 'casualisation' and it is common for organisations to 'contract out' even key functions. Clearly, where the contract provides for benefits such as pension rights, or for the worker to be subject to internal dismissal procedures, these factors will be indications of employee status. However, the absence of these factors will not normally carry any significant weight (see, eg *Young v Woods Ltd v West* [1980] IRLR 201). In SP-IT/1/04 (Revised April 2011) the Revenue Commissioners express the (surely correct) view that a contract of engagement which stipulates that an individual has no rights to statutory employee entitlements is not *prima facie* evidence that the said individual is self-employed, since an individual's right to statutory employee entitlements such as holidays, holiday pay, etc is not a test of whether he is an employee but rather is a *consequence* of his being an employee.

In *Re Sunday Tribune Ltd* [1984] IR 505 (a non-tax case) Carroll J did however invoke the integration test, citing the dictum of Lord Denning in *Stephenson, Jordan & Harrison Ltd v MacDonald* [1952] ITLR 102:

> One feature which seems to run through the cases is that under a contract of service a man is employed as part of the business and his work is done as an integral part of the business; whereas under a contract for services his work, though done for the business, is not integrated into it but only accessory to it.

The label that parties choose to attach to their contract cannot override its true legal nature (see also *Young v Woods Ltd v West* [1980] IRLR 201). However, the expressed intention of the parties may be a significant factor in ambiguous or unclear cases. The arrangements entered into by the parties regarding PAYE, etc will usually be evidence of their intentions.

In *O'Coindealbhain v Mooney* IV ITR 45 the taxpayer entered into a contract with the Department of Social Welfare to act as the branch manager of a local employment exchange. His remuneration consisted of a combination of allowances and fixed-rate fees, related to the volume of work to be performed. He was obliged to provide and furnish his own premises and to employ a competent deputy and such clerical assistance as was necessary. The premises and the employees had to be approved by the Department. The duties of the taxpayer were clearly defined and the exchange had to be open at stipulated times. The Department could terminate the contract on three-months' notice.

Blayney J considered each of the three conditions laid down by McKenna J in the *Ready Mixed Concrete* case. Firstly, he held that the control exercised by the department and the taxpayer was limited in its scope; while the contract laid down what had to be done, it did not generally direct how it was to be done or when it was to be done (while the office had to be open during stipulated hours there was no requirement as to when the balance of work had to performed). The learned judge also stated that the power of dismissal, while inherent in a master-servant relationship, could also frequently be found in a contract for services. Similarly (and perhaps more significantly) the characteristics of the contract were inconsistent with a contract of service. The learned judge said:

> The second test to be applied is whether the respondent is in business on his own account. In my opinion he is. I have no doubt that he is running a business, the nature of the business

> being to provide a particular service for the Minister. His profit is the amount by which his remuneration exceeds his expenses; the lower he can keep his expenses the greater his profit. If he employs no one other than a deputy, and does a substantial amount of the work himself, his profit will be much greater than if he does little of the work himself and employs another person to do it instead. Similarly, the amount of his profit will also depend on how much rent he has to pay for his premises, and how well he succeeds in keeping down his other expenses. All these matters require management decisions and in making them the respondent is working for himself and not for the Minister. So it seems to me that he is clearly in business on his own account as the profit he makes from the contract depends on how he decides to perform the work which has to be done.

The learned judge also added that it was significant that the taxpayer had to provide and furnish his own premises, Finally, the learned judge held that there was no obligation on the taxpayer to perform the work under the contract personally. It seems that this feature on its own could arguably have sufficed to negate the presence of a contract of service.

Blayney J also indicated in *Mooney* that where all the terms of the contract have been reduced to writing and have not been varied by the subsequent conduct of the parties, then the court must confine itself to consideration of the written contract (see *Narich Pty v Payroll Commrs* [1984] ICR 286); contrast however *Denny v Minister for Social Welfare*, discussed below. It would seem to follow from Kenny J's dicta in *Mara v Hummingbird* (see **2.204**) that in such an instance the issue is to be treated as one of law and not as one of fact (see *Davies v Presbyterian Church of Wales* [1986] IRLR 194; *McManus v Griffiths* [1997] STC 1089). Where the contract is only partly reduced to writing, then it seems the issue will be one of fact, except to the extent that the decision involves interpretation of the written element (see *Denny v Minister for Social Welfare*, discussed below).

In *McAuliffe v The Minister for Social Welfare* V ITR 94 (a social welfare case), Barr J stressed that:

> Having regard to the wide range of particular circumstances from case to case, it is not possible to devise any hard and fast rule as to what constitutes a servant and what constitutes an independent contractor. Each case must be considered on its own special facts in the light of the broad guidelines which the law provides.

The case itself concerned an individual who was previously employed, but who then entered into a series of short-term, non-exclusive contracts with the same paymaster to deliver newspapers. The individual used his own vehicle, paying all overheads, providing relief drivers where necessary, and accepting liability for any losses or delays. On these facts, it was held that he was self-employed.

The remarks of Barr J in the *McAuliffe* case were echoed in the UK case of *Hall v Lorimer* [1994] STC 23 where Nolan LJ concurred with the view expressed by Mummery J in the High Court to the effect that:

> In order to decide whether a person carries on business on his own account it is necessary to consider many different aspects of that person's work activity. This is not a mechanical exercise of running through items on a check list to see whether they are present in, or absent from, a given situation. The object of the exercise is to paint a picture from the accumulation of detail. The overall effect can only be appreciated by standing back from the detailed picture which has been painted, by viewing it from a distance and by making an informed, considered, qualitative appreciation of the whole. It is a matter of evaluation of the overall effect of the detail, which is not necessarily the same as the sum total of the individual details. Not all details are of equal right or importance in any given situation.

The court held in *Hall v Lorimer* that a vision mixer who worked under a series of one- and two-day contracts for a wide range of paymasters, but who employed no staff and provided none of his own equipment, was self-employed. The court emphasised that an individual exercising a profession or vocation would often not exhibit the usual trappings of a business. The findings of the Special Commissioners are highly pertinent in this regard. They stated:

> … the taxpayer provides no equipment (ie he has no tools). He provides no 'work place' or 'workshop' where the contract is to be performed, he provides no capital for the production, he hires no staff for it … But that is not his business. He has his office, he exploits his abilities in the market place, he bears his own financial risk, which is greater than that of one who is an employee, accepting the risk of bad debts and outstanding invoices and of no, or an insufficient number, of engagements. He has the opportunity of profiting from being good at being a vision mixer. According to his reputation there will be a demand for his services for which he will be able to charge accordingly. The more efficient he is at running the business of providing his services the greater is his prospect of profit.

For a somewhat startling decision in favour of the taxpayer see also *Barnett v Brabyn* [1996] STC 716 (note the critical comments by Frank Carr at [1996] ITR 298).

It may be noted that the UK Special Commissioners have also distinguished *Fall v Hitchen* in the case of actors hired under a standard equity contract, and that their finding has since been accepted by the Inland Revenue. The views of the Revenue Commissioners on the indicators of employment and self-employment in the context of tax and PRSI are included in 'A Guide For Tax and Social Insurance – Employed or Self-Employed'.

In *Henry Denny & Sons v Minister for Social Welfare* V ITR 238, a social insurance case, the Supreme Court held that the Social Welfare Appeals Officer was entitled to find that a demonstrator of food products at supermarkets was an employee. The employer had the right to direct and control the employee as to how, when and where she worked and the right of dismissal; it also supplied the materials with which she worked and set specific work targets for her. Per Keane J:

> The amount of money she earned was determined exclusively by the extent to which her services were availed of by the appellants: she was not in a position by better management and employment of resources to ensure for herself a higher profit from her activities

Furthermore, the employee could not delegate her duties to others, although, with the approval of the employer, she could arrange for a substitute in exceptional circumstances. It may be seen that these factors would be expected to outweigh the facts that the employee was not paid for holidays or illness, was not a member of the employer's pension scheme, and was free to refuse to work and to undertake work for others (unless it was in competition with the employer). The legal reality of the arrangements was not altered by the fact that the contract stated that it was not to be construed as one of employment (particularly as the employee had little option but to sign it on those terms).

In the High Court, Carroll J emphasised the incontrovertible point that the fact the local inspector of taxes had agreed to treat one contract as being one 'for services' was not conclusive (adding that this was particularly so as it was merely a temporary 'holding' arrangement on his part, but this aspect of matters does not in fact appear to be in point). Per Keane J, the fact that a Circuit Court judge had held that a similar (but not the same) contract was one 'for services' for the purposes of wrongful dismissal was not binding on the Appeals Officer (it is not clear in fact why the difference in statutory context is significant, if one accepts that the contract of/for services dichotomy is an issue of general law).

Interestingly, in contrast to the *Mooney* case (see above), the court held that in this instance the terms of the written contract did not constitute the whole of the relationship between employer and employee; thus, for example, it did not indicate the manner in which the demonstrations were to take place or the skills which the employee would be required to exercise when carrying out the demonstration.

In *Lynch (Inspector of Taxes) v Neville Brothers Ltd* VI ITR 757 an individual provided his services as a 'merchandiser' to a Neville Brothers Ltd (the 'paymaster') which supplied certain goods (bread and confectionery) to supermarket stores. The individual was responsible for delivering goods to the stores concerned and ensuring that the paymaster's products were continuously on display. He was required to be available each day with the exception of Sunday; however, he could appoint individuals to work on his behalf, and was not under any obligation to perform these services personally. The contract also stated that the individual was not to be subject to directions from the paymaster as to the manner in which he performed his work. In practice, the individual did delegate the work to third parties without requiring prior permission. The contract between the paymaster and the individual stated that he was to be regarded as an independent contractor and that he was solely responsible for any income tax, VAT and PRSI liabilities in relation to the payments received by him.

The inspector of taxes argued that the individual was an employee on the basis that he did not supply any equipment, took no financial risk; received remuneration fixed by contract and had no responsibility for investment and management of the business. Counsel for the paymaster pointed to the lack of control exercised by the paymaster; in fact, in the authors' view, the fact that the individual was not required to render his services personally should have sufficed to negate the existence of a contract of service. The individual's counsel also pointed out that the individual was not integrated into the paymaster's organisation, given that he did not work at the paymaster's premises (although, in the authors' view, this is not uncommon in many cases of employment), was not a member of the paymaster's pension scheme, did not have prospects of promotion and was not subject to employee disciplinary procedures; in this connection, counsel also pointed to the fact that the individual also provided services to other paymasters (again in the authors' view this is a factor which in its own right points to being in business on one's own account rather than relating to the 'integration test' per se). Counsel for the paymaster also invoked the 'economic reality' test, pointing out *inter alia* that the individual provided his own transport, wore a special coat owned by himself, and hired and supervised his own helpers. Further, he could profit from sound management by increasing his income through providing merchandising services to a number of companies, merchandising products for other merchandisers to their mutual advantage and by paying helpers less than the amount he received himself. In the authors' views, these are powerful indicators of self-employment (compare *Hall v Lorimer*).

Carroll J, declining to disturb the finding of the Circuit Court that the individual was self-employed (and therefore that the paymaster was not liable to account for PAYE and PRSI in relation to payments under the contract), observed:

> It is correct that the relationship between the Respondent and the merchandiser cannot be defined merely by labelling it as a contract for services in the contract between them but the reality of the situation is that there is nothing in the contract or in the factual matrix of this case to cast doubt on the designation of the relationship in the contract.

> Case law shows that there is a variety of tests. No single test is decisive. The question is whether this court is persuaded by the Appellant that no reasonable judge would have come to the conclusion that the merchandiser is an independent contractor on the facts and evidence set out in the case stated. In my opinion the Appellant have not discharged that onus. It was in my opinion entirely reasonable for the learned Circuit Court judge to come to the conclusion (which he did) that this was a contract for services.

It appears that the Revenue Commissioners take the view, following a decision of the Circuit Court, that part-time lecturers working for the professional accountancy institutes are employees (see [1996] ITR 49). While each case must be decided on its particular facts, it may be noted that a part-time college lecturer was held to be an employee in both *Sidey v Phillips* [1987] STC 871 and *Walls v Sinnott* [1987] STC 236. The Revenue Commissioners have stated that where lecturers/teachers give 'once off' lectures, Sch E does not apply but they do not accept 'once off' or 'guest' lectures for the same body can fall outside Sch E; this approach appears to be unduly dogmatic.

In *Tax Briefing 82*, the Revenue Commissioners express the view that doctors engaged under the 'Doctors Out of Hours Service' and locum pharmacists will be engaged under a contract of service but adopt a more non-committal approach otherwise. However, in practice, following a decision in their favour by the Appeal Commissioners, it appears that the Revenue Commissioners are taking a more intransigent stance and are refusing to register locums in general as self-employed.

In *Cooke v Blacklaws* [1985] STC 1, the taxpayer, who was a dentist, contracted to provide his services to a non-resident company. The company in turn contracted to provide his services to a dental practice for whom he had previously worked as a self-employed person. The High Court upheld the Appeal Commissioners finding of fact that the taxpayer's contract with the company was one for services, notwithstanding that such a contract was illegal under NHS regulations. It might well seem that if a contract is void for illegality, then by definition there cannot be a contract of service in existence. In *FÁS v Minister of Social Welfare, Abbott and Ryan*, Egan J in the High Court held that no employee PRSI contributions were due in respect of an illegal contract of service. In the Supreme Court, it was held that the contract in question was *ultra vires* the employer rather than illegal (consequently the court was able to exercise its discretion and refused to invalidate the contract).

It may be that some self-employed individuals with substantial overseas activities may now wish to incorporate their businesses for tax planning purposes; incorporation for these purposes will however be pointless, unless the individual can demonstrate that he has a valid contract of service with his company, (see *CITB v Labour Force Ltd* [1970] 3 All ER 220 and *Minister of Labour v PMPA* III ITR 505 for a discussion of the kind of contracts entailing an obligation to provide services to third parties, which were held not to constitute contracts of services). Note also *Muscat v Cable & Wireless plc* [2006] ECWA Civ 220 where on the specific facts it was found that there was an implied contract of service between the end-user and the individual providing services to it through an agency.

In *Louth v Minister for Social Welfare* IV ITR 311, it was held that the formation of an association under which individuals who worked on a rota basis pooled their earnings did not affect the contractual arrangement between each employee and the main employer. This was not a case where the association had contracted to supply the services of the individuals to a third party (as in *Minister of Labour v PMPA*).

The categorisation of casual workers raises special consideration, since such workers are unlikely to display many entrepreneurial characteristics, while the nature of their relationship with their 'paymaster' may still not be regarded as consistent with a contract of service. In *O'Kelly v Trust House Forte* [1983] 3 WLR 505 (a non-tax case), the workers concerned were so-called 'regular casuals' working in a hotel, who were given preference in the hotel's work rotas over other casual workers. The House of Lords upheld the finding of the Employment Appeal Tribunals that they were not employees as one of fact, on *Edwards v Bairstow* principles. The tribunal found that the most significant factor which was inconsistent with a contract of service was the lack of mutual obligation: the hotel was not bound to provide work, and the workers were not bound to accept work, if offered.

In *Wickens v Champion Employment* [1984] ICR 365, casual agency workers were held not be employees, even though they operated no business of their own, because of the 'lack of continuity and care' which were thought to be the hallmark of an employer/employee relationship (see also *Interlink Express Parcels Ltd v Night Trunkers Ltd* [2001] RTR 338). However, the necessary element of mutuality and continuity may be inferred from an ongoing course of conduct (see eg *Nethermere (St Neots) Ltd v Taverna* [1984] IRLR 240 a case concerning homeworkers, and also *Byrne v Gartan Ltd* (1983) EAT 1048/83, a case heard by the Irish Employment Appeals Tribunal where a hotel worker described as a 'permanent casual' was held to be an employee; the 'integration test' was held to be a significant indicator in these instances; note also the comments of the Revenue Commissioners in *Tax Briefing 31*).

In *Brightwater Selection (Ireland) Ltd v Minister for Social and Family Affairs* [2011] IEHC 510, it was confirmed that there could not be a contract of service in the absence of mutuality of obligation.

It may be noted that special arrangements have been agreed between the Revenue Commissioners and courier companies. Under these arrangements, the courier will be accepted as being self-employed but where the courier company operates a voluntary system of deducting PAYE from payments made to couriers engaged by them, the courier will be allowed to claim the employee tax credit, as well as a special allowance of 45 per cent of their income if they use motorbikes (20 per cent if they use push bikes).

The Employment Status Group have issued a 'code of practice' (Updated June 2010) which is designed to be applied in determining the employment/self-employment status of individuals (see *Tax Briefing 43*).

The distinction between an office and an employment is generally of lesser importance than that between a profession and an employment, since offices and employments will both normally fall within Sch E. However, the question as to whether emoluments are earned by an office holder or employee of a company may still be relevant in a number of contexts. For example, earnings from a directorship (or other office) held with an Irish incorporated company will always fall under Sch E but earnings from employments with such companies may fall under Sch D Case III. The distinction between director's emoluments and employment earnings may also be relevant for double tax treaty purposes (see **14.210**; **14.211**).

It is possible for an individual to hold separate offices and employments with the same company (see eg *Lee v Lee's Air Farming Ltd* 3 WLR 758). This case demonstrates that is possible for an individual who is a director and majority shareholder of a company to be an employee of that company, although this will not be the case if on the facts the company cannot exercise any control over the relevant activities, in which case he may be self-employed in respect thereof: see the discussion at **11.202**.

It will depend on the facts as to whether particular activities of an office-holder constitute a different office or employment, or an extension of an existing one. In

Goodwin v Brewster 3 STC 80, it was accepted that the taxpayer occupied the posts of both director and managing director, but both posts were held to represent offices. Jenkins LJ commented:

> I have no doubt that matters might have been so contrived that Mr Goodwin did hold the office of director in England and was also appointed to serve the company as manager or technical supervisor [overseas] … but I feel that was not in fact what did occur.

The position of managing director raises some interesting issues. Normally, the articles of a company provide that the holder operates under a contract of service in his capacity as managing director, while concurrently holding office as a director. However, as *Goodwin v Brewster* demonstrates, while the managing director may not be a director in his capacity as managing director, he nevertheless holds an office in that capacity. The case also demonstrates that it can be possible for an employment also to be an office. However, a director cannot be an employee in respect of his directorship, since the autonomy and independence required of a director is inconsistent with working under a contract of service, (which generally implies subordination to the control of another). In practice, if a director undertakes senior managerial functions, these will often be regarded as relating to his directorship, unless he can show that the functions are performed under a distinct contract of (or for) services. In *Taylor v Provan* [1974] STC 168 where the taxpayer was given a directorship as part of his consultancy agreement, all services rendered thereunder were held to attach to his directorship (see *Mudd v Collins* 9 TC 297, to similar effect in reference to an *ex gratia* payment and *Shipway v Skidmore* 16 TC 748; in *Venables v Hornby* [2003] UKHL 65, [2003] All ER (D) 86, a majority of the House of Lords held that on the facts a majority shareholder who acted as the main executive director (although not managing director as such) held a directorship concurrently with a contract of service notwithstanding there was no written documentation to this effect.

See also *Parsons v Parsons* [1979] ICR 271, but compare *Stakelum v Canning* [1976] IR 314, both employment law cases.

A related area of difficulty can be in determining who is the employer, where the employee is assigned or seconded to work for a third party. It would appear that where the employment contract between the original employer and the employee continues unbroken then the original employer will remain such (see *IRC v Morris* 44 TC 685; *Caldicott v Varty* 51 TC 403; *Customs & Excise v Tarmac Roadstone Holdings Ltd* [1987] STC 610). The position is different where the individual is assigned to hold a directorship since (as noted above) a director cannot also be an employee in his capacity as a director. Thus, it seems that an individual who personally receives director's emoluments (eg from an Irish subsidiary) will receive them as a director and not as a seconded employee (eg of the overseas parent), thus falling potentially within the scope of Sch E (see **13.607**). In SP-IT/1/04 (Updated April 2011), the Revenue Commissioners express the (surely correct) view that where a member holding an office on a statutory board mandates his remuneration to a company owned, in whole or in part, by him, the payment belongs to the individual in his capacity as officeholder and, as such, must be taxed in the same way as if the payment is made directly to him or her (see *O'Coindealbhain v Gannon* III ITR 484, discussed at **1.403**).

It may be noted that the OECD has suggested that double tax treaties should be applied on the basis of the concept of the 'economic' employer, rather than that of the 'legal' employer (see **14.210**).

10.104 Emoluments from office or employment

Once it is established that a person holds or exercises an office or employment chargeable under Sch E, the next question is what are the emoluments of that office or employment that are to be taxed under the Schedule? This question is now examined in the context of TCA 1997, s 112 which charges to tax 'all salaries, fees, wages, perquisites or profits whatsoever therefrom', ie from the office or employment. It is considered first without any reference to those other provisions in the Income Tax Acts mentioned in **10.101** which have been added over the years to widen the scope of taxation under Sch E. If a particular payment or other benefit is not within the main charging words of TCA 1997, s 112 just quoted the possibility that it may still be taxable under Sch E by virtue of any of those added provisions has then to be considered as a separate matter.

There is usually little difficulty in accepting that any payments in cash as salaries, bonuses (including exceptional payment awards) whether contractual or non-contractual (see *Denny v Reed* 18 TC 254) round sum allowances (see *Ferguson v Noble* 7 TC 176, as discussed in *Marchioness Conyngham v Revenue Commissioners* I ITR 231) or reimbursement of personal expenses (*Sanderson v Durbridge* 36 TC 239) made to the holder of an office or employment are emoluments taxable under Sch E. The Revenue Commissioners have issued a precedent stating that allowances lodged to the credit card account of an employee are indistinguishable from wages lodged to the employee's bank account, a pronouncement which is beyond any dispute.

Difficulties can arise where an employee carries out tasks outside the normal scope of his duties. In *Fuge v McLelland* 36 ITC 571, a teacher who took night classes under a separate contract with the same local authority which employed her, was held to fall within Sch E in respect thereof. In *Mitchell and Eden v Ross* 40 TC 11 it was held that a hospital consultant, who was otherwise self-employed, was also held liable under Sch E in respect of fees for voluntarily undertaking domiciliary visits which did not form part of his consultancy contract.

In contrast to the above cases, *Donnelly v Williamson* [1982] STC 88 concerned a teacher who was reimbursed for the cost of attending parent's meetings outside school hours. It was held that the reimbursements were not referable to her duties as an employee. Possibly the taxpayer was assisted by the fact that her duties were the subject of a rigidly drawn, nationally-based service agreement, which clearly excluded the activities involved.

The Revenue Commissioners have issued a precedent to the effect that payments made to employees who introduce potential new employees are taxable on the basis that such payments 'arise from the employment'; this analysis may well be open to challenge, depending on the facts, given that such introductions would not normally form part of an employee's job description.

Nevertheless, it remains true that the greater bulk of litigation has centred on the words 'perquisites or profits whatsoever' which have been the cause of considerable litigation resulting in a number of important court decisions affecting the scope and limitations of Sch E. In order to get a better understanding of the types of payments or other benefits that may or may not be taxed under Sch E as perquisites or other profits of an office or employment, it is necessary to review a number of the more important tax cases on this subject.

It may be helpful to break down this subject under a number of subheadings described somewhat loosely either by reference to different principles which have emerged from the cases or by a common subject heading. It is to be noted that this division is somewhat approximate and arbitrary. A number of the cases are relevant under more than one subheading and various principles that have been established in earlier cases are seen to be referred to time and again in the judgments of later cases. These various subheadings now appear in **10.105–10.116**.

10.105 Perquisites taxable whether money or money's worth

It has been accepted for a long time that the words 'perquisites or profits whatsoever' cover a very wide range of payments or other benefits that may be made to or conferred on the holder of an office or employment. In *Tennant v Smith* 3 TC 158, Lord Watson made the statement that has been quoted directly or indirectly in many cases that followed. He said that the words denote something acquired which the acquirer becomes possessed of and can dispose of to his advantage, in other words, money or that which can be turned to pecuniary account.

Tennant v Smith made it clear that the main charging words of Sch E (now contained in TCA 1997, s 112) are only applicable to tax money or money's worth. It is accepted that unless the benefit or advantage acquired by the employee is capable of being turned to pecuniary account, ie converted into money, then it is not a perquisite or other profit of his office or employment. In *Tennant v Smith* it was held that the value of a residence as part of a bank premises which a bank manager was required by his employer to occupy was not a perquisite of his office. In his judgment, Lord McNaghten said:

> No doubt if the appellant had to find lodgings for himself he might have to pay for them. His income goes further because he is relieved from that expense. That the person is chargeable for income tax under Sch D, as well as under Sch E, not on what saves his pocket but on what goes into his pocket. And the benefit which the appellant derives from having a rent free house provided for him by the bank brings in nothing which can be reckoned up as a receipt or properly described as income.

Under current law, the provision by an employer of living accommodation for an employee normally results in the employee having additional income taxable under Sch E. This is not due to the main Sch E charging words in TCA 1997, s 112, but arises under the separate benefit in kind rules which come into operation when the employer incurs expense in providing a benefit for the employee in a form that cannot be converted into money (see **Division 10.2**).

In fact, there are many ways in which a perquisite or benefit may be given to an employee in a form that may be converted into cash. Examples are the transfer of ownership of an asset by an employer to an employee, allowing an employee to subscribe for shares in an employer company at a price below market value, the discharge by the employer of an employee's personal debt, the provision of vouchers, etc In any such case it is the market value of the perquisite or benefit on the date on which it is given that is taxable under Sch E, and not the cost to the employer of providing the benefit.

In *Wilkins v Rogerson* 39 TC 44, Mr Rogerson's employer company arranged for a tailor to provide certain employees with a suit overcoat or raincoat up to a cost of £15. The employee was to order the article and the tailor was to present the bill to the company. Mr Rogerson ordered a suit costing just under £15 and this amount was paid to the tailor by the company. The Crown assessed him under Sch E on £15 on the grounds that he had got the right to the payment of that amount. The Court of Appeal confirmed the Commissioners' finding that the emolument to be taxed was not the cost of the suit to the company but the price the employee would get if he sold it, ie its market value. In this case, the market value was less than the cost to the company, but this does not affect the principle; if the market value had exceeded the £15 cost to the company the higher figure would have been taken.

In *Wilkins v Rogerson*, the Crown had argued that the reasoning in two earlier cases – *Hartland v Diggines* 10 TC 247 and *Nicoll v Austin* 19 TC 531 – should be applied to support the assessment. Both those cases provide authority for the principle that, if an employer discharges a debt that is the personal liability of an employee then the employee must be treated as receiving emoluments in money or money's worth equivalent to the debt discharged. Lord Evershed MR rejected that argument. He held that it was only when the suit was delivered that Mr Rogerson had got something that was his own, ie the suit, and which he could convert into money. This was not a case in which he was entitled to call upon the company to pay some sum of money on his behalf. In this case, what the employee received was a present of a suit and until he received that he got nothing. It was the suit that was convertible into money's worth.

In *Hartland v Diggines* a company paid the income tax in respect of an employee's salary, although it had entered into no agreement, written or verbal with him to do so (note also *Perro v Mansworth (Insp of Taxes)* [2001] STC (SCD) 179, where the UK Special Commissioners held that a tax equalisation payment paid by an overseas employer was liable to tax in so far as it referred to emoluments which were themselves taxable).

The House of Lords held that the tax so paid must be treated as a Sch E emolument. In *Nicoll v Austin*, a managing director of a company (who happened to have a controlling interest in it) was requested by the company for its convenience and the prestige of its business to continue to reside in a large residence, which would otherwise have been too costly for him to maintain himself, on the understanding that the company undertook to pay all outgoings in respect of the house and to maintain the house and garden in proper condition. It was held that what the director had got from this arrangement in money's worth was the sum actually expended by the company on the upkeep, etc of the house and gardens, ie the amounts paid in discharge of liabilities personal to him.

In the Irish case of *Connolly v McNamara* 3 ITC 341, the respondent occupied a house as a weekly tenant of the Middleton Urban District Council. The rent payable by him under his letting agreement with the council was paid by the company which employed him. The company had entered into an arrangement with the council for the provision of houses for certain of its employees. The respondent was not obliged as a condition of his employment to live in the house. It was held by the High Court that the respondent was correctly assessable under Sch E on the rent paid by the company. Teevan J decided that, by contrast with the position in *Tennant v Smith*, it was the payments of rent which were provided by the company and not the house itself. Since the rent was a liability of the tenant under his agreement with the council, he held that the decision in *Hartland v Diggines* was directly in point and he would follow it.

In *Ableway Ltd v IRC* SpC 00294 (a National Insurance case), the UK Special Commissioners held that where an employer discharged school fees for its' employees' children, this was on the facts the discharge of a pecuniary liability of the employees concerned.

In *Glynn v IRC* [1990] STC 227, a Privy Council case concerning the Hong Kong equivalent of TCA 1997, s 112, it was held that where an employer assumed the legal liability for the school fees of an employee's children under the terms of his service contract, the sums paid to the school fell within the principle in *Hartland v Diggines*.

Although the decision contains some wide ranging observations, it may perhaps simply be accepted as authority for no more than the principle that money paid at the direction of an employee is equivalent to money paid to the employee.

Under general income tax principles, a taxpayer remains liable to tax on his income, even though he is legally bound to apply it for the benefit of a third party. Thus, in *Dolan v K* I ITR 656 a teaching nun remained liable on her earnings, even though she was obliged to hand over all of them to her order (see also *Parker v Chapman* 13 TC 677 and *Hibbert v Fysh* 40 ATC 220. In *Perkins v Warwick* 25 TC 419, it was held that an assignment of his future emoluments by an employee was an application, and not an alienation, of income (see also *Hadlee* [1993] STC 294, discussed at **4.501**). In *Smyth v Stretton* 5 TC 36, it was held that where employees were obliged to place part of their salary in a provident fund, that part remained taxable as their earnings under Sch E (contrast *Edwards v Roberts* 19 TC 618).

Similarly, in the earlier case of *Mahon v McLoughlin* 11 TC 83, the taxpayer was held to be taxable on that part of his earnings out of which he was obliged to pay the cost of his board and lodgings. Rowlatt J said:

> If a person is paid a wage with some advantage thrown in, you cannot add the advantage to the wage for the purpose of taxation unless that advantage can be turned into money. That is one proposition. But when you have a person paid a wage with the necessity – the contractual necessity if you like – to expend that wage in a particular way, then he must pay tax upon the gross wage, and no question of alienability or inalienability arises …

The Court of Session case of *Murray Group Holdings Ltd and others v Revenue and Customs Commissioners* [2016] STC 468 dealt with what is referred to as the 'redirection principle' and concerned the use of employee benefit trusts. The arrangement typically operated as follows. An Employees' Remuneration Trust ('the Principal Trust') was established. A company in the Murray Group which wished to benefit one of its employees made a cash payment to the Principal Trust in respect of that employee. The paying company recommended the trustee of the Principal Trust to resettle the sum in question on to a sub-trust, and would ask that the income and capital of the sub-trust should be applied in accordance with the wishes of the employee. The beneficiaries of the sub-trust were chosen by the employee, and were generally the members of his family. In practice the trustees of the sub-trusts invariably gave effect to the wishes of the employee. The employee would be appointed protector of the sub-trust, and the trustee of the sub-trust would then lend the employee the money that had been advanced to the sub-trust from, ultimately, his employer. The First-tier Tribunal held that the trustee of the Principal Trust had a genuine discretion as to how to apply the funds advanced to it, and the settlement on to the sub-trust merely represented the exercise of that discretion. Thus the benefit enjoyed by the employee and his family resulted from the exercise of a discretionary power by the trustee of the sub-trust. HMRC asserted that the cash payment made by the employing company to the trustee of the Principal Trust was in consideration of services by the employee, and thus had been earned by the employee. The employee was content to take the risk that he might not benefit if the trustee of the Principal Trust chose not to follow the recommendation of the employer. Nevertheless, the employer arranged for a letter of wishes from the relevant employee to be passed to the trustee of the Principal Trust, and also an application for a loan by the trustee of the sub-trust to the employee. HMRC's fundamental argument was that the cash payment to the Principal Trust was part of the remuneration package of the employee, comprising salary and bonuses; it had been earned for work done. The Court of Session agreed with that approach.

Lord Drummond Young noted at paras 56 and 57 of his decision in *Murray Group* that '...if income is derived from an employee's services qua employee, it is an emolument or earnings, and is thus assessable to income tax, even if the employee requests or agrees that it be redirected to a third party. That accords with common sense. If the law were otherwise, an employee could readily avoid tax by redirecting income to members of his family to meet outgoings that he would normally pay: for example, to a trust for his wife, as in *Hadlee* [this is a reference to *Hadlee v CIR* [1993] STC 294 which is mentioned earlier], or to trustees to pay for his children's education or the outgoings on the family home. It follows that, if the principle applies, it is irrelevant that the redirection is through the medium of trust arrangements. It is equally irrelevant that the trustees who receive the payment, at whatever remove, exercise a genuine discretion as to what happens to the funds. The funds are ultimately derived as consideration for the employee's services, and on that basis they are properly to be considered emoluments or earnings. Indeed, in *Brumby v Milner*, the existence of a discretion in the trustees as to the benefits taken by employees was taken as a factor pointing towards the conclusion that the payments were derived from employment ... This principle is ultimately simple and straightforward—indeed, so straightforward that in cases where elaborate trust or analogous relationships are set up it can easily be overlooked.' It must be noted that Lord Drummond Young goes on at para 58 to note 'In applying this principle to the facts of a particular case, one further general legal principle is of importance. In assessing the liability of a transaction to taxation, it is imperative in every case to determine the true nature of the transaction, viewed realistically: *Barclays Mercantile Business Finance Ltd v Mawson (Inspector of Taxes)* [2004] UKHL 51, [2005] STC 1, [2005] 1 AC 684 (at [32], [36]), quoting *Collector of Stamp Revenue v Arrowtown Assets Ltd* [2003] HKCFA 46, (2003) 6 ITLR 454 (at [35]) ...'. The reference to a review of the facts 'realistically' is important as arguments could be made that this requires a review of the facts in a manner other than their legal form which is something that the Irish courts may not be inclined to do other than in cases involving the general anti-avoidance rule.

By way of contrast in *Reade v Brearley* (see **1.408**) the taxpayer acted as the headmaster of a school established by a congregation of secular priests, of which he was a member. The congregation had agreed that none of their members should receive any personal remuneration. Subsequently, new government regulations required that all teachers should be employed under written contracts. As a consequence, an agreement was executed, formally appointing the taxpayer to the headmastership at an annual salary. In the accounts of the school, the salary was charged as an expense, but a corresponding amount was entered as a donation to the congregation; no cash was actually paid to the taxpayer. The court rejected the Revenue's contention that the taxpayer had received a taxable salary and had subsequently applied it for the benefit of his congregation. It was held that the agreement was purely cosmetic and that the 'salary' always belonged to the congregation (in effect a 'sham' but an innocent one – see **1.408**).

In *Heaton v Bell* 46 TC 211 the taxpayer elected to join a scheme whereby employees were provided with a car for their personal use only, in return for what was described as a 'weekly reduction' in their wages. An employee could leave the scheme on giving two-weeks' notice, after which the 'reduction' would no longer operate. The House of Lords (Lord Reid dissenting) held that the 'reduction' was merely an application of the taxpayer's wages and thus had to be added back to ascertain his gross, taxable remuneration. However, Lord Reid and two other Law Lords (Lords Morris of Borth-y-Gest and Diplock) also held that, failing this, the benefit of the car would have been 'convertible' because the taxpayer could have enjoyed additional wages by (a) withdrawing from the scheme (per Lords Reid and Morris) or (b) withdrawing from or rejecting the scheme (per Lord Diplock).

In Richardson v Worrall; Westall v McDonald [1985] STC 693 the Inland Revenue argued that the benefit of private petrol was convertible into money because the taxpayer could either siphon the petrol out of his car or use it to provide lifts to the public for a fee. The court rejected this proposition, on the basis that the Revenue were not allowed to assume dishonest or unlawful actions on the part of an employee. In the same case the taxpayer had the choice of having a personal expense either (i) incurred by and paid for by his employer or (ii) incurred by himself and subsequently reimbursed by his employer. Option (i), taken in isolation clearly fell under the protection of the principle in *Tennant v Smith*, while option (ii) equally was clearly a taxable emolument. Applying *Heaton v Bell*, Scott J held that because the taxpayer could have foregone option (i) and taken option (ii) instead, option (i) was thereby 'convertible' into cash and was thus itself a taxable emolument.

In *James H Donald (Darvel) Ltd & Ors v Revenue and Customs Commissioners* [2015] UKUT 514 (TCC). A company was set up, 'Services', and the shares of which were issued to the company, 'Darvel', which employed a director and a number of employees. The Upper Tribunal held the total sums received by the subscribers from Services, whether by wage or salary or dividend, represented emoluments of their employment with Darvel.

In *Revenue and Customs Commissioners v Smith & Williamson Corporate Services Ltd & Ano*r [2015] UKUT 666 (TCC) Warren J noted that the word 'from' in the expression 'earnings from employment' in s 9(1) of ITEPA (Income Tax (Earnings and Pensions) Act) denoted a relevant link or connection between the payment to the employee and their employment, and furthermore a causal connection between the payment and the employment.

In *Revenue and Customs Commissioners v Apollo Fuels Ltd & Ors* [2016] EWCA Civ 157 a corporate group leased cars to employees on arm's length commercial terms, including lease charges at full market value in order to enable the employees to carry out their duties. HMRC argued that, although the employees did not derive any financial benefit from the lease and paid a full price by way of lease charges, they were still chargeable to income tax. The Court of Appeal noted that the word 'benefit', without a definition altering its ordinary meaning intended that, before a charge to income tax arose then there had to be a benefit to the employee in the ordinary sense of that word. The Court of Appeal held that the employees in the present case received no benefit.

With effect from 31 January 2008, TCA 1997, s 118B statutorily enshrined the principle in *Heaton v Bell* by providing that the remuneration foregone under a salary sacrifice arrangement is to be taxed as emoluments of the employee TCA 1997, s 118B(2)(b)). However the section also provides that in limited circumstances a salary sacrifice shall not be treated as an application of emoluments. For these purposes, a salary sacrifice is defined as any arrangement under which an employee forgoes the right to receive any part of their remuneration due under their terms or contract of employment, and in return their employer agrees to provide him or her with a benefit

(TCA 1997, s 118B(1)). The exemptions apply to salary sacrifice arrangements specifically approved by the Revenue Commissioners in relation to:

(i) travel passes issued by an approved transport provider under TCA 1997, s 118(5A) (see **10.204**);

(ii) exempt shares appropriated to employees under an approved profit sharing scheme under TCA 1997, Pt 17, Ch 1 (see **11.4**) (TCA 1997, s 118B(2)(a)); and

(iii) bicycles and safety equipment within TCA 1997, s 118(5G) (see **10.210**).

These exceptions will not apply if there is an arrangement or scheme in place whereby the employee is recompensed, wholly or partly, by the provision of the otherwise relevant benefit together with a compensating payment (TCA 1997, s 118B(4)). Furthermore, the exemptions will also be disapplied where a salary sacrifice agreement is entered into in respect of any right, bonus, commission or any other emolument which arises to an individual after the end of the year of assessment concerned (TCA 1997, s 118B(5)). Finally, the exemptions will not apply where an otherwise relevant benefit is provided to the spouse, civil partner or dependant of, or a person connected with, the individual who has entered into a salary sacrifice arrangement (TCA 1997, s 118B(3)).

Where an employer and employee agree that the employee's level of remuneration will be reduced in the future but that the employer will instead provide a benefit it would not appear that this arrangement constitutes a salary sacrifice under general principles or by virtue of TCA 1997, s 118B; this follows, since no contractual right to the remuneration arises in these circumstances. A discretionary bonus which an employee has indicated in advance that he would wish to be paid in whole or part as a benefit, would not appear to be a salary sacrifice since the employee never acquires entitlement to the cash sum in question. Where there is an entitlement to a bonus but there is an option to take all or part thereof as an employer's contribution to a pension, then even if the option to convert the bonus arises prior to the right to receive the remuneration, this would seem to fall foul of the decision in *Heaton v Bell* 46 TC 211 as now embodied in (TCA 1997, s 118B).

For the treatment of salary sacrifices in the context of pension schemes, see the discussion at **16.108** and in the context of Approved Profit Sharing Schemes see **11.402**.

In the case of the award of cash vouchers, these will give rise to an emolument equal to their cash value. In the case of non-cash vouchers, the realisable value may be zero (eg if they can only be used in exchange for personal services and are non-assignable) or may reflect the realisable value of the goods which they can be used to acquire (eg shopping vouchers). Similar considerations apply to bonus bonds. The benefit-in-kind rules will however normally bring into charge the actual cost to the employer of providing the voucher, bonus bond, etc: see **10.205**.

10.106 The source of emoluments

Decisions in a number of tax cases have shown that a person holding an office or employment may receive payments or other benefits in money or money's worth which, although he would not have received them if he had not held the position, do not amount to perquisites or other profits of the office or employment. In the words of Younger LJ in *Cowan v Seymour* 7 TC 372 the employment may be a '*causa sine qua non*' of the benefit but not the '*causa causans*'; it is only when the employment is the '*causa causans*' that the amount is taxable. In *Hochstrasser v Mayes* 38 TC 673, Lord Radcliffe expressed this alternatively by holding that while it is not sufficient to render a payment assessable that an employee would not have received it unless he had been an employee, it is assessable if paid to him in return for 'his acting, as or being, an employee'.

In *Hochstrasser v Mayes* in a passage which Viscount Simmonds in the House of Lords considered, in the same case, to be a good summary of the law on the point. Upjohn J said:

> In my judgment, the authorities show this, that it is a question to be answered in the light of the particular facts of every case whether or not a particular payment is or is not a profit arising from the employment … not every payment made to an employee is necessarily made to him as a profit arising from his employment. Indeed, in my judgment the authorities show that for there to be a profit arising from the employment the payment must be made in reference to the services the employee renders by virtue of his office, and it must be something in the nature of a reward for services past, present or future.

In that case, a company operated a housing scheme for married employees whom it transferred from one part of the country to another. Under the scheme an employee might be offered a loan to assist in the purchase of a house, and provided the house was maintained in good repair, if on being transferred the employee incurred any loss in selling the house for less than its original purchase price, the employee would be compensated for the loss. Mr Mayes entered into an agreement under the scheme and, having sold his house at a loss on a later transfer, he received a payment from the company to compensate him for the loss. He had not known of the housing scheme when he joined the company. It was held that this payment was not taxable under Sch E as a profit accruing to Mr Mayes by virtue of his office or employment.

The House of Lords considered the scheme in its own right, ie as something independent of the employee's contract of service. Thus, Viscount Simonds spoke of the scheme as a 'bargain and as good bargains should be thought by each side to be worthwhile. Accordingly, the source of a payment was the housing agreement itself. Lord Cohen held that the housing agreement constituted a genuine bargain, advantageous no doubt to the [taxpayer] but also not without its advantages to the [employer]. He added: 'I see no reason for disregarding [the agreement] as the source of a payment sought to be taxed'. Lord Cohen also emphasised that the sum was received 'not under the [taxpayer's] service agreement but under an indemnity contained in the housing agreement'. Viscount Simonds and Lord Radcliffe both emphasised that an employee's salary was not reduced as a result of his decision to enter the scheme; presumably, if this had in fact been the case, the housing agreement would then have been properly regarded as forming part of the employee's terms and conditions of service In *Laidler v Perry*, Lord Hodson described *Hochstrasser v Mayes* as a case which 'depended on its own peculiar facts, there being a collateral agreement between the employer and the employee quite outside their contracts of service.

Lord Radcliffe considered on the other hand that the scheme was 'in substance a free benefit' but held that the payment under the scheme was 'no more taxable than a profit from [the taxpayer's] employment than would be a payment out of a provident or a distress fund set up by an employer for the benefit of employees whose personal circumstances might justify assistance'. Viscount Simonds considered that there was nothing express or implicit in the agreement between the company and Mr Mayes that suggested that the payment was a reward for services except the single fact of the relationship of the parties. He stated that it was clear from *IRC v Duke of Westminster* 19 TC 490 that relationship alone would not justify such a conclusion. The employer/ employee relationship may have been the '*causa sine qua non*' of the payment, but in his view it was not in this case the '*causa causans*'. The conclusions of the House of Lords in this respect are discussed further in **10.107**.

The distinction between 'causa causans' and 'causa sine qua non' is neatly illustrated in *McManus v Griffiths* [1997] STC 1089. In that case, the taxpayer was an employee of a golf club. She was required as part of her duties to provide catering services at the club. She was responsible *inter alia* for purchasing, preparing and presenting the food, for hiring and paying catering staff and for setting prices. She was entitled to the profits and had to bear any losses arising from the catering operation. Lightman J held accordingly that the taxpayer was self-employed in relation to the catering operations (see **10.103**). Furthermore, while the opportunity to carry on self-employment was attributable to her employment (ie the employment was the *causa sine qua non* of her profits), the profits themselves arose out of her self-employed activities (ie the employment was not the *causa causans* of her profits).

The decision in *Hochstrasser* may be compared with that in *Clayton v Gothorp* 47 TC 168, where the principal sum due under a loan agreement between the taxpayer and her employer was waived once the taxpayer had completed a prescribed period of service. The benefit of the waiver was held to be taxable under Sch E. Although the loan agreement was legally distinct from the employee's contract of service, the consideration for the waiver was the completion of the period of service by the employee. The benefit was clearly consideration for past services, and therefore necessarily arose 'from' the employment.

While Upjohn J's words in *Hochstrasser v Mayes* above have been quoted as the basis of, or in the reasoning leading up to, the decision in a number of other cases, they should not be taken as a substitute for the actual words in the Act. In *Laidler v Perry* 42 TC 351, Lord Reid in the course of his judgment in the House of Lords said:

> There is a wealth of authority on this matter, and various glosses on or paraphrases of the words in the Act appear in judicial opinions including speeches in this House. No doubt they were helpful in the circumstances of the cases in which they were used, but in the end we must always return to the words in the statute and answer the question – did this profit arise from the employment? The answer will be no if it arose from something else.

Laidler v Perry concerned a case of a group of companies which gave their employees and pensioners every Christmas a gift voucher to be used at a shop of their choice for the purchase of goods up to the value of £10. The appellant had relied on the decision in *Hochstrasser v Mayes*. He had submitted that the only reasonable conclusion from the evidence was that the gift of the vouchers did not constitute a reward for services but rather a gesture of Christmas goodwill. This argument was rejected and the decision of the Special Commissioners that the vouchers were given in return for services was upheld. Lord Reid went on to say:

> I think that, although the word 'reward' has been used in many of the cases, it is not apt to include all the cases which can fall within the statutory words. To give only one instance, it is clear that a sum given to an employee in the hope or exception that the gift will produce good service by him in future is taxable. But one can hardly be said to reward a man for something which he has not yet done and may never do.

The concept of 'reward for services' also seems to be particularly inapt to cover cases where a payment relates to a change in the terms or conditions of the employment.

In *Hamblett v Godfrey* [1987] STC 60, payments made to member of GCHQ in recognition of the withdrawal of their rights to join a trade union were held to constitute emoluments. Neill LJ said:

> The removal of the rights involved changes in the conditions of service. The payment was in recognition of the changes in the conditions of service. I have been driven to the conclusion that the source of the payment was the employment. It was paid because of the employment and because of the changes in the conditions of employment and for no other reason. It was referable to the employment and to nothing else. Accordingly, in my judgment, the [sum] was a taxable emolument …

Similarly, the concept of 'reward for services' would not cover the case of an inducement payment made by a third party who could not benefit from the employee's future services and who accordingly, could not in any sense be said to be attempting to reward them. Thus, in *Shilton v Wilmshurst* [1991] STC 88, a footballer was paid a large sum by his current employer to induce him to sign for another club. Lord Templeman commented:

> … an emolument arises from employment if it is provided as a reward or inducement for the employee to remain or become an employee and not for something else.

The Revenue Commissioners do take the point that Upjohn J's dictum is too narrowly framed (*Tax Briefing 32*). In fact, Lord Templeman's formulation is itself too narrow, being clearly framed with regard to the specific facts of the *Shilton* case. Thus, payments made to an individual for having been or having acted as an employee are clearly also taxable emoluments: see *Brumby v Milner*, discussed at **10.100**.

In *Sports Club and others v Insp of Taxes* [2000] STC (SCD) 443 it was held that payments made *inter alia* in respect of promotional ('image') rights by the employer of a sportsman did not relate to the services which he was required to render under his employment contract and accordingly were not liable as emoluments under general principles.

In *O'Leary v McKinlay* [1991] STC 492, the taxpayer was a professional footballer employed by Arsenal Football Club Ltd. His previous contract of employment having come to an end, the taxpayer decided to negotiate his new contract in what he hoped would be a tax-efficient manner. To this end, a third party established a Jersey trust of which the taxpayer was the sole life tenant. The capital settled by the third party was purely nominal in amount. However, Arsenal proceeded to lend the Jersey trustees the sum of £266,000 free of interest and repayable on demand. The trustees then invested this amount in a deposit account at a Jersey bank. The interest earned on this account was approximately £29,000 pa, to all of which the taxpayer was beneficially entitled. This figure had been taken into account when setting the level of the taxpayer's emoluments under his employment contract. Clearly, the taxpayer's position had to be protected in these circumstances; accordingly, the employment contract was terminable at his option if Arsenal demanded repayment of their loan to the trustees.

The net effect of these arrangements in economic terms was to leave the taxpayer in the same position as if he had negotiated a straightforward contract of employment. On a strict legal analysis however, the taxpayer had transformed part of what would otherwise have been wages into income arising under an overseas trust. The taxpayer contention was that this income arose from a foreign possession (namely the underlying Jersey bank account (see *Baker v Archer-Shee* discussed at **15.301**) and was therefore eligible for the remittance basis since the taxpayer was non-UK domiciled (the equivalent Irish provisions are discussed at **Division 13**). The whole point of the scheme, naturally, lay in the fact that the taxpayer did not remit any such income to the UK, thus (it was hoped) escaping tax entirely on the amount of £29,000.

Vinelott J in the High Court upheld the Revenue's contention that the trust income constituted emoluments of the taxpayer's employment, chargeable under Sch E and not under the UK equivalent of Sch D Case III. The learned judge stated:

> The practical effect of these arrangements was that the taxpayer became entitled to receive the interest on the deposit with the bank so long and only so long as he continued play for the club. Of course, in theory the club might have called on the trustee to repay the loan during the currency of the agreement and the taxpayer might nonetheless have decided not to terminate the agreement; and the club might have left the loan outstanding even though the agreement expired or was terminated by agreement on some ground other than a demand for repayment of the loan by the club. But these possibilities are merely theoretical. The scheme was set up in order to provide the taxpayer with additional income while he continued to play for the club under the terms of the agreement and for no other purpose.

The decision seems to be correct since the payments would not have been received unless the taxpayer had been an employee of Arsenal; further, the payments were not received in respect of any consideration provided by the taxpayer other than his services; they were not actuated by altruistic or disinterested motives on the part of the employer who directly financed them; on the contrary, as a substitute for wages, they were clearly designed to reward the services of the taxpayer.

The case is primarily of interest in demonstrating that the courts will look at the substance of the matter in determining the source of an emolument *inter alia*. This does not mean that the courts will ignore the legal rights and obligations arising under the arrangements under review, but that they will look at the practical consequences of those arrangements taken as a whole. Thus, for example, if Arsenal had agreed to leave the loan outstanding for a fixed period, irrespective of whether or not the taxpayer continued in his employment it would have been much more difficult to argue that the trust income derived from the employment (ie since it would have been legally due whether or not the taxpayer was an employee at the time: compare *IRC v Duke of Westminster* 19 TC 490, discussed in Ward: Taxation of Contractual Termination Payments 1998 ITR 407). Naturally, such an arrangement would normally be commercially impracticable. In Ireland, even if such a scheme were to succeed, it would be necessary to consider *inter alia* the provisions of TCA 1997, s 806 (**Division 17**).

In their statement on vehicle leasing issued on 21 July 1981, the Revenue Commissioners dealt with the situation where a trader pays excess leasing charges in respect of a vehicle in order to enable the lessor to provide the vehicle at an undervalue to an employee or director at the end of the leasing period. The Revenue Commissioners state that the individual 'may be liable under the provisions of Sch E on any benefit he obtains'. It is clear that the source of the emolument for the employee would be the arrangements made and funded by the employer. Accordingly, it would normally follow that such an emolument arose 'from' the employment. The benefit-in-kind provisions could also be relevant if these gave rise to a higher tax liability on the employee (see **10.203**).

10.107 Voluntary payments

A person holding an office or employment may receive payments or other benefits in money's worth to which he has no legal right under his contract of service. The fact that such payments or benefits are given to him entirely voluntarily on the part of the giver, not necessarily the employer, does not of itself mean that they are not taxable under

Sch E. Any voluntary payment that is made to a person by virtue only of his office or employment (ie on account of his having been/acted as or being/acting as or becoming/agreeing to act as an employee) is taxable. On the other hand, a payment made on purely personal, compassionate or altruistic grounds is not taxable as an emolument.

In Wing v O'Connell 1 ITC 170, a jockey who had just won a race received from the horse's owner a sum of £400 as a present. The jockey was normally remunerated for each race by a scale fee fixed by the Turf Club and had no entitlement to the present. However, the Supreme Court held that the sum of £400 was an emolument which accrued to the jockey by reason of his vocation and as a reward for his services and should, therefore, be included in computing his income.

A similar decision was reached in the UK case of *Calvert v Wainwright* 27 TC 475 where a taxi driver was employed by a company receiving a definite wage and tips were no part of the bargain. It was held that he was assessable under Sch E on the tips which he received from passengers since a tip is in the ordinary way given as remuneration for services rendered. It follows that waiters in hotels and restaurants, hotel porters, etc are also taxable in respect of tips which they receive. In practice, it is usual for a round sum to be agreed as the estimate of the total tips taxable for any year.

The fine distinction between a payment made to the employee for no other reason than that he is an employee and a payment made on personal grounds was expressed as follows by Atkinson J in the *Calvert* case:

> Suppose somebody who has the same taxi every day, which comes in the morning as a matter of course to take him to his work, and then takes him home at night. The ordinary tip given in those circumstances would be something which would be assessable, but supposing at Christmas, or, when the man is going for a holiday, the hirer says: 'You have been very attentive to me, here is a 10s note,' he would be making a present, and I should say it would not be assessable because it has been given to the man because of his qualities, his faithfulness and the way he has stuck to the passenger. In those circumstances, it would, in my opinion, be a payment of an exceptional kind.

A number of cases in this area also emphasise the principle that the question of the taxability of a receipt must be resolved from the standpoint of the employee. Thus, for example, whatever the motives or purposes of the payer, the receipt will be an emolument if it arises on foot of a custom or practice which attaches to the employment (the regular tip paid to a taxi driver discussed above in *Calvert v Wainwright* being an archetypal example) To put it somewhat simplistically the test is: does the receipt 'come with the job?'

Thus, *Herbert v McQuade* 4 TC 489 was concerned with an annual grant of money paid to a beneficed clergyman out of the diocesan fund which could be used by the diocesan council to supplement the stipends of clergy within the diocese. It was held that the appellant had received the grants as perquisites of his office taxable under Sch E. Sir Richard Collins MR said:

> That seems to me to be the test; and if we once get to this, that it has come to him by virtue of his office, accrued to him in virtue of his office, it seems to me that it is not negatived, that it is not impossible merely by reason of the fact that there was no legal obligation on the part of the persons who contributed the money, to pay it.

Similarly, in *Cooper v Blakiston* 5 TC 347 it was held that the Easter offerings paid by a church to its vicar accrued to him by reason of his office (see also *Corbett v Duff* 23 TC 763 where a lump sum benefit received by a footballer was held to be taxable since it was customary and expected; in other words 'it came with the job').

In *Cooper v Blakiston,* Lord Ashbourne observed:

> It was suggested that the offerings were made as personal gifts to the vicar as a mark of esteem and respect. Such reasons no doubt played their part in obtaining and increasing the amount of the offerings, but I cannot doubt that they were given to the vicar as vicar, and that they formed part of the profits occurring by reason of his office.

In *Wright v Boyce* 38 TC 160, a huntsman received presents of cash every Christmas, generally from followers of the hunt. It was held that all such gifts (except those received from persons unconnected with the hunt) were taxable emoluments. Jenkins LJ said:

> … [the custom] is a custom to make presents of cash at Christmas time to the person for the time being holding the office or employment of huntsman. It is the huntsman as such by virtue of his office or employment who is the object of the custom.

In *Reed v Seymour* 11 TC 625, the taxpayer was a professional cricketer who had given long and distinguished service to the Kent Cricket Club. He was granted a benefit on the understanding that he allowed the proceeds to be invested in the name of trustees of the club during the pleasure of the committee. It was, however, always the practice for such benefits to be handed over to the cricketer concerned at the end of his career. On the facts of this case, it was held that the benefit was not assessable as a profit or perquisite arising from his employment but was a personal gift or testimonial by way of recognition of the pleasure that had been afforded over the years to the patrons of the club due to the qualities of his play (compare *Moorhouse v Dooland*, discussed at **10.110**).

In *Cowan v Seymour* 7 TC 372 money paid by the shareholders of a company to its secretary and liquidator out of the surplus available for distribution in the liquidation after his office had ceased was held to be in the nature of a testimonial. The facts that the payment was a 'once off' sum, payable after the office had terminated, and was unsolicited, all indicated that it was in the nature of a personal gift; note also *IRC v Morris* 44 TC 685.

In *Ball v Johnson* 47 TC 155, a payment made to an employee by his employer to mark his success in his professional examinations was held not to be a taxable emolument but made to mark a meritorious achievement. In a 1982 decision, the Appeal Commissioners held that payments made routinely to bank officials to compensate them for their distress following armed raids were not taxable emoluments.

In *Mulvey v Coffey* I ITR 618, an additional sum of £1,000 paid to the retiring President of University College, Dublin, on top of the maximum pension and gratuity to which he was entitled under the relevant statute of the College was held to be non-taxable. In *Mulvey v Coffey*, emphasis was placed on the fact that the governing body of the College had remunerated Dr Coffey as fully as it could and that, under the College statutes, it could neither remunerate him further for his services nor increase his pension or gratuity on his retirement. The additional £1,000 paid out of the general funds of the College was considered to be in the nature of a personal gift or testimonial to him on his relinquishing office so that it was not taxable as an emolument of that office.

In *Moore v Griffiths* 48 TC 388, for playing in the World Cup, Bobby Moore received match fees and expenses paid by the Football Association through his club which deducted PAYE. Before the Cup began, the Association resolved to pay a bonus to be divided among the members of the team in the event of their winning the cup, but that was not known to the appellant until after it was won. This last fact coupled with the facts that this was a most exceptional event with no foreseeable likelihood of recurrence (as subsequent events have amply demonstrated!) and that there had been no advance expectation of this additional reward, led to the decision that the payment was not taxable. Brightman J said:

> I think it would be wrong to regard the payment to Mr Moore as being something in the nature of a reward or remuneration for services. The true purpose of the payment was to mark his participation in an exceptional event, namely, the winning of the World Cup Championship … In other words, the payment had the quality of a testimonial or accolade rather than the quality of remuneration for services rendered.

In *Bridges v Bearsley* 37 TC 289 a gift of shares made by the principal shareholders to a director who had played a key role in building up the business was held to be non-taxable. The case is discussed more fully at **10.113**.

In *O'Reilly v Casey* I ITR 601 the taxpayer's father bequeathed him 10 per cent of the income from the properties held in his estate (plus a percentage of the sale proceeds or market value, as appropriate, of any property disposed of). The bequest was payable only for so long as the taxpayer continued to manage the properties, but the estate trustees could only remove him from his responsibilities for 'good cause'. The Supreme Court held that the bequest was a gift subject to a condition, and not a reward for services rendered. The Supreme Court's decision relied primarily on the fact that there was no contract between the taxpayer and the estate trustees (see also *Baxendale v Murphy* 9 TC 46, but note *Dale v IRC* 34 TC 468).

Hochstrasser v Mayes 38 TC 673, the facts of which are related in **10.106** is a difficult case. As discussed above, the House of Lords expressed the view that in the scheme there was a genuine bargain, distinct from the contract of services. On that analysis, the source of the profit made by the taxpayer was the consideration given by him under the scheme and not the employment. However the House also made it clear overall that even if the payment was a gift, then it was made to alleviate potential hardship and not to reward services.

In fact, it might have appeared that the approach in cases such as *Wright v Boyce* should have proven fatal to the taxpayer in *Hochstrasser*. If the sum in question were to be properly regarded as a free benefit, then it was one which was offered to a very wide range of employees and of which prospective employees might well be aware (although the taxpayer in this particular instance was not so aware), making it look suspiciously like a perk of the job. On this basis, the reason why the taxpayer received the sum was simply for being an employee and for nothing else. The House of Lords emphasized that employees in similar organisations which did not operate a housing compensation scheme received similar remuneration to the taxpayer; arguably all that this proved was that the taxpayer's employer offered additional perks compared to its competitors. In fact the House of Lords seem to have considered that because the benefit of the housing scheme was not provided as a substitute for salary, and was therefore not a reward for services in the sense of disguised remuneration, therefore it was not taxable. This was a flawed approach and arguably led to an incorrect decision.

A number of employers operate staff suggestion schemes under which employees may be rewarded for suggestions which result or may result in improved performance by the employer. Depending on the facts, it may not follow that payments under such schemes fall within Sch E. While the employee would not be in a position to receive such a payment if he was not an employee, the payment may not be made in return for being or acting as an employee where the suggestion falls outside the scope of his duties ie the employment will be the *causa sine qua non* but not the *causa causans* of the payment (note *Donnelly v Williamson*, discussed at **10.104**). The Revenue take the view that all such payments strictly fall within Sch E and as such are liable to PAYE. However, prior to 1 January 2004 in practice, the Revenue did not seek to tax those payments where certain conditions were met. In broad terms, the main conditions required that there should be a formally constituted scheme, the relevant suggestion should fall outside the scope of the employee's normal duties (ascertained in accordance with Revenue guidelines), the awards should be related to the financial benefits of the proposal (unless £100 or less) and should not exceed 10 per cent of the employee's gross salary for the year in which the suggestion is adopted; there was an overriding limit of £5,000 per employee per annum. The Revenue reserved the right to take any appropriate steps where they consider tax avoidance is involved (*Tax Briefing 32*).

10.108 Pre-commencement or post-cessation payments

In *Bray v Best* [1989] STC 159, the employee's company had set up a trust to buy shares in the company on behalf of the employees. In 1979, following a take-over, the employees were re-employed by Fisons plc. Shortly before the re-employments became effective, the trustees wound up the trust and distributed the net proceeds among the eligible employees, based on length of service and salary levels. In 1979–80, Mr Best, who had been employed by the company from 1958 until the take-over, received payments from the trustees. The Special Commissioners determined that although the sums derived from the employment, they could not be attributed to any year other than 1979–80, and since the employment had ceased, there was no source from which the emoluments arose in the year of assessment; accordingly, there could be no charge to tax under Sch E.

This decision should be contrasted with that in *Heasman v Jordan* 35 TC 518 where, on the particular facts, it was held that a 'one-off' lump sum payment specifically designed to compensate an employee for under-remuneration in previous years could be allocated to those years (see also *Griffin v Standish* [1995] STC 825). As explained in **10.102** above, an 'earnings' basis generally applies for Irish Sch E purposes; however, lump sum receipts, which cannot be related to earlier (or future) years can only be treated as arising in the year in which they fall due.

As a consequence of the decision in *Bray v Best* TCA 1997, s 112 now provides that emoluments arising in a tax year before the employment commences will be taxed in the tax year in which the employment commences and emoluments arising in a tax year after the employment has ceased will be taxed in the year in which the employment ceased. Rather oddly, s 112 defines 'emoluments' for these purposes as 'anything assessable to income tax under Sch E'. The whole point of *Bray v Best* however was that the emoluments in question were not so assessable!

10.109 Payments on commencement of employment

As already discussed in **10.108**, a payment made to induce a prospective employee to accept a new employment will represent a taxable emolument. On the other hand, if a payment is made for a consideration outside the employment, or in recognition of a factor other than the mere taking up of the employment, it will not represent a taxable emolument. In some cases, such a payment may however give rise to other tax considerations, eg potential exposure to capital gains tax if the consideration for the payment is the loss or surrender of goodwill (see eg *Hose v Warwick* 10 TC 459). The 'golden handshake' provisions, discussed in **10.111** may also sometimes be relevant.

In *Jarrold v Boustead* 41 TC 701, a lump sum of £3,000 paid by a Rugby League club to Mr Boustead as a signing on fee was held to be a once and for all inducement to him to give up for ever his amateur status and was not paid in consideration for undertaking to play rugby football for the Hull Football Club. In reaching this conclusion, the Court of Appeal held that, to ascertain the nature of the signing on fee, it was necessary to look at the bye-laws of the Rugby League. Under bye-law 24, a player was entitled to receive a signing on fee only when first registering as a professional player; apart from giving up his amateur status for life, he could not on any subsequent occasion receive a signing on fee for any other club.

In *Glantre Engineering Ltd v Goodhand* [1983] STC 1, the Chancery Division upheld a decision of the Special Commissioners that a payment of £10,000 by a company to a chartered accountant working for an international firm of accountants was an inducement held out to him to enter into the company's services, formed part of his contract of service and was properly charged to tax under Sch E. The Crown contended that the real purpose of the payment was to obtain the accountant's services in the future on the terms agreed and that payments made under agreed terms of appointment were, on established principles, chargeable to tax under Sch E. For the taxpayer company (taxed under the PAYE regulations), it was argued that the payment was separable from the contract of service and was made to compensate the accountant for sacrificing his professional status as an independent chartered accountant and for giving up the chance of a partnership in the international firm. The Special Commissioners held that the taxpayer's argument did not justify a conclusion that the payment in this case was made otherwise than in consideration for the future services of the accountant. The court held that the Commissioners' decision was a reasonable one based on, and not inconsistent with, the facts before them; in essence the payment was made to compensate the taxpayer for the risk entailed in taking up his new employment rather than to compensate him for a loss of a substantive asset or advantage.

Another case concerning a chartered accountant changing his position was *Pritchard v Arundale* 47 TC 680. Mr Arundale was a senior partner in a firm of chartered accountants who agreed in 1962 to serve a company as joint managing director for seven-years commencing on 1 January 1963 at a salary of £5,500 per year. He only consented to accept the position if a shareholding in the company was provided for him. The service agreement to which he, the company and Mr L (who held most of the 51,000 shares in the company) were parties, provided that in consideration of Mr Arundale's undertaking to serve the company, Mr L would forthwith after the execution of the agreement transfer to him 4,000 shares. The Special Commissioners decided that the transfer of the 4,000 shares was not in the nature of a reward for future services, thus effectively accepting the contention that the shares were compensation to the taxpayer for the loss of his established position. It was held that there was ample evidence on which the Commissioners could reach their conclusion.

In distinguishing Mr Arundale's case from that of the chartered accountant in the *Glantre Engineering Ltd* case, Warner J noted three main points. First, in Mr Arundale's case there was a transfer of shares by a third party and not a payment by the employer. Secondly, Mr Arundale was not merely changing from one employment to another, but was exchanging the status of a senior partner in his firm for that of joint managing director and shareholder in a company. Thirdly, the tripartite agreement under which he entered the service of the company and received the shares was so framed that he was entitled to the transfer of the shares 'forthwith' after executing the agreement but was not to enter the service of the company until some months later. He might, for example, have died after receiving the shares but before commencing his office with the company. None of these factors were conclusive; it is to be noted that both these cases were ones where the court could not set aside the Commissioners' decision unless it was inconsistent with the only reasonable conclusion that could be drawn from the evidence (see *Edwards v Bairstow* 36 TC 207).

Pritchard v Arundale was distinguished in *Shilton v Wilmshurst* [1991] STC 88 (see **10.106**); in the latter case the only consideration provided by the taxpayer was an undertaking to take up his new employment. It followed that the payment which he received was referable to his future employment and to nothing else.

In *O'Connor v Keleghan* [2001] 2 IR 490, the taxpayer (K), disposed of his shares in G Ltd to S Ltd as part of a takeover under which G Ltd became a subsidiary of S Ltd. On the same date as the share purchase agreement, K executed a service agreement with the Purchaser as required by the provisions of the share purchase agreement. Under the service agreement Mr Keleghan was bound to serve the Purchaser for a term of 18 months and thereafter until termination by either party giving three-months' notice to the other of them. Whilst the agreement provided that K 'shall serve the company as sales director' it was also stated that:

> In pursuance of his duties hereunder [K] shall perform such services for subsidiary companies or any parent company and (without further remuneration unless otherwise agreed) accept and hold for the duration of this agreement such offices or appointments in such subsidiary companies as the general manager may from time to time reasonably require.

In a side-letter K acknowledged that £250,000 of the consideration paid to him under the share purchase agreement 'was paid as an inducement for me to enter into the service contract and accordingly in the event of my not complying with the terms of the said service contract the [sum] will become repayable by me to S Ltd'.

In the event, K continued to act as sales director for G Ltd but did not take up any new employment with any other member of the S Ltd group.

In the Supreme Court, Murphy J endorsed the reasoning in *Shilton v Wilmshurst* and held that the inducement payment fell within what is now TCA 1997, s 112, notwithstanding that K had not actually taken up employment with S Ltd. The learned judge observed:

> … regard must be had to the fact that [K] expressly and in writing agreed to enter into a service contract with [S Ltd] and for that was paid a sum of £250,000. There was also the provision for the repayment of that sum if the transaction was not consummated. Whilst there is no specific finding in relation to it, I understand that it is agreed that the [repayment] of that sum was never sought or made. If it had been repaid the question of taxation would not arise. Whilst tax legislation frequently proceeds on the basis of legal fictions, as has already been noted, and legitimate tax avoidance arrangements may well demand the implementation of transactions which would not be justified on purely commercial considerations, I think that the Court must infer that [S Ltd] were satisfied to accept the continued service of [K] with [G Ltd] as compliance with the terms of his service agreement … The alternative interpretation would be to treat the payment as one made for a consideration which wholly failed or else as a gift the validity of which might be open to question. These alternatives are neither attractive nor compelling. In my view the payment of £250,000 by S Ltd or the treatment of that sum as having been so paid in accordance with the provisions of the side letter resulted in a taxable emolument in the hands of K.

Revenue's view with regard to the taxability of inducement payments is set out in *Tax Briefing 32*. They express the view there that 'payment made to an individual as an inducement to take up employment is liable to income tax'. However, this blanket view fails to accord due weight to the decisions in *Jarrold v Boustead* and *Pritchard v Arundale*.

In *Teward v IRC* [2001] STC (SCD) 36, the UK Special Commissioners decided that a payment by a new employer to compensate for the taxpayer's no longer being able to participate in his previous employer's share option scheme was a taxable emolument of the new employment. While the payment in question was not a term of the new employment contract, it clearly formed part of the package of arrangements under which the taxpayer accepted the new employment.

10.110 Payments by third parties

On balance, a payment by 'third party' (ie somebody other than the employer) is less likely to be an emolument than a payment made by the employer. This follows from the fact that an employer's transaction with his employee will tend to be coloured by the employer/employee relationship. However, each particular case must be looked at in the light of its own specific facts, and it would be dangerous to place too much weight on the isolated circumstance that the payment is made by a third party. This is particularly true where the third party has an interest in promoting or securing the future services of the employee.

In *Laidler v Perry* 42 TC 351, Lord Reid observed that, notwithstanding this principle, the purposes of the employer would always be significant. There does not in fact seem to be any good reason why the purposes of a third party in making a payment should be any more or less significant per se than those of the employer. In fact, the better view seems to be that the purposes of the payer, be it employer or a third party may often be of no or limited relevance (see eg *Wright v Boyce* discussed at **10.107**). As discussed above, it is well-established that the issue of taxability under Sch E must be adjudicated from the standpoint of the employee; the purposes of the payer are therefore only likely to be significant in equivocal cases.

In *Cowan v Seymour* 7 TC 372, the issue was whether or not a voluntary payment made in recognition of the past services of a liquidator by the shareholders of the liquidated company was taxable. Lord Green MR said:

> … looking at [the facts] … I find the very important factor of the office having terminated … and the other almost equally important factor that the payment is made not by the employers but by somebody else, though in this case perhaps that is not quite so important as there is a close connection between the employer … and the persons who gave the money.

In *Pritchard v Arundale* the third party making the payment was the controlling shareholder of the employer company and thus it seems that despite Warner J's comments in the *Glantre Engineering* case (cited in **10.109**), the fact that the payment was made by a third party probably should not have been very significant in these circumstances. In *Bootle v Bye* [1996] (SCD) STC the UK Special Commissioners held on the facts that a payment made by a company closely associated with the employer was an emolument.

In *Moorhouse v Dooland* 36 TC 1 the taxpayer was a professional cricketer whose contract entitled him to take collections from spectators whenever he had achieved particular feats in the course of a match. The contractual nature of his right to receive the payments was held to be conclusive by the Court of Appeal. Per Sir Raymond Evershed MR:

> the right … was part of the consideration for his services flowing from his employers;

it followed that the sums which accrued to the taxpayer, whenever that right crystallised, arose 'from' the employment. Per Birkett LJ, the existence of the right was 'decisive'; he observed:

> the monies given … by the cricketing public from whatever motive seem to me to be governed for tax purposes by the provisions of the contract and it is the recipient and not the giver who is the concern of the tax collector

It may be argued that even in the absence of a contractual term entitling the taxpayer in *Moorhouse* to receive and retain collections, he should still have been liable thereon under Sch E. This is on the basis that, if such payments had been customary and regular (albeit non-contractual), they could have been fairly regarded as 'perks of the job'; ie the taxpayer would have received those payments by reason solely of the fact that he was an employee. The collections would have been analogous to the Christmas presents in *Wright v Boyce* (indeed, given that the sums received in *Moorhouse* were linked to the performance of the employee's duties, albeit only if carried out at a particularly notable level, the argument for taxability would probably have been even stronger than in *Wright v Boyce*).

Shilton v Wilmshurst (discussed in **10.106**) shows that even payments made by a third party with no interest in the future services of the taxpayer may be taxable, although, the facts there, where the third party benefited financially as a result of the taxpayer taking up his new employment, were somewhat unusual. Another example is *Brumby v Milner* [1976] STC 534, where a profit-sharing trust was wound up, following a take-over of the employer company. The distributions of the trust capital to current and former employees were held to be taxable emoluments in their hands. The sole reason for making the payments was because the recipients were or had been employees. The fact that the payments were made by trustees with no interest in the performance of the services by the employees was not regarded as a material factor.

10.111 Payments for loss of office and other compensation payments

Lump sum payments are sometimes made to compensate a person who has held an office or employment for the loss of that office or employment which may arise in certain circumstances. Alternatively, it may happen that such payments may be made in consideration for a person's surrendering or otherwise agreeing to change the rights he has, whether expressed or implied, under an existing contract of service. In any of these types of case, the question again arises as to whether or not the payment is to be treated as a perquisite or other profit of the office or employment so as to be taxable under the main charging rule of Sch E in TCA 1997, s 112. If the payment is not directly chargeable to income tax under that rule, it remains necessary to consider whether, and if so to what extent, it may be charged to income tax under TCA 1997, s 123 which deals specifically with payments in connection with the termination of an office or employment not already taxable under Sch E (see **Division 10.4**).

The discussion here is concerned solely with the question of whether the compensation, etc payments are chargeable under Sch E as a perquisite by TCA 1997, s 112 without reference to TCA 1997, s 123 or any other provision of the Income Tax Acts. It may be noted that lump sum or other payments made under the Redundancy Payments Act 1967, s 46 are expressly exempted (TCA 1997, s 203); in addition there are reliefs and exemptions in relation to compensation payments in relation to certain business reorganisations and pay restructuring agreements as well as the provision of retraining courses as part of a redundancy package in prescribed circumstances (see **10.407**).

Taking, firstly, payments made as compensation for the loss of an office or employment, it may as a general rule be taken that such a payment is taxable as a profit under TCA 1997, s 112 if it is paid as a result of any term in the contract of service or in the conditions of employment. Otherwise, such a payment is not generally taxable under the main Sch E charging rule. In *Henry v Foster* 16 TC 605, the respondent was a director of a company. He had no written contract of service with the company, but the company's articles of association provided that in the event that any director, who had held office for not less than five years, died, resigned or ceased to hold office, the company should pay to him or his personal representatives by way of compensation for loss of office a sum equal to the total remuneration received by him during the preceding five years. The respondent resigned as director after more than five years' service and the lump sum compensation payment as provided for in the articles was made to him. It was held by the Court of Appeal that this compensation payment was correctly assessed under Sch E as a profit of the office of director; since the compensation payment was provided for in the articles of association it was in effect a term of his service (see also *Allan v Trehearne* 22 TC 15, where a lump sum due under similar arrangements and which became payable on the death of the director, was again held to be a taxable emolument even though he was not alive to receive it and note *Wilson v Daniels* 25 TC 473).

Hunter v Dewhurst 16 TC 605 concerned the same company as *Henry v Foster*, but the facts were slightly different. Here the respondent wished to retire from active management of the company, but his co-directors wished to continue to consult him. It was agreed that he should resign the office of Chairman, receive a lump sum in consideration for surrendering his right to the compensation payment provided for in the articles, and remain on the board at a reduced remuneration. It was held by the House of Lords that the sum received was not income assessable to income tax. In this case, the lump sum was not received by Mr Dewhurst under the term of his service implied by the articles, but rather under a separate agreement for giving up his right to the benefit of the provision in the articles. This is a rather odd decision since it is generally accepted that a payment made in lieu of a taxable emolument is itself a taxable emolument (see, for example, *Bird v Martland*, discussed below). This is logical, since the only consideration provided by the employee was located in the subsisting employment contract itself and the taxpayer's rights thereunder. The fact that it could be said that the employer was paying the sum to remove a contingent liability (a factor on which the court placed some weight) is irrelevant if it is accepted that the issue must be resolved from the standpoint of the taxpayer; in this case, the employee received his payment in lieu of future emoluments. The reasoning of the Law Lords in *Dewhurst* was clearly influenced by the now outmoded concept that for an emolument to be taxable, it had to constitute a reward for services and could not be taxable under any other circumstances (see **10.106** above). Lord Atkin accepted in *Dewhurst* that *Henry v Foster* was correctly decided. However, he held that the lump sum in *Dewhurst* was:

> not paid for past remuneration, for the condition of its becoming payable … never was performed. It was not paid for future remuneration for that was expressed to be £250 pa.

Lord Wright also observed that:

> no part of the [lump sum] represented salary retained either in the past or the future

Lord Thankerton accepted that the lump sum in *Henry v Foster* was contractually part of the consideration for his services as a director but added that there:

> remained the question as to whether it was income or not … I find it unnecessary to resolve that question.

The concept that a sum received as a reward for services might not be taxable underscores the peculiarity of the decision in *Dewhurst*. Accordingly, it would be unwise to regard *Dewhurst* at best as other than a case decided by reference to its own special facts.

The decision in *Dewhurst* was in fact followed in *Duff v Barlow* 23 TC 633, where a managing director received a lump sum as compensation for loss of remuneration following the removal of his responsibility for managing a subsidiary. The decision that the lump sum was not taxable seems difficult to sustain given the taxpayer's continuance in office. The decision certainly does not seem reconcilable with *Prendergast v Cameron* discussed below.

In *Dale v de Soissons* 32 TC 118, the taxpayer was entitled by the terms of his service agreement to a salary and a commission. The agreement also provided that the company should be entitled to terminate his appointment at the end of the first or second year of the three years covered by the agreement by three-months' notice, whereupon a lump sum would become payable to the taxpayer by way of compensation for loss of office. The company exercised that right at the end of the first year and paid the agreed sum of compensation to him. It was held that the compensation payment was profit arising from his employment taxable under Sch E as his entitlement to it arose under the terms of the service agreement.

There are a number of cases, however, of payments held not to be taxable under Sch E as being, in effect, payments made to compensate a director or employee for the loss of his position. In *Henley v Murray* 31 TC 351, the taxpayer was employed as managing director of a company under a service agreement terminable at the earliest on 31 March 1944. For certain reasons, it became desirable from the company's point of view that he should leave the service of the company. He did so on 6 July 1943 and in consideration for doing so was paid £2,000, an amount equal to that to which he would have been entitled under his service agreement had his employment continued until 31 March 1944. It was held that this sum, being payable in consideration of the abrogation of his contract of employment, and not under that contract, was not assessable as a profit of the employment. In *Du Cros v Ryall* 19 TC 444, the whole of a lump sum paid as 'agreed damages' in settlement of the taxpayer's action against a company for wrongful repudiation of a service agreement and for arrears of salary and commission, was held to be a capital payment as damages for compensation for breach of the service agreement, and was not assessable to income tax. *Henley v Murray* was followed in *Glover v BLN Ltd (No 2)* [1973] IR 432.

In *Wilson v Clayton* [2004] EWHC 898(Ch), the taxpayer's employer had terminated his employment contract in 1997 and had then re-employed him on terms which excluded his previous car allowance. An employment tribunal made an award of damages for unfair dismissal to the taxpayer which was in fact outside its jurisdiction and also ordered that his employer should reinstate him. The proceedings were compromised and the employer made a payment under a negotiated settlement based on the tribunal's decision. The High Court held that the payment did not refer to services rendered under the original or the subsequent contract and did not constitute a profit from the employment and was therefore not taxable as an emolument (although it did fall within the UK equivalent of TCA 1997, s 123: see **10.4**).

In some cases depending on the facts, it may be possible to argue that the payment of a lump sum arises under a variation of the original contract. This argument was raised by the Revenue authorities, but rejected on the facts in two Privy Council cases: *CG of Inland Revenue v Knight* [1973] AC 428 and *CIR v Sutherland* [1952] AC 469.

In *Williams v Simmonds* [1981] STC 715, the taxpayer held a directorship under which he was contractually entitled to a lump sum as compensation for loss of office. In addition, it was provided that he should lose his office on the happening of certain events unless he elected otherwise. One of these events materialised, but the taxpayer decided to forego his right of election as his fellow directors wished him to leave, and so took his lump sum. Vinelott J, holding that the lump sum was taxable, commented:

> The result is unfortunate, in that, if the taxpayer [had made the election] and … had subsequently bowed to the pressure which was being exerted upon him and had resigned his employment and had then agreed to accept, as compensation for the abrogation of his rights under the service agreement, a sum equal to the [lump sum] compensation which would have been payable if he had not [made the election] the sum so payable might well not have attracted tax …

In *Antelope v Ellis* [1995] STC (SCD), the taxpayer had agreed to forego compensation for breach of his employment contract in return for a contractual right to a lump sum if he subsequently decided to take a new job (which is in fact what happened). The Special Commissioner held that the lump sum was a taxable emolument, being received as part of the taxpayer's (amended) terms of employment. It might be argued however that, in these unusual circumstances, full consideration had been given for the right to receive the lump sum (namely the foregoing of compensation which would not itself have been a taxable receipt).

In *Mairs v Haughey* [1993] STC 569, the taxpayer was one of a number of employees of Harland and Wolff (H & W). As part of the privatisation of H & W, these employees were offered new employments with the successor to H & W, H & W 1989, as an alternative to redundancy. The terms of the new employments entailed the ultimate discontinuance of a non-statutory redundancy scheme operated by H & W as part of the employees' terms and conditions of employment. Employees who accepted the offer of a new employment on these terms were to be entitled to a '*ex gratia*' lump sum. The courts were asked to decide *inter alia* whether: (a) any payments under the existing redundancy scheme would have been taxable and (b) if the answer to (a) was yes, whether the lump sum paid in lieu of the right to those payments was itself taxable.

In the light of the overwhelming bulk of the previous case law, the answer should have been in the affirmative in both cases. This conclusion follows simply because the right to the redundancy payments was part and parcel of the taxpayer's conditions of employment (as eg in *Moorhouse v Dooland*). It is extremely difficult to see how such a right could not refer to the employment itself. If and when the taxpayer was made redundant, this would have been simply the occasion on which that right would have crystallised into an unconditional entitlement to the appropriate payment. It is at this point that the charge under Sch E would have arisen (see *Edwards v Roberts* 19 TC 618). The court laid some emphasis on the fact that pensions are not taxable, albeit the right to them may be granted under a contract of service. This misses the point that a pension is regarded as a distinct stream of income which derives from that right: see **10.112**.

The House of Lords held that payments made under a contractual redundancy scheme were not taxable emoluments, since the purpose of the scheme was to compensate an employee for the loss of his livelihood. The only judgment was delivered by Lord Woolf. Lord Woolf firstly found that the purpose of a redundancy payment was to compensate an employee:

> for the consequences of his not being able to earn a living in his former employment.

He noted:

> redundancy … involves an employee finding himself without a job through circumstances over which he has no control. It is also a quality of redundancy that it does not give rise to a right to compensation unless the employee has been employed for a minimum period and the right … subsequently reduces until eventually the employee loses any right to payment on reaching normal retirement age.

The learned Law Lord then proceeded to cite Lord Radcliffe's observation in *Hochstrasser v Mayes* that the sum paid in that latter case was:

> no more taxable as a profit … than would be a payment out of a provident or a distress fund.

With respect, Lord Woolf's observations pay insufficient attention to the fact that in contrast with the housing agreement in *Hochstrasser v Mayes*, the redundancy scheme formed part of the terms and conditions of the taxpayer's employment. This should have been conclusive of the taxability of payments under the scheme. Lord Woolf sought to reconcile his conclusions with decisions such as *Henry v Foster* discussed above, saying:

> *Prima facie*, a payment made after the termination of employment is not an emolument from that employment. It can be, however, an emolument from the employment if for example it is a lump sum payment in the nature of deferred remuneration. As Lord Hanworth MR indicated in *Henry v Foster*, in order to determine whether this is the situation it is necessary to look at the substance of the matter. If a payment relates to the services rendered then the fact that the payment is made after the employment comes to an end does not mean that it is divorced from the employment. The distinction between the deferred payments of wages or salary and a redundancy payment may be narrow but is nonetheless real. In the case of the deferred payment once the employment comes to an end the right to payment will inevitably accrue. In the case of a redundancy payment, the sum is only payable in limited circumstances and there would be no entitlement if for example the employee leaves the employment of his own accord.

Firstly, it may be noted that a payment made after the termination of an employment will always be taxable if made to the employee on account of his employment, even if it cannot be described as deferred remuneration (see *Bray v Best* [1989] STC 159). Since everything will depend on the precise facts, to say that a payment is or is not *prima facie* taxable is probably unhelpful.

Secondly, it may be noted that when Lord Hanworth asserted in *Henry v Foster* that it was necessary to look to the 'substance of the matter' he was in fact no more than reiterating the truism that the label which the parties chose to attach to a transaction cannot override its true nature. Thus, in *Foster* the parties had described the payment under review as 'compensation for loss of office', clearly an unsustainable description.

Lord Hanworth proceeded to conclude that the payment was made in fact under the terms of the taxpayer's contract of service and expressly contrasted that payment with a:

> charitable payment wholly detached from any contract entered into between the director and the company and wholly independent of any services received by the company from the director.

Thirdly, it may be noted that the concept that a lump sum would only constitute 'deferred remuneration' where it will 'inevitably accrue' on the termination of the employment is inconsistent with the facts in *Henry v Foster* itself, where there would have been no entitlement to the lump sum payment if the taxpayer had lost his office due to misconduct, bankruptcy, lunacy or incompetence. On the other hand, it was not essential to Lord Woolf's reasoning that any element of contingency would remove the payment from the general scope of Sch E. The thrust of his judgment indicated that the circumstances under which the relevant contingency will crystallise must indicate an underlying purpose, such as the relief of hardship or distress. However, the fact that hardship is the occasion on which a contractual right to payment is triggered off seems should be properly regarded as a matter of timing and not one of causation.

Thus, in *CG of Inland Revenue v Knight* [1973] AC 428, Lord Wilberforce, delivering the judgment of the Privy Council implicitly accepted that *Henry v Foster* was authority for the proposition that a sum received under a contract of employment was taxable per se. This view is irreconcilable with the reasoning in *Haughey*. Lord Wilberforce's speech was in fact delivered in the context of the taxability of redundancy payments, albeit under Malaysian tax law where, in order to be taxable, a sum had to be 'paid or granted in respect of the employment'. Although Lord Woolf sought to diminish the relevance of *Knight* by noting that Malaysian legislation was 'not identical but only similar' to UK legislation, Lord Wilberforce had in fact expressly rejected the notion that the difference in wording was material.

Even if it is assumed for the sake of argument that the fact that the redundancy payment was part of the contractual rights granted under the taxpayer's contract of services is not conclusive, it is still by no means clear that the reason why the employee received the payment could have been other than on account of his employment. The redundancy payments were after all available to all employees and could have been fairly regarded as a perk of the job. If this view is correct, then since matters must be viewed from the standpoint of the employee, the reason why the employer set up the redundancy scheme would have been irrelevant (as in *Wright v Boyce*).

It might be added that even if it were to be accepted that the purpose of the employer was relevant, then it may be noted that Lord Woolf apparently applied an objective test, ie holding that the characteristics of the redundancy scheme in question was such that payments under it were necessarily made to compensate for hardship. It is arguable that it is the actual purposes of the employer which should be taken into account (as seemingly was the position in *Hochstrasser v Mayes*) and that it should not be automatically assumed that the employer was motivated by a desire to alleviate distress.

Once it had been held that the redundancy payments were not taxable under the general Sch E rules, then it followed that a lump sum paid to buy out the right to such payments was equally non-taxable. It was therefore a purely hypothetical issue as to whether, if the redundancy payments had been taxable, the lump sum might nevertheless have been non-taxable on the strength of *Hunter v Dewhurst*. As noted above, the decision in *Hunter v Dewhurst* is impossible to reconcile with the principle that the tax characterisation of lump sum payments must be determined under Sch E from the standpoint of the employee. Lord Woolf indicated that he was not persuaded that *Hunter v Dewhurst* was wrongly decided. On the other hand, the learned Law Lord asserted that:

> a payment made to satisfy a contingent right derives its character from the nature of the payment which it replaces.

These two comments are, with respect, completely inconsistent with each other.

In practice, the Revenue Commissioners accept that payments in lieu of notice are not emoluments so long as they do not exceed the pay which would have been received in the required period of notice (Employer's Guide to PAYE, para 5.12) The PAYE Guide does not address the question as to whether such a payment should be treated as taxable if paid under the terms of the employee's contract. It would seem that such a payment should be taxable in principle, although this is subject to the correctness of the decision in *Mairs v Haughey* (discussed below). It is in fact far from clear that even if *Mairs v Haughey* were regarded as correctly decided that the principle there would necessarily extend to a contractual payment in lieu of notice.

The decision in *Mairs v Haughey* was readily distinguished in *Allen v IRC*; *Cullen v IRC* [1994] STC 943, where the employing company agreed to make supplementary redundancy payments to employees on the cessation of its business. Some employees were made redundant, but the company was subsequently acquired by a purchaser which agreed to make, supplementary redundancy payments to all the employees including those who were kept on in employment (including the taxpayers). The court held that payments made irrespective of redundancy could not be regarded as compensation for an anticipated loss of employment. The payments had been made to the taxpayers in return for acting as employees, and were consequently taxable emoluments arising from their employment.

In *EMI Group Electronics Ltd v Coldicott* [1997] STC 1372, the contracts of services between the employer (EMI) and its senior employees provided that EMI would give the employees six-months' notice of dismissal, but reserved the right of EMI to make a payment in lieu of such notice (hereafter referred to as a PILON). The Crown argued that the payment was directly comparable with the sum received in *Dale v de Soissons* 32 TC 118, where, under the terms of the relevant service agreement, the employer was entitled to terminate the employment prematurely on payment of an agreed lump sum. In that case, the court held that the sum was taxable because '… [the taxpayer] surrendered no right … he got exactly what he was entitled to under the contract of employment' (note also *Williams v Simmonds* [1981] STC 715).

Neuberger J in the High Court held that the PILON was in fact taxable, for the following reasons:

(a) The payment was due under a contract of service; while this was not sufficient in itself (ie in the light of *Mairs v Haughey*), it was a factor which suggested that the PILON was offered as 'part of a package of benefits … offered to the employees to induce him to take up the employment.'

(b) The terms on which an employment contract could be ended appeared to be self-evidently an inherent part of the contractual relationship between the employer and the employee. The determination of the employment coupled with the election to pay a PILON was merely the occasion on which the payment arose and not the cause thereof.

(c) Payment of a PILON was not personal to any particular employee or dependent on the personal circumstances of the employees.

(d) Since the payment of a PILON was made in lieu of earnings which would otherwise be taxable, it would be surprising if a PILON were not itself taxable.

(e) The payment of a PILON was similar to the payment in *Dale v de Soissons*.

(f) The characteristics of redundancy payment were such that it might be regarded as compensation for loss of the employee's stake in his employment or else a payment to relieve distress; a PILON on the other hand was part of the standard agreed machinery used to terminate the employment.

Reasons (a) to (c) above seem to be equally applicable to the facts in *Mairs v Haughey*. It may be noted incidentally that the learned judge seems to have thought that the housing scheme in *Hochstrasser v Mayes* had in fact been incorporated into the terms and conditions of the taxpayer's employment there, but this (as discussed above) does not seem to be correct. Reason (d) may be somewhat circular. If the PILON had been regarded as analogous to the payment in *Mairs v Haughey* (ie as a payment designed to relieve hardship or distress), then the court could have as easily said that the wages foregone were simply the measure of the hardship suffered by the employee. Reason (e) does not in itself explain why the logic of *Dale v de Soissons* was not applied in *Mairs v Haughey*.

Reason (f) seems in fact to represent the real nub of the matter: a contractual redundancy payment, although, in one sense, a subset of contractual termination payments in general, does have special characteristics which mark it out as potentially as a payment designed to relieve distress. These are noticeably absent in the case of a PILON. This kind of reasoning strongly suggests that the UK Courts are unlikely to regard contractual termination payments such as those in *Dale v de Soissons* or *Williams v Simmonds* as now falling within the scope of the decision in *Mairs v Haughey*. The Court of Appeal upheld the decision in *Coldicott* ([1999] STC 803). Chadwick LJ distinguished *Mairs v Haughey* on the basis that 'Notice of intention to terminate … or a payment in lieu of notice is not intended to relieve the hardship consequent upon becoming unemployed'. The Court of Appeal's approach is discussed more fully in Ward, '*Coldicott v EMI*: A Pilon is Flattened' in [1999] British Tax Review.

The UK case of *Richardson v Delaney* [2001] STC 1328 extended the scope of the decision in *Coldicott*. The facts of the case were that the taxpayer was employed by a company from 1 December 1994 on a salary of £60,000 a year. His service agreement provided for 18-months' notice but the employer could terminate immediately if it paid salary in lieu of notice. On 1 December 1995 the taxpayer was given notice of termination by letter. A second letter of the same date marked 'without prejudice' set out the employer's proposals concerning the termination. The employee was placed on 'gardening leave' and started negotiations with the employer following which the employment was terminated by mutual agreement and he accepted a sum of £75,000 in settlement, which was broadly equivalent to what he would have received by way of salary in lieu of notice. The taxpayer appealed against a Sch E income tax assessment on the lump sum of St £75,000 as an emolument of his employment taxable under the UK equivalent of TCA 1997, ss 112 and 123) on the basis that the lump sum represented compensation for breach of contract. The taxpayer's argument was rejected by the High Court.

It was held that a payment in lieu of notice pursuant to a contractual provision such as existed in this case was an emolument of the employment (following *EMI Group Electronics Ltd v Coldicott (HM Inspector of Taxes)*). What the taxpayer received was not identical to what was provided for under the contract, but it was not fundamentally different. In the present case, on the facts and on the evidence, there were no grounds for finding that the company was in breach of contract. The employer had acted in accordance with the contract in giving notice. Such notice was not immediately effective to terminate the employment and the termination by subsequent mutual agreement did not constitute a breach by the employer.

The decision does not seem to imply that lump sums received by way of settlement on the termination of a contract are taxable as emoluments per se; rather, the rationale seems to be that where a sum is received which equates to what would otherwise have been received under the terms of the employment contract, and in the absence of a breach of contract there is a strong inference that the source of the payment is the employment itself.

In *Cerberus Software v Rowley* [2001] IRLR 160, an employment law case, the employment contract included a clause under which the employer had a discretion to make a PILON. The court upheld the right of the employer not to exercise its discretion but to breach the contract instead (the damages arising being less than the sum payable under the PILON). It seems clear that a payment of the kind made in the *Cerberus* case would not be taxable on general principles under TCA 1997, s 112.

The UK Inland Revenue take the view that non-contractual PILONs may be treated as emoluments where such sums are paid automatically following a termination. Whatever the merits of this argument or indeed the likelihood of such a practice being established, it may be prudent in some cases for employers to lay down a clear policy that every case will be treated on its merits.

In *Tax Briefing 22*, the Revenue Commissioners state that where there is a prior entitlement to a termination payment 'and it is in the nature of a supplement to remuneration' then TCA 1997, s 112 applies. This statement does not indicate whether the Revenue would accept the analysis in the *Haughey* case that the redundancy payment was not in the nature of a supplement to remuneration.

Tax Briefing 22 also makes clear that where there is an arrangement under which an employee is made 'redundant' and is then immediately re-engaged the Revenue will look to the real nature of the agreement between the parties. *Tax Briefing 44* reproduced the article originally set out in *Tax Briefing 22*. A 'redundancy' arrangement under which it was intended to maintain the existing employment relationship would seem to be in the nature of a sham (see **1.408**).

Payments of 'wages' made after the contract of employment had ceased were held to fall outside the equivalent of TCA 1997, s 112 in *Clayton v Lavender* 42 TC 607 (compare *Hoffman v Wadman* 27 TC 192, a decision which is difficult to support). The position where an employee serves out his period of notice without being required to carry out any further services (so-called 'garden leave') seems to be distinguishable, ie on the basis that the contract of service nevertheless still endures (see the non-tax case of *Delaney v Staples* [1992] 2 WLR 451). In *Redundant Employee v McNally* [2005], the taxpayer was made redundant by her employers. Her contract provided for a three-month notice period. The letter confirming the termination of employment stated that the termination took effect 'from today', but that her 'continuing duty of confidentiality' remained under the terms of her contract, after her employment had terminated. She was paid a sum described as salary for the three months, but was not required to attend her employer's office, although she was told to make herself available for work if required. The taxpayer did not in fact return to the office. The UK High Court held that reading the letter as a whole, in light of the factual background, the most convincing of the possible interpretations was that the taxpayer had been given three-months' notice and had been put on garden leave. The letter would have conveyed to an ordinarily reasonable employee that the company was enforcing her contract rather than breaking it, because: pay was to be made in the normal manner via the payroll each month; she was required to be available for work; and she had been reminded of her continuing duty of confidentiality during the three-month period. Accordingly, the payments made to her were taxable emoluments arising from her employment.

However, post-employment receipts if not emoluments may alternatively be annual payments falling under Sch D Case III. In *Asher v London Film Productions Ltd* [1944] KB 133, the taxpayer agreed to take an annual percentage of the profits of certain films as compensation for the cancellation of his service contract. It was held that the payments arose under the agreement for the cancellation of his contract and were not remuneration for past services; instead they were annual payments chargeable under Sch D Case III (see also *McMann v Shaw* 48 TC 530).

A payment in lieu of notice, which represents compensation for breach of contract, should again fall outside TCA 1997, s 112. Where the contract of service itself provides for such a payment, it would seem that the payment is a taxable emolument (although if *Mairs v Haughey* were to be upheld in Ireland, some doubt might be cast on this latter proposition).

Mairs v Haughey was distinguished in *Allen v IRC* [1995] STC 945. There, the employer company, which was due to be taken over and which expected that its employees would not be retained by the new management, made so-called 'supplementary redundancy payments' to its employees. Because the taxpayer received her payment, irrespective of whether or not she was actually made redundant, it was held to be a taxable emolument in her hands under general principles.

Another type of case is that in which a lump sum is paid in consideration for an individual's relinquishing rights under a service agreement, but where he continues in the office or employment after he receives the payment. In this regard, a useful case to consider is *Wales v Tilley* 25 TC 136, in which a managing director of a company with an existing service agreement under which he agreed to continue to serve as managing director at a salary equal to one third of his previous salary. Under the new agreement, he also released the company from a right he had under the old agreement to a pension for ten years after he ceased to be employed by the company. In consideration for taking the reduced salary and for giving up his future pension rights, he was paid a lump sum of £40,000. The House of Lords held that, contrary to the view of the Court of Appeal, it was permissible to separate the part of the agreement dealing with the pension rights from that dealing with the reduction in salary. It was held that so much of the £40,000 as related to the commutation of the pension was not taxable, but that so much as was paid in compromise of the reduction of salary was taxable as a profit of the office of director (note also the discussion on *O'Siochain v Morrissey* IV ITR 407).

Earlier in the Court of Appeal, Lord Greene MR said:

> If a man agrees to serve in consideration of a lump sum and no periodical salary or a small periodical salary, that lump sum is just as much remuneration and taxable as such as a periodical salary or a larger periodical salary would have been ... Indeed, the only real argument that was presented on behalf of the appellant on this aspect of the case consisted of an endeavour to draw a distinction between a lump sum paid at the beginning of the service and a lump sum paid, as in the present case, in consideration of an agreement to continue to serve for a reduced salary. There is no substance in this distinction.

This may be taken as a clear statement of the law as it still stands in relation to lump sums paid in consideration for a person's agreeing to continue to serve but at a reduced salary. The decision on this point in *Wales v Tilley* followed a similar decision in *Prendergast v Cameron* 23 TC 122. In the latter case, the respondent was a director of a company and wished to resign his position and so obtain greater ease of life. His fellow directors urged him not to do so and an agreement was made between the company and himself under which his salary was reduced from £1,500 to £400 per year, but he also received a lump sum of £45,000. The House of Lords decided that the latter amount was a profit from the directorship assessable under Sch E. Similarly, payments for loss of perquisites under the employment contract will be taxable emoluments; this is logical, since the sole source of such payments is the employment itself (note also *Holland v Geoghegan* 48 TC 482, where bonuses paid in respect of loss of salvage rights in order to induce striking barmen to return to work were held to be taxable emoluments).

In *Bird v Martland* [1982] STC 603, the taxpayer enjoyed the use of a company car, a facility which was provided to all employees of his employer company above a certain level of seniority. The facility was eventually withdrawn from a number of employees, including the taxpayer. The employer paid all the employees affected an *ex gratia* lump sum which was held to be taxable for present purposes. Walton J observed:

> … the employees received the money because they were employees having perquisites which were going to be taken away from them in future.

(Note also *Bolam v Muller* 28 TC 471; *McGregor v Randall* [1994] STC 223; *Holland v Geoghegan* 48 TC 482 discussed above.)

Beecham Group Ltd v Fair [1984] STC 15 is an interesting 'borderline' case. There, the taxpayer company employed a number of salesmen, all of whom were obliged to garage their company cars. The company granted each employee a garage allowance in return for discharging this obligation. Walton J held that the allowances constituted taxable emoluments; this was on the basis that the allowances were paid to the employees for carrying out a contractual duty to protect their employer's property, and not in their capacity as garage owners. The learned judge observed that matters would have been different if each employee had instead granted a lease or licence over his garage to the employer in return for the sums involved. This seems to be correct, since in that case it would have been possible to identify a separate and valuable consideration moving from the employee other than the rendering of services (of course the sums would not thereby have lost their income character).

In *Porter v HMRC* (2005) SpC 501, the taxpayer was entitled to have shares vested in him on the third anniversary of his commencing employment under a stock incentive scheme. The conditional right to receive the shares was subject to forfeiture if the employment was terminated within the three-year period, but subject to the discretion of the scheme committee which could take into account factors such as loyalty (ie not subsequently joining a competitor). The taxpayer was made redundant and negotiated to have his rights maintained under the stock incentive scheme, enabling the shares to vest in him in the future, subject to the continued discretion of the plan's committee. The taxpayer did not join a competitor and the committee duly exercised its discretion to vest the shares in him.

The UK Special Commissioners found that the vesting of the shares arose firstly from the terms of settlement reached as a result of the ending of his employment agreement. It was not paid under the term of his employment agreement, but rather under the terms of the termination agreement. This reflected the fact that his employment agreement had been ended, that he was no longer in employment, and that he might have enjoyed claims as a result of that termination. Secondly, it was paid in recognition of the fact that he had conducted himself as a loyal ex-employee. Accordingly, it was not an emolument arising from his employment, although it was clearly 'in connection with the termination of' his employment and thus subject to the UK equivalent of TCA 1997, s 123 (see **10.4**). As the shares were regarded as being acquired by reason of the settlement between the employer and the taxpayer and not by reason of the employment, then in similar circumstances in Ireland, TCA 1997, s 122A would not have been in point (see **10.113**).

There has been some debate concerning the correct treatment of payments under employment protection legislation and the Revenue Commissioners' position on such payments; (see [2003] ITR 219). It is clear that payments under such legislation which consist of compensation in the form of arrears of remuneration eg for failure to provide equal pay are taxable under general principles. However, it is difficult to see that payments to compensate an employee for acts of discrimination or victimisation are made in return for acting or being an employee. While such payments are made in the context of the employment and are only granted by statute because of the fact of employment, these factors would only seem to render the fact of employment the *causa sine qua non* rather than the *causa causans* of the payments. It is submitted that the source of such payments is not the employment itself but rather the statutory right to redress in respect of wrongs suffered by the employee; while the line is not easy to draw with precision, these rights seem distinguishable from those in *Hamblett v Godfrey* which was concerned with the regulation of the employer-employee relationship and where there was in effect a modification of the terms and conditions of the employees' service contracts (see **10.106**) (note also the decision of the Special Commissioners in *Walker v Adams* [2003] STC (SCD) 269).

In any event, TCA 1997, s 192A, provides statutory exemption for many payments of this nature; this does not mean that where the section does not apply that a payment must necessarily be taxable on general principles. The section exempts any payment under a 'relevant Act', to an employee or former employee by their employer or former employer, as the case may be, which is made, on or after 4 February 2004, in accordance with a recommendation, decision or a determination by a relevant authority in accordance with the provisions of that Act (TCA 1997, s 192A(1)(b)).

A 'relevant Act' means an enactment which contains provisions for the protection of employees' rights and entitlements or for the obligations of employers towards their employees;

A 'relevant authority' means any of the following:

(a) a Rights Commissioner;
(b) the Director of the Equality Tribunal,
(ba) an adjudication officer of the Workplace Relations Commission,
(bb) the Workplace Relations Commission,
(bc) the District Court;
(c) the Employment Appeals Tribunal;
(d) the Labour Court;
(e) the Circuit Court; or
(f) the High Court (TCA 1997, s 192A(2)).

In addition, the TCA 1997, s 192A applies to:

(a) a payment made in accordance with a settlement arrived at under a mediation process provided for in a relevant Act as if it had been made in accordance with a recommendation, decision or determination under that act of a relevant authority (TCA 1997, s 192A(3));

(b) a payment:

(i) made, on or after 4 February 2004, under an agreement evidenced in writing, being an agreement between persons who are not connected with each other (as defined by TCA 1997, s 10: see **12.304**), in settlement of a claim which:

(I) had it been made to a relevant authority, would have been a *bona fide* claim made under the provisions of a relevant Act,

(II) is evidenced in writing, and

(III) had the claim not been settled by the agreement, is likely to have been the subject of a recommendation, decision or determination under that Act by a relevant authority that a payment be made to the person making the claim,

(ii) the amount of which does not exceed the maximum payment which, in accordance with a decision or determination by a relevant authority (other than the Circuit Court or the High Court) under the relevant Act, could have been made under that Act in relation to the claim, had the claim not been settled by agreement, and

(iii) where:

(I) copies of the agreement and the statement of claim are kept and retained by the employer, by or on behalf of whom the payment was made, for a period of six years from the day on which the payment was made, and

(II) the employer has made copies of the agreement and the statement of claim available to an officer of the Revenue Commissioners where the officer has requested the employer to make those copies available to him or her.

It is a requirement under (b) that on being so requested by an officer of the Revenue Commissioners, an employer shall make available to the officer all copies of:

(I) such agreements entered into by or on behalf of the employer; and

(II) the statements of claim related to those agreements;

kept and retained by the employer as required thereunder.

(The Revenue may examine and take extracts from or copies of the documents concerned (TCA 1997, s 192A(4).) The requirements under (b) are both onerous and studded with uncertainty requiring as they do the parties to stand in the shoes of the relevant authority and guess at the outcome of a hypothetical set of proceedings.

The exemption will not apply in relation to payments, however, described, of remuneration including arrears thereof or to any payments falling within TCA 1997, s 123 (Termination payments: see **10.4**) or TCA 1997, s 480(2)(a) (Payments to compensate for a reduction in emoluments or changes in working conditions, etc: see **10.407**) (TCA 1997, s 192A(5)) or to a payment of compensation paid in accordance with an order made under the Employment Permits Act 2003, s 2B (TCA 1997, s 192A(5A)). Under the Employment Permits Act 2003 a foreign national may not be employed in the State without an employment permit. Notwithstanding the absence of such a permit, and the consequent illegality of the employment, under the Employment Permits Act 2003, s 2B a foreign national may take a civil action for compensation against such an employer. Such payments are by virtue of TCA 1997, s 124A treated as profits or gains accruing from an office or employment chargeable to tax under Sch E and emoluments to which PAYE must be applied.

Legal costs

Legal costs recovered by an employee from his employer as part of proceedings to obtain compensation for loss of office, etc may be regarded as a taxable receipt where the compensation itself is taxable under Sch E, although this does not necessarily follow if for example it is possible to differentiate the award itself from the costs to which the employee was put as a result of a wrongful act on the part of the employer. The Revenue Commissioners apparently take the view that the taxable nature of the costs follows that of the event; however, the Revenue Commissioners will not seek to impose tax where costs are paid directly to the former employee's solicitor in discharge of costs related solely to the relevant proceedings under a specific term of the agreement (*Tax Briefing 51*). The reference to 'former' employee may imply that the purported concession only applies to termination cases.

10.112 Pensions and sickness benefits

Sch E charges tax in respect of every annuity, pension or stipend payable out of the public revenue of the State (other than any annuity chargeable under Sch C) and any other pension from an Irish source (TCA 1997, s 19(1), Sch E, paras 1 and 2). In applying Sch E, the word 'pension' is used as including a pension that is paid voluntarily or is capable of being discontinued, as well as a pension payable under a legal obligation; the word 'annuity' is given a correspondingly extended meaning (Sch E, para 3).

In *Wales v Tilley* 25 TC 136, Viscount Simonds, who delivered the majority speech, rejected the argument that a pension was 'deferred remuneration'. Thus, it may be seen that the right to receive a pension, although it may be incorporated into a taxpayer's service contract, represents a distinct source of income (see also the discussion of *IRC v Duke of Westminster* 19 TC 490 in Ward: Taxation of Contractual Termination Payments [1998] ITR 407). The House of Lords held in *Wales v Tilley* that a pension was a separate subject matter of taxation apart from employments or offices, and thus a sum paid in commutation of pension rights was not taxable as an emolument. Under the foregoing analysis, the provision of TCA 1997, s 19(1) (which brings pensions into charge as discrete items) simply recognises that a pension is necessarily a separate subject matter for taxation; on this basis, the only effect of s 19(1) is to translate the taxation of such pensions generally from Sch D to Sch E (see also *Westminster Bank v Barford* 38 TC 68). The Revenue Commissioners have issued a precedent stating their view that it may be possible for a *bona fide* sum paid to compensate an employee for changes in the benefit structure of a pension scheme to be paid 'free of tax' (but presumably subject to TCA 1997, s 123: see **10.4**).

In *Stedeford v Beloe* 16 TC 505, the House of Lords held that a pension paid voluntarily by the governing body of a school out of the school funds to a headmaster on his retirement was not taxable under Sch E. In that case, there was no pension scheme in existence under which the headmaster could have qualified for the pension and the governing body had the right at any time to cease making payments to him should it decide to do so. The extended meanings of 'pension' and 'annuity' set out in Sch E para 3, as mentioned above, and the further provision of TCA 1997, s 790 were brought in to prevent the decision in *Stedeford v Beloe* taking a voluntary pension or annuity out of the income tax net. TCA 1997, s 779 charges all pensions paid under approved retirement benefit schemes (see **16.110**) under Sch E.

TCA 1997, s 790 provides that any pension, annuity or other annual payment made to a person who has ceased to hold an office or employment, or to the widow(er), surviving civil partner, child or child of surviving civil partner or any relative or dependant of that person, is deemed to be income assessable to income tax under Sch D or Sch E, as the case may require. The pension, etc is taxable as income notwithstanding that it may be paid voluntarily or may be capable of being discontinued. It may be payable by the former employer or other person under whom the office or employment was held, or by the heirs, executors, administrators or successors of that employer or other person. If the pension, annuity or annual payment is from an Irish source, it is taxable under Sch E, but any pension, etc from a foreign source is income within Sch D Case III (see **13.106**). Any lump sums on the commutation of, or compensation for the loss of such a pension would again be non-taxable on general principles albeit potentially within TCA 1997, s 123 if paid in connection with the termination of an employment, etc (see **10.401**).

In short, an individual is taxable under Sch E (except for unapproved foreign pensions) on any pension, annuity, annual payment or other allowance paid to him, whether it is paid voluntarily or under a legal obligation, through an approved or unapproved pension scheme, or otherwise. It is sufficient that it is payable in consequence of or following the holding of a prior office or employment. The taxpayer may have ceased to hold the office or employment as a result of retirement, or of some other cause such as redundancy or disability: *Johnson v Holleran* [1989] STC 1. The term 'pension' however does not extend to an annual payment made by way of compensation for loss of office (*McMann v Shaw* 48 TC 530). The person taxable is the actual recipient, whether he is the person who held the office or the employment or he is the spouse, civil partner, child, dependant, etc of that person.

The reference in TCA 1997, s 19 Sch E para 2 to any annuity or pension payable out of the public revenue of the State brings within the charge to tax under that Schedule not only pensions payable to former civil servants, members of the Defence Forces and the Garda Síochána, etc, but also the various pensions and other long term benefits payable under the Social Welfare Acts such as the retirement pension, the widow's (now survivor's) (contributory) pension, the orphan's (contributory or non-contributory) allowance, the old age (contributory) pension, the invalidity pension and the deserted wife's benefit. The orphan's (contributory) allowance is, however, the income of the child and not that of the parent or guardian who receives it on his behalf (*O'Coindealbhain v O'Carroll* IV ITR 221). The Revenue Commissioners accept that a similar analysis applies to the orphans (non-contributory) allowance. In *O'Siochain v Neenan* ITR 472, Smyth J applied the decision in *O'Carroll* and held that the addition in the widow's social welfare contributory pension in respect of a dependent child was the income of the child. This decision, which relied on an avowedly (and most dubious) purposive approach to the legislation, was reversed by the Supreme Court in 1998.

In practice, short term social welfare benefits are generally not taxed, but it is understood that it is the Revenue's view that any benefit payable at regular intervals may be taxed if the period of payment extends over a full year or more. This excludes from taxation such benefits as the death grant and other social welfare benefits which are payable only once or for periods which do not normally amount to one year or more. In practice the Revenue will not seek to tax the Supplementary Welfare allowance or the Family Income supplement.

By virtue of TCA 1997, s 126 the following benefits are generally rendered taxable irrespective of whether receivable in the long term or short term:

(a) unemployment benefit;
(b) injury benefit comprised in occupational injuries benefit;
(c) disability benefit; and
(d) pay-related benefit.

With effect from 1 July 2013, maternity benefit, adoptive benefit and health and safety benefit are all liable to tax under Sch E. Paternity benefit is equally liable from 1 August 2016 (inserted into TCA 1997 by Paternity Leave and Benefit Act 2016 and commenced by SI 435/2016). Disability and Occupational Injury benefit, Unemployment Benefit and Pay-Related benefit (now replaced by Jobseeker's benefit and Jobseeker's allowance) are all generally taxable (SI 66/1993; SI 19/1994). However, by virtue of TCA 1997, s 126(3)(b), any amount referable to a qualifying child as defined by SWCA 2005, s 2(3) is not brought within the charge to tax. The first €13 per income tax week of unemployment benefit, excluding amounts referable to a qualifying child will be disregarded (TCA 1997, s 126(4)). For years prior to 2012 disability and/or injury benefit payable for the first 36 days of a claim in the year of assessment was also exempt (TCA 1997, s 126(5) deleted by FA 2012). The three 'waiting days' for which disability benefit is not payable and Sundays were not counted towards the 36 days; where there is more than one period of absence, then the 'waiting days' referable to each such period were normally disregarded (confirmed in *Tax Briefing 26*).

Unemployment benefit paid to a person in 'short-term' unemployment is also exempt (TCA 1997, s 126(3)(c) as inserted by FA 2007, s 10; short-term unemployment is defined as for the purposes of the Social Welfare Acts; SWCA 2005, s 2(1) defines short-time employment as one where for the time being the number of days actually worked are less than those of a normal working week for the employment concerned and this occurs on a systematic basis.

TCA 1997, s 126(2) provides that the widow's contributory pension (now replaced by the survivor's contributory pension), the orphan's contributory allowance (now replaced by the Guardian's Payment (Contributory)), the retirement pension (now replaced by the State Pension (Transition)) and old age contributory pensions (now replaced by the State Pension (Contributory)) are deemed to be emoluments to which TCA 1997, Pt 42 Ch 4 (the PAYE system) applies. TCA 1997, s 126(7) permits the Revenue Commissioners to modify the PAYE regulations in order to collect tax due in relation to these benefits, including a power to allocate tax reliefs between those benefits and other emoluments received by the individual. While PAYE is not in practice directly deducted from these benefits, the recipient remains entitled to the employee tax credit (see **3.310**).

In *Cronin v C* IV ITR 135, the assignment of a pension to a third party in return for a lump sum was held to be effective for income tax purposes. A different view was expressed by the Special Commissioners in *Meredith-Hardy v McCellan* [1995] STC (SCD) 26, citing *Hadlee v CIR* [1993] STC 294 as a general authority that the assignment of a mere right to income cannot alter the incidence of tax. In fact, as noted at **4.501**, the ratio of the decision in *Hadlee* was narrower than this. However, it may be noted that in some cases there will be a legal bar against the assignment of a pension (see eg Social Welfare Consolidation Act 2005, s 283).

Sick pay paid to an employee by his employer while he is unable to work is fully taxable under general Sch E principles. In some cases, employers and employees may contribute jointly into a sickness scheme; in such cases the Revenue will generally only seek to tax the excess of any payments from the fund over and above the employee's contributions.

Permanent health insurance schemes (PHI)

As discussed in **3.317**, contributions to permanent health insurance schemes approved by the Revenue Commissioners under TCA 1997, s 125 will qualify for deductions in computing an individual's taxable income (subject to prescribed limits). Contributions paid by an employee subject to PAYE are deducted at source from the employee's emoluments; PAYE will only be applied to the net amount of the emoluments (TCA 1997, s 986(1)(g)(i)). Any benefits received under a scheme are deemed to arise from an employment and are to be computed in accordance with TCA 1997, s 112, see **10.102**; the PAYE rules are to apply accordingly (TCA 1997, s 125). As noted in **3.317**, contributions paid on an employee's behalf by the employer are taxable as a benefit under the normal rules of Sch E (see **10.203**); however, the employee may claim a deduction as if he had paid the contribution himself (TCA 1997, ss 125(2), (3)).

10.113 Shares and share options

Award of shares under general principles

A person holding an office or employment with a company may sometimes be given an opportunity of acquiring shares in that company or, perhaps, in its parent company at a favourable price. This may be done simply by allowing him to subscribe for the shares at a price less than their market value on the date in question; alternatively, he may be given an option to apply for shares in the company at a stated price at any time within a stated period. Depending on the terms of the agreement in the particular case, once the shares are acquired he may either have unrestricted rights to dispose of them at any time or he may be restrained from disposing of them for a certain minimum period. Normally, in such cases an emolument taxable under the main Sch E charging rule is deemed to arise if the employee is not required to pay to the company the full market value of the shares allotted or of any other valuable right to which he may become entitled in relation to the shares. However, for the benefit to be taxable, it must have arisen from the office or employment under the general principles discussed above.

In *Weight v Salmon* 19 TC 174, the respondent was the managing director of a company entitled under a service agreement to a fixed salary. In addition, the directors of the company by resolution each year gave him the privilege of applying for certain unissued shares in the company at their par value, which was considerably less than their current market value. He duly applied for and was allotted the shares. He was assessed to tax under Sch E on the difference between the market value of the shares taken up and the par price actually paid for them. There was no restriction imposed on the transferability of the shares after they were allotted. It was held in the House of Lords that this privilege for subscribing for the shares at less than their market value represented money's worth and was assessable as a profit of his office as managing director.

The position is problematic when the founder (or founders) of a company receives shares at a valuation below that at which shares are issued to outsiders (such as venture capitalists). Assuming that the founder will also be directors and/or employees of the company, the issue of a potential Sch E charge under TCA 1997, s 112 arises. Where there is a significant delay between the initial issue of shares to the founder(s) and the issue of shares to the outsiders, it may be that value has flowed into the company in the meanwhile. This could arise as a result of the founder's own participation in the company, eg where he has entered into an employment contract with the company. It could also arise where the founder(s) have in the meanwhile assembled a project with high financial potential. In the absence of factors such as these, it will be highly debatable whether the benefit of the shares received at undervalue were received by an individual in his capacity as founder (ie as initiator of the corporate project) or as director/employee (in anticipation of future services).

In *Tyrer v Smart* [1979] STC 34, the taxpayer was entitled to apply for a public issue of shares at a pre-arranged price which was likely (but by no means certain) to prove favourable. In the event the taxpayers derived a considerable benefit from these arrangements. The House of Lords upheld the finding of the Appeal Commissioners that this benefit derived from the taxpayer's employment and not from his decision to invest as one of fact; it seems that a finding to the opposite effect would equally well have been upheld.

One case in which the gift of shares in a company to a director was held to be a gift or personal testimonial, and not remuneration for services rendered, was *Bridges v Bearsley* 37 TC 289. This case was heard jointly with that of *Bridges v Hewitt*. Both Mr Bearsley and Mr Hewitt were directors of Meccano Ltd. They had served respectively as managing director and director and in other capacities for many years and had greatly helped in building up the business and in running it when it had become established. Both respondents had been under the impression that the former principal shareholder would bequeath them shares by his will, but he had not done so.

Subsequently, the sons of the deceased owner, acting under a sense of moral obligation, agreed to execute a deed binding them to transfer some of their own shares to the taxpayer. The taxpayer's solicitor, who was anxious to ensure that the deed would be binding, inserted an additional clause expressing the transfer to be in consideration of the taxpayer continuing to serve as a director for a prescribed period. The Revenue argued that his clause was conclusive on the issue of whether or not the transfer of shares was an emolument.

The majority judges in the Court of Appeal held that the arrangement was in reality a conditional gift: the fulfilment of the period of service was merely the contingency which had to be satisfied before the taxpayer's entitlement to the shares could crystallise.

Thus, the transfer of shares was not in any sense an inducement for services to be rendered in the future. In arriving at this conclusion, the court looked at the legal realities of the arrangements and not merely at the terminology used in the documents. Morris LJ stated:

> … [the sons] made it a condition of their promise that [the taxpayer] would go on serving the company … It was for the [taxpayer] and for the company to decide whether he should continue. [The taxpayer] … could not therefore contract with [the sons] in positive terms that they would serve the company.

As discussed in **10.110** the fact that shares may be given to employees by a third party, ie a person other than the employer company, is not of itself sufficient to take the gift out of the tax net. In *Patrick v Burrows* 35 TC 138, a trust was created by a director of a company to hold and, at the discretion of the trustees, to distribute 2,000 of the company's shares among employees to whom it was expedient to give an interest in the business in consideration of past or future services and with a view to the prosperity of the company. Assessments on one of the employees in respect of shares distributed to him were upheld. The same principle would apply to distributions of shares directly to employees by an Employee Share Ownership Plan within TCA 1997, s 519.

In any case involving the acquisition of shares or of a right to subscribe for shares, the date on which the employee is regarded as receiving the perquisite or profit of the employment is important as it is on that date that the market value of the shares or other right must be ascertained, and compared with any price paid by the employee, to determine the amount that is taxable. In *Bentley v Evans* 39 TC 132, certain employees of an English company were offered shares in its Canadian parent company at a price 15 per cent below the market value of the shares on 1 October 1953. The purchase price was to be paid by instalments which, in the absence of other arrangements, were recoverable by deductions from pay. At the end of any month in which the parent company had received sufficient funds to pay the purchase price of at least three shares, the company would issue those shares to the employee. On 7 October 1953, Mr Evans accepted this offer to buy 15 shares. He was allotted three shares in each of the months March, July and October 1954 financed by deductions from pay. In November 1954 he paid cash and was allotted his remaining six shares.

The Crown contended that the profits from his employment arose when the shares were actually allotted to Mr Evans and that, in consequence, the amounts assessable were to be calculated by reference to the difference between the offer price and the market values of the shares obtainable in March, July, October and November 1954 respectively. This was rejected and it was held that the taxable perquisite should be calculated by reference to the market value of the 15 shares on 7 October 1953. Although the shares were only freely transferable after they had been paid up and issued, Mr Evans had when he accepted the company's offer on 7 October 1953 acquired a legally enforceable right to the shares and he could have paid them up more quickly if he had wanted to.

In *Tyrer v Smart* [1979] STC 34 (discussed above), the taxpayer was entitled to apply for a public issue of shares in his employer company at a pre-arranged price. The House of Lords held that he was liable on the benefit of the difference between the price which he paid for his shares and their value at the date his application was accepted (any fluctuations in value between that date and the date of issue being accordingly disregarded). This analysis depended on identifying the perquisite as crystallising at the point where the taxpayer acquired an enforceable legal right. In strictness, the granting of priority allocations of shares to employees in respect of public offers of shares issued at a discount to current market value could attract a similar analysis for Sch E purposes.

An important case concerning the granting of a share option to an employee is *Abbott v Philbin* 39 TC 82. The appellant, the secretary of a company, paid £20 on 7 October 1954 for an option granted to him by the company under which he became entitled to purchase up to 2,000 shares in the company for the then market price of the shares (£3.42 per share). The terms of the option, which was non-transferable, permitted the appellant to exercise it at any time within 10 years. On 28 March 1956, he applied for and was allotted 250 shares at the option price of £3.42, the market value per share then being £4.10. The Crown assessed him for 1955–56 on the excess of that market price of the 250 shares (£1,025) over the sum of the option price (£855) paid for them and a proportion of the 20 paid for the option.

The House of Lords held, by a 3–2 majority, that the benefit of the share option contract was a perquisite of the appellant's office taxable in the year in which the option was granted (1954–55) and not, as the Crown had contended in the later year (1955–56) in which it was exercised. This meant that the amount of the perquisite to be assessed under Sch E had to be measured as the excess of the market value on 7 October 1954 (date of granting option) of the right to purchase the shares at the fixed price over the £20 paid for the option. Since the option price was the same as the market value on that date, and as it was quite possible that the price of the shares in the next 10 years could go down as well as up, the value of the perquisite at 7 October 1954 was likely to be significantly lower than the alternative sought unsuccessfully by the Crown.

The majority decision of the House of Lords in *Abbott v Philbin* overruled an earlier decision on a similar point by the Scottish Court of Session which had held, in *Forbes' Executors v IRC* 38 TC 12, that a non-transferable share option had no value until it was exercised and that it was only then that the taxpayer had received something which he could convert into money. In his judgment in *Abbott v Philbin*, Viscount Simmonds (one of the three Law Lords giving the majority decision) rejected the Crown's argument in seeking to tax the value of the option when it was exercised, as that implied that the appellant had not acquired a perquisite at the date the option was granted. He considered there could not be one perquisite at that date and another perquisite when the shares were taken up. The better view is that this does not imply that the perquisite represented by the original option must necessarily have had a monetary value. Viscount Simmonds observed:

> … it was, in my opinion, a perquisite at the date of grant and, if it had no value, there was nothing to tax and that is the end of the matter.'

The court, in fact, held that when the appellant was granted the option he then had something which could be turned to pecuniary account. While the non-transferability of the option was a feature which might reduce its value, this did not alter the fact that it was a valuable right that could be converted into money.

Viscount Simmonds and Lord Radcliffe also held that the capital appreciation enjoyed by the taxpayer subsequent to the date of grant of the option was (in the words of Lord Radcliffe):

> … an advantage which accrued to the (taxpayer) … as the holder of a legal right which he had obtained in an earlier year, and which he had exercised as option holder against the company. The quantum of the benefit, which is the alleged taxable receipt, is not in such circumstances the profit of the service; it is the profit of his exploitation of a valuable gift.

This reasoning was followed in *Wilcock v Eve* [1995] STC 18, where it was held that an *ex gratia* payment to compensate a taxpayer for the loss of such capital appreciation on the premature termination of a share option-scheme, was itself not taxable under Sch E.

The decision in *Abbott v Philbin* may be contrasted with that in the earlier case of *Edwards v Roberts* 19 TC 618, where under the terms of his service agreement, a fund was set up for the benefit of the taxpayer, to which his employer made yearly contributions. In broad terms, the taxpayer was entitled to the assets of the trust (which were, again, shares in his employer company), subject to his completing five years' service with his employer. The Court of Appeal held the employer's yearly contributions did not in themselves constitute emoluments, and that an emolument only accrued to the taxpayer when and if the assets of the fund vested in him. It followed that the amount of the benefit which he received was based on the value of the fund assets at the time of vesting (ie inclusive of all capital appreciation up to that time). No question arose as to whether the taxpayer's conditional rights to acquire the fund assets in the future should have been regarded as taxable perquisites (see also *Bootle v Bye* [1996] STC (SCD) 58 where the UK Special Commissioners came to a similar conclusion in respect of an agreement to make a payment to directors, contingent on a take-over taking place).

In order to counter the effect of *Abbot v Philbin* TCA 1997, s 128 now charges tax under Sch E by reference to the market value of the shares at the date of exercise of the option, but subject to an exception for share options granted (and exercised) in accordance with the terms of a share option scheme approved by the Revenue Commissioners.

Where an employer or other person awards shares (including stock or securities as defined by TCA 1997, s 135, ie including securities not creating or evidencing a charge on assets) to an employee or director, and income tax under either Sch D or Sch E may be chargeable on the recipient, the person concerned must submit relevant particulars to the Revenue Commissioners on or before 31 March after the end of the tax year in which the award was made or the forfeiture occurred (TCA 1997, s 897B, inserted by FA 2010, s 18, with effect for shares awarded on or after 1 January 2009). The requirement will not apply if the person concerned is otherwise obliged to provide such particulars to the Revenue Commissioners. Failure to make a return attracts the penalties appropriate to returns within TCA 1997, Sch 29, Column 3 (see **2.701**).

Restricted Shares

Following the principle established in *Wilkins v Rogerson* (see **10.105**), the value of the shares received by way of taxable emoluments should normally be taken as the amount of cash into which they could be converted. Where the shares are subject to a genuine restriction (or 'clog') on their disposal, it would seem that the value of the shares should be reduced accordingly (see *Ede v Wilson & Cornwell* 26 TC 381, a case preceding *Wilkins v Rogerson*, in which the court also expressed the view that it was the value to the particular taxpayer which had to be taken into account). The Revenue Commissioners traditionally took the view that such a restriction could not be taken into account in valuing the shares concerned but only in valuing the benefit to the employee (ie net of any consideration paid by the employee) (*Tax Briefing 31*). This view seemed neither logical nor correct as a matter of general principle. TCA 1997, s 128D, as amended by FA 2010, s 17 with effect from 20 November 2008, however, makes clear that the restriction is taken into account in arriving at the amount chargeable to income tax, *viz* the value of the shares concerned before any deduction for consideration payable by the employee.

Prior to the enactment of TCA 1997, s 128D the Revenue Commissioners in practice operated a sliding scale under which they reduced the benefit arising on receipt of the shares by reference to the number of years during which the shares cannot be disposed of, as follows:

Number of years	*% Reduction*
1	10
2	20
3	30
4	40
5	50
6 and above	55

The Revenue Commissioners however generally required arrangements of this kind to be approved in advance and for the shares to be held in trust or under similar arrangements in order to ensure that the clog on disposal was effective. They also required that the clog should be absolute in nature (presumably meaning that the clog must apply in all circumstances); again, this requirement does not appear to be justified in law. They reserved the right to withdraw what they view as a concession where a clog is imposed for tax avoidance as opposed to genuinely commercial reasons (*Tax Briefing 35*).

The Revenue stated that where a restriction attaching to shares is subsequently removed or amended the original income tax charge would be correspondingly revised (*Tax Briefing 31*). This approach again seemed wrong in principle, since the value of the shares at the date of receipt is an issue of fact to be resolved by reference to the circumstances prevailing at the time. The correct issue would seem to be whether the subsequent removal or amendment of a restriction (which will result in an increased value in the shares concerned) is itself a pecuniary benefit; in principle there seems to be no persuasive reason why not.

TCA 1997, s 128D inserted by F(No2)A 2008, s 12, as amended by FA 2010, s 17, provides a statutory code from 2009 onwards in relation to clogs on disposal and other restrictions. The section applies where a director or employee, as widely defined by TCA 1997, s 770(1), ('employee' hereafter) acquires in their capacity as such *restricted shares* in their employing company or in a company which controls (within the meaning of TCA 1997, s 432) their employer company (TCA 1997, s 128D(2). These provisions apply to shares granted directly to employees other than under TCA 1997, Sch 11 (Profit Sharing Schemes: see **11.4**), Sch 12 (ESOTs: see **11.5**), Sch 12A (Approved Savings-Related Share Option Schemes: see **11.5)** or Sch 12C (Approved Share Option Schemes: see **11.7)** and also to shares granted on the exercise of an option, chargeable under TCA 1997, s 128 (see below) (TCA 1997, s 128D(7)).

Restricted shares are shares or stock where:

(a) there is a written contract or agreement in place under the terms of which the employee cannot assign, charge, pledge as security for a loan or other debt, transfer, or generally otherwise dispose of the shares for a specified period of not less than one year (the '*specified period*'). There is an exception for disposals:
   (i) on the death of the employee, or
   (ii) as a consequence of the employee agreeing to:
      (I) accept an offer for the shares (in this clause referred to as the 'original shares') if the acceptance or agreement would result in a new holding (within the meaning of TCA 1997, s 584) being equated with the original shares for the purposes of capital gains tax,
      (II) a transaction affecting the shares or such of the shares as are of a particular class if the transaction would be entered into pursuant to a compromise, arrangement or scheme applicable to or affecting all the ordinary share capital of the company in question or, as the case may be, all the shares of the same class as the shares acquired by the director or employee, or
      (III) accept an offer of cash, with or without other assets, for the shares if the offer forms part of a general offer made to holders of shares of the same class as the shares acquired by the employee or of shares in the same company and made in the first instance on a condition such that if it is satisfied the person making the offer will have control (within the meaning of TCA 1997, s 432) of that company; and

(b) the contract or agreement is in place for bona fide commercial purposes and does not form part of a scheme or arrangement of which the main purpose or one of the main purposes is the avoidance of tax;

(c) during the specified period, the shares are held in a trust established by the employer for the benefit of employees or held under such other arrangements as the Revenue Commissioners may allow (TCA 1997, s 128D(3); with effect from 4 February 2010, the trust must be established in the State or another EEA state and the trustees must be resident in the State or another EEA state (TCA 1997, s 128D(2) as inserted by FA 2010, s 16);

Where the section applies:

(a) the amount chargeable to income tax under Sch E (and computed in accordance with TCA 1997, s 112 (general Sch E charging provisions) or TCA 1997, s 128 (taxation of share options etc; see below) or under Sch D Case III, on the acquisition of the shares, shall be reduced by an amount determined by the formula A x (B/10),

where:

A is the amount of the income chargeable to tax under Sch E or Sch D Case III; and

B is the number of specified years up to a maximum of six (TCA 1997, s 128D(4)(a)).

This contrasts with Revenue practice where the maximum reduction was 55 per cent where the shares were restricted for six years or more. The amount chargeable to income tax will be computed by reference to the open market value of the shares (as ascertained under TCA 1997, s 548) at the date of acquisition but without regard to the restriction on the freedom of the employee to assign charge, pledge as security for a loan or other debt, transfer, or otherwise dispose of the shares (TCA 1997, s 128D(4)(b)).

There will be a recapture of any reduction of income tax claimed under these provisions where subsequently but before the expiry of the specified period, either:

(a) any of the restrictions enumerated above is removed or varied; or

(b) the shares are disposed of under one of the exceptions described above (eg on a qualifying share-for-share takeover). The income tax charge on acquisition of the shares will be adjusted to reflect the actual period during which the restriction applied. The adjustment of liability may be made at any time whether by means of an assessment, an additional assessment or otherwise (TCA 1997, s 128D(5)).

Where in any year:

(a) a person awards restricted shares to an employee or the employee acquires restricted shares on the exercise of an option within TCA 1997, s 128 previously granted by that person; or

(b) an event occurs which requires a recapture of a reduction in income tax previously granted under the section (*presumably, though not stated, where the shares were originally awarded by the person in question*),

that person must submit relevant particulars to the Revenue Commissioners on or before 31 March after the end of the tax year in which the award was made or the event occurred (TCA 1997, s 128D(8)).

Forfeitable Shares

It is understood that the Revenue Commissioners adopted a similar approach to that applied by them to restricted shares (see immediately above) in the case of shares awarded to employees which are subject to forfeiture. Again, TCA 1997, s 128E inserted by F(No2)A 2008, s 12 provides a statutory code in respect of shares acquired from 20 November 2008 onwards where an employee, as widely defined by TCA 1997, s 770(1), ('employee' hereafter) acquires in his capacity as such, forfeitable shares in his employing company or another company. These provisions apply to shares granted directly to employees and also to shares granted on the exercise of an option, chargeable under TCA 1997, s 128 (see below) (TCA 1997, s 128E(2)).

Forfeitable shares are shares or stock where:

(a) there is a written contract or agreement (*prima facie* including the Articles of a company) under the terms of which:
   (i) there will be a forfeiture of the shares, if certain circumstances arise or do not arise,
   (ii) as a result of the forfeiture, the employee will cease to have any beneficial interest in the shares, and
   (iii) the employee will not be entitled to receive, directly or indirectly, consideration in money or money's worth in respect of the shares on their forfeiture in excess of the consideration given by the employee for the acquisition of the shares; and

(b) the contract or agreement is in place for bona fide commercial purposes and does not form part of a scheme or arrangement of which the main purpose or one of the main purposes is the avoidance of tax; (TCA 1997, s 128E(3)).

Shares will not be treated as forfeitable shares only because they are unpaid or partly paid shares which may be forfeited for the non-payment of calls (TCA 1997, s 128E(4)).

Where under the terms of the relevant contract or agreement the shares are in fact subsequently forfeited, then:

(a) the employee will be treated, for the tax year in which the shares were acquired, as if he did not acquire the shares; and
(b) such adjustment shall be made by repayment or otherwise as the case may require, on receipt of a claim from the employee.

The claim must be made within four years from the end of the tax year in which the shares are forfeited (TCA 1997, s 128E(6)). The normal time limits for repayments of tax under TCA 1997, s 865(6) will not apply in these circumstances (TCA 1997, s 128E(7)).

Where in any year:

(a) a person awards forfeitable shares to an employee; or
(b) such shares are in fact subsequently forfeited (*presumably, though not stated, where the shares were originally awarded by the person in question*),

that person must submit relevant particulars to the Revenue Commissioners on or before 31 March after the end of the tax year in which the award was made or the forfeiture occurred (TCA 1997, s 128E(9)). There is no provision under this heading for the case where the employee acquires forfeitable shares on the exercise of an option within TCA 1997, s 128 previously granted by that person,

Shares acquired at an undervalue/disposed of at overvalue

TCA 1997, s 122A seeks to impose a tax charge on certain acquisitions and disposals by employees which might otherwise fall outside the income tax code. Firstly, TCA 1997, s 122A(2) applies where an employee or a person connected with an employee acquires any shares at an undervalue in pursuance of a right or opportunity available by reason of his employment.

An 'employee' is defined as for the purposes of TCA 1997, s 122 (the 'preferential loan' rules); this definition is discussed at **10.211** under 'employee'. As noted there, the definition prior to 1 January 2005 implied that only employees liable to tax under Sch E were subject to these provisions; however, TCA 1997, s 122A(7) again clearly envisages that Sch D employees also fall within the scope of the charge.

The definition of a 'connected person' is that within TCA 1997, s 10 (see the discussion thereof at **12.304**).

Shares are deemed to be acquired at an undervalue where they are acquired for nothing or for an amount which is less than the market value (as defined under the capital gains tax rules of TCA 1997, s 548 in terms of open market value) of fully paid up shares of the class of shares in question. It is immaterial whether or not the person acquiring the shares is obliged to make any payment at a time in the future (TCA 1997, s 122A(3)(a)). Shares include securities as defined by TCA 1997, s 135 (ie including securities not creating or evidencing a charge on assets) (TCA 1997, s 122A(1)); the shares can relate to any company, not merely the employing company (TCA 1997, s 122A(2)). The shares can be acquired by subscription assignment or any other means (TCA 1997, s 122A(1)).

Where shares are issued at an undervalue only to employees (or a class of employees), it will be very difficult to rebut the inference that the acquisition of those shares was not in pursuance of an opportunity available by reason of the employment (note the discussion in *IRC v Herd* [1992] STC 264 and compare *Cheatle v IRC* [1982] STC 376. In *Wilcock v Eve* [1995] STC 18 Carnwath J suggested that the expression 'by reason of the employment' differed little, if at all, from the general 'source' principle under Sch E (discussed in **10.106**).

Where the above conditions are met, TCA 1997, s 122A(2) deems the employee to have received an interest-free loan falling within TCA 1997, s 122 (see **10.211** below) and a benefit in kind arises accordingly. The amount of the loan is equal to the 'under-value on acquisition' to the extent that this is not already chargeable to tax as an emolument (ie as a profits arising from the individual's employment) (TCA 1997, s 128(1) and (4)). The principle established in *Weight v Salmon* 19 TC 174 would result in an employee being taxed by reference to the actual market value of shares received by him if the receipt thereof constituted a profit 'from the employment'; however, in the case of shares in a private company the open market value rule applicable under TCA 1997, s 122A under TCA 1997, s 548 will normally lead to a higher valuation. In theory therefore, if such shares are received in pursuance of a right or opportunity available 'by reason of the employment', the excess of open market value over actual market value could be caught under TCA 1997, s 122A.

The 'under-value on acquisition' for these purposes is the market value of fully paid-up shares of the same class, less any payment made for the acquisition (TCA 1997, s 128(3)(b)); payment can involve any consideration whether in money or money's worth and whether made under a legal obligation or not (TCA 1997, s 122A(11)). Thus, it is not permissible to discount the market value of the shares by reference to the fact that they do not have to be fully paid-up on subscription.

TCA 1997, s 122A(2) accordingly will apply to issue of partly paid-up shares, and to acquisitions of fully paid shares at an undervalue by persons connected to the employee (if the acquisition is in pursuance of a right or opportunity available by reason of the employee's employment). The acquisition of fully paid-up shares by the employee himself by reason of his employment would normally be taxable under general principles in any event. There are three main exceptions to this proposition. Firstly, the benefit of shares acquired by an employee under an approved profit sharing scheme will be exempt (see **11.4**); however, TCA 1997, s 122A is expressed to be subject to the profit-sharing provisions contained in TCA 1997, Pt 17 Ch 1. Secondly, the benefit of shares acquired under approved option schemes within FA 1986, s 10 (ie in respect of options granted between 6 April 1986 and 28 January 1992) will also escape taxation. In practice, the Revenue will not take this point and will not apply the provisions of either TCA 1997, s 122(2) or s 122A(6) (see below) to shares acquired under s 10 schemes (*Tax Briefing 32*). Finally, the benefit of shares acquired where a Revenue approved Save As You Earn (SAYE) share scheme is also exempt (see **11.6**).

The notional loan is deemed to remain outstanding until one of four events arises; however, the amount thereof will be reduced by any subsequent payments made for the shares concerned (TCA 1997, s 122A(4)). The wide definition of payment within TCA 1997, s 122A(4) again applies. The four events are as follows:

(a) the whole amount of the amount outstanding is made good by means of payments or further payments made for the shares;
(b) the case being one in which the shares were not at the time of acquisition fully paid up, any outstanding or contingent obligation to pay for them is released, transferred or adjusted so as no longer to bind the employee or any connected person;
(c) the shares are so disposed of by surrender or otherwise that neither the employee or any connected person no longer has a beneficial interest in the shares; and
(d) the employee dies (TCA 1997, s 122A(5)).

The wide definition of 'payment' within TCA 1997, s 122A(11) again applies. Where events (b) or (c) occurs, the employer is treated as releasing the notional loan, then giving rise to a tax charge on the amount deemed to be released under TCA 1997, s 122(3): see **10.211** (TCA 1997, s 122A(6)).

The charge applies regardless of whether the employment has been terminated at the time of the event in question (TCA 1997, s 122A(8)). However, no charge will apply if the employee has died prior to the event in question (TCA 1997, s 122A(9)).

The provisions of TCA 1997, s 122A(2) apply to interests in shares including an interest in the proceeds of sale of part of the shares, but not to share options (already dealt with under TCA 1997, s 128: see below) (TCA 1997, s 122A(10)). The references to shares, and the market value of shares, etc in the provisions mentioned above are extended to cover interests in shares (TCA 1997, s 122A(10)(a)–(d)). The provisions of TCA 1997, s 122A(7) apply with effect from 4 March 1998 irrespective of when the shares were acquired; any notional loan arising is deemed to commence on that date equal to the amount then outstanding (FA 1998, s 14(2)(a)–(b)).

TCA 1997, s 122A(7) contains a second charging provision. It applies where any shares (including securities within TCA 1997, s 135, ie including securities not creating or evidencing a charge on assets) which have been acquired in pursuance of a right or opportunity available by reason of an individual's employment (as defined by TCA

1997, s 122A(2): see above) are subsequently disposed of, so that neither the employee or any connected person (again as defined by TCA 1997, s 10) retains any beneficial interest therein, for a consideration in excess of their market value (again as defined by TCA 1997, s 548). It is again not necessary that the shares should be shares of the employing company; the shares again may have been acquired by subscription, assignment or any other means. However, in this case it is irrelevant whether or not the shares were originally acquired at an undervalue.

In *Grays Timber Products v HMRC* [2010] UKSC 4, a company director was entitled to an enhanced proportion of the proceeds on the sale of a controlling stake in the company pursuant to a shareholders' agreement. The rights were personal to him and could not be passed on to a subsequent hypothetical purchaser. Accordingly, the consideration received was in excess of the market value of the shares and was taxable under the UK equivalent of TCA 1997, s 122A(7).

Where the conditions set out above are met, the excess of the consideration over the market value of the shares is deemed to be an emolument from the employee's employment in the tax year of disposal (TCA 1997, s 122A(7)). The legislation states that a charge under Sch D or Sch E will arise accordingly; however, as already noted, it is not clear that Sch D Case III employments fell within the scope of TCA 1997, s 122A prior to 1 January 2005. It does seem clear however, that if the employment in question is outside the scope of Irish taxation in the tax year in question, no liability can be imposed under TCA 1997, s 122A(7).

The provisions of TCA 1997, s 122A(10) which extend the scope of the section to interests in shares for the purposes of TCA 1997, s 122A(2) (see above) apply equally to the charge under TCA 1997, s 122A(7). The provisions of TCA 1997, s 122A(10) could be in point for example where an employer operates 'stop loss' arrangements in favour of an employee's shareholdings (ie it binds itself to buy the shares at an agreed price, thus protecting the employees from the consequences of a fall in value in the relevant shares). The provisions of TCA 1997, s 122A(7) apply in respect of disposals made on or after 4 March 1998 (ie irrespective of the date of acquisition) (FA 1998, s 15(2)(c)).

Treatment of share options under TCA 1997, s 128

TCA 1997, s 128 deals generally with the income tax and capital gains tax consequences which ensue where a person obtains a right or option as a director of a company or as an employee to acquire shares in any company or any other asset or assets. In principle, it charges him to income tax under Sch E if and when he exercises, assigns or releases his right or option (and not when it is granted) by reference to the market value of the shares or other asset(s) at the date the option is exercised (but with a deduction for the option price paid for the acquisition of the shares, etc and for the consideration, if any, paid for the granting of the option).

The discussion which follows in the rest of this subdivision relates only to the tax treatment of share options (other than under approved share option schemes: see **11.7** and options acquired under a Save As You Earn (SAYE) share scheme: see **11.6**, which provide exceptions to the s 128 regime) and of other rights to acquire assets granted to directors and employees by reason of their offices or employments.

The rules of TCA 1997, s 128 are expressed as applying to any right obtained by a person as a director of a company or as an employee. The word 'right' is defined as a right to acquire any asset or assets including shares in any company. 'Shares' are defined as including stock as well as securities (as defined by TCA 1997, s 135, ie including securities not creating or evidencing a charge on assets).

Since in practice the most likely form of right to be affected is the option to acquire shares, the discussion which follows refers mainly to the taxation of share options, but the wider application of TCA 1997, s 128 to any right obtained by a person as a director or employee to acquire assets (of any kind) should not be overlooked. This contrasts with the legislation for approved share option schemes (see **11.7**) which covers only ordinary shares and not any other shares or assets.

For the purposes of TCA 1997, s 128, a person is regarded as acquiring a share option or other right 'as a director of a company or as an employee' if, by reason of his office or employment, it is granted either to him or to any other person who assigns it to him. Once it is established that the option or right has been granted by reason of the taxpayer's office or employment, the section applies notwithstanding that it may be granted either before he commences the office or employment or after he ceases to hold the office or employment. In *Wilcock v Eve* [1995] STC 18 Carnwath J suggested that the expression 'by reason of the employment' differed little, if at all, from the general 'source' principle under Sch E (discussed in **10.106**).

Territorial scope in respect of options granted prior to 5 April 2007

Prior to the amendment of TCA 1997, s 128(2) on the coming into force of FA 2005, s 16 (see further below) with effect from 5 April 2007, TCA 1997, s 128 simply provided that a person would only be regarded as obtaining an option as an employee or director if the income from his foreign office or employment was *not* taxable on the remittance basis under TCA 1997, s 71(3) on the individual acquiring the option or right (TCA 1997, s 128(1)(b)(ii)(II)). In other words, an individual not domiciled in the State (or an Irish citizen not ordinarily resident in the State) was not affected by TCA 1997, s 128 in respect of a share option or right to acquire assets which arose from his foreign office or employment (see **13.402**). With effect from 1 January 2006, it has to be borne in mind that to the extent that any duties of the office or employment were performed in Ireland, the remittance basis did not apply (see **10.101**), In SP IT/1/07, the Revenue Commissioners express the view that where *part* of the emoluments of a foreign office or employment is taxable under Schedule E on the arising basis, TCA 1997, s 128 will apply. It is by no means clear that this is a correct interpretation, since the office or employment is not one to which s 71(3) does not apply, albeit it does not apply *completely* to it.

It would also seem that it is the applicability of TCA 1997, s 71(3) at the time when the option is granted which is material since the exclusion is directed to the occasion on which the individual acquires the relevant right. Revenue Commissioners have expressed their own views on the territorial scope of TCA 1997, s 128 as it stood prior to the coming into operation of FA 2005, s 16 in *SP IT/1/07*. They take the view that it is the residence status of the employee at the time the option is granted which is critical. They argue that accordingly an individual who was resident in the State at the date of grant of an option is chargeable to tax on the exercise thereof even if he has ceased to be resident. Presumably, the Revenue would accept that this analysis cannot apply to a resident who was taxable on the remittance basis in respect of the employment concerned (see above). The Revenue also generally accept that a non-resident who has been granted an option in relation to an employment outside the scope of Irish taxation will not be liable on the exercise of the option even if the exercise occurs at a time when he has become resident in the State so long as the time the option was granted it was not contingent on, or connected with the duties of the office or employment being performed in the State. There is a strong inference to be drawn from the exemption granted in respect of employments taxable on the remittance basis that an option granted in respect of an employment altogether outside the scope of Irish taxation at the time of grant should not be covered by TCA 1997, s 128 irrespective of the residence status of the individual at the date of exercise. If this is indeed the case, then the Revenue position may well merely reflect the correct legal analysis.

Territorial scope in respect of options granted from 5 April 2007 onwards

With effect for share options granted on or after 5 April 2007, TCA 1997, s 128(2) provides that a charge will be imposed 'notwithstanding that [the taxpayer] was not resident in the State on the date on which the right was obtained'. This is a clumsy piece of drafting, equivalent to providing that a benefit will be taxable notwithstanding that it is not taxable. The declared intention of the Revenue Commissioners is to modify the territorial basis of TCA 1997, s 128 so that it falls into line with the limits imposed under Ireland's Double Tax Agreements and OECD principles (see **14.210**). In essence, this means that the Revenue take the view that Ireland now has a right to tax options granted prior to an individual becoming resident in the state where those options are exercised after the date on which he becomes resident; this is subject to the provisions of any relevant Double Tax Treaty.

It is by no mean apparent that the revised wording achieves this aim since it leaves the territorial scope of the section extremely unclear. The fact that a person who is non-resident at the time the option was granted may be chargeable to tax cannot mean that all non-residents who exercise share options are therefore within the charge to Irish tax (eg it is clear that an individual who has never been resident in the State and who has never been liable to Irish tax in respect of his employment income cannot be caught; but there is no obvious basis for saying that an individual who was liable to Irish tax on his employment income in a tax year subsequent to the year in which he received the option is so caught).

It does seem clear that the position regarding taxpayers liable on the remittance basis is unaffected by the change since TCA 1997, s 128(2) as amended applies only in relation to a right obtained as an employee or director; the effect of TCA 1997, s 128(1)(b)(ii)(II) is to treat the remittance taxpayer as *not* acquiring the right in that capacity.

In *SP IT 1/07*, the Revenue Commissioners provide numerous worked examples showing the interaction of the typical employment article in Double Tax Treaties.

In applying this section, the words 'director' and 'employee' are given the same meanings as they have in TCA 1997, s 770 in relation to approved retirement benefit schemes (see **16.103**). The 'market value' of any shares or other assets is to be determined in accordance with the capital gains tax valuation rules in TCA 1997, s 548. In principle, the latter section defines 'market value' as the price which the shares or assets might reasonably be expected to fetch on a sale in the open market, but it contains certain further rules relating respectively to the market value of shares quoted on stock exchanges, unquoted shares and unit trusts.

The charge to tax

The legislation provides for charging tax under two main headings – on any gain realised on the exercise, assignment or release of the share option or other right and also, in the case only of 'seven-year options' (see below), on the granting of the option or right. For options or rights other than seven-year options, tax is generally only chargeable in respect of the exercise, assignment or release of the option by the person to whom it is granted. However, there are certain anti-avoidance rules which charge tax in certain other circumstances (see below).

TCA 1997, s 128 charges tax under Sch E on the gain (if any) realised by the exercise of any share option or other right to acquire shares or other assets. It also charges any gain realised by the assignment or release of any such option or right. For this purpose, the release of an option or right includes an agreement to a restriction on the exercise of the option. The amount of the gain, as computed in the manner described in the next paragraph, is assessable for the tax year in which it is realised (and not for the year in which the option is granted).

TCA 1997, s 128 requires the taxable gain on the exercise of a share option or right to acquire assets to be calculated as the excess of:

(a) the market value of the shares (or other assets) the subject of the option or right at the date of their acquisition; over
(b) the aggregate of the value of the consideration given for the acquisition of the shares (or assets) and the price (if any) paid for the granting of the option or right.

'Market Value' follows the capital gains tax definition in TCA 1997, s 548 (TCA 1997, s 128(1)(a): see above).

In the case of an assignment or release of the option or right, the taxable gain must be taken as the excess of the consideration received for the assignment or release over the price (if any) paid for the grant of the option or right. If the shares are subject to a restriction on disposal, then the Revenue Commissioners will apply the percentage reductions described under General Principles above to the gain and not to the consideration; as discussed above, the correctness of this approach is open to question. A worked example of the Revenue approach is provided in *Tax Briefing 31*.

Where necessary, the inspector is authorised to make any just apportionment of any entire consideration given in part for the granting of the option and in part for something else, whether for the purposes of calculating the gain on an assignment or release of the option or that on its exercise. The services of the director or employee in his office or employment are not to be regarded as providing any consideration either for the grant of the option or for the grant of the option and something else (TCA 1997, s 128(4)).

TCA 1997, s 128(3) provides that, if income tax may become chargeable under the section in respect of any gain realised on the exercise of an option or a right to acquire shares or other assets, income tax is not to be charged under any other rule in the Tax Acts in respect of the receipt of the same option or right (except in the case of a 'seven-year option', see below). In other words, the general principle confirmed in the *Abbott v Philbin* case, that income tax may be charged on the excess of the value of the option at the time granted over any price paid for the option, is no longer applicable in the case of options (except for a seven-year option). The use of the word 'may' in the two places in TCA 1997, s 128 makes it clear that no income tax is chargeable in respect of the granting of any option or right, even if no tax actually becomes chargeable on its exercise (eg due to a fall in the market value of the shares or other asset) or if the option is simply allowed to lapse so that no gain is realised.

In addition to the tax charge under TCA 1997, s 128 on any gain from the exercise, assignment or release of a share option or right to acquire assets, TCA 1997, s 128 permits tax to be charged in respect of the grant of an option or right if, but only if, it is capable of being exercised more than seven years after the date it is granted. For convenience, any such option or right is referred to in this sub division as a 'seven-year option'. Any tax charged under this rule on the granting of a seven-year option is deductible from any tax that is chargeable on the gain (if any) taxed under TCA 1997, s 128 in respect of the subsequent exercise, assignment or release of the seven-year option.

In principle, the amount chargeable to tax in respect of the granting of a seven-year option is determined under the provisions of the Tax Acts in force before the enactment of TCA 1997, s 128. In other words, tax is chargeable under Sch E on the market value of the seven-year option taken normally at the date it is granted, but reduced by the price (if any) payable for it. TCA 1997, s 128(5)(b) makes it clear that the value of the option is to be not less than the market value of the shares or assets (the subject of the option) taken at the date the option is granted as reduced by the option price at which the shares or assets may be acquired on the exercise of the option. If the option price is a variable one, the amount by which the market value of the shares, etc may be reduced is to be taken as the lowest possible option price.

The use of the words 'not less than' should be noted. It is possible that the terms of an option may be such that the value of the option at the date it is granted may be greater than the excess of the market value of the shares or assets at that date over the option price. If this should be the case, the inspector may be able to charge tax under TCA 1997, s 128(5) by reference to that market value. In this regard, it is worth noting that the decision in *Abbot v Philbin* makes it clear that an option (or any other right) should be valued at the date of its grant and not the date on which it is first exercisable.

Payment of tax

The previous option under TCA 1997, s 128A to defer payment of income tax for up to seven years was abolished in the case of share options exercised after 28 March 2003: see the 2009 edition of this book. TCA 1997, s 128B now applies to accelerate the payment of tax on option gains relative to other income where a person is chargeable to tax under TCA 1997, s 128 on the exercise of an option on or after 30 June 2003.

Under TCA 1997, s 128B, the taxpayer is required to pay a sum of 'relevant tax' which is to be an amount equal to the taxable gain under TCA 1997, s 128(4) charged at the higher rate of income tax in force for the year in which the right is exercised (TCA 1997, s 128B(2)). TCA 1997, s 531AS(1A) provides that 'relevant tax' includes USC at the higher rate in force for the year in which the right is exercised. Thus relevant tax payable includes USC. PRSI due in respect of share options must also be paid at the same time as relevant tax (Social Welfare (Consolidated Contributions and Insurability (Amendment) Regulations 2012, SI 229/2012). There is a provision for the taxpayer to apply to the Revenue Commissioners on the basis that they are likely to be only chargeable at the standard rate of income tax or a lower rate of USC. Where the Revenue Commissioners are so satisfied, the rate of income tax used in the calculation of relevant tax will be the standard rate (TCA 1997, s 128B(14)) and the rate of USC the lower rate applicable (TCA 1997, s 531AS(1A)(b)).

The relevant tax must be paid to the Collector-General within 30 days after the exercise of the option. A return, in a form prescribed by the Revenue Commissioners, detailing the amount of the gain and the income tax arising on that gain together with any other details that might be required, must accompany each payment of relevant tax. The return will include a declaration that the return is correct and complete (TCA 1997, s 128B(3), (4), (5)).

The Revenue has the power to raise an estimated assessment in circumstances where it considers that a return does not contain full details of relevant tax due. In such circumstances interest will be charged on late payment of the relevant tax from the original date on which it was due to be paid. Any assessments, adjustments or set-offs may be made as are required to arrive at the true liability to relevant tax. The provisions of the Income Tax Acts in relation to assessments, appeals, collection and recovery of income tax apply equally to the assessment, collection and recovery of the relevant tax (TCA 1997, s 128B(7), (8), (9)).

The relevant tax paid may be set against any other income tax liability of the taxpayer for the same year of assessment, and where the relevant tax is in excess of the income tax liability for the year of assessment, the taxpayer can claim a refund of the excess. The relevant tax is not to be treated as a payment of, or on account of, preliminary tax for the purposes of the Taxes Consolidation Act 1997, ss 959AN and 959AO (thus eg it must be disregarded in deciding whether or not the 90 per cent or 100 per cent test has been met under TCA 1997, s 959AO(2)): see **2.104**) (TCA 1997, s 128B(10), (11), (12)).

The normal requirements for a chargeable person to make a return under Taxes Consolidation Act 1997, s 959I continue to apply to gains arising from the exercise of share options in respect of which relevant tax is payable (TCA 1997, s 128B(13)).

Self-assessment is extended to any person who is chargeable to Sch E under TCA 1997, s 128, unless the person has been given an exemption by an inspector from the obligation to file a return under TCA 1997, s 959N (TCA 1997, s 128(2A)).

Example 10.113.1

On 24 April 2001, Falcon Ltd granted a share option to an employee, Mr A Bird, to purchase 1,000 shares in its parent company, Hawk Ltd, at an option price of €3.50 at any time between 1 July 2001 and 30 August 2015. The share option is non-transferable and no restrictions are placed on the disposal of any shares which may be acquired under the option. Mr Bird paid Falcon Ltd the sum of €125 for the option.

The market value of the shares in Hawk Ltd on 24 April 2001 (the date of granting the option) is €4.80 per share. On 1 August 2015, Mr Bird exercises his option and acquires the 1,000 shares in Hawk Ltd at the option price of €3.50 per share. The market value of the shares at 1 August 2015 is €6.25 per share. Since the latest possible date for exercising the option was more than seven years after 24 April 2001, tax is chargeable in respect of the granting of the option and, subject to the credit for that tax, on the gain realised on the exercise of the option.

Mr Bird is chargeable to tax under Sch E for the relevant tax years as follows:

	€	€
2001 (under TCA 1997, s 128(5)(a))		
Value of option at 24/4/2001[1]		
Market value of shares 1,000 x €4.80	4,800	
Less:		
Option price 1,000 x €3.50	3,500	
	1,300	
Less:		
Price for grant of option	125	
Amount taxable 2001	1,175[2]	
Income tax payable €1,175 x 42%		493
2015 (under TCA 1997, s 128(2))		
Gain realised on exercise of option:		

Market value of shares 1,000 x 6.25	6,250	
Less:		
Option price for shares 1/8/2014 1,000 x 3.50	3,500	
	2,750	
Less:		
Price for grant of option	125	
Amount taxable 2015	2,625	
Income tax payable €2,625 @ 40%		1,050
Less:		
Credit for tax chargeable under TCA 1997, s 128(5)(a)		(493)
Net balance payable 2015		557

Notes:

1. It is assumed here that the inspector does not seek to attribute any additional value to the option other than that due to the excess of the market value of the shares at 24 April 2001 over the option price.
2. The amount taxable in 2001 (ie the year the option is granted) is added to Mr Bird's total income for that year. It is assumed that the full amount is charged at his top rate for that year of 42 per cent.
3. TCA 1997, s 128B provides that the balance of tax due, including USC and PRSI, must be paid by 31 August 2015.

Anti-avoidance

TCA 1997, s 128(6)–(9) contain further rules intended to prevent the avoidance of the main provisions of the section. For example, a director or employee (hereafter for simplicity, 'employee') might arrange for an option to be granted to another person who is not an employee. Alternatively, the employee might assign his share to another person for a low consideration in an effort to reduce his own gain. In either case, TCA 1997, s 128(6) applies to charge the employee in respect of the gain realised by the other person. It also charges the employee in respect of any gain realised by a person connected with him (at the time the gain is realised) on the exercise, reassignment or release of an option assigned to the connected person, notwithstanding that the assignment to him may have been for a full arm's length consideration. In these last two situations, where the right was divested from the employee by operation of law on bankruptcy or otherwise, any gain arising on exercise of the right will not be taxed on the employee but instead on the other person under Sch D Case IV (TCA 1997, s 128(7)). With effect from 20 November 2008, the anti-avoidance rules also apply if the employee benefits directly or indirectly from the exercise, assignment or release ('disposal' hereafter, for simplicity) of the right by another person. With effect from 20 November 2008, a gain realised by another person shall include a gain where that person exercises the right in question as nominee or bare trustee of the other person, or otherwise on behalf of the other person.

In the case of a tax charge under TCA 1997, s 128(6) on the employee in respect of any assignee's gain, or with effect from 20 November 2008, in relation to a person from whose disposal the employee derives any benefit, the taxable amount is reduced by the amount of any gain previously chargeable to income tax under TCA 1997, s 128(2). This applies whether the assignment has been one made to any person for a non-arm's-length consideration or whether it has been one made between connected persons for any (or no) consideration or under the circumstances where the employee derives a benefit from the disposal. In determining whether any two persons are connected, the connected person rules of TCA 1997, s 10 are applied (see **12.304**).

Where a right (the 'original right') is assigned or released and the whole or part of the consideration for the assignment or release consists of or comprises another right (the 'new right') the new right will not be treated as consideration for the assignment or release; but the charging provisions will apply in relation to the new right as they apply to the original right on the basis that the consideration for its acquisition did not include the value of the original right but *did* include the amount or value of the consideration given for the grant of the original right in so far as that has not been offset by any valuable consideration for the assignment or release other than the consideration consisting of the new right. From 20 November 2008, this is not to prevent a charge arising on any gain realised by the exercise of the original right. (TCA 1997, s 128(8), inserted by F(No2)A 2008, s 10). These provisions also apply where the employee ceases to hold a right as a result of two or more transactions and he or a person connected to him come to hold another right under any circumstances, and one or more of those transactions formed part of arrangements involving two or more persons holding rights chargeable under TCA 1997, s 128. The transactions may involve an assignment preceding, coinciding with, or subsequent to the acquisition of a right (TCA 1997, s 128(9)).

Information returns

TCA 1997, s 128(11) as amended by FA 2014, s 4 requires the person concerned to give particulars to the Revenue Commissioners, in an electronic format approved by them, of any of the following events:

(a) the granting of a share option or other right in respect of which tax may become chargeable under the section (whether or not the option or right is exercised);

(b) the allotment of any shares or the transfer of any asset in pursuance of any such option or right;

(c) the giving of any consideration for the assignment or release, in whole or in part, of any such option or right; and

(d) the receipt of written notice of the assignment of any such option or right.

The relevant notice in electronic format must be given no later than the 31 March in the year of assessment following the end of the tax year in which the particular event occurs. It must be given respectively by the person granting the option, etc, the person allotting shares or transferring any asset, the person giving the consideration or the person receiving the notice of assignment. The failure by any person required to notify the inspector to do so renders him liable to a penalty for a 'column 2 offence' under TCA 1997, Sch 29 (see **2.701**). TCA 1997, s 128(12) extends the reporting requirement of TCA 1997, s 128(11) to non-resident companies, where the right is obtained by a director or an employee of a company which is resident in Ireland or which is not resident in the state but which carries on a trade through a branch or agency in Ireland. The obligation to make the return will fall as appropriate on the resident company or on the agent, manager, factor or other representative of the branch or agency of the non-resident company.

Employment-related securities

TCA 1997, s 128C, inserted by FA 2008, s 16, provides generally for a tax charge under Schedule E on the happening of a *chargeable event* in relation to *employment-related, convertible securities*. An *employment-related security* is one acquired either by an employee or director (as defined for occupational pension purposes by TCA 1997, s 770) as a director or employee of the employer company or of any other company (TCA 1997, s 128C(3)(a)) *or* by any other person by reason of the director's or employee's office or employment, including a former or prospective employment (TCA 1997, s 128C(2)). At face value, this wording implies that a security acquired by the director or employee personally in respect of a former or prospective employment is not covered by the definition. Thus, shares given to a relative of an employee by the employer company, irrespective of whether or not those shares are in the employer company, may fall within the section if the shares were given 'by reason' of the employee's employment (see **10.107** for a discussion of the scope of this phrase); the tax charge will however be imposed on the employee or director and not the holder of the securities in such a case.

At the time of acquisition, the securities must be convertible securities or an interest in such securities (TCA 1997, s 128C(3)(b)); in other words, the section is intended to extend to cases where a mere interest in a convertible security is acquired. For these purposes an 'interest' includes one which comprises less than full beneficial ownership and an interest in the proceeds of the sale of the securities, but does not include a right to acquire securities (typically an option) (TCA 1997, s 128C(1)).

The term 'security' is extensively defined to include:

(a) shares and stock;

(b) securities within the meaning of TCA 1997, s 135 (ie including securities not creating or evidencing a charge on assets);

(c) debentures, debenture stock, loan stock, bonds, certificates of deposit, and other instruments (including certificates and warrants) creating or acknowledging indebtedness, including certificates and other instruments providing for a share in the profits of a company;

(d) options (other than options to acquire securities, except where such options are acquired under arrangements of which the main purpose or one of the main purposes is the avoidance of income tax, corporation tax or capital gains tax) and financial and commodity futures (within the meaning of the Investment Intermediaries Act 1995);

(e) warrants and other instruments entitling their holders to subscribe for securities;

(f) certificates and other instruments conferring rights in respect of securities held by persons other than persons on whom the rights are conferred and the transfer of which may be effected without the consent of those persons; and

(g) units in a collective investment scheme, defined as any scheme or arrangement made for the purpose, or having the effect, of providing facilities for the participation by persons, as beneficiaries, in profits or income arising from the acquisition, holding, management or disposals of assets.

The term does *not* include cheques or other bills of exchange, bankers' drafts or letters of credit, statements showing balances in current, deposit or savings accounts, or leases and other dispositions of property (TCA 1997, s 128C(1)).

Securities will be regarded as *convertible* if:

(a) they confer on the holder an entitlement (whether immediate or deferred and whether conditional or unconditional) to convert them:

   (i) into securities of a different description, or

   (ii) into money or money's worth;

   or

(b) a contract, agreement, arrangement or condition:

   (i) authorises or requires the grant of such an entitlement as is referred to in (a) to the holder if certain circumstances arise or do not arise, or

   (ii) provides for the conversion of the securities, otherwise than by the holder, into securities of a different description or into money or money's worth (TCA 1997, s 128C(4)).

The term 'securities of a different description' is not further defined. It is arguable that where eg shares can acquire enhanced dividend rights at some point in the future, that entitlement inheres in those shares and the shares subsequent to the enhancement do not alter their identity. Certainly, it would not appear that the section will apply if it is the case that the value of employment-related shares are enhanced as a consequences of other shares in the same company suffering a diminution of their rights.

A '*chargeable event*' is defined by reference to four subheadings:

(a) the conversion of the employment-related securities (or the securities in which they are an interest) into securities of a different description in circumstances in which the holder is beneficially entitled to the securities into which the employment-related securities are converted;

(b) the release for consideration of the entitlement to convert the employment-related securities (or the securities in which they are an interest) into securities of a different description;

(c) the disposal for consideration of the employment-related securities or any interest in them by the holder at a time when such securities are still convertible securities; or

(d) the receipt by the holder of a benefit in money or money's worth in connection with the entitlement to convert (other than securities acquired on the conversion of the employment-related securities or consideration referred to in paragraphs (b) and (c)) (TCA 1997, s 128C(7)).

The 'chargeable amount' on which tax under Sch E is payable is to be determined by the formula:

$$A - B,$$

where:

A is the amount of any gain realised on the occurrence of a chargeable event (see below); and

B is the total of any consideration given for the entitlement to convert the employment-related securities and the amount of any expenditure incurred by the holder of the employment-related securities in connection with the relevant chargeable event (ie the conversion, disposal, release or receipt of a benefit described respectively under (a), (b), (c) and (d) above (TCA 1997, s 128C(8)(a)). For these purposes, consideration is to be treated as given for the entitlement to convert the employment-related securities only to the extent that the amount of any consideration given for the acquisition of the employment-related securities exceeds the market value of such securities ((as defined by TCA 1997, s 548 but determined as if the employment-related securities were not convertible securities) at the time of their acquisition (TCA 1997, s 128C(9));

'A' in the formula is in turn to be determined on the conversion of the securities under (a) above by the formula:

$$C - (D + E),$$

where:

C is the market value (as defined by TCA 1997, s 548) at the time of the chargeable event of the securities into which the employment-related securities are converted and where those securities are themselves convertible, their market value is to be determined as if they were not convertible. Where the individual holds an interest in employment-related securities, then C is the same proportion of that market value as the market value of the interest in the securities bears to the market value of those securities;

D is the market value (as defined by TCA 1997, s 548) of the employment related securities at the time of the chargeable event, determined as if they were not convertible securities or an interest in convertible securities; and

E is the amount of the consideration given for the conversion of the securities (TCA 1997, s 128C(8)(b)(i)).

In effect, the formula for 'A' in this case is designed to catch the increase in value of the employment-related securities attributable to the conversion. Thus, for example if employment-related securities are converted into other (non-convertible) shares valued at €100,000 and the market value of the securities at the date of conversion on the assumption that they were not convertible was €40,000, the gain would be €60,000. If the employee had paid €20,000 for the securities at a time when their market value on the assumption that they were non-convertible was €15,000, the excess of €5,000 could be deducted from the gain, reducing it to €55,000.

'A' in the above formula is to be determined on the release of the securities under (b) above as the amount of consideration received for the release (TCA 1997, s 128C(8)(b)(ii)).

In the case of a disposal under (c) above, 'A 'is to be determined by the formula:

$$F - G,$$

where:

F is the amount of consideration given on disposal of the employment-related securities; and

G is the market value (as defined by TCA 1997, s 548) of the employment-related securities at the time of the chargeable event, determined as if they were not convertible securities or an interest in convertible shares (TCA 1997, s 128C(8)(b)(iii)).

In the case of the receipt of a benefit under (d) above, 'A' in the formula is to be determined as the amount of money received or else the open market value (as defined by TCA 1997, s 548) of the benefit received (TCA 1997, s 128C(8)(b)(iv)).

For these purposes, any consideration given for the acquisition of employment-related securities and any consideration given for the entitlement to convert shall not be taken to include the performance of any duties in or in connection with the office or employment (which of course is entirely logical). Furthermore, it is expressly provided that no part of the amount or value of any consideration may be deducted more than once (TCA 1997, s 128C(10)).

The issue of convertible shares to employees at an undervalue may be chargeable under general Sch E principles by virtue of TCA 1997, s 112. In addition, the notional gain on the acquisition of convertible shares on the exercise of an option may fall to be taxed by virtue of TCA 1997, s 128. Finally, the provisions of TCA 1997, s 122A may apply where convertible shares are deemed to be acquired at an undervalue. Clearly, if the enhancement in value of those shares attributable to their rights of conversion were taken into account for the purposes of those provisions, this would give rise to an element of double-counting. Accordingly, in such cases, the market value of the securities must normally be determined as if they were not convertible (TCA 1997, s 128C(5)(a)). However, this relaxation does not apply if the securities are acquired under arrangements of which the main purpose or one of the main purposes is the avoidance of income tax, corporation tax or capital gains tax. In this case, the market value of the securities must generally be determined as follows, but only if this yields a *higher* value than would otherwise be the case (TCA 1997, s 128C(5)(b)):

(i) in the case of securities with a right of the holder to conversion into securities of a different description, on the assumption that the entitlement to convert was immediate and unconditional (if such is not already the case, which would be highly unusual);
(ii) in the case where a contract etc. authorises or requires a right of the holder to conversion into securities of a different description, on the assumption that the entitlement to convert was immediate;
(iii) in the case of securities with a right of the holder to conversion into money or money's worth or in the case where a contract etc. provides for a person other than the holder to conversion into securities of a different description or into money or money's worth, on the assumption that provision was made for their immediate conversion (TCA 1997, s 128C(5)(c)).

In all cases the securities will be deemed to be 'immediately and fully convertible', *viz* convertible immediately after the acquisition of the securities so as to obtain the maximum gain that would be possible on a conversion at such time without giving any consideration for the conversion or incurring any expenses in connection with it (TCA 1997, s 128C(5)(b)).

Where the market value of the securities determined in accordance with these principles applies, the chargeable amount arising on a conversion etc is reduced by an amount found by the following formula:

$$H - I,$$

where:

H is the excess of the market value thus applied over what it would have been if those principles had not applied (ie on the basis that the securities did not carry conversion rights); and

I is the amount of any reduction already given in relation to any prior chargeable events in respect of that excess (TCA 1997, s 128C(8)(c)).

There is an exclusion from the scope of TCA 1997, s 128 where the following conditions are met:

(i) the securities concerned are shares belonging to a specific class;

(ii) all the shares of that class are convertible securities;

(iii) all the shares of that class are affected by an event similar to that which constitutes a chargeable event in relation to the securities (ie conversion); and

(iv) immediately before the event which would otherwise be a chargeable event, the majority of the company's shares of the class are not employment-related securities (TCA 1997, s 128C(11)(a)).

For the purposes of (iii), shares are affected by an event similar to that which is a chargeable event in relation to employment-related securities, if they are either:

(I) in a case where subheading (a) of the definition of a chargeable event applies (see above), the securities are converted into securities of a different class; or

(II) in a case where subheading (b) applies, the entitlement to convert them into securities of a different description is released; or

(III) in a case where subheading (c) applies, the securities are disposed of; or

(IV) in a case where subheading (d) applies, a similar benefit is received in respect of the entitlement to convert the securities (TCA 1997, s 128C(12)).

There is also an exclusion from the scope of TCA 1997, s 128 where at the time the securities *are acquired*, the emoluments from the office or employment are not within the charge to tax under Sch E or Sch D.

Where a person is chargeable for any tax year under TCA 1997, s 128C, then he will be deemed to be a chargeable person under the self-assessment system even if this would not otherwise be the case, unless specifically exempted under TCA 1997, s 959I (TCA 1997, s 128C(13)).

Where in any tax year, either:

(a) a person awards employment-related securities to an employee or director (or to any other person by reason of the director's or employee's office or employment) within TCA 1997, s 128C; or

(b) a chargeable event occurs in relation to employment-related securities so awarded;

then that person must deliver particulars of the awards or the chargeable event to the Revenue Commissioners on or before 31 March in the year following the year in which the award was made or the chargeable event occurred, as the case may be (TCA 1997, s 128C(14)(b).

10.114 Restrictive covenants

TCA 1997, s 127 is, broadly speaking, aimed at the situation where an employee receives a sum in return for entering into a restrictive covenant, typically a covenant not to compete with the individual's employer after leaving his employment. The relevant provisions are designed to override the decision in *Beak v Robson* 25 TC 33 where the individual was held not to be liable under Sch E in respect of such a sum. The rationale for that decision was in effect that the employee had provided full consideration (other than his services as an employee) in return for the sum received.

The section applies where a sum is received in return for the individual giving or fulfilling (partly or wholly) an undertaking in connection with an office or employment 'the tenor or effect of which is to restrict him as to his conduct or activities'. The section applies whether the individual held the office or employment when the undertaking was given, or if he had previously held it or was about to hold it. Even if the undertaking is not one which is legally enforceable against him, or if it is not an absolute, but a qualified undertaking, the section still applies. Further, the individual who gives the undertaking remains taxable even if the sum or any part of it was paid to any other person, eg his spouse, grandson, charity, etc.

The following further points should be noted in connection with TCA 1997, s 127 payments, namely:

(a) the value of any consideration given otherwise than in the form of money for the restrictive covenant is taxable under these rules in the same way as money consideration;

(b) if the individual dies after the undertaking has been given, but before the sum has been paid, the sum is treated as part of his total income for the year in which he dies as if it had been paid immediately before his death.

Where the section applies, all of the sum (or consideration) received is treated as taxable earnings (if not already so taxable) under Sch E (or Sch D Case III if the relevant employment or office is a 'foreign possession' see **13.104**). Where Sch E applies, PAYE must be operated.

The payment must be made 'in respect of' the relevant undertaking, so that the restriction on the individual's activities must be something over and above that which is already implicit in exercising the employment or office (*Vaughan-Neil v IRC* [1979] STC 644, where a payment by his new employer to a barrister to compensate him for ceasing to practice at the bar was held to fall outside the equivalent of TCA 1997, s 127 since taking up the employment prevented him from so practising in any event). The requirement that the undertaking must be 'in connection with' the holding of the office or employment is rather vague, but it is probably necessary to demonstrate a direct linkage for TCA 1997, s 127 to apply.

Common-sense suggests that a departing employee who executes a restrictive covenant and who also receives a termination payment at the same time, should ensure that the two transactions are kept separate otherwise it may not be clear that all of the sums received do not fall within TCA 1997, s 127.

10.115 Relief for non-remitted earnings

As noted in **10.101**, emoluments from foreign employments attributable to duties performed in the State were brought within Schedule E from 2006 onwards. A major consequence was that non-domiciled individuals were no longer eligible to claim the benefit of the remittance basis on such emoluments. TCA 1997, s 825B, as inserted by F(No 2)A 2008, s 13, provides a limited form of remittance basis in certain tightly-defined circumstances.

The relief does not generally apply for the year 2012 onwards, but will continue to be available to those who had an entitlement to relief in the years 2009 to 2011 as follows, subject to all other conditions being satisfied:

(a) If an individual was first entitled to relief for 2009, he shall continue to be entitled to relief for 2012 and 2013;

(b) If an individual was first entitled to relief for 2010, he shall continue to be entitled to relief for 2012, 2013 and 2014;

(c) If an individual was first entitled to relief for 2011 tax year, he shall continue to be entitled to relief for 2012, 2013, 2014 and 2015.

Where an individual makes a claim for relief s 825B, no relief will be given under in respect of the Foreign Earnings Deduction (TCA 1997, s 823A), the Special Assignee

Relief Programme (SARP) (TCA 1997, s 825C), or Research and Development relief (TCA 1997, s 472D).

The relief may apply where a *relevant employee*:

(a) becomes resident in the State;
(b) is required by his *relevant employer* to exercise the duties of his employment in the State;
(c) exercises those duties in the State on behalf of the relevant employer or an *associated company* for a period of at least one year; and
(d) while so exercising those duties, continues to be paid *relevant emoluments* from abroad by the relevant employer or associated company.

A relevant employee is an individual who, in a given tax year is resident, but not domiciled, in the State, and who, prior to becoming so resident:

(i) was resident in a jurisdiction which is not a member of the EEA, but which has a tax treaty in force with Ireland (hereafter, 'Qualifying Jurisdiction');
(ii) was employed in that jurisdiction by the relevant employer or an associated company; and
(iii) had exercised the greater part of his employment in that jurisdiction.

A *relevant employer* is a company which is incorporated *and* resident, in a qualifying jurisdiction.

An *associated company* is a company which is that employer's associated company within the meaning of TCA 1997, s 432 and which is incorporated *or* resident in a qualifying jurisdiction (this seems anomalous given the requirement that the employer company should be both resident and incorporated in the qualifying jurisdiction). *Relevant emoluments* are emoluments as defined for PAYE purposes, in effect any amount subject to tax under Schedule E which are:

(a) paid by a relevant employer or its associated company to a relevant employee; and
(b) are in fact subject to PAYE (TCA 1997, s 825B(1)).

Where the foregoing conditions are satisfied, then after the end of any tax year in respect of which the relevant emoluments are paid, the relevant employee may claim to have the tax due on the relevant emoluments re-computed for the tax year on the *greater* of—

(i) the relevant emoluments received in, or remitted, to the State in that year:
 (I) either directly or indirectly,
 (II) through any property imported,
 (III) through any money or value received on credit
 or on account, to the State in that tax year; and
(ii) an amount equal to €100,000 plus 50 per cent of the relevant emoluments in excess of €100,000.

FA 2010, s 10 amended TCA 1997, s 825B so as to relax the conditions for relief in the case of non-domiciled individuals who after 1 January 2010:

(i) become resident in the State for the first time, and
(ii) exercise the duties of their employment in the State for the first time.

In these cases the definition of qualifying jurisdiction is amended so that it no longer excludes EEA members. As a result employees resident in EEA states are potentially capable of qualifying for the relief.

The definition of remittances is not restricted to cash sums brought into the State and this combined with the vague reference to 'directly or indirectly' suggests that the scope of the term is potentially far more wide-reaching than that in TCA 1997, s 71(3) (see **13.402**). (TCA 1997, s 825B(2)). The anti-avoidance provisions of TCA 1997, s 72 are stated to apply with any necessary modifications (see **13.404**) (TCA 1997, s 825B(3)). In addition, all PAYE deductions from relevant emoluments will be deemed to be remitted to the State for the tax year to which such deductions refer. Any excess tax will then be repaid to the relevant employee (TCA 1997, s 825B(4)). If relevant emoluments are remitted to the State in a tax year after the tax year in which they were earned, and the individual has received a repayment under sub-s (2) of any tax originally deducted from those emoluments, the individual will be liable to tax on those emoluments from the date on which the tax was originally deducted (TCA 1997, s 825B(5)(a)). The Revenue Commissioners may raise an additional assessment for these purposes under TCA 1997, s 959AB within four years after the end of the tax year in which the emoluments were so remitted (TCA 1997, s 825B(5)(b)). Where a relevant employee has claimed a repayment of tax under these provisions but fails to comply with the one year minimum period requirement described above then that employee shall, whether or not requested to do so by a Revenue officer and within two months of that failure, repay to the Revenue Commissioners any tax repaid under these provisions (TCA 1997, s 825B(6)).

If a Revenue officer is not satisfied with the information provided by a relevant employee making a claim under these provisions, he may refuse the claim (TCA 1997, s 825B(7)). There is no right of appeal granted against this decision, so presumably the only potential avenue of redress is by means of Judicial Review (see **2.206**).

10.116 Special Assignment Relief Programme

TCA 1997, s 825C provides for income tax relief on a proportion of income earned by relevant employees who, having worked with a relevant employer for a minimum period of 6 months (12 months for employees who arrived in the State before 2015), are assigned to the State to work for that employer, or an associated company, in the State. The relief can be claimed for a maximum period of five consecutive tax years and applies in the case of employees who are first assigned to the State in the years 2012 to 2020 (inclusive). Where certain conditions are satisfied an employee can make a claim to have part of his income from his relevant employment exempted from income tax. The income is not exempt from the USC or PRSI. The conditions relating to the years 2015 to 2020 are slightly relaxed compared to the earlier years.

A 'relevant employer' means a company that is incorporated, and tax resident in a country or jurisdiction with which the State has a double taxation agreement or a tax information exchange agreement (TCA 1997, s 825C(1)).

A 'relevant employee' is an individual who:

In the case of an individual who arrives in the State in any of the tax years 2012, 2013 or 2014:

(a) was a full time employee of a relevant employer and exercised the duties of employment with that relevant employer outside the State for the whole of the 12 months immediately prior to arrival in the State;

(b) arrives in the State at the request of their relevant employer to:

(I) perform the duties of their employment in the State for that relevant employer, or

(II) take up employment in the State with an associated company of the relevant employer;

(c) performs the duties of their employment in the State for that relevant employer or that associated company for a minimum period of 12 consecutive months from the date of their arrival in the State, and

(d) was not resident in the State for each of the five tax years immediately prior to the tax year in which he first arrives in the State for the purpose of performing those duties (TCA 1997, s 825C(2)).

For these purposes, any duties performed outside the State that are merely incidental to the performance of the duties in the State are treated as performed in the State.

In the case of an individual who arrives in the State in any of the tax years 2015 to 2020:

(a) was a full-time employee of a relevant employer and exercised the duties of employment with that relevant employer outside the State for the whole of the six months immediately prior to arrival in the State;

(b) arrives in the State at the request of their relevant employer to:

  (I) perform duties of their employment in the State for that relevant employer, or

  (II) take up employment in the State with an associated company of the relevant employer and to perform duties in the State for that company;

(c) performs the duties of their employment in the State for that relevant employer or that associated company for a minimum period of 12 consecutive months from the date of their arrival in the State;

(d) was not resident in the State for each of the five tax years immediately prior to the tax year in which he first arrives in the State for the purpose of performing those duties; and

(e) in respect of whom the relevant employer or associated company certifies to the Revenue Commissioners within 30 days of the employee's arrival in the State that the individual complies with conditions (a), (b) and (c) (TCA 1997, s 825C(2A)).

As can be seen from the above the definition of 'relevant employee' for those who arrive in the State in 2015 has been changed in two ways. Firstly for employees who arrived in the State in 2012, 2013 and 2014, requirement (b) was that they should perform 'the duties' of their employment in the State. For this purpose any incidental duties performed outside the State were treated as performed in the State. Requirement (b) for employees who arrive in 2015 is that they should perform 'duties' of their employment in the State. Thus, there is no restriction on the amount of duties which the employee can perform outside the State, although if emoluments from such duties are liable to tax in another country and double taxation relief is due in respect of such tax relief, relief under TCA 1997, s 825C is restricted (see below). Although it would seem from the legislation that the relaxation on the duties which can be performed outside the State only applies to employees who arrive in 2015 to 2020, Revenue guidance notes state that the relaxation applies regardless of when the relevant employee arrived in the State. Secondly, for employees who arrive in the State in 2015 to 2020, they will only be entitled to the relief if the employer provides the necessary certification to Revenue within 30 days. For employees who arrived in the State before 2015 the necessary certification by the employer only had to be provided when a claim was made by the employee. A 'relevant employment' is an employment held by a relevant employee with a relevant employer. An 'associated company' is a company which is employer's associated company within the meaning of TCA 1997, s 432 (TCA 1997, s 825C(1)).

Where for a tax year a relevant employee:

(a) is resident in the State for tax purposes and is not resident elsewhere; with effect from the tax year 2015 the reference to 'not resident elsewhere' is removed.

(b) performs, in the State, duties of their relevant employment or the duties of an employment with an associated company, and

(c) has relevant income from their relevant employer (or associated company) which is not less than the annualised equivalent of €75,000 (before 2015 the requirement was that relevant income was not less than €75,000), and

(d) makes a claim for the relief,

he or she shall be entitled to have a 'specified amount' of income from that employment disregarded for income tax purposes (but not USC or PRSI). The relief will continue for not more than five consecutive tax years commencing with the tax year for which he is first entitled to the relief. For employees who were assigned before 2015, claims had to be accompanied by a certificate from a relevant employer (or associated company) confirming that the employee is a relevant employee (TCA 1997, s 825C(3)). Claims by employees assigned before 2015 were made using form SARP 1 which included the employer's certification. For employees assigned in 2015 to 2020 certification must be made by the employer to Revenue within 30 days of the employee's arrival using form SARP 1A.

'Relevant income' in relation to a relevant employee and a tax year means income, profits or gains from the employment concerned, net of expenses and excluding the following: amounts represented by general benefits-in-kind; the value of the benefit-in-kind in respect of a car; amounts in respect of preferential loans; severance payments; amounts in respect of restrictive covenants; any bonus, commission or other similar payments, whether contractual or otherwise; amounts arising from the exercise of share options; and any form of share based remuneration (TCA 1997, s 825C(1)).

The 'specified amount' is the amount determined by the formula:

$$(A-B) \times 30\%,$$

where:

A is the amount of the relevant employee's income, profits or gains from their employment in the State with a relevant employer or associated company excluding any amount that is not assessed to tax in the State and any amount in respect of which double taxation relief is available and net of any superannuation contributions and tax deductible expenses. For the tax years 2012, 2013 and 2014 where this amount exceeds €500,000 it is €500,000, the 'upper threshold'; and

B is €75,000, the 'lower threshold' (TCA 1997, s 825C(1)). Income from the relevant employment shall be deemed not to include any amount paid in respect of expenses incurred in the performance of the duties of the relevant employment which would be deductible under TCA 1997, s 114, TCA 1997, s 825C(12)).

The upper threshold is removed for the tax years 2015 to 2020.

A relevant employee's first year of entitlement to relief under TCA 1997, s 825C in general, will be the year he arrives in the State to carry out the duties of employment. However, where in a year of arrival a relevant employee is not tax resident in the State or is tax resident in the State and also tax resident elsewhere that employee is first entitled to claim relief in the year following the year he arrived in the State to carry out the duties of the employment (TCA 1997, s 825C(4)). The reference to tax resident elsewhere is removed for the tax years 2015, 2016 and 2017 so that once the employee is resident in the State for that year he is entitled to claim the relief. For 2014 and previous years where a relevant employee performed the duties of their employment in the State with the relevant employer (or associated company) for less than an entire tax year the upper and lower thresholds (ie €500,000 and €75,000) were reduced proportionately (TCA 1997, s 825C(5)). The purpose of this restriction was to restrict the relief where non-incidental duties of the employment were carried on outside the State. As outlined above, for 2015 and subsequent years there is no restriction on the duties which may be carried on outside the State. For 2015 and subsequent years the €75,000 threshold is only reduced proportionately where the period of employment in the first and last years in which the employee is entitled to relief is less than a full tax year.

In any tax year in respect of which a relevant employee is entitled to make a claim for relief under TCA 1997, s 825C, the payment or reimbursement of the following by the relevant employer (or associated company) will not be chargeable to tax:

(a) the reasonable costs associated with one return trip from the State for the relevant employee, their spouse or civil partner, and a child of the relevant employee or of the relevant employee's spouse or civil partner to:
   (i) the country of residence of the relevant employee prior to their arrival in the State;
   (ii) the country of residence of the relevant employee at the time of first employment by the relevant employer, or
   (iii) the country in which the relevant employee or their spouse is a national, and

(b) the cost of school fees, not exceeding €5,000 per annum for each child of the relevant employee or for each child of their spouse or civil partner, paid to a school established in the State which has the approval of the Minister for Education and Skills for the purposes of providing primary or post-primary education to students (TCA 1997, s 825C(6)).

Where an individual makes a claim under TCA 1997, s 825C no relief will be given in respect of the Foreign Earnings Deduction (TCA 1997, s 823A), Cross Border Relief (TCA 1997, s 825A), or Research & Development relief (TCA 1997, s 472D).

In addition the remittance basis does not apply to income from the employment where relief under TCA 1997, s 825C is claimed (TCA 1997, s 825C(7)).

Any individual making a claim under this section will be deemed to be a chargeable person for the purposes of TCA 1997, Pt 41A and is therefore required to file a return of income for the years of assessment to which the claim relates (TCA 1997, s 825C(8)).

Following an application from a relevant employer (or associated company) a Revenue officer may confirm in writing to the relevant employer (or associated company) that no deduction of tax need be made under the PAYE system on the specified amount for a relevant employee (TCA 1997, s 825C(9)).

Where for a tax year a relevant employer (or associated company), certifies that an employee is a relevant employee, the relevant employer or associated company must deliver by 23 February following each tax year an annual return to the Revenue Commissioners setting out the following details in respect of each employee certified:

(a) name and PPS number;

(b) nationality,

(c) country in which the relevant employee worked for the employer before his arrival in the State,

(d) job title and brief description of his new role and

(e) if relevant, the amount of income, profits or gains in respect of which PAYE was not deducted because of the relief.

The 23 February deadline for filing a return was only inserted in the legislation with effect from 1 January 2015.

In addition the relevant employer (or associated company) must provide their employer registration number and details of the increase in the number of employees, or details of the number of employees retained by the company as a result of the operation of the relief (TCA 1997, s 825C(10)). *Revenue eBrief No 66/16* notes that *Tax and Duty Manual* Part 34-00-10 in relation to the operation of the Special Assignee Relief Programme has been updated primarily to include Appendices which provide examples on the correct completion of the Form 11, Form SARP 1A, the Employer SARP return and the Form P35 for SARP cases.

10.117 Granting of vouchers

Previously there was a small benefit concession that Sch E did not apply to one off incentives of €250 per annum. TCA 1997, s 112B serves to put this concession on a statutory footing from 22 October 2015. It provides that a qualifying incentive shall be exempt from income tax and shall not be reckoned in computing income for the purposes of the Income Tax Acts. A 'qualifying incentive' is defined as follows:

'qualifying incentive' means either a voucher or a benefit that is given to an employee by his or her employer in a year of assessment where the following conditions are satisfied:

(a) the voucher or the benefit does not form part of a salary sacrifice arrangement;

(b) the voucher can only be used to purchase goods or services and cannot be redeemed, in full or in part, for cash;

(c) the voucher or the benefit cannot exceed €500 in value;

(d) not more than one voucher or benefit can be given to that employee in any year of assessment.

It should be noted that although voucher is not explicitly defined (see below) for the purposes of the section 'benefit' is so defined as meaning 'a tangible asset other than cash'. Therefore, the combination of voucher and benefit is wide. It can be seen that reference is made to an 'employee' above and the question arises as to whether this can include an office holder. 'Employee' is not defined for the purposes of this section and a comparison can be had to TCA 1997, s 116 which deals with benefits in kind and was amended by FA 2013, s 13 to include the definition '"employee" includes the holder of an office'. On that basis it would appear arguable that the section is relevant only for employees and will not apply to company directors who are not so regarded. That said, Revenue have confirmed that that the exemption applies to all directors.

Paragraph (a) notes that the voucher or the benefit does not form part of a salary sacrifice arrangement. Such arrangement is defined in the section as follows '"salary sacrifice arrangement" means any arrangement under which an employee forgoes the right to receive any part of his or her remuneration due under his or her terms or contract of employment and in return his or her employer agrees to provide him or her with a qualifying incentive.' It can be seen that reference is not had to TCA 1997, s 118B and such reference would appear unnecessary given that that section has its own definition which is very similar save the reference to 'qualifying incentive' is to 'a benefit'.

Earlier reference was made to voucher not being explicitly defined for the purposes of the section. That is because of para (b) above which restricts its meaning to its use being restricted to non-cash activities.

Para (c) and (d) are important in that the qualifying incentive is limited to €500 in a year of an assessment. Say in June 2016 an employee is given a voucher for €400 but in December that year he obtains another voucher from his employer for €100. The total amount of vouchers in that year received by the employee is €500 which meets the quantum test imposed by the section but the employee has received two vouchers in the same year of assessment. Arguably, this means that the employee has breached condition (d) above and therefore neither the €400 nor €100 vouchers can be regarded as a qualifying incentive for the purposes of this section. This would appear an anomalous result in that the employee could have obtained one voucher for €500 and the tax exemption in this section would have applied.

However, IA 2005, s 18 provides that the singular can be read as the plural and vice versa unless s 4 of that Act regards the context as otherwise applying and it's submitted that should not be the case in this instance.

10.2 Expenses Payments, Benefits in Kind etc

10.201 Persons chargeable

TCA 1997, Pt 5, Ch 3 charges to income tax under Sch E expense payments (expenses) and benefits in kind when paid or given to any director of a body corporate or an employee earning €1,905 or more, but only if the expenses or benefits are not otherwise chargeable to income tax as income of the director or employee concerned. The charging rules are contained in TCA 1997, s 117 for expenses and TCA 1997, s 118 for benefits in kind, (which treats the cost of providing benefits as a payment of expenses falling within TCA 1997, s 117). Each section is worded in terms of expenses paid or benefits in kind provided by a body corporate. However, TCA 1997, s 120 provides that TCA 1997, Pt 5, Ch 3 is to be read as applying in a corresponding way to tax also expenses paid or benefits in kind provided by other kinds of employer, namely unincorporated societies and other bodies, as well as any partnership or individual carrying on any trade or profession. TCA 1997, s 120 was amended by FA 2013, s 13 to include a definition of a 'public body'. The section now specifically provides that benefits in kind arise where a public body incurs an expense in relation to a person who holds an office or employment in that public body. The vast majority of taxable benefits are subject to the PAYE system (see **11.1**).

The expenses and benefit in kind rules of TCA 1997, Pt 5, Ch 3 apply to any director of a body corporate, irrespective of the level of the emoluments of his office. TCA 1997, s 116(1) defines 'director' in relation to a body corporate primarily as a member of the board of the directors or similar body which manages the affairs of the body corporate including the case where there is only a single director or similar person. A '*de facto*' director, ie a person who is held out by the body corporate as a director and who undertakes the functions of a director but who is not validly appointed as such does not appear to fall within this definition. However, the definition is extended to include a so-called 'shadow' director, ie any person in accordance with whose directions or instructions the directors of a body corporate (as defined above) are accustomed to act. A person is not however, deemed to be a director just because the directors may act on advice given by him in a professional capacity. This does not prevent such a professional advisor, eg a company's solicitor or financial advisor, from being treated as a director if the directors are in fact accustomed to act on his directions or instructions given otherwise than as professional advisor. There are a number of UK and Irish company law cases dealing with the equivalent definition of 'shadow director' for those purposes. The definition is almost identical, except that for company law purposes, it is necessary to consider the relationship between the person concerned and *all* the directors, *including* any '*de facto*' directors. In *Re Unisoft Group Ltd (No 3)* [1994] 1 BCLC 609, it was held that the shadow director must be in effect '*the puppet master controlling the actions of the board*' (see also *Australian Securities Commission v AS Nominees Ltd* (1995) 133 ALR 1). In *Secretary of State v Deverell* [2000] WLR 907, it was held that 'direction or instructions' can include mere advice (although whether an Irish Court would stretch the statutory language to this extent may be doubted) and that such advice need not extend to all of the company's activities. Most recently in *Ultraframe v Gary Fielding* [2005] EWHC 1638, it was held that it must be shown that all, or at least a consistent majority, of the board of directors must have been accustomed to act on the person's directions, etc as part of a regular course of conduct over a period of time, and not merely on one occasion.

A person who is not a director of a body corporate is not subject to the expenses and benefit in kind rules unless he is employed 'in an employment to which this Chapter applies'. TCA 1997, s 116(3), (4) defines this as an employment the emoluments of which, including any expenses and benefits in kind taxable as income under the rules of TCA 1997, Pt 5, Ch 3, are €1,905. For this purpose, the emoluments are to be estimated in accordance with the provisions of the Income Tax Acts before making any deduction to which the employee may be entitled for any expenses wholly, necessarily and exclusively incurred in performing the duties of his employment. It may be noted that both TCA 1997, ss 117, 118 apply only to expenses and benefits provided to individuals who are currently directors or employees, as opposed to former or prospective directors or employees.

The word 'employment' as used in these provisions is defined by TCA 1997, s 116(1) as any employment the emoluments of which fall to be assessed under Sch E. While this definition does not include a foreign office or employment assessable under Sch D Case III, a resident person is chargeable under that Case on expenses and benefits in kind arising from a foreign office or employment (see **13.105**). Any person who takes part in the management of the affairs of a body corporate, but who is not a director, is treated as an employee for the purposes of TCA 1997, Pt 5, Ch 3 even if not directly employed by the body. By contrast, a partner in a partnership or an individual who is a sole trader does not as such have an employment to which the Chapter applies even though he clearly takes part in the management of his business. The employees of a partnership or of a sole trader are within the definition of 'an employment to which this Chapter applies', if the €1,905 minimum emoluments test is met.

Example 10.201.1

P Ltd employs Mr A and Mrs B neither of whom is a director, on a part-time basis to carry out a door-to-door canvass for its products. In the period ended 31 December 2016, Mr A is paid a salary of €1,700 and Mrs B €1,300. The company reimburses them for actual expenses incurred and also pays directly bills charged up by them for meals supplied by a local public house. Mr A and Mrs B are required to repay to the company one half of the costs of the meals.

Based on the above salaries and the expenses and meal costs shown below the emoluments of each employee used to determine whether the €1,905 minimum is reached for 2016 are as follows:

	Mr A	*Mrs B*
	€	€
Salary paid in year	1,700	1,300

Expenses reimbursed in year	200	160
Benefit in kind:		
One half of meal bills	120	140
	2,020	1,600

For 2016, Mr A has an employment to which TCA 1997, Pt 5, Ch 3 applies as his total emoluments for the year arrived at under the TCA 1997, s 116(3) test exceed €1,905. It is therefore necessary in this case to consider whether, and if so, to what extent he may be taxed under the expenses and benefit in kind rules as applicable to his employment with P Ltd. On the other hand, Mrs B does not have emoluments amounting to €1,905 and is not therefore subject to these rules in respect of this employment, at least not in 2016.

It is to be noted that the full amount of the expenses reimbursed must be included in applying this test, even if it subsequently turns out that the employee can deduct all the expenses as being wholly, necessarily and exclusively incurred by him. On the other hand only the net benefit in kind – ie after deducting the part of the cost made good by the employee (see **10.205**) is included.

A person may have two or more employments with the same employer (whether or not a company) or he may have an employment with one company and a second (or third, etc) employment with one or more other companies in the same group. In any such case, the emoluments of all these employments must be added together to see whether the €1,905 test is met. Alternatively an individual may be the director of a company and have at the same time one or more employments with that company or with other companies in the same group. If so, not only do the expenses and benefit in kind rules apply to him in relation to his office as director, but the other employments are treated as employments to which TCA 1997, Pt 5, Ch 3 applies irrespective of the level of emoluments from them (TCA 1997, s 116(3)).

In applying the dual (or multiple) employment rules mentioned in the last paragraph, one company is in the same group as another company if either has control of the other or if both are under the control of a third company. 'Control' is defined by TCA 1997, s 116(1) in relation to a body corporate in exactly the same words as those used in the first test of control contained in TCA 1997, s 312, except that the term 'body corporate' is used instead of 'company'. For the definition given by the latter section, see **6.105**, but note that the second test of control used in TCA 1997, s 312 is not applied in the TCA 1997, s 116(1) definition.

In certain circumstances, a partnership carrying on a trade or profession may have control over a company or other body corporate. If so, TCA 1997, s 120 provides two further rules. First, if any director of the body corporate is an employee of, as distinct from a partner in, the partnership, then that employment is one to which TCA 1997, Pt 5, Ch 3 applies. Secondly, if a person is an employee of both partnership and the body corporate, his emoluments from each such employment must be added together to see whether the €1,905 test is met.

Example 10.201.2

Mr C and Mr D are in partnership as chartered accountants. The partnership assets include a 60 per cent holding in the ordinary share capital of a company, R Ltd. Mr G is employed by the partnership on a part time basis with emoluments in 2016 of €860. He is also employed by R Ltd with emoluments for that year of €1,400. Since the partnership controls R Ltd and as the emoluments from both employments total €2,260, ie in excess of €1,905, both employments are covered by the TCA 1997, Pt 5, Ch 3 expenses and benefit in kind rules.

10.202 Expenses payments

The payment by a company or other employer to a director or employee of an allowance for expenses is taxable as a perquisite of the office or employment under the main Sch E charging rule of TCA 1997, s 112, but only if and to the extent that the allowance exceeds the actual expenses incurred. It has been held in various cases (*Owen v Pook* 45 TC 571) that the reimbursement by an employer of actual business expenses incurred by an employee without any profit element accruing to the employee was not a perquisite taxable under the main charging rule of Sch E. By contrast, in *Perrons v Spackman* [1981] STC 739, a mileage allowance paid in respect of an employee using his car on the employer's business was held to be a taxable perquisite; in this case, the allowance included a significant contribution to the employee's private use of the car, ie it considerably exceeded the business expense element.

TCA 1997, s 117 is designed to remove the difficulty which the Revenue previously had in seeking to assess directors and employees on expenses payments by the employer which might contain an element of personal benefit to the recipient, but which it was claimed approximated to the actual business expenses incurred. TCA 1997, s 117 does this by deeming any sum paid in respect of expenses to be a perquisite chargeable under Sch E (if not already taxable under TCA 1997, s 112), if paid to a director or to an employee earning €1,905 or more. It is then left to the director or employee to claim such a deduction (if any) in respect of the expenses actually paid by him as are allowable under the Sch E expenses rules discussed in **10.302–10.303**.

It is to be emphasised that TCA 1997, s 117 *prima facie* covers any sum paid by the company or employer to the director or employee in respect of expenses properly incurred for the purposes of the employer's business. However, in *Luke v IRC* 40 TC 630, Lord Reid expressed a different view, in respect of a similar wording under ITA 1952, s 160(1), saying that the term 'expenses' could not cover '... a sum which conferred no benefit of any kind on the director'. However, this (*obiter*) view seems to involve reading on a limitation to the words of the statute which it is difficult to justify.

It would seem highly arguable that the terms 'expenses' in its ordinary sense only refers to expenditure incurred by the employee; thus, if the employee discharges a liability of the employer (for example, paying a supplier out of his own pocket) and is subsequently reimbursed for so doing, TCA 1997, s 117 may not be in point. If, however, the liability incurred by the employer relates to the provision of a benefit to the employee then TCA 1997, s 118 (see **10.203**) would come into play in any event.

The term 'expenses' does not appear apt either to cover the making good of losses incurred by an employee (as decided in *Hochstrasser v Mayes* 38 TC 673, where the employer had reimbursed the employee for the shortfall on the sale of his house). Expenses paid by third parties (ie other than the company or employer) are not covered by TCA 1997, s 117.

TCA 1997, s 117 also includes any sum which the employer puts at the disposal of, and which is paid out for expenses by, the director or employee (TCA 1997, s 117(2)). It does not cover expenses paid directly by the employer to a third party, eg travelling or hotel expenses for directors or employees where the bills are sent by the travel company, hotel, etc direct to the employer. However, to the extent that expenses paid directly by the employer to a third party provide a personal benefit for the director or employee, this may again give rise to the latter's being charged on a benefit in kind under TCA 1997, s 118 (see **10.203**).

If applied strictly, TCA 1997, s 117 would require all payments in respect of expenses of any kind paid to a director or employee to be included in his gross emoluments chargeable under Sch E and to leave it to the individual to claim (and agree with the inspector) his appropriate expenses deduction (if any) in each year. In practice, the Revenue Commissioners are generally prepared to accept that payments made by the employer that are no more than direct reimbursement of vouched expenses actually and necessarily incurred in the performance of the duties may be disregarded and PAYE accordingly need not be applied to such payments (SP IT/2/07). Round sum payments including car allowances (as opposed to acceptable or approved mileage payments: see below) are however to be treated as gross emoluments and are accordingly subject to PAYE.

The Revenue Commissioners' practice in respect of mileage allowances is set out in their SP IT/2/07. There the Revenue Commissioners state that they will accept two types of flat rate schemes of reimbursement in respect of allowable business journeys, where the employee bears all of the expenses concerned, namely:

(a) a flat rate up to, but not exceeding, the current schedule of civil service mileage rates; (see below); and
(b) a flat rate based on any other schedule of rates and related conditions of travel and subsistence which do no more than reimburse the employee for actual expenditure necessarily incurred.

The current relevant rates are set out on the Revenue Commissioners' website.

Reimbursements under (a) may be applied without specific Revenue approval, so long as there is a satisfactory recording and internal control system in operation. Employees would be expected to provide their employer with a record showing for each business journey:

(a) the date of the journey;
(b) the reason for the journey;
(c) the mileage involved;
(d) details of starting point and finishing point of the journey; and
(e) the basis for reimbursement.

All such records must be retained for at least six years.

In most cases, an employee will be based largely, or virtually exclusively, in an office, etc in his employer's business premises. In other cases, an employee may spend substantial periods away from those premises. The Revenue Commissioners state in SP IT/2/07 that the employee's 'normal place of work' will be regarded as the employer's business premises where travelling is a requirement in the course of the job or an integral part of the job, eg a salesperson or service engineer keeping daily appointments with customers or a coach driver. This reflects the Revenue's view that travelling expenses may only be allowable where an employee is temporarily away from his place of work, an analysis not supported by the case law (see **10.303**). The better view is that where travelling is an integral part of the duties of the employment, expenditure thereon is necessarily incurred in performing those duties, irrespective of whether the employee has a base or otherwise. However the Revenue Commissioners do reach the same conclusion, albeit by circuitous logic. The Revenue Commissioners also accept that an employee who is required to work at a number of locations on a daily basis will incur allowable travelling expenditure.

They also state that 'the employee's home would not be regarded as his normal place of work unless there is an objective requirement that the duties of the office or employment must be performed at home, ie it is not sufficient for an employee merely to carry out or opt to carry out some of the duties … at home'. The case law in this area is discussed at **10.302**, **10.303**. In practice, the Revenue Commissioners will treat payments of travel expenses to employees with specialist skills who are required to give instructions away from their place of work in cases of grave emergency as non-taxable. Payments of travel expenses made to employees to attend at urgent and serious emergencies (as defined) outside normal working hours will also be exempted in practice, in respect of a maximum of 60 incidents per annum. Exemption is also extended to employees attending to emergencies at a customer's premises outside of normal working hours. Finally, the provision, or payment, for taxis or other transport, for irregular work-to-home journeys not exceeding 60 per annum may be made tax-free where an employee is required to finish work at a time between 10 pm and 6 am.

The Revenue state that where an employee makes a business journey directly from home to a 'temporary place of work' (rather than from his normal place of work) or returns from a temporary place of work directly to home, the business mileage should be taken as the lower of:

(a) the distance between home and temporary place of work; and
(b) the distance between his normal place of work and temporary place of work (for a discussion of the case law principles, see **10.303**).

A reduced mileage rate applies to individuals who are not obliged to travel in the normal course of their duties but who occasionally use their cars on business journeys (the logic apparently being that they should not be entitled to relief for the standing costs of running their cars).

It is important to note that a standard mileage allowance scheme is not acceptable where an employer also reimburses specific motoring costs of the employee (eg insurance) since the employee in such a case is no longer bearing all of his motoring expenses. The Revenue state that the employer's tax office should be approached in such cases in order to agree the appropriate tax treatment of such expenses, including cases where the employer covers the financing costs of the vehicle (these are not allowable costs for Sch E purposes). As the Revenue Commissioners point out in SP IT/2/07, it remains open for an employee to insist on the strict statutory treatment of his mileage allowances, so that the allowances will be taxable under TCA 1997, s 117. The employee can then claim his deductible motor expenses under TCA 1997, s 114, and any capital allowances which are due (see **10.305**).

The Revenue Commissioners practice in relation to subsistence expenses is set out in *Leaflet IT 54* (amended by *eBrief* No 63/2015). They state:

> Where an employee performs the duties of the employment while temporarily away from his normal place of work or is working abroad on a foreign assignment, allowable subsistence expenses can be reimbursed on the basis of:
>
> (a) acceptable flat rate-allowances, or
>
> (b) actual expenses which have been vouched with receipts.
>
> … Where an employee's allowable expenses are reimbursed free of tax by an employee, then, an income tax claim by the employee for those expenses does not arise.

The Revenue's view of what constitutes allowable subsistence expenses is also open to question. The position as it emerges from the case law in this area is discussed in **10.302**, **10.303**.

The Revenue Commissioners grant tax-free status to the reimbursement of travel and subsistence expenses paid to temporary assignees posted to the State for a period not exceeding 12 months, subject to a number of highly restrictive conditions (see SP IT/2/07).

The Revenue Commissioners make the point (similar to that made by them in relation to travel expenses) that where an employee proceeds on a business journey directly from home (rather than commencing the business journey from the normal place of work) or returns home directly, any subsistence expenses should be calculated as the lesser of the subsistence expenses actually incurred and those which would have been incurred if the journey had started and finished at the normal place of work.

The Revenue Commissioners again point out that it remains open to an employee to opt for the strict statutory treatment. Under this, any subsistence expenses reimbursed by the employer (including any flat-rate allowance) will be treated as emoluments; a deduction will be granted in relation to allowable expenses actually incurred by the employee.

Reference should also be made to the question of the reimbursement of business entertainment expenses discussed in **10.304**. At one stage, some inspectors of taxes were suggesting that direct reimbursements by employers to employees of business entertainment expenses should be included in emoluments subject to PAYE, even where no benefit to the employee resulted. It now appears as if the Revenue is not pursuing this particular approach in the case of *bona fide* business entertainment expenses.

Exempt payments

Reasonable flat rate travel and subsistence expenses paid to Members of the European Parliament are exempt under EU law (*Lord Bruce of Donnington v Aspden* [1981] STC 761). Annual allowances payable under the Courts of Justice Act 1953, s 5 to members of the judiciary are exempted by TCA 1997, s 196.

TCA 1997, s 196A (as inserted by FA 2005, s 12) provides an exemption for allowances and emoluments granted to an officer of the State and certified by the Minister for Finance, having consulted with the Minister of Foreign Affairs or any other Minister as he deems appropriate, as representing compensation for the extra cost of living outside the State in order to perform his duties (TCA 1997, s 196A(1)). 'Emoluments' are defined for these purposes as restricted to those falling within TCA 1997, s 985A, ie benefits-in-kind subject to PAYE (See **11.1**). Normal salary is therefore not eligible for the exemption (TCA 1997, s 196A(2)).

An 'officer of the State' is defined as:

a Civil Servant as defined by Civil Service Regulation Act 1956, s 1(1):

(a) a member of the Garda Síochána; or

(b) a member of the Permanent Defence Force (TCA 1997, s 196A(2)).

TCA 1997, s 196B (as inserted by FA 2007, s 18) provides an exemption for allowances and emoluments granted to an employee of a designated agency and certified by the Minister for Finance, having consulted with the Minister of Foreign Affairs or any other Minister as he deems appropriate, as representing compensation for the extra cost of living outside the State in order to perform his duties (TCA 1997, s 196B(1)). 'Emoluments' are defined for these purposes as restricted to those falling within TCA 1997, s 985A, ie benefits-in-kind subject to PAYE (See **11.1**). Normal salary is therefore not eligible for the exemption (TCA 1997, s 196B(2)).

TCA 1997, s 195A (as inserted by FA 2007, s 12) exempts payments made by a *non-commercial body* to or on behalf of a *member* of the body in respect of expenses of travel and subsistence incurred by the member in the attendance at meetings of the body to the extent that such payments do not exceed the current civil service rates, (TCA 1997, s 195A(2), (3)).

For these purposes, a 'body' is defined as an unincorporated body of persons or a body corporate, being either:

(a) any board, council or committee, however expressed; or
(b) any [subsidiary] body of persons exercising some or all of the functions of such a board, council or committee.

The duties of the office of members of the body must be wholly discharged in the course of meetings of the body concerned, or in the course of preparation for such meetings; however, incidental duties (such as attendance at conventions or meetings as delegates on behalf of the body) may be disregarded for this purpose (TCA 1997, s 195A(1)).

A 'non-commercial' body is one:

(a) which is organised solely for purposes other than profit, where the declared purposes of the body can be ascertained from documents of record;
(b) which in fact, operates solely for purposes other than profit and, for this purpose, any activity generating income carried on by the body:
    (i) which is carried on for the purposes of assisting the body to achieve its purposes, and
    (ii) the income of which is used for those purposes, shall be regarded as operating for purposes other than profit;

    and
(c) any benefit, or part of the income or accumulated income, of which, cannot be paid to, or cannot otherwise be made available to, any officer, employee or member of the body for the personal benefit of that person or a person connected with that person other than by way of:
    (i) any wages, salaries, fees or honorariums for services rendered to the body but only if the amounts paid are no more than reasonable amounts that would be paid in a transaction at arm's length for similar services by a body organised solely for purposes other than profit, being a body operating in accordance with (b) above;
    (ii) any payment to which TCA 1997, s 195A itself applies,
    (iii) any payment made to officers, employees or members to assist in the covering of expenses to attend conventions or meetings as delegates on behalf of the body where such attendance is to further the purposes of the body, and
    (iv) where the officer, employee or member concerned, or a person connected with such officer, employee or member, is also an object of the purposes of the body, a benefit which is in furtherance of the purposes of the body (TCA 1997, s 195A(1)).

A 'member' of a body is a person holding office as a member of that body:

(a) who has no other duties directly or indirectly, whether as an employee of the body or of a person connected with that body, in relation to that body; and
(b) whose annualised amount of the emoluments from the office for the year of assessment 2006 and for each subsequent year in which the person is a member

of the body, other than payments to which TCA 1997, s 195A itself applies, does not exceed:

(i) in the case of a member who is the chairperson of the body, other than a subsidiary body (see definition of 'body' above) €24,000, and

(ii) in any other case, €14,000 (TCA 1997, s 195A(1)).

In addition, the Revenue Commissioners state in SP IT/2/07 that reimbursement of travel and/or subsistence expenses to voluntary unpaid workers made by philanthropic organisations will be exempt, subject to meeting certain conditions.

10.203 Benefits in kind

General

TCA 1997, s 118 (as amplified by TCA 1997, s 120) charges tax on benefits in kind, ie benefits provided by an employer for a director or employee which would not otherwise be caught as a perquisite or other profits of the office or employment under the main Sch E charging rule. TCA 1997, s 118 applies in any case where:

> a body corporate [or other employer] incurs expense in or in connection with the provision, for any of its directors or for any person employed by it in an employment to which this chapter applies, of living or other accommodation, of entertainment, of domestic or other services, or of other benefits or facilities of whatever nature.

In *Templeton v Jacobs* [1996] STC 991, it was held that a benefit was 'provided' at the point in time when it became available to be enjoyed by the taxpayer, and not when the cost of providing the benefit had been incurred. It may be argued that TCA 1997, s 118 imposes a charge where the employer incurs expense in (or in connection with) the provision of a benefit, while its UK counterpart (ICTA 1988, s 154) imposes a charge where a benefit is provided. However, it is considered that TCA 1997, s 118 presupposes that a benefit is actually provided to the employee. If this view is correct then logically the section can only become operative at the time the benefit is so provided. If this view is not correct, an expense incurred in year one in order to provide a benefit to an employee in year two is chargeable on the employee in year one even if he ceases to be an employee before the commencement year (and thus enjoys no benefit at all).

In *Williams v Todd* [1988] STC 676, the taxpayer was relocated from Wigan to London and received an interest free loan from his employer in order to enable him to buy a house there. The court rejected an argument that, the loan did not confer a benefit on the taxpayer but simply compensated him for having to move to a more expensive house. Per Peter Gibson J:

> One looks to the loan and the benefit thereof and nothing else.

TCA 1997, s 122, which deals with preferential loans, does not (unlike its UK counterpart) include any reference to a 'benefit' being conferred on the employee, (see **10.211**).

The scope of the term 'facility' in the context of TCA 1997, s 118 is questionable. In ordinary usage, it denotes the equipment or means for doing something; it is unclear in what circumstances a facility would not represent a benefit in any event.

A benefit would appear to arise when an employee acquires an entitlement to avail of facilities, even if in practice he makes limited or no use of that entitlement. The Revenue Commissioners cite as an example an individual who is granted an annual subscription to a golf club but who is then unable to avail of it due to sickness. The position would be different where an employee's entitlement only arises for part of the tax year when an appropriate apportionment of the annual expense would be required.

It is the incurring of the expense by the employer that triggers off the operation of TCA 1997, s 118 and, unlike the position with perquisites and other profits taxed directly by TCA 1997, s 112, it is not necessary for the Revenue to establish that the source of the benefit to the director or employee is his office or employment. Any expense incurred by the employer in providing benefits, etc for the spouse, civil partner, family, servants, dependants or guests of the director or employee is treated as if incurred in providing the benefit to the director or employee himself (TCA 1997, s 116(2)). Any reference here to expense incurred for the benefit of a director or employee should, therefore, be read in this wider sense.

In *Wicks v Firth* [1983] STC 25 the Court of Appeal held that the expression 'benefits and facilities of whatsoever nature *(whether or not similar to any of those mentioned above)*' was wide enough to catch a cash payment made by an educational trust established by the taxpayer's employer to the minor child of a taxpayer. In *Mairs v Haughey* [1992] STC 495, [1993] STC 569, the Northern Ireland Court of Appeal took the view that the expression also covered a cash payment made directly to the taxpayer. The latter finding was logical in the light of *Wicks v Firth*, since there seems to be no justification for distinguishing between the making of cash payments made to the employee as opposed to those made to his spouse, family, etc.

It remains open whether *Wicks v Firth* would be followed on this point in Ireland (bearing in mind that the italicised words above do not appear in TCA 1997, s 118). There seems to be a strong argument to the contrary, in that the words 'other benefits or facilities of whatsoever nature' are preceded by an itemisation of non-cash benefits (ie living or other accommodation, etc). Under the *ejusdem generis* rule of statutory interpretation there is a presumption that the width of the expression 'other benefits or facilities of whatsoever nature' should be limited by reference to the class of items preceding it. It may be noted that TCA 1997, s 118 provides an exemption for a benefit consisting of the provision of (*inter alia*) a pension or lump sum on retirement or death. This might be taken to imply that cash payments do fall within the scope of TCA 1997, s 118 (ie since otherwise this exemption would be unnecessary). However, it is suggested that TCA 1997, s 118 would still be necessary, even if direct cash payments were outside the scope of TCA 1997, s 118, since it would exempt the expense of funding future retirement benefits.

It will be apparent that if this view is wrong, and TCA 1997, s 118 can extend to all cash payments, then, this will provide the Revenue with an additional argument for taxability under Sch E in some cases (if they choose to take the point). Thus, eg it would be possible to argue that the payment in *Ball v Johnson* (see **10.107** above) was taxable as a sum paid by the employer. In practice the Revenue Commissioners will allow such payments to be made tax-free, subject to their prior approval.

In *Wicks v Firth*, Lord Templeman also expressed the view that the payments made to the taxpayer's child were 'at the cost of' the employer. He said:

> All the trusts, powers and discretions and other authorised activities of the trustees emanate from and were established and defined by [the employer]. The capital moneys necessary for the performance by the trustees of their duties were provided by [the employer]. The income of the trust fund was sacrificed by [the employer] to the same purpose …

The test in the context of Irish tax law is whether the expense of providing the benefit in question was incurred by the employer (TCA 1997, s 118), but the principles involved seem to be identical. For these purposes it is debatable whether it should be permissible to 'look through' a trust and attribute payments made by the trustees out of settled funds to the settlor. It certainly seems doubtful that the income foregone by the employer on the capital now held by his trustees could properly be treated as 'expense incurred' by the employer (see also the discussion of *Pepper v Hart* in **10.404**).

In certain circumstances expenses incurred by the trustees would in any event be deemed under Irish tax law to be incurred by the employer (TCA 1997, s 118(7)). While a distribution made by the trustees would not normally be thought of as an 'expense' incurred by them, a wide meaning should probably be attributed to the term 'expense' in this context. The specific statutory rules now dealing with educational trusts are discussed at **10.212**.

TCA 1997, s 118 does not, however, apply if and to the extent that, the expense incurred by the employer is already chargeable to income tax as income of the director or employee: for example, if a benefit is given in a form convertible into money and has as its source the relevant office or employment, it will be taxable already under TCA 1997, s 112. Where the expense incurred on providing a pecuniary benefit exceeds its market value, the Revenue are likely to seek to tax the market value under TCA 1997, s 112 and the excess under TCA 1997, s 118. Further, the provision of a benefit in kind through the employer's making a motor car available for the private use of a director or employee is not taxable under TCA 1997, s 118, but under the separate rules of TCA 1997, s 121 (see **10.207**).

TCA 1997, s 118 operates by treating the director or employee as if (i) he had incurred an amount equal to the expense incurred by the employer in providing the benefit, reduced by any part of that expense made good by the director or employee to the employer and (ii) this amount had been refunded to him by way of expenses. This has the effect of bringing the employer's net expense in providing the benefit within TCA 1997, s 117 (see **10.202**) and thus within the charging words of TCA 1997, s 112 so that it becomes assessable under Sch E on the director or employee. In *Mairs v Haughey* [1992] STC 495, the Northern Ireland Court of Appeal held that the expense could be made good by a non-cash transaction, including the surrender of valuable rights.

In determining the expense incurred by the employer, regard must be had to the benefit in kind valuation rules of TCA 1997, s 119(1), (2) which, in some circumstances, deem certain expenses to have been incurred or require other expenses to be ignored. These valuation rules are discussed generally in **10.205** and, in relation to the provision of living accommodation, in **10.206**.

TCA 1997, s 118 deals with the case where a director or employee of one body corporate, or his spouse, civil partner, family, dependants, etc may be provided with a benefit not by the body corporate employing him, but by some other person connected with that body corporate. If the expense in providing the benefit is incurred by such a connected person, this subsection deems that expense to have been incurred by the employer so that the director or employee is taxed in the same way as if the employer had actually incurred the expense.

TCA 1997, s 118 defines 'connected person' for the purpose of this rule. It provides that, if the employer is a body corporate, a connected person may be the trustee of a settlement made by that body corporate or another body corporate, but only if the trustee or other body corporate would be regarded as connected with the employer within the connected person rules of TCA 1997, s 10. A 'settlement' is as defined by TCA 1997, s 794(1) as including any disposition, trust, covenant, agreement, arrangement, etc (see **15.402**).

Similarly, if the employer is an unincorporated body, a partnership or a sole trader, TCA 1997, s 118 applies to treat in the same way expenses incurred by a person connected with that employer as if they had been incurred by him. Again, the connected person may either be the trustee of a settlement made by the employer or any body corporate connected with him within the rules of TCA 1997, s 10 (TCA 1997, s 118 as applied by TCA 1997, s 120). For example, if a company controlled by the partners of an accounting firm should provide benefits in kind for the employees of the partnership, TCA 1997, s 118 applies to tax the employees in respect of those benefits as if they had been provided directly by the firm.

Example 10.203.1

Plum Ltd and Pear Ltd are each controlled by a Mr R E D Cherry through his holdings of 54 per cent and 70 per cent respectively in their voting share capitals. Orange Ltd is a wholly owned subsidiary of Pear Ltd and is, in consequence, regarded as being controlled also by Mr Cherry. Mr A Mandarin is employed by Orange Ltd at a salary of €10,000. Mr Mandarin lives in a house owned by Plum Ltd for which he pays a nominal rent only.

Since the employer company (Orange Ltd) and the company providing the living accommodation (Plum Ltd) are controlled by the same person (Mr Cherry), these two companies are regarded as being connected with each other by TCA 1997, s 10. TCA 1997, s 118 therefore applies to deem the expense incurred by Plum Ltd, less the nominal rent paid by Mr Mandarin, as being expense incurred by Orange Ltd. This net expense to Plum Ltd is therefore taxable as a benefit in kind on Mr Mandarin although his employment is with Orange Ltd.

An employer may incur expenses partly in or in connection with the provision of benefits in kind for one or more directors or employees and partly in connection with other matters. In any such case, TCA 1997, s 118(6) requires a proper apportionment of these expenses so that only the proportion attributable to the benefit in kind is included in arriving at the taxable benefit in kind in each case. Similarly if expenses incurred in providing benefits for more than one director or employee cannot be directly allocated between them, an apportionment in some appropriate manner should be made. In *Rendell v Went* 41 TC 641, the employer incurred expense on legal fees in defending the taxpayer on a serious criminal charge. The employer's purpose in so doing was to attempt to avoid losing the benefit of the taxpayer's services if he were sent to jail. It was held that no apportionment could be made in this case. All of the expense related to the provision of a benefit for the employee and the fact that it was also designed to benefit the employer was irrelevant. *Rendell v Went* was distinguished in *Westcott v Bryan*, discussed in **10.206**.

In some cases an employer will bear the cost of medical examinations for its employees. It may be argued that this is done in the commercial interests of the employer but it also clearly entails the provision of a benefit to the employee. In the Employer's Guide to PAYE Revenue state that the provision of one medical check-up per annum at the expense of the employer will not be regarded as a taxable benefit.

When an employer apportions expenses under this rule, then to the extent that the apportionment is relevant for the return under TCA 1997, s 897(2) of employees' emoluments, etc (see **10.213**), the return must specifically mention that one or more sums in it result from apportionments. The inspector of taxes may then, if he considers it necessary for any tax assessment, request the employer to give him full particulars of the apportionment and the manner in which it was made. If the inspector is not satisfied with any such apportionment of expenses, he may apportion them in the manner he thinks fit in making his assessments on each director and employee affected. Any reapportionment by the inspector of expenses for this purpose is subject to the normal appeal procedure (TCA 1997, s 897(6)).

Medical and long-term care insurance paid by employer

Qualifying medical insurance and long-term care insurance policies (up to 2009) attract tax relief by reduction of the premiums payable at the standard rate of income tax (see **3.314**). Where an employer bears the cost of the premiums on behalf of an employee this will constitute a taxable benefit in the normal manner (ie based on the gross premium net of any contribution made by the employee). However, it is also provided that the employee will be entitled to a tax credit equal to the gross premium multiplied by the standard rate of income tax. The employer will be obliged to refund to the Revenue the benefit of the tax reduction which it will receive on payment of the premiums (TCA 1997, s 112A). Further to F(No 2)A 2013, the maximum tax credit is €200 for premiums paid for an adult and €100 for premiums paid for a child with effect from 1 January 2014.

Example 10.203.2

Gráinne Tuohy is employed by Academia Ltd. In 2016, Academia Ltd pays qualifying medical insurance premiums on her behalf of €800, ie a gross premium of €1,000 net of standard rate tax of €1,000 x 20% = €200. Gráinne contributes €300 towards the cost of the premiums.

Gráinne will be taxed on a benefit of € (1,000 – 300) = €700 but will be entitled to a personal tax credit of €1,000 x 20% = €200 for 2016.

Where an employer provides the benefit to an individual who qualifies for the age-related tax credit in respect of such premiums (see **3.324**), the aggregate of the age-related tax credit and the credit due under TCA 1997, s 470 due in respect of the payment may not exceed the income tax charged on the benefit (TCA 1997, s 470B(6)).

10.204 Benefits in kind not subject to tax

TCA 1997, s 118 does not apply to tax as a benefit in kind expense incurred by an employer for any of the following purposes:

(a) the provision of living accommodation for an employee (who is not a director) in part of the employer's business premises that includes living accommodation, but only if:
   - (i) the employee is required by the terms of his employment to reside in the accommodation in order to enable him to perform his duties properly, and
   - (ii) it is necessary in the type of trade carried on by the employer for employees of the class in question to reside in premises of the class in question or the accommodation is provided in accordance with a common practice in existence prior to 30 July 1948 (TCA 1997, s 118(3));

(b) the provision for a director or employee, in any of the employer's business premises, of any accommodation, supplies or services, but only if provided for the director or employee himself and if used by him solely in performing the duties of his office or employment (TCA 1997, s 118(2));

(c) the provision of meals in any canteen in which meals are provided for the staff generally (TCA 1997, s 118(4));

(d) the provision for a director or employee himself, or for his spouse, civil partner, children or children of civil partner or dependants, of any pension, annuity, lump sum, gratuity or similar benefit to be given on his death or retirement other than an expense incurred by way of a contribution by the body corporate to a PRSA (within the meaning of Pt 2A, Ch 30): for the treatment of PRSAs see **16.3** (TCA 1997, s 118(5));

(e) expenditure incurred by an employer in connection with the provision, to an employee or director of a monthly or annual bus pass or railway pass by an operator as defined by Dublin Transport Authority Act 2008, s 2, by a licence holder under Public Transport Regulation Act 2009, Pt 2 or a person operating a ferry service holding a valid passenger safety certificate, boat licence or high-speed craft safety certificate issued by the Minister for Transport, Tourism and Sport.

(f) with effect up to 2010, the provision of childcare services by an employer on behalf of its employees or directors in a qualifying premises, ie premises which comply with the requirements of Article 9, 10 or 11 as appropriate of the Child Care (Pre-School) Regulations 1996 and which are made available solely by the employer or made available either jointly by the employer or by third parties where the employer is wholly or partly responsible either for financing and managing the provision or for capital expenditure on the construction or refurbishment of the premises concerned; in the last-named case the exemption is limited to the amount of capital expenditure incurred (TCA 1997, s 120A);

(g) the provision of the use of a mobile phone (as defined) where any private use (see below) is incidental to business use (see below); the exemption applies even if the mobile phone is supplied in respect of a car or van the provision of which itself gives rise to a taxable benefit in kind (TCA 1997, s 118(5C) inserted by FA 2004, s 8);

(h) the provision of a high-speed internet connection (as defined) to the home of the director or employee where any private use (see below) is incidental to business use (see below); (TCA 1997, s 118(5D) inserted by FA 2004, s 8);

(i) the provision of the use of computer equipment (to include a fax machine, hardware such as personal computers, laptops, printers, scanners, modems, disc drives, discs as well as software, where any private use (see below) is incidental to business use (see below) (TCA 1997, s 118(5E);

(j) with effect up to 2010, the payment or reimbursement of annual membership fees to a professional body on behalf of an employee where membership of the body concerned is 'relevant' to the employer's business, ie necessary for the performance of the duties of the employment or facilitates the acquisition of knowledge which is necessary or directly related to the performance of those duties or would be necessary or directly related to prospective duties of the employment (TCA 1997, s 118(5E) inserted by FA 2004, s 8); in practice, the Revenue Commissioners are prepared to continue to treat the reimbursement of certain annual membership fees paid to a professional body as non-taxable benefits: see *e-Brief 19/11*);

(k) the provision of certain vans (see **10.210**);

(l) with effect from 1 January 2009, the provision of certain bicycles and bicycle safety equipment (see **10.210**).

For the purposes of (g) and (h) above, 'business use' is defined as use in the performance of the duties of the employment (there is no requirement that such use should be 'necessarily' in the performance thereof) and private use is defined as all use other than business use (TCA 1997, s 116(1) inserted by FA 2004, s 8).

TCA 1997, s 236 also provided an exemption up to 2009 from the charge to benefit in kind in respect of expenses incurred by a company in providing an 'art object' on loan to a director or employee provided the 'art object' is kept in a building or garden approved for relief under TCA 1997, s 482 and reasonable access thereto is afforded to the public. Further details on this exemption are included in the 2012 and earlier editions of this book.

Each of these exceptions to the main benefit in kind charging rule of TCA 1997, s 118 only operate if the conditions of their application are strictly met. Thus, eg exception (c) would not apply if meals are provided in a canteen which is open to directors only or, say, to directors and certain senior employees, but not to the staff generally.

Exception (a) does not apply to expense incurred by a body corporate in providing living accommodation in its business premises for any of its directors, or provided for an employee who is a director of another body corporate that is connected with the body corporate providing the accommodation. For this purpose, the body providing the accommodation and the other body are connected if either has control of the other or if both are under control of the same person.

The limits to this exception were considered in *Butter v Bennett* 40 TC 402. This case concerned a mill manager who was required by his employing company to live in a house provided by it. His service agreement provided that the company was to be solely responsible for the cost of all coal, coke, gas and electricity reasonably required for the heating or lighting of the house, for all rent, rates, and taxes payable in respect of the house and for the upkeep of any garden attached. The manager had to be available if required night and day, including weekends, and it was accepted that it was necessary for him to have to live in the house which was beside the mill in order to perform his duties properly.

It was held by the Court of Appeal that the exemption for expense incurred in or in connection with the provision of living accommodation for an employee required to reside in the employer's premises is restricted to the expenditure necessary to provide and maintain immovable property as a residence. Lord Denning MR drew the distinction between the expense of providing the living accommodation (including the expense of maintaining it so as to make it habitable) as distinct from the expense of inhabiting the accommodation. Only the former type of expense was covered by the exemption. He held that the expense of providing and maintaining the accommodation included any rent expense, rates and repairs, but that the expenses of coal and electricity and of keeping the garden were costs of inhabiting the accommodation provided and had to be included in calculating the benefit in kind when incurred by the employer.

The Revenue Commissioners have expressed the view that an employee will be required to occupy living accommodation in order to properly perform his duties where he is required to be on call outside normal working hours, he is in fact frequently called out and the accommodation is provided so as to permit quick access to the place of employment. The Revenue give as examples of such circumstances managers or night staff in residential or respite centres (other than nursing facilities); governors and chaplains in prisons and genuine, full-time caretakers living on the relevant premises and au pairs who are required under their terms of employment to 'live in'. The Revenue have also expressed the view that the exemption would not normally apply to hotel staff, but (for reasons that are unclear) that it would apply to student nurses engaged in grant-funded diploma programmes under the auspices of the Department of Health and/or a Health Authority.

The Revenue also express the view (correctly in the writer's opinion) that the exemption would not apply to accommodation provided to employees who are obliged to work late and stay over occasionally away from home.

In respect of exemption (e), the Revenue Commissioners will agree that, subject to conditions, a salary sacrifice will be allowed to fund the provisions of travel passes on a tax free basis. The conditions are:

(a) there must be a *bona fide* and enforceable alteration to the terms and conditions of the existing employment contract;
(b) the alteration cannot be retrospective, and must be in writing;
(c) once the alteration is made there can be no entitlement to forgo the benefit in favour of cash;
(d) the choice to amend the terms and conditions of employment cannot be made more frequently than once a year. An exception to this may be made on the occurrence of a 'significant life event', but with the employer's agreement.

Arguably, once conditions (a)–(c) are met, the decision in *Heaton v Bell* would no longer be potentially applicable in any event: see **10.105**. Since 31 January 2009, TCA 1997, s 118B prescribes the conditions under which the Revenue Commissioners will not treat a 'salary sacrifice' as taxable emoluments in this context: see **10.105.** As that section does not appear to extend the scope of *Heaton v Bell,* in the writer's view it is arguable that in fact these are superfluous.

The specific statutory rules dealing with educational trusts are covered in **10.212**.

Personal security assets and services

TCA 1997, s 118A, as inserted by FA 2005, s 10, provides for an exemption from TCA 1997, s 118(1) where:

(a) there is a credible and serious threat to the physical personal safety of a director or employee arising wholly or mainly from his office or employment (TCA 1997, s 118A(2));
(b) expenditure otherwise within TCA 1997, s 118(1) is incurred by the employer in relation to the provision of *assets,* or the use of *services* for the improvement of the individual's security in order to meet the threat to their personal physical security; and
(c) the assets or services are provided with the sole object of meeting that threat (but note that there is in fact provision for apportioning the cost of providing assets for mixed purposes: see below) (TCA 1997, s 118A(3)).

For these purposes an 'asset' includes equipment or a structure but *not* any mode of transport or a dwelling or the grounds attached thereto and 'service' does not include the use of a dwelling or the grounds attached thereto (TCA 1997, s 118A(1)).

The exemption extends to expenditure connected with, as well as directly incurred in, the provision of assets or use of the services (eg running costs associated with provision of an asset). It also applies where any of the costs concerned are incurred by the individual and are reimbursed by the employer. Where the employer intends an asset to be used solely to improve the individual's personal physical security, any incidental usage will be ignored (TCA 1997, s 118A(5)). However, where the employer intends an asset to be used only partly in order to improve the personal physical security of the individual, the exemption from the charge under TCA 1997, s 118(1) will only apply in relation to that portion of the expenditure which is attributable to that intended use (TCA 1997, s 118A(6)). The section does not provide how this rather problematic apportionment is to be made; it may be noted that it is the subjective intention of the employer which counts not the actual effect of the expenditure.

The exemption will only apply in relation to a service where the benefit resulting to the individual consists wholly or mainly of an improvement in their personal physical security (ie this is an 'all or nothing' test, without any possibility of apportionment) (TCA 1997, s 118A(5)).

The exemption will not be denied by reason of the fact that an asset becomes permanently attached to a premises (whether or not a dwelling), or that the individual is, or subsequently becomes, entitled to ownership of that asset, or to any estate or interest in premises to which the asset is attached as a fixture. Nor will the exemption be denied by reason of the fact that the asset or service improves the personal physical security of members of the individual's family or household as well as himself (TCA 1997, s 118A(8)).

Revenue concessions

The Revenue Commissioners also concessionally exempt the payment of certain removal and relocation expenses in accordance with their Statement of Practice SP IT 1/91 (such expenses are clearly not incurred in the performance of the employee's duties: *Friedson v Glynn-Thomas* 8 TC 302). The concession applies both to relocations within the same organisation and relocations in order to take up a new employment. The main conditions for obtaining approval are as follows:

(a) the reimbursement or payment is made by, or borne directly by, the employer in respect of expenses actually incurred by the employee;
(b) the expenses are reasonable in amount;
(c) the payment is properly controlled; and
(d) moving house must be 'necessary' in the circumstances (ie necessary in practical terms as opposed to necessary under the strict terms of the Sch E expenses rule: see **10.302**).

It is not necessary to obtain the prior approval of the local tax office before the employer can make qualifying relocation payments free of tax. However, the employer must retain all relevant records for six years unless instructed otherwise by an inspector (*Tax Briefing 31*).

In general, the expenses which can be reimbursed without giving rise to a charge to tax would be those incurred directly as a result of the move and would include:

(a) auctioneer's and solicitor's fees and stamp duty arising from moving house;
(b) removal of furniture and effects;
(c) storage charges;
(d) insurance of furniture and effects in transit or in storage;
(e) cleaning stored furniture;
(f) travelling expenses on removal;
(g) temporary subsistence allowance (subject to a limit of 10 nights at the appropriate rates set out on the Revenue website), while looking for accommodation at the new location; and

(h) vouched rent of temporary accommodation for a period of up to three months, but excluding any period covered by above.

The Revenue Commissioners state that, with the exception of any temporary subsistence allowance, all payments must be matched with receipted expenditure. The inspector of taxes must be satisfied that the amount reimbursed or borne by the employer does not exceed expenditure actually incurred. Any reimbursement of the capital cost of acquiring or building a house or any bridging loan interest or loans to finance such expenditure would be subject to tax.

It appears that the Revenue Commissioners also exempt in practice costs of certain training expenses borne by the employer and long service awards in the form of a tangible article with a value not exceeding €50 per year of service (such period of service to be at least 20 years and no similar award having been made in the previous five years) (see *Tax Briefing 48*). It may also be noted that where an employee, etc falls ill or suffers injury while abroad on his employer's business and the employer bears or refunds the costs of medical treatment abroad, the Revenue will not usually charge the employee to tax, so long as the scale of the benefit provided is reasonable.

The Revenue have also indicated that they will not treat the following as giving rise to taxable benefits:

(a) provision of car parking facilities by an employer; (but see **10.209** re the Parking Levy)

(b) provision of taxi transport on an irregular basis to an employee required to work after 10 pm where such transport is provided to ensure the safety of the employee;

(c) provision of a licensed carrier to transport workers from home to work where the service is available to employees generally and the main use of the service is for such journeys or journeys between workplaces;

(d) provision of staff parties, special occasion meals or other inclusive events, such as sports days for staff, where the expenses involved are reasonable in amount;

(e) provision of sports and recreational facilities on the employer's premises which are available to staff generally;

(f) provision of medical check-ups which employees are required to undergo by their employer; in addition contributions by employers to make up shortfalls under in-house medical plans or payments by employers to retain the services of a general medical practitioner may be disregarded;

(g) payment or reimbursement of exam fees where the course undertaken is 'relevant' to the employer's business (in the sense applied to professional subscriptions); similar treatment applies to examination awards conditional on passing an exam or acquiring a business-related qualification, where the amount of the award can be reasonably regarded as doing no more than covering the costs of studying and sitting for the relevant exam, etc. Any bonus or additional increments granted on passing an exam, etc are of course fully taxable in the normal way;

(h) provision of newspapers, periodicals, etc which are generally related to the employer's business;

(i) provision of protective clothing or clothing either bearing logos or of such colour or design as to be readily identifiable as a uniform (in fact, even if technically a benefit, it seems clear that the notional expense would be incurred wholly, exclusively and necessarily in the performance of the duties: see **10.302**);

(j) provision of a second home telephone account by the employer who bears the cost thereof, where private use is incidental to business use (presumably the definition in TCA 1997, s 116 applicable in relation to mobile phones and computer equipment (see above) applies);

(k) contributions by the employer into a sickness insurance scheme jointly funded by the employer and employees subject to obtaining a ruling from the appropriate Regional Revenue office;

(l) a once-off benefit up to €250 per employee per annum (€150 prior to 1 January 2005); any benefit in excess of this limit or a second benefit of any amount provided in the same tax year is taxable in full;

(m) annual membership or stamp duty payable in respect of a corporate charge card but only where the card is provided exclusively for business use;

(n) private use of lorries, ie any commercial vehicle with a gross laden weight in excess of 3,500 kg; and

(m) the costs incurred by an employer in respect of an employee's entry visa or work permits.

In *Tax Briefing 60*, Revenue Commissioners state that they are prepared to regard the payment of legal fees incurred by an employee or director and paid on their behalf by an employer as tax-free if those fees relate to an investigation/disciplinary procedure instigated by an employer and all of the following conditions are met:

(a) the fees are due to a member of the legal profession arising from representing the employee/director;

(b) the payment on behalf of the employee/director represents a full or partial discharge of legal fees incurred by the employee/director only in connection with the investigation/disciplinary procedure instigated by her/his employer;

(c) the legal fees are paid by the employer directly to the employee's/director's legal representative and only after having had sight of the invoice relating to such fees (ie on sight of the invoice issued to the employee/director by the employee's/director's legal representative); and

(d) where the investigation/disciplinary procedure instigated by the employer, or the action taken by an employee/director, results in a settlement being made to the employee/director by the employer, the discharge of the legal fees on behalf of the employee/director must form part of a specific term of any such settlement agreement.

10.205 Valuation of benefits in kind: general rules

There are two main steps in arriving at the amount of the taxable benefit in kind. First, the gross amount of the expense incurred or deemed to have been incurred by the employer in providing the benefit is ascertained. Secondly, any payment or other reimbursement to the employer made by the director or employee in respect of the employer's expense of providing the benefit is deducted. In *Mairs v Haughey* it was held that payments in kind (including the surrender of valuable rights) were eligible for deduction. However, the value of services rendered by the employee to the employer is naturally not eligible (if this were not the case the whole basis of charging benefit-in-kind would be undermined: *Stones v Hall* [1989] STC 138). The taxable benefit in kind, to be included in the recipient's total income assessable under Sch E, is the net expense after this deduction. If the employer's expense is fully or more than fully repaid, there is no benefit in kind to be taxed. If the director or employee makes no reimbursement to the employer, the full amount of the employer's expenses is assessable as the benefit in kind.

The general rule is that it is the actual expense incurred in the tax year by the employer (or by a connected person) that is brought into the benefits computation for that year as the gross expense. This general rule applies in every case except to the extent that it is varied by any of the rules contained in TCA 1997, s 119. This section deals with three types of case – the first where the benefit takes the form of the transfer of the property in any asset owned by the employer, the second where the benefit is provided through giving the director or employee the use of an asset which remains the property of the employer and the third when the benefit takes the form of services. In applying any of the benefit in kind valuation rules, expense is regarded as being incurred when the employer's liability to pay arises, even if payment is in fact made on a different date or in another tax year.

TCA 1997, s 119(2) deals with the case where a taxable benefit in kind arises as the result of the transfer of the property in any asset of the employer that has been used or has depreciated. In such a case, the valuation of the benefit in kind is made on the assumption that the employer had incurred expense in providing the benefit equal to the value of the asset at the date of the transfer. In fact, in most cases where an asset is transferred by an employer to a director or employee for less than its market value, the excess of the market value over the amount (if any) paid to the employer is taxable as a perquisite under the main Sch E charging rule. TCA 1997, s 119(2) precludes the possibility that the excess of employer's capital cost in providing the asset over its market value at the date of transfer might be taxed as a benefit in kind under TCA 1997, s 118, ie in addition to the perquisite taxable under the main charging rule (as discussed in **10.203**).

Example 10.205.1

L Ltd purchased a car at a cost of €8,500 on 10 May 2016 which it sold to one of its directors, Mr M, on 30 May 2016 for a consideration of €5,000. Although the car had not been used by any of the company's employees or directors prior to the sale to Mr M, it was agreed that it had depreciated in value to €7,800 by 30 May 2016. Mr M is taxable under TCA 1997, s 112 for 2016 on a perquisite of €2,800, the excess of €7,800 over the consideration of €5,000 paid by him to L Ltd. Were it not for TCA 1997, s 119(2), then it seems that Mr M would also be taxable for 2016 under TCA 1997, s 118 on a benefit in kind of €700, ie on the excess of the €8,500 expense incurred by the company in purchasing the car over the sum of the €5,000 consideration paid by him and the €2,800 already taxable under TCA 1997, s 112.

However, since it is accepted that the company's asset has depreciated in value before the transfer to Mr M, TCA 1997, s 119(2) requires the €7,800 market value at 30 May 2016 to be substituted for the actual expense of €8,500, with the following consequences:

	€
Expense in providing asset:	
Deemed by TCA 1997, s 119(1) to be	7,800
Less:	
Amount paid by Mr M	5,000
	2,800

Less:	
Amount taxable as perquisite by TCA 1997, s 112	2,800
Benefit in kind under TCA 1997, s 118	Nil

If an asset which is transferred to an employee can be converted into cash for a consideration in excess of the cost to the employer (a relatively unusual circumstance), the employee will be taxed on the resale value under general principles (see **10.105**). In practice, the Revenue will accept the figure for cost to the employer where the difference between it and the resale value of the asset in question is unlikely to be significant.

Example 10.205.2

Mr Morrow's employer sells goods to him which it holds as trading stock for €7,100. The goods would normally be sold by his employer for €9,400. The cost to the company of buying the goods was €3,200. If Mr Morrow were to sell the goods himself he would receive only €5,300 because they are now second hand. There is no taxable emolument as the price paid for the goods (€7,100) exceeds the resale value (€5,300); similarly there is no benefit-in-kind under TCA 1997, s 118, as set out below:

	€
Expense in providing asset:	3,200
Less:	
Amount paid by Mr Morrow	7,100
Benefit in kind under TCA 1997, s 118	Nil

Assume now that Mr Morrow could resell the goods for €8,000; in this case, a taxable emolument arises under general principles, because the resale value €8,000 exceeds the price paid for the goods (€7,100), ie resulting in a perquisite of €900. No charge arises under TCA 1997, s 118 as the calculation above remains unchanged.

Assume now that the facts in the previous paragraph stay the same but that the goods were manufactured rather than purchased by Mr Morrow's employer. The tax consequences remain unchanged; the only issue may be the correct basis for the calculation of the cost of the manufactured goods. The Revenue have expressed the view that in this kind of case, the expense incurred by the employer would normally be lower than the amount which the goods would realise if sold on the open market, but this will always depend on the precise facts.

In the case of vouchers, the realisable value may be zero or below the cost to the employer (see **10.105**); TCA 1997, s 118 will operate in such cases to bring into charge the full cost to the employer. The Revenue Commissioners have stated that in a case where the realisable amount would not significantly exceed the expense incurred by the employer, the latter amount may be taken as the measure of the benefit. The provision of vouchers, etc will often in practice be paid on a 'grossed up' basis, ie where the employer bears the cost of the associated PAYE/PRSI liabilities: see **11.1**.

There are two special rules to consider when the benefit in kind is provided by giving a director or employee the use of an asset which remains the property of the employer. First, TCA 1997, s 119(1) provides that any expense incurred by the employer in the acquisition or production of the asset in question is to be left out of account. Secondly, TCA 1997, s 119(3) deems the expense incurred by the employer to be the sum of the annual value of the use of the asset and any other expense actually incurred by the employer in connection with the asset (except acquisition, etc expense excluded by TCA 1997, s 119(1)). For this purpose, expense incurred in connection with an asset is limited to expense in providing the benefit to the director or employee. If the asset is used as well for other purposes, the appropriate proportion of both the annual value and of the other expenses should be excluded from the benefit in kind calculation.

The first rule clearly excludes from the benefit calculation any capital cost to the employer in acquiring the asset so long as it remains the employer's property. It has also been held that expenditure of a kind that would normally fall on the owner of an asset, as distinct from the user, should also be excluded (*IRC v Luke* – see also **10.206**). While the latter decision was made in the context of premises provided as living accommodation, it is possible that the same principle could, in appropriate circumstances, be applied where other types of asset are involved. Expenditure on the improvement or alteration of an asset which continues to belong to the employer should generally be excluded. On the other hand, repairs should normally be included, but there could be cases where the director or employee might argue that he should not be taxed on repairs incurred by the employer as owner.

It is provided that in the case of an asset other than premises, the annual value thereof will be five per cent of the market value of the asset (as defined by TCA 1997, s 548 for CGT purposes) when it was first provided to a director or employee (not necessarily the same director or employee who is currently enjoying the use of the asset). The definition of market value per TCA 1997, s 548 is the price which the asset might reasonably be expected to fetch on a sale in the open market; it seems therefore that it is resale value and not the original cost which is always relevant.

TCA 1997, s 119(3) does provide that however, in a case where the asset made available to the director or employee has been rented or hired by the employer, if the rent or hire payable by the employer exceeds the annual value of the use of the asset, then the actual rent or hire payable is used instead of the annual value. Should the rent or hire charge be less than the annual value, the rent or hire is ignored and the annual value is included. In either event, the other expenses (excluding the rent or hire charge) must also be brought in.

The definition of annual value which applies for premises is discussed at **10.206**.

Example 10.205.3

A Dublin firm of chartered accountants opens a new office in Wexford. It employs a manager who has already his own house in Wexford. In order to help him create a better image when entertaining the firm's clients in his home, the firm purchased new quality furniture and carpets at a total cost of €7,000 and it handed them over to the manager for use in his home, starting on 6 July 2015. It is assumed that their resale value at that time equates to their cost to the employer. The manager agrees to pay the firm €200 per annum for the use of the furniture and the carpets. The firm agrees to pay for cleaning the carpets from time to time, but there is no arrangement about repairs. The firm retained ownership.

During the tax year 2016, the furniture is damaged in an exceptional accident and the firm pays €1,200 in having the furniture restored and repaired; it also pays €200 in having the carpets cleaned.

The benefit in kind on which the manager is taxable for 2015 and 2016 is determined as follows:

	2015	*2016*
	€	€
Annual value of use of furniture:		
5% x market value €7,000 for 6 months	175	
5% x market value €7,000 for 1 year		350
Other expenses incurred by employer:		

Expenses of repairs[1]	Nil	600
Cleaning carpets	Nil	200
Gross cost of providing benefit	175	1,150
Less:		
Rent payable by manager	100	200
Taxable benefit in kind	75	950

Note:

1. It is assumed that the manager claimed that the full cost of repair (€1,200) of the carpets were owner's expenses and should not be included in computing the benefit in kind assessment (*IRC v Luke* 40 TC 630), but that after an argument with the inspector it was agreed that only one half (€600) should be excluded for this reason.

Where a benefit takes the form of services (eg the provision of a gardener), then the expense incurred by the employer is the measure of the taxable benefit under TCA 1997, s 118 in the normal way.

In *Pepper v Hart* [1992] STC 898, [1994] IJOT 40, the taxpayer's employer was a school which granted his children places at heavily discounted fees. The majority of the House of Lords held that under traditional principles of statutory interpretation, the UK equivalent of TCA 1997, s 118 meant that the expense incurred by the school was a proportion of the total costs of educating all the students at the school. However, the House then departed from previous UK judicial practice and proceeded to hold that they could refer to Hansard (the official record of parliamentary proceedings). On the basis that there was an ambiguity or obscurity in the relevant provisions (for a critique of this justification see Ward: *Pepper v Hart* [1992] STC 898, [1994] IJOT 40), Hansard demonstrated that the original intention of the promoters of the relevant Finance Act was only to impose tax on a marginal cost basis. Accordingly, it was decided that the taxpayer was only taxable in respect of the additional costs incurred by the school in providing places for his children (net of fees paid by him).

As discussed at **1.404**, the Irish courts have not generally referred to Irish parliamentary proceedings in order to resolve interpretative doubts (although this is not an inflexible practice). Nevertheless, it appears that, in practice, an inspector will normally accept that a marginal cost basis does apply. However, in discussions with the Irish Taxation Institute, the Revenue Commissioners have expressed the view that in a case where the recipient of a benefit was displacing a customer who would otherwise be paying the full fee, the marginal cost would be the fee foregone.

However, there does not seem to be any justification in law for substituting notional opportunity costs for actual expense incurred (to which effect see the speech of Lord Griffiths in *Pepper v Hart* but compare that of Lord Browne-Wilkinson; the case is discussed more fully in Ward: *Pepper v Hart* [1992] STC 898, [1994] IJOT 40). It may be argued that the legislature has implicitly accepted that an opportunity cost is not an expense incurred by the employer in the context of 'preferential loans' to employees, which are subject to a specific tax regime (this would be superfluous if the interest forgone on such loans fell within TCA 1997, s 118): see **10.211**. However, if the employer deliberately incurs expense in order to provide goods or services to both customers and employees, ie the provision to employees is not merely incidental, it is highly arguable that such expense should be apportioned under TCA 1997, s 118.

The principle in *Pepper v Hart* could seem to be equally applicable to costs incurred in connection with assets applied by an employer and which are provided for the employee's use. However, the benefit of the use of the asset would seem to fall outside the decision in *Pepper v Hart* given the specific wording of TCA 1997, s 119(3) (see above).

Example 10.205.4

Dumb Ltd which hires out sophisticated electronic equipment allows Eli, one of its employees, the free use of such equipment when it is not required by customers. The equipment cost €90,000 when new but its market value when first provided to Eli was €40,000 Eli has the use of the equipment for three months during 2016. Dumb Ltd provided the services of its in-house repairman to Eli free of charge when the equipment broke down while he had the use of it. Dumb Ltd pays the repairman a fixed salary of €18,000 pa; the repairman incurred additional travel cost of €80 (travel expenses and spare parts at cost) in repairing the equipment for Eli.

Eli's benefit in kind for 2016 should it seems be calculated as follows:

	€
Annual value of equipment €40,000 x 5% x 3/12 =	500
Additional costs incurred in respect of repairs (following *Pepper v Hart*)	80
Total benefit in kind	580

The Revenue Commissioners accept that where an employee is allowed to retain the benefit of air miles arising as a result of his business travel, there is no cost to the employer involved in such an arrangement and that accordingly no taxable benefit arises.

Where expenditure is incurred in order to provide a benefit to a number of employees, an apportionment is clearly required. The Revenue have indicated that in the case of so-called '*en bloc*' payments made to provide a benefit on behalf of employees generally, the expense should be attributed equally amongst the employees entitled to avail of that benefit, but excluding those who specifically indicate that they do not wish to, and will not avail of the benefit. This is probably a tenable approach on the basis that the benefit consists of the right to use the facilities and not the actual quantum of use *per se*.

The apportionment of costs of providing facilities such as sporting facilities which are not concessionally regarded as tax exempt (see above) will have to be carried out on a 'just and reasonable' basis, subject to negotiation.

In practice, the Revenue will be prepared to accept that where a home telephone is paid for by the employer and there is mixed business and private that 50 per cent of the total cost (inclusive of line rentals) should be treated as private; it remains open to the taxpayer to establish a lower proportion of private use.

10.206 Living accommodation

In any case in which premises belonging to the body corporate or other employer are used in providing living accommodation or other benefits in kind, the annual value of the use of the asset is given a particular meaning. The term 'premises' is defined to include lands (TCA 1997, s 116(1) as amended by FA 2005, s 7). The principal effect is that the annual valuation basis applicable to premises will apply also to adjoining grounds.

TCA 1997, s 119(4) defines the annual value of the use of the premises as being the rent which might reasonably be expected to be obtained if the tenant had a letting on the following assumptions:

(a) the letting is on a year to year basis;

(b) the tenant undertakes to pay all the usual tenant's rates; and

(c) the landlord undertakes to bear the costs of the repairs, insurance and any other expenses necessary for maintaining the premises in a state to command that rent.

If the employer's interest in the premises is itself a lease for which he (or it) pays a rent greater than the annual value of the use of the premises, the actual rent payable is used instead of the annual value. In any event, if the employer incurs any other non-capital expense in connection with the premises, ie expense other than the landlord's expenses mentioned in (c) above, then that additional expense must also be included in the benefit in kind calculation. Since the landlord's expenses are deemed to be included in the assumed market value rental, it is accepted in practice that these expenses are not included again, irrespective of the actual amounts incurred by the employer. Should the director or employee as tenant actually incur without reimbursement any of these landlord's expenses, then it seems logical that practice should also permit the assumed rental brought into the benefit calculation to be reduced by the actual landlord's expenses paid by the tenant.

The Revenue Commissioners usually seek to apply a rule of thumb approach by assuming that the expected market value rent to be taken as the annual value of the premises is equal to eight per cent of the market value of the premises at the beginning of the relevant tax year. This approach has no statutory basis. It is therefore always open to the director or employee concerned, or his employer on his behalf, to satisfy the inspector that there should be a lower annual value, if he can substantiate that the facts would justify a lower market value rental. The Revenue give the example of an auctioneer's estimate of the rent likely to be obtained. Since a year-to-year letting is assumed, the market value rent taken as the annual value should be reviewed each year.

Example 10.206.1

GFE Ltd owns a house and grounds purchased several years ago for €180,000 which it makes available as a residence for the manager of its branch in a country town. Under its tenancy agreement with its current manager, Mr DC, the company undertakes to pay the ground rent, insurance and all repairs, internal and external. In addition, it also agrees to have the company's general handyman to look after the grounds at the company's expense. Mr DC agrees to pay the company a rent of €5,560 per annum in 2016. In the period ended 31 December 2016, GFE Ltd paid the following expenses in connection with the house:

	€
Ground rent	60
Insurance	670
External repairs	530
Internal repairs and decorating	1,540
Wages, etc of handyman (proportion allocated to keeping garden)	610
	3,410

The market value of the house and grounds at 1 January 2016 is agreed to be €290,000. Initially, the inspector seeks to take the annual value of the use of the house as being €23,200, ie eight per cent of €290,000. However, an almost identical house in the same neighbourhood had just been rented on a year to year basis for €17,800 in an arm's length transaction made in February 2016. In that case the terms of the letting were similar except that the tenant had undertaken to pay the internal repairs.

In Mr DC's case, the inspector accepts that the notional annual value of the use of the company's house should be taken at €18,800, ie a rent comparable to the €17,800 payable in the arm's length letting increased by €1,000 to allow for the fact that Mr DC has no responsibility for internal repairs. It was agreed that the actual internal repairs of €1,540 incurred in 2016 were more than would normally be expected. In calculating the benefit in kind enjoyed by Mr DC for the tax year 2016, the ground rent, insurance, external and internal repairs are left out of account as these are all landlord's expenses necessary to provide and maintain the house to command the assumed market value rent of €18,800 pa. The benefit in kind assessment for 2016 is now calculated as follows:

	€
Annual value of use of house:	
Assumed rent for year per the rule in TCA 1997, s 119(4)	18,800
Costs of maintaining garden	610
Expense incurred by company	19,410
Less:	
Rent payable to company	5,560
Benefit in kind for 2016	13,850

In *IRC v Luke* 40 TC 630, it was held by the House of Lords that expenditure on repairs (being of a kind which would normally fall on an owner and not on a tenant) and improvements to a house let to a director was incurred by the company in the acquisition or production of an asset which remained its own property, and was therefore by reason of the UK equivalent of TCA 1997, s 119(1) not taxable as a benefit in kind. The Crown had argued that the words 'acquisition or production of an asset' could only refer to the original purchase or building of a house and that improvements, renewals or repairs could not be covered by those words. In rejecting this, Lord Pearce gave his view of the intention of the legislation to be that:

> the expenses that go to acquiring or producing the 'living accommodation' shall not be charged against the director as a benefit in kind, but the annual value of it enhanced, of course, as it will be by any renewals or repairs, shall be charged against him ... Any money spent which enhances the value of the 'living accommodation' goes to produce an asset. If a man possesses a derelict house, the cost of putting it into repair may be said to be expense that produces an asset; the resulting asset is a house in good repair.

In fact, *IRC v Luke* was decided under UK legislation which did not provide for taking a notional rent on the basis now in the Irish TCA 1997, s 119(4) which makes it clear that all the expenses such as insurance, landlord's repairs, improvements, etc in providing the living accommodation are to be treated as covered by the assumed market value rental. In another UK case, decided about the same time, *Doyle v Davison* 40 TC 140, it was held that expenditure by a company on the repairs of a house let to a director were properly assessable as a benefit in kind on him. In distinguishing that case in his judgment in *IRC v Luke*, Lord Reid noted that on the facts in *Doyle v Davison* the repairs were of a nature that would normally fall on the tenant.

The question of the apportionment of expenses under the UK equivalent of TCA 1997, s 118 (see **10.203**) was considered in *Westcott v Bryan* 45 TC 476. In that case, Mr Bryan was the managing director of a pottery company, the factory of which lay in a rural area in Staffordshire. Although he wished to live in London, the company insisted that he occupy a large rambling house owned by the company in Staffordshire at which he could entertain customers. Customers were in fact entertained in the house and on various occasions stayed overnight. It was held by the Court of Appeal that it was proper to apportion expenses incurred by the company in connection with the provision of accommodation in the house as between use for the benefit of the managing director on the one hand and on use for the benefit of the company on the other. The Crown's contention that benefits derived from the concurrent enjoyment of accommodation, etc by a director and his company were not severable was rejected. The basis for apportionment should it seems be on a 'just and reasonable' basis (see *Bennion* at [1995] BTR 325).

The Revenue Commissioners have stated that where two or more employees share living accommodation, the annual value should be apportioned between them.

While most cases of the use of a company's premises by a director or employee are concerned with living accommodation, other uses may give rise to benefit in kind assessments. Although not specifically defined for the purposes of TCA 1997, Pt 5, Ch 3, the normal meaning of the word 'premises' may be taken as including land as well as building. If, for example, a director of a company owning farm land and buildings is given the use of that land to farm on his own private account at less than a proper market value rent, the benefit in kind rules apply in a similar way to that discussed for living accommodation. The taxable benefit in kind is again calculated by taking the assumed annual value or notional rent calculated under TCA 1997, s 119(4) (or the actual rent paid by the company, if higher) plus any other expenses incurred by the company in providing the benefit (other than those landlord's expenses deemed to be covered by the notional rent).

10.207 Motor cars

General

The rules concerning the taxation of the benefits arising from the provision of motor cars were substantially overhauled with effect from 1 January 2004 and subsequently revamped from 2009 onwards. The position prior to 1 January 2004 is fully set out in the 2003 edition of this book. The position prior to 1 January 2009 is fully set out in the 2008 edition.

TCA 1997, s 121 as amended by F(No 2)A 2008, s 6 has effect, for any tax year, in relation to a person chargeable to tax in respect of an employment, where any car is, by reason of his employment, made available (without a transfer of the property in it) to him, if the car is in that year available for his private use (TCA 1997, s 121(2)(a)).

A transfer of a part-interest in a car to an employee was held not to constitute a transfer of 'the property' (ie construed as denoting full ownership) therein in *Christensen v Vasili* [2004] EWHC (Ch) 476 (discussed further below). 'Employment' is defined as meaning an office or employment of profit such that any emoluments (within the meaning of TCA 1997, s 113) thereof would be chargeable to tax (TCA 1997, s 121(1)(a)). A 'car' excludes a motor-cycle (defined as a mechanically propelled vehicle with less than four wheels and an unladen weight of 410 kilograms or less-a motor-cycle which exceeds this criterion is treated as a car for benefit in kind purposes), a van (as defined by TCA 1997, s 121A: see **10.210** below) and a vehicle of a type not commonly used as a private vehicle and unsuitable to be so used (on which, see *Gurney v Richards* [1989] STC 682). The Revenue have stated that the definition includes all cars within the ordinary meaning of the term, crew cabs and jeeps but excludes hearses and lorries. It will also include motor-cycles with an unladen weight in excess of 410 kilograms.

TCA 1997, s 113 defines emoluments in terms of all salaries, fees, etc arising from an office or employment, and without reference to whether the office or employment is held or exercised in the State. Consequently, the car benefit rules apply both where the office or employment is taxable under Sch E and where it is a foreign office or employment taxable under Sch D Case III. The rules apply both to directors and to employees, irrespective of the level of their incomes from their offices or employments.

For a charge to arise under TCA 1997, s 121, the car must be made available to the employee, by reason of his employment and it must be available for his private use. In *Wilcock v Eve* [1995] STC 18 Carnwath J suggested that the expression 'by reason of the employment' differed little, if at all, from the general 'source' principle under Sch E (discussed in **10.106**). In a situation where a car is owned jointly by the employer and employee, it is highly arguable that the car is available to the employee in consequence of his rights as a co-owner. This argument was rejected (without much analysis) by the UK High Court in *Christensen v Vasili* [2004] EWHC (Ch) 476. The court seemed to take the view that the alternative interpretation was tenable and should be preferred since this meant tax would not be avoided in these circumstances (an approach which seems contrary to the basic principles of the interpretation of tax law: see **1.401**).

Where a car is made available to an employee by his employer (or by a person connected with his employer) it is automatically deemed to be made available by reason of the employment. There is one exception. A car is not to be treated as made available by reason of the employment if, where the employer is an individual, the car is made available, for example, to the employer's wife or son, in the normal course of the employer's domestic, family or personal relationships (TCA 1997, s 121(1)(b)(i)(II)).

Where the provision of a car meets these conditions, TCA 1997, s 121(2)(b)(i) ensures that TCA 1997, ss 117, 118 can no longer apply. TCA 1997, s 121 does not deal with the position where the costs of providing the car would be caught under TCA 1997, s 112(1) as a perquisite convertible into cash. This could arise, for example, where the employee was personally liable to pay for repairs, but the employer discharges this liability. It is thought that in practice the Revenue would confine themselves to the application of TCA 1997, s 121.

With the exception of pool cars (see **10.207**), a car made available in any year to the employee by reason of his employment is deemed to be available in that year for his private use, unless the terms on which the car is made available prohibit private use and no such use is actually made of the car in that year (TCA 1997, s 121(1)(b)(i)(I)). A car is also available for an employee's private use if it is available to any of his spouse, civil partner, his sons and daughters and children of his civil partner and their spouses, his partners and his servants, dependants and guests (TCA 1997, s 121(1)(b)(i)(III)).

Once a car is available to the employee for his private use, it does not matter whether in fact he makes any private use of it nor does the amount of his private mileage affect the amount of his taxable benefit. The fact that he is permitted to use it for non-business purposes is sufficient. Conversely, even if he is not strictly permitted to do so, if he uses the car at all for private purposes in any tax year, he is chargeable to tax under the rules of TCA 1997, s 121. 'Private use' is defined as any use of the car other than business use; 'business use' means travelling in the car which the person is necessarily obliged to do in the performance of the duties of his employment (TCA 1997, s 121(1)(a)).

The question of whether there was private use of a car was considered under the comparable UK legislation in *Gilbert v Hemsley* [1981] STC 703. A director of a plant hire company had duties including the maintenance and repair of engineering plant which involved his travelling from the company's yard to its building sites, from his home to the sites and directly from the sites to his home, as well as from his home to the company's yard. He did not have an office in his employer's premises. A car was made available to him by the company and, because of the risk of vandalism and lack of space at the company's premises, the taxpayer was required to take the car home at night. He was told the car was for business use and that he was not expected to use it for private purposes. He had a car of his own for private use and he did not in fact use the company car for any domestic purposes.

It was held in the Chancery Division that it could be inferred from the facts found by the Commissioners that the taxpayer's home was his working base and that he was travelling in the performance of his duties whenever he used the company's car. The Commissioners were therefore entitled to hold that he did not actually use the car for private purposes in the tax year in question. On the second condition that had to be satisfied so that the car should not be deemed available for his private use, the Commissioners had accepted the taxpayer's contention that, as the company told him he was 'not expected' to use the car for private purposes, he was in fact prohibited from making such use of it. The court held that this was the reasonable conclusion which the Commissioners were, on the particular facts before him, entitled to make.

The facts in *Gilbert v Hemsley* were somewhat exceptional. It is clear from the various cases which decided that the expenses of travelling from home to work were not deductible in computing Sch E income that, in the normal case, any use of an employer-provided car in travelling from home to work or from work to home would be regarded as private use of the car. In *Gurney v Richards* [1989] STC 682 it was held that a fire officer who travelled from his home to work, and was in frequent telephone contact with his employers while he so travelled, was potentially within the scope of the UK equivalent of TCA 1997, s 121. It was held that he was merely performing some of his duties while he travelled, as opposed to travelling 'in the performance' of his duties. Unlike the doctor in *Owen v Pook* 45 TC 571, (discussed in **10.302**), he was not required by the very nature of his employment to carry out his duties at two places of work. The fact that the taxpayer was on call at home and might on occasions give advice on the telephone from there meant only that he was obliged to be available or to give advice from wherever he happened to be at the time.

The constitutionality of the motor car benefit-in-kind provisions was upheld in *Browne & Ors v Attorney General* IV ITR 323.

Exception for pool cars

The foregoing rules for taxing employees on the benefit of employer provided cars made available to them do not apply at all to cars in a car pool if certain conditions are met. For this purpose, 'car pool' treatment is given to any car if the inspector of taxes is satisfied that it has for the year in question been included in a car pool for the use of the employees of one or more employers (TCA 1997, s 121(7)(a)). A claim for this treatment may be made by any of the employees concerned or by the employer on behalf of all of them (TCA 1997, s 121(7)(d)). There is a right of appeal available to any person aggrieved by a decision of the inspector on any question relating to this car pool treatment; notice must be given to the inspector within two months of receiving his decision. The normal appeal procedures apply thereafter (TCA 1997, s 121(7)(e)).

In order that any particular car may be given car pool treatment for any tax year, all of the following conditions must be met in that year:

(a) it must be available to, and actually used, by more than one of the employees concerned;

(b) in the case of each employee it must be available to him by reason of his employment;
(c) it must not ordinarily be used by any of the employees concerned to the exclusion of the others;
(d) in the case of each of the employees concerned, any private use of the car made by him was merely incidental to his other use of it in the year; and
(e) it must not normally be kept overnight on or in the vicinity of any residential premises where any of the employees reside, except where it is kept overnight on premises occupied by the employer or other person making the car available to them (TCA 1997, s 121(7)(b)(iii)).

In practice, the Revenue apply these conditions strictly and does not concede car pool treatment unless all conditions are fully met. It may be seen that there must be at least a minimum of two employees (which could include directors) entitled to use the pool car or cars for the whole of the tax year. A car pool may, however, consist of one car only if all the conditions are satisfied. Incidental private use might, for example, include an employee's taking a pool car home occasionally, but probably only if that is to enable him to set off from home on the employer's business. Any practice of allowing an employee to use the car privately, say at a weekend prior to setting off on business on a Monday morning, would probably disqualify the car from pool treatment.

10.208 Calculation of taxable motor car benefit

When it is established that an employee (or director) is taxable in any tax year in respect of a car made available by reason of his employment, TCA 1997, s 121(2)(b)(ii) treats as emoluments of the employment an amount equal to the excess of the 'cash equivalent' of the benefit of the car for that year over the aggregate of the amounts which the employee is required to make good, and actually makes good for that year, to the employer in respect of the costs of providing or running the car. The calculation of the taxable motor car benefit for any tax year involves the following steps:

(a) ascertain the appropriate 'cash equivalent percentage' for the year and the 'original market value' (OMV) of the car(s) available to the employee during the year;
(b) apply the appropriate cash equivalent percentage to the original market value to determine the cash equivalent of the benefit of the car ('the cash equivalent') for the full year, reduced proportionately where the vehicle has been available only for part of the year;
(c) ascertain the aggregate of the amounts which the employee makes good to the employer ('the employee's contribution') in the manner explained below; and
(d) determine the taxable motor car benefit by deducting the employee's contribution from the cash equivalent of the benefit (as adjusted, if relevant, in step (c)).

The original market value to which the cash equivalent percentage has to be applied must in all cases be taken as the price which the car might reasonably have been expected to fetch if sold in the State singly in a retail sale in the open market immediately before the date of its first registration, ie when it was new. The retail price used is one inclusive of all relevant customs and excise duties and value added tax (TCA 1997, s 121(1)(b)(iii)) (in practice, list price net of the customary cash discount is used). Even if the employer first acquires the car second-hand, or if he does not purchase but leases it, the retail price of the particular make and type of car when it was new before its first registration remains its open market value for all subsequent years. The Revenue Commissioners state in *Tax Briefing 28*, that in the case where an exceptionally large discount is granted on a car purchase, or if the discount cannot be determined (ie in the case of a trade-in) then the discount normally obtainable in respect of a single retail sale should be used. Revenue go on to state that they feel that such discounts do not normally exceed 10 per cent.

With effect from 1 January 2014, FA 2013, s 11 provides for car BIK to be calculated using the metric system (kilometres) rather than the imperial system (miles). This change should have no impact in practice on employees' tax liabilities. The cash equivalent percentage is the percentage by which the open market value (OMV) is multiplied to arrive at the cash equivalent of the car benefit for a full year. In the case of cars first provided prior to 1 January 2009, where annual business mileage is 24,000 kilometres or less, the percentage is 30 per cent. The percentage is not affected by the extent (if any) to which the running costs of the car (including fuel, insurance, repairs, servicing or road tax) are borne by the employee. Where in the case of such a car, the employee's mileage on business use for a tax year exceeds 24,000 kilometres, the cash equivalent percentage which would otherwise apply for that year becomes a lower percentage figure as set out in the 'high mileage' Table below.' (TCA 1997, s 121(4)).

Business mileage		*% of Original Market Value*
lower limit (kilometres)	*upper limit (kilometres)*	
24,000	32,000	24
32,000	40,000	18
40,000	48,000	12
48,000	not applicable	6

In the case of a car first provided on or after 1 January 2009, the Table to be applied by TCA 1997, s 121(4B) incorporates both mileage and CO2 emission factors, as follows (TCA 1997, s 121(4B)).

Business mileage		*% of Original Market Value*	*% of Original Market Value*	*% of Original Market Value*
lower limit (kilometres)	*upper limit (kilometres)*	*Vehicle Category*	*Vehicle Category*	*Vehicle Category*
		A,B C	D,E	F,G
-------	24,000	30	35	40
24,000	32,000	24	28	32
32,000	40,000	18	21	24
40,000	48,000	12	14	16
48,000	not applicable	6	7	8

The Vehicle Categories above are graded in accordance with their level of officially confirmed levels of Vehicle CO2 Emissions (CO2 g/km), as follows:

A: 0g/km up to and including 120g/km;
B: More than 120g/km up to and including 140g/km;
C: More than 140g/km up to and including 155g/km;
D: More than 155g/km up to and including 170g/km;
E: More than 170g/km up to and including 190g/km;

F: More than 190g/km up to and including 225g/km;
G: More than 225g/km.

The replacement of the table to be applied by TCA 1997, s 121(4B) by a table incorporating both mileage and CO_2 emission factors will not take effect until the issue of a commencement order by the Minister for Finance. Until this order is issued a company car BIK is to be calculated without taking into account the CO_2 emission levels of the car.

Where a taxpayer fails to return particulars of the value of a car and/or details of his business or private mileage or the inspector is not satisfied with the return, the inspector is obliged to make an estimate of the amounts involved to the best of his judgement. The inspector is required to assume that the minimum non-business mileage for the tax year is 8,000 kilometres, so that the business mileage figure is arrived at by deducting 8,000 kilometres from the total kilometres travelled in the year, unless sufficient evidence to the contrary is produced (TCA 1997, s 121(6)(b)). Consequently, if any employee wishes to claim that his private mileage for the year is less than 8,000 kilometres, it would be essential for him to keep a full log of all his business journeys, with details of their purpose and mileage on each. There is a specific right of appeal in relation to the value of the car and or the relevant mileages in relation to an assessment made in respect of the employment concerned (TCA 1997, s 121(6)(d)).

If a car provided by the employer is made available to a particular employee for part only of a tax year, the cash equivalent percentage contained in the high mileage Table is reduced by a factor equal to the number of days in the part of the year during which the car was available (including non-working days) divided by 365. The mileage figures in the Table are also scaled down correspondingly.

The Revenue Commissioners have stated that where use of a company car is restricted to a limited number of days per week, is only used by the employee or any member of his household during those days, and the vehicle concerned is otherwise kept on the employer's premise, they will accept that that the car is only available in respect of the days in question.

The Revenue Commissioners have also stated in *Tax Briefing 21* that they will not regard a car as being available for private use for any part of the year in which the employee (or director) is outside the State for the purpose of performing his duties, subject to the following conditions:

(a) the aggregate number of days spent outside the State for the purpose of performing the duties of the office or employment is at least 30 complete days in the tax year (any holiday leave period abroad should be excluded); a day for this purpose must include an overnight stay;
(b) the director/employee travels abroad without the car; and
(c) the car is not available for use by the director's/employee's family or household during the director's/employee's period of absence outside the State.

Where, the employee has business mileage of less than 24,000 kilometres per annum, but the car is available for only part of the year, the cash equivalent must be apportioned in the same ratio as the part of the year in which it is available bears to the whole year (TCA 1997, s 121(3)(b)); in this case there is no statutory formula expressed in terms of days, but the calculation would seem to be virtually identical to that required in respect of the high mileage Table.

A special relief is available to an employee whose business mileage exceeds 8,000 kilometres in the year of assessment and who spends 70 per cent or more of the time spent in performing his duties away from his employer's place of business; it is to be expected that the 8,000 business mileage floor would be scaled down where the employee takes up his post during the tax year (TCA 1997, s 121(5)). The relief is not available, however, if the time spent on his duties is less than 20 hours per week on average over the tax year.

Where the employee so elects in writing to the inspector, the cash equivalent will be calculated as 80 per cent of the amount otherwise assessable (ie disregarding the high mileage Table), so resulting in an effective percentage of 24 per cent. The employee must furnish his 'relevant log book' within 30 days of the inspector requesting it; failure to do so leads to loss of the relief for the relevant year of assessment.

A 'relevant log book' is defined as a daily record of the employee's business mileage in relation to any relevant car or cars, containing details of distances travelled, the nature and location of business transacted, and the amount of time spent away from the employer's place of business. The employer must certify the relevant log book as being true and accurate to the best of his knowledge and belief (TCA 1997, s 121(1)(a)).

TCA 1997, s 121(2)(b)(ii) permits the employee (or director) to a deduction for his contribution (if any) to the employer's costs of providing and running the car for the relevant tax year. This deduction is made as the final step in computing the taxable benefit, ie as a deduction from the cash equivalent of the benefit (as reduced, if relevant, for part year use only and/or the 'off-site workers' factor). For any expenses to be deducted by the employee under this heading, the rule requires that they must be expenses which the employee is required to make good directly to the employer and which he actually does so make good.

Example 10.208.1

Tangent Ltd purchased a new car for €12,000 in June 2010 for the use (including private use) of the company's sales manager, Mr R H Angle. Mr Angle had agreed to bear personally all the petrol costs related to his private use of the car, as well as reimbursing to Tangent Ltd all the costs of repairs and servicing. Tangent Ltd bore all the costs of business petrol, insurance and road taxes. Mr Angle's business mileage from 1 January 2015 to 30 November 2015 was 23,790 kilometres.

On 1 December 2015, Tangent Ltd sold the car and acquired a replacement immediately for Mr Angle's use. The retail price of the replacement car on the date of its first registration in November 2015 was €16,600. Mr Angle made a lump sum contribution of €4,150 towards the cost of acquiring the car. Mr Angle's business mileage for December was 833 kilometres. Petrol costs for the year were €2,050 and repair/servicing costs for the year amounted to €950.

Mr Angle's assessable motor car benefit for the year 2015 is computed as follows:

(1) Company owned car (to 30/11/2015)	*2015*
Original market value June 2010 (€12,000) =	€12,000
Mileage threshold exceeded: 24,000 x 334/365 =	21,962
Annual percentage per table	24%
Time-apportioned percentage: 24% x 334/365 =	21.96%
Cash equivalent:	
OMV €12,000 x 21.96% =	€2,635
Company owned car (from 1/12/2015)	
Original market value (Nov 2015)	€16,600

Mileage threshold: 24,000 x 31/365 =	2,038
Annual Percentage (not high mileage as below 2,038)	30%
Time-Apportioned Percentage: 30% x 31/365 =	2.55%
Cash equivalent:	
OMV €16,600 x 2.55%=	€423
Aggregate of cash equivalents	€3,058
Less: Deduction for contributions made to employer by Mr Angle	
Repairs/servicing Costs:	(€950)
Private petrol – not deductible as not paid directly to employer	-
	€2,108
Lump sum contribution €4,150, restricted to	(€2,108)
Taxable motor car benefit	Nil
Balance of lump sum contribution carried forward for offset against cash equivalent in 2016: €4,150 – 2,108 =	€2,042

Example 10.208.2

Jim Gallagher is provided with a car with an original market value of €24,000. His employer, Foyle Ltd, bear all the costs of running the car and Jim contributes €2,400 per annum directly to Foyle Ltd as his contribution towards those costs. Jim's business mileage for 2015 is 10,000 kms. Jim works 35 hours per week and spends 90 per cent of his time working at the premises of clients. Jim's taxable benefit for 2015 is computed as follows:

	2015
Cash equivalent of benefits:	€
€24,000 x 30%=	7,200
Adjust by 'offsite worker' relief €7,200 x 80% =	5,760
Deduction for expense made good to employer	(2,400)
Taxable motor car benefit	3,360

10.209 Parking levy

By virtue of TCA 1997, Pt 18B inserted by F(No 2)A 2008, s 4, a flat-rate parking levy will potentially apply to every employee who has an *entitlement to use a parking space* for parking a *specified vehicle* in *designated urban areas* which is provided directly or indirectly *by their employer*. TCA 1997, s 531P provides that the Minister for Finance can make an order providing the commencement date for Pt 18B. At the time of writing no order has yet been made. Hence, the information is provided here on the basis that an order could be made at any time. The levy will potentially apply irrespective of whether or not the vehicle concerned is already subject to a benefit-in-kind charge. The levy cannot be claimed as a deduction in computing emoluments and applies even where the employee pays for the parking privileges in question. This section will become effective once the ministerial order setting out the urban areas to which the levy is to apply is granted.

As outlined below, there are a number of exceptions and exemptions to the charge. For the purpose of the levy, the terms 'employee' and 'employer' effectively mean respectively *any* person who receives emoluments which are liable to deductions under the PAYE system and any person who is liable to deduct PAYE from such emoluments under the PAYE system. Deductions of the levy will be spread under the PAYE system throughout the year in line with the frequency of salary payments. The levy will apply to parking spaces provided in designated areas within the major urban centres of Cork, Dublin, Galway, Limerick and Waterford. The designated areas in which the levy will apply will be designated by Orders of the Minister for Finance following consultation with the city councils.

An employee is regarded as having *an entitlement to use a parking space* where any one or more of the following circumstances apply: the employee holds or has been issued with any type of authorisation to use a parking space or is given any type of permission (including arrangements or agreements with the employee) to use a parking space; the employee holds or has been issued with any form or means of access to a parking space; the employee has been allocated a dedicated parking space; the employee has been allocated a parking space on a shared basis or other similar arrangement; the availability of a parking space to the employee is on a first-come – first-served basis.

Specified vehicles generally include private cars and vans used as private vehicles (ie where such vans are not required to be used by an employee in the performance of their duties of employment). Jeeps and other vehicles constructed with rear passenger seats are also liable. In general, motor bikes are excluded from the levy. Certain cars owned or provided by the State, the Garda Síochána, the Defence Forces and certain other services such as the fire and ambulance service and the Customs service are excluded where the employee is required to use the vehicle in the performance of his duties. A van is excluded from the levy where the employee is required by the employer to use the van in the performance of their duties of employment.

In general, an employer is regarded as *providing a parking space to an employee* where the parking space is provided directly or indirectly, including where: the employer provides the parking space at its own premises; the parking space is provided at the premises of a person with whom the employer is connected (as defined by TCA 1997, s 10); the employer enters into an arrangement or agreement with an employee or some other person to provide a parking space; in the case of a public sector employee, the person providing the parking space is funded directly or indirectly by the employer (eg parking spaces provided by a school funded by the Department of Education which pays the salary of certain teachers and other staff).

An employee can disclaim entitlement to use a parking space by notifying their employer in writing or in an electronic format. Additionally, the employee should return whatever form of authorisation he or she holds and any form or means of access to a parking space, and cease actual use of the parking space. The disclaimer provision is not designed for periods of annual leave or short periods where an employee does not make use of a parking space. Revenue have stated, however, that they will look sympathetically at situations where use of the disclaimer provision may be appropriate for practical reasons. Periods of unpaid leave may be considered in this context. In circumstances where entitlement to use a parking space lapses or is withdrawn for any reason, the levy will no longer apply so long as the employee returns whatever form of authorisation he or she holds and any form or means of access to a parking space, and ceases actual use of the parking space.

The amount of the levy will be a flat rate amount of €200 for a full year. The Revenue interpret the legislation as restricting the charge to €200 in relation to any number of parking spaces provided by the same employer but imposing a separate charge of €200 in relation to parking spaces provided in different employments. In the first year of the levy, the amount of the levy payable will be reduced on a pro-rata basis to reflect the period of the year in which the levy is effective. A reduced levy applies where parking spaces are shared between employees provided that the ratio of employees (who have an entitlement to park) to each parking space is 2:1 or more. In these circumstances, the levy for employees with an entitlement to park will be reduced to €100. Where an employee's normal pattern of work is on the basis of part-time or job-sharing arrangements, then the levy amount payable is reduced pro-rata but not below a minimum of 50 per cent of the amount payable.

Where an employee's entitlement to use a parking space applies for only *part* of a year, then the amount of the levy payable by the employee is to be reduced on a pro-rata basis. This is designed to cover situations such as where an employee starts or finishes work during the year. For example, if an employee's entitlement to use a space commences on 1 December in a year, then only 1/12th of the levy will apply for that year. This would mean that a person who is given, say, a dedicated space would pay €16.66 for the month of December (ie €200 x 1/12th).

The amount of the levy is also reduced where an employee is on maternity leave; the 26 week period of maternity leave to which she is entitled together with the 10 week period immediately prior to the commencement of maternity leave is disregarded for the purposes of calculating the levy.

The amount of the levy is also reduced in the case of shift workers. Anyone starting or finishing work after nine o'clock in the evening or before seven o'clock in the morning will have the part of the year during which they are on shift work involving those hours disregarded for the purposes of calculating the levy. For example, someone doing such shift work for three months of the year would be liable to pay €150 (ie €200 less ¼ excluded because of shift work).

There is no reduction in the amount of the levy for contributions made by an employee to their employer towards the cost of a parking space.

There are exemptions for:

(i) holders of a valid disabled person's parking permit;

(ii) employees of the emergency services where the use of a space relates solely to a response to an emergency situation required by the employer;

(iii) retired persons no longer in employment where a space continues to be provided to them for occasional use;

(iv) employees who do not otherwise have entitlement to use a parking space, but are occasionally permitted to use a space that the total number of days (including part-days) for which permission is granted any year does not exceed ten.

Employers are obliged to deduct the levy from employees' net salary payments after income tax, PRSI, and the Universal Social Charge are deducted and remit it to the Office of the Collector-General at the same time and in the same manner as the employer currently remits deductions made under the PAYE system. Employers will be obliged to keep records, for each year, in relation to: the location(s) at which parking facilities are provided, including the number of parking spaces provided at each location; the name and PPSN of each employee who has, or ceased to have, an entitlement to use a parking space, and evidence of the deduction of the parking levy from relevant employees. A penalty of €3,000 applies where an employer fails: to deduct the levy from employees or remit the levy to Revenue; to keep the required records, or to provide the required details on the Form P35. A separate penalty potentially applies in relation to each offence.

10.210 Motor vans and bicycles

Motor vans

TCA 1997, s 121A applies in relation to a person chargeable to tax in respect of an employment, where any van is, by reason of his employment, made available (without a transfer of the property in it) to him, if the van is in that year available for his private use (TCA 1997, s 121A(2)(a)). The question of when a van is made available to an employee and what constitutes private use thereof is decided on the same criteria as applicable to motor cars (TCA 1997, s 121A(4)(a) (see **10.207**).

For these purposes TCA 1997, s 121A(1) as amended by FA 2004, s 8 defines a 'van' as a mechanically propelled road vehicle which is designed or constructed solely or mainly for the carriage of goods or other burden, which has a roofed area or areas to the rear of the driver's seat, which has no side windows or seating fitted in that roofed area or areas and with a laden weight of no more than 3,500 kilograms. The Revenue take the view that a vehicle cannot change its status from a car to a van as subsequent adaptation cannot alter the original purpose of design or construction.

TCA 1997, s 121A(2)(b) applies the charge to tax on the cash equivalent of the benefit of the van, subject to a deduction in respect of any amount made good by the employee towards the cost of providing or running the van. This subsection also provides that the general benefits in kind charge contained in TCA 1997, Pt 5, Ch 3 does not apply in relation to the expenses (petrol, insurance, repairs and servicing, etc) incurred in the provision of the van concerned, ie as in the case of motor cars.

The cash equivalent of the benefit of a van is computed as five per cent of the original market value (ascertained as in the case of motor cars: see **10.207**). The percentage is fixed, irrespective of the level of business mileage in the year. The benefit is reduced proportionately where a van is only available for part of a year, as in the case of motor cars (TCA 1997, s 121(3)(b) applied by TCA 1997, s 121A(4)).

There is an exception for pooled vans identical to that applicable in the case of motor cars (TCA 1997, s 121(7) applied by TCA 1997, s 121A(4)): see **10.207**.

In addition TCA 1997, s 121A(2A) provides an exemption where there is private use of a van, but:

(a) the van made available to the employee is necessary for the performance of the duties of the employee's employment;

(b) the employee is required by the person who made the van available to keep it, when not in use in the performance of the duties of the employee's employment, at or in the vicinity of the employee's private residence;

(c) apart from travel between the employee's private residence and workplace, other private use of the van is prohibited by the person making the van available and there is no such other private use; and

(d) in the performance of the duties of their employment, the employee spends at least 80 per cent of their time engaged on such duties away from the premises of the employer to which the employee is attached.

Example 10.210.1

Shaun McIntyre is employed by SeeWater Ltd from 1 July 2016. He is allowed unrestricted private use of a van in respect of which he will incur business mileage of 26,000 miles per annum. SeeWater Ltd bears all the costs of running the van except private petrol which Shaun pays himself. Shaun contributes €20 per month towards the running costs of the van. The van had a market value of €14,500 when first registered on 6 May 2010.

The taxable benefit for 2015 in respect of Shaun's van will be computed as follows:

	€	€
Open Market Value	14,500	
Cash Equivalent	€14,500 x 5% x 6/12 =	363
Less: Contributions by employee	€20 x 6 =	120
Taxable benefit		243

Bicycles

TCA 1997, s 118(5G), inserted by F (No 2) A 2008, s 7 provides exemption for the provision of a bicycle and/or *bicycle safety equipment* by an employer to a director or employee ('employee' hereafter) with effect from 1 January 2009, up to a cost of €1,000, subject to meeting the following conditions:

(i) they are unused and not second-hand;
(ii) the employee uses them mainly for *qualifying journeys*;
(iii) and they are made available generally to employees.

A '*bicycle*' is defined as a pedal cycle, namely;

(i) a bicycle or tricycle which is intended or adapted for propulsion solely by the physical exertions of a person or persons seated thereon; or
(ii) a pedelec,

ie a bicycle or tricycle which is equipped with an auxiliary electric motor having a maximum continuous rated power of 0.25 kilowatts, of which output is progressively reduced and finally cut off as the vehicle reaches a speed of 25 kilometres per hour, or sooner if the cyclist stops pedalling, but does not include a moped or a scooter. '*Bicycle safety equipment*' includes:

(i) bicycle bells and bulb horns;
(ii) bicycle helmets that conform to European product safety standard CEN/EN 1078;
(iii) bicycle lights, including dynamo packs;
(iv) bicycle reflectors and reflective clothing; and
(v) such other safety equipment as the Revenue Commissioners may allow.

A '*qualifying journey*', employee, is defined as the whole or part of a journey:

(i) between the employee's home and *normal place of work*, or
(ii) between the employee's normal place of work and another place of work,

where the employee is travelling in the performance of the duties of his employment. A '*normal place of work*' means the place where the employee normally performs the duties of his employment;

An employee will not be exempted under these provisions more than once in any period of five consecutive tax years of assessment, commencing with the year of assessment in which he is first provided with a bicycle and/or bicycle safety equipment. It would appear that if the bicycle is scrapped or stolen that the exemption would not apply for a replacement within five years of the original purchase, which appears harsh. If the provision of the bicycle and/or equipment is subject to a salary sacrifice arrangement, no tax will be charged on the salary foregone if the conditions of TCA 1997, s 118B are satisfied.

10.211 Loans to employees and directors

Following *Tennant v Smith* (see **10.105**), the grant of a loan which is repayable on demand to an employee at a low (or zero) interest rate would not be taxable as an emolument under general principles (see also *O'Leary v McKinlay* [1991] STC 492). Furthermore, in general it would usually be impracticable to apply the general benefit-in-kind rules (see **10.203**) due to the difficulty of identifying the cost of providing the loan incurred by the employer. Accordingly, a special tax regime applies to the provision of loans (as widely defined) to employees and directors.

TCA 1997, s 122(2) applies where in relation to an individual there is a preferential loan outstanding for the whole or part of a tax year. Section 122(2) charges the individual (or the individual's spouse or civil partner in the case where he/she is the chargeable spouse under joint assessment under TCA 1997, s 1017) to tax under Sch E or Sch D III as appropriate on the benefit derived from the 'preferential loan'.

TCA 1997, s 122(3) additionally charges an individual to tax under Sch E or Sch D III as appropriate on any amount of any loan (whether or not a preferential one) made to him directly or indirectly by his employer or by a person who subsequently becomes his employer and which is released or written off or on any amount of any liability to interest payable on any such loan that is released or written off.

In each case, the value of the benefit to the employee or director, as determined under the rules of TCA 1997, s 122, is treated as if it were a perquisite of his office or employment. This perquisite is chargeable to income tax under the main Sch E charging rule of TCA 1997, s 112 except, if the office or employment with the employer is or would be a foreign one, it is stated to be chargeable under Sch D Case III (TCA 1997, s 122(2), (3) but note the comments below on the position prior to 1 January 2005).

Before giving the definition of a preferential loan for the purpose of the charge to tax under the section, some other definitions relevant to it should be given.

'Employee'

'Employee' is defined, in relation to an employer, as meaning an individual employed by the said employer in an employment within TCA 1997, Pt 5, Ch 3, ie one 'such that any emoluments thereof would fall to be assessed under Sch E (TCA 1997, s 116(1))' or, with effect from 1 January 2005, an employment 'the profits or gains of which are chargeable to tax under Sch D Case III' (TCA 1997, s 122(1) as amended by FA 2005, s 9). Prior to 1 January 2005, when there was no reference to Sch D Case III, it was difficult to see how the section could apply to foreign employments, although, as noted above, such a charge is envisaged under TCA 1997, s 122(2), (3). The Revenue Commissioners apparently take the view that the charge under Sch D Case III was effective under the previous legislation. If the employer is a body corporate, the term 'employee', includes a director of the body corporate (as defined by TCA 1997, s 116: see **10.201**) (TCA 1997, s 122(1)(a)). Each reference in this Chapter, including any already made, to an 'employee' is to be taken as including a reference to a director unless the context requires otherwise.

'Employer'

'Employer' is defined, in relation to an individual, as meaning any of the following:

(a) a person of whom the individual or his spouse or civil partner (but *not* any other relative) is an employee (as defined above);

(b) a person of whom the individual or his spouse or civil partner ((but *not* any other relative) was previously an employee (in respect of loans made on or after February 2004, following the enactment of FA 2004, s 10);

(c) a person of whom the individual (but not the individual's spouse or civil partner) becomes an employee subsequent to the making of a loan by the person to the individual and while any part of the loan or of another loan replacing it is outstanding); or

(d) any person connected with a person who is an employer under (a), (b) or (c) (TCA 1997, s 122(1)(a)).

It would appear that loans which are left outstanding after the cessation of an employment remain within the section during the lifetime of the employee concerned. There is no requirement that the individual must be employed in the tax year of charge. However, a loan made to a former employee prior to 4 February 2004 falls outside the section (other than a loan replacing a loan made prior to or during the employment: see below).

Under limb (c) it would appear that if the person who made the loan (or another person connected with that person) becomes the individual's employer after the loan was made, no tax charge can arise under TCA 1997, s 122 for any tax year prior to that in which the actual employer/employee relationship commences.

For the purposes of the rules of the section, a person is treated as being connected with an employer if he would be so regarded for the purposes of TCA 1997, s 250. This in fact requires the connected person rules of TCA 1997, s 10 to be applied (see **12.304**). For example, if the actual employer is an individual, any loan made by a relative (as defined in the latter section) of the actual employer or by a company controlled by him is treated as a loan made by an employer. Another example, if an individual is an employee of a company, any other company controlled by the employer company or of which the employer company has control is also regarded as the employer of the individual.

Further, TCA 1997, s 250(5)(b) treats a person (the 'first person') as being connected with any other person to whom he (or, if a company, it) has made any loans or advanced any money, except in the case where any such loan or advance has been made in the ordinary course of a business which includes the lending of money carried on by the first person. Consequently, a loan made to an employee of a given employer by another person to whom the employer has made any loan or advanced any money (other than in the ordinary course of a business of lending money) is treated as a loan made by the actual employer.

'Specified rate'

For every loan made by an employer (or person connected with the employer) to an employee (or to his spouse or civil partner), it is necessary to ascertain the specified rate for each tax year in which any of that loan remains outstanding. This is necessary first to determine whether or not that loan is a preferential loan and, then if it is, the specified rate is used in measuring the amount of the perquisite on which the employee is charged to income tax.

For the tax year 2015, TCA 1997, s 122(1)(a) provides that the specified rate, in relation to a loan made by an employer to an employee, is:

(a) 4 per cent per annum (the qualifying loan rate) if the loan is a *qualifying loan* within the meaning of TCA 1997, s 244(1)(a) (see **Division 3**) (and is not one to which the rate in (c) applies);
(b) 13.5 per cent per annum (the general rate), if the loan is not a *qualifying loan* (and is not one to which the rate in (c) applies)); or
(c) a rate equal to the arm's length rate (if lower than the qualifying loan rate), but only if all the conditions mentioned under '*arm's length rate*' discussed further below in the text immediately following **Example 10.211.1** are met.

Prior to the tax year 2010 for category: (a) to apply, it was a requirement of TCA 1997, s 122 that any interest paid on a preferential loan had to qualify for relief under TCA 1997, s 244. For 2010 onwards, it is merely necessary that the loan constitutes a qualifying loan. As a result the qualifying loan rate will apply to an individual who has a qualifying loan but who no longer qualifies for relief on the interest paid. Both the qualifying loan rate and the general rate, as set out above, are liable to be changed from time to time. This may be done in the Finance Act in any year or, alternatively, the Minister for Finance is empowered to prescribe by regulations a different rate for either or both of these rates. A change in the rate for qualifying loans also affects the determination of the arm's length rate in any case in which that rate may be relevant (see below).

The qualifying loan rate applies as the specified rate – except in a case where the 'arm's length rate' rate in (c) applies – where the interest is paid by the borrower on a qualifying loan. It is not necessary that all of the interest should qualify ie the fact that relief in relation to the interest would be restricted under the rules of TCA 1997, s 244 would not be material.

In any case where the employer loan is not a qualifying loan and is not a case to which the arm's length rate in (c) applies, the specified rate is the general rate (the highest and least favourable rate). Since the cases where the rate in (c) applies are less common, the choice of specified rate is normally between two rates – the qualifying loan rate and the general rate.

'Preferential loan' defined

'Preferential loan' is defined in relation to an individual as a loan, in respect of which either no interest is payable or interest is payable at a preferential rate, made directly or indirectly to the individual or to his spouse or civil partner by a person who in relation to the individual or his spouse or civil partner is an employer. From 26 January 2011, the definition is altered to refer to interest paid rather than payable; the effect of this alteration is obscure given that interest may be payable in one tax year and paid in another. For the exception to this definition, see below. In a case where an individual's spouse or civil partner receives a loan from a person who subsequently becomes the individual's employer, that person is not the spouse's or civil partner's employer under limb (c) of the definition of 'employer' discussed above. The definition of 'preferential loan' effective from 1 January 2005 onwards does not overcome this limitation as the loan was not deemed to be made by a person who was the individual's employer at the time the loan was made.

'Preferential rate', in relation to any loan by an employer to an employee (or spouse or civil partner), is defined by TCA 1997, s 122(1) as meaning a rate of interest which is less than the specified rate. This means a rate less than the qualifying loan rate, the general rate or the arm's length rate, whichever is appropriate to the particular loan. Therefore, a preferential loan is any such employer loan on which the interest is payable at a rate lower than the specified rate appropriate to the type of loan or, alternatively, an interest free loan from the employer.

Since the specified rate, whether the qualifying loan rate or the general rate, normally remains unchanged throughout the whole of a tax year, but as the rate of interest actually payable may change during a tax year, it is possible that a given employer loan may be a preferential loan for one part of the year (if the rate of the interest payable in that part falls below the specified rate), but may not be a preferential loan in another part of the year (if the rate payable in the other part equals or exceeds the specified rate).

An exception to the above definition of 'preferential loan' may apply where the employer making a loan for any purpose to an employee or his spouse or civil partner is a bank, building society or other lending agency which, in the course of its trade, makes equivalent loans for similar purposes to persons other than employees or their spouses or civil partners. In any such case, the loan to the employee or spouse is not a preferential loan if the rate of interest charged on the loan is no lower than the rate charged on the equivalent loans for equivalent purposes at arm's length to non-employees (TCA 1997, s 122(1)(a)(ii)).

'Loan' includes any form of credit, and references to a loan include references to any other loan applied directly or indirectly towards the replacement of another loan. In *Harvey v Williams* (1995) STC (SCD) 329 the taxpayer's employer granted him an interest-free loan to purchase a house. The Special Commissioner rejected the taxpayer's argument that the loan ceased to be a loan because the obligation under the agreement was to repay not the principal sum, but instead a fixed proportion of the ultimate sale proceeds of the house. The Special Commissioner stated that a loan could not be transmuted into something else merely because it would be discharged by an amount greater or less than the sum originally borrowed.

In *Williams v Todd* [1988] STC 676 it was held (unsurprisingly) that an advance of salary repayable by instalments fell within the definition of a 'loan'. In strictness, similar considerations should presumably apply to cash 'floats' provided to employees to cover their business expenses; it is not thought, however, that an inspector would wish to take this point where reasonable amounts were involved.

In *Horner v Hasted* [1995] STC 766, the taxpayer received a severance payment of £90,000. The taxpayer's employer also agreed to maintain his life insurance cover on the basis that if the taxpayer should die before the age of 65 a sum of £90,000 out of the insurance proceeds would be paid to the firm. Lightman J held that the contingent obligation to pay the latter sum was a distinct and separate matter which could not alter the legal character of the severance payment (which was not repayable in any circumstances). Accordingly the severance payment remained exactly that and was not a loan.

In *Stephens v T Pittas Ltd* [1983] STC 376 (a case concerning the close company anti-avoidance rules governing loans to participants: (TCA 1997, s 438) it was held that a misappropriation of funds by a director was not a 'loan' since it lacked the necessary element of consensus between the parties. However, unpaid purchase money left outstanding, which does not constitute a loan as such (*Ramsden v IRC* 37 TC 619) would be caught as a form of credit. In *Grant v Watton* [1999] STC 330, the taxpayer formed a company (of which he was a director) to provide services to his business as a sole trader. The fees for the company's services were paid annually. The court held that the company had provided credit to the taxpayer since payment was not demanded until a time later than that at which the services were supplied.

Any reference in the section (and in this text) to a loan being made by a person includes a reference to a person assuming the rights and liabilities of the original lender; it also includes a reference to a person arranging, guaranteeing or in any way facilitating a loan or the continuation of a loan already in existence (TCA 1997, s 122(1)). It follows from this extended meaning that, for example, if an employer (or a person connected with the employer) guarantees a loan made by another person to one of the employer's employees, and if the rate of interest charged on the loan is less than the specified rate, then the loan is treated as a preferential loan made by the employer. Similarly, a loan with interest charged at a rate less than the specified rate made by a person other than the borrower's employer becomes a preferential loan if the employer (or a person connected with the employer) takes over the loan.

Example 10.211.1

Mr B White is a director of Water Ltd (the actual employer). Another company, Ground Ltd, owns more than 50 per cent of the ordinary share capital of Water Ltd. Ground Ltd is therefore a person connected with the actual employer so as to be an 'employer' for the purposes of the preferential loan rules of TCA 1997, s 122. Neither company's trade involves the making of loans to persons other than employees or their spouses or civil partners (so that there is no 'arm's length' rate to consider).

Mr White and his wife have each received loans as follows:

(a) Mr White: loan of €30,000 made by Water Ltd on 15 February 2010 applied by him towards the cost of the couple's principal residence in Dublin (ie a qualifying loan). Interest is charged on this loan at a fixed rate of 3.5 per cent.

(b) Mrs White: loan of €15,000 made by Ground Ltd on 22 March 2010 applied by her in carrying out improvements on a bungalow in County Wexford used as the couple's second and subsidiary residence (not a qualifying loan). Interest is charged on this loan between 1 January 2014 and 30 June 2015 at a rate of 11 per cent, but this is increased to 14 per cent with effect from 1 July 2015 (and continues unchanged).

The status of these loans (ie whether preferential or not) for each of the tax years 2014 and 2015 is determined as follows:

Loan to employee (Mr White) by employer:	*2014*	*2015*
Specified rate (qualifying loan rate)	4.0%	4.0%
Actual rate charged (whole year)	3.5%	3.5%
Preferential loan (if actual rate is the lower)	Yes	Yes
Loan to spouse of employee by 'employer':		
Specified rate (general rate)	13.5%	13.5%
Actual rate charged all tax year 2014	11%	
period 1/1/2015 to 30/6/2015		11%
period 1/7/2015 to 31/12/2015		14%
Preferential loan (if actual rate the lower)		
All tax year 2014	Yes	
period 1/1/2015 to 30/6/2015		Yes
period 1/7/2015 to 31/12/2015		No

In summary, Mr White's loan from Water Ltd (his actual employer) is a preferential loan for the whole of 2014 and 2015. Mrs White's loan from Ground Ltd (deemed to be her employer as being connected with her spouse's employer) is a preferential loan for all of 2014 and for

2015 up to 30 June 2015 also. For the way in which their respective benefits from these loans are taxed, see **Example 10.211.3**.

'Arm's length rate'

TCA 1997, s 122(1)(a)(ii) provides that a rate lower than the qualifying loan rate is to be used as the specified rate in any case where all of the following conditions are met:

(a) a preferential loan is made to an employee by an employer;

(b) the making of loans for the purpose of purchasing a dwelling house for occupation by the borrower as a residence, for a stated term of years at a rate of interest which does not vary for the duration of the loan, forms part of the trade of the employer; and

(c) the rate of interest at which the employer in the course of its trade, at the time the preferential loan is made, makes loans at arm's length to persons other than employees, for the purpose of purchasing a dwelling house for occupation by the borrower as a residence is less than four per cent for 2015.

In any case where all the above conditions are met, the specified rate for the preferential loan to the employee becomes the rate at which the employer, at the time that loan was made, was making loans at arm's length to persons who are not his/its employees for the purpose of purchasing a dwelling house for occupation by the borrower as a residence. For convenience, this rate for non-employees may be referred to as the 'arm's length rate'.

It may be seen that the circumstances in which the 'arm's length rate' becomes the specified rate are in fact very restricted. First, it is only necessary to consider the possibility of this rate applying if the loan to the employee (or spouse or civil partner) is not already excluded from the definition of 'preferential loan' by the exception mentioned earlier, ie where the lender is a bank, building society or other lending agency and where the rate of interest on the employer loan is not any lower than the rate charged to non-employees on equivalent loans for similar purposes.

Secondly, the loan made by the employer must be one made to the employee himself. A loan made to the spouse or civil partner of an employee cannot have the arm's length rate as its specified rate (so that the specified rate for the spouse or civil partner loan is either the qualifying loan rate or the general rate). This is because the arm's length rate is relevant only for a loan made to an employee. Although the definition of employer includes the employer of the spouse or civil partner of the individual whom it is sought to tax, the definition of an employee does not include the employee's spouse or civil partner.

Thirdly, a specified rate equal to the arm's length rate can only occur in a case where the employer carries on a trade which includes the making of loans for the purposes of purchasing a dwelling house for occupation by the borrower as a residence ('home purchase loans'). In effect, this restricts the use of the arm's length rate to cases where the employer making the loan to the employee is a bank, building society or other type of lender which has a trade of or including the making of home purchase loans.

Fourthly, even if the employer makes such home purchase loans in the course of such a trade, the arm's length rate does not apply unless that trade includes the making of home purchase loans which are loans for a stated term of years and which have a rate of interest which does not vary for the duration of the loan. It is not essential that the making of such 'fixed rate' loans is a major part of the trade of the bank, building society, etc, but it must be at least some part of that trade.

Finally, it is to be noted that, in applying condition (c) to determine the specified rate for any tax year in respect of any particular preferential loan for which conditions (a) and (b) are met, the lender's arm's length rate (for non-employees) as applying at the date the particular loan was made is compared with the qualifying loan rate in force in the tax year. In a case where the bank, etc offers loans at different rates depending on the terms and conditions of the loan (as will invariably be the case) it seems to be open to select the lowest rate on offer. An alteration to the terms of a loan will not generally give rise to a new loan in this context: *West v O'Neill* [1999] STC 147.

Example 10.211.2

Assume that on 1 May 2016 a bank made a loan in the course of its trade to Mr X, an employee of the bank, for the purchase of a new house to be used as his sole residence (ie a qualifying loan). The bank also makes house purchase loans at arm's length to non-employees, some of which are for stated terms of years with interest at a fixed rate for the duration of the loans. The bank charges interest at 3.5 per cent per annum on this loan to Mr X. On 1 May 2016 (date of loan to Mr X), the bank's lowest variable rate of interest on its house purchase loans to non-employees is 3.5 per cent (but this rate is increased to 4.5 per cent on 25 May 2016.

Since the per cent rate being charged by the bank to non-employees on the date the loan to Mr X was made is less than 4 per cent (the qualifying loan rate for 2015), and since conditions (a) and (b) are also met, the specified rate for Mr X's loan is 3.5 per cent (ie the arm's length rate applies). The fact that the non-employees' rate is increased above 4.0 per cent soon after the loan to Mr X was made has no bearing on the matter.

Exception for family etc loans

The rules of TCA 1997, s 122 relating to employer loans do not apply to any loan made by an employer, if that employer is an individual, which can be shown to have been made in the normal course of his domestic, family or personal relationships (TCA 1997, s 122(5)). For example, if Mr Jones makes an interest free loan to his daughter (who happens to be an employee of his) on the occasion of her marriage to help her purchase furniture for her new home, this is not regarded as a preferential loan so that no tax charge arises on the interest benefit (nor on any release or write off of any part or all of the loan).

Tax charge for interest on preferential loan

In any case where an employee or his spouse or civil partner has, at any time during a tax year, a preferential loan from a person who is his employer, TCA 1997, s 122 charges income tax on him in respect of the benefit derived in that tax year from the preferential loan.

The value of the perquisite from a preferential loan for any tax year is the excess (if any) of:

(a) the interest which would have been payable in that year on the preferential loan if interest had been charged on that loan at the specified rate per annum (the 'notional interest'); over

(b) the interest (if any) paid or payable in that year on the preferential loan (TCA 1997, s 122(2)).

If an individual has two or more preferential loans at any time in a tax year from the employer, the amount chargeable to tax in respect of the two or more preferential loans is the excess (if any) of the aggregate of the notional interest for that year on those loans over the aggregate of the interest paid or payable in that year on those loans.

Where the benefit of a loan enjoyed by one spouse or civil partner is attributable to the employment of the other spouse, the benefit will normally be subject to PAYE in relation to the earnings of the employee spouse or civil partner (see **11.1**). In the rare case where PAYE does not apply, then if the individual in receipt of the perquisite(s) from a preferential loan or loans is a wife or civil partner whose husband or civil partner is assessed to tax under TCA 1997, s 1017 in respect of their joint incomes, the husband or civil partner shall be the person charged to tax in respect of his wife's or civil partner's perquisite(s). Similarly, should any such joint assessment under that section be made on the wife or civil partner, then she is charged to tax in respect of any perquisites which her husband or civil partner may have from any preferential loan or loans made to him.

Although treated as a taxable perquisite of the office or employment, any interest benefit chargeable under TCA 1997, s 122 does not count as emoluments for the purpose of entitling the employee (or director) to the PAYE tax credit under TCA 1997, s 461 (TCA 1997, s 122(6)). However, in most cases the employee would have sufficient other income taxable under Sch E to claim the full PAYE allowance.

Example 10.211.3

Continue with the facts of **Example 10.211.1** where it is established that Mr B White and his wife each have preferential loans connected with his employment (directorship) in Water Ltd, although his wife's loan comes from that company's parent company (deemed to be an employer), Ground Ltd.

TCA 1997, s 122 requires Mr and Mrs B White to be charged to tax under Sch E in respect of the 'perquisites' derived from their respective preferential loans. The information on which the amounts taxable are calculated is as follows:

(a) Mr White's outstanding loan balance at 1 January 2014 is €24,000. Mrs White's loan at 1 January 2014 stands at its original balance of €15,000.

(b) Mr White reduces his outstanding loan by repayments of €1,000 on 30 June and 31 December in each tax year. He pays interest on the same dates on the loan balance outstanding for the previous six months.

(c) As indicated in **Example 10.211.1**, the specified rate of interest on Mr White's loan (a qualifying loan) is 4% for 2014 and 2015 and he is charged interest at the rate of 3.5 per cent per annum throughout both periods.

(d) Mrs White reduces her loan by repayments of €2,500 on 31 December of each tax year starting with 31 December 2014 and pays interest annually on 31 December each year.

(e) As indicated in **Example 10.211.1**, the specified rate of interest on Mrs White's loan (not a qualifying loan) is 13.5% for 2014 and 2015. She is charged interest at 11 per cent pa between 1 January 2014 and 30 June 2015 and then at 14 per cent pa from 1 July 2015 to 31 December 2015.

The amounts of the perquisites chargeable for each of the tax years 2014 and 2015 are computed as follows:

	Loan to Mr BW	*Loan to Mrs BW*
Year 2014 Notional interest at relevant specified rate:	€	€
Mr White		
€24,000 x 4.0% x 6/12 (6 mths to 30/06/2014)	480	
€23,000 x 4.0% x 6/12 (6 mths to 31/12/2014)	460	
	940	
Mrs White		

€15,000 x 13.5%		12,025
Less:		
2014 Interest actually payable in year:		
Mr White		
€24,000 x 3.5% x 6/12 (6 mths to 30/06/2014)	420	
€23,000 x 3.5% x 6/12 (6 mths to 31/12/2014)	403	
	823	
Mrs White		
€15,000 x 11%		1,650
2014 Amount taxable as perquisite:		
Excess of notional interest over interest payable	117	375
Year 2015 Notional interest at relevant specified rate:		
Mr White		
€22,000 x 4% x 6/12 (6 mths to 30/06/2015)	440	
€21,000 x 4% x 6/12 (6 mths to 31/12/2015)	420	
Mrs White – up to 30/6/2015		
€12,500 x 13.5% x 6/12=	—	844
	860	844
Year 2015 Interest actually payable in year:		
Mr White		
€22,000 x 3.5% x 6/12 (to 30/06/2015)	385	
€21,000 x 3.5% x 6/12 (to 31/12/2015)	368	
Mrs White		
€12,500 x 11% x 6/12 (6 months to 30/06/2015)		688
	753	-
Amount taxable as perquisite in 2015:		
Excess of notional interest over interest payable	107	156

Tax charge on release of employer loan

TCA 1997, s 122(3) charges tax in respect of any part of any loan from an employer (as defined above), or any interest payable on such a loan, that is released or written off. The amount that is written off in any tax year is taxed under TCA 1997, s 112 as if it were a perquisite of the relevant office or employment received in that year, ie it is taxable under Sch E as additional emoluments for that year. In the event that an employment with the person releasing or writing off the loan is, or would be, a foreign employment, then the amount written off is taxable under Sch D Case III as if it were additional income chargeable under that Case received in the year of the release or write off, (subject again, to the doubt caused by the definition of 'employee' effective prior to 1 January 2005 as discussed above).

It is to be noted that the tax charge under TCA 1997, s 122 arises where there is a release or write off of the loan and/or interest on any employer loan, whether or not it is a preferential loan giving rise to a tax charge under TCA 1997, s 122. TCA 1997, s 122 applies in respect of any loan made to the individual directly or indirectly by an employer (as defined above). The employer/employee (including director) relationship must be one that existed either at the time the loan was made or at a subsequent time or, in the case of loans made on or after 4 February 2004 only, at a time prior to the making of the loan.

In a case where an individual's spouse or civil partner receives a loan from a person who subsequently becomes the individual's employer, that person is not the spouse's or civil partner's employer under limb (c) of the definition of 'employer' discussed above. However, TCA 1997, s 122(3) will cover this situation as the person will have become the employer of the spouse or civil partner within limb (a) of the definition of 'employer' discussed above.

It is worth noting that loan waivers may in some cases be chargeable in any event under the general Sch E provisions, since a discharge of the employer's liability is equivalent to a cash payment. In *Clayton v Gothorp* 47 TC 168 the taxpayer's employer agreed to waive a loan if the taxpayer remained in its employment for 18 months. The waiver once made was held to fall within the then UK equivalent of TCA 1997, s 112; the source of the cash benefit to the taxpayer was evidently the employment (see **10.106**). Clearly, in such cases, no question of double taxation can arise as a matter of principle. Similar considerations should apply where the release of a loan falls within TCA 1997, s 439 (release of loan to participators). The choice between alternative tax charges would seem to lie with the inspector (see *Speyer Bros v IRC* [1908] AC 92, discussed at **1.405**).

Although treated as a taxable perquisite of the office or employment, any amount of loan principal or interest written off or released and chargeable under TCA 1997, s 122 does not count as emoluments for the purpose of entitling the employee (or director) to the PAYE allowance under TCA 1997, s 472 (TCA 1997, s 122(6)).

Example 10.211.4

Take the case of Mr B White from **Examples 10.211.1**, **10.211.3**. Assume that he had also a second qualifying loan from Water Ltd granted in 2010 and used to defray the expenses of an extension to his main residence. The outstanding balance on this loan at 1 January 2015 was €5,000. Interest is payable annually on 31 March.

Mr White is due to make a repayment of €1,800 in respect of the outstanding balance on 31 March 2015 when the interest on that balance for the 12 months to that date is also payable. The rate of interest on this loan is 3.5 per cent per annum, ie less than the relevant specified rate in 2015 (4 per cent), so that the loan is a preferential loan in 2015.

On 1 April 2015, Water Ltd releases Mr White from his obligation to make the repayment of €1,800 and writes off altogether that amount of this loan as well as the 12 months' interest due to have been paid on 31 March 2015, but leaves the balance of €3,200 outstanding as a debt due by Mr White. The rate of interest is increased to 5 per cent from 1 April onwards so at that point the loan ceases to be preferential for 2015.

Mr White is assessable under TCA 1997, s 122 for 2015 in respect of the amount of principal and the interest written off in that year on this loan. He is also assessable for that year under TCA 1997, s 122 in respect of the benefit of interest at the preferential rate. The amounts chargeable to tax for 2015 in respect of the €5,000 loan (in addition to the amounts taxable on the other two preferential loans, see **Example 10.211.3**), are calculated as follows:

	€
Amount of loan released 1/4/2015	1,800

Interest for year due on 31/3/2015 written off 1/4/2015:	
€5,000 x 3.5%	175
Amount taxable under TCA 1997, s 122(3)	1,975
Notional interest at specified rate (2015)	
€5,000 x 4% x 3/12=	50
Interest payable for year[1]	
€5,000 x 3.5% x 3/12=	44
Amount taxable under TCA 1997, s 122(2) (excess of notional over actual)	6

In summary, the Sch E perquisites to be included in Mr White's total income for 2015 in respect of this preferential loan from Water Ltd are as follows:

	€
Release of interest payable 31/3/2015	175
Excess of notional interest over interest payable	6
	181
Release of repayment due 31/3/2015	1,800
Total assessable	1,981

Notes:

1. Although Mr White did not in fact pay any interest on this loan in 2015 (due to the release of the interest on 1 April 2015), the interest was payable and is therefore deductible from the notional interest in computing the perquisite taxable under TCA 1997, s 122.
2. If no repayment of capital had been due, but if the company had written off €1,800 from the outstanding loan balance, the same amount would have been assessable under TCA 1997, s 122.

Tax relief for notional interest

When an individual is charged to tax under TCA 1997, s 122 on an interest benefit from a preferential loan or is charged under TCA 1997, s 122 on an amount of interest released or written off in respect of any employer loan, he is deemed by TCA 1997, s 122(4) to have paid an amount of interest on the loan equal to the amount of the perquisite on which he so charged. This means that, if the preferential loan or employer loan is a 'qualifying loan' within TCA 1997, s 244, the individual is entitled to claim relief under that section: see **3.205**.

10.212 Educational trusts

On general Sch E principles, if an educational trust set up by the taxpayer's employer makes payments to one of the taxpayer's family members, then such payments are the income of the family member and not that of the taxpayer (*Barclays Bank v Naylor* 39 TC 256).

However, as discussed in **10.203** the House of Lords held in *Wicks v Firth* that payments made to the taxpayer's child by an educational trust established by his employer did rank as a 'benefit' for the purposes of the UK equivalent of TCA 1997, s 118. As further discussed in **10.203**, it is debatable whether this conclusion should be followed in Ireland. Notwithstanding the House of Lord's conclusion, the taxpayer in *Wicks v Firth* avoided any liability under Sch E. This was because the Law Lords further concluded (albeit by a 3–2 majority) that the terms of the UK equivalent of TCA 1997, s 193, which in its original form granted a blanket exemption to scholarship income, also overrode the benefit-in-kind charge under the equivalent to TCA 1997, s 118 (a conclusion itself open to debate, but which will be assumed to be correct for the purposes of the discussion which follows).

The statutory predecessor to TCA 1997, s 193 was subsequently amended to limit severely the exemption afforded under that section to employer-funded educational trusts (the transitional provisions are dealt with in the 1997/98 edition of this book: see TCA 1997, s 193(6)). TCA 1997, s 193 in its present form assumes that the first conclusion of the House of Lords in *Wicks v Firth* was correct, and that TCA 1997, s 118 is therefore capable of applying to payments made by such trusts. TCA 1997, s 193 accordingly ensures that the general exemption for scholarship income can apply only to the individual holding the scholarship, thus reversing the decision in *Wicks v Firth*.

TCA 1997, s 193 however preserves the exemption in respect of income arising from a 'relevant scholarship' (as defined below) which is both:

(a) provided by a trust fund or under a scheme; and
(b) held by a full-time student.

However, the exemption applies only if not more than 25 per cent of the total payments made to full-time students by the fund or scheme in the particular year of assessment relates to 'relevant scholarships' (TCA 1997, s 193(4)). A 'relevant scholarship' is defined by TCA 1997, s 193(1) as one which is

(a) a scholarship provided directly or indirectly by a 'relevant body', or by a person connected (as defined by TCA 1997, s 10: see **12.304**) to that relevant body; and
(b) under which payments are made (either directly or indirectly) to:
   (i) an employee or director of that relevant body, or
   (ii) the spouse or civil partner, family, dependants, servants or children of the civil partner of such an employee or director.

The term 'scholarship' is defined by TCA 1997, s 193(1) as including an exhibition, bursary, or other similar educational endowment. A 'relevant body' is defined by TCA 1997, s 193(1) as a body corporate, unincorporated body, partnership or other body. In effect therefore if any such body provides a scholarship to one of its employees or directors or to his spouse/civil partner, family, etc, there will be a 'relevant scholarship'. The same will apply if the person providing the scholarship is a body corporate, unincorporated body, partnership or other body which is connected to the employer, as defined by TCA 1997, s 10. In addition, there will also be a 'relevant scholarship' if the person providing it is a trustee of a settlement (as defined by TCA 1997, s 794(1): see **15.402**) made by the employer or a person who is connected to the employer under TCA 1997, s 10. For a discussion of the definition of a 'connected person', see **12.304**.

As noted above, only income arising under a 'relevant scholarship' held by a 'full-time student' can qualify for the exemption; furthermore in applying the 25 per cent test, only payments made in respect of 'full-time students' are taken into account. If any question arises as to whether or not an individual is a full-time student, the Revenue Commissioners may consult the Minister for Education (TCA 1997, s 193(5)).

Example 10.212.1

Multi Global (Ireland) plc has established an educational trust primarily for the benefit of its own employees. The trust also makes some grants to persons who are not their employees and who are not related to, or connected with their employees ('third parties'). The trust is not connected to Multi Global plc for the purposes of TCA 1997, s 10. In 2016 the trust awards total scholarships as follows:

	Full-Time Students	*Part-Time Students*
	€	€
Employees	30,000	5,000
Employees' children	44,000	6,000
Third parties	20,000	4,000

Full-time students

The grants of €30,000 to employees who are full-time students, even if they fall potentially within TCA 1997, s 118 are exempt under TCA 1997, s 193(2) since they are the persons holding the scholarships. The grants of €44,000 to employees' children do not qualify for exemption under TCA 1997, s 193(4). This is because out of a total of €94,000 in grants made to full-time students, €(30,000 + 44,000) = €74,000 (ie 79 per cent) relates to 'relevant scholarships'. The grants made to the children are not taxable in their hands, by virtue of TCA 1997, s 193(2). If *Wicks v Firth* was correctly decided in this respect, a charge under TCA 1997, s 118 will be imposed on the parents of the children on benefits-in-kind totalling €44,000. The grants of €20,000 made to the third parties will be exempt in their hands by virtue of TCA 1997, s 193(2).

Part-time students

TCA 1997, s 193 is irrelevant in relation to these students, since it applies only to full-time students. The grants of €5,000 paid to employees who are part-time students will be taxable in their hands as trust income (see **15.304**). This is on the basis that even if TCA 1997, s 118 can cover direct cash payments, the 'expense' of providing the payment is chargeable in any event. The payment of €6,000 to employees' children will *prima facie* be taxable in their hands as trust income. However, if *Wicks v Firth* was correctly decided, TCA 1997, s 118 applies because the 'expense' of providing the payments is not chargeable as income of the employee. This implies that the payments must be taxed on the employees and that, accordingly, cannot be taxed on the employees' children (see the discussion in **1.405**: Presumption against double taxation). Presumably, in practice, the inspector would grant the credit for standard rate tax which normally attaches to trust income to the employees. The grants made to the third parties will be taxed as trust income in their hands (see **15.304**).

TCA 1997, s 897(2)(d) imposes an obligation to furnish particulars of relevant scholarships in relation to employees or directors when so required by an inspector (see **10.213**).

10.213 Returns

The Income Tax Acts contain provisions requiring employers, and employees (including directors) to make returns to the inspector of taxes in respect of expenses payments and benefits in kind taxable under TCA 1997, Pt 5, Ch 3, of cars made available to employees which may give rise to taxation under TCA 1997, s 121 of preferential loans within TCA 1997, s 122, and of relevant scholarships within TCA 1997, s 193.

The return of employees (including directors) which an employer is required by TCA 1997, s 897(2) to make, when required to do so by notice from an inspector, must include for each director and employee details of payments made to him in respect of taxable expenses within TCA 1997, s 117 and the amount of any benefit in kind taxable under TCA 1997, s 118, other than those already dealt with under the PAYE system (which will in practice cover the vast majority of such items). The benefit of preferential loans which remain outstanding after the termination of an employment will be outside the scope of the PAYE system as will the grant of certain shares (see **11.1**), contributions by an employer to a PRSA, and the notional benefit arising where an employee fails to repay excess deductions under the PAYE system (see **11.1**) and will all therefore require to be included in form P11D (see below).

The return under TCA 1997, s 897 (Form P11D) must also give particulars of any car made available to any employee or director by reason of his employment within TCA 1997, s 121 (see **10.207**) All cars so available to all directors and employees must be included in this return, whether or not available for their private use, as must cars in a car pool (see **10.207**). All this information is necessary to enable the inspector to raise such questions as he considers necessary to satisfy himself regarding cars said to be unavailable for private use or that the car pool treatment is justified. The employer's return under TCA 1997, s 897 is also required to give particulars if relevant, of any preferential loan within TCA 1997, s 122 which is made by him, or which is released or written off by him in whole or in part (see **10.211**) He is also required to give particulars of any interest released, written off, or refunded by him in respect of any such preferential loans. TCA 1997, s 897 also requires particulars of any relevant scholarship within TCA 1997, s 193 in relation to employees or directors (see **10.212**). TCA 1997, s 897B (as inserted by FA 2010, s 18) requires an employer to make a return of any shares awarded to a director or employee by 31 March in the year following that in which the shares are awarded, if the award is not otherwise required be reported by the Tax Acts.

However, although TCA 1997, s 897 says that all of the above information must be provided, in practice Form P11D states that only non-cash benefits in respect of which PAYE/PRSI/USC has not been deducted need be included on the form. Details of cars provided to employees where no benefit arises or cars or loans provided where any BIK arising has been subject to PAYE need not therefore be included in Form P11D.

Apart from the duty to include in his annual income tax return particulars of any taxable expenses payments or benefits in kind, TCA 1997, s 121 imposes a duty on any employee or director who is taxable under that section in respect of the benefit of a car or van made available by his employer (or by other person connected with his employer) to deliver in writing to the inspector particulars of the vehicle, its original market value and of his business and private mileage for each relevant year of assessment (TCA 1997, s 121(6); s 121A(4) applying s 121(6)). This statement is required to be made no later than 30 days after the end of the year. In strictness, failure to do so carries the threat of a penalty under TCA 1997, s 1052.

10.3 Expenses and Other Deductions

10.301 Introduction

TCA 1997, s 112 requires the full amount of all emoluments arising from an office or employment within Sch E to be charged to tax, subject only to the deduction of any duties or other sums payable on or chargeable against such emoluments as are permitted by any statute, provided that such duties or other sums have been really and *bona fide* paid and borne by the person assessable on the emoluments. TCA 1997, s 113 provides that any deduction from emoluments allowed by the Taxes Consolidation Act for the purposes of a Sch E assessment is to be made by reference to the amount of the expenses or other deductible sum as relates to the particular emoluments that are the subject of the tax charge for the relevant tax year.

In short, no deduction is given from the emoluments chargeable under Sch E, unless and to the extent that the deduction is permitted by some specific provision in the Income Tax Acts. The deductions that are permitted in taxing Sch E income are limited to the following:

(a) expenses wholly, exclusively and necessarily incurred by the holder of an office or employment in the performance of the duties of that office or employment (see **10.302**), but subject to certain exceptions and restrictions (see **10.303**);

(b) employee contributions to an exempt approved pension scheme, and in the case of a non-pensionable office or employment, premiums paid under certain approved retirement annuity contracts as well as certain contributions to PRSAs (see **16.111**, **16.202**, and **16.301**); and

(c) capital allowances in respect of any machinery or plant (eg a motor car) belonging to the employee and in use by him for the purposes of his office or employment (see **10.305**).

10.302 Expenses wholly, exclusively and necessarily incurred

TCA 1997, s 114 is the main rule governing the deductibility of expenses from Sch E emoluments. Since it has been the subject of many tax cases and has often been quoted and analysed in detail in the course of judgments, it is worth setting out in full, as follows:

> If the holder of an office or employment is necessarily obliged to incur and defray out of the emoluments thereof the expenses of travelling in the performance of the duties of the office or employment, or otherwise to expend money wholly, exclusively, and necessarily in the performance of the said duties, there may be deducted from the emoluments to be assessed the expenses so necessarily incurred and defrayed.

The words of this rule regarding the deductibility of expenses against Sch E emoluments have been said to be 'notoriously rigid, narrow and restricted in their operation' (Vaisey

J in *Lomax v Newton* 34 TC 558). For travelling expenses to be deductible, the holder of the office or employment must be 'necessarily obliged' to incur them 'in the performance of' the duties of that office or employment. For expenses other than travelling expenses, the deduction is given for money expended 'wholly, exclusively, and necessarily' in the performance of those duties. In either case, it is to be noted that the words 'necessarily obliged' and 'wholly, exclusively and necessarily' are directly linked to the performance of the duties.

An important authority on TCA 1997, s 114 is the House of Lords decision in the case of *Ricketts v Colquhoun* 10 TC 118. That case concerned a barrister, who resided and practised in London but held the Recordership of Portsmouth. It was held that he was not entitled to deduct from the emoluments of his office as Recorder either the costs of travelling between London and Portsmouth in order to attend the Quarter Sessions or his hotel expenses at Portsmouth. In his judgment on the question of the travelling expenses, Viscount Cave LC said:

> they must be expenses which the holder of an office is necessarily obliged to incur that is to say, obliged by the very fact that he holds the office, and has to perform its duties and they must be incurred in, that is, in the course of, the performance of those duties. The expenses in question in this case do not appear to me to satisfy either test.

He went on to indicate that the expenses were incurred, not because the appellant held the office of Recorder of Portsmouth, but because he had to travel to that place before he could begin to perform his duties as Recorder and, having concluded those duties, desired to return to his home. The expenses were incurred, not in the course of performing the duties, but partly before he entered upon them and partly after he had fulfilled them. However, whereas the actual performance of the office of Recorder in *Ricketts v Colquhoun* did not involve any travelling, Viscount Cave recognised that:

> No doubt the Rule contemplates that the holder of an office may have to travel in the performance of his duties and therefore there are offices of which the duties have to be performed in several places in succession, so that the holder of them must necessarily travel from one place to another.

Then, in *Nolder v Walters* 15 TC 388, Rowlatt J said:

> Some offices and employments do involve the duty of travelling. It is not a question of getting to the place of employment, but the employment may be actually to travel, as in the common case of the commercial traveller, and, as some people say, in the case of the Member of Parliament. The duties may actually be to travel, and this gentlemen's duty is to travel; therefore he is allowed the expenses of so travelling.

In relation to the hotel expenses, in *Ricketts v Colquhoun* Viscount Cave stated that the rule imposed two limitations – first, that the deduction is confined to expenses incurred in the performance of the duties of the office and, secondly, that the deduction is further limited in operation by the emphatic qualification that the expenses must be wholly, exclusively and necessarily so incurred. He stated that a man must eat and sleep somewhere, whether he has or has not been engaged in the administration of justice. He went on to state:

> and if he elects to live away from his work so that he must find board and lodging away from home, that is by his own choice and not by reason of any necessity arising out of his employment;

Again, this prohibition against subsistence expenses does not apply where they are 'part and parcel' of the costs of travelling in the performance of the duties (see under *Wholly and exclusively*, below).

Lord Blanesburgh, in the same case, commenting on the meaning of 'necessarily' in the context of the performance of the duties, said:

> the language of the Rule points to the expenses with which it is concerned as being confined to those which each and every occupant of the particular office is necessarily obliged to incur in the performance of its duties, to expenses imposed upon each holder ex necessitate of his office and to such expenses only.

He went on to state that the rule is objective and that deductible expenses do not extend to those which the holder has to incur mainly because of circumstances in relation to his office which are personal to himself or are the result of his own volition. *Ricketts v Colquhoun* was followed in the Irish case of *Phillip v Keane* I ITR 64. In the latter case, the claim by a National School teacher to deduct part of the expenses of a pony and trap which he kept to convey him to and from the school and his residence five miles apart, as he could not procure a suitable residence any nearer, was rejected.

The cases indicate that the rigour of the rule is more attributable to the phrase 'in the performance of the duties', than to the objective test of necessity as formulated by Lord Blanesburgh. This follows because an expense incurred in actually carrying out the agreed duties of an employment will not normally be of a kind which is referable to the personal circumstances or volition to the taxpayer (see Limits of the 'objective test', below). The objective test of necessity will, however, still be very much in point where an expense is incurred 'in the performance', but the amount of the expense is excessive or unduly extravagant (as in *Marsden v IRC* 43 TC 326, where a claim for travelling expenses was restricted on the basis that the taxpayer could have used public transport rather than his own car).

In *Elwood v Utitz* 42 TC 482 it was accepted that for reasons of prestige it was essential that the taxpayer had to use a first-class hotel when making business visits to London. Lord MacDermott made the following instructive remarks in the course of his judgment:

> … the word 'necessarily' attaches to the expenditure and the circumstance that there are several ways of getting or buying what is requisite does not meet to me, or itself, to make the choice of way or method a determining consideration. I say, 'of itself', because the word 'necessarily' may rule out one of several forms of expenditure for other reasons, eg excessive or unreasonable cost.

The test of necessity also governs the word 'incurred'. Thus, in *HF Kelly v H* II ITR 460, gratuities paid to a batsman by a military officer were held to be disallowable since there was no legal obligation to pay them.

In *MacDaibheid v SD* III ITR 1, the taxpayer's claim was rejected because he had failed to show that he could not have recovered them from his employer. Per McWilliam J:

> … it was entirely for [the taxpayer] to establish that he was necessarily obliged to incur these expenses out of his emoluments.

The observations in *Ricketts v Colquhoun* have been invoked as the basis for the decisions in a number of other cases. In *Humbles v Brooks* 40 TC 500, the respondent was the headmaster at a primary school and in this capacity was required to teach various subjects including history. He attended a series of weekend lectures in history at a college of adult education for the purposes of improving his background knowledge. He contended that the fees paid for this course were an allowable deduction under the Sch E expenses rule. The Commissioners upheld this view and allowed his appeal, but their decision was reversed in the High Court (Chancery Division) where it was held that no deduction was due.

Ungoed-Thomas J, in his judgment, stated that, to be within the words 'necessarily obliged in the performance of the said duties', the taxpayer must be obliged by the very fact that he holds the office and has to perform its duties. He referred to *Ricketts v Colquhoun* as support for his statement that the test is not a personal test, but an objective one. He referred also to Donovan LJ who, in the Court of Appeal in *Brown v Bullock* 40 TC 1, stated that the test is whether the duties impose the expense,

> in the sense that the duties cannot be performed without incurring a particular outlay.

Having reviewed these and several other authorities, he concluded that, in attending the course of lectures, the respondent was not acting in the performance of his duties within the meaning of the Sch E expenses rule. Further, even if getting information and material at the course could be regarded as part of the preparation of his own lectures, the expense incurred was not an expense which passed the objective test put forward by Lord Blanesburgh and Donovan LJ.

Brown v Bullock (see above) concerned the manager of a West End branch of a bank who became a member of a club. It was virtually a condition of appointment that the manager should join a club suited to the purpose of fostering local contacts and the bank paid the annual subscription to the club. He was already a member of another club at an annual subscription of £12, but here some personal advantage from his membership was admitted and the bank only paid one half of this subscription. The amounts totalling £27 paid by the bank were included as the manager's emoluments under Sch E. The manager contended that the amount paid should be allowed as an expenses deduction. The court of Appeal held that the expenses were not deductible as they were not necessarily incurred in the performance of his duties as a bank manager. The manager's argument that it was necessary for him to incur the expense as his employer required him to be a member of the club was rejected. The test was not whether the employer imposed the expense, but whether the duties could or could not be performed without incurring the expense. It had to be accepted that, even if the expense had not been incurred, the duties as bank manager could still be performed.

In *Blackwell v Mills* 26 TC 468, a student assistant in the research laboratory of the company was required by his employer to attend classes in preparation for a university degree. He claimed to deduct the expenses he incurred in travelling to and from the classes and in the purchase of text books. The Commissioners allowed the claim, but the court held that the expenses were not incurred in the performance of the duties of the employment so that no deduction was admissible. In his judgment, Macnaghten J said:

> The duties of his employment were as a student assistant in the research laboratories of the General Electric Company. It seems to me impossible to say that, when he was listening to the lecture at the Chelsea Polytechnic, he was performing the duties of a student assistant at the laboratories of the company.

In *Shortt v McIlgorm* 26 TC 262 a fee paid to an employment agency for obtaining a job was held (unsurprisingly) not to be incurred in the performance of that job; similarly, in *Eagles v Levy* 19 TC 23, the costs of suing for the recovery of wages were disallowed. However, in *Mitchell v Child* 24 TC 511, a rector had opposed a bill giving the

Government power to compulsorily purchase his parsonage. As a result the bill was amended, ensuring that a new parsonage would be provided in place of the old one. The costs of opposing the bill were held to be allowable, since it was the taxpayer's duty as a corporation sole to protect the corporation from the loss of its property. In contrast, in *Jardine v Gillespie* 5 TC 263 the costs of a minister of religion in petitioning for an increase in the stipend attaching to his ministry was held to be disallowed; the benefit of any increased salary would have accrued to the holders of the ministry, and not to the ministry itself.

The expenses of hiring somebody else to carry out an employee's duties will not generally be deductible. In *Lothian v Macrae* 2 TC 65, a minister had grown too old to attend personally to all his duties; contributions towards the stipend of an assistant were held to be inadmissible under the rule. Lord Adam observed that:

> the expenses are incurred not to enable (the taxpayer) to perform his duty, but to enable another person to perform part of his duty for him.

Similarly, in *Jardine v Gillespie* 5 TC 263 a minister was refused a deduction for the cost of pulpit supply during holidays. It is thought that, in practice, an inspector would normally allow the costs of essential substitutes or locums in comparable circumstances.

There is certainly no reason in principle why an employee should not be allowed the cost of remunerating a subordinate whose services are essential to the proper performance of his duties. In a case where a senior executive or director takes his spouse on a business journey, the inspector will normally be prepared to allow his spouse's expenses, where it can be established that she has some special skill or practical qualifications directly associated with her spouse's work which she uses to assist him regularly (but not necessarily full-time) during a tour of duty. The Revenue, will, however, also have regard to the 'wholly and exclusively' criterion (discussed below), if they consider that there is a 'holiday' element in the journey. In practice, it will also be pertinent that the employer has required the employee to take his spouse with him.

The requirement that expenditure be incurred 'in the performance' of the duties denied a claim for the cost of journals by a medical officer who had to keep up to date with developments in his specialisation, in *Simpson v Tate* 9 TC 314; (see also *O'Broin v Meidhre* II ITR 366 and *Hamilton v Overy* 35 TC 73, where a doctor's professional insurance premiums were disallowed). This type of reasoning was extended by the House of Lords in *Smith v Abbot* [1994] STC 237 to deny the cost of newspapers purchased by journalists in order to brief themselves before deciding on each day's news agenda. The decision in *Smith v Abbot* does however seem dubious. This is because the newspapers were not acquired in order to equip the taxpayers there with the skill and knowledge needed to carry out their duties; rather, they were in the nature of materials consumed in the course of carrying out such duties. The main rationale for the decision can probably be found in the following words of Lord Templeman:

> … the reasons for the strictness of the rule governing deductible expenses is not hard to find. If a journalist or other employee were allowed to deduct expenses incurred by him in his spare time in improving his usefulness to his employer the imposition of income tax would be distorted and the amount of the expenses would depend entirely on his own choice.

This analysis seems to depend more on speculative considerations of policy rather than adherence to the statutory text. Moreover, it assumes the conclusion which it seeks to justify, ie that the expenses concerned were incurred in the employee's 'spare time', rather than in the performances of his duties.

In practice, the Revenue do not in fact seek to tax the benefit of newspapers, periodicals, etc provided by an employer where these are generally related to the business of the employer; similarly they will not treat the payment or reimbursement of course fees or examination fees by the employer as giving rise to a benefit where the course concerned is relevant to the employer's business. Up to 2010, a statutory exemption applied to certain professional subscriptions paid for or borne by the employer (see **10.204**); in practice, the Revenue Commissioners are prepared to continue to treat certain annual membership fees paid to a professional body as deductible under TCA 1997, s 114 and correspondingly any reimbursements thereof as non-taxable benefits: see *e-brief 19/11*). The Revenue also issue a list of flat rate expense allowances which will be granted automatically to employees falling within prescribed categories (ranging from cardiac technicians to dockers). It is, of course, open to any employee entitled to such an allowance to make a claim instead based on his actual deductible expenditure, if greater.

Limits of the 'objective test'

It must be borne in mind that Lord Blanesburgh's observations above were framed in the context of an office which had firmly defined duties, and which would be passed from holder to holder. Even at the time this represented a narrow context; it is even narrower in the modern era, when many employments are fluid and open-ended in nature and where 'control' has become a less prominent feature of many employer-employee relationships (see **10.103**).

These aspects of the expenses rule have been recognised in a number of cases. In *McLean v Trembath* (discussed below) it was said:

> … in connection with directors their duties are seldom stereotyped and you cannot find out what a director's duties are without studying the resolutions of the directors.

In *White v Higginbottom* [1983] STC 143, Vinelott J observed:

> … it may be in the case of an office the duties of which are not stereotyped or precisely defined the decision by the holder of the office as to the extent of his duties … for instance in the case of a clergyman … the number of services he is required to perform … could not at least within broad limits be challenged.

As Vinelott J's remarks suggest, where an employee exceeds the bounds of discretion inherent in his employment and proceeds to undertake an activity, 'off his own bat', then he will not be acting 'in the performance of [his] duties'. Thus, in *Owen v Burden* 47 TC 476, a county surveyor was denied the costs of attending an overseas conference incurred entirely on his own initiative, notwithstanding that his purposes in so doing were purely work-related (see also *Thomson v White* 43 TC 261 and compare *McLean v Trembath* which indicates that a controlling director may have some latitude in assigning himself special duties, so long as these are duly authorised).

The UK case law indicates that travel between 'two places of work' or 'bases' may itself arise 'in the performance' of the duties (as in the case of the Member of Parliament cited by Rowlatt J above, ie because he is based at Westminster and also his constituency). A number of these cases also indicate that the objective nature of the Sch E expenses rule does not mean that expenses must automatically be disallowed where the personal circumstances or the volition of the taxpayer have influenced the structuring of the terms and conditions of the employment.

In *Owen v Pook* 45 TC 571, the taxpayer was a doctor who carried on a general practice at his residence-cum-surgery but who also held a part-time appointment at a distant hospital. The taxpayer was required to be on standby in his surgery at prescribed times. His responsibility for a patient commenced as soon as he received a telephone call from the hospital, and the instructions which he gave over the telephone were as indispensable to the treatment of patients as his subsequent attendance (if required) at the hospital. The taxpayer duly claimed the costs of travel between his home and the hospital, a claim upheld by the House of Lords by a 3–2 majority. The key to the decision seems to lie in the fact that the employee's contract genuinely required him to use his home as a 'place of work'.

Lord Wilberforce said:

> … what is required is proof … that the taxpayer in a real sense … had two places of work

Lord Guest said:

> It is noteworthy that under … [the taxpayer's] terms and conditions of service the hospital is referred to [as] the place 'where his principal duties lie'. There were thus two places where his duty is performed.

Lord Pearce observed that:

> it was as a doctor practising in [his surgery] that [the taxpayer] was appointed to his standby duty,

again declining to probe behind the contractual realities (compare *Gurney v Richards*, discussed in **10.207**).

It is apparent that the employer in *Owen v Pook* only contracted on the basis which it did because the taxpayer would, for purely personal reasons, have refused to base himself solely at the hospital. However, as Lord Wilberforce pointed out:

> … the choice in the matter, if any exists, lies not with the doctor who is there in his practice, but with [his employer] which decides, however near or far he works, to appoint him and to require him to discharge a part of his duty at his practice.

The Revenue Commissioners have set out a rather idiosyncratic interpretation of the decision in *Owen v Pook*, in Statement of Practice SP IT/2/07, stating their view that case law has established that employees with 'specialist' skills may be working from the time they receive notification to attend their normal place of work in order to deal with an emergency. This follows in their view because such an employee must give instructions to those present at the situation and retains responsibility for handling the emergency while travelling to his normal place of work. With effect from 1 January 2006, the travel expenses (ie the cost of taxis or mileage expenses up to the appropriate civil service mileage rate) to and from their normal place of work in these circumstances may be paid tax-free up a maximum of 60 emergencies per annum (any more than this number will require the employer to notify the relevant inspector of taxes who will review the position). The Revenue state that an 'emergency' in this context is dependent on the nature of the industry concerned, but, in general, encompasses an unforeseen or sudden event requiring immediate or urgent attention; and that would have serious consequences if left until the individual commenced normal working hours. An emergency does not include an event where staff are required to attend their normal place of work outside their normal working hours to, for example to replace a scheduled member of staff who fails to attend work; or to assist with an increased volume of work; or to attend for a non-emergency or other routine event. The Revenue state that whether a 'call out' is in respect of a genuine emergency is a question of fact, having regard to relevant facts and circumstances supported by the records kept relating to the event. As the Revenue apparently accept that the principle is one based on case law, then claims may be possible in respect of periods prior to 1 January 2006.

The decision in *Gilbert v Hemsley*, discussed in **10.207**, again demonstrates that a taxpayer's home may double up as a base. The decision in that case can be contrasted with that in *Elderkin v Hindmarsh* [1988] STC 267, where the taxpayer was required to undertake a continuous series of short-term assignments at various locations throughout the UK. Although the taxpayer did not have an office at his employer's premises, no argument was raised that the taxpayer's home was his base. Vinelott J simply expressed the view that the taxpayer's travel between his home and work locations was analogous to that of the taxpayer in *Ricketts v Colquhoun*. The decision in *Hindmarsh* may be viewed with some reservations, as the case for the taxpayer was presented rather weakly (by the taxpayer himself!) (see the discussion in Ward, '*Elderkin v Hindmarsh*' [1989] British Tax Review 24; note also the decisions in *Bhadra v Ellam* [1983] STC 289 and *Parikh v Sleeman* [1990] STC 233, although decided by reference to deemed employments under UK legislation, for which there is no Irish equivalent).

In *Taylor v Provan* 49 TC 579, the taxpayer succeeded in establishing that his work as a brewery director was divided between the UK and his bases in the overseas countries where he resided. This was notwithstanding that, in the words of Lord Wilberforce (this time, one of the dissenting Law Lords):

> the centre of gravity of [the taxpayer's] … work was clearly in the United Kingdom.

Two of the majority Law Lords took the view that the relevant contractual obligations could not be rewritten by the courts. Lord Borth-y-Gest said:

> When analysed, it seems to me that the contention of the Crown must amount to a contention that the [employer] … need not have made the arrangement that … [the taxpayer] would do all his work in England. But there is no evidence that they ever could have made such an arrangement. All the indications are that they would never have secured the … [the taxpayer's] services on terms other than those which were made: and the fact remains that they did make the arrangements as found.

Lord Salmon was even more forthright, asserting that:

> When you are considering where the duties of a man's employment require him to work you look first at the term of his employment. These normally are conclusive. A term which may appear to be rather more for the man's benefit than for the benefit of their employers is still a term of employment.

The third majority Law Lord, Lord Reid took a rather different tack, basing his judgment on the proposition that the crucial aspect of the case was that it was a practical necessity in the circumstances for the employer to contract on the terms agreed. However, logically, the question of necessity must be adjudged from the viewpoint of the employee, and this can only be done by reference to the terms of his contract of employment as they exist in reality. The emphasis on 'reality' here is important: it emerges clearly from the speeches of both Lord Morris of Borth-y-Gest and Lord Salmon that the obligations concerned must have a genuine commercial justification and be more than mere 'shams', designed to circumvent the expenses rule.

There is strong authority, therefore, that the 'objective test' as expressed by Lord Blanesburgh should be applied pragmatically, based on the specific contract actually agreed between the parties (see Ward, 'Subjective Objectivity the Schedule and Expenses Rule' [1988] British Tax Review 6).

In *Miners v Atkinson* [1997] STC 58, it was held that the taxpayer, who was a controlling shareholder/director of W Ltd was not entitled to the expenses of travel between his home (from which he ran W Ltd, and which was accepted to be his base) and the offices of his main client 80 miles away. Arden J, relying largely on Lord Reid's opinion in *Taylor v Provan*, took the view that it was not necessary for the taxpayer's work to have been carried out at his home, since it 'could have been done anywhere'. Accordingly, the learned judge held that the travel expenses were non-deductible. The basis for the decision seems in fact to suffer from the same flaw as Lord Reid's approach in *Taylor v Provan*. The key issue should have been whether the taxpayer was required to use his home or his base under the terms of his employment and not whether it was necessary for the company to impose that requirement.

As pointed out by Carr in [1997] ITR 124, it would still not necessarily have followed that all the cost of the travelling between the taxpayer's home and the customer's office would have been deductible. The taxpayer would still have had to establish that the performance of his duties made it necessary to undertake any particular journey. It is arguable that this requirement could be tested by asking: 'If the taxpayer had a residence which was not also his base, would he still have been obliged to travel between his base and his client's office, or would he have travelled directly from his residence to the other location?'.

A clearer case arose in *Warner v Prior* where the taxpayer was a supply teacher who carried out her duties at a number of schools in the Kent area. The Special Commissioner accepted that it was objectively necessary for her to have a place of work outside those schools in order to prepare lessons, mark students' work, etc. She used her own home for these purposes. She was refused a claim for the costs of travelling from her home to the various schools. The Special Commissioner commented as follows:

> … the location of [her] other place of work at her home has no bearing on her appointment to her job or her ability to perform it. If she moved, at least within the Kent area, there is no evidence to suggest that Kent County Council would have any objection. The result would be that she might have further to travel to some schools and less far to travel to others. It would make no difference to her ability to do the job. The significant factor is that her secondary place of work at home is dictated by where she lives and not by the requirements of the job itself. In contrast, [the taxpayer in *Owen v Pook*] was appointed because he worked in a particular place, Fishguard, where he could be contacted by the hospital in emergencies and from which he could reach the hospital in a reasonable time. The location of his secondary place of work was dictated by the hospital job. (Spc 3040/2002).

In *Kirkwood v Evans* [2002] STC 231 (discussed below) the costs of travelling from home to work where the taxpayer had volunteered to work from home was disallowed.

In *Baird v Williams* [1999] STC 635 it was accepted that the taxpayer (who was a clerk to the UK General Commissioners) was required to maintain his own office. However, the court denied his claim for interest on borrowings to acquire the property which he used as an office. The court held that it was not necessary for him to purchase the property outright. Furthermore,) the borrowing of moneys and the payment of interest thereon could not be said to have been carried out 'in the performance of the duties'.

The 'wholly and exclusively' test

The 'wholly and exclusively' element of the Sch E expenses rule may preclude claims where the expenditure concerned serves a dual purpose; this mirrors the position on the Schedule D expenses rule, where a similar wording is used (see **5.305**).

In *Lucas v Cattell* 48 TC 353, it was held that an employee could deduct the business proportion of his telephone dialling charges, but not a corresponding share of the fixed cost of his telephone rental. In practice, an inspector of taxes would be likely to agree an apportionment of the rental in these circumstances (normally a global deduction for both call and line rental costs in the order of 50 per cent is granted). In *Hillyer v Leeke* [1976] STC 490, the taxpayer was a computer engineer who was required to attend at a client's premises in formal clothing. The suits which he wore on these occasions were not worn by him outside of work. The nature of his job resulted in his clothing suffering acute wear and tear. The taxpayer claimed the additional expense incurred as a consequence of not being in a position to wear more durable clothing while at work.

Goulding J rejected the claim, saying:

> If a taxpayer works in an occupation where ordinary civilian clothing is worn of the sort that is also worn off duty … the individual is wearing clothing for his own purposes of cover and comfort conveniently with wearing it in order to have the appearance which the job requires.

The learned judge also stated that the fact that the suits were retained exclusively for wearing when the taxpayer was at work made no difference because:

> where the clothing worn is not of a special character dictated by the occupation as a matter of physical necessity but is ordinary civilian clothing of a standard required for the occupation; you cannot say one purpose (ie warmth and decency) is incidental to the other (ie to have the appearance which the job requires).

In practice, the Revenue will accept that costs associated with protective clothing or uniforms (ie clothing bearing a logo or of a style, etc so that they are readily identifiable as uniforms) fall within the Sch E expenses rule.

The learned judge also decided the case on the alternative ground, that even though the taxpayer wore the suits exclusively for work purposes, it was not necessary for him to do so, and therefore he fell foul of the objective test of necessity. This reasoning has been rightly criticised; the test of 'necessity' is complementary to the 'wholly and exclusively' test; the rule does not demand that the expenditure should be necessarily 'wholly and exclusively' incurred (see [1983] British Tax Review 189).

Hillyer v Leeke was followed in *Woodcock v IRC* [1977] STC 405), a case in which the taxpayer did heavy and dirty work in his capacity as an engineer. He was refused his claim for the cost of ordinary clothing which he wore at work.

In *Ward v Dunn* [1979] STC 178, the taxpayer was employed as an assistant surveyor and in the course of his duties was required to visit construction sites. The taxpayer claimed a deduction for the wear and tear suffered on the clothing. Walton J dismissed his claim on the basis that:

> when the taxpayer purchases a suit he purchases it may be partly with a view to going round the sites but at any rate partly with a view to wearing it in the ordinary course, as one wears clothing for comfort and for covering ones nakedness.

This is a very clear enunciation of the 'subjective' purpose test and indeed the leading Sch D case *Caillebotte v Quinn* was cited as a precedent. The Revenue Commissioners have expressed the view that claims for gym membership and special foods would not be deductible in the case of an employed sportsperson, on the basis that there could be no differentiation between the part of the expense incurred for the purposes of playing sport and the part incurred to keep the individual fit and healthy. This view appears to be in keeping with the case law.

In *O'Broin v MacGiolla Meidhre* and *O'Broin v Pigott* (taken together at III ITR 235), claims by a County Engineer (in the first case) and by a Chief Assistant Engineer (in the second case), each employed by the Clare County Council, for expenses deductions under what is now TCA 1997, s 114 in respect of *inter alia*, costs of telephone at home and certain other items were held to be non-deductible. Referring to Vaisey J's statement in *Griffiths v Mockler* 35 TC 135 that the words of the rule defining allowable expenses were 'notoriously narrow in their application', Teevan J concluded that each case stated failed to give facts showing that the expenses related 'exclusively' to the performance of the duties of the office.

The treatment of subsistence expenses also requires consideration. In *Sanderson v Durbridge* 36 TC 239, a local government officer was obliged to attend at committees during certain evenings. On those evenings he had to buy his meals at a restaurant. His claim for the excess costs of these meals over what he would otherwise have spent if he had been able to eat at home was refused by Wynn-Parry J, on the grounds that he was only engaged in his duties while actually in attendance on the committee.

However, in general, subsistence costs should be allowed if they are regarded as an inherent element of the expense of travelling. In *Nolder v Walters*, Rowlatt J observed:

> I think it always has been agreed, that when you get a travelling office, so that travelling expenses are allowed, those travelling expenses do include the extra expense of living which is put upon a man by having to stay at hotels and inns, and such places, rather than stay at home.

The question of hotel expenses incurred while travelling on the employer's business raises a further question related to 'home savings'. While Rowlatt J accepted that the extra expense which the employee had to incur on hotel, etc expenses were deductible under Sch E, he considered that the cost of food and lodging was not wholly and exclusively laid out in the performance of the duties, but only the extra part of the cost. This view seems to overlook the fact that the Sch E expenses rule does not impose a 'wholly and exclusively' requirement in respect of travelling expenses. Further, it seems likely that if the 'wholly and exclusively' rule did apply, the duality principle would strictly mean that no part of the cost should be allowed (see **5.305**).

Nevertheless based on the decision in *Nolder v Walters*, it could be argued that where a person incurs a material amount of hotel expenses incurred in performing his duties, any deduction for the hotel expenses should be restricted by an amount representing at least the cost which he would have otherwise incurred in respect of food. In practice, fixed flat-rate subsistence allowance paid in accordance with rates approved by the Revenue Commissioners, will be treated as non-taxable (thus making the issue of a corresponding claim for expenses academic) (see the discussion of SP IT/2/07 at **10.202**), and note the discussion of travelling expenses in **10.303**.

It would appear that subsistence costs incurred by an employee when staying away from home temporarily in the course of his duties should also be allowable, as in *Elwood v Utitz* 42 TC 482 (company director visiting London in order to hold meetings here with suppliers). In *McLean v Trembath* 36 TC 653, the taxpayer, a controlling director of his employer company, was allowed the costs of visiting Australia in order to gain knowledge of business methods which it was considered would benefit the company. Again, this analysis appears to be accepted by the Revenue Commissioners, who will normally permit flat rate allowances in respect of such absences which are paid in accordance with approved rates to be treated as non-taxable (see **10.202**).

The former situation needs to be distinguished from the case where an employee is posted for a limited period to a new base as in *Evans v Richardson* 37 TC 178 (where the taxpayer was refused a claim for the cost of renting additional accommodation during a one year assignment away from his usual place of work). This distinction is reflected in Revenue practice, which will not normally permit flat rate allowances to be paid tax free for periods in excess of twelve months within Ireland, subject only to short extensions of this period in certain cases (see **10.202**). Details of the position for persons working outside Ireland are set out in **10.202**).

The 'living away' subsistence expenses of the taxpayer in *Elderkin v Hindmarsh* (discussed above) were similarly disallowed, seemingly on the basis that the taxpayer there did not possess a normal place of work or 'base' and simply worked at a number of consecutive temporary locations. For the Revenue Commissioners treatment of 'country money' and analogous payments in practice, see below.

In SP IT/2/07, the Revenue Commissioners take the view that where an employee carries out his duties at the various premises of his employer's customers, the employer's premises will not constitute his normal place of work 'unless he carries out 'substantive duties' there.' Similarly, they will not regard an employee's home as his base unless there is an objective requirement that his duties must be performed there. The case law suggests that this denotes an objective requirement that 'substantive' duties be performed at home (see above). In SP IT/2/07, Revenue suggest that such cases are confined to situations where a person with specialist skills must give instructions from the time he is contacted in dealing with a grave emergency.

As discussed above, this analysis seems to be based on an overly narrow interpretation of the decision in *Owen v Pook* 45 TC 571. It would follow that unless the employee can establish that his home is also his 'base', any 'living away' subsistence expenses would be non-deductible (no question would arise accordingly of the employee being entitled to receive a flat rate allowance tax free under the terms of SP IT/2/07). However, the Revenue recognise the special position of construction industry workers, who do not generally have a fixed base (see *Elderkin v Hindmarsh,* discussed above), and permit 'country money' payable under Registered Employment Agreements to be paid tax-free to such workers working more than 20 miles from their employer's base (or from the GPO in the case of Dublin-based workers if so elected). The exemption is subject to stringent conditions. Payments to workers recruited 'on site' or where the employer provides board and lodgings or transport to and from the site are excluded from the exemption. Exemption may also apply to certain on-site eating allowances for such workers subject to a maximum of €5 per day or to the provision of temporary accommodation and meals at temporary locations.

Domestic expenses

In general, additional domestic or living expenses incurred as a result of holding an office or employment will not meet the requirements of the Sch E expenses rule. Such expenses are not incurred in the performance of the duties but in order to enable an employee to perform them (equally they are not 'necessary' in the sense that they are imposed not by the obligations of the employment but by the personal circumstances of the employee). In many cases the expenses will also fail the 'wholly and exclusively' element of the Rule.

In *Bowers v Hardings* 3 TC 22, a man and his wife were jointly appointed as master and mistress of a school. It was accepted that to enable the wife to work at the school it was essential to employ a servant to carry on the household duties. Pollock B held that the outlay was 'merely a deprivation of a portion of their income in order that they might accept the office'.

In *Halstead v Condon* 46 TC 284, a widower claimed the cost of childminders who looked after his children while he was at work. Megarry J held that the expense was 'nothing to do with the way in which he performed his function as a clerk'. The learned judge accepted that this case could be distinguished from *Bowers v Harding* because in that case an alternative course of action was open to the taxpayers (being husband and wife) whereas in the present case, if the childminders had not been employed, the taxpayer (being a widower) would have had to give up work altogether. The learned judge appeared to accept that accordingly the expenses met the test of 'necessity'. With due respect to the learned judge this cannot be so; it was clearly an expense which arose solely by virtue of the personal circumstances of the taxpayer. It would seem in fact that both *Bowers v Harding* and *Halstead v Condon* could also have been decided on the basis of the objective test of necessity (although it must be borne in mind that the former case preceded *Ricketts v Colquhoun*).

In *Bolam v Barlow* 31 TC 136, there was a finding by the Appeal Commissioners that the taxpayer's duties included receiving and giving instructions outside office hours, a telephone having been installed in his lodgings for this purpose by his employers. Croom-Johnson J held that the additional costs of accommodation incurred by the taxpayer, as a result of having to live near his work could not be claimed as representing the expense of an office. The learned judge commented that 'many of us have to take work home … but that is not what the rule says'. Similarly, in *McKie v Warner* 40 TC 65, the payment of rent on a flat by a senior employee, part of whose duties included the entertainment of foreign buyers there, was held to be non-deductible. Plowman J stated that the taxpayer 'was not performing the duties, not doing the job … by living in the flat'.

It is also noteworthy that a special allowance is granted to clergymen of ministers of religion in respect of the rent of their dwelling houses under TCA 1997, s 837. It is understood that a decision of the Appeal Commissioners took cognisance of this provision in deciding that a travelling salesman was not allowed to deduct the cost of any part of the rent of his private residence. The inference clearly was that if rental payments fell within the Sch E expenses rule it would not have been necessary to create this specific allowance for one class of taxpayer.

In *Newlin v Woods* 42 TC 649, where the taxpayer had failed to establish that this home was also an office, the general commissioners nevertheless allowed him a proportion of his heating and lighting costs. The court did not disturb this finding as a question of fact (and note also *Elwood v Utitz* 42 TC 482, at p 495). The costs of a 'home office' (which are normally allowable under Sch D: see **5.306**) may perhaps be justified under the Sch E expenses rule if it is a genuine requirement of the employment to do some work at home (as in *Baird v Williams* discussed above where however a deduction was refused in respect of mortgage interest). In *Kirkwood v Evans* [2002] STC 231 it was held that a civil servant who lived in Norfolk and who chose to adopt a home working scheme under the terms of which he was required to travel one day each week to his employer's office in Leeds was not entitled to deduct the costs of heating and lighting his home office. This was on the rather pedantic grounds that the home working scheme was optional, not requiring the taxpayer to work from home and because it was not a requirement of the scheme that he should maintain a separate room for work. However, it is submitted that once the scheme had been adopted, it was thereafter necessary in practical terms for the employee to incur those costs in performing his duties in the manner agreed with his employer.

In practice, the Revenue Commissioners will not challenge reimbursed expenses of up to €3.20 per day in respect of the costs of heat and light. This does not mean however that the taxpayer's home will therefore automatically qualify as a 'place of work' or 'base'. This is because the employer is not requiring him to work at a particular location but simply to work 'out-of-office' hours, wherever his home happens to be (see eg *Warner v Prior* discussed above). Furthermore, the duties are unlikely to be sufficiently substantial to justify such a finding (see *Owen v Pook* discussed above).

10.303 Travelling expenses

The general principles governing the deductibility of travelling and other expenses have been discussed in **10.302**. It is clear, accordingly that, in general, travel between the taxpayers' home and his place of work is not carried out in the performance of his duties (*Ricketts v Colquhoun* 10 TC 118). This remains the case even if the taxpayer uses his car (rather than public transport) to get to his place of work in order that he can subsequently use the car for business journeys (*Burton v Rednall* 35 TC 435). On the other hand, travel between two places of work or bases undertaken in order to perform the duties of the employment at both locations is deductible (as in the case of the Member of Parliament travelling between his constituency and Parliament, or a solicitor's clerk with duties split between two offices). This principle holds good even if one of the places of work is also the taxpayer's home, although this may be difficult to establish on the facts (see *Owen v Pook*; *Taylor v Provan*; *Gilbert v Hemsley*, but compare *Miners v Atkinson*, all discussed at **10.302**).

A 'place of work' or base is it seems a fixed location where the employee is required to work and to carry out duties of substance (*Owen v Pook*).

Travelling between a base and a temporary work location (eg to visit a customer or even to attend a conference) will equally be carried out 'in the performance of his duties' (as in *Gilbert v Hemsley* and *McLean v Trembath*, discussed at **10.302**). Again (as in *Gilbert v Hemsley*) the taxpayer's home can also be his base. If the employee does not have a base (as effectively conceded by the taxpayer in *Elderkin v Hindmarsh*, discussed at **10.302**) then such travelling expenses will it seems not be allowable (these were not even claimed by the taxpayer in *Elderkin v Hindmarsh*).

In their SP IT/2/07, the Revenue Commissioners state that where an employee travels directly from home to a temporary place of work (rather than travelling to there from his base) the allowable business mileage will be the lesser of:

(a) the distance between his home and the temporary place of work; and
(b) the distance between his base and the temporary place of work.

In effect, this rule ensures that the employee can never claim any additional mileage where his home is further from the temporary place of work than his base. The rule seems generally consistent with the case law, but it should probably not be extended to 'itinerant employees' (see below).

Employees who hold 'itinerant' employments seem to form a distinct category. An itinerant employment may be said to exist where the job literally is to travel (eg the airline pilot in *Nolder v Walters*) or where the duties by their very nature 'have to be performed, in several places in succession (*Charlton v IRC* 27 SLR 647). In other words these employees must travel between a number of temporary workplaces dispersed over their area of operations. Common examples within this category are commercial travellers and roving inspectors. It is arguable that it is irrelevant whether such employees have a fixed base or not since in a sense their job is to travel.

In the Sch D case of *Horton v Young* 47 TC 60 (see **5.306**) it was held that the travelling expenses of an itinerant bricklayer between his home and the various building sites on which he worked was allowable. In the court of first instance, Brightman J decided in favour of the taxpayer on the grounds that his trade was by its nature itinerant, irrespective of whether or not he carried on any business activity at home. It is submitted that Brightman J's reasoning is persuasive also in the context of the Sch E expenses rule.

It would also follow that even if an itinerant employee does not have a fixed base, he should normally be entitled to claim the cost of travelling from home notwithstanding that it is not a place of work (see, for example, *Jardine v Gillespie* 5 TC 263).

Lord Simon of Glaisdare had this to say of such situations in *Taylor v Provan* 49 TC 579:

> In such cases the taxpayer may well be travelling in the performance of his duties from the moment of leaving home to the moment of his return … a visit to any head office might well be incidental or fortuitous.

In *SP IT/2/07*, the Revenue Commissioners state that they will regard an employee's normal place of work as being his employer's premises where 'travel is an integral part of the job involving daily appointment with customers'. Presumably the same principle would apply to roving inspectors, who do not have dealings with 'customers' as such. Accordingly, the Revenue view subsistence expenses of such an employee as deductible, since he will be regarded as being absent from his normal place of work. The better view, seems to be that such expenses should be regarded as an inherent part of the costs of travelling; as noted above, the deductibility of such travelling costs in the case of an itinerant employee should probably not depend on the existence or otherwise of a fixed base. Nevertheless, the Revenue analysis will nearly always lead to the same conclusion, namely that the subsistence costs in question are deductible. Flat rate subsistence allowances of this nature paid within approved limits may be paid tax-free under the terms of *SP IT/2/07*.

In *Gilbert v Hemsley* [1981] STC 703 Vinelott J drew a similar inference to that of Lord Simon in *Taylor v Provan* from the case of *Burton v Rednall* 35 TC 435. In that case, the taxpayer was the secretary of a cattle society who was obliged to make frequent visits to outlying farms, some of which were closer to his home than to his place of work. On occasions, the taxpayer drove from home firstly to one or more of the nearby farms and from there on to his place of work. Vinelott J pointed out that no dispute was raised to the deductibility of the expenses of travel between home and the nearby farm. However, Vinelott J did not refer to the position vis-à-vis the subsequent expense of travelling from the outlying farms on to the taxpayer's place of work, and he may in fact have overlooked this aspect of the case. It is arguable that the journey from the taxpayer's home to his place of work via the nearby farms was a combination of 'home and work' and 'necessary' travel. On this view only the extra expense of deviating from the direct route from home to work in order to visit the outlying farms should have been allowable. This would apparently equate with the Sch D position, see *Sargent v Barnes* [1978] STC 322 (discussed at **5.306**).

In *SP IT/2/07* the Revenue Commissioners express the view that where an employee undertakes business journeys directly from/to home, any travel/subsistence expenses should be computed as the lower of:

(a) the expenses actually incurred; or

(b) the expenses which would have been incurred if the journey had been undertaken form the normal place of work to the destination concerned.

In strict law, a director who is on the board of two or more companies within the same group is not entitled to claim the cost of travelling or related subsistence expenses between the place of business of one group company to another. This is because each directorship represents a separate and distinct office. However, as set out in *SP IT/2/07* the Revenue Commissioners will in practice regard directors in this position as having one place of employment at which he normally performs his duties (ie 'head office') and he will be entitled to a deduction for the expenses from travelling from there to other places of business within the group. A 'group' for these purposes will include 'associated' companies, ie companies on whose board the group is represented because of its shareholding or other financial interests. Employees as well as directors are entitled to this concession, where appropriate. Similar treatment will be granted to individuals who hold directorships in non-related companies as part of the duties of their office or employment. It may be observed that in a case where an employee is seconded by his employer to work part-time for another organisation on its behalf (while remaining throughout an employee of his original employer (see **10.103**), he may well be regarded as having two places of work on the authority of *Owen v Pook* (see above).

The Revenue is currently carrying out what has become known as 'The Contractor's Project'. It originally started in the South West Region and has since been extended nationwide. The project involves, *inter alia*, a review of the expenses claimed by employees of one-man companies. It seems that there was a practice of claiming unvouched expenses amongst certain sectors. Two *Tax Briefings* issued on this matter during 2013, in July and November and both are available on the Revenue website. *Tax Briefing 3* of 2013, is entitled 'Reimbursement of Travel and Subsistence Expenses by Intermediaries' and it sets out the Revenue position of travel and subsistence expenses where an individual provides their services through an intermediary.

The Revenue have been taking a strong stance on this issue with a starting point of 'deliberate default' in cases that have been identified for audit. It is understood that their basis for doing this is that they assert that the cases selected for audit appear to have serious issues around expenses. However, where it transpires during the course of an audit that there was no deliberate default, they have accepted that the 'careless behaviour' category is the appropriate category.

One of the main issues that arises in these cases is the travel expenses that can be claimed tax free. It has always been the case that travel from home to work was not allowable. However, as technology has moved on, it has become easier for people to work from home and as a result substantial duties of an employment are frequently carried on at an employee's home and indeed an individual's home is often their office. Therefore, travelling from that office to another place of work should be allowed. The author considers there are situations that the Revenue are incorrect in disallowing travel expenses – for example, where an employee gave up their office due to the downturn and are now working from a purpose-built office in their garden. Each case should be considered in detail prior to engaging with the Revenue. The payment of travel expenses to non-executive directors has been a very topical issue recently. The Revenue issued an *e-brief (61/14)* in June 2014 in which they stated that in their opinion if a company pays travel and subsistence expenses to directors (including non-executive directors) for their attendance at board meetings, such expenses are subject to PAYE/USC. In the case of non-executive directors although some preparatory work for a board meeting may be undertaken at the director's home, it does not mean that any travelling expenses to attend the board meetings are allowable as a deduction under TCA 1997, s 114. This treatment has now been superseded in that the matter was legislated for in FA 2015 with the insertion of TCA 1997, ss 195B and 195C which is discussed below.

Motor expenses

As discussed in **10.202**, the reimbursement of motor expenses on a scale approved by the Revenue Commissioners will normally be disregarded for the purposes of TCA 1997, s 117; correspondingly no claim in respect of motor expenses actually incurred will be allowable under TCA 1997, s 114. However, it always remains open to an employee to insist that the statutory basis should apply even in these circumstances. Further, where reimbursements are made on a scale which is not approved by the Revenue Commissioners the employee will be assessed therein under TCA 1997, s 117 and will need to make the appropriate claim under TCA 1997, s 114 (as well as usually also claiming capital allowances in respect of the relevant motor vehicle: see **10.305**).

The restriction applied by TCA 1997, s 376 which imposed a restriction on the deduction otherwise available for the expenses of running a private motor car with a 'relevant cost' in excess of a specified amount was deleted by FA 2002, s 28(1) as regards expenditure incurred in an accounting period ending on or after 1 January 2002. The restriction of a deduction for motor expenses in respect of lease or hire of a car in the context of the computation of the Sch D Case I (or Case II) profits of a trade (or profession), is discussed in **5.312**. Prior to the deletion of this section TCA 1997, s 376(1)(a)(ii) applied a corresponding restriction to any deduction claimed by an employee (or director) in respect of the running expenses of a private car used by him in the performance of the duties of his office or employment. There is a statutory prohibition on any deduction for the parking levy. This will be relevant when it is introduced (see **10.209**).

Certain expense payments for non-executive directors

TCA 1997, s 195B contains an exemption for the payment of travel and subsistence expenses incurred by a 'relevant director' for the attendance at a 'relevant meeting'.

> A 'relevant director' is defined as 'in relation to a company, means a director who is not resident in the State and is a non-executive director of that company;'

A director has the same meaning as it has in TCA 1997, s 770 which reads as follows:

> 'director', in relation to a company, includes—
>
> (a) in the case of a company the affairs of which are managed by a board of directors or similar body, a member of that board or body,
>
> (b) in the case of a company the affairs of which are managed by a single director or similar person, that director or person,
>
> (c) in the case of a company the affairs of which are managed by the members themselves, a member of that company,
>
> and includes a person who is to be or has been a director;

A 'relevant meeting' is defined as meaning 'a meeting attended by a relevant director in his or her capacity as a director for the purposes of the conduct of the affairs of the company;'

Expenses for the purposes of this section mean vouched expenses and travel is widely defined to mean 'travel by car, motorcycle, taxi, bus, rail, boat or aircraft'.

The section applies to payments made by a company to or on behalf of a relevant director of that company in respect of expenses of travel and subsistence incurred by the relevant director, on and from 1 January 2016, solely for the purpose of the attendance by him or her at a relevant meeting. It is of note that 'director' is defined for the purposes of the section but not a non-executive director but either way that person must be a director of the company concerned. CA 2014, s 167 deals with audit committees and sub-s (10) thereof applies the following definition for that section 'a non-executive director is a director who is not engaged in the daily management of the large company or body concerned, as the case may be'. This would concur with the application of that expression in practice which is typically one who does not engage in the day-to-day management of the organisation, but is involved in policy making and planning exercises. Further the director must not be resident in the State and this is of note given that TCA 1997, s 195B(3) is to be exempt from income tax and is not to be reckoned in computing income for the purposes of the Income Tax Acts. This means that a resident non-executive director travelling to the same meeting as a non-resident non-executive director will have differing tax treatments of travel expenses with the former being taxable in accordance with Revenue guidance and the latter not. Revenue *eBrief* 61/14 notes that it had updated Part 05-02-19 of the Income Tax, Capital Gains Tax and Corporation Tax manual on the Revenue website to:

1. set out the position in relation to the tax treatment of expenses of travel and subsistence incurred by non-executive directors in attending board meetings,
2. confirm that, generally speaking, no deduction is due to a non-executive director in respect of such expenses, and
3. confirm that where such expenses are met by a company on a director's behalf or are reimbursed to him, PAYE/USC must be deducted.

The wide definition of director in TCA 1997, s 770 to include a person who has been or will be a director is curious for the purposes of this section but arguably nothing turns on this given that presumably that person will not be attending a board meeting unless that person is a director in the first instance. However, there may be instances where reliance could be had on this expanded provision.

TCA 1997, s 195D was brought about by FA 2016, s 3 and applies to payments made by a company to or on behalf of a relevant director of that company in respect of expenses of travel and subsistence incurred by the relevant director, on and from 1 January 2017, solely for the purpose of the attendance by him or her at a 'relevant meeting'. A 'relevant director' for the purposes of that section is a 'relevant director' in relation to a company, meaning a person holding office as a non-executive director of that company:

(a) who is resident in the State, and
(b) whose annualised amount of the emoluments from the office for the year of assessment 2017 and for each subsequent year in which the person is a relevant director of the company, other than payments to which this section applies, does not exceed €5,000.

This differs from the definition in TCA 1997, s 195B in that it applies for 'resident' non-executive directors. The monetary restriction of €5,000 is of some note and its theme is continued in sub-s (3) which will be discussed further below. Further it defines a 'civil servant' as having the meaning assigned to it by the Civil Service Regulations

Act 1956. Section 1 of that Act explains the term as meaning '...a person holding a position in the Civil Service, and includes a member of the staff of the Houses of the Oireachtas'. TCA 1997, s 195D(3) differs from the exemption in TCA 1997, s 195B and reads:

> So much of a payment to which this section applies, as does not exceed the upper of any relevant rate or rates laid down from time to time by the Minister for Public Expenditure and Reform in relation to the payment of expenses of travel and subsistence of a civil servant, shall be exempt from income tax and shall not be reckoned in computing income for the purposes of the Income Tax Acts'.

Such restrictions are not in place for non-resident directors. Further Revenue manual 07-01-36 notes that as a consequence of the income tax exemption, payments which come within the exemption are also exempt from USC and PRSI.

Certain expense payments for State Examinations Commission examiners

TCA 1997, s 195C contains an exemption for the payment of travel and subsistence expenses by the State Examinations Commission to an 'examiner' for 'examination purposes'. The following definitions are relevant:

> 'civil servant' has the meaning assigned to it by the Civil Service Regulation Act 1956; and that Act defines same in s 1 as 'a person holding a position in the Civil Service, and includes a member of the staff of the Houses of the Oireachtas'.
>
> 'employee' has the same meaning as in s 983;

In that section an employee is defined as 'meaning any person in receipt of emoluments with emoluments being defined therein anything assessable to income tax under Sch E and references to payments of emoluments include references to payments on account of emoluments;

> 'examination purposes' means:
>
> (a) the development of examination papers or other examination materials;
>
> (b) the marking of such papers or other such materials; or
>
> (c) the carrying out of invigilator duties at an examination;
>
> 'examination' means any examination standing specified for the time being in Sch 2 to the Education Act 1998; that schedule contains the following listing of examinations:
>
> - Leaving Certificate Examination
> - Junior Certificate Examination
> - Technological Certificate Examination
> - Trade Certificate Examination
> - Certificate in Commerce Examination
> - Ceardteastas Gaeilge Examination
> - Teastas i dTeagasc na Gaeilge Examination
> - Typewriting Teachers Certificate Examination
> - Commercial Instructors Certificate Examination
>
> 'examination paper' includes any paper, plan, map, drawing, diagram, pictorial or graphic work or other document and any photograph, film or recording (whether of sound or images or both)—
>
> (a) in which questions are set for answer by candidates as part of an examination or which are related to such questions, or

(b) in which projects or practical exercises are set which candidates are required to complete as part of an examination or which are related to such projects or exercises;

'examiner' means, other than a person employed as an Examinations and Assessment Manager, a person who is an employee of the relevant employer for examination purposes;

'relevant employer' means the State Examinations Commission;

'travel' means travel by car, motorcycle, taxi, bus or rail.

TCA 1997, s 197C applies to payments made by the relevant employer to or on behalf of an examiner in respect of expenses of travel and subsistence incurred by the examiner, on and from 1 January 2016, for examination purposes. So much of any payment to which this section applies, as does not exceed the upper of any relevant rate or rates laid down from time to time by the Minister for Public Expenditure and Reform in relation to the payment of expenses of travel and subsistence of a civil servant, shall be exempt from income tax and shall not be reckoned in computing income for the purposes of the Income Tax Acts. Although brought about by the same Finance Act 2015 as TCA 1997, s 197B this exemption does not require expenditure to be vouched. Revenue manual 07-01-37 notes that as a consequence of the income tax exemption, payments which come within the exemption are also exempt from USC and PRSI.

10.304 Business entertainment expenses

TCA 1997, s 840(2)(c) prohibits any deduction at all under TCA 1997, s 114 for any expenses incurred in providing business entertainment. TCA 1997, s 840 prevents an employee (or director) from obtaining any deduction not only for business entertainment expenses paid out and borne by him personally, but also for all part of any sum reimbursed to him by the employer in respect of business entertainment expenses that is included in his taxable emoluments under the rule of TCA 1997, s 117 (see **10.202**). The fact that the employee may have incurred these expenses wholly, exclusively and necessarily in the performance of his duties is not sufficient to permit him any deduction under TCA 1997, s 114.

'Business entertainment' is defined by TCA 1997, s 840 as meaning:

> entertainment (including the provision of accommodation, food and drink or any other form of hospitality in any circumstances whatsoever) provided directly or indirectly.

TCA 1997, s 840 makes it clear that the rule covers any sum paid by the employer to, or on behalf of, or placed by him at the disposal of a member of his staff for the purpose of defraying expenses incurred or to be incurred by that employee in providing business entertainment. This links up with TCA 1997, s 117 which deems any such sum put at the disposal of an employee (or director) to be a perquisite chargeable to tax on him under Sch E, just as it does for any reimbursement by the employer of expenses incurred by the employee. In practice, the Revenue Commissioners do not seek to impose a tax liability on an employee who receives a properly vouched reimbursement of business entertainment expenses; in such a case, the employer will incur a disallowance under TCA 1997, s 840 on the amount of the reimbursement.

10.305 Capital allowances

In practice, it is relatively unusual for a person holding or exercising an office or employment to have any capital allowances to offset against his emoluments taxable under Sch E. However, he is entitled to claim a wear and tear (or annual) allowance under TCA 1997, s 284 (plant and machinery) or s 291 (computer software) in respect of relevant capital expenditure. This wear and tear allowance is given against the person's emoluments from the office or employment for each tax year in which he continues to use the plant for the purposes of the office or employment.

It is to be noted that the wear and tear allowance is given without the qualification that the plant must be used wholly, exclusively and necessarily in the performance of the duties of the employment. It is given in terms of the Sch D words 'for the purposes of' as set out in TCA 1997, s 284(1) but as extended to offices and employments by TCA 1997, s 301(1). The question of capital allowances in this context tends to occur in relation to motor cars, but it is capable of extending to any other type of plant which the employee may acquire for use for the purposes of his employment.

In the case of a motor car, two types of restriction affecting the amount of the capital allowances given are likely to arise in most cases. First, if the employee continues to use his own car, it is most unlikely that he will use it solely for the purposes of his employment. Assuming there is at least some use for other (normally private) purposes, the actual wear and tear allowance given for any tax year is computed by restricting the normal allowance otherwise available by reference to the ratio of the business use to the total use (but note the discussion at **6.203**: Conditions for wear and tear allowance).

In practice, this ratio is normally taken as the proportion which the business mileage bears to the total mileage in the relevant year. However, in computing the tax written down value of the plant at the end of one tax year, ie to arrive at the amount on which the wear and tear allowance for the next year is computed, the expenditure should be written down by the normal wear and tear allowance for the full year.

Secondly, if the capital expenditure in purchasing the car exceeds the relevant capital limit (the maximum capital cost eligible for capital allowances where motor cars are concerned), or with effect from 1 July 2008, the CO_2 emission level of the car exceeds a prescribed threshold the rules for restricting or denying the wear and tear allowances to be given each year are applied in the manner discussed fully in **6.212**.

When any item of plant in respect of which wear and tear allowances have been obtained in respect of use for an office or employment comes to be sold, or otherwise ceases permanently to be used for the purposes of the employment, a balancing allowance or balancing charge has to be computed applying the rules already discussed in **6.207**. In applying the rules discussed in **6.212** in relation to plant used for an employment, any reference to a 'trade' should be replaced by a reference to an 'employment'.

10.306 Foreign earnings deduction

TCA 1997, s 823A as amended by FA 2016 provides for relief from income tax for individuals who are resident in the State but who spend *qualifying days* in one or more *relevant states*. The relief was extended for the years 2017, 2018, 2019, 2020 and expanded to include an additional three countries. It had previously applied for the tax years 2015, 2016 and 2017 only. The relief is disregarded for the purposes of calculating the charge to Universal Social Charge and PRSI. The relief is granted on foot of a claim from a taxpayer who is resident in the State by providing a proportional tax deduction (the *specified amount)* based on the number of qualifying days worked in the relevant states. The deduction is made against the income, profit and gains from all offices or employments chargeable under either Sch E or Sch D Case III. The maximum that can be deducted from all such income etc, in any tax year is €35,000 (TCA 1997, s 823A(3)).

A '*qualifying day*' means a day on or after 1 January 2012, the whole of which is spent in one of the *relevant states*, which is one of at least three consecutive days of presence in a relevant state for the purpose of the performance of the duties of a *relevant office or employment*. For tax years before 2015 a qualifying day was one of at least four consecutive days. This was reduced to three by FA 2014. No day will be counted more than once. For 2015 and subsequent years a day includes travelling time from Ireland to the relevant country or from one relevant state to another relevant state. A '*relevant state*' means as regards the year of assessment 2012 Brazil, Russia, India, China or South Africa, from 2013 includes Egypt, Algeria, Senegal, Tanzania, Kenya, Nigeria, Ghana and the Democratic Republic of Congo, from 2015 includes Japan, Singapore, the Republic of Korea, Saudi Arabia, United Arab Emirates, Qatar, Bahrain, Indonesia, Vietnam, Thailand, Chile, Oman, Kuwait, Mexico and Malaysia and from 2017 includes Colombia and Pakistan. A '*relevant office or employment*' means an office or employment part of the duties of which are performed in a *relevant state* on a *qualifying day*;

'*The specified amount*' is an amount determined by the formula:

$$\frac{D \times E}{F}$$

where:

D is the number of qualifying days in the year of assessment in relation to the individual;

E is the income in the tax year from a relevant office or employment, and includes so much of any gain realised by the exercise, assignment or release of a right obtained by the individual as an office holder or employee in the relevant office or employment, after deducting any contribution or qualifying pension premium but excluding the amount of:

(a) any benefit in kind under general BIK provisions;

(b) any benefit in kind arising by virtue of a car being made available by reason of the employment;

(c) any benefit in respect of a preferential loan;

(d) any gratuitous lump sum termination payments;

(e) any payments under restrictive covenants; and

(f) is the total number of days in the tax year that the individual held a relevant office or employment (TCA 1997, s 823A(1)).

The amount of income, profits or gains arising to the individual from a relevant office or employment does not include amounts in respect of expenses paid or recouped by the claimant (TCA 1997, s 823A(4)).

The claimant must have worked at least 30 (previously 60 for the years of assessment 2012–2014 and 40 for 2015–2016) qualifying days in a tax year or in a relevant period, ie a continuous twelve month period, part of which falls in the tax year to which the claim relates. No period can be included as part of more than one relevant period, no overlap between relevant periods is permitted. The total number of qualifying days may relate to one or more than one relevant office or employment.

The relief potentially applies to all directors and employees in the private sector and to those employed in the commercial semi-state sector, but does not apply to those working in the civil and public service. The relief is not available in respect of income from an office or employment which is chargeable on the remittance basis or in respect of income to which:

(a) TCA 1997, s 472D applies (Research and Development credit);
(b) TCA 1997, s 822 applies (Split year treatment);
(c) TCA 1997, s 825A applies (Relief for income earned outside the State);
(d) TCA 1997, s 825C applies (Special Assignee Relief Programme) (TCA 1997, s 823A(2)).

Where an individual is entitled to double tax relief under TCA 1997, Pt 35 for tax suffered in a relevant state, the specified amount is reduced by an amount equal to the amount of income on which such tax was paid (TCA 1997, s 823A(5)).

10.307 Relief on retirement for earnings of designated sportspersons

TCA 1997, s 480A provides that sportspersons specified in TCA 1997, Sch 23A may on retirement claim deductions from their total income for 10 years based on their earnings from the sport concerned. The sportspersons concerned are athletes, badminton players, boxers, cricketers (with effect from 2012 onwards), cyclists, footballers, golfers, jockeys, motor racing drivers, rugby players, squash players, swimmers and tennis players.

Where the individual retires on or after 1 January 2014 he can claim the deduction from income arising in any ten of the fifteen tax years before retirement (including the year of retirement). Individuals who retired before 1 January 2014 could claim the deduction from income arising in any 10 years from 1990/91 onwards, including the year of retirement. The deduction is computed for any given tax year as 40 per cent of the gross receipts included in the profits of the basis period of that year which arose wholly or exclusively ie deriving directly from the actual carrying on of his profession, such as match or performance fees, prize moneys and appearance moneys paid as a direct consequence of participating in the sport concerned but not other earnings such as sponsorship fees, advertising or promotional income, media fees, or fees for personal interviews or appearances, magazine articles, the use of the sportsperson's image or name for promotional or endorsement purposes etc (TCA 1997, s 480A(6)).

Example 5.317.1

Pat Golden is a professional rugby player who retired from rugby in 2015. Of the fifteen years (2001 to 2015 inclusive) before he retired, the 10 years in which his salary from playing rugby were highest were the years 2008–2012 and 2002–2006 and so Pat's claim for relief under TCA 1997, s 480A will be made for those years. Pat's taxable income for 2012 was as follows:

	€
Salary	250,000
Employment expenses	(5,000)
Net Schedule E Income	245,000
Case IV: Sponsorship income	10,000
Total/Taxable Income	255,000

Pat will be entitled to claim a deduction of €100,000 (40% of €250,000) from his taxable income for 2012 which will give rise to a refund of €41,000 (€100,000 at 41%). Similar relief will be claimed and tax refunds due for the years 2008–2011 and 2002–2006.

Because USC is calculated on income without regard to any amount deductible in calculating total income (TCA 1997, s 531AM(1)(b) (see **3.404**)), the individual remains liable to USC on his income before the relief is given. PRSI also continues to be payable because it is charged on income before deductions (see **3.402** and **11.2**).

An individual can only claim the relief where he is resident in the State, an EEA state (ie EU Member States plus Iceland, Liechtenstein and Norway) or an EFTA state (ie Iceland, Liechtenstein, Norway and Switzerland) in the retirement year. Individuals who retired prior to 1 January 2014 had to be resident in the State in the year of retirement in order to claim the relief. In addition for individuals who retired before 1 January 2014 the deduction could only be claimed for tax years in which the individual was resident in the State. This is no longer a requirement for individuals who retire on or after 1 January 2014. Such individuals must only be resident in the State, an EEA or EFTA state in the retirement year. The retirement year is the year in which the individual proves to the satisfaction of the Revenue Commissioners that he has ceased permanently to be engaged in carrying on his sporting profession or occupation. When the individual ceases permanently is a matter of a fact to be determined by examining the circumstances in each particular case. In order to be entitled to claim the relief the individual must cease to carry on the sport as a profession or as an employee, the fact that the individual continues to participate in the sport in question as an amateur would not preclude him from claiming the relief. Furthermore, the relief is only available to an individual who complied with the Income Tax Acts. In the author's view this potentially gives the Revenue Commissioners discretion to disallow a claim where the individual making the claim has at some point not been income tax compliant.

Where the individual is required to file a return for the year in which the individual retires, the relief must be claimed in the return for the year in which the sportsperson retires. An individual who qualifies for relief under TCA 1997, s 480A is required to file a return electronically under ROS (see **2.105**) however the online Form 11 does not cater for relief claimed in respect of years prior to the current year and any claim included in the Form 11 is treated as a claim in respect of income for the current year. In practice therefore an individual must claim relief under TCA 1997, s 480A by writing separately to Revenue. If an individual is not required to file a return for the year in which the individual retires, TCA 1997, s 480A(7) provides that he can submit a claim for the relief to the Revenue Commissioners. The claim must be made within four years from the end of the retirement year (TCA 1997, s 480A(3)). The normal four-year time limit on claiming repayments under TCA 1997, s 865 will not apply (TCA 1997, s 480A(4)).

The relief cannot create or augment a loss under Sch D Case II; this seems to follow in any event from the fact that the relief is granted as a deduction from total income (TCA 1997, s 480A(8)(c)). The relief will not affect the calculation of the sportsperson's net relevant earnings as defined for the purposes of TCA 1997, s 787 (level of allowable contributions for the purposes of retirement annuity contracts: see **16.2**) (TCA 1997, s 480A(9)). The relief will be given by way of repayment of tax subject only to any right of offset under TCA 1997, s 960H (see **2.617**) but will not carry interest. (TCA 1997, s 480A(8)). Provision is made to withdraw the relief by way of a Sch D Case IV assessment at any time for the tax years in respect of which the relief was originally given if the person subsequently recommences to be engaged in that sport, though this does not prevent a subsequent claim for the relief if and when the sportsperson finally does retire at a later time (TCA 1997, s 480A(10)).

10.4 Termination Payments

10.401 Payments chargeable under TCA 1997, s 123

Scope of the charge

Certain payments may be made by a company or other employer to a person holding an office or employment, or to a past holder, in a form which may not be taxable as the emoluments or perquisites of the office or employment under the main Sch E charging rule contained in TCA 1997, s 112. In particular, it was at one time possible for lump sum payments, which could be substantial, to be made tax free to a person as a personal gift or testimonial on retirement from his office or employment (see eg *Reed v Seymour* and *Mulvey v Coffey* discussed in **10.107**) or, in the case of a person's removal from an office or employment, as compensation for the loss of the office or employment (see **10.111**). It was thought possible that certain payments in connection with a change in the nature of a person's office or employment could be made without being taxed as a perquisite under TCA 1997, s 112. The scope for such payments looks narrow in view of the decision in *Hamblett v Godfrey*, although the facts in *Mairs v Haughey* (if that decision is in fact correct) may represent one example (see **10.111**). Following *Wales v Tilley 25 TC 136*, sums paid in commutation of pension rights are also outside TCA 1997, s 112 because pensions form a separate taxable category in their own right (see **10.111**).

In *Walker v Adams* [2003] STC (SCD) 269, a case heard by the UK Special Commissioners, the taxpayer had been constructively dismissed on the basis of religious discrimination. The Northern Ireland Fair Employment tribunal awarded him two lump sums under the relevant anti-religious discrimination laws. The first sum, which related to loss of earnings and pension rights was held to fall within the UK equivalent of TCA 1997, s 123. The Special Commissioners rejected the argument that the source of this payment was the act of unlawful discrimination and therefore outside TCA 1997, s 123, holding that the discrimination had caused the termination of the contract and the compensation awarded by the Tribunal was therefore paid in consequence of or otherwise in connection with the termination of the taxpayer's employment. They observed that the wording of TCA 1997, s 123(1) did not impose a strict causation test, particularly in light of the phrase 'or otherwise'. The second sum was awarded for injury to the taxpayer's feelings but the Inland Revenue conceded that this fell outside TCA 1997, s 123.

The provisions of TCA 1997, s 123 are equally capable of applying in the case of a foreign office or employment taxable under Sch D Case III (although if the employee is, or has been, taxed on the remittance basis, the exemptions and reliefs granted in relation to foreign service is always likely to be relevant: see **10.406**). It is likely that lump sum payments of a kind which would escape taxation on general principles under Sch E would enjoy the same treatment under Sch D Case III. Even if the employment in question is taxable under Sch D Case III, the charge under TCA 1997, is imposed under Sch E.

In order to deal with these types of payment, TCA 1997, s 123(2) charges income tax under Sch E in respect of any payment (not otherwise chargeable to tax) which is made, whether or not under any legal obligation, either directly or indirectly in consideration or in consequence of, or otherwise in connection with any of the following:

(a) the termination of an office or employment;

(b) any change in the functions or emoluments of an office or employment; or

(c) the commutation of any annual or periodical payments which would otherwise have been made in connection with such termination or change (TCA 1997, s 123(1)).

For ease of explanation, any payment (or other valuable consideration) chargeable to tax by TCA 1997, s 123 falling under any of these three headings are referred to here as 'termination payments', although, as indicated, the section extends to payments in connection with certain changes which may not involve the termination of an office or employment. However, any payment which is already chargeable to income tax under TCA 1997, s 112 (or under any other rule apart from TCA 1997, s 123 itself) is not a 'termination payment', even if it arises in connection with the termination of an office or employment. This distinction is important since the exemptions and reliefs from tax under TCA 1997, s 123 provided by TCA 1997, s 201 and Sch 3 are not given in respect of any payment or other valuable consideration chargeable to tax otherwise than under TCA 1997, s 123.

It should also be noted that statutory redundancy payments are not chargeable under either TCA 1997, s 112 or s 123.

Subject to the exemptions provided by TCA 1997, s 201, tax is charged under TCA 1997, s 123 whether the termination payment is made to the holder or past holder of the office or employment, to his spouse or civil partner or to any dependant of his, or to his executors or administrators. The payment may be made by the person under whom the office or employment is or was held, or by any other person. Once it is established that the payment, by whoever made, is not already taxable under Sch E (or Sch D Case III in the case of a foreign office or employment) and is directly or indirectly connected with the termination of the office or employment, or with a change in its functions, etc, it is taxable as the income of the holder or past holder of the office or employment. Any valuable consideration other than money is taxable as if it were a payment of money equal to the value of that consideration at the date it is given.

Any payment or other valuable consideration taxable under TCA 1997, s 123 is deemed to be emoluments of the holder or past holder of the office or employment and is assessable to income tax under Sch E (and subject to PAYE – see **11.105**) (TCA 1997, s 123(3)). Except for a payment in commutation of annual or other periodical payments, the termination payment is treated as income received on the date of the termination or change in respect of which it is made, whether it is in fact paid on that date or on any other date. A payment in commutation of annual or other periodical payments is treated as income received on the date on which the commutation is effected (TCA 1997, s 123(4)).

In *George v Ward* [1995] STC (SCD) 230, the taxpayer's termination payment included the right to the use of a car for the following nine years. The Special Commissioner held that the use of a car, although arguably not convertible into cash, should be valued at the amount a reasonable person would be prepared to pay in order to enjoy that benefit. The Special Commissioner also held that the taxpayer could only be taxed to the extent that the car(s) in question were actually provided to the taxpayer. This latter conclusion seems arguable, since a contractual right to a future benefit would appear to constitute consideration in itself. Where an interest-free (or low-interest) loan is made to a taxpayer following the termination of his employment (and which falls, as will usually be the case in those circumstances in the case of loans made prior to 4 February 2006, outside TCA 1997, s 122) the reasoning in *George v Ward* suggests that the commercial benefit of that loan could fall within TCA 1997, s 123. However, if the loan is repayable on demand (so that the legal value of the taxpayer's legal rights in relation to the loan is negligible), it is again arguable whether TCA 1997, s 123 could in fact bite.

If the holder or past holder of the office or employment dies, any tax which would have been chargeable on him by TCA 1997, s 123, if he had not died, must be assessed and charged on his executors or administrators; any such tax is a debt due and payable out of his estate (TCA 1997, s 123(5)) (see also the discussion at **15.103**). In such a case, the calculation of the amount of the tax assessable on the executors or administrators is made by reference to the deceased person's own total income, allowances, etc for the tax year for which the termination payment is treated as income. For example, if an individual has been removed from his office as a director of a company on 15 March 2015, and dies on 1 April 2015 and if the company pays, say, €20,000 to his widow on 15 June 2015 as the compensation to which he would have been entitled for the loss of the office if he had not died, then the tax assessable on his executor is calculated by including the non-exempted part of the termination payment as part of the deceased individual's 2015 income to the date of his death.

PRSI and the Universal Social Charge

It should be noted that termination payments are not 'reckonable earnings' for the purposes of employee contributions. The Universal Social Charge is chargeable on the excess of the termination payment over the basic and increased exemptions and, Standard Capital Superannuation Benefit (SCSB) (see **3.404**). The treatment of termination payments under the PAYE system is discussed at **11.105**.

Exempted payments

TCA 1997, s 201(2) exempts the following payments from the charge to income tax under TCA 1997, s 123:

(a) any payment in connection with the termination of an office or employment due to the death of the holder;

(b) any payment made on account of injury to or disability of the holder of an office or employment;

(c) any benefit (eg a permitted lump sum payment in part commutation of a pension) under an approved pension scheme, a statutory scheme or a scheme set up by a foreign government for the benefit of its employees as referred to in TCA 1997, s 778(1)), subject to the exclusions listed in TCA 1997, s 201(3) noted below;

(d) any benefit provided under an unapproved retirement benefit scheme where the holder of the office or employment was chargeable to tax by TCA 1997, s 777 in respect of contributions by the employer to provide the benefit (see **16.104**); and

(e) any sum paid as consideration to a current, past or future holder of an office or employment for a restrictive covenant which is chargeable to tax under TCA 1997, s 127 (see **10.114**).

TCA 1997, s 201(3) denies the exemption in (c) above to termination and severance allowances payable to the following:

(a) members of the Oireachtas;
(b) Ministers of State;
(c) parliamentary office holders.

With effect for all payments made on or after 1 January 2011, an overriding maximum €200,000 applies to the amount by which a termination payment may be reduced by reference to the basis exemption and the standard capital superannuation benefit. The limit may operate retrospectively since it operates as a lifetime limit, taking into account reductions of termination payments which were made prior to 1 January 2011. Where two or more termination payments within TCA 1997, s 123 are made to or in respect of the same person in respect of the same office or employment, or in respect of different offices or employments, the cap of €200,000 will apply as if those payments were a single payment of an amount equal to the aggregate of all such payments (TCA 1997, s 123(8)). FA 2013, s 14 introduced a number of amendments to TCA 1997, s 201 and Sch 3. It was confirmed that the cap of €200,000 also applies to payments made in connection with the termination of an office or employment by virtue of death or on account of injury or disability to the holder of the office or employment. The cap of €200,000 is a life time cap.

In addition, special severance gratuities paid to certain civil servants are also denied the exemption provided in (c) as are benefits paid under a statutory scheme which exceeds the benefits customarily payable thereunder, and which relate to the termination of employment as a consequence of (broadly speaking) internal rationalisations or reorganisations. The benefits regarded as customarily payable include enhanced benefits as a result of the purchase of 'added years' and also 'short service gratuities' previously paid on an administrative basis. The exclusion applies to any statutory scheme established or amended after 10 May 1997.

Under exemption (b), it is necessary that the payment be made on account of the injury to or disability so that a redundancy payment which happens to be made to a disabled person does not qualify (*O'Cahill v Harding* IV ITR 233). However, an *ex gratia* payment made on an employee's decision to retire as a result of severe ill health was held to qualify in *O'Shea v Mulqueen* V ITR 134. The court rejected the argument that the payment must be made directly on account of the disability and not on account of retirement due to disability. In *Horner v Hasted* [1995] STC 766, Lightman J held that the UK equivalent of exemption (b) required that a relevant disability, etc should be established as an objective fact, and that the payer's motive in making the payment (ie whether or not on account of the disability) should be established as a subjective fact.

TCA 1997, s 203(2) exempts from income tax under Sch E any lump sum, weekly or other payment to an employed or unemployed person under the regulations to Redundancy Payments Act 1967, s 46. Consequently, although such sums might otherwise be a payment in connection with the termination of an office or employment, they have to be left out of account entirely in applying the charge to tax under that section. Any such payments within the Redundancy Payments Act, therefore, must first be deducted from any termination payment before applying any of the rules just discussed.

It is important to note, however, that this exemption is specifically limited to the statutory redundancy payments. If as frequently happens, any person becoming redundant negotiates any additional compensation payment over and above the statutory amount, then that additional amount will fall within the rules of TCA 1997, s 123 (and its supporting provisions).

TCA 1997, s 201(4) exempts certain payments in respect of an office or employment where the holders' service included a substantial amount of foreign service (see **10.406**).

With effect for training made available on after 13 March 2008, TCA 1997, s 201(1A), inserted by FA 2008, s 22, provides that the cost of a qualifying retraining course to an 'eligible employee' made available as part of a redundancy package (including any scheme of compensation made on the termination of the employment) will be exempt from the scope of TCA 1997, s 123 up to an amount of €5,000. An eligible employee is one who has completed at least two years continuous service (or is treated as doing so under the redundancy legislation) prior to being made redundant. The training course must be designed to impart or improve skills or knowledge, relevant to, or intended to be used in obtaining gainful employment or in setting up a business. The course must be primarily devoted to the teaching or practical application of such skills or knowledge and must be completed within six months of the termination of the employment. The employer must also make such retraining available to all eligible employees. No relief is granted in relation to retraining provided to the spouse or civil partner and/or any dependants of the employee. Furthermore, the relief is denied where there is any arrangement or scheme in place under which the employee can receive the cost of the training wholly or partly and directly or indirectly in money or money's worth and he does in fact receive that cost.

Scheme of the legislation

TCA 1997, s 123(4) requires the amount of any termination payment that is taxable under the section to be treated as emoluments of the holder or past holder of the office or employment assessable to income tax under Sch E. The taxpayer is entitled however firstly to reduce the sum otherwise chargeable by the amount of the 'basic exemption' (discussed at **10.402**). The taxpayer is entitled by TCA 1997, s 201(6), to claim certain other reliefs provided for in Sch 3, to the extent that they apply to his case. There were two forms of relief in respect of payments made up to 31 December 2013: first, a further reduction (in addition to the basic exemption) may be available to reduce the sum chargeable to tax; secondly, there may have been a further relief given as a reduction of the income tax payable on the sum in question (known as top slicing relief). Any claim for these reliefs must be made by notice in writing to the inspector before the end of the fourth tax year after the end of the tax year for which the termination payment is treated as income. The second relief, top slicing relief was abolished by F(No 2) A 2013, s 4 for all termination payments made on or after 1 January 2014.

Several preliminary points should be made. First, any relief given by TCA 1997, Sch 3 is restricted, if necessary, so that it does not reduce the taxpayer's liability to satisfy the income tax he is entitled to deduct from annual payments, etc, which rank as charges on his income (TCA 1997, Sch 3). Secondly, in applying any provision in the Income Tax Acts which requires any particular income to be treated as the highest part of a person's income, that provision is to be read as if no part of any termination payment taxable under TCA 1997, s 123 were included in his total income (TCA 1997, s 201(7)). Thirdly, in reading the various paragraphs of Sch 3, any reference to a payment chargeable under TCA 1997, s 123 is to be taken as a reference only to the net amount of the termination payment after deducting the basic exemption or, if there are connected termination payments, the part of that exemption applicable to the payment in question (TCA 1997, Sch 3 para 2).

In the absence of any claim for the TCA 1997, Sch 3 reliefs, the computation of the income tax chargeable is straightforward. Assuming only one termination payment is involved, that payment is reduced by the basic exemption and the resulting net termination payment is included in the taxpayer's total income for the relevant tax year; income tax is then computed in the ordinary way. If more than one termination payment from the same office or employment (or from associated employers) arises, eg as for Mr GX in **Example 10.402.1**, the appropriate part of the basic exemption is deducted from each payment. No further comment is thought necessary where no Sch 3 reliefs are claimed.

The main complications in calculating the tax chargeable under TCA 1997, s 123 arise in connection with the computation of the TCA 1997, Sch 3 reliefs. It is proposed to deal with the matter separately in two stages. First the determination of the net amount chargeable, ie the net termination payment as reduced by the TCA 1997, Sch 3 reliefs given in reducing the amount chargeable, is covered in **10.402** and **10.403**. Secondly, top slicing relief which may be available by way of reduction in the tax payable, in respect of payments made prior to 1 January 2014, is discussed in **10.404**. In explaining these TCA 1997, Sch 3 reliefs, it is assumed that only one termination payment is involved. The variations which may occur where there are connected payments from the one employer (or from associated employers) are dealt with in **10.405**, while the rules in respect of foreign service are discussed in **10.406**.

It should be noted that there is no provision for deductions other than those specified in TCA 1997, Sch 3. Thus, in *Warnett v Jones* [1980] STC 131, a claim for legal expenses to be set off against damages received for wrongful dismissal under the UK equivalent of TCA 1997, s 123 was rejected. Where a claim for damages is settled, the employer may agree to reimburse part or all of the employee's legal expenses under the terms of the settlement. Where the case goes to court, legal costs may be awarded in favour of the employee. In strictness such amounts reimbursed must be included in the amount assessable under TCA 1997, s 123, but with no right to a corresponding deduction following *Warnett v Jones*. However, the Revenue Commissioners will not seek to impose tax where costs are paid directly to the former employee's solicitor in discharge of costs related solely to the relevant proceedings under a specific term of the agreement (*Tax Briefing 51*).

10.402 The basic exemption

TCA 1997, s 201(5) provides that tax is not chargeable under TCA 1997, s 123 on a termination payment that does not exceed the basic exemption. Under TCA 1997, s 201(1)(a) the basic exemption is equal to €10,160 plus €765 for each complete year of service by the employee up to the 'relevant date.' Where a termination payment is made to an employee and the payment is stated to be in respect of employment within a number of group companies Revenue have stated (see Revenue Manuals Part 05.05.19 paragraph 5.1.2) that the employee's years' service in all group companies can be taken into account in determining the employee's period of service.

The 'relevant date' is the date of the termination of the office or employment (or, if appropriate, the date of the change in its functions or emoluments) in respect of which the termination payment is made. It seems that where the termination is caused by a breach of the contract the date of termination is the date of the breach (*Micklefield v SAS Technologies* [1991] 1 All ER 275). If the payment is one made in commutation of annual or other periodical payments, the relevant date remains the date of the termination of the office or employment (or the date of the change in its functions or emoluments) in respect of which those payments are being made. It may be noted that the relevant date for such a commutation payment applies notwithstanding that the commutation payment is treated as income arising on the date the commutation is effected (TCA 1997, s 201(1)(a)). In computing the basic exemption it will be necessary to establish the period of service relevant to the employment in question. In some cases an employee may have worked for the same employer in a number of different capacities (eg as a result of being promoted). It is thought that the inspector would normally accept that the period of service commenced from the date on which the individual took up his initial employment. The position may be more problematic where there has been a change of employer but the rights and obligations of the employment contract have not been carried over by virtue of the Acquired Rights Directive (EC 77/187) (and see European Communities (Protection of Employees on Transfer of Undertakings) Regulations 2003, SI 131/2003).

For a payment that exceeds the basic exemption, tax is only chargeable in respect of the excess of the payment over that basic exemption. The basic exemption is, however, applicable to all payments chargeable under TCA 1997, s 123 made to the same person (including his spouse or civil partner relatives, etc) in respect of (a) the same office or employment, (b) different offices or employments held under the same employer, and (c) different offices or employments held under associated employers. TCA 1997, s 201(5)(b) requires all such payments to be added together and the basic exemption applied as if the person in question had received a single payment equal to the aggregate amount of all the payments. Then, in applying the basic exemption, the following rules are adopted:

(a) the basic exemption is deducted rateably from the payments in proportion to their respective amounts, unless the payments are treated as income of different tax years; and

(b) in the latter event, the basic exemption is deducted first from any payment(s) treated as income of an earlier year before any payment(s) treated as income of a later year.

Where two different employments are concerned the amount of the basic exemption may be different in each case. TCA 1997, s 201 gives no guidance as to which amount should be used in the calculation.

Two or more offices or employments are treated as being held under associated employers: (a) if one of those employers is under the control of the other, (b) if both employers are under the control of a third person, or (c) if one of the employers is under the control of a third person who is himself under the control of the other employer (TCA 1997, s 201(1)(c)). For this purpose, 'control' in relation to a body corporate means the power of a person to secure, by means of the holding of shares, the possession of voting power, or by virtue of any powers conferred by the articles of association or any other document, that the affairs of the body corporate be conducted in accordance with the wishes of that person. 'Control', in relation to a partnership, means the right to a share of more than 50 per cent of the assets or of the income of the partnership (TCA 1997, s 201(1)(a)) (see **12.304**).

Any two or more termination payments are treated as coming from associated employers if, on the date which is the relevant date in relation to any of those payments, the above 'common control' connection exists. The definition of 'relevant date' is that already noted above. For example if Mr X receives from A Ltd a termination payment the relevant date of which is 15 May 2014, and if he receives from B Ltd a termination payment with a relevant date of 28 February 2015, then if A Ltd and B Ltd have become associated employers following a take-over on 5 November 2014, the basic exemption has to be deducted rateably from the termination payments. The fact that there was no connection between the two companies on the relevant date for the first payment does not matter.

TCA 1997, s 201 gives no guidance as to how to deal with the situation where the amount of the basic exemption differs in respect of different employments. This could arise for example, in a case where the employee's period of service differs in respect of each employment. The most practical solution appears to be to calculate the basic exemption in respect of each employment concerned and to scale down the amount thus calculated in proportion to the respective amount of the payment received in respect of that employment. This is the approach which has been adopted in the example below and throughout the text which follows.

Example 10.402.1

Mr GX who has held a number of different pensionable offices and employments within a group of companies since 12 October 1994, retired as managing director of the parent company on 15 November 2014, but remained an employee of one of its subsidiary companies, S Ltd, as well as continuing to be a non-executive director of the parent company until his full retirement on 1 November 2015.

He received a lump sum of €10,000 on 2 January 2015 as a 'golden handshake' following his retirement as managing director. On his final retirement, he was paid lump sums of €14,000 and €6,000 respectively attributed to his continued employment with S Ltd and his directorship of the parent company. These payments were made respectively on 1 November 2015 and 23 December 2015. The inspector of taxes accepts that none of these payments is taxable under the main Sch E charging rule of TCA 1997, s 112.

Subject to the basic exemption, all three payments are chargeable as Sch E income under TCA 1997, s 123 – the €10,000 being subject to TCA 1997, s 123 in 2014 by reference to the date of his retirement as managing director on 15 November 2014, although the payment was not made until a date in the next tax year. The basic exemption is deductible from the three payments as follows:

	Payment	*Exempted*	*Taxable*[3]
	€	€	€
2014:			
Payment on 15/11/2014[1]	10,000	(10,000)	Nil
2015:			
Payment from parent company on 1/11/2015[2, 3]	6,000	(4,638)[4]	1,362
Payment from S Ltd on 23/12/2015	14,000	(10,822)	3,178

Notes:

1. The full amount of the payment taxable for 2014, being an earlier tax year, is exempted as being within the basic exemption.

2. The basic exemptions in relation to the payments made in 2015 are as follows:

   Payment 1/11/2015 €10,160 + (€765 x 20) = €25,460

   Payment 23/12/2015: €10,160 + (€765 x 20) = €25,460.

3. It is assumed that Mr GX is not entitled to the increase in the basic exemption as discussed below.

   € (25,460 – 10,000) x 6,000/ (6,000+14,000) = €4,638

   € (25,460 – 10,000) x 14,000/ (6,000+14,000) = €10,822

4. Mr GX may be able to claim an enhanced reduction by virtue of the Standard Capital Superannuation Benefit Rules (see **10.403** below).

Increase in basic exemption

TCA 1997, Sch 3 para 8 entitles the person who has made the claim under TCA 1997, s 201(6) in respect of a particular termination payment, but who has not previously made any claim for relief under TCA 1997, s 201 in the previous 10 years of assessment, to have the basic exemption increased by the lower of:

(a) €10,000; and

(b) the excess (if any) of €10,000 over 'the relevant capital sum'.

For this purpose, 'the relevant capital sum' is defined in the same manner as applies in the calculation of the Standard Capital Superannuation Benefit (see below); in broad terms it refers to a tax free lump sum to which the employee is entitled under the terms of a pension scheme related to the relevant office or employment.

Thus, where a person has made no claim for relief in the previous 10 years of assessment under TCA 1997, s 201, his basic exemption may be increased by €10,000 if he is not entitled to a relevant capital sum under a pension scheme connected with the office or employment from which the present termination payment arises. If, for example, he receives a tax free lump sum of €10,000 or more, his basic exemption will not be increased. Should he receive a tax free lump sum from the pension scheme of say, €2,700 (at its present day valuation), then his basic exemption is increased by the excess of €10,000 over €2,700, ie € 7,300. Should he have made any claim for this relief in the previous 10 years of assessment, under TCA 1997, s 201, this revision is not available so that the maximum exemption for the present termination payment remains the basic exemption.

10.403 Standard capital superannuation benefit

TCA 1997, Sch 3 para 6 entitles a person to have the net termination payment reduced by the amount (if any) by which the standard capital superannuation benefit exceeds the basic exemption (increased as appropriate) under TCA 1997, Sch 3 para 8 (see above). In effect, this means that the net chargeable amount of the termination payment to be taxed as additional Sch E income is the actual termination payment as reduced by the higher of the standard capital superannuation benefit and the basic exemption.

The 'standard capital superannuation benefit' (SCSB) is defined, in relation to any office or employment, in a manner which can conveniently be converted into the following formula:

$$E \times \frac{n}{15} - L = SCSB$$

where:

E= the average for one year of the taxpayer's taxable emoluments from the office or employment for the last three years of his service before the relevant date;

n= the whole number of complete years of his service in the office or employment; and

L= any tax free lump sum received or receivable by him out of any approved pension scheme, statutory scheme or foreign government scheme in respect of the office or employment (TCA 1997, Sch 3 para 1).

The 'relevant date' is as defined by TCA 1997, s 201(1)(a) in the same manner as for the basic exemption (see **10.402**). Some of the issues which may arise when seeking to establish the employee's period of service are discussed at **10.402**. The Revenue Commissioners have issued a precedent stating that it is the last three years of paid service which should be taken into account, so that eg career breaks will not be counted for these purposes.

Prior to FA 2014 the definition of E in the formula above was the average emoluments from the office or employment for the last three years, ie the word 'taxable' was only inserted by FA 2014, Sch 3(1)(g). The Appeal Commissioners had held that the term 'emoluments' was to be given its ordinary meaning disregarding the definition thereof as 'anything assessable under Sch E' within TCA 1997, s 112(2). Accordingly, the value of shares appropriated to an employee under an approved profit sharing scheme (and thus exempt from tax under Sch E: see **11.406**) were properly included in the calculation of emoluments under TCA 1997, Sch 3 para 1 (9 AC 2000). Certainly while there is nothing to suggest that the definition in s 112(2) should be applied for purposes beyond those of s 112; there is indeed a separate definition for the purposes of TCA 1997, s 113. The term 'emoluments' is undefined in Sch 3 and before FA 2014 there was no compelling reason it should have been read as referring only to taxable emoluments. The matter has been clarified following FA 2014.

Revenue has stated (see Revenue Manual Pt 05.05.19, Para 5.5.5, updated May 2016) that Finance Act 2014 amended Sch 3 para 1(1) in the definition of SCSB (Standard Capital Superannuation Benefit) by amending 'emoluments' to 'taxable emoluments'. This amendment has no effect on the established method of computing the SCSB. Taxable emoluments means any income that is assessable under Sch E including such income where it is relieved by another provision of the Act, such as:

- the travel pass scheme,
- the value of any shares appropriated to employees and directors under an approved profit sharing scheme,
- the cycle to work scheme, and
- contributions to pension schemes by employees and office holders.

The Revenue Commissioners have issued a precedent stating that they will disregard gaps in service such as a career break when ascertaining the average emoluments for the previous three years; in such cases, it will therefore be necessary to go back further than 36 months prior to the relevant date.

Where a termination payment is made to an employee and the payment is stated to be in respect of employment within a number of group companies Revenue have stated (see Revenue Manuals Pt 05.05.19 Para 5.1.2) that the employee's years' service in all group companies can be taken into account in determining the employee's period of service.

The tax free lump sum from an approved pension scheme, etc that has to be brought into account as L in the standard capital superannuation benefit contribution and, if relevant, in the TCA 1997, Sch 3 revision of the basic exemption, may be either of the following:

(a) any lump sum which the employee elects to take in commutation of part of his pension (if the termination payment arises on his retiring and taking his pension entitlements – see **16.110**). This includes the value of any option which, whether exercised at some future date or not, will result in the pension or part of it being commuted in favour of a tax free lump sum. However, if the employee, in accordance with the pension agreement, irrevocably surrenders his option then the optional value will not be included in the total comprising 'L' in the SCSB formula Sch 3 para 1(2)); or

(b) the present value (as actuarially computed) of the maximum lump sum commutation payment to which the employee would be entitled at normal retirement age in respect of the office or employment (if the termination payment arises on his ceasing his employment with his present employer before becoming entitled to take his pension).

The question of whether or not any refund of an employee's contributions to the scheme (repayable to him where his employment ceases before normal retirement date), which is subject to the 20 per cent tax charge levied on the administrator under TCA 1997, s 780 (see **16.109**), is to be treated as a tax free lump sum was the subject of a case heard by the Appeal Commissioners in 1985 (see [1986] ITR 214). Prior to that case, the Revenue Commissioners had taken the view that such a refund of employee's contributions was a tax free lump sum receivable by him so as to reduce his standard capital superannuation benefit (and to reduce the increase in the basic exemption – see above). However, the Appeal Commissioners held that the refund is not receivable 'tax free' and should not, therefore, reduce the standard capital superannuation benefit (or the increase in the basic exemption).

It is to be noted that there is no lump sum to be taken into account under heading (b) if the employee, having reached pension date, opts to take his full pension without any commutation. However, if the termination payment arises in circumstances where the employee terminates his employment and becomes entitled to a deferred pension (usually payable from normal retirement age) or if he transfers his built up future pension benefits to a new employer's pension scheme, the Revenue Commissioners insist that the sum mentioned under heading (b) be taken into account. In this case, the maximum lump sum commutation payment is determined by reference to the taxpayer's salary, etc from the office or employment at the date of the event giving rise to the current termination payment. As noted above, the lifetime cap of €200,000 was introduced by FA 2011. FA 2013, s 14 provides that no SCSB relief is available on any payment over €200,000, ie the SCSB cannot be applied to the excess.

Example 10.403.1

Mr R Rolls retires from his office as managing director of Afford Ltd on 1 July 2015 after 12.5 years' service with the company. He has just reached his 63rd birthday which under the company's pension scheme entitles him to take his pension. Although entitled to commute part of his pension benefits for a lump sum, he elects not to do so and to take his full pension instead.

On 7 September 2015, the directors of the company resolve that, in recognition of the exceptional contribution which Mr Rolls made to the development and growth of the company, a special lump sum *ex gratia* payment of €60,000 should be made to him. Following ratification of this proposal by the company in its annual general meeting on 19

November 2015, the sum of €60,000 is paid to Mr Rolls on 26 November 2015 (but subject to the deduction of PAYE).

Mr Rolls' emoluments from his office with the company for the three years ended 30 June 2015, ie before 1 July 2015 (the relevant date), are:

	Year ended 30/06/2013	*Year ended 30/06/2014*	*Year ended 30/06/2015*
	€	€	€
Director's fee	1,000	1,000	1,500
Salary	21,400	21,900	26,300
Benefits in kind	3,600	4,100	3,200
	26,000	27,000	31,000

Mr Rolls makes the appropriate claim under TCA 1997, s 201(6) for the TCA 1997, Sch 3 reliefs. The first stage of deducting the basic exemption and the further reliefs by way of reduction of the sum chargeable work out as follows:

	€	€
Basic tax exemption[1]		19,340
Add:		
Maximum addition	10,000	
Less: tax free lump sum from pension scheme	Nil	
		10,000
Revised basic exemption		29,340
Standard capital superannuation benefit:		
E = average emoluments for 3 years to 30/6/2015		
(€26,000 + €27,000 + €31,000) ÷ 3 =		28,000
N = number of whole years' service =		12 years
L = tax free sum from pension scheme =		Nil
SCSB= €28,000 x 12/15= €22,400	SCSB	
Amount of termination payment chargeable:		
Ex gratia payment (before any deduction)		60,000
Less: revised basic exemption (as above)		(29,340)
Net termination payment		30,660
Less:		
Excess of SCSB	22,400	
Over revised basic exemption	(29,340)	
		N/a
Net amount chargeable		30,660

Notes:

1. Basic exemption is €10,160 + (12 x €765) = €19,340.

10.404 Relief by reduction of tax ('Top Slicing Relief') in respect of payments made prior to 1 January 2014

As noted earlier, top slicing relief was abolished by F(No 2)A 2013, s 4 in respect of payments made on or after 1 January 2014. Details of how the relief operated prior to 1 January 2014 are set out below.

TCA 1997, Sch 3 para 10 entitled the person liable to tax in respect of a termination payment to a further relief which is given as a reduction in the income tax chargeable on the payment. The method of computing this relief is set out in a formula which, for ease of explanation and without altering the result, can be modified slightly to the following:

$$(A - B) - P \times \frac{T}{I} = \text{amount of relief}$$

where:

A= the tax chargeable before any relief under TCA 1997, Sch 3 para 10 in respect of the taxpayer's total income (including the net amount chargeable under TCA 1997, s 123);

B= the amount of tax which would be chargeable in respect of his total income if no termination payment had been made;

P= the net amount chargeable under TCA 1997, s 123 (ie the termination payment less any relief given by reduction of the sum chargeable);

T= the aggregate of the amounts of the tax chargeable in respect of total income for the three years (five years prior to 1 January 2005) immediately preceding the tax year for which the termination payment is taxable (before any credit relief for foreign tax);

I= the aggregate of the taxpayer's taxable income for the same three (five) preceding tax years.

The formula does not seem to address the situation where a married couple are assessed jointly, but the spouse in receipt of the TCA 1997, s 123 payment is not the chargeable person (see **2.102**) for some or all of the relevant tax years. In practice, however, the Revenue apply the formula to the total income which is subject to joint assessment, irrespective of which spouse is the chargeable person. In *Tax Briefing Issue 67*, the Revenue Commissioners stated that they would accept a computation based on a notional separate assessment (see **3.504**) of a couple who were jointly assessed (ie by reference to the total income and tax payable attributable to the spouse in receipt of the termination payment) if that produced a more favourable result. A worked example is provided in *Tax Briefing 67*.

FA 2013, s 14 provided that top slicing relief does not apply to any payment in excess of €200,000 in respect of payments made on or after 1 January 2013. (TCA 1997, Sch 3 para 13).

Example 10.404.1

Mr A Martin retired on 1 July 2013 from Car Ltd. It has been established that the termination payment of €70,000 made in respect of his retirement from office on 1 July 2013 was reduced to a net chargeable amount of €30,660.

In order to calculate the TCA 1997, Sch 3 para 10 relief, the symbols in the formula have to be evaluated. P is already known, ie it is the €30,660 net chargeable amount. A and B are now determined by computing the income tax chargeable in respect of Mr Martin's total income for 2013 taken respectively as including the net chargeable amount (ie €30,660) and as excluding that amount, assuming that he is a single person and that his various income figures, personal tax credits, etc are as follows:

	2013 inclusive chargeable amount	*2013 exclusive chargeable amount*
	€	€
UK dividends	2,800	2,800
Other overseas income (subject to 15% withholding tax)	1,000	1,000
Emoluments from Car Ltd to 30/6/2013 (salary, fee, benefits, etc for 6 months)	17,100	17,100
Pension for 6 months to 31/12/2013	5,250	5,250
Termination payments (as chargeable)	30,660	
	56,810	26,150
Less:		
Qualifying annual payment to niece	(500)	(500)
Total income = taxable income	56,310	25,650

Income tax chargeable:[1]

A 2013 inclusive of chargeable amount		
€ 32,800 @ 20%	6,560	
€ 23,510 @ 41%	9,639	
€56,310		
B 2013 exclusive of chargeable amount		
€25,650 @ 20% =	-	5,130
	16,199	5,130
Less: credits say	(3,120)	(3,120)
Less: DTR on overseas income	(150)	(150)
A =	12,929	
B =		1,860

The necessary income, allowances, etc figures for the three preceding tax years to determine T and I for the formula are assumed to have been as follows:

	2010	*2011*	*2012*	*Total*
	€	€	€	
Total income	22,000	29,100	31,200	82,300
Less:				
Annual payment	(500)	(500)	(500)	

Statutory total income = taxable income	21,500	28,600	30,700	
Income tax:				
(after personal tax credits but before any DTR credits)	1,980	3,292	3,576	8,848

The relief may now be computed by assembling the figures for the five symbols in the formula as follows:

A = €12,929

B = €1,860

P = €30,660

T = €8,848 (tax for 3 years to 2012)

I = €82,300 (taxable income for 3 years to 2012)

It may be seen that the effective rate in respect of the previous three tax years is €8,848/ €82,300 = 10.75%, which is less than the marginal rates of 20 per cent and 41 per cent which apply when the chargeable termination payment is added to total income for 2013; accordingly relief will be due.

Additional tax on termination payment: (€12,929 – €1,860) = €11,069

Tax on Termination Payment at average rate for three prior tax years: [€30,660 x (€8,848/€82,300)] = €3,296

Relief due: €11,069 – €3,296= €7,773

After applying the TCA 1997, Sch 3 para 10 calculation, one can now calculate Mr Martin's final income tax liability for 2013 as follows:

	€
Other income (except TCA 1997, s 123 amount)	26,150
Net amount chargeable (TCA 1997, s 123)	30,660
	56,810
Less: Annual payment	(500)
Taxable income	56,310
€ 32,800 @ 20%	6,560
€ 23,510 @ 41%	9,639
€56,310	
	16,199
Less: Tax credits	(3,120)
	13,079
Less:	
TCA 1997, Sch 3 para 10 relief on retirement payment	(7,773)
	5,306
Less: Double tax relief	(150)
	**5,156
Add: Tax withheld on annual payment	100
Final income tax payable	5,256

**(subject to credit for PAYE on Sch E income, including retirement payment)

Notes:

1. In calculating the income tax chargeable in determining A, B and T, the tax on charges on income (the annual payment) is ignored.

10.405 Relief where connected payments

Connected payments in same year

The treatment of the basic exemption where a person benefits from two or more termination payments from the same employer or from associated employers has been dealt with in **10.402**. TCA 1997, Sch 3 para 7 contains corresponding rules modifying the TCA 1997, Sch 3 deduction in respect of the standard capital superannuation benefit in the case of any two or more such connected termination payments. It provides that TCA 1997, Sch 3 para 6 is to be applied by treating all such connected payments as a single payment equal to their aggregate amount, and by taking the standard capital superannuation benefit as being an amount equal to the sum of the standard capital superannuation benefits for each separate office or employment in respect of which the payments are made.

The matter is very simple where both connected payments are treated as Sch E income for the same tax year: only one calculation of the TCA 1997, Sch 3 para 6 relief is necessary and the deduction for the excess of the standard capital superannuation benefit(s) over the basic exemption may be made from the aggregate of the net termination payments. The net amount chargeable under TCA 1997, s 123 to be brought into the TCA 1997, Sch 3 para 10 calculation of the relief by reduction of the tax chargeable is the single aggregate figure after deducting the TCA 1997, Sch 3 para 6 relief.

Connected payments in different years

Where connected termination payments are treated as income of different tax years, the calculation of the separate net amounts chargeable under TCA 1997, s 123 for each year involved is slightly different. While the aggregate of the net amounts chargeable should be the same, the inclusion of the separate amounts as additional income in two (or more) tax years is likely to result in a difference in the final tax chargeable. The calculation of the TCA 1997, Sch 3 para 6 relief in such a case can best be explained by an example.

Example 10.405.1

Mr FY who has for many years been director of G Ltd and H Ltd, each wholly owned subsidiaries of K Ltd is dismissed from his offices on 1 February 2012 and 20 April 2013 respectively. He is paid €16,000 by G Ltd and €12,000 by H Ltd as compensation for loss of office. Assume that his SCSB in respect of G Ltd is €14,700 and in respect of H Ltd is €9,780 and that he is only entitled to a single basic exemption of €13,000 in relation to both offices (see **10.402**).

The net amounts chargeable under TCA 1997, s 123 in respect of the two compensation payments are computed as follows:

Tax year 2012:	€
Compensation payment (G Ltd)	16,000
Less: basic exemption	13,000
Net termination payment	3,000

Less:		
SCSB	14,700	
Less: basic exemption	13,000	
Sch 3 Pt 2 relief		(1,700)
Net amount chargeable 2012		1,300
Tax year 2013:		
Compensation payment (H Ltd)		12,000
Compensation paid to date: (16,000 + 12,000)	28,000	
Basic Exemption	Used 2012	
SCSB (14,700 + 9,780) = 24,480		
Less: Basic Exemption (13,000)	11,480	
Used 2012	(1,700)[1]	
SCSB 2013: (10,780 – 1,700) =		(9,780)
Net amount chargeable 2013		2,220[2]

Notes:

1. The aggregate of the total TCA 1997, Sch 3 para 6 relief is made by reference to the aggregate of the two net termination payments, ie €28,000 and the sum of the SCSBs, (€14,700 + €9,780) = €24,480 less the basic exemption, €13,000 = €11,480. However, the amount of this relief to be deducted in 2013 from the H Ltd payment is arrived at by deducting the €1,700 relief already obtained in 2012 on the G Ltd payment.
2. The net amounts chargeable may be summarised:

	€
2012: G Ltd payment	1,300
2013: H Ltd payment	2,220
	3,520

Relief by reduction of tax

As noted at **10.404**, this relief also known as 'top slicing relief' is no longer available in respect of payments made on or after 1 January 2014.

Where the tax is chargeable in the one tax year in respect of two or more connected payments, whether in relation to the same or associated offices or employments, the relief under TCA 1997, Sch 3 para 10 for the relevant year is computed by treating these payments as if they were a single payment equal to their aggregate amount (TCA 1997, Sch 3 paras 10, 11). The TCA 1997, Sch 3 para 10 computation is applicable without any modification to this aggregate amount.

For connected payments taxable in different years of assessment, the TCA 1997, Sch 3 para 10 formula is applied separately in each year by reference to the different net amounts chargeable in each year. For example, on the facts of **Example 10.405.1**, separate calculations of the TCA 1997, Sch 3 para 10 relief have to be made for 2012 (where P in the formula is €1,300) and for 2013 (where P is €2,220). In making the computation for 2012, both T and I in the formula would be based on the three tax years ended 31 December 2011. For the 2013 computation, the three years to 31 December

2012 would be used, including in the 2012 figures the G Ltd net chargeable amount of €1,300 and the tax payable on it.

10.406 Effect of foreign service

Foreign service relief only applies to payments made before 27 March 2013, the date of passing of FA 2013. For payments made after that date the relief has been abolished.

The European Commission asked Ireland (Case no 2011/4124) to change its legislation stating that it was contrary to the free movement of workers set out in the Treaties and the European Economic Area Agreement. The Commission stated that Irish law takes account of the number of years of service in group companies in Ireland, but not the years of service in group companies in other Member States and EEA countries (Norway Liechtenstein and Iceland). A press release of 9 December 2014 on the EU website states that the case was closed on 25 September 2014 following a change in legislation. It would appear that the Commission was referring to the Revenue practice whereby in determining an individual's period of service for the purpose of calculating the basic exemption and SCSB, where a termination payment is stated to be in respect of employment within a number of group companies Revenue allowed periods of service within a group to be taken into account. However, only service within Irish group companies could be taken into account. This practice would have been put in place at a time when relief would have been available for termination payments attributable to foreign service.

The Revenue's revised Pt 05.05.09 of their Manuals now states that the employment does not have to commence in Ireland and gives the example of an individual who worked for a Belgian company and then moved to a group company in Ireland after 10 years. It states that these 10 years can be included for the purposes of calculating the basic exemption and for the number of years' service for the SCSB relief.

The rules as they applied prior to 27 March 2013 are set out below.

'Foreign service' is defined, in relation to an office or employment, as service such that:

(a) tax was not chargeable in respect of the emoluments of the office or employment;

(b) in the case of an office or employment within Sch E, tax under that Schedule was not chargeable in respect of the whole of the emoluments thereof; or

(c) in the case of an office or employment that is a foreign possession within the meaning of Sch D Case III (see **13.104**), tax did not fall to be computed on the basis of the income arising from the office or employment under TCA 1997, s 71(1) (TCA 1997, s 201(1)(a)).

Generally, this means that for service in any period to be treated as foreign service, it is necessary that the holder of the office or emolument be resident in that period outside the State and exercise the office or employment outside the State. However, a resident person whose emoluments come from a foreign office or employment in respect of which he is taxable on the remittance basis (see **13.401**) will be treated as having foreign service even if he was carrying out his duties in the State up to 31 December 2005 (see **13.104**). A resident person who may be working outside the State for a period, but whose remuneration from his employment is paid within the State so as to be fully assessable under Sch E, is not regarded as having any foreign service in that period.

A director of an Irish incorporated company whose remuneration as a director is always taxable under Sch E (see **13.104**) does not have any period of foreign service in relation to his office as director, even if he should carry out most or all of his duties of the office abroad. However, this does not prevent such a director's having a period of foreign service in respect of any executive employment outside the State if he is paid separately for his duties in that employment, and if any of the above conditions for foreign service are met in respect of that employment.

The legislation charging termination payments under TCA 1997, s 123 excludes, in effect, from the charge to tax any termination payment attributable to 'foreign service' made up to the 27 March 2013 (date of the passing of FA 2013). It does so in two ways. First, TCA 1997, s 201(4) exempts altogether any payment in respect of an office or employment in which the holder's total service included foreign service of a prescribed minimum length (which may include one or more separate periods of foreign service). Secondly, where the length of the foreign service is insufficient to qualify for the total exemption, TCA 1997, Sch 3 para 9 provides an additional deduction in arriving at the net amount chargeable under TCA 1997, s 123 which excludes the proportion of that amount attributable to the foreign service.

TCA 1997, s 201(4) exempts the total payment where the length of the foreign service comprised:

(a) 75 per cent of the whole period of service down to the relevant date (in any case);

(b) the whole of the last 10 years (where the total period of service to the relevant date exceeded 10 years); or

(c) 50 per cent of the total period of service, provided that it includes any 10 of the last 20 years, down to the relevant date (where the total period of service exceeded 20 years).

The 'relevant date' is defined by TCA 1997, s 201(1)(a) in the same manner as applies for the basic exemption (see **10.402**). Several examples to illustrate the rules of TCA 1997, s 201(4) may be useful. In each case, it is assumed that the employee terminates his employment on 31 December 2012 (the relevant date) and that he receives a termination payment that would be taxable if it is not exempted due to his foreign service.

Example 10.406.1

Mr X joined the company on 1 January 2007. His periods of foreign service (overseas selling companies) and service in the company's Dublin office were as follows:

	Foreign	*Home office*
	Months	*Months*
1/1/2007 to 31/3/2008		15.0
1/4/2008 to 15/10/2012	54.5	
16/10/2012 to 31/12/2012		2.5
	54.5	17.5

Since this foreign service comprises = 54.5/ (54.5 + 17.5) = 75.7 per cent of his total six years' service, the foreign service exemption applies in respect of the termination payment.

Example 10.406.2

Mr Y joined the company on 1/1/1981. His periods of foreign and home service were as follows:

	Foreign	*Home office*
	Months	*Months*
1/1/1981 to 30/11/2001		251
1/12/2001 to 31/12/2012	133	

Although only approximately one third of his total service is foreign, his foreign service has exceeded 10 years and the whole of the last 10 years have been on foreign service. Therefore, the foreign service exemption applies.

Example 10.406.3

Mr Z joined the company on 1 October 1989. His periods of foreign and home service have been as follows:

	Foreign	*Home office*
	Months	*Months*
1/10/1989 to 31/12/1990		15
1/1/1991 to 31/12/2003	156	
1/1/2003 to 31/3/2010		87
1/4/2010 to 30/9/2012	42	
1/10/2012 to 31/12/2012		3
	198	105

Since the total period of service (22 years 3 months= 267 months) exceeded 20 years, and as the foreign service periods totalled more than 50 per cent of the total period of service, the foreign service exemption applies.

In *Nichols v Gibson* [1996] STC 1008, it was held that the UK equivalent of TCA 1997, s 123 was an independent charging provision and that its territorial limits were contained in the UK equivalent of TCA 1997, s 123(4) and not in the general Sch E charging provisions. It followed that a payment, even though made to a non-resident who exercised no duties in the UK in the relevant tax year, fell within the section. The 'stand alone' nature of the TCA 1997, s 123 charge is underlined in the Irish context by the fact that it can impose a Sch E charge in respect of a Sch D Case III employment.

As noted above, no foreign service relief applies in respect of payments made on or after 27 March 2013, the date of passing of FA 2013.

Relief for non-exempted foreign service

TCA 1997, Sch 3 para 9 provides relief in calculating the net amount chargeable under TCA 1997, s 123, in addition to the deductions otherwise available, where a termination payment is made in respect of an office or employment which has included foreign service, but where the amount of that service was insufficient to qualify for the TCA 1997, s 201(4) total exemption. Before making this additional deduction under TCA 1997, Sch 3 para 9, any other deduction to which the holder (or past holder) of the office or employment is entitled is first given to arrive at a provisional net amount chargeable. This provisional amount is then reduced by TCA 1997, Sch 3 para 9 by an amount equal to the sum that bears the same proportion to the provisional net amount chargeable as the length of the foreign service bears to the length of the total service before the relevant date.

Example 10.406.4

Mr G Mander was dismissed from his position with Soft Soap Ltd on 30 September 2012 after 18 years' service during which his periods of foreign and home office service were as follows:

	Foreign *Months*	*Home office* *Months*
1/10/1994 to 31/3/1999		54
1/4/1999 to 31/3/2012	156	
1/4/2012 to 30/9/2012		6
	156	60

Mr Mander's foreign service (156/ (156 + 60) = 72.2 per cent) is less than 75 per cent of his total period of service, he did not have the whole of his last 10 years' service in foreign service and, as his total service did not amount to 20 years, the fact that more than 50 per cent of the service was foreign service does not help him. He does not qualify for the total exemption under TCA 1997, s 201(4).

Mr Mander was paid a sum of €36,000 as compensation for the loss of his employment. He does not receive any tax free lump sum under any approved pension scheme, etc. He has not previously made any other claim for relief under TCA 1997, Sch 3. His standard capital superannuation benefit (SCSB) is determined to be €35,500.

Based on these facts, the net amount chargeable on him under TCA 1997, s 123 (after he has claimed relief under TCA 1997, s 201(4), Sch 3 is calculated as follows:

	€	€
Compensation payment		36,000
Less:		
Basic exemption €10,160 + (€765 x 18) =	23,930	
Increase under TCA 1997, Sch 3 para 8	10,000	
		33,930
Net termination payment		2,070
Less: SCSB	35,500	
Less: basic exemption	33,930	
		(1,570)
Provisional net amount chargeable		500
Less:		
Deduction under TCA 1997, Sch 3 para 9:		
Length of foreign service: 156 months		
Length of total service: 216 months		
Deduction is €500 x 156/216		361
Final net amount chargeable under TCA 1997, s 123		139

(Mr Mander is also entitled to relief under TCA 1997, Sch 3 para 10 by way of reduction of the tax payable in respect of this chargeable amount of €139.)

10.407 Compensation for business reorganisation, pay restructuring etc

Business reorganisations

TCA 1997, s 480 provides a different form of relief in respect of certain sums chargeable to tax under the normal rules of Sch E, ie sums which are treated as emoluments, perquisites, etc under the main charging rule of TCA 1997, s 112, although it seems unlikely that such a payment could fall outside TCA 1997, s 112 (see **10.111**). The application of the relief to any payment chargeable to tax under TCA 1997, s 123 is specifically excluded. The relief cannot be claimed by a part-time director or employee or by a proprietary director or employee (ie a director or employee able, either directly or indirectly, to control more than 15 per cent of the ordinary share capital of a company making the payment in question).

Subject to these exceptions, the relief may be claimed in respect of any payment chargeable to tax under Sch E made to the holder of an office or employment to compensate for a reduction or a possible reduction of future remuneration arising from:

(a) a reorganisation of the business of the employer;

(b) a change in the working procedures, working methods, duties or rates of remuneration of the office or employment; or

(c) a change in the place where the duties of the office or employment are performed.

The relief from tax given by TCA 1997, s 480 is in all cases granted by way of repayment (TCA 1997, s 480(5)(a)). The employer making any such compensation payment is required to deduct income tax from the full amount of the payment under the normal PAYE procedure. The individual in receipt of the payment is then entitled, on making a claim and proving the relevant facts to the satisfaction of the inspector, to have his total income tax liability for the tax year reduced to the sum of the two following amounts:

(a) the amount which would have been payable by him for that year if he had not received the payment; and

(b) an amount equal to tax on the whole of the payment computed at a special rate (TCA 1997, s 480(3)).

The special rate at which the compensation payment is taxed is determined by taking the additional income tax payable on the assumption that one third of the payment only is added to the individual's total income (excluding the payment) for the relevant tax year, and by dividing this notional additional tax payable by a sum equal to one third of the payment (TCA 1997, s 480(4)). The application of this special rate may not always lead to a reduction of the income tax otherwise payable. If the effect of including only one third of the payment in total income in the notional tax computation has the result that the special rate is lower than the rate(s) at which the payment would, assuming it to be the highest part of the individual's total income, otherwise be taxed, then there should be a net reduction in the final income tax payable.

Example 10.407.1

Mr EZ, a single person is paid €3,000 on 24 October 2016 to compensate him for a likely reduction in his future earnings in his present employment following a major reorganisation of his employer's business. It is accepted that the payment of €3,000 is taxable under TCA 1997, s 112 as a profit of his employment.

Mr EZ, whose income for the year 2015 totals €14,000 apart from this compensation payment, claims relief under TCA 1997, s 480. This relief is computed as follows:

	Income for year	*Income including 1/3 of payment*	*Income excluding payment*
	€	€	€
Income (apart from payment)	14,000	14,000	14,000
Compensation payment:			
Full amount	3,000		
One third		1,000	
Taxable income	17,000	15,000	14,000
Income tax payable before tax credits, etc:			
At 20%	3,400	3,000	2,800
	3,400	3,000	2,800

Special rate for TCA 1997, s 480 relief:

Additional tax due to including 1/3 of payment €3,000 – €2,800 = €200

Special Rate= [Additional Tax/ (1/3 x Payment)] x 100

Final income tax payable 2016:	€
Tax on income (excluding payment):	
As above	2,800
Tax on compensation €3,000 x 20%	600
Final income tax payable	3,400

Special Rate= [200/ (1/3 x 3000)] x 100= 20%.

On the assumption that Mr EZ has already paid tax of €3,400 under PAYE in respect of his total income for the year (including the €3,000 compensation payment), he is not entitled to any repayment under TCA 1997, s 480.

10.408 Returns by employer

Any employer or other person who makes any payment chargeable to tax under TCA 1997, s 123 is required to deliver particulars of it in writing to the inspector of tax no later than 14 days after the end of the tax year in which the payment is made (TCA 1997, s 123(6)). For example, if a payment is made to an employee on 14 May 2015 by way of compensation for loss of office, the person who made the payment must advise the inspector no later than 14 January 2016. Failure to give this notice to the inspector may give rise to a penalty of €3,000 (TCA 1997, s 1052).

TCA 1997, s 201(2A) provides for the obligatory reporting to the Revenue Commissioners, within 46 days of the end of the tax year, of details of any lump sum payments treated as exempt under TCA 1997, s 201(2)(a) (payments made on death, or on account of injury to or disability of the employee). The particulars to be furnished are:

(a) the name and address of the person to whom the payment was made;

(b) that person's personal public service number (PPS no);

(c) the amount of the payment; and

(d) the basis on which the payment is not chargeable to tax under Taxes Consolidation Act 1997, s 123, indicating, if the payment is made on account of injury or disability, the extent of the relevant injury or disability.

10.409 Damages

In *BTC v Gourley* [1955] 3 All ER 796, a personal injury case, the House of Lords held that where an award of damages included an amount based on loss of future taxable earnings, and the damages themselves were not taxable, then the amount of those damages had to be reduced to reflect the tax which would have been deducted from the earnings in question.

In *Glover v BLN Ltd (No 2)* [1973] IR 432, the plaintiff received damages for loss of office based on loss of future salary. These were subject to the termination payment rules of TCA 1997, s 123 and TCA 1997, s 201 as they stood at the relevant time, which granted a fixed exemption of £3,000. Kenny J applied the principle in *Gourley* to the first £3,000 of the damages awarded. The learned judge also held that the difficulties of estimating the impact of taxation in subsequent years of assessment on the plaintiff's future earnings would not prevent the exercise being undertaken, and indicated that current tax rates and allowances should be used for this purpose, (but note the approach of the Supreme Court in *Griffiths v Van Raaj* [1985] ILRM 582). The learned judge also made clear that there was no basis for distinguishing between the treatment of damages received in personal injury cases and those received in wrongful dismissal cases.

In *Lynsdale Fashion Manufacturers v Rich* [1973] STC 32 the taxpayer, who had been wrongfully dismissed, was awarded damages for loss of sales commission which he would otherwise have earned (the principle in *Gourley* clearly applied). It was held that the tax which he would have paid on that commission should be computed on the difference between:

(a) the tax payable on the taxpayer's notional income, inclusive of the earnings forgone; and

(b) the tax payable on his income exclusive of those earnings.

In effect, therefore the income foregone was treated as the taxpayer's top slice of income in a notional computation, with any deduction or reliefs (or additional amounts thereof) attributable to the income set off against such income.

The reverse side of the coin to the decision in *Gourley* case is that where the damages in question are subject to tax, no adjustment will be required. This is obviously a rather rough form of justice, since the potential impact of tax on the income foregone may differ significantly from the actual impact of tax on the damages received. However, this approach has the merit of sparing the court from becoming involved in complex and speculative tax calculations (see *Deeny v Gooda Walker* [1996] STC 299, discussed at **5.204**).

An issue which has not been satisfactorily resolved by the UK courts is the treatment of damages only part of which is eligible for exemption (as indeed was the position in the *Glover* case). In *Glover* it was held that the *Gourley* principle should apply only to the element of the damages which were tax exempt. Logically, this should be achieved by firstly applying the *Gourley* principle to all of the damages (ie so that they are based on net of tax earnings). If the amount thus computed is less than the exemption available under TCA 1997, s 201 then no further adjustment is needed. If the amount thus computed exceeds the exemption available under TCA 1997, s 201, the excess falls outside the *Gourley* principle and should be adjusted accordingly (ie should be based on pre-tax earnings).

A modified version of this approach was adopted in *Stewart v Glentaggart* 42 TC 318 and followed in *Shove v Downs Surgical* [1984] IRLR 17. This again entailed firstly computing the damages taking account of the notional tax which would have been suffered by the plaintiff on the earning's foregone. The amount thus calculated was then grossed up by the amount of any tax charged under the equivalent of TCA 1997, s 123.

In *Cooke v Walsh* [1984] ILRM 208, the *Gourley* principle was applied in a personal injury case. The damages in that case were based on the plaintiff's earnings net of tax and the levies (see also *Allen v O'Suilleabhain* (11 March 1997) SC).

For a discussion of the taxation of damages in the context of trading (and professional) profits see **5.204**.

Division 11 PAYE, PRSI and Profit Sharing Schemes

11.1 PAYE

11.101 Emoluments subject to PAYE

TCA 1997, Pt 42 (ss 983–987) requires a person making any payment of any emoluments to which that Chapter applies to deduct or repay income tax (as the case may require) and to account for it to the Revenue Commissioners in accordance with the rules of the PAYE system (TCA 1997, s 985). This obligation imposed on the employer to operate the PAYE system exists in every case where there is a payment of emoluments, those emoluments are chargeable to tax under Sch E, and the emoluments in question are not excluded from the application of PAYE by the rules of TCA 1997, s 984 (see **11.102**). The deductions made by the employer in accordance with the PAYE system are treated as discharging an equivalent amount of the salary or wages due to the employee (TCA 1997, s 997(2)). In addition, as explained in **11.2**, the collection of employees' and employers' PRSI contributions (including the Universal Social Charge) is fully integrated into the PAYE system. Accordingly, all references to the operation of PAYE hereafter are to the collection thereunder of income tax together with the associated PRSI and Universal Social Charge. FA 2008, s 17 inserted TCA 1997, s 986(1)(k) which enables the Revenue Commissioners to make regulations for the collection and recovery, to the extent that they deem appropriate and if the employee does not object, of tax in respect of income other than emoluments which has not otherwise been recovered during the year. In other words, this provides statutorily that the tax on minor amounts of non-PAYE income may be collected through the PAYE system rather than the self-assessment system, unless the employee requests that this should not occur. Minor amounts of income are net income of less than €3,174.

The Universal Social Charge operated on a 'stand alone' basis for 2011 and was computed on a non-cumulative week one or month one basis as appropriate. Unless the employee had been in continuous employment with the same employer throughout the tax year any consequent overpayments of the Universal Social Charge were required to be claimed from the Revenue Commissioners either by submitting a prescribed form or availing of the online facility on the Revenue Commissioners' website. From 2012 the USC is deducted on a cumulative basis in the same way as PAYE is deducted based on USC rates and thresholds as provided by Revenue in the employee's tax credit certificate. Detailed guidance on the operation of the Universal Social Charge is available on a FAQ sheet which may be downloaded from the Revenue Commissioners' website and for further reading see **3.404**.

The term 'emoluments', as used in TCA 1997, Pt 42, is defined as anything assessable to income tax under Sch E, and any reference to the payment of emoluments is to be taken as including a payment on account of emoluments (TCA 1997, s 983). It therefore includes all payments of salaries, fees, wages, perquisites, etc, whether taxable directly under the main Sch E charging section (TCA 1997, s 112) or by virtue of any other provision in the Income Tax Acts which requires the particular payment to be taxed under Sch E (see **10.101**).

Payment in respect of expenses taxable under TCA 1997, s 117 (see **10.202**) made in the form of a round sum allowance, is a payment of emoluments to the employee under general principles and should be included in gross and taxable pay. In practice, payments made according to an approved scale are not included in 'taxable pay'. For a fuller discussion of the position see **10.202**.

Payments by the employer to the employee as a direct reimbursement of actual expenses incurred wholly, exclusively and necessarily by the employee in performing the duties of his employment are not, in practice, normally included in taxable pay subject to PAYE (reg 10(3)). Reimbursements of other expenses such as qualifying professional subscriptions, certain course fees and exam fees, home telephone expenses (up to 50 per cent), etc may also be treated as non-taxable items: see **10.204**.

The term also includes any pension or similar payment that is chargeable under Sch E. It was generally accepted that although the term 'payment' is wide enough in some contexts to include non-pecuniary payments, only payments from which it was practicable to deduct tax fell within the scope of the PAYE system under TCA 1997, s 985 until legislation was brought in under TCA 1997, s 985A to treat the provision of benefits in kind (apart from certain awards of shares made before 31 December 2010 and employer's contributions to a PRSA) as notional payments to which the PAYE system applies.

The notional pay which is subject to PAYE in respect of a taxable benefit must be based on the 'best estimate' which can reasonably be made by the employer, generally at the time at which the benefit is provided, by reference to the valuation rules set out in TCA 1997, s 118 to s 122A see **10.205–10.212** inclusive. In many cases the calculation of the benefit may be straightforward but in some cases the valuation may be problematic, for example, in a case where the valuation of the benefit of a car will vary in relation to the level of business mileage in the tax year or where apportionment is required in respect of benefits enjoyed concurrently by a number of employees. The Revenue will accept that a 'best estimate' has been made where a genuine attempt has been made to calculate the taxable benefit based on all relevant details available to the employer at the time and where it has been reviewed prior to the end of the tax year where appropriate (for example, in the case of a car with potentially high business mileage: see **10.208**).

In most cases, PAYE must be operated at the time the benefit is provided. However, in the case of benefits consisting of the private use of a company car, a company van, a preferential loan or the use of accommodation or other assets provided by the employer, the notional pay may spread over the period in the tax year during which the relevant asset is made available (reg 17A).

The Revenue guidelines make clear that in the case of the discharge of pecuniary liabilities of employees it is the date on which the relevant payment or payments are made which determines when PAYE should be deducted.

The PAYE liability thus arising will be deducted from the first available cash payments made to the employee concerned (reg 16A). Where the liability exceeds the cash payments the employer is still obliged to pay over any excess PAYE which he is required but unable to deduct (reg 16A). The employee will be entitled to a credit for such excess PAYE against any assessment made on him for the tax year in which the excess arose (TCA 1997, s 985A(4A)).

The employer is entitled to recover the excess from the employee by deduction from subsequent payments of emoluments or by way of direct reimbursement. If the employee fails to make good the excess before the end of the relevant tax year (extended to the following 31 March in practice), the excess will itself be treated as a notional payment for PAYE purposes in the following tax year (reg 16B). If the employee has left the employment before the following 31 March, any unrecouped excess should instead be returned on Form P11D (see **10.213**). The Revenue Commissioners will not seek to apply the preferential loan rules (see **10.211**) to the amount of any unrecouped excess.

It is provided by TCA 1997, s 985B (inserted by FA 2004, s 9) that employers may make arrangements with the Revenue Commissioners to account directly to the Revenue for tax payable in respect of minor and irregular benefits. Before sanctioning such arrangements, the Revenue Commissioners are statutorily obliged to take account of a number of factors including the total amount of emoluments covered by the relevant arrangement, the total number of employees covered by the arrangement and their respective rates of income tax, together with any such other matters as are agreed to be relevant between the Revenue and the employer in respect of the emoluments concerned (TCA 1997, s 985B(5)). The Revenue have made clear that arrangements of this kind will not apply to payments of wages or bonuses, round sum allowances or significant benefits such as company cars or preferential loans granted to individual employees.

Where the arrangements apply, PAYE must be calculated by reference to the 'grossed up' equivalent of the relevant benefit, ie so that the grossed up amount net of PAYE is equal to the value of the benefit received; the calculation must be carried out by reference to each individual employee's income tax and, if relevant, PRSI rate. The benefits in question will not be treated as income of the employees involved for income tax or PRSI purposes nor will the employees be entitled to any credit for the income tax accounted for under the arrangement by the employer nor for the PRSI in respect of their contributions record.

Where an employer otherwise wishes to provide benefits to employees on a 'tax paid' basis, and the benefits are not treated as minor and irregular as described above, PAYE and PRSI must be calculated by reference to the grossed-up amount of the benefit using the employee's marginal tax rate(s) but the notional payment thus calculated will count as part of the employee's income for the year and he will be entitled to a credit for the income tax so deducted (see PAYE reg 25).

Share Awards

FA 2011, s 10 inserted TCA 1997, s 985A(1B) to provide that certain shares awarded after 1 January 2011 are subject to PAYE. The shares in question are any form of shares including stock, but only if the shares, etc are shares in the employer company or in a company which has control (as defined by TCA 1997, s 432) over the employer company (TCA 1997, s 985A(1A) inserted by FA 2004, s 9). Exemption from employee's PRSI only applies for 2011 where the share-based remuneration agreements were the subject of a written agreement between the employer and the employee executed prior to 1 January 2011. Therefore with effect from 1 January 2011, where an employer makes notional payments to employees in the form of shares, it is obliged to account for income tax, USC and PRSI on the value of those shares. It is the net value of the shares awarded which is to be treated as notional pay at the time the shares are given to the employee. With effect from 1 January 2012, if the employee does not otherwise provide the employer with sufficient means to do so the employer is entitled to withhold and to realise sufficient shares to fund that income tax liability. Even though the employee has not actually received the shares, he is treated as if the value of the shares had been paid by the employer (TCA 1997, s 985A(4B)).

Application of PAYE

The Revenue Commissioners Employer's Guide to PAYE states that remuneration voted to a director which is credited to an account with the company on which he is free to draw is his pay for PAYE purposes (para **5.10**). Similarly, a payment applied in the reduction of a debt due to the company by the director is treated as pay.

In *Garforth v Newsmith Stainless Ltd* [1979] STC 129, the court held that where a company credited bonuses to directors' accounts on which they were free to draw at any time, this equated to payments. The court noted that different considerations would have applied if the right to draw on the account had been contingent (eg on the passing of a resolution by the board of directors or at a general meeting of company members). Note, in this regard, the decision in *Macpherson v Bond* [1985] STC 678, discussed at **8.102**. The decision in *Garforth* was approved at first instance in *Dormers Building (London) Ltd v C & E* [1984] STC 735, a VAT case.

Payments on account, or in advance, of director's remuneration are also treated as pay. Where the remuneration is subsequently voted to the director in such a way as to constitute pay (see above) only the excess is treated as pay (paras 28, 29). It may not always be easy to decide whether or not payments to a director are on account of remuneration where the director does not have a service contract. This is particularly true if the director's account with the company is in credit at the time the payment is made.

A sum described as an advance of salary which was repayable on demand (albeit primarily repayable by way of deduction from future payments of salary) was held not to be a payment 'on account of' emoluments in *Williams v Todd* [1988] STC 676. The key point was that a sum repayable on demand was in the nature of a loan and could not be a repayment of salary; the legal realities accordingly prevailed over the label given to the transaction by the parties (see **1.407**).

Third party liabilities paid by a company on behalf of a director have been held by an Appeal Commissioners' decision (12 March 2013) to be subject to PAYE/PRSI on the amounts actually paid by the company. The Revenue Commissioners had sought the payments to be taxed on a re-grossed basis. It is understood that the Revenue have expressed dissatisfaction with the decision.

For the purposes of TCA 1997, Pt 42 (and for the relevant regulations (Income Tax (Employments) (Consolidated) Regulations 2001 (as subsequently amended)); 'Regulations' hereafter), TCA 1997, s 983 defines the word 'employee' as any person in receipt of emoluments and 'employer' as any person paying emoluments. It is clear that in many cases, the references in the regulations to an 'employer' must be to the actual employer or at the very least, to the person who pays emoluments to the employee on an ongoing basis (eg reg 11(2) which requires the inspector to send the 'employer' a certificate of tax credits': see **11.103**). In *Booth v Mirror Group of Newspapers plc* [1992] STC 615, it was held that any person (in this case a company connected to the employer which paid emoluments) had to operate PAYE, even where a 'one off' payment was concerned. Consistently with this analysis, the Revenue Commissioners have expressed the view that where a car distributor makes awards for sales performance directly to individuals who are the employees of other garage businesses, the distributor is liable to account for PAYE in respect of such awards.

Given that the payer in this kind of case would not hold a Certificate of Tax Credits and Standard Rate Cut-Off Point (see **11.103** below), he would have to operate PAYE on an emergency basis. In *Hearne v O'Cionna* IV ITR 113, it was similarly held that where a company paid emoluments on behalf of a partnership it was liable to account for PAYE thereon. Where an individual is placed by an employment agency with a client who becomes the employer of that individual, it follows that the employment agency will be liable to operate PAYE if it pays the individual's wages or salary to him (see *Tax Briefing 31*). In some cases, however, the individual may be regarded as employed with neither the agency or the client: see **10.103**. It remains debatable as to whether the obligation to deduct PAYE can apply to every person who pays emoluments, including, say, a person who gives a tip to a waiter (although, naturally, the Revenue Commissioners would not wish to take the point in those circumstances). In *Figael v Fox* [1992] STC 83, it was held that an employer who distributed tips received from customers to his employees was liable to account for PAYE thereon. This was despite the fact that the employer never had a legal interest in the money paid as tips. It is understood that the Appeal Commissioners reached a contrary decision in an appeal heard in 1992, concerning the distribution of gratuities paid by credit card to hotel employees. Revenue have since clarified, in their FAQs to the Employer's Guide to PAYE, that where tips are given to the employer, PAYE/PRSI must be applied to the amount paid to the employee. If paid by credit card, the employer must deduct PAYE/PRSI when distributing to the employee. If an employee receives the tips directly there is no obligation on the employer to operate PAYE/PRSI, however the employee is obliged to include the tips received in their annual income tax return. The author is aware of two Appeal Commissioners' decisions on the issue of tips. In each case, the employer argued that a troncmaster was in place and therefore they had no obligations as regards PAYE/PRSI on the tips. The Appeal Commissioners found, on a question of fact, for the employer in one case and the Revenue in the other. It is understood that the employer won in the case where it could be demonstrated that the troncmaster system operated properly and adequate records were maintained.

One important example of where the context clearly seems to require an exception to be made to the wide definition of 'employer' is provided by reg 3. This states (broadly) that where an employee (E) works under the 'general control and management' of a person (A), as opposed to his immediate employer (B), then A will be deemed to be the 'principal employer' and will be responsible for the operation of PAYE in respect of E's emoluments. Where B actually pays the emoluments, then B must pay the correct net amount of emoluments to E, and A must then adjust the amount reimbursed to B in respect of E's emoluments accordingly (it is highly arguable that the regulation is accordingly intended only to apply where the cost of the emoluments falls on the third party).

The reference to the 'immediate employer' seems to be to the legal employer and not merely the person who happens to be the paymaster (since the regulation envisages that the immediate employer may pay emoluments to the employee, but that he may not necessarily do so). This was the view taken by Hobhouse J in *Booth v Mirror Group of Newspapers plc* [1992] STC 615 (but note that in *Andrews v King* [1991] STC 481 the Inland Revenue conceded, apparently for the purposes of that case only, that a paymaster could be regarded as the 'immediate employer'). One practical effect of reg 3 therefore seems to be that where an employee is seconded to work for a third party, the third party and not the legal employer will be responsible for PAYE in respect of emoluments paid under the arrangement, irrespective of who actually pays them (although, as noted above, where the immediate employer pays the emoluments, this seems to apply only where the immediate employer recovers the cost of the emoluments from the third party).

Transnational employees

In *IRC v Herd* [1993] STC 436, the House of Lords held that PAYE did not apply to the payment of a single sum, only part of which was liable to tax under Sch E. It may therefore have been arguable, for example, that in strictness PAYE should not have been operated on the Sch E earnings of a non-resident individual, only part of whose duties are exercised in the State (see **13.607**); in practice, the Revenue would have always been likely to vigorously resist any such contention. In any case since 1 January 2006, the earnings from a foreign-source employment held by either an Irish resident or (although subject to argument: see **13.607**) a non-resident are taxable under Sch E to the extent that they are attributable to Irish duties, (FA 2006, s 15). This development under which an employment may be partially taxable on duties performed in the State (TCA 1997, s 18(2) as amended by FA 2006) under Sch E and partially under Sch D Case III raises the issue in particularly acute form. Consequently, TCA 1997, s 985E provides a statutory basis for applying PAYE in cases where an employment is exercised only partly within the State.

TCA 1997, s 985E applies in relation to an employee who works or will work (ie performs or will perform the duties of his office or employment: TCA 1997, s 985D(1)) in the State in a tax year and also works or is likely to work outside the State in the same tax year (TCA 1997, s 985E(2)); for convenience, in this text, he will be referred to as a 'transnational employee'. Where in such circumstances it appears to the inspector of taxes that some of the transnational employee's income will be taxable under Sch E but an as yet unascertainable proportion of his income may not be so taxable, the inspector may issue a direction determining the proportion of the payments in that year which should be subject to PAYE. The determination will be made only on an application by the 'appropriate person', ie the person designated by the employer for these purposes or failing this, the employer itself. In *SP IT/3/07* (as amended in December 2017, see **11.102**), the Revenue Commissioners indicate that apportionment on a time basis between Irish and non-Irish duties will be the appropriate method to be used by the employee and that the need to apply for a direction should only arise relatively rarely, *viz* in a case where the employer is uncertain as to the correct split between those respective duties. They also set out their view of the method of computation required where tax equalisation arrangements apply in respect of a transnational employee, together with some worked examples. In effect the net 'take home' pay attributable to Irish duties must be grossed up to the amount which after deduction of Irish PAYE income tax (and if relevant employee's PRSI and/or the Universal Social Charge) corresponds to the amount of take home pay.

'Payments' are those made of income, or on account of, income of the employee (which presumably includes income taxable in part under Sch D Case III on the arising or remittance basis or 'income' which is partly non-taxable, eg where a non-resident with an Irish employment performs some duties within the State and some outside the State). Taken literally, the section applies to all payments made to a transnational employee, whether of employment earnings or not, but logically it can only refer to payments of earnings as such. Where a direction has been issued, then the due proportion of payments made in the year will be treated as emoluments for the purposes of the PAYE regulations (TCA 1997, s 985E(7)). In the absence of a direction, all payments of, or on account of, income made to a transnational employee must be treated as emoluments for the purposes of the PAYE regulations (TCA 1997, s 985E(4)). The section provides that references to payments made by the employer include payments made by a person acting on behalf of the employer and at the expense of the employer or of a person connected (within the meaning of TCA 1997, s 10) with the employer (TCA 1997, s 985E(1)(b)); in fact there are no such references in the section which seems simply to treat payments of earnings to transnational employees as consisting wholly of PAYE emoluments in the absence of a determination to the contrary.

An application for a direction must provide such information as is available and is relevant to the giving of the direction (TCA 1997, s 985E(4)). The direction must:

(a) specify the employee to whom and the year of assessment to which it relates;
(b) be given by notice to the appropriate person; and
(c) may be withdrawn by notice to the appropriate person from a date specified in the notice (TCA 1997, s 985E(5)).

The specified date may not be earlier than 30 days from the date on which the notice of the withdrawal is given (TCA 1997, s 985E(6)). The section makes clear that any deductions of PAYE under its provisions are without prejudice to:

(a) any assessment in respect of the income of the employee, or
(b) any right of the employee to repayment of income tax overpaid and any obligation to pay income tax underpaid (TCA 1997, s 985E(4)).

In a case where s 985D applies (see **11.102**), ie where non-resident persons default on their obligation to deduct PAYE, with the result that the person for whom the transnational employee works (the relevant person) is obliged to operate PAYE, it is provided that the reference to the employer in the definition of 'appropriate person' above includes a reference to the 'relevant person'. In other words, the person for whom the employee actually works and who has become responsible for operating PAYE under TCA 1997, s 985D may designate the appropriate person or itself act as the appropriate person in applying for a determination from the inspector (TCA 1997, s 985E(10)(a)). It is also provided that references to payments made by the employer include payments deemed to have been made by the 'relevant person' (TCA 1997, s 985E(10)(b)). In fact, as noted above, there are no such references in the section.

Payments by intermediaries

With effect from 31 March 2006, TCA 1997, s 985C as inserted by FA 2006, s 16, provides that where any payment of emoluments is made to an employee by an intermediary of the employer (which latter term again presumably denotes 'employer' in the strict legal sense, as opposed to any person which pays emoluments), the employer will be liable to account for any PAYE which falls due if the intermediary fails to account for it in accordance with the PAYE regulations (TCA 1997, s 985C(1), (2)). An intermediary is defined for these purposes as either:

(a) a person acting on behalf of the employer, where the payment of emoluments is made at the expense of the employer (or of a person connected with the employer as defined by TCA 1997, s 10); or
(b) a trustee holding property for a group, or class, of persons which includes the employee (TCA 1997, s 985C(4)).

If the amount paid by the intermediary is the amount to which the employee is entitled after deduction of tax, the employer is treated as making a payment of the total of the amount paid and the tax due in respect of that amount; otherwise he is treated as making a payment of the gross amount paid by the intermediary (TCA 1997, s 985C(3)).

These provisions are aimed primarily at artificial structures (typically involving the use of offshore trusts to pay remuneration) designed to take advantage of the principle established in *Clarke v Oceanic Contractors* [1983] STC 35 (discussed in **11.102**).

Mobile workforce

TCA 1997, s 985F (inserted by FA 2006, s 16) applies where it appears to the Revenue Commissioners that:

(a) a person (the 'relevant person') has entered into, or is likely to enter into, an agreement that employees of another person ('the 'contractor') will in any period work (ie carry out the duties of their office or employment: TCA 1997, s 985D(1)) for the relevant person, but not as its employees;
(b) payments of emoluments are likely to be made either by or on behalf of the contractor to the employees in respect of work done in the period concerned; and
(c) PAYE should be operated on such payments but it is likely that in fact PAYE will not be properly deducted or accounted for (TCA 1997, s 985F(1)).

In these circumstances, the Revenue Commissioners may give a direction that PAYE should be deducted where any payments are made by the relevant person in respect of work carried out by employees of the contractor during the period (TCA 1997, s 985F(2)); this is to be done on the basis that so much of the payments as are attributable to the work done by each of the contractor's employees are to be treated as emoluments of that employee (TCA 1997, s 985F(5)). The Revenue Commissioners' direction must:

(a) specify the relevant person and the contractor to whom it relates;
(b) be given by notice to the relevant person; and may
(c) be withdrawn at any time by notice to the relevant person (TCA 1997, s 985F(3)).

The Revenue Commissioners must take such steps as are reasonably practicable to ensure that the contractor is supplied with a copy of any notice issued to the relevant person which relates to the contractor (TCA 1997, s 985F(4)).

These measures are designed to tackle potential evasion rather than avoidance and it is hoped that they will be exercised with due restraint.

Social welfare benefits

Any person paying a pension taxable under Sch E, eg a former employer or the trustees of a pension scheme, is an employer for PAYE purposes. Strictly, applying the general rule that all payments of Sch E emoluments should be subject to PAYE (unless specifically excluded), it would appear that long term social welfare benefits liable under Sch E (see **10.112**) should also be paid less PAYE deductions. However, in practice, the Revenue accept that the Department of Social Community and Family Affairs may pay these benefits gross by virtue of TCA 1997, s 984 (see **11.102**) and it is left to the individual recipient to pay any tax due by him thereon to the Revenue. This may be done by direct assessment or, if the individual is in receipt of other Sch E emoluments subject to PAYE, by a reduction in his tax credits (see **11.103**).

Certain short-term benefits which have been rendered liable to tax under Sch E (unemployment and pay-related benefits; disability and injury benefits (see **10.112**)) are subject to the PAYE system. From 1 January 2012, employers are required to deduct PAYE from taxable illness benefit (including occupational injury benefit) paid by the Department of Social Protection. Such benefits are not subject to PRSI or USC. Prior to 1 January 2012 the first six weeks (36 days) of illness benefit was exempt from tax. Additional payments made to claimants in respect of qualifying children, known as Child Dependant additions are exempt for tax purposes.

FA 2013, s 8 has amended TCA 1997, s 126 to provide that maternity benefit, adoptive benefit and health and safety benefit payable from 1 July 2013 are subject to PAYE but such payments are not liable to PRSI or USC. Employers will be required to operate PAYE and will receive updated tax credit certificates to reflect the payment being made to the employee.

Local Property Tax

Finance (Local Property Tax) Act 2012 as amended by Finance (Local Property Tax) (Amendment) Act 2013 provides that the Revenue Commissioners may direct an employer to deduct Local Property Tax (LPT) from an employee's net emoluments from 1 July 2013. An employee can elect for the payment of LPT to be made by deduction from his net emoluments. Alternatively, the Revenue Commissioners can direct an employer to withhold LPT where an individual has failed to file an LPT return containing an election for a specified method of payment. In addition, if an individual files a return but fails to make the relevant payment, the Revenue Commissioners can direct the employer to withhold the tax. The LPT is required to be paid over to the Revenue Commissioners and reported in the monthly or quarterly P30. The LPT amount will be notified to the employer by way of revised Tax Credit Certificates (P2C). The Finance (Local Property Tax) Act 2012 also provides that TCA 1997, Pt 42, Chs 1A to 1D will apply to the collection and recovery of LPT.

Payment obligations

The total income tax deducted and the total PRSI contributions and Universal Social Charge (the amount deducted from pay plus the amount payable by the employer) ('PAYE' hereafter) must generally be paid over by the latest on the 14th of the calendar month following the month in which the deductions were made (the exception for certain small businesses is described below). Employers who file their returns and make their tax payments on ROS have until 23rd of the month to do so.

Payment may be made by sending the PAYE due with the completed Form P30/Payslip to the Collector-General. Alternatively the return can be filed online on the Revenue Online Service (ROS). The employer must additionally submit an annual PAYE Return Form P35 by 15 February following the end of the tax year, extended to 23 February if filing and paying on ROS. Alternatively, payment may be made by direct debit on a monthly basis, together with the submission of the annual return Form P35. A single direct debit instruction can be used for both PAYE and VAT. There is a more flexible direct debit option for seasonal business, which allows for payment of varying amounts to be paid each month. The employer should ensure that the amounts paid by direct debit are likely to be sufficient to cover his ongoing liability for the year, and where necessary adjust the direct debit amounts to achieve this. At the end of the year if a shortfall arises, the balancing payment should be made when submitting the annual return P35. Where insufficient amounts were paid by direct debit and as a result, the balance of tax payable with the annual return is more than either:

(a) 20 per cent of the annual liability for VAT; or
(b) 10 per cent of the annual liability for PAYE/PRSI,

interest will be charged, backdated to the mid point of the year.

Employers whose total PAYE and PRSI payments for the year are €28,800 or less will have the option of accounting for PAYE and PRSI on a quarterly basis. Payments for 2015 will accordingly fall due on 14/23 April 2015, 14/23 July 2015, 14/23 October 2015 and 14/23 January 2016.

11.102 Excluded emoluments and foreign aspects

TCA 1997, s 984 provides that where the deduction of tax under the PAYE system is impracticable, the emoluments may be excluded.

In the event that an employer fails to apply PAYE to any emoluments which he thinks are covered by an exclusion from PAYE, but where he has not received any notice from the Revenue to this effect, he runs the risk of being held accountable for any tax deductible, but which was not deducted, from the emoluments. Consequently, it is always advisable for the employer to make sure, if possible, that the application for the appropriate exclusion notice is made in good time before the emoluments in question are due to be paid.

If a person is employed abroad by an Irish employer, all of the duties are performed abroad and the individual will be non-resident in the tax year (or is treated as non-resident for these purposes under the 'split-year' rule of TCA 1997, s 822: see **13.504**), a PAYE Exclusion Order will normally be issued. Full details in writing must be submitted by the employer to the appropriate Revenue office.

Regulation 22, which requires an employer to operate the emergency procedure if he pays any Sch E emoluments to a person from whom he has not obtained a certificate of tax credits, does not apply in either of the following two types of case:

(a) where the employee performs the duties of his employment wholly outside the State; or
(b) where the employee is outside the State and the emoluments are paid outside the State (reg 22(7)).

Consequently, an employee in either position may be paid his emoluments without having income tax deducted under PAYE, if the employer has not received a certificate of tax credits and standard rate cut-off point, a tax deduction card, etc.

Revenue eBrief No 119/15 notes that where there is simultaneous deduction of Irish tax and non-refundable foreign tax at source from the same income, Revenue is prepared to consider, on a case-by-case basis, granting tax relief in 'real time' through the PAYE system in respect of the non-refundable foreign tax deducted in accordance with the practice set out as part of that ebrief. Prior to that instruction relief in respect of simultaneous deduction of Irish tax and non refundable foreign tax at source from the same income was granted by Revenue at the end of the year.

Non-resident employers

TCA 1997, s 984 excludes from the operation of PAYE any emoluments in respect of which the employer has been notified by the inspector that they are emoluments from which, in his opinion having regard to the circumstances of the office or employment, the deduction of income tax under PAYE is impracticable. Before an employer can refrain from deducting PAYE on the payment of any emoluments for this reason, he must receive the authority to do so by a notice from the Revenue Commissioners. In practice, very few such notices are issued.

One type of situation where the Revenue were prepared, if necessary, to accept that the deduction of income tax is impracticable was where a non-resident employer paid emoluments outside the State to one or more employees in respect of a Sch E office or employment. Unless the non-resident employer was prepared to comply voluntarily with the Irish PAYE rules, it was not generally possible for the Revenue to force him/it to do so. It would appear that in many cases the territorial limits of Irish taxation meant that the employer was in any event outside the scope of the PAYE regulations (see *Clarke v Oceanic Contractors* [1983] STC 35; *Agassi v Robinson* [2004] EWCA Civ 1518 and also *Bootle v Bye* [1996] STC (SCD) 58). In such a case, the employee would have received his emoluments gross, but remained chargeable on them by direct assessment under Sch E. In most cases prior to 1 January 2006, the fact that the emoluments were paid outside the State by a non-resident caused them to be Sch D Case III income not subject to PAYE. However with effect from 1 January 2006, the earnings from such a foreign-source employment are taxable, under Sch E to the extent that they are attributable to duties performed in the State (although this may in fact be arguable in the case of non-resident employees: see **13.607**) (TCA 1997, s 18(2), as amended by FA 2006, s 15).

The effects of the decision in *Clarke v Oceanic Contractors* have been restricted with effect from 31 March 2006 by the insertion of TCA 1997, s 985D by FA 2006, s 16. Section 985D applies where:

(a) an employee, during any period, works (ie performs duties of an office or employment (TCA 1997, s 985D(1))) for a person (the 'relevant person') who is not his employer (which presumably must mean 'employer' in the strict legal sense as opposed to any person who pays emoluments: see the discussion of TCA 1997, s 985C above);
(b) a payment of emoluments is made to him for such work by his employer or by an intermediary of either the employer or of the relevant person;
(c) the payer or, if the payer is an intermediary, the employer is not resident in the State; and
(d) income tax is not deducted or accounted for in accordance with the PAYE Regulations by the payer or, if the payer is an intermediary, by the employer (TCA 1997, s 985D(2)).

The word 'or' in both (c) and (d) presumably must be read as denoting 'and/or', ie in a case where payment of emoluments is made by an intermediary, then the provisions apply where both the intermediary and the employer are non-resident and where PAYE is not accounted for by either the intermediary or the employer. The employer would be *prima facie* liable under TCA 1997, s 985C if the intermediary defaulted, but the liability might be non-enforceable in the light of *Clarke v Oceanic Contractors*.

In the circumstances outlined above, where the amount of emoluments paid to the employee is the amount to which the employee is entitled after deduction of tax, the 'relevant person' is treated as making a payment of the total of the amount paid and the tax due in respect of that amount; otherwise the 'relevant person' is treated as making a payment of the gross amount of the emoluments paid to the employee (TCA 1997, s 985D(3), (4)). Notional payments in relation to benefits in kind under TCA 1997, s 985A (see above) are treated as gross payments (TCA 1997, s 985D(5)).

An intermediary is defined for these purposes in similar terms to TCA 1997, s 985C (see above) as either:

(a) a person acting on behalf of the employer, where the payment of emoluments is made at the expense of the employer (or of a person connected with the employer as defined by TCA 1997, s 10); or
(b) a trustee holding property for a group or a class of persons which includes the employee (TCA 1997, s 985D(6)).

In practice, TCA 1997, s 985D will most commonly occur in situations where an employee is seconded by his foreign employer to work for an Irish employer (typically an Irish subsidiary of an overseas corporation). As an Irish resident, the employee will be fully subject to Sch E on his earnings, assuming all the duties of the employment are carried out in Ireland (see **13.104** and also the discussion of TCA 1997, s 985E below, which covers the specific situation where the part of the earnings of an employment in fact fall outside Sch E). Accordingly, the Irish employer may become liable to operate PAYE even though all of the employee's earnings are paid by the parent company.

Non-resident employees

Payments to a non-resident individual in respect of emoluments taxable under Sch E, Sch E emoluments from an Irish office, employment or pension have always been subject to PAYE in the normal way. With effect from 1 January 2006, the earnings from a foreign-source employment are taxable, under Sch E to the extent that they are attributable to duties performed in the State (although this may in fact be arguable in the case of non-resident employees: see **13.607**) (TCA 1997, s 18(2), as amended by FA 2006, s 15).

A non-resident person due to receive any emoluments taxable under Sch E and subject to PAYE requires a certificate of tax credits to give to the employer paying the emoluments in the same way as a resident person. If the employer has not received either this certificate or a tax deduction card for the non-resident, the employer must account for tax under the emergency procedure. Depending on the circumstances, a non-resident may be able to claim either all, or a proportion of, the personal reliefs/tax credits available to resident taxpayers: see **13.610**. These will be incorporated in the individual's certificate of tax credits; after the year end, if the non-resident is married and living with his spouse, the Revenue will where appropriate grant the aggregation relief described in **13.610** which may result in a refund of PAYE.

While perhaps open to argument, the Revenue Commissioners take the view that Sch E applies to the earnings of a non-resident with a foreign-source employment to the extent that they refer to Irish duties (see **13.607**).

It is clear that even where an individual may be exempt from Irish taxation on his earnings under a double tax treaty (see **14.210**), PAYE should in strictness be operated if the earnings are emoluments taxable under Sch E under Irish domestic law. In *SP IT/3/07* (as amended in December 2016), the Revenue Commissioners have stated that they will not require an employer to operate PAYE where the following criteria are satisfied:

(a) the individual employee is resident in a country with a double taxation agreement with Ireland and he is not resident in Ireland for tax purposes for the relevant tax year;
(b) there is a genuine foreign office or employment;
(c) the individual is not paid by, or on behalf of, an employer resident in Ireland;

(d) the cost of the employees' earnings is not borne, directly or indirectly, by a permanent establishment of the foreign employer located in the State; and

(e) the duties of that office or employment are performed in the State for not more than 60 working days in total in a year of assessment and, in any event, for a continuous period of not more than 60 working days.

Conditions (a), (c) and (d) mirror the typical requirements for exemption under double tax treaties, although they do not deny relief where the employee is resident in the State under Irish law but is regarded for treaty purposes as a resident of the other treaty State. Condition (c) was expanded by the December 2016 edition of the statement of practice and is discussed below. A treaty will also provide exemption for periods of work of up to 183 as opposed to 60 days; as discussed at **14.210**, the UK Revenue in practice seek to deny exemption under tax treaties where the cost of the employee's services are recharged to a UK employer and the employee is present in the UK for more than 60 days (namely the highly questionable concept of the 'economic employer'); however there was previously no reference to the recharging issue in the Revenue statement and it was unclear as to whether the Revenue Commissioners would attempt to invoke the 'economic employer' argument in some circumstances. However, see the amendment made by the December 2016 version of SP-IT/3/07.

The additional requirement that there is a genuine 'foreign' office or employment is puzzling; presumably the concession will still apply if the employment is Irish-source, for example, because payments are made directly from an Irish bank account (see **13.104**). The fact that the concession was introduced on foot of the changes introduced by FA 2006, s 16 reflects the fact that the Revenue Commissioners take the view that the liability under Sch E applies to earnings referable to Irish duties in the case of non-residents holding foreign employments. The concession will be denied where arrangements are undertaken for tax avoidance purposes.

Where the concession does not apply because the employee is present for more than 60 days, PAYE need not be operated where the assignee is subject to the equivalent of PAYE in his home jurisdiction and various stringent conditions are met (see *SP IT/3/07*).

The December 2016 version of SP IT/3/07 added the following comment in relation to point (c) above as follows:

> As regards (c) above, Revenue, in line with OECD guidance (commentary on Article 15 of the OECD Model Tax Convention on Income and on Capital), is not prepared to accept, for the purposes of granting a release from the obligation to operate the PAYE system, that the remuneration is paid by, or on behalf of, an employer who is not a resident of the other State where the individual is;
>
> - working for an Irish employer where the duties performed by the individual are an integral part of the business activities of the Irish employer, or
> - replacing a member of staff of an Irish employer, or
> - gaining experience working for an Irish employer, or
> - supplied and paid by an agency (or other entity) outside the State to work for an Irish employer.
>
> Also, the release from the obligation to operate the PAYE system will not be granted (i) simply because the remuneration is paid by a foreign employer and charged in the accounts of a foreign employer or (ii) where the remuneration is paid by a foreign employer and the cost is then re-charged to an Irish employer.

The above conditions create uncertainty in connection with the application of the PAYE concession. It can be seen that reference is made above to the 'integral' nature of the service provided. The OECD commentary on the model convention notes that whether services rendered by an individual may properly be regarded by a State as rendered in an employment relationship rather than as a contract for services concluded between two enterprises is not always clear. It notes that the nature of the services rendered by the individual will be an important factor since that 'it is logical to assume that an employee provides services which are an integral part of the business activities carried on by his employer'. The reference to 'integral' there is of some note and it continues that a 'key consideration will be which enterprise bears the responsibility or risk for the results produced by the individual's work. Clearly, however, this analysis will only be relevant if the services of an individual are rendered directly to an enterprise. Where, for example, an individual provides services to a contract manufacturer or to an enterprise to which business is outsourced, the services of that individual are not rendered to enterprises that will obtain the products or services in question'.

The reference to 'gaining experience working for an Irish employer' as outlined as part of the above conditions is a difficult one if the experience gained is not one that it is 'integral' to the business of the employer. That said the approach adopted by SP-IT/3/07 is a novel one vis-à-vis previous practice.

In the September 2007 version of *SP IT/3/07* the Revenue Commissioners also state that PAYE need not be deducted where a non-resident employee from a non-treaty country performs incidental duties for no more than 30 days in total in a tax year. A day is counted if it is one in which any duties are performed in the State. Again, this concession will be denied where arrangements are undertaken for tax avoidance purposes. This was updated in the December 2016 version of the statement of practice as follows: 'Where a non-resident employee performs in the State incidental duties and performs those incidental duties in the State for no more than 30 days in aggregate in a tax year, PAYE need not be deducted in respect of income attributable to such duties.' It can be seen that the reference to a non-treaty country has been removed in the updated guidance. Where PAYE is deducted on this basis and a treaty applies then a refund should be available.

Pensions to certain non-residents

A non-resident individual in receipt of a pension chargeable under Sch E (eg from the administrator of the approved pension scheme of his former Irish company employer) may be exempted from Irish income tax on this pension under the terms of a double taxation agreement concluded between the country in which he is now resident and the Republic of Ireland. In such a case, on being satisfied as to his entitlement to this exemption, the Revenue Commissioners may notify the 'employer' paying the pension (eg the administrator of the pension scheme) that income tax is not to be deducted under PAYE from the pension. This notice has the same effect as a notice under TCA 1997, s 984(1), (2) and the employer should pay the pension gross without applying PAYE. In practice, the Revenue also exempt pensions referable to substantial periods of overseas service (**16.110**).

Revenue will not however grant PAYE exclusion orders in respect of non resident individuals who are in receipt of a distribution from an ARF. PAYE must be withheld on all payments of distributions from an ARF and where it is paid to a non resident individual such individual must apply separately to Revenue for a repayment. The repayment claim form (Form IC9) includes a declaration which must be made by the tax authorities in the country of residence of the individual to confirm that tax is payable on such income in that country before a repayment will issue from the Irish Revenue. The individual will also need to provide Revenue with a notice of assessment showing that the income has been taxed in the country of residence.

11.103 PAYE in brief

TCA 1997, s 985 imposes the obligation on every employer making any payment of any Sch E emoluments (other than excluded emoluments) to deduct income tax from, or to make a repayment of income tax in respect of, the payment in question. The amount of the income tax to be deducted or repaid is determined in accordance with the procedure laid down in regulations which the Revenue Commissioners are authorised by TCA 1997, s 986 to make regarding the assessment, charge, collection and recovery of tax under the PAYE system. The regulations made under TCA 1997, s 986 are the Income Tax (Employments) (Consolidated) Regulations 2001, as amended by the Income Tax (Employments) Regulations 2002, Income Tax (Employments) Regulations 2003, Income Tax (Employments) Regulations 2008, Income Tax (Employments) Regulations 2009 and Income Tax (Employments) Regulations 2012 ('the Regulations').

The Regulations contain the following Parts:

- Part 1: General;
- Part 2: Register of employers and register of employees;
- Part 3: Tax credits and standard rate cut-off point;
- Part 4: Deduction and repayment of tax;
- Part 5: Payment and recovery of tax, etc;
- Part 6: Assessment;
- Part 7: Contributions by employees to certain superannuation funds and schemes;
- Part 8: Special provisions where employees are in receipt of or are entitled to receive certain benefits payable under the Social Welfare Acts; and
- Part 9: Miscellaneous.

FA 2008, s 17 has inserted TCA 1997, s 986(6A) which enables the Revenue Commissioners to notify an employer that it is not necessary for him to comply with one or more regulations.

The system of Pay As You Earn has been designed to ensure so far as possible that the total income tax deducted from each employee's emoluments paid during each tax year approximates to the income tax payable by him for that year in respect of all his Sch E income. It does this through a system which spreads each employee's personal tax credits and other allowances evenly through the year and by the set of PAYE tax tables under which tax is deducted from his net taxable pay at the rate or rates estimated according to his expected income level for the year.

The main features of the system may be summarised under the following headings:

Registration by employers

Every employer who makes payments of emoluments to one or more employees at a rate exceeding €8 a week, or to any employee with other employments at a rate exceeding €2 a week, is required to register as an employer with the Revenue Commissioners. Income Tax (Employments) Regulations 2012 provide that such registration can be carried out by electronic means. If employees are paid monthly or at longer intervals, the employer must register if the rate of emoluments exceeds €36 a month for full time employees or €9 a month for employees with other employments (reg 7). These figures also form the threshold of PAYE for any individual employee, ie the employer should not apply PAYE to the emoluments paid to any employee not exceeding these weekly or monthly rates (or their equivalent for emoluments paid at other intervals). PAYE need not be applied by an individual paying emoluments of less than €40 per week to a domestic employee (TCA 1997, s 986(6); reg 9). A 'domestic employee' is defined as an employee employed solely on domestic duties (including the minding of children) in the employer's private dwelling house. The domestic employee must be the only such employee of the individual (although there is nothing in principle preventing more than one family member availing of this relaxation of the PAYE thresholds).

Any employer who pays, or starts to pay, emoluments in excess of the relevant amounts must, if he is not already registered for PAYE, notify his local district tax office of his name and address and of the fact that he is paying such emoluments within nine days from when he first pays the emoluments. An employer is also required to maintain a register of employees, outlining their name, address, PPS number, the date of commencement and the date of cessation, where relevant (reg 8).

The employer is thereafter required to implement the PAYE procedure in respect of all emoluments paid by him and also in respect of all notional payments in respect of taxable benefits provided by him and to account monthly (or quarterly) to the Collector General for all tax so deducted as well as any PAYE due in respect of notional payments which cannot be recouped from the pay of employees. An employer who fails to account for any PAYE so due may be held directly liable to account therefor, but there are some relieving provisions in certain cases. The employer is also required to make returns of employees and tax deducted at the end of each tax year. If an employer pays the tax deducted by direct debit, a single end of year return only is required.

TCA 1997, s 988 provides that the Revenue Commissioners may register as an employer any person who they believe is liable to register as an employer (but who has not done so) and serve a notice of registration on that person. If the person claims he is not obliged to register, he should object in writing to the inspector within 14 days from the date of service of the notice of registration; F(TA)A 2015, s 39, which was subject to Ministerial Order (SI 110/2016 appointed 21 March 2016 as the day on which the Finance (Tax Appeals) Act 2015, came into operation), requires the notice to be sent to the Appeal Commissioners. An employer who fails to comply with any provision of the PAYE regulations under TCA 1997, Pt 42, Ch 4 (apart from the filing of the end of year P35), or to remit income tax to the Collector-General or to make any deduction or repayment in accordance with TCA 1997, s 986(1)(g), is liable under TCA 1997, s 987(1) to a penalty of €4,000; if the employer is a body of persons, the secretary is liable to a separate penalty of €3,000 (TCA 1997, s 987(2)). A separate penalty applies for the late submission of Forms P35 – initially €1,000 increasing over a four-month period to €4,000. TCA 1997, s 987(1) also provides that the penalty of €4,000 applies where an employer does not register with the Revenue Commissioners and fails to keep and maintain a register of employees in accordance with the Income Tax (Employments) (Consolidated) Regulations 2001 (regs 7 and 8).

An employer to which the PAYE system applies, should notify the inspector if he ceases to be an employer within 14 days from the date of that cessation. In practice, this notice should only be given if the cessation is expected to be permanent and where it is unlikely that the employer will have any employees in the foreseeable future. If an employer, being an individual, dies and his business is discontinued so that there are no longer any employees, his personal representatives should notify the inspector of this fact. Should the personal representatives continue the business, or retain any employees to help with its winding up, the employer's registration is continued in their name so long as there are any employees being remunerated in excess of the PAYE threshold.

Certificates of tax credits and standard rate cut-off point

The inspector is required to determine the amount of tax credits and the standard rate cut-off point appropriate to an employee for a given tax year. The standard rate cut-off point, is the standard rate band of income tax as reduced generally by the value of benefits in kind (and possibly other non-Sch E income) and increased to reflect the value of tax reliefs allowable at the higher rate (eg allowable expenses of the employment).

For these purposes the inspector is entitled to have regard to any of a number of matters, including the amount of the employee's emoluments, the income tax reliefs to which the employee will be entitled for the year and any other income accruing to the employee; however in the last two cases the employee may request the inspector to disregard any particular relief or item of income. The inspector may also have regard to reliefs effective at the higher rate of tax, any overpayments or underpayments of tax from prior years, and any other adjustments necessary to secure that tax on the employee's emoluments for the year is collected under the PAYE system (reg 10). This procedure allows the income tax deductible (or repayable) by the individual's employer to be calculated. Adjustments may also be made where an individual has more than one employment. The inspector must send a notice of determination of the tax credits and standard rate cut-off point to the employee and a corresponding certificate or tax deduction card incorporating such a certificate to the employer (reg 11).

An employee, who is not satisfied with the inspector's determination of his tax credits, etc, may give notice in writing of his objection to the inspector, stating the grounds of his objection within 21 days of the date on which the inspector notifies him of his credits. If the matter cannot be settled by agreement between the inspector and the employee, the employee may appeal to the Appeal Commissioners who are then required to determine the amount of the tax credits, etc. The decision of the Appeal Commissioners on the question is final; there is no right to any subsequent rehearing or further appeal (reg 12).

In practice, it is seldom necessary to take the determination of credits as far as the Appeal Commissioners. Almost invariably, any point of initial difference arises because the inspector has not previously been informed of all the facts about the employee's personal circumstances. On being given the necessary particulars to establish the employee's right to additional credits, the inspector usually adjusts the amounts concerned automatically and issues an amended certificate to the employee (with a copy to the employer). FA 2005, Ch 3 has introduced new provisions designed to facilitate the extension of the benefits of the Revenue Online Service (ROS) to PAYE taxpayers, known as PAYE Anytime as well as a number of telephone-based self-service options (see below) which permit most such matters to be dealt with on an automated basis.

An employee who becomes entitled to additional credits during a tax year, etc, is entitled to be given an amended certificate of tax credits on supplying the necessary particulars to the Inspector (reg 13). An employee is not required to notify the Inspector of a change in his circumstances during the tax year.

The employer normally uses a tax deduction card supplied by the Inspector for each employee for calculating the PAYE deduction (or repayment) for each pay period throughout the year (reg 17). This card provides for the calculation of cumulative taxable pay for each period. The application of the relevant rate to the cumulative taxable pay produces the cumulative tax payable at the end of the period. The tax actually deductible by the employer for a given pay period (eg month ending 31 August) is the excess of the cumulative tax payable at the end of that period over the corresponding figure of cumulative tax payable at the end of the previous period (eg month ending 31 July). If the cumulative tax payable at the end of the previous period should exceed the cumulative tax payable at the end of the current period, the employer should repay the excess to the employee on paying his emoluments for the current period (reg 17).

Emergency card procedure

There is provision for the employer to deduct income tax through the emergency card procedure in any case where he has not received from the employee the necessary certificate of tax credits or, alternatively, an employment cessation certificate on form P45 from a previous employer. This emergency card procedure only gives the employee minimum tax credits for the first four weeks of a new employment (and no credits thereafter until the necessary certificate is received). Both standard rate and higher rate tax may be deducted on the basis that the standard rate cut off point equates to the standard rate band for a single person (reg 22). It is very important for all employees to ensure that they comply with the necessary formalities so that they can obtain their proper tax credits as soon as possible. When the proper certificate is obtained, the employee is entitled to be repaid any excess tax suffered through the emergency procedure.

Net pay arrangements

Where an employee makes tax-deductible contributions to an approved pension scheme (see **16.108**), a PRSA (see **16.3**) or a payment under a qualifying retirement annuity contract (see **16.2**) or makes contributions to a Permanent Health Insurance Scheme which are deductible from his Sch E emoluments (see **3.317**), such contributions will be deducted by the employer from the employee's gross pay and PAYE will be operated on the net amount (reg 41).

Electronic filing

Following the introduction of TCA 1997, ss 917D to 917N in FA 1999 it is possible to file monthly P30 PAYE returns and the Annual P35 PAYE Return as well as Part 1 of Form P45 electronically. TCA 1997, s 917EA makes provision for mandatory electronic filing by specified persons. This section enables the Revenue Commissioners to make regulations requiring certain categories of taxpayers to file tax returns and pay tax liabilities electronically.

Electronic and telephonic claims

Since 2005 the Revenue Commissioners have been able to offer improved customer service, including e-filing of returns and automated self service options, to PAYE taxpayers. This improved customer service is based on an enhanced telephone service and an electronic communications system. TCA 1997, s 864A provided enabling powers for the Revenue Commissioners to introduce facilities, including automated facilities, for PAYE taxpayers to make electronic (including telephone) claims for reliefs which are to be used in the operation of the PAYE system or in relation to repayments of tax paid under that system. The particular type of claims that can be made in accordance with the section must be specified by the Revenue Commissioners. In general, these claims are in respect of all the main personal tax credits and reliefs, including notifications and notices in relation to the taxpayer's circumstances, for example, change in personal circumstances or details and, in the case of married couples, in relation to their preferred taxation option, ie single treatment, joint assessment or separate assessment. In the case of automated telephone claims, claims have been restricted to low risk tax credits, for example, age allowance and medical expenses. The electronic system permits PAYE taxpayers to view their tax details and to request balancing statements.

The statutory requirements under TCA 1997, ss 458, 459 that claims for relief should be accompanied by returns of income will not apply in relation to reliefs that are to be used in the operation of the PAYE system including a case where the claim is in relation to repayment of tax deducted under PAYE. Provision is also made to modify TCA 1997, s 865 to permit the Revenue Commissioners to refund, without a formal claim, PAYE tax which they are satisfied has been overpaid. As a corollary to these relaxations of the law, TCA 1997, s 886A, as inserted by FA 2005, s 25, imposes, with effect from 25 March 2005, an obligation on taxpayers claiming tax reliefs to retain underlying records for the longer of six years from the end of the tax year to which the claim relates or the period ending on the date when any enquiry made into the claim is completed. These provisions are discussed more fully in **Division 2**.

Compliance Code for PAYE Taxpayers

Even though the employer is responsible for the deduction of PAYE and USC from an employee's wages, it is the employee's responsibility to ensure that Revenue have accurate information on the tax credits and reliefs to which an employee is entitled. Revenue's Compliance Code for PAYE Taxpayers sets out the obligations of PAYE taxpayers to ensure that they are paying the correct amount of tax and how they can regularise their tax affairs in the event they have been granted credits to which they are not entitled.

The Compliance Code which came into effect on 18 November 2013 also outlines the categories of default which can apply to a PAYE taxpayer which are similar to those provided for in the Revenue Audit Code of Practice, and the types of interventions which can be used by Revenue to ensure that the taxpayer is declaring the correct amount of income and is entitled to all the credits, reliefs and allowances claimed. This code provides that if a taxpayer is selected for an audit, the Code of Practice for Revenue Audits will apply. In all other cases the Compliance Code for PAYE Taxpayers will apply to determine the settlement of any additional tax liability and the interest and penalties due.

11.104 Emoluments of different years and unpaid remuneration

The general principle that the tax to be deducted from, or repaid to, the employee is computed by reference to the cumulative emoluments and the cumulative credits at the date of each successive payment within the tax year is not altered by the fact that a particular payment is of emoluments earned in a different tax year. 'Cumulative emoluments' is defined, in relation to any date, as the sum of all payments of emoluments *made* by the employer to the employee from the beginning of the year up to and including that date (reg 2). Consequently, if an individual is not paid a part of his salary which has accrued due to him for the year ended 31 December 2014 until, say, 14 February 2015, then his employer must apply PAYE to the amount paid on the latter date as if it were emoluments for the PAYE month ending 28 February 2015, ie in the tax year 2015. The fact that PAYE may have been deducted in one tax year from emoluments earned in a different year does not cause those emoluments to be included in the employee's total income for a year other than that in which they were earned. For the purpose of the calculation of the employee's final tax liability for any year made after the end of the year, it is necessary to include the full Sch E income actually earned in that year irrespective of the year in which it was paid and PAYE deducted. If the timing of the actual payments has resulted in the deduction of insufficient PAYE in one year, or too much in another year, any necessary adjustment to bring the tax actually paid into line with the final liability for each year is made when the full position is known. The validity of this procedure was upheld in *Bedford v H* II ITR 588. The issue is only likely to arise in relation to payments of wages, salaries, bonuses, commissions and the like; the provision of benefits which are treated as notional payments for PAYE purposes (see **11.101**) are normally taxable under Sch E as and when they are provided to the employee (see **10.203**).

In the absence of any special provision, it would be possible for an employer to secure a deduction in arriving at its Sch D Case I trading income for remuneration due to directors and/or employees by accruing the expense in the accounts, but to delay the payment of the remuneration to prevent the Revenue's collecting the tax under PAYE until, perhaps, a year to two later. Since interest on tax deductible under PAYE is normally only chargeable after the employer has failed to remit tax, which he is required to deduct on the actual payment of emoluments, the delay in making the payments meant that no interest could be charged in respect of the tax on the accrued (but unpaid) remuneration.

TCA 1997, s 996 accordingly discourages delay by employers in paying remuneration and enables the Revenue to charge interest retrospectively on the PAYE attributable to any remuneration to which the section applies. It does this by deeming the remuneration in question to have been paid on a certain date ('the relevant date') and deems that remuneration to be emoluments subject to PAYE as if it had been paid on that date. This means that interest on the PAYE due in respect of the unpaid remuneration starts to run from the ninth day after the end of the PAYE month in which the relevant date falls.

The remuneration to which TCA 1997, s 996 applies is limited to emoluments that are:

(a) salaries, fees, wages, perquisites or profits whatsoever from an office or employment;
(b) deductible as an expense in computing for Sch D purposes the profits or income of a trade or profession for any accounting period or period of account; and
(c) still unpaid at the end of six months after the relevant date (or, if earlier, six months after the date of cessation of the office or employment from which the unpaid remuneration arises).

The 'relevant date' is normally the last day of the period of account or, in the case of a company, the last day of the accounting period for which the remuneration has been accrued. In other words, if the remuneration for the period of account or accounting period has not been paid or otherwise credited to the director or employee within six months after the closing balance sheet date, TCA 1997, s 996 applies to make the employer accountable for the PAYE that would have been deducted if the accrued remuneration had been paid on that balance sheet date. This means that interest on the unpaid tax can be charged retrospectively from the due date of the employer's PAYE remittance for the PAYE month in which the balance sheet date falls.

In the event that any remuneration is accrued (but not paid) over more than one accounting period or period of account, TCA 1997, s 996 is applied on the basis that there are two separate relevant dates, ie one relevant date on the last day of the first period and another relevant date on the last day of the second period. Interest can therefore be charged on the PAYE due in respect of the unpaid remuneration for the first period by reference to its closing balance sheet date up to the actual date on which the relevant PAYE is remitted by the employer. Similarly, interest can be charged in respect of the PAYE for the second period by reference to its closing balance sheet date.

In the case where the director or employee entitled to the unpaid remuneration ceases to hold the office or employment before the end of the relevant period of account or accounting period, the unpaid remuneration is deemed to have been paid on the date on which the office or employment ceased. Consequently, interest on any unpaid PAYE attributable to the accrued remuneration may be charged retrospectively from the due date for the employer's PAYE remittance for the PAYE month in which the office or employment ceased, but only if the remuneration is not paid within six months after the date of cessation.

Finally, if the employer carrying on the trade or profession accrues remuneration as an expense in a period of account that exceeds 12 months in duration, the provisions of TCA 1997, s 996 apply to enable interest to be charged on the PAYE attributable to the part of any unpaid remuneration that has accrued at the end of the first 12 months of the period of account, unless that remuneration is paid no later than 18 months after the first day of the period of account.

Example 11.104.1

Melody Ltd makes up its accounts annually to 31 March, but has delayed making up its accounts for both of the years to 31 March 2013 and 31 March 2014. It has paid its managing director, Mrs I Theme, €800 a month on account of her salary for each year. It accrues the balance of her final remuneration (as shown below) in the accounts for each year, but only pays the unpaid remuneration on 31 December 2014 and remits the PAYE on it on 14 January 2015 with its other PAYE remittances for the month ended 31 December 2014.

TCA 1997, s 996 is applied as follows:

	€
Year to 31/03/2013:	
Final remuneration (as charged in accounts)	15,000
Less: paid on account (subject to PAYE)	9,600
Remuneration paid 31/12/2014	5,400
Year to 31/03/2014:	
Final remuneration (as charged in accounts)	18,000
Less: paid on account (subject to PAYE)	9,600
Remuneration paid 31/12/2014	8,400

TCA 1997, s 996 deems the unpaid remuneration to have been paid as follows:

	€
Deemed paid on 31/03/2013:	
Unpaid remuneration in accounts to that date	5,400
(accrued from 1/4/2012 – 31/03/2013)	
Deemed paid on 31/03/2014:	
Unpaid remuneration in accounts to that date	8,400
(accrued from 1/04/2013 to 31/03/2014)	

Assuming that the PAYE which would have been deducted on the €5,400 accrued in the accounts to 31/03/2013 would have been €2,538 if that sum had been paid on 31/03/2013, the Collector General may charge interest on €2,538 for the 21 months from 14 April 2013 (due date for tax on remuneration deemed paid on 31 March 2013) to 14 January 2015 (date of payment).

Similarly, if the additional PAYE that would have been due on the unpaid remuneration of €8,400 accrued in the accounts to 31 March 2014 would have been €3,948 the Collector General may charge interest on €3,948 for the nine months from 14 April 2014 to the date of payment on 14 January 2015.

11.105 PAYE and termination payments

The subject of certain retirement, etc payments has been discussed in **Division 10.4**. It was indicated there that the basic exemption €10,160 (as possibly enhanced) plus the sum of €765 for each complete year of service, of a payment chargeable to tax by virtue of those provisions is normally exempted (except if there are other connected payments made by the same or a connected employer) and that it is possible for relief to be given by certain other reductions in the sum chargeable (see **10.403**). Then, as set out in **10.404**, further relief was available in respect of payments made prior to 31 December 2013, for top slicing relief, as a reduction in the amount of income tax payable in respect of the net termination payment chargeable. Top slicing relief was originally restricted to ex-gratia lump sums of less than €200,000 with effect from 1 January 2013, however it has been completely abolished for termination payments made from 1 January 2014. In addition foreign service relief, dealt with at **10.406** is no longer available on payments made after 27 March 2013.

Since such payments in respect of the termination of an office or employment or payments made in respect of a change in its functions or emoluments, are treated by TCA 1997, s 123 as emoluments chargeable under Sch E, the payments are subject to PAYE. Any such payment must, to the extent that it exceeds the available exemptions, be included in the employee's (or former employee's) gross pay for the PAYE week or month in which the payment is made. Allowance is, however, available at the time the payment is being made for any relief given by TCA 1997, Sch 3 by way of reduction of the tax payable, such as the SCSB. For any payment to which top slicing relief was available prior to 31 December 2013, the employee (or former employee) must make his own claim for any such relief available when he is finalising his income tax position after the end of the year.

It should be borne in mind that payments to the extent that they relate to restrictive covenants undertaken by the employee (or former employee) are fully taxable under Sch E (see **10.114**).

11.106 Employee's position at year end

TCA 1997, s 997 provides that an assessment under Sch E need not be made except where:

(a) the employee so requires by notice in writing; or

(b) the emoluments paid in the year differ in amount from the emoluments taxable for the year (eg where a sum earned in one tax year is paid in a later tax year); or

(c) there is reason to suppose that the taxpayer is liable to the higher rates of tax.

The Inspector can accordingly use his discretion not to issue an assessment if one is not required by the taxpayer under (a) in a case where there is no outstanding liability for the year concerned (*City of Limerick VEC v Carr and The Revenue Commissioners* (25 July 1998) HC.

Where paragraph (a) applies, the taxpayer must request the assessment within four years of the end of the tax year concerned (previously five years in respect of the tax year 2002 and earlier tax years. Where para (b) or (c) applies, the assessment must be made within four years of the end of the tax year concerned (TCA 1997, s 997(1A), inserted by FA 2003, s 17(1); SI 508/2003). Where any assessment is made, credit is to be given for the actual amount of tax deducted from the emoluments concerned (TCA 1997, s 997(1), as amended by FA 2003, s 17(1); SI 508/2003). Previously the reference was to tax deducted or 'estimated to be deductible', but see the Appeal Commissioners' determination at 24 AC 2000 to the effect that the inspector was entitled to confine himself to the amount of tax actually deducted. The normal rights of appeal apply in relation to such assessments (reg 38).

The inspector may therefore make an assessment on the employee after the year end to recover any excess of the employee's Sch E liability over PAYE suffered by him. If there is a net liability payable and the inspector does not propose to recover it by reducing the employee's tax credits for a later year, the inspector may require the employee to remit the balance due to the Collector General (reg 39). If there is a net refund due to him, the employee has the right to require it to be repaid to him. In any case where the inspector does not propose to make an assessment, including the case where the employee has overpaid tax under PAYE, the inspector is required to send to the employee, as soon as possible after the year end, a statement showing the calculation of his liability for the year and how it is proposed to deal with any overpayment or underpayment of tax (reg 37).

TCA 1997, s 997(3) provides that where an inspector issues a statement under reg 37, he may give notice in, or together with, the statement that it is to be treated as if it were in all respects an assessment raised on the employee. Accordingly, all the provisions of the Income Tax Acts relating to appeals against assessments and collection and recovery of tax charged in an assessment will apply to the statement.

It is worth noting that no interest can be charged by the Revenue Commissioners on the employee in respect of any tax underpaid through PAYE during the year prior to tax year 2005, since the rules of TCA 1997, s 1080 as they stood prior to amendment by TCA 1997, s 145 had only provided for interest to run on tax charged by an assessment. With effect from 2005, if the inspector does make an assessment (or a statement under reg 37 which is treated as such) after the year end to recover any tax underpaid, then the interest on overdue tax rules are applied in the ordinary way to the tax charged on that assessment, etc.

The position of Sch E employees who are 'chargeable persons' under the PAYE system is dealt with under **Division 2**. For those employees whose income consists exclusively, or virtually exclusively, of PAYE income and who therefore do not generally qualify as 'chargeable persons' (with the exception of certain directors and their spouses, see **2.102**), most of the provisions of the old 'pre-self assessment' regime remain relevant.

TCA 1997, s 960 provides that tax is payable on assessments raised for any year of assessment, not later than 30 September in that year or in respect of an assessment made after 30 September not later than one month from the date on which the assessment is raised.

TCA 1997, s 948 also grants full rights of appeal against the amount of tax deducted from Sch E emoluments (as opposed to the amount assessable under Sch E for the year).

The 'discovery' provisions of TCA 1997, s 924 (which is only relevant for years of assessment prior to 2013) remain relevant to 'non-chargeable persons'. If an Inspector discovers that any taxable income has been omitted from earlier assessments or that the taxpayer has not given a full and proper statement of his income or that he has been undercharged to tax in some way, the inspector may make such one or more additional assessments as is or are necessary to remedy the position. Any such additional assessments are subject to the same rules, rights of appeal, etc as the first assessments (TCA 1997, s 924).

TCA 1997, s 924 begins with the words 'Where the inspector discovers that ...' before going on to provide for the making of the additional assessment in the case of specified types of 'discovery'. The meaning of the word 'discovers' and the extent to which an inspector might make such a 'discovery' was the subject of a number of cases in relation to additional assessments under the old system.

The word 'discovers' was held to have a wide meaning and covers not only the case where the inspector finds out new facts, but also that:

> where no new fact has come to light but the Revenue authorities have formed the opinion that upon a mistaken view of the law, the taxpayer has been undercharged in his original assessment ... I can see no reason for saying that a discovery of an undercharge can only arise where a new fact has been discovered. The words are apt to include any case in which for any reason it newly appears that the taxpayer has been undercharged, and the context supports rather than detracts from this interpretation.

The above extract from the judgment from Viscount Simmonds in the House of Lords in *Cenlon Finance Co Ltd v Ellwood* 40 TC 176 was quoted with approval in the Irish case of *W Ltd v Wilson* II ITR 627. In the latter case, heard in 1974, Kenny J in the High Court held that an Inspector of taxes was entitled to raise additional assessments notwithstanding that previous inspectors had agreed the profits of the taxpayer company, having accepted certain deductions, in arriving at those profits.

Kenny J held that another inspector could validly raise additional assessments when he had occasion to look back over the previous years' computations and came to the conclusion that the deductions were not allowable. The taxpayer company had contended that the deductions in question were shown in the company's accounts as prepared for tax purposes, that nothing had been concealed by the company in relation to the matter and that a change of opinion by the inspector was not a discovery entitling him to make the additional assessment. Kenny J rejected this argument. Discovery, therefore, could be taken as including a case where an inspector comes to the conclusion that a previous view taken on the application of the law was incorrect.

In *Hammond Lane Metal Co Ltd v O'Culacháin* IV ITR 187, it was held that where an appeal was compromised under TCA 1997, s 933(3)(b), so that the assessment was to be treated as one in respect of which no appeal had been made, the inspector was entitled to make a discovery in respect of the subject matter of the assessment. The position is presumably different where a particular issue is determined by the Appeal Commissioners under TCA 1997, s 933(4) (or by the Circuit Court judge under TCA 1997, s 942(3): see *Cenlon Finance Co Ltd v Ellwood* 40 TC 176, albeit decided on a more explicit form of wording). The foregoing rules relating to the time limit for making an assessment for 1987–88 or any earlier year are equally applicable to any current or future assessment to be made for any such year as they were earlier. They also apply to income outside the self-assessment system.

TCA 1997, s 959AB (for years of assessment 2013 *et seq*, prior to that s 924(2)(d)) provides that the four-year time limit for discovery assessments (which applies in the absence of fraud or neglect) (ten years prior to 1 January 2005) (see **2.111**) runs from the end of the year in which Sch E emoluments are received (and not the year in which they are *earned*, if different). This provision is designed to ensure that payments made, for example, in year four which relate (wholly or partly) to year zero remain assessable (see *Heasman v Jordan* 35 TC 518).

In any case where any form of fraud or neglect has been committed by or on behalf of a taxpayer in relation to the tax to be assessed, an assessment may validly be made *at any time* without any time limit (TCA 1997, s 959AD(5)).

'Neglect' is defined as negligence or failure to give any notice, to make any return, statement or declaration, or to produce or furnish any list, document or other information required by the Acts (TCA 1997, s 959AD(1)). Fraud occurs, broadly, if a taxpayer (or a person acting on his behalf) deliberately makes any incorrect statement in any tax return, other statement or declaration, or deliberately omits to return any income or deliberately misrepresents his position in any way. If the Revenue Commissioners, or one of their officers allowed an extended time for a person to do some act normally required to be done within a prescribed time limit, and if this act was (or is) done within the extended time, there is no neglect. Further, if a person had a reasonable excuse for not doing some act, there is no neglect if he in fact did that act without unreasonable delay after the excuse had ceased to apply.

For assessments made to charge income outside the self-assessment system, TCA 1997, s 933(1)(a) requires the notice of appeal to be given within 30 days from the date of the Inspector's notice of assessment in all cases.

11.107 Recovery of underpaid tax and shareholders' emoluments

Where the employer does not account for the full amount of the PAYE which should have been paid over in respect of an employee's emoluments including any notional payments in respect of taxable benefits in any month, and if the Revenue Commissioners are satisfied that the employer took reasonable care to comply with the PAYE regulations and that the underpayment was due to an error made in good faith, they may direct that the under-deduction shall be recovered from the employee. If this direction is made, the employer ceases to be liable to remit the amount in question to the Collector General (reg 28(3) as substituted by Income Tax (Employments) Regulations 2003).

Any employer who deliberately does not account for the full amount of PAYE which he is required by the regulations to deduct from an employee's emoluments in any month or to remit in respect of notional payments where the full amount of tax thereon cannot be recouped from an employee's pay, faces the likelihood that he will be called upon to make good the deficiency to the Revenue. However, if the Revenue Commissioners are of the opinion that the employee has received his emoluments knowing that his employer wilfully failed to make the full deduction or remit the unrecouped tax, the Revenue may direct that the amount under deducted or not remitted is to be recovered directly from the employee (see, eg *R v IRC ex parte Chisholm* [1981] STC 253, *R v IRC ex parte Sims* [1987] STC 211 and *R v IRC ex parte Cook* [1987] STC 434). Should they make this direction, the employer is absolved from his liability to remit the amount in question to the Collector General (reg 28(4) Income Tax (Employments) Regulations 2003).

The Revenue's direction is not open to appeal, but in appropriate cases, it may be subject to judicial review (see **2.206**). If the Revenue does not make the direction, it is debatable whether or not the employer could be allowed to recover the tax from subsequent payments to the employee; it is clear however that no such recovery is possible unless the employer has actually paid the tax (*Bernard & Shaw Ltd v Shaw*

[1951] 1 All ER 267 and see Watson [1994] British Tax Review 82). FA 2008, s 17 has inserted TCA 1997, s 986(1) which now enables the Revenue Commissioners to make regulations for the collection and recovery, from the employee rather than from the employer of any amount of tax that they consider should have been deducted by the employer from the employees' emoluments.

Where the employer has deducted the tax but failed to account for it to the Revenue Commissioners, there seem to be no grounds on general principles for refusing a credit for the tax so deducted in any assessment made on the employee TCA 1997, s 997(1); see also the discussion in [1993] *Irish Tax Review* 441.

In the case of a director-controlled company it may not, however, always be clear whether payments were in fact made net or gross (see *R v IRC ex parte McVeigh* [1996] STC 91, where an internal bookkeeping entry was held to be insufficient to establish that a payment had been made net of tax in circumstances where there had been a total disregard of the PAYE regulations and it was not possible to demonstrate that there was a pre-existing entitlement to a gross amount).

Special rules apply under TCA 1997, s 997A to directors or employees who have a 'material interest' in the employer company. An individual is treated as holding a 'material interest in a company' if:

(a) the individual on his own;
(b) the individual together with any connected person(s); or
(c) any connected person(s);

beneficially owns, or is able directly or through the medium of other companies or by any other indirect means, to control more than 15 per cent of the ordinary share capital of the company (TCA 1997, s 997A(1)(a)).

'Control' has the same meaning as in TCA 1997, s 432 and 'connected person' is as defined by TCA 1997, s 10 (see **12.304**). 'Ordinary share capital', in relation to a company, means all the issued share capital (by whatsoever name called) of the company. This definition displaces the standard definition in TCA 1997, s 2 which excludes share capital with a right to a fixed rate dividend but without a right to share in profits of the company (TCA 1997, s 997A(1)(a)).

No credit will be given to an individual for income tax deducted from his emoluments by a company in which he has a material interest in any assessment or any statement issued under reg 37 (see **11.106**) unless there is documentary evidence that the tax deducted has been remitted by the company to the Collector-General in accordance with the PAYE Regulations (TCA 1997, s 997A(3)).

Any tax remitted by the company to the Collector-General will in the first instance be treated as deducted from the emoluments of employees or directors of the company without a material interest therein (TCA 1997, s 997A(4)).

Where tax is deducted from emoluments paid to two or more directors or employees with material interests in the employer company and it is remitted to the Collector-General, it will be treated as deducted from the emoluments paid to each such individual in the same proportion as the emoluments paid to that individual bears to the aggregate amount of emoluments paid by the company to all those individuals (ie any shortfall in remittance of PAYE will be allocated between them in proportion to their total emoluments subject to PAYE) (TCA 1997, s 997A(5)). From 2010 onwards, where the tax so allocated exceeds the amount actually deducted in any case, then only the *latter* amount may be credited against the individual's income tax liability (TCA 1997, s 997A(5) inserted by FA 2010, s 8). Changes made from 1 January 2012 provide that any amounts remitted by a company are allocated firstly to PRSI employment contributions, next to the Universal Social Charge and lastly to income tax (TCA 1997, s 997A(7) inserted by FA 2010, s 15). With effect from 1 January 2012, an appeal against a decision by the Revenue Commissioners in relation to TCA 1997, s 997A is subject to the same provisions as apply in TCA 1997, s 949 in relation to claims under TCA 1997, s 864. F(TA)A 2015, which was subject to Ministerial Order (SI 110/2016 appointed 21 March 2016 as the day on which the Finance (Tax Appeals) Act 2015, came into operation) inserted a new sub-s (1A) into TCA 1997, s 864 (and to which TCA 1997, s 864(1) is subject) which requires any person aggrieved by a determination under sub-s (1) on any claim, matter or question referred to in that subsection may appeal the determination to the Appeal Commissioners within the period of 30 days after the date of the notice of that determination. This is subject to TCA 1997, s 949I and Ch 6 of Pt 41A, which deals with appealing determinations of the Appeal Commissioners.

TCA 1997, ss 989, 990, empower the Revenue Commissioners to serve notice on an employer that an amount of tax estimated by the Commissioners to be due has not been remitted to the Collector General by the employer, or has not been fully remitted. An employer upon whom such a notice is served may, within 14 days from the service of the notice, give notice in writing to the Revenue Commissioners claiming that the amount of tax estimated to be due is not correct and may require the matter to be referred to the Appeal Commissioners for a final decision on the matter; F(TA)A 2015, s 39, which was subject to Ministerial Order (SI 110/2016 appointed 21 March 2016 as the day on which the Finance (Tax Appeals) Act 2015, came into operation), requires an appeal under TCA 1997, s 989 to be made directly to the Appeal Commissioners within the above mentioned 14 days and under TCA 1997, s 990 the timeframe is 30 days both of which were the same as the original timeframes in the respective sections. If no notice of appeal is given, the tax estimated to be due and specified in the notice given to the employer becomes due and payable on the fourteenth day after the service of the notice. If an appeal is made, the amount of the tax found to be due by agreement on the determination of the appeal becomes due and payable on the date the matter is agreed or determined by the Appeal Commissioners. TCA 1997, s 991(2) extends the charge to interest on unremitted tax to include the tax estimated to be due under a notice under TCA 1997, s 989 or 990. Where the tax is recoverable under a s 989 notice, the interest charge generally runs from the latest due date for the remittance of the tax deducted under PAYE for the month specified in the notice. In the case of tax recoverable for a tax year under a TCA 1997, s 990 notice, the interest is generally calculated from the latest due date for the remittance of PAYE for the last PAYE month in the year of assessment to which the notice relates. TCA 1997, s 991(1A) further provides that where amounts of PAYE are paid later than 14 days after the end of the tax year and exceed 10 per cent of the employer's full year liability, interest will be chargeable on the amount paid from the mid point of the year. TCA 1997, s 991A applies these provisions to cover direct debit arrangements within reg 29. Interest is charged under TCA 1997, s 991 at a rate of 0.0274 per cent per day with effect from 1 July 2009.

Notice is given under TCA 1997, s 989 where the Revenue Commissioners have reason to believe that an employer was liable to remit tax in relation to any particular income tax month (or for more than one month), but where the employer has not in fact remitted any tax for that month(s). In this case the Commissioners' estimate specified in the notice is of the tax that should have been remitted by the employer in respect of emoluments paid in that month. Notice is given under TCA 1997, s 990 where the

Revenue Commissioners have reason to believe that the total amount of tax which the employer was liable to remit in respect of all the months in a tax year is greater than the amounts of tax (if any) actually remitted by the employer for the various months in the year. The notice served should specify the total tax estimated to have been remittable for the year, the total tax (if any) remitted by the employer over the year, and the balance of tax remaining unpaid. The constitutionality of the statutory precursor to TCA 1997, s 989 was upheld in *Kennedy v Hearne* III ITR 590.

Where an employer furnishes a declaration of the amount due in respect of monthly PAYE or makes a P35 (annual return of PAYE liability) in accordance with reg 31 and pays the sum outstanding inclusive of any related interest and costs, the Notice under s 988 or s 989, as the case may be, will be discharged. Where however underpaid PAYE is the subject of court proceedings or recovery proceedings under TCA 1997, s 962, the discharge shall not apply until the proceedings have been completed unless the Revenue Commissioners otherwise direct. With effect from 28 March 2003, there is provision for additional estimates to be raised where a previously estimated amount has been paid without submission of the requisite declaration or annual return or the Revenue Commissioners have reason to believe that the original estimate understated the true liability (TCA 1997, s 989(3)(e) inserted by FA 2003, s 157(a)).

TCA 1997, s 993 applies the various collection powers contained in the Income Tax Acts to enable the Revenue Commissioners to enforce payment of any tax which any employer is liable to remit but neglects or fails to do so. In particular, the provisions of TCA 1997, s 963, (TCA 1997, s 962(1)–(3)), TCA 1997, s 962 (recovery by Sheriff or County Registrar), TCA 1997, s 963 (power of Collector to sue), TCA 1997, s 966 (High Court proceedings) and TCA 1997, s 998 (recovery by suit of Attorney General) may all be used as appropriate to recover the tax and interest from a defaulting employer. In any proceedings brought to recover tax and interest, a certificate signed by an officer of the Revenue Commissioners which certifies that a stated amount of tax is due and payable by the employer is, unless and until the contrary is proved by the defendant, evidence that the amount is so due and payable.

TCA 1997, s 993 extends these powers of collection to enable the recovery of any estimated amount of tax (and interest) that is specified by a notice under TCA 1997, s 989 or 990 as being due. In such a case, TCA 1997, s 993 is applied as if the amount so estimated as being due, or any balance of tax so estimated and remaining unpaid, were an amount of tax for which the employer was liable under the PAYE regulations.

TCA 1997, s 994 includes an employer's unpaid liability for tax deducted under PAYE (and interest) among the debts which are to be paid in priority to all other debts in the distribution of the property of a bankrupt, arranging debtor or person dying insolvent, but only to the extent that this liability relates to the last 12 months. This period to which the priority claim relates is the period of 12 months immediately prior to the date on which the order of adjudication of the bankrupt was made, the petition of arrangement of the debtor was filed or the person died insolvent, whichever was the case. In arriving at the amount of the priority debt, the total tax which the employer was due to deduct from emoluments paid is reduced by the total of all repayments of tax which he was due to make to employees, etc in the same 12-month period.

In the case of a company in liquidation, Companies Act 1963, s 285 makes the company's liability for tax deductible under PAYE in the 12 months immediately before the date of winding up a priority debt in the liquidation of the company. Again, any interest chargeable on this 12 months' liability is included in the priority debt, while any tax which the company was liable to repay to employees under PAYE in the same period is deducted. For this purpose, the relevant date up to which the 12-month period is measured is:

(a) the date of the passing of the resolution for the winding up of the company (unless it is a compulsory winding up);

(b) the date of the appointment (or first appointment) of a provisional liquidator or, if no such appointment was made, the date of the winding up order (if the company has been ordered to be wound up compulsorily).

In the case of a company where either a receiver is appointed on behalf of the holders of any debentures of a company secured by a floating charge, or possession is taken by or on behalf of those debenture holders of any property subject to such a charge, then, if the company is not already in the course of being wound up, Companies Act 1963, s 98 makes the company's liability to account for PAYE in respect of the last 12 months a priority debt. Again, interest on the liability for the last 12 months is included in the priority debt, while any repayments of tax to employees due in the same period are deducted. Here the priority is for the PAYE debt to be paid (as one of all such priority debts), out of any assets coming into the hands of the receiver or any other person taking possession of the property secured by the floating charge, before any claim for the principal or interest in respect of the debentures. The 12-month period is that immediately before the appointment of the receiver (or the taking of possession).

The provisions of TCA 1997, s 1001 should also be noted in this context.

11.108 Revenue powers

An officer of the Revenue Commissioners, if authorised by them in writing for the purpose, may attend at any premises of any employer and may request the production for inspection of all documents and records whatsoever relating to the calculation or payment of the emoluments of the employer's employees. If so requested, the employer or any employee of his at the premises must produce all wages sheets, certificates of tax credits, tax deduction cards and any other relevant documents as may be in his possession or power or procure. The authorised Revenue officer must, if so requested, produce his authority in writing to the person required to produce the records, etc (reg 32(1) and (2)).

Regulation 32(3) requires every employer to retain all the wages sheets, tax deduction cards (or their equivalent in an 'own system'), and all other documents and records that relate to the calculation or payment of the emoluments of his employees or to the deduction of tax from these emoluments. All these records, documents, etc must be retained by the employer for six years after the end of the tax year to which they refer, unless the Revenue Commissioners specifically authorise in writing a shorter retention period. This retention requirement does not, however, extend to the certificates of tax credits, nor to the temporary tax deduction forms or emergency cards.

TCA 1997, s 987 imposes a penalty of €4,000 on any employer who fails to comply with any provision of the Employments Regulations requiring him:

(a) to send any return, statement, notification or certificate (other than the end of year P35);

(b) to remit any tax deducted to the Collector General;

(c) to make any deduction or repayment of tax which he should have made in paying any emoluments;

(d) to register with the Revenue Commissioners; or

(e) to keep and maintain a register of employees.

If the defaulting employer is a company, the secretary of the company is liable to a separate penalty of €3,000 in addition to the penalty on the company (TCA 1997, s 987(2)). There is a separate graduated penalty on an employer for late submission of form P35. This is an initial €1,000 increasing over a four-month period to €4,000. The due date for filing P35s is 46 days after the end of the tax year which is extended to the 23rd of the month if the return is filed and payment is made on ROS. If the return is not filed by the due date, any interest will be charged from the 14th of the month. A €3,000 penalty also applies to company secretaries. As with other penalties under the Tax Acts generally, the Revenue Commissioners have discretion as to whether or not to impose the penalties provided for or to remit or reduce the amount of the penalty. Any penalty imposed on an employer for failure to deduct any tax is payable in addition to any tax (and interest) for which the employer is liable.

In practice, penalties are only likely to be imposed if there is wilful failure to comply with the regulations, etc or if the employer is seriously negligent in complying.

Powers of Inspection – PAYE

TCA 1997, s 903 grants extensive power to the Revenue to investigate and verify that proper procedures under the PAYE system are in operation. These powers include the right to:

(a) enter a premises or place where an officer believes an activity is or has been carried on by an employer in his capacity as such, or where emoluments, benefits-in-kind or perquisites are or have been, paid or received, or where any relevant records (as widely defined) are, or may be, kept;

(b) demand the production of all records and documentation;

(c) search the premises for other records if those at (b) above are not adequate and take copies as required; and

(d) seek assistance in this examination from the employer or any other person on the premises (other than a customer).

By virtue of TCA 1997, s 906, the authorised officer may be accompanied by a member or members of the Garda Síochána when entering the premises. Any such member(s) may arrest without warrant any person who obstructs or interferes with the officer in his enforcement of his duties under TCA 1997, s 903. A person who does not comply with the requirements of the authorised officer will be subject to a penalty of €4,000 (TCA 1997, s 903(5)).

There is also a requirement that relevant records should be retained for a period of six years after the end of the year to which they refer or such shorter period as the Revenue Commissioners may authorise in writing to the employer (TCA 1997, s 903(6)).

11.2 PRSI

11.201 General

Employers and employees are liable to make pay related social insurance ('PRSI') employed contributions in respect of the employees' emoluments from insurable employments exercised in the State. The primary legislation is Social Welfare Consolidation Act 2005 ('SWCA 2005'), as amended by subsequent Social Welfare Acts (SWAs supplemented by Social Welfare (Consolidated Contributions and Insurability) Regulations, 1996 ('SW Regs') as subsequently amended.

For emoluments chargeable under Sch E including notional payments in relation to taxable benefits in kind (see **11.101**), the collection of these contributions is fully integrated into the PAYE system. Further, the Universal Social Charge in respect of these emoluments (as computed for the purposes thereof) are also collected as part of the total PAYE deduction made from their emoluments. For the treatment of emoluments chargeable under Sch D Case III, see *Foreign offices, employments and pensions* below.

Strictly, the subject of pay related social insurance may not be directly relevant to a book on income tax, but since the PRSI contributions are similar to a tax on employment income and in view of their integration with PAYE, it may be useful to give a very broad outline of the main aspects of PRSI contributions.

Every employer who pays emoluments chargeable to tax under Sch E is required to account to the Collector General for pay related social insurance contributions at the same time as he is due to remit the income tax deductible from the emoluments under the PAYE system (SWCA 2005, s 13, SW Regs Art 8). The employer is liable to pay to the Collector General, both the employees' and his own PRSI contributions in respect of the emoluments paid to the employees in each month (ending on the end date of each calendar month). The employer deducts each employee's PRSI contribution from the emoluments paid to that employee each month. The €127 weekly exemption which was disregarded when calculating an employee's PRSI liability has been abolished with effect from 1 January 2013.

In contrast to the PAYE Regulations, there is no general provision for imposing liability on 'intermediate' employers: see *Hearne v O'Cionna* IV ITR 113 (although there is such provision in the case of non-PAYE employees: SW reg 39, paralleling the provisions of PAYE reg 3 discussed at **11.101**).

There is no ceiling on the amount to which the employer's PRSI contribution is charged and as such it is chargeable on the total gross emoluments of each employee; a full deduction applies for the purposes of employers' PRSI in the case of the pension levy incurred by public sector workers. In the case of the benefits arising on certain share-based remuneration, including share awards and the exercise of non-exempt share options, although generally subject to PRSI from 1 January 2011 unless granted in writing prior to that date, there is an exemption from employer's PRSI. The shares in question are any form of shares including stock, but only if the shares, etc are shares in the employer company or in a company which has control (as defined by TCA 1997, s 432) over the employer company (TCA 1997, s 985A(1A)).

Employees and individuals in receipt of an occupational pension, who are under 66, who have unearned income such as dividends, rental income and deposit interest are liable to PRSI on this income from 1 January 2014. The individual must be a chargeable person, as defined in TCA 1997, s 959A. Revenue *Tax Briefing 62* provides that an individual is not a chargeable person if their gross non employment income is less than €50,000 and such assessable income is less than €3,174 and is fully coded against their tax credits so that all such income is taxed under the PAYE system. Such individuals are not required to file a tax return and as such their unearned income is not subject to PRSI. An individual whose gross non employment income is over €50,000 and net assessable income is over €3,174 is required to file a tax return and such income is subject to PRSI from 1 January 2014. In addition, modified rate payers, individuals who pay PRSI under class B, C or D have been brought within the charge to PRSI from 1 January 2013 if they have income from a trade or profession.

Social insurance contributions

The social insurance element of the employee's and employer's PRSI contribution is levied on all 'reckonable earnings' of 'employed contributors' in 'insurable employments', but not on any earnings from other employments. The two main conditions to be satisfied before any liability arises for either employee or employer to make contributions are, therefore, that there be an insurable employment and that the person who derives emoluments from that employment fall within the definition of an employed contributor.

The question of what is an insurable employment is discussed in more detail in **11.202**. Here, it is sufficient to say that an insurable employment normally involves employment under a contract of service. It is not limited to employments the emoluments of which are chargeable to income tax under Sch E and may include an employment treated for income tax purposes as a foreign employment (see below). Further, while the office of director is not an insurable employment as such, a director may in certain circumstances be regarded as having an insurable employment with the company of which he is a director (see **11.202**).

An 'employed contributor' is defined as any person who, if over the age of 16 years and under pensionable age, is employed in an insurable employment (SWCA 2005, s 12(1)). Since 'pensionable age' is defined as the age of 66 years (SWCA 2005, s 2(1)), the definition may be simplified to mean a person in an insurable employment who has passed his 16th birthday, but who has not yet reached his 66th birthday. Every person who becomes an employed contributor for the first time thereby becomes insured under the Act and thereafter continues throughout his life to be so insured, but if he ceases to be employed in an insurable employment, he ceases to be obliged to make social insurance contributions so long as this position continues.

The term 'employed contributor', as used in the Social Welfare Acts, may be taken also as including any person, regardless of his age, who is employed in insurable (occupational injuries) employment, but this has effect only with regard to employment contributions, claims, benefits, etc related to occupational injuries insurance. It does not operate to make a person under 16 or over 66 liable to make social insurance contributions. The employer is liable to make the occupational injuries contribution (as part of his total PRSI contribution) in respect of any employee in an insurable (occupational injuries) employment.

Since the majority of employments exercised in the State are both insurable and insurable (occupational injuries) employments, the discussion in the rest of this part of this chapter does not distinguish the latter type of employment.

The rules relating to the liability of individuals for self-employment social insurance contributions on reckonable emoluments (as defined for those purposes), as well as on other self-employment income, are dealt with in detail in **3.402**. The obligation imposed on employers paying reckonable emoluments (as defined) to deduct self-employment contributions are covered in **3.403** and **3.404** where it is noted that the PAYE/PRSI collection system, as discussed in this Division, is used as the mechanism for collecting self employment contributions on Sch E emoluments also.

Employers' PRSI exemption

From 16 September 2003 to 1 May 2009, exemption was granted from employer's PRSI contributions in respect of qualifying employees under the Back to Work Allowance Scheme. The employees were exempt from PRSI (and also income tax) in respect of allowances received under the scheme but remained liable in the normal way to employee's PRSI in respect of their earnings from the employment.

11.202 Insurable employments

An 'insurable employment' is defined as employment such that a person, over the age of 16 years and under pensionable age, employed in it would be an employed contributor (SWCA 2005, s 2(1)). For an employment to be one in respect of which such a person would be an employed contributor, it must be one of the employments specified in SWCA 2005, Sch 1 Pt 1, but it must not be one of the excepted types of employment specified in SWCA 2005, Sch 1 Pt 2. Consequently, in order to arrive at the real meaning of the term, it is necessary to turn to SWCA 2005, Sch 1.

SWCA 2005, Sch 1 Pt 1 para 1 sets out the main definition of an insurable employment in the following terms:

> Employment in the State under any contract of service or apprenticeship, written or oral, whether expressed or implied, and whether the employed person is paid by the employer or some other person, and whether under one or more employers, and whether paid by time or by the piece or partly by time and partly by the piece, or otherwise, or without any money payment.

The two principal elements for there to be an insurable employment within this definition are that the employment be in the State and that it be one under a contract of service. Unless both these elements are present, the office, employment or other relationship that may exist between the person paying the emoluments and the person receiving them is not an insurable employment; consequently, no social insurance contributions are payable in respect of the emoluments. There is no qualification in this definition to exclude an employment under a contract of service made abroad. Consequently, an employment that is in fact carried on in the State under such a foreign contract is just as much an insurable employment as one under a domestic contract.

SWCA 2005, Sch 1 Pt 1 para 2 includes as an insurable employment, or deemed employment, an employment under a contract of service as either the master or a member of the crew of an Irish ship or the captain or a member of the crew of an Irish aircraft. Again, the relevant contract of service may be written or oral, expressed or implied and the remuneration of the employment may be paid either by the employer or some other person. SWCA 2005, Sch 1 Pt 1 para 2 defines an Irish ship or an Irish aircraft in identical terms, namely:

(a) any ship (or aircraft) registered in the State; or

(b) any other ship or vessel (or aircraft) of which the owner either resides or has his principal place of business in the State.

In the event that there is more than one owner of the ship, vessel or aircraft, the ship or aircraft is an Irish one for this purpose if the managing owner or manager resides or has his principal place of business in the State. It is to be noted that SWCA 2005, Sch 1 Pt 1 para 2 does not make it a condition of insurable employment that the employment be exercised in the State. Consequently, any employment within that paragraph is an insurable employment, even if the Irish ship or aircraft on which the employment is exercised spends all its time in international or other foreign transport and does not dock or land at an Irish port or airport.

SWCA 2005, Sch 1 Pt 1 paras 3–12 detail other employments or deemed employments that are insurable employments. These include permanent public sector employees, eg civil servants, members of the Defence Forces and of the Garda Síochána, local or public authority employees, as well as several miscellaneous other types of employment. These employments need not necessarily be exercised in the State, eg a civil servant or member of the Defence Forces serving abroad continues to have an insurable employment.

Agency workers

With effect from 1 April 2003, where an individual agrees with an employment agency to perform work or services for a third party, it appears that he will be deemed to be performing the work, etc in the course of an employment, notwithstanding that in law he may be self-employed (see **10.103**) (SWCA 2005, Sch 1 Pt 1 para 13). This provision will apply irrespective of whether or not the third party is a party to the contract in question and whether or not the third party pays the wages or salary of the employee. The actual wording of the section is less than ideal, since taken at face value, it seems to presuppose that there is an employment in existence and that a payment of wages and salary is being made, but without expressly deeming this state of affairs to exist for the purposes of PRSI.

At the time of writing, the Department of Social & Family Affairs does not accept that this is in fact the effect of the legislation. However, assuming that the provision does in fact operate as described above, the person who is liable to pay the individual's salary or wages (normally the agency) will be deemed to be the individual's employer (SWCA 2005, s 12(4)). If the agency worker is a non-PAYE worker but is operating under the control and management of a third party, the 'intermediate employer' rules contained in SW Reg 39 would indicate that the third party is legally liable for any PRSI liabilities arising out of the deemed employment. While in practice the employment agency is likely to account for PRSI in these circumstances, the third party will it seems remain liable for any default by the agency in these circumstances.

Non-insurable employments

SWCA 2005, Sch 1 Pt 2 lists a number of excepted employments which, even if under a contract of service, are not insurable employments. The most significant of these are:

(a) employment with an employer who is the husband or wife of the employee (SWCA 2005, Sch 1 Pt 2 para 1);

(b) employment of a casual nature, but with the exception that casual employment for the purpose of the employer's trade or profession or any game or recreation where the persons employed are engaged or paid through a club, remain insurable employments (SWCA 2005, Sch 1 Pt 2 para 2);

(c) employment specified in regulations as being of such a nature that it is ordinarily adopted as subsidiary employment only and not as the principal means of livelihood (SWCA 2005, Sch 1 Pt 2 para 4, SW Regs Art 89);

(d) employment by a prescribed relative in the common home of the employer and employee or in corresponding circumstances as defined by Regulation (SW Regs Art 93);

(e) employment 'of inconsiderable extent' as defined by Regulations generally speaking where gross reckonable earnings are less than €38 pw (SW Regs Art 90); and

(f) employments under the Community Employment Scheme administered by FÁS entered into prior to 6 April 1996 (SW Regs Art 88);

(g) employment in a company where the employed person is either the beneficial owner of that company, or able to control 50 per cent or more of the ordinary share capital of that company. (SWCA 2005, Sch 1 Pt 2 para 7 as inserted by SWP(MP)A 2013). See below for meaning of 'contract of service'.

The distinction between an employee acting under a contract *of* service and a self-employed person with a contract *for* services has previously been discussed in **10.103** in the context of the Sch E definition of an employment. The remarks there are equally applicable in the present context. If it is established that the individual is acting under a contract for services, even if he does not provide such service in the course of a regular trade or profession, he does not have an insurable employment.

Directors

As discussed in **10.104**, a director of a company is not, in his capacity as director, employed under a contract of service. Consequently, if his duties for the company are performed solely in the capacity of director, he does not have an insurable employment with the company. However, if he has also a distinct executive or other position in the company in respect of which he has a contract of service with the company, this generally means that he has an insurable employment with the company (subject to the treatment of 'proprietary' directors discussed in the next paragraph). If he has such a position, social insurance contributions are payable in respect of his emoluments for his services as an executive, but not in respect of remuneration/fees paid solely for acting as a director (this aspect is considered more fully at **10.103**).

The Department of Social & Family Affairs take the view that a director who is a majority shareholder in the company of which he is a director, or who is otherwise able to exercise such a degree of control over the affairs of the company that he is able to decide the services he will perform for the company, and the manner and timing of rendering those services does not have a master/servant relationship with the company. On the basis of this view the Department consider that a director in this position – a 'proprietary' director – does not have an insurable employment even if some of his services are of the same nature as would be performed by an ordinary executive director. Consequently, neither the proprietary director nor the company is liable for employed social insurance contributions in respect of his emoluments (although the company remains liable to deduct his Universal Social Charge, and self-employed PRSI and to account for them to the Collector General under the PAYE/PRSI system).

This view has been solidified by an amendment to SWCA 2005, Sch 1 Pt 2 (as amended by the SWP(MP)A 2013, s 12) which provides that a person employed in a company, where that person is the beneficial owner of the company or is able to control 50 per cent or more of the ordinary share capital of the company will not be regarded as being insurable as an employed contributor in the company. The individual will be deemed to be engaged under a contract for services and liable to Class S PRSI contributions.

It remains unclear, however, where a director holds less than 50 per cent of the ordinary share capital, as to whether they are insurable under Class A1 or Class S. The decision in such cases is left to Scope Section of the Department to decide.

The view taken by the Department with regard to a controlling shareholder, does not seem to be consistent with the decision in *Lee v Lee's Air Farming Ltd* [1961] AC 112, where it was held that a controlling director could nevertheless enter into a contract of service with his company. In *SSTI v Bottrill* [1999] ILRL 326, the Court of Appeal made the following pertinent observations:

> Whether an employer/employee relationship exists can only be decided by having regard to all the relevant facts. If an individual has a controlling shareholding that is certainly a fact which is likely to be significant in all situations and in some cases it may prove to be decisive. However, it is only one of the factors which are relevant and certainly is not to be taken as determinative without considering all the relevant circumstances.

The court in *Bottrill* indicated that a crucial element was whether or not the director in question could realistically be dismissed; if not, then there would be no effective control on the part of the company. Nevertheless, if the board included genuinely independent directors alongside the majority shareholder, it would be perfectly possible for the power of dismissal to exist.

It would seem likely that the UK case law, which is based to a large extent on the principle of the separate legal personality of a company, would be upheld by the Irish courts. However, in practice, the Department's view overrides what may strictly be the correct legal position. The criteria applied by the Department in the classification of executive directors emerge clearly in Form INS 1 the questionnaire issued in relation to an application for a decision on the insurable status of a director). It appears that the Chief Appeals Officer decided that three brothers who were directors with roughly one-third shareholdings each and an equal say in the running of, their company, were not in insurable employment (*Tax Fax* 11.7.1997).

The PRSI analysis applied by the Department is not necessarily inconsistent with the general income tax treatment, since in many cases the activities of a director will be treated as referable to his office and thus taxable under Sch E whether or not they are treated as carried out in the course of an employment.

In *Neenan Travel Ltd v Minister for Social and Family Affairs* [2011] IEHC 458, a non-tax case, the court held that a director who held 16.7 per cent of the shares in his employer company, received a monthly salary and who accepted that he could have been contractually dismissed for unsatisfactory performance was held to be working under a contract of service.

Continental shelf employment

The Geneva Convention on the High Seas giving the state rights to natural resources, etc on the Irish sector of the continental shelf, and the Continental Shelf Act 1968 whereby the Government may, by statutory order, declare areas on the continental shelf as designated areas for the purpose of the exploration and exploitation of natural resources, are referred to in **13.606**. The Social Welfare (Continental Shelf) Regulations 1978 (SI 1978/19), a statutory order made under the latter Act, provides that certain employment in a designated area is to be an insurable employment for the purposes of the Social Welfare Acts, notwithstanding that the employment is outside Irish territorial waters and not, therefore, within the State.

The employment specified in this Regulation that is to be treated as an insurable employment is:

> employment in a designated area on or about any drillship, rig, platform or similar installation in the exploration of the seabed or subsoil or in the exploitation of their natural resources which would, if such employment were in the State, be insurable employment.

Consequently, employees exercising such an employment in a designated area (and their employers) are liable to pay social insurance contributions under the same rules as apply to employments in the State. However, a foreign employee working temporarily in a designated area for a foreign employer (and the employer himself) may be exempted by the Department of Social & Family Affairs from liability to contributions, but only if the same conditions apply as exempt a foreign employee working temporarily in the State (see **11.205**).

11.203 Reckonable earnings

The employed social insurance elements of both employee's and employer's PRSI contributions are calculated on the employee's 'reckonable earnings', as defined under the Social Welfare Consolidation Act 2005.

SWCA 2005, s 2(1) defines 'reckonable earnings' as being:

> subject to regulations, earnings derived from insurable employment or insurable (occupational injuries) employment.

SW Regs then defines reckonable earnings more narrowly for the purposes of collecting contributions from employees under the PAYE system as emoluments derived from insurable employment or insurable (occupational injuries) employment, to which TCA 1997, Pt 42, Ch 4 applies, but without regard to s 1015 of that Act, reduced by so much of the allowable contribution referred to in regs 41 and 42 (inserted by the Income Tax (Employments) Consolidated Regulations 2001) (ie 'net pay' on which PAYE is due: see **11.103**) as is deducted on payment of those emoluments.

The exclusion in respect of non-pecuniary emoluments which had previously applied was removed with effect from 1 January 2004, ie bringing into charge all notional payments in respect of taxable benefits in kind.

Employees who make contributions to PRSAs other than by means of deduction from their gross pay are no longer be entitled to have their reckonable earnings reduced accordingly in calculating the employee's PRSI contribution from 1 January 2011; prior to 31 December 2011 the employer's contribution was calculated on the basis of a deduction of 50 per cent of the amount of the contribution. With effect from 1 January 2012 the PRSI relief of 50 per cent from employer PRSI for employee contributions was removed.

The Revenue Commissioners have confirmed that where an employer's PRSA contribution does not give rise to a tax liability after taking into account the corresponding relief due to the employee, then neither PAYE on income or PRSI (for either employee or employer) will apply; the Universal Social Charge will however apply to the full benefit-in-kind (*e-Brief 36/11*).

From 1 January 2011, employee's PRSI applies to the initial market value of shares appropriated to an employee under an approved profit sharing scheme (see **11.406**) as well as both the value of the right to acquire shares under an approved SAYE scheme (see **11.601**) and any notional gain accruing on the exercise of such a right under TCA 1997 s 128 (see **10.113**). In practice, it appears that the Revenue Commissioners will seek only to impose a charge on the latter gain, since otherwise an element of double taxation would arise. Employers' PRSI should not apply in these circumstances as noted above.

In the case of 'special contributors' (ie non-PAYE contributors), the definition of reckonable earnings is more expansively framed to include:

> salaries, wages and other similar remuneration derived from insurable employment or insurable (occupational injuries) employment, to which the provisions of TCA 1997 (other than Ch 4 of Pt 42) apply or would apply if the employed contributor in receipt of remuneration were resident in the state, but without regard to s 1015 of that Act.

It may be noted that termination payments whether or not taxable under Sch E are not liable to PRSI contributions; however, any taxable element remains liable to the Universal Social Charge (see **3.402**).

In short, the employer paying emoluments (or providing taxable benefits) of an insurable employment that are chargeable to income tax under Sch E (so that he is obliged to deduct income tax under PAYE) is required to deduct also the employee's total PRSI contribution as well as the Universal Social Charge in respect of 'relevant emoluments'. The employer has then to pay over the amount deducted, together with the employer's own PRSI contribution, at the time of lodging the Form P30 within fourteen days of the end of the income tax month or 23rd of the month if filing and paying on the Revenue Online Service (ROS) (subject to the provisions for certain small businesses to account for PAYE on a quarterly basis or availing of the direct debit facility noted at **11.101**). The employee's and employer's contributions are calculated at the relevant rates for the employee's contribution class (see **11.204**). The employer is not entitled to deduct the employer's contribution from an employee's remuneration (or otherwise to recover the contributions from the employee), and any contractual agreement to that effect is void (SWCA 2005, s 13(6)). Where the employer makes a deduction within SWCA 2005, s 13(6) or attempts to do so, he commits a criminal offence (SWCA 2005, s 252(1)(b)). The employer must deduct the employee's contributions at the time of payment, otherwise, he will be liable to bear the cost personally.

In the case of an employee taken on after a previous employment with another employer during the contribution year, the employee's Form P45 from his previous employer should indicate his total net pay since the commencement of the previous tax year to the date of leaving that employment. The new employer should continue to account for both the employee and the employer PRSI contributions at the rates appropriate to the employee's cumulative reckonable earnings for the year from both his current employment and his previous employment(s).

In the event that any employee has two or more separate employments (or offices) running concurrently, each employer is required to account for the employee PRSI contributions separately.

11.204 Rates of PRSI contributions

A summary of PRSI rates for 2015 is set out below.

	Rate		*Income limit*
Employer's PRSI	10.75%	1	No limit
Employee's PRSI	4%	2	No limit
Self-employed PRSI	4%	3	No limit

Notes:

1. Employer's PRSI is 8.5 per cent on income of €376 per week or less, prior to 1 January 2016 the income threshold was €356 per week.
2. There is no employee's PRSI on income of €352.00 per week or less, calculated on a non-cumulative basis. From 1 January 2016 for gross earnings between €352.01 and €424, the amount of the PRSI charge at 4% is reduced by a new tapered weekly PRSI Credit. The maximum weekly PRSI Credit of €12.00 applies at gross weekly earnings of €352.01. For gross weekly earnings over €352.01, the maximum weekly PRSI Credit of €12.00 is reduced by one-sixth of weekly earnings in excess of €352.01. There is no PRSI Credit once gross weekly earnings exceed €424.
3. No self-employed PRSI if income from all sources is less than €5,000 pa.

The rate of the employee's and the employer's total PRSI contributions varies depending on the particular contribution class in which he is insured. There are numerous contribution classes each applying to certain types of employment and providing cover for a different range of social insurance (including occupational injuries and redundancy) benefits.

A detailed analysis of the PRSI regime is outside the scope of this book. Accordingly, it is not proposed to give details of the rates of contribution for all classes, but only for a class A1 employees, which in fact covers the majority of employees.

It should be noted that from 1 January 2013, the exemption from employee's PRSI which applied to the first €127 of weekly earnings was abolished. Therefore all income, for employees earning over €352 per week is subject to employee's PRSI. From 1 January 2011, the employer's contribution ceiling was removed so that the employer is liable to contribute at the rate of 10.75 per cent on all earnings of each employee's reckonable earnings (reduced to 8.5 per cent where earnings are below €356 per week). The employer's social insurance contribution is not payable on earnings other than reckonable earnings (but see **11.201** for the liability to PRSI for employees who are chargeable persons, and modified rate contributors from 1 January 2014 and 1 January 2013 respectively and **3.403** for the liability to self-employment contributions).

11.205 Foreign aspects

The general principle that the employee's (and the employer's) liability for social insurance contributions depends solely on whether the employment is exercised in the State is, in practice, subject to a number of exceptions. These relate to cases where an employee, who normally resides and works in the State, is sent abroad by his employer for a temporary period or, in the reverse case, where a person comes from a foreign country to work in the State for a foreign employer. The treatment applied in practice in each type of case depends on whether the temporary transfer of employment is to or from either another Member State of the European Community or an EEA state (or Switzerland) or a country with which Ireland has entered into a bilateral social security agreement. Discussion of these issues is outside the scope of a work dealing with income tax, but it should be noted that in some cases employees posted to the State may be permitted to remain outside the Irish social security system for periods of up to five years.

Sch D Case III emoluments

Foreign offices, employments and pensions

The fact that the emoluments of a foreign office, employment or pension are chargeable to income tax under Sch D Case III does not necessarily mean that no PRSI contributions are payable by the employee or employer. For the purpose of the social insurance element of the PRSI contribution (including the employer's redundancy and occupational injuries contributions), the sole test is whether there is an insurable employment which is, in fact, exercised within the State by a person over 16 and under 66. If there is, the place where the contract of employment was concluded, the residence or non-residence of the employer and the place where the emoluments are paid do not affect the issue. If the employment is exercised within the State both the employee and employer must pay the normal social insurance contributions in respect of the full reckonable earnings. As noted above, in practice, the definition of reckonable earnings for non-PAYE employees ('Special Contributors') is applied in a similar manner to the definition applicable to PAYE employees.

Since 1 January 2006, the earnings from a foreign-source employment held by an Irish resident are in any event, generally taxable under Sch E to the extent that they are attributable to duties performed in the State (TCA 1997, s 18(2) as amended by FA 2006, s 15) under Sch E and subject to PAYE accordingly.

However, since income tax on the emoluments chargeable under Sch D Case III is not normally collected through the PAYE system, some other procedure is required to collect the social insurance contributions.

The social insurance contributions for both the employee and the employer in respect of the employee's reckonable earnings should be made directly, usually by the employer, to the Department of Social Protection, PRSI Special Collections Section. The employer should use a 'special contributor's' form with each remittance, giving the necessary particulars of the employees in respect of whom the contributions are made. PRSI in respect of employees with PAYE Exclusion Orders is required to be returned to the Revenue with the P30/P35 since 1 January 2011.

The Universal Social Charge in respect of employment emoluments taxable under Sch D Case III are all collected by the Collector General by direct demand. This demand is based on the individual's 'relevant income', ie on all the income in respect of which he is assessable to income tax, but excluding any relevant emoluments subject to PAYE.

11.3 Employees' Share Purchase Scheme

11.301 How the relief is granted

TCA 1997, s 479 entitled an individual, if he was a full-time director or a full-time employee of a qualifying company or of its 75 per cent subsidiary, to tax relief in respect of his subscription(s) for eligible shares, ie new ordinary shares meeting certain conditions, issued by the qualifying company. The relief was given by way of a deduction from the individual's total income for the year of assessment in which the shares are issued (TCA 1997, s 479(2)). The total deduction given to any one individual in respect of all amounts subscribed for eligible shares issued to him in *all* tax years from 1996–97 onwards was €6,350.

The relief has been abolished in respect of all subscriptions for shares made on or after 8 December 2010. A full description of the nature of the relief, the manner in which it was granted and the limits to the deduction are fully covered in the 2010 edition of this work.

11.4 Approved Profit Sharing Schemes

11.401 Introduction

TCA 1997, Pt 17 Ch 1 (ss 509–518) enables a body corporate ('the company concerned') to establish a 'profit sharing scheme' under which shares in the company or in a connected company may, if certain conditions are met, be appropriated income tax free to eligible employees or directors. With effect from 1 January 2011 the value of shares appropriated to participants under the scheme is subject to USC and PRSI. These amounts are required to be collected by the employer company under the PAYE system.

The object of the provisions under TCA 1997, Pt 17 Ch 1 (ss 509–518) is to facilitate the acquisition of shares by employees in their employer companies, but to do so under a scheme the form of which has to be approved by the Revenue Commissioners and under rules which withdraw, in whole or in part, the tax benefit to the employee if he does not retain the shares for at least three years.

The profit sharing scheme ('the scheme') must be one set up by the company concerned under a trust deed providing for the establishment of a body of persons resident in the State ('the trustees') responsible for administering the scheme. The trustees have to acquire the shares in the company concerned (or, if relevant, in a connected company) that are to be appropriated to the individuals eligible to participate ('the participants') out of moneys paid to them by the company concerned or, if there is a group scheme, by another participating company. Usually, the shares acquired by the trustees ('the scheme shares') are new shares issued by the company concerned (or a connected company) for which the trustees subscribe directly, but the scheme shares may also be existing shares in the company (or a connected company) purchased by the trustees.

The trustees have the duty to appropriate the scheme shares to the participants in accordance with their respective entitlements under the terms of the scheme, but the value of the shares appropriated to any one participant in any tax year may not exceed €12,700. This limit was increased by FA 1999, on a once off basis, to €38,100 in respect of shares which previously had been held in an Employee Share Ownership Trust (ESOT) for a minimum period of 10 years where those shares were held in an ESOT as security for its borrowings by the ESOT for a minimum period of five years. The tax regime applicable to ESOTs is explained in **11.5**.

FA 2000, s 24 further modified this section to enable this period to be reduced by order of the Minister of Finance, with the prior approval of Dáil Éireann. This limit is measured by reference to the 'initial market value' of all the shares appropriated by the trustees under the scheme to the participant in the year in question. The initial market value of any shares is normally their market value at the date of appropriation to the participant (but see **11.407**). The chargeable value for the purposes of PRSI and USC is the initial market value of the shares being appropriated. The employer is required to deduct such amounts when the funds are being given to the trustees to purchase the shares. Revenue has confirmed in *Tax Briefing 02/2011* that it is not intended that the requirement to fund the USC and PRSI should impact on the current annual limit on the value of shares that can be appropriated of €12,700.

FA 2001 amended the legislation to facilitate the establishment and operation of ESOTs and Approved Profit Sharing Schemes in TSB Bank and ICC Bank in the context of their impending sale. In each case the ESOT/APSS was limited to the current employees of those companies even after they were taken over. Provision was also made to ensure that the employees would be entitled to benefit from ESOT/APSSs established by the respective companies taking over these banks with normal limits (as outlined above) applying to the aggregate of all shares appropriated in any year. Certain other amendments were introduced to this legislation by FA 2002. Its effects are four-fold:

It amends the definition of 'shares' as contained in TCA 1997, s 509(1) to include 'specified securities'. The purpose of this amendment is to ensure that the transfer or appropriation of shares or securities (other than ordinary shares) to the participants of an APSS/ESOT in the circumstances of certain takeovers may take place in a manner which preserves the tax benefits of the participants. The takeovers are ones to which TCA 1997, s 586 applies and which occur after the APSS/ESOT was established. TCA 1997, s 586 prescribes the rules to be adhered to under a company's amalgamation by exchange of shares and was enacted to outlaw the kind of schemes involved in *Furniss v Dawson* [1982] STC 267 and *Floor v Davis* [1979] STC 379.

The legislation brought into being by FA 2002, s 13 provides that the tax benefits enjoyed by the participants in the APSS/ESOT may carry through in the event of the reorganisation of share capital under TCA 1997, s 584 where such companies have no ordinary share capital or insufficient ordinary share capital available to them:

(a) It also provides that income receivable on the type of securities mentioned above may be used to reinvest in other such securities.

(b) It restates TCA 1997, s 511A to ensure that the three-year retention period for which the shares must be held to benefit from the relief will be satisfied if the total combined time that such shares are held in an APSS or an ESOT exceed this three-year limit.

(c) It includes ACC Bank and the company that acquired control of the Irish National Petroleum Corporation Limited under the definition of 'relevant company' in TCA 1997, Sch 12 para 1(1). This amendment allows the original employees to participate in both the original APSS/ESOT and, if necessary, a second APSS, subject to the overall APSS limit of €12,700 per annum.

Other principal features of the legislation are:

(a) each participant is bound under contract to permit his scheme shares to remain in the ownership of the trustees for at least a minimum 'period of retention' (normally two years, but see **11.407**), and not to assign, charge or otherwise dispose of his beneficial interest in his shares during that retention period;

(b) if a participant is to remain entirely free of income tax in respect of his scheme shares, he should let the shares remain in the names (ie legal ownership) of the trustees until the third anniversary ('the release date') of the day on which the particular shares were appropriated to him and, further, he should not dispose of his beneficial interest in the shares (which he acquires when they are appropriated to him) before the release date (the 'release date' was the fifth anniversary prior to 10 May 1997: see TCA 1997, s 511(2));

[This three-year retention is not however necessary where the shares had previously been held for at least three years in an ESOT of which the participant was at all times a beneficiary. Furthermore, where the shares were held in an ESOT for less than three years the three-year APSS requirement is reduced pro-rata.]

(c) if a participant's shares should be disposed of or if he should derive certain other capital benefits from them before the release date, he is charged to income tax under Sch E, usually on an amount arrived at as a percentage (which reduces the longer the shares are held) of the market value of the shares on the date of appropriation;

(d) should the participant breach his obligation and assign (or otherwise dispose of) his beneficial interest in scheme shares before the end of the retention period, he is chargeable to tax under Sch E on the full market value of the shares as at the date of assignment;

(e) the death of the participant before the release date does not, however, cause any income tax liability to arise in respect of his scheme shares;

(f) dividends and other distributions received by the trustees in respect of the participant's scheme shares must be paid to him as they arise (so as to be taxable as his income);

(g) for any scheme to be approved by the Revenue Commissioners, they must be satisfied that the conditions set out in TCA 1997, Sch 11 and the further requirements of TCA 1997, s 511 are met (see **11.402–11.405**); and

(h) no scheme may be approved by the Revenue Commissioners unless it is open to every employee and director satisfying a minimum qualification period (other than certain 'proprietary' directors or employees).

With the intention of tackling potential avoidance schemes, FA 2001, s 16(a) amended para 4(1A)(b) of TCA 1997, Sch 11, redefining a group of companies and also inserted the new para (13B). This was to tackle the possibility of the scheme being manipulated to benefit directors or higher paid employees of the company. There was a danger that the normal rules (stating that the scheme must not wholly or mainly benefit these directors or highly paid executives) could be circumvented by transferring the directors or employees concerned to a company outside the 'group' as was previously defined. To this end, the definitions of 'group of companies' has been extended to cover associated companies which would not normally fall within the group.

With effect from 4 February 2010, shares in service companies (as defined) are no longer be eligible for relief, and approval will not be granted to any scheme where there are arrangements in place to provide loans or other forms of credit to participants in the scheme.

The establishment of a profit sharing scheme may be complemented by an employee share ownership trust (TCA 1997, s 519; Sch 12). The rules governing the deductibility for corporation tax purposes of payments to the trustees of an approved scheme and expenditure on establishing an approved scheme are contained in TCA 1997, ss 517 and 518, respectively.

11.402 Approval by Revenue Commissioners

The Revenue Commissioners are required to approve a profit sharing scheme if, on the application of the company which has established the scheme (the company concerned), they are satisfied that the scheme complies with the conditions necessary for approval as set out in TCA 1997, Sch 11. The application for approval must be in writing containing such particulars and supported by such evidence as the Commissioners may require. Before outlining and discussing the conditions which have to be met, it is necessary to distinguish between the 'single company scheme' and the 'group scheme'.

A single company scheme is one established for the benefit only of employees and directors of the company concerned. A group scheme is a scheme which by its terms is expressed as extending to all or any of the companies of which the company concerned setting up the scheme has control. A group scheme is for the benefit of the employees and directors of both the company concerned and each controlled company to which the scheme is extended. In dealing with a group scheme, the legislation uses the term 'participating company' as meaning either the company concerned or any controlled company that is within the scheme (TCA 1997, Sch 11 para 3). Please note the comments above and the redefinition of 'group of companies' contained at TCA 1997, Sch 11 para 4(1A)(b) and (1B).

The conditions which the profit sharing scheme must satisfy before the Revenue Commissioners can approve it, so that the participants may benefit from the tax free appropriation of scheme shares to them, may be summarised as follows:

(a) the scheme must be one which complies with both TCA 1997, Sch 11 para 3(3) and (4) (see below);

(b) the Revenue Commissioners must be satisfied that every employee or full-time director of the company concerned, or of each participating company in a group scheme, is eligible to participate on similar terms as provided for in TCA 1997, Sch 11 para 4 (unless he is ineligible under any of the rules of TCA 1997, Sch 11 Pt 4);

(c) the Revenue Commissioners must be satisfied that, whether under the terms of the scheme or otherwise, every participant in the scheme is bound in contract with the company concerned to comply with the matters set out in TCA 1997, s 511; and

(d) the scheme must not contain any features which appear to the Revenue Commissioners to be neither essential nor reasonably incidental to the purpose of providing benefits in the nature of interest in shares for employees and directors.

It may be noted that for schemes approved prior to 10 May 1997, the reference in condition (b) to 'employee' was to 'full-time employee'.

TCA 1997, Sch 11 para 3(3) requires that the scheme provide for the establishment of a body of persons resident in the State ('the trustees'):

(a) who, out of monies paid to them by the company concerned, are required by the scheme to acquire shares that meet the 'conditions as to shares' set out in TCA 1997, Sch 11 Pt 3 (see **11.404**);

(b) who are under a duty to appropriate the shares acquired to individuals who, not being ineligible under TCA 1997, Sch 11 Pt 4 (see **11.403**), participate in the scheme; and

(c) whose functions are regulated by a trust constituted under Irish law the terms of which are embodied in a trust instrument that complies with the provisions of TCA 1997, Sch 11 Pt 5 (see **11.405**).

In the case of a group scheme, the monies to be applied by the trustees in acquiring the shares may be provided by any one or more of the participating companies. In practice, the rules of TCA 1997, s 517 for the deduction of its contributions to the scheme in calculating each participating company's taxable income should mean that each company will normally contribute to the cost of the scheme more or less in proportion to the share benefits derived by its own employees and directors (see **11.414**).

TCA 1997, Sch 11 para 3(4) requires the scheme to provide that the total initial market value of the shares appropriated by the trustees to any participant in any one tax year is not to exceed an upper limit of €12,700 or €38,100 in certain circumstances (TCA 1997, s 515(1)(b)). The €38,100 limit applies where the following conditions are satisfied:

(a) shares allocated to an individual have been transferred to the trustees of the APSS scheme by the trustees of an approved ESOT;

(b) at the time of the transfer of the shares from the ESOT to the APSS, the shares must have been held as security for borrowings by the ESOT for a period of at least ten years;

(c) at all times in the five years since the ESOT was established, 50 per cent of the securities held by the ESOT trustees (or less if allowed by the Minister for Finance) were pledged as security for borrowings (the Minister for Finance may reduce this five year period by order, with effect from 6 April 2000 (FA 2000, s 24);

(d) none of the shares pledged at any time since the ESOT was transferred have been transferred from the trustees of the ESOT to the trustees of the APSS because they have been pledged for the period of 10 years or more referred to above.

The €38,100 limit may only be applied in the first year of assessment in which the 'encumbered period' has elapsed and then only in respect of shares allocated after the encumbered period has elapsed.

TCA 1997, s 515(2) contains technical provisions dealing with situations where a participant is allocated shares in two or more schemes. There is, however, no reason why the terms of a scheme may not permit a participant to have shares appropriated to him in each successive year with an initial market value not exceeding the limit for that year. For the meaning of 'initial market value' see **11.407**.

TCA 1997, Sch 11 para 4 requires the Revenue Commissioners to be satisfied that every employee or director of the company concerned (in a single company scheme) is eligible to participate on similar terms if:

(a) he is at the time an employee or full-time director of the company concerned (see above); and

(b) he has been such an employee or director throughout a qualifying period prescribed by the scheme (which may not exceed three years) (with effect from 25 March 1999, previously five years); and

(c) he is chargeable to tax in respect of his office or employment under Sch E;

provided that he is not rendered ineligible to participate by any of the rules of TCA 1997, Sch 11 Pt 4 (see **11.403**).

In the case of a group scheme, the Revenue Commissioners must be satisfied that every employee or full-time director in each participating company must be eligible to participate subject to the same conditions. The requirements of TCA 1997, Sch 11 para 4 do not necessarily mean that an employee or director some or all of whose emoluments are from a foreign office or employment with the company (or a participating company) is ineligible to participate, should the terms of the scheme permit it to do so. It is not, however, essential that an individual with emoluments taxable under Sch D Case III be included in the employees and directors eligible to participate.

The requirement of TCA 1997, Sch 11 para 4 is that every individual eligible to do so must be able to participate on similar terms. This does not prevent the scheme from providing that the number of shares that may be appropriated to the participants should vary by reference to different levels of remuneration, length of service or similar factors (TCA 1997, Sch 11 para 4(2)). However, the Revenue Commissioners take the view that where levels of remuneration are used as a reference point, these should relate to basic salary only (ie exclusive of bonuses, overtime, etc – *Tax Briefing 20*). Shares may be allocated on the basis of salary banding within strict limits and may be allocated by reference to a formula which takes both salary and length of service into account; allocation on the basis of performance/appraisal schemes is also permitted subject to strict conditions. The allocation of shares on the basis of age, status or seniority of grade will not be acceptable (*Tax Briefing 56*).

The ability of every single employee or director of the company concerned (or participating companies in a group scheme) to participate, should he wish to do so, is an absolute requirement. The Revenue Commissioners will not, and cannot, approve a profit sharing scheme that is open to some classes of employees and/or directors (eg sales representatives and factory workers) and not to others (eg directors and head office staff). Furthermore, approval will not be available where it is considered that a scheme is established only for the benefit of a group of higher paid employees and directors, for example, if such persons were reorganised into one company within a group and the scheme was only to apply to this company.

TCA 1997, s 511(4) prevents the approval of a profit sharing scheme unless the Revenue Commissioners are satisfied that every participant in the scheme is bound in contract with the company concerned:

(a) to permit his shares to remain in the hands of the trustees throughout the period of retention (as **11.407**);

(b) not to assign, charge or otherwise dispose of his beneficial interest in his shares during the period of retention;

(c) if he should direct the trustees to transfer the ownership of his shares to him at any time before the release date (see **11.407**), to pay to the trustees a certain sum (see **11.410**); and

(d) not to direct the trustees to dispose of his shares before the release date otherwise than by a sale for the best money consideration that can reasonably be obtained.

TCA 1997, s 511(6) permits certain specified exceptions to the foregoing. The participant's contractual obligation with the company does not prevent his directing the trustees to accept an offer for his shares as part of a general offer (eg on a take-over) for the shares of the company as a whole. It does not prevent his directing the trustees to accept a new holding of shares and/or securities as part of a reconstruction, amalgamation, etc. The consequences of these permitted exceptions to the participant's obligations under TCA 1997, s 511(4) are discussed further in **11.408** (disposals of scheme shares before release date) and in **11.412** (company reconstructions etc).

With effect for schemes approved on or after 4 February 2010, the Revenue Commissioners must be satisfied that there are no arrangements connected in any way, directly or indirectly, with the scheme, which make provision for a loan or loans to be made to some or all of the eligible participants (TCA 1997, Sch 11 para 4 (1C), inserted by FA 2010, s 19(1)(a)).

Salary sacrifice/contributory schemes

Historically, the Revenue Commissioners have approved a number of profit sharing schemes which are partly funded by salary sacrifices on the part of the participating employees.

In *Tax Briefing 20*, the Revenue have indicated the guidelines which they apply in deciding whether to grant approval to such schemes as follows:

(a) the salary foregone must form only a subsidiary element of the overall scheme;
(b) the salary foregone should be optional for each participant;
(c) the maximum amount of salary that may be foregone is 7.5 per cent of basic salary;
(d) where it is intended to include a provision for a minimum amount of salary to be foregone, that minimum amount cannot exceed €127 or one per cent of basic salary;
(e) where varying percentages are included in a scheme the same choice must be given to all participants; and
(f) in respect of each participant there must be at least a 1:1 ratio between the shares appropriated in lieu of salary foregone and the shares funded by the other monies provided by the company.

For these purposes, shares funded by discretionary bonuses, will concessionally be regarded as part of the employer-funded element of a scheme so long as the bonuses are based on objective criteria and are payable to all employees and directors as a basis of entitlement under an approved scheme. The Revenue Commissioners have announced that they will not approve new schemes which utilise non-discretionary ('fixed') bonuses as a basis of entitlement nor permit existing schemes to incorporate fixed bonuses as a basis of entitlement; bonuses payable under so-called 'flex plans' (agreements to restructure pay and working arrangements) are not acceptable from 2005 onwards (*Tax Briefing 56*).

In the case of a salary sacrifice scheme it is understood that the Revenue Commissioners would not have sought to apply the decision in *Heaton v Bell* (see **10.105**) in order to tax the employees on the salary foregone as an application of their salary, rather than as an effective waiver of salary. With effect from 31 January 2008, the position regarding salary sacrifices in relation to profit-sharing schemes is placed on a statutory footing by TCA 1997, s 118B (see **10.105**).

In *Tax Briefing 20*, the Revenue Commissioners also indicate that a 'contributory element' may be included in profit sharing schemes. This refers to the situation where participants in a scheme are required by the employer company to purchase shares out of after-tax (or 'net') salary in order to receive free shares under the scheme. The following guidelines will be applied in deciding whether approval be granted to such schemes:

(a) the 'contributory' amount must form only a subsidiary element of the overall scheme;
(b) the maximum amount of shares purchased out of 'net' salary cannot exceed 7.5 per cent of basic salary;
(c) where it is intended to include a minimum amount in respect of a participant's contribution that minimum amount cannot exceed €127 or one per cent of basic salary;
(d) each participant must receive at least one free share for each share purchased;
(e) while the 'purchased' shares do not form part of an approved profit sharing scheme they must be retained for the employee by nominees/trustees for a minimum period of two years.

The Revenue emphasise that the granting of approval to salary sacrifice or contributory schemes is purely concessional and that each scheme will be considered according to its own particular rules. Thus, adherence to the guidelines will normally be a necessary condition for approval but is not a guarantee of approval. The normal monitoring and review procedures will apply to such schemes.

11.403 Individuals ineligible to participate

TCA 1997, Sch 11 Pt 4 sets out certain sets of circumstances which, if they apply to him, make an individual *ineligible* to have scheme shares appropriated to him in any tax year affected by the particular circumstances.

Shares may not be appropriated under the scheme to an individual in any given tax year:

(a) unless he is at the time of appropriation, or was within the preceding 18 months, a director or employee of the company concerned (or, if a group scheme, of a participating company) (TCA 1997, Sch 11 para 12), (there is one exception to this rule, with effect from 25 March 1999, appropriation of shares made by the trustees of an APSS is permitted to an individual at any time if those shares were transferred to the trustees of the scheme by the trustees of an ESOT and the individual is at that time or was within the previous 30 days, a beneficiary);
(b) if, in the same tax year, shares have previously been appropriated to him under another approved scheme established by either:
   (i) the company concerned,
   (ii) a 'connected company',
   (iii) a company which is a member of a consortium that owns the company concerned, or
   (iv) a company which is owned in part by the company concerned in its capacity as a member of a consortium (TCA 1997, Sch 11 para 13); and
(c) if he has at the date of the appropriation, or had at any time within the 12 months preceding that date, an interest of more than 15 per cent in the ordinary share capital of a close company which is either:
   (i) the company of which the shares are to be appropriated ('the scheme company'), or
   (ii) a company that has control of the scheme company, or
   (iii) a company which is a member of a consortium which owns the scheme company (TCA 1997, Sch 11 para 14(1)).

For the purposes of (b) above, a 'connected company' is either a company controlling or controlled by the company concerned, or is a company which is controlled by a third company which also controls the company concerned.

In the case of appropriations of shares made on or after 23 March 2000, the limitation under (b) may not apply where shares are issued under an approved scheme by a company which has acquired control, or is part of a consortium which has acquired ownership, of the company which has previously issued approved scheme shares to the individual; this exception will only apply where the requisite control or ownership is acquired under a scheme of reconstruction or amalgamation, as defined by TCA 1997, s 587. The Revenue Commissioners take the view that a reconstruction entails an undertaking being transferred from one company to another company consisting substantially of the same shareholders and that an amalgamation entails the blending of two undertakings into one undertaking with the shareholders of each company becoming substantially the shareholders in the company carrying on the blended undertaking. The limits of €12,700 or €38,100, as the case may be, apply to the aggregate value of the shares issued by both companies in the tax year (TCA 1997, Sch 13A inserted by FA 2000, s 25).

For the purposes of (c) above, a 'close company' is given the meaning attributed to the term by TCA 1997, s 430, except that the term includes both a non-resident company which would be a close company if resident in the State and also a company which only escapes being a close company because 35 per cent or more of its voting power is held by the 'public' through shares quoted on a stock exchange.

For the purposes of the foregoing rules, the term 'control' in relation to a company is given the same meaning as in TCA 1997, s 432. A company is a member of a consortium owning another company if (a) it is one of not more than five companies which between them beneficially own 75 per cent or more of the other company's ordinary share capital and (b) each member of the consortium beneficially owns no less than five per cent of that share capital.

11.404 Conditions as to shares

TCA 1997, Sch 11 Pt 3 prescribes the conditions which must be met by the shares that are acquired by the trustees for the purposes of an approved profit sharing scheme ('the scheme shares'). These conditions are:

(a) the scheme shares must form part of the ordinary share capital of:

  (i) the company concerned,

  (ii) a company which has control of the company concerned,

  (iii) a company which is a member of a consortium that owns either the company concerned or a company controlling the company concerned, and itself beneficially owns at least 15 per cent of the company so owned, or

  (iv) a company which issued the shares to the trustees of an ESOT to which TCA 1997, s 519 applies, in an exchange to which TCA 1997, s 586 applies, which shares were transferred to the trustees of an approved scheme by the trustees of the ESOT;

(b) any reference in (a)(iv) above to shares shall include shares which were issued to an ESOT as a result of a reorganisation or reduction of share capital in accordance with TCA 1997, s 584 which occurred subsequent to the exchange referred to therein and which represent:

(i) the shares referred to in (a)(iv),

(ii) the specified securities issued in such an exchange as is referred to in the definition of 'specified securities' contained in TCA 1997, s 509(1) (see **11.401**);

(c) the scheme shares must be either:

(i) shares of a class quoted on a recognised stock exchange, or

(ii) shares in a company which is not under the control of any other company, or

(iii) shares in a company which is under the control of a company whose shares are quoted on a recognised stock exchange (but only if the controlling quoted company is neither a close company nor a company which would, if resident in the State, be a close company) (TCA 1997, Sch 11 para 9);

(d) the scheme shares must be fully paid up, not redeemable, and not subject to any restrictions which do not apply to all shares of the same class, other than 'authorised restrictions' (see the commentary below) (TCA 1997, Sch 11 para 10); and

(e) if the company in which the scheme shares are held has more than one class of ordinary share capital, the majority of the issued shares of the class of ordinary shares of which the scheme shares form part must be held by persons *other than*:

(i) persons who acquired their shares through a right conferred or an opportunity afforded as a director or employee of the company concerned or of any other company (except as a result of a public offer),

(ii) trustees holding shares on behalf of persons who acquired their beneficial interests in the shares in the manner described in (i), and

(iii) any company that controls, or is an associated company of, the company in which the scheme shares are held (but only if the scheme shares are unquoted shares in a company that is under the control of a non-close quoted company) (TCA 1997, Sch 11 para 11).

In applying condition (a)(iii), a company is a member of a consortium that owns another company if the same two conditions mentioned in the last paragraph of **11.403** are met. With regard to condition (d), the effect is to prevent the scheme shares from being in a separate class of ordinary shares if the majority of the holders of issued shares in that class is made up of the trustees of the profit sharing scheme and/or individuals who acquired their shares as a result of the profit sharing scheme and/or, if (iii) above applies, a controlling or associated company. If there is only one class of ordinary share capital in the company in which the scheme shares are held, there is no need to consider condition (d).

In applying condition (c), the exception for 'authorised restrictions' applies to schemes approved on or after 10 May 1997. TCA 1997, Sch 11 para 10(2) provides that the scheme shares may be subject to a *restriction* imposed by the articles of the company, requiring:

(a) all shares held by directors or employees of the company or controlled subsidiaries to be disposed of when they cease to be directors or employees, and

(b) anyone who has never been or is no longer an employee or director to dispose of shares when they acquire them in pursuance of rights obtained by employees or directors (eg personal representatives on the death of an employee).

The restriction, however, must be such that:

(a) any disposal required by the restriction will be by way of sale for money on terms specified in the company's Articles; and

(b) the Articles require all shares of the same class (whether or not acquired under the scheme) to be sold on the same terms as specified under (a) above (TCA 1997, Sch 11 para 10(3)).

Furthermore, the restriction must not require a person to dispose of his beneficial interest in the scheme shares prior to the release date, unless she has already acquired the legal ownership of those shares from the trustees (TCA 1997, Sch 11 para 10(4)).

Also, in applying paragraphs (i) and (ii) of condition (d), the persons to be excluded from the required majority include persons who acquired their shares in the scheme class by the exercise of a share option granted by reason of their office or employment (see **10.113**) or by an acquisition under the employees' share purchase scheme.

'Ordinary share capital' – for the purposes of the above and of the profit sharing scheme rules generally – bears the meaning attributable to the term by TCA 1997, s 2(1). This defines ordinary share capital, in relation to a company, as:

> all the issued share capital (by whatever named called) of the company, other than capital the holders of which have a right to a dividend at a fixed rate, but have no other right to share in the profits of the company.

An 'associated company' – for the purposes of (d)(iii) above – is (TCA 1997, Sch 11 para 11(c)) as defined in TCA 1997, s 432. TCA 1997, s 432(1) provides that one company is an associated company of another company at any given time if, at that time or at any time within one year previously, one of the two has control of the other, or both are under the control of the same person or persons. 'Control' is again given the same meaning as in the rest of TCA 1997, s 432.

It may be noted that, while only the company establishing the scheme and companies controlled by it (ie excluding any company that controls it) can be participating companies in a group scheme, there is no reason why the scheme shares may not be in the parent company of the company concerned, or in a group scheme, in the parent company of all the participating companies. Generally, if there is a group of companies, it is in fact the parent company that establishes the scheme for its employees and directors and for those of any of its subsidiaries it wishes to include as participating companies in a group scheme.

There is no reason why the scheme shares may not be shares in the ordinary share capital of a non-resident company, provided that all the conditions of TCA 1997, Sch 11 Pt 3 as to the scheme shares are met. For example, an Irish resident subsidiary of a UK resident company quoted on the London Stock Exchange could establish an approved profit sharing scheme for its own employees and directors (or a group scheme to include its own subsidiary companies) and provide that the trustees may acquire ordinary shares in the UK parent company for appropriation under the scheme.

In the case of shares appropriated on or after 4 February 2010, they must not be shares in a 'service company'. A service company is defined as one company where the business carried on by that company consists wholly or mainly of the provision of the services of persons employed by that company and the majority of those services are provided to either: (i) a person or persons who have, control of the company, or (ii) a company associated with the company, or (iii) a partnership associated with the company. For these purposes, a company is associated with another company where either (i) both companies are under the control of the same person or persons, or (ii) it could reasonably be considered that either: (I) both companies act in pursuit of a common purpose, or (II) any person or any group(s) of persons having a reasonable commonality of identity have or have had the means or power, either directly or indirectly, to determine the trading operations to be carried on by both companies or (III) both companies are under the control of any person or any group(s) of persons having a reasonable commonality of identity. A partnership is associated with a company where the partnership and the company act in pursuit of a common purpose.

A 'person' includes a partnership, and where a partner, or a partner together with another person or persons, has control of a company, the partnership is to be treated as having control of that company. 'Control' throughout bears the meaning given by TCA 1997, s 432.

The prohibition is extended to shares in a company which controls a service company but, in a proviso of stunning obscurity, only if that company is under the control of a persons or persons referred to in relation to the service company provisions (*viz* persons who a person or persons who control the service company and who are in receipt of the majority of its services) (TCA 1997, Sch 11 para 8B, inserted by FA 2010, s 19).

11.405 Requirements as to trust deed

TCA 1997, Sch 11 Pt 5 provides that the trust instrument or deed, which must relate to a trust under Irish law, must:

(a) require the trustees to notify each participant, as soon as practical afterwards, of any shares appropriated to him, specifying both the number and description of those shares and their initial market value (TCA 1997, Sch 11 para 15);

(b) prohibit the trustees from disposing of any shares appropriated to any participant before the end of the relevant period of retention (except on a direction from the participant in question in connection with a general offer, scheme of arrangement or other capital reconstruction);

(c) prohibit the trustees from disposing of any shares after the end of the period of retention and before the release date, except under a direction given by the participant or any person in whom his beneficial interest in the shares is for the time being vested, and by a transaction which does not involve a breach of the participant's contractual obligation under TCA 1997, s 511(4)(c), (d) (TCA 1997, Sch 11 para 16(2));

(d) require the trustees to pay over to the participant any dividends, money or money's worth received in respect of any of his shares, and to deal with any right to be allotted other shares, securities or rights (in respect of his shares) only if, and as, directed by the participant or, if relevant, by any other beneficial owner of the shares (TCA 1997, Sch 11 para 17); and

(e) impose on the trustees an obligation to maintain such records as are necessary to enable them to carry out their responsibilities under the profit sharing scheme rules, and to inform the participant of the facts relevant to his liability under Sch E if any event occurs giving rise to such a liability (TCA 1997, Sch 11 para 18).

11.406 The individual's tax exemption

TCA 1997, s 511(4) provides that the appropriation of shares by the trustees under an approved profit sharing scheme to an individual participating in the scheme is exempted from any charge to income tax that would otherwise be made on him under any provision in the Income Tax Acts. In the absence of this rule, it is more than likely that an appropriation or transfer to him of a beneficial interest in any shares of the company (or a connected company) in which he holds his office or employment would be taxable as a prerequisite under Sch E (or under Sch D Case III, if a foreign office or employment) unless he pays full market value for the appropriation or transfer (see **10.113**). While an appropriation of shares by the trustees is exempt from income tax, PRSI and USC apply to the initial market value of the shares appropriated after 1 January 2011.

Assuming that the profit sharing scheme has been properly established by the company concerned and approved by the Revenue Commissioners, the participant acquires his beneficial interest in the scheme shares at the date of their appropriation to him completely free of income tax, but subject to the USC and PRSI. If he allows the shares to remain in the legal ownership of the trustees, and does not assign, charge or otherwise dispose of his beneficial interest before the release date (or if earlier, his death), he can become the legal owner without incurring any income tax liability.

The participant may, however, incur a liability to income tax in respect of any shares appropriated to him under the scheme, if, before the earlier of the three-year release (five-years release prior to 10 May 1997: see TCA 1997, s 511(2)) and his death, any of the following 'taxable events' occurs:

(a) he sells, gifts, assigns, charges or otherwise disposes of his beneficial interest in the shares appropriated to him;
(b) he directs the trustees to transfer the ownership of his shares (or any of them) to him (which he is entitled to do at the end of the compulsory retention period);
(c) the trustees dispose of any of his shares (which they are only permitted to do if directed by him) whether by sale in the market or as the result of a take-over of the company concerned or otherwise (except as part of a reconstruction, amalgamation, share exchange, etc within TCA 1997, s 514 – see **11.412**);
(d) otherwise than as a result of a disposal of shares within (c) above, the trustees or the participant becomes entitled to any 'capital receipts' within TCA 1997, s 513; or
(e) despite the rules of the scheme, the initial market values of all the shares appropriated to him in any one tax year exceeds the maximum permitted limit for that year or, if the trustees should appropriate shares to him at a time when he is ineligible to participate in the scheme.

In the case of a distribution in specie from a demerged company where shares have been appropriated to participants of an Approved Profit Sharing Scheme and the Release Date for those shares has not been reached, no charge to income tax will arise where all of the following circumstances apply:

(a) the relevant scheme shares have been appropriated to participants of the scheme and the scheme shares have not reached their Release Date;
(b) the scheme shares are retained by the Trustees until the Release Date;
(c) the scheme is continued by the company; and
(d) the distributed shares are retained by the Trustees and not passed to the participants until the Release Date.

It is necessary to furnish extensive particulars in relation to the demerger and to formally request prior approval in order to be granted this treatment (*Tax Briefing 54*).

FA 2000, s 51 further modified TCA 1997, s 519A in order to ensure that the tax treatment of the company operating the scheme and their employees is the same, whether a trust is used or not. It provides that where a company uses a dedicated trust or subsidiary company as part of an SAYE scheme to hold 'scheme shares', that trust or company will not be liable to capital gains tax on any disposal of such shares to employees under the terms of the scheme. The base cost to the employees for capital gains tax purposes of the scheme shares is being set at the price actually paid by them and the company will not be entitled to a corporation tax deduction in respect of any expenses incurred by it enabling the trust or subsidiary company to acquire scheme shares.

With effect from 25 March 1999 the provisions of TCA 1997, s 511A have been modified. TCA 1997, s 519A provides for a reprieve from the necessity to hold shares for three years where shares are acquired from an ESOT. It is not necessary for the trustees of an APSS to comply with the three-year holding requirement (ending on the release date) where the following conditions are met:

(a) the shares allocated to a participant in an APSS were transferred by the trustees of an approved ESOT to the trustees of an APSS;
(b) the shares were held in the ESOT for at least three years immediately prior to that transfer; and
(c) the participant was a beneficiary of the ESOT for the full three-year period ending on the date of allocation.

TCA 1997, s 511A as amended by FA 2001, s 17 also provides that if the shares were held in the ESOT for less than a three-year period, the three-year holding requirement in the APSS will be reduced *pro rata*.

11.407 Definitions relevant to taxable events

Before discussing the treatment of the various events which generally result in a participant becoming chargeable to income tax under Sch E, it is necessary to give the following definitions.

Period of retention

This is the minimum period for which the participant is legally bound by contract to retain his beneficial interest in the scheme shares and to permit the legal ownership to remain in the names of the trustees. There is a separate period of retention for each successive appropriation of scheme shares to each participant. The period of retention begins on the date of the appropriation of the particular shares and ends on the second anniversary of that date, unless any of the following events occur before that second anniversary:

(a) the participator ceases to be a director or employee of the company concerned (or, in a group scheme, of any of the participating companies) by reason of either (i) injury or disability or (ii) dismissal by reason of redundancy;
(b) the participant reaches 66 years of age; or
(c) the participant dies.

In other words, if none of these exceptions apply, the period of retention is two full years from the date of appropriation. If any of the events mentioned in (a), (b) or (c) occur before the end of the two-year period, the period of retention ends instead on the date on which the event in question occurs. If more than one of these events occur, the retention period ends on the date of the first of them (TCA 1997, s 511(1)).

Release date

This is the third anniversary of the date on which scheme shares were appropriated to a participant (TCA 1997, s 511(2)). However, none of the rules which charge tax in respect of an event occurring before the release date do so after the date of the participant's death, if that occurs earlier. Accordingly, a participant may now dispose of or otherwise deal with his scheme shares after the third anniversary without incurring any charge to income tax under Sch E.

Initial market value

This is the market value of the scheme shares on the date on which the particular shares were appropriated to a participant, unless the Revenue Commissioners and the trustees of the scheme agree in writing that the market value at an earlier date is to be taken instead (TCA 1997, s 510(2)). In the latter event, the initial market value is the market value of the shares on the earlier date stated in the agreement with the Revenue Commissioners.

'Market value' is as defined by TCA 1997, s 548 which, taking the general definition from TCA 1997, s 548(1) means the price which those shares might reasonably be expected to fetch on a sale in the open market (TCA 1997, s 509(1)). TCA 1997, s 548 also contains certain other rules which may be relevant, depending on whether the scheme shares are quoted or unquoted shares.

Locked in value

On their appropriation to a participant, the scheme shares acquire a locked in value equal to their initial market value. The shares in question retain this locked in value until the release date (after which it ceases to be relevant), unless the participant becomes chargeable to income tax in respect of any 'capital receipt' within TCA 1997, s 513 which is referable to those shares (see **11.411**). In the latter event, the locked in value is reduced by the amount of that capital receipt to arrive at a new locked in value (TCA 1997, s 512(1)).

Example 11.407.1

Mrs P Pan, an employee of Darling Holdings Ltd, had 1,000 shares in that company appropriated to her on 21 September 2012 by the trustees of the company's approved profit sharing scheme. The market value of those shares on that date was agreed to be €0.82 per share. On 18 March 2015 the company made a rights issue to all its shareholders. The trustees, on the direction of Mrs Pan, sold the rights in respect of the 1,000 shares held for her for the sum of €80 (a capital receipt – see **11.411**).

The locked in value of the 1,000 shares held by the trustees for Mrs Pan is determined as follows:

	€
Between 21/9/2012 to 18/3/2015:	
1,000 shares at initial market value at 21/9/2012:	
1,000 x 0.82	820
Less:	
Capital receipt (sale of rights – 18/3/2015)	80

Locked in value (from 18/3/2015 to 20/09/2015) (unless reduced by subsequent capital receipts)	740

Appropriate percentage

This is the percentage which is applied to the 'gross taxable amount' in respect of which a participant may be chargeable under Sch E on the occurrence of any of the taxable events mentioned in **11.406**.

TCA 1997, s 511(3)(a) applies an appropriate percentage of 100 per cent generally to taxable events.

In any case where the taxable event occurs after the participant has ceased to be an employee or director of any relevant company by reason of injury, disability or redundancy (but not otherwise), or after he has reached the age of 66, the appropriate percentage is reduced to 50 per cent. For this purpose, a relevant company is the company which established the scheme (the company concerned) or, in the case of a group scheme, any of the participating companies in that scheme.

An appropriate percentage below 100 per cent may not be allowed in certain cases irrespective of the date of the taxable event – see **11.409** (disposals within retention period) and **11.413** (disposals of unauthorised shares).

11.408 Disposals of scheme shares before release date but after the retention period

TCA 1997, s 512(2) charges the participant to income tax under Sch E if the trustees dispose of any of his shares at any time before the release date, but not if the participant has died before the disposal. The tax is charged for the year of assessment in which the disposal is made. The amount of 'income' chargeable is computed as being equal to the locked in value of the shares disposed of at the date of the disposal multiplied by the appropriate percentage (see **11.407**). However, if the proceeds of the disposal are less than the locked in value, the net taxable amount is computed instead by applying the appropriate percentage to these proceeds. If the disposal is not at arm's length (eg a gift), the Revenue may direct that the proceeds of disposal be taken as being equal to the market value of the shares at the date of disposal (TCA 1997, s 512(8)(b)).

Example 11.408.1

Take the facts of **Example 11.407.1** and assume that Mrs Pan, who is short of cash following the loss of her job through redundancy, instructs the trustees to sell her 1,000 shares in Darling Holdings Ltd for the best possible price. The shares are sold on 25 August 2015 for €480.

Mrs Pan is charged to income tax under Sch E for 2015 on an amount calculated as follows:

	€
Locked in value of shares 25/8/2015:	
As per **Example 11.407.1**	740
Sale proceeds 25/8/2015	480
Appropriate percentage 25/8/2015:	
Before 3rd anniversary (and not within period of retention) (due to redundancy)	50%
Gross taxable amount:	
Lower of locked in value and sale proceeds	480

Net taxable amount (Sch E income 2015):	
Gross taxable amount €480 x 50%	240

A disposal of scheme shares out of a holding of shares appropriated to a participant at different times must be treated on a first in/first out basis (TCA 1997, s 512(6)). This is for the purpose of determining, for any relevant purpose of TCA 1997, Pt 17 Ch 1, the initial market value, the locked in value and the appropriate percentage.

Example 11.408.2

Take the facts of **Example 11.407.1**, but ignore those of **Example 11.408.1** and assume that Mrs Pan continued to be employed by Darling Holdings Ltd. On 24 March 2015, the trustees appropriated an additional 800 shares to her when the shares had a market value of €2 per share. She now has a total holding of scheme shares with locked in values as follows:

			Locked in value
			€
Appropriated 21/9/2012 –	1,000	shares	740
Appropriated 24/3/2015 –	800	shares	1,600
	1,800		2,340

Assume that on 20/8/2015 Mrs Pan sells her beneficial interest in 1,200 of these shares for a sum of €2,760 (ie for €2.30 per share). TCA 1997, s 512(6) requires the rules to be applied on the basis of disposals of shares as follows:

	Locked in value	*Sale proceeds*
	€	€
Out of shares first appropriated (21/9/2012):		
1,000 shares	740	2,300
Out of shares next appropriated (24/3/2015):		
200 shares	400	460

Since 200 of the shares in respect of which Mrs Pan has assigned her beneficial interest have not been held for the two-year retention period from 24/3/2015, TCA 1997, s 511(7) requires Mrs Pan to be taxed under TCA 1997, s 515 by reference to their market value (€460) on 20/8/2015 (see **11.409**).

Since the assignment of the beneficial interest in the 1,000 shares appropriated on 21/9/2012 is made before the third anniversary of that date, the appropriate percentage to be applied is 100 per cent (the redundancy assumption of **Example 11.408.1** no longer is applicable). The amount chargeable under Sch E in respect of the 1,000 shares, is therefore, computed as follows:

	€
Locked in value (lower than proceeds €2,300)	740
Net taxable amount (Sch E: 2014)	
€740 x 100%	740

The total amount assessable for 2015 in respect of the 1,200 shares is:

On 200 shares	460
On 1,000 shares	740
	1,200

In principle, the rules of the scheme must prohibit any disposal at all of the shares appropriated to any participant within the period of retention relevant to the shares in question, but TCA 1997, s 511(6) makes certain exceptions. It permits the trustees, if directed to do so by the participant, to accept an offer for the shares which results in a new holding of shares within TCA 1997, s 584 (which deals with company reconstructions, mergers, etc on a 'share for share' basis). It also permits the trustees, if directed by the participator, to accept an offer of cash (with or without other assets) for his shares, if the offer forms part of a general offer made to holders of shares of the same class or to holders of shares generally in the same company.

In the event that the trustees dispose of a participant's shares for cash as the result of such an offer, the ordinary rules of TCA 1997, s 512 for disposals before the release date are applied, notwithstanding that the disposal may occur within two years of the date of appropriation (or within any shorter retention period that may apply). The participant is charged to tax under Sch E on an amount equal to the appropriate percentage of the locked in value of the shares (or of the disposal proceeds, if lower). If the event occurs within the retention period, the appropriate percentage is 100 per cent (or if the participant is entitled to the disability, redundancy or pensionable age relief, 50 per cent).

In the case where the disposal by the trustees is solely for a new holding of shares (and/or securities) within TCA 1997, s 584, there is no charge to tax on the participant (or the trustees), whether or not the event occurs within the retention period. The rules of TCA 1997, s 514 apply as regard any subsequent application of TCA 1997, Pt 17 Ch 1 to the new holding now held by the trustees for the participant (see **11.412**).

11.409 Disposal of participant's beneficial interest

The participant may sell, gift or otherwise dispose of his beneficial interest in any scheme shares held for him by the trustees, without necessarily consulting them or having the legal ownership transferred out of their hands (although this usually follows in due course). In any such case, the shares in question are treated for all purposes of TCA 1997, Pt 17 Ch 1 as if they were disposed of by the trustees at the time the participant disposed of his beneficial interest in them (TCA 1997, s 512(7)). This means that, if this deemed disposal of the shares occurs before the three-year release date and during the participant's lifetime, he is charged to income tax under Sch E under the general rules of TCA 1997, s 512 (see **11.408**), but subject to certain further rules which may be relevant. The treatment varies depending on whether or not the beneficial interest was disposed of within the retention period.

If the participant sells his beneficial interest in his scheme shares in an arm's length transaction after the end of the retention period, he is charged under Sch E on a net taxable amount equal to the appropriate percentage of the locked in value of the shares (or, if lower, of the proceeds of this sale). If he has gifted the beneficial interest, or has otherwise disposed of it not at arm's length, the appropriate percentage is applied to the lower of the locked in value or the market value of the shares at the date of the disposal.

No tax charge arises if the beneficial interest is not disposed of until after the release date or after the participant's death.

Any disposal by the participant of his beneficial interest in scheme shares *before* the end of the retention period is in breach of his contractual obligation under the scheme not to make any such assignment. In the event of any such breach of this obligation, TCA 1997, s 511(7) requires the participant to be treated as if he had acquired the shares in question as 'unauthorised shares' within TCA 1997, s 515.

The effect of the rules of TCA 1997, s 512, as they are modified by those of TCA 1997, s 515 in relation to the unauthorised shares the beneficial interest in which has been disposed of, is that the participant is chargeable to tax under Sch E on the full market value of those shares at the date of the disposal of the beneficial interest. The normal locked in value of the shares related to their market value at the date of appropriation is replaced by the market value at the date of disposal (TCA 1997, s 515(6)), the appropriate percentage is always 100 per cent (TCA 1997, s 515(4)) and the proceeds of the disposal are taken as equal to the market value at the date of the disposal (TCA 1997, s 512(8)).

Example 11.409.1

Mr R Roy, a director of Kenilworth Ltd the wholly owned subsidiary of Midlothian Ltd (both Irish companies), is a participant in the approved group scheme established by the latter company and in which the former company is a participating company. On 9 July 2014, the trustees of the scheme appropriated to Mr Roy 2,000 C ordinary shares in Waverley Holdings plc, a UK public company holding all the share capital of Midlothian Ltd. On 9 July 2014, these shares were valued at €4,800 (€2.40 per share). The employer company deducted PRSI and USC based on the market value of the shares at the date of appropriation and paid this to the Revenue.

On 15 August 2015, Mr Roy (now in financial difficulties) assigns his beneficial interest in 1,200 of these shares for a consideration of €3,000 (€2.50 per share), although the market value of the shares on that date was €3,600 (€3 per share). Since this assignment is made within the two-year retention period (he is aged 57 and continues to be a director of Kenilworth Ltd), he is chargeable under Sch E for 2015 on an additional amount of income computed as follows:

Locked in value of 1,200 shares (15/8/2015):	€
Normally initial market value (9/7/2014)	
1,200 x €2.40 = €2,880	
but TCA 1997, s 515(6) substitutes market value 15/8/2015	3,600
Proceeds of disposal (15/8/2015):	
Actual proceeds €3,000	
but TCA 1997, s 512(8)(c) substitutes market value	3,600
Net taxable amount chargeable under Sch E	
100% x €3,600	3,600

In practice, it is not necessary to go through this full computation and the additional Sch E income can be taken simply as the market value of the shares in question, ie €3,600.

Example 11.409.2

Take the facts of **Example 11.409.1**, but assume that Mr Roy had reached his 66th birthday on 11 August 2015 (for which he had waited before assigning his beneficial interest in the 1,200 shares on 15 August 2015). On these facts, the retention period has ended on 11 August 2015 so that the TCA 1997, s 515 modifications no longer apply and his appropriate percentage related to the assignment on 15 August 2015 is 50 per cent (over age 66, before 3rd anniversary of appropriation of shares).

Mr Roy is now charged under Sch E on an amount computed as follows:

	€
Locked in value of 1,200 shares initial market value	2,880
Proceeds of disposal actual amount received	3,000
Net taxable amount 2015: 50% x 2,880	1,440

11.410 Transfer of ownership to participant

After the end of the period of retention, the participant may (if he wishes) direct the trustees to transfer the full ownership of schemes shares to him, but if this transfer takes place before the release date, he is charged to tax under Sch E according to the rules of TCA 1997, s 512 on the same amount as if the trustees had sold the shares for their market value at the date of the transfer (TCA 1997, s 512(8)(a)). Normally, there is no need for a participant to request this transfer of the legal ownership as he continues to have the beneficial interest and to receive the dividends, etc in respect of the shares. Should he wish to sell any of the shares after the retention period has ended, he can always direct the trustees to do so without previously having had the legal ownership transferred into his name.

Should he in fact decide to direct the trustees to transfer the ownership of any shares to him, he must before the transfer takes place, pay to the trustees a sum equal to income tax at the standard rate on the appropriate percentage of the locked in value of the shares at the time he gives the direction (TCA 1997, s 511(4)(c)). This requirement to pay such a sum to the trustees does not apply to the personal representatives of a deceased participant who may, on producing a copy of probate, require the trustees to transfer the ownership of scheme shares to them, irrespective of when this direction is made (TCA 1997, s 511(5)).

Two further consequences ensue from a transfer of ownership from the trustees to the participant before the release date. First, the trustees are chargeable to income tax at the standard rate under Sch D Case IV on the same amount as that on which the sum payable to them by the participant was calculated, thereby making them liable to pay over to the Revenue the sum received from him (TCA 1997, s 516(a)).

Secondly, the net taxable amount on which the participant is chargeable to tax under Sch E is treated (TCA 1997, s 516(b)) as if it were an amount from which income tax has been deducted at the standard rate under the rules of TCA 1997, s 238. This means that the income tax deemed to have been deducted is allowed as a credit against the income tax chargeable on his taxable income for the year (which includes the net taxable amount).

The amount of this credit should equal the sum paid by the participant to the trustees, except if the market value of the shares at the date of the direction to the trustees was less than their locked in value at that date. In the latter event, the sum paid to the trustees is still calculated on the appropriate percentage of the locked in value, but the net amount taxable is computed on the same percentage of the market value; the credit against the tax chargeable is also based on the lower figure.

Example 11.410.1

On 21 July 2013, the trustees of the approved profit sharing scheme of Fairford Ltd appropriated 600 ordinary shares which they had previously acquired in the company to Mr D Latimer, an employee participant in the scheme. The market value of the shares on that date was €960 (€1.60 per share), thus giving the opening locked in value. The employer company deducted PRSI and USC based on the market value of the shares at the date of appropriation and paid this over to the Revenue.

Assuming no events occur to affect the locked in value until August 2015 when Mr Latimer directs the trustees to transfer the ownership of 500 of these shares to him, at which time the market value is €5 per share, the consequences are as follows:

(1) Before the transfer can take place, TCA 1997, s 511(4)(c) requires Mr Latimer to pay to the trustees the sum of €160, computed as follows:

	€
Locked in value (August 2015): 500 shares x €1.60	800
Appropriate percentage:	
Transfer after 2nd anniversary of 21/7/2013	100%
Sum to pay (€800 x 100%) x 20%	160

(2) The trustees are chargeable under Sch D Case IV for 2014 on the sum of €800 so that they pay tax to the Revenue of €160, ie €800 assessed at the standard rate.

(3) The participant, Mr Latimer, is assessed under Sch E for 2015 (in addition to any other Sch E income) in respect of the 500 shares transferred (not the entire 600), as follows:

	€
Locked in value (August 2015): as above	800
Disposal proceeds (August 2015) taxed as marked value 500 shares x €5	2,500
Net taxable amount €800 (the lower figure) x 100%	800

(4) Assuming the additional Sch E income of €800 is taxed at his top marginal rate for 2015 of 40 per cent, the additional income tax payable by him is computed:

	€
Additional income €800 x 40%	320
Less:	
Income tax deemed paid per TCA 1997, s 516(b):	
€800 x 20%	160
Additional tax payable	160

11.411 Capital receipts before release date

TCA 1997, s 513 charges a participant to income tax under Sch E if, before the release date, either the trustees or the participant become entitled to a capital receipt in respect of any of the participant's shares. The amount chargeable is equal to the appropriate percentage of the capital receipt or, if it is lower, of the locked in value of the shares immediately before the entitlement to the receipt arose. This charge to tax is not, however, made if the capital receipt does not exceed €13, nor if the entitlement to it does not arise until after the participant's death. TCA 1997, s 531AUA provides that where USC is chargeable on the initial market value of the shares on appropriation, it shall not be charged where there is a capital receipt within the meaning of TCA 1997, s 513(1).

For the purpose of this charge to tax under TCA 1997, s 513, a 'capital receipt' is defined as any money or money's worth to which the trustees or the participant become entitled in respect of, or by reference to, the participant's shares, but excluding any money or money's worth if and to the extent that:

(a) it is income for the purposes of income tax in the hands of the recipient;

(b) it is the proceeds of a disposal of shares falling with TCA 1997, s 512 (see **11.408**); or

(c) it consists of new shares forming a new holding or part of a new holding as defined in TCA 1997, s 514 (see **11.412**).

Perhaps the most likely type of capital receipt to arise, particularly if the scheme shares are quoted on a stock exchange, occurs where the company in which the shares are held offers its existing shareholders (including the trustees holding scheme shares for the various participants) the opportunity of subscribing for additional shares at a price below the normal quoted price. If the participant does not wish to subscribe for the additional shares offered to him, he can instruct the trustees to sell his rights to those shares on the market. The proceeds of any such sale of rights is a capital receipt within TCA 1997, s 513 so that the participant is normally chargeable under Sch E on the appropriate percentage of the proceeds of the sale.

A participant may wish to have the trustees take up his rights to the new shares, but may not have the cash available to subscribe for them. TCA 1997, s 513(3) provides that if the trustees, on the direction of a participator, dispose of some of the rights arising on the rights issue and use the resulting proceeds to enable the other rights to be exercised, the sale proceeds so applied are not treated as capital receipts.

A capital receipt within TCA 1997, s 513 may also arise if, in a company reconstruction, etc, the trustees or the participant become entitled before the release date to any cash or other consideration in addition to any new shares making up a new holding. Any such other consideration that is taxable as a distribution is not of course, treated also as a capital receipt.

Finally, the amount or value of every capital receipt that is brought into a computation of tax chargeable under TCA 1997, s 513 is deducted from the locked in value of the relevant scheme shares (TCA 1997, s 512(1)). The amount deducted is the full capital receipt, ie before the reduction (if any) made by the appropriate percentage in arriving at the net amount taxable. Consequently, the maximum amount that can be charged to tax under Sch E on a subsequent taxable event before the release date (other than one in the retention period) is reduced to the revised locked in value.

11.412 Company reconstructions etc

TCA 1997, s 514 provides rules for dealing with any case where scheme shares held by the trustees for a participant ('the original holding') are the subject of a transaction (a 'company reconstruction') which results in a new holding (as that term is defined in TCA 1997, s 584). Such a new holding arises, for example, if the company in which the shares are held makes a bonus issue of new shares to its existing shareholders (or to shareholders of a particular class) so that the original shares plus the bonus shares make up a new holding.

The object of the provisions of TCA 1997, s 514 is to equate the new holding held immediately following the company reconstruction with the original shares held immediately before it. TCA 1997, s 514(1) defines the 'new shares' as the shares comprised in the new holding issued in respect of, or otherwise representing, the shares comprised in the original holding; it defines 'the corresponding shares' as the shares in respect of which the new shares were issued. It is proposed here to use the term 'the original shares' instead of 'the corresponding shares' used in the section. In the case where the company reconstruction was a bonus or rights issue, it may be seen that the term 'new shares' means both the original shares and the bonus or rights shares.

TCA 1997, s 514(4) contains the following provisions affecting the application of the rules of TCA 1997, Pt 17 Ch 1:

(a) a company reconstruction does not involve any disposal of the original shares;
(b) the new shares are deemed to have been appropriated to the participant on the same date as the original shares were appropriated; and
(c) the conditions as to qualifying scheme shares (see **11.401**) are treated as satisfied with respect to the new shares if they were met for the original shares.

Consequently, if any event taxable under any of these provisions occurs after the company reconstruction in respect of any part of the new holding, the computation of the net taxable amount is made by reference to the locked in value of the original shares. The appropriate percentage to be applied is similarly determined by the period of time that has elapsed between the date of appropriation of the original shares and the date of the taxable event in respect of the new shares. Similarly, if the company reconstruction has occurred before the end of the retention period, the participant's obligations to permit his shares to remain in the hands of the trustees and not to dispose of his beneficial interest extends to all the shares in the new holding.

If there is a disposal of any of the shares in a new holding that has resulted from a rights issue, it is necessary to take into account any payment that the participant may have made to the trustees to enable them to take up the rights and to subscribe for the additional shares. The locked in value of the enlarged holding of shares after the rights issue is not altered, but TCA 1997, s 512(4) provides that the proceeds of the disposal are to be reduced by a proportion of the payment made to the trustees. The proceeds of the disposal are not, however, to be reduced by any amount that arises from the sale of some of the rights to enable the other rights to be taken up (TCA 1997, s 512(5)).

The effect may well be to produce a disposal value for the part of the new holding that is sold which is lower than the locked in value. Consequently, when tax is charged under TCA 1997, s 512 (see **11.408**), the application of the appropriate percentage to the lower disposal value results in a smaller net taxable amount. The amount to be deducted from the proceeds of disposal in respect of the payment to the trustees, or to the aggregate of the payments (if more than one) is determined as follows:

$$\text{payment(s) to trustees} \times \frac{\text{market value of shares disposed of}}{\text{market value of all participants shares}}$$

Example 11.412.1

On 15 May 2014, the trustees of the approved profit sharing scheme of Brian Boru Ltd appropriated 1,000 ordinary shares in the company to one of the participants, Mrs I Bordiseer. The market value of the shares at that date was €4,000 (€4 per share). The employer company deducted PRSI and USC based on the market value of the shares at the date of appropriation and paid this over to the Revenue. On 23 July 2014, Brian Boru Ltd made a rights issue to all its shareholders (including the profit sharing scheme participators) under which each shareholder could subscribe for one new share for every 5 shares held at a subscription price of €3 per share.

Assuming that the rights to subscribe for the new shares can be sold on the market for €1 per share, Mrs Bordiseer instructs the trustees to subscribe for 150 new shares, but to sell her rights to the other 50 shares to help finance the acquisition. The trustees, therefore, subscribe €450 for the 150 new shares from funds provided as follows:

Sales of rights to 50 shares:	€
€1 x 50	50

Payment received from participant	400
Subscription for 150 shares (at €3)	450

Early in 2015, Mrs Bordiseer has a serious motor accident and on 18 May 2015 she ceases entirely to be an employee (she is not a director) of Brian Boru due to the serious injuries she has received, thus terminating her period of retention (which would not otherwise have ended until 15 May 2016). On 29 June 2015, the trustees on her direction sell 800 of the new holding of 1,150 ordinary shares which resulted following the July 2015 rights issue. The ordinary shares of Brian Boru Ltd (quoted) are valued at €3.50 on 29 June 2015.

The amount on which Mrs Bordiseer is charged under Sch E for 2015 in respect of this disposal is determined as follows:

	€
Disposal proceeds (29/6/2015): 800 shares x €3.50 (realised)	2,80
Reduce for payment to trustees (not counting proceeds of sale of rights to 50 shares):	
€400 x (€2,800/€4,025)=	(278)
Proceeds as reduced per TCA 1997, s 512(4)	2,522
Locked in value of shares sold:	
4,000 (MV 15/5/2014) x 800/1,150 =	2,783
Appropriate percentage (ceased through injury before 3rd anniversary of 15/5/2014)	50%
Net taxable amount €2,522 (lower figure) x 50%	1,26

Notes:

1. Market value of 800 shares disposed of is taken at €3.50 per share (€2,800); and the market value of the total post-rights issue holding of 1,150 shares is also taken at the €3.50 date of disposal value (€4,025).

11.413 Excess and unauthorised shares

The trustees of the profit sharing scheme may, possibly without realising they are doing so, appropriate shares with an initial market value exceeding the €12,700 or €38,100 upper limit, whichever is appropriate. Ignoring the €38,100 limit for the moment, which is dealt with below; this might happen, for example, if the shares are unquoted and if the Revenue subsequently establish that their proper market value at the date of appropriation was greater than €12,700 despite the trustee's earlier estimate of a market value not exceeding €12,700. Alternatively, an individual may be a participant in two or more profit sharing schemes and may have shares appropriated to him in the same year from more than one scheme and it may turn out that the aggregate of the initial market values exceed €12,700.

The term 'excess shares' is used to refer to any share or shares which cause the limit €12,700 to be exceeded in any tax year (TCA 1997, s 515(1)). If shares are appropriated to a participant on more than one occasion in any year, the respective initial market values are marked off against the €12,700 limit in the order the shares are appropriated. For example, if shares valued at €10,000 are appropriated to Mr A on 1 January 2015 and if shares valued at €4,000 are appropriated to him on 1 March 2015, none of the shares appropriated first are excess shares but 1300/4000ths of the second appropriation are excess shares.

The trustees of a scheme may, usually unintentionally, appropriate shares to an individual at a time when he is not eligible to participate in the scheme (see **11.403**). For example, an individual who was previously eligible to participate may, unknown to the trustees, have just inherited additional ordinary shares which brings his total ordinary share capital of the company concerned (a close company) to more than 15 per cent. Any shares appropriated to this individual after he becomes ineligible as a 'proprietary' employee or director are referred to as 'unauthorised shares', as are shares appropriated to any other individual at a time when he is ineligible to participate (TCA 1997, s 515(3)).

The actual appropriation of any excess or unauthorised shares does not itself cause the individual who benefits to be taxed, but TCA 1997, s 515(4)–(7) ensures that the individual is charged at a later date to income tax under Sch E on the full market value of the excess or unauthorised shares (referred to here collectively as 'the unapproved shares'). First, if any of the unapproved shares are disposed of before the release date or before the individual's death, he is charged to tax by TCA 1997, s 512 (as modified by TCA 1997, s 515) on the full market value of the shares at the date of the disposal. If any capital receipts within TCA 1997, s 513 arise to the trustees or the participant, he is taxed by TCA 1997, s 513 (as modified by TCA 1997, s 515) on the full amount of those capital receipts as they relate to the unapproved shares. Similarly, on any transfer of ownership of the shares from the trustees to the participant, tax is charged on the full market value of the unapproved shares as at the date the individual directs the trustees to make the transfer.

The retention of the unapproved shares in the ownership of the trustees until after the release date or the participant's death does not, unlike the position with scheme shares in the normal case, result in the individual escaping free of income tax. TCA 1997, s 515(5) provides that, if any of the unapproved shares have not been disposed of before the release date, the participant is charged under Sch E an amount equal to the full market value at the release date of the shares in question. If the individual has died before the release date, he is still charged at the date of death on the full market value of the unapproved shares still retained. In this event, the amount taxable is included with the deceased individual's other income for the tax year up to the date of death so that his personal representatives have to pay the additional tax liability when discharging all his tax liabilities to the date of death (see **15.103**).

When any taxable event occurs under any of the profit sharing provisions affecting a holding of shares comprising both unapproved shares and other scheme shares ('approved shares'), this event is taken as relating first to the approved shares and then, as to the balance of the holding, to the unapproved shares (TCA 1997, s 515(4)(b)). This does not, however, alter the normal rules of TCA 1997, s 512(6) which requires the initial market value, the locked in value and the appropriate percentage (relevant to taxable events affecting the approved shares) to be determined on the 'first in first out' basis in the case of a disposal of shares appropriated at different time (see **11.408**).

Example 11.413.1

The trustees of an approved profit sharing scheme set up by an unquoted company appropriated shares in the company to a participant, Mr D Lillwall, separately on 15 July 2013 and 15 September 2013. The trustees estimated the market value of the shares appropriated at each date to be €2.50 per share, but following negotiations with the Revenue it was accepted that the shares should have been valued at €3.18 per share at each date. The employer company deducted PRSI and USC based on the market value of the shares at the date of appropriation and paid this over to the Revenue. A further payment in respect of the shortfall of PRSI and USC was made after discussions with Revenue on the valuation of the shares.

The shares appropriated (as revalued) were:

Date appropriated		*No of shares*	*Initial market value*
			€
15/7/2013	3,600 x €2.50[1]	3,600 x €3.18	11,448
15/9/2013	700 x €2.50	700 x €3.18	2,226
		4,300	13,674

Assume that Mr Lillwall instructs the trustees to sell 4,100 of these shares on 25 September 2015 (ie just after the end of the retention period for the second appropriation). These shares are sold at their full market value at the time of €20,500 (€5 per share). Assume that Mr Lillwall dies on 29 December 2015 when his remaining 200 shares are valued at €700 (€3.50 per share).

The tax consequences are as follows:

(1) No income tax is charged in respect of the appropriation of the 4,300 shares at the times of their respective appropriations in 2013.

(2) The total holding of 4,300 shares is divided between approved shares and unapproved (excess) shares as follows:

	Initial market value
Approved shares:	€
3,600 shares (15/7/2013) x €3.18	11,448
394 shares (15/9/2013) x €3.18	1,252
3,994	12,700
Unapproved shares:	
306 shares (15/9/2013) x €3.18	974
Total	
4,300 shares	13,674

(3) The sale of the 4,100 shares on 25/9/2015 is taken first as a sale of the approved shares (3,994) and only as to the balance (106) out of the unapproved shares. Assuming that he has passed his 66th birthday, he is chargeable under Sch E for 2015 on a taxable amount of €6,880 (at his relevant rate of tax), computed as follows:

Appropriate percentage:	
Approved shares (less than 3 years)	50%
Unapproved shares[2]	100%
Locked in value:	€
Approved shares[3]	12,700
Market value (25/9/2015): unapproved shares sold[4]	
106 x € 5 =	530
Amount taxable	
Approved shares €12,700 x 50%	6,350
Unapproved shares €530 x 100%	530
	6,880

(4) If any of the approved shares had been still held by the trustees on Mr Lillwall's death, no tax charge would arise in respect of those shares (but there were none left after the 25/9/2015 disposal).

However, his estate is taxable for 2015 in respect of the 200 unapproved (excess) shares still held by the trustees on his death on 29 December 2015. TCA 1997, s 531AUA provides that where USC is chargeable on the initial market value of the shares on appropriation, it shall not be charged where an income tax charge arises under TCA 1997, s 512(2) on the death of a participant. The amount chargeable under Sch E for 2015 is computed:

Market value at 29/12/2015	€
200 shares x €3.50 =	700

Notes:

1. TCA 1997, s 512(6) requires the appropriate percentage (individual after 66th birthday) to be taken first on the 3,600 shares acquired on 15/7/2013 and then on the later appropriation of the 400 (part of 700) shares acquired on 15/9/2013. In this case, the percentage is the same (before 3rd anniversary) for all the 3,994 approved shares.
2. The appropriate percentage for unapproved shares is always 100 per cent.
3. The amount taxable for the 3,994 approved shares sold is based on their locked in value (€3.18 per share).
4. The full market value (€5 per share) at the date of sale of the 106 unapproved shares sold is taxable.

€38,100 limit

With regard to the €38,100 limit, this can only be applied in the first year of assessment during which the 'encumbered period' has elapsed and then only in respect of shares allocated after the encumbered period has elapsed.

The €38,100 limit is available on a once off basis in respect of shares allocated to an individual (via trustees of an APSS) by the trustees of an approved ESOT where the following conditions are met:

(a) at the time of the transfer a period of at least ten years (or, with effect from 31 January 2009 such lesser period as the Revenue Commissioners may allow on a case-by-case basis: TCA 1997, s 515(2A) as amended by FA 2008, s 13) commencing with the date the ESOT was established and ending at the time when all pledged shares became unpledged ('the encumbered period') has elapsed;

(b) at all times in the five years (or such lesser period as the Minister for Finance may prescribe by order: FA 2000, s 24) since the ESOT was established 50 per cent of the securities, or such lesser amount as the Minister may allow, held by the trustees at the time were pledged as security for borrowings by the ESOT; and

(c) none of the shares pledged at any time since the ESOT was established have been transferred from the trustees of the ESOT to the APSS because they have been pledged for the period of ten years or more referred to above.

There are also provisions to deal with situations where an individual participates in more than one scheme.

11.414 Trustees' tax position

TCA 1997, s 510(6) prevents the scheme trustees from being charged under TCA 1997, s 805 to the discretionary trust undistributed income surcharge on any dividends received on shares acquired for the purposes of the scheme, provided that the same three conditions are met. Any dividends received after the appropriation of the shares are the income of the participant, but if the trustees receive dividends or other distributions on the scheme shares before the appropriation of the shares, they are liable to income tax; at the standard rate on them (subject to relief for the tax credit attaching to distributions from resident companies).

If the trustees fail to appropriate any shares within the 18-month period, or should they sell any shares before appropriating them to participants, these exemptions cease to apply. Thus, any dividends received by the trustees after the acquisition of the shares, but before their sale or later appropriation to a participant, may be subject to the income tax surcharge under TCA 1997, s 805. It is therefore important that the trustees ensure that all scheme shares acquired by them are appropriated within the 18-month period. In applying these rules, shares of the same class are treated as being appropriated on the 'first in first out' basis.

11.415 Revenue powers and withdrawal of approval

The Revenue Commissioners are empowered to require any person, by giving him notice in writing, to furnish them such particulars as they think necessary to enable them to carry out their functions in respect of profit sharing schemes. In particular, they may require any information considered necessary to enable them to determine whether to approve a scheme or to withdraw an approval previously given; and to determine any liability to income tax and/or capital gains tax of any participant in an approved scheme (TCA 1997, s 510(7)).

Failure by any person to comply with a request for information served by the Revenue Commissioners under this rule renders the person liable to the penalties applying to a column 2 (TCA 1997, Sch 29) offence (see **2.701**).

The Revenue Commissioners are empowered to require any person, by giving him notice in writing, to furnish them such particulars as they think necessary to enable them to carry out their functions in respect of profit sharing schemes. In particular, they may require any information considered necessary to enable them to determine whether to approve a scheme or to withdraw an approval previously given; and to determine any liability to income tax and/or capital gains tax of any participant in an approved scheme (TCA 1997, s 510(7)).

Failure by any person to comply with a request for information served by the Revenue Commissioners under this rule renders the person liable to the penalties applying to a column 2 (TCA 1997, Sch 29) offence (see **2.701**).

With effect for tax year 2008 onwards, TCA 1997, s 510(7) (inserted by FA 2008, s 19), provides that a return in a prescribed form must be made automatically by 31 March following the end of the tax year; the penalties for failure to make returns under TCA 1997, ss 1052 and 1054 will apply.

The Revenue Commissioners may withdraw the approval previously given to a profit sharing scheme for any of the following reasons (TCA 1997, Sch 11 para 5(1)):

(a) a participant (or participants) breaches his (their) contractual obligations under TCA 1997, s 511(4)(a), (c) or (d);

(b) with respect to the operation of the scheme, there is any contravention of any provision of Ch 1, or of the scheme itself or the terms of the trust under which it is established;

(c) any shares of a class of which shares have been appropriated to participants receive different treatment in any respect from the other shares of that class; or

(d) the Revenue Commissioners cease to be satisfied that the scheme remains open to every eligible employee or director in the manner set out in TCA 1997, Sch 11 para 4.

No alteration in the scheme or the terms of the trust under which it is established can be made without the approval of the Revenue Commissioners. If any such alteration should be made after the scheme has been approved, the whole scheme ceases to be an approved scheme after the date of the alteration, unless the Revenue Commissioners have approved of the alteration (TCA 1997, Sch 11 para 5(2)).

11.416 Appeals

If the company concerned is aggrieved by (a) the failure of the Revenue Commissioners either to approve a scheme or to approve of an alteration made in the scheme or (b) the withdrawal of approval, the company may make an application to have its claim for relief from that decision heard and determined by the Appeal Commissioners. This appeal must be made by notice in writing given to the Revenue Commissioners within 30 days from the date on which the company is notified of their decision.

The Appeal Commissioners are required to hear and determine the claim in the same way as an appeal made against an income tax assessment. All the provisions of the Income Tax Acts relating to such appeals apply to the company's application. Consequently, there is a right to a rehearing by the Circuit Court judge and to the statement of a case for the opinion of the High Court on any point of law (TCA 1997, Sch 11 para 6). F(TA)A 2015, s 41 which was subject to Ministerial Order (SI 110/2016 appointed 21 March 2016 as the day on which the Finance (Tax Appeals) Act 2015, came into operation), replaces TCA 1997, Sch 11, para 6 in its entirety noting 6. A company aggrieved by a decision of the Revenue Commissioners made in respect of that company—(a) to not approve of a scheme under para 3(1), (b) to not approve of an alteration to a scheme or the terms of a trust under para 5(2), or (c) to withdraw approval of a scheme under para 5(1), may appeal the decision to the Appeal Commissioners, in accordance with s 949I, within the period of 30 days after the date of the notice of that decision. The reader is directed to **2.207** for a review of the appeal provisions brought about by F(TA)A 2015.

11.5 Employee Share Ownership Trusts

11.501 Introduction

Employee share ownership trusts, (ESOTS), if approved by the Revenue Commissioners, enjoy certain tax advantages. For the purposes of this book, it is assumed that the term ESOT relates to Revenue approved ESOTs.

ESOTs are trusts established for the benefit of 'all employees and full-time directors' (see below re eligible participants) who acquire shares in a 'founding company' for distribution to beneficiaries. ESOTs can be funded by contributions from a company or by borrowings. As an ESOT becomes a shareholder it can also receive dividends on the shares held in the company.

ESOTs have a degree of autonomy to build up an employee stakeholding in a company. Typically they operate in tandem with approved profit sharing schemes as a method to transfer shares to employees tax free. In the case of private companies, ESOTs can act as a market maker for shares.

Provided the trustees of ESOTs meet certain conditions as to what they do with the money received by an ESOT (eg on sale of shares or receipt of dividends), there are exemptions from income tax and capital gains tax available. Furthermore, a company can, subject to qualifying conditions, obtain tax deductions for the cost of establishing an ESOT and for contributions to the trustees of an ESOT.

FA 2001 amended TCA 1997, s 519 and Sch 12 in order to provide for exemption from tax in respect of any payment of money or a transfer of securities by the trustees of an Employee Share Ownership Trust (ESOT) to the personal representatives of a deceased beneficiary of the trust. Until this enactment such a payment or transfer would have given rise to a charge to capital gains tax on the trustees in the event that any securities were sold to fund any payment and an income tax charge would also arise for the personal representatives on any net proceeds received. This exemption is conditional on the deceased beneficiary having been a participant in an Approved Profit Sharing Scheme (APSS) through which the securities would have passed to the beneficiary had he lived.

11.502 Tax reliefs available under ESOT legislation

TCA 1997, s 519 sets out the tax reliefs for ESOTs. The following is a summary of these reliefs (and is on the assumption that Revenue approval remains intact):

(a) A company establishing an ESOT may claim a corporation tax deduction for the costs of establishing an ESOT, and contributions to the trustees of an ESOT. (Certain conditions apply as to timing, how contributions to the trustees should be expended, etc) (TCA 1997, s 519(2)–(5)).

(b) Dividend income accruing to the trustees of an ESOT is exempt from income tax if and to the extent that it is spent by the trustees in an 'expenditure period' on one or more 'qualifying purposes' as defined in TCA 1997, Sch 12 para 13 which deals with Revenue approval for ESOTs (TCA 1997, s 519(7)).

Furthermore, ESOT trustees are exempt from the income tax surcharge in respect of the undistributed income of discretionary trusts. (Unlike the case where shares have been allocated to individuals under an APSS, where shares have been notionally allocated to beneficiaries by ESOT trustees, dividends accruing to those shares are the income of the trustees of the ESOT while the shares remain in the ESOT. Such income can be used to contribute to the funding of further acquisitions of shares for employees).

(c) Where the trustees of an ESOT sell securities on the open market, any gain accruing to such a sale shall not be liable to capital gains tax as long as the proceeds are used to repay monies borrowed by the trustees, to pay interest on borrowings or to pay a sum to the personal representatives of a deceased beneficiary (TCA 1997, s 519(7A) as amended by FA 2001, s 13).

(d) There is an exemption from capital gains tax to ESOT trustees on the transfer of shares to the trustees of an APSS (for onward allocation to employees) (TCA 1997, s 519(8)).

(e) Securities transferred by the trustees of an ESOT to the personal representatives of a deceased beneficiary shall not give rise to a chargeable gain (TCA 1997, s 519(8A)).

(f) The payment of any sum or the transfer of any securities to the personal representatives of a deceased beneficiary shall be exempt from income tax (TCA 1997, s 519(8B)).

All of the above reliefs are not applicable to any ESOT where approval has been withdrawn. The reliefs cease to apply from the effective date of the withdrawal.

11.503 Approval of ESOTs

TCA 1997, Sch 12 contains the rules governing the approval of ESOTs. A summary of the main provisions of TCA 1997, Sch 12 is set out below. The rules are in relation to the approval process, the appointment of trustees, the eligibility of beneficiaries and the functions of trustees.

ESOTs are not restricted to single companies and can extend to groups. For the purposes of ESOTs, a company falls within the founding company's (the company establishing the scheme) group if it is either the founding company or at a particular time, is controlled by it and is included as a group company in the ESOT. It may also fall within the founding company's group if it is a relevant company or is controlled by a relevant company. A 'relevant company' means:

(a) a company into which a trustee savings bank has been reorganised under the Trustee Savings Banks Act 1989, s 57;

(b) ICC Bank plc;

(c) ACC Bank plc; or

(d) a company which acquired control of the Irish National Petroleum Corporation Ltd (Sch 12 para 1(1) as amended by FA 2002, s 13(1)).

It is important to note that Revenue approval will not be obtained if the Revenue Commissioners are not satisfied that the ESOT would not have the effect of benefiting wholly or mainly the directors, the highest or higher paid employees of a group of companies. Revenue approval can be withdrawn if any of the rules relating to approval contained in TCA 1997, Sch 12 are broken, if shares received by the ESOT trustees are treated differently to other shares of the same class or if there is an unapproved alteration to the ESOT (in which case approval ceases automatically).

TCA 1997, Sch 12 para 3(4) provides that the Revenue Commissioners can request information from any person which will assist them to determine whether to approve or withdraw approval of an ESOT and to determine a beneficiary's tax liability under an ESOT. TCA 1997, Sch 12 para 4 provides for appeals.

Approval rules

Trust deed

An ESOT must be established under a trust deed by the founding company. At the time the trust is established the founding company must not be under the control of another company.

Trustees

The trust deed must provide for the establishment of a body of trustees, falling within one of three alternative forms, as follows:

(a) Majority employee representation:

The trust deed must provide that at any time in its existence there must be at least three trustees, all of the trustees must be resident in the State and of whom:

(i) one must be a professional trustee (a trust corporation, a solicitor or member of another professional body approved by the Revenue Commissioners);

(ii) a majority of whom are not, and never have been, directors of either the founding company or any group company;

(iii) a majority of whom must be representatives of the employees of the founding company or of a group company and who neither have nor ever had a material interest (more than five per cent control of ordinary share capital, directly or indirectly) in the founding company or any group company. Such trustees are required to have been chosen by a majority of employees of the founding company or a group company at the time of selection (TCA 1997, Sch 12 para 8(2));

(b) Paritarian trust with equal company/employee representation.

For this type of structure the ESOT trust deed appoints the initial trustees. It is also provided that the ESOT trust deed will contain rules governing the retirement, removal and appointment of additional and replacement trustees.

Under this structure:

(i) there must be at least three trustees, all of the trustees must be resident in the State and of whom at least one must be a professional trustee (see structure (1) above) who must not be an employee or director of either the founding company of a group company, and who when appointed as an initial trustee was chosen by persons who were subsequently appointed as the initial non-professional trustees, or in the case of an additional or replacement trustee was selected by persons who at that time were the non-professional trustees;

(ii) at least two of the trustees must be non-professional trustees, of whom at least half are required to be employees (who must never have had a material interest) in the founding company or a group company. In addition such trustees are to be selected either by a process under which, in so far as is reasonably practicable, all employees of the founding company and group companies are afforded the opportunity to put themselves forward for selection and to vote for those standing or by persons elected to represent those persons (TCA 1997, Sch 12 para 9(2)–(7));

(c) Single corporate trustee with equal company/employee representation on its board of directors.

A 'single trustee' is a company. The 'trust company' must be resident in the State and be under the control of the founding company. As is the case in (2) above, the ESOT trust deed must provide for the appointment of the initial trustee and contain rules for the removal and appointment of a replacement trustee.

There are a number of conditions relating to the board of directors of a single trustee (TCA 1997, Sch 12 para 10(3)–(8)). The trust company's board of directors is made up in the same manner as the trustees in (2) above.

Beneficiaries

ESOTs are for 'all employees', as defined. This is in accordance with other schemes which attract favourable tax treatment (eg approved profit sharing schemes (see **11.4**) or save as you earn schemes (see **11.6**)).

TCA 1997, Sch 12 para 11(2)–(9) set out the rules regarding who is eligible to be a beneficiary of an ESOT and provide that:

(a) All employees and full-time directors of the founding company or a group company, who have been so for a qualifying period of up to three years and who are chargeable to income tax under Sch E (must be eligible to be beneficiaries of the ESOT). A full-time director is one who works for the company concerned for at least 20 hours a week, ignoring holidays and sick pay. The trust deed may provide that a person is a beneficiary at a given time if he would qualify as a beneficiary were it not for the requirement to be chargeable under Sch E;

(b) With effect from 25 March 1999, certain former employees and directors of the founding company or a group company, for up to five years from the time they ceased their employment or the company has ceased to be a group company, may be beneficiaries where the trust deed provides accordingly on the basis that the following conditions are met:

   (i) the person must have been an employee or director of the founding company or a company within the founding company's group:

      (I) during a qualifying period; and

      (II) on the date the ESOT was established, within nine months prior to that date or any time in the period of five years beginning with that date;

   (ii) at all times in the five years from the time the ESOT was established (ie from execution of the ESOT trust deed) (or in the case of an ESOT approved on or after 23 March 2000, such lesser period as the Minister for Finance may prescribe by order (FA 2000, s 26), 50 per cent (or such lesser amount as may be approved by the Minister for Finance) of the shares held by the ESOT trustees were pledged as security for ESOT borrowings; and

   (iii) the ESOT has been established for at least 20 years, amended by F(No 2)A 2013, previously 15 years.

   The trust rules must provide that everybody who meets the above conditions is eligible to be treated as a beneficiary (TCA 1997, Sch 12 para 11(2C); 11A(7) as amended by FA 2004, s 15);

(c) The former employees and directors of the founding company or a group company may also be beneficiaries where the trust deed provides accordingly on the basis that either they have ceased employment within the previous 18 months or the company has ceased to be a group company and the case where the founding company is the ESB and as respects all securities acquired by the trustees on or before 31 December 2001, where the person was an employee or director of a company within the founding companies group on 1 January 1998. The trust rules must provide that everybody who meets the above conditions is eligible to be treated as a beneficiary, with effect from 1 January 2004;

(d) Any employee or director who has held a material interest (more than five per cent) in the company within the previous 12 months is precluded from being a beneficiary;

(e) In certain circumstances charities can be beneficiaries where an ESOT is being wound up;

(f) FA 2001, s 17 inserted TCA 1997, Sch 12 para 11A to allow employees or directors of a 'relevant company' as described above to become beneficiaries of an ESOT. The conditions are broadly similar to those outlined at (a) to (e) above.

Apart from the above list, no-one else can be a beneficiary of an ESOT.

Trustees' functions

TCA 1997, Sch 12 para 12 deals with the functions of trustees which must be provided for in an ESOT trust deed. The general functions are as follows:

(a) to receive sums from the founding company and other sums, by way of loan or otherwise;

(b) to acquire securities (generally via purchase);

(c) to grant rights to acquire shares to persons who are beneficiaries of the ESOT in question;

(d) to transfer securities or sums (or both) to persons who are beneficiaries of the ESOT, also to pay any sum or transfer any securities to the personal representatives of deceased persons who were beneficiaries under the terms of the trust deed;

(e) to transfer securities to the trustees of an APSS (as a means of getting shares to employees tax efficiently); and

(f) pending transfer, to retain and manage the securities by exercising voting rights or otherwise.

Sums received by the ESOT

TCA 1997, Sch 12 para 13 deals with sums of money received by the ESOT trustees. Essentially it requires that the trustees are actively dealing with sums on a qualifying basis.

The ESOT deed must provide that any sum received by the trustees shall:

(a) be expended within the 'expenditure period' (ie within the nine-month period starting, where the sum is received from the founding company or a group company, from the end of the accounting period in which the sum was expended by the company, and in any other case, the day the sum is received); and

(b) be expended only for one or more 'qualifying purposes' (ie acquiring shares in the company which established the trust; repaying borrowings (including interest on borrowings); the payment of any sum to a beneficiary of the ESOT; or the meeting of expenses); and

(c) any sums received by the trustees must, while retained by them, be kept either in cash or with a relevant deposit taker (see **Division 2**).

The ESOT trust deed is required to provide that in determining whether a particular sum has been expended, expenditure of sums received by the trustees is deemed to be on a first-in-first-out basis.

Finally, any payments to beneficiaries are to be on 'similar terms'. This does not mean that all beneficiaries are to receive the same amount. The amount receivable is permitted to vary in relation to remuneration levels, length of service or similar factors.

With effect from 25 March 2005, TCA 1997, s 130(2)(f), inserted by FA 2005, s 18, provides that surplus dividend income (as defined) which has to be distributed to the beneficiaries of the ESOT as a cash payment, will be treated as a dividend and taxable as such under Sch F, in the hands of the beneficiaries.

Conditions as to shares

As in the case of 'approved' schemes generally, the shares in question must meet qualifying conditions. These are set out in TCA 1997, Sch 12 para 14.

The shares must be:

(a) part of the ordinary share capital of the founding company;
(b) fully paid up;
(c) not redeemable; and
(d) not subject to any restrictions other than restrictions which attach to all shares of the same class or an authorised restriction in connection with cessation of employment, see below.

The following are authorised restrictions, provided that disposal is by way of sale for money in accordance with terms set out in the company's Articles of Association in certain circumstances:

(a) a restriction which requires directors or employees of a company (or a company controlled by that company) to dispose of their shares when they cease to be director or employees; and
(b) a restriction which requires persons who are not, or have ceased to be such directors or employees, to dispose of, on acquisition, shares which they have acquired in pursuance of rights or interests obtained by such directors or employees.

ESOT trustees are not allowed to pay in excess of market value for shares in the founding company. Furthermore, shares in the founding company may not be acquired by the trustees at any time when the founding company is under the control of another company.

Miscellaneous rules

There are various other features which an ESOT trust should contain, including the following:

(a) shares must be transferred to the beneficiaries of an ESOT on qualifying terms (ie as an 'all employee' scheme);
(b) shares must be transferred to beneficiaries not more than 20 years after their acquisition by the ESOT trustees (this is looked at on a first-in-first-out basis);
(c) the trust is not to contain superfluous provisions to those which are essential or reasonably essential to the purposes of the ESOT (ie to acquire or transfer sums or securities to beneficiaries and transferring shares to an APSS);

(d) in the case of permitted acquisitions of shares in other companies as a result of an amalgamation or reconstruction, the 'new shares' received in exchange for the 'old shares' are deemed to step into the shoes of the old ones; and

(e) there are also provisions to deal with how to determine when shares have been acquired (TCA 1997, Sch 12 paras 16–18).

Returns

With effect for tax year 2008 onwards, TCA 1997, Sch 12 para 3(5) inserted by FA 2008, s 19, provides that a return in a prescribed form must be made automatically by 31 March following the end of the tax year; the penalties for failure to make returns under TCA 1997, ss 1052 and 1054 will apply.

11.6 Save As You Earn (SAYE) Schemes

11.601 Introduction

Save as you earn (SAYE) schemes were introduced by FA 1999, s 68, with effect from 6 April 1999. The legislation governing SAYE schemes is contained in TCA 1997, Pt 17 Ch 3 (ss 519A–519C) and in TCA 1997, Schs 12A–12B.

TCA 1997, s 519A sets out the essence of SAYE schemes. Where an individual is granted the right and exercises that right to obtain shares in his employing company under an *approved* savings related share option scheme, no income tax arises on the grant of the option or the exercise of the option. The shares must be paid for out of the proceeds of a 'certified contractual savings scheme'.

An SAYE scheme allows employees to save a part of their after tax salaries (up to a maximum of €500 a month) over a defined period, at the end of which the savings can be used to purchase shares in the employing company. Regardless of whether the proceeds are so used, any interest earned or terminal bonus is tax free and no DIRT is payable thereon. With effect from 1 January 2011, any gain realised by the exercise of a right to obtain shares under a savings related share option scheme is liable to PRSI. The employer is responsible for withholding PRSI from current employees and remitting this to the Collector General. In respect of former employees, the employee is required to pay the PRSI to Revenue through the self-assessment system. There is no charge to employer PRSI on share based remuneration.

A charge to USC under TCA 1997, s 531AM(1) arises on the exercise of the right to obtain shares under a SAYE scheme and also falls within the PAYE system. Any bonus or interest earned is not liable to PRSI or USC.

SAYE schemes can include a discounted option price, of up to 25 per cent of the market value of the shares at the beginning of the savings period, without giving rise to adverse tax consequences.

The savings must be contractual savings schemes with 'qualifying savings institutes', as listed (TCA 1997, s 519C).

A company can claim a tax deduction for the costs of establishing an SAYE scheme (TCA 1997, s 519B). However under FA 2000, s 51 (TCA 1997, s 519B), the company operating the scheme is denied a corporation tax deduction for expenses incurred in enabling shares to be acquired by a trust or subsidiary company.

There are various conditions which must be complied with in order to obtain Revenue approval. These are dealt with in TCA 1997, Sch 12A and include conditions as to eligibility, type of shares, exercise of rights, shares price etc.

11.602 Approval by Revenue Commissioners

Revenue approval is required in order that the beneficial tax treatment of approved SAYE schemes is available. A company must apply for approval in writing and the application should contain whatever particulars and be supported by whatever evidence is required by Revenue (TCA 1997, Sch 12A para 2(1)–(2)).

It is possible to set up a group scheme in cases where a company controls (within the meaning of TCA 1997, s 432) one or more companies. A 'group of companies' means:

(a) a company and any other companies of which it has control or of which it is associated; and

(b) a company shall be associated with another company if it can reasonably be considered that:

   (i) both companies are in pursuit of a common purpose,

   (ii) any person or any group of persons having reasonable commonality of identity have or had the means of power, either directly or indirectly to determine the trading operations carried on by both companies, or

   (iii) both companies are under the control of any person or group of persons having reasonable commonality of identity.

The Act does not define the term 'commonality of identity' and as such this term should be taken to have its ordinary meaning (see also the discussion of 'Associated Companies' at **18.106**).

In the case of group schemes, a participating company is either the one which established the scheme or a company over which the founding company has control and is a participating company under the terms of the scheme (TCA 1997, Sch 12A para 2(3)–(4)).

The Revenue Commissioners will not approve a scheme which contains features which they consider not to be essential nor reasonably incidental for the purposes of providing benefits for employees in the nature of rights to acquire shares. Furthermore, as is similarly the case for approval of profit sharing schemes (see **11.402**), a scheme must have no features which would discourage any employee from participating, or if the company seeking approval is a member of a group of companies, that approval of that scheme would result in benefits being conferred wholly or mainly on the higher or highest paid directors or employees in the group of companies (TCA 1997, Sch 12A para 3(2)).

Withdrawal of approval

TCA 1997, Sch 12A para 4 provides that if any of the requirements of Sch 12A cease to be complied with, or if the grantor of the options fails to provide the information requested of it under TCA 1997, Sch 12A para 6 (see below), Revenue approval may be withdrawn. The tax relief on exercise of the option (TCA 1997, s 519A(3)) shall however continue to apply as if the scheme remained approved to rights obtained before the withdrawal of approval which are exercised after such withdrawal. Approval should be obtained for any alterations to an SAYE scheme as unapproved alterations will invalidate Revenue approval.

Appeals

An appeal procedure is provided for in TCA 1997, Sch 12A para 5, where the Revenue Commissioners refuse to give approval to a scheme, refuse to approve an alteration to a scheme, withdraw their approval to a scheme or refuse to decide that a condition subject to which approval was given has been satisfied. A company can appeal, by notice of appeal in writing, to the Revenue within thirty days of notification of the decision taken by the Revenue Commissioners. The appeal is effectively treated as an appeal against an assessment to income tax and must be heard by the Appeal Commissioners. F(TA)A 2015, s 41, which was subject to Ministerial Order (SI 110/2016 appointed 21 March 2016 as the day on which the Finance (Tax Appeals) Act 2015, came into operation), replaces para 5 in its entirety noting that a grantor aggrieved by a decision of the Revenue Commissioners made in respect of that grantor:

(a) to not approve of a scheme under para 2(1);
(b) to not approve of an alteration to a scheme under para 4(2); or
(c) to withdraw approval of a scheme under para 4(1), may appeal the decision to the Appeal Commissioners, in accordance with s 949I, within the period of 30 days after the date of the notice of that decision. The reader is directed to **2.207** for a discussion of the appeal provisions brought about by F(TA)A 2015.

Information required by Revenue

TCA 1997, Sch 12A para 6 sets out that the Revenue Commissioners may, by written notice, require a person to provide within 30 days any information they consider necessary, to enable them to make a decision as to whether to approve a scheme; or to withdraw approval granted earlier. This information may also be required to enable the Revenue Commissioners to determine a participant's tax liability or to administer the scheme or to alter the rights of the scheme. As is the case for many such Revenue powers, the Revenue Commissioners may nominate any of their officers to perform acts and discharge functions on their behalf which are authorised by TCA 1997, Sch 12A.

11.603 Individuals eligible to participate

Certain persons are not eligible to participate in approved SAYE schemes. A person is not eligible if he has, or has had at any time in the previous 12 months, a material interest in a close company which is either the company whose shares may be acquired under the SAYE scheme or in a company controlling that company or in a company which is a member of a consortium owning the company whose shares may be acquired under the scheme.

A 'close company' is defined as where a person holds a material interest in a company, ie if he owns more than 15 per cent of the company's ordinary share capital. TCA 1997, Sch 12A para 8(3) provides for the definition of 'associate' for the purposes of establishing whether a person holds a material interest.

Subject to the material interest test, TCA 1997, Sch 12A para 9 provides that SAYE schemes are 'all employee' schemes, that is, participation in the scheme must be open to every person (ie to obtain and exercise rights under it) on similar terms. This applies to every person who:

(a) is a full-time director or an employee of the company which established the scheme or of a participating company of a group scheme;
(b) has been so during a qualifying period as set out in the scheme rules (max three years); and
(c) is chargeable to tax under Sch E in respect of his office or employment (eg not a consultant taxed as a self-employed person).

Similar terms do not require each person to have identical rights. Rather, it means that people in the same circumstances should be treated equally. This means that if a company does not want absolute equal treatment for employees, it can differentiate by reference to their level of remuneration, length of service or similar factors.

Except in certain circumstances, as set out in TCA 1997, Sch 12A para 9(3), a person shall not be an eligible participant if he is not an employee or director of the establishing company of the scheme or of a participating company.

11.604 Conditions as to the shares

The shares which may be acquired under option under an approved SAYE scheme must meet a number of qualifying conditions, as set out in TCA 1997, Sch 12A paras 10–15.

The scheme shares must form part of the ordinary share capital of:

(a) the company which established the scheme;

(b) a company which has control of the company which established the scheme; or

(c) a company which either is or has control of a company which is a member of a consortium owning the company which established the scheme (or a company having control of that company), and which beneficially owns 15 per cent or more of the ordinary share capital of that company.

Scheme shares must be fully paid up, not redeemable and not subject to any restrictions, except for restrictions which apply to all shares of the same class or, an 'authorised restriction' as set out in TCA 1997, Sch 12A para 13(2) (in connection with the cessation of employment).

TCA 1997, Sch 12A para 14 deals with how to determine whether scheme shares are subject to any restrictions. If any 'contract, agreement, arrangement or condition by which such person's freedom to dispose of the shares or of any interest in them or of the proceeds of their sale or to exercise any right conferred by them is restricted or by which such a disposal or exercise may result in any disadvantage to that person or a person connected with that person', they will be deemed to be restricted.

TCA 1997, Sch 12A para 15 deals with situations where a company has more than one class of issued ordinary share capital. Where this is the case, the majority of the issued shares of the class used in the scheme must be held by persons other than:

(a) persons who acquired their shares because of a right conferred on them or an opportunity made available to them as a director or employee of the company establishing the scheme or any other company and not as a result of any offer to the public;

(b) trustees holding shares on behalf of persons who acquired their beneficial interests in the shares as a result of the above opportunity or rights; and

(c) where the shares are unquoted but are shares of a company which is under the control of another company (not being a close company) whose own shares are quoted, companies which control the first-mentioned company or associated companies of the first-mentioned company.

11.605 Exchange provisions, reconstructions etc

TCA 1997, Sch 12A para 16 deals with 'exchange provisions' and permits a scheme's rules to contain provisions allowing option holders to exchange their options in certain circumstances, where the acquiring company:

(a) obtains control of a company whose shares are scheme shares as a result of a general offer to acquire the whole of one or more classes of the scheme company's shares;

(b) obtains control of a company whose shares are scheme shares following a compromise or arrangement sanctioned by the court under the Companies Act 1963, s 201; or

(c) becomes bound or entitled to acquire shares in a company whose shares are scheme shares under the Companies Act 1963, s 204.

Where the above applies, participants in a scheme are given an opportunity to exchange 'old rights' for 'new rights' in the acquiring company within an 'appropriate period', as defined below.

The 'appropriate period' is:

(a) a period of six months commencing when control has been obtained and when any condition attaching to the offer is satisfied;

(b) a period of six months commencing when the court sanctions the compromise or arrangement; or

(c) the period during which the acquiring company remains bound or entitled.

The shares for which the 'new rights' are granted must also meet the necessary conditions for approval and must be exercisable in the same way as the old ones. Similarly, the value and aggregate subscription price of the new rights on acquisition must be identical to the value and aggregate subscription price of the old rights on disposal. For the purposes of the Scheme, the new rights effectively step into the shoes of the old ones and are treated as having been granted at the time of the old rights.

11.606 Exercise of rights

Shares acquired under an SAYE scheme can only be paid for with the repayments (contributions and bonus) payable and any interest under the certified contractual savings scheme, as defined.

Except in certain situations (see below) rights cannot be capable of being exercised before the 'bonus date' (the date on which repayments are due to be paid). At the time a participant in a SAYE scheme obtains his rights, he is required to decide whether repayments to be used to buy the shares are to include the bonus or not, and where so, whether it is to be the maximum bonus payable on the earliest date the maximum bonus is payable, or in relation to any other bonus, the earliest date that bonus is payable (TCA 1997, Sch 12A para 18).

There are certain provisions which must be included in a scheme in connection with the death of participants. Where a person dies before the bonus date, the scheme must provide for those rights to be exercisable within 12 months of the date of death. If the person dies within six months after the bonus date, the scheme is required to provide for the rights to be exercised within 12 months of the bonus date.

Scheme rules must also provide for 'good leavers' who cease to hold an eligible office or employment due to injury, disability, redundancy, or retirement or reaching what legislation refers to as the 'specified age', to allow their rights to be exercised within six months of cessation. FA 2000 introduced the concept of the specified age, which replaces 'pensionable age' and for the purposes of the scheme means any age between 60 and 66.

For all other leavers of the company the position is different. If a participant leaves within three years of obtaining rights, those rights must lapse, except in certain situations where the office or employment is in a company of which the grantor ceases to have control, or that office or employment relates to a business or part of a business which is transferred to a person who is neither an associated company of the company establishing the scheme nor a company of which that company has control. If a person leaves more than three years after obtaining his rights, either they must lapse, or be exercisable within six months of cessation.

In the case of participants who continue to work after reaching the specified age, they must be allowed exercise their rights within six months of reaching the specified age (TCA 1997, Sch 12A para 21).

TCA 1997, Sch 12A para 22 sets out a number of factors which may also be provided for in a set of approved scheme rules (but see **11.608** in relation to tax implications), as follows:

(a) if any person acquires control of a company whose shares are scheme shares as a result of making a conditional general offer to acquire the whole of the issued ordinary share capital of the company to the effect that it is satisfied that it will obtain control of the company, or a general offer to acquire all the shares in the company in the class of the scheme shares, then rights obtained under the SAYE scheme may be exercised within six months of the time when the offeror obtains control of the company and other conditions of the bid have been satisfied;

(b) if a compromise or arrangement for the purposes of reconstructing a company under the Companies Act 1963, s 201 is sanctioned by the court, and the plan relates to the company whose shares are scheme shares, or its amalgamation with any other company or companies, rights acquired under the scheme may be exercised within six months of the court sanction;

(c) where any person becomes bound or entitled to acquire shares in a company whose shares are scheme shares under the Companies Act 1963, s 204, rights obtained under the scheme can be exercised at any time when the person remains so bound or entitled;

(d) if a company, whose shares are scheme shares, passes a resolution for a voluntary winding up, within six months of the passing of the resolution participants may exercise their rights to acquire shares in the company;

(e) if a person's office or employment ceases because either:
   (i) it is in a company of which the company establishing the scheme ceases to have control, or
   (ii) it relates to a business or part of a business which is transferred to a person who is neither an associated company of the company which established the scheme nor of a company of which the company which established the scheme has control,

   then it is permissible to allow such persons to exercise their rights within six months of cessation; and

(f) where, at the bonus date, a participant who obtained rights under a scheme, holds an office or employment in a company which is not a participating company but which is an associated company which established the scheme, or a company over which the establishing company has control, those rights may be exercised within six months of the bonus date.

Control for the purposes of (a) to (f) above includes where a person and others acting together have obtained control of a company.

The rights obtained under an SAYE scheme are generally not transferable or capable of being exercised more than six months after the bonus date. This does not however apply where, (under TCA 1997, Sch 12A para 19), a person's rights may pass to their estate and be exercisable within one year of death, or if death occurs within six months after the bonus date, be exercised within 12 months of the bonus date (TCA 1997, Sch 12A para 23).

In determining whether a person shall be treated as ceasing to hold an office or employment for the purposes of TCA 1997, Sch 12A para 20 or 20(1)(e), the person will not be treated as ceasing to hold his office or employment until he ceases to hold an office or employment in the company which established the scheme or in any company controlled by that company or in any associated company.

11.607 Acquisitions of shares, share price, options etc

The rationale behind SAYE schemes is that employees are saving to buy shares in their employer company at a fixed price in the future. In this regard, TCA 1997, Sch 12A para 25 requires that contributions made by employees must be sufficient, as nearly as possible, to generate a repayment of capital and interest which is enough to pay for the participant's option shares. There is a minimum and maximum amount of monthly contributions which can be made by participants of €12 and €500 per month respectively, ie employees can save between these two amounts each month in saving up their option price. The above limits are subject to variation by the Minister for Finance.

The exercise price of the shares to be acquired by an individual under an SAYE scheme must be stated at the time those rights are obtained. It is possible to set the price at a discount of up to 25 per cent of the market value of the shares of the same class at that time or at an earlier time or times agreed in writing between the Revenue Commissioners and the company which has established the scheme. The scheme rules can provide for variation of the subscription price as necessary to take account of any variation in the share capital of which the scheme shares form part.

TCA 1997, Sch 12A para 27 is a technical paragraph and deals with technical issues relating to material interests.

11.608 Certified contractual savings schemes

TCA 1997, Sch 12B contains provisions enabling the Minister for Finance to specify the requirements in relation to the operation of the certified contractual savings scheme. The 'qualifying savings institutions' which may operate contractual savings schemes are set out in TCA 1997, s 519C.

The Minister for Finance is empowered to specify the requirements to be imposed in respect of certified contractual savings schemes *vis-à-vis* the classes of persons who may enter into savings contracts under a scheme, the level of contribution to be made and the sum to be paid or repaid to individuals.

TCA 1997, Sch 12B also deals with the withdrawal and specification of certified contractual savings schemes (TCA 1997, Sch 12B paras 3–4). It also gives the Revenue Commissioners the power to require certain information, on serving written notice, to determine whether to certify a scheme, to determine a participant's liability to tax under a scheme or to enable them to administer the scheme and any alteration of the terms of a scheme. This information must be provided within 30 days.

TCA 1997, s 519A provides that where an individual obtains a right to acquire shares in his employer company (or another company) by reason of his office or employment, that individual being an employee or director, and the right is obtained under a Revenue approved SAYE scheme on or after 6 April 1999 (in respect of which approval has not been withdrawn) no tax will be charged on receipt of the right. The provisions of TCA 1997, s 128 which generally give rise to an income tax charge on an 'paper gain' on exercise of share options in an employer company do not apply in the case of Revenue approved share option schemes.

The above exemption from tax does not however apply where a right being exercised is exercised within three years of being granted and has become exercisable for one of the following reasons (see TCA 1997, Sch 12A para 22):

(a) a person obtaining control of the company as a result of a general offer to acquire all of one or more classes of shares;

(b) an amalgamation or reconstruction of the company in certain circumstances;

(c) a person becoming bound or entitled to acquire shares in the company in certain circumstances;

(d) a resolution being passed for the winding up of the company; or

(e) the sale out of the group of the part of the company or business or the company for which an option holder worked.

A corporation tax deduction is also available for the cost of setting up an SAYE scheme which has been approved. Certain conditions apply:

(a) the cost must have been incurred on or after 6 April 1999;

(b) no employee or director has obtained rights prior to obtaining Revenue approval.

TCA 1997, s 519B also deals with SAYE scheme set-up expenses in management or assurance companies and how to claim a deduction for establishment expenses where approval is obtained after the period of account in which the costs are incurred (TCA 1997, s 519B(2)–(3)).

TCA 1997, s 519C deals with interest earned on individual's savings under an approved SAYE scheme. Interest on a terminal bonus earned on an individual's savings under a certified contractual savings scheme used only in conjunction with an approved SAYE scheme is exempt from tax. Furthermore, DIRT does not apply to such interest.

Only specified financial institutions may operate certified contractual savings schemes. Those that can include the following:

(a) branches in the State of all licensed banks and certain other institutions excluded from the requirement to hold a licence from the Central Bank (eg building societies, trustee savings banks, ACC Bank plc, ICC Bank plc, ICC Investment Bank Limited, the Post Office Savings Bank and credit unions);

(b) branches in the State of financial institutions who hold a licence or other similar authorisation under the law of another EU State which corresponds to a Central Bank licence; and

(c) other financial institutions as may be added to this list by an order of the Minister for Finance.

TCA 1997, s 519C(4) defines a contractual savings scheme as a scheme:

(a) which provides for the making of periodical contributions by individuals to a qualifying savings institution for a specified period;

(b) where the individuals above are eligible participants in an approved SAYE scheme; and

(c) which is certified by the Revenue Commissioners as qualifying for an exemption from tax (or interest and terminal bonus) in accordance with TCA 1997, Sch 12B.

Returns

With effect for tax year 2008 onwards, TCA 1997, Sch 12A para 6A (inserted by FA 2008, s 19), provides that a return in a prescribed form must be made automatically by 31 March following the end of the tax year; the penalties for failure to make returns under TCA 1997, s 1052 and 1054 will apply.

11.7 Revenue Approved Share Option Schemes

11.701 Introduction

In the normal course of events, when an employee exercises a share option, a charge to income tax will arise under TCA 1997, s 128 (see **10.113**) based on the excess of the value of the shares over the option price. The tax charge arises at the time of exercise even where the employee might actually retain the shares (although deferral of the payment of the tax liability may be available in these circumstances). However, the provisions contained in TCA 1997, s 519D and the cognate Sch 12C offered favourable tax treatment for options granted under a Revenue approved share option scheme.

Under an approved scheme, employees were not chargeable on either the grant or the subsequent exercise of the option but were instead chargeable to capital gains tax on the full gain (ie the difference between the amount paid for the shares and the amount received) on a disposal of the shares.

These exemptions have been abolished in respect of all grants of options or gains accruing from the exercise of options arising on or after 24 November 2010. A full description of the nature of the scheme, the manner in which it was granted and the qualifying conditions for approval are covered in the 2010 edition of this work.

Division 12 Immovable Property

12.1 Schedule D Case V

12.101 Introduction

Apart from its use for farming, woodlands and related activities, the ownership of land may be exploited in various ways to produce profits or gains that are chargeable to income tax or corporation tax. It is convenient to group together and deal in this division with the main uses of lands, buildings and other interests in land giving rise to income (other than their use as fixed assets in a trade or profession the profits of which are taxable under Sch D Cases I and II).

The first subject discussed is the taxation under Sch D Case V of rents and certain other receipts from leases (and subleases) of lands, buildings and similar premises, as well as from rights in or over lands. The main principles of Sch D Case V, including the rules for computing the income taxable and those relating to the basis of its assessment, are covered in **12.1**.

Apart from rents receivable and receipts from easements, a person leasing land, buildings, etc may derive what is effectively income if he receives a premium on granting a lease since, due to the payment of the premium by the lessee, the rent payable by him is normally lower than it would otherwise be. There are rules under which premiums on leases are taxable as if they were additional rental income under Sch D Case V, as well as for charging certain other gains resulting from certain types of transactions involving leases. These rules, contained in TCA 1997, ss 98–100, are dealt with in **12.2**.

In general, there is no relief for capital expenditure on lands and buildings from which the rental income taxable under Sch D Case V is derived. There are, however, several exceptions to this general rule. Industrial buildings allowances may be claimed in respect of qualifying capital expenditure incurred on the construction or refurbishment of leased industrial buildings (see **6.5**). Wear and tear allowances may be claimed on the cost of leased machinery and plant provided that the burden of wear and tear falls on the lessor (see **6.3**). Special allowances may be available for capital expenditure on the construction, conversion or refurbishment of certain leased industrial, commercial and residential properties located within tax incentive areas and incurred within the appropriate time limits (see **Division 19** in the 2009 edition of this book). There may be a restriction on the carry forward of such unused capital allowances (discussed at **6.107**), TCA 1997, Pt 12, Ch 4A, ss 409F–409G).

Another important subject is the taxation of profits from dealing in or developing land. A building contractor or dealer in or developer of land may derive all his business income from the carrying on of a normal trade, in which case, he is taxable under the ordinary rules of Sch D Case I. On the other hand, due to the particular nature of transactions involving disposals of interests in land, it is possible for persons dealing in or developing land to realise profits in a quasi-capital form which, in the absence of any other rules, would not be taxable as income either as Sch D Case I trading receipts or under any other Case or Sch. The special rules to deal with such profits, contained mainly in TCA 1997, Pt 22 are dealt with in **12.3**.

The special rules in relation to the exploitation of minerals are discussed in **12.4**.

12.102 The income charged

TCA 1997, s 75(1) charges to tax under Sch D Case V the profits or gains arising from:

(a) any rent in respect of any premises; and
(b) any receipts in respect of any easement,

but with the exception that rents or other receipts from premises or easements used in connection with certain mining, quarrying, etc concerns (see **12.401**) are not taxable under Sch D Case V (TCA 1997, s 75(1)).

For the purposes of the charge to tax under this Case, TCA 1997, s 96(1) defines certain terms, as follows:

> 'premises' means any lands, tenements or hereditaments in the State;
>
> 'easement' includes any right, privilege, or benefit in, over or derived from premises (ie from lands, etc in the State);
>
> 'rent' includes:
>
> (a) any rent charge, fee farm rent and any payment in the nature of rent, notwithstanding that the payment may relate partly to premises and partly to goods or services, and
>
> (b) any payment made by a lessee to defray the cost of work of maintenance or of repairs to the premises, not being work required by the lease to be carried out by the lessee.
>
> 'lease' includes an agreement for a lease and any tenancy, but does not include a mortgage; and
>
> 'lessee' and 'lessor' derive their meanings from 'lease' and the terms include, respectively, the successors in title of a lessee or a lessor.

The income chargeable is, it should be noted, the profits or gains that arise from the rent or the receipts in respect of the easement. This implies that expenses in earning the rent, etc are deductible from the gross receipts, but TCA 1997, s 97 goes on to specify the type of expenses to which the deduction is limited (see **12.104**). It is, therefore, appropriate to use the term 'gross rents', or simply the 'rents', to denote the total rent receipts and to refer to the amount of income actually chargeable under Sch D Case V as the 'net rental income'. Further, except where it is necessary to refer specifically to receipts from easements, references in this Part to net rental income are to be taken as including any net receipts from easements which the taxpayer may have.

Under general principles, only receipts in the nature of income fall within Sch D Case V. In *Lowe v Ashmore* 46 TC 597, payments for the right to remove turves were held to be income derived from rights over land; in this case the turves were regarded in effect as fruits of the land. By way of contrast, in *McClure v Petre* [1988] STC 749, the receipt of a lump sum payment in return for allowing subsoil to be dumped onto the taxpayer's land was held to be capital in nature, since it related to the sterilisation of one aspect of the utility of the land. However, there are statutory exceptions to this principle in the case of certain premiums and analogous sums (see **12.2**).

In *IRC v John Lewis* [2001] STC 1118, the UK High Court held that a lump sum received in return for the right to receive future rents was capital in nature, following *Paget v IRC* 21 TC 677. This decision was upheld in the Court of Appeal (*IRC v John Lewis* [2003] STC 117). In the absence of legislation to the contrary the fact that the lump sum was a capital receipt under general principles provided the opportunity for individuals who paid income tax (as well as PRSI and levies) on their rental income to reduce their exposure to tax by selling the right to receive the rent. TCA 1997, s 106A was introduced to ensure that a capital sum received by a person (other than a company) after 5 February 2003 in return for the right to receive future rents is taxable as income under Sch D Case IV.

Rental income normally arises where a person owning an interest in land (either the freehold interest or any leasehold interest, whether derived from the freehold interest or from any superior leasehold interest) gives another person the use of the land and/or any buildings on the land under a lease, sublease or tenancy agreement. It is not, however, essential for there to be a formal lease or tenancy agreement to make any rents receivable by a person for the use of his land, buildings, etc taxable under Sch D Case V. Income derived by a person from, say, an informal letting of his house, holiday cottage, etc constitutes a rent chargeable to tax (see also the Appeal Commissioner's decision, noted in [1995] ITR 1333).

Further, it may be seen from the definition of 'rent' that, should a tenant incur expense which under the terms of his lease or tenancy agreement is the landlord's responsibility, the cost borne by the tenant should be included in the landlord's gross rent in his Sch D Case V computation. If the payment by the tenant in consideration for the right to occupy any premises includes a payment for goods and/or services which the landlord has agreed to provide under the terms of the lease or the tenancy agreement, that payment must also be included in the rent receipts in the Sch D Case V computation. An example of this is a sum paid as rent under a lease for the benefit of services such as cleaning, heating, caretaker, etc provided by the landlord (note *Property Holding Co v Clark* [1948] 1 KB 630).

Receipts from easements arise if a person owning an interest in land grants another person, for a consideration in money or money's worth which is in the nature of income, any right to use the land or any part of it in a way that does not amount to a lease or tenancy. Receipts from granting a licence to occupy land as well as receipts from fishing, shooting, etc rights in or over a person's land are examples of receipts from easements. Another example is a payment received for allowing an advertising hoarding or sign to be put on a person's land or buildings (see also *Jeffries v Stevens* [1982] STC 639). It is arguable that damages recovered in respect of loss of rent, while not rent as such, are receipts from an 'easement'; if not liable under Case V they will still be taxable as income (presumably under Sch D Case IV): *Raja's Commercial College v Gian Singh* [1976] STC 282.

The Revenue Commissioners take the view that income from conacre lettings of farmland is in 'the nature of rent' and thus falls to be taxed under Sch D Case V (*Tax Briefing 21*). This view is said to be based on the Northern Ireland rating case of *Taylor v Commissioner of Valuation* [1981] NILR 236, where it was held that the conacre 'tenant' was the occupier of the land. However, that decision also upheld the long-established principle that a conacre 'tenant' is not in fact a tenant in law. Since rent is in law the consideration given for a tenancy, it would seem that the Revenue's view is dubious ('rent' is in fact defined by Deasy's Act s 51 as including 'any sum or return in the nature of rent'). However, it seems that the Revenue view may be justified alternatively on the basis that income from a conacre 'letting' is a receipt in respect of the 'landlord's' rights of ownership over land and accordingly falls within TCA 1997, s 96 (note also the capital gains tax case *O'Coindealbhain v Price* IV ITR 1).

In addition to the actual rents receivable under any lease or tenancy agreement, the income chargeable under Sch D Case V includes a proportion of any premium that is required on the granting of a lease if, but only if, the duration of the lease does not exceed 50 years. Normally, the appropriate proportion of the premium is included in the lessor's Sch D Case V computation as if it were an additional payment of rent received in the tax year in which the lease is granted. The rules for determining the amount to be included in the Sch D Case V computation for any year in respect of such a premium are discussed in detail in **12.2**, as are those relating to certain transactions connected with leases which may give rise to a tax charge under Sch D Case IV.

It is to be noted that TCA 1997, Pt 4, Ch 8 (ss 96–106A) deal only with the taxation of rents, receipts from easements and other payments treated as rent that are derived from premises situated in the State (see definition of 'premises' above). Rents and any other income from the leasing of lands and buildings situated abroad are taxable under Sch D Case III as income from foreign possessions. In general, such foreign rental income is taxed in a similar way, but the special rules of TCA 1997, ss 98–100 which charge tax on lease premiums and other amounts do not apply to tax such items if the leased land and buildings are situated abroad (see **Division 13**).

Sums received under interest cap arrangements do not qualify as rental income, since they are not sourced in immovable property but simply arise under an extraneous financial arrangement. Nevertheless, where the cost of acquiring interest cap protection is treated as deductible in computing rental profits (see below), the Revenue Commissioners will in practice agree to take it into account in computing Sch D Case V profits (*e-brief* 62/09).

Deduction at source

Where a tenant pays rent (or other income assessable under Sch D Case V) to the agent of a non-resident landlord, the landlord will be assessable in the name of the agent by virtue of TCA 1997, s 1034 (discussed in the context of trading income in **13.603**). Where, however, a tenant pays rent directly to a landlord whose usual place of abode is outside the State, TCA 1997, s 1041(1) requires the tenant to withhold standard rate tax from the payments concerned (see the discussion at **2.308**). The landlord may be able to claim a full or partial repayment of the tax thus withheld in appropriate circumstances (TCA 1997, s 1041(2): see the discussion at **13.609**). Payments of rent in these circumstances will fall within TCA 1997, s 1041, even if paid in the State (for example, into an Irish bank account of the landlord (TCA 1997, s 1041(1)). No liability can arise under TCA 1997, s 1034 in this case, even if the landlord has an Irish agent who would otherwise fall within that provision.

In fact the TCA 1997, s 1041 procedure extends also to:

(a) income arising under a lease to a person other than the lessor which is chargeable under Sch D Case IV; and

(b) any other payments which would be chargeable to tax under Sch D Case V if they had arisen to the person who entered into the contract or disposition giving rise to those payments (TCA 1997, s 1041).

'Rent-a-room' relief

TCA 1997, s 216A provides an exemption for 'relevant sums' derived from the letting of a 'qualifying residence'. A 'relevant sum' is one which arises in respect of the use as residential accommodation of a room or rooms of a qualifying residence; it includes any payments in respect of meals, cleaning and laundry and similar goods or services which are incidental to the letting (TCA 1997, s 216A(1)). A 'qualifying residence' is a residential premises (defined in turn as a building or part thereof used as a dwelling) located in the State and used by the individual claiming the relief as his sole or main residence during the tax year concerned (TCA 1997, s 216A(1)). If the word 'during' is construed as meaning 'at some time in' as opposed to 'throughout', then receipts from letting all the rooms in a residence during a period of temporary absence could qualify as relevant sums. The Revenue Commissioners take the view that the relevant sums must be received while the individual concerned is occupying the residence as his sole or main residence. They also take the view moreover that the relief only applies to the letting of rooms as such and cannot cover the letting of an entire residence; they accept however that receipts from letting a self-contained unit within a residential premises may qualify for relief (*Tax Briefing 44*). TCA 1997, s 216A(3A) inserted by FA 2007, s 14 provides that the exemption will not apply to rent payable by a child of the individual. Further, *eBrief* No 21/2015 notes in the accompanying guidance that 'the room or rooms must be used for the purposes of residential accommodation, ie the occupants are effectively using the room on a long-term basis, either on its own or in conjunction with other parts of the residence, as a home. The relief does not apply to rooms that are used for business purposes. Income from the provision of accommodation to occasional visitors for short periods, including, for example, where the accommodation is provided through online accommodation booking sites, does not qualify for relief as the visitors use the accommodation as guest accommodation rather than for residential purposes. Income from guest accommodation such as a bed and breakfast or a guesthouse operation is generally treated as trading income (Case I) and not rental income (Case V). This type of income, even where it is under the relevant limit, does not qualify for rent-a-room relief'.

The relief extends to relevant sums chargeable under Sch D Case V and also Case IV (possibly relevant if services are charged for separately) (TCA 1997, s 216A(2)). The relief applies to relevant sums (before deducting any related expenses) up to a limit of €14,000 for 2017 and subsequent years, (€12,000 per annum from 2015, €10,000 per annum in 2014) (TCA 1997, s 216A(5)); somewhat anomalously, no relief at all is due if the relevant sums exceed the limit for the tax year (TCA 1997, s 216A(2)). However, the relief is only given in relation to the net profit arising from such relevant sums and no relief is available in respect of losses arising in relation thereto (TCA 1997, s 216(2)); where the relief is claimed, any potential claim for capital allowances under TCA 1997, s 284 shall be deemed to have been made, thus leading to an enforced 'waste of allowances'. Where more than one individual is entitled to relevant sums from the same qualifying residence, the above limits are apportioned equally between the individuals concerned (TCA 1997, s 216A(7)). The relief will apply unless the individual specifically elects otherwise for the tax year concerned prior to the tax return filing date for that year (which would be advisable if losses are incurred) (TCA 1997, s 216A(3)).

Where the relief applies, the receipt of relevant sums will not affect any entitlement to relief for qualifying mortgage interest under TCA 1997, s 244 (TCA 1997, s 216A(8)).

Example 12.102.1

Mr Doyle has a spare room in his house in Waterford City. He decided to let the room for the calendar year 2015 for €850 per month. Mr Doyle will also provide cleaning services to the tenant for €100 per month. The relevant sums that Mr Doyle will receive in 2017 are as follows:

Rental income	(€850 x 12)	=	€10,200
Cleaning services	(€100 x 12)	=	€1,200
Total			€11,400

The income is exempt under TCA 1997, s 216A as the relevant sums are less than the limit of €14,000 for 2017.

With effect from 2010, the relief will not apply where either the individual or a person connected with the individual is an office holder, or employee, of either: (I) the person making the rental payments, or (II) a person connected with the person making the payments, and irrespective of whether such payments are made directly or indirectly. This anti-avoidance measure is designed to prevent employers channelling tax-free sums to employees by paying them rents for the use of part of their property (TCA 1997, s 216A(3B), inserted by FA 2010, s 13).

12.103 Basis of assessment

TCA 1997, s 75(3) provides that tax under Sch D Case V is to be charged on the full amount of the profits or gains arising within each year of assessment. Thus an individual is assessed under Sch D Case V for the tax year 2015 on all his income chargeable within Case V which arises in the year ending 31 December 2015.

TCA 1997, s 75(2) requires all profits or gains within Sch D Case V to be treated as if they all issued from a single source.

The full amount of profits or gains within Sch D Case V arising in any tax year is the aggregate of the taxpayer's surpluses of rent over deductible expenses occurring in that year in respect of each lease, rental or easement to which he is entitled, as reduced by the aggregate of any rental deficiencies in that year. For the detailed rules used in computing the surplus or deficiency from each separate lease or rent, etc, see **12.104**.

Example 12.103.1

Mr Quincy Lewis owns two houses in Dublin, one converted into two flats and the other left as a single residence. He has lived in the single residence for some years, but has let the two flats on separate leases which commenced respectively on 1 January 2015 and 1 July 2015. On 1 September 2015, his employment required him to move to live in Waterford. He then rented out the house used as his residence for an 18-month period commencing 1 September 2015.

For the years ending 31 December 2015 and 31 December 2016, the Sch D Case V rental surpluses or deficiencies from the three separate lettings are computed, applying the rules explained in **12.104** (but details not given here), as follows:

	Year of assessment 31 December 2015	*Year of assessment 31 December* 2016
Flat no 1	€	€
Surplus in each year	9,000	9,000

Flat no 2		
Surplus in year to 31/12/2015	7,000	
Deficiency in period to 31/12/2016		(1,400)
House		
Surplus in 4 months to 31/12/2015	6,000	
Surplus in 12 months to 31/12/2016		18,000
Net rental surpluses	22,000	25,600

Mr Lewis is assessed under Sch D Case V for 2015 and 2016 on the full amount of his income from all his Case V sources arising in each year. The amounts assessable are therefore:

Year of assessment 2015:	€
Income arising in year to 31/12/2015	22,000
Year of assessment 2016:	
Income arising in year to 31/12/2016	25,600

12.104 Computation of income

TCA 1997, s 97(1) requires the computation of the total Sch D Case V income actually arising in each period of assessment to start with separate calculations of the surplus or deficiency in respect of each separate rent and the total receipts from easements. The total Sch D Case V income arising in the year (assessable to income tax according to the basis of assessment rules already discussed) is then arrived at as the aggregate of all the surpluses as reduced by the aggregate of all the deficiencies, but any surplus or deficiency from a letting excluded by TCA 1997, s 75(4) must be ignored (see **12.107**).

The computation of the surplus (or deficiency) in respect of each rent arising from each separate lease or tenancy agreement, is made by taking the full rent receivable in the relevant tax year and by deducting the outgoings in respect of that rent to the extent authorised by TCA 1997, s 97(2) and by any other relevant provisions of the Income Tax Acts. If any premium on the granting of the lease from which a particular rent arises has been obtained in the year, the part of that premium taxable by TCA 1997, s 98 must be included in arriving at the final surplus or deficiency in respect of the rent in question.

The rent to be brought into account is that receivable in the year to 31 December for which the computation is made, whether or not the rent is actually received in that period. However, if the person chargeable claims and proves that the whole or part of a rent is not in fact received due to its being irrecoverable on the default of the person liable, or due to his having waived payment of the rent without consideration and in order to avoid hardship, then the rent not recovered is excluded from the Sch D Case V computation (TCA 1997, s 101).

In any case where the person chargeable proves that a rent is irrecoverable, on either of these grounds, after it has been included in a tax assessment, he is entitled to have the assessment adjusted and to receive any appropriate repayment. Conversely, if, after relief has been granted under this provision, the amount written off is subsequently received, the inspector is entitled to revise the assessments or make any new assessments to recover any tax underpaid. In practice the Revenue Commissioners will allow bad debt provisions on a similar basis to that applicable to Sch D Cases I and II.

Deductible expenses

TCA 1997, s 97(2) permits the person receiving any rent under a lease or tenancy agreement to deduct from the rent receivable any of the following expenses:

(a) any rent payable by him in respect of the premises or part of them;
(b) any sums actually borne by him, in accordance with the conditions of the agreement, in respect of county, municipal or other rates;
(c) the cost to him of any services rendered or goods provided by him for which he receives no separate consideration, but only where he is legally bound under the agreement to provide them;
(d) the cost of maintenance, repairs, insurance and management of the premises borne by him, except for any expenses of a capital nature (the prohibition against capital expenditure would follow from general principles in any event); and
(e) interest on borrowed money employed in the purchase, improvement or repair of the premises, subject to the limitation set out immediately below.

In the case of interest on loans for expenditure on the purchase, improvement or repair of a residential premises, TCA 1997, s 97(2J) as inserted by FA 2009 restricted the allowable amount to 75 per cent of what it would otherwise have been; for these purposes, interest is deemed to accrue on a daily basis. FA 2016 replaced TCA 1997, s 97(2J) in its entirety and outlined the proportionate interest deductions that can be taken in this regard as follows:

Period	*Allowable interest fraction*
7 April 2009 – 31 2016	75%
Year to 31 December 2017	80%
Year to 31 December 2018	85%
Year to 31 December 2019	90%
Year to 31 December 2020	95%

TCA 1997, s 97(2J) notes that it is not to apply in respect of interest accrued on or after 1 January 2021 which would mean that at that time one has to have regard to TCA 1997, s 97(2)(e) which allows a full interest deduction on borrowed money employed in the purchase, improvement or repair of the respective premises.

Where an individual borrows money to acquire land and to finance the construction of a residential premises on the land, the aggregate of all such borrowings will be treated as being incurred on the purchase of residential premises. Where a premises is not wholly residential, then the restriction shall apply only to the part of any borrowings which is attributable to the residential proportion on a just and reasonable basis. A 'residential premises' is any building or part of a building used or suitable for use as a dwelling and any outbuildings, garden, etc, usually enjoyed with that building (TCA 1997, s 96(1)). It would seem that holiday cottages fall squarely within this definition. The previous interest restriction under TCA 1997, s 97(2A) provided an explicit let-out for holiday cottages, absent in these provisions. In the case of nursing homes, there is likely to be at least some de facto residential use. However, some parts of the building may not constitute useable accommodation and there may accordingly be a good case for excluding those elements. The treatment for rates purposes might also be a relevant factor.

The Revenue Commissioners have indicated in *Tax Briefing 26* that it is *not* their practice to allow a deduction for management expenses equal to a percentage of gross rental income (although percentage commissions charged by a letting agent will normally be allowable on general principles). In *Tax Briefing 25*, the Revenue Commissioners express the view that accountancy fees incurred on preparing rental accounts arguably relate more to the management of the landlord's financial affairs than that of the premises; further, they are arguably not an expense of the transaction of letting. Nevertheless, in practice the Revenue will allow claims for such fees included in computations submitted after the publication of *Tax Briefing 25*, but will not reopen returns submitted prior to that. In *Tax Briefing 53*, the Revenue Commissioners state that they recognise that financial institutions insist that mortgage protection policies are put in place when sanctioning borrowings. A mortgage protection policy operates so that the full amount of the outstanding borrowings is repaid if the policyholder dies. Despite the fact that such a policy has more to do with the management of the landlord's financial affairs than the management of the premises and that an argument could be made that the payment is of a capital nature, Revenue will allow a deduction for the premiums. This treatment applies to returns submitted after 1 January 2002.

In The *Revenue Commissioners v Collins* [2016] IEHC 748 the Irish High Court held the answer to the question as to whether the Non-Principal Private Residents (NPPR) charge pursuant to the Local Government (Charges) Act 2009 was deductible against rental profits under TCA 1997, s 97(2) as being 'any rate levied by a local authority' in the affirmative. The wording used in TCA 1997, s 97(2)(b) is that a deduction shall be allowed for

> … any sums borne by the person chargeable –
>
> (i) in the case of a rent under a lease, in accordance with the conditions of the lease, and
>
> (ii) in any other case, relating to and constituting an expense of the transaction or transactions under which the rents or receipts were received,
>
> in respect of any rate levied by a local authority, whether such sums are by law chargeable on such person or on some other person;

Reynolds J notes at para 17 of his judgment that 'Where there is no definition of the word "rate" or "levy" in the Taxes Consolidation Act, 1997 the Court must look to the ordinary meaning of the phrase "any rate levied by a local authority". Clearly the use of the word "any" suggests that the provision was not limited to a particular category of a rate but was providing prospectively for rates which might be contemplated by the legislature at some point in the future.' He went on to rely on the dicta in *Inspector of Taxes v Kiernan* [1981] 1 IR 117 that 'any rate levied by a local authority' should be given its ordinary or colloquial meaning and would therefore include the NPPR charge. It is understood at the time of writing that Revenue will appeal this decision.

In the case of receipts from easements, where it is necessary to calculate the surplus or deficiency in respect of the total receipts, deductions may be claimed under TCA 1997, s 97(2) for any rates, the cost of services rendered or goods provided and for the cost of maintenance, repairs, insurance and management, but only in so far as they relate to and constitute an expense of the transaction(s) from which the receipts from the easements are received. For example, if a landowner receives payments for the right to fish and/or shoot on his lands and if he provides certain services in part consideration for the payments received, he should be able to deduct the costs borne by him in providing those services. To the extent it is necessary for him to incur expense in maintaining the land, river bank, etc as an essential part of the transaction he should also be able to deduct those expenses.

TCA 1997, s 97(3) provides that the amount of the expenses referred to in s 97(2) which can be deducted in the Sch D Case V computation, is the most which could be deductible in computing the profits of a trade taxable under Sch D Case I. For this purpose, the receipt of the rent is deemed to be the equivalent of a trade carried on during the currency of the relevant lease (if the rent is received under a lease) or, in any other case, during the period throughout which the taxpayer is entitled to the rent. This has a number of consequences, including:

(a) the expenses should normally be deductible on an accruals basis, in line with the principles discussed in **5.302**;

(b) the expense to be deductible must be incurred wholly and exclusively for the purpose of earning the rent, etc (see **5.305**; **5.306**);

(c) the expense to be deductible must be revenue rather than capital in nature; (TCA 1997, s 97(2)(d) already prohibits capital expenditure on maintenance, etc), while general principles would prevent a deduction for capital expenditure, the question of what is revenue or capital must be decided on Sch D Case I/II principles, by reference to the notional trade carried on during the period of the lease, etc. One example of items which would be disallowable as capital are the rent charges incurred in *IRC v Land Securities Investments Trust Ltd* 45 TC 495 (see **5.307**);

(d) any cost incurred in repairing, insuring or maintaining the premises before the lease under which the rent is payable commences is the equivalent of pre-trading expenses, not deductible in principle; the Revenue Commissioners have indicated in *Tax Briefing 31* their view that pre-letting expenses are not allowable under TCA 1997, s 82 as it is merely the quantum of the deduction under TCA 1997, s 97(2) which is determined in accordance with Case I/II principles; the requirement that such costs must be expenses 'of' the leasing transaction, etc may act as a barrier against claiming such expenses in any event;

(e) any expense incurred after the termination of the lease is not deductible;

(f) any business entertainment expenses which might otherwise be deductible as part of the management expenses cannot be deducted (TCA 1997, s 840 prohibits any such deduction as it does in the case of a trade – see **5.313**); the restrictions of TCA 1997, ss 380M–380O relevant to the deductions for any leasing costs for private cars costing more than the 'relevant capital limit' are applied in the same way as for a trade (see **5.312**); and

(g) contributions by the person chargeable to an exempt approved pension scheme in respect of employees engaged in the maintenance, management, etc of the leased property are deductible as part of the expenses of management, etc (TCA 1997, s 774(6), Sch 32 para 26 – applicable as for a trade: see **16.108**).

When any expenses or other payments are made by the taxpayer that are attributable partly to the premises from which the rent is obtained and partly to other premises, the inspector of taxes is required to make such apportionment as, to the best of his knowledge and judgment, is appropriate in arriving at the amount of that expense deductible under these rules (TCA 1997, s 97(4)). Further, no deduction is allowed for any part of any expense that is otherwise deductible in computing the income of the person chargeable (or any other person) for income tax or corporation tax purposes (TCA 1997, s 97(5)).

For example, the taxpayer may have employees working in his trade or profession who are also involved in the maintenance or management of his rented premises. Clearly, if and to the extent that, their remuneration and other costs are deducted in the Sch D Case I or Case II computation, no further deduction for the same expense can be made in the Sch D Case V computation. On the other hand, a reasonable apportionment of any such expenditure between the computation of the trading profits and that of the Sch D Case V rental income is generally acceptable (see **5.305**).

The Sch D Case I trade expense test must, strictly, be applied separately to each lease or tenancy agreement. If, for example, a lessor in receipt of a number of rents under different leases grants a lease of a new property for the first time, expenses incurred in respect of the new property for any period before its first lease commences should be disallowed in computing the taxable surplus or deficiency from the rent in question. For the expenses to be deductible, it is necessary that they be incurred during the currency of the particular lease notwithstanding that the taxpayer may be in receipt of rents from other properties for a number of years. It may be noted that a 'lease' is defined as including an agreement for lease (see **12.102**); consequently, it may be possible in some cases to regard expenses incurred after the agreement for lease is made as expenses incurred in the currency of the lease.

Expenses incurred during the period immediately after the termination of a lease, but before the granting of a new lease to the same premises, are deemed to have been incurred during the currency of the lease just terminated, provided that three conditions are met. These expenses are therefore deductible in computing the surplus or deficiency from that lease. The three conditions are:

(a) the expenses would otherwise be deductible under TCA 1997, s 97(2);

(b) the person who was the lessor immediately before the termination of the lease was not in occupation of any part of the premises during the post-termination period, but was entitled to possession of the premises; and

(c) the premises become subject to another lease granted by the same lessor at the end of that period (TCA 1997, s 97(3)).

In *GH Ltd v Browne* III ITR 95, the High Court held that an auctioneer's letting fee and a solicitor's costs incurred in negotiating leases were deductible under TCA 1997, s 97(2)(d) as expenses of management of the premises in respect of which the leases were made. The Revenue had argued that the expenses in question were of a capital nature on the grounds that they were incurred in the creation of a capital asset (the lease) and not as expenses of management. In rejecting this argument, Mr Justice McWilliam said:

> I am of the opinion that the capital of the appellant consists of the premises known as Stephen Court (and not the lease) and that its business is both the letting of the premises and the collection of the rent reserved rather than that the capital is some sort of landlord's interest in the lease divorced from the ownership of the premises so that the business to be managed consists solely in the collection of rent.

The deduction given by TCA 1997, s 97(2)(e) is for interest payable on money borrowed for the purpose of the purchase, improvement or repair of the leased premises. Interest on a loan to acquire an option over a premises which was subsequently exercised would for example not be deductible under this heading. In *Tax Briefing 50* Revenue indicated that interest on any part of a loan relating to stamp duty or legal fees is not deductible.

The accuracy of Revenue's interpretation is questionable since the legislation allows a deduction for borrowed money employed in the purchase of the premises and stamp duty and legal costs are clearly costs of purchase. There is no restriction on the maximum amount of interest that may be deducted under this rule for non-residential properties, provided that it can be established that the money borrowed was in fact employed for one of these stated purposes. Where joint owners of a property fund their acquisition of their respective interests by separate loans, such interest should be deductible against their respective shares of rental income arising from that property.

Interest accruing after 5 February 2003 on borrowings used to purchase a rented residential premises from an individual's spouse is not allowable in computing the profits chargeable under Sch D Case V (TCA 1997, s 97(2G); (2H) inserted by FA 2003, s 16(1)). A 'rented residential premises' is defined at TCA 1997, s 96(1) as a 'residential premises' in respect of which the taxpayer is entitled to any rent or payment from easements. 'Residential premises' is any building or part of a building used or suitable for use as a dwelling and any outbuildings, garden, etc, usually enjoyed with that building. This restriction does not apply in the case of arrangements between separated or divorced spouses.

For 2006 and subsequent years of assessment interest on borrowings used to purchase, improve or repair a rented residential premises will not be deductible unless the registration requirements of the Private Residential Tenancies Board are complied with in respect of *all* tenancies which existed in relation to the premises in the year of assessment (TCA 1997, s 97(2I) inserted by FA 2006, s 11(1)(a)). A written communication from the Private Residential Tenancies Board to the chargeable person which confirms the registration of a tenancy in relation to the residential premises is accepted as evidence of compliance with the registration requirement. (See *Tax Briefing 63*).

On the basis that capital expenditure is disallowable, there is in fact a theoretical question mark over the allowability of interest on long term loans (see the discussion at **5.315**, where the view is taken that such interest is in fact allowable on general principles). In practice, the point is not normally taken by the Revenue Commissioners in any event.

In strictness, interest on a loan which replaces a loan incurred for a qualifying purpose is not eligible for relief. In practice, Revenue are prepared to overlook this point. In the case of replacement loans for residential property the interest will be deductible provided that the loan is replaced for genuine commercial reasons on an arm's length basis and not for the avoidance of tax. As regards replacement borrowings for commercial property it is no longer necessary to seek Revenue pre-approval for the interest to be deductible. The general position, however, is that the interest on a loan that directly replaces an existing loan for a commercial property may be allowed where the replacement of the original loan is for genuine commercial reasons and is not part of a scheme the main purpose of which is to avoid tax. Where loans are amalgamated, it is necessary that the capital and interest in respect of each property can be traced back to the original borrowings. The current Revenue practice in relation to replacement borrowings for both residential and commercial properties is covered in more detail in *Revenue Instruction 4.8.6*. Only interest payable during the period for which the premises are leased is deductible (but this may include interest for a period of temporary vacancy after the termination of one lease – see above and TCA 1997, s 97(3)). If, for example, money is borrowed to help finance the purchase of premises intended for leasing as soon as a suitable tenant can be found, no deduction is available for the interest payable for the period prior to the commencement of the first lease.

In fact, a further rule has to be considered in this connection. TCA 1997, s 105 prohibits the deduction either of interest paid on borrowed money or rent payable for any period prior to the date when the premises are first *occupied* by a lessee for a trade or undertaking or for use as a residence. That section was introduced primarily as an anti-avoidance measure to counteract an arrangement whereby a lease might nominally start on one date, but where the tenant did not really enter into occupation until a later date, with perhaps only the payment of a nominal rent to the lessor between the two dates. The Appeal Commissioners decision 01TACD2016 looked at a particular fact pattern, and having referred to TCA 1997, s 105 makes the point that 'it is incumbent on the Appellant to demonstrate, on the balance of probabilities, that the interest was payable from the date on which the lessee commenced occupation of the premises'.

In *Tax Briefing 25* the Revenue Commissioners state that they will treat a payment for an interest cap as part of the interest expense relating to a loan in computing profits under Sch D Case V. In *e-brief 62/09* they confirm that consequently the 75 per cent restriction will also apply to such payments in the cases of residential property loans. An interest cap is a payment in return for protection against rising interest rates for a specified period of time because the cap specifies the maximum amount of interest that can be charged by the bank. Revenue clarified in *Tax Briefing 50* that in the case of a once off cap fee the payment should be spread over the term of the loan so that it is matched to the periods to which it relates.

TCA 1997, s 109 provides that the employer's lump sum redundancy payment under the Redundancy Payments Act 1967, s 46 may be deducted as an expense of maintaining or managing leased premises, provided that the payment is made in respect of an employment involved wholly in maintaining or managing leased premises producing rents taxable under Sch D Case V. This applies only to the statutory lump sum payable; any additional redundancy payment in excess of this amount met by the employer is not covered by TCA 1997, s 109.

Example 12.104.1

Mr L Danrold, who has for a number of years sublet two shops in each of which he holds a leasehold interest, decides to rent out his former residence in the suburbs on acquiring a flat in the city. He borrows €50,000 on 21 March 2016 to pay for structural alterations to the house in order to render it suitable for letting. He incurs €1,500 on having the property repainted in May 2016.

On 1 July 2016, he grants a five-year tenancy of the house commencing on that date under which the tenant agrees to pay a rent of €100 for the first three months and a rent of €18,000 per annum thereafter. The tenancy agreement provides that the tenant is to be responsible for all internal repairs, but that the landlord is to bear the ground rent, insurance and all external repairs. The tenant does not occupy the house until 15 September 2016. The subleases of the two shops require Mr Danrold as lessor to pay the rates, insurance and external repairs. The rents receivable and the outgoings actually paid by Mr Danrold in respect of the full year ended 31 December 2015 for each of the shops and the house are as follows:

	Shop 1	*Shop 2*	*House*
	€	€	€
Rents receivable:			
Shops	9,000	4,000	
House – 1/7/2016 to 30/9/2016			100

– 1/10/2016 to 31/12/2016			4,500
Outgoings paid:			
Structural alterations[1]			50,000
Repainting prior to letting[1]			1,500
Loan interest (285 days)			1,952
Rents paid to freeholder	2,900	1,800	
Ground rent			80
Insurance	460	170	240
External repairs*	720	1,250	50
Local authority rates	2,500	1,800	

*The tenant of shop 1 also paid €300 in respect of external painting the cost of which should have been borne by the landlord.

The computation of Mr Danrold's surplus/deficiency for each rent for the year ended 31 December 2016 is as follows:

	Shop 1	*Shop 2*	*House*
Rents receivable:	€	€	€
Per leases	9,000	4,000	4,600
External repairs paid by tenant[2]	300		
	9,300	4,000	4,600
Deductible expenses:			
Rents payable	2,900	1,800	
Ground rent payable[3]			23
Insurance[4]	460	170	120
External repairs[2]	720	1,250	50
Local authority rates	2,500	1,800	
Loan interest (107 days) 733[5] x 75%=			550
	6,580	5,020	743
Surplus	2,720		3,857
Deficiency		(1,020)	

His net rental income arising in the year to 31 December 2016 is now determined:

Surpluses –	€
Shop 1	2,720
House	3,857
	6,577
Less:	
Deficiency – shop	(1,020)
Sch D Case V income 2016	5,557

Notes:

1. No deduction is given for the structural alterations (capital expenditure in any event) and the repainting carried out before the house lease commenced.

2. The cost of external painting borne by the tenant of shop 1 (not his responsibility under the lease) is treated as additional rent received see definition of 'rent' in

12.102. A corresponding deduction can be claimed as it represents allowable expenditure if incurred by the landlord.

3. Although the house lease commenced on 1/7/2015, no deduction is given for the proportion of the year's ground rent payable up to 15/9/2015 (the date of first occupation as a residence by the tenant) – TCA 1997, s 105.

4. The part of the year's insurance payable in respect of the house attributable to the pre-letting period to 1/7/2015 is not deductible.

5. Since the tenant of the house did not occupy the premises as a residence prior to 15/9/2015, the loan interest payable for the 147 days from 21/4/2015 to 14/9/2015 is not allowable (TCA 1997, s 105). As it relates to residential premises, only 75 per cent of the amount otherwise allowable can be deducted.

Interest on property let for social housing purposes

The detailed rules in connection with this relief are contained in TCA 1997, s 97(2K). From 1 January 2016 a person chargeable who leases residential property for a period of three years to tenants in receipt of social housing supports (qualifying tenants) may, notwithstanding subsection TCA 1997, s 97(2J) which restricts the deduction for interest on borrowings used to purchase, improve or repair rented residential property, deduct all of the interest accruing during that three-year 'specified period' when computing their taxable rents from the respective property.

The conditions that must be met in claiming relief under this subsection are outlined in TCA 1997, s 97(2K)(f):

(i) a residential premises is let under a qualifying lease for one or more than one specified period, and

(ii) a relevant undertaking in respect of that premises for each specified period is submitted to and registered by the Board.

Revenue guidance on this subsection notes that 'given the definition of "specified period" there can be no more than two such periods in respect of a property' presumable on the basis of a specified period being three years as discussed above. Regard would need to be had to the conditions which apply where a qualifying tenancy terminates for reasons outlined below and where 'replacement' tenants can be found.

There are a significant number of definitions in this subsection with the following being key for an understanding of same.

'lease' means any lease or tenancy in respect of a residential premises required to be registered by the person chargeable under Pt 7 of the Residential Tenancies Act 2004.

Part 7 of the aforementioned act requires a landlord of a dwelling to apply to the Board to register the tenancy of the dwelling with the Private Residential Tenancies Board (PRTB).

'qualifying lease' means a lease granted by the person chargeable to a qualifying tenant;

'qualifying tenant', in relation to a qualifying lease, means—

(i) a household in respect of which rent is payable by a housing authority—

(I) in accordance with Pt 4 of the Housing (Miscellaneous Provisions) Act 2014, or

(II) under a contract under s 19 of the Housing (Miscellaneous Provisions) Act 2009, between the housing authority and the person chargeable,

or

(ii) an individual in respect of whom a rent supplement is payable by, or on behalf of, the Minister for Social Protection;

'relevant borrowings' means borrowed money employed in the purchase, improvement or repair of a premises or a part of a premises which, at a time interest accrues on the borrowings, is a residential premises let under a qualifying lease;

'relevant interest', in relation to relevant borrowings and a specified period, means the amount by which the aggregate deductions authorised by sub-s (2)(e) are reduced by the application of sub-s (2J) in respect of that part of the chargeable periods (within the meaning of s 321) that falls within the specified period and, for the purposes of this definition, interest shall be treated as accruing from day to day;

TCA 1997, s 97(2J) restricts the interest deductions permitted under sub-s (2)(e). It will be seen below that specified period is defined as a particular period certain of three years (see below). Revenue guidance on this subsection gives the following example.

Example 12.104.2

A person chargeable (who is an individual) undertakes to rent a residential property to a qualifying tenant for a three-year period ending on 31 December 2018. The interest on borrowings used to purchase the property is €1,000 in each of the tax years 2016 – 2018 inclusive. The aggregate amount of the interest on the borrowings over the three-year period, computed as if all of the interest is deductible is €3,000.

'relevant undertaking', in relation to a residential premises, means an undertaking under para (b)(i);

The undertaking referred to in para (b)(i) reads as follows:

an undertaking to the effect that the person chargeable will let a residential premises under a qualifying lease for the duration of a specified period commencing on:

(I) in the case of a qualifying lease commencing on or after 1 January 2016, the date of commencement of that lease, or

(II) in the case of a lease that commenced prior to 1 January 2016, which would, if the lease commenced on that date, be a qualifying lease, 1 January 2016.

'specified period' means a continuous period of three years commencing on or after 1 January 2016 but not later than 31 December 2019.

The specified period definition permits a landlord to which the conditions in TCA 1997, s 97(2K) applies to grant qualifying leases to qualifying tenants at any time during that period.

As noted above a taxpayer seeking to claim unrestricted interest relief under this subsection must submit a 'relevant undertaking' in such form and containing such information as prescribed. The PRTB must register a relevant undertaking in the register of private residential tenancies maintained by it. A relevant undertaking must be submitted to the PRTB as follows:

- where a lease commences on or after 1 January 2016, the undertaking must be submitted at the same time as the person chargeable is required to make an application to register the tenancy in accordance with s 134 of the Residential Tenancies Act 2004 (in general this must be within 1 month of the start of the tenancy);
- in any other case by 31 March 2016.

TCA 1997, s 97(2K)(b)(iv) looks at the position where a person chargeable submits a relevant undertaking to the PRTB in respect of a specified period ('first period') and, following the end of that period, submits an undertaking in respect of a further three-year period ('second period'). This subparagraph provides that the date on which the second period commences is:

(A) the date of a qualifying lease which commences on or after the date following the end of the first specified period, or

(B) the day immediately following the end of the first specified period where the new qualifying lease commences prior to the end of that period.

Secondly, the subparagraph provides that the relevant undertaking for the second period in respect of a qualifying lease commencing after the end of the first period must be submitted to the PRTB at the same time as the person chargeable is required to register the new tenancy with the PRTB. In any other case, the undertaking must be submitted within three months after the second period commences.

A lease which commences before 1 January 2016 and which would be a qualifying lease if it were to commence on that date is treated as a qualifying lease commencing on 1 January 2016 where a relevant undertaking is submitted to, and registered by, the PRTB. This means that a person who, on 1 January 2016, was leasing residential property to a qualifying tenant which started before that date can avail of the relief as if it were a qualifying lease on 1 January 2016. Absent this statutory fiction it is arguable whether the relief could have applied to that taxpayer in the first instance.

Where a qualifying lease terminates during a specified period, eg the tenant leaves the property, then the currency of that lease 'shall be deemed' to include 'a period' following the lease's termination which the legislation refers to as the 'intervening period' if at the end of the intervening period, the person chargeable grants a subsequent 'qualifying lease' in respect of the residential premises ('subsequent lease') and during the intervening period:

A. the premises was not let under a lease that was not a qualifying lease;

B. the person chargeable immediately before the termination was not in occupation of the premises or any part of the premises but was entitled to possession of the premises; and

C. a person connected with the person chargeable was not in occupation of the premises or any part of the premises.

The reference to a connected person is a reference to a person who would be regarded as connected with the person chargeable under TCA 1997, s 10. Examples of such connected persons include the chargeable person's spouse, brother or sister etc.

Where the above conditions are met then the first lease and the subsequent new lease are taken together and treated as one 'qualifying lease'. It is noted that there may be more than one subsequent lease granted but obviously the above conditions would have to be met for the subsection to continue to apply. Where a tenant ceases to be a qualifying tenant during a specified period then the lease continues to be treated as a qualifying lease, ie a lease occupies to reside in the property under the lease. Revenue guidance on the subsection notes that an example of the above applying would be one where the tenant's situation has improved presumably such that the allowances mentioned earlier are no longer payable to the tenant. This ensures that the person chargeable does not need to have constant vigilance on the tenant's circumstances.

The following example is taken from Revenue guidance on the subsection

Example 12.104.3

Take the case of a person chargeable who is an individual where the specified period in relation to a property ends on 31 December 2018. In this scenario, the relevant interest is deemed to accrue on 1 January 2019 and is taken into account, along with the actual interest accrued in 2019, in computing the taxable rents from the property in question of that year. Subsection (2J), which restricts the deduction for interest on borrowings on residential property does not apply to relevant interest.

The relevant interest of a specified period is not taken into account in computing the relevant interest of a subsequent specified period. A claim for relief under this subsection must:

- include a statement to the affect that the conditions of para (f) are met; and
- be submitted electronically in the manner provided for by the Revenue Commissioners.

Where a residential property is let partially under a qualifying lease (which is a lease between a person chargeable and a qualifying tenant) and partially under another lease, the deduction for interest on borrowings under sub-s (2)(e) is computed by apportioning the interest between the respective leases on a just and reasonable basis. The retention period for records and linking documents provided for in TCA 1997, s 886 (which is concerned with the obligation on taxpayers to retain certain records) commences on the last day of the specified period in respect of which a claim is made under this subsection.

Capital allowances

The availability of Industrial Buildings Allowances for offset against Sch D Case V income is covered in **Division 6.5**. The extension of those allowances to premises in the various tax incentive areas is covered in **Division 19** of the 2009 edition of this text, as are the special reliefs available for expenditure on qualifying residential premises in those areas. The restrictions on carry forward of unused capital allowances (discussed at **6.107**) apply to these reliefs (TCA 1997, Pt 12, Ch 4A, ss 409F–409G).

In general, where rental income assessable under Sch D Case V relates in part to the letting of machinery or plant, wear and tear allowances should be available in respect thereof and should be offsettable against that income so long as the burden of wear and tear falls on the lessor (see **6.3**).

In the case of furnished residential lettings, prior to 6 April 1997 there was in strictness no entitlement to capital allowances on furniture, fixtures, etc, since they were not being used for the purposes of a trade. In practice, the Revenue Commissioners granted capital allowances on fittings on the same basis which applied to plant and machinery used in a trade; alternatively, a claim equal to one-twelfth of gross rents could be made up to a maximum €254 in respect of all Sch D Case V sources for the relevant year of assessment (*Tax Briefing 9*). TCA 1997, s 284(6) (with a consequential amendment to TCA 1997, s 284(7)) placed the Revenue practice in relation to capital allowances on a statutory basis. TCA 1997, s 284(7) provides that wear and tear allowances are available in respect of capital expenditure incurred on the provision of plant and machinery, where:

(a) the expenditure is incurred wholly and exclusively in respect of a house which is used solely as a dwelling which is (or is to be) let as a furnished house; and

(b) that house is provided for renting or letting on *bona fide* commercial terms in the open market.

The Revenue Commissioners have stated that items eligible for capital allowances will include furniture, kitchens, and bathroom suites. The rate of wear and tear allowances on capital expenditure incurred on the provision of plant after 3 December 2002 is 12.5 per cent pa over an eight-year period. The normal provisions in relation to balancing allowances, charges, etc apply (see **6.2**).

TCA 1997, s 300(4) provides that any wear and tear allowance claimed by virtue of TCA 1997, s 284(6) is to be made in charging the person's income to tax under Case V. This means that the allowances may be offset against the individual's Case V income for the year of assessment and, where allowances are not fully utilised in the year in which they arise, they may be carried forward to the following year for use against Case V income arising in that year. TCA 1997, s 406 provides that the excess Case V allowances (claimed under TCA 1997, s 284 in respect of fixtures and fittings for furnished residential accommodation) may not be offset against other income.

12.105 Controlled rents

Special provisions previously governed rents controlled by the Rent Restrictions Acts by virtue of ITA 1967, s 82 (see the 1996/97 edition of this book). These provisions are now obsolete.

12.106 Relief for Sch D Case V losses

A Sch D Case V rental loss occurs if the aggregate of the rent deficiencies arising in any year of assessment exceeds the aggregate of the surpluses in the same year. The deficiencies and surpluses taken into account in determining whether there is a (and, if so, the amount of the) Sch D Case V loss are arrived at in the manner explained in **12.104**. Any surplus or deficiency from any letting excluded by TCA 1997, s 75(4) must, however, be ignored (see **12.107**).

Any person chargeable to income tax in respect of Sch D Case V rental income is, where a loss arises in any tax year, entitled to relief for that loss in the manner discussed below. The question of any additional relief for industrial buildings allowances is discussed separately in **6.505**.

A Sch D Case V loss must be carried forward and set off against Sch D Case V income arising for the next subsequent year, and thereafter against the Sch D Case V income for the following years (TCA 1997, s 384(2)).

A Sch D Case V loss carried forward must be set off against any Sch D Case V income assessable in the next year to the extent of such income and any unrelieved balance is carried forward for set off in the next available year. There is no time limit and any unrelieved Sch D Case V loss can be carried forward indefinitely until fully relieved. Further, unlike the position with trading losses carried forward, the carry forward does not cease if there is a cessation of Sch D Case V source income followed by a resumption of Sch D Case V income in some later year (TCA 1997, s 384(3)).

Unlike the TCA 1997, s 381(1) claim available in respect of losses under Sch D Cases I and II, there is no provision under which the taxpayer may elect to set off a Sch D Case V loss against income from other sources. This contrasts with the claim which may be made under the TCA 1997, s 305(1)(b) to set off against income from other sources the excess of capital allowances for leased industrial buildings over the taxpayer's net Sch D Case V rental income (see **6.505**).

Any excess capital allowances brought forward under TCA 1997, s 305(1)(a) are to be offset in priority to unused rental losses brought forward (TCA 1997, s 384(4) as inserted by FA 2010, s 15(b), with statutory effect from 2010.

12.107 Excluded lettings/Uneconomic lettings

TCA 1997, s 75(4) deals with any case where a person derives a rent under a lease which is insufficient, taking one year with another, to meet the lessor's costs of fulfilling his obligations under the lease and covering his expenses of maintenance, repairs, insurance and management of the leased premises. It provides that the letting in question is to be left out of account altogether in applying the rules of TCA 1997, ss 75(1)–(3), 97 (regarding the assessment of Sch D Case V income) and also those of TCA 1997, s 384 (in giving relief for Sch D Case V losses). Consequently, any surplus or deficiency on such an 'excluded letting' should be completely ignored for all purposes of tax under Sch D Case V.

It is to be noted that the evaluation of whether or not the rent is sufficient to meet the lessor's obligations and expenses has to be determined 'taking one year with another'. Consequently, the fact that a surplus happens to arise in any particular year does not, of itself, mean that the letting ceases to be an excluded one. Further, if the rent is sufficient to cover the lessor's obligations under the lease and his expenses of maintenance, etc, the fact that a deficiency will arise in most years due to other deductible items apart from those mentioned in TCA 1997, s 75(4) (for example due to interest on a loan to purchase the premises) does not make the letting an excluded one.

In determining whether or not there is sufficient income to meet the lessor's obligations, etc, an appropriate sum in respect of any premium payable under the lease is to be included with the rent, but only if the duration of the lease does not exceed 50 years. The section does not specify what is an appropriate sum, but it appears that it might be appropriate to include an annual amount arrived at by dividing the premium by the number of years in the lease period. If the sum of the annual rent and this annual amount in respect of the premium is sufficient to cover the lessor's expected annual outgoings to meet his obligations, etc, the letting should not be an excluded one.

12.108 Apportionments on sale of premises

TCA 1997, s 106 contains the tax rules for dealing with the apportionments of receipts and outgoings that are usually made between vendor and purchaser in the event of the sale of premises from which rents taxable under Sch D Case V are receivable. The rules ensure that the apportionments made between the parties to the sale are given the same effect for tax purposes so that the vendor and purchaser are, respectively, taxable on the receipts and entitled to deduct the following outgoings to the extent actually apportioned to each of them.

The section applies in any case where, by virtue of a contract for the sale of an estate or an interest in premises, any receipt or outgoing is apportioned between the parties to the sale. Two types of apportionment are covered. First, a receipt (eg rent due) or an outgoing (eg local authority rates) covering a period starting before and ending after the date of completion of the sale (the date by reference to which the apportionments are made) may be due for payment before that date. In this instance, the vendor normally receives the rent or pays the outgoing, but is due to account to the purchaser for the proportion of it attributable to the period after the date of completion. The appropriate adjustment is usually made as a decrease or increase in the cash payment made by the purchaser for the acquisition of the premises.

TCA 1997, s 106 deals with this first type of case. Assume that a person owns a 21-year leasehold interest in premises which he has sublet on a yearly tenancy for a rent of

€12,800 per annum payable half yearly (in advance) on 1 May and 1 November. On 1 October 2014, he contracts to sell his 21-year leasehold interest for a consideration of €50,000 with completion of the contract taking place on 31 December 2014. The half year's rent of €6,400 covering the period 1 November 2014 to 30 April 2015 is dealt with as follows in the apportionment account:

	€
Due to vendor:	
2/6ths of €6,400	2,133
Due to purchaser:	
4/6ths of €6,400	
(period 1/1/2015 to 30/4/2015)	4,267
Adjust purchase consideration:	
Agreed sale price	50,000
Less:	
Rent receivable by vendor due to purchaser	4,267
Net cash due to vendor from purchaser	45,733
(subject to any other apportionments)	

TCA 1997, s 106 requires the part of the rent becoming due for payment between the date of making the contract and the date of completion that is apportioned to the purchaser (which is, in effect, received by the vendor in trust for the purchaser) to be treated, for the purposes of Sch D Case V, as if received on behalf of the purchaser immediately after the completion of the sale. In other words, the part of the receipt apportioned to the purchaser (the €4,267 in the above example) is his rent for Sch D Case V purposes and not that of the vendor who actually received it. TCA 1997, s 106 applies in the same way to an outgoing that becomes payable before the date of completion where a part of the payment is made by the vendor in trust for the purchaser. The purchaser is treated as if he had paid the part apportioned to him immediately after the date of completion; consequently, if the outgoing is an expense deductible from Sch D Case V rents, the purchaser is entitled to deduct the part paid on his behalf by the vendor in computing his Sch D Case V surplus (or deficiency) from the rent in question.

TCA 1997, s 106 deals in exactly the same way with any apportioned receipt or outgoing that becomes due for payment before the date on which the contract for sale is made. If in the previous example, the half-yearly rent receivable for the period beginning before and ending after the completion date was due on 1 September 2014 (ie before the contract date of 1 October 2014 in respect of the six months to 28 February 2015), the contract is deemed to have been made before the receipt (or outgoing) is due and the rule in TCA 1997, s 106 is then applied in the way explained above. In other words, the purchaser is deemed to receive immediately after the completion date (1 January 2015) the 2/6ths part of the rent received by the vendor in trust for the purchaser for the period 1 January 2015 to 28 February 2015.

TCA 1997, s 106 deals with the other type of apportionment that may be made, namely that of a receipt or outgoing becoming due to or payable by the purchaser after the completion date, but covering a period spanning that date. For example, assume that the holder of the above 21-year leasehold interest that is the subject of the sale has to pay an annual rent of €1,800 due on 1 April (in arrears) each year to the freeholder. The rent payable for the year to 1 April 2015 (payable by the purchaser) is dealt with as follows in the apportionment account:

	€
Liability of vendor:	
9/12ths of €1,800	1,350
(period 1/4/2014 to 31/12/2014)	
Liability of purchaser:	
3/12ths of €1,800	450
Adjustment to purchase consideration:	
As above (after adjustment re rent receivable)	45,733
Less:	
Rent payable by purchaser on behalf of vendor	1,350
Final cash due to vendor	44,383

TCA 1997, s 106 requires the part of the rent payable that is apportioned to the vendor to be treated for Sch D Case V purposes as if it had actually been paid by him immediately before the completion of the sale. Consequently the vendor is entitled to treat that part of the outgoing as if it were an expense so that, if allowable, that part (ie the €1,350 in the example) may be deducted in computing the vendor's final Sch D Case V surplus (or deficiency) from the rent in question up to the date of completion. TCA 1997, s 106 would operate in a corresponding manner to attribute to the vendor the apportioned part of any rent receivable after the completion date that is attributable to the period before that date. It also requires that the part of any such receipt or outgoing apportioned to the vendor must be deducted from the actual amount received or paid out by the purchaser, for the purpose of his Sch D Case V computation of the surplus (or deficiency) from the date of acquisition of the premises.

12.109 Returns by letting agents, managers of premises and certain public bodies

TCA 1997, s 888, as supplemented by TCA 1997, s 894, requires all agents and managers of premises who receive rent or other payments (arising from the premises) on behalf of another person to furnish a return to the inspector of taxes detailing:

(a) the full address of the premises;
(b) the local property tax number of each such premises that is a residential property;
(c) the name and address of the person to whom the premises belongs;
(d) the tax reference number of every such person;
(e) the amount of rent or other receipts arising from each premises; and
(f) any other information relating to the premises as may be requested by the inspector of taxes.

Points (b) and (d) above were added by FA 2015 but subject to Ministerial Order; it also requires a person referred above who manages any premises or is in receipt of rent or other payments arising from any premises shall request from every person to whom such premises belongs:

(i) the person's tax reference number; or
(ii) where the person does not have a tax reference number, confirmation to that effect.

TCA 1997, s 888 requires that any Minister of the Government (ie Government department), the Health Service Executive, or any local authority or other board or authority, or other similar bodies, established under statute which makes a payment in the nature of rent or rental subsidy must also furnish a return providing the above details.

12.110 Deduction for capital expenditure on student accommodation/qualifying residential accommodation

Student accommodation

TCA 1997, Pt 10, Ch 11 (ss 372AK to 372AV) provided relief for lessors for capital expenditure incurred on the provision of certain residential accommodation including student accommodation.

In summary, the relief for student accommodation provided for a deduction for qualifying capital expenditure against the rental income of the property in question; any excess of expenditure over that rental income was set against other Case V rental income of the same year and any remaining excess was carried forward against total Case V rental income of the next and succeeding years until exhausted. Only Irish rental income is charged under Case V; non-Irish rental income is charged under Case III, so the relief was available only against Irish rental income.

Relief was available for eligible expenditure incurred on qualifying student accommodation in the qualifying period. The original qualifying period was from 1 April 1999 to 31 March 2003. The end of the qualifying period was extended to 31 December 2006 provided the planning authority acknowledged that it received a valid application for full planning permission by 31 December 2004. If the work involved is an exempted development for planning purposes the extension to 31 December 2006 also applies provided that three conditions are satisfied by 31 December 2004; a detailed plan in relation to the development work is prepared, a binding contract in writing under which the expenditure is incurred is in existence, and work to the value of five per cent of the development costs is carried out.

Where the extension of the qualifying period to 31 December 2006 applied then a further extension to 31 July 2008 was also to be available provided that work to the value of not less than 15 per cent of the actual cost was carried out by 31 December 2006 and the person claiming the relief can show that this condition is satisfied. Where expenditure was incurred after 31 December 2006 the amount of expenditure treated as having been incurred in the qualifying period for the purposes of granting the relief was reduced. If the expenditure was incurred during the calendar year 2007 then the expenditure qualifying for relief was 75 per cent of the amount that would otherwise qualify for relief. If the expenditure was incurred in the period from 1 January 2008 to 31 July 2008 then the amount that qualified for relief was reduced to 50 per cent.

To qualify for the relief expenditure must have been incurred on the construction, conversion or refurbishment of a qualifying premises. With some exceptions noted below, the provisions of TCA 1997, Pt 10, Ch 11 as they applied to rented residential property relief under the 1999 Urban Renewal Scheme apply to student accommodation relief. These measures are discussed in detail in **19.6** of the 2009 edition of this book and readers should refer to that discussion.

The main difference between the rented residential property relief in urban renewal areas described in **19.6** of the 2009 edition of this book and student accommodation relief is the provision that enables the Minister for Education and Science to issue guidelines for the purpose of student accommodation relief. The guidelines may include provisions with regard to such matters as the design, construction, conversion or refurbishment of houses, the total floor area and dimensions of rooms within houses, the provision of ancillary facilities and amenities, the granting of certificates of reasonable cost and certificates of compliance, the designation of qualifying areas, the terms and conditions relating to qualifying leases and the educational institutions and the students attending those institutions in respect of whom the accommodation is provided. The legislation provides that a house will not be a qualifying premises for the purpose of the relief unless it is used for letting to and occupation by students in accordance with the guidelines (TCA 1997, s 372AM(9)) and the floor area of the house complies with the guidelines (TCA 1997, s 372AM(4)). A lease will not be a qualifying lease unless it complies with the requirements in the guidelines (TCA 1997, s 372AO(4)(c)).

The Minister issued guidelines in relation to student accommodation in 1999. An educational institution is defined in the guidelines as an institution in the State which provides courses to which a scheme approved by the Minister for Education and Science under the Local Authorities (Higher Education Grants) Acts 1968 to 1992, applies or an institution that offers an approved course for the purpose of TCA 1997, s 474 (now obsolete). All of the main third-level educational institutions (Universities, Institutes of Technology, Teacher Training Colleges, Art and Design Colleges, Business Colleges, Blackhall Place, King's Inns) are contained in the list of the educational institutions in the guidelines. A student is a person who is a registered student of, and is pursuing a full-time course of study at an educational institution.

The relief was available in respect of a qualifying development which is defined in the guidelines as a development of at least 20 bedspaces that is certified by an educational institution. The certification includes the name of the individual or company which owns the development and the number of units and bedspaces to be provided for the students of the educational institution. This certification must be produced when any claim for relief is subject to a Revenue audit.

A qualifying area means the campus area of the educational institution or areas within an 8 km radius of the main campus, which are approved by the educational institution for the purposes of the development.

The floor area of qualifying premises are also set out in the guidelines. Accommodation must be provided by groupings of study bedrooms in 'house' units. Each unit must have at least 3 bedspaces (minimum gross floor area 55 sq metres) up to a maximum of 8 bedspaces (maximum gross floor area 160 sq metres). Units of study bedrooms will share a kitchen/dining/living room area based on a minimum of 4 sq metres per bedspace in the unit. Kitchen units, sink, cooker and fridge must be installed. The minimum areas for bedrooms depend on the bathroom arrangements. Bathrooms are either ensuite or separately provided to serve a maximum of three bedspaces. Minimum bedroom size will be 8 sq metres (single bedroom/no ensuite), 12 sq metres (single room/ensuite), 15 sq metres (twin room/no ensuite), 18 sq metres (twin room/ensuite) or 15 sq metres (single disabled room/ensuite). Where the residences are not on campus, adequate open space should be provided or, where this is not possible, other alternatives should be provided (for example roof gardens).

Communal service facilities should also be provided. A qualifying development includes ancillary units such as a caretaker/security office and apartment, centralised storage, laundry facilities, drying rooms, utility rooms and seminar rooms. The floor area of these facilities must not exceed 12 per cent of the area of the total development and the cost of these facilities must not exceed 12 per cent of the total qualifying expenditure.

Internet services must be available to each study. Bedspace and minimum technical requirements in this regard are set out in the guidelines.

A qualifying lease means a lease for the whole of the academic year (defined as the academic year of a course, including examinations, being pursued by the student by whom the unit is occupied) governed by the provisions of the Landlord and Tenant code granted to students *or* a lease granted to the educational institution which then on-lets the units to students. TCA 1997, s 372AM provides that all of the rent payable in respect of the letting of the house must be paid to the investor where the expenditure qualifying for relief is incurred on or after 18 July 2002. The explanatory guidance issued by Revenue in this regard is discussed below. The units may be let to non-students for periods outside the academic year. These requirements apply for the usual 10-year 'relevant period'; non-compliance with these requirements prior to the end of the 10 year relevant period will result in a clawback of the relief.

A Certificate of Reasonable Cost must have been issued by the Department of the Environment and Local Government and must accompany all claims for tax relief, other than in the case of newly constructed, converted or refurbished units which are purchased from a builder. Where a unit is purchased from a builder a certificate of compliance was required.

In order to prevent a situation whereby investors' rental income from student accommodation was effectively not taxable TCA 1997, s 372AM was amended to provide that the following conditions had to be satisfied for a house to comprise qualifying student accommodation for the purposes of the relief:

(a) All of the rent payable in respect of the house during the 10-year relevant period must be payable to the investor. If two or more investors incurred the expenditure in relation to the house then the gross rent must be apportioned between them in the same proportion as they incurred the expenditure in relation to the house.

(b) Any borrowings used for the construction, conversion, refurbishment or purchase of the house must be borrowed directly by the investor from a financial institution (within the meaning in TCA 1997, s 906A). The borrower must be personally responsible for the repayment of capital, the payment of interest and the provision of security in relation to the borrowings. There must be no agreement or arrangement whereby any person agrees to be responsible for the investor's obligations in relation to the loan.

(c) Any management or letting fees payable by the investor throughout the 10-year relevant period must comprise *bona fide* fees which reflect the level and extent of the services provided and the aggregate amount of the fees cannot exceed 15 per cent of the gross rents receivable or received in relation to the house.

These additional conditions applied in respect of expenditure incurred on or after 18 July 2002 unless a binding contract for the construction, conversion, or refurbishment of the house was evidenced in writing before that date. In addition the conditions in relation to the recipient of the rent and the management fees did not apply if the Revenue Commissioners issued an opinion in writing prior to 6 February 2003 stating that the lease of the house between the investor and an educational institution would be a qualifying lease for the purpose of the relief.

Revenue issued an explanatory note in January 2004 to clarify the Revenue practice in relation to the three conditions set out above. Revenue is prepared to accept arrangements whereby the college or a management company enter into tenancy agreements with students provided that the net rent secured and taxable in the hands of the investors is the same as if the investors had contracted directly with the students. The college or the management company can guarantee investors a minimum level of rent provided that this does not fall below the rent actually received from the students less allowable deductions. All borrowing must be from a financial institution and expenditure that is funded partly by an interest free loan and partly from a financial institution will disqualify all of the expenditure from relief. If the management and letting fees exceed 15 per cent of the rental income the claim for relief will not be invalidated but the fees in excess of 15 per cent will not be deductible in arriving at the taxable rental income. Revenue also outlined what they regard as management and letting fees. Management fees include fees for the maintenance of the accommodation (ie inspecting the premises to ensure that repairs are carried out but not including the repair costs), collecting rent and changing the names on utility bills when lettings change. Letting fees include advertising to find suitable tenants, obtaining and verifying references, drawing up legal agreements including legal fees, taking deposits from tenants, setting up tenant names on utility bills and setting up direct debits between tenants and landlords. In order to get a deduction for management and letting fees up to the 15 per cent limit the investor, college or management company must be able to show that they are *bona fide* and reflect the level and extent of the services provided.

A college or a management company may wish to allocate the rent appropriate to each investor without doing a separate calculation in each case. Revenue allow rent pooling in respect of rents received from students in the academic year provided that the arrangement is entered into for genuine commercial reasons. Rent pooling schemes devised using an allocation of rent based on bed spaces are acceptable. These rent pooling arrangements applied with effect from 1 January 2004.

Another difference between the rented residential property relief in urban renewal areas and student accommodation relief is the provision which allows an investor to claim relief on the relevant price paid even if the house was let prior to the purchase by the investor. Where qualifying student accommodation which has been let for a period of less than one year is sold by a builder in the course of a trade after 4 December 2001 the purchaser was entitled to relief equal to the relevant price paid, ie costs of construction, conversion or refurbishment and a portion of the builder's profit (TCA 1997, s 372AP(10)) calculated as follows:

$$\text{Purchase} \times \frac{\text{Cost of construction/conversion/refurbishment}}{\text{Cost of construction/conversion/refurbishment plus site cost}}$$

This catered for the situation where the builder let a house prior to its sale. In the absence of this provision the purchaser's entitlement to relief would be limited to the lower of the actual cost of construction, conversion or refurbishment, or the relevant price paid by the purchaser.

The changes made in Finance Act 2012 to guillotine the ability to claim unused capital allowances beyond 2014 do not apply to student accommodation.

Example 12.110.1

In January 2005, Mr Jones purchased a dwelling in a student accommodation development from Mr Dempsey, a builder. The development is located in the vicinity of University College Galway and satisfies all of the conditions in relation to student accommodation relief. The purchase price of the dwelling was €180,000. Mr Dempsey's cost of construction was €105,000. The site cost was €17,700. The net rental income from the house in 2005 amounts to €6,000. Mr Jones has rental income after allowable expenses from a commercial property in the amount of €47,500.

The qualifying expenditure is calculated as follows:

$$\text{Purchase price} \times \frac{\text{Cost of construction}}{\text{Cost of construction plus site cost}}$$

$$180{,}000 \times \frac{105{,}000}{105{,}000 + 17{,}700} = 154{,}034$$

Mr Jones Rental income computation for 2005 is as follows:

	Student accommodation	*Commercial property*
	€	€
Net Rental income	6,000	47,500
Student accommodation relief	(154,034)	-
Taxable Rental income	(148,034)	47,500

The case V sources are aggregated so that the loss on the student accommodation shelters the rental income from the commercial property. The loss carried forward in the amount of €100,534 will be available to offset Mr Jones' Irish rental income in subsequent years.

Qualifying residential accommodation

There was a countrywide scheme of relief for lessors in respect of refurbishment expenditure incurred on certain residential buildings referred to as 'special qualifying premises'. In common with other reliefs for capital expenditure incurred on residential accommodation the legislative provisions for this scheme are contained in TCA 1997, Pt 10, Ch 11.

A person who incurred refurbishment expenditure on a house that is a special qualifying premises and who made a claim, was entitled to an annual deduction of 15 per cent of the expenditure incurred in the qualifying period in computing the rental surplus or deficiency from the premises. TCA 1997, s 97(1) provides that Irish rental profits are computed by deducting the aggregate rental deficiencies from the aggregate rental surpluses. As a result the deduction granted by TCA 1997, s 372AP(3) was available against a taxpayer's total Irish rental income. The annual deduction was first given in the year in which the expenditure was incurred or if the premises was not let in that year the relief was delayed until the year of first letting. Relief was also given for any subsequent year in which the premises was a special qualifying premises. The aggregate deduction could not exceed 100 per cent of the expenditure.

The relief applied in respect of expenditure on the refurbishment of a special qualifying premises. For these purposes refurbishment means any works of construction, reconstruction, repair or renewal, including the provision or improvement of water, sewerage or heating facilities, carried out in the course of repair or restoration (including by way of maintenance) of the building or for the purpose of complying with the requirements of the Housing (Standards for Rented Houses) Regulations 1993 (SI 147/1993). Expenditure attributable to any part of the building that is not a house will not qualify for relief (TCA 1997, s 372AN(5)). Any expenditure that is met by the State, by any board established by statute or by any public or local authority was not regarded as incurred by a person with the result that relief could not be claimed in respect thereof.

A special qualifying premises is a house that was comprised in a special specified building, which was used solely as a dwelling and which on completion of the refurbishment to which the expenditure relates was let (or if not let on that date, was, without having been used after that date, first let) under a qualifying lease and thereafter throughout the remainder of the relevant period (except for temporary disuse between lettings) continued to be let under such a lease. A special specified building was one in which before and after the refurbishment to which the relevant expenditure relates there was at least one house. For this purpose a house includes any building or part of a building used or suitable for use as a dwelling and any out office, yard, garden or other land enjoyed with the building.

A house was not a special qualifying premises if the lessor had not complied with all of the requirements of the Housing (Standards for Rented Houses) Regulations 1993 (SI 147/1993), the Housing (Rent Books) Regulations 1993 (SI 146/1993) and the Residential Tenancies Act 2004, Pt 7 in respect of all tenancies relating to that premises.

Any house on which expenditure was incurred that qualified or would have qualified for relief under TCA 1997, s 372AP, ie the urban renewal, rural renewal, town renewal scheme, etc was not a special qualifying premises.

The qualifying period in relation to a special specified building was the period from 6 April 2001 to 31 July 2008. Where the expenditure was incurred after 31 December 2006 the amount that was to be treated as expenditure incurred in the qualifying period was reduced. If the expenditure was incurred during the calendar year 2007 the amount of that expenditure that qualified for relief was reduced to 75 per cent. If the expenditure was incurred in the period from 1 January 2008 to 31 July 2008 the portion of that expenditure that qualified for relief was reduced to 50 per cent.

The relevant period was the period of 10 years beginning on the date of completion of the refurbishment to which the expenditure relates, or if the premises was not let under a qualifying lease on that date, the period of 10 years beginning on the date of first letting after completion.

A claw back of the relief is outlined in TCA 1997, s 372AP(7) and arises if at any time in the relevant period either:

(a) a house ceases to be a special qualifying premises; or
(b) the ownership of the lessor's interest in the house passes to any other person but the house does not cease to be special qualifying premises.

The clawback operates by treating the taxpayer as being deemed to have received on the day before the day of the occurrence of the event an amount as rent from that premises equal to the amount determined by the formula—

$$A - B$$

where—

A is the amount of the deduction or, as the case may be, the aggregate amount of the deductions in respect of eligible expenditure incurred on or in relation to the premises, and

B relates to Case V losses under TCA 1997, s 384 and is that part of the amount of any excess (within the meaning of section 384) that is attributable to the deduction under TCA 1997, s 372AP in respect of eligible expenditure incurred on or in relation to the premises and which has been carried forward under s 384 to the year of assessment in which either of the events above occurs.

Where a claw back occurs as a result of the ownership of the lessor's interest passing to another person the purchaser is treated as having incurred refurbishment expenditure equal to the amount treated as eligible refurbishment expenditure in relation to the house.

This relief is subject to the restrictions applicable to high income individuals discussed at **3.111** from tax year 2007 onwards.

Interaction with Capital Gains Tax

TCA 1997, s 372AP was amended with retrospective effect by FA 2015, s 12 by the insertion of a new sub-s (13A) into that section in relation to an event outlined in TCA 1997, s 372AP(7) occurring on or after 1 January 2012. The events specified in sub-s (7) comprise where a house is a qualifying premises or a special qualifying premises and at any time during the relevant period in relation to the premises either of the following events occurs:

(a) the house ceases to be a qualifying premises or a special qualifying premises, as the case may be, or

(b) the ownership of the lessor's interest in the house passes to any other person but the house does not cease to be a qualifying premises or a special qualifying premises, as the case may be.

Where the amendment applies then TCA 1997, s 555 will apply as if a deduction in accordance with TCA 1997, s 372P were a capital allowance. TCA 1997, s 555 provides the restriction of capital losses for capital gains tax purposes by excluding from the deductible expenditure any capital allowance or renewals allowances which have been 'or may be made' in respect of that expenditure. However, the amendment also provides that the reference to 'A' in the formula outlined in TCA 1997, s 372AP(7) and discussed above was a balancing charge. This means that the clawback will effectively reduce the capital loss restriction.

12.111 Receiverships and rental income

TCA 1997, s 96(3) deals with certain receivership issues. It states that 'where the estate or interest of any lessor of any premises is the subject of a mortgage and either the mortgagee is in possession or the rents and profits are being received by a receiver appointed by or on the application of the mortgagee, that estate or interest shall be deemed for the purposes of this Chapter to be vested in the mortgagee, and references to a lessor shall be construed accordingly; but the amount of the liability to tax of any such mortgagee shall be computed as if the mortgagor was still in possession or, as the case may be, no receiver had been appointed and as if it were the amount of the liability of the mortgagor that was being computed.' Revenue's operational manual was published in October 2015 and dealt with the tax consequences of receiverships and Mortgagee in Possession (MIP). It deals with issues arising across the tax heads but this will look to the income tax consequences only.

The manual notes that the appointment of a receiver is one of the ways by which a lender can enforce a mortgage or charge with various types of receivers, eg a fixed charge receiver who is appointed under a mortgage in respect of a particular asset. It continues that a floating charge receiver is a receiver who takes control of a person's assets generally, or of certain categories of assets (for example, debtors or stock).

A receiver's main purpose is to realise the assets over which they have been appointed for the benefit of the charge holder and may often continue to trade, rent property etc pending a sale of the property or the relevant assets. A receiver may also be appointed by court order where, for example, the lender does not have a power to appoint a receiver under the mortgage deed and is deemed an officer of the court and owes duties to the court. TCA 1997, s 1049 looks at court appointed receivers so what follows looks at receivers and mortgagees in possession (MIPs), other than court appointed receivers.

Para 3.1 looks at TCA 1997, s 96(3) and notes that it:

> provides that tax on net rental income from property in receivership, or from property where the mortgagee has taken possession, is chargeable on the mortgagee. This includes tax on any balancing charge arising or on 'section 23' type relief clawed back on a sale of property. This means that the mortgagee (not the receiver) has to make a return in respect of, and pay the tax liability on, such income. For each individual letting, rental profit should be calculated as if the borrower was still in possession. This has a number of consequences, including the need to take into account in the calculation the borrower's–
>
> - other income;
> - losses and allowances, current or brought forward;
> - tax credits, if the borrower is an individual; …
>
> However, it should be noted that unconnected receivership losses, or losses etc from other activities of the mortgagee, cannot shelter such rental profits … A consequence of this is that, where the letting of the property in receivership gives rise to a loss, the loss is not available to the borrower to utilize against other rental income. Any such loss is, however, available to the mortgagee in question when calculating its liabilities under section 96(3) in respect of the rental property of that borrower only.

The question of the availability of balancing allowances etc being available to the MIP has been one of debate and Revenue's view is clearly stated in the above.

12.2 Premiums on Leases etc

12.201 Premiums treated as rent

In the absence of any rule to the contrary, it would be possible for a person to lease premises for a low annual rent but to obtain a full economic return by also taking a premium, ie a lump sum consideration for the grant of the lease (see *Clarke v United Real (Moorgate) Ltd* [1988] STC 273). On general principles this would be a capital sum not chargeable to income tax. The distinction between such a capital sum and an advance payment of rent can in some situations be extremely fine: see *Flynn v John Noone Ltd* II ITR 222 and *O'Sullivan v P* II ITR 464. Both cases underline the principle that the description or 'label' which the parties to a transaction attach to it cannot override its true legal effect (see **1.407**).

While it is a perfectly valid commercial arrangement for a lessor to take some part of the return on his investment in the property by way of a premium on the granting of a new lease, TCA 1997, s 98 contains rules to ensure that the lessor is charged to tax on a proportion of the premium or any like sum (TCA 1997, s 96(1)) determined by reference to the duration of the lease. It also taxes premiums and certain other amounts received during the currency of a lease. The rules do not apply to other capital sums received in respect of rights over land.

TCA 1997, s 98(1) requires an additional amount to be included in the computation of the surplus (or deficiency) arising from the rent under any lease as defined by TCA 1997, s 96(1) if:

(a) the payment of any premium is due under the terms subject to which a lease is granted; and

(b) the duration of the lease does not exceed 50 years.

The amount in question is treated as an amount of rent (in addition to any actual rent) that is deemed to be received on the date the lease is granted. In applying this rule, any sum paid in connection with the granting of a lease that is not rent is presumed to have been paid as a premium unless, and to the extent that, other sufficient consideration is shown to have been given for the sum paid (TCA 1997, s 98(6)).

The amount included as additional rent is an amount equal to the premium reduced by two per cent of the premium for each complete period of 12 months comprised in the term of the lease, but with the exception that the full premium is included in the case of a lease granted for a term of less than two complete years. For leases with durations of between 2 and 50 years, the computation of the additional rent (the 'taxable amount') can be set out conveniently in the following formula:

$$\text{Taxable amount} = P \times \frac{(51 - n)}{50}$$

where

P= the amount of the premium; and

n= the number of each complete period of 12 months comprised in the term of the lease.

No taxable amount arises where the term of the lease exceeds 50 years. For rules defining the duration (ie the term) of a lease, see **12.210**.

Example 12.201.1

On 1 January 2015, Mr LD grants a lease for 35 years and nine months to Mr TN in consideration of an annual rent of €40,000 (subject to review every seven years) and a premium of €200,000. Mr LD has been in receipt of Sch D Case V rental income from other lettings for a number of years.

The calculation of the surplus in respect of the rent from Mr TN for the year ending 31 December 2015 (to be included in his total Sch D Case V income for 2015) is made as follows:

	€
Rent receivable: €40,000	40,000
Additional rent in respect of the premium:	
€200,000 x (51–35)/50=	64,000
	104,000
Less:	
Deductible expenses, say	40,000
Surplus on lease to Mr TN	64,000

Notes:

1. The calculation of the additional rent in the manner actually set out in the Act is:

	€
Amount of premium	200,000
Number of complete years in lease period = 35 years	
Reduction is:	
€200,000 x (35 – 1) x 2% =	(136,000)
Additional rent (same as above)	64,000

12.202 Amounts deemed to be premium

TCA 1997, s 98(2)–(4) deems the payment of a premium to the lessor to be required by a lease in certain specified circumstances. In any such case, TCA 1997, s 98(1) is applied to the amount deemed to be a premium with the result that an additional 'rent' amount must be brought into the computation of the relevant surplus (or deficiency). The (51–n)/50 fraction is applied to the deemed premium, but the value of *n* is varied in any case within either TCA 1997, s 98(3) or (4), but not one under TCA 1997, s 98(2).

TCA 1997, s 98(2) deems a lease to have required the payment of a premium to the lessor if the terms on which it is granted impose on the lessee an obligation to carry out any work on the premises, except if the work is such (eg repairs) that the cost would be a deductible expense to the lessor if he (and not the lessee) were required to undertake it. The deemed premium is taken as an amount equal to the enhancement in value of the lessor's interest in the premises that would have resulted if the work required had been carried out immediately after the commencement of the lease. Normally, the increase in value of the lessor's interest is measured as a capitalisation of the increase in rent which, if he had carried out the work himself, the lessor could have demanded. While TCA 1997, s 98(2) does not apply to other forms of consideration provided by the lessee, these might be regarded in some cases as constituting premiums under general principles (see the non-tax case of *Elmdene Estates v White* [1960] 1 All ER 306).

Example 12.202.1

AX grants a 21-year lease on 1 November 2015 to YB, a sole trader, at an annual rent of €24,000 (payable monthly in arrears) and a premium of €120,000. The lease contains a term requiring the lessee to double glaze all windows and to insulate all exterior walls and the roof space (capital expenditure not normally deductible). The cost of the work is estimated to be €50,000 and it is further estimated that if AX had done this work itself, he could have demanded an additional rent of €8,000 per annum. If the double glazing, etc had been done on 1 November 2015, it is assumed that the lessor's interest in the premises would have been €56,000 greater (ie the additional rent capitalised at seven years' purchase). The lease is, therefore, deemed by TCA 1997, s 98(2) to have required a further premium of €56,000 (in addition to the actual premium).

AX is required to include in his total Sch D Case V income for 2015 the following surplus in respect of his lease to YB:

	€
Rent receivable: 24,000 x 2/12 =	4,000
Additional rent re premium:	
€120,000 x (51–21)/50	72,000
Additional rent re deemed premium:	
€56,000 x (51–21)/50	33,600
Surplus for 2015 (no expenses assumed)	109,600

TCA 1997, s 98(3) deems a lease to have required the payment of a premium if the terms on which it is granted provide for a sum becoming payable by the lessee either:

(a) in lieu of the whole or a part of the rent for any period; or

(b) as consideration for the surrender of the lease.

In this case, the deemed premium is taken as equal to this sum, but the additional rent (the taxable amount) in respect of this deemed premium is brought into the Sch D Case V computation for the period in which the sum is actually payable. Further, if the sum is payable in lieu of the whole or a part of the rent for any period (ie alternative (a) above), the computation of the taxable amount is made on the assumption that the term of the lease is limited to the period in respect of which the nil or reduced rent is payable. This means that the TCA 1997, s 98(1) formula has to be applied on the basis that n is equal to the number of complete periods of 12 months comprised in that period (and not in the full term of the lease).

Example 12.202.2

Take the facts of **Example 12.201.1**, but assume that the terms under which the lease was granted provided that Mr TN (the lessee) would pay Mr LD (the lessor) a lump sum of €40,000 on 1 July 2015 in consideration for the lessor accepting a reduced rent of €30,000 per annum for the first five years from 1 January 2015 to 31 December 2019.

In addition to the amount of additional rent of €64,000 brought into the computation of the surplus to 31 December 2015, as shown in **Example 12.201.1**, TCA 1997, s 98(3) now requires an additional amount of rent to be included in the computation of the surplus for the year to 31 December 2015, ie by reference to the date (1/7/2015) on which the sum of €40,000 is payable. The additional rent in respect of this lump sum payment is computed as follows:

Lump sum 40,000 x (51–5)/50=	€36,800

TCA 1997, s 98(4) deems a lease to have required the payment of a premium if any sum, other than as a rent, becomes payable by the lessee as consideration for the variation or waiver of any of the terms of the lease. In this case, the additional rent is deemed to be received on the date the agreement for the variation or waiver is entered into; and the computation of the taxable amount is made on the assumption that the term of the lease is only the length of the period during which the variation or waiver has effect. In *Banning v Wright* 48 TC 421, a tenant's option to renew a lease was forfeited due to his breach of a covenant under the lease. It was held that a sum paid to the landlord to reinstate the option fell within the UK equivalent of TCA 1997, s 98(4). The court held that although the landlord's rights under the lease remained unchanged (so that the landlord could still have forfeited the option if there had been any subsequent breaches of the covenant) a waiver of the exercise of rights as a result of a breach fell within these provisions.

Example 12.202.3

Mr DNT occupies premises under a 21-year lease granted on 1 May 2010 under which he pays a rent of €8,000 per annum. On 1 October 2015, Mr DNT enters into an agreement with the current lessor (who had acquired it by purchase in 2011) which provides that, in consideration for a lump sum of €11,000, the lessor (PQ Ltd) will accept a reduced rent of €4,500 per annum for the next four years beginning 1 January 2016.

Based on the deemed term of the lease (four years), the amount of additional rent deemed by TCA 1997, s 98(4) to be received by PQ Ltd on 1 October 2015 (date of the agreement) is computed:

Lump sum €11,000 x (51–4)/50 =	€10,340

12.203 Premiums to persons other than the lessor

TCA 1997, s 98(5) deals with any case where either a premium on the granting of a lease (TCA 1997, s 98(1)), a sum in consideration for a reduced rent for any period (TCA 1997, s 98(3)), or a sum in consideration for the variation or waiver of any of the terms of a lease (TCA 1997, s 98(4)) is payable to a person other than the lessor. In any such case, one reason for not making the premium or other lump sum payment to the lessor could have been an attempt to avoid the charge to tax under TCA 1997, s 98, for example, by making the payment to a person connected with the lessor. A payment may also be made to a person other than the lessor where a lease is granted and the terms of the lease permit the lessee to sublease the premises on condition that the sub lessee pay a premium to the original lessor (who is not, however, the lessor in relation to the sublease).

In any case to which it applies, TCA 1997, s 98(5) requires the person to whom the premium or other sum is paid to be taxed under Sch D Case IV on an amount equal to the 'additional rent' which the lessor would have had to include in his Sch D Case V computation if the payment had been made to him. In other words, the amount taxable under Sch D Case IV is equal to the premium or other relevant sum multiplied by the appropriate (51–n)/50 fraction, depending on whether the premium or other sum arises under TCA 1997, s 98(1), (3) or (4).

In the case where the deemed premium payable to the non-lessor arises under TCA 1997, s 98(4), under an agreement for the variation or waiver of any of the terms of a lease, TCA 1997, s 98(5) only applies to tax the recipient if he is a person connected with the lessor. If this sum is paid to an unconnected person, presumably under some genuine commercial arrangement, the charge to tax under TCA 1997, s 98(5) is not made. In determining whether a person is connected with the lessor for this purpose, the connected person rules of TCA 1997, s 10 are applied.

12.204 Reverse premiums

In broad terms a reverse premium is a payment in return for a tenant agreeing to enter into a tenancy. Prior to the introduction of TCA 1997, s 98A (in FA 2002) there was no specific legislation governing the income tax treatment of reverse premiums. Accordingly general principles, in particular the principles used to distinguish revenue and capital receipts, had to be used to determine the correct income tax treatment. In the New Zealand case of *CIR v Wattie* [1998] STC 1160 it was held that a reverse premium was of a capital nature notwithstanding that it was 'commercially, financially and mathematically' linked to an increased rental payable by the lessee. It should be noted that a sum paid in return for a tenant entering into a new lease would not normally give rise to a gain for capital gains tax purposes as the tenant would not be disposing of any property in return for the sum received.

The charging provisions

TCA 1997, s 98A defines a reverse premium as a payment or other benefit received by a person by way of inducement in connection with a transaction under which he or a person connected with him is granted an estate or interest in land or a right in or over land (a relevant transaction). TCA 1997, s 98A(2) provides that a reverse premium is to be regarded as a revenue receipt with the result that it will fall within the scope of income tax. As a general rule the amount or value of a reverse premium is to be treated as rental income. Accordingly, if a reverse premium is paid in connection with a relevant transaction over Irish land the amount or value would be assessed under Sch D Case V whereas if the relevant transaction related to non-Irish land the charge would be under Sch D Case III. There are a number of exceptions to the general rule, however. If the recipient is the person who enters into the lease, and does so for the purpose of a trade or profession which he carries on or will carry on, the reverse premium is taken into account in computing the profits of the trade or profession under Sch D, Case I or II as appropriate. Where a reverse premium is received by an assurance company that carries on life business which is not taxable under Sch D, Case I the amount or value of the reverse premium is deducted from the company's expenses of management.

Example 12.204.1

Mr Quirke entered into a 2-year lease of a commercial property on 2 January 2015. The annual rental income under the lease amounted to €50,000. In return for entering into the lease Mr Quirke received €18,000. Mr Quirke sub-let the property to Mr Johnson on 1 April 2015 for rent of €60,000 per annum. Mr Quirke's rental income computation for 2015 is as follows:

Rental income		€
Reverse premium		18,000
Rental income	(€60,000 x 9/12)	45,000
Outgoings		
Rent	(€50,000 x 9/12)	(37,500)
Case V income		25,500

The timing of the charge

In the normal case TCA 1997, s 98A is silent as regards the timing of the charge to tax. Where the reverse premium is treated as a receipt of a trade or profession it should be accounted for in accordance with the accepted principles of commercial accounting. UITF 28 provides that a lessee should recognise the aggregate benefit of incentives as a reduction of the rental expense. The benefit of a reverse premium should be allocated over either the term of the lease, or if shorter than the full term, the date to the first rent review that would adjust the rent to the prevailing market rate. The allocation should be on a straight line basis unless another systematic basis is more representative of the time pattern of the lessee's benefit from the use of the leased asset.

TCA 1997, s 98A prescribes the timing of the charge in two instances. Where two or more people who enter into relevant arrangements are connected with each other and the terms of the arrangement are not at arm's length the charge to tax on the amount or value of the reverse premium is accelerated. Relevant arrangements means a relevant transaction and any arrangements entered into in connection with it whether before, at the same time or after it. In such a case the amount or value of the reverse premium is brought into charge in the period in which the relevant transaction is entered into. There is an exception to this rule in the case where the relevant transaction is entered into by the person in receipt of the reverse premium for the purpose of a trade or profession that has not yet commenced in which case the reverse premium will be treated as accruing in the period in which the trade or profession commences. This provision prevents connected persons from achieving a tax advantage by creating long leases on a non-arm's length basis and spreading the reverse premiums over an unrealistic period. The second instance at which TCA 1997, s 98A prescribes the timing of the charge is where a reverse premium is received by an assurance company whose profits are taxable otherwise than under Sch D, Case I. In this case the reverse premium should be deducted from the assurance company's expenses of management in the period in which it is received.

Exclusions from the charge

The charge to tax on reverse premiums does not apply in certain instances. Firstly if the payment or benefit is received by an individual in connection with taking an interest in a premises which will be the individual's only or main residence a charge under TCA 1997, s 98A will not arise. There is also an exclusion from the charge on a payment or benefit to the extent that it is consideration for the sale in a sale and leaseback arrangement. This is defined as an arrangement under which a person disposes of the full interest in land to another person and the terms subject to which the disposal is made provide for the grant of a lease to that person. The exemption only applies where a sale and leaseback arrangement is entered into on *bona fide* commercial terms. Finally if a reverse premium received by a lessee as an inducement to enter into a lease comprises a revenue receipt under general principles and is taxable in computing the profits of a trade or profession under Sch D, Case I or II the provisions of TCA 1997, s 98A will not apply. The payment of contributions towards a trading lessee's revenue expenditure as an inducement to enter into a lease such as a contribution towards relocation costs would comprise revenue receipts under general principles.

The scope of the charge

A reverse premium takes the form of a payment or other benefit received by way of inducement in connection with entering into a relevant transaction. Typical examples of payments caught by TCA 1997, s 98A would be lump sum cash payments or contributions towards a lessee's cost of fitting out the building in order to induce the tenant to enter into a lease. The meaning of the term 'other benefits' is not defined for the purpose of TCA 1997, s 98A but prima facie would include the supply and installation of the tenant's trade fixtures or payments to third parties to meet the lessee's obligations. Arguably the definition of reverse premium infers that where provision is made for a payment or benefit in the lease agreement it will not comprise a reverse premium. On this basis, the provision in a lease agreement for rent free or reduced rent periods of occupation would not comprise a reverse premium since the benefit would be a term of the lease rather than a benefit received as an inducement in connection with entering into the lease. Even if this point is challenged, it would seem that the legislation is directed only where there is a cash outlay on the part of the landlord. It should also be borne in mind that outlay of a nature which results in the landlord being enabled or entitled to charge a higher rent would not normally be caught on the basis that no benefit would accrue to the tenant in these circumstances. A contribution to tenant's fitting out costs might be caught by the legislation in principle (either because it is not a term of the lease or it is ultimately held that this is not a relevant factor); however, if the rent charged under the lease is enhanced to reflect the value of the landlord's contribution, the section should not apply.

TCA 1997, s 98A will not give rise to a charge to tax on the sale of a freehold interest. The reason for this is that a relevant transaction is a transaction in which a person is granted an estate or interest in land or a right in or over land. As a freehold interest is the superior interest in land it cannot be the subject of a grant and its disposal therefore does not comprise a relevant transaction.

There is no reference in TCA 1997, s 98A to the person who will provide the payment or other benefit as an inducement in connection with entering into a relevant transaction. In most cases the payment or benefit will be provided by the grantor of an estate or interest in land, or a right in or over land. However, the provision of a payment or other benefit by any other person as an inducement in connection with entering into the transaction will also fall within the scope of TCA 1997, s 98A.

12.205 Assignment of lease granted at undervalue

TCA 1997, s 99(1) charges income tax under Sch D Case IV on any profit or gain realised on the assignment of any lease that was granted at an undervalue, but this does not apply to any lease the duration of which exceeds 50 years. For this purpose, a lease is treated as having been granted at an undervalue if, having regard to values prevailing at the time it was granted, it should have required a greater premium than the premium (if any) that was in fact obtained at that time. In determining the amount of the premium that should have been paid, it must be assumed that the negotiations for the lease had been at arm's length.

In the absence of TCA 1997, s 99, it would be possible for the lessor to grant the lessee (probably a person connected with him) a very favourable lease (ie one with a rent below a normal market rent) without charging him an adequate premium to compensate for the low rent. The lessee would, in consequence, have a valuable asset which he could sell and realise a capital profit not subject to income tax. The fact that the assignment of the lease is now the disposal of an asset subject to capital gains tax (not the position when TCA 1997, s 99 was originally enacted) does not prevent the operation of TCA 1997, s 99 for income tax purposes.

TCA 1997, s 99 taxes the person assigning the lease on a proportion of the excess of the consideration received for the assignment over the premium (if any) for which the lease was granted (the 'excess consideration'), but only to the extent that the excess consideration is equal to or less than the 'amount forgone' on the granting of the lease. The amount forgone is the additional premium, ie over the actual premium (if any), the lease would have required if it had been granted as the result of an arm's length transaction. If there was no premium on the granting of the lease, the amount forgone is taken as the full premium which would have been charged in an arm's length transaction.

The part of the excess consideration or, if it is lower, of the amount forgone that is treated as income of the assignor chargeable under Sch D Case IV is determined by the same formula used by TCA 1997, s 98 to tax premiums on the granting of leases (see **12.201**). In other words, the proportion that is taxable reduces by two per cent for each full year in the term of the lease (except the first). This is quite logical since the taxable income arises because of the amount of the additional premium that could have been obtained when the lease was granted. The amount taxable is chargeable in the tax year in which the assignment takes place.

Example 12.205.1

On 8 May 2015, Mr A O'Brien granted a 21-year lease in certain premises to O'Brien Ltd for an annual rent of €1,000 and a premium of €18,000. On 25 October 2015, O'Brien Ltd sells the 21-year lease to an unconnected company for €50,000. The 21-year lease granted in May 2015 would have commanded a premium of €36,000 in an arm's length transaction. Clearly, the lease is one granted at an undervalue.

Mr O'Brien is charged under TCA 1997, s 98(1) on an additional rent of €10,800 (receivable 8/5/2015) by reference to the actual premium obtained of €18,000. TCA 1997, s 99 applies to charge O'Brien Ltd as the assignor under Sch D Case IV for its 12-month accounting period to 31 December 2015 on a taxable amount of €10,800, computed as follows:

	€
Consideration for assignment of lease (25/10/2015)	50,000
Less: actual premium paid (8/5/2015)	18,000
Excess consideration	32,000
Amount forgone (8/5/2015):	
Arm's length premium	36,000
Less:	
Actual premium paid	18,000
Amount forgone	18,000

Number of complete years in term of lease: 21 years

€18,000 x (51–21)/50 =	10,800

Notes:

1. The TCA 1997, s 98(1) formula is applied as if the premium (P) were the lower of the excess consideration (€32,000) and the amount forgone (€18,000), ie the latter figure.

So far only the first assignment of a lease granted at an undervalue has been considered. Unless the excess consideration on the first assignment equals or exceeds the amount forgone on the granting of the lease (as it did in **Example 12.205.1**), TCA 1997, s 99 applies again if the first assignee should sell or otherwise assign the lease to another person (the second assignee) for a consideration in excess of his own cost of acquiring it. In such a case, TCA 1997, s 99 charges the first assignee (now the assignor) to tax under Sch D Case IV, but the amount chargeable may be reduced by the rule of TCA 1997, s 103 which applies in the case of successive taxable events under TCA 1997, ss 98–100 (see **12.207**).

The amount chargeable in respect of the second assignment (before applying TCA 1997, s 103) is arrived at as follows:

(a) ascertain the excess of the consideration received by the first assignee over his cost of acquiring the lease;

(b) determine the revised amount forgone by deducting from the original amount forgone (date of granting lease) the excess consideration on the first assignment; and

(c) compute the amount chargeable by applying the TCA 1997, s 98(1) formula to the lower of the excess consideration on the second assignment and the revised amount forgone.

In the event that the second assignee should sell the lease in question to a third assignee, the same procedure should be followed to determine the second assignee's chargeable amount (before TCA 1997, s 103), and so on. However, once the amount of the premium forgone on the granting of the lease has been reduced to nil by one or more assignments, TCA 1997, s 99 ceases to have any application.

A person who assigns or otherwise sells a leasehold interest in premises in the course of a trade of dealing in or developing land normally brings the full sales proceeds into his accounts as a trading receipt in calculating the profits of the trade that are taxable under Sch D Case I. If such a person is chargeable by TCA 1997, s 99 under Sch D Case IV on the assignment of the same leasehold interest granted at an undervalue, the amount assessable under Sch D Case IV is deducted from the trading receipts included in arriving at the Sch D Case I profits (TCA 1997, s 99(2)).

For example, if O'Brien Ltd in **Example 12.205.1** had assigned the lease in the course of a trade of property dealing, the sale proceeds to be included as a trading receipt in its Sch D Case I computation for 2015 would be €39,200 (ie the actual consideration received of €50,000 reduced by the Sch D Case IV taxable amount of €10,800).

12.206 Sale of land with right to reconveyance or lease

TCA 1997, s 100(1) charges tax under Sch D Case IV on a person (the vendor), who sells an estate or interest in land, if the terms of the sale entitle the vendor or a person connected with him, to either the reconveyance at any future date of the interest sold or the grant of a lease directly or indirectly out of the interest sold (other than a lease starting within one month of the sale). The object of the section is to prevent the vendor's making a tax free gain by selling his interest in the land at one price and by reacquiring it at a later date at a lower price or by getting the use of the property again by a lease on favourable terms.

TCA 1997, s 100 deals with a sale with the right to a reconveyance. The Sch D Case IV taxable amount is based on the excess of the consideration for the sale of the interest in the land (the sale price) over the price at which it is to be reconveyed (the reconveyance price). If the earliest date on which, under the terms of the sale, the interest is due to be reconveyed is less than two years after the date of the sale, the taxable amount is the full excess of the sale price over the reconveyance price.

If the earliest reconveyance date possible is two complete years or more after the sale, the taxable amount is determined in a manner which can be reduced to the following formula:

$$\text{Taxable amount} = E - (E \times (n - 1) \times 2\%)$$

where

E= the excess of the sale price over the reconveyance price; and

n= the number of complete years in the period between the sale and the earliest reconveyance date.

In other words, the taxable amount is the amount of the excess reduced by two per cent of that excess for each complete year, other than the first, between the sale and the earliest reconveyance date.

Example 12.206.1

Mr A Winner sells his 35-year leasehold interest in a warehouse for €100,000 on 1 September 2015 under a sales agreement which requires the purchaser (X Ltd) to reconvey that interest to Mrs C Loser (his daughter, a connected person) for a consideration of €67,000 at any time between three and five years after the date of the sale (if requested by six-months' notice in writing).

TCA 1997, s 100(1) applies so that Mr Winner is charged to income tax under Sch D Case IV for 2015 (the tax year of the sale) on a taxable amount of €31,680, computed as follows:

	€
Sale price (1/9/2015)	100,000
Less:	
Reconveyance price	67,000
Excess (= E)	33,000
Earliest date of reconveyance is 1/9/2018: n = 3 years	
Taxable amount: €33,000 – (€33,000 x (3 – 1) x 2%) =	31,680
(subject to any possible claim under TCA 1997, s 100 – see below)	

TCA 1997, s 100 provides two further rules which may be relevant in any case where the reconveyance date is not fixed under the terms of the sale. First, if the reconveyance price varies depending on the date of the reconveyance, the lowest possible reconveyance price under the terms of sale is brought into the calculation of the taxable amount TCA 1997, s 100(2)(a)). Secondly, if the reconveyance takes place at a later date than the earliest possible date, the vendor is entitled to have the original Sch D Case IV assessment recalculated and any excess tax repaid. The revised taxable amount is made by taking n in the above formula as equal to the number of complete years (if more than one) from the date of the sale to the actual reconveyance date (and by taking the reconveyance price as the price payable on that date) (TCA 1997, s 100(2)(b) as amended by FA 2008, Sch 6). Any claim for a repayment under TCA 1997, s 100(2)(b) may be made at any time no later than four years after the actual date of the reconveyance without prejudice to the general four-year repayment time limit under TCA 1997, s 865(4). It may be made whether or not the reconveyance price varies with the date of the reconveyance (eg as in **Example 12.206.1** where the reconveyance could take place at any time between three and five years after the date of the sale). It is not, however, relevant if the actual reconveyance takes place less than two complete years after the sale.

Example 12.206.2

Take the facts of **Example 12.206.1**, except to assume that the sale agreement provided for a reconveyance price of €59,000 if the reconveyance is made between three and four years after the sale by Mr Winner, but for a reconveyance between four and five years the price is to be €70,000.

Assume that the reconveyance is made by X Ltd to Mrs Loser (the connected person) on 15 September 2019, ie over four complete years after the sale on 1 September 2015. The original assessment under TCA 1997, s 100(2)(a) on Mr Winner, and the revised assessment by reference to which he is entitled to claim repayment of excess tax under TCA 1997, s 100(2)(b), are now made as follows:

(1) Original Sch D Case IV assessment:	€
Sales price (as before)	100,000
Less:	
Lowest possible reconveyance price	(59,000)
Excess	41,000
Earliest date of reconveyance: 1/9/2018 (n = 3 years)	
Taxable amount: €41,000 – (€41,000 x (3 – 1) x 2%) =	39,360
(2) Revised Sch D Case IV assessment (reconveyance 15/9/2019):	
Sales proceeds (as before)	100,000
Less:	
Reconveyance price (between 4 and 5 years)	(70,000)
Excess	30,000
Actual reconveyance date: 15/9/2019 (n = 4 years)	
Taxable amount: €30,000 – (€30,000 x (4 – 1) x 2%) =	28,200

Assuming Mr Winner paid income tax in 2015 at the top marginal rate of 40 per cent on the full amount of the original Sch D Case IV assessment (€39,360), he is entitled to claim repayment of €4,464, ie (€39,360 – €28,200) x 40 per cent.

TCA 1997, s 100(3) applies where the terms of the sale of an estate or interest in land provide for the granting of a lease out of that interest. It provides that the amount taxable under Sch D Case IV as income of the vendor is to be calculated under the rules of TCA 1997, s 100(1) just illustrated, but on the following assumptions:

(a) that the grant of the lease out of the interest in land sold is treated as if it were a reconveyance of that interest; and

(b) that the reconveyance price is equal to the sum of the premium (if any) payable for the granting of this lease and the value, at the date of the sale, of the right to receive a reconveyance of the reversion (ie of the superior interest to that lease) immediately after the lease begins to run.

TCA 1997, s 100(3) does not apply at all in any case where the lease is granted, and actually begins to run, within one month after the sale. This exception is provided to allow for a genuine sale and leaseback transaction which may be made without the vendor being charged to tax under Sch D Case IV, provided that the leaseback has been completed within the one-month deadline. The vendor may, however, incur a liability to capital gains tax if any chargeable gain arises from the sale, but that is another matter.

The sale of an interest in land subject to a right of reconveyance (or granting of the lease) may sometimes be made in the course of a trade of dealing in or developing land carried on by the vendor. If so, the proceeds of the sale included as trading receipts in the vendor's Sch D Case I computation is reduced by the amount on which he is taxable under Sch D Case IV due to the rules of either TCA 1997, s 100(1) or (3). In the event that the property dealer or developer subsequently claims under TCA 1997, s 100(2)(b) to have the Sch D Case IV taxable amount recomputed by reference to the date of the actual conveyance (or granting of the lease), his Sch D Case I computation for the relevant period of account must be revised retrospectively to reflect the lower deduction for the reduced amount taxable under Sch D Case IV (TCA 1997, s 100(4)).

Example 12.206.3

Take the facts of **Example 12.206.2**, but assume that Mr A Winner sold the 35-year leasehold interest in the warehouse in the course of a trade of property dealing. He makes up accounts annually to September and has carried on this trade for a number of years.

The amount credited in the Sch D Case I computation of the property dealing trading profits for the 12-month period of account ended 30 September 2015 is €60,640, computed:

	€
Actual sale proceeds per **Example 12.206.2**	100,000
Less:	
Amount taxable under Sch D Case IV (TCA 1997, s 100(3))	
per **Example 12.206.2** – original assessment	39,360
	60,640

Assume that Mr Winner makes his claim under TCA 1997, s 100(2) (b) to have the Sch D Case IV assessment for 2015 revised on 20 December 2019 (well within the four years after the actual reconveyance on 15 September 2019). He is entitled to the repayment of the €4,464 excess tax paid under Sch D Case IV for 2015, as per **Example 12.206.2**. The Case I profits for 2015 (based on accounts of the year to 30/9/2015) must be increased, and additional income tax becomes payable for that year when assessed in 2019, computed as follows:

Increase in Sch D Case I profits	€
Sch D Case IV taxable amount (as originally deducted)	39,360
Less: Sch D Case IV taxable amount as revised (now to be deducted)	28,200
Additional Sch D Case I profits	11,160

12.207 Successive taxable events (TCA 1997, ss 98–100)

Any one of the events giving rise to an amount chargeable to tax under TCA 1997, s 98 (premium on granting of lease, etc), TCA 1997, s 99 (assignment of lease granted at undervalue) or TCA 1997, s 100 (sale with right to reconveyance, etc) may be followed by a later event in relation to the same premises that is also within the provisions of TCA 1997, ss 98–100. If, in any such case, the later event occurs in relation to either (a) a lease granted out of the lease, estate or interest of or in the premises in respect of which the prior taxable event arose, or (b) a sale, assignment or other disposition of the said lease, estate or interest, then the rules of TCA 1997, s 103 come into operation as regards the later event.

Examples of such successive taxable events are:

(a) Mr A grants a 21-year lease to Mr B at a premium of €40,000 (amount taxable under TCA 1997, s 98, €24,000), and Mr B later grants a 10-year sublease to Mr C at a premium of €8,000 (also within TCA 1997, s 98);

(b) X Ltd grants a 15-year lease to Y Ltd at a premium of €10,000 (chargeable under TCA 1997, s 98, but with premium forgone of €30,000), and Y Ltd later sells this 15-year lease to Z Ltd for €20,000 (assignment within TCA 1997, s 99);

(c) Z Ltd subsequently resells the same 15-year lease to Dombey & Sons for €36,000 (assignment also within TCA 1997, s 99); and

(d) Mr PC sells his freehold interest in an office building for €200,000 with the right to a reconveyance in five years' time at a price of €150,000 (amount taxable under TCA 1997, s 100, €46,000) and following its reconveyance to him he grants a 21-year lease of the ground floor to Mr GS at a premium of €33,000 (within TCA 1997, s 98).

TCA 1997, s 103 applies to reduce the amount that would otherwise be chargeable under TCA 1997, ss 98–100 in respect of the later event ('the later chargeable amount') but does not have any effect on the amount chargeable in respect of the prior event ('the prior chargeable amount'). It provides that the amount chargeable under TCA 1997, ss 98–100 (whichever is the case) in respect of the later event is determined as follows:

	€
Later chargeable amount	A
Less:	
prior chargeable × $\frac{\text{relevant period L}}{\text{relevant period P}}$	B
Taxable amount (TCA 1997, ss 98–100)	C

where

relevant period L = the relevant period for the later chargeable amount; and

relevant period P = the relevant period for the prior chargeable amount (TCA 1997, s 103).

TCA 1997, s 103 defines 'relevant period' separately in relation to any chargeable amount depending on whether that amount arises under TCA 1997, ss 98–100, as follows:

(a) amount chargeable under TCA 1997, s 98: the full duration of the lease (see **12.210**);

(b) amount chargeable under TCA 1997, s 99: the part of the duration of the lease that remains at the date of the assignment that gave rise to the particular Sch D Case IV charge on the assignor; and

(c) amount chargeable under TCA 1997, s 100: the period beginning on the date of the sale giving rise to the Sch D Case IV tax charge and ending on the date fixed by the sale agreement as the date for the reconveyance or the grant of the lease (but if no such date is fixed, the relevant period ends on the earliest date at which the reconveyance or grant could be made).

Example 12.207.1

Take the facts of **Example 12.201.1** where Mr LD granted a 35 year nine months lease on 1 January 2015 to Mr TN for a premium of €200,000. Assume that, on 1 May 2015, Mr TN grants a 10-year sublease to Mr SL for an annual rent plus a premium of €80,000. The 'additional rent' which TCA 1997, s 98 requires to be included in the computation of Mr TN's Sch D Case V income arising in the year to 31 December 2015 (the later chargeable amount) is determined as follows:

		€
Later chargeable amount (on 1/5/2015 sublease):		
€80,000 x (51–10)/50 =		65,600
Prior chargeable amount (on 1/1/2015 lease):		
€200,000 x (51–35)/50 =		64,000
Relevant period L: duration of sublease	10	
Relevant period P: duration of lease	35.75	
Additional rent: later chargeable amount		65,600
Less:		
Prior chargeable amount €64,000 x 10/35.75		17,902
Additional rent taxable		47,698

Example 12.207.2

On 1 July 2015, Siegfried granted a 15-year lease of a commercial property to Tristan, for an annual rent of €2,000 (with no rent reviews) and a premium of €24,000. Siegfried is therefore charged under TCA 1997, s 98 on an additional rent (receivable 1/7/2015) of €17,280 (the prior chargeable amount), computed as follows:

€24,000 x (51–15)/50=	€17,280

On 1 September 2015, Tristan assigns the 15-year lease to Darrowby for a consideration of €73,000. If the lease had been granted in an arm's length transaction on 1 July 2015 it would have commanded a premium of €60,000. The lease is, therefore, one granted at an undervalue and, in consequence, TCA 1997, s 99 applies to tax Tristan on the assignment.

The amount chargeable on Tristan as Sch D Case IV income for 2015 is calculated:

	€
Consideration for assignment (1/9/2015)	73,000
Less: actual premium paid (1/7/2015)	(24,000)
Excess consideration	49,000
Amount forgone (1/7/2015): arm's length premium	60,000
Less: actual premium paid	24,000
Amount foregone	36,000
Taxable amount (TCA 1997, s 99):	
€36,000[1] x (51–15)/50 =	25,920
(Subject to TCA 1997, s 103)	

Since this taxable amount of €25,920 (the later chargeable amount) arises as the result of Tristan's disposition of the 15-year lease by reference to which the prior chargeable amount of €17,280 was taxable, TCA 1997, s 103 applies to reduce the amount chargeable under TCA 1997, s 99 in respect of the assignment, as follows:

	€
Relevant period L:	
1/9/2015 (date of assignment) to 30/6/2030 (end of lease)	
ie 14 years 10 months (14.83 years)	
Relevant period P:	
1/7/2015 to 30/6/2030	
ie 15 years (duration of lease)	
Taxable amount (1/9/2015):	
Later chargeable amount	25,920
Less:	
Prior chargeable amount €17,280 x 14.83/15	17,084
Sch D Case IV income[2]	8,836

Notes:

1. The TCA 1997, s 98 fraction used in computing the amount taxable under TCA 1997, s 99 (before the TCA 1997, s 103 reduction) is applied, in this case, to the amount forgone (€36,000) as it is less than the excess consideration (€49,000).
2. In this case, the charge to tax on Tristan under Sch D, Case IV may not be the end of the matter. Unless it can be shown that Tristan acquired the lease on 1 July 2015 as an investment, the dealing profit will be taxable under Sch D, Case I.
3. If it should be appropriate to tax Tristan under Sch D, Case I, the dealing profit would be computed:

	€
Consideration for assignment (1/9/2015)	73,000
Less: Sch D Case IV taxable amount	8,836
Net consideration	64,164
Less: cost of acquiring lease (premium paid 1/7/2015)	24,000
Sch D Case I profit	40,164

12.208 Deduction for premiums etc: Sch D Cases I and II

TCA 1997, s 102 entitles the person occupying premises under a lease in respect of which an amount was previously charged to tax (usually on another person) under any of the rules of TCA 1997, ss 98–99 to a deduction in computing his Sch D Case I or Case II trading income (or trading loss). Similarly, TCA 1997, s 102 also allows a Sch D Case I or Case II deduction to the person occupying premises as the holder for the time being of an interest in premises (eg freehold, leasehold, etc) which having previously been sold with the right to a reconveyance or to the grant of a lease, resulted in the vendor being charged to tax under TCA 1997, s 100. The full amount that was charged under TCA 1997, ss 98–100 is eligible for the Sch D Case I or Case II deduction, but it has to be spread over the 'relevant period' related to the particular chargeable event.

TCA 1997, s 102 gives a separate meaning to the 'relevant period' depending on whether the amount previously chargeable on the lessor, assignor or vendor arose under TCA 1997, ss 98–100. In each case, the relevant period is the same period as that defined in TCA 1997, s 103 already set out in **12.207**. For example, in the case of a taxable amount under TCA 1997, s 98 in respect of a premium obtained by a lessor on the granting of a lease, the relevant period is the full duration of the lease. Here, it is to be noted that the length of the TCA 1997, s 98 relevant period used in computing the TCA 1997, s 102 deduction for the periods of account affected remains the full term of the lease in all cases; the fact that a shorter period is applied as n in the TCA 1997, s 98 formula in computing the amount taxable under TCA 1997, s 98(3), (4) does not affect the calculation of the deduction for the Sch D Case I or II computation.

For a deduction to arise under TCA 1997, s 102 in any period of account, the taxpayer must occupy the premises in that period wholly or partly for the purpose of his trade or profession. Further, the interest in the premises held by him must be the same lease, estate or interest in respect of which the amount taxable under TCA 1997, ss 98–100 arose. He may, for example, be the original lessee who paid the premium in respect of which the lessor was charged to tax under TCA 1997, s 98. Alternatively, he may be any other subsequent lessee who acquired the lease from the original lessee, whether by purchase, succession on death or otherwise.

The TCA 1997, s 102 deduction in the Sch D Case I or Case II computation for any period of account (or part of a period) falling within the 'relevant period' is calculated as a proportion of the amount that was taxable on the lessor, assignor or vendor (the 'taxable amount'). The deduction given in each period of account is an amount equal to the proportion of the taxable amount that is represented by the ratio of the length of that period of account to the total length of the relevant period. No deduction is given neither for any period of account falling wholly outside the relevant period nor for any period in which the current holder of the relevant lease or interest does not occupy the premises for his trade or profession.

When the amount deductible under TCA 1997, s 102 has been determined for any period of account, the person carrying on the trade or profession is treated as if he had paid an amount of rent (in addition to any actual rent paid) in respect of the premises in question. Consequently, if only part of the relevant premises is used for the trade or profession in that period, so that only a proportion of any actual rent would be a deductible expense, then only a corresponding proportion of the full TCA 1997, s 102 deduction is given in the Sch D Case I or II computation. The same rules apply whether the trade or profession is carried on by a person chargeable to income tax or by a company chargeable to corporation tax.

No Sch D Case I or Case II deduction is given for any period of account in which the premises concerned are not used at least partly for a trade or profession. However, once a tax charge has been made under TCA 1997, ss 98–100, the entitlement to the deduction under TCA 1997, s 102 remains throughout the relevant period so that any person, not necessarily the first user after the taxable event, occupying the premises for a trade or profession at any time during the relevant period is entitled to the appropriate deduction for any period of account within the relevant period.

Example 12.208.1

Take the facts of **Examples 12.201.1** and **12.202.2** respectively where Mr LD granted a 35 year, 9 month lease on 1 January 2015 for an annual rent of €36,000 (for the first seven years) and under which the following amounts were taxable on the lessor:

	Premium/ deemed premium	*Taxable amount (TCA 1997, s 98)*
Premium on granting lease:	€	€
TCA 1997, s 98	200,000	64,000

Deemed premium: TCA 1997, s 98 (sum for reduced rent for first 5 years)	40,000	36,800
Additional rent receivable (1/1/2015)		100,800

Assume that the lessee, Mr TN, spends a few months fitting out the leased premises before commencing to trade in them on 1 March 2015. He makes up his first accounts for the 10-month period ended 31 December 2015 and prepares accounts annually thereafter. However, he maintains a flat in the top floor of the building and it is agreed with the inspector that one fifth of the rent payable is attributable to this non-trading use of the premises.

Mr TN is entitled to the following deductions (apart from other allowable expenses) in his Sch D Case I computations for his first two periods of account:

	10 months to 31/12/2015	*Year to 31/12/2016*
Reduced rent payable:	€	€
€30,000 x 10/12	25,000	
Reduced year's rent		30,000
TCA 1997, s 102 deductions[1]		
TCA 1997, s 98:		
Taxable amounts (total) €100,800		
Relevant period (TCA 1997, s 98) 35.75 years		
Deduct (in addition to rent)		
10 months to 31/12/2015 (0.83 years)		
€100,800 x 0.83/35.75	2,340	
Year to 31/12/2016		
€100,800 x 1/35.75		2,820
Deduction (if no private use)	27,340	32,820
Restrict for private use:		
ie reduce by 1/5th	(5,468)	(6,564)
Final deduction	21,872	26,256

Notes:

1. Any lessee occupying the premises under the 35 year, 9 month lease for a trade or profession continues to be entitled to an TCA 1997, s 102 deduction at the rate of €2,820 for each 12-month period of account throughout the duration of the lease (but subject to any restriction in respect of private use, etc).

The fact that the lessor, assignor or vendor may occasionally be a person on whom the amount otherwise taxable under TCA 1997, ss 98–100 is not in fact charged to tax, due to an exemption, does not affect the entitlement of the person occupying the premises for a trade or profession to the TCA 1997, s 102 deduction. This might be relevant, for example, if the lessor who granted a lease at a premium was a charity (see **Division 18.2**), the trustees of an exempt approved pension scheme (see **Division 16**) or a life assurance company exempted from corporation tax on the investment income of its approved pension fund business. Further, the Sch D Case I or II deduction is not affected by a reduction in the amount taxable under TCA 1997, ss 98–100 by reason of TCA 1997, s 103. The effect of such a reduction is illustrated in the context of the corresponding TCA 1997, s 103 deduction against Sch D Case V income (see **12.209**).

A person entitled to a Sch D Case I or II deduction under TCA 1997, s 102 may not necessarily be aware of this or of the amount of his entitlement. Further, if the inspector should assess the lessor, assignor or vendor under TCA 1997, ss 98–100 on an amount lower than that which could be charged, he may be depriving the lessee, assignee or purchaser (or his successor) of part of subsequent TCA 1997, s 102 deductions.

TCA 1997, s 947(1) requires the inspector of taxes intending to make a charge on a lessor, assignor or vendor under TCA 1997, ss 98–100 to give notice in writing to the lessee, assignee or purchaser of the amount which the inspector determines to be chargeable under the relevant section. The lessee, assignee or purchaser, whose deduction may be affected by the inspector's determination, has then the right to object to the inspector's determination by giving notice in writing within 21 days after the date of the inspector's notice to him. This gives the lessee, etc (whose TCA 1997, s 102 deduction depends on the amount charged on the lessor, etc) access to the normal appeal procedure in determining the matter. F(TA)A 2015, s 35, which was subject to Ministerial Order (SI 110/2016 appointed 21 March 2016 as the day on which the Finance (Tax Appeals) Act 2015, came into operation), inserts a new TCA 1997, s 100A which deals with appeals made under TCA 1997, ss 98 to 100. It has similar provisions as those contained in TCA 1997, s 947. F(TA)A 2015 brings about a new Pt 40A regarding appeals taken after the commencement of that Act (SI 110/2016 appointed 21 March 2016 as the day on which the Finance (Tax Appeals) Act 2015, came into operation); the explanatory note to its insertion refers to TCA 1997, s 100A as a 'relocated and updated version of section 947'.

If the lessee, assignee or purchaser does not object to the proposed determination within this time limit, he has to accept the amount finally charged on the person liable as being the amount on which his TCA 1997, s 102 deductions are calculated. However, any person to whom no notice is sent under this rule has the right to appeal against the inspector's determination in so far as the amount chargeable affects his liability to tax. All such persons affected may take part in the proceedings before the Appeal Commissioners and in any other appeal arising out of those proceedings. All persons to whom notices were sent are bound by the determination made in the proceedings or on appeal, and their successors in title are also bound by it.

12.209 Deduction for premiums etc: Sch D Case V

TCA 1997, s 103 gives a corresponding deduction in computing Sch D Case V income to a person deriving rental income from premises in which he is the holder for the time being of the lease, estate or interest in respect of which an amount was chargeable to tax under TCA 1997, ss 98–100. The deduction is given under TCA 1997, s 97 in computing the surplus (or deficiency) in respect of the rent from the premises in question as if the person claiming the deduction paid a further amount of rent (in addition to any actual rent payable by him). This deduction is only available during any part of the 'relevant period' in which he is entitled to the particular lease, estate or interest that gave rise to the amount taxable on the lessor, assignor or vendor.

The 'relevant period' is, as explained in **12.207**, defined separately by TCA 1997, s 103 depending on whether the amount taxable arose under TCA 1997, s 98, 99 or 100. The taxable amount is, so far as the person claiming the deduction is concerned, treated as rent accruing on a day to day basis over the entire relevant period for the amount in question. For example, if Mr G sold his 21-year leasehold interest in an office building to Mr H for €100,000 with a right to a reconveyance for €70,000 in three years' time,

TCA 1997, s 100 requires Mr G to be assessed on an amount of €28,800 (€30,000 – (€30,000 x (3 – 1) x 2%) – see **12.206**).

If Mr H derives rental income from leasing the premises to the tenant (Mrs K) for the whole of these three years (the TCA 1997, s 100 relevant period), Mr H is entitled to a deduction under TCA 1997, s 103 of €28,800 spread over the three years (ie €9,600 per annum).

The position is more complicated if, due to two events each giving rise to amounts chargeable under TCA 1997, ss 98–100, the amount chargeable on the second event (the later chargeable amount) has been reduced under TCA 1997, s 103 by the appropriate fraction of the amount (the prior chargeable amount) chargeable in respect of the earlier event (see **12.207**). In such a case, the amount of the TCA 1997, s 103 deduction in the lessor's Sch D Case V computation following the second event is determined in one of two ways, depending on the circumstances, as follows:

(a) if the later chargeable amount (ie before applying TCA 1997, s 103) exceeds the appropriate fraction of the prior chargeable amount, the TCA 1997, s 103 deduction is given for the prior chargeable amount only (spread over the relevant period), and no deduction at all is given in respect of the later chargeable amount; or

(b) if the appropriate fraction of the prior chargeable amount exceeds the later chargeable amount (before TCA 1997, s 103), two separate TCA 1997, s 103 deductions are given, as follows:

   (i) the later chargeable amount (before the TCA 1997, s 103 reduction) is deductible in full (spread over its relevant period); and

   (ii) a reduced prior chargeable amount (spread over its relevant period) is deductible, computed as:

$$PCA \times \frac{F - L}{F}$$

where

PCA = the prior chargeable amount;

F = the appropriate fraction of the PCA; and

L = the later chargeable amount.

In effect, it appears that the result of these rules is to give a TCA 1997, s 103 deduction that cannot in any circumstances exceed the prior chargeable amount, but which will (in total) be less than the prior chargeable amount if the relevant period for the later event is shorter than that for the prior one.

Example 12.209.1

Take the facts of **Example 12.207.2** where the events there may be summarised as follows:

On 1 July 2015:

(a) Siegfried granted a 15-year lease to Tristan for a premium of €24,000 (but with a premium foregone of €36,000);

(b) Siegfried was charged under TCA 1997, s 98 on an amount of €17,280 (the prior chargeable amount).

On 1 September 2015:

(c) Tristan assigned this undervalue lease to Darrowby for a consideration of €73,000 and was assessed under TCA 1997, s 99 on an amount of €25,920 (the later chargeable amount), but which was reduced by TCA 1997, s 103 to a final taxable amount (Sch D Case IV) of €8,836.

Assume that Tristan had sublet the premises leased under the main lease for a full market rental of €10,000 per annum with effect from 1 July 2015 (the date the main lease was granted). Darrowby, which had purchased the main lease (now subject to the sublease) from Tristan on 1 September 2015, then became the lessor entitled to the €10,000 per annum rent.

TCA 1997, s 103 entitles Tristan to an 'additional rent' deduction by reference to the prior chargeable amount (€17,280) in computing its Sch D Case V surplus or deficiency from the premises in each of the tax years spanning its period of ownership of the 15-year lease (ie the period 1/7/2015 to 01/09/2015).

The TCA 1997, s 103 deduction for the tax year 2015 for Tristan is computed as follows:

	€
Prior chargeable amount €17,280	
Relevant period P (TCA 1997, s 98)	
1/07/2015 to 30/06/2030 (end of lease) ie 15 years	
2 months to 31/8/2015 (all in relevant period)	
ie 0.17 years	
TCA 1997, s 103 deduction for 2015:	
€17,280 x 0.17/15	*196*

TCA 1997, s 103 entitles Darrowby to an 'additional rent' deduction with effect from 1 September 2015 onwards (ie from the date of its purchase of the 15-year lease), but only for so long as it remains the holder and continues to derive Sch D Case V income from it.

Darrowby's TCA 1997, s 103 deduction for the tax year 2015 is computed as follows:

	€
Prior chargeable amount (PCA) (TCA 1997, s 98)	17,280
Later chargeable amount (TCA 1997, s 99)	25,920
Relevant period P (TCA 1997, s 98)	
1/7/2015 to 30/6/2030 (end of lease)	
ie 15 years	
Relevant period L (TCA 1997, s 99)	
1/9/2015 to 30/6/2030	
ie 14.83 years	
Appropriate fraction of PCA	
€17,280 x 14.83/15	17,084

Since the later chargeable amount (€25,920) exceeds the appropriate fraction of the prior chargeable amount (€17,084), TCA 1997, s 103 denies Darrowby any deduction in respect of the later chargeable amount. However, Darrowby remains entitled to the normal TCA 1997, s 103 deduction in respect of the prior chargeable amount, computed as follows:

	€
Prior chargeable amount	17,280
Relevant period (P) – 15 years	
4 months to 31 December 2015, ie 0.333 years	
TCA 1997, s 103 deduction for 2015:	
€17,280 x 0.333/15	384

Example 12.209.2

Take the facts of **Example 12.207.2** and **Example 12.209.1**, but assume that the Sch D Case IV assessment (TCA 1997, s 99) on Tristan in respect of the assignment to Darrowby of the undervalue lease on 1 September 2015 was calculated on the following figures:

	€
Consideration for assignment (1/09/2015)	73,000
Less: actual premium (1/7/2015)	24,000
Excess consideration	49,000
Amount forgone (1/7/2015) arm's length premium (assumed now to be)	40,000
Less: actual premium paid	24,000
Amount forgone	16,000
Taxable amount (TCA 1997, s 99)	
€16,000 x (51–15)/50 =	11,520
€11,520 is the later chargeable amount	
Less:	
TCA 1997, s 103 reduction	
€17,280 x 14.83/15	(17,084)
Final Sch D Case IV amount – TCA 1997, s 99	Nil

Siegfried has been charged under TCA 1997, s 98 in respect of the original lease premium (€24,000) on an amount of €17,280 (the prior chargeable amount). Tristan would have been charged on the above €11,520 (the later chargeable amount) but for the effect of TCA 1997, s 103 which has reduced the TCA 1997, s 99 charge to nil.

T's TCA 1997, s 103 deductions between 1/7/2015 and 31/8/2015 are the same as those shown in **Example 12.209.1**.

Since the appropriate fraction (€17,084) of the prior chargeable amount exceeds the later chargeable amount (€11,520), Darrowby's TCA 1997, s 103 deduction – as the current holder of the 15-year lease – is based on two separate amounts, namely:

	€
Later chargeable amount	11,520
(To be spread over the TCA 1997, s 99	
relevant period of 14.83 years from 1/9/2015)	
Prior chargeable amount (as reduced)	
€17,280 x (€17,084 – €11,520) / €17,084 =	5,628
(To be spread over the TCA 1997, s 98 relevant period of 15 years from 1/7/2015)	

Darrowby's first TCA 1997, s 103 deduction, for the tax year 2015 is calculated as follows:

	€
On later chargeable amount €11,520 x 0.333/14.83	259
On prior chargeable amount €5,628 x 0.333/15	125
	384

12.210 Duration of lease

TCA 1997, s 96(2) contains rules for determining the length of the term of a lease for the purpose of applying the charging rules of TCA 1997, ss 98–100 and for computing the deductions under Sch D Cases I, II and V given by TCA 1997, ss 102–103. In the normal case, the duration of a lease is the term specified in the lease or tenancy agreement for which it is to last, commencing from the date on which it is stated to be effective. However, TCA 1997, s 96(2) deals with special factors which may apply to require the duration of the lease to be treated as either longer or shorter than it purports to be.

The three main rules, intended mainly as anti-avoidance measures, are:

(a) if any of the terms of the lease or any other circumstances render it unlikely that the lease will continue beyond a date earlier than the stated end of the lease term, and if the premium on granting the lease was not substantially greater than it would have been if the lease were due to expire on that earlier date, the duration of the lease has to be limited to a term ending on the earlier date;

(b) if the terms of the lease include a provision under which the lessee is entitled, by giving notice, to obtain an extension of the lease beyond its stated term or beyond any other given date, the duration of the lease may be determined by taking account of any circumstances making it likely that the lease will be so extended; and

(c) if the lessee, or a person connected with him, is or may become entitled to a further lease of the same premises, or of premises that include the whole or part of the same premises, the term of the lease may be treated as not expiring before the end of the term of the further lease.

In applying the foregoing rules, all the facts known or ascertainable at the time the lease is granted are to be taken into account. It is to be assumed that all the parties concerned are acting as they would in an arm's length relationship. If, by the lease or other arrangements in connection with the granting of it, payments are made or other benefits conferred that would not have been expected in an arm's length agreement, these factors may be taken into account under any of the above rules in determining the duration of the lease.

12.3 Profits from Dealing in or Developing Land

12.301 Introduction

One of the more complicated areas of tax legislation in the State over the years has been that related to the taxation of income derived from dealing in or developing land. A person carrying on a trade of dealing in or developing land is chargeable to income tax under Sch D Case I on the profits or gains of his trade. This is, of course, no different to the position with any trade. However, the law contains a number of additional provisions which have been found necessary to define the types of activity which may be taxed under Sch D Case I as part of a trade or business of dealing in or developing land and to deal with the computation of the amount of the taxable profits or gains.

TCA 1997, ss 639–646 contain the additional rules which are superimposed upon the normal rules of Sch D Case I where transactions in land dealing or development are involved. TCA 1997, ss 639–646 may be subdivided into separate parts. TCA 1997, s 639 gives a number of important definitions and other rules for interpreting the provisions of these parts.

TCA 1997, s 640 brings within Sch D Case I certain activities of a business of dealing in or developing land which would not otherwise be treated as a trade taxable under that Case. TCA 1997, ss 641–642 superimpose certain special rules on the normal Sch D Case I computational rules; these special rules are applied, where relevant, in computing the Sch D Case I profits (or losses) of any trade or business of dealing in or developing land. TCA 1997, s 646 provides for the payment by instalments of the tax on the profits from certain types of sale and leaseback transactions. These various provisions are dealt with in **12.305–12.309**.

TCA 1997, s 643 seeks to tax as income under Sch D Case IV certain gains of a capital nature (not otherwise taxable as income) realised from the disposal of land and/or certain other property deriving its value from land. TCA 1997, s 644 and s 645 are supplementary to s 643. TCA 1997, ss 643–645 are covered in **12.310–12.315**.

TCA 1997, s 644A was historically a relieving provision which applied a reduced 20 per cent rate of income tax to profits from dealing in or developing residential development land. TCA 1997, s 644B was a similar provision which applied to companies. TCA 1997, s 644A ceased to apply for individuals with effect from the 2009 year of assessment and subsequent years. Similarly TCA 1997, s 644B no longer applies to companies in respect of accounting periods ending after 31 December 2008.

The rules in TCA 1997, ss 639–646 (with the exceptions of s 644A and s 644B) are primarily directed against tax avoidance schemes devised over the years and have been modified on several occasions since their original introduction to deal with new schemes seeking to get round the legislation as it developed. As they now stand, they are derived from FA 1981, s 28 and s 29 which substantially amended the previous legislation. The current rules became effective as regards profits, gains or losses in any period that ended after 5 April 1981.

Before discussing the rules of TCA 1997, ss 639–646 generally, it will be useful to give a brief outline of the main landmarks in the development of the legislation over the years. Apart from helping to explain some of the complications that may arise in transactions involving interests in land, the notes on the historical background which follow may show at least some of the reasons why it was felt necessary to bring in TCA 1997, ss 639–646.

12.302 Historical background

Birch v Delaney I ITR 515

A builder acquired by lease certain plots of ground, each for a term of 500 years and subject to a ground rent. On these plots he built houses which he disposed of by way of subdemise, ie sublease, for periods varying from 450 to 495 years in consideration of fines, ie lump sums and ground rents. The inspector of taxes assessed him under Sch D for the four years to 1932–33 on the basis of including, as trading receipts, the fines received plus the capitalised value of the excess of the ground rents receivable under the subdemises over the original ground rents.

The High Court upheld the Revenue argument, O'Byrne J commenting as follows:

> the respondent is a speculative builder and … he acquired these parcels of land for the purposes of his business as such … namely for the purposes of building houses and disposing of same in such a manner as to make a profit by such disposition and it seems to me to be quite immaterial for the purposes of this case whether the Respondent disposed of the houses in such a way as to exhaust his interest in the land on which they were built or to retain an interest by way of reversion or otherwise.

This conclusion was consistent with the approach of the UK Courts in *Emery & Sons v IRC* 20 TC 213 and subsequently in *Utting v Hughes* 23 TC 174.

However, the Supreme Court took an opposing view. Fitzgibbon J said:

> The fundamental fallacy in the judgments of the High Court is the assumption that if an adventure can be described as a trade its profits must be charged by and assessable under Sch D, and cannot be charged by or assessable in accordance with Sch A, although they in fact arise out of the ownership or occupation of lands.

Thus, the law in Ireland following the decision in *Birch v Delaney* was that the disposal of an interest in land by a land developer (or a land dealer) which was less than the full interest in the land held by him could not be taken into account for the purposes of computing his income under Sch D Case I. Any receipts attributable to the disposal were taxable only (if at all) under the former Sch A in respect of the ownership of land (by reference to a low, notional annual value).

FA 1935, s 6

This section, introduced to counteract the *Birch v Delaney* decision, provided for the taxation under Sch D Case I of the profits or gains from any building operation or from the sale or demise of any lands acquired by the trader with the intention either of selling, demising or developing them by any building operation. This section also brought in a rule that, in the event of a disposal by way of demise or lease, the capitalised value of the rent reserved on the demise should be included as a trading receipt in addition to any fine, premium or other amount that was actually included in the consideration for the demise.

Swaine v VE II ITR 472

The taxpayer purchased certain lands in 1937. At the date of purchase he was a builder, but shortly after that date he retired from building and used the lands for farming. It was found as a fact that at the time of purchase he had formed the intention of retiring from business and that he did not purchase the lands with the intention of selling or demising them nor with the intention of developing them by the erection or reconstruction of buildings. In 1948, having decided to develop the lands and to resume building he built a number of houses and shops on the lands and sold them by way of subdemise for a long term in consideration of fines and ground rents.

The Supreme Court held that, because he had not acquired the lands with the intention of selling, demising or developing them, FA 1935, s 6 could not be applied to tax him either on the fines or the capitalised value of the ground rents. Walsh J concluded that the words of FA 1935, s 6 were not in fact wide enough to cover the case where the land was not acquired as a trade asset, ie acquired otherwise than as trading stock of the business.

The decision in *Swaine v VE* was clearly justifiable in the light of the specific wording of FA 1935, s 6. However, it does not seem correct as a matter of general law that land can only form the stock in trade of a dealer or developer where it is originally acquired as such.

In *Taylor v Good* 49 TC 277 Russell LJ observed:

> If of course you find a trade in the purchase and sale of land, it may not be difficult to find that properties originally owned (for example) by inheritance, or bought for investment only, have been brought into the stock in trade of that trade … But where … there is no question at all of absorption into a trade of dealing in land or lands previously acquired with no thought of dealing, in my judgement there is no ground at all for holding that activities … designed only to enhance the value of the land in the market, are to be taken as pointing to, still less establishing, an adventure in the nature of trade.

The principle of 'appropriation to stock' (sometimes known as 'supervening trading') was in fact applied in *O'hArgain v B Ltd* III ITR 9 where a company (B Ltd) had engaged in land development activities but also owned farmland which had been let out on conacre for some time; it was held on the facts by the Appeal Commissioners that the farmland had been acquired solely for farming purposes. The farmland was subsequently rezoned for development. In response to an enquiry by the Revenue as to whether the company had ceased its development activities, the company's accountant indicated that all available sites had been sold but that it was possible that the farmland might also be developed, albeit this was not in current contemplation. A and B were shareholder/directors of B Ltd. The court held that, because A was an architect (and thus familiar with the development possibilities), an inference arose that the company had definitely formed the intention to exploit the land for development and thus appropriate it to its (existing) trade of development once it had been rezoned.

If B Ltd had simply gone on to develop and sell the land, it would have followed from the court's analysis that the sale should have been regarded as a trading transaction. However, what happened in fact was that C and D arranged for B Ltd to be put into liquidation. Following this, B Ltd's land was sold to R Ltd, a company formed by C and D in order to sell and develop the land. The rationale behind this series of arrangements was that since B Ltd would never have engaged in developing its land, the profit on the sale of the land to R Ltd would be of a non-trading nature (and, under the law as it stood then, entirely tax-free). The court held however that the decision to liquidate B Ltd and to form R Ltd was 'merely the manner in which … [B Ltd] … chose to carry out the development'.

The court's conclusion in this respect seems to have been based on an incorrect application of the (it is submitted, correct) principle of supervening trading, since it is impossible to see how B Ltd could embark on a trade of developing land by providing an opportunity for a *different* company to develop its land and to reap all of the consequent profits. It should be noted that where land is appropriated to trading stock TCA 1997, s 641(2)(d) now expressly provides that the cost of the land for Sch D Case I purposes is the market value of the land at the date of appropriation.

TCA 1997, ss 639–646

These provisions were the subject of considerable amendments when they were first introduced but have appeared in their current form since the enactment of FA 1981. TCA 1997, s 640 is designed to overcome the gaps in the previous law exposed by the decisions in *Birch v Delaney* and *Swaine v VE*. The scope of TCA 1997, s 640 is dealt with in **12.305**.

TCA 1997, s 641 modifies the normal rules of Sch D Case I for calculating the taxable profits of any trade of dealing in or developing land (or of an activity deemed by TCA 1997, s 640 to be such a trade). TCA 1997, s 643 covers not only gains realised directly or indirectly through the sale of shares in land dealing, etc companies, but also gains realised through selling an interest in a trust or in a partnership. TCA 1997, ss 644, 645 are used to bring in certain additional administrative and information rules. TCA 1997, s 644A, 644B relate to profits from dealing in or developing residential development land by individuals or other persons and companies respectively. These sections no longer apply following FA 2009. All other provisions of TCA 1997, ss 639–646 are applicable both to individuals and other persons liable to income tax and to companies chargeable to corporation tax.

12.303 Definitions

TCA 1997, s 639 defines various terms used in these provisions and contains other provisions to be used in interpreting its rules. It provides that TCA 1997, Pt 22, Ch 1 is to apply where there is a business of dealing in or developing land notwithstanding any provisions to the contrary in TCA 1997, Pt 4, Ch 8 dealing with the taxation of rents and certain other payments (TCA 1997, s 639(3)).

Land

The Interpretation Act 2005 provides that the word 'land' includes tenements, hereditaments, houses and buildings, land covered by water and any estate, right or interest in or over land.

Development

In relation to any land the term 'development' means: (a) the construction, demolition, extension, alteration or reconstruction of any building on the land or (b) the carrying out of any engineering or other operation in, on, over or under the land to adapt it for materially altered use. The words 'developing' and 'developed' are to be construed in a corresponding manner. Apart from the obvious case where a house, factory or other building is constructed, a development of land takes place if, for example, farming land is cleared and drains suitable for housing are put down. Should the land be sold after such an operation has been wholly or partly completed, the sale is one of land that has been developed, even if someone else undertakes all the main construction work at a later time.

Disposal of an interest in land

Clearly there is such a disposal where a person sells, gifts or otherwise transfers the entire interest that he holds in the land. A disposal of an interest in land is also treated as taking place where the owner of the interest creates any other interest in the same land, except in the case where a lease of the land is granted on terms which do not require the payment of any fine, premium or similar lump sum. The conveyance or transfer of an interest in land by way of security, for example, where the land is mortgaged as security for a loan, is not to be regarded as a disposal.

An option or other right to acquire or dispose of any interest in land is deemed to be an interest in the land. In fact, an option is such an interest in any event (*George Wimpey & Co v IRC* [1974] STC 300). Consequently, if the owner of (say) a freehold interest grants another person an option either to buy the freehold or to take a lease of the land, this is treated as a disposal of an interest in the land by the person granting the option. On general principles, the mere grant of a licence to occupy land would not amount to an interest in land.

Example 12.303.1

Mr BA, who owns the freehold interest in certain lands that have recently been developed grants a 35-year lease to Mr AS, in consideration of a premium of €500,000 and an annual rent of €25,000. This is a disposal of an interest in the land within the meaning of the phrase for the purposes of TCA 1997, ss 639–646.

Mr OR, in a similar position to that of Mr BA, grants a 35-year lease to Mr TEM in consideration only of an annual rent of €45,000. Since the terms of this transaction do not require the payment of any fine, premium or similar sum, the grant of this lease is not a disposal of an interest in land within TCA 1997, ss 639–646.

Trading stock

This term is given the same meaning as that in TCA 1997, s 89 (see **5.4**). In the context of a trade of dealing in or developing land, or of a business treated by TCA 1997, ss 639–646 as such a trade, trading stock may therefore be taken as including any land and/or interest in land (including any buildings on the land) sold, or intended to be sold, in the ordinary course of the trade or business, whether in its existing state or on the completion or part completion of their development. Trading stock also includes building, etc materials used or intended to be used in the development of the land and/or buildings in the course of the trade or business.

Market value

This means, in relation to any property, the price which that property might reasonably be expected to fetch if sold in the open market.

This is similar to the definition contained in TCA 1997, s 548. However, it may be noted that there is no provision equivalent to TCA 1997, s 548, which states that the market value of assets must not be reduced on the assumption that all of the assets will be placed on the market simultaneously. There is substantial UK case law on the concept of open market value in the context of estate duty, inheritance and capital gains tax. A detailed discussion of the case law would be out of place in the current text. However, the following salient points are worthy of note:

(a) Where there is a restriction on the disposal of an asset (eg a covenant against the assignment of an interest in land) the open market value must nevertheless be ascertained on the hypothesis that the asset can be freely disposed of but that the person buying the asset on this hypothesis would then be subject to the same restriction. Accordingly the restriction must be taken into account when valuing the asset, (*IRC v Crossman* [1936] 1 All ER 762 and see also *Alexander v IRC* [1991] STC 112 where the fact that a hypothetical sale would have resulted in the lifting of the restriction was disregarded). Where an asset is subject to an option to acquire it for an amount below market value, it follows that this will depress the 'open market value'. It must be borne in mind, however, that the grant of an option will itself be a disposal for the purposes of TCA 1997, s 639 (see above).

(b) It is necessary to take into account the existence of all potential purchasers including 'special purchasers', ie persons for whom the property concerned has an enhanced value. In *IRC v Clay; IRC v Buchan* [1914] 3 KB 466 it was observed:

> To say that a small farm in the middle of a wealthy landowner's estate is to be valued without reference to the fact that he will probably be willing to pay a large price, but solely with reference to its ordinary agricultural value, seems to me absurd. If the landowner does not at the moment buy this farm, land-brokers or speculators will give more than its purely agricultural value with a view to reselling it at a profit to the landowner.

This does not imply that the special purchaser would be willing to pay the full difference between the value to him and the value to the rest of the market place.

In *IRC v Gray* [1994] STC 360, Hoffman LJ observed:

> It cannot be too strongly emphasised that although the sale is hypothetical, there is nothing hypothetical about the open market in which it is supposed to have taken place. The concept of the open market involves assuming that the whole world was free to bid, and then forming a view about what in those circumstances would in real life have been the best price reasonably obtainable. The practical nature of this exercise will usually mean that although in principle no one is excluded from consideration, most of the world will usually play no part in the calculation. The inquiry will often focus on what a relatively small number of people would be likely to have paid. It may have to arrive at a figure within a range of prices which the evidence shows that various people would have been likely to pay, reflecting, for example, the fact that one person had a particular reason for paying a higher price

> than others, but taking into account, if appropriate, the possibility that through accident or whim he might not actually have bought. The valuation is thus a retrospective exercise in probabilities, wholly divorced from the real world but rarely committed to the proposition that a sale to a particular purchaser would definitely have happened.

(c) It should be assumed that the sale in the open market will be conducted as advantageously as possible. Thus it might involve for example, dividing land up into smaller parcels or conversely selling a particular parcel of land in conjunction with another parcel of land. However, a notional combining or dividing up of assets for the purposes of optimising the sale price is only permissible where this would not entail substantial expenses and/or work in order to achieve it (*Duke of Buccleuch v IRC* [1967] 1 AC 506).

Settlement

A settlement is defined in TCA 1997, s 10 in the same wide-ranging terms as used in the anti-avoidance provisions covering settlements, in favour of minors. Thus, it includes any 'disposition, trust, covenant, agreement or arrangement', and 'any transfer of money or other property or of any right to money or other property'. The scope of this definition is discussed in **15.402**.

The general definition of 'settlor' from TCA 1997, s 10 also applies, ie:

> Settlor ... in relation to a settlement, means any person by whom the settlement was made ... or entered into directly or indirectly, and, in particular (but without prejudice to the generality of the preceding words) includes any person who has provided or undertaken to provide funds directly or indirectly for the purpose of the settlement, or has made with any other person a reciprocal arrangement for that other person to make or enter into the settlement.

This definition closely resembles the equivalent definition in the UK settlement anti-avoidance provisions. It is therefore particularly likely that the UK decisions on the meaning of the term 'settlor' in cases such as *Mills v IRC* 49 TC 367 and *Crossland v Hawkins* 39 TC 493 will be relevant in the context of TCA 1997, Pt 22, Ch 1 (see the discussion of these cases in **15.402**).

Connected persons

The 'connected person' rules are discussed separately in **12.304**, as is the meaning of 'control' in TCA 1997, s 432 as it is applied in relation to a company which may be a connected person.

12.304 Connected persons' and 'control'

The definition of 'connected person' has been standardised for all income tax purposes by TCA 1997, s 10 (replacing similar but not identical provisions contained in predecessor to TCA 1997, Pt 22, Ch 1). The circumstances in which TCA 1997, s 10 requires one person to be treated as connected with another person are set out in the form of seven rules, referred to below as rules 1 to 7, as follows:

Rule 1: general

Any provision in rules 2 to 7 to the effect that one person is connected with another person is to be taken as meaning that they are connected with one another (TCA 1997, s 10(2)). For example, if A Ltd is connected with Mr B, it follows that Mr B is connected with A Ltd.

Rule 2: individuals

The following persons are connected with an individual:

(a) the individual's husband or wife or civil partner;
(b) any relative (see definition below) of the individual;
(c) any relative of the individual's husband or wife or civil partner;
(d) the husband or wife or civil partner of a relative of the individual (eg his brother's wife); and
(e) the husband or wife or civil partner of a relative of the individual's spouse or civil partner (eg his wife's sister's husband) (TCA 1997, s 10(3)).

A separated spouse but not a widow(er), or an ex-spouse, is a husband or wife for these purposes.

A 'relative' of an individual is defined as meaning brother, sister, ancestor (eg father, grandmother, etc) or lineal descendant (eg daughter, grandson, etc), but not nephews or nieces, uncles or aunts, although these latter categories are included for capital gains tax purposes. An adopted child is treated in the same way as a natural child and is deemed to have the same relationships with other persons as a natural child (TCA 1997, s 6); see also TCA 1997, s 8 which applies the Status of Children Act 1987 for tax purposes. An individual may also be connected with other persons under rules 3, 4, 5 and 7.

Rule 3: partners

A person is connected with any person with whom he is in partnership and with the husband, wife or relative of any individual with whom he is in partnership (TCA 1997, s 10(5)). If a company or a trustee of a settlement is a partner in a partnership, that company or trustee (in his capacity as trustee) is similarly connected with any other partner, or that partner's husband, wife or relative. There is an exception for acquisitions or disposals of partnership assets under *bona fide* commercial arrangements. In this situation, the partners will not be regarded as connected persons so that the actual price agreed between them will not be displaced by a notional market value.

Rule 4: trustees

A person in his capacity as trustee of a settlement (as defined above) is connected with any individual who is a settlor in relation to the settlement (there may be more than one settlor) and with any person (whether an individual, company or trustee of another settlement) connected with an individual who is a settlor (TCA 1997, s 10(4)). For example, if Sean Kelly is the trustee of a settlement of which John Smith is the settlor, Sean Kelly (as trustee, but not personally) is connected with John Smith, as well as with John Smith's wife, any relative of John Smith, any company controlled by John Smith and the trustee of any other settlement of which John Smith is a settlor.

In addition, a trustee will be connected to a body corporate which is deemed to be connected with that settlement in any accounting period or year of assessment as appropriate. A body corporate will be deemed to be connected with the settlement if at any time in the relevant period or year it is a close company (or would be a close company if resident in Ireland) and the participators include either:

(a) the trustees of the settlement; or
(b) a beneficiary of the settlement.

'Close company' is defined as for the purposes of TCA 1997, ss 430, 431. However, the term 'participator' is not defined for the purposes of TCA 1997, s 10 although presumably it was intended that the 'close company' definition in TCA 1997, s 433 would apply.

For example, if Susan Moore is the trustee of the Coakley Settlement and Alan Keegan is a beneficiary of that settlement, then the settlement is deemed to be connected with Reed Ltd (a close company) if Alan holds shares in that company. As a result, Susan (in her capacity as trustee) will be connected with Reed Ltd.

Rule 5: companies

A company is connected with another person (whether an individual, another company or a trustee of a settlement) if either that other person has control of the company, or that other person *and* persons connected with him together have control of the company (TCA 1997, s 10(7)).

For example, Mr B is connected with A Ltd (and A Ltd is connected with Mr B) if Mr B and his sister (a relative) have between them sufficient of the voting shares in A Ltd to give them control of the company within the TCA 1997, s 432 definition of 'control' (see below). In this event, A Ltd is also connected with Mr B's sister, since she and a person connected with her (her brother) together have control of A Ltd.

If A Ltd controls a second company, S Ltd, not only are A Ltd and S Ltd connected with each other, but Mr B and his sister are each also connected with S Ltd, as they together can control its affairs through their control of A Ltd.

Rule 6: companies under common control

Apart from being connected with each other under rule 5, two companies are also connected with each other in any of the following cases:

(a) if the same person has control of both companies;

(b) if one person has control of one company and either persons connected with him or that person *and* persons connected with him have control of the other company; or

(c) if a group of two or more persons has control of each company and if each group either consists of the same persons or would be regarded as consisting of the same persons if one or more members of either group were to be replaced by a person (or persons) with whom the replaced member is connected (TCA 1997, s 10(6)).

For example, if Mr D controls P Ltd and the trustees of a settlement of which Mr D is the settlor control Q Ltd, then P Ltd and Q Ltd are connected persons (under (b) above). If R Ltd is controlled by Mr A, Mr G and N Ltd and if S Ltd is controlled by Mr A, Mr G and Mr L, each person holding 33.3 per cent of the shares in each company, R Ltd and S Ltd are connected persons if Mr L controls N Ltd. In this latter event, the two groups of shareholders would consist of the same persons if N Ltd were replaced in the first group by Mr L (or if Mr L were replaced in the second group by N Ltd) – R Ltd and S Ltd will then be connected with each other under (c) above.

Rule 7: persons acting together to control/acquire holdings in a company

Any two or more persons acting together to secure or exercise control of a company or to acquire a holding in a company, are treated, in relation to that company, as connected with one another and with any person acting on the directions of any of them to secure or exercise control of the company or to acquire a holding in the company as appropriate (TCA 1997, s 10(8)).

The question as to whether 'secure' in this context means 'obtain' as opposed to 'safeguard' was left open in *Steele v EVC* [1996] STC 785. In the *Steele* case it was also held, on the facts, that two parties operating under a shareholders' agreement were acting together to exercise voting control over the company concerned.

For this rule to connect otherwise unconnected persons, more is required than the fact that their respective interests in the company add up to more than 50 per cent of the voting power or other form of control in the company; the persons in question must actually act together to control the company. If two or more persons satisfy this latter requirement, the rule does connect those persons, but not for any purpose other than in relation to the company concerned.

Example 12.304.1

Mr A and Mr B, two otherwise unconnected persons, hold respectively 30 per cent and 25 per cent of the only issued share capital of H Ltd. Mr C who is not connected with either Mr A or Mr B holds the remaining 45 per cent of the shares.

Mr A and Mr B do not like the approach of Mr C (the managing director) in running the affairs of H Ltd and they agree that they will regularly vote together to outvote Mr C and run the company in accordance with their own wishes. They in fact carry out this agreement. Rule 7 applies so that Mr A and Mr B are treated as connected persons in relation to the affairs of H Ltd.

In view of this connection, it follows that Mr A is also connected with H Ltd (ie by virtue of rule 5) as he and Mr B (now connected with him) together have control of the company; for the same reason, Mr B is also connected with H Ltd. Should Mr A and Mr B have similar holdings in another company, JK Ltd, but do not act together to control the affairs of that company, then their connection with each other in relation to H Ltd does not make them connected persons so far as JK Ltd is concerned.

'Control' of company

The definition of 'control' to be applied for the purposes of the 'connected person' rules is the same as the very broadly drawn definition laid down by TCA 1997, s 432 for the purposes of the close company legislation (note in this regard the decision in *R v IRC ex parte Newfield Developments* [2001] STC 901). TCA 1997, s 432(2) provides that a person has control of a company if the person exercises, or is able to exercise or is entitled to acquire control, whether direct or indirect, over the company's affairs. In particular a person has control of a company if the person possesses or is entitled to acquire:

(a) the greater part of the share capital or issued share capital of the company or of the voting power in the company;
(b) such part of the issued share capital as would entitle the person to receive the greater part of the amount distributed on the distribution of all of the income of the company to the participators (other than loan creditors); or
(c) such rights as would entitle the person to receive the greater part of the assets of the company which would be available for distribution to the participators on a winding up.

Example 12.304.2

The issued share capital of Space Ltd is divided into 10,000 A ordinary shares of €1 each and 10,000 B ordinary shares of €1 each. The A shares carry one vote per share, the B shares are non-voting. Apart from voting rights, the two classes of share capital rank *pari passu* in all respects. The shares are held as follows:

	Total	*A ord*	*B ord*
Mr ET	6,000	3,000	3,000
Mrs ET (his wife)	1,000	-	1,000
Trustees of settlement			
(Settlor – Mr ET's brother in law)	2,000	1,000	1,000
Meteor Investments Ltd			
(Owned 100% and thus controlled by Mr & Mrs ET)	1,500	-	1,500
	10,500	4,000	6,500
Other shareholders			
(not connected with Mr ET)	9,500	6,000	3,500
	20000	10,000	10,000

There are no loan creditors (as defined by TCA 1997, s 433). The beneficiaries in the settlement have no interests in either Space Ltd or Meteor Investments Ltd.

Mr ET and persons connected with him (the three other shareholders named above) have the right to more than 50 per cent of the income available to participators (as well as of the net assets in a winding up) due to their holding of 10,500 out of the 20,000 A and B ordinary shares. This conclusion is not altered by the fact that they do not have sufficient voting power to ensure that the affairs of the company be conducted in accordance with their wishes.

In view of this control, Mr ET is a person connected with Space Ltd (rule 5 above). Mrs ET is similarly treated as controlling Space Ltd and is therefore a person connected with that company. The trustees of the settlement are connected with both Mr and Mrs ET – Mrs ET is a relative (sister) of the settlor and Mr ET is also connected with him (husband of his relative – rule 2) so that rule 4 applies to connect each of them with the trustees.

Assuming that Mr ET's brother in law has no shares or other interest in Meteor Investments Ltd, he is not connected with that company. The trustees of the settlement cannot, therefore, be connected with Meteor Investments Ltd under rule 4. Assuming that the trustees do not hold any shares in Meteor Investments Ltd, they are not connected with it under rule 5 either.

The combined holdings in Space Ltd of Meteor Investments Ltd and of persons connected with that company (Mr ET and Mrs ET) amount to 4,000 A (voting) and 5,500 B (non-voting) shares. This is insufficient to give Meteor Investments Ltd and persons connected with it control of Space Ltd under any of the tests of control in TCA 1997, s 432. Space Ltd and Meteor Investments Ltd are not, therefore, connected persons.

The trustees of the settlement and persons connected with them (again Mr ET and Mrs ET) hold 4,000 A (voting) shares and 5,000 B shares in Space Ltd (out of the total 20,000 shares); the settlor does not hold any shares in Space Ltd. Consequently, the trustees do not control Space Ltd and are not, therefore, connected with it.

Several other comments may be useful in relation to the 'connected persons' rules. First, while rule 1 makes it clear that a statement that one person is connected with another person always means that the two persons named are each connected with each other, the fact that A is connected with B (and B with A) and that B is connected with C (and C with B) does not connect A with C (or C with A). It is quite possible that there may be another connection between A and C, but it is always necessary to test separately for any such relationship in such a case.

Secondly, an interesting point arises in determining whether a company is connected under rule 5 with a person (eg a spouse) connected with the controlling shareholder of the company. The company is not connected with any person connected with the controlling shareholder *unless* that other person has at least some shares, voting power or other means of control in the company. For example, if Mr P Smith and Mr R Smith (brothers) own 80 per cent of the total share capital, voting power, etc in Smith Ltd and all the other shares are held by unconnected persons, Mr P Smith's wife who holds no shares is not connected with Smith Ltd under rule 5. However should Mrs P Smith hold one share, she is then connected with Smith Ltd as she and persons connected with her have control of the company.

Finally, it may be noted that the Revenue Commissioners may in practice be prepared to treat persons who are technically connected with each other under the above rules as being non connected, where there are no direct personal or business links between them.

12.305 Extension of Sch D Case I to certain activities

TCA 1997, s 640 extends Sch D Case I to tax the profits of certain activities of a business of dealing in or developing land. TCA 1997, s 640 brings under Sch D Case I any such activities which:

(a) would not, in the absence of the section, be regarded as carried on in the course of a trade within Sch D; but

(b) would be so regarded if every disposal of an interest in land which is included among the activities of the business (*including a disposal of [the taxpayer's] ... full interest in the land*) were treated as fulfilling both of two conditions, namely;

  (i) it is a disposal of the full interest in the land which the person carrying on the business had acquired, and

  (ii) the interest in land had been acquired in the course of the business by the person making the disposal.

In the Supreme Court decision in the case of *Mara v Hummingbird* II ITR 667 which was decided before the provision in italics was inserted by FA 1981, Kenny J stated in the course of his judgment:

> The activity which is brought within the tax net by section 17 is one in which the taxpayer has disposed of a lesser interest than he had. But in this case, the sale was of the whole of the taxpayer's interest in the land and the section therefore does not apply to the sale of the ... premises.

Thus, TCA 1997, s 640 specifically requires the two conditions to be applied even where the disposal by the person carrying on the business of dealing in or developing land is a disposal of the full interest, as well as where it is the disposal of a lesser interest.

Following the logic of the *Hummingbird* decision, it is arguable that TCA 1997, s 640 does not cover the case where the taxpayer has actually acquired his interest in land in the course of a business of dealing or development. This is because sub-s (2) requires the taxpayer to be treated *as if* he had met condition (b)(ii); this seems to imply that, in the absence of this deeming provision, the taxpayer must not be able to meet this condition, ie the section only brings in an activity where the taxpayer did not acquire the land in the course of a business of dealing, etc. This point was not addressed by the amendments made by FA 1981.

Thus, if the facts in *Birch v Delaney* (see **12.302**) arose now, it is open to question whether the disposal by the builder by way of sub-lease would necessarily have to be treated as a trading activity. However, even if TCA 1997, s 640 fails to achieve its obvious intention, and does not catch such a transaction, the profit made by the builder would probably fall within TCA 1997, s 643 (although not it seems, if the land was outside the State) (see **12.310**).

TCA 1997, s 640 does clearly catch cases where a business is not treated as a trade because the relevant disposals of land fail to meet both of the above two conditions. Thus, if the facts in *Swaine v VE* (see **12.302**) arose today, the taxpayer who came out of retirement to build (and sell) houses on the land on which he had been farming would be deemed by the section to have acquired the land for the business of development and resale, and to have disposed of his full interest therein. Accordingly, his profits would be brought within Sch D Case I.

TCA 1997, s 640 does not apply to treat any person as carrying on a trade or to deem certain activities to be trading activities, unless the person in question undertakes the relevant activities in the course of a business and that business is one of dealing in or developing land. The term 'business' is not defined anywhere in the Tax Acts, although the term has been discussed in a number of statutory contexts. In *IRC v Marine Steam Turbine* 12 TC 174 Rowlatt J defined business as 'an active occupation … continuously carried on', although he qualified this in *IRC v South Behar Railway Co* 12 TC 657 by saying:

> When I said business involved activity, I merely meant something you describe by way of an active verb – something positive.

In the latter case, Lord Simons observed that the term 'business' implies a 'repetition of acts'.

The references to the qualities of 'continuity' and 'repetition' imply that an isolated transaction will not constitute a 'business' as such. In *Rolls v Miller* [1884] 27 Ch D 71 (cited by Judge Sheridan in *AE v Revenue Commissioners* V ITR 686) Lindley LJ stated:

> The word means almost anything which is an occupation as distinguished from a pleasure – anything which is an occupation or duty or which requires attention in a business.

Thus, it appears that an activity carried out by an individual in his personal capacity, will not constitute a 'business'. For example, a person who buys a house as a residence, perhaps extends it once or twice, and later sells it on acquiring a new residence, cannot in the normal case be regarded as selling it in the course of a business. On the other hand, if a person buys a house, converts it into flats and rents out the flats, whether or not involving any fine or premium, this would generally be regarded as a business activity.

The position in relation to a company will normally be different since a company cannot act in a 'personal' capacity but generally acts, instead, for the benefit of its shareholders. In *American Leaf Blending v Director-General* [1978] STC 561 (a Privy Council case) Lord Diplock, said:

> In the case of a private individual it may well be that the mere receipt of rents from property that he owns raises no presumption that he is carrying on a business. In contrast, in their Lordships' view, in the case of a company incorporated for the purpose of making profits for its shareholders any gainful use to which it puts any of its assets *prima facie* amounts to the carrying on of a business.

The significance of 'continuity' in the definition of business will be critical when facts arise such as those in *Spa Estates v O'hArgain* (1975) HC. There a company acquired land for development with a view to its eventual disposal. In the event, the land was sold off before the development commenced. Kenny J observed:

> It is an oversimplification to say that Spa was formed to carry on business as builders. The trade which the directors of Spa intended to carry on was that of developing lands, building houses on them and selling the houses. The purchase of the lands and the applications for planning permission seem to me to have been acts preparatory to the carrying on of a trade and not to be evidence that a trade was being carried on. This view is supported by the decision in *The Birmingham & District Cattle By-Products Co Ltd v IRC* 12 TC 92. It is true that houses cannot be sold without selling the lands on which the houses are situate. But when no development has been done and no houses have been built, the purchase of the land for the purpose of building does not involve the consequence that the taxpayer was dealing in land. In my view, the only possible conclusion on the facts in this case was that Spa never commenced to carry on the trade of developing lands, building houses on them and selling the houses nor did they commence the business of dealing in land.

This decision can be contrasted with that in the UK case of *Shadford v Fairweather* 43 TC 291 where the facts were broadly similar. In the latter case the taxpayer's original intention was to exploit the developed land in the most profitable manner possible, but it had not decided whether this was to be by way of lease or sale. In the absence of a definite intention to hold the land as an investment the court held in these circumstances that the company had undertaken an adventure in the nature of trade. Buckley J commented as follows:

> It is perfectly clear that the intention was to develop this property with a view to commercial profit; whether this was achieved by selling or letting it does not seem to me to be of any particular importance. The transaction was a commercial transaction and was a transaction in nature of trade.

Assuming that *Spa Estates* was correctly decided, it remains open to question whether or not the facts in the *Spa Estates* case would now be caught by TCA 1997, s 640. This is because it is doubtful whether a simple isolated transaction of this kind can constitute a 'business of … dealing' (see above concerning the definition of 'business'). However, TCA 1997, s 643 (see **12.310** *et seq*) would now presumably catch this transaction (although not, it seems, if the land was situated outside the State).

TCA 1997, s 640 also provides that any person who secures the development of any land can, in applying this provision, be treated as if he developed the land himself. Consequently, if a person secures the development of land as part of the activity of a business not otherwise treated as a trade within Sch D Case I, TCA 1997, s 640 can be applied, if all the other circumstances fit, to treat that business as a trade. This provision ensures, *inter alia*, that property developers in the wider, everyday sense, as well as speculative builders, are brought within the potential scope of TCA 1997, s 640.

It is highly arguable that TCA 1997, s 640 does not apply unless the business of development is one which is undertaken with a view to realisation at a profit.

In *Mara v Hummingbird* II ITR 667 the taxpayer was a company that acquired property which it intended to develop and thereafter let as a long-term investment. Shortly after development had commenced, the company received an attractive offer for the property which it subsequently sold at a substantial profit. The Supreme Court upheld the Appeal Commissioners' finding of fact that the acquisition and sale did not represent an 'adventure in the nature of trade' on general principles. The Revenue had contended before the Appeal Commissioners that the effect of TCA 1997, s 640 was *inter alia* to catch:

> ... transactions which would be regarded as trading transactions but for the circumstance that the interest in land disposed of had not been acquired with a view to re-sale at a profit. In other words ... where the full interest was sold, the question whether the purchase and sale of the land amounted to trading was to be determined as if [the taxpayer] had acquired the land with the intention of carrying out the operation which it did in fact carry out ie the partial development *and sale of the land at a profit* (emphasis added).

However, TCA 1997, s 640 requires that the disposal of the relevant interest in land should be one which is 'included among the activities of the business [of development]'. In the *Hummingbird* case, the taxpayer's business was one of development for *investment* purposes, followed by an unanticipated sale which did *not* form part of the business activities concerned. It was unnecessary for the Supreme Court to explore these issues, in view of its conclusion that the section (as it then stood) only applied to disposals of less than a full interest in the land. However, it is submitted that if a disposal does not form part of the activities of development, TCA 1997, s 640 should not be in point.

Example 12.305.1

Planet Ltd, a company trading as a manufacturer of electronic components for the aerospace industry, has owned a large country house which has been occupied as the residence of its managing director for the last 10 years. On the retirement of the managing director in February 2015, the company decides to redevelop the house as an office block with the intention of realising it in the manner most suitable to maximise profits.

When the redevelopment has been completed, Planet Ltd disposes of the building by granting a 99-year lease to an insurance company in consideration for a lump sum of €2,750,000 plus a nominal rent. In the absence of TCA 1997, s 640, Planet Ltd could argue that the profits from this development and subdemise of the premises would not be taxable as income under Sch D Case I, because:

(a) Planet Ltd had not acquired its freehold interest in the house as trading stock of any trade of dealing in or developing land, (however, the Revenue could argue that, on the retirement of the Managing Director, Planet Ltd had then appropriated the property to a new trade of development);

(b) it did not dispose of its full freehold interest in granting the 99-year lease; following *Birch v Delaney* this argument could not be countered.

TCA 1997, s 640 now has to be considered. First, there seems little or no doubt that Planet Ltd's redevelopment and subdemise of the house has been undertaken as part of an overall 'business' of developing land with a view to disposal. Would the subdemise by granting the 99-year lease be regarded as an activity carried on in the course of a trade?

If both the assumptions required by TCA 1997, s 640 are made – ie conditions (i) and (ii) in (b) mentioned in the discussion above are met, then, it appears that the inspector has a strong case that the development and subdemise of the property has to be treated as carried on in the course of a trade. If the inspector succeeds in this argument, Planet Ltd becomes taxable under Sch D Case I on its profits derived from the redevelopment and subdemise. For the rules to be applied in computing the Sch D Case I profit in this type of case see **12.307**.

Example 12.305.2

Take the facts of **Example 12.305.1**, but assume that Planet Ltd redeveloped the country house as offices with the intention of using the ground floor and certain outhouses as additional offices and letting the other two floors on short leases to suitable tenants. After two years, the company acquires new offices in the nearby town and sells the redeveloped building at a substantial profit.

On these facts, Planet Ltd's redevelopment of the house is again properly regarded as being carried on as a business activity. If it is assumed – for the purposes of this example – that the redevelopment is part of a business of developing land, then on making the two assumptions required by TCA 1997, s 640(2), can the profit realised on the eventual sale of the building be taxed under Sch D Case I as the profits of a trade?

On the above facts, Planet Ltd should be able to establish that the redevelopment of the property was carried out with the intention of providing offices for the company (a fixed asset) and perhaps also, in part, a property investment. Assuming that this is the case, the profit on the sale should not be capable of being brought within Sch D Case I by TCA 1997, s 640.

Normally, the question of whether there is, or is not, a dealing in land or a development of land is clear and needs no special definition. TCA 1997, s 640 makes it clear that, for the purposes of this provision, a dealing in land is regarded as taking place in any case where a person, having an interest in any land, disposes either of that interest or of any interest derived from it. This applies whether the interest disposed of relates to the whole or any part of the land in which the interest is held. For example, a person who has acquired a 35-year leasehold interest in an acre of land can be treated as dealing in that land whether he sells his 35-year lease, or alternatively, grants (say) a 21-year sublease out of it.

A person who had originally acquired land for non-trading purposes, but who then disposes of it in a 'business like' way, (eg by obtaining planning permission and then selling off the land in smaller, more marketable parcels) may perhaps be more exposed to a potential charge under TCA 1997, s 640. However, it is arguable that a distinction should be made between a business of dealing (ie an activity involving the systematic acquisition, and possibly appropriation, of land with a view to disposal for profit) and the mere disposal of land in a businesslike manner.

12.306 Disposals of land in course of winding up

Under ordinary principles, a trade is normally regarded as ceasing when a company goes into liquidation, whether, compulsorily, due to the company being insolvent or, voluntarily, by a resolution of its shareholders to wind up. While it is possible in certain circumstances for a liquidator to be held to be trading (see **4.104**) this is a relatively unusual case – generally the liquidator is regarded as doing no more than realise the assets of the company to the best possible advantage. Although a contrary decision was reached in *O'hArgain v B Ltd*, the correctness of the decision is open to doubt (see **12.302**). Consequently, it was usually possible at one time for the profits of a trade of dealing in or developing land to escape a charge to tax if the disposal did not take place until after a company had gone into liquidation.

TCA 1997, s 640(3) therefore provides that where an interest in land is disposed of in the course of the winding up of a company, the company is deemed, for the purposes of TCA 1997, s 640, not to have ceased to carry on the trade or business which it carried on before the commencement of the winding up. The trade or business is deemed to continue until the completion of the last disposal of an interest in land by the liquidator. It requires the question whether any such disposal was made in the course of the business of dealing in or developing land to be determined without regard to the fact that the company is being wound up. This applies whether the business is itself a trade or is deemed to be a trade by TCA 1997, s 640.

It follows that in any case where tax would have been charged either under the normal rules of taxing the profits of a trade under Sch D Case I, or by those rules as extended by the provisions of TCA 1997, s 640, the charge to tax cannot be avoided by the company going into liquidation. However, it remains necessary to ask the question as to whether that business was a trade or, if not, whether it would be regarded as a trade if the two conditions of TCA 1997, s 640(2) are assumed to be met.

12.307 Computation of taxable profits: Sch D Case I

TCA 1997, s 641 provides certain special rules for computing the Sch D Case I taxable profits (or losses) of a business of dealing in or developing land, whether that business is itself a trade within Sch D Case I or is deemed by TCA 1997, s 640 to be a trade. TCA 1997, s 642 adds two further rules which are relevant if there is any transfer of an interest in land between the person carrying on the trade or business and any other person connected with him.

TCA 1997, s 641 contains some additional general computational rules more likely to be relevant in the normal case while TCA 1997, s 642 contain anti-avoidance measures discussed separately in **12.308**. The rules of TCA 1997, ss 641, 642, as well as one further matter, are now dealt with under the following headings:

(a) trading receipts, including treatment of lease premiums;
(b) trading stock, its acquisition and retention; and
(c) valuation of trading stock after disposal of part of interest in land.

Trading receipts

The trading receipts to be credited in the Sch D Case I computation must include the full consideration received for every disposal of an interest in land that is made in the course of the trade or, if relevant, in carrying out the activity that is treated by TCA 1997, s 640 as a trade or part of a trade. However, to the extent that the consideration for any disposal includes rent or any part of a lease premium or other sum treated as rent by TCA 1997, s 98 (see **12.201**), then that rent or amount treated as rent should be excluded from the Sch D Case I computation. Where part of a premium or other sum deemed to be a premium is taxable as rent under TCA 1997, s 98, the balance of the premium or other sum excluded from the Sch D Case V income by TCA 1997, s 98 must be brought in as a trading receipt (TCA 1997, s 641(2)(a)).

Example 12.307.1

PD Ltd, a property developing company, disposes of an interest in a building it has just developed by granting a 35-year lease in consideration for a premium of €120,000 and an annual rent of €10,000. TCA 1997, s 641(2)(a) requires the company to include in its Sch D Case I computation a trading receipt of €81,600, determined as follows:

	€
Premium on granting lease	120,000
Less:	
Amount treated as rent by TCA 1997, s 98:	
€120,000 x (51–35/50)=	38,400
Trading receipt	81,600

Notes:

The annual rent of €10,000 excluded from the Sch D Case I computation is taxable under Sch D Case V, as is the €38,400 deducted above.

When a person taxable under Sch D Case I in respect of a trade or business of dealing in or developing land disposes of an interest in land to a person connected with him, and if the price in the transaction is less than the market value of the interest in land, then the market value must be substituted for the actual price paid in computing the Sch D Case I profit or loss. The term 'price' includes premiums, fines, etc payable for the grant of a lease. A gift is treated as a disposal at a nominal price so that similarly, the market value must again be included as the trading receipt if the disposal to the connected person is by way of gift. The substitution of the market value is not, however, required if the person connected with the vendor also carries on a trade or business of dealing in or developing land and is entitled to debit the actual purchase price paid in computing his own Sch D Case I profits (TCA 1997, s 642(2)).

When the person carrying on the taxable trade or business purchases any interest in land from another person with whom he is connected, and if the price in the transaction is greater than the market value of the interest acquired, then the market value must instead be taken as the acquisition cost of the land acquired as trading stock (TCA 1997, s 642(1)). This rule does not, however, apply if the person from whom the trader acquires the land includes the sale consideration as a trading receipt of a business of dealing in or developing land. For an acquisition at less than market value from any unconnected person, the actual price paid in the transaction must be used as the cost of the trading stock acquired and the purchaser is not entitled to substitute the market value.

It seems that gifts or sales at wholly unrealistic under (or over) valuations should, in any event, be treated as transfers of market value under the principle laid down in *Sharkey v Wernher*, (see **5.101**).

The capital gains tax position should also be borne in mind. Disposals between 'connected persons' as defined by TCA 1997, s 10 as it applies to capital gains tax, or by way of a bargain other than at arm's length are treated as taking place at market value (TCA 1997, s 547). Thus, even where TCA 1997, s 642 does not apply (eg because there is a transaction between two land dealing entities) and assuming that on the facts the Revenue Commissioners do not seek to apply the decision in *Sharkey v Wernher* TCA 1997, s 547 may still be in point. Transfers of land between members of the same capital gains tax corporate group will however give rise to a nil gain/nil loss outcome (TCA 1997, s 617), so that a transfer between land dealing companies in a capital gains tax group may avoid a charge to both income tax and capital gains tax.

The position is more complicated where there is a transfer between a company trading in land (a 'dealer') and a company not trading in land (an 'investor') and both companies are members of the same capital gains tax group. Where there is a transfer by an investor to a dealer, the dealer is treated as acquiring the land on a nil gain/nil loss basis in the usual way, but is then deemed to appropriate the land as trading stock at its market value, thus triggering a capital gain/loss (TCA 1997, s 618(1)). The dealer has however the right to have the capital gain untaxed and instead deduct it from the cost of the land for Sch D Case I computational purposes (TCA 1997, s 596).

Example 12.307.2

A Ltd and B Ltd are members of the same capital gains tax group. A Ltd is an investor in land while B Ltd is a dealer in land. A Ltd sells a parcel of land to B Ltd, details of which are as follows (ignore indexation):

	€
Cost for capital gains tax purposes	10,000
Market value	
(as agreed for capital gains tax and TCA 1997, s 642 purposes)	21,000
Sale price	25,000

For the purposes of Sch D Case I, TCA 1997, s 642(1) deems B Ltd to acquire the land at its market value of €21,000. For the purposes of capital gains tax, B Ltd acquires the land at €10,000 but is then deemed to appropriate it at its market value of €21,000 generating a gain of €11,000. B Ltd can then either pay any resultant corporation tax on the gain (or capital gains tax in the case of development land as defined by TCA 1997, s 648) or else deduct the gain of €11,000 from the cost of the land for Sch D Case I purposes, ie reducing the cost to €10,000. This will of course increase the Sch D Case I profit on a subsequent disposal of the land.

Where a 'dealer' transfers land to an 'investor' in the same capital gains tax group, the dealer is firstly deemed to have appropriated the land as a capital asset at the value at which is brought into the Sch D Case I computation (TCA 1997, s 618). It is this latter value which then forms the basis for the deemed nil gain/nil loss acquisition by the 'investor' company.

Example 12.307.3

C Ltd and D Ltd are members of the same capital gains tax group. C Ltd is a dealer in land while D Ltd is an investor in land. C Ltd sells a parcel of land to D Ltd, details of which are as follows:

	€
Cost	10,000
Market value	21,000
Sale price	12,000

TCA 1997, s 642 will deem C Ltd to sell the land for €21,000 for Sch D Case I purposes. For capital gains tax purposes, C Ltd will be deemed to have acquired the land for €21,000. The land will, correspondingly, be deemed to be acquired by D for the same amount, ie €21,000.

Any consideration received by the trader for the granting of any right in relation to the development of any land must be included as a trading receipt (TCA 1997, s 641(2)(e)). This prevents a person otherwise taxable under Sch D Case I from realising a tax free gain by disposing of his right to develop the land for a valuable consideration, instead of developing it himself.

Trading stock

Where the person carrying on the taxable trade or business has acquired an interest in land before the trade commenced, or if he has acquired land otherwise than as trading stock and only appropriates it as trading stock at a later date, the interest in land must be brought into the accounts as trading stock at an assumed cost equal to its market value at the time of that appropriation (TCA 1997, s 641(2)(d)). By virtue of TCA 1997, s 596, the appropriation of a capital asset to trading stock is treated as a disposal of that asset at its market value, thus triggering off a capital gain (or capital loss). However, the taxpayer may elect for the gain to be untaxed and deducted instead from the cost of the land for Sch D Case I computational purposes. If land, or an interest in land is acquired otherwise than for a consideration in money or money's worth, eg on an inheritance, its cost as trading stock is taken as being equal to its market value at the time of its acquisition or, if later, on the date it is appropriated as trading stock (TCA 1997, s 641(2)(c), (d)).

Example 12.307.4

On 11 February 2005, Mr A Builder inherited 100 acres of farm land (market value at the time of €800,000) from the estate of his deceased uncle. He continued to farm the land under a manager until after it was rezoned and available for development in July 2015. Some years earlier Mr A Builder had purchased a house with several acres of amenity land in the same area for €200,000; he used the house as his residence for a number of years.

On 1 January 2015, Mr Builder who had previously been the employee of a building contractor, commenced to trade on his own account as a speculative builder. He purchased a new residence and appropriated the old one and its lands to this trade and commenced to redevelop the land. On 1 July 2015, he appropriated the farm lands to his building trade. He makes up accounts annually to 31 December.

Based on the market values assumed below, TCA 1997, s 641 treats Mr Builder as having acquired interests in land as trading stock of his business of developing land, as follows:

Year to 31/12/2015:	€
Acquisition as trading stock (1/1/2015) of former residence and Amenity lands	
Market value at 1/1/2015	500,000
Acquisition as trading stock (1/7/2015) of former farm lands	
Market value at 1/7/2015	1,500,000

Notes:

1. Since the former residence was appropriated as trading stock immediately after the trade commenced, the market value at the date of the commencement is taken.
2. Although the trade had been in existence for six months, the former farm lands were not appropriated as trading stock until 1/7/2015, so that the market value at that date is taken.

Example 12.307.5

In 2004, Mrs N Battery purchased the freehold interest in a cottage which she converted into premises for use in her ladies' hairdressing business. The cost of acquisition and the total conversion cost was €30,000. On 15 November 2015, she moved her business to a new premises and sold the old one to Battery Construction Ltd a company carrying on a building trade, for a consideration of €500,000 (when the market value of the premises was €450,000).

Battery Constructions Ltd acquires the premises to demolish them and to build offices for resale. The share capital of the company, all a single class of ordinary shares, is held as follows:

	%
Mr N Battery (husband)	47
Mrs N Battery	2
Mr A Pile (brother of Mrs Battery)	2
	51
Other unconnected persons	49
	100

Since Battery Constructions Ltd is controlled by Mrs Battery and persons connected with her, she and the company are connected persons (see **12.304**). Battery Constructions Ltd is, therefore, required by TCA 1997, s 642(1) to bring the premises acquired into its trading stock at their market value of €450,000 (lower than the actual purchase price).

Any interest in land which has been acquired as trading stock, or which is appropriated as trading stock on some date after its acquisition, continues to be regarded as trading stock until either it is fully disposed of in the course of the trade or business of dealing in or developing land or that trade or business is permanently discontinued, whichever happens first (TCA 1997, s 641(2)(b)). This means that, if the person carrying on the trade or business withdraws land or any interest in land from his trading stock, applies it for some other purpose while retaining ownership, and then sells it at a later date while the trade or business continues, he is required to bring in the full sale proceeds as trading receipts. In the event that the trade should be discontinued before the land is fully disposed of, it must be included in the closing trading stock valuation on the date of the discontinuance of the trade in accordance with the rules of TCA 1997, s 89(2) (see **5.603**). However, where the stock is transferred from one trader to another connected trader, such stock is to be valued at the price which would have been received if the transfer had occurred between independent, non-connected parties. If that price however, exceeds the amount of the book value of the stock and the amount of the actual transfer price, the connected parties can elect to have the stock valued at the higher of those two amounts.

In the case of a trade or business of dealing in or developing land carried on by a company which, under the rule of TCA 1997, s 640(3), is regarded as still continuing despite the fact that the company is being wound up (see **12.306**), TCA 1997, s 641 treats all unsold interest in land acquired as trading stock as continuing to be trading stock until finally disposed of by the liquidator.

Valuation of retained interest

When the person carrying on the trade or business disposes of an interest in land that has been acquired or appropriated as trading stock, but does not dispose of the entire interest, the interest that is retained continues to be trading stock of the business. For example, should a builder who has developed houses on land held freehold, demise them on long leases under which he remains entitled to ground rents, then he must continue to include at an appropriate value the freehold interest in the land which he has retained.

Consequently, it is necessary to apply the normal Sch D Case I rules for valuing the interest retained as trading stock at the lower of its cost or net realisable value at the balance sheet date. In determining the 'cost' of the interest retained for this purpose, the so called 'Emery' formula is used. This formula, first put forward in the UK case of *John Emery & Sons v IRC* [1937] AC 91, 20 TC 213 and first applied in *Hughes v BC Utting & Co Ltd* 23 TC 174, is:

'cost' of interest retained = D x (A/ (A+B))

where

A = the market value of the interest retained at the date the inferior interest is created;

B = the consideration received for the part of the interest in land disposed of;

D = the cost to the trader of the entire interest acquired including the development costs allocated to it.

Example 12.307.6

Battery Constructions Ltd, a building company, acquired the freehold interest in a plot of ground for €500,000 and erected a shop on it at an *additional* cost of €250,000. On 14 September 2015, the company granted a 99-year lease of the shop for a lump sum of €950,000 (= B) and the right to receive an annual rent of €1,300. The market value of the rent reserved at 14 September 2015 is agreed to be €10,400 (= A).

The taxable profit on the development of the shop and its disposal by the 99-year lease, to be included in the Sch D Case I computation of the company's building trade for its accounting period made up to (say) 31 December 2015, is determined as follows:

	€	€
Consideration for 99-year lease (14/9/2015)		950,000
Add:		
Trading stock value (31/12/2015) of interest retained:		
€750,000 x (10,400/(10,400 + 950,000)=	8,122	
		8,122
Less:		
Cost of development		
Site cost	500,000	
Building, etc costs	250,000	
		750,000
Taxable profit		208,122

Notes:

1. The freehold interest retained must continue to be brought forward as trading stock at its 'cost' of €8,122 (or at 'market value', if lower at any balance sheet date) so long as the company's building trade continues.

12.308 Prevention of artificial deductions

TCA 1997, s 641(3) contains anti-avoidance rules intended to prevent the person carrying on the trade or business of dealing in or developing land from obtaining an artificial deduction in computing the Sch D Case I taxable profit (or loss). TCA 1997, s 641(3) provides that no account is taken in the Sch D Case I computation of any sum (the 'relevant sum') which is paid or payable at any time by the trader as consideration for the forfeiture or surrender of the right of any person to an annuity or other annual payment, unless the annuity or other annual payment arises under either a testamentary disposition (eg a will or an intestacy), or in a manner such as can only be attributed to certain genuine non-avoidance reasons.

In the absence of this rule, it might be possible for the trader to arrange for land to be charged with the payment of an annuity on some non-arm's length basis so that, if the trader at a later date pays a lump sum to the annuitant in consideration for the latter's surrendering his right to the annuity, he could claim a deduction for this lump sum as a business expense in computing his Sch D Case I profits. TCA 1997, s 641(3) prevents this arrangement.

Apart from the annuity or other annual payment arising under a testamentary disposition, TCA 1997, s 641(3) does not prevent the deduction in the Sch D Case I computation of a sum otherwise deductible that is paid by the trader as consideration for an annuitant or other person forfeiting or surrendering his right to an annuity or other annual payment, if that right arises under a liability incurred either for:

(a) valuable and sufficient consideration all of which is treated as taxable income of the person to whom the payment is made; or
(b) consideration given to a person meeting the conditions mentioned in the next paragraph.

These conditions are that the person to whom the consideration for the forfeiture or surrender is given is a person who:

(a) has not at any time carried on a business of dealing in or developing land which is, or is to be regarded as, a trade or a part of a trade; and
(b) is not, and was not at any time, connected with any of the following persons:
    (i) the trader,
    (ii) a person who is, or was at any time, connected with the trader, and
    (iii) any other person who, in the course of a relevant business, holds or held an interest in land upon which the annuity or other annual payment was charged or reserved ('relevant business' for s 641(3) is one of dealing in or developing land which is either a trade or regarded by TCA 1997, s 640 as a trade or a part of a trade).

TCA 1997, s 641(4) contains a somewhat similar measure to deal with the case where a person other than the trader pays a sum to any person as consideration for that person's forfeiture or surrender of his right to an annuity or other annual payment. For this subsection to be applicable, two other conditions must both be met. First, it only applies if the trader has incurred any expenditure ('the cost') in acquiring any interest in land upon which the annuity or other annual payment in question has been reserved or charged. Secondly, the sum paid for the forfeiture or surrender must not be a sum which the person to whom it is payable is required to bring into account as a trading receipt in computing the Sch D Case I profits of his own trade or business of dealing in or developing land.

Assuming that all the conditions for its application are met, TCA 1997, s 641(4)(b) treats the trader as if the cost of acquiring the interest in land subject to the annuity or other annual payment were equal to the cost he would have incurred if the right to the annuity, etc had not been forfeited or surrendered. Further, the excess of the cost of the interest in land over what the cost would have been, if the right had not been forfeited or surrendered, has to be dealt with under TCA 1997, s 641 as if payable by the trader as consideration for the forfeiture or surrender of the right (ie it is not deductible in the Sch D Case I computation).

Example 12.308.1

A builder is about to acquire an interest in land with a market value of €100,000 on which an annuity with a capitalised value of €18,000 is charged. Before the acquisition is made, another person (who happens to be the builder's son) pays the annuitant €21,000 for giving up his right.

TCA 1997, s 641(4) requires the builder's acquisition cost to be taken as the amount he would have paid if the right to the annuity had not been surrendered, ie a deductible acquisition cost of €82,000 (and not the €100,000 paid).

Further, the excess of the actual price paid over the €82,000, ie €18,000, is treated as if it had been an amount paid by the trader himself in consideration for the surrender of the annuity by the third person. In other words, the builder cannot deduct this €18,000 in computing his Sch D Case I profits, unless the annuity surrendered arose under a testamentary disposition, or a liability incurred for valuable and sufficient consideration, etc (see above).

12.309 Postponement of tax: certain leasebacks

TCA 1997, s 646 entitles a person carrying on a trade of dealing in or developing land ('the trade') to pay by instalments over a 10-year period a part of the tax on the profits from certain types of sale and leaseback transactions. The provision is worded specifically in terms of income tax and applies in any case within its ambit to allow the postponement of the part of the tax in question to an individual or other person chargeable to income tax. For a company chargeable to corporation tax in respect of this type of trade, TCA 1997, s 647 provides an almost identical form of tax postponement given in corresponding circumstances.

TCA 1997, s 646 only grants the tax postponement in a case where the consideration for the sale by the person carrying on the trade ('the vendor') includes a sum which represents the value of any right of the vendor to be granted a lease ('the leaseback') of the premises sold. Further, *all* of the following other conditions must also be met for the section to apply:

(a) the disposal by the vendor must be made in the course of his trade and must consist of the full interest in the land previously acquired by him;
(b) the purchaser must not be a person connected with the vendor;
(c) the vendor's right to the leaseback must be contained in the terms of the sale;
(d) the leaseback must in fact be granted by the purchaser to the vendor within six months after the date of the sale;
(e) the vendor must retain the leasehold interest acquired by him from the purchaser as a result of the transaction; and
(f) the vendor must not dispose of any interest derived from that leasehold interest (eg by granting a sublease), whether of the whole or any part of the land concerned.

The amount of the tax that is payable by instalments ('the tax postponed') is not the tax payable on the total profit from the sale and leaseback transaction, but is the additional tax payable resulting from the inclusion in the sales consideration of the sum representing the value of the vendor's right to a leaseback. The rest of the taxpayer's income tax liability for the year of assessment affected is payable on its normal due date. The tax postponed is payable in nine equal instalments at yearly intervals commencing on the 1 January in the calendar year following that in which the tax charged by an assessment on the profits of the trade would normally be due and payable.

The amount of the tax postponed is equal to 90 per cent of the additional tax attributable to the vendor's right to the leaseback. Its calculation may be expressed conveniently by the following formula:

$$\text{Tax postponed} = 90\% \times (A - B)$$

where:

A = the total income tax payable by the vendor for the relevant tax year calculated in the ordinary way on his taxable income (including the value of the right to the leaseback); and

B = the total income tax that would be payable by the vendor for the same year on his taxable income (assuming the value of the right to the leaseback is excluded).

Example 12.309.1

Mr BLD, who trades as a property developer, buys a site freehold and pays a building contractor to erect a block of flats on it at a total cost of €1,250,000. When the construction is completed, Mr BLD sells the freehold interest in the developed property to an insurance company in consideration for a cash payment of €1,500,000 plus the right to be granted a 35-year lease at an annual rent of €100,000 for the first seven years (with five-year rent reviews on an arm's length basis thereafter).

The sale by Mr BLD to the insurance company is made on 25 February 2015 and the insurance company grants the 35-year lease to Mr BLD on 23 May 2015 (ie well within the six-month limit).

Mr BLD's building trade accounts for his accounting year to 31 March 2015 (assessable 2015) result in Sch D Case I taxable profits (after capital allowances) of €500,000 after crediting the sales price of €1,500,000, but before adding on the additional trading receipt that must be included for the value of Mr BLD's right to the leaseback on the above terms. It is agreed that this right should be valued at €75,000, this increasing the final Sch D Case I profits for the year to €575,000. Mr BLD's income tax liability for 2015 is determined on income including the additional €75,000 and on income excluding that amount, as follows:

	Including	*Excluding*
	€75,000	€75,000
	€	€
Sch D Case I profits (builder)	575,000	500,000
Other income	3,000	3,000
	578,000	503,000
Deductions in arriving at total income (say)	(30,500)	(30,500)
Taxable income 2015	547,500	472,500
Income tax payable 2015		
Married person's table		
Tax on		
€ 42,800 @ 20% = 8,560		
€504,700 @ 40% = 201,880		
€547,500	210,440	
Tax on		
€ 42,800 @ 20% = 8,560		
€429,700 @ 40% = 171,880		
€472,500		180,440

The tax postponed is, therefore, calculated as:

90% x (210,440 – €180,440) = €27,000

Consequently, Mr BLD's income tax liability for 2015 is payable on the following dates:

	€	€
31/10/2016 (due date for tax under self assessment, disregarding preliminary tax paid by 31/10/2015):		
Liability for year	210,440	
Less:		
Tax postponed	27,000	
		183,440

1/01/2017	
Tax postponed – first instalment	
€27,000 x 1/9	3,000
1/01/2018	
Tax postponed – second instalment	3,000
and 7 subsequent annual instalments of €3,000	
each on 1 January 2019 to 2025:	
€3,000 x 7 =	21,000
Total tax liability	210,440

Notes:

1. An adequate amount of preliminary tax would have to be paid on or before 31/10/2015 in order to avoid incurring interest charges (see **2.104**).

TCA 1997, s 646(4) provides that, after there has been any postponement of tax under the section, the balance of the income tax still unpaid becomes due and payable forthwith if any of the following events occur:

(a) the vendor ceases to retain the leasehold interest acquired by him from the purchaser;
(b) the vendor disposes of any interest derived from that leasehold interest (whether as regards the whole or any part of the land involved);
(c) the vendor, if he is an individual, dies; or
(d) the vendor, if a company, commences to be wound up.

12.310 Gains of a capital nature

TCA 1997, s 643 is a close, although not exact, reproduction of what at the time was ICTA 1970, s 488 *et seq* (currently, ICTA 1988, s 776 *et seq*) in the UK. The UK provisions were enacted primarily in response to the decision in *Ransom v Higgs* [1974] STC 539. In that case, a number of companies controlled by the taxpayer (H) and his wife, the H group, undertook an avoidance scheme. The H group firstly sold land at an undervalue to a partnership in which a family trust (T) had an interest. T subsequently sold its interest in the partnership to the promoter of the scheme. This sale effectively realised the difference between the cost of the land and the estimated development value, (less a fee for the scheme promoter). It was hoped that this gain would be treated as capital in nature, on the basis that it had transformed a disposal of trading land into a disposal of a partnership interest held as a capital asset. Following the sale, C, a development company owned by H, effectively developed the land on behalf of the promoter.

The Inland Revenue argued that H had engaged in trade and that the trustees were taxable on the basis that they had received the profits of this sale (see **15.303**). The contention that H was a trader was bound to fail once it was accepted that the legal entities involved in the scheme were not acting merely as his agents. The fact that he had procured those entities to play their part in the scheme was insufficient. As Lord Wilberforce commented:

> In the whole course of these transactions (H) bought nothing, sold nothing and ventured nothing.

TCA 1997, s 643 charges certain gains of a capital nature obtained from the disposal of land or of other property deriving its value from land as income under Sch D Case IV. It is stated to apply to any person, whether resident in the State or not, if all or any part of the land is situated in the State. This wording implies that transactions relating to land outside the State do not fall within the scope of the section, even if they are carried out by an Irish resident. Even if the wording should be said to be unclear, any doubt should presumably be resolved on the basis that the legislature has failed to impose a clear charge in respect of land outside the State (see **1.406**). The wording employed also illustrates the difficulties which arise when supplementary charging provisions are enacted which do not clearly define their territorial limits (see **1.405**). The section clearly *does* apply if there is a disposal of land in the State through the sale of any foreign asset that derives its value from that land.

Under general principles, a company is clearly a 'person', while trustees and personal representatives are clearly 'persons' (see **1.302**). TCA 1997, s 643(16) states that not only trustees and personal representatives but that also partners are to be regarded as persons distinct from the individuals or other persons who are trustees, personal representatives or partners for the time being. This deeming provision seems designed in particular to enable the Revenue to look at the activities of a partnership as a whole (ignoring any intervening changes in the composition of the partnership) in order to decide whether or not those activities fall within the section. It may be noted however that, under general law, any change in partners leads to the creation of a new partnership. Apart from this, the section is silent on how Case IV income attributed under the section to a partnership as such is to be allocated between the members of the partnership.

There are three tests to determine whether TCA 1997, s 643 applies to charge tax under Sch D Case IV; each is discussed in more detail in **12.311** but may be summarised as follows:

(a) either land must have been acquired, held or developed for one of three specified purposes, or property deriving its value from land ('PDVL') must have been acquired with the object of realising a gain from a disposal of the land (the 'purpose' test);

(b) a gain of a capital nature must have been obtained from a disposal of land as widely defined (the 'transaction' test); and

(c) the person realising the gain must be either the person who acquired, held or developed the land or a person connected with him or, in the case of an arrangement or scheme involving the land, a person concerned in the arrangement or scheme (the 'relevant person' test).

For these purposes 'land' is defined as including any interest in land, and 'PDVL' is to be regarded as including:

(a) any one of the following assets deriving its value, or the greater part of its value, directly or indirectly, from land:
   (i) any shareholding in a company; or
   (ii) any partnership interest; or
   (iii) any interest in settled property; and

(b) any option, consent or embargo affecting the disposition of land (TCA 1997, s 643(1)).

A shareholding in a company, a partnership interest or an interest in settled property is, therefore, treated as PDVL if more than 50 per cent of its value is attributable to land. In determining whether and to what extent the value of any property or right is derived from land or any other property or right, value may be traced through any number of companies, partnerships and trusts; and the property held by any company, partnership or trust is to be attributed to its shareholders, partners or beneficiaries at each stage in whatever manner is considered just and reasonable (TCA 1997, s 643(14)).

There is no guidance provided in the more complex cases to determine whether or not an asset is 'PDVL'. In broad terms, it would appear that in the case of a trading company, the value of goodwill should be taken into account, when deciding whether or not the greater part of the value of that company can be attributed to any interest in land which it may hold. The correct treatment of liabilities may be arguable in any situation where the company owns both land and other assets. Current liabilities should probably be offset against current assets in order to ascertain a figure for net working capital. However, there is a strong case for saying that longer term liabilities, such as loans, should not as a rule be set off against specific assets (with a possible exception where a liability is secured on a specific asset).

The concept of PDVL also appears in the Irish capital gains tax legislation, where TCA 1997, s 29 impose a charge on non-residents in respect of disposals of unquoted shares 'deriving their value or the greater part of their value directly or indirectly from ... [land in the State]'. In that context the Revenue Commissioners have argued *inter alia* that the liabilities of a company should be set off firstly against all of its assets *other than land*. This approach is inherently biased against the taxpayer, and seems impossible to justify under normal valuation principles.

Before going on to discuss the circumstances in which these provisions may apply to charge tax on certain gains of a capital nature, it may be useful to give some examples of how a shareholding in a company, an interest in a partnership or an interest in settled property may be regarded as deriving the greater part of its value from land.

Example 12.310.1

Assume the following facts:

(a) The trustees of a settlement own 80 per cent of the shares in A Ltd,

(b) A Ltd is a partner in a partnership with an entitlement to 90 per cent of all the firm's profits or losses on income and on capital account,

(c) The partnership (A, B and Partners) owns 75 per cent of the shares in B Ltd (not a partner),

(d) B Ltd is the parent company of C Ltd (in which it owns 100 per cent of the share capital, voting rights, etc), and

(e) C Ltd's only asset is 100 acres of land scheduled for development valued at €2,000,000 (and it has no liabilities).

From the above facts, and assuming the values of the other assets of each person as stated below, and assuming it is just and reasonable to attribute to each person its share of the land held by C Ltd on the basis of the above percentages, the following position emerges:

	Land	*Other assets*	*Total*
	€	€	€
C Ltd	2,000,000		2,000,000
B Ltd			
100% of C Ltd's assets	2,000,000		2,000,000
Other assets	-	500,000	500,000
	2,000,000	500,000	2,500,000
Partnership			
75% of B Ltd's assets	1,500,000	375,000	1,875,000

Other assets	-	125,000	125,000
	1,500,000	500,000	2,000,000
A Ltd			
90% of partnership assets	1,350,000	450,000	1,800,000
Other assets	-	50,000	50,000
	1,350,000	500,000	1,850,000
Settlement			
80% of A Ltd's assets	1,080,000	400,000	1,480,000
Other assets	18,000	840,000	858,000
	1,098,000	1,240,000	2,338,000

Conclusions:

(a) the shares in C Ltd held by B Ltd are clearly PDVL since the former company's net assets consist solely of land;

(b) the shares in B Ltd held by the partnership (and the other 25 per cent held by the other shareholders) are also PDVL (80 per cent of the value of B Ltd is land);

(c) A Ltd's interest in the partnership is PDVL (75 per cent of the value of the partnership is land);

(d) the settlement's shares in A Ltd is PDVL (73 per cent of the value of A Ltd is land); but

(e) any interest in the settlement attributed to any beneficiary is not PDVL as only 46.9 per cent of the settlement's total value of €2,338,000 is attributable to land.

12.311 Conditions for application

The three sets of conditions, each one of which must be satisfied before tax can be charged under Sch D Case IV as a result of TCA 1997, s 643, have been summarised in **12.310** as:

(a) the 'purpose' test;
(b) the 'transaction' test; and
(c) the 'relevant person' test.

The 'purpose' test

The purpose test is satisfied in relation to the disposal of any land if *any* of the following conditions are met:

(a) the land or PDVL was acquired with the sole or main object of realising a gain from disposing of the land;
(b) the land was held as trading stock; or
(c) the land was developed *by a company* with the sole or main object of realising a gain from disposing of the land when developed.

Condition (a) requires the object of realising a gain from the disposal of the land to have been present at the time the land or the PDVL was acquired. If it was acquired for another purpose (eg land acquired for farming) and the decision to dispose of the land to realise a gain was made later, TCA 1997, s 643 cannot be applied under condition (a). However, irrespective of the intention at the time of acquisition, the purpose test is satisfied under condition (b) if the land is subsequently appropriated as trading stock before the disposal or, under condition (c), if the land is developed by a company for the purpose of realising a gain from the disposal of the land when developed.

It is to be noted that condition (c) is only relevant where the development is made by a company, whereas either of the other two conditions may apply whether the person who acquired the land or the PDVL or who held the land as trading stock, is an individual, a company or any other person.

In the case of PDVL, it is not necessary that *all* of the underlying interests in land should have been acquired with the requisite object.

The 'sole or main object' test appears to require a *subjective* approach, ie it is necessary to determine the object or purpose which the acquiror or developer had at the time of the acquisition. Thus, evidence given by a person of his actual intentions will always be material. However, this does not mean that such evidence will be conclusive of the absence of a profit-making object (or vice versa). In fact TCA 1997, s 643(13) expressly provides that the intentions, objects and powers of any company, partners or trustees set out in any document are not conclusive evidence. The tribunal of fact, ie the Appeal Commissioners (or the Circuit Court judge as appropriate) must consider all of the factual evidence, including the person's own evidence, and then deduce from this what were likely to have been his intentions. In practice, therefore, the test to be adopted is likely to be similar to the test which is supposed to be used in deciding whether or not an 'equivocal transaction' is an adventure in the nature of trade (see **4.102**).

However, for a case where it was effectively held that a purchase and resale undertaken for tax avoidance purposes could have the necessary 'object', but yet not be a trading transaction, see *Sugarwhite v Budd* at **12.314**. This finding could perhaps be justified on the basis that the transaction was insufficiently commercial to be regarded as trading on an objective analysis (see the discussion in **4.102**). Alternatively, there may be a distinction between the objective of realising a gain and a genuine profit motive (which presumably implies the objective of making a profit on one's own behalf and not merely as a step in a larger scheme designed ultimately to benefit somebody else).

The 'transaction' test

This test may be broken down into two conditions which must be satisfied. Condition (a) requires that there must be a disposal of the land in question (ie land in respect of which the 'purpose' test is met). In considering this condition, the special meaning attributed by TCA 1997, s 643(5) to the expression 'disposal of land' has to be applied. Condition (b) requires that a gain of a capital nature must be obtained from that disposal. Here, it is to be noted that the word 'obtained' is used in relation to the gain, rather than the more usual 'realised'. These two questions are now discussed:

TCA 1997, s 643(5) defines 'disposal of the land' so as to include *inter alia* the 'effectual disposal' of either 'the property in', 'or control over', the land in question. Thus, for example, if shares giving control (presumably as defined by TCA 1997, s 432 (see **12.304**)) over a company owning land as an investment are acquired, with the sole or main object of realising a gain on the sale of the shares, condition (a) will be met. This is because PDVL (ie the shares) has been acquired with the object of effectively disposing of control over the company and thus, control over the land which it owns (see below).

Similarly, if a controlling shareholding in a company which holds land as trading stock is sold, condition (b) will be met, in this case irrespective of the objective behind the original acquisition of that shareholding (the tax charge is in this case subject to a potential exception discussed in **12.312** below).

In fact, a disposal of land could also be regarded as taking place if the majority shareholder in a land-owning company sells sufficient of his shares to reduce his holding to a point where he can no longer exercise control of the company. For example, if Mr A owns 51 per cent of the controlling shares in X Ltd, and Mr B owns 49 per cent, a sale by Mr A to Mr B of 1.1 per cent of these shares would transfer control over the land and, therefore, amount to a disposal of the land within these provisions. On the other hand, if Mr A owned 73 per cent and Mr B 27 per cent, a sale by Mr A to Mr B of 22.9 per cent of his holding would not result in a change of control over the land so that, if this is the only transaction, it does not amount to a disposal of the land.

As discussed at **4.102**, the courts are generally slower to regard transactions in shares as being adventures in the nature of trade than they are transactions in land. However, this does not necessarily mean that an isolated purchase and sale of shares in a land-dealing or land-developing company can never be treated as a trading transaction.

In *Associated London Properties Ltd v Henriksen* 26 TC 46, A Ltd, a property-dealing company, sold land which it held as trading stock to P Ltd, a development company owned as to 50 per cent by itself, and 50 per cent by a third party, H Ltd. Subsequently, in accordance with a shareholders' agreement, A Ltd sold its shares in P Ltd to H Ltd at a considerable profit. The court held that the transfer of land to P Ltd and the subsequent sale of shares to H Ltd were merely a 'special method of dealing with the land', and that the profit accordingly derived from the company's trade of property-dealing. By treating A Ltd's interest in P Ltd as an interest in P Ltd's assets the Court seems to have effectively disregarded the separate legal personality of P Ltd, thus preferring 'substance' over 'form' (see **1.407**).

In the *Fundfarms Development* case (discussed below) it was held that the critical factor in the *Associated London Properties* case was that the real source of the profit was land originally acquired as trading stock. Even if the court's approach in the latter case was not correct, it is arguable that the disposal of the shares as such could still properly have been treated as an 'adventure' in the nature of trade. This is because those shares were acquired with a view to a quick realisation, and the transaction clearly exploited the taxpayer's special commercial expertise (see **4.102**).

If a controlling shareholding in a company which holds land as an investment is acquired, and the new shareholders arrange for the land to be subsequently developed, with the object of selling the shares at a profit, condition (c) will be met. TCA 1997, s 643(5) thus seeks to eliminate the difficulties raised for the Revenue by the decision in *Fundfarms Development Ltd v Parsons* 45 TC 707. In that case a property-dealing company, F Ltd, acquired all of the shares in a land-owning company, G Ltd, following which F Ltd's parent company developed G Ltd's land. The court held that F Ltd's profit on the subsequent disposal of its shares in G Ltd did not arise in the course of its trade of property dealing. As noted above, the court distinguished the decision in the *Associated Properties* case, on the basis that the land in the latter case had originally been held as trading stock. The court left open the position as to whether the purchase and sale of shares looked at as a distinct transaction in its own right could have been regarded as an 'adventure in the nature of trade' (for a case where the sale of shares in a holding company which had been formed to develop properties owned by its subsidiaries and other associated companies was held *not* to be a trading transaction, see *Beautiland v IRC* [1991] STC 467; there was no evidence that the owner of the holding company had intended to 'trade in land via shares').

The following two important points must be noted:

(1) *'Disposal of land'*: A disposal of land is regarded as taking place whether it occurs as a result of either one or more transactions or any arrangement or scheme. The transaction(s), arrangement or scheme may concern the land itself

or any PDVL in question. Any number of transactions may be regarded as constituting a single arrangement or scheme if a common purpose is discerned in them, or if there is other sufficient evidence of a common purpose (TCA 1997, s 643(6)).

Where the transaction, arrangement or scheme concerns a shareholding in a company or an interest in a partnership or in settled property, TCA 1997, s 643 only applies if both control over the land changes and the greater part of the value of the shareholding or interest actually arises from the land. It is possible, for example, for a person to sell a controlling interest in a partnership that carries on a trade of dealing in land, but which also carries on other activities not relating to land. Should the greater part of the value of the partnership be attributable to its non-land assets, the sale of the controlling interest is not treated as a disposal of land and the transaction test is not met.

The disposal of land or of control over the land may take place in any manner whatsoever. TCA 1997, s 643(7) provides that account must be taken of any method, direct or indirect, by which any property or right is transferred or transmitted to another person, or by which the value of any property or right is enhanced or diminished. Consequently, the occasion of the transfer or transmission of any property or right, or the occasion on which the value of any property or right is enhanced or diminished, may be treated as an occasion on which tax becomes chargeable under these provisions (assuming that both the '*purpose*' and '*person*' tests are also met).

TCA 1997, s 643(8) then elaborates on these provisions and enumerates a number of ways in which any property (meaning any asset of any kind) may be transferred to another person or in which the value of any property or right may be enhanced or diminished (so as to constitute a disposal). It makes it clear that TCA 1997, s 643 is to apply, in particular, to:

(a) sales, contracts and other transactions made for less than full consideration or for more than full consideration (sales, etc for full consideration are already included directly by this subsection);

(b) any method by which any property or the control over any property may be transferred to any person by assigning:
    (i) share capital or other rights in a company,
    (ii) rights in a partnership, or
    (iii) an interest in settled property;

(c) the creation of any option, consent or embargo affecting the disposition of any property; and

(d) the disposal of any property on the winding up, dissolution or termination of any company, partnership or trust.

(2) *Gain of a 'capital nature'*: This expression is defined indirectly. TCA 1997, s 643(1) in fact defines the term 'capital amount' as meaning any amount in money or money's worth which, were it not for these provisions, would not be included in any computation of income for the purposes of income tax or corporation tax under the Tax Acts. It goes on to provide that any other expressions in TCA 1997, ss 643, 644 which include the word 'capital' are to be given a corresponding meaning.

It may, therefore, be taken that any disposal of land (within the above very wide definition) that gives rise to the receipt by any person of any amount that exceeds the expenditure properly attributable to the relevant transaction is, to the extent of that excess, a gain of a capital nature; the sole exception arises where the amount of the receipt falls to be included in the computation of income under the Tax Acts. For example, in *Yuill v Wilson* (see below), the sale by a share dealing company resident in Guernsey was regarded as giving rise to a gain of a capital nature because the proceeds of the sale were not, due to the non-residence of the company, included in any computation of income for UK tax purposes. The fact that the Guernsey company, if resident in the UK, would have been taxed on the gain as the income did not prevent the attribution of the character of 'capital' to the gain under the corresponding UK legislation.

The 'relevant person' test

Assuming that it has been established that there has been a gain of a capital nature obtained from the disposal of land, and that the purpose test has also been satisfied, these provisions enable tax to be charged if the gain has been 'obtained' from the disposal by any of the following persons, either for him or for any other person, namely:

(a) the person acquiring, holding or developing the land;
(b) any person connected with that person; or
(c) any person who is a party to, or concerned in, any arrangement or scheme effected as respects the land which enables the gain to be realised (whether directly or indirectly by any transaction or by a series of transactions).

In determining whether a gain has been obtained by a person connected with the person acquiring, holding, or developing the land, the connected person rules of TCA 1997, s 10 are again applied (up to 5 April 1996 slightly different rules applied). Where shares in a landowning company are sold, the shareholders will not be 'relevant persons' unless they are 'connected to' the company (see **12.304**). It should be borne in mind that two or more persons acting together to secure or exercise control of a company may be treated as connected with each other in relation to that company. Thus a group of minority shareholders who are otherwise unconnected with each other but who join together in the sale of a company may be 'relevant persons' by virtue of this latter provision. The circumstances in which a person obtains the gain for himself do not need further comment, but TCA 1997, s 643(6)(a) explains how a person is regarded as obtaining a gain for another person. This occurs if one person *makes available* to another *the opportunity of realising a gain*. This opportunity may be provided directly in any manner whatsoever, but one particular method, ie a premature sale, is given as an example. In any such case, the person who obtained the gain for the other person, ie by providing the opportunity for that other person to realise the gain, is the person to be taxed (TCA 1997, s 643(11) – see also **12.313**).

A good example of the very wide reach of these provisions and, in particular, of the sort of circumstances in which a taxpayer may be taxable due to having provided another person with an opportunity to realise a gain, was that in the UK case of *Yuill v Wilson* [1980] STC 460, decided on the corresponding provisions of the UK Taxes Act (currently ICTA 1988, s 776 *et seq*).

In that case, an individual (Mr Y) was a substantial shareholder in Y Ltd, a building company. His shares together with the shares of trustees of family settlements created by him constituted a controlling interest in Y Ltd. A number of years before the transactions giving rise to the case, two other companies (the 'land holding companies') controlled by Mr Y and his family interests acquired various interests in land expected to be used in due course by Y Ltd in its building business. In September 1972, Mr Y created a new settlement with trustees resident in Guernsey for the benefit of members of his family. These trustees formed two companies resident in Guernsey, M Ltd and C Ltd; the trustees held all the shares in, and had complete control of, these two companies.

Between December 1972 and March 1974, M Ltd and C Ltd acquired several holdings of UK land from the two land holding companies and sold these lands to Y Ltd at substantial profits. It was accepted that the profits were not taxable as trading income in the UK (see **12.314**). The Inland Revenue assessed Mr Y under ITA 1970, s 488 on the grounds that he, either directly or through his companies and with the help of his Guernsey trustees, obtained the gains for M Ltd and C Ltd by making available to them the opportunity for realising the gains. The House of Lords unanimously held that this was the correct view.

More often than not, TCA 1997, s 643 is likely to be relevant where the gain of the capital nature is obtained by the person acquiring, holding or developing the land or by some other person connected with him. Unless there is an arrangement or scheme, it is not possible for any unconnected person to be charged under this section in respect of the gain. In any case where there is, or has been, an arrangement or scheme carried out as respects the land, two further questions have to be answered in the affirmative before such an unconnected person can be charged by it.

First, was the person who has obtained the gain of a capital nature from the disposal of the land either a party to the arrangement or scheme, or was he concerned in it? Secondly, did the arrangement or scheme enable the gain to be realised directly or indirectly? Clearly, a person is a party to an arrangement or scheme if he is either a transferor or a transferee in any one or more of the transactions which together make up the scheme, but a person may sometimes be concerned in a scheme even if he is not a party to any of the transactions in the scheme or is not involved in its documentation.

In the UK case of *Winterton v Edwards* [1980] STC 206, the ownership of land acquired with the sole or main object of realising a gain was transferred by L to a company in which he held 90.5 per cent of the share capital. The transfer was accomplished by a series of transactions in a manner designed to defer L's income tax liability on the disposal of the land. After the acquisition of the land, but before execution of the scheme, L agreed with the taxpayer, W, that the latter would be given a 4.5 per cent share in the proceeds of the sale. The scheme was in due course implemented and Mr W was paid his share of the sale proceeds.

W was assessed under the UK provisions corresponding to TCA 1997, s 643 on his share of the proceeds. Although he was not a party to any of the documentation related to the sale of the land to the company, it was held that he was 'concerned in' the scheme, since it had been agreed he would receive a share of the proceeds and as L had by letter executed a declaration of trust confirming W's interests. On the second question as to whether the scheme effected by L had enabled W to realise a gain, the fact that he subsequently received a proportionate share of the proceeds of sale was held to be sufficient to answer the question in the affirmative. The taxpayer was held to be correctly assessable.

In *Page v Lowther* [1983] STC 799, the taxpayers were trustees of settled land. They decided that this land should be developed for residential purposes, but wished to ensure that the development was in keeping with the local area. A development company was prepared to undertake the project, but not at the price the trustees wished. It was therefore arranged that the trustees would grant a long lease to the company and the company undertook that when it granted an underlease to the ultimate occupiers they would pay a premium directly to the trustees. No tax avoidance motives were involved in these arrangements which, although elaborate, were designed purely to secure the best price for the trustees in the circumstances.

The court held that the UK equivalent of TCA 1997, s 643 applied. Firstly, condition (c) of the 'purpose' test was satisfied, since the company had developed the land with the required objective. Secondly, conditions (a) and (b) of the 'transaction' test were met, since 'capital' gains were obtained by the trustees from the disposal of the developed land by way of the underleases. Finally, condition (c) of the 'relevant person test', was met since the grant of the long lease was an 'arrangement … as respects the land' which enabled gains to be realised, and to which the trustees were a party.

Two points need to be made in connection with the decision in *Page v Lowther*:

(a) It seems that the trustees could have avoided liability under the equivalent of TCA 1997, s 643 by ensuring that they had full legal entitlement to consideration from the developer prior to the development taking place. In this case, condition (c) of the 'transaction' test should not have been met, since the gains would have been obtained from the disposal of the land in its original, undeveloped state. This would still be the case even where the ultimate sale price varied according to a formula which reflected the developer's ultimate profits.

(b) TCA 1997, s 643 would not apply given the same facts, but assuming that the development had been undertaken by an entity other than a company.

It may also be noted that the Minister of Finance made the following observations in the Dáil on 14 May 1981:

> If it transpires that the anti-avoidance provisions now proposed operate in practice so as to impose a charge where it would not be just and reasonable that such charge should be imposed, the Revenue Commissioners will make use of any means open to them within the limits of their role in the care and management of the taxes not to apply the new legislation to such cases. If this is not possible, amending legislation will be introduced to ensure that genuine commercial transactions which have no tax avoidance elements are not jeopardised by the new legislation. The essential object of his legislation is to ensure that real profits are taxed in a just and reasonable manner.

The extent to which the Revenue are in fact entitled to apply concessionary treatments to taxpayers is discussed in **2.206**.

12.312 Exceptions

TCA 1997, s 643(2) excludes from the charge to tax under the section any gain accruing to an individual (but not to any other person) from the disposal of a dwelling house in circumstances in which the gain qualifies for exemption from capital gains tax under TCA 1997, s 604.

There are two other exceptions to the full charge to tax under Sch D Case IV, notwithstanding that the three tests above are all satisfied. Firstly, if the 'purpose' test is satisfied because of the development of land by a company with the object of realising a gain from disposing of the land when developed, this section does not apply to tax part of the gain that is fairly attributable to the period before the intention to develop the land was formed (TCA 1997, s 643(10)). This exception cannot, however, be availed of if the land was previously acquired with the object of realising a gain from its disposal or if it was held as trading stock. In other words, if the land was acquired to realise a dealing gain or was held as trading stock of a land dealing business, the fact that a subsequent decision is made to develop the land before the disposal, does not operate to exclude any part of the gain from the charge to tax under Sch D Case IV.

Secondly, the section does not apply in certain circumstances where there is a disposal of shares in either a company which holds land as trading stock or a company which owns directly or indirectly 90 per cent or more of the ordinary share capital of another company which holds land as trading stock. For the tax charge to be excluded in any such case where it would otherwise apply, three further conditions must all be met, namely:

(a) all the land held as trading stock by the company concerned must be disposed of in the normal course of its trade by that company;
(b) the disposal of the land must be made in such a way as to ensure that all opportunity of profit in respect of the land arises to that company only; and
(c) the gain must not be one obtained by any person who is a party to, or concerned in, any arrangement or scheme effected as respects the land (TCA 1997, s 643(12)).

Where a land-dealing company sells its trading stock, a subsequent disposal of shares in the company will be outside the scope of TCA 1997, s 643. This remains the case even though the value of the shares derives from the property originally held by it (see *Chilcott v IRC* [1982] STC 1).

12.313 How the tax is charged

TCA 1997, s 643 requires the whole of the gain of a capital nature from the disposal of the land to be treated as income chargeable to tax arising at the time the gain is realised. It is, therefore, taxable under Sch D Case IV in the year of assessment in which the gain is realised.

Person chargeable

The person chargeable to tax under Sch D Case IV is normally the person by whom the gain is realised on the particular disposal of land giving rise to the gain. This person is unlikely to be the person who acquired, held or developed the land with the object of realising a gain from disposing of the land since, in the event of this person's making an actual disposal of the land (as distinct from a deemed disposal), he or it would almost always be assessable under Sch D Case I either directly or as a result of TCA 1997, s 640 (see **12.305**). The person chargeable is more likely to be a person who effects a disposal of land by selling or otherwise transferring PDVL, eg by an individual selling his controlling interest in the parent company (an investment company) of another company that has developed the land with the object of realising a gain.

TCA 1997, s 643(11) provides an exception to the normal rule that it is the person actually realising the gain who is chargeable. It is relevant in any case where a gain within these provisions accrues to any person if all or any part of the gain is derived from either value or an opportunity of realising a gain provided directly or indirectly by some other person. In any such case, TCA 1997, s 643 is applied to tax the person who provided the value or made available the opportunity of realising a gain for the other person; the person actually realising the gain is not then taxable under the section.

In *Yuill v Wilson* (see **12.311**), the assessment under the corresponding UK legislation was made on Mr Y who had provided the two Guernsey companies with the opportunity of realising the gains of a capital nature from the disposal of land in the UK.

Computation of taxable gain

No precise rules are provided for computing the amount of the gain of a capital nature that is chargeable under Sch D Case IV. TCA 1997, s 643(9) requires the adoption of such a method of computation as is just and reasonable in the circumstances. It then gives a few guidelines which are to be applied. The value of any consideration of any kind obtained for the disposal of the land is to be brought into account, and only such expenses as are attributable to the land disposed of may be deducted. It is to be inferred from the definition of 'capital amount' (see **12.311**) that any part of the consideration falling to be included in the computation of any income otherwise chargeable under the Tax Acts should be excluded in computing the amount of the gain. The time when a gain is realised must be determined by using the normal meaning of these words. In *Yuill v Wilson*, the sale proceeds were only payable in instalments on the occurrence of specified contingencies. The House of Lords held that the proceeds could only be brought into account as they were received. However, this conclusion was based on the express wording of ICTA 1988, s 777(13) which is *not* repeated in the Irish legislation.

In applying these guidelines, it should be noted that the consideration, or other capital amount received, may be in respect of the disposal of shares in a company or of other PDVL. In this type of case, the deductible expenses should normally include the cost of acquiring the property disposed of (eg the shares), as well as any reasonable expenses incurred in connection with the disposal. However, the requirement to use any appropriate 'just and reasonable' method leaves the matter open to the inspector to disallow any deduction he does not consider appropriate in all the circumstances of the case. Any decision of the inspector on this or any other method of computing the amount taxable under Sch D Case IV is, of course, open to the normal appeal procedure when the inspector makes his assessment to income tax or corporation tax.

Clearly, due to the very wide scope of these provisions and to the variety of possible circumstances in which a gain of a capital nature within them may arise, it would not be possible to provide for all matters to be taken into account in the computation of the taxable gain in all circumstances. Several other points are, however, mentioned. First, TCA 1997, s 643(9)(a) provides that, if the transaction(s) involve or include the acquisition of an interest in land and the retention of the reversion on a subsequent disposal, the approach that would be taken in such a case under Sch D Case I *may* be taken into account (ie the 'Emery' formula – see **12.307**). It could well be necessary, in an appropriate case, to attribute a value to the reversion retained (to be credited in the Sch D Case IV computation, as if a closing trading stock).

Secondly, in any case where the 'purpose' test is met due only to the development of land by a company with the sole or main object of realising a gain from disposing of the land when developed, TCA 1997, s 643(10) requires the computation of the taxable amount of the gain to exclude any part of the gain that is 'fairly' attributable to the period (if any) before the intention to develop the land was formed. In applying this rule, the subsection requires that account *shall* be taken of the treatment under Sch D Case I of a person who appropriates land as trading stock. In effect, this means that the opening value of the land (or of the property deriving its value from the land) that is debited as the 'acquisition cost' in the computation of the taxable gain should be its market value at the date the intention to develop the land is formed.

Example 12.313.1

Mr P Robert owns 60 per cent of the ordinary share capital of Robert Holdings Ltd ('RH Ltd'), which shares he purchased in June 1986 for a euro equivalent of €200,000. The remaining 40 per cent are held by a merchant banking company (with which Mr Robert is not connected). RH Ltd's only asset is an 80 per cent holding in the ordinary share capital of SJ Ltd. The latter company has traded for many years as a wholesaling and warehousing company.

On 1 March 2011, SJ Ltd ceased its original trade and by 1 May 2011 had disposed of all its trading assets and had paid off most of its liabilities. Its only remaining assets were its land and buildings valued in May 2011 at €260,000 and a bank balance of €210,000. On 1 June 2011, the decision was taken that SJ Ltd would demolish the existing buildings on its freehold land and would redevelop the site by erecting three modern factory units with the intention of selling them off at a profit when developed.

The development is completed on 30 September 2015 at which date the balance sheet of SJ Ltd is as follows:

	€	€
Freehold land and buildings:		
at cost	150,000	
cost of redevelopment	450,000	
		600,000
Balance at bank		25,000
		625,000
Less:		
Liabilities (including loan to help finance development)		230,000
Net assets		395,000
Represented by:		
Share capital and reserves		395,000

On 1 October 2015, the market value of the developed factory units was certified by professional valuers as being €950,000. Owing to the financial climate, it was difficult to find purchasers for the buildings at the right price and it was decided to delay selling the factories. However, Mr P Robert wished to realise his investment in RH Ltd. The merchant bank purchased his 60 per cent holding for €325,000.

The consequences are as follows:

(a) Although no actual disposal of the developed factory sites has taken place, the sale by Mr Robert of his controlling shareholding in RH Ltd (which controls the company that developed the land) is a sale of property deriving its value from land which transfers the control over SJ Ltd's developed land. It is, therefore, a disposal of land within TCA 1997, s 643 and enables the 'transaction' test to be satisfied.

(b) Since the land was developed by SJ Ltd, (a company), with the object of realising a gain on its disposal when developed, the 'purpose' test (see condition (c) in **12.311**) is met.

(c) Since the gain from the deemed disposal of the land (the sale of the RH Ltd shares) is obtained by Mr Robert as a person (the controlling shareholder) connected with the company which developed the land (SJ Ltd), the 'relevant person' test is also met.

(d) TCA 1997, s 643 applies to limit the amount chargeable to the part of Mr Robert's gain attributable to the post 1 June 2011 period, ie after the intention to develop the land was formed. In determining this part of the gain, the market value of the land at that date (when it was appropriated as trading stock by SJ Ltd) has to be brought into the computation.

(e) The following is the authors' suggestion as to how the gain taxable under TCA 1997, s 643 in respect of the sale of Mr Robert's 60 per cent holding in RH Ltd should be calculated:

	€	€
Sale price for 60% holding (1/10/2015)		325,000
Assumed cost of 60% holding:		
Taken as equal to market value of the holding at 1/6/2011[1]	184,416	
Expenses of negotiating sale, say	15,400	
		(199,816)
Gain taxable under Sch D Case IV		125,184

Notes:

1. The value of Mr Robert's holding in RH Ltd at 1/6/2011 has been determined, after bringing in SJ Ltd's land at its market value at that date (ie applying the Sch D Case I rule for land appropriated as trading stock) as follows:

	€
Value of SJ Ltd:	
Land and buildings at market value 1/6/2011	260,000
Balance in bank	210,000
Less: liabilities	(18,000)
Value of 100% holding	452,000
Value of RH Ltd:	
Market value of 80% holding in SJ Ltd	
€452,000 x 80%	361,600
Value of Mr Robert's shares at 1/6/2011:	
Market value of 60% holding in RH Ltd	
€361,600 x 60%	216,960
Less: 15% discount (say[2])	(32,544)
say market value at 1/6/2011	184,416

2. It has been assumed that it is appropriate to take a 15 per cent discount, compared with the full underlying market value of the assets, in valuing the 60 per cent holding.
3. The exclusion from the tax charge provided by TCA 1997, s 643(12) is not available as RH Ltd (the company whose shares are disposed of) is not the company that holds the land as trading stock and it does not own 90 per cent or more of the ordinary share capital of SJ Ltd (see **12.312**). Also, even if SJ Ltd subsequently disposes of the developed land in the course of its trade, this would not have deprived Mr Robert of his opportunity to realise a profit from the earlier disposal of his shares in RH Ltd.

Recovery of tax from person realising gain

When TCA 1997, s 643 is applied so that a person who provided value, or who made available an opportunity for another person to realise a gain, is taxable in respect of a gain realised by that other person, TCA 1997, s 644 entitles the person so taxable (the first named person) to recover from the other person (the second named person) any of the tax so charged that the first named person has paid. In calculating the amount of tax so recoverable, it is assumed that the amount charged as income under TCA 1997, s 643 was taxed as the highest part of the first named person's income for the tax year in question.

The first named person is entitled to request the inspector of taxes to furnish him with a certificate specifying the amount of income in respect of which he has paid tax, and the amount of tax so paid. He may present this certificate to the second named person when seeking to recover the tax. On the other hand, if any part of the tax assessable on the first named person has not been paid by him within six months from the due date of the tax, the Revenue Commissioners are entitled to recover the tax from the person who actually realised the gain.

For the circumstances in which a person is taxable under these provisions in respect of a gain realised by another person in consequence of an opportunity made available by the person taxable, see the discussion of the 'person' test in **12.311**.

12.314 Non-residents

Any non-resident individual, company or other person may be charged to tax under Sch D Case IV in the same circumstances and in the same manner as a resident person, but only if the land actually disposed of is situated in the State (TCA 1997, s 643(17)). The position of non-residents who carry out transactions in respect of Irish land raises a number of complex issues. Thus, for example, a non-resident who acquires Irish land, develops it for resale and then disposes of it is clearly carrying on a trade, or an adventure in the nature of trade. It seems clear that the profits from such a trading activity 'in substance' arise in Ireland (see *Rhodesia Metals Ltd v IRC* [1940] AC 774, approved in *CIR v HK-TVB International Ltd* [1992] STC 723, and the discussion of this issue in **13.602**). The gain is therefore of an income, not a capital nature, so that it appears TCA 1997, s 643 should not apply. The Revenue Commissioners may however have difficulty in collecting any tax due unless perhaps the company operates through an Irish resident agent (see **13.603**). The withholding tax imposed by TCA 1997, s 980 should not apply once the inspector is satisfied that the disposal does not give rise to a capital gains tax liability (ie since some or all of the consideration is included in the computation of the taxpayer's income tax liability: TCA 1997, s 551).

The position becomes more complex where the non-resident is resident in a country with which Ireland has a double tax treaty. It may be that the company can demonstrate that its development activities constitute an 'enterprise', but one which does not operate through a 'permanent establishment' in Ireland, and thus, that any profits arising are exempted under the treaty (see **14.201**). If this is the case then, although the matter is not beyond doubt, it would seem likely that the profits which arise are 'capital' within the definition of TCA 1997, s 643. The treaty exemption should also extend to protecting the non-resident company against any charge under TCA 1997, s 643. However, it is not clear whether it will protect an Irish resident who is deemed to receive the company's gain (see the discussion of *Willoughby v IRC* and *Bricom v IRC* at **17.209**).

Where a non-resident acquires and sells land in order to make a quick profit, this will normally be an 'adventure in the nature of trade'. It is probable that the profits of this adventure will again 'in substance' arise in Ireland and will thus be liable within Sch D Case I (see *Wilson v Hooker*, a case not directly decided on this point, which is discussed at **13.603**). However, the question of treaty protection will again need to be considered. In this situation, it may be argued that a one-off dealing transaction does not constitute an 'enterprise', so that the permanent establishment Article of the treaty (see **14.201**) cannot be invoked (compare *Thiel v FCT*: see **14.106**). However, it does not seem that

Irish taxing rights could be established under either the 'capital gains' or 'income from immovable property' articles of a typical treaty. In this case, the profits would usually fall under the 'other income' article (which again would normally preclude Ireland from taxing the gain).

If the non-resident undertakes a purchase and sale of Irish land which is an adventure in the nature of trade, but the profits are regarded as arising *outside* Ireland, then the gain realised would be a 'capital sum'. This is because the gain would relate to an overseas source in the hands of a non-resident (see **1.501**). The gain would not be liable to capital gains tax because it is the profit of a trade, even though it is not actually chargeable to Irish income tax (TCA 1997, s 551). It seems that in this situation the gain would fall within TCA 1997, s 643 (see *Yuill v Wilson* where the Inland Revenue could not enforce liability under the equivalent UK provisions against the Guernsey companies but succeeded in taxing a UK resident individual as the person who provided them with the opportunity of realising their gains).

In *Sugarwhite v Budd* [1988] STC 533 an individual who was unable to sell a surplus property eventually sought assistance from his solicitor who introduced him to a Bahamian company. The taxpayer sold the property to the company for £25,000, but 11 days later the property was sold on for £33,500. The profit was split between the company, the other Bahamian companies and the taxpayer. The taxpayer was held to be assessable on the company's profit of £8,500 as he was knowingly party to an arrangement whereby the company obtained a capital profit. The Bahamian company had clearly acquired the land with the object of disposing of it at a profit. An argument that the Bahamian company was trading in the UK and therefore the gain was not capital in nature was rejected on the grounds that the taxpayer had not produced any evidence for this contention before the Appeal Commissioners (see **2.204**). Clearly, the court had in mind the possibility that the overriding purpose behind the Bahamian company transaction was simply to act as a means of diverting profits out of the UK tax net rather than to deal in land. The significance of the taxpayer's actual intention in the question of trading is discussed at **4.102**.

While it is the situation of the land that is the determining factor for liability, a non-resident person remains chargeable where the disposal is made through the sale of any property deriving its value from the land in the State. The fact that this property, eg the shares in a company or an interest in a partnership, may be an asset situated outside the State does not of itself prevent the non-resident from being assessable.

However, if it appears that TCA 1997, s 643 is potentially applicable, to tax a non-resident person on a gain realised through the sale (or alienation) of any PDVL (eg shares in a company, be it resident or non-resident), the double taxation agreement between the State and the foreign country of which the person in question is a resident should be consulted. It may be that the relevant article dealing with capital gains on the alienation of assets other than land will apply to exempt the non-resident from any Irish tax on the gain. It is not unusual for a double tax agreement to provide that the resident of the other country is not to be subject to Irish tax on gains realised from the sale of shares in companies. Although TCA 1997, s 643 charges the gain arising as *income*, it is arguable that the context of the double tax treaty indicates that the term 'capital gain' should be given a general meaning common to both contracting states, rather than its technical Irish tax meaning (see **14.106**). Article 13 of the Commentary to the OECD Model Double Tax Convention also indicates that it is purely a question of domestic law as to whether capital gains should be taxed and, if taxable, *how* they should be taxed.

However, it may be noted that not all double tax agreements provide this exemption if the gain is from shares owing the greater part of their value to land in the State.

In any case where a person chargeable to tax under these provisions is resident outside the State, it is likely to be difficult for the Revenue to enforce payment of the tax by direct assessment. In such a case, TCA 1997, s 644(2) empowers the Revenue Commissioners to direct that the TCA 1997, s 238 collection of tax at source procedure (see **2.304**) is to be applied to any payment due to be made to the non-resident person that forms part of any consideration or amount that is chargeable to tax under these provisions. There is, however, no specific requirement for any person making such a payment to a non-resident to withhold income tax under this rule, unless the Revenue Commissioners actually make this direction. In a case concerning the equivalent UK provisions, it was held that the tax authorities could only make a direction at a time when the non-resident party was legally entitled to the relevant consideration (*Pardoe v Energy Power Development Corp* [2000] STC 286).

In any case where this direction is made by the Revenue Commissioners the person making any payment that is covered by the direction is required to deduct income tax at the standard rate (20 per cent for 2015) from the actual amount being paid. The non-resident person who suffers this withholding of tax at source is entitled to recover any excess of the tax withheld over the amount of his actual liability to tax under the provisions of TCA 1997, s 643. The recovery can, however, only be made after the non-resident has submitted the necessary returns and other information and has agreed his actual liability with the inspector of taxes. As the tax is withheld from the gross amount of the payment, without allowing any deductions which may be due, this is likely to act as an incentive to the non-resident to make the necessary returns.

A non-resident person who claims that, due to a relevant provision in the double tax agreement between the State and his country of residence, he is exempted from any Irish tax in respect of a gain within TCA 1997, s 643 may apply to the Revenue Commissioners for the withdrawal of any direction under TCA 1997, s 644(2) (if such a direction is made). If the Revenue Commissioners are satisfied that the non-resident is in fact entitled to such an exemption, it is to be expected that they would withdraw the direction (or refrain from making it, if advised in advance).

12.315 Miscellaneous points

Power to obtain information

TCA 1997, s 645(1) empowers an inspector of taxes by notice in writing to require any person to furnish such particulars as the inspector may think necessary for the purpose of applying TCA 1997, ss 643, 644. The particulars which may be requested by the inspector by this notice include particulars related to various matters which are set out in TCA 1997, s 645(2). These matters include information as to whether the person served with the notice has taken part in any transactions or arrangements of a kind specified in the notice. The information may be requested as regarding such matters whether the person in question is or was, acting on his own account or on behalf of other persons.

TCA 1997, s 645(3) provides an exception which excludes a solicitor from having to furnish information as regards any transactions or arrangements in respect of which his only involvement was to give professional advice to a client in connection with the transactions or arrangements. However, if the solicitor has done more than give professional advice and has otherwise involved himself in any way, he is not excused from giving full information in relation to his other involvement. In relation to anything done on behalf of a client, the solicitor cannot be compelled to do more than state that he is or was acting on behalf of the client, and give the name and address of the client.

Tax on capital gains

A transaction involving the disposal of land (including property deriving its value from land) is generally also a disposal of an asset within the Capital Gains Tax Acts. In the more straightforward case, where the person charged under these provisions is also the person within the charge to tax on capital gains as the disponer of the asset in question, the normal rules of capital gains tax apply to prevent a double assessment to tax. Any amount in money or money's worth that is included as a receipt in calculating an amount of income chargeable under these provisions is excluded from the consideration receivable in computing the chargeable gain. Similarly, any expenditure deductible in the TCA 1997, s 643 calculation cannot be deducted again in the computation of the capital gain.

TCA 1997, s 644(5) extends the capital gains tax rules preventing double assessment (TCA 1997, ss 551, 554) to cover the case where the person assessed to income tax (or corporation tax) under these provisions is not the person who actually realises the gain. This is relevant where the person is so charged due to having provided value or an opportunity for another person to realise the gain. In making any computation for capital gains purposes in such a case, any receipt or expenses included or deducted in the computation under these provisions of the person providing the value or the opportunity to realise the gain is excluded from the capital gains computation of the person who actually disposed of the asset and realised the gain.

TCA 1997, s 644(4) deals with the case where TCA 1997, s 643(10) has applied to exclude from the computation of the gain under that section the part attributable to a period before the intention to develop the land was formed. It provides that any land or other property appropriated as trading stock in the computation under that section at the time the intention to develop (and to realise a gain from the developed land) was formed is to be regarded, in applying the capital gains tax computational rules of TCA 1997, s 596, as having been appropriated as trading stock at the same time. In effect, this means that the person treated as appropriating the land as trading stock may be charged to tax on a capital gain computed by reference to a deemed disposal of the asset at its market value at that date (see **12.307**: *Trading Stock*).

Deeming provisions

TCA 1997, s 644(3) states that TCA 1997, s 643 is subject to any provision which deems income accruing to one person to belong to another. Thus, for example, by virtue of TCA 1997, s 791, a gain within TCA 1997, s 643 realised by trustees could be attributed to the settlor of the relevant trust.

12.316 Flat rate tax on profits from dealing in residential land

With effect from 1 December 1999 TCA 1997, s 644A charged income tax at a flat rate of 20 per cent on certain profits from dealing in or developing residential development land. TCA 1997, s 644A(6) inserted by FA 2009, s 6(a) terminated this regime with effect from 2009 onwards. A full description of this historic regime is provided in the 2012 edition of this text.

12.317 Windfall tax

FA 2014, s 30 ceased the operation of the windfall tax regime with effect from 2015. Full details of the windfall tax regime as it applied to trading land disposals during income tax years 2010 to 2014 are set out below.

Charging provisions

With effect from 2010, TCA 1997, s 644AB, as inserted by National Asset Management Agency Act 2009, Pt 10, and as amended by FA 2010, s 25, imposes a 'windfall tax' on specified land development profits, subject to the exemptions described below (TCA 1997, s 644AB(4)).

TCA 1997, s 644AB applies where a profit arises from a trade or part of a trade of dealing in or developing land which is subject to income tax, if some or all of that profit is attributable to a *'relevant planning decision'* (TCA 1997, s 644AB(2)).

A *'relevant planning decision'* is either:

(a) a change in the zoning of land in a development plan or a local area plan made or varied under the Planning and Development Act 2000, Pt 11 from non-development land-uses to development land-uses or from one development land-use to another development land-use, including a mixture of such uses, which is made on or after 30 October 2009; or

(b) a decision to grant permission, in accordance with the Planning and Development Act 2000, s 34(6) or s 37(2) for a development which would materially contravene a development plan, made on or after 4 February 2010. For these purposes, 'non-development land-use' means a land-use which is agricultural, open space, recreational or amenity use or a mixture of such uses, and 'development land-use' means residential, commercial or industrial uses or a mixture of such uses (TCA 1997, s 644AB(1)).

A special 80 per cent flat rate of income tax applies to that part of the profits which is attributable to a relevant planning decision. Where an apportionment of profits, amounts receivable or expenses incurred is required to be made, such apportionment is to be made in a manner that is just and reasonable (TCA 1997, s 644AB(8)).

The 80 per cent rate will also apply to such part of the profits arising from a business of dealing in or developing land which is treated as a trade by virtue of TCA 1997, s 640 (see **12.305**) and to such part of any gain of a capital nature arising directly or indirectly from the disposal of land which is liable to income tax under Case IV of Sch D by virtue of TCA 1997, s 643: see **12.310**) (TCA 1997, s 644AB(2)).

Exemptions

Qualifying Land

There are certain exemptions for any profits or gains which are attributable to 'qualifying land' such as disposals of sites of one acre (0.047 hectares) or less, or the market value of which does not exceed €250,000, so long as any disposal of the land does not form part of a larger transaction or series of transactions. It would seem that transfers made on foot of a single contract will be regarded as part of a larger, transaction while contracts which are legally interdependent will constitute a series of transactions (compare the UK Stamp Duty case of *Attorney General v Cohen* [1937] 1 All ER 27). The definition of qualifying land also extends to land disposed of to an authority possessing compulsory purchasing powers where the Revenue Commissioners are satisfied that the disposal would not have been made but for the exercise of those powers or the giving by the authority of formal notice of its intention to exercise those powers (TCA 1997, s 644AB(7)(b)).

Construction Profits

Similarly, no account is to be taken of profits or gains which are attributable to construction operations (as defined by TCA 1997, s 530(1) on the land: see **2.311**) (TCA 1997, s 644AB(7)(a)). Where an apportionment of profits, amounts receivable or expenses incurred is required to be made, such apportionment is to be made in a manner that is just and reasonable (TCA 1997, s 644AB(8)).

'Construction operations' are defined as for the purposes of TCA 1997, s 530 (see **2.311**).

Effect on total income; losses

Where the 80 per cent rate applies to land dealing or development profits, those profits are excluded from the taxpayer's total income (TCA 1997, s 644AB(4)(b)). Any losses attributable to a relevant planning permission are only available for carry forward against windfall profits or gains, taking the earliest available profits first (TCA 1997, s 644AB(5)).The provisions governing the assessment, collection and recovery of income tax and of any associated interest or penalties continue to apply (TCA 1997, s 644AB(4)(b)).

The levies

Profits liable to tax under the windfall gain provisions and dividends paid out of such profits (see **9.1**) are exempt from self-employed PRSI (TCA 1997, s 644AB(6), (10)). Profits liable to tax under the windfall gain provisions are automatically excluded from the definition of total income and dividends paid out of such profits (see **9.1**) are exempt from income tax; accordingly neither will be liable to the Universal Social Charge.

12.318 Taxation of release of debts in land dealing or developing land trades

TCA 1997, s 87B, was introduced into the Tax Acts by Finance Act 2013, s 18 to target individuals who carry on a trade of dealing in or developing land or a business which is deemed to be a trade under TCA 1997, s 640(2)(a), collectively referred to in the section as carrying on a 'specified trade'.

The aim of the provision as confirmed in Revenue *eBrief No 31/14* is to 'ensure that individuals engaged in the trade of dealing in and developing land do not obtain the benefit of losses for tax purposes when they have not, in fact incurred any economic loss'. This would arise for example in a case where an individual had borrowed on a limited recourse or non-recourse basis. In this scenario, the amount owed to the financial institution would be limited to the value of the land or property over which the bank has security. The individual would not be held personally liable for any shortfall between the value of the original loan and the value realised for the land or property.

The objective of this new section is to treat a release or write off of the whole or part of a 'specified debt' as a taxable trading receipt of the particular 'specified trade'. TCA 1997, s 87B(1), defines a specified debt as meaning 'any debt incurred by an individual in respect of borrowed money employed in the purchase or development of land held as trading stock (within the meaning of TCA 1997, s 89) of a specified trade'. This would include loans from financial institutions but would also include loans from a land dealer's company or from his relatives.

Therefore to the extent that financial institutions or other lenders agree to release or write off borrowings of land dealers or developers, the amount of the debt released or written off must be taken into account in calculating that individual's Sch D Case I trading profits or losses for the relevant basis period of that trade.

In order to come within the scope of the section, the borrowings in question must have been employed in the purchase or development of land held as trading stock within the meaning of TCA 1997, s 89. Trading stock is defined under this section as meaning 'property of any description, whether real or personal, which is either:

(i) property such as is sold in the ordinary course of the trade in relation to which the expression is used or would be so sold if it were mature or if its manufacture, preparation or construction were complete; or

(ii) materials such as are used in the manufacture, preparation or construction of property such as is sold in the ordinary course of that trade'.

Accordingly, any debt release caught by this section must be in relation to borrowings which have been taken out either to purchase land or to fund any subsequent construction or development work carried out on the land. The author considers that the section applies not only to the loan principal but also accrued interest which has not been paid.

The provision applies in respect of any 'specified debts' which are released on or after 13 February 2013. Therefore any 'specified debts' which were released before this date do not come within the scope of this provision. For the purposes of this new provision, the release of the whole or any part of a specified debt will be treated as having been effected on the *earliest* of the following dates, TCA 1997, s 87B(4):

(a) the date when the lender has confirmed that release to the borrower;

(b) the date on which the lender and borrower either formally or informally agree that the debt or part of the debt is no longer required to be paid;

(c) where the original loan agreement provided for a future release or non-collection of the debt or part of the debt, the date when the conditions necessary for that release or non-collection are first satisfied; for example in the case of a limited recourse or non-recourse loan, or

(d) in a case where the release or write off is as a result of:

   (i) a discharge from bankruptcy, or

   (ii) a discharge from debt under the provisions of the Personal Insolvency Act 2012,

   the date of that discharge.

The Revenue has confirmed in its *Revenue Operational Manual*, Pt 4.6.22 that in practice, they will accept the date of final distribution in the case of a bankruptcy as being the date of release, where this falls after the date of discharge.

In view of the above, it will be important to document any future debt releases with the relevant lender from the point of view of determining the relevant accounts basis period in which the debt release is to be recognised for income tax purposes.

The new legislation also caters for a situation where any debt releases or write offs are agreed in a subsequent year of assessment following a permanent discontinuance of the relevant specified trade. In this scenario, the amount of the debt released will be treated as a sum received after the discontinuance of the trade and is taxed in accordance with TCA 1997, s 91 as a post cessation receipt arising after the discontinuance of the trade. Under this section, where any trade has been permanently discontinued, tax is charged under Case IV of Sch D in respect of any sums to which TCA 1997, s 91 applies, subject to the normal Case I deductions (including capital allowances) that would have been received had the trade not been permanently discontinued.

It is difficult to predict the impact of the above section as each individual land dealer or developer will have their own particular fact pattern and circumstances. However, normally, you would expect a corresponding write down in the cost of the trading stock where there is a debt release and therefore any taxable receipt arising as a result of the debt write down should be matched by the loss created by the corresponding write down of the trading stock. It will be of particular relevance to developers who have non-recourse loans as once the land is sold the debt write off will automatically occur, thereby crystallising a taxable trading receipt.

Example 12.318.1

Mr Land Dealer has been carrying on a land dealing trade for the past number of years. In 2006, he purchased a land bank for €10 million which he intended to develop. The purchase was funded by 100% bank borrowings. The site is still reflected in his accounts at its original cost of €10 million. Mr Land Dealer makes up his accounts to 31 December each year. In March 2016, the bank agreed to release €5 million of the original loan on the basis that this represents the current market value of the site.

Mr Land Dealer's net accounting loss for 2016 has been arrived at as follows:

	€	€
Turnover[1]		
Opening Stock	10,000,000	
Purchases	0	
Less: Closing Stock	(5,000,000)	(5,000,000)
Less: Interest	500,000	
Professional fee	20,000	(520,000)
Other income		5,000,000
Net Loss per Accounts		(520,000)

Mr Land Dealer's Sch D Case I Computation:

	€
Net loss per the accounts	(520,000)
Sch D Case I loss	(520,000)

Note:

1 The write off by the bank of €5 million of a loan which was applied by Mr Land Dealer in the purchase of trading stock is treated as a taxable receipt in accordance with s 87B and is therefore not adjusted out of the Schedule D Case I tax computation. In this scenario, there is no overall Case I profit arising as a result of the write down of debt on the basis that Mr Land Dealer makes a corresponding write down of the site in his accounts.

To the extent that the relevant land dealer or land developer has already written down the value of their trading stock in their trading accounts to the lower of cost and net realisable value, a subsequent debt release may result in a taxable receipt for the individual depending on the relevant facts and circumstances. For example, if the individual had written down his trading stock in his accounts in prior basis periods or income tax years of assessment and in the same year made a TCA 1997, s 381 claim to offset the resulting Sch D Case I trading losses against other income, this particular individual is likely to be liable to income tax, PRSI and the Universal Social Charge on the amount of the debt released. In this scenario, the new provision may discourage certain individual land dealers from availing of the personal insolvency options in the Personal Insolvency Act 2012 as any debt written off under such arrangements will be subject to tax. The Revenue have confirmed that in the case of a personal insolvency arrangement and in a bankruptcy situation, any tax liability which may arise under TCA 1997, s 87B will be the responsibility of the taxpayer. Therefore no provision for its payment should be made in agreeing the final Personal Insolvency Arrangement or as part of the bankruptcy proceedings. Where a tax liability arises as a result of either process, it will be up to the taxpayer to discuss appropriate payment arrangements with the Office of the Collector General.

Example 12.318.2

Take the example from **12.318.1** above but assume that Mr Land Dealer had previously written down the cost of the site to €5 million in his accounts in 2011. Mr Land Dealer made a s 381 claim in the same year electing to set off this loss of €5,000,000 against other income.

Mr Land Dealer's accounts for 2016 will now look as follows:

	€	€
Turnover		
Opening Stock	5,000,000	
Purchases	0	
Less: Closing Stock	(5,000,000)	0
Less: Interest	500,000	
Professional fee	20,000	(520,000)
Other income		5,000,000
Net Profit per Accounts		4,480,000

Mr Land Dealer's Sch D Case I Computation for 2016:

	€	€
Net profit per the accounts		4,480,000
Adjusted Sch D Case I profit		4,480,000

However, if any prior write down of the trading stock resulted in the generation of a Schedule D Case I trading loss which was not otherwise used in reducing the relevant individual's Schedule D Case I land dealing profits nor formed part of a prior year TCA 1997, s 381 claim, this trading loss carried forward should be available to reduce any taxable trading profit arising as a result of a future debt release under TCA 1997, s 382. This trading loss should eliminate any income tax or Universal Social Charge liability which would otherwise have arisen on the amount of the debt release. However, as trading losses carried forward are not taken into account in calculating PRSI, the relevant individual will be liable to PRSI in this particular scenario on the amount of the debt release which appears harsh given the underlying commercial position. There is a further complication where the trading losses brought forward arose prior to 2009 and relate to residential development land. In this scenario, TCA 1997, s 644AA(8) only permits taxpayers to utilise these losses on a value basis. Specifically loss relief for residential development land losses which arose prior to 2009 is only given in the form of a tax credit which is calculated by multiplying the relevant loss by 20/100. This tax credit may only be offset against the tax payable on the profits arising in the combined trade in subsequent tax years. This loss relief provision is dealt with in **4.411**.

Example 12.318.3

Take the example from **12.318.2** above but assume that Mr Land Dealer did not make any loss relief claim under s 381 in respect of the Sch D Case I loss which arose in 2011 as a result of the write down of the land bank in his accounts to the lower of cost and net realisable value. This loss is available for carry forward against future taxable profits arising from the same trade (TCA 1997, s 382).

Mr Land Dealer's accounts for 2016:

	€	€
Turnover		
Opening Stock	5,000,000	
Purchases	0	
Less: Closing Stock	5,000,000	0
Less: Interest	500,000	
Professional fee	20,000	(520,000)
Other income		5,000,000
Net Profit per Accounts		4,480,000

Mr Land Dealer's Sch D Case I Computation for 2016:

	€
Net profit per the accounts	4,480,000
Sch D Case I profit	4,480,000
Less:	
Section 382(1) loss relief claim	(4,480,000)
Net Sch D Case I profit/loss	Nil

Note:

1 Mr Land Dealer is entitled to set off his trading loss carried forward from 2011 against his taxable Sch D Case I profit arising in 2016 under s 382(1). Accordingly, Mr Land Dealer will not have to pay any income tax or Universal Social Charge on his 2015 Sch D Case I profit. However, Mr Land Dealer will be required to pay PRSI on his Sch D Case I profit of €179,200 (€4,480,000 x 4%) on the basis that trading losses are not taken into account in calculating PRSI.

It should be noted that this provision is stated as only having application to individuals which presumably also extends to land dealing and developing partnerships in which an individual is a partner(s). However, losses in most land dealing partnerships would have been restricted by TCA 1997, s 1013 and therefore the losses forward should be available to reduce the taxable receipt on a debt write off subject to the comments above. Companies are excluded from the ambit of this specific section.

12.319 Restriction of loss relief

Finance Act 2013, s 18 also introduced a new provision (TCA 1997, s 381A) with the intention of restricting loss relief under TCA 1997, s 381 in specific circumstances for certain individuals carrying on a land dealing or developing trade or business deemed to be a land dealing or developing trade under TCA 1997, s 640(2)(a), such trades being collectively referred to under the new legislation as a 'specified trade'.

Not all land dealers or developers will be caught by this provision. The provision is specifically stated to apply to individuals whose 'aggregate income' for the relevant tax year and the two immediately preceding tax years deriving from the specified trade is less than 50 per cent of the total individual's 'aggregate income' for the same three tax years. The meaning of aggregate income for the purposes of this provision is taken from one of the Universal Social Charge provisions, TCA 1997, s 531AL. In this section, 'aggregate income for the tax year' is defined in relation to an individual and a tax year as meaning the aggregate of the individual's:

(a) relevant emoluments in the tax year; and
(b) relevant income for the tax year.

Both relevant emoluments and relevant income are defined in TCA 1997, s 531AM for the purposes of the Universal Social Charge and are discussed in detail in **3.404**.

While the above exclusion from this section is welcomed, it is assumed that a limited number of land dealers or developers would fall within this exclusion on the basis that many land dealers or developers are currently generating trading losses in the current environment.

The new provision provides for the restriction of a claim under TCA 1997, s 381 where the claim relates to a 'specified loss' as defined and the specified loss does not satisfy certain criteria. The effect of this provision is to disallow certain specified losses from being available for offset against other sources of income.

The term 'specified loss' is defined in TCA 1997, s 381A, as meaning any loss sustained in the course of the specified trade, which is referable to a deduction allowed in computing the profits or gains of the trade, in respect of either or both:

(a) Interest on borrowed money employed in the purchase or development of land which is held as trading stock (within the meaning of TCA 1997, s 89) of the trade, and
(b) Any reduction in the value of land held as trading stock (within the meaning of TCA 1997, s 89).

TCA 1997, s 381A(2) sets out two scenarios in which a 'specified loss' will be restricted in making a TCA 1997, s 381 claim as follows:

1 Where the land dealing or developing loss is attributable to a deduction allowed for interest on borrowed money employed in the purchase or development of land held as trading stock as defined in TCA 1997, s 89, where such interest has not been paid *prior to the claim being made*. In order to make a valid claim under TCA 1997, s 381, the claim must be made no later than two years after the end of the year of assessment, TCA 1997, s 381(6).

For example, where a land dealing loss arises in the 2015 year of assessment, and part of the loss consists of a tax deduction taken for interest on a loan drawn down to purchase trading stock, this interest must be paid by 31 December 2017 for a valid TCA 1997, s 381 claim to be made for the 2015 income tax year of assessment.

Accordingly in this scenario, any claims under TCA 1997, s 381 would need to be delayed until such time the interest is paid subject to the time limit described above.

2 A claim will similarly be restricted where the loss is in respect of a reduction in the value of land, unless the loss has been realised by way of a disposal of the land prior to the claim being made.

It follows that any write downs of land held as trading stock in accordance with standard accounting principles will not be allowed to form part of the relevant claim. The land in question will need to be disposed of to an unconnected party in order to generate an allowable loss for the purposes of claiming this particular loss relief as TCA 1997, s 381A(3) excludes any disposals of the land to connected persons within the meaning of TCA 1997, s 10.

TCA 1997, s 381A(4) and (5) set out specific computational rules which need to be taken into account in the application of this section.

Firstly, in determining the amount of any interest which has been paid and which is referable to a 'specified loss' sustained in any particular tax year, the interest is to be treated as having been paid in respect of an earlier tax year in preference to a later tax year.

Secondly, in determining the amount of a 'specified loss' sustained in any particular tax year which is referable to a deduction allowed in respect of either interest or a reduction in land value, the following rules should be taken into account:

(a) the deduction allowed in respect of interest is treated as being deducted after all other deductions, and

(b) the deduction allowed in respect of a reduction in the value of land is treated as being deducted immediately prior to the deduction allowed in respect of interest.

This new section is deemed to take effect in respect of any interest becoming payable or a reduction in land value which occurs on or after 13 February 2013. Therefore any reduction in land values which occurred prior to this date should not be affected by this section although presumably such reductions in land value will need to be reflected in prior year trading accounts or proven by the taxpayer (by way of written independent valuation) to have occurred within the period from 1 January 2013 to 12 February 2013. In the former scenario, the amendment of prior year accounts to reflect a reduction in land value will only be of benefit to the taxpayer in the context of making a TCA 1997, s 381 claim if the relevant time limit for making the claim can still be satisfied, ie within two years of the relevant year of assessment affected. The onus of proof will also be on the individual taxpayer to support the basis for amending prior year accounts to reflect a reduction in land value whether this be by way of independent valuation report or otherwise.

It should be noted that to the extent the above provision applies to an individual, such losses which are disallowed for the purposes of the TCA 1997, s 381 claim, will still be available to carry forward against any future profits arising from the same trade under TCA 1997, s 382.

12.4 Mining Rents and Other Matters

12.401 Rents from mining, quarrying, dock undertakings etc

TCA 1997, s 104 charges tax under Sch D Case IV on rents, tolls, duties royalties and annual or periodical payments in the nature of rent received in respect of premises or easements used, occupied or enjoyed in connection with any of the types of concern enumerated in Sch D Case I (b) (TCA 1997, s 18(2) (see **4.101**)). In effect the charge covers any payment received in return for rights to work or use the land concerned or any element thereof. The concerns in question are those which derive profits or gains arising out of lands, tenements and hereditaments which are taxable under Sch D Case I (b) in respect of any of the activities enumerated in that Case, including:

> quarries of stone, slate, limestone, etc, mines of coal, tin, lead, copper, etc, ironworks, gasworks, waterworks, docks, canals, inland navigations and other concerns of a like nature having profits from or arising out of any lands, tenements or hereditaments.

These rents, royalties, etc have been referred to elsewhere for short as 'mining, etc rents' (see **2.302** – where it was indicated that they are included among the types of payment subject to deduction of income tax at source). They are the sole exception to the normal rule that all rents and receipts from easements from lands, tenements and hereditaments in the State are taxable under Sch D Case V. The charge to tax under Sch D Case IV in respect of these mining, etc rents is, therefore, relevant where the owner of the lands, etc in question derives a rent, royalty or any yearly interest, annuity, or other annual payment for allowing the lands to be used for mining, quarrying, inland waterways, docks, etc. On the meaning of the term 'easement' see *Stratford v Mole* 24 TC 20 and *Duke of Fife's Trustees v George Wimpey & Co* 22 ATC 275.

Although chargeable under Sch D Case IV, the recipient of these mining, etc rents normally receives them as taxed income and they are dealt with as such in his income tax (or corporation tax) computations. They are always taxable on a current year basis, ie in the tax year in which they are receivable. However, any rent in respect of the premises or easements in question that is paid in kind, ie in produce of the concern in question (eg in limestone quarried) is taxed under Sch D Case IV on its market value as it is outside the scope of the rules for deduction of tax at source.

12.402 Expenses allowance for mineral rights

TCA 1997, s 111(1) entitles the person owning rights to work minerals in the State, who derives rents or royalties from leasing or otherwise allowing another person to work those minerals, to claim a deduction for expenses which he (the lessor) incurs wholly, exclusively and necessarily in managing or supervising the minerals. This allowance for those expenses is one made by repayment of the tax which the lessor has paid or suffered in respect of the rent or royalties in question. The allowance is given for the expenses incurred in the relevant tax year against the actual rents or royalties receivable in that year.

No repayment of tax is, however, made under this section:

(a) unless the lessor proves that he has actually paid tax on the aggregate amount of the rent or royalties receivable in the tax year or accounting period; or

(b) if, and to the extent that, the said expenses have in any other way been allowed to the lessor as a deduction in computing his income for purposes of income tax.

The lessor must specifically claim this allowance by giving notice in writing to the inspector within 24 months of the end of the relevant tax year. The normal rights of appeal to the Appeal Commissioners etc are open to the lessor if the inspector objects to his claim under this section.

12.403 Capital sums for sale of scheduled mineral assets

TCA 1997, s 683 charges tax under Sch D Case IV on any person who realises a capital sum as the whole or part of the net proceeds of sale of any scheduled mineral asset. A 'scheduled mineral asset' is defined as either a deposit of scheduled minerals, land comprising such a deposit or an interest in or right over such a deposit or land. 'Scheduled minerals' are defined as:

> barytes, felspar, serpentinous marble, quartz rock, soapstone, and ores of copper, gold, iron, lead, manganese, molybdenum, silver, sulphur and zinc. (TCA 1997, s 672(1) Table).

TCA 1997, s 672(3) provides that the Minister for Finance may lay regulations before the Dáil, adding minerals occurring in non-bedded deposits of such minerals to the table.

The amount chargeable under Sch D Case IV (the taxable amount) in respect of the sale of any scheduled mineral asset is the amount of the capital sum that comprises the consideration for the sale (or part of such consideration if the sale is only partly for a capital sum), *reduced by* the amount of any capital sum previously paid by the vendor on his acquisition of the scheduled mineral asset. Any part of the consideration for the sale consisting of a royalty or similar payment that is already taxable as income is excluded from the computation. The same applies to deny the deduction of any part of the vendor's previous acquisition cost that consisted of a royalty.

TCA 1997, s 683 charges to tax under the same rules any capital sum received in consideration (or as part of the consideration) for the grant of a licence to work scheduled minerals (TCA 1997, s 683(1)). In other words, the granting of a licence by the holder of rights to work scheduled minerals is treated as a sale of part of his rights if, but only if, a capital sum, is included in the consideration received. If the only consideration for the licence is a royalty, the provision has no application.

The rules for taxing capital sums in respect of the sale of scheduled mineral assets (or for the grant of a licence to work scheduled minerals) are similar to those applicable for the sale of patent rights (or for the licensing of patents) already discussed in **8.303** (resident vendor) and **8.304** (non-resident vendor). However, TCA 1997, s 683(2) provides that the vendor is assessable in respect of the capital sum for the year of assessment in which he receives the sum. If the person chargeable is an individual (but not otherwise) he is entitled to elect to have the amount on which he is chargeable spread equally over the tax year in which the sum is received and each of the next five tax years.

An individual who wishes to make this election must do so in writing no later than 24 months after the end of the tax year in which the sum is paid. A company chargeable to corporation tax has no right to make this election.

A non-resident vendor of the scheduled mineral asset is also chargeable under Sch D Case IV, but the person paying the capital sum to him is required to deduct Irish income tax at the standard rate and to account to the Revenue Commissioners under TCA 1997, s 238 for the tax deducted. On making any necessary returns to the inspector of taxes, the non-resident vendor is entitled to have his liability in respect of the capital sum adjusted to allow the deduction as an expense for any capital sum previously paid by him on his acquisition of the asset. If he is an individual, the non-resident vendor may make the same election as a resident individual to have his liability under TCA 1997, s 683 spread over six years of assessment.

12.404 Allowances for mining development, exploration etc

The subject of capital allowances was dealt with in **Division 6**. One other type of capital allowance, that is available for certain mining development, exploration, etc expenditure and for mineral depletion, has not been considered elsewhere in this work. Although these allowances are only given to persons carrying on the trade of working mines (taxable under Schedule D Case I), it is not entirely inappropriate to deal with them in this Division which is concerned with the taxation of income from land. While persons carrying on mining activities are almost invariably companies, the subject is probably one more appropriate for a book on corporation tax, but – for the sake of completeness – it is dealt with, albeit fairly briefly, in the following paragraphs. For a comprehensive review of the tax regime for mining operations see A Crawford, 'Mining Taxation' IOT Seminar, May 1997.

There are two sets of provisions to consider. First, TCA 1997, s 670 provides for a mining development allowance to any person (whether chargeable to income tax or corporation tax) who is carrying on the trade of working a mine and who has incurred capital expenditure in the development of that mine and on the construction of certain works for the purpose of that mining operation. Secondly, TCA 1997, ss 672–682 provide capital allowances for mining development expenditure and for exploration expenditure, as well as certain other allowances, to a person carrying on the trade of working a 'qualifying mine' (see below). The latter rules for these qualifying mine development and exploration allowances are more generous and, as they cover most (if not all) of the types of mining currently carried on in the State, it is proposed to concentrate on them.

A 'qualifying mine' is defined as a mine that is being worked for the purpose of obtaining scheduled minerals. The types of minerals treated as 'scheduled minerals' are those set out in TCA 1997, s 672(1) Table (see **12.403**). Other important definitions are:

'Development expenditure', is defined in TCA 1997, s 672(1) as meaning capital expenditure:

(a) on the development of a qualifying mine; or

(b) on the construction of any works in connection with a qualifying mine which are of a nature that, when the mine ceases to be operated, they are likely to have little or no value;

and includes interest on money borrowed to meet such capital expenditure, but does not include any expenditure on the acquisition of the site of the mine or of rights in or over the site, and excludes also any expenditure on acquiring any scheduled mineral asset.

'Exploration expenditure' means capital expenditure on searching in the State for deposits of scheduled minerals, on testing such deposits, or on winning access to them, but does not include either expenditure on operations in the course of working a qualifying mine or any development expenditure.

The main allowances given by TCA 1997, ss 672–682 are now discussed under the following headings:

Development expenditure allowance

A person carrying on the trade of working a qualifying mine is entitled by TCA 1997, s 673(1) to claim a mine development allowance in respect of development expenditure incurred after 5 April 1974. The allowance is given in taxing the profits of the trade of working that mine for the chargeable period in which the expenditure is incurred or, if it was incurred before the trade commenced, it is given as if the expenditure had been incurred on the day the trade commenced. On the assumption that the person entitled to the allowance is a company chargeable to corporation tax, this means that the allowance is given for the company's accounting period in which the expenditure was incurred or, if later, in the accounting period in which the trade commenced.

The amount of the allowance for development expenditure given in the relevant chargeable period is equal to the total amount of the development expenditure *as reduced by* the amount which, in the opinion of the inspector, the assets representing that expenditure are likely to be worth at the end of the estimated life of the qualifying mine. In order to obtain this allowance, the person working the qualifying mine must make an application for the allowance under the rules of TCA 1997, s 670, which has to be made to the inspector no later than 24 months after the end of the chargeable period for which it is claimed.

Exploration allowance

A person carrying on the trade of working a qualifying mine is also entitled by TCA 1997, s 673(1) to claim a mine development allowance under TCA 1997, s 670 equal to the full amount of the exploration expenditure incurred. This allowance may be claimed whether or not a deposit of scheduled minerals is found as a result of the exploration expenditure in question. There is, however, an exception to this. No mine development allowance can be claimed for any unsuccessful exploration expenditure that was incurred prior to 1 April 1990 and more than 10 years before the person concerned commenced to carry on the trade of working a qualifying mine.

The mine development allowance in respect of the exploration expenditure is given for the chargeable period in which the expenditure is incurred or, if the person claiming the allowance does not commence his trade of working a qualifying mine until later, the allowance is given for the chargeable period in which that trade is commenced. Again, the allowance is obtained by an application to the inspector no later than 24 months after the end of the relevant chargeable period. The allowance is given in taxing the trade of working the qualifying mine. If the profits of the trade for the relevant chargeable period are insufficient to absorb the allowance fully, any unused part of the allowance is carried forward and treated as a mine development allowance for the next chargeable period, and so on.

The same carry forward rule applies to any part of the allowance given for mining development expenditure that cannot be used in the relevant chargeable period.

Exploration investment allowance

A person carrying on the trade of working a qualifying mine is entitled to an investment allowance, in addition to its mine development allowance, in respect of exploration expenditure incurred by it prior to 1 January 2011. This allowance is of an amount equal to 20 per cent of the relevant exploration expenditure (TCA 1997, s 677(1)). The relevant exploration expenditure is that on which the mine development allowance has been claimed within the above 24-month time limit; the investment allowance is given for the same chargeable period as that for which the mine development allowance is available.

The addition of the investment allowance to the mine development allowance (100 per cent) on the exploration expenditure gives the person working the qualifying mine a total allowance equal to 120 per cent of the exploration expenditure for the same chargeable period. Any part of the total allowance unused in that year is available for carry forward for set off against future taxable profits from the qualifying mine. It is to be noted, however, that there is no investment allowance in respect of development expenditure (so that the write off of the costs of developing the mine cannot exceed 100 per cent).

Abortive exploration expenditure

A person carrying on the trade of working a qualifying mine is entitled by TCA 1997, s 674 to an allowance for exploration expenditure incurred otherwise than in connection with that qualifying mine but no account is taken of expenditure incurred before 1 April 1990 if that expenditure was incurred more than 10 years before the person commenced to carry on that trade. The rationale for this allowance is that it may well be necessary for a person intending to carry on mining operations to carry out exploration which may prove to be abortive before there is success in finding suitable mineral deposits. In any such case, but subject to one qualification, the person who incurred the abortive exploration expenditure within that 10-year period is entitled to an allowance equal to the total of such abortive expenditure in that period. This 100 per cent allowance is given for the chargeable period in which he commences to carry on the trade of working the qualifying mine.

The right to this allowance is, however, restricted to exclude any case where the person commencing to carry on the trade of working the qualifying mine has not itself incurred the exploration expenditure in connection with that mine. In other words, for the abortive exploration allowance to be given, it is in effect an essential prerequisite that the person in question should have also had successful exploration expenditure resulting in the discovery of the mineral deposits for the qualifying mine.

Mining depletion allowance

A person carrying on the trade of working a qualifying mine is entitled by TCA 1997, s 680 to an annual allowance for capital expenditure incurred on the acquisition of a scheduled mineral asset which gives it the right to work deposits of scheduled minerals. The allowance is only given if the person who incurred the acquisition expenditure actually commences to work the mineral deposits in connection with its trade. Where the person incurred the expenditure before the trade commenced, he will be deemed to incur the expenditure on the first day of trading (TCA 1997, s 680(2)).

This allowance, referred to as the mineral depletion allowance, is given under the rules of TCA 1997, s 670 relating to the mine development allowance. The inspector is required to estimate to the best of his judgement the estimated life of the mineral deposits but this estimated life cannot exceed 20 years. He is then required to estimate also the likely residual value of the mineral deposits at the end of this estimated life. The mineral depletion allowance for each chargeable period during the estimated life of the deposits is computed as the appropriate proportion (on a time basis) of the excess of the acquisition cost of the scheduled minerals over their estimated residual value at the end of the estimated life.

For the purpose of this allowance, a 'scheduled mineral asset' is defined as a deposit of scheduled minerals or land comprising such a deposit or any interest in or right over such deposit or land. The interest acquired in the mineral deposits by the person claiming the allowance must, of course, be one which entitles him to work the mineral deposits.

Unlike the case for most assets in respect of which capital allowances are given there is no requirement to calculate a balancing charge if the scheduled mineral assets are subsequently sold for more than their tax written down value, but no balancing allowance can be claimed if they are sold for less. The rules requiring tax to be charged under Schedule D Case IV on the sale of the assets for a capital sum in excess of their acquisition cost (unaffected by any mining depletion allowances previously obtained) has been discussed in **12.403**. In computing the amount of the capital sum taxable on such a sale, no deduction is allowed for any part of any mine development or exploration expenditure.

Sale of assets representing exploration

TCA 1997, s 676 applies to enable a purchaser of assets representing exploration expenditure incurred by another person to a capital allowance in respect of the other person's expenditure, but only if the following conditions are met:

(a) the other person (the prospector) incurred exploration expenditure which resulted in the finding of a deposit of scheduled minerals;

(b) the prospector sells any assets representing that expenditure without having carried on a trade consisting of or including the working of *that* deposit;

(c) the purchaser carries on a trade consisting of or including the working of that deposit; and

(d) the working of the deposit in question results in the production of scheduled minerals in reasonable commercial quantities.

If these four conditions are all met, the person carrying on the trade of working the qualifying mine (including the deposits purchased) is given a mine development allowance equal to 100 per cent of the exploration expenditure incurred by the prospector or, if it is lower, of the price paid to the prospector for the assets in question. The additional exploration investment allowance under TCA 1997, s 677 is not however, given.

Mining machinery and plant

TCA 1997, s 678 gives a 20 per cent investment allowance for capital expenditure incurred on new machinery or new plant for the purposes of a trade of working a qualifying mine incurred prior to 1 January 2011. This allowance, enabling a 120 per cent write off of the qualifying expenditure, is given in addition to the ordinary capital allowances for machinery and plant (wear and tear, etc). It is only given if the person carrying on the trade incurs the expenditure himself, ie it is not available for leased plant. Further, no investment allowance may be claimed for private motor cars, commercial or other road vehicles.

Rehabilitation of mines

TCA 1997, s 681 provides for an allowance in respect of expenditure incurred on the rehabilitation of a qualifying mine following the closure of the mine. A qualifying mine is one being worked for the purpose of obtaining scheduled minerals (within the meaning of TCA 1997, s 672), dolomite, dolomitic limestone, calcite and gypsum, or (with effect from 6 April 1998) fireclay or coal.

Where such rehabilitation expenditure is incurred after the cessation of trade in the working of a mine, it is treated as if it were incurred at the date of cessation. Accordingly an allowance may be made for that period.

Where a company is obliged to make a contribution to a mine rehabilitation fund under the terms of a license, the aggregate amount of those payments will be allowed over the estimated life of the mine. This is subject to the condition that cumulative allowances at any time may not exceed the total of payments made at or before that date, to the fund.

Payments by the fund holders to a person for the purpose of a rehabilitation of the mine are treated as taxable income of that person, but the actual expenditure on rehabilitation of the mine will be allowed for tax purposes in the manner set out above.

Division 13 Foreign Aspects

13.1 Foreign Possessions and Securities

13.101 Introduction

The territorial limits of Irish income taxation have been referred to in **1.501** – namely, for tax to be charged on that income there must generally either be a person resident in the State who can be charged or, if the person entitled to (or in receipt of) the income is not so resident, the income must arise from a source situated in the State. An individual who is not resident but who is *ordinarily* resident in the State remains liable in respect of foreign income, but excluding:

(a) income from a trade, profession, office or employment carried on wholly outside the State; and
(b) foreign investment income not exceeding €3,810 pa (see **13.504**).

This Division deals with the main foreign aspects of the Irish income tax system under two main headings, respectively the taxation of resident persons on income from foreign possessions and securities and the liability of non-resident persons to Irish tax on Irish source income. The treatment in this chapter of these two main aspects is largely confined to the rules as they stand under domestic tax law, ie before considering any modifications which may be imposed by the terms of double taxation agreements with other countries. The effects of double taxation agreements are dealt with separately in **Division 14**.

The first issue addressed in this chapter is the distinction between foreign source and domestic source income in respect of the different types of income. This distinction is important from several points of view. Firstly, if the source of the income is regarded as foreign, it is always assessable under Sch D Case III, irrespective of whether it arises from a trade, profession, office, employment, rented properties, patent royalties or any other source. Secondly, in the case of non-domiciled individuals, foreign income is taxable on the remittance basis.

Finally, if the income is from a foreign source, it is not chargeable at all to Irish tax if received by a person who is not resident in the State (subject to the position regarding non-resident but ordinarily resident individuals noted above).

13.102 Foreign income charged under Sch D Case III

Sch D Case III charges income tax, *inter alia*, on income arising from securities outside the State (unless charged under Sch C) and income arising from possessions outside the State (see also **8.101**). Based on the wording in the Sch to the Act of 1799 which imposed income tax in Great Britain, it is usual to refer to the income taxed by this provision as being income from foreign possessions and foreign securities. In determining the income on which income tax may be imposed by this rule, it is necessary to consider the meaning of the terms 'possession' and 'security'. They are not given any special definition in the Income Tax Acts, but their respective meanings have been the subject of various judgments in the courts over the years.

In one of the most frequently quoted passages on the subject, Lord Macnaghten in his judgment in *Colquhoun v Brooks* 2 TC 490 said:

> … I am, therefore, forced to the conclusion that in the expression 'foreign possession' as used in the Act of 1799 the word 'possession' is to be taken in the widest sense possible as denoting everything that a person has as a source of income.

He went on to hold that a taxpayer resident in England was liable to UK income tax in respect of his share of profits in a Melbourne firm in which he was a partner and which was engaged in a trade carried on entirely outside the UK. This case is established authority for the principle that a foreign trade is a foreign possession, as well as providing this very clear meaning of 'possession'.

It was observed in *Singer v Williams* 7 TC 419 that, broadly, a *foreign security* is a debt or claim outside the State which is in some way secured or which gives the taxpayer a right to resort to some fund or property situated outside the State. Examples of foreign securities might be a loan note or other instrument evidencing a debt that is secured on property situated in another country or a foreign government stock which entitles the holder (ultimately) to resort to the funds of that government for payment.

It is probably no longer necessary to focus much attention on the meaning of the word 'security' in this connection since it is accepted that a foreign security is just one class of foreign possession. At one time, there were certain differences in the tax treatment of foreign securities and of foreign possessions, but this is no longer the case and the distinction has ceased to have any relevance.

In short, the income from foreign securities and possessions charged under Sch D Case III includes the annual profits or gains arising from any kind of property whatsoever, including trades, professions, offices, employments located outside Ireland, ie from everything the person possesses that is a source of income, other than a source situated within the State. The principles governing the classification of the various sources of income as Irish or foreign are discussed in the remaining sections of this division.

The question of whether any particular income is from an Irish or a foreign source is important for an individual who is neither resident nor ordinarily resident in the State since, unless it is from an Irish source, it is not normally assessable to Irish tax on him under any Case or Sch. For an individual who is ordinarily resident, but not resident in the State, there is the possibility of avoiding Irish taxation on non-Irish sources which fall within the exclusions noted above.

TCA 1997, s 71(1) charges tax on the full amount of the income arising to a resident person from all his foreign securities and possessions, whether the income has been or will be received in the State or not. In other words, it is normally of no consequence whether the resident person remits any or all of his foreign source income back to the State as it arises, or in a later year, or simply spends or invests it all abroad. This general principle is subject to the exception that a person not domiciled in the State may claim to be taxed only on remittances into the State of non-Irish income otherwise taxable under Sch D Case III. From 1 January 2006, earnings from foreign-source employments are charged under Sch E to the extent that they are attributable to the performance of duties in the State; this in effect generally denies the possibility of the remittance basis to such earnings. Prior to 1 January 2008, the remittance basis was not available in respect of UK income.

From 2009 onwards a restricted form of the remittance basis was introduced in certain limited cases to individuals with foreign employments entailing Irish duties. (TCA 1997, s 825B as inserted by F(No 2)A 2008). However, this section ceased to apply for the tax year 2012 and subsequent tax years unless the relevant employee had an entitlement to the relief for tax years 2009, 2010 or 2011 in which case the relevant employee can continue to claim the relief for a maximum of five years from the first year of claim. From 2012, there is a new Special Assignee Relief Programme that is available which replaces the above regime. A more detailed analysis of both regimes is provided in **10.115** and **10.116** of this book.

TCA 1997, s 1004 empowers the Revenue Commissioners, if satisfied that any particular foreign source income cannot, by reason of legislation in the country in which it arises or of executive action of the government of that country, be remitted to the State, to exclude the amount of that income from the taxpayer's income tax assessment. The onus is placed on the taxpayer of proving to the Revenue Commissioners that the income is unremittable for the reasons stated. The Revenue Commissioners may call for such information as they consider necessary to come to their decision on the matter. If dissatisfied with their decision, the taxpayer has the right of appeal to the Appeal Commissioners with the same rights to a rehearing by the Circuit Court judge, etc as if he were appealing against an assessment to tax. F(TA)A 2015, s 39, which was subject to Ministerial Order (SI 110/2016 appointed 21 March 2016 as the day on which the Finance (Tax Appeals) Act 2015, came into operation), removes the right of a rehearing to the Circuit Court and the references in that section to an appeal to the High Court.

Before the unremittable income can be excluded under this rule, it is necessary that there first be an assessment to tax for the relevant year of assessment and the tax assessed on the unremittable income has not been paid. If, after foreign income has been excluded from any assessment under this rule, the Revenue Commissioners cease to be satisfied that the particular income cannot be remitted, the income in question must be reinstated in the assessment and the additional tax now due becomes payable. It is the assessment for the year of assessment for which the income would have been taxable normally in the absence of the TCA 1997, s 1004 exclusion that has to be amended, even if the foreign income only becomes remittable in a later year.

In the ordinary way, income arises in the State if the source of the income is situated in the land area of the State or in its territorial waters. However, TCA 1997, s 13 treats as domestic source income any profits or gains from exploration or exploitation activities on the Irish section of the continental shelf outside Irish territorial waters. It also treats a person performing the duties of an office or employment on that part of the continental shelf as if he had performed those duties in the State so that, if the resulting emoluments are paid wholly or partly within the State, the emoluments are taxable under Sch E (and not under Sch D Case III).

These rules relating to continental shelf activities are relevant mainly to the taxation of non-residents – since a resident person is taxable on the income therefrom in any event – and are discussed further in **13.605** (trades) and **13.607** (employments).

13.103 Foreign trades and professions

For a trade or profession carried on by a resident person to be classified as a foreign trade or profession so as to be taxable under Sch D Case III, it must be carried on wholly outside the State. A trade (or profession) carried on wholly within, or partly within and partly outside the State, is not a foreign possession so that any profits or gains arising from it are assessable under Sch D Case I or Case II, and not under Sch D Case III. It is the Revenue Commissioner's view that professions are always taxable under Case II and that it is not possible to have a Case III profession (refer Revenue *eBrief No 06/14*). The author does not agree with this interpretation. It is the author's view that it is possible to have a Case III profession where it can be demonstrated that it is carried on wholly outside the State. The practicalities of ensuring that the profession is carried on wholly outside the State will be difficult to manage when you factor in the use of mobile phones and emails but it is still possible.

It might at first sight be thought that the charging words of Sch D Case I in TCA 1997, s 18(2) referring to 'any trade' would be sufficient to bring a foreign trade within Sch D Case I. However, it was held by the House of Lords in *Colquhoun v Brooks* (see also **13.101**) that, as stated by Lord Macnaghten in 2 TC 490 at page 508:

> there are other provisions which it is not necessary to go through which seem to show that the 'first case' (Case I), though clearly applying to a trade carried on partly abroad and partly in Great Britain, was not intended to apply to a trade carried on exclusively abroad.

This principle that a trade carried on wholly abroad is a foreign possession giving rise to taxation under Sch D Case III, whereas a trade carried on at least partly within the State is taxable under Sch D Case I, has always been accepted and applied by the Revenue Commissioners. These circumstances in which a trade (or profession) is regarded as being carried on wholly outside the State require consideration. Clearly, any resident individual, partnership or company which carries on its main business within the country, but which has one or more foreign branches, is taxable under Sch D Case I (and not Sch D Case III) on the profits of its foreign branches. Not all cases may be so clear cut and it is necessary to examine the matter further.

A useful review of the principles involved is contained in several of the judgments of the House of Lords in *The Egyptian Hotels Ltd v Mitchell* 6 TC 542. Lord Parker said:

> … in considering whether the principle of *Colquhoun v Brooks* applies to any particular circumstances it is also necessary to bear in mind your Lordships' decision in the case of *The San Paulo (Brazilian) Railway Company Ltd v Carter 3* TC 407 to the effect that a trade or business cannot be said to be wholly carried on abroad if it be under the control and management of persons resident in the United Kingdom although such persons act wholly through agents and managers resident abroad. Where the brain which controls the operations from which the profits and gains arise is in this country, the trade or business is, at any rate partly, carried on in this country.

Lord Sumner said in the same case:

> … where a resident in the United Kingdom is proprietor of a profit earning business wholly situated and carried on abroad he is chargeable to income tax under [Case III] of Sch D, if he takes no part in earning those profits, and if he takes any part is chargeable under Sch D Case I. This is true whether the proprietor is a natural or an incorporated person; whether he takes part in earning the profits in his own person or only by agents or servants.

Applying these principles to Irish tax, it may generally be taken that a trade or profession that is under the management and control of a proprietor who is resident in the State, or one in the management of which that proprietor takes an active part, is not one carried on wholly outside the State, irrespective of where the actual operations take place. The reason for the decision in *Colquhoun v Brooks* that the taxpayer's income arose from a foreign possession was that the UK resident partner did not in fact take any part in the management of the business of the Australian firm.

In another case, *Ogilvie v Kitton* 5 TC 338, a warehousing business in Canada was held not to be carried on wholly abroad where the UK sole proprietor regularly exercised a general oversight of the business which was otherwise carried on entirely by managers in Toronto on his behalf. The fact that he did not actually intervene in the running of the business so long as everything went smoothly was not considered sufficient to upset this conclusion.

In *Executors and Trustees of AC Ferguson (deceased) v Donovan* I ITR 183, the taxpayers were trustees (three of whom resided in the State and two of whom resided in England) holding the legal interest in an Australian farming business. They had delegated all powers of management of the farm by power of attorney to Australian residents. The Supreme Court held, following *Egyptian Hotels v Mitchell*, that the trade was not carried on in either Ireland or England, but in Australia. *Ogilvie v Kitton* was distinguished on the basis that in the former case the taxpayer had executed oversight of the trade, albeit this was passive in nature. In the *Ferguson* case, the taxpayers did not even have the legal right to intervene in the running of the business.

Some caution should, however, be exercised before drawing the conclusion that control or management by a resident person of trading operations carried on outside the State means that there can never be a foreign trade taxable as a foreign possession under Sch D Case III. If the resident person, whether an individual, or a company acting through its board of directors, takes part in the actual management or running of the trading operations from his 'seat' within the State, then the conclusion that there is a trade taxable under Sch D Case I (and not Sch D Case III) normally holds good.

However, the facts of each particular case must be examined. If, for example, an individual whose home is in Donegal in the State owns a retail business in Derry in Northern Ireland (say about 20 miles away), and if he travels each day to manage and run that business entirely from his office in Derry, it would probably be accepted that he is carrying on that business wholly outside the State, so that its profits are taxable under Sch D Case III as income from a foreign possession. The same conclusion should be arrived at if we assume the same facts but instead of a retail business it was a GP's practice, ie a profession being exercised wholly in Northern Ireland. In these days of high speed air travel, it is likely that there are other instances of businesses being carried on wholly abroad by individuals resident in the State.

There may also be cases where an individual is resident in the State for tax purposes in a given year of assessment, but may in fact only be physically present there for relatively brief and/or casual periods. If, for example, an individual left the State on 31 December 2014 in order to set up a sole tradership in Ruritania and if he returned to the State for say 32 days during 2015 solely in order to visit family and friends, he might well be resident for 2015 under the rules of TCA 1997, s 819 (see **1.502**). It would seem difficult in such circumstances to sustain an argument that the individual's trade was partly carried on in the State in 2015.

13.104 Foreign offices and employments

In determining the location of an office or employment, different considerations apply depending on whether the source of income is a 'public office or employment of profit' referred to in Sch E para 1 or is any other office or employment, ie one that is not a 'public' office or employment.

Public offices

The emoluments of any public office or employment of profit within the State are taxable under Sch E and the office or employment in question is never a foreign source, even if some or all of the duties of the office are performed outside the State. A list of public offices and employments is provided by TCA 1997, s 19(2) (see **10.103**); the final category is 'all other public offices or employments of profit of a public nature', which is perhaps somewhat question-begging. It is clearly established that the directorship of a company is public in nature; this is because the company and its organs are creations of statute (*McMillan v Guest* 24 TC 190).

The question of the locality of a company directorship was first addressed in the context of similar UK provisions in *McMillan v Guest*. The taxpayer in that case was a director of a limited company resident in the UK, but who exercised no functions as a director in the UK. Lord Atkin (Lord Roche concurring) said:

> The office of director of an English company the head seat and directing power of which is admitted to be in the United Kingdom seems to me of necessity to be located where the company is.

Lord Porter also emphasised that the employing company was resident and managed in the United Kingdom. Lord Wright approved the dictum of Lord Greene MR in the Court of Appeal that the office was held in the United Kingdom, on the basis that:

> Every right which a director has and every duty which the law general or special imposes on the director is to be exercised in the [United Kingdom] and nowhere else.

Lord Greene's conclusions seem to reflect the fact that the *duties* of a director of a UK resident company would necessarily be carried out in the United Kingdom.

In *McMillan v Guest*, Lord Greene had expressly left open the position in relation to the case of a directorship of a United Kingdom non-resident company incorporated in the United Kingdom. Exactly such a case came before the Irish High Court in *Tipping v Jeancard* II ITR 68, where the taxpayer was the director of an Irish company resident in France who carried out no duties in the State. Maguire J approved Lord Wright's citation of Lord Greene's observations in *McMillan v Guest*, but made no reference to the fact that it had been delivered expressly in the context of a UK resident company.

The ratio of *Jeancard* would seem to be best captured in the following passage of Maguire J's speech:

> It is abundantly clear that the office was set up in accordance with Irish law and that it exists under its protection. The directors or any of them were entitled to have recourse to the courts in Ireland to enforce specifically the exercise of their rights and to enable them to discharge their duties. They were entitled to the protection of the courts to maintain them in their office against unlawful ouster or interference. This position remained unaltered during the existence of the company.

The above passage implies that a directorship of a non-Irish incorporated but Irish resident company is not held within the State (it may be noted that Maguire J also commented that the location of a director's office was not the same issue as the residence of a company). However, the Revenue may seek to argue otherwise on the strength of some of the judicial dicta (such as that of Lord Atkin) in *McMillan v Guest*. It is also necessary to bear in mind that TCA 1997, s 112(1) imposes a Sch E charge on persons 'having *or exercising* an office or employment of profit mentioned in' Sch E. In *Tipping v Jeancard*, Maguire J approved the following dictum of Wrottesly J in

Archbishop of Thyateira v Hubert 25 TC 249, commenting on the observations of Lords Atkin and Wright in *McMillan v Guest* on this phrase:

> Both alike lay stress, therefore, on the distinction to be drawn between the office and the officer. Both alike hold the view that the place of exercise does not govern, that is to say it is not necessarily the test. Neither goes so far as to say that the place of exercise must necessarily be excluded. The rule says 'Having or exercising' and a man may have his office in one place and exercise its duties in another.

(In the *Archbishop of Thyateira* case it was in fact held that an archbishop appointed under a decree of the Orthodox Greek Church to a seat in London held an office in the United Kingdom, a decision difficult to reconcile with that in *Jeancard*).

It seems arguable therefore that a public office created under non-Irish law, but the duties of which are carried out in the State, may fall within Sch E. In *Tipping v Jeancard*, Maguire concluded:

> I am of opinion the office of director … was held in Ireland by Mr Jeancard while I am satisfied he never exercised that office here. It is enough to satisfy the requirements of Sch E that he held the office in Ireland.

With effect from 1 January 2006 onwards, the earnings from a *foreign* office held by an Irish resident, to the extent that they are attributable to duties which are performed in the State, are taxable under Sch E from that date (TCA 1997, s 18(2)(f) as inserted by FA 2006). A fuller discussion of the post-1 January 2006 rules are discussed below under *Foreign Employments*.

The position in respect of public employments may, in theory, be different. In *Robinson v Corry* 18 TC 411, it was held that a deputy cashier at a naval base situated outside the United Kingdom held 'a public office or employment'. In *McMillan v Guest* Lord Greene MR expressed the view that it was in fact a mere employment (which seems to be correct, in view of the general definition of an office (see **10.103**). Lord Greene commented that it was not possible to regard an employment as being 'held' anywhere, so that the place of exercise was the solely decisive factor. However, the Revenue Commissioners take the view that generally civil servants remain within Sch E, even when posted outside the State.

General offices and employments

The rules for determining the location of the source of emoluments from all other, ie 'non-public' offices and employments, are different. In explaining these rules, it is proposed to use the single term 'employment' to cover all positions affected by them, whether offices or employments.

The case law relevant in deciding whether the income from any particular employment is taxable under Sch D Case III or Sch E consists in the first instance of a line of UK cases on the subject. However, these case law principles are qualified from 1 January 2006 onwards. From that date, earnings from an employment which constitutes a foreign source are nevertheless taxed under Sch E, to the extent that such earnings (as computed under the Sch E rules) are attributable to duties performed in the State (although this may in fact be arguable in the case of non-resident employees: see **13.607)** (TCA 1997, s 18(2)(f) as inserted by FA 2006).

In *Pickles v Foulsham* 9 TC 261, the emoluments of an agent in West Africa of a British company were assessed to tax as income from a foreign possession. His duties were performed wholly in West Africa, but under his agreement with the company the commission which formed the bulk of his remuneration was payable by the company in the UK. The House of Lords held that the earnings were not income from a foreign possession as the source of income was not wholly abroad. In his judgment, Lord Dunedin (Lord Atkinson concurring) referred to the income coming from the contract of employment made in the UK, which was one factor, but went on to qualify this in the following words:

> When I say 'made in the United Kingdom', I am not referring to the place where the signing of the contract took place. I am referring to the source of the profit, which is the payment which the employers covenanted to make. This was payable and paid in Liverpool.

Lord Buckmaster said:

> The source of his income was the money paid by a [UK] company into a UK bank in pursuance of an agreement for service made in this country.

All the Law Lords placed heavy reliance on the fact that Sch D Case V (Irish Sch D Case III) at that time was assessable on the remittance basis in the hands of *all* taxpayers, ie irrespective of their domicile, etc. This was taken to imply that such income must have been payable abroad in the first instance.

In *Bennett v Marshall* 22 TC 73, which reached the Court of Appeal, the taxpayer was vice-president of a company both incorporated and resident in the US. Part of the taxpayer's duties involved supervising the affairs of a UK subsidiary. His contract had been made in the US and he was also paid from there; at his request, payment was made to his bank account in Canada. The Inland Revenue did not in fact seek to argue that the taxpayer *exercised* a public office within the UK and thus fell within Sch E (however, it is worth noting the comments on Maguire J's approach in this connection in *Tipping v Jeancard*, as discussed above).

Lord Greene in the Court of Appeal indicated that the effect of the decision in *Pickles v Foulsham* was to prescribe the test for ascertaining the source of income, whether from a domestic or foreign source, as being:

> to look for the place where the income really comes to the employee.

He also noted that:

> It is perfectly true that Lord Buckmaster there referred not merely to the UK character of the company but also to the place where the agreement for service was made. I do not regard the mention of these circumstances as involving any difference in views between Lord Buckmaster and Lord Dunedin.

Lord Greene then concluded that the source of the payment was Canada. This conclusion is inconsistent with *Pickles v Foulsham*, which established that the place of the payment and not the place of receipt was critical. In *Bray v Collenbrander* (see below), Lord Morton described this conclusion as a 'slip', and stated that in fact the source of the payment was the United States. In the same case, Romer LJ observed:

> The House of Lords, as it seems to me, in *Pickles v Foulsham* have definitely decided that, in the case of an employment, the locality of the source of income is not the place where the activities of the employee are exercised, but the place either where the contract for payment is deemed to have a locality or where the payments for the employment are made, which may mean the same thing.

In *Bray v Collenbrander*; *Harvey v Breyfogle* 34 TC 138, two cases were heard together in the House of Lords. In the former case, the taxpayer was a journalist based in London, employed by a Dutch company. He was paid in Holland under a contract made there, although he had arranged with his employers that they would remit certain sums to the

UK. In the latter case, the taxpayer was a senior bank official employed by a US company. He was assigned to carry out various special functions in the UK, including monitoring economic and monetary policy developments there. He was paid in the US under a contract which had been made there. The House of Lords held that in both cases the employments constituted 'foreign possessions'.

Lord Nomand, with whom all the other Law Lords agreed, affirmed the reasoning of Sir Wilfred Greene in *Bennett v Marshall*, noting that:

> In the interval between 1938 and 1950 many people must, I should think, have entered into contracts of employment with a tract of future time in the faith that the *place of payment* of their salary was *conclusive* in settling whether they would have to pay non [UK] income tax … (emphasis added).

In the Court of Appeal, it was held that all of the taxpayer's salary in *Bray v Collenbrander* was payable in Holland, notwithstanding that some of it had been subsequently remitted into the UK by the employer. This situation was distinguished from one where the taxpayer was entitled under the terms of his contract to call for payment in the UK. In practice, the payment of a salary out of funds made available to any branch, suboffice or agent in the State will be treated as paid in the State. In *Archbishop of Thyateira v Hubert* (discussed above), the Inland Revenue were prepared to accept that *voluntary* payments made in the UK, but which arose from a foreign office, would not lead to that office losing 'foreign possession' status.

The UK case law therefore provide strong authority that the location of the paypoint is the initial criterion in determining 'foreign possession' status. Nevertheless, a note of caution should be struck, particularly bearing in mind that the UK cases were all concerned with a situation where, apart from the fact that the duties of the employment were carried out in the UK, the contract of employment had no connection with the UK. The Irish courts might therefore regard the judgments in these cases as being too widely stated and as being capable of being distinguished on different sets of facts.

Furthermore, it may be noted that in *Pickles v Foulsham* the court approached the question of the locality of the source in a way that fits uneasily with decisions under other heads (see in particular the remarks of Lord Hailsham in *Westminster Bank Executor & Trustee Co (CI Ltd) v National Bank of Greece* SA 46 TC 491 and compare the approach of the courts to the location of sources of income, discussed at **2.302**, **2.303** and **13.108**).

It appears that in practice the Revenue Commissioners may well challenge the existence of 'foreign possession' status, even in the case of an employment with a foreign paypoint, where the employer is Irish resident, unless *all* of the duties are carried out overseas (see **13.607**). It seems also likely that the Revenue Commissioners would argue similarly that an employment with a UK employer constituted a UK source of income, even if the paypoint was located outside the UK; this would be material prior to 1 January 2008 when UK sources of income were ineligible for the remittance basis.

As noted above, with effect from 1 January 2006, earnings from an employment which constitutes a foreign source are nevertheless taxed under Sch E in the hands of an Irish resident individual to the extent that such earnings (as computed under the Sch E rules) are attributable to duties performed in the State (TCA 1997, s 18(2)(f) as inserted by FA 2006). From 2009 onwards a restricted form of the remittance basis applied in certain limited cases to individuals with foreign employments entailing Irish duties (TCA 1997, s 825B as inserted by F(No 2)A 2008). This restricted form of the remittance basis generally ceased to apply (subject to certain exceptions) with effect from 1 January 2012. Please refer to **10.115** for further details.

The Revenue Commissioners have stated in *e-brief 9/2006* that they will accept that bonuses in relation to foreign-source employments which were earned in respect of periods prior to 1 January 2006 but which were paid after that date are outside the PAYE system (this follows from the fact that Schedule E operates on an earnings basis and that such bonuses are taxable therefore as income of 2005; the principle applies in fact to any earnings which arise prior to 1 January 2006, but which are paid after that date. As discussed in **13.607**, it appears that earnings from a foreign-source employment received by an individual who is non-resident fall outside the scope of Irish taxation on general principles, even if some duties are performed in the State (subject to the provisions of TCA 1997, s 821 in the case of ordinarily resident individuals), although the Revenue Commissioners will undoubtedly challenge this analysis.

Where emoluments arise from a foreign office or employment in the sense outlined above which are not taxable under Sch E, they are received before the deduction of any Irish income tax, since the employer's obligation to deduct income tax under the PAYE procedure does not apply to emoluments taxable under Sch D Case III. Of course, for a non-domiciled but resident individual, non-Irish Sch D Case III earnings will be taxable on the remittance basis.

Where an Irish resident employee has a foreign source employment where part of the related earnings (ie those attributable to duties performed in the State) fall within Schedule E and the remainder fall within Sch D Case III, special rules apply with effect from 1 January 2006 to determine the amount of income subject to PAYE: see **11.102**).

13.105 Foreign benefits in kind

TCA 1997, s 57(1) applies the Sch E expenses payments and benefit in kind rules of TCA 1997, Pt 5 Ch 3 to charge to tax expenses payments made to, or benefits in kind provided for, a person holding a foreign office or employment the emoluments of which are taxable under Sch D Case III. TCA 1997, s 57(1) operates if, in any year of assessment, such a person receives from his employer (or a person connected with the employer) any sum in respect of expenses or derives any benefit which, if he were taxable under Sch E, would be taxable under TCA 1997, Pt 5 Ch 3 (see **10.202, 10.203**).

In any case where TCA 1997, s 57 applies, the amount of income taxable in respect of the expenses payment or benefit in kind is calculated in exactly the same way as if the emoluments of the office or employment were chargeable under Sch E. In the case of payments by the employer to the employee (or director) in respect of expenses, this means that the full amount paid by the employer is taxable as a perquisite of the foreign office or employment, but the employee is entitled to claim an expenses deduction against his foreign emoluments in the same way and to the same extent as he could for an office or employment chargeable under Sch E (see **Division 10**). In other words, only expenses incurred wholly, exclusively and necessarily in the performance of the duties of the foreign office or employment are deductible (with no deduction for business entertainment expenses, etc; see **10.304**).

In the case of a benefit in kind (other than that referable to a 'company car' or preferential loan), the general principle is that the measure of the benefit is the amount of the expense incurred by the employer (or connected person), unless varied by the rules of TCA 1997, s 119 already discussed in the context of Sch E in **10.204** and **10.205**. The foreign benefit in kind assessable is, as with one under Sch E, the gross benefit as reduced by the amount of the employer's cost (if any) that is made good to the employer by the employee.

The net amount of the benefit in kind is then, as is the amount taxable in respect of expenses, included with the other emoluments of the foreign office or employment arising in the period in which the payment in respect of expenses is received or the benefit in kind derived. In other words, it is treated as additional Sch D Case III income assessable according to the Sch D Case III basis of assessment rules, on the current year basis. If the office or employment is a foreign one under a foreign employer, but the expense in providing a benefit in kind is incurred in the State by a person connected with the employer (for example, an Irish subsidiary of a foreign corporation), the benefit remains a foreign benefit taxable under Sch D Case III.

Example 13.105.1

Mr PQ, who is Irish resident and domiciled, is employed by a UK company to work in the UK commencing on 1 April 2016. Mr PQ's remuneration is all paid by the UK company at the rate of €4,445 a month. In addition, the UK company pays him out of the same account a round sum expense allowance of €381 a month.

In addition, on the instruction of the UK company, its Irish subsidiary leases a house in London in which Mr PQ and his family live so long as he is working for the company. In paying Mr PQ's remuneration, the UK company deducts €127 a month which it is agreed he is to contribute towards the cost of leasing the house. Mr PQ pays all the normal tenant's outgoings (other than the lease rent). The lease rent (€794 a month) paid by the Irish subsidiary in the tax year 2016 is accepted as being a proper arm's length rent.

Mr PQ is assessable under Sch D Case III for 2016 as follows:

	€	€
Salary paid by UK company:		
€4,445 x 9		40,005
Expense payments by UK company:		
€381 x 9		3,429
Benefit in kind provided by connected company:		
Lease rent €794 x 9	7,146	
Less:		
Contributed by Mr PQ €127 x 9	(1,143)	
		6,003
Total emoluments		49,437
Less:		
Expenses paid by Mr PQ wholly, exclusively and necessarily in his employment (excluding business entertainment), say		(1,816)
Net emoluments chargeable under Sch D Case III		47,621

TCA 1997, s 57(2) directs that the amount which would be chargeable under Sch E in respect of a benefit '*shall* be charged to tax' under Sch D Case III (emphasis added). It seems unlikely therefore that a taxpayer who is entitled to the remittance basis in respect of his salary could in strictness argue that the remittance basis should be extended to benefits covered by TCA 1997, s 57. Nevertheless, it is likely that in practice, an Inspector would accept that a benefit enjoyed outside the State should not be taxed in the hands of an individual who is entitled to the remittance basis in respect of his salary.

'Company car'

TCA 1997, s 121, discussed in the context of Sch E, at **10.207–10.210**, is stated to apply to any person chargeable to income tax in respect of an office or employment 'such that any emoluments … would be charged to tax' (TCA 1997, s 121(1)(a)). The effect of TCA 1997, s 121(2)(b) is to treat the cash equivalent of the benefit of an 'employer-provided' motor car as an emolument of the individual's employment and accordingly 'chargeable to income tax'. This wording does leave open the question whether the computation of the taxable emolument is subject to the remittance basis in the hands of an individual entitled to that basis. In practice, the inspector would once more usually only be prepared to apply the remittance basis where the motor car was provided outside the State.

Preferential loans

TCA 1997, ss 122 and 122A charge under Sch D Case III any interest benefit (ie any interest paid at less than the 'specified rate') on a preferential loan (under s 122) or a notional loan (under s 122A) obtained by an individual from his employer (or from a connected person) in any case where the emoluments of his office or employment are taxable under Sch D Case III (ie where the office or employment is a foreign one).

Similarly, in the case where the relevant office or employment is a foreign one, TCA 1997, s 122 charges under Sch D Case III any amount written off a loan from the employer (or from a connected person), as well as any amount written off or waived in respect of interest on such a loan. It is open to question whether or not the wording of TCA 1997, s 122 (which is also applied by TCA 1997, s 122A) in fact achieved this intention prior to 1 January 2005 (see the discussion in **10.211**).

13.106 Foreign pensions

In the normal case, pensions are treated as having a foreign source giving rise to taxation under Sch D Case III where they are payable by a person resident outside the State; if payable by a resident person, they are usually assessable under Sch E (and subject to PAYE) as income from a domestic source. The first of these two rules is subject to an important exception if any pension is payable under a pension scheme approved under TCA 1997, Pt 30 Ch 1 established by a non-resident employer. As indicated in **16.110**, TCA 1997, s 779(1) requires strictly that any pension payable under such an approved scheme should be taxed under Sch E irrespective of the residence, place of incorporation, etc of the employer.

A pension need not necessarily arise from a former employment. In *Forbes v Dundon* II ITR 491, a retirement pension paid out of the UK was held to be income from a foreign possession taxable under Sch D Case III. It had been argued on behalf of the taxpayer that his right to a retirement pension was not provided for by any deed, agreement or legal document and that, in consequence, he did not have any foreign possession from which he could derive income taxable in the State.

In his High Court judgment, Kenny J rejected this argument, taking the view that the taxpayer did have a legal right under the UK National Insurance Act 1946 enforceable by proceedings before the Minister or the tribunals established under the Act, the decisions of which could be reviewed by the High Court in England. He went on:

> In my opinion, a legal right to which a person resident in this country is entitled and which is situated outside Ireland and which may be enforced by legal proceedings in a country outside Ireland is either a security or 'a possession' … and income which comes from such

> a right is either income arising from securities in a place out of Ireland or income arising from possessions in a place out of Ireland.

(see also *Aspin v Estell* [1987] STC 723; *Albon v IRC* [1998] STC 1181).

The question of whether a voluntary annual allowance paid by an English company to a former managing director could be taxable as income from a foreign possession arose in *McHugh v A* II ITR 393. It was argued on behalf of the taxpayer that she had no foreign possession as she had no enforceable right to compel the company to pay the allowance if it decided to stop making it. It was held by the High Court that FA 1932, s 4 (now TCA 1997, s 790 – see **10.111**) had the effect of creating a foreign possession in the case of a voluntary pension or allowance to an ex-employee when paid by a foreign company. Teevan J, going back to Lord Macnaghten's words in *Colquhoun v Brooks*, said that 'the word 'possessions' is to be taken in the widest sense possible, as denoting everything that a person has as a source of income', and concluded:

> In my view therefore, for present purposes, 'foreign possession' means a source abroad from which is derived this income of the respondent, non-assessable but for section 4 of the 1932 Act. The monies must have some source and that must be looked to in considering the standard and method of assessment.

The Revenue have stated their view that disability benefits received under US insurance policies are also taxable under Case III. As such benefits do appear to be in the nature of income, this view looks correct.

TCA 1997, s 200(2) provides exemption for foreign pensions or similar benefits which:

(a) are given in respect of past services in an office or employment or which correspond to provisions of Pt 2, Chs 15, 18 or 19 or Pt 3, Chs 4 or 6 of the Social Welfare Consolidation Act 2005;

(b) if they were received by a person who, under the tax laws of the state in which the pension, etc, arises, was regarded as resident there (and not also as resident elsewhere), would be disregarded for income tax purposes.

TCA 1997, s 200(2A), inserted by FA 1998, s 18, disapplies the exemption with effect from 6 April 1998 to a pension to which Art 18 para 1(b) of the 1997 Ireland-US Double Tax Treaty applies (ie a US Social Security pension paid to a resident of Ireland).

13.107 Distributions from non-resident companies

Any dividend or other distribution of income from a company that is not resident in the State is income from a foreign possession taxable under Sch D Case III. Thus, a dividend from any foreign incorporated company that is resident for tax purposes in the State is treated as having a domestic source and is chargeable under Sch F. Conversely, dividends, etc from a company incorporated under Irish law that is not resident in the State for tax purposes (on which see **1.504**) are chargeable as foreign source income under Sch D Case III.

The question of whether the country of incorporation of a company should be a decisive factor in determining the source of dividends paid by the company was considered by the House of Lords in *Bradbury v English Sewing Cotton Co Ltd* 8 TC 481. In this case, it was held that a company incorporated in New Jersey, USA, but resident for tax purposes in the UK, was a UK source of income and not a foreign possession. Viscount Cave, in the course of his judgment at page 508, said:

> The question, therefore, arises whether the locality of shares of a company is to be determined by its place of incorporation and registration or by its place of residence and trading. After some doubt, I have come to the conclusion that the latter is the true view.

This principle is now subject to the rules which treat certain Irish incorporated companies as resident in the State (subject to certain exceptions): see **1.504**.

Since cases of persons chargeable to income tax receiving dividends, etc from foreign incorporated companies resident in the State are rare, it is proposed to use the term 'foreign company' to refer to any company that is non-resident so that its dividends and other distributions of income ('dividends') are chargeable under Sch D Case III in the hands of a recipient resident in the State. Such foreign company dividends are not, of course, subject to Irish income tax if received by a non ordinarily resident shareholder.

The special rules in TCA 1997, s 130 (and the supporting TCA 1997, ss 131–135) giving an extended meaning to the term 'distribution' are expressly stated as being for the use of that term as it appears in the Corporation Tax Acts (TCA 1997, s 130(1)). Since the term 'distribution' is used in those Acts in the context of resident companies only, the special meaning of 'distribution' is not directly relevant to the taxation of persons in receipt of dividends etc from non-resident companies. Consequently, in determining whether any distribution received from a foreign company is to be taxable as income in the hands of a resident shareholder, it is necessary to apply general principles to distinguish income distributions (taxable) from distributions received in the form of capital (non-taxable).

In the great majority of cases, it is quite clear that dividends, etc received from foreign companies are distributions of income so as to be chargeable as income from foreign possessions. On the other hand, any payments made as a return of capital or as some other form of distribution of capital by a foreign company are not taxable as income, unless received as a trading receipt in the course of a trade of dealing in investments. Clearly, a return of the shareholder's capital in the winding up of a foreign company is always a receipt on capital account (again, except for the dealer in investments), but not all cases are so self evident.

In ascertaining whether or not a distribution from a foreign company is income in the hands of a resident shareholder, the critical question is whether the shareholder's capital in the foreign company is left intact after the distribution is made. If it is, as in almost all cases of dividends paid, the distribution is received as income from the foreign possession, irrespective of how the payment may be described by the foreign company.

For example, in *IRC v Trustees of Joseph Reid deceased* 30 TC 431, a South African company paid a 'capital' dividend out of capital profits and, although at that time a corresponding capital dividend from a UK resident company would not have been taxed as income in the hands of the UK shareholder, the House of Lords held that the capital dividend was income from the foreign possession as the capital of the distributing company was left intact. Both before and after the capital distribution, the shareholder held the same number of shares and there was no question of any return or repayment of share capital.

The question of whether a payment by a foreign company to a resident shareholder is to be treated as income or as a return of capital has to be decided by reference to the nature of the payment according to the general or company law of the country in which the paying company is incorporated. In *Rae v Lazard Investment Co Ltd* 41 TC 1, an

American company transferred part of its business to a second American company in exchange for shares in the latter. The first company then distributed to its shareholders these shares in the second company. The House of Lords held that a UK company shareholder in the first US company did not receive this distribution as income although it continued to hold the same number of shares. The reason for this decision was that, under the law of the State of Maryland (where the distributing US company was incorporated), the distribution was made as a 'distribution on partial liquidation'. It was thereby impressed with the quality of a return of capital and was capital for all purposes so that it could not be assessed to UK tax as income (note also *Memec v IRC* [1998] STC 754).

In another UK case, *Courtaulds Investments Ltd v Fleming* 46 TC 111, a distribution by an Italian company out of its share premium reserve was held to be a return of capital. Under Italian law, the distributing company was required to allocate a certain percentage of its net annual profits to a legal reserve (the share premium reserve) until it reached 20 per cent of its share capital. Since under Italian law, the share premium reserve had at all times to be treated in the same way as if it were paid up capital of a company, the distribution out of that reserve was endowed with the quality of capital and could not be taxed as income in the hands of the UK company shareholder.

On the basis of these principles, it seems likely that the surplus arising on the purchase of its own shares at a premium over the subscription price by a non-Irish resident company will be capital in nature where the domestic company law system operates in accordance with Anglo-Irish principles. This follows because in the words of Lord Reid in the *Lazard* case:

> In deciding whether a shareholder receives a distribution as capital or income, our law goes by the form in which the distribution is made rather than the substance of the transaction.

In the case of a share buyback, the form of the transaction literally takes the sale of shares which in the absence of any domestic general or corporate law provisions to the contrary is inherently capital in nature, notwithstanding that the economic substance involves funds representing accumulated profits of the company being transferred to shareholders.

It is generally accepted that the principles laid down in these decisions of the House of Lords are equally applicable in corresponding circumstances affecting an Irish resident shareholder in a foreign company. If it can be established that the distribution is a return of capital (as determined by the law of the relevant foreign country) it should not be taxable as income from the foreign possession. However, if this cannot be established, the distribution payment will be taxable under Sch D Case III (unless it takes the form of a bonus issue of shares or a similar capitalisation of profits).

The taxation of shares issued in lieu of dividends in relation to a non-resident company is subject to the special rules contained in TCA 1997, s 816 (see **8.208**).

13.108 Other types of foreign income

General

Income from immovable property, for example, lands, buildings, mining or other extracting rights, farming, forestry, etc is taxable under Sch D Case III as foreign income if the property is situated outside the State. Other types of income not specifically covered (see **13.103–13.107**) are generally taxable as income from foreign possessions if the legal right to enforce payment of the income is situated in a foreign country. It has been clearly established by various court decisions that income arising from a foreign chose in action or a foreign contract, ie one enforceable in the courts of another country, is taxable income from a foreign possession (unless treated as the receipt of a trade or profession carried on in Ireland). For example, in *Chamney v Lewis* 17 TC 318 it was held that an annuity payable to a UK resident under a deed of separation executed in India (and enforceable there) was income from a foreign possession, even though the annuity was paid by bankers in London. Similarly, in *CIR v Anderstrom* 13 TC 482 it was held that a yearly maintenance payment imposed on a husband by a court in Sweden in giving a divorce decree was income from a foreign possession taxable on the UK resident recipient.

Copyright royalties payable to an Irish resident person by a London publisher would, if not trading receipts of a profession carried on wholly or partly in the State, normally be income from a UK (foreign) possession (*Alloway v Phillips*, discussed at **8.201**; note also the discussion at **2.307**), in relation to payments of interests, annual payments and patent royalties.

Foreign deposit interest

TCA 1997, s 267M provides that with effect from 1 January 2005, certain interest on EU deposit accounts, termed 'specified interest', is taxed at the 'appropriate rate' and, with effect for interest received on or after 8 February 2012, certain interest on non-EU deposit accounts, termed 'foreign deposit interest', is taxed at the 'appropriate rate' to the extent the interest would otherwise be liable to tax at the standard rate. 'Specified interest' and 'foreign deposit interest' is interest which would be deposit interest subject to deposit interest retention tax (DIRT) if it were payable in Ireland. Under the DIRT provisions contained in TCA 1997, s 256 (see **2.401**), interest on relevant deposits (as defined) held with relevant deposit takers (again as defined) is subject to DIRT, levied at the 'appropriate rate', 41 per cent for interest paid on or after 1 January 2014.

Section 267M(1)(a) adopts the definition of *relevant deposit* for the purposes of identifying 'specified interest' and 'foreign deposit interest', subject to some amendments. TCA 1997, s 256(1)(c) excludes deposits held at non-Irish branches of Irish resident lending institutions (eg the UK branch of an Irish bank) from the scope of the DIRT provisions and TCA 1997, s 256(1)(d) excludes deposits held at non-Irish branches of non-Irish resident lending institutions (eg the UK branch of a French bank) from the scope of the DIRT provisions. Both of these provisions are deemed to be deleted in applying the definition of relevant deposit for the purpose of identifying foreign deposit interest (ie non-EU deposit interest). For the purpose of identifying 'specified interest' (ie EU deposit interest) ss 256(1)(c) and 256(1)(d) are substituted so that 'specified interest' does not include deposits held at the non-EU branches of lending institutions resident in an EU Member State (eg the Russian branch of a German bank) and non-EU branches of lending institutions resident outside the EU (eg the Chinese branch of a Australian bank). Before s 267M was amended by FA 2012 to include non-EU deposit interest, such interest would not have been liable to tax at the appropriate rate under TCA 1997, s 267M. However, such interest, post-FA 2012, while not coming within the definition of 'specified interest' will fall within the definition of 'foreign deposit interest' because it arises in a territory other than a Member State of the EU, and will be liable to tax at the appropriate rate under TCA 1997, s 267M.

TCA 1997, s 256(1)(g) relates to Irish currency deposits of foreign residents – this is disregarded for the purposes of TCA 1997, s 267M.

Section 267M(1)(b) adopts and amends the definition of *relevant deposit taker* for the purposes of identifying specified interest and foreign deposit interest. TCA 1997, s 256(1) defines this term as meaning a bank (which already includes EU banks), a building society (which is defined separately to include EU building societies), and a trustee savings bank, a credit union or the Post Office Savings Bank. Thus TCA 1997, s 267M is extended to deposits held with bodies equivalent to trustee savings banks, etc. established under the laws of any other EU Member State and to bodies established outside the EU which are authorised under the laws of the country in which they are established to accept deposits of money.

TCA 1997, s 267M(2) provides that specified interest (EU interest) is chargeable to tax at the appropriate rate (see table below) whereas foreign deposit interest (non-EU interest) is chargeable to tax at the appropriate rate to the extent that it would otherwise be chargeable to tax at the standard rate.

Year of assessment	*Rate of tax*
2017	39%
2018	37%
2019	35%
2020 and subsequent years	33%

The above seeks to ensure that 'specified interest' is subject to tax in Ireland in the same way to that of similar Irish interest so as to ensure discrimination. FA 2016, s 21 notes that notwithstanding the above, where any liability of the individual for a year of assessment in respect of the specified interest or foreign deposit interest has not been discharged on or before the specified return date for the chargeable period for that year, then the part of taxable income, equal to that specified interest or that foreign deposit interest, shall be chargeable to tax at the rate of tax described in the table to TCA 1997, s 15 as the higher rate, being the higher marginal rate of income tax.

13.2 Computation of Foreign Income

13.201 General

The general principle is that the amount of income arising from any particular foreign source chargeable to tax is computed by applying the same rules as if the income arose from a source within the State. TCA 1997, s 71(1) provides that the income tax chargeable under Sch D Case III on income from foreign securities and possessions is to be computed on the full amount arising, whether the income has been or will be received in the State or not. It goes on to say that, in the case of income not received in the State, the amount of the income chargeable to tax is to be reduced by:

- (a) the same deductions and allowances as if the income had been received in the State;
- (b) any income tax paid in respect of the income in the country of the source; and
- (c) any annuity or other annual payment (or certain annual interest) payable out of the income to any non-resident person.

The significance of this wording, which can be traced back to the ITA 1842, is notably obscure. The purpose of limb (a) seems to be to ensure that foreign income which is not physically received in the State attracts the same allowances and deductions as income which is so received. The problem is that there are in general no express provisions in the Income Tax Acts for deduction and allowances to be made against foreign income which *is* received in the State.

Whatever may be the literal interpretation of TCA 1997, s 71(1), it is established practice that, in determining the amount of income from foreign sources for assessment on a resident person, the computational rules of the particular Sch or Case are used that would apply if the particular foreign income had arisen in the State.

For example, if a resident person carries on a trade or profession wholly abroad, the amount of the annual profits or gains assessable as Sch D Case III income in respect of any period of account is computed in accordance with the Sch D Case I computational rules that would apply if the trade were carried on in the State. The same capital allowances are given (or balancing charges made) in taxing those profits as for a trade or profession chargeable under Sch D Case I or II.

The deductions and allowances against foreign source income are discussed further in **13.202**. Another important factor in taxing foreign source income is the need to translate the actual income and expenses, which are usually received or incurred in foreign currency, into euro. This is dealt with generally in **13.203**, but is covered in more detail in relation to trades and professions in **Division 13.3** where the difficult question of exchange gains and losses is considered in some depth. In passing, it is noted here that the subject of exchange gains and losses is as much relevant to the Sch D Case I or II computations of a trade or profession carried on in the State which has transactions in foreign currencies, as it is for foreign trades and professions.

13.202 Deductions from foreign income

Deductions in computing income

Since what is assessed under Sch D Case III is the 'annual profits or gains arising' from the foreign securities or possessions, it follows that expenses of a revenue nature that have to be incurred before an annual profit can be realised are normally deductible in arriving at the amount of the income accruing from the foreign source. Then, after the foreign income has been determined, it may be possible – depending on the facts – to deduct certain allowances in computing the net foreign income that is actually taxable.

A brief summary of the main factors likely to be relevant in respect of different types of foreign income is now given, as follows:

Foreign trade or profession:

(a) The trading income taxable under Sch D Case III is computed in the same way as for a trade (or profession) carried on in the State, except that no stock relief is available since farming carried on wholly outside the State is not a 'qualifying trade' within TCA 1997, Pt 23 Ch 2. In some cases, overseas farming activities may not in any event strictly rank as a trade (note the discussion at **7.101**). Capital allowances may generally be claimed in exactly the same way as for a trade in the State. However, it should be noted that in the case of industrial buildings allowances, there are specific restrictions which are set out in TCA 1997, s 268(5) which considerably limit the circumstances in which industrial buildings allowances may be claimed.

(b) The same relief is available for trading losses (computed in the same way as profits) under TCA 1997, ss 381 and 382 regardless of whether the trade/ profession is assessable under Case I/II or Case III (see Revenue *eBrief No 06/ 14*).

Foreign office or employment:

(a) The income assessable under Sch D Case III (ie attributable to non-Irish duties only, with effect from 1 January 2006 as discussed above) includes all salaries, wages, fees, perquisites or other profits of a revenue nature earned in or accruing from the foreign office or employment. In addition, any benefits in kind (including motor car benefits), amounts taxable in respect of expenses payments by the employer and any interest etc benefits from employer – provided loans (see **13.105**) are assessable.

(b) The same deductions may then be made for expenses incurred in performing the duties of the foreign office or employment, but only if the same conditions as those set out in TCA 1997, s 114 for Sch E offices, etc are met (see **10.302**); also for employee contributions to any exempt approved pension scheme, approved retirement annuity contracts etc; also for any relevant capital allowances for any machinery or plant used for the purposes of the foreign office or employment (see **10.305**). The same prohibition and restrictions on the deduction of business entertainment apply as are relevant for a Sch E office or employment (see **10.304**).

(c) A deduction could formerly be claimed under TCA 1997, s 823 by an individual from the income of a foreign office or employment if he had 90 or more qualifying days absent from the State in the performance of the duties of that office or employment (or in performing the duties of any other office or employment within TCA 1997, s 823). For the circumstances in which this deduction could be claimed and for the calculation of the amount of the deduction, see **10.306** in the 2003 and earlier editions of this book. This foreign earnings deduction was re-introduced in a more limited format by FA 2012 to apply to Irish resident employees working in certain countries (TCA 1997, s 823A). A detailed analysis of the relief is provided in **10.306** of this book.

Foreign rental income:

(a) The computation of the net rental income taxable under Sch D Case III is made by deducting from the gross rent receivable the same deductions as would apply under TCA 1997, s 97 if the income were from premises in the State taxable under Sch D Case V (see **12.104**), as confirmed in the Revenue Commissioners' *Guide to the Irish Tax Implications of Foreign Property Ownership*. It may be noted however that the anti-avoidance rules concerning premiums as opposed to reverse premiums (see **12.204**) are not extended to Sch D Case III.

(b) TCA 1997, s 71(4) makes it clear that the deduction given by TCA 1997, s 97(2)(e) for interest on borrowed money employed in the purchase, improvement or repair of the foreign situated premises is generally deductible on Case V principles in computing the net rental income taxable under Sch D Case III.

    There is no statutory provision for the relief of Case III rental losses; in practice the Revenue Commissioners will allow losses on foreign rental properties to be offset against profits from foreign rental properties and any overall loss in relation to foreign rental properties in a tax year to be carried forward against future profits on such properties.

(c) If the foreign rented property is an industrial building, the same industrial buildings allowances may be claimed as for a leased industrial building situated in the State, subject however to the extensive restrictions contained in TCA 1997, s 268(5) (see **6.401**). Where the building is leased to a trading tenant, then capital allowances will be available in respect of plant and machinery where the burden of wear and tear falls on the tenant in accordance with TCA 1997, s 298, subject to the ring-fencing provisions of TCA 1997, s 403 (see **6.305**).

If the foreign rented property is residential, then it appears in strictness that capital allowances will not be available for fixtures and fittings used therein as TCA 1997, s 284(6), (7) apply only for the purposes of Sch D Case V (see **12.104**); however, in practice the Revenue Commissioners do not take this point and allow a deduction against rental income for capital allowances in respect of fixtures and fittings.

Deduction for foreign tax

TCA 1997, s 71(1)(b) permits the deduction of foreign income tax paid where the foreign income arises, in arriving at the amount of that income which is chargeable to tax under Sch D Case III, but only if the recipient is not entitled to any foreign tax credit in respect of that income (or elects not to take any such credit) under a relevant double taxation agreement. TCA 1997, Sch 24 para 7(3)(a) provides that no deduction for foreign tax is given to the extent that foreign tax credit (which reduces the tax payable) is taken in respect of the income in question. For the circumstances in which a credit for foreign tax against the Irish tax payable is given, see **14.301**.

In practice, if the income arises in a country with which there is a double taxation agreement, the credit for the foreign tax against tax payable is usually taken as it is likely to give a lower final tax liability. The taxpayer is not, however, compelled to take an available credit for foreign tax, and may elect not to do so (TCA 1997, Sch 24 para 10). If no credit against Irish tax payable is available for the foreign tax (ie because there is no relevant double taxation agreement) or if the taxpayer elects not to take any available credit, the foreign tax paid in the country in which the income arises should be deducted in arriving at the amount of the foreign income chargeable under Sch D Case III. The foreign tax which may be deducted is limited to the tax actually paid on the income arising in the other country, whether this has been paid by deduction at source or by direct assessment. In *Yates v GCA* [1991] STC 157 it was held (in a broadly similar statutory context) that it was only the amount of profits which 'in substance arose' in the overseas territory (see **13.602**) which was eligible for relief and not the amount of profits (if different) on which foreign income tax was payable. The question of whether a foreign tax 'corresponded' to UK income tax was also considered in the case (the Irish legislation refers simply to 'income tax' incurred in the place where the income arises, but the reasoning in *Yates* may have persuasive value).

Deduction for annuity, annual payment etc

TCA 1997, s 71(1) permits the deduction from the taxpayer's total income from foreign sources of any annuity or other annual payment payable out of that income to a person (or persons) not resident in the State.

For an annuity or other annual payment (or annual interest to the extent previously allowable) to be deductible from any foreign source income, all of the following conditions must be met:

(a) it must be an annual payment in the sense defined in **2.302**;
(b) it must be payable out of the foreign source income;
(c) it must not be payable to any person resident in the State; and
(d) it must not be an annual payment of income which is deemed by any of the provisions of TCA 1997, Pt 31 to be the income of the payer (see **15.4**).

In practice, condition (b) is generally accepted as being met if the total foreign source income from which it is sought to make the deduction is equal to or greater than the amount deductible, even if the actual payment is made from some other funds (see *Allchin v Coulthard* [1942] 2 KB 228; *Postlethwaite v IRC* 41 TC 224). However, the prudent taxpayer should apply the actual foreign income received to make the annual payment or, at the least, arrange matters so that the annual payment can be shown to have been made out of funds or an account into which the foreign income has been lodged.

13.203 Translation of income etc from foreign currency

Income for Irish tax purposes is always assessed in euro (with effect from 1 January 2002). Consequently, if income of any kind is earned or if a transaction relevant to the computation of taxable income taxes place in a foreign (ie non-euro) currency, it is necessary to translate the figures into euro.

For items of income such as dividends, interest rents, and other payments receivable from foreign (ie non-euro) sources that are in fact converted into euro shortly after their receipt, the matter is straightforward and the actual amount received in euro, on the lodgement to the taxpayer's bank account is strictly the figure to take. In practice, however, particularly if the items are numerous (for example, where the taxpayer receives dividends from a portfolio of foreign investments), the inspector is likely to accept a translation of the foreign currency amounts at an average of the relevant exchange rates that prevailed during the period over which the income was paid.

For types of foreign income earned over a period of time, for example, a salary paid outside the State in foreign currency in respect of an employment exercised abroad, the strictly correct treatment is probably to translate each periodic payment at the exchange rate in force on the date of payment. In practice, the inspector of taxes is likely to accept any reasonable method of translating the foreign currency figures into euro, whether an actual rate for each payment or an average rate taken over the period the income was earned. For example, a foreign salary earned in US dollars for the six months ended 30 June 2015 might be converted at an average US dollar/euro exchange rate for those six months; alternatively, if paid monthly, each month's payment might be converted at the relevant month end rate.

When any type of foreign income is computed as the excess of receipts over deductible expenses and where most of the transactions involved are carried out in the foreign currency, the best approach may be to compute the taxable income first in the foreign currency and then to translate the resulting net income (or net loss) into euro at an appropriate rate of exchange. The choice is usually between the exchange rate at the end of the period of computation and an average exchange rate for the period. Whichever method is used, it should be applied consistently from period to period, unless circumstances change to make a different method more suitable. For example, if a foreign rented property remains unlet for five months in one year, it may be more appropriate to translate the rents receivable at an average exchange rate for the other seven months even if in previous years the translation had been at the average exchange rate over the whole year.

Where the taxpayer is a person who incorporates the results of the foreign activity in its Irish financial statements, the method used in those statements for translating the foreign profits (or losses) from foreign currency into euro is almost invariably followed for tax purposes. If, for example, an individual has a foreign trading branch the accounts of which are kept in a foreign currency, and if the branch profit and loss account is translated into euro at the year end exchange rate for the currency in question, then the same rate of exchange should be used in adding back any disallowable expenses charged in those accounts in foreign currency. The treatment of foreign branches is covered in more detail in **13.307**.

For capital allowance purposes, any qualifying expenditure in a foreign currency should be translated into euro at the exchange rate current at the date the expenditure is incurred (the transaction rate). This rule applies irrespective of the exchange rate(s) used for translating the foreign branch profits or other type of foreign income from which the capital allowances are deducted. Once the capital expenditure has been converted at the transaction rate, all initial and subsequent capital allowances are based on the euro figure. If in due course any sale or other proceeds of realisation are received in a foreign currency, the balancing allowance or balancing charge is computed by reference to those proceeds translated at the rate of exchange prevailing at the date the sales proceeds were realised.

In certain cases, not only may the accounts of a foreign branch be in a foreign currency, but a person carrying on a trade in the State may prepare the accounts of the business in a foreign currency. Should a business which prepares its accounts in a currency other than euro (or a foreign branch with its account in a foreign currency) incur a loss for any accounting period, that loss has to be translated into euro at the same exchange rate (yearend rate or average rate) as would be used to translate a profit if there were one. If the loss is being carried forward for set off against future profits of the same trade in a later year or accounting period, it is the amount as translated into euro at the exchange rate applicable for that year or period which is carried forward.

13.3 Foreign Currency Translation

13.301 General

The subject of translating income, expenses, assets, liabilities, etc received, paid or expressed in terms of foreign (ie non-euro) currencies is particularly relevant in relation to the taxation of trades (and professions) where the activities of the business involve or include transactions in foreign currencies. This subject is not limited in its application to cases where there is a resident taxpayer deriving income from a foreign trade, ie from one carried on wholly abroad. In fact, it has to be considered in practice much more frequently in the case of a business carried on wholly or partly in the State, but which has transactions involving buying and selling in foreign currencies or which trades through a branch or branches in one or more foreign countries.

The discussion in this Division deals separately with two main topics. Firstly, it considers the treatment of exchange gains and losses arising in the course of a trade carried on in the State as a result of transactions involving foreign currencies. Such transactions may be in the purchase and sale of goods outside the country, or in incurring expenses for services, etc provided by foreign suppliers or in providing services to foreign customers. They may also involve incurring liabilities on capital account for the purchase of fixed assets or the borrowing of capital repayable in foreign currency. Secondly, it discusses the way in which the results of the trading activities of foreign branches are translated into euro and are dealt with for tax purposes.

The taxation treatment of exchange gains and losses, as well as that of the translation of foreign branch results, cannot be fully understood without at least some knowledge of the accounting treatment of transactions in foreign currencies. Consequently, although this is not intended to be a textbook in accountancy, it is thought necessary to summarise the main accounting principles as set out in FRS 102 *Section 30 Foreign Currency Translation*. FRS 102 is mandatory for accounting periods beginning on or after 1 January 2015 for entities which prepare accounts intended to give a true and fair view, other than listed entities

The standard accounting treatment as prescribed in FRS 102 *Section 30 Foreign Currency Translation* is discussed separately in the context of exchange gains and losses generally in **13.302** and, as regards the treatment of foreign branches, in **13.306**.

13.302 Exchange differences: accounting treatment

Exchange gains and losses (collectively referred to as 'exchange differences') are relevant in the case where a person carrying on a trade or profession wholly or partly in the State has business transactions involving foreign currencies. An exchange difference arises where euro are converted into a foreign currency to settle a liability payable in that currency that was previously recorded in the books at a different rate of exchange to that applicable when the liability is settled. Alternatively, an exchange difference occurs where an amount owed in foreign currency to the trader is settled and the currency received is converted into euro at a different exchange rate to that used in translating the original transaction that gave rise to the debt.

Apart from transactions fully concluded in the one period of accounts, exchange gains or losses may also arise at the end of any period of accounts when any assets or liabilities denominated in any foreign currency are translated into euro at the balance sheet date. If the rate of exchange at the balance sheet date is different to that at which the relevant asset or liability was translated into euro when the original transaction was previously recorded in the books, an exchange difference arises which has to be debited (if a loss) or credited (if a gain) before the accounts for the period are finalised.

In summary, an exchange difference may arise either on the settlement of a debt due by or to the trader when foreign currency is actually converted into euro or vice versa or, alternatively, where for accounting purposes it is necessary to translate the outstanding balance payable or receivable in the foreign currency at an accounting date. The distinction between the terms 'conversion' and 'translation' should be noted. A foreign currency is 'converted' into euro, or vice versa, when a person holding one currency actually changes it into the other currency. A foreign currency is said to be 'translated' into euro in the records or accounts of a business as part of the procedure for producing the financial statements of the business in terms of euro.

FRS 102 *Section 30 Foreign Currency Translation* uses the term 'functional currency', which it defines in para 2 as the currency of the primary economic environment in which the entity operates. Since the topic discussed here concerns the taxation of the business of an Irish resident person, the functional currency for present purposes is the euro. The main accounting principles in FRS 102 *Section 30 Foreign Currency Translation* relevant to the consideration of the treatment of exchange gains and losses in the Sch D Case I (or Sch D Case II) computation are:

(a) purchases, sales, expenses, etc in a foreign currency should be translated into euro at the spot exchange rate in operation on the date the transaction occurs (the transaction rate);
(b) at each balance sheet date, monetary assets and liabilities in foreign currency should be translated into euro at the spot exchange rate (the closing rate) at the balance sheet date;
(c) foreign currency expenditure in acquiring fixed assets or other non-monetary assets should be converted at the transaction rate and retained in the books at the resulting euro figure by reference to which subsequent depreciation and other writing off is made; and
(d) exchange gains or losses on settled transactions and unsettled monetary items should be reported as part of the profit or loss for the year from ordinary activities (unless resulting from transactions treated as extraordinary items).

'Monetary items' are money held and amounts to be received or paid in money. Non-monetary items include fixed assets, accumulated depreciation, stock in trade and work in progress, investments, intangible assets (for example, goodwill, patents, etc) and prepaid expenses.

Realised and unrealised exchange gains etc

For tax purposes, it is necessary to distinguish between realised and unrealised exchange gains or losses. A realised gain or loss occurs when a monetary asset or a liability in a foreign currency is disposed of or discharged at a different rate of exchange from the transaction rate used when the asset or liability was originally booked in euro. An unrealised gain or loss arises when a monetary asset or a liability in a foreign currency is translated into euro at the balance sheet date at a closing rate different from the original transaction rate or, if relevant, from the closing rate used for the same asset or liability at the previous balance sheet date. No exchange difference arises in respect of a fixed asset or other non-monetary item, but an exchange gain or loss may occur in respect of the liability to the person from whom the item was acquired.

Example 13.302.1

AB & Co, a trading partnership, purchases trading stock on credit from a UK supplier for Stg£100,000 on 29 March. The company pays for the goods as to Stg£60,000 on 15 May and the balance of Stg£40,000 on 15 July.

AB & Co makes up its annual accounts and balance sheet to 30 June. The relevant exchange rates for the UK pound in terms of the Irish pound are assumed to be:

29 March:	€1=Stg£0.82
15 May:	€1=Stg£0.84
30 June:	€1=Stg£0.81
15 July:	€1=Stg£0.85

The company debits its purchases (or cost of sales) and credits its supplier's account with €121,951, ie with Stg£100,000 translated at the 29 March transaction rate of €1=Stg£0.82. In discharging Stg£60,000, ie 60 per cent, of the liability on 15 May when the exchange rate is €1=Stg£0.84, the company realises an exchange gain, as follows:

	€
Amount of liability repaid (part only):	
€121,951 x 60,000/100,000	73,170
Cost of foreign currency to pay supplier:	
Stg£60,000 at €1 = Stg£0.84	(71,429)
Exchange gain (realised)	1,741

In preparing its accounts for the year ended 30 June, AB & Co finds that all the goods purchased from the UK supplier are still in its trading stock which, as a non-monetary asset, retains its 'cost' value of €121,951. It still has to translate the balance of Stg£40,000 still due to the supplier at the year end exchange rate at 30 June. This results in the following position:

	€
Original liability	121,951
Less: part repaid in May (as above)	(73,170)
Creditor at 30 June (before adjustment)	48,781
Liability translated at closing rate (30 June):	
Stg£40,000 at €1=Stg£0.81	(49,383)
Exchange loss (unrealised)	(602)

Finally, when the balance of Stg£40,000 is repaid on 15 July, the exchange difference realised is computed by reference to the 30 June liability in the accounts in euro, as follows:

	€
Liability per 30 June balance sheet	49,383
Amount of foreign currency to pay supplier:	

Stg£40,000 at €1=Stg£0.85 (rate at 5 July)	(47,059)
Exchange gain (realised)	2,324

Example 13.302.2

C & D & Co, a trading partnership, purchased an item of machinery as a fixed asset on 10 January 2015 from a US supplier for $200,000. Extended credit terms are obtained and the partnership undertakes to pay the full purchase price in dollars on 10 May 2016 (over a year later). The partnership makes up its annual accounts and balance sheet to 31 March in each year. The relevant exchange rates for dollars in terms of the euro are assumed to be:

10 January 2015: US$1.37

31 March 2015: US$1.35

31 March 2016: US$1.30

10 May 2016: US$1.36

The cost of the machinery is debited to the fixed asset account at the 10 January 2015 transaction rate. The machinery therefore has an original cost value for all future accounting, depreciation and tax purposes of €145,985, ie $200,000 converted at US$1.37. The treatment of the US creditor in the accounts of the partnership to 31 March 2015 and 31 March 2016 is as follows:

	€
Accounts Y/E 31/3/2015	
Less: Liability translated at 31/3/2015 balance sheet rate:	
$200,000 translated at 1.35	148,148
Exchange loss (unrealised) in accounts to 31/3/2015:	2,163
Accounts Y/E 31/3/2016	
Liability as at 1/4/2015	148,148
Liability translated for 31/3/2016 balance sheet:	
$200,000 translated at 1.30	(153,846)
Exchange loss (unrealised) in accounts to 31/3/2016:	5,698

When C & D & Co pays the US supplier on 10 May 2016, the partnership realises an exchange gain (to be credited in its next profit and loss account for the year ended 31 March 2017), as follows:

	€
Liability to supplier as per 31/3/2016 balance sheet	153,846
Less:	
Cost of foreign currency (10/5/2016):	
US$200,000 translated at 1.36	(147,059)
Exchange gain (realised)	6,787

13.303 Exchange differences: taxation treatment

The treatment of exchange gains and losses in the Sch D Case I or II income tax computation depends on whether the exchange difference arises on 'circulating' or on 'fixed' capital and whether it is a realised or an unrealised gain or loss. Briefly, the rules may be summarised as follows:

(a) an exchange gain realised on circulating capital account is always taxable as a trading receipt;
(b) an exchange loss realised on circulating capital account is always deductible as a trading expense;
(c) exchange gains, whether realised or unrealised, on fixed capital account are never taxable as trading receipts, while no exchange loss on fixed capital account is deductible as a trading expense; and
(d) strictly speaking, unrealised exchange gains and losses on circulating capital account should be excluded from the tax computation, but this may not always be followed in practice (see below).

In order to apply these rules in the Sch D Case I computation for the relevant period of account, the net credit for the excess of exchange gains over exchange losses (or the net debit if there is an excess of exchange losses), as included in the financial accounts for the period, should be analysed as between:

(a) exchange gains on circulating capital account;
(b) exchange losses on circulating capital account;
(c) exchange gains on fixed capital account; and
(d) exchange losses on fixed capital account.

If the financial accounts have been prepared in accordance with the accounting requirements of FRS 102 *Section 30 Foreign Currency Translation*, the net credit or net debit for exchange differences should appear as a single entry in arriving at the pre-tax accounting profit. For accounting purposes, it is generally unnecessary to distinguish between realised and unrealised gains and it is not usually significant whether the accounting gains and losses are on circulating or fixed capital account. Consequently, it is usually desirable, if possible, to arrange for the accounting records to keep separately the necessary analysis of the exchange differences to be used in preparing the tax computations at the end of the year.

Assuming that all exchange differences have been credited or debited in arriving at the pre-tax accounting profit, any exchange losses on fixed capital account must be added back in the Sch D Case I computation, while any fixed capital exchange gains must be deducted. In either case, this applies whether the fixed capital exchange differences are realised or unrealised ones. In the event that the accounting treatment required by FRS 102 *Section 30 Foreign Currency Translation* is not followed and any exchange differences on *circulating* capital account are not entered in the profit and loss account, the appropriate add back (exchange gain) or deduction (exchange loss) must be made in the Sch D Case I computation.

The treatment of unrealised exchange differences on circulating capital account is less clear cut. Applying strict tax principles, any unrealised circulating capital gains should be excluded from the Sch D Case I taxable profit and any unrealised circulating capital losses disallowed. This is on the principle that a profit is not taxable until it is realised and a loss is not deductible until it has actually been incurred. However, this principle does not appear to be always followed in practice, particularly in cases where the circulating capital foreign currency transactions are numerous. The practical approach often taken in such cases is discussed further below.

Circulating and fixed capital distinguished

The distinction between circulating and fixed capital has been considered in the context of the rules governing the deductibility of trading expenses and for the taxability of trading receipts.

Broadly, the circulating capital of a trader is the capital employed in the normal trading operations of the business and which is regularly turned over in the course of those operations. Circulating capital includes trading stocks, debts and other receivables on income account, as well as current and deposit account bank balances if held for the purposes of the trading activities. Accounts due to trade creditors for trading stock purchased or for disbursements on income account are also circulating capital items. The status of loans is more problematic and is discussed separately in **13.304** under the heading 'foreign currency borrowings'. Capital which is not circulating capital is fixed capital and includes machinery, equipment, premises and other items (eg investments) that are not turned over in the course of the trading operations, but are held and used for the purposes of those operations or, perhaps, simply as investments (eg leased premises).

A reference to two UK tax cases may be useful. In *Imperial Tobacco Co v Kelly* 25 TC 292, the company held large amounts of dollars prior to the beginning of each leaf buying season. The dollars were held to be used in buying leaf in the United States for the purpose of the company's business of tobacco manufacture. At the outbreak of war in September 1939, the company stopped all further purchases of tobacco leaf in the United States. The company had in hand a holding of dollars which had been accumulated between January and August 1939. When sold for sterling these dollars realised a gain to the company due to the appreciation of the dollar. The company's contention that the profit was a realised appreciation of a temporary investment in foreign currency, and not a profit of its trade, was rejected. It was held to be a profit of trade to be taxed as a trading receipt.

In *Davies v The Shell Company of China Ltd* 32 TC 133, the company required its Chinese agents to deposit with it sums in Chinese currency to secure any sums due to it by the agents. The deposits were converted into sterling until the agencies were eventually closed down when the agents were repaid in Chinese currency, which had depreciated against sterling in the meantime. It was held that, on the facts of the case, the company had been free to use the deposits for investment as part of its fixed capital and that it did in fact so use them, and that the resulting exchange gains were not taxable as trading receipts.

In his judgment in the Court of Appeal, Jenkins LJ considered the real question to be whether the deposits from the Chinese agents were trading receipts received by the company in the course of its trade or whether they were to be regarded simply as loans received by the company and therefore receipts of a capital nature. He agreed with the Special Commissioners who had taken the latter view. In his conclusion, he said:

> … it (the conversion of the deposits into sterling and the subsequent repurchase of Chinese dollars at a lower rate) was simply the equivalent of an appreciation in a capital asset not forming part of the assets employed as circulating capital in the trade.

In contrast, Lord Greene MR in the *Imperial Tobacco Co* case, in holding that the exchange gain was taxable, said:

> We have here a finding of fact as to the purpose for which the dollars were bought. The purchase of the dollars was the first step in carrying out an intended commercial transaction,

namely, the purchase of tobacco leaf. The dollars were bought in contemplation of that and nothing else.

The company had contended that, although the dollars were purchased for the purpose of its trade they ought, as matters turned out, to be regarded as having been purchased for the purpose of making a 'temporary investment in foreign currency' and not, therefore, connected with its trade (see *McKinlay v H T Jenkins & Son Ltd* 10 TC 372). This argument was rejected on the facts of the case. Lord Greene concluded:

> … and its seems to me quite impossible to say that the dollars have lost the revenue character which attached to them when they were originally bought, and in some mysterious way have acquired a capital character.

Example 13.303.1

Take the facts of **Example 13.302.1** in which AB & Co had the following exchange gains and losses:

	€
Year 1:	
Realised gain on part payment to UK supplier	1,741
Unrealised loss on translating year end liability to supplier	(602)
Exchange gains credited in P & L a/c	1,139
Year 2:	
Realised gain on paying balance to supplier (credited in P & L a/c)	2,324

These three exchange differences are all on circulating capital account, since they have arisen from the liability to the supplier of goods acquired as stock in trade. The correct treatment in the company's Sch D Case I computation is as follows:

	€
Year 1: Add to accounting profit unrealised loss at 30 June	602
Year 2: Deduct from accounting profit unrealised loss at previous year end	(602)

Notes:

1. The exchange gains credited respectively in the accounts and the Sch D Case I computations are reconciled as follows:

	Per Accounts	*Sch D Case I Computation*
	€	€
Year 1	1,139	1,741
Year 2	2,324	1,722
Net exchange gains (losses)	3,463	3,463

2. In practice, the approach in **Example 13.303.3** below can be taken.

Example 13.303.2

Take the facts of **Example 13.302.2** in which C & D & Co's accounts included the following exchange gains and losses:

	€
Y/E 31/3/2015:	
Unrealised loss re liability to supplier of machinery	(2,163)

Y/E 31/3/2016:	
Unrealised loss re same liability	(5,698)
Y/E 31/3/2017:	
Realised gain on discharging liability	6,787

All three exchange differences arise on fixed capital account, since they relate to the liability on the purchase of a fixed asset to be used in the business to generate income, rather than to be resold in the course of trade. The unrealised losses debited in the P & L account in each of the first two years must, therefore, be added back in the respective Sch D Case I computations.

The exchange gain of €6,787 realised in the year ended 31 March 2017, and credited in the P & L account in accordance with FRS 102 *Section 30 Foreign Currency Translation*, is deducted in the Sch D Case I computation since it is a capital and not a trading receipt.

Unrealised differences on circulating capital account

In practice, the distinction between realised and unrealised exchange differences on circulating capital account is not always made, particularly where the trader's foreign currency transactions on income account are numerous. In practice all exchange differences on circulating capital account, as actually credited or debited in the profit and loss account, may be treated respectively as trading receipts or deductible expenses for tax purposes, irrespective of whether realised in the particular period of account. Where debtors and creditors payable in foreign currencies are usually settled within a few months of invoicing, this is generally a satisfactory way of dealing with the matter. However, if there should be any unusual or particularly large unrealised exchange loss debited in the accounts, an inspector of taxes might well seek to add it back and only allow it in the period in which the loss is realised.

Example 13.303.3

Take the facts of **Example 13.303.1** above. If AB & Co regularly purchases goods on credit from its foreign suppliers, it is likely that in practice the exchange gains and losses shown in that example would be dealt with for tax purposes as they were included in the profit and loss account, ie as follows:

	€
Year 1:	
Gains on circulating capital realised and unrealised as credited in accounts	1,079
Year 2:	
Gains on circulating capital realised and unrealised as credited in accounts	2,324

Deposits, etc in foreign currencies

A trader who regularly carries out foreign currency transactions may retain balances in foreign currency for limited periods to meet the normal requirements of his trade. In most cases, such funds are likely to be held on circulating capital account to pay suppliers, etc so that any exchange differences either on the application of the funds or on their year end translation into euro for accounting purposes are dealt with for tax purposes as being on income account. Any translation gain or loss on such funds for the year end balance sheet is an unrealised one, but when the funds are applied to make a purchase or pay a creditor an exchange gain or loss is usually realised.

When the foreign currency in the 'hold' account has been obtained specifically to purchase a capital asset, for example, new machinery for the factory, any exchange gain or loss on application of the funds or on a year end translation is on fixed capital account and should be excluded from the Sch D Case I computation. Such a gain on holding the foreign currency is a capital gain and the question of tax on capital gains has to be considered.

13.304 Foreign currency borrowings

The income tax treatment of exchange gains or losses in respect of borrowings in foreign currency is determined by the principles already discussed. The question of whether a loss on exchange on the repayment of a foreign currency loan is deductible in the Sch D Case I computation depends on whether the loan is one on circulating or fixed capital account. The taxability or otherwise of an exchange gain is similarly determined. This issue is discussed at **5.203**.

Following the principles already established, all realised or unrealised exchange gains on foreign currency borrowings on fixed capital account should be excluded from the Sch D Case I computation, while all corresponding exchange losses deducted in the profit and loss account should be added back. All *realised* gains in respect of foreign currency borrowings on circulating capital account must be included in the Sch D Case I computation as trading receipts, while all corresponding exchange losses are deductible as trading expenses.

On the other hand, unrealised exchange losses on circulating capital borrowings are not deductible, nor are the corresponding unrealised exchange gains taxable. Even if it may not be the practice to exclude from the Sch D Case I computation unrealised exchange differences in respect of ordinary debtors and creditors on circulating capital account, there is not the same argument for not adding back unrealised losses or deducting unrealised gains, ie translation differences, in respect of foreign currency borrowings on circulating capital account. Normally, an exchange difference is only realised on a loan in foreign currency when that loan is repaid either wholly or in part.

13.305 The *Marine Midland* case

An important decision on foreign currency translation was given by the House of Lords in *Pattison v Marine Midland Ltd* [1984] STC 10. The case concerned a UK company (a subsidiary of an American bank) which carried on the business of borrowing and lending money in dollars and other foreign currencies. The main part of its trading income consisted of the excess of interest received from its customers on loans and deposits (its assets) over the interest it paid on loans and deposits given to it (its liabilities).

In October 1971, the UK company issued subordinated loan stock to the value of US$15 million to two US subsidiaries of its parent company in consideration of loans made by them to it. The proceeds of these loans were used by the UK company to make dollar deposits at interest in the normal course of its business. The loan proceeds were never converted into sterling, but were retained throughout the relevant years in US dollars so that the company's liability of $15 million to the holders of the loan stock was always matched by $15 million in dollar deposits.

The tax issue with which the case was concerned arose in June 1976 when the UK company purchased (for cancellation) the loan stock for $15 million from the US company holders, using for the purpose $15 million realised by withdrawing $15 million from its dollar deposits. During the period October 1971 to June 1976, the UK company's accounts were expressed in sterling and, for the purpose of these accounts, assets and liabilities denominated in foreign currency (including the loan stock and the matching dollar deposits) were translated into sterling at the spot rate of exchange at the balance sheet date. To the extent that loans and deposits made by the UK company were matched by borrowings in the same currency, so that any exchange profit or loss on the assets was balanced by an equal exchange loss or profit on the corresponding liabilities, nothing was brought into the profit and loss account for changes in their sterling values. This was the position with the $15 million loan stock and the matching dollar deposits between October 1971 and June 1976.

For the accounting period in which the loan stock was repaid by its purchase and cancellation by the UK company, the Crown assessed the company on the basis that the excess of the sterling value (£8.465 million) of the dollar deposits repaid by the company's customers over the original sterling value (£6.024 million) of the $15 million placed on deposit with them in October 1971 was an income profit chargeable to corporation tax.

The Crown further argued that the corresponding translation loss on the repayment of the $15 million loan stock to the US company holders in June 1976, ie the currency loss of £2.441 million between the original sterling value on the issue of the loan stock and sterling value at the date of its repayment, was a loss on fixed capital account and was not, therefore, deductible in the tax computation. In other words, although the company had in the ordinary commercial sense avoided any real or reported exchange profits or losses in respect of the $15 million, it was faced with a possible taxable profit of £2.441 million in addition to its real and admitted profit on the interest on the application of the foreign currency borrowings.

In the Chancery Division, the decision went in favour of the Crown. In the course of his judgment Vinelott J discussed in some detail some of the previous cases which dealt with the question as to when borrowings were on circulating capital and when on fixed capital account. He concluded that the borrowing of $15 million was of fixed capital so that the exchange translation loss on the repayment of the loan stock was not deductible, while he held that the translation profit on the dollar deposits arose on circulating capital account and was taxable.

However, both the Court of Appeal and the House of Lords took a broader view and held that, since the company did not at any time convert any of the $15 million into sterling, no profit or loss was attributable to its dollar assets that were equal to (or matched with) its dollar liabilities. Consequently, it followed that the company made neither a capital or any other loss when it redeemed the loan stock with funds withdrawn from its dollar assets, nor did it realise any income or other profit when it received from its customers the $15 million which it had loaned to them.

The *Marine Midland* decision is of interest primarily to a company or other person that carries on an international banking business involving borrowing and lending in foreign currencies. It has established that, where 'matched' foreign currency transactions are concerned, no taxable profit or loss arises due solely to the translation of the foreign currency into the local currency of the taxpayer. There seems no reason to doubt that this decision would be applied in corresponding circumstances if the currency translation was into euro. The decision does not, of course, alter the fact that the normal circulating *v* fixed capital rules still have to be considered where there are foreign currency liabilities that are not matched with corresponding foreign currency assets.

For a company chargeable to corporation tax for any accounting period beginning after 31 December 1994, the Irish tax treatment of any exchange gains or losses on any borrowings in foreign currencies and related hedging contracts is governed by TCA 1997, s 79.

13.306 Foreign branches: accounting treatment

The ASC accounting standard (SSAP 20) on 'Foreign Currency Translation' prescribed two methods which may be used in accounting for the trading results, assets and liabilities of a foreign branch. These are the 'closing rate' (or 'net investment') method and the 'temporal' method. With effect from 1 January 2015 entities which prepare accounts intended to give a true and fair view, other than listed entities, must prepare accounts based on a new single Reporting Standard, FRS 102, which replaces existing Irish GAAP including all SSAPs. The temporal method allowed under SSAP 20 is not provided for under FRS 102 *Section 30 Foreign Currency Translation* only allows for the closing rate method.

Closing rate method of accounting

The closing rate method is based on the concept that the investment of the resident person is in the net worth of the foreign enterprise rather than a direct investment in its assets and liabilities. For a foreign branch, this method of accounting involves preparation of the branch's profit and loss account and balance sheet initially in the foreign (ie non-euro) currency and, after the end of the accounting period, the complete accounts of the branch are translated into euro for inclusion in the main profit and loss account and balance sheet.

For this purpose, FRS 102 *Section 30 Foreign Currency Translation* requires the year end balance sheet of the foreign branch to be translated at the rate of exchange current on the balance sheet date, ie at the closing rate. It permits the figures in the branch profit and loss account to be translated either at the closing rate or at an appropriate average rate for the accounting period, but requires the method selected to be applied consistently from period to period.

For a branch, the resident entrepreneur's net investment in foreign currency is the balance on the head office account as shown in the branch balance sheet, ie the excess of the branch's assets over its liabilities. Apart from any movements on the head office account over the year, the net investment in foreign currency at the year end is increased or decreased, as the case may be, by the net profit or loss of the branch (as reduced by any provision for foreign tax).

When the year end balance sheet of the branch is translated into euro at the closing rate, an exchange difference is thrown up in respect of the opening net investment (the opening balance on the head office account) which had been included in the previous balance sheet at the closing rate then applicable. An exchange difference also arises if the branch profit and loss account has been translated at an average rate different from the closing rate, but no such difference occurs if the branch profit and loss account is converted at the closing rate.

Any transactions during the year between head office and the branch are normally credited or debited to the head office account in the branch records (in the branch's local currency) at the relevant transaction rate, thus increasing or decreasing the net investment in foreign currency. If the closing rate is different, a further exchange difference is reflected on the translation of the year end balance on the account.

For example, if additional cash of €20,000 is injected by the head office in mid-year into its UK branch when the exchange rate is Stg£1.25, the head office account is increased by Stg£16,000; if the closing rate is Stg£1.20, the corresponding euro value at the year end in respect of that capital injection is €16,667. In other words, as a result of the increase in the value of the UK currency against the euro, the net investment in the branch has increased by €20,667 (taking the effect of the additional cash invested on its own).

For accounting purposes, FRS 102 *Section 30 Foreign Currency Translation* requires any exchange differences, whether gains or losses, that are attributable to the net investment, ie due to the translation of the head office current account into euro, to be treated as movements on the reserves and not as credits or debits in the main profit and loss account. Should the branch itself have transactions with outside parties in foreign currencies other than that in which it prepares its accounts, for example, a UK branch selling goods invoiced and payable in US dollars, its own profit and loss account would include (in sterling) any resulting exchange gains or losses (to be converted at the year end into euro at the same exchange rate as is applied to all the branch's profit and loss account items).

13.307 Foreign branches: taxation treatment

The general rule is that, unless any principle of taxation requires otherwise, (and subject to any relevant statutory exemptions or disallowances) the ordinary principles of commercial accounting are to be applied in determining the taxable profit or loss of the foreign branch of a person resident in the State (see **5.102**). Assuming that the business of the foreign branch is part of a trade (or profession) carried on partly within the State, the foreign branch profits are taxable under Sch D Case I or II along with the profits earned in the State.

Since, under normal accounting principles, the branch results should already have been incorporated in euro in the main profit and loss account and balance sheet of the business, a separate tax computation for the branch is only necessary if there is a claim for a credit for foreign tax paid on the branch profits. The taxable profit or loss of the branch and any relevant capital allowances are, in effect, merged into those of the entire trade so as to arrive at a single adjusted tax profit or loss for the whole business.

The Sch D Case I tax computation for the trade, including the results of all foreign branches, therefore starts in the normal way with the net profit before tax taken from the accounts in which the figures for the branches have been incorporated under whichever method of accounting is used. In making any necessary add backs or deductions to arrive at the adjusted tax profit or loss, the receipts and expenses of each foreign branch must be analysed for non-trading receipts and disallowable expenses in the same way as the corresponding items in the domestic trading activities are dealt with, thus, for example, any business entertainment expenses incurred by a foreign branch will be disallowed.

Exchange gains and losses

Since under the closing rate method of accounting the complete branch profit and loss account as prepared in the foreign currency is translated intact into euro, no exchange gains or losses on individual transactions have to be considered in the tax computation, unless the branch accounts included any exchange differences as a result of its own transactions involving foreign currencies other than that of the country in which the branch carries on its own activities.

Any such exchange differences in the branch accounts will have been translated into euro in the same way as any other trading receipts or expenses of the branch as part of the procedure for merging the branch results into the accounts of the main business, ie usually at the closing exchange rate between the euro and the branch's local currency (unless an average rate for the year is used). Any such exchange differences are dealt with under the normal rules, ie all branch exchange differences on fixed capital account are excluded from the Sch D Case I computation and all realised exchange differences on circulating capital account are included.

Apart from the branch's own exchange differences (if any), the only other item to consider is the exchange gain or loss that arises from translating the net investment in foreign currency, ie the branch's head office account, into euro at the year end. The exchange difference under this heading is, in fact, no more than an accounting adjustment that does not have any relevance in arriving at the taxable profit or loss since the full branch profit and loss account has already been translated into euro. The fact that the accounting treatment under the closing rate method required by FRS 102 *Section 30 Foreign Currency Translation* deals with this exchange difference through the reserves of the company is a clear indication that accepted accounting practice regards it as a non-trading item.

Foreign tax paid

An Irish resident person trading through a branch in a foreign country is almost certain to be liable to pay tax in that country on the profits earned by the branch. If the foreign country is one with which there is a double taxation agreement, the foreign tax paid should be available for credit against the appropriate Irish tax payable on the foreign branch profits. If there is no double taxation agreement, the foreign tax paid is deductible in arriving at the amount of the foreign branch profits chargeable to Irish tax (see **13.202**).

Strictly, the credit or the deduction (whichever is appropriate) for the foreign tax should be the amount paid in the foreign currency translated into euro at the exchange rate on the actual date of payment. When the closing rate method of accounting has been used for the branch accounts, in practice the appropriate credit or deduction for the actual foreign tax paid, as translated into euro at the same exchange rate as that used in translating the branch's profit and loss account for the year in respect of which that tax is payable.

13.4 Foreign Income: Remittance Basis

13.401 Persons entitled to remittance basis

TCA 1997, s 71(2), as mostly recently amended by FA 2013, s 6, entitles an individual resident but not domiciled in the State to be taxed in respect of his foreign source income taxable under Sch D Case III on the remittances into the State out of that income, instead of the full amount of the income arising from the foreign source(s). Prior to 1 January 2008, UK income was not eligible for the remittance basis (TCA 1997, s 73(2)(a) repealed by FA 2008, s 18). In *e-brief 11/10*, the Revenue Commissioners have indicated that they are prepared to review on a case-by-case basis repayment claims by individuals eligible for the remittance basis in relation to UK income assessed on the arising basis for years prior to 2008, subject to the usual statutory time limits (see **2.106**).

The 'remittance basis' of taxing foreign source income may be claimed for a particular tax year if the individual satisfies the Revenue Commissioners that he is not domiciled in Ireland in that year. For tax years prior to 2010, the remittance basis also applied to an individual who could establish that, although resident, he was an Irish citizen and was not ordinarily resident in the State for that year. It seems clear that the latter provision, by favouring Irish nationals, was discriminatory for the purposes of EU law (see **1.410**); the European Commission in fact formally requested Ireland to amend its legislation accordingly.

The onus is on the individual to establish that he meets the requisite conditions; (see *Proes v Revenue Commissioners* V ITR 481). It may be noted that it will not always be necessarily favourable for an individual who is strictly entitled to the remittance basis to actually claim it.

The meaning of 'domicile' has been discussed in **1.505**. In the case of an individual who is not domiciled in the State, his citizenship is not and has never been, a relevant factor. In returning his remittances into the State out of his foreign income, it is normally sufficient to give the total of such remittances made in the year, but the description 'remittances of foreign source income' should be added. In certain circumstances, eg if the taxpayer is claiming credit relief for foreign taxes paid on any income qualifying for such relief, it may be necessary to give a breakdown of the different classes of foreign income from which the remittances have been made.

Revenue Commissioners should, if they are not satisfied that a person claiming to be taxed on the remittance basis is domiciled outside the State (as the case may be), notify the claimant to this effect. If the taxpayer is aggrieved by their decision on any question as to his domicile, he is entitled to have his claim for relief under TCA 1997, s 71(2) heard and determined by the Appeal Commissioners (TCA 1997, s 71(5), (6)). All the other provisions relating to appeals also apply.

13.402 What remittances are taxable?

An individual resident in the State, but who establishes that he is domiciled in any foreign country is taxable on his full income arising from all Irish sources, but is taxable only on his income from foreign sources to the extent that it is remitted into the State in a relevant tax year.

In arriving at the total remittances taxable for any year only remittances of income, as distinct from remittances of capital, are included (*Kneen v Martin* 19 TC 33). Any sums, etc brought into the State out of capital sources or out of foreign capital gains are not chargeable to income tax and should be excluded from the total remittances shown in the individual's income tax returns. Remittances of foreign capital gains may give rise to capital gains tax, but that is a separate matter, outside the scope of this work.

References to 'income' in the Taxes Acts are to income which is within the scope of Irish income tax, unless the contrary is stated (see *Astor v Perry* 19 TC 255). The effect of TCA 1997, s 71(3) is that the tax chargeable 'in respect of income [from foreign possessions]' is to be computed not on the 'full amount arising', (which would otherwise be the position by virtue of TCA 1997, s 71(1)) but instead is to be computed on 'the full amount of the actual sums [ie of income] received in the State …'. Thus, while there is no actual judicial decision on this point, it would seem that there is a strong argument that accumulations of foreign income which arose at a time when an individual was neither resident (nor deemed to be resident on the grounds of ordinary residence status – see **1.502**) should be treated as capital in nature. It is believed that the Revenue accept that the remittance basis acts as a limitation on the 'arising' basis and cannot increase the overall amount of a taxpayer's assessable income in comparison with what it would have been under the 'arising' basis. However, if an individual becomes a resident in the year of his arrival, remittances out of foreign source income earned between 1 January (the first day) of that year and the date of arrival in the country are taxable as remitted income, subject to relief available under TCA 1997, s 822 in relation to split-year relief arising on employment income.

Thus, for the remittance basis taxpayer who continues to be resident in the State for a number of years, any capital saved or acquired before the first year of residence, whether out of income or otherwise, should retain their status as capital. Remittances can be made out of such capital without giving rise to an Irish income tax liability provided that it is not mixed with any foreign source income earned on or after 1 January in the first year of residence, apart from employment income to which TCA 1997, s 822 applies which can also be regarded as capital. In the case of any 'mixed fund', ie one consisting of both capital and income elements, any remittances are normally presumed by the Revenue to have been made first out of the income part of the fund until that income has been fully remitted. This approach was followed in *Scottish Provident Institution v Allan* 4 TC 91, but the existence of a general presumption to this effect was doubted in *Kneen v Martin* 19 TC 33.

In order to avoid this mixed fund problem, an individual who has capital funds at the time of his arrival should endeavour to keep those funds separate from any foreign source income he may earn while resident in the State. For liquid funds, this may usually be done quite simply by keeping two separate accounts in a bank or other financial institution outside the State. The capital funds are kept in a 'savings' account and any foreign source income earned following 1 January in the first year of residence in the State is lodged to an 'income' account. In order to prevent the savings account (so long as it lasts) from becoming a mixed fund, any interest credited to it should be transferred immediately to the income account, ideally on foot of explicit instructions to the bank concerned that this procedure was to be followed. The individual is then in a position to choose whether he takes any particular remittance out of capital or out of income by having the transfer to his Irish bank account made out of the appropriate fund.

Sums of income do not lose their character when they are used to acquire investments. Thus, if the sale proceeds of such investments are remitted to the State, they will be treated as consisting of the original sums of income (*Patuck v Lloyd* 26 TC 284). Accordingly, any such sums arising during periods of residence will be subject to tax.

In *O'Sullivan v O'Connor* II ITR 61, a citizen of the US was resident in the State for several years during which she had income from US securities which were lodged in a US bank. She was compelled by the Minister for Finance under the Emergency Powers Orders to transfer his dollar balances to him through his bank in the State. It was claimed that the sums received in the State were not remittances of income, but were in the nature of compensation for the enforced surrender of the dollar balances. The High Court held that the sums were taxable as remittances since the fact of the compulsory transfer did not alter their essential character as foreign income.

It is an anomalous feature of the legislation that once an individual becomes domiciled then the arising basis applies from that point. Accordingly, remittances of income arising prior to becoming Irish domiciled can thereafter be made free of tax.

Example 13.402.1

Mr F Demonal, who is domiciled abroad takes up residence in Ireland on 6 May 2015 where he continues to be employed by a US company to carry out non-Irish duties. Mr Demonal is treated as present for 195 days in the State in 2015 and is consequently regarded as Irish resident for that year. Between 1 January 2015 and 5 May 2015 (before his arrival in the State), Mr Demonal had lodged his US remuneration to his overseas bank account. The transactions on that account between 1 January 2015 and 6 May 2015 are summarised as follows in terms of overseas currency:

	$	$
Funds to credit of account at 1/1/2015		18,400
Add:		
Salary lodgements 1/1/2015 to 5/5/2015	22,500	
Less: drawings for living expenses	(9,500)	
		13,000
Balance at 5/5/2015		31,400

On 1 May 2015, Mr Demonal opened a separate savings account with the same bank and instructed it to transfer to that account on 6 May 2015 the final balance on the other account at the close of business on 5 May 2015. It is noted here that the $31,400 transferred includes the net $13,000 left out of his overseas earnings in the Irish tax year 2015 up to 5 May 2015.

He then arranged for the overseas corporation to pay his remuneration from 6 May 2015 onwards by direct lodgement to his original current account. The transactions on these two accounts between 6 May 2015 and 31 December 2015 were as follows:

	Savings account	*Current account*
	$	$
Transfer from current account – 6/5/2015	31,400	
Interest credited by bank – 31/12/2015	440	

Salary credited May 2015/December 2015			34,500
Less:			
Remittances to Ireland			
6/5/2015 to 31/12/2015		(18,000)	(16,000)
Balances at 31/12/2015		13,840	18,500

Assuming that all his remittances are converted into euro at an exchange rate of \$1.20 = €1, Mr Demonal is treated as having made the following remittances of foreign source income, commencing on 6 May 2015, to be assessed under Sch D Case III for 2015:

	€
Out of savings account:	
Interest credit 31/12/2015 deemed first remitted after that date[1]	
\$440 at \$1.20[1,2]	367
Out of current account:	
All \$16,000 at \$1.20[3]	13,334
Total remittances of income	13,701

Notes:

1. Following the *Scottish Provident* case (but see above), the first \$440 remitted out of the saving account (a mixed fund) prior to 31/12/2015 is treated as a remittance of interest income, ie as made out of the interest credited to the account on that date.
2. Since all the income (less the living expenses paid out of it) lodged to the savings account was received prior to 5 May 2015 is employment income, Mr Demonal is entitled to split-year relief under TCA 1997, s 822, as such, this income is treated as capital).
3. The \$16,000 remittance (€13,334) made out of the current account fed by employment income received in the US after 5 May 2015 are clearly taxable as remittances of income.
4. If Mr Demonal invested \$6,000 out of his current account in IBM foreign shares, and if at any time later while still resident in Ireland he sells those shares for \$8,000 and subsequently remits all the proceeds to the State, the first \$6,000 would be treated as a remittance of income.
5. The example does not take into account the possibility where appropriate of double tax relief. This could take the form of an exemption for earnings arising while Mr Demonal was resident in the other treaty country, or a credit for overseas tax incurred in respect of such earnings (described at **13.405**).

The precise wording of TCA 1997, s 71(3) merits further comment. The section provides that the income tax charged under Sch D Case III is to be computed in such a case on the full amount of the actual sums *received* in the State from one of four sources:

(a) remittances payable in the State;

(b) property imported [ie into the State];

(c) money or value arising from property not so imported; and

(d) money or value so received [ie in the State] on credit or on account in respect of such remittances, property, money or value brought into the State.

Given the reference to 'actual sums' received, it seems that TCA 1997, s 71(3) only applies to the extent that income is received in the State in the form of money:

> whether … sent in bullion, or in bank notes or through the ordinary banking mechanism.

(*per* Maguire J in *O'Sullivan v O'Connor* II ITR 61). It is however possible that the Revenue Commissioners could challenge this assumption.

The unilateral crediting of a sum which is due to a taxpayer in his accounts does not constitute a remittance, if no funds have actually been received in the State (*Gresham Life Assurance Society v Bishop* 4 TC 464).

The drafting of TCA 1997, s 71(3) is somewhat awkward. Thus, for example to speak of sums received 'from' remittances payable in the State seems rather odd, since the sums received under heading (a) would consist of the actual remittances themselves. It is suggested that the four headings (a) to (d) act as a limitation on the words 'sums received in the State', so that it is necessary to show that the sum received falls within one of the four headings. This was the approach of Lord Reid in *Thomson v Moyse* 39 TC 291. However, in the same case, Lord Radcliffe suggested that the four headings were merely illustrative and thus could not limit the scope of the expressions 'sums received [in the State]'. He added that the wording of the UK equivalent of TCA 1997, s 71(3) was unclear and that the headings (a) to (d) should be 'construed according to their general sense and without too much nicety of language'. This approach seems to stray too far from the principle that tax liability must be imposed by 'clear words' (see **1.406**).

In the UK case of *IRC v Gordon* 33 TC 226, an individual lodged foreign earnings in the overseas branch of a London bank, and was allowed by the London head office to overdraw his London account with the bank (the overdraft was transferred periodically to the overseas branch to be offset by earnings lodged there once it had reached £500). The overdrafts were not secured on the taxpayer's foreign income and there was no finding that they were made on account of or on credit for that income. The House of Lords held that the taxpayer had made no remittances of foreign earnings to London and that the monies received by the taxpayer from the bank in London were advances of capital. This decision followed a similar one in the earlier case of *Hall v Marians* 19 TC 582. The decisions in favour of the taxpayer in these two cases led to the enactment of provisions to prevent a remittance basis taxpayer from obtaining loans on capital account to meet his current living expenses while using unremitted foreign earnings to offset or repay the loan abroad (see **13.404**). It is unclear to what extent these anti-avoidance provisions were in fact necessary given the subsequent approach of the House of Lords in *Thomson v Moyse* 39 TC 291. In that case, the taxpayer, resident in the UK, but domiciled in the US, was entitled to foreign income from certain foreign trusts, which income was paid into his New York bank account. He asked two UK banks to purchase certain cheques from him which he had drawn in their favour in dollars on the New York bank. The UK bank then sold the cheques to the Bank of England, and credited the taxpayer's account with the sale proceeds. The taxpayer's cheque when cashed resulted in his dollars being credited to the Bank of England's US account. It was held that the proceeds received by the taxpayer in the UK were remittances of US income.

In his judgment, Lord Radcliffe said:

> … The computation in respect of income from foreign securities depends simply on the question, what is the amount of sums which have been or will be received in the UK in the year of assessment. No doubt proper construction of those words requires that the sums

> computable must be sums 'of' the income, by which I would understand 'sums of money derived from the application of the income to achieving the necessary transfer.

The taxpayer argued that because all his income still remained in the US at the time he received the proceeds of the sale of his cheques none of that income had been remitted. Lord Radcliffe (with whom Viscount Simonds and Lord Cohen agreed) held that the taxpayer had merely emptied 'one pocket of dollars in order to fill another pocket with sterling'.

All of the Law Lords who heard *Thomson v Moyse* agreed that the sums received were within heading (c) of the UK equivalent of TCA 1997, s 71(3), ie as arising from 'money or value arising from property not imported'. The 'property not imported' consisted of the balances of the US dollars, the rights to which the taxpayer had assigned in order to create equivalent 'money or value' in the UK. There was no requirement that such money or value should itself have arisen outside the UK and have been subsequently imported into the UK. Lord Radcliffe took the view that the sums concerned were also probably within heading (a), as 'remittances payable in the UK'.

In *Thomson v Moyse*, Lord Normand sought to reconcile the decision in that case with *IRC v Gordon* on the basis that in the latter case there was 'no nexus between [the money or value received] and the income receipt in Ceylon'. On this view, the sums received in *Gordon* could not be traced back to the overseas income. Lord Radcliffe doubted whether there had been a correct finding of fact in *Gordon*. Indeed, given the circumstances in *Gordon*, it is hard to resist the inference that the loans there were advances against the overseas income concerned. Lord Radcliffe also added rather ominously:

> In essence [the decision] adopted the view you could, as it were, take the debt over to the income instead of bringing the income to the debt. Whether that is the right way to treat the facts when the creditor is a bank with London and overseas branches is not now of any importance.

Lords Reid and Denning left the correctness or otherwise of the decision in *Gordon* unresolved.

It is difficult to draw firm conclusions where there has been such a diversity of judicial views, in the context of particularly obscurely-drafted provisions. However, it would clearly be inadvisable for those individuals outside the reach of TCA 1997, s 72 (see **13.404**) to place too much reliance on *IRC v Gordon* as a precedent.

In *Carter v Sharon* 20 TC 229 it was held that where a sum was gifted by the taxpayer to a third party prior to its transmission to the UK, the UK equivalent of TCA 1997, s 71(3) did not apply. This was on the basis that at the time of receipt in the UK the moneys no longer represented the income of the taxpayer. It may be noted that a gift by way of cheque is regarded as having been perfected only when the cheque is cashed (*Re Owen (Deceased)* [1949] 1 All ER 901; *Parkside Leasing Ltd v Smith* [1985] STC 63). Accordingly, if a non-domiciled individual makes a gift of a cheque drawn on an overseas account to another individual who then cashes it in Ireland, this will count as a remittance into the State. It may be noted that it is not necessary that the non-domiciled individual should receive the proceeds; it is sufficient that they are remitted to the State while still in his ownership.

In *Timbrell v Lord Aldenham's Exors* 28 TC 293, the taxpayers (who were UK resident) applied overseas income in paying up capital due to an overseas partnership. The partnership used these funds to repay a trading debt to the taxpayers, the repayment being received in the UK. The court held in effect that the overseas income had ceased to belong to the taxpayers once it had been transferred to the partnerships. Accordingly, the repayment of the debt could not be treated as a remittance of the overseas income. The decision can probably be justified, even in the light of *Thomson v Moyse*, on the basis that it was the elimination of the debt which was the source of the remittance.

In *Harmel v Wright* 49 TC 149, a taxpayer domiciled in South Africa was employed in the UK by a South African company. He applied part of his salary paid in South Africa in subscribing there for shares in A Ltd (a company he controlled). A Ltd applied from time to time the exact monies so subscribed as a loan to L Ltd (not controlled by him), which in turn lent the same money to him in London. While L Ltd was not bound to on-lend the monies on to the taxpayer, the taxpayer had selected its shareholders and had ensured that, if it had failed to do so, the moneys lent to it by A Ltd would have been immediately recalled.

Templeman J held that the sums in question, being clearly traceable to the appellant's salary, were remittances of his South African salary. Since the sums of money received in the UK could clearly be seen to have been derived from the application of the taxpayer's income in South Africa to achieving the necessary transfers which led to his receiving the money, Lord Radcliffe's test set out in *Thomson v Moyse* was met.

Harmel v Wright was not concerned with the UK equivalent of TCA 1997, s 71(3), and it was not therefore necessary to consider within which of the four headings (a) to (d) above it fell. However, it would appear that since the result of the chain of transactions was to move funds representing income from South Africa to the UK the sums received would have fallen within the heading (a), ie 'remittances payable in [Ireland]'. In *Grimm v Newman & Anor* [2002] STC 84, it was held that an accountant had correctly advised a UK resident who was domiciled in the USA that he could give his wife USA investments (representing foreign income taxable in the UK on the remittance basis) to enable her to purchase a half share in a UK house jointly with him without giving rise to a constructive remittance. The Court of Appeal held that following the transfer the investments became the absolute property of the taxpayer's wife and thereby lost the characteristics which made them potentially liable to UK tax in the taxpayer's hands. The legislation dealing with constructive remittances did not entitle the court to treat husband and wife as the same person. Interestingly, the Finance Act 2013 inserted a new anti-avoidance measure subsection, TCA 1997, s 71(3B) to counter such arrangements. Specifically, the section treats as foreign income remitted by the non-domiciled individual sums received in the State on or after 13 February 2013 which derive from foreign income which has been loaned or transferred to a spouse or civil partner or used to acquire property which was subsequently transferred to a spouse or civil partner outside the State.

TCA 1997, s 71(3B)(b) prescribes that such sums received can come in four different ways as follows:

1 remittances payable in the State,
2 property imported;
3 money or value arising from property not imported; or
4 money or value so received on credit or on account in respect of such remittances, property, money or value.

However, overall there must be link between the sums received and the original loan, money or property transfer which arose as a result of an application of foreign income. The legislation refers to a remittance which is derived from the transfer abroad. Where this link can be established, the relevant sums received will be treated as a remittance by the individual who applied the foreign income in the first instance, ie the non domiciled individual who is entitled to claim the remittance basis of taxation under TCA 1997, s 71(3).

While this section is stated as only applying to sums received in the State on or after 13 February 2013, it will be necessary for non domiciled individuals availing of the remittance basis of taxation to review the origin of funds remitted to the State to ensure that they are not caught by this section. It would seem that this new legislation could have retrospective effect on the basis that an individual may receive sums in the State which derive from a historic application of foreign income which was subsequently transferred to a spouse or civil partner whether it be by way of loan or gift or property transfer.

The wording of the legislation does not give any guidance as to how far back an individual would be required to trace the origins of funds remitted by their respective spouse. The logical conclusion is that the section should only have application to foreign income which arose in a tax year during which the relevant individual was either resident or ordinarily resident in the State where that income was subsequently transferred to the spouse or civil partner. This is on the basis that the non domiciled individual should only be liable to Irish income tax in respect of their remitted foreign income to the extent he or she is resident or ordinarily resident in the State. Therefore any deemed remittances of income under this new section should only derive from the application of foreign income arising during periods of residence or ordinary residence of the relevant individual.

Conversely, if a sum is subsequently received at a time when the individual ceases to be resident or ordinarily resident in the State, he or she should equally not come within the ambit of this section.

Where an individual acquires goods or services in Ireland using a foreign credit card and subsequently discharges his liability to the credit card company out of income held in a foreign bank account, it would appear that this is likely to amount to a constructive remittance on the basis that the overseas income will have been applied indirectly in discharging a pecuniary liability of the individual in Ireland (see the analysis of the credit card transaction in the UK Sch E case of *Richardson v Worrall* [1985] STC 693).

13.403 Basis of assessment

The normal Sch D Case III rule of TCA 1997, s 70(2) is that income tax is assessed on the full amount of the income within Case III which arises in the relevant year (see **8.102**). However, in the case of the foreign income of a remittance basis taxpayer, TCA 1997, s 70(4) varies this rule by providing that the reference in the normal rule to the income arising in a tax year is to be read as if it were a reference to income received in the State in that tax year. In other words, the remittance basis taxpayer's liability to income tax in respect of his foreign income for any relevant tax year (eg 2015) is based on the total amount of such income remitted into, and received in, the State in that year.

The foreign income taxed on the remittance basis is treated by TCA 1997, s 70(1) as part of the Sch D Case III 'single source' together with any other income which the remittance basis taxpayer may have from Sch D Case III sources (for example, interest on Irish government securities, etc). Finance Act 2013 inserted a new subsection TCA 1997, s 70(1A) which provides that a foreign rental loss cannot be offset against other foreign income. The subsection applies for the tax year 2013 and subsequent tax years. The wording 'Income or profits chargeable under Case III of Sch D shall … be deemed to issue from a single source ...' in TCA 1997, s 70(1) was open to the interpretation that a taxpayer could net their Case III income or profits. However, the Revenue Commissioners have always stated that this was never the correct position.

Example 13.403.1

Ms Sara Smiles, who has been a resident in Ireland since 2013, but is domiciled in Australia, has the following Sch D Case III income from Irish sources arising in the two years 2015 and 2016:

	Tax year 2015	*Tax year 2016*
	€	€
Interest on Irish government stocks	6,800	5,000

On 13 April 2015, Ms Smiles remitted €2,000 to Ireland being part of a director's fee from an Australian company originally lodged to a savings account in Sydney when it was paid on 18 December 2014. She also received dividends from Australian companies of the equivalent of €7,500 in the tax year 2015 and €6,900 in the tax year 2016 (mandated to a bank account in Jersey, Channel Islands). She makes no remittances to reland from these dividends in 2015, but transfers €2,975 from them to her Dublin bank account in 2016.

Ms Smiles isassessed under Sch D Case III for 2015 and 2016, all as income from a 'single source', as follows:

	2015	*2016*
Income taxed on full amount arising in each year:	€	€
Interest on Irish government stocks	6,800	5,000
Income taxed on amount received in the State in each year:		
From director's fees[1]	2,000	Nil
From Australian dividends [2]	Nil	2,975
Total Sch D Case III income for each year	8,800	7,975

Notes:

1. Although the director's fee remitted in 2015 arose in 2014, it has to be included in Ms Smiles' Irish total income for the year in which the remittance was made. Income earned in any tax year of Irish residence is liable to be included in the year of actual remittance (so long as she remains resident and non-domiciled in the year of remittance).
2. Again, it is the amount actually remitted in 2016 out of the Australian dividends which is taxable in that year, notwithstanding that some of these dividends were declared and paid in the previous year.
3. If the director's fee had been originally received before 1 January 2014, ie before the start of her first tax year of Irish residence, it would not have been included as a taxable remittance (and the remittance would have been completely free of Irish tax).

13.404 Loans and the remittance basis

TCA 1997, s 72, as introduced by FA 1971, s 4, was intended to counteract the type of loan arrangement used in the *IRC v Gordon* case mentioned in **13.402**, but the provisions of the section were more widely drawn to cover a number of other variations on the same theme. TCA 1997, s 72 originally required income arising from foreign securities and possessions which is applied outside the State *by a person ordinarily* *resident in the State* for certain specified purposes to be treated as if it were remitted into the State by him for the purposes of TCA 1997, s 71(3).

By virtue of TCA 1997, s 72(5), these provisions also apply to individuals who are resident without being ordinarily resident in the State in respect of debts incurred on or after 20 February 1997, or debts incurred in order to satisfy such debts in whole or in part. In the remainder of this section, the term 'resident' will be used to denote an individual who falls within the scope of TCA 1997, s 72.

The foreign source income is deemed to have been remitted into the State if, and to the extent that, it is applied outside the State by a person resident in the State in or towards the satisfaction of:

(a) any debt or money lent to the individual in the State or any interest on money so lent;
(b) any debt for money lent to him outside the State which is remitted into the State; or
(c) any debt incurred to satisfy wholly or partly a debt falling within (a) or (b) above.

It may be noted that TCA 1997, s 72 does not extend to debts incurred other than in relation to loans of money.

Example 13.404.1

Mr O Labiche, who is domiciled in the Canton of Zug, Switzerland, took up residence in the State on 1 January 2008. He has a part-time employment with a Swiss company working outside the State.

On 20 December 2015, Mr O Labiche borrowed the equivalent of €7,200 from a bank in Zurich and on 5 January 2016 transferred this sum to his new Irish bank account in Dublin. His salary continued to be paid by his employer.

Mr Labiche instructs his Swiss employer to deduct from his salary, and transfer to the Zurich bank by way of repayment of the loan, the equivalent of €600 on the 15th of each month each month starting in February 2016. The bank charges interest on the loan each quarter which Mr Labiche meets by withdrawals from a second bank account in Zurich into which the balance of his monthly salary is lodged and from which he makes some remittances to the State each year.

Since his Swiss paid salary is applied as to €600 per month (until the loan is finally repaid on 1 January 2016) in repaying the loan obtained in Zurich, the proceeds of which were remitted into the State, TCA 1997, s 72 deems Mr Labiche to make the following remittances of foreign income into Ireland (in addition to remittances directly out of the salary):

Tax year 2015:	€
no remittances	-
Tax year 2016:	
€600 x 11 months =	6,600
	6,600

Note:

1. The use of the foreign paid salary to meet the interest payments outside the State is not treated as a remittance in the case of money lent outside the State.

Example 13.404.2

On 10 April 2016, Mr O Labiche took out a further loan, this time from an Irish branch of a US banking corporation which had another branch in Geneva, Switzerland. He borrowed €6,000 in Dublin and agreed to repay the bank by transferring €250 a month from his

Swiss paid salary to the bank's branch in Geneva. He also arranged to pay the interest on the loan six monthly commencing on 30 September 2016 by making further payments to the Geneva branch out of his Swiss salary.

In addition to his other taxable remittances of Swiss income, TCA 1997, s 72 deems him to make the following remittances of Swiss income:

	€
Tax year 2016	
€250 x 9 months	2,250
Interest paid 30/9/2016	405
	2,655

Example 13.404.3

Paul Rowlandson, who is UK domiciled, arrived in the State on 6 November 2015. He did not elect to be treated as Irish resident for tax year 2015 under TCA 1997, s 819 (see **1.502**). Mr Rowlandson borrowed £15,000 from a UK bank on 1 December 2015 and received a further loan of £10,000 from the same bank on 1 March 2016. All the borrowed sums were brought into the State on the date on which they were borrowed.

Mr Rowlandson has income from German investments, which was used to make repayments to the UK bank as follows (he has no other foreign source income):

	2015	*2016*
Loan 1/12/2015	€	€
– Principal	1,500	6,000
– Interest	300	810
Loan 1/3/2016		
– Principal	___	4,000
– Interest	___	240

Mr Rowlandson is not liable to Irish tax on his German income for tax year 2015 since he is not resident in the State for that tax year (see **1.502**). Mr Rowlandson is resident, for tax year 2016. Accordingly, TCA 1997, s 72 applies to the loan made on 1 December 2015 and the loan made on 1 March 2016. Mr Rowlandson will accordingly be taxed under Sch D Case III on the remittance basis in the amount of €10,000 (again the use of foreign source income to meet interest payments outside the State is not treated as a remittance in the case of money lent outside the State).

TCA 1997, s 72(3) deals with the case where money is borrowed abroad, but where the debt for the money is wholly or partly satisfied out of foreign source income before the money received as a result of the loan is actually remitted into the State. It provides that any remittances out of the original loan proceeds, made after the foreign income has been applied towards the satisfaction of the loan, are to be treated as remittances out of the foreign income made at the time when the sums in question were actually brought into the State. In the case of individuals who are resident but not ordinarily resident in the State this rule applies to debts lent on or after 20 February 1997 or debts incurred in order to wholly or partly satisfy such debts (TCA 1997, s 72(5)).

Example 13.404.4

Mr F Rouge, who is domiciled in Belgium but resident in the State, borrowed the equivalent of €2,000 from a bank in Brussels on 1 February 2016. He repays €1,500 of that loan on 1 March 2016 out of his dividend income from Belgian and French companies. He has lodged the original €2,000 loan proceeds to a bank account in an Amsterdam bank.

On 15 April 2016, Mr Rouge instructed the Amsterdam bank to transfer the full €2,000 to his account in a Dublin bank. TCA 1997, s 72 deems the first €1,500 of that transfer to be a remittance of foreign income (out of the Belgian and French dividends).

On 17 July 2016, Mr Rouge applies another French dividend to repay a further €350 of the debt due to the Belgian bank and a few days later discharges the final outstanding balance with money received from a legacy. TCA 1997, s 72 deems him to make a remittance on 17 July 2016 into the State of €350. Since the legacy used to clear off the final loan balance is not income for income tax purposes, its use does not give rise to a taxable remittance.

TCA 1997, s 72(4) deals with the case where any foreign income is applied, by the person indebted for money lent to him, in such a way that the cash or any property representing the income is held by the lender on behalf of the borrower in such circumstances that the cash or property is available to the lender to satisfy or reduce the debt by set off or otherwise. It provides that any foreign income so applied is to be treated as if it had actually been used in or towards the satisfaction of the debt if, under any arrangement between the borrower and the lender, the amount of the loan depended directly or indirectly on the amount or value held by the lender and available to him to satisfy or reduce the debt.

Example 13.404.5

Take the facts of **Example 13.404.4**, but assume that instead of using the Belgian and French dividends to make the loan repayment of €1,500 on 1 March 2016, Mr F Rouge applied €2,200 of his foreign dividend income in purchasing a Belgian government bond.

By agreement with the Brussels bank which had advanced him the equivalent of €2,000, he deposited the bond with the bank and agreed that if he did not otherwise repay the loan, the bank could realise the bond and apply the proceeds to satisfy the balance then outstanding (and repay him any surplus).

The agreement also provided that, if the market value of the bond fell more than 10 per cent below the balance of the loan outstanding at any time, Mr Rouge would on demand from the bank make a repayment of the loan to reduce the outstanding balance to the then market value of the bond. Although only €2,000 is borrowed, the full €2,200 of the foreign income is represented by the property (the Belgian government bond) held by the lender to cover his advance.

Consequently, TCA 1997, s 72(4) treats Mr Rouge as if he had applied on 1 March 2016 the full €2,200 of the foreign income used to purchase the bond. Then, when he subsequently makes the transfer of the €2,000 loan proceeds to his Dublin bank account on 15 April 2016, TCA 1997, s 72 applies to deem this €2,000 to be a remittance of foreign income made on the latter date.

It is the application of foreign income for any of the purposes stated in TCA 1997, s 72 that is necessary before there is deemed to be a remittance of that income. If the debt for the money lent, whether in or outside the State, is satisfied out of capital or even out of income from Irish sources (already subject to tax), there is no remittance taxable under any of the provisions of TCA 1997, s 72(2).

13.405 Double tax relief

The non-domiciled individual may have borne foreign tax on the foreign source income in the country where it arose (the source country). If there is a double taxation agreement between the Republic of Ireland and the source country, the article in that agreement dealing with the elimination of double taxation normally provides for the granting of a credit for tax borne in the other country to be set off against the Irish tax payable in respect of income arising in that country.

The rules regarding the granting of credits for foreign tax against Irish tax are contained mainly in TCA 1997, Sch 24, are discussed in detail in **Division 14**. The principles explained there, in the context of foreign income fully chargeable to income tax, have to be modified slightly where the foreign income is taxable only on the basis of remittances into the State.

For the remittance basis taxpayer, TCA 1997, Sch 24 para 7 requires the amount of the relevant foreign income that is included in his total income to be computed as the amount remitted into the State grossed up by the amount of the foreign tax which is allowed as the credit against his Irish income tax liability. If the remittances are made out of more than one source of foreign income, a separate double taxation relief computation has to be made for each separate source by reference to the amount of the remittances made from each source.

In practice, it is not usually difficult to identify the particular source from which remittances are made. For individuals working in the State for foreign owned or controlled businesses, the main source of remittances is usually the foreign paid remuneration. In such cases, the source country may not tax the remuneration at all since, under its own tax laws, income from employments exercised outside its territory by persons residing in other countries may not be subject to its taxes. Clearly, in such a case, no credit for foreign tax can be claimed against the Irish tax on the remittances.

When remittances are made out of a mixed fund of different types of foreign income, the Revenue Commissioners are normally prepared to accept that the remittances may be attributed first to the class of income that has paid foreign tax at the highest rate, then from the next highest taxed foreign income, and so on, thus permitting the most favourable credit against the Irish tax on the total remittances.

When the amount actually remitted into the State out of particular foreign income (carrying the right under a double taxation agreement to a credit against Irish tax) has been determined, the procedure summarised in **14.302** is followed.

Example 13.405.1

Mr H Schmidt is an individual domiciled in the Federal Republic of Germany, but resident in the State for a number of years. He is employed by an Irish company and is paid a salary that is fully taxable in the ordinary way under Sch E. In addition, he regularly makes remittances into the State out of his bank account in Frankfurt.

In the tax year 2015, Mr Schmidt remitted a total of €20,300 out of the Frankfurt bank account. It is assumed that the funds lodged to that bank account were made up as follows:

	€
Dividends from German companies (after 15 per cent German withholding tax)	16,300
Dividends from Dutch companies (after 15 per cent Dutch withholding tax)	18,500
Deposit interest (not subject to any non-Irish tax)	1,400
	36,200

Under the Ireland/Germany tax treaty, Mr Schmidt as a resident of Ireland is entitled to a foreign tax credit at the lower of the German or Irish effective tax rates to the extent he is taxed on dividends from German companies. Under the Ireland/Netherlands tax treaty, he is only entitled to a credit for Netherlands tax against his Irish tax at a maximum of 15 per cent.

He is assessable to Irish tax for tax year 2015 on his remittances made in that year. His effective rate of Irish tax for 2015 is assumed to be 32.5 per cent. In accordance with accepted Revenue practice his €20,300 remittances are deemed made in the year 2015 in the following order:

First:	€
German dividends (effective rate of German tax including underlying tax (see **14.311**) – 39 per cent)	16,300
Next:	
Dutch dividends (effective rate of Dutch tax – 15 per cent)	4,000
	20,300

Applying the grossing up procedure explained in **14.302**, Mr Schmidt includes in his final total income assessable to Irish tax for 2015 the following foreign source income amounts:

	€
Remittances from German dividends:[1]	
$16{,}300 \times \frac{100}{100 - 32.5}$	24,148
Remittances from Dutch dividends: [2]	
$4{,}000 \times \frac{100}{100 - 15}$	4,705
	28,853

Notes:

1. The German dividend remittances are grossed up at the effective Irish rate (32.5 per cent – lower than the 39 per cent German rate – see **14.310**).
2. The Dutch remittances are grossed up at the effective Netherlands rate (only 15 per cent on portfolio dividends).
3. The example ignores the USC (see **14.302**).

13.406 PRSI and the Universal Social Charge

In addition to income tax, a resident but non-domiciled individual may be liable to pay 'pay related social insurance' (PRSI) contributions, and the Universal Social Charge in respect of their income. It is appropriate to discuss the extent of the non-domiciled individual's liabilities to these additional charges separately under each heading.

PRSI on employment income

The subject of pay related social insurance on employment income has been dealt with in **11.202** where it was indicated that both employees and employers are liable to make PRSI contributions to the Department of Social Welfare in respect of all emoluments paid in respect of insurable employments (the 'reckonable earnings' – see **11.202**). In some cases, however, employees posted to the State may be entitled to continue to contribute to their home country social security system (see **11.205**). Subject to these exceptions, it is the place where the employment is actually exercised that determines whether or not PRSI contributions are payable. The fact that the contract of employment may have been executed entirely abroad between a foreign employer and the employee does not alter the question of liability if the employment is exercised in the State, nor does payment of the emoluments wholly abroad.

Consequently, a non-domiciled individual remains fully liable for the employee's PRSI contributions at the appropriate rate on his emoluments from any insurable employment, even if he is taxable under Sch D Case III on a lower amount of remittances of foreign paid emoluments. The employer, whether foreign or Irish resident, is similarly fully liable for the employer's contribution in respect of the employee's full emoluments in the insurable employment. From 1 January 2006, earnings from foreign employments held by an Irish resident will in any event be chargeable under Sch E to the extent that they are attributable to duties performed in the State (as discussed above) and will consequently be subject to PAYE.

Since any earnings from a foreign employment to the extent that they are assessable under Sch D Case III are not subject to PAYE, special arrangements have to be made by the foreign employer for the payment of both the employees' contributions and the employer's contributions in respect of such emoluments in so far as they relate to insurable employments exercised in the State. The foreign employer remains liable under the Social Welfare Consolidation Act 2005, s 13(4) to make these contributions, and is entitled to recover the employee's contributions from the employees concerned [mixed employments]. The employer should pay both the employee and the employer contributions directly to the Department of Social and Family Affairs. Strictly, payments should have been made monthly, but it is understood that the Department has, in appropriate cases, accepted the remittances from the foreign employer on a quarterly or other suitable basis to be agreed with the Department.

PRSI on self-employment income

The remittance basis taxpayer is also liable to pay the self-employed social insurance (PRSI) contributions for any contribution year (ending 31 December) for which he is within the definition of a 'self-employed contributor' (see **3.402**). He is liable to pay the self-employment contributions on his reckonable income and his reckonable emoluments (if any) under the same rules as any other self-employed contributor.

However, since 'reckonable income' is defined as including income from all sources 'as estimated in accordance with the provisions of the Income Tax Acts' (although with certain modifications, see **3.402**), it follows that the remittance basis taxpayer is only liable to the contributions on his Sch D Case III foreign source reckonable income to the extent that it is remitted into the State.

Universal Social Charge

The remittance basis taxpayer is also liable to pay the Universal Social Charge on his relevant income and relevant emoluments for each tax year under the same rules as any other taxpayer. These rules are discussed in **3.404.** Since 'relevant income' together with 'relevant emoluments' comprise the aggregate of an individual's income from all sources as estimated for income tax purposes, subject to certain exceptions, it follows that income falling outside those exceptions and which is eligible for the remittance basis is chargeable only to the extent of the remittances actually made. The actual remittances into the State out of the foreign source income made in the tax year are included in the relevant income and relevant emoluments for that year.

13.5 Miscellaneous Foreign Matters

13.501 Employments exercised outside the State

FA 1998, s 13 inserted TCA 1997, s 825A, provides a relief available against Irish tax payable on income arising to a *resident* individual from a qualifying office or employment which is held outside the State. There is already case law which indicates the criteria for deciding where an office is held, but the position regarding the situs of an employment is less clear (see **13.104**).

A qualifying employment is an office or employment which:

- (a) is held in a country with which Ireland has a double tax treaty;
- (b) is held for a minimum continuous period of 13 weeks;
- (c) the emoluments of which are not paid out of the revenue of the State; and
- (d) is not held with any body, statutory or otherwise, established under Irish statute (TCA 1997, s 825A(1)).

The definition is further stated to include a directorship of a non-resident company which would be chargeable to corporation tax if resident in the State and which carries on a trade or profession. This provision seems designed to extend the relief to a directorship of a non resident, but Irish incorporated, trading company; such an office would automatically be regarded as held in the State following *Tipping v Jeancard* II ITR 68 (see **13.104**). The company in which the directorship is held must itself carry on the trade or profession. A directorship of a holding company which does not carry on a trade or profession is not a qualifying employment, even if all the companies of which it is the holding company carry on trades or professions. However, such a director may qualify for the relief if he has a qualifying employment with one or more of the trading companies in the group (but only in respect of the emoluments from such an employment). This situation is clearly anomalous.

The condition that the company would, if resident, be within the charge to corporation tax precludes the relief for a director of any such company which would be exempted from corporation tax by any provision of the Corporation Tax Acts. Thus, a directorship in a non-resident company is a qualifying employment if that company carries on a trade or profession, whether or not in the State, and provided that it would not come under an exemption from corporation tax were it to be resident in the State.

When claiming the relief, the individual must also show that his duties are carried out wholly in a treaty country, but also that he is present in the State on at least one day out of every week in which he is absent for the purposes of the qualifying employment (thus, eg he would not be required to establish presence during a period of absence from the State while on holiday) (TCA 1997, s 825A(3)(e)). An individual is deemed to be present in the State for the day if he is present there at any time during the day (prior to 2010, if present at the end of the day, ie midnight (TCA 1997, s 825A(7) as most recently amended by FA 2010, s 11)). If incidental duties are carried out in the State, they will be treated as performed outside the State (TCA 1997, s 825A(4)); on the meaning of 'incidental duties' note the discussion of *Robson v Dixon* at **13.504**.

In addition, the full amount of the income from the qualifying employment must be subject to tax in the country where the employment is held or where the duties thereof are performed, and must not be exempt or otherwise relieved from such charge to tax (TCA 1997, s 825A(3)(c)). Logically, this must require simply that the relevant overseas jurisdiction imposes a full tax charge on the income of the employment as computed under its tax laws; the fact that it might treat some element of remuneration which would be regarded as taxable in Ireland as non-taxable should not prejudice the availability of the TCA 1997, s 825A relief. The taxpayer must have paid the overseas tax on the income from the qualifying employment and must not either have received or be entitled to receive a refund thereof (TCA 1997, s 825A(3)(d)).

The relief may not be claimed where income from the qualifying employment:

(a) is chargeable to tax on the remittance basis under TCA 1997, s 71(3) (see **13.4**);

(b) falls within TCA 1997, s 822 by virtue of the individual taking up or ceasing residence in the year (see **13.503**); or

(c) is earned by a proprietary director (as defined by TCA 1997, s 472A: see **3.310**) or his spouse (TCA 1997, s 825A(2)).

The relief is also denied where either:

(d) a seafarer allowance under TCA 1997, s 472B (see **3.312**) is claimed in the year; or

(e) the foreign earnings deduction under TCA 1997, s 823 (see **10.306**) is claimed, no longer relevant for 2004 onwards (TCA 1997, s 825A(5)).

The relief takes the form of reducing the amount of the tax which would otherwise be payable in respect of the individual's total income to the 'specified amount', ie assuming that the latter amount is lower (TCA 1997, s 825A(3)). Although the reference is to tax payable, it can only sensibly refer to the tax charged on the individual before taking into account tax deducted at source (eg PAYE) or tax credits available for offset against tax chargeable under Sch F (ie 'A' in the formula below). The 'specified amount' is determined according to the formula:

$$\frac{A \times B}{C}$$

Where:

A = the income tax *chargeable* on the individual after taking into account any tax reductions (see **3.106**) but disregarding any double tax relief; tax deducted at source (eg PAYE) or tax credits available under Sch F in computing tax payable are to be disregarded in principle; and

B = the total income of the individual for the year of assessment concerned, but *excluding* income from the qualifying employment; and

C = the total income of the individual for the year of assessment concerned.

There is a theoretical difficulty with this formula where the individual is married and subject to joint assessment under TCA 1997, s 1018, but is not the chargeable spouse; in such a case his total income is deemed to be that of his spouse and the tax for the year is chargeable not on him, but his spouse (see TCA 1997, ss 1017(1)(a); 1019(3)). In practice, the Revenue will apply the formula, irrespective of whether or not the individual concerned is in fact the chargeable spouse, by reference to the total income of the couple. However, it should be noted that the benefit of the TCA 1997, s 825A relief may be enhanced in some cases if the couple choose to be taxed as single persons. The same considerations as relate to married couples will apply *mutatis mutandis* to civil partners following the enactment of Finance (No 3) Act 2011.

Where the TCA 1997, s 825A relief applies, the individual will not be entitled to double tax relief in relation to the qualifying employment income (TCA 1997, s 825A(6)). This implies that the individual claiming the relief should be entitled to compute his qualifying employment income net of the overseas tax, since the prohibition under TCA 1997, Sch 24 para 7 against deducting such tax where relief is given by way of credit does not apply. However, there is no warrant for computing the 'specified amount' on this basis. 'C' in the formula for determining the specified amount refers simply to total income and not total income computed on the hypothesis that no treaty relief would be available. Accordingly, total income should be computed on normal principles, so that it would include qualifying employment income *before* deducting overseas tax for which a treaty credit would be due; the fact that 'A' in the formula is computed as the tax chargeable *before* granting treaty credit merely recognises that such credit would otherwise be available in computing income tax chargeable, and is not a direction to assume that such credit is not available.

The income from a qualifying employment to be taken into account is after excluding any amounts paid in respect of expenses incurred wholly, exclusively and necessarily in the performance of the duties of the office or employment (TCA 1997, s 825A(8)). As explained in **10.202**, amounts which are paid by an employer to a director or employee in respect of expenses incurred by the employee are treated as income from the office or employment, but the director or employee is then entitled to claim a deduction against his emoluments to the extent that such expenses were incurred wholly, exclusively and necessarily in the performances of the duties of the office or employment. Since the net effect in terms of the assessable amount of Sch E emoluments is nil, the purpose of this provision is unclear.

Example 13.501.1

Paul Doolin lives in Donegal but works full-time in Derry for a UK supermarket chain. He is liable to UK PAYE on all of his earnings. He returns home every evening after finishing his work. His wife, Noelle, works as a teacher in Donegal. The couple are jointly assessed under TCA 1997, s 1018, Paul being the chargeable spouse. Paul had earnings of €37,418 (converted from sterling) in 2015, suffering UK PAYE of €5,613 (converted from sterling) which equated exactly to his UK liability for the period. He also received UK Dividends of €4,603 (converted from sterling). Noelle had earnings of €47,052 in 2015, suffering Irish PAYE of €3,760. The first step is to compute Paul's income tax chargeable and payable for 2015, on normal principles, as follows:

	€	€
Noelle – Sch E (Irish employment)		47,052
Paul – Sch D Case III (UK employment)		37,418
Paul – Sch D Case III (UK Dividends)		4,603
Total Income/Taxable income		89,073
Tax chargeable:		
€67,600 x 20% =	13,520	

€21,473 x 40% =	8,589	22,109
€89,073		
Less:		
Personal tax credit:	3,300	
PAYE tax credits	3,300	(6,600)
		15,509
Less: Double Tax Relief[1]		(5,613)
		9,896
Less: PAYE		(3,760)
Tax Payable		6,136

The 'Specified Amount' is computed as follows:

[€89,073 – €37,418]/ €89,073 x €15,509 = €8,994

Paul's tax chargeable and payable for 2015 can now be recomputed on the basis that a claim under TCA 1997, s 825A(3) is made, as follows:

	€	€
Noelle – Sch E (Irish employment)		47,052
Paul – Sch D Case III (UK employment) (€37,418 – €5,613) =		31,805
Paul – Sch D Case III (UK Dividends)		4,603
Total Income/Taxable Income		83,460
Tax Chargeable:		
€67,600 x 20% =	13,520	
€15,860 x 40% =	6,344	19,864
€83,460		
Personal tax credit	3,300	
PAYE tax credits	3,300	(6,600)
		13,264
Less: TCA 1997, s 825A relief[3]		(4,270)
		8,994
Less: PAYE		(3,760)
Tax payable		5,234

Notes:

1. The UK effective rate (€5,613/€37,418) = 15 per cent is less than the Irish effective rate (€15,509/€89,073) = 17.41% per cent, so that a full credit is available (see **14.306**).

2. Mr Doolin is entitled to deduct the UK tax from his UK earnings on the basis that no claim for credit relief is made; however, the tax chargeable will be reduced to the specified amount in any event.

3. The amount of the TCA 1997, s 825A relief is calculated as the amount which will reduce the tax chargeable (net of tax reductions) to the specified amount.

4. In the present case, because the normal double tax relief does not fully cover the Irish tax liability on Paul's UK income, the s 825(A) relief is beneficial.
5. The above example ignores the USC. Where TCA 1997, s 825A applies the total income for the purposes of the USC is reduced. The reduction is equal to the amount by which the income would have to be reduced by in order to arrive at the same tax liability as the liability due after relief under TCA 1997, s 825A has been granted (TCA 1997, s 531AM(b)(iv)). See also Revenue Operation Manual 18D–00–01. In the example above in order for the income tax liability to be €8,994, total income would have to be €72,785 (ie €83,460 – (€4,270/40%)). Income liable to USC will therefore be €72,785.

13.502 Seafaring employments

The rules of TCA 1997, s 819 defining when an individual is resident for tax purposes have been covered in **1.502**.

Clearly, a seafarer whose ship travels regularly in and out of Irish ports on a daily basis and who normally stays at his home in the State will generally have sufficient days in the State (present at any time during a day to count) to be resident. For the seafarer whose ship is regularly away from the State for a week or more at a time, it is more than likely that he may not have sufficient days presence in the State to be resident, even under the look back rule.

In summary, a seafarer (like any other individual) is now regarded as resident for a tax year if either:

(a) he is present in the State on 183 or more days in that year; or
(b) he is present in the State on 280 or more days in that year and the immediately preceding tax year (disregarding periods of less than 30 days presence in the tax year).

From 2009 onwards the test of present for a day has changed from being present in the State at midnight to present in the State at any time during the day (FA 2008, s 15).

If the seafarer does not meet either of these two tests, he is not resident at all for the tax year. It is irrelevant whether or not he has any place of abode in the State. However, should he be on board a ship that is in an Irish port on any day, that day counts towards the 183, 280 days or 30 days, as the case may be.

Once it is established whether a seafarer is resident or not resident for a tax year, the question of the extent of his liability (if any) to Irish income tax on the emoluments of his seafaring employment for that year can be examined. The discussion which follows is only concerned with that income. If he has income from other sources, he is liable or not liable, as the case may be, under the normal principles of the Income Tax Acts.

In general, the seafarer who is resident in the State for a tax year is fully liable on all the emoluments from his seafaring employment, whether it falls under Sch E (Irish source) or Sch D Case III (foreign source). Normally, if the employment is with an Irish resident shipping company, it will be taxed under Sch E and subject to PAYE. It would also usually fall under Sch E if paid by a non-resident employer through an office in the State, but would otherwise usually be within Sch D Case III in so far as the duties are carried on outside the State. (see **13.104**).

Under TCA 1997, s 472B (inserted by FA 1998, s 14) an Irish resident seafarer may be entitled to claim an additional personal allowance of €6,350 (or the amount of income from the 'qualifying employment', if lower) where he is absent from the State for at least 161 days in the tax year (see **3.312**).

In the case of non-resident seafarers it is arguable that if the non-resident taxpayer has a 'foreign employment' then none of his earnings therefrom should be taxable irrespective of the fact that his ship(s) may call on Irish ports. This derives from the general territorial limits of Irish taxation whereunder a non-resident will not normally be subject to tax on foreign-source income (TCA 1997, s 18(2)(f) as inserted by FA 2006 does not appear to alter the foreign-source nature of overseas employments incorporating Irish duties). This interpretation is not accepted by the Revenue Commissioners.

13.503 Changes in residence: immigration

An individual who is resident in the State for a tax year is, in principle, liable to Irish income tax on his income from both Irish and foreign sources (ie world-wide income) for that tax year. On the other hand, an individual who is not resident in the State for a tax year is not, in principle, liable on any foreign source income subject only to the special provisions which apply to individuals who are not resident, but who are ordinarily resident. These principles, which are explained at **1.502**, are clear enough where an individual is resident or non-resident, as the case may be, for the whole of a tax year, but what happens when an individual changes his residence during a tax year?

Certain special considerations arise in the tax year in which a previously non-resident individual becomes resident in the State and, in the opposite case, where an individual who has been resident ceases to be resident. It is appropriate to consider some of the factors involved in a change of residence. This chapter deals with the case where an individual becomes resident during a tax year ('immigration'), while **13.504** covers the case where an individual ceases to be resident during a tax year ('emigration'). The tax consequences of immigration and emigration under the tax rules applicable in 1993–94 and earlier tax years are dealt with in the 1994–95 edition of this book.

The circumstances in which an individual is regarded as being resident in the State for 1994–95 and subsequent tax years – as prescribed by TCA 1997, s 819 – are explained in **1.502**. Also covered there are the rules for determining an individual's 'ordinary residence' as they apply from 1994–95 onwards. As noted there, the tests for residence in the State for a tax year are (broadly speaking) either 183 or more days present in the State for that year or 280 or more present in the State in that year and the preceding tax year combined.

An individual who has not spent any days in the country before he moves in does not become resident for the year of the move unless he has at least 183 days presence in the State in that year.

On the other hand, if the new resident has a minimum of 183 days presence in the State in the year of the move, he is – in principle – treated as resident for the whole of the tax year. The 183 days may be made up of any days present in the State in the tax year before the actual move as well as the remaining days present during the rest of the year ending 31 December. For example, the individual may come into the country for some days before making the move to see about living accommodation or might even spend a few weeks holiday in the country during the earlier part of the year. All such days are counted, if he is present at any time during the day(s) in question.

An individual who arrives in a tax year too late to have enough days present in the State to be resident for that year is, however, entitled by TCA 1997, s 819 to elect to be treated as if resident for that year, provided that it was his intention to be resident for the following tax year (see **1.502**). The decision whether or not to make this election is entirely a matter for the individual and, if he does not elect to be resident, that is the end of that matter and he is taxed for the year of arrival as a non-resident.

An individual who is resident for the tax year of his arrival in the State is, in principle, liable to Irish income tax (and the Universal Social Charge and, if relevant, the self-employed PRSI contribution: see **Divisions 3** and **11**) on his world-wide income for the whole of that tax year. This principle is subject to two possible exceptions:

(a) 'split-year residence' may be claimed for the year of arrival with the effect that income from any employment is treated as that of a non-resident to the extent that it arises prior to the date of the individual's arrival in the State; and
(b) if the individual is not domiciled in the State, any foreign source income is only taxable on the amount remitted into the State.

TCA 1997, s 822 provides for the split-year residence rules for the year of arrival, but limits its application to the income, profits or gains of an employment. There is no split-year residence treatment for the income from an office such as a directorship, nor for any other type of income (for example, income from a trade or profession or investment income). In practice, the Revenue apply the split-year treatment to UK pensioners in the case of individuals coming from the UK; the better view is that this income would be exempt in any event under the Ireland/UK Double Tax Agreement (see **Example 13.503.1**: *Note 2*).

In order to benefit from the split-year residence rules for the year of arrival (the relevant year), the individual must satisfy an authorised officer that he meets the following conditions:

(a) he must not have been resident in the previous tax year;
(b) he must satisfy the inspector of taxes that he has arrived in the State with the intention, and in such circumstances, that he will be resident in the State for the following tax year; and
(c) he must be resident in the State for the relevant year (apart from the effect of the section).

The Revenue Commissioners have stated that where there is no reason to doubt the reliability of the taxpayer's evidence of his intentions (eg an employment contract or a letter from his employer) the split-year assessment should be granted. In this respect, regard must be paid to the presumption of the taxpayer's honesty embodied in the Revenue Customer Service Charter.

The Revenue Commissioners have also stated that where an individual intends to reside in the State in the year following arrival but fails to fulfil that intention due to unforeseen circumstances (eg domestic or health reasons, or the cancellation of an employment contract) a ruling that the split-year treatment should apply will not be withdrawn. The Revenue Commissioners have also stated that in the exceptional case where the taxpayer is unable to satisfy the inspector that he meets the relevant conditions, the position will be reviewed at the end of the tax year following the year of arrival. If it transpires that at that stage the individual does in fact meet the residence requirements of TCA 1997, s 822 the split-year treatment will be granted. This approach is arguably generous, since a taxpayer who is in fact resident in the year following the year of arrival may not in fact have originally intended to be such.

An individual who is aggrieved by a determination of an authorised officer (ie an officer of the Revenue Commissioners authorised by them in writing for the purposes of this provision (TCA 1997, s 818), may appeal within two months from notice of the determination; the usual appeal provisions apply (TCA 1997, s 824).

Once the individual has satisfied the authorised officer that he meets these conditions, the following consequences ensue:

(a) the individual is deemed – for the purposes of taxing his income from an employment or employments – to be resident in the State only for that part of the relevant year from the date of his arrival in the State (ie from the date of arrival to the following 31 December: the 'pre-arrival' period);

(b) the individual's earnings, to the extent that they arise in the part of the relevant year before the date of his arrival in the State are treated as those of a non-resident; and

(c) any other income of the individual for the relevant year is taxable normally by reference to the income arising in the full tax year.

It would seem logical that the 'date of arrival' should be the date in which the individual commences to take up a settled pattern of residence sufficient to demonstrate that he has formed the required intention regarding his residence. Thus, earlier, short visits to the State in order to make preliminary arrangements should not usually be taken into account for these purposes. The Revenue Commissioners have stated that they will review all such cases on an individual basis.

In a case where an employee arrived in Ireland to take up employment on 1 July with an Irish subsidiary, stayed in Ireland one week and then spent three months overseas with the parent company, the Revenue accepted that 1 July constituted the 'date of arrival' for the purposes of TCA 1997, s 822 (see Revenue Precedents).

The split-year treatment will generally exempt the pre-arrival earnings from a foreign employment. An exception will arise in the unusual situation where the individual is ordinarily resident in the State and some of the (non-incidental) duties of the foreign employment are carried out in the State in the pre-arrival period (see TCA 1997, s 821). The terms of any relevant double tax treaty would be required to be considered in such a situation. Where a non-resident individual holds a foreign employment, but performed Irish duties before arrival in the State, the Revenue Commissioners take the view that he will be taxable on earnings therefrom under Sch E although this interpretation may be open to question (see **13.607**).

Where the relevant employment represents an Irish source (ie so that Sch E applies) then the split-year treatment will exempt the pre-arrival earnings to the extent that the duties of the employment in the pre-arrival period are performed outside the State (see **13.607**). These pre-arrival earnings are also not subject to the USC. In the case of a public office or employment within Sch E the split-year treatment will provide no relief (see **13.607**) although the terms of any relevant double tax agreement should be consulted in such circumstances.

Example 13.503.1

Ms CTR Westhill, who was not resident or ordinarily resident in the State for the tax year 2014 but who is Irish domiciled, arrives in the State on 15 June 2015 with the intention of living there indefinitely. Her income for the whole tax year 2015 is as follows:

Employment with Tabby (UK) Ltd:	€
Salary from 1/1/2015 to 14/6/2015	15,000
Directors fees (English Rum Ltd):	
From 1/1/2015 to 14/6/2015	3,000

From 15/6/2015 to 31/12/2015	5,000
Employment with Tabby (Ireland) Ltd:	
Salary from 1/7/2015 to 31/12/2015	17,500
Investment income (UK):	
From 1/1/2015 to 14/6/2015	4,400
From 15/6/2015 to 31/12/2015	3,200

Ms Westhill takes 14 days holidays in Switzerland in December 2015, but otherwise is present in the State for the rest of the 2015 tax year. This gives her 186 days present in the State in the tax year 2015. She is therefore resident for 2015 under the normal 183 day current year rule. She meets the other conditions for split-year residence under TCA 1997, s 822.

Ms Westhill's total income for 2015, applying the split-year rules to her foreign employment income, is made up as follows:

	£
Salary to 14/6/2015 (Tabby UK Ltd)[1]	-
Directors fees (English Rum Ltd) – full year[2]	8,000
Salary to 31/12/2015 (Tabby Ireland Ltd)	17,500
Investment income – full year[2]	7,600
Total income for 2015 (assuming she has no deductions)	33,100

Notes:

1. Her salary from the UK employment earned before her arrival in the State is dealt with as if she were non-resident for the part of the year before 15 June 2015, ie it is not chargeable to Irish tax as it is foreign income in the hands of an individual treated as non-resident for these purposes.

2. There is no exclusion for the UK directors' fees nor for the UK investment income earned before the date of the arrival in the State. The split-year residence treatment is given only for employment income. However, because Ms Westhill was a resident of the UK in the pre-arrival period, she should be able to claim exemption from Irish tax in respect of her UK income under the Ireland/UK Double Tax Treaty (see **14.105**).

The split-year residence rules may apply somewhat differently in the case of an individual who, although resident in the State in the year of arrival, is not domiciled in the State in the year of arrival. Such an individual is entitled to be taxed under TCA 1997, s 71(3) on the remittances into the State out of the income from an employment sourced outside the State and taxable under Sch D Case III as well as on his remittances of any other foreign income (see **13.401**).

If such an individual qualifies for the split-year treatment, then he will be treated as a non-resident in respect of any pre-arrival remittances of such foreign earnings. This generally results in such remittances being exempt. An exception will arise in the unusual case where the individual is ordinarily resident in the State in the year of arrival *and* some of the (non-incidental) duties of the foreign employment are carried out in the State in the pre-arrival period (see TCA 1997, s 821).

Example 13.503.2

Dr SP Personality, an individual domiciled in Canada, arrives to take up residence in the State on 1 July 2015. He is employed as a senior manager by a Canadian company and is transferred to be the general manager of its Irish subsidiary for a three-year period. He continues to draw a salary from the Canadian company in respect of non-Irish duties, paid into his bank account in Montreal from which he makes remittances into his Irish bank account, as follows:

Remitted before arrival:	€	€
1 May 2015 (to pay furnishing expenses in a Galway apartment)	5,300	
25 June 2015	2,800	8,100
Remitted on and after arrival:		
1 July 2015	2,000	
1 August 2015 to 31 December 2015 (in monthly amounts)	17,000	19,000

Dr Personality satisfies the inspector that he is entitled to split-year residence treatment for 2015 as the year of his arrival in the State. He is charged to Irish tax for the tax year 2015 on his foreign salary as follows:

Salary from Canadian company:	€
Amount remitted into State	
Before 1 July 2015 – €8,100 exempted	-
From 1 July 2015 to 31 December 2015	19,000

13.504 Change in residence: emigration

An individual, who is resident in the State and who leaves in the course of a tax year to take up residence in another country, is – in principle – regarded as resident in the State for the whole of that tax year. Similar considerations arise in the year of departure in cases of such 'emigrations' as occur for the year of arrival of individuals in the State to take up residence (see **13.503**), but with more possible complications since there may be a need to distinguish between cases of temporary departure from those of longer term or permanent future absence from the country.

An individual who leaves the State may or may not be *resident* in the State for the tax year in which he departs to take up residence elsewhere, dependent on whether he is present in the State for 183 days (or more) in the year of departure or, alternatively for 280 (or more) days in the year of departure and the previous year combined. Although an individual may have had an aggregate of 280 or more days present in the State in the year of departure 2015 and the previous tax year 2014, he is *not* resident in the State for the year of departure unless he has had a minimum of 31 days (more than 30) present in the State in the year of departure itself (TCA 1997, s 819(2)).

Example 13.504.1

Ms S Stringbow, who has been resident in the State for several years, leaves the country on the morning of 19 May 2015 to take up residence in the UK. She retained her apartment in Dublin until its sale in June 2015. She does not come back to the State for any other days before 31 December 2015. Her days in the State in 2015 and 2014 are noted as follows:

2015:	
1/01/2015 to 19/5/2015	139
2014:	
Full year except for holidays in Spain	342

Ms Stringbow is resident in the State for the tax year 2015 (the year of departure) because she has 481 days (more than 280 days) in that year and the previous tax year, although less than 183 days in 2015.

Example 13.504.2

Take Ms S Stringbow's case from **Example 13.504.1**, except assume that she had advanced her departure to the morning of 26 January 2015. She does not spend any more days in the State before 31 December 2015. Her total days present in the State in 2015 is therefore the 26 days from 1 January 2015 to 26 January 2015. Although Ms Stringbow has a total of 368 days in the State in 2015 (26 days) and the previous year 2014 (342 days), she is not resident in the State for 2015 as she has less than 31 days present in the State in 2015.

Example 13.504.3

Take the facts of Ms S Stringbow's case as assumed in **Example 13.504.2**. Add the further assumption that she comes back to the State in December 2015 for the purpose of medical tests in a Dublin hospital (where she was previously treated for the same illness). She is in Dublin from the evening of 14 December to the morning of 18 December 2015 when she flies out again.

This visit counts as five days present in the State. When added to the 26 days in January 2015, this gives a total of 31 days present in the State in 2015. Since this is more than the 30 days minimum she no longer escapes from the 'look back' test of residence and the effect of the total of 373 days (more than 280) present in the two years is that she is resident for 2015.

When an individual is resident in the State for the year of departure, the individual would, in the absence of any other rule, be liable to Irish income tax (and the various additional taxes such as the Universal Social Charge on income) on his world-wide income for the whole of that year, whereas if not resident for the year of departure the individual would be liable only on his Irish source income (and his foreign source income for the whole of the year would not be chargeable at all) subject to the special rules which apply to individuals who are not resident but who are ordinarily resident (see below).

However, there are some additional rules to be considered in relation to an individual ceasing to be resident in the relevant tax year. These are now discussed under two main headings, namely:

(a) the effects of TCA 1997, s 822 which provides a similar 'split-year residence' rule for the year of departure to that explained in **13.503** for an individual arriving to take up residence; and
(b) the effects of TCA 1997, s 820 which normally continues an individual's 'ordinary residence' in the State for three tax years after he has ceased to be resident in the State.

Split-year residence

TCA 1997, s 822 entitles an individual to claim the benefit of 'split-year' treatment in respect of his income, profits and gains from any *employment* in the tax year in which he is leaving the State if he satisfies an authorised officer that he meets the following conditions:

(a) he is not leaving the State merely for a temporary purpose;
(b) he is departing with the intention that he will not be resident in the State for the following tax year; and
(c) he is resident in the State for the year of departure (apart from the effects of the section).

In practice, the Revenue will accept that, where the individual intends to spend sufficiently few days in Ireland in the tax year following the year of departure, so that he will be non-resident in that tax year (thus fulfilling condition (b)), then the 'temporary purpose' test will be met. There is UK case law which, while decided on different statutory wording, does suggest that a period of absence of a year may reflect a non-temporary purpose (*Reed v Clark* [1985] STC 323). Since the test is one of purpose, a taxpayer who subsequently makes an early return to the State as a result of events beyond his control should not thereby forfeit the benefit of the 'split-year' treatment.

If an individual satisfies the authorised officer that he meets the above conditions for split-year residence for any tax year (the relevant year), the following consequences ensue:

(a) the individual is deemed – for the purposes of taxing his income from an employment or employments – to be resident in the State only for that part of the relevant year from 1 January up to the date of his departure from the State;
(b) the individual's earnings from any employment, to the extent that those earnings arise in the part of the relevant year after the date of his departure from the State (the 'post-departure' period) are treated as those of a non-resident; and
(c) any other income of the individual for the relevant year is taxable normally by reference to the income arising in the full tax year (subject, in the case of the post-departure income, to the terms of any relevant double tax treaty).

An individual who is aggrieved by a determination of an authorised officer (ie an officer of the Revenue Commissioners authorised by them in making for the purposes of this provision (TCA 1997, s 818) may appeal within two months from notice of the determination: the usual appeal provisions apply (TCA 1997, s 824).

The implications of being treated as a non-resident for the post departure period are the mirror image of those of being treated as a non-resident for the pre-arrival period. Thus, the split-year assessment will generally exempt the post-departure earnings from a foreign employment otherwise taxable under Sch D Case III. An exception will arise in the situation where the taxpayer is ordinarily resident in the State and some of the (non-incidental) duties of the foreign employment are carried out in the State in the post-departure period (see TCA 1997, s 821). The terms of any relevant double tax treaty would again be required to be considered in such a situation.

Where the relevant employment represents an Irish source, then the split-year treatment will exempt the post-departure earnings to the extent that the duties of the employment in the post-departure period are performed outside the State. Where however the individual receives income after he has left the State but which relate to the pre-departure period, eg bonuses or arrears of pay, the income remains Irish source income liable to tax under Sch E. These post departure earnings are also not subject to the USC (see Revenue ebrief No 52/14). This will not apply however where the source is an Irish public office or employment where the split-year treatment will not afford any relief (see **13.607**); however, the terms of any relevant double tax agreement should be consulted.

Again, the split-year residence rules may apply somewhat differently in the case of an individual who, although resident in the State in the year of departure, is not domiciled in the State. Again, such an individual is taxed under TCA 1997, s 71(3) on the remittances into the State out of the earnings from a foreign employment.

Example 13.504.4

Dr Personality (see **Example 13.503.2**) leaves the State on 1/7/2015 to work full time overseas; but remaining on the payroll of the Canadian company. He is resident for 2015 under the 'look back' rule.

Relevant details of his earnings are as follows:

	€
Canadian company	
Remitted 1/1/2015 – 30/6/2015	6,400
Remitted 1/7/2015 – 31/12/2015 (on a short holiday to visit Irish friends)	1,500

Dr Personality satisfied the inspector that he is entitled to split-year residence treatment for 2015 as the year of his departure from the State. He is charged to Irish tax for 2015 on his foreign salary as follows:

Salary from Canadian company:

	€
Amount remitted into State	
Before 30/6/2015	6,400
After 30/6/2015 – exempt	-

In *Tax Briefing 17 and Part (42–04–01) of the Revenue Manual dealing with PAYE-Exclusion Orders*, the Revenue Commissioners stated that they will grant PAYE exclusion orders where an individual with a Sch E employment who has left the State to carry out his duties overseas qualifies for the split-year treatment. The exclusion order will indicate the date from which it is effective and will include the following statement: 'This exclusion order is effective only for the period in which the employee resides abroad to perform the duties of the employment.' The exclusion order will have the effect that PRSI will cease to be deductible under the PAYE system. In some cases, the employee will continue to be insurable in the State and in such cases, employers will be required to remit PRSI directly to the Department of Social Welfare. Copies of exclusion orders will be sent automatically to the Department.

Further, *eBrief* no 3/2015 deals with the position where Irish resident employers carry on some or all of their trade or profession in foreign jurisdictions and recruit non-resident employees to work in the foreign jurisdiction. It clarifies that 'These employees generally reside locally in the area in which the trade or profession is being carried on and carry out all the duties of their employment in the foreign jurisdiction and never set foot in Ireland. To obviate the necessity for such a non-resident employee to apply for a PPS number and for the employer to apply for an Exclusion Order, Revenue is prepared to accept that the employer is released from the obligation to make the appropriate deductions under the PAYE system from the employee's remuneration where the employee:

- is not resident in the State for tax purposes;
- has been recruited abroad;
- carries out all the duties of employment abroad;
- is not a director of the employer; and
- is outside the charge to tax in the State.

Position when ordinarily resident but not resident

TCA 1997, s 820 provides that an individual, who is ordinarily resident in the State for a tax year, does not cease to be ordinarily resident until after three complete tax years of non-residence following the end of the last year for which he was resident in the State (see **1.502**). This principle, when taken in conjunction with other rules in the Taxes Consolidation Act 1997, has the effect of keeping the still ordinarily resident individual within the charge to Irish income tax in respect of certain sources of income for which he would otherwise have no liability due to being not resident in the State.

The following rules are relevant to the taxation of an individual who is ordinarily resident, but not resident, in the State:

(a) the rules of TCA 1997, s 821 which allow the individual to be taxed under Sch C or Sch D on certain types of foreign source income which would otherwise escape due to his non-residence; and

(b) the rules of TCA 1997, s 153(4), (6) which leaves such an individual liable in full to income tax on any Sch F income he may have in a year of ordinary residence (see **9.101**) this is however subject to any treaty relief available.

TCA 1997, s 821

The rules of TCA 1997, s 821 are particularly significant when taken in conjunction with TCA 1997, s 820. As explained in **1.502**, TCA 1997, s 820 prevents an individual who has been ordinarily resident in the State from ceasing to be ordinarily resident until after he has had three complete tax years in which not resident in the State. The exception – where the individual has left the State in 1993–94 or an earlier tax year with the intention of making his permanent home outside the State – has also been dealt with in **1.502**.

TCA 1997, s 821 provides that an individual who is not resident, but who is ordinarily resident, in the State in a tax year remains chargeable to Irish income tax in respect of income within either Sch C or Sch D in the same way as if the individual were resident in the State. However, there is an exclusion for income from a foreign trade or profession, ie one carried on wholly outside the State, and the income from any office or employment, *all* the duties of which are performed outside the State (disregarding merely incidental duties – see below).

In effect, this extends the charge to tax – in the case of the non-resident individual who remains ordinarily resident – to all foreign income within either Sch C (tax on public revenue dividends including foreign public revenue dividends when collected by an Irish bank or paying agent as charged by TCA 1997, Pt 3, see **2.309**) and to all foreign source income to the extent which it is charged under Sch D III by TCA 1997, s 18(1) (other than the income from an excepted trade, profession, office or employment). However, persons whose income from these sources is less than €3,810 are exempt (TCA 1997, s 821(1)(b)). The Revenue Commissioners have confirmed in *Tax Briefing 25* that they accept that Irish income is not counted towards the €3,810 limit.

In essence, the intention is to retain the individual's liability to Irish tax where he has foreign investment income and any income from non-excepted trades, employments, etc. totalling in excess of €3,810 so long as he continues to be ordinarily resident in the State. It does not affect the charge to tax on Irish source income under any heading which has always been, and continues to be, chargeable to tax on non-resident persons under existing principles (but see **13.607** regarding Sch E income from an office or employment exercised outside the State). Where any income from a foreign-source employment falls outside Sch D Case III because it is attributable to Irish duties, TCA 1997, s 821 (see TCA 1997, s 18(1) as amended by FA 2006) has no application to such income. Further, it is arguable that no charge can arise in respect of such income because it retains its character as foreign-source income received by a non-resident, notwithstanding that it is chargeable under Sch E. This interpretation is not accepted by the Revenue Commissioners.

It is to be noted that, for an office or employment of the non-resident but ordinarily resident person to be covered by the exception and thereby excluded from being charged to Irish tax by TCA 1997, s 821, the condition is that the duties of that office or employment must be performed outside the State. In determining whether *all* the duties of an office or employment are performed outside the State, any duties performed in the State which are merely incidental to the performance of the duties outside the State are deemed to be performed outside the State (TCA 1997, s 821(2)). In *Robson v Dixon* 48 TC 527 it was held that duties were not 'merely incidental' if they formed an essential element of the employee's duties even though they were of brief duration. Accordingly, a small number of flights to UK Airports by an international pilot were held to be more than merely incidental to the performance of his overseas duties. In practice, an Inspector may agree to adopt a less stringent approach to what constitutes 'merely incidental' duties. Where those duties of an employment which are performed in the State do not take up more than 30 days each year, the Revenue Commissioners will usually accept that these are merely incidental in nature (see *Tax Briefing 17*). Another possible exception may occur if the individual who is ordinarily resident, but not resident in the State, becomes a resident of another State with which the Irish government has concluded a double taxation agreement (see **Division 14**). If the terms of any such treaty provide that some or all of the non-Irish income otherwise chargeable to Irish income tax by TCA 1997, s 821 is to be taxed only in the other treaty State, then the terms of the double taxation agreement take precedence and the particular income ceases to be chargeable to Irish tax.

The result of TCA 1997, s 821 is that an individual who is ordinarily resident either in the tax year of departure from the State, or in the previous tax year (if not resident in the year of departure), must continue to make income tax returns, pay preliminary tax, etc under the self-assessment procedure for the following three tax years after the last year in which resident. However, the income to be returned is limited to the individual's relevant foreign income, and only then if it exceeds €3,810, as well as any continuing Irish source income (other than an Irish employment exercised wholly outside the State).

Should the non-resident individual's income in any year of ordinary residence consist only of income from a foreign trade, no part of which is carried on in the State and/or income from a foreign office or employment all the duties (other than incidental duties), of which are performed outside the State, then the individual has no need to file a tax return or pay any preliminary tax for that year.

Although an ordinarily resident but non-resident individual may be taxable on his foreign investment and non-excepted foreign trade, employment income, etc chargeable under Sch D Case III (and any relevant Irish source income), he is not entitled to any personal allowances against that income or any tax credits in calculating his tax liability, unless he falls within any of the exceptions provided by TCA 1997, s 1032, or under a double taxation agreement with his new country of residence. In principle, an individual must be a resident to be entitled to any personal allowances – ordinary residence on its own is not sufficient. For the cases in which, and the extent to which, personal allowances and tax credits may be given to non-residents, see **13.610**.

Example 13.504.5

Mr RY Riggs, an Irish domiciled citizen, who has been resident and ordinarily resident in the State for a number of years, leaves the country on 15 September 2014 to take up residence in Ecuador (with which Ireland does not have a Double Tax Treaty) for the next five years where he works for a US oil company (no duties in Ireland). He is resident in the

State for 2014 (more than 280 days presence in 2014 and the previous year), but will not be resident for any subsequent tax year.

TCA 1997, s 820 has the effect of continuing Mr Riggs' ordinary residence for the tax years 2015, 2016 and 2017, but he will cease to be ordinarily resident in 2018 (as he will then have had three successive years of being non-resident, assuming no change of mind or return to reside in Ireland before 1 January 2018).

Based on his income from all sources (including all foreign income) in the tax year 2015 as shown below (translated where necessary into €), Mr Riggs, as a non-resident but ordinarily resident individual, has the following income chargeable to Irish tax for 2015:

Income from Irish sources:	€
Sch F income[1]	4,300
Sch D Case V rental income[2]	7,900
Income from foreign sources:	
Salary from Taxoil Inc €85,000 (not taxable)[3]	-
Dividends from UK companies[4]	2,300
Interest on US municipal bonds (tax exempt in US)[4]	1,600
'Total income' for Irish tax	16,100

Notes:

1. The Sch F dividends will be subject to withholding tax at 20 per cent (see **9.101**).
2. He is subject to Irish tax on the Irish dividend and the Irish rental income.
3. His salary from Taxoil Inc is excluded from the effect of TCA 1997, s 821 since the duties of that employment are performed wholly outside the State.
4. The UK dividends and US municipal bond interest (although from foreign sources) exceed €3,810 and are all fully taxable due to his ordinary residence in the State and to the effect of TCA 1997, s 821.
5. Since Mr Riggs is an Irish citizen, he is entitled to a proportion of the tax credits available to a resident individual applying the rules of TCA 1997, s 1032 (see **13.610**).

13.505 Married persons: one spouse non-resident

The taxation of married persons living together is covered in **Division 3**. It is indicated there that they are jointly assessable (in the name of the husband) under TCA 1997, s 1017 if an election for joint assessment is made under TCA 1997, s 1018(1) or is deemed by TCA 1997, s 1018(4) to have been made, unless either spouse has elected to be taxed as a single person. The spouses may elect instead for the joint assessment to be made on the wife. If relevant, the following comments may be read with the wife substituted for the husband.

TCA 1997, s 1017, when applied, then requires the husband to be assessed not only on his own total income (if any) for the relevant tax year, but also on his wife's total income (if any) for that year. This application presents a problem if only one spouse is resident and if the non-resident spouse has foreign source income so that his total income is not in fact chargeable to Irish income tax. Given the change to the test for residence introduced by FA 2008, s 15 (see **Division 1.5**), this situation is likely to become more common.

The Revenue Commissioners have generally taken the view that the spouses must be assessed as single persons unless the total aggregate income of the married couple is in fact assessable to Irish tax. Consequently, if the non-resident spouse has income from any source(s) outside the State, the resident spouse is assessed on his own total income as a single person, ie he is only given the single person's personal tax credit; similarly his taxable income is charged at the single person's rates of tax. If the non-resident spouse has any income from Irish sources, he is taxable on it in the same way as any non-resident single person (see **13.610**, where the correctness or otherwise of the Revenue view is also considered).

This type of case may arise, for example, where the married couple lives together outside the State (for example, in Northern Ireland or Great Britain) and one spouse works in the State without the other spouse being present in the State in such a way as to make him (or her) a resident. In any such case, if the inspector is satisfied that the non-resident spouse either has no income or, alternatively, has only Irish source income which has been fully returned so as to be chargeable to tax, the inspector will apply the joint assessment rules of TCA 1997, s 1017 and should make any necessary assessments on the resident spouse (whether the husband or the wife), unless there is an election for assessment as single persons.

However, if the non-resident spouse does have some income from foreign sources, then the inspector will assess the resident spouse on his total income only, granting the single person's personal tax credits and applying the single person's rates of tax. However, this is not necessarily the end of the matter.

The same considerations as relate to married couples will apply *mutatis mutandis* to civil partners following the enactment of the Finance (No 3) Act 2011.

Aggregation relief

If the result of the foregoing treatment is that the tax payable by the resident spouse exceeds the amount that would have been payable if the total incomes of both spouses (including the foreign source income of the non-resident spouse) had been assessed on the joint basis, then the inspector is authorised to give relief if certain conditions are met, a long-standing practice confirmed in *Tax Briefing Issue 67*. These conditions are that the spouses jointly elect under TCA 1997, s 1017 for relief on the 'aggregation' basis, and that the spouses have made returns of their respective total incomes from all sources, including the non-resident spouse's foreign income (and Irish source income, if any).

Although the inspector still assesses the resident spouse as a single person, he allows him 'aggregation relief' by reducing the final tax liability so that it equals the tax which would have been payable on the resident spouse's total income if the aggregate of the total incomes of both spouses were assessable jointly under TCA 1997, s 1017. This involves two computations – first, the computation of the actual income tax payable (before aggregation relief) by the resident spouse as a single person; secondly, the computation of income tax that would be payable (the notional income tax liability) if the aggregate of the total incomes from all sources (world incomes) were assessable jointly under TCA 1997, s 1017. In carrying out this second computation, Irish tax rules must be applied to the foreign sourced income (so, for example, payments to a foreign non-authorised medical insurer (see **3.314**) would not qualify for a deduction).

It is then necessary to determine the part of the notional income tax liability that is attributable, by a pro-rata apportionment, only to the resident spouse's total income. If the actual income tax payable (before aggregation relief) exceeds this part of the notional income tax liability, the necessary relief is given to eliminate the excess. Should the notional income tax liability attributable to the resident spouse's total income be greater than the actual income tax payable as a single person, the latter figure is the final income tax liability (and the notional liability ceases to have any relevance). No claim for aggregation relief can be made if husband and wife are not living together.

Example 13.505.1

Frank and Mary Ballintrae have a house in Northern Ireland where they live with their family (now grown up and working). Frank is a commercial traveller working in the Republic of Ireland for his employer, a company resident there. It is accepted that he is a resident in the State for income tax purposes, but Mary is resident in Northern Ireland only.

Apart from his employment earnings, Frank has Sch D Case V income from a leased warehouse in Dublin, but has no other income. Mary has income consisting of interest on an Irish government security (exempted from Irish tax as she is resident outside the State) and has also UK dividends and certain other UK income, Frank and Mary claim the relief on the 'Aggregation basis' and submit full details of all their income to the Irish inspector.

Frank's income tax liability (USC & PRSI ignored) for the tax year 2015 as a single person is computed, based on the income stated below, as follows:

Sch E:	€	€
Emoluments from employment		33,900
Sch D Case V:		
Net rental income		8,500
Total income/Taxable income		42,400
Income tax payable (single rate table)		
€33,800 x 20%		6,760
€ 8,600 x 40%		3,440
€42,400		10,200
Less credits		
single person's basic		(1,650)
PAYE tax credit		(1,650)
Actual income tax payable (before relief)		6,900

In order to compute the TCA 1997, s 1017 'aggregation' relief, the following notional computation is made based on joint total incomes (including Mary's income as stated below) as follows:

Frank's total income:		€
As above		42,400
Mary's income:		
Irish government loan interest	1,300	
UK Dividends	900	
Other UK income	5,600	
		7,800
Notional total taxable income (joint) (carried forward)		50,200
Income tax (married rate table)		
€50,200 x 20%		10,040
Less credits		
married person's tax credit		(3,300)
PAYE tax credit		(1,650)
Notional income tax liability		5,090

Frank's tax liability for 2015 is then determined finally as follows:

Notional income tax liability attributable to his total income €42,400 chargeable to Irish tax:

	€
€5,090 x €42,400 /€50,200 =	4,299
Actual income tax payable as a single person:	
As calculated above (before aggregation relief)	6,900
Therefore give aggregation relief of €2,601 to reduce final liability to	4,299

13.506 Lloyd's underwriters

A number of Irish resident individuals are members of Lloyd's underwriting syndicates and derive income (or may incur losses) from this membership. A Lloyd's underwriting syndicate carries on a trade of underwriting insurance risks, usually on a world-wide basis, under the collective business name of Lloyd's. Each member of a syndicate shares in its underwriting profits or losses, as well as in the syndicate's investment income and capital gains or losses. Each syndicate is run by the syndicate managers who are professional underwriting agents. The individual members (referred to as 'Names') do not generally participate in the management of the syndicate, but are required to put up a certain amount of capital (either directly or through guarantees) and are paid out their shares of the syndicate's underwriting income (less losses), investment income and capital gains (less losses).

Underwriting income

It may be noted that a syndicate is not a partnership in strict legal terms. In particular, each member of a syndicate is liable only for his personal share of syndicate debts (ie there is no joint and several liability). The Revenue Commissioners' general practices in respect of Irish resident names are set out in *Tax Briefing 19* and *Tax Briefing 24*, and these are reflected in the text below.

Lloyd's underwriting syndicates are managed and controlled in the UK and each Irish resident Name is treated for tax purposes, both in the UK and in the Republic of Ireland, as carrying on a trade in the UK through a permanent establishment there. He is, therefore chargeable to UK income tax on his share of the underwriting income of each syndicate of which he is a member, as well as on his share of the syndicate's investment income. The investment income is treated as being effectively connected with the underwriting business of the syndicate carried on by it through the 'permanent establishment' in the UK and is, therefore, taxable as if it were business profits in the UK in accordance with the Ireland/UK double taxation agreement (see **14.201**). The Name is also liable to UK capital gains tax on his share of the syndicate's capital gains (but not in respect of gains on UK government securities held by the syndicate for more than 12 months).

Capital gains (or losses) on syndicate investments are treated as an element of underwriting profits (or losses). The Irish resident Name is treated, for Irish tax purposes, as carrying on a trade wholly abroad since the Name does not take any part in the management of the trade of the one or more underwriting syndicates of which he is a member (see **4.102**: *Agency arrangements*). The Name is, therefore chargeable to income tax under Sch D Case III on his underwriting income, including his share of the syndicate investment income, and he is entitled to claim loss relief under TCA 1997, s 381 in respect of his share of syndicate underwriting losses. The syndicate investment income and syndicate capital gains arise from the investment of the syndicate's surplus cash; since it receives insurance premiums at an early stage and has only to meet claims later on, each syndicate usually has a significant amount of cash to invest, which it places mainly in UK government securities.

The method of accounting for the syndicate's underwriting business involves keeping accounts on a calendar year basis, but each year's account is kept open until the end of the second calendar year following the particular accounting year. For example, the accounts for the year ended 31 December 2015 will not be closed until 31 December 2017. This is to enable the details of underwriting claims arising in the year of account to be established as accurately as possible and to be fully provided for in those accounts. It is then normal for the Name to be advised of his share of the underwriting profit (or loss) and of the syndicate's investment income, capital gains, etc for the accounting year (eg 2015) about six months after the accounts are finally closed (eg about June 2018). The Name should, however, be given details of his Lloyds fund investment income, capital gains, etc in the year following that in which they arise.

The fact that the syndicate results are not available for about two and a half years after the end of the accounting year necessitates special arrangements for dealing with the Irish resident Name's taxation position in respect of his Lloyd's income. In order to deal with this and other complications arising from the nature of the activity, the Revenue Commissioners have devised special arrangements to deal with all members of Lloyd's resident in the State in respect of their Lloyd's income. These special arrangements had to be changed to fit in with the self-assessment system after it was introduced by FA 1988, Pt I, Ch II (see **Division 2**).

Accordingly, underwriting profits or losses are assessed in the year *following* the year in which the relevant account is closed. Thus the underwriting profit or loss for the Lloyds Account 2015 (which ends on 31 December 2015 and is closed off on 31 December 2017) will be assessed in 2018.

As the Lloyds account is made up on a calendar year basis, it is coterminous with the year of assessment. Accordingly, there is no requirement to apportion profits in the opening and closing years (see **4.206**).

Computation of underwriting income or loss

In arriving at the underwriting profit or loss for any tax year, the Revenue Commissioners accept that the figure as computed for UK tax purposes for the relevant Lloyd's year, and as agreed by each syndicate with the UK Inland Revenue, is to be taken for Irish tax purposes. This effectively applies the normal Sch D Case I rules that would be used in calculating the taxable profits or loss of any other trade. It is normal for each syndicate's own accountants to submit the syndicate accounts to the Inland Revenue and to agree the underwriting profit or loss for the year, as well as the syndicate's investment income, capital gains, etc as chargeable to UK tax. Damages received by underwriters in respect of negligence by their managing and members' agents were held to be taxable as receipts of their underwriting trades in *Deeny & Ors v Gooda Walker Ltd* [1996] STC 299.

A taxpayer is allowed to deduct (for both UK and Irish tax purposes) payments made to a 'special reserve fund', designed to finance underwriting losses. Correspondingly, any withdrawals from the fund are treated as trading receipts. The income and gains attributable to investments held in a special reserve fund are treated as exempt for both UK and Irish tax purposes.

The taxable underwriting profit or loss can be ascertained by reference to the taxation advice issued by Lloyd's Central Services Unit (a reproduction of which is included in *Tax Briefing 19*). The relevant figure is shown on line 14 of the advice, but this will be further adjusted by reference to:

(a) Costs incurred by the Name in his own right such as bank/guarantee charges, letter of credit fees and 'stop loss' premiums (ie a policy taken out by the Name to limit his potential underwriting losses). A number of other possible deductions are discussed below.

(b) Recoveries receivable under stop loss policies (taxed for the year of assessment in respect of which the loss is declared); withdrawals from the Special Reserve Fund; rebates of members' special contributions; income exempt from UK taxation (eg interest on 3.5 per cent war loan stock, not taxable in the hands of non-residents).

Additional expenses which may be claimed include:

(a) the initial annual subscription but not the entrance fee;

(b) subscriptions to the Association of Lloyd's Members (ALM) and any related expenses;

(c) interest on loans taken out to fund underwriting losses; presumably interest or loans to meet cash calls or fund other Lloyd's liabilities should also be allowed (however if the Name ceases to underwrite, the interest expense can only be set off against Lloyd's underwriting post-cessation receipts (see **5.607**).

The Revenue also accept that travel and accommodation costs in attending meetings of ALM in Ireland are allowable if incurred 'wholly and exclusively for the purposes of the trade' (given that the Name is not actually carrying on the trade in question, this treatment may be generous). The Revenue Commissioners do not accept that the cost of travelling between a Name's home and London is allowable, following *Newsom v Robertson* (see **5.306**: *Travelling and subsistence expenses*), but may be prepared to allow relief where the cost of overnight accommodation in London is shown to be a 'necessary business expense … which satisfies the wholly and exclusively test'. In fact, it is difficult to see how the cost of an overnight stay can be deductible if the cost of the related travelling is not (either the visit is for exclusively trading purposes or it is not). However, given that the Name is not actually carrying on the trade, the willingness of the Revenue to grant any deductions may again be seen as a reasonable compromise. The UK Revenue have also accepted that subscriptions to various Lloyd's Action Groups are allowable.

Credit relief for overseas tax, including UK tax, is available subject to the normal rules (see **14.3**). Overseas taxes which have been treated as deductions in the computation of underwriting income (see line 10 of the Lloyd's advice) may need to be added back and an appropriate claim for a tax credit made instead. Credit relief is, of course, only available to the extent that the overseas tax is not subsequently refunded (eg under the terms of a tax treaty). The Revenue state that where a taxpayer is uncertain about the amount of overseas tax which will be refunded, it may be possible to avail of the 'expression of doubt' provisions under TCA 1997, s 959P (see **2.105**). Relief for payment of retirement annuity premiums (see **16.202**) is available in practice to all names in respect of both underwriting income and income from funds at Lloyd's even though they may not be actively engaged in underwriting (notwithstanding the strict legal position that such income is not 'relevant earnings', as established in *Koenigsberger v Mellor* [1995] STC 547). Losses incurred by a Name are eligible for relief under TCA 1997, s 381 (or s 385 if appropriate): see **13.202**.

In the case of Names who take up residence in Ireland, or who leave Ireland to take up residence elsewhere, the appropriate treatment will normally depend on the relevant double tax treaty (see **14.105**). The Revenue have stated their practice in non-treaty cases as follows:

(a) Generally, Names who emigrate will continue to be charged to Irish income tax at the standard rate, with any tax credit relief confined to that rate, for each of the three years following emigration. Thus, a Name emigrating in 2015 would remain assessable for tax years up to and including 2018 covering underwriting years up to and including the 2018 account.

(b) However, it is recognised that this approach would give rise to anomalous results in Ireland, where a Name had been resident for a period of, say, less than six years. For example, a Name resident in Ireland for three tax years might under the above treatment be assessable for six tax years, covering six underwriting accounts. These situations will be dealt with by the Revenue on a case by case basis, the general intention being to ensure that the Name is not assessable for years in excess of those of actual residence.

The Revenue have also stated their practice in relation to deceased Names as follows (updated in terms of references for years of assessment):

> A deceased Name will be taxed in the year of assessment in which death occurs, following the normal rules. Thus, a Name dying in October 2015 will be assessable for 2015 on the results of the 2012 underwriting account. Certain underwriting accounts will not be closed at the time of death and therefore some profits or losses will remain to be established for the Lloyd's activities. The latter income will be assessed on the executors for each of the subsequent years of assessment for which underwriting profit or losses remain to be determined. Thus, in the example given above, the executors would be assessable for 2016 on the results of the 2013 account, for 2017 on the results of the 2014 account and so on. Personal allowances, tax credits and reliefs would not be available.
>
> Where a deceased Name has underwriting losses carried forward as at the date of death, these may be carried forward to his executors for offset against any subsequent underwriting profits assessable in their name.
>
> Terminal loss relief will also be available to the executors on losses arising in the final year of assessment of Lloyd's income. This relief may be carried back for offset against Lloyd's income in earlier years including the year of assessment in which death occurred subject to the three year rule. Any losses on underwriting accounts not closed at the date of death and assessed on the executors are relievable only against other Lloyd's related income and not against any other income assessable on the executors as part of the Estate.

Tax Briefing 19 sets out reproductions of (i) the Lloyd's Taxation Advice, together with (ii) the statement required for Irish tax purposes.

It is to be noted that the figures provided by the syndicates are quoted in pounds sterling. Therefore, in making his return, the Name should convert them into euro at the appropriate rate of exchange for the closing date of the relevant Lloyd's accounting year. The question arises as to the date on which the pound sterling/Irish pound exchange rate is to be taken to translate the pounds sterling figures into euro. The Irish Revenue practice seeks to use the exchange rate prevailing at the end of the calendar year in which the earlier Lloyd's accounting year is closed (for example, the rate at 31 December 2017 for the Lloyd's year ended 31 December 2015).

This practice could be open to question. It seems that a case could be made for translating the sterling figures into euro at the exchange rate prevailing on the closing date of the relevant Lloyd's accounting year, ie the year end rate for the accounting year in which the income is earned (even though the underwriter may not actually receive the income until it has been quantified some years later).

Funds at Lloyd's

The income from Lloyd's funds, although treated for UK and Irish tax purposes as underwriting income is not included in the Lloyd's taxation advice. However, such income must be reported, noting that it is assessable on normal principles (ie the three year delay does *not* apply to such incomes). Similarly, any capital gains arising in respect of Lloyd's funds continue to be liable to Irish tax in the normal way.

The Name is required to maintain a deposit (the 'Lloyd's deposit') at a prescribed minimum consisting of approved investments. In addition, the Name is likely to have investments made for him by the syndicate on account of his own 'Lloyd's funds', which he is expected to build up and have retained by the syndicate as a cushion against possible future underwriting losses. The Lloyd's deposit and the personal reserve are known collectively as 'Lloyd's funds'. Investment income and capital gains or losses from Lloyd's funds are also treated as income or capital gains effectively connected with the Lloyd's permanent establishment in the UK so as to be subject to UK tax. Capital gains realised on investments held outside the UK are not, however, subject to UK capital gains tax, provided that the Name is not domiciled in any part of the UK. These UK exempt capital gains, however, remain subject to Irish capital gains tax.

Lloyds reconstruction and renewal scheme

The Revenue Commissioners have set out how they intend to deal with the tax implications of the Lloyds reconstruction and renewal scheme in *Tax Briefing 24*. Payments received under the Estate Protection Plan in order to meet losses are taxed as trading receipts, as are any return premiums payable under the terms of the Equitas reinsurance contract (these will be attributed to the tax year beginning in the calendar year in which the return premium is received, or to the tax year of receipt for Names who have ceased to trade at Lloyds). The impact of the reconstruction and renewal proposals on recoveries under stop loss policies is also covered. Finally, the Revenue Commissioners note that some other Irish tax issues may arise which are particular to individuals; each Irish case will be looked at on a case-by-case basis.

13.6 Taxation of Non-Residents

13.601 General

The territorial limits of Irish taxation have been discussed in Ch 1. In broad terms, non-residents are taxable only in respect of income from Irish sources, although individuals who are not resident but who are ordinarily resident may also be liable in respect of certain non-Irish sources (see **13.504**).

In many cases, the assessment of a non-resident in respect of Irish source income is under one of the Cases of Sch D (depending on the type of income involved), but distributions received from Irish resident companies are taxable under Sch F (see **13.608**) and income from offices, employments and pensions in the State are chargeable under Sch E (see **13.607**).

The treatment of a non-resident discussed in this Division is in the context of a person chargeable to income tax. A non-resident company that carries on a trade in the State through a branch or agency is chargeable to corporation tax (and not to income tax) on the resulting trading income and on any other income that is properly attributable to that trading branch or agency.

A non-resident company that does not trade in the State remains chargeable to income tax under the rules summarised above or, even if it trades in the State, on any Irish source income other than that attributable to the trading branch or agency. To the extent that a non-resident company is chargeable to income tax on any such income, the discussion which follows (other than that relating to the personal allowances and the higher rate of income tax) is equally applicable as to any other non-resident person.

A non-resident person (other than an individual taxable as such) is liable to income tax at the standard rate only and is not entitled to any personal allowances or reliefs. However, he will be able to claim amounts specifically deductible in computing the income (eg trading or rental expenses) as well as deductions for losses and other payments, subject to the normal rules for allowability. A non-resident individual is chargeable to income tax at the standard rate and, if their total income from Irish sources is high enough, at the higher rate. The treatment of individuals is dealt with further in **13.610** where the circumstances in which a non-resident individual may be entitled to claim some personal allowances are discussed.

An important qualification needs to be made regarding the matters discussed in this part of this chapter. The non-resident person may be a resident of another country which has concluded a double taxation agreement (a 'tax treaty') with the government of the Republic of Ireland. If so, the principles described here may be subject to some modification by one or more of the provisions of the relevant tax treaty.

For example, the treaty may provide that certain types of Irish source income are not to be taxable in the State, but only in the country in which the foreign resident person is resident or, alternatively, it may limit the rate of Irish tax that may be imposed on the foreign resident in respect of certain types of Irish source income. It is, therefore, important to note that the treatment of non-residents discussed in the rest of **Division 13** is, unless indicated otherwise in relation to any particular point, based on the tax law of the State before considering the effects of any relevant tax treaty.

13.602 Trades exercised within the State

A non-resident person is chargeable to tax on the profits from any trade or profession exercised within the State or from the sale of goods manufactured or partly manufactured in the State (TCA 1997, s 18(1)). The profits from a trade are taxed under Case I and those from a profession under Case II (TCA 1997, s 18(2)). While the issue arises much more frequently for a trade than it does for a profession, it is of course quite possible for a non-resident to carry on his profession partly or wholly in the State. Consequently, although for convenience the discussion which follows is expressed mainly in terms of a trade, most of it is equally applicable (with any necessary modifications in wording) to a profession exercised within the State by a non-resident person(s).

The question of when a non-resident person carries on a trade within the State so as to be chargeable to Irish income tax is one which requires consideration of some of the more important tax cases that were decided in the UK. The principles which have been clearly established by those cases are, it has always been considered, equally applicable (assuming similar circumstances) in helping to decide the issue for Irish tax purposes. It should, of course, be emphasised that it is important to look carefully at the facts of any particular case before coming to any definite conclusions as to its outcome. The decided tax cases do, however, provide a number of principles which should be applied wherever appropriate to the facts.

For the non-resident to be assessable to tax on a trade in the State, it is required that he should exercise the trade 'within' the State. Lord Herschell, in *Grainger & Sons v Gough* 3 TC 462 drew attention to the distinction that has to be made, when he said:

> In the first place, I think there is a broad distinction between trading *with* a country, and carrying on a trade *within* a country. Many merchants and manufacturers export their goods to all parts of the world, yet I do not suppose anyone would dream of saying that they exercise or carry on their trade in every country in which their goods find customers … If all that a merchant does in any particular country is to solicit orders, I do not think he can reasonably be said to exercise or carry on his trade in that country.

The *Grainger & Son* case concerned a French wine merchant who appointed an English firm as his sole agents in England for the sale of champagne. The English agents obtained orders, which they transmitted to their principal abroad. The French wine merchant exercised his discretion as to executing the orders. The wine ordered was forwarded from France direct to the purchasers at their expense and risk. Payments were mainly made directly to the French wine merchant, though sometimes they were made through the agents. All receipts were sent by the French wine merchant to the customers directly. The English agents were paid by commission.

It was held in the House of Lords that the French wine merchant did not exercise a trade within the UK. The important facts behind the Lords' decision were that the contracts for the sale of the champagne were not made in the UK either by, or on behalf of, the French wine merchant, but only when he accepted in France the orders canvassed by his UK agents, and (to a much lesser extent) that the delivery of the goods to the customers was made in France on the dispatch of the goods direct from Rheims. Lord Watson added:

> There is, in my opinion, a very broad distinction between the case of a foreigner making contracts in England with his English customers for the sale of his wines, either personally or through a representative, and the case of his making similar contracts with those customers in his own country. In the present instance the orders forwarded to Louis Roederer were, in law, nothing more than offers to purchase, until the contract between him and each offeror was completed by his acceptance at Rheims; and he fulfilled his part of the contract by making delivery of the wine sold to the purchaser, and at his risk in Rheims.

The *Grainger & Sons* case was one where all (or, at least, most) of the main factors – place of conclusion of contracts, place of delivery and place of payment – were all outside the country, thus leading to the conclusion that the non-resident wine merchant was only trading with, and not within, the country. In practice, many actual cases are equally clear in the opposite direction (*Pommery and Greno v Apthorpe* 2 TC 182, discussed below).

Thus, for example a non-resident individual may operate in the State through a branch office which both buys and sells goods in the State or which maintains a stock of imported goods from which its locally based staff execute orders and supply goods to the customers. In such a case, the non-resident is clearly exercising a trade within the State and the profits realised from that trade are assessable to income tax.

The importance of the place where the contracts for sale are concluded in the case of a merchanting business has been emphasised in a number of other decided cases. For example, in *Maclaine & Co v Eccott* 10 TC 481 at page 574, Viscount Cave LC made the following observation:

> The question whether a trade is exercised in the UK is a question of fact, and it is undesirable to attempt to lay down any exhaustive test of what constitutes such an exercise of trade; but I think it must now be taken as established that in the case of a merchant's business, the primary object of which is to sell goods at a profit, the trade is (speaking generally) exercised or carried on … at the place where the contracts are made. No doubt reference has sometimes been made to the place where payment is made for the goods sold or to the place where the goods are delivered, and it may be that in certain circumstances these are material considerations; but the most important, and indeed the crucial, question is where the contracts of sale made?

The determination of the place where the contract of sale is concluded will normally be made under Irish legal principles. This determination may be of considerable significance in the context of electronic commerce. Thus, for example an Irish customer may order goods through the internet from a non-resident supplier. If the non-resident communicates acceptance of the order to the Irish customer via the internet, the contract will be concluded in the State and the non-resident will accordingly be trading in the State. In practice, it would not be difficult to organise matters so that contracts were in fact concluded outside the State.

Where a non-resident simply purchases goods within the State and uses those goods to fulfil contracts made outside the State to supply goods to another non-resident person, this does not amount to exercising a trade in the State (see *Sulley v Attorney General* 2 TC 149).

The same principles which have been applied in the case of merchanting operations, have been extended to international communication and transport operations. Thus, in *Erichsen v Last* 4 TC 422, a non-resident telegraph company possessing a world-wide system of cables was held to exercise a trade within the UK in respect of telegraphic communication services to foreign countries on the grounds that the contracts were made in the UK.

Cotton LJ, observed:

> … the trade or business which the company carries on is a business of collecting messages for transmission to various parts of the world: that is to say entering into contracts for money paid to them to transmit telegraphic messages to various parts of the world. That business might be carried on by them even although they have no lines at all of their own.

A non-resident shipping or airline business transporting passengers or goods from ports or airports within the country to foreign countries is, for similar reasons, regarded as exercising a trade within the State to the extent that its business is derived from contracts concluded or tickets sold in the State (see *Cunard Steam Ship Co Ltd v Herlihy* I ITR 330).

Atkin LJ in *Greenwood v Smidth* 8 TC 193 at page 203, while accepting the importance of the place of the contracts, suggested a more fundamental test, namely:

> I think that the question is, where do the operations take place from which the profits in substance arise?

In *Greenwood v Smidth* 8 TC 193 a Danish company, which sold machinery to UK customers had a UK-based employee who solicited orders and who was involved in the preliminary negotiation of contracts (all of which were however concluded by the non-resident trader). The employee also supervised the installation of the machinery in the UK. It was held that the profits 'in substance arose' in Denmark. The activities carried out by the employee in the UK, were regarded as merely ancillary to the exercise of the trade in Denmark where 'the goods were bought and sold'.

This more broadly based test proposed by Atkin LJ appears more pertinent in the non-merchanting context. Thus, where goods are manufactured in the State, but are shipped and sold abroad it would seem logical on *general principles* that the profits therefrom are attributable to operations carried on in the State.

In *Greenwood v Smidth*, however, Atkin J did not quite so far as fully endorsing this proposition when he observed:

> I can imagine cases where the contract of resale is made abroad and yet the manufacture of the goods, some negotiation of the terms and complete execution of the contract take place [in the UK] under such circumstances that the trade was in truth exercised here.

The reference to the negotiation and execution of the contract as additional prerequisites may seem unduly cautious. In *Firestone Tyre & Rubber Co v Llewellin* 37 TC 111 (discussed below), a manufacturing operation carried on in the UK was held to constitute trading in the UK although the master contract under which all sales were made had been concluded outside the UK. In *Pommery and Greno v Apthorpe* 2 TC 182 the taxpayers manufactured champagne in France, but sold stocks through a branch office located in the UK. It was held that the taxpayers were trading in the UK on the basis that they were habitually entering into sale contracts there. No weight was placed on the fact that the product in question was manufactured outside the UK, although Lord Denman implied in his judgment that it would be necessary to exclude the manufacturing element of the profits concerned (see the discussion in **13.604**).

In *Commissioners of Taxation v Kirk* [1900] AC 588 (a case concerning similar issues in the context of Australian tax law), the taxpayer extracted ore and converted it into a marketable product in one jurisdiction, but sold it in a different jurisdiction. It was held that the taxpayer was carrying on its trade in the first jurisdiction.

In *Rhodesia Metals Ltd v IRC* [1940] AC 774, (a case concerning Rhodesian tax) it was held that profits from purchasing, developing and selling property in a particular jurisdiction arose in that jurisdiction, irrespective of the fact that the contracts of purchase and sale were concluded in a different jurisdiction. It is difficult to extract a single, clear principle from the non-merchanting cases. It may well be that on general principles the carrying on of manufacturing or like operations *or* the regular entering of sales contracts in the State is sufficient to establish a trade in the State. The point is largely academic in the case of pure manufacturing operations carried on in the State since TCA 1997, s 18(1) imposes tax under Sch D Case I on non-residents in respect of profits from the sale of goods, wares or merchandise manufactured or partly manufactured by them in the State.

There are also some cases which shed light on the location of profits arising from the performance of professional services. In *IRC v Brackett* [1986] STC 521, the taxpayer entered into a contract of service with a non-resident company as a property consultant. The taxpayer was the company's only employee and the consultancy was its only trade. The taxpayer referred potential clients to the company and the clients then contracted with the company. It was held that, because the consultancy activities were carried out in the UK and these represented the essential operations of the company's trade, the company was trading within the UK (the issue became academic, since the taxpayer was held to be assessable on the company's profits under the UK equivalent of TCA 1997, s 806 (see **17.203**).

In *Yates v GCA* [1991] STC 157, the taxpayer entered into a consultancy agreement in Venezuela under which part of the services thereunder were performed in the UK and part in Venezuela. The case was not directly concerned with the UK equivalent of TCA 1997, s 18, but it is relevant, because the test propounded by Atkin LJ in *Greenwood v Smidth* was applied in order to see if profits arose in Venezuela. Scott J held that on these facts the profits from the contract arose in substance where the services were performed – ie partly in the UK and partly in Venezuela. Interestingly, the point was kept open as to whether or not the profits from a consultancy contract concluded in the UK by a non-resident where the services were carried out principally outside the UK would be taxable under the UK equivalent to TCA 1997, s 18. If the answer were in the affirmative, this would imply that a non-resident performing professional services will be taxable in the State if either the service contract is concluded in the State or the services are performed in the State (but only to the extent that they are performed there). This would be similar to the position which as suggested above may apply to manufacturing and like activities (although in the latter case the profits attributable to manufacturing outside the State would be excluded).

In *CIR v HK-TVB International Ltd* [1992] STC 723, the Privy Council applied the 'where the profits in substance arise' test in the context of intellectual property under a provision of Hong Kong tax law. The taxpayer company was based in Hong Kong, from where it carried on a trade of granting sublicences in respect of its overseas copyright interests in various films. In general, the taxpayer sent its representatives abroad to solicit business and to negotiate with potential customers. The sublicences were granted in Hong Kong in consideration of fixed sums to the overseas customers. These sums were not linked in any way to the profits subsequently made by the taxpayers' customers. The Privy Council held that the taxpayer did not render any services in the relevant overseas territories, since this implied positive activity on the part of the taxpayer. Instead, the taxpayer had as a result of granting the licences, merely refrained from preventing its customers exploiting the films which it had licensed to them. Further, the fact that the licences were exercisable overseas was irrelevant, in the absence of any participation in the licensees' profits by the taxpayer. The Privy Council concluded accordingly that the operations which gave rise to the taxpayer's profits were carried out in Hong Kong and not overseas.

The decision in *CIR v HK-TVB* distinguished the earlier case of *CIR v Hang Seng Bank* [1990] STC 733. In the latter case, the Privy Council held that profits on the purchases and sale of foreign currency executed outside Hong Kong arose outside Hong Kong. Interestingly, Lord Bridges remarked:

> The broad governing principle, attested by many authorities, is one looks to see what the taxpayer has done to earn the profits in question. If he has rendered a service or engaged in an activity such as the manufacture of goods, the profit will have arisen or derived from the place where the *service was rendered*, or *the profit making activity was carried on* …
>
> But if the profit was earned by … dealing in commodities or securities by buying and reselling at a profit, the profit will have arisen where the contracts of purchase and sale were effected (emphasis added)

The latter reference to contracts of 'purchase and sale' may simply reflect the particular facts of the Hong Kong case, rather than detract from the importance of the location of the contract of sale in relation to merchanting-type operations.

In *CIR v Orion Caribbean* [1997] STC 923 (another case on Hong Kong law) the profits from loans which were made outside Hong Kong but where the corresponding borrowings were raised in Hong Kong and which were also negotiated, approved and serviced in Hong Kong were held to arise in substance in Hong Kong.

The position is further complicated by the fact that the non-resident may trade within the State through an intermediary such as an agent.

The term 'agency' in contract law denotes a relationship under which the agent binds the principal on whose behalf he is acting; where a person who is acting on behalf of a principal, but does not bind him by the contract which he makes (as in *Ireland v Livingston* 1872 LR 5 HL 395) then he is not a true agent in the contract law sense (albeit described as a 'commission agent' in *Ireland v Livingston*: see *Bowstead & Reynolds on Agency* (16th edn, Sweet and Maxwell, 1996) at 1.019). However, the term 'agency' may have a wider meaning in other contexts. In *Customs & Excise v Johnson* [1980] STC 624 it was held that an agent was a person who acts on behalf of another; it is submitted that, similarly, for the purposes of Sch D Cases I/II, the test for an agent is whether the person concerned is carrying on trading activities on his own behalf or on behalf of another (the principal).

Thus, a non-resident may be trading in the state through an agent, even where the agent is selling the goods in question as a principal: *Weiss, Bilheller and Brook v Farmer* 8 TC 381 (following the wide usage of the term in *Ireland v Livingston*). This principle was also applied in *Firestone Tyre & Rubber Co v Llewellin* 37 TC 111 where a subsidiary company was held to be manufacturing and selling goods on behalf of its overseas parent (thus rendering the parent liable on the full manufacturing profits, less a small commission). The key point here was that the parent company exercised comprehensive control over its subsidiary in such a manner as to direct the conduct of its trading and to ensure that it obtained the profits therefrom (see also the discussion of this case at **1.407** and also *IRC v Brackett* discussed above). It must also be borne in mind that the use of an agent or employee based in the State does not necessarily imply that the non-resident is trading in the State (note *Greenwood v Smidth*, discussed above).

A finding of agency being one of fact, will however depend on the exact circumstances of each case.

One further point: if the non-resident is entitled to benefit under a double taxation treaty between his country of residence and the State, he is only likely to be liable to Irish tax on his trading profits to the extent that they are attributable to a trade exercised in the State through a permanent establishment, even if the contracts for sales are concluded in the State. Similarly, the treatment of a foreign shipping or airline business may sometimes be protected by the article regarding international transport in a relevant tax treaty (see **14.203**).

13.603 Assessment of non-residents

TCA 1997, s 1034 provides that any non-resident person may be assessed to tax in the name of any trustee, guardian, or committee, or in the name of any factor, agent, receiver, branch, or manager. This assessment is to be made and the tax charged in the same way as if the non-resident person were a resident. It may be made whether or not the factor, agent, etc actually receives the profits or gains on which the assessment in his (or, if a company, its) name is made on the non-resident.

TCA 1997, s 1035 provides that any non-resident person is to be charged to tax on any profits or gains arising, whether directly or indirectly through or from any factorship, agency, receivership, branch or management; the tax so chargeable is assessable in the name of the factor, agent, receiver, branch or manager. These provisions appear to be saying almost the same thing twice, but it may be they are intended to be complementary to each other. TCA 1997, s 1034 ensures that the non-receipt by the factor, agent, branch, etc of the profits does not prevent him being assessed on behalf of the non-resident. TCA 1997, s 1035 expressly limits the assessment that may be made to the profits or gains realised, whether directly or indirectly, by the factorship, agency, branch, etc by means of which the non-resident exercises the trade in the State.

In *IRC v Brackett* (see above) Hoffman J upheld a finding of fact by the Special Commissioners that the sole employee of a non-resident company carrying on a trade in the State was a 'branch or agency' of that company. Hoffman J added:

> for the purposes of [the UK equivalent of TCA 1997, s 1035] I do not think that it is necessary that an agent should be a person who is empowered to enter into contractual relations on behalf of the non-resident company … I find it difficult to imagine how a non-resident company which carries on a trade with any degree of continuity in the UK can do so otherwise than through a [factorship, agency, receivership, branch or management].

In *Hafton Properties Ltd v McHugh* [1987] STC 16, it was held that it was possible for a non-resident to trade in the UK without a branch or agency there. In the instant case it was unclear whether a non-resident bank in this situation, and which had made a number of loans to UK residents, had concluded the loan contracts in the UK; however, irrespective of the contractual position, the Appeal Commissioners were held to be entitled to find that no business was being carried on in the UK. It may be said perhaps that the profits 'in substance' arose from the ongoing provision of funds made by the overseas offices of the bank rather than at the point of contract.

At first sight, it might appear as if, once the non-resident has an agency, branch, etc in the State, TCA 1997, s 1035 would permit that person to be assessed on all profits arising directly or indirectly through the agency, branch, etc, even if the sales contracts (and any other relevant factors) take place abroad. This is not in fact the case. The House of Lords held in *Greenwood v Smidth* (see **13.602**) that the UK equivalent of TCA 1997, s 1035 did not have the effect of extending in this way the general principles under which a non-resident is chargeable to tax. It was not considered to be a charging section, but rather one relating to the machinery or method for collecting the tax payable by virtue of the main charging rules of Sch D; (see also *IRC v Commerzbank* [1990] STC 285.)

Consequently, it may be taken that TCA 1997, ss 1034, 1035 can only be applied to enable an inspector to assess a non-resident in the name of an agent, branch, etc, if, and to the extent that profits arise from a trade exercised in the State by, or on behalf of, the non-resident.

With effect from 1 January 2003, TCA 1997, s 1035A removes the potential liability to Irish tax which would otherwise arise where a non-resident avails of the services of an authorised agent who is resident in the State in order to carry on a financial trade in the State. An authorised agent is essentially a person carrying on investment business services and which is authorised under the Investment Intermediaries Act 1995 or the Stock Exchange Act 1995 or under equivalent legislation in another Member State of the EU, including a credit institution within the EU. Since 2010, an authorised agent also includes a company which is authorised under any laws of the State that implement the relevant Directives (as defined by the section) and which carries on a trade which consists of or includes the management of unit trust, common contractual funds or investment companies, or any combination of the three, each of which is a relevant UCITS as defined by the section. The definition of 'authorised agent' was further expanded with effect from 1 January 2016 to include Alternative Investment Fund Managers (AIFMs) having the same meaning as in TCA 1997, s 747G which are: Irish authorised AIFMs, or an Irish branch or agency of an AIFM authorised under the laws of an EEA state. In broad terms, to qualify for exemption, the agent must:

(a) be acting in the ordinary course of the agent's business;
(b) be acting in an independent capacity; (the Revenue Commissioners interpret this as meaning that the commercial relationship between the agent and the non-resident person must be at arm's length);
(c) must have a limited economic involvement in the financial trade of the non-resident (generally no greater than a 20 per cent entitlement to the profits of the trade, including the interests of persons connected with the agent); and
(d) must not otherwise act for the non-resident person.

In addition to the provisions of TCA 1997, s 1035, TCA 1997, s 1036 may give rise to a liability where:

(a) a non-resident person exercises substantial control over a resident person;
(b) there is a close connection between the non-resident person and the resident person; and
(c) owing to (a) and (b), the business which is carried on between the resident person and non-resident person in pursuance of their close connection is arranged so that the resident person makes either no profits, or less than the ordinary profits, which would be expected from that business.

Where TCA 1997, s 1036 applies, two consequences follow:

(a) the non-resident person is treated as carrying on a notional trade in the State through the agency of the resident person; and

(b) the non-resident is assessable on the profits from that notional trade in the name of the resident person.

TCA 1997, s 1036 is accordingly both a charging section and also a machinery section for the collection of the tax charged (see *Gillette Safety Razor Ltd v IRC* [1920] 3 KB 358).

TCA 1997, s 1036 does not apply where the non-resident person is either an Irish citizen, an Irish firm or company, or a branch of a non-resident person thereof. An 'Irish' company is one incorporated in the State (*Egyptian Delta Land & Investment Co v Todd* 14 TC 119). The granting of preferential treatment to Irish nationals is likely to conflict with the non-discrimination article in any relevant double tax treaty (see **14.219**) and also with the right to freedom of establishment under EU law (see **1.410**).

TCA 1997, s 1039 imposes a further restriction on the circumstances in which a non-resident may be charged to tax in the name of an agent or other similar person. It provides that no assessment can be made under TCA 1997, Pt 45 Ch 1 in respect of profits arising from sales or transactions carried out through either a broker or general commission agent or an agent who is not an authorised person carrying on the regular agency of the non-resident person.

In *Nielsen, Andersen & Co v Collins* 13 TC 91 it was held that the expression 'not being an authorised person carrying on the non-resident's regular agency' limited the scope of the terms 'broker' and 'general commission agent' as well as the term 'agent'. This is a somewhat surprising conclusion, and its correctness is open to question. If it is correct, it means that it is not sufficient for the taxpayer to show that he is trading as a broker or general commission agent in order to fall outside TCA 1997, s 1039; he must *also* show that he is not carrying on the regular agency of the non-resident trader. The effect of the provision is not that the non-resident person cannot be charged to tax if his or its activities in the State amount to the exercising of a trade there, but simply that the assessment cannot be made on any broker, general commission agent or other agent in question within TCA 1997, s 1039.

TCA 1997, s 1039 specifies that it does not apply to a resident person who is deemed to be an agent for the purposes of TCA 1997, s 1036. The terms 'broker' and 'commission agent', which first appeared in tax legislation in 1915, have their origins in 19th century mercantile law. A broker was generally a selling agent who did not have possession of the goods being sold (although a stockbroker is a long-established exception to this principle) while a 'commission agent' (or 'factor') was a selling agent who had such possession and who normally sold the goods in his own name (see JF Avery-Jones & D A Ward, 'Agents as Permanent Establishments under the OECD Model Convention' [1993] BTR 341). In *Wilcock v Pinto* 9 TC 111 it was observed that a broker was 'essentially a negotiator between two parties'.

The term '*general* commission broker' is however, a creation of tax law. In *Fleming v London Produce* 44 TC 582 Megarry J observed:

> … the word 'general' itself must have some import, and in the context I think the most likely sense is that of a commission agent who holds himself out as being ready to work for clients generally and who does not in substance confine his activities to one principal or an insignificant number of principals.

While the statutory wording of ITA 1952, s 373 (the UK counterpart of TCA 1997, s 1039 at that time) is not directly comparable to that of TCA 1997, s 1039, this observation may still carry persuasive weight in the Irish context.

In the case of *Gavazzi v Mace* 10 TC 698, it was held on the facts that UK agents were really working for a non-resident firm and that they were not, in consequence, acting as brokers or general commission agents. Rowlatt J referred to the fact that the agents in that case had accepted a bill of exchange that enabled the non-resident firm to give its money in advance and said:

> … This differentiates them entirely, and must differentiate them, from the position of a general commission agent. It was contended as I understand it, that because they were remunerated by a commission, and by the full commission which is earned in this trade, therefore there was no reason to consider them being anything else, they were merely general commission agents. I do not think that this is possible, I think they were doing something clearly outside the scope of general commission agents …

In *Belfour v Mace* 13 TC 539 an agent who had undertaken not to act for his principal's competitors, and who received a commission on some sales which were not negotiated by him, was held not to qualify as a 'general commission agent' (see also *Boyd & Sons v Stephen* heard concurrently).

In *Wilcock v Pinto* 9 TC 111, a UK individual who was appointed agent for the UK market by an overseas trader (and who did not act for other traders, although at liberty to do so) was held to act as a 'regular agent' of the non-resident (see also *Nielsen, Andersen & Co v Collins* (noted above)).

In *Firestone Tyre & Rubber Co v Llewellin* (see above) the UK company there was held to be assessable as a regular agent of its non-resident parent as in *IRC v Brackett* above, the resident agent did not enter into contracts on behalf of the non-resident principal.

In *Wilson v Hooker* [1995] STC 1142, it was said that a 'regular agency' was an agency which was other than casual or occasional. Vinelott J proceeded to hold that the taxpayer, who had arranged for the purchase and sale of a parcel of UK land on behalf of a non-resident company, acted as the company's 'regular' agent. Although the company had only undertaken one trading transaction, the taxpayer was the person through whom all the transactions of [the non-resident] in the UK were carried out during the relevant period. The logic of the decision (which is open to question) is that somebody who acts for a trader who does not trade regularly is more likely to be found to be a regular agent!

TCA 1997, s 1039(2) prevents a resident agent or any other resident person from being assessed (on behalf of a non-resident) in respect of profits arising from sales or transactions which the non-resident makes with other non-resident persons (the so called 'double foreigner' exemption). This means that the resident agent may in the course of an agency business act for non-resident principals and arrange or carry out transactions on their behalf with non-resident customers without being assessable under TCA 1997, s 1034 on the profits made on behalf of the non-resident principals. The resident agent is, of course, assessable directly in respect of any agency profits earned through commissions received in respect of the business arranged abroad. The protection of TCA 1997, s 1039(2) extends only to agents and other relevant individuals and not for example to the Irish branch of a non-resident trader (*Muller v Lethem* 13 TC 126).

In *Maclaine & Co v Eccott* 10 TC 481, Viscount Cave stated that the 'double foreigner' exemption applied only in cases where the agent did not actually receive the profits in question. This dictum was explicable by virtue of the fact that FA 1915, s 31(7) (which brought in the 'double foreigner' exemption) did so only by reference to FA 1915, s 31(1) (which expressly extended the power to assess resident agents to cases where they did not receive the profits in question). However, ITA 1967 General Rules 5,

6 and 11 (the precursors of TCA 1997, ss 1034–1036), although part of a consolidation Act, did not limit the scope of the double foreigner exemption in this manner. Accordingly, it would seem that Viscount Cave's dictum is no longer valid.

In *Puddhu v Doleman* [1995] STC (SCD) 236, the UK Special Commissioner held (*inter alia*) that the fact that all of a non-resident's trading operations were carried out in the UK did not mean that he was trading there through a 'branch'.

It is not always easy to apply these long-established principles to electronic commerce. It is considered that an internet service provider (ISP) which provides a web site and internet access to a non-resident trader will not normally constitute an agent thereof. This follows because the ISP will simply be providing facilities to the non-resident, enabling the latter to conduct his trading operations. This issue will only be relevant of course if the non-resident is trading 'within' Ireland (see the discussion at **13.602**).

13.604 Computation of non-residents' trading income

A non-resident person is assessable (in the name of the resident agent, etc) on the profits of the trade which he (or, if a company, it) exercises in the State. In principle, the assessable profits are computed in accordance with the rules of Sch D Case I and the non-resident is entitled to the same capital allowances as a resident person (but only in respect of capital expenditure on qualifying assets used for the part of his trade in the State). While these principles are quite clear, it may not always be quite so easy to determine what are the profits properly attributable to the trade in the State if that is only part of his entire trade (note in this regard *Yates v GCA* [1991] STC 157). Some further comments are, therefore, necessary.

Ideally, the non-resident should make up a separate set of accounts setting out the total sales of the trade exercised in the State (usually a branch or agency), and deducting the cost of sales after adjusting for the opening and closing trading stocks and all the expenses incurred to the extent attributable to the trade carried on by or through the branch or agency. If such a set of accounts is available, the Sch D Case I computation is made in the same way as for a trade carried on by a resident person with such adjustments (add backs and deductions) as are necessary to arrive at the taxable profit or loss (see **4.202**).

To the extent that the expenses charged include an allocation of the total expenses of the non-resident's whole business, this should be disclosed to the inspector in submitting the accounts. The inspector will require to be satisfied that the apportionment of the expenses had been made on a reasonable basis to arrive at the best possible estimate of the expenses incurred for that part of the total trade that is exercised in the State.

In the event that the non-resident's branch or agency in the State sells goods previously manufactured or purchased by the business outside the State, the inspector may wish to be satisfied that the price at which these goods are charged to the branch (and debited in its accounts as part of the cost of sales) is a fair and proper one. If the goods have been purchased outside the State by the non-resident, the amount debited in the branch's cost of sales should be the cost of purchase plus any transport costs, excise and/or import duties payable, etc and should not include any profit element. If the goods have been manufactured or produced by the non-resident outside the State, then the non-resident is entitled to debit in the branch's cost of sales such an amount as is necessary to limit the profit made on the sale of those goods by the branch to the profit which might reasonably be expected to be realised by an independent merchant or retailer (whichever corresponds to the type of business carried on by the branch) (TCA 1997, s 1038).

In cases where separate accounts are not prepared for the part of the trade that is carried on in the State, the inspector is likely to request a copy of the accounts of the non-resident's entire trade and to seek to ensure that the proper proportion of the non-resident's total trading profit or loss is attributed to the branch or agency in the State. This proportion could, in the absence of special factors, possibly be based on the proportion that the sales of the branch or agency in the State bear to the total sales of the entire trade.

Again, it is necessary to make any add backs or deductions for disallowable expenses (eg business entertainment expenses) or other items to reflect the rules of Sch D Case I. If the branch sells goods manufactured or produced outside the State by the non-resident person's own business, the non-resident may again apply under TCA 1997, s 1038 to have the branch's taxable profit attributable to those sales limited to the profit which an independent merchant or retailer would expect to realise if carrying on a similar type of business.

TCA 1997, s 1037(1) provides that where the inspector or (following an appeal) the Appeal Commissioners take the view that the true amount of the trading profits of a non-resident person who is chargeable in the name of a resident person cannot be readily ascertained, then he may be assessed on a 'percentage of turnover' basis. If either the non-resident or the resident person is dissatisfied with the percentage adopted, there is a right of appeal to a referee or board of referees appointed specially by the Minister of Finance. The decision of the referee or board is final and conclusive. In practice, however, TCA 1997, s 1037 is most unlikely to be invoked.

One further point should be noted. If the non-resident person is a resident of a country with which there is a double taxation agreement, the terms of that agreement and particularly the article dealing with business profits (see **14.202**) should be consulted. It may contain provisions relevant to the computation of the taxable profits (or loss) of the non-resident's trade in the State.

13.605 Non-residents and partnership trades

References in this Chapter to a non-resident person carrying on a partnership trade in the State may be taken as including carrying on a profession in the State in partnership.

A non-resident may trade in the State as a partner in a partnership with one or more resident partners or, alternatively, part of a trade operated by a partnership of two or more non-resident persons may be exercised in the State in the same way as in the case of the non-resident person previously discussed. In any such case, the rules for taxing partnership trades apply in a similar way to that discussed in **Division 4**.

Each non-resident partner is separately assessable for the relevant tax year as if his share of the partnership profits were the profits of a separate ('several') trade carried on by him solely. Normally, the non-resident partner is assessable for a tax year on his share of the firm's taxable profits for the firm's 12-months accounting year ending in the same tax year. If the partnership's trade or profession is one carried on primarily outside the State, but with a branch or agency in the State, each non-resident partner is only taxable on his share of the taxable profits of the branch or agency in the State. Capital allowances related to the firm's trade are dealt with similarly (see **4.505**).

If the non-resident person has recently joined the firm or if he ceases to be a partner, the rules of Sch D Cases I and II relating to the commencement or cessation of a trade (see **4.205**, **4.206**) are applied by reference to the non-resident's date of commencement or cessation as if his several trade were a trade on its own (see *Taxing of several trades* in **4.503**).

In determining when the several trade of the non-resident partner is to be regarded as commencing or ceasing, his position in relation to the partnership trade as a whole is the relevant factor, and not the time the partnership trade first commenced or ceased to be exercised in the State. Similarly, in determining when the partnership trade as such commences or ceases, regard is made to the position of the trade as a whole.

One interesting question relates to the treatment of a non-resident partner in partnership with one or more resident partners carrying on a trade that is exercised partly in the State and partly abroad. Is the non-resident partner's share of that part of the profits attributable to the trade outside the State chargeable to Irish tax? The Income Tax Acts do not provide any specific guidance on the point which has, therefore, to be considered from general principles. If the partnership trade is carried on mainly in the State, and if the majority of the partners are residents, it would seem that the non-resident partner is chargeable to Irish tax on his share of the total profits. This is on the general principle that a trade controlled by a resident person or persons is not to be treated as a foreign possession (see **13.103**) so that, in consequence, the non-resident's share of the firm's trading income earned abroad remains income from a trade exercised in the State.

On the other hand, if it can be shown that the control is exercised by non-residents, and if the partnership has branches both in the State and abroad, it would appear that each non-resident partner should only be chargeable under Sch D Case I to the extent that his share of the firm's profits is derived from that part of the trade exercised in the State. In practice, such cases are rare and it is probably not possible to make any general statement which could determine the issue whenever it arises. Each actual case must be considered on its own facts.

One other possibility should be mentioned. It may happen that a non-resident person may be a partner in a firm which carries on a trade in the State through one branch therein and carries on trade in one or more other countries through other branches in those countries. If in such a case, the non-resident's share of the firm's profits (or losses) is solely related to the profits (or losses) of one or more of the branches outside the State, then the non-resident would not normally be chargeable to any Irish tax on his share.

13.606 Continental shelf activities

The Geneva Convention on the High Seas (29 April 1958) entitles the State to exercise rights outside Irish territorial waters with respect to the seabed, subsoil and their natural resources on that part of the continental shelf recognised by that Convention as attributable to the State. The Continental Shelf Act 1968 ('CSA 1968') provides that areas of the continental shelf outside Irish territorial waters may be designated by statutory order as areas in which the State may exercise the rights of exploration for and exploitation of natural resources. Any areas so designated on the Irish sector of the continental shelf are referred to as 'designated areas'.

The Petroleum and Other Minerals Development Act 1960 ('POMDA 1960') authorises the Minister for Energy to grant licences that permit the holder either to explore or to exploit the natural resources in a specified part or parts of any designated area. In practice, the Minister is prepared to grant exploration licences to suitable persons entitling the grantee to explore in the particular area covered by the licence. In the event that oil, gas or other minerals should be discovered in any area explored under such a licence, the State is then prepared to negotiate terms with the licence holder or his assignees for the exploitation of those resources.

The CSA 1968 recognises that the Irish sector of the continental shelf within which the State may exercise rights is not, so far as it is outside territorial waters, a part of the State. Consequently, in the absence of any other law, any income derived by a non-resident person from exploration or exploitation activities undertaken on the continental shelf outside territorial waters would, in most instances, be outside the scope of Irish taxation as income from foreign possessions. TCA 1997, s 13, Sch 1 deal with the matter, in respect of both trades involving or connected with exploration and/or exploitation in any designated area and offices or employments the duties of which are performed in any designated area.

TCA 1997, s 13(1) contains certain definitions which apply in interpreting these provisions. These are as follows:

> *'Exploration or exploitation activities'*:
>
> activities carried on in connection with the exploration or exploitation of so much of the seabed and subsoil and their natural resources as is situated in the State or in a designated area;
>
> *'Exploration or exploitation rights'*:
>
> rights to assets to be produced by exploration or exploitation activities or to interests in or to the benefit of such assets;
>
> *'Designated area'*:
>
> an area designated by order under CSA 1968, s 2.

TCA 1997, s 13 refers specifically to income tax, but TCA 1997, s 76 applies income tax law and principles for the purposes of corporation tax so that, if a company is within these provisions, the rules discussed here are equally applicable in charging that company to corporation tax. In fact, apart from the application of TCA 1997, s 13(5) to employments (see **13.607**), its rules (and those of TCA 1997, Sch 1) are more likely to be applied to companies chargeable to corporation tax, as continental shelf exploration and exploitation activities are generally undertaken by companies rather than by individuals or other unincorporated persons.

TCA 1997, s 13(2) provides that any profits or gains from exploration or exploitation activities in a designated area, or from exploration or exploitation rights, are to be treated for tax purposes as income from activities or property in the State. This means that any income derived in the course of a trade by any person (whether resident or non-resident) is taxable under Sch D Case I as income from a trade carried on in the State. If the income is derived in some other way by a resident person, for example, as royalties received for allowing another person to use his exploration or exploitation rights, that income is taxable under the appropriate Case of Sch D as Irish source income.

TCA 1997, s 13(3) goes on to deal specifically with non-residents. It provides that any profits or gains arising to a non-resident person from exploration or exploitation activities carried on either in the State or in a designated area, or from exploration or exploitation rights, are taxed as the profits or gains of a trade carried on by that person in the State through a branch or agency. This clearly puts the non-resident person in the same position as if he carried on the relevant trade in the State so that the various rules (TCA 1997, Pt 45 Ch 1) discussed in **13.603**, **13.604** apply. It is to be noted that, in the case of the non-resident, all forms of income within the section (including any non-trading income from exploration or exploitation rights) are taxable as the trading income of the assumed branch or agency in the State, ie they are taxable under Sch D Case I and not under any other Case of Sch D.

In order for TCA 1997, s 13 to be applicable to either a resident or non-resident person, two conditions must be met. Firstly, he (or, if a company, it) must actually carry on an activity in a designated area (or otherwise derive income from rights in a designated area). Secondly that activity must be either exploration or exploitation or any other activity in connection with exploration or exploitation. This makes it clear that it is not only the licence holder, or any other person on his behalf, actually exploring for or exploiting the natural resources that is within the section. Any other person carrying on any other activities that can be said to be 'in connection with' the actual exploration or exploitation is also covered, but only in respect of such connected activities as take place in a designated area.

For example, a company (whether resident or non-resident) with an exploration licence may contract with one or more other persons (resident or non-resident) for services such as test drilling, analysis of samples, the leasing of exploration ships and equipment, catering and similar services for the personnel working in the exploration ships, etc. Any such support activities are within the definition of exploration and exploitation activities so that any income derived by the persons undertaking them are taxable under Sch D Case I, if carried on in a designated area. However, if a non-resident person undertaking, say, the analysis of seabed or subsoil samples, provides this service wholly outside both the State and the designated areas (eg in Aberdeen, Scotland), that person is not within TCA 1997, s 13 and is not subject to any Irish tax on the profits from this activity.

TCA 1997, s 13(4) provides that the holder of the exploration or exploitation licence granted under POMDA 1960 is deemed to be the agent of any person who carries on any exploration or exploitation activities on the licence holder's behalf. This means that, if the person carrying on the relevant activities in a designated area (or in the State) is a non-resident, the rules of TCA 1997, ss 1034, 1035 apply so that the inspector of taxes is entitled to assess the non-resident's profits in the name of the licence holder. In practice, the inspector is normally prepared to assess the non-resident directly, but if the non-resident does not submit to assessment or make returns of the profits from the relevant activities, the inspector will make the assessments in the name of the licence holder.

In order to enable the inspector to tax all non-resident persons performing exploration or exploitation activities in the State or in designated areas, TCA 1997, Sch 1 empowers the inspector to serve a notice requiring information on the holder of any licence granted under POMDA 1960. If served with such a notice, the licence holder is required to give to the inspector such particulars as may be required of transactions in connection with the licensed activities as a result of which any other person is, or may be, liable to tax by virtue of TCA 1997, s 13 and of emoluments payable in respect of duties performed in any designated area in connection with those activities. The licence holder is required to take any reasonable steps to obtain the necessary information.

TCA 1997, Sch 1 para 2 goes further. It entitles the Revenue Commissioners to recover from the licence holder any tax payable, but unpaid, by a non-resident person in respect of profits from exploration or exploitation activities connected with the activities for which the licence holder is licensed. This provision is enforced, where necessary, by the service by the Revenue Commissioners of the appropriate notice on the licence holder requesting him to pay the tax due by the non-resident, together with any interest payable. This notice may be served if the tax payable by the non-resident has not been fully paid within 30 days after it became due and payable. This rule does not, however, apply to tax payable in respect of emoluments for duties performed in designated areas (TCA 1997, Sch 1 para 3).

A licence holder may be able to obtain a clearance certificate exempting him (or, if a company, it) from the liability under TCA 1997, Sch 1 to pay any unpaid tax (and/or interest on the tax) due by the non-resident person. To obtain this certificate, the non-resident person (not the licence holder) must apply to the Revenue Commissioners for it. If satisfied that the non-resident will comply with the obligations imposed by the Tax Acts to make returns and to pay any tax due in respect of the own profits from the activities in the designated area, the Revenue Commissioners should issue the clearance certificate to the licence holder (TCA 1997, Sch 1 para 5).

The licence holder may then cease to be concerned about the possibility of having to pay tax or interest on tax due by the non-resident in question, so long as the certificate continues to be valid. An exemption certificate given under TCA 1997, Sch 1 para 5 continues to be valid indefinitely unless, and until, the certificate is cancelled. The Revenue Commissioners are authorised to cancel any such certificate by giving notice of cancellation to the licence holder; such cancellation takes effect from the date specified in this notice, but this date cannot be earlier than 30 days after the service of the cancellation notice (TCA 1997, Sch 1 para 6).

For the treatment of emoluments for duties performed in a designated area by a non-resident employee, see **13.607**.

13.607 Offices and employments of non-residents

A non-resident person is chargeable to tax under Sch E (normally subject to PAYE) in respect of the emoluments from any public office in the State, irrespective of where he performs the duties of the office (TCA 1997, s 19(1)). For example, any fees or other emoluments in respect of the office of a director of an Irish incorporated company accruing to a non-resident remain taxable under Sch E, even if the non-resident director performs all his duties abroad (*Tipping v Jeancard* – see **13.104**). Similarly, as discussed in **13.104**, the Revenue take the view that all of the emoluments of an Irish civil servant exercising the duties of his employment wholly outside the State (for example, as the member of a diplomatic mission to a foreign country) are taxable under Sch E, whether or not he is a resident. This is on the basis that he holds a public employment of profit within TCA 1997, s 19(2).

As discussed in **13.104**, it may be that a public office *held* outside the State but *exercised* within the State is also within TCA 1997, s 19(1), (eg a director of a non-Irish incorporated but Irish resident company, who attends board meetings in the State).

TCA 1997, s 19 extends the potential scope of Sch E to non-residents who have an office or employment which is neither:

(a) a public office or employment held or exercised within that State (ie is not otherwise within TCA 1997, s 19(1)); or

(b) a 'foreign possession' taxable under Sch D Case III.

The legislature has adopted a rather circuitous route in order to produce this result. TCA 1997, s 19(1) brings into charge any 'office, employment or pension' which would be chargeable to tax under Sch D 'but for the paragraph 2 of that Sch'. Paragraph 2 retains within Sch D only those 'offices, employment or pensions' which fall within Case III, ie those which constitute 'foreign possessions', but with effect from 1 January 2006 excludes any earnings which are attributable to the performance of duties within the State (see **13.104**). Thus, it becomes necessary to look to TCA 1997, s 18(1) to discover to what extent offices or employments are taxable in the case of non-residents.

Irish employments and non-public employments

So far as employments are concerned, TCA 1997, s 18(1)(a)(iii) charges tax on 'any person, whether a citizen of Ireland or not, although not resident in the State, from any ... employment exercised in the State.' Thus, if the non-resident exercises an Irish-source employment which falls within TCA 1997, s 19(1) entirely outside the State he is not taxable in respect of the income therefrom. Conversely, if the non-resident exercises an Irish-source employment entirely within the State, he is fully taxable in respect of the related earnings. Logically, where the non-resident exercises an Irish-source employment partly within the State and partly outside the State, then he is liable on a proportionate part of the earnings therefrom. Offices are not explicitly mentioned within TCA 1997, s 18(1)(a)(iii) but would seem to fall within TCA 1997, s 18(1)(b) which charges 'all ... other annual profits or gains not charged under ... Sch E ...' (although the effect of TCA 1997, s 19(1) will then be to bring them within Sch E). It would seem that in strictness, any office which falls outside TCA 1997, s 19(1) and which is not a foreign possession must by definition be an Irish office, regardless of where it is exercised. In practice, the Revenue are likely to treat such offices held by a non-resident in the same way as employments – ie charging the earnings to tax to the extent that the relevant duties are performed in the State.

Foreign employments and non-public offices up to 31 December 2005

Where a non-resident held a foreign office or employment within Sch D Case III, then (subject to the rule in TCA 1997, s 821: see below) he was outside the scope of Irish taxation, in accordance with the generally accepted territorial limits of Irish taxation (see **1.405**). At first sight this analysis appears to be inconsistent with TCA 1997, s 18(1) which charges tax on non-residents in respect of profits or gains 'arising or accruing from any property whatever in the State or from ... any employment exercised in the State'. As a result it would seem possible to argue that the scope of a potential liability under Sch D Case III is identical to that under Sch E, ie the non-resident is chargeable on his earnings to the extent that the relevant duties are performed in the State (subject to the possible application of the remittance basis: see **13.503**).

The root of the problem was that TCA 1997, s 18(1) clearly implies that to the extent that an employment is 'exercised in the State' it is an Irish source in relation to a non-resident, while the decision in *Bray v Collenbrander* (see **13.104**) established the principle that the place where the employment is exercised has no bearing on the location of the employment. It is not possible to argue that the implication of the wording in TCA 1997, s 18(1) and the decision in *Bray v Collenbrander* can both be correct. On the assumption that the principle in *Bray v Collenbrander* is correct, it must be accepted that the apparently wide wording of TCA 1997, s 18(1) is necessarily limited by reference to the structure of the individual cases within Sch D. The contrary argument, even on its own terms, does not seem capable of applying to a foreign office (which is not also an employment) held by a non-resident; this is because TCA 1997, s 18(1)(a)(iii) refers only to *employments* exercised in the State.

Foreign employments and non-public offices up from 1 January 2006

As noted above, earnings from a foreign possession to the extent that they are attributable to duties performed in the State are chargeable under Sch E with effect from 1 January 2006. The territorial principles of Irish taxation would arguably seem to imply that a non-resident who holds a foreign-source employment is not generally within the scope of Irish taxation in respect of his earnings therefrom, irrespective of where the duties are performed and whether or not those earnings would be otherwise chargeable under Sch D Case III or Sch E. On this analysis, a non-resident with a foreign employment will remain outside the scope of Irish taxation on his earnings therefrom notwithstanding that he carried out some or all of his duties in the State. This view is not accepted by the Revenue Commissioners and it will be generally assumed hereafter that non-residents will be taxable under Sch E in these circumstances.

Apportionment of earnings

As noted above, if the non-resident does in fact perform any of his duties of an Irish-source employment (or seemingly, with effect from 1 January 2006, of a foreign-source employment) within the State, he is chargeable to tax under Sch E on so much of his emoluments as are attributable to the duties in the State, but not in respect of duties performed abroad. If only some of the duties are carried out in the State, the total emoluments must be apportioned in some appropriate manner, most logically, (in the absence of any counter-indications in the contract of service itself) in the ratio of the number of the working days in the State to the total number of working days in the tax year (note the UK Special Commissioners decision in *Perro v Mansworth* [2002] STC (SCD) 413). Where the contract expressly provides for different levels of remuneration in respect of Irish and non-Irish duties, it will be difficult for the Revenue Commissioners to challenge this arrangement unless it can be shown to be a sham.

An individual who is not resident, but who is ordinarily resident, in the State will fall within the scope of TCA 1997, s 821. This means that he will normally be liable under Sch D Case III in respect of emoluments from any foreign employment in respect of which some of the duties (other than incidental duties) are performed in the State (see **13.504**). However, to the extent that the emoluments relate to the performance of Irish duties, they will fall under Sch E with effect from 1 January 2006 and TCA 1997, s 821 will therefore not apply to them. As discussed above, it would appear that an individual who is resident outside the State but who performs some duties there for a non-resident employer will often qualify for exemption under the terms of a relevant double tax treaty (see **14.210**).

The non-resident exercising the duties of his office or employment in the State who is chargeable under Sch E in respect thereof will be subject to PAYE in the usual manner. Where a non-resident employee has an employment where part of the related earnings (ie those attributable to duties performed in the State) fall within Sch E and the remainder are non-taxable, special rules apply with effect from 1 January 2006 to determine the amount of income subject to PAYE: see **11.104**.

Continental Shelf

TCA 1997, s 13(5) treats any emoluments from an office or employment in respect of duties performed in a designated area of the Continental Shelf in connection with exploration or exploitation activities in the same way as if they were emoluments in respect of duties performed in the State. This means that any non-resident employee is chargeable to tax in respect of such emoluments in accordance with the rules just mentioned – ie under Sch E if the employment is Irish and, in the view of some inspectors, under Sch D Case III, if the employment is foreign. TCA 1997, s 13(5) only treats the duties in the designated area as being performed in the State, and does not alter the *source* of the emoluments.

If a non-resident person performing the duties of an office or employment in the State (or in a designated area) is a resident of a country with which there is a double taxation agreement, the employment article in that agreement should be consulted. In certain circumstances, that article may provide that the emoluments arising in respect of the office or employment may not be taxable in the State, notwithstanding the place where the duties are performed (see **14.210**).

13.608 Distributions from resident companies

The taxation under Sch F of dividends and other distributions of companies resident in the State has been covered in **9.101**.

13.609 Other sources of income within the State

Among the other sources of income not already referred to which the non-resident may have in the State are the following:

(a) rental income from lands, tenements and hereditaments in the State assessable under Sch D Case V (see **Division 12**);

(b) income from patents, including, where relevant, capital sums from the sale of Irish patents (see **Division 8**);

(c) income from leasing machinery, etc in the State (see **8.206**);

(d) annuities or other annual payments which are regarded as arising from an Irish source (see **2.302–2.304**); and

(e) interest income from loans, debt claims, etc which are regarded as Irish sources, (see **2.306**).

In general, the Revenue Commissioners do not seek to assess non-residents directly in respect of many of these miscellaneous types of Irish source income but the system of deduction of income tax at source already covered in **Division 2** requires resident persons making payments under various headings to persons residing outside the State to deduct income tax at the standard rate and to account for that tax to the Collector General. In general, it would be impracticable to make direct assessments on non-residents in many cases. Assessments on a resident factor, agent, etc under TCA 1997, ss 1034, 1035 (see **13.603**) are usually confined to cases where the non-resident exercises a trade or profession in the State, or where an agent collects rent on his behalf (see **12.102**: *Deduction at source*; note also the discussion of copyright royalties paid to non-residents at **8.207**).

Not all payments of or on account of income made by a resident to a non-resident are subject to withholding tax at source. There is, for example, no requirement for a resident payer to deduct income tax from copyright royalties (as distinct from patent and mineral royalties), nor has income tax to be withheld on paying rents for leased machinery (as distinct from rents on real estate). Interest paid by banks, etc (see (i) below) may also be paid gross to non-residents but such income will strictly remain liable to Irish tax (subject to the provisions of any relevant Double Tax Agreement).

It may be useful to summarise here the types of payment from which a person making the payment in the State is required to deduct income tax at the standard rate, namely:

(a) annuities and other annual payments chargeable under Sch D (see **2.302**);
(b) royalties and other sums paid in respect of the use of a patent (see **2.302**);
(c) mining rents, royalties and similar annual payments (**2.302**);
(d) yearly interest charged under Sch D (**2.306**);
(e) rents in respect of any lands, tenements or hereditaments in the State (**2.308**);
(f) any capital sum paid for the purchase of patent rights under an Irish patent (**2.302** and **8.304**);
(g) any capital sum for the purchase of scheduled mineral assets (**2.301**);
(h) public revenue interest, dividends, etc assessable on the payer under Sch C, but not including interest on certain Irish government and other public corporation stocks paid gross **2.309**); and
(i) interest paid or credited by a bank, building society, trustee savings bank or other relevant deposit taker, but only if the non-resident's declaration has not been made by or on behalf of the non-resident entitled to the interest (see **2.401**, **2.402**).

Rental income: deduction of expenses, etc

A non-resident who receives rent in respect of leased real property in the State may have incurred expenses by way of rates, repairs, maintenance, management, etc and may perhaps also be paying interest on money borrowed to purchase, improve, etc the leased property. These are all expenses which the non-resident would be entitled to deduct in arriving at the net rental income assessable under Sch D Case V but the person paying the rent to a non-resident normally has to deduct income tax at the standard rate from the gross rent (TCA 1997, s 1041). This income tax suffered may be greater than the tax the non-resident would have to pay if assessed directly under Sch D Case V.

The non-resident is entitled to claim to be assessed under Sch D Case V and to recover the amount (if any) by which the income tax payable by him on the assessment exceeds the income tax suffered by deduction from the rent. However, to claim relief for these rental expenses, the non-resident must make a return of his total income from all Irish sources, including the net rental income computed under the rules of Sch D Case V. The total Irish income tax liability has to be computed on the non-resident's total Irish source income. It is only if the income tax suffered by deduction from the rental income in the relevant tax year exceeds the income tax payable on the total Irish source income that the non-resident is entitled to any repayment of the excess income tax suffered.

Effect of double taxation agreements

A resident of a foreign country or state which has a double taxation agreement with the State and who receives income from any of the above Irish sources after the deduction of income tax at the standard rate, should consult the relevant article in the double taxation agreement. It may be that the agreement may entitle the foreign resident to be either exempted from Irish tax or taxed at a rate lower than the standard rate, in respect of the source of income in question.

If so, the resident of the foreign state should apply to the Revenue Commissioners for a repayment of the excess (if any) of the Irish income tax withheld by the person paying the income over the foreign resident's liability to Irish tax (if any) in accordance with the double taxation agreement. If the foreign resident is due to receive similar payments in the future, he may request the Revenue Commissioners to authorise the resident payer to deduct tax in future at the lower 'treaty' rate (or, if the treaty exempts the non-resident from Irish tax, not to make any deduction).

Exemptions

In certain cases, Irish source income is expressly exempted in the hands of non- resident and/or domiciled persons (see **1.306**).

13.610 Rates of tax, personal tax credits etc

A non-resident person who is not an individual is, in principle, always chargeable to Irish income tax at the standard rate in respect of Irish source income. The higher rate of income tax applies to individuals only and is never charged on any person other than an individual taxable in his own right. A non-resident person (including an individual) in receipt of Irish source income in a fiduciary or representative capacity, for example, as the trustee of a settlement or as the executor or administrator of a deceased person, is similarly chargeable only at the standard rate (TCA 1997, s 15). Any non-resident person may, however, be taxed at a rate lower than the standard rate in respect of a particular type of income, or may be exempted, if that is specifically provided for in a double taxation agreement under which the non-resident is entitled to benefit.

A non-resident individual is, in principle, liable to income tax on his total income (ie all income) from Irish sources and is taxable at the standard rate and, if his total Irish income is high enough, at the higher rate. This general rule is subject to any exemption provided for by any special rule in the Tax Acts (for example, the exemption for interest on certain Irish Government for non-residents and other public corporation securities, where the individual is also not resident in the State).

The limitation of the non-resident individual's taxable income to his total income from Irish sources is varied for any tax year for which he is ordinarily resident in the State. In any such case, TCA 1997, s 821 applies to make the non-resident but ordinarily resident individual also liable to Irish tax on certain income from certain foreign trades, professions, offices or employments and on any other income which he may have in that tax year but only if that latter income is in excess of €3,810 (see **13.504**).

For the discussion in the rest of **13.610** it is assumed – unless stated otherwise that the non-resident individual is not ordinarily resident in the State for the same tax year.

Rates of tax: individuals

The non-resident individual's taxable income for any year of assessment is his total income from all Irish sources for that year, as computed in accordance with the rules of the relevant Schedule or Case, but excluding all non-Irish source income. The non-resident may be entitled to deductions in respect of trading losses under TCA 1997, s 381(1) etc, or for example annuities or other annual payments which will also reduce his total income (see below). Except to the extent that he can claim personal allowances and reliefs (see below), his total income from Irish sources is also his Irish taxable income.

Charges on income etc

In arriving at his total income chargeable to Irish tax, a non-resident individual is entitled to the same deductions as a resident person in respect of annuities or other annual payments made by him, but only to the extent that they are paid wholly out of his income chargeable to income tax in the State (see **3.103**). For these purposes, it seems to be sufficient that the amount of the Irish income will cover the payment in question (see *Allchin v Coulthard* [1942] 2 KB 228). In other cases, it will be necessary to see whether the particular rules for deductibility require that the payment should be chargeable to Irish tax in the hands of the recipient, and, if so, whether the non-resident status of the payer affects the issue of Irish chargeability.

A non-resident may not set off a charge against Sch F income in respect of which he is exempt (TCA 1997, s 153(4)(b) inserted with effect from 6 April 1999 by FA 1999, s 28). This could result in a liability to account to tax under TCA 1997, s 238 (see **2.304**).

Tax credits etc

TCA 1997, s 1032(1) provides that a non-resident individual is not entitled to any of the tax credits or reliefs specified in TCA 1997, s 458 (see **Division 3**). However, TCA 1997, s 1032(2) grants certain non-resident individuals a proportion of those tax credits and reliefs available to residents.

TCA 1997, s 1032(2) gives a non-resident individual the appropriate proportion of the tax credits and reliefs, etc if, but only if, he proves to the satisfaction of the Revenue Commissioners that:

(a) he is a citizen of Ireland;
(b) he is resident outside the State for the sake of his health or that of a member of his family who lives with him (provided that he was resident in the State prior to such residence abroad);
(c) he is a citizen, subject, or national of another Member State of the European Union;
(d) he is a citizen, subject, or national of a country whose citizens, subjects or nationals are for the time being exempted by an order made under the Aliens Act 1935, s 10 from the provisions of that Act (this covers most citizens of the Commonwealth); or
(e) he is a person who, prior to 5 April 1935, was either:
    (i) a British subject,
    (ii) a person employed in the service of the British Crown,
    (iii) a resident in the Isle of Man or the Channel Islands, or
    (iv) a widow whose deceased husband was in the service of the British Crown.

A non-resident individual, who satisfies the Revenue Commissioners (through the inspector) that he falls into any of these categories, is entitled to deduct from his total income from Irish sources a proportion of the personal allowances and reliefs) as well as a proportion of any relevant tax credits to which he would be entitled if a resident. The relevant proportion is determined as follows:

$$\text{Tax credits/reliefs} \times \frac{A}{B}$$

where

A = the individual's total income chargeable to Irish income tax; and
B = his 'world' income, ie total income from all sources as calculated in accordance with Irish tax principles (including income not subject to Irish tax).

The reference in 'B' to income not subject to Irish tax is imprecise but would seem apt to cover income not charged to Irish tax by virtue of the residence and domicile status of the individual (including income exempted under the terms of a double tax treaty), but not income which is expressly exempt under the Income Tax Acts.

TCA 1997, s 1032(3) grants unrestricted personal allowances reliefs and tax credits to a non-resident individual where the following conditions are satisfied:

(a) he is a resident of another Member State of the European Union; and
(b) the amount of the individual's income which is subject to Irish tax (note comments above) as a proportion of his world-wide income is 75 per cent or greater.

A non-resident individual, who does not fall into any of the categories enumerated in TCA 1997, s 1032(2), may be entitled to tax credits and allowances, etc if he is a resident of a country with which there is a double taxation agreement (tax treaty). Most of the tax treaties made between the Republic of Ireland and other countries contain an article providing that an individual who is a resident of the other country is entitled to the same personal allowances, reliefs and other deductions as are available to an Irish citizen resident outside the State.

This means that a non-resident individual, who is a resident of a country with which there is a tax treaty containing this form of article, is entitled to the same deductions in computing taxable income and tax reductions in respect of personal tax credit, etc as is given by TCA 1997, s 1032 to the Irish citizen resident abroad. In order to qualify for this benefit under a tax treaty, the non resident must fall within the particular definition of 'resident of' the country in question (see **14.105**).

Thus, eg an individual who is a resident of Belgium can claim full tax credits and reliefs for tax year 2015, if his Irish taxable income is 75 per cent or more of his world-wide income. If his income falls below the 75 per cent threshold, then the due proportion of personal allowances, etc can be claimed under TCA 1997, s 1032 if the individual is a national of Ireland or of any other EU Member State. If the individual is not an EU National (and does not otherwise fall within s 1032(2)) he could in fact still claim proportionate personal allowances, etc under the terms of the Ireland/Belgium Double Tax Treaty.

Example 13.610.1

Mr X O'Mahony, an Irish citizen resident in the UK and employed by a UK company, is a director of its Irish subsidiary, attending board meetings in Waterford. He is not ordinarily resident in the State. He is a single person. His income from all sources (as computed under Irish tax principles) for the tax year 2015 is as follows:

	€	€
Income from Irish sources:		
Sch E director's salary		3,500
Sch D Case V:		
Net rental income from Irish flat		5,200
		8,700
Interest on Irish government securities[1]		1,200
Income from foreign sources:		
Employment in UK	15,000	
UK dividends	3,100	18,100
World income (all sources)		28,000

Mr O'Mahony's Irish taxable income for the year 2015 is computed as follows:

	€
Sch E – director's salary	3,500
Sch D Case V	5,200
Total income chargeable to Irish tax[1]	8,700
Taxed as follows	
€8,700 x 20%	1,740
Less:	
Proportion of tax credits[2]	
€3,300 x 8,700/28,000[3]=	(1,025)
Tax payable	715

Notes:

1. Since Mr O'Mahony is not – resident in the State, he is exempted from Irish tax on the government securities interest (he would also be exempt as a UK resident under the interest article in the Ireland/UK tax treaty).
2. His tax credits for 2015 are made up as follows:

	€
Personal tax credit	1,650
PAYE tax credit (director's fees)	1,650
	3,300

3. The exempt Irish government securities interest is included in the income from all sources (€28,000) used as the denominator in the 'A/B' fraction.

Example 13.610.2

Mr D Toulouse, a French national (ie a EU national) is a resident of Spain (another EU Member State), and is neither resident or ordinarily resident in Ireland, in the tax year 2015. He has substantial rents from Irish land and buildings and is also a part-time executive director of an Irish company. He is a married man; none of his wife's income is subject to Irish income tax.

Mr Toulouse's world-wide income for 2015 is made up as follows:

	€
Income subject to Irish tax:	
Sch E Director's fees	20,000
Sch D Case V net rents	35,000
	55,000
All other world income	18,000
Total world income	73,000

Mr Toulouse would, if resident in the State for 2015 be entitled to a single persons tax credit of €1,650, (see *Marriage and Non-residents* below) and a PAYE tax credit of €1,650 – ie total credits of €3,300.

Since the €55,000 income subject to Irish tax is 75.34 per cent of the €73,000 total world income, and since Mr Toulouse is a resident of another EU Member State, Mr Toulouse is entitled to claim under TCA 1997, s 1032 for the full personal tax credits of €3,300 (to be deducted from the tax on his Irish income calculated at the rates applicable to single persons). Mr Toulouse could however claim aggregation relief if this were favourable, (see *Marriage and Non-residents* below).

It may be noted that in some cases the conditions on which a personal tax credit is granted themselves require the individual concerned to be resident (eg the seafarer's allowance: see **3.312**), so that a non-resident will not become entitled thereto on the basis of TCA 1997, s 1032(2) or (3) (both of which simply remove the blanket prohibition under TCA 1997, s 1032(1)).

Marriage and non-residents

A resident individual, if married and living with his spouse, is entitled to elect to be assessed jointly under TCA 1997, s 1017 in respect of their joint total incomes. In that case, the married personal tax credit and the married person's standard tax rate band table are applied. In the case of a non-resident individual, even if living with his spouse, the Revenue take the view that this election for joint assessment cannot be made unless the total income from all sources of each spouse is chargeable to Irish tax. This would only be the position, if despite their being non-residents, neither spouse has any income other than income that is chargeable to Irish tax.

If either non-resident spouse has some income that is not chargeable to Irish tax (which is usually the position), the Revenue view is that the spouse with Irish source income must be assessed as a single person on his Irish taxable income (the same would apply to the other non-resident spouse if he also had income subject to Irish tax). In other words, the income tax payable on each spouse's Irish income is calculated according to the single person's tax bands and credits. Then, if either non-resident spouse is entitled under TCA 1997, s 1032 personal tax credits (or a proportion thereof), only the single person's personal tax credits (or a proportion thereof) is included in the computation (with any other relevant reliefs appropriate to a single person).

In *Fennessy v McConnelogue* V ITR 129 the taxpayer was a UK resident who had earnings from an employment exercised in Ireland. His wife (who was also UK resident) had a roughly comparable level of earnings from the employment exercised in the UK. The Revenue succeeded before the High Court in their argument that TCA 1997, s 1017 cannot apply where the taxpayer's wife is non-resident and has non-Irish income. This was on the basis that the wife's non-Irish income fell outside the territorial scope of Irish tax, with the result that her 'total income', could not be subjected to Irish tax. Accordingly, a claim under TCA 1997, s 1018 could not take effect since the wife's total income could not be assessed jointly or otherwise.

It is suggested that this argument did not in fact deserve to succeed. A taxpayer's 'total income' comprises his income *as estimated for Irish tax purposes* (TCA 1997, s 3(1)). Thus, eg TCA 1997, s 188 declares that for the purpose of the small income exemption limits, 'total income' has the same meaning as in TCA 1997, s 3(1), but *also* includes income arising outside the State which is not chargeable to tax. TCA 1997, s 188 accordingly recognises that in the absence of a special deeming provision, 'total income' excludes non-chargeable income.

From this it follows that the 'total income' of the non-resident spouse, as defined by TCA 1997, s 3(1) is perfectly capable of being the subject of a joint assessment. The Revenue's argument that the spouse's 'total income' is not so capable, depends on treating 'total income' as meaning 'total income whether chargeable to Irish tax or not'. In the absence of any deeming provision such as TCA 1997, s 188, this is not a permissible interpretation.

It would appear that the denial of the right to joint assessment is probably not in breach of European law (see **1.410**).

It would seem that, in any event, the requisite degree of comparability which is required to establish discrimination was absent in the specific facts of *McConnelogue* case. This is because the taxpayer's spouse received sufficient income to avail fully of the benefit of personal allowances (and her own single rate band) in the UK.

The same considerations as relate to married couples will apply *mutatis mutandis* to civil partners following the enactment of the Finance (No 3) Act 2011.

Aggregation relief

On the basis of their view (now the law, following *Fennesy v McConnelogue)* that each non-resident spouse with any Irish source income subject to income tax is to be assessed as a single person, the Revenue Commissioners have always been prepared to grant 'aggregation relief' on similar lines to those explained in **13.505** in the case of one resident and one non-resident spouse, as confirmed in *Tax Briefing Issue 67.*

This aggregation relief is available if the spouse liable to Irish tax on Irish source income can show that the income tax payable by him in the single person assessment on that income exceeds the 'notional income tax' (payable were a joint assessment to be made under TCA 1997, s 1017 on the aggregate of their respective 'world' total incomes) which is attributable to that spouse's total income chargeable to Irish tax. The relief is then given by reducing the amount of the income tax payable on the single person assessment so as not to exceed the said attributable notional income tax.

Aggregation relief is only given if the non-resident married couple elects under TCA 1997, s 1017 for the aggregation basis to apply and the spouses make a satisfactory return to the inspector of their respective world incomes.

Division 14 Double Taxation Relief

14.1 Double Taxation Agreements: General

14.101 Introduction

Division 13 has explained the general principle that a person resident in the State is normally liable to Irish tax in respect of his worldwide income, ie irrespective of whether the income arises from sources in the State or from sources in other countries. In the case of foreign source income, the government of the country in which any particular income arises usually has the right under its own tax laws to subject the income to its own income tax, corporation tax etc. Consequently, in the absence of any other provisions in the tax law of either country, the foreign source income of an Irish resident person would be taxed twice, once in Ireland and again in the other country.

Conversely, a person not resident in the State who has Irish source income is, under general principles of Irish tax law, liable to Irish income tax and the Universal Social Charge on that income. At the same time, the government of the country in which he resides is likely to subject him to its own income tax (or equivalent tax). Again, in the absence of any other rules in either country, the same income is likely to be taxed twice, once in the country of source (Ireland) and a second time in the country in which the person in question is resident.

In order to prevent these (and other) forms of double taxation, or at least to minimise their effects, the government of Ireland has negotiated a series of double taxation agreements with the governments of other countries. These agreements contain rules which may vary the normal taxation laws of the two countries. A double taxation agreement or 'convention' (frequently referred to as a 'tax treaty') is, therefore, a bilateral agreement between the governments of two countries containing rules generally aimed at avoiding the double taxation of income flowing from sources in one of the countries to residents of the other, or vice versa. A tax treaty may also contain measures to relieve or prevent the double taxation of capital gains or of capital.

This Division starts by discussing the way in which a tax treaty with another country fits in with the normal tax laws of the State ('domestic tax law'). It then describes the scope of tax treaties generally, deals with the definition of the term 'resident' as it is usually applied in a tax treaty and with certain other definitions used in most tax treaties. The methods employed in tax treaties for avoiding double taxation are then outlined in principle.

It is a general principle of double taxation agreements that the particular treaty between the State and the other country that is a party to that treaty applies to persons who are residents of either of the two countries ('the contracting states'). Each treaty contains a series of 'articles', each dealing with a particular class of income and setting out the respective taxation rights of each contracting state, or the limitations imposed by the treaty on those rights, where a resident of one of the countries has income of the class in question in the other country.

Each treaty usually contains an article providing for the exchange of information between the tax authorities of the respective countries to assist in the prevention of tax evasion or tax fraud. While it is always necessary in considering the tax position of any particular taxpayer to look at the relevant articles in the double taxation agreement affecting him, the various articles in the different treaties dealing with the particular classes of income, capital gains, etc have many features in common. The approach taken in the different articles is discussed generally in **Division 14**.

From the point of view of the person resident in the State with foreign source income, the matter of most practical significance is the manner in which he obtains relief for foreign tax paid or borne on that income. Generally, the double taxation agreements negotiated by the government entitle him to have the foreign tax credited against the Irish tax otherwise payable on that income. While the entitlement to this 'foreign tax credit' is provided by the relevant agreement, the method by which the actual amount of the credit is computed is prescribed by the Income Tax Acts (mainly in TCA 1997, Sch 24). The rules for the calculation of foreign tax credits are discussed in detail in **Division 14**.

14.102 Legal status of agreements

By virtue of Article 29.5 of the Constitution, every international agreement must be laid before Dáil Éireann. Further, by virtue of Article 29.6 no such agreement can become part of Irish domestic law (thus conferring direct rights on individual taxpayers) unless the Oireachtas has so determined. In the context of double tax agreements, this is achieved by TCA 1997, s 826(1), as substituted by FA 2007, s 35 and most recently amended by FA 2010, s 157, which provides inter alia that, with effect generally from 2 April 2007, where:

(a) the Government by order declare that arrangements specified in the Order have been made with the Government of any territory outside the State in relation to:

  (i) affording relief from double taxation in respect of (I) income tax, Universal Social Charge ... and any taxes of a similar character, imposed by the laws of the State or by the laws of that territory, and

  (ii) and in the case of taxes of any kind or description imposed by the laws of the State or by the laws of that territory:

    (I) exchanging information for the purposes of the prevention and detection of tax evasion, or

    (II) granting relief from taxation under the laws of that territory to persons who are resident in the state for the purposes of tax,

    (III) collecting and recovering tax (including interest, penalties and costs in connection with such tax) for the purposes of the prevention of tax evasion,

  and that it is expedient that those arrangements should have the force of law; or

(b) the order so made is referred to in TCA 1997, Sch 24A, Pt 1,

then, subject to this section and to the extent provided in this section, the arrangements shall, notwithstanding any enactment have the force of law as if each such Order were an Act of the Oireachtas on and from the date ... of the insertion of a reference to the order into TCA 1997, Sch 24A, Pt 1.

Similar provisions apply to arrangements with other countries for the purposes of prevention and detection of tax evasion or other such matters relating to the relief of double taxation as the Government consider appropriate, in which case the relevant order must be inserted in Sch 24A, Pt 2 (TCA 1997, s 826(1B)). A number of agreements with tax haven countries are currently in force. It is also provided that once Ireland signs the Convention on Mutual Administrative Assistance in Tax Matters, the Convention and any subsequent protocols are to have the force of law as if each related order were an Act of the Oireachtas on and from the date of the insertion of a reference to the order into TCA 1997, Sch 24A, Pt 4 (TCA 1997, s 826(1C), inserted by FA 2010, s 56). FA 2015 inserted a new TCA 1997, s 826(1D) to enable arrangements to be entered into with a non-governmental representative authority for the purpose of preventing double taxation and providing for the exchange of information and, here necessary, for the recovery of tax. Such arrangements will have the force of law in Ireland once an Order approved by Dáil Éireann has been made and the Oireachtas enacts legislation that makes the Order part of Irish law by an insertion into TCA 1997, Sch 24A.

All the tax treaties currently in force between Ireland and other countries derive their legal status from statutory orders made by the government under this authority conferred by TCA 1997, s 826(1), as now amended to require a reference to the relevant Order in TCA 1997, Sch 24A. In the case of each particular agreement, the terms are first negotiated between officials of the respective governments and are then in due course put before the respective parliaments for ratification. On the Irish side, the full terms of the treaty to be ratified are set out in a draft statutory order that is laid before Dáil Éireann. On the approval of this Order by a resolution of Dáil Éireann, and the enactment by the Dáil of an incorporation of a reference to the Order in TCA 1997, Sch 24A, the agreement will acquire the force of law. The agreement will normally enter into force on the exchange of the instruments of ratification, but may then take retrospective effect if so agreed.

Several phrases in the above extract from TCA 1997, s 826 merit further comment. First, the authority given by the section, apart from the various 'exchange of information' powers mentioned above, is for the Government to make arrangements 'to afford relief from double taxation'. Then, when the required statutory order setting out the agreement with a particular country has been made, the terms contained in it are 'notwithstanding anything in any enactment' given 'the force of law', but this is *inter alia* 'subject to the provisions of this section'.

It is generally accepted that the terms of a treaty may vary the normal domestic tax law in a way which provides relief from taxation, whether for the benefit of a resident of the State or for a resident of the other country, but it cannot impose any new or additional taxation to that already provided for in the domestic law. This point is worth making since it is not unusual for some of the articles in treaties to state that one (or both) of the contracting states 'may' tax specified income in a particular way. Such a provision means that the country in question is given the right to tax the income in that way, should it wish to do so, but it does not itself impose any additional taxation to that already existing under the domestic tax laws of the country in question.

The reference to the tax treaty arrangements having the force of law is made 'subject to the provisions of this section'. In effect, there are only a few additional provisions to be considered. TCA 1997, s 826(2) requires the rules of TCA 1997, Sch 24 to be applied in connection with the calculation of any foreign tax credit permitted under any relevant treaty. TCA 1997, s 826(3) approves any provision in a treaty which allows relief from tax for a period prior to the actual conclusion of that treaty. TCA 1997, s 826(5) permits the Government to revoke any existing treaty by a subsequent statutory order (which must first be approved by a resolution of Dáil Éireann).

TCA 1997, s 826(9) authorises the Revenue Commissioners, if they think fit, to make regulations relating to the implementation of any double taxation agreements; to date, the Revenue Commissioners have not, it would appear, thought it necessary to make any regulations affecting any double taxation agreement covered by TCA 1997, s 826.

14.103 OECD Model Double Taxation Convention

Each double taxation agreement concluded between two countries normally follows to a greater or less extent a number of principles which have a fairly wide international acceptance regarding the way in which relief for double taxation should be provided. The Organisation for Economic Cooperation and Development ('OECD') approved in 1963 the text of a draft double taxation convention on income and capital which had been prepared by its Fiscal Committee. In 1977, the OECD Council approved the Revised Model Double Taxation Convention on Income and Capital – 1977 and recommended that OECD member countries should conclude any new tax conventions in accordance with that Convention. The Convention and the accompanying commentary have been updated since on a regular basis. In 2010, the latest version of the Model Convention was published. The OECD Council approved the contents of a new update to the OECD Model Tax Convention in July 2014. A revised version of the Model Tax Convention is due to be published incorporating the 2014 update. The fact that the OECD Convention may serve as a model for tax treaties negotiated between different countries does not mean that there cannot or should not be variations in individual treaties negotiated between countries which accept its general principles. Variations can and do occur as it is always necessary to have regard to the particular tax laws and the policies of the governments concerned in any bilateral treaty negotiations. As noted above, the Model Convention is published with a detailed commentary on each of its articles. This commentary is particularly useful in elaborating on and explaining the intention behind each article.

14.104 'Scope' of agreements and 'taxes covered'

Each double taxation agreement which follows the general lines of the OECD Model Convention starts off with the 'personal scope' article which provides that the agreement applies to persons who are residents of one or both of the contracting states. It had generally been thought that the treaties which do not contain this article (most of the older treaties) are similarly applicable only to the residents of the two countries concerned.

However, in *IRC v Cummerbund* [1990] STC 285, it was held that a person resident in a third state could take advantage of a double tax treaty to which his state of residence was not a party, if the wording of the treaty did not preclude this happening. This type of situation is unlikely to arise in the context of a modern treaty, which will usually follow art 1 of the Model Convention which expressly provides that 'this convention shall apply to persons who are residents of one or both of the contracting states' (the same wording was also used in the earlier versions of the Model Convention). It may be noted that TCA 1997, Sch 24 confines credit relief (but not exemptions) to resident persons.

The first instance decision on this point in the *Cummerbund* case is controversial and might not be followed by an Irish court (see eg Baker, *Double Taxation Conventions and*

International Tax Law (1994) at page 75). It is understood, however, that the Revenue Commissioners have, in fact, conceded the point in the context of a tax exemption available under the previous Ireland – USA treaty. The position is now also subject to the ECJ decision in *Saint Gobain* (Case C–307/97).

It may also be noted that the non-discrimination article in treaties applies also to the *nationals* of the contracting states.

Every double taxation agreement contains an article, usually headed 'taxes covered', specifying the particular taxes of each of the two contracting states to which the agreement is to apply. The treaties concluded from 1976 onwards (including the treaties amended subsequently) specify the Irish taxes covered as including income tax. The earlier treaties that still remain in force specify the Irish taxes as including income tax and surtax, but provide that the treaty is to apply also to any identical or substantially similar taxes which may subsequently be imposed in addition to, or in place of, those in existence at the date the treaty was made. From 2011 onwards this will include the Universal Social Charge (USC). It would appear clear that the USC will be covered in treaties which extend their coverage to taxes that are identical or substantially similar to income tax and a number of foreign tax administrations have already stated their acceptance of this analysis.

In applying any pre-1976 treaty that remains in force, the references in the 'taxes covered' article (and anywhere else) to the Irish surtax are no longer relevant. Surtax has long been replaced by the higher rates of income tax. Consequently, any reference in a treaty to surtax may now be taken as applying in a corresponding manner to the higher rates of income tax.

Subnational taxes in other countries

A number of foreign countries charge income (and, sometimes, capital gains) to taxation at the state or municipal level in addition to that levied under the federal or national law. For example, many of the different states in the US and the cantons and municipalities in Switzerland impose income taxes on persons resident and/or income having its source there. The question as to whether a person resident in Ireland is entitled to any relief in respect of such subnational foreign taxes depends on whether the state, municipal, etc taxes are specifically listed in the 'taxes covered' article in the relevant treaty.

Penalties and interest

In certain cases a treaty excludes from the Irish tax and the overseas tax covered by the treaty any penalty or interest imposed under the law of either country in relation to their respective taxes (eg the Ireland/New Zealand and Ireland/Australia treaties). Consequently, if for example Ireland is permitted to tax a certain type of income arising in Ireland to a resident of New Zealand up to a maximum rate of, say, 15 per cent, and if any penalty or interest should be imposed on the New Zealand resident for failure to pay the 15 per cent tax on time, the interest or penalty remains chargeable notwithstanding that the maximum permitted rate of tax has already been reached. This clause almost certainly only serves to make clear what is already the position under all treaties.

14.105 'Resident of' contracting state defined

In general, the majority of the articles in all the tax treaties are expressed as affecting the taxation by the contracting states of income (or capital gains) from sources in one of the contracting states when earned by a resident of the other state. Each treaty normally defines the term 'resident of' a contracting state in the way that this term is to be applied wherever it is used in the treaty. Usually, the treaty defines 'resident of Ireland' and 'resident of (say) France' separately, but in some cases the same wording is used for each definition.

It is important to note that the treaty definition of a 'resident of Ireland' may not always coincide exactly with the meaning of the term 'resident' as it is applied for Irish tax purposes in cases not affected by a double taxation agreement. It is possible, in some circumstances, for a person to be resident *in* Ireland under Irish domestic tax law without him falling within the definition of 'resident *of* Ireland' as contained in a particular tax treaty. Conversely, a person may be resident in the other contracting state under its laws without necessarily being a resident *of* that state within the definition of the term in its treaty with Ireland. While the treaty definition has to be used where it is applied in any relevant treaty article, it does not alter either state's domestic tax law definition of 'resident' for other purposes.

The pre-1976 treaties, except that with Japan, define a 'resident of Ireland' as a person who is resident *in* Ireland for the purposes of Irish tax and who is not resident *in* the other contracting state for the purposes of its taxation. In other words, it is necessary to apply the ordinary Irish rules of residence first (see **1.502** to **1.504**), and then to confirm that the person is not considered by the other state as being resident in its territory (as the concept of residence is understood under its laws). It is possible in some cases for an individual to be treated as resident in both countries. Such a 'double resident' is not entitled to benefit from any article in a particular treaty expressed as applying specifically to a resident 'of' one of the states.

The treaty with Italy varies the normal older treaty definition slightly by treating a person as a resident of Italy, provided the other conditions are satisfied, even if that person is resident in Ireland for Irish tax, provided that the period or periods spent in Ireland does not exceed 91 days in the relevant tax year. That treaty similarly permits a person to be regarded as a resident of Ireland if their period(s) spent residing in Italy does not exceed 91 days in the year. For these purposes a day of presence is to be construed in line with the definition in TCA 1997, s 819, denoting any time during the day (prior to 2009 it was presence at midnight) (*Kinsella v The Revenue Commissioners* [2007] IEHC 250).

The treaty with Japan takes a different approach. It allows Ireland and Japan to apply their respective domestic tax laws first, but if that results in an individual being considered resident in both countries, the treaty then requires the 'Competent Authorities' of the two countries to determine, by mutual agreement, the country of residence that is to apply for the purpose of the treaty. Unlike the later agreements (see below), the treaty with Japan does not prescribe any specific tests to determine the issue, but it is thought that in practice similar tests to those in the later treaties would probably be used by the respective competent authorities.

TCA 1997, s 821 treats individuals who are ordinarily resident, but not resident in the State, as if they were resident in respect of certain overseas income only (see **13.504**). Such individuals do not appear to be 'resident in Ireland' for treaty purposes in these circumstances, given the limited scope of TCA 1997, s 821. Accordingly, an individual who is, for example, resident in Germany for German tax purposes, and who is ordinarily resident, but not resident in Ireland should be able to claim the appropriate benefits of the Ireland/German treaty (pre-1976 treaty) as a 'resident of Germany'. It is not known if the Revenue Commissioners share this view.

The later treaties each contain a 'fiscal domicile' article in the form used in the OECD Model Convention. This starts by defining 'resident of a contracting state' as meaning any person who, under the laws of that state, is liable to tax there by reason of his domicile, residence, place of management or any other criterion of a similar nature. A person is not, however, treated as a resident of a contracting state if the only reason he is liable to tax in that state is because he derives income (or capital gains) from sources there. In this case an individual who is not resident, but who is ordinarily resident, in Ireland *does* appear to be a 'resident of Ireland'. This is because 'ordinary residence' is a criterion similar to 'residence', and the individual is liable to Irish tax (albeit to a limited extent) by reason of that criterion. This analysis is in practice adopted by the Revenue Commissioners, albeit only in relation to income which is potentially chargeable by virtue of TCA 1997, s 821. However, the treaty 'tiebreaker clause' (see below) will normally deem the individual to be a resident of the other contracting State for treaty purposes. Where the individual is treated as resident in Ireland for treaty purposes he will nonetheless not be strictly entitled to credit relief for tax suffered in the other treaty country since he is not resident in the State for Irish tax purposes (see **14.301**). However, the Revenue Commissioners, grant concessional credit relief in these circumstances.

The application of each contracting state's own tax laws (the main test of residence) may sometimes result in an individual being regarded as resident in each of the two states. If so, the 'fiscal domicile' article in the later treaties goes on to provide a series of supplementary tests to determine the residence of the individual for purposes of the relevant treaty (his 'treaty residence'). There are four supplementary tests to enable the individual to be classified either as a resident of Ireland or as a resident of the other contracting state (whichever is the case), so that the treaty articles may be applied accordingly. The four tests, which must be applied in the order they appear, until the 'double resident' is regarded as a resident of one of the states only, are:

Test A:

(a) if he has a permanent home available to him in one of the states only, he is deemed to be a resident of that state (and not of the other state), but
(b) if he has a permanent home available to him in both the states, he is deemed to be a resident of the state with which his personal and economic relations are closer (ie the state in which he has his 'centre of vital interests');

Test B:

if the individual's treaty residence cannot be determined under test A, he is deemed to be a resident of the state in which he has an habitual abode;

Test C:

if he has an habitual abode in both states, or in neither of them, he is deemed to be a resident of the state of which he is a national; and

Test D:

if he is a national of both states, or of neither of them, the competent authorities of these two states must settle the question by mutual agreement.

Once the individual's treaty residence has been determined, it is not necessary (or permitted) to apply any of the tests further down in the order. For example, if an individual has a permanent home in both states, it may well be possible to decide the matter on the grounds that his centre of vital interests is clearly in one of the states. If so, the location of the individual's habitual abode or the question of his nationality (generally identified with citizenship) is irrelevant.

The commentary to art 4 of the Model Convention states that in the case of Test A, any form of home may be taken into account (ie including a house, apartment or furnished room owned or rented by the individual). However, it adds that the home must be available on a continuous basis. In *O'Brien v Quigley* [2013] IEHC 398, the appellant had no intention of occupying the building as a permanent home or keeping the building available for his permanent use (works had been commissioned rendering the building unavailable for residential use). The High Court held that the decision of the appeal commissioner was correct in finding that the appellant did not have a permanent home available to him in Ireland.

The commentary also suggests that in determining an individual's 'centre of vital interests', regard should be had to his family and social relations, his occupations, his political, cultural and other activities, his place of business and the place from which he administers his assets, etc.

The commentary states that Test B tips the balance in favour of the state where the individual spends most time (including time spent elsewhere than in his permanent home (if any)). The comparison between his length of stays in the states must cover a sufficient length of time to decide whether his 'abode' is 'habitual'.

Where an individual changes residence during a tax year, so that he is only doubly resident for part of a tax year, the commentary to art 4 of the Model Convention indicates that the tiebreaker tests are only relevant to the period of double residence. Thus, for example, an individual who leaves the UK in March 2015 and becomes resident in Ireland in 2015 would normally be liable under Irish tax law on all of his income for 2015, (subject to the limited exemption available under the 'split year treatment': see **13.503**; **13.504**). It seems that such an individual should be able to claim exemption from Irish tax in respect of all of his pre-arrival, non-Irish income under the terms of the Ireland/UK tax agreement.

The main rule of the fiscal domicile article in the later treaties treats a company or other person(s) not being an individual, as being a resident of the contracting state in which it is liable to tax by reason of its domicile, residence, place of management or other criterion of a similar nature (but liability to tax in either state due only to having income or capital with its source in that state does not count). In the event that the application of this main rule would result in a company being a resident of both contracting states, then a supplementary rule provides that it is to be deemed to be a resident of the state in which its place of effective management is situated. In the US treaty, a mutual agreement procedure applies instead of this rule.

The UK Inland Revenue take the view that, in some cases, the place of effective management can differ from the place of central management and control. They give as a possible example a company run by executives based overseas, but where the final directing power is exercised in the UK by non-executive directors.

Under UK domestic tax law provisions, a company incorporated in the UK is generally treated as resident there. Where the company's place of effective management is located in a treaty partner state (eg Ireland) so that it is treated as resident in the partner state for the purposes of the treaty, it is then treated as UK resident for all UK domestic tax law purposes as well (UK FA 1994, s 249).

In the older treaties, the general approach is to treat a company as a resident of Ireland if its business is managed and controlled in Ireland, irrespective of the country of its incorporation. In some of the treaties, the reference is to the country in which the effective management of the company is situated, but this usually has the same effect (see above). The treaty with Japan is slightly different. Each country is to apply its own tests of residence first, and should these result in a company being resident in both Japan and Ireland, it is deemed for purposes of the treaty to be a resident of the country in which its head office or main office is situated.

The treaties with Federal German Republic, Luxembourg, Norway and Finland each provide that a company is a resident of the foreign country if it is either managed and controlled in the foreign country or incorporated there (except if it is managed and controlled in Ireland). For example, a company which is incorporated under Luxembourg law is treated as a resident of Luxembourg if it is managed and controlled in any third country (eg France), but not if it is managed and controlled in Ireland (in which case it is deemed to be a resident of Ireland).

The Model Convention does not contain any specific provisions dealing with partnerships. The issue arises therefore whether a partnership should be treated for treaty purposes as a 'body of persons' or whether the partners should be treated as separate individuals. The potential significance of this distinction is underlined by the case of *Padmore v IRC* [1989] STC 493. That case concerned the application of the UK-Jersey Double Tax Treaty to a partnership business which was managed and controlled, and physically carried on in Jersey, but where there were a number of UK-resident partners. Under the terms of the treaty, a business enterprise carried on by a 'person' who was resident in Jersey, but *not* resident in the UK, was exempt from UK taxation if it did not have a 'permanent establishment' in the UK. The Court of Appeal held that the Jersey partnership was a 'body of persons' and that it was resident where it was managed and controlled, ie in Jersey. Accordingly, all of the profits of the partnership, including the share attributable to the UK resident partners, were exempt from UK taxation.

The income tax definition of a 'body of persons' (see TCA 1997, s 2(1) in Ireland) is 'any body politic, corporate or collegiate, and any company, fraternity, fellowship and society of persons, whether corporate or not corporate'. It does not seem that this definition can include a partnership. However, even assuming that the income tax definition does not include a partnership, it is by no means certain that the income tax definition of 'body of persons' should necessarily take precedence over the general meaning of the term (the term 'body of persons' in its normal sense would have included partnerships in both the UK and Jersey). Under most treaties, terms not otherwise defined assume their domestic tax meaning 'unless the context otherwise requires' (see **14.106**). In *Padmore*, the court felt that it was unlikely that it was intended to exclude coverage of partnerships, given their widespread use in both the relevant jurisdictions.

It is unclear as to how far the decision in *Padmore* depends on the fact that the definition of the term 'person' in the UK-Jersey treaty referred to a 'body of persons, *corporate or not corporate'*, (the words in italics are *not* employed in the Model Convention). The significance of the words in italics is that they demonstrated that the term 'body of persons' could not have been meant to refer back to the UK tax definition (since it would have been unnecessary in that case to add the words 'corporate or not corporate', which are already contained in the tax definition).

Nevertheless, from an Irish tax viewpoint, the concept of a partnership as a body of persons and thus a taxable person, in its own right, with its own place of residence, seems difficult to sustain. By virtue of TCA 1997, s 1008, each partner is deemed to carry on a 'several trade' on his own (in the UK a partnership was generally treated (at the time that the facts in *Padmore* arose) as a separate entity for assessment purposes). Further, there is no reference in the income tax legislation to the residence of a partnership (again, in contrast to the position in the UK). The better view therefore seems to be that a partnership *as such* cannot be a resident of Ireland for tax treaty purposes, and consequently, cannot avail of any treaty exemptions or credits. In practice, this is the analysis which is adopted by the Revenue Commissioners.

It follows that each Irish resident partner in a mixed residence partnership should be entitled in his capacity as an individual or as a company (in the case of a corporate partner) to avail of the treaty in his/its own right (compare the tax treatment of Lloyd's Underwriters at **13.506**, albeit Lloyd's syndicates are not, strictly speaking, partnerships as such). In some cases, a treaty will deal expressly with the treatment of partnerships on this basis. Thus, for example art III(2) of the Germany/Ireland Treaty expressly provides that a partner resident (for treaty purposes) in one treaty state will be taxable in the other state only on his share of the profits arising in that other state (ie assuming that the partnership is trading there through a 'permanent establishment' (see **14.201**).

The taxation of trusts raises similar problems to those encountered in the case of partnerships. Both the Model Convention and the accompanying commentaries remain silent as to their appropriate treatment. The discussion below concentrates on the portion of 'non-transparent' trusts, ie where the beneficiaries are not absolutely entitled to the trust income as it arises (see **15.304**). If the decision in *Dawson v IRC* [1989] STC 473 were to be upheld in Ireland, it would again be difficult to sustain the concept of the trust as a taxable 'person' in its own right, for Irish income tax purposes. This is because *Dawson* decided that it is generally the *trustees* who are taxable in respect of trust income, and not the *trust* as a distinct and separate entity. The position is different in respect of capital gains tax, where:

(a) the trustees are taxed a continuing body of persons; and
(b) there are statutory rules for determining the residence of that body (TCA 1997, s 574).

The Irish income tax position of trustees (on the continuing assumption that *Dawson v IRC* would be upheld in Ireland) differs from that of a partnership in so far as that where there are two or more trustees, they are liable to tax on a joint basis, ie they are taxable collectively as 'persons'. Thus, if all of the trustees are Irish resident, they can be classed as 'persons' resident in Ireland (subject to the point noted in the next paragraph), and should therefore potentially qualify for relief as Irish residents under any relevant treaty (ie taking the term 'person' to include the plural 'persons' in accordance with the Interpretation Act 2005, s 18(a)). However, if one or more of the trustees are not Irish resident, then it would appear that they cannot qualify for treaty relief as 'persons' all of whom are resident in Ireland. This outcome seems logical, given that the trust will be in effect treated as non-resident for Irish domestic tax purposes (again assuming that *Dawson* would be followed in Ireland).

Notwithstanding the above, where a treaty states that a 'person' comprises (ie consists *only* of) 'an individual, company or body of persons' in strictness then the argument that the trustees are 'persons' does not seem possible (since trustees are not 'individuals' but 'persons' for tax purposes, and the tightness of the definition does not allow one to include *other* taxable 'persons').

Trustees are clearly not a body of persons within the income tax definition of TCA 1997, s 2(1), but on the strength of the decision in *Padmore*, it is arguable that the context requires that the ordinary meaning of the term should be used. A 'body of persons' in its ordinary sense would generally include trustees (see *IRC v Reids Trustees* 30 TC 431), but it must be noted that in *Revenue Commissioners v ORMG* III ITR 28, the Supreme Court held that two persons could not constitute a 'body of persons' in the normal sense of that expression (the court did not specify a minimum number). However, even if the trustees *were* to be regarded as a 'body of persons' for treaty purposes but included both Irish resident and non-resident trustees then, following *Dawson* it seems that the trust should again be regarded as non-resident in Ireland, and thus precluded from the treaty relief available to Irish residents.

In practice, the Revenue Commissioners have traditionally regarded a trust as a body of persons with a distinct residence status of its own. Where the trustees were individuals, then if they were all resident in Ireland, the trust would be regarded as resident in Ireland: this leads to the same end-result as the analysis in *Dawson*. Where some of the individual trustees were resident outside Ireland, then the trust would usually be regarded as resident where the effective administration of the trust took place: this may lead to a different result from the analysis in *Dawson*. In the case of professional trustees, the residence of the settlor at the time the trust was established (or at the time of his death in the case of a will trust) was attributed to the trust (see McAteer *et al*: *Income Tax* Ch 14); again this may lead to a different result from the analysis in *Dawson*.

If a 'mixed residence' trust is regarded as an Irish resident body of persons under traditional Revenue practice, (and the taxpayer does not challenge this position on the basis of *Dawson*), the Revenue should usually accept that the trust is eligible for treaty relief. Where a trust is accepted to be Irish resident for treaty purposes, there remains the possibility that it will also be regarded as resident in the other treaty state under its domestic laws.

Where trustees are regarded as resident under the domestic law of both treaty countries, the tie-breaker clause relating to 'individuals' does not seem to be appropriate. This is again because trustees *in their capacity as such* are regarded as 'persons' rather than individuals, for Irish tax law purposes. Under the later treaties therefore it seems that the trustees should be regarded as resident in the state where the effective management of the trust takes place (*see Wensleydale's Settlement Trustees v IRC* [1996] STC (SDC) 241, where it was held that the test to be applied was where the centre of top level management was located). Under the older treaties, the trustees will generally continue to be regarded as resident 'in' both jurisdictions and will not therefore qualify as a resident 'of' Ireland or of the other jurisdiction for the purposes of the relevant treaty.

The Revenue Commissioners manuals set out the following guidelines for applying the 'tiebreaker' rules to trusts in the context of the Ireland/UK Double Taxation Agreement:

(a) if the trustees are all individuals residing in one country only that country should be accepted as the place of effective management;

(b) if the trustees are all individuals but not all residing in one country:

   (i) the country in which the individual who generally controls and supervises the work of administering the trust (ie keeps the accounts, conducts the correspondence, arranges the meetings of the trustees and puts into effect the decisions taken at such meetings) resides should be taken,

   (ii) if there is no such individual the dates and places of all meetings held should be established and the country in which the majority of the meetings were held regarded as the place of effective management;

(c) if a professional body is acting as trustee either alone or in conjunction with individuals the place of business of that professional body should generally be presumed to be the effective place of management of the trust;

(d) if the professional body acting as trustee is a United Kingdom bank with a branch or subsidiary in this country and the work of administering the trust is carried out by that branch or subsidiary this State should be regarded as the country of residence, and vice versa in the converse situation.

It may be noted that limb (b)(i) of the Revenue's guidelines would appear to put undue emphasis on the administrative functions of the trust as opposed to the top level decision-making function.

Similar considerations apply to personal representatives as to trustees. Where all of the personal representatives are resident in Ireland, the Revenue have generally regarded them as a body of persons resident in Ireland. Where some of the personal representatives are resident outside Ireland, then the place where the effective administration of the estate takes place would usually determine the issue. The Revenue apply similar guidelines to those applicable to trustees for these purposes.

Article 4 of the Model Treaty makes it clear that the State itself, as well as any political subdivision or local authority thereof, is a resident of the contracting State concerned.

14.106 Other definitions

Each tax treaty contains definitions of a number of other terms that are used in the course of the treaty. These definitions are in a fairly standard form in most of the treaties, but it remains essential to check the precise wording used in the particular treaty that is relevant to the position of any person claiming relief under that treaty. Some exceptions to the standard wording are noted below.

Reference may be made here to the following definitions which appear in more or less common form in the treaties generally.

Territory of contracting state

This is defined in each treaty for each of the two contracting states. The definition usually consists of the name of the country concerned, but in some of the treaties, eg those with Australia, France and the US, the foreign country is stated as including specified overseas departments or territories. For example, the term 'Australia' is defined as meaning the Commonwealth of Australia and, when used in a geographical sense, includes such exotic sounding places as Norfolk Island, Christmas Island, Cocos (Keeling) Island etc.

A number of the treaties contain definitions which extend the territories of the contracting states to include that part of the continental shelf within which each state is entitled to exercise exploration, exploitation, etc rights with respect to the seabed and subsoil and their natural resources. It has become the normal practice to include this extension in treaties concluded from the early 1970s onwards. In the absence of any specific extension to bring in the continental shelf or any overseas territories, the territory of a country for purposes of a treaty is limited to its recognised land area (including any islands included therein) and its territorial waters (in the case of Ireland, see Article 2 of the Constitution).

Enterprise of a contracting state

This is defined simply as an enterprise carried on by a resident of either one of the states, depending on the context. For example, the reference in art 6 of the Ireland/Switzerland Treaty to an enterprise of a contracting state carrying on business in the other contracting state through a permanent establishment there may be taken as applying either to (a) an enterprise carried on by a resident of Ireland through a permanent establishment in Switzerland or (b) an enterprise carried on by a resident of Switzerland through a permanent establishment in Ireland.

The commentary to the Model Convention states that the question whether a commercial activity is to be considered as part of an enterprise, or as an enterprise in itself, is a matter of domestic law. In *Thiel v FCT* [1990] 90 ATC 4717, the Australian High Court held in effect that an adventure in the nature of a trade carried on by a resident of a treaty state could constitute an 'enterprise'. The practical result was that the resident of the treaty partner state was entitled to claim exemption from Australian tax under the relevant treaty, since he did not have a 'permanent establishment' in Australia. The decision may have been influenced by the fact that the treaty would not have provided exemption if the profit in question had been regarded as a capital gain (the normal capital gains article was not included in the treaty). It is open to question how persuasive a precedent the *Thiel* case would be in the eyes of an Irish court.

Contracting state

This is defined in each treaty as meaning either of the states whose governments have concluded the treaty, as the context may require. For ease of reference in this chapter, the phrase 'treaty country' is used synonymously with 'contracting state'.

Person

This term generally is to be taken as 'including' an individual, a company and any other body of persons. There are some exceptions, for example, the German treaty defines a person as including individuals and companies and all other entities treated as taxable units under the laws of the respective contracting states. Some treaties (eg that with the UK) defined the term as comprising, rather than including, an individual etc. This is a narrower definition, the implications of which are explained at **14.105**.

Company

This term is defined in most of the treaties as including any body corporate or any entity which is treated as a body corporate for tax purposes. The commentary to art 3 of the OECD Convention indicates that it is the treatment as a body corporate according to the tax laws of the contracting state in which the entity is organised that determines the matter. It is unclear why the tax law of the State of incorporation or registration, should be decisive, since the relevant entity could be formed in one state but be tax resident in a different state.

The general approach under Irish tax law would be to regard an overseas entity which has a separate legal personality under its own system of law as a body corporate for tax purposes (see *Dreyfus v IRC* 14 TC 560; *Memec v IRC* [1998] STC 754). This case is discussed in more detail at **14.304** as part of the House of Lords discussion in *Anson v HMRC* [2015] UKSC 44. In other cases, where an entity is treated by the other contracting state as a body corporate resident for tax purposes in that state, then that entity should be capable of qualifying as a 'resident of' the latter state (see **14.105**).

Potential problems in this area concerning the treatment of partnerships are discussed in the commentaries to arts 1 and 10 of the Model Convention.

Nationals

The term 'national' is generally defined as an individual possessing nationality of a treaty state or any legal person, partnership of association deriving its status as such from the laws in force in a contracting state. Thus, a company which is incorporated in Ireland is an Irish national, regardless of where it is resident.

In relation to the United Kingdom, 'nationals' means citizens of the United Kingdom and Colonies, British subjects under specified provisions in the British Nationality Acts (subject in some cases to time limits), British protected persons within the British Nationality Act 1948 (this Act has now been repealed), and all legal persons, associations or other entities deriving their status as such from the law in force in the United Kingdom.

Irish tax

This term refers to any or all (as appropriate) of the Irish taxes listed in the 'taxes covered' article. For example, if a particular treaty article provides a relief from Irish tax in respect of capital gains, the article may be taken as applying either to capital gains tax or corporation tax on chargeable gains. If the 'taxes covered' article applies the treaty to any identical or substantially similar taxes introduced after the treaty was signed, the term 'Irish tax' may be given a similar extended meaning.

Each treaty usually contains a corresponding definition of the 'tax' of the other treaty country. For example, the term 'Swiss tax' in art 2 of the Ireland/Swiss Confederation Agreement refers to the Swiss federal, cantonal and communal taxes listed in that article.

Terms not defined

The treaties generally contain a clause providing that any term not specifically defined in any treaty is to be given the meaning which it has under the laws (or, sometimes more narrowly the tax laws) of the contracting state relating to the taxes which are the subject of that treaty, unless the context requires otherwise. It remains an open question as to how widely or narrowly the context of the treaty should be construed for these purposes. Presumably it must at least include those materials which can normally be taken into account when interpreting the treaty in question (see eg JF Avery-Jones 'Article 3(2) of the OECD Model Convention, etc' [1993] European Taxation 252; JF Avery-Jones et al, 'The interpretation of tax treaties et' [1984] BTR 14, 90; C Van Raad 'Interpretation and Application of Tax Treaties by the Courts' [1996] European Taxation 3.

The application of this clause has already been noted with regard to *Padmore v IRC* [1989] STC 493, where the UK Court of Appeal suggested that the context of the treaty indicated that the wider legal definition of the term 'body of persons' might have to be applied rather than the narrower tax definition. As the terms of the clause indicate, the domestic tax law definition to be applied is that which is relevant to the particular tax provisions which are the subject of treaty relief. Thus, for example, where a term is defined differently for the purposes of income tax and capital gains tax, the income tax definition should be applied in respect of income subject to potential double taxation, etc (but this general principle may not apply where there is a specific treaty definition provision: see *Steele v EVC* [1996] STC 785). The principle still applies even if a term used in tax law simply carries its general legal meaning (see the discussion of 'employment' at **14.210**). Article 3 of the Model Treaty was amended to state that the meaning of a term under the applicable tax laws of the contracting state should prevail over any other legal meaning in that state. This seems to make clear what is already implicit in this clause; nevertheless Ireland has reserved the right to exclude this amendment in its future treaties.

It is of course possible that a domestic tax law definition will be altered subsequent to the conclusion of a treaty. This raises the question as to which definition should apply: the definition in force when the treaty was concluded, or the definition in force when the treaty is being applied at some later date. Article 3 of the Model Treaty was also amended to state that undefined terms should be given their meaning 'at the time' the treaty is applied. This seems to be a sensible approach. Thus, for example, the term 'resident in Ireland' in a treaty should reflect the new definition of 'residence' for individuals introduced by FA 1994, with general effect from 1994–95 onwards.

The commentary does indicate however that there are limits to the 'ambulatory approach'. Thus, the context of the treaty may indicate that the incorporation of a new domestic tax definition would 'impair the balance or effect the substance' of the treaty in such a way that the new definition should *not* be adopted. The commentaries also suggest that where a new tax definition is incorporated into the treaty the treaty states 'can settle any difficulties that may emerge from the new system of taxation', ie under the 'mutual agreement' procedure (see **14.221**).

An unresolved point of difficulty concerning the 'terms not defined' clause arises where the two treaty states apply conflicting domestic tax law definitions. The Revenue Commissioners have indicated that where there is a treaty and the country of source has exerted taxing rights on the basis of having classified the income differently from Irish law, double tax relief will still be granted. In some cases, a treaty will expressly provide that a particular term has to be defined by reference to the general law or to the tax law of one of the treaty states. Thus, for example, art 6 of the Model Convention states that immovable property is to have the meaning which it has under the law of the treaty state in which the relevant property is situated (this format is generally adopted in Ireland's tax treaties: see **14.208**). Similarly, the term 'dividends' is defined in some treaties as including 'income from other corporate rights assimilated to income from shares by the taxation law of the state of which the company making the distribution is a resident' or even more widely 'as any income or distribution assimilated to income from shares' (see **14.206**).

In *Travers v Ó'Síocháin* IV ITR 159, Carroll J discussed the correct approach to the interpretation of the expressions 'local authority in the UK' and 'functions of a governmental nature' contained in art 18 of the Ireland/UK Tax Treaty. Neither expression was defined in the treaty, but the 'terms not defined' clause was not relevant, since neither expression was defined in the context of Irish tax law. Given that the status of a 'local authority' is dependent on the laws of the State in which it is established, that expression had to be interpreted in the light of its legal meaning in the UK. On the other hand, the concept 'functions of a governmental nature' did not bear a technical legal meaning. Accordingly, Carroll J, decided that it had to be interpreted generally in such a way as to give it the same meaning in both treaty jurisdictions (this is in accordance with art 33(3) of the Vienna Convention which states that the terms of a treaty are presumed to have the same meaning in each text).

Certain other terms, eg 'permanent establishment', 'international traffic', etc are discussed in **14.2** in the context of the particular articles to which they are relevant.

14.107 Elimination of double taxation

The elimination of double taxation through tax treaties is dealt with in two stages. First, each treaty contains articles dealing with specific classes of income, capital gains (if covered by the treaty) etc arising from sources in either of the two treaty countries (the 'country of source') earned by a person who is a resident of the other country (the 'country of residence'). These articles lay down rules defining whether and, if so, to what extent the country of source may tax a resident of the other country in respect of the type of income, capital gains etc covered. Depending on the particular treaty and the type of income, gain, etc, the country of source may be permitted by the treaty to tax it fully or up to a specified maximum rate of tax or, alternatively, may be required to exempt it from its tax altogether.

Secondly, each treaty contains an article, usually headed 'elimination of double taxation'. This article sets out the manner in which each contracting state has agreed to grant double taxation relief to any person resident in its territory if he has borne or paid tax in the other state in respect of income arising there. In general, the country of residence is only required by this article to give relief for tax which the other country is entitled to charge in accordance with the specific income, etc articles in the treaty. It is to be noted that Irish tax law applies this article, where appropriate, to give double taxation relief for the relevant foreign tax if the person claiming the relief is resident *in* Ireland, even if he is not a 'resident of' Ireland within the treaty definition of that term.

The OECD Model Convention provides two principal ways in which the elimination of double taxation article in a tax treaty may operate. These are referred to as the 'exemption' and 'credit' methods of double taxation relief. Under the exemption method, the country of residence does not tax any item of income which, in accordance with the treaty article dealing with the type of income in question, may be taxed in the country of source. Under the credit method, the country of residence includes the full income arising in the other country in the resident person's total income chargeable to its income tax (or corporation tax), but grants a credit for the foreign tax paid in the other country on the income. It is not necessary that the two contracting states to any one treaty should adopt the same method. One country may agree to apply the exemption method, while the other may give the necessary double taxation relief by the credit method.

All the double taxation agreements which the Irish government has made with other countries adopt the credit method of granting double taxation relief to Irish resident persons who have paid tax in the other treaty country, but only for taxes properly paid in accordance with that country's 'primary taxing rights' provided for in the specific income, etc articles in the relevant treaty (note the discussion at **14.106**: *Terms not defined*). On the other hand, the method used by the other country in giving its residents relief for Irish taxes properly paid in accordance with the relevant treaty varies with the practice and law of the country concerned. For example, the UK adopts the credit method, while Germany adopts the exemption method.

The elimination of double taxation article in each treaty concluded by the State requires the Irish Revenue to grant the credit for the relevant foreign tax against the Irish tax on the particular foreign income 'subject to the provisions of the law of Ireland regarding the allowance as a credit against Irish tax of tax payable in a territory outside Ireland'. A similar rule applies where, under a relevant treaty, a resident person is entitled to a credit against Irish tax for tax paid in the other country on a capital gain realised in that country. The Irish tax law regarding the manner in which credits are given for foreign tax against the corresponding Irish tax is contained mainly in TCA 1997, Sch 24, which also has rules affecting the amount of the relevant foreign income (or capital gain) that is brought into the Irish resident's total income (or total chargeable gains). There is no provision in Irish law for granting relief in respect of self-employed PRSI, (see **Division 3**), notwithstanding that this is effectively a tax on income.

The foreign tax credit rules of TCA 1997, Sch 24 do not permit a credit against Irish tax for any tax paid in the other country that is not one of the taxes mentioned in the 'taxes covered' article in the treaty with that country, nor do they allow any credit for any tax paid in a country with which there is no tax treaty. Any such non-creditable foreign taxes are, however, usually deductible in arriving at the amount of the income (or capital gain) on which the relevant Irish tax is charged (see **13.202**). Any tax levied by the other country on any income in excess of the tax that country is allowed to charge under the relevant treaty article is not eligible for credit against Irish tax. The Irish resident must seek a refund from the tax authorities of the other country of any such excess tax paid.

For a full discussion of the Irish rules for granting credits for foreign tax against Irish income tax and the Universal Social Charge, see **14.3**.

14.108 Interaction with anti-avoidance provisions

In many cases, domestic tax law imposes legal fictions, typically deeming provisions, in order to prevent perceived tax avoidance strategies. Thus, for example, in certain circumstances the income of a trust may be deemed to be that of the settlor (see **15.4**) or the income of an offshore entity may be deemed to be that of a person who made a transfer of assets resulting in income accruing to that entity (see **17.2**). The general anti-avoidance provision, TCA 1997, s 811C, in particular may permit the Revenue Commissioners inter alia to recharacterise avoidance-based transactions in whatever manner is appropriate in order to counter tax advantages (see **17.3**). The interaction between such provisions and those of double tax agreements is discussed in **15.403**, **17.209**, **17.210** and **17.302** respectively.

The OECD model commentary to art 1 ('Persons covered') states the view that 'substance over form', 'economic substance' and general anti-abuse rules forming part of the basic domestic rules for determining which facts give rise to a tax liability are not affected by tax treaties. On this analysis, there will generally be no conflict between domestic anti-avoidance rules and the provisions of a double tax treaty. Notwithstanding this broad assertion it will always be necessary to take into account the specific wording of relevant anti-avoidance provisions and to also bear in mind the relative precedence of domestic and international law in issues of interpretation (see the observations on the commentary to this effect by Ireland).

14.2 Articles in Double Taxation Agreements

14.201 Business profits: permanent establishment

Each double taxation agreement contains an article dealing with 'business profits', the heading used in the OECD Model Convention. This article, frequently heading 'industrial or commercial profits' in Ireland's tax treaties, should be read with the definition of 'permanent establishment' given either as a separate article or included in the 'definitions' article, depending on the treaty concerned.

The general principle adopted in all the treaties is that the industrial or commercial (or business) profits of an enterprise carried on by a resident of one of the contracting states shall not be subject to tax in the other state, unless that enterprise carries on business in that other state through a permanent establishment situated there. Consequently, an individual, company or other person who is a resident of Ireland is not taxable on any business profits earned in, say, France (eg through selling goods there) unless he carries on business in France through a permanent establishment situated in France. Conversely, a resident of France must carry on business through a permanent establishment in Ireland if he is to be subject to any Irish income tax or corporation tax on his business profits.

Thus, there may be circumstances in which a non-resident person would be taxable under Irish law (eg if he sells goods in the State under contracts made here), but where the transactions are not part of or connected with a trade carried on in the State through a permanent establishment. In such a case, the non-resident cannot be taxed on the profits from the transactions, provided that he is a resident of a country with which there is a tax treaty. In each case, the 'permanent establishment' definition contained in the relevant treaty must be applied.

Permanent establishment

This term is defined in each tax treaty as meaning a fixed place of business through which the business of an enterprise is wholly or partly carried on. Each treaty gives its own list of examples of what can be regarded as constituting a permanent establishment, eg a place of management, a branch, an office, a factory or a workshop; a mine, quarry or other place of extraction of natural resources. This list may vary in different treaties, but in each treaty it should be read in the context of the general definition quoted above. For example, a resident of Belgium may have an office in Dublin, but this office is not treated by the Ireland/Belgium treaty as a permanent establishment if no business is carried on through that office.

The commentary to art 5 of the OECD Model Convention provides a lengthy and helpful discussion of the definition of 'permanent establishment'. According to the Commentary, the definition should be applied in the light of the following salient considerations:

(a) The term 'place of business' covers any premises, facilities or installations, whether or not used exclusively for the business of the enterprise and whether they are owned, rented or otherwise placed at the disposal of the enterprise (including facilities made available by another enterprise).
(b) The place of business must be fixed to a specific geographical location for a purpose which is not merely temporary. However, premises used for a short-term project, or for a long term project which is subsequently cut short or aborted, may still fall within the definition (the Revenue Precedents give the example of a bookmaker's stand at a racecourse as a permanent establishment).

The commentary also deals with the time when a permanent establishment should be treated as commencing or ceasing to exist, and discusses some of the specific issues raised by leasing operations.

Most of the treaties refer to a mine, oil well or other place of extraction or exploitation of natural resources within the State as being a permanent establishment. While some of the treaties do not mention a mine, etc it is considered that the exploitation of natural resources carried out through a mine, quarry, etc in the State is clearly an activity through a fixed place of business. In other words, there is a permanent establishment within the general definition of the term.

The Irish tax rules regarding the taxation of non-resident persons carrying out exploration or exploitation activities on the Irish sector of the continental shelf are dealt with in **13.606**. A non-resident person carrying on such activities on the continental shelf outside Irish territorial waters may be exempted by a tax treaty from Irish tax on his trading profits therefrom, depending on the terms of the treaty with his country of residence. The question depends on how the particular treaty defines the 'territory of Ireland' or 'Ireland'. Many of the modern treaties provide that the term 'Ireland' includes any area outside Irish territorial waters which in accordance with international law has been or may hereafter be designated, under the laws of Ireland concerning the continental shelf, as an area within which Ireland may exercise rights with respect to the seabed and subsoil of the continental shelf.

The permanent establishment article in these latter cases either includes in its definition a mine, quarry or other place of extraction of natural resources, or specifically provides that activities carried on in the State in connection with the exploration or exploitation of the seabed, subsoil or their natural resources in the State are to be treated as activities of a business carried on through a permanent establishment in the State.

Consequently, where any treaty takes this approach, the resident of the other treaty country remains liable to Irish taxation under TCA 1997, s 13 on the profits derived from its Irish continental shelf activities. In some cases, activities of short duration may be excluded (see eg the treaty with Sweden).

Where a treaty does not extend the definition of the territory of Ireland, a resident of the other treaty country is not liable to Irish taxation under TCA 1997, s 13 (or under any other rules) in respect of the profits which he may earn from any exploration or exploitation activities carried on by him outside Irish territorial waters, even if on the Irish sector of the continental shelf. This assumes that the non-resident in question does not have any fixed base or other place of business in the State itself from which the continental shelf activities are carried on. In the absence of any such fixed place of business within the State, he does not have a permanent establishment in Ireland (as defined in the treaty with his country of residence).

It is almost certain that, when any of the treaties which do not treat 'Ireland' as including the continental shelf are renegotiated, the definition of the territory of Ireland in each new or amended treaty will be extended to include the Irish sector of the continental shelf.

The treatment of building sites and construction/installation projects is also dealt with by the commentary to art 5 of the OECD Model Convention. Article 5 provides that such works will not constitute a permanent establishment, even if there is an installation such as an office or workshop associated with them, so long as they last only for a period of 12 months or less. The commentary suggests also that the office, etc of an enterprise which provides planning and supervisory services for the purposes of such works lasting 12 months or less, will not constitute a permanent establishment, if such an office, etc, is used exclusively for those purposes. The commentary also deals at some length with the rules for determining whether the 12-month period has been exceeded where roads are being built and the activities performed at each particular spot are part of a single project. The project itself will be a permanent establishment if it exceeds 12 months. These rules apply to the builder and also the person developing the land (although the latter point is not absolutely clear).

A number of Ireland's treaties do not deal expressly with the treatment of building sites, etc, or else incorporate a shorter period than 12 months in their definition of permanent establishment (eg the treaties with New Zealand and the UK which applies a cut-off point of six months). The Ireland/UK treaty previously did not deal with the position of building sites. In *Tax Briefing 26*, the Revenue Commissioners stated their view that since the Ireland/UK agreement did not specify a time period, every building site which was a fixed place of business through which the business of a UK enterprise was wholly or partly carried on was a permanent establishment.

In this context, the Revenue Commissioners regarded the 'fixed place of business' as the site itself if either:

(a) the contractor was present on the site for two months or longer;
(b) the contractor brought a significant amount of plant, machinery or equipment on to the site; or
(c) the contract was 'significant', generally denoting a value of £500,000 or more.

The Revenue Commissioners also took the view that in the case of road building, the building site was any point along the roadway or proposed roadway where machinery might be left at night. These criteria are somewhat arbitrary (particularly limb (c), which appeared to be entirely irrelevant) and it was perfectly possible that the UK Inland

Revenue might have taken the view that any Irish tax suffered as a result would not have been imposed if the treaty had been correctly interpreted by the Revenue Commissioners. The Revenue Commissioners noted that in these circumstances the differences between the two Revenue authorities should have been resolved under the mutual agreement provisions (art 24 of the Ireland/UK Treaty): see **14.221**.

All the treaties provide that an agent or other person (including an employee) acting in one of the contracting states on behalf of an enterprise of the other contracting state may, if certain conditions are present, be deemed to be a permanent establishment of that enterprise in the former state. With the exception of a broker, general commission agent or other agent of independent status (see below), an agent or other representative of the foreign enterprise is deemed by all the treaties to be a permanent establishment of that enterprise in a contracting state if he has and habitually exercises in that state an authority to conclude contracts in the name of the enterprise. However, if he does no more than purchase goods or merchandise for the enterprise, that is not on its own sufficient to render him a permanent establishment.

The expression 'contracting in the name of' is based on civil law principles, rather than on common law principles. Under the common law of contract, it is possible for an agent to bind a principal while still contracting in his own name. However, it seems clear that the expression in the OECD Model Convention implies the ability of the agent to conclude contracts on behalf of the relevant non-resident enterprise. The commentary to art 5 of the OECD Model Convention bears out this interpretation. It may be noted that the UK has added an observation to the commentary to the effect that this is how it intends to apply the article in practice.

The commentary to the OECD Model Convention indicates that, for the non-resident to be taxable in the State, the agent's authority should extend to concluding contracts other than those relating to matters that are merely internal to the non-resident's business. For example, if the agent's authority only extends to engaging employees for the non-resident's business, this would not be sufficient, on its own, to constitute the agent as a permanent establishment. Generally, it may be taken that the agent's authority must extend to concluding contracts for sales. The OECD commentary also emphasises that the authority to conclude contracts must be habitually exercised for there to be a permanent establishment. Article 5 of the OECD Model Convention makes explicit that once an agent falls to be treated as a permanent establishment, then all activities which he undertakes for the relevant enterprise are treated as relating to that permanent establishment.

There is no requirement that the agent etc should be resident in the state. In *Tax Briefing 26*, the Revenue Commissioners state that where a sole trader or a member of a partnership habitually enters into contract in the State, he will be regarded as an agent of the sole tradership/partnership for the purposes of the article.

Some treaties deem an agent to be a permanent establishment of the foreign enterprise if either he has, and habitually exercises, authority to conclude contracts for the enterprise or if he has a stock of goods or merchandise from which he regularly fills orders on its behalf. For example, if a Japanese company has an agent in Ireland without any authority to conclude sale contracts, but who holds a stock of the Japanese company's goods within the country from which he fills orders from the company's customers, then the company is deemed to carry on business through a permanent establishment in the State, ie through the agent.

It may be however that the Japanese company is not trading *in* Ireland under Irish domestic law (see the discussion in **13.602**). Because a double tax treaty cannot impose a tax charge, the Japanese company would remain non-taxable in respect of its trade *with* Ireland.

The treaties, generally provide that the term 'permanent establishment' excludes a 'broker', 'general commission agent', or any other 'agent of independent status' who acts for the non-resident enterprise in the ordinary course of his business. Again, the terms 'broker' and 'general commission agent', which were based on UK legislation (and are to be found in TCA 1997, s 1039, etc) do not fit easily with a civil law framework (see JF Avery-Jones 'Agents as Permanent Establishments under the OECD Model' [1993] BTR 341. The commentary to art 5 of the OECD Model Convention indicates that an agent will be excluded from permanent establishment status only if he:

(a) is independent of the non-resident enterprise legally and economically, and
(b) acts in the ordinary course of his business when acting on behalf of the enterprise.

The commentary suggests that where an agent's activities are subject to detailed and comprehensive control by the enterprise or where the preponderance of entrepreneurial risk falls on the enterprise rather than the agent, then the agent will not be independent. The commentary also suggests that where an agent performs activities which belong to the enterprise's sphere of activities, rather than to his own business operations, he will not be acting 'in the ordinary course of his business'. Thus, a person acting as a permanent agent with the authority to conclude contracts could constitute a permanent establishment.

One important point should be noted. If a non-resident enterprise has a fixed place of business, this will constitute a permanent establishment even if none of the persons employed there can be classed as agents (for example, because they cannot conclude contracts on behalf of the non-resident enterprise). In other words, the agency criterion is an *alternative* to the 'fixed place of business' criterion. If either criterion is satisfied the non-resident enterprise will have a permanent establishment in the State.

The treaties also generally provide that the fact that a company is controlled by another company does not *in itself* make the former permanent establishment of the latter. However, if a subsidiary in fact acts as an agent of its parent company then the normal rules set out above will apply.

The increased growth of electronic commerce will clearly require refinement of the concept of a 'permanent establishment'. A web site on the internet may be accessed from virtually any location in the world in order to place orders for goods or services. The web site as such does not seem to constitute a fixed place of business although it does enable the seller of the goods or services in effect to establish a 'presence' in the jurisdiction where the good or services are ordered. The position may arguably be different if the trader maintains a computer server with a web site on it in the relevant jurisdiction (particularly if the web site contains advanced software allowing it to process and conclude contracts).

There is apparent support for the argument that a service web site may constitute a permanent establishment in a German decision (see *Tax News Service* 17 March 1997) which held that underground pipelines located in Germany and which were used to deliver crude oil to German customers constituted a 'fixed place of business'; this was notwithstanding the fact that the pipelines were fully operated by a computer located in Holland and the taxpayer had no employees in Germany. The decision has been much criticised and does seem dubious, given that all the business activity of the taxpayer was conducted outside Germany. Accordingly, it seems difficult to justify the proposition that the pipeline was a location through which all or part of the business of the Dutch taxpayer was carried on (see Lamp 'Broadening the definition of a permanent establishment: The pipeline decision' [1998] European Taxation 67).

In any event, the argument as to the status of a computer server is likely to prove academic since a server can be located virtually anywhere in the world (or in the case of satellite servers, literally out of this world). In their extremely useful report 'Electronic commerce and the Irish tax system (June 1999)', the Revenue Commissioners observed feelingly:

> The very concept of permanent establishment may be ill-adapted to e-commerce, as the concept is based on physical presence and could be considered meaningless in the electronic environment

This observation seems particularly pertinent in the context of sales of digitised products where the latter can be downloaded directly from the internet, removing the need to establish sales outlets in the customers' territories.

The commentary on the OECD Model Convention reflects the view that a website *per se*, lacking as it does any tangible presence, cannot constitute a fixed place of business. The commentary takes the view that only physical equipment such as a server may be so regarded. However, the commentary accepts that where a website is hosted on a server, the server will not usually be at the disposal of the enterprise carrying on business through that website. On the other hand, the commentary takes the view that an enterprise which owns or leases its own server may thereby have a fixed place of business in the jurisdiction where the server is located, even if it does not employ or otherwise engage any personnel within that jurisdiction. The UK has expressed a dissenting observation on this point. This would depend on, for example whether the server can be regarded as being fixed at a particular location and whether any business functions of the enterprise are carried out by means of the server. The commentary recognises that in any event there will be no permanent establishment where the server is dedicated to merely preparatory or auxiliary activities such as advertising or market research.

14.202 Business profits: amount taxable

When a resident of a country with which there is a double taxation agreement carries on a trade or profession through a permanent establishment in Ireland, the business profits article in the relevant treaty entitles Ireland to tax that foreign resident on his business profits, but only on so much of them as are attributable to the permanent establishment. In principle, the amount of the taxable profits of the business (the foreign enterprise) is ascertained under the ordinary rules of Sch D Cases I and II, but the business profits article in the treaty may add some additional rules to be applied to the extent relevant.

Ireland's treaties generally require the taxable profits of the permanent establishment of the foreign enterprise to be calculated on the assumption that the business of the permanent establishment is carried on as a distinct and separate enterprise, ie as one dealing wholly independently with the enterprise of which it is the permanent establishment. In other words, the taxable profits are computed on the basis that the prices charged to, or by, the permanent establishment for goods or services supplied by, or to, its foreign head office are the same as would apply in dealings between independent unconnected parties.

Most of the treaties also add a provision that, in calculating the taxable profits of the permanent establishment, deductions may be made for expenses incurred for the purposes of the permanent establishment including executive and general administration expenses, irrespective of whether incurred in the taxing state or elsewhere. The commentary to the OECD Model Convention indicates that in the case, for example, of general administration expenses incurred at the head office of the enterprise, it may be appropriate to deduct a proportionate part based on an appropriate ratio, eg the ratio of the turnover of the establishment to that of the enterprise as a whole. In practice, the taxation authorities of the country in which the permanent establishment is situated usually require to be satisfied that the amount charged for these expenses is fair and reasonable having regard to all the circumstances of the particular case.

The dividing line between the situations where the head office incurs expenses which are attributable to the permanent establishment and where it provides services to the permanent establishment (on which an arm's length mark-up should be applied) may not always be clear.

An issue that has arisen in a number of jurisdictions is whether a permanent establishment can claim a notional amount of interest in respect of finance provided by head office. The general consensus seems broadly to be that no claim may be made for such interest, but that where the head office incurs actual borrowings for the purpose of the permanent establishment then the associated interest costs may be deductible. This is in line with the analysis provided in the commentary to the OECD Model Convention (with an exception for certain financial institutions). It is understood that this is also the approach adopted by the Revenue Commissioners.

The term 'industrial and commercial profits' is separately defined in a few of the treaties, but in the absence of any special reference in a treaty, it may be taken as including the taxable profits of all forms of trading activity except for types of income covered in separate articles. Almost all the treaties deal with the profits from ships and aircraft operated in international traffic under a separate article (see **14.203**). The treaty with Germany provides that industrial and commercial profits include rents and royalties in respect of cinematography (including television) films, whereas the treaty with Pakistan specifically excludes such rents or royalties from business profits. A number of the treaties deal in a separate article with the profits from professional and other independent personal services, whereas other treaties regard such income as coming under the industrial and commercial profits article.

While items of income dealt with under other articles in a treaty are not normally treated as business profits, most of the treaties provide that dividends, interest or royalties received by a resident of one of the countries are, if effectively connected with a permanent establishment in the other country, to be taxed as part of the profits of that permanent establishment under the business profits article. In such a case, this article operates in priority to the relevant dividend, interest or royalty article.

14.203 Shipping and air transport

The business of operating ships or aircraft in international traffic is generally dealt with separately in double taxation agreements from that of other types of trade. Owing to the special nature of the business, the permanent establishment rule applied for other businesses is not considered suitable. An international shipping or air transport operation usually involves the enterprise in having offices and/or other facilities in a number of countries and in concluding contracts in more than one country to carry passengers and/or cargo between two or more countries. In the absence of special treatment in double taxation agreements, an international transport enterprise could be liable to tax on its profits in a number of countries in respect of the same activities (due to having permanent establishments, eg a booking office, in each). As these rules are generally relevant only to companies, they are not discussed further in this book.

14.204 Associated enterprises

All the treaties contain an article headed 'associated enterprises'. This article may be relevant in any case where two associated enterprises trade or have other commercial or financial dealings with each other on terms different from those which would apply in similar transactions or dealings between independent enterprises. An enterprise of one contracting state is treated, for the purposes of this article, as associated with the enterprise of the other state if:

(a) either one of the two enterprises participates directly or indirectly in the management, control or capital of the other enterprise; or
(b) the same persons participate directly or indirectly in the management, control or capital of each of the two enterprises.

If, as a result of any non-arm's length transactions between two such associated enterprises, any profits do not accrue to one of the enterprises (say that resident in treaty country A) which would have accrued if their dealings had been at arm's length, then the 'associated enterprises' article in the treaty between the two contracting states permits the state prejudiced (country A) to include the 'missing' profits in the taxable profits of its resident enterprise. The area in which this rule is likely to have the most frequent application is in relation to the pricing of goods passing between associated enterprises in the course of their trading activities, but it may apply also to inter-company services, interest on loans, royalties for the use of patents, leasing of equipment, etc.

Example 14.204.1

Lille-Chartres SA, a French incorporated and resident company is owned by the Irish resident members of a partnership, Corklily and co, which is the distributor in Ireland for goods manufactured by the French parent company. During the partnership's period of account ended 31 December 2016, it has the following transactions in goods purchased from Lille-Chartres SA:

	€	€
Sales by Corklily partnership		210,000
Less:		
Purchases from Lille-Chartres SA	130,000	
Trading expenses, etc	45,000	
		175,000
Sch D Case I profits		35,000

Following correspondence with the Irish inspector, Corklily and co has to accept that a proper arm's length price for the goods purchased from Lille-Chartres SA would have been €90,000. Article 5 (associated enterprises) of the Ireland/France treaty appears to permit the Irish inspector to adjust the Sch D Case I profits of Corklily and co as follows:[1]

	€
Sch D Case I profits (as above)	35,000

Add:

'Missing' profits due to non-arm's length pricing	
€130,000 – €90,000	40,000
Revised Sch D Case I profits	75,000

Note:

1. As mentioned in **14.102**, an article in a tax treaty may permit a contracting state (in this case, Ireland) to tax income in a particular way, but it is also necessary that the domestic tax law of the state in question must contain rules to implement the taxation in the particular circumstances. In the absence of any more specific provisions in the Irish tax legislation, it appears that the inspector *may* be able to implement the rules of art 5 by disallowing €40,000 of the cost of purchase of the goods on the grounds that part of the cost is not an expense incurred wholly and exclusively for the trade (see **5.305**). In addition, a transfer pricing regime based on the OECD Guidelines was introduced with effect from 1 January 2011. It applies to both domestic and international trading transactions carried out between associated entities (as defined). The regime does not apply to contracts or terms and conditions agreed before 1 July 2010. The provisions will not apply to small and medium-sized enterprises (as defined). Accordingly, these provisions are far more likely to impact on inter-group corporate transactions as opposed to transactions within the sphere of income tax. A fuller account of the scope of these provisions is therefore more appropriate to a work on corporation tax.

In a case such as that just illustrated, the 'missing' profits, assessed on the enterprise that is the subject of the adjustment in treaty country A were, of course, already included in the profits of the associated enterprise in the other contracting state (say, treaty country B). Unless the tax laws or practice of treaty country B permit the taxable profits of the latter enterprise to be adjusted downwards to compensate for the taxation of the missing profits in treaty country A, the same part of the aggregate of the profits of the two enterprises will be taxed twice, once in each country.

The majority of Ireland's tax treaties do not require the contracting state in the treaty country B position to make any compensating adjustment to the taxable profit of, or to the tax payable by, the associated enterprise resident in its territory. There are a growing number of exceptions, for example, the treaties with Australia, New Zealand, Sweden and the UK, in each of which there is a provision requiring the B contracting state to give such relief.

In the Ireland/Australia treaty, art 10(4) (associated enterprises) requires the country B contracting state (Ireland or Australia, as the case may be) to make an appropriate adjustment (downwards) to the amount of its tax that is otherwise chargeable on the profits of the associated enterprise resident there. In determining the amount of this adjustment, due regard must be had to the other provisions in the treaty and, if necessary, the Irish and Australian Revenue authorities may consult each other on the matter. Article 10(2) of the treaty with Sweden and art 11(2) of the treaty with New Zealand are in the same form.

The double taxation agreement with the UK also requires the contracting state in the treaty country B position to make the compensating adjustment by a reduction in the tax payable by the associated enterprise resident in its territory. The adjustment is made through an extension of the foreign tax credit rules under the elimination of double taxation article (art 21) in the agreement.

In any case where the contracting state in the treaty country A position makes this adjustment to the taxable profits of the country A enterprise, art 21(4) (elimination of double taxation) requires treaty country B (the United Kingdom or Ireland, as the case may be) to make a compensating adjustment (downwards) in the tax payable by the associated enterprise resident in its territory (the country B enterprise). This adjustment starts from the fact that the 'missing profits' are included in the accounting and taxable profits of the country B enterprise that are subject to tax in country B as a result of the pricings actually used in the transactions between the two associated enterprises. Article 21(4) deems an amount equal to the 'missing' profits taxed by country A on the country B enterprise to be income which the latter enterprise has earned in country A.

The country B enterprise is then assumed to have paid the additional country A tax on those 'missing' profits that was actually paid by the country A enterprise due to the adjustment to its taxable profits made under the power given in the 'associated enterprises' article in the treaty. The Revenue authorities of country B are then required to allow the country B enterprise credit for the country A tax which that enterprise is deemed to have borne on the 'missing' profits. In granting this credit, country B applies its normal rules for determining the amount of the credit for the foreign tax against its own tax. If, for example, Ireland is in the country B position, this means that the computational rules of TCA 1997, Sch 24 are applied (see **14.302**).

The commentary to the Model Convention suggests that even where there is not any express provision for compensatory adjustments, these should nevertheless be made under the 'mutual agreement' article (see **14.221**). There would however appear to be no legal basis for this generally in Irish tax law. However, the European Convention on the elimination of double taxation in connection with the adjustment of profits of associated enterprises (90/436/EEC) provides a framework for the making of adjustments, involving where necessary, the appointment of an advisory commission by the contracting states concerned. The Convention has been ratified by all of the EU states, including Ireland (see SI 1994/88). The protocol to the convention provides that the original convention will be renewed automatically every five years unless any Member State objects at least six months prior to the renewal date (SI 2004/40, taking effect from 1 January 2000).

14.205 Dividends, interest and royalties: general

The domestic tax laws of most countries impose withholding taxes on dividends, interest and royalties paid from sources within their territories to persons resident in other countries. Irish tax law requires income tax at the standard rate to be withheld in the case of annual interest paid to a person whose usual place of abode is outside the State (subject to certain exemptions) (see **2.306**) and for patent royalties paid to a non-resident (see **2.307**). Irish tax law requires income tax to be withheld at the standard rate from dividends or other distributions paid by resident companies to non-residents subject to certain exemptions. TCA 1997, s 172D states that dividend withholding tax will not apply where a company resident in the State makes a relevant distribution to a qualifying non-resident person. A qualifying non-resident person is a person beneficially entitled to the distribution, not being a company, who is neither resident nor ordinarily resident in the State but is resident in another EU Member State or tax treaty country. A certificate must be obtained from the tax authority of the appropriate territory certifying that the person is resident in that territory (TCA 1997, Sch 2A para 8) (see **9.106**). Further, dividend withholding tax will not apply where a company resident in the State makes a relevant distribution to a company which is not resident in the State and which satisfies certain conditions (TCA 1997, s 172D(3)(b); see also TCA 1997, s 831 in relation to dividends paid by Irish resident subsidiaries to non-resident parent companies) (see **9.106**).

All the tax treaties contain articles which vary the domestic rules of taxation in each of the contracting states in respect of dividends, interest and royalties. In general, these articles provide that the contracting state in which the income arises should either exempt the income from its taxes or tax the income at a reduced rate if the beneficial owner of the income is a resident of the other state. In practice, some countries operate a procedure whereby this treaty relief or exemption may be obtained at the point of payment of the relevant income, whereas in other cases the normal withholding taxes are imposed and the resident of the other country has to make a repayment claim to the tax authorities of the country of source.

In the case of interest and royalties from Irish sources, the Revenue Commissioners have been prepared to authorise the Irish resident person making the payment not to withhold any income tax or to apply a lower treaty rate (whichever is appropriate under the relevant treaty). In order to satisfy the Revenue Commissioners that he is entitled to such a benefit, the resident of the other country should obtain a claim form from the Residence Branch of the Revenue Commissioners. He should complete this form and have it certified by the tax authorities of his country of residence to the effect that he is a resident of it and entitled to benefit from the relevant article in the treaty. This certified form should then be presented to the Residence Branch which if satisfied, will then instruct the payer of the interest or royalty to make the payment gross or at the appropriate reduced rate. This procedure implies that the requirement to withhold tax is not overridden by exemptions granted under a double tax treaty (but note *inter alia* TCA 1997, s 246 which applies a withholding requirement only to interest 'charged to tax under Sch D', note also TCA 1997, s 826(9) which refers to the situation where tax has not been deducted from periodical payments in order to comply with a double tax agreement).

In considering whether one of these treaty articles applies, reference should be made in each case to the definition given to the type of income involved. Variations do occur between some of the treaties as to precisely what is covered by the terms 'dividend', 'interest' and 'royalties'.

It may be noted that because the meanings of 'dividends', 'interest' and 'royalties' are specifically defined for the purposes of the treaty, they do not fall within the scope of the rule for 'terms not defined' (see **14.106**).

The requirement that the resident of a contracting state who receives the income should be the 'beneficial owner' of the income raises some potential difficulties in the case of trusts. Under Irish tax law, trust income payable to a beneficiary who is absolutely entitled to that income, should be treated as accruing to him from the underlying source (see **15.304**). Thus, for example, an individual with a life interest in an Irish resident trust which owns shares in an Irish resident company should normally be treated as 'beneficial owner' of any dividends arising. If the individual is resident in a treaty state, Ireland should therefore apply the appropriate treaty article in respect of these dividends (net of any attributable trust expenses). It is thought that the inspector would normally be prepared to attribute the trust expenses to the non-dividend income in priority to the dividend income in these circumstances.

In other cases, for example where an accumulation or discretionary trust is involved, the income is initially received by the trustees, and is only subsequently received (if at all) by the beneficiaries by virtue of powers or discretions exercised by the trustees. The commentary to the OECD Model Convention suggests that the term 'beneficial owner' should be given a wide meaning in order to prevent misuse of the treaty and that it is designed primarily to prevent tax relief being improperly obtained through the use of agents or nominees. However, under Irish trust law (and tax law) the trustee(s) in these circumstances cannot strictly be regarded as the beneficial owner(s) of the trust income. It is unclear whether the context of the treaty requires that a wider meaning as opposed to the narrower Irish legal meaning should be adopted (see **14.106**: *Terms not defined*, above). In *Indofood International Finance Ltd v JP Morgan Chase Bank NA London Branch* [2006] EWCA Civ 158, a non-tax case, one of the issues at stake was whether a conduit company through which interest payments were being funnelled in order to reduce withholding taxes, could be reasonably treated as not being the 'beneficial owner' of the interest which it received for double tax treaty purposes and which was subject to very tight contractual undertakings. The company had little operational freedom, being required to pass on the interest received by it to the ultimate recipients almost instantaneously. The UK Court of Appeal agreed that that the term '"beneficial ownership" should be accorded an "international fiscal meaning" not derived from the domestic laws of Contracting States', and that in the circumstances it was likely the relevant tax authority could have relied on this to deny the benefits of the treaty concerned. In practice, the Revenue Commissioners may be prepared to 'look through' discretionary distributions of income to the underlying trust income, and to treat the recipients as beneficial owners of the income distributed to them. Thus, for example, if the trustees of a UK discretionary trust make a distribution out of Irish dividend income to a UK resident individual he will be treated as 'beneficial owner' of that income and the dividend article in the Ireland/UK treaty would normally be applied to him. To the extent that such income is accumulated by UK trustees, the Revenue Commissioners should be prepared to treat the trustee as beneficial owners of that income for treaty purposes.

It should be noted that the meaning of beneficial ownership is one of the subjects addressed in the 2014 update of the OECD Model Tax Convention. This new update has not yet been formally incorporated into the next revised edition of the OECD Model Tax Convention at the date of writing.

14.206 Dividends: specific points

Most treaties generally permit the country of source to tax the dividend, but limit its right to tax to a maximum rate per cent. In the other treaties, the resident of the other treaty country receiving a dividend from an Irish resident company was exempt from the higher rates of Irish tax (referred to usually by its former name of 'surtax'). A number of the more recent treaties entitle an Irish resident company holding a minimum proportion of the share capital in the distributing company to an even lower maximum rate of tax or, in some cases, to a complete exemption. For example, the maximum rate of Swiss tax payable on Swiss company dividends to shareholders who are residents of Ireland is 15 per cent, but if the recipient is a company controlling directly or indirectly at least 25 per cent of the voting power in the Swiss company paying the dividend, the Swiss tax is limited to a maximum 10 per cent (art 9(4), as amended, in the Ireland/Switzerland agreement).

Article 10(3) of the OECD Model Convention extends the definition of dividends for the purpose of that article to include 'income from other corporate rights which is subjected to the same taxation treatment as income from shares by the laws of the State of which the company making the distribution is a resident'. This definition has been incorporated in a number of Ireland's treaties. Some of the older treaties (eg that with France) define 'dividends' in a similar way, but may define the term in a way which it seems is to be regarded as excluding distributions which are not dividends in the strict sense (*see Murphy v Asahi Synthetic Fibres* III ITR 246). The application of this definition in the context of Irish tax law would have the effect of including as a dividend any distribution of an Irish resident company that is treated as such by TCA 1997, s 130 where the source can be regarded as rights enshrined in the constitution (ie normally the articles and memorandum) of the company concerned. This definition would not normally be apt to cover payments of interest. A broader definition of 'dividend' namely as 'any income or distribution assimilated to income from shares has been adopted in later (eg the treaties with Australia, Finland and Hungary). Where this definition has been incorporated in the treaty, it would have the effect of treating as a dividend *any* distribution of an Irish resident company within TCA 1997, s 130. Conversely, in applying the relevant treaty to a dividend from a company resident in the foreign country, the term 'dividend' would be given its extended meaning under the tax law of the country in question.

The term 'dividend' is defined by art 11(3) of the Ireland/UK treaty for Irish tax purposes, as any item which under the law of Ireland is treated as a distribution and as including, for UK tax purposes, any item which under the law of the UK is treated as a distribution. It is not clear why Irish distributions are expressed to be treated as such for 'Irish tax purposes' and not for the purposes of the treaty (and similarly for UK distributions). Despite this obscurity of expression it is accepted that any provision in art 11, which grants a relief or exemption to a UK resident in respect of Irish tax on a dividend from an Irish resident company, is to be taken as giving the same relief or exemption on a payment that is a 'distribution' within the meaning of that term under TCA 1997, s 130 and its supporting sections. The same will apply in reverse to a distribution from a UK resident company to a resident of Ireland.

It may be noted that while the purchase of its own shares by a company resident in a treaty state may be treated as a distribution in that state, it will normally be treated as a capital gain in Ireland, following *Rae v Lazard Investment Co Ltd* 41 TC 1 (see **13.107**); see the discussion of *Murphy v Asahi Synthetic Fibres* III ITR 246 in **14.207**.

All the later treaties, and most of the older ones, exclude from the operation of the 'dividend' article any dividends (and other distributions within the 'dividend' definition) paid on any shares, etc the holding of which is 'effectively connected with' (or, in some treaties, 'attributable to') a business which the beneficial owner of the dividends carries on through a permanent establishment in the country of source. In any such case, the dividends may be taxable in the country of source under the 'business profits' article in the relevant treaty. This means that the foreign resident is no longer entitled to claim the repayment of tax credits otherwise available under the later treaties.

Article 24(4) of the Ireland/Sweden treaty provides an exemption from Swedish tax for dividends paid by an Irish resident company to a Swedish resident company, but only where such dividends would be exempt from Swedish tax if both companies were Swedish companies. A Swedish company is entitled, by applying the appropriate rules of Swedish law applicable to inter-company dividends between Swedish companies, if its holding in the Irish resident company is held otherwise than as a portfolio investment. Generally, a holding of at least 25 per cent of the voting power in the Irish company is sufficient to satisfy this condition, but lesser holdings may qualify a Swedish resident company for the exemption in certain circumstances.

14.207 Interest and royalties: specific points

Interest

Virtually all the treaties give the main right of taxing interest income to the country of residence of the recipient, but some treaties, for example that with Belgium, allow the country of source the right to a limited measure of taxation. For example, a resident of Belgium in receipt of interest income from an Irish source is subject to Irish tax at a rate of 15 per cent instead of the normal Irish standard rate; conversely, a resident of Ireland in receipt of Belgian source interest income is subject to a Belgian withholding tax on interest income at a maximum rate of 15 per cent. The treaty with New Zealand allows each contracting state a maximum tax of 10 per cent on interest and royalties arising in its territory payable to a resident of the other state.

The treaty with Pakistan requires the country of residence of the recipient to exempt the interest from its tax if the interest has been taxed under the domestic laws of the country of source. In the case of interest paid or guaranteed by the government of the country of source, the treaty gives the sole taxing right to that country. Since Ireland does not impose any taxation on interest on government securities when beneficially owned by a person not resident in the State (see **2.309**), it appears that a resident of Pakistan may be free of both Irish and Pakistani tax on interest from Irish government securities.

The term 'interest' is generally given a fairly standard form of definition, although the exact words used may vary a little from treaty to treaty. An example of the type of wording used may be taken from the definition of 'interest' given in art 9(3) of the Ireland/Netherlands agreement, namely:

> income from Government securities, bonds or debentures, whether or not secured by mortgage and whether or not carrying a right to participate in profits, and debt claims of every kind as well as all other income assimilated, by the taxation law of the State in which the income arises, to income from money lent.

However, the later treaties exclude as 'interest' any income which is treated as a dividend under the relevant dividends article (eg interest on certain securities treated by TCA 1997, s 130 as a distribution).

In the absence of such a provision, the treaty rules which relate to interest will continue to apply, even if the interest is treated as a distribution for Irish tax purposes (*Murphy v Asahi Synthetic Fibres* III ITR 246). The fact that the interest article is applied for *treaty* purposes has no bearing on the treatment of the interest as a distribution for *Irish* tax purposes: Tax treaties do *not* require that the treaty states should recharacterise transactions under their domestic tax provisions. Each state must firstly apply its own domestic tax rules to a transaction and only then must it look to the treaty to see if it must grant exemption or tax credits, etc, in respect of that transaction. In practice, however, where a provision of the kind mentioned is not included in a treaty, the Revenue Commissioners will be prepared to treat interest paid by an Irish resident company to a resident of the treaty state as if it were not a distribution. This allows the Irish resident company to claim the interest as an expense, but it then remains liable to deduct tax therefrom at the treaty rate.

Royalties

Most of the treaties provide that royalties which a resident of one of the contracting states derives from sources in the other country are to be taxable only by the country of residence. A few of the treaties give a limited taxation right to the country of source. For example, the treaties with Australia and Japan permit the country of source to charge tax at a rate up to 10 per cent of the gross amount of the royalties.

The definition of 'royalty' covered by the royalty article tends to vary from treaty to treaty. A fairly commonly used definition is that in the Ireland/Switzerland agreement, namely:

> payments of any kind received as consideration for the use of, or the right to use any copyright of literary, artistic or scientific work, including cinematograph films or films or video tapes for use in connection with television, any patent, trademark, design or model, plan, secret formula or process, or for the use of or the right to use, industrial, commercial, or scientific equipment, or for information concerning industrial commercial, or scientific experience

This form of definition is broadly in line with that in the OECD Model Convention. The commentary to that Convention makes it clear that this definition is intended to include not only copyright and patent royalties, but also lease rentals for the use of plant, machinery, equipment or other industrial properties. In fact, it is generally accepted that Irish tax law does not require any income tax to be withheld at source from copyright royalties; clearly no such requirement applies to lease rents in respect of movable property paid to non-residents. However, this form of article makes it clear that the resident of the other treaty country has no liability to Irish tax (or only a limited liability in some cases) on any royalty payments, whether by deduction at source or by direct assessment.

The commentary on the Model Convention reflects the view that where a customer downloads digitised products (eg software) for personal use and enjoyment, the payment made by the customer is essentially consideration for a product rather than for the right to use a copyright. The commentary distinguishes this situation from one where the customer acquires the right to commercially exploit the digitised product. The commentary also deals with numerous other permutations which are possible in the context of e-commerce.

Interest and royalties

In the case of interest and royalties, a resident of one of the contracting states is generally entitled to the treaty exemption (or, if relevant, to the reduced rate of tax) if the interest or royalty arises in the other state. The later treaties usually required that the resident person is the 'beneficial owner' of the interest or royalties (see the discussion at **14.205**). In general, the person making the payment does not have to be a resident of the source country. For example, a resident of Germany is entitled to receive free of any Irish tax any Irish-source interest or patent royalties paid by an Irish manufacturing branch of, say, a Bermuda company (for a discussion of the criteria in determining the location of the source of such payments under Irish law, see **2.302–2.304**). However, the Ireland/Sweden treaty, for example, provides that, for the purpose of each article, the interest/royalties are normally deemed to arise in the contracting state of which the payer is a resident or, where the payer is the state itself or a political sub-division or a local authority of a state, in that state. However, where the payer (whether or not he is a resident of either contracting state) has a permanent establishment or fixed base in one of the contracting states (eg Ireland), the interest or royalties are deemed to arise in that State (Ireland) if the interest or royalties arise on indebtedness or an obligation connected with the permanent establishment or fixed base and if the interest or royalties are borne by the permanent establishment or fixed base.

The application of the relevant interest or royalty article to exempt the resident of the other country from tax in the country of source (or to limit the rate of tax) may be restricted if there is a special relationship between the payer (in the country of source) and the recipient (in the country of residence). Most of the treaties provide that, in such a case, any interest or royalty paid in excess of a fair and reasonable consideration for the use of the money or of the other benefits provided is not entitled to benefit from the treaty, so that such excess interest or royalty is subject to normal taxation in the country of source.

There is a recent tendency to incorporate anti-avoidance clauses into the royalty and interest articles. Thus, for example, art 12(5) of the Ireland/UK treaty provides that art 12 ('interest') will not apply 'if it was the main or one of the main purposes of any person concerned with the creation or assignment of the debt claim in respect of which the interest is paid to take advantage of this article by means of that creation and assignment': under the previous wording, there was an exception for transactions undertaken for *bona fide* commercial reasons. This test raises similar difficulties of interpretation and application to blanket anti-avoidance clauses in other contexts (see the discussion at **18.111**: *Prevention of misuse*). The Ireland/New Zealand treaty contains similar clauses in arts 13 and 4 (interest and royalties respectively).

These types of clause are aimed mainly at so called 'treaty shopping' operations. Typically, these arise where, for example, a company (A) in state A is liable to withhold tax on interest payments to a company (B) in state B. State A and state B may not have concluded a tax treaty, or else the treaty between them may not eliminate the withholding tax. In such a case, the companies may decide to interpose company C, resident in state C, which would borrow money from company B and lend it on to company A. Assume that the tax treaty between state A and state C allows company A to pay interest free of withholding tax to company C and that the domestic law of state C allows company C to pay interest free of withholding tax to company B. The interposition of company C therefore allows interest to flow indirectly from company A to company B, free of withholding taxes, ie in the absence of an appropriate 'anti-avoidance' clause. Note also *Indofood International Finance Ltd v JP Morgan Chase Bank NA London Branch* [2006] EWCA Civ 158 discussed at **14.205**.

Almost all of Ireland's tax treaties exclude from the operation of the 'interest' article any interest on any debt claim that is 'effectively connected with' (or, in some treaties, 'attributable to') any business which the recipient of the interest carries on through a permanent establishment in the country of source. Similarly, these treaties exclude from the operation of the 'royalty' article any royalty arising from any right or property effectively connected with (or attributable to) such a business. In any such case, the interest or royalty is taxable in the ordinary way under the 'business profits' article and the treaty exemption (or reduced tax rate) given for interest or royalties does not apply.

14.208 Income from immovable property

All the treaties contain an article dealing with income from immovable property. In each case, the state in which the immovable property is situated is given the right to tax the income under its own laws without any restriction. This article applies to all income from immovable property, normally defined as comprising income derived from the direct use, letting, or use in any other form of the property.

The treaties all state that the term 'immovable property' is generally to be given the meaning which it has under the law of the contracting state in which the property is situated. This is designed to avoid difficulties of interpretation in different countries as to whether an asset or an interest in property is to be regarded as immovable property or not. A form of definition common to most treaties states that the term includes:

> property accessory to immovable property, livestock and equipment used in agriculture and forestry, rights to which the provisions of general law respecting landed property apply, usufruct of immovable property and rights to variable or fixed payments as consideration for the working of, or the right to work mineral deposits, sources and other natural resources …

It follows that a resident of the other treaty country is liable to full Irish taxation including, in the case of an individual, the higher rates of income tax, if he derives income from farming land in the State, from rental or other income taxable under Sch D Case V, or from any royalties or other income for the right to work mineral deposits or other natural resources situated in the State.

Article 7(4) of the Ireland/Sweden treaty provides that a lease of land or any other interest in or over land, and any right to payments for the working of mineral deposits, etc, is to be regarded as situated where the land, mineral deposits, oil or gas well, natural resources, etc are situated. This is primarily an anti-avoidance measure so that the granting of a lease or other interest in or over land, mineral deposits, etc cannot be used to deny the country in which the land, etc is situated its right to tax all forms of income from that immovable property. A similar provision appears, for example, in the Ireland/New Zealand treaty.

It is to be noted that the treaty with Pakistan deems interest on debts secured by mortgages on immovable property to be income derived from such property. Consequently, a resident of Pakistan is subject to full Irish income tax on interest income from a debt secured by a mortgage on land situated in Ireland.

The tax laws of both Ireland and the UK contain similar rules exempting from their respective income taxes investment income received by a body of persons or trusts established for charitable purposes only (see **18.203**). Similarly, each country exempts from its income taxes the investment income of certain approved superannuation or pension schemes and of certain approved trust schemes which provide retirement annuities for self-employed persons. Thirdly, each country exempts from liability to corporation tax the income from investments and deposits of the part of a life assurances' company life assurance and annuity funds that is attributable to its pension business (in Ireland, see TCA 1997, s 717).

The Ireland/UK tax treaty contains several special measures under which each of the contracting states extends additional reliefs (not available to other person) to charities, superannuation schemes and life assurance companies (in respect of pension business) resident in the other state. These special measures are contained in art 14A covering *inter alia* income from immovable property and capital gains from the alienation of such property.

In each case, the Commissioners of Inland Revenue (United Kingdom) or the Revenue Commissioners (Ireland) must certify that the relevant income is not subject to tax in the country of residence of the charity, superannuation scheme etc.

Article 14A is expressed as applying notwithstanding the rules of art 7. That article entitles the country of source to tax residents of the other state in respect of income from immovable property (art 7 by reference to the situation of the immovable property). It is not unusual for superannuation schemes and life assurance companies resident respectively in the United Kingdom and Ireland to invest in immovable property situated in the other country. In the absence of art 14A, an Irish superannuation scheme, etc fully exempted from tax in Ireland would have been left liable to UK tax in respect of its income from immovable property in the United Kingdom (and vice versa for the UK resident scheme). Article 14A avoids this result, and extends the same treatment to charities resident in the respective countries.

'Superannuation schemes' entitled to the benefit of art 14A are defined in the same way as those entitled to the dividends exemption of art 11(3) (see above). The term 'immovable property' is, in referring to such property situated in either of the states, given the meaning that it has under the domestic law of the state in question and is to be taken as including also property accessory to immovable property, livestock and equipment used in agriculture and forestry and rights to variable or fixed payments as consideration for the working of, or the right to work, mineral deposits or other natural resources (ie the definition in art 7(2) applies).

Consequently, the charity, superannuation scheme, etc exemption of art 14A includes not only rental income from immovable property situated in the other state, but it covers all farming income, income from woodlands, as well as mineral, etc rents and royalties.

14.209 Professional services ('independent personal services')

All the treaties, except those with Pakistan, the UK and the US, contain an article dealing with income derived from professional services or other independent activities of a similar character. Most of these treaties indicate that the term 'professional services' (or the other term used, 'independent personal services') is to include especially independent scientific, literary, artistic, educational or teaching activities as well as the independent activities of physicians, lawyers, engineers, architects, dentists and accountants. The commentary to the OECD Model Convention indicates that these are intended to be examples of typical liberal professions, but that the list given is not necessarily exhaustive.

Broadly, the activities covered by the independent personal services article in these treaties correspond with those assessable to Irish tax under Sch D Case II. They are to be distinguished from 'dependent personal services', ie services given by persons as employees of other persons, which are dealt with in most treaties under one or more separate articles (eg income from employments, governmental functions, and directors' fees). The 'professional services' article generally provides that a resident of one of the contracting states (eg France) is to be taxable only in his country of residence unless he has a fixed base regularly available to him in the other contracting state (eg Ireland) for the purposes of performing his activities. If he has such a fixed base in the other country, the income may be taxed there, but only to the extent that the income is attributable to that fixed base. The commentary to art 14 of the OECD Model Convention makes it clear that the principles which apply to the computation of profits attributable to a permanent establishment extend also to the profits attributable to a 'fixed base'.

The term 'fixed base' is not defined in any of the treaties, but is for the person carrying on a profession or other independent activity the equivalent of the permanent establishment of a person carrying on a trade. The OECD Convention commentary indicates that the term would cover, for instance, a doctor's consulting room or the office of an architect or a lawyer.

In the treaty with Pakistan, income from professional services is dealt with in the same article as income from employments. In the US agreement, professional services are covered in the same way as personal services generally. In both these cases, each country has the right to tax income from professional service performed in its territory by a resident of the other country, even where there is no fixed base, but only if the person is present in that territory for more than 183 days in the relevant tax year. Under the agreement with the UK, independent professional services are covered by the business profits article, ie the permanent establishment test is applied.

Article 6(3) of the Ireland/New Zealand treaty deems professional services carried on in connection with the exploration and exploitation of the sea bed, etc in one of the countries to be services performed in a fixed base regularly available to him in that country. This avoids any doubt that such specified activities might not otherwise be included in the definition of activities carried on through a permanent establishment or fixed base (so as to be taxable in the country in which the permanent establishment or fixed base is situated). A similar provision appears in the Ireland/Sweden treaty (subject to a let out for activities lasting less than 30 days over a 12-month period).

Article 16 of the Ireland/New Zealand treaty goes further than the normal article dealing with independent personal services. Apart from giving the country of source the right to tax the profits from such services performed through a fixed base in its territory, any income derived by a resident of the other country in respect of professional services or other activities of an independent character carried on in the country of source may be taxed in that country if the individual is present therein for 183 days or more in any consecutive period of 12 months (even if he does not have a fixed base in the country of source).

14.210 Income from employments

A non-resident person is, in principle, liable to Irish tax on any income from an Irish employment that is exercised within the State; if such an employment is only partly exercised in the State, he is liable on that part of the employment income attributable to the duties performed in the State (see **13.607**). A non-resident who holds a foreign employment will generally be outside the scope of Irish taxation unless he is ordinarily resident in Ireland and he performs some duties (other than incidental duties) in Ireland (see **13.607**). Accordingly, it will be possible that some individuals who 'may' be taxed on their employment income in Ireland under the terms of the treaty will in fact not be taxable thereon under Irish tax law. This could be significant where the other treaty state grants exemption from tax on employment income where Ireland has the right under the treaty to tax such income (irrespective of whether it has the right to do so under Irish tax law).

All of the treaties contain an 'employments' article (in some treaties referred to as 'dependent personal services') which maintains the general principle that a non-resident remains taxable in respect of his Irish duties, but which exempts a resident of one of the contracting states from taxation in the other state on his employment income if certain conditions are met. The 'employments' article in its most common form contains a clause which exempts a resident of the other contracting state from Irish tax on the remuneration from an employment exercised in Ireland, but only if *all* of the following conditions are satisfied:

(a) the recipient is not present in Ireland for more than a total of 183 days in the tax year concerned;

(b) the remuneration is paid by, or on behalf of, an employer who is not a resident of Ireland; and

(c) the remuneration is not borne by a permanent establishment or a fixed base which the employer has in Ireland.

The 'employment' article fails to specify which territory's fiscal year is to be taken into account. The 'terms not defined' clause in the definitions article (see **14.106**) dictates that each State should apply its own tax law in deciding this question, unless the context otherwise requires. If two states with different fiscal year-ends were to apply the article according to their own domestic tax laws, then in some cases, each state could reach a different conclusion as to whether or not the exemption applied. The OECD takes the view that the context (ie the right or otherwise to exemption of the taxpayer's activities in the state where the activities are undertaken) makes clear that it is the tax year of the state of activity which is relevant. Thus, an individual who spends less than 183 days in the State in an Irish tax year will meet condition (a).

In applying the 183-day rule the Revenue Commission will include a part of a day in their calculation. Days of sickness will also be included in the calculation, unless they prevent the individual from leaving the state and he would otherwise have qualified for the exemption.

Article 15 of the OECD Model Convention states that the 183-day test must be met in respect of any period of 12 months. This change is reflected in the treaty with Israel.

Where an employee is seconded temporarily to an Irish resident company by a company which is resident in a treaty state, it may be necessary to decide which company is the employer. In strict legal terms, it would appear that the seconding company will normally remain the employer (see **10.103**). The commentary to art 15 of the OECD Model Convention suggests that the term 'employer' should be understood as meaning the person having the rights over the work produced and bearing the relative responsibility and risks in relation to the employee (ie the 'economic' employer, a term not actually used by the commentary). This suggestion is made specifically in the context of preventing the abuse of the exemption clause by the use of overseas employment companies.

The Inland Revenue in the UK have sought to invoke the concept of the 'economic employer' in order to justify denying the exemption in any case where the employee is seconded to work for a UK resident company and the cost of the employee's services is then recharged to the UK company. The Inland Revenue's approach seems to be dubious, since the context of the treaty does not seem to justify any departure from the normal domestic tax meaning of the term 'employer'. The term as used in UK (and Irish) tax law is neither ambiguous nor obscure, and clearly denotes the *legal* and not the economic employer. Accordingly, there seems to be no reason to refer to the commentary to the OECD Model Convention for clarification of the meaning of the term; even if this were not the case, the status of the commentary as a form of *travaux prepatoires* implies that only the version of commentary in force *at the time the treaty was concluded* can be used as supplementary material for interpretative purposes (see **1.411**).

Where the normal 'employments' article applies, it is not essential that the employer be a resident of, or resident in, the other country of which the employee is a resident, provided that the employer is not a resident of Ireland. The treaty with Pakistan, however, only grants the exemption if the employee's services are performed for a resident of Pakistan.

Although the point is not beyond doubt, the Revenue Commissioners regard remuneration as being borne by the employer's permanent establishment or fixed base in Ireland if the cost of that remuneration is debited in computing the taxable profit (or loss) of that permanent establishment or fixed base (see **14.202**).

The employments article in tax treaties generally contains a special rule dealing with remuneration from an employment exercised aboard a ship or aircraft engaged in international traffic. In most cases, this rule permits the country in which the place of management of the international transport enterprise is situated to tax the relevant employment income. The treaty with Norway extends this provision to include remuneration from an employment exercised aboard a fishing, sealing or whaling vessel. The treaty with the Netherlands differs by giving the sole taxing right to the country of residence of the person employed aboard the ship or aircraft.

The fact that a treaty gives taxing rights to the country in which the place of effective management of the international transport enterprise is situated does not necessarily mean that tax is always levied by that country. Under Irish tax law, a non-resident employee of an international shipping or airline enterprise that has its place of effective management in Ireland is only taxable if and to the extent that he exercises his employment in the country. If his ship or aircraft does not dock in an Irish port or land at an Irish airport on any occasion, the non-resident employee cannot be made liable to Irish tax solely by the terms of a double taxation agreement. For a discussion of the normal Irish approach to income from seafaring employments, see **13.502**.

Article 16(3) of the Ireland/Sweden treaty provides that the remuneration derived by a resident of Sweden in respect of an employment exercised aboard an aircraft operated in international traffic by Scandinavian Airlines System (SAS) will be taxable only in Sweden. This provision is necessary as SAS operates as a partnership of which only one of the partners is a resident of Sweden (see the discussion on art 9 on 'shipping and air transport').

Article 6(4) of the Ireland/New Zealand treaty enables salaries, wages, etc earned by a resident of one of the countries in an employment in the other country (the country of source), to be taxed in the country of source if, and to the extent that, the employment is exercised in connection with exploration and exploitation activities in that country. This liability to tax in the country of source applies under this article, notwithstanding that art 17 (dealing with employment income generally) might otherwise apply to deny the country of source the right to tax the employment income (eg because the employee is present in that country for less than 183 days in a tax year). A similar provision appears in the Ireland/Sweden treaty.

Where a treaty does not extend the definition of Ireland to cover the Irish continental shelf, then duties performed there will not be performed 'in Ireland' for the purposes of the treaty. Accordingly, the treaty will override the charge imposed by TCA 1997, s 13 (see **13.607**).

The exercise of share options raises complex issues. Where domestic law treats any gains on the exercise of such options as employment income (as will usually be the case in Ireland: see **10.113**), the better view is that such gains do fall within the employment article of a relevant treaty. This in turn raises interesting questions where an employee is granted an option while resident and employed in Ireland but subsequently exercises the option at a time when he has relocated to another (treaty) state. Prior to the amendment of the tax treatment of share options mentioned further below, the Revenue Commissioners regarded the gain as fully liable to Irish tax under domestic law. It may be argued that the notional employment income arises in a year when the individual is not exercising his employment in Ireland and is therefore exempt under the treaty. The alternative view, supported by international practice, is that the income should be attributed proportionately to the Irish duties of the employment in respect of which the gain arises. The OECD Model Convention calls for a facts-and-circumstances determination of whether and to what extent an employee stock option is derived from employment exercised in a particular state. It states that as a general rule, an employee option should not be considered to relate to any services rendered after the period of employment required to grant the employee the right to exercise the option (ie after the option vests). Thus, a period of time that is merely a delay in exercising the option generally should not be taken into account. It also states that as a second principle, an option should only be considered to relate to services rendered before its grant if the option is a specific reward for those services. Finally, in case where an option is derived from employment in more than one state, the benefit should be apportioned on the number of days the worker is employed in each state (which in the author's view can produce anomalous results if the work done is not of equal value eg following a promotion).

One of the problems inherent in this type of approach is that the capital appreciation attaching to the option does not necessarily accrue evenly over the period of the relevant employment. The Irish tax treatment of share options was amended in an apparent attempt to bring it into conformity with OECD principles: see the discussion at **10.113**. The Revenue Commissioners have set out their views on the practical implications of this regime in *SP 1/07*.

14.211 Directors' fees

Directors will generally receive some remuneration in their capacity as directors. In the case of non-executive directors, this will usually consist of fees for attendance at board meetings, etc. In the case of executive directors, the remuneration which they receive in their capacity as directors may also refer to senior managerial functions which they perform (see **10.103**). It is also possible for an executive director to receive remuneration in a separate capacity, acting as an employee (if he is operating under a 'contract of services') or possibly as an independent consultant (if he is operating under a 'contract for services'). Where an individual receives remuneration in his capacity as a director then this is not employment income under Irish law. This follows because the inherent autonomy and independence of a director's office means that a director in his capacity as such cannot be a servant of his company (see the discussion at **10.103**). However, art 15 of the OECD Model Convention (director's fees), which is expressed to be 'subject to' art 16 (employment income), thereby implies that directors' fees would otherwise be treated as relating to 'dependent personal services'. It may be noted however that, for example, the Ireland/UK treaty specifically provides that directors' remuneration should be treated 'as if' it were employee remuneration (ie implying that otherwise it would not be so regarded).

Most of the treaties follow the OECD Model Convention and contain a separate article dealing with directors' fees and similar payments. This article usually provides that directors' fees and similar payments derived by a resident of one of the contracting states in his capacity as a member of the board of directors of a company which is a resident of the other contracting state may be taxed in that other state. This form of article makes no reference to the place where the duties of the director are actually performed. It is not necessary that the payment of the fees, etc should be made by the company of which the individual is a director.

The commentary to the OECD Convention indicates that the wording in the 'directors' fees' article is not intended to cover remuneration paid for other functions which the director may perform for the company, eg as an ordinary employee or consultant. Consequently, remuneration for such other functions are normally taxable under the 'employments' or 'professional services' articles. The treaty with Sweden in fact deals with this point by specifically providing in the 'directors' fees' article that a director's remuneration for executive, managerial or technical functions is to be dealt with under the 'employments' article or 'professional services' article as appropriate.

Where a director's remuneration refers in part to the carrying out of his senior managerial functions (ie where these are not remunerated separately) it is not clear whether (and if so, how) an apportionment should be made between remuneration referable to his purely 'directorial' functions and to his other functions.

The article does not cover the situation where a non-resident individual receives director's remuneration from an Irish incorporated, but non-resident, company. Under Irish tax law, such remuneration is taxable under Sch E, irrespective of where the directors' duties are performed (see **13.104**). As discussed above, it is arguable whether such remuneration will fall under the 'employment' article (in which case the remuneration may be exempt). An alternative argument is that such remuneration is an item of income which falls under the 'income not expressly mentioned' article, if such an article is included in the relevant treaty.

The agreements with Pakistan and the UK do not contain a separate article dealing with directors' fees, but require all directors' remuneration to be dealt with under the 'employments' article in the relevant agreement. It is usually difficult to establish that a director of an Irish resident company is not exercising his duties as director in Ireland. However, should he be able to establish this, the 'employments' article in these treaties would appear to exclude that remuneration from liability to Irish tax. Any such case is likely to be very closely examined by the Irish Revenue before the exemption is granted.

14.212 Governmental functions

All the treaties have an article dealing with remuneration paid to an individual by the government of one of the contracting states for services rendered to that state in the discharge of governmental functions. Article 19 of the OECD Model Convention makes it clear that the article is designed to apply only to employees (and ex-employees) of the state concerned. In most cases, the article provides that such remuneration, including pensions, is to be taxable only by the state making the payment. A number of the treaties extend this rule to remuneration and pensions for services to a political subdivision or local authority of the state in question, eg a German municipality, a Swiss canton or an Irish or UK local authority.

In *Travers v Ó'Síocháin* IV ITR 54, Carroll J said of the term 'functions of a governmental nature':

> In my opinion, it means 'related to governing the country', which would include the functions of the ordinary civil service and of local government administrators. It may go even further than that but would not include everyone paid out of the public purse. A dentist employed to pull a tooth is not thereby discharging 'functions of a governmental nature'. Likewise a nurse providing nursing care is not, in my opinion, contemplated by (the) Article.

The Financial Secretary to the UK treasury has said that services rendered to a state agency, board or statutory body are not rendered to the government or local authority concerned (Hansard Vol 151, Col 601, 27/4/1990).

When this form of article applies, an employee of the government (or of the political subdivision, etc) of one of the contracting states who is working in and/or resident in the other state cannot be taxed by the other state in respect of his governmental remuneration, even if he performs all the duties of his employment in its territory. Similarly, a former governmental employee of one of the states who has retired and is a resident of and/or resident in the other state, is taxable only by the former state on his pension payable in respect of his former governmental service for that state.

Some treaties (eg that with Sweden, New Zealand, UK and the USA) start with the usual rule that the contracting state *for* which the services are rendered is the only state permitted to tax the government services income, but then goes on to provide an exception. This gives the other state (ie the state *in* which the services are rendered) the sole taxing rights if:

(a) the services are rendered in that other state by an individual; *and*

(b) that individual; either

  (i) is a national of that other state, or

  (ii) did not become a resident of that other state solely for the purposes of rendering the services.

In order for a clause in this form in a tax treaty article to take the sole taxing rights for governmental services income away from the contracting state (or subdivision thereof) for which the services are rendered, the individual's residence status must first be determined by applying the residence article of the relevant treaty. If the individual is determined to be a resident of the other state, the state for which the services are rendered will retain its sole taxing rights if the individual became a resident of the other state solely for the purposes of exercising his governmental functions, unless he is a national of the other state. If he is such a national, the other state has the taxing rights even if he became a resident of that other state solely for the purposes of rendering the services. A clause of this kind was held not to contravene the law in Gilly v Directeur des Services Fiscaux de Bas-Rhin [1998] STC 1014. The ECJ held that it was legitimate for Member States to allocate their taxing powers between themselves, particularly where this was in accordance with international practice and the OECD Model Convention.

The agreements generally exclude from the 'governmental functions' article any remuneration and pensions in respect of services rendered in connection with any trade or business carried on by a contracting state or by a local authority or political subdivision (the Swiss treaty is one exception). In these cases, the treaty articles dealing with employments, directors' fees or pensions, whichever is relevant, are applied. This exclusion would apply, for example to remuneration for services to state owned railways, broadcasting stations, nationalised industries, etc. However, service in a country's military forces are regarded as service in the discharge of governmental functions.

14.213 Pensions

Almost all of Ireland's treaties provide that, with the exception of pensions covered by the 'governmental functions' article, an individual who is a resident of one of the contracting states is to be taxable only in his state of residence on any pension or similar remuneration paid to him in respect of past employment, even if that employment was from a source in the other state. This varies the normal Irish tax law under which a non-resident person in receipt of a pension from an Irish source is liable to Irish income tax under Sch E. Normally, in such a case, the former employer, the trustees of the relevant pension scheme or the other person paying the pension is required to deduct Irish income tax under PAYE (see **11.101**). A resident of another country entitled to benefit under such a treaty article may, on proof of the facts to the Revenue Commissioners, have his pension paid without any PAYE deduction. Alternatively, he may claim a repayment of any tax deducted. It seems that the term 'pension' will not generally cover payments made as compensation for loss of office. Such payments, if taxable, should fall to be considered as employment income or directors' fees, as appropriate.

The Pakistan agreement differs from the normal pattern by permitting the country of source to tax a pension or annuity from a superannuation fund approved or recognised under the tax laws of the source country, but follows the general practice with regard to other pensions.

A number of treaties deal with life annuities under the 'pensions' article. A common form of definition of 'annuity' for this purpose is 'a stated sum payable periodically at stated times during life or during a specified or ascertainable period of time under an obligation to make the payments in return for adequate and full consideration in money or money's worth'. The other treaties do not specifically mention life annuities in the 'pensions' article. This may not be significant if such a treaty contains an 'income not expressly mentioned' article which also gives the sole right of taxation to the country of residence.

14.214 Artistes, athletes, entertainers etc

All of the treaties contain an article dealing with income derived by entertainers such as theatre, motion picture, radio or television artistes, musicians and athletes. In these treaties, the 'entertainers' article permits the state in which the taxpayer derives income from his personal activities under this heading to tax that income. This article normally states that it is to apply to the exclusion of any other article that might otherwise deal with the income in question. Thus, for example, the exemption available to certain employees (see **14.210**) will not apply.

While in practice, there may sometimes be difficulty in levying Irish income tax on the income earned within the state by a visiting individual entertainer, TCA 1997, s 18(1), (3) contains the power to assess him in respect of income from his profession or employment to the extent that it is exercised within the State. This is subject again to the point that in strict law, it appears that a non-resident is not chargeable in respect of the income from a foreign employment, irrespective of where his duties are performed (see **13.607**). The power of the Revenue to assess a resident agent or manager, etc, under TCA 1997, s 1034 in respect of a trade or profession exercised *through* that agent or manager, etc is unlikely to be of relevance, given the fact that the services in question will be rendered personally by the entertainer.

Some agreements (including those with Australia, New Zealand, Sweden and the UK) contain an additional rule entitling the state where the services are performed to tax the income from the personal activities of an entertainer or athlete notwithstanding that it may have accrued to some other person, eg a so-called 'loan out' company (where the entertainer forms a company purely to exploit his services).

Where the entertainer supplies his services through a 'loan out company', then his services are likely to represent a trading activity on the part of that company. Ireland's right to tax the profit from this activity would normally be relinquished under the 'permanent establishment' article of the treaty. However, if the treaty includes the anti-avoidance rule noted above, this will restore Ireland's taxing rights in this respect.

14.215 Professors, teachers and researchers

Most of the treaties provide that a professor or teacher from one of the contracting states who visits the territory of the other state for the purpose of teaching for a period not exceeding two years, at a university, college, school or other education institution, is to be exempted from tax in the contracting state he is visiting in respect of his remuneration for such teaching. The two-year period runs from the date he first visits the State for the relevant purposes (so that if he makes more than one visit, the clock runs from the date of the first visit); further, where the visit(s) exceed two years, the exemption is entirely lost (ie even in relation to the first two years: *IRC v Vas* [1990] STC 157). In *Devai v IRC* [1996] STC (SCD) 31, the UK Special Commissioner held that a change of employer did not bring a visit to an end (it was also indicated that a return home to the State for holiday purposes also will not bring a visit to an end). It may be noted that there are a number of Revenue precedents dealing with this Article.

Of the treaties providing the exemption, all except those with Japan extend this exemption on the same conditions to the remuneration which an individual of one of the states earns for undertaking advanced study or research at a high level at a university, research institute, school, college or other similar establishment in the other contracting state. The agreement with Japan does give a similar exemption for research, but only where the individual is the recipient of a grant, allowance, or award for the primary purpose of conducting the research. In some cases the exemption does not apply if the research is undertaken primarily for the private benefit of a specific person or persons (see eg the treaties with Spain and the Czech Republic). A number of treaties specifically require the individual to have been a resident of his home contracting state immediately before his temporary sojourn in the other country. While the other treaties do not refer to this specific point, it is thought that in practice most countries would require this condition to be satisfied before granting the exemption to a visiting resident of the other country.

When a professor, teacher or other individual who has been resident in Ireland visits another country for the purpose of teaching, advanced study or research, he may not be liable to Irish tax on his remuneration from the date of his departure (see **13.504**). In such a case he may avoid liability to tax on his remuneration in both states. It should be noted, however, that the article does not provide an exemption from tax in the country being visited in respect of any other income which that individual might have that is subject to tax under the laws of that country.

14.216 Students and apprentices

All of the treaties contain an article exempting students and business apprentices from one of the contracting states from taxation in the other state on certain payments. The exempted payments are those made for the purpose of the student's maintenance, education or training when he visits the other state for the purpose of that education or training. For the exemption to apply, the payments must be made from sources outside the country being visited. Should the student or apprentice be in receipt of a scholarship in the country he is visiting, the question of whether the scholarship income is taxable in that country depends on whether its law taxes such scholarships.

A number of the treaties also contain a provision exempting the visiting student or apprentice from tax in the country being visited in respect of remuneration earned from labour or personal services performed in that country in order to acquire practical experience related to his studies or training. The treaties which give this additional benefit all have limits to the extent it can be made use of. For example, under the Netherlands treaty the period worked must not exceed 100 days in any tax year, while in a number of the others the limit is 183 days. In the Belgian agreement, this 183-day limit applies, but there is a further condition that the remuneration must not exceed 8,000 Belgian francs per month (circa €198 per month) or its equivalent in Irish pounds.

14.217 Income not expressly mentioned ('other income')

A number of Ireland's treaties contain a 'sweeper' article which generally provides that where, a resident of one of the contracting states derives an item of income that is not expressly mentioned in the relevant treaty, that income is to be taxable only in the state of which the recipient is a resident. Some of the treaties indicate that this article only applies to items of income arising in the other contracting state (eg the treaties with Belgium, Cyprus and Japan). Other treaties do not impose this limitation to the application of this article (eg the treaties with Austria, France, Switzerland and the UK). Under the treaties of the latter type, only the country of residence of the taxpayer is entitled to tax the otherwise unmentioned income, whether it arises in the other state or in a third country.

If a treaty does not contain an 'income not expressly mentioned' article, it generally follows that the country of source is entitled to tax any such income according to its domestic tax laws. In such a case, the country of residence is required to give the appropriate double taxation relief either by the credit or the exemption method (whichever it applies). The agreement with Australia does contain an article dealing with income not otherwise mentioned, but it permits the country of source to tax any such income. It appears in this case, therefore, that the article is only of relevance to income arising in a third country.

The treaty with New Zealand is different in that it permits either contracting state to tax any income not expressly mentioned in the treaty *only* where that income arises from a source in its territory. If the recipient of the income is a resident of the other state, that state is required to grant the double taxation relief (relief by the credit method in both countries). Subject to this provision, the income not expressly mentioned is only taxable in the recipient's country of residence. The effect of the article in this treaty in giving the country of residence the sole taxing right is, therefore, limited to income arising in third countries. The country of residence has, under normal principles, the right to tax its own residents on income arising in its own territory.

Article 22(2) of the Ireland/Sweden treaty is typical of later treaties in that it excludes any such 'other income' derived by a permanent establishment or fixed base in one of the contracting states (through which a resident of the other contracting state carries on business or performs independent personal services) where that other income is effectively connected with the permanent establishment or fixed base. Any such other income, eg income arising in a third country, may be taxed in the contracting state (Ireland or Sweden) in which the permanent establishment or fixed base is situated under the rules of art 8 (business profits) or art 15 (independent personal services). For example, a Swedish resident company carrying on trade through a permanent establishment in Ireland may be taxed in Ireland in respect of, say, interest or royalty income arising from third country sources if effectively connected with that permanent establishment.

The Ireland/UK treaty contains an anti-avoidance provision (art 20(3)). This states that the provisions of the other income article will not apply 'if it was the main purpose or one of the main purposes of any person concerned with the creation of or assignment of the rights in respect of which income is paid to take advantage of this article by means of that creation or assignment'. This test raises similar difficulties of interpretation and application to blanket anti-avoidance clauses in other contexts (see eg the discussion at **18.111**: *Prevention of misuse*). The test is narrowly framed in so far as it focuses exclusively on the creation or assignment of the rights in question.

The position of discretionary trusts which are Irish resident, and which distribute Irish income to beneficiaries who are resident in a treaty State, merits special consideration. Unless the treaty has an article explicitly covering trusts, such distributions will, it is suggested, fall to be treated as 'income not expressly mentioned' and would thus not normally be subject to Irish tax under the treaty. It seems that tax deducted at source from such payments should accordingly be refundable to the non-resident. It seems however that the Revenue Commissioners take the view that such payments are distributions of net income (see **Division 15**); on this view, it is the underlying sources of income which must be referred to in order to determine eligibility for double tax relief (see **14.205**).

The suggested analysis however may give a better Irish tax result for the non-resident than any general 'look through' treatment which may be available. Thus, eg if an Irish discretionary trust distributes Irish rental income to a resident of a relevant treaty state, on this analysis the tax at source should be refunded. If the Revenue Commissioners had 'looked through' the distributions to the underlying rental income, no refund would be due since – Ireland always retains the right to tax such income under its tax treaties. Both Ireland and the UK have in fact entered a reservation to art 21 of the Model Convention, reserving their right to tax the income of domestic trusts and estates. In Ireland's case this is possibly a purely protective measure and should not be read as meaning that the Revenue accept the analysis suggested (the position is clearer under UK law). The Ireland/UK treaty in fact excludes trust income from the 'income not expressly mentioned' article (see also, eg the Ireland/Sweden treaty).

Annual payments within TCA 1997, ss 237, 238 (see **2.302–2.307**) will normally fall within the 'other income' article of a treaty. In such cases, the Revenue may direct the payer to make the payment without deduction of tax (see **14.205**). Where an individual obtains relief at the basic rate by withholding and retaining tax under TCA 1997, s 237, a direction of this kind could lead to the loss of this relief. It is thought that the inspector would be prepared to make a compensatory adjustment in the taxpayer's computation in such circumstances.

14.218 Limitation of treaty relief

A number of treaties either contain an article under this heading or include a clause in the 'definitions' article which is intended to cover the case of an Irish resident who, because he is not domiciled in Ireland, is taxable on his foreign income on the remittance basis (see **Division 13**). This article or clause in a treaty provides that any article which requires the country of source to exempt the resident of the other country from tax on certain types of income, or to charge such income at a reduced rate, is only applicable to the amount of that income remitted to, or received in, the country of residence. The country of source is entitled to charge its normal taxation on the remainder of the income.

Example 14.218.1

Mr Gene O'Connor, an individual domiciled in the State of New Jersey, USA, is resident in Ireland for the tax year 2016. In view of his foreign domicile, TCA 1997, s 71(2) entitles him to be assessed to Irish tax on his foreign source income to the extent only that it is remitted to, or received in, Ireland. In the year 2015, he has income from patent royalties (sources in Australia) and his remittances to Ireland from that income are as follows:

	Income arising	*Remittances to Ireland*
	€	€
Australian patent royalties	5,000	3,200

Article 13(2) of the Ireland/Australia tax treaty limits the tax which Australia may charge on royalties paid to a resident of Ireland to 10 per cent of the gross amount of the royalties, but in the absence of a tax treaty Australian tax at say the rate of 27 per cent would be withheld on royalties paid to a non-resident. Article 6 of the treaty limits the treaty relief to the part of the royalties remitted to Ireland. Mr O'Connor is, therefore, chargeable to Australian tax on the royalty income as follows:

	€
Royalties remitted to Ireland:	
€3,200 x 10%	320
Unremitted royalties:	
€1,800 x 27%	486
	806

The Ireland/US treaty also contains a comprehensive 'limitation of benefits' provision (art 23). In general this does not apply to individuals.

14.219 Non-discrimination

Ireland's tax treaties generally contain a clause under this article which provides that the nationals of either contracting state shall not be subjected in the other contracting state to any taxation, or to any connected requirements which is more burdensome than the taxation and connected requirements to which nationals of that other state in the same circumstances are or may be subjected. The term 'nationals' is usually defined separately, as all citizens of that country and all legal persons, partnerships and associations deriving their status as such from the law in force in the country concerned (see **14.106**). It is a vexed issue as to whether this article falls within the authority conferred by TCA 1997, s 826 for the Government to enter into 'arrangements … in relation to affording relief from double taxation'.

This article generally also contains a clause providing also that a permanent establishment which an enterprise of one of the contracting states has in the other state shall not be less favourably taxed in that other state than an enterprise of that other state carrying on the same activity.

The commentary to the OECD Model Convention makes it clear that the first clause in the 'non-discrimination' article dealing with 'nationals' is solely designed to prevent discrimination in tax treatment on the grounds of nationality. It does not require, for example, either of the contracting states to give nationals of the other state, who are not resident in its territory, the full personal allowances against its taxes if it does not give the full personal allowances to its own non-resident nationals. However, it must be borne in mind that under EU law, discrimination against non-residents may be regarded as equivalent to discrimination against non-nationals. Such discrimination will be impermissible in the absence of an acceptable justification (see *R v IRC ex parte Cummerbund* [1991] STC 27, [1993] STC 605).

The commentary also notes that, if one of the contracting states should grant special taxation privileges either to its own public bodies or public service, or to private non-profit making institutions whose activities are performed for purposes of public benefit specific to its own territory, the 'non-discrimination' article is not to be construed as obliging that state to extend the same privileges to the public bodies or public services of the other state or to any such private institutions in the other state.

The commentary, in referring to the clause relating to permanent establishments, states that its purpose is to end all discrimination in the treatment in one of the states of the permanent establishment there of the enterprise of the other state, but only as compared with the treatment of resident enterprises belonging to the same sector of activities. It indicates that the clause does not mean that the state in question may not apply a different practical approach to the taxation of the permanent establishment, provided that the final result is not to impose more burdensome taxation than on similar resident enterprises.

The commentary admits that experience in applying 'non-discrimination' articles in tax treaties has shown that it is often difficult to define clearly exactly how this principle of equal tax treatment should operate. The main reason for this difficulty appears to lie in the actual nature of the permanent establishment, which is not a separate legal entity but only a part of an enterprise that has its head office in another state.

14.220 Allowances for non-residents

Most of Ireland's tax treaties contain an article providing that a resident of the other contracting state is entitled to the same personal allowances, reliefs and reductions for the purposes of Irish tax as Irish citizens who are not resident in Ireland (one exception is the treaty with Australia). Conversely, these treaties usually provide also that a resident of Ireland is, for the purposes of tax in the other country, entitled to the same personal allowances, reliefs and reductions as nationals of that country who are not resident there.

In the case of Ireland, an article in this form entitles a resident of the other treaty country who has income from Irish sources to claim a deduction under the rules of TCA 1997, s 1032, for the appropriate proportion of the Irish allowances and reliefs relevant to his personal circumstances (see **13.610**). However, in applying the fraction 'Irish source income: worldwide income' to the available allowances, etc, any Irish source income in respect of which the resident of the other country is exempted from Irish tax by the relevant income article in the treaty is excluded from the numerator of the fraction. On the other hand, any Irish source income which the treaty requires to be taxed at a reduced rate is included in the numerator as it remains 'subject to Irish tax' (see TCA 1997, s 1032). An individual who meets the requirements of TCA 1997, s 1032 will be entitled to full allowances in any event (see **13.610**).

As discussed at **13.610**, the Revenue Commissioners view that a non-resident is generally not entitled to the benefit of joint assessment has been upheld in *Fennessy v McConnelogue* V ITR 129 (although it is debatable as to whether this principle may breach European law in some circumstances (see **1.410**)); in practice the Revenue will allow a non-resident so-called 'aggregation relief'. The Revenue also take the view that since the married person's tax credit and tax rate bands are not available to the non-resident Irish citizen, the treaty article cannot put the resident of the other treaty country in any better position than that of such an Irish citizen.

The same considerations as relate to married couples will apply *mutatis mutandis* to civil partners following the enactment of Finance (No 3) Act 2011.

14.221 Mutual agreement procedure

Most of Ireland's tax treaties contain an article under this heading which entitles inter alia a resident of either of the contracting states to invoke the assistance of the 'competent authority' of the state of which he is a resident to resolve any problems in the application of any of the provisions in the relevant treaty to his own particular case. The 'mutual agreement procedure' article in a treaty is normally worded in terms of giving the resident of the state in question the right to seek this assistance if he considers that the actions of the competent authority of either or both of the contracting states result, or will result, in him being taxed other than in accordance with the terms of the particular treaty.

Under an article of this type, the taxpayer in question is required to present his case to the competent authority of his country of residence (in Ireland, the Revenue Commissioners). The competent authority is then required to examine the case and, if the claim appears to it to be justified and if it is not itself able to arrive at an appropriate solution, that competent authority should endeavour to resolve the case with the competent authority of the other contracting state. There is, however, no obligation on the competent authorities to actually reach a solution. However, a taxpayer who considered that the Revenue Commissioners were failing to meet their obligations in this respect would have the right to seek judicial review (see **2.206**). This recourse to the mutual agreement procedure is usually available to the taxpayer aggrieved in addition to any of the remedies provided by the national laws of the two states (eg in addition to the normal appeal procedure in Ireland). In practice, it is likely that the Revenue Commissioners would allow an appeal, etc to remain open until the mutual agreement procedure had been exhausted. Regard should be had to **2.207** for details of the appeal measures brought about by F(TA)A 2015 which were subject to Ministerial Order (SI 110/2016 appointed 21 March 2016 as the day on which the Finance (Tax Appeals) Act 2015, came into operation).

Tax treaties which adopt this form of article include those with Austria, Australia, France, Switzerland and the UK. Among the treaties which use a somewhat different form of wording are those with Belgium, Germany and Pakistan, each of which entitles the resident of either state, who considers that the actions of either or both contracting states result, or will result, in double taxation prohibited by the agreement in question, to seek the assistance of the competent authority of his country of residence. In effect, it is a very similar approach and, in fact, highlights the intention that the article is usually applicable where there is actual or potential double taxation conflicting with the terms of the treaty.

The commentary to the OECD Model Convention contains a useful discussion of the intentions behind this type of article in tax treaties. It mentions, *inter alia*, that the most frequent applications of the procedure in practice are likely to relate to the interpretation of articles in the treaty designed specifically to avoid double taxation. Such problems might relate, for example, to the rules for the attribution to a permanent establishment in one country of a proper proportion of the executive and general administration expenses incurred by the head office of the enterprise in the other country. Problems might relate also to cases where lack of information as to the taxpayer's actual position has led to misapplication of the agreement, eg as to the determination of residence or as to the existence of a permanent establishment.

The commentary also indicates that the right of the taxpayer to seek the assistance of the competent authority of his country of residence should be available, whether or not he has exhausted all the remedies available to him under the domestic law of each of the two states. The commentary also notes that the competent authority in question is obliged, if it appears that the taxpayer's complaint is justified, to take the appropriate action.

If the complaint is regarded as justified and if the competent authority accepts that it is due wholly or in part to the laws of the state of residence, the commentary to the OECD Model Convention indicates that it should take the necessary action as speedily as possible and to make such adjustments or allow such reliefs, ie to avoid the double taxation, as appear to be justified. If the complaint is due to tax provisions in the country of source, then the competent authority of the state of residence must make every effort to resolve the issue with the competent authority of the other country.

In practice, recourse to the mutual agreement procedure through the competent authorities of contracting states seems to occur very rarely at present. Possibly, with the continuing expansion of international trading between residents of different countries, it may occur more frequently in future.

Many of the mutual agreement articles also contain a clause directing Ireland and the other treaty state to resolve by mutual agreement any difficulties or doubts arising as to the interpretation or application of the Convention. The commentary to the OECD Model Convention indicates that this provision authorises the competent authorities to:

(a) complete or clarify the definition of doubtful terms used in the treaty;
(b) settle any difficulties arising out of changes to the internal tax laws of either contracting state; and
(c) determine the application of 'thin capitalisation' rules.

In *IRC v Cummerbund* [1990] STC 285, the UK High Court held that an interpretation agreed by the Revenue authorities of the two contracting states under the 'Mutual Agreement' article of the UK/USA treaty did not 'confer any binding or authoritative effect on the view or statements of the competent authorities in the English Courts'. However, it is arguable that an agreed interpretation should at least be 'taken into account' by virtue of the principles set out in art 31(3) of the Vienna Convention on the Law of Treaties (see **1.411**).

14.222 Exchange of information

Tax treaties which follow the OECD Model Convention contain an article providing for the exchange of information between the competent authorities of the two contracting states under two broad headings. Under the first heading, the two contracting states to a treaty undertake to exchange such information as is 'reasonably foreseeable' for carrying out the provisions of the tax treaty in question. Under the second heading, they agree to exchange such information as is necessary for carrying out the provisions of their respective domestic tax laws.

All of Ireland's tax treaties (except that with Switzerland) contain an article under which the two contracting states agree to exchange such information as is necessary for carrying out the provisions of the relevant treaty. However please note that on 26

January 2012 a new protocol was entered into with Switzerland inserting a new art 26 to exchange information with similar wording to the other treaties. This protocol became effective on 1 January 2014. Some of the treaties, follow the OECD Model Convention and provide also for the exchange of such information as is necessary for the carrying out of the domestic laws of the two states. The type of article adding this second provision generally limits the exchange of information under it to the taxes covered by the agreement in question and, then only, in so far as the taxation under the relevant domestic laws is not contrary to anything in the agreement.

The OECD Model Convention, and the treaties following its approach, each contain a supplementary clause in the 'exchange of information' article which limits the application of the article so that it does not impose on either contracting state any obligation:

(a) to carry out administrative measures at variance with its own laws and administrative practice or with those of the other state;
(b) to supply information which is not obtainable under its own laws or in the normal course of its administration or of those of the other state; or
(c) to supply information which would disclose any trade, business, industrial, commercial or professional secret or trade process, or information, the disclosure of which would be contrary to public policy.

The OECD commentary gives examples of the type of information which might be exchanged under either of the two headings of this form of article. One example mentioned in connection with the application of the article to the implementation of the relevant tax treaty is a request by state A for information from state B (in which the payer of a royalty is resident) as to the amount of royalty actually paid to a recipient resident in state A (who may, perhaps, not have declared the full amount of the royalty received in his tax return in state A). An example of a request for information by state A in implementing its own domestic tax laws could arise where a company in state A sells goods through a third country (possibly a low tax country) to a company in state B. State A may use this form of article to request information from state B regarding the price paid for the goods by the company in state B. The most recent version of the article seeks to make clear that a contracting state should provide such information notwithstanding that it has no 'domestic interest' therein (ie it would not normally make the enquiries concerned since they would have no relevance to any tax liability under its own laws. The position has been clarified in Ireland by the insertion of TCA 1997, s 912A (see below). The latest version of art 26 also contains a specific override in relation to any domestic banking secrecy laws. The Finance Act 2013 extends the remit of TCA 1997, s 912A to include requests under the Convention on Mutual Administrative Assistance in Tax Matters and any protocol to the Convention.

Some of the treaties (eg that with Australia) contain an additional subclause to the effect that the information that may be exchanged is not to be restricted by the 'personal scope' article in the treaty. In other words, although the treaty may contain an article providing that the agreement as a whole is to apply to persons who are residents of one or both of the contracting states, the inclusion of that subclause permits either state to seek information from the other state regarding persons not resident in either state. Such information about non-residents may, however, only be sought within the same limitations of the article as apply to information about residents of either state.

A number of the older treaties (eg those with Belgium and Germany provide a different second heading to the type of information which the contracting states must, if requested, supply to each other. This second heading is not quite as wide as information exchanged to enable the states to implement their own domestic tax laws generally, but in many instances it may have a similar effect. Under it, information may be exchanged that is necessary either for the prevention of fraud or for the administration of statutory provisions against legal avoidance ('tax planning') in relation to the taxes that are covered by the relevant treaty. As with the newer form of article, the ordinary tax treaty relating to income taxes (and/or capital gains taxes) does not permit either state to request information from the other state for other taxes (eg value added tax or a sales tax).

It is normal for the 'exchange of information' article to require each contracting state to observe the same requirements as to secrecy regarding the information exchanged as must be observed under the respective domestic tax laws of the two states. The information must not be disclosed other than to persons or authorities (including courts and administrative bodies) involved in the assessment or collection of the taxes covered by the treaty, or to persons involved in the enforcement of, or in the determination of appeals in relation to, those taxes.

TCA 1997, s 826(7) authorises the Irish Revenue Commissioners to disclose to any authorised officer of the government of another contracting state to a treaty such information as is required to be disclosed under the terms of that treaty. Otherwise, the Irish laws relating to the secrecy of tax information would prevent the Revenue Commissioners from making such a disclosure to the other state. The effect of the EC Directive on Mutual Assistance is discussed at **1.205**. The Finance Act 2013 has amended TCA 1997, s 826(7) and the Revenue Commissioners are now authorised to disclose to any authorised officer of the government of another contracting state to any protocol to the treaty such information as is required to be disclosed under the terms of that protocol to the treaty.

As noted above, TCA 1997, s 826(1B) enables the Government to enter into Tax Information Exchange Agreements, ie agreements with the governments of other jurisdictions for the exchange of information on request between the tax authorities of each jurisdiction in order to prevent and detect the evasion of income taxes, capital gains taxes and corporation taxes (and taxes of a similar character). Where the Government enters into such an agreement, it will acquire the force of law subject to the same procedures as a double tax treaty. It may be noted that an OECD Model Agreement on Exchange of Information for Tax Purposes was issued in April 2002.

As a complementary measure, TCA 1997, s 912A, provides that the Revenue may request information under various heads of the TCA 1997, where it is required for the purposes of determining a tax liability in a state with which Ireland has a double tax treaty or a tax information exchange agreement.

The following provisions (see **2.6**) now apply not only to Irish tax liabilities, but also in relation to tax liabilities arising in such treaty countries:

TCA 1997, ss 900, 901	concerning the power to call for a taxpayer's books;
TCA 1997, s 902	concerning access to information of third parties;
TCA 1997, s 902A	concerning access to information concerning third parties by way of application to the High Court;
TCA 1997, s 905	inspection of documents and records;
TCA 1997, s 905	TCA 1997, s 905
TCA 1997, s 907	concerning access to information of financial institutions by way of an application to the Appeal Commissioners;

TCA 1997, s 908	concerning access to information of financial institutions by way of an application to the High Court.

Under TCA 1997, s 902A, 907 and 908, as they apply for Irish tax purposes, information can also be sought in relation to a group or class of persons whose individual identities are not known; this extension of powers is excluded in the case of information in respect of treaty state tax liabilities.

14.3 Credits for Foreign Tax

14.301 General

TCA 1997, s 826 requires the rules of TCA 1997, Sch 24 to be applied in any case where a credit for a foreign tax is to be given against Irish tax (for present purposes Income Tax and the Universal Social Charge) under any double taxation agreement given the force of law by a government order made under the section. The discussion which follows in this Division covers the rules of TCA 1997, Sch 24.

The credit for foreign tax against the Irish tax chargeable on any income is given by reducing the relevant Irish tax by the amount of the credit (TCA 1997, Sch 24). It is to be noted that the credit for foreign tax paid on any item of income is only given against the Irish tax payable on the same income. If, for example, the foreign tax on one item of income exceeds the foreign tax credit limit for that income (see **14.302**), but if the foreign tax on another item of income is less than the limit for that income, the spare part of the latter credit limit cannot be used to cover the excess foreign tax on the first item of income. The credit is applied first in reducing the income tax in respect of that income before then determining the amount available for credit against the USC (TCA 1997, Sch 24 para 2A).

'Foreign tax', for individuals for the purposes of TCA 1997, Sch 24 is limited to any foreign tax that is properly chargeable under the laws of another country with which there is a double taxation agreement and is a tax for which the agreement with the relevant country permits a credit against Irish tax (TCA 1997, Sch 24 para 1(1)). Further, the elimination of double taxation article in most treaties provides that the credit is for taxes paid in the other treaty country 'in accordance with this Convention'. In other words, if the treaty with country X permits it to levy a maximum 15 per cent tax on interest paid to a resident of Ireland, but if the withholding tax actually imposed is 20 per cent, the foreign tax creditable against Irish tax cannot exceed 15 per cent. The taxpayer affected must seek a repayment from country X of the excess 5 per cent.

It is not an essential condition for the credit for foreign tax that the income on which it is paid be treated under Irish tax law as income from a foreign possession, ie income that is taxable under Sch D Case III. While it is frequently the case that the foreign tax is payable on such foreign income, this is not always the case.

For example, an Irish resident individual carrying on a trade in the State may have a trading branch in the United Kingdom. Any UK tax paid on the profits of the UK branch is eligible for credit against the Irish income tax payable by the individual, notwithstanding that the UK branch profits are treated as part of the profits of the trade carried on in the State and are taxable under Sch D Case I.

No credit for foreign tax against any of the Irish taxes is given unless the person making the claim is resident in the State (TCA 1997, Sch 24 para 3). If the credit is against income tax, the taxpayer must be resident for the tax year in which the relevant income is taxable.

The requirement in the elimination of double taxation article is for the person claiming the credit to be resident *in* Ireland, as distinct from being a 'resident of Ireland' as defined in the relevant tax treaty (see **14.105**). Consequently, a person who is not a 'resident of Ireland' under, for example the Federal German tax treaty, due to him being resident *in* both Ireland and Germany, is entitled to a credit for German tax paid on, for example his German source interest income for set off against his Irish tax payable on this income. The fact that he cannot claim exemption from the German tax under the 'interest' article (as he is not a resident *of* Ireland) does not prejudice his foreign tax credit claim for the German tax so long as he is resident *in* Ireland for the relevant tax year.

14.302 Principles of computation

The principles set out in TCA 1997, Sch 24 are applied to determine:

(a) the amount of the foreign income subject to income tax in respect of which the foreign tax credit is first claimed.

(b) the limit to the amount of the credit for the foreign tax against income tax.

(c) the amount of the foreign income subject to the USC in respect of which the balance of the foreign tax credit is then claimed.

(b) the amount of the credit for the foreign tax against the USC.

The credit for foreign tax is applied first in reducing the income tax chargeable in respect of the foreign income. It is therefore necessary to determine the amount of the foreign tax credit used against income tax before considering the USC. To do this separate income tax and USC calculations must be done.

The income subject to the foreign tax is first taken as the amount chargeable to Irish income tax under the rules of TCA 1997, s 71(1), ie after any of the deductions permitted by that subsection or the amount taxable under Sch D Case I for profits of a trade carried on in the State (see **Example 14.302.1**). In any case where a credit is claimed by an Irish resident person for tax paid in the other treaty country in respect of income arising there, TCA 1997, Sch 24 para 7(3) adds the following rules which must be applied in arriving at the amount of the foreign income finally chargeable to Irish tax:

(a) no deduction is allowed for any foreign tax on the same or any other income (except to the extent required by (c) below); and

(b) if the income is a dividend in respect of which the taxpayer is entitled to a credit for underlying or indirect taxes (see **14.303**), the amount of the foreign income on which he is chargeable to Irish tax is increased by the foreign indirect tax for which the credit is given; but

(c) any 'excess foreign tax' (including, if relevant, any indirect foreign tax) is deducted in arriving at the amount of the foreign income on which he is finally chargeable.

In order to simplify the explanation of the computations relating to the credit for foreign tax against Irish tax, certain phrases are used in this Division. These phrases and the meanings assigned to them are as follows:

Foreign taxes available for credit:

the foreign tax for which the relevant tax treaty permits a credit to be given against any Irish tax (subject to any limit imposed under TCA 1997, Sch 24);

Foreign tax credit limit:

the upper limit to the amount of the foreign tax that may be set off against the Irish tax payable on any item of foreign income (relevant in any case where the foreign taxes available for credit exceed the amount of the relevant Irish tax attributable to that income);

Excess foreign tax:

the excess of the foreign taxes available for credit in respect of any item of income over the foreign tax credit limit for that income;

Effective rate of foreign tax:

the rate of the foreign taxes available for credit expressed as a percentage of the foreign income (as grossed up by the foreign taxes available for credit);

Effective rate of Irish income tax:

the rate of the Irish resident person's income tax payable (before any credit for foreign tax) for the relevant tax year expressed as a percentage of his total income.

The rules of TCA 1997, Sch 24 para 7(3) noted above present an apparent conflict. The amount of the foreign income to be included in the total income of the resident person claiming the credit must be reduced by any excess foreign tax in respect of the income. However, the foreign tax credit limit (which determines whether there is any excess foreign tax) is itself dependent on the amount of the foreign income finally included in total income. In fact, there is a reasonably simple procedure for dealing with this problem. The grossing up procedure is the procedure used and involves grossing up the 'net foreign income' by the lower of the effective rate of foreign tax and the effective rate of Irish income tax. First, it produces the amount of the foreign income that is included in the resident person's total income by reference to which the Irish tax payable is finally computed (before setting off the foreign tax credit). Secondly, by applying the lower of the two effective rates of tax (the Irish or the foreign rate, as the case may be), it secures that the excess (if any) of the foreign taxes available for credit over the foreign tax credit limit is automatically deducted in arriving at the grossed up foreign income (see note 3 in **Example 14.302.1** below).

The 'net foreign income' brought into the grossing up calculation is the amount of the relevant item of income (as determined under Irish tax law) *after* deducting the foreign taxes actually paid (or payable) in respect of that income, and *before* adding back any foreign indirect taxes that may be available for credit against Irish tax (see **14.303**). For example, if the relevant item of income is a dividend paid by a company resident in a treaty country of a gross amount of €1,000 from which 15 per cent overseas tax of €150 has been withheld by the paying company under the overseas tax laws and in accordance with the treaty concerned, the net foreign income is €850. No deduction is made for any Irish tax that has been deducted by the Irish paying agent under the deduction at source rules (see **2.310**).

The formula for determining the grossed up foreign income ('final foreign income') in respect of any item of foreign income is as follows:

$$\text{Final foreign income} = \text{net foreign income} \times \frac{100}{100 - r}$$

where

r = the lower of the effective rate of foreign tax and the effective Irish income tax rate.

The amount of the foreign tax for which the credit against Irish income tax is finally given is the excess of the final foreign income over the net foreign income. It may be useful to note that the amount of the final foreign tax credit may also be arrived at in either of the following ways:

(a) foreign tax credit = net foreign income × $\frac{r}{100 - r}$

or

(b) foreign tax credit = grossed up foreign income × $\frac{r}{100}$

Example 14.302.1

Mr Art Dreech, a chartered accountant, has a branch office in country X with which there is a double taxation agreement. This entitles him to a credit against Irish tax for any taxes payable in country X on profits earned there from his profession to the extent they are attributable to a fixed base (his office) in that country (see **14.209**).

For his 12-month period of account ended 31 December 2015 (assessable to Irish tax for 2015), Mr Dreech's taxable profit from his country X branch are agreed under the respective tax laws of country X and Ireland as follows:

	€
Taxable profits per country X rules	22,000
Taxable profits per Irish tax rules	21,000

Country X charges tax of €7,200 on the branch profits as computed in accordance with its laws. This is the foreign tax available for credit against Irish tax to which the rules of TCA 1997, Sch 24 have to be applied. The effective foreign rate (the country X rate) is computed as follows (see also **14.305**):

	€
Country X tax payable	7,200
Country X branch profits (as computed under *Irish* rules)	21,000
Effective foreign rate:	
€7,200/€21,000 x 100 =	34.285%

Assuming that Mr Dreech's 2015 effective rate of Irish tax for the year for which the profits are taxable is computed as 27 per cent (applying principles explained in **14.306**), then the final country X branch profits for inclusion in his total income for 2015 and the foreign tax credit to be set off against the Irish tax payable are calculated as follows:

	€
Country X branch profits	21,000
Less:	
Country X tax payable (34.285%)	7,200
Net foreign income	13,800
Effective rates of tax:	€
Foreign rate (country X) 34.285%	
Irish rate 27%	

Gross up net foreign income at the lower rate (27%)

€13,800 x (100/ (100–27) =	18,904
Foreign tax credit: €18,904 – €13,800	5,104

Notes:

1. The final amount of the country X branch profits of €18,904 is included in Mr Dreech's total income for 2015.
2. The credit for the country X tax available for credit (€7,200) has been restricted to €5,104 (the foreign tax credit limit in this case) due to the fact that the effective Irish rate (27 per cent) is lower than the effective foreign rate (34.285 per cent).
3. The 'excess foreign tax' of €2,096 (ie €7,200 less €5,104) has in effect been deducted from the country X branch profits that are finally included in Mr Dreech's total income for 2015. This may be shown as follows:

	€
Country X branch profits (as first computed for Irish tax)	21,000
Less:	
Excess country X tax	2,096
Final country X branch profits (as above)	18,904

4. The foreign tax credit for the country X tax could, alternatively, have been arrived at either as:

$$13{,}800 \times \frac{27}{100 - 27} = 5{,}104$$

or

$$18{,}904 \times 27\% = 5{,}104$$

5. The above example ignores the USC.

The changes introduced in the Finance Act 2013 ensure that the USC is now separately taken into account when granting credit for foreign taxes. TCA 1997, Sch 24 para 5A sets out the formula for determining the amount of foreign tax available for credit against the USC (see **Example 14.308.1**) and an apportionment of the credit between spouses and civil partners where the income is jointly owned. TCA 1997, Sch 24 para 7A(3)(b) increases the amount of the income liable to the USC by the amount of the indirect taxes (see **Example 14.308.1**). There is no provision in TCA 1997, Sch 24 para 7A to give any reduction in the income subject to the USC for unused credits. This contrasts with the position for income tax where relief is given by way of a reduction of the income chargeable through the use of the grossing up procedure (see **Example 14.302.1**) discussed above.

The procedure for granting credit for foreign taxes against Irish income tax and the USC may be summarised as follows:

1 ascertain the foreign taxes available for credit in respect of the income including, if relevant, any indirect taxes (see **14.303**);

2 calculate the effective rate of foreign tax (see **14.305**);

3 calculate the effective rate of Irish income tax under TCA 1997, Sch 24 para 5 by dividing the income tax payable (assuming the individual was taxable on the

gross foreign income, ie net foreign income plus foreign direct taxes only) by the total income (see **14.306**);

4 revise the foreign income to be assessed to Irish income tax. This is done by using the lower of the effective rate of Irish income tax and the foreign effective tax rate to gross-up the net foreign income. Where the revised foreign income is less than the gross foreign income, the difference is the amount of relief which has been given by way of a reduction (see **14.307**);

5 calculate the amount of the foreign tax credit by subtracting the 'regrossed foreign income' from the 'net foreign income' for each item of income (see **14.307**);

6 calculate the revised income tax position using the revised foreign income under 4 above and the foreign tax credit as determined by 5 above (see **14.307**);

7 establish the tax value of the relief given by way of a reduction. This is done by subtracting the tax payable under 6 above from the tax payable had a reduction not applied. When determining the tax payable had the reduction not applied use the gross foreign income instead of the revised foreign income per 4 above. Gross foreign income for this purpose includes indirect foreign taxes (see **14.308**);

8 determine the amount of foreign tax available for credit against the USC. This figure is obtained by subtracting the foreign tax determined by 5 above and the amount of the tax value of the relief given by way of a reduction (7 above) from the total foreign tax amount (includes both direct and indirect foreign taxes) (see **14.308**);

9 apportion the balance of foreign tax available for credit against the USC between each foreign income source. The apportionment is done on the basis of each foreign income source's share of the reduction. This is the difference between the amount assessed for each foreign income source to Irish income tax under 5 above and the amount which would have been assessed had the net foreign income been grossed up by the effective rate of foreign tax including indirect taxes (see **14.308**);

10 calculate the effective rate of the USC using gross foreign income (including both direct and indirect foreign taxes) (see **14.308**);

11 determine the amount of the USC that applies to each source of foreign income by multiplying the effective rate of the USC by each source of gross foreign income (including both direct and indirect foreign taxes) (see **14.308**);

12 deduct from 11 above the amount apportioned to each foreign income source under 9 above (see **14.308**).

14.303 Foreign taxes available for credit

It has been shown that the first step in the foreign tax credit calculation for any item of income is to determine the foreign taxes available for credit. For this purpose, it is necessary to look carefully at the double taxation agreement with the country concerned. Most of the treaties provide credits in respect of direct taxes, ie for the taxes payable to the other contracting state either directly on, or by deduction from, specific items of income arising in the other state, but only to the extent that the relevant treaty permits that state to tax that income.

In addition to the credit for foreign direct taxes, most of Ireland's tax treaties also permit the Irish resident person to claim a credit for certain foreign indirect taxes in certain circumstances. 'Indirect' or, as it is often termed 'underlying'; foreign tax is the foreign corporation tax (or any other equivalent tax) which a company resident in the other contracting state has paid or is due to pay on its profits out of which its dividends are paid. The question of a credit for any indirect foreign tax against Irish tax only arises where the Irish resident person receives dividends and, then, it is only relevant to him if the treaty with the contracting state in which the distributing company is resident specifically provides that an indirect tax credit may be given (as well as the normal credit for any foreign direct taxes borne on the dividends).

Some of the treaties grant an indirect tax credit for *any* dividends paid to any person resident in Ireland by a company resident in the other country, but in most of these cases the credit for the indirect taxes is only given in respect of an ordinary dividend or any participating element in a participating preference dividend. A number of the treaties only grant the credit for indirect taxes where the foreign dividends are received by an Irish resident company holding a minimum (or greater) percentage of the voting share capital or of the ordinary share capital in the company paying the dividend.

If the relevant treaty includes in its 'taxes covered' article any taxes payable to a political subdivision, municipality, local authority, etc of the foreign country, the treaty may provide for the taxes available for credit to include any such indirect subnational taxes to the extent payable on the distributing company's profits. For example, the Ireland/Federal German Republic agreement permits the credit for foreign tax to include the German trade tax (*Gewerbesteuer*), a municipal tax, but only to the extent that it is based on profits.

14.304 'Same profits' subject to double taxation for credit relief purposes

The Anson case

In *Anson v HMRC* [2015] UKSC 44 the UK Supreme Court was concerned as to whether the same profits had been subject to double tax for which double tax relief could be available. The conclusion of that court was that Mr Anson was subject to tax on the same profits as the LLC such that double tax relief was available. It should be noted that the First Tier Tribunal held for Anson as did the Supreme Court but both the High Court and the Court of Appeal both held for HMRC effectively saying that the LLC at issue was opaque. Therefore, the matter of an Irish court's view on same is not beyond doubt but the UK Supreme Court decision would be persuasive. Also it may be possible to distinguish this case on the facts given the possibility of disparate LLC agreements and HMRC have said this to be the case. Indeed one commentator noted 'as a result of the Supreme Court's decision there seems clear potential to draft either a "transparent" or "opaque" LLC for tax purposes'.

Mr Anson was a member of a Delaware limited liability company which was classified as a partnership for US tax purposes and he was liable to US tax on his share of the profits. Mr Anson was UK resident but non-domiciled such that he was liable to UK tax on a remittance basis subject to double tax relief. He remitted his share of the profits to the UK and HMRC decided that Anson was not entitled to any double taxation relief on the basis that the income which had been taxed in the US was not his income until such time as it was distributed to him and until that time the profit remained that of the limited liability company. For the purposes of double tax relief for US tax suffered by Anson the Supreme Court focused on the relevant provisions of the UK/US Tax Treaty and specifically as to whether Anson was subject to UK tax on the 'same profits or income' on which he had already suffered US tax. Given the case may be distinguished on its facts then the Supreme Court citing the FTT's findings at paras 10-11 of its decision in connection with the LLC itself are of importance:

(i) The LLC was a legal entity which was brought into existence by executing a certificate of formation, filing of that certificate with the Delaware Secretary of State, and entering into an LLC agreement.

(ii) The business of the LLC was carried on by the LLC itself, rather than by its members, in the sense that the LLC as an entity with separate legal existence was engaged in business. The members were however active in the business, each member being required by the LLC agreement to devote at least 90 per cent of his full business time to the advancement of the LLC's business and interests.

(iii) The assets used for carrying on the business of the LLC belonged beneficially to the LLC and not to the members.

(iv) The LLC was liable for the debts incurred as a result of carrying on its business. The members had no liability for the liabilities of the LLC.

(v) A Delaware 'limited liability company interest' is defined by ss 18-101(8) of the LLC Act as 'a member's share of the profits and losses of a limited liability company and a member's right to receive distributions of the limited liability company's assets'. (It should be noted here that articles IV and V of the LLC agreement noted respectively that 'all gross income and gains ... realized during the period in question ... shall ... be credited, and all losses, deductions and expenses ... during the period in question ... shall ... be debited, to the respective capital accounts of the members pro rata, in accordance with ratios prescribed in the agreement' and 'Subject to the provisions of this article V, to the extent cash is available, distributions of all of the excess of income and gains over losses, deductions and expenses allocated in accordance with s 4.2 with respect to any calendar year will be made by the company at such time within seventy-five (75) days following the end of such calendar year and in such amounts as the managing members may determine in their sole discretion. The managing members may from time to time in their discretion make additional distributions in accordance with the provisions of this article V'). Indeed, para 18 of the Supreme court's decision notes that '... article IV allocated the profit to the members as it arose and article V required payment to be made'.

(vi) That interest is in principle assignable, except as provided in the LLC agreement. The assignee has no right to participate in the management of the business except as provided in the agreement and with the approval of all the other members. An assignee does not become a member but becomes entitled to the same economic interest as the assignor.

(vii) In the present case, the LLC agreement provided that a member's interest could not be transferred except for sales by a former member (a) under provisions giving the LLC a right of first refusal before any such sale, (b) to a person engaged in the full time business of the LLC, with the written consent of the managing members and two-thirds of the other original members, or (c) on death.

(viii) Section 18–503 of the LLC Act provides that 'the profits and losses of a limited liability company shall be allocated among the members, and among classes or groups of members, in the manner provided in a limited liability company agreement'.

(ix) 'A limited liability company interest is personal property. A member has no interest in specific limited liability company property' (s 18–701 of the LLC Act).

(x) Subject to the LLC agreement, the members manage the LLC and vote in proportion to their interest in profits.

(xi) The LLC agreement provided that the operation and policy of the LLC was vested in the managing members, who had power to contract on its behalf, but certain matters, such as mergers and incurring liabilities of more than $500,000 in a year, required the consent of the members.

(xii) The interest of a member in the LLC was not similar to share capital, but was more similar to partnership capital in an English partnership.

The Supreme Court had regard to the decision of *Memec plc v IRC* [1998] STC 754 which has been affirmed in the Irish High Court decision of *Harris v Quigley & Anor* [2008] IEHC 403. Harris did not deal with the 'same profits' question but rather whether Mr Harris was a 'limited partner' as defined in para (d) of its definition in TCA 1997, s 1013(1), and the court responded in the negative. The question as to whether the Cook Islands partnership at issue carried on a trade was not a concern for the Irish High Court. It dealt only with the s 1013 issue.

Memec plc ('Plc') was a partner in a German silent partnership (Stille Gesellschaft). The partnership had no separate legal personality but was a contractual arrangement under which Plc had the right to receive a share of the profits of the business carried on by the other partner, in return for a capital payment. The other partner, Memec GmbH ('GmbH'), was a German company, wholly owned by Plc. It alone carried on the business of the silent partnership. It alone owned the assets of the business, and the income from those assets as it accrued. It had wholly owned subsidiaries, which were also German companies. The subsidiaries paid dividends to GmbH, and that income formed the principal source of the profits of the partnership, which were shared between the partners in accordance with their agreement. The question was whether Plc could claim credit under the double taxation agreement for German taxes paid by the subsidiaries of GmbH on their trading profits.

Lord Reed in *Anson* criticised the Court of Appeal's approach to *Memec* in *Anson* by providing as follows:

> … First and foremost, the court did not directly address the only relevant question, namely whether the UK tax was computed by reference to the same profits or income by reference to which the US tax was computed. It began by identifying that question, but then appears to have been diverted by a consideration of the issue which it understood to have been decided in *Memec*, and the approach adopted in that case. As a consequence, the remainder of its judgment focused on the question whether Mr Anson had a proprietary right to the profits of the LLC as they arose. That question not only appears to demonstrate the persistence of the conceptual confusion between profits and assets, but does not address the critical point, namely whether the income taxed in one country is the same as the income taxed in another.

He went on to note that Memec dealt with the article of a German treaty which looked at giving a credit for underlying tax on the profits borne by a company which would not have been available in this instance because of Anson being an individual and not a company. That said he noted, albeit obiter, at para 108:

> … if, for example, the taxpayer were Anson plc, a UK resident company holding at least 10% of the voting power in the LLC, and the question was whether it was entitled to relief from corporation tax in respect of underlying tax paid in the US by subsidiaries of the LLC

> – then it would be necessary, as in *Memec*, to consider whether Anson plc could be treated as having been paid the dividends received by the LLC from its subsidiaries. But that is not this case.

Therefore Lord Reed did not disagree with dicta in Memec but rather noting that it had a different question before it and so was limited by its own facts.

Anson was concerned with interpreting the UK/US tax treaty only from the perspective of the meaning attached to 'same profits' without regard to the form the LLC took (ie transparent or opaque). In fact the Supreme Court cited the decision of the FTT at para 32 where Lord Reed noted that the FTT said it would apply *Memec* but 'preferred to concentrate on the words of the treaty rather than as whether the LLC was transparent or opaque'. That said Lord Reed in citing the findings ascertained by the First Tier Tribunal at para 11 of his decision noted that 'the interest of a member in the LLC was not similar to share capital but was more similar to partnership capital in an English partnership'. At para 32 of his decision he noted that 'it was in their view on the partnership side of the dividing line, particularly in relation to its income'. The latter dictum would at least imply that the LLC could be a partnership for income and something else from a capital perspective but the previous dictum would at least indicate that would not be the case in this instance.

Lord Reed gave a three-stage analysis to the question at hand. It can be seen that this makes no reference to the transparent or opaque nature of the LLC. He notes at para 113 as follows with the numbering being the author's own for ease of discussion:

> 1. Giving the words used in article 23(2)(a) their ordinary meaning, it is necessary to identify the profits or income by reference to which the taxpayer's UK tax liability is computed. That is primarily a question of UK tax law (I say 'primarily', because the meaning of terms used in the Convention may not be a question of UK tax law: 'United Kingdom tax', for example, is a defined term).
> 2. It is then necessary to identify the profits or income from sources within the US on which US tax was payable under the laws of the US and in accordance with the Convention. That is primarily a question of US tax law.
> 3. It is then necessary to compare the profits or income in each case, and decide whether they are the same. The words 'the same' are ordinary English words. It should however be borne in mind that a degree of pragmatism in their application may be necessary in some circumstances if the object of the Convention is to be achieved, for example where differences between UK and foreign accounting and tax rules prevent a precise matching of the income by reference to which tax is computed in the two jurisdictions. It appears that some potential difficulties of this kind are in practice avoided by the Commissioners' accepting that the profits on which foreign tax is computed and in respect of which relief can be claimed are not confined to those arising under UK tax principles in individual UK chargeable periods …

The main factor in determining whether the 'same profits' were at point was whether the profits belonged to the members of the LLC as they arose or whether the members of the LLC were entitled to a distribution of the profits. The former is the determining factor. Therefore as can be seen from the FTT's findings as discussed earlier – see points (v), (viii) and (ix) – it is the provisions of the Delaware Act and the LLC agreement which give the right of the profits to the members as they arise. Paragraph 10 of the FTT decision is cited at para 18 of Lord Reed's decision regarding the references to 18-101 and 18.503 of the LLC Act noted above as follows:

> This means that the profits do not belong to the LLC in the first instance and then become the property of the members because there is no mechanism for any such change of ownership, analogous to the declaration of a dividend. It is true, as Mr Talley has said, that the assets representing those profits do belong to the LLC until the distribution is actually made but we do not consider that this means that the profits do not belong to the members … Conceptually, profits and assets are different, as is demonstrated by the reference to both in the definition of 'limited liability company interest' [in section 18-101(8) of the LLC Act]. There is a corresponding liability to the members evidenced by the allocation to their capital accounts … Accordingly, our finding of fact in the light of the terms of the LLC operating agreement and the views of the experts is that the members of [the LLC] have an interest in the profits of [the LLC] as they arise.

In particular Lord Reed points out at para 119 of the judgment as follows: 'It is relevant to note, in the first place, that the rights of a member of the LLC were found to arise from the LLC Act, combined with the LLC agreement. Secondly, that agreement was not a contract between the LLC and its members: the LLC was not a party to it, but was brought into being by it, on the terms set out in it and in the provisions of the LLC Act. It was thus the constitutive document of the LLC. It was against that background that the FTT made findings which contradict the premise that the profits belong to the LLC in the first instance and are then transferred by it to the members. Their conclusion, on the contrary, was that, under the law of Delaware, the members automatically became entitled to their share of the profits generated by the business carried on by the LLC as they arose: prior to, and independently of, any subsequent distribution. As the FTT stated:

> The profits do not belong to the LLC in the first instance and then become the property of the members … Accordingly, our finding of fact in the light of the terms of the LLC operating agreement and the views of the experts is that the members of [the LLC] have an interest in the profits of [the LLC] as they arise.

Commenting specifically on the Court of Appeal's decision, Lord Reed cites para 71 of that decision as follows:

> Delaware law governs the rights of the members of [the LLC] as the law of the place of its incorporation, and the LLC agreement is expressly made subject to that law. However, the question whether those rights mean that the income of [the LLC] is the income of the members is a question of domestic law which falls to be determined for the purposes of domestic tax law applying the requirements of domestic tax law …

Lord Reed then goes on to illustrate the difficulties with this as follows at para 51 of his judgment:

> The reasoning … appears to elide two distinct issues. First, the questions whether the members had a right to the profits, and as to the nature of that right, were questions of non-tax law, governed by the law of Delaware. The FTT's conclusion, whether correctly construed as a finding that Delaware law had the effect of conferring on the members of the LLC an automatic statutory (or contractual) entitlement to the profits of the LLC, or as a finding that Delaware law vested the members with a proprietary right to the profits as they arose, was on either view a finding of fact. Secondly, domestic tax law – in this case, the relevant double taxation agreements as given effect in UK law – then fell to be applied to the facts as so found. This approach was explained by Robert Walker J in *Memec* ….

One can see the difference in approach but it was held in the Supreme Court that the Court of Appeal was wrong to treat the question of whether the income of the LLC was the income of the members as a question of domestic law—it was a question of Delaware law which had been found as a fact by the FTT.

As can be seen from the above, the main issue in the *Anson* decision was attempting to attach a meaning to the term 'same profits' per the relevant provision of the UK/US tax treaty. This issue was determined using Delaware law in conjunction with the LLC agreement. *Anson* did not reject *Memec* and indeed the FTT before it had looked to *Memec* in arriving at its conclusion that on balance the LLC at issue in *Anson* was akin to a partnership from the income tax point of view. *Memec* has been affirmed in the Irish courts and it may be that the Irish courts may wish to remain with analysing the facts by reference to dicta in *Memec* given the aforementioned affirmation.

14.305 Effective rate of foreign tax

The effective rate of foreign tax for any income is determined by expressing the foreign taxes available for credit in respect of that income as a percentage of the aggregate of the net foreign income and the foreign taxes available for credit. This is straightforward when the relevant treaty provides only for a credit for direct tax in respect of any foreign income that is paid less a foreign withholding tax (eg dividends, interest, royalties, etc). The effective foreign rate is simply the ratio of the tax withheld to the gross dividend, interest, etc (expressed as a percentage). In these cases, the effective foreign rate is more often than not the maximum rate which the relevant treaty permits the foreign country to levy on the type of income in question, but the effective foreign rate can never exceed the rate actually charged.

When the income is directly assessed in the foreign country, eg on the profits which an Irish resident person derives from a trading branch in that country, the effective foreign rate may be determined by the formula:

$$\frac{FT}{NFI + FT} \times 100$$

where:

FT = the foreign taxes actually payable on the foreign branch profits; and

NFI = the net foreign income computed by deducting the actual foreign taxes payable from the branch profits (as determined under Irish tax rules and after deducting any capital allowances).

Example 14.305.1

Mr A Trader, an Irish resident, trades through a branch, ie a permanent establishment, in France. The branch accounts for the year ended 31 December 2015 show a trading profit of €13,187. For French tax purposes, the accounting profits are adjusted to taxable profits of €16,572 and French tax €5,966 became payable at a rate of 36 per cent (assumed rate).

Mr Trader is assessed to Irish income tax on those profits for the year 2015. The assessable profits computed under the rules of Sch D Case I, and the relevant capital allowances for 2015, are as follows:

	€
Profits per branch accounts	13,187

Add:	
Disallowable expenses (Irish rules)	3,241
	16,428
Less:	
Capital allowances 2015	2,648
Net branch profits (before French tax)	13,780
Less:	
French tax payable	5,966
Net foreign income	7,814

Effective rate of French tax:

$$\frac{5,966 \times 100}{7,814 + 5,966} = 43.29\%$$

The calculation of the effective foreign rate is more complicated if the foreign income is a dividend in respect of which the Irish resident person is entitled by the relevant tax treaty to include the foreign underlying tax in the tax credit computation. In such a case, the effective rate of foreign tax is a combination of the rate of direct tax withheld by the distributing company on paying the dividend (not exceeding the maximum rate permitted by the treaty) and the rate of the underlying tax payable by the distributing company on the profits out of which the dividend has been paid (the 'relevant profits').

The below illustrates how the effective rate of foreign tax is computed when the underlying tax rate is known. Assuming that the underlying tax rate has been determined as 40 per cent and that the dividend is payable less a withholding (direct) tax of 10 per cent, the effective rate of foreign tax is arrived at as follows:

	per 100
Distributable profits of foreign company (before foreign tax)	100
Rate of underlying tax	(40)
Available for dividend	60
Foreign withholding tax on dividends:	
Dividend 60 x 10%	(6)
Net foreign income	54
Effective rate of foreign tax (direct tax 6% + indirect tax 40%)	46%

14.306 Effective rate of Irish tax

TCA 1997, Sch 24 para 5 sets the upper limit to the amount of foreign tax that may be credited against Irish income tax in respect of any item of foreign income (the foreign tax credit limit). It provides that the credit is not to exceed the sum which would be produced if the foreign income in question were to be charged to income tax – at a rate determined in the manner prescribed in that paragraph (as affected by certain further rules contained in TCA 1997, Sch 24). The rate determined in this manner is the effective rate of Irish income tax previously mentioned in **14.302**. The rules for computing this effective rate of Irish tax are now explained.

The effective rate of Irish tax is computed for each year of assessment for which the Irish resident person claims a credit for foreign tax. Only one effective Irish rate calculation is made each year, whether the taxpayer concerned is entitled to a credit in respect of a single source of foreign income or two or more credits on different sources with varying rates of foreign tax. The effective Irish rate is computed in a 'provisional' income tax computation for each year. Although the income tax payable and total income figures used in this provisional computation may differ in some respects from those that appear in the 'final' income tax computation (see **14.307**), the effective Irish income tax rate remains that as determined in the provisional computation.

The effective rate of Irish income tax – (effective Irish rate) for an individual for any tax year is computed as follows:

$$\text{Effective rate} = \frac{\text{Income tax payable}}{\text{Total income}} \times 100$$

The 'income tax' and the 'total income' figures used in this formula are determined in the provisional income tax computation that is made in the ordinary way by reference to the individual's income from all sources, deductions, personal allowances, etc for the year in question, but with certain modifications.

TCA 1997, Sch 24 para 7 as supplemented by TCA 1997, Sch 24 para 5, defines the two terms as follows:

'income tax payable':

the income tax payable for the year calculated on the provisional taxable income arrived at by deducting the individual's normal allowances and reliefs from his provisional total income (see below), but before making any reduction for any foreign tax credits due to be set off against income tax; and

'total income':

the individual's total income including, if he is assessable jointly under TCA 1997, s 1017 as a married person, his spouse's total income, each calculated in the normal way, except that:

(a) there is no reduction in computing the foreign income for any excess foreign tax which cannot be allowed as a credit against Irish tax; and
(b) any foreign indirect tax is ignored (although, in the final income tax computation, it may be wholly or partly included in the foreign income finally chargeable).

The income tax payable figure taken from the provisional computation is the individual's total income tax (provisional) for the year, but excludes any income tax which he is entitled to charge against any other person (ie income tax deductible under TCA 1997, s 237 on annual payments etc made by him).

For an individual subject to the high earners restriction, the effective rate of Irish income tax is determined by dividing the income tax payable by the amount of the individual's adjusted income (see **3.111**). Prior to Finance (No 2) Act 2013 the effective rate of Irish income tax was calculated before taking account of the high earners restriction. The effect of this was that the tax relief given for foreign tax was not in line with the tax relief provided for by the double taxation agreements. The Revenue Commissioners have stated in Revenue *eBrief No 75/14* and its Revenue Operation Manual 15–02A–05 that the change is retrospective and applies to tax returns submitted on or after 1 January 2008. A taxpayer entitled to a greater tax credit may make a claim for repayment of tax. As ROS will not calculate the correct double tax relief, each claim should be supported by calculations showing how the additional claim to double taxation relief was arrived at.

Example 14.306.1

Mr XR, an Irish resident assessed jointly on the income of himself and his wife under TCA 1997, s 1017 for the year 2015, claims credit for foreign taxes on the following income from investments in countries with which there are tax treaties:

	Gross foreign income	*Foreign direct tax*	*Net foreign income*
	€	€	€
Canadian loan interest[1] (Self)	600	90	510
Belgian company dividends[2] (Self)	5,000	750	4,250
Netherlands company dividends[1] (Self)	2,600	391	2,209
	8,200	1,231	6,969

Mr XR's effective Irish rate of income tax for 2015 is calculated by reference to his above foreign income (after adding back the foreign direct taxes, but before adding on any foreign indirect tax in respect of the Belgian company dividends for which he is entitled to an indirect tax credit) and by reference to his other income, deductions, tax credits and reliefs etc as set out in the following provisional income tax computation.

Assessable income 2015:	€	€
Sch D Case I (self)		83,900
Sch D Case III (Irish source) (self)		3,300
Sch F (including Dividend Withholding Tax €480) (self)		2,400
Sch E (wife's salary, subject to PAYE)		5,600
		95,200
Foreign income subject to DTR as above		
Net foreign income	6,969	
Add: Foreign direct taxes only	1,231	
		8,200
		103,400
Less:		
TCA 1997, s 381 loss claim (self)	8,600	
Charges on income (deed of covenant to incapacitated sister)	1,500	10,100
Total taxable income (provisional)		93,300
Income tax payable (provisional):[3]		
€48,400 x 20%	9,680	
€44,900 x 40%	17,960	27,640
€93,300		
Less:		
Married person's tax credit	(3,300)	
Miscellaneous credits	(3,373)	
Employee tax credit-max.	(1,120)	(7,793)
Income tax		19,847
Effective rate of Irish income tax 2015: 19,847/93,300=		21.27%

Notes

1. Direct tax credits only are available in respect of the Canadian loan interest and the Netherlands dividends.
2. Direct and indirect tax credits are available under the Belgian treaty for the dividends from companies in that country but the indirect taxes are ignored in this provisional computation.
3. No addition to the (provisional) income tax payable is made for the tax of €300 which Mr XR deducted under TCA 1997, s 237 from the €1,500 annual payment to his sister. No deduction is made for either the Dividend Withholding Tax or, the PAYE on his wife's salary.
4. For the computation of Mr XR's final total income for 2015 and of the income tax and Universal Social Charge finally payable by him, see **Example 14.307.1** and **14.308.1**.

14.307 Final income tax computation

When the Irish resident individual's Irish effective rate has been determined for the relevant tax year, as well as the effective foreign rates applicable to the various items of foreign income, steps (4), (5) and (6) of the procedure outlined in **14.302** can be completed. If the individual has foreign income from various sources for which he is entitled to a credit for foreign tax at more than one effective foreign rate, the grossing up procedure (step (4)) has to be applied separately to each item. For some items, the foreign rate may be lower than the Irish rate so that the net foreign income is grossed up at the foreign rate; for other items, the reverse may be the case.

The individual's final income tax computation is then prepared. The total income tax on the final taxable income is then calculated in the ordinary way at the appropriate rate(s) of income tax and the total of the credits for foreign taxes (see step (5)) in **14.302**) is then set off against the income tax chargeable. Any other credits against income tax are also deducted (eg income tax suffered at source etc) in order to arrive at the final income tax balance payable for the year (or, possibly if the other credits are large enough, the balance of the tax refund due to him).

In determining the individual's final total income for the year, each item of foreign income is brought in at the re-grossed figure resulting at the end of step (4). In the case of any foreign dividend in respect of which an indirect tax credit is given under the relevant treaty, the amount finally chargeable may be higher than that used in the provisional computation to determine the effective Irish rate; in certain instances, it may be lower due to the individual having a low effective Irish rate. For foreign income other than such dividends, the amount finally chargeable will be lower than that taken in the provisional computation if the effective Irish rate is less than the foreign direct tax rate but cannot be higher than the amount provisionally taken in.

In calculating the individual's final taxable income, all his deductible charges and reliefs should be deducted from his final total income. In this connection, any relief or deduction which is given from, or is restricted by reference to, total income must be dealt with on the basis of the final total income (including the foreign income as re-grossed). If the final total income is not the same as that in the provisional computation, the relief or deduction finally given may also be different.

TCA 1997, Sch 24 para 6 provides that the total credit for foreign tax to be allowed against any person's Irish income tax liability for any year of assessment must not exceed the total income tax payable by him for that year, *as reduced by* any income tax which he is entitled to charge against any other person (ie income tax deducted by him from annual payments, etc within TCA 1997, s 237). This 'overall' limit refers to the total of all the credits for foreign tax to which the individual would otherwise be entitled in respect of all his sources of foreign income.

Example 14.307.1

Take the facts of Mr XR's case as set out in **Example 14.306.1** in which his Irish effective rate for 2015 was calculated as being 21.27 per cent. As indicated there, he is entitled to credits under TCA 1997, Sch 24 in respect of the direct taxes (only) in respect of the Netherlands dividends and for the Canadian loan interest, but he is entitled to a credit for both direct and indirect taxes in respect of the Belgian dividends.

The net foreign income from each source, the effective rates of foreign tax applicable in each case and the effective Irish rate for the year are summarised as follows:

	Net foreign income	*Effective rates*	
		Foreign %	*Irish %*
	€		
Canadian loan interest	510	15	21.27
Netherlands dividends	2,209	15	21.27
	2,719		
Belgian company dividends[1]	4,250	44	21.27
	6,969		

The first two types of income all have the same effective foreign rate (15 per cent) which is lower than the effective Irish rate (21.27 per cent) and can therefore be re-grossed in the one calculation. The Belgian dividends have a separate effective foreign rate, but the effective Irish rate is lower. The foreign income to be included in Mr XR's final income tax computation for 2015 is now computed as follows:

Calculate the final income tax position under step 6 of the procedure outlined in **14.302.**	€
Netherlands dividends and Canadian loan interest re-grossed at the lower foreign rate:	
€2,719 x (100/ 100–15)=	3,199
Belgian company dividends re-grossed at lower Irish rate:	
€4,250 x (100/ 100–21.27)=	5,398
	8,597

The credits for foreign tax in respect of the different items of foreign income available for set off in the final income tax computation are as follows:

	€
Netherlands dividends and Canadian loan interest	
€3,199 x 15% =	480
Belgian company dividends	
€5,398 x 21.27%	1,148
Total foreign tax credits	1,628

Mr XR's final income tax computation for 2015 may now be set out as follows:

	€	€
Income from Irish sources:		
As per **Example 14.306.1**		95,200
Foreign source income (with credits for foreign tax): as above		8,597
Income from all sources		103,797
Less:		
Deductions as per **Example 14.306.1**		(10,100)
Total taxable income		93,697
Income tax payable:		
€48,400 x 20%	9,680	
€45,297 x 40%	18,119	27,799
€93,697		
Less: Tax Credits as per Example **14.306.1**		(7,793)
Double Tax Relief		(1,628)
		18,378
Less credits against tax: PAYE on wife's salary (say)	130	
Dividend Withholding Tax	480	
		(610)
		17,768
Add: Income tax on charges €1,500 x 20% =		300
Final income tax payable		18,068

Notes:

1. The effective rates of tax on the Belgian dividends are those accepted by the Irish Revenue for portfolio investments in Belgium (see **14.310**).

14.308 Foreign tax credit against the USC

Once the Irish resident individual's final income tax payable has been determined for the relevant tax year, steps 7 through to 12 of the procedure outlined in **14.302** can be completed.

The first of these steps is to establish the tax value of the relief given by way of a reduction. Where the revised foreign income to be assessed to Irish tax is less than the gross foreign income, the difference is the amount of relief which has been given by way of a reduction. The tax value of the relief given by way of a reduction equals the tax payable under step 6 (see **Example 14.307.1**) less the tax payable had the reduction not applied. However, for the purposes of calculating the tax payable had the reduction not applied the gross foreign income includes indirect foreign taxes.

Example 14.308.1

Take the facts of Mr XR's case as set out in **Example 14.306.1**.

Net foreign income	*Foreign %*	*Gross*
€		€
510	15	600

2,209	15	2,600	
4,250	44	7,589	
		10,789	

	€	€
Income from Irish sources:		
As per **Example 14.306.1**		95,200
Foreign source income (with credits for foreign tax including indirect tax): as above		10,789
Income from all sources		105,989
Less:		
Deductions as per **Example 14.306.1**		(10,100)
Total taxable income		95,889
Income tax and Universal Social Charge payable:		
€48,400 x 20%	9,680	
€47,489 x 40%	18,995	28,675
€95,889		
Less: Tax Credits as per **Example 14.306.1**		(7,793)
Double Tax Relief		(1,628)
		19,254
Less: credits against tax: PAYE on wife's salary (say)	130	
Dividend Withholding Tax	480	
		(610)
		18,644
Add: Income tax on charges €1,500 x 20% =		300
Final income tax payable without reduction		18,944
Final income tax payable with reduction per **Example 14.306.1**		(18,068)
Tax value of reduction		876

For the above example, it was not necessary to do the income tax computation again as it was evident that the reduction was taxed at 40%. Simply, the reduction of €2,192 (€10,789 minus €8,597) multiplied by 40% gives the tax value of reduction (€876).

Once the tax value of reduction has been calculated the amount of foreign tax available for credit against the USC (step 8) can be determined by subtracting the tax value of the reduction and the foreign tax credit used in the final income tax computation (See **14.307**) from the total amount of foreign taxes (including indirect taxes).

	€
Withholding tax – direct tax	1,231
Indirect tax[1]	2,589
Total	3,820
Subtract	
Total credit under step 5 refer example **14.307.1**	(1,628)
Tax value of reduction	(876)
Foreign tax available against USC	1,316

Note

1 net dividend received €4,259 re-grossed @44% = €7,589 – €5,000 (gross dividend received) = €2,589

When the foreign tax available against USC has been calculated, it needs to be apportioned between each foreign income source (step 9). This is done on the basis of each foreign income source's share of the reduction.

Apportionment of foreign tax credit to each income source

		Reduction given in IT computation	*Foreign tax available for credit against USC*	*Allocation of foreign tax to each income source*
		€	€	€
Canadian loan interest (Self)		0	1,316 x 0 / 2,143 =	0
Belgian company dividends (Self)	Regrossed at 44%(€7,589–€5,398) subject to income tax	2,191	1,316 x 2,191 / 2,191 =	1,316
Netherlands company dividends (Self)		0	1,316 x 0 / 2,143 =	0
		2,191		1,316

Once the foreign tax credit has been apportioned to each income source, it is necessary to calculate the effective rate of USC using gross foreign income (ie including both direct and indirect taxes).

				€
Calculate the effective rate of USC				
Total Irish Income (Self) per **Example 14.306.1**				
Sch D Case I (self)				83,900
Sch D Case III (self)				3,300
Sch F (self)				2,400
Canadian loan interest (Self)				600
Belgian company dividends (Self)				7,589
Netherlands company dividends (Self)				2,600
Total				100,389
USC	12,012	@ 1.5%	180	

	5,564	@ 3.5%	195
	52,468	@ 7%	3,673
	29,956	@ 8%	2,396
	389	@11%	43
			6,487
Effective rate of USC			6,487 / 100,389 = 6.46%

Once the effective rate of USC has been determined, the amount of USC that applies to each income source can be calculated by multiplying the effective rate (eg 6.46 per cent) by each source of gross foreign income.

USC on foreign income sources	*Gross foreign income*			*USC thereon*	*Credit*	*USC due after credit for foreign tax*
	€			€	€	€
USC on Canadian loan interest	600	@	6.46%	39	0	39
USC on Belgian company dividends	7,589	@	6.46%	490	1,316	Nil
USC on Netherlands company dividends	2,600	@	6.46%	168	0	168
				697	1,316	207

Summary of USC	€
USC per computation	6,487
Credit against USC on Belgian company dividends	(490)
USC due	5,997
Summary of final income tax & USC liability	
Final income tax payable	18,06
USC due	5,99
	24,06

14.309 Double taxation relief: trustees and other persons

The discussion of the rules relating to the granting of credits for foreign tax against the Irish income tax and Universal Social Charge payable by a resident person has so far dealt only with the treatment of individuals. It is necessary now to cover the position of other resident persons chargeable to income tax in respect of foreign source income which has suffered tax in any of the countries with which Ireland has double taxation agreements. This includes persons in receipt of such foreign source income in a fiduciary or representative capacity (eg the personal representatives of a deceased person, the trustees of a settlement, etc), as well as unincorporated bodies of persons not exempted from Irish income tax. The entitlement generally of trustees and personal representatives to double tax relief is discussed at **14.105**. It must be borne in mind that in some cases it may be the beneficiaries of the trust rather than the trustees who will claim the double tax relief (see **14.205**).

In fact, the principles of computation explained in **14.302** are implemented for such other persons in the same way as for individuals, but with the exception that the effective rate of Irish tax is nearly always the standard rate of income tax. This is because only individuals are chargeable to income tax at the higher rates and are the only persons entitled to personal allowances, etc which may produce an effective Irish rate of less than the standard rate. There is one exception which is dealt with separately in **15.310** in the context of trustees who are subject to the Irish discretionary trust surcharge of TCA 1997, s 805, but that is an exceptional type of case and is ignored here.

TCA 1997, Sch 24 para 5 limits the credit for the foreign tax (including, where relevant, any underlying foreign tax in respect of any dividend) to the sum produced by charging the foreign income in question to Irish income tax at the basic rate, but the credit cannot of course be greater than the actual foreign taxes available for credit in respect of each relevant item of foreign income. There is, therefore, no need to make the provisional income tax computation that is necessary in arriving at an individual's effective Irish rate. The computation of the foreign income finally chargeable to Irish tax may be made straight away by grossing up the net foreign income by the lower of the foreign rate or the Irish basic rate.

TCA 1997, Sch 24 para 6 operates, where relevant, in the same way as for individuals to impose an overall limit to the total credits for foreign tax in any one tax year. Again, this ensures that the foreign tax credits cannot be used to offset any income tax deductible by the resident person from annual payments, etc within TCA 1997, s 237.

Example 14.309.1

Mrs YS and the ZT Banking Co Ltd are the executors and trustees of the estate of the late Mr GS who died on 1 April 1999. They continue to carry on his former trade as the business has been left in trust for his son (a minor) contingently on the son reaching his 21st birthday.

The executors' income from Mr GS's estate, as taxable for the year 2015, includes dividends from Belgian companies carrying an effective foreign rate of 44 per cent, and the computation of the taxable Belgian income and the credits for tax against Irish tax are as follows:

		€
Gross dividends		6,000
Less: Belgian tax withheld at 15%		(900)
Net foreign income		5,100
Effective rate of Belgian tax	44%	
Effective rate of Irish tax (standard rate)	20%	
Gross up at the lower rate (Irish)		
€5,100 x (100/ 100–20)=		6,375
Sch D Case I (trade continued):		
Adjusted profits		Nil
Other income		4,500
Income from all sources		10,875
Less:		

TCA 1997, s 381 trading loss claim	5,800	
Annuity payable under will	3,000	(8,800)
Total income (final)		2,075
Income tax payable by executors:		
€2,075 x 20% =		415
Less:		
Credit for Belgian tax €6,375 x 20%[1]	1,275	
But credit limited to[2]		(415)
		0
Add: tax on charge €3,000 x 20% =		600
Final tax payable		600

Notes:

1. The amount of the credit for Belgian tax (before the overall limit is applied) is equal to the re-grossed Belgian dividends multiplied by the lower effective rate (in this case 20 per cent).
2. TCA 1997, Sch 24 para 6 applies to limit the total credit for foreign taxes to the total income tax payable (€415) excluding the tax on the charges on income (€600).

14.310 Portfolio investments

In determining the effective rate of foreign tax in respect of dividends for which the relevant double taxation agreement entitles the Irish resident shareholder to a credit for the foreign underlying tax, two types of case may be distinguished – namely dividends from 'portfolio' investments and dividends from 'direct' investments. A portfolio investment in a company is generally a shareholding representing a small proportion of the company's issued share capital. It is usually, but not necessarily, an investment in a quoted company and, in many cases, is one of a number of such investments held by the taxpayer concerned. In general, direct investments (ie larger shareholdings, typically representing at least 10 per cent of issued share capital or ordinary shares or voting power) are held by companies; those which are held by individuals are not normally entitled to enhanced double tax relief. The tax treatment of direct investment will accordingly be treated as falling outside the scope of this book.

Dividends received by Irish resident persons from portfolio investments in foreign companies are, more often than not, subject to direct or withholding taxes in the country of source, although some countries do not levy such tax as a result of a provision either in their tax treaty with Ireland or in their own domestic tax laws. In all cases where there has been a withholding tax (within the terms of the relevant tax treaty), the credit against Irish tax includes the withholding tax.

14.311 Effective foreign rate

Dividends from other countries

It may be difficult for the portfolio investor to ascertain the proper effective rates of foreign tax for dividends carrying the right to a credit for the foreign underlying tax (in addition to any direct tax) against Irish tax. There is usually no problem about the rate of the foreign withholding tax (if any) as this is normally indicated on the counterfoil or advice sent with the dividend. This rate is in most cases the maximum rate specified in the relevant tax treaty. The Irish resident should, however, check that the rate of foreign tax actually withheld from his dividend does not exceed the maximum treaty rate, since some countries charge a higher rate and leave it to the Irish resident to reclaim any excess tax withheld. It may be noted that not all countries necessarily charge the maximum withholding tax permitted by the treaty.

The foreign underlying taxes to be included in the Irish resident's foreign tax credit computation may, if the relevant treaty permits it, include any subnational (eg municipal or state) taxes payable on the distributing company's profits. This may in some cases increase the underlying foreign tax rate quite significantly. For example, a company resident in Germany is chargeable to the municipal trade tax (*Gewerbesteuer*) on its income (and on capital) in addition to the national corporation tax. Article 6 of the Ireland/Federal German Republic tax treaty restricts the German withholding tax on dividends paid to a resident of Ireland to 15 per cent. Article 22(1) entitles the resident of Ireland to a credit against his Irish tax of both the German direct tax and the German underlying taxes consisting of the national corporation tax and the trade tax to the extent payable on the distributing company's income (but not that on its capital).

The treaties with the countries set out below give an Irish resident portfolio investor a credit for the underlying tax (in addition to the direct tax) on ordinary dividends from companies resident in the country in question. The current effective foreign rates which will be accepted by the Revenue Commissioners (as stated most recently at 1 January 2009) are as follows:

Belgium	44%	Japan	44%
Germany	28%	Luxembourg	34%
France	43%	Italy	38%

The treaties with Cyprus, Pakistan, Russia and Zambia also provide for underlying tax credits, but the Revenue Commissioners have indicated that it is not practicable to publish a standard effective rate in these instances.

14.312 Excess relief

If it should happen that excess double tax relief has been granted, either due to a failure to tax the full grossed-up amount of foreign income or due to an incorrect calculation of the credit for foreign tax, any necessary additional assessment to tax may be made under Sch D Case IV to rectify the position (TCA 1997, Sch 24 para 11).

Division 15 Estates and Settlement

15.1 Estates of Deceased Persons

15.101 Introduction

On the date of an individual's death, all his property passes to his personal representatives and he ceases to have any source of income. His personal representatives are responsible for administering his estate, ie for collecting his assets, paying his liabilities, funeral and other testamentary expenses, discharging any legacies, devises, etc as provided for in his will (if there is one) and for ensuring that his residuary estate is transferred in due course to the person(s) entitled to it. The personal representatives have not only to agree the deceased person's income tax liabilities on all his income up to the date of his death, but they are in principle chargeable in their representative capacity on all income arising from his estate during the period of their administration.

The deceased person's personal representatives may be his executor(s) or his administrator(s), depending on whether he has died testate (ie leaving a valid will) or intestate (ie without leaving a will or if any will has been declared invalid by the High Court). If he dies testate, the personal representative(s) appointed by his will is his 'executor(s)'; if he dies intestate, his personal representative(s) is his 'administrator(s)'. An administrator is appointed to an intestate estate by the High Court on the application of the deceased's next of kin or of some other person interested in his estate. Before the executors or administrators can commence to act, a grant of representation must be obtained. Where there is a valid will, this is the grant of probate; if the deceased dies intestate, it is the grant of letters of administration by the court that authorises the administrator to carry out his function.

It is immaterial for any purpose of income tax whether the personal representatives are executors appointed by a will or administrators acting under letters of administration. All the relevant provisions in the Tax Acts are expressed in terms of the taxation of personal representatives. Consequently, any reference to them in this Division (or elsewhere) should be taken as referring equally to an executor or an administrator or, if relevant, to two or more executors or administrators where more than one is appointed. In practice, it is more usual to be dealing with an executor than with an administrator, so that the text may contain some references to an executor without mentioning an administrator. Apart from the fact that some matters (eg a will trust) are not encountered in intestate estates, most references to executors could apply equally to an administrator dealing with the same matter. An extended definition of 'personal representative' applies for the purpose of taxing the beneficiaries of an estate (see **15.203**).

The taxation of a deceased person's estate falls to be discussed under four main headings, namely:

(a) the agreement by the personal representatives of the deceased's income tax liabilities up to the date of his death;

(b) the taxation of the personal representatives during the administration period;

(c) the taxation of non-residuary beneficiaries during the administration period; and

(d) the taxation of residuary beneficiaries during and at the end of the administration period.

The deceased person, his personal representatives and each beneficiary who becomes entitled under the will or the rules of intestacy to a source of income from the deceased's estate are taxed as separate persons. This means in particular that the appropriate basis of assessment must be applied to income within Sch D Cases I and II.

15.102 Allocation of income on death

The Apportionment Act 1870 may require income (eg dividends, interest on securities, rents, etc) not received until after the date of death, but which accrued wholly or partly before that date, to be apportioned to the pre-death and post-death periods by reference to the period over which it accrues or in respect of which it was payable. This apportionment is required, unless specifically excluded by the deceased person's will, if different persons have interests respectively in the capital and the income of the estate, eg if there is a life tenant entitled to the income and another person due to succeed to the capital on the life tenant's death. Any income allocated by the rules of apportionment to the pre-death period is treated for distribution purposes as capital, while only the income allocated to the post-death period is distributable as income.

Example 15.102.1

Mr AB died on 31 March 2015. In his will, he left a life interest in all his estate to his widow with remainder (ie entitlement to capital on her death) to his two daughters in equal shares. His estate includes a holding of an Irish government stock on which the half yearly interest of €490 is payable on 31 December and 30 June. It also includes a holding of ordinary shares in an Irish company.

Between the date of death and 31 December 2015, Mr AB's executor received the following interest and dividends on the dates stated:

	€
Interest on government stock:	
6 months to 30/06/2015 (paid 30/06/2015)	490
6 months to 31/12/2015 (paid 31/12/2015)	490
Dividend on ordinary shares in Company Z for its Y/E 31 May 2015 (paid 21/09/2015)	
Gross Amount	3,250

Since Mr AB's will does not exclude the rules of apportionment, the Apportionment Act 1870 applies so that the above income is allocated between the pre-death and post-death periods as follows:

	Pre-death (capital)	Post-death (income)
	€	€
Government stock interest to 30/06/2015:		
Period 1/01/2015 to 31/03/2015		
490 x 90/181 days	244	-
Period 1/4/2015 to 30/06/2015		
490 x 91/181 days	-	246
Government stock interest to 31/12/2015:		
All post-death		490
	244	736
Dividend in Company Z for year to 31/5/2015:		
Period 1/6/2015 to 31/03/2015		
3,250 x 304/365 days	2,707	
Period 1/4/2015 to 31/5/2015		
3,250 x 61/365 days		543
	2,951	1,279

Taxation of Income on Executors

In general, Sch D income is taxed as and when it is received, although there are exceptions to this rule (in particular, Sch D Cases I and II where, generally, an earnings basis applies: see **5.201**; **5.302**, and Sch D Case V where an 'entitlement' basis applies: see **12.103** and also the discussions at **8.102; 8.202**; **8.205**). Sch F income is also normally taxed on a receipts basis, but dividends are treated as being paid when they are due and payable (see **9.101**).

Where income is taxed on a receipts basis, then amounts not received until after the date of death, if received by the personal representatives in the administration period, are always taxable as *their* income (in their representative capacity), and not as that of the deceased person. The Apportionment Act 1870 has no application, even if part of the income had accrued in respect of the pre-death period. For example, since an Irish company dividend (as noted above) does not arise as income to any person until it is due and payable, the whole of a dividend declared after the death is taxable as the income of the personal representatives, even if it is paid in respect of a period falling wholly before the date of death.

Traditionally, interest accrued on bank deposit accounts up to the date of death has been in practice treated as an exception to this general principle. This was on the basis that the depositor could in theory have closed his account at any time and received the interest accrued to date. The justification for this practice is open to question, since all interest in strictness accrues on a 'day-to-day basis' (see *Schaffer v Cattermole* [1980] STC 650; *Orange Personal Communications v Girvan* [1998] STC 567). In the case of interest subject to DIRT (see **8.204**), TCA 1997, s 261 expressly provides that 'any *payment* of relevant interest shall be regarded as income chargeable under Sch D Case IV'.

In *IRC v Henderson's Executors* 16 TC 282, the executors used the Apportionment Act to claim that certain dividends and interest received by them under deduction of tax after the date of death should be apportioned on a time basis over the period in respect of which they were paid. If successful, the claim would have enabled them to recover income tax previously paid by the deceased person by apportioning income to the pre-death period to be offset by unused personal allowances. The court confirmed the income tax principle that income is chargeable when the income arises and upon the person receiving it and that, in consequence, no part of the dividends and interest which had become due after the date of death could be treated as the income of the deceased.

Similarly, in *Bryan v Cassin* 24 TC 468, where a portion of the quarterly instalment of an annuity had accrued to, but had not been paid by, the date of the annuitant's death, it was held that no part of this quarterly instalment formed any part of the deceased's income. It had been contended by the annuitant's executor that the case was distinguishable from the *Henderson* case in that there were no income producing assets, but the deceased had simply been entitled for his life to an annuity which ceased to exist when he died. It was argued that the executor was therefore collecting the part of the annuity accrued to the date of death as a debt due to the deceased and not as an annuity due to the executor. In rejecting this claim, MacNaghten J stated the tax principles very clearly, as follows:

> The legal personal representative of a deceased person can assert any right to repayment of tax which the deceased possessed at the time of his death. There is no doubt or dispute as to that. But in respect of a sum of money which formed no part of the income of the deceased because it did not come to him in his lifetime … the legal personal representative cannot maintain any claim for the repayment of tax, notwithstanding the fact that the deceased, if he had received the money in his life time, could have done so.

It should be noted, however, that an annual payment within TCA 1997, s 237 which is paid after the date it falls due will be treated as arising on the due date.

Sch E income is normally assessable on an 'earnings basis' (see **10.102**). Thus, emoluments received after an employee's death, but which relate to services rendered before the date of death, should be treated as income of the deceased employee. Where emoluments from an employment are received after the date of death, but before the end of the tax year, and cannot be related back to the period before the date of death, TCA 1997, s 112 would again seem to impose a charge in respect thereof on the deceased employee. TCA 1997, s 112 has the effect that emoluments received in a tax year following the year of death are to be treated as emoluments of the year of death. The question of whether emoluments which cannot be related back prior to the date of death, can be assessed on the personal representatives, is discussed in **15.105**.

It is clear, therefore, that in general, investment income received by the personal representatives after the date of death is chargeable to income tax in their hands, whether or not the Apportionment Act is applicable to treat any part of that income as capital of the estate. However, if there is a life tenant, any part of the income apportioned to capital is excluded from the income of the residuary estate in respect of which the life tenant is taxable under TCA 1997, s 800 (see **15.205**) as he cannot benefit from it. The part of the income attributable to capital should, after deducting the part of the executor's income tax liability attributable to it, be reinvested to become part of the capital of the estate. If all the deceased's estate is left absolutely to one or more beneficiaries, there is no need to make any apportionments and all the income received after the death is included in arriving at the residuary estate income distributable to the residuary beneficiaries (see **15.205**).

Example 15.102.2

Take the facts of **Example 15.102.1** and assume that the €3,250 dividend from Company Z is subject to dividend withholding tax of €650. Mr AB's executor is taxable for 2015 on the full income received (without apportionment) in the period from the date of death (31 March 2015) to 31 December 2015.

Executor's income tax liability:

	€
Schedule D income	
Government stock interest (paid 30/6/2015)	490
Government stock interest (paid 31/12/15)	490
Schedule F income	3,250
Total income	4,230
Income tax at 20%	846
Less DWT	650
Net income tax due	196

The executor must, however account separately for the pre-death (capital) and post-death (income) parts of the income and must allocate his income tax liability between the capital and income in a corresponding manner.

The figures for the period 31 March 2015 to 31 December 2015 work out as follows:

	Executor's income	*Apportioned to capital*	*Income*
	€	€	€
Sch F income:			
Dividend received[1]	3,250	2,707	543
Sch D Case III[1]	980	244	736
Total income	4,230	2,951	1,279
Income tax at 20%	846	590	256
Less: DWT	650	541	109
Net income tax due	196	49	147

Having apportioned the gross income of the estate for the period between capital and income and having allocated the executor's income tax liability in corresponding proportions, the executor's net income for allocation between the capital of the estate and the life tenant (income) is made as follows:

	Capital	*Income*
	€	€
Dividend received	2,707	543
Interest on government stock	244	736
	2,951	1,279
Less:		
Income tax payable (as above)	49	147
Net income after tax[2]	2,902	1,132

Notes:

1 The capital and income parts of the dividend and the Government loan interest received are those as apportioned in **Example 15.102.1**.

2 The net income after tax is dealt with: €2,902 – Reinvest or use as capital. €1,132 – Distributable to life tenant as net income (subject to any executor's expenses chargeable against income).

15.103 Taxation of deceased to date of death

The personal representatives of a deceased person are responsible for agreeing all his liabilities to income tax on all income received by him up to the date of his death. They are also responsible for paying out of the estate all outstanding income tax liabilities and any interest or penalties that may be properly charged on it. They should also look into the possibility that the deceased may have overpaid income tax in one or more previous years, and if necessary, they should make any outstanding claims for relief from income tax (eg a loss relief claim under TCA 1997, s 381 not made by the deceased before he died, or a terminal loss relief under TCA 1997, s 385 where there is a discontinuance of a trade on death). The personal representatives have similar responsibilities in relation to capital gains tax on chargeable gains from disposals of assets by the deceased before his death.

An exception to the general position may arise where the deceased and his spouse were jointly assessed and the surviving spouse was the spouse assessed on the income of the couple under TCA 1997, s 1017. In such a case, the surviving spouse normally remains assessable on the total income of the couple for the year of death (including the income of the deceased spouse up to the date of his death). However, by virtue of TCA 1997, s 1022(6), the surviving spouse (or if appropriate his personal representatives) may disclaim further responsibility for any unpaid income tax of the deceased spouse for any year of assessment in respect of which he was jointly assessed under TCA 1997, s 1017. For these purposes, the income tax liabilities of the deceased spouse are deemed to be the amounts on which he would have been assessed if an election for separate assessment under TCA 1997, s 1023 had been in force for the relevant years of assessment (TCA 1997, s 1022(1)).

FA 2000, s 29 introduced certain amendments to TCA 1997, s 1022(6)–(8) to make the application of the section gender neutral, ensuring that the section is equally applied where the assessable person is the husband or wife. The provisions apply to all assessments affected by TCA 1997, s 1022 from 10 February 2000.

Where the surviving spouse wishes to make a disclaimer under TCA 1997, s 1022, he or she must give notice thereof to both the inspector and to the deceased's personal representatives, specifying the latter's names and addresses. The notice must be given within two months of the grant of probate or letters of administration or at any later date if the deceased's personal representatives so consent (TCA 1997, s 1022(6), (7)). Once a valid disclaimer has been made the inspector will proceed to raise assessments on the deceased spouse under the provisions of TCA 1997, s 1022 in the normal manner (see **3.502**). It should also be borne in mind that, even if the surviving spouse does not make a relevant disclaimer, the Revenue Commissioner have the power to recover unpaid tax attributable to the deceased spouse from his personal representatives under the general provisions of TCA 1997, s 1022(1). This treatment has been extended to civil partners under TCA 1997, s 1031G where the civil partners had been jointly assessed by virtue of a claim for joint assessment under TCA 1997, s 1031C.

The effect of the death of a spouse on the tax treatment of a married couple is fully dealt with in **3.506**.

The question of whether the joint or single person assessments are made in the year of the death of one spouse or civil partner is normally determined by the form of assessment that applied in the preceding year. If that assessment had been a joint one, a similar assessment will be made on the joint incomes in the year of the death unless either the joint election had been withdrawn by either spouse or civil partner before the death or by the surviving spouse or civil partner before the end of the tax year or the spouses or civil partners had ceased to live together before the death. Conversely, if the couple although living together, had been assessable as single persons for the preceding year (through electing out of joint assessment), similar assessments would be made for the year of death unless a new election for joint assessment is made before the end of that year. Although TCA 1997, s 1018 and TCA 1997, s 1031D dealing with the making and withdrawing of an election for joint assessment does not specifically say so, it would appear that any election open to a married individual or civil partner while alive may be exercised, before the end of the year, by his personal representatives to affect the assessment of the deceased person for the tax year in which he died.

In order to agree a deceased person's income tax position, the personal representatives should as a first step complete an income tax return in respect of the deceased's income for the period from the previous 1 January to the date of death. If the deceased had carried on a trade or profession, the personal representatives must see that proper accounts of the business are prepared up to the date of the death and submitted to the inspector with computations of the Sch D Case I or II profits and of capital allowances, balancing charges, etc. Some of the factors relevant to the taxation of both the deceased and the personal representatives in respect of a trade or profession are dealt with separately in **15.108**.

In computing the deceased person's total income for the tax year in which he dies, any relevant cessation rules under which the income falls must be applied; this is generally only relevant for income taxable under Sch D Cases I and II, (see **4.206**).

In a case where the deceased had traded, or carried on a profession, in partnership, the personal representatives should seek from the precedent acting partner details of the deceased's share of the firm's taxable profits (or losses) and capital allowances for all relevant periods of account to enable the taxable profits (or losses) of the deceased's 'several' trade as a partner be determined up to the date of death (see **4.503**). Since a partner's several trade ceases on his death, the income tax assessment for the year of death is based on his actual profits to the date of death; the assessment on the penultimate year should be reviewed and, if necessary, increased to charge the actual profits of the several trade for that year (if higher).

The personal representatives of a deceased person who has incurred tax losses in a trade or profession prior to the date of death should consider how best to obtain relief for those losses for the benefit of the estate. Tax losses incurred prior to the death cannot be carried forward for set off against subsequent profits of a trade or profession that continues to be carried on after the death by the personal representatives or by another person succeeding to the trade. Capital allowances and losses carried forward from earlier years should be set off, if possible, against any subsequent taxable profits made by the deceased from his trade up to the date of his death. For a trading loss incurred in the year of death, or in the preceding tax year, a claim under TCA 1997, s 381 against the deceased's total income may be available assuming the anti-avoidance provisions introduced by Finance Act 2014 do not apply (see **4.404**). Alternatively, for a trading loss incurred in the 12 months prior to the death, it may be appropriate to make a terminal loss claim under TCA 1997, s 385 (see **4.410**).

If the deceased person had carried on the trade of farming similar considerations arise regarding claims for losses, unused capital allowances, etc, but this is subject to any of the special rules which might apply to restrict relief for farming losses, etc.

The personal representatives should also look into the question as to whether the deceased might have had unused losses and/or capital allowances carried forward under Sch D Case V (rental income), Sch D Case IV (miscellaneous activities) or Sch D Case III (foreign trade, foreign rental, etc); any such losses, etc carried forward are only available for set off against income of the same class in any later tax year up to the date of the death, but not after it.

15.104 Assessments on income of deceased person

TCA 1997, s 1047 provides the statutory authority which makes the personal representatives liable for the income tax already charged on the income of a deceased person up to the date of his death. TCA 1997, s 1048(1) provides that the personal representatives may be assessed in respect of any income which arose or accrued to the deceased before his death, whether by way of an assessment or an amended assessment. The assessment may be made on the income chargeable for any tax year for which the deceased could have been assessed if the assessment had in fact been made immediately before his death, or if he were still living at the time. This enables the inspector to assess the personal representatives on the deceased's income under the normal rules of TCA 1997, Pt 41A, Ch 5 (see **2.108**).

Where a sum is received after the date of death but forms part of the deceased's income prior to the date of death (ie the 'receipts' basis does not apply: see **15.102**), it would seem that this sum is also chargeable where it would have been included in an assessment if the deceased had still been living. Similar considerations apply to adjustments to a taxpayer's Sch D Case I/II profits arising as a result of a discontinuance (see TCA 1997, s 67, 69). Post-cessation receipts of a trade or profession which are not included in profits assessable up to the date of death are assessable on the personal representatives under a special regime (**5.605**). The position regarding Sch E emoluments which are received on death (as in *Allen v Trehearne* 22 TC 15), or which are received after the date of death is less clear. Where such receipts can be related back to the period before death under the 'earnings basis' (see **10.102**), it seems that they should be treated as 'arising' before the date of death. In the case of receipts which cannot be so related back, it is not clear whether the personal representatives can be assessed thereon (see **15.105**).

If the personal representatives neglect or refuse to pay any tax, they may be proceeded against in the same way as any other person. In view of the presumption of innocence until proof of guilt, the imposition of a penalty which is criminal in nature on a dead person has been held to be incompatible with the European Convention on Human Rights which has been incorporated into Irish Law (*AP, MP and TP v Switzerland* (71/1996/690/8802): see **1.412**. This principle has been enshrined in TCA 1997, s 1077D, with effect from 26 December 2008, which provides that penalties may only be recovered from a deceased person's estate where, *during their lifetime*, (a) the person (or a person acting on their behalf) either agreed in writing to pay the penalty, or agreed in writing with an opinion or amended opinion of a Revenue officer that he was liable to a penalty, or (b) a relevant court has determined that the person was liable to a penalty. In all other cases, the institution of any proceedings against the personal representatives is subject to the same time limits as apply to assessments of tax in relation to pre-death income (see above).

The personal representatives are entitled to deduct all payments made by them in respect of the deceased's income tax liabilities (including interest and penalties) out of the assets and effects of the estate. As a matter of general law, the personal representatives are not liable for the taxes and other debts of the deceased to the extent that the assets of the estate are insufficient to meet them.

TCA 1997, s 1048(2) imposes time limits within which assessments can be made on the income of a deceased person, even under the rules of TCA 1997, s 959AA. If the grant of probate or letters of administration was made in the same tax year as that in which the death occurred, the basic rule is that the assessment must be made no later than three years after the end of that year. If the grant was not made in the year of death, the basic time limit is two years after the end of the year in which it was made. The basic time limit for the assessment under either of these rules is, however, extended if the personal representatives lodge either an additional affidavit required by the CATCA 2003, s 48 or lodge a corrective affidavit where required to do so by the Revenue Commissioners. In any such case, the assessment or amended assessment on the deceased's income may be made up to, but no later than, two years after the end of the tax year in which the additional or corrective affidavit was lodged. If a personal representative liable to deliver an additional affidavit under CATCA 2003, s 48 does not in fact deliver it after being required to do so by the Revenue Commissioners, the time limit for the assessment remains open.

Example 15.104.1

Mrs A Morte, a widow, dies on 1 October 2014; probate is obtained on 2 March 2015. She had prior to her death made full income tax returns for all years since her husband's death in 2004. She always made returns prior to the return filing date. In looking back over his files in June 2015 when considering the assessments to be made on her executors in respect of her pre-death income, the inspector discovered that Mrs Morte had been under-assessed to income tax for each of the years 2007 and 2009.

The inspector accepts that the under-assessment was due solely to an error regarding the law on the part of the Revenue. Accordingly, TCA 1997, s 959AA(1) would only have permitted an amended assessment to be raised within four years following the end of the year in which the return is delivered (see **2.108**). Thus, in the case of income assessable for 2007 (return was delivered in October 2008, ie in 2008; thus no amended assessment could have issued after 31 December 2012, while in the case of income assessable for 2009 (return delivered in October 2010, ie 2010) no assessment could have been issued after 31 December 2014. Since the amended assessment for 2009 could have been raised immediately before Mrs Morte's death, the inspector may raise that assessment at any time up to 31 December 2017 (two years after the end of the year of assessment in which probate was obtained).

Example 15.104.2

Take the facts of **Example 15.104.1** but assume that the estate is a complicated one and the two additional affidavits are lodged for capital acquisitions tax purposes on 20 June 2016 and 8 August 2017.

If no additional affidavits had been required, the inspector would have had until 31 December 2017 to make an assessment on Mrs Morte's income for 2009. However, since the last additional affidavit was lodged in the tax year 2017, the inspector has until 31 December 2019 to make any necessary assessment.

The time limits set down by TCA 1997, s 1048 apply even in cases of fraud or neglect, notwithstanding that TCA 1997, s 959AD provides that in such cases an assessment may be raised at any time. Irrespective of whether the liability arises under the self-assessment regime or not, TCA 1997, s 1048 is the only authority for making an assessment on the personal representatives and therefore any assessment must comply with the conditions laid down therein (as conceded in *Harrison v Willis* (43 TC 61)). TCA 1997, s 959AA expressly declares that the provisions in that section do not affect the operation of s 1048.

Example 15.104.3

Charlie Chancer died on 5 June 2014 and probate was extracted in October 2014. Charlie had substantial under-declared trading income in the tax years 1986–87 to 1988–89 inclusive, the proceeds of which he placed in a single premium life assurance policy in 1990. By the time Charlie died, the policy had been cashed in and the money spent or disbursed to various members of Charlie's family. The undeclared income comes to the attention of the Revenue Commissioners on 10 January 2018. There is nothing disclosed which would require an additional affidavit under Capital Acquisitions Tax Consolidation Act 2003, s 48 (on which see: O'Hara: 'Bogus Non-Resident Offshore Accounts of Deceased Taxpayers' 2004 ITR 398). The Revenue could have raised amended assessments on Charlie for 1986–87 to 1988–89 if he had still been alive; however, they are unable to raise those assessments on his personal representatives since the three-year time limit set by TCA 1997, s 1048 has elapsed and as there was no error or omission in the original affidavit filed there is no possibility of the time limits being extended under TCA 1997, s 1048(2).

If the undeclared income had come to the attention of the Revenue Commissioners on 10 January 2016 an assessment could be made on the personal representatives before 31 December 2016 in respect of the undeclared income of the tax years 1986–87 and 1988–89 under TCA 1997, s 959AD.

If on the other hand Charlie held a significant undeclared offshore bank account which was in existence when he died and was not included in the original affidavit, Revenue could request an additional affidavit be lodged under CATCA 2003, s 48 and could raise an assessment for underpaid income tax for up to two years after the end of the year of assessment in which the additional affidavit is lodged.

15.105 Taxation of executors etc in administration period

The personal representatives of a deceased person are taxable in their representative capacity on the Sch D income from his estate during the period of their administration as the persons in receipt and control of the estate income under TCA 1997, s 52 (as confirmed in *Moloney v Allied Irish Banks* III ITR 477). Similar considerations apply to Sch F (TCA 1997, ss 20, 136). The position on Sch E emoluments which arise on death (as in *Allen v Trehearne* 22 TC 15) or which arise after the date of death and which cannot be related back to the period prior to the date of death under the earnings basis (see **15.102**), is obscure. Such earnings do not appear to be caught by TCA 1997, s 1048 since the profits or gains cannot be said to have accrued *before* the death of the taxpayer. The personal representatives should not be liable under TCA 1997, s 112, which imposes liability under Sch E upon the person 'having or exercising' the relevant employment.

The estate income is assessable to income tax on the executor or administrator separately from, and without any reference to, any income in respect of which he may be taxable in his own personal capacity. Assessments on personal representatives are always made at the standard rate of income tax on the income chargeable, without any deduction for personal allowances or other reliefs from income tax that are expressed as being available only to individuals. The assessments are made under the normal Schedules and Cases with deductions available, to the extent relevant to the personal representatives, from the total assessable income for such items as excess capital allowances on industrial buildings claimed under TCA 1997, s 305(1).

The personal representatives are taxable for each year of assessment, or part of a year, that falls within the administration period (see **15.106**). In the case of income assessable under any of Sch D Case I and II the relevant basis of assessment rules must be applied. The personal representatives are regarded as having a commencement of the source on the date of death (at the earliest) and as having a cessation of the source on the last day of the administration period (at the latest).

The personal representatives may in appropriate circumstances arrange for some or all of the income to which a beneficiary is entitled to be paid directly to him before the end of the administration period. Alternatively, they may assent to the transfer of an income producing asset to a beneficiary entitled without necessarily waiting to complete their administration. If this is properly done so that the personal representatives do not in fact receive the income in question, then that income is excluded from any assessments on the personal representatives and becomes taxable directly in the hands of the beneficiary. For the circumstances in which a residuary beneficiary with an absolute interest in an estate may be assessed directly from the date of death onwards, see **15.204**.

The discussion so far has assumed that the personal representatives of the deceased person are resident in the State throughout the administration period. It is the residence of the executor or administrator that determines the extent of his liability to Irish income tax on the income from the estate. If he is resident in the State, the worldwide income of the estate is within the charge to income tax (unless any specific exemption applies); if he is not resident for any tax year, only the Irish source income of the estate may be assessed for that year. The residence of the deceased person before his death does not affect the liability of his personal representatives to income tax.

The residence of the executors was one of the factors in the UK case of *Wood v Owen* 23 TC 541 under comparable law. In that case the appellant was the executor of an individual who before his death had been resident in Guernsey and not in the United Kingdom. During his lifetime the deceased had been entitled as life tenant to certain income from the trustees of Guernsey settlements. After the life tenant's death, his executor, who was resident in the United Kingdom, received from the Guernsey trustees the apportioned part of the settlement income due to the life tenant to the date of his death. It was held that the settlement income, to the extent received by the executor, was chargeable to UK income tax on him as personal representative because of his UK residence. The fact that the deceased had in his lifetime been exempted from UK income tax due to his Guernsey residence did not alter the executor's position.

15.106 Meaning of administration period

The administration period is the period commencing on the date of the deceased person's death and ending when the residue of the estate has been ascertained, ie when the personal representatives have completed the administration of the estate and have thereby discharged their function. The question of when the administration has been completed is one to be determined on the facts of each particular case. In general, the residue is not ascertained until all the debts of the deceased, including those for outstanding taxes of all kinds, have been quantified, agreed and in most cases discharged. All non-residuary legacies (ie bequests of personal property) and devises (bequests of real property) must have been paid or otherwise implemented. If any annuity is payable to any beneficiary under the will, specific sums or investments must have been appropriated to provide for the annuity. It is also necessary for the personal representatives to agree the income tax (and capital gains tax) liabilities in respect of income received (or chargeable gains realised) by them in the course of their administration.

In *Daw v IRC* 14 TC 58, a will provided that the residue of an estate was to be divided when the youngest son of the deceased became 25 years old, and until then the executors were to apply the surplus income to reduce mortgages on certain properties. The executors did not, however, divide the property and continued to apply the surplus income to reduce mortgages for a number of years after the youngest son's 25th birthday. It was held that so long as the mortgage debts remained unpaid the executors were entitled to retain any assets coming into their hands, that the beneficiary did not enforce conveyance to himself of his share of the residue, and that in consequence the administration had not been completed.

In a not dissimilar case, *IRC v Sir Aubrey Smith* 15 TC 661, where the respondent was entitled to a share in a residuary estate against which mortgages were still outstanding, it was held that the decision in *Daw v IRC* did not establish any rule of law precluding the Commissioners from finding that the estate had been administered, and that the question of ascertainment of the residue was a question of fact which the Commissioner should determine. The Special Commissioners had earlier considered they were bound by the *Daw* decision and did not therefore make any determination on the facts. The Court of Appeal did not decide whether or not the residue had been ascertained, but remitted the case to the Commissioners for them to come to their conclusion on the question of fact.

In a large or involved estate, the administration period during which the personal representatives continue to function as such may last for a number of years. One particular reason for this lies in the complications of the tax system generally, especially in the areas of capital gains tax and capital acquisitions tax where difficult issues can take years to resolve. Clearly, if any income tax, capital gains tax or capital acquisitions tax (eg on lifetime gifts) liability of the deceased person has not been finally agreed, or if there is an outstanding tax issue affecting the liability of the personal representatives, the residue cannot normally be ascertained until such matters have been dealt with.

When the personal representatives assent to the passing of the residuary estate to the residuary beneficiaries or, where there is a will trust, to the trustees, the administration is completed and the administration period ends. While the personal representatives' assent may take the form of some express action on their part, it has been established in various cases that the assent of the executor to the residue's passing may be inferred where there is clearly nothing more to be done by way of administration. The fact that the property of the estate may remain in the possession of the executor after this point has been reached does not put back the end of the administration period until possession is actually transferred. In his judgment in the *Sir Aubrey Smith* case (see above) Lawrence LJ said:

> The property which on the death of the testator vests in the *executor* does not remain vested in him for ever. So soon as he assents to the dispositions of the will becoming operative and the trusts taking effect, the estate vested in him as executor is divested and vests under the dispositions of the will in the *trustees* of the will. The assent of an executor may be given informally and may be inferred from his conduct. In my opinion, it is a pure question of fact whether such an assent has been given or not, depending on the particular circumstances of

each case, and no other case with different facts can form any guide for the determination of the question.

The fact that a will may appoint the same person(s) to be both executor(s) for the purpose of administering the estate and trustee(s) to hold the residuary estate (when it is ascertained) on trusts provided for in the will does not alter the principle, so clearly enunciated by Lawrence LJ, that the function of the executor must at some time come to an end so that the job of the trustee can begin. When this happens, as already indicated, any remaining source(s) of income of the executor ceases and the trustees (even if the same persons) taking over the same income have a commencement of source(s).

15.107 Relief for interest paid by executors

The executor (or administrator) of a deceased person may take over, among the liabilities of the estate, loans or other interest bearing debts or may himself obtain loans in the course of his administration. The various rules under which relief for interest paid may be obtained have been summarised in **3.201** and have been discussed in more detail in **3.202–3.210**, mainly in the context of individuals. Since a person acting in the capacity of executor is not treated as an individual for tax purposes, it may be useful to discuss how and to what extent an executor may obtain relief for interest paid by him against the income of the estate assessable on him.

First, an executor is entitled in the same way as an individual or any other person to deduct all interest paid by him for the purpose of any trade or profession under the ordinary rules of Sch D Case I or II, should he continue to carry on the deceased person's trade or profession after the death (see **15.108**). No Sch D Case I or II interest deduction is, however, available for interest paid if the executor does not continue the trade or profession or for interest payable for any period after the executor has ceased to trade. Should the executor be assessable under Sch D Case IV on post cessation receipts arising from the trade or profession, he should be able to claim under TCA 1997, s 91(4) to deduct from the Sch D Case IV assessment any interest paid which, if there had been no cessation, would have been deductible as a trade expense.

Secondly, the executor is entitled to the same deduction as any other person under Sch D Case V for interest paid on money borrowed for the purchase, improvement, repair, etc of rented premises. He is entitled to a similar deduction under Sch D Case III for interest on borrowings for foreign rented premises. In each of these instances, the deduction is only available against the rental income assessable under the relevant Case. The deduction is available whether the loan on which the interest is paid was obtained by the deceased before his death or was taken out by the executor in the course of the administration.

Thirdly, an executor may be able to claim a tax deduction or equivalent relief at source for interest paid on a qualifying residence loan in the circumstances referred to in TCA 1997, s 244 (subject to the maximum allowable amount and to the formula for determining the relievable amount applicable to a single person). The extent to which an executor is entitled to relief is in fact very limited.

The definition of a 'qualifying loan' (TCA 1997, s 244(1)), as it applies in relation to an individual paying interest, was given in **3.202** and continues to permit an executor to obtain relief for interest paid by him on a loan that was applied solely to meet the cost of the purchase, repair, development or improvement of a residential premises situated in an EEA State as of 1 January 2015 (previously the State, Northern Ireland or Great Britain), but only if certain conditions are met.

Two types of case have to be considered. The first one is where the residential premises as previously defined in **3.202** (referred to here for simplicity as 'the house') were used by the deceased as his sole or main residence at the date of his death. In this first type of case, any interest paid by the executor on any loan applied for the purchase, etc of the house (or in paying off another loan used for such a purpose) is eligible for relief, if:

(a) on the assumption that the deceased had not died and had been the borrower, he would have been eligible for relief in respect of the interest; and
(b) at the time the interest was paid by the executor, the house in question was used as the sole main residence of either the deceased's widow or widower or any dependent relative (see **3.202**) of the deceased (TCA 1997, s 245(6)).

The second type of case is where the house on which the loan proceeds have been applied is not one that was used as the sole or main residence of the deceased at the date of his death. This could, for example, be a house used at that date by the former or separated spouse or by a dependent relative of the deceased. It could also be a new house purchased by the executor to replace the deceased's former residence for the use of the widow or widower, or it could be a new house purchased for a former spouse or a dependent relative of the deceased. It is to be assumed that any such new house is purchased by the executor in implementing the terms of the will.

In this second type of case, the interest paid by the executor is eligible for relief if, on the assumption that the deceased had not died and had been the borrower, the deceased would have been eligible for relief. This means that the executor is only entitled to the relief if the house is occupied as the sole or main residence of either the deceased's widow or widower, a former or separated spouse of the deceased, or a dependent relative of the deceased. As in the case of a loan in respect of the deceased's sole or main residence at his death, 'dependent relative' is limited by the narrow definition given in **3.202** and it is also necessary that the house be provided rent free and without any other consideration (TCA 1997, s 245(6)).

In both situations, it is to be noted that the tests for eligibility for interest relief are applied by reference to the house in connection with which the loan is obtained and to the person using it as a residence. The relief may be claimed by the executor, once the relevant tests are satisfied, whether the qualifying loan on which the interest is paid is one taken over by the executor on the date of death or is a new loan obtained by him for a qualifying purpose.

15.108 Effect of death on trade; post cessation receipts etc

When an individual who has carried on a trade (including the trade of farming) or a profession dies, a number of points arise for consideration in connection with the deceased's taxation position and with that of the personal representatives and/or the beneficiaries of his estate. These concern the computation of the profits (or loss) of the trade or profession up to the date of death, the treatment of capital allowances in that connection, whether the trade or profession may be continued after the death and the question of possible post cessation receipts. For simplicity, the discussion which follows refers only to a trade, but it could be taken as applying equally to a profession, unless the text states otherwise on any particular point.

Cessation of trade by deceased

Except only for the concessional treatment given in certain circumstances to a succession by a widow or widower (see below), the death of a trader always involves a cessation of his trade for tax purposes, even if his executor (or administrator) or a beneficiary of his estate in fact continues the trade. The accounts of the business should be made up for the period from the last accounting date before the trader died to the date of death. The same accounting principles as previously applied should continue to be used in preparing these accounts. These accounts then form the basis of the Sch D Case I or Case II computation for the deceased's final period of accounts to the date of death.

The closing trading stock of the business at the date of death should be valued in the ordinary way at the lower of cost or net realisable value (see **5.603**). The special stock valuation rules of TCA 1997, s 89 normally applicable on a cessation of trade are specifically excluded in the case of the trade of a sole trader that ceases on his death. Where it was customary to prepare accounts before the death on a full earnings basis (as distinct from an acceptable conventional basis – see **5.502**), the normal accounting accruals should be made for all trading receipts and expenses still receivable or payable on the date of death in arriving at the accounting profit (or loss) for the final period of account. If a conventional basis of accounting had previously been used, the same basis should be applied for the final period.

Capital allowances; balancing charges

In addition to the requirement to apply the Sch D Case I cessation rules to the adjusted trading profits to determine the amount assessable for the final tax year to the date of death, and for the two preceding tax years, the capital allowance computations for the years up to the date of death must be adjusted as for any other cessation of trade. Further, the relevant balancing allowance or balancing charge must be computed on any machinery or plant in use for the trade at the date of death if capital allowances were previously obtained on that plant.

If the relevant plant, etc is sold at or about the time of the death, or within a reasonable time after it, these balancing adjustments should be calculated by reference to the actual proceeds realised (assuming the sale was at market value or higher). Should the plant, etc be retained by the executors, or be used by a beneficiary of the estate or by any other person succeeding to the trade, the market value of the plant at the date of death should be used in the computation. The market value should also be used if the plant is sold at less than market value (TCA 1997, s 289).

For the purposes of industrial buildings allowances the beneficiary steps into the shoes of the deceased as the beneficiary has acquired a relevant interest in the building for capital allowances purposes (see **6.409**).

The widow(er)'s concession

The concession under which the Revenue may permit a widow/widower who succeeds absolutely on his spouse's death to his trade to elect to be assessed on a continuing trade business has been discussed in **4.207**. If the surviving spouse makes this election, it means that the Sch D Case I cessation rules are not applied in assessing the profits of the trade on the deceased spouse's death, but the assessments continue to be made on a preceding year basis. It also avoids any revision of the capital allowance computations and no balancing allowance or charge arises due to the death. The capital allowances for the tax year in which the death occurs are computed in the ordinary way by reference to the normal basis period for that year (usually the accounting year ended in the previous tax year). These capital allowances (and any balancing charges) are then apportioned on a time basis between the deceased and the widow(er) by reference to the date of death in the same way as the Sch D Case I profits.

Trading by personal representatives

The question of whether the executor (or administrator) continues to carry on the trade or profession of the deceased person after his death is one to be determined on the facts of the particular case. Frequently, the executor does no more than realise the assets and pay off the liabilities of the business. The realisation of assets and paying of liabilities, as distinct from continuing to trade, does not expose him to income tax under Sch D Case I or Case II on any profits he may make on the disposal of the assets (see the full discussion at **4.104**). The executor may, however, be liable to income tax under Sch D Case IV on post cessation receipts in accordance with the rules of TCA 1997, s 91 (see below).

Post cessation receipts

Unless the executor continues to carry on the deceased's trade or profession so as to be assessable under Sch D Case I or Case II on any profits after the death, he is taxable under Sch D Case IV to the extent that he receives during the administration period any post cessation receipts within the rules of TCA 1997, s 91 (see **5.605**). This is more likely to happen if the deceased had accounted for profits before his death on a conventional basis than if accounts had been prepared on a full accruals basis, but even in the latter case a Sch D Case IV assessment may be made on the executor if any trading receipts that accrued prior to the death, but which were not taken into the accounts to the date of death, are received by the executor.

In the event that the executor is assessable on any post cessation receipts, he should see if the deceased had any unused trading losses or capital allowances carried forward from previous years or from the year of the death. If there is no more advantageous way of using those losses or capital allowances (eg by a TCA 1997, s 381 claim against the deceased's total income of the tax year before the death), the executor can offset them against the assessment on the post cessation receipts.

It is also possible that the executor may incur expenses in collecting outstanding receipts due to the estate in respect of the trade. For example, he may retain some of the trader's staff to help him collect the monies due and, perhaps, to complete certain contracts of the business to enable it to be wound up more advantageously. If and to the extent that any such expenses would have been deductible in computing the trading profits if the trade had not ceased, then the executor should be able to deduct them from the post cessation receipts under TCA 1997, s 91(4).

The executor is entitled to elect under TCA 1997, s 95 to have the post cessation receipts taxed as if they were received on the day trading ceased, ie on the date of death, instead of in the tax year in which actually received (see **5.605**). In deciding whether or not to make this election, the executor should have regard to the deceased's marginal rate of income tax for the year of his death, whether he had any unused allowances or other deductions for that year, and any other relevant factors affecting the deceased's liability up to the date of his death. If, after taking all the relevant factors into consideration, it appears more advantageous to have the receipts taxed as part of the deceased's income, rather than that of the executor, then the election should be made.

15.2 Beneficiaries of Deceased Person's Estate

15.201 Introduction

The income received by the personal representatives during the administration period is distributable to the beneficiaries of the estate in accordance with their respective entitlements under the will or, in an intestate estate, under the rules of intestacy. Any expenses paid by the executor or administrator, in so far as properly chargeable against income, are borne by him out of the income subject to tax in his hands, so that only the net income after these expenses is distributable between the beneficiaries. Except for any income which is assessed directly on any beneficiary, any distribution of income during or at the end of the administration period reaches the beneficiary concerned as taxed income, ie as income which has suffered income tax at source in the hands of the executor at the standard rate.

The beneficiaries of a deceased person's estate may be divided into two main classes – non-residuary and residuary beneficiaries. Non-residuary beneficiaries may be subdivided into pecuniary legatees, specific legatees and annuitants. A residuary beneficiary may be entitled either to an absolute or a limited interest in the whole of the residuary estate, or there may be two or more residuary beneficiaries with absolute or limited interests, depending on the terms of the will. The taxation of beneficiaries in respect of the income of the estate depends on their respective entitlements and on the nature of their interests in the estate.

15.202 Taxation of non-residuary beneficiaries

Pecuniary legatees

A beneficiary left a sum of money is not normally entitled to receive any interest on it and is not therefore liable to any income tax (although he may be liable to capital acquisitions tax on the legacy). He may be entitled to interest on the legacy if the will specifically provides that interest should be paid or if the legacy is not paid within one year from the date of death. If any such interest is paid to the pecuniary legatee out of the income of the estate, it is treated as a distribution of part of that income and reaches him as taxed income, thus reducing the estate income distributable to the other beneficiaries.

Specific legatees

A specific legatee is one to whom a specific item of property has been left by the will. Unless the will provides otherwise, a specific legatee is entitled to the income (if any) arising from that property from the date of death onwards. Although the income may not be paid over to him until later, it is treated retrospectively as always having been the specific legatee's income for the tax year(s) in which it arises (*IRC v Hawley* 13 TC 327). The income cannot, however, be assessed on him until his entitlement to it is established, but in these circumstances it should then be related back to the relevant tax year(s). Unless the income from the specific property is mandated over to him any earlier, the specific legatee usually receives this income in one sum at the time the executor assents to the transfer of the specific property to him. To the extent that the income on his specific legacy is first received by the personal representatives, it is chargeable to income tax on them so that – when duly distributed to the specific legatee – he receives it as taxed income.

If the specific legacy is a non-income producing item (eg a painting), or if it is an item which does not yield any income between the date of death and the date of assent by the executor, the legatee is not usually entitled to any of the other income of the estate. Clearly, in such a case, no question of income tax liability on the specific legatee in respect of his legacy arises.

The position in *IRC v Hawley* may be distinguished from that in *Dewar v IRC* 19 TC 561, where no moneys had been set aside to meet a pecuniary legacy (so that no interest actually arose thereon in the period between death and the payment of the legacy). It was held that the taxpayer, although entitled to receive interest on his legacy could not be taxed until and unless he actually received it. In other words, this was a case where the income would have arisen only on a payment being actually made by the personal representatives. It seems that if the interest had been paid to the taxpayer it would all have been fully taxable in the year of receipt (see the discussion in **8.102**).

Annuitants

A beneficiary may be left an annuity by the will either for his life or for a specific number of years, although the former is the more common. Unless the will provides otherwise, the annuity is payable from the date of death onwards. An annuity under a will is payable net of income tax at the standard rate. In order that the executor may complete his administration, it is usual for him to appropriate a capital sum or a specific investment out of the residuary estate so that the income from it will be sufficient to pay the annuity. Alternatively, the executor may purchase the annuity from a life assurance company. It is to be noted that such a purchased annuity, whether or not made as the result of a direction in the will to purchase it, does not qualify for the favourable tax treatment given to purchased life annuities by TCA 1997, s 788 (see **16.401**).

If there is a definite direction in the will to purchase an annuity for a beneficiary who is of full age and contractual capacity, the beneficiary has the right to require the capital sum that would be needed to purchase the annuity to be paid to him instead. This follows from a principle of trust law established in the case *of Saunders v Vautier* [1841] Cr & Ph 240, 10 LJ Ch 354. In such a case, the beneficiary receives a capital sum which he may, although he is not bound to, use to purchase a life annuity for himself so that he may receive the capital element of the annuity without any liability to income tax under TCA 1997, s 788. The annuitant does not have this right if the will simply provides for him to be paid an annuity without making such a specific direction to purchase one.

The beneficiary to whom an annuity is payable under the will, or for whom an annuity is actually purchased, whether or not under a direction in the will, must include the full gross amount of the annuity in his total income each year, but is entitled to credit any income tax deducted by the executors or trustees of the will against his total income tax liability. This is the case whether or not the full annuity is paid out of income of the estate. Since the annuity has the character of income in the hands of the annuitant, it does not matter that the executor or trustee may have had to use capital if the estate income was not sufficient to pay the annuity (*Brodie's Will Trustees v IRC* – see **15.306**).

One further point should be mentioned with regard to annuities. The annuitant is entitled to require the executors to appropriate a capital sum to secure his annuity. If the capital of the estate is not large enough to provide the necessary capital sum, the annuitant is, as a matter of general law regarding the administration of estates, entitled to a capital sum out of the residue of the estate. This capital sum is taken as the actuarial valuation of the annuity at the date of death abated with the other legacies provided for in the will. For example, if the actuarial value of the annuity is €60,000, the other legacies €10,000 and the available capital of the estate €56,000, then the annuitant would be entitled to a capital sum of €48,000, ie 6/7ths of €56,000.

In such a case, the intended annuitant receives his benefit fully in the form of capital without any liability to income tax (although he may be liable to capital acquisitions tax on his inheritance). This was held to be the position in *IRC v Castlemaine* 25 TC 408. Even though the executors had made payments on account of the annuity before it was appreciated that the capital of the estate was insufficient, those payments were held to have been made, in effect, as instalments of the capital sum and were not liable to income tax in the hands of the beneficiary.

15.203 Residuary beneficiaries: general

Although the Succession Act 1965, s 10(3) states that the personal representatives hold the deceased's estate 'as trustees' for the beneficiaries, this simply denotes that they are acting in a fiduciary capacity; the residuary beneficiaries do not become entitled to the assets of the estate until it is fully administered (see Delany, *Equity and the Law of Trusts in Ireland* (5th edition, Round Hall, 2011)).

TCA 1997, ss 799–804 deals with the liability to income tax of the residuary beneficiaries on their shares of the residuary income of a deceased person's estate. The residuary income is, in effect, the total income of the estate received by the personal representatives during the administration period, but reduced by any of that income paid to non-residuary beneficiaries and by certain other annual payments and expenses properly chargeable to income. The treatment of residuary income payable to a residuary beneficiary depends on whether he has an absolute or a limited interest in the residue. There is also a distinction made between the way in which the residuary income of a foreign estate is taxed compared with an Irish estate. The terms 'absolute interest', 'limited interest', 'Irish estate' and 'foreign estate', as well as certain other general principles, are now explained before going on to deal with the rest of this topic.

Absolute interest in residue

A beneficiary has an absolute interest in the residue of an estate in the course of administration, or in a part of the residue, if the *capital* of the residue or of that part of it would, if the residue had been ascertained, be properly payable to him or to another person on his behalf or for his benefit (TCA 1997, s 799(2)(a)). For example, if Mr X died on 21 May 2015 leaving a will under which a one half share of his residuary estate is to be payable to his son, John. As soon as the residue is ascertained, John is treated as having an absolute interest in one half of the residue with effect from 21 May 2015 (the testator's date of death) even if the residue is not actually ascertained until several years later. The fact that John may be a minor so that his share of the capital cannot be paid over to him until he becomes of age does not affect the matter. On the other hand, if Mr X's will had first left his widow a life interest in the residuary estate, John's interest would only be a reversionary one, ie he would not be entitled to have his share of the capital paid to him until his mother dies; he would not, therefore, have an absolute interest in the residue during her lifetime.

Limited interest in residue

A beneficiary is regarded as having a limited interest in the residue of an estate or in a part of the residue, during any period (other than one during which he has an absolute interest in that residue or in that part of it), if the *income* of the residue or of that part of it would, if the residue had been ascertained at the commencement of that period, be properly payable to him or to another person on his behalf or for his benefit (TCA 1997, s 799(2)(b)). For example, if Mrs Y died on 29 July 2014 leaving a will under which her widower is entitled to receive the income, but not the capital, from the residuary estate during his life-time (ie as a life tenant), and if Mr Y himself dies on 18 June 2015, then he is treated as having a life interest in the residue in each of the periods 29 July 2014 to 31 December 2014 (2014 tax year), 1 January 2015 to 18 June 2015 (2015 tax year) even though the residue of Mrs Y's estate may not be ascertained until, say, 14 December 2015.

Irish estate

A deceased person's estate is an Irish estate in any year of assessment, if for that year the income of the estate consists entirely of income which has borne Irish income tax by deduction or in respect of which the personal representatives are directly assessable to Irish income tax. This is subject to the exception that, if any part of the income of the estate is income in respect of which the personal representatives are entitled to claim exemption from Irish income tax by reference to the fact that they are neither resident nor ordinarily resident in the State, then the estate is not an Irish estate (TCA 1997, s 799(1)(a)).

In effect, this means that an estate is an Irish estate if the executor or administrator is resident in the State so as to be taxable on the worldwide income of the estate. It also means that there may be an Irish estate where the executor or administrator is not resident in the State, but only if the income of the estate for the relevant tax year consists *solely* of Irish source income in respect of which the non-resident personal representative is chargeable to Irish income tax. If a non-resident personal representative has any non-Irish source income, this prevents the estate from being treated as an Irish estate. The residence status of personal representatives and their eligibility for double tax relief is considered at **14.105**.

Foreign estate

A foreign estate is defined as any estate that is not an Irish estate. The usual example of a foreign estate is one where the deceased died abroad with personal representatives resident outside the State, but which has one or more resident residuary beneficiaries. However, as indicated in the last paragraph, if *all* the income of such an estate for any tax year is chargeable to Irish income tax, whether by deduction or by assessment, the estate is not a foreign estate for that year. If the personal representatives are not resident, it is only necessary for them to have one single item of non-Irish source income for the estate to be a foreign estate. If they are non-resident and entitled under a double taxation agreement to exemption from Irish income tax in respect of a particular type of income included in the estate income (eg Irish source interest income), this would generally seem sufficient to make the estate a foreign one for the purposes of TCA 1997, ss 799–804 (since the non-resident executor has at least some income not liable to Irish income tax) by reference to their non-resident status (the position where personal representatives who are resident under Irish tax law claim exemption by virtue of being regarded as residents of a treaty state for the purposes of the relevant treaty, may be different).

Personal representatives

The definition of a 'personal representative' for the purposes of TCA 1997, ss 799–804 is provided by TCA 1997, s 799(1)(a). He is defined as being the personal representative of a deceased person within the meaning of the Succession Act 1965, s 3(1), but also includes any person who takes possession of, or intermeddles with, the property of the deceased.

Sums paid etc

For the purpose of the rules for taxing residuary beneficiaries in respect of their shares of the residuary estate income of the administration period, any reference to 'sum paid' in TCA 1997, s 799–804 is taken as including a reference to the transfer of an asset or the release of a debt (due by a beneficiary to the estate); the amount of the sum paid in any such case is taken as the value of the asset transferred, or the amount of the debt released, at the date of the transfer or release. Similarly, a reference to 'sums payable' includes a reference to assets to which an obligation to transfer exists on the completion of the administration. The appropriation of an asset by a personal representative to himself, or the release of a debt due by him to the estate, ie where he is a beneficiary himself, is similarly treated (TCA 1997, s 799(1)(b)).

Although the transfer of an asset to a residuary beneficiary is treated as a sum paid to him, it does not follow that the entire sum paid is a payment of or on account of income. It may, of course, be a payment on account of the residuary estate capital to which he is entitled, alternatively, it may be a payment consisting partly of capital and partly of income. TCA 1997, s 801(3) provides that any sum paid to a beneficiary with an absolute interest in residue is to be treated as paid first on account of income, but only to the extent that the sum in question (or the aggregate of that sum and any other sums payable previously) does not exceed the beneficiary's share of the net residuary estate income up to (and including) the tax year in which that sum is paid (see also step 4 in **15.204**).

Example 15.203.1

Mr P Pacific died on 11 October 2014 leaving the residue of his estate absolutely to his daughter, Atlanta. Before the residue is ascertained, his executor is required by the will to provide for an annuity to his widow and to implement certain trusts regarding a specified part of his estate in favour of certain former employees. On 15 November 2015, the executor transfers 1,000 shares in Baltic Ocean Research Ltd to Atlanta on account of her share in the residuary estate. On 30 December 2015, the executor pays her €1,000 in cash as a distribution of net income of the estate. No other distributions of any kind are made to Atlanta between 11 October 2014 and 31 December 2015. The residuary income of the estate (all due to Atlanta) up to 31 December 2015 is determined ('step 2' in **15.204**) to be:

	€
Period 11/10/2014 to 31/12/2014	1,390
Year to 31/12/2015	7,630
	9,020

The 1,000 Baltic Ocean Research Ltd shares are valued at €10,000 at 15 November 2015. Applying 'step 4' described in **15.204**, the 'sums paid' to Atlanta up to 31 December 2015 are divided as between income and capital receipts as follows:

Sums paid in 2015:	€
Value of BOR Ltd shares (15/11/2015)	10,000
Cash paid (30/12/2015)	1,000
	11,000
Treated as:	
On account of residuary income up to 31/12/2015	9,020
(ie up to full amount of residuary income from 11/10/2014 to 31/12/2015)	
On account of residuary estate capital	1,980
(ie the balance of the sums paid)	-
	11,000

Charges on residue

These are defined as certain specified liabilities properly payable out of the estate of a deceased person, and interest payable in respect of those liabilities. The liabilities in question are funeral, testamentary and administrative expenses and debts; general legacies, demonstrative legacies and annuities; and any other liabilities of the personal representatives in that capacity (TCA 1997, s 799(1)(a)). However, any such liability (and any interest payable on it) that falls exclusively or primarily either upon any property that is the subject of a specific disposition (see definition below) or upon a legacy or annuity, is only a charge on residue to the extent that it falls ultimately upon the residue.

Specific disposition

This is defined as a specific devise (of real property) or bequest (of personal property) that, under the law of the State or that of any other country, has an effect similar to that of a specific devise or bequest (TCA 1997, s 799(1)(a)). However, if real estate is included in a residuary gift made by the will of a testator, it is treated as part of the residue of the estate and not as the subject of a specific disposition (TCA 1997, s 799(2)(c)).

For example, an estate may include land that is the subject of a mortgage as the security for a bank loan. If the will devises that land (subject to the mortgage) to Mr Red, but leaves the residue of the estate to Mr Black, there is a specific disposition of the land (subject to the mortgage). However, if the testator by his will leaves a share of the residue (including the land subject to the mortgage) to Mr Red, then this is a residuary gift and not a specific disposition. In the former case, neither the bank loan nor any interest payable on it is a charge on the residue of the testator's estate, unless and to the extent that the value of the land is insufficient to cover the loan so that part of the loan has to be met out of the residue. In the second case, the loan and the interest payable are charges on the residue.

Where it is necessary to recover excess tax relief given to a beneficiary during the administration period because his final share of taxed income from the estate works out at less than the share previously allocated to him (on which he may have claimed relief for tax suffered at source), this may be effected by means of an assessment under Sch D Case IV (TCA 1997, s 804(2)).

15.204 Absolute interests in residue

Before discussing the statutory procedure for taxing beneficiaries with absolute interests in residue, it should be noted that the inspector of taxes may, if the estate is a straightforward one, adopt a simpler approach and tax the residuary beneficiary directly on all the income of the estate received from the date of death onwards. In such a case, no assessments are made on the personal representatives and the beneficiary is taxable each year in the same way as if he had received the estate income from its various sources directly himself. This approach is usually only suitable if there are only one or two beneficiaries absolutely entitled to the residue and if there are no annuitants, life tenants or any other persons entitled to any of the income of the estate. It is not used if the residuary beneficiary is not resident in the State as the inspector could have difficulty in enforcing assessments against a non-resident.

The statutory procedure, which applies where the simpler approach is not suitable, is set out in TCA 1997, s 801, backed up by certain supplementary provisions in TCA 1997, s 802. In effect, a beneficiary with an absolute interest in the residue is taxable on his share of the residuary estate income for each of the tax years in the administration period by reference to the income arising from the date of death onwards, but no assessment can be made on him before the end of the administration period unless and to the extent that sums have been paid to him on account of his absolute interest. At the end of the administration period, he is assessable on any balance of his residuary estate income not previously assessed on him in the manner outlined below.

The TCA 1997, s 801 procedure may be broken down into a number of steps. In explaining these steps, an Irish estate is assumed. To the extent that there are differences for a foreign estate, these are dealt with separately in **15.207**. The steps are as follows:

Step 1

The 'aggregate income of the estate' for each year of assessment and for each broken part of a year of assessment in the administration period is determined.

The aggregate income of the estate for any tax year is defined by TCA 1997, s 799(1)(b) as the aggregate of the income from all sources of the personal representatives for that year. The income to be included from any source is the amount on which income tax falls to be borne for the year in question.

Example 15.204.1

Mrs EF died on 10/10/2012 and her executor is an Irish resident. The total income on which income tax is chargeable on the executors for the period of administration is as follows:

	€
2012 (part of year from 10/10/2012)	910
2013 (full year)	5,486
2014 (full year)	4,720
2015 (part of year to 8/4/2015)	1,120
	12,236

The aggregate income of the administration period is accordingly €12,236.

Step 2

The 'residuary income' of the estate for each tax year is ascertained by deducting from the aggregate income for each year the sum of the following amounts:

(a) any annual interest, annuity or other annual payment for that year, but only if it is a charge on residue;

(b) the amount of any payment made in the year in respect of expenses incurred by the personal representatives in the management of the assets of the estate, but only such expenses as, in the absence of any express provisions in the will to the contrary, would be properly chargeable to income; and

(c) any of the aggregate income for the year to which a legatee or devisee is entitled under a specific disposition (see **15.203**).

No deduction may be made under either (a) or (b) for any interest, annuity or other payment allowable in computing the aggregate income of the estate. In fact, there are no longer any categories of interest which qualify as deductions against the total income of personal representatives. Further, not all charges on residue are deductible, but only the annual interest, annuities, etc specifically mentioned in (a).

The amount paid in respect of expenses in (b) should be taken as the total of the expenses in question grossed up by the standard rate of income tax. This is because the personal representatives have to bear income tax at the standard rate on that part of the estate income which has to be used to meet the expenses.

Example 15.204.2

Continue on from the facts of **Example 15.204.1** and assume that Mrs EF's will provided for the payment of an annuity to her sister of an amount which after the deduction of income tax at the standard rate will leave €285. Assume that the actual expenses chargeable to income paid in each tax year were respectively €66, €121, €131 and €86.

The residuary income of the estate for each tax year of the administration period may be determined as follows:

Standard rate of tax	20%	20%	20%	20%
	2012	*2013*	*2014*	*2015*
	€	€	€	€
Aggregate income of estate	910	5,486	4,720	1,120
Deduct:				
Annuity to sister (gross)				
285 x 100/(100 – 20)	(81)[1]	(356)	(356)	(96)[2]
Expenses paid (grossed)				
Actual x 100/(100 – 20)	(82)	(151)	(164)	(108)
Residuary income of estate	747	4,979	4,200	916

Notes:

1. Annuity for 83 days from 10/10/2012 to 31/12/2012: €285 x 100/(100–20) = €356 x 83/365 = €81
2. Annuity for 98 days from 1/1/2015 to 8/4/2015: = €356 x 98/365 = €96.

Step 3

The residuary income of the estate for each tax year in the administration period is allocated to the one or more beneficiaries with absolute interests in the residue, ie to arrive at each beneficiary's residuary income for each such year.

If the residuary estate is left absolutely to one beneficiary only, the whole of the residuary estate income becomes that beneficiary's residuary income for each tax year in the administration period (assuming he holds that interest throughout the period). If two or more persons are left the residue absolutely between them in certain shares, then the residuary estate income is allocated between them in those shares. If a limited interest exists in any part of the residue in any tax year, the appropriate proportion of the residuary estate income cannot be allocated to an absolute beneficiary. If for example, Mr Q is left a life interest in one half of the residue of Mr X's estate, and if Mr P and Mrs T are left the other half absolutely between them in equal shares, then so long as Mr Q survives, the shares in the residuary estate income attributable to the absolute interests are:

Mr P's residuary income: 1/2 share of 1/2 share of residuary estate income, ie a 1/4 share.

Mrs T's residuary income: same as Mr P's, ie a 1/4 share.

Step 4

The income tax liability of any beneficiary to whom any sum or sums are paid during the administration period on account of his absolute interest in residue is *provisionally* determined for each relevant tax year on the following basis:

(a) each sum paid (including the value of any assets transferred, see **15.203**) is deemed to have been paid as net income, but only to the extent that the sum or the aggregate of such sums does not exceed that beneficiary's share of the net residuary estate income up to and including the tax year in which the sum is paid;

(b) that beneficiary's share of the net residuary estate income for any tax year is to be taken as his residuary income (per step 3) less income tax at the standard rate for the year in question;

(c) to the extent not exceeding that share, each sum paid as net income per (a) above is deemed to represent gross income equal to that sum grossed up at the standard rate of income tax for the tax year to which the sum is attributed; and

(d) any sum paid on account of the beneficiary's absolute interest, or the aggregate of such sums, is attributed to tax years as if applied in satisfying that beneficiary's residuary income in the order in which it accrued.

Example 15.204.3

Continue on from the facts of **Example 15.204.2** and assume that on 13 October 2014 Mrs EF's executor paid to the sole residuary legatee, Ms GF, the sum of €6,195 on account of her absolute interest in the residue and at the same time released Ms GF from a debt of €500 which she had borrowed from Mrs EF during her lifetime.

In calculating Ms GF's income tax position up to the end of the year 2014, the 'sums paid' on 13 October 2014, a total of €6,695, are deemed to be applied in satisfying her right to net residuary income as it has accrued up to 2014. In this case, her 100 per cent share of the gross residuary estate income is taken for each of the tax years 2012 to 2015 as set out on the bottom line of **Example 15.204.2**.

The sums paid of €6,695 are appropriated to the tax years, as follows:

	2012	*2013*	*2014*
	€	€	€
Ms GF's share of gross income	747	4,979	4,200
Less:			
Income tax at standard rate (20%)	149	996	840
Net residuary income	598	3,983	3,360
Sums paid appropriated (€6,695)[1]			
First	(598)		

Next		(3,983)	
Next			(2,114)
Net residuary income c/f[2]	Nil	Nil	1,246

Ms GF's total income for each tax year up to 2014 must be adjusted (with appropriate additional assessments) to include her provisional taxed income from Mrs EF's estate, as appropriated to the tax years, as follows:

	€
2012: €598 grossed up at 20%	747
2013: €3,983 grossed up at 20%	4,979
2014: €2,114 grossed up at 20%	2,642

Notes:

1. On the assumption that there were no previous sums paid to Ms GF since the date of death, the total sums paid on 13/10/2014 must first be attributed to the earlier years in the administration period to the full extent of the net residuary income for those years.
2. If any further sum was paid to Ms GF during a continued administration period, it would be appropriated first to satisfy the €1,246 net residuary income carried forward at 31/12/2014.

Step 5

On the completion of the administration, the computations of the income tax liabilities of each beneficiary with an absolute interest in the residue are revised so that he is taxed, for each tax year during which he had that interest, as if his residuary income for each such year had actually been paid to him as taxed income for that year. Any necessary adjustments of assessments, relief claims, etc may then be made to adjust for any differences in the final income tax payable by (or refundable to) the residuary beneficiary.

Example 15.204.4

Take the residuary income of the estate (all due to Ms GF) as finally determined in **Example 5.204.2** for each year in the administration period, as follows:

	2012	*2013*	*2014*	*2015*
	€	€	€	€
Her residuary income (final)	747	4,979	4,200	916
Compare with provisional assessments in **Example 15.204.3**	747	4,979	2,642	—
Additional income to be assessed on Ms GF	Nil	Nil	1,558	916

Additional assessments of €1,558 and €916 are required respectively for 2014 and 2015, but Ms GF is entitled to credit against her additional income tax payable on these assessments the income tax treated as paid by her executor on these amounts, ie a credit for 2014 of €312 (20% of €1,558) and a credit for 2015 of €183 (20% of €916).

TCA 1997, s 802(2)(b) requires the beneficiary's residuary income to be recomputed if, at the end of the administration period, it turns out that the aggregate of the benefits received in respect of his absolute interest is less than the aggregate of his residuary income for all relevant years. In such a case, the beneficiary's residuary income for each year is reduced in the same proportion as the deficiency bears to the aggregate of his residuary income for all years. This would require a further revision of the beneficiary's income tax assessments for the relevant tax years, ie step five is repeated with the reduced residuary income figures inserted. In this case, the normal four-year time limit for repayments of tax under TCA 1997, s 865(4) (see **2.104**) will not apply (TCA 1997, s 804(2)(a) as amended by FA 2008, Sch 6).

In fact, since a beneficiary with an absolute interest in residue is entitled to both capital and income, and as the term 'benefits received' is defined in TCA 1997, s 802(2)(a) as all sums paid before, or payable on, the completion of the administration in respect of his absolute interest, whether these sums are on account of capital or of income. It very seldom happens that the aggregate of the benefits received is less than the aggregate of the residuary income. It could happen in the case of an insolvent estate where the personal representatives have to use some or all of the income they may receive after the death to meet the liabilities of the deceased person which cannot be covered by his assets. In the UK case of *IRC v Mardon* [1956] 36 TC 565, a taxpayer tried to argue that 'benefits received' meant only payments to him of an income nature. This was rejected by the court which held that the phrase covered benefits of both capital and of income.

15.205 Limited interests in residue

The procedure for taxing a beneficiary with a limited interest in residue is set out in TCA 1997, s 800 and is, generally, somewhat simpler than that for a residuary beneficiary with an absolute interest. In the normal case, the person with the limited interest is a life tenant who is entitled to the residuary estate income, or to a proportionate share of that income, although it is possible for a testator to leave a person a limited interest in the residue for a defined period. A person may only be able to receive income from the residue if the executor should exercise a discretion in his favour under discretionary powers in the will; such a person does not have a limited interest in the estate. For the treatment of such a discretionary beneficiary, see **15.206**.

A beneficiary whose limited interest extends to the whole of the residue is entitled to receive the balance of the full income of the estate after deducting any of that income that is applied to pay any annuities provided for in the will, any interest payable on legacies, debts of the estate, etc and any expenses of the personal representatives that are properly chargeable against income in accordance with the terms of the will. The full income of the estate is taken after excluding any income apportioned under the Apportionment Act 1870 to capital, ie to the period prior to the death of the deceased (see **15.102**). A beneficiary with a limited interest in part only of the residue (eg a one third share) is entitled to receive a corresponding part (one third) of the balance of the full income computed in the same way.

TCA 1997, s 800 prescribes the following procedure for taxing a beneficiary with a limited interest in the residue of an Irish estate:

Step 1

During the administration period, every sum paid in respect of that limited interest is grossed up at the standard rate of income tax for the tax year in which it is paid for inclusion in the beneficiary's total income as taxed income for that year. The beneficiary's income tax liability for each tax year in which any such sums are paid is calculated provisionally by reference to that total income.

Step 2

On the completion of the administration of the estate, any further sum payable to the beneficiary in respect of his limited interest up to the date of ascertainment of the residue, ie the balance of net income due to him, is added to the aggregate of all sums paid to him during the administration period to arrive at his total income for the whole of that period.

Step 3

The beneficiary's total net income for the administration period is then deemed to have accrued to him from day-to-day, ie evenly, during the whole of that period, or if his limited interest existed for a part of that period only, during that part of the period.

Step 4

The beneficiary's income tax liability for each tax year in the administration period, as previously calculated provisionally in step one, is recalculated by adjusting his total income to include the grossed up equivalent of the part of his total net income deemed in step three to have accrued in that year. Any necessary additional assessments, adjustments of earlier assessments, relief claims, etc must then be made to finalise the beneficiary's income tax position for each tax year affected. In this case, the normal four-year time limit for repayments of tax under TCA 1997, s 865(4) (see **2.104**) will not apply (TCA 1997, s 804(2)(a) as amended by FA 2008, Sch 6).

Example 15.205.1

Mr JK died on 2 May 2013, leaving his widow, Mrs OK, a life interest in one half of the residue of his estate. He directed in his will that the Apportionment Act 1870 should not apply, thus enabling Mrs OK to receive her one half share of the income attributable to the residuary estate from the date of death onwards without having to apportion to capital any part of that income attributable to the period before Mr JK's death.

Mr JK's executors completed the administration of the estate on 30 June 2015. During the administration period they made the following payments to Mrs OK on account of her life interest:

	€	€
15/07/2013	1,200	
18/12/2013	900	
		2,100
5/06/2014	2,000	
1/12/2014	2,500	
		4,500
4/02/2015		1,000
		7,600

The income from the estate to be included in the provisional computations required by step 1 would be as follows:

	2013	*2014*	*2015*
	€	€	€
Sums paid to her (total €7,600)	2,100	4,500	1,000

include in total income:

2,100 x 100/(100–20)	2,625		
4,500 x 100/(100–20)		5,625	
1,000 x 100/(100–20)			1,250
Credit for income tax deemed paid	(525)	(1125)	(250)

On the completion of the administration (30/6/2015), the executors work out the total net income of the estate payable to Mrs OK in respect of her one half life interest, as follows:

		Period 2/5/2013 to 31/12/2013	*Year to 31/12/2014*	*Period 1/1/2015 to 30/6/2015*
		€	€	€
Executors' total income		15,600	12,430	3,900
Less:				
Executors' income tax				
€15,600 x 20%		(3,120)		
€12,430 x 20%			(2,486)	
€3,900 x 20%				(780)
Expenses chargeable to income		(1,422)	(1,270)	(514)
Executors' net income		11,058	8,674	2,606
One half due to Mrs OK (total €11,169)		5,529	4,337	1,303

This total net income of €11,169 due to Mrs OK for the whole administration period (€7,600 already paid and a balance of €3,569 payable on 30 June 2015) is now allocated to the tax years in the administration period, and is grossed up at the standard rates assumed, as follows:

	2013	*2014*	*2015*
	€	€	€
Days in administration period (total 789)	243	365	181
€11,169 x 243/789	3,440		
€11,169 x 365/789		5,168	
€11,169 x 181/789			2,561
Gross up for inclusion in Mrs OK's total income:			
€3,440 x 100/80	4,300		
€5,168 x 100/80		6,460	
€2,561 x 100/80			3,201
Credit for income tax deemed paid	860	1,292	640

Final adjustments

Mrs OK's income tax liabilities for 2013 to 2015 are now recomputed by adding to her total income from other sources the final grossed up income from her life interest in her late husband's estate and by giving her the revised tax credits on that income. Additional assessments arise (with a corresponding adjustment in the credits for the tax paid by the executors) as follows:

	2013	*2014*	*2015*
	€	€	€
Income assessed provisionally	2,625	5,625	1,250
Income finally assessable	4,300	6,460	3,201
Additional income assessable at end of	1,675	835	1,951
Administration period			
Additional credit for income tax paid:			
€1,675 x 20%	335		
€ 835 x 20%		167	
€1,951 x 20%			390

15.206 Discretionary trusts etc in wills

The terms of a will may give the executors the discretion as to whether or not, and if so as to how much, to pay income to or for the benefit of one or more beneficiaries who have neither an absolute nor a limited interest in the residue at the time the discretionary payment is made. This could occur if the will leaves the residuary estate, or a part of it, in the form of a discretionary trust under which the capital and/or the income is to be paid to, or applied for the benefit of, such one or more of a class of named beneficiaries as the executors or trustees should in their discretion decide. Alternatively, the will might leave a beneficiary a contingent interest in the residue (as distinct from a vested interest) and might give the executors or trustees the discretion to apply income for his benefit before the contingency occurs. The distinction between a contingent and a vested interest is discussed in the context of settlements in **15.307**; the same principles apply, if relevant, in the case of property settled by a will.

In any case where any income of the residue of a deceased person's estate for any part of the administration period is paid to, or applied for the benefit of, a beneficiary of the estate as a result of the exercise of a discretion, the actual sum paid is deemed to be received as taxed income of that beneficiary for the tax year in which the payment was made. It represents the amount of income which, after deducting income tax at the standard rate for the year of payment, equals the sum paid (TCA 1997, s 803(3)). Even if a number of discretionary payments are made to the same beneficiary, there is no question of having to allocate any part of such payments to a different tax year from that in which each payment is made.

Example 15.206.1

Take Mr JK deceased's estate dealt with in **Example 15.205.1**. Assume that, subject to Mrs OK's life interest in one half of the estate, the residue is left by the will on a discretionary trust under which the executors and trustees (who are the same persons in this case) are given absolute discretion as to the distribution of capital and income, as and when they think fit, between a class of beneficiaries. The potential beneficiaries in this class are Mrs OK, two sons, one daughter and their respective spouses and issue.

Assume that the executors and trustees exercise their discretion and make the following payments out of the one half of the residuary income not appropriate to Mrs OK as life tenant:

	Mrs OK	*John K Jnr (minor son)*
	€	€
19/08/2013: school fees		1,300
15/11/2013: cash	520	
10/01/2015: school fees		1,600

TCA 1997, s 803(3) applies to treat Mrs OK and John K junior as receiving respectively taxed income from the estate (in addition to the taxed income attributable to Mrs OK's life interest) as follows:

	Mrs OK	*John K Jnr*
Year to 31/12/2013:		
Cash payment €520 x 100/80[1] (tax paid €130)	650	
School fees €1,300 x 100/80[1] (tax paid €325)		1,625
Year to 31/12/2015:		
School fees €1,600 x 100/80[1] (tax paid €400)		2,000

Notes:

1 The payments made to or for the benefit of the discretionary beneficiaries are grossed up at the standard rate of 20 per cent.

15.207 Foreign estates

A beneficiary resident in the State entitled to the whole or a part of the residuary income of a foreign estate, whether his interest is an absolute or a limited one is chargeable to Irish income tax broadly in the same way as if he had a corresponding interest in an Irish estate. If he has an absolute interest in the residue, the TCA 1997, s 801 procedure discussed in **15.204** is applied; if his interest in the residue is a limited one, then the TCA 1997, s 800 procedure described in **15.205** is followed. In either case, there are certain differences compared with the treatment of the residuary income of an Irish estate to deal with the fact that the personal representatives, being non-resident, are not chargeable to Irish income tax on any income of the estate that arises from foreign sources.

The most important difference is that any sum paid as income during or at the end of the administration period to a residuary beneficiary of a foreign estate is deemed to be income of an amount equal to the actual sum paid (ie without grossing up). This amount is assessable to Irish income tax on the beneficiary (if resident) under Sch D Case III as foreign source income (TCA 1997, s 800(4)(b); 801(6)). In principle, this means that the beneficiary receives the income as untaxed income and, unlike the position with an Irish estate, there is no credit for income tax suffered at source. However, if any part of the aggregate income of the foreign estate has borne Irish income tax, TCA 1997, s 800(5) provides a relief to the beneficiary in respect of the Irish tax borne by the personal representatives (see below). While TCA 1997, s 800(5) deals specifically with the limited interest beneficiary, the same relief is extended by TCA 1997, s 801(7) to a beneficiary with an absolute interest, and by TCA 1997, s 803(3)(b) to a discretionary beneficiary.

The 'aggregate income of the estate' for a foreign estate for any tax year comprises the total income of the personal representatives for that year from all sources, whether foreign or Irish, but the amount of income included in respect of any particular source depends on whether or not it is chargeable to Irish income tax in the hands of the personal representatives. If the income is chargeable to Irish tax by deduction or otherwise, ie if it arises from an Irish source, the gross income on which that tax is borne for the year in question is included. Where any part of the tax deducted at source is refunded (eg following a claim for expenses under TCA 1997, s 97(2) against Irish rental income subject to withholding tax under TCA 1997, s 1041 or under the terms of a double tax treaty). It seems that only the tax net of the refund should be regarded as being 'borne' (see *IRC v Herdman* 45 TC 394). In the case of foreign source income, the amount to be included in the aggregate income for any tax year is the full amount of that income actually arising in that year, computed in accordance with Irish tax principles and after such deductions as would have been allowable if it had been charged to Irish income tax.

Example 15.207.1

Mr FRG died in Ruritania on 1 May 2014. By his will he appointed Mr GDR, a resident of Ruritania, as the administrator of his estate and he bequeathed a one half share in the residue of his estate absolutely to Ms IRL, a single person, who is resident and domiciled in the Republic of Ireland. The income-producing assets of the estate consist only of shares in Ruritanian companies, a shareholding in an Irish resident company and ground rents in Galway (no expenses incurred).

Assuming that Ruritania only taxes the administrator at a flat rate of 25 per cent on the Ruritanian income and does not tax him at all on the other income, the aggregate income of the estate for 2014 based on the income figures assumed below is calculated as follows:

	€	€
Income chargeable to Irish tax:		
Dividend from Irish company (paid 14/9/2014)		2,000
(inclusive of Dividend Withholding Tax €400)[1]		
Rental from Galway property (gross)[2]		1,000
(received less Irish tax €200)		
Other income:		
Ruritanian dividends	6,667	
Less: Ruritanian tax[3]	1,667	
		5,000
Aggregate income of estate		8,000

Notes:

1. The Ruritanian administrator is chargeable to Irish income tax on the gross amount of the Irish company dividend paid (see **13.608**).

2. The gross rental income is included as Irish tax was borne by deduction on this amount (see **13.609**).

3. Although not chargeable to Irish tax, the Ruritanian dividends must be included in computing the aggregate income, but as reduced by the foreign tax paid.

A residuary beneficiary with an absolute interest in the residue of a foreign estate is, as with an Irish estate, taxable on his share of the residuary income for each year of the administration period. He is taxable provisionally in respect of sums paid on account during the period (as per step 4 in **15.204**) and any such provisional assessments are reviewed on the completion of the administration (as per step 5), but on the basis of including the sums paid as untaxed Sch D Case III income (subject to any relief for Irish tax paid – see below). In this case, the normal four-year time limit for repayments of tax under TCA 1997, s 865(4) (see **2.104**) will not apply (TCA 1997, s 804(2)(a) as amended by F(No 2)A 2008, Sch 6).

In arriving at the total residuary income of the foreign estate, the aggregate of the income of that estate is reduced by the same types of deduction (annual interest, annuities, etc) as are allowed for an Irish estate, irrespective of the country in which the payments are made.

Similarly, the approach to the taxation of a residuary beneficiary with a limited interest in the residue of a foreign estate is the same in principle as that for an Irish estate (see **15.205**), but the sums paid on account and at the end of the period again are brought in as gross income assessable under Sch D Case III and subject to any relief for Irish tax paid – see below. The apportionment of the aggregate of all sums paid to the beneficiary over the entire administration period to arrive at the amount treated as accruing on a day-to-day basis in each tax year of that period is, therefore, an apportionment of untaxed income. This contrasts with the position at the corresponding stage in dealing with an Irish estate where it is the aggregate net income that is apportioned (see step 3 in **15.205**).

Relief for Irish tax paid

Where any part of the aggregate income of a foreign estate has borne Irish income tax by deduction or otherwise, any beneficiary who is chargeable to Irish tax on income from that estate, whether his interest is an absolute, limited or discretionary one, is entitled to relief by TCA 1997, s 800(5) for the Irish tax. This relief is given on proof of the facts and no time limit is specified within which the relief must be claimed, but clearly the beneficiary should claim the relief before the assessments on him in respect of the foreign estate income are finalised at the end of the administration period.

The calculation of the TCA 1997, s 800(5) relief involves two further steps. First, the beneficiary's share of the total income of the foreign estate, as included as Sch D Case III income for each relevant tax year, is reduced by an amount bearing the same proportion to that share of the total estate income as the amount of the estate income chargeable to Irish tax (ie Irish source income included in the aggregate income of the estate) bears to the aggregate income of the estate. In any case where this deduction in respect of the Irish tax is made for any tax year, the second and final step is to treat the beneficiary as receiving, in addition to the reduced Sch D Case III income from the foreign estate, an amount of Irish taxed income equal to the amount of the TCA 1997, s 800(5) deduction as grossed up by the standard rate for the year (TCA 1997, s 800(6)). He is then entitled to the usual credit against his total income tax chargeable for the Irish tax deemed to have been deducted from this taxed income.

Example 15.207.2

Take the facts of **Example 15.207.1** and assume that Mr GDR completed his administration of Mr FRG's estate on 9 June 2015 when he distributes the net residuary income for the whole administration period and completes the transfers of the estate assets to the beneficiaries entitled. Taking the income figures already stated and assuming the other income, expenses and payments mentioned below, the residuary income of the estate and its allocation for each of the periods 1 May 2014 to 31 December 2014 and 1 January 2015 to 9 June 2015 are as follows:

	Period to 31/12/2014	*Period to 31/12/2015*
	€	€
Ruritanian income:		
Dividends less Ruritanian tax	5,000	1,200
Income chargeable to Irish tax:		
Dividend from Irish company	2,000	-
Rental from Galway property (gross)	1,000	300
Aggregate income of estate	8,000	1,500
Less:		
Annuity payable under will	(340)	(64)
Administration expenses	(260)	(186)
Total residuary income	7,400	1,250
Less:		
Irish income tax:		
Dividend withholding tax	(400)	
Deducted at source from rent	(200)	(60)
Net distributable income of estate	6,800	1,190
1/2 share due to Ms IRL	3,400	595

Ms IRL is taxable in each of the two tax years involved on her share of the residuary estate income, and on her other income assumed below (none of which is Sch D Case III income from any other source), as follows:

	2014	*2015*
	€	€
Income from foreign estate (Sch D Case III)		
Her 1/2 share as above	3,400	595
Less:		
TCA 1997, s 800 deduction:		
€3,400 x 3,000/8,000[1]	(1,275)	
€595 x 300/1,500[2]		(119)
Sch D Case III foreign estate income finally Taxable	2,125	476
Taxed income from foreign estate:		

€1,275 x 100/80[3]	1,594	
€119 x 100/80[3]		149
Income from other sources	36,391	19,152
Total income	40,110	19,777
Income tax payable (single rate tables)		
€32,800 x 20%	6,560	-
€7,310 x 41%	2997	-
€19,777 x 20%		3,955
	9,557	3,955
Less: Personal tax credit	(1,650)	(1,650)
Less:		
Income tax deemed paid[4]		
€1,594 x 20%	(319)	
€ 149 x 20%	-	(30)
Final income tax payable	7,588	2,275

Notes:

1. The TCA 1997, s 800(5) deduction is in the ratio of the administrator's Irish source income for 2014 to the aggregate income of the estate for that year.
2. The TCA 1997, s 800(5) deduction for 2015 is in the corresponding ratio for that year.
3. The taxed income from the foreign estate for each year is equal to the TCA 1997, s 800(5) deduction for that year grossed up at the standard rate.
4. The credit for each year is taken as tax at the standard rate on the taxed income from the foreign estate (see note 3).

15.3 Trustees, Settlements and Their Beneficiaries

15.301 General

Broadly, there is a trust or settlement where any property is transferred by its owner (the settlor or testator) on trusts to another person (the trustee or trustees) who is required to hold the legal title to the property and to deal with the capital and/or income in accordance with the terms of the trust, usually for the benefit of one or more named beneficiaries (the '*cestui que* trust'). In general, the trust will be created by a deed, will or other instrument although oral trusts are also possible in some cases. A trust may be set up during the lifetime of the settlor in which case the responsibilities of the trustees begin as soon as any property is transferred to them. Alternatively, a trust may be established by a will to become effective after the death of the testator; in this case, the responsibilities of the trustees as such normally only commence on the ascertainment of the residue of the testator's estate when the executors (who may or may not be the same persons) assent to the passing of the residuary estate to the trustees.

The trustees of a settlement must act in accordance with the terms of the trust. A settlement may take a number of forms and may provide for the payment of benefits in a variety of ways. In some trusts, the trustees may be required to apply the income each year as it arises by distributing it all to the beneficiaries in specified shares, whether by direct payments or by applying the income for their benefit for specified purposes. In other cases, the trustees may be given a discretion to decide how and when the capital and the income of the trust is to be divided amongst a number (or class) of beneficiaries, not all of whom may necessarily benefit. Again, the trustees may have a discretion to accumulate all or some of the trust income, either to be added to the capital of the trust fund or to be retained for distribution in a subsequent year. The trustees may also have powers to vary the terms of the trust or to appoint capital and income to particular beneficiaries. The distinction between a discretion and a power is explained more fully in Keane, *Equity and the Law of Trusts in the Republic of Ireland* (2nd edn, Bloomsbury Professional, 2011), ch 6.

From an income tax perspective, a key distinction is whether or not the terms of the trust are such that any beneficiary (or beneficiaries) is/are entitled to the trust income as it arises. In this case the trust income will be regarded as that of the beneficiary, irrespective of whether or not the trustees actually distribute the income to him (subject only to the discharge of trust expenses).

A beneficiary will normally be regarded as being entitled to the income where he has a vested interest in the income, that is an immediate and unconditional right to the income (eg a life tenant). Exceptionally, this principle will not apply where the beneficiary's interest in the income is defeasible, ie can be subsequently defeated by a power of the trustee(s) to accumulate his income as capital for the benefit of others (*IRC v Berrill* [1981] STC 784). Where a receipt is regarded as capital for trust law purposes then even if it is regarded as income for tax purposes, an income beneficiary is not normally to be regarded as being entitled thereto. The fact that trust income may be treated as that of the beneficiary does not however convert trading profits earned by the trustees into earned income in his hands.

Where the beneficiary's interest in the income is merely contingent, for example where he will only become entitled to it on reaching a certain age, then the income once again does not accrue to him for tax purposes. Naturally, in the case of a discretionary trust, where any particular beneficiary has no more than a hope ('spes') of receiving income if the trustees so see fit, the same principle applies. Where the trustees exercise their discretion and distribute income to a beneficiary then he will be taxable on that distribution (seemingly as an annual payment: see the discussion below): *Drummond v Collins* 6 TC 525.

The fact that income is accumulated does not mean necessarily that the income is not that of the beneficiary. If the beneficiary is entitled to the income as it arises, then as noted above, it is his income for tax purposes whether or not the trustee actually distributes it to him. (*Baker v Archer-Shee* 11 TC 749; *IRC v Hamilton Russells Exors* 25 TC 200).

If, however, the income is being accumulated as capital to which a beneficiary may become entitled on satisfying a particular contingency (eg reaching age 25) then this will not be the case. The same of course applies if the income is being accumulated and the trustees have a discretion to distribute the accumulated income amongst a number (or class) of beneficiaries as and when they see fit. The tax treatment of accumulated income is discussed more fully at **15.307**.

In principle, any person who receives income as a trustee or otherwise in a fiduciary capacity is chargeable to income tax on that income, although only at the standard rate (TCA 1997, s 15). Except in the case of a trustee for an incapacitated individual (and, in some cases at least, the trustee of a non-resident) no deductions for any personal allowances or for any other reliefs that are granted to individuals only are given in taxing the income of a trustee. He is assessed as trustee separately from, and without any reference to, his own or his spouse's income, personal allowances, etc. A company may be the trustee of a settlement or may otherwise act in a fiduciary capacity. If so, the company is assessable to income tax on any trust income received by it in exactly the same manner as a non-corporate trustee. A company is not chargeable to corporation tax on any income that accrues to it in a fiduciary or representative capacity, except only if and to the extent that it has a beneficial interest in the income (TCA 1997, s 26(2)).

In general, therefore, the effect of a settlement is to transfer the liability for income tax on the income from the settled property away from the settlor and on to the trustees and/or the beneficiaries to whom income accrues or to whom it is distributed. In the absence of any rules to the contrary in the Income Tax Acts, the transfer of capital and/or income to trustees by way of settlement would give considerable scope to individuals, particularly those with high incomes, for avoiding income tax by splitting their incomes in various ways through the use of trusts. In order to prevent this happening in ways considered to be unacceptable, TCA 1997, ss 791–798 contains various rules which, in any case to which they apply, negate the effect of the settlement for income tax purposes by deeming the income to be that of the settlor and not that of the trustee, beneficiary or any other person. These anti-avoidance rules are dealt with separately in **15.4**, but the taxation of trustees and beneficiaries of settlements not affected by them is now dealt with in this division.

15.302 Liability of trustees

The statutory provisions explicitly governing the taxation of trustees are scanty and often obscure. TCA 1997, s 1034 enables the Revenue Commissioners to assess a non-resident person in the name of the trustee of such a person. TCA 1997, s 1045 empowers the Revenue Commissioners to assess a trustee on behalf of any incapacitated person (defined by TCA 1997, s 3(1) as any minor or person of unsound mind) where the trustee has direction, control or management of that person's property. TCA 1997, s 1046(1) renders the trustee who is chargeable on behalf of a non-resident person or in respect of an incapacitated person answerable for all matters required to be done under the Income Tax Acts for the purpose of assessment and payment of tax. TCA 1997, s 1034 and TCA 1997, s 1045 are collection provisions only, and do not extend the scope of the liability of the non-resident or incapacitated person on whose behalf the trustee is taxed (see *Greenwood v Smidth* 8 TC 193). It follows that the non-resident or minor may be assessed directly, where it is practicable to do so (*R v Newmarket Commrs ex parte Huxley* 7 TC 49).

TCA 1997, s 1050 provides protection for a trustee who has authorised the receipt of trust income by the person entitled thereto (or by that person's agent). The trustee, so long as he delivers a return under TCA 1997, s 890 of the name, address and profits of the relevant person is not required 'to do any other act for the purpose of the assessment of that person', unless the Revenue Commissioners require his testimony. In *Singer v Williams* (discussed below) Scrutton J held in the Court of Appeal that the equivalent provision in ITA 1842, s 42 released a trustee from the possibility of assessment, but only in the case of UK resident and non-incapacitated beneficiaries in view of the express equivalents to provisions of TCA 1997, s 1034. However, the better view may be that TCA 1997, s 1050 is a purely mechanical provision, concerned with limiting the administrative responsibilities of trustees. In *Lord Advocate v Gibb* 5 TC 194, the Court of Session opined that the equivalent provision in the ITA 1842 applied only to trustees who were not directly assessable under the equivalent provisions to TCA 1997, s 1034 and TCA 1997, s 1046(1). In *Singer v Williams*, the House of Lords seems to have regarded the provision as implicitly substantiating the proposition that the beneficiary is the person who is generally assessable, ie it did not relate to the liability of the trustees as such (see Viscount Cave, at p 411; Lord Phillimore, at p 417, and Lord Wrenbury, at p 414).

If it is correct that the trustee of a non-resident may be assessed in respect of the latter's income, irrespective of whether or not the trustee falls within the terms of TCA 1997, s 1050, this still leaves open the question of what is meant by the trustee '*of* a non-resident'. It may be noted that ITA 1918, General Rule 5, (the predecessor of TCA 1997, s 1034) clearly restricted the assessability of trustees to those 'having the direction, control or management of the property or concern' of the non-resident.

An important decision on the general principles governing taxation of trustees and beneficiaries was that of the House of Lords in two cases heard jointly, *Singer v Williams* and *Pool v Royal Exchange Assurance* 7 TC 387. In each case, trustees domiciled and resident in the United Kingdom held shares in a foreign company for the benefit of an individual resident abroad. Dividends on those shares were not received by the trustees, but were mandated and paid direct to the beneficiary abroad. It was held that the trustees were not liable to UK income tax on those dividends and, as the beneficiary was not resident and the income did not arise in the United Kingdom, he was not liable either. Some remarks from the judgment of Viscount Cave LC, may usefully be quoted as helping to explain the taxation of a trustee and the beneficiary:

> The fact is that, if the Income Tax Acts are examined, it will be found that the person charged with tax is neither the trustee nor the beneficiary as such, but the person in actual receipt and control of the income which it is sought to reach. The object … is to secure for the state a proportion of the profits chargeable, and this end is attained (speaking generally) by the simple and effective expedient of taxing the profits where they are found. If the beneficiary receives them, he is liable to be assessed upon them. If the trustee receives and controls them, he is primarily so liable … but in cases where a trustee or agent is made chargeable with the tax, the statutes recognise the fact that he is a trustee or agent for others, and he is taxed on behalf of and as representing his beneficiaries or principals.

Accordingly, the trustees of a settlement may be charged to income tax under Sch D on any income which they receive in that capacity or which they are entitled to, and which is chargeable under that Schedule (TCA 1997, s 52). If resident in the State, the trustees may be assessed under Sch D both on income from Irish sources within that Schedule and on all income from foreign sources (but see below for the position where there is a non-resident beneficiary). The criteria for deciding the residence of trustees and their eligibility for double tax relief is discussed at **14.105**.

The position under Sch F is set out in TCA 1997, s 20 which provides that a distribution made by an Irish resident company is to be taxed unless specially excluded from income tax. It is arguable, that in the case of a beneficiary who is entitled to the trust income as it arises, any Sch F distributions included in that income can only be assessed on the beneficiary (except to the extent that such income is used to defray trust expenses, when it is not regarded as the beneficiary's income: *Aikin v MacDonald's Trustees* 3 TC 306, discussed below). This follows because there is no provision under Sch F equivalent to TCA 1997, s 52, which charges tax under Sch D on the persons receiving income as well as the persons entitled to it. In practice, in these circumstances, Sch F income which is actually received by the trustees may be taxed in their hands (as illustrated in the text). The position regarding non-resident trustees in receipt of Sch F distributions is discussed at **9.101**.

Singer v Williams is also authority for the proposition that trustees are not liable on general principles in respect of income which they do not receive, (but, subject it seems to the specific provisions of TCA 1997, s 1045 and also, arguably TCA 1997, s 1034, as discussed above). In *Reid's Trustees v IRC* 14 TC 512, Lord Clyde suggested that trustees who mandate income to a beneficiary might still be said to be 'entitled' to that income, but this can hardly be correct in a case where the beneficiary is absolutely entitled to the income.

Singer v Williams is also generally accepted as authority for the wider proposition that trustees are not liable in respect of non-Irish income to which a non-resident beneficiary is entitled as it arises, on the basis that such income falls outside the territorial scope of Irish taxation (see **1.501**).

In *Reid's Trustees v IRC* 14 TC 512, Lord Clyde observed:

> … trustees, albeit only the representatives of ulterior beneficial interests, are assessable generally in respect of the trust income … but … just because they represent those

> beneficial interests – they may have a good answer to a particular assessment, as regards some share or part of the income assessed, on the ground that such share or part arises or accrues *beneficially* to a *cestui que trust* in whose hands it is not liable to income tax eg a foreigner.

This limitation on the liability on the trustees will only apply where the income falls outside the ambit of Irish taxation. It is no answer to an assessment on the trustees for them merely to say that since the income does not belong beneficially to *any* person, the trustees therefore cannot be taxed in a representative capacity (*Reid's Trustees*, confirmed by *Moloney v Allied Irish Banks* III ITR 477).

In *Kelly v Rogers* 19 TC 692, the respondent, a woman of American birth, but married to an Englishman and resident in England, was appointed under the American will of her mother, a US citizen, as trustee for her incapacitated sister who lived with her in England. The trust fund consisted mainly of US stocks, shares and securities. It was held by the Court of Appeal that the respondent, as a UK resident being in receipt and control of the income of the trust fund as trustee, was liable to UK tax on the whole of that income and not merely on the part of it applied for the benefit of her sister. In this case, there was no question of any non-resident beneficiary being entitled to the balance of the foreign income. It would seem however, that where a beneficiary is not domiciled in the State, any overseas income which is not remitted to the State should not be assessable on either the trustee or the beneficiary.

The exemption of the income of the non-resident income beneficiary in *Singer v Williams* was followed by the decision in *Baker v Archer-Shee* 11 TC 749, which confirmed the principle that any beneficiary who has the right to be paid the income of a trust as it arises, even if subject to the trustees' expenses, is taxable as if the income receivable by him arises from the specific securities, stocks, shares, rents or other property comprising the trust fund.

These two decisions have led the Revenue Commissioners generally to seek to tax resident beneficiaries, and not the trustees directly, on that part of the trust income each beneficiary is entitled to receive as it arises, even in cases where the trust income is *not* mandated directly to the beneficiary. However, if in the latter circumstance the beneficiary in question cannot be assessed or does not pay his liability, the Revenue will assess the trustees in respect of any trust income actually received by them, ie as the persons in receipt of the income. (There is authority for this in *Reid's Trustees* although it has to be said that the point is not entirely beyond doubt: see, for example, the comments of Nicholls LJ in the Court of Appeal in *Dawson v IRC* [1988] STC 684: the source of the doubt is whether trustees who are obliged to pay over income to a beneficiary as it arises can really be said to be in 'receipt and control' of the trust income, but support for the approach in *Reid's Trustees* can also be found in *Brown v IRC* 42 TC 42 and *Aplin v White* [1973] STC 322). The Revenue Commissioners would normally seek to assess the trustees in respect of income accruing to a non-resident beneficiary, given the difficulties in enforcing an assessment against a non-resident person. The extent of the liability of trustees in relation to non-residents is discussed above. In practice, where a trustee is assessed to tax, a return under TCA 1997, s 890 is not required (see **2.605**).

In any case where income of a settlement is assessed as that of the trustee, any distribution to a beneficiary out of that income is treated as taxed income in respect of which the trustee should issue to the beneficiary the appropriate form R 185 made by the trustee under a discretion or power conferred by the trust deed. Where a beneficiary is entitled to the income as it arises, then he receives that income net of expenses and the tax borne thereon by the trustees; he receives credit for the tax suffered at source by 'grossing up' the net amount received at the standard rate (ie by 100/80 for 2013). In other cases, it seems that payments made by the trustee are strictly speaking annual payments (see *Drummond v Collins* 6 TC 525; *Cunard's Trustees v IRC* 27 TC 122) thus subject to compulsory deduction of tax under TCA 1997, s 238 to the extent that they exceed the income of the trust for the year of assessment. In practice, the Revenue Commissioners normally regard such payments as distributions out of taxed income and would only seek to invoke TCA 1997, s 238 where a payment in the nature of income is made out of trust capital. This is the approach followed in the appropriate examples in the text.

Where the trustees receive the income, then even if one or more beneficiaries are entitled to the income of the settlement, the trustee must retain sufficient income to enable him to pay the expenses of administration incurred each year (to the extent that the expenses are properly chargeable against income). The trustee remains assessable on the amount of the trust income used each year to pay these expenses. Further, since the trustee must also apply income to pay his resulting income tax liability, the minimum assessment on the trustee is normally made on an amount equal to the expenses grossed up at the standard rate of income tax. For the exception to this principle where there is a non-resident beneficiary entitled to trust income which includes foreign source income, see below.

Where trustees receive the income but the beneficiary or beneficiaries entitled to trust income are assessed directly, it is still necessary to allocate the income from the various sources between the trustee (to meet his expenses and income tax liability) and the beneficiary(ies) entitled to income. Normally, the trustee's expenses (and income tax liability) are treated as payable out of each different source of trust income in the ratio which the income from that source bears to the total trust income. The balance of the trust income from each source is then allocated to the beneficiary(ies) so that it is assessed on him/them according to the rules for each type of income. For example, if the trust income includes Sch F dividends, the beneficiary is given the benefit of the withholding tax attributable to his allocated share of those dividends.

Two questions require to be considered regarding the method of allocating the trust income between the trustee and the beneficiary(ies) to be assessed directly. First, should the trustee's 'share' of the income to meet the expenses incurred in a particular tax year be determined by reference to the income from the various sources *arising* in that year or to the income which would be *chargeable to tax* for that year if the trustee were to be assessed in respect of the full income? While the matter may not be free from all doubt, it is considered here that the apportionment between the various sources of income should be made on the income arising basis. Once the income is allocated between the trustee and the beneficiary on this basis, the appropriate basis of assessment rules for the different types of income are applied separately to the trustee and to the beneficiary in respect of their respective shares. This is normally only an issue in respect of the commencing and closing years of a trade or profession within Sch D Case I and II.

The second question is whether the apportionments should be made on a gross or net income basis. If the gross method is used, the actual expenses paid or incurred in the year are first grossed up at the standard rate of income tax for that year. For example, for 2015 if the actual expenses are €80, the grossed up amount is €100 to pay those expenses and the income tax of €20 payable by the trustee on the gross income. The amount of each type of income allocated to the trustee to pay the expenses (and income tax) is then determined by multiplying the gross income from the source in question by the fraction:

$$\frac{\text{administration expenses incurred in year (grossed up)}}{\text{total net income arising in year (grossed up)}}$$

This gross method may not be suitable in all cases. For example, the trust income may include French dividends received less the 15 per cent French withholding tax in respect of which an Irish resident person is entitled to a foreign tax credit not only for the French withholding tax, but also for the underlying French corporation tax; this treatment also applies in the case of a limited number of other double tax agreements (see **14.310**). Since the trustee's credit for the total French tax cancels out any Irish tax liability in respect of these French dividends (see **14.308**), the net dividends received are fully available to the trustee towards his expenses. Where the trust income includes any French dividends or any other types of income in respect of which the trustee does not actually pay Irish income tax at the standard rate, the net method of allocating the different sources of income may be preferable.

The net method requires the determination of the net amount of income from each source after deducting the actual Irish income tax payable on the income from that source. Since it is the trustee's share of the net income needed to pay the expenses which is the critical issue, the net income from each source is determined on the assumption that Irish tax is charged on the full income from that source, but after allowing any credits against tax to which the trustee would be entitled if assessable on the full income from that source (eg the withholding tax on Sch F income or credits for foreign tax). The amount of net income from each source allocated to the trustee is then arrived at by multiplying the net income from each source by the fraction:

$$\frac{\text{administration expenses incurred in year (actual)}}{\text{total net income arising in year}}$$

Example 15.302.1

Mr AB is the Irish resident trustee of a settlement made some years ago under which all the available income is payable each year to the three adult grandchildren (all Irish resident) of the settlor (a Mr Y Zedd) in equal shares. The trustee is authorised to pay all normal costs of administration of an income nature out of the trust income and is then required to distribute the balance of income to the beneficiaries after setting aside sufficient funds to meet his expected income tax liabilities as trustee.

Although all the trust income is received by Mr AB as trustee, the inspector has for some years adopted the practice of assessing the beneficiaries directly on their respective shares, but he assesses the trustee in respect of the part of the income used to pay the administration expenses. This requires the trust income received in each year to be apportioned between the trustee on the one hand and the three beneficiaries on the other.

In the tax year 2015, the trustee incurs trust administration expenses of €1,091 on income account. The total trust income arising in the tax year 2015 is made up as follows:

	€
Sch F income	3,608
Sch D Case V:	
Net rental income	6,400

Sch D Case III:	
Interest from Japanese company (gross)	918
French dividends (gross)	1,400
	12,326

The €918 of Japanese interest has been received less 10 per cent Japanese tax which is not refundable under the Ireland/Japan tax treaty, but which is available for credit against Irish tax. The €1,400 of French dividends has been received less 15 per cent French tax (**14.310**) which is similarly available for credit against Irish tax in addition to the underlying French corporation tax.

14.310

In order to apportion the income from the different sources between the trustee (for the expenses) and the beneficiaries entitled to income (the balance), it is necessary to reduce each source of income to its net amount on the assumption that all the income is to be assessed on the trustee (although the beneficiaries' shares are to be assessed directly on them).

The net income from each source, after deducting the income tax which would be payable on that income if fully assessed on the trustee, is as follows:

	€	€
Sch F income	3,608	
Less: Dividend Withholding Tax at 20%	(722)	2,886
Sch D Case V	6,400	
Less:		
Tax at 20%	(1,280)	5,120
Sch D Case III		
Japanese interest (net)[1]		734
French dividends (net)[2]		(1,190)
Total net income		9,930

The trustee's share of the net income from each source is now determined by applying to the above net income figures a multiplier determined as follows:

$$\frac{\text{Administration expenses}}{\text{Total net income}} = 1{,}091/9{,}930 = .1099$$

The total net income arising in the tax year 2015 is now allocated between the trustee (to pay the expenses) and the three beneficiaries (taken together) as follows:

	Total	*Trustee*	*Beneficiaries*
	€	€	€
Sch F income (net)	2,886	317	2,569
Sch D Case V (net)	5,120	563	4,557
Sch D Case III (net):			
Japanese interest	734	80	654
French dividends	1,190	131	1,059
	9,930	1,091	8,839

The manner in which the trustee is assessed on his share of the trust income is shown in the next example. The treatment of the beneficiaries is shown in **Example 15.304.1** (which uses the same facts as in this example).

Notes:

1. The actual Japanese interest received is €826, ie gross interest of €918 less €92 Japanese tax. The Irish tax is calculated at 20 per cent on the gross interest, but with a credit for the €92 Japanese tax suffered. The Irish tax of €92 (€184 less €92) reduces the net income figure to €734.

2. The gross French dividends of €1,400 are received less 15 per cent French tax (€210), ie amount received €1,190. The latter figure is the net income figure as there is no further Irish tax due to the credits for the French 15 per cent withholding tax and the underlying French corporation tax (see **14.308**).

Trustees' position where beneficiary is non-resident

The determination of a resident trustee's liability to income tax in respect of trust income is different if there is a non-resident beneficiary entitled to be paid the trust income (or a share of it) as it arises each year. If the non-resident beneficiary is entitled to all the trust income in any year (subject to the trust expenses) the assessment on the trustee is limited to the settlement's Irish source income even if any foreign source income is received by the trustee, the *Singer v Williams* decision (see above) is applied to exclude all the foreign source income from the assessment. Since in this case the trustee is taxable only as representing the beneficiary, the general principle that a non-resident person is not liable to Irish income tax on any foreign income is applied (subject to the provisions of TCA 1997, s 821, where the beneficiary is not resident but is ordinarily resident in the State). Any trust expenses paid out of the non-resident beneficiary's share of the exempt foreign income is treated as a disbursement of that income, and not as the trustee's income.

If a non-resident beneficiary is entitled to a share (but not all) of the trust income, the corresponding share of the foreign source income is fully excluded from the assessment on the trustee. The balance of the trust income from all sources, whether payable to any resident beneficiary absolutely entitled to it or distributable only at the discretion of the trustee, remains assessable on the trustee (except to the extent that the beneficiary is assessed directly).

One further point is worth mentioning. The income of a settlement may include interest on Irish government securities which have been issued with the condition that no Irish tax is to be charged if the securities are beneficially owned by a person not ordinarily resident in the State (TCA 1997, s 43, see **2.309**). In this case, a beneficiary who is not ordinarily resident in the State, and who is absolutely entitled to the income (if not the capital) of the settlement, is treated as if he were the beneficial owner of the relevant securities to the extent that the interest on those securities actually accrues to him. To this extent, no assessment is made either on the trustee or on the non-resident beneficiary in respect of that interest. However, as the interest is Irish source income, the trustee remains assessable to tax in respect of any part of the interest which is applied to pay the trustee's expenses (and his resulting tax liability). Since the non-resident beneficiary is not entitled to be paid that part of the interest, the TCA 1997, s 43 exemption does not apply to it.

Example 15.302.2

Mr MN and A Bank Ltd are the Irish resident trustees of a will trust. Mrs G St Ouen, an individual resident and ordinarily resident in France, is entitled as a life tenant to all the trust income after the trustees have deducted their expenses properly chargeable against income. No income is mandated directly to the beneficiary and the inspector assesses the trustees where possible. The trust income arising and the trustees' expenses paid in the tax year 2015 are as follows:

	€
Irish source income:	
Sch D Case V net rents	3,760
Interest on €18,300 11% National Loan	1,838
Foreign source income:	
UK dividends	1,800
French dividends (net after 15% withholding tax)	3,060
Trustees' expenses paid:	
On income account	620
On capital account	1,040

Since the only beneficiary (Mrs St Ouen) is resident outside the State, the trustees can only be assessed on the Irish source income of the trust, ie on the Sch D Case V net rents and the Sch D Case III government stock interest. In order to determine the amount of the assessment, the income from the Irish and foreign sources must be apportioned between the amount required to cover the trustees' expenses on income account (and any Irish tax payable on this amount) and the balance of the income due to the non-resident beneficiary.

In this apportionment calculation, the income from each foreign source is brought in as the net amount received after any foreign tax suffered. No double tax relief credit or repayment is available to the trustee since the beneficiary is not a resident of Ireland. Further, as the Irish source income is taxable subject to the exemption for the beneficiary's share of the Irish government stock interest, the apportionment must be made on a 'net' basis. This involves bringing in all the Irish source income net after Irish tax at the standard rate.

The apportionment computation is as follows:

	Total	*Expenses*	*Beneficiary*
	€	€	€
Expenses (on income account only):	620	620	
Irish source income (net after tax at 20%)			
Sch D Case V			
Gross €3,760 x 80%	3,008	200	2,808
National Loan interest			
Gross €1,838 x 80% =	1,470	98	1,372[2]
Foreign source income:			
UK dividends	1,800	119	1,681[3]
French dividends	3,060	203	2,857[4]
Total trust income (net)	9,338	620	8,718

The assessment on the trustees for 2015 is now made as follows:

	€	€
Sch D Case III (government loan interest):		
Share to meet expenses		
€98 grossed up (x 100/80)		123
Beneficiary's share		
€1,372 grossed up (x 100/80) = €1,715[2]		
(exempted TCA 1997, s 43)		Nil
		123
Sch D Case V		
Share to meet expenses		
€200 grossed up (x 100/80)	250	
Beneficiary's share		
€2,808 grossed up (x 100/80)	3,510	
		3,760
Total assessable on trustees		3,883

Notes:

1. The trustees' 'share' of the net trust income from each source required to pay the expenses is determined as follows:

$$\frac{\text{Administration expenses}}{\text{Total net income}} = 1{,}091/9{,}930 = .1099$$

(eg trustees' share of net National Loan interest = €1,470 x 0.0664= €98)

The beneficiary's share is the balance (eg share of net National Loan interest is €1,470 less €98 = €1,372).

2. Although all the National Loan interest is included in the apportionment calculation on a net basis, no Irish tax is actually charged by deduction or otherwise on the non-resident beneficiary's share. Mrs St Ouen is therefore entitled to a €1,372/0.8 = €1,715 share of the gross interest.

3. The non-resident beneficiary's share of the UK dividends is not chargeable to Irish tax.

4. The non-resident beneficiary's share of the net French dividends is not chargeable to Irish income tax.

The actual cash amount available for distribution to the non-resident beneficiary is made up as follows:

	€
Beneficiary's share of:	
Irish government stock interest (untaxed)[2]	1,715
Irish net rents (after 20% tax assessed on trustees)	2,808
UK dividends (no Irish tax charged)[3]	1,681
French dividends (no Irish tax charged)[4]	2,857
Net cash distributable	9,061

15.303 Basis of assessment on trustees

The normal income tax basis of assessment rules are applied in taxing the income of trustees. This will usually be relevant only to the extent that the beneficiaries are not assessed directly. Consequently, income taxable under Sch D Cases I and II is taxed on the basis of the income arising in the current tax year, except where the rules of commencement or cessation are applicable. If relevant, these rules are applied by reference to the later when the trustee commences or ceases to trade, etc.

In computing the income on which the trustee is chargeable under any particular Sch or Case, the same deductions are available as for any other person liable to income tax. In most cases, the total of the trustee's income from all sources is also the total income on which he is chargeable to income tax (ie his taxable income), as he is not entitled to any personal allowances as trustee, nor is the trust income aggregated with any income to which he is beneficially entitled (*Aplin v White* [1973] STC 322). However, if relevant in any particular case, a trustee may be entitled to deduct any Sch D Case I or Case II loss claimed under TCA 1997, s 381 (see **Division 4**) subject to the anti-avoidance provisions which were introduced by Finance Act 2014 which require an active participation by the relevant person carrying on the trade in order to avail of loss relief under TCA 1997, s 381, any excess capital allowances in respect of leased industrial buildings claimed under TCA 1997, s 305(1) (see **6.5**), any excess capital allowances in respect of leased machinery or plant claimed under TCA 1997, s 305(1) (but see **6.305** for restrictions) and any interest paid by the trustee that is eligible for relief.

The rules regarding relief for interest paid by a trustee of a settlement are the same as those for interest paid by the personal representatives of a deceased person's estate, except that relief under TCA 1997, s 244 in respect of interest on a qualifying residence loan is only available if the settlement is one made by the will of a deceased person (see **15.107**).

Except where deductible in computing income from a particular source (eg repairs to a leased property taxable under Sch D Case V), no allowance is given for any expenses of administration, management, etc incurred by a trustee in arriving at the income on which he is taxable (*Aikin v MacDonald's Trustees* 3 TC 306). However, these administration expenses as well as the income tax payable by the trustees for each tax year have to be deducted from the income received by them in that year in order to arrive at the net income distributable to the beneficiaries. For this purpose, it is also necessary to deduct any interest paid by the trustee that was not allowed in computing his income chargeable to income tax. Although such interest may not reduce the trustee's income tax liability, it remains an outgoing against income and, by reducing the amount distributable to the beneficiaries, any income tax payable at the higher rates on the net income in the hands of the beneficiaries is reduced.

Example 15.303.1

The trustees of the late Mr L Shower's will trust assumed responsibility for his residuary estate on the completion of its administration by the executors on 6 May 2015. The estate assets consisted of Irish government securities and certain leased premises. The residuary estate was left on discretionary trusts which permitted the trustees at their discretion to distribute the income between the widow and the deceased's two children or, if the trustees thought fit, to accumulate it during the lifetime of the widow.

During the period 6 May 2015 to 31 December 2015, the trustees paid the following:

	€
Interest on loan to improve Sch D Case V leased commercial premises	1,700
Overdraft interest (not allowable)	220
Management expenses (all chargeable to income)	1,140

Based on the income received in the period 6 May 2015 to 31 December 2015 as assumed below, the trustees' taxable income, income tax payable and distributable income for this period are determined as follows:

	€	€
Sch D Case V:		
Net rental income 6/5/2015 to 31/12/2015		10,800
Less: interest paid (TCA 1997, s 97)		(1,700)
		9,100
Sch D Case III:		
Interest on Irish government securities		7,400
Assessable income		16,500
Less:		
Income tax payable 2015:		
€16,500 x 20%	3,300	
Management expenses paid	1,140	
Overdraft interest	220	
		4,660
Distributable income		11,84

Note:

Assuming that the trustees decide to distribute in full the distributable income for the period to 31 December 2015 to Mrs Shower (widow), she receives taxed income as follows:

	€
Net amount distributed €11,840/0.8 =	14,800

Mrs Shower is entitled to credit for tax suffered at source of €2,960 (€14,800 – €11,840).

A resident trustee who is assessed on income arising from a source in a foreign country which has a double taxation agreement with Ireland may be entitled to the credit for foreign tax given in accordance with the terms of that agreement. No credit under this heading is given to the trustee in respect of any part of the trust income that is assessed directly on a beneficiary and not on the trustee.

The normal rule that the trustee of a settlement is only assessable at the standard rate is subject to the exception that income otherwise available for distribution, but which is not distributed to any beneficiary within a certain period, is chargeable to an additional tax at the rate of 20 per cent. The circumstances in which this undistributed income surcharge is made and the way in which it is computed are covered in **15.308–15.310**.

A non-resident trustee assessable to Irish income tax in his own right is so assessable only on any income accruing to him from sources in the State, whether the settlement is one made under Irish or foreign law. The question of where the settlor was resident at the time he made the settlement, or that of where he is resident when the income accrues, does not affect the trustee's liability to income tax. In the event that there are two or more trustees of any settlement, and one or more of them are resident in the State, the question arises as to whether it is open to the Revenue Commissioners to assess the resident trustees on the world-wide income of the settlement, notwithstanding the non-residence of one or more trustees. In this type of case, the Revenue have usually sought to tax all of the trust income if the general administration of the settlement is carried on in the State. However, in *Dawson v IRC* [1989] STC 473 the House of Lords held that because trustees are jointly liable to tax *all* of them had to be resident in order for the trust to be treated as resident. The logic of the decision seems to be equally persuasive in the Irish context (at least, if it is accepted that the trustees are not taxable as a distinct 'body of persons' (see **1.302**)). It is understood that the Revenue Commissioners do in fact regard the decision in *Dawson* with some reservations.

The question of the residence status of trustees and their eligibility for double tax relief as Irish residents is discussed at **14.105**.

If the trustees of a settlement are resident in a country which has a double taxation agreement with the State, they may be able to avail themselves of any relevant article in that agreement which exempts or relieves a resident of that country from normal Irish taxation on certain types of income (eg Irish source interest income). This depends on the wording of the article in question. If it is expressed in terms of giving relief to a resident of the other country without any other condition, then the trustees are entitled to benefit from the article. The position where it gives the relief to a resident of the other country only if he beneficially owns or is beneficially entitled to the income in question is discussed at **14.205**.

15.304 Taxation of beneficiaries

As already discussed, where a beneficiary receives a distribution of income at the discretion of the trustees, this is treated as taxed income in his hands. In strictness, such a distribution seems to be an annual payment, but in practice this point does not seem to be taken by the Revenue. Accordingly, it seems that the distribution should normally be assessed in the year of receipt (as discussed in **8.205**).

In a case where a beneficiary is entitled to the income as it arises, the following scenarios are possible:

(a) the trustees mandate all of the income to the beneficiary and the inspector assesses the beneficiary directly;

(b) the trustees receive and then distribute the income and either:

  (i) the inspector nevertheless assesses the beneficiary directly, or

  (ii) the inspector assesses the trustee and the beneficiary in full on their respective incomes;

and

(c) the trustees receive and accumulate the income for the benefit of the beneficiary.

Under scenarios (a) and (b)(i) the beneficiary is taxed as if the trust's income from the various sources (or his proportionate share thereof) was his. Under scenario (a), where all of the income is mandated directly to the beneficiary, he will be taxable on the full amount thereof. Under scenario (b)(i) the beneficiary will be taxed on the income net of expenses with the trustee remaining taxable on the income required to cover the trust expenses, (see **Example 15.302.1** above and **Example 15.304.1** below). Under scenarios (a) and (b)(i) the beneficiary's income from the settlement is included with any other income which he may have taxable under the same schedules and cases, so that the basis of assessment rules are applied by reference to the beneficiary's own circumstances and not those of the trustee. This is normally only relevant in respect of the commencing and closing years of a trade or profession within Sch D Cases I or II.

Under scenario (b)(ii), it would appear that in strictness, the beneficiary should again be taxed on the income arising in the tax year (net of the trustee's expenses and subject to credit for tax on that income already borne by the trustees), and that such income should again be attributed to the various underlying sources (see *Baker v Archer-Shee* discussed at **15.301**). However, in practice, the net income generally is treated as taxed income assessable under Sch D Case IV which is brought into the beneficiary's total income when it is actually paid to him (ie in the same manner as that applicable in practice to distributions from a discretionary trust).

Scenario (c) is considered at **15.306** below. As discussed at **15.302**, special considerations may apply where the beneficiary is a non-resident or an incapacitated person (including an infant).

Example 15.304.1

Example 15.302.1 shows a case where the inspector assessed the beneficiaries directly on their respective shares of the trust income, but charged the trustee on that part of the trust income applied to meet the trustee's expenses. It allocated the different types of income received by the trustees in the year 2015 between the trustees (to cover the expenses) and the three beneficiaries (the balance of the income).

Miss Wendy Zedd is one of the three grandchildren entitled in equal shares to receive the income each year from Mr Y Zedd's settlement. She has other income in her own right of €520 per annum from an Irish government security assessable under Sch D Case III and a salary from an employment.

Wendy is entitled to a one third share of the net trust income available for the beneficiaries each year after the proportion of the total net income required to meet the trust expenses has been deducted. Since she is to be assessed directly, she must first be allocated her one third share of each item of net income as shown in the 'beneficiaries' column in each of the tables set out respectively at the end of **Example 15.302.1** (year to 31 December 2015).

Wendy's one third share of each item of net income is as follows:

	Year ended 31/12/2015
	€
Sch F	856
Sch D Case V (net)	
Net rental income	1,519
Sch D Case III (net)	
Japanese interest	217
French dividends	353
	2,945

Her share of net income from each source is re-grossed to give the following gross income:

		Year ended 31/12/2015
	€	€
Dividends received	856	
Dividend withholding tax (20/80ths)	214	1,070
Sch D Case V		
Net rental income 1,519/0.8 =		1,899
Sch D Case III		
Japanese interest		
Net amount received	217	
Japanese tax withheld (10%)	24	241
French dividends		
Net amount received	353	
French tax withheld (15%)	62	415
		3,625

Wendy is chargeable to income tax both on her share of the trust income from various sources and on her personal income.

Her income tax liability for the year 2015 is now calculated as follows:

Sch F income:		€
income in year to 31/12/2015 (trust)		1,070
Sch D Case V:		
income in year to 31/12/2015 (trust)		1,899
Sch D Case III		€
income in year to 31/12/2015		
Japanese interest (gross) (trust)		241
French dividends re-grossed (trust)		
353 x (100/100–20)[1]		441
Government loan interest (her own)		520
Sch E		
Income in year to 31/12/2015 (her own)		15,760
Total income 2015		19,931
Income tax payable 2015		
19,931 x 20%		3,986
Less: Personal tax credits, say	1,650	
Dividend withholding tax	214	
Credit for foreign tax		
Japanese tax: €241 x 10%	24	
French tax: €441 x 20%	88	
Credit for PAYE suffered	852	
		2,828
Net income tax payable		1,158

Note:

1. The net French dividends received are re-grossed at Wendy's own effective rate of Irish tax for 2015 (20 per cent) as it is lower than the effective French rate of 43%. The calculation of her Irish effective rate follows the principles explained in **14.306**. In this example it is assumed that the Japanese interest and the French dividends were received by the trustees otherwise than through an Irish bank so that no Irish income tax was deducted on the receipts (see **2.310**). If Irish tax had been deducted on the receipts, the income would have been assessed as taxed income (Sch D Case IV, and not as Sch D Case III income).

Example 15.304.2

The trustees of a will trust, the residue of which was ascertained a number of years ago, are assessed on the trust income which arises from sources taxable respectively under Sch D Case III and Sch F. They are charged with the payment of an annuity of €2,000 from which they deduct income tax at 20 per cent under TCA 1997, s 237. After deducting the expenses of administration, the trustees are required to distribute the balance of income to two sisters, Marie and Maeve.

In this case, the two beneficiaries are minors and the inspector assesses the trustees in respect of the entire trust income so that Marie and Maeve receive their respective shares of the trust income (after the trustees' expenses) as taxed income. The trust income assessable to income tax for 2015 on the trustees and the income tax payable are as follows:

Sch F income (year to 31/12/2015):	€
Distributions received	4,620
Dividend withholding tax (20/80ths)	1,155
	5,775
Sch D Case III (year to 31/12/2015):	
Untaxed interest (government securities)	2,800
Total taxable income	8,575
Income tax:	
€8,575 x 20%	1,715
Less:	
Dividend withholding tax	(1,155)
Final tax payable by trustees	560

The trustees make up accounts for the year ended 31 December 2015, bringing in the actual income received in that year and deducting the net annuity and the expenses of administration paid out in the amounts shown below. After providing for their income tax liability (as above), they distribute the balance of the actual income received in the year to 31 December 2015 between Marie and Maeve. The accounts are made up in terms of the actual receipts and payments in respect of the year, as follows:

Income received:	€	€
Dividends from Irish companies (as above)		4,620
Untaxed interest		2,800
		7,420

Payments out:		
Annuity (€2,000 less tax at 20%)	1,600	
Trustees' expenses	420	
		(2,020)
		5,400
Trustees' income tax 2015:		
As above		560
		4,840
Distributable to beneficiaries:		
Marie ½	2,420	
Maeve ½	2,420	
		(4,840)

The two sisters as beneficiaries and the annuitant should each be given form R185E by the trustees certifying the following income distributions actually made out of the trust income received in the year ended 31 December 2015, but in practice taxable on the beneficiaries as taxed income in the year of receipt by them:

	Gross payment	*% Rate of tax*	*Tax deducted*
	€	€	€
Annuitant: annuity for 2015	2,000	20	400
Marie: share of trust income 2015	3,025	20	605
Maeve: share of trust income 2015	3,025	20	605

*(gross payment = net payment 2,420 x 100/80 = €3025)

Alienation of income

A beneficiary who alienates his income in favour of a third party will not be taxable in respect of such income. However, where the income of a beneficiary is merely applied in a prescribed manner it remains taxable as his income (*Curtis-Wilson v IRC* 31 TC 422 and note also *Smyth v Stretton* 5 TC 36 and *Edwards v Roberts* 19 TC 618 (distinguished in the *Curtis-Wilson* case)).

15.305 Trustees' expenses and the beneficiaries

The treatment of the trustees' expenses of administering their trusts sometimes causes difficulty in relation to the taxation of the beneficiaries and needs to be considered further (this is not really an issue where the income is mandated directly to the beneficiaries: see **15.304**). The discussion up to this point has assumed that the expenses incurred by the trustees have been properly chargeable against the trust income. To the extent that this is the case, the expenses are an effective deduction from the income on which the beneficiaries may be taxed and, as already indicated, the trustees must as a minimum bear income tax on an amount of income equal to those expenses grossed up at the standard rate of income tax.

In fact, not all expenses paid by trustees are permitted to reduce the amount on which the beneficiaries are taxable. For example, if a beneficiary has an absolute interest in both capital and income of settled property, the trustee is effectively acting as a bare trustee for the beneficiary. In this case, any expenses incurred by the trustee related to the beneficiary's interest are treated as if incurred on behalf of the beneficiary personally. It follows that this beneficiary is taxable on the total income of the trust, or on his share of it, without any deduction for expenses except for any expenses deductible under ordinary income tax rules in computing income from a particular source (eg Sch D Case V income).

The position may be more complicated if the beneficiary has some form of limited interest in the trust property. In such a case, the expenses incurred by the trustees in administering or managing the trust are generally, but not always, a charge on the trust income for the tax year in which they are incurred. Any beneficiary entitled to receive the trust income, or a proportionate share of it, is normally only entitled to the net income of the year (or his share of it) after the trustees' expenses and any income tax payable by the trustees have been deducted. This principle has been firmly established by such cases as *Murray v IRC* 11 TC 133 and *McFarlane v IRC* 14 TC 532. It does not, of course, apply to a beneficiary entitled to an annuity of a stated amount which, in the absence of a specific provision to the contrary in the trust instrument, is payable without any deduction for trust expenses (but subject to the deduction of income tax).

An important exception is that expenses paid by the trustees in providing a benefit for a beneficiary, even if in the course of administering the trust in accordance with the trust deed, are not deducted in arriving at the amount of trust income to be distributed among the beneficiaries. Such payments are treated as if they were paid out to the beneficiary on account of his share of the income. For example, in *Lady Miller v IRC* 15 TC 25, the trustees of a will were directed to hold and retain certain lands and estates and to pay all duties, burdens, costs of repair, maintenance, etc and to allow the deceased's widow to occupy the estate house during her lifetime free of rent, taxes, etc. The widow, Lady Miller, occupied the house and in carrying out these trusts the trustees paid certain rates on the house occupied by her. It was held that the monies paid by the trustees for rates were paid for her benefit and ought to be included in her total income on which super tax was then payable.

Lord Tomlin said:

> The rates fall primarily on the respondent as occupier and so far as the money for this liability is provided by the trustees, it is in my opinion, money paid for her benefit which, with the income tax upon it, ought to be included in her total income for super tax purposes.

However, in *Marchioness Conyngham v Revenue Commissioners* I ITR 231 it was held that yearly sums expended on the maintenance and upkeep of Slane Castle were not assessable on the taxpayer who enjoyed the right to use and occupy that property for life under a trust. The Supreme Court took the view that the maintenance of the property was for the benefit of the remainderman of the trust and not of the taxpayer (compare *Shanks v IRC* 14 TC 249; *Sutton v IRC* 14 TC 662).

In determining whether or not particular expenses must be deducted in arriving at the net income to which a beneficiary is entitled, regard must be had to the terms of the trust deed or will. No deduction may be made for expenses which the deed or will directs to be paid out of capital. Apart from expenses incurred in providing a benefit (eg the *Lady Miller* case) and expenses chargeable against capital, the test to apply is whether or not the trustees are obliged to incur the expense before the beneficiary is entitled to require the income to be paid over to him. If the trustees pay expenses after the beneficiary's entitlement to the income has vested, no deduction for those expenses may be taken in assessing the beneficiary.

For example, in *Earl Howe v IRC* 7 TC 289, where the terms of a trust were established by a trust deed, a loan to a beneficiary was made, and as security, an insurance policy was taken out on the beneficiary's life. Since the beneficiary was entitled under the trust deed to the income before the premium became payable, it was clear that his entitlement was to the net income before deducting the insurance premium. By contrast, in a rather unusual case, *Lord Wolverton v IRC* 16 TC 467, trustees paid premiums on a life policy under an obligation to do so imposed by certain trust deeds made in a family arrangement to alter the terms of a will. In the special circumstances of the case, which it was thought were unlikely to recur in another case, the premiums were held by the House of Lords to be a proper deduction in arriving at the net income available to the beneficiary.

The treatment of capital allowances, where there are beneficiaries absolutely entitled to the trust income, merits a brief mention. In general, the trustees alone will in strictness have the right to claim capital allowances, since they will be the persons to whom the relevant asset will 'belong' or will be the persons entitled to the relevant interest therein (see eg **6.403**; **6.409**). On the other hand, trust income required to cover any related depreciation charges in the trust accounts is by definition income to which the beneficiary is not entitled. The most practical approach would be to cut through these complexities and simply treat each beneficiary as assessable on his share of trust income as reduced by any capital allowances claimed by the trustees and increased by his share of any balancing charges (but even this approach creates anomalies as in the case where the beneficiary who is taxed on the balancing charges did not receive all (or any) of the benefit of the allowances. The Revenue position in this area is not known to the writer. It does seem clear at least that the beneficiary cannot take the benefit of excess capital allowances in order to offset these against his non-trust income. The Revenue Commissioners have followed this analysis in a precedent dealing with urban renewal allowances under TCA 1997, s 342. Similarly, where a trust incurs a loss under Sch D Case I, such a loss is not available to a beneficiary who is entitled absolutely to the income of the trust under TCA 1997, s 381 (see **4.404**), ie he may not utilise the loss in a claim against his total income. This follows because the beneficiary does not satisfy the requirement under TCA 1997, s 381 that he should be the person carrying on the trade (*EF Fry v Shiels Trustees* 6 TC 583).

15.306 Trust distributions: capital or income?

A beneficiary may, depending on his interest(s) in settled property according to the trust instrument, receive distributions out of capital as well as out of income. Sometimes he may receive a distribution out of income accumulated in previous years that has been reinvested and has become an effective addition to the capital of the trust fund. The fact that a benefit is paid out of capital does not necessarily mean that it cannot be taxed as income in the hands of the beneficiary. Conversely, while payments or other benefits provided for a beneficiary out of current income are almost invariably taxable income of the beneficiary, payments out of accumulated income may in certain circumstances be non-taxable capital receipts of the beneficiary (see **15.307**).

It has been held in various tax cases that it is the character of the payments in the hands of the beneficiary, and not whether paid as income or capital by the trustee, that is the determining factor as to whether or not the distribution is taxable income of the beneficiary. For example, in *Brodie's Will Trustees v IRC* 17 TC 432, amounts paid by will trustees in a number of consecutive years out of capital of an estate to bring the total sums paid to the deceased's widow up to £4,000 a year, when the income from the part of the residue charged with this annuity was insufficient to meet it fully, were held to be income of the widow. In his judgment, Finlay J said:

> Of course, if certain sums of capital were simply handed over by the trustees to the lady and received by the lady as capital, it is quite clear that income tax was not attached, but it is, to my mind, not less clear that, if the sums were paid to the lady and were received by the lady as income, then it is immaterial what they may have been in the hands of the trustees who pay them.

Similar decisions were reached in *Michelham's Trustees v IRC* 15 TC 737, *Lindus and Hortin v IRC* 17 TC 442 and *Cunard's Trustees v IRC* 27 TC 122. In *Lindus and Hortin*, as a result of a deed of family arrangement following a will, the trustees were not specifically directed to make payments out of capital but were authorised in their absolute discretion to do so to the extent that they considered it necessary and proper for the maintenance of a beneficiary and her home. In each of five successive tax years, the trustees paid the beneficiary sums out of the capital of the trust fund in addition to the income of the fund, while they also paid rates, other household expenses, etc on behalf of the beneficiary. It was argued on the latter's behalf that, as she had no enforceable right to the payments out of the capital, they were voluntary payments and were not therefore taxable on her. Finlay J in his judgment said:

> I think that where you get the relation of trustee and '*cestui que* trust' and where you get payments made which constitute income of the recipient, then it matters not whether the payments were made because the trustees were directed by their deed to make them, or whether they were made pursuant to a discretion they exercised…

In *Postlethwaite v IRC* 41 TC 224, the taxpayer was entitled to a so called 'capital annuity' consisting of £1,000 pa up to a maximum of £15,000; there was provision for accelerating the payments (up to the maximum of £15,000) and any balance of the amount of £15,000 unpaid on the taxpayer's death was payable as a lump sum to his children. It was held by Wilberforce J that the annuity was in the nature of income, albeit that it was referenced to a capital amount by virtue of the fact that it was payable for a fixed period. The learned Judge distinguished *IRC v Ramsey* 20 TC 29 which involved the sale of a business in return of a series of annual payments.

In *Stevenson v Wishart* [1987] STC 266, trustees appointed 22 sums totalling £109,000 out of capital over a period of two years to a single beneficiary. The sums were used to defray the costs of medical treatment and residential care incurred by the beneficiary who was elderly and unwell. The Court of Appeal held that the sums were not income in nature. Fox LJ observed:

> Applying the test of the 'reality' of the matter, the position was this. [The beneficiary] was a woman of very advanced age who needed nursing home care. That was exceedingly expensive. It seems to me quite unreal to regard it as an ordinary income expense. Certainly it involved day-to-day maintenance expenditure, but it was expenditure of very substantial amounts which would be quite outside normal income resources … That was the sort of expenditure which, if it is to be met at all, is in practice met either from the patient's own capital, or from family capital … The result, in my opinion, is that there is nothing in the present case which indicates that the payments were of an income nature except their recurrence. I do not think that is sufficient. The trustees were disposing of capital in exercise of a power over capital. They did not create a recurring interest in property. If, in exercise of a power over capital, they chose to make at their discretion regular payments of capital to deal with the special problems of [the beneficiary's] last years rather than release a single

sum to her of a large amount, that does not seem to me to create an income interest. Their power was to appoint capital. What they appointed remained capital.

Each of the *Brodie's Will Trustees*, *Michelham's Trustees* and *Lindus and Hortin* cases concerned assessments by the inspector under ITA 1918, rule 21 (the forerunner to the Irish TCA 1997, s 238). In each case, the assessments were made on the trustees on the part of the payments to each beneficiary that was made out of capital to bring up the beneficiary's income from the trust to the required level. In each case, the amounts paid out of capital were held to be annual payments made otherwise than out of income brought into charge to tax so as to be correctly assessable under ITA 1918, rule 21. In corresponding circumstances under current law, similar payments to the extent made out of capital would be assessable under TCA 1997, s 238 (see **2.304**).

15.307 Accumulated income

The treatment of trust income which is accumulated, rather than being paid out to, or applied for, the immediate benefit of any beneficiary, depends on the nature of the rights given by the trust instrument to the beneficiaries. In particular, it depends on whether any beneficiary has a vested interest in the income or whether the interest of the beneficiary is only a contingent interest. Broadly, a beneficiary has a vested interest in income receivable by trustees if he is absolutely and beneficially entitled to that income so as to be able to call upon the trustees to pay the income over to him or to apply it for his benefit. A minor who has a vested interest in capital, eg if the capital is his absolutely even if held by trustees until he comes of age, is regarded as having a vested interest in the income from that capital, whether the income is applied for his benefit or is accumulated for him until he comes of age. If a minor beneficiary does not have a vested interest in the capital, but is or may be entitled to the accumulated income on, say, becoming 21 or on the happening of some other future event, his interest is only a contingent one.

Any beneficiary (including a minor) who has a vested interest in income is treated as if the income is his year by year as it accrues and is taxable on him accordingly, irrespective of whether the income is paid to him, or is accumulated by trustees for payment to him at some later date (*IOT v Longford* VI ITR 691 and *Gascoigne v IRC* 13 TC 573). For example, in *Gascoigne v IRC*, the appellant's grandfather by his will devised certain estates to trustees, the property of which was left absolutely to her, but was to be managed during her minority by the trustees who were required to accumulate the rents from the estates and to pay the accumulated income to her on her 21st birthday. Assessments made on her for the various years during which she was a minor, based on her total income for each year that included the gross income from the estates, were upheld on the grounds that she had been left the capital absolutely and that her interest in the income was, therefore, a vested one. (See also *Spens v IRC* 46 TC 276: this treatment does not contravene the principle that investment income is not generally taxable until it is received (see **8.102**) as the trustees receive the income in question on behalf of the beneficiary).

By contrast, when a beneficiary has only a contingent interest in income received by trustees, that income is not regarded as his so long as it is accumulated by the trustees in accordance with their trusts (*Stanley v IRC* 26 TC 12). If, however, during the period before the happening of the event on which the interest is contingent, the trustees should apply some or all of the income for the maintenance, education or other benefit of the beneficiary, the amount so applied is taxable on the beneficiary as a distribution of net income from the trust. To the extent that income in which there is no vested interest is accumulated, it is effectively added to the corpus of the trust fund and is treated as capital, and not as income, in the hands of the beneficiary who becomes entitled to it on the happening of the contingency.

It is therefore important to distinguish between cases where there is a genuine contingent interest in income from those in which the interest is vested but the beneficiary's right to receive the income is merely postponed until a later date or the happening of a specified event. A useful test is to consider what would happen to the accumulated income if the contingency did not occur. For example, assume a trust instrument which requires the trustees to accumulate income until a beneficiary becomes 25 years of age, but which gives them the discretion to apply up to 50 per cent of the income each year for his maintenance. If the terms of the deed are such that, should the beneficiary die before his 25th birthday, the accumulated income is to form part of his estate so as to pass under his will or intestacy, the beneficiary's interest is a vested one. On the other hand, if the accumulated income would pass on his death under the terms of the trust deed to another person, the beneficiary's interest is a contingent one.

Where income vests in a beneficiary at the time it accrues, but the trustees can divest it subsequently through the exercise of a power to accumulate it for the benefit of other beneficiaries, the beneficiary's interest in such income is regarded as contingent. Accordingly, the income is treated as belonging to the trustees only (*Stanley v IRC* 26 TC 12). Where the power of accumulation subsequently lapses, it seems that all of the income which was previously subject to that power accrues to the beneficiary at the time the power lapses (*IRC v Berrill* [1981] STC 784).

When income is being accumulated for a beneficiary with a vested interest, the inspector will normally seek to assess him directly each year. Even if he is a minor, if his taxable income including both his income from the settlement and any other income he may have is high enough, he is chargeable at the higher rates to the extent appropriate. He is entitled to his normal personal allowances, etc. If the beneficiary is an incapacitated person such as a minor, the inspector is entitled under TCA 1997, s 1045 to assess the trustees in receipt of the income.

In any case where there is a contingent interest in income arising under a trust, the inspector always assesses the trustees on that income. This applies whether the settlement is an accumulation and maintenance trust contingent on, say, one or more beneficiaries' attaining a specified age or marrying or is a discretionary trust where the contingency is the decision of the trustees to exercise a discretion to appoint capital or income to a beneficiary. If and to the extent that any payments are made by the trustees out of income for the maintenance, education, etc of a beneficiary with a contingent interest, the beneficiary is entitled to set off his personal allowances against his total income including the grossed up amount of the payments made for his benefit. This may result in the beneficiary being entitled to a repayment of a whole or a part of the tax assessed on the trustees if his total income is low enough.

Example 15.307.1

On 29 April 1990, Mr LR settled shares in an Irish company on trust under which the capital and accumulated income was to accrue in equal shares to his twin grandchildren, Patrick and Jane, contingently on their attaining the age of 25. In the event of either child's not surviving to that age, his share of the trust fund was to be paid absolutely to their mother (the settlor's daughter). The trustees were permitted to apply income for the maintenance, etc of the grandchildren in any year, but were not bound to do so.

Patrick and Jane each became 25 on 7 January 2015, on which date their interests in the trust fund vested so that each became entitled to receive his share of the capital and accumulated income (all in the form of a capital receipt). In the year ended 31 December 2015, the trustees had incurred administration expenses of €862 and had distributed a net €800 each to Patrick and Jane towards their maintenance, but had retained the balance of income (subject to the TCA 1997, s 805 surcharge – see **15.308**) as an addition to the capital of the trust fund to be distributed between them as capital. Based on the trust income below, the trustees' income tax position for 2015 was as follows:

	€
Sch F income:	
Dividends received	7,200
Dividend withholding tax	1,800
	9,000
Sch D Case III	1,600
Total income	10,600
Income tax payable	
€10,600 x 20%	2,120
Less: Dividend withholding tax	1,800
Net tax due by trustees	320

The application of the trust income received in the year ended 31 December 2015 is as follows:

	€	€
Dividends received (net)		7,200
Sch D Case III received gross:		1,600
		8,800
Less:		
Payments		
Trustees' income tax	320	
Trustees' expenses	862	
Maintenance Patrick/Jane		
Cash €800 x 2	1,600	
		2,782
Balance accumulated (subject to surcharge)[1]		6,018

For the tax year 2015, Patrick and Jane are each treated as receiving taxed income from the settlement of €1,000, ie the €800 paid to each grossed up at the standard rate of income tax.

Notes:

1. Since the undistributed income for 2015 is due to be paid out to the twins on 7 January 2015 as capital (and not as income) on the happening of the contingency, ie their becoming 25, it remains subject to the TCA 1997, s 805 surcharge, even if the capital payment was made immediately. To calculate the amount subject to the surcharge, this amount needs to be regrossed as a deduction is not available for the 20% income tax liability when calculating the surcharge.

15.308 Surcharge on trust income

TCA 1997, s 805 imposes an additional 20 per cent income tax charge on certain trust income. The income in question must be 'income which is to be accumulated or which is payable at the discretion of the trustees or any other person, whether or not the trustees have power to accumulate it' (TCA 1997, s 805(2)(a)). In *IRC v Berrill* [1981] STC 784, it was held that this definition extends to income which, although it vests in beneficiaries as it arises, is subject to divestment through the subsequent exercise of a power of accumulation in favour of other beneficiaries. Such income would be treated as that of the trustees for income tax purposes (see **15.307**).

The reference to 'income' in TCA 1997, s 805(2)(a) is clearly to income as recognised for the purposes of trust law since it is only income for those purposes which the trustees may dispose of. Accordingly, in the absence of any statutory provision to the contrary, receipts which are regarded as capital for trust law purposes (and to which a life tenant would accordingly not be entitled) but which are deemed to be income for tax purposes do not fall within the definition in TCA 1997, s 805(2)(a) (see *Howell v Trippier* [2007] STC 1245, where this general principle was upheld, although the court also took the view that the UK legislation treating 'stock dividends' as income did in fact extend the definition in the UK equivalent of TCA 1997, s 805(2)(a); the corresponding Irish provisions in TCA 1997, s 816 (see **8.208**) do not appear capable of being interpreted in this way).

TCA 1997, s 805 excludes the following income from the surcharge:

(a) any income which before being distributed is the income of any person other than the trustees (ie a beneficiary). This exception covers income which vests in a beneficiary, (and is thus his income for tax purposes: see **15.307**), but which is accumulated subject to a power to make payments for his benefit; this would typically arise in the case of a settlement in favour of a minor;

(b) any income that is treated for any of the purposes of the Income Tax Acts as the income of a settlor (eg income covered by certain special rules relating to settled or transferred income);

(c) income arising under a trust established for charitable purposes only; and

(d) income from investments, deposits or other property held for the purposes of a fund or scheme established for the sole purpose of providing pensions and related benefits on retirement, death, etc for employees, directors, etc which fall within the definition of relevant benefits in TCA 1997, s 770.

Dividends on qualifying shares acquired by the trustees of an approved profit sharing scheme, and appropriated by them for the purposes of the scheme within eighteen months of acquisition are exempt from the surcharge (TCA 1997, s 510). Dividends on shares held by an approved Employment Share Ownership Trust are also exempt from the surcharge (TCA 1997, s 519). TCA 1997, s 737 exempts the income of Special Investment Schemes.

In any case where trustees have income that is potentially liable to the surcharge, ie income that is not excluded from surchargeable income by (a) to (d) above, it is firstly necessary to determine the amount of the surchargeable income that arose in the tax year under consideration. The surchargeable income for any tax year ending 31 December is arrived at as follows:

(a) ascertain the total income actually arising to the trustees in the year;

(b) if relevant, deduct any of the total income arising that is to be excluded under (a) to (d) above;

(c) deduct the amount (if any) of the total income arising that is used to meet expenses incurred in the year by the trustees so far as those expenses are properly chargeable to income; s 805 (2)(d); and

(d) deduct the amount (if any) of the total income arising that is distributed as income to one or more persons either during the year or within 18 months after the end of the year. (TCA 1997, s 805 (2)(e)).

The total income arising to the trustees is the aggregate of the trustees' income from all sources as determined in accordance with the computational rules of the various Schedules and Cases under which it is assessable. It must also include any taxed income received, even if not the subject of any direct assessment on the trustees. The object is firstly to ascertain the amount of the income actually arising in the tax year that is available for distribution (the result at the end of step (c) above) and then to apply step (d) above to see how much of that income (if any) remains undistributed at the end of the 18 months distribution period. This undistributed balance is the surchargeable income and the 20 per cent surcharge is levied on that amount.

By virtue of TCA 1997, s 805 the surcharge is to apply only to the extent that the potentially chargeable income 'exceeds the income applied in defraying the expenses of the trustees in that year which are properly chargeable to income, or would be so chargeable but for any express provisions of the trust'. Unfortunately, it is not possible to give a sensible interpretation to these words if they are taken at face value. This is because it is inconceivable that the legislation is envisaging a situation where the trustees would apply income in defraying expenses which could not be properly charged against income under the express provisions of the trust (a course of action which would be clearly unlawful).

In *Carver v Duncan* [1985] STC 356 the Court of Appeal held that UK equivalent to s 805(2)(d) should be given a 'secondary meaning' (the 'golden rule' of interpretation is discussed at **1.405**) in order to resolve this difficulty. The court held that the legislature had envisaged two distinct situations. Firstly, there was the case where the trust deed contained no express provisions concerning the allocation of expenses, ie as between income and capital. This situation was covered by the first limb of TCA 1997, s 805 which allowed a deduction only for 'expenses … which are properly chargeable to income', ie under the general law. Secondly, there was the case where the trust deed contained express provisions concerning the allocation of expenses. This situation was covered by the second limb of TCA 1997, s 805 which allowed a deduction only for 'expenses … which would be [properly] chargeable [to income] but for any express provisions of the trust'. The court held that this limb was to be interpreted as allowing a deduction only for expenses properly chargeable to income under general law, disregarding the terms of the trust. Thus, the fact that the trust might direct 'capital' expenses to be treated as 'income' expenses (or vice versa) would be immaterial.

The question of what expenses are properly chargeable to income is one of trust law rather than of tax law. In *Carver v Duncan*, the question also arose as to whether the payments of life assurance premiums were expenses 'properly chargeable to income'. Oliver LJ commented as follows:

> Obviously, individual trusts will vary, but the universal answer is, I should have thought, that one has to look in each case at the person or group of persons for whose benefit the policy is in fact being maintained under the relevant trust. If on such an investigation it is perfectly plain that the policy is being maintained as an investment of capital and for the benefit of capital, then I should have thought that it must inevitably follow that the premiums paid by

the trustees, in the absence of express direction in the trust, would be chargeable to capital and not to income.

Where the life assurance policy concerned is in the nature of an investment then it may well be that the premiums paid in order to build up its value are not 'expenses' at all and indeed may represent accumulations of income. This point was left open in *Carver v Duncan*.

In the same case, it was held that the fees for investment advice concerning the trust funds as a whole were properly chargeable to capital. The Revenue Commissioners concessionally treat the annual charge on discretionary trusts as being deductible for the purposes of the surcharge; this concession does not extend to any capital gains tax liabilities incurred by the trust (*Tax Briefing 33*). In any case income tax payable by the trustees is not deductible when calculating the surcharge which gives an effective tax rate of 40 per cent on the income of the trust which is subject to the surcharge.

Since the surcharge is levied on 'gross' income, the actual trustees' expenses paid and the cash paid to or applied for the benefit of the beneficiaries on account of income must be grossed up at the standard rate of income tax. With regard to the distributions to or for the beneficiaries, only amounts paid in circumstances resulting in the treatment of the income distributed as income for tax purposes in the hands of the recipient are deductible. For example, if an individual becomes entitled to the capital and accumulated income on his 21st birthday, and if the amount is distributed to him in one capital sum, then no part of this distribution is deductible in computing the surchargeable income, even if it includes income that arose to the trustees within the normal 18 months' distribution period.

Example 15.308.1

Mr RS Thornbird, who died on 15 June 1999, by his will left his residuary estate on trust giving the will trustees (AB Bank Trustee Company Ltd and his solicitor, Mr PT Sharpclaw) the discretion to distribute the capital and income among the beneficiaries in such manner and at such time or times as they in their discretion think fit. The beneficiaries are named as his widow, Anne, his two sons, Robert (born 19 May 1983) and Stanley (born 22 August 1989), his sister and her children and two charities.

On 25 July 2003, following the completion of the administration of the estate, the trustees appointed an annuity of €5,000 (before tax) to the widow to be paid out of the income of the trust fund comprising the residue of the estate. On 1 January 2014, the trustees appointed a life interest in one half of the trust fund (subject to the annuity) in favour of Robert, but with power to enlarge this life interest into an absolute interest at any future time should they think that appropriate. The rest of the residuary estate remains subject to the discretionary trusts.

In the year 2015, the trustees received the following income in respect of the entire estate (as computed under the rules of the relevant Schedules and Cases):

	€	€
Sch F income:		
Dividends Received	7,840	
Dividend Withholding Tax	1,960	9,800
Sch D Case III:		
Interest on Irish government securities	5,400	
Dividends from UK companies	2,000	7,400

Sch D Case IV:	
Taxed interest from Irish company loan	
Stocks	2,000
Sch D Case V:	
Net rents	4,070
Total income arising in year	23,270

The other relevant facts related to 2015 are as follows:

(a) The trustees have not set up separate funds for Mrs A Thornbird's annuity nor for Robert's life interest (so that the annuity has to be paid out of the trust income and so that Robert is entitled to be paid out one half of the net trust income after expenses have been discharged and the annuity paid);

(b) The expenses incurred by the trustees in the year were;

	€
Expenses chargeable to income	1,658
(1/2 chargeable to Robert's income)	
Expenses chargeable to capital	740
(not relevant to surchargeable income)	

(c) Net annuity paid to Mrs Thornbird

(€5,000 less tax at 20%)	4,000

(d) Robert is paid his one half share of the trust income (after the annuity and expenses);

(e) During the year 2015 the trustees in the exercise of their discretion made the following cash payments for Stanley's maintenance and benefit:

	€€
Out of income of year to 2013	
Paid 29/06/2015[1]	2,000
Out of income of year 2014	
Paid 24/04/2015[1]	1,400
Out of income of year 2015	
Paid 21/07/2015	1,000
Paid 15/12/2015	900

Assuming that no further distributions are made out of the income arising in the year 2015 within the next 18 months ending 30 June 2017, the surchargeable income of the settlement is calculated as follows:

	€	€
Total income arising in year (gross):		23,270
Less: Annuity paid to Mrs Thorn (gross)		5,000
Balance of income after annuity		18,270
Less: One half due to Robert[2]		9,135
		9,135
Less: Trustees' expenses (1/2)[3]	829	
Distributions for Stanley's maintenance[1]	1,900	
	2,729	

Cash amounts grossed up	
€2,729 x 100/80[4]	3,411
Surchargeable income[5]	5,724

Notes:

1. It has been assumed that the trustees appropriated the €2,000 maintenance payment made on 29 June 2015 to the income of the year 2013 so as to reduce the surchargeable income of that year (payment just in time!). It is not therefore relevant to the calculation of the surchargeable income for the year 2015. The same applies to the €1,400 payment made out of the income of the year ended 2014.
2. Since Robert has a life interest in one half of the trust fund, he is entitled as of right to a one half share of the trust income (a vested interest). Therefore this share of income must be excluded in arriving at the surchargeable income.
3. The one half of the expenses chargeable to Robert's share of the income is not deductible in computing the surchargeable income.
4. The actual expenses and the cash distributed for Stanley's maintenance are grossed up at the standard rate of income tax for the year for which the surchargeable income is being calculated (ie at the 20 per cent rate for 2015).
5. The surchargeable income in respect of the year to 2015 may be reduced further if the trustees make further distributions out of the income of the year no later than 30 June 2017 (18 months after 31 December 2015).

Deposit interest subject to retention tax

The income arising to trustees in a tax year may include deposit interest from which the deposit interest retention tax has been deducted (referred to as 'relevant interest') under the rules of TCA 1997, s 257 (see **2.401–2.403**).

TCA 1997, s 261 provides that relevant interest is to be regarded as chargeable under Sch D Case IV and included in the total income of the person entitled thereto. In the case of individuals, their liability on such income is generally set at the appropriate rate while credit for the retention tax is given by the application of TCA 1997, s 59 (thus ensuring no additional liability can arise, on that income). While it is accepted that no assessment at the standard rate applies to the trustees in respect of relevant interest, the discretionary surcharge is an additional duty of income tax, liability in respect of which does not depend on the trustees being otherwise assessable to income tax (see, in a different context, *IRC v Regent Trust* [1980] STC 140). It follows that relevant interest should be included in the trustees' surchargeable income. The Revenue Commissioners do take this point.

15.309 Assessment of surcharge

TCA 1997, s 805 provides that, in addition to being chargeable to income tax at the standard rate for the tax year for which it is so chargeable, the income to which the section applies shall be charged to an additional duty of income tax at the rate of 20 per cent. This additional duty is the 'surcharge' and it is applied to the surchargeable income (if any) as separately determined in respect of each tax year.

As explained in **15.308**, the surchargeable income for any year ending 31 December is determined under TCA 1997, s 805 by taking the income arising to the trustees from all sources in that year (excluding any income to which any other person is entitled) and, then, by deducting any of that income applied in meeting the trustees' expenses in that year and in making distributions to the beneficiaries within the 18 months after the end of that year. Since the trustees are given this 18-month distribution period within which to distribute the income of any particular year, clearly no assessment for the surcharge can be made until after the end of the distribution period.

TCA 1997, s 805 goes on to apply the other provisions of the Income Tax Acts to the surcharge in a corresponding manner to the way in which they apply to the assessment of income, except that TCA 1997, s 805 provides that no relief or repayment in respect of the surcharge shall be given to any person to whom the income is distributed after it has become liable to the surcharge. In other words, if any income is distributed after the end of the 18-month distribution period, it is taxable fully in the hands of the recipient subject to a credit only for income tax at the standard rate, but with no credit or other relief for the surcharge. The surcharge is applied within the self-assessment system for the collection of income tax.

TCA 1997, s 805 provides that the Inspector may give notice to the trustees requiring that any return of income made in respect of income arising to them shall include particulars of the manner in which the income has been applied, including particulars as to the exercise by them of any discretion and of the persons in whose favour it has been exercised. Failure by the trustees to comply leaves them liable to the same penalties as may be applied for failure to make a return of income. If the trustees do not provide the Inspector with the necessary information to make accurate assessments, he is empowered to make such assessment(s) as he considers appropriate to the best of his judgment. The normal procedure relating to appeals, specified payments, etc apply to the surcharge assessments.

TCA 1997, s 805 provides that the surcharge in respect of income arising in a year of assessment ('the year of income') shall be charged on the trustees for the year of assessment in which the 18-month distribution deadline for the year of the income occurs (the 'year of charge'). This surcharge is deemed to be income tax chargeable for the year of charge. In other words, the surcharge is added to the income tax payable by the trustees at the standard rate on the income arising in the year of charge and the trustees must pay the surcharge as part of their self-assessment liability for that year. The year of charge is always the second tax year after the year of the income. TCA 1997, s 805 does not deal with the situation where a trust is wound up (so that there are no trustees on whom to assess the surcharge in a subsequent tax year).

The consequences as the result of the application of the self-assessment rules (see **2.104–2.107**) are as follows for 2015:

(a) the trustees should make a payment of preliminary tax (due by 31 October 2015) of an amount which, if interest on tax is to be avoided, should be at least equal to the lower of:

  (i) 90 per cent of the trustees' final income tax liability for the same year, determined as in (c) below, or

  (ii) 100 per cent of the trustees' final income tax liability for the immediately preceding year similarly determined (ie 2014),

  (iii) 105 per cent of the final income tax liabilities for the pre-preceding tax year (ie 2015), subject to meeting the requirements to avail of this option;

(b) the trustees must make a return of income (due no later than 31 October in the tax year following the year of the return) which:

  (i) must give details of all the income actually arising in the year of the return, and

   (ii) should either have attached a computation of the surchargeable income (if any) arising in the tax year two years earlier or give full details of how the income arising in that tax year has been applied (to enable the surcharge to be assessed);

(c) the trustees' final income tax assessable is the aggregate of:

   (i) the income tax payable at the standard rate on the income actually arising in the year (net of any tax credits), and

   (ii) the surcharge payable at 20 per cent on the surchargeable income (if any) arising in the tax year two years earlier; and

(d) the trustees should pay the balance of income tax (including any surcharge), ie the excess (if any) of the final income tax in (c) over the preliminary tax paid, no later than 31 October in the following tax year, ie 31 October 2016 in relation to the tax year 2015.

Example 15.309.1

Take the facts of **Example 15.308.1**. The surcharge payable as additional income tax under TCA 1997, s 805 in respect of the trustees' income arising in the year 2015, and not distributed within the 18 months ending 30 June 2017, is computed as follows:

Surchargeable income:	€
As per **Example 15.308.1**	5,724
Surcharge thereon:	
€5,724 x 20%	1,145

TCA 1997, s 805 requires the surcharge in respect of the income arising in the tax year 2015 to be treated as income tax payable for the tax year 2017 (the tax year in which the 18-month distribution deadline for that income ends).

15.310 Surcharge: miscellaneous points

Personal representatives

The undistributed income surcharge of TCA 1997, s 805 is only made on persons acting as trustees, whether as the trustees of a settlement made during the lifetime of a settlor or of a trust created by a testator's will which has effect after his death. TCA 1997, s 805 makes it clear that the word 'trustees' does not include 'personal representatives' within the meaning of that term as defined in TCA 1997, s 799 (see **15.203**). Consequently, the personal representatives of a deceased person cannot be assessed to the surcharge in respect of any income received by them during the administration period (see **15.106**).

This is not necessarily the end of the matter. TCA 1997, s 805 goes on to deal with the case where, on or before the completion of the administration of the estate, the personal representatives pay to trustees any sum representing income which, if the personal representatives were trustees, would be surchargeable income. In this event, that sum is deemed to be received by the trustees as net income that has borne income tax at the standard rate. This rule may be relevant in any case where the residue of the estate has been left by the deceased person's will in such a way that the entire income of the estate is not the subject of either an absolute or a limited interest (see **15.203**). This is likely to be where the residue of the estate, or a part of it, is left in the form of a discretionary trust or, perhaps, as a trust with power to accumulate income.

If income in which no beneficiary has a vested interest has been received by the personal representatives during the administration period, but has not been distributed to any beneficiary or applied to meet expenses on income account before the end of that period, the rule in TCA 1997, s 805 comes into play. The trustees are treated as receiving the undistributed income as taxed income on the date of ascertainment of the residue or, if earlier, on the date on which the sum is paid to them by the personal representatives. Consequently, the sum paid (which may include the value of any asset(s) transferred to the trustees) as grossed up at the standard rate is treated as part of the total income arising to the trustees in the relevant tax year so that, if not distributed by the trustees to a beneficiary as income within the 18-month distribution period, is included in their surchargeable income.

Example 15.310.1

Mr H I Manor died on 31 December 2013, leaving a widow, two daughters (ages 23 and 21) and a minor son (born 28 February 2004). Since his wife has substantial assets and income of her own, by his will Mr Manor left all his residuary estate to trustees to be held in the form of a discretionary trust under which the trustees were, at their discretion, authorised to apply income for the maintenance, education, etc of the minor son and to accumulate the balance of the income not required for this purpose. When the son attains his 21st birthday, the trustees are to appoint the capital and any accumulations of income absolutely between the two daughters and the son in equal shares.

During the administration period which ran from 1 January 2014 to 21 July 2015 (the date of ascertainment of the residue), the executors received income and applied it as follows:

	1 January 2014 to 31 December 2014	*1 January 2015 to 21 July 2015*
	€	€
Sch F income (gross)	2,800	Nil
Sch D Case III	2,600	2,100
Sch D Case V	5,700	3,400
Total income from all sources	11,100	5,500
Income tax paid by executors:		
€11,100 x 20%	2,220	
€5,500 x 20%[1]		1,100
Less:		
Dividend Withholding tax	(560)	
	1,660	1,100
Distributable income:		
€(11,100 – €2,220) =	8,880	
€(5,500 – €1,100) =		4,400
Less:		
Expenses paid (income)	(982)	(610)
Maintenance of son	(3,400)	(1,210)
Undistributed income (net)	4,498	2,580

In June 2015, the executors invested the undistributed income of €4,498 in respect of the year 2014 in a holding of government stock. Among the assets which passed from the executors to the trustees on the completion of the administration on 21 July 2015 was this holding and a cash balance which included the €2,580 undistributed income up to 21 July

2015. TCA 1997, s 805 applies and the trustees are deemed to receive the following income on 21 July 2015:

	€	€
Sum representing income of executors:		
Government stock (value 21/7/2015)	4,580	
Limited to income invested		4,498
Cash representing income		2,580
		7,078
Gross up at 20%		
€7,078 x 100/80		8,848

This taxed income of €8,848 must be added to the other income arising to the trustees in computing their surchargeable income arising in the period 21 July 2015 to 31 December 2015 with the result that, if it is not distributed *as income* to a beneficiary before 30 June 2017 the tax payable by the trustees for 2015 will be increased by €1,770 (€8,848 x 20%).

Double tax relief and the surcharge

The income included in the surchargeable income of trustees may include foreign source income which has suffered foreign tax that is eligible for double tax relief by credit against the Irish income tax chargeable. In most cases, the foreign tax available for credit will have been fully used in reducing the Irish income tax in the normal standard rate assessment made on the trustees. In this type of case, no question of any double taxation relief arises from computing the surcharge under TCA 1997, s 805. However, if the income of the trustees includes any foreign source income carrying an effective rate of foreign tax available for credit, in excess of the Irish standard rate for the year in which the income arises, the trustees are entitled to an additional credit for the foreign tax against the surcharge.

Example 15.310.2

The total income arising to the trustees of a discretionary settlement in the year ending 31 December 2015 chargeable at the standard rate is made up as follows:

	€	€
French dividends:		
Gross amount paid	10,000	
Less: French tax deducted at 15%	1,500	
Net amount received in State	8,500	
Grossed up at Irish standard rate		
€8,500 x 100/80[1]		10,625
Sch F income:		
Distributions Received	6,400	
Dividend withholding tax	1,600	8,000
Total income		18,625

The income tax payable by the trustees at the standard rate for 2015 on this income is calculated as follows:

	€	€
Income tax chargeable:		
€18,625 x 20%		3,725

Less:		
Dividend Withholding tax	1,600	
Double tax relief: French dividends[3]	2,125	3,725
Net income tax payable		Nil

The trustees apply a cash amount of €520 from the trust income for the year 2015 to discharge administration expenses (properly chargeable against income). Cash distributions totalling €4,500 are made to beneficiaries out of the same income by 30 June 2017 (the 18-month distribution deadline for the year 2015).

Since there is undistributed income for the year 2015 remaining on 30 June 2017, the 20 per cent surcharge has to be made under TCA 1997, s 805 for the tax year 2017 in respect of that income. The effect of that surcharge will be to increase the effective rate of Irish tax on the surchargeable income to 40 per cent (Irish standard rate income tax for 2015, 20 per cent, plus the 20 per cent surcharge). Since the effective rate of French tax available for credit under the Ireland/France tax treaty is also in excess of the 20 per cent rate used in giving double tax relief against the standard rate assessment, the trustees are entitled to further double tax relief in assessing the surcharge.

The total amount of double tax relief to which the trustees are entitled in respect of the French dividends is tax at the lower of the Irish and French effective rates (see **14.308**). In computing the double tax relief to be given against the surcharge the French effective rate in respect of dividends paid by French companies in the year 2015 (inclusive of withholding tax) is taken to be 43 per cent.

TCA 1997, s 805 does not provide any rules for dealing with the double tax relief computation in his type of case, but it is suggested that the following procedure meets the principles for giving relief for foreign tax by way of credit against Irish tax (see **14.302**):

(a) Allocate the trustee's expenses and the net distributions, ie a total of €5,020, between the French dividends and the other trust income in the ratio of the respective 'gross' incomes (as included in the standard rate assessments as above):

	€
Expenses/distributions out of French dividends	
$5{,}020 \times \frac{10{,}625}{18{,}625}$	2,864
Expenses/distributions out of other income	
$5{,}020 \times \frac{8{,}000}{18{,}625}$	2,156
	5,020

(b) Deduct from the net income (after standard rate income tax) arising respectively from the French dividends and the other income the actual expenses/distributions as just apportioned to each type of income, as follows:

	French dividends	*Other income*
	€	€
French dividends – net received	8,500	
Sch F income – net		6,400
Less:		
Income tax assessed at standard rate[2]	Nil	Nil
	8,500	6,400

Deduct:		
Expenses/distributions (as allocated)	2,864	2,156
Net surchargeable income	5,636	4,244

(c) The amount on which the surcharge is levied is the gross income equivalents of these two net surchargeable figures. The gross equivalent for the other income involves grossing up the €4,244 amount at the standard rate for 2015 (20 per cent).

The gross equivalent for the French dividends is determined by grossing up the net surchargeable income attributable to those dividends by the lower of:

(i) the Irish effective rate, including the surcharge, of 40 per cent; and

(ii) the effective French rate assumed to be 43 per cent.

(iii) The final surchargeable income is therefore arrived at as follows:

	€
French dividends:	
Net amount (after expenses) grossed at 40%	
€5,636 x 100/60	9,393
Other income:	
Net amount (after expenses) grossed at 20%	
€4,244 x 100/80	5,305
Surchargeable income	14,698

(iv) The surcharge and the further double taxation relief for the French tax is now calculated as follows:

	€
Surcharge before DTR:	
€14,698 x 20%	2,940
Less:	
Credit for French tax	
€9,393 x (40% – 20%)[3]	(1,879)
Final surcharge payable	1,061

Notes:

1. For the standard rate assessment, the net French dividends are grossed up at the lower of the Irish standard rate (20 per cent for 2015) and the effective French rate (assumed to be 43 per cent). The gross up is therefore at the rate of 20 per cent.

2. The credit for French tax (double tax relief) is an amount equal to the excess of the grossed up French dividends (€9,393) over the net amount received in the State (€8,500).

3. All the income tax charged at the standard rate is effectively levied on the other income since the credit for French tax equals the tax at 20 per cent on the grossed up French dividends included in the total income.

4. The credit for French tax against the surcharge is calculated on the grossed up undistributed French dividends at the excess of the lower effective rate (in this case the 40 per cent Irish rate) over the rate used in computing the double tax relief in the standard rate assessment.

It is to be noted that the effective rates of Irish and foreign tax used in the double tax relief computations are always the rates to which the income is subject and not the rates in the tax year for which the surcharge is levied.

As the example shows, in any case where the effective rate of foreign tax available for credit against Irish tax equals or exceeds the aggregate of the Irish standard rate and the surcharge rate, the further double tax relief will reduce the part of the surcharge attributable to the foreign dividends to nil. The amount of surcharge payable in such a case will be confined to the part of the undistributed income apportioned to the other income (which could include other foreign income carrying an effective foreign rate lower than the aggregate of the Irish standard rate and the surcharge rate).

15.311 Exempt trusts

Trusts which are established for charitable purposes are exempt in relation to most categories of income; exemptions may also apply to trusts if they qualify as an approved Sports Body, qualifying Human Rights Organisation or a qualifying trust for incapacitated persons: see **18.2**. Because these exemptions are expressed to apply to income tax and the discretionary trust surcharge is constituted as an additional duty of income tax, it follows that no surcharge can arise on non-distributed income which qualifies for exemption under the relevant provisions.

15.4 Anti-Avoidance

15.401 General

TCA 1997, Pt 31, Chs 1 and 2 (ss 791–798) contain some important rules restricting the ways in which a person may reduce his own taxable income by settling or by transferring in some other way any income, the right to any income or the capital or other source producing the income. TCA 1997, Pt 31, Ch 1 (ss 791–793) deals with income transferred by revocable settlements, etc and with other dispositions of income not made for valuable and sufficient consideration. TCA 1997, Pt 31, Ch 2 (ss 794–798) applies to certain settlements, arrangements etc made by an individual under which income is or may be paid to, or may be accumulated for the benefit of minors. Chapter 2 also deals with certain transfers of trade to children, discussed at **15.409**. The rules of these two chapters are now discussed in more detail.

The rules of TCA 1997, Pt 31, Chs 1 and 2 operate, broadly speaking, in the same way. They deal with income which 'by virtue or in consequence of' a disposition (Ch 1) or a settlement (Ch 11) is paid to or otherwise dealt with for the benefit of a person other than the person who made the disposition or settlement. Such income is, in the circumstances in which the relevant rule applies, treated as the income of the person who made the disposition or settlement, and not as the income either of the person who receives it or of any other person. The right of the beneficiary, trustee or other person entitled to the income under the terms of the disposition or settlement is not affected, but he may be called upon by the person taxed on the income to reimburse the tax (see **15.410**).

TCA 1997, Pt 31, Ch 1 is applicable to a disposition made by any person which results in income being transferred to any other person. Its main operating provisions are contained in TCA 1997, s 792(1) which first sets out the general rule that makes all such income transfers ineffective for tax purposes but which then, by way of exception, permits outright transfer of capital and certain specified types of annual payments to have effect. TCA 1997, s 791(2) is largely supportive to TCA 1997, s 792; it may be relevant if a person disposes of a source of income or makes a covenant to pay income to another person while, at the same time, retaining a right of revocation or some other power which may allow the disponer to take back the beneficial enjoyment of the income.

TCA 1997, Pt 31, Ch 2 is applicable specifically to any settlement in favour of minors of the settlor or which includes one or more minors (as defined) among its actual or potential beneficiaries. TCA 1997, s 795(1) starts off with the presumption that the settlor is the person to be taxed if, at the time the income arises, there is any minor who may be a beneficiary at any time, but TCA 1997, s 796 permits income to be accumulated in certain circumstances without being treated as the settlor's income.

15.402 Meaning of 'settlement' and 'settlor'

(i) 'Settlement'

TCA 1997, Pt 31, Ch I (revocable dispositions/short-term dispositions)

TCA 1997, Pt 31, Ch 1 refers to 'dispositions' rather than to 'settlements'. The term 'disposition' in normal usage is imprecise, but would presumably include any transaction whereby a person divests themselves of present or prospective property rights.

TCA 1997, s 794(1), which defines the term 'settlement' for the purposes of TCA 1997, Pt 31, Ch 2 (discussed below), states that it includes *inter alia* 'any disposition … *and* any transfer of money or other property or of any right to money or other property' (emphasis added). It is unlikely that the phrasing of TCA 1997, s 794(1) can justify an inference that an outright transfer of property or property rights cannot be a 'disposition' for the purposes of TCA 1997, Pt 31, Ch 1.

In *EG v MacShamhrain* II ITR 352, the taxpayer had a life interest in the income of a settlement made by her father. In exercise of a power conferred on her by that settlement, she appointed part of her income to her minor daughter. Teevan J said of the exercise of the power:

> Is it a 'disposition' or 'transfer'? It could be termed either but more certainly the latter.

The appointment was therefore regarded as a settlement in favour of the taxpayer's daughter (see also *IRC v Buchanan* 37 TC 365). In *Young v Pearce* [1996] STC 743, Vinelott J said:

> It is impossible to conceive of circumstances in which a transfer of assets would not also amount to a disposition.

A court order was held to fall outside the definition of 'settlement', unless it created a trust in favour of a beneficiary, in *Yates v Starkey* 32 TC 38.

It seems clear that the waiver of a dividend where the taxpayer is already legally entitled to receive the dividend is a disposition (the taxpayer will also be liable to tax on the dividend since the waiver will be in this case an application, and not an alienation, of income). It is questionable whether a waiver in other circumstances is a 'disposition' as such, as opposed to an act which merely prevents future property rights accruing. However, it may be that in some cases the waiver could form part of an 'arrangement' (on which, see the discussion of *Copeman v Coleman* immediately below).

By virtue of TCA 1997, s 791(1) the term 'disposition' is extended to include 'any trust, covenant, agreement or arrangement'. The word 'arrangement' is particularly wide in its scope, since there need not be any legally binding links between the transactions which make up the 'arrangement'.

In *Copeman v Coleman* 22 TC 594, the taxpayers (a married couple) were the controlling shareholders of a company. The company passed resolutions, creating a new class of preference shares, and then issued some of these shares to the taxpayer's children. Each share had a nominal value of £200, of which £190 remained as uncalled capital. The company shortly afterwards declared a dividend of £40 per preference share. It was held that this series of transactions constituted an 'arrangement' by virtue of which income accrued to the taxpayers' children (the taxpayers were held to be the settlors: see (ii) below). *Copeman v Coleman* was followed in *Young v Pearce* [1996] STC 743. A similar analysis was applied in *Donovan and McLaren v HMRC* [2014] TC03188 where the controlling shareholders in the company waived their right to dividends over a number of years which then caused a dividend larger than that payable in the absence of the waiver to be paid to their spouses. Blewitt J stated:

> We found the irresistible inference from the facts of these appeals to be that the Appellants waived their entitlement to dividends as part of a plan to ensure that the dividend income became payable to their wives. We agreed with Sir Stephen Oliver QC in *Buck v R&C Commrs* that:
>
> '… there is no need for any formal legal trust or settlement to bring the statutory provisions into operation … a definite plan, including a relatively simple one, to use a company's shares to divert income falls within the meaning of an arrangement …'

In *Crossland v Hawkins* 39 TC 493, the taxpayer was an actor who entered into a service agreement with a newly formed company. The service agreement allowed the company to exploit his services on terms which ensured that it would make substantial profits. A few months later, the so called 'slave' company was acquired by trustees of a settlement for the benefit of the taxpayer's children. The taxpayer was aware that steps were being taken in order to save tax but was not consulted at the time the deed of settlement was made. Eventually, dividends were paid by the company to the trustees, who subsequently applied them for the benefit of the taxpayer's children. Donovan LJ observed:

> I think there is sufficient unity about the whole matter to justify it being called an 'arrangement' for this purpose, because, as I have said, the ultimate object is to secure for somebody money free from what would otherwise be the burden, or the full burden, of tax. Merely because the final step to secure this objective is left unresolved at the outset and decided upon later does not seem to me to rob the scheme of the necessary unity to justify it being called an 'arrangement'.

There was therefore an 'arrangement' and thus a 'settlement', by virtue of which income accrued to the taxpayers' children. The question of whether or not the taxpayer was the 'settlor' in relation to the arrangement is discussed under (ii) below.

In *Butler v Wildin* [1989] STC 22 the taxpayers were two brothers who formed a company issuing shares to themselves and to their minor children. The taxpayers acted as unpaid directors of the company. Under their direction, the company commenced a profitable trade of land development, financed by a bank loan guaranteed by the taxpayers. The court held that dividends subsequently paid by the company to the taxpayers' minor children accrued to them by virtue of an 'arrangement' orchestrated by the taxpayers. This 'arrangement' was said in effect to consist of: (i) the incorporation of the company; (ii) the issue of shares; and (iii) the provision of services and the assumption of risk, free of charge by the taxpayers. The court also held that a transfer of shares by one of the taxpayers to a new born nephew was not part of the arrangement because it had not been contemplated at the time of the formation of the company (the transfer of shares would itself be caught under current Irish law, which applies to all settlements (as defined) in favour of minors: See **15.406**).

In *O'Dwyer v Cafolla* II ITR 82, the taxpayer, who had been a sole trader, took his sons and mother-in-law, M, into partnership with him. M played no active role in the partnership, and she alone of all the partners was entitled to assign her share in the partnership. Four days after the formation of the partnership, M assigned her partnership share in trust for the benefit of the minor children of the taxpayers. M's solicitor gave evidence that M had originally intended to leave her share in her will to the taxpayer's children but subsequently changed her mind on his advice. A 3–2 majority in the Supreme Court upheld the Appeal Commissioner's finding of fact that the formation of the partnership and the assignment by M were not part of a single arrangement. Accordingly, the income accruing for the benefit of the taxpayer's minor children was attributable to the assignment by M, and could not be related back to the formation of the partnership by the taxpayer (under current Irish law, any income arising under a trust in favour of minors would be caught: see **15.406**).

The requirement of bounty

TCA 1997, s 792(1)–(4) ('income under dispositions for short periods') explicitly excludes any disposition made for 'valuable and sufficient consideration'. However, it has been held that, in any event, only transactions with an element of bounty will normally fall within the settlement provisions. (See also *IRC v Plummer* [1979] STC 793 where a tax-saving objective was held to be commercial in this context and the arrangements in question therefore lacked 'bounty'; *IRC v Levy* [1982] STC 442).

In *IRC v Leiner* 41 TC 589, the respondent's mother (M) was, following a series of loan transactions, owed £34,000 by T Ltd, a company in which the taxpayer (L) had an interest. M then executed a settlement under which L, his wife and his minor son had discretionary interests. Subsequently, T Ltd repaid the £34,000 due to M. On the same day, M paid the £34,000 to the trustees to be held on the trusts of their settlement. A few days later, the trustees lent the £34,000 to L at six per cent interest and he in turn lent £34,000 to T Ltd, interest-free. The trustees applied the loan interest received from L for the benefit of L's minor son. It was held that the trustee's loan interest income arose from a 'settlement' by L and was therefore correctly assessed as his income.

In his judgment, Plowman J felt he could not disassociate the interest-free loan to T Ltd from the other transactions which had preceded it. Looking at the arrangement as a whole, he found it impossible to say that L did not provide the trustees with an income equal to the interest on the loan of £34,000 in the sense required, ie as a transaction involving an element of bounty. *IRC v Leiner* again illustrates the wide scope of the term 'arrangement'.

In *O'Dwyer v Cafolla* (discussed above), the taxpayer's sons each received a share of partnership profits in the sum of £2,602 pa whereas previously they had received £150 pa as employees of the business. In the Supreme Court, O'Byrne J (Geoghegan J concurring) said:

> The entire income consists of the profits arising from the partnership business and the portions of this income, which the inspector seeks to treat as income of the father, are the shares of these profits which under the terms of the Partnership Deed, are payable to the three children. In no way can these shares of the profits of the business be said to be paid or payable to the children by virtue of a settlement by the father. Until the Partnership Deed was entered into, there was no partnership and there could be no partnership profits. That Deed, at one and the same moment, created the partnership and provided for the distribution of the profits of the business to be carried on by the partners. In law, and subject to the express terms of the Partnership Deed as to the distribution of profits and otherwise, all the partners are equal and Joseph Cafolla cannot be regarded as settlor any more than any of the other partners.

The other majority judges did not comment directly on this aspect of the case. It is implicit in the remarks of O'Byrne J that the actual division of partnership profits in *Cafolla* did not entail bounty and that this sufficed to dispose of the Revenue argument that a settlement existed. However, it is clear that the initial creation of the partnership was a disposition involving an act of bounty, as a result of which partnership profits accrued to the taxpayer's children. The fact that the disposition gave rise to a new source of income (ie partnership profits in the hands of each partner) does not seem to negate the true nature of the taxpayer's disposition.

While TCA 1997, s 798 reverses the decision in the *Cafolla* case it only applies to the creation of interests in favour of the taxpayer's children. Accordingly, the correctness (or otherwise) of the approach taken by the majority judges in *Cafolla* is still a relevant issue.

TCA 1997, Pt 31, Ch 2 (dispositions in favour of minors)

ITA 1967, Pt XXVIII, Ch II defines 'settlement' as including 'any disposition, trust, covenant, agreement or arrangement, and *any transfer of money or other property or of any right to money or property'*. The definition is therefore in substance the same as that which applies to Pt XXVIII, Ch I, with the addition of the words in italics (see the discussion above). In *Thomas v Marshall* 34 TC 178, a transfer of money was held to be a settlement for these purposes. A contention that the definition only applied to transfers which were in the nature of a 'settlement' in its everyday sense of a 'trust' was rejected (see also *Hood Barrs v IRC* 27 IRC 385: gift of shares held to be a settlement).

There may well be difficulties in tracing income to a 'settlement' which consists of an outright transfer of capital, especially where the beneficiary regularly turns over his investments. If the capital is used to discharge a pre-existing liability, then it will obviously not give rise directly to any income. However depending on the facts, the Revenue might be able to argue that the initial incurring of the liability was itself part of a 'wider' arrangement.

(ii) 'Settlor'

TCA 1997, Pt 31, Ch I does not refer to a 'settlor' as such, but rather to the person who 'makes' the disposition, whether directly or indirectly (TCA 1997, s 791(2);792(1)(b)). TCA 1997, Pt 31, Ch 2 simply refers to the 'settlor' (TCA 1997, ss 795; 794(5); 797) without any distinction between 'direct' and 'indirect' settlors. In *EG v MacShamhrain* II ITR 352, Teevan J rejected an argument that the term 'settlor' should effectively be construed as equivalent to 'trustee'. He said:

> If transfers, disposition or contracts are to be treated as settlements, I would think that the transferors, disposers or contractors as the case may be must be regarded as settlors …

Accordingly, where an individual appointed away her interest in income under the terms of a trust *she* was the settlor in respect of that income and not the individual who had established the original trust.

In *Chinn v Collins* [1981] STC 1, trustees exercised a power of appointment under the terms of a discretionary trust in favour of the taxpayers. The House of Lords held that the exercise of this power completed the bounty of the original settlor. *Chinn v Collins* may be distinguished from *EG v MacShamhrain* on the basis that in the latter case the person exercising the trust power thereby relinquished a beneficial interest in the trust.

Where the 'disposition' or 'settlement' is in the nature of an arrangement, the identity of the settlor can be more difficult to resolve. In *Copeman v Coleman* (see above) it was held that the taxpayer's exercise of their control over 'their' company in order to pass the necessary resolutions represented an 'indirect' settlement by them.

The definition of 'settlor' in the equivalent UK provisions is expressly stated to include *inter alia* 'any person who has provided or undertaken to provide funds directly or indirectly for the purposes of the settlement'. In the *MacShamhrain* case, Teevan J was of the view that the lack of such an explicit definition in the Irish provisions *strengthened* the Revenue Commissioner's position, but this point still remains open.

In *Mills v IRC* 49 TC 367, the taxpayer was party to a scheme similar to that undertaken in *Crossland v Hawkins* (see above). The House of Lords held that she was a settlor because, by entering into a service agreement with the 'slave' company, she had indirectly provided the trust with funds (ie the source of the dividends received by the trust was money paid to the company held by the trust, which otherwise would have been paid to the taxpayer for her services).

In *Butler v Wildin* (see above) the taxpayers were treated as settlors because the source of the dividends paid to their children was their unpaid exertions and assumptions of risk. This decision has been criticised on the basis that the taxpayers provided expertise rather than funds to their children's company.

In *Garnett v Jones* [2005] EWCA Civ 1553 the UK Court of Appeal, reversing the decision of the High Court, distinguished the decisions in *Mills v IRC* and *Butler v Wildin*. The taxpayer in that case had set up a company with the initial shareholding being held equally by himself and his wife. The taxpayer was the sole director of the company and held the casting vote as a shareholder. All of the company's income was attributable to service contracts undertaken by the taxpayer, although his wife also undertook significant administrative tasks. Apart from two years in which the taxpayer received a full salary and his wife received no salary (as a result of other tax considerations), the taxpayer and his wife received nominal salaries. The profits of the company were subsequently distributed as dividends equally between the taxpayer and his wife. At the time that the company was incorporated, it was not carrying on a trade and the taxpayer had not yet obtained any service contracts. The Court of Appeal held that the arrangements (consisting of the incorporation of the company, issuing of shares to the taxpayer and his wife and the appointment of the taxpayer as sole director) lacked the requisite element of bounty; this followed because at the time the arrangements came into being, it was not known what salary the taxpayer might charge and whether there would in fact be any profits available for distribution or whether any such profits would even be subsequently distributed. Furthermore, given this fluidity and uncertainty, it was not legitimate to combine the initial arrangements with subsequent events and treat them as an overall arrangement.

However, the House of Lords [2007] UKHL 35 subsequently rejected this analysis. Lord Hoffmann, giving the leading judgement, accepted the proposition that the acquisition of the company and the transfer of a share to the taxpayer's wife, enabling her to receive the dividends which were expected to be paid, was an arrangement. It was not a transaction at arm's length because the taxpayer would never have agreed to the transfer of half the issued share capital, carrying with it an expectation or hope of substantial dividends, to a stranger who merely undertook to provide the paid services which his wife provided. In his view, that provided the necessary 'element of bounty'. He also took the view that what happened subsequently to the arrangement, namely the earning of money by the company – which was expected but not guaranteed – could not be part of the initial arrangement because it was still at that time contingent (in contrast to *Crossland v Hawkins* where the income stream for the company was already guaranteed because it was to receive income from a film which was already arranged). Nevertheless, it constituted income which arose under the arrangement as originally expected and foreseen.

It remains an open question as to what weight the Irish courts might give to the decisions in cases such as *Mills v IRC*, *Butler v Wildin* and *Garnett v Jones*. The approach taken by the Supreme Court in *O'Dwyer v Cafolla* seems to imply that where a new source of income is created by the disposition, then one looks at the position immediately after the creation of that source. Thus, for example, it would be open for the taxpayer to argue in a case such as *Mills v IRC* that the 'slave' company was fully entitled to all of the profits which it made, and that there was accordingly no settlement in relation to *those* profits. It may be that the courts would not follow *Cafolla*, or would else seek to distinguish it in the light of different sets of factual circumstances.

In *IRC v Wachtel* 46 TC 353, the taxpayer arranged for an overdraft to be granted to a trust. He guaranteed the overdraft and deposited a sum sufficient to cover it with the lending bank. It was agreed that the taxpayer's deposit would carry no interest and that the overdraft would be charged interest at a rate of only one per cent. The overdraft was used by the trust to acquire income-bearing investments. The court held that the taxpayer was a settlor on the basis that he had directly or indirectly provided funds for the purposes of the trust. In the Irish context, the correct analysis would seem to be that the taxpayer's foregoing of interest on his deposit was a disposition and that the trust income arose indirectly as a consequence of that disposition.

The legislation does not provide for the situation where there are two or more settlors. This could have the effect of making the provisions unworkable where it is not possible to apportion the contributions of the settlor, in the light of *Vestey v IRC* (discussed at **17.202**); see also *IRC v Herbert* 25 TC 93.

In *IRC v Clarkson-Webb* 17 TC 451 two individuals made an arrangement to execute covenants in favour of each other's children. It was held that each individual was a settlor in respect of the income accruing to his own child.

15.403 Income subject to power of revocation

TCA 1997, s 791(2) provides that income must be treated as the income of a person if he has, directly or indirectly, made a disposition by virtue or in consequence of which he has retained any power of revocation, power of appointment or any other means by which he is able, without the consent of any other person, to obtain for himself the beneficial enjoyment of that income. In other words, if the disponer has not divested himself irrevocably of the beneficial enjoyment of the income, that income remains his income for tax purposes as it arises.

TCA 1997, s 791(2) is capable of applying to tax the disponer whether the income itself was the subject of the disposition or if the income arises from capital of which the disponer has not divested himself absolutely by an irrevocable transfer or settlement. Even if there has been an irrevocable transfer of the capital, if the disponer retains any power of appointment over the income so that he can recall it for his own beneficial enjoyment, the section applies to tax him on the income. The retention of a power of appointment or power of revocation which the disponer cannot exercise in any way other than to appoint or cause the income to be paid to or applied for the benefit of any person other than himself does not cause TCA 1997, s 791(2) to apply.

If it is possible for the disponer to obtain the beneficial enjoyment of the income through the exercise by his spouse (and not by himself) of the power of appointment, revocation, etc, the power is deemed to be exercisable by the disponer so that he (or she) remains the person taxable (TCA 1997, s 791(4)). On the other hand, the section does not apply if the power of appointment, revocation, etc is provided for on the basis that it may only be exercised by the disponer if he obtains the consent of another person. This other person may not, however, be the disponer's spouse, unless they are living apart either by agreement or under a court order (TCA 1997, s 791(3)).

In *D'Ambrumenil v IRC* 23 TC 440, the appellant covenanted to pay certain sums to trustees who were required by deed to hold the sums upon trust to accumulate them by investment, to pay to another person out of the income arising to the fund such sums as the appellant should direct, and to accumulate the balance. The sums due for investment were to be invested as the appellant might direct, but the trustees were required to advance to him, on his request, any part of the funds in their hands for such period and upon such terms as he chose. The trustees were not to be liable for any loss of monies so advanced. It was held (*inter alia*) that, as the appellant had in effect the power to obtain for himself the beneficial enjoyment of the income arising to the trustees by requiring them to advance the income to them, he remained taxable on the income under the former UK equivalent of TCA 1997, s 791(2).

In *IRC v Firth* 17 TC 603 it was held that a settlement which could be revoked on the settlor's first obtaining the written consent of his accountant 'or of some person appointed by me other than a wife of mine' fell outside the equivalent of TCA 1997, s 791.

In *Hughes v Smith* I ITR 411 the taxpayer, a nun, transferred funds into a trust under which the income was to be applied for various religious and charitable purposes. The trust deed provided that in the event of the taxpayer leaving her religious order, she was to take an absolute interest in the trust funds, subject to (*inter alia*) discharging various long-term commitments out of the trust income.

The High Court held that the taxpayer could, as a consequence of the terms of the trust deed, obtain the trust income by leaving her order (this bringing her within the equivalent of TCA 1997, s 791). The court rejected an argument that the means of obtaining the trust income had to be analogous to a power of appointment or a power of revocation. The court did not consider it material that the taxpayer would not have been able to obtain the immediate beneficial enjoyment of the income on leaving her order. Hanna J (dissenting) likened the taxpayer's rights to the existence of a power of revocation which was exercisable only at a future date (when, in his view, the equivalent of TCA 1997, s 791 could not apply).

In *O'Dwyer v Cafolla* (see above) a 3–2 majority in the Supreme Court rejected the argument that TCA 1997, s 791 applied to a partnership deed under which the individual who had initiated the partnership could terminate it at any time and recover possession of all of the partnership assets for his own use. The court held that once the taxpayer had terminated the partnership there could no longer be any partnership income for him to enjoy. As noted above, the majority of judges were heavily influenced by the fact that the partnership represented a source of income distinct from the taxpayer's sole tradership.

Foreign element

It has been held in the United Kingdom that the reference to income in the former UK FA 1922, s 20 (the equivalent of the present Irish TCA 1997, s 791) excluded any income not within the charge to UK income tax (*Ormonde v Brown* 17 TC 331, as upheld by the House of Lords in *Astor v Perry* 19 TC 255). Lord Macmillan said in the *Astor* case:

> The result of the process of 'deeming' which the section directs is, in my opinion, not to bring into tax income not previously chargeable but to substitute one person for another as

> the person liable to be charged in respect of income already chargeable. To justify reading the section as on the one hand imposing a charge on income not at present subject to charge and on the other hand as exempting from charge altogether income which is at present chargeable – for that is the result of the Crown's contention – would, in my view, require much more express and precise language than the section contains'.

As indicated by Lord Macmillan, it also generally follows that neither will TCA 1997, s 791 apply to deem the non-Irish income of B (who is Irish resident) to be the income of A (who is non-Irish resident): *Becker v Wright* 42 TC 591. The scope of the decision in *Astor v Perry* must however be considered in the light of TCA 1997, s 821, which imposes a liability in certain cases in respect of non-Irish income accruing to individuals who are not resident, but who are ordinarily resident, in the State. (See **13.503**, **13.504**). There may also be room to doubt whether the Irish courts would necessarily uphold Lord MacMillan's purposive approach which is tantamount to a presumption that a deeming provision cannot alter the taxable status of income in the absence of explicit words to that effect.

Where non-resident trustees receive income from foreign possessions and there are no Irish beneficiaries absolutely entitled to the income, that income is outside the normal territorial limits (see **1.501**) of Irish taxation. Accordingly, such income cannot be attributed to an Irish resident settlor under TCA 1997, s 791. However, the provisions of TCA 1997, s 806 may apply in these circumstances to a settlor who is resident or ordinarily resident in the State (see **Division 17**). It also follows that TCA 1997, s 791 does not permit income from foreign possessions which accrues to an Irish resident to be attributed to a non-resident settlor, so that it would thereby fall outside the scope of Irish taxation (see *Becker v Wright* discussed in **15.404**).

It would seem that the principle in *Astor v Perry* does not apply where the income of the trustees would be exempt in their hands only by virtue of a double tax treaty. This is because it would seem that one must firstly arrive at the final tax position under Irish domestic tax law, and only once that point is reached does it become necessary to determine the effects of any relevant double tax treaty. The issue also arises as to whether a settlor to whom income is imputed under TCA 1997, s 791 can claim the benefit of double tax treaty: see **17.209**.

15.404 Income under dispositions for short periods

TCA 1997, s 792(1)(b) provides that, subject to stated exceptions, income must be treated as the income of the person who has made any disposition (other than one for valuable and sufficient consideration) which has resulted in that income becoming payable to or applicable for the benefit of any other person. There is a Revenue precedent to the effect that pensions paid to former partners by a partnership may in principle be regarded as being incurred for valuable and sufficient consideration (ie so that TCA 1997, s 792 will not apply).

An individual, or any other person is not permitted in any circumstances to reduce his own taxable income by giving away the income or the source from which it arises *unless* either:

(a) the income arises from capital of which the disponer has divested himself absolutely in favour of the person to whom the income is payable or applicable; or

(b) the income is payable under a deed of covenant or other legally binding instrument to certain individuals or to certain other specified persons for a stated minimum period.

The precise import of the requirement that the taxpayer should have 'divested' himself 'absolutely' of the capital transferred is uncertain. It seems clear that a 'revocable disposition' within TCA 1997, s 791 would not meet this requirement. Further, some settlements which fall outside TCA 1997, s 791 will not meet the requirements. An obvious example is a settlement which can be revoked with the consent of a third party (other than the settlor's spouse). Other examples include settlements where capital reverts to the settlor at the end of a fixed period, and or possibly also those which incorporate powers of revocation exercisable only at some future date (*see* the remarks of Hanna J in *Hughes v Smith* discussed in **15.403**). Waivers of dividends to the extent they may fall within the settlement provisions would also fall outside exception (a), as would other assignments of income (some assignments may not be effective for tax purposes in any event, irrespective of TCA 1997, s 792; see eg *Hadlee v CIR* [1993] STC 294; *O'Coindealbhain v Gannon* III ITR 484 and *Parker v Chapman* 13 TC 677).

It will be necessary for the purposes of applying TCA 1997, s 792 to identify the capital which is the subject of the settlement. The UK case law suggests that the assets of a company which is held by a trust cannot normally be treated as assets of the settlement (*IRC v Chamberlain* 25 TC 317).

Where there is an outright transfer of capital by way of gift or settlement, etc, the income arising after the date of transfer will normally be taxable as the income of the recipient. However, income arising from gifts or settlements in favour of minors will generally continue to be treated as that of the settlor (see **15.406**).

If the settlor has not divested himself absolutely of the underlying capital or if the transfer is one of income (typically by means of a deed of covenant) then the income will be deemed to be that of the settlor unless it is income payable to an individual for his own use, or income that is applicable for the benefit of a named individual, if so payable or applicable for a period which exceeds or may exceed six years. It is understood that the Revenue Commissioners may be prepared to treat the research arm of a charity as a 'college' for these purposes, subject to the satisfaction of certain conditions.

While it may be possible to create 'short term' settlements by means other than a deed of covenant (eg through a 'fixed term' trust or in some cases by an assignment of income), in practice the limits noted below will impact primarily on deeds of covenants. Accordingly, the term 'deed of covenant' will be treated hereafter as being synonymous with 'short-term settlement of income'.

Covenants will generally be effective only if they are either in favour of an individual who is either:

(a) permanently incapacitated by reason of mental or physical infirmity: this exception does *not* apply to the minor children (including adopted children, stepchildren and illegitimate children) of the covenantor which will fall within TCA 1997, s 795: see **15.406**; or

(b) aged 65 or older.

In situation (b), the payment under the covenant is effective only up to an amount equal to five per cent of the covenantor's total income.

TCA 1997, s 792 does not permit income to be transferred for tax purposes to any person who is not an individual. However, income may be covenanted to trustees if they are required to pay or apply the income for the benefit of an individual for the required period.

In drafting a deed of covenant, care should be taken to ensure that the wording clearly provides for the payments of income to continue for at least the required minimum period. The fact that the payments may cease on the happening of certain contingencies before the end of the period does not invalidate the deed of covenant provided that, at the time the deed was made, there was no certainty that the contingency would happen before the end of the period. For example, the fact that the deed provides for the payments to cease on the death of either party or, say, on a future change in the tax law affecting the covenantor's tax position, does not affect the covenant. On the other hand, a covenant made by an uncle on his niece's 18th birthday to pay her £100 each year up to and including her 21st birthday is not effective for tax purposes as the payments cannot continue for more than six years.

In determining whether or not income is payable in excess of six years, the principle was established by the Court of Appeal in *IRC v St Luke's Hostel Trustee* 15 TC 682 that the period must be calculated from the due date of the first payment until the due date of the last payment as provided for in the relevant deed or other instrument. In that case, a deed provided for payments for a seven-year period from 6 April 1926, with the first payment to be made on 31 December 1926 and the subsequent payments on each succeeding 31 December in the period. The deed was not in fact executed until 3 February 1927. Although the seven-year period ran from 6 April 1926 up to 5 April 1933, the period over which the annual payments were made had to be measured from 3 February 1927 (date of first payment) to 31 December 1932 (last payment), ie a period of only five years and eleven months. This was a UK case where income covenanted to a charity for a period exceeding six years was deductible from the covenantor's income; there is no corresponding deduction under Irish tax law for covenants in favour of a charity.

A covenant in favour of an individual should provide for the payments to continue for a period of seven years from the date of execution of the deed and the first payment should be made on that date and no later. If not, the Inspector may be able to disallow the income transfer, as in the *St Luke's Hostel* case. Payments need not necessarily be paid once a year. A covenant may provide for payments on a half yearly, quarterly or monthly basis, but it is always necessary to ensure that there is the required time interval between the first and last payments. The Revenue Commissioners have indicated that they will follow the UK decisions in this area.

A retrospective variation of a covenant will not usually be effective for tax purposes: see *Morley-Clarke v Jones* [1985] STC 660, discussed at **1.408**.

The rules of TCA 1997, s 791 (see **15.403**) apply to disallow for tax purposes any transfer of income made by a deed of covenant (or other instrument) if the covenantor retains any power of revocation or similar right by which, without the consent of any other person, he may cease to make the payments before the end of the period of the covenant. As discussed, it is possible to include a term which would permit him to stop the payments if he obtains the permission of a named third party other than his spouse.

The amount of income which a person covenants to pay each year is treated as an annual payment. Consequently, if paid wholly out of the covenantor's income brought into charge to income tax, each payment is a payment to which TCA 1997, s 237 applies so that the payer is entitled to deduct and retain income tax at the standard rate (see

2.303). If it is not paid wholly out of income charged to income tax, the payer is required by TCA 1997, s 238 to deduct income tax at that rate and to account for the tax to the Revenue Commissioners (see **2.304**). In either case, the payer's total income for each relevant tax year is reduced by the grossed up amount of the payments made in that year (up to the amount of that total income) in question in accordance with the terms of the covenant. The recipient includes the gross payments in his total income for the same year and is entitled to credit the income tax deducted against his own income tax liability and, if appropriate, to obtain a repayment of any excess income tax for which he is not liable.

Where a payment under a deed of covenant is expressed as being 'free of tax', the amount payable (say €800) should be grossed up at the appropriate standard rate in force (ie equivalent to €1,000 gross where the standard rate is 20 per cent). However, where the recipient is entitled to a repayment of part or all of the tax withheld at source by the covenantor, the repayment should be handed back to the covenantor (*Re Pettit Le Feure v Pettit* [1992] 2 Ch 765, followed in *Re Cochrane* [1953] IR 160 and *Re Vestey Deceased* [1958] IR 268). The position is different where the payment is expressed as being 'free of tax at the standard rate', when any repayment of the tax withheld can be retained by the recipient (*Nolan v Nolan* [1958] 92 ILTR 94).

Treatment of receipt

The person who receives a covenanted payment, which is within the income transfers permitted by TCA 1997, s 792 includes the grossed up amount as taxed income in his total income for the tax year in which it is paid. He is then entitled to credit the income tax payable for the year in question. If the recipient's income including the covenanted payment is insufficient to give rise to any income tax liability, or if the tax deducted from the covenanted payment exceeds his total income tax liability (as reduced by any other credits against tax), he is entitled to be repaid the tax suffered or the excess over the total liability (whichever is appropriate).

The recipient must make a return of his total income for the relevant tax year if he is to obtain a repayment of the tax suffered (or of any part of that tax). If he has income from other sources, he is likely to be sent the necessary income tax return by the appropriate inspector and he should submit the completed return to that inspector in the ordinary way. If he has no other income or has not been sent an income tax return by any inspector, the best approach may be for the covenantor to ask his inspector for a tax return form on behalf of the recipient.

The Revenue Commissioners issued a draft deed of covenant together with guidance notes (although these need to be interpreted in the light of legislation). There are also a number of Revenue Precedents published in this area.

Foreign element

Similar considerations apply as in the case of revocable settlements. Thus, in *Becker v Wright* 42 TC 591, an individual by a deed executed in Trinidad covenanted to pay to an English bank in trust for his daughter annual sums for three years. The covenantor was resident outside the United Kingdom, but his daughter was resident with her husband in England. Her husband claimed that, as the period of the payments did not exceed six years, the payments were deemed to be the income of the non-resident covenantor. It was held (following *Astor v Perry*: see **15.403**) that, as the covenantor's foreign income was not capable of being charged to UK income tax, the UK equivalent of TCA 1997, s 792 could not deem the income to be his instead of that of his daughter to whom the payments were made. The annual payments were therefore properly assessable on her husband. Again, the decision in *Becker v Wright* needs to be considered in the light of TCA 1997, s 821 which imposes a liability in certain cases in respect of non-Irish income accruing to individuals who are not resident but who are ordinarily resident in the State.

15.405 Restriction on covenanted payments

As explained in **15.404**, it will often be the case that the amount of income which may, for tax purposes, be transferred by an individual in any tax year by deed of covenant or similar instrument cannot exceed five per cent of his total income. The amount by which the gross amounts of all covenanted payments made in the year exceeds this five per cent limit is deemed for all purposes of income tax to be the covenantor's income and not that of the persons receiving the payments. The Revenue Commissioners do not seek to apply the decision in *Ang v Parrish* [1980] STC 341, where in the context of similar, but not identical, wording it was held that the full amount of the covenanted payment should be allowed as a charge, and that the amounts falling within the equivalent of TCA 1997, s 792 would be added to the settlor's income. In other words, in practice, only a part of these income transfers is effectively allowed as a deduction in arriving at the covenantor's total income; the other part is disallowed. The Revenue Commissioners also take the view that TCA 1997, s 237 do not apply to covenanted payments which do not qualify as allowable charges: [1997] ITR 90.

Since an individual's total income is his total income from all sources as estimated in accordance with the provisions of this Act (TCA 1997, s 3(1)), the five per cent limit must accordingly be calculated by reference to the covenantor's total income *after* deducting any income that is validly transferred to become part of another person's total income. Applying the legislation in its strict sense, therefore, in making the computation, any fully allowable covenanted payments should first be deducted to arrive at a provisional total income figure before the payments which are subject to the five per cent restriction. The TCA 1997, s 792 limit is then calculated as 5/105ths of this provisional total income. In the case of a married couple assessed jointly under TCA 1997, s 1017, the aggregate of their covenanted payments to descendants is only deductible up to a maximum of five per cent of their joint total income, irrespective of which spouse entered into the covenants. The interaction between payments subject to the five per cent restriction with retirement annuity relief is described in **16.208**.

When the TCA 1997, s 792 limit applies to restrict the covenantor's income transfers in any tax year, the amount of the income transferred that is included in each convenantee's total income is correspondingly reduced. If a restricted covenanted payment has only been made to one covenantee, the amount included in that person's total income for the year is the same as the restricted income transfer allowed to the covenantor. If there are restricted covenanted payments to more than one person in a year, each such person includes in his total income a proportionate part of the restricted deduction allowed to the covenantor. Each person's proportion is taken in the ratio which the covenanted payments he is entitled to receive bears to the total of the covenanted payments which the covenantor is liable to make to all the descendants.

Example 15.405.1

Mr and Mrs Adam-Eve, assessed jointly under TCA 1997, s 1017 for the year 2015 on the income set out below, paid the following amounts under deeds of covenant during the year:

	Amount paid	*Grossed-up equivalent*
	€	€
Mary Abel (grandmother, aged 68)	898	1,122
John Adam-Eve (grandfather, aged 74)	674	843
Peter Adam-Eve (unmarried son, aged 19)	449	561
Cecil Adam-Eve (incapacitated son, aged 23)	730	913

The covenant in favour of Peter is ineffective for tax purposes as he is neither incapacitated nor elderly. The amounts deductible in arriving at Mr and Mrs Adam-Eve's total income for 2015 in respect of the other covenanted payments are as follows:

	€	€
Salary – husband		24,000
– wife		14,000
Sch D Case III income – husband		1,200
– wife		4,500
		43,700
Less:		
		4,000
Interest on qualifying loan to acquire interest in partnership		
Payment to Cecil (unrestricted)	913	
		4913
Total income (before payments under covenants to elderly adults)		38,787
Less:		
Covenants to Mary and John:		
€1,122 + €843	1,965	
Deduction restricted to:		
€38,787 x (5/105)[1]=		1,847
Total income (final)		36,940

Notes:

1. The use of the fraction 5/105 applied to the provisional total income figure enables the limit to the total deduction for the covenants to Mary and John to be arrived at. In practice, the inspector may be prepared to accept a computation with the 5/105 fraction being applied to total income before all covenanted payments (ie €(38,787+ 913) = €39,700.

2. Mary and John between them therefore must include in their respective separate total incomes a total of €1,847 (which works out at five per cent of Mr and Mrs Adam Eve's total income of €38,787). This income of €1,847 is apportioned between Mary and John in the ratio, as follows:

   Mary: €1,847 x 1,122/(1,122 + 843)= €1,055

   John: €1,847 x 843/(1,122 + 843)= €792

15.406 Settlements on minors

TCA 1997, s 795(1) treats as the income of a settlor (and not as that of any other person) any income arising by virtue or in consequence of a settlement made by him if, during his lifetime, either:

(a) that income is paid to or for the benefit of a person who at the time of payment is a minor; or

(b) that income is so dealt with that it, or assets representing it, will or may become payable or applicable in the future to or for the benefit of a person who, at the time the income is so dealt with, is a minor. ('minor' is defined in accordance with the Age of Majority Act 1985: TCA 1997, s 7).

Rule (a) is quite clear and requires little comment. Rule (b) is more involved and is subject to an important exception in that it does not apply to income accumulated for the future benefit of a minor if the settlement is one made by an 'irrevocable instrument' (see **15.407**). For rule (b) to apply, it is not essential that the minor should still be under the age of majority and unmarried when the benefit may ultimately accrue to him, nor has he to have a definite entitlement to benefit in the future. It is sufficient that he may benefit, whether this is on the fulfilment of a condition, or on the happening of a contingency, or by the exercise of a power or discretion conferred on the trustees or any other person, or in some other way.

The terms of a settlement may require or permit income to be accumulated, but may not require the accumulated income to be allocated to any particular beneficiary. In such a case, TCA 1997, s 795(2)(b) requires any income which the trustees are not required to allocate to be treated for the purposes of rule (b) as if paid, at the time the income is accumulated, in equal shares to each person to, or for whose benefit, the income will or may become payable or applicable.

This notional allocation of the unallocated income is made between all the persons included as actual or potential beneficiaries, whether or not they are minors. Then, unless the exception for an irrevocable settlement applies, the share of the income notionally allocated to each minor is treated by TCA 1997, ss 795 as the income of the settlor (and not of the trustees) as if received by him in the tax year in which the income is so dealt with.

Example 15.406.1

On 3 January 2013, Mr X gave his son John a 15th birthday present of €2,000 (nominal) 12 per cent Exchequer Stock 2000. The annual interest of €2,400 on this holding has since that date been paid to John.

Since a settlement may include a gift (see **15.404**), TCA 1997, s 795 applies to treat the €2,400 interest received by John in each of the tax years 2013, 2014 and 2015 as Mr X's income for all income tax purposes. From 3 January 2016 (John's 18th birthday) onwards, TCA 1997, s 795 ceases to apply and any of the Exchequer Stock interest paid after that date is John's income for tax purposes. Mr X is entitled to recover from John the income tax he (Mr X) pays on the €2,400 Exchequer Stock interest treated as his income by TCA 1997, s 795 (see **15.410**).

Example 15.406.2

On 12 February 2009, Mr Y transferred shares in an Irish company to trustees on trust under which they are, in their absolute discretion, to apply the income of the trust fund and the capital for the benefit of such one or more of a class of named beneficiaries in such proportions as the trustees should decide, either by paying out some or all of the income arising in any year or by accumulating it or any part of it as an addition to the capital.

No beneficiary is entitled to require the trustees to make any distribution of income or capital in his favour. The class of beneficiaries consists of Mr Y's married daughter (Anne), his son (Patrick aged 9 in 2009), his daughter (Susan aged 7 in 2009) and his wife (whose inclusion as a potential beneficiary during his life prevents the trust being treated as an irrevocable one (see **15.407**)).

In the year ended 31 December 2014, the trustees receive net Irish dividends from the company totaling €8,000 (net of Dividend Withholding Tax of €2,000) and they pay out administration expenses of €356. On 31 December 2014, the trustees exercise their discretion and distribute all the available net income, as follows:

Anne – 1/2 share to be paid direct to her

Patrick – 1/4 share to be paid towards his maintenance

Susan – 1/4 share to be paid towards her maintenance

TCA 1997, s 795 requires the part of the trust income that is paid to or for the benefit of the two minors to be taxed as the income of Mr Y, and not as that of either beneficiary or of the trustees. The income payable to Anne is not affected by this rule and, as this is a discretionary trust, her share would be assessed on the trustees and distributed to her as taxed income. The trustees are also assessable on the part of the trust income applied to meet their expenses.

In a case such as this, it may be easier to work out the tax position in terms of gross income, as follows:

	€	€
Income received by trustees:		
Dividends		8,000
Dividend withholding tax		2,000
Sch F income		10,000
Less:		
Trustees' expenses grossed up		
€356 x 100/80		445
Balance available for distribution		9,555
Distribution of balance:		
Anne – 1/2	4,777	
Patrick – 1/4	2,389	
Susan – 1/4	2,389	
		(9,555)
Income accumulated		Nil

Mr Y is therefore treated by TCA 1997, s 795 as if he received in the year 2014 (when the income was distributed) the Sch F income allocated to Patrick and Susan, ie a gross €4,777. He is entitled to the benefit of the Dividend Withholding Tax attributable to this amount (€955, ie 20 per cent of €4,777).

Example 15.406.3

Take Mr Y's settlement again. Assume that in the year 2015, the trustees distribute €1,300 in cash to Anne (the married daughter), but decide to accumulate the surplus income.

Taking the income received and the outgoings paid in the year as assumed below, the allocation of the income is worked out as follows:

	€	€
Income received by trustees:		
Dividend		8,000
Dividend Withholding Tax		2,000
Sch F income		10,000
Sch D Case III:		
Untaxed interest		2,000
Total income		12,000
Less:		
Trustees' expenses	623	
Distribution to Anne (net)	1,300	
	1,923	
Gross up:		
€1,923 x 100/80		2,404
Income accumulated		9,596

Since the trustees are not required to allocate the undistributed income, the notional allocation of TCA 1997, s 795 between the persons who may benefit is:

	€
Anne – 1/4 share	2,399
Patrick – 1/4 share	2,399
Susan – 1/4 share	2,399
Wife – 1/4 share	2,399

Mr Y was therefore treated as receiving income in the year 2015 of €4,798 (the shares of Patrick and Susan, the minors). For the purposes of assessment, this is broken down in proportion to the different types of income received by the trustees, as follows:

	€
Sch F income:	
€4,798 x 10,000/12,000	3,998
Sch D Case III:	
€4,798 x 2,000/12,000	800
	4,798

Although €4,798 of the accumulated income was notionally allocated to Anne and Mrs Y, TCA 1997, s 795 does not cause it to be taxed as the settlor's income as neither are minors. Since neither Anne nor Mrs Y actually received the income, it does not form part of their taxable income. Anne's only taxable income from the settlement in 2015 was the €1,625 (net €1,300) actually distributed to her.

The very wide scope of TCA 1997, s 795 is narrowed down somewhat by the following exceptions:

(a) income from trust property settled by an irrevocable instrument is not taxed as the income of the settlor to the extent that it is accumulated (see **15.407**);

(b) income paid to a minor, or otherwise dealt with for his future benefit, after the death of the settlor is not affected and is assessable as appropriate, either on the trustees or the minor; and

(c) as noted above, the section does not apply to any income paid to or otherwise dealt with or for the benefit of a permanently incapacitated minor, other than a child (as defined above) of the settlor (TCA 1997, s 794(4)).

Foreign income

'Income' for the purposes of TCA 1997, Pt 31, Ch 1 is not restricted to income taxable in Ireland. This is because TCA 1997, s 794(1) overrides the decision in *Astor v Perry* (see **15.403**) by defining income as 'any income chargeable to income tax by deduction or otherwise and any income which would have been so chargeable if it had been received in the State by a person resident or ordinarily resident in the State'. However, TCA 1997, s 795 does not apply in respect of income for which the settlor is not taxable as a resident in the State for the relevant tax year (TCA 1997, s 794(3)). Accordingly, TCA 1997, s 794(1) would allow overseas income received by non-resident trustees to be imputed to a resident settlor. On the other hand, the section will not apply in any case where the settlor is not resident. It may be noted in this connection that TCA 1997, s 821, which states that TCA 1997, s 18(1) is to apply as if 'an individual ordinarily resident were resident in the State' does not deem such an individual to be resident in the State. The issue also again arises as to whether a settlor to whom income is attributed under TCA 1997, s 791 can claim the benefit of double tax treaty: see **17.209**.

15.407 Income accumulated for minors under irrevocable instruments

TCA 1997, s 796(2) provides that income accumulated in any tax year for the benefit of a minor is not to be treated by TCA 1997, s 795 as the settlor's income if it arises from property vested in or held by the trustees of a settlement made by an *irrevocable* instrument. Any person making a settlement under which it is intended that income should or may be accumulated for the future benefit of any individuals who are still minors at the time he makes it should, therefore, ensure that the terms of the settlement are such as to make it an 'irrevocable' one (see below). TCA 1997, s 796(2), does not, however, apply to enable a settlor to escape liability to tax on income accumulated by the trustees that consists of annual or other periodical payments secured either by the covenant of the settlor or by a charge made by him on any part of his property or on any part of his future income (TCA 1997, s 796(1)).

Income accumulated under an irrevocable settlement within TCA 1997, s 796 is taxable as the income of the trustees by reference to the tax year in which it arises (but subject to the relevant basis of assessment rules where Sch D Case I and II income is involved). TCA 1997, s 795 remains applicable to treat as the settlor's income any settlement income that is actually paid to or for the benefit of any of his minors, whether the payment is made out of income arising in the same year or from income accumulated in a previous year. Further, a payment out of capital to a minor may also be taxed as the settlor's income to the extent TCA 1997, s 796(1), (2)(b) applies (see below).

In the absence of any other provision, the trustees of an irrevocable settlement could avoid the effect of TCA 1997, s 795, by accumulating income and paying it out at a later date in the form of capital (eg by winding up the trust) to benefit one or more minors. TCA 1997, s 796(1), (2)(b) contains the necessary anti-avoidance provision. It provides that *any sum whatsoever* paid under the trusts of an irrevocable instrument to or for the benefit of a person, who at the time of this payment, is a minor, is deemed to be paid as income (so that TCA 1997, s 795 applies to treat it as the income of the settlor). This rule applies irrespective of whether the payment is made out of income, accumulations of income or out of the capital of the trust fund, but is subject to the limitation described in the next paragraph. It follows that TCA 1997, s 795 does not cover payments in the form of capital to an individual when he is no longer a minor.

A sum cannot be deemed by TCA 1997, s 796(2)(b) to be paid as income to the extent that it exceeds the aggregate of all income that has accrued to the trustees since the settlement was made, as reduced by the aggregate of all previous payments (if any) made to or for the benefit of the same minor or of any person who was a minor at the beginning of the year of assessment on which the payment was made.

In the first instance, a settlement must, be 'irrevocable' within the normal meaning of the term (*Jenkins v IRC* 26 TC 265) subject to the statutory extensions and exceptions laid down by TCA 1997, s 794(5). Thus for example, a settlement containing a power to terminate its trusts would clearly be 'revocable' on general principles. The term 'irrevocable' is extended by TCA 1997, s 794(5) to apply to a settlement where any of its terms may permit:

(a) the settlor to be a beneficiary during the life of any person who is or may be entitled to benefit from any income or accumulations of income from the settlement;

(b) the spouse of the settlor to be a beneficiary, while the settlor is alive, during the life of any such person;

(c) the trusts of the settlement to be terminated by the act or on the default of any person; or

(d) the payment by the settlor of a penalty in the event of his failing to comply with the provisions of the instrument.

Apart only from the exceptions mentioned in the next paragraph, if the trust deed or other instrument of settlement contains any clause which would permit the settlor or his spouse (during his lifetime) to benefit from any capital, income or accumulations of income in any circumstances whatsoever, so long as any person who may benefit is alive, the settlement is not an irrevocable one for the purposes of TCA 1997, s 796. A clause permitting the settlor or his spouse to be a beneficiary after the deaths of all the persons included as actual or potential beneficiaries would not prevent the deed being treated as an irrevocable instrument, nor would one permitting the settlor's widow or widower to be a beneficiary after the death of the settlor. Because a power of revocation must be provided by the 'trusts' of the relevant instrument, the ability to obtain the assets of a company which is owned by the trust under the terms of that company's articles or memorandum should fall outside TCA 1997, s 794(5) (compare the case of *Wolfson v IRC* 31 TC 158, decided to this effect, although by reference to different statutory wording).

A settlement is not prevented from being an irrevocable instrument for the purposes of TCA 1997, s 796 by reason only of the fact that it may contain provisions which permit any of the following:

(a) any capital, income or accumulations of income to be payable to or for the benefit of the settlor or his spouse if:

   (i) the person for whose benefit income or accumulation of income may be payable should become bankrupt, or

(ii) such a person should make any assignment of or a charge on the capital, income or accumulations of income; or

(b) the termination of the trusts in such circumstances that, it would not, during the lifetime of any such person, benefit anybody other than the person, his spouse or his issue.

A taxpayer who seeks to avail of one of these exceptions must bear in mind the provisions of TCA 1997, s 792 which impose a liability on the settlor in respect of income which arises from capital of which he has not divested himself absolutely (see **15.403**). However, income which is accumulated for the benefit of a minor with a vested interest in the trust income is the income of the minor for tax purposes (see **15.307**) and is correspondingly outside the scope of the surcharge (see **15.308**).

It is not necessarily a disadvantage for trust income to be taxable as the income of the settlor. Since the introduction of the 20 per cent surcharge on undistributed trust income (see **15.308**), income that is accumulated by the trustees of a discretionary or other settlement permitting accumulations is now generally subject to income tax at a combined rate of 40 per cent. If for any tax year, the settlor's other income is such that his marginal rate of income tax is less than 40 per cent, it could be advantageous for him to request the trustees of the irrevocable settlement to distribute income to one or more of the minor unmarried beneficiaries.

There is a further point to be borne in mind. The trustees must pay the surcharge if the income is not distributed within 18 months after the end of the tax year in which it arises and, if distributed later, the surcharge already payable cannot be refunded (TCA 1997, s 805) (see **15.308**).

15.408 Basis of assessment on settlor

When any of the above provisions apply to treat the income of a settlement as that of the settlor, it is the actual income received by the trustees that is attributed to the settlor. Consequently, the basis on which the settlor is assessed on the trust income has to be considered separately for each relevant Schedule or Case under which the trust income falls.

15.409 Transfer of interest in trade to children

TCA 1997, s 798 in its original form was brought in to counter the decision in *O'Dwyer v Cafolla* II ITR 82. TCA 1997, s 798(1) deems the transfer of a trade or of an interest in a trade by an individual to one or more of his children to constitute a settlement for the purposes of TCA 1997, s 795 (and its supporting sections). There is such a transfer of a trade where, by any means or steps whatsoever a trade which, before those steps were taken, was carried on by the individual solely or in partnership becomes, as a result of those steps, carried on either by one or more of his children or in a partnership in which the individual and one or more of his children are partners. The means or steps adopted which result in such a change in the person(s) carrying on the trade may be direct or indirect and may include or consist of a series of operations.

The effect of TCA 1997, s 798 is to cause any profits or share of profits from the trade accruing to a child of the settlor who is a minor to be treated by TCA 1997, s 795 as the income of the parent who transferred the interest in the trade and who, in consequence, is deemed to be a settlor. This is subject to one qualification. If the child or children whose profits are deemed to be the income of the parent work in the business, the income of the parent resulting from this section is reduced by an amount equal to the salary that would have been appropriately payable to the child if he had been an employee. This notional salary is deemed to be income taxable under Sch E in the hands of the child.

It may be noted that TCA 1997, s 798 does not apply to professions or to minors who are not children of the taxpayer.

15.410 Recovery of tax from trustees

Any person who has been charged to, and has paid, income tax on any income treated as his by TCA 1997, ss 795, 796 is entitled to recover this tax from the trustees or any other person (eg his minor child) to whom the income is actually payable (TCA 1997, s 797(1)). Conversely, if the settlor obtains any repayment of income tax as a result of the treatment of the settlement income as his, he is required to pay over to the trustee or other person entitled to the income the amount of the tax repaid (TCA 1997, s 797(2)). The settlor could for example, obtain a repayment of tax for a year in which the addition of the relevant settlement income to his other income enables him to use personal allowances or some other form of relief (eg a TCA 1997, s 381 loss claim subject to new anti-avoidance provisions, TCA 1997, ss 381B and 381C) which, because his own income was not high enough, would not otherwise have been fully utilised. If there would have been some repayment of tax before adding the settlement income, only the extra repayment is refundable to the trustee or other person.

Similarly, if a person has been charged to and has paid income tax on income arising from a disposition which, by reason of TCA 1997, s 792 is treated as his income (see **15.404**), that person is entitled to recover this income tax from any trustee or other person to whom the income is actually payable (TCA 1997, s 793(1)). Correspondingly, any repayment or additional repayment of income tax obtained by the person chargeable by TCA 1997, s 792 must be paid over to the person to whom the income is in fact payable (TCA 1997, s 793(2)). In determining the amount recoverable from, or refundable to, the trustee or other person by the settlor (TCA 1997, s 797) or by the person who made the disposition (TCA 1997, s 793), the relevant extra income is treated as if it were the highest part of the income of the settlor or disponer (TCA 1997, s 793(3); s 797(4)). The Revenue Commissioners are required, where any of these rules apply, to give the settlor or disponer a certificate specifying the additional income treated as his and the amount of tax paid; this will be evidence thereof, unless the contrary is proved (TCA 1997, ss 793(1)(b); 797(1)(b)).

Example 15.410.1

Mr A Mann who is aged 68 executed a discretionary settlement under an irrevocable instrument some years ago. In the years 2014 and 2015 the trustees had total incomes of €9,000 and €10,000 respectively from the trust property all subject to tax at source. After paying trust expenses of €560 and €640 in those years, the trustees paid out cash of €1,871 in 2014 and €1,692 in 2015 towards the school fees of Mr Mann's 15 year old nephew, but the balance of the income (after the trustees' income tax and expenses) is accumulated.

The payments for the school fees are treated as paid out of taxed income for inclusion in Mr Mann's total income for each year as follows:

	€
2014:	
€1,871 x 100/80	2,339
2015:	
€1,692 x 100/80	2,115

Mr and Mrs Mann's only income of their own arises from a trade carried on by him assessable under Sch D Case I. They are assessed jointly under TCA 1997, s 1018. Assuming the income and allowances set out below, their income tax position (including the distributions of the settlement income taxable under TCA 1997, s 795) is as follows:

	2014	*2015*
	€	€
Sch D Case I:	82,800	33,500
Income from settlement (TCA 1997, s 795):		
Taxed income (as above)	2,339	2,115
Total income		35,615
	85,139	
Income tax payable:		
€41,800x 20%	8,360	
€43,339 x 41%	17,769	
Age income exemption applies		Nil
	26,129	
Less: Tax Credits – Personal	(3,300)	-
Age	(490)	
Less:		
Income tax on taxed income €2,339 x 20%/€2,115 x 20%	(468)	(423)
Net income tax payable 2014	21,871	-
Income tax refund due 2015		(423)

For 2014, the €2,339 income from the settlement, as taxed as the highest part of his income, resulted in an increase in Mr Mann's total income tax liability by €959 (€2,339 x 41%) in respect of which €468 tax was deducted at source. He is now entitled to recover from the trustees the additional tax of €491 actually paid by him (€959 less €468).

For 2015 without the addition of the settlement income, Mr Mann would not have had any income tax repayment claim; accordingly, he is required to pay over the full income tax refund of €423 to the trustees.

Division 16 Retirement Plans

16.1 Overview and Occupational Pension Schemes

16.101 Introduction

The Tax Acts contain various rules which facilitate the funding during an individual's working life of a pension or retirement annuity (and certain related benefits including tax-free cash lump sums) payable on his retirement, or otherwise on his death or in his old age. In addition, certain individuals may retain part of their retirement funds without converting them into a pension or annuity, subject to prescribed conditions. Individuals in employment and their employers are permitted to make tax-deductible contributions to approved pension or superannuation schemes, PRSAs and qualifying overseas pension plans, while self-employed and certain other individuals are entitled to tax relief for their contributions to approved retirement annuity plans, PRSAs and qualifying overseas pension plans. Further, the investment income and capital gains resulting from the investment of the funds of approved pension schemes, retirement annuity plans and PRSAs are exempted from taxation, thus enhancing the value of the funds available to provide the required pensions and other benefits.

In providing this favourable tax regime, the legislation aims to encourage employers, employees and self-employed individuals to put money aside during the earning life of the individuals to secure their income in retirement. This has the advantage of relieving the State of a potential future obligation to provide for the individuals in their old age.

The Income Tax Acts do not, however, allow unlimited or uncontrolled tax free funding of pension scheme and retirement plan benefits. The legislation is drafted to ensure that the pension schemes and retirement plans follow certain well defined parameters within government policy. The Acts do this by only granting the benefits of favourable tax treatment to pension schemes or retirement plans that are approved by the Revenue Commissioners as meeting a number of conditions specified in the legislation regarding the type and level of benefits provided, the level of contributions etc. One other compelling reason for following the approved pension scheme route is the rule which treats contributions by an employer to an unapproved scheme as additional taxable emoluments of the employees, albeit subject to a number of exceptions (see **16.104**).

In principle, an approved pension scheme, retirement plan or PRSA must provide benefits for the individuals covered in the form of pensions or retirement annuities, which are taxable as income when received after retirement. However, the legislation permits an approved scheme or plan to allow an individual to elect, on his retirement, to commute a limited proportion of his pension or retirement annuity for a tax free lump sum. Further, an approved scheme or plan may provide for a tax free capital sum to be payable to the individual's dependants or personal representatives in the event of his death before his pension or retirement annuity becomes payable.

Furthermore, a number of additional options are available to the self-employed, five per cent directors (20 per cent directors prior to 6 April 2000) holders of AVCs and with effect from 6 February 2011 other individuals in defined contribution schemes. These options are discussed in more detail in **16.4**. Similar options apply to funds held within a PRSA (see **16.3**). Finance Act 2013 allows individuals to withdraw funds in AVCs prior to retirement (see **16.114**).

The subject of approved pension schemes and retirement annuity plans requires to be discussed under four separate headings. First, occupational pension schemes, ie schemes provided by employers for their employees (and, in the case of a company, for its directors), are dealt with in **16.102** onwards. Secondly, self-employed retirement plans which are available not only to self-employed individuals, but also to any individual who has earnings from an office or employment that is not a pensionable office or employment are covered in **16.2**. Thirdly, personal retirement savings accounts (PRSAs), which are effectively portable pension schemes and which may be available to self-employed or individuals in employment are covered in **16.3**. Fourthly, the relief available for contributions by migrant workers to a qualifying overseas pension plan is set out in **16.6**.

The legislation limits the quantum of the tax-relieved pension benefits and lump sums and these are outlined at **16.5**.

Finally, although they are separate and distinct from pension schemes and retirement plans it is convenient to discuss also in this chapter the subject of purchased life annuities (see **Division 16.7**).

16.102 Approved pension schemes: general principles

TCA 1997, Pt 30, Ch 1 contains the main rules under which the Revenue Commissioners may approve occupational pension schemes. It also deals with the taxation treatment of contributions by employers and employees to, and of benefits arising from, such schemes.

TCA 1997, Pt 30, Ch 1 in fact provides tax relief for contributions to two types of 'retirement benefit scheme' (the term used in the legislation to denote an occupational pension scheme – see **16.103**). These are the 'approved scheme' and the 'statutory scheme'. The discussion which follows is concerned almost entirely with approved schemes only (except for a few brief references to statutory schemes). The subject of statutory schemes – relating to individuals in government service, certain semi-state bodies and other employments which provide a superannuation scheme as the result of a public statute – is dealt with briefly in **16.113**.

Before dealing with the subject in more detail, it may be useful to give a brief summary of the more important tax rules affecting retirement benefit schemes as follows:

(a) the contributions (if any) of an employee (or of a director of a company) to an 'exempt approved scheme' (see **16.103**) are deductible (within set limits) in computing that employee's emoluments chargeable to income tax (see **16.108**);

(b) the contributions of an employer paid to an exempt approved scheme are deductible in computing the employer's profits chargeable to tax (whether income tax or corporation tax) from his trade, profession etc (see **16.108**);

(c) the income and capital gains from the investments or deposits of an exempt approved scheme are exempted respectively from the taxes on income and chargeable (capital) gains (see **16.111**);

(d) any payments made by an employer, under a retirement benefits scheme, to provide any 'relevant benefits' (see **16.103**) for any of his employees (or for a director) is taxable as income of the employee (or director), *unless* paid under an approved scheme or is subject to a statutory or concessional exception (see **16.104**); and

(e) pensions paid under an approved scheme are generally chargeable to income tax and are subject to the PAYE deduction at source procedure (see **16.110**).

The detailed rules regarding the application of these principles are now discussed in **16.103–16.113**.

Finally, it may be noted that all approved schemes come within the regulatory framework of the Pensions Act 1990, together with the Pensions Act 1996, Pensions (Amendment) Act 2002 and Social Welfare and Pensions Act 2012 and supplementary regulations. (It should be noted that the provisions of that Act apply also, with certain modifications, to members of UK pension schemes with Irish service: SI 238/1994.)

16.103 Definitions

TCA 1997, Pt 30, Ch 1 provides the following definitions of various terms used for the purposes of the rules relating to retirement benefit schemes:

Retirement benefits scheme: any scheme for the provision of benefits consisting of or including relevant benefits, but not including any scheme under the Social Welfare Consolidation Act providing such benefits. For this purpose, a 'scheme' includes a contract, deed, agreement, series of agreements, or other arrangements providing for relevant benefits notwithstanding that it or they relates or relate only to a small number of employees or a single employee or the payment of a pension starting immediately on the making of the arrangements (TCA 1997, s 771(1)).

Relevant benefits: any pension, lump sum, gratuity or other like benefit to be given on retirement or on death, or in anticipation of retirement, or, in connection with past service, after retirement or death, or to be given on or in anticipation of or in connection with any change in the nature of the service of the employee in question, but any benefit to be provided solely by reason of the death or disability of a person resulting from an accident connected with his office or employment is not a relevant benefit (TCA 1997, s 770(1)). The term 'retirement' is not defined but is clearly not intended to include dismissal or redundancy.

Approved scheme: a retirement benefits scheme for the time being approved by the Revenue Commissioners for the purposes of TCA 1997, Pt 30, Ch 1 (TCA 1997, s 770(1)).

Statutory scheme: a retirement benefits scheme established by or under any enactment.

Exempt approved scheme: any approved scheme that is:

(a) shown to the satisfaction of the Revenue Commissioners to be established under irrevocable trusts;

(b) an overseas pension scheme; or

(c) a scheme which, having regard to any special circumstances, the Commissioners direct shall be an exempt approved scheme (TCA 1997, s 774(1)).

Administrator: the person or persons, established in a Member State of the European Communities, having the management of a retirement benefits scheme (including, if relevant, a person resident in the State responsible for discharging all the duties imposed on the administrator of a scheme of a non-resident employer) (TCA 1997, ss 770(1), 772(2)(c)(ii)).

Company includes any body corporate or any unincorporated body of persons other than a partnership.

Employee includes, in relation to any employer, a person who is to be or has been an employee and, in relation to a company, includes any director or other officer of the company and any other person taking part in the management of its affairs (TCA 1997, s 770(1)).

Employer is given a corresponding meaning to that of an 'employee', ie as the person employing the employee or as the company of which he is an officer, director, etc (TCA 1997, s 770(1)).

Director: in relation to a company, includes any member of the board of directors or similar body that manages the affairs of a company, any single director or similar person who manages the affairs of a company, or any member of a company the affairs of which are managed by the members themselves (and the term includes also any person who is to be or has been a director) (TCA 1997, s 770(1)).

Overseas Pensions scheme: means a retirement benefits scheme, other than a state social security scheme, which is:

(a) operated or managed by an Institution for Occupational Retirement Provision (IORP) as defined in Article 6(a) of the EU Pensions Directive 2003/41/EC; and

(b) which is established in an EU Member State (other than Ireland) which has implemented the Directive in its national law.

Overseas pension schemes that are being marketed in Ireland by providers in other EU Member States must be regulated under the Directive.

State Social Security Scheme: means a system of mandatory protection put in place by the government of a country or territory, other than Ireland, to provide a minimum level of retirement income or other benefits, the level of which is determined by that government.

Pension adjustment order: means an order made in accordance with either Family Law Act 1995, s 12, Family Law (Divorce) Act 1996, s 17 or the Civil Partnership and Certain Rights and Obligations of Cohabitants Act 2010, s 121.

Proprietary director: means a director who, either alone or together with their spouse and minor children is or was, at any time within three years of the date of:

(a) the specified normal retirement date;

(b) an earlier retirement date, where applicable;

(c) leaving service; or

(d) in the case of a pension or part of a pension payable in accordance with a pension adjustment order, the relevant date in relation to that order;

the beneficial owner of shares which, when added to any shares held by the trustees of any settlement to which the director or their spouse had transferred assets, carry more than five per cent (20 per cent prior to 6 April 2000) of the voting rights in the company providing the benefits or in a company which controls that company.

It should be noted that under the Revenue practice notes certain restrictions are imposed on 20 per cent directors. The Revenue have confirmed these restrictions will continue to apply only to 20 per cent directors and will not be extended to five per cent directors.

Relevant date: means in relation to a pension adjustment order, the date on which the decree of separation or the decree of divorce, as the case may be, was granted, by reference to which the pension adjustment order in question was made.

Pension includes also an annuity (TCA 1997, s 770(1)).

Service means service as an employee (as defined above) of the employer in question (TCA 1997, s 770(1)). Other expressions related to service, eg 'retirement', are to be construed accordingly.

Personal Retirement Savings Account or PRSA: see **16.3**.

Additional Voluntary Contribution means voluntary contributions made under the rules of a retirement benefits scheme (the 'main scheme') or under a separate scheme associated with the main scheme over and above the level of contributions specified in the main scheme (TCA 1997, s 770(1)). The separate scheme may be a PRSA ('AVC PRSA') (TCA 1997, s 787A) (see **16.3**).

16.104 Unapproved schemes

TCA 1997, s 777 charges an employee to tax under Sch E in respect of any payments made by his employer to provide any relevant benefits for the employee, the employee's spouse, widow, widower, children, dependents or personal representatives. TCA 1997, s 778(1), however, provides that the employee is not chargeable under that rule if the employer's payments are to any retirement benefits scheme that is either an approved scheme, a statutory scheme, or a scheme set up by a foreign government for the benefit of its employees. Any scheme to provide relevant benefits which is not one of these three types of scheme mentioned in TCA 1997, s 778(1) is referred to here as an 'unapproved scheme'.

Under art 17A of the UK/Ireland Double Tax Treaty, where an individual is seconded to work in the State for a period of up to a maximum of ten years (five years if he was not resident in the UK immediately prior to taking up employment in Ireland) for an associated employer (as defined), the UK pension scheme may be treated as if it were approved under the corresponding Irish legislation (equivalent treatment applies to individuals seconded to the UK: see **16.107**). The employee must not have been resident in the State immediately before taking up the employment. Similar treatment applies for secondments up to five years under art 18 of the US/Ireland Double Tax Treaty, but provision is made for scaling down the deductibility of contributions made to the extent that the employee avails of the remittance basis.

TCA 1997, s 778 provides a further exception from the charge to tax under Sch E in respect of the employer's payments to an unapproved scheme. No tax is to be charged by TCA 1997, s 777 if the employee for whom the payments to secure the relevant benefits are made is either not assessable to income tax on the emoluments of his employment or is only assessable on those emoluments on the remittance basis. The first of these exceptions is relevant for a non-resident employee exercising the duties of his employment wholly abroad; the second applies if the employee's emoluments derive from a foreign possession and he is domiciled outside the State.

With effect from 1 January 2006, an Irish resident who holds a foreign source office or employment is taxed under Schedule E to the extent that his earnings are attributable to duties performed in the State. In computing such earnings, normal Schedule E rules apply which would generally mean that contributions to a foreign (and thus normally non-approved) pension scheme would be taxable as a benefit in kind; equally, employee contributions to such schemes would be non-deductible (see also **16.108**). The Revenue Commissioners have however set out in *SP IT/3/07* a concession which may be available in these circumstances. They state that this will apply in '*bona fide*' cases where the employee:

(i) has been seconded by a foreign company to work in the State for that company or for a connected company;

(ii) was, prior to coming to work in the State, employed outside the State for a period of not less than 18 months by the foreign company (or a foreign company connected to that company);

(iii) is either not Irish domiciled or, being an Irish citizen, is not ordinarily resident in the State at the time the pension contributions are made;

(iv) had, prior to coming to work in the State, been making contributions to the foreign pension scheme for a period of not less than 18 months;

(v) is not resident in the State for a period of more than five years;*

and the foreign employer:

(I) is resident for tax purposes in an EU Member State or in a country with which the State has a double taxation treaty;

(II) has, prior to the individual coming to work in the State, been making contributions to a foreign pension scheme on behalf of the employee for a period of not less than 18 months.

In addition the foreign pension scheme must be a statutory scheme based in an EU Member State or treaty country but not a state social security scheme, or is a scheme in respect of which tax relief is available in that state or country; furthermore, both the employer and employee contributions must comply with the rules of that foreign pension scheme.

In these circumstances, the Revenue Commissioners will treat contributions made by the employer to the pension scheme as non-taxable and will allow relief for the pension contributions made directly by the employee (subject to the normal income percentage limits).

* Where an individual is resident in the State for a period of more than five years, ignoring any periods prior to 1 January 2003, written permission of the local Revenue Commissioners office will be required for the continuation of the above treatment of pension contributions beyond a period of five years.

With effect from 1 January 2005 a statutory scheme of relief has been inserted into TCA 1997, Pt 30, Ch 2B to relieve pension contributions paid to an overseas pension plan in another EU Member State by or on behalf of migrant workers. This means that EU-based employers who carry on a trade only partly in the State should not need to set up an Irish approved pension scheme. Subject to meeting the conditions for the relief in Ch 2B the migrant employee should be in a position to claim tax relief for the contributions paid to the overseas pension plan as if it were an exempt approved scheme (see **16.6**).

An existing practice allows an employee to claim relief for their contributions to an overseas employer's scheme where the employee has been transferred to Ireland to work for an associated employer provided that the period of secondment does not exceed ten years, the scheme is a trust scheme and the benefits provided by the scheme are within Irish approvable limits. Contributions made by the employer are chargeable to tax as emoluments but a corresponding deduction will be granted; however the total of employer and employee contributions will be subject to the annual earnings limit, namely €115,000 since 2013.

TCA 1997, s 777(2) also charges to tax under Sch E as income of the employee an amount equal to the cost of securing the provision by a third person of any relevant benefits for the employee, his wife, widow, children, etc. This charge is made where the employee has a right or expectation to benefit under any form of retirement benefits scheme, but where the provision of the benefits is not fully secured in advance by payments by the employer. For example, an employer may enter into an agreement or arrangement with an employee that he (the employer) will purchase a life annuity from an assurance company for the employee on the latter's retirement. Such an annuity to be given on retirement is clearly a 'relevant benefit' within the definition in TCA 1997, s 770(1) and, as the word 'scheme' is defined by TCA 1997, s 771(2) as including any agreement or arrangement, the cost of purchasing this annuity is assessable on the employee in the manner prescribed in TCA 1997, s 777. No tax charge on the employee is, however, to be made under this rule if any of the exceptions in TCA 1997, s 778 apply (see above).

TCA 1997, Sch 23, Pt 1 para 3 requires any employer operating for any of his employees a retirement benefits scheme, which is neither an approved scheme nor a statutory scheme, to give particulars of that scheme to the inspector of taxes within three months from the date on which the scheme first comes into operation. The wide definition of 'retirement benefits scheme', ie as one which may be by deed, but which may equally be no more than an arrangement or agreement with the employee(s) concerned to provide retirement benefits, should be borne in mind when considering the extent of this requirement. It is thought that the definition, although wide ranging, does not cover a simple decision to grant a termination payment to a retiring employee; it may be noted that the definition expressly refers to provisions for pension payments as being covered, even though the payments commence immediately on the making of the arrangements. This implicitly acknowledges that an arrangement is something which provides a framework within which payments are made and amounts to something more than the mere making of a payment itself. Further, if required to do so by a notice given by the inspector, the employer must furnish the inspector with particulars of any such unapproved scheme and of the employees to whom it relates. The administrator (if any) of such a scheme is also required to give any particulars relating to the scheme that the inspector may by notice request.

16.105 Approval of pension schemes

In order to secure exemption for his employees from liability to income tax in respect of any contributions he makes to a retirement benefits scheme, the employer must have the scheme approved by the Revenue Commissioners under TCA 1997, Pt 30, Ch 1. Any arrangement constituting a retirement benefits scheme (see **16.103**) which meets the conditions for Revenue approval (see **16.106**) may be approved so as to secure this exemption.

There is, however, a distinction between a simple 'approved scheme' and an 'exempt approved scheme'. While every exempt approved scheme is an approved scheme and attracts the tax advantages summarised in paragraphs (a) to (c) in **16.102**, as well as exempting the employees from tax under TCA 1997, s 777, an approved scheme which is not an exempt approved scheme does no more than provide the latter exemption. Consequently, in discussing the approval of retirement benefit or pension schemes, it is proposed to assume that the employer wishes to establish an exempt approved scheme. In practice this is almost invariably what is required.

In the majority of cases, for an Irish pension scheme to be approved as an exempt approved scheme it must be established under an irrevocable trust. The trust deed would provide for the appointment of a trustee or administrator and he would be charged with the management of the scheme, the investment of the trust funds, the payment of pensions and other benefits, etc in accordance with the rules of the scheme. In special circumstances, the Revenue Commissioners may direct that an approved scheme not established under an irrevocable trust is to be treated as an exempt approved scheme. An example is an annuity purchased beneficially for the employee shortly before their retirement (a so-called 'Hancock' annuity) where a direction may be made, unless the employer objects. Similar considerations apply in the case of a 'single premium' scheme established shortly before retirement. With effect from 1 January 2005 an overseas pension scheme may also be approved as an exempt approved scheme. This enables the Revenue Commissioners to approve an overseas pension which is structured otherwise than on a trust basis. This should enable Irish employers and employees to contribute in a tax efficient manner to pension plans provided by an institution for occupational retirement provision (IORP) based in other EU Member States.

On the other hand where an IORP established in Ireland is authorised and approved by the Pensions Board to accept contributions from an undertaking located in another EU Member State in respect of a retirement benefits scheme established under irrevocable trust, then certain exemptions from income tax will be allowed in respect of the investments or deposits of the scheme. This provision is set out in TCA 1997, s 790B and came into operation by ministerial order (SI 570/2005).

TCA 1997, Sch 23, Pt 1 para 1 requires the application for approval of any retirement benefits scheme to be made in writing by the administrator of the scheme to the Revenue Commissioners ('the Commissioners') in such form and manner as they may specify. This application should be made before the end of the first tax year for which the approval is required. In practice, however, the Commissioners are prepared to accept an application for approval made no later than three months after the last day of the tax year for which the approval is first required.

TCA 1997, Sch 23, Pt 1 para 1 also provides that the application for approval of a new scheme must be supported by:

(a) a copy of the instrument or other document constituting the scheme (eg the trust deed);

(b) a copy of the rules of the scheme; and

(c) such other information and particulars (including copies of any actuarial report or advice given to the administrator or employer in connection with the setting up of the scheme) as the Commissioners may consider relevant.

In the case of an existing retirement benefits scheme, a copy of the accounts of the scheme for the last year to which such accounts have been made up is also required.

It is not always practical for the employer and/or his professional advisors to have the final trust deed (referred to as the 'definitive deed') containing all the rules of the scheme ready within the above time limit for the approval application. In such a case, the Commissioners are normally prepared to grant the tax reliefs for the employer's and the employees' contributions from the first year of operation of the scheme based on an application for approval supported by an interim deed. The tax relief is given provisionally on the understanding that the definitive deed is in a form capable of being approved by the Commissioners and will be submitted within a reasonable time.

The interim deed actually establishes the scheme by creating an irrevocable trust (the normal requirement for 'exempt approved' status) in relation to the monies, etc to be held by the administrator or trustee(s) on behalf of the scheme. The interim deed must also set out the main purpose of the scheme, usually the provision of pensions and other retirement and/or death benefits for the employees. It is not, however, required to detail the rules of the scheme, which must be included in the definitive deed. Before granting tax relief provisionally under this interim deed procedure, the Commissioners must be satisfied that the principal features of the scheme have been communicated in writing to every employee who has a right to be a member.

The interim deed should be submitted to the Revenue Commissioners, Retirement Benefits District, before the end of the first tax year for which the Revenue approval is required. Again, the Commissioners are in practice prepared to grant a further three-month period of grace for the submission of the interim deed. Assuming that the interim deed and the other necessary particulars are in fact sent in within this period, and provided that the definitive deed is submitted in due course, the approval of the scheme is formally backdated to the beginning of the first year.

Where there is provision for employees to make additional voluntary contributions (ie in order to enhance their benefits under the scheme in question), it is often the case that such provision is catered for under a separate deed. However, even if this is the case, arrangements for payments of additional voluntary contributions (AVCs) will continue to be treated as an element of the overall scheme.

With effect from 2 April 2007, blanket approval may be given to generic occupational pension scheme products where a qualifying promoter provides a single member scheme, using standard documentation approved in advance by the Revenue Commissioners. A qualifying promoter is a person lawfully carrying on life annuity business and which is either: (a) resident in the State; (b) is trading in the State through a fixed place of business; or (c) is an insurance undertaking authorised to carry out insurance business in the State under Directive 2002/83/EC. Any subsequent alterations to the scheme must be approved by the Revenue, failing which, approval for the scheme will lapse. The Revenue Commissioners may withdraw approval at any time from such date as they specify, if in their opinion this is warranted by the facts; in such a case they may also make such assessments as are appropriate to withdraw any tax relief already obtained. It is a requirement that the aggregate employer and employee contributions to the scheme in any tax year must not exceed the limit for allowable employee contributions in that year (TCA 1997, s 772A inserted by FA 2007, s 17(1)(a)).

16.106 Conditions for approval

TCA 1997, s 772(1) requires the Revenue Commissioners to approve any retirement benefits scheme which satisfies all of the conditions related to the purpose of the scheme, etc as set out in TCA 1997, s 772(2) and all the conditions in TCA 1997, s 772(3) as respects the benefits to be provided by the scheme. TCA 1997, s 772(4) gives the Revenue Commissioners a certain discretion to approve particular schemes which do not comply fully in certain respects with those conditions. The conditions for approval may, therefore, be subdivided into the 'basic' conditions which, if met by the proposed retirement benefits scheme, entitle that scheme to automatic approval by the Revenue Commissioners, and the 'discretionary conditions' which may vary the basic conditions if, and only if, the Commissioners agree to them in the particular case.

Basic conditions for approval

The basic conditions which, if all are met, entitle the employer to have the retirement benefit scheme approved under TCA 1997, s 772(1) without having to depend on any discretion of the Revenue Commissioners, are:

(a) Conditions as to purpose (TCA 1997, s 772(2)):

(i) the scheme is *bona fide* established for the sole purpose of providing relevant benefits in respect of service as an employee, being benefits payable to the employee or to his widow(er), surviving civil partner, children, dependants, personal representatives or children of his surviving civil partner,

(ii) the scheme is recognised by the employer and employees to whom it relates,

(iii) every employee who is, or has a right to be, a member of the scheme has been given written particulars of all essential features of the scheme which concern the employee,

(iv) the administrator of an overseas pension scheme has either entered into a contract with the Revenue Commissioners in relation to the discharge of all duties and obligations imposed on the administrator under TCA 1997, Pt 30, Ch 1, Ch 2C and Stamp Duties Consolidation Act 1999, s 125 or there is a person resident in the State appointed by the administrator who will be responsible for the discharge of those duties and obligations. Any contract between the Revenue Commissioners and an administrator of the overseas scheme is to be governed by the laws of the State and the courts of Ireland are to have exclusive jurisdiction in determining any dispute arising under such contracts. Where an administrator opts to appoint a person resident in the State to discharge the duties and obligations, the appointment and identity of that person must be notified to the Revenue Commissioners,

(v) the employer is a contributor to the scheme (there is no requirement for the employee to be a contributor, but he may be),

(vi) the scheme is established in connection with some trade or undertaking carried on in the State by a person resident in the State (which may include a profession, an investment company or the management of property rents); however, 20 per cent directors (see **16.107** *Repayment of employee's contributions*) of an investment company (other than a company holding and co-ordinating its trading subsidiaries) cannot be members of an approved scheme,

(vii) no repayment can be made of any employee's contributions under the scheme;

(b) Conditions as to benefits: General (TCA 1997, s 772(3)):

(i) the maximum benefit for an employee is a pension on retirement not exceeding two thirds of his final remuneration (as defined), but for service of less than 40 years the maximum pension is:

$$\frac{n}{60} \times \text{final remuneration}$$

where n = the number of years of service,

(ii) the pension must be one payable on retirement at a specified age not earlier than 60 (prior to 1991–92 a lower age limit of 55 applied to women) and not later than 70 (except on earlier retirement due to incapacity),

(iii) any pension payable to a widow(er), surviving civil partner, children, dependants or children of a surviving civil partner of an employee who dies before retirement must not exceed the maximum pension to which that employee would have been entitled if he had continued to serve in the employment until the normal retirement date at a remuneration equal to his final remuneration before his death,

(iv) any lump sums payable to the widow(er), surviving civil partner, children, dependants or personal representatives of an employee or children of a surviving civil partner of an employee who dies before retirement must not exceed, in the aggregate, four times the employee's final remuneration,

(v) any benefit for a widow(er), surviving civil partner, children or dependants or children of a surviving civil partner of an employee payable on his death after retirement must be a pension and must not exceed any pension payable to the employee,

(vi) the maximum lump sum (subject to (c) below) which an employee may take, if permitted to do so under the terms of the scheme, is an amount equal to 1.5 times his final remuneration, but for service of less than 40 years the maximum lump sum is,

$$\frac{n \times 3}{80} \times \text{final remuneration}$$

where n = the number of years of service; and

(vii) no other benefits, other than those specified above, can be payable under the scheme;

(c) Conditions as to benefits: Proprietary Directors and Holders of AVCs:

The Revenue Commissioners may not approve a scheme unless it provides that any individual entitled to a pension under the scheme who is:

(i) a proprietary director (or spouse or former spouse or civil partner or former civil partner where part of the pension is payable in accordance with a pension adjustment order) of a company to which the scheme relates, or

(ii) an individual entitled to rights arising from additional voluntary contributions to the scheme,

may opt, on or before the date on which that pension would otherwise become payable, for the transfer, on or after that date to:

(i) the individual, or

(ii) an approved retirement fund,

of an amount determined by the formula:

$$A - B$$

where:

A is the amount equal to the value of the individual's accrued rights under the scheme which relates to additional voluntary contributions paid by the individual exclusive of any part of that amount paid by way of lump sum in accordance with TCA 1997, s 772(3)(f) in conjunction with the scheme rules, and

B is the amount, if any, required to be transferred to an approved minimum retirement fund in accordance with TCA 1997, s 784C or applied in purchasing an annuity payable to the individual with effect from the date of the exercise of the option.

With effect from 6 April 2000, the definition of 'proprietary director' was amended to refer to five per cent voting rights in the relevant company instead of 20 per cent as previously applied (see **16.103**).

TCA 1997, s 772(3B)(b) specifies that in the case of a proprietary director where the election under TCA 1997, s 772(3A) is made, the maximum tax free lump sum for a proprietary director is calculated by reference to 'a lump sum not exceeding 25 per cent of the value of the pension which would otherwise be payable' as opposed to the normal 3/80th for each year of service specified in TCA 1997, s 772(3)(f) subject to a limit of €200,000.

Although TCA 1997, s 772(3A) applies to schemes approved on or after 6 April 1999 (in the case of proprietary directors) or 6 April 2000 (in the case of individuals who make Additional voluntary contributions) a scheme approved before those dates can be altered to incorporate the options described above.

TCA 1997, s 772(3C) provides that where the rules of a retirement benefits scheme provide for the purchase of an annuity, references in TCA 1997, s 772(3A) to the date a pension would otherwise become payable (see above) shall be construed as references to the latest date on which such an annuity must be purchased in accordance with those rules. This amendment took effect from 6 April 1999 and was designed to cover the situation where the purchase of an annuity was deferred for five years under a small self-administered scheme or in the case of an individual working beyond normal retirement age, who although he has drawn the lump sum, had deferred drawing his annuity. In both of these cases the individual is entitled to opt for the transfer of the funds to avail of the options outlined above provided the annuity has not been purchased.

In effect, therefore, a scheme will not be approved unless it provides that a proprietary director or a holder of AVCs is entitled to the same retirement options as apply under Retirement Annuity contracts; the Revenue Commissioners may not exercise their discretion to waive this requirement (TCA 1997, s 772(4)(c)). The same conditions which apply in relation to Approved Retirement Funds and Approved Minimum Retirement Funds apply in the context of Approved Occupational Pension schemes (TCA 1997, s 772(3B)(a)).

With effect from 8 February 2012, the inclusion of a provision for the encashment option under TCA 1997, s 787TA (see **16.504**) in the rules of an occupational pension scheme won't affect Revenue approval of the scheme (TCA 1997, s 772(3H)(a)).

The benefits referred to in these conditions are maximum benefits (subject to such discretionary additional benefits which the Revenue Commissioners may accept under their discretionary powers). It is not a condition for approval that any given scheme provide for benefits up to these levels, nor that it provide all the types of benefit mentioned. For example, a scheme may provide only for a pension on retirement to an employee and may limit that pension to (say) one half of final remuneration. It may provide only a reduced widow(er)'s or civil partner's pension or no widow(er)'s or civil partner's pension. It need not provide any death in service benefit and may provide a lower benefit equal to (say) one year's remuneration. It is not necessary that a scheme should be open to all employees; indeed, at the extremes, it is possible to operate a 'one man' approved scheme. Part-time and temporary employees may be included in a scheme.

Transfers to Personal Retirement Savings Account (PRSA) (TCA 1997, s 772(3D))

With effect from 7 November 2002, a retirement benefits scheme won't cease to be an approved scheme because of any provision in the rules of the scheme whereby, either or both:

(a) a member's entitlement under the scheme, other than an amount referred to in paragraph (b) below, may, either on the member's changing employment or on the scheme being wound up, be transferred to one or more than one PRSA to which that member is the contributor if the following conditions are satisfied, that is to say:

  (i) benefits have not become payable to the member under the scheme, and

  (ii) the period or the aggregate of the periods for which the individual has been a member of the scheme or of any other scheme related to that individual's employment with, or with any person connected with, the employer immediately before the said transfer is 15 years or less;

(b) an amount equal to the accumulated value of a member's contributions to the scheme, which consist of additional voluntary contributions made by the member, may be transferred to one or more than one PRSA to which that member is the contributor. (TCA 1997, s 772(3D) inserted by Pensions (Amendment) Act 2002, s 4, as implemented by SI 502/2002).

The first point to note is that there is no restriction on employees transferring their AVCs to a PRSA irrespective of the length of service. This will result in a possible split transfer of benefits for AVC funds and main scheme benefits, whereas previously split transfers in general were not permitted.

In relation to main scheme benefits they can only be transferred to a PRSA where the employee is changing employment or the scheme is being wound up and the period of service for which the individual was a member of the pension scheme is 15 years or less. There is no definition of 'changing employment' so if an employee was promoted or seconded to another group company, etc it is unclear whether this would allow a transfer to a PRSA. Presumably if a new contract of employment were given there would be a change of employment. It should also be noted that it is not service with the employer but service as a member of the pension scheme that counts. This provision would appear to also restrict an employee transferring benefits on or after normal retirement date to a PRSA as the benefits would have become payable under the scheme.

Provision for borrowing

Prior to 25 March 2004 (the date of passing of FA 2004) the Revenue Commissioners did not approve schemes that included provision for borrowing in their rules. With effect from 25 March 2004 TCA 1997, s 772(3E) provides that the Revenue will not be prevented from approving a retirement benefits scheme that has the power to borrow funds. Furthermore a retirement benefits scheme will not cease to be an approved scheme if the scheme rules make provision for borrowing. The provision enables Revenue to approve a scheme which has the power to borrow. It does not require Revenue to approve such a scheme.

The Occupational Pension Schemes (Investment) Regulations 2005 (SI 593/2005) provide that pension schemes, other than 'one member arrangements' can only borrow money for liquidity purposes and on a temporary basis. The trustees of a 'one member arrangement' may borrow. A 'one member arrangement' is a scheme which:

(a) is established for one person only;
(b) that one person will always be the only member (other than where the scheme is subject to a Pensions Adjustment Order); and
(c) that member has discretion as to how the resources of the scheme are invested.

The Regulations came into effect on 23 September 2005.

The Revenue Pensions Manual (Ch 5.5) sets out the following rules that apply to scheme borrowings:

(a) only assets purchased by borrowings may be used to provide security to the lender. Cross collateralisation is not permitted;
(b) the assignment of rental income to the lender is not permitted;
(c) life cover in the amount of the debt may only be provided outside the scheme;
(d) interest only loans and loans for a period in excess of 15 years are not permitted. The loan must be repaid in full prior to normal retirement age;
(e) the use of scheme assets to clear residual debt is not permitted.

Commutation of pension benefits (TCA 1997, s 772(3F))

A retirement benefits scheme will not cease to be an approved scheme nor will the Revenue Commissioners be prevented from approving a scheme because of any provision in the rules of the scheme whereby a member's entitlement under the scheme may be commuted, to such extent as may be necessary, for the purpose of discharging the tax liability in connection with that entitlement under Ch 2C (see **16.5**).

Pre-Retirement Access to AVCS

Finance Act 2013, s 17 provided for pre-retirement access to AVCs in limited circumstances (see **16.114**).

A retirement benefits scheme will not cease to be an approved scheme where the trustees of the scheme allow a member or as the case may be, where the scheme is subject to a pension adjustment order, the spouse, former spouse, civil partner or former civil partner of the member to avail of an option to access AVCs.

16.107 Revenue Commissioners' discretionary powers

TCA 1997, s 772(4) empowers the Revenue Commissioners, if they think fit, having regard to the facts of any particular case, to approve a retirement benefits scheme that does not satisfy any one or more of the prescribed conditions. These discretionary powers may be used to permit the approval of a scheme which varies in certain ways which the Commissioners consider acceptable from the basic conditions, whether the scheme is to be an exempt approved scheme or, simply, an approved scheme which only gives exemption from tax to the employees in respect of the employer's contributions.

In particular, TCA 1997, s 772(4) authorises the Commissioners to approve a scheme which:

(a) permits a pension to be paid to an employee, his widow(er), civil partner, dependants, children of a deceased civil partner or personal representatives, or a payment to an employee on his retirement in commutation of part of his pension rights, computed in either case by reference to the maximum payment for 40 years' service, even though the actual service has been for a less period;

(b) allows benefits to be payable on early retirement within 10 years before the specified age or on earlier incapacity;

(c) permits a repayment in certain contingencies (eg leaving service) of an employee's contributions and the payment of interest (if any) on those contributions; or

(d) relates to a trade or undertaking carried on only partly in the State and by a non-resident person.

In applying their discretionary powers under TCA 1997, s 772(4), the Commissioners may impose such conditions, if any, as they think proper to attach to their approval. TCA 1997, s 772(4), while it specifies the main areas in which the Commissioners may approve variations from the basic conditions for approval, does not necessarily prevent the approval of modifications in other respects. In practice, however, the Revenue Commissioners have drawn up a number of guidelines within which they normally exercise their discretionary powers given by the subsection. The Revenue Commissioners produce a Revenue Pensions Manual which covers in some detail the Revenue's current practice in exercising its discretionary powers. This has been recently updated on 17 July 2014 (ebrief No 56/14). A full discussion of Revenue practice is outside the scope of this book, but a number of the more salient points may usefully be mentioned.

Maximum total benefits

The aggregate of all benefits payable under an approved scheme to an employee who retires at normal retirement age, after 40 or more years' service with the same employer, must always be restricted by the rules of the scheme so as not to exceed two thirds of his final remuneration. In applying this maximum benefits limit, any lump sum or other benefits payable otherwise than as a pension, as well as any pension, are to be measured in terms of an annual amount payable for life. This two-thirds limit represents the definitive upper limit to the benefits which may be provided on the employee's retirement.

While the maximum pension that may be paid on an employee's retirement at normal retirement date can never exceed two thirds of his final remuneration, the granting of 'inflation adjustments' (see below) may in fact increase the pension actually payable subsequently above the two-thirds figure. Also, in certain circumstances, an employee who remains in service after normal retirement date may be permitted to earn an increased pension (not to exceed forty-five sixtieths of final remuneration at the actual date of retirement); certain restrictions apply to 20 per cent directors (see *Repayment of employees' contributions* below).

In some cases, a scheme may calculate 'defined' benefits on a formula other than that set out by the Revenue Commissioners. Such schemes are approvable if the benefits fall below the maximum total benefits permitted. The trustees of a scheme may also purchase a 'buy out' bond in the name of a beneficiary who has left the employer's service, ie an insurance policy or bond in lieu of the beneficiary's benefit entitlements under the scheme (alternatively the trustees may assign an existing policy or bond held by them to the beneficiary). Various rules apply to the operation of such bonds.

Service of less than 40 years

The normal condition that an employee's maximum benefits, when expressed in terms of an annual pension for life, cannot exceed one sixtieth of final remuneration for each year of service (the '*n* sixtieths' rule) may, in certain circumstances, be varied. The Commissioners are usually prepared to approve a scheme which provides for pension benefits of up to two thirds of final remuneration for employees who, by reason of age at the date of entry to the scheme, cannot complete 40 years' service before the normal retirement date in the scheme in question.

For a scheme permitting the full 'two thirds pension' to be paid to such 'late entrants', it is an absolute requirement of the Commissioners that the employee concerned have not less than ten years of potential service before the normal retirement date. Where the maximum potential service is between six and ten years, the Commissioners may approve a scheme permitting pension benefits on an 'uplifted sixtieths' basis, ie one where the pension exceeds one sixtieth of final remuneration for each year of service, as follows:

Years of service to normal retirement date	*Maximum pension (before commutation) expressed as fraction of final remuneration*
6	8/60ths
7	16/60ths
8	24/60ths
9	32/60ths
10 or more	40/60ths

A late entrant to an approved scheme may have previously been a member of another employer's retirement benefit scheme, or he may have paid premiums under a retirement annuity contract deductible from his 'relevant earnings' in respect of an earlier non-pensionable employment or self-employment (see **16.2**). In any case where the employer seeking approval for his retirement benefits scheme wishes to provide for uplifted pension benefits for late entrants, it is a Revenue requirement that the rules of the scheme restrict the scheme benefits so that, when aggregated with the pension equivalent of the retained benefits from any previous approved scheme, PRSAs or retirement annuity contract, they do not exceed two thirds of the employee's final remuneration.

For this purpose, the 'retained benefits' must be taken as the sum of such of the following items as are relevant:

(a) the pension(s) retained by the individual under other approved or statutory schemes, whether still deferred or currently being paid, including any parts of those pensions which are commutable or which have been commuted;

(b) benefits (current or deferred) under any retirement annuity contracts under TCA 1997, s 784 in respect of any previous non-pensionable employment or self-employment;
(c) benefits (current or deferred) under schemes relating to overseas employment;
(d) benefits (current or deferred) under 'buy out bond' policies referable to a previous employment; and
(e) benefits arising from PRSA's contracts.

However, small deferred pensions not exceeding in aggregate €330 pa, lump sums not exceeding €1,270 in aggregate and refunds of contributions may be ignored. Benefits under statutory or approved schemes or under retirement annuity contracts in relation to concurrent employments may also be left out of account. There is no mention of benefits under a PRSA relating to a concurrent employment.

The provision of uplifted pension benefits for late entrants is usually an expensive matter. Consequently, an employer may wish to limit the extent to which he includes any such benefits in the retirement benefits scheme he is establishing. He is not, of course, obliged to depart from the normal '*n* sixtieths' formula at all. If he does do so, he may wish to limit the uplifted benefits to certain key personnel (eg senior management) whom it may be necessary for the good of the business to recruit at a later stage in their working lives than is normal. The Revenue Commissioners are normally prepared to approve any scheme which provides uplifted benefits for certain categories of employees only.

Commutation of pension benefits

The normal rule is that an approved scheme may permit an employee, if he wishes, to commute on his retirement a part of his pension benefits in the form of a tax free lump sum which must not exceed three eightieths of his final remuneration for each year of service (see above). In a normal case, it may be taken that a lump sum commutation payment reduces the pension becoming payable on retirement to the employee by an annual amount (before income tax) of approximately one-ninth of the lump sum. However, this factor will vary with age and may also be adjusted where there is an entitlement to, or expectation of, post-retirement 'cost of living' increases in the pension.

The Commissioners are normally prepared to approve a scheme which entitles a late entrant to elect to commute part of his pension benefits at a higher rate, provided that the individual has at least a potential nine years' service to normal retirement age when he joins the scheme. However, there must again be a restriction so that the aggregate value of any lump sum commutation taken from the current scheme and any lump sum retirement benefits in respect of service with previous employers can never exceed 120/80 times final remuneration from the current employer.

The maximum lump sum commutation available to the late entrant may normally only be provided at the 120/80 rate if he has a potential 20 or more years' service with the current employer. For service of between nine years and 19 years, the maximum commutation of pension from the current employer increases on a sliding scale from 30/80ths for nine years' service up to 108/80ths of final remuneration for 19 years' service.

Where a proprietary director elects under TCA 1997, s 772(3A) to avail of the new retirement options (see **16.106**) the maximum tax free lump sum is calculated by reference to 25 per cent of the value of the pension which would otherwise be payable.

Provision may also be made for commutation of a pension at a time when the recipient is in exceptional circumstances of ill health, ie where the expectation of life is unquestionably very short. The decision to commute should be reported to the Retirement Benefits Division only in the case of 20 per cent directors or members of small self-administered schemes (see below).

In some cases (usually involving public sector schemes) provision may be made for a specified lump sum and a non-commutable pension on retirement. In such cases, the accrual rate for the maximum approvable pension will be restricted correspondingly (thus eg if the lump sum is based on the 3N/80ths formula, the maximum accrual rate for the pension would become N/80 instead of N/60).

Where life assurance cover continues to be provided after retirement or leaving the employment, the value of that benefit must be taken into account for the purpose of determining the maximum permitted benefits under the scheme.

Repayment of employee's contributions

While TCA 1997, s 772(2)(f) imposes the basic condition that no repayments may be made of an employee's contributions to an approved scheme, almost all schemes to which the employees contribute (but not, of course, non-contributory schemes) permit the repayment of the employee's contributions if he leaves the service of the employer with less than two years qualifying service. The inclusion of a rule in the scheme permitting the repayment of the employee's contributions in this event, together with interest at a reasonable rate, is usually approved by the Commissioners without question. However, where employees have paid additional voluntary contributions (AVCs) under separate arrangements (see **16.103**) such contributions will not be refundable if the main scheme is non-contributory. The right to the repayment may be an absolute one or, alternatively, the scheme may permit the employee to choose whether to take a repayment or a deferred pension payable on his normal retirement date or to transfer to a PRSA.

For the tax treatment of repayments of employees' contributions (and interest) on withdrawal from service, see **16.109**. With regard to the level of interest, most schemes where repayments are permitted provide for compound interest at a rate between three per cent and five per cent per annum. Since a scheme once established may have to last indefinitely or at least for many years, the rate of interest allowed by the rules is usually conservatively based.

Alternatively, a scheme may be approved if, instead of a direct refund of the employee's contributions plus interest, it provides a sum equal to the surrender value of a policy of assurance appropriate to the contributions. In either event, any interest or enhanced value in excess of the actual contributions is treated only as an element in the calculation of the benefit from the scheme; it is not regarded as interest for tax purposes in the hands of the employee.

Where an employee receives a refund of contributions the amount thereof (net of any tax charge: see **16.109**) counts as part of the maximum lump sum which may be approved in respect of all schemes relating to the employment concerned.

One exception exists to the rule permitting an employee leaving an employment to elect for a refund of contributions. If the employer is a company, the Commissioners are not prepared to allow a member of that company's exempt approved scheme to take any refund of contributions on leaving the company's service if he is a '20 per cent director'.

For these purposes, a '20 per cent director' is one who is or, at any time within three years of the specified normal retirement date or earlier retirement or leaving the company's service, was, the beneficial owner of shares carrying more than 20 per cent of the voting rights in the company providing the benefits (or in a company controlling that company). In applying this test, it is necessary to include with the director's own shareholding any shares held by his spouse, by any minor children or by the trustees of any settlement to which the director and his spouse has transferred any assets. This restriction (and any other restrictions imposed on a 20 per cent director) do not apply to the spouse of such a director, although the Revenue Commissioners may wish to ensure that he is a genuine employee/director.

Deferred benefits/transfer payments

Where an employee leaves the employer's service (other than on retirement under the rules of the scheme) and does not receive a refund of their contributions, he may be provided with either:

(a) a deferred pension and/or lump sum;
(b) the payment of a transfer value to the scheme of a subsequent employer (see SI 604/2005 – Occupational Pension Schemes (Preservation of Benefits) (Amendment) Regulations 2005);
(c) the purchase of a deferred annuity and/or 'buy out' bond (see above) under *Maximum total benefits*; or
(d) assuming the conditions in TCA 1997, s 772(3)(d) are satisfied (see **16.106**: *Transfers to PRSAs*) transfer to a PRSA.

Detailed rules apply to the operation of all four options, as described in the Revenue Pensions Manual.

Final remuneration

This is relevant in determining the maximum benefits under a number of the headings discussed above. TCA 1997, s 770(1) defines final remuneration as the average annual remuneration of the last three years' service, but in practice this definition is frequently departed from within the discretionary conditions approvable by the Revenue Commissioners. Except in relation to benefits for 20 per cent directors, the Commissioners accept that the rules of a scheme may provide for final remuneration to be computed on any one of the following bases:

(a) remuneration for any one of the five years preceding the date of retirement, death, etc as appropriate, plus the average of any fluctuating emoluments over 3 or more consecutive years ending on that date;
(b) the average of the total remuneration for any three or more consecutive years ending not earlier than ten years before the retirement date etc; or
(c) the basic rate of pay at the retirement date, etc or at any date within the year ending on that date plus the average of any fluctuating emoluments (but with certain exceptions).

For a 20 per cent director, the scheme is not permitted to adopt either of bases (a) or (c) and basis (b) is available only subject to conditions.

Special provisions apply to individuals receiving long-term sick pay and part-time employees.

'Remuneration' or 'pensionable pay' should be specifically defined in the rules of each scheme. For purposes of Revenue approval, it may be taken as including all emoluments chargeable to income tax under Sch E (or, in the case of a foreign employment, under Sch D Case III) and may include any benefits in kind or expenses payments treated as income under the rules of Sch E (or, if relevant, under Sch D Case III), as well as the taxable gain arising on the exercise of a share option under TCA 1997, s 128.

Inflation adjustments

The Commissioners are prepared to approve schemes which contain rules providing for an increase in the pensions payable by reference to inflation after the employee has retired and taken his pension. Similarly, any widow's, civil partner's or dependant's pension payable under the scheme, whether following the employee's death in service or after retirement, may be increased for the same reason. The Commissioners are prepared to allow guaranteed increases in pensions of up to three per cent per annum (*or* the rate of increase in the Consumer Price Index) to be built into the pension benefits under the rules of any scheme.

A scheme may also be permitted to increase pensions on a discretionary basis up to the rate of increase in the Consumer Price Index (or similar agreed index). One other form of increase permitted by the Commissioners is the 'parity' increase. Here the Revenue permits the level of the pension to be increased to the amount that would be payable based on the *present* remuneration of a holder of the same office as the pensioner held immediately prior to his retirement. A corresponding parity increase may be made in the pension being paid to the widow, civil partner or dependant of a former employee.

Any permitted inflation adjustment is made by reference to the actual pension which commences to be payable on the individual's retirement date or, in the case of a widow's or a dependant's pension, to the pension taken by the widow or dependant at the date of the individual's death. For example, assume the case of an individual who retires on 31 March 2009 after 40 years' service with a final remuneration of €75,000, entitling her to a two-thirds pension of €50,000. Assume also that she opts to commute €20,000 of that pension for a tax free lump sum so that her actual pension which commences on 1 April 2009 is €30,000 per annum. If the scheme rules permit an inflation adjustment (based on the CPI) of five per cent, the increased pension becoming payable a year later on 1 April 2010 would be €31,500 per annum (ie €30,000 – and not €50,000 – increased by five per cent).

Voluntary contributions

In practice, the rules of many approved schemes define remuneration or final remuneration in a way that restricts the pension and related benefits to amounts below the maximum capable of being approved within the Commissioners' discretionary powers. It may not always be considered practical to include such fluctuating elements as overtime, discretionary bonuses, taxable benefits in kind etc. An approved scheme may contain a rule permitting an employee to make voluntary additional contributions to the scheme to enable him to increase the level of future benefits and, at the same time, to secure tax relief on the additional contributions.

In any such case, the Commissioners require that the voluntary contributions be restricted, if necessary, to ensure that the individual's aggregate benefits from the scheme remain within approvable limits. However, if the normal contributions of the employer and of the employee (if he makes any) are based on pensionable pay below the maximum approvable amount, it is likely that there is scope for the additional contributions by the employee without the risk of breaching the limits to the approvable benefits. Further, the age related limits to the employee's tax deductible contributions applies to the aggregate of their compulsory and voluntary contributions including contributions to an AVC PRSA (see **16.3**) each year (see also **16.108**).

Normal retirement age

Any normal retirement age within 60 to 70 is usually acceptable, and in exceptional cases a retirement age outside these limits may be agreed (but *not* in the case of '20 per cent directors'). Different retirement ages can apply to individual employees or categories of employee. In a number of cases, Revenue have accepted that the normal retirement age is less than 60.

Early retirement

Voluntary early retirement is generally permissible only at age 50 at the earliest, in which case special rules are used to calculate entitlement to pension and the tax-free cash lump sum. Early retirement may also be allowed on grounds of ill health, in which case the pension and lump sum entitlements may be based on assumed service up to normal retiring date.

Delayed retirement

An employee who remains in employment after the normal retiring date may take his entitlements on that date or take his cash lump sum only or defer both his cash lump sum and his pension; in the case of deferral, the deferred benefits can be uprated within prescribed limits.

Death benefits

On death in service before normal retirement age, a lump sum not exceeding the greater of €6,350 or four times the deceased employee's final remuneration may be paid to a nominated person or at the discretion of the scheme's trustees. A refund of the employee's contributions (plus interest, if so wished) may also be paid.

Payment of lump sums is not generally permitted on death after retirement. One exception is the payment of a lump sum to make up any shortfall between the pensions payable to dependants and the value of the member's contributions towards those benefits (plus reasonable interest).

Group schemes

The Revenue Commissioners are prepared to approve group schemes operated by closely associated employers (as defined) or by certain trade groupings, trade associations or professional associations. Various conditions and rules apply.

Non-resident employer

The circumstances in which the Commissioners use their discretionary powers to approve a retirement benefits scheme of a non-resident employer are dealt with separately in **16.112**.

Employees seconded within Ireland

An employee who is seconded (temporarily) within Ireland (or who is otherwise temporarily absent from their employment) may continue to be a member of an approved scheme subject to meeting various conditions (primarily that he does not become a member of another approved scheme other than one relating to a concurrent employment). Periods of absence in excess of five years require approval from

Retirement Benefit Division, which will normally be granted if the employee is not a member of another scheme and there is a clear expectation of return.

Employee seconded overseas

Where an employee is temporarily seconded to work overseas for a non-resident employer and can be deemed to remain on the payroll of his Irish employer, the Revenue Commissioners will permit the employee to remain a member of the Irish employer's pension scheme. Similar treatment applies to certain other transfers from an Irish resident parent company to overseas subsidiaries where the employee remains under the control of the parent company. The treatment will not apply to transfers between subsidiaries of a common parent. The overseas companies in question must reimburse the Irish employer for its contributions unless the Retirement Benefits Division agrees otherwise. In these circumstances the employee will need to consider the tax treatment of their Irish pension scheme arrangements in the overseas jurisdiction. Under the pensions protocol to the UK/Ireland double tax treaty, where an individual is seconded for a period of up to ten years to work in the UK for an associated employer, the UK will generally treat the Irish pension scheme as if it were approved under the corresponding UK legislation (equivalent treatment applies to individuals seconded to Ireland: see **16.104**).

16.108 Tax relief for pension scheme contributions

The most immediate consequence of having a retirement benefits scheme approved by the Revenue Commissioners as an exempt approved scheme (as distinct from a simple approved scheme) is that the employer's and employee's contributions qualify for tax relief respectively under TCA 1997, ss 774(6) and 774(7). The rules under which this tax relief is given are now discussed separately for the employer and the employee.

Employer's contributions

It is a requirement for approval that the employer should contribute to the scheme. The Revenue Commissioners previously required that at normal retiring age the employer have borne at least 1/6th of the costs of the benefits provided. In the case of a 'defined contribution' scheme this meant that the employer had to contribute 1/6th of total contributions on an ongoing basis. Where there were separate schemes designed for additional voluntary contributions, these also were counted in for the purposes of the '1/6th' criterion. Retirement Benefits District issued revised guidance in April 2002 regarding the level of employer contributions to defined benefit and defined contribution pension plans. The Revenue Commissioners will now approve schemes where the employer contributions are '*meaningful*'. The Revenue Commissioners would regard the following as meaningful,

(a) where the employer bears the cost of establishment of the scheme and ongoing operation costs in addition to meeting the cost of provision of death in service benefits; or

(b) where the employer contributions are not less than 10 per cent of the total ordinary annual contributions to the scheme exclusive of employee voluntary contributions.

The Revenue Commissioners are open to discussions as to the circumstance of particular schemes.

The legislation originally was expressed so as to allow any contribution made by an employer under an exempt approved scheme to be deducted as an expense in the year in which it was paid in arriving at the employer's taxable income from his trade or profession within Sch D Case I or II. Despite the apparently clear wording, it was thought that a deduction might still be obtainable in respect of provisions for future personal contributions (ie in accordance with the principle set out in *Southern Railways of Peru Ltd v Owen* 37 TC 602, discussed at **5.302**). Accordingly, the legislation was amended to make it clear that a deduction is available only for payments actually made and not for any additional provisions. TCA 1997, s 775 seeks to ensure that no deduction will be allowed for sums paid into pension schemes to the extent that provisions have already been allowed which exceed the amount of contributions actually paid into the scheme.

There are a number of points to note in relation to employer contributions. First, the deduction is only allowed to the extent that the contributions relate to employees in the trade or profession in respect of which the employer is assessable to income tax under Sch D Case I or II (TCA 1997, s 774(6)(c)).

Secondly, any contribution by the employer that is not an ordinary annual contribution is to be treated, depending on how the Commissioners direct either as an expense incurred in the year in which the sum is paid, or as an expense spread over a period of years that the Commissioners consider to be appropriate (TCA 1997, s 774(6)(d)). This refers to special contributions that are made in addition to the employer's ordinary annual contributions (eg to provide benefits for back service not already funded or to augment benefits already secured). Analogous treatment applies to the outright purchase of a 'Hancock' annuity or single premium schemes which are granted exempt approved status. (It should be borne in mind that payment of such an annuity is normally deductible in full under general principles: ie without any obligatory 'spreading'). No spreading is required where special contributions are payable by instalments over a period of five years or longer, or are paid annually on a basis which is not expected to produce substantial variations. Further, no spreading is required to the extent that special contributions are made to finance cost-of-living increases for existing pensioners. In practice, no spreading of the deduction for special contributions in any year is required if the aggregate of all special contributions made by the employer in that year to their exempt approved scheme(s) does not exceed the higher of €6,350 or the aggregate of ordinary annual contributions made by the employer in that year for all their employees.

In *Kelsall v Investment Chartwork* [1994] STC 33, it was held that the exercise of the equivalent discretion of the Board of Inland Revenue to apportion contributions was not reviewable by the Appeal Commissioners; this followed, because their role is appellate and not supervisory. It remains open for a taxpayer to seek redress by way of judicial review in appropriate circumstances (see **2.206**).

In any case where this limit is exceeded, the period over which the special contributions for any year must be spread is determined by dividing the aggregate of those special contributions by the aggregate ordinary annual contributions payable in the same year (or, if higher, by €6,350). If the quotient is between 1 and 2, the special contributions are spread over two years; in any other case, the number of years' spread is rounded down if the quotient includes a fraction of half a year or less, and rounded up if more than half of a year. However, the maximum period of the spread is five years.

Example 16.108.1

Employer Special Contribution

Employers A, B, C and D, who are unrelated, make the following annual and special contributions to their respective approved pension schemes for the year ended 31 December 2014:

	Employer A	*Employer B*	*Employer C*	*Employer D*
	€	€	€	€
Ordinary annual contribution	50,000	50,000	50,000	50,000
Special contribution	45,000	55,000	115,000	140,000
Relief on special contributions is calculated as follows:				
Years of spread				
Special/annual	.9 years	1.1 years	2.3 years	2.8 years
Rounded to	1 year	2 years	2 years	3 years
Tax deduction				
Year 1	45,000	50,000	57,500	50,000
Year 2	-	5,000	57,500	50,000
Year 3	-	-	-	40,000
Total	45,000	55,000	115,000	140,000

Notes:

1. If special contribution does not exceed the ordinary annual contribution relief is granted fully in year of payment.
2. If fraction achieved when special contribution is divided by ordinary contribution is between 1 and 2, relief is spread over two years. In all other cases it is rounded up or down to nearest whole number.
3. After determining the number of years of spread the amount allowable in each year will be the higher of the special contribution divided by the number of years of spread or the ordinary annual contribution.

Once the spread has been calculated no further adjustment shall be made irrespective of changes in the ordinary annual contribution in later years. If a further special contribution is made before relief has been granted in full, a recalculation is required. The recalculation is based on adding the new special contribution plus the unrelieved portion of the previous special contribution and carrying out the steps outlined above. In certain cases it may be advantageous to 'force' (by making a small special contribution) a recalculation where the ordinary annual contribution has increased which would result in a lower spread.

An employer making contributions to an approved scheme that is not an exempt approved scheme may still be entitled to deduct those contributions under the ordinary rules of Sch D Case I or II, but only if the contributions satisfy the 'wholly and exclusively' and 'not of a capital nature' requirements of TCA 1997, s 81(2) (see **5.305–5.307**). If the employees for whom the employer makes the contributions are related to the employer or, where the employer is a company, are persons having a substantial beneficial interest in its share capital, the inspector dealing with the employer's accounts is likely to examine the whole position closely. If not satisfied that the contribution is made wholly and exclusively for the purpose of the employer's trade or profession, the inspector may seek to disallow the contribution either in whole or in part.

In practice, ordinary annual contributions paid on a regular basis are likely to be allowed, but the position regarding special contributions may give rise to difficulty in securing a Sch D Case I or II deduction. Clearly it is preferable that any approved scheme be an exempt approved one to avoid these possible difficulties.

Special provisions apply to one-man arrangements and insured schemes using earmarked policies.

Employee's contributions

TCA 1997, s 774(7)(a) allows an employee to deduct any ordinary annual contribution to an exempt approved scheme from his emoluments of the relevant office or employment in respect of which he is taxable under Sch E. This deduction is allowed as an expense in the tax year in which the contributions are paid but the amount deductible in any tax year cannot exceed a specified percentage (see below) of the employee's total remuneration for the year from the office or employment in respect of which the contributions are paid.

Age at any time during the tax year	*% Contribution*
Under 30	15%
30–39	20%
40–49	25%
50–54	30%
55–59	35%
60 or over	40%

The contribution limit in excess of 30 per cent for individuals aged 55 or over applies with effect from 1 January 2006.

For this purpose, total remuneration includes all emoluments chargeable under Sch E, including benefits in kind, expenses payments, etc. The Revenue do not accept that the element of a termination payment chargeable as emoluments under TCA 1997, s 123 (see **10.4**) is a component of remuneration for this purpose. In unusual cases, an employee's contributions may be restricted in order to keep their benefits within the approved limits or to ensure that the employer's contribution does not fall below a meaningful contribution (as defined above). Contributions after normal retirement age may be permitted provided the individual continues to work (subject to these constraints).

An earnings limit of €115,000 has applied since 2011 to income that qualifies for relief in respect of pension contributions to occupational pension schemes, retirement annuity contracts, PRSAs and overseas pension plans. For subsequent years the earnings limit was due to increase by an earnings adjustment factor designated by the Minister for Finance. There has been no increase as at 1 January 2015.

Prior to 6 February 2003, TCA 1997, s 774(7)(b) allowed an employee to deduct as an expense in computing his emoluments assessable under Sch E any special contribution (ie one that is not an ordinary annual contribution), but empowered the Revenue Commissioners to direct, as they thought fit, either that the contribution be treated as an ordinary annual contribution deductible in the year in which paid, or that it should be apportioned and deducted over the number of years they considered appropriate. No deduction was, however, allowed in any tax year to the extent that the aggregate of the employee's ordinary annual contributions in that year and the amount of any special contribution allocated to that year exceeded the appropriate contribution limit of total remuneration, the benefit test and the requirement that the employer contributions should be 'meaningful' (see above). In practice, where it was not possible to spread forward the relief the Revenue Commissioners would normally allow special contributions to be spread back and set off against the remuneration of the previous ten years; fuller details of Revenue practice are set out in the 2002 edition of this book. In this case, the normal four-year time limit for repayments of tax under TCA 1997, s 865(4) (see **2.104**) will not apply (TCA 1997, s 774(7A), (2) (inserted by FA 2008, Sch 6).

With effect from 6 February 2003, the spreading back of special contributions is confined to:

(a) contributions made on retirement, following an application in writing by the employee before 6 February 2003 to contribute, towards the purchase of pension benefits within Revenue limits in respect of actual service by the employee for the period before the employee became a member of the scheme (TCA 1997, s 774(7)(b));

(b) contributions deducted from a lump sum payable on retirement to provide for dependants' benefits (TCA 1997, s 774(7)(ba)); and

(c) contributions made on retirement to pay back a previous refund of contributions or to pay back benefits previously provided to the member of a pension scheme [such as a marriage gratuity], where the contributor had previously left the employment related to the pension scheme (TCA 1997, s 774(7)(ba)).

Special contributions paid for a tax year between the end of the tax year and the return filing date for that year will, subject to the annual limits, be allowed to be set against the income for the tax year where a claim is made by the return filing date (TCA 1997, s 774(8)). Any contributions which cannot be allowed due to an insufficiency of remuneration in a given tax year will be carried forward and treated as if they had been paid in the subsequent tax year (TCA 1997, s 774(7)(d)). Any amount still unrelieved will be carried forward in the same manner to subsequent tax years (TCA 1997, s 774(7)(e)).

There is no provision in the Income Tax Acts to allow an employee any deduction or other tax relief in respect of contributions to an approved scheme that is not an exempt approved scheme. Further, no tax relief is available under TCA 1997, s 774(7) in respect of an employee's contribution to an unapproved scheme.

Salary sacrifices

The Revenue Commissioners state categorically in their Pensions Manual that salary sacrifices made in return for equivalent employer's contributions are *applications* of an employee's salary and not an expense of the employer. Thus for example an employee who 'waives' €x in return for an employer's contribution of €x to a pension scheme remains taxable under Sch E on the €x (see *Dolan v K* I ITR 656). The employer (who is seeking to fund their contributions out of the employee's income) is also thereby prejudicing the approved status of the scheme.

The manual also states that such arrangements are subject to the provisions of TCA 1997, s 118B. Where the section applies the employer contribution is treated as a payment of emoluments subject to income tax. The legislation has been amended at TCA 1997, s 116 with effect from 1 January 2013 to include directors in the definition of employees. In other circumstances, arrangements which fall within the scope of the decision in *Heaton v Bell* 46 TC 211 may also be treated as involving an effective application of income (see **10.105**).

Contributions on termination

Where an employee is ceasing employment, the employer may agree to enhance his pension entitlements by making a special contribution to the pension fund. It is thought that so long as the sum paid by way of special contribution had not previously been awarded to the employee (in which case the enhancement would in fact be funded by him and not the employer), no objection would be raised by the Revenue Commissioners. It is also considered that the Revenue would not in these circumstances seek to invoke the provisions of TCA 1997, s 123 (see **10.401**).

Returns by employers in relation to pension products

Regulation 31 of the Income Tax (Employments) (Consolidated) Regulations 2001 provides that an employer must make an annual return (P35) detailing the total amount of emoluments paid to or on behalf of each employee in a tax year and the total tax deducted. TCA 1997, s 897A provides that for the year of assessment 2005 and subsequent years the employer will be obliged to include the following details on Form P35:

1. the number of employees in respect of whom the employer deducted an employee pension contribution, an RAC premium (see **16.2**) or a contribution to a PRSA (see **16.3**) from the employees' emoluments in the year for which the return is being made;
2. the number of employees in respect of whom the employer made an employer pension contribution or a PRSA employer contribution in that year;
3. the total amount of the employee contributions deducted from the emoluments due to the employee in that year; and
4. the total amounts of the employer pension contributions made in the year.

Penalties will be imposed for failure to make the return.

16.109 Taxation of pension scheme refunds

The payment of contributions to an exempt approved scheme results, as indicated in **16.108**, in the employer's and the employee's ability to deduct those contributions in arriving at their respective taxable incomes. The object of the contributions is to procure the payment in the future of pensions and other related benefits to the employees and/or their dependants. In certain circumstances, either the employer or the employee may receive a refund of contributions or some other payment out of the pension fund other than a pension or other benefit within the main purposes of the scheme. In any such case, the question of the taxation of the refund or other payment has to be considered.

Repayment of employee's contributions

TCA 1997, s 780(2) charges tax on the repayment to an employee during his lifetime of any of his previous contributions to an exempt approved scheme, except that no tax is charged if the employee receiving the repayment exercised his employment outside the State. With effect from 1 June 2002 only employees with less than two years of qualifying service will be entitled to a repayment of pension scheme contributions. The tax is charged at the standard rate of tax (previously 25 per cent for payments made prior to 5 December 2001) on the full amount of the contributions repaid, including the interest (if any) paid on the contributions to the employee at the time of the repayment. The tax is charged under Sch D Case IV on the administrator of the scheme, and not on the employee, with the result that no part of the repayment (including any interest) is treated as part of the employee's income for tax purposes. Where the contributions are transferred to a PRSA the tax is avoided.

The circumstances in which an employee may receive a repayment of contributions, ie on leaving the service of the employer, have been referred to in **16.107**. A refund of contributions, usually with interest, may also be received by the employee's personal representatives if the employee dies before becoming entitled to the pension (although some schemes pay a separate death benefit secured by a life assurance policy). It is to be noted that the Sch D Case IV tax charge on the administrator is only made where the repayment is made during the lifetime of the employee. If a repayment of contributions is made to the personal representatives of an employee who died in service, the repayment (including any interest) is entirely free of income tax.

Although the administrator of the scheme is the person chargeable to tax on the lifetime repayment to the employee, the employee may be required to bear the tax charge. In many cases, the rules of the pension scheme in question entitle the administrator to deduct an amount equal to the standard rate of income tax charged on him in paying over the refund of contributions to the employee leaving the employer's service. In such a case, the employee receives a net payment equal to, currently 80 per cent, of the total refund of their contributions (and interest) out of the pension fund. However, this is not a legal requirement and the rules of a pension scheme may be drawn up so as to permit 100 per cent of the total refund to be paid to the employee leaving (so that the tax remains a charge on the pension fund).

It is to be noted that TCA 1997, s 780(7) authorises the Minister for Finance to increase or decrease the flat rate of tax charged on these repayments. He may do so at any time by statutory order approved by a resolution of Dáil Éireann.

The tax charge on the administrator is made in respect of all the employee's contributions repaid, including any contributions paid to the scheme before it became an exempt approved scheme, but no tax is charged in relation to any contribution that was made to a retirement scheme after it ceased to be an exempt approved scheme (TCA 1997, s 780(4)). However, this exception does not apply if the scheme becomes an exempt approved scheme again, even if the contributions now being repaid were made to it at the time when it was not such a scheme.

In applying the other exception provided by TCA 1997, s 780(3), ie a repayment of contributions to an employee whose employment was carried on outside the State, the Revenue manual sets out how the Revenue interprets this condition. The manual indicates that the exemption from the tax charge under TCA 1997, s 780(3) will be given in any case where the employee worked abroad throughout at least 75 per cent of the period during which he was a member of the scheme. However, if the contributions refunded consist partly of contributions first made to another scheme and later included in a transfer payment to the scheme making the repayment, the 75 per cent test must be applied to his period of membership of both schemes taken together.

Refunds to employer

TCA 1997, s 782(1) requires any payment made, or becoming due, to an employer out of funds held for the purposes of an exempt approved scheme related to a trade or profession carried on by the employer to be treated as a receipt of that trade or profession. The payment is taken into account in computing the taxable income of the trade or profession for the period of account in which it becomes due for payment to the employer (whether or not actually paid to him in that period). However, if the employer had ceased to carry on his trade or profession before the repayment became due, it is included as a receipt on the last day on which the trade or profession was carried on.

The fact that the payment became due out of the funds of the retirement benefits scheme at a time when it was not an exempt approved scheme does not prevent the application of TCA 1997, s 782 in this way, if the scheme was at any time previously an exempt approved scheme. However, any repayment which became due to the employer before the scheme first became an exempt approved scheme is not taxable under this rule (TCA 1997, s 782(2)). In applying TCA 1997, s 782, any transfer of assets or other transfer of money's worth made or becoming due to the employer out of the funds of a scheme are to be treated in the same way as any payment, ie included as trading receipts (TCA 1997, s 782(3)).

An employer who carries on an undertaking other than a trade or profession may receive or become entitled to payments out of the funds of an exempt approved scheme established for the purposes of his undertaking. In any such case, TCA 1997, s 782(1)(b) charges him to tax under Sch D Case IV on the amount of the payment (or any transfer of assets, etc treated as a payment). However, to the extent that the payment represents contributions by the employer under the scheme which were not allowable as deductions for tax purposes, no tax is charged under Sch D Case IV on the proportion of the payment represented by those disallowed contributions.

It is to be noted that TCA 1997, s 782 refers to any payment to the employer out of the trust funds, and not merely to repayments of the employer's contributions. For example, an employer may receive a payment out of the contributions of an employee refundable on the latter's leaving the employer's service under a rule entitling the employer to be reimbursed out of the employee's refund for a financial loss caused by the fraud or negligence of the employee. Any such reimbursements to the employer must be treated as a trading receipt of their trade or profession or, if relevant, must be charged to tax on the employer under Sch D Case IV.

16.110 Taxation of pension scheme benefits

TCA 1997, s 779 requires all pensions paid under any scheme, including an overseas pension scheme, which is approved or is being considered for approval under TCA 1997, Pt 30, Ch 1 to be charged to tax under Sch E and paid subject to the deduction of income tax under the PAYE procedure. While pension payments to Irish residents from a foreign source would normally be taxable under Case III of Sch D, TCA 1997, s 779(1) makes it clear that any pensions paid from an overseas pension scheme approved, or being considered for approval, by the Revenue Commissioners are to be considered taxable under Sch E and that the PAYE system will apply.

This applies to pensions paid under a simple approved scheme as well as to those under an exempt approved scheme. It affects pensions paid both to the individual who was a member of the scheme before his retirement and to any widow, civil partner, child, other dependant or personal representatives of a deceased employee or pensioner.

The person responsible for paying the pensions under an approved scheme – whether he is the administrator of the scheme, any life assurance company with which the scheme has been insured or from which an annuity under the scheme has been purchased, or any other person – is treated as the 'employer' responsible for deducting income tax at the time of payment to the extent required under the PAYE procedure (see **Division 11**). The taxation of approved scheme pensions under Sch E (subject to PAYE) applies even if the pensioner was, before his retirement, paid the emoluments of this employment outside the State in circumstances where the emoluments were taxable under Sch D Case III (see also **16.112**).

The fact that the person receiving the pension may be resident outside the State does not, in principle, affect their liability to Irish tax under Sch E. Any pension paid as a result of contributions to a scheme approved under TCA 1997, Pt 30, Ch 1 is income from a source within the State and chargeable to Irish income tax irrespective of the country of residence of the pensioner at the time he receives it. However, if the pensioner is a resident of a country with which Ireland has a double taxation agreement, the terms of that agreement may entitle him to exemption from Irish income tax (see **14.213**). The Revenue Commissioners have confirmed in the most recent Pensions Manual that payments from an ARF, AMRF or vested PRSA are not payments of pension and as such all payments from such arrangements to a non-resident individual are subject to tax as emoluments and it is not possible to obtain a PAYE exclusion order.

Further, if the pensioner is resident outside the State, the Revenue Commissioners in practice allow the pension to be exempted from Irish income tax in the case of an individual whose service in respect of which the pension is paid was abroad, provided that either:

(a) the last ten years of that service were abroad; or

(b) one half of the total of that service was abroad and at least 10 of the last 20 years of that service were also abroad.

On the other hand, irrespective of the amount of the foreign service, any pension from an approved scheme payable to a pensioner who is now resident in the State is fully taxable under Sch E within TCA 1997, s 779. Further, the fact that TCA 1997, s 779 does not deal with any pensions or annuities payable under unapproved retirement benefit schemes does not mean that such pensions, etc are free of income tax in the hands of a resident pensioner. Such pensions are chargeable to income tax under other rules in the Income Tax Acts (see **10.101**).

Commutation payments

The rules of most approved schemes permit an employee to opt on his retirement to commute a part of his pension for a lump sum, but subject to a maximum lump sum calculated by the '3*n* eightieths' formula or 'uplifted sixtieths' basis (see **16.107**) or 25 per cent of the value of the pension in the case of proprietary directors who elect to the options under TCA 1997, s 772(3A) (see **16.107**). If the employee exercises this option, the lump sum received is tax free in his hands within prescribed limits.

Two other forms of commutation of pension benefits may be permitted by the rules of a scheme approved within the Revenue Commissioners' discretionary powers. Firstly in the case of trivial pensions the rules may permit the full commutation of an employee's pension. If the aggregate benefits payable to the employee under the scheme and any other scheme relating to the same employment do not exceed the value of a pension of €330 per annum full commutation is permitted. Alternatively with the agreement of the scheme beneficiary and the trustees, Revenue do not object to the payment of once-off pensions. This may take place where the total of all funds available for pension benefits, following the payment of lump sum benefit, is less than €20,000. The quantum of retirement benefits from all sources must be taken into account in calculating the limit of €20,000. Prior Revenue approval is not required and any such sums received are liable to tax under Sch E. The Revenue Commissioners have confirmed in the revised Pension Manual that these options also apply to RACs and PRSAs.

Secondly if at the time the pension becomes payable the individual is in 'exceptional circumstances of serious ill health' it may be possible to take a full commutation of the pension: see **16.107**.

TCA 1997, s 781 charges tax under Sch D Case IV in respect of any lump sum payments received by an employee in commutation of his pension benefits under either the trivial pensions rule or the exceptionally serious ill health rule. However, the amount on which the tax is charged by TCA 1997, s 781 is normally the amount of the commutation payment as reduced by the maximum commutation payment of the part of the pension that could have been opted for under the rules of the scheme in question.

Alternatively, the actual commutation payment taxable under TCA 1997, s 781 may be reduced by the amount (if it is higher) determined as the maximum commutation payment the individual could have received if the scheme contained a rule limiting the maximum payment to that set out in the basic conditions relating to benefits in TCA 1997, s 772(3). Under this alternative, the strict 3*n* eightieths rule (without discretionary modification) must be applied to the final remuneration determined as the average of the last three years' remuneration. Where a pension is commuted, for example, on grounds of ill health, but the scheme also provides separately for a lump sum based on 3*n*/80ths of final remuneration, the whole of the commutation sum will be taxed.

In a case where this provision applies to tax trivial (other than once off pension payments of less than €15,000) or serious ill health commutation payments, the tax is charged on the administrator of the approved scheme at the flat rate of 10 per cent provided for in TCA 1997, s 781(3). As in the case of the similar rule for taxing the repayments of an employee's contributions (see **16.109**), the amount taxable on the administrator is not treated as the employee's income for any purpose of income tax. Further, under the same conditions as for repayments of employees' contributions, TCA 1997, s 781 does not charge any tax on commutation payments where the employee's employment was carried on outside the State (TCA 1997, s 781(2)).

Benefits for dependants

Income tax is not charged on any death benefits, (other than a pension) that become payable under the rules of an approved scheme to the widow, civil partner, children or other dependants, or to the personal representatives of a deceased employee. On the other hand, any benefit from an approved scheme payable in the form of a pension to the widow, civil partner, children, dependants, etc of a deceased employee or pensioner is taxable on the recipient under Sch E and subject to PAYE under TCA 1997, s 779.

Deemed pension payments

With effect from 2 February 2006 where the assets of a retirement benefits scheme which is approved or is being considered for approval are used in connection with any transaction which would, if the assets were the assets of an approved retirement fund, be regarded under s 784A as giving rise to a distribution, then the use of the assets will be regarded as a pension paid under the scheme. Any amount which is regarded as a pension paid under the scheme or any property, the acquisition or sale of which is regarded as giving rise to a pension payment, will not be regarded as an asset of the scheme.

Finance Act 2014 inserted a new TCA 1997, s 790E with effect from 23 October 2014 which provides that any transaction referred to in TCA 1997, s 784A(1B)(h) shall also be treated as a deemed pension payment. This refers to a transaction whereby a pension arrangement of an individual connected to the ARF holder has acquired units in a fund, trust or scheme in which the ARF has also invested and the value of the units held by the pension investor increases, or may increase due in whole or in part to the units held by the ARF investor.

16.111 Tax exemption of pension scheme funds

A retirement benefits scheme operates by investing the ordinary annual contributions and the special contributions (if any) of the employer and the employees (if they contribute). The investments produce income and, in the event of changes in investments or their ultimate sale to pay the scheme benefits, capital gains (or capital losses). Alternatively, if the scheme is arranged through a life assurance company as part of that company's pension business, the contributions are invested by the life company which derives the income and capital gains (or losses), but which is responsible for applying funds in due course to meet the pensions and other scheme benefits which it has contracted to assure.

One of the most important consequences of having an exempt approved pension scheme (as distinct from a simple approved one) is that the investment income of the scheme funds is entirely free of income tax with one exception which is discussed below. This permits the funds consisting of the employer's and employees' contributions, plus previous income and less any benefits paid out, to build up at a faster rate than if income tax was payable, thereby permitting the funding of the benefits at lower contribution levels than would otherwise be necessary.

TCA 1997, s 774(3) provides the exemption from income tax for the exempt approved scheme in respect of all income derived from the investments or deposits of the scheme, but only to the extent that the Commissioners are satisfied the investments or deposits are held for the purposes of the scheme. TCA 1997, s 774(5) provides a similar exemption from income tax in respect of underwriting commissions otherwise chargeable under Sch D Case IV to the extent that the Revenue Commissioners are satisfied that those commissions are applied for the purposes of the scheme. In either case, the administrator or a person acting on his behalf must claim the exemption by applying to the Retirement Benefits District.

In *Clarke v Trustees of British Telecom Pension Scheme et al* [2000] STC 222 the taxpayers were trustees of exempt approved pension schemes and were paid sub-underwriting commissions which were applied for the purposes of the schemes. The taxpayers successfully claimed that the commissions would have been taxable under the UK counterpart to Sch D Case IV rather than as trading income. The Court of Appeal held that if the legal or commercial characteristics of a transaction pointed unequivocally to trading, the trader's subjective purpose or motive could not change the character of the transaction. However, its character might be ambiguous until resolved by reference to purpose or motivation. Therefore, it was necessary to consider the relationship between the taxpayers' sub-underwriting and investment activities, and the weight to be given to their intentions. The Appeal Commissioners, while recognising that the taxpayers' activities had features indicative of a trade had not treated these as decisive. It was not unreasonable for the Appeal Commissioners to conclude that the activity of sub-underwriting was an integral part of the taxpayer's investment activities and took its colour from them as non-trading in nature.

No exemptions are given, however, for any income arising at a time when the scheme is not an exempt approved scheme (TCA 1997, s 774(2)). In some cases, only partial exemption will be available, for example in the case of a foreign scheme of a non-resident employer where only a part of that scheme, ie the part relating to benefits provided for employees in the State, is approved under TCA 1997, Pt 30, Ch 1 (see **16.112**).

TCA 1997, s 256(1) permits exempt schemes to open deposit accounts on which interest will be paid gross, without deduction of deposit interest retention tax subject to the scheme furnishing the deposit taker with the reference number assigned to the employer by the Revenue Commissioners.

The trustees (or the administrator) of an exempt approved scheme are also entitled to receive dividends from Irish resident companies free of dividend withholding tax (TCA 1997, s 172C(1)). If the fund investment income includes any taxed income (eg annuities receivable or interest on company loan stocks), the administrator or trustees may reclaim the income tax deducted at source from that income.

One final point in relation to the income tax exemption of the exempt approved scheme should be made. In certain circumstances, the trustees of a scheme may invest funds in immovable property and may even become involved in the development of such property. It is important to note that the exemption given by TCA 1997, s 774(3) only relates to income from investments. Consequently, should the trustees carry out any transactions by way of dealing in or developing immovable property, in such a way as gives rise to trading profits taxable under Sch D Case I, the pension scheme exemption does not apply. Therefore, the trustees should if at all possible make sure that their activities in relation to developing property go no further than developing with an intention to hold as an investment. Rental income from immovable property earned by an exempt approved scheme is exempt from income tax. However, there is no exemption for pension schemes from local property tax and NPPR.

A pension scheme may invest all of its assets in an insurance contract or the assets may be under the control of the scheme trustees themselves (a 'self-administered scheme'). Where the benefits of an exempt approved scheme are assured through a contract with a life assurance company, TCA 1997, s 717(1) provides that exemption from corporation tax is given in respect of income, chargeable gains, investments and deposits of any life assurance company's funds, but only to the extent that they relate to its pension business. For this purpose, a life assurance company's 'pension business' is defined by TCA 1997, s 706 as including contracts for the purposes of an exempt approved scheme under TCA 1997, Pt 30, Ch 1 (as well as approved retirement annuity plans, approved retirement fund and approved minimum retirement funds and PRSAs), but does not include any contracts or other business connected with any unapproved retirement benefit scheme.

Special requirements apply to '*small self-administered schemes*' (SSAS), defined by the Revenue Commissioners generally as a scheme with less than twelve members. The Revenue state that these requirements are necessary to ensure that the scheme is one which is '*bona fide* established for the sole purpose of providing relevant benefits' within TCA 1997, s 772(2) and 'not a scheme designed for avoidance.'

The Revenue Commissioners state in their Pensions manual that:

> A scheme designed primarily for a few family directors, to whom are added some relatively low paid employees with entitlement to only insignificant benefits, included to bring membership to 12 or more, or a scheme with more than 12 members where most or all of the members are *20 per cent directors* (eg where subsidiary or associated companies are included) will both be regarded as small. Conversely, it might not be necessary to regard a scheme with fewer than 12 members as small if all the members are at arm's length from

each other, from the employer and the trustees. A small insured scheme which becomes self-administered after approval must from the change-over date, comply with the special requirements.

They add that:

> Irrespective of the number of members involved a scheme will be regarded as small at any time when 65 per cent or more of the value of the investments of the scheme relate to the provision of benefits for 20 per cent directors of the sponsoring employer(s) and for their spouses, civil partners and dependants.

Revenue requirements in connection with SSAS include the following:

(a) the trustees must include a 'pensioneer trustee', ie an individual or body widely involved with occupational pension schemes and their approval, who is prepared to give an undertaking to the Retirement Benefits Division that he will not consent to any termination of a scheme of which he is trustee, otherwise than in accordance with the approved terms of the 'winding up rules' laid down by the Revenue. Where there are non-pensioneer trustees they must not be permitted to outvote the pensioneer trustee on issues relating to the termination of the scheme. Corporate trustees must have pensioneer trustees as a majority of their controlling directors;

(b) the investment powers of the SSAS trustees are limited, to exclude:

 (i) loans to members of the scheme or any other individual with a contingent interest in the scheme (eg a dependant) or to the employer,

 (ii) a proposal to acquire real property as an investment can be approved subject to the following:

  (I) the vendor is 'at arm's length' from the pension scheme, the employer and the employer's directors and associated companies,

  (II) the acquisition is not for disposal or letting to the employer, its directors or its associated companies,

  (III) the scheme investments overall match the scheme liabilities and that the investment does not compromise the liquidity of the scheme. Where the main or only asset is property, it is considered that the concentration of investments in an asset not readily realisable does not satisfy the requirement to match investment assets with a scheme's liabilities,

  (IV) the disposal of the property is on an arm's length basis,

  (V) the purchase of holiday homes is not allowed,

  (VI) the purchase of overseas property will only be acceptable if the penioneer trustee is able to maintain control over the asset to ensure that Revenue rules are complied with,

  (VII) property development with a view to disposal is not acceptable (but this prohibition applies generally in any event: see above),

  (VIII) any proposal that involves the diversion of the sponsoring employer's taxable activity into the scheme is not acceptable;

(c) 'self-investment' in property or other fixed assets from the employer or shares and securities of an employing company, whether by subscription or purchase is not acceptable;

(d) schemes are not permitted to invest in 'pride in possession articles' such as works of art, jewellery, yachts, vintage cars, etc (but excepting intangibles such as shares, copyrights and financial futures); and

(e) investments in shares in 'private companies' must be limited to 5 per cent of the scheme assets and to 10 per cent of the private company's share capital.

With effect from 23 September 2005 a SSAS other than a 'one member arrangement' cannot borrow other than for liquidity purposes and only on a temporary basis (see **16.106**).

Various conditions also apply in connection with the purchase of pension annuities, death benefits, approval of commutation on grounds of exceptionally serious ill-health, funding, actuarial reports and accounts. The Retirement Benefits Division will not respond to hypothetical enquiries concerning an SSAS.

Finally, it may be noted that, where an approved pension scheme ceases to meet the conditions for approval, the scheme will thereby become an unapproved scheme; however, depending on the circumstances, there may be no clawback of any tax exemptions obtained during the period in which it enjoyed approved status.

16.112 Non-resident employers' schemes

TCA 1997, s 772(4)(b)(iv) authorises the Revenue Commissioners to approve a scheme relating to a trade or undertaking carried on only partly in the State by a non-resident person. From the point of view of such a non-resident employer's employees who come to Ireland to exercise their employment in the State, it may be desirable that any payments by the non-resident employer should be made through a scheme approved within TCA 1997, Pt 30, Ch 1. The fact that an employee's emoluments may be taxable under Sch D Case III does not absolve the employee from liability to Irish tax under TCA 1997, s 777 except to the extent that he is eligible for the remittance basis (see **16.104**).

In any event, with effect from 1 January 2006, emoluments of a foreign employment to the extent attributable to the performance of Irish duties are chargeable under Schedule E. (TCA 1997, s 18(2)(f) as inserted by FA 2006).

Further, if the non-resident employer wishes to operate a scheme with 'exempt approved status' so as to benefit from the exemption from income tax and capital gains tax in respect of the scheme's investment income and capital gains, he may set up the scheme for the Irish employees so as to qualify as an exempt approved scheme under TCA 1997, s 774. However, it may be noted that an employee's contributions are deductible only against Sch E (not Sch D Case III) earnings (TCA 1997, s 774(7)). Again, this will not usually be an issue given that with effect from 1 January 2006, emoluments of a foreign employment to the extent attributable to the performance of Irish duties will be chargeable under Schedule E (TCA 1997, s 18(2)(f) as inserted by FA 2006). For a description of the concessional reliefs granted in relation to certain secondments from abroad, see **16.104**. Types of exempt approved scheme may be established by the non-resident employer – an 'Irish' scheme and an 'overseas' scheme. An Irish scheme is one operated through a trust fund held by trustees resident in the State. Such a scheme which meets the conditions for approval, either under the basic conditions or within the Commissioners' discretionary powers, may be approved as a single scheme if it relates wholly to persons employed in the State.

If it relates partly to employees in the State and partly to employees abroad, it is regarded as being two separate schemes of which one only, ie that relating to persons employed in the State, can be approved within TCA 1997, Pt 30, Ch 1. In this event, only the separate approved scheme qualifies for the tax benefits (no income tax or capital gains on scheme investments, etc). If both the approved scheme and the unapproved scheme (for employees abroad) operate through a single trust fund, the income and capital gains arising from the investments of the single fund have to be apportioned between the two separate schemes to determine the application of the tax reliefs appropriate to the approved scheme only.

A non-resident employer's overseas scheme is one established abroad and operated by non-resident trustees. Such a scheme which relates at least partly to employees exercising their employment in the State may be approved by the Commissioners under TCA 1997, Pt 30, Ch 1. No approval is, however permitted for a non-resident employer's overseas scheme where all the employees are abroad. In the more likely case where there are employees both in the State and abroad, the scheme is regarded as two separate schemes and the scheme relating to employees in the State is approvable separately in the same way as a non-resident employer's Irish scheme.

In the case of the overseas scheme, it is an invariable condition of approval that a person resident in the State must be appointed to act for the non-resident trustees or administrator and to be responsible for all the duties and liabilities of an approved scheme under Irish tax rules and practice. It is also a requirement that all pensions becoming payable under the approved scheme be paid through the Irish resident representative (subject to the application of the PAYE rules). However, where the individual in question has subsequently ceased to be Irish resident, the pension would normally be exempt from Irish tax under the terms of any relevant double tax treaty. The Revenue operate an exemption for other non-resident individuals so that PAYE may not need to be operated in these circumstances (see **16.110**).

In the case of an overseas scheme, it is likely that the terms and rules will be those corresponding to the law and practice in the country in which the scheme is established. In order that such a scheme may be approved by the Commissioners as an approved scheme within the Irish legislation so far as its employees in the State are concerned, it is necessary that the rules of the scheme applicable to those employees conform to the conditions capable of approval within the Commissioners' discretionary powers.

In many cases, it is more than likely that the rules of the overseas scheme do not conform to those necessary for approval in the State. In this event, the matter may be dealt with by the execution by the non-resident employer and administrator or trustees of a supplementary deed which contains the rules as to contributions, benefits, etc for the Irish resident employees covered by it. This supplementary deed should be in a form suitable for approval under Irish law and practice.

16.113 Statutory schemes

TCA 1997, s 776 deals with statutory schemes, ie with any retirement benefits scheme established by or under any enactment. Compared with the position with regard to approved and exempt approved schemes, the rules are very straightforward. No question arises as to the terms of the scheme nor of obtaining the approval of the Revenue Commissioners after the scheme is enacted. Since any statutory scheme is set up by a public statute, it is to be assumed that its terms and the benefits it may provide are acceptable within the public policy at the time of the relevant enactment.

TCA 1997, s 776(2)(a) requires any ordinary annual contribution paid under a statutory scheme by any officer or employee to be deducted as an expense in assessing him to tax under Sch E. The deduction is given in the tax year in which the contribution is paid. For any contribution paid or borne by any officer or employee other than as an ordinary annual contribution, an expense deduction is similarly given under Sch E, but the Commissioners may, if they think fit, direct that the contribution should be apportioned over such years as they may direct.

With effect from 6 February 2003, the spreading back of special contributions is confined to:

(a) contributions made on retirement, following an application in writing by the employee before 6 February 2003 to contribute, towards the purchase of pension benefits within the standard Revenue limits in respect of actual service by the employee for the period before the employee became a member of the scheme (TCA 1997, s 776(2)(b));
(b) contributions deducted from a lump sum payable on retirement to provide for dependants' benefits (TCA 1997, s 776(2)(ba)(i)); and
(c) contributions made on retirement to pay back a previous refund of contributions or to pay back benefits previously provided to the member of a pension scheme [such as a marriage gratuity], where the contributor had previously left the employment related to the pension scheme (TCA 1997, s 776(2)(ba)(ii)).

Similar to the position for an employee's contributions to an exempt approved scheme, the maximum deduction in respect of both ordinary annual contributions and any special contribution apportioned to any year must not exceed the aged related contribution limit (**16.107**) of the total remuneration derived from the relevant office or employment in the year in question.

16.114 Pre-retirement access to AVCs

With effect from 27 March 2013, TCA 1997, s 782A and TCA 1997, Sch 23C introduced by Finance Act 2013 allow for access to AVCs before retirement age. The pre-retirement transfer option is the transfer by the administrator of the scheme to the relevant individual before retirement, of an amount not exceeding 30 per cent of the value at the time of the transfer of the relevant individual's AVC fund. The amount transferred will be subject to PAYE at the higher rate of income tax (40 per cent with effect from 1 January 2015, previously 41 per cent) unless the administrator has received a certificate of tax credits and the standard rate cut off point or a tax deduction card for that year in respect of the individual (TCA 1997, s 782A(4)). No USC or PRSI is payable (FA 2013, s 2).

The amount transferred is deemed not to be a benefit crystallisation event (see **16.502**).

The relevant individual may during the period of three years from 27 March 2013 irrevocably instruct in writing the administrator of their AVC fund to exercise on one occasion only the above transfer under TCA 1997, s 782A(2). Finance (No 2) Act 2013 amended TCA 1997, s 782A(2) to ensure that the relevant individual can exercise the pre-retirement access option notwithstanding that the scheme rules may prohibit transfers pre-retirement. This will avoid scheme rules having to be amended to facilitate pre-retirement transfer. The change is effective from 27 March 2013, the date Finance Act 2013 was enacted.

A relevant individual means a member of the scheme who has an AVC fund and, as the case may be, where the AVC fund is subject to a pension adjustment order includes the spouse, former spouse, civil partner or former civil partner of the member. An AVC fund includes an AVC PRSA fund provided the benefits have not already become payable to the member under the main approved or statutory scheme of the member. It excludes ordinary contributions to an approved occupational pension scheme and does not include any voluntary contributions to purchase notional service.

The administrator must deliver within 15 working days of the end of each quarter commencing with the quarter ending 30 June 2013 to the Revenue Commissioners the following information:

(a) the number of transfers made;
(b) the aggregate value of the transfers made; and
(c) the tax deducted from the aggregate transfers made.

The early access will assist individuals who may be in financial difficulties and who are not close to retirement. It is also of benefit to individuals who are likely to have pension funds exceeding the standard threshold and who can avoid the higher tax rates associated with a benefit crystallisation event on retirement.

16.2 Retirement Annuities

16.201 Introduction

TCA 1997, Pt 30, Ch 2 deals with the tax relief given for premiums or other consideration paid by an individual to secure a retirement annuity. Due to the fact that the individuals principally interested in paying premiums for retirement annuities are individuals carrying on a trade or profession on their own account or in partnership, ie self-employed individuals, this form of relief is frequently referred to as self-employed retirement relief. It is not, however, limited to self-employed individuals, but may be claimed by any individual exercising an office or employment that is not a 'pensionable' office or employment, as well as by certain other persons with 'relevant earnings' (see **16.202**).

In order to secure tax relief for their premiums or contributions to any 'self-employed retirement plan' (the term used to describe any contract or arrangement qualifying for tax relief under TCA 1997, Pt 30, Ch 2), the taxpayer must pay the premium or other consideration either under a life annuity contract that has been approved by the Revenue Commissioners or to a 'trust scheme' approved by the Commissioners. When a retirement annuity contract or a trust scheme has been approved by the Commissioners, a further advantage is secured in that the income from the investments representing the premiums on the approved annuity contracts or the contributions to the trust scheme are permitted to accrue free of income tax. It may be seen, therefore, that there are a number of similarities to the treatment of the contributions to, and the income or capital gains of, exempt approved pension schemes.

The subject of retirement annuities may, perhaps, best be discussed by dealing first with the question of who may claim the tax relief that is given by deduction under TCA 1997, s 787 from the individual's relevant earnings. This question is dealt with in **16.202** (where the meaning of 'relevant earnings' should be particularly noted) and in **16.203**.

The conditions which must be satisfied by a retirement annuity contract (or other relevant contract) to which qualifying premiums are paid, before the approval of the Revenue Commissioners is given, are discussed in **16.204**. As is the case with approved occupational pension schemes, the Commissioners are given certain discretionary powers to approve contracts for self-employed, etc retirement annuity contracts that vary from the basic conditions. The question of the approval of trust schemes, ie schemes under irrevocable trusts to provide retirement annuity benefits for individuals in a particular occupation or group of occupations, is then covered in **16.205**.

TCA 1997, s 787 is the actual relieving section and it grants tax relief in the form of a full deduction (but with certain limits) from relevant earnings for qualifying premiums paid by an individual entitled to the relief. The manner in which the relief is granted and the limits to it are dealt with in **16.206**, while the question of carrying forward qualifying premiums exceeding the limits in any one tax year is covered separately in **16.207**. For ease of explanation, the relief given by TCA 1997, s 787 is referred to throughout the rest of this Division as 'retirement annuity relief'.

The important concept of 'net relevant earnings' is explained (and illustrated) in some detail in **16.208**. Since the maximum tax deduction for qualifying premiums in any one tax year is based on the computation of net relevant earnings. The remaining articles (**16.209–16.210**) deal respectively with claims for retirement annuity relief, the taxation of retirement annuities and related benefits including the retirement options introduced in FA 1999 and the tax exemption given in respect of the income and capital gains from investments held for the funds of self-employed, etc retirement plans.

16.202 Who may claim relief?

TCA 1997, s 784(1) entitles certain individuals to claim tax relief, in the manner granted by TCA 1997, s 787, in respect of qualifying premiums paid under certain types of approved annuity contracts. Previously in order to claim this relief in any tax year, the individual had to be chargeable to income tax for that year in respect of 'relevant earnings' from a trade, profession, office or employment. With effect from 1 January 2002, it is only necessary that the individual previously had a source of 'relevant earnings', ie even if the source of relevant earnings has ceased, the individual is still permitted to make contributions. If an individual carries or (previously carried) on a trade or profession or holds or previously held an office or employment which would normally generate relevant earnings, but which does not do so in any given year due to an insufficiency of income, he may still pay qualifying premiums in that year and may carry forward the premiums for relief in subsequent tax years.

TCA 1997, s 784(4) permits an individual to claim tax relief under TCA 1997, s 787 in respect of contributions to an approved trust scheme established to provide retirement annuities and related benefits for individuals (and their dependants) engaged in any particular occupation. Again, relief for such contributions depends on the individual having or previously had relevant earnings from a trade, profession, office or employment. If he has, relief is given for the trust scheme contributions in exactly the same way as for qualifying premiums on approved retirement annuity contracts.

Any references in the following pages relating to the treatment of qualifying premiums to approved annuity contracts may, therefore, be taken as applying equally to contributions to an approved trust scheme. The only real technical difference between an approved retirement annuity contract and an approved trust scheme is that the former involves the payment of a premium to a person lawfully carrying on in the State a business of granting annuities on human life (almost invariably a life assurance company), whereas in the latter case the contributions are made to trustees established under irrevocable trusts.

In short, retirement annuity relief may only be claimed by an individual for any tax year if he carries or previously carried on any trade or profession in that year capable of generating relevant earnings, or if he holds or exercises in that year an office or employment that produces relevant earnings (not all offices and employments do). The definition of 'relevant earnings' is, therefore, the critical matter.

Relevant earnings

TCA 1997, s 783(3) defines 'relevant earnings' as being any income of the individual chargeable to tax for the tax year for which the retirement annuity relief is claimed, but only in so far as such income consists of:

(a) income chargeable under Sch D immediately derived by the individual from the carrying on of his trade or profession either as a sole trader or as an active partner;

(b) the emoluments of any *non-pensionable* office or employment held by the individual; or

(c) income from any property attached to or forming part of the emoluments of any such non-pensionable office or employment.

In *Bucks v Bowers* 46 TC 267, Pennycuick J held that certain taxed interest and dividends received by merchant bankers was not 'immediately derived' from the carrying on of the trade, saying:

> Quite apart from authority, I do not think that, in the context of an income tax statute, one would naturally treat income received under deduction by a trader in the carrying on of his trade as 'derived', still less 'immediately derived', from the carrying on of that trade. It is certainly derived by him in the course of that trade, but the word 'from' suggests that the trade must be the source of the income, and that is not so in the case of income charged by deduction. The source of interest is not the trade but the loan obligation from which the interest springs.

Pennycuick J's dictum seems doubtful; the fact that income taxed at source should not be included in a Sch D Case I/Case II computation does not necessarily mean that it would not also be a trading receipt on general principles. If it would be such, then it should clearly rank as 'earned income'. The same decision could have been reached simply on the basis that the income there was not of a trading nature. The decision in *Bucks v Bowers* was followed by Templeman in *Northend v White and Leonard* [1975] STC 317, in which interest on moneys held on general deposit accounts was received by a solicitor. The taxpayer's right to retain the interest arose from the provisions of the UK Solicitors Act 1965 and was said to be in the nature of a recompense for the task of looking after the client's moneys. Templeman J commented as follows:

> Of course, if the Solicitors Act 1965 had not been passed, or if the firm had not carried on the exercise of the profession of solicitors, there would have been no deposit account and no interest. But it does not follow that the interest was 'immediately derived' from the carrying on of the profession. To produce the interest there must be an intervening event which could not be described as the carrying on of the profession of a solicitor, namely, the loan of money by a customer [ie the solicitor] to a bank …

Both of the above passages were approved by Murphy J in *Kerrane v Hanlon* III ITR 633.

The reference to an 'active' partner (ie one 'personally acting' in a partnership) means that the profit share of a limited partner cannot qualify as 'relevant earnings'; the same will normally hold true of a so-called 'sleeping partner' (see **4.501**). The profits of an individual who owns but who does not carry on a trade (ie he leaves the entire management and control of the trade to their agent(s): see **4.102**) equally do not qualify as 'relevant earnings' (*Koenigsberger v Mellor* [1995] STC 547, in which retirement annuity relief was denied to a non-working Lloyd's name, see **13.506**).

In *Pegler v Abell* [1975] STC 23, it was held that a pension paid to a retired partner was not derived from the previous conduct of his trade, but from the contractual liability of the existing partners to pay the pension to him. Accordingly, the pension did not qualify as 'relevant earnings' (compare *Peay v Newton* 46 TC 653).

TCA 1997, s 783(4) provides that a married woman's or civil partner's relevant earnings (if she has any) must be calculated separately from those of her husband or civil partner (if he has any). This applies notwithstanding that her income chargeable to tax is treated as the income of her husband or civil partner or vice versa (in a case where they are assessable jointly under TCA 1997, s 1017). Consequently, any reference hereinafter to an individual with relevant earnings entitled to claim relief under TCA 1997, s 787 in respect of qualifying premiums is, in the case of a married individual or civil partner assessed jointly with their spouse or civil partner, to be taken as referring to whichever spouse or civil partner has the relevant earnings. If both spouses or civil partners have relevant earnings, the reference to the individual is to the spouse or civil partner whose position is under consideration at the particular time.

The relevant earnings from a trade or profession for any year of assessment are the adjusted Sch D Case I or II profits arising in the basis period for that year (eg a 12-month accounting period ended 30 September 2015 assessable in 2015). Relevant earnings are taken before deducting capital allowances (but see **16.208** for the deduction of capital allowances in arriving at *net* relevant earnings).

The trade or profession giving rise to relevant earnings may either be one carried on by the individual as a sole trader or one carried on by a partnership in which the individual is an active partner. The trade may be one of farming or any other type of trade, including one of dealing in or developing land, the profits of which are chargeable under Sch D Case I (or Sch D Case III, if a foreign trade). Similarly, if a profession is involved, it may be one carried on in the State assessable under Sch D Case II, or a foreign profession chargeable under Sch D Case III.

The emoluments of an office or employment only qualify as relevant earnings if the office or employment is not a pensionable office or employment. TCA 1997, s 783(2) defines a 'pensionable office or employment' as one in which the individual's service is service to which a sponsored superannuation scheme relates. It is, therefore, necessary to determine what is a 'sponsored superannuation scheme'. This latter expression is defined in a single sentence (consisting of more than 100 words!) by TCA 1997, s 783(1) which it is not proposed to repeat in full here.

In short, a 'sponsored superannuation scheme' is any scheme or arrangement relating to service in particular offices or employments that has as its object the provision of future retirement and related benefits (eg death benefits) for persons serving therein. However, the term does not include any unapproved scheme or arrangement, ie one where any part of the cost of providing the benefits is taxable on the employees under TCA 1997, s 777. Broadly, therefore, a pensionable office or employment can be taken as one for which there exists any retirement benefits scheme excluded by TCA 1997, s 778 from the charge to tax under TCA 1997, s 777 – ie any approved scheme, any statutory scheme and any foreign government scheme (see **16.104**). With effect from 1 January 2003, an employee who is a member of an employer sponsored occupational pension scheme or statutory pension scheme for risk benefits within TCA 1997, s 772(3)(b), (c), (ie death in service, pension to surviving spouse, children or dependants) only, will not be regarded as being in pensionable employment for these purposes (TCA 1997, s 783(2)(a)). Any employee contributions made under the scheme will however be treated as if they were retirement annuity premiums in computing the limits to the relief available (see **16.206**).

It follows that an individual in an office or employment where there is either no retirement benefits scheme at all, or only a 'risk benefit' scheme or an unapproved scheme, is entitled to take out an approved retirement annuity contract and to obtain tax relief under TCA 1997, s 787 for his qualifying premiums. An individual may also pay qualifying retirement annuity premiums notwithstanding that there is an approved scheme open to him in his office or employment, but where he elects not to participate in that scheme by exercising any option to that effect available to him.

The relevant earnings from a non-pensionable employment may include any amounts treated as emoluments of that employment under the rules of Sch E (see **10.101**). This means that such items as expenses payments treated as emoluments and benefits in kind (see **10.202**, **10.203**) and amounts taxable under TCA 1997, s 122 in respect of preferential employer loans (see **10.211**) can be treated as relevant earnings *provided that* they are derived from a non-pensionable employment (or office). It would appear that, in strictness, termination payments in respect of an office or employment to the extent that they are brought into charge by TCA 1997, s 123 (see **10.401**) do not constitute 'relevant earnings'. This is because while such payments are deemed to be emoluments chargeable under Sch E they are not emoluments 'of' the office previously held by the taxpayer (nor are they deemed to be so): note also the decision in *Nichols v Gibson* [1996] STC 1008.

There is no wording in TCA 1997, s 783(3) to restrict relevant earnings to remuneration derived only from employments in the State. Consequently if an individual has any remuneration or other emoluments from a foreign employment, that remuneration counts as relevant earnings provided that:

(a) the employment is not a pensionable employment (within the Irish definition under TCA 1997, s 783(2) – see above); and

(b) the remuneration in question is actually charged to Irish income tax in the hands of the individual (eg foreign (non-UK) source remuneration not remitted into the State by an individual liable to Irish tax only on remittances of foreign (non-UK) income is not relevant earnings, see **Division 13**).

A proprietary director or employee of an investment company may have a non-pensionable office or employment with that company, but TCA 1997, s 783(3) provides that any remuneration from that office or employment is not to be treated as 'relevant earnings'. Consequently, he is not entitled to take out an approved retirement annuity contract to provide any tax relief related to that remuneration. A 'proprietary director' or 'proprietary employee' is a director or employee of the company beneficially owning, or able to control directly or indirectly, more than 15 per cent of the ordinary share capital of the company (as defined by TCA 1997, s 2(1)).

An individual who has a pensionable office or employment may sometimes have an additional office or employment which is not pensionable. For example, the managing director of a company, who is a member of that company's approved pension scheme, may be a director of several other unconnected companies from which he receives directors' fees. Assuming that he does not participate in the approved pension schemes of the other companies, his directors' fees from them are 'relevant earnings' within TCA 1997, s 783(3); he is, therefore, entitled to retirement annuity relief for any qualifying premiums he may pay related to those relevant earnings (subject to the normal limits). Similarly, an individual with relevant earnings from a trade or profession has additional relevant earnings if he also receives any salary, director's fee or other emoluments from any non-pensionable office or employment which he may hold.

Medical practitioners may have a mixture of GMS fees and private fees. TCA 1997, s 773 provides that income from the GMS is to be treated as remuneration from a pensionable office or employment, ie excluded from 'relevant earnings'. This strictly requires that all GMS fees (net of an appropriate proportion of practice expenses) should be deducted from the practitioner's Sch D Case II assessable profits in computing 'relevant earnings'.

This would not give rise to any inequity where all of the GMS fees are superannuable. The Revenue give an example of how they deal with this situation in *Tax Briefing 5* (slightly modified for updating purposes).

Example 16.202.1

A doctor, aged 29, receives gross GMS fees of €50,000 (all of which are allowable net of 10 per cent Health Board Contribution) and has gross private practice fees of €15,000. His overall allowable practice expenses are (say) €25,000, leaving a net taxable income from the practice of €40,000.

The maximum retirement annuity relief allowable in relation to private practice is calculated as follows:

$$\text{Net relevant earnings} = \frac{40{,}000}{(50,\ 000 + 15,\ 000)} \times 15{,}000 = 9{,}230$$

Maximum retirement annuity relief is therefore:

$$€9{,}230 \text{ x } 15\% = €1{,}385$$

Neither the income nor the contributions in respect of the pension scheme for doctors in the GMS come into the reckoning. If retirement annuity premiums in excess of €1,385 were paid for the tax year, any balance above the 15 per cent maximum can be carried forward to future tax years.

In practice, GMS income will usually include a proportion of 'non-capitation' income, which is not superannuable. The Chief Inspector of Taxes has indicated that from 1996–97 onwards, in such cases, the practice expenses may be offset firstly against the non-capitation income. Only the balance of expenses not so offset will be apportioned between GMS capitation income and private income: see [1997] ITR pp 400–402.

Example 16.202.2

Assume the same facts as in **16.202.1**, except that the GMS fees include non-capitation fees of €16,800. The relevant earnings can be computed using the following formula in order to achieve the order of offset of practice expenses described above:

$$R = \frac{I \times P}{(P + C)}$$

Where:

R = Relevant earnings;
I = Sch D Case II adjusted profits, net of capital allowances;
P = Private income; and
C = Capitation income

Accordingly, the relevant earnings in this instance are:

$$40{,}000 \times \frac{15{,}000}{(15{,}000 + 33{,}200)} = 12{,}448$$

Maximum retirement annuity relief is therefore €12,448 x 15% = €1,867.

16.203 Qualifying premiums

Premiums paid by individuals with relevant earnings from a trade, profession, office or employment may be qualifying premiums under either TCA 1997, s 784 or TCA 1997, s 785, referred to here respectively as 's 784 premiums' and 's 785 premiums'. In each case, the premiums must be paid under a contract made by the individual with a person lawfully carrying on in the State the business of granting annuities on human life and which meets the other conditions for approval by the Revenue Commissioners under TCA 1997, Pt 30, Ch 2.

In order to qualify as a s 784 premium, the premium or other consideration paid by the individual must be under an approved annuity contract which secures, as its main benefit, a life annuity for the individual himself in his 'old age' or the new options under TCA 1997, s 784(2A). In the normal case, this means that the annuity must be one commencing at any time on or after the individual's 60th birthday and no later than his 70th birthday (75th in respect of contracts approved after 6 April 1999). For certain occupations Revenue have agreed that the annuity may commence at an earlier age. Usually, contracts under TCA 1997, s 784 permit the individual to select the actual commencement date of the annuity within these two ages. The individual does not actually have to retire before the annuity commences.

In order to qualify as an s 785 premium, the premium or other consideration paid by the individual must be under an approved contract which provides either:

(a) as the main benefit secured subject to the new retirement options available under TCA 1997, s 784(2A) by the contract, a life annuity for the wife, husband, civil partner or for any one or more of the dependants of the individual who paid the premiums; or

(b) as the sole benefit secured by the contract, a lump sum payable only on the death of the individual to his personal representatives (which lump sum must usually be one payable on the death of the individual before he attains the age of 70 or 75 in respect of contracts approved on or after 6 April 1999).

TCA 1997, s 785 enables an individual with relevant earnings, if he wishes, to enter into a contract to provide an annuity directly for his spouse or civil partner (as distinct from the survivorship annuity which may be provided by a TCA 1997, s 784 contract payable only to a widow or widower or civil partner after the individual's death). Alternatively, or as an additional contract, he may contract to secure what is in effect a whole life assurance to provide a capital sum payable to his personal representatives to be distributed to their heirs or successors in accordance with his will (or under the rules of intestacy). An individual may take out both TCA 1997, s 784 and TCA 1997, s 785 contracts, or may contract under the latter section only. Qualifying premiums may be paid annually on the same retirement annuity contract or may be single premiums paid on one or more separate contracts. It is, of course, quite possible for an individual to take out more than one contract involving annual premiums. The annual premium contract has the advantage that the individual has a commitment to make the contribution for his future retirement and/or old age on a regular basis and, once he has made the contract, he will receive a regular reminder each year in the form of the premium notice from the life assurance company with which the contract is made. While the individual's relevant earnings and, therefore, the desired level of retirement annuity contributions, are likely to increase as the years go by, additional annual premium contracts or, possibly, a single premium one may be added as required.

Most of the life assurance companies are also prepared to accept single premium retirement annuity contracts, but usually only for a minimum premium of at least €3,000. Normally, the only upper limit to the single premium acceptable is the maximum amount that the individual can reasonably expect to be deductible from his relevant earnings over a period of years. Although the amount deductible in any one tax year cannot normally exceed the contribution limits of net relevant earnings, the facility to carry forward 'excess premiums' for deduction from relevant earnings in later years may sometimes make it advantageous to pay higher premiums than can be deducted immediately.

For an individual with relevant earnings from a trade or profession which tend to vary from year-to-year, the payment of single premiums under separate contracts each year offers the advantage of flexibility. It enables the amounts contributed each year to be adjusted, if required, having regard to fluctuations in the level of the individual's net relevant earnings (which determine the maximum deduction in any one tax year). The individual may also, if he wishes, have one or more annual premium contracts with contributions to provide retirement annuities relating to their average expected earnings and may, in years when their net relevant earnings are higher than normal, pay single premiums for additional annuity contracts to top up their future retirement annuity benefits.

There are many alternative options open to the individual with relevant earnings, whether from a trade, profession, office or employment. There is no limit to the number of approved retirement annuity contracts that he may take out. The only limit relates to the maximum amount of qualifying premiums that may be deducted in any one tax year (but see **16.207**).

16.204 Conditions for approval

Prior to 1 January 2005 the Revenue Commissioners were only authorised to approve retirement annuity contracts under TCA 1997, s 784, and approvable annuity contracts or contracts for life cover under TCA 1997, s 785, if the contracts are made with a person lawfully carrying on in the State the business of granting annuities on human life. With effect from 1 January 2005 the section specifies that, where a provider is not established in the State, it must be an insurance undertaking authorised to transact such business in the State under the relevant EU directive. The conditions for approval are different depending on whether a TCA 1997, s 784 or a TCA 1997, s 785 contract is involved. The appropriate conditions are now discussed separately under each heading.

TCA 1997, s 784 contracts

The conditions which a TCA 1997, s 784 contract must satisfy to be certain of approval by the Revenue Commissioners are set out in TCA 1997, s 784(2). These are the 'basic' conditions as to the nature and form of the benefits which may be provided by the contract. However, the Commissioners are authorised by TCA 1997, s 784(3) in their discretion to approve a contract which varies in one or more stated respects from, but otherwise complies with, the basic conditions. In exercising their discretion in approving a contract which varies in any respect from the basic conditions, the Commissioners may impose any additional conditions they consider to be appropriate.

The basic conditions of TCA 1997, s 784(2) as to the benefits and the possible modifications which may be approved under the discretionary powers given by TCA

1997, s 784(3) need not be repeated in full here as they are clearly set out in the Act. It may, however, be helpful to note some of the main points, as follows:

(a) the only payment that may be made under a TCA 1997, s 784 contract during the lifetime of the individual who paid the qualifying premiums is an annuity payable to the individual himself (but subject to (b) and (c) below);

(b) the contract may permit the individual to elect, at the time the annuity commences to be payable, to take a lump sum in commutation of part of the annuity, provided that this lump sum does not exceed 25 per cent of the value of the annuity;

(c) In respect of contracts approved on or after 6 April 1999 the Revenue Commissioners will not approve a contract unless it provides that the person entitled to the annuity under the contract is entitled to exercise an option for the transfer to himself or to an approved retirement fund an amount determined by the formula:

$$A - B$$

where:

A is the amount of the individual's accrued rights under the contract exclusive of any lump sum paid ((b) above), and

B is the amount of the value of assets which the person with whom the contract is made is required to transfer to an approved minimum retirement fund or to apply towards the purchase of an annuity payable to the individual.

(d) the annuity payable to the individual must (as previously indicated) commence between the ages of 60 and 75 years;

(e) apart from the payment of an annuity to the individual, the only other sums that may be paid out by the life assurance company are:
   (i) an annuity to the individual's widow or widower or civil partner (or, at the Commissioners' discretion, dependants), or
   (ii) sums payable to the individual's personal representatives by way of return of premiums, reasonable interest thereon or bonuses out of the assurer's profits;

(f) any annuity paid under the contract must be one payable for the life of the annuitant, whether the individual is a widow, widower or dependant, but the Commissioners have the discretion to approve a contract providing an annuity for a term certain (which must not exceed 10 years) even if the annuitant should die within that term;

(g) apart from the commutation rights in (b) and (c) above, the contract must not contain any provision permitting any annuity payable under it to be capable of surrender, commutation or assignment;

(h) with effect from 7 November 2002, a contract will not cease to be an approved contract where there is a legal right to a transfer of assets to one or more PRSA contracts (whether or not such right is contained in the contract) (TCA 1997, s 784(2C));

(i) a retirement annuity contract will not cease to be an approved contract nor will Revenue be prevented from approving a contract notwithstanding that the contract provides for the annuity secured by the contract for an individual to be commuted to the extent necessary for the purpose of discharging the tax liability under the provisions of Ch 2C (**16.5**) (TCA 1997, s 784(2D)); and

(j) with effect from 8 February 2012, the provision of the encashment option in a contract (as provided for in TCA 1997, s 787TA) (see **16.504**) will not affect existing Revenue approval of the contract nor prevent Revenue from approving such a contract (TCA 1997, s 784(2E)).

FA 2016, s 14(1)(a) enacts a new TCA 1997, s 784(2F). That Act introduced a new definition into TCA 1997, s 787) being a 'vested RAC'. That definition reads:

> 'vested RAC' means a relevant pension arrangement of a kind referred to in paragraph (b) of the definition of that term in this subsection [being effectively an approved pension scheme under TCA 1997, s 784] in respect of which—
>
> (a) payment of the annuity to the individual entitled to the annuity under the contract *has not commenced*, or
>
> (b) a transfer *has not been made* under section 784(2A), [being a transfer to the individual or to an ARF]
>
> on or before the date on which the individual attains the age of 75 years.

TCA 1997, s 784(2F) states that a retirement annuity contract shall not cease to be an approved contract where the insurance undertaking with which the contract is made –

i. commences to an annuity or pays a retirement lump sum to the contributor, or
ii. transfers an amount to the contributor or to an ARF

on or before 31 March 2017, or to discharge any liability to chargeable excess tax under Ch 2C of Pt 30 arising as a result of the deemed vesting of the annuity contract. For these provisions to apply paras (b) and (c) of TCA 1997, s 784(2F) note that for (i) above the contract 'is' deemed to be a vested RAC in accordance with TCA 1997, s 787O(6) and for (ii) above the contract 'is' a vested RAC. TCA 1997, s 787O(6) deems a relevant pensions arrangement to be a vested RAC where the individual referred to in the definition of 'vested RAC' becomes 75 years of age before the passing of FA 2016, being 25 December 2016.

The wording used to in paras (b) and (c) of TCA 1997, s 784(2F) is curious in that for example, para (c) notes 'insofar as subparagraph (ii) ... is concerned, the annuity contract is a vested RAC'. Revenue guidance on the section would seem to indicate that this means that the paragraph will apply where the contract is a vested RAC but another (albeit strained) reading could be that where the tests in (ii) are met then the contract 'is' a vested RAC. Clearly that is not the intent in that Revenue would appear to view the contract to be a vested RAC before this subsection goes on to say that that fact in addition to the above tests will not prevent the contract from being a Revenue approved one.

TCA 1997, s 784(7) notes that where an annuity contract is a vested RAC as defined above then the TCA 1997, s 784A(4) is to apply to the cash and other assets representing the individual's accrued rights under the contract at the time of death of the individual as if that cash and those other assets were assets of an approved retirement fund.

TCA 1997, s 785 contracts

The conditions which a TCA 1997, s 785 contract for a spouse's, civil partner's (or a dependant's) annuity must satisfy to be certain of approval by the Revenue Commissioners are set out in TCA 1997, s 785(1). However, TCA 1997, s 785(3) authorises the Commissioners, if they think fit, to approve such a contract even if it does not satisfy all those conditions. Unlike the corresponding discretionary powers given in the case of TCA 1997, s 784 contracts, TCA 1997, s 785 does not detail the areas within which the basic conditions may be modified. The question of what variation (if any) from the basic conditions may be approved is, therefore, left entirely within the Commissioners' discretion.

The basic conditions to be satisfied by a s 785 contract for a spouse's, civil partner's (or dependant's) annuity are:

(a) any annuity payable to the spouse (or a dependant) of the individual must be one commencing on the death of the individual (rather than by reference to the age of the annuitant);

(b) any annuity payable under the contract to the individual himself cannot commence until at least the individual's 60th birthday and must normally, commence no later than his 75th birthday (but an annuity payable to him on the death of the spouse or dependent may commence on a later date);

(c) apart from any annuity payable to the individual's spouse, civil partner or dependant or to the individual himself, the contract must not provide for any payment by the assurer of any sum except that, if no annuity at all becomes payable under the contract, the assurer may make payments by way of return of premiums, reasonable interest thereon or as bonuses out of profits in respect of those premiums;

(d) the contract may not provide for the payment of any annuity otherwise than for the life of the annuitant; and

(e) no annuity payable under the contract shall be capable of surrender, commutation or assignment (and there is no corresponding right to that of a s 784 contract to commute up to 25 per cent of the value of any annuity).

While TCA 1997, s 785 refers to a contract to provide an annuity for the spouse, civil partner (for a dependant) of the individual with the relevant earnings, the fact that any annuity to a spouse, civil partner or dependant can only be one commencing on the individual's death means that the contract is primarily one to secure a death benefit in the form of an annuity. One reason for using part of the individual's TCA 1997, s 787 deduction for this type of contract to provide a spouse's, civil partner's annuity, rather than one for the individual himself (with perhaps a survivorship annuity to the widow or widower or civil partner on his death), could be in a case where the individual's life expectancy is significantly less than that of his spouse or civil partner.

The other type of s 785 contract, which provides a capital sum payable only on the death of the individual, may be a useful alternative to additional life assurance. It has the advantage that the qualifying premium is fully deductible (subject to the normal limits), whereas there is no income tax relief on life assurance premiums.

16.205 Trust schemes

TCA 1997, s 784(4) provides the same tax relief for contributions to an approved trust scheme by an individual with relevant earnings as is given for s 784 premiums paid under an approved retirement annuity contract. For this purpose, the Revenue Commissioners are empowered to approve a trust scheme if that scheme meets the following conditions:

(a) it is established for the benefit of individuals engaged in or connected with a particular occupation (or a group of occupations) for the purpose of providing retirement annuities for them, with or without subsidiary benefits for their families or dependants;

(b) it is established under the law of, and administered in, the State;

(c) it is established under irrevocable trusts by a body of persons comprising or representing the majority of the individuals engaged in a particular occupation (or group of occupations) in the State; and

(d) the benefits which may be provided by the scheme must be within the same limits as those capable for approval under a retirement annuity contract.

TCA 1997, s 785(5) similarly permits the same form of relief for contributions to an approved trust scheme as applies for s 785 premiums paid under an approved retirement annuity contract. For this purpose, the Revenue Commissioners are empowered to approve a trust scheme (or part of a trust scheme) that satisfies conditions (a), (b) and (c) mentioned in the last paragraph in relation to a scheme for providing retirement annuity benefits, but which has as its main purpose the provision of annuities for the spouses, civil partners and dependants of the individuals contributing to the scheme, or the provision of lump sums payable on death to the personal representatives of the individuals. Normally, a trust scheme is set up to provide both retirement annuity benefits approved under TCA 1997, s 784 and these annuities or lump sums for spouses, civil partners' dependants and the personal representatives within TCA 1997, s 785, but it is possible to have a trust scheme providing benefits only under one of these two sections.

When a trust scheme is set up for a particular occupation or group of occupations, there is no requirement that all of the individuals eligible to join the scheme actually participate in it. It remains open for any such individual to enter into his own approved annuity contracts or contracts for annuities and or lump sums for his spouse, civil partner, dependants or personal representatives. It may, however, sometimes be possible for him to secure the same benefits at a lower premium under a group scheme. An example of a trust scheme approved by the Revenue Commissioners is that established by the Institute of Chartered Accountants in Ireland for its members. Any member of that Institute with relevant earnings from a trade or profession or from a non-pensionable office or employment may become a contributor to that scheme and obtain tax relief for their contributions.

16.206 Manner of granting and limits to relief

TCA 1997, s 787 contains the rules determining the manner of granting, and the limits to, retirement annuity relief in respect of qualifying premiums paid under approved contracts, as well as for contributions to approved trust schemes. There is no difference between the treatment of qualifying premiums to approved contracts and that of contributions to an approved trust scheme.

In order to simplify the explanations, the discussion which follows refers only to qualifying premiums, but it may be taken that the same rules apply in all respects for trust scheme contributions. Consequently, any reference to a s 784 premium may refer equally to a contribution to a trust scheme for the purpose of providing a retirement annuity for the individual making the contribution. Similarly, a reference to a s 785 premium may include also a trust scheme contribution by the individual to secure a spouse's or civil partner's annuity, a dependant's annuity or a lump sum payable on death to personal representatives.

How the relief is granted

TCA 1997, s 787(6) grants relief by deducting the amount of the qualifying premium(s) paid by the individual in any year of assessment from the relevant earnings for that year his trade or profession, or non-pensionable office or employment. The relevant earnings for any year are those chargeable to income tax under the appropriate basis of assessment rules for the Sch or Case involved. For this purpose, relevant earnings are taken before giving effect to any deduction for any loss (eg a trading loss carried forward from an earlier year) or for any capital allowances for any year TCA 1997, s 787(1)).

Relief is only given by TCA 1997, s 787 if a claim is made to, and allowed by, the inspector of taxes (TCA 1997, s 787(15); see also **16.209**). The individual is not obliged to claim the relief in any year, but if not claimed for the year in which the premium is paid, it cannot be used in any other tax year (see also **16.207**).

When a husband and wife or civil partners each have relevant earnings taxable in the same year, each must take his respective deductions (if any) separately from his own respective relevant earnings. Similarly, in applying the rules limiting the deductions from relevant earnings to percentages of net relevant earnings (see below), these limits must be calculated separately for each spouse or civil partner. If one spouse's or civil partner's qualifying premiums exceed his maximum deduction in any year, and if the other spouse or civil partners does not pay sufficient qualifying premiums to use up fully his maximum deduction, there is no facility for setting off one spouse's, or civil partner's excess premiums against the other's relevant earnings.

Since the relief for a qualifying premium is given as a deduction from the relevant earnings of the tax year in which the premium is paid, the deduction (where claimed) is made before arriving at the claimant's total income. In some cases, this may bring the individual's total income below his 'small incomes exemption limit' (see **3.322**) so that he becomes fully exempt from income tax for the year in question.

Election to backdate relief

Normally, retirement annuity relief is, as just indicated, given for qualifying premiums and/or approved trust scheme contributions actually paid by the individual within the tax year for which the relief is claimed. However, TCA 1997, s 787(7) permits the individual to elect that qualifying premiums/trust scheme contributions paid after the end of a tax year but prior to the relevant return filing date (ie the following 31 October) may be deducted in that year (and not in the tax year in which they are paid). The election must itself be made on or before the relevant return filing date.

The ability to make this election may be particularly useful to an individual carrying on a trade or profession who finds that, for any year of claim, their relevant earnings turn out to be higher than expected. This may be due to their being slow in making up accounts for his relevant basis period for the year of claim. He may then, if he wishes, pay additional qualifying premiums or trust scheme contributions to avail of the increased limits to his maximum TCA 1997, s 787 relief for the year of claim.

To the extent that the qualifying premiums in respect of which this election is made, when added to the qualifying premiums actually paid in the year of claim, exceed the limits to the relief available to him for that year, the election has no effect with regard to that excess (which remains allowable under the normal rules as a TCA 1997, s 787(6) deduction in the tax year in which the premiums are actually paid).

Limits to relief

There are two elements determining the limits to relief:

(a) age related contribution rates; and
(b) upper earnings cap.

Firstly, it may be noted that the contribution rates increase, based on an individual's age during the year of assessment.

Age	*% Contribution*
Under 30	15%
30–39	20%
40–49	25%
50–54	30%
55–59	35%
60 or over	40%

The contribution limits in excess of 30 per cent for individuals aged 55 or over apply in respect of contributions made on or after 1 January 2006. In relation to certain specified occupations, primarily sporting occupations, (TCA 1997, Sch 23A) the contribution rate is 30 per cent irrespective of age for all ages up to 54.

An individual's net relevant earnings cannot exceed the earnings limit. TCA 1997, s 790A provides that the earnings limit is €115,000 for 2011 (this has not changed for 2012, 2013, 2014 or 2015) and for any backdated payments made in 2011 in respect of 2010. This limit applies to the aggregate of the remuneration and net relevant earnings that qualifies for relief in respect of pension contributions to occupational pension schemes, retirement annuity contracts, PRSAs and overseas pension plans.

16.207 Carry forward of excess premiums

TCA 1997, s 787(10) provides that any excess qualifying premiums paid in one tax year and carried forward are treated, for the purposes of retirement annuity relief, as if they were qualifying premiums paid in the next year. This applies to any part of any qualifying premiums which cannot be deducted from relevant earnings in the year of payment because the total qualifying premiums exceed the overall limits.

For this purpose, the 'excess qualifying premiums' is the amount by which the total qualifying premiums paid in a tax year (as increased by any unused premiums carried forward from a previous year) exceed the relevant limits.

It is to be noted that there is no carry forward available for the premiums which do not exceed the relevant limit in the case where the TCA 1997, s 787 deduction in any year reduces the individual's total income below his small incomes exemption limit. However, excess qualifying premiums not deducted in arriving at total income are available for carry forward notwithstanding that the individual may have obtained the small income exemption for a tax year.

Any qualifying premium carried forward is added to the qualifying premiums actually paid in the next tax year and is deductible from the relevant earnings for that year, but subject to the same limits. Any part of any qualifying premium carried forward which cannot be allowed in the next year is then carried forward to the next following year, and so on to succeeding years until fully deducted from relevant earnings (TCA 1997, s 787(11)).

This carry forward rule is particularly useful for an individual carrying on a trade or profession whose business profits and/or capital allowances tend to fluctuate from year-to-year. It also enables an individual, if he can afford to do so, to contribute a large (or larger than normal) premium in one year to an approved annuity contract or approved trust scheme, and then to make no contributions or smaller contributions in subsequent years. The fact that qualifying premiums are invested by the assurer (or by the trustees of a trust scheme) to earn tax free income to enhance the value of the annuity ultimately payable may justify the earlier outlay of the higher premium, even if the individual does not secure full tax relief for it until several years later.

Example 16.207.1

Mr A Counter, a partner, aged 47 on 31 December 2012, in a firm of chartered accountants took out an approved retirement annuity contract in April 2012 under which he pays an annual premium of €7,000 on 1 April in each year. On 15 July 2012, he pays a single premium of €5,000 on another approved retirement annuity contract.

Mr Counter's net relevant earnings for the tax years 2012 to 2015 (based on his relevant earnings from his share of the partnership's profits) and the respective overall limits for each of these years are as follows:

Tax years	*Net relevant earnings*	*Overall limit*	
	€	€	
2012	25,000	6,250	(25%)
2013	30,000	7,500	(25%)
2014	40,000	10,000	(25%)
2015[1]	100,000	30,000	(30%)

The total deduction obtained in each tax year (as affected by the limits) and the premiums carried forward may be set out as follows:

	Total
2012:	€
Annual premium paid[2]	12,000
TCA 1997, s 787 deduction	(6,250)
c/f to 2013	5,750
2013:	
Annual premium paid	7,000
Available for deduction	12,750
TCA 1997, s 787 deduction	(7,500)
c/f to 2014	5,250
2014:	
Annual premiums paid	7,000
Available for deduction	12,250
TCA 1997, s 787 deduction	(10,000)
c/f to 2015	2,250
2015:	
Annual Premium Paid	7,000
Available for deduction	9,250
TCA 1997, s 787 deduction	(9,250)
c/f to 2016	Nil

Notes

1. Mr A Counter is aged 50 during the 2015 tax year thus 30 per cent limit applies.
2. Including single premium of €5,000.

16.208 Meaning of 'net relevant earnings'

It is necessary to determine the amount of an individual's net relevant earnings subject to the earnings limit for each year of assessment in which he pays qualifying s 784 and/or s 785 premiums in order to compute the limit to his retirement annuity relief for each such year. As indicated in **16.206**, the total deduction for any year for qualifying premiums cannot exceed the relevant contribution limit.

In arriving at an individual's net relevant earnings for any year, his position has to be distinguished from that of his spouse or civil partner who may have separate relevant earnings of her (or his) own. A married woman's or civil partner's relevant earnings are not treated as her husband's or civil partner's relevant earnings, notwithstanding that her income is, if an election for joint assessment under TCA 1997, s 1017 is made, treated as his income (or vice versa) (TCA 1997, s 783(4)). Consequently, if the spouses or civil partners both pay qualifying premiums in respect of their own separate relevant earnings, each has to compute a separate net relevant earnings figure, whether or not they have elected to be assessable jointly.

TCA 1997, s 787(2) defines an individual's 'net relevant earnings' for any year as the amount of their relevant earnings for that year (as defined by TCA 1997, s 783(3) – see **16.202**), *less* the amount of any deductions falling to be made from those relevant earnings in computing his total income for that year, being either:

(a) deductions made in respect of payments made by him (see below); or

(b) deductions in respect of losses and/or capital allowances which arise from activities ('relevant activities') which, if profitable, would generate relevant earnings of the individual or of the individual's spouse;

subject to the earnings limit of €115,000.

The items to be deducted from relevant earnings in computing an individual's net relevant earnings therefore fall under two main headings – the deductions in respect of 'payments' (the paragraph (a) deductions) and those for capital allowances and losses (the paragraph (b) deductions). For both paragraph (a) and paragraph (b) deductions, the amount to be brought into account for each item is the amount actually deducted in arriving at the individual's total income (but not exceeding the amount treated under TCA 1997, s 787(4) as made out of relevant earnings – see below). If the amount of any item deductible in computing total income is restricted, then there is a similar restriction to the amount taken into account for the deduction from relevant earnings.

Deductions in respect of payments

The payments to be deducted under paragraph (a) refer to payments made by the individual which are actually deducted in the calculation of his total income, but these payments are only deducted from relevant earnings to the extent that their total exceeds the individual's other income (see also below). Retirement annuity premiums are not deducted from relevant earnings in arriving at net relevant earnings. Further, payments which give rise to a deduction *from* total income in arriving at taxable income, eg business expansion scheme subscriptions (see **18.106**), are not deducted in computing net relevant earnings.

The payments which are deducted, to the extent that they are treated as made out of relevant earnings, include:

(a) interest paid on a loan to purchase an interest in a partnership, deductible under TCA 1997, s 253 (see **3.208**);

(b) interest on a loan to purchase shares in a company in which the individual has a material interest (see **3.206**);

(c) annuities and other annual payments to the extent deductible as charges on income (see **3.103**, **15.404–15.405**);

(d) qualifying payments in respect of certain historic and other significant buildings for which a deduction is given under TCA 1997, s 482 (see **18.301**);

(e) maintenance payments made by a party to a marriage following a dissolution, annulment or separation within TCA 1997, s 1025 (see **3.507**); and

(f) payments made as gifts for public purposes within TCA 1997, s 483 (see **18.302**).

TCA 1997, s 787(4) requires the payments made by the individual to be treated as deductions first from income *other than* relevant earnings. This means that an individual who has sufficient other income (before deducting any of the payments) to cover all the payments in question does not have their relevant income reduced by any paragraph (a) deductions. If he has some other income, only the excess of the payments made over that income are deducted in arriving at their net relevant earnings.

In the case of a married couple or civil partnership, only payments made by the individual (whether the wife or the husband or either civil partner) whose net relevant earnings are being determined are deducted from her or his relevant earnings (to the extent that such payments exceed her or his other income). The individual is not allowed set off any excess of her or his payments made over her or his other income against her or his spouse's or civil partner's income; any such excess must be deducted from the individual's own relevant earnings. The fact that there is a joint assessment under TCA 1997, s 1017 does not alter this position; the words in TCA 1997, s 787(2) refer to payments made by the individual.

An interesting point arises with regard to annual payments made under covenants to elderly persons or to qualifying bodies. As indicated in **15.405**, the amount of such covenanted payments (income transfers) deductible from the payer's income for any tax year cannot exceed five per cent of his total income for that year. Total income for this purpose is *after* deducting the covenanted payments. It is therefore necessary to compute the limit to the deduction for those payments as 5/105ths of total income before that deduction (but after all other deductions in computing total income).

If the aggregate of the individual's paragraph (a) payments exceeds their other income, the amount to be included in that aggregate in respect of covenanted payments to the descendants cannot exceed 5/105ths of his total income before deducting those covenanted payments, but after his final deduction for his qualifying retirement annuity premiums. In other words, in order to determine the upper limit to the deduction for the covenanted payments to descendants, it is necessary to know the individual's net relevant earnings (since the deduction for his retirement annuity premiums is the lower of the actual premiums or the relevant per cent of net relevant earnings). However, the ascertainment of net relevant earnings cannot be finalised without knowing the final figure for the paragraph (a) payments which include the covenanted payments. A solution to this dilemma is provided by Statement of Practice IT/2/90 which states that retirement annuity relief is to be computed as the relevant per cent of net relevant earnings *after* deducting restricted annual payments.

Deductions for capital allowances, losses

The amounts to be deducted from relevant earnings under paragraph (b) include all capital allowances given in taxing the profits of the trade or profession from which the relevant earnings are derived. For an individual with relevant earnings from a non-pensionable employment, if he has any capital allowances in respect of machinery or plant (eg a motor car) used for that employment, the amount of those allowances for the relevant tax year are similarly deducted from those relevant earnings.

The deduction from relevant earnings in respect of capital allowances attributable to relevant activities may either be allowances for the same tax year or any unused capital allowances carried forward from a previous tax year. In each of these cases, the capital allowances are so deducted without any reference to any other income which the individual may have. In certain cases, an individual may claim under TCA 1997, s 392 to use capital allowances in excess of the current year's taxable profits by including them in a loss set off against total income in a s 381 claim (see **4.405**). In any such case, the capital allowances so included are treated as part of the loss to which the rules of TCA 1997, s 787(2) discussed in the following paragraphs apply.

The deductions from relevant earnings in respect of losses of a trade or profession may be for an unused loss carried forward from a previous tax year under TCA 1997, s 382 (see **4.402**), a loss (including capital allowances) carried back in a terminal loss claim under TCA 1997, s 385 (see **4.409**) or a loss deductible from income from all sources in a claim under TCA 1997, s 381 (including, if appropriate, any capital allowances added under TCA 1997, s 392) (see **4.405**).

In the case of losses carried forward or carried back respectively under TCA 1997, s 382, only losses from the trade or profession of the individual concerned are material. Any losses so carried forward or back in respect of any trade or profession of the individual's spouse or civil partner may only be set off against any relevant earnings of that spouse or civil partner. This limit to the use of losses carried forward or back arises from the rules that such losses are only deductible from future or past profits of the same trade or profession and cannot be set off against any other income.

TCA 1997, s 787(3) requires that any losses or capital allowances in respect of 'relevant activities' which could be offset wholly or partly against either relevant earnings or 'other income' must be deducted firstly from relevant earnings. In the case of losses set off against an individual's income from all sources in a claim under TCA 1997, s 381 (a 's 381' claim), this rule has to be read in conjunction with the rules of the latter section relating to the order in which such losses are to be relieved.

In computing the total income of an individual assessed as a single person, the s 381 losses (including any capital allowances added) are set off first against their earned income and then, to extent of any balance, against their unearned income.

'Earned income' for these purposes is as defined by TCA 1997, s 3(2) to include *inter alia:*

(a) emoluments from an employment or office or a pension paid in respect thereof;
(b) any income from property attached to an office or employment;
(c) any income from a trade or profession carried on as a sole trader or as an 'active' partner;
(d) any annuity payable under an approved retirement annuity policy; and
(e) any sum not included above which is chargeable under Sch E.

It follows that earned income for s 381 purposes may sometimes include income other than relevant earnings (eg a pension or a salary from a pensionable employment) and if so has to be dealt with as such in applying TCA 1997, s 787, ie the s 381 loss which is set off against the taxpayer's earned income must be set off primarily against any relevant earnings (eg income from a non-pensionable employment which he also holds) included in that amount of earned income.

In arriving at the total income of an individual assessed jointly with his spouse or civil partner under TCA 1997, s 1017, the individual's s 381 losses (and any capital allowances added) are set off against their spouse's or civil partner's income from all sources in the following order:

firstly: against the individual's earned income;

next: against their unearned income;

next: against their spouse's or civil partner's earned income; and

lastly: against their spouse's or civil partner's unearned income.

In applying TCA 1997, s 787(3) to the case of a married couple or civil partners assessed jointly where one spouse or civil partner (say, the husband) has a s 381 loss for a tax year and the other spouse (the wife) has relevant earnings from one or more sources, the order in which the husband's loss is set off to affect each spouse's net relevant earnings is as follows:

firstly: against the husband's relevant earnings (eg income from a non-pensionable employment which he also holds);

next: against the balance of his earned income;

next: against his unearned income;

next: against his wife's relevant earnings (as reduced by any capital allowances or losses from her own relevant activities);

next: against his wife's earned income other than relevant earnings; and

lastly: against his wife's unearned income.

Capital allowances and losses from other activities

No deduction from relevant earnings is made for any capital allowances (or losses) given in respect of any activity or source of income which is not a 'relevant activity'. This is the case both for capital allowances given directly in taxing the source of income (eg capital allowances on leased buildings in an urban renewal area allowed against Sch D Case V rental income – see **Division 19** of the 2009 edition of this book) and for any excess capital allowances over non-relevant earnings in respect of which the individual has the right to set it off against their income from all sources (eg capital allowances on leased industrial buildings deductible under TCA 1997, s 305: see **6.505**). However, by reducing the individual's income other than relevant earnings, these 'other' capital allowances reduce the income available to absorb the paragraph (a) payments which are set off firstly against the other income. This may result in deduction from relevant earnings for such payments, where otherwise none would have arisen. Alternatively, it may cause a higher deduction from relevant earnings for those payments than would otherwise have been necessary.

Summary: single person assessment

It may be useful to provide a summary of the steps to be taken by a single person (or a married person or civil partner assessed as a single person under TCA 1997, s 1016) to determine their net relevant earnings for any tax year. The steps are as follows:

(a) calculate relevant earnings for the year (which, as previously mentioned, are taken before any deduction for capital allowances or losses);

(b) deduct from the relevant earnings any capital allowances or losses that will reduce the individual's total income for the year in question to the extent that those allowances or losses are attributable to their relevant activities (both the allowances or losses directly deductible and those included in any s 381 claim for the year);

(c) ascertain the total of any deductions due to be made in computing the individual's total income in respect of paragraph (a) payments made by him;

(d) allocate the total of the deductions referred to in (c) so far as possible against any income other than relevant earnings which the individual may have for the year;

(e) deduct from relevant earnings any balance of the payments referred to in (c) which cannot be absorbed by the other income at step (d);

(f) the individual's net relevant earnings for the year will be the balance of relevant earnings as reduced by the deductions made at steps (b) and (e)*; and

(g) the earnings limit is €115,000 and this limits the amount of all income qualifying for relief in respect of pension contributions to occupational pension schemes, retirement annuity contracts, PRSAs and overseas pension plans.

* In the event that any amount has been carried forward under the rule of TCA 1997, s 787(3) in respect of capital allowances or losses deducted from income other than relevant earnings in any previous tax year (see below), the net relevant earnings determined at step (f) must be reduced further by that amount.

Example 16.208.1

Mr V R Triste, a widower, aged 58, makes contributions totalling €35,000 in the year ending 31 December 2015 to an approved trust scheme established for the benefit of individuals in his profession. He also receives directors' fees from a number of directorships (all non-pensionable offices). For the tax year 2015, his total income *before* retirement annuity relief is determined as follows:

Sch D Case II (share in partnership):	€	€
Adjusted profits year to 31/12/2015		108,000
Sch E:		
Directors' fee year to 31/12/2015		34,000
Sch D Case III:		
UK dividends year to 31/12/2015		15,000
Sch D Case V:		
Leased industrial buildings		64,000
Income from all sources		221,000
Deductions – against particular sources of income:		
Capital allowances (Sch D Case II)	11,000	

Capital allowances (Sch D Case V)	42,000	
TCA 1997, s 382 loss (Sch D Case II)	33,000	(86,000)
		135,000
Deductions in computing total income:		
Annual payment to elderly mother (deed of covenant)	4,000	(4,000)
Total income (before TCA 1997, s 787 relief)		131,000

The calculation of Mr Triste's net relevant earnings for 2015 requires the deductions (€86,000 + €4,000 = €90,000) to be allocated between his relevant earnings and his other income for the year in accordance with the rules of TCA 1997, s 787(4). The computation is as follows:

	Relevant earnings	*Other income*
	€	€
Relevant earnings:		
Sch D Case II	108,000	
Sch E (non-pensionable)	34,000	
Other income:		
Sch D Case III		15,000
Sch D Case V	-	64,000
	142,000	79,000
Deductions:		
Capital allowances (Sch D Case II)[1]	(11,000)	
Capital allowances (Sch D Case V)		(42,000)
TCA 1997, s 382 loss (Sch D Case II)[1]	(33,000)	
Payment – deed of covenant[2]	-	(4,000)
Net relevant earnings/Other income after deductions 2015	98,000	33,000

Notes:

1. The capital allowances (Sch D Case II only) and the TCA 1997, s 382 loss claim arise from a relevant activity and must, therefore, be deducted from relevant earnings.
2. The deduction for payments totalling €4,000 is applied to reduce the other income.
3. Mr Triste's retirement annuity relief under TCA 1997, s 787 for 2015 is, therefore, limited to €34,300 (ie 35 per cent of net relevant earnings €98,000) so that his final total income for the year is calculated as:

	€
Total income (before TCA 1997, s 787 relief)	98,000
Less:	
TCA 1997, s 787 deduction	34,300
Total income (final)	63,700

Note: The deduction for the annual payment was not restricted as the amount paid (€4,000) was less that the limit calculated as follows:

€135,000 x 5/105 = €6,428.

As noted above, this limit is not recalculated even though total income has been reduced by the retirement annuity premium: SP 11/2/90.

4. His trust scheme contribution carried forward to 2016 is €700 (ie €35,000 paid less €34,300 allowed in 2015).

Summary: married person's or civil partner's joint assessment

In principle, in the case of a joint assessment under TCA 1997, s 1017 where both spouses or civil partners have sources of net relevant earnings, the steps to be taken in arriving at the net relevant earnings of either or both husband and wife or either or both civil partners are the same as those in a single person assessment, but a few additional points have to be taken into account. In the case where only one spouse or civil partner has a source or sources of relevant earnings, the steps in arriving at their net relevant earnings are exactly the same as for the single person and no further comment is necessary.

In the case of a joint assessment where both spouses or civil partners have sources of relevant earnings, the steps outlined for a single person are followed separately for each spouse or civil partner, but with certain modifications as follows:

(a) calculate relevant earnings for the year (ie as for a single person);

(b) deduct from the relevant earnings any capital allowances or losses that will reduce the individual's total income for the year in question to the extent that they relate to their relevant activities (ie as for a single person); however, it is necessary to deduct also from the relevant earnings of each spouse or civil partner the amount (if any) by which the other spouse's or civil partner's capital allowances and/or losses from their relevant activities exceed that other spouse's or civil partner's income from all sources which is available to absorb such allowances or losses;

(c) ascertain the total of any deductible 'paragraph 'a' payments' made by the individual (ie as for a single person);

(d) allocate the payments in (c) so far as possible against income other than relevant earnings (ie as for a single person);

(e) deduct from relevant earnings any balance of the payments in (c) which cannot be absorbed by other income in step (d) (ie as for a single person);

(f) each spouse's or civil partner's net relevant earnings for the year will be the balance of their own relevant earnings as reduced by the deductions made at steps (b) and (e);* and

(g) the earnings limit for each spouse or civil partner is €115,000. This limit applies to the aggregate of all income qualifying for relief in respect of pension contributions to occupational pension schemes, retirement annuity contracts, PRSAs and overseas pension plans.

* In the event that any amount has been carried forward under the rule of TCA 1997, s 787(3) in respect of either individual's capital allowances or losses deducted in any previous tax year from income other than relevant earnings** (see below), the net relevant earnings of that individual as determined at step (f) must be reduced further by that amount.

** The deduction in the previous year for the capital allowances or losses may have been one made from the income other than relevant earnings either of the individual affected by the carry forward or of their spouse or civil partner.

Example 16.208.2

Mr and Mrs Smith, a married couple assessed jointly to income tax under TCA 1997, s 1017, and both aged 45, pay qualifying TCA 1997, s 784 premiums in the year ending 31 December 2015 – he pays €5,000 and she pays €1,500. His relevant earnings come from a non-pensionable employment and hers from a trade as a florist.

Mrs Smith incurs a tax loss of €10,455 in the year ending 31 December 2015. Relief for this loss is claimed under TCA 1997, s 381 against Mr and Mrs Smith's income from all sources for 2015.

Mr and Mrs Smith's respective total incomes (before claiming relief under TCA 1997, s 787) for 2015 are as follows:

	Mr Smith	*Mrs Smith*
	€	€
Sch D Case I (profit)		Nil
Sch E (non-pensionable)	24,000	
Sch D Case III	3,825	5,460
Income from all sources	27,825	5,460
Deductions in computing total income:		
TCA 1997, s 381 loss (€10,455) set off:		
Against Mrs Smith's earned income		Nil
Against Mrs Smith's unearned income		(5,460)
Against Mr Smith's earned income	(4,995)	
Separate total incomes	22,830	Nil
Joint total income under TCA 1997, s 1017 (before TCA 1997, s 787 relief)		22,830

The respective computations of net relevant earnings for Mr Smith and Mrs Smith are as follows:

	Mr Smith		*Mrs Smith*	
	relevant income	*other income*	*relevant income*	*other income*
	€	€	€	€
Relevant earnings:				
Sch D Case I			Nil	
Sch E	24,000			
Other income:				
Sch D Case III	-	3,825	-	5,460
	24,000	3,825	Nil	5,460
Deductions:				
TCA 1997, s 381 loss	(4,995)[1]			(5,460)[2]
Other income after deductions	-	3,825	-	Nil
Net relevant earnings 2015	19,005		Nil	

Mr and Mrs Smith's separate TCA 1997, s 787 deductions, etc for 2015 are now finally determined as follows:

	Mr Smith	Mrs Smith
	€	€
Qualifying premiums paid in year:	5,000	1,500
25% of net relevant earnings:		
Mr Smith 25% x €19,005	4,751	
Mrs Smith 25% x €Nil		Nil
Amount of TCA 1997, s 787 deduction:		
Mr Smith lower of €5,000 and €4,751.	4,751	
Mrs Smith lower of €1,500 and €Nil.		Nil
Amount to carry forward to 2016 under TCA 1997, s 787(10):		
Mr Smith	249	
Mrs Smith		1,500

Notes:

1. Since all of the €4,995 of Mrs Smith's loss set off against Mr Smith's income was covered by his relevant earnings, there is no amount to be carried forward in his case.
2. Mrs Smith's TCA 1997, s 381 loss in the amount of €5,460 has been deducted from her other income (and not from relevant earnings). The rule in TCA 1997, s 787(3) does not apply to reduce her net relevant earnings in future years as she was not entitled to claim relief under TCA 1997, s 787 in 2015.

Carry forward re certain capital allowances, losses

TCA 1997, s 787(3) provides a special rule which applies if all the following circumstances exist for any tax year:

(a) an individual claims and is allowed relief for that year under the section in respect of qualifying retirement annuity premiums;

(b) a deduction in respect of capital allowances or losses from any relevant activity of the individual (ie a paragraph (b) deduction) falls to be made in computing either the total income of the individual or the total income of the individual's wife or husband or civil partner and

(c) the said deduction (the 'paragraph (b) deduction') or any part of it falls to be made from income other than relevant earnings.

In any case where all three conditions for the application of the subsection are met, TCA 1997, s 787(3) requires the carry forward to the next tax year of a sum equal to the amount of the paragraph (b) deduction which was deducted from the income other than relevant earnings. The amount so carried forward is then deducted from the individual's net relevant earnings for the next year so as to reduce those earnings and, therefore, to lower the deduction for a retirement annuity premium in the next year.

Further, once an amount is carried forward in respect of a particular individual's loss or capital allowances, and if it exceeds that individual's net relevant earnings for the next year to which it is carried forward, then the excess must be carried forward again to the year after that. The excess carried forward is applied to reduce his net relevant earnings of the later year, and so on until completely used up.

The carry forward rule of TCA 1997, s 787(3) is only capable of applying to losses or capital allowances of a relevant activity which are set off in a claim under TCA 1997, s 381 against income from all sources (and only then if conditions (a) and (c) are also met). The carry forward rule cannot apply to losses and/or capital allowances carried forward or carried back under the rules of TCA 1997, ss 382 and 385 for which relief is only given by deduction from the income of the same trade or profession (and not from any other income). Further, capital allowances (or losses) related to sources of income other than relevant activities do not give rise to any carry forward under TCA 1997, s 787(3) although deducted from income other than relevant earnings.

It is to be noted that this special rule, if it should apply in the case of a married couple or civil partners assessed jointly, refers to the loss or capital allowances of the spouse or civil partner who claims the retirement annuity relief ('the claimant'). However, the rule may come into play either where losses or capital allowances deducted from income other than relevant earnings are a deduction in computing the total income of the claimant or where they are deducted in determining the total income of the claimant's spouse or civil partner. If both spouses or civil partners have relevant earnings and each obtains retirement annuity relief for the year under review, the question as to whether there are any losses or capital allowances deducted from other income has to be considered separately for each spouse or civil partner treating each in turn as the claimant.

In fact, it appears that the circumstances in which a carry forward under the rule of TCA 1997, s 787(3) may arise are very restricted. In the more usual case where an individual has a deduction under TCA 1997, s 381 in computing total income for losses and/or capital allowances in respect of his relevant activities which are set off against his other income, it will only be after his relevant earnings have been reduced to nil. In such a case, he will not be allowed any retirement annuity relief for the year (ie condition (a) will not be met) since net relevant earnings will be nil thereby restricting his deduction under TCA 1997, s 787 to nil. Therefore, the rule of TCA 1997, s 787(3) does not apply in this case.

It is open to question whether there are any circumstances at all in which a s 381 loss (or capital allowances included in such a claim) will fall to be set off against income other than relevant earnings and in which the individual will have any relevant earnings left (after deducting the loss, etc) to enable him to have a valid claim for a deduction under TCA 1997, s 787. Is it possible that the carry forward rule of TCA 1997, s 787(3) was included to cover a situation which could arise at the time when the retirement annuity relief was first introduced, but which may not now arise with the current rules regarding the order for setting off losses or capital allowances in a s 381 claim.

16.209 Claim for relief

TCA 1997, s 787(15) requires a claim for retirement annuity relief to be made to the inspector of taxes and the claim must be allowed by the inspector before any relief can be given under TCA 1997, s 787. The normal method of claim is to complete the relevant section in the individual's income tax return giving details of the retirement annuity contracts or trust scheme premiums that the individual and their spouse or civil partner paid in the relevant tax year. The Revenue Commissioners are empowered to make regulations under TCA 1997, s 986(1)(g) to extend the 'net pay arrangement' to cases where an employer deducts contributions to a Retirement Annuity Contract (RAC) from an employee's salary.

When a life assurance company makes a qualifying contract with an individual, whether under TCA 1997, s 784 or 785, it is standard practice for the company to issue the individual with a form RAC setting out the main particulars of the contract. These particulars contain all the necessary information to enable the individual to claim the retirement annuity relief under TCA 1997, s 787.

Only one form RAC is issued for each separate TCA 1997, s 784 or TCA 1997, s 785 contract, whether the premium is annual or single. In the case of annual premiums, the one form RAC is sufficient to establish the individual's entitlement to the relief for the annual premiums payable throughout the term of the contract. It is, however, necessary for the individual to continue to claim the relief in his income tax return for each subsequent year for every qualifying premium or approved trust scheme contribution. Should he cease to pay the premium he naturally ceases to be entitled to the relief.

The claim for retirement annuity relief should be included on the individual's income tax return for the year of assessment to which the claim relates. The exceptional case where an individual elects under TCA 1997, s 787(7) to claim relief for a particular tax year in respect of a premium paid after the end of that year has been dealt with separately in **16.206**.

An individual's claim for TCA 1997, s 787 relief may be allowed by the inspector based on the assessments and other data in relation to the individual's income existing at a particular time, but the assessments may be adjusted or additional assessments made to reflect changes in the relevant facts. For example, an individual may have obtained relief under TCA 1997, s 787(6) for qualifying premiums paid in the tax year 2015 based on the relevant earnings from his trade in the 12 months ended 31 October 2015. If he ceases to trade on (say) 30 November 2015, the relevant earnings from the trade for 2015 must be revised in line with the cessation rules.

The result of any change in the individual's income for this or any other reason may well alter the amounts of his relevant earnings and/or net relevant earnings on which the TCA 1997, s 787 relief was previously based. In any such case, TCA 1997, s 787(13) requires any necessary consequential adjustments to be made in the amount of the TCA 1997, s 787 relief given, thereby increasing or decreasing (whichever is the case) the individual's income tax payable for the year or years affected.

TCA 1997, s 787(14) provides that, once relief is claimed and allowed for any tax year in respect of any payment, relief must not be given again in respect of that payment under any other provision of the Income Tax Acts. Further, no other relief may be given in respect of any other premium or consideration for an annuity under the same contract.

16.210 Taxation of retirement plan benefits

Any annuity payable under an approved retirement annuity contract or under an approved contract to provide an annuity for a spouse, civil partner or a dependant, or under an approved trust scheme, is taxable under Sch E on the recipient as income of the tax year in which it is paid (TCA 1997, s 784(7)).

Any annuity payable to an individual under an approved annuity contract or trust scheme is treated as earned income of the recipient to the extent to which the annuity is payable in return for any amount on which retirement annuity relief was given under TCA 1997, s 787 (TCA 1997, s 3). This applies whether the recipient is the individual who paid the qualifying premiums, or is the widow, civil partner or dependant of that individual. In fact, the distinction between earned and unearned income has now little significance so that the treatment of a retirement annuity as earned income should not affect the tax position of the recipient. An individual who, at the time his annuity is due to commence, exercises the right now provided by most retirement annuity contracts and trust schemes to commute up to a maximum of 25 per cent of the annuity, receives the resulting lump sum free of income tax. This part commutation option is only available to the individual who paid the premiums in respect of his relevant earnings under a TCA 1997, s 784 annuity contract. There is no corresponding commutation option for a spouse's, civil partner's or a dependant's annuity under a TCA 1997, s 785 contract.

In the event that the intended annuitant dies before any annuity due to s 784 premiums becomes payable, the payment made under the annuity contract or trust scheme to his personal representatives is received by them free of income tax and capital gains tax. This applies whether the payment made is a return of premiums or other contributions (including reasonable interest or bonuses out of the assurer's profits) or is, as is usual with unit linked contracts, a capital sum determined by the value at the date of the relevant death of the units in the life assurance company's investments purchased by the individual's premiums under the contract with which those investments are linked.

16.3 Personal Retirement Savings Accounts (PRSAs)

16.301 Overview

TCA 1997, Pt 30, Ch 2A deals with the tax relief for premiums or other forms of consideration paid by an individual to secure a PRSA. The PRSA regime commenced on 7 November 2002, when the Pensions (Amendment) Act 2002, s 4 was implemented by Ministerial Order SI 502/2002. PRSAs are portable investment vehicles designed to cover the pension provision for employees, self-employed and a variety of other categories of individuals. They are designed to enable individuals to maintain their pension provision in situations where they move between periods of employment and self-employment, including also periods of unemployment. Similarly to an RAC the PRSA is a contract between the PRSA provider and the individual. PRSAs are highly regulated and are designed to provide a low cost, transparent vehicle for pension funding. The Pensions Authority (formerly the Pensions Board) and the Revenue Commissioners jointly approve PRSAs (TCA 1997, s 787K).

The PRSA legislation is primarily modelled on the legislation regarding retirement annuities but with some important differences. It should be noted that under the PRSA legislation there is no provision for trust schemes or schemes similar to s 785 schemes.

Key features of the PRSA regime are as follows:

(a) Contributions can be offset against 'relevant earnings' of the year in which the contributions are paid within the same percentage limits of 'net relevant earnings' (and subject to the combined earnings limit: see below) as apply in the case of occupational pension schemes and retirement annuity contracts (TCA 1997, s 787C(1), (2)). The definitions of 'relevant earnings' and 'net relevant earnings' are identical to those applicable to retirement annuity contracts with the exception the relevant earnings *include* remuneration from an office or employment of profit held by the individual irrespective of whether it is a pensionable office or employment (TCA 1997, s 787B).

(b) An employee in pensionable employment may only pay into a PRSA by way of Additional Voluntary Contribution (AVC) PRSAs in relation to the earnings from that employment (see **16.103** for the definition of AVCs) (TCA 1997, s 787E(3)). With effect from 1 January 2003, an employee who is a member of an approved occupational pension scheme or statutory pension scheme for risk benefits within TCA 1997, s 772(3)(b), (c) (ie death in service, pension to surviving spouse, civil partner, children or dependants) only, is not regarded as being in pensionable employment for these purposes (TCA 1997, s 787E(3)).

(c) As in the case of retirement annuity contracts and occupational schemes, contributions paid in any year in excess of the maximum tax deductible contribution may be carried forward and claimed in future years subject to the annual limit for those years (TCA 1997, s 787C(4), (5)). Similarly, contributions paid while unemployed may be carried forward and claimed against future earnings on return to paid employment subject to the annual limits.

(d) The tax relief is non-transferable between spouses or civil partners in line with existing rules for retirement annuity contract and occupational pension scheme contributions (TCA 1997, s 787B(7)).

(e) As in the case of retirement annuity contracts and occupational schemes, contributions paid after the end of the tax year and before the return filing date for that year may be claimed for that tax year (TCA 1997, s 787C(3)).

(f) An employer is obliged to provide access to a 'Standard' PRSA where some or all of its employees are not entitled to join the existing pension plan after more than six months' service and/or where they do not have access to make AVCs. A standard PRSA is differentiated only by reference to the requirements of the pension legislation that there is a requirement that standard PRSAs should be operated through the employer's payroll on a 'net pay' basis.

(g) Tax relief will be granted in respect of annual contributions of up to €1,525 irrespective of the level of net relevant earnings except in the case of an employee who is a member of an occupational pension scheme or of a statutory pension scheme (TCA 1997, s 787E(4)).

(h) The additional retirement options applicable to retirement annuity contracts and certain employees in pensionable employments (see **16.4**) apply similarly to PRSAs (TCA 1997, s 787H, applying TCA 1997, ss 784A–784D). Further, where the PRSA holder dies prior to retirement the assets in the PRSA fund will pass free of income tax to his estate (TCA 1997, s 787G(3)(c)). Where the contributor dies after benefits have commenced, the taxation rules for the PRSA fund will be similar to the taxation rules for an ARF on death (TCA 1997, s 787G(6)).

FA 2016, s 14(1)(b) inserted a new TCA 1997, s 787G(4B) such that for the purposes of TCA 1997, s 787G(6), the administrator of a PRSA, in respect of which the PRSA contributor has attained the age of 75 years where, up to and including the date on which the contributor attained that age, no assets of the PRSA have been made available to, or paid to, the PRSA contributor or to any other person, other than a transfer of part of the assets to another PRSA to which the contributor to the first mentioned PRSA is the contributor, shall be treated as making the assets of the PRSA available to the PRSA contributor on the date the contributor attains the age of 75 years or, where the contributor attained the age of 75 years prior to the date of passing of the Finance Act 2016 (25 December 2016), on the date of passing of that Act (25 December 2016).

In terms of portability, the following key aspects of the PRSA regime should be noted:

(a) Refunds of contributions (with interest where applicable) paid out from occupational schemes may be transferred to a PRSA without a tax charge; otherwise such refunds are charged to tax at the standard rate: see **16.109**. The transfer to the PRSA will not attract any further relief (TCA 1997, s 787F).

(b) Transfers from a retirement annuity contract to a PRSA will be allowed; again, the transfer to the PRSA will not attract any further relief (TCA 1997, s 787F).

(c) Transfers from an occupational pension scheme or a statutory scheme to a PRSA will be allowed where the member has been in the scheme for 15 years or less and either:

    (i) the scheme is being wound up, or

(ii) the member is changing employment,

the value of AVC contributions to an occupational pension scheme may be transferred to a PRSA without regard to the foregoing restrictions; again, the transfer to the PRSA will not attract any further relief.

(d) Transfers between PRSAs must be permitted (TCA 1997, s 787L).

16.302 PRSAs in relation to employments

As explained in **16.301**, an employer must provide access to a 'Standard PRSA' in certain circumstances. In such cases, the employer, if so requested by the employee, is required to operate the 'net pay' system, ie to make payroll deductions in respect of the employee's PRSA contributions. The 'net pay' system means that all PRSI contributions (both employer's and employee's) and health contributions are based on earnings net of the employee's contributions. Similar treatment applies in the case of AVC PRSAs. The net pay arrangement may of course only be applied to contributions within the allowable limits. AVC PRSAs, taken together with contributions to the main scheme, may not provide benefits in excess of those which are permissible under TCA 1997, s 772 (see **16.106/16.107**) (TCA 1997, s 787E(3)(d)).

Unlike the position for an AVC PRSA, an employer may itself make contributions to a standard PRSA on behalf of an employee. In such a case, the payment by the employer will constitute a taxable benefit in kind (TCA 1997, s 118(5)) (see **10.203**). However, the employee will be entitled to relief as if he made a corresponding contribution (TCA 1997, s 787E(2)). The employer will apply the 'net pay' arrangement to the amount of the benefit net of the amount of the employee's notional contribution which is eligible for relief (ie by reference to the appropriate limits). Even where the employer makes all the contributions to the PRSA, the employee will still be regarded as the contributor for the purposes of the PRSA regime (TCA 1997, s 787A(1)).

The advantage of an employer contribution to an occupational pension scheme over an employer contribution to a PRSA is that no employer PRSI applies to the former.

Any sum paid by an employer by way of contribution under a PRSA contract of an employee will be allowed as an expense in the year in which it was paid in arriving at the employer's taxable income from his trade or profession within Sch D Case I or II. A deduction is only allowed to the extent that the contributions relate to employees in the trade or profession in respect of which the employer is assessable to income tax or corporation tax (TCA 1997, s 787J(3)).

Unlike employer contributions to occupational pension plans, no distinction is made between ordinarily annual contributions and special contributions.

For PRSA purposes, an employment includes any contract whereby an individual agrees with an employment agency to work for a third party (whether or not the third party is a party to the agreement); in that case the person who is liable to pay the wages of the individual will be deemed to be the employer (TCA 1997, s 787A(1)).

Since 2005 an employer is obliged to give details on Form P35 of the number of employees in respect of whom PRSA contributions were deducted from their emoluments during the year, the number of employees in respect of whom a PRSA employer contribution was paid in that year, the total amount of contributions deducted from the employee's emoluments and the total amount of employer contributions paid in the year (TCA 1997, s 897A).

16.303 Extent of relief

The maximum annual relief for contributions to PRSAs is based on a percentage of an individual's net relevant earnings that varies depending on the individual's age during the year of assessment. The contribution rates are as follows (in line with those applicable to occupational pension schemes and retirement annuity contracts):

Age	*% Contribution*
Under 30	15%
30–39	20%
40–49	25%
50–54	30%
55–59	35%
60 or over	40%

The contribution limit in excess of 30 per cent for individuals aged 55 or over applies in respect of contributions made on or after 1 January 2006. An earnings limit of €115,000 applies since 2011 to all remuneration and net relevant earnings in respect of which relief can be claimed for pension contributions to occupational pension schemes, retirement annuity contracts, PRSAs and overseas pension plans (TCA 1997, s 790A).

In relation to certain specified occupations (mainly of a sporting nature) (TCA 1997, Sch 23A) the contribution rate of 30 per cent applies for all ages up until age 55. From age 55 onwards the higher contribution limits would apply.

Example 16.303.1

Mr Green aged 43 has the following sources of income in 2015:

	€
Director fees (non pensionable)	34,000
Sch D case I income	36,000

He is currently paying an annual premium to a retirement annuity contract of €10,000, Mr Green is entitled to make a contribution to a PRSA contract as follows:

Relevant Earnings

	€
Director fees	34,000
Sch D case I	36,000
Total	70,000
Deductions	Nil
Net Relevant Earnings	70,000
Allowable contribution @ 25%	17,500
Less contribution to RAC	10,000
Net allowable contribution	7,500

Example 16.303.2

George Riddle is aged 53. He has the following income in the year 2015:

	€
Pensionable employment (Sch E)	100,000
Trading profits (Sch D Case 1)	200,000
Total	300,000

He made the following pension contributions in 2015:

	€
Occupational Pension Scheme	30,000
PRSA contract	7,500

The maximum allowable contributions for 2015 are €115,000 x 30% = €34,500. The total contributions paid are in excess of this amount. The contributions in the amount of €3,000 in excess of the limit will not be deductible in 2015 and must be carried forward.

16.304 Miscellaneous matters

Conditions for approval of PRSA products

The conditions for approval of a PRSA contract are similar to those applicable to retirement annuity contracts as outlined in **16.204** (TCA 1997, s 787K). The main exception is that the Revenue Commissioners have discretion to approve a contract where in the case of an individual who is an employee, the payment to the individual is of an annuity or other sum, or the making available of the assets of the PRSA to an individual commencing on retirement at age 50 or over. The individual must have retired in order to access the PRSA.

This presumably is to cater for AVC PRSAs so the benefits can be taken at the same time as the benefits under an approved or statutory scheme under the early retirement provisions. The position will presumably be clarified by the Revenue Commissioners.

FA 2016, s 14(1)(c) inserted a new TCA 1997, s 787K(2D). It notes that an approved PRSA shall not cease to be an approved product where, notwithstanding anything contained in the terms of the product as approved—

(a) the PRSA administrator—

(i) on or before 31 March 2017—

(I) commences payment of an annuity to the PRSA contributor,

(II) pays a lump sum to the PRSA contributor,

(III) makes assets of the PRSA available to the PRSA contributor, or

(IV) transfers assets of the PRSA to an approved retirement fund,

or

(ii) in priority to any payment, making of assets available or transfer referred to in subparagraph (i), makes available from the PRSA assets, to such extent as may be necessary, an amount for the purposes of discharging a tax liability in relation to the PRSA contributor under the provisions of TCA 1997, Pt 30, Ch 2C in respect of the PRSA,

(b) insofar as subparagraph (i) of paragraph (a) is concerned, the PRSA is deemed to be a vested PRSA in accordance with TCA 1997, s 790D(1A), and

(c) insofar as subparagraph (ii) of paragraph (a) is concerned, the PRSA is a vested PRSA within the meaning of paragraph (c) of the definition of 'vested PRSA' in TCA 1997, s 790D(1).

Revenue guidance on the provision notes as follows that:

> An approved PRSA product which becomes a 'vested PRSA' (within the meaning of section 790D(1)) when the contributor attains the age of 75 years without having drawn down benefits, shall not cease to be an approved product where a PRSA administrator–
>
> - in the case of a contributor who was 75 years of age prior to 25 December 2016 (i.e. the date on which Finance Act 2016 was passed)–
>   - O pays an annuity or a retirement lump sum to the contributor, or
>   - O transfers the PRSA assets to the contributor or to an ARF
>
>   on or before 31 March 2017, or
> - regardless of whether the PRSA becomes vested on the date the contributor attains the age of 75 years or on 25 December 2016, uses the PRSA assets to discharge any liability to chargeable excess tax under Chapter 2C of Part 30 arising as a result of the deemed vesting of the PRSA.

The wording used to in paras (b) and (c) of TCA 1997, s 787K(2D) is curious in that for example, para (c) notes 'insofar as subparagraph (ii) ... is concerned, the PRSA is a vested PRSA'. Revenue guidance on the section would seem to indicate that this means that the paragraph will apply where the PRSA is a vested PRSA but another (albeit strained) reading could be that where the tests in (ii) are met then the contract 'is' a vested PRSA. Clearly that is not the intent in that Revenue would appear to view the contract to be a vested PRSA before this subsection goes on to say that that fact in addition to the above tests will not prevent the contract from being a Revenue approved one.

A PRSA product will neither cease to be an approved product nor will the Revenue Commissioners be prevented from approving a product notwithstanding that the product permits the PRSA administrator to make available from the PRSA assets an amount for the purpose of discharging the tax liability under Ch 2C in connection with a relevant payment to the PRSA contributor. With effect from 8 February 2012, the provision of the encashment option in a PRSA product (as provided for in TCA 1997, s 787TA) (see **16.504**) will not affect existing Revenue approval of the contract nor prevent Revenue from approving such a contract (TCA 1997, s 787K(2B)).

Tax exemption of PRSA plan funds

A similar regime applies to that applicable in the case of retirement annuity contracts and occupational pension plans (TCA 1997, s 787I).

Benefits from PRSA contracts

As noted at **16.301**, the retirement options available to retirement annuity contracts apply similarly to PRSA contract.

It is important to note that for a PRSA to which additional voluntary PRSA contributions were made, the tax-free cash entitlement is based on the 80ths scale or uplifted scale of final salary and not 25 per cent of the fund (TCA 1997, s 787G(3)(a)).

This would appear to suggest that if at any stage a PRSA has received additional voluntary PRSA contributions then the 25 per cent cash entitlement is lost. In the author's view this would appear to be a drafting error or, if not, a potential trap for the unwary.

Taxation of payments from a PRSA

Subject to the exceptions below, the amount or value of any assets that a PRSA administrator makes available to, or pays to, a PRSA contributor or to any other person (including the releasing of funds for the purchase of an annuity) are liable to tax under Sch E and the provisions of Pt 42 Ch 8 apply accordingly (TCA 1997, s 787G(1)).

Where the PRSA administrator has not received a certificate of tax credits and standard rate cut-off point or tax deduction card for the relevant year the administrator is obliged to deduct tax at the higher rate of tax.

The exceptions are:

(i) the tax-free lump sum of 25 per cent of the value of the PRSA or in the case of a PRSA where additional voluntary PRSA contributions were made then the lump sum calculated on the 80ths scale or uplifted scale;

(ii) where the assets are transferred to an ARF or AMRF;

(iii) on death where the assets are passed to the personal representatives of the PRSA contributor;

(iv) where the assets are transferred to an approved scheme or statutory scheme provided the lump sum at (i) above has not been taken; and

(v) an amount made available from a vested PRSA (within the meaning of TCA 1997, s 790D(1)) for the purpose of reimbursing a pension scheme administrator for tax paid by that administrator on a chargeable excess relating to the PRSA contributor (TCA 1997, s 787G(3)).

16.305 Vested PRSAs

TCA 1997, s 790D, which applies for the tax year 2012 onwards, provides for the taxation of imputed distributions from both Approved Retirement Funds (ARFs) and vested PRSAs on a composite basis where the ARF or vested PRSA holder is 60 years of age or over for the whole tax year. Where the aggregate value of the assets held in an ARF(s) and/or a vested PRSA(s) on 30 November 2015 is €2 million or less, the rate of the imputed distribution is 4 per cent of the value of the assets. This rate of imputed distribution was reduced from 5 per cent in Finance Act 2014. However, where the ARF or vested PRSA holder is age 70 years or over for the whole of the tax year, the previous rate of imputed distribution applies, ie 5 per cent. Where the aggregate value is in excess of €2 million, irrespective of whether the ARF or vested PRSA holder is over age 70 or not, the rate is 6 per cent of the entire aggregate value. TCA 1997, s 790D applies to ARFs created on or after 6 April 2000 – the date that the existing gross roll-up regime for ARFs was introduced – and to PRSAs vested on or after 7 November 2002 – the date that PRSA products were introduced. Prior to 2012, the imputed distribution regime related only to ARFs and was dealt with under TCA 1997, s 784A(1BA). Details of the legislation governing the earlier regime can be read in the 2011 edition of this book.

A 'Vested PRSA' is a PRSA from which assets of the PRSA have been made available to the PRSA owner or any other person. This was amended by FA 2016, s 14 to include the following 'a PRSA in respect of which the PRSA contributor has attained the age of 75 years where, up to and including the date on which the contributor attained that age, no assets of the PRSA have been made available to, or paid to, the PRSA contributor or to any other person, other than a transfer of part of the assets to another PRSA to which the contributor to the first mentioned PRSA is the contributor;'

The following will *not* constitute the making available of assets for these purposes:

(i) an amount transferred to an ARF/AMRF;

(ii) an amount made available to a personal representative of the PRSA holder (ie to purchase an annuity for the individual's widow, widower or civil partner);

(iii) the transfer from one PRSA to another.

The second part of the definition ensures that where assets are in a PRSA AVC, vesting is deemed to take place at the time benefits are taken from the main occupational pension scheme (ie at the point of retirement).

It should be noted that TCA 1997, s 790D(1A) states that where a PRSA contributor of a kind referred to in para (c) of the definition of 'vested PRSA' above (as inserted by FA 2016) attains the age of 75 years in the circumstances referred to in that paragraph prior to the date of passing of the Finance Act 2016 (25 December 2016), the PRSA is deemed to become a vested PRSA on the 25 December 2016.

16.4 Taxation of Additional Retirement Options Introduced in FA 1999, s 19

16.401 Introduction

In respect of retirement annuity contracts approved on or after 6 April 1999, there are a number of additional retirement options available over and above the standard entitlement to receive up to 25 per cent of the retirement fund as cash and to apply the balance in purchasing an annuity. The new rules can also apply to contracts or schemes approved prior to 6 April 1999 provided the relevant scheme rules are amended.

These additional options are also available to proprietary directors and holders of AVCs in relation to occupational pension schemes (see **16.106**), to holders of PRSAs (see **16.3**) and with effect from 6 February 2011, to all members of defined contribution schemes.

The two additional options are:

Option 1

(a) take up to 25 per cent of the value of the fund;

(b) mandatorily transfer up to €63,500 to an approved minimum retirement fund or purchase an annuity; and

(c) take the balance of fund as taxable cash.

Option 2

(a) take up to 25 per cent of the value of the fund;

(b) mandatorily transfer up to €63,500 to an approved minimum retirement fund or purchase an annuity; and

(c) transfer balance of fund to an approved retirement fund.

The taxation of Approved Retirement Funds and Approved Minimum Retirement Funds differ depending on whether the assets were accepted into the fund before or after 6 April 2000. As pre-6 April 2000 funds remain in existence the rules for pre and post 6 April 2000 funds are described separately below. With effect from 2012, the legislation provides for imputed distributions for both Approved Retirement Funds (ARFs) and vested PRSAs on a composite basis. Vested PRSAs are PRSAs where benefits have commenced, normally by way of a 'tax-free' lump sum being taken by the PRSA contributor.

16.402 Approved Minimum Retirement Fund (AMRF): pre-6 April 2000

An approved minimum retirement fund means a fund managed by a qualifying fund manager (QFM) within the meaning of TCA 1997, s 784A and which complies with the conditions of TCA 1997, s 784D.

In general, qualifying fund managers (TCA 1997, s 784A) would include a bank, building society, credit union, collective investment undertakings, life assurance companies, stockbrokers and other persons approved by the Minister for Finance. There are onerous requirements for the qualifying fund manager in relation to records, annual statements and returns to the Revenue.

An AMRF is designed to be a safety net for individuals in retirement. There is a requirement for an individual after taking the tax free cash to put a minimum amount of €63,500 in this fund, although this requirement is not needed where at the time of drawing benefits:

(a) the individual is age 75 or over;

(b) the individual has specified income over €12,700;

(c) the individual instead uses €63,500 to purchase an annuity; or

(d) the individual had previously transferred €63,500 to an AMRF.

Specified income is defined as a pension or annuity which is payable for the life of the individual, including a pension payable under the Social Welfare (Miscellaneous Provisions) Act 1963 and any pension to which the provisions of TCA 1997, s 200 apply.

Both husband and wife's or civil partners' specified income is treated separately and each must satisfy the above test separately.

Under an AMRF the individual remains the beneficial owner of the assets. The AMRF automatically becomes an ARF on the individual reaching age 75 or on his earlier death (TCA 1997, s 784C(6)).

Any realised income and gains arising in the AMRF are taxable on the individual subject to the normal provisions of the Income Tax Acts and the Capital Gains Tax Acts (TCA 1997, s 784C(7)). Any withdrawal from the income and gains account does not give rise to a further tax liability.

On TCA 1997, s 784A(4), a distribution made following the death of the individual beneficially entitled to the assets in an ARF is treated as the income of that individual for the year of death and PAYE applies to the payment unless it is made to an ARF in the name of the deceased's spouse or civil partner or it is made to or for the sole benefit of a child of the deceased, or any child of the civil partner of the deceased. (TCA 1997, s 784A(4)(a), (b)). With effect from 1 January 2011 however, a distribution made to a child aged 21 or over from the ARF of the deceased, or made from an ARF in the name of a surviving spouse or surviving civil partner funded by the ARF of the deceased spouse or civil partner (other than such a distribution to a child aged under 21 years of the surviving spouse or surviving civil partner), is subject to an income tax charge under Case IV of Sch D at a rate of 30 per cent. The amount so charged will not form part of the individual's total income, and is computed without regard to any deductions allowed in computing taxable income; similarly, no reliefs, deductions or tax credits may be set against the amount so charged or against the tax payable on that amount, and the income tax exemption limits and marginal relief will not apply as regards the income tax so charged (TCA 1997, s 784A(4)(c)). The reporting and collection provisions that apply to excess lump sums pursuant to TCA 1997, s 790AA will also apply, with necessary modifications to such distributions (TCA 1997, s 784A(4)(d)).

Example 16.402.1

Mr Jones aged 70 draws on his retirement fund; the value of the retirement fund is €50,000. He elects to receive his maximum tax free cash of 25 per cent of the fund. He is in receipt of a Social Welfare pension of €5,000 pa and his wife is in receipt of an occupational pension of €10,000 pa.

After taking his maximum tax free cash of €12,500 the balance of the fund is €37,500. As his specified income is less than €12,700 and he is aged under 75 he must put the balance of the fund of €37,500 into an AMRF.

If Mr Jones invests his €37,500 through a QFM in a government stock, assuming six per cent stock at par, he will be liable to income tax on the interest of €2,250 at his marginal tax rate irrespective of whether he draws down the income.

If Mr Jones were to have any further retirement fund the maximum additional amount that needs to be transferred to an AMRF is €26,000 (€63,500 less amounts previously transferred to the AMRF).

Certain events could cause a pre-6 April 2000 AMRF to fall into the post-5 April 2000 Rules, namely:

(a) where the AMRF is switched to a new qualifying fund manager; and
(b) on death where the AMRF is passed (as an ARF) to the individual's spouse.

As outlined in options 1 and 2, an individual can take the balance of his pension fund as taxable cash. The steps would be:

(a) take the 25 per cent of the fund as tax free cash;
(b) meet the requirements in relation to an AMRF; and
(c) take the balance of funds as taxable cash.

Where the individual withdraws his balance of the fund, he is subject to marginal rate tax on the withdrawal. The original fund transferred to an AMRF can be withdrawn after age 75.

Example 16.402.2

Assume Mr Jones in the previous example draws on another retirement fund which is valued at €200,000. His specified income position remains unchanged, so that he must still meet the AMRF test. The following steps apply:

		€
(1) Tax free cash 25% x €200,000	=	50,000
(2) To AMRF (top up to €63,500)	=	26,000
(3) Balance – taxable	=	124,000

Thus, Mr Jones' income will include €124,000 from the full withdrawal of his pension. This amount is taxable under Sch D Case IV (or Sch E in the case of proprietary directors).

At age 75 Mr Jones could if so wished withdraw his €63,500 from his AMRF, again subject to marginal rate tax.

16.403 Approved Retirement Fund (ARF); pre-6 April 2000

An 'approved retirement fund' means a fund which is managed by a qualifying fund manager and which complies with the conditions of TCA 1997, s 784B.

An approved retirement fund operates in a similar fashion to an AMRF except that there is no restriction on withdrawals from the fund. Again, the individual is the beneficial owner of the assets and is subject to the normal income and capital gains tax provisions on all realised income and gains irrespective of whether the income or gains are withdrawn.

There are two elements:

(a) residue account; and
(b) realised income and gains account.

Any withdrawals are deemed first to come from the income and gains account.

The residue is the original amount transferred to the ARF, or the amount reduced by reference to previous withdrawals from the residue. Any withdrawal from the residue is liable to marginal rate tax and taxable under Sch D Case IV (or Sch E for proprietary directors).

Any realised income and gains are subject to normal income and capital gains tax rules irrespective of whether the income or gains are withdrawn.

Example 16.403.1

Mr Smyth (who is not a proprietary director) retires and accesses his retirement fund valued at €300,000 on 1 January 2000. He elects to take the maximum tax free cash of €75,000, leaving €225,000 available to transfer to an ARF. There is no requirement to transfer to an AMRF as his specified income exceeds €12,700. Because Mr Smyth's ARF was set up pre 6 April 2000 he is taxed under the pre 6 April 2000 regime.

Mr Smyth has the following activity in his ARF during 2015 and does not draw down any income or gains in that year:

ARF

€125,000 invested in 6% government stock (at par)

(payable half-yearly on 1 December and 1 July)

€50,000 deposit (at 3% gross)

€50,000 shares: (dividends received €800 net of withholding tax)

His income for 2015 is as follows:

	€
Sch D Case III Government interest	7,500
Sch D Case IV Deposit interest – gross DIRT	1,500
DIRT	(615)
Sch F Gross	1,000
Dividend Withholding tax	(200)

The above amount must be included in Mr Smyth's tax return for 2015 and assessed to tax accordingly.

Example 16.403.2

Assume the facts in **Example 16.403.1** but that on 31 December 2015 Mr Smyth withdraws €50,000.

To establish the tax on the withdrawal we must track his income and gains:

	Residue account	*Income and gains account*
	€	€
1 January 2015	225,000	
Income:		
Government interest		7,500
Deposit interest net of (DIRT)		885
Dividends		800
Total	225,000	9,185
Withdrawal (€50,000)	40,815	9,185

Position 31 December 2015	184,305	Nil
Thus, Mr Smyth's income for 2015 would also include:		
Sch D Case IV		40,815

Certain events could cause a pre-6 April 2000 ARF to fall into the post-5 April 2000 rules, namely:

(a) where the ARF is switched to a new qualifying fund manager; and
(b) on death where the ARF is passed to spouse.

Pre-6 April 2000 ARFs can still accept further retirement funds after that date.

Death provisions: approved funds pre-6 April 2000

Where an individual dies and assets are held in an ARF or AMRF at the time of death, the tax position will be as follows:

ARF inherited by:	*Income tax:*	*CAT:*
Surviving spouse	None	None
Children:		
under 21	None	Normal CAT rules
over 21	Marginal rate tax on residue	None

Where an ARF passes on death to a surviving spouse, the provisions on the subsequent death of the spouse are as follows:

ARF inherited by:	*Income tax:*	*CAT:*
Children:		
under 21	None	Normal CAT rules
over 21	25% of Residue	No
Others	25% of Residue	Normal CAT rules

16.404 Approved Minimum Retirement Fund (AMRF): post-6 April 2000

In the case of an AMRF set up post-6 April 2000 there are fundamental changes in how income and gains arising in the fund are taxed.

For post-6 April 2000 funds:

(a) all income and gains accumulate tax free in the fund; and
(b) all withdrawals are liable to Sch E tax, deductible under the PAYE system (TCA 1997, s 784A(3)): for the definition of 'withdrawal' see the discussion of ARFs below

The QFM is responsible for operating PAYE. The definitions of a QFM is amended to include certain investment intermediaries approved under the Investment Intermediaries Act 1995, s 10. With effect from 28 March 2003, QFMs are required to notify the Revenue Commissioners within one month of commencing to act as a QFM; managers acting in this capacity prior to 28 March 2003 were required to notify the Revenue Commissioners within three months of that date. Failure by a QFM to notify the Revenue Commissioners that they are acting in that capacity will be subject to civil penalties. In 2015 an individual must be in receipt of specified income of €12,700 and if this is not the case the amount to be contributed to an AMRF is €63,500 (TCA 1997, s 784C(4)(a)) or the alternative is to purchase an annuity for this amount.

Historically the income amount and the AMRF amount have varied. With effect from 3 February 2005, TCA 1997, s 784C(4)(a) provided that an individual must be in receipt of specified income of €12,700 pa, as opposed to having a future entitlement to that income in order to avoid the transfer to an AMRF. In the case of individuals retiring on or after 6 February 2011, this amount was increased to a sum equivalent to 1.5 times the maximum annual rate of the then-current State Contributory Pension (circa €18,000). The income requirement may be satisfied at any point before age 75 allowing conversion of the AMRF into an ARF at that point. In the case of individuals who retired prior to 6 February 2011 and who held an AMRF prior to that date or having availed of the deferred annuity purchase facility opted to make a transfer to an ARF prior to 5 March 2011, the previous income guarantee limit of €12,700 will continue to apply for a period of three years.

Further in the case of individuals retiring on or after 6 February 2011, the amount which had to be transferred to an AMRF if the income threshold was not met was increased to a sum equivalent to 10 times the maximum annual rate of the then-current State Contributory Pension (circa €119,800). Transitional relief applies to individuals who have availed of the deferred annuity purchase facility prior to 6 February 2011. However, FA 2013 effectively reversed the 2011 changes to €12,700 for specified income and if this is not met the amount to be contributed to an AMRF is €63,500. These limits will also apply to anyone who opted for the ARF option post FA 2011 and who could not avail of the lower limits under the transitional rules. This meant that any AMRF which had funds in excess of €63,500 converted the excess to an ARF on 27 March 2013.

Withdrawals from Approved Minimum Retirement Fund – post 6 April 2000

Finance Act 2014, s 19(2)(b) provides, with effect from 1 January 2015, for an annual withdrawal from an AMRF up to 4 per cent of the value of the assets of the fund at the time of the payment. While the imputed distributions from the ARF are compulsory (see **16.405** below), a withdrawal from an AMRF is at the option of the AMRF holder. The option can be availed of on one occasion only in the year and will be subject to income tax operated in the same way as a distribution from an ARF.

16.405 Approved Retirement Fund (ARF): post-6 April 2000

In the case of an ARF set up post-6 April 2000 there have been corresponding fundamental changes in how income and gains arising in the fund are treated.

For post-6 April 2000 funds:

(a) all income and gains accumulate tax free in the fund; and
(b) all withdrawals are liable to Sch E tax, with tax deductible under the PAYE system other than transfers on death to a spouse or civil partner or on death to or for the sole benefit of any child of the individual or of the individual's civil partner (TCA 1997, s 784A(3), (4)).

The QFM is responsible for operating PAYE on distributions from the fund. The definition of a QFM is amended to include certain investment intermediaries approved under the Investment Intermediaries Act 1995, s 10.

A withdrawal is deemed to take place whenever there is a distribution by a QFM in a sum equal to the amount or value of that distribution. For these purposes a distribution includes any payment or transfer of assets out of the fund or any assignment of assets out to the fund whether to the individual himself or to any other person (TCA 1997, s 784A(1)(d)).

Finance Act 2014 amended TCA 1997, s 784A to insert various anti-avoidance provisions in relation to ARFs. In particular, it states that any assignment of the fund or of assets out of the fund will be deemed to be a distribution from the ARF and thus subject to income tax. It also states that any distribution from an ARF will be deemed to have been made by the QFM, thus placing an obligation on the QFM to operate PAYE on the distribution.

With effect from 6 February 2003, a distribution is treated as taking place (at the respective amount stated) in so far as the assets of the ARF are used in connection with the transactions in (a) to (f) below. With effect from 2 February 2006 a distribution is regarded as taking place where the ARF assets are used in connection with the transaction at (g) and with effect from 23 October 2014 where ARF assets are used in connection with the transaction at (h):

(a) the making or securing of a loan to the individual or a connected person (amount equal to the value of the assets in the ARF used to make or secure the loan);

(b) the acquisition of property from the individual or a connected person (amount equal to the value of the assets in the ARF used in connection with the acquisition);

(c) the sale of ARF assets to the individual or to a connected person (amount equal to the value of the assets being sold);

(d) (i) the acquisition of holiday property or of property to be used immediately as a private residence by the individual or a connected person (amount equal to the value of the assets in the ARF used in connection with the acquisition),

(ii) following the acquisition of property acquired on or after 6 February 2003 for some other purpose [eg letting], its subsequent use as a holiday property or as a residence by the individual or a connected person (amount equal to the value of the assets in the ARF used in connection with the acquisition of the property together with any assets used in the improvement or repair of the property up to the date of such use);

(e) the acquisition of shares or other interests in a close company, or a company which would be a close company if resident in Ireland, in which the individual or a connected person is a participator (amount equal to the value of the assets in the ARF used in connection with the acquisition);

(f) the acquisition of tangible moveable property (amount equal to the value of the assets in the ARF used in connection with the acquisition);

(g) (i) the acquisition (on or after 2 February 2006) of property to be used immediately in connection with any business of the individual or a connected person (amount equal to the value of the assets in the ARF used in connection with the acquisition),

(ii) following the acquisition of property acquired on or after 2 February 2006 for some other purpose its subsequent use in connection with any business of the individual or a connected person (amount equal to the value of the assets in the ARF used in connection with the acquisition of the property together with any assets used in the improvement or repair of the property up to the date of such use), and

(h) the acquisition (on or after 23 October 2014) of units or shares in any fund, trust or scheme whereby a pension arrangement of an individual connected to the ARF holder has also invested and the value of the units held by the pension investor increases, or may increase due in whole or in part to the units held by the ARF investor.

For these purposes, market value is as determined for capital gains tax purposes under TCA 1997, s 548 (TCA 1997, s 784A(1E)). The definition of 'close company', 'participator' and 'connected person' follow those of TCA 1997, ss 430, 433 and 10 respectively (TCA 1997, s 783(1)).

In so far as ARF assets are treated as having been distributed they are no longer regarded as ARF assets; similarly, where the acquisition of assets is treated as giving rise to a distribution, the assets acquired will not be regarded as assets in the ARF (TCA 1997, s 784A(1C), (1D)).

With effect from 8 February 2011, a distribution from an ARF which is used to reimburse a pension scheme administrator for tax paid by that administrator on a chargeable excess under TCA 1997, Pt 30, Ch 2C (Limit on Tax-Relieved Funds) relating to the ARF holder will not be treated as a payment to the ARF holder for the purposes of sub-s (3).

Imputed distributions: approved retirement funds post-6 April 2000

TCA 1997, s 790D, which applies for the tax year 2012 onwards, provides for the taxation of imputed distributions from both Approved Retirement Funds (ARFs) and Vested PRSAs (see **16.305**) on a composite basis where the assets were first accepted into the fund after 6 April 2000 and the ARF or vested PRSA holder is 60 years of age or over for the whole tax year, (TCA 1997, s 790(3)). The aggregate of all ARFs and Vested PRSAs held by the individual is termed the 'Relevant Fund'.

Where the individual is beneficially entitled to the assets in a relevant fund, then an amount referred to as a specified amount will be treated as a distribution not later than the second month of the tax year following the tax year in which the specified amount is determined. The specified amount for a year of assessment from 2012 onwards is determined by the formula:

$$[A \times B\%] - C$$

Where:

A is the value of the assets in the Relevant Fund on 30 November in year of assessment, excluding the value of assets retained by the PRSA administrator as would be required where appropriate to be transferred to an AMRF if the holder had elected under TCA 1997, s 787H(1);

B is 4 per cent where the individual is not over age 70 for the whole of the tax year and the relevant value, ie the value of the relevant fund on the specified date (ie 30 November in the tax year concerned) is not greater than €2,000,000, 5 per cent where the individual is over age 70 for the whole of the tax year and the relevant value is not greater than €2,000,000 or otherwise 6 per cent;

C is the aggregate of the amounts or values of the distributions from ARFs or AMRFs and/or assets made available from a PRSA, other than excluded distributions made by the relevant QFM or PRSA Administrator as the case may be in respect of the Relevant Fund (TCA 1997, s 790D(1)).

Excluded distributions comprise:

(a) a specified amount regarded as a distribution from an ARF or AMRF or making available of assets from a PRSA;

(b) a transfer of all of the assets in an ARF to another ARF in the same beneficial ownership;

(c) a transaction which is regarded as a distribution from an ARF under TCA 1997, s 784A(1A);

(d) a transfer under TCA 1997, s 784C(5)(a). This section was amended by FA 2014 to include a withdrawal from an AMRF as outlined in **16.404** above;

(e) a transaction which is regarded as the making available of assets from a PRSA under TCA 1997, s 787G(3). TCA 1997, s 787G(3) was amended by FA 2014 to include payment by the QFM of the appropriate share of a non-member of income tax charged on a chargeable excess, ie following a pension adjustment order (see **16.504**);

(f) a transaction which is deemed to be the making available of assets from a PRSA under TCA 1997, s 787G(4A); or

(g) a distribution made for the purpose set out in TCA 1997, s 784A(3A), ie one which is used to reimburse a pension scheme administrator for tax paid by that administrator on a chargeable excess under TCA 1997, Pt 30, Ch 2C (Limit on Tax-Relieved Funds) (TCA 1997, s 787O(1)). TCA 1997, s 784A(3A) was amended by FA 2014 to include payment by the QFM of the appropriate share of a non-member of tax charged on a chargeable excess, ie following a pension adjustment order (see **16.504**).

The value of any assets in a relevant fund will be determined under the open market value rules of TCA 1997, s 548 (TCA 1997, s 790D(2)).

Where an individual has more than one ARF and/or PRSA and they are managed by different qualifying fund managers (QFMs) and/or PRSA administrators, one of the QFMs or PRSA administrators may be appointed as a nominee to discharge the obligations in relation to the withholding of tax on the specified amount. The appointment of a nominee is optional where the relevant fund has a value of €2m or less but is otherwise compulsory. Where the Relevant Fund consists of a mixture of ARFs and vested PRSAs and the QFM and the PRSA administrator are the same person, the specified amount is regarded as a distribution from an ARF. Where they are not the same person and the individual appoints a nominee (see above), then it will depend on whether the nominee is a QFM, a PRSA administrator, or both, in which case the specified amount will be considered to be a distribution from an ARF, a PRSA and an ARF respectively. If no nominee is appointed, each QFM and PRSA administrator must operate in isolation and apply the relevant per cent notional distribution to the relevant ARF(s) or PRSA(s) they manage/administer (TCA 1997, s 790D(4), (5)).

Where an individual appoints a nominee, he or she must advise the other QFMs and/or PRSA administrators of that fact and provide the name, address and telephone number of the nominee (TCA 1997, s 790D(6)). Where the appointment of a nominee is compulsory the individual must advise the other manager(s) that the appointment of the nominee is a compulsory appointment and that the reason for the appointment is that the aggregate value of the assets in the ARFs or PRSAs is greater than €2m and therefore attracts the 6 per cent rate of tax. The other manager/managers must provide the nominee with a certificate for that year, stating the aggregate value of the assets in, and relevant distributions from, the ARFs or PRSAs they manage within 14 days of the specified date (ie by 14 December of a tax year). In the case of a PRSA fund, the certificates should exclude any amount retained by the PRSA administrator for AMRF purposes, as these do not form part of the asset base for the specified amount. The nominee must retain the records for six years for production to the Revenue Commissioners if required (TCA 1997, s 790D(7)).

Where the nominee receives a certificate(s) from the other manager(s), the nominee must determine the specified amount as if the value of the assets and the relevant distributions stated in each certificate so received were the value of assets in, and relevant distributions from, an ARF or a vested PRSA managed or administered by the nominee. This will apply even if the nominee only receives some but not all of the required certificates (TCA 1997, s 790D(8)). Where the relevant fund value is €2m or less and a nominee is appointed but where the nominee receives no certificates at all from the other manager or managers, the nominee and the other manager(s) must each determine the specified amount in respect of the ARFs/PRSAs that they manage in isolation, as if the individual's relevant fund comprised solely of the ARFs/PRSAs that each manages. Where the nominee has received some certificates but not all of them, the managers who failed to provide certificates must determine the specified amount in isolation as above. As the nominee will have received at least one or more certificates from the compliant manager(s), the nominee must calculate the specified amount in respect of the nominee and the other managers that provided certificates. For situations where the relevant value of the assets in the individual's relevant fund is greater than €2m any specified amount calculated in isolation is to be based on 6 per cent of the value of the fund (TCA 1997, s 790D(10)).

In situations where the individual's relevant fund comprises ARFs and/or PRSAs that are not managed or administered by the same QFM and/or PRSA administrator and because the value of the assets in the relevant fund does not exceed €2m, the individual opts not to appoint a nominee, each QFM and/or PRSA administrator must determine the specified amount in respect of the ARFs/PRSAs that they manage in isolation as if the individual's relevant fund comprised solely of the ARFs/PRSAs that each manages (TCA 1997, s 790D(11)).

Death provisions: approved funds post-6 April 2000

A distribution made following the death of the individual beneficially entitled to the assets in an ARF is treated as the income of that individual for the year of death and PAYE applies to the payment unless it is made to an ARF in the name of the deceased's spouse or civil partner or it is made to or for the sole benefit of a child of the deceased, or any child of the civil partner of the deceased. (TCA 1997, s 784A(4)(a), (b)). With effect from 1 January 2011 however, a distribution made to a child aged 21 or over from the ARF of the deceased, or made from an ARF in the name of a surviving spouse or surviving civil partner funded by the ARF of the deceased spouse or civil partner (other than such a distribution to a child aged under 21 years of the surviving spouse or surviving civil partner), is subject to an income tax charge under Case IV of Sch D at a rate of 30 per cent. The amount so charged will not form part of the individual's total income, and is computed without regard to any deductions allowed in computing taxable income; similarly, no reliefs, deductions or tax credits may be set against the amount so charged or against the tax payable on that amount, and the income tax exemption limits and marginal relief will not apply as regards the income tax so charged (TCA 1997, s 784A(4)(c)).

The reporting and collection provisions that apply to excess lump sums pursuant to TCA 1997, s 790AA will also apply, with necessary modifications to such distributions (TCA 1997, s 784A(4)(d)).

Where an individual dies and the assets are held in an ARF or AMRF at the time of death the tax position will therefore be as follows:

ARF inherited by:	*Income tax:*	*CAT:*
Surviving spouse	None	None
Children:		
under 21	None	Normal CAT rules
over 21	30%	None
Others	Marginal rate of tax	Normal CAT Rules

Where an ARF passes on death to a surviving spouse, the provisions on the subsequent death of the spouse are as follows:

ARF inherited by:	*Income tax*	*CAT*
Children:		
under 21	None	Normal CAT rules
over 21	30%	None
Others	Marginal rate of tax	Normal CAT rules

Buy-Out Bonds

Revenue *eBrief 72/16* supersedes *eBrief 72/11* of 28 November 2011. Its purpose was to advise of a policy change announced by the Minister for Finance on 22 June 2016, to the effect that individuals with a Buy-Out Bond (BOB) that originated from a defined benefit pension scheme may, where benefits are taken on or after that date, access the Approved Retirement Fund (ARF) option in respect of the BOB in question. As a result of this change, access to the ARF option will apply to benefits in respect of all BOBs with effect from 22 June 2016 regardless of whether the transfer value to the BOB comes from a Defined Contribution (DC) or a Defined Benefit (DB) scheme and regardless of when the transfer occurs (ie whether before or from that date). Notwithstanding the above change in respect of BOBs originating from DB schemes, it should be noted that the position regarding ARF access for DB main scheme benefits remains unchanged, ie such access is available to proprietary directors only.

In the case of Buy-Out Bonds (BOBs), access to the ARF option in respect of main scheme benefits under the occupational pension scheme arrangement from which the transfer value to the BOB originated can be summarised as follows:

Defined Benefit (DB) Schemes: With effect from 22 June 2016, the ARF option is available in respect of transfer values from all DB occupational schemes to BOBs where benefits are taken on or after that date and regardless of when the transfer occurs, ie whether the transfer to the BOB took place before that date or from that date. Prior to 22 June 2016, the ARF option applied only where the scheme member had the right to exercise the option under the scheme rules prior to the date of transfer to the BOB, ie where he or she met the proprietary director test before the date of transfer (see *eBrief 72/11*).

Defined Contribution (DC) Schemes: With effect from 26 May 2014, the ARF option is available in respect of transfer values from all DC occupational schemes to BOBs regardless of when the transfer occurs. Prior to 26 May 2014, the ARF option was not available in respect of transfers to BOBs which occurred before 6 February 2011 (the date of passing of Finance Act 2011 which extended the ARF option to the main scheme benefit from DC schemes) – other than in the case of proprietary directors.

16.5 Limit on Tax-Relieved Pension Funds

16.501 Overview

TCA 1997, Pt 30, Ch 2C limits the quantum of pension benefits that an individual can take from a relevant pension arrangement (**16.502**). It also limits the lump sums that may be drawn from any of those schemes (**16.505**). A cap was introduced on 7 December 2005 on the value of accumulated pension assets at retirement. If the pension fund exceeds this cap, any value in excess of the cap is taxed immediately at the marginal income tax rate (currently 40 per cent for 2015). This is termed the *chargeable excess*. When the balance of the fund is withdrawn it is subject to normal income tax, USC and PRSI depending on age.

The excess over the cap suffers an effective tax rate of up to 68 per cent and higher where PRSI applies.

Example 16.501.1

Michael is aged 68 and has €100,000 of pension assets at retirement in excess of the cap of €2,000,000.

The tax arising on the excess is as follows:

	€
Excess pension fund over cap	100,000
Income tax @ 40%[1]	(40,000)
Balance	60,000
Tax on drawdown	
Income tax 40%	(24,000)
USC[1]	(4,200)
Net income	31,800
Total tax suffered	68,200
%	68.2%

Notes

1. Assumes that Michael has other income which utilises lower USC bands and 20% income tax band.

The cap known as the *Standard Fund Threshold* was initially set at €5,000,000 on 7 December 2005. It was indexed in 2007 and 2008 and remained at €5,418,085 from 2008 to 7 December 2010 when it was reduced to €2,300,000. It has been reduced with effect from 1 January 2014 to €2,000,000.

An individual whose pension assets were in excess of the €5,000,000 cap on 7 December 2005 could apply to Revenue for this higher value, ie their *Personal Fund Threshold*. Similarly when the cap reduced on 7 December 2010, if an individual's pension value was between €2,300,000 and €5,418,085 they could apply to Revenue for the higher value to apply.

If an individual's pension fund value was in excess of €2,000,000 at 1 January 2014 they can apply to Revenue for the higher value subject to it not being in excess of €2,300,000, being the cap that applied to that date.

It is relatively easy to value a pension fund which is a defined contribution fund. It is the value of any lump sum payable plus the value of the remaining assets and cash that will be transferred to an ARF or used to purchase an annuity. However, a defined benefit scheme or a public pension does not have specific assets for each pension holder. These funds are valued using the annual pension payable multiplied by a valuation factor known as the *relevant valuation factor* plus any lump sum payable. In the majority of cases the valuation factor up to 31 December 2013 had been 20.

Finance (No 2) Act 2013 has introduced variable valuation factors which vary according to age at retirement. These range from 37 at age 50 to 22 at aged 70 and over. The higher factors will lead to a higher value been place on the pension and therefore increased risk that it will exceed the Standard Fund Threshold of €2,000,000. There are transitional measures to protect pensions which have accrued at 1 January 2014 known as the *accrued pension amount*. These are to be valued using the old valuation factor of 20. These are outlined in more detail below.

Example 16.501.2

Mary is aged 58. She has worked for 33 years and is entitled to a public pension at normal retirement age 65. Her pension if she retired on 1 January 2014 would be €70,000. Her pension at aged 65 will be €90,000.

Her accrued pension amount at 1 January 2014 is calculated as follows:

€70,000 x 20 = €1,400,000

At normal retirement the deemed value of her pension will be the accrued pension amount at 1 January 2014 of €1,400,000 plus €520,000 (€90,000 – €70,000) x 26[1]) = €1,920,000.

As this is under the Standard Fund Threshold of €2,000,000 assuming it has not changed in the interim there will be no chargeable excess taxable at 40%.

Note

1 Factor from Table for person aged 65.

From 1 January 2011 any tax payable at the standard rate on a lump sum taken at retirement can be used as a credit against the excess fund tax TCA 1997, s 787RA.

Revenue issued a summary guidance note on the changes to the Standard Fund Threshold regime contained in Finance (No 2) Act 2013 on 25 October 2013. This note outlines the background to the threshold and provides worked examples and is a very useful reference.

16.502 Definitions

TCA 1997, s 787O sets out a large number of the definitions for the purposes of Ch 2C and Sch 23B.

The limitation on pension benefits applies to benefits from a *relevant pension arrangement*. This is defined as:

(a) a retirement benefits scheme within the meaning of TCA 1997, s 771, for the time being approved by the Revenue Commissioners (**16.103**);

(b) an annuity contract or a trust scheme approved by the Revenue Commissioners under TCA 1997, s 784 (**16.201**);

(c) a PRSA contract within the meaning of TCA 1997, s 787A, in respect of a PRSA product (**16.301**);

(d) a qualifying overseas pension plan within the meaning of Ch 2B (**16.6**);

(e) a public service pension scheme within the meaning of the Public Service Superannuation (Miscellaneous Provisions) Act 2004, s 1; or

(f) a statutory scheme within the meaning of TCA 1997, s 770(1) (**16.113**).

The *administrator* is the person having the management of the relevant pension arrangement and includes:

(a) an administrator of a retirement benefits scheme (**16.103**);

(b) a person lawfully carrying on the business of granting annuities on human life (**16.204**);

(c) a PRSA administrator; and

(d) a person specified by the Regulations as the administrator of a public service pension scheme or a statutory scheme.

Accrued Pension amount means the part (if any) that has accrued to the individual at 1 January 2014 calculated in accordance with TCA 1997, Sch 23B para 1.

The *maximum tax-relieved pension fund* is the overall limit on the amount that may be crystallised by a benefit crystallisation event(s) on or after 7 December 2005 without giving rise to a chargeable excess.

A *benefit crystallisation event* is defined in TCA 1997, Sch 23B, para 2 as occurring where:

(a) the individual becomes entitled to any one of the following benefits:

(i) a pension,

(ii) an annuity,

(iii) a lump sum;

(b) the individual exercises an option under TCA 1997, ss 772(3A), 784(2A) or 787H(1) for the transfer on the annuity or pension payment date of an amount to either of:

(i) the individual,

(ii) an ARF, or

(iii) an AMRF;

(c) a payment is made to an overseas pension fund at the direction of the individual under the Occupational Pension Schemes and Personal Retirement Savings Accounts (Overseas Transfer Payments) Regulations 2003;

(d) the individual, having become entitled to a pension under a relevant pension arrangement on or after 7 December 2005, becomes entitled to the payment of that pension, other than in *excepted circumstances*, at an increased annual amount which exceeds by more than the *permitted margin* the annual amount at which it was payable on the day the individual became entitled to it;

(e) (with effect from 24 February 2010) the individual does not elect to exercise an option in accordance with TCA 1997, s 787H(1) and instead retains the assets of the PRSA in that or any other PRSA (see **16.301**) (TCA 1997, Sch 23 para 2 as amended by FA 2010, s 16); or

(f) (with effect from 25 December 2016 – date of passing of FA 2016):

(i) the individual is a PRSA contributor and the PRSA becomes a vested PRSA of a kind referred to in paragraph (c) of the definition of 'vested PRSA' in TCA 1997, s 790D(1),

(ii) the relevant pension arrangement becomes a vested RAC within the meaning of TCA 1997, s 787O(1).

The *permitted margin* is the amount by which the annual amount of the pension would be greater if it had been increased by whichever of calculation A and calculation B gives the greater amount. Calculation A means a calculation that increases the annual amount of a pension at five per cent pa for the period beginning with the month in which the individual became entitled to the pension and ending with the month in which he or she becomes entitled to payment of the pension at an increased annual amount. Calculation B means a calculation that increases the pension by two per cent pa plus the movement in the CPI starting in the month in which the individual first became entitled to the pension and ending in the month when he or she becomes entitled to the pension at an increased annual amount.

Excepted circumstances are circumstances such that the increase in the annual amount of pension payment is directly related to the increase in the rate of remuneration of all persons or of a class of persons employed in the sector in which the individual was employed and in respect of which employment the individual was entitled to the pension under the relevant pension arrangement.

If more than one benefit crystallisation event occurs in relation to the individual on the same day, the individual will decide the order in which they are deemed to occur (TCA 1997, s 787O(3)).

The *amount crystallised by a benefit crystallisation event* is defined in TCA 1997, Sch 23B, para 3 (as most recently amended by F(No 2)A 2013, s 18) as:

(a) subject to (aa) below where the benefit crystallisation event is the individual becoming entitled to a pension, an amount determined by the formula:

$$P \times A$$

where:

P is the amount of pension which would be payable to the individual, on the assumption that there is no commutation of part of the pension for a lump sum, in the period of 12 months beginning with the day on which the individual becomes entitled to it and on the assumption that there is no increase in the pension through that period, and

A is the relevant age-related factor;

(aa) where the benefit crystallisation event is the individual becoming entitled to a pension and the administrator of the relevant pension arrangement is satisfied, based on information and records available to the administrator, that there is an accrued pension amount in respect of that event, an amount equivalent to the amount determined by the formula:

$$(APA \times B) + ((P - APA) \times A)$$

where 'P' and 'A' have the meanings given to them respectively in the formula in subparagraph (a) and where:

APA is the accrued pension amount, and

B is the relevant valuation factor on the specified date,

and the administrator shall keep and preserve for a period of six years after the date of the event such information and records as may be required for the purposes of demonstrating to the satisfaction of an officer of the Revenue Commissioners that there was an accrued pension amount in respect of the event;

(b) where the benefit crystallisation event is the individual becoming entitled to an annuity, the aggregate of the cash sums and the market value of such of the other assets under the relevant pension arrangement as are applied towards the purchase of the annuity;

(c) where the benefit crystallisation event is the individual becoming entitled to a lump sum, the amount of the lump sum paid to the individual;

(d) where the benefit crystallisation event is the individual exercising an option to transfer funds to the individual, an ARF or an AMRF, the aggregate of the amount of so much of the cash sums and market value of the assets as are to be transferred following the exercise of the option;

(da) where the benefit crystallisation event is the individual not electing to exercise an option in accordance with TCA 1997, s 787H(1) and instead retaining the assets of the PRSA in that or any other PRSA, the aggregate of cash and the market value of assets held by the relative PRSA(s).

(db) where the benefit crystallisation event is an event of a kind referred to in paragraph 2(bb), the aggregate of the amount of any cash sums and the market value of the assets in the PRSA at the date the individual attains the age of 75 years or, where the individual attained the age of 75 years prior to the date of passing of the Finance Act 2016 (25 December 2016), on that date,

(dc) where the benefit crystallisation event is an event of a kind referred to in paragraph 2(bc), the aggregate of so much of the cash sums and the market value of such of the other assets representing the individual's rights under the relevant pension arrangement at the date the individual attains the age of 75 years or, where the individual attained the age of 75 years prior to date of passing of the Finance Act 2016 (25 December 2016), on that date,

(e) where the benefit crystallisation event is the payment to an overseas arrangement, the amount of the payment made or as the case may be the market value of the assets transferred;

(f) where the benefit crystallisation event is an increase in the annual pension an amount determined by the formula:

$$A \times IP$$

where:

A is the relevant age-related factor, and

IP is the amount by which the increased annual pension exceeds the annual amount on the day the individual became entitled to it, as increased by the permitted margin. If a crystallisation event previously occurred by reason of the individual having become entitled to a payment of the pension at an increased annual amount then the amounts crystallised by those events will be deducted in arriving at the amount crystallised by the event.

Where the individual's pension arrangements are subject to a pension adjustment order made or subsequently varied under either Family Law Act 1995 or Family Law (Divorce) Act 1996, any designated benefits payable or actually paid thereunder must be disregarded in calculating the amount which has been crystallised.

The *relevant valuation factor* in relation to a relevant pension arrangement was fixed at 20 up until 1 January 2014. Prior to FA 2011, the administrator could, with the prior agreement of Revenue, use valuation factors other than 20 where they were satisfied that the factor of 20 was clearly inappropriate, and the alternative factor would be appropriate to use in the circumstances. From 1 January 2014 the valuation factor will depend on the age of the individual at retirement. The valuation factors are set out in the Table inserted after Sch 23B para (5) by Finance (No 2) Act 2013. There are transitional arrangements where part of the pension has been accrued at 1 January 2014. The part accrued at 1 January 2014 – referred to as the accrued pension amount, will be valued using a factor of 20 and the part accrued after 1 January 2014 will be valued using the age-related factor contained in the Table.

The *uncrystallised pension rights* on any date are the pension rights in respect of which the individual was not entitled to the payment of benefits on that date.

The *amount of uncrystallised pension rights on the specified date* (eg 1 January 2014) is defined in TCA 1997, Sch 23B, para 1 as the aggregate of the amount of such rights on that date in respect of each of the relevant pension arrangements of which the individual is a member. If the relevant pension arrangement is a defined contribution scheme (ie one that provides benefits calculated by reference to an amount available for the provision of benefits to or in respect of the member, whether the amount is determined solely by reference to contributions made by or on behalf of the member and the investment return on those contributions or otherwise, and includes an annuity contract or a trust scheme under TCA 1997, s 784 and a PRSA contract under TCA 1997, s 787A) the individual's uncrystallised pension rights are the aggregate of the cash sums and the market value of any other assets held for the purpose of the arrangement on the specified date and as represent the individual's rights under the arrangement.

In the case of a defined benefit scheme (ie a relevant pension arrangement other than a defined contribution scheme) the uncrystallised pension benefits are determined by the formula:

$$(RVF \times AP) + LS$$

where:

RVF is the relevant valuation factor as defined above on the specified date;

AP is the annual pension which the person would on the valuation assumptions be entitled to on the specified date if the individual acquired an actual right rather than a prospective right to receive a pension in respect of the uncrystallised pension rights. This calculation is done on the valuation assumption that the individual had reached the age to enable him to take the benefits without reduction on account of age and on the assumption that the right to receive the benefits had not been occasioned by incapacity of mind or body;

LS is the amount of any lump sum to which the individual would on the valuation assumptions be entitled to under the arrangement on the specified date (otherwise than by way of commutation of pension) if, on that date the individual acquired an actual rather than a prospective right to payment of a lump sum in respect of their rights.

The amount of the standard fund threshold or personal fund threshold that is available for a current event is defined in TCA 1997, Sch 23B, para 4 as:

(a) if prior to the current event, no benefit crystallisation event has occurred in relation to the individual on or after the specified date, the whole of the standard or personal fund threshold;
(b) if prior to the current event one or more benefit crystallisation events occurred on or after the specified date and the previously used amount is greater than the standard or personal fund threshold, none of the threshold is available; and
(c) in any other case, so much of the threshold as is left after deducting the previously used amount.

The *previously used amount* is defined in TCA 1997, Sch 23B, para 5 as:

(a) where one benefit crystallisation event occurred before the current event, the amount crystallised by the previous event multiplied by the higher of 1 and A/B where:
   A is the standard or personal fund threshold at the date of the current event, and
   B is the standard or personal fund threshold at the date of the previous benefit crystallisation event;
(b) where two or more benefit crystallisation events have occurred before the current event, the aggregate of the amounts crystallised by each previous crystallisation event each of those being adjusted by the higher of 1 and A/B where:
   A is the standard or personal fund threshold at the date of the current event, and
   B is the standard or personal fund threshold at the date of the previous benefit crystallisation event.

A *current event* is a benefit crystallisation event occurring on or after the specified date. The *date of the current event* is the date on which:

(a) the individual acquires an actual entitlement to the payment of a benefit in respect of the current event under the relevant pension arrangement, whether or not the benefit is paid on that date;
(b) the annuity or the pension would otherwise become payable under a relevant pension arrangement where the person exercises the option to transfer funds to the individual, an ARF or an AMRF;
(c) a payment or transfer is made to an overseas arrangement by the direction of the individual;
(d) the individual having become entitled to a pension under a relevant pension arrangement on or after the specified date becomes entitled to an increased annual amount which exceeds the permitted margin; or
(e) the annuity or the pension would otherwise become payable under a PRSA, where the individual does not elect to exercise an option in accordance with TCA 1997, s 787H(1) and instead retains the assets of the PRSA in that or any other PRSA.

For the purpose of Ch 2C, market value is construed in accordance with TCA 1997, s 548.

The Table inserted by F(No 2)A 2013 in Sch 23B after para 5 is:

TABLE

Age (1)	Relevant age-related factor (2)
Up to and including 50	37
51	36
52	36
53	35
54	34
55	33
56	33
57	32
58	31
59	30
60	30
61	29
62	28
63	27
64	27
65	26
66	25
67	24
68	24
69	23
70 and over	22

FA 2016, s 14(1)(d) brings about a new definition of 'vested RAC' as follows:

> 'vested RAC' means a relevant pension arrangement of a kind referred to in paragraph (b) of the definition of that term in this subsection in respect of which—
>
> (a) payment of the annuity to the individual entitled to the annuity under the contract has not commenced, or
>
> (b) a transfer has not been made under section 784(2A), on or before the date on which the individual attains the age of 75 years.

Revenue guidance on the above notes as follows '"vested RAC" is a retirement annuity contract … from which the owner has not taken retirement benefits, either by way of an annuity, a retirement lump sum or a transfer under the ARF options, on or before the date of his or her 75th birthday …' Further, a new sub-s (5) was inserted which Revenue guidance explains 'Under subsection (6), where an RAC owner attains the age of 75 before 25th December 2016 (ie the date of passing of Finance Act 2016), without having taken benefits, the RAC is deemed to become a vested RAC on 25th December 2016. There are similar provisions in section 790D(1) in relation to "vested PRSAs"'.

16.503 Limit on tax-relieved pension funds

TCA 1997, s 787P provides that an individual's maximum tax-relieved pension fund cannot exceed:

(a) the *standard fund threshold*. This is €2,000,000 from 1 January 2014. It was previously €2,300,000 between 7 December 2010 and 31 December 2013. When it was first introduced on 7 December 2005 it was €5,000,000 and this was indexed in 2007 and 2008 and remained at €5,418,085 from 2008 to 7 December 2010); or

(b) the *personal fund threshold*, where the Revenue Commissioners have issued a certificate or a revised certificate following a notification in writing made by the individual on the authorised form that he or she had a personal fund threshold and supplying prescribed details, including full name, address and PPS number and particulars of the relevant pension arrangements with a schedule setting out the computation of the personal fund threshold. The notification must have been made by the individual on the appropriate form to Financial Services (Pensions) Branch before 7 June 2011 or where the benefit crystallisation event occurred after 7 December 2010 but before 7 June 2011 the notification must have been made before the first benefit crystallisation event. There is provision for the Revenue Commissioners to issue a revised certificate where they are not satisfied that the computation of the personal fund threshold contained in the notification is in fact correct.

From 1 January 2014 the individual must notify the Revenue Commissioner by such electronic means (within the meaning of TCA 1997, s 917EA) as are required by the Commissioners, within the period of 12 months from the date the electronic means are made available by the Commissioners, or before the first benefit crystallisation event occurs after the 1 January 2014, whichever is the earlier, that he or she is entitled to a personal fund threshold and provide the following information (in this section referred to as the 'PFT notification'):

(i) their full name, address, telephone number and PPS Number;

(ii) the following particulars of each relevant pension arrangement in respect of which the personal fund threshold arises:

  (I) the name, address and telephone number of the administrator;

  (II) the name and reference number of the arrangement;

  (III) whether the arrangement is a defined benefit or defined contribution arrangement:

  (IV)

    (A) the amount of the individual's pension rights in respect of the arrangement as certified by the administrator, and

    (B) where the arrangement is a defined benefit arrangement, the annual amount of pension the individual would be entitled to on 1 January 2014 as certified by the administrator;

  and

  (V) such other information and particulars as the Revenue Commissioners may reasonably require.

The above information must be retained and if required made available for a period of six years after the date of the benefit crystallisation event.

Revenue issued an *ebrief 50/14* on 1 July 2014 confirming that the electronic system was available and that applications would be accepted by electronic means from that date until 2 July 2015. Applications for a personal fund threshold must be made through ROS or PAYE Anytime. Revenue *eBrief* 64/2015 advised of an extension, to 31 July 2015, of the deadline for making an electronic PFT notification to Revenue for pension purposes given the original time limit for making a notification was due to expire on 2 July 2015.

16.504 Taxation of chargeable excess

Chargeable excess

TCA 1997, s 787Q(1) provides that income tax is charged on a sum referred to as the 'chargeable excess' where a benefit crystallisation event occurs on or after 7 December 2005 in relation to an individual who is a member of a relevant pension arrangement and either of the following conditions are met:

(a) all or part of the individual's standard or personal fund threshold is available at the date of the current event but the amount of the event exceeds the standard/personal fund threshold which is available at that date; or

(b) none of the individual's standard or personal fund threshold is available at the date of the benefit crystallisation event.

The amount of the standard or personal fund threshold that is available at the date of the current event is determined in accordance with TCA 1997, Sch 23B (**16.502** above).

The chargeable excess is the amount of the current event or the amount by which that event exceeds the amount of the standard or personal fund threshold that is available at that date in relation to the individual. Where all or part of the tax arising on the chargeable excess is paid by the administrator of the relevant pension arrangement then the tax paid is treated as part of the chargeable excess unless the individual's rights under the relevant pension arrangement (defined benefit scheme) are reduced so as to fully reflect the amount of the tax paid or the individual reimburses the administrator for the tax so paid (TCA 1997, s 787Q(5)).

On the other hand where the administrator of a public service pension scheme or a statutory scheme pays the tax on the chargeable excess then the amount of tax paid is a debt due to the administrator from the individual and the administrator shall be reimbursed by the individual for the tax paid under one of the following options: (TCA 1997, s 787Q(7)–(8)).

Where the chargeable excess tax paid does not exceed 20 per cent of the lump sum payable to the individual reduced by the amount of tax payable on the lump sum (referred to as the net lump sum):

(a) by appropriating that percentage from the net lump sum;

(b) by payment by the individual of a sum equivalent to the tax paid to the administrator;

(c) by any combination of the above; or

(d) by way of a reduction in the gross annual pension payable to the individual over a period not exceeding 20 years. This is an additional option that was introduced in Finance (No 2) Act 2013.

Where the chargeable excess tax paid is greater than 20 per cent (previously 50 per cent) of the net lump sum:

(a) by appropriating not less than 20 per cent of the net lump sum or such higher percentage as the administrator and the individual agree;

(b) by payment by the individual of a sum not less than 20 per cent of the net lump sum to the administrator or such higher percentage as the administrator and the individual agree; or

(c) by any combination of the above; and

(d) by recovering any balance by reducing the gross pension payable over a period not exceeding 20 years (previously 10 years);

(e) alternatively by way of a reduction in the gross pension payable to the individual over a period not exceeding 20 years. This is an additional option under Finance (No 2) Act 2013.

Income tax on chargeable excess

TCA 1997, s 787R(1) provides that the whole amount of the chargeable excess is liable to income tax at the marginal rate (currently 40 per cent) under Sch D Case IV. No relief, reduction or deduction is allowable in computing the tax on the chargeable excess. The income exemption and the age exemption will not apply as regards tax charged on the excess. When the individual comes to draw benefits from the pension fund (say from an ARF) he will be subject to income tax again. This means that the funds in excess of the standard or personal fund threshold are subject to double taxation by the time they are withdrawn.

The administrator of the relevant pension arrangements and the individual are liable for the income tax on the chargeable excess and their liability is joint and several.

The administrator may request the individual to make a declaration in writing which contains:

(a) the individual's name, address and PPS number;

(b) the date of the event and the amount crystallised on the event;

(c) in relation to benefit crystallisation event(s) that are due to occur from the date of the declaration the expected date of each such event and the estimated amount crystallised by each event;

(d) the amount of the individual's personal fund threshold and the certificate or revised certificate issued by the Revenue Commissioners under TCA 1997, s 787P(7) or s 787P(8); and

(e) such other information as the Revenue may reasonably require for the purpose of TCA 1997, Pt 30, Ch 2C.

Where an individual who has been requested to provide a declaration to the administrator fails to provide that declaration then the administrator may:

(a) withhold the payment of any benefit or increase in the annual pension where the benefit crystallisation event is an individual becoming entitled to a pension, an annuity, a lump sum or an increased pension in excess of a permitted margin until the declaration is made;

(b) refuse to make the transfer of funds to the individual, an ARF, an AMRF or an overseas arrangement or refuse to make assets of the PRSA available to the PRSA contractor until the declaration is made.

FA 2016, s 14(1)(e) brings about a new ss (5A) to TCA 1997, s 787R. Revenue guidance on that subsection points out that where the owner of a Retirement Annuity Contract

(RAC) or a PRSA does not take benefits from the RAC or PRSA by age 75, such benefits are treated as commencing on the date of the owner's reaching 75 years of age or on 25 December 2016 (ie the date Finance Act 2016 was passed), if he or she is 75 years of age before 25 December 2016, notwithstanding that benefits have not actually commenced by the date in question. An individual whose RAC or PRSA vests in these circumstances must provide a declaration to his or her administrator within 30 days from the date of the deemed vesting, regardless of whether or not the declaration is requested by the administrator. Where an individual fails to provide a declaration, the administrator must assume that the individual's Standard Fund Threshold or Personal Fund Threshold, if applicable, is fully 'used up' and, accordingly, the entire value of the benefit crystallisation event (BCE) is treated as a 'chargeable excess' and taxed at the higher rate of income tax in force for the year in which the BCE arises.

The administrator must keep and retain the declarations for a period of six years. The administrator is required to make the declarations available to the Revenue should they request them.

Pension benefits subject to a pension adjustment order

Finance Act 2014 made a number of amendments to TCA 1997, Pt 30, Ch 2C to address an imbalance in the treatment of the member spouse and the non-member spouse of a pension scheme when an excess fund tax arises following a pension adjustment order. Previously, the member spouse was solely responsible for any excess fund tax that arose, however following this amendment, the excess fund tax will be split between the member spouse and the non-member spouse in proportion to their share of the fund.

A number of definitions have been inserted into TCA 1997, s 787O(1). The member spouse is referred to as the *relevant member* and is defined as:

(a) a member of a relevant pension arrangement in respect of whose retirement benefit under the arrangement a pension adjustment order has been made in favour of a non-member, or

(b) a member of a relevant pension arrangement to which a sum representing that member's accrued rights under the relevant pension arrangement referred to in paragraph (a) has been transferred, or subsequently transferred.

The non-member spouse is defined as an individual (other than a dependent member of the family within the meaning of the Family Law Act 1995, s 2 and the Family Law (Divorce) Act 1996, s 2) in whose favour a pension adjustment order in respect of the retirement benefit of a member of the arrangement has been made.

TCA 1997, s 787R(2A) sets out how the excess fund tax will be split between the relevant member and the non-member on a benefit crystallisation event. It provides that where an excess fund tax arises on a benefit crystallisation event, the excess fund tax shall be apportioned between the relevant member and the non-member such that each party's share of the tax shall not exceed such part of the tax as would bear to that tax the same proportion as each party's share of the retirement benefit bears to that retirement benefit having regard to the designated benefit payable to the non-member pursuant to the pension adjustment order. TCA 1997, s 787R(2A)(c) sets out the formula for calculating each party's share of the excess fund tax as follows:

In the case of the non-member:

(a) where the relevant pension arrangement is a defined benefit arrangement and is the arrangement in respect of which the pension adjustment order has been made, it shall be the designated benefit on which the transfer amount was calculated; and

(b) in any other case, it shall be the transfer amount.

And

In the case of the relevant member, it shall be an amount equivalent to the amount determined by the formula:

$$A - B$$

where –

A is the retirement benefit arising under the benefit crystallisation event giving rise to the tax; and

B is the non-member's share determined in accordance with clause (I) or (II) of subparagraph (i).

The persons liable for the tax in relation to the relevant member shall be the administrator of the relevant pension arrangement and the relevant member. In relation to the non-member spouse, where no transfer amount has been applied, it shall be the administrator of the relevant pension arrangement and the non-member. Where a transfer amount has been applied, it shall be the subsequent administrator and the non-member. The liability of the subsequent administrator shall not exceed the lesser of the non-member's appropriate share and the amount or value of the assets in the transfer arrangement or the ARF or vested PRSA if the benefits have crystallised.

A number of administrative provisions have been put in place to deal with this and it places a heavy burden on pension scheme administrators.

Pay and file obligation for tax on chargeable excess

TCA 1997, s 787S(1)(a) provides that the administrator of the pension arrangement concerned must make a return on Form 787S to the Collector General within three months following the end of the month in which a benefit crystallisation event occurs, setting out:

(a) the name and address of the administrator;

(b) the individual's name, address and PPS number;

(c) details of the relevant pension arrangement(s);

(d) the amount of, and the basis of calculation of, the chargeable excess arising in respect of the benefit crystallisation event;

(e) the amount of tax which the administrator is required to account for in relation to the chargeable excess and where the administrator is the administrator or a relevant pension arrangement subject to a pension adjustment order, the return shall also contain:

  (i) where no transfer amount has been applied –

    (I) the name address and PPS Number of the non-member, and

    (II) details of the relevant member's and non-member's appropriate share of the tax which the administrator is required to account for,

  and

  (ii) where a transfer amount has been applied,

    (I) the name address and telephone number of the subsequent administrator,

(II) the name, last known address and PPS Number of the non-member, and

(III) the relevant member's appropriate share of the excess fund that the administrator is required to account for and the non-member's appropriate share of the excess fund tax that the subsequent administrator is required to account for by way of a separate return.

Finance Act 2014 also inserted TCA 1997, s 787S(1A) placing an obligation on the subsequent administrator of a transfer arrangement following a pension adjustment order to file a similar return within three months from the end of the month in which the benefit crystallisation event occurs or on other specified dates such as the receipt of a certificate from the relevant administrator advising of a benefit crystallisation event in the relevant pension arrangement, to make a return to the Collector General. This return shall set out:

(a) the name, address and telephone number of the subsequent administrator,
(b) the name, address and PPS Number of the non-member,
(c) the name, address and telephone number of the administrator of the relevant pension arrangement from which the transfer amount arose,
(d) the amount of and basis of calculation of the non-member's appropriate share of the tax, and
(e) the amount of the non-member's share of the tax which the subsequent administrator is required to account for.

The tax on the chargeable excess is due to be paid at the same time as the return is due (TCA 1997, s 787S(3)). Interest on late payment runs at a rate of 0.0219 per cent per day from 7 December 2010.

If Revenue are dissatisfied with any return or if they feel that tax on a chargeable excess has not been included in a return they can make an assessment on the person liable for the tax. Where any sum is incorrectly included in a return as a chargeable excess Revenue may make such assessments, adjustments and set-offs as are required for securing that the resulting tax liabilities are what they would have been if the item had not been included.

TCA 1997, s 787S(7) provides that the provisions of the income tax acts in relation to assessments to income tax, appeals against assessments and the collection and recovery of income tax apply in relation to the assessment, collection and recovery of tax on the chargeable excess. F(TA)A 2015, s 38, which was subject to Ministerial Order (SI 110/2016 appointed 21 March 2016 as the day on which the Finance (Tax Appeals) Act 2015, came into operation), deletes the above reference to appeals in TCA 1997, s 787S(7) and inserts a new sub-s (7A) into the section. The latter provides that where a person aggrieved by an assessment made on that person under the section may appeal the assessment to the Appeal Commissioners within the period of 30 days after the date of the notice of assessment. However, where, a person is required to make a return and account for appropriate tax to the Collector-General, then no appeal lies against an assessment until such time as the person makes the return and pays or has paid the amount of the appropriate tax payable on the basis of that return.

Discharge of administrator from tax liability on chargeable excess

TCA 1997, s 787T provides that the administrator can apply in writing to have the tax liability or the excess liability discharged where he or she reasonably believed that a benefit crystallisation event did not give rise to an income tax liability or that the amount of the income tax liability was less than the actual amount. Where Revenue are of the opinion that it would not be just and reasonable for the administrator to be made liable for the tax on the chargeable excess they may discharge him or her from that liability. The notification of discharge will be in writing.

Encashment Option

TCA 1997, s 787TA allows individuals who have private and public sector retirement funds with effect from 8 February 2012 to cash in their private fund entitlements on a once-off basis. The purpose is to enable such individuals to do so in whole or in part, from age 60 (or earlier, where retirement is due to ill health), with a view to eliminating or minimising the chargeable excess that would otherwise arise when their public service pension rights crystallise. The exercise of this option attracts income tax (which is ring-fenced) at the point of encashment on the full value of the rights at the individual's marginal rates of tax plus a liability to Universal Social Charge at 4 per cent. In general, no tax-exempt lump sum can be taken from a scheme in respect of which the encashment option has been exercised. The administrator of the scheme will be primarily responsible for deducting and remitting the tax due on encashment to the Revenue Commissioners. Transitional arrangements apply to affected individuals who may have drawn down their private sector pensions before 8 February 2012, but who remain members of a public sector scheme on or after that date.

Given the complex and specialised nature of these provisions, space does not permit further discussion of the detailed measures which they contain.

Penalties

TCA 1997, s 787TB as inserted by Finance (No 2) Act 2013 imposes a penalty of €3,000 on a person who fails to comply with any of the obligations imposed on that person under Pt 30, Ch 2C and Sch 23B. The penalty of €3,000 applies to each failure.

16.505 Limit on lump sums

A lump sum is a sum that is paid to an individual under the rules of a relevant pension arrangement by means of commutation of part of a pension or annuity. For 2011 and subsequent years the lifetime tax free lump sum limit will be €200,000. The excess over the tax free limit is subject to a flat rate tax of 20 per cent under Sch D Case IV, up to an amount of €300,000 (previously €375,000 pre-1 January 2014); this excess does not form part of the individual's total income. The administrator of the relevant pension arrangements and the individual are liable for the income tax on this excess and their liability is joint and several. The administrator must submit a return on Form 790AA to the Collector General and pay the tax by EFT within three months of the end of the month in which the lump sum is paid. The administrator will normally deduct the tax from the lump sum paid to the individual or (less likely) can seek a reimbursement thereof; if the administrator bears the cost of the tax this will be treated as an addition to the lump-sum. Any excess over a sum of €500,000 (€575,000 up to 1 January 2014) is included in the taxpayer's total income and consequently subject to tax at his marginal rate. This excess is subject to the operation of PAYE by the administrator. The scheme administrator is obliged to deduct tax from the excess payment at the higher rate of tax for the year in question unless he has received a certificate of tax credits and standard rate cut off point or a tax deduction card in respect of the individual for the year.

In the case of the first lump sum paid to the individual on or after 7 December 2005 the excess lump sum is the amount by which the current lump sum exceeds the lump sum limit. Where one or more lump sums were paid on or after 7 December 2005 but before the current lump sum is paid then:

(a) where the amount of the earlier lump sum is less than the lump sum limit, the excess lump sum is the amount by which the earlier lump sum(s) and the current lump sum exceed the limit; and

(b) where the earlier lump sum is equal to or greater than the lump sum limit, the excess lump sum is the amount of the current lump sum.

Where lump sums are paid on the same day but at different times, the earlier sum shall be treated as being paid first. If two or more lump sums are paid simultaneously, the individual can decide the order in which they are deemed to have been paid. The restriction on lump sum benefits does not apply to death-in-service benefits which may be payable to the widow, widower, surviving civil partner, children, dependents or personal representatives or children of a civil partner of a deceased individual. As outlined at **16.110** TCA 1997, s 781 charges income tax on a commutation of an entire pension in excess of the normally commutable amount. TCA 1997, s 790AA does not override s 781. The impact of this is that the commutation of pension benefits in excess of the lump sum limit will be exposed to double tax.

16.6 Overseas Pension Plans: Migrant Member Relief

16.601 Overview

TCA 1997, Pt 30, Ch 2B provides a statutory scheme of relief for contributions paid by a migrant worker or their employer to a qualifying overseas pension plan. The purpose of this chapter is to allow the migrant worker who comes to the State to continue to contribute to a pre-existing overseas pension plan concluded in another EU Member State. The provisions in the chapter are effective from 1 January 2005.

16.602 Definitions

The relief applies to contributions made to a qualifying overseas pension plan. An overseas pension plan means a contract, an agreement, a series of agreements, a trust deed or other arrangements, other than a state social security scheme, which is established in, or entered into under the law of, a Member State of the European Communities, other than the State. A qualifying overseas pension plan is an overseas pension plan:

- (i) which is established in good faith for the sole purpose of providing retirement benefits similar to retirement benefit schemes (Ch 1), retirement annuity contracts (Ch 2) or PRSA's (Ch 2A);
- (ii) in respect of which tax relief is available for contributions paid under the law of the EU Member State in which the plan is established; and
- (iii) in relation to which the migrant member of the plan provides certain supporting evidence and information to the Revenue Commissioners.

The Revenue Commissioners will not have a role in approving an overseas plan as this will have been set up on the basis of the laws of the EU Member State in which it was established. The inclusion of the 'sole purpose' test in the definition of qualifying overseas pension plan enables the Revenue Commissioners to deny relief for contributions paid to an overseas pension plan if they are not satisfied that the scheme is set up for the sole purpose of providing retirement benefits.

Relief is given in respect of contributions made by or on behalf of a relevant migrant member of a qualifying overseas pension plan. A relevant migrant member is defined as an individual who:

- (i) is a resident of Ireland;
- (ii) was a resident of another EU Member State at the time he or she first became a member of the plan and was entitled to tax relief on contributions paid under the plan under the law of that Member State;
- (iii) was a member of the plan at the beginning of the year in which the individual became a resident of Ireland;
- (iv) was resident outside of the State for a continuous period of three years immediately before becoming a resident of the State; and
- (v) is a national of an EU Member State or, if not, was resident in an EU Member State immediately before becoming a resident of the State.

TCA 1997, s 787N(2) gives discretion to the Revenue Commissioners to treat an individual as a relevant migrant member notwithstanding that he or she was not resident outside the State for a continuous period of three years immediately before becoming resident of Ireland.

In order to comprise a qualifying overseas pension plan the relevant migrant member is required to provide certain supporting evidence and information to the Revenue Commissioners. TCA 1997, s 787M(2) outlines these requirements. The migrant member is required to provide such evidence as the Revenue Commissioners may reasonably require to verify that the plan is established for the sole purpose of providing retirement benefits and that the contributions to the plan are eligible for tax relief in the Member State in which the plan is established. The member is also required to make the following specific information in relation to the plan available:

- (i) the name, address and tax reference number of the institution operating or managing the plan;
- (ii) the policy reference number;
- (iii) the date on which the relevant migrant member became a member of the plan;
- (iv) the date on which the first contribution was paid to the plan; and
- (v) the date on which the benefits under the plan first become payable.

The migrant member would obtain this information from the administrator of the plan. The Revenue Commissioners can seek this information in such form and manner as they can specify which would enable them to request, for example, to have the documents made available in English.

TCA 1997, s 787M(2)(b) requires the relevant migrant member to irrevocably instruct the administrator of the plan to provide to Revenue such information as they may reasonably require in relation to any payments made under the plan. Payments under the plan will be taxable in Ireland if the relevant migrant member is resident here at the time the payments are made. TCA 1997, s 787N(3) gives Revenue the power to seek information on the payments by way of notice in writing to the administrator.

A certificate of contributions is required in order to claim tax relief for the contribution. Such a certificate would set out the following information:

- (i) the relevant migrant member's name, address, PPS number and policy reference number;
- (ii) the contributions paid by the relevant migrant member under the plan in that year; and
- (iii) where relevant, the contributions if any paid by the relevant migrant member's employer.

16.603 Relief for contributions

TCA 1997, s 787N(1) provides that where a relevant migrant member makes contributions to a qualifying overseas pension plan or where contributions are made in respect of such a member by their employer, then, where the relevant migrant member has provided a certificate of contributions to the Revenue Commissioners, relief will be available on such contributions under the relevant provisions of TCA 1997, Pt 30 Ch 1, 2 or 2A as the case may be, and with any necessary modifications:

- (i) as if the qualifying overseas pension plan was an exempt approved scheme (ie retirement benefits scheme), approved annuity contract or approved PRSA product under those Chapters; and

(ii) as if the relevant migrant member was an employee or an individual referred to in those Chapters.

The earnings limit for 2014 of €115,000 applies to the aggregate of all income in respect of which contributions to occupational pension schemes, retirement annuity contracts, PRSAs and overseas pension plans can be made (TCA 1997, s 790A).

16.7 Purchased Life Annuities

16.701 Definition

In the ordinary way, any person to whom an annuity is payable by any other person receives it as taxed income, ie as a net amount after the person paying it has deducted income tax at the standard rate from the full (or gross) amount of the annuity. TCA 1997, Pt 30, Ch 3 provides for 'purchased life annuities' which are treated for income tax purposes as containing both a capital (non-taxable) element and an income element (taxable). This recognises the fact that, when an annuity has been purchased for a full consideration, the payments made annually to the annuitant consist partly of a repayment of the purchase consideration and partly of income derived by the immediate investment of the full purchase consideration by the grantor of the annuity.

In order for this favourable tax treatment to apply to any annuity, it must be a purchased life annuity to which TCA 1997, s 788 applies. A 'purchased life annuity' is defined in TCA 1997, s 788(1) as a life annuity granted for a consideration in money or money's worth in the ordinary course of a business of granting annuities on human life. In effect, this means that a purchased life annuity within TCA 1997, s 788 is almost invariably one acquired from a life assurance company.

A 'life annuity' is defined in the same subsection as:

> an annuity payable for a term ending with (or at a time ascertainable only by reference to) the end of a human life, whether or not there is provision for the annuity to end during the life on the expiration of a fixed term or on the happening of any event or otherwise, or to continue after the end of the life in particular circumstances.

TCA 1997, s 788(2) excludes from the application of the section certain annuities which, even if purchased from a life assurance company, must always be treated fully as taxable income in the hands of the annuitant. These excluded annuities – which should not, therefore, be treated as including any capital (non-taxable) element – are:

(a) any annuity where the whole or part of the consideration for the grant of the annuity consisted of premiums qualifying for retirement annuity relief under TCA 1997, s 787 (see **16.2**);

(b) any annuity purchased under a direction in a will, or to provide for an annuity payable under a will or settlement out of income of property disposed of by the will or settlement;

(c) any annuity purchased under or for the purposes of any sponsored superannuation scheme (see **16.202**), or any trust scheme approved under TCA 1997, s 784 (see **16.205**);

(d) any annuity purchased by any person in recognition of another person's services (or past services) in any office or employment (eg an annuity provided by an employer by way of an *ex gratia* pension);

(e) any annuity which, under the ordinary tax rules relating to annuities and other annual payments, would be treated as including the payment or repayment of a capital sum (eg the discharge of the purchase price for a business by means of an annuity);

(f) any annuity where the whole or part of the consideration for the grant of the annuity consisted of assets which, at the time of application of the said assets for the purchase of the annuity, were assets in an approved retirement fund, within the meaning of TCA 1997, s 784A, or in an approved minimum retirement fund, within the meaning of TCA 1997, s 784C; or

(g) Any annuity where the whole or part of the consideration for the grant of the annuity consisted of assets which, at the time of the application of the said assets for the purchase of the annuity, were PRSA assets (see **16.3**).

It may be noted that any purchased life annuity within the TCA 1997, s 788(1) definition, other than any annuity excluded by TCA 1997, s 788(2), qualifies for the capital or income treatment. Unlike the requirement for qualifying premiums entitled to tax relief under TCA 1997, s 787 payable to secure a retirement annuity, it is not essential that the business of granting annuities on human life be one carried on in the State by a life assurance company (or other person). The purchased life annuity may be one purchased from a foreign life company carrying on its business wholly abroad.

16.702 Capital and income elements

A purchased life annuity to which TCA 1997, s 788 applies (ie one other than an annuity excluded by TCA 1997, s 788(2)) is, for all purposes of the Income Tax Acts relating to tax on annuities and other annual payments, treated as containing a capital element. This has the following consequences:

(a) the capital element is not treated as an annual payment;

(b) the person who purchased the life annuity and who receives its payment each year excludes the capital element of the annuity from his total income and, therefore, is not chargeable to any income tax on it;

(c) the recipient of the annuity must, however, treat the balance of the annuity, ie the income element, as income chargeable to income tax in the ordinary way; and

(d) the person paying the annuity (normally a life assurance company) is entitled to deduct the full annuity (including the capital element) in computing profits, gains or losses chargeable to tax in any circumstances where he would be entitled to deduct a lump sum payment.

TCA 1997, s 788(4) requires the amount of the capital element in any purchased life annuity within the section to be determined by reference to the amount or value of the consideration paid for the grant of the annuity. The proportion which the capital element bears to the total amount of the annuity must be a constant proportion for all payments on account of the same annuity.

If the term and the amount of the annuity depend only on the duration of a human life or lives, the capital element is to represent the same proportion of each annuity payment which the total value of the consideration for the grant of the annuity bears to the actuarial value of the annuity payments. If either the term or the amount of the annuity depends partly on any other contingency, the capital element is to be the proportion of the whole annuity that may be just having regard to all the circumstances.

In fact, the calculation of the capital element by reference to the actuarial value of the annuity payments is a complex technical matter. TCA 1997, s 788(5)(c) provides that the actuarial value of the annuity payments is to be taken as their value as at the date when the first of the payments begin to accrue. That actuarial value is to be determined by reference to the tables of mortality prescribed by the Revenue Commissioners in the regulations relating to purchased life annuities. If the one consideration is given both for the grant of an annuity and for something else, any necessary apportionment of the consideration must be made.

The life assurance company from which any purchased life annuity within TCA 1997, s 788 was acquired must, if it made the annuity contract in the course of a business carried on in the State, deduct income tax on making any payment on account of the annuity. However, it only deducts income tax (at the standard rate) from the income element of the annuity, ie from the balance of the payment after subtracting the capital element. The recipient must include in his total income, as taxed income for the year in which each payment is received, an amount equal to the income element of each such payment (ie the gross income element before the deduction of tax by the payer).

In the event that a purchased life annuity within TCA 1997, s 788 is received by a resident individual from a foreign source, again the recipient only brings the income element into his income for tax purposes. Should it happen that the foreign payer has deducted foreign tax from the full annuity under the tax laws of the country of source, any credit or other relief against Irish tax for the foreign tax suffered is restricted to the proportion of that tax attributable to the income element of the annuity.

16.703 Uses of purchased life annuities

The two most frequently purchased life annuities, the rules of which are outlined in TCA 1997, Pt 30, Ch 3 are discussed briefly. First, there is the purchase by an individual, usually a person who has passed middle age, of an annuity to be payable for the rest of his life. Secondly, a purchased life annuity may be used as the basis of shorter term investment. In each type of case, the purchaser of the annuity receives his return in a form that includes a tax free capital element. Although both forms involve the purchase of a life annuity, it is proposed to distinguish them in the following discussion by referring to them respectively as an 'annuity for life' and a 'shorter term annuity investment'.

The individual purchasing an annuity for life pays a capital sum to a life assurance company which contracts, in exchange, to pay the purchaser an annuity of a stated amount for the rest of his life. Normally, there is no provision for any part of the purchase price to be repaid, but the contract may provide for the annuity to be paid for a guaranteed period, eg for 10 years, so that if the annuitant should die before the end of the term provided, his heirs or personal representatives may continue to receive the annuity payments or may be able to commute for a capital sum the annuity payments still due to be made within the term certain.

For the older purchaser of a life annuity, the capital element constitutes a high proportion of each payment on account of the annuity. The capital proportion increases progressively depending on the age of the purchaser at the time of purchase. The rates of annuity payable per (say) €1,000 invested vary with the prevailing interest rates and other factors relevant at the time of purchase.

Example 16.703.1

Mrs Old, aged 70 on her last birthday on 31 December 2014, purchased a life annuity for a capital sum of €50,000 on 1 January 2015. The life assurance company contracts to pay her a life annuity of €6,400 containing a capital element of €3,540, but the contract is for a guaranteed period of five years (in contrast to the type of annuity assumed in the table). The annuity is payable half-yearly on 30 June and 31 December. Assume that Mrs Old, a widow, has already sufficient taxable income to be liable at the top rate of income tax on any additional income. The additional income tax payable by her in the tax year 2015 as a result of the annuity is computed as follows:

	€
Annuity payable (gross)	6,400
Less:	
Capital element	3,540
Taxable part of annuity (income element)	2,860
Income tax payable:	
€2,860 at 40% (top rate)	1,144
Less:	
Tax deducted by payer	
€2,860 at 20%	572
Net income tax due	572

There are two main forms of shorter term annuity investment – the guaranteed income bond and the guaranteed growth bond, but only the income bond normally involves the payment of any annuity. The growth bond involves the application of the purchaser's capital payment to purchase a deferred life annuity not to become payable before the end of a specified period of years. It contains a cash option which permits the purchaser to take a capital sum at the end of the specified period in exchange for his right to the annuity due to commence at that time. Should the deferred annuity be taken up in lieu of the cash option, the rules relating to that annuity having a capital and income element start to apply to the annuity then becoming payable. If the holder of a growth bond takes the cash option at the end of the specified investment period, he is paid a tax free capital sum which is guaranteed by the life assurance company and stated in the annuity bond issued to him shortly after the purchase of the bond. This cash sum represents the repayment of the original purchase consideration plus 'rolled up' interest over the investment period. In the case of the growth bond, no payments are made to the holder during this period. However, should he die before the end of the period, the terms of a normal growth bond are likely to entitle his personal representatives to be paid the original purchase money invested plus a certain amount in respect of interest to the date of death. This 'death benefit' is also free of income tax and capital gains tax.

In the case of a guaranteed income bond, the purchase consideration paid to the life assurance company is applied by the company in two parts. One part purchases a temporary annuity which becomes payable immediately (but usually six months in arrears) to the purchaser. The annuity is expressed as being payable during the lifetime of the annuitant (thus falling within the 'life annuity' definition of TCA 1997, s 788 – see **16.701** but provides for the payments on account of the annuity to cease at the end of a stated number of years (ie at the end of the 'investment' period). If the investment period is, say, five years, the purchaser therefore receives the temporary annuity for this five-year period only. Each payment on account of the temporary annuity is received as payment of a purchased life annuity within TCA 1997, s 788 so that only the income element in each payment is taxable as the income of the recipient.

The second part of the purchase consideration is applied to purchase a deferred annuity due to commence at the end of the investment period. As with the deferred annuity in the case of the guaranteed growth bond, the purchaser has the right to take a guaranteed cash sum at the end of the investment period in lieu of the deferred annuity. Alternatively, he may take the deferred annuity which is payable for the rest of his life after the end of the investment period. Any such annuity taken is again a purchased annuity within TCA 1997, s 788 containing both capital and an income element and is taxed accordingly in each year in which received.

In the case of the income bond, the guaranteed cash sum that may be taken at the end of the investment period instead of the deferred annuity is usually an amount equal to the actual sum invested originally to purchase the annuity bond. In effect, it gives the investor the refund of his original capital invested and is not subject to any tax in his hands. The cash used to fund the payments of the temporary annuity during the investment period is, in effect, the interest which the life assurance company earns on the purchase consideration invested. These payments represent the return to the investor on his outlay which, as indicated, is then repaid to him in full through the exercise of the cash option.

16.704 Administrative matters

TCA 1997, s 789(1) requires the inspector of taxes to determine whether an annuity is a purchased life annuity to which TCA 1997, s 788 applies and, if so, to determine what is the capital element in the annuity. Any person aggrieved by the decision of the inspector on either of these matters is entitled to appeal within the prescribed time to the Appeal Commissioners. F(TA)A 2015, s 38, which was subject to Ministerial Order (SI 110/2016 appointed 21 March 2016 as the day on which the Finance (Tax Appeals) Act 2015, came into operation) amends the above and notes that any person aggrieved by any determination of the inspector on any such question may appeal the determination to the Appeal Commissioners, in accordance with s 949I, within the period of 30 days after the date of the notice of that determination. TCA 1997, s 789(3) authorises the Revenue Commissioners to make regulations prescribing the procedure to be adopted for giving effect to the rules of TCA 1997, Pt 30, Ch 3 including the time limit for appeal against the inspector's decision.

The Regulations

The Income Tax (Purchased Life Annuities) Regulations 1959 (SI 152/1959) operate to prescribe rules for implementing TCA 1997, s 788 (which was originally FA 1959, s 22). Among the matters covered in these regulations are:

(a) a claim for the application of TCA 1997, s 788 to an annuity must be made in writing to the inspector by the payee (ie by the person beneficially entitled to the payments on account of the annuity (reg 2);

(b) the inspector may then require the payer of the annuity to furnish such particulars relating to the annuity as he may require to make his determination in the matter (reg 4);

(c) on receipt of the payee's claim, the inspector is required to determine whether the annuity is a purchased life annuity to which TCA 1997, s 788 applies and, if so, to determine what proportion of each payment on account of the annuity constitutes the capital element (reg 5).

This regulation prescribes the tables of mortality to be used in making the necessary actuarial calculations – TCA 1997, s 788, see **16.702** – as being the select tables in the volume of tables published in 1953 at the University Press, Cambridge for the Institute of Actuaries and the Faculty of Actuaries, entitled 'The a (55) Tables for Annuitants'.

The inspector is required to give a notice of his determination ('the original determination') to the payee and (normally) to the payer of the annuity.

(d) If the payee is dissatisfied with the determination of the inspector, he is entitled to give notice to the inspector of his intention to appeal against the determination. This notice of intention to appeal must be given within 21 days from the date of the service of the inspector's notice of determination. It must also specify the grounds of the appeal (reg 6).

If this appeal under regulation 6 is not withdrawn or settled by agreement, it is to be heard by the Appeal Commissioners who, for the purpose, have all the powers they would have in relation to an appeal against an income tax assessment under Sch D.

(e) If the original determination by the inspector is amended on appeal, any amount of tax overpaid by the payee, whether by deduction or by assessment on him, in respect of payments on account of the annuity based on the original determination is to be repaid to the payee. If the payee has underpaid tax due to the amendment of the original determination by the Appeal Commissioners, the inspector is required to recover the tax underpaid by assessing the payee under Sch D Case IV for each relevant tax year (reg 13).

The payer is required to implement the inspector's determination immediately once he has been notified in accordance with reg 5 as to whether or not the annuity is a purchased life annuity within TCA 1997, s 788 and of the capital element (if any) of the annuity. The payer must then deduct income tax on the income element of all payments on account of the annuity, whether or not the inspector's original determination is to be the subject of an appeal to the Appeal Commissioners (TCA 1997, s 788(6)). As prescribed by reg 13, if this results in an incorrect tax charge having regard to the outcome of the subsequent appeal, the tax overpayment or underpayment is adjusted retrospectively.

In the event that the payer is making any payment on account of a purchased life annuity and has not received any notification from the inspector as to the amount of the capital element, he is required to deduct income tax at the standard rate from the full amount of the payment (TCA 1997, s 788(7)). This makes it all the more important that the claim by the payee to have the annuity treated as a purchased life annuity within TCA 1997, s 788 should be made at the earliest possible date. In practice, the payee's claim to have the annuity treated as a purchased life annuity under TCA 1997, s 788 is usually drawn up for his signature by the life company or other person granting the annuity (or by any professional brokers acting on behalf of the payee) at the time he pays the purchase consideration.

A form PLA1 is used for the payee's claim for TCA 1997, s 788 treatment of his purchased life annuity. Part A of the form must be completed and signed by the payee. It gives personal details of the payee including his name, address, income tax district reference number, etc and requires confirmation that the source of the annuity is not such that it would prevent the rules of TCA 1997, s 788 from applying. Part B, which is a declaration of the amount of the annuity and a statement of the payer's calculation of the capital element contained in it, is completed and signed by the payer of the annuity.

The completed form is then sent to the claimant's district inspector. If satisfied that the annuity is one to which the section applies and that the capital element in part B is correctly stated, the inspector should give his notice of determination to this effect to the payee (with a copy to the payer). Since the amount of the capital element is taken directly from the prescribed annuity tables, the approval of a claim submitted by a recognised life assurance company is, in practice, given almost automatically.

Regulation 15 deals with the case of a foreign payer of a purchased life annuity. For this purpose, a foreign payer is a person granting the annuity in the ordinary course of a business of granting annuities on human life, but who is not resident in the State and pays the annuity other than through a branch or agency of his business in the State. A non-resident life assurance company paying the annuity through a branch or agency in the State is treated as any other payer in accordance with the rules already mentioned. In effect, reg 15 applies the other regulations, with relatively minor modifications, in the same way to a foreign payer as to any other payer. In other words, any resident payee who wishes to have the foreign annuity treated as a purchased life annuity containing a capital element under TCA 1997, s 788 must make the appropriate claim to his inspector of taxes with all the necessary particulars.

The foreign payer does not have any obligation to deduct and account for Irish income tax to the Revenue Commissioners when making any payment on account of the annuity. The possibility that the annuity may suffer a foreign withholding tax in the payer's country has already been mentioned. The foreign paid annuity may, however, suffer the deduction of Irish income tax by the paying bank collecting the annuity under the rules of Sch D (see **2.310**). Since any such deduction by the paying agent will not have distinguished the capital element of the annuity, reg 16 provides for the repayment to the payee of any excess income tax suffered by deduction in this way.

TCA 1997, s 789(5) provides for a penalty of €3,000 which may be imposed in the event that any person knowingly makes any false statement or false representation, whether for the purpose of obtaining for himself or for any other person any relief from or repayment of tax under the purchased life annuity rules of TCA 1997, Pt 30, Ch 3.

Division 17 Anti-Avoidance

17.1 Transactions in Securities etc

17.101 Introduction

The Income Tax Acts contain various anti-avoidance rules designed to prevent persons chargeable to income tax or corporation tax from obtaining tax advantages from different types of transaction involving the purchase and sale of stocks, shares and other securities. The terms 'bond washing', 'dividend stripping' and 'reverse bond washing' are sometimes used to refer to the types of transaction in question, but – in the author's view – these terms are frequently loosely applied and do not always convey exactly what is involved. It is not, therefore, intended to do more than mention them here. In dealing with the rules relevant to the different types of transaction, it is more appropriate to describe the effects of the sections in the Income Tax Acts dealing with each.

Some of the rules have already been dealt with in **Division 8**. It is now proposed to cover the remaining rules in this Division. For the sake of completeness it may be useful to enumerate here the various sections in the Acts containing anti-avoidance rules relating to transactions in securities (using the word 'securities' in the broad sense to include all stocks, shares and securities). The various provisions and the places in this work where they are dealt with are as follows:

Statute	*General heading*	*Reference*
TCA 1997, ss 748–751	purchase and sale (ex div) of securities	**17.102–17.103**
TCA 1997, ss 752–753	purchase of shares by share dealers and exempted persons	**17.104**
TCA 1997, s 812	transfer of right to receive interest, etc from securities	**8.210**
TCA 1997, s 815	sales of government securities cum div	**8.213**

The two sets of rules now to be discussed – those respectively of TCA 1997, ss 748–751 and of TCA 1997, ss 752–753 – have several features in common. Each set of rules concerns a dealer in shares and securities (a 'share dealer') and concerns ways in which an artificial trading loss (or reduction in trading profits) may be created so that, in the absence of anti-avoidance rules, the share dealer would be able to obtain relief for that loss so as to secure a tax advantage which the legislature did not intend him to have.

Each set of rules also deals with persons exempted from income tax (eg a charity or an approved pension scheme) who might otherwise be able to obtain an unintended repayment of income tax deducted from interest on securities. These rules also covered the repayment of tax credits attaching to Sch F income for periods up to 5 April 1999. There are also provisions to prevent a person carrying on a non-share dealing trade from obtaining relief for trading losses against income created by the type of scheme covered by these rules.

17.102 Purchase and sale (ex div) of securities

The anti-avoidance rules of TCA 1997, ss 748–751 apply only where *all* of the following conditions are met:

(a) if a person purchases any 'securities' and subsequently resells them ex div, ie so that the person in question – referred to as 'the first buyer' – is entitled to receive the 'interest' becoming payable on the securities sold;

(b) if the time elapsing between the purchase of the securities by the first buyer and his taking steps to dispose of them does not exceed one month (or, in any case where the purchase and sale are not genuine transactions each effected at current market price, six months); and

(c) the first buyer is either:
   (i) a dealer in securities within TCA 1997, s 749,
   (ii) a person otherwise exempted from income tax in respect of the interest (eg a charity), or
   (iii) a person carrying on a trade not within TCA 1997, s 749 otherwise entitled to obtain relief for a trading loss by set off against his total income (including the interest).

For the purpose of these rules, the term 'securities' includes stocks and shares. The term 'interest' includes a distribution as defined for the purposes of the Corporation Tax Acts as well as all other dividends.

In measuring the time elapsing between the date of the purchase of the securities and the date the first buyer takes steps to dispose of them, the latter date is normally the actual date of the sale. However, if the first buyer sold the securities in the exercise of an option he had acquired to do so, he is regarded as taking steps to dispose of them on the date he acquired the option (TCA 1997, s 748(5)(a)). In order for the shorter one-month period to be brought into play it is necessary that the Revenue Commissioners be of the opinion that the purchase and the sale were each effected at current market prices, and that the sale was not effected pursuant to an agreement or arrangement made before, or at, the time of the purchase (TCA 1997, s 748(3)(b)).

The sale may be either of the same securities purchased or of similar securities (TCA 1997, s 748(6)(a)). Similar securities are those which entitle the holder to the same rights against the same persons as to capital and interest and the same remedies for the enforcement of those rights, notwithstanding any difference in the total nominal amounts of the respective securities or in the form in which they are held (TCA 1997, s 748(1)).

Where parcels of similar securities are bought at different times, any subsequent sale of any of the similar securities are, so far as may be, related to the securities purchased on a 'last in first out' basis (TCA 1997, s 648(6)(a)). However, a person who sells similar securities is not taxable to a greater extent than if he had sold the original securities (TCA 1997, s 748(6)(b)).

When the first two conditions above are met, ie where the sale which leaves the first buyer with the right to receive the interest is not made more than one month (or, if necessary, more than six months) after the purchase, it is then necessary to apply whichever of the charging sections TCA 1997, ss 749–751 as is relevant (if any of them is). Each of these sections operates, in their respective ways, to disallow the tax benefit which the first buyer would otherwise obtain as a result of the transaction.

The separate rules require either an add back (TCA 1997, s 749), an exclusion from exempted income (TCA 1997, s 750) or an exclusion from income available to relieve a loss (TCA 1997, s 751), of the appropriate amount of the interest receivable by the first buyer. For these purposes, the 'appropriate amount' is taken as defined in TCA 1997, Sch 21. While the rules for determining the appropriate amount of any interest vary slightly depending on whether the rules of TCA 1997, s 749 or, alternatively, the rules of either TCA 1997, s 750 or 751 apply, the common object in every case is to arrive at (and to disallow from relief) the element of accrued interest in the original purchase price of the securities sold.

Two types of securities are distinguished in the 'appropriate amount' computation rules of TCA 1997, Sch 21. First, there are those stocks, shares, and securities which are quoted on a stock exchange at prices which include the accrued interest element without separating it from the underlying capital price of the security. This includes all shares of companies and most other securities except those falling within the second category. It also includes all other unquoted shares and securities. In all cases of securities within this first category, the appropriate amount of the interest receivable by the first buyer is determined as being the 'appropriate proportion' of the interest becoming payable.

TCA 1997, Sch 21, para 3 provides the rules for computing the appropriate proportion of any interest within this first category. While the 'appropriate amount' (the disallowable amount) in a TCA 1997, s 749 application requires the appropriate proportion of the net interest to be taken and TCA 1997, ss 749 and 751 deal with the appropriate proportion of the gross interest, the rules of TCA 1997, Sch 21, para 3 are common to both and may, therefore, be explained here. The procedure for computing the appropriate proportion of any interest (whether net or gross) may be condensed to the following formula:

$$\text{interest (or distribution)} \times \frac{\text{length of period A}}{\text{length of period B}}$$

where:

A = the number of days *between* the earliest date on which the securities could have been quoted 'ex div' in respect of the last interest paid before the interest included in the first buyer's purchase price began to accrue, *and* the day before the first buyer purchased the securities; and

B = the number of days *between* the first date referred to in the definition of period A, *and* the day before the earliest date on which the securities could have been quoted 'ex div' in respect of the interest receivable by the first buyer.

In any case where the interest receivable by the first buyer was the first interest (or distribution) payable in respect of the securities, the opening date of both period A and period B in the above formula is to be taken as the first day of the period for which the interest (or distribution) was payable. If the full capital amount of the relevant securities was not paid up at the beginning of that period, there are further rules in TCA 1997, Sch 21, para 3(3) to deal with this position. Further, if the securities involved are not the subject of a quotation in the official list of the Dublin Stock Exchange, the Appeal Commissioners are empowered by TCA 1997, Sch 21, para 3(4) to prescribe the appropriate periods to be taken respectively as period A and period B. F(TA)A 2015, s 41, which was subject to Ministerial Order (SI 110/2016 appointed 21 March 2016 as the day on which the Finance (Tax Appeals) Act 2015, came into operation), amends para 3(4) above to put the calculation of interest payable on certain securities on a self-assessment basis by removing the reference to the opinion of the Appeal Commissioners.

TCA 1997, Sch 21, para 4 deals with the second category of securities. It applies where the securities that are the subject of the purchase and sale within these provisions are securities of a kind which, in accordance with usual practice, are sold at a bargain price which is increased by reference to gross interest accruing before the bargain date. This rule does not refer to all securities which pay interest without the deduction of tax, but it relates to those short dated government and similar securities which are, by stock exchange practice, quoted at all times at the underlying 'capital' price plus (or minus) '*n*' days' interest. In these cases, '*n*' is the number of days between the date of the payment of the previous half-year's interest and the date of the relevant bargain.

In any case of any securities in this second category, TCA 1997, Sch 21, para 4 requires the appropriate amount of the interest (the amount of relief disallowed) to be taken as the actual increase in the bargain price made for the number of days' gross interest added on. Since this is an accurate determination of the actual accrued interest element (already separated from any variations in the underlying capital value of the securities), no apportionment calculation is necessary. In practice, it is understood that the Dublin Stock Exchange quotes all government securities in this way if they have less than five years to run before their maturity date.

Example 17.102.1

The trustees of the exempt approved pension scheme of Old and New Enterprises Ltd purchased €10,000 nominal of a short dated 12 per cent government stock on 17 August 2015 at a bargain price of 98 plus 140 days' interest. The security went *ex div* on 24 August 2015 prior to the payment of the half-yearly interest due on 30 September 2015. The trustees of the pension scheme sold its entire €10,000 of the security on 1 September 2015 at a sales price of 98.15 minus 30 days interest.

The financial results of this transaction are as follows:

		€
Sale of security 1/9/2015: 10,000 @ 98.15		9,815
Less:		
Adjustment to bargain price: €10,000 x 12% x 30/365 (30 days' interest)		99
Final sales price		9,716
Purchase of security (17/8/2015): 10,000 x 98	9,800	
Add:		
Adjustment to bargain price: €10,000 x 12% x 140/365 (140 days' interest)	460	
Final purchase price		(10,260)
Loss on sale of security		(544)
Interest received on security sold: €10,000 x 12% x 6/12 (half-year's interest payable 30/9/2015)		600
Net book gain on transaction		56

Since the purchase and sale resulting in the payment of the 30 September 2015 interest to the trustees were within one month of each other, and as the trustees are exempt from income tax in respect of the pension scheme investment income under TCA 1997, s 774 (see **16.111**), the provisions of TCA 1997, s 748–751 are applicable. Therefore, it is necessary to deal under that section with the 'appropriate amount' in respect of the 30 September 2015 interest receivable by the trustees.

TCA 1997, Sch 21, para 4 applies in this case as the securities are of the kind (maturity within five years) where the bargain price is increased by reference to the gross interest accruing before the bargain date for the purchase. The 'appropriate amount' is, therefore, €460 – ie the 140 days' accrued interest to the date of purchase added to the bargain price.

For the treatment under TCA 1997, s 750 of the trustees of the pension scheme in respect of this amount, see Example **17.103**.1.

With effect in respect of securities purchased on or after 1 January 2003, TCA 1997, s 749 will not apply to short term purchases of Irish Government securities or overseas securities where these are purchased in the ordinary course of the dealer's trade and all of the interest is taken into account as a trading receipt in computing the dealer's profits for the chargeable period. Additionally, in the case of overseas securities the dealer must elect in writing, by return filing date for the chargeable period in question, that credit for foreign tax on those securities, which might otherwise be due under a double taxation agreement or under any unilateral or other provision, is not to be allowed. This election is to be made annually in writing and submitted along with the dealer's self-assessment tax return (TCA 1997, s 749(2A)).

17.103 The rules of TCA 1997, ss 749–751

TCA 1997, ss 749–751 deal with the taxation of the first buyer who is respectively a dealer in securities, a person exempted from tax, and a person carrying on a trade (other than as a dealer in securities) who claims relief for a trading loss against his total income. The three sections are now examined separately as to how each of them deals with the 'appropriate amount' of the relevant interest (as determined in the manner explained in **17.102**).

Dealers in securities

TCA 1997, s 749 applies to the case of the first buyer who carries on a trade consisting of dealing in securities. It requires the appropriate amount in respect of the interest (or distribution) becoming payable, as a result of the purchase and sale transaction, to be deducted from the purchase price paid by the first buyer. Apart from a transaction involving a security within TCA 1997, Sch 21, para 4, the amount of the deduction from the first buyer's purchase price is an amount equal to the appropriate proportion of the *net* interest (TCA 1997, Sch 21, para 1). If the interest is a distribution from a resident company, the purchase price is reduced by the appropriate proportion of the actual distribution (ie before adding the tax credit).

In the absence of this adjustment, the result of the purchase and the sale of the securities would normally be to create an artificial trading loss because the purchase price (including the accrued interest element) exceeds the sales price (which excludes the value of the interest extracted by the securities dealer). On the other hand, the securities dealer has received interest in respect of which he may be able to claim a repayment of income tax deducted at source.

For transactions involving securities paying gross interest and where the bargain price is increased by the actual number of days' accrued interest (ie one within TCA 1997, Sch 21, para 4), the actual accrued interest added to the bargain price (for the first buyer's purchase) is deducted from the purchase price.

In practice, the easiest way of making the adjustment required by TCA 1997, s 749 is simply to credit (ie add back) the appropriate amount of the interest (or distribution) in the share dealer's Sch D Case I computation. By increasing the Sch D Case I profit (or by reducing the loss) by the appropriate amount, this achieves the same result without having to adjust the figure for purchases in the share dealer's accounts.

There are two exceptions to the application of TCA 1997, s 749. First, no reduction in the purchase price of the securities is required if the first buyer is, in the opinion of the Revenue Commissioners, either a member of a stock exchange in the State recognised by the committee of that stock exchange as carrying on the business of a dealer, or a person *bona fide* carrying on the business of a discount house in the State. In either of these cases, the adjustment is not required, provided that the securities are bought in the ordinary course of the share dealing business of the stockbroker or the discount house (TCA 1997, s 749(2)). Secondly, no adjustment under TCA 1997, s 749 is required if the interest (or distribution) is within the anti-avoidance rules of TCA 1997, s 752, in which event the rules of that section apply (see **17.104**).

Persons exempted from tax

TCA 1997, s 750 applies in the case of the first buyer who would otherwise be exempt from tax in respect of the interest received as a result of the transaction. It disallows the exemption to the extent to which it relates to the appropriate amount in respect of the interest. In this case, TCA 1997, Sch 21, para 2 provides that the appropriate amount in respect of the interest is the *grossed up* equivalent of the appropriate proportion of the net interest receivable by the first buyer. Again, this is subject to the exception provided by TCA 1997, Sch 21, para 4 which, when applicable, requires the exempted first buyer to be taxed on the actual gross interest added to the bargain price.

Example 17.103.1

Take the facts of **Example 17.102.1** where the trustees of an exempt approved pension scheme purchased and sold a holding of a short dated 12 per cent government stock at a bargain price increased by the gross interest accruing before the date of the purchase (ie a security within TCA 1997, Sch 21, para 4).

In the absence of TCA 1997, s 750, the pension scheme trustees (exempt from income tax by TCA 1997, s 774) would not be chargeable to income tax (or any other tax) on any part of the ?600 half-yearly interest received on 30 September 2015. However, TCA 1997, s 750 applies so that the trustees of the pension scheme are taxable as follows:

	€
Interest received on stock sold ex div	600
Appropriate amount of 'gross' interest[1] (no longer exempt)	460
Income tax payable (at standard rate)[2]	
460 x 20%	92

Notes:

1. In the event that the interest had been received after the deduction of income tax (which it was not) TCA 1997, s 750 still requires the appropriate amount to be computed by reference to the 'gross' interest (by contrast with the rule in TCA 1997, s 749 which uses the net interest).

2. The fact that the trustees' net book gain on the transaction was only €56 does not prevent the charge to tax on the appropriate amount of €460. The trustees are not entitled to any relief in respect of the €544 loss on the sale of the security (as this is a capital loss).

Other traders with loss claims

TCA 1997, s 751 applies if the first buyer carries on a trade other than one of dealing in securities within TCA 1997, s 749, and claims under TCA 1997, s 381 to set off a loss sustained in that trade against his total income which includes the interest resulting from the transaction. In any such case, in determining the amount of the relief to be given under the TCA 1997, s 381 claim, TCA 1997, s 751 provides that the computation of the repayment takes no account of either the appropriate amount in respect of the interest, or of any tax paid on that appropriate amount.

In applying these rules, TCA 1997, Sch 21, para 2 requires the appropriate amount in respect of the interest to be taken as the gross amount corresponding to the appropriate proportion of the net interest. Again, this is subject to the exception provided by TCA 1997, Sch 21, para 4 which, when applicable, treats the appropriate amount in respect of the interest as being equal to the actual gross interest added to the bargain price.

Where TCA 1997, s 751 applies, it affects the computation of the income tax repayable in respect of the trading loss in two ways. First, it requires the amount of the loss that is deducted in arriving at the taxpayer's total income to be restricted so that the deduction does not exceed the total income (before the loss) as reduced by the 'appropriate amount' in respect of the interest that is within s 751. It does not, however, reduce the full amount of that interest that is included in the taxpayer's total income.

Secondly, in calculating the repayment of tax to be made as a result of the loss claim, the excess of the tax borne in the original computation of tax liability (ie based on total income before deducting any loss) over the tax borne in the final computation (based on the total income as reduced by the loss deducted) must be restricted by an amount equal to the tax paid on the appropriate amount of the relevant interest. In any case where the appropriate amount is in respect of taxed interest it is to be noted that the computation of the repayment should be made before taking any account of the credits against tax due for the income tax suffered at source on the taxed interest.

17.104 Dividends received by share dealers etc out of accumulated profits

TCA 1997, s 752 contains anti-avoidance rules intended primarily to prevent a person carrying on a trade as a dealer in shares or other investments from creating a trading loss (or reducing his Sch D Case I profits) by the device of purchasing shares in a company and by extracting dividends from profits of the company accumulated before he acquired the shares. With the abolition of refundable tax credits in relation to dividends with effect from 6 April 1999, these provisions are now largely obsolete. For a full discussion of these provisions, see the 2002 edition of this book.

17.2 Transfer of Assets Abroad

17.201 Introduction

TCA 1997, s 806 was enacted in its original form (FA 1974, s 57) in an attempt to counter certain forms of offshore tax planning. These exercises typically involved the transfer by resident individuals, usually with relatively high incomes taxable at the higher rates of income tax, of assets and thereby income, to non-resident companies, trustees, etc. This could be done in various ways which resulted in the non-resident person's company receiving the income from the assets (usually in a low tax or nil tax country), but which left the resident individual in a position to benefit directly or indirectly from the income or capital, usually in a tax-free form.

Two examples will illustrate some of the more straightforward strategies involved. Firstly, an individual could transfer funds to a non-resident trust which would invest in non-Irish assets. Accordingly, the trustees would be outside the scope of Irish taxation and they could accumulate the trust income, subject only to overseas taxation (if any). The individual transferring the assets would have no liability to Irish taxation so long as: (i) he was not entitled to the trust income as it arose (see **15.307**); and (ii) the anti-avoidance rules of what are now TCA 1997, Pt 31, Chs 1 & 2 did not apply so as to deem the trust income to be his (see **Division 15**). The individual could in due course arrange for the trustees to distribute the accumulated income to him or to other nominated beneficiaries (typically his spouse or children). A distribution in these circumstances would normally rank as a capital receipt and would thus be outside the scope of income tax.

Alternatively, an individual might incorporate a non-resident company and transfer funds or assets to it, eg in exchange for debentures. The non-resident company would invest in non-Irish assets (or possibly even carry on a non-Irish trade). The income of such a company would of course again fall outside the scope of Irish taxation. The accumulated profits of the company might eventually be extracted, for example, by redemption of the debentures (which could be held by the individual and/or other family members). The redemption of the debentures would not give rise to any income tax consequences. Funds might also be extracted by way of loan, free of any tax liability, unless the recipient was a director or employee of the company, or of a person connected to the company, when a benefit-in-kind charge would arise (see **10.211**).

Following *Vestey v IRC* (discussed further below) it was clear that TCA 1997, s 806 did not catch transfers which did not result in actual or potential benefits accruing to the individual making the transfer or to his spouse.

In the *Vestey* case, Lord Wilberforce stated that 'The UK equivalent of TCA 1997, s 806 was 'directed against persons who transfer assets abroad … attacking those who *removed* assets abroad so as to gain tax advantages while residing in the United Kingdom' (emphasis added).

However, the reasoning in the *Vestey* case was in no way concerned with the geographical situation of the transferred assets. Lord Wilberforce's reference to a 'removal' of assets was clearly no more than a convenient form of shorthand, adopted to avoid repeating the lengthy preamble contained in the section, currently enacted as TCA 1997, s 806(3) in Ireland (see below). The charging provision of TCA 1997, s 806 has been (somewhat belatedly) remedied by the insertion of TCA 1997, s 807A by FA 1999, s 60 with effect from 11 February 1999. These provisions are dealt with in **17.210** below.

TCA 1997, s 806 incorporates a statement of its purpose, previously cast in the form of a 'preamble' or 'foreword' in the antecedent legislation (FA 1974, s 57), which requires to be read with, and used to help interpret, the main charging rules. It is worth quoting in full:

This section shall apply for the purpose of preventing the avoiding by individuals *resident or* ordinarily resident in the State of liability to tax by means of transfers of assets by virtue or in consequence whereof, either alone or in conjunction with associated operations, income becomes payable to persons resident or domiciled out of the State. (TCA 1997, s 806(3)).

The words in italics, which greatly extend the potential scope of the section, take effect in relation to income arising on or after 12 February 1998 (FA 1998, s 12(1)(a)(i), (2)). The section as it previously applied (ie to ordinarily resident individuals only) is discussed in the 1997/98 edition of this book. The question of when income arises should it seems be decided by reference to normal Irish tax law principles (see *Chetwode v IRC* [1977] STC 64, discussed at **17.209**).

This preamble, when read with the two charging subsections, spells out the conditions which must be met before TCA 1997, s 806 can apply. These can be summarised as follows:

(a) there must be a transfer of assets (here referred to as *'the relevant transfer'*);

(b) the relevant transfer must have been made by an individual resident or ordinarily resident in the State in the current year (here referred to as *'the chargeable individual'*);

(c) income must become payable, by virtue or in consequence of the relevant transfer, either on its own or in conjunction with associated operations, to a person resident or domiciled outside the State (*'the foreign person'*);

and either:

(d) (i) the chargeable individual or his spouse has, as a result of the relevant transfer and any associated operations, the *'power to enjoy'*, whether immediately or in the future, any income of the foreign person (TCA 1997, s 806(4)), or

(ii) the chargeable individual receives or is entitled to receive any *'capital sum'* the payment of which is any way connected with the relevant transfer or with any associated operation (TCA 1997, s 806(5));

and

(e) in the case of TCA 1997, s 806(4), only, the income of the foreign person would be taxable on the chargeable individual if it were received by him in the State, whether by deduction at source or by assessment. The purpose of this requirement is obscure and does not seem to add anything to the scope of the charging provisions.

In the case where liability to tax arises because the chargeable individual has power to enjoy any income of a foreign person (ie case (i) of (d) above), TCA 1997, s 806(4) deems that income to be the income of the individual for all the purposes of the Income Tax Acts. Similarly, if the chargeable individual is brought within the section due to his receiving or becoming entitled to receive a capital sum (ie case (ii) of (d) above), TCA 1997, s 806(5) deems the relevant income of the foreign person to be the income of the resident individual for all Irish income tax purposes. These two subsections are alternatives; the individual becomes taxable under TCA 1997, s 806 if he falls within the conditions of *either* subsection.

The circumstances and manner in which tax is chargeable under TCA 1997, s 806 are examined in more detail in **17.202–17.210**. TCA 1997, s 806(8) which prevents a charge to tax under either TCA 1997, s 806(4) or (5) if there has been a transfer of assets without any tax avoidance purpose or as a *bona fide* commercial transaction, is discussed in **17.207**.

It may be noted that in the appropriate circumstances it is arguable that the provisions of TCA 1997, s 806 *et seq* may be in breach of the freedom of establishment enshrined in EU Law, particularly in the light of the *Cadbury Schweppes* Case C–196/04 which indicated that such anti-avoidance measures must be proportionate and accordingly confined to wholly artificial arrangements and not extended to situations where genuine economic activities are carried on in the host Member State.

The same considerations as relate to married couples will apply *mutatis mutandis* to civil partners following the enactment of Finance (No 3) Act 2011.

17.202 Transfers of assets and chargeable individuals

The headnote to TCA 1997, s 806 is entitled 'Charge to income tax on transfer of assets abroad'. While many of the asset transfers likely to give rise to a tax charge under TCA 1997, s 806 may indeed involve the transfer of one or more assets out of the State, it is not an essential pre-requisite for the application of the section that there actually be a transfer of an asset from the State to a foreign country. The requirement is that there be some transfer of assets (any asset(s)) and that the transfer, whether with or without any associated operations, should have the result that income becomes payable to a foreign person (ie to any person who is either not resident or not domiciled in the State).

The asset transferred may already be situated in a foreign country or, alternatively, it may be situated in the State at the time of the transfer and remain there either temporarily or permanently. For example, an individual may transfer the ownership of land in the State to the trustee of a settlement who is and remains resident in the State. The trustee may then, as an associated operation (see **17.203**), incorporate a company in Guernsey, to which he transfers the Irish land. The transfer by the individual does not involve any physical transfer of the land or of its ownership outside the State. Although the later transfer by the trustee still does not involve the physical transfer of the asset abroad, the result of the individual's transfer and the later associated operation carried out by the trustee is to cause the income from the land to become payable to a foreign person (the Guernsey company).

The requirement that it must be the chargeable individual, ie the individual who has made the relevant transfer (or his spouse, see below) who meets the 'power to enjoy' or 'capital sum' conditions reflects the House of Lord's decision in *Vestey v IRC* [1977]

STC 414, [1980] STC 10, reversing the House's previous decision in *Congreve v IRC* 30 TC 163. The House of Lords in *Vestey* effectively decided that the references to 'an individual' in the charging provisions, TCA 1997, s 806(4) and (5) referred back to the equivalent provision to TCA 1997, s 806(3) taken as a whole.

Thus, Lord Wilberforce (Lords Salmon and Keith concurring) commented:

> [TCA 1997, s 806 is to be interpreted] … as having a limited effect; to be directed against persons who transfer assets abroad; who by means of such transfers avoid tax, and who yet manage when resident in the United Kingdom to obtain or to be in a position to obtain benefits from those assets.

In the *Vestey* case, the taxpayers concerned were all beneficiaries of a non-resident discretionary trust. It followed that each of them had, as a consequence, 'power to enjoy' *all* of the income of the trust (see **17.205** below). The *Congreve* case had decided that *any* individual with 'power to enjoy' was within the scope of the then UK equivalent TCA 1997, s 806(5), ie irrespective of whether they had made, or had been a party to, the relevant transfer. Thus, if *Congreve* had been correctly decided, this meant that *each* of the taxpayers in the *Vestey* case was potentially liable in respect of all of the trust income.

The Revenue argued in *Vestey* that they had a managerial discretion which enabled them to assess one or more (or all) of the beneficiaries as they thought fit, subject only to the limitation that they could not assess an aggregate amount in excess of the total trust income. If this were correct, then the normal appeal procedures would have been closed off. The only possible redress for the taxpayer would, it seems, have been to seek judicial review where the Revenue had acted unreasonably or unfairly (see **2.206**).

The House of Lords vigorously rejected the Revenue argument. Lord Wilberforce observed:

> Taxes are imposed on subjects by Parliament. A citizen cannot be taxed unless he is designated in clear terms by a taxing act as a taxpayer, and the amount of his liability is clearly defined. A proposition that whether a subject is to be taxed or not, or that, if he is, the amount of his liability is to be decided (even though within a limit) by an administrative body, represents a radical departure from constitutional principle.
>
> When Parliament imposes a tax, it is the duty of the commissioners to assess and levy it on and from those who are liable by law. Of course they may, indeed should, act with administrative common sense. To expend a large amount of taxpayer's money in collecting, or attempting to collect, small sums would be an exercise in futility; and no one is going to complain if they bring humanity to bear in hard cases. I accept also that they cannot, in the absence of clear power, tax any given income more than once. But all of this falls far short of saying that so long as they do not exceed a maximum they can decide that beneficiary A is to bear so much tax and no more, or that beneficiary B is to bear no tax.
>
> This could be taxation by self-asserted administrative discretion and not by law. As (Walton J at first instance) well said, '*One should be taxed by law, and not be untaxed by concession*'. The fact in the present case is that Parliament has laid down no basis on which tax can be apportioned where there are numerous discretionary beneficiaries.
>
> If your Lordships do not follow me so far (ie agree that only individuals who make transfers are caught) then, in view of the consequences which would result from the extension of *Congreve* into a case where there are discretionary beneficiaries, I would hold that it cannot be applied to such a case, that no method for levying the tax in such cases has been prescribed by Parliament, that this gap cannot be filled by administrative decision and in that the tax and the assessments of it fail (emphasis supplied).

Lord Wilberforce's references to the 'unconstitutional' nature of the Revenue's purported powers need to be set in the context of the UK legal system where Parliament is sovereign (subject only to the transfer of certain legislative powers to the EU) and theoretically could, if it so wished, delegate its taxing powers in favour of the Inland Revenue. The position is different in Ireland where any such delegation of powers would be in breach of Article 15.2.1 of the Constitution (see **1.409**). It should also be noted that the Inland Revenue were *not* merely seeking the ability to grant Extra Statutory Concessions in the *Vestey* case. No 'concession' is involved where one person's tax saving automatically becomes another person's tax bill; this exercise entails not a remission of tax, but an allocation of tax between individuals.

If *Congreve* were correctly decided, then as the *Vestey* case demonstrates, TCA 1997, s 806 will be unworkable in very many cases. These are not restricted to situations where discretionary beneficiaries are concerned, but also, eg where individuals hold varying interests (eg different classes of shares or combinations of shares and debentures) in a non-resident company. The interpretation in *Vestey* therefore seems far preferable to that in *Congreve*, if only because it maintains the workability of the section.

Lord Wilberforce also adverted in his speech to the injustice of taxing individuals 'who had no hand in the transfer, who may never benefit from it, who cannot escape from it'. In *Madigan & Madigan v Attorney General* III ITR 127, the taxpayer argued that it was unconstitutional that his eligibility for relief from Residential Property Tax should depend on the income of his household, over which he had no control. The Supreme Court did not dispute the principle involved but held that in reality the household members would (or should) contribute to the running of the family home. It could be argued therefore that the *Congreve* interpretation produces unfairness, on a scale which constitutes an unjust attack on property rights under the Constitution. If this view is accepted, the *Vestey* interpretation should again be preferred to that in *Congreve*, given the general presumption in favour of the constitutionality of a statute (see **1.409**).

Finally, there are strong arguments in favour of the *Vestey* interpretation based on the wording of the section. TCA 1997, s 806(2) states that 'a reference to an individual shall be deemed to include the wife or husband of the individual'. The primary purpose behind this provision is to ensure that if A makes a relevant transfer and A's spouse, B, rather than A, acquires 'power to enjoy' or receives a 'capital sum', then the section still bites. As Viscount Dilhorne pointed out 'If the decision in *Congreve* is right, it is not easy to attach significance to [s 806(2)]'.

This is because under the *Congreve* interpretation the section would operate regardless of s 806(2), ie B would be assessable, irrespective of the identity of the transferor.

It is considered most likely therefore that the Irish courts would follow the decision in *Vestey* and this division of the text has accordingly been written on the basis that *Vestey* represents a correct statement of the law for Irish tax purposes. It is understood that this also reflects the approach of the Revenue Commissioners.

The *Vestey* decision is, however, subject to one significant qualification. In *Congreve*, the judgment of the Court of Appeal contained an alternative ratio to that subsequently struck down in *Vestey*. The court took the view that the equivalent of TCA 1997, s 806 could also bite where the execution of the transfer was *procured* by the individual concerned. The Court of Appeal held that this principle applied in *Congreve*, since the transfers in question were made by a company under the control of the taxpayer. It is not clear that this 'alternative ratio' was in fact adopted by the House of Lords. However, in

Vestey, Lord Wilberforce seemed to accept that the House of Lords as well as the Court of Appeal 'had accepted an alternative argument that (the taxpayer) had organised or engineered (the transfer)'.

Lord Wilberforce also observed that the equivalent of TCA 1997, s 806 only applied where the taxpayer 'made, or maybe, was associated with the transfer'. The words 'associated with' although apparently wide, cannot have been intended to extend the scope of the phrase 'organised or engineered' earlier employed by Lord Wilberforce. Lord Edmund-Davies and Lord Keith also expressly approved the 'alternative ratio' in *Congreve*.

In *IRC v Pratt* [1982] STC 756, the Inland Revenue sought to tax three individuals who were both directors and shareholders of a company which had made a transfer of assets. The individuals between them formed only a minority of the board of directors and of the company's shareholders. Walton J described *Congreve* as a case where:

> because (the taxpayer) could, by the exercise of her voting strength in the company, get it to do whatever she wanted, (she) was a quasi-transferor.

In the instant case, however:

> there was no question of any of the three taxpayers, either alone or in concert being able to 'procure' (the company) to do anything.

Walton J rejected an attempt by the Revenue to rely on the use of such words as 'associated with' in *Vestey*, saying:

> Nor, however widely one construes any wording to be found in [TCA 1997, s 806] is the substance of a person being 'associated with' or 'having a hand in' a transfer necessarily equivalent in any way to that person himself making the transfer.

Accordingly, it was held that it was the *company* and not the individuals concerned which had made the transfer.

It does seem clear therefore that an individual who has engineered, organised or brought about the transfer is likely to fall within TCA 1997, s 806. It may be open to the Revenue to raise this point in appropriate circumstances where an individual seeks to stay outside TCA 1997, s 806 by arranging for a third party (typically a family member) to set up an offshore structure for his subsequent use. Further, any subsequent transactions between the taxpayer and entities in the offshore structure could lead to him being treated as a transferor or quasi-transferor.

Multiple transferors

The *Pratt* case also demonstrates that, even following *Vestey*, the lack of any mechanism for apportioning income between two or more individuals may still render the section unworkable. In *Pratt*, the Inland Revenue had firstly argued that the three taxpayers there should all be treated as 'constructive' or 'quasi' transferors. They proceeded to contend that because each of them had power to enjoy *all* of the income of the foreign person, that income should be apportioned between them on a 'just and reasonable' basis. While (as noted above) Walton J rejected the Inland Revenue's initial argument, he also addressed this latter proposition, stating:

> As a matter of law, it appears to me that in the case of a plurality of transferors, if it is impossible to separate out their respective interests so as to be able to say, 'the first transferor transferred A per cent of the interest transferred, the second B per cent and so on, the series adding up to 100, I do not think [TCA 1997, s 806] bites at all. I put my

qualification in the manner I have done because I can see an argument open to the Crown, under many circumstances, that such a dissection is possible.

Without in any way deciding that this is indeed the position, I can well see that if A and B own an asset jointly, and transfer it abroad, then one might for this purpose be able to separate out their beneficial interests as being equal, or, if the transfer was in fact a sale, according to the division between them of the purchase money. Something of the sort might even be possible in the case of quasi-transferors, where two or three of them own the company which makes the transfer, but where it is not possible to do just that TCA 1997, s 806 does not bite at all.

Of course, counsel for the Crown recognised the difficulties in his way. Those difficulties simply are that, in the circumstances put, the section provides no machinery whatsoever for attributing anything less than the whole of the income referred to any transferor. Where an identifiable portion of the asset transferred can be attributed to a particular transferor then, of course – any rate in any normal case – that part actually transferred will produce a similar part of the income, and in no case is there any difficulty in applying the section, since one will apply it separately to each of the individual transfers, or each identifiable portion.

But if there is no such identifiable portion, then what one is dealing with is, in the case of each individual, 'the transfer' and all the consequences which it produces, leading to the results that each individual transferor or quasi transferor is liable to tax on precisely the same income.

Walton J dismissed the notion that a 'just and reasonable' basis for apportionment could be adopted, saying:

All this is, in my view, completely bogus. It was really dealt with by Lord Wilberforce in the *Vestey* case, because precisely the same problem arose as to apportionment – or suggested apportionment – in relation to discretionary beneficiaries, but what was going to be apportioned, if apportionment was going to take place, was the very same income with which I am now dealing.

Walton J finally cited Lord Wilberforce to the effect that 'In the absence of any such basis (ie for assessing discretionary beneficiaries), the tax must fail'.

Walton J also pointed out that the relieving provisions of TCA 1997, s 806(3) (see **17.207**) depend on a purpose or purposes of ascertaining 'the transfer', making it impracticable to apply TCA 1997, s 806 where there are two or more transferors each with their own potentially distinct purposes. However, this point loses its force if the test of purpose is objective and the actual purposes of the individual transferor are accordingly irrelevant (see **17.207**).

As may be seen, Walton J left open the circumstances in which an apportionment might be feasible. An interesting case in this connection is *Shanks v IRC* 14 TC 249 where a sum was payable under a will trust towards the upkeep of a house jointly occupied by two taxpayers. The Court of Appeal decided that the allocation of this sum between the taxpayers was an issue of fact; thus, the income of each consisted of a share of the total figure involved.

Russell LJ observed:

This question of the proportion properly attributable to (the taxpayer) seems to me to be a question for the (Appeal) Commissioners whose conclusion we cannot disturb even if we wished to do so. For myself unless very clear evidence were addressed to show that in fact (the benefit) had been shared unequally, I would conclude that a moiety was the proper proportion to attribute to (the taxpayer).

It may be noted that the apportionment in *Shanks* was regarded as one which *could* be satisfactorily resolved on the basis of factual evidence. Where this is not possible, then (as in *Vestey*) it follows logically that the charge to tax must fail (this indeed was the conclusion of Rowlatt J at first instance in *Shanks*). (For the view that apportionment is not possible even in the case of joint incomes, see the dissenting judgment of McCarthy J in *Revenue Commissioners v ORMG* III ITR 28).

It must be borne in mind, however, that the arguments in *Pratt* lose their force where there is a joint transfer by husband and wife, since TCA 1997, s 806(2) directs spouses to be treated as one and the same individual. Finally, it should be noted that for the purposes of TCA 1997, s 806 it is immaterial whether the spouses are no longer living together, or are assessed separately for income tax purposes under TCA 1997, s 1016, however, widow(er)s are not included (*Vestey's Executors v IRC* 31 TC 1).

In *IRC v Herdman* 45 TC 394, the Court of Appeal held that the chargeable individual need not be ordinarily resident at the time the transfer was made (at that time the equivalent to TCA 1997, s 806(3) referred only to ordinarily resident individuals). The Court of Appeal's approach in *Herdman* was plainly influenced by the main ratio in *Congreve*; however, the conclusion can still be justified, even when the support of the decision in *Congreve* is removed. The contrary view would mean that the single reference to an individual ordinarily resident in the UK must simultaneously bear two different meanings, ie 'an individual ordinarily resident at the time of the transfer' and 'an individual ordinarily resident in the relevant year of assessment'. However, in *IRC v Willoughby* [1995] STC 143, [1997] STC 995 the House of Lords overturned the decision in *Herdman*. The Law Lords seemingly took the view that ordinary residence status was a stable underlying characteristic of the individual who made the transfer and who was also potentially liable under the equivalent of TCA 1997, s 806. It could well be argued that ordinary residence status does not attach to an individual in this way, and is instead something to be determined on a year-to-year basis. However, in relation to income arising on or after 12 February 1998, it is expressly provided that nothing in TCA 1997, s 806(3) is to be taken as implying that either s 806(4) or (5) applies only if the individual in question was resident or ordinarily resident at the time the transfer was made (FA 1998, s 12(1)(a)(ii);(2)).

TCA 1997, s 806(2) provides that the term 'assets' includes property or rights of any kind and that the word 'transfer', in relation to any rights, includes the creation of those rights. The asset transferred may simply be cash or it might be the right to receive income without necessarily involving any transfer of the assets that actually produce that income. For example, a life tenant may transfer his right to receive the income from a deceased person's estate or an annuitant his right to an annuity. The incorporation of a company and the subscription for shares in it, whether or not actually paid up, is a transfer of assets as it involves the creation of rights. Another example is the grant to a person of an option to acquire shares in a company or to purchase any other property. The granting of a lease or a sublease is also a transfer of assets.

In *IRC v Brackett* [1986] STC 521 it was held that an individual who entered into an employment contract with a non-resident company thereby created rights in favour of the latter. Accordingly, he had made a 'transfer of assets' for the purposes of the UK equivalent of TCA 1997, s 806.

Transfers of a distinct interest in a larger asset are clearly within the definition (see *Latilla v IRC* 25 TC 107, which concerned the sale of interests in a partnership trade and *Vestey's Executors v IRC* 31 TC 1, which concerned a settlement of rent receivable under a lease). A distinction must be drawn, however, between such interests, and interests in a single asset held by two or more individuals: see *IRC v Pratt* [1982] STC 756, discussed above. In *Pratt*, Walton J also remarked that 'a bare transfer of the legal title' to an asset would not suffice.

It is hard to see that a loan, at least one which is repayable on demand, could constitute a 'transfer of assets' as there is no surrender or creation of any ownership rights on the part of the lender. In *Fynn v IRC* [1957] 37 TC 629, the Inland Revenue did not seek to treat such a loan as a transfer but instead tried to link it to an earlier, admitted transfer as an 'associated operation' (see below).

It appears that the expression 'transfer of assets' comprises the entire transaction whereby the relevant assets are transferred, not merely the transfer itself taken in isolation. Thus, for example where an individual incorporates a non-resident company by transferring income-bearing assets to it in exchange for shares and/or debentures in that company, two consequences arise simultaneously from the transaction: (i) income becomes payable to a non-resident person, *and* (ii) the transferor in his capacity as a shareholder or debenture holder acquires 'power to enjoy' the income of the non-resident person (as discussed below). Thus in *IRC v Brackett* (above), the execution of the employment contract entailed a transfer of assets, but was also regarded as resulting in the taxpayer at the same time acquiring 'power to enjoy' the income of the non-resident company (see **17.205**).

The person to whom the transfer of assets is made by the chargeable individual need not, as shown above, be a foreign resident or domiciled person. He may, for example, be resident in the State at the time the chargeable individual makes the transfer to him, but the operation of TCA 1997, s 806 may be triggered by him taking up residence outside the State at a later date. Alternatively, the original transferee (whether or not resident in the State) may have made a further transfer of the assets or of any assets representing them so that income becomes payable to the second (or third, etc) transferee who is a foreign resident or domiciled person. Assuming that these events after the original transfer by the resident individual are associated operations in relation to that transfer, tax may be charged under TCA 1997, s 806 if the other conditions summarised in **17.201** are met.

In *Corbett's Exors v IRC* 6 TC 305, the taxpayers transferred assets to a UK resident company (W Ltd) in exchange for shares in W Ltd. W Ltd subsequently sold some of its assets to a non-resident company, D Ltd, in exchange for shares and debentures in D Ltd. The relevant transfer to W Ltd followed by the associated operation (ie the onward sale of W Ltd's assets to D Ltd: see **17.203**) resulted in income becoming payable to D Ltd, a 'foreign person'. The result of the relevant transfer and the associated operation was that the taxpayers had 'power to enjoy' the income of D Ltd (see **17.205**).

17.203 Associated operations

An individual's liability to income tax under TCA 1997, s 806 arises also when income becomes payable to a foreign person as a result of a relevant transfer taken in conjunction with associated operations (if the relevant transfer on its own does not produce this result). He may have power to enjoy such income due to associated operations taken in conjunction with a relevant transfer or, alternatively, due to his receiving or being entitled to receive a capital sum which is in any way connected with any associated operation or with the relevant transfer. It is, therefore, important to define what is an associated operation.

TCA 1997, s 806(1) defines 'an associated operation', in relation to any transfer of assets, as being:

(a) an operation of any kind;
(b) effected by any person; and
(c) in relation to:
   (i) any of the assets transferred, or
   (ii) any assets representing, whether directly or indirectly any of the assets transferred, or
   (iii) the income arising from 'any such' assets, ie presumably assets within (i) and (ii), or
   (iv) any assets representing, whether directly or indirectly, the accumulations of income arising from any such assets.

TCA 1997, s 806(1) elaborates on how the phrase 'assets representing any assets' is to be interpreted. It is to include shares in or obligations of any company to which those assets are or have been transferred. It includes also any obligations of (eg a debt) any other to whom those assets are or have been transferred. Similarly, the phrases 'assets representing any income' or 'assets representing accumulations of income' include shares in or obligations of any company (or any unincorporated association) to which, or obligations of any other person to whom, that income or those accumulations are or have been transferred.

It is not necessary that the shares or obligations should originally have been issued in exchange for the transferred assets. Thus, for example if a taxpayer sells an asset to a non-resident company, leaving the sale price outstanding on loan account, any subsequent dealing in the shares of that company would be an 'associated operation' in relation to the relevant transfer (ie the initial sale of the asset).

With effect for any associated operation carried out on or after 1 February 2007, it is provided that it is immaterial whether the operation is effected before, after, or at the same time as the transfer. This probably is no more than a statement of what was already implicit in the existing wording and seems of little practical import. It would appear that any transactions in relation to shares in a company to which there is a subsequent transfer of assets would not be associated operations, since the shares would not represent the assets at the time the transactions occurred.

In *Vestey v IRC* [1977] STC 414, it was held at first instance that the term 'accumulations' was wide enough to include sub-accumulations; thus assets representing income derived from the investment of income (and so on) fell within (iv) above).

It seems that an asset may 'represent' a transferred asset (or the income therefrom, etc), even if the value of the former asset is not entirely attributable to the transferred asset, etc. Thus, eg if a relevant transfer is made to a company which already has assets of its own, any subsequent dealing in the shares or that company is very likely to rank as an 'associated operation' in relation to the relevant transfer.

The scope of the expression 'directly or indirectly' is uncertain; it is presumably apt to cover operations carried out in relation to the holding company of a company to which there has been a relevant transfer.

It may be seen that the 'associated operations' definition is an extremely wide one. In particular, it should be noted that the associated operation may be effected by *any* person, including but not necessarily limited to the individual who made the relevant transfer, the person to whom that transfer was made and any person with power to enjoy the income etc.

The breadth of the words 'operations of any kind' can be seen in a number of cases. In *Latilla v IRC* 25 TC 107, the taxpayers transferred their interests in a mining partnership to a non-resident company in exchange for debentures in that company. The non-resident company then carried on the partnership with the remaining partner. The taxpayer argued that the share of profits which accrued to the company did so, not as a result of the transfer, but was solely attributable to the activities of the partnership in exploiting its mine. It was held that the turning of the business assets to account was itself an associated operation in relation to those assets.

It could not have been argued in the *Latilla* case that the income which accrued to the company did so as a result of the associated operation 'alone', rather than as a result of the associated operation 'in conjunction with' the original transfer. This is because (in broad terms) the income in question could not have accrued to the company, if the original transfer had not been made. The taxpayers fell within the then UK equivalent of TCA 1997, s 806 because: (i) the relevant transfer to the non-resident company, together with the associated operation noted above, resulted in income accruing to a 'foreign person'; (ii) the transfer resulted in the taxpayers receiving debentures from a 'foreign person' and thus acquiring 'power to enjoy' the income of that foreign person (see below).

In *Beatty's Exors v IRC* 23 TC 574, two brothers transferred assets to different non-resident companies in exchange for shares and debentures in each of those companies. Each brother then executed a deed of gift of his shares and debentures in favour of the other brother. Both brothers were held liable under the then UK equivalent of TCA 1997, s 806. For the sake of simplicity, the court's reasoning is presented in terms of one of the brothers (A) only, as follows: (i) A made a relevant transfer to A Ltd; (ii) as a result of the relevant transfer, income accrued to A Ltd a 'foreign person'; (iii) when A made a gift of his interest in A Ltd, this was an associated operation since it was carried out in relation to assets (shares in A Ltd) which 'represented' the transferred assets; (iv) A received a 'gift' of his brother B's interest in B Ltd, in return for A's 'gift' under (iii); (v) A as a shareholder of B Ltd had 'power to enjoy' the income of a foreign person (ie B Ltd); (see **17.205** below). This conclusion depended on looking at the *actual* transaction carried out by the taxpayers, ie the exchange of their interests in A Ltd and B Ltd, and meant disregarding the 'label' of a 'gift' which was attached by the taxpayer to each side of their reciprocal transaction (see **1.407**).

In *Banbridge v IRC* 36 TC 313, the taxpayer's mother had held shares in a non-resident company (K) to which she had previously transferred assets. The taxpayer inherited these shares as a residuary beneficiary of her mother's will, thus acquiring 'power to enjoy' the income of K. It was held that the death of the taxpayer's mother in itself could not constitute an associated operation. However, it was the contingency upon which effect was given to her mother's will, the making of which *was* an associated operation (ie it was an operation 'in relation to' the shares in K, which 'represented' the assets which had been the subject of the original transfer by the taxpayer's mother). Following *Vestey* (see below) the taxpayer in *Banbridge* would in fact have been outside TCA 1997, s 806 as she was not responsible for the original transfer.

In *Congreve*, it was held that where assets had been transferred to a resident company which subsequently became non-resident, the change of residence was itself an associated operation in relation to the assets transferred. In the Court of Appeal, this was justified on the grounds that the associated operation had altered the incidence of taxation in relation to the income of those assets. In the House of Lords, Viscount Simonds seemed to rely on the wide definition of an associated operation, implying that the operation was somehow related to the *shares* in the company, which further 'represented' the transferred assets for these purposes. This seems dubious, and may reflect the tendency of the UK courts at that time to interpret these provisions as punitively as possible.

It does appear that the word 'operation' must denote some degree of positive activity. Thus, for example, if in the *Banbridge* case the shares had devolved on the taxpayer on an intestacy, there are *obiter dicta* which strongly suggest that such devolution would *not* have amounted to an associated operation.

In *IRC v Herdman* 45 TC 394, it was left open to question whether or not the accumulation of its income by a company, and the subsequent management of assets representing that income in such a way as to leave funds available for the taxpayer to draw upon, were associated operations. Correspondingly, it would appear that the accumulation of income arising from a transferred asset by trustees, as well as a subsequent appointment to beneficiaries out of such accumulated income, might both rank as associated operations. It may be noted that at the time the above cases were decided, the UK legislation equivalent to TCA 1997, s 806 required that the power to enjoy income should arise '*by means of* any (relevant transfer), either alone or in conjunction with associated operations'. The phrase 'by virtue or in consequence of' which is used in TCA 1997, ss 806(4), (5) seems in fact to be wider in its potential scope.

However, the width of the 'associated operations' provision is not unlimited. In this respect, the words 'in relation to' are significant. In *Fynn v IRC* [1957] 37 TC 629, the taxpayer had transferred assets to a non-resident company (C Ltd) in exchange for shares. The taxpayer then divested himself of his shares in favour of his children. C Ltd secured an overdraft on the assets transferred, and the taxpayer subsequently lent money to the company which it was free to use as it chose, but which had the immediate effect of reducing its overdraft. It was held that the charging of the overdraft on the transferred assets *was* an 'operation' in relation to those assets and was, therefore, 'associated' with the relevant transfer. However, the making of the loan could not be said to be carried out in relation to the transferred assets (nor indeed to any asset representing them). If the loan had been made for the specific purpose of freeing the assets from the bank's charge on them, it seems that the case would almost certainly have been decided differently.

The significance of the reasoning in the *Fynn* case was that the taxpayer: (i) had made a transfer which resulted in income becoming payable to a foreign person (C Ltd), and; (ii) had as a result of the loan to a foreign person (again C Ltd) 'power to enjoy' the income of that foreign person (see **17.204** below). However, the equivalent of TCA 1997, s 806(4) did not apply because the taxpayer's 'power to enjoy' the income in question did not arise either as a result of the relevant transfer (since he no longer owned the shares acquired as a result of that transfer) nor as a result of any associated operation in relation to the relevant transfer.

It is clear that the Revenue must be able to identify one particular 'relevant' transfer as the starting point for imposing a charge under TCA 1997, s 806. However, they are free to select different associated operations, if appropriate, for the purposes of satisfying each of conditions (c) and (d): see **17.201**. In this respect, the Revenue are also free to select which out of a number of related transactions they wish to take as the 'transfer' (and indeed, they may put forward alternative contentions (see, eg *Philippi v IRC* 41 TC 75). Thus, for example if an individual receives a gift of shares from an uncle, which she subsequently transfers to a non-resident trust of which she and her children are the beneficiaries, she cannot argue that it is the original gift which *must* be regarded as the transfer. If the individual was entitled to make this argument, then her uncle would be the transferor and since he would have no power to enjoy the income of the non-resident trust (the 'foreign person'), TCA 1997, s 806 could not apply.

17.204 'Income becoming payable' to a 'foreign person'

TCA 1997, s 806 does not bite unless income becomes payable to a 'foreign person' as a result of a relevant transfer together with any associated operations (conditions (c)). Furthermore, the liability of an individual is measured either by reference to the income of a foreign person which he has 'power to enjoy' (condition (d)(i)), or income which becomes payable to the foreign person, where he receives a capital sum, etc (condition (d)(ii)).

The first problem which the legislation addresses is that created by the fact that the overseas income of a non-resident person is not 'income' for Irish tax purposes (see *Astor v Perry* 19 TC 255). However, both TCA 1997, s 806(5), (4) (which incorporate conditions (d)(i) and (d)(ii) respectively), make clear that income can be imputed to an individual 'whether it would or would not have been chargeable to tax apart from the provisions of this section'. This provision does not necessarily cover capital sums which are deemed to be income for Irish tax purposes only (see *IRC v McGuckian* [1997] STC 908); specific provisions apply in relation to offshore income gains (TCA 1997, s 746(5)).

The definition of 'foreign person' is also important. TCA 1997, s 806(4) and (5) refer to 'persons resident or domiciled out of the State'. TCA 1997, s 806(2)(a) requires that any body corporate incorporated outside the State is to be treated as resident outside the State whether in fact it is so resident or not (in any event, such a company would seem to be a non-domiciled person: *Gasque v IRC* 23 TC 210).

The UK courts have held that where income accrues to a trust, it is the personal residence of the trustees which is decisive. Thus, it is not a question of imputing a notional residence to the trust as a body of persons distinct from the trustees themselves (see *Vestey v IRC* [1977] STC 414). This is consistent with the decision in *Dawson v IRC* [1989] STC 473. In *Dawson*, the House of Lords decided that where some of the trustees of a discretionary trust were resident in the UK and some were not, they could not be assessed on foreign income under the equivalent of TCA 1997, s 18. This was because liability under those provisions required such income to accrue either to a person resident in the UK, or where (as here) it accrued *jointly* to a group of persons, to persons *all of whom were UK resident* (see the discussion at **14.105** and note the reservations of the Revenue Commissioners on this case discussed there).

The issue in *Dawson* arises in mirror image form in the context of TCA 1997, s 806. It seems to follow that the references therein to income accruing 'to persons resident outside the UK' must mean 'to persons *all of whom are* resident outside the UK' If this is so, then it would seem that a discretionary trust with a mixture of Irish and non-Irish trustees escapes income tax on non-Irish sources, (ie on the authority of *Dawson*) but is also outside the terms of TCA 1997, s 806. In fact, this very point was made by counsel for the Revenue in the *Dawson* case. It may be noted that if the trustees were all resident, but non-domiciled, in Ireland the definition of 'foreign persons' means that TCA 1997, s 806 would be potentially in point again. Finally, it may be noted that TCA 1997, s 806 does not apply to entities which, while resident under Irish law, are treated as non-resident under the terms of a double tax treaty (ie 'dual resident' entities).

There is no requirement that the foreign person should be non-resident (or non-domiciled) either at the time that the relevant transfer (or any associated operation) is effected, or at the time that income first becomes payable to that person. In *Congreve v IRC*, Viscount Simonds remarked:

> The transfer of assets aimed at is not expressed to be a transfer to a (foreigner). I should suppose that it is deliberately not so expressed, for I cannot think that so simple an expedient as the transfer of assets to a company resident in the UK and the immediate removal of that company outside it would not occur to the draftsman (emphasis added).

There does not appear to be anything in the decision in *Vestey* which undermines this conclusion, nor does there seem to be any contextual justification for limiting the words of the section in this fashion. Even if this view is incorrect, then it is possible that change of status from resident to non-resident may itself be an 'associated operation', but as discussed above this seems rather dubious (see **17.203**).

17.205 Liability if 'power to enjoy' income

TCA 1997, s 806(4) taxes the chargeable individual (or spouse) who made the relevant transfer, on the income of the foreign person where, by virtue or in consequence of that transfer (and any associated operations), the chargeable individual has power to enjoy any income of the foreign person. In any such case, the chargeable individual is charged to Irish income tax in the same way as if the income of the foreign person were the individual's own income received by him in the State.

With effect for transactions taking place on or after 1 February 2007, it is specifically provided that any income which becomes payable to, or has become income of, the foreign person by virtue or in consequence of: (i) the transfer, (ii) one or more associated operations, or (iii) the transfer and one or more associated operations must be taken into account for these purposes (TCA 1997, s 806(2)(d), (e) inserted by FA 2007, s 44). This wording is designed seemingly to rule out beyond doubt any argument that on the facts the income arising to the foreign person or the creation of the transferor's power to enjoy is attributable only to an associated operation and not to the combined effect of the transfer and associated operation taken together (eg in the latter case where assets are transferred to a non-resident company in which the transferor has no interest and shares are issued to him at a later date at which point he obtains power to enjoy the company's income). It must be emphasised that it is *not* the case that the foreign person to which income becomes payable as a result of the relevant transfer, etc, must be the same foreign person in respect of which the chargeable individual has 'power to enjoy' its income. This is illustrated by the decision in *Beatty Exors* case noted in **17.203** above, where A made a transfer of assets to A Ltd, but ended up with 'power to enjoy' the income of B Ltd.

It is, however, essential, under both TCA 1997, ss 806(4) and (5) that the income becomes payable to the foreign person *as a result of* the transfer (together with any associated operations) *or*, as noted above, with effect from 1 February 2007 as a result of the associated operations alone (TCA 1997, s 806(2)(e) inserted by FA 2007, s 44). Thus, if a chargeable individual purchases shares in an existing non-resident company with which he has not been previously associated, there has been a relevant transfer (ie of funds to the vendor) as a result of which the individual has in his capacity as shareholder 'power to enjoy' the income of the company (see below). However, the income which accrues to the company is attributable to the past transactions of that company and its previous owners and has no relationship to the relevant transfer or to any associated operation involving the assets of, or shares in, the company.

A similar logic applies where a chargeable individual transfers funds to a non-resident discretionary trust of which he is a beneficiary and the trustees subsequently acquire a controlling shareholding in an existing non-resident company, with which neither the individual nor the trustees have been previously associated. The individual has 'power to enjoy' the income of that company (see below) in these circumstances. However, once again the income which accrues to that company cannot be related back to the relevant transfer. In *IRC v McGuckian* [1997] STC 908, Lord Browne-Wilkinson suggested that in fact TCA 1997, s 806(4) could bite in these circumstances since dividends would be (potentially) payable to the trustees; with respect, income which *might* become payable to the trustees cannot be said to be 'payable' in any ordinary sense of that term. Clearly, however, were the company to subsequently pay a dividend to the trust, the dividend income of the trust would then clearly be attributable to the relevant transfer and an associated operation (ie the trustee's subsequent investment of the relevant funds in the shares of the non-resident company (see **17.203**)).

TCA 1997, s 806(7) directs that in deciding whether or not an individual has 'power to enjoy' income, 'regard shall be had to the substantial result and effect of the transfer and any associated operation'. In *IRC v Vestey's Exors* 31 TC 1, Lord Normand took the view that this provision would allow the courts to equate an individual with a company under his complete control, so that a benefit received by the latter could be treated as being received by him. Such control would, however, have to be legally based (eg through voting power) and not merely on a *de facto* basis, eg through personal influence. This is a fairly conservative analysis and seems to represent only a small movement away from the 'form over substance' principle in *IRC v Duke of Westminster* 19 TC 490 (see **1.407**).

In *Vestey's Exors*, the Law Lords also refused the invitation of the Revenue to treat certain trust powers as non-fiduciary merely on the basis that they had been created with an eye to tax-avoidance. In other words, a trust created to save tax is as binding on the trustees as any other form of trust and cannot be discounted by virtue of TCA 1997, s 806. Moreover, they held that any benefits received as a result of the *abuse* of such powers could not be received 'by virtue of rights' possessed by the taxpayer. It is suggested that this latter finding is correct, since the language of the statute itself demanded a strictly legally-based analysis. In *Vestey v IRC* [1978] STC 567, the Special Commissioners partly relied on the words contained in the UK equivalent of TCA 1997, s 806 in holding that a beneficiary of a discretionary trust had 'rights' to the income of the trust. This contention was rejected out of hand by the House of Lords.

TCA 1997, s 806(7) also requires that 'all benefits which may at any time accrue to the individual (whether or not he has rights at law or in equity to such benefits) as a result of the relevant transfer and any associated operations must be taken into account'.

TCA 1997, s 806 makes it clear that tax may be charged if the power to enjoy the relevant income of the foreign person is either a power to enjoy it 'forthwith' or a power to enjoy it 'in the future'. Consequently, in applying each of the deeming provisions of paras (a) to (e) above, the question has to be asked in respect of the income becoming payable to the foreign person (in each year to 31 December) whether any of those provisions are applicable to treat the resident individual as having the power to enjoy that income either immediately or at any time in the future.

In most cases, if an individual has such a power in respect of the income of one tax year, it is more than likely that the same deeming provision will be applicable in the same way for the next and subsequent years. However, it is possible that in some cases the circumstances that deem the individual to have power to enjoy the relevant income may come to an end. In any such case, the fact that the chargeable individual was taxable under TCA 1997, s 806 for one or more tax years does not mean that he continues to be so taxable in later years after his power to enjoy the income has come to an end (*Vestey v IRC* [1980] STC 10, at p 15). It is, of course, possible that such an individual may remain taxable due to him having received or having been entitled to receive a 'capital sum' (see **17.206**).

There are five circumstances in which an individual is deemed to have 'power to enjoy' the income of a 'foreign person'. These are discussed in turn below. As will emerge, the taxpayer may fall within more than one (indeed, occasionally all) of these definitions.

(a) The income is in fact so dealt with by any person as to be calculated, at some point of time, and whether in the form of income or not, to ensure for the benefit of the individual.

The accumulation of income by the directors of a company would, it seems constitute a 'dealing' for these purposes (see *Chetwode v IRC* [1977] STC 64). Thus, a shareholder or debenture holder in a company would fall within (a) (as well as within most, or all, of the other definitions as well (see below). In *IRC v Botnar* [1999] STC 711, the Court of Appeal held that the retention and reinvestment of income by a company for future use constituted a dealing in that income. The court also held that the funds in question enured for the benefit of the taxpayer concerned where he intended to use them ultimately to fund philanthropic (or other) activities rather than for personal consumption.

(b) The receipt or accrual of the income operates to increase the value to the individual of any assets held by him or for his benefit.

In *Ramsden v IRC* 37 TC 619, it was held that the receipt by a foreign company of a dividend from an investment transferred to the company by a UK resident individual operated to increase the value of a debt owed by the company to the individual as it increased the value of his right to recover the debt. He was, therefore, held to have power to enjoy the income of the company under the rule of para (b). In this case, the appellant had at one time been a director of the company and the sole beneficial owner of its issued share capital, but some years before the company received the dividend he had resigned his directorship and transferred his shareholding in the company to his son. The debt due by the company was his only interest in it when the relevant income became payable to the company.

It is debatable if this analysis should apply where the debt is amply secured on the assets of the foreign person or where the foreign person has substantial reserves. The Revenue could argue that no debt can ever be entirely risk-free and that any income received by the debtor therefore must serve to increase the value of such a debt. There may be a counter-argument based on the requirement of TCA 1997, s 806(7) to have regard to substance, but there are *dicta* by Walton J to the contrary effect in *IRC v Vestey* [1978] STC 567.

The term 'assets' bears its extended sense throughout TCA 1997, s 806. Thus it includes property or rights of any kind. The term 'asset' is, however, not apt to cover the holding of a fiduciary power of appointment from which the taxpayer cannot personally benefit (see *Vestey's Exors*).

(c) The individual receives or is entitled to receive, at any time, any benefit provided or to be provided out of that income or out of moneys which are or will be available for the purpose by reason of the effect or successive effects of the associated operations on that income and on any assets which directly or indirectly represent that income.

In *Lee v IRC* 24 TC 207, a shareholder in a company was held to be within (c) as he was entitled to receive dividends out of its income. In *Lord Howard de Walden v IRC* 25 TC 121, repayments of loans financed out of income were held to fall within both (b) and (c).

TCA 1997, s 806(1) states that the term 'benefit' is to include a 'payment of any kind'. Thus, a payment in satisfaction of a pre-existing obligation, even one incurred for full consideration (as in *de Walden*) falls within (c). In *IRC v Brackett* [1986] STC 521, it was held that cash payments received from the sale of unmarketable properties by the taxpayer to a non-resident company represented a benefit by way of 'provision or liquidity'. It would seem, however, that the fact that a payment had been made should have sufficed, irrespective of (arguably, rather nebulous) considerations of liquidity.

It was also held in *Brackett* that a salary paid to the taxpayer out of the trading income of a non-resident company was a 'benefit' for these purposes. However, if the taxpayer's salary is deductible before arriving at the (net) income of the foreign person (see **17.208**), it is hard to see how it can be payable '*out of*' that income.

The word 'payment' does not seem apt to include a loan as such (although TCA 1997, s 806(5) may be relevant, since it deems a 'capital sum' to include a loan (see **17.206**)). However, while TCA 1997, s 806(1) defines a benefit to *include* a 'payment of any kind' this does *not* limit the normal meaning of the term. Thus, other forms of benefit, which do not involve a payment, would still be caught, for example, the benefit of a loan offered on uncommercially favourable terms.

In *Vestey's Executors v IRC* 31 TC 1, the House of Lords held that there could be no power to enjoy income under para (c) (nor under para (a)) unless there was a clear and explicit finding of fact that the individual actually received or was definitely entitled to receive a benefit.

One common example, where definition (d) clearly applies, is the case where a non-resident trustee of a discretionary trust receives income as the result of a relevant transfer and where, under the terms of the trust deed, the class of potential beneficiaries to whom the trustees may, if they think fit, appoint income or capital, includes the individual who (or whose spouse) made the transfer. The fact that the non-resident trustee had the power to appoint income to the individual (or to the individual's spouse) means that the individual has power to enjoy the income of the trust.

(d) The individual has power by the means of the exercise of any power of appointment or power of revocation or otherwise to obtain for himself, whether with or without the consent of any other person, the beneficial enjoyment of the income or may in the event of the exercise of any power vested in any other person become entitled to the beneficial enjoyment of the income.

It may be that the interests of individuals who are *currently* discretionary beneficiaries would in any event fall also under some of the earlier paragraphs. Thus, for example under (b), the accrual of income to the discretionary trustees arguably increases the value of assets which are held for the benefit of the beneficiaries (bearing in mind that

TCA 1997, s 806(7) directs that 'all benefits which may at any time accrue' must be taken into account).

It is debatable whether or not the 'power to enjoy' which is exercisable by the individual or vested in any other person, must be *ejusdem generis* with powers of appointment or revocation (contrast the wording in *Hughes v Smith* I ITR 411).

It seems that where a discretionary trust has *complete* control of a company, the income of that company can be treated as that of the trustees for the purposes of para (d) (per Viscount Dilhorne in *Vestey v IRC*); but note the comments of the Special Commissioner in *IRC v Botnar* [1998] STC 38). This follows from the requirement of TCA 1997, s 806 that 'regard should be had to the substantial result and effect' of the arrangements involved. Thus, a settlor who is a potential beneficiary of the trust in these circumstances has 'power to enjoy' the income of the company.

In *IRC v Botnar* [1999] STC 711, the Court of Appeal held that the UK equivalent of TCA 1997, s 806(6)(d) (TCA 1997, s 478(5)(d)) applied where the settlor could have benefited under a trust which owned shares in a non-resident company to which assets have been transferred by the taxpayer. The court did not in fact rely on the argument suggested above that the income of the company could be treated as the income of the trust. Instead, the court took the view that once the relevant powers could be exercised so as to constitute the taxpayer as a beneficiary of the trust income, he was accordingly able to obtain the beneficial enjoyment of the company's income. The fact that it would also have been necessary for the company to declare dividends in favour of the trustees was not expressly addressed; it may be perhaps taken as read that this would simply have constituted one further exercise of a power (ie on the basis that the reference to 'power' in TCA 1997, s 806(6)(d) can be extended to include the plural 'powers' per the Interpretation Act (see **1.106**)); in *Botnar* itself it would have been necessary for two successive powers to have been exercised to grant a beneficial interest in the trust funds to the taxpayer.

The court in *Botnar* also rejected an argument of the taxpayer that the UK equivalent to TCA 1997, s 806(6)(d) could not apply because what the taxpayer had potential power to enjoy was not the income of the company, but the capital accumulated of the trust (albeit constituted out of the company's income).

Morrit LJ observed:

> [TCA 1997, s 806(6)(d)] is looking at possibilities at any time in the future. The words 'the income' clearly require that of which the transferor has beneficial enjoyment in the future to be identified as having been the income of the companies in the year of assessment in which the transferor is taxed.

It is interesting to note that a power reserved to a UK resident individual to appoint by will or codicil any interest in a fund settled by him in favour of his widow was held, again in the *Vestey's Executors* case, not to be sufficient to give either the individual or his wife the power to enjoy the income of the settled fund. The House of Lords overruled an earlier decision of the Court of Appeal in *IRC v Gaunt* 24 TC 69 and held that the word 'wife' did not include 'widow'.

In ruling to this effect, Lord Morton of Henryton said (in relation to a different section dealing with settlements, but which was considered to be equally valid in relation to the UK equivalent of TCA 1997, s 806):

> To my mind, if a payment is to come within the subsection it must be made to a lady who answers the description of a wife at the time of payment. No such payment could ever be made (in this case) because no payment could be made until after the death of William (the

individual who made the relevant transfer); the income then becomes payable not to his wife but to his widow.

Paragraph (d) was also considered (in the form of its UK equivalent) in the *Vestey's Executors* case in relation to a provision in Lord Vestey's (William's) Settlement under which the trustees were required to invest the settlement income at the direction of certain 'authorised persons' specified in the trust deed. At the material times, the authorised persons were Lord Vestey and his brother Edmund. The Inland Revenue had claimed, *inter alia*, that this enabled Lord Vestey (as the resident individual) to direct that accumulated income might be invested by way of loan to himself at a low rate of interest, ie that he could control the application of the income of the non-resident trustees so as to give him power to enjoy that income.

The House of Lords held that the power given by the deed to direct the manner of the investment had to be exercised in a fiduciary capacity and could not, in the circumstances of the case, be exercised in a way to give the individual any personal benefit (at least not without a breach of trust).

(e) The individual is able, in any manner whatsoever, whether directly or indirectly, able to control the application of the income.

Paragraph (e) would clearly cover a taxpayer who was a controlling director of a non-resident company, or the trustee of a non-resident settlement with, eg a power of accumulation or a discretion to distribute income.

In *Lee v IRC* 24 TC 207, it was held that the holder of the majority voting power in a company was also within (e); MacNaghten J observed:

> Since (the taxpayer) has power to make and unmake the directors he is able by use of that power to control the application of the income.

In *IRC v Schroder* [1983] STC 480, Vinelott J distinguished such a power from that of replacing and appointing trustees, at least where there was no evidence that the taxpayer could ensure that the trustees would act in disregard of their fiduciary duties (note also the decision in *IRC v Botnar* [1998] STC 38).

In *Vestey's Exors*, Lord Morton (with whom Lord Simonds and Lord Normand concurred on this point) held that a special power of appointment was not within (e), since the taxpayer:

> could only make an appointment in the shape of a capital payment in favour of (the specified beneficiaries) and if such a power were intended to be caught it would have been included in (d) which deals expressly with powers of appointment.

This reasoning may now perhaps be doubted, since it seems income is capable of including capitalised income. Furthermore, the wide degree of overlap between the paragraphs does not lend much support to the notion that (d) and (e) should be treated as mutually exclusive.

In *Vestey's Exors*, it was held that a fiduciary power to direct how investments should be made was not a power to control 'an application of income'. A power to make loans (even at uncommercial rates or interest) may not be an application of income (according to Viscount Simonds in *Vestey's Exors*). However, the receipt of a loan by the chargeable individual (or his spouse) would potentially be within TCA 1997, s 806 (see **17.206**). There does not, however, appear to be any requirement that the application of the income should be for the benefit of the taxpayer himself.

The *quantum* of the benefit to be assessed under TCA 1997, s 806 raises some difficult issues. In *Lord Howard de Walden v IRC* (above) the taxpayer was treated as having power to enjoy the income of a company of which he was a mere creditor. Furthermore, his liability extended to the *entire* income of the company, because it was this which was deemed to enhance the value of his rights to repayment. An argument that he should only have been taxed on the economic value of the actual benefit which he enjoyed was rejected by the Court of Appeal. It is suggested that this conclusion must be correct, since TCA 1997, s 806(4) focuses on the income which the taxpayer has power to enjoy.

Nevertheless, it is arguable that it is only the income which the chargeable individual actually has power to enjoy, and not necessarily *all* of the income accruing to the foreign person, which should be taken into account. Thus, for example if an individual has power to appoint 1/3rd of the assets of a trust to himself, para (e) should, on this analysis, apply *only* in respect of 1/3rd of the trust income. In *Vestey v IRC* [1977] STC 414, trust assets were split into two funds, each subject to powers held by two different individuals. The Special Commissioners rejected in principle an argument that each individual could only be assessed on the income of his fund, ie as opposed to that of the trust as a whole. It is suggested that this conclusion is open to question.

Interestingly TCA 1997, s 807(4) provides that an individual 'shall be chargeable' on the whole of the amount or value of (the benefit mentioned in para (c))', except to the extent that it is derived (directly or indirectly) from income previously caught under TCA 1997, s 806. This implies that despite the widely-drawn wording of para (c), it is only the amount of benefit actually received (or receivable) which can be taxed. In *Botnar* [1999] STC 711, the Court of Appeal expressed the *obiter* view that the UK equivalent to TCA 1997, s 807(4) was in fact a charging section which superseded the UK equivalent of TCA 1997, s 806(6)(c).

A further possible limitation on the quantum of income assessable is that it should be restricted to that which can be 'traced back' to the original transfer. This view has attracted some judicial sympathy, and the Revenue may be persuaded to apply it in practice. However, although the outcome in *de Walden* has been criticised in subsequent cases, it has a reasonable basis in law. The requirement of TCA 1997, s 806(4) is that the result of the transfer, etc should be that the taxpayer has power to enjoy income, not that it should result in income which the taxpayer has power to enjoy. The contrast with the wording of TCA 1997, s 806(5) should be noted, where the liability is measured by reference to the income which accrues to a foreign person by virtue or in consequence of the transfer.

Finally, it may be that the issue of quantum can cut both ways. Thus, for example, an individual may inherit all of the shares in a non-resident company and subsequently make a transfer of further assets to the company by way of gift. Arguably, this transfer does not result in him having power to enjoy income of the company as he already had that power (under all of the circumstances set out above) prior to the transfer. Against this, it might be objected that his power to enjoy the *additional* income which relates to the transferred assets is attributable to his transfer. However, this objection seems inconsistent with the view that the origins of the foreign person's income are irrelevant under TCA 1997, s 806.

The situation where there are multiple transferors also raises interesting issues. In *Corbett's Exors v IRC* 6 TC 305, the residuary beneficiaries of an estate sold their respective interests to a company, as a result of which (taking into account a further 'associated operation') they *all* came to acquire 'power to enjoy' the income of the *same* non-resident company. In such a case *each* of the individuals concerned could potentially be deemed to have 'power to enjoy' the *entire* income of the non-resident.

Unless it was considered practicable to apportion the income between them, TCA 1997, s 806 would accordingly seem to be inoperable (see the discussion of *IRC v Pratt*, at **17.202** above).

Finally, an important question which potentially affects all of the five paragraphs above, is the correct treatment of situations where the *means* of the 'power to enjoy' income are held jointly by two or more persons. In the *Vestey's Exors* case, the taxpayer held a fiduciary power jointly with another individual. As noted above, the House of Lords held that the possession of such a power did not fall within any of the paras (a) to (c). However, the House of Lords also held *inter alia* that a 'power to enjoy' must be held by an individual in his own right.

Lord Simonds observed:

> The Interpretation Act cannot be invoked to convert singular into plural. The context does not admit of it. Just as it is the income of an individual that is being assessed so it is the right of that individual that must be regarded. Whatever view, then, is taken of the right to direct investment, that was not a right of (the taxpayer) alone and it cannot be said that by virtue of that right he is brought within the section.

Lord Reid said:

> I agree that a right which an individual can only exercise in conjunction with some other person is not a right by virtue of which he has power to enjoy anything within the meaning of this section. I think that it is plain in [s 806] the singular 'individual' does not include the plural. The section is referring to the individual whose taxable income is being determined and to him alone.

The UK legislation at that time required the chargeable individual to have 'rights' by virtue of which he acquired his 'power to enjoy' the relevant income. However, the reference to 'rights' was subsequently deleted from the UK provisions and does not appear in the Irish legislation. This, however, does not seem to detract from the validity of the observations of Lords Simonds and Reid above.

It is arguable therefore that if either 'the benefit' mentioned in paras (a) or (c) or the 'assets' mentioned in para (b), or the ability to control the application of income mentioned in para (e), is held jointly, then TCA 1997, s 806 cannot apply. The position regarding para (d) is more complex. The power exercisable by the individual mentioned therein is one which is exercisable 'with or without the consent of any other person'. It is unclear whether this wording would automatically cover jointly held powers.

17.206 Liability if 'capital sum' receivable

TCA 1997, s 806(5) taxes the chargeable individual who (or whose spouse) made the relevant transfer on the relevant income where, whether before or after any such transfer, the individual either receives or is entitled to receive any capital sum which is in any way connected with the relevant transfer or with any associated operation. The relevant income, which is deemed by this subsection to be the individual's income, is all the income which has become payable to any non-resident person by virtue or in consequence of the transfer of assets (or as a result of any associated operations).

With effect for transactions taking place on or after 1 February 2007, it is specifically provided that any income which becomes payable to, or has become income of, the person by virtue or in consequence of: (i) the transfer, (ii) one or more associated operations, or (iii) the transfer and one or more associated operations must be taken into account for these purposes (TCA 1997, ss 806(2)(d) inserted by FA 2007, s 44). This wording is designed seemingly to rule out beyond doubt any argument that on the facts the income arising to the foreign person is attributable only to an associated operation and not to the combined effect of the transfer and associated operation taken together.

For this purpose, the term 'capital sum' is defined as:

(a) any sum paid or payable by way of loan or repayment of loan; and
(b) any other sum paid or payable otherwise than as income, being a sum which is not paid or payable for full consideration in money or money's worth. TCA 1997, s 806(5)(c) (as inserted by FA 1999, s 60(1)(a)(iii)) now provides that an individual will be deemed to receive (or be entitled to receive) a capital sum where a third party receives (or is entitled to receive) such a sum at the direction of that individual or by virtue of the assignment by that individual of his right to such a sum. This extension of the charge applies to any capital sum which a third party receives (or becomes entitled to receive) on or after 11 February 1999 (FA 1999, s 60(2)(b)).

It is not necessary that the capital sum should be payable by the transferee, so that devices such as the exchange of shares in the *Beatty Exors* case (see **17.203**) would be equally ineffective for the purposes of TCA 1997, s 806(5) as they are for TCA 1997, s 806(4). In contrast to TCA 1997, s 806(4) there is not even a requirement that the capital sum should be payable *by* a foreign person. Again, because TCA 1997, s 806(5) imposes liability by reference to an *individual* in his own right, it would appear that a capital sum which is received jointly by two or more individuals falls outside TCA 1997, s 806 (see **17.205**).

While this definition of 'capital sum' is a wide one, it was held in *Ramsden v IRC* 37 TC 619 that a debt constituting the unpaid balance of the purchase consideration (for assets transferred), due to the individual who made the transfer, is not a loan within part (a) of this definition. Consequently, the fact that the individual receives or is entitled to receive the payment of the purchase price is not, on its own, sufficient to cause the individual to be taxed under TCA 1997, s 806(5). However, as already indicated in **17.205**, the individual who made the relevant transfer in that case was taxable under TCA 1997, s 806(4) as he had the power to enjoy the relevant income.

A similar decision was reached in *Lee v IRC* 24 TC 207 where it was held that the amount payable to an individual under promissory notes issued, in full consideration for a transfer of assets, was not a 'capital sum' within the UK equivalent of TCA 1997, s 806(5). Again, however, the taxpayer lost the case as he was held to have had the power to enjoy the income of the foreign company to which the assets had been transferred, due to the application of TCA 1997, s 806(4) – see **17.205**.

In the *Fynn* case (discussed in **17.203**) it was held that the loan to the company made by the taxpayer – was not connected with the relevant transfer, so that the right of repayment fell outside TCA 1997, s 806(5). In *IRC v Botnar* [1998] STC 38, the UK Special Commissioner held that the right to use an asset was not a capital sum for these purposes.

Example 17.206.1

C establishes the C settlement (of which is he not a beneficiary), entailing the conveyance of his foreign securities to Irish resident trustees. The trustees subsequently decide to exchange the trust's securities for all of the shares in C Ltd, a newly formed non-resident investment company, to the trustees.

C Ltd eventually pays a dividend to the C settlement, which subsequently uses that income net of Irish tax, to make a loan on commercial terms to C. The inspector of taxes accepts that the commerciality of the loan means that C has not received a benefit from the

> trust within TCA 1997, s 806(4). However, the inspector seeks instead to impose liability under TCA 1997, s 806(5). C has made a relevant transfer (to the C settlement). The exchange by the trustees of the transferred assets for shares in C Ltd is an associated operation in relation to that transfer; the payment of C Ltd of dividends out of the income arising from those assets is a further associated operation. The relevant transfer and the *first* associated operation has resulted in income becoming payable to a 'foreign person' (C Ltd) (as noted above, any argument that the income becomes payable only as a result of the associated operation and not as a result of the combined effect of the transfer and the associated operation will lose whatever force it had for transactions undertaken on or after 1 February 2007). C has received a capital sum (the loan) which is clearly connected with the receipt of the dividend, ie the second 'associated operation' in relation to the relevant transfer. Accordingly, TCA 1997, s 806(5) applies and C is taxable on all of the income of C Ltd.

For tax to be charged under TCA 1997, s 806(5) under the 'capital sum' rule, it is not necessary that the individual or his spouse have, or be deemed by any of the rules of (repealed) FA 1974, s 54(5) to have, any power to enjoy the income of the foreign person. While the receipt of a capital sum (or the individual becoming entitled to receive it) may occur before the relevant transfer, or at any time after that transfer, the capital sum must be connected in some way either with the relevant transfer or with an associated operation.

In *Ramsden* and *Lee* above, the assets had been sold to the respective foreign companies for a full consideration so that neither the entitlement to be paid the outstanding balance of the purchase consideration (*Ramsden*) nor the later discharge of the promissory notes (*Lee*) was treated as capital sums. However, if the assets had been transferred to the respective companies at other than a full consideration, then part (b) of the 'capital sum' definition would have applied to give different results in both of those cases. Also, it is to be noted that if instead of leaving the purchase consideration outstanding as a debt, Mr Ramsden (or his wife) had loaned an identical sum to the company to enable it to purchase the assets, Mr Ramsden would have been entitled to receive a capital sum, ie the repayment of the loan, so as to have been within TCA 1997, s 806(5).

Once the resident individual has received or becomes entitled to receive any capital sum (however small) that is connected with the relevant transfer or any associated operation, it appears that *all* of the income becoming payable to the foreign person may thereafter be treated as the income of the resident individual. TCA 1997, s 806(5) clearly refers to 'any' capital sum and does not limit the income attributable to the individual either as to its aggregate amount or as to any time in the future. Since TCA 1997, s 806(5) stands on its own, the fact that the resident individual may not have any power to enjoy any of the income, and although he may not have any entitlement to receive any other capital sum there is nothing in the legislation to prevent the individual from being taxed under the subsection, either in the same or any subsequent year, on income which may be considerably in excess of the actual capital sum receivable.

Again, the grossly disproportionate relationship between the tax charged and the benefit enjoyed, which could well arise in some circumstances, may raise doubts as to the constitutionality of these provisions (see **1.409**).

TCA 1997, s 806(5) attributes to the chargeable individual any income which has become payable to a foreign person 'by virtue or in consequence of' the relevant transfer together with an associated operation. The effect is to limit the amount of the foreign person's income that can be attributed to the resident individual to the income that is traceable, directly or indirectly and whether or not through any associated operations, to the transfer(s) of assets made by that individual (and/or his spouse). In most cases, it is probable that this will include all the income of the foreign person since the type of tax avoidance scheme now caught by TCA 1997, s 806(5) usually involves transfers of assets by only the one individual. However, if there should be any case where the foreign person only has other income that is not traceable to or is not in any other way connected with the individual's transfer of assets and/or associated operations, then – it is suggested – that other income should not be deemed to be that individual's income.

While the receipt of a capital sum may result in an individual being taxed under TCA 1997, s 806(5) on the foreign person's income for all subsequent years, at least to the extent that the income is traceable to the relevant transfers and/or associated operations, it does not have retroactive effect. No income accruing to the foreign person prior to the date on which the capital sum first becomes receivable by him (or by his spouse) can be taxable on him under TCA 1997, s 806(5). It is, of course, necessary to ask whether the individual had previously any power to enjoy the foreign person's income due to a relevant transfer and any associated operations. If so, liability to tax could arise under TCA 1997, s 806(4).

Authority for the statement that TCA 1997, s 806(5) does not operate retroactively can be found in Viscount Dilhorne's remarks as *obiter dicta* in *Vestey v IRC* [1977] STC 414, [1980] STC 10:

> While the income of the non-resident trustees would be deemed to be income of his wife on her receipt of the £100,000 on 2nd May 1966 in that and subsequent financial years, I see nothing in sub-s (2) which gives it retroactive effect. It does not provide that the income of the non-resident in any year before a person receives or is entitled to receive it (the capital sum) is to be deemed that person's income.

In strictness, it appears that the income of the foreign person may be deemed to be that of the chargeable individual without any time limit, starting from the date the capital sum of entitlement thereto arises. This seems to be the case even where the capital sum consists of a loan which has been subsequently repaid.

It is possible that an individual could fall foul of *both* TCA 1997, s 806(4) and (5) in a single year. However, in *Vestey v IRC* [1977] STC 414, [1978] 567 it was accepted that the subsections are alternatives to each other. The Revenue will presumably elect for the subsection which imposes the higher liability in the particular circumstances (*Speyer Bros v IRC* [1908] AC 92: see **1.405**).

17.207 Exceptions to TCA 1997, s 806

In *Vestey v IRC* a number of the Law Lords made references (based on the terms of the then equivalent to TCA 1997, s 806(3)) to the transferor as the person who 'avoided or sought to avoid income tax' by means of his transfer. Taken at face value, these references imply that the transferor (and the transferor *alone*) must have had the intention to avoid income tax. However, too much should probably not be read into such expressions, particularly as the decision in *Vestey* was not concerned with the motivation of the transferor as such. More significantly, TCA 1997, s 806(8) provides two express exceptions to the operation of TCA 1997, s 806, based broadly on the absence of intention to avoid *any* form of taxation. TCA 1997, s 806(8) would serve no purpose if TCA 1997, ss 806(4), (5) were limited to transfers made in order to avoid income tax (for a contrary view see the decision of the Special Commissioner in *IRC v Botnar* [1998] STC 38). However, in relation to income arising on or after 12 February 1998, any doubt is removed by TCA 1997, s 806(5A)(b) inserted by FA 1998, s 12(1)(a)(ii). This states that nothing in TCA 1997, s 806(3) is to be taken as implying that TCA 1997, ss 806(4) or (5) apply only if the avoidance of liability to income tax was the purpose, or one of the purposes, for which the transfer was effected.

TCA 1997, s 806(8) provided two limiting rules (hereafter the 'Old Rules'), either one of which (if applicable in any particular case) prevents the Revenue's charging tax under either charging subsection. It would appear that if the Revenue Commissioners decide that the rules apply, then the taxpayer cannot challenge their finding (see the obiter dicta to this effect in *HMRC v Anson* [2012] UKUT 59 (TCC) where the taxpayer sought to demonstrate that the rules did not prevent the UK equivalent of TCA 1997, s 806 from applying, in order to establish his entitlement to double tax relief. Strangely, HMRC did not challenge his right to do so notwithstanding the grave misgivings voiced by the judge. In the event, the court found that the limiting rules were in point. These rules have now been displaced by new TCA 1997, s 806(10) (the 'new rules') with effect from 1 February 2007, subject to transitional provisions contained in new TCA 1997, s 807B inserted by FA 2007, s 44, discussed further below.

The old rules: general considerations

The old rules provide that no tax is to be charged under TCA 1997, s 806(4), (5) on any individual if he can show either:

(a) that the purpose of avoiding liability to taxation was not the purpose or one of the purposes for which the transfer of assets or associated operations or any of them was effected ('old rule 1'); or
(b) that the transfer and any associated operations were *bona fide* commercial transactions and were not designed for the purpose of avoiding liability to taxation ('old rule 2').

In other words, the onus is placed on the individual assessed under TCA 1997, s 806 (or threatened with an assessment) to satisfy the Revenue Commissioners that at least one of these exceptions are applicable to the transfer of assets or associated operations. However, if the Revenue Commissioners do not accept that either exception in TCA 1997, s 806(8) is applicable, the taxpayer is entitled to appeal against their decision to the Appeal Commissioners on the matter. The Appeal Commissioners are then required to hear and determine the appeal as if it were an appeal against an assessment to tax. Consequently, the taxpayer has the right to a rehearing by the Circuit Court judge, and either the taxpayer or the Revenue Commissioners have the right to require the statement of a case for the opinion of the High Court, etc on a point of law (TCA 1997, s 806(4)).

An important point must be noted in respect of 'associated operations' and 'tax avoidance' purposes. It is *only* those associated operations which have to be taken into account for the purposes of establishing potential liability under TCA 1997, s 806 which are relevant for these purposes (*IRC v Herdman* 45 TC 394, as interpreted in the light of subsequent amendments to the statutory wording).

Example 17.207.1

A makes a transfer to an overseas trust, T, of which she is also a discretionary beneficiary. This transfer will, of course, result in income accruing to a foreign person and will also result in A having power to enjoy such income. Assuming that A can establish that she had no tax-avoidance purpose under old rule 1 (perhaps an uphill, but not impossible task), then even if the trustees were for example subsequently to enter into a capital gains tax avoidance scheme in respect of the trust assets, the defence available to A under TCA 1997,

> s 806(8)(a) would not be prejudiced. This assumes that: (i) the trust was not in fact set up to facilitate the CGT avoidance scheme, and (ii) the CGT scheme does not affect the taxpayer's relationship to the trust, thus leaving her with identical rights granting 'power to enjoy' income before and after the scheme.

It will be critical in the case of both the old rules to establish what is denoted by the 'purpose' of a transaction. the recent case of *Carvill v IRC* [2000] STC (SCD) 143 (the facts of which are outlined further below), the Special Commissioner followed pre-existing authority to the effect that it is the actual (ie 'subjective') purpose of the relevant person(s) which counts and not what a reasonable person might infer from the facts the purpose of the transaction concerned was likely to be (ie the 'objective purpose' of the transaction(s): *Philippi v IRC* 41 TC 75). In *IRC v Willoughby* [1997] STC 995, Lord Nolan did somewhat cryptically observe:

> Where the taxpayer's chosen course is seen upon examination to involve tax avoidance (as opposed to tax mitigation), it follows that tax avoidance must be at least one of the taxpayer's purposes in adopting that course, whether or not the taxpayer has formed the subjective motive of avoiding tax.

However, this obiter remark seems merely to be drawing the distinction between the taxpayer's personal intentions and his personal view of his intentions; in other words, the fact that the taxpayer might not have regarded what he was doing as tax avoidance is irrelevant. It is the taxpayer's personal (subjective) intentions which are to be ascertained in the first instance; the issue as to whether or not those intentions amount to an avoidance purpose is a matter of classification for legal tax purposes to be determined objectively. In terms of the practical application of this test, evidence given by the taxpayer as to his personal intentions may be material but will never be conclusive; all the surrounding facts will need to be considered and evaluated. Thus, evidence from third parties and an objective assessment of the likelihood of the taxpayer being unaware of, or uninfluenced by, tax-saving considerations are very likely to be relevant.

A further potential obstacle to the effective application of a purely subjective test arises in the case of multiple transferors, since each may have their own distinctive purpose for making the transfer. This may not be that critical in practice since multiple transferors may fall outside the scope of the TAA provisions in any event (see *IRC v Pratt*, discussed at **17.202**).

Another crucial but even more problematic issue is the precise significance of the term 'tax avoidance' under the old rules. Firstly, it is to be noted that, while TCA 1997, s 806(3) is expressed in terms of avoiding the liability to 'income tax', TCA 1997, s 806(8) requires under both of the Old Rules that the individual should show that the transactions, etc were not for the purpose of avoiding liability to '*taxation*'. There is authority that the word 'taxation' extends to all forms of Irish taxation (eg capital gains tax, capital acquisitions tax, stamp duty, etc: see *Sassoon v IRC* 25 TC 154). Consequently, even if no avoidance of income tax is involved, the fact that the relevant transfer and/or associated operations result in the avoidance of some other form of Irish tax may be sufficient to deny the individual the benefit of the TCA 1997, s 806(8) exclusions. However, it appears that a transfer effected in order to avoid *overseas* taxation is not liable as such (*IRC v Herdman* 45 TC 394). This may constitute a potential defence for individuals coming to Ireland who had previously established offshore structures in order to avoid tax in their previous home jurisdiction (but not if, eg made in contemplation of relocating to Ireland).

In *Carvill v IRC* [2000] STC (SCD) 143, the Appeal Commissioners accepted Lord Nolan's interpretation of 'tax avoidance' contained in *IRC v Willoughby* [1997] STC 995 as '... a course of action designed to conflict with or defeat the evident intention of Parliament'. In *Willoughby* it was held on the facts that investment in a 'personal portfolio' offshore fund (which was the subject of express statutory provisions equivalent to those discussed in **17.403**, although at that time with no specific provisions to penalise personal portfolio policies) did not constitute tax avoidance. Lord Nolan, further observed that:

> The hallmark of tax avoidance is that the taxpayer reduces his liability to tax without incurring the economic consequences that Parliament intended to be suffered by any taxpayer qualifying for such reduction in his tax liability. The hallmark of tax mitigation, on the other hand, is that the taxpayer takes advantage of a fiscally attractive option afforded to him by the tax legislation, and genuinely suffers the economic consequences that Parliament intended to be suffered by those taking advantage of the option ...

Lord Nolan further observed that it would be absurd to describe merely taking advantage of a tax-free opportunity deliberately provided by the Parliament as tax avoidance. This may have been a generous analysis, since the offshore fund provisions appear to be more in the nature of anti-avoidance measures designed to counter the fact that the underlying income of such funds is outside the territorial scope of domestic taxation.

Analysis of avoidance given by Lord Nolan is similar to the approach adopted in *Queen v Canada Trustco Mortgage Co* [2005] SCC 54, where the Canadian Supreme Court held that:

> In general, abusive avoidance will be found where the relationships and transactions as expressed in the relevant documentation lack a 'proper basis' relative to the object, spirit or purpose of the provisions that are purported to confer the tax benefit, or where they are wholly dissimilar to the relationships or transactions contemplated by the provisions.

This passage was specifically endorsed by the High Court in *Revenue Commissioners v O'Flynn Construction Ltd et al*, albeit in the context of TCA 1997, s 811 (see **17.302**). Assuming that this general approach commends itself to the Irish courts in the context of the TAA (Transfer of Assets Abroad) provisions, the scope of its application to unique sets of factual circumstances will clearly have much latitude for debate in practice.

It may perhaps be inferred therefore from the decision in *Willoughby* that the choice of a 'straightforward', but tax-efficient, structure to carry out a transaction primarily motivated by non-tax considerations may well not be 'tax avoidance' for present purposes. However, presumably this is likely *not to* be the case where the structure is regarded as 'artificial' or 'contrived', ie where the transaction is dominated or explicable primarily by tax considerations. In *IRC v Brackett* [1986] STC 521, the taxpayer who had previously carried on business as a property consultant in the UK, subsequently agreed to carry on those activities as the employee of a non-resident company. The Special Commissioners found that the purpose of the new arrangements was the avoidance of the tax liabilities which would have otherwise have continued to be incurred by the taxpayer.

Conversely, in *Beneficiary v IRC* [1999] STC (SCD) 134, the Special Commissioners found that an elderly Japanese settlor who undertook: (a) the transfer to Jersey of substantial cash assets previously situated in the UK (and therefore liable to UK inheritance tax); and (b) the creation of a Jersey trust to take custody and control of the cash (thereby placing those assets outside the scope of UK Inheritance Tax) was not practising 'tax avoidance' but 'tax mitigation'. Parliament was adjudged to have effectively made an offer of freedom from UK inheritance tax to non-domiciled individuals by explicitly exempting property situated outside the UK when in the ownership of such individual.

Old rule 1: specific considerations

Old rule 1 is on the face of it the harder to satisfy but unlike old rule 2 is not limited to commercial transactions. At one time, in the corresponding UK legislation it was sufficient if the resident individual could show that the transfer of assets in question was effected mainly for some purpose other than the purpose of avoiding liability to taxation (eg see *Latilla v IRC* 25 TC 107). However, the rule contained in the Irish TCA 1997, s 806(8)(a) follows the more stringent wording which has been in force in the United Kingdom for many years. The test in TCA 1997, s 806(8)(a) is only satisfied if it can be shown that the avoidance of liability to taxation was not one of the purposes (even a subsidiary one) of either the transfer of assets or of any operation associated with it.

It is important to note that even where the original transfer was carried out purely for non-tax reasons, TCA 1997, s 806(8)(a) will provide no protection if any of the associated operations is tainted by a tax-avoidance purpose. It will be recalled furthermore, that an associated operation may be carried out by any person, not merely the transferor. Therefore it is implicit in TCA 1997, s 806 that a chargeable individual may be entirely innocent of any intention to avoid tax and yet still fall within TCA 1997, s 806.

Old rule 2: specific considerations

The test in TCA 1997, s 806(8)(b) is a dual one. Firstly, it must be shown that the relevant transaction and any associated operations which are relevant to the operation of s 806 were *bona fide* commercial transactions. The term '*bona fide*' seems to mean simply 'genuine', ie not a sham (see eg Viscount Dilhorne in *IRC v Plummer* [1979] STC 793). The term 'commerce' is somewhat indeterminate and tends to derive its colour from its context. In a very narrow sense it may relate simply to transactions carried out in the course of buying and selling. There is a number of UK cases decided in the context of a similar (but not identical), motive test in ICTA 1988, s 703 (the 'transactions in securities' provisions) which suggest that the wider meaning of 'relating to business' is more appropriate (see *IRC v Brebner*, discussed at **17.302**, where the test of commerciality was not satisfied and *IRC v Goodwin* [1976] STC 28, where it was held that the retention of control of a closely-held company was a commercial transaction where this was conducive to the future success of the company's trade).

The UK ICTA 1988, s 703 cases indicate that it may be necessary to consider a transaction not in isolation, but in the light of all the relevant circumstances. Thus in *Clark v IRC* [1978] STC 28, it was held that the realisation of shares in a tax-efficient fashion met the test of commerciality, since the proceeds were to be used in the acquisition of a farm. (See also *Marwood Homes v IRC* (1997) STC (SCD) 37). Arguably, the approach in *Re Clark* was generous to the taxpayer, given that the investment in the farm was independent of the transaction in which the tax advantage was obtained.

The ICTA 1988, s 703 provisions expressly distinguish between 'commercial' transactions and those carried out in the ordinary course of 'making or arranging investments'. In the absence of such explicit wording in TCA 1997, s 806(8)(b), it is debatable whether or not the term 'commercial' therein can be construed in a very wide sense, as relating to anything undertaken for financial return or with a view to profits (*see* in a different context, *Wannell v Rothwell* [1996] STC 450). However, even the most generous interpretation of the term could not embrace bounteous transactions such as transfers into family trusts.

Whatever the precise scope of the term 'commercial', it is clear that it is necessary under TCA 1997, s 806(8)(b) for the taxpayer to demonstrate a positive commercial purpose underlying the transaction (*see IRC v Goodwin* [1976] STC 28). Secondly, even when this can be shown, it must also be established to the satisfaction of the Revenue Commissioners (or, on appeal, to the Appeal Commissioners, etc) that the transfer and any associated operations were not designed for the purpose of avoiding liability to taxation. (F(TA)A 2015, s 38(8), which was subject to Ministerial Order (SI 110/2016 appointed 21 March 2016 as the day on which the Finance (Tax Appeals) Act 2015, came into operation), removes the abovementioned satisfaction requirement from TCA 1997, s 806(10)(b) such that it becomes an objective test).

In *Carvill*, the taxpayer had established a UK company and also various other trading companies operating in the reinsurance business one of which specialised in the US market. It was decided to form a Bermudan holding company and this was effected by way of a share for share exchange. The taxpayer relied on the UK equivalent of TCA 1997, s 806(8)(b) as a defence against an assessment under the UK equivalent of the TAA provisions. With regard to the facts before them, the Appeal Commissioners held that the purpose of the share for share transaction and establishment of the Bermudan company was to set up a vehicle which would manage the group from a neutral territory. This was a strategic move in relation to its US operations since the Bermudan company could obtain US business without being regarded as competing from the UK with the established US brokers (this made it easier inter alia to attract senior US personnel). Accordingly it qualified as a *bona fide* commercial transaction. It was also held that in view of the fact that transactions may have more than one purpose, it was the main purpose of the transaction in question which should be examined and that exemption under TCA 1997, s 806(8)(b) was available where tax avoidance was a minor purpose. In the present case it was held that in fact there were no tax avoidance purposes involved.

As noted above, TCA 1997, s 806(8)(a) makes it clear that the transfer and each associated operation must pass the 'no tax avoidance purpose' test. However, it seems that this is also the position under TCA 1997, s 806(8)(b), ie the relevant transfer and each of the associated operations must be a *bona fide* commercial transaction, not designed for the purpose of avoiding taxation (see *Cottingham's Exors v IRC* 22 TC 344). If this is correct, then a transaction undertaken for commercial reasons may fall outside the protection of TCA 1997, s 806(8)(b), if either the transfer alone or one of the associated operations relevant to the operation of the TAA provisions can be shown to have been designed in order to avoid tax.

However, if the transfer and the associated operations are simply integral steps making up a larger commercial transaction, in which any tax-avoidance elements are subsidiary, then it seems highly arguable that it is the purpose of the larger transaction which should be material. In other words, in these circumstances the steps which make up a single transaction cannot logically have purposes distinct from the purpose of the transaction itself (see *IRC v Brebner* 43 TC 705). This implies that such a transaction might well meet the test under TCA 1997, s 806(8)(b) (but presumably not the test under TCA 1997, s 806(8)(a), since any tax-avoidance purpose is fatal thereunder).

New rules: general considerations

TCA 1997, s 807(10)(b) provides exemption from the operation of TCA 1997, s 806 and by extension TCA 1997, s 807A (see **17.210**) where the taxpayer shows in writing or otherwise to the satisfaction of the Revenue Commissioners (F(TA)A 2015, s 38(8), which was subject to Ministerial Order (SI 110/2016 appointed 21 March 2016 as the day on which the Finance (Tax Appeals) Act 2016, came into operation), removes the abovementioned satisfaction requirement from TCA 1997, s 806(10)(b) such that it becomes an objective test) that either:

(i) it would not be reasonable to draw the conclusion, from all the circumstances of the case, that the purpose of avoiding liability to taxation was the purpose, or one of the purposes, for which the transfer and any associated operations [the 'relevant transactions'] or any of them were effected ('new rule 1'); or

(ii) all the relevant transactions (I) were genuine commercial transactions, and (II) it would not be reasonable to draw the conclusion, from all the circumstances of the case, that any one or more of those transactions was more than incidentally designed for the purpose of avoiding liability to taxation ('new rule 2').

New rule 2 is expressed to be applicable only if the conditions in new rule 1 are not met.

One of the most significant aspects of the new provisions is the move from what had been held to be a subjective purpose test under the old rules (although it may be observed that HMRC in the UK believe that *Carvill* was wrongly decided on this point). Under both new rule 1 and new rule 2, it must now be shown that 'it would not be reasonable to draw the conclusion, from all the circumstances of the case…' that a tax avoidance purpose etc existed. However, this does not import a purely objective test, since it is additionally provided that:

> the intentions and purposes of any person who, whether or not for consideration: (i) designs or effects the relevant transactions or any of them, or (ii) provides advice in relation to the relevant transactions or any of them, are to be taken into account in determining the purposes for which those transactions or any of them were effected (TCA 1997, s 806(10)(c)).

Clearly, therefore, the intentions of the person who carries out the transfer of assets or any associated operation will need to be taken into account, as will those of third parties such as family members who have dictated or influenced those transactions and also professional advisors. In the last case the personal intention of the professional advisor will be presumably to earn a fee; however it may argued on the facts that his immediate intention is to devise a plan to avoid tax (in order to secure that fee). This wording is also clearly apt to cater for a situation involving multiple transferors, if this should prove necessary (see comments above)

How will a hybrid test of this nature work in practice? One hypothesis is that the test should be viewed as being primarily objective, somewhat along the lines of the observations by Lord Denning in the context of the Australian General Anti-Avoidance Rule in *Newton v FCT* [1958] 98 CLR, when he observed:

> In order to bring the arrangement within the section, you must be able to predicate – by looking at the overt acts by which it was implemented – that it was implemented in that particular way so as to avoid tax. If you cannot so predicate, but have to acknowledge that the transactions are capable of explanation by reference to ordinary business … dealings, without necessarily being labelled as a means to avoid tax, then the arrangement does not come within the section.

Thus, if a transaction was only explicable in the context of a material tax avoidance purpose, the TCA 1997, s 807(10) defences would not apply. If the facts were equivocal, the subjective elements might then be invoked to resolve the issue. In practice, the analysis is unlikely to be so clearcut and it will probably be the case that all the evidence will be thrown into the melting-pot. Professional advisors should certainly be on guard not to inadvertently compromise their clients' prospects of a successful claim under TCA 1997, s 806(10) when drafting their advice.

It is also provided that any associated operation which would otherwise be ignored must be taken into account if:

(i) that associated operation, or

(ii) that associated operation taken together with the transfer or any one or more other associated operations, would fail to satisfy the conditions of the New Rules.

This reverses the effect of the decision in *IRC v Herdman* noted above, so that on the facts of **Example 17.207.1**, no defence under the new rules would be available from the time the 'tainted' associated operation was carried out. A limited form of relief may be available under certain circumstances in the case of TCA 1997, s 806 only by virtue of new TCA 1997, s 807C (see discussion under: *Relief where exemption is lost due to subsequent associated operation* below).

New rule 1: specific considerations

Apart from these changes, the import of new rule 1 is identical to that of old rule 1.

New rule 2: specific considerations

The requirement under new rule 2 that the commercial transaction should be 'genuine' as opposed to '*bona fide*' under the old rules seems to be no more than a clarification of the previous terminology.

However, new rule 2 does include some further, substantive modifications to old rule 2. Firstly, for the purposes of new rule 2, a 'commercial transaction' is now stated not to include:

(i) a transaction on terms other than those that would have been made between independent persons dealing at arm's length; or

(ii) a transaction that would not have been entered into in the first place between independent persons dealing at arm's length (TCA 1997, s 806(10)(a)).

'Independent persons' are defined as persons who are not connected with each other (within TCA 1997, s 10); there is no prohibition on transactions between connected persons as such. The reference to independent persons in fact seems irrelevant, since once it is the position that parties are dealing at arm's length then the degree of connection between them is immaterial. While, as discussed above, bounteous arrangements could never have qualified as commercial transactions under the old rules, the test is perhaps rendered rather more concrete under the new rules. Having said this, if parties acting at arm's length simply happen to conclude a bad bargain (ie at a price which would be the norm in these circumstances) it is difficult to see that the transaction should fall foul of this proviso.

Secondly, new rule 2 further provides that a relevant transaction is a commercial transaction only if it is effected:

(i) in the course of and for the purposes of a trade or business; or

(ii) with a view to setting up and commencing a trade or business and for the purposes of such trade or business (TCA 1997, s 806(10)(d)).

The scope of the term 'business' is notoriously elusive and has been the subject of considerable commentary elsewhere.

In the absence of any words of limitation it would seem that a transaction will qualify if it is carried out in the course of trade or business by either party to the transaction. In *IRC v Willoughby* 1995 [STC] 143, it was accepted by the Court of Appeal that a private investment by an individual in a personal portfolio life insurance policy qualified as a commercial transaction (since the policy was issued in the course of the provider's trade) and thus fell within the UK equivalent of TCA 1997, s 806(8)(b). While the issue was however left open in the House of Lords, the conclusion would seem to be correct and, if so, to still hold good under the terms of TCA 1997, s 807(10)(b).

Thirdly, a departure from the approach under Old Rule 2 is that the definition of 'commercial transaction' is explicitly restricted, so that the making and managing of investments is not regarded as a trade or business except to the extent that:

(i) the person by whom it is done; and
(ii) the person for whom it is done are independent persons (as defined above) dealing at arm's length (TCA 1997, s 806(10)(e)).

Accordingly an investment transaction carried out between connected persons cannot be regarded as a commercial transaction. It would seem that the fact that a transaction is at arm's length between non-connected persons does not mean that it automatically qualifies as commercial and that it remains necessary that it should be carried out in the course of a trade or business etc.

New rule 2 requires in terms that 'any one or more' of the relevant transactions meets the tax avoidance purpose condition; this seems to do no more than render the position under old rule 2 explicit (as noted above).

Finally, it may be recalled that the previous requirement under old rule 2 was that the relevant transactions should not be 'designed for the purpose of avoiding liability to taxation' (interpreted in *Carvill*, as noted above, to infer that the main purpose should not be tax avoidance). Under new rule 2, it is necessary to show that each of the relevant transactions was 'not more than incidentally designed for the purpose of avoiding liability to taxation'. This is a notably vague and subjective criterion, but on the face of it offers less latitude than the previous wording, at least as interpreted in *Carvill*. Nevertheless if it can be demonstrated that an offshore structure was clearly the best or only option in the circumstances without regard to Irish tax factors, then notwithstanding that Irish tax benefits were also foreseeable, it seems that new rule 2 should apply.

Transitional provisions

A 'new transaction' means a *relevant* transaction (ie the original transfer of assets and any associated operations) effected on or after 1 February 2007; an 'old transaction' means a relevant transaction effected before 1 February 2007. As one would expect, where all the relevant transactions are old transactions, the old rules continue to apply; if all the relevant transactions are new transactions, then the new rules will apply (TCA 1997, s 807B(2)(a)). However, if the relevant transactions are a mixture of old and new transactions, then the rules set out in TCA 1997, s 807B(3) must be considered. Where any or all of the old transactions fail to meet the old rules then, as before, no exemption will be available (TCA 1997, s 807B(3)(a)). Where the old transactions do satisfy the old rules, but all or any of the new transactions fail to satisfy the new rules, the exemption will again be lost, but subject to transitional measures. The effect of these measures is that any income arising before 1 February 2007 to a person resident or domiciled out of the State which would otherwise be taxed as the income of the individual effecting the transfer will be disregarded up to that date (TCA 1997, s 807B(3)(b)(i)). As TCA 1997, s 806 taxes income as it arises, the effect is simply to exclude income arising in January 2007.

In the case of TCA 1997, s 807A (see **17.210**), there is no disregard of income arising prior to 1 February 2007, but where a benefit is received by an individual in 2007, that part which relates to the period prior to 1 February 2007 (ascertained on a time-apportionment basis) is to be disregarded (TCA 1997, s 807B(3)(b)(ii)). If a benefit was received in full prior to 1 February 2007, it seems highly arguable that time-apportionment is irrelevant and that such a benefit should be wholly exempt.

Relief where exemption is lost due to subsequent associated operation

TCA 1997, s 807C provides a restricted possibility of relief from liability under TCA 1997, s 806 (but not TCA 1997, s 807A (see **17.210**)) where exemption which had been obtained under old rule 2 and/or new rule 2 is lost as a result of a subsequent associated operation with a non-incidental tax avoidance purpose. The precise requirements are as follows:

(a) TCA 1997, s 806 applies because the conditions in new rule 2 are not satisfied (TCA 1997, s 807C(2)(a)); since, as noted above, new rule 2 only comes into play when the conditions of new rule 1 are not satisfied, this necessarily implies that new rule 1 was also failed;

(b) since the original transfer of assets, there have been one or more tax years where the individual was not liable under TCA 1997, s 806 because either old rule 2 or new rule 2 applied to all the relevant transactions up to the end of that year (or would have applied but for an absence of income to be attributed to the individual) (TCA 1997, s 807C(2)(b)), this will be termed for convenience a 'rule 2' year;

(c) the income taxable under TCA 1997, s 806 is attributable:

  (i) partly to relevant transactions which satisfied old rule 2 or new rule 2 in the last exempt year; and

  (ii) partly to other associated operations ('chargeable operations') (TCA 1997, s 807C(2)(c)).

An 'exempt year' is a 'rule 2' year where there was no earlier tax year in which the individual was liable to TCA 1997, s 806 (or would have been liable but for an absence of income to be attributed to the individual) (TCA 1997, s 807C(1)). It seems this restriction applies to any liability of the individual under TCA 1997, s 806, not just in relation to the arrangements concerned. In relation to requirement (b), if exemption had been obtained under old rule 1 or new rule 1, the relief will not apply.

Where the conditions are met, the liability of the individual will be computed on the basis of so much of the income as appears to the Revenue Commissioners to be justly and reasonably attributable to the chargeable operations in all the circumstances of the case (TCA 1997, s 807C(3)). F(TA)A 2015, s 38(8), which was subject to Ministerial Order (SI 110/2016 appointed 21 March 2016 as the day on which the Finance (Tax Appeals) Act 2016, came into operation), amends this provision to remove the reference to how the matter appears to the Revenue Commissioners making it a more objective test. The factors to be taken into account for the purposes of this apportionment (if any) include whether, and to what extent, the chargeable operations or any of them directly or indirectly affect—

(a) the character, description or amount of any income of any person;
(b) any person's power to enjoy any income; or
(c) the character, description or amount of any income which a person has power to enjoy (TCA 1997, s 807C(4)).

This is a strikingly vague prescription. There is no provision for an appeal against the Revenue's decision under the normal statutory mechanisms. The relief would not apply in relation to **Example 17.207.1**, as exemption had been obtained under old rule 1 rather than old rule 2.

Example 17.207.2

In 2004, Mr Butler subscribes for all the issued shares on the incorporation of Sam Inc a company resident in Erewhon, where it subsequently earns profits from its trading operations. He owns 100 per cent of the shares in Sam Inc. Erewhon does not have a double tax treaty with Ireland. It is accepted that the transaction is commercial and has only minor tax avoidance purposes, so that old rule 2 applied up to and including tax year 2014. In July 2015, Mr Butler transfers his shares to a non-resident discretionary trust of which he is one of the beneficiaries; the main purpose of the settlement is to avoid Irish taxation and thus this associated operation automatically fails both new rule 1 and new rule 2. In this case, the chargeable operation (the settlement on the trust) does not alter the income accruing to Sam Inc nor does it enlarge Mr Butler's power to enjoy the income of the company, although it *does* alter the heading under which he will be treated as having power to enjoy the income of Sam Inc (so that arguably the decision in *Herdman* would not have applied in any event). It would appear therefore that there is a very strong case that no income should be attributed to the chargeable operations in this situation and that no liability should arise under TCA 1997, s 806. However, there will be no protection from TCA 1997, s 807A (see **17.210**) in these circumstances.

The EU exemption in TCA 1997, s 806(11)

This exemption was brought about by FA 2015, s 21 and coming into operation on 1 January 2016. This does not mean that transactions entered into before this date could not argue a fundamental freedom has been impinged in a manner which was contrary to EU law before that date. Section 806(11) will be looked at below but some background is necessary.

The UK equivalent of TCA 1997, s 806 was most recently referred to in the UK First Tier Tribunal (FTT) decision of *Fisher & Ors v HMRC* [2014] UK FTT 804 (TC). The facts of the case as outlined in the first few paragraphs of the tribunal's decision were as follows:

Before internet betting became as widely available as a means of betting as it is now, there was 'telebetting', the placing of bets by telephone. The Fisher family, of which Anne, Stephen and Peter Fisher were each members, built up a successful and well-known bookmaking business under the Stan James brand over a number of years. It was one of the first in its sector to recognise and exploit the possibilities of the fast developing market for telebetting in the mid-1990s. Over the course of 1999/2000, a number of bookmakers based in the UK who also offered telebetting, including Stan James, moved their operations to Gibraltar. The move of so many industry players over a relatively short timescale excited ongoing coverage not just in the industry press but the wider media at the time and speculation as to whether and if so when the UK would make changes to its betting duty regime. At the time the betting duty regime was considerably more favourable in Gibraltar than in the UK. This appeal concerned the application of the anti-avoidance code on transfer of assets abroad legislation to the transfer of the telebetting business to Stan James Gibraltar Limited and income which subsequently arose to that company. Stan James (Abingdon) Limited ('SJA'), a UK resident company of which Anne, Stephen and Peter were each shareholders, sold its telebetting business to Stan James Gibraltar Limited ('SJG'), a Gibraltarian resident company of which the appellants were also shareholders (in different proportions). Of interest for our purposes is that Anne Fisher had an Irish nationality. The court held for the appellants (ie that the transfer of assets abroad legislation did not apply in this instance) on various grounds but when it came to Anne Fisher the EU law argument again raised its head.

The tribunal notes at para 638 et seq as follows:

> Anne Fisher's situation as an Irish national establishing in another part of the 'UK' is, in our view, analogous to the non-Belgian Member State nationals, resident in Belgium, whose rights to establish in another part of Belgium were held to be infringed .... The relevance of Anne Fisher's nationality may be masked by the many years during which she has lived in the UK but it is not clear to us at all why it should make a difference in principle how long she has been in the UK. There was no legal authority from the cases we were referred to for the suggestion that she should lose her freedom to establish into a Member State different to the Member State of which she was a national just because she has exercised other rights and has become resident/established in the UK .... The relevance of Anne Fisher's nationality is not so much that by virtue of it she has exercised free movement or freedom of establishment rights into the UK, but that her rights as a national of one Member State to establish in a Member State other than that of her origin (and in this case a particular part of the 'UK') are preserved not extinguished .... The conclusion at this point therefore is that the European law arguments are relevant to Anne Fisher but not to Stephen Fisher and Peter Fisher.

The tribunal proceeded for this part of the decision on the basis that the UK and Gibraltar were, for the purposes of the freedom of establishment and free movement of capital, to be treated as different parts of the same Member State, ie the UK. In relation to Anne, the tribunal was clear at para 649 that she was a national of one Member State (Ireland) who was 'dissuaded from establishing in part of another Member State (the UK for the purposes of this argument) by being charged to UK tax on the profits of SJG and being charged at a higher personal tax rate'.

An infringement of a fundamental freedom does not mean that it is incompatible with EU law. There are instances where such infringements can be justified and if justified then for it to be compatible the legislative response must be a proportionate response. In both these instances the tribunal held that EU law had not been complied with. It is noted at para 653 that HMRC argued that the transfer of assets abroad legislation was justified and proportionate and made reference to 'justifications of balanced allocation of taxation, fiscal cohesion and/or the fight against tax avoidance' but the tribunal noted that only the fight against anti-avoidance was elucidated upon by the HMRC. Although not mentioned in the decision these three justifications have their basis in EU law. For example, the CJEU in *Marks & Spencer plc v Halsey (Her Majesty's Inspector of Taxes)* (Case C-446/03) which dealt with cross border group loss relief made the following similar points at paras 42 and 43:

> the United Kingdom and the other Member States which submitted observations put forward three factors to justify the restriction. First, in tax matters profits and losses are two

> sides of the same coin and must be treated symmetrically in the same tax system in order to protect a balanced allocation of the power to impose taxes between the different Member States concerned. Second, if the losses were taken into consideration in the parent company's Member State they might well be taken into account twice. Third, and last, if the losses were not taken into account in the Member State in which the subsidiary is established there would be a risk of tax avoidance.

That said, as noted by the tribunal only the anti-avoidance issues were developed by the HMRC. The tribunal referred to the European Court's decision in *Cadbury Schweppes plc, Cadbury Schweppes Overseas Ltd v Commissioners of Inland Revenue* (Case C–196/04) which dealt with Controlled Foreign Companies (CFC) legislation which is not too dissimilar, at least conceptually, from the legislation at issue in this case (in that if certain conditions are not met then certain elements of a foreign subsidiary's results can be subjected to tax in the parent's jurisdiction) citing:

> As suggested by the United Kingdom Government and the Commission at the hearing, that finding must be based on objective factors which are ascertainable by third parties with regard, in particular, to the extent to which the CFC physically exists in terms of premises, staff and equipment .... If checking those factors leads to the finding that the CFC is a fictitious establishment not carrying out any genuine economic activity in the territory of the host Member State, the creation of that CFC must be regarded as having the characteristics of a wholly artificial arrangement. That could be so in particular in the case of a 'letterbox' or 'front' subsidiary ...

In this case the tribunal found that SJG was a real operation with premises, staff and equipment. It was not a letter box company and 'there can be no question in our minds that it falls within the artificial arrangements envisaged by "avoidance" as understood in European law terms ... It follows from *Cadbury-Schweppes* that this behaviour does not amount to avoidance in European law terms and that the justification of fighting against tax avoidance understood in those terms does not serve to justify the [Transfer of Assets Abroad] legislation which is cast in far wider terms.'

Finance Act 2015 amendments

The explanatory memorandum which accompanied the Finance Bill as initiated explained the amendment discussed below that it 'amends the provisions in relation to the:

> 'transfer of assets abroad' legislation. This legislation is an anti-avoidance provision which was introduced in 1974. It provides, inter alia, that if arrangements are put in place such that income arises to a non-resident but a resident individual has the power to enjoy that income, then that resident individual is chargeable to income tax in respect of that income. The first amendment in this section is to ensure that the provision is compatible with the Treaty on the Functioning of the European Union.

So the EU law intention is clear.

FA 2015, s 21(1) inserts a new sub-s (11) into TCA 1997, s 806. It defines 'non-resident person', 'relevant Member State' and 'relevant transactions' and then adds in the following provision:

> Where a non-resident person is resident in a relevant Member State, sub-s (10) shall apply as if the following were substituted for paragraphs (b), (c), (d) and (e) of that subsection:
>
> (b) Subsections (4) and (5) shall not apply where the individual concerned shows in writing or otherwise to the satisfaction of the Revenue Commissioners that—
>
> (i) it would not be reasonable to draw the conclusion that the relevant transactions

form part of any arrangement or scheme of which the main purpose is, or one of the main purposes is, the avoidance of a liability to tax, and

(ii) genuine economic activities are carried on by the non-resident person in the relevant Member State.

TCA 1997, s 806(10) outlines certain exemptions from the application of the charging provisions in TCA 1997, s 806(4) and (5) discussed in **17.207** under the 'new rules'. It is curious that sub-s (11) leaves sub-s (10)(a) undisturbed given that it has definitions therein which are not relevant for the interpretation of sub-s 1 but it also has the definition of 'relevant transactions' which is so used thereby necessitating some of that subsection to remain.

TCA 1997, s 806(11) notes that where the person, resident or domiciled outside Ireland, to whom income becomes payable is resident in the EU or EEA then the charging provisions in sub-ss (4) and (5) will not apply where a 'main purpose or one of the main purposes' test is met and 'genuine economic activities are carried on by the non-resident person in the relevant Member State'.

Note the similarity between this limb and the suggested conforming interpretation outlined by counsel for HMRC with which the Court of Appeal agreed with in *Vodafone 2* in respect of a controlled foreign company: 'if it is, in that accounting period, actually established in another member state of the EEA and carries on genuine economic activities there'. The choice of expression 'genuine economic activities' is initially intriguing in both instances and produces a more positive tone than the negative 'wholly artificial arrangements' but it was also used by the CJEU in *Cadbury Schweppes plc, Cadbury Schweppes Overseas Ltd v Commissioners of Inland Revenue* (Case C-196/04) so has its basis in dicta of the European courts.

The above reference to *Vodafone 2* is to *Vodafone 2 v Revenue and Customs Commissioners* [2005] STC (SCD) 549 which was heard by the Special Commissioners in June 2008. The point at issue was the implications of the decision in *Cadbury Schweppes plc, Cadbury Schweppes Overseas Ltd v Commissioners of Inland Revenue* (C-196/04) at the CJEU and whether the motive test outlined in the UK's CFC legislation was sufficient to deal only with 'wholly artificial arrangements' as outlined in *Cadbury*. There the court noted:

> As suggested by the United Kingdom Government and the Commission at the hearing, that finding must be based on objective factors which are ascertainable by third parties with regard, in particular, to the extent to which the CFC physically exists in terms of premises, staff and equipment .... If checking those factors leads to the finding that the CFC is a fictitious establishment not carrying out any genuine economic activity in the territory of the host Member State, the creation of that CFC must be regarded as having the characteristics of a wholly artificial arrangement. That could be so in particular in the case of a 'letterbox' or 'front' subsidiary ....

The link between 'genuine economic activity' and 'wholly artificial arrangements' can be clearly seen above.

In *Vodafone 2* the two Commissioners had differing views, but a casting vote confirmed the answer to the question posed, ie, that the motive test dealt could be construed as only dealing with such arrangements. The matter went as far as the Court of Appeal in May 2009 in that the High Court before it agreed with the taxpayer that it was not possible to interpret the CFC legislation so as to conform with the freedom of establishment as declared by the CJEU's decision in *Cadbury*. The Court of Appeal disagreed with the approach taken by the Special Commissioners but in the end took the view that the CFC legislation could be interpreted in a way that conformed with EU law. It's just the way that such conformation actually occurred in this instance isn't based on the motive test alone.

Sir Andrew Morritt C giving the leading judgment at the Court of Appeal noted the exceptions to the CFC rule as follows:

> … Section 748 is headed 'Cases where section 747(3) does not apply'. Section 748(1) provides: 'No apportionment under section 747(3) falls to be made as regards an accounting period of a controlled foreign company if—There follow in paras (a) to (e) a series of exceptions. They relate to the CFC and may be summarised as those CFCs as pursue (a) an acceptable distribution policy, (b) engage in exempt activities, (c) satisfy a public quotation condition, (d) make profits of less than £50,000 or (e) are resident in a territory specified in regulations to be made by HMRC subject to any conditions HMRC might specify. The exceptions specified in paras (a), (b) and (c) are further elaborated in the applicable parts of Sch 25. It is clear that these exceptions are not mutually exclusive.

On para (3) he noted that:

> With regard to the exception in para (e) regulations were made by HMRC in December 1998 …The schedule to the Regulations has two lists of specified territories. The other conditions to be satisfied in order to be entitled to the benefit of this exception differ according to which list the territory falls into. A number of member states of the EU come within the first list. Luxembourg and other member states fall within the second but the relevant conditions are not satisfied by [the company at issue in this decision] ….

He went on to cite s 748(3) below which he noted differs from the other exceptions outlined above in that 'it depends on the subjective intention behind the relevant transactions or the existence of the CFC, not the objective existence of specific circumstances' (ie the motive test).

> Notwithstanding that none of the paragraphs (a) to (e) of ss(1) above [exceptions from the application of the CFC legislation] applies to an accounting period of a controlled foreign company, no apportionment under s 747(3) falls to be made as regards that accounting period if it is the case that:
>
> (a) insofar as any of the transactions the results of which are reflected in the profits arising in that accounting period, or any two or more transactions taken together, the results of at least one of which are so reflected, achieved a reduction in UK tax, either the reduction so achieved was minimal or it was not the main purpose or one of the main purposes of that transaction or, as the case may be, of those transactions taken together to achieve that reduction, and;
>
> (b) it was not the main reason or, as the case may be, one of the main reasons for a company's existence in that accounting period to achieve a reduction in the United Kingdom tax by diversion of profits from the United Kingdom ….

However, as noted earlier, it is important to note that the High Court concluded that it was 'impossible to construe [the motive test in the CFC legislation] so as to make it conform to the right of establishment under art 43 EC'. It must be recalled that the CJEU in *Cadbury* had opined at para 72 of its decision as follows: 'In this case, it is for the national court to determine whether, as maintained by the United Kingdom government, the motive test, as defined by the legislation on CFCs, lends itself to an interpretation which enables the taxation provided for by that legislation to be restricted to wholly artificial arrangements …'. The reference to 'wholly artificial arrangements' is clear but the Court of Appeal held that it was not bound by the motive test alone with Sir Andrew Morritt C noting para 36 as follows 'This court is entitled and bound to consider all parts of the CFC legislation in ascertaining whether it is amenable to a conforming interpretation'. This is an important point in that having looked at the whole of the CFC legislation the judge took the view that an interpretation which conformed to EU law could be arrived at. This is because counsel for HMRC suggested, which the court ultimately agreed with, that 'all that is required is to introduce an additional exception in respect of a controlled foreign company: "if it is, in that accounting period, actually established in another member state of the EEA and carries on genuine economic activities there." Such an exception could be an additional lettered paragraph in s 748(1) or an additional alternative in s 748(3)'. But how the suggestion of implying additions to legislation stands so as to conform with EU law if it isn't in the law already?

Sir Andrew, at para 37 of his decision summarised 'the principles to be observed in looking for a conforming interpretation in either the European Community or human rights contexts ... The principles which those cases established or illustrated were helpfully summarised by counsel for HMRC in terms from which counsel for V2 did not dissent. Such principles are that:

> In summary, the obligation on the English courts to construe domestic legislation consistently with Community law obligations is both broad and far-reaching. In particular:
>
> (a) It is not constrained by conventional rules of construction ...
>
> (b) It does not require ambiguity in the legislative language ...
>
> (d) It permits departure from the strict and literal application of the words which the legislature has elected to use ...
>
> (e) It permits the implication of words necessary to comply with Community law obligations ... and
>
> (f) The precise form of the words to be implied does not matter ...
>
> The only constraints on the broad and far-reaching nature of the interpretative obligation are that:
>
> (a) The meaning should 'go with the grain of the legislation' and be 'compatible with the underlying thrust of the legislation being construed.' ... An interpretation should not be adopted which is inconsistent with a fundamental or cardinal feature of the legislation since this would cross the boundary between interpretation and amendment; ... and
>
> (b) The exercise of the interpretative obligation cannot require the courts to make decisions for which they are not equipped or give rise to important practical repercussions which the court is not equipped to evaluate ...

Counsel for the taxpayer objected to the interpretation which allowed for insertion of the additional exception into the CFC provisions under three grounds all of which were obviated by the Court of Appeal. The arguments, which could be made to an Irish court should a similar matter arise '(1) such an interpretation would not conform with the scheme and essentials of the CFC legislation; (2) such an interpretation would create two regimes, one for CFCs established within the EEA and ... (3) any such interpretation would be retrospective in its operation, involve legal or economic policy decisions and would fail to satisfy the test of legal certainty'.

In the end the Court of Appeal allowed the conforming interpretation in that, inter alia, it 'does not alter the impact on other CFCs which are not excepted by any other exception. Certainly it provides an additional exception but, as counsel for HMRC submitted, the grain or thrust of the legislation recognises that the wide net cast by s 747(3) is intended to be narrowed by s 748. Further the terms of various exceptions were not intended to be either mutually exclusive or immutable as the ability to amend the conditions contained in various parts of Sch 25 and the terms of para (e) of s 748(1) show.

The Irish courts have taken a similar approach in *Murphy v Bord Telecom Éireann* [1989] ILRM 53 but it is not beyond doubt that they would go as far as *Vodafone 2*. There Keane J looked at legislation which although not specifically designed to implement EU legislation, was in conflict with what was then Art 119 of the EC treaty and noted that '... the Oireachtas is presumed not to legislate in a manner which is in breach of rights protected under community law. Those rights already existed in our domestic law by virtue of s 2 of the European Communities Act 1972 when the Act was passed by the Oireachtas. In the present case, in the light of the ruling of the Court of Justice of the EC, this court should seek if possible to adopt a teleological construction of the relevant sections of the Act ... one which looks to the effect of the legislation rather than the actual words used by the legislature'. He then went on to insert additional words by reference to the clear objectives of Art 119 of the EC treaty. The principle in *Marleasing* (which was invoked in Sir Andrew Morritt C in *Vodafone 2*) was also invoked in *Byrne v Conroy* [1995] HC where it was held that an ambiguity should be resolved in favour of the construction which was consistent with the EU treaty.

A similar point was made in the Irish Supreme Court in *Albatros Feeds v Minister for Agriculture and Food & Ors* [2006] IESC 52 where it was noted 'the Court is under an obligation to interpret national law, so far as possible, in the light of the Community law provisions it is designed to implement. The important qualification is: so far as possible. The European Court does not interpret national law. It is a fundamental principle that the Community law respects national procedural autonomy. The national court is subject to the obligation of "conforming interpretation," as the court described it in its judgment in Case C–105/03 *Criminal proceedings against Maria Pupino* (judgment delivered 16 June 2005). There are, however, limits to that obligation. Most recently, the European Court in its judgment in Case C–212/04 *Adeneler v ELOG*, repeated that "the obligation on a national court to refer to the content of a directive when interpreting and applying the relevant rules of domestic law is limited by general principles of law, particularly those of legal certainty and non-retroactivity, and that obligation cannot serve as the basis for an interpretation of national law contra legem.' It should be noted that *Albatros* looked to a regulation which was bound by s 3 EU Act 1972 rather than an article in the EU treaty which would be bound by s 2 of that Act which says that 'the treaties governing the European Communities and the existing and future acts adopted by the institutions of those Communities shall be binding on the State and shall be part of the domestic law thereof under the conditions laid down in those treaties'.

The key point here is that a conforming interpretation in *Vodafone 2* was applied in order to arrive at the conclusion that the CFC provisions could be read in accordance with EU law. However, that interpretation was not based on the motive test alone but rather the full CFC legislation which has other exceptions.

It is unclear whether an Irish court would go as far as the Court of Appeal did in *Vodafone 2* in that it would mean the Irish court effectively ignoring the 'main purpose' test or reading it objectively which the UK court admitted had its difficulties.

17.208 Assessment and computation of income

TCA 1997, s 807(1) charges the chargeable individual under Sch D Case IV on any income of any foreign person that is deemed by either TCA 1997, s 806(4) or (5) to be his income. The issue of how that income should be computed was examined in *Lord Chetwode v IRC* [1974] STC 474, where the relevant income consisted of foreign dividends received by a foreign company. It was held by the House of Lords that the resident individual was not entitled to any deduction for the company's management and other expenses. If the taxpayer had received the dividends himself, he would not have been allowed any deduction for his expenses of managing the investments, but only for the costs of collecting the foreign dividends.

In *Lord Chetwode's* case, it was held that the resident individual's liability to income tax should be computed on the dividends as they came in, ie on the 'gross' income of the foreign company, and not on the net income of the company after deducting the expenses. The House of Lords rejected the taxpayer's argument that he had no power to enjoy that part of the company's income which was spent in paying the expenses.

In the course of his judgment, Lord Wilberforce indicated that the UK equivalent of TCA 1997, s 806, being part of an Act which dealt comprehensively with all aspects of income tax in the United Kingdom, was concerned with individuals ordinarily resident there. He then went on:

So one should start with a disposition to interpret 'income' as the word is used in our tax legislation. There has never been any definition in our tax code. What is chargeable with income tax is left to be determined under the particular heads of charge under the Schedules. Dividends received from foreign companies are income arising from possessions out of the United Kingdom, taxed as such under Case V of Sch D. If for the purpose of applying section [TCA 1997, s 806] it is sought to claim some deduction against that 'income' before the tax is imposed, some warrant must be found for the deduction.

Lord Wilberforce quoted with approval the following words of Viscount Radcliffe in *IRC v Frere* 42 TC 125:

> In principle it is gross income as reduced for the purposes of assessment by such deductions only as are actually specified in the tax code or are granted by way of reliefs … No doubt the assessment of profits under Sch D has come to require a rather different approach, since in that case the basic figure for assessment is the balance between receipts and expenditure …

The reference in these quotations to the heads of charge under the Schedules suggest strongly that the amount of the foreign person's income that is deemed by TCA 1997, s 806 to be the income of the chargeable individual should be determined in accordance with the computational rules of the relevant Schedule or Case. For this purpose, the relevant Schedule or Case is the one under which the individual would be chargeable in respect of the income in question if he were to receive it directly. If, on that assumption, the individual would be entitled to deduct certain expenses, etc if paid by him in arriving at his income for tax purposes, then any expenses of the same kind incurred by the foreign person in relation to the income should be deductible in arriving at the amount chargeable on the individual under Sch D Case IV as a result of TCA 1997, s 806.

Example 17.208.1

> In January 2014, Mr T X Voider, who is domiciled and resident in Ireland, had transferred immovable property situated in Brazil to Minesweeper Ltd, a company incorporated and resident in Gibraltar. In consideration, Mr Voider was issued 1,000 shares in Minesweeper Ltd (its entire share capital). From May 2014 onwards, Minesweeper Ltd derived a rental income from the villas under leases which required it to meet the expenses of insurance and all maintenance, repairs, etc. The company also incurred a certain amount of expenses each

year in managing the villas. It is assumed that Mr Voider cannot avail of either of the defences under TCA 1997, s 806(10).

In view of Mr Voider's power to enjoy the income of Minesweeper Ltd, TCA 1997, s 806 requires the income of Minesweeper Ltd to be treated as his income from 2014 onwards. For the three tax years 2014, 2015 and 2016, the receipts and expenses of Minesweeper Ltd were as follows:

	Year ended 31/12/2014	*Year ended 31/12/2015*	*Year ended 31/12/2016*
	€	€	€
Gross rental income	14,000	16,000	17,500
Expenses payable:			
Insurance	800	900	1,000
Repairs & maintenance (Revenue)	2,500	7,000	4,600
Improvements (capital)	1,500	12,000	–
Management expenses	820	950	1,100
	5,620	20,850	6,700
Brazilian tax payable	4,900	3,100	5,200
	10,520	23,950	11,900
Net distributable income			
After tax	3,480		5,600
Net deficit		(7,950)	

If Mr Voider had received the income from the Brazilian holiday villas himself, he would have been assessed under Sch D Case III on the net rental income, ie after deducting the insurance, repairs and maintenance (revenue), and management expenses, but would not have been given any deduction for the expenses of improving the property. He would also in practice have been allowed to deduct the Brazilian tax payable (see **17.209** for the treatment of foreign taxes).

Mr Voider is, therefore, assessable under Sch D Case IV on the income of Minesweeper Ltd, computed as follows for each of the three tax years 2014, 2015 and 2016.

	2014	*2015*	*2016*
	€	€	€
Gross rental income	14,000	16,000	17,500
Deductions:			
Insurance	800	900	1,000
Repairs & maintenance	2,500	7,000	4,600
Improvements			
Management expenses	820	950	1,100
Brazilian tax payable	4,900	3,100	5,200
	9,020	11,950	11,900
Net chargeable Sch D Case IV	4,980	4,050	5,600

Following that decision in *Latilla v IRC* 25 TC 107, and *IRC v Brackett* [1986] STC 521, it is clear that trading profits are 'income' for the purposes of TCA 1997, s 806. It should, however, be easier to establish that a trading operation falls within the exceptions to TCA 1997, s 806 (see **17.207**). It should be possible to reduce the relevant income by charging director's remuneration, at least up to a level which does not run foul of the principle enunciated in *Copeman v Flood* 24 TC 53.

The interposition of the 'foreign person' might in some cases convert what would have otherwise been a series of capital gains into trading income. For example, a company may be regarded as a trader where the individual with the power to enjoy its income might not have been (see, eg *Lewis Emmanuel and Son Ltd v White* 42 TC 369). On the other hand, the interposition may convert what would otherwise have been by a UK trade into a foreign trade (see *Ogilvie v Kitton* 5 TC 338).

In *Latilla v IRC* it was held that the Revenue were not entitled to go behind the accounts of a partnership in which a non-resident company was a member. Per Lord Green MR:

> The income *payable* to a partner is his share of the partnership profits which the partners in accordance with the partnership agreement determine to *divide* … the Crown was bound to accept the *actual* amounts *received* by the company as being the correct basis for the assessment [emphasis added].

However, it is suggested that Lord Greene's emphasis on the word 'payable' was misplaced and that the term should be understood as meaning something like 'accrue to'. Thus, in *IRC v Brackett*, Hoffman J observed of the decision in *Latilla*:

> Although there are references in the speeches to the income having been paid out of partnership funds, I do not think that this was an essential element in the reasoning. A partnership is not, after all, a separate legal entity … the profits of the partnership arise to the partners in exactly the same way as in the case of a sole trader.

TCA 1997, s 807(2) entitles the chargeable individual to the same deductions and reliefs in computing his liability to tax as if the foreign person's income deemed to be his income had actually been received by him. This provision seems to be designed to ensure that although the income in question is only notional, it is to be treated as if he had actually received it in computing his personal income tax liability. This is of particular relevance to the treatment of overseas taxes suffered on the income concerned: see **17.209**.

TCA 1997, s 807(3) prevents the same resident individual being charged to income tax twice on the same income. It provides that, if he has been assessed under Sch D Case IV on any relevant income of a foreign person due to the deeming of that income by TCA 1997, s 806 to be his income, and if that income is actually received by him subsequently, then on the occasion of the subsequent receipt, the income is deemed not to be his income.

Clearly, this rule is essential since, as has been indicated previously, the charge to tax under TCA 1997, s 806 arises when income becomes payable to the foreign person, whether or not any actual distributions of the income are made to the individual when it is received. If, for example, a resident individual previously charged under Sch D Case IV due to TCA 1997, s 806 on interest income received in the year ended 31 December 2014 by a Jersey investment company, to which he transferred assets a number of years earlier, is paid a dividend on 19 September 2015 by that company out of that interest income, then TCA 1997, s 807(3) applies to exclude that dividend from his taxable income.

TCA 1997, s 807(4) deals specifically with the case where the resident individual is treated by TCA 1997, s 806 as having power to enjoy an income of a foreign person due to that individual having received any such benefit as is mentioned in TCA 1997, s 806(6)(c). This arises where the individual receives any benefit provided out of the income of the foreign person (or out of monies available for the purpose by reason of the effect(s) of associated operations on that income or on assets representing it).

The case of *R v Dimsey* (2001) UK HL 46 considered the question of whether income of a foreign transferee which is deemed to be income of a UK resident transferor under the provisions of the UK equivalent TCA 1997, s 806, is for tax purposes regarded as not being the income of the foreign transferee. It is important to note that the UK legislation is not identical to the Irish equivalent legislation contained in TCA 1997, s 806 but is largely the same. The case was by way of an appeal against criminal proceedings against the appellant where he had been found guilty of an offence conspiring to cheat the Inland Revenue of corporation tax payable by offshore companies to which assets had been transferred. An unusual aspect of the case was that the offshore company was held by the Court of Appeal to be UK tax resident. The appellant argued that the Income and Corporation Tax Acts 1988, s 739(2) (equivalent to TCA 1997, s 806), which deems the income of the foreign transferee to be the income of the transferor, imputes that such income is not deemed to be the income of the foreign transferee since it is taxable in the transferor's hands. Accordingly, he argued that on that basis the companies were not liable to pay UK corporation tax on its profits and he could not therefore be guilty of the offence of cheating or conspiring to cheat the Revenue of corporation tax payable by the companies.

The two issues to be considered by the court were whether the income of the offshore companies, which was deemed for income tax purposes to be the income of the transferor, results in such income not being regarded as the income of the transferee companies and, secondly, if the answer to the first issue is in the negative, whether this position is at variance with the right to property guaranteed by Article 1 of Protocol Number 1 of the European Convention for the Protection of Human Rights and Fundamental Freedoms. The House of Lords considered these questions in isolation. Clearly if assets are transferred to a company which is tax resident in Ireland, TCA 1997, s 806 does not apply and although the Court of Appeal had decided in this case that the transferee companies were UK tax resident the House of Lords considered the ICTA 1988, s 739 point in isolation.

Lord Scott of Foscote delivering the leading judgment in this case considered that the first question was a matter of construction of ICTA 1988, s 739 (2). In reaching his decision he referred to the fact that the legislation provides for the income of the offshore company to be deemed to be the income of the UK tax resident transferor does not necessarily result in such income not being regarded as the income of the offshore company. He referred to other statutory provisions, including settlements made in favour of minor children where the legislation specifically provides that the income is not deemed to be the income of the other person. The argument put forward by the appellant against double taxation was also dismissed. In construing the legislation, he noted that there was no provision in the legislation prohibiting the taxation of the income in the hands of a transferee company despite the fact that such deemed income would have been taxable in the hands of the transferor. In this regard, he commented as follows:

> This however is a more theoretical point than a real one. It is in practice highly unlikely that UK tax can be recovered from a ICTA 1988, s 739 transferee. Transferees are chosen by tax avoiders in order to avoid UK tax. Non resident and foreign domiciled transferees are likely to be chosen. They do not submit tax returns to the Revenue. In the present case, it is only because Mr Chipping, the transferor, so involved himself in the affairs of his offshore companies that they became resident in the UK that their liability to corporation tax arose.

> Accordingly, the double taxation possibilities that the Revenue's case undoubtedly leaves theoretically open do not seem to carry weight in considering the correct construction of ICTA 1988, s 739(2).

The court also dismissed the principle contained in *IRC v Vestey* (1980) AC 1148 as having application to the current case and held that there was no constitutional difficulty in providing for the income to be taxable both in the transferee's hands and in the transferor's hand.

With regard to the second issue before the court, namely the application of the European Convention on Human Rights, the court dismissed this argument as not being relevant and dismissed the appeal by the appellant.

This decision has been criticised by a number of commentators and it is highly questionable whether it would be followed in Ireland. The decision would have application where the foreign transferee company is resident in Ireland, for example if the offshore company had an Irish branch. However, if the branch carries on a *bona fide* trade and can satisfy the Revenue Commissioners that the transfer of any assets to the offshore company was for *bona fide* commercial reasons and not for the avoidance of tax the provisions of TCA 1997, s 806 would not apply. The decision may have application if a non Irish non treaty resident company, for example a Jersey company, has Irish source income. In this instance the company would have an Irish source tax liability and this income would also be deemed to be the income of the Irish transferee under the provisions of TCA 1997, s 806(2). If the decision of *R v Dimsey* is followed in Ireland this would result in both the Irish source income being subject to Irish tax in the Jersey company's hands and the same income would also be subject to tax in the Irish transferor's hands under the provisions of TCA 1997, s 806(2). However, the decision in *R v Dimsey* may not be upheld in Ireland on constitutional grounds.

When TCA 1997, s 807(4) applies, the individual is chargeable under Sch D Case IV for the tax year in which the benefit is received on the full amount or value of the benefit, *unless* and to the extent that it can be shown that the benefit is derived directly or indirectly from income on which he has already been charged to tax for the same or any previous year of assessment. It would appear that this rule is intended to deal primarily with a case where the individual does not otherwise have power to enjoy the relevant income, but where a benefit (which may include a payment of any kind) is in fact provided for him out of that income.

In any case where the individual is only regarded as having power to enjoy any relevant income due to the operation of TCA 1997, s 806(6)(c), it appears to be the intention of the rule in TCA 1997, s 807(4) to limit the income assessable under Sch D Case IV so that it does not extend to the full income of the foreign person, but is confined to the actual amount or value of the benefit. However, it seems as if this limitation does not apply in any other case where there is power to enjoy the relevant income under any of the other paragraphs of TCA 1997, s 806(6), or where the charge to tax arises due to the individual receiving or becoming entitled to receive a capital sum. The implications of TCA 1997, s 807(4) have been discussed more fully at **17.205**.

The latter part of TCA 1997, s 807(4) is – like TCA 1997, s 807(3) – designed to avoid a double charge to tax. However, it differs from the rule in TCA 1997, s 807(3) in that it puts the specific onus on the individual to satisfy the inspector that the benefit is derived from income on which he has already been taxed. By contrast, under TCA 1997, s 807, the requirement not to tax the same income again is mandatory on the inspector.

An individual who is resident in the State, but who has a foreign domicile, is entitled to be assessed to Irish tax on his foreign source income on the basis only of the remittances of that income into the State (see **Division 13**). Prior to the insertion of TCA 1997, s 807(5) by FA 1999, s 60(1)(b), a resident but non-domiciled individual could nevertheless be taxed under the rules of TCA 1997, s 806 on the full amount of the income becoming payable to the foreign person in the same way as an individual who is both ordinarily resident and domiciled in the State, assuming of course that either the 'power to enjoy' or 'capital sum' conditions were also satisfied. This was made clear by the fact that the charge to tax under TCA 1997, s 806 is imposed under Sch D Case IV to which the remittance basis does not apply. The fact that, if he had not made the transfer of assets, he could have avoided Irish income tax on the foreign income simply by not remitting it into the State, did not prevent him being assessed on *all* the relevant income, whether or not actually remitted into the State. However, TCA 1997, s 807(5) provided with effect from 12 February 1998 that a non-domiciled individual is not to be chargeable on income deemed to be his under TCA 1997, s 806, if he would not have been chargeable to tax on that income if it had actually been his income. However, TCA 1997 s 807(5) was deleted by FA 2015, s 21(2B) applying to income arising on or after 1 January 2016. It is understood that such deletion was brought about to counter artificial structures surrounding certain employment income. A consequence of this deletion is that a non-domiciled person who has assets abroad with power to enjoy income from those assets may avail of the remittance basis but a person who transferred assets abroad with power to enjoy income from such transferred assets may now be within the application of s 806 where the latter is within the purpose of that section in first instance. As a result of such deletion the reader is directed to earlier editions of this text for a fuller discussion of TCA 1997, s 807(5).

Where the income of the foreign person includes Irish distributions taxable under Sch F, entitlement to any associated tax credit (relevant only up to 5 April 1999) will flow through to the individual (TCA 1997, s 136).

17.209 Double tax treaties and treatment of foreign taxes

The interaction of double tax treaties with TCA 1997, s 806 raises a number of important (and vexed) issues. The first issue is whether or not an Irish resident individual can claim the benefit of a double tax treaty between Ireland and the country in which the foreign person is resident. Thus, for example, assume that A transfers assets to A Co, a company resident in a jurisdiction which has a double tax treaty with Ireland. Assume also that under the terms of the treaty, A Co's investment income is taxable only in the other jurisdiction. On one view, the exemption under the treaty applies to the income of A Co which is deemed under TCA 1997, s 806 to be that of A personally. The reasoning behind this view is that by virtue of TCA 1997, s 826(1) the exemption under the treaty 'shall, notwithstanding anything in any enactment have the force of law'. Thus, the exemption under the treaty overrides the charge otherwise imposed by TCA 1997, s 806.

The alternative view is that the notional income attributed to the taxpayer under TCA 1997, s 806 forms a different taxable subject-matter from the income which is actually received by the foreign person. It may be said that the foreign person's income is simply the *measure* of the income to be assessed on the chargeable individual.

In *IRC v Willoughby* [1995] STC 143, the taxpayer had invested in 'personalised' investment bonds (ie single premium insurance policies carrying a right to select the underlying investments) with an insurance company which was resident in the Isle of Man, and which did not have a permanent establishment in the UK (as defined for the purposes of the UK – Isle of Man treaty). Article 3(2) of the treaty provided, in effect, that the business profits of an Isle of Man enterprise would be exempt from UK tax, unless those profits accrued through a UK permanent establishment. The Inland Revenue sought to assess the taxpayer under the UK equivalent of TCA 1997, s 806 on the income accruing to the Isle of Man company in relation to the premiums paid by the taxpayer in respect of his bond. The taxpayer argued that this income formed part of the business profits of the company, which were exempt under the treaty, and thus could not be taxed upon him (ie as a UK resident entitled to the benefit of the treaty).

The Special Commissioners, rejecting the taxpayer's claim, held that it was not permissible to apply the treaty twice, or to two different persons. It is not clear why, as a matter of principle, if a jurisdiction were to seek to tax the same income twice over, it should not also be obliged to grant treaty exemption twice over as well. In fact, the issue may not arise in the present context since, where the relevant conditions are met, TCA 1997, s 806 deems the income of a non-resident/non-domiciled person to be that of a-resident or ordinary resident individual 'whether [that income] ... would or would not have been chargeable to ... tax apart from the provisions of ... [s 806]'. The word 'would' implies that income taxed under TCA 1997, s 806 is no longer capable of being charged under any of the other provisions of the Income Tax Acts. Indeed, even if it could be said that the language of s 806 is ambiguous, there is a very strong interpretative presumption against double taxation: see **1.405** (note also TCA 1997, s 807(3), discussed above, which, in effect exempts income paid by a non-resident, etc entity out of income already charged to tax on the taxpayer under that section; if the section rules out 'economic' double taxation, it seems highly unlikely that 'legal' double taxation is contemplated thereby); note also the comments of Lord Steyn in *IRC v McGuckian* [1994] STC 888. The position is unclear where there are overlapping anti-avoidance provisions each of which are capable of attributing income which actually accrues to one person to a different person for income tax purposes, as was the position in the *McGuckian* case. The Special Commissioner in *Willoughby* also observed:

> In my opinion there is a distinction between actual income of an individual and actual income of another person which is deemed to be income of the individual.

The Special Commissioner distinguished *Padmore v IRC* [1989] STC 493 where a UK resident partner in a Jersey-based partnership was held to be exempt in respect of his individual share of profits. This in turn relied on the Court's conclusion that the partnership as such was entitled to exemption on its profits under the UK/Jersey Double Tax Treaty (see **14.105**).

The crucial distinction between *Willoughby* and *Padmore*, according to the Special Commissioner, was that the taxpayer in *Padmore* had a 'real share in real profits of a real partnership' (in fact the decision in *Padmore* was rather paradoxical: the Jersey partnership was held in effect to be a distinct entity for double tax treaty purposes, but to be an entirely transparent entity for domestic tax purposes). The Special Commissioner expanded on this point as follows:

> [The attributed] ... income is not industrial or commercial profits of the individual nor quoad [ie regarding] the individual is it deemed to be industrial profits or deemed to be his income as if it were such profits.

It may be doubted if the recharacterisation argument deserved to succeed in *Willoughby*. This is because the provision for assessment under Sch D Case IV appears to be primarily mechanical in nature (although admittedly, it would seem to prevent a non-domiciled individual claiming the benefit of the remittance basis in respect of foreign source income, since TCA 1997, s 71(3) applies only to Sch D Case III income). In *Chetwode v IRC* [1977] STC 64 Lord Wilberforce indicated that 'income' for TCA 1997, s 806 purposes must generally be calculated according to domestic tax principles, by reference to the rules of the Schedule and Case under which it would fall if it had been taxed directly on the chargeable individual.

On the face of it, the rather special facts of *Willoughby* did seem to give rise to a mismatch between the treaty-exempt income and the income assessable under the UK equivalent of TCA 1997, s 806. This is because the UK Inland Revenue argued that the taxpayer should be treated as having 'power to enjoy' the gross income accruing on the funds which represented his original investments; however, it was only the net trading profit in respect of his investments (ie after *inter alia* providing for the payouts on the bonds) which would have been eligible for treaty exemption. However, the apparent mismatch may disappear if it is accepted that the taxpayer could in fact only have been assessed on the net profit figure (since it was that amount which represented the 'income' of the non-resident person, and that what is assessable under s 806 (see *Chetwode v IRC* [1977] STC 64, at p 68j; 69a).

In *Bricom Holdings v IRC* [1996] STC (SCD) 228, the Special Commissioners were concerned with the application of the 'Controlled Foreign Company (CFC)' legislation in the UK, which (very broadly speaking) attributes the profits (subject to some exceptions of certain non-resident subsidiaries to their UK resident parent). In this case, the non-resident subsidiary was resident in the Netherlands and received UK interest which was exempt in its hands under the UK/Netherlands Double Tax Treaty. The UK parent argued that this exemption extended to the profits attributed to it under the CFC rules.

The Special Commissioners held that the interest in question was simply an ingredient in the computation of the profits assessable under the CFC rules and thereby lost its character as 'interest'. They observed:

If it had been the original interest which had been apportioned to [the parent ...] *as interest,* this might not in itself have prevented the treaty from applying to it. But it has already lost its character as interest before being apportioned. The situation is analogous to that found in *IRC v Willoughby*. Income which was 'industrial and commercial profits' of one person was deemed by [Irish TCA 1997, s 806] ... to be income of another person, but its character as industrial and commercial profits was not preserved as it was charged to tax in the hands of the deemed recipient under Case IV of Sch D [Irish Sch D Case IV] (emphasis added).

The 'recharacterisation' argument accepted by the Special Commissioners in *Bricom* has subsequently been rejected by the Court of Appeal in *Bricom* [1997] STC 1179. The court held in favour of the Revenue on different grounds, namely that the interest was only an element in the calculation of a notional profit figure assessed on the taxpayer. This would not seem to be a valid point in relation to TCA 1997, s 806, where the income of the foreign person is directly imputed to the chargeable individual.

Another important argument was raised by the Inland Revenue before the Special Commissioner in *Willoughby*. This was to the effect that the exemption under the UK/ Isle of Man Treaty was 'personal to the Manx enterprise', ie the treaty in exempting the profits of the Manx enterprise was in effect exempting the Manx enterprise to which those profits accrued. *Padmore* would only be an apparent exception to this principle, since, in that case, the individual partners and the Jersey partnership were one and the same (although, as already noted, this logic was not pursued in deciding whether or not the Jersey partnership as such qualified for treaty exemption).

The issue of the availability (or otherwise) of double tax relief was not pursued when *Willoughby* came before the UK Court of Appeal. The Court of Appeal in *Bricom* appeared to accept in principle that a treaty exemption could be extended to persons other than the actual recipient of the income at issue. However, no definitive judicial guidance in the UK or Ireland exists on this point, which remains open to debate. It may be noted however that the Inland Revenue have historically commented on this issue, as reported in CCAB TR 500 (issued 10/3/83), in the context of CGTA 1992, s 13 (the UK equivalent to TCA 1997, s 590):

> CGTA 1992, s 13 … can impose a charge on a parent company on capital gains arising from disposals by its overseas subsidiary if the latter would be a close company if it were resident in the UK. The Inland Revenue has confirmed that, where the overseas subsidiary is resident in a territory with which the UK has a double taxation agreement and there is an article exempting residents of that territory from a charge to UK capital gains tax then such an article may prevent the imposition of a charge under s 13.

Although the reference is to a corporate shareholder, it appears that the Inland Revenue accept that the same principle applies to individual shareholders.

At first sight, the Inland Revenue's position as set out in CCAB TR 590 appears to be inconsistent with the approach which they adopted in *Willoughby*. The source of the distinction made by the Inland Revenue may lie in the typical wording of the capital gains article in double tax treaties. This usually provides that gains other than those mentioned elsewhere in the article (typically the article will mention gains in respect of immovable property located in one of the contracting states) may be taxed only in the state of which the person making the disposal ('the alienator') is resident. The inference seems to be that the article confines the taxing rights to the state where the alienator is resident, ie irrespective of where the associated capital gains might be taxable under the domestic laws of the contracting states.

It may be objected that this distinction is rather artificial, on the basis that it is implicit that the alienator will normally be the person to whom any gains will actually accrue. Following the Inland Revenue's own line of argument in *Willoughby*, the benefit of the treaty article should therefore be confined to the alienator. It is interesting that the Inland Revenue appear to have decided that this is not a good point in the instant context.

It is also noteworthy that the Inland Revenue's approach in CCAB TR 500 embodies an acceptance that gains taxable under the equivalent of TCA 1997, s 590 are the same gains as those eligible for exemption under a relevant double tax treaty (so that the 'recharacterisation' point, raised in *Willoughby* and *Bricom*, does not apply).

Assuming that exemption is not available, this raises a second issue, ie whether or not the chargeable individual is entitled to credit by reference to a relevant double tax treaty for overseas tax imposed on the income of the 'foreign person'. TCA 1997, s 807(2) states that in computing the chargeable individual's liability in respect of the income assessed under TCA 1997, s 806, 'the same deductions and reliefs shall be allowed as if the income had actually been received by him'. In practice, it is thought that the Revenue Commissioners would accept that the taxpayer can accordingly claim credit relief under a treaty, although only to the extent that the overseas tax suffered equals that which would have been suffered by the taxpayer if he had received it directly. The fact that TCA 1997, s 807(2) does not expressly deem the taxpayer to have paid the foreign tax does not appear to be a critical factor.

In order to demonstrate this point, it may make it easier to use a specific example. Take the facts of **Example 17.208.1** but assume that the rental income received by the

Gibraltar company had arisen from immovable property situated in France and that the company had paid French tax on that income. In the event that the resident individual (Mr Voider) had received the French rental income himself, he would have been entitled to double taxation relief in the form of a credit for the French tax paid in respect of that income to be offset against his liability to Irish tax. Again, it appears that the Revenue will accept that TCA 1997, s 807(2) should entitle the resident individual to the same relief – ie a credit against Irish tax – for the French tax payable on the French rental income deemed to be his income as if that income had been payable to him (instead of to the Gibraltar company).

In support of this conclusion, it may be observed that art 21(b) of the Ireland/France double taxation agreement entitles an Irish resident person to a foreign tax credit in respect of the French tax payable directly or by deduction from income arising from French sources, but subject to the Irish tax rules relating to the granting of credits for foreign tax against Irish tax. These latter rules, contained in TCA 1997, Sch 24 (see **Division 14**), allow the credit for the relevant foreign tax in respect of the foreign income that is assessable to Irish tax. The reference in both art 21(b) and in TCA 1997, Sch 24 are each to the income that has suffered the relevant foreign tax. Since in the present case the relevant foreign tax (French tax) would have been paid on the income deemed by TCA 1997, s 806 to be Mr Voider's income for all Irish tax purposes, it is suggested that TCA 1997, s 807(2) may be interpreted as entitling Mr Voider to a credit for the French tax by way of double taxation relief under the rules of TCA 1997, Sch 24.

The foreign person may pay income tax in the country in which he or it is resident or domiciled in respect of relevant income arising in another country. For example, a company resident in Switzerland may in consequence of a relevant transfer of assets by an Irish resident individual receive income from sources in France (eg French dividends and rental income) and may pay Swiss income tax on it. In such a case, the Irish resident individual assessable to tax under TCA 1997, s 806 in respect of the French dividends and rental income does not – if the legislation is interpreted strictly – appear to have any right under TCA 1997, s 807(2) to a credit for the Swiss tax payable. If he had received the French dividends and rental income himself, he would not have had to pay any Swiss tax at all.

The final issue is whether, if the foreign tax is incurred in a jurisdiction with which there is no double tax treaty, can the chargeable individual deduct the foreign tax paid from the amount of his assessable income under TCA 1997, s 806? A similar approach to that extended to the issue of treaty relief should normally apply. TCA 1997, s 71(1) allows – in the case of any foreign income received in the ordinary way by a resident person – the deduction of any foreign income tax paid in respect of the income in question – in the country in which that income arises. Since TCA 1997, s 807(2) entitles the individual chargeable under TCA 1997, s 806 to the same deductions and reliefs as if the relevant income had actually been received by him, it seems that the TCA 1997, s 71(1) deduction should be available for the foreign tax paid by the foreign person in respect of the relevant income. There again seems to be no requirement under TCA 1997, s 71(1) that the overseas tax should have been paid by the individual in receipt of the overseas income.

17.210 Extension of charge to non-transferors

As noted in **17.201** the *Vestey* decision meant that an individual could transfer assets offshore without infringing TCA 1997, s 806 so long as neither he (nor his spouse) could benefit potentially from the income attributable to the transfer. TCA 1997, s 807A (inserted by FA 1999, s 60) is accordingly designed to extend the charge to non-transferors (although arguably in some cases it is wide enough to extend the charge to transferors who fall outside TCA 1997, s 806: see below).

The main charging provisions

The provisions of TCA 1997, s 807A apply where two main preconditions are satisfied, namely that:

(a) income arises to a person resident or domiciled out of the State (hereafter an 'foreign person') as a result of either:
   (i) a transfer of assets, or
   (ii) a transfer of assets together with associated operations (TCA 1997, s 807A (1)(a)); and

(b) an individual who is resident or ordinarily resident in the State and who is not liable to tax under TCA 1997, s 806 by reference to the [same] transfer receives a benefit provided out of assets which are available for the purposes [ie of providing such a benefit] as a result of the [same] transfer or of any associated operations (TCA 1997, s 807A(1)(b)).

With effect for transactions taking place on or after 1 February 2007, it is specifically provided that any income which becomes payable to, or has become income of, the foreign person by virtue or in consequence of:

(i) the transfer;
(ii) one or more associated operations, or
(iii) the transfer and one or more associated operations must be taken into account for these purposes (TCA 1997, ss 806(2)(d) inserted by FA 2007, s 44).

This wording is designed seemingly to rule out beyond doubt any argument that on the facts the income arising to the foreign person is attributable only to an associated operation and not to the combined effect of the transfer and associated operation taken together.

The extended definitions of 'transfer', 'assets' and 'associated operations' (but not that of 'income') which apply for the purposes of TCA 1997, s 806 are also imported into TCA 1997, s 807A (TCA 1997, s 806(1), as amended by FA 1999, s 60(1)(a)(i)). The same definition of 'benefit' (ie as including a 'payment of any kind') also applies.

The first of these two preconditions (a), is similar to that implicit in TCA 1997, s 806(4), (5). However, unlike TCA 1997, s 806, there is no implicit requirement that the person making the transfer should be resident or ordinarily resident in the relevant year of assessment; that person need not be an individual so that, for example, a transfer by a *company* could trigger off these provisions. The second precondition (b), laid down in TCA 1997, s 807A(1)(b) represents a significant departure from the second precondition contained in TCA 1997, s 806(4), (5). These latter provisions operate (in broad terms) by deeming the income of the relevant 'foreign person' to be the income of the person making the transfer where he has power to enjoy such income (see TCA 1997, s 806(6)) or a capital sum connected with the transfer accrues to him or her (see TCA 1997, s 806(5)) as amended by FA 1999, s 60(1)(a)(iii), discussed above).

By way of contrast, TCA 1997, s 807A(1)(b) is targeted at non-transferors (but note the discussion on this issue, below). Further, it is designed to operate effectively on a receipts basis, ie individuals will fall within the scope of the section only to the extent (broadly speaking) that they actually receive benefits provided out of relevant assets. It may also be noted that there is no requirement that the assets should represent income which has accrued to the 'foreign person'. The rules governing the quantum of the charge (see below) are however designed to ensure that only benefits received out of offshore income are in fact subject to tax under TCA 1997, s 807A.

Finally, it should be noted that the let-outs for 'non-tax avoidance' transactions contained in TCA 1997, s 806(8) as displaced with effect from 1 February 2007 by TCA 1997, s 806(10) which apply for the purposes of TCA 1997, s 806, are also imported into TCA 1997, s 807A (TCA 1997, s 807A(7)): (see **17.207**, which also includes a discussion of the transitional provisions as they affect s 807A). The additional 'EU law' let out contained in TCA 1997, s 806(11) is also imported into TCA 1997, s 807A(7) applying for income arising on or after 1 January 2016. It may be seen that the recipient of a benefit may be liable under TCA 1997, s 807A, notwithstanding that he has no involvement whatsoever with the transfer or any associated operation and is utterly innocent of any intention to avoid tax.

Example 17.210.1

On 1 January 2015, Mr Thin, who is resident in the State, settled €500,000 on a Jersey resident discretionary trust. One of his purposes in making the settlement was to avoid Irish income tax. The beneficiaries of the trust comprise Mr Thin's wife and his adult son, Slim, both of whom are resident and domiciled in the State.

No distributions of income or any other form of benefit or payment were made by the trustees in the tax year 2015. The trustees received income of €16,000 in 2015. The provisions of TCA 1997, s 806 will apply so that all of the income of the trust (ie €16,000) will be deemed to be the income of Mr Thin. TCA 1997, s 807A has no relevance, since Slim receives no benefits from the trust. If the trust had in fact provided a benefit to Mr Thin's wife, this would not fall within TCA 1997, s 807A, since Mr Thin is already fully liable on the income of the trust under TCA 1997, s 806.

Example 17.210.2

Assume the same facts as in **Example 17.210.1**, except that the beneficiaries comprise only Mr Thin's son, Slim, and his adult daughter Tina (who is also Irish resident and domiciled). In this case, neither the provisions of TCA 1997, s 806 or TCA 1997, s 807A will apply.

It may be noted that the assets which are available in order to provide a benefit within precondition (b) need not necessarily be held by the offshore entity to which the income accrues within precondition (a).

Example 17.210.3

On 1 January 2015, Mrs Nox, who is resident and domiciled in the State, settled €600,000 on an Irish resident discretionary trust. One of her purposes in making the settlement was to avoid Irish income tax. The trustees invested all of the funds by subscribing for shares in a newly-formed offshore investment company. The beneficiaries of the trust (who are all resident and domiciled in the State) comprise the adult children of Mrs Nox. The company received income for a number of years and was then liquidated. The trustees subsequently made capital payments to the beneficiaries out of the liquidation proceeds. It would appear that precondition (a) is met (income arises to the offshore entity as a result of the initial transfer and the subsequent associated operation of setting up the offshore entity; any argument that the income becomes payable only as a result of the associated operation and not as a result of the combined effect of the transfer and the associated operation will lose whatever force it had for transactions undertaken on or after 1 February 2007: TCA 1997, s 806(2)(d)) *and* that precondition (b) is also met since the capital payment is provided out of trust assets which are available as a result of the transfer and the associated operation.

As discussed above at **17.208** FA 1999, s 60(a)(iii) has, with effect from 11 February 1999, extended the definition of a receipt of a capital sum for the purposes of the charging provisions of TCA 1997, s 806 to include 'any sum … which a third person receives … at the individual's direction or by virtue of the assignment by the individual of the individual's right to receive it'. This breadth of wording does not apply for the purposes of TCA 1997, s 807A, although it should be borne in mind that the concept of receipt is not construed narrowly for income tax purposes (see *O'Coindealbháin v Gannon* III ITR 484).

The quantum of the charge

In the first instance, the taxpayer who receives a benefit falling within the potential scope of TCA 1997, s 807A is liable at most on 'the amount or value of any benefit' received by him (TCA 1997, s 807A(2)): there is no liability under TCA 1997, s 807A to the extent that the benefit is already chargeable to income tax.

Example 17.210.4

On 1 January 2015, Mr Fat, who is resident in the State, settled €810,000 on a Jersey resident discretionary trust. One of his purposes in making the settlement was to avoid Irish tax. The beneficiaries of the trust comprise Mr Fat's adult sons, Rambo and Aubrey, both of whom are resident and domiciled in the State. In 2015 the trustees made a distribution out of trust capital to Rambo amounting to €10,000 and a distribution out of the trust income amounting to €5,000 to Aubrey.

Aubrey will be taxable on the distribution of income on general principles under Sch D Case III (see *Drummond v Collins* 6 TC 525). Rambo is most unlikely to be subject to income tax on his receipt under general principles (note: *Stevenson v Wishart* [1987] STC 266). Accordingly, Rambo will be liable to tax on the benefit which he receives, up to an amount of €10,000, but limited by reference to the quantum of the 'relevant income', (discussed immediately below).

The amount of the benefit which is taxable under TCA 1997, s 807A cannot exceed the amount of the 'relevant income'. This is defined in relation to any given individual as income which arises to an 'offshore entity' and which as a result of the relevant transfer of assets or associated operations can directly or indirectly be used to provide (or enable the provision of) a benefit to that individual (TCA 1997, s 807A(3)).

Example 17.210.5

Assume the same facts as in **Example 17.210.4**, except that Rambo is not entitled to any income arising under the trust (whether or not it is accumulated as trust capital). It would appear that TCA 1997, s 807A cannot apply to Rambo since the income of the trust cannot be used directly or indirectly to provide him with a benefit and cannot therefore constitute 'relevant income'.

Various rules apply in relation to the matching of benefits with relevant income. Firstly, a benefit is treated as taxable to the extent to which it can be matched against the relevant income arising for all tax years up to the end of the tax year in which the benefit is received (TCA 1997, s 807(2)(a)). Where the value of the benefit exceeds the amount of that relevant income, the excess is matched against the relevant income arising in subsequent tax years and so on (TCA 1997, s 807(2)(b)).

Example 17.210.6

Assume the facts as in **Example 17.210.4**. Assume also that the income arising in the trust during 2015 amounted to €12,000. The relevant income in relation to Rambo for 2015 is €12,000 less €5,000 actually distributed to Aubrey (which therefore cannot be used to provide a benefit to Rambo). The benefit received by Rambo is valued at €10,000 but he can only be taxed up to the amount of the relevant income (ie €7,000) for 2015. On the assumption that income arising to the trust was €9,000 in 2016 and that no distributions were made to Aubrey in that tax year, Rambo would be chargeable on the untaxed balance of the benefit in that tax year (ie €10,000 less €7,000 taxed in 2015 = €3,000). The amount of €3,000 is covered by relevant income of €9,000. The relevant income arising in 2016 which was not matched against benefits received by Rambo, ie €(9,000 – 3,000) = €6,000 would be effectively carried forward to 2017 and future tax years. Any future benefit received by Rambo would be matched against this amount of €6,000 plus any other relevant income which had accrued subsequently up to the end of the tax year in which the benefit concerned was received.

Relevant income arising prior to 11 February 1999 is disregarded. However, relevant income arising on or after that date will be taken into account, irrespective of the date of the transfer or associated operations concerned (TCA 1997, s 807A(8)). There is no transitional relief which allows benefits to be matched against relevant income arising prior to 11 February 1999.

Where a benefit exceeds the relevant income available to match it, it is possible that all or part of the excess may be treated as a capital payment for the purposes of the newly-enacted TCA 1997, s 579A (attribution of gains of offshore trusts), as supplemented by TCA 1997, s 579F(2) (attribution of gains of migrant trusts). In these circumstances, the amount of the excess so taken into account will not also be taken into account for the purposes of TCA 1997, s 807A (TCA 1997, s 807A(6)). Thus, for example if a benefit of €10,000 was received in a tax year in which there was no relevant income and €6,000 of that benefit was taken into account under TCA 1997, s 579A, only the balance of €4,000 would be carried forward to be matched against the relevant income of subsequent tax years under TCA 1997, s 807A.

The final issue to be considered under this heading is that of the valuation of the benefits. This is clearcut where the benefit takes the form of straightforward monetary payment. However, TCA 1997, s 807A does not lay down rules on valuing benefits-in-kind. It is unclear eg whether such benefits should be valued according to what the recipient would have paid in order to obtain the benefit or according to what the recipient would receive if he were to sell or assign the benefit. Thus, for example, an individual may receive an interest-free (or low interest) loan from an offshore entity which has ‘relevant income’. It seems that the loan itself does not confer rights of any value if it is repayable on demand (note in this regard *O'Leary v McKinlay* [1991] STC 492). The UK Revenue take the view that the benefit of the loan should be valued by reference to the interest which the taxpayer would otherwise have had to pay in respect thereof. The contrary view is that this benefit is merely a notional saving which is incapable of being converted into cash and therefore has a zero value (see the Sch E case of *Tennant v Smith* 3 TC 158). The decision in the UK capital gains tax case of *Billingham v Cooper* [2001] STC 1177 lends support to the views of the Inland Revenue.

In the case of an interest-free (or low-interest) loan which is immediately repayable, it is also debatable whether or not the benefit (if such it is) of the interest avoided by the taxpayer is provided out of the assets of the foreign entity (as required by TCA 1997, s 807A(1)(b): see above). While the money advanced may represent part or all of the available assets, the benefit would seem to consist simply of the use of that asset: the assets themselves remain intact. Obviously, the same argument potentially applies where an individual enjoys the use of any asset free of charge on a revocable or ‘at will’ basis.

The UK Inland Revenue do accept that the grant of a life interest in the funds held by an offshore entity is not provided ‘out of the assets’ of that entity. This is however a more clear-cut situation since the assets remain wholly within the trust in the sense that the beneficiary has no proprietary interest in the specific assets held by the trust.

The remittance basis

As in the case of TCA 1997, s 806 the charge where TCA 1997, s 807A applies is also imposed under Sch D Case IV. In the absence of any special provisions, this would imply that the remittance basis is not available to non-domiciled individuals who fall within the scope of TCA 1997, s 807A.

TCA 1997, s 807A(5) previously provided, that an individual domiciled outside the State would not be taxable under TCA 1997, s 807A by reference to relevant income which, as a result of his non-domiciled status, would not have been taxable if it had actually been received by him. This is similar to the wording of the relief under TCA 1997, s 807(5) on which see the discussion at **17.207**. However, TCA 1997, s 807A(5) was deleted by FA 2015, s 21(2)(b) applying to income arising on or after 1 January 2016. It is understood that such deletion was brought about to counter artificial structures surrounding certain employment income and as a result of such deletion the reader is directed to previous editions of this text for a fuller discussion of the then applicable TCA 1997, s 807A(5).

Is multiple taxation possible?

It is clear that, taken at face value, TCA 1997, s 806 and s 807A carry the potential to impose double taxation (ie in the domestic and not the international sense of the expression). This matter has been drawn to the attention of the Revenue Commissioners by the Irish Taxation Institute.

Example 17.210.7

> Assume the same facts as **Example 17.210.1**, except that the trustees provide a benefit valued at €3,000 to Slim in 2015. As discussed, Mr Thin is liable on the full income of the trust under TCA 1997, s 806. However, Slim would also seem to be liable on the benefit received by him under TCA 1997, s 807A (paid out of the same income on which Mr Thin is taxable).

It is submitted that there is however a strong presumption against double taxation under well-established fiscal principles. This was stated (in the context of the UK equivalent of TCA 1997, s 806) by Lord Steyn in *IRC v McGuckian* [1997] STC 908, when he observed: 'That the Revenue authorities should have overlapping taxing powers is a non-remarkable consequence … such a construction cannot cause unfairness to the taxpayer since he cannot be taxed twice on the same income'. Perhaps, more importantly, double taxation of the same income would appear to be arbitrary and unfair to a degree which would render the provisions in question unconstitutional.

The difficulty, however, is that in the present example there is no guidance as to how the income which is potentially subject to double taxation is to be apportioned between Mr Thin and Slim. The equivalent UK legislation (ICTA 1988, s 744) expressly provides that the same income cannot be taxed more than once under the equivalents to TCA 1997, ss 806 and 807A. It also authorises the Inland Revenue to resolve any potential double taxation issues on a 'just and reasonable basis' (subject to a right of appeal). In the absence of these kind of provisions, the only practical solution would be for the Revenue Commissioners to apportion the income at their own discretion. It would appear, however, that any attempt to do so in the absence of express statutory authority would fall outside the administrative function of the Revenue (see *Vestey v IRC* [1980]

STC 10) and would therefore be *prima facie* unconstitutional. The consequences would seem to be that the legislation may simply be unworkable in the face of facts such as those described in **Example 17.210.8**.

Can s 807 apply also to transferors?

So far it has been assumed that TCA 1997, s 807A can apply only to non-transferors. However, the position is unclear where a non-domiciled transferor escapes taxation under TCA 1997, s 806 because the relevant offshore entity receives non-Irish income which is not remitted to the State. If the transferor receives a benefit in the State which is available to him as a result of the transfer (and which does not itself result in forfeiture of the exemption under TCA 1997, s 807(5)), can TCA 1997, s 807A apply to the benefit? It may be recalled that TCA 1997, s 807A can apply only to an individual who is 'not liable to tax' under TCA 1997, s 806.

In the circumstances described above, the transferor is 'not liable' under TCA 1997, s 806 in the sense that he is not actually chargeable in respect of the particular income concerned. On the other hand it may be argued that he is liable to be taxed under TCA 1997, s 806, ie in the sense that he falls within the general scope of the section, albeit subject to the exemption available under TCA 1997, s 807(5). There is no clear answer to this interpretative dilemma. It is perhaps worth pointing out, however, that the UK equivalent of TCA 1997, s 807A was enacted to cure the deficiencies identified in the *Vestey* case in relation to non-transferors and not to extend the scope of pre-*Vestey* provisions to transferors.

Is double taxation relief available?

There is a strong argument that if income which accrues to an offshore entity is exempted under the terms of a double tax treaty, then the benefit of that exemption should be extended to any charge which would otherwise arise under TCA 1997, s 806. The point here is that the income of the offshore entity is deemed to be that of the transferor for income tax purposes (TCA 1997, s 806(4), (5)(a)); accordingly (it is argued) there is nothing to prevent the treaty exemption carrying on through to the transferor (note *Bricom Holdings v IRC* [1997] STC 1179).

In the case of TCA 1997, s 807A, however, tax is not charged on the basis of a statutory fiction that the income of the offshore entity is that of the recipient of the benefit. Instead, TCA 1997, s 807A(2) charges tax on the amount or value of the benefit received as if it were income received by him. The 'relevant income' received by the offshore entity (which may arguably be exempt under the terms of a double tax treaty) determines the quantum of the potential charge but is not treated as the income of the individual as such. It also follows that no credit will be available for overseas taxes suffered in relation to the relevant income out of which a benefit is provided (contrast TCA 1997, s 807(2) which applies for the purposes of TCA 1997, s 806).

It may be noted that if a transferor can indeed escape the clutches of TCA 1997, s 806 by virtue of the terms of a double tax treaty, the question arises as to whether he could be taxed under TCA 1997, s 807A if he were to receive a benefit out of the relevant income concerned (note the discussion of *Multiple Taxation* above).

17.211 Exclusion of certain exemptions

TCA 1997, s 809 makes it clear that the resident individual's liability to tax under TCA 1997, s 806 (and with effect from 1 February 1999 TCA 1997, s 807A) in respect of any relevant income of a foreign person cannot be avoided on the grounds that the income is of a type specifically exempted from Irish tax because it is received by a person not resident, or not ordinarily resident or neither domiciled nor ordinarily resident in the State. Since the income of the foreign person which may be deemed by TCA 1997, s 806 to be the income of the resident individual is, in principle, income determined in accordance with the Irish Income Tax Acts, it might otherwise be possible to argue that if the foreign person is exempted from tax on any particular income, then that income should not be treated as the income of the resident individual.

TCA 1997, s 809 provides that the foreign residence, foreign domicile and/or foreign ordinary residence of the foreign person in receipt of any income is not to be the grounds for excluding that income from assessment under the rules of TCA 1997, ss 806–808. In particular, TCA 1997, s 809 is stated as referring to interest, dividends, etc on certain types of stocks and securities referred to in the undermentioned provisions, but without restricting the generality of the rule. The interest, etc payments covered specifically by TCA 1997, s 809 are:

(a) income from any stock or other security to which TCA 1997, ss 43, 47, 49, or 50 apply (see **2.309**);

(b) income consisting of public revenue dividends, interest, etc of any foreign territory payable in the State for which a non-resident person can normally claim exemption under TCA 1997, s 35 (see **2.309**); and

(c) other foreign dividends payable in the State, normally subject to the deduction of income tax by the paying agent where payable to a non-resident person normally entitled to claim exemption under TCA 1997, s 63 (see **2.310**).

TCA 1997, s 809 does not, however, remove any exemption from tax that is given to an individual by any of the rules of the Tax Acts for particular types of income, provided that the exemption in question does not distinguish between resident and non-resident (or non-domiciled) persons. For example, if the relevant income of a foreign person, otherwise within the rules of TCA 1997, s 806 or s 807A, includes exempt woodlands income, that income retains its tax exempted status. Even if deemed by TCA 1997, s 806 to be the resident individual's income, it remains income that is to be left out of account for all purposes of the Income Tax Acts.

17.212 Administrative provisions

Rules for assessment, collection etc

TCA 1997, s 810 applies all the normal administrative rules of the Income Tax Acts, with any necessary modifications, to the charge, assessment, collection and recovery of tax under TCA 1997, s 806 (and, with effect from 11 February 1999, TCA 1997, s 807A). Similarly, the ordinary rules relating to appeals against assessment (including where applicable the taxpayer's right to a rehearing by the Circuit Court judge) and to cases to be stated for the opinion of the High Court on a point of law (with the right to appeal to the Supreme Court) apply to tax assessed under TCA 1997, s 806 or s 807A, as they do to income tax assessments generally. For the rules on appeals and interest, see **Division 2**.

Power to obtain information

TCA 1997, s 808 authorises the Revenue Commissioners, or any officer appointed by them, to serve notice in writing requiring 'any' person to furnish them with such particulars as they think necessary for the purposes of TCA 1997, s 806, 807, 807A,

807B, 807C and 809. The notice should specify the time within which the particulars are to be supplied, but this must not be less than 28 days from the date of the notice.

This notice requiring information may, of course, be sent directly to the individual the Revenue Commissioners have in mind to assess, but the section is also drafted to enable the Revenue Commissioners to seek any relevant information from persons such as accountants, stockbrokers, solicitors, banks etc. The Commissioners are entitled to require any person on whom they serve a notice under TCA 1997, s 808 to supply the information requested in the notice including particulars:

(a) as to transactions where the person is or was acting on behalf of others;
(b) as to transactions which, in the opinion of the Revenue Commissioners or of any officer appointed by them, it is proper that they should investigate for the purposes of the relevant sections (even though the person to whom the notice is given is of the opinion that no liability to tax arises under the sections); and
(c) as to whether the recipient of the notice has taken any part in transactions of a kind specified in the notice (and if so, as to what part he has taken).

Solicitors

TCA 1997, s 808(4) limits, to some extent, the particulars which a solicitor may be required by a 's 808 notice' to furnish. A solicitor is not regarded as having taken part in a transaction by reason only that he has given professional advice to a client in connection with that transaction. Therefore, if he has done no more than give such professional advice, he is not to be required to furnish particulars of the transactions with respect to which he was giving such advice.

Further, a solicitor cannot, unless with the consent of his client, – in relation to anything done by him on behalf of a client – be compelled by a s 808 notice to do more than state that he is or was acting on behalf of a client, give the name and address of his client, and also supplies certain further information in relation to certain matters (set out in TCA 1997, s 808(4) – not repeated here).

Banks

TCA 1997, s 808(6) provides some limitation on the particulars which a bank may be required to furnish by a s 808 notice. Such a notice cannot impose on any bank the obligation to furnish any particulars of any ordinary banking transactions between the bank and a customer carried out in the ordinary course of banking business. However, this exclusion from the obligation to supply the particulars required by a s 808 notice does not apply if a bank has acted or is acting on behalf of any customer in connection with either:

(a) the formation or management of any body corporate which is either resident or incorporated outside the State, and would be, were it resident in the State, a 'close company' as defined in TCA 1997, ss 430 and 431; or
(b) the execution of the trusts of any settlement (as defined by TCA 1997, s 10) by virtue of or in consequence whereof income becomes payable to a person resident or domiciled outside the State.

For the exclusion under TCA 1997, s 808(6) from the requirement to comply with a s 808 notice to apply to a bank, it is therefore necessary that the transactions on behalf of the customers be both ordinary or normal banking transactions and, also, be carried out in the ordinary or normal course of a banking business. A bank carrying on an ordinary banking business may, on occasions, carry out transactions for customers which are not normal banking transactions; if so, particulars relating to those transactions, the customers involved, etc must be given by the bank if served with a notice for particulars under the section.

In the event that a bank has acted or is acting on behalf of any customer in connection with the formation or management of such a foreign body corporate or a trust as is mentioned above, it ceases to be entitled to withhold any particulars requested in a s 59 notice relating to ordinary banking transactions with the customers in question. Even if the bank has not acted on behalf of a customer in connection with such matters, the onus remains on the bank to show that any transactions involved were ordinary banking transactions. It was held in *Royal Bank of Canada v IRC* 47 TC 565 that the exclusion from disclosure did not apply to banking transactions that were not 'ordinary' banking transactions.

The question of what were ordinary banking transactions in particular circumstances came up for consideration in an Irish case, the *Royal Trust Co (Ireland) v Revenue Commissioners* [1982] ILMR 459. In that case, the High Court held that certain types of transactions were in fact entitled to the exclusion from disclosure, but that certain other types of transaction carried out by the same bank could not, in the circumstances of the particular bank, be regarded as coming within the exemption of TCA 1997, s 808(6). In this judgment, McWilliam J commented, at p 465:

> I would add that it appears to me that, once an institution has been duly licensed as a bank, I must consider whether a particular transaction is an ordinary banking transaction carried out in the ordinary course of the banking business of that type of banking institution. It does not appear to me that I should be tied to the type of ordinary banking transaction carried on by the older banks operating cheque accounts.

Surcharge

FA 2014 introduced a surcharge as part of the new general anti-avoidance provisions (New GAAR), (TCA 1997, s 811D) and is stated to apply specifically to TCA 1997, ss 806 and 807A.

Under this provision, where a taxpayer submits a tax return or otherwise seeks to obtain the benefit of a tax advantage and the transaction that gives rise to the tax advantage is caught by TCA 1997, s 806 or s 807A, the taxpayer maybe liable to the 30 per cent surcharge under TCA 1997, s 811D. The surcharge only applies to transactions which commenced on or after 24 October 2014. The surcharge and the ways to mitigate the surcharge are discussed further in **17.302.2**.

Payment notices

With effect from the date of passing of FA 2014, 23 December 2014, TCA 1997, ss 817S and 817T were inserted. Normally no tax will be payable or repayable following a determination by the Appeal Commissioners if the decision is subject to a rehearing by the Circuit Court or an appeal on a point of law to the High Court (see **2.202**). However, TCA 1997, s 817S provides that in cases where a taxpayer has entered into a transaction to which either TCA 1997, s 806 or s 807A applies, it should be borne in mind that in the event that an assessment is raised by Revenue withdrawing part or all of the tax advantage gained by entering into the transaction any additional tax may be collected by Revenue when any appeal has been heard and determined by the Appeal Commissioners by the issue of a payment notice. This is the case even if the taxpayer has requested a rehearing by the Circuit Court or lodged an appeal to the High Court. F(TA)A 2015, s 38, which was subject to Ministerial Order (SI 110/2016 appointed 21 March 2016 as the day on which the Finance (Tax Appeals) Act 2015, came into operation), removes the possibility of a rehearing at the Circuit Court. Furthermore, Revenue can issue a payment notice requesting immediate payment of tax due in such an assessment if a similar transaction has been the subject of an Appeal Commissioners' determination which resulted in the issue of a payment notice to another taxpayer (see under Payment notices in **2.618**, Disclosure of certain tax avoidance transactions).

17.3 General Anti-Avoidance

17.301 Introduction

Prior to FA 2014, TCA 1997, s 811 was the comprehensive anti-avoidance provision which was capable of being applied, if the circumstances which permit its application were found to exist in relation to any 'tax avoidance transaction', whichever of the taxes were involved (income tax, corporation tax, capital gains tax, capital acquisitions tax, value-added tax, etc). It gave the Revenue Commissioners the power to attack and withdraw or deny any 'tax advantage' resulting from any such transaction in the manner and to the extent prescribed in the section. The provisions of this section are dealt with in **17.302.1**. TCA 1997, s 811C replaced TCA 1997, s 811 for tax avoidance transactions which commenced on or after 24 October 2014. The provisions of this new general anti avoidance section are explained in detail in **17.302.2**.

TCA 1997, s 817 is intended to counteract schemes, involving closely controlled companies and their shareholders, which convert profits available for distribution (chargeable to income tax on the shareholder) into a capital receipt not chargeable to income tax. The provisions of this section are discussed in **17.304**.

TCA 1997, s 242 is intended to defeat tax avoidance schemes involving the device of 'reverse annuities'. Under this type of scheme, a taxpayer undertakes to make annual payments (annuities) to a finance company in return for a capital sum. The result, in the absence of any special rule to the contrary is that the tax-payer receives a non-taxable capital sum while the annuity paid is in effect a deduction in arriving at his total income so that his income tax liability is reduced. The rules of this section to prevent this position are dealt with in **17.305**.

For the new rules governing the mandatory disclosure of certain tax avoidance transactions see **2.618**.

17.302 General measure to counter tax avoidance transactions

The position prior to the introduction of the general anti-avoidance provisions

As discussed in **1.401**, the Irish courts traditionally refused to adopt an 'equitable' style of interpretation in relation to tax statute. In particular, the doctrine of 'substance over form' was roundly rejected in such cases as *O'Sullivan v P* II ITR 464 and *McGrath v McDermott* III ITR 683, following the seminal UK case of *IRC v Westminster* 19 TC 490.

This restrained approach to the interpretation of tax statute permitted taxpayers a relative degree of certainty in organising their affairs tax efficiently, at the cost of some leakage of tax revenue through the exploitation by taxpayers of loopholes in the law unanticipated by the legislature. Historically, these loopholes, (or at least, the more glaring examples) have been plugged on a reactive basis, ie by means of specific anti-avoidance rules designed to counteract particular schemes or classes of schemes.

However, in the 1970s, a climate of aggressive tax planning developed in the UK, which threatened to undermine the integrity of the tax system there.

Typically, this type of planning, involved elaborate pre-packaged schemes, aimed purely at generating tax reliefs and losses. Such schemes were normally 'circular' in nature, giving rise to no economic consequences whatsoever.

Prior to the introduction of its own general anti-avoidance legislation on 17 July 2013, the UK relied on a court developed doctrine. The landmark case for the type of scheme discussed above was *Ramsay v IRC* [1981] STC 174. The scheme in *Ramsay* consisted of a series of transactions which generated both a gain and counterbalancing loss; the gain was designed to arise under circumstances whereby it attracted a tax exemption, while the loss was designed to be fully allowable. The success of such schemes relied on the legally distinct nature of the various steps comprised in them. In the absence of any general 'associated operations' rule (such as that contained in TCA 1997, s 806) the principle set out in the *Westminster* case meant that the courts were bound to attach tax consequences to each step in its own right and were not entitled to look at the end result (which, in this case, was non-existent in economic terms). It was reasonable to infer that the legislature would not have intended such paper schemes to give rise to tax benefits, but no such principle could be discovered in the tax rules themselves.

Prior to *Ramsay*, the House of Lords had maintained the traditional *Westminster* approach in the face of a different, but typically circular, scheme in *IRC v Plummer* [1979] STC 793 (This type of scheme is now expressly nullified in Ireland by virtue of TCA 1997, s 242). Under the scheme, the taxpayer, P, covenanted to make a series of annual payments to the scheme promoter, H, in return for a lump sum. P was contractually obliged to apply the lump sum in purchasing promissory notes, which were then deposited as security for his annual payments. The notes were subsequently used to discharge the annual payments to H as they fell due. As the law then stood, annual payments of a revenue nature were deductible for income tax purposes.

The point of the scheme in *Plummer* was to enable the taxpayer to obtain a tax deduction, although his net economic position would be unaffected. The Revenue argued, *inter alia* that the annual payments were in fact capital in nature, a contention rejected by the House of Lords. Lord Wilberforce commented:

> The plan now involved was explained by the [promoters] in great detail, and its intended accomplishment set out, with timetables, in almost military precision. This … entitles and requires us to look at the plan as a whole. It does not entitle us to disregard the legal form and nature of the transactions carried out … While it may be true that an annuity bought for a capital sum has the character of income and while there was such an annuity in this case, it was said that the concomitant arrangements, in particular the arrangements for security, changed the character of the repayments. The capital sum paid by H remained in existence – in the form of promissory notes – and it was this sum, in that form which was paid back to H. Instead of receiving an annuity H was simply receiving back its own capital instalments … If it were possible to disregard the *legal form* of the documents and to look behind them for an *underlying substance* there would be attractions – beyond those of ingenuity – in this argument [emphasis added].

However, in *Ramsay*, the House of Lords executed a subsequent *volte face*, and treated the scheme there as a 'fiscal nullity', ie as a 'non-event' for tax purposes. On this occasion, Lord Wilberforce observed:

> To say that a loss (or gain) which appears to arise at one stage in an indivisible process and which is intended to be and is cancelled out by a later stage so that the end of which was …

> a single continuous operation is not such a loss (or gain) as the legislation is dealing with, is in my opinion well, and indeed essentially, within the judicial function.

Lord Wilberforce accordingly argued that 'what appears to be' a 'new approach' was no more than the application of *old* principles to a *new* legal phenomenon. However, it is evident that the approach taken by Lord Wilberforce in *Ramsay* was truly 'new', and quite incompatible with the views expressed by the same judge in *IRC v Plummer*. This fact was ultimately acknowledged by the House of Lords in *Moodie v IRC* [1993] STC 188, when another taxpayer, who had also used the scheme in *Plummer*, was denied a deduction for his payments in the light of the *Ramsay* decision. The court held that, although the facts in both cases were identical, *Plummer*, was not a true precedent since the 'new approach' had not been considered there.

The new approach was extended in *Furniss v Dawson* [1984] STC 153, where the taxpayers, D, had agreed in principle to sell a block of shares to W. As part of a pre-planned arrangement, designed to defer a tax charge on the capital gain arising on the sale, D exchanged their block of shares in exchange for shares in G, a non-resident company wholly owned by them. G then immediately sold the shares to W. Unlike the position in *Ramsay*, the arrangement in *Furniss v Dawson* did not consist of a series of ultimately self-cancelling steps but in fact achieved a commercial objective – ie the sale of shares to W. Nevertheless, the House of Lords held that, despite the lack of circularity in Dawson, it was entitled to deny any independent effect to a step or steps inserted into a preordained series of transactions, where the sole purpose of such steps was the avoidance of tax. Lord Brightman, who delivered the main judgment in *Dawson*, stated:

> In this case the inserted step was the introduction of G as a buyer from D and as a seller to W. That inserted step had no business purpose apart from the deferment of tax, although it had a business effect. If the sale had taken place … before capital gains tax was introduced, there would have been no …[G].

(In fact, the 'insertion' of G seems strictly not to have been a step in itself but rather was an element in the splitting of what would have been a single sale transaction into two separate transactions – the sale by D to G and the sale by G to W. *Neither* of these steps would have taken place in the absence of potential capital gains tax charge).

As a result of its extension of the 'new approach' to so-called 'linear schemes', the court in *Dawson* was faced with the task of *recharacterising* the two separate transactions which had actually taken place as a notional, single (or 'composite') transaction. Moreover, they were bound to do this in a manner which was consistent with the actual results of the arrangement, undertaken by the taxpayers, since these results carried 'permanent legal, practical and fiscal consequences' (eg the funds held by G would no longer be at D's personal disposal, and any subsequent dividends paid by G to D would be liable to income tax). The court held that the arrangement should be recharacterised as a three-way contract whereby D had sold the shares directly to W (thus incurring a capital gain) in exchange for W transferring the sale proceeds to G.

Encouraged by the development of the 'new approach' by the UK courts, the Revenue Commissioners brought a blatant tax avoidance scheme before the Irish courts in the case of *McGrath v McDermott*. It is worthy of note that the stated case submitted to the court included the finding that 'the series of transactions [concerned] was avowedly a tax avoidance scheme and had no other purpose'. The scheme used in *McGrath* consisted of a series of self-cancelling purchases and sales of shares designed to manufacture a capital loss. The Supreme Court unanimously and forcibly rejected the

Revenue's contention that the 'new approach' should be applied in the Republic. Finlay CJ said:

> The function of the courts is confined to ascertaining the plain meaning of each statutory provision … The courts have not got a function to add or to delete from express statutory provisions so as to achieve objectives which to the courts appear desirable.
>
> It was contended that the real as distinct from what is described as the artificial nature of the transaction should be looked at by the court and that if there was no real loss the section should not apply. This contention is rejected. To do otherwise would constitute the invasion by the judiciary of the powers and functions of the legislature, in plain breach of the constitutional separation of powers.

The Chief Justice also added pointedly that 'the Revenue Commissioners have the expertise to deal with tax avoidance schemes,' and noted the existence of general anti-avoidance provision in Canada and Australia. McCarthy J referred scathingly to 'the mental gymnastics necessary to conclude that *Ramsay v IRC* did not reverse *IRC v Duke of Westminster'*.

In the House of Lords decision in *MacNiven v Westmoreland Investments Limited* [2001] STC 237, the House of Lords reconsidered the Ramsay principle and moved closer to the Irish approach contained in *McGrath v McDermott*. Westmoreland Investments Limited (WIL) was owned by the trustees of an exempt approved superannuation scheme to whom it owed substantial sums of money and as a result had a huge accrued interest liability. WIL borrowed funds from its parent to enable it to pay the interest liability and thereby crystallised tax losses which could be sold to a third party purchaser. The Inland Revenue disputed WIL's interest deductions as a charge both on technical grounds and on the basis that the *Ramsay* principle applied since the transactions had no commercial purpose and were purely for the purpose of avoiding tax. The Special Commissioners held that the interest had been paid and that as such an allowable deduction was available. The Inland Revenue appealed to the High Court where the court, in applying the *Ramsay* principle, held that the interest was not deductible since there was no commercial purpose to the transaction apart from the avoidance of tax. The Court of Appeal held for the taxpayer, ruling that the *Ramsay* principle did not apply and that the interest deduction was available. The Inland Revenue appealed to the House of Lords.

Lord Hoffman in delivering the leading judgment rejected the Revenue's argument that the *Ramsay* principle applied. In considering the *Ramsay* principle he commented that:

> [(the *Ramsay* principle)] does not look to me like a principle of construction at all. There is ultimately only one principle of construction, namely what Parliament meant by using the language of a statute. All other 'principles of construction' can be no more than guides which past judges have put forward, some more helpful or insightful than others, to assist in the task of interpretation … the courts have no constitutional authority to impose such an overlay upon the tax legislation. (p 386)

He explained the decision of Lord Wilberforce in *Ramsay* as treating:

> … statutory words 'loss' and 'disposal' as referring to commercial concepts to which a juristic analysis of the transaction treating each step as an autonomous and independent, might be determined. What was fresh and new about *Ramsay* was the realisation that such an approach need not be confined to well recognised accounting concepts such as profits and loss but could be the appropriate construction of other taxation concepts as well. (p 388)

In reinforcing his decision that the courts had no constitutional authority to legislate on tax matters and in restoring this position to parliament he said:

> It has occasionally been said that the boundary of the *Ramsay* principle can be defined by asking whether the taxpayer's actions constituted (acceptable) tax mitigation or (unacceptable) tax avoidance. Where the statutory provisions do not contain words like 'avoidance' or 'mitigation', I do not think that it helps to introduce them. The fact the steps taken for the avoidance of tax are acceptable or unacceptable is the conclusion at which one arrives by applying the statutory language to the facts of the case. It is not a test for deciding whether it applies or not.

He stated that in interpreting tax legislation a distinction must be made between commercial and legal concepts and that where tax is imposed by reference to a commercial concept that the overall scheme should be considered.

He stated that 'to have regard to the business 'substance' of the matter is not to ignore the legal position but to give effect to it.' (p 390)

Therefore according to the decision unless tax is imposed by reference to a commercial concept the substance and motive to the matter is not relevant and only the legal position should be considered in interpreting the section. This House of Lords decision although it does not per se overrule the *Ramsay* and *Furniss v Dawson* decisions has explained them in a new light and its impact will ultimately depend on future judgments.

With regard to the case before him he stated that the question of whether the interest was 'paid' pursuant to ICTA 1988, s 338 was a legal concept and did not have some other commercial meaning. Therefore the purpose of the payment was irrelevant since this was not required by the statute for a tax deduction to be available for interest as a charge. All that was required was for the interest obligation to be discharged. He held that this had been done and that how WIL financed this payment was irrelevant once the interest had been 'paid'. It was therefore immaterial that the payment had been funded by the lender and that the scheme was essentially 'circular' in nature.

Lord Hoffman's judgment makes it clear that the fact that there is a tax avoidance motive to a transaction does not necessarily result in the transaction being recharacterised. It provides that the tax payable is based on the proper legal analysis of the transaction in question and that in construing statutory provisions it is necessary to consider whether the individual section contains a commercial or legal concept and to interpret the legislation accordingly.

The Revenue's response to their disappointment in *McGrath* was to secure the enactment of TCA 1997, s 811, a general or 'blanket' anti-avoidance provision. TCA 1997, s 811 borrowed heavily from the equivalent provision in Canada (ITA s 245).

However, it also imports some elements from other jurisdictions, notably the UK (ICTA 1988, s 703 *et seq*) and Australia (ITAA 1936, Pt IV(a)) while also incorporating a number of 'homegrown' innovations. The Explanatory Memorandum issued with Finance Bill 1989 gives a useful summary of the intention of FA 1989, s 86, the antecedent to TCA 1997, s 811, as follows:

> The purpose of the section is to counteract certain transactions which have little or no commercial reality but are carried out primarily to create an artificial tax deduction or to avoid or reduce a tax charge. Such a transaction is referred to in the section as a tax avoidance transaction.

Although no statement in the Explanatory Memorandum is binding, it is possible that it could be invoked by a court in cases of doubt (see **1.404**). This statement should certainly be borne in mind when the question is considered whether any particular transaction is likely to be attacked by the Revenue Commissioners under s 811 as a tax avoidance transaction.

Revenue Commissioners v O'Flynn Construction Ltd [2011] IESC 47 is the only case on TCA 1997, s 811 which has been decided by the Supreme Court. Following the *O'Flynn Construction Ltd* case it can be said that the approach of the Irish courts in TCA 1997, s 811 cases is to look at the economic substance or financial result of a transaction as well as the legal form. In *O'Flynn Construction Ltd* a company purchased the benefit of tax-exempt reserves from another company which had initially qualified for the exemption in order to pay tax-free dividends out of its own accumulated reserves. The High Court held in favour of the Revenue Commissioners that this transaction was caught by TCA 1997, s 811 and rejected the argument that the purpose of the transaction was to effect the purchase of reserves albeit in a tax-efficient form. In the Supreme Court, the decision of the High Court was upheld by a 3–2 majority. Donnelly J delivering the majority decision observed:

> It is possible to admire the ingenuity with which the scheme was devised and efficiency with which it was executed but lament the fact that such skills are put to use for the sole objective of avoiding tax. The reason each party was able to become involved in this scheme, and why companies and advisors were able to devote time and considerable sums of money to the scheme, was that in effect, if successful it would be paid for by the tax avoided by the shareholders in OFCL. It is probably unnecessary to observe that the scheme is entirely artificial. It has no commercial logic. Its only purpose was to permit an ESR dividend to be paid to the shareholders in the company that supplied the original funds. The artificiality of the scheme is not in any way denied by the taxpayers. Indeed, they put the matter with disarming bluntness:
>
> > 'In the transactions here, Mitchelstown sold these reserves to the appellant company, for cash. The shareholders in the appellant company, who are the individuals ... then received ESR dividends ... the ultimate effect of the transaction was that the shareholders of the appellant company received ESR dividends originally earned by Mitchelstown but purchased by the appellant company.'
>
> This was undoubtedly the commercial reality of the transaction. It is, however, worth noting at least two things: first, at no stage of the transaction did the appellant company (OFCL) deal directly with Mitchelstown; and second, not one of the steps in this transaction could constitute 'a sale' by any party, at least as a matter of law. Notwithstanding the artificiality of the scheme, the appellant tax payer says that it was perfectly lawful. In the end, franked dividends earned legitimately by an ESR company, passed through a series of companies to the shareholders in Magmac and the appellants herein. Nothing (the Appellants contend) in the ESR scheme required that the shareholders receiving such dividends should be shareholders at any time in the ESR earning company, or indeed be shareholders in the related company, at the time when the profits were earned.

TCA 1997, s 811(3)(a)(ii) provided that Revenue shall not regard a transaction as being a tax avoidance transaction if it is not, inter alia an abuse or misuse of an existing relief or allowance. It was not contested that the transaction was a tax avoidance transaction. The key point to be determined was in the circumstances whether the effective sale of ESR dividends to a third party constituted a misuse or abuse of the ESR provisions. O'Donnell J held that the form of the transaction was highly artificial and contrived. The scheme, which allowed the shareholders of a non ESR company benefit from ESR on the profits of the non-exporting company, was a misuse or abuse of the ESR provisions. Interestingly he took the view that if *the appellant company h*ad bought the

ESR company in a bona fide commercial transaction and subsequently the shareholders of *the appellant company* received ESR dividends that this would arguably be consistent with the ESR provisions.

The minority decision given by McKechnie J disagreed as the ESR dividend exemption had been so wide and unregulated for years he could not conclude that the transaction was an abuse of the exemption. McKechnie stated that as no attempt had been made over 35 years to regulate the tax status of dividends (other than salary sacrifice situations) and concluded this was part of a deliberate policy supporting the total tax exemption of ESR profits from tax. The author finds it difficult not to agree with the minority decision.

Notwithstanding the Revenue Commissioner's success in the *O'Flynn* case at Supreme Court level, a number of amendments were made in FA 2014 to the operation of the general anti-avoidance provisions. The provisions of TCA 1997, s 811 will continue to apply to a transaction which was commenced on or before 23 October 2014. The new general anti-avoidance provision (TCA 1997, s 811C) will apply to tax avoidance transactions which commence after this date. Full details regarding the operation of this new general anti-avoidance provision are set out in further detail in **17.302.2**. However, in the meantime, the key provisions of the original anti-avoidance provision (s 811) which will remain effective for historic transactions are summarised below.

Summary of original general anti-avoidance provision

The main provisions of TCA 1997, s 811 may be summarised as follows:

(a) the Revenue Commissioners may, at any time, form the opinion that a particular transaction is a 'tax avoidance transaction' (if the transaction is within the definition of that term) (TCA 1997, s 811(4)); alongside the commencement of the 20 per cent surcharge regime (see sub-heading below) the Revenue Commissioners are empowered to make any enquiry at any time in connection with TCA 1997, s 811 or s 811A (TCA 1997, s 811A(1A), inserted by FA 2008, s 140); however, in *Revenue Commissioners v Droog* [2011] IEHC 142 it was held that the four-year time-limits for imposing additional tax liabilities under TCA 1997, s 955(2) and making enquiries under TCA 1997, s 956(1)(c) in relation to self-assessment taxpayers, override TCA 1997, s 811(4). The Revenue Commissioners have appealed the decision to the Supreme Court. A similar matter came before the High Court in *Revenue Commissioners v Lacey* [2015] IEHC 529. This involved a film fund where film relief claimed in 1995 was sought to be withdrawn by assessment in July 2005. The High Court looked at *Droog* and in the end held for the taxpayer. TCA 1997, s 481(19) says that 'Where any relief has been given under this section which is subsequently found not to have been due, it shall be withdrawn by making an assessment to corporation tax or income tax, as the case may be, under Case IV … notwithstanding anything in the Tax Acts such an assessment may be made at any time'. Arguably this is more specific than the matter in *Droog* given the reference to 'notwithstanding' but the court held accordingly. With effect for any assessments or amendments to assessments made on or after 28 February 2012, any time limits in relation to assessments, amendments to assessments, liabilities or additional tax liabilities shall not apply to tax arising on an opinion under s 811 becoming final and conclusive. (TCA 1997, s 811(5A)). The Irish Supreme Court held in 2016 similarly to the High Court in *Droog*.

(b) where they form this opinion about any transaction, the Revenue Commissioners are then required to give notice in writing of this opinion to any person from or to whom a 'tax advantage' resulting from the transaction is to be withdrawn or denied if the Revenue's opinion becomes final and conclusive (TCA 1997, s 811(6));

(c) the said notice must specify:

  (i) the transaction which is a tax avoidance transaction (in the opinion of the Revenue Commissioners),

  (ii) the tax advantage, or part thereof, which is to be withdrawn from or denied to the person to whom the notice is given (if the opinion becomes final and conclusive),

  (iii) the steps to be taken by the Revenue Commissioners to withdraw from or deny to that person the tax advantage resulting from the transaction in so far as it refers to him (if the opinion becomes final and conclusive), and

  (iv) the amount of any double taxation relief calculated by the Revenue Commissioners which they propose to give to the person if the opinion becomes final and conclusive (TCA 1997, s 811(6));

(d) any person to whom a notice of the Revenue's opinion is given is entitled to appeal to the Appeal Commissioners against the opinion provided that he does so within 30 days of the date of the notice of the opinion; with effect from 19 February 2008, the grounds for appeal are restricted unless a full and timely protective notification has been made to the Revenue Commissioners (TCA 1997, s 811(7));

(e) the Revenue's opinion that any transaction is a tax avoidance transaction becomes final and conclusive either:

  (i) if no appeal is made under sub-s (7) within the 30-day time limit against any matter or matters specified or described in the notice of opinion, or

  (ii) as and when all appeals against any such matter or matters have been finally determined and if none of the appeals have been determined by an order to the effect that the opinion of the Revenue Commissioners is void (TCA 1997, s 811(5)(e));

(f) if and when their opinion that a transaction is a tax avoidance transaction becomes final and conclusive, the Revenue Commissioners are authorised to make all such adjustments and to do all such acts as are *just and reasonable* in order to withdraw from or deny to any person concerned the tax advantage which would otherwise result from the tax avoidance transaction (TCA 1997, s 811(5)(a));

(g) unless an opinion of the Revenue Commissioners becomes final and conclusive in either of the ways mentioned in (e) above, no tax charge or no adjustment of any other matter affecting tax can be made under TCA 1997, s 811;

(h) with effect from 19 February 2008, interest and a 20 per cent surcharge (previously 10 per cent) will apply to tax payable as a result of the application of TCA 1997, s 811 unless a full and timely protective notification has been made to the Revenue Commissioners (TCA 1997, s 811A as amended by FA 2008, s 140).

TCA 1997, s 811 applies to counteract the effects of tax avoidance transactions in relation to any one or more of the taxes, duties, levies or charges and any interest penalty or other amount payable in accordance with or pursuant to the provisions of any of:

(a) the Tax Acts;
(b) the Capital Gains Tax Acts;
(c) the Value-Added Tax Consolidation Act 2010 and the enactments amending or extending that Act;
(d) the Capital Acquisitions Tax Consolidation Act 2003 and the enactments amending or extending that Act;
(e) the statutes relating to stamp duty and;
(f) the Taxes Consolidation Act 1997, Pt 18D and any instruments made thereunder.

'Transaction' and 'tax advantage'

Before considering what constitutes a tax avoidance transaction, two other definitions must be considered in advance as set out below. It should be noted that both definitions have been transposed word for word into the new replacement anti-avoidance provision TCA 1997, s 811C which is discussed in detail at **17.302.2**.

'*Transaction*' is defined as

(i) any transaction, action, course of action, course of conduct, scheme, plan or proposal;
(ii) any agreement, arrangement, understanding, promise or undertaking, whether express or implied and whether or not enforceable or intended to be enforceable by legal proceedings; and
(iii) any series or combination of the circumstances referred to in paragraphs (i) and (ii), whether entered into or arranged by one person or by two or more persons:
    (I) whether acting in concert or not,
    (II) whether or not entered into or arranged wholly or partly outside the State, or
    (III) whether or not entered into or arranged as part of a larger transaction or in conjunction with any other transaction or transactions. (TCA 1997, s 811(1)(a)).

The definition, while evidently striving to cover all possibilities, does leave open the question as to whether or not a series of related steps *must* be viewed as a whole, or whether each step can be considered as a transaction in its own right.

A similar definition to that used in TCA 1997, s 811(1)(a) appears in the Australian General Anti-Avoidance Rule (ITAA 1936, Pt IV). In *FCT v Peabody* 94 ATC 4663, the Australian High Court held that a 'transaction' (or 'scheme' as it is termed in the Australian legislation) does not include a *part* of a transaction. The High Court took the view that a set of circumstances would not constitute a 'scheme' where they were 'incapable of standing on their own without being robbed of all practical meaning'.

In reaching this conclusion, the court relied on the decision in *IRC v Brebner* 43 TC 705 (from which the phrase cited above was drawn, albeit with reference there to the *wording* of the legislation and not the 'scheme' under review), a case concerning the application of what is now ICTA 1988, s 703, ('Transactions in Securities') in the UK. ICTA 1988, s 703 does not apply where the relevant:

> transaction or transactions were carried out … for *bona fide* reasons … and none of them had as their main object or one of their main objects to enable tax advantages to be obtained.

In the *Brebner* case, the taxpayers were directors of a company with which they did business on favourable terms. Following a take-over bid for the company, the taxpayers made a successful counter-offer and acquired shares in the company, primarily in order to protect their own business interests. The acquisition of the shares was financed by a bank overdraft which was subject to early repayment. It was always intended that the repayment would be funded out of the assets of the company itself. Following a gap of approximately two years, assets were duly extracted from the company and the overdraft was repaid. The method used to extract the assets was a scheme of capital reduction, selected to minimise the tax liability of the taxpayers. The Revenue argued that the share acquisition and the capital reduction scheme should be treated as two distinct transactions and that the main object of the latter transaction was to obtain a 'tax advantage'. The House of Lords upheld the Appeal Commissioners' finding of fact that the share acquisition and the capital reduction should be regarded as a *single* transaction, the main object of which was commercial. Lord Pearce said 'The method of carrying out (the single transaction) was intended as one part of a whole which was dominated by other considerations'.

Despite their citation of *IRC v Brebner*, the Australian High Court in the *Peabody* case did in fact hold that the devaluation of shares, undertaken as part of a larger plan to float the shares of a company in a tax-effective fashion, *could* be regarded as a separate transaction. The court also accepted that the Revenue authorities could 'pick and choose', ie they could attack the narrower 'transaction' within a wider 'transaction' (as in *Peabody*), or attack the wider transaction itself. The court's approach in *Peabody* is inconsistent with that in *Brebner*, where the House of Lords accepted that it was a question of fact whether a given set of events constituted a single transaction or two or more transactions.

However, in view of the fact that TCA 1997, s 811(1)(a) defines a 'transaction' so variously and widely, it seems that the approach taken in *Peabody* would be more appropriate than that taken in *Brebner*. This is particularly so given that a 'transaction' is stated to retain its character as a 'transaction':

> whether or not entered into or arranged as part of a larger transaction or in conjunction with any other transaction or transactions.

Some of the elements contained in the definition of a 'transaction' have been the subject of judicial discussion both in Ireland and in other jurisdictions. It is doubtful whether these precedents have much value in the context of TCA 1997, s 811 and also its replacement TCA 1997, s 811C (discussed below), which, for example, envisages a transaction 'entered into or arranged by one person or by two or more persons … *whether acting in concert or not*' (emphasis added). In addition, the fact that 'any series' or 'any combination' of 'transactions' may *itself* be treated as a transaction extends the potential scope of the term. Thus, if, for example 'transaction' A is succeeded by 'transaction' B, and in the normal sense of the various words used to define a 'transaction', transactions A and B would be regarded as separate and distinct from each other, the extended definition of 'transaction' nevertheless allows the Revenue to treat the two transactions as if they were a single transaction.

The concept of a series of transactions has been defined very restrictively by the House of Lords in the context of the 'new approach'. In *Craven v White* [1988] STC 476 the House of Lords considered a similar scheme to that which had been struck down in *Dawson* (discussed above). In this case, however, the taxpayers carried through the initial exchange of their shares with their subsidiary, M, while negotiations with the ultimate purchaser, O, were still in progress. As events turned out, those negotiations broke down, but were eventually resumed successfully at a later date. The court held that, in contrast to *Dawson*, the required degree of preordainment was absent. Lord Oliver stated:

> It does seem to me to be essential at least that the principal terms ... (of the composite transaction) should be agreed to the point at which it can be said that there is no practical likelihood that the transaction which actually takes place will not take place. Nor is it sufficient in my opinion that the ultimate transaction which finally takes place, though not envisaged at the intermediate stage as a concrete reality, is simply a transaction of the kind that is then envisaged.

However, there seems to be no persuasive reason why such a narrow approach should prevail in the context of TCA 1997, s 811 and its replacement TCA 1997, s 811C.

It is arguable that the rather vague expressions 'course of action' and 'course of conduct' are capable of including a deliberate failure to act, (eg where a shareholder allows his shares to be devalued as a result of a reorganisation of share capital without invoking his statutory rights to prevent this happening). There seems to be no reason why a deliberate failure to act should not form part of an arrangement or scheme (see *Floor v Davis* [1979] STC 379(3), where shareholders who refrained from voting against a winding up order in furtherance of a tax avoidance scheme were held in the circumstances to have 'exercised' their shareholding control).

The making of a will is clearly a 'transaction' as defined, although the act of dying presumably is not (see *Banbridge v IRC* discussed at **17.203**).

In *Inland Revenue v Yick Fung Estates Ltd* 1999, the Hong Kong Court held that the alteration of a trader's accounting date could amount to a transaction (defined in this context as 'including any transaction, operation or scheme'). It may be noted that TCA 1997, s 811 and its replacement TCA 1997, s 811C specifically envisages a transaction carried out by one person only.

'Tax advantage' is defined as:

(a) a reduction, avoidance or deferral of any charge or assessment to tax, including any potential or prospective charge or assessment; or

(b) a refund of or a payment of an amount of tax, or an increase in an amount of tax refundable or otherwise payable to a person, including any potential or prospective amount so refundable or payable,

arising out of, or by reason of, a transaction, including a transaction where another transaction would not have been undertaken or arranged to achieve the results, or any part of the results, achieved or intended to be achieved by the transaction.

It seems that the term 'reduction' is used in order to cover cases of partial avoidance of tax. There will be a reduction or avoidance of an *actual* (as opposed to a potential or prospective) tax charge where, eg the taxpayer generates a loss or claim to a deduction by means of a transaction and then offsets that loss against income which would otherwise be taxed. It would seem that it will also apply to the reduction, etc of any tax liability which would otherwise be generated by the transaction itself, eg an investment which attracts tax reliefs or exemptions (see further below).

The references to reductions, etc of 'potential' tax charges echoes the wording of ICTA 1988, ss 703–9 ('Transactions in Securities') in the UK. It seems that the rationale behind such references is to cover the situation where the taxpayer seeks to achieve a particular economic result or outcome, but does so by structuring the relevant transaction in a particular *form* which reduces or eliminates the tax liability which would otherwise arise. Thus, for example, under ICTA 1988, ss 703–9 a taxpayer who extracts profits from a company in the form of capital receives a 'tax advantage' because he could potentially have received those profits in the form of taxable income, ie as dividends (see *Brebner v IRC* discussed above). In *Revenue Commissioners v O'Flynn Construction Ltd et al* [2011] IESC 47, the Supreme Court held that a tax advantage arose when a company effectively purchased the benefit of tax-exempt reserves from a company which had initially qualified for the exemption in order to pay tax-free dividends out of its own accumulated reserves; the court rejected the argument that the purpose of the transaction was to effect the purchase of reserves albeit in a tax-efficient form.

The term 'prospective' bears the dictionary meaning of 'future' or 'expected'. The reference to 'prospective' tax liabilities therefore may be aimed at the situation where a particular, existing state of affairs would give rise to ongoing tax liabilities, but the taxpayer undertakes a transaction in order to rearrange his affairs in a manner designed to prevent such liabilities arising in the future. In *Revenue Commissioners v O'Flynn Construction Ltd et al* [2006] ITR 81, the High Court rejected the argument that there must be an actual tax charge or significant probability of a tax charge which is subsequently avoided for the section to apply. McKechnie J in his dissenting Supreme Court judgment in that case stated that *O' Flynn Construction* avoided an ACT charge on the payment of dividends.

In *IRC v USS* [1997] STC 1, it was held in the specific context of the UK 'transactions in securities' provisions that a repayment generated by reference to the exempt status of the recipient (a charity) could constitute a tax advantage. The different statutory context of TCA 1997, s 811 still invites the question as to whether a repayment to an exempt person arises 'out of, or by reason of a relevant transaction', or merely by virtue of the exempt status of that person *per se*. The answer is likely to be in the affirmative, since there would be no repayment in the absence of the transaction concerned.

The reference to a transaction, where another transaction would not have been undertaken to achieve the same results, etc, emphasises the point that TCA 1997, s 811 would not have been confined to transactions where the taxpayer achieves a given result by structuring his transaction in a particular form which results in his obtaining a tax advantage. Thus, transactions which are undertaken (wholly or partly) in order to save tax and, where accordingly *no* equivalent transactions would have been undertaken in the absence of the hoped-for tax savings would also have fallen within the potential scope of TCA 1997, s 811. This principle is also seemingly capable of extending to transactions which would not be economically practicable in the absence of tax savings, and which again would accordingly not have been undertaken in the absence of such savings. However, it may well be that these latter transactions would not have usually fallen within the scope of TCA 1997, s 811, on the basis that their main purpose is not to gain a tax advantage (see below).

It may be noted that the tax advantage must arise from the transaction which is treated as a tax avoidance transaction, but since the term 'transaction' is so widely defined, the circumstances in which the tax advantage may occur are equally widely defined. Also, the tax advantage which is the subject of the tax avoidance transaction may be a reduction, avoidance, deferral, etc of any of the taxes noted under '*Taxes covered*'; note also that a transaction which results in a reduction of interest or penalty in respect of *any* of the taxes covered may also be treated as giving rise to a tax advantage.

The above commentary also has equal relevance from the point of view of interpreting replacement anti-avoidance provision TCA 1997, s 811C.

Tax avoidance transactions

For TCA 1997, s 811 to have applied at all, there must be a tax avoidance transaction undertaken by one or more persons. For the purpose of the section, a tax avoidance transaction is defined by TCA 1997, s 811(2), subject to sub-s (3), as a transaction in respect of which the Revenue Commissioners, having regard to the factors noted in the next paragraph, form the opinion that:

(a) it gives rise to a tax advantage; and
(b) it was not undertaken or arranged *primarily* for purposes other than to give rise to a tax advantage [emphasis added].

In forming this opinion, the Revenue Commissioners are to have regard to any one or more of the following:

(a) the results of the transaction;
(b) the use of the transaction as a means of achieving those results; and
(c) any other means by which the results or any part of the results could have been achieved.

The term 'tax avoidance' taken in isolation is highly ambiguous. In *Mangin v IRC* (a case concerning the application of the New Zealand General Anti-Avoidance Provision) Lord Wilberforce observed:

> What is tax avoidance – whether the concept extends to any transaction if it is carried out in a way calculated to minimise the tax payable; and within the field of tax avoidance whether there is a distinction between 'proper' and 'improper' tax avoidance – are questions on which a wide variety of views are possible.

In *CIR v Challenge Corporation* [1986] STC 548, (a case concerning the same provision) Lord Templeman held that 'tax mitigation' had to be distinguished from 'tax avoidance', saying:

> In the former case, the taxpayer merely reduces his income or incurs expenditure in circumstances which reduce his assessable income or entitle him to a reduction in his tax liability … Thus, when a taxpayer executes a covenant and makes a payment under the covenant he reduces his income … the tax advantage results from the payment under the covenant … [on the other hand] … the taxpayer engaged in tax avoidance does not reduce his income or suffer a loss or incur expenditure but nevertheless obtains a reduction in his liability to tax as if he had … In an arrangement for tax avoidance the financial position of the taxpayer is unaffected (save for the costs of devising and implementing the arrangement) and by the arrangement the taxpayer seeks to obtain a tax advantage without suffering the reduction in income, loss or expenditure which other taxpayers suffer and which Parliament intended to be suffered by any taxpayer qualifying for a reduction in his liability to tax.

Lord Templeman's distinction therefore leans very heavily on the House of Lords 'new approach'. Transactions which are 'fiscal nullities', as in *Ramsay* (and presumably also tax-avoiding steps inserted into pre-ordained transactions as in *Furniss v Dawson*) represent 'tax avoidance'. All other tax-saving exercises are, by definition, examples of 'tax mitigation'. Because Lord Templeman's distinction is based on the 'new approach', it would appear to be of little persuasive value outside the UK.

The scheme of TCA 1997, s 811 is designed to rule out vague distinctions between 'tax minimisation/tax mitigation' and 'tax avoidance', or 'proper' avoidance and 'improper' avoidance. Thus, it firstly defines a 'tax advantage' in a neutral fashion (see above); secondly, it defines a 'tax avoidance transaction' by applying this definition of 'tax advantage' in conjunction with an objective 'main purpose' test. Whether this approach in fact succeeds in dispelling uncertainty seems very much open to question.

It is to be noted that it seems the factors outlined above are the only ones to which the Revenue Commissioners may have regard (except that they are also required to have regard to both the form and the substance of the transaction and of any connected or related transaction as provided by sub-s (3) (see *Second exclusion* below)). These factors are results-related and it appears that the Revenue Commissioners are not allowed take into account the taxpayer's subjective motive behind the transaction (the point was not contested in *Revenue Commissioners v O'Flynn Construction Ltd* [2011] IESC 47. If the provision is to be effective, it must be accepted that there is a necessary implication that the Revenue Commissioners must *also* weigh up the economic results achieved against the *tax advantages* involved, since presumably the term 'results' does not include the tax consequences of the transaction concerned. The Australian equivalent to TCA 1997, s 811 expressly includes the tax consequences of the transaction under review as one of the factors to be taken into account.

It is arguable that this purpose test resembles that stated by Lord Denning in the context of the Australian General Anti-Avoidance Rule in *Newton v FCT* [1958] 98 CLR, when he observed:

> The section is not concerned with the motives of individuals. It is not concerned with their desire to avoid tax, but only with the means which they employ to do it. In applying the section you must look at the transaction *itself* and see which is *its* effect – which *it* does – irrespective of the motives of the persons who made it. Williams J put it well when he said: The purpose of a (transaction) must be what it is intended to effect and that intention must be ascertained from its terms. Those terms may be oral or written or may have to be inferred from the circumstances but, when they have been ascertained, their purpose must be what they effect.
>
> In order to bring the arrangement within the section, you must be able to predicate – by looking at the overt acts by which it was implemented – that it was implemented in that particular way so as to avoid tax. If you cannot so predicate, but have to acknowledge that the transactions are capable of explanation by reference to ordinary business or family dealing, without necessarily being labelled as a means to avoid tax, then the arrangement does not come within the section.

In *Mangin v IRC* [1971] 1 All ER 179, Lord Wilberforce observed in the context of the New Zealand General Anti-Avoidance Rule:

> [Lord Denning's speech in Newton] … properly interpreted, does not mean that every transaction, having as one of its ingredients some tax-saving feature thereby becomes caught by the section. If a *bona fide* business transaction can be carried through in two ways, one involving less liability to tax that the other, their Lordships do not think that (the section) can properly be invoked. Indeed, in the case of a company, it may be the duty of the directors *vis-à-vis* their shareholder so to act. Again, trustees may in the interests of their beneficiaries, deliberately choose to invest in Government securities issued with some tax-free advantage, and to do so for the express purpose of securing it. They do not thereby fall foul of the section.

If this is the correct approach to the interpretation of TCA 1997, s 811, then the mere fact that a taxpayer chooses to carry out an economic transaction in a tax-efficient manner should not suffice to stamp it as a 'tax avoidance' transaction.

In *IRC v Brebner* (discussed above) Upjohn J observed:

> When the question of carrying out a genuine commercial transaction, as this was, is considered, the fact that there are two ways of carrying it out – one by paying the maximum amount of tax, the other by paying no, or much less tax – it would be quite wrong as a necessary consequence to draw the inference that in adopting the latter course one of the main objects is, for the purposes of the section, avoidance of tax. No commercial man in his senses is going to carry out commercial transactions except upon the footing of paying the smallest amount of tax involved.

While Upjohn J's remarks were made in the context of a *subjective* purpose test, this factor does not seem to detract from the general principle involved.

In their Guidance Notes to Form PN1 (Protective notifications under TCA 1997, s 811A, discussed under *Interest and 20 per cent Surcharge Regime* below), the Revenue Commissioners observe:

> The comparison of routes, that could have been chosen to achieve the results of a transaction, is the principal guide to the purpose of the route chosen:
>
> For example, in undertaking a business transaction, a taxpayer is not obliged to choose the most tax-costly route from routes A, B and C. Route B may involve the acquisition of a business asset with tax-deductible interest on borrowings whereas route A would involve a purchase with own funds. Although Route B involves a tax saving there would not normally be a tax avoidance transaction involved. If route C is a circuitous route that appears to have been primarily arranged for tax purposes, then it may be a tax avoidance transaction even though, as with routes A and B, a business asset is acquired.

The *Mangin* case in fact concerned a scheme whereby the taxpayer established a short-term trust for the benefit of his family members and then diverted what would otherwise have been his income into the trust by means of non-arm's length rental arrangements. The Privy Council held that these arrangements lacked any 'business reality', ie they took the view that there was no economic rationale to the transaction (other than saving tax); accordingly, it could be inferred that they were devised mainly in order to reduce the tax liability which, would otherwise have been incurred in respect of the taxpayer's income (it might be argued, however, that arrangements designed to transfer income to family members are by no means necessarily economically unreal).

Before the Revenue Commissioners can form the opinion that a given transaction is a tax avoidance transaction within this sub-s (2) definition, TCA 1997, s 811(3)(b) has also to be considered. TCA 1997, s 811(3)(b) states that, in forming their opinion under sub-s (2) whether (or not) a transaction is a tax avoidance transaction, the Revenue Commissioners shall have regard to:

(a) the form of that transaction;
(b) the substance of that transaction;
(c) the substance of any other transaction or transactions to or with which that transaction may reasonably be regarded as being directly or indirectly related or connected; and
(d) the final outcome and result of that transaction and any combination of those other transactions which are so related or connected.

The references to 'form' and 'substance' seem designed to ensure that the Revenue Commissioners are not bound by the doctrine of 'form over substance' (see **1.407**) when arriving at their opinion. However, the requirement for the Revenue Commissioners to have regard to the 'results' of a transaction (see above) may in any event be wide enough to encompass all of the legal and economic outcomes of a transaction. It may be noted that TCA 1997, s 806 contains a similar direction to take 'substance' into account, but that this has had limited effect in practice (see **17.205**).

Exclusions

TCA 1997, s 811(3)(a) has also to be considered. That subsection commences by stating that it is not to prejudice the generality of the definition in sub-s (2) (see previous two paragraphs). It then goes on to say that the Revenue Commissioners shall not regard a transaction as a tax avoidance transaction if they are satisfied that either one of two sets of circumstances apply to the transaction. These two 'exclusions' are now described. In *Revenue Commissioners v O'Flynn Construction Ltd et al* [2006] ITR 81, the High Court held that in an appeal the onus lay on the taxpayer to establish the matters necessary for the exclusions to apply.

First exclusion

A transaction is not to be regarded as a tax avoidance transaction if the Revenue Commissioners are satisfied that both of two conditions are met, namely:

(a) that the transaction was undertaken or arranged by the person sought to be taxed with a view, directly or indirectly, to the realisation of profits in the course of the business activities of any trade, profession or vocation carried on by that person; and

(b) that the transaction was not undertaken or arranged primarily to give rise to a tax advantage.

If the Revenue Commissioners are satisfied that both these conditions are met, then they are not to regard the transaction as a tax avoidance transaction notwithstanding that the purpose of the transaction could have been achieved by some other transaction which would have given rise to a greater amount of tax being payable. This exclusion may be described as the 'business profits' exclusion. For it to apply, not only must the transaction be undertaken in the course of the business in question, but, apart from an intention to realise profits (which may, it seems, be income or capital profits), the transaction must also have as its primary purpose some definite objective other than to secure a tax advantage.

Second exclusion

This exclusion may be referred to as the 'relief without misuse or abuse' exclusion. A transaction is not to be regarded as a tax avoidance transaction if the Revenue Commissioners are satisfied that:

(a) the transaction was undertaken or arranged to obtain the benefit of any relief, allowance or other abatement from tax available under any provision of the Acts; and

(b) the same transaction does not result directly or indirectly in a misuse or abuse of the relief, allowance or abatement having regard to the purposes for which that relief, allowance or abatement was intended.

It is clear that a transaction which falls clearly within the conditions to benefit from either of the first or the second exclusions in sub-s (3) should not be regarded as a tax avoidance transaction notwithstanding the 'without prejudice to' opening words of the subsection.

At first sight, exclusion (i) seems to subtract nothing from the basic definition of a 'tax avoidance transaction'. This is because, if a transaction is one which is 'not undertaken or arranged primarily for purposes other than to give rise to a tax advantage', it is difficult to see how it can be saved by an exemption confined to transactions 'not undertaken or arranged primarily to give rise to a tax advantage'. Whatever the scope of the first exclusion, it will be limited to business transactions undertaken with a view to profit and will not apply, for example to bounteous family arrangements.

It is also unclear how much substance is contained in exclusion (ii). Thus, for example an individual may have invested in the shares of a company qualifying for relief under the Employment and Investment Incentive (EII). Assume that subscription for the shares costs €10,000 and that the expected present value of the return on that investment is only €8,000, (ie yielding a negative net present value of (€8,000–€10,000) = €2,000. In the absence of the tax relief obtained under the EII, (the value of which, it is assumed will be €4,100, disregarding any timing issues) the investment is not economically viable and thus, would not be undertaken. Once the tax relief is factored into the equation, the cost of the shares falls to €5,900 and the investment becomes economically viable, (ie yielding a positive net present value of (€8,000 – €5,900) = €2,100). This assumes for the sake of simplicity that the pricing of the shares is not affected by the availability of the tax relief.

There are at least three ways of viewing this situation. The first is to argue that the taxpayer is simply exercising a commercial choice between alternative investments within the framework of the existing tax system, ie in the same way as the trustees who invest in exempt securities, alluded to by Lord Wilberforce in *Mangin v IRC* (see above). If this argument is correct, then the primary purpose of the EII investment is not to save tax, but instead to make an economically viable investment. The second is to argue that the return of €8,000 is greater than the amount of the tax break concerned, ie €4,100, and thus the primary purpose of the transaction is not to obtain the latter benefit. The third way of viewing this situation is to argue that the particular investment makes a projected loss in pre-tax terms, and thus, the primary purpose for undertaking it must be to obtain the tax advantage under the EII. This runs counter to the authorities cited above and would bring everyday economic transactions into the scope of TCA 1997, s 811. A straightforward transaction of this nature could hardly constitute an abuse or misuse of the legislation.

A further example is that of a leasing arrangement where the lessor factors in the tax benefits of the capital allowances which he obtains into the lease rentals which he charges to customers. This is a transaction which is inherently commercial, but where the values involved have to be calculated in the light of the tax environment. In other words, it is not legitimate to compare a *post-tax* rental stream with the *pre-tax* cost of investment (note the UK decision in *Barclays Mercantile Business Finance Ltd v Mawson* [2002] EWCA Civ 1853). Even if this argument was not accepted (which seems highly unlikely), exclusion (ii) would presumably have applied in any event, ie on the basis that the purpose of the capital allowances rules is to stimulate the provision of qualifying assets (see, eg *Ben-Odeco v Powlson* [1978] STC 360).

In *FCT v Spotless Services* 96 ATC 5201, the High Court of Australia (the final court of appeal), ruled on the application of the Australian general anti-avoidance rule (ITAA 1936, ss 177A–177B) in the context of a tax-effective investment. The taxpayer in the *Spotless* case had $40 million dollars available for short-term investment. These funds were deposited with a bank based in the Cook Islands. The interest on these funds was subject to a 5 per cent withholding tax in the Cook Islands. Under Australian tax law (as it then stood) this should have entitled the taxpayer to an exemption from Australian tax on the interest income. The rate of return on the funds was four per cent less than that offered by Australian banks (reflecting the tax advantages attached to those deposits). The High Court held that the transaction to be considered was the act of depositing the funds in question with the Cook Islands bank and not the overall transaction of investing to achieve the best after tax return. A similar analysis should arguably have applied to TCA 1997, s 811, in so far as the question to be asked in cases such as this is: why was *this* particular transaction undertaken?

The conclusion of the Australian High Court seems closest to the third view expressed above. However, taken at face value, it goes even further, in that any transaction which would not have been undertaken in the absence of tax advantages seems to fall within the principle enunciated there. Apart from the staggeringly wide implications of the decision in *Spotless,* it is difficult to reconcile it with the dicta of Lord Wilberforce in *Mangin v IRC* and those of Upjohn J in *IRC v Brebner*. However, it may be that the court's approach in *Spotless* was coloured by the facts; namely that:

(a) the arrangements were promoted commercially as a tax-avoidance scheme; and
(b) in order to provide security for the funds a complex set of banking arrangements were entered into under which the funds never in fact left the Australian bank in which they were originally deposited (see Krever 'The ghost of the Duke of Westminster laid to rest in Australia?' [1997] *Canadian Tax Journal* 122.

In *Appeal Case 86/08* (decided under TCA 1997, s 811) the taxpayers owned a company (X Ltd) which held cash in the region of €4 million but which for unexplained reasons was unable to pay dividends. The taxpayers subsequently formed a new company (Y Ltd) to which they sold the shares in X Ltd for a consideration of €4 million. The funding for the consideration was provided by a loan from X Ltd itself. The taxpayers gave evidence that the company could have been liquidated but as a matter of practicality and convenience they preferred to keep it going. The Appeal Commissioners held that a notion of a comparator transaction was implicit in the notion of a tax advantage and that it had to be possible to point to some actual or potential charge to tax, which had been avoided. They concluded that the payment of a dividend was too speculative and uncertain to qualify as a true comparator and that recharacterising the transaction as a liquidation (a comparison which would not have entailed any comparative tax saving) was the closest and most appropriate comparator to what had actually occurred, *viz* the stripping out of the cash reserves. It is difficult to see why the payment of a dividend could not as easily have been used as a means of stripping out cash reserves, although it appears that in fact this route was not available to the company (a matter not further commented upon by the Appeal Commissioners).

A contention made by the Revenue Commissioners that the extraction of the surplus cash by way of directors' remuneration was dismissed by the Appeal Commissioners. As they forcefully and correctly pointed out, the purpose of such remuneration could only be to reward services rendered to the company. The Revenue Commissioners have appealed the case to the High Court.

The terms 'misuse' and 'abuse' as used in exclusion (ii) are at first blush rather vague. In *Revenue Commissioners v O'Flynn Construction Ltd et al* [2006] ITR 81, (see above), the High Court relied on *McCann Ltd v O'Culacháin* III ITR 304 to hold that the purpose of the exemption under the export sales relief legislation was to encourage the creation of employment and the promotion of exports and not to be a commercially available product. As discussed at **1.402**, the interpretative approach in *McCann* was arguably over-expansive. In any event, it is not clear that the ability to sell on the benefit of a tax exemption does anything more than enhance its utility for the companies engaged in export activities. In the Supreme Court, the majority took a broader approach and held that invocations of the purpose behind the relief 'can be deployed almost rhetorically on either side of this case'. Instead it was necessary to interpret TCA 1997, s 811 in the context of its leglislative history, which was clearly directed towards the reversal of the decision in *IRC V Duke of Westminster in Ireland.* As discussed in **1.401**, and **1.402**, because the court's role is confined to one of interpretation, this means they must rely mainly on the statutory text itself in order to ascertain statutory purposes. While the courts may also take into account such factors as the generally-known background to a tax statute, and the general principles of tax law, they are not entitled to speculate about the probable motives of the legislature. The Irish courts do not refer even in cases of doubt to the record of the Dáil proceedings (see the discussion at **1.404**). TCA 1997, s 811 cannot compel or authorise the courts to depart from their constitutional role as interpreters of statute. However, the court felt entitled to place TCA 1997, s 811 in its historical context and confirmed that a purposive approach was appropriate even for fiscal statute.

Accordingly the Revenue Commissioners were obliged to apply the exclusion by reference to the general scheme and overriding purpose of TCA 1997, s 811; given the artificial and contrived nature of the arrangements, that their sole purpose was to avoid tax and the substance thereof was to enable a non-exporting company to avail of ESR, then by definition it represented a misuse or abuse of the relief.

In many cases, it will be extremely difficult for the courts to establish the statutory purposes with any degree of precision. As suggested in previous editions of this book, it now appears that in such circumstances the courts will be prepared to assume that manifestly 'artificial' transactions (perhaps particularly those which involve little, or no, net economic outlay by the taxpayer) could never have been contemplated by the legislature as being entitled to tax relief. The Supreme Court did indicate however that in the case of highly detailed and prescriptive legislation, conformity with the literal requirements laid down might suffice without any wider consideration of purpose.

In *Appeal Cases 162 to 164/07*, the taxpayers entered into a leasing scheme under which they incurred expenditure on student accommodation which was then leased to a college; the college lent the taxpayers the funds to finance this expenditure and entered into option agreements which together with complementary security deposit arrangements effectively ensured that they were guaranteed to recover their expenditure at a predetermined date. The outgoings payable on the loan by the taxpayers were covered to an extent by the rent receivable by them under the lease; the rationale of the arrangement being that the taxpayers' net outgoing was the price they paid for obtaining capital allowances on their expenditure under TCA 1997, s 372AP. The Appeal Commissioners held that there was nothing in TCA 1997, s 372AP which required that the expenditure should be borne by the taxpayer nor was there any requirement that the taxpayer should incur financial risk. Accordingly they found that the inferred purpose of TCA 1997, s 372AP to encourage the construction and renovation of student accommodation had not been violated and there had not been abuse of that provision. Whether this decision is consistent with that in *O'Flynn Construction Ltd* is debatable. The Revenue Commissioners have appealed the case to the High Court.

In *McNichol v The Queen* 97 DTC 111, a case concerning the Canadian general anti-avoidance rule (see above), the Canadian tax court held that a 'teleological' approach should be adopted in the construction of a similar exclusion. The court then took the view that something less than an 'extreme undermining of the statutory purpose', as well as what might be described as 'ordinary tax planning', could amount to an abuse or misuse of a statutory provision. In *McNichol* the Canadian tax court held that the transaction there (see above) was 'a classic example of surplus stripping', since the scheme of the tax legislation was to require corporate distributions to be treated as income. It followed that the transaction entailed an abuse of the legislation. Whether the Irish courts would adopt such a radically purposive approach to the Taxes Acts when applying TCA 1997, s 811 is questionable. In *O'Flynn Construction Ltd*, the Supreme Court made clear that no assistance was to be drawn from the Canadian jurisprudence in this area.

In *Ensign Tankers v Stokes* [1992] STC 226, a film production company resident in the USA sought to raise finance in the UK from a number of passive investors. These included the taxpayer, E, a resident trading company. It was necessary to offer considerable tax benefits to the investors in order to induce them to participate. Accordingly the following steps were (in essence) undertaken:

(a) E and some other investors formed a Ltd partnership, V;

(b) V agreed to finance the production and exploitation of a film. The rights to the film negatives were assigned to V by L, which was to produce the film on behalf of V. V invested 25 per cent of the projected capital expenditure on the film out of their own funds (the 'initial investment');

(c) The balance of expenditure ('the residual investment') was provided by way of a loan from L. L immediately reacquired the funds lent to V in its capacity as producer. Under the loan agreement, L's right of repayment was limited to the net receipts which accrued to the partnership from the distribution of the film (a so-called 'non-recourse' loan); and

(d) Under a separate distribution agreement, V granted exclusive distribution rights to S1 and S2, two wholly owned subsidiaries of L. Under this agreement, the loan from L was to be repaid out of 75 per cent of the net receipts from the film, until such time as the initial investment had been recouped out of the remaining 25 per cent of the net receipts. Thereafter, V was to receive 25 per cent of the net receipts, with the remaining 75 per cent going to S.

V claimed capital allowances in respect of the total capital expenditure on the film. In economic terms, this meant that, if successful, V would have received allowances based on an amount of four times the initial investment.

The House of Lords held, however, that the 'new approach' applied, and that V could only claim allowances on the 'initial investment'. The scheme was one which included the achievement of a 'legitimate' commercial end, ie the making of the 'initial investment'. However, the court held that the loan by L to V, the making of the residual investment and the distribution agreement were all 'inserted' steps adopted with the sole purpose of generating additional tax depreciation claims. Looking at the final position, once the various agreements were completed, it can be seen that V's legal obligations and rights regarding the loan and the corresponding residual investment were self-cancelling. The obligation to repay the loan did not impinge upon V's shares of profits or put at risk any other of V's income or assets. The mere fact that non-recourse loan finance is used would not of itself justify the application of the 'new approach' (see *Peterson v Commissioner of Inland Revenue* [2005] STC 448).

It seems likely that the scheme in *Ensign* would also in principle fall foul of TCA 1997, s 811 (leaving aside the specific anti-avoidance rules contained in TCA 1997, s 1013). Although the scheme had a commercial 'result', (ie the making of the initial investment) the means to achieve that result were adopted in order to obtain a 'tax advantage', (ie the additional claim for capital allowances in respect of the residual investment on the part of V). It also seems most unlikely that exclusion (ii) would be in point, since the claim for capital allowances in respect of a share in an asset where the risk and rewards of ownership had been effectively transferred to a third party would seem to be *prima facie* an abuse or misuse of the legislation.

In *Airspace Investments Ltd v Moore* V ITR 3, a similar scheme was upheld by Lynch J, who noted however that TCA 1997, s 811 was not applicable since the scheme was concluded before that section took effect.

It may also be noted that exclusion (ii) does not seem to cover claims for *deductions* in computing income. It is also open to question whether the remittance basis constitutes an 'abatement' for these purposes. The taxpayer who falls outside the territorial scope of Irish taxation as a result of a transaction will clearly be unable to invoke the exclusion. Further, the recasting of a transaction to bring it within capital gains tax, as opposed to income tax would not seem to qualify. The term 'relief' does however seem sufficiently broad to cover exemptions (see *IRC v USS* [1997] STC 1).

Double tax treaties

TCA 1997, s 826 (which is the vehicle for incorporating double tax treaties into Irish law) and TCA 1997, s 811 are expressed to apply 'notwithstanding anything in any enactment' and 'notwithstanding any other provision of the Acts' respectively. The better view seems to be that in this case the construction which is compatible with Ireland's treaty obligations should be preferred. On this footing TCA 1997, s 826 should take precedence over TCA 1997, s 811. The same principles should equally apply to its replacement provision TCA 1997, s 811C (see **17.302.2**). The decision in *Bricom Holdings v IRC* [1997] STC 1179 suggests that the protection of a double tax treaty may apply not only to the person who is actually in receipt of the income in question but also to a person to whom that income is attributed under a deeming provision. However, *Bricom* suggests that where income or gains are recharacterised or simply form an element in the measurement of a notional amount of income, the benefit of treaty exemption may be lost (see the discussion at **17.209**).

Formation, issue and effects of opinion

When the Revenue Commissioners form the opinion that a transaction is a tax avoidance transaction under TCA 1997, s 811, they must at the same time:

(a) calculate the tax advantage which they consider arises from the transaction;
(b) determine the tax consequences of the transaction (to be applied if the Revenue Commissioners' opinion becomes final and conclusive); and
(c) calculate the amount of any relief from double taxation which they propose to give to any person affected by their opinion as required by subsection (TCA 1997, s 811(6)).

It may be seen that where a transaction either creates a loss, or results in the increase in the valuation of an asset, it will be impossible to quantify the resulting tax advantage until the loss is the subject of a claim (or the relevant asset is disposed of). Thus, while a transaction may give rise to a tax advantage in the sense of a potential tax saving, it is only possible for the Revenue to invoke the section in the face of an actual tax advantage. There will inevitably be other situations where it will only be possible for the Revenue to quantify a tax advantage in the light of events which take place subsequently to the alleged 'tax avoidance' transaction. Moreover, where a transaction generates tax savings over an indefinite future tract of time, the Revenue would have been put to some difficulty. For example, if A had diverted an ongoing stream of income to B, and assuming that TCA 1997, s 811 had applied, would this have given rise to an annual 'notice of opinion' (see below) by the Revenue? It is worth noting that under TCA 1997, s 811A, the Revenue may have been required to set out the dates on which tax would have been due and payable if the tax avoidance transaction had not been undertaken: see *Interest and 20 per cent Surcharge Regime* below.

The calculation of the 'tax advantage' may be reasonably straightforward in other instances. Thus, for example, on the facts in the *Ensign Tankers*, case the 'tax advantage' could presumably be identified as the tax attributable to the additional claim for capital allowances made in respect of the 'residual investment' by V. This is a reasonably clear-cut issue, because in the absence of the scheme adopted in *Ensign Tankers*, V would have been entitled only to a claim in respect of the 'initial investment'.

However, particularly where more complex 'linear' transactions are involved, the identification of the 'tax advantage' may be much more controversial. If the Revenue is confronted with a transaction which achieves economic results, but where no other transaction would have been carried out in order to achieve those particular results, and where it is not possible to point to the exploitation of a specific exemption or relief, it may well lack a benchmark against which to measure the tax advantage which arises. Logically, in these kind of circumstances, tax can only be avoided or reduced if it is possible to point to a situation where more tax would have been paid in a comparable situation, or in the absence of the exemption or relief.

There will also be considerable room for argument where a particular economic result could be achieved by a number of methods, each of which gives rise to a different tax cost. Are the Revenue entitled to choose as the 'benchmark' the method which would generate the highest tax cost, thus maximising the tax advantage obtained by the taxpayer? This was in fact the approach taken in the context of the UK 'Transactions in Securities' legislation (ICTA 1988, s 703 *et seq*) in *Ansyz v IRC* [1978] STC 296. There, the relevant 'tax advantage' was computed by comparing (i) the (non-taxable) transaction which the taxpayer actually carried out against; (ii) a theoretical and highly improbable, but taxable, transaction.

The 'tax consequences', in relation to any tax avoidance transaction are defined as such adjustments and acts as the Revenue Commissioners propose to make and do in order to withdraw or deny the tax advantage resulting from that transaction (TCA 1997, s 811(1)(a)). The tax consequences may apply to such one or more persons who would otherwise derive a tax advantage from the transaction.

Once the Revenue Commissioners form the opinion that a transaction is a tax avoidance transaction, they must *immediately* give notice in writing of the opinion to any person or persons from or to whom a tax advantage is to be withdrawn or denied or to whom relief from double taxation is to be given if the opinion becomes final and conclusive (TCA 1997, s 811(6)(a)).

The reference to double taxation appears to be in the domestic, rather than the international, context since the double taxation concerned must 'arise by virtue of any adjustment made or act done by the Revenue Commissioners'. This provision seems designed to meet the type of situation where a notice of opinion is served upon B, as the person from whom the tax advantage is withdrawn, attributing income of A to B by way of adjustment. TCA 1997, s 811 envisages that a notice of opinion may also be sent to a person (here A) other than that from whom the tax advantage is to be withdrawn, specifying the amount of double taxation relief which the Revenue propose to allow him. This seems to underline the domestic nature of the double taxation impost, since it is hard to see why relief should be granted for overseas taxation in respect of a person not otherwise affected by the section. In the present example, the relief would presumably take the form of striking out the tax on A's income. This would all make perfect sense if, eg B had been attempting to divert income to A who paid tax at lower rates than B, (assuming that the various other stipulations of TCA 1997, s 811 are met).

It would appear logical that the relief for 'double taxation' can apply only where the same income or gains would otherwise be attributed to two (or more) persons (see the general discussion of 'double taxation' – in **1.405**: *Presumption against double taxation*). It remains unclear therefore whether any relief is available where other, additional types of tax liabilities are incurred as a result of a tax avoidance transaction. A very simple example might be a scheme under which an individual restructures his affairs in order to save income tax of €100,000 but in so doing incurs a VAT liability for €20,000. It is arguable that the Revenue Commissioners can nullify the tax advantage of €100,000 leaving the VAT liability of €20,000 intact, since there is no question of levying tax twice on income. Would the status of the VAT liability depend on the nature of the Revenue Commissioners adjustments, (eg if they deem that the VATable transaction never took place in order to recapture the individual's tax liability of €100,000, would they then be obliged to repay the VAT, but not otherwise?).

The opinion of the Revenue Commissioners does not have any effect until it becomes final and conclusive. This occurs either:

(a) 30 days after the date of the notice of the opinion, if no appeal is made under sub-s (7) within that time against any matter or matters specified or described in the notice of opinion; or
(b) on the final determination of any appeal or, if more than one appeal is made, on the determination of all appeals, against any such matter or matters (provided that none of the appeals has been determined by an order to the effect that the opinion of the Revenue Commissioners is void) (TCA 1997, s 811(5)(e)).

TCA 1997, s 811(1)(c) as inserted by FA 2006, s 126 provides in this connection that all appeals made under TCA 1997, s 811(7) if they have not otherwise been so determined (eg by the Appeal Commissioners, etc) shall be deemed to have been finally determined when:

(a) there is a written agreement, between the taxpayer and the inspector that the notice of opinion is to stand or is to be amended in a particular manner;
(b) the terms of such an agreement that was not made in writing have been confirmed by notice in writing given by the taxpayer to the inspector or vice versa *and* 21 days have elapsed since the giving of the notice without the recipient giving notice that he desires to repudiate or withdraw from the agreement; or
(c) the taxpayer gives notice in writing to the inspector that the person desires not to proceed with the appeal.

When the opinion of the Revenue Commissioners becomes final and conclusive (if it does so), then they may make all such adjustments and do all such acts as are just and reasonable (in so far as such adjustments and acts are specified in the notice of the opinion) to withdraw or deny the tax advantage from or to any person concerned (TCA 1997, s 811(5)(a)). The fact that only an adjustment or act specified in the opinion may be made or done enables any person concerned to appeal against the adjustment or act before the opinion becomes final and conclusive.

The adjustments or acts to disallow the tax advantage may, without prejudice to the generality of the statement in the first sentence of the last paragraph, include:

(a) allowing or disallowing, in whole or in part, any deduction or other amount which is relevant in computing tax payable, or any part thereof;

(b) allocating or denying to any person any deduction, loss, abatement, allowance, exemption, income or other amount, or any part thereof; or

(c) recharacterising for tax purposes the nature of any payment or other amount (TCA 1997, s 811(5)(b)).

In Revenue Commissioners v O'Flynn Construction Ltd et al [2006] ITR 81, the High Court held that while these provisions gave TCA 1997, s 811 primacy over other provisions, it still enabled other provisions to be taken into account as appropriate. McKechnie J also referred to this matter in his dissenting Supreme Court judgment.

Where any adjustment is made or any act is done to withdraw or deny a tax advantage, and if that adjustment or act would otherwise result in any double taxation, the Revenue Commissioners are required to afford the appropriate relief from that double taxation (TCA 1997, s 811(5)(c)). Since the amount of the relief to be given must be specified in the notice of opinion given under sub-s (6), the person entitled to the relief has the opportunity of appealing against the amount of the relief proposed before the opinion becomes final and conclusive, if he considers the proposed relief is inadequate.

It remains an open question as to whether the Revenue Commissioners' power to form an opinion and to create or extinguish tax liabilities thereby is taxation by administrative discretion as opposed to taxation by law. In *Marshall Castings Ltd v IRC* 34 TC 122, where similar powers were granted by the Inland Revenue under the former UK excess profits tax legislation, Wrottesley J did not deny that such powers were far reaching and 'came perilously near exposing the subject to such taxation as the Commissioners of Inland Revenue might choose to impose'.

The delegation of taxing powers to the Revenue Commissioners (or indeed to any appellate body, including the courts) would of course represent a breach of the constitutional separation of powers, under which legislation is the sole preserve of the legislature (Article 15.2: see **1.409**). The constitutional validity of TCA 1997, s 811 may therefore depend on whether or not the courts would view the discretion granted to the Revenue Commissioners as simply administrative in nature, (ie merely giving effect to the policy laid down in the statute: see *Cityview Press v AnCo* [1980] IR 381). The issue was not the subject of separate proceedings in *Revenue Commissioners v O'Flynn Construction Ltd et al* [2011] IESC 47.

In *Revenue Commissioners v McNamee* [2012] IEHC 500, the High Court held that the notice of opinion was given immediately after the nominated officer formed the opinion that the transactions in question were tax avoidance transactions. The applicant had claimed that the Revenue Commissioners had treated him and 25 other tax payers who had entered into similar type transactions as a group and once they had formed the necessary opinion immediately thereafter all 26 tax payers should have been issued with notice of opinions. For this reason the applicant claimed that the opinion was tainted by pre-judgement and bias. The High Court found that there was no evidence that the necessary opinion had been formed or could be formed in respect of the 26 as a group. The taxpayer's appeal was dismissed by the Supreme Court in 2016 ([2016] IESC 33).

Appeals

Any person aggrieved by an opinion formed or, in so far as it refers to him, a calculation or determination made by the Revenue Commissioners, is entitled to appeal to the Appeal Commissioners against the opinion. Any such appeal must, if it is to be valid, be made within 30 days of the date of the notice of the opinion. An appeal only applies on one or more of the following grounds:

(a) that the transaction specified in the notice of opinion is not a tax avoidance transaction; or
(b) that the amount of the tax advantage specified in the opinion is incorrect; or
(c) that the adjustments or acts specified in the opinion to withdraw or deny the tax advantage are not reasonable to withdraw or deny that advantage; or
(d) that the amount of relief from double taxation proposed is insufficient or incorrect (TCA 1997, s 811(7)).

Any such appeal is made on the basis that, having regard to all the circumstances, any of the said grounds exist. The circumstances to be considered include any facts or matters which were not known to the Revenue Commissioners when they formed their opinion or made the calculation or determination appealed against.

The Appeal Commissioners are required to hear any appeal made in due time as if it were an appeal against an assessment to income tax (see **2.204**). Further, all the provisions of TCA 1997, relating to the rehearing of an appeal by the Circuit Court judge and the statement of a case for the High Court on a point of law are to apply with any necessary modifications (see **2.205**) (TCA 1997, s 811(8)). F(TA)A 2015, s 38(8), which was subject to Ministerial Order (SI 110/2016 appointed 21 March 2016 as the day on which the Finance (Tax Appeals) Act 2015, came into operation), amends TCA 1997, s 811(8) to say that in adjudicating and determining an appeal, the Appeal Commissioners shall not enquire into any grounds of appeal other than those specified in sub-s (7) as outlined above.

There are several additional rules relating to an appeal against an opinion of the Revenue Commissioners under TCA 1997, s 811. No ground of appeal may be gone into other than those specified in subparagraphs (a) to (d) above. If there is more than one appeal against the same opinion, calculation or determination, the appeals of two or more appellants may be heard or reheard together if the appellants in question so request. The Revenue Commissioners do not, however, have the right to require the appeals of different appellants to be heard together.

TCA 1997, s 811(9)(a) contains further rules to be observed by the Appeal Commissioners on their hearing of an appeal against an opinion, determination or calculation of the Revenue Commissioners. The Appeal Commissioners must have regard to all matters to which the Revenue Commissioners may or are required to have regard under any of the provisions of TCA 1997, s 811.

The Appeal Commissioners must therefore have regard to any one or more of the results of the transaction the subject of the appeal, the means of achieving those results and any other means by which those results could have been achieved (TCA 1997, s 811(2)). Also, they are to take into account both the form and the substance of the transaction, the final outcome and result of the transaction, as well as the substance, final outcome and result of any other transaction(s) with which the transaction under appeal may reasonably be regarded as being connected (TCA 1997, s 811(3)(b)).

Further, in determining the appeal under any of the permitted grounds of appeal, TCA 1997, s 811(9)(a) prescribes the alternative determinations which may be made by the Appeal Commissioners. The available determinations vary according to which of the grounds of appeal is the subject of the determination.

For a determination on an appeal on the grounds that a transaction is not a tax avoidance transaction, there are two alternative bases for the Appeal Commissioners' decisions. The first, narrower, basis applies where the transaction is potentially subject to the 20 per cent surcharge regime (broadly speaking, where a transaction or part thereof has been effected on or after 19 February 2008 or would otherwise generate a tax advantage by reference to events on or after that date and where a timely protective notification has *not* been submitted: see *Interest and 20 per cent Surcharge Regime* below).In these circumstances, the decision may be any one of three depending on the view of the Appeal Commissioners, or a majority of them, namely:

(a) where they consider that there are grounds on which the transaction, or any part of it specified or described in the notice of opinion could *reasonably* be considered to be a tax avoidance transaction, an order that the opinion is to stand good to the effect that the transaction specified in the notice of opinion is to stand in relation to that transaction or part thereof; or
(b) where they consider, subject to such amendment or addition as they deem necessary and specify, that there are grounds on which the transaction, or any part of it specified or described in the notice of opinion could *reasonably* be considered to be a tax avoidance transaction, an order that the opinion is to stand good subject to such amendment or addition in relation to that transaction or part thereof; or
(c) an order that the opinion is void in relation to the transaction being a tax avoidance transaction (TCA 1997, s 811A(1C), inserted by FA 2008, s 140).

The standard of reasonableness under (a) and (b) appears to resemble that enumerated in *Edwards v Bairstow* 36 TC 207 (see **2.204**); if this is correct, the onus on the taxpayer to dislodge a Revenue opinion will be daunting.

The second alternative basis applies in all other circumstances and again the decision may be any one of three, depending on the view of the Appeal Commissioners or a majority of them, namely:

(a) an order that the opinion is to stand good to the effect that the transaction specified in the notice of opinion is a tax avoidance transaction (or that, in so far as a part of the transaction is a tax avoidance transaction, that the opinion is to stand good as regards that part); or
(b) an order that the opinion is to stand good subject to such amendment as the Appeal Commissioners, or a majority of them, deem necessary and specify (or similarly for an opinion standing good in relation to a part of the transaction subject to such amendment); or
(c) an order that the opinion is void in relation to the transaction being a tax avoidance transaction.

Under both alternatives, the power of an appellate body to add to the substance of the Revenue Commissioners' opinion, and thus impose a new basis for liability on the taxpayer (as opposed to the power to increase a liability already assessed) is striking. Under the equivalent Canadian provisions, any additional tax liability can be imposed only 'to the extent that it may reasonably be regarded as relating to the (tax avoidance) transaction'. The fact that under the first alternative basis above the taxpayer must furthermore establish the unreasonableness of a Revenue opinion in order to rebut it compounds the situation.

If the Appeal Commissioners determine under alternative (c) on either of the alternative bases above that the opinion of the Revenue Commissioners is void, that is the end of the matter (unless the Revenue Commissioners require a case to be stated under TCA 1997, s 941 for the opinion of the High Court on a point of law, see **2.205**). The opinion simply never becomes final and conclusive (unless the High Court or, if the matter is taken there, the Supreme Court reverses the decision of the Appeal Commissioners on a point of law).

It may be accepted that the transaction is a tax avoidance one, or the Appeal Commissioners may determine that it or part of it is a tax avoidance one. Then, it is necessary for the Appeal Commissioners to determine any appeal(s) on any one or more of the other permitted grounds of appeal. For an appeal on the grounds that the amount of the tax advantage specified in the opinion is incorrect, the Appeal Commissioners must determine the appeal by ordering either:

(a) that the amount of the tax advantage, or the part thereof specified in the opinion shall stand good; or
(b) that the amount of the said tax advantage is to be increased or reduced by such amount as they shall direct.

For an appeal on the grounds that the adjustments, etc to withdraw or deny the tax advantage are not reasonable, the Appeal Commissioners may determine either that the adjustments, etc are to stand good or that they are to be altered or added to in such manner as the Appeal Commissioners direct. Similarly, for an appeal on the grounds that the amount of relief from double taxation proposed is insufficient or incorrect, the Appeal Commissioners may direct that the amount of relief is to stand good or is to be increased or reduced to the extent to which they so direct.

Rehearing by Circuit Court judge, Appeal to High Court etc

TCA 1997, s 811(9)(b) applies all the foregoing rules in relation to the hearing of an appeal by the Appeal Commissioners to a rehearing by the Circuit Court judge. Similarly, it applies the same rules to the extent necessary to the determination by the High Court of any question or questions of law arising on the statement of a case for the opinion of the High Court. In short, the same matters have to be determined by the Circuit Court judge or by the High Court (or Supreme Court) in relation to the opinion of the Revenue Commissioners, dependent on the particular grounds or alternative grounds of appeal, but neither the High Court or the Supreme Court may alter any decision on any point of fact (as distinct from on a point of law). F(TA)A 2015, which was subject to Ministerial Order (SI 110/2016 appointed 21 March 2016 as the day on which the Finance (Tax Appeals) Act 2015, came into operation) removes the reference to a Circuit Court rehearing from the section.

Amendment of opinion

TCA 1997, s 811(10) authorises the Revenue Commissioners at any time to amend, add to or withdraw any matter specified in a notice of opinion by giving 'notice of amendment' in writing to each and every person affected by the amendment, addition or withdrawal. Where such a notice of amendment is issued, all the rules of the section are applied as if that notice were a notice of opinion and as if any matter specified in the notice of amendment were specified in a notice of opinion.

In other words, the notice of amendment will become final and conclusive if no appeal against it is made within 30 days. Also, the same rights of appeal to and the same procedures for the hearing, rehearing, etc of appeals to the Appeal Commissioners, Circuit Court, etc exist in relation to the notice of amendment as do for the original notice of opinion. However, no amendment, addition or withdrawal of, to or from the notice of opinion is allowed to set aside or alter any matter which has become final and conclusive as the result of the determination of an earlier appeal made with regard to that matter. On the other hand, an amendment, etc to a notice of assessment which had previously become final and conclusive due to failure to make any appeal may be the subject of an appeal if the appeal against the notice of amendment is made within the 30-day time limit.

Interest and 20 per cent surcharge regime

The better view is that TCA 1997, s 811 in isolation was insufficient to justify imposing interest on any payments of tax ultimately found to be due as a result of applying the section. TCA 1997, s 811A, inserted by FA 2006, s 126 and subsequently amended by FA 2008, s 140 imposes interest and a 20 per cent (previously ten per cent) surcharge on tax which becomes payable (including recoupments of refunds or repayments previously made to the taxpayer) as a result of adjustments or acts carried out by the Revenue Commissioners under TCA 1997, s 811(5). Such adjustments and acts will follow once their opinion that a transaction is a tax avoidance transaction within TCA 1997, s 811 (or their opinion as amended, or added to, on appeal where relevant) has become final and conclusive (TCA 1997, s 811A(1)(a), (2)). The interest and surcharge regime applies to any tax avoidance transaction where all or any part of the transaction is undertaken or arranged on or after 2 February 2006. It also applies to any tax avoidance transaction even where all of it was undertaken or arranged before that date, if that transaction would have but for TCA 1997, s 811 either:

(a) given rise to any avoidance, reduction or deferral of tax and such tax would only have arisen as a result of one or more other transactions carried out wholly on or after 2 February 2006; or
(b) given rise to a refund or repayment of tax (or an additional refund or repayment) due on or after 2 February 2006 (TCA 1997, s 811A(7)).

The rate of surcharge generally increases from 10 per cent to 20 per cent where all or any part of the transaction is undertaken or arranged on or after 19 February 2008 and on or before 23 October 2014. It also applies to any tax avoidance transaction even where all of it was undertaken or arranged before that date, if that transaction would have but for TCA 1997, s 811 either:

(a) given rise to any avoidance, reduction or deferral of tax and such tax would only have arisen as a result of one or more other transactions carried out wholly on or after 19 February 2008; or
(b) given rise to a refund or repayment of tax (or an additional refund or repayment) due on or after 19 February 2008.

The above interest and surcharge regime will cease to apply to transactions which commence after 23 October 2014. This regime has essentially been replaced by a more penal 30 per cent surcharge regime which has been introduced in tandem with the new general anti-avoidance provision TCA 1997, s 811C. Full details of the new surcharge regime is set out in **17.202.2**.

The scope of the term 'arranged' as opposed to 'undertaken' is open to doubt, not least given the very wide definition of transaction in TCA 1997, s 811(1)(a) which itself includes 'arrangements' and 'undertakings' as well as larger transactions containing these elements.

The interest and 20 per cent surcharge regime will not apply generally, however, if the Revenue Commissioners have received a 'protective notification' of the relevant transaction before the 'relevant date'. The taxpayer will be treated as making the notification:

(a) solely to prevent the application of the first, narrower basis for the determination of an appeal described above and any possibility of a surcharge or interest becoming payable by that person; and

(b) wholly without prejudice as to whether any opinion by the Revenue Commissioners that the transaction concerned was a tax avoidance transaction would be correct (TCA 1997, s 811A(3)(a), (b) as amended by FA 2008, s 140).

In relation to the 20 per cent surcharge, the relevant date is determined as follows:

(a) where the whole or any part of the relevant transaction, is undertaken or arranged on or after 19 February 2008, the later of:
   (i) 90 days after the date on which the transaction commenced, or
   (ii) 19 May 2008;

(b) where the whole of the transaction is undertaken or arranged before 19 February 2008, and would but for TCA 1997, s 811 have given rise to any avoidance, reduction or deferral of tax and such tax would only have arisen as a result of one or more other transactions carried out wholly on or after 19 February 2008:

   90 days after the date on which the first of those other transactions commenced;

and

(c) where the whole of the transaction is undertaken or arranged before 19 February 2008, and would but for TCA 1997, s 811 have given rise to a refund or repayment of an amount of tax (or an additional refund or repayment) due on or after 19 February 2008:

   90 days after the amount concerned became due (TCA 1997, s 811A(3) as amended by FA 2008, s 140).

The cut-off dates for the ten per cent surcharge regime are set out in the 2007 edition of this book. It should be noted that where a protective notice was filed in relation to a transaction before the relevant date for the purposes of the ten per cent surcharge regime, then the 20 per cent surcharge regime will not apply to it (even though such a transaction undertaken prior to 19 February 2008 generates a reduction of tax by reference to a transaction undertaken after that date).

A protective notification must be delivered in the form prescribed by the Revenue Commissioners (Form PN1) and must contain:

(a) full details of the relevant transaction, including any part of that transaction that has not been undertaken before the protective notification is delivered;

(b) full reference to the provisions of the Acts which the taxpayer considers to be relevant to the treatment of the transaction for tax purposes; and

(c) full details of how, in the opinion of the taxpayer, each such provision,

applies, or does not apply, to the transaction (TCA 1997, s 811A(6)(a)).

It is specifically provided that an 'expression of doubt' in a tax return within TCA 1997, s 959P (see **2.105**) is not to be regarded as, or as equivalent to, a protective notification (TCA 1997, s 811A(6)(b) as amended by FA 2008, s 140). This does not mean that an expression of doubt may still not be in point in relation to at least some aspects of the transaction, depending on the circumstances of the case.

Under the 20 per cent surcharge regime, the Revenue Commissioners are debarred from forming an opinion after two years have expired from the relevant date or date of submission of the notification if earlier; this is without prejudice to their right to make enquires at any time in connection with TCA 1997, s 811 or s 811A (TCA 1997, s 811A(1B), inserted by FA 2008, s 140).

Where the Revenue Commissioners form the opinion that a transaction is a tax avoidance transaction but believe that a protective notification in accordance with the requirements of TCA 1997, s 811(6)(a) has not been delivered by the relevant date, they must give notice of their belief when giving their opinion. TCA 1997, s 811 is to be construed with all necessary modifications as if TCA 1997, s 811(7) included the delivery of a protective notification as one of the grounds of appeal against a Notice of Opinion. TCA 1997, s 811(9) is to be construed as providing that an appeal on these grounds must be determined by ordering either that the protective notification either was, or was not, delivered (ie there is no middle ground) (TCA 1997, s 811(6)(c)).

The disclosure requirements laid down for a protective notification in relation to the details of the transaction itself are onerous taken at face value, given the ambivalence and in some instances downright obscurity of TCA 1997, s 811. On first principles, there may even be ample scope for disagreement between the taxpayer and the Revenue Commissioners as to what constitutes the relevant transaction and when indeed it commenced (pertinent to establishing if the 90-day deadline has been met). The particular requirements regarding the taxpayer's opinion in relation to the tax analysis of the transaction would appear to be rather ambitious. If a taxpayer fails to ventilate particular lines of argument which are unhelpful to his cause, it will usually be difficult to demonstrate any deliberate default on his part. In their Guidelines to Form PN1, the Revenue Commissioners state that they are not likely to challenge submissions 'made in good faith'. There is no onus on the Revenue Commissioners to respond to Form PN1 and until and unless they decide to issue a Notice of Opinion at some indefinite time in the future, the taxpayer will not know if the Revenue Commissioners will regard it as valid.

Where interest falls due, it becomes necessary to set a due date from which it will run. Accordingly, the determination of tax consequences, contained in the notice of opinion issued under TCA 1997, s 811(6) is to include specification of:

(a) a date or dates which are just and reasonable to ensure that tax is deemed to be due and payable not later than if the transaction had not been undertaken; no account is to be taken of any contention that another transaction would not have been undertaken or arranged to achieve the results, or any part of the results, achieved or intended to be achieved by the transaction; and
(b) where there is a recoupment of an earlier refund or repayment of tax made to the taxpayer (or of an additional refund or repayment) the date on which that refund or repayment was made, set off or accounted for.

The formulation in (a) is problematic: see the discussion in *Formation, Issue and Effects of Opinion* above. It may also be noted that TCA 1997, s 1080(2) implies that prior to 1 January 2005, only tax charged by an assessment to tax falls within its ambit. There are no provisions within TCA 1997, s 811A deeming the tax payable under TCA 1997, s 811 to have been charged by an assessment for these purposes. There is no provision made for the fact that in some cases the effect of a notice of opinion may be to substitute a different set of tax liabilities wholly or partly for pre-existing tax liabilities, so that in equity credit should be given for payments of the liabilities which would now be cancelled.

It is made clear that the above dates must be specified without any regard to:

(a) the date on which an opinion of the Revenue Commissioners that the transaction concerned was a tax avoidance transaction was formed;

(b) the date on which any notice of that opinion was given; or

(c) the date on which the opinion (as amended, or relevant) became final and conclusive (TCA 1997, s 811A(4)(a)).

There is provision for an appeal by the taxpayer against the notice of opinion on the grounds that the dates specified are not just and reasonable (TCA 1997, s 811A(4)(b), (c)).

Notwithstanding the delivery of a protective notice, interest will run on payments of tax under TCA 1997, s 811 made after the date on which the opinion of the Revenue Commissioners becomes 'final and conclusive'. The 20 (or 10) per cent surcharge, if relevant, will also become due and payable on the date that the Revenue opinion becomes 'final and conclusive'. Interest will run on late payment of the surcharge as if it were part of the related tax payable under the notice of opinion (TCA 1997, s 811A(3)); all the normal provisions relating to the recovery of tax correspondingly apply (TCA 1997, s 811A(2)(a)). The surcharge is clearly not a fine or penalty for the purposes of TCA 1997, s 1086 ('Publication of Names of Tax Defaulters': see **2.705**). The Revenue Commissioners have acknowledged this in their Guidance Notes to Form PN1.

The date on which the Revenue opinion is treated as becoming final and conclusive is:

(a) where no appeal is made under TCA 1997, s 811(7): 31 days after the date of the Notice of Opinion; or else

(b) the date on which all appeals made under TCA 1997, s 811(7) have been finally determined, provided that none of the appeals has been determined by an order to the effect that the opinion of the Revenue Commissioners is void (in which eventuality TCA 1997, ss 811 and 811A cease to be relevant).

The date on which an appeal settled by agreement, etc with the Revenue Commissioners is treated as having been finally determined is covered in *Formation, Issue and Effects of Opinion* above.

Secrecy rules

TCA 1997, s 811(11) makes a further exception to the rules in the Tax Acts in relation to the obligation of officials of the Revenue Commissioners to keep the tax affairs of each taxpayer secret from other taxpayers and from all other persons (other than where specifically varied by another statutory provision) (see **1.205**).

This exception applies where the Revenue Commissioners form the opinion that a transaction is a tax avoidance transaction and where, pursuant to that opinion, the Revenue Commissioners are required by TCA 1997, s 811(6) to give notices of opinion to two or more taxpayers. In any such case, the Revenue Commissioners (and their relevant officials) are absolved from the normal secrecy rules of TCA 1997, s 857 and any other relevant statute in so far as the following actions are concerned:

(a) the giving of the notices of opinion (or notices of amendment) to two or more persons affected by the same notice; and

(b) the performance of any acts or the discharge of any functions authorised under TCA 1997, s 811 (including any act or function in relation to an appeal made under sub-s (7) of the section.

Qualifying Avoidance Disclosure

Finance Act 2014 amended TCA 1997, s 811A affording taxpayers with an opportunity to settle with the Revenue Commissioners, avoiding the imposition of the 10 per cent or 20 per cent surcharge and also availing of a reduction in interest which would otherwise be levied under this section if the Revenue Commissioners were to form an opinion that the taxpayer had undertaken a tax avoidance transaction within the meaning of TCA 1997, s 811.

In order to avoid the surcharge, the relevant taxpayer must deliver a 'qualifying avoidance disclosure' to the Revenue Commissioners on or before 30 June 2015.

TCA 1997, s 811A(2A)(a) sets out what is meant by a 'qualifying avoidance disclosure' for the purposes of avoiding the surcharge. In summary, it must be a disclosure that the Revenue Commissioners are satisfied is a disclosure of complete information in relation to a transaction that is a tax avoidance transaction or a transaction that would have given rise to a tax liability under TCA 1997, s 811 had the Revenue formed an opinion that the transaction is a tax avoidance transaction.

The disclosure must be made in writing and signed by or on behalf of the taxpayer. It must also be accompanied by:

(i) a declaration, to the best of that person's knowledge, information and belief, made in writing, that all matters contained in the disclosure are correct and complete, and

(ii) a payment of any tax due and payable in respect of any matter contained in the disclosure and the interest payable on the late payment of the tax.

Provided a full and complete qualifying avoidance disclosure has been made by the requisite deadline, ie by 30 June 2015, the 20 per cent surcharge should not apply to the transaction and also any amount of interest payable shall be reduced by 20 per cent.

17.303 New general anti-avoidance provision

TCA 1997, s 811C replaces the original general anti-avoidance provision, TCA 1997, s 811 and will apply to transactions which take place after 23 October 2014.

While the essence of the new general anti-avoidance provision is similar in many respects to TCA 1997, s 811, there are some important procedural or operational differences to take note of which are set out in more detail below.

The original TCA 1997, s 811 definitions of 'the Acts', 'tax advantage', and 'transaction' have been replicated in the new provision, therefore the commentary provided previously in **17.202.1** in respect of these definitions is equally relevant in the context of interpreting and applying such definitions when considering the potential application of this provision. There has been a slight change to the definition of 'tax' to remove the reference to penalty.

The definition of a 'tax avoidance transaction' has been rearranged in the main with some differences which have been highlighted below.

TCA 1997, s 811C(2)(a) states that subject to paragraph (b), for the purposes of this section, a transaction shall be a 'tax avoidance transaction' if having regard to the following matters:

(i) the form of that transaction;

(ii) the substance of that transaction;

(iii) the substance of any other transaction or transactions which that transaction may reasonably be regarded as being directly or indirectly related to or connected with; and

(iv) the final outcome of that transaction and any combination of those other transactions which are so related or connected; and

having regard to any one or more of the following matters –

(I) the results of the transaction;

(II) its use as a means of achieving those results;

(III) and any other means by which the results or any part of the results could have been achieved,

it would be reasonable to consider that –

(A) the transaction gives rise to, or but for this section would give rise to, a tax advantage; and

(B) the transaction was not undertaken or arranged primarily for purposes other than to give rise to a tax advantage.

The key differences in the wording of this definition from the old definition of a 'tax avoidance transaction' is the removal of the requirement of the Revenue having to form an opinion that a transaction is a tax avoidance transaction taking all the factors referred to above into account. This new definition states that a transaction shall be a tax avoidance transaction if taking into account all relevant matters described above, it would be reasonable to consider that the transaction gives rise to a tax advantage and was not undertaken primarily for non-tax advantage motivated purposes.

Previously it was necessary for the Revenue to form an opinion in a specific manner within a set time limit as to whether a transaction was a tax avoidance transaction. The removal of this requirement is intended to reduce the number of possible taxpayer challenges to the application of the general anti-avoidance provisions based on a technicality, ie for example the Revenue may not have abided by the relevant time limit to form their notice of opinion. In *McNamee v Revenue Commissioners* (2012) the taxpayer unsuccessfully challenged a notice of opinion given by the Revenue Commissioners on the basis that it had not been immediately given after the relevant officer had formed the opinion that the transaction in question was tax avoidance transaction (required under TCA 1997, s 811(6)). In *McNamee*, the taxpayer's appeal was dismissed by the Supreme Court in 2016 ([2016] IESC 33).

The insertion of a 'reasonableness test' into the revised definition for 'tax avoidance transaction' should also be borne in mind. The addition of this wording is not considered a welcome addition for the taxpayer on the basis that there will be a higher burden of proof on the taxpayer to evidence that the transaction is not a tax avoidance transaction. The Revenue guidance notes on this 'reasonableness' test published in January 2016 explains 'Whether or not it is reasonable to consider that the transaction gives rise to, or but for Section 811C, would give rise to, a tax advantage and whether or not it is reasonable to consider that the transaction was not undertaken or arranged primarily for purposes other than to give rise to a tax advantage, are objective tests and not subjective ones. Therefore, it is not enough for a taxpayer to say "I reasonably consider that I did not undertake this transaction primarily for the purposes of avoiding tax". That would be applying the test in a subjective manner. An objective test involves asking oneself a hypothetical question of what a reasonable person would reasonably consider, given the facts of the case.' The matter is not beyond doubt in that Smyth J at the High Court before the Supreme Court's decision in *Revenue Commissioners v O'Flynn Construction Ltd* [2011] IESC 47 (which dealt with the application of s 811 being the pre-cursor to s 811C) when he said that, '… it was common case that whether or not a tax avoidance transaction existed, such must be determined objectively. Accordingly, the taxpayers' motivation in entering into the transaction is absolutely irrelevant.' There is no reference to 'motivation', 'intent', 'intentions' or other synonyms thereof in s 811(2) or s 811C(2) as they are in s 806(10), for example, but rather only to, inter alia, the results of entering into the transaction. That said the High Court judge continued that 'On the appeal, the taxpayer has the option and right to give evidence in support of the case that he is making. In the absence of such evidence, it is necessary to infer, solely from objective considerations, for what purpose the transaction has been undertaken or arranged …'. Therefore arguments exist that reference to a taxpayer's motivation may not be ruled out in that if a taxpayer were to give evidence it is likely that its motivations behind the transaction could be aired. It is of note that the TCA 1997, s 811C(2) brings about a reasonableness test whereas the TCA 1997, s 817DA which looks at the specified descriptions for mandatory disclosure, when it comes to loss schemes, refers to the duties of an 'informed observer, having examined it, could reasonably conclude …' the transaction is of a specified description.

The above-mentioned Revenue guidance brings about a reasonable man test which differs from the Revenue opinion that existed in s 811 in that the latter would have a detailed knowledge of the law at issue. Looking now at the 'reasonable to consider' test, the case of *Vieira Ltd v The Revenue Commissioners* [2015] IESC 78 is of note. It dealt, not with a reasonable to consider test but with a reasonable to believe test. This was an Irish Supreme Court decision and dealt with VATA 1972, s 23 which allowed the raising of an assessment where a relevant Revenue official has 'reason to believe' that the total amount of VAT properly payable is greater than the tax actually paid. Clarke J noted that there may be two aspects to the 'reasonable to believe' test and noted at para 6.4 *et seq* as follows:

> 6.4 The point might be explained in this way. If ground (a) and ground (b) are entirely independent bases for making a decision, and if the decision maker has properly and sustainably found ground (a) to exist, then the decision may well be justified irrespective of how the decision maker addressed ground (b). In such a case, the decision maker was not required to consider ground (b) at all, for ground (a) provided a self-contained basis for reaching the decision concerned. Even if some legitimate criticism can be made of the way in which ground (b) was considered, that may not have any effect on the validity of the decision, for it could not have influenced the question of whether ground (a) was found to be present, and ground (a) would, in and of itself, be sufficient.
>
> 6.5 In contrast, one might envisage a case where a decision maker was required to have regard both to factor (a) and factor (b) in reaching an overall decision. The decision maker may have properly considered factor (a) and found that it weighed heavily in favour of making the decision. On the other hand, some significant flaw may be exposed in the way in which the decision maker considered factor (b). In such a case, it may well not be clear as to whether the same decision could or should have been made had factor (b) been properly taken into account, for a consideration of that factor was required to form part of the mix in any event. If that factor was not properly considered, then it might have been that, no matter what view was taken of factor (a), a different decision would have been made. Even if there might be an argument that the same decision would have been reached in any event based on the weight to be attached to factor (a) alone, there would still be a strong argument that the decision as a whole was tainted…For those reasons, there will be cases where, provided that

(iii) allocate or deny any credit, deduction, loss, abatement, relief, allowance, exemption, income or other amount, or any part thereof;

(iv) recharacterise for tax purposes the nature of any payment or other amount.

It is stated that relief will be given if an adjustment made by the Revenue officer results in double taxation for the taxpayer.

Alternative assessment

An alternative assessment means an assessment made under the Tax Acts, other than pursuant to TCA 1997, s 811C(4), the effect of which is to withdraw or deny the tax advantage. The Revenue officer has the power to make or amend an alternative assessment at the same time as making or amending an assessment under section TCA 1997, s 811C(4). A taxpayer may not use the fact that an assessment was made pursuant to TCA 1997, s 811C(4) as grounds for appeal against an alternative assessment or vice versa. Where an assessment and an alternative assessment are made by the Revenue officer, only one of the assessments will become final and conclusive. Which assessment becomes final and conclusive is either decided by agreement with the taxpayer or by way of a determination on appeal.

Time limit

A Revenue officer may at any time, in connection with TCA 1997, ss 811C and 811D, do any of the following:

(a) make an enquiry;

(b) take any action;

(c) make or amend an assessment;

(d) collect or recover any amount of tax.

The exception to this is where a protective notice has been made under TCA 1997, s 811D. Where a valid protective notice has been made, the normal time limits would apply.

Previously, the Revenue Commissioners had to abide by and operate within the confines of certain time limits before an assessment could be made to collect or recover any tax. This is on the basis that an assessment could not be made until such time as the Revenue's opinion became final and conclusive. In order for the Revenue's opinion to become final and conclusive, the notice of opinion would need not to have been appealed within the relevant time limits or if appealed would have needed to have been finally determined upon through the courts. In the latter scenario, it could be years before a Revenue opinion could become final and conclusive by virtue of waiting for the outcome of the relevant appeals and hence a delay in the making of an assessment.

Accordingly, the replacement anti-avoidance provision facilitates the making of an assessment at a much earlier date once a tax avoidance transaction has been identified by the Revenue Commissioners.

Secrecy rules

TCA 1997, s 811C(7) makes a further exception to the rules in the Tax Acts in relation to the obligation of officials of the Revenue Commissioners to keep the tax affairs of each taxpayer secret from other taxpayers and from all other persons (other than where specifically varied by another statutory provision) (see **1.205**).

This exception applies with respect to:

(i) the making of any adjustment, the performance of any other acts or the discharge of any functions authorised by this section to be made, performed or discharged by a Revenue officer; or

(ii) the making of any adjustment, the performance of any other acts or the discharge of any functions (including any act or function in relation to an appeal made which is directly or indirectly related to the adjustment, acts or functions so authorised.

Where the exception applies, the Revenue Commissioners (and their relevant officials) are absolved from the normal secrecy rules of TCA 1997, s 857 and any other relevant statute.

Appeals

Unlike its predecessor, TCA 1997, s 811C is silent on the appeals procedure other than the reference to the interaction of appeals. However, it is understood that the standard appeals procedures (see **2.2**) should apply where a Revenue officer has denied or withdrawn a tax advantage pursuant to TCA 1997, s 811C(4).

Surcharge

FA 2014 introduced another new section TCA 1997, s 811D, to replace the previous surcharge and interest section, TCA 1997, s 811A which applied as a consequence of coming within the general anti-avoidance provision TCA 1997, s 811. The specific rules governing the imposition of the original surcharge and interest provision is discussed in detail in **17.202.1**. The main change to the surcharge provisions is namely the introduction of a higher surcharge equal to 30 per cent (previously 20 per cent) of the tax advantage, where the taxpayer has sought the benefit of the tax advantage either by filing a tax return or by some other way and the transaction is caught by TCA 1997, s 811C.

It should also be noted that the surcharge provided for under TCA 1997, s 811D is not just confined to transactions coming within the general anti-avoidance provision. The surcharge has also been extended to transactions which are subject to specific anti-avoidance provisions as set out in TCA 1997, Sch 3.

As the author noted in *Irish Tax Review, issue* 2 of 2015, the specific anti-avoidance provisions listed in this Schedule can be summarised as outlined below with the type (a) and (b) designations being those of the author:

		Type (a)	Type (b)
TCA 1997, s 381B	Restriction of loss relief — passive trades	X	
TCA 1997, s 381C	Restriction of loss relief — anti-avoidance		X
TCA 1997, s 546A	Restrictions on allowable losses		X
TCA 1997, s 590	Attribution to participators of chargeable gains accruing to non-resident company		X**
TCA 1997, s 806	Charge to income tax on transfer of assets abroad		X
TCA 1997, s 807A	Liability of non-transferors		X
TCA 1997, s 811B	Tax treatment of loans from employee benefit schemes	X*	X*

TCA 1997, s 812	Taxation of income deemed to arise from transfers of right to receive interest from securities	X	
TCA 1997, s 813	Taxation of transactions associated with loans or credit	X	
TCA 1997, s 814	Taxation of income deemed to arise from transactions in certificates of deposit and assignable deposits	X	
TCA 1997, s 815	Taxation of income deemed to arise on certain sales of securities	X	
TCA 1997, s 816	Taxation of shares issued in place of cash dividends	X	
TCA 1997, s 817	Schemes to avoid liability to tax under Schedule F		X
TCA 1997, s 817A	Restriction of relief for payments of interest		X
TCA 1997, s 817B	Treatment of interest in certain circumstances		X
TCA 1997, s 817C	Restriction on deductibility of certain interest	X	

* Note: On a strict reading s 811B would be a type (b) provision due to its 'mechanistic' nature however *e-Brief* 39/13 brings about some subjectivity to its application and is so characterised above as a result.

**TCA 1997, s 590 would have been a type (a) provision until a main purpose test was inserted therein by FA 2015.

The difference between the two types of provision is the prima facie absence of an explicit avoidance purpose in the former such that type (a) are mechanical in their approach with type (b) involving some element of subjectivity. Put another way:

- Type (a) provisions operate to say that if a taxpayer engages in a particular transaction then the tax consequences outlined in that section follow; and
- Type (b) provisions say that if a taxpayer engages in a particular transaction, with tax as a primary purpose or without a bona fide intention or similar wording to that effect, then the consequences outlined in that section follow.

It is submitted that type (b) provisions would be closer in their conceptual approach to that of s 811C given the subjective assertions that have to be made as part of their application in that arguments exist as to the absence of looking to a taxpayer's motive in arriving at the conclusion that the transaction is one of avoidance for the purposes of that section. Revenue's Manual [33.01.01] *Tax Avoidance 'Main purpose' Tests* – created March 2015 makes the following point regarding the 'new' GAAR. It notes as follows:

> Section 811C provides that when determining whether or not a transaction is a tax avoidance transaction one must consider whether or not, having regard to a number of factors, it would be reasonable to consider that the transaction gives rise to a tax advantage and that the transaction was not arranged primarily for purposes other than giving rise to that tax advantage. Furthermore, the factors which one must consider are in themselves objective: for example, one must look to the form and substance of the transaction and to the results of the transaction. The subjective intention of the taxpayer is not something which can be considered or inferred. Therefore, this is also an objective test in that the results are used to

determine motive, rather than trying to actually determine what was in the taxpayer's mind at the time of the transaction.

However, Smyth J at the High Court in *O'Flynn Construction* (which dealt with the application of s 811 being the precursor to s 811C) said that, '... it was common case that whether or not a tax avoidance transaction existed, such must be determined objectively. Accordingly, the taxpayers' motivation in entering into the transaction is absolutely irrelevant.' There is no reference to 'motivation', 'intent', 'intentions' or other synonyms thereof in s 811(2) or s 811C(2) as they are in s 806(10), for example, but rather only to, inter alia, the results of entering into the transaction. That said the High Court judge continued that '... On the appeal, the taxpayer has the option and right to give evidence in support of the case that he is making. In the absence of such evidence, it is necessary to infer, solely from objective considerations, for what purpose the transaction has been undertaken or arranged...'. Therefore arguments exist that reference to a taxpayer's motivation may not be ruled out in that if a taxpayer were to give evidence it is likely that its motivations behind the transaction could be aired.

Taking this view means that some conceptual similarity can be seen between the type (b) provisions mentioned above and the GAAR in s 811C. That said, s 811C now possesses a 'reasonable to consider' test without dictating the person doing the considering thereby confirming a subjective element in its application and indeed s 806 which deals with transfer of assets abroad has a similar reasonableness test therein. The 'cash tax' difference between the GAAR and SAARs from a tax payable perspective is that no protective notification option is available when a SAAR is in point. Although the s 811D surcharge may apply (which wouldn't have applied before where a SAAR was in point) that taxpayer may still be able to rely on the Qualifying Avoidance Disclosure (QAD) mechanism to reduce the surcharge, discussed further below. However, the tax is still payable under a QAD which is not the case under a protective notification at least until an assessment has been raised and one which ultimately the courts agree with if it is appealed.

In short, a failure to apply a type (b) provision could be the result of the taxpayer taking a particular view on the non-tax purpose or bona fides of the transaction whereas a failure to apply a type (a) provision would not. That said the surcharge can now apply to either type (a) or (b) provisions which may be indicative of a policy shift by allowing the s 811D surcharge apply in both instances.

The provisions of TCA 1997, Pt 47, Ch 3A with regard to penalty notifications and court determinations, will apply to the surcharge with any necessary modifications as they apply to penalties.

The 30 per cent surcharge does not apply where the taxpayer has either carelessly or deliberately filed an incorrect return pursuant to TCA 1997, s 1077E(2) or TCA 1997, s 1077E(5) and the relevant penalty applies. The tax geared penalty in such cases is equal to 100 per cent of the under-declared tax.

The 30 per cent surcharge will also not apply where a transaction is found to be a tax avoidance transaction and a protective notification has been made by the taxpayer or on their behalf. It should be noted that this protective notification can only be made in respect of transactions coming within the general anti-avoidance provision TCA 1997, s 817C and does not appear to apply to transactions falling within specific anti-avoidance provisions.

Protective notification

A protective notification must be delivered in the form prescribed by the Revenue Commissioners to such office of the Revenue Commissioners as is prescribed in the form. The relevant form for a protective notification under TCA 1997, s 811A was a Form PN1. For transactions entered into on or after 24 October 2014, the protective notification must be made pursuant to TCA 1997, s 811D.

A protective notification must contain:

(a) full details of the relevant transaction, including any part of that transaction that has not been undertaken before the protective notification is delivered;

(b) full reference to the provisions of the Acts which the taxpayer considers to be relevant to the treatment of the transaction for tax purposes;

(c) full details of how, in the opinion of the taxpayer, each such provision applies, or does not apply, to the transaction;

(d) full details of why, in the opinion of the taxpayer, TCA 1997, s 811C does not apply.

The protective notification must also include copies of all documentation pertaining to the transaction. To be a valid protective notice it must be received by the Revenue Commissioners within 90 days of the transaction commencing and must not relate to a disclosable transaction (within the meaning of TCA 1997, s 811D). Where part of the transaction is undertaken after the aforementioned 90 days, provided copies of documents pertaining to that part are submitted within 30 days of their execution the conditions relating to a protective notification will be deemed to have been complied with.

The benefits of filing a protective notification include the following:

- TCA 1997, s 811C(6) which allows a Revenue officer to make enquiries and assessments outside the normal time periods is dis-applied;
- the 30 per cent surcharge does not apply where the transaction is found to be a tax avoidance transaction;
- where the transaction is found to be a tax avoidance transaction, the tax is due and payable within 30 days of the assessment. This is in-line with the timeframe for payment of tax in cases where a valid expression of doubt is made. Accordingly, the interest clock does not start running until such time that the tax becomes due and payable.

It is specifically provided that an 'expression of doubt' in a tax return within TCA 1997, s 959P (see **2.105**) is not to be regarded as, or as equivalent to, a protective notification (TCA 1997, s 811D(2)(b)).

Furthermore, it is provided that a taxpayer shall be treated as having made a protective notification by virtue of TCA 1997, s 811D(4)(a)(ii) solely to avoid interest and the 30 per cent surcharge without prejudice as to whether the transaction is a tax avoidance transaction. (TCA 1997, s 811D(6))

A taxpayer has a right of appeal to the Appeal Commissioners if a Revenue officer commences carrying out enquiries or makes or amends an assessment outside the normal time periods (as permitted under TCA 1997, s 811C(6)(a) and (c)) and the taxpayer is of the belief that a valid protective notification was made. The relevant rights of appeal are as provided for with any necessary modifications in TCA 1997, ss 959Z and 959AF respectively.

Reduction in surcharge

Where a protective notification has not been made, TCA 1997, s 811D also allows for a reduced surcharge where a taxpayer makes a 'qualifying avoidance disclosure'. The amount of the reduction depends on when the disclosure is made and whether the transaction is a 'disclosable transaction' or not. This reduction in surcharge also applies to transactions which fall within specific anti-avoidance provisions and not just tax avoidance transactions within the meaning of the general anti-avoidance provision TCA 1997, s 811C.

'Qualifying avoidance disclosure' means a disclosure that a Revenue officer is satisfied is a disclosure of complete information in relation to, and full particulars of, all matters occasioning a liability to tax that gives rise to the 30 per cent surcharge, made in writing to the Revenue officer and signed by or on behalf of that person and which is accompanied by:

(a) a declaration, to the best of that person's knowledge, information and belief, made in writing, that all matters contained in the disclosure are correct and complete, and

(b) a payment of any tax due and payable in respect of any matter contained in the disclosure and the interest payable on the late payment of that tax.

A disclosable transaction has the same meaning as under the Mandatory Disclosure regime (see **2.618**) with certain exceptions. For the purposes of TCA 1997, s 811D, a transaction is not a disclosable transaction if:

- the transaction was disclosable by the promoter pursuant to the Mandatory Disclosure regime and not by a person who enters into a transaction which is disclosable under TCA 1997, s 817F, s 817G or s 817H;
- the transaction was not assigned a transaction number or the taxpayer was not provided with a transaction number by the promoter or marketer;
- the taxpayer provides a Revenue officer with specified information within the meaning of the Mandatory Disclosure regime; and
- the taxpayer without unreasonable delay provides a Revenue officer with any other information that the officer may reasonably require for the purposes of deciding if an application should be made to the relevant court to impose a penalty under the Mandatory Disclosure regime.

Where a taxpayer makes a qualifying avoidance disclosure in relation to a transaction which is not a disclosable transaction the amount of the surcharge is as follows (TCA 1997, s 811D(5)(a)):

- Nil – if the disclosure is made prior to a Revenue officer commencing an enquiry into the transaction and within a period of 24 months from the end of the chargeable period in which the transaction commenced;
- 3 per cent – if the disclosure is made prior to a Revenue officer having withdrawn or denied the tax advantage either under TCA 1997, s 811C or one of the specific anti-avoidance provisions referred to in TCA 1997, Sch 33;
- 5 per cent – if the disclosure is made after a Revenue officer has withdrawn or denied the tax advantage either under TCA 1997, s 811C or one of the specific anti-avoidance provisions but before an appeal has been made;
- 10 per cent – if the disclosure is made after a Revenue officer has withdrawn or denied the tax advantage either under TCA 1997, s 811C or one of the specific

anti-avoidance provisions but before the appeal has been heard by the Appeal Commissioners;
- 30 per cent – if the case does not fall into any of the above.

Where a taxpayer makes a qualifying avoidance disclosure in relation to a transaction which is a disclosable transaction the amount of the surcharge is as follows:

- 3 per cent – if the disclosure is made prior to a Revenue officer commencing an enquiry into the transaction and within a period of 24 months from the end of the chargeable period in which the transaction commenced;
- 6 per cent – if the disclosure is made prior to a Revenue officer having withdrawn or denied the tax advantage either under TCA 1997, s 811C or one of the specific anti-avoidance provisions as listed in TCA 1997, Sch 33;
- 10 per cent – if the disclosure is made after a Revenue officer has withdrawn or denied the tax advantage either under TCA 1997, s 811C or one of the specific anti-avoidance provisions but before an appeal has been made;
- 20 per cent – if the disclosure is made after a Revenue officer has withdrawn or denied the tax advantage either under TCA 1997, s 811C or one of the specific anti-avoidance provisions but before the appeal has been heard by the Appeal Commissioners;
- 30 per cent – if the case does not fall into any of the above.

'Main purpose or one of the main purposes' tests

Revenue Operational Manual [33.01.01] was published in March 2015 and outlines what is meant by a main purpose test and it divides its commentary between 'objective' and 'subjective' tests. The manual notes that a main purpose test is a mechanism used by the Tax Acts to prevent taxpayers claiming a relief if they are claiming it for tax avoidance purposes. The manual gives the following examples:

(a) Many of the specific anti-avoidance provisions within the Tax Acts provide that certain reliefs or deductions will not be available if the main purpose, or one of the main purposes, of an arrangement is to secure a tax advantage.

(b) Section 811C applies to withdraw or deny a tax advantage that a person seeks to gain from entering into a tax avoidance transaction. A transaction is only a tax avoidance transaction, for the purposes of s 811C, if it would be reasonable to consider that it was not undertaken primarily for purposes other than to give rise to a tax advantage.

(c) A transaction is only disclosable under the Mandatory Reporting regime (Ch 3 of Pt 33) if the main benefit, or one of the main benefits, of the transaction is obtaining a tax advantage.

Taking point (c) above. The definition of disclosable transaction in TCA 1997, s 817D is one that, inter alia, '... is such that the main benefit, or one of the main benefits, that might be expected to arise from the transaction or the proposal is the obtaining of that tax advantage'.

The case of *Crown Bedding Co Ltd and South Wales Flock Co Ltd v CIR* (1945–1953) 34 TC 107 dealt with a 'main benefit' test in excess profits tax legislation. In essence a loss making company was acquired which could reduce the profits of the existing company. In addition, Lord Greene noted that 'There was evidence in the Case that the directors thought ... that it would be advantageous to the Crown Bedding Company, and to the South Wales Flock Company ... to get rid of the minority shareholding ...' and this was argued as a commercial benefit of the transaction. In this regard, he continued that 'The commercial benefit to which the Special Commissioners referred in that finding is quite clearly the commercial benefit to be expected from the elimination of the minority shareholders, and they find as a fact–and there is no possible ground for differing from them in this Court–that that benefit was so small as to be practically negligible. There is ample evidence on which they could come to that finding and we could not possibly disturb it.' It can be seen that a comparison was made between the tax benefit and other commercial benefits such that the tax benefit was the main benefit in this instance and he added later in the decision that 'The Special Commissioners, in their finding, quite clearly are finding as a fact that, in their opinion, a tax benefit was to be expected and, comparing that benefit with the alleged commercial benefit, they take the view that the tax benefit was the main benefit.' Like the 'main purpose' cases discussed below, a comparison is made between various results of a transaction and the main one ascertained.

The decision of the High court in *Jarvis Robinson Transport Ltd v Commissioners of Inland Revenue* (1961–1964) 41 TC 410 dealt with a legislative provision which read 'having regard to the provisions of the law relating to the profits tax other than this section which were in force at the time when the transaction or transactions was or were effected, the main benefit which might have been expected to accrue from the transaction or transactions in the three years immediately following the completion thereof was the avoidance or reduction of liability to the tax, the avoidance or reduction of liability to the profits tax shall be deemed for the purposes of this section to have been the main purpose or one of the main purposes of the transaction or transactions'. It can be seen that this links the benefit with a tax avoidance purpose where the 'main benefit' is a tax benefit. The court affirmed the test to be met as outlined by the Special Commissioners as follows:

> … it was pointed out by Lord Greene, MR, with reference to those provisions in Crown Bedding Co Ltd … that the test to be applied in considering Section 32 (3) is the objective test: Would a reasonable man in fact expect that the main benefit which would accrue from these transactions would be the avoidance of tax? It seems to me to be manifest that that is what an independent, objective third party would think was the main benefit to be expected from it. It was not a certainty, but it was, to my mind, more than a possibility. It was, indeed, a probability.

The bringing about of a '*reasonable man*' (often referred to as 'the man on the Clapham Omnibus') test brings about a subjective element but nonetheless the conclusion would appear to be to assess all benefits of the transaction such that a comparison can be made. This subjective element is recognised in HMRC's guidance on the UK General Anti-Abuse Rule (GAAR) at para C.510 *et seq* dealing with the meaning of the expression in the GAAR that looks at transactions being abusive where entering into same 'cannot reasonably be regarded as a reasonable course of action in relation to the relevant tax provisions …' as follows:

> C5.10.1 The double reasonableness test ('cannot reasonably be regarded') is the crux of the GAAR test. It does not ask whether entering into or carrying out the arrangements was a reasonable course of action in relation to the relevant tax provisions. Instead it asks whether there can be a reasonably held view that entering into or carrying out the tax arrangements in question was a reasonable course of action.
>
> C5.10.2 Applying this in the context of an appeal to a tribunal or court, the test does not require the judge to give a view on whether the tax arrangements were a reasonable course of action. Instead the judge is required to consider the range of reasonable views that could be held in relation to the arrangements. This means that the arrangement would not be

regarded as abusive, and hence the GAAR will not apply, if the judge considers in all the circumstances that the arrangements could reasonably be regarded as a reasonable course of action, even if the particular judge does not himself or herself regard it as a reasonable course of action.

C5.10.3 In other words, in respect of any particular arrangement there might be a range of views as to whether it was a reasonable course of action: it is possible that there could be a reasonably held view that the tax arrangements were a reasonable course of action, and also a reasonably held view that the arrangement is not a reasonable course of action. In such circumstances the tax arrangements will not be abusive for the purposes of the GAAR.

C5.10.4 It is important to note, however, that some person's view that the tax arrangements are a reasonable course of action (whether the view of a Queens Counsel (QC), an accountant, solicitor or anyone else) will not inevitably lead to the conclusion that the arrangement is not abusive. It will be necessary to test that view to see whether that view itself can be regarded as reasonable, having regard to the purposes of the GAAR legislation and the factors that it requires to be taken into consideration.

C5.10.5 The reason for this is the recognition that some individuals may hold extreme views. These views may, for example, be based on the proposition that all taxation is state-sponsored theft, or that the Government cannot be trusted to spend citizens' money sensibly. Such views, even if held by individuals who would otherwise be regarded as reasonable, cannot be regarded as reasonable for the purposes of the GAAR. This is because the GAAR is based on the premise that taxation is the principal means by which the necessary functions of the state are funded.

C5.10.6 There are less obviously extreme views – which may be commonly held – that nonetheless cannot be regarded as reasonable for the purposes of the GAAR. Perhaps the clearest example is the view that it is the function of HMRC and the Parliamentary drafter to get the legislation right, and that if they fail to do so there is nothing wrong with individuals or companies exploiting defects in the drafting. However, this is wholly inconsistent with one of the basic purposes of the GAAR, namely to deter or counteract the deliberate exploitation of shortcomings in the legislation. Accordingly, even if such views are held by someone who would ordinarily be regarded as reasonable, and indeed may be eminent in a field of work (such as accountancy or the legal professions), those views themselves would not fall to be regarded as reasonable for the purposes of the GAAR.

The recognition of the difficulties of the 'reasonable man' test are clear in this instance. Irish Revenue in its guidance on objective tests note that:

objective tests can be phrased in a number of ways. For example, they can require that something be reasonable, invoking the bonus paterfamilias or 'reasonable man' test. Two examples of objective 'main purpose' tests in the Tax Acts are:

(i) Disclosure of a transaction under the mandatory disclosure regime is, in some cases, linked to what an 'informed observer' would conclude. For example, a loss scheme is disclosable if an informed observer could reasonably conclude that the creation of an income tax loss is a main outcome of the transaction. This test is objective in that what the taxpayer actually intended is irrelevant. What an informed observer would reasonably conclude, from the facts, is the test in law.

(ii) Section 811C provides that when determining whether or not a transaction is a tax avoidance transaction one must consider whether or not, having regard to a number of factors, it would be reasonable to consider that the transaction gives rise to a tax advantage and that the transaction was not arranged primarily for purposes other than giving rise to that tax advantage. Furthermore, the factors which one must consider are in themselves objective: for example, one must look to the form and substance of the transaction and to the results of the transaction. The subjective intention of the taxpayer is not something which can be considered or inferred. Therefore, this is also an objective test in that the results are used to determine motive, rather than trying to actually determine what was in the taxpayer's mind at the time of the transaction.

Revenue in their guidance notes on the General Anti-Avoidance Rule (GAAR) published in January 2016 note on the 'reasonable to consider' test in TCA 1997, s 811C(2)(a) that:

> it is not enough for a taxpayer to say:
>
> 'I reasonably consider that I did not undertake this transaction primarily for the purposes of avoiding tax'. That would be applying the test in a subjective manner. An objective test involves asking oneself a hypothetical question of what a reasonable person would reasonably consider, given the facts of the case.

It can be seen that the reasonable person test is, in Revenue's view, to be applied in arriving a conclusion on the 'reasonable to consider' test in that section. It is of some note that an 'informed observer' is mentioned in connection with loss schemes in the Mandatory Disclosure Rules; that is because TCA 1997, s 817DA(5) requires an 'informed observer' to reasonably conclude that the main outcome of a transaction was the creation of losses. The guidance notes on Mandatory Disclosure note that 'An informed observer is a person who is independent and has knowledge of the various taxation codes, such as an Appeal Commissioner. He need not necessarily be a tax practitioner'. This is of some note in that the legislature has distinguished an informed observer in Mandatory Disclosure but no such requirement exists in TCA 1997, s 811C or indeed 'main purpose' tests within the taxes Acts. Given the intricacies of TCA 1997, s 811C and that its predecessor in TCA 1997, s 811 was referred to by the majority judgment in *O'Flynn Construction* as a 'provision of mind numbing complexity' then there must be grounds for making such reasonable consideration therein to be made by an 'informed observer'.

Revenue Operational Manual [33.01.01] notes that many of the reliefs with TCA 1997 contain subjective tests and notes that they contain 'contain a provision to the effect that relief will not be available if part of what has to be done to claim that relief was 'not for bona fide commercial purposes and was part of a scheme or arrangement the main purpose, or one of the main purposes of which, was the avoidance of tax'. These tests are generally subjective in nature. See for example s 489(7). The latter example relates to the Employment and Investment Incentive Scheme (EIIS) and reads:

> Where by reason of its being wound up, or dissolved without winding up, the company carries on relevant trading activities for a period shorter than 4 months, then subsection (4)(a) shall apply as if it referred to that shorter period but only if it is shown that the winding up or dissolution was for bona fide commercial reasons and not as part of a scheme or arrangement the main purpose or one of the main purposes of which was the avoidance of tax.

In Revenue's view this is subjective in its nature.

The case of *Snell v HMRC* [2006] 78 TC 294 was a UK High Court decision where the main or one of the main *purposes* of a transaction was under scrutiny. The facts of that case were as follows: Mr Snell entered into an agreement in December 1996 to sell his 91 per cent interest in Sovereign Rubber Plc to Inhoco 564 Ltd. The consideration was £7,317k comprising £6,580k in loan stock of three separate classes, £537k in deferred consideration and £200k in respect of costs. Mr Snell left the UK in April 1997, initially for the Isle of Man and then at the end of 1997 for the Cayman Islands.

Mr Snell redeemed £5,630k of the loan stock in July 1997. Mr Snell was assessed to CGT in respect of that part of the sale of his shares made in return for the deferred consideration and the monies in respect of his costs. However, in respect of the loan stock he claimed the benefit of the UK equivalent of s 586 (although, unlike its current Irish equivalent, the UK law allowed share for loan type transactions) being treated as the same asset as the original shares for which the loan stock had been exchanged, until the loan stock was redeemed. The effect of this treatment was to render the redemption of the loan stock CGT-free for the now non-resident Mr Snell. The High Court held that (1) the exchange in question was effected for bona fide commercial purposes but (2) it was part of a 'scheme or arrangements of which the main purpose, or one of the main purposes, is avoidance of liability to capital gains tax … '. Ireland's s 586(3)(b) has a similar two pronged test.

The judge at the High Court broke down s 586(3)(b) (ie was the exchange part of a scheme or arrangements of which the main purpose, or one of the main purposes, was the avoidance of liability to capital gains tax) into two separate questions being:

1. was the exchange part of a scheme or arrangements and if so what were they?
2. did the purposes of such scheme or arrangements include the purpose of avoiding a liability to capital gains tax and if so was it a main purpose?

Revenue argued and the judge concurred that the scheme or arrangements included 'the issue of each of the loan stocks with the purpose of becoming non-resident and redeeming them while non-resident.' The judge continued that 'If that was the scheme or arrangements then it is obvious that a main purpose was, subject to a point of construction on which Mr Snell relies, the avoidance of a liability to capital gains tax for there could have been no other.' The conclusion here is that a comparison is made between the purposes of the transaction.

The point of construction at issue above was explained by a reference to Lord Nolan's decision in the case of *Willoughby* which sought to explain the difference between 'tax avoidance' and 'tax mitigation' but Sir Andrew Morritt in *Snell* would have none of it in that he noted as follows:

> … No such distinction is drawn in s 137 [not unlike the Irish s 586(3)(b)]. Section 137 is concerned with the terms on which a liability to capital gains tax may be deferred. It provides for a right of deferral to be lost if it is to be used for the purpose not of deferral but of avoidance altogether. If that is a main purpose of the scheme or arrangements it matters not whether the scheme etc. was formed for purposes of tax mitigation, avoidance or indeed evasion. The plain fact is, as the Special Commissioners recognised in the concluding sentence in para 6 of their decision, that the main purpose of the scheme is the avoidance of a liability to capital gains tax.

It can be seen from all of the above that deferral in this transaction was replaced by a complete avoidance of the tax deferred by virtue of the paper for paper transaction earlier.

In the end the judge agreed with the Special Commissioners' decision in that 'the plain fact is … that the main purpose of scheme is the avoidance of a liability to' CGT in that instance. He referred to para 6 of the Special Commissioners' decision in this regard which read as follows:

> It is one thing for a person to enter into an exchange knowing that the consequence may be that as a result of a relief (on death, setting the gain against losses or annual exemptions, becoming non-resident or non-domiciled) no tax will ultimately be paid. It is another for a person to enter into the exchange with the main purpose that no tax should be paid as a

result of obtaining a particular relief in a later year. It must be within the evident intention of Parliament that reliefs may result in no tax being paid in the future. But it does not follow that that is within the evident intention of Parliament that one can enter into an exchange with the specific purpose of deferring tax so as to obtain a particular relief in a subsequent year. We see nothing inconsistent with these two propositions. In the year of the exchange the relief is not applicable and the exchange is effected solely with the purpose of deferring the charge to tax until the particular relief is available. There is no reason why Parliament should intend this. Accordingly, we reject [counsel for Mr Snell]'s contention on the meaning of tax avoidance. In principle, if one of the Appellant's main purposes of effecting the arrangements is that capital gains tax should not be paid because the loan stocks will be redeemed while he is non-resident, that is avoidance of liability to capital gains tax within s 137.

It can be seen from the above that the judge and the Special Commissioners concluded that the 'main purpose' of the transaction was one of avoidance without explaining what was meant by such an expression. It appears that the court thought it was 'obvious' that tax avoidance was the main purpose but no detailed analysis of that expression is conducted there.

The expression 'main purpose' was addressed in *Commissioners of Inland Revenue v Sema Group Pension Scheme Trustees* [2002] 74 TC 593. In that instance, the High Court judge (the case went to the Court of Appeal but the description here is useful) described a tax advantage as not being 'a main object' of the transaction if it is the 'mere icing on the cake'. This expression is also used in Revenue's operation manual 33.01.01. In this regard he referred to an *obiter dictum* of Cross J in *Commissioners of Inland Revenue v Kleinwort Benson Ltd* 45 TC 369 as authority in favour of a holding that the obtaining of the tax credit was not a main object. Cross J noted as follows:

> Here there was only a single indivisible transaction and it was an ordinary commercial transaction, a simple purchase of debenture stock … When a trader buys goods for £20 and sells them for £30, he intends to bring in the £20 as a deduction in computing his gross receipts for tax purposes. If one chooses to describe his right to deduct the £20 (very tendentiously be it said) as a 'tax advantage' one may say that he intended from the first to secure this tax advantage. …

A point of note is that Revenue in their manual give the following initial summary:

> there are some general principles, having regard to established case law, which are helpful in applying these tests:
>
> - There is a difference between something being the sole or main purpose of a transaction and being one of the main purposes of that transaction. That a transaction has a genuine commercial motive as the main purpose does not mean it does not have obtaining a tax advantage as one of the main purposes.
> - Where a tax advantage is simply 'the icing on the cake' then it is not a primary purpose or main benefit of the transaction.
> - It is often obvious whether or not a primary purpose or main benefit of a transaction was to give rise to a tax advantage.

The first point has a cautionary tone. The manual later illustrates 'Where a taxpayer has a commercial goal in mind, but something in the way the transaction is carried out has a tax avoidance purpose, then the transaction may also fail a 'main purpose' test. For example:

- the price paid may be set at an artificial level; or
- artificial, complicated and unnecessary steps may be introduced

so as to gain a tax advantage. In these cases, the main purpose of the transaction may be a genuine commercial purpose. However, the main purpose of structuring the transaction in an artificial way is to obtain a tax advantage. Therefore, one of the main purposes of the transaction, as a whole, is to obtain a tax advantage.' It can be seen from the second point above that Revenue reference the *Revenue Commissioners v O'Flynn Construction & Ors* [2011] IESC 47 case, which dealt with a transaction which was ultimately countered by the general anti-avoidance rule in TCA 1997, s 811 as opposed to the operation of a 'main or one of the main purposes' test. That case dealt with a particularly complex transaction and it will be recalled that O'Donnell J at the Supreme Court said that 'more than 40 individual steps were taken over a period of 50 days …'.

17.304 Sch F avoidance schemes

Capital gains are taxable at 33 per cent and still attract the benefit of indexation relief up to 31 December 2002, whereas Schedule F distributions received by persons liable to income tax are potentially chargeable at an effective rate of up to 55 per cent (ie including as appropriate the Universal Social Charge and Self-Employed PRSI). Accordingly, the attractions of extracting cash from companies in a capital form for tax purposes are self-evident. TCA 1997, s 817 is broadly designed to prevent taxpayers avoiding tax by converting dividends into capital receipts.

For the purposes of illustrating the application of the section and the various issues raised by its wording, regular reference will be made to the hypothetical facts set out in **Example 17.304.1** immediately below.

Example 17.304.1

Eleven individuals (none of whom are associates of any other shareholder within the meaning of TCA 1997, s 433(3)) set up a trading company, Gaucho Ltd, to acquire, develop and sell a specific block of non-residential Irish land. Each individual owns 9.1 per cent of the Ordinary Share Capital; there is only one class of shares in existence. Six of the shareholders are directors; none of the other shareholders are involved in the management of the company. The land is sold with the profits being taxed at 12.5 per cent. At this point, the shareholders are deliberating whether to undertake a further project of the same kind in the future, but in any event would not wish to conduct this through a company which has substantial cash holdings potentially available to creditors. They therefore conclude that whatever is decided in future they do not wish to retain cash in Gaucho Ltd. The shareholders decide against Gaucho Ltd paying out a dividend because of the tax costs and instead decide to liquidate the company, which they hope will give rise to a capital gain taxed at 33 per cent. Ignoring timing effects, the overall tax rate on the development profit would then be 41.375 per cent. ie [(12.5%) + 33% (100%–12.5%)]. Six months following the completion of the liquidation of Gaucho Ltd, nine of the same individuals together with three other individuals (again, none of whom are associates of any other shareholder within the meaning of TCA 1997, s 433(3)) do in fact incorporate another company, Goldteeth Ltd and undertake a similar project. Each individual owns 8.3 per cent of the Ordinary Share Capital; there is only one class of shares in existence. Five of the shareholders are directors; none of the other shareholders are involved in the management of the company.

The statutory purpose

TCA 1997, s 817(2), as inserted by FA 2006, s 24, states that the section is to apply:

> for the purposes of counteracting any scheme or arrangement undertaken or arranged by a close company, or to which the close company is a party, being a scheme or arrangement the purpose of which, or one of the purposes of which, is to secure that any shareholder in the

> close company avoids or reduces a charge or assessment to income tax under Sch F by directly or indirectly extracting, or enabling such extracting of, either or both money and money's worth from the close company, for the benefit of the shareholder, without the close company either paying a dividend, or … making a distribution, chargeable to tax under Sch F [(apart from TCA 1997, s 817(4), *viz* the main charging section itself)].

This replaces the previous wording discussed in the 2005 edition of this book.

The first point to address is whether TCA 1997, s 817(2) is to be construed as a substantive provision (so that only transactions of the kind described by it may be caught), subject to any further limitations imposed by other provisions within the section, or simply as an interpretative guide. In *Page v Lowther* [1983] STC 799, the UK provisions which equate to Irish TCA 1997, s 643 (Certain gains on disposal of land to be taxed under schedule D Case IV), contained a provision in the nature of a preamble (for simplicity, hereafter referred to as 'the preamble') which stated that:

> This section is enacted to prevent the avoidance of tax by persons concerned with land or the development of land.

In the High Court, the learned judge held that the charging provisions applied nevertheless to a transaction where it was arguable that no tax avoidance was involved, stating:

> I do not doubt that the provisions … must be interpreted in the light of the purpose … as stated … After all, any legislation must be interpreted in the light of its purpose in so far as that purpose is discernible from the legislation itself, and it would be perverse to refrain from applying that principle where the legislature has taken the trouble expressly to state its purpose at the outset. I do not, however, think that entitles one to treat as ambiguous, with a view to bending their meaning, words … that are in themselves clear. What constitutes tax avoidance is … very much a matter of opinion, and it would, in my judgment, be dangerous in the extreme for a judge to take it upon himself to modify the meaning of words … according to his own conception of what does and does not constitute tax avoidance.

This is itself a questionable decision which probably rendered the preamble almost entirely meaningless. Certainly, judges in subsequent cases have met the challenge of defining the scope of tax avoidance notwithstanding the lack of a statutory definition (see eg the discussion of *IRC v Willoughby* below). TCA 1997, s 817(2) is furthermore extremely detailed and explicit, going far beyond what would be appropriate as a mere interpretative aid. It may be inferred that the Revenue share this view of the status of TCA 1997, s 817(2), given the significant rewording of TCA 1997, s 817(2) by FA 2006, making clear inter alia that there is no requirement that the close company should possess distributable reserves in order for TCA 1997, s 817 to apply. The Revenue Guidance Notes to FA 2006 in fact state that:

> The new wording refocuses the purposive subsection (2) and seeks to pre-empt the type of argument that has been made by taxpayers in defence of certain arrangements.

On the assumption that TCA 1997, s 817(2) is indeed substantive in nature, the first point to note is that there must be a 'scheme or arrangement' in place. Neither the term 'scheme' or 'arrangement' is defined for the purposes of TCA 1997, s 817 (compare the extremely open-ended definition of 'transaction' within general anti-avoidance provision TCA 1997, s 811C). One typical dictionary definition of a scheme is 'A systematic plan or arrangement for achieving a particular object or effect', while a typical dictionary definition of 'arrangement' is 'a structure or combination of things for a purpose'. While neither definition necessarily implies that the transactions which

circumstances occur (ie notwithstanding that these might not give rise to a disposal for capital gains tax purposes under the appropriate relieving provisions):

(a) there is an arrangement between a close company (the 'first company') and its shareholders or some of them;
(b) the arrangement is similar to an arrangement entered into for the purposes of or in connection with a scheme of reconstruction and amalgamation;
(c) another close company (the 'second company') issues shares to those shareholders in respect of or in proportion to their holdings in the first company; and
(d) the shares in the first company are either retained by the shareholders or are cancelled.

In any such case, each shareholder mentioned in (a) is treated for purposes of TCA 1997, s 817 as making a disposal or a part disposal, whichever is the case, of the shares in the first company in exchange for the shares actually held by him as a result of the arrangement.

Preconditions at date of disposal

It is important to note that s 817 only has effect in relation to cash or assets extracted from close companies, as defined above. Section 817(4) imposes the tax charge 'at the time of the disposal by the close company to the shareholder. It must follow that if the company is not a close *company at the time of disposal*, as determined under the CGT rules, TCA 1997, s 817 cannot apply. In the case of a sale of shares this will normally be the date of the contract or the date of a condition precedent being satisfied or the exercise of an option if relevant (TCA 1997, s 542(1)(a), (b)). In the case of a liquidation, there will be a separate deemed disposal on the receipt of each capital distribution (TCA 1997, s 583(2)). On the facts of **Example 17.304.1** given above, because the directors hold the majority of shares in Gaucho Ltd, they are deemed to control it and thus Gaucho Ltd is a close company. However, if two of the shareholders had resigned as directors before the first distribution of assets by the liquidator, Gaucho Ltd would not have been a close company at the time of disposal and thus TCA 1997, s 817 could not apply.

The fact that a non-resident company is excluded from the definition of a 'close company' also leaves a significant lacuna in the coverage of TCA 1997, s 817. Thus, if an individual resident in Ireland received cash from the redemption of shares in a UK resident company as part of a scheme undertaken with the purpose of avoiding Irish tax on UK dividends (potentially taxable under Sch D Case III), TCA 1997, s 817 would not be in point. The question of whether a payment by a non-resident company to a resident shareholder is to be treated as income or as a return of capital has to be decided by reference to the nature of the payment according to the general or company law of the country in which the paying company is incorporated (*Rae v Lazard Investment Co Ltd* 41 TC 1: see **13.107**). Accordingly, the fact that the payment might be treated as a distribution for UK tax purposes has no relevance for Irish tax purposes; this is unaffected by the existence of any double tax treaty between Ireland and the state of residence of the company concerned (*Murphy v Asahi Synthetic Fibres Ltd* III ITR 246: see **14.207**).

TCA 1997, s 817 generally only applies to any disposal of shares if the shareholder's interest in any trade or business (the 'specified business' hereafter) carried on by the close company at the time of the disposal is not significantly reduced (subject to an extension in the case of certain mere holding companies (on which see under significant reduction test below). The fact that the close company in question does, or does not, carry on the specified business after the disposal has no relevance (TCA 1997, s 817(3)). As discussed above, the time of disposal is generally accepted as being determined by the relevant capital gains tax rules. Accordingly, TCA 1997, s 817 does not apply where the close company ceased to carry on any trade or business prior to the disposal. However, with effect for disposals from 26 January 2011, the holding of money by a company will be deemed to be a business carried on by the company, regardless of how that money was contributed to, or acquired by, the company.

Returning to **Example 17.304.1**, the Revenue Commissioners might seek to claim that the operations undertaken by Goldteeth Ltd represent a continuation of the trade of Gaucho Ltd. This seems *prima facie* unlikely on the basis of the facts presented but a fuller analysis would be required to assess the validity of such a proposition. Even if the Revenue Commissioners were to succeed in such a claim, it would seem probable on the facts presented that the trade concerned was at least in abeyance by the time the first distribution was made by the liquidator, so that it was not being carried on by Gaucho Ltd at the time of disposal. On this basis, TCA 1997, s 817 should not be applicable.

Significant reduction test

TCA 1997, s 817(1)(c), as supplemented by TCA 1997, s 817(1)(ca), as inserted by FA 2005, s 39 lays down the test to be applied to determine whether or not there is a significant reduction in the shareholder's interest in the specified business. In fact, this test is a negative one, ie it describes the circumstances (the only circumstances) in which the shareholder's interest is to be regarded as being not significantly reduced. In other words, if the circumstances so described do not apply, then his interest in the specified business is regarded as significantly reduced with the result that, TCA 1997, s 817 cannot be applied.

The test is applied by reference to the close company carrying on the specified business at any given time (not necessarily the company in respect of which the disposal was made) and looks at the shareholder's percentage beneficial ownership of, or beneficial entitlement to:

(a) the ordinary share capital of that close company;

(b) any profits of that close company which are available for distribution to equity holders; and

(c) any assets of that close company which would be available for distribution to equity holders on a winding up.

The shareholder's percentage of each of the said ordinary share capital, profits or assets at any time after the disposal (the later percentage) is compared with his percentage of the corresponding item at any time prior to the disposal (the earlier percentage). Then, if the later percentage of each of the three items is not significantly reduced compared with the earlier percentage respectively for each of the corresponding items, it has to be concluded that the shareholder's interest in the specified business is not significantly reduced.

The requirement that the comparison is to be made 'at any time' either side of the disposal must presumably be subject to some limitation. Taken literally, a person who had originally acquired his shares after the formation of the company could not pass the test since at a time prior to the test he would have owned no shares in the close company. Having said this, it is difficult to state what form such limitation should take; logically, one would expect that any comparison should have been required immediately before and after the execution of the scheme or arrangement, since this is what the section is focusing on. The Revenue state in their Guidance Notes that the absence of any limitation is 'to prevent temporary reductions of interests being arranged to get round the section' and it may be that in practice they will interpret the wording of the section in this narrow light.

In order to satisfy the test, it is therefore necessary that there should be a significant reduction in the shareholder's percentage of each of ordinary share capital, entitlement to distributable profits and entitlement to assets distributable in a winding up. Should there be the necessary significant reduction in the percentage of one or two of the items (say ordinary share capital and distributable profits), but not in the third item (entitlement to assets), then there is not a significant reduction in the interest in the specified business. While there is no statutory definition of what is to be taken as a 'significant reduction' in any of the three items, in practice it is generally accepted that a reduction by a factor of 25 per cent is significant for the purposes of s 817.

A critical limitation is that the significant reduction test cannot come into play if, following the relevant disposal, there is not a close company carrying on the specified business. Thus, if the shareholders acquire the specified business in their own right as a consequence of the scheme or arrangement and it is not subsequently transferred to a close company, the significant reduction test will not be failed. In terms of **Example 17.304.1**, the two original individuals who did not subscribe for shares in Goldteeth Ltd will of course satisfy the significant reduction test. The other nine original shareholders will only have reduced their respective interests in the putative specified business by 9 per cent; by introducing a further three additional equal shareholders, they could have reduced their interests by 25 per cent. However, on the facts as presented, Goldteeth Ltd is not a close company and so long as this remains the case, s 817 cannot be in point (if Goldteeth Ltd were to become close at a later date, then, as discussed above, it may be that the Revenue would not seek to apply s 817 if they were to take the view that this did not form part of a temporary arrangement designed to circumvent the section).

TCA 1997, s 817(1)(ca)(i) provides that following the relevant disposal or scheme, the shareholder's interest in the specified business after the relevant disposal is deemed to include any such interest held by persons connected with him (as determined under TCA 1997, s 10) but only where that would result in the shareholder's interest not being 'significantly reduced'. This drafting leaves something to be desired since the concept of a connected person's 'interest in the [specified business]' is not actually defined.

Example 17.304.2

Walter Fagan owns 100 per cent of the shares in Dubco Ltd, a trading company. On 1 April 2016 he sells his shares for cash to NewDub Ltd, a company owned 50 per cent by himself and 50 per cent by his wife Marie. Looked at in isolation, Walter has significantly reduced his interest in the specified business carried on by Dubco Ltd from 100 per cent to 50 per cent. On a literal view, Marie has no interest in the specified business in the ordinary sense of that term and there is nothing to deem her to have such interest, so that TCA 1997, s 817(1)(ca)(i) does not potentially apply. It would probably be unwise to rely too heavily on this argument, since despite the poor quality of the draftsmanship, the intention of the legislature is clear. This is especially so given the clear sanction for purposive construction provided by Interpretation Act 2005, s 5 (which only provides an exception for penal, as opposed to fiscal, statutes).

TCA 1997, s 817(1)(ca)(ii) provides that following the relevant disposal or scheme a shareholder's interest in the specified business is deemed not to have been 'significantly reduced' where the following two conditions are met:

(a) the business of the close company is wholly or mainly that of holding shares in another company or companies carrying on a trade or business; and
(b) the interest of the shareholder in any such trade or business (whether or not it continues to be carried on by the same company) is not significantly reduced.

Thus, for example, the liquidation of a holding company (which necessarily entails the termination of its specified business) will nevertheless potentially fall within TCA 1997, s 817 if a shareholder in the holding company acquires all or part of the shareholdings of the holding company in the course of the liquidation and as a consequence continues to hold an indirect interest in a business or trade owned by one or more of those companies. The interests of persons connected with the shareholder are not relevant for the purposes of this provision.

TCA 1997, s 817(1)(ca)(iii) provides that following the relevant disposal or scheme a shareholder's interest in the specified business is deemed not to have been 'significantly reduced' where the gain realised by the shareholder from the disposal of the close company concerned is wholly or mainly attributable to payments or other transfers of value to the close company from any other company (or companies) controlled by either (i) the shareholder on his own or (ii) the shareholder together with persons connected with him (but not a company controlled only by persons connected with the shareholder). With effect for disposals made on or after 26 January 2011, the above wording is amended to provide that following the relevant disposal or scheme a shareholder's interest in the specified business is deemed not to have been 'significantly reduced' where the gain realised, or the proceeds in either or both money or money's worth received, by the shareholder on that disposal is or are wholly or mainly attributable to payments or other transfers of value from another company or companies, which is or are controlled (within the meaning of TCA 1997, s 432) by that shareholder or by that shareholder and persons connected with him or her, to the close company.

Finally, TCA 1997, s 817(1)(ca)(IV) provides that following the relevant disposal or scheme a shareholder's interest in the specified business is deemed not to have been 'significantly reduced' where:

(a) there would be no 'significant reduction' if the shareholder were treated as beneficially entitled to any shares held by a trust, and to which he could become entitled at any time on the exercise of a discretion by the trustees;
(b) the acquisition of the shares by the trust was directly or indirectly related to a disposal (including a prior or subsequent disposal) of such shares by the shareholder; and
(c) the shares were acquired by the trustees with the direct or indirect financial assistance of a company or companies controlled by (i) the shareholder or (ii) the shareholder and persons connected with him (but not a company controlled only by persons connected with him).

The definition of 'connected person' is once more in accordance with TCA 1997, s 10 (see **12.304**). This provision does not apply where the shareholder has a life interest only in a trust. The position where the shareholder is excluded as a beneficiary but could subsequently be included as a beneficiary on the exercise of a trust power is open to debate.

It is therefore necessary that there is a significant reduction in the shareholder's percentage of each of ordinary share capital, entitlement to distributable profits and entitlement to assets distributable in a winding up. Should there be the necessary significant reduction in the percentage of one or two of the items (say ordinary share capital and distributable profits), but not in the third item (entitlement to assets), then there is not a significant reduction in the interest in the specified business.

One interesting point: there is no definition of what is to be taken as a 'significant reduction' in any of the three items. It therefore may be necessary to satisfy the inspector that any reduction in each of the percentages is significant in the context of the facts of the particular case. However, in practice, it is generally accepted that a reduction by a factor of 25 per cent is significant for the purposes of s 817.

In determining the percentage of ordinary share capital, distributable profits or assets distributable in a winding up which a shareholder beneficially owns or is beneficially entitled to, the rules and definitions used in TCA 1997, ss 413–415, 418 (which relate to group relief for companies) are to be applied with any necessary modifications (TCA 1997, s 817(1)(c)). However, the rule of TCA 1997, s 411(1)(c) (which restricts the application of the above sections to companies resident in the State in relation to group relief) is not to make a similar restriction in applying the said sections for purposes of TCA 1997, s 817.

It is not proposed to give all the details of TCA 1997, ss 413–415, 418 as they are applied in relation to whether there is a significant reduction in the interest in the specified business, but the following points are noted:

- (a) an equity holder of a company is a person who either holds ordinary shares in the company or is a loan creditor in respect of a loan which is not a commercial loan (TCA 1997, s 413);
- (b) ordinary shares are all shares other than fixed-rate preference shares (TCA 1997, s 413);
- (c) for the definition of 'fixed-rate preference shares' as used in the definition of ordinary shares, see TCA 1997, s 413;
- (d) for the determination of the shareholder's percentage of profits available for distribution to equity holders, see TCA 1997, s 414;
- (e) for the determination of the shareholder's percentage share of assets available for distribution to equity holders on a winding up, see TCA 1997, s 415; and
- (f) a shareholder's percentage of distributable profits or of assets distributable on a winding up is the percentage thereof to which he is entitled either directly or through another company or other companies or partly directly and partly through another company or other companies (TCA 1997, s 418).

Exemption for commercial transactions

TCA 1997, s 817 provides that the section does not apply to a disposal of shares where it is shown to the satisfaction of the inspector that:

- (a) the disposal was made for *bona fide* commercial reasons; and
- (b) the disposal was not a part of a scheme the purpose, or one of the purposes, of which was the avoidance of tax (TCA 1997, s 817(7)); 'tax' means income tax in the case of individuals (TCA 1997, s 3(1)).

If the inspector is not satisfied on either or both counts and assesses the taxpayer to income tax by applying the section, there is a right of appeal to the Appeal Commissioners and to a rehearing by the Circuit Court judge (TCA 1997, s 817(7)).

F(TA)A 2015, s 38, which was subject to Ministerial Order (SI 110/2016 appointed 21 March 2016 as the day on which the Finance (Tax Appeals) Act 2015 came into operation), removes the reference of an appeal to the Circuit Court.

The test in TCA 1997, s 817(7) is a dual one. Under the first element, it must be shown to the satisfaction of the Inspector (or Appeal Commissioner or Circuit Court judge as appropriate) that the disposal was made for *bona fide* commercial reasons. F(TA)A 2015, s 38, which was subject to Ministerial Order (SI 110/2016 appointed 21 March 2016 as the day on which the Finance (Tax Appeals) Act 2015, came into operation), removes the reference to satisfaction of the Inspector or Appeal Commissioners making it a more objective test. The term '*bona fide*' seems to mean no more than 'genuine', ie not a sham (see eg Viscount Dilhorne in *IRC v Plummer* [1979] STC 793). The term 'commercial' is somewhat indeterminate and tends to derive its colour from its context. In a very narrow sense, it may relate simply to transactions carried out in the course of buying and selling. There is a number of UK cases decided in the context of a similar (but not identical) motive test in ICTA 1988, s 703 (the 'transactions in securities' provisions) which suggest that the wider meaning of 'relating to business' is more appropriate (see *IRC v Brebner* 43 TC 705 and *IRC v Goodwin* [1976] STC 28). In fact, because the 'transactions in securities' provisions expressly distinguish between 'commercial' transactions and those carried out in the ordinary course of 'making or arranging investments', it would seem that the term 'commercial' in TCA 1997, s 817(7) should be construed in an even wider sense, as relating to anything undertaken with a view to financial gain. In *IRC v Willoughby 1995* [STC] 143, it was accepted by the Court of Appeal that an investment by an individual in a personal portfolio life insurance policy qualified as a commercial transaction within the then UK equivalent of TCA 1997, s 806(8)(b); the issue was however left open in the House of Lords. The reference to the 'reasons' for the disposal strongly indicates that it is the actual motives of the person(s) who bring about the disposal which are relevant, ie this element is premised on a subjective test (which is consistent with the analysis of the term 'purpose' below). It is considered that it will therefore be necessary to consider the complete background to the disposal including any related scheme or arrangement in order to determine whether there is a genuine commercial motivation behind it.

It does seem clear at least therefore that a disposal which is no more than a means of extracting cash for the benefit of shareholders in tax-efficient form without any ulterior business rationale is most unlikely to satisfy the '*bona fide* commercial' test (see *IRC v Goodwin; Hasloch v IRC*; a similar conclusion appears to have been reached in relation to a scheme to sell the benefit of export-sales relieved reserves in *Revenue Commissioners v O'Flynn Construction Ltd et al*, albeit in the different statutory context of TCA 1997, s 811: see **17.302**).

The second element of the test in TCA 1997, s 817(7) requires that it must be shown to the satisfaction of the Inspector (or Appeal Commissioner or Circuit Court judge as appropriate) that the disposal was not made 'as part of a scheme or arrangement the purpose or one of the purposes of which was the avoidance of tax'. The meaning of the terms 'scheme or arrangement' has already been discussed.

The wording of the second element is very close to that of TCA 1997, s 806(8)(a), which provides an exemption from the 'Transfer of assets abroad' provisions where the 'purpose of avoiding liability to taxation was not the purpose or one of the purposes for which the transfer … was effected', discussed at **17.207**. The conclusion there is that it may be inferred from the decision in *IRC v Willoughby* [1997] STC 995 that the choice of a 'straightforward', but tax-efficient, method to carry out a commercially motivated transaction may well not constitute avoidance within the meaning of provisions such as TCA 1997, s 817(7). However, matters will presumably be otherwise where the method employed is viewed as 'artificial' or 'contrived', ie where the overall shape of the transaction concerned is regarded as being dominated or explicable primarily by tax considerations.

The dividing line between simply availing of a choice implicit in the tax code (suffering tax at 33 per cent on a capital gain as opposed to suffering tax, PRSI and the USC at say 55 per cent on income profits) and engineering an unintended loophole in defiance of the supposed will of the legislature is of course as arbitrary as the distinctions made by the tax code itself. *IRC v Brebner* 43 TC 705 (a case discussed more fully at **17.302**), Lord Upjohn famously observed:

> My Lords, I would only conclude my speech by saying, when the question of carrying out a genuine commercial transaction, as this was, is reviewed, the fact that there are two ways of carrying it out – one by paying the maximum amount of tax, the other by paying no, or much less tax – it would be quite wrong, as a *necessary* consequence, to draw the inference that, in adopting the latter course, one of the main objects is, for the purposes of this section, avoidance of tax. No commercial man in his senses is going to carry out commercial transaction except upon the footing of paying the smallest amount of tax that he can. The question whether in fact one of the main objects was to avoid tax is one for the (Appeal Commissioners) to decide upon a consideration of all the relevant evidence before them and the proper inferences to be drawn from that evidence.

It should be borne in mind that the observations in *Brebner* were delivered in the context of deciding whether a 'main purpose' of a transaction was the avoidance of tax whereas under s 817 (as under TCA 1997, s 806(8)(a)) it will suffice that 'one of the purposes' was the avoidance of tax. However, this distinction is unlikely to be significant in practice. This is because under the relevant UK provisions there can be more than one 'main' purpose, so that the word 'main' must be used in the specialised sense of important or material.

McNichol v The Queen 97 DTC 111, a case concerning the Canadian general anti-avoidance provisions, illustrates a judicial approach to drawing this vexed dividing line which is particularly pertinent in the context of a discussion of TCA 1997, s 817: see the discussion at **17.302**.

This leaves open the question as to whether in a case where there is found to be avoidance, such avoidance was the purpose of the transaction. There is authority in the case law on ICTA 1988, s 703 that it is the actual (ie 'subjective') purpose of the relevant person(s) which counts and not what a reasonable person might infer from the facts the purpose of the transaction concerned was likely to be (ie the 'objective purpose' of the transaction(s): see discussion at **17.207**. A similar approach was applied by the UK Courts in interpreting the exemption clause under the 'transaction in securities' provisions. In *IRC v Brebner* 43 TC 705, Lord Upjohn noted that the issue as to whether a main object was to obtain a tax advantage was a subjective matter of the intention of the parties. This was often the intention of the taxpayers concerned, but it sufficed if it was the intention of those in control of carrying out the relevant transaction(s).

In terms of **Example 17.304.1**, the lack of premeditation which would make it difficult to identify an arrangement would equally cast doubt as to whether there could be a tax avoidance purpose involved; a decision to wind up a company when it has reached the end of its useful shelf-life without any definite intention to resume operations of a similar kind in the future looks purely commercial in nature. The position would be more problematic if the liquidation of Gaucho Ltd and the subsequent incorporation of Goldteeth Ltd had been all part of a predetermined plan and there was clear evidence of the continuity of the underlying specified business. It could then be argued that these transactions were an artificial alternative to simply carrying on the specified business through the same company and distributing surplus profits by way of dividend. Against this, it could be contended that it is the tax code itself which creates an artificial distinction between capital gains and dividends and that the use of a straightforward liquidation mechanism is simply availing of a choice implicitly offered by the legislation.

Treatment as distribution

Once it is established that the section applies to a particular disposal of shares in a close company, TCA 1997, s 817 requires the disposal to be treated, *for all purposes of the Tax Acts*, as if it were a distribution (within the meaning of the Corporation Tax Acts) made, at the time of the disposal, by the close company to its shareholder. In other words, the amount of this deemed distribution (as 'grossed up' by the appropriate tax credit) is taxable as income under Sch F as income of the shareholder (see **Division 9**).

The amount deemed to be a distribution is *the lowest* of:

(a) the proceeds in money and/or money's worth received by the taxpayer in respect of the disposal of shares in the close company concerned;

(b) the excess of those proceeds over any new consideration previously received by the close company for the issue of those shares (TCA 1997, s 817(4)); or

(c) the amount of the capital receipt or, if relevant, the aggregate of the capital receipts received by the taxpayer in respect of the disposal (or received by reason of any act done pursuant to any scheme of which the disposal is a part) (TCA 1997, s 817(5)(b)).

In other words, the maximum amount which is to be treated as a distribution (ie before 'grossing' for the tax credit) cannot exceed the excess of the disposal proceeds over the amount subscribed (ie paid up) as new consideration when the shares were issued. The new consideration may or may not have been paid by the shareholder who makes the disposal. It is irrelevant if the distributable reserves of the company are less than the amount of the distribution.

However, the amount of any purchase price paid by the shareholder in acquiring the shares from any other person is not relevant. 'New consideration' is given the same meaning as the term has in TCA 1997, s 135; it is normally the actual cash subscribed for the shares, but subject to any special rules in that section.

'Capital receipt' is defined as any amount of money and/or money's worth (other than shares issued by the close company concerned) which is received by the taxpayer as consideration for the disposal of shares by reason of any act done under a scheme or arrangement of which the disposal is a part *and* which would not be chargeable to income tax if TCA 1997, s 817 were not to apply (TCA 1997, s 817(5)(a)).

'Money's worth' is defined as the market value at the time of its receipt of any item received in money's worth as distinct from money (TCA 1997, s 817(1)(d)). This may be relevant in quantifying the proceeds of the disposal of shares or the amount of any capital receipt. Note that the time of the receipt of money's worth at which the market value is taken may not necessarily be the same as the date or time of the disposal.

The amount of any deemed distribution resulting from an arrangement similar to a scheme of reconstruction or amalgamation within TCA 1997, s 817(1)(b)(ii) (see above) is the lowest of the three amounts mentioned above. The 'proceeds' in money or money's worth (the paragraph (a) amount) and the 'capital receipts' (the paragraph (c) amount) for this purpose are both taken as the market value (at the date the arrangement is effected) of the shares held by the shareholder concerned as a result of the arrangement. These shares will be the new shares issued by the second company plus any of the shareholder's shares in the first company which are retained (and not cancelled) immediately after the arrangement is completed.

Tax credits

Tax credits have been abolished with effect from 6 April 1999. Earlier editions of this book should be consulted for the position prior to that date.

Surcharge

FA 2014 introduced a surcharge as part of the new general anti avoidance provisions (New GAAR), (TCA 1997, s 811D) which is stated to apply specifically to TCA 1997, s 817.

Under this new provision, where a taxpayer submits a tax return or otherwise seeks to obtain the benefit of a tax advantage and the transaction that gives rise to the tax advantage is caught by TCA 1997, s 817, the taxpayer may be liable to the 30 per cent surcharge under TCA 1997, s 811D. The surcharge only applies to transactions which commenced on or after 24 October 2014. The surcharge and ways to mitigate the surcharge are discussed further in **17.302**.

Payment notices

With effect from the date of passing of FA 2014, 23 December 2014, TCA 1997, ss 817S and 817T were inserted. Normally no tax will be payable or repayable following a determination by the Appeal Commissioners if the decision is subject to a rehearing by the Circuit Court or an appeal on a point of law to the High Court (see **2.202**). However, TCA 1997, s 817S provides that in cases where a taxpayer has entered into a transaction to which TCA 1997, s 817 applies, it should be borne in mind that in the event that an assessment is raised by Revenue withdrawing part or all of the tax advantage gained by entering into the transaction any additional tax may be collected by Revenue when any appeal has been heard and determined by the Appeal Commissioners by the issue of a payment notice. This is the case even if the taxpayer has requested a rehearing by the Circuit Court or lodged an appeal to the High Court. F(TA)A 2015, s 38, which was subject to Ministerial Order (SI 110/2016 appointed 21 March 2016 as the day on which the Finance (Tax Appeals) Act 2015, came into operation), removes the possibility of a rehearing at the Circuit Court. Furthermore, Revenue can issue a payment notice requesting immediate payment of tax due in such an assessment if a similar transaction has been the subject of an Appeal Commissioners' determination which resulted in the issue of a payment notice to another taxpayer (see under Payment notices in **2.618**, Disclosure of certain tax avoidance transactions).

17.305 Anti-avoidance: annuity schemes

TCA 1997, s 242 is intended to counteract the so called 'reverse annuity' scheme. Under this type of scheme, a person would undertake to make annual payments to a finance company in consideration for a capital sum paid by the finance company. The lump sum was not taxable, but the person was entitled to deduct the amount of the annual payment in arriving at his total income for each year for which it continued to be paid. Further, while, the finance company had to include the annual payments received by it as part of its profits, this was offset by the fact that the lump sum paid by it was deductible as an expense of the trade.

TCA 1997, s 242 now denies any deduction in computing the income or total income of the payer of any interest, annuity or other annual payment to which the section applies. It further provides that any interest, annuity or other annual payment to which the section applies must be paid without the deduction of income tax and shall not be allowed as a charge on income for corporation tax purposes.

TCA 1997, s 242 provides that the section applies to any annuity or other annual payment (other than certain excepted payments) which:

(a) is charged with tax under Sch D Case III; and
(b) is made under a liability incurred for consideration in money (or money's worth) where all of the consideration is not required to be brought into account in computing the taxable income of the person making the payment.

The section does not apply to any of the three following types of payments (the excepted payments):

(a) interest;
(b) an annuity granted in the ordinary course of a business of granting annuities; or
(c) a payment made to an individual under a liability incurred in consideration of his surrendering, assigning or releasing an interest in settled property to or in favour of a person having a subsequent interest.

There is a Revenue Precedent to the effect that 'pensions' paid to former partners by a partnership may in principle fall outside the scope of TCA 1997, s 242.

17.306 Anti-avoidance: restrictions of relief for payments for interest

FA 2000 introduced the general anti-avoidance provision contained in TCA 1997, s 817A on restriction of relief for payments of interest made pursuant to a tax avoidance scheme. It provides that a tax deduction for the payment of interest, including interest as a charge for income, shall not be allowable if a scheme has been effected or arrangements have been made where the 'sole or main benefit' is for a reduction of tax liability to arise. The section applies in respect of interest paid from 29 February 2000.

The section is undoubtedly intended to disallow 'up fronting' of interest payments and 'circular schemes' which result in the borrower being in the same economic position as he was prior to the borrowing of the funds and effected for the sole reason of obtaining a tax deduction. This section is discussed in **5.315**.

Surcharge

FA 2014 introduced a surcharge as part of the new general anti avoidance provisions (New GAAR), (TCA 1997, s 811D) which is stated to apply specifically to TCA 1997, s 817A.

Under this new provision, where a taxpayer submits a tax return or otherwise seeks to obtain the benefit of a tax advantage and the transaction that gives rise to the tax advantage is caught by TCA 1997, s 817A, the taxpayer may be liable to the 30 per cent surcharge under TCA 1997, s 811D. The surcharge only applies to transactions which commenced on or after 24 October 2014. The surcharge and ways to mitigate the surcharge are discussed further in **17.302**.

Payment notices

With effect from the date of passing of FA 2014, 23 December 2014, TCA 1997, ss 817S and 817T were inserted. Normally no tax will be payable or repayable following a determination by the Appeal Commissioners if the decision is subject to a rehearing by the Circuit Court or an appeal on a point of law to the High Court (see **2.202**). However, TCA 1997, s 817S provides that in cases where a taxpayer has entered into a transaction to which TCA 1997, s 817A applies, it should be borne in mind that in the event that an assessment is raised by Revenue withdrawing part or all of the tax advantage gained by entering into the transaction any additional tax may be collected by Revenue when any appeal has been heard and determined by the Appeal Commissioners by the issue of a payment notice. This is the case even if the taxpayer has requested a rehearing by the Circuit Court or lodged an appeal to the High Court. F(TA)A 2015, s 38, which was subject to Ministerial Order (SI 110/2016 appointed 21 March 2016 as the day on which the Finance (Tax Appeals) Act 2015, came into operation), removes the possibility of a rehearing at the Circuit Court. Furthermore, Revenue can issue a payment notice requesting immediate payment of tax due in such an assessment if a similar transaction has been the subject of an Appeal Commissioners' determination which resulted in the issue of a payment notice to another taxpayer (see under Payment notices in **2.618**, Disclosure of certain tax avoidance transactions).

17.307 Employee benefit schemes

Introduction

Finance Act 2013 introduced TCA 1997, s 811B to counteract arrangements being used by employers to avoid paying taxable remuneration to employees. The arrangements involved trust structures, funded by employers, passing benefits or making loans to employees at favourable interest rates or at no interest rate at all. The trust structures were typically offshore and the loans ultimately were intended to be written off without a creating a tax charge. The concern for the Revenue Commissioners at the time was that the existing benefit-in-kind provisions could not impose a tax charge on the benefits being received from the trust. The section applies from 1 January 2013 and makes a distinction between benefits made on or after 13 February 2013 and benefits made before that date. The section does not apply to Profit Sharing Schemes, Employee Share Ownership Trusts and Occupational Pension Schemes approved by the Revenue Commissioners. Although the section does not contain a motive test, it is generally understood that the Revenue Commissioners will likely only use the provisions to target tax avoidance transactions.

The charge to tax for benefits made on or after 13 February 2013

A charge to income tax under Sch D Case IV arises where an individual, being an employee, former employee, prospective employee or any person connected to that individual, receives directly or indirectly from a benefit scheme a payment, a benefit or an asset and that scheme was directly or indirectly funded by that employee's employer, former employer or future employer. The charge under Case IV of Sch D will be levied either on the amount of the payment, the greater of the cost of providing the benefit or the value of that benefit at the date of provision and the value of the asset. The charge only applies to the extent the amount is not otherwise chargeable to income tax and in the case of a prospective employee the amount is not liable to income tax in another country with which Ireland has a double tax agreement. The charge is not confined to Irish tax resident individuals.

An 'employee' includes a director and any person who is an employee as defined in TCA 1997, s 983, ie any person in receipt of emoluments (meaning anything assessable to income tax under Sch E). An 'employer' includes any person connected with an employer and an employer is defined in TCA 1997, s 983 as meaning any person paying emoluments. The question of whether a person is connected with another person is to be determined in accordance with TCA 1997, s 10. A 'payment' is stated as including a loan and an 'asset' includes the loan of an asset as well as the provision of the use of an asset.

For the purposes of the provision, a 'benefit scheme' is defined subject to the exceptions set out in TCA 1997, s 811B(2)(c), as meaning a trust, scheme or other arrangement and includes any settlement, disposition, covenant, agreement, transfer of money or transfer of other property or of any right to money or of any right to other property.

Offset or repayment of tax in respect of benefits made on or after 13 February 2013

Given that the charge to income tax under the section will typically exceed the charge to income tax under the normal benefit-in-kind provisions, the section incorporates a balancing provision. The section provides that an individual is entitled to relief by way of an offset or repayment of tax where he repays all or part of a loan, or ceases for a period of at least 12 months to have use of the asset or ceases for a period of at least 12 months to have use of the benefit in respect of which the charge under the section arose. The amount of the repayment in the case of a loan repaid in full (or where the use of an asset/benefit has ceased) is the difference between the tax charged under this section and the tax that would have been charged had the benefit-in-kind provisions applied up to the date the loan was repaid (or the use of the asset/benefit ceased). Where the loan has not been repaid in full the amount of the offset or repayment is the difference between the tax charged under this section attributable to the amount of the loan repaid and the tax that would have been charged had TCA 1997, s 122 applied in respect of the amount of the loan repaid. There is anti-avoidance to ensure that this relief does not apply in situations where the employer or former employer of the individual directly or indirectly funds the loan repayment.

An individual has four years from the end of the year of assessment in which the loan (or part of the loan) is repaid or the use of the benefit/asset ceases to make a claim for repayment. For this relief to apply the individual must have paid the full amount of tax due under the section.

The charge to tax for benefits made prior to 13 February 2013

Loans or the provision of an asset (including a loan of an asset) made prior to 13 February 2013 are also caught by the section. A charge to income tax under Case IV of Sch D will arise for 2013 and each subsequent year where the benefit remains outstanding at any time during the year of assessment. The amount chargeable in respect of a benefit being a loan is the interest that would be payable on the loan had the notional benefit-in-kind rate of interest under TCA 1997, s 122 applied less any interest actually paid by the individual. There is anti-avoidance measures included to ensure that a deduction is only allowed where the interest is actually borne by the individual and not just added to the outstanding balance of the loan. The amount chargeable in respect of a benefit being a loan of an asset or use of an asset is the amount that would have been chargeable as an expense, emolument or perquisite had the normal benefit-in-kind provisions applied. Given the amount chargeable to tax is the same as the amount determined under the normal benefit-in-kind provisions there is no mechanism for claiming a repayment of tax where the arrangements cease.

Surcharge

FA 2014 introduced a surcharge as part of the new general anti-avoidance provisions (New GAAR), (TCA 1997, s 811D) which is stated to apply specifically to TCA 1997, s 811B.

Under this new provision, where a taxpayer submits a tax return or otherwise seeks to obtain the benefit of a tax advantage and the transaction that gives rise to the tax advantage is caught by TCA 1997, s 811B, the taxpayer may be liable to the 30 per cent surcharge under TCA 1997, s 811D. The surcharge only applies to transactions which commenced on or after 24 October 2014. The surcharge and ways to mitigate the surcharge are discussed further in **17.302**.

Payment notices

With effect from the date of passing of FA 2014, 23 December 2014, TCA 1997, ss 817S and 817T were inserted. Normally no tax will be payable or repayable following a determination by the Appeal Commissioners if the decision is subject to a rehearing by the Circuit Court or an appeal on a point of law to the High Court (see **2.202**). However, TCA 1997, s 817S provides that in cases where a taxpayer has entered into a transaction to which TCA 1997, s 811B applies, it should be borne in mind that in the event that an assessment is raised by Revenue withdrawing part or all of the tax advantage gained by entering into the transaction any additional tax may be collected by Revenue when any appeal has been heard and determined by the Appeal Commissioners by the issue of a payment notice. This is the case even if the taxpayer has requested a rehearing by the Circuit Court or lodged an appeal to the High Court. F(TA)A 2015, s 38, which was subject to Ministerial Order (SI 110/2016 appointed 21 March 2016 as the day on which the Finance (Tax Appeals) Act 2015, came into operation), removes the possibility of a rehearing at the Circuit Court. Furthermore, Revenue can issue a payment notice requesting immediate payment of tax due in such an assessment if a similar transaction has been the subject of an Appeal Commissioners' determination which resulted in the issue of a payment notice to another taxpayer (see under Payment notices in **2.618**, Disclosure of certain tax avoidance transactions).

17.4 Offshore Funds

17.401 Background

TCA 1997, Pt 27, Ch 11 ('the offshore funds legislation') is designed to counteract tax avoidance by Irish residents who invest in 'offshore funds'. An offshore fund may take the form of a non-resident company, a unit trust scheme with non-resident trustees or an arrangement made under foreign law creating rights of co-ownership (TCA 1997, s 743(2)). Income tax was avoided by allowing an investment in such a fund to 'roll up' ie accumulate over several years as the profits were reinvested. The owner of the units would realise his investment when the units had increased sufficiently in value. He would also claim:

(a) that the profit element of the sale price was a capital (as opposed to an income) gain;
(b) that he was entitled to the appropriate annual allowance against his total capital gains for any tax year, including capital gains derived from the sale of units in offshore funds; and
(c) that he was entitled to the benefits of capital gains tax indexation relief, ie the gain (if any) on which he would be taxed would be the gain after removing the part of the gain directly attributable to the increase in the Irish inflation rate during the period in which the asset disposed of increased in value.

Investors in such funds who would not normally have used their annual capital gains tax allowance could transform income which would have been taxable over several years into a single tax free capital gain at the end of the investment period, assuming their final gain was below the annual capital gains tax allowance. Investors could convert annual gains taxable at the higher rate of income tax into a single capital gain taxable at a lower rate.

TCA 1997, Pt 27, Ch 2 provides that, gains accruing as a result of disposing of a 'material interest' in a 'non qualifying offshore fund' will be taxed as income rather than capital gains and indexation relief will not apply to the gains. A non-qualifying offshore fund is essentially a fund which accumulates (or rolls up) its profits, ie it does not distribute the annual profits to its investors – the investor realises his gain at the *end* of the investment period. With effect from 1 January 2001, a special regime applies to offshore funds based in an 'offshore state' (as defined); see **17.407**.

17.402 Material interest in an offshore fund

Material interest

A person's interest in an offshore fund is a 'material interest', if when it was acquired, it could reasonably be expected that the value of the interest could be realised within seven years beginning at the time of the acquisition (TCA 1997, s 743(2)). In this division, a material interest in an offshore fund will generally be referred to as units in that fund, unless the context otherwise requires.

An owner of units in an offshore fund will not be able to claim that he cannot sell his units, for example, as a result of the terms of the purchase contract. The owner is deemed to be capable of realising the value of his material interest if he can realise an amount (in money *or* assets of equivalent value) which is roughly equal to the proportion of the underlying assets of the offshore fund which his interest represents (TCA 1997, s 743(3)), ie the interest in the fund must be assets-based. The fact that a person's interest in an offshore fund may at any time be worth more on the open market than the value of the underlying assets, does not mean that he is to be regarded as being able to realise such an amount (TCA 1997, s 743(4)(b)). The purpose of this last provision seems to be to ensure that *inter alia* an investment in a company with substantial goodwill (as opposed to a company which is a mere investment vehicle) does not fall within the definition of a 'material interest' (this presupposes that 'goodwill' is not to be regarded as an asset of the company, although this point is not made clear by the legislation).

The following are not regarded as material interests in an offshore fund:

(a) a normal commercial loan from a bank (TCA 1997, s 743(5)(a));

(b) a right under an insurance policy (TCA 1997, s 743(5)(b));

(c) a shareholding held in a non Irish resident company for the purpose of developing the trade of that overseas company. The shares must entitle the holder to least 10 per cent of the voting rights (or 10 per cent of the net break-up value of the company) and no more than 10 persons may hold shares in the overseas company. In this context, 'break-up value' means the net value of the company in the event of a winding up after all debts and liabilities have been paid. In addition, the company holding the shares must have been expecting at the time of the acquisition that within the next seven years it could only realise the value of the shares by requiring the other participators to buy its shares (ie a buyout agreement was contemplated at that time). Alternatively, there may have been an agreement between the shareholder and the other participators that the overseas company would be wound up within seven years (TCA 1997, s 743(6)); and

(d) an interest in an overseas company where the holder has the right to have the company wound up, and upon such a winding up, is entitled to more than 50 per cent of the net assets after debts have been paid (TCA 1997, s 743(8)).

TCA 1997, s 743(9) provides that the CGT market value rules of TCA 1997, s 548 generally apply in computing the value of a material interest in an offshore fund: the interest is valued at the price which the units might reasonably be expected to realise on sale in the open market. However, where there are published buying and selling prices for the units, the market value is the *lower* price as published on the relevant date.

Material time

This is defined, in relation to a material interest, as a time after 5 April 1990, or if it is later, the earliest date on which 'relevant consideration' is given for the interest, ie consideration which would be taken into account under the normal capital gains tax rules in computing the amount of the gain or loss (TCA 1997, s 741(7)).

17.403 Non-qualifying offshore funds

Introduction

All offshore funds are automatically deemed to be 'non-qualifying' offshore funds, unless the Revenue Commissioners certify that the fund is a 'distributing fund', ie a fund which distributes to its unit holders (ie holders of material and other interests) at least 85 per cent of the income of the fund for the period and that total distribution is not less than 85 per cent of the 'Irish equivalent profits' for the period (ie the amount on which corporation tax would be chargeable). In addition the distribution must be made during, or within six months of the end of the 'account period', and it must be made in such a form that, if received by a resident person other than in the course of a trade or profession, it would be taxed under Sch D Case III.

In particular, the following are non-qualifying offshore funds:

(a) funds where more than 5 per cent of the value of the assets consist of interests in other offshore funds (TCA 1997, s 744(3)(a));

(b) funds where more than 10 per cent of the value of the assets consists of interests in a single company (TCA 1997, s 744(3)(b)). Such an interest must be valued when the fund acquired (or most recently added to) the interest. An interest acquired as a result of a share exchange transaction involving company reorganisation or merger activity will be disregarded so as not to affect qualification provided no net consideration has been given (TCA 1997, s 744(4)). An interest in a *bona fide* banking company will be similarly disregarded for the purposes of this test (TCA 1997, s 744(5));

(c) funds whose assets include a shareholding of 10 per cent or more in any company (TCA 1997, s 744(3)(c)); and

(d) funds which have several classes of units some of which do not receive proper distribution benefits as defined by TCA 1997, s 744(7) (TCA 1997, s 744(3)(d)). These do not include units held by managers of the assets of the funds which carry (i) no right to share in the assets of the fund or (ii) no right to receive anything other than the return of the price paid for the units (TCA 1997, s 744(6)). The fact a fund may have several classes of unit does not necessarily mean that those units shall receive proper distribution benefits unless if each class of unit were in a separate offshore fund each such fund could be certified as distributing more than 85 per cent of its profits (TCA 1997, Sch 19, Pt 1).

The purpose of the foregoing provisions is to ensure that the charge to tax is not avoided by accruing an offshore income gain at one further remove from the investor. For example, if fund A reinvests its investors' money in fund B, provided fund B 'rolled up' (ie accumulated) the income accruing, fund A would have no income to distribute and would pass the distribution test. Gains arising to investors disposing of their interests in fund A (see **17.404**) would not be chargeable as income.

Disposal of material interest in non-qualifying offshore funds

The offshore funds legislation applies to the disposal of units in a non-qualifying offshore fund, ie a fund which has not passed the 'distribution test' which is set out in TCA 1997, Sch 19 Pt 1. The legislation also applies to the disposal of assets in an *Irish resident* company (or unit trust scheme) if before 1 January 1991 the company (or unit trust scheme) was non-*resident* and the asset constituted a material interest in the fund. TCA 1997, s 741(2) applies the capital gains tax legislation in ascertaining whether an asset has been disposed of for the purposes of the offshore funds legislation. Where necessary, the capital gains tax legislation has been modified to prevent it being used to avoid the charge to income tax under the offshore funds legislation.

TCA 1997, s 573 provides that death is not to be regarded as giving rise to a disposal for the purposes of capital gains tax. This provision is suspended for the purposes of the offshore funds legislation, ie death is an occasion of charge. Where a person dies, and the assets 'of which he was competent to dispose' include units in an offshore fund, then the units are deemed to have been disposed of by the deceased for a market value consideration (TCA 1997, s 741(3)).

TCA 1997, ss 586 and 587 allow that 'paper for paper' transactions in company reconstructions/takeovers and amalgamations may not be regarded as disposals for capital gains tax purposes. This relief does not apply for the purposes of the offshore funds legislation where the acquiring company (a distributing fund) issues shares or debentures of another company (a non distributing fund). The exchange of shares, debentures or other interests is regarded as being a disposal of units in the offshore fund at a market value price, at the time of the exchange (TCA 1997, s 741(5)).

Offshore income gains: charge to income tax

(a) Irish residents

TCA 1997, s 745(1) provides that an offshore income gain will be charged to tax under Sch D Case IV as income arising to the person making the disposal. The income is deemed to arise at the time of the disposal. TCA 1997, s 745(2)–(4) go on to apply the capital gains tax residence rules to such gains. Resident individuals are chargeable in respect of all offshore income gains, while non-residents are not generally liable to tax unless the underlying assets consist of land or mineral or exploration rights located within the State. Offshore income gains arising to resident individuals who are not domiciled in the State are treated in the same way as gains arising to such individuals from assets located outside the State, ie a gain arises only to the extent that the profits are remitted into the State.

Charities are exempt from income tax in respect of offshore income gains provided the gain is applied for charitable purposes – TCA 1997, s 745(5). A charity is as defined for income tax purposes, ie any body or trust established 'for charitable purposes only', (see **Division 18**). Where a property (representing directly or indirectly an offshore income gain) held on charitable trusts ceases to be held on charitable trusts, the trustees will be treated as if they disposed of and immediately reacquired the property at market value and any gain accruing will be treated as not accruing to a charity. This provision is designed to prevent situations arising where a (qualifying) charity which has availed of the exemption from income tax becomes involved in non charitable activities and begins to apply the accumulated income (or assets) for business or other purposes. If such a situation occurs, the tax advantage which the charity had gained as a result of its charitable status is automatically withdrawn (TCA 1997, s 745(5)(b)).

The position regarding trusts is designed to reflect that applicable under the capital gains tax code. TCA 1997, s 745(6) deals specifically with the case where the interest in the offshore fund is settled property (as defined for the purposes of the Capital Gains Tax Acts). If for the purposes of those Acts the trustees (or a majority thereof) are regarded as resident and ordinarily resident outside the State *and* the general administration of the trust is regarded as being carried on outside the State, then there will be no charge to income tax on any offshore income gains arising on the disposal of

income gain shall be reduced to the amount of the unindexed gain (TCA 1997, Sch 20, para 8). If a disposal involving an equalisation element results in 'no gain, no loss' (other than due to indexation relief) to the person making the disposal, the 'no gain, no loss' rules shall not apply in determining the unindexed gain (TCA 1997, Sch 20, para 8(3)).

17.404 Qualifying offshore funds

Introduction

An offshore fund is regarded as a 'qualifying' offshore fund if:

(a) it is certified by the Revenue Commissioners as a 'distributing' fund, ie it has passed 'the distribution test' set out in TCA 1997, Sch 19, Pt 1. Only offshore funds which pursue a 'full distribution policy' will be capable of being certified as distributing funds; and

(b) it does not breach *any* of the four special conditions set out in TCA 1997, s 744(3) (see above).

The distribution test is applied in respect of an account period, which is not defined in the offshore funds legislation but is, broadly speaking, a period to which the offshore fund makes up its accounts, ie an accounting period, however, the account period could be more closely defined as the income accrual period (or the period when the income to be distributed was earned). It is therefore possible to have one or more account periods ending within a single accounting period. TCA 1997, s 744(8)–(10) set out when an account period is deemed to begin, and when an account period is deemed to end.

An account period of an offshore fund begins:

(a) on 6 April 1990, or if later when the fund begins to carry on its activities; or

(b) once the activity has commenced, when the previous account period ends.

An account period ends on the earliest of:

(a) 12 months after the beginning of the account period; or

(b) on the offshore fund's accounting date; or

(c) the date of cessation of the fund's activities.

An account period of a company resident outside the State ends when the company becomes resident in the State. An account period of a unit trust scheme (where the trustees are not resident in the State) ends when the trustees become resident in the State (TCA 1997, s 744(10)).

The distribution test

TCA 1997, Sch 19, para 1(1) states that an offshore fund is said to be pursuing a 'full distribution policy' if a distribution is made for an account period and that distribution:

(a) represents at least 85 per cent of the income of the fund for the period;

(b) is not less than 85 per cent of the fund's Irish equivalent profits (see below) for the period in question;

(c) is made in such a form that if received by an Irish resident (otherwise than as trading income) it would be taxable under Sch D Case III; and

(d) is made during or within six months of the end of the account period.

An offshore fund which has no income (and no Irish equivalent profits) for the account period will be regarded as pursuing a full distribution policy, ie such a fund will be a qualifying fund provided it meets the other conditions (TCA 1997, Sch 19, para 1(2)). A fund which does not make up accounts for an account period will be regarded as *not* pursuing a full distribution policy, ie such a fund will not be a qualifying fund (TCA 1997, Sch 19, para 1(3)). There is a Revenue precedent to the effect that where the level of income of an offshore fund does not exceed one per cent of the average value of the fund assets held in the relevant accounting period, the fund would still be regarded as qualifying for certification (see **17.405**) even though no distributions were made in the period.

TCA 1997, Sch 19, para 1(4) sets out several rules relating to accounting periods which contain two or more account periods.

(a) the income in the accounts must be apportioned on a time basis between those account periods; and

(b) a distribution made for a period which includes two or more account periods must be apportioned between the two account periods on a time basis.

Where a distribution is made out of specified income, but not for a specified period, it must be attributed to the account period of the fund in which it in fact arose and the distribution will accordingly be treated as made for that period. In the event that a distribution is made neither out of specified income *nor* for a specified period it must be treated as made for the last account period of the fund before the distribution was made.

Should a situation arise where the distribution for an account period exceeds the income for that period (and the distribution is made for a period which includes two or more account periods and is accordingly apportioned between the two account periods on a time basis) the excess must be reapportioned to another account period which also ends within the *accounting* period for which the distribution was made. In such a situation, the excess is to be treated as an additional distribution for preceding account periods (in which the distributions would normally be less than the income for the period). The excess must continue to be applied to previous account periods (commencing with the immediately preceding account period) until the excess is used up (TCA 1997, Sch 19, para 1(5)).

TCA 1997, Sch 19 goes on to provide that offshore funds which are restricted by the law of a foreign territory from making a distribution for an account period, by reason of an excess of losses over profits, will be allowed a deduction (in determining the fund's income for the 'undistributable' period) for any amount which cannot be distributed as a result of such restriction.

Equalisation arrangements

As discussed in **17.403**, certain offshore funds do not pay 'income' to the unit holders and instead operate 'equalisation arrangements'. Equalisation arrangements have the result that where an initial investor in the fund's units subsequently becomes entitled to distribution that includes a *payment of capital* which is paid into a separate (equalisation) account. The size of the distribution payment is determined by reference to the income which had accrued to the fund up to the date the new purchaser bought the units.

Thus, if a fund is operating equalisation arrangements, it means that when the fund redeems units in the fund, the proceeds of redemption will include the accrued part of the next distribution to the holder of the units. If a person then wants to buy those units from the fund, he will have to pay for the right to receive the pre-acquisition part of the distribution from the fund. When the next distribution arrives, the new owner's distribution will be equal to that given to all other unit holders ('equalisation') however that distribution, (because it will include the accrued pre-acquisition part of the distribution) effectively includes a part refund of his payment to acquire the interest. Such refund is not treated as income of the new owner, ie to the extent that the distribution is a repayment of part of the purchase price it is ignored for the charge to income tax.

Where a fund which operates equalisation arrangements also pursues an 85 per cent distribution policy only the 'equalisation' part of the redemption proceeds (not the entire proceeds) will be treated as income, ie the income accrued to the date of redemption (TCA 1997, Sch 19, para 2(1)). In deciding whether the fund satisfies the 85 per cent test, the distribution income included in the disposal proceeds of such interests is taken into account.

This applies to a disposal of a material interest in the offshore fund concerned

(a) whether or not the units disposed of were in an offshore fund which operates equalisation arrangements;

(b) provided:

  (i) before the disposal, the income has been arising to resident companies or individuals chargeable to tax under Sch D Case III in respect of their interests (or if the income is derived from assets within the State, it would be taxable if the assets had been outside the State), and

  (ii) the disposal does not take place during a period 'relevant to the arrangements' when the person initially buys the units; and

(c) which is a disposal to the fund itself or to the fund's managers in their capacity as such (TCA 1997, Sch 19, para 2(2)).

The 'accrued income' is defined by TCA 1997, Sch 19, para 2(3) as the amount which would be credited to the equalisation account of the offshore fund where on the disposal date another person first bought the same material interest.

TCA 1997, Sch 19, para 2(4) goes on to provide that where units in an offshore fund are disposed of in the foregoing circumstances, the amount of accrued income to the date of disposal must have deducted from it the amount credited to the fund's equalisation account on the last such acquisition, no matter how many initial purchases of the material interest have taken place within that account period.

Distributions made by an offshore fund in the foregoing circumstances will be regarded as:

(a) chargeable to tax under Sch D Case III (if received by an Irish resident person otherwise than as trading income);

(b) paid out of the fund's income for the account period in which the disposal occurs; and

(c) paid immediately before the disposal to the unit holder at that time (TCA 1997, Sch 19, para 2(5)).

In the case of funds that operate equalisation arrangements, TCA 1997, Sch 19, para 2(6) provides that distributions made to the fund's managers in their capacity as such are ignored for the purposes of the 85 per cent of income and 85 per cent of Irish equivalent profits tests.

Sch D Case III income

TCA 1997, Sch 19, para 3 provides that in the event that the unit holders in an offshore fund (other than a non-resident company, ie a unit trust scheme or an arrangement under the law of a foreign territory) receive income in such a form that:

(a) they are chargeable under Sch D Case III in respect of their interests (or if the income is derived from assets within the State would be so chargeable if the assets had been outside the State); and
(b) they would be chargeable under Sch D Case III if they were resident in the State (not being resident companies or individuals),

then, if the income (as described above) is not distributed within the account period (or within six months after the end of the account period), the income will be deemed to be distributed within the prescribed time limit and also deemed to be paid to the unit holders to which the income refers.

Commodity income

An offshore fund which derives some of its profits from dealing in commodities (tangible assets dealt with on a commodity exchange other than currency, stocks, shares, debts or financial assets) is permitted by TCA 1997, Sch 19, para 4 to omit one half of its commodity dealing profits in calculating its income for the purposes of the 85 per cent of income test and also for the purposes of the 85 per cent of Irish equivalent profits test. 'Dealing' in this context includes dealing by way of futures contracts and traded options. Similarly, an offshore fund with some commodity dealing income is permitted, in carrying out either of the aforementioned 85 per cent distribution tests, to apportion the fund's expenditure between the profits from dealing in commodities and other income. TCA 1997, Sch 19, para 4(3)(b) goes on to state that in deciding what expenditure is to be regarded as deductible in computing the fund's Irish equivalent profits, the non commodity dealing part of the business is regarded as being carried on by a separate company.

Funds which operate equalisation arrangements are given a corresponding '50 per cent' reduction relief where the profits which become transmitted to the unit holder via accrued 'income' (which is credited to the offshore fund's equalisation account) are treated as being reduced by half.

Irish equivalent profits

On the temporary assumptions that:

(a) an offshore fund is an Irish resident company for the account period;
(b) the account period corresponds to the company's accounting period; and
(c) dividends (or distributions) receivable by the company as franked investment income which would normally be left out of the company's corporation tax computation are in fact *included* in the computation as if they were distributions of a non-resident company (TCA 1997, Sch 19, para 5(3)).

then the 'Irish equivalent profits' of the offshore fund are defined by TCA 1997, Sch 19, para 5(1), (2) as the total profits of the fund (not including chargeable gains) on which corporation tax *would* be chargeable. In particular, 'Irish equivalent profits' includes interest on Irish government securities which has been received by the offshore fund without tax being deducted.

Continuing the foregoing assumptions. TCA 1997, Sch 19, para 5(4) provides that the corresponding deductions available against the offshore fund's profits include:

(a) a deduction for an amount which would form part of the fund's income which the fund is prevented by the law of a foreign territory from distributing;
(b) the total amount of income tax paid by way of withholding tax (or otherwise) in respect of the income of the account period, provided the tax has not been repaid to the offshore fund – in this context, income tax paid by deduction does not include a tax credit to which the person suffering the deduction is entitled; and
(c) a deduction for foreign tax which was taken into account in calculating the fund's income for the account period, where the income was not remitted into the State.

17.405 Certification procedure

Application for certification

An offshore fund wishing to be certified as a distributing fund must apply to the Revenue Commissioners for certification, enclosing copies of the relevant financial accounts and any information which the Revenue Commissioners may reasonably require in connection with the application (TCA 1997, Sch 19, para 15(1)). Should the Revenue Commissioners subsequently discover that the accounts or information accompanying the application did not make a full and true disclosure, they must notify the offshore fund accordingly, stating the account period concerned. In such circumstances, the original certificate that the fund was a qualifying fund is automatically withdrawn as if it had never been issued (TCA 1997, Sch 19, para 15(5)).

The application must be made by or on behalf of an officer (or trustee) of the offshore fund within six months of the end of the account period to which the application relates. If the Revenue Commissioners refuse to certify the fund as a distributing fund, they must inform the applicant (TCA 1997, Sch 19, para 15(2), (3)).

Appeals

Where the Revenue Commissioners have refused an application for certification as a distributing fund (or where an application has been withdrawn following the discovery of further information which casts doubt on the accounts or information accompanying the original application) the aggrieved applicant may appeal against the refusal. The appeal must be made to the Appeal Commissioners within 30 days of the refusal notification, and it must be made by an officer or trustee of the fund.

The appeal will be heard by the Appeal Commissioners in the same manner as an appeal against an assessment to income tax, and all the provisions of the Income Tax Acts in relation to appeals apply (including the appellant's right to further hearings in the Circuit Court, High Court and Supreme Court). Where they see fit to do so, the Appeal Commissioners are expressly permitted to review any decision of the Revenue Commissioners (TCA 1997, Sch 19, para 16(3)).

Uncertified funds

The essential consequence of an offshore fund not receiving certification is that the capital gain arising to the unit holder which would otherwise have been assessable to tax as a chargeable gain, is instead taxed as income, without the inflation indexation relief which the capital gains tax legislation allows up to 31 December 2002 (TCA 1997, s 745(1), Sch 20, para 5).

TCA 1997, Sch 19, paras 17–18 set out several supplementary provisions which are designed to assist taxpayers who suffer unnecessary amounts of tax because a disinterested offshore fund has failed to apply to the Revenue Commissioners for certification. A taxpayer may *not* claim that he is not assessable to tax simply on the grounds that the Revenue did not certify a particular offshore fund as a distributing fund. Nevertheless, he may (provided the offshore fund has not already applied for certification) require the Revenue Commissioners to determine whether the fund in question should be certified. When the Revenue Commissioners receive such a request from a taxpayer, they must 'invite' the offshore fund which has not applied for certification to apply for certification.

The Revenue Commissioners are not obliged to request an application from the uncertified offshore fund before the expiry of the account period (for which the application was not made). If it is to be in time, the offshore fund's subsequent application must be submitted within 90 days of receipt of the Revenue Commissioners' request that it apply for certification. Failure to submit the application within that 90-day period will mean that the Revenue will decide the issue of certification 'as if such an application had been made'.

In the event that the Revenue Commissioners receive several notices from different aggrieved taxpayers on the grounds that such taxpayers have (in their own view, unnecessarily) paid tax because a particular offshore fund has not applied for certification, provided the Revenue Commissioners have dealt with *one* of the notices (in the manner outlined above) they will be treated as having dealt with *all* the notices.

In determining whether an offshore fund should be certified 'as if such an application had been made', the Revenue Commissioners shall regard any accounts or information submitted with the notice from the aggrieved taxpayer as if those accounts and information had been submitted with an application for certification from the fund itself. If, following an application from an aggrieved taxpayer, the Revenue Commissioners have refused to certify a fund, and that person subsequently sends information or accounts to the Revenue Commissioners which was not enclosed with the original application, the Revenue Commissioners will be obliged to reconsider the original determination in the light of the fresh information and if necessary, they must certify the fund accordingly.

The Revenue Commissioners are also obliged to notify the aggrieved taxpayer of their decision as to whether the fund in question has been certified or not. A fund which has failed to apply for certification as a distributing fund is precluded from appealing against a determination made by the Revenue Commissioners following such a request by an aggrieved taxpayer.

Official secrecy

Although the Revenue Commissioners are obliged by the Official Secrets Acts not to disclose any information they may have in relation to any taxpayer's affairs, TCA 1997, Sch 19, para 19 expressly permits the Commissioners to disclose details of any determination made by the Revenue or Appeal Commissioners as to whether an offshore fund should be certified as a distributing fund. However, such details may only be disclosed 'to any person appearing to them to have an interest in the matter'.

Delegation of duties

TCA 1997, Sch 19, para 20 permits the Revenue Commissioners to nominate any of their officers to carry out any duties which TCA 1997, Sch 19 obliges the Commissioners to perform.

17.406 Relaxation of conditions for certification

Investments in a secondary (distributing) offshore fund

A situation may arise where, during an account period, the assets of an offshore fund (the 'primary fund') include a holding of units in another offshore fund (the 'secondary offshore fund') and as a consequence of having such an investment the offshore fund fails to qualify as a distributing fund (because such interests exceed the 5 per cent limit for investments in other offshore funds, or because one company owned more than 10 per cent by value of the fund's assets, or because the fund itself owned more than 10 per cent of the share capital of any company). Nevertheless the secondary offshore fund may still be certifiable as a distributing fund because it is distributing more than 85 per cent of its income (and more than 85 per cent of its Irish equivalent profits) and the offshore fund in question has not contravened any of the aforementioned 5 per cent or 10 per cent holding limits set out in TCA 1997, s 744.

In such circumstances, TCA 1997, Sch 19, para 6 allows the primary fund's investments in the secondary (qualifying) fund to be ignored for the purposes of the '5 per cent' (and '10 per cent') tests in deciding whether the primary fund is certifiable as a distributing fund. Nevertheless, the primary fund's interests in the secondary fund must not be omitted in any calculations where it is necessary to compute the total value of the fund's assets.

In particular, where a primary offshore fund has investments in a secondary (distributing) offshore fund (or any company whether an offshore fund or not) and it is necessary to decide, as already mentioned, whether such an interest prevents the primary fund being regarded, as a distributing fund then the primary fund's share of that interest must be treated as an additional asset of the primary fund.

Excess income

In deciding whether the primary fund passes the 85 per cent of Irish equivalent profits test, TCA 1997, Sch 19, para 8 provides that it may also be necessary to have regard to the 'excess income' of the secondary (qualifying) offshore fund. 'Excess income' in this regard means the amount by which the Irish equivalent profits of the secondary fund exceed its distributions for that period. Where the secondary fund's distributions *do* exceed its Irish equivalent profits for an account period, the Irish equivalent profits of the primary fund are allowed to be increased (but only for the purposes of the 85 per cent test) by the primary fund's share of the excess income (of the secondary fund) which is attributable to that period.

If the account periods of the primary and secondary funds coincide, the procedure is relatively simple. The excess income of the secondary fund is attributable to that period of the primary fund. Where the account periods of the primary and secondary funds do *not* precisely coincide, the 'appropriate fraction' of the excess income of the secondary (qualifying) fund is attributed to the account period of the primary fund. This fraction is calculated as being the number of days common to the account period of the primary fund and the secondary fund, divided by the number of days in the account period of the secondary fund.

TCA 1997, Sch 19 allows an averaging 'appropriate fraction' calculation to be performed for the purposes of the TCA 1997, s 744(3) 5 per cent and 10 per cent holding tests. Because the underlying assets of an offshore fund may constantly change in value, it would be unfair to penalise a primary fund whose investments in a secondary (qualifying) fund exceeded the 5 per cent limit for (say) three days of an account period lasting 90 days. The purpose of this relief is to allow such a primary fund to 'average' the value of its holdings in the secondary (qualifying) fund over the length of the account period. This will generally have the effect of allowing a primary fund which has briefly exceeded the 5 per cent (or 10 per cent) holding in a secondary (qualifying) fund to still qualify itself as a distributing fund.

Investment in trading companies

Where an offshore fund invests in a single trading company (which does not deal in commodities, futures contracts, traded options, stocks, shares, or financial assets or money lending) TCA 1997, Sch 19, para 10 permits the TCA 1997, s 744(3) test be varied to allow the fund to hold up to 20 per cent of the issued share capital of the trading company (in contrast with the 'normal' strict limit of 10 per cent).

Wholly owned subsidiaries

TCA 1997, Sch 19, para 11 allows an offshore fund which 'wholly owns' a subsidiary to be entitled to regard a share (proportionate to its shareholding in the issued share capital of the subsidiary) of receipts, expenses, assets and liabilities of the subsidiary as its (the offshore fund's) own receipts, expenses, etc. This means that for the purposes of the TCA 1997, s 744(3) 5 per cent and 10 per cent tests, the net assets of the wholly owned subsidiary must be included in those of the 'owning' offshore fund. In computing the 'owning' offshore fund's income (and Irish equivalent profits) for the purposes of the 85 per cent tests set out in TCA 1997, Sch 19, para 1, the offshore fund in question must deduct the net profit of the wholly owned subsidiary from its own net profit. The resulting profit figure is the profit figure to be used for the purposes of the 85 per cent tests (TCA 1997, Sch 19, para 11(4)).

The offshore fund in question will be regarded as wholly owning a subsidiary only if it 'directly and beneficially' owns the subsidiary ie it is not permitted to own the subsidiary via an intermediary person or persons, for example, through a company which in turn owns the subsidiary. Similarly, where it is the case that the offshore fund in question is a unit trust scheme, it will be regarded as wholly owning a subsidiary only if the trustees directly own the subsidiary for the benefit of the fund. If the offshore fund is of the final variety, ie an arrangement under the law of a foreign State, it must directly own the subsidiary in 'a corresponding manner' (TCA 1997, Sch 19, para 11(2)). In addition, TCA 1997, Sch 19, para 11(3) provides that in order to qualify as wholly owning a subsidiary which has only one class of shares issued, the 'owning' offshore fund must own at least 95 per cent of those shares.

Dealing and management companies

An offshore fund which wholly owns a subsidiary whose entire business is managing and administering the fund (by way of dealing in units in the fund) is allowed (by TCA 1997, Sch 19, para 12) to disregard its holding in that subsidiary for the purposes of the TCA 1997, s 744(3) 10 per cent holding (in another company) test, ie the 'owning' offshore fund is allowed to ignore its holding in the dealing and management company in deciding whether it (the holding offshore fund) is a qualifying (distributing) fund. The following conditions must also be observed:

(a) the dealing and management subsidiary company must not be entitled to any distribution in respect of the units it holds; and
(b) the 'owning' offshore fund must 'directly and beneficially' own the subsidiary dealing and management company, ie the subsidiary must not be owned via an intermediary individual or individuals, or via intermediary trusts, companies or other arrangements.

Where a subsidiary management company, which is *not necessarily wholly* owned:

(a) holds property occupied or used in connection with the administration (or management) of the offshore fund; and
(b) provides administrative and management services to the offshore fund (or any other offshore fund which has an interest in the management company),

then, provided the payment the management company receives for the services it provides is not excessive (ie above arm's length prices) the same relaxation of the TCA 1997, s 744(3) 10 per cent holding test may apply.

17.407 Offshore funds based in offshore states

TCA 1997, Pt 24, Ch 4 as amended by F (No 2) A 2008, s 27 and FA 2009 provides a special regime for the taxation of investors in offshore funds based in designated 'offshore states'. An offshore state is defined as either a Member State of the EU or the EEA, or an OECD state with which Ireland has a double taxation agreement (TCA 1997, s 747B(1)).

A fund is regarded as based in an offshore state if it is a company resident in such a state, a trust where the trustees are resident in such a state or consists of co-ownership type arrangements which take effect under the law of such a state (TCA 1997, s 747B(2)). The Revenue Commissioners have nevertheless expressed their view that they have the option of continuing to treat arrangements such as co-ownerships as transparent for tax purposes under general principles, although this interpretation is open to challenge. They apparently also take the view that this treatment extends to limited liability partnerships notwithstanding that they possess a separate legal personality under their domestic law of registration. However, with general effect for income and gains arising on or after 20 February 2007, the special regime will no longer apply to any offshore fund unless it falls under one of the following categories of entity ('regulated funds' hereafter for convenience):

(a) (i) is an undertaking for collective investment formed under the law of an offshore state;
(ii) is similar in all material respects to an investment limited partnership (within the meaning of the Investment Limited Partnership Act 1994); and
(iii) holds a certificate authorising it to act as such an undertaking, being a certificate issued by the authorities of that state under laws providing for the proper and orderly regulation of such undertakings;
(b) is authorised by or under any measures duly taken by a Member State for the purposes of giving effect to:
(i) Council Directive 85/611/EEC on the coordination of laws, regulations and administrative provisions relating to undertakings for collective investment in transferable securities (UCITS), or

(ii) any amendment to that Directive;

(c) (i) is a company formed under the law of an offshore state;

(ii) is similar in all material respects to an authorised investment company (within the meaning of Part XIII of the (Companies Act 1990);

(iii) holds an authorisation issued by the authorities of that state under laws providing for the proper and orderly regulation of such companies and that authorisation has not ceased to have effect; and

(iv) is an investment company:

(I) which raises capital by promoting the sale of its shares to the public, or

(II) each of the shareholders of which is an investor which, if the company were an authorised investment company within the meaning of Part XIII of the Companies Act 1990 would be a collective investor within the meaning of TCA 1997, s 739B; or

(d) (i) is a unit trust scheme, the trustees of which are not resident in the State;

(ii) is similar in all material respects to an authorised unit trust scheme (within the meaning of the (Unit Trusts Act 1990);

(iii) holds an authorisation issued by the authorities of that offshore state under laws providing for the proper and orderly regulation of such schemes and that authorisation has not ceased to have effect, and

(iv) provides facilities for the participation by the public, as beneficiaries under the trust, in profits or income arising from the acquisition, holding, management or disposal of securities or any other property whatsoever (TCA 1997, s 747(2A) inserted by (FA 2007, s 39).

A non-regulated offshore fund in an offshore state will not be subject to the general offshore fund regime (TCA 1997, s 747AA inserted by FA 2007, s 39(1)(b)); the taxpayer will therefore be liable to tax at his marginal rate on income therefrom in the normal manner. Transitional relief applies so that the special regime will continue to apply where a person held a material interest in a non-regulated fund on 20 February 2007 which would not be a personal portfolio investment within TCA 1997, s 739BA (see below) (FA 2007, s 39(2)).

Payments from an offshore fund – non personal portfolio investment

Where an individual investor receives a payment from a regulated fund, and the payment is not made in consideration of the disposal of an interest in an offshore fund, it will be liable to income tax at a rate of 41 per cent from 1 January 2014 regardless of whether it is a 'relevant payment' or not. The rate of tax remains at 41 per cent for 2015 notwithstanding a reduction in the marginal rate of income tax to 40 per cent. Prior to the changes introduced by Finance (No 2) Act 2013, the rate that applied to a 'relevant payment' was different to the rate that applied to a non-relevant payment. A 'relevant payment' is a payment made annually or more frequently but otherwise than on the disposal of all or part of the individual's interest in the fund. A relevant payment received before 1 January 2014 was liable to income tax at 33 per cent. A payment received before 1 January 2014 from a regulated fund which was not for the disposal of an interest in the fund and which was not a relevant payment (ie received less frequently than annually) was liable to income tax at 36 per cent.

Payments from an offshore fund – personal portfolio investment

The definition of a personal portfolio investment is extremely complex; in broad terms, it is an investment under which the investor or a person acting on his behalf ('agent') or a person connected with the investor or with his agent, can select or influence the selection of assets which is used to determine some or all of the benefits conferred by the investment. The legislation also aims to cover cases where the right to make or influence a selection is contingent on (a) the exercise of an option or (b) the exercise of its discretion by the undertaking or (c) a right to request a change in the terms of the policy so as to create rights of selection or (d) the right to require the undertaking to appoint an investment advisor in relation to the selection process. If certain conditions are met, investment will not be a personal portfolio investment. Firstly, the opportunity to select a particular item of land (including interests in land and unquoted shares deriving all or most of their value from land) or to select any other assets falling within a specified category must be identified clearly and be marketed as being generally available to the public. Secondly, the investment undertaking must deal on an equal basis with all those persons who have an opportunity to make or influence the selection process; furthermore, where the investment undertaking is marketed on the basis that a majority of the assets concerned will consist of land (including interests in land and unquoted shares deriving all or most of their value from land) and the total amount to be invested by the public is predetermined, each investment by an individual investor must not exceed 1 per cent of that total amount (TCA 1997, s 739BA).

In the case of personal portfolio investments, payments on or after 1 January 2014 from a regulated fund, other than payments for a disposal of an interest in the fund, will be liable to income tax at a rate of 60 per cent. For such payments before 1 January 2014 the rate was 56 per cent. Where the full amount of the payment is not included in the individual's tax return and the return is submitted by the due filing date, or the return is filed late, the payment will become liable to income tax at a rate of 80 per cent. Such payments before 1 January 2014 were liable to income tax at the individual's marginal rate plus 33 per cent. The rate of income tax on such payments remains at 60 per cent and 80 per cent respectively for 2015.

Disposal of interest in an offshore fund

Where the individual disposes of the whole or part of his interest in the fund then the amount of the gain on disposal is computed in accordance with CGT principles, but without the benefit of indexation relief. With effect from 31 March 2006, there will be a deemed disposal and reacquisition at market value of the individual's interest in the fund on the occurrence of every 8th anniversary of the acquisition of the interest in the fund. This provision is designed to create a level playing field with the treatment of Irish CIUs (see **8.401**). With effect for disposals on or after 1 January 2014, all gains arising on an actual or deemed disposal will be liable to income tax at 41 per cent. The rate of tax remains at 41 per cent for 2015 notwithstanding a reduction in the marginal rate of income tax to 40 per cent. Gains arising on disposals before 1 January 2014 were liable at 36 per cent. In the case of a personal portfolio investment (see above) a disposal of a material interest in the fund on or after 1 January 2014 will be liable to income tax at a rate of 60 per cent (TCA 1997, s 747E). The rate of income tax remains at 60 per cent for 2015. Such disposals before 1 January 2014 were liable to income tax at 56 per cent. The 60 per cent rate only applies in the case of a personal portfolio investment where the individual includes details of the disposal in the individual's tax return and the return is filed on time. Where the return is filed late or the details are not included in a return filed on time the gain is liable to income tax at an 80 per cent rate of tax. This more penal rate of income tax applies with effect from 1 January 2015.

An interest in an offshore fund is treated as having been disposed of and acquired immediately before the death of the person holding that interest (TCA 1997, s 747B(3)). With effect from 1 January 2004, a disposal of a material interest in an offshore fund (the 'old interest') in return for the receipt of a material interest in another offshore fund (the 'new interest') in connection with a scheme of reconstruction or amalgamation will not give rise to a gain and the new interest will be treated as having been acquired at the same time and at the same cost as the old interest. A scheme of reconstruction or amalgamation is defined as an arrangement under which the new interest must be acquired in respect of, or in proportion to (or as nearly as may be in proportion to) the value of, the old interest and where the value of the old interest must become negligible (TCA 1997, s 747F).

Generally where a loss arises on a disposal or a deemed disposal no loss is deemed to arise (TCA 1997, s 747E(3)). Losses arising on the disposal of interests in offshore funds are therefore not available to offset against any other gains arising to the individual. However, where tax is payable on foot of a deemed disposal under TCA 1997, s 747E(6) on an eight-yearly relevant event (see above) and a loss arises on a subsequent actual disposal of the interest in the fund, a refund may be claimed so that the total tax payable in respect of the interest is the same as if TCA 1997, s 747E(6) had not been enacted; the normal four-year time limit for claims under TCA 1997, s 865 does not apply (see **2.104**) (TCA 1997, s 747E(3)(b) inserted by FA 2006, s 51)). This provision is necessary to avoid the inequity of tax being paid on a notional disposal when a monetary loss has been incurred over a longer period of ownership of the interest in the fund.

Miscellaneous

Further, no claims against such gains are permitted in respect of trading losses under TCA 1997, s 381 (see **4.4**) or Case IV losses under TCA 1997, s 383 (see **8.2**) (TCA 1997, s 747E(4)).

Income treated as accruing on such a disposal as well as any payments received in respect of a material interest in an offshore fund referred to in TCA 1997, s 747D are also exempt from self-employed PRSI (SI 428/2004). All payments liable to income tax under TCA 1997, Pt 27, Ch 4 are excluded from the Universal Social Charge (see **3.404**).

Division 18 Exemptions and Reliefs

18.1 Employment and Investment Incentive and Seed Capital Scheme

18.101 The main features

The Employment and Investment Incentive (EII) scheme was introduced for shares issued in the period 25 November 2011 to 31 December 2020. The qualifying period was extended to 31 December 2020 by Finance Act 2013, s 22 and SI 497/2013. The EII scheme replaces the Business Expansion Scheme (BES) (described in the 2011 edition of this text) with effect from 25 November 2011. In the case of shares issued between 25 November 2011 and 31 December 2011 an election could be made for relief to be claimed under the provisions of the BES.

The EII and BES rules are broadly similar although the list of relevant trading activities is far more extensive under the EII and relief under the EII is claimed in two tranches. Assuming a marginal rate of 40 per cent, 30 per cent is claimed in Year 1 and assuming the company meets certain employment criteria or has increased research and development expenditure in Year 3, 10 per cent is claimed in Year 4. Under the EII, the eligible shares must be held for four years (subject to a Ministerial Order and previously three years), a reduction from five years under BES. The extension of the period from three years to four years was introduced by Finance Act 2014 but was subject to a Ministerial Order. Instead of a Ministerial Order issuing Finance Act 2015, s 18(1) amended the commencement date in Finance Act 2014 such that it has effect in respect of shares issued on after 13 October 2015. The purpose of the scheme remains unchanged. Relief is available on a claim by a qualifying individual (specified individual for seed capital) who subscribes for eligible shares issued by a qualifying company. The shares must be issued for relevant trading activities carried on or to be carried on by the qualifying company or its qualifying subsidiary. As entitlement to a claim for the additional 10 per cent is based on employment numbers at the end of Year 3, this implicitly discriminates against a start-up company which by its nature is more risky than an existing company seeking to expand its trade.

TCA 1997, Pt 16 contains the legislation which entitles individuals to claim tax relief under the Employment and Investment Incentive (EII) and Seed Capital Scheme (SCS). The relief is subject to various conditions and restrictions and it is vital that the reader has a full understanding of the various definitions and restrictions which apply.

The relief is available in respect of money subscribed for ordinary shares in unquoted trading companies incorporated within the EEA, and which are either resident in the State or else resident in another EEA country and carry on business through a branch or agency in the State. When the EII was originally introduced the initial 30/40ths (usually this gives rise to income tax relief at 30 per cent) of the relief was a specified relief and subject to limitation in the hands of high income individuals discussed at **3.111**. A claim for the initial 30/40ths of the relief was removed from the schedule of specified reliefs by Finance (No 2) Act 2013 in respect of a subscription for eligible shares in the period 16 October 2013 to 31 December 2016. FA 2016, s 20 permanently ensured that the 30/40 tranche is not subject to the high income restriction discussed above. A claim for the second 10/40ths is not a specified relief.

For years of assessment prior to 2015, relief was claimed at 30/41sts and 11/41sts. The change in relief from 30/41 and 11/41 to 30/40 and 10/40 was amended by FA 2014, s 27(1)(b) and per FA 2014, s 27(2)(a) applies for the year of assessment 2015 and subsequent years. This implies that 10/40 is the appropriate fraction where a claim is made for the second tranche of relief in any year from 2015. However, Revenue take the view that the change only applies for investments made from 1 January 2015. For example, if an EII investment was made in 2014 a claim for the second tranche of relief in 2017 would be based on 11/41 and not 10/40.

TCA 1997, s 489(1) requires that, before the relief is granted the money provided by the individual for eligible shares in the qualifying company either was used, is being used or is intended to be used for one of two stated purposes (see below). In addition, the section requires that the money is used with a view to the creation or maintenance of employment in the company.

The purposes for which the money subscribed may be used by the qualifying company are:

(a) for the purpose of carrying on r*elevant trading activities* (see **18.104**); and
(b) in the case of a company which has not commenced to trade, in incurring expenditure on research and development within the meaning of TCA 1997, s 766.
(c) in the case of a company that owns and operates a qualifying nursing home, for the purposes of enlarging the capacity of the qualifying nursing home (with effect for shares issued on or after 13 October 2015).

A qualifying nursing home is explained in TCA 1997, s 488(1) as meaning:

(a) a nursing home within the meaning of s 2 of the Health (Nursing Homes) Act 1990 and which is registered under s 4 of that Act; and
(b) where applicable, a qualifying residential unit constructed on the site of, and operated by, a nursing home within the meaning of paragraph (a), but does not include any nursing home or qualifying residential unit which is subject to any power on the exercise of which the nursing home or residential units, or any part or interest in the nursing home or residential units, may be revested in the person from whom it was purchased or exchanged or in any person on behalf of such person.

Reference is made above to a 'qualifying residential unit' which is also defined in TCA 1997, s 488(1) as meaning a house which:

(a) is constructed on the site of, or on a site which is immediately adjacent to the site of, a registered nursing home,

(b) is—

(i) a single storey house, or

(ii) a house that is comprised in a building of one or more storeys in relation to which building a fire safety certificate under Part III of the Building Control Regulations 1997 (SI No 496 of 1997) is required, and prior to the commencement of the construction works on the building, is granted by the building control authority (within the meaning of section 2 of the Building Control Act 1990) in whose functional area the building is situated where—

(I) the house is, or (as the case may be) the house and the building in which it is comprised are, designed and constructed to meet the needs of persons with disabilities, including in particular the needs of persons who are confined to wheelchairs, and

(II) the house consists of one or two bedrooms, a kitchen, a living room, bath or shower facilities, toilet facilities and a nurse call system linked to the registered nursing home,

and

(c) is comprised in a development where—

(i) those units are operated or managed by the registered nursing home and an on-site caretaker is provided, and

(ii) back-up medical care, including nursing care, is provided by the registered nursing home to the occupants of those units when required by those occupants.

There is a Revenue Precedent in respect of the BES to the effect that shares issued to raise money in order to repay bank borrowings incurred for trading purposes may be eligible for relief. The shares must be issued for money and not money's worth so that, for example, an issue of shares in exchange for a transfer of assets will not qualify (*Thompson v Hart* [2000] STC 281). Similarly, an issue of shares in discharge of a debt due from the company would not qualify; there is a statutory relaxation of this rule in respect of the SCS: see **18.112**.

One of the conditions to be satisfied by the company issuing the eligible shares, if it is to be a qualifying company, is that it may only have a subsidiary company or companies which meet the requirements prescribed by TCA 1997, s 505. Broadly, it may only have a subsidiary company if that company itself carries on relevant trading activities or carries on a trade of buying or selling goods for, or of rendering services to, the qualifying company or fellow subsidiaries. The conditions to be met by a qualifying subsidiary company are covered in more detail in **18.105**.

TCA 1997, Sch 10 provides that shares issued by a qualifying company may, instead of, or as well as, being issued for the purpose of raising money for relevant trading activities of the issuing company, be issued for the purpose of raising money for relevant trading activities carried on by a qualifying subsidiary. In any case where shares are issued wholly or partly for the trade of a qualifying subsidiary, TCA 1997, ss 488(1), 489(1)(c), (5), (6) and (8) are to take effect as if the references therein to 'the company' included references to the subsidiary. Therefore, the purpose test of TCA 1997, s 489(1) may be satisfied if the money subscribed for the eligible shares in the qualifying company is used or is intended for use to enable a qualifying subsidiary to undertake or expand relevant trading activities with a view to the creation or maintenance of employment in the subsidiary company.

The other key conditions for obtaining the relief are as follows:

(a) the individual must be 'an individual who qualifies for the relief' (see **18.102**);

(b) the shares for which the individual's subscription is made must be eligible shares in a qualifying company (see **18.103**);

(c) the shares must be issued by the qualifying company for the purpose of raising money for relevant trading activities (see **18.104**) carried on or intended to be carried on either by the qualifying company or by a qualifying subsidiary company (see **18.105**);

(d) the qualifying company must satisfy the Revenue Commissioners as required that the money subscribed for the eligible shares is being used or is intended to be used for one or more of the purposes specified in TCA 1997, s 489(1) (see below);

(e) the qualifying company (or a qualifying subsidiary) must be carrying on relevant trading activities at the time the shares are issued or, alternatively, must commence to carry it on within two years (depending on the circumstances) after the issue of the shares or meet conditions regarding the amount of its expenditure on research and development (see **18.104**);

(f) the amount raised by the issue of eligible shares and which qualifies for the relief does not exceed the prescribed capital limits (see **18.106**);

(g) the eligible shares must be retained by the individual for at least four years (subject to a Ministerial Order and previously three years) after the date of their issue (see **18.108** for the effect of an earlier disposal or of certain other events which require the withdrawal of relief previously given); and

(h) there must not be any value received or replacement capital (**18.111**).

A modified version of the scheme applies to certain seed capital investments (SCS) by new entrepreneurs. The intention of the SCS is to encourage employees to set up their own businesses with the tax refund(s) from the backdated relief being available to help capitalise the new business (see **18.112**).

18.102 Individuals qualifying for relief

In order that an individual can qualify for EII relief in a qualifying company, TCA 1997, s 492 prescribes that he must meet the following conditions:

(a) he must make a subscription for the eligible shares on his own behalf (except see **18.110** for an investment through a designated investment fund); and

(b) he must not be connected with the qualifying company, or with any subsidiary company of the qualifying company (TCA 1997, Sch 10), at any time in the specified period (see the definition below). The exception to this is if the aggregate of all amounts subscribed for the issued share capital and loan capital does not at any time during the specified period exceed €500,000.

There is provision for shares to be subscribed for and/or held by a nominee; any disposal by the nominee will be treated as being that of the beneficial owner (TCA 1997, s 506(1)); this may be done through the medium of a holding in joint names, as accepted by a published Revenue Precedent in relation to the BES.

TCA 1997, s 488(1) defines what eligible shares are for the purposes of the relief. For the shares issued to the qualifying individuals to be 'eligible', they must be new ordinary shares and they must, throughout the 'relevant period' (see **18.103**), carry no present or future preferential right to dividends or to a company's assets on its winding up and no present or future preferential right to be redeemed. The shares may, however, have any normal non-preferential right to dividends or to share in the company's assets in a winding up.

Example 18.102.1

ABC Limited issues 50,000 Ordinary Shares and 50,000 A Ordinary Shares. The shares rank *pari passu* except the A Ordinary Shares are entitled to an annual 3% dividend in preference to the payment of dividends on any other class of shares. In these circumstances the A Ordinary Shares would be regarded as preferred shares and would not be eligible shares for EII purposes. The Ordinary Shares should qualify for relief provided the other conditions of the scheme are met.

'Ordinary shares' are any shares forming part of a company's ordinary share capital (TCA 1997, s 488(1)). 'Ordinary share capital' has the meaning given by TCA 1997, s 2(1), namely: all the issued share capital (by whatever name called) of the company, other than capital the holders whereof have a right to a dividend at a fixed rate, but have no other right to share in the profits of the company.

A company may issue ordinary shares qualifying as eligible shares at different times. If it does, each separate issue of eligible shares has its own separate period in which there must be no preferential right to dividends, assets, etc attaching to the shares in question. Further, in applying any other rule in the legislation which relates to the date of issue of eligible shares, the rules have to be applied separately to each issue of eligible shares. However, for ease of explanation, the discussion in **Division 18** generally assumes that there is only one issue of eligible shares involved (except if indicated otherwise to the contrary at any particular point).

In addition, the individual must not dispose of the eligible shares before the end of the specified period if he is to retain the relief. If he disposes of the shares at any time during that period, TCA 1997, s 492 normally applies to deny or reduce the right to the relief and to cause the retrospective withdrawal of any excess relief already granted. Also no relief is available if the individual acquires an option or grants an option to any other person the effect of which is either to bind another person to purchase the shares or to bind the individual to dispose of the shares at a price other than market value (TCA 1997, s 496). For more details of these rules, see **18.108–18.109**.

'Specified period'

TCA 1997, s 488(1) defines 'the specified period', as that term is used in TCA 1997, ss 492, 496, 497, 498, 499 in relation to relief in respect of any eligible shares by a company, as meaning the period beginning two years before the date on which the shares were issued or, if it is later, on the date of incorporation of the company, and ending four years after the issue of the shares. The extension of the period from three years to four years was introduced by Finance Act 2014 but is subject to a Ministerial Order. For a company which makes more than one issue of eligible shares on different dates, a separate 'specified period' applies for each issue of eligible shares.

The specified period is normally longer than four years, as it is unusual for eligible shares to be issued on the date of incorporation. For example, if a company incorporated on 1 May 2014 issues eligible shares on 1 July 2015, the specified period runs for the five years and two months from 1 May 2014 (date of incorporation) until 30 June 2019 (four years after the date of issue). On the other hand, if that company was incorporated on 1 May 2013 (more than two years before the date of issue), the specified period runs for the six years from 1 July 2013 (two years before the date of issue) to 30 June 2019 (four years after the date of issue).

Connection with company

An individual is only entitled to claim relief in respect of his subscription for eligible shares in the qualifying company if he is not at any time during the specified period connected with that company or with any subsidiary of that company (TCA 1997, s 492). It is to be noted that the establishment of the connection between an individual and the qualifying company (or any subsidiary) *at any time* during the specified period related to the particular issue of eligible shares is sufficient to disqualify the individual from entitlement to the relief in respect of his subscription for those shares (see *Wild v Canavan* [1997] STC 966).

For example, an individual may subscribe for eligible shares in a qualifying company at a time when he is not connected with that company (or any subsidiary) and may be allowed the relief for the tax year in which those shares were issued to him. However, should he become connected with that company say, three years and 364 days after the shares were issued (ie still within the four-year specified period), he loses his entitlement to the relief for that investment. The necessary assessment under Sch D Case IV must, therefore, be made on the individual to withdraw the relief previously given (see **18.108**).

TCA 1997, s 492 (supported by TCA 1997, Sch 10 in relation to any subsidiary company) prescribes the circumstances in which an individual has to be regarded as connected with the qualifying company. Subject to the exceptions provided by TCA 1997, s 495 (see below), an individual is treated as connected with a qualifying company when any of the following circumstances exists at any time in the specified period:

(a) the individual, or any associate of his, is:
  (i) a partner of the qualifying company or of any subsidiary of the company, or
  (ii) a director or employee of either the qualifying company, a company which is a partner of the company or of any subsidiary of the company who, during the three years after the date the eligible shares are issued, receives any 'non-arm's length' payment from the company or any subsidiary (TCA 1997, s 492(2));

(b) the individual directly or indirectly possesses or is entitled to acquire more than 30 per cent of any of:
  (i) the issued ordinary share capital of the qualifying company or of any subsidiary of the company, or
  (ii) the loan capital (as defined) and the issued share capital of the qualifying company or of any subsidiary, or
  (iii) the voting power in the qualifying company or of any subsidiary (TCA 1997, s 492(4));

(c) the individual directly or indirectly possesses or is entitled to acquire such rights as would, in the event of the winding up of the qualifying company or of any subsidiary or in any other circumstances, entitle him to receive more than 30 per cent of the assets of the company or the subsidiary that are available at the relevant time for distribution to the equity shareholders of the company or the subsidiary as determined by TCA 1997, s 413; s 415 but without regard to TCA 1997, s 411(1)(c) (TCA 1997, s 492(6));

(d) the individual has control of the qualifying company within the meaning of TCA 1997, s 11 (TCA 1997, s 492(7));

(e) the individual has at any time in the relevant period had control within TCA 1997, s 11 of another company which has, since that time and before the end of that relevant period, become a subsidiary of the qualifying company (TCA 1997, Sch 10);

(f) the individual, if not already connected with the qualifying company under any of the foregoing rules, subscribes for shares in the company as part of any arrangement which provides for another person to subscribe for shares in another company, but only if the individual or any other individual who is a party to the arrangement is connected with that other company (TCA 1997, s 492(11)).

In *Cook v Billings* [2001] STC 16, seven associated individuals each acquired 10 per cent of the share capital of a company. The Court of Appeal held that each of the shareholders had to have all of the shareholdings of his six associates attributed to him so that *all* of the shareholders were consequently each deemed to hold more than 30 per cent of the share capital of the company.

There is a Revenue Precedent that where the original promoters (who will typically own 100 per cent of the company on incorporation) hold less than 30 per cent of the shares in the company following the relevant EII issue, the 30 per cent rule will not be applied in respect of their promoter's shareholdings; accordingly they will be able to claim relief in respect of their subscription under the EII issue.

TCA 1997, s 492(8)(a)(i) provides an exception to rules (b), (c) and (d) above. An individual is not connected with a company under any of these three rules if the aggregate of the amounts subscribed for the company's issued share capital (counting all classes) and loan capital does not, at any time during the specified period (in relation to the particular issue of eligible shares) exceed €500,000.

This exception now enables an individual to obtain the relief in respect of subscriptions for eligible shares to any such 'small company' regardless of the percentage of the shares, loan capital and/or voting power held by him and whether or not he controls the company. However, this small companies' exception still does not allow the relief to an individual who is connected with the qualifying company under any of rules (a), (e) or (f).

A specified individual is not debarred from relief under the SCS (see **18.112**) by reason only of the fact that he:

(a) directly or indirectly possesses or is entitled to acquire more than 30 per cent of any of:
   (i) the issued ordinary share capital of the qualifying company or of any subsidiary of the company,
   (ii) the loan capital and the issued share capital of the qualifying company or of any subsidiary, or
   (iii) the voting power in the qualifying company or of any subsidiary;

(b) directly or indirectly possesses or is entitled to acquire such rights as would, in the event of the winding up of the qualifying company or of any subsidiary or in any other circumstances, entitle him to receive more than 30 per cent of the assets of the company or the subsidiary that are available at the relevant time for distribution to the equity shareholders of the company or the subsidiary; or

(c) has control of the qualifying company.

For the purpose of rule (a)(ii) above, a 'non-arm's length' payment is any payment from the qualifying company or its subsidiary other than a payment representing full and proper consideration for any services rendered to the company or the subsidiary or for any goods supplied to, or for money loaned or invested in, the company or its subsidiary. The fact that an individual is a director or employee of a company does not of itself connect him with the company, nor is he connected under rule (a)(ii) if the only payments he receives are no more than full and proper remuneration for his services as a director or employee or for goods supplied, money loaned, etc. Also, note that it is only non-arm's length payments in the three years after the date of issue of the eligible shares that cause the connection (any such payments in the part of the specified period before the issue of the shares are not counted in applying rule (a)(ii)).

For the purpose of rules (d) and (e), an individual is treated by TCA 1997, s 11 as having control of a company if he has the power to secure that the affairs of that company are conducted in accordance with his wishes. This applies whether he has this power by means of the holding of shares or the possession of voting power in or in relation to that company or any other company or by virtue of any powers conferred by the articles of association or other document regulating that company or any other company.

In applying rules (a), (b) and (c) in relation to a subsidiary of the qualifying company, it does not matter whether the subsidiary has become a subsidiary before, during or after the year of assessment in which the individual makes his subscription for the eligible shares (TCA 1997, Sch 10). For example, if the individual has or is entitled to acquire a greater than 30 per cent holding of the ordinary shares, of all the share and loan capital or of the voting power in a company which is a subsidiary of the qualifying company for part only of the specified period, but subscribes for the eligible shares in a different part of the specified period, he is treated as connected with the qualifying company and disqualified from the relief for that subscription.

Similarly, if an individual (or his associate) is, at any time in the specified period, a partner, director or employee of a company which is a subsidiary of a qualifying company at any time in the specified period, and if the individual (or associate) receives a non-arm's length payment from the subsidiary in the three years after the issue of the eligible shares, the individual is connected with the qualifying company. The fact that the partner, employee or director relationship exists at a different time in the specified period does not prevent rule (a) from denying the relief to the individual (TCA 1997, Sch 10).

Example 18.102.2

ZW Ltd, a manufacturing company incorporated in 2010, issues eligible shares on 11 January 2015 to obtain EII finance when it has no subsidiary company. The specified period for this issue of eligible shares runs from 11 January 2013 (two years before 11 January 2015) to 10 January 2019.

One of the subscribers, who subscribes €15,000 for his eligible shares, is a Mr A Andrew who is an executive director of another manufacturing company, TH Ltd, which, at the time the eligible shares are issued, has no connection with ZW Ltd. Mr Andrew is not himself connected in any way with ZW Ltd on 11 January 2015 and, on that date, meets all the conditions to be an individual qualifying for relief so far as the said share issue is concerned.

On 2 January 2016, ZW Ltd acquires all the ordinary share capital of TH Ltd so that the latter becomes a subsidiary of ZW Ltd (a qualifying subsidiary, see **18.105**). Since this has occurred during ZW Ltd's relevant period in respect of the share issue of 11 January 2015, it will be necessary to ascertain whether Mr Andrew is now connected with ZW Ltd through his directorship/employment with TH Ltd.

The following facts are now ascertained:

(a) on 17 December 2016, Mr Andrew retires from TH Ltd and resigns his directorship;

(b) Mr Andrew does not, and has not held since 2010, any shares in TH Ltd (nor has he at any time since 2010 owned any loan capital or voting power in the company); and

(c) on 1 April 2016, Mr Andrew when a director of TH Ltd received a payment of €10,000 from the company for goods then worth €5,000 sold to the company (ie a payment in excess of the market value of the goods).

Since Mr Andrew was a director of TH Ltd for part of the specified period (from 11 January 2013 to 17 December 2016) in relation to ZW Ltd's issue of eligible shares on 11 January 2015, and since TH Ltd has become a subsidiary of ZW Ltd during a part of the specified period (from 2 January 2016), the rule of TCA 1997, s 492 may deem Mr Andrew to be connected with ZW Ltd.

By itself, Mr Andrew's directorship/employment with TH Ltd does not connect him with ZW Ltd. However, Mr Andrew has received a non-arm's length payment (the payment mentioned in (c) above) within the four years after the date the eligible shares were issued (11 January 2015). This means that he must be treated by rule (a) as being connected with ZW Ltd during the specified period and results in his ceasing to be an individual qualifying for the relief so that the relief given for his €15,000 subscription for the eligible shares in ZW Ltd has to be withdrawn (see **18.108**).

'Associate' defined

The term 'associate' is given the same meaning for the purpose of the EII legislation as it has in TCA 1997, s 433, *except* that a relative of an individual is not treated as an associate of his TCA 1997, s 488(1). Therefore the shareholding of a husband and wife are counted separately.

Under this definition, an associate of any person (say Mr X) may be any of:

(a) a partner of Mr X;

(b) the trustee of any settlement of which either Mr X or any relative of his (living or dead) was the settlor; or

(c) if Mr X is interested in any shares or obligations of a company which are either subject to any trust or are part of the estate of a deceased person, any other person with an interest in the same shares or obligations.

It is to be noted that the trustee of a settlement made by a relative of Mr X is an associate of Mr X under (b) notwithstanding that the relative is not his associate (unless treated as such under either (a) or (c)). Further, for a person to be treated as an associate of Mr X under (c) in relation to the affairs of a given company, the shares or obligations subject to the trust or being part of the estate of a deceased person must be shares or obligations in that company, its subsidiary or its parent company.

Other supporting rules

There are other supporting rules which may be relevant in determining whether or not an individual is connected with a company. In attributing to an individual any shares, loan capital or voting power which he is entitled to acquire, he is deemed to be entitled to acquire anything which he is entitled to acquire at a future date or will at a future date be entitled to acquire. Also, there must be attributed to the individual any rights or powers which any other person who is an associate of his has or is entitled to acquire (TCA 1997, s 492(9)). For example an individual who holds 25 per cent of the share capital of the company and has options to acquire a further 15 per cent would be regarded as connected.

The loan capital of a company is treated as including any debt incurred by the company for any money borrowed or capital assets acquired, for any right to receive income or for consideration the value of which to the company, at the time the debt was incurred, was substantially less than the amount of the debt (TCA 1997, s 492(5)). Debts for goods (other than capital assets) or services (other than the lending of money) supplied to a company are not part of its loan capital. The definition of loan capital excludes a bank overdraft. This can make it more difficult for an individual to avoid the 30 per cent connected person rule.

18.103 The 'qualifying company'

TCA 1997, s 494 sets out the requirements which must be met by a company if it is to be a qualifying company able to issue eligible shares for EII purposes, as follows:

(a) the company must be incorporated in the State or, in any other EEA state (TCA 1997, s 494(2));

(b) the company must, throughout the relevant period (see definition below), be an unquoted company that is resident in the State or resident in another other EEA country and which carries on business in the State through a branch or agency (TCA 1997, s 494(3)(a));

(c) the company must be a micro, small or medium sized enterprise as defined (TCA 1997, s 494(4)) within the meaning of annex 1 to Commission Regulation (EU) No 651/2014; for shares issued on or after 13 October 2015 a new TCA 1997, s 494(4A) was inserted. This states that a company that does not meet the requirements of paras 5 and 6 of Art 21 of Commission Regulation (EU) No 651/2014 of 17 June 2014 shall not be a qualifying company. *E-Brief* No 107/15 notes that any company which had received EII outline approval from Revenue prior to 13 October 2015 but had not raised EII funding by that date must consider, before issuing shares, whether or not it is a qualifying company under the amended scheme. Investors should note that outline approval issued prior to 13 October 2015 may no longer be valid. They should confirm with the potential investee company that it complies with the new requirements of the scheme. The main change which is likely to exclude companies which may have been qualifying companies prior to 13 October 2015 is the new requirement that a qualifying company must now meet the conditions of paras 5 and 6 of Article 21 of Commission Regulation (EU) 651/2014 of 17 June 2014. These paragraphs are reproduced below for ease of reference:

> 5. Eligible undertakings shall be undertakings which at the time of the initial risk finance investment are unlisted SMEs and fulfil at least one of the following conditions:
>
> (a) they have not been operating in any market;
>
> (b) they have been operating in any market for less than 7 years following their first commercial sale;

(c) they require an initial risk finance investment which, based on a business plan prepared in view of entering a new product or geographical market, is higher than 50% of their average annual turnover in the preceding 5 years.

6. The risk finance aid may also cover follow-on investments made in eligible undertakings, including after the 7 year period mentioned in paragraph 5(b), if the following cumulative conditions are fulfilled:

(a) the total amount of risk finance mentioned in paragraph 9 is not exceeded;

(b) the possibility of follow-on investments was foreseen in the original business plan;

(c) the undertaking receiving follow-on investments has not become linked, within the meaning of Article 3(3) of Annex I with another undertaking other than the financial intermediary or the independent private investor providing risk finance under the measure, unless the new entity fulfils the conditions of the SME definition.

Revenue's operation manual 16.00.08 outlines a number of frequently asked questions in relation to the above as follows:

Do these new rules make it harder for a company which is more than 7 years old to raise EII funding for the first time?

Yes. Where a company is looking to raise risk finance aid (EII) for the first time more than 7 years after its first sale, then it can only do so if it comes within paragraph (5)(c) of GBER. That is, it must be entering into a new market (either geographic or product) and the amount that the company wants to raise under EII is greater than 50% of the company's average annual turnover in the preceding 5 years.

… Do these new rules make it harder for a company to raise EII funding for the second time?

Yes. There are two sets of conditions to be met. Firstly, a company is only eligible to raise EII funding a second time if it previously raised funding through BES/EII/seed capital relief (all of which are found in Part 16 TCA 1997) where, at the time of that funding it met the conditions of paragraph (5) of GBER. For most companies, that will mean that they raised EII, BES or seed capital funding within 7 years of their first sale. Other companies will meet this test as they used EII funding to expand into new markets and met the 50% of turnover threshold. So a company must ask itself: Would I have satisfied one of the conditions in paragraph (5) of GBER at the time of my EII/BES/seed capital funding? Where the company can answer yes to that question then the next condition is that the business plan at the time of the first EII/BES/Seed capital funding round foresaw this second (or subsequent) funding round. Where the initial business plan foresaw this second or subsequent round of financing, the total financing to be raised cannot exceed €15,000,000 and the company cannot have become linked' to another company/companies unless together they remain SMEs.

… My company raised share capital when it was less than 7 years old, but relief under BES wasn't claimed. It is now 15 years old. Can my company qualify for EII funding?

No. The company must have raised BES/EII/seed capital funding at a time when it would have qualified under paragraph (5) of GBER and the business plan from that funding round must have foreseen this new funding.

(d) it must, throughout the relevant period, satisfy any *one* of the following three tests as to the nature of its business:

  (i) it must exist wholly for the purpose of carrying on relevant trading activities at least some of which are carried on from a fixed base in the State (see **18.104**),

  (ii) it must be a company whose business consists wholly of the holding of shares or securities of, or the making of loans to, one or more *qualifying subsidiaries* (see **18.105**), or

  (iii) it must be a company whose business consists wholly of both the holding of such shares or securities or the making of such loans as are referred to in (ii) above, for the purpose of carrying on relevant trading activities at least some of which are carried on from a fixed base in the State (TCA 1997, s 494(3));

(e) the company's share capital must not, at any time during the relevant period, include any issued shares that are not fully paid up (TCA 1997, s 494(11));

(f) throughout the relevant period, the company must not be controlled by any other company (other than NAMA or a 75 per cent subsidiary of NAMA) and must not control any other company (except any qualifying subsidiary) (see *Conditions as to control* below);

(g) the company must not be disqualified by reason of the provisions of TCA 1997, s 494(13) (see below);

(h) if the company's trade is or includes that of a tourist traffic undertaking, it must meet certain requirements to be approved by the National Tourism Development Authority (TCA 1997, s 494(6) – see **18.104**);

(i) the company must not be put into liquidation before the end of the relevant period (except for *bona fide* commercial reasons);

(j) the company must not be regarded as a firm in difficulty for the purposes of the Community Guidelines on State Aid for rescuing and restructuring firms in difficulty (TCA 1997, s 494(18)); and

(k) if the company's trade comprises of internationally traded financial services it must be in receipt of an appropriate certificate from Enterprise Ireland. This provision was introduced by Finance Act 2014 in respect of 2015 and subsequent years. Its introduction is subject to a Ministerial Order.

In general, the above conditions have only to be complied with up to the end of the four-year relevant period, but note that there is a different period involved in applying TCA 1997, s 494(13) in condition (g) (see below). In determining, for the purposes of condition (c), whether a company (or qualifying subsidiary or branch or agency) is located in an assisted area the location shall be determined by reference to the place where the relevant trading operations are carried on (TCA 1997, s 494(5)).

Fáilte Ireland is responsible for approving tourism applications. If it approves the application it issues a certificate of approval to the company. Guidelines for the approval process are available on Fáilte Ireland's website. The application process is regarded as a consultative process with applicants given an opportunity to provide additional information to support an application. A business plan must be submitted which should include five years' financial projections and a three-year marketing plan. Upper limits apply to the level of land and buildings as a percentage of total assets.

'Relevant period'

TCA 1997, s 488(1) defines 'the relevant period', as that term is applied in TCA 1997, s 494 in relation to relief in respect of any eligible shares issued by a company, as meaning the period beginning with the date on which those shares were issued and ending four years after that date or, if the company or a qualifying subsidiary was not at that date carrying on relevant trading activities, four years after the date on which the company or a qualifying subsidiary subsequently began to carry on such a trade. The Finance Act 2014 extended the relevant period from three years to four years in respect of 2015 and subsequent years. The changes introduced by Finance Act were subject to a Ministerial Order and instead of such order issuing Finance Act 2015, s 18(1) amended the commencement date in Finance Act 2014 such that it has effect in respect of shares issued on after 13 October 2015. The date on which the relevant trading activities are commenced by the qualifying company (or by a qualifying subsidiary) is, therefore, an important factor.

The definition of the four-year relevant period in TCA 1997, s 488(1) does not itself cover the case where the relevant trading activities are carried on not by the qualifying company, but by a qualifying subsidiary. TCA 1997, Sch 10 deals with this matter. It provides that, where the shares issued by the qualifying company are issued for the purpose of raising money for relevant trading activities carried on or intended to be carried on by a subsidiary, then TCA 1997, ss 488(1), 489(1), (5), (6), (8) are to be applied as if references there to the company are, where necessary, to be taken as including references to the subsidiary. In the case where the end of the relevant period is based on the date a subsidiary commenced relevant trading activities, both the qualifying company and the subsidiary must continue to satisfy the conditions for treatment respectively as a qualifying company (TCA 1997, s 495) and as a qualifying subsidiary (TCA 1997, s 505) for the whole of that relevant period.

Example 18.103.1

XY Ltd was incorporated in the State on 23 August 2013 for the purpose of carrying on relevant trading activities in the State from a fixed base in the State and for the holding of shares in subsidiary companies carrying on separate relevant trading activities carried on from fixed bases in the State. On 13 January 2015, XY Ltd issued 100,000 eligible shares to a number of different persons for the purposes of raising finance for the relevant trading activities of XY Ltd and its qualifying subsidiaries.

On 1 April 2015, the first of the relevant trading activities was commenced by one of the subsidiaries, X Ltd and, on 10 June 2015, XY Ltd commenced its relevant trading activities. The relevant four-year period for the purpose of the qualifying company rules of TCA 1997, s 494 (and also for the rules of TCA 1997, s 505) is, therefore, the period beginning on 13 January 2015 (ie the date of issue of the eligible shares) and ending on 31 March 2019 (ie four years after the first relevant trading activities was commenced by X Ltd).

Micro, Medium and Small Enterprises

Finance Act 2014, s 27 amends the definition of a qualifying company to include all medium-sized enterprises as defined. This change is due to take effect from 2015 but is subject to a Ministerial Order. Prior to Finance Act 2014, s 27 a medium-sized enterprise was a qualifying company if it was not beyond start-up stage as defined by the EU Commission or a medium sized enterprise as defined by the EU Commission located in an assisted area of the State. Assisted areas of the State are defined as all counties except Dublin, Kildare, Wicklow, Meath and Cork excluding Cork Docklands.

Unquoted company

The condition that the company issuing the eligible shares must be an unquoted company is met if none of its shares (of any class), stocks or debentures is listed in the official list of a stock exchange or is dealt in on an unlisted securities market (TCA 1997, s 488(1)).

However, a qualifying company may, without infringing the unquoted company condition, obtain a listing of an official stock exchange or be dealt in on an unlisted securities market at any time *after* the end of the *four*-year relevant period.

A company may also enter the Enterprise Exchange of the Irish Stock Exchange without prejudicing its status as a qualifying company for EII purposes. The company's shares may also be listed on any similar or corresponding market of the stock exchange of one or more members of the EU. However, this broadening of the exception applies only where the company obtained its listing on the Irish Enterprise Exchange of the Irish Stock Exchange before or at the same time as the listing on the similar foreign exchange.

Conditions as to control

TCA 1997, s 494 provides that, apart from qualifying subsidiaries within TCA 1997, s 505 (see **18.105**), a company is not a qualifying company if, at any time during the *four*-year relevant period, either:

(a) it alone or together with any connected persons, controls any other company;

(b) it is under the control of any other company alone or together with persons, connected to that company other than NAMA or a 75 per cent subsidiary of NAMA within TCA 1997, s 616(1)(g));

(c) it is a 51 per cent subsidiary of any other company other than NAMA or a 75 per cent subsidiary of NAMA within TCA 1997, s 616(1)(g)); or

(d) it has a 51 per cent subsidiary itself.

No arrangements must be in force during the relevant period by virtue of which the company could fall within (a), (b), (c) or (d).

In determining whether any company is controlled by any other company, the definition of 'control' given in TCA 1997, s 432(2)–(6) is used (TCA 1997, s 488(1)–(3)). This is the so called 'close company' definition of control explained in **12.304**.

A company is a 51 per cent subsidiary of another company if *more than* 50 per cent of its ordinary share capital is owned beneficially directly or indirectly by that other company. 'Owned directly or indirectly' means ownership whether direct, through another company or other companies, or partly directly and partly through another company or other companies (TCA 1997, s 9 as applied by TCA 1997, s 494). For the purpose of defining a 51 per cent subsidiary, 'ordinary share capital' has the meaning given by TCA 1997, ss 1(1), 2, 4 as set out under *Eligible shares* in **18.101**.

Effect of winding up

TCA 1997, s 494(9) states the general rule that a company will normally cease to be a qualifying company if, at any time before the end of the relevant *four*-year period, either a resolution is passed, or an order is made, for the winding up of the company or the company is dissolved without winding up. This general rule is subject to the exception provided by TCA 1997, s 494(10) that the company does not cease to be a qualifying company by reason of being wound up or dissolved, provided that:

(a) it is shown that the winding up or dissolution is for *bona fide* commercial reasons and not part of a scheme or arrangement which has, as one of its main purposes, the avoidance of tax (see also **18.111**); and
(b) the company's net assets are distributed to its members before the end of the relevant period or, in the case of a winding up, before the end of three years from the commencement of the winding up (if this is after the *four*-year relevant period).

Just as the event of an individual's ceasing to qualify for the relief within the *four*-year relevant period requires *his* EII relief to be withdrawn retrospectively, the cessation by a company or, if relevant, by a qualifying subsidiary, to meet the necessary qualifying conditions within the *four*-year relevant period results in the retrospective withdrawal of any relief previously granted. In this case, however, the withdrawal of the relief affects *all* the individuals to whom relief has previously been granted in respect of subscriptions for eligible shares in the company in question.

Disqualification for pre-existing trades

TCA 1997, s 494(13) provides in respect of SCS that a company (the first company) is not a qualifying company in any case where:

(a) any individual has acquired a controlling interest in the first company's trade or in the trade of any subsidiary of the first company;
(b) the same individual has or has had, at any time in the period mentioned below, a controlling interest in another trade (which may be a trade of a company, partnership or any other person or persons); and
(c) the trade carried on by the first company or its subsidiary is of the same or a similar type to the other trade mentioned in (b) (see below).

For the purpose of (a) and (b), an individual is regarded by TCA 1997, s 495 as having a controlling interest in a trade carried on by a company (whether the first company, its subsidiary or a company carrying on the other trade mentioned in (b)) in any of the following circumstances:

(a) where he controls the company carrying on the trade (see below);
(b) where:
    (i) the company carrying on the trade is a close company, and
    (ii) the individual or an associate of his is a director of the company and is the beneficial owner of, or able directly or through other companies or by any other means to control, more than 30 per cent of the ordinary share capital of the company; or
(c) where not less than 50 per cent of the trade would be regarded as belonging to him if TCA 1997, s 400 were applied.

The period in question is the period beginning two years prior to the date on which the shares were issued, or if later, the date on which the company began to carry on the trade and ending three years thereafter.

In determining whether an individual controls a company for the purpose of (a) above, the term 'control' has to be construed under the provisions of TCA 1997, s 432 (TCA 1997, s 488(1)). The circumstances in which those provisions deem a person to have control of a company are discussed in **12.304**. One point to note here is TCA 1997, s 432 attributes to any person any shares, rights, etc in a company which are held by any associate of his. Now, although the definition of an 'associate', where referred to specifically in the EII rules, excludes a relative, the application of the TCA 1997, s 432 definition of 'control' must be read as a whole so that shares, etc held by a relative are treated as held by the individual to whom it may be sought to attribute control of a company under TCA 1997, s 494.

It follows that, in looking at a trade carried on by a company (whether the company seeking the EII finance or another company carrying on the similar trade), any shares or rights to control held by a relative of any relevant individual must be taken into account in determining whether the individual has a controlling interest in the company's trade. However, in looking at any trade carried on by a person other than a company, any share in the profits or assets of that trade held by a relative of an individual with a controlling interest in the EII company are not taken into account (unless the trade is carried on by a partnership in which both the related individuals are partners).

In determining whether an individual has a controlling interest in a company's trade through the application of TCA 1997, s 400, it is necessary to ascertain the proportion of that company's ordinary share capital which is held by the individual. The effect of that subsection is to treat a trade carried on by a company as belonging to the persons beneficially owning the ordinary share capital of that company in the proportion to their respective beneficial holdings of that capital. Consequently, any individual who beneficially owns 50 per cent or more of the ordinary share capital is treated as owning 50 per cent or more of the company's trade and, therefore, as having a controlling interest in that trade.

In the case where a trade is carried on by a company which is a 75 per cent (or greater) subsidiary of another company (the parent company), that trade is regarded by TCA 1997, s 400 as belonging to the persons holding ordinary shares in the parent company in proportion to their beneficial holdings of such shares. Consequently, any individual who beneficially owns 50 per cent or more of the ordinary share capital of the parent company is treated as having a controlling interest in the trade of the 75 per cent subsidiary. For this rule to apply, the parent company must hold, directly or through another company or companies 75 per cent or more of the ordinary share capital of the subsidiary.

For the purpose of (b) above, an individual is regarded as having a controlling interest in a trade carried on by a person other than a company if he is entitled to 50 per cent or more of either of the assets used for the trade or of the income arising from the trade (TCA 1997, s 494(14)). If any associate of the individual is entitled to any share of such assets or income of the trade, then that associate's share is added to the individual's share to determine whether the 50 per cent share of either assets or income is reached to give the individual the controlling interest in the trade in question (TCA 1997, s 494(15)).

For the purposes of (c) above, the trade carried on by the first company or its subsidiary (the first trade) is regarded as being of the same or a similar type to the other trade in which the same individual has a controlling interest if either:

(a) the first trade, or a substantial part of it, is concerned with the same or similar types of property (or parts thereof) or provides the same or similar services or facilities as the other trade; or

(b) the first trade serves substantially the same or similar outlets or markets as the other trade.

Disqualification for green energy companies

A company whose relevant trading activities includes green energy activities will cease to be a qualifying company unless it has expended all of the money subscribed for eligible shares on such activities, within a period ending one month before the end of the relevant period (TCA 1997, s 494(7)). 'Green energy activities' means activities undertaken with a view to producing energy from renewable sources (TCA 1997, s 488(1)).

Disqualification for qualifying nursing homes

A company whose relevant trading activities includes operating a qualifying nursing home and is engaged in enlarging its capacity shall cease to be a qualifying company unless it has expended all of the money subscribed for eligible shares on such activities, within a period ending 30 days before the end of the relevant period (TCA 1997, s 494(7A)). A qualifying nursing home is explained in TCA 1997, s 488(1) as meaning:

(a) a nursing home within the meaning of section 2 of the Health (Nursing Homes) Act 1990 and which is registered under section 4 of that Act, and

(b) where applicable, a qualifying residential unit constructed on the site of, and operated by, a nursing home within the meaning of paragraph (a), but does not include any nursing home or qualifying residential unit which is subject to any power on the exercise of which the nursing home or residential units, or any part or interest in the nursing home or residential units, may be revested in the person from whom it was purchased or exchanged or in any person on behalf of such person.

Reference is made above to a 'qualifying residential unit' which is also defined in TCA 1997, s 488(1) as meaning a house which—

(a) is constructed on the site of, or on a site which is immediately adjacent to the site of, a registered nursing home,

(b) is—

(i) a single storey house, or

(ii) a house that is comprised in a building of one or more storeys in relation to which building a fire safety certificate under Part III of the Building Control Regulations 1997 (SI No 496 of 1997) is required, and prior to the commencement of the construction works on the building, is granted by the building control authority (within the meaning of section 2 of the Building Control Act 1990) in whose functional area the building is situated where—

(I) the house is, or (as the case may be) the house and the building in which it is comprised are, designed and constructed to meet the needs of persons with disabilities, including in particular the needs of persons who are confined to wheelchairs, and

(II) the house consists of one or two bedrooms, a kitchen, a living room, bath or shower facilities, toilet facilities and a nurse call system linked to the registered nursing home,

and

(c) is comprised in a development where—

(i) those units are operated or managed by the registered nursing home and an on-site caretaker is provided, and

(ii) back-up medical care, including nursing care, is provided by the registered nursing home to the occupants of those units when required by those occupants.

Disqualification for companies funding R & D expenditure

Where a company raised funds through the scheme at a time when it had not commenced to trade, and such funds were used to fund expenditure on research and development, that company will cease to be a qualifying company unless it has within a period ending one month before the end of the relevant period: (a)(i) expended all the funds raised on research and development, and (a)(ii) disposed of a specified intangible asset within TCA 1997, s 291A which has arisen as a result of such research and development, to another person for the purposes of that other person's trade, or (b) within two years of the date on which the eligible shares were issued has commenced to carry on relevant trading activities and has expended all the funds raised on those relevant trading activities or on research and development before the end of the relevant period (TCA 1997, s 494(8)).

There may be some inconsistencies in the EII legislation as regards R&D companies because R&D is no longer deemed to be a trading activity unlike the BES regime. If we take the example of an R&D company which undertakes research with a view to developing a product but after 12 months the project collapses.

TCA 1997, s 489(4) provides that relief shall be given on a claim and shall not be allowed in the case of a company which has not commenced to carry on relevant trading activities at the time the shares are issued unless the company commences to carry on trading within two years or spends not less than 30 per cent of the money subscribed for shares on R&D activities connected with and undertaken with a view to carrying on of the relevant trading activities

TCA 1997, s 501(1)(ii) provides that a claim for relief for the 30/40ths (30/41 for years prior to 2015) deduction shall be made no earlier than the time of disposal, in the case of a company which has not commenced trading when the shares were issued and does not begin to carry on relevant trading activities, or otherwise four months after trading has commenced.

There seems to be an inconsistency between TCA 1997, ss 489(4) and 501(1)(ii) as set out above in that the former clearly envisages a claim being allowed when 30 per cent of R&D funds are spent but the latter states there cannot be a claim until there is a disposal of shares if there is no commencement of trading.

TCA 1997, s 489(8) provides that a company which has not commenced to trade and raises money for R&D ceases to be a qualifying company unless it spends all of its money on R&D within one month before the end of the relevant period and disposes of a 'specified intangible asset' which is connected with and arises from those R&D activities to another person for the purpose of a trade carried on by the other person or commences to trade within two years and has spent all of the money on those activities on R&D before the end of the relevant period. However, what is the relevant period for an R&D company which has not commenced to trade? Relevant period is defined in TCA 1997, s 488 as commencing when the shares are issued and ending three years after the company commences to trade? If the R&D company does not commence to trade the relevant period never ends. Under the BES legislation R&D activities were deemed to be a trade so this type of issue did not arise.

18.104 The relevant trading activities

Under the old BES legislation there was a restricted definition of what constituted a qualifying trade. If a trade was not included in the definition relief was not available. In contrast the EII relief is written on the basis that all Case I trades qualify unless it is specifically excluded from the relief.

The legislation provides that the money raised by the issue of the ordinary shares of the qualifying company must be applied for the purposes of relevant trading activities or of related research and development carried on either by the company issuing the shares or by a subsidiary company which meets certain further qualification tests (see **18.105**). The trades which are excluded from the definition of relevant trading activities are specified as follows:

(a) adventures or concerns in the nature of trade;

(b) dealing in commodities or futures or in shares, securities or other financial assets;

(c) financing activities;

(d) the provision of services, which would result in a close company (within the meaning of TCA 1997, s 430) which provides those services being treated as a service company if that close company had no other sources of income

(e) dealing in or developing land;

(f) the occupation of woodlands within the meaning of TCA 1997, s 232;

(g) operating or managing hotels, guest houses, self-catering accommodation or comparable establishments or managing property used as an hotel, guest house, self-catering accommodation or comparable establishment except where (from 1 January 2013) the operation or management of such a premises is a tourist traffic undertaking;

(h) Prior to 2015 operating or managing nursing homes or residential care homes or managing property used as a nursing home or residential care home. The deletion of paragraph (h) from the list of excluded relevant trading activities from 2015 was included in Finance Act 2014 but its introduction is subject to a Ministerial Order;

(i) operations carried on in the coal industry or in the steel and shipbuilding sectors;

(j) the production of a film (within the meaning of TCA 1997, s 481);

but including tourist traffic undertakings (TCA 1997, s 488(1)).

A 'tourist traffic undertaking' comprises:

(a) with effect from 1 January 2013 the operation of tourist accommodation facilities for which Fáilte maintains a register in accordance with the Tourist Traffic Acts 1939 to 2003;

(b) the operation of such other classes of facilities as may be approved of for the purposes of the relief by the Minister for Finance in consultation with the Minister for Tourism, Culture and Sport on the recommendation of Fáilte Ireland in accordance with specific codes of standards laid down by it; or

(c) the promotion outside the State of any one of the foregoing facilities, including such hotels, guest houses and self-catering accommodation so registered.

For the purposes of exclusion (c), 'financial activities' means the provision of, and all matters relating to, the provision of, financing or refinancing facilities by any means which involves, or has the effect equivalent to the extension of credit; 'financing or refinancing facilities' includes:

(a) loans, mortgages, leasing, lease rental, and hire-purchase, and all similar arrangements;
(b) equity or other investment;
(c) the factoring of debts and the discounting of bills, invoices and promissory notes, and all similar instruments; and
(d) the underwriting of debt instruments and all other kinds of financial securities.

'Financial assets' includes shares, gilts, bonds, foreign currencies and all kinds of futures, options and currency and interest rate swaps, and similar instruments, including commodity futures and commodity options, invoices and all types of receivables, obligations evidencing debt (including loans and deposits), leases and loan and lease portfolios, bills of exchange, acceptance credits and all other documents of title relating to the movement of goods, commercial paper, promissory notes and all other kinds of negotiable or transferable instruments (TCA 1997, s 488(1)).

Commencement of relevant trading activities

For the EII relief to be given in respect of the issue of any eligible shares, the relevant trading activities must be carried on by the qualifying company (or by its qualifying subsidiary) at the time those shares are issued or, if not carried on at that time, it must commence within:

(a) in the case where the qualifying company (or a qualifying subsidiary) had already commenced relevant trading activities at the date on which the eligible shares were issued, unless and until the company has carried on those activities for four months; or
(b) in the case where the qualifying company (or a qualifying subsidiary) had not already commenced relevant trading activities at the date on which the eligible shares were issued, unless the company begins to carry on relevant trading activities within the following two years or expends not less than 30 per cent of the money subscribed for shares on research and development activities which are connected with and undertaken with a view to the carrying on of the relevant trading activities (TCA 1997, s 489(4)).

The four month qualifying period in (a) will be reduced to the period during which the company carried on relevant trading activities if this ended by reason of the winding up or dissolution of the company for *bona fide* commercial reasons where this was not part of a scheme or arrangement which had, as one of its main purposes, the avoidance of tax (TCA 1997, s 489(7)).

A company carrying on green energy activities will be deemed to have commenced relevant trading activities when it has made an application for a grid connection agreement. (TCA 1997, s 489(11)). A 'grid connection agreement' means an agreement with the transmission system operator (as defined by the Electricity Regulation Act 1999) or distribution system operator, or an offer from the transmission system operator or distribution system operator to enter into an agreement for connection to, or use of, the transmission or distribution system. (TCA 1997, s 488(1)). 'Green energy activities' means activities undertaken with a view to producing energy from renewable sources; 'energy from renewable sources' means energy from renewable non-fossil sources, that is to say wind, solar, aerothermal, geothermal, hydrothermal and ocean energy, hydropower, biomass, landfill gas, sewage treatment plant gas and biogases and includes the development of any facilities for the storage of energy from renewable sources (TCA 1997, s 488(1)).

18.105 Qualifying subsidiary companies

TCA 1997, s 505 permits a qualifying company to have one or more subsidiary companies without prejudicing its status as a qualifying company, but only if each subsidiary meets certain conditions specified in TCA 1997, s 505 regarding its status and purpose and regarding the nature of the control held by the qualifying company. Any subsidiary company satisfying all these conditions is a 'qualifying subsidiary company' for the purposes of the EII legislation.

TCA 1997, s 505 defines a qualifying subsidiary company as a subsidiary company which, throughout the whole of the *four*-year relevant period, either:

(a) is a company which itself exists wholly for the purposes of carrying on relevant trading activities from a fixed place of business in the State; or
(b) is a company existing *solely* for the purpose of carrying on any trade consisting *solely* of any one or more of the following trading operations:
    (i) the purchase of goods or materials for use by the qualifying company or its subsidiaries,
    (ii) the sale of goods or materials produced by the qualifying company or its subsidiaries, or
    (iii) the rendering of services to or on behalf of the qualifying company or its subsidiaries.

In order to be a qualifying subsidiary by meeting the first of these two tests (ie test (a) above), the subsidiary must exist wholly for the purpose of carrying on relevant trading activities (as defined in **18.104**) and carry on at least part of those activities from a fixed base in the State. It is also necessary that the subsidiary be, and remain throughout the relevant period, an unquoted company resident in the State or resident in another EEA country and carry on business through a branch or agency in the State. For a subsidiary to qualify under test (b) it does not have to be a resident company. However, the condition that the trade of the subsidiary must be confined solely to the types of operation specified in subparagraphs (i) to (iii) of test (b) must be strictly adhered to.

TCA 1997, s 505 requires *all* of the following three conditions to be met throughout the whole of the relevant period by each subsidiary if it is to be a qualifying subsidiary:

(a) the subsidiary must be a 51 per cent subsidiary (see **18.103**) of the qualifying company;
(b) no other person must have control of the subsidiary within the meaning of TCA 1997, s 11 (unlikely when condition (a) is met, but theoretically possible); and
(c) no arrangements must exist by virtue of which conditions (a) and (b) could cease to be satisfied.

TCA 1997, s 505(3) provides that a *bona fide* winding up or dissolution without winding up of either a qualifying subsidiary or the qualifying company is not to cause the withdrawal of the relief due to the subsidiary's ceasing to meet the above conditions as to status and control. For this rule to apply, the winding up or dissolution must be shown to be for *bona fide* commercial reasons and not part of a scheme or arrangement that has as any of its main purposes the avoidance of tax (see the discussion at **18.111**). Further, the net assets of the company being wound up or dissolved must be distributed to its members before the end of the *four*-year relevant period or, in the case of a winding up, before the end (if later) of three years from the commencement of the winding up. In the absence of this rule, a winding up (or dissolution without winding up) within the relevant period would cause the EII relief to be withdrawn.

18.106 Granting and limiting of relief

In principle, TCA 1997, s 489(2) gives the relief to the qualifying individual by allowing the amount subscribed for the eligible shares as a deduction from his total income (ie in arriving at his taxable income) in two tranches, equal to 30/40ths and 10/40ths of the total amount invested respectively (prior to 2015 it was 30/41sts and 11/41sts), for the tax year in which the shares are issued and for the tax year following the date on which the relevant period ends. The relevant period for the purposes of granting relief for the second tranche is three years from the date the shares were issued provided the company was carrying on relevant trading activities on that date. If not, the relevant period is three years from the date the company subsequently began to carry on relevant trading operations.

Example 18.106.1

Mr A subscribes €50,000 for eligible shares in a qualifying company in 2015. The company meets all the conditions of the relief. Mr A will be entitled to the following deductions from his taxable income

2015	€50,000 X 30/40 =	€37,500
2018	€50,000 X 10/40=	€12,500

The relief is available at Mr A's marginal rate of income tax in each year. An investor subscribing for eligible shares must have sufficient income in both 2015 and 2018 to obtain maximum deductions.

In *National Westminster Bank plc v IRC* [1994] STC 580, the House of Lords held by a 3–2 majority that shares were not issued until they had been finally registered, following application and allotment. In a powerful dissenting speech, Lord Jauncey (Lord Woolf concurring) observed:

> The purpose of the [EII] is relatively simple, namely, to encourage smaller business to commence or expand by raising capital from investors who, but for the inducement of tax relief, would be unlikely to put money into such concerns. What is therefore important for the purposes of the scheme is that the investor should have irrevocably paid over the money to the company in question and should have acquired the rights and assumed the liabilities of a shareholder. When the company has raised the money and the investor is fully committed, expansion can take place and the purpose of the scheme has been achieved.

There is a Revenue Precedent in relation to the BES to the effect that the decision in *National Westminster Bank* would be followed by the Revenue.

The second tranche of relief will not be available under TCA 1997, s 489(2)(b) unless in relation to a qualifying company either: '(a)(i) the employment relevant number exceeds the employment threshold number by at least one qualifying employee, and (ii) the relevant amount exceeds the threshold amount by at least the total emoluments of one qualifying employee in the year of assessment in which the relevant period ends, or (b) the amount of expenditure on research and development incurred by the qualifying company in the specified relevant period (as defined by TCA 1997, s 766) ending in the year of assessment preceding the year of assessment in which, in relation to the subscription for eligible shares, a relevant period ends, exceeds the amount of expenditure on research and development incurred by the qualifying company in the specified relevant period ending in the year of assessment preceding the year of assessment in which the subscription for eligible shares was made.

'*Employment relevant number*' means the total number of *qualifying employees* in receipt of emoluments (within the meaning of TCA 1997, s 983), from the qualifying company in the year of assessment in which, in relation to a subscription for eligible shares, a relevant period ends. '*Employment threshold number*' means the total number of *qualifying employees* in receipt of emoluments from the qualifying company in the year of assessment preceding the year of assessment in which the subscription for eligible shares was made.

The 'relevant amount' means total emoluments (other than non-pecuniary emoluments) paid by a qualifying company to qualifying employees as referred to in the definition of 'employment relevant number', in the year of assessment in which, in relation to a subscription for eligible shares, a relevant period ends.

The 'threshold amount' means the total of the emoluments (other than non-pecuniary emoluments) paid by a qualifying company to the qualifying employees referred to in the definition of 'employment threshold number', in the year of assessment preceding the year of assessment in which the subscription for eligible shares was made but where there was a general reduction in the basic pay rate of qualifying employees then the threshold amount shall be reduced accordingly.

'*Basic pay rate'* in relation to a qualifying employee of a qualifying company, means the employee's emoluments (other than non-pecuniary emoluments) per hour from the company in respect of an employment held with the company.

A 'qualifying employee', in relation to a qualifying company, means an employee (within the meaning of TCA 1997, s 983), other than a director, of that company—(i) who throughout his or her period of employment with that company is employed by that company for at least 30 hours duration per week, and (ii) his or her employment is capable of lasting at least 12 months.

Example 18.106.2

Company ABC issues eligible shares in March 2016 and undertakes relevant trading activities for the three-year relevant period. Qualifying investors claimed relief and received refunds in respect of 30/40ths of their investments. They now wish to establish whether they are entitled to a further 10/40ths of relief. The following information is relevant:

Employee Numbers	*2016*	*2019*
Full time Directors	2	2
Full time employees	10	11
<30 hours per week employees	0	18
Salaries	*2016*	*2019*
Full Time Directors	€100,000	€150,000
Full Time Employees	€350,000	€450,000
<30 hours per week employees	0	€400,000

The appropriate tests follow:

Employment Relevant Number:	11
Employment Threshold Number:	10

Relevant Amount:	€450,000
Threshold amount:	€350,000
	Excess €100,000

As noted earlier there are two elements to the first test that must apply before the second tranche of relief will be available. In the above example the employment relevant number exceeds the employment threshold number by at least one qualifying employee and the relevant amount exceeds the threshold amount but the question to be asked is whether the latter excess is at least the total emoluments of one qualifying employee. This question would appear to require a factual as opposed to an average result. If we assume in the above example that the one qualifying employee is paid €50,000 then this test is also met such that the second tranche of relief should be available.

The total amount in relation to which relief may be granted to by any individual is limited to €150,000 in relation to shares issued in any given tax year, or €100,000 in the case of the SCS (but a husband and wife are entitled to separate limits of up to €150,000 or €100,000 each for their separate subscriptions) (TCA 1997, s 490(2)).

However, for any subscription for eligible shares through a designated investment fund within TCA 1997, s 506, the individual may elect to claim the relief by reference to the year in which he makes the subscription to the fund, provided that the eligible shares are issued to the fund no later than the end of the next tax year. Any such election must be made by notice in writing to the inspector (TCA 1997, s 489(3)). If no such election is made, the normal rule applies. TCA 1997, s 489(3A) notes that where an investment through a fund in accordance with TCA 1997, s 506 was made in the period from 1 January 2014 to 31 December 2014 and the fund invests in shares in the month of January 2016, then, notwithstanding sub-s (3), the individual may elect by notice in writing for relief to be available either in the 2014 or 2016 year of assessment.

The amount of the relief granted under the EII (referred to herein as 'the amount of the relief') is normally by reference to the appropriate fraction (either 30/40 or 10/40 as the case may be) of the total of the amounts subscribed by the individual for all eligible shares issued to him in the relevant tax year, but the amount of the relief given in any year cannot exceed the limit imposed by TCA 1997, s 490 (see below). The relief may be claimed, subject to that limit, for subscriptions for eligible shares in any one or more qualifying companies.

Relief is given by way of a personal relief (TCA 1997, s 458); accordingly a non-resident individual may be entitled only to restricted relief or to no relief at all: see **13.610**.

Further, TCA 1997, s 459(1) applies, where relevant, to limit the deduction so that the amount of the relief in any tax year does not offset any charges on income retained in the individual's income tax assessment, ie so that he still has to pay over the income tax deducted at source on any annual payments made to other persons. TCA 1997, s 459(2) also applies so that the relief may be given either by discharge or reduction of any assessment, or by repayment of any excess income tax previously paid.

Individual's limits to relief:

TCA 1997, s 490 limits the amount of the relief under the EII which any one individual may claim for any tax year to a maximum deduction calculated as the appropriate fraction (either 30/40 or 10/40) of €150,000 or €100,000 in the case of the SCS.

The amount of the deduction for any tax year is also limited to the individual's total income for that year. The amount of the relief for any year is, therefore, the lowest of the following amounts:

(a) the appropriate fraction of the total amount subscribed for eligible shares issued in a given tax year (subject to the election to include the amount subscribed in the year to designated investment funds for shares issued before the end of the following year);
(b) the individual's total income for that year; or
(c) the appropriate fraction of €150,000.

For the rules which permit the carry forward of unused relief to be treated as a subscription for eligible shares available for relief in a later year, see below.

Each spouse/civil partner is only entitled to a deduction by reference to the amount of his qualifying subscriptions from his total income of the relevant tax year. Even in the case of a joint assessment under TCA 1997, s 1017, ie where the husband/civil partner is charged to tax on both his own and his wife's/civil partner's total income, TCA 1997, s 489(2), 493(2) quite specifically allows the deduction to each spouse/civil partner as 'an individual' from 'his' total income. There is no rule to enable one spouse's/civil partner's excess deduction over his total income to be set off against the other spouse's/civil partner's total income.

The first (30/40) tranche is not a specified relief in respect of a subscription for eligible shares in the period 16 October 2013 to 31 December 2016 and is not subject to the restrictions applicable to high income individuals discussed at **3.111**. FA 2016, s 20 permanently removed para no 47A from TCA 1997, Sch 25B such that the 30/40 tranche is not subject to the high income restriction discussed above.

Minimum subscription

TCA 1997, s 490 provides that no EII relief is to be given in respect of an individual's subscription for eligible shares in a particular company unless the total amount subscribed by him in the year of claim for those shares in that company is €250. This minimum subscription limit applies separately to each qualifying company in which he may subscribe for shares in any one tax year. For example, if during 2015 an individual subscribes €199 for eligible shares separately in each of three qualifying companies, then although his total investment in the year is €597, he is not entitled to any relief under TCA 1997, s 489(3), (6) for any of these subscriptions. Two separate investments of €298 and €299 in two of the companies would, however, allow him relief for the full €597 invested.

In applying this minimum subscription rule in the case of a husband and wife assessed jointly under TCA 1997, s 1017 for the tax year in question, the amount subscribed by the wife for eligible shares in any company is deemed to have been subscribed by the husband. This permits the relief to be given in respect of both the husband's and the wife's subscription if, when aggregated, the subscriptions of both spouses in the company concerned is €250 or more. This does not alter the general rule that the wife's subscription can only be deducted from her total income and the husband's subscription from his total income. The same rule applies to civil partners.

This minimum subscription rule does not apply to deny an individual the relief in respect of a subscription for eligible shares in any qualifying company when made by the managers of a designated investment fund as nominees of the individual (see **18.110**).

Carry forward of relief

TCA 1997, s 490(3) contains rules permitting the carry forward of any part of the total amount subscribed for eligible shares which cannot be deducted in the tax year to which it relates because it exceeds the lower of the individual's total income or the appropriate fraction of €150,000 (the 'unused relief'). These rules enable the unused relief for any tax year to be carried forward so as to be eligible for relief in the next tax year. If not fully used in that year, the unrelieved balance is carried forward to the year after that, and so on, except that no deduction is given for any tax year later than the year of assessment 2020.

The unused relief for any tax year (eg 2014), whether claimed for a direct subscription or for one made to a designated investment fund, is carried forward and treated as if it were a direct subscription for eligible shares issued in the immediately following year (2015). It is then allowed as a deduction for that year in priority to the amount of the relief for any qualifying subscriptions otherwise deductible in that year (2015).

Company's limit

TCA 1997, s 491 provides limits on the amount raised by a company which can qualify for relief under the EII and/or the SCS.

TCA 1997, s 491(2) applies a formula, 'A – B' to be used in respect of an issue of eligible shares. 'A' and 'B' in the formula have the following meanings:

A is: €15,000,000 (Finance Act 2014 increased the limit from €10,000,000 to €15,000,000 from 2015 subject to its commencement by a Ministerial Order); and

B is the lesser of:

(a) the amount of 'A'; and

(b) the aggregate amount of all previous issues of eligible shares since 6 April 1984.

This is subject to the restriction that no more than €5,000,000 (again the annual limit was increased from €2,500,000 from 2015 by Finance Act 2014 subject to its commencement by a Ministerial Order) may be raised by a single issue or in aggregate within any period of 12 months (TCA 1997, s 491(4)).

Associated companies

In any case where a company wishes to raise funds by the issue of eligible shares and that company is associated with one or more other companies, 'B' in the formula 'A–B' in TCA 1997, s 491(2)(a) is amended by TCA 1997, s 491(3)(a) to take account of any amounts raised by the issue of eligible shares by the company planning the current issue and any of its associates. 'A' in the formula is as previously explained. 'B' is the lesser of:

(a) the amount of 'A'; and

(b) the aggregate amounts of all previous issues of eligible shares made by the Company *or by any of its associated companies*.

TCA 1997, s 491(5) ensures that, in determining by how much the revised limits to the amounts which a company may raise by the issue of eligible shares should be reduced by reference to previous issues of eligible shares, no account should be taken of any shares previously issued where the person receiving the shares did not qualify for EII/Seed

Capital relief or where some of the amount subscribed by a qualifying person did not qualify for relief because it exceeded (or fell below) the amount stipulated under TCA 1997, s 490 which may qualify for relief in any one year.

A company is regarded as associated with another company where it could reasonably be considered that that company *or* any of its qualifying subsidiaries, and the other company *or any of its* qualifying subsidiaries meet one of the following criteria:

(a) both companies act in pursuit of a common purpose;
(b) any person or any group(s) of persons having a reasonable commonality of identity have or have had the means or power, either directly or indirectly, to determine the trading operations to be carried on by both companies; and
(c) both companies are under the control of any person or any group(s) of persons having a reasonable commonality of identity.

Thus, if a qualifying subsidiary of A Ltd pursues a common purpose with B Ltd (or with a qualifying subsidiary of B Ltd) A Ltd and B Ltd will be associated for these purposes.

A 'qualifying subsidiary' is defined as for the general purposes of the EII (see **18.105**), but also includes a company which was at any time a qualifying subsidiary of another company.

A company will, however, not be considered to be associated with another company *only* by reason of the fact that a subscription for eligible shares in both companies is made by a person or persons having the management of an investment fund designated under TCA 1997, s 506 (see **18.110**) as nominee for any person, group of persons or groups of persons. 'Control' (as is generally the case in relation to the provisions of the scheme) is as defined by TCA 1997, s 432.

Again, only issues of eligible shares for which relief was obtained by an individual under the scheme are included in 'B'. Where necessary, relief is allocated between individuals.

It may be noted that these wide-ranging rules apply to all issues of eligible shares, even those made before these rules came into force. However, it seems clear from the wording of TCA 1997, s 491 that a company must be associated with the issuing company at the time the relevant issue is made, if the amounts raised through issues of eligible shares by the former company under the scheme are to be taken into account.

Thus, for example, if the companies in question had previously acted 'in pursuit of a common purpose' but no longer do so at the time of the relevant issue, they should not be associated for these purposes. Similarly, if the companies in question are not under common control (as defined) at the time of the relevant issue they should not be associated. However, if any person or group(s) of persons with a reasonable commonality of identity have *previously* had the power to determine the trading operations (to be) carried on by both companies, those companies will be associated.

In a case heard by the Appeal Commissioners (15 AC 2000), two companies had been formed by the same promoters to operate hostels located in adjoining premises. The shares in each company were issued to different sets of shareholders and there were no agreements in place between those shareholders. Initially, the trading operations of the two companies were little differentiated but thereafter the companies were operated as separate identities. All the shareholders claimed relief under the corresponding provisions of the BES scheme. The Appeal Commissioners held that the companies were not acting in pursuit of a common purpose (which seems an inevitable conclusion on the facts as stated) but that they were under the control of persons having a reasonable commonality of identity. The latter finding seems odd; it would seem

However, that the promoters had had the power to determine the trading operations of both companies so that criterion (b) above would have been met.

There are also some Revenue Precedents in connection with the corresponding BES provisions; these infer that the Revenue take the view that *any* shared purpose will suffice to activate criterion (a), and that it is not necessary that the companies should share a main or overriding purpose in relation to the totality of their activities.

Disposal of shares/clawback

TCA 1997, s 496(4) provides that where an individual holds shares of the same class and EII relief has been claimed on some of the shares then any disposal is treated as first coming out of the shares that EII relief was claimed. However, this does not apply where there is a clawback of relief under an Approved Profit Sharing Scheme TCA 1997, s 512(2). There shall be no clawback of EII or SCS relief on the basis that the shares disposed of under the Approved Profit Sharing Scheme will not be treated as eligible shares issued under the EII or SCS. Of course, the remaining shares will then still include the EII or SCS shares, so unless they are held for the prescribed relevant period, there is still the risk of clawback of the EII or SCS relief if any further shares are sold.

18.107 Procedure for claiming relief

Every individual claiming the relief in respect of eligible shares in any company must submit, with his claim, a certificate issued by the company in question certifying that the conditions for the relief, so far as they apply to the company and the trade, are satisfied TCA 1997, s 501(3). No claim for relief can be allowed to any individual unless he furnishes this 'certificate of compliance' with his claim. If the individual has subscribed for eligible shares in more than one qualifying company, he must furnish a separate certificate of compliance from each company.

Before any qualifying company may issue certificates of compliance to the various individuals who have subscribed for its eligible shares, the company must obtain the approval of the inspector of taxes to the issue of the certificates (TCA 1997, s 501(3)). In order to obtain the inspector's approval, the company must give a statement in prescribed form to the inspector which contains all the information which the Revenue Commissioners may reasonably require and must include a declaration that it is correct to the best of the company's knowledge and belief (TCA 1997, s 501(5)). If a company either makes this statement to the inspector or issues any certificate of compliance to any individual fraudulently or negligently, the company is liable to a penalty of up to €4,000. A penalty may also be imposed if the company issues any certificate of compliance without the approval of the inspector.

TCA 1997, s 501(1)(a) prescribes the earliest dates on which a claim may be made for the relief:

(a) In respect of the first tranche (30/40) of relief in the case of an investment under the EII, if a company has not commenced relevant trading activities at the time the eligible shares were issued and does not begin to carry on relevant trading activities, the time of the disposal and in any other case the end of the period of four months, following the commencement of trading. In respect of the second tranche (10/40) the date is the end of the relevant period.

(b) In the case of an investment under the SCS the date on which the company commences to carry on relevant trading activities or the company has expended not less than 30 per cent of the relevant investment on research and development activities which are connected with and undertaken with a view to the carrying on of relevant trading activities.

TCA 1997, s 501(1)(b) prescribes the latest dates on which a claim may be made for the relief:

(a) two years after the end of the year of assessment in which the shares were issued, or if the company had not been carrying on relevant trading activities for at least four months when the shares were issued and the four-month period ended after the year of assessment, two years after the end of the four-month period, TCA 1997, s 489(4)(a); or

(b) three months after the date that the statement, in the required format, is furnished to the Revenue Commissioners, by the qualifying company or its agent, where such statement is furnished within the three months prior to the expiry of the time specified in (a).

An individual claiming relief in respect of eligible shares issued by any qualifying company to the managers of a designated investment fund must also make his own claim, but this should be accompanied by the certificate from the managers of the fund referred to in **18.110**.

An individual who has claimed EII relief is, if he is taxable under PAYE in respect of Sch E emoluments, entitled to have his certificate of tax credits for the relevant year increased to include the amount of the deduction to which he is entitled for the year. However, the relief can only be taken into account after the claim has been admitted by the inspector under the procedure explained above (TCA 1997, s 501(7)).

TCA 1997, s 1080 charges the individual with interest if his income tax liability (or any preliminary tax) is not paid when it is due and payable. There are also rules relating to the payment of interest on overdue tax after an amended assessment has been raised or an appeal has been determined.

For the purposes of these interest rules of TCA 1997, s 1080, the claim for EII relief under TCA 1997, s 489(3), (6) is, in effect, treated as a payment on account of income tax made on the date on which the claim is actually made (TCA 1997, s 501(8)). This only applies if the individual's income tax liability for the year of claim is already due and payable, and if that income tax has not already been paid. It also assumes that the claim for relief is in due course accepted by the inspector. If no claim has yet been made, or if the first four months of trading by the qualifying company have not yet been completed, any income tax due and payable on a given date remains subject to the normal interest rules if not paid on time, notwithstanding that a valid claim for relief may be made at a later date. Once the claim has been made, the interest ceases to run.

When determining if an adequate amount of preliminary tax has been paid by reference to the liabilities of the preceding or pre-preceding tax years as appropriate, those liabilities must be recomputed if necessary in order to disregard any relief obtained under the scheme (see **2.104**).

18.108 Withdrawal of relief

TCA 1997, s 489(6) requires any EII relief that has been allowed to any individual to be withdrawn if by reason of any subsequent event, whether affecting the individual or any relevant company, it is found that he is not entitled to the relief. In any such case, TCA 1997, s 502(1) provides for the withdrawal of the relief by way of an assessment under Sch D Case IV to be made for the tax year for which the relief was given. This means that the individual's liability for the original year of claim has to be recomputed and any additional tax found to be due (having regard to his tax rates, etc for the year of claim) paid to the Collector General. Although the assessment is made under Case IV, because it is not an assessment on income as such, in the author's opinion no relief for any Case IV losses arising in the relevant tax year will be available for set off against such an assessment.

Effect of death

There is no provision deeming death to give rise to a disposal. TCA 1997, s 502(4) prevents the making of any assessment to withdraw relief previously granted to any individual where the disqualifying event occurs after the death of the individual in question. If, for example, all the conditions for relief were met by both the individual and the qualifying company up to the date of the individual's death, a post-death event causing the company to cease to be a qualifying company within the relevant period cannot result in any assessment under Sch D Case IV, whether on the personal representatives or the individual's heirs. However, if the disqualifying event occurs during the individual's lifetime, any assessment required to withdraw relief given to him may, if necessary, be made on his personal representatives.

In the ordinary case, the tax chargeable by any amended assessment becomes due and payable 30 days after the date of the assessment. TCA 1997, s 502(7) varies this normal rule, for the purposes of the interest on unpaid tax under TCA 1997, s 1080, where the assessment is one under TCA 1997, s 502 to withdraw EII relief previously given. It specifies a different 'due and payable' dates for the tax charged by the TCA 1997, s 502 assessment, depending on the nature of the event causing the withdrawal of the relief.

Interest where relief withdrawn

In general, the additional tax charged by the Sch D Case IV assessment withdrawing the relief is deemed to be due and payable on the date of the particular disqualifying event which results in the individual losing his entitlement to the relief. In effect, this means that the tax becomes due and payable and, in consequence, interest becomes chargeable at the rate for the time being applicable under TCA 1997, s 1080 immediately the event occurs, even if the inspector of taxes does not get round to making his assessment until some time later.

For example, if the relief has to be withdrawn due to an event occurring within the appropriate relevant period, whether affecting the individual or the qualifying company, the due date of the additional tax payable as a result of the TCA 1997, s 502 assessment is the date on which that disqualifying event occurs. Similarly, if relief has to be withdrawn, whether wholly or in part due to the individual's disposing of some or all of the eligible shares in respect of which the relief was previously granted, the due date of the additional tax payable is the date on which the shares were sold (or otherwise disposed of).

In short, although the individual may have had the benefit of the reduced income tax liability between the date on which his claim for relief was granted and the date of the subsequent disqualifying event, he is not liable to pay interest on the tax 'recaptured' in respect of the period between these two dates. There is, however, one exception to this rule.

This exception applies if the relief is withdrawn as the result of the rule in TCA 1997, s 500 ('prevention of misuse' – see **18.111**). In this event, the due date of the tax is normally the date on which the relief was actually granted, so that the interest on the tax now reassessed is charged with retrospective effect from that date to the date of payment. For this purpose, it is assumed that the relief was granted on the date of the repayment (if any) of tax that gave effect to the relief, or if there was no such repayment, the due date is assumed to be the date on which the inspector notified the claimant of the amount of the tax payable after giving effect to the relief now withdrawn (TCA 1997, s 502).

Assessment to withdraw relief

Any assessment made under TCA 1997, s 502 for withdrawing the relief as the result of an event occurring after the date of any claim must, normally, be made within four years of the end of the tax year in which the disqualifying event occurred; (TCA 1997, s 502(3)). However, if any form of fraud or neglect by any person was involved in connection with the matter, the assessment withdrawing relief may be made at any time without time limit under TCA 1997, s 924 (see **2.111**).

If the relief previously granted was allowed in an assessment on a married couple taxed jointly under TCA 1997, s 1017, any assessment made subsequently by reason of an event causing the withdrawal of the relief is normally made also on the assessable spouse. However, in the case of the withdrawal of relief as the result of a disposal of the shares, if that spouse is no longer assessable under TCA 1997, s 1017 in respect of the joint incomes of the spouses, the assessment under TCA 1997, s 502 is made on the person making the disposal. In this case, the person on whom the assessment is made has to pay the full amount of the tax 'recaptured', even if the relief originally granted had been apportioned between husband and wife in a claim for separate assessment under TCA 1997, s 1023 (see **3.504**) (TCA 1997, s 502(2)(a); TCA 1997, s 1018). Similar provisions apply in the case of a civil partnership (TCA 1997, s 502(2)(b)).

It is to be noted that this last rule (contained in TCA 1997, s 502(2)) only applies where the disqualifying event is a disposal of the eligible shares by the individual (whether spouse or civil partner) who subscribed for them. If the assessment under TCA 1997, s 502 is being made as the result of any other disqualifying event (eg the qualifying company's ceasing to carry on its relevant trading activities within the relevant period), the assessment must be made on the spouse or partner who was jointly assessable for the year of claim in respect of his own and his spouse's income. The fact that the spouses or partners may no longer be jointly assessable at the time this event occurs does not affect the matter.

In any case where the relief originally granted has to be withdrawn in full, the amount of tax recaptured should always be equal to the tax saved as a result of the claim previously granted, whether a joint assessment or a single person assessment is involved. If relief is only partially withdrawn (eg due to a sale of eligible shares at less than cost – see **18.109**), the additional tax becoming due is computed at the rate(s) of tax that result from adding on the income recaptured to that taxed originally (after the relief). In any case where the relief was originally granted to either spouse or civil partner in a single person assessment, any withdrawal of relief under TCA 1997, s 502 is always made as an additional assessment on the spouse who originally obtained the relief.

If relief is withdrawn due to a disposal of eligible shares in an arm's length bargain, the amount of the deduction disallowed is limited to the consideration receivable for the disposal (see **18.109**). If this consideration is less than the amount of the relief in respect of the shares, there will be a balance of the EII deduction unaffected by the disposal. TCA 1997, s 502(5) provides that, if an individual has disposed of *all* his ordinary shares in the qualifying company, no further assessment to withdraw this balance of the relief is to be made as a result of any subsequent disqualifying event unless it occurs at a time when he is connected with the qualifying company. However, if the individual becomes connected with the sponsoring company within the relevant period, the balance of the relief is then withdrawn.

Options etc for disposals at other than market value

TCA 1997, s 496(3) applies to deny relief for subscriptions for eligible shares where the individual enters into any option or similar agreement the effect of which is to enable him to dispose of those shares at a price other than the market value of the shares at the time of the disposal. This subsection applies if the agreement in question is entered into at any time in the relevant period.

The intention of the subsection is to prevent the type of EII which would otherwise enable the subscribing individuals to be 'taken out' of the scheme after the end of the specified period at a price which would guarantee them against a loss.

TCA 1997, s 496(3) provides that no EII relief is to be given to an individual for a subscription for any eligible shares where at any time during the specified period that individual directly or indirectly enters into any type of option or agreement mentioned in the subsection.

The types of option or agreement mentioned in TCA 1997, s 496(3) are, in *relation* to any specific eligible shares, any of the following:

(a) an option acquired by the individual where the exercise of the option would bind the person from whom the option is acquired (or any other person), or would cause that person (or any other person) to purchase, or otherwise acquire, the eligible shares at a price other than their market value;

(b) an agreement entered into by the individual which binds the other party (or any other person), or causes the other party (or any other person) to purchase, or otherwise acquire, the eligible shares at a price other than their market value;

(c) an option granted by the individual to any person where the exercise of it would bind the individual to dispose, or cause to dispose, of the eligible shares to the person to whom the option is granted (or to any other person) at a price other than their market value; or

(d) an agreement entered into by the individual which binds or causes the individual to dispose of the eligible shares to the person with whom the agreement is made (or to any other person) at a price other than their market value.

'Market value', for the purpose of the foregoing is the market value of the eligible shares in question at the time those shares are actually purchased from the individual or are disposed of by him under the relevant agreement. In practice, the inspector of taxes dealing with the tax returns of the individual affected may examine after the disposal the consideration actually paid to the individual to ensure that he does in fact receive a market value consideration at the relevant time.

The individual's right to be bought out on the exercise of an option, or the other person's right to buy him out, at a price other than market value may be given under the terms of the option itself. Alternatively, it may be given under the terms of any arrangement or understanding subject to which or otherwise in connection with which the option is acquired or granted. Similarly, in the case of an agreement other than an option, the rights may be given either under the agreement itself or under any arrangement or understanding subject to which or otherwise in connection with which the agreement is made.

In applying these rules, the references in TCA 1997, s 496 to an option or agreement are extended to include also references to any right or obligation to acquire or grant an option or enter into an agreement. References to the exercise of an option include references to the exercise of an option which may be acquired or granted by the exercise of such a right or under such an obligation (TCA 1997, s 496(3)(a)).

It may be seen that the anti-avoidance rules of TCA 1997, s 496(3) are very widely drawn. Consequently, if the terms of a particular EII are to include any form of option or agreement providing for the buying out of the individual subscribing for the eligible shares, then these terms must be very carefully drawn up to ensure that they are not capable of being applied directly or indirectly to provide for the buy-out price at other than market value. The same of course applies to any form of option or agreement drawn up separately at any time during the specified period for the eligible shares in question.

There is no objection to having a 'take out' option or agreement the terms of which provide that the buying or selling price must be the market value of the shares at the date on which the individual actually disposes of the shares through the exercise of the option or under the agreement. Of course, there is no need for an EII to have any 'take out' agreement in which case the provisions of TCA 1997, s 496(3) are not relevant.

It is not unusual that the qualifying investors and the promoters of the EII company, enter into put and call options over the eligible shares exercisable immediately after the end of the specified period at market value. If the eligible shares have a limit placed on the quantum of dividends and assets receivable on a winding up then they are likely to be less valuable than a full ordinary share with no such restrictions. For example there can be two classes of shares in issue. The EII shares may only be entitled to cumulative dividends and surplus assets on a winding up equal to 110 per cent of the amount subscribed. The EII shares can never have preferential rights but they can have inferior rights to other shares issued by the qualifying company.

18.109 Disposal of shares

TCA 1997, s 496(1) deals with the position where an individual disposes of any eligible shares before the end of the specified period. It distinguishes two types of disposal – first, a disposal otherwise than by way of a bargain at arm's length (eg a gift or other disposal for less than market value) and, secondly, any other disposal (ie a sale at market value).

Any disposal of eligible shares made otherwise than in an arm's length bargain, if made before the end of the relevant period, results in the individual's losing entirely his right to any relief in respect of the shares disposed of (TCA 1997, s 496(1)(a)). If the relief has been granted to him before the disposal was made, the necessary Sch D Case IV assessment under TCA 1997, s 502 must be made on him to withdraw in full the amount of the credit previously granted. If the individual has claimed the relief but it has not yet been granted, he should notify the inspector of the disposal and withdraw his claim.

In the case where a disposal of eligible shares within the relevant period is a bargain made at arm's length, the amount by reference to which the individual is entitled to relief is reduced by the amount (or value) of the consideration which he receives for them (TCA 1997, s 496(1)(b)). Consequently, if the arm's length consideration received is less than the amount which the individual subscribed for the shares disposed of, the individual remains entitled to the relief in respect of the excess of the amount subscribed over the sales price realised. Again, if the relief has already been granted, the Sch D

Case IV assessment required to withdraw the relief, to the extent necessary, must be made.

A disposal of eligible shares within the relevant period by one spouse or civil partner to the other, if made at a time when husband and wife, or civil partners, are living together, does not cause any loss of relief. However, if the transferee (wife, husband or civil partner, as the case may be) subsequently disposes of the shares to a third person before the end of the relevant period, the relief is then lost to the extent provided (TCA 1997, s 496(2)). If some only of a holding of eligible shares acquired at the same time are disposed of, the individual only loses his entitlement to the proportionate part of the total relief attributable to the part of the entire holding that is disposed of.

Example 18.109.1

If an individual subscribes €1,000 for 1,000 eligible shares (€1 per share) on 1 June 2014, and if he sells 600 of these shares for their market value of €450 (€0.75 per share) on 1 May 2015, the amount finally available to be relieved for 2014 (the year of issue of the 1,000 shares) is determined as follows:

600 shares sold (1 May 2015):	€
Amount subscribed (€1 per share)	600
Consideration for sale (arm's length)	(450)
	150
400 shares retained:	
Amount subscribed (€1 per share)	400
Amount available to be relieved	550

An individual may hold a number of ordinary shares in a qualifying company, but only part of this holding may be eligible shares for which he is entitled to the relief. Where the eligible and non-eligible shares are of the same class (if there is more than one class of ordinary share), any disposal of any of these shares is treated as made first out of the eligible shares in priority to any of the other shares (TCA 1997, s 496(4)).

For example, an individual may sell 3,500 A ordinary shares on 1 February 2015 out of a total holding of 10,000 A ordinary shares in a company. If 7,000 shares out of the total holding have been held by him since 1986 (not eligible for relief) and only 3,000 shares are eligible shares (subscribed for on 10 May 2013), he is deemed to have sold all his eligible shares and only 500 non-eligible shares. Any relief previously granted on the 3,000 eligible shares is, therefore, withdrawn to the extent necessary.

An individual may have subscribed for eligible shares issued at different times by the same qualifying company. In such a case, any disposal of any shares out of the total holding of shares of the same class is treated as made on a 'first in first out' basis – shares issued earlier are deemed to be disposed of before shares issued later (TCA 1997, s 496(5)). In applying this rule, as well as TCA 1997, s 496(5), shares in a company are treated as being of the same class if, but only if, they would be so treated if dealt with on a stock exchange in the State (TCA 1997, s 496(7)).

The 'first in first out' rule of TCA 1997, s 496(5) enables an individual to dispose of part of a total holding of eligible shares without loss of relief, but only up to the number of eligible shares issued earlier, after the specified period has expired for that issue, even if the specified period for the later issue is still current. It may also affect the calculation (and the tax year) of the amount of relief to be withdrawn if the part of the total holding disposed of comes out of eligible shares issued at different times.

An individual holding eligible shares for which he is entitled to relief under TCA 1997, s 489(3), (6) may receive additional shares from the same company as the result of a bonus or rights issue. He is, thereby, regarded as having a 'new holding' consisting of both the original holding of eligible shares and the additional shares allotted to him in respect of those shares as a result of the bonus or rights issue. In the case of a bonus issue (but not in that of a rights issue which involves a payment for the allotment of the additional shares), TCA 1997, s 496(6) requires the entire new holding to be treated as consisting of eligible shares so that, if he disposes of any part of the new holding within the specified period, the rules relating to the withdrawal of relief are applied accordingly.

In the event that the bonus issue also results in the allotment of additional shares in respect of non-eligible shares in the original holding, it clearly follows that the part of the new shares attributable to the non-eligible shares must also be treated as non-eligible shares. In the case of a rights issue, there is no special rule. Consequently, if there is a disposal of any part of the new holding, the normal rules of TCA 1997, s 496 are applied (see above).

18.110 Designated investment funds

An investment qualifying for relief under the EII is of a venture capital nature and, in consequence, involves a greater or lesser element of risk depending on the business of the qualifying company, the strength of its management, etc. Some investors may prefer to invest in a number of companies so as to spread the risk. Further, the average investor without special financial knowledge may find it difficult to identify suitable unquoted companies prepared to issue eligible shares in which he can invest. For these reasons, an individual wishing to make an investment that will enable him to obtain the relief and, at the same time, spread his risk over a number of companies might consider subscribing through a designated investment fund.

TCA 1997, s 506 entitles an individual to claim EII relief for money subscribed to acquire eligible shares in one or more qualifying companies through a designated investment fund approved by the Revenue Commissioners. The individuals who subscribe through such an investment fund ('the participants') have eligible shares in qualifying companies purchased on their behalf by the managers of the investment fund who hold the shares as nominees of the individuals. The managers allocate to each participant units in the fund which represent that participant's proportionate share of each investment held by the fund to which he has subscribed. Each participant is paid out his proportionate share of the return received by the managers on the fund investments, less the managers' commission (see below).

When an individual has shares in qualifying companies purchased on his behalf and held by the managers of the fund as his nominees, the €250 minimum subscription required by TCA 1997, s 490(1) for a direct subscription does not apply. The rules of the fund itself may only allow the managers to accept subscriptions from participating individuals of minimum and/or maximum amounts, but that is a matter for the persons establishing the fund to decide and is not affected by any rule in the legislation.

Broadly, the same rules apply for claiming relief in respect of a qualifying subscription through a designated investment fund as they do for a direct subscription by the individual for eligible shares (see **18.107**). The individual concerned must make his own claim directly to his inspector of taxes; it is not done by the managers of the investment fund on his behalf. The time limits provided by TCA 1997, s 501 within which the individual's claim for relief must be made, in respect of each qualifying company in which the managers of the fund have invested his subscription, are applicable. If his subscription has been invested in more than one qualifying company, different time limits may apply for each such investment, depending on the date on which the company in question issued its shares to the managers of the fund and on the date that company started to trade.

The individual claiming relief for a qualifying subscription made through an approved investment fund must supply a certificate in the form authorised by the Revenue Commissioners issued to him by the managers of the fund (TCA 1997, s 506(5)). This managers' certificate must contain the information required by the Revenue Commissioners in respect of each qualifying company covered by it. It must also certify that the managers hold certificates of compliance issued to them by each of the companies covered by the managers' certificate.

Each qualifying company in which the managers of the approved investment fund subscribe for eligible shares must furnish to the managers, and not to the individuals participating in the fund, the certificate of compliance referred to in TCA 1997, s 501) (see **18.107**). Clearly, the managers of the fund can only issue their certificate to the individual participants to cover such companies as have provided them with certificates of compliance.

Exactly the same limits to the maximum relief which may be claimed by any individual in the one tax year apply whether he subscribes for eligible shares in one or more qualifying companies through an approved investment fund, by direct investment himself, or partly in one way and partly in the other. These limits have been noted in **18.106**.

Again, the rules relating to the withdrawal of relief and the circumstances in which this may occur are the same as for direct investments in eligible shares by the individual himself (see **18.108**). In the event that an individual participant in an investment fund disposes of all his units in the fund representing more than one qualifying company investment, the rules of TCA 1997, s 496 are applied separately to the individual's proportionate holding (via the managers) in each company. If his disposal concerns only his shares in one qualifying company, the withdrawal of relief is limited to his holding in that company. Equally, if relief has to be withdrawn because one of the qualifying companies in which his subscription to the fund is invested ceases to meet the qualifying conditions, the individual only loses his entitlement to relief to the extent attributable to that company.

TCA 1997, s 506(8) requires the Revenue Commissioners to designate a fund as an approved investment fund if, but only if, they are satisfied that:

- (a) the fund is established under irrevocable trusts;
- (b) it is so established for the *sole* purpose of enabling individuals who qualify for the relief (see **18.102**) to invest in eligible shares of one or more qualifying companies; and
- (c) the terms of the trust contain provisions setting out the purpose of the fund and a number of specified rules regarding the operation and management of the fund.

The required rules, which are an essential condition for approval of the investment fund as a designated fund, are set out in TCA 1997, s 506(8). It is not, therefore, proposed to restate them here.

The Revenue Commissioners may, by notice in writing given to the managers of any designated fund, withdraw the designation (ie the approval). If this notice is given, the fund ceases to be a designated fund as regards any subscriptions from participants made after the date of publication of the withdrawal in *Iris Oifigiúil*. This withdrawal of designation does not prejudice the participants' rights for the relief for subscriptions made prior to this publication of the withdrawal.

TCA 1997, s 489(3A) notes that where an investment through a fund in accordance with TCA 1997, s 506 was made in the period from 1 January 2014 to 31 December 2014 and the fund invests in shares in the month of January 2016, then, notwithstanding sub-s (3), the individual may elect by notice in writing for relief to be available either in the 2014 or 2016 year of assessment.

18.111 Anti-avoidance

TCA 1997, ss 497–500 contain a number of additional rules which are anti-avoidance measures to prevent individuals from obtaining EII relief in circumstances outside the intended scope of the scheme.

Value received from company by an investor

Section 497 is designed to ensure that amounts subscribed for qualifying shares are retained by the company and are not returned to the qualifying individual by repayment of loans, transfers of assets and other benefits. Where a qualifying individual who has subscribed for eligible shares in a company receives value from that company in his 'specified period', TCA 1997, s 497 imposes a clawback of the relief obtained in respect of those shares. The specified period is the period from two years before the issue of the eligible shares (or date of incorporation if later) and four years after the issue. Finance Act 2014 extended the period from three years to four years with effect from 2015 but the extension is subject to a Ministerial Order. The clawback operates by withdrawing relief for the qualifying individual up to the amount of value received.

For those purposes, value is received if the company:

(a) repays, redeems or purchases any of the individual's shares or securities or pays him for giving up rights to his shares, etc on their cancellation or extinction; the amount of the value received is the amount receivable, or the market value of the shares, etc, if greater;

(b) repays any debt owed to the individual on or after the date the relevant shares are issued, except:

   (i) an ordinary trading debt incurred by the company, or

   (ii) any other debt incurred by the company on or after the earliest date on which he subscribed for the eligible shares (any debts which replaced debts incurred prior to the issue of the eligible shares do not qualify for this exception) (TCA 1997, s 497(3)(b)),

   an 'ordinary trade debt' is defined as any debt for goods or services supplied in the ordinary course of a trade or business where the credit period does not exceed six months *and* is not longer than that normally applicable to the company's customers (TCA 1997, s 497(1)); the amount of the value received is the amount receivable, or the market value of the debt, if greater (TCA 1997, s 497(6)(a));

(c) makes a payment to the individual for giving up a right to a debt on its extinguishment, other than a debt which would be excepted under (b) above, or a debt in respect of the supplies of goods or services within TCA 1997, s 955(1), (2)(a) (ie such that the receipt of moneys in respect thereof would be disregarded in deciding whether a director or employee of the company was connected with the company: see **18.102**) TCA 1997, s 497(3)(c)); the amount of the value received is the amount receivable or the value of the debt, if greater. (TCA 1997, s 497(6)(a));

(d) releases or waives the individual's liability to the company or discharges a liability of the individual to a third party: where a liability is not discharged within 12 months, it is deemed to have been released or waived (TCA 1997, s 497(3)(d)) – the amount of the value received is the amount released or waived (TCA 1997, s 497(6)(b));

(e) makes a loan or advance to the individual; a loan includes for these purposes a debt incurred by the individual directly to the company or to a third party and which is subsequently assigned to the company TCA 1997, s 497(3)(e)); the amount of the value received is the amount of the loan, advance or debt (TCA 1997, s 497(6)(c));

(f) provides a benefit or facility for the individual; the expression 'benefit or facility' bears its ordinary, wide-ranging meaning (see the Sch E case law, considered at **10.203**) TCA 1997, s 497(3)(f)); the amount of the value received is the cost of providing the benefit net of any consideration given for it by the individual, (the Revenue Commissioners apparently accept that marginal cost is generally the correct measure of a benefit in the Sch E context (see **10.204**) (TCA 1997, s 497(6)(d)));

(g) transfers an asset to the individual for no consideration (or for consideration less than its market value) or acquires an asset from the individual for consideration in excess of its market value (in strictness therefore it is not sufficient to demonstrate that the transaction was an arm's length bargain, if the price agreed is out of line with market value, as defined by TCA 1997, s 548(1): see TCA 1997, s 952) TCA 1997, s 497(3)(g)); the amount of the benefit is the difference between the market value of the relevant asset and the consideration paid (TCA 1997, s 497(6)(e)); or

(h) makes *any* other kind of payment to the individual other than:
   (i) a payment within TCA 1997, s 955(1), (2) (ie any payment which would be disregarded in deciding whether or not a director or employee of the company was connected with the company: see **18.102**); or
   (ii) a repayment of an ordinary trading debt (as defined under (b) above) TCA 1997, s 497(3)(h)); the amount of the value received is the amount of the payment (TCA 1997, s 497(6)(f)).

Payments and transfers made to an individual are to include those which are made to him indirectly or to his order or for his benefit. Furthermore, payments and transfers to an *associate* of an individual are treated as if made to him. Payments and transfers made by a person connected with the company are treated as if made by the company (TCA 1997, s 497(2)). 'Associate' is again defined as for the purposes of TCA 1997, s 433, while the rules of TCA 1997, s 10 are applied to determine who is connected with the company for these purposes: see **12.304**).

In addition, TCA 1997, Sch 10 provides that the 'value received' rules apply to a subsidiary of the company in question in the same way as they do to the company itself. The company need only have been a subsidiary at some point during the relevant period (as defined above) and need not be a subsidiary at the time at which value is received.

Example 18.111.1

(i) George, who has subscribed €20,000 for eligible shares in Dinky Ltd, also holds redeemable preference shares in that company. The redemption of those shares for €5,000 during the 'relevant period' will constitute 'value received' of €5,000 under (a) above.

(ii) (I) Liam lends €10,000 to Derry Ltd and subsequently subscribes €20,000 for eligible shares in Derry Ltd. Two years later Derry Ltd repays the loan to Liam. The repayment, which falls within the specified period, constitutes 'value received' of €10,000.

(II) Liam, instead of lending €10,000 to Derry Ltd, lends the sum instead to Gerard who owns 80 per cent of the voting shares of Derry Ltd. The repayment of the loan following Liam's subscription for eligible shares in Derry Ltd will again count as value received of €10,000 since Gerard is connected with Derry Ltd (a company which is controlled by him).

(iii) (I) Assume the same facts as in (ii)(I), except that, instead of repaying the loan to Liam, Derry Ltd gives him consideration valued at €9,000, in return for agreeing to extinguish the company's indebtedness to him. The consideration will again constitute 'value received' of €10,000 (assuming that this is the market value of the debt).

(II) Assume the same facts as (iii)(I) except that the loan was made by Liam's wife, Sara. The consideration for the extinction of the loan (now receivable by Sara) will again be 'value received' of €10,000 since Sara is an associate of Liam.

(iv) (I) Neil has subscribed €20,000 for eligible shares in Magee Ltd. Neil owes €3,000 to Magee Ltd a sum which is waived by the company during the specified period. The waiver gives rise to 'value received' of €3,000.

(II) Assume the same facts as in (iv)(I) except that the loan and subsequent waiver relates to Jordanstown Ltd, which becomes a subsidiary of Magee Ltd, at some time later, but during the specified period. The waiver again gives rise to 'value received' of €3,000, since Jordanstown Ltd is treated as if it were Magee Ltd for these purposes.

(v) Monica subscribes €30,000 for eligible shares in Hoodo Ltd. During the specified period, Hoodo Ltd allows Monica to obtain goods from it at a substantial discount while still making a profit on the transaction. This is the provision of a benefit under (f) above, but the value of the benefit would appear to be nil, since the company recovers its costs in full.

(vi) Maeve subscribes for eligible shares in Macca Ltd. She subsequently lets a warehouse to the company at a rent of €6,000 pa. The rental would in strictness count as value received of €6,000 under (h) above, as a payment which does not fall under any of the specified exceptions. Maeve is strictly not entitled to a deduction for the value provided by her (ie the grant of the tenancy).

TCA 1997, s 497(5) provides that an individual also receives value if he obtains any payment or asset on a winding up or dissolution of the company within TCA 1997, s 494(10) (ie a *bona fide* commercial winding up, etc which does not lead to the company being treated as non-qualifying: see **18.103**). The amount of the value received in this case is the amount of the payment or market value of the asset as appropriate (TCA 1997, s 497(7)(g)).

Finally, TCA 1997, s 497(6) treats an individual as receiving value if any person connected with the company as widely defined by TCA 1997, s 492 (see **18.102**) either:

(a) purchases any of the share capital, or securities, in the company from the individual; or

(b) makes a payment to the individual for giving up any right in relation to such share capital or securities.

The amount of the value received in these cases is the amount receivable or the market value of the shares or securities if greater (TCA 1997, s 497(7)(h)).

Example 18.111.2

Nuala subscribes €200,000 for eligible shares in Argyll Ltd. She already owns debentures in the company and she sells these for €3,000 (their market value) to Brian during the relevant period. Brian is a non-executive director of Argyll Ltd and receives fees which are in excess of reasonable and necessary remuneration. Nuala is regarded as receiving value of €3,000 since Brian is connected with Argyll Ltd for the purposes of TCA 1997, s 492.

For the purposes of identifying the shares in respect of which relief is to be withdrawn, TCA 1997, s 492 provides that this is to be done where necessary on a 'FIFO' basis.

Where a specified individual within the SCS (see **18.112**) makes a loan to a company and coverts that loan into eligible shares within one year of the making of the loan, then the conversion of the loan may be treated as the making of a relevant investment by that individual on the date of the making of the loan. Furthermore, TCA 1997, s 497(3)(b) will not apply so as to treat the discharge of the loan as giving rise to a receipt of value by the individual. However, it is necessary for the auditor of the company to certify that in their opinion the money raised by the company was used exclusively for the qualifying purposes set out in TCA 1997, s 493(1)(d).

Value received from company by third parties

A clawback of relief is also imposed on a qualifying individual who has subscribed for eligible shares, if in the specified period either:

(a) shareholders who have *not* qualified for relief under the EII receive a repayment in respect of their share capital; or

(b) shareholders in the company receive value from the company.

The specified period is the period two years before the issue of the eligible shares (or the date of incorporation if later) and four years after the date of issue of the shares. The four years was extended from three years with effect from 2015 in the Finance Act 2014 but its introduction is subject to a Ministerial Order.

TCA 1997, s 499 applies where the company repays, redeems or repurchases any of its share capital (but not its securities) belonging to any person *other than* either the individual who has claimed relief, or any other individual who as a result is subject to a clawback of relief under TCA 1997, s 499 (see above). The section also catches payments made in respect of the cancellation or extinguishment of the company's share capital (TCA 1997, s 499(1)). It may be noted that TCA 1997, s 499, does not apply to a purchase of the company's shares by a person connected with the company. Where there is a repayment of share capital within TCA 1997, s 499 the relief granted to the individual is reduced by the greater of the amount receivable by the shareholders concerned or the nominal value of their shares, if greater (TCA 1997, s 499(4)). Where relief has to be withdrawn from more than one individual under this provision, it is withdrawn in proportion to those individuals' entitlements to relief (TCA 1997, s 499(4)).

There is an exclusion in respect of share capital where the redemption rate was fixed before 26 January 1984 (TCA 1997, s 499(2)). There is also an exclusion in respect of the redemption of shares issued to comply with the Companies (Amendment) Act 1983, s 6 (public company not to do business unless requirements as to share capital satisfied). The shares must be redeemed within 12 months of the date of the issue of the eligible shares (TCA 1997, s 499(3)).

TCA 1997, s 499 applies to a qualifying individual who has subscribed for eligible shares in a company where other shareholders receive or are entitled to receive value from the company. A person is treated as entitled to receive anything which he is entitled to receive in the future or which he will be entitled to receive in the future (TCA 1997, s 499(9)). For the purposes of TCA 1997, s 499 a shareholder receives value if he falls within heading (d) to (h) inclusive of TCA 1997, s 499 above. However, for these purposes (h) will not apply where the payment received is in return for full consideration (TCA 1997, s 499(8)). Thus, the lease of premises at a market rental to the company by a shareholder in the company cannot trigger off a clawback under TCA 1997, s 499.

Where a shareholder including a qualifying individual who has subscribed for eligible shares and who is therefore liable to a clawback under TCA 1997, s 499 receives value from the company, each qualifying individual who has subscribed for eligible shares must recalculate his percentage of ordinary share capital for the purposes of TCA 1997, s 492 (the rule under which an individual who directly or indirectly possesses or is entitled to acquire more than 30 per cent of the issued ordinary share of the company, etc, is deemed to be connected with the company: see **18.102** (TCA 1997, s 499(5))).

For these purposes the share capital is divided into two parts, namely:

(a) the part of the ordinary share capital which the individual possesses directly or indirectly or which he is entitled, to acquire as defined by TCA 1997, s 492; and

(b) the remaining part of the ordinary share capital.

Both (a) and (b) must then be reduced where appropriate by multiplying them by the formula to be found in TCA 1997, s 499, ie:

$$\frac{S - V}{S}$$

where

S = the amount subscribed for the shares in question;

V = the amount of the value received by the shareholders in question (as ascertained for the purposes of TCA 1997, s 499: TCA 1997, s 499).

The amount of the ordinary share capital is treated as the sum of (a) and (b): TCA 1997, s 499(6).

Example 18.111.3

The shareholdings in Cherids Ltd are as follows:

	Nominal value	*Subscription price*
	€	€
Maurice	20,000	120,000

Sean	20,000	120,000
Patrick	40,000	160,000
Marianne	40,000	300,000
	120,000	700,000
Veronica	40,000	200,000
	160,000	900,000

Cherids Ltd only has ordinary shares in issue. Veronica had obtained relief under the EII for her investment in the company (spread over a number of years). The company waived loans to Maurice, Sean and Patrick totalling €194,400 during Veronica's specified period (this gives rise to value received of €194,400: TCA 1997, s 499(3)(d)). As a result, TCA 1997, s 499 requires Veronica's percentage of share capital to be recalculated as follows:

	Notional value
(a) Veronica's ordinary share capital: no change	€
(since no value received by her)	40,000
(b) Remainder of ordinary share capital:	
120,000 x (700,000 – 194,400)/700,000 =	86,674
Revised ordinary share capital for the purposes of TCA 1997, s 492	126,674

Veronica is now regarded as holding 40/126.67 (ie 31.5 per cent) of the company's issued ordinary share capital. Accordingly she has become connected with the company for the purposes of TCA 1997, s 492 and relief will therefore be withdrawn in full. Where TCA 1997, s 499 results in withdrawal of relief, TCA 1997, s 499(10) provides that is to be done where necessary on a 'FIFO' basis.

TCA 1997, s 499 is a far-reaching section and a passive EII investor may have his relief clawed back through the actions of the directors of the company. The EII shareholder may not be aware that value was given to another shareholder. For this reason it is prudent for an EII investor to seek an indemnity from the directors of the company when making the investment.

Replacement of capital (TCA 1997, s 498)

This section is intended to prevent individuals from obtaining the relief in respect of subscriptions for share capital in circumstances where the investment is, in effect an indirect replacement of capital in an existing trade. It provides that the relief is not to be given in respect of shares in a company where, at any time in the specified period in relation to the eligible shares, the company or any of its qualifying subsidiaries takes over a trade or the whole or greater part of the assets of a trade, and where the individual claiming relief (or a group of persons of which the individual is one) has or had more than a 50 per cent interest in, or control over, the trade concerned. The specified period is two years before the eligible shares are issued (or date of incorporation if later) and four years after the shares are issued. The period of four years was extended from three years with effect from 2015 in the Finance Act 2014 but its introduction is subject to a Ministerial Order. For the section to apply to deny the relief to any individual, it is also necessary that the individual in question (or a group of persons of which he is one) to have more than a 50 per cent interest in, or control over, the qualifying company (or any of its subsidiaries) to which the trade or the assets of the trade have been transferred (TCA 1997, s 498(2), (3)(a)). For these purposes, the attribution of ownership of a trade or a share in a trade is made in accordance with the rules of TCA 1997, s 400 'Company Reconstructions without change of ownership' (TCA 1997, s 498(5)); further, any interests, rights or powers of the associate of any person will be attributed to that person (as defined by TCA 1997, s 488(1)). 'Trade' for these purposes includes any business, profession, vocation and references to a trade previously carried on and includes references to a part of a trade (eg where a division of a previous trade is taken over by a new company) (TCA 1997, s 498(1)).

Relief is also denied in a case where the individual is a person or one of a group of persons who controls, or who had previously controlled, the company and had at any time also controlled another company which had carried on the trade (TCA 1997, s 498(3)(b)).

Finally, provision is made to deny relief where a company acquires all the issued share capital of another company in the relevant period and the individual is a person or one of a group of persons who controls, or who had previously controlled, the company and who controls, or who has at any time in the relevant period controlled, that other company (TCA 1997, s 498(4)).

Prevention of misuse (TCA 1997, s 500)

This section is short and may be quoted in full. It provides that an individual is not entitled to relief in respect of any shares unless the shares are subscribed for and issued for *bona fide* commercial purposes, and not as part of a scheme or arrangement the main purpose or one of the main purposes of which is the avoidance of tax. It seems unlikely that merely obtaining the tax benefits provided by the EII in itself could constitute 'tax avoidance' in any ordinary meaning of that phrase. It is suggested that tax can only be 'avoided' if there is a tax liability which is in some sense otherwise due and payable. However, it is the tax laws alone which can determine what that liability should be; as discussed at **1.401** there is no 'equity' attaching to taxation and thus no predetermined relationship between a taxpayer's economic circumstances and his liability to tax which determines how much tax he 'ought' to pay (see also *IRC v Willoughby* discussed at **17.207**; note also *Barclays Mercantile Industrial v Melluish* [1990] STC 314, decided in the context of claims for capital allowances).

It would seem therefore that this anti-avoidance provision is likely only to apply to arrangements which exploit the benefits of the EII but which, taken as a whole, are regarded as disproportionately driven by tax considerations. This is, in effect, a general 'sweeper' clause which the Revenue Commissioners might seek to apply in a case where some scheme is devised to utilise the provisions of the EII legislation in a way not compatible with what the Commissioners consider to be intended by the legislation, but where none of the other anti-avoidance rules are sufficient to counter the scheme.

Risk-free schemes

This section is intended to ensure that only individuals who invest with some degree of business risk become entitled to the EII relief. It is designed to counteract certain tax avoidance schemes usually involving designated investment funds where the potential investors would be guaranteed a certain minimum return on their investment. This was seen as being contrary to the spirit of the EII legislation and relief has now been restricted where there is little or no risk to the investor.

TCA 1997, s 489(9) provides that where any agreement, arrangement or understanding exists which could reasonably be considered to eliminate the risk to the beneficial owner of the shares that he might not receive a return on his investment, then relief will not be allowed to the subscriber for the shares. 'Beneficially owned', in this regard, includes shares owned by the shareholder and also any person 'connected' with him. There are a small number of Revenue Precedents in respect of BES in this area which appear to demonstrate a relatively pragmatic approach to the issue of risk.

18.112 Seed capital investment by new entrepreneurs

The scope of the EII relief is widened to provide a refund of tax already paid by an individual who sets up and takes employment in a new qualifying company (referred to in the legislation as 'the relevant investment'). The relief is to encourage individuals currently or formerly in employment to set up new business ventures. The legislation relating to this relief is incorporated into the provisions of the relief for the EII as outlined in **18.101** to **18.111** with additional requirements (and also some relaxations) of the EII rules, as outlined below.

The relief is granted where:

(a) a specified individual makes a relevant investment;

(b) the shares issued to the specified individual are issued for the purposes of raising money by a qualifying company for the benefit of its activities referred to in (d) below;

(c) the activities carried on by the qualifying company are a *qualifying new venture*;

(d) the money was used, is being used or is intended to be used for the benefit of a *qualifying new venture* for the purpose of carrying on relevant trading activities, or in the case of a company that has not commenced qualifying trading activities, incurring expenditure on research and development within the meaning of TCA 1997, s 766;

(e) the use of the money set out in (d) will contribute directly to the creation or maintenance of employment in the company.

A *'specified individual'* is an individual who makes a relevant investment and who meets a number of qualifying conditions set out in TCA 1997, s 495.

A *'relevant investment'* is the total amount subscribed by a specified individual in a year of assessment for eligible shares in a qualifying company (both as defined for the EII) which carries on or intends to carry on relevant trading activities (as defined for EII purposes) (TCA 1997, s 488(1)),

A *'qualifying new venture'* means a venture consisting of relevant trading activities which are set up and commenced by a new company other than:

(a) activities which were previously carried on by another person and to which the company has succeeded; or

(b) a venture, the activities of which were previously carried on as part of another person's trade or profession (TCA 1997, s 488(1)),

The amount to be deducted by any individual in the year of assessment is limited to €100,000. The relief will be allowed as a deduction from the total income of a specified individual for the tax year in which the eligible shares are issued and the company commenced to trade. However, the individual may elect to have the relief deducted from his total income of any of the six years immediately prior to the tax year in which the shares are issued. This election will result in an immediate refund to the taxpayer TCA 1997, s 493(3)(a). This is a very valuable relief although it should be noted that in most cases that part of the relief will usually be claimed at the standard rate of tax unless the claimant has very significant taxable income.

Furthermore, TCA 1997, s 493(3) also provides that an individual may elect to have a second qualifying investment in the same company treated in this way provided the second investment is made no later than in the second year of assessment following the year in which the first relevant investment was made. Thus, if an individual makes a first investment and receives eligible shares in 2013, he may make a second relevant investment up to 31 December 2014 which he may elect to have deducted from his total income for any year back to 2007 (ie six tax years prior to the year in which the original eligible shares were issued, in 2013), subject to there being sufficient total income remaining in those years following his claim in respect of the original investment. Any unabsorbed relief in respect of both the first and second seed capital investments is carried forward to the tax years nominated by the individual for this purpose between the tax year originally nominated and the tax year in which the shares actually issued in respect of the first such investment. Any relief still outstanding in respect of the first or second seed capital investment is given in the year in which the shares are actually issued or in a subsequent year as normal EII relief. The SCS relief is only available in respect of two relevant investments made by a specified individual in all tax years.

In the case of a specified individual, 'the relevant period' is the period beginning on the share issue date and ending one year after that date, or where the company was not at that date carrying on relevant trading activities, one year after the date it commenced to carry on such operations (compared to three years for the EII).

The specified individual must take up a relevant employment, ie full-time employment for a specified period of twelve months in the company in which he has made his seed capital investment (being the first tranche of such an investment) (TCA 1997, s 488(1); s 493(7)).

The relief must be claimed and is not allowed unless and until the qualifying new venture commences to carry on relevant trading activities or in the case of a company that has not commenced the carrying on of qualifying trading activities, has expended not less than 30 per cent of the relevant investment on research and development activities which are connected with and undertaken with a view to the carrying on of relevant trading activities (TCA 1997, s 493(5)). Relief will be withdrawn where an event occurs within the appropriate relevant period which results in the claimant not being entitled to relief (TCA 1997, s 493(6)).

Relief is denied in respect of amounts subscribed for shares in a company where the shareholder or a person connected with the shareholder is either:

(a) assured of recovering part or all of the capital subscribed, other than a distribution as defined by the Corporation Tax Acts; or

(b) assured of receiving an agreed distribution or a shareholder is assured of recovering capital invested or of receiving a dividend. A shareholder is assured of recovering capital invested or of receiving a dividend where by virtue of an agreement, arrangement or understanding it could reasonably be considered that the risk element has been eliminated (TCA 1997, s 493(9)).

Where a specified individual claims relief under the SCS, no relief will be granted to that individual under the EII in respect of the same qualifying company (TCA 1997, s 493(10)).

The Revenue Commissioners may require the qualifying company to provide evidence as they consider necessary and may consult with such persons or body of persons as in their opinion may be of assistance to them, to enable them to verify that the conditions necessary for the claiming and granting of relief have been satisfied (TCA 1997, s 493(11)):

(a) In each of the three years of assessment immediately preceding the year of assessment that the relevant investment is made and in which the new employment commences, his total income from sources other than employment income (Sch E) or foreign employment income (Sch D Case III) cannot exceed the lesser of:
   (i) the amount of income thus assessed under Sch D Case III and Sch E, or
   (ii) €50,000;

   The income test applies for each of the three tax years before the tax year preceding the tax year in which the individual makes his first SCS investment. There is no restriction on the source of the individual's income in the year which immediately precedes the year in which he makes that investment;

(b) Must possess throughout his relevant period at least 15 per cent of the issued ordinary share capital of the company in which the relevant investment is made. The relevant period in this regard is one year from the date the shares were issued or one year from the date the company commenced carrying on the relevant trading activities if later. Where an individual makes two seed capital investments this requirement applies in respect of both. An individual is not regarded as ceasing to comply with the requirement to retain at least a 15 per cent ownership of the company for the relevant period referred to where he does so by reason of the company concerned being wound up for bona fide commercial reasons and not because of a tax avoidance scheme;

(c) Not have possessed or possess more than 15 per cent of the issued ordinary shares or the aggregate of the issued ordinary shares and loan capital or of the voting power of or in any other company at the date he commenced employment or within the previous 12 months; this restriction is relaxed by TCA 1997, s 495(6), if the individual exceeds the threshold in one other company where that company which exists wholly or mainly for the purpose of carrying on relevant trading activities with a turnover in each of the three accounting periods immediately preceding the period in which the date of the individual's investment falls of less than €127,000; the restriction is also waived if the individual holds more than 15 per cent of a non-trading dormant company.

   A company is treated as carrying on wholly or mainly relevant trading activities, where it receives not less than 75 per cent of its total income from the trade over a period of three accounting periods (as defined by TCA 1997, s 27) in the case of tourist traffic undertakings and 90 per cent of its total income from the trade over a period of three accounting periods in the case of other relevant trading activities.

Breach of these conditions will lead to a withdrawal of any relief previously granted.

18.113 Miscellaneous matters

Information

TCA 1997, s 503, contains various provisions which require information to be furnished to the inspector in certain circumstances and also enable the inspector to seek information in relation to matters relevant to the application of the relief, its withdrawal etc.

TCA 1997, s 503(1) requires an individual who ceases to qualify for relief under any of the rules of TCA 1997, s 492, or whose relief previously given falls to be withdrawn by either TCA 1997, s 496 or TCA 1997, s 497, to notify the inspector of the fact. This notice must be given by the individual within 60 days of his coming to know of the event requiring the withdrawal of the relief. This notice must be given in writing.

TCA 1997, s 503(2) requires the inspector to be notified of any event requiring the relief to be withdrawn in respect of any shares in a company due to any of the provisions of TCA 1997, s 494, TCA 1997, s 495, or any of the anti-avoidance rules of TCA 1997, ss 497–500. In this case the company is required to give notice of the event in writing to the inspector within 60 days of the occurrence of the event affecting the company (or any qualifying subsidiary). Any other person connected with the company who has knowledge of the matter is also required to give notice of it to the inspector (but presumably if that other person, eg a director, is aware that the appropriate notice is being given on behalf of the company, he need not repeat the notice).

TCA 1997, s 503(3) empowers the inspector, if he has reason to believe that any person has not given a notice required by either TCA 1997, s 503(1) or (2), to serve the person in question with notice in writing requiring him to furnish such information relating to the relevant event as the inspector may reasonably require. The information should be supplied within the time specified in the inspector's notice; this time must not be less than 60 days.

TCA 1997, s 503(4) entitles the inspector to require by notice in writing any person concerned with any arrangement or scheme mentioned in TCA 1997, ss 492, 494 or 500, to furnish information related to that arrangement or scheme.

TCA 1997, Sch 29 applies the general penalty rules provided in TCA 1997, ss 1052, 1053(1)–(4), 1054(2)–(4), for failure to comply with the information requirements of this section. An individual, company or other person who fails to give the necessary notice within TCA 1997, s 503(1) or (2) is subject to the penalties for a TCA 1997, Sch 29 'column 3 offence', whereas the failure of any person to comply with the inspector's notice requesting information under TCA 1997, s 503(3) or (4) is a 'column 2 offence'.

In addition, nominees may be required to provide details of the beneficial owner of payments or assets which may constitute value received under the anti-avoidance provisions described above or the beneficial owner of any shares in respect of which relief has been claimed (TCA 1997, s 503(6), (7)).

Finally, an inspector will not be prevented by his obligations to maintain secrecy from disclosing to a company that relief has been given or claimed in respect of a particular number or proportion of its shares (TCA 1997, s 503(8)).

TCA 1997, s 507 enables the inspector to require a qualifying company or the managers of a designated fund to furnish such information as the Revenue Commissioners may reasonably require for the purposes of compiling annual reports under European State Aid rules. An inspector will not be prevented by his obligations to maintain official secrecy from disclosing this information. There is provision for penalties for non-compliance.

Finance Act 2014 has introduced a provision which was subject to Ministerial Order that the company must meet the requirements of holding a tax clearance certificate before a claim to EII relief or seed capital relief is allowed (TCA 1997, s 501(9)). This was substituted by FA 2015, s 18 and now provides that the amendment was to have effect in respect of shares issued on or after 13 October 2015. It should be noted that a company does not have to hold a tax clearance certificate but to qualify for a tax clearance certificate. In practice this will mean that a company must have its taxes up to date before EII approval or seed capital relief is received.

Appeals

The EII legislation does not specifically provide for appeals against any decision of the inspector or the Revenue Commissioners in the implementation of the relief. However, TCA 1997, ss 864(1), 949 apply to enable an individual to appeal against any decision of the inspector or the Revenue Commissioners not to give relief to an individual who considers he is entitled to it (see **2.206** *et seq*). F(TA)A 2015, which was subject to Ministerial Order (SI 110/2016 appointed 21 March 2016 as the day on which the Finance (Tax Appeals) Act 2015, came into operation) inserted a new sub-s (1A) into TCA 1997, s 864 (and to which TCA 1997, s 864(1) is subject) which requires any person aggrieved by a determination under sub-s (1) on any claim, matter or question referred to in that subsection may appeal the determination to the Appeal Commissioners within the period of 30 days after the date of the notice of that determination. This is subject to TCA 1997, s 949I and Ch 6 of Pt 41A, which deals with appealing determinations of the Appeal Commissioners. Any assessment under Sch D Case IV to withdraw relief previously given is a new assessment to income tax so that the individual assessed has the right to appeal against it in the same way as any other assessment to income tax; but in any such case, the due date for payment of the tax assessed by reference to which interest is chargeable is the date provided by TCA 1997, s 502 (which date varies dependent on the particular disqualifying event which causes the withdrawal of relief, see **18.108**).

18.2 Exemptions for Charities, Sports Bodies etc

18.201 Introduction

TCA 1997, s 207(1), (2), 207A, 208 grant exemption from the charge to income tax under Schs C, D and F in respect of specified types of income accruing to certain bodies of persons or trusts established for charitable purposes. In general, this exemption is only given to the extent that the income in question is applied for charitable purposes. TCA 1997, s 76 extends these exemptions so that a body corporate that is established for charitable purposes only is exempted from corporation tax in respect of the same types of income in corresponding circumstances.

The tax exemptions given to such charitable bodies and trusts (referred to collectively as 'charities') are limited to those specifically provided in these sections. There is no general exemption given to charities as such, so that any charity which should have income not specifically covered by these exemptions remains liable to tax on it in the ordinary way. For example, there is no exemption for any income taxable under Sch E (although it would be rather unusual for a charity to have any Sch E income). A charity may, in certain circumstances, also be taxable on income derived from a trade carried on by it. Further, a charity may be taxed on income from a source normally exempt to the extent that such income is not applied for charitable purposes only.

The exemptions given to charities are discussed in **18.203** and the question of trading by charities in **18.204**, while the question of when income is applied for charitable purposes only is covered in **18.205**. First, however, it is necessary to explain what the terms 'charity' and 'charitable purposes' mean for the purposes of the tax exemptions. This involves some examination of the general law relating to charities which is one of the more complex branches of the law of equity. In attempting a general explanation of this subject in **18.202**, the surface is only touched to give a broad background against which the tax issues can be considered.

Another important tax exemption is that given by TCA 1997, s 235 which exempts from income tax all the income of certain approved 'sports bodies' to the extent that income is applied solely for the purpose of promoting athletic or amateur games or sports. This topic is covered in **18.206**.

The exemptions given by TCA 1997, ss 211(1)–(4), 213(1)–(2) respectively to friendly societies and trade unions are discussed in **18.208**. The exemptions given from income tax by all these sections is extended to corporation tax by TCA 1997, s 76 if the exempted person is a body corporate chargeable to corporation tax.

Finally, the exemption given by TCA 1997, s 215 (also extended to corporation tax) for the profits from exhibitions or shows held by societies or institutions established for the purpose of promoting the interests of agriculture, horticulture, livestock breeding, or forestry, are mentioned in **18.209**.

18.202 Meaning of 'charity' and 'charitable purposes'

TCA 1997, s 207(1), (2) grants its exemptions – to the extent applicable (see **18.203**) – to bodies of persons and trusts established for charitable purposes only. TCA 1997, s 208 provides its exemptions for any 'charity', which it defines as any body of persons or trust established for charitable purposes only (TCA 1997, s 208(1)). Apart from this latter statement, the Tax Acts do not attempt any definition either of 'charity' or 'charitable purposes'. It is, therefore, necessary to find the definition of 'charitable purposes' out of the general law relating to charities. If it can be established that a body of persons meets this 'charitable purposes' test, it may be regarded as a 'charity'. Until the enactment of the Charities Act 2007, there was no formal system of registration for charities in Ireland. However, registration under the Act does not necessarily imply that the body concerned is eligible for the tax exemptions described below, which remains the sole province of the Revenue Commissioners. Equally, the acceptance by the Charities Section of the Revenue Commissioners that a body is entitled to those exemptions is not conclusive evidence of such status under general law, but will provide certainty in respect of all tax issues. However, any organisation in receipt of charitable tax exemptions from the Revenue Commissioners on the day the register was established will be automatically entered in the register of charities.

A claim for exemption must be made under TCA 1997, s 864 or in the case of certain foreign charities (see below) under TCA 1997, s 208A. With effect from 2010 onwards, any such claim must be supported by such information as the Revenue Commissioners may reasonably require in order to determine whether the exemptions apply. The Revenue Commissioners published a booklet entitled CHY 1 updated in July 2014. This booklet outlines what constitutes a charity for exemption purposes and provides guidance on completing the application for exemption from tax. A charity which has received a favourable determination is obliged to provide such information as the Revenue Commissioners may request in relation to the charity's activities in any subsequent financial years (TCA 1997, s 208B(3)). Any such information must be submitted in English or Irish (TCA 1997, s 208B(4)). The Revenue Commissioners may appoint a qualified person (in effect a recognised auditor) to verify all such information (TCA 1997, s 208B(5)). The expenses incurred by any such person may be recovered by the Revenue Commissioners from the charity trustees (who are to be jointly and severally liable) or where this is not practicable from the charity itself (TCA 1997, s 208B(6)). This provision seems to be misdrafted since presumably it is recovery of the costs incurred by the Revenue Commissioners in engaging the qualifying person which they want to pass on to the charity.

In his *Irish Land Law* (4th edn, Bloomsbury Professional, 2010), JCW Wylie, in discussing charitable trusts, starts his definition of 'charity' by quoting Gavan Duffy J in *Re Howley's Estate* [1940] IR 109:

> 'Charity' is in law an artificial conception, which during some 300 years, under the guidance of pedantic technicians, seems to have strayed rather far from the intelligent realm of plain common sense; thus, the textbooks tell us that charity in the eyes of the law includes a bequest for a 'home for lost dogs', as an institution for domestic animals must benefit the human race which they serve, and a legacy to further 'conservative principles', if combined with zeal for mental and moral improvement ...

Wylie goes on to indicate that the starting point of modern charity law, and, in particular, a guide to the definition of charity is the list of charitable purposes contained in the Statute of Charitable Uses (Ireland), 1634 (10 Ch I sess 3, c 1). That Act provided that dispositions:

> … for the erection, maintenance or support of any college, school, lecture in divinity, or in any of the liberal arts or sciences, or for the relief or maintenance of any manner of poor, succourless, distressed or impotent persons, or for the building, re-edifying or maintaining in repair of any church, college, school or hospital, or for the maintenance of any minister and preacher of the holy word of God, or for the erection, building, maintenance or repair of any bridges, causeways, cashes, paces and highways, within this realm, or for any other like lawful and charitable use and uses, warranted by the laws of this realm, now established and in force, are and shall be taken and construed to be good and effectual in law.

Although that Act has been repealed, it has been settled that it, along with its English counterpart, the Statute of Charitable Uses 1601 (43 Eliz 1, c 4), is a guide to the Irish courts in determining whether a particular trust comes within the category of charitable trusts. The early law on the subject was concerned principally with the control and administration of charitable trusts which had become common by the end of the Tudor period. The principles laid down in the Charitable Uses Statutes, and adopted in judicial decisions over many years, as to what types of disposition were to be regarded as valid gifts for charitable purposes, are broadly the principles to apply in deciding what are (or are not) charitable purposes for the tax exemptions.

The leading tax case on the subject is still the early case of *IT Comrs v Pemsel* 3 TC 53 in which Lord Macnaghten, in an often quoted judgment, grouped charitable purposes into four general categories, namely:

(a) relief of poverty;
(b) advancement of education;
(c) advancement of religion; and
(d) other purposes beneficial to the community not falling within the other three categories.

Although *Pemsel's* case was an English one, the four general categories of charitable purposes enumerated by Lord Macnaghten have been accepted by the Irish courts as a proper classification for the purposes of Irish law generally and for tax law in particular. There have, however, been some variations between the decisions of the English and the Irish courts in relation to particular matters coming within one or more of these classifications. In particular, the Irish courts have tended to accept a somewhat wider range of objects as charitable under the heading of the advancement of religion.

As a general rule, a trust is considered to be charitable only if it satisfies each of the following three criteria:

(a) it must be of a charitable character, so that it comes within the courts' interpretation of the essence of the Statutes of Charitable Uses (see above);
(b) it must be solely charitable within that interpretation; and
(c) its effect must be the promotion of some public benefit.

'Public benefit' criterion

While a disposition must generally promote some public benefit if it is to have a charitable purpose, this is not necessary to the same extent if the relief of poverty is involved. In *Re Scarisbrick, Cockshott v Public Trustee* [1951] 1 All ER 822, Jenkins LJ stated the following general propositions:

(a) as a general rule, a trust or gift in order to be charitable in the legal sense must be for the 'benefit of the public' or 'some section of the public';
(b) an aggregate of individuals ascertained by reference to some personal tie (eg of blood or contract) such as the relations of a particular individual, the members of a particular family, the employees of a particular firm, etc does not amount to the public or a section thereof for the purposes of the general rule;
(c) there is, however, an exception to the general rule, in that trusts or gifts for the relief of poverty have been held to be charitable, even though they are limited in their application to some aggregate of individuals ascertained as in (b); and
(d) this exception cannot be accounted for by reference to any principle, but is established by a series of authorities of long standing.

While the requirement that the object of the disposition must involve benefit to the public, or to some section of the public, (except to some degree where the relief of poverty is involved) is a fundamental one, this alone is not sufficient. An object may be for the public benefit but yet not regarded as a charitable one. The benefit must be of a kind which is regarded in law as charitable (ie within one of Lord Macnaghten's four main categories). It is now appropriate to consider each of these categories separately.

Relief of poverty

For a trust or body of persons to be regarded as charitable under this heading, the objects of the charity do not necessarily have to be for, or to be confined to, the relief of the destitute. In *Re Coulthurst* [1951] All ER 774, a fund for the benefit of widows and orphans of deceased officers of a bank most deserving of assistance by reason of their financial circumstances was held to be charitable. In that case, Evershed MR in referring to the 'poor', said:

> It is a word of wide and somewhat indefinite import; it may not unfairly be paraphrased for present purposes as meaning persons who have to 'go short' in the ordinary acceptance of that term, due regard being had to their status in life and so forth

In *Re Wall, Pomeroy v Willway* [1889] 43 Ch D 510, gifts to the poor limited to the members of a particular church were held to be charitable. In that case, as in the case of *Re Coulthurst*, the beneficiaries may not have been within the public or a section of the public to meet the normal 'for the public benefit' test, but the purposes were held to be charitable under the less stringent requirements of the relief of poverty category of charitable purpose.

With regard to this public benefit element in relation to a trust for the relief of poverty, Lord Greene MR in *Re Compton, Powell v Compton* [1945] Ch 123, said:

> There may perhaps be some special quality in gifts for the relief of poverty which places them in a class by themselves. It may, for instance, be that the relief of poverty is to be regarded as in itself so beneficial to the community that the fact that the gift is confined to a specific family can be disregarded.

Advancement of education

For objects to be charitable under this heading, it has been held that 'education' is to be taken in a wide sense and the term is not limited to formal instruction. Clearly, the maintenance of and the provision of support to colleges, schools, etc are directly within the words of the Statute of Charles I (and of the Statute of Elizabeth I in England). The fact that a school may charge fees and be primarily for the reasonably well off does not prevent its support and maintenance from being a charitable purpose, provided that it is not run for the purpose of making a profit (*Campbell College v Commissioners of Valuation* NI [1964] NI 107.

The advancement of education has also been held to include 'the promotion or encouragement of those arts and graces of life which are, perhaps, the first and best part of the human character' (Vaisey J in *Re Shaw's Will Trust* [1952] 1 All ER 49). A disposition for the promotion of annual chess tournaments for boys has been held to be a valid trust for the advancement of education (*Re Dupree's Deed Trusts* [1944] 2 All ER 443), as has one for the encouragement of choral singing in London (*Royal Choral Society v IRC* 25 TC 263).

These cases each had the necessary element of public benefit involved, an essential prerequisite of a charitable purpose where the advancement of education is concerned. The Londoners who might benefit from the advancement of music were clearly a section of the public, as were the boys who might benefit from the improvement in their ability to play chess as a result of the tournaments. The other essential ingredient – the advancement of education, in its wider sense – was also present in each case.

In contrast, a trust for the advancement of education in political matters in the interests of one political party only was held not to be for charitable purposes (*Bonar Law Memorial Trust v IRC* 17 TC 508). Although political education is within the meaning of 'education' and a public benefit may have been involved, the decision of the Special Commissioners was upheld to the effect that the political party limitation was so strong as to become the primary object of the trust, thereby preventing it from being a charitable trust for the advancement of education.

Advancement of religion

For a trust or body of persons to be a charity under this heading, it must be established for the advancement of religion and must contain a sufficient element of public benefit (but see below re the Charities Act 1961). The purpose must be wholly and exclusively religious. The question of whether trusts for religious purposes meet the public benefit test has given rise to difficulties in the past in a number of cases, both under English and Irish law. In this area in particular, differences in interpretation have arisen from time to time in the two countries and, in contrast to the tendency in most matters where the laws are similar in the two countries, it should not be assumed that an English precedent is necessarily valid in Ireland.

It has been held in Ireland that a gift in perpetuity for Masses is a valid charitable gift, ie for a charitable purpose, whether the Masses are to be celebrated in public or in private or whether for the benefit of an individual or a class (*O'Hanlon v Cardinal Logue* [1906] 1 IR 247). Other purposes held to be charitable under this heading have included a general gift for religious purposes (*Arnott v Arnott* [1906] 1 IR 127), the advancement and benefit of the Roman Catholic religion (*Copinger v Crehane* [1877] 11 IR Eq 429) and the benefit of Presbyterian missions and orphans (*Jackson v Attorney General* [1917] IR 332).

On the other hand, a gift to 'His Holiness the Pope and his successor' was held not to be charitable, because the Pope had a wide discretion on the application of monies and could apply them for non-charitable purposes. One other area of difficulty has arisen in connection with gifts for contemplative nuns and other closed religious orders. In England, such gifts have been held not to be charitable on the grounds that the necessary 'public benefit' is not present. In Ireland, the matter has been less certain and there have been conflicting decisions in different cases.

A religious community is not itself a charitable object and, broadly, the position appears to be that the application of a gift (or of income) for the benefit of the religious community is not for charitable purposes, unless the objects of that community itself are charitable and the gift is to be devoted for the purposes of the community. A gift to the Dominican nuns was held not to be charitable because the object of the community was the provision of their own religious welfare, not a valid charitable purpose (*Cocks v Manners* [1871] LR 12 Eq 574, an English decision which has been applied in several Irish cases in the past).

However, it appears as if the *Cocks* case may no longer be a valid precedent in view of the Charities Act 1961. Section 45 of that Act provides that, in determining whether or not a gift for the purpose of the advancement of religion is a valid charitable gift, it shall be conclusively presumed that the purpose includes and will occasion public benefit. The effect seems to be that, once it has been established that the purpose of the gift is the advancement of religion, the other requirement to show a public benefit no longer has the same significance. Section 45(2) added that, in construing the effect of a valid charitable gift for the advancement of religion, the laws, canons, etc of the religion concerned are to be used in the particular case.

The Interpretation of Charities Act 1961, s 45 in relation to whether any particular trust or body of persons is charitable under the advancement of religion heading is a matter for professional legal advice.

Other purposes beneficial to the community

For a trust or body of persons to be a charity under this heading, it is necessary to show that its purposes come within the spirit of the old Statutes of Charitable Uses. As Viscount Cave LC said in *Attorney General v National Provincial Bank* [1924] AC 262:

> It is not enough to say that the trust in question is for public purposes beneficial to the community or for the public welfare; you must also show it to be a charitable trust.

The preamble to the English Statute of 43 Eliz 1, c 4, includes as a charitable purpose 'the repair of highways and bridges' (while the Irish Statute of 10 Ch 1, sess 3, c 1, includes a similar purpose). By analogy, this has been held in various cases to include the improvement of a town, the provision of a water supply, a cemetery and a workhouse, the establishment of a house of rest for nurses of a hospital, lifeboats, public libraries, museums and a village hall. On the other hand, the suppression of vivisection was held by the House of Lords not to be charitable on the grounds, *inter alia,* that its purposes were not beneficial to the community (*IRC v National Anti-Vivisection Society* 28 TC 311).

In *IRC v Temperance Council of the Christian Churches of England and Wales* 10 TC 748, which is quoted from time to time in judgments in other cases, the Council was constituted by resolution at a meeting of representatives of the temperance organisations of the Christian churches of England and Wales. Its purpose, as stated in the resolution forming the Council, was stated to be 'united action to secure legislative and other temperance reform'. While it was not denied that the promotion of temperance might be regarded as for the benefit of the community, it was held that the Council was instituted mainly with the direct purpose to effect changes in the law, not a charitable purpose. It was, therefore, held that the Council was not entitled to the income tax exemption it claimed as it was not established for charitable purposes only.

In *Pharmaceutical Society of Ireland v Revenue Commissioners* I ITR 542, it was held that one of the main purposes of the society in question was the protection and furtherance of the pharmaceutical profession. Accordingly, the society did not qualify as a charity, even though its other main purpose, the relief of the sick, was beneficial to the community and thus charitable; it is necessary that purposes of the body in question are *solely* charitable (see **18.205**). In *IRC v White* 55 TC 651, Fox J considered whether the promotion of industry and commerce could be a charitable object. He observed:

> ... the promotion or advancement of industry (including a particular industry such as agriculture) or of commerce is a charitable object provided that the purpose is the advancement or benefit of the public at large and not merely the promotion of the interests of those engaged in the manufacture and sale of their particular products.

The court held in *White* that a charity which provided subsidised workshops to individuals commencing a craft trade was charitable; although the arrangements benefited the individuals in question, they were merely the means by which the object of preserving the craft was implemented (this object being considered to be one which was beneficial to the public). In *IRC v Yorkshire Agricultural Society* 13 TC 58, it was held that a society formed to promote agriculture and to hold an annual exhibition to this end was charitable (note the statutory exemption discussed in **18.209**). The exhibition was held for a public purpose rather than merely to benefit the members of the society (see also *Crystal Palace Trustees v Minister of Town and Country Planning* [1951] Ch 132).

In contrast to these decisions, it was held in *Hadaway v Hadaway* [1955] 1 WLR 16, that a trust which provided financial assistance to businesses within a particular industry was not charitable, since it was primarily directed at benefiting private individuals. In *IRC v Oldham Training and Enterprise Council* [1996] STC 1218, an organisation which provided support and advice to businesses in a particular area (Oldham) was held not to be charitable. It was held that while the services concerned would have helped the businesses receiving them to become more profitable and thus improve employment levels in Oldham, the benefits to the community were too remote. The primary purpose of the organisation was to confer private benefits on the businesses in question (for a critique of this decision see Roycroft [1997] British Tax Review 59.

In the *Oldham TEC* case, it was also held that where the objects of an institution were comprehensively set out in its constitution, then it was necessary to refer to that constitution alone, without reference to the motives of the founders of the institution. However, evidence of what the institution had actually done was admissible in order to ascertain the practical consequences of implementing the institution's objects.

Charitable Regulatory Authority

TCA 1997, s 207A was enacted by FA 2015, s 24 and has retroactive effect from 16 October 2014. It states that the 'Charities Regulatory Authority' shall, in relation to 'relevant income', be deemed to be a body that has made a claim for, and has been granted, such exemption from income tax as is to be allowed under s 207, ie exempt status for charities. Relevant income means income from the Common Investment Fund (formerly known as the 'The Commissioners Common Investment Fund') established by the Commissioners of Charitable Donations and Bequests for Ireland under s 46 of the Charities Act 1961 with effect from 23 April 1985 and vested in the Charities Regulatory Authority on the establishment of that Authority on 16 October 2014.

18.203 Exemptions for charities

Any body of persons (whether corporate or incorporated) established for charitable purposes or any trustee for charitable purposes is a 'person' and is, therefore, subject to tax (whether income tax or corporation tax) on all sources of income, unless and to the extent specifically exempted by any provisions in the Tax Acts. This general statement is made here to make it clear that the acceptance by the Revenue Commissioner that any body of persons or trust has 'charitable status' does not mean that it can thereupon assume that it is exempt from income tax (or corporation tax). If it has any non-exempt income (eg trading income, but in certain circumstances only – see **18.204**), it can be assessed on that income in the same way as any other person.

The charitable exemptions, which are provided for income tax by TCA 1997, ss 207(1), (2), 208, may conveniently be stated separately by reference to the Sch and types of income for which they are given. The exemptions from income tax discussed in the following paragraphs also apply in corresponding circumstances to exempt from corporation tax the same types of income received by a company or other body corporate established for charitable purposes only (TCA 1997, s 76). Consequently, although TCA 1997, ss 207(1), (2), 208 both only mention 'income tax', the following explanations use the word 'tax' to denote either income tax or corporation tax (whichever is appropriate).

The types of income and the circumstances in which the charitable exemptions are given are as follows:

Schedule C

TCA 1997, s 207(1), (2) exempts from tax any interest, annuities, dividends or shares of annuities chargeable to tax under Sch C, but only if:

(a) that income forms part of the income of a body of persons or trust established for charitable purposes only; or

(b) that income is, according to the rules or regulations established by statute, charter, decree, deed of trust or will, applicable to charitable purposes only;

and only so far as that income is in fact applied to charitable purposes only.

Schedule D: interest and annual payments

TCA 1997, s 207(1), (2) also exempts from tax yearly interest or annual payments chargeable under Sch D in the same circumstances as outlined in the previous paragraph for Sch C interest, annuities, etc. This exemption is not limited to yearly interest and annual payments received from sources in the State, but extends also to any such income from foreign sources. Any charity entitled to this exemption can obtain a repayment of any retention tax deducted from deposit interest (if it has not avoided the deduction by making the charity's declaration under TCA 1997, s 266 (see **Division 2**)).

Schedule F

The exemption from tax is also granted by TCA 1997, s 207(1) for any distributions from resident companies, but again only if those distributions are part of the income of a body of persons or trust established for charitable purposes only (or is income applicable to such purposes according to rules, etc established by statute, trust, will, etc), and again only so far as the income is applied for charitable purposes only.

Schedule D: rents and other income

TCA 1997, s 207(1), (2) exempts from tax income chargeable under Sch D in respect of the rents and profits of any property:

(a) which belongs to any hospital, public school or almshouse; or
(b) which is vested in trustees for charitable purposes, but only so far as those rents or profits are applied to charitable purposes only.

At one time, the exemption given by TCA 1997, s 207(1), (2) was applicable only to such rents and profits from any such property chargeable to tax under either the old Sch A or the old rules relating to the taxation of rental income in the State. However, when the Income Tax Acts were being amended following the abolition of the old Schs A and B (by FA 1969), the wording was changed so that the charitable exemption is now extended to cover both rents chargeable under Sch D Case V and also the profits from 'any property' chargeable under Sch D. Since the word 'property' in the main Sch D charging section (TCA 1997, s 18(1), (3)) is given a very wide meaning, it seems clear that the same word, as used in ITA 1967, s 331(1)(a), must be similarly construed.

In short, apart from the profits of any trade which may – as explained in **18.204** – be taxable on the charity, the view appears to be accepted now that the charitable exemption extends to all types of income from any property or other asset that is chargeable to income tax (or corporation tax) under Sch D. This of course assumes that the income in question is actually applied to charitable purposes only, the overriding condition which must be met irrespective of the type of income or the Schedule or Case under which it normally falls.

Schedule C: income applied for certain purposes

The exemption from income tax is given by TCA 1997, s 207(1), (2) for any interest, annuities, dividends or shares of annuities chargeable under Sch C in the names of trustees applicable solely towards the repairs of any cathedral, college, church or chapel, or any building used solely for the purposes of divine worship, but only so far as the said income is applied to those purposes.

Schedule D: trading income

The treatment of income from trading is dealt with separately in **18.204**. At this point, it is sufficient to mention that a charity is, in principle, taxable under Sch D Case I on any income that it may derive from carrying on a trade, but TCA 1997, s 208 grants an exemption from this charge to tax in certain circumstances. In the case of a trade of farming, this exemption is given in any case where the profits realised by the charity (as defined) are applied solely to the purposes of the charity; for other trades, the position is not quite so straightforward and is explained later.

Repayments of tax

The body of persons or trust established for charitable purposes only normally receives any Sch C income or any annual payments chargeable under Sch D net after income tax has been deducted at the source. Similarly, if yearly interest chargeable under Sch D is received from a company resident in the State, income tax is usually deducted by the company under TCA 1997, s 246(1), (2), (4) (see **2.306**). Further, if the charity receives any foreign dividends, it is likely that tax may be deducted by the paying banker or other collecting agent in the State under the rules of TCA 1997, ss 60–63 (see **2.310**).

In any case where a charity receives any taxed income in respect of which it is exempted from tax under any of the rules of TCA 1997, s 207(1), (2), the charity is entitled to reclaim in full the income tax so deducted. For the right of a charity to reclaim any deposit interest retention tax suffered under TCA 1997, s 257, see **8.204**. Similarly, if the charity receives any distributions from resident companies (Sch F income), it is entitled to exemption from dividend withholding tax (see **9.104**).

TCA 1997, s 207 requires every claim made by a qualifying charity for exemption from income tax, whether in respect of taxed income or Sch F income, to be verified by an affidavit confirming that the charity continues to be entitled to the relevant exemption and that the income in respect of which the claim is made has been applied for charitable purposes only. For the exceptions to a charity's right to exemption, applicable under the anti-avoidance rules of TCA 1997, ss 750, 752, see **17.103–17.104**.

Any body of persons or trust established for charitable purposes only is, if resident in the State, entitled to claim exemption from UK Income Tax any dividends it may have from UK resident companies under art 11(3) of the Ireland/UK double taxation agreement if it can produce a certificate from the Revenue Commissioners confirming that it is exempted from Irish tax in respect of those dividends under the rules applicable to charities.

Foreign charities

The provisions of TCA 1997, s 208 apply only to charities which are 'established' within the State for the various exemptions (*Dreyfus (Camille & Henry) Foundation Inc v IRC* 36 TC 126). The scope of the term 'established' in this context is unclear. A trust which is subject to the jurisdiction of the Irish courts, or a company incorporated in Ireland should be regarded as meeting this requirement. However, in practice, the Revenue Commissioners will usually treat a branch of a foreign charity as established in the State if its activities are managed and controlled entirely within the State. TCA 1997, s 208A now supplements TCA 1997, ss 207 and 208 following representations by the European Commission in the light of the decision in *Stauffer* (Case C–386/04) where the ECJ held that an Italian charitable foundation in receipt of rental income from a German investment property should not be liable to German tax in circumstances where a similar charitable foundation established in Germany was exempt from tax.

With effect from 2010 onwards, TCA 1997, s 208A(2) provides that a person or trust established in an EEA or EFTA state may seek a determination from the Revenue Commissioners that if that person or trust were established in the State, it would qualify for exemption on its income falling within TCA 1997, ss 207 and 208. Every such claim must be verified by a sworn document corresponding or equivalent to an affidavit sworn in the State and proof of the claim may be given by the treasurer, trustee or any duly authorised agent (TCA 1997, s 208A(5)). The Revenue Commissioners must issue a written notice of a favourable determination (TCA 1997, s 208A(4)).

Third world charities

TCA 1997, s 848A provided a relief for charities having as their sole object relief and development in countries on the list of aid recipients produced by the Development Committee of OECD.

A list of designated third world charities is provided in *Tax Briefing 22*. To this list should be added The Church of Ireland Bishop's Appeal Fund for Relief and World Development (*Tax Briefing 23*), and Bóthar (*Tax Briefing 27*). These charities are within the 'Approved Bodies' regime described in **18.304**.

18.204 Trading by charities

TCA 1997, s 208(2) exempts any body of persons or trust established for charitable purposes only (a 'charity') from tax chargeable under Sch D in respect of the profits of any trade carried on by it, but only if:

(a) the profits are applied solely to the purposes of the charity; and
(b) either:
   (i) the trade is exercised in the course of the actual carrying out of a primary purpose of the charity, or
   (ii) the work in connection with the trade is mainly carried out by beneficiaries of the charity.

This rule is, however, varied if the trade carried on by the charity is the trade of farming. In this event, the exemption is given if the profits of the trade are applied solely to the purposes of the charity (TCA 1997, s 208(3)). It is not necessary for the charity's farming trade to satisfy either part of condition (b) above. This amendment to the general rule relating to trading by charities was brought in by TCA 1997, s 683 (but was made effective retrospectively from 6 April 1974 onwards, ie from the commencement of the taxation of farming profits).

Apart from this exception for farming, any charity carrying on a trade that is not exempted, because it cannot satisfy either part of condition (b), is taxable on the profits of the trade under the ordinary rules of Sch D Case I. It should be borne in mind that the term 'trade' includes adventures in the nature of a trade, and that even 'one off' events could fall to be taxed. However, in *Leaflet CHY 7* which was withdrawn, the Revenue Commissioners had set out a concession in respect of profits arising from small-scale activities which have been run to raise funds for charitable purposes only.

The following conditions must be satisfied:

(a) the trading activities are not carried on regularly;
(b) the trading activities carried on are not in competition with other commercial traders;
(c) the public support the trading activities because they believe that the profits are intended for application to charitable purposes only; and
(d) the profits are applied for charitable purposes only.

The Revenue stated that each activity would be considered on its merits, provided that it is small in scale. In deciding what is considered to be 'small-scale', several factors must be considered together:

(a) the level of both turnover and profit;
(b) the degree of commercial organisation involved;
(c) the level of input by outside bodies including professional fundraisers and well known personalities, including individuals giving their services voluntarily; and
(d) the numbers of people attending.

The Revenue stated also that relief will normally extend to all of the profits of an activity including:

(a) admission charges;
(b) sale of refreshments;
(c) sale of programmes; and
(d) sale of advertisements, eg in a programme.

However, every source of income must form part of the overall event and contribute to the total profits earned. In any case where a source of income constitutes a separate profit-making activity the profits generated will be taxable.

Another point to note is that income derived from the use of land and buildings will normally be taxed as rental income under Sch D Case V. In certain situations where the use of land is provided as part of a package of services it may rank as trading income (see **4.102**: *Income from property rights*). In *Leaflet CHY 7*, the Revenue Commissioners expressed the view that the provision of ancillary services, such as caretaking services, might mean that what would otherwise constitute rental income could be classed as trading income. It would seem however, that the services concerned should be more substantial in nature than *CHY 7* would suggest before this would become an issue.

The Revenue Commissioners had also accepted that the sale of donated goods by charity shops (or by way of auction or jumble sale) is not generally a trading activity. They stated that:

> An increasing number of charities are raising funds by selling donated goods and this activity may take place on a regular basis through a shop or on an occasional basis at jumble sales or auctions. The feature which distinguishes this activity from a commercial retail business is the way in which the goods being sold are acquired – charity shops merely realise the value of a gift which they have received, whereas a commercial venture buys goods specifically for resale at a profit. On this basis, the sale of donated goods is not regarded as being a trade for tax purposes and will not attract a liability. The goods donated may be cleaned and/or repaired prior to sale and this will not affect the tax treatment. However, if donated goods are subjected to a major refurbishment or to a process which alters their condition fundamentally, the sale of the goods may be regarded as being a trade. For example, if a manufacturer donates a roll of cloth and the charity converts this into items of clothing for sale then the operation will be treated as a commercial trade.

It is not clear following the withdrawal of CHY 7 if the Revenue will continue to follow the above concessions. In an earlier version of *'Applying for relief from tax on income and property of charities resident in the State'* CHY 1 published in February 2013, under the heading 'Trading', outlined that a separate exemption is required in connection with trading activities and that the applicant was requested to attach a statement showing how it will advance the objectives of the body. It also requested details of any trading activities already being carried on.

There are a number of tax cases where it has been held that a body of persons, admitted to be established for charitable purposes only, is taxable on the profits of a trade carried on by it, even where all the profits are applied solely to its charitable purposes. However, in reviewing any cases on this issue, it is to be noted that the exemption now given in TCA 1997, s 208(2) for a trade exercised in the course of carrying out a primary purpose of the charity was only introduced in Ireland by FA 1955, s 3. The corresponding exemption for such a 'primary purpose' trade was brought into the UK legislation in 1927. Consequently, any decision in the UK before 1927, or any Irish decision before 1955, may not necessarily be a valid precedent for a corresponding case occurring now in which the primary purpose test is satisfied.

In *Brighton College v Marriot* 10 TC 213, the House of Lords held – in 1925 – that the surplus fees over expenses of a company, limited by guarantee, formed to carry on a public school, were profits or gains arising from the carrying on of a trade by the college in respect of which the college was assessable under Sch D Case I. It had been accepted that the college was a trustee for charitable purposes and had, as a result, been granted a repayment of income tax suffered on its rents and dividends. Further, the profits from its trade had been applied solely to its charitable purposes. In the course of his judgment, Viscount Cave LC said:

> It has also been decided, both in the courts and in this House, that a charitable institution which carries on a trade at a profit is chargeable with income tax in respect of its profits or gains in that trade, notwithstanding that they are and can only be applied to the purposes of the charity.

A similar decision was reached in the Irish case of *Davis v Superioress, Mater Misericordiae Hospital, Dublin* I ITR 387. In this case, a hospital established for the relief of the sick who were poor also admitted paying patients for treatment in an annexe. The hospital and the annexe were administered as one undertaking and the costs of running the entire undertaking significantly exceeded the income from the paying patients in the annexe. However, although the whole undertaking was accepted as a charitable institution, the Supreme Court held – in 1933 – that the acceptance of private patients was the carrying on of a trade and the resulting profits from it were taxable. Since the rest of the undertaking was non-trading, it was not permissible to set off the excess expenses of the non-trading activities against the trading profits.

It is understood that the UK amendment in 1927 bringing in the 'primary purpose' trade exemption was made to overcome the difficulty arising from the decision in the *Brighton College* case in 1925. It was clearly felt that surplus fees arising in the case of a school run by a charitable trust (a clear charitable purpose) should be exempt if applied solely to that or any other charitable purpose. The parallel Irish amendment in 1955 was brought in to deal particularly with the position of educational and hospital charities, but applies now to any charity trading in the course of the primary purpose for which it is established.

It is not uncommon for schools to be established in the State as companies limited by guarantee which, in their memoranda of association, set out their objects as being the advancement of education. If the constitution of the company also requires the whole of the income and property of the company to be applied solely towards the promotion of that object, the school should – in the absence of any other factors to the contrary – be accepted as a body of persons established for charitable purposes only. If so, any trading profits from running the school are exempted from tax.

In *Dean Leigh Temperance Canteen Trustees v IRC* 38 TC 315, a canteen was carried on by trustees nominated by the local branch of a temperance organisation (not itself a charity). The trustees were appointed under a deed which provided that any receipts of the business should be applied to the running and maintenance of the canteen, to the provision of similar canteens in Hereford or elsewhere or towards any other objects which tended to promote temperance. All profits not required for carrying on and maintaining the canteen were in fact given to temperance organisations or invested.

It was held in the Chancery Division that the trust was established for charitable purposes only, namely the promotion of temperance generally by charitable means, and that the canteen was run in the carrying out of that charitable purpose. The profits were, in consequence, exempted from income tax under the UK equivalent of (TCA 1997, s 208(2)). On the basis that the promotion of temperance was an accepted charitable purpose, Harman J was satisfied that the appellants in the case had met the test which he stated to be:

> Therefore what the appellants must show is that their trust is a trust for the promotion of temperance and that the carrying on of this canteen is a means to that end – in other words

that it is a trust to promote temperance by running a canteen; and this must be the sole purpose the promotion of temperance, and the running of the canteen the means to that end.

In *Leaflet CHY 7*, which has now been withdrawn, the Revenue Commissioners gave as examples of 'primary purpose' trades:

(a) an art gallery or museum holding an exhibition and charging an admission fee;
(b) a school providing an educational service on a fee paying basis;
(c) a theatre selling tickets for a production which it is staging; and
(d) a hospital providing health care services on a fee paying basis.

The Revenue Commissioners also accepted that trades which were ancillary to the carrying of a primary purpose trade would qualify for charitable exemption. They gave as examples:

(a) a theatre selling food and drink in a bar and/or restaurant to members of the audience attending a performance being staged;
(b) a school providing accommodation for students on a rental basis;
(c) a hospital selling papers, flowers and toiletries to patients and their guests; and
(d) a museum or art gallery selling food in a coffee shop to visitors attending an exhibition.

The Revenue also stated that situations may arise where a trade may be carried on which could not be classified as being solely a primary purpose activity although certain elements of it could be included in that category. They gave as an example of such a situation an educational charity which provides accommodation for students on a fee basis during school terms and rents out the same buildings to tourists during holiday periods. In these circumstances, they stated that it is likely that the trade would not qualify for exemption because it is not solely a primary purpose activity. However, in practice, it would be accepted that the profits of the trade would be exempt where:

(a) that part of the trade which is not a primary purpose activity is small, relative to the overall trading activity; and
(b) the turnover of that part of the trade which is not a primary purpose activity is not greater than 10 per cent of the entire trading turnover.

The Revenue stated that in any situation where these conditions are not fulfilled, *all* of the profits arising will be liable to tax, including that part which is a primary purpose activity. However, it must be borne in mind that it remains open to the taxpayer to argue in appropriate cases that the 'non-primary purpose' activity is a separate trade, or that it is not a trading activity at all (as may be the case for a letting activity).

An example of a case of a trade carried on by a charity exempted due to the fact that the work in connection with the trade is mainly carried on by beneficiaries of the charity is *Brighton College v Marriot* 10 TC 213. The convent was a branch of a religious order established for the sanctification of its members by worship and by labour for the benefit of their fellow creatures, particularly by the Christian education of young girls and the care of the sick. In addition to their training in matters of religion, the nuns were educated to take part in carrying on the school or other work of the convent of which they were members. The main work of the convent was to carry on the school. The nuns were held to be beneficiaries of the charity so that it was, therefore, entitled to the tax exemption in respect of the trading profits of the school.

In *Leaflet CHY 7*, the Revenue Commissioners had stated that where the work undertaken by the beneficiaries of the charity has an educational or remedial purpose, it will often qualify in any event as a 'primary purpose' activity. They commented further as follows:

> However, even if the work is not a primary purpose activity it will still qualify for exemption from tax as a trade where the work is carried out mainly by the beneficiaries. In order to obtain exemption from tax, it is necessary to prove that the greater part of a trade carried on by a charity is undertaken by the beneficiaries – particularly where there are others involved, eg employees or volunteer workers who are not beneficiaries. There is nothing to prevent the charity paying the beneficiaries as employees. An example of such a trade would be the sale of goods manufactured by the beneficiaries of a charity established for individuals suffering from disability.

Mining, quarrying etc profits

TCA 1997, s 208(2)(a) exempts any charity from tax chargeable under Sch D Case I by TCA 1997, s 18(2), (3) where the profits or gains so chargeable arise out of lands, tenements or hereditaments which are owned and occupied by the charity. This applies where the lands, etc are occupied by the charity for the purposes of mining, quarrying or any of the other concerns enumerated in Sch D Case I(b). In this case, there is no further condition imposed, other than that the charity must be a body of persons or trust established for charitable purposes only.

18.205 'Charitable purposes only'

The various tax exemptions provided by TCA 1997, ss 207(1), (2), 208 require – in nearly all cases – that the charitable body or trust show (a) that it is established for charitable purposes only and (b) that the income to be exempted is applied for charitable purposes only. While the meaning of 'charitable purposes' has been discussed in some detail in **18.202**, several other questions must be dealt with. First, what is necessary for the charitable purposes 'only' condition to be met? Is it possible for the test to be satisfied if the body of persons or trust has any purpose that is not strictly charitable, even if its main purposes are charitable? Secondly, what counts as the 'application' of income to charitable purposes?

Before accepting that a body of persons or trust has 'charitable status', so that any repayment of tax or exemption from assessment may be given, the Revenue Commissioners require to be satisfied that the 'established for charitable purposes *only*' test is, in fact, met. This does not necessarily mean that the charity may not have some ancillary objects which would not, on their own, be regarded as charitable, but any such ancillary objects must be incidental and/or subsidiary to the attainment of the primary charitable purposes of the charity. This links in with a rule of the general law relating to charities that a gift may have a non-charitable object if it is only incidental to a larger charitable purpose.

It is important to note that any body of persons or trust established with objects which include one or more objects not within the legal concept of 'charitable purposes' (other than permitted ancillary objects) is not entitled to the tax exemptions available to charities. In deciding whether to grant any relevant exemption in any case, the Revenue looks primarily at the main statute, charter, deed of trust or, in the case of a company, its memorandum of association to determine what are the objects of the body of persons or trust concerned.

If this charter, deed of trust, memorandum of association etc includes any primary object which is not 'charitable', the Revenue should decline to grant the charitable status and reject any claim for the repayment of tax. In particular, any suggestion in the objects that it is possible, even if only remotely, for any income or profits to be applied for purposes other than those of the charity (eg for the distribution of any profits or the payment of any benefit to any person other than a genuine beneficiary) the tax exemption is not given.

A body of persons or a trust may be established for proper charitable purposes, but the attainment of those purposes (its primary objects) may sometimes involve the promotion of objects which are not in themselves strictly charitable. In any such case, this should not take away the charitable status provided that it is clear that any non-charitable objects which might be involved are no more than subsidiary and/or ancillary to the attainment of the primary objects. Clearly, it is not possible to make any precise statement as to when objects may have this ancillary nature that does not cause the charity to be regarded as established other than for charitable purposes only. Each particular case must be considered on its own facts.

One tax case where the question of ancillary purposes was considered is *Incorporated Council of Law Reporting for England and Wales v Attorney General* 3 All ER 1029, 47 TC 321. The Council's primary object, as set out in its memorandum of association and to which all the other objects were ancillary, was the preparation and publication in a convenient form at a moderate price, and under gratuitous professional control, of reports of judicial decisions in the courts in England. The Council's income and property were applicable solely towards the promotion of its objects and were not transferable to the members by way of dividend or otherwise.

The Council had contended that its purposes were charitable either as being fo advancement of education or, alternatively, as being otherwise beneficial to community. For the Crown, it was contended that the purposes of the Council were n wholly charitable because they amounted to no more than carrying on the trade c publishers and sellers of law reports and because one of the Council's main purposes was to advance the interests of the legal profession by supplying it with the tools of its trade.

The Court of Appeal held that the Council was established for charitable purposes only, those purposes being either the advancement of education or, if not, other charitable purposes beneficial to the community. In commencing his judgment, Russell LJ (at page 334) indicated:

> In order to see for what purposes the Association was established and whether those purposes are exclusively charitable, attention must be focused upon its memorandum and articles of association, bearing in mind, of course, that purposes merely ancillary to a main charitable purpose which if taken by themselves would not be charitable, will not vitiate the claim of an institution to be established for purposes that are exclusively charitable.

In the course of his judgment, Buckley LJ (at page 349) said:

> The fact that the Council's publications can be regarded as a necessary part of a practising lawyer's equipment does not, in my judgment, at all prevent the Council from being established exclusively for charitable purposes. The practising lawyer and the judge must both be lifelong students in that field of scholarship for the study of which the Law Reports provide essential material and a necessary service … It also helps the lawyer to earn his livelihood, but that is incidental to or consequential on the primary scholastic function of advancing and disseminating knowledge of the law, and does not, in my judgment, detract from the exclusively charitable character of the Council's object …

A charity may be accepted as having charitable purposes only, but the availability of the exemptions depends also on the actual application of the income for which the exemptions are claimed to charitable purposes only. The use of the income to meet the normal running expenses of the charity (including proper remuneration for the employees) has always been accepted as an application for the charitable purposes as, clearly, is any application for the benefit of the primary objects of the charity, eg to provide relief for the 'poor' or to advance education (possibly by paying good salaries to secure good teachers or possibly by way of giving scholarships).

What is the position with the reinvestment of income or with the transfer of income to another charitable body? Both these issues were considered by the Court of Appeal in *IRC v Helen Slater Charitable Trust Ltd* [1980] STC 150. Two companies – 'the Trust' and 'the Foundation' – were incorporated in 1970 exclusively for charitable purposes, and were intended to work in tandem, the Trust's main function being to raise funds for the Foundation. In the years 1973 to 1975, the Trusts donated substantially its whole income to the Foundation, most of which the Foundation added to its general funds which were not distributed. The Revenue rejected the Trust's claim to charitable exemption for the income on the ground that the money had not been 'applied' for charitable purposes.

It was held that such a transfer by a charitable corporation, acting *intra vires*, to any other company established exclusively for charitable purposes, in such a manner as to pass the transferee full title to the money, must be said to have been an 'application' of the money for charitable purposes. This conclusion was not upset by the fact that the transferee added the money to its general reserves for expenditure in the future. This decision was given on the basis that the transferor knew that the money would be applied in due course for charitable purposes by the transferee or, at least, that the transferor had no reason for thinking that the money would not be so used.

One of the arguments of the Crown rejected by the Court of Appeal was that money subject to charitable trusts is not 'applied' unless it is actually expended on the expenses of managing the charity or in making distribution for the attainment of particular charitable objects. It was suggested that the investment of the monies was not an 'application' for the required purposes. On this point, Oliver LJ, in rejecting the Crown's point, said:

> Charitable trustees who simply leave surplus income uninvested cannot, I think, be said to have 'applied' it at all, and, indeed, would be in breach of trust. But if the income is reinvested by them and held, as invested, as part of the funds of the charity, I would be disposed to say that it is no less being applied for charitable purposes than if it is paid out in wages to the secretary.

In *Nightingale v Price* [1996] STC (SCD) 116 the taxpayer was a charity which owned a number of trading subsidiaries which covenanted their profits to it. The taxpayer made loans back to the subsidiaries equal to the sums received under the covenant arrangements at high rates of interest. The Special Commissioner held that the taxpayer had a deliberate policy designed to increase its financial resources and the loans were not merely made on an automatic basis to offset the covenanted sums paid by the subsidiaries. Accordingly, the making of the loans was an application of the taxpayer's income for charitable purposes.

18.206 Exemption of certain sports bodies

TCA 1997, s 235 exempts from income tax any income accruing to any unincorporated body of persons which has been established, and exists, for the sole purpose of promoting athletic or amateur games or sports. However, the exemption from tax is only given in respect of so much of the income of the 'sporting body' as is shown to the satisfaction of the Revenue Commissioners to be income which has been, or will be, applied to the sole purpose of promoting athletic or amateur games or sports.

Although a sporting body may be exempted from income tax on its income by TCA 1997, s 235, it suffers the retention tax on any deposit interest paid or credited to it by a bank, building society or other relevant deposit taker (see **8.204**). Unlike an exempted charity, the sporting body is not entitled to any repayment of the deposit interest retention tax, nor is it able to avoid the deduction of this tax by making the declaration available to an exempted charity.

TCA 1997, s 235 starts by using the term 'approved body of persons' to denote any body of persons established for and existing for the sole purpose of promoting athletic or amateur games or sports ('the qualifying sporting purpose'), as well as any body of persons entitled to the exemption for 1983–84 or earlier years. It then goes on to exclude from an 'approved body of persons' any such sporting body to which the Revenue Commissioners serve notice in writing that it does not qualify for the sporting bodies exemption. Upon service of this notice, the body in question ceases to be entitled to the exemption and becomes taxable under the ordinary rules with effect from a date which depends on the reasons for the notice (see below).

TCA 1997, s 235, in defining an 'approved body of persons', takes the line that any body of persons established and existing for the sole purpose of promoting athletic or amateur games or sports (any one such purpose will do), or any such body of persons to which the exemption was granted prior to 1984–85, is within the exemption for 1984–85 unless and until it has been served with a notice withdrawing its approval. While this may appear to confer '*prima facie*' approval unless and until such a 'notice of disapproval' has been served, it does not mean that a sporting body on which no such notice of disapproval has yet been served may continue to enjoy the exemption after it has ceased to be entitled to it. The notice of disapproval may be served with retrospective effect (see below).

In order to be entitled to the exemption as an approved body of persons, a sporting body to which no exemption was granted before 1984–85 must show that it has been established for one or more of the qualifying sporting purposes. It must also satisfy the Revenue Commissioners that it does not have any other purpose. In making their decision on this matter, the Revenue Commissioners generally require to examine the detailed constitution, rules, etc of the sporting body concerned to make a determination as to whether they meet the sole sporting purpose test or, alternatively, as to whether they have other purposes which will prevent its obtaining the exemption under TCA 1997, s 235.

The sporting body may be a particular club (eg a rugby football club or a basketball club) or it may be an association representing some or all of the clubs participating in a certain sport (eg the Dundrum and District Croquet Clubs Association). Further, while the word 'amateur' appears, it is linked only with the word 'games' and does not prevent a body of persons with a sole purpose of promoting athletic games or other sports which may have some element of professional participation. However, if the making of profits is a primary purpose of the sporting body, this is likely to disqualify it from the exemption. On the other hand, a club or association which might make a profit on its activities is not debarred from the exemption, provided that its rules make it clear that any such profit can only be applied for the purposes of promoting the sports, games, etc.

The Revenue Commissioners are empowered to give a notice in writing to any body of persons stating, if it is their opinion to that effect, that the body either:

(a) was not established for the sole qualifying sporting purpose, or was established wholly or partly for the purpose of securing a tax advantage; or
(b) being established for the sole qualifying sporting purpose, either no longer exists for such purpose or commences to exist wholly or partly for the purpose of securing a tax advantage.

TCA 1997, s 235 provides that, where the notice is served under heading (a), it has effect to deny the sporting body the benefit of the exemption from the tax year in which it was established or if later, from the tax year 1984–85. This provision is designed to counteract the perceived abuse of the exemption which might have followed from the approach of the courts in *Revenue Commissioners v ORMG* III ITR 28.

In the case of a notice of disapproval within heading (b), the sporting body ceases to be entitled to the exemption with, if necessary, retrospective effect to the tax year in which it ceased to exist for the sole qualifying sporting purpose, but not for any year earlier than 1984–85.

TCA 1997, s 235 allows a body of persons aggrieved by a notice given to that body by the Revenue Commissioners to appeal the notice to the Appeal Commissioners within the period of 30 days after the date of the notice; this was brought about by F(TA)A 2015, s 35(7) and was subject to Ministerial Order (SI 110/2016 appointed 21 March 2016 as the day on which the Finance (Tax Appeals) Act 2015, came into operation).

18.207 Human rights organisations

TCA 1997, s 209 extended charitable status to any body of persons having consultative status with the United Nations Organisation or the Council of Europe which:

(a) has as its sole or main object the promotion or observance of the provisions of the Universal Declaration of Human Rights or the implementation of the European Convention for the Protection of Human Rights and Fundamental Freedoms, or both; and
(b) is precluded by its rules or constitution from the direct or indirect payment or transfer, otherwise than for valuable and sufficient consideration, to any of its members of any of its income or property by way of dividend, gift, division, bonus or otherwise howsoever by way of profit.

This exemption was designed primarily to provide charitable status to Amnesty International, which would not otherwise qualify (*McGovern v Attorney General* [1981] 3 All ER 493). From 6 April 2001, qualifying organisations are brought within the 'Approved Bodies' regime described in **18.304**.

18.208 Friendly societies and trade unions

Friendly societies

TCA 1997, s 211(1)–(4) exempts a registered friendly society from tax in respect of all income otherwise chargeable under Schs C, D and F, but only if the following conditions are *all* met:

(a) the society is precluded, by statute or by its rules, from assuring to any person a sum exceeding €1,270 by way of gross sum, or €70 a year by way of annuity;

(b) the society was established for any or all of the purposes set out in the Friendly Societies Act 1896, s 8(1), and not for the purpose of securing a tax advantage; and

(c) the society has, since its establishment, engaged solely in activities directed to achieving the purposes for which it was so established and has not engaged in trading activities (other than by way of insurance in respect of its members) with a view to the realisation of profits.

A friendly society is a society established to provide, by the voluntary subscriptions of its members, for the relief or maintenance of the members and their families during sickness or old age, and their widows and orphan children. A friendly society is normally registered under the Friendly Societies Acts, in which case, it acquires corporate status under those Acts and is, in consequence, chargeable to corporation tax on its income (unless within the exemption provided by TCA 1997, s 211(1)–(4)). A friendly society may remain unregistered. In this event, it is an unincorporated body of persons liable to income tax on any income it may earn on its deposits, investments, etc.

In the case of the registered friendly society, the Revenue Commissioners may, after considering any evidence in relation to the matter submitted to them by the society, determine – if the circumstances warrant – that the society does not satisfy either or both of the conditions (b) and (c) stated above. If the Commissioners make this determination for any tax year, the society's exemption from tax under TCA 1997, s 211(1)–(4) ceases to apply for that tax year and subsequent tax years. The society then becomes liable to tax on its income from all sources in the ordinary way.

If a friendly society is aggrieved by such a determination of the Revenue Commissioners, the society is entitled to appeal to the Appeal Commissioners. The Appeal Commissioners are then required to hear and determine the appeal as if it were an appeal against an assessment to income tax or corporation tax. The normal provisions regarding the rehearing of the appeal by the Circuit Court judge, and for the statement of a case for the opinion of the High Court on a point of law (see **Division 2**), apply also (TCA 1997, s 211(1)–(4)). However, the rehearing to the Circuit Court was removed by F(TA)A 2015, s 35(7) but such adjustment was subject to Ministerial Order (SI 110/2016 appointed 21 March 2016 as the day on which the Finance (Tax Appeals) Act 2015, came into operation).

Although it may be exempted from income tax on its income, a registered friendly society is liable to the DIRT on any deposit interest paid or credited to it by a bank, building society or other relevant deposit taker. The registered friendly society is not entitled to claim any repayment of this deposit interest retention tax (TCA 1997, s 261).

Trade unions

TCA 1997, s 213(1), (2) exempts a registered trade union from tax in respect of interest and dividends otherwise chargeable under Schs C, D and F, but only if the trade union is precluded, by statute or by its rules, from assuring to any person either a sum exceeding €10,160 by way of gross sum, or €2,540 a year by way of annuity.

This exemption is only given in respect of the trade union's interest and dividends which are applicable, and are in fact applied, solely for the purpose of provident benefits. 'Provident benefits' are defined as including:

> any payment expressly authorised by the registered rules of the trade union, which is made to a member during sickness or incapacity from personal injury or while out of work, or to an aged member by way of superannuation, or to a member who has met with an accident, or

has lost his tools by fire or theft, and includes a payment in discharge or aid of funeral expenses on the death of a member, or the wife of a member, or as provision for the children of a deceased member.

There is a Revenue precedent to the effect that provident benefits may include dental, optical and legal benefits.

Although it may be exempted from income tax in respect of interest and dividends, a trade union is liable to the DIRT on any deposit interest paid or credited to it by a bank, building society or other relevant deposit taker. A trade union is not entitled to claim any repayment of this deposit interest retention tax (TCA 1997, s 261).

18.209 Agricultural societies: exhibitions and shows

TCA 1997, s 215 exempts an agricultural society from tax on any profits or gains arising from an exhibition or show held for the purposes of the society, but only if they are applied solely to the purposes of the society. For this exemption, 'agricultural society' is defined as any society or institution established for the purpose of promoting the interests of agriculture, horticulture, livestock breeding, or forestry.

The question of whether a particular society was entitled to this exemption as an agricultural society within the above definition was considered in the case of *The Trustees of the Ward Union Hunt Races v Hughes* I ITR 538. In that case, a committee (the Trustees) set up to hold horse races annually at Fairyhouse, Co Meath, was held not to be a society or institution established for the promotion of livestock breeding (and it did not qualify under any of the other headings of the definition of 'agricultural society'). The Circuit Court judge (on a rehearing) accepted that the body of trustees was a 'society' and was 'established', but that it was not an agricultural society within the meaning of the relevant exemption (the forerunner to TCA 1997, s 215). The High Court upheld that decision as it was a finding of fact supported by valid evidence.

18.210 Special trusts for permanently incapacitated individuals

TCA 1997, s 189A provides an exemption from income tax in respect of most forms of non-trading income for 'qualifying trusts'. A '*qualifying trust*' is a trust established by deed in respect of which it is shown to the satisfaction of the inspector or, on appeal, to the Appeal Commissioners (the requirement that it be shown to the satisfaction of the Inspector or Appeal Commissioner is removed by F(TA)A 2015, s 35(7) but such adjustment was subject to Ministerial Order) (SI 110/2016 appointed 21 March 2016 as the day on which the Finance (Tax Appeals) Act 2015, came into operation), that:

- (a) the trust has been established exclusively for the benefit of one or more specified *incapacitated individual* or individuals, for whose benefit *public subscriptions* have been raised;
- (b) the trust requires that:
  - (i) the *trust funds* be applied for the benefit of such individual(s) at the discretion of the trustees, and
  - (ii) in the event of the death of such individual(s), the undistributed part of the trust funds should be applied:

  where the individual or last surviving individual as the case may be is survived by a child, spouse, or civil partner, be appointed in favour of the estate or the deceased individual (inserted by Finance Act 2014, s 10) or otherwise be applied for charitable purposes or be appointed in favour of the trustees of charitable bodies; and

(c) none of the trustees is connected (within the meaning of TCA 1997, s 10: see **12.304**) with such individual(s) (TCA 1997, s 189A(1)). A 'permanently incapacitated individual' is one who is permanently and totally incapacitated by reason of mental or physical infirmity, from being able to maintain himself or herself.

'*Public subscriptions*' are subscriptions in the form of money or other property raised, following an appeal made in that behalf to members of the public, for the benefit of one or more incapacitated individuals, whose identity or identities are known to the persons making the subscriptions. In addition, the subscriptions must meet *either* of the following conditions:

(a) the total amount of the subscriptions does not exceed €381,000; or

(b) no amount of the subscriptions, at any time on or after the specified return date (see **2.105**) for the chargeable period for which exemption is *first* claimed (for either income tax or capital gains tax) constitutes a subscription made by any one person that is greater than 30 per cent of the total amount of the subscriptions.

It may be noted that in applying the 30 per cent rule there is no provision for aggregating the subscriptions made by connected persons; thus, eg a husband and wife could each make subscriptions just below the 30 per cent threshold (assuming that neither spouse is acting as an agent or nominee for the other and on the basis that TCA 1997, s 811 is not in point). '*Trust funds*' are defined as:

(a) public subscriptions, raised for the benefit of the incapacitated individual(s) who are the subject (s) of the trust; and

(b) all moneys and other property derived directly or indirectly from such public subscriptions (ie including reinvested income and capital gains).

The exemption from income tax under TCA 1997, s 189A extends to dividends or other income which would otherwise be chargeable under Sch C, Sch D Case III, IV (by virtue of TCA 1997, s 59: see **2.309**, TCA 1997, s 745: see **17.403,** or with effect from 1 January 2007, TCA 1997, s 747E: see **17.407**), Sch D Case V or Sch F (TCA 1997, s 189A(2)).

A beneficiary in receipt of income from a qualifying trust may also be exempt from tax thereon: see **1.307**.

18.3 Miscellaneous Reliefs

18.301 Expenditure on certain significant buildings

TCA 1997, s 482(1)–(7), (10) allows 'loss relief' to any person (whether an individual, company or other person) who has incurred *qualifying expenditure* in respect of an *approved building* that is either owned or occupied by him. The relief is given by treating the full amount of the qualifying expenditure as if that amount were a loss from a trade sustained in the tax year in which the expenditure was incurred. It is given without regard to whether or not the person claiming the relief is in fact carrying on any trade at all. This relief is potentially subject to the restrictions applicable to high income individuals discussed at **3.111**.

Relief will only be allowed if details of the dates and times when the building is open to the public are provided to Fáilte Ireland by 1 November in the tax year for which the claim is made. This condition must also be fulfilled in the shortest of the following periods:

(a) all tax years since 23 May 1994;
(b) all tax years since approval was given;
(c) all tax years since an approved building was purchased or occupied; or
(d) the five tax years prior to the period for which the claim is made (TCA 1997, s 482).

This information is provided to Fáilte Ireland on the understanding that it may be published for the promotion of tourism. In addition, where the building is in use as a tourist accommodation facility, (ie guest house accommodation, registered with Bord Fáilte under the Tourist Traffic Act 1939, Pt III, or under Tourist Traffic Act 1957, s 9) that the registration or listing was maintained throughout the tax years described above (TCA 1997, s 482(2)(b)).

Relief will not apply for any tax year prior to that in which the application is made to the Revenue Commissioners.

The effect of granting the relief for the qualifying expenditure on approved buildings in this way is that, if the claimant is an individual or other person chargeable to income tax in respect of his total income, the amount of the 'loss' is deducted under the rules of TCA 1997, s 381 in arriving at his total income for the tax year in which the expenditure is incurred (see **4.404**). Consequently, if the person incurring the qualifying expenditure is a husband or wife assessable jointly under TCA 1997, s 1017, any part of the qualifying expenditure which cannot be fully absorbed by that person's own income from all sources may be offset against his spouse's income for the tax year in question.

Of course, in the case of an approved building which is a 'tourist accommodation facility' the individual will in fact be carrying on a trade in the building. However, a strict reading of the relieving provision (TCA 1997, s 482(2)) still requires that the qualifying expenditure be treated as if it were a loss carried on in a trade separate to any trade actually carried on by the individual.

Where qualifying expenditure is incurred in a tax year, but due to an insufficiency of income in that period the notional trading loss cannot be fully utilised, the unused part of the loss may be carried forward to the subsequent tax year and, if still not fully utilised in that year, any unused element may be carried forward to the next subsequent tax year, but not to any subsequent tax years. The amount carried forward in each such case is treated as a loss in a separate trade carried on by the claimant in the tax year into which the relief is carried forward. Any unutilised relief carried forward must be utilised in priority to any relief due in the current tax year. Relief carried forward from an earlier year must also be utilised in priority to relief carried forward from a later year (TCA 1997, s 482(3)).

From 1 January 2002, subject to certain transitional arrangements, the amount of the relief under TCA 1997, s 482 was restricted to €31,750 in the case of an individual participating in a passive investment scheme. The relief will only be available for tax years 2010 and 2011 in relation to work which was completed or under way before 4 February 2010 or else carried out under a contractual commitment entered into prior to 4 February 2010 and evidenced in writing where the work commenced after that date. Broadly, a passive investment scheme is defined as a scheme under which:

(a) a person (who will make a claim under TCA 1997, s 482 as owner or occupier) takes an interest in a building from its then owner;

(b) at that time, or in the next five years, the building is determined to be an approved building for the purposes of TCA 1997, s 482; and

either:

(c) (i) arrangements exist at the time of the transfer such that the original owner or a person connected with him:

 (I) retains the right to determine how any expenditure on the building is to be incurred,

 (II) is entitled to participate directly or indirectly in the tax benefits, or

 (III) may reacquire the transferee's interest, or

 (ii) the transfer is made for the sole or main purpose of facilitating the claim.

For these purposes, any relevant arrangements may be express or implied and need not be legally enforceable (TCA 1997, s 409C(2)).

Where relief is restricted under TCA 1997, s 409C(4), ie because the amount of the notional trading loss exceeds €31,750, the excess is treated as if it arose due to an insufficiency of taxable income (TCA 1997, s 409C(5)). Accordingly, such excess will be carried forward to the following tax years (up to a maximum of two) as described above, but subject always to the overriding limit of €31,750 pa.

Approved building

First, the relief is only allowed if the building is one owned or occupied by the person claiming the relief. Secondly, the building must be one which – following an application by the person claiming the relief – is determined by the Minister for Arts, Heritage and the Gaeltacht to be a building which is intrinsically of significant scientific, historical, architectural or aesthetic interest. Thirdly, the Revenue Commissioners must determine that the building is one to which reasonable access is afforded to the public (TCA 1997, s 482(1)–(7)) or which is in use as a tourist accommodation facility for at least six months in each calendar year, including at least four months in the period from 1 May to 30 September (TCA 1997, s 482(1)–(7)).

For the building to be one to which reasonable access is afforded to the public, the following further conditions must be met:

(a) the access to the public must be to the whole or a substantial part of the building at the same time;

(b) the access to the public must be afforded for not less than 60 days in any year for at least four hours per day (subject to temporary closure necessary for the repair, maintenance or restoration of the building). Of these 60 days, 40 days must be during the period 1 May–30 September each year and with effect for expenditure incurred on or after 8 February 2012, must include any days which comprise National Heritage week which fall within that period. In cases where determinations have been made on or after 23 March 2000 (date of passing of the FA 2000), 10 out of the 40 days must fall on Saturdays or Sundays. In cases where determinations have been given before 23 March 2000, the requirement to comply with the new 10 day/weekend rule will apply where qualifying expenditure is incurred in a chargeable period beginning on or after 1 October 2000; and

(c) the price (if any) paid by the public for that access must, in the opinion of the Revenue Commissioners, be reasonable in its amount (TCA 1997, s 482(1)–(7)).

For these purposes, an approved building includes land occupied or enjoyed with that building as part of its garden or ornamental grounds (TCA 1997, s 482(1)(c)).

Qualifying expenditure

This term means expenditure incurred (a) on the repair, maintenance or restoration of an approved building or (b) on the maintenance or restoration of any land occupied or enjoyed with an approved building as part of its garden or grounds of an ornamental nature. Any part of such expenditure is to be treated as qualifying expenditure if and to the extent that it is not met directly or indirectly by the State, any public or local authority, by any other person or under any contract of insurance or by way of compensation or otherwise (TCA 1997, s 482(1)–(7)). TCA 1997, s 482 provides for it to be treated as having been incurred only to the extent that it is attributable to work actually carried out in that tax year. This amendment has effect as respects qualifying expenditure incurred on or after 12 February 1998. With regard to qualifying expenditure incurred before that date, the amount incurred in a tax year is gauged by reference to the amount payable in the year.

Withdrawal of relief

The entitlement to relief for qualifying expenditure on an approved building may be withdrawn in one of three sets of circumstances. First, if due to either (a) any alteration made to the building or (b) any deterioration of the building, the Minister for Arts, Heritage and the Gaeltacht considers that the building is no longer one that is intrinsically of significant scientific, historical etc interest, they may by notice in writing to the owner or occupier revoke their previous determination. This revocation has effect from the date on which they consider that the building ceased to have the required qualities. No expenditure on the building after that date may qualify for any relief.

Secondly, if reasonable access to the building ceases to be afforded to the public, the Revenue Commissioners may, by notice in writing to the owner or occupier, revoke their previous determination. This revocation has effect from the date on which they consider that such access ceased.

Thirdly, if the building ceases to be used as a tourist accommodation facility for the period of at least six months in any calendar year, the Revenue Commissioners may revoke, by notice in writing, their previous determination with effect from the date on which the building ceased to be used as a tourist accommodation facility.

Where the Revenue Commissioners revoke the approved building status for this reason, no expenditure after the effective date of the revocation qualifies for relief. Further, any relief given in respect of qualifying expenditure incurred on that building in the five years immediately preceding that date is withdrawn. Consequently, the taxpayer's income tax (or corporation tax) liabilities affected by that withdrawal of the relief have to be recomputed for all relevant years of assessment (or accounting periods of a company). Any necessary assessments or additional assessments may be made by the Revenue to recover any tax underpaid as a result of the withdrawal of the relief (TCA 1997, s 482(1)–(7)).

TCA 1997, s 482(1)–(7) allows for a switch of use of an approved building. Where the building was previously approved on the basis that reasonable access is afforded to the public, it may switch to use as a tourist accommodation facility; similarly, where the building has been approved on the basis of being a tourist accommodation facility, it may cease to be put to this use and may become a building which provides reasonable access to the public. In either of these circumstances, a new determination will be made by the Revenue Commissioners and this will be effective from the date of the first determination.

Claim for relief

The relief for qualifying expenditure on approved buildings is only given if the person entitled specifically makes a claim for that relief. The claim must be in the form prescribed by the Revenue Commissioners. It should be accompanied by the statements in writing regarding the qualifying expenditure, including any statements by persons to whom payments were made, that are indicated by the Revenue's prescribed form (TCA 1997, s 482(10)).

While TCA 1997, s 482 does not itself prescribe any time limit within which this claim must be made, the time limit provided by TCA 1997, s 381(2)–(7) (see **4.404**) applies if the claim is made by a person chargeable to income tax. In each case, the claim must be made no later than two years after the end of the chargeable period in which the qualifying expenditure is incurred. The normal time four-year time limit for claims to repayments under TCA 1997, s 865(4) does not apply.

Approved garden

TCA 1997, s 482(1)(a), (9) extends the qualifying expenditure to include the cost of maintenance or restoration of gardens that are not attached to an approved building but are determined to be of significant horticultural, scientific, historical, architectural or aesthetic interest by the Minister for Arts, Heritage and the Gaeltacht and where the Revenue Commissioners determine that reasonable access is afforded to the public.

Approved object

TCA 1997, s 482(1) treats expenditure on certain approved objects in an approved building to qualify as expenditure incurred on that building. The relief is to cover expenditure of up to an aggregate of €6,350 per annum attributable to works carried out in the relevant tax year on:

(a) the repair, maintenance or restoration of approved objects in an approved heritage building/garden, provided the objects are on display for two years from the year the relief is first claimed;
(b) the installation, maintenance or replacement of an alarm system in an approved heritage building/garden; and
(c) public liability insurance for the above premises.

An approved object means an object (including a picture, sculpture, print, book, manuscript, piece of jewellery, furniture or other similar object or a scientific collection) owned by the owner/occupier of an approved building/garden which is determined to be of significant national, scientific, historical or aesthetic interest by the Minister for Arts, Heritage and the Gaeltacht. The determination may be revoked by the Minister with effect from the date he considers the object has ceased to qualify (TCA 1997, s 482(6)(c)). It must also be determined by the Revenue Commissioners that reasonable access is afforded. Where the approved building housing the object is a tourist accommodation facility, the object must be displayed in a part of the building to which all patrons have access (TCA 1997, s 482(6)(b)(i)); in any other case, access must be afforded on the same basis as applies to the approved building and the price charged for access to the object must be reasonable and non-prohibitive in amount (TCA 1997, s 482(6)(b)(ii)). The Revenue Commissioners may revoke their determination where the access conditions cease to be met or the object ceases to be owned by the individual concerned; any relief for expenditure incurred in the two years up to the date of such revocation will be withdrawn (TCA 1997, s 482(6)(d)).

18.302 Gifts for public purposes

Where a person makes a gift to the Minister for Finance for any purpose for which, or towards the cost of which, public moneys are provided then he may claim a deduction equal to that amount in computing his total income in the year of the gift (TCA 1997, s 483(1)–(3)). It is necessary however, that the Minister should accept the gift. 'Public moneys' are defined as any moneys charged on or issued out of the Central Fund or provided by the Oireachtas. For the purposes of a joint assessment on a spouse under TCA 1997, s 1017, the assessable spouse's total income (which is deemed to include the total income of his spouse) is to be calculated after deducting both his own and his spouse's net qualifying gifts. However, it appears that the husband's and wife's separate net gifts are only deductible to the extent that their respective total incomes are sufficient to cover their own net gifts.

18.303 Reliefs for gifts of heritage items

Gifts to approved bodies

TCA 1997, s 1003, as most recently amended by FA 2004, s 85, FA 2006, s 121 and FA 2008, s 131 provides for relief by way of a non-refundable credit against certain tax liabilities of an individual or other person where that person makes a 'relevant gift' of a 'heritage item' to an 'approved body'.

A 'heritage item' is defined as any kind of cultural item, including any archaeological item, archive, book, estate record, manuscript, painting and any collection of cultural items and any collection of such items in their setting on which the 'selection committee' (see below), has made a determination that the item, or collection of items, is:

(a) an outstanding example of the type of item involved, pre-eminent in its class, and the export of which from the State would constitute a diminution of the accumulated cultural heritage of Ireland or (following the enactment of FA 2002, s 124) whose import into the State would constitute a significant enhancement of the accumulated cultural heritage of Ireland; and
(b) suitable for acquisition by an approved body (TCA 1997, s 1003(2)).

An 'approved body' is defined as:

(a) the National Archives;
(b) the National Gallery of Ireland;
(c) the National Library of Ireland;
(d) the National Museum of Ireland;
(e) the Irish Museum of Modern Art;
(f) the Crawford Art Gallery Cork Limited (from 2 April 2007);
(g) in relation to the offer of a gift of a particular item or collection of items, any other such body owned or funded wholly or mainly by the State as approved by the Minister for Arts, Heritage, Gaeltacht and the Islands, with the consent of the Minister for Finance (TCA 1997, s 1003(1)(a)).

A 'relevant gift' is one in respect of which no consideration (other than TCA 1997, s 1003 relief itself) is received from any person by the person making the gift either directly or indirectly. The 'selection committee' consists of the directors or chairpersons as appropriate of the approved bodies (or their nominees as necessary). There is provision for the chairperson of the committee to be appointed by the Minister for Transport, Tourism and Sport. An application for relief must be made in writing to the selection committee. The selection committee will reach their final determination after having consulted such persons or bodies of persons as they deem appropriate and after consideration of any evidence put forward by the donor. The committee must also seek and consider the opinion in writing of (I) the approved body to which it is intended to make the gift and (II) the Heritage Council and the Arts Council.

The member of the selection committee representing an approved body to which it is intended to make the gift may still participate in the discussion of the application concerned but may not participate in the making of the actual decision in respect of that application.

Where an application relates to a collection of items, the committee may not make a determination in respect of the collection unless it is satisfied that it could also, if required, make a determination of at least one individual item in that collection. However, the committee is not required to actually make a formal determination in regard to that item. This requirement does not apply in the case of a collection consisting wholly of archival material or manuscripts, which was either assembled or created over time by one individual, family or organisation and constitutes a collection of archival material or manuscripts where each item has been in such collection for a period of not less than 30 years and merits maintenance as a collection.

The committee must request Revenue Commissioners to furnish them with the market value of the heritage item. The value is the price which, in the opinion of the

Revenue Commissioners, the item would fetch if sold in the open market in such manner so as to obtain for the vendor the best price for the property at the date the application is made. Where the item was acquired at auction by the donor, the market value will be deemed to include the auctioneer's fees, inclusive of any non-recoverable VAT or any equivalent overseas tax (following the enactment of FA 2002, s 124) (TCA 1997, s 1003(3)(d)). The Revenue Commissioners may authorise a person to inspect the heritage item and the person in possession or in custody of the item must give that person access to the item at such reasonable times as the Revenue Commissioners deem necessary. The Revenue must bear the costs of valuation (TCA 1997, s 1003(3)(b)).

The selection committee may not make a determination in any case where the market value of the item is less than €150,000 (€100,000 prior to 25 March 2004). With effect from 25 March 2004, in the case of a collection, at least one item in the collection must have a minimum value of €50,000. However, the €50,000 minimum value does not apply in the case of a collection consisting wholly of archival material or manuscripts. The selection committee will be permitted only to make determinations in favour of items up to a total value of €6,000,000 (€3,800,000 prior to the enactment of FA 2002, s 124) in any one year for all taxpayers (TCA 1997, s 1003(2)(c)).

Where relief is granted, a credit equal to 80 per cent of the market value of the heritage item can be set off against the income tax, capital gains tax and capital acquisitions tax liabilities of the donor (TCA 1997, s 1003(5)). With effect from 1 January 2006, the 'market value' for these purposes is the lower of:

(i) the open market value as ascertained by the Revenue Commissioners on the assumptions stated above; or

(ii) (I) the open market value as tendered by the donor on the same assumptions, or

(II) the amount paid for the property by the donor, if the donor so elects;

(TCA 1997, s 1003(3)(a) as substituted by FA 2006, s 121).

The income tax liabilities in question do not include PAYE or the withholding tax on 'relevant contracts' (see **2.311**).

The credit, which is non-refundable, is set off in the following order:

(a) tax liabilities in respect of years prior to the tax year in which the relevant gift is made (including any interest and penalties relating to that tax; the arrears of earlier periods are taken in priority to those of later periods (by reference to the due date for payment of the outstanding liabilities);

(b) any tax liability arising in the year of assessment in which the relevant gift is made and which is nominated by the individual; and

(c) any tax liability arising in future years of assessment and which is nominated by the individual (TCA 1997, s 1003(6), (7)).

No interest is payable in respect of any overpayment of tax generated by the relief (TCA 1997, s 1003(10)). Relief for the gift may not be claimed under any other provision (TCA 1997, s 1003(11)).

In order to obtain the relief, a certificate affirming that the gift has actually been made must be issued by an appropriate officer of the approved body or, failing this, a nominee of the Minister for Arts, Heritage and the Gaeltacht (TCA 1997, s 1003(4)). There are provisions for revoking a determination where the prospective donor disposes of the item other than to the relevant approved body or notifies the selection committee in writing of his intention not to proceed with the gift. The property will also cease to be a heritage item if the individual fails to make the gift within the calendar year following the year in which the determination is made (TCA 1997, s 1003(2)(d)).

The Revenue Commissioners are obliged to compile an annual list of heritage items, including descriptions and valuations, in respect of which relief has been granted under the section; such list must be included in their annual report notwithstanding the obligations to secrecy imposed on them by the Tax Acts and the Official Secrets Act 1963 (TCA 1997, s 1003(12)).

Gifts to Irish Heritage Trust or Office of Public Works

TCA 1997, s 1003A, as most recently amended by FA 2013, s 25, provides for relief by way of a non-refundable credit against certain tax liabilities of an individual or other person where that person makes a 'relevant gift' of 'heritage property' to The Irish Heritage Trust Limited (the 'Trust') (TCA 1997, s 1003A(2); SI 521/2006), or from 2010 onwards, to the Office of Public Works ('OPW'). The relief has been restricted by FA 2013, s 25.

'Heritage property' means a building or garden which, following a written application by a person who owns the building, is determined by the Minister for Arts, Heritage and the Gaeltacht ('the Minister') or the OPW to be a building which is an outstanding example of the type of building or garden involved, pre-eminent in its class, and intrinsically of significant scientific, historical, national, architectural or aesthetic interest, and is suitable for acquisition by the Trust or OPW, as appropriate. The written consent of the Minister will be required before any property can be accepted by the OPW under the scheme, and such acceptance will be subject to such conditions as specified by the Minister in each case.

For these purposes, a 'building' includes:

(i) any associated outbuilding, yard or land where the land is occupied or enjoyed with the building as part of its garden or designed landscape and contributes to the appreciation of the building in its setting;
(ii) the contents of the building (defined by TCA 1997, s 1003A(1) as furnishings historically associated with the building where the Minister or OPW is satisfied they are important to establishing the historic or aesthetic context of the building) TCA 1997, s 1003A(2)(a)); and
(iii) land necessary for the provision of access to the building or for the provision of parking facilities for visitors to the building.

Finance Act 2013, with effect from 27 March 2013 amended the relief to include (iii) above and in addition lands donated which are required for access or parking where the heritage property was owned by a different owner.

A 'relevant gift' is one in respect of which no consideration (other than TCA 1997, s 1003A relief itself) is received from any person by the person making the gift either directly or indirectly (TCA 1997, s 1003A(1)). In considering the owner's written application, the Minister or OPW, as appropriate, shall consider such evidence as the owner submits therewith (TCA 1997, s 1003A(2)(b)). On receipt of the application, the Minister or OPW must also request the Revenue Commissioners to value the heritage property (TCA 1997, s 1003A(2)(c)). For the purposes of this section, the market value of property shall be estimated to be the lesser of:

(i) the price which, in the opinion of the Revenue Commissioners, the property would fetch if sold in the open market on the valuation date in such manner and subject to such conditions as might reasonably be calculated to obtain for the vendor the best price for the property, and

(ii) (I) the open market value which, in the opinion of the person making the gift, the property would fetch on the valuation date on the same assumptions as under (i); or

(II) if that person so elects, the amount paid for the property by that person.

The 'valuation date' is the date of the written application made by the owner for a determination by the Minister or the OPW (though the latter is not stated explicitly) (TCA 1997, s 1003A(1)).

The market value of the property shall be ascertained by the Revenue Commissioners in such manner and by such means as they think fit, and they may authorise a person to inspect the property and report to them the value of the property and the person having custody or possession of the property shall permit the person so authorised to inspect the property at such reasonable times as the Revenue Commissioners consider necessary (TCA 1997, s 1003A(3)(b)).

Where the Revenue Commissioners require a valuation to be made by a person authorised by them, they must bear the associated costs (TCA 1997, s 1003A(3)(c)).

The Minister or OPW will not be permitted to make a determination in favour of heritage property where its open market value (as determined by the Revenue Commissioners) when added to the relevant valuations of all heritage property for which determinations were made (and not subsequently revoked) in the same calendar year would exceed €6,000,000 (increased to €10,000,000 for tax year 2007 only and to €8,000,000 for tax year 2008 only) (TCA 1997, s 1003A(2)(d)). The fact that the owner's valuation might be lower than the Revenue Commissioners' valuation and could result in the €6,000,000 annual threshold not being exceeded does not seem to be relevant.

Where a relevant gift is made to the Trust or OPW, it must issue a certificate to the donor, in such form as the Revenue Commissioners may prescribe, certifying the receipt of that gift and the transfer of the ownership of the heritage property to it; it must also transmit a duplicate of the certificate to the Revenue Commissioners (TCA 1997, s 1003A(4));

When the donor submits the certificate to the Revenue Commissioners, he is treated as if he had at that time made a payment on account of tax equal to 50 per cent of the open market value of the heritage property (as defined above); (prior to 27 March 2013 the relevant percentage was 80 per cent). This can be set off against his income tax, capital gains tax and capital acquisitions tax liabilities; the income tax liabilities in question do not However, include PAYE or the withholding tax on 'relevant contracts' (see **2.311**) (TCA 1997, s 1003A(1); TCA 1997, s 1003A(5)).

The credit, which is non-refundable, is set off in the following order:

(a) tax liabilities in respect of years prior to the tax year in which the relevant gift is made (including any interest and penalties relating to that tax; the arrears of earlier periods are taken in priority to those of later periods (by reference to the due date for payment of the outstanding liabilities); and

(b) any tax liability arising in the year of assessment in which the relevant gift is made and which is nominated by the individual;

(c) any tax liability arising in future years of assessment and which is nominated by the individual (TCA 1997, s 1003A(1), (6), (7), (9)).

No interest is payable in respect of any overpayment of tax generated by the relief (TCA 1997, s 1003A(10)). Relief for the gift may not be claimed under any other provision (TCA 1997, s 1003A(11)).

There are provisions for revoking a determination where the prospective donor disposes of the item other than to the Trust or OPW or notifies the Trust or OPW in writing of his intention not to proceed with the gift. The property will also cease to be a heritage item if the individual fails to make the gift within the calendar year following the year in which the determination is made (TCA 1997, s 1003A(2)(e)).

The Revenue Commissioners are obliged to compile an annual list of heritage properties, including descriptions and valuations, in respect of which relief has been granted under the section; such list must be included in their annual report notwithstanding the obligations to secrecy imposed on them by the Tax Acts and the Official Secrets Act 1963 (TCA 1997, s 1003A(12)).

18.304 Donations to approved bodies

TCA 1997, s 848A and Sch 26A provide for tax relief for donations to charities and approved bodies. The section gives relief for donations by individuals and companies. The minimum donation in any year is €250. The pre-FA 2001 regime for donations to public bodies, etc is dealt with in the 2000/01 edition of this book. This relief was potentially subject to the restrictions applicable to high income individuals discussed at **3.111** from tax year 2007 onwards. However, FA 2013 amended this relief significantly. The relief no longer applies for a donation made after 1 January 2013. Post-FA 2013 the different treatment between self-employed individuals and those under PAYE has been removed and the approved body will now obtain a specified amount of the donation rather than the self-employed individual obtaining a tax deduction for the donation. The specified rate reclaimable by the approved body has been set at 31 per cent. This is in contrast to a possible 41 per cent previously for individuals subject to PAYE. This has led to a reduction in revenue for some approved bodies. The aggregate qualifying donations in any one year for any individual has been capped at €1,000,000.

Approved bodies

TCA 1997, Sch 26A (as most recently amended by FA 2008, s 34) which supplements TCA 1997, s 848A lists the approved bodies and the conditions which they must satisfy in order to be approved.

The list of bodies is as follows:

(1) a body approved for education in the arts (see below);

(2) a body approved as an eligible charity (see below);

(3) an institution of higher education within the meaning of the Higher Education Authority Act 1971, s 1, or any body established for the sole purpose of raising funds for such an institution;

(4) an institution in the State in receipt of public funding which provides courses to which a scheme approved by the Minister for Education and Science under the Local Authorities (Higher Education Grants) Acts, 1968 to 1992, applies or any body for the sole purpose of raising funds for such an institution;

(5) an institution of higher education which provides courses which are validated by the Higher Education Training and Awards Council under the provisions of the Qualifications (Education and Training) Act 1999;

(6) an institution or other body which provides primary education up to the end of the sixth standard, based on a programme prescribed or approved by the Minister for Education and Science;

(7) an institution or other body which provides post-primary education up to the level of either or both the Junior Certificate and the Leaving Certificate based on a programme prescribed or approved by the Minister for Education and Science;

(8) a body to which TCA 1997, s 209 applies which is a body for the promotion of the observance of the Universal Declaration of Human Rights or the implementation of the European Convention for the Protection of Human Rights and Fundamental Freedoms or both the promotion of the observance of that Declaration and the implementation of that Convention; and

(9) US-Ireland Alliance Limited (Company incorporated under the Companies Acts, 1963 to 2001 on 30 January 2003).

Prior to 1 February 2007, it was an additional requirement for the bodies listed in (3)–(7) above that they should be established in the state.

TCA 1997, s 848A(14) states that where any approved body for education in the arts or body approved as an eligible charity has been approved or holds an authorisation, under any enactment and, that approval or authorisation has not been withdrawn prior to 6 April 2001, such body will be deemed to be an approved body for the purposes of this section.

Approved body for education in the arts

An 'approved body' means any body or institution which may be approved by the Minister for Finance and which:

(a) provides any course one of the conditions of entry to which is related to the results of the Leaving Certificate examination or the Matriculation examination of a recognised university in the State or an equivalent examination held outside the State (prior to 1 February 2007, it was an additional requirement that the course should be provided in the State); or

(b) (i) is established on a permanent basis solely for the advancement of one or more approved subjects (prior to 1 February 2007, it was an additional requirement such advancement should be wholly or mainly in the State),

(ii) contributes to the advancement of such subject(s) on a national or regional basis, and

(iii) is prohibited by its constitution from distributing to its members any of its assets or profits.

The 'approved subjects' are as follows:

(1) the practice of architecture;
(2) the practice of art and design;
(3) the practice of music and musical composition;
(4) the practice of theatre arts;
(5) the practice of film arts; or
(6) any other subject approved for this section by the Minister for Finance.

TCA 1997, Sch 26, Pt 2, para 2 states that the Minister for Finance may, by notice in writing given to the body or institution, withdraw the approval of any body or institution. Notice of its withdrawal shall be published as soon as may be in *Iris Oifigiúil*. On the giving of the notice the body or institution shall cease to be an approved body from the day after the date of the notice referred to above.

Approved body as an eligible charity

An 'eligible charity' means any body which holds an authorisation which is in force. The Revenue Commissioners may on application to them by a body and obtaining such information as they may reasonably require issue that body with an authorisation as an eligible charity. The authorisation shall be for such period as the Revenue Commissioners may determine but for a period not exceeding five years. Where the Revenue Commissioners are satisfied that an eligible charity has ceased to comply with the requirements, they are empowered to withdraw the authorisation by notice in writing served by registered post on the charity. With effect from 1 January 2015 the withdrawal will have effect on such date which is not earlier than when the charity ceased to comply. This wording was inserted by Finance Act 2014, s 18. This allows for retrospective withdrawal. Prior to 1 January 2015 the wording only allowed for retrospective withdrawal. As a consequence of this amendment the section has been amended to ensure that donors are still allowed a deduction for donations made in good faith before the notice had been served on the charity (TCA 1997, s 848A(3B)).

In order for the authorisation to be issued it must be shown to the satisfaction of the Revenue Commissioners that:

(a) it is a body of persons or a trust established for charitable purposes only;
(b) the income of the body is applied for charitable purposes only;
(c) before the date of making the application it has been granted exemption from tax as a charity (TCA 1997, s 207) or in the case of a body established outside the state has a received a notice of determination granting it exempt status under TCA 1997, s 208A (see **18.203**) for a period of not less than two years;
(d) it provides such other information to the Revenue Commissioners as they may require for the purposes of their functions under this part of the Act; and
(e) it complies with such conditions (if any) as the Minister for Social, Community and Family Affairs may from time to time specify for this part of the Act.

TCA 1997, Sch 26A, Pt 3, para 4 states that an eligible charity must publish information in the manner reasonably required by the Minister for Finance including audited accounts comprising an income and expenditure account or a profit and loss account, as appropriate, for its most recent accounting period and a balance sheet as at the last day of that period. The Revenue Commissioners may make available to any person the name and address of an eligible charity despite any obligations as to secrecy or other statutory restriction on the disclosure of information.

Relevant donations

In order for a taxpayer to qualify for relief the donation must be a relevant donation. A relevant donation is defined in TCA 1997, s 848A(1) (as amended by FA 2006, s 20) as a payment by a donor consisting of a sum(s) of money or designated securities amounting to, or with a market value of, at least €250. In the case of an individual, the donation must be made to an approved body in a year of assessment. 'Designated securities' are defined as shares (including stock) and debentures of a class quoted on a recognised stock exchange. Where relief is claimed under s 848A in respect of a donation of quoted securities, relief from capital gains tax on the disposal of the securities under TCA 1997, s 611 is disallowed.

The donation must also satisfy the requirements of TCA 1997, s 848A(3). These requirements are as follows:

(1) the donation is not subject to any condition of repayment;

(2) neither the donor nor any person connected with him receives a benefit in consequence of making the donation directly or indirectly;

(3) it is either not conditional on, or associated with, or part of an arrangement involving the acquisition of property by the approved body, otherwise than by way of gift, from the donor or a person connected with him;

(4) the donation is not otherwise deductible in computing for the purposes of corporation tax the profits or gains of a trade or profession and it would not be an expense of management deductible in computing the total profits of a company;

(5) in respect of a donation made by an individual, the individual must be resident in the State for the year of assessment in which the relevant donation is made; and

(6) the individual, must give an annual certificate or enduring certificate in relation to the donation to the approved body and must have paid the tax referred to in such a certificate and is not entitled to a repayment of that tax or any part of that tax.

TCA 1997, s 848A(3A) provides that where the aggregate of donations made by an individual in any year of assessment to approved bodies with which he is associated exceeds 10 per cent of his total income for that year, or the aggregate of the amounts of all donations made by an individual in any year of assessment to approved bodies is in excess of €1,000,000 the amount of the excess in either case will be disregarded for the purposes of the relief. An individual will be treated as associated with an approved body if at the time the donation is made he is an employee or member of the approved body, or of another approved body which is associated with the first approved body. An approved body is associated with another approved body if it could reasonably be considered that the same person or the same group of persons or the same groups of persons having a reasonable commonality of identity:

(i) has, have or had the means or power, either directly or indirectly, to determine the activities carried on or to be carried on by both bodies; or

(ii) or exercise, or can exercise, control over both bodies.

From 1 January 2013 an individual donor is required to certify in an annual certificate that:

(i) donation satisfies the conditions for the relief;

(ii) the individual has paid or will pay tax at the specified rate of 31 per cent on the grossed up amount of the donation; and

(iii) the donor acknowledges that the tax repaid to the approved body is not regarded as tax paid by the donor.

Individuals can provide enduring certificates that can be renewed. These will apply for five consecutive years of assessment and can be renewed. The same information is required as for the annual certificates outlined above and should include the year of assessment for which it applies and the individuals PPS no. Revenue issued *e-Brief No 55/13* on 23 December 2013 with copies of the Enduring Certificate (CHY3 Cert) and the Annual Certificate (CHY4 Cert). These forms should be sent to the approved body.

Self-assessed individuals

From 1 January 2013 there is no distinction between self-employed and PAYE individuals. The following text outlines the historic position for tax years up to and including 2012. The legislation differentiates between the treatment of donations made by PAYE individuals and self-assessed individuals. Where the donation is made in a year of assessment which is less than 12 months, the relevant donation was proportionately reduced (TCA 1997, s 848A(6)).

PAYE individuals

TCA 1997, s 848A(9) outlined the treatment of donations made by PAYE individuals.

The relief was given on a 'grossed-up basis' on a donation. TCA 1997, s 848A(1)(b) defined the 'grossed up amount' as the amount which after deducting income tax at the standard rate or at the higher rate or partly at the standard rate and partly at the higher rate, as the case may be, for the relevant year of assessment leaves the amount of the donation. The relevant year of assessment was the year of assessment in which the relevant donation is made.

Therefore, for whatever amount the individual donated, the approved body was deemed to receive a grossed up amount with a credit for tax at the donor's rate of tax. If the donor was a 41 per cent taxpayer and gave a donation of €590 to an approved body, the body was deemed to have received €1,000 less tax amounting to €410.

The approved body was treated as if the grossed up amount of the donation was an annual payment received as income by it under deduction of tax, in the amounts and at the rates specified in the appropriate certificate for the relevant year of assessment. The donor had to supply an appropriate certificate for the approved body to reclaim the tax. If the amount of tax referred to in the appropriate certificate was not paid, the amount of the repayment did not exceed the amount of tax actually paid by the donor (TCA 1997, s 848A(9)).

The 'appropriate certificate' is a certificate in such form as the Revenue Commissioners may prescribe and must contain the following statements (TCA 1997, s 848A(1)(a)):

(a) The donation satisfies the requirements of TCA 1997, s 848A(3) – (see above).

(b) The donor has paid or will pay income tax to the Revenue Commissioners which is equal to income tax at the standard rate or the higher rate or partly at the standard rate and partly at the higher rate as the case may be, for the relevant year of assessment on the grossed up amount of the donation.
However, the income tax will not be:
   (i) income tax which the donor is entitled to charge against any other person or to deduct, retain or satisfy out of any payment which the donor is liable to make to any other person, or
   (ii) appropriate tax within the meaning of TCA 1997, Pt 8, Ch 4 (Interest payments by certain deposit takers).

(c) A specification of how much of the grossed up amount has been or will be liable to income tax at the standard rate and the higher rate for the relevant year of assessment.

(d) The donor's PPSN (personal public service number).

When the body makes the repayment claim, details contained in the 'appropriate certificates' must be given to the Revenue Commissioners in electronic format approved by them. A declaration by the approved body, on a form prescribed or authorised for that purpose by the Revenue Commissioners, to the effect that the details are correct and complete must accompany the appropriate certificate (TCA 1997, s 848(10)).

Where the Revenue Commissioners are satisfied that the approved body does not have the facilities to give the details contained in an 'appropriate certificate' in electronic format, these details can be given in writing in a form prescribed or authorised by them and accompanied by a declaration made by the approved body to the effect that the claim is correct and complete (TCA 1997, s 848A(11)).

Example 18.304.1

Michael is single and has Sch E income of €39,100 from his employment for the year 2012. He makes a donation to an approved body during 2012 of €4,500.

His income tax position for 2012 is as follows:

	€	€
Sch E income		36,500
Income tax payable		
€32,800 @ 20 per cent		6,560
€ 3,700 @ 41 per cent		1,517
€36,500		8,077
Less: Personal tax credit	1,650	
PAYE tax credit	1,650	(3.300)
Income tax payable		4,777
(before credit for PAYE paid)		

The donation paid during year 2012 to an approved body is €4,500. The 'grossed-up' payment is calculated as follows:

	€	€
Part taxed at 41 per cent		3,700
Cash amount of donation paid		
(€3,700 – €1,517)	2,183	
Balance of cash amount paid out of income taxed at 20 per cent		
€4,500 – €2,183 = €2,317		
Gross up €2,317 at 20 per cent		
€2,317/0.8		2,896
Grossed up amount of relevant donation		6,596
Tax deemed to be suffered by approved body:		
€3,700 @ 41 per cent	1,517	
€2,896 @ 20 per cent	579	2,096
Net donation received		4,500

The approved body reclaims €2,096 and therefore receives €6,596 (ie €4,500 + €2,096). Michael's tax has not changed.

Self-assessed individuals

TCA 1997, s 848A(7) outlined the procedure applicable to self-assessed individuals. There was no grossing-up arrangement as for PAYE individuals. Instead the individual claimed an income tax deduction in their tax return for the year of assessment in which the donation was made (TCA 1997, s 848A(8)).

The donation was set off against any income of the individual chargeable to tax in the year of assessment in which the donation was made and tax was discharged or repaid where necessary. The donation could be claimed by either spouse in the case of jointly assessed married couples. For the purposes of calculating retirement annuity relief, the donation was not taken into account in determining a person's or as the case may be, the individual's spouse's net relevant earnings (TCA 1997, s 848A(7)).

Example 18.304.2

Taking the same figures as in the previous example except that Michael's income for the year 2012 is Case I income. He makes a relevant donation amounting to €4,500 to an approved body.

His income tax payable for 2012 is as follows:

	€
Sch D Case I income	36,500
Less:	
Relevant donation	4,500
Taxable income	32,000
Income tax payable	
€32,000 @ 20 per cent	6,400

The approved body does not receive any tax refund but receives the actual €4,500 donation.

Michael's tax has been reduced by the tax applicable to the donation deducted which amounts to €1,677 (ie €800 @ 20 per cent + €3,700 @ 41 per cent).

Therefore, the self-assessed individual with the same income as the PAYE individual has reduced his income tax liability by €1,677 with a donation of €4,500 and the PAYE individual has not received any reduction in his liability. However, if both individuals intend that the approved body should receive the same net benefit (ie inclusive of any tax refund if appropriate), then they will end up in a similar post-tax position.

18.305 Donations to approved sports bodies for approved projects

TCA 1997, s 847A with effect from 1 May 2002, provides for a scheme of tax relief for donations to certain sports bodies for the funding of capital projects to be approved by the Minister for Tourism, Sport and Recreation 'the Minister'). The approved sports body concerned must apply to the Minister for approval in respect of the project. The Minister may then give an approval certificate but not in any case in respect of a project which will cost in excess of €40,000,000. The Minister may revoke a certificate previously given by notice in writing and the project will cease to be an approved project for the purposes of the relief from the date of the Minister's notice (TCA 1997, s 847A(4)). This relief will be potentially subject to the restrictions applicable to high income individuals discussed at **3.111** from tax year 2007 onwards.

A qualifying project must comprise one or more of the following:

(a) purchasing, constructing or refurbishing a building or structure or part thereof for use for sporting or recreation activities provided by the approved sports body;

(b) purchasing land for use by the approved sports body in providing sporting or recreation facilities;

(c) purchasing permanently based equipment (excluding personal equipment) for use by the approved sports body in providing such facilities;
(d) improving the playing pitches, surfaces or facilities of the approved sports body; and
(e) repaying money borrowed (and paying interest on such money) by the approved sports body on or after 1 May 2002 for any of the above-mentioned purposes (TCA 1997, s 847A(1)).

The sports body must hold a certificate from the Revenue Commissioners stating that the body is, in their opinion, a body of persons to which TCA 1997, s 235, applies, ie its income is exempt from tax because it is a body established for and existing for the sole purpose of promoting athletic or amateur games or sports and such income is applied solely for those purposes (and such exemption has not been withdrawn). The body must also possess a valid tax clearance certificate issued for the purposes of the section (TCA 1997, s 847A(1), (3)).

The donation must amount to at least €250 in any tax year (TCA 1997, s 847A(1)). The methods of giving relief for individuals liable to PAYE and self-employed individuals respectively follow the pre 2012 rules applicable under TCA 1997, s 848A in the context of donations to approved bodies (see **18.304**).

A donation will qualify for relief only if the following conditions are met:

(a) it is made to the approved sports body for the sole purposes of funding an approved project;
(b) it is or will be applied by that body for that purpose;
(c) it is not otherwise deductible in computing the profits or gains of a trade or profession or deductible as an expense of management in computing the profits of a company;
(d) it is not a relevant donation relievable under s 848A of the Taxes Consolidation Act, 1997 (see **18.304**);
(e) it is not subject to repayment;
(f) neither the donor nor any person connected (as defined in TCA 1997, s 10) with the donor receives a benefit, whether directly or indirectly, as a result of making the donation;
(g) the donation is not conditional on or related to the acquisition of property by the approved sports body (otherwise than by way of gift) from the donor or any person connected with the donor; and
(h) the individual is resident in the State for the year of assessment in which the donation is made, and in the case of a taxpayer who is not within the self assessment system, the individual has given an appropriate certificate to the approved sports body in relation to the donation and has paid the tax referred to in such certificate and is not entitled to a repayment of that tax or any part of that tax (TCA 1997, s 847A(5)).

The Minister for Tourism, Sport and Recreation may request in writing a return of the aggregate of relevant donations received by any approved sports body (TCA 1997, s 847A(14)).

Approved sports bodies are required to issue receipts to persons making relevant donations which must contain specified details (TCA 1997, s 847A(16)). However, an approved sports body is not obliged to issue such a receipt to an individual donor who is not within the self assessment system (TCA 1997, s 847A(17)).

Relief will not be given in respect of a relevant donation to an approved sports body where that sports body had already received relevant donations of €40,000,000 in respect of the approved project (TCA 1997, s 847A(18)).

Where relief has been granted under this section and the donation concerned has not been used for the purpose of the approved project or where the relief was otherwise found not to have been due, the relevant donation in respect of which the relief was granted will be regarded as taxable income in the hands of the sports body concerned (TCA 1997, s 847A(19)).

18.306 Exemption in respect of water conservation grant

TCA 1997, s 192E with effect from 21 December 2015, being the date of passing of FA 2015, provides for a tax relief for a payment made under s 5 of the Water Services Act 2014 and shall be exempt from income tax and shall not be reckoned in computing income for the purposes of the Income Tax Acts. Revenue *eBrief No 10/16* notes that Tax and Duty Manual Part 07-01-38 summarises the provision which in turn notes that the provision 'provides that the water conservation grant, to be paid on an annual basis to households registered with Irish Water, will be exempt from income tax. As a consequence of the income tax exemption, water conservation grant payments are also exempt from USC and PRSI.'

18.4 Relief for Investment in Films

18.401 Introduction

An individual investor was entitled to relief in respect of an investment in a film production company, subject to various complex conditions being satisfied. This relief was potentially subject to the restrictions applicable to high income individuals discussed at **3.111.** The scheme of film relief, as it applied to individual investors is described in detail below. Finance Act 2013 overhauled the relief entirely following an economic impact assessment. Film relief is no longer available to individual investors from 1 January 2015. The new rules commenced with effect from 12 January 2015 by SI No 4/2015

Instead the relief will be in the form of a payable tax credit of 32 per cent to film producer companies. The tax credit will reduce their tax liability for the previous year with any excess available to fund the film project which will be carried out through a special purpose subsidiary of the film company. FA 2013 also extended the scheme until 31 December 2020 and was contingent on EU approval. As the new scheme from 2015 only applies to corporates it is outside the remit of this publication. The position for individuals up to the changes in FA 2013 are outlined in detail below.

18.402 Definitions and conditions to be met by film company

Film relief under TCA 1997, s 481 is available to a qualifying individual in respect of a relevant investment in a qualifying company (a film production company) made in the qualifying period. An understanding of the circumstances in which film relief may be claimed by the investor requires giving the definitions of the terms in the last sentence. The definitions are given in TCA 1997, s 481.

Qualifying individual

A 'qualifying individual' is defined, in relation to the film production company in which the relevant investment is made, as an individual who is not connected with that company Relief is given by way of a personal relief against total income (TCA 1997, s 458); accordingly a non-resident individual may be entitled only to restricted relief or to no relief at all: see **13.610**.

In determining whether an individual investor is connected with the film production company in which the investment is made, the 'connected person' rules of TCA 1997, s 10 are applied. In applying these rules, it appears that it may be sufficient for film relief that the investor is not connected with the film company at the time the relevant investment is made. There is no rule corresponding to that under the Employment and Investment Incentive Scheme where the individual must remain unconnected with the BES company for a defined period (see **18.102**). It is highly unlikely that it is necessary for the investor to remain unconnected until after the claim is made on the grounds that the Revenue could not make the repayment to a person connected at the time when the repayment is made.

Qualifying period

The qualifying period ran to 31 December 2014. The author is aware that Revenue granted an extension for films where the funds went into the production company pre-13 February 2015.

New certification procedures

TCA 1997, s 481(1) (as amended by FA 2004, s 28; FA 2005, s 36) provides that all applications for certification by a 'qualifying company' (see below) should be made to the Revenue Commissioners and not as heretofore to the Minister for Arts, Heritage and the Gaeltacht (the Minister with overarching responsibility is now the Minister for Tourism, Culture and Sport who must authorise the Revenue Commissioners (subject to various conditions) if they are to consider the application. Reference should be made to the previous edition of this book for a description of the pre-2005 regime.

Relevant investment

A relevant investment is defined, in effect, as a sum of money paid to a qualifying company by a qualifying investor in the following circumstances:

(a) the sum must be paid to acquire shares in the qualifying company;
(b) it must be paid in the qualifying period;
(c) it must be paid by the investor on his own behalf directly to the qualifying company;
(d) it must be paid for the purpose of enabling the qualifying company to produce a qualifying film in respect of which the qualifying company has received from the appropriate authorised officer of the Revenue Commissioners the notice in writing mentioned in (f) below;
(e) it must actually be used by the qualifying company within two years of its receipt for the purpose specified in (d);
(f) the relevant authorised officer has issued a notice in writing that the Revenue Commissioners are satisfied for the time being that a written application under TCA 1997, s 481 has been made in the form prescribed by the Revenue Commissioners and containing all such information as is specified under the accompanying statutory regulations authorised by sub-s (2E) (see below); and
(g) the terms under which the sum is paid must not include any provision for the repayment of that sum other than in the event that the Revenue Commissioners do not give a certificate for the film.

The requirement in the definition that the investment must be 'in respect of shares' in the qualifying company does not specify the type of shares. Consequently, an investment in any type of share, ordinary, preference, deferred, etc may qualify for a deduction from total income. In practice, schemes for obtaining s 481 investments in qualifying film companies are almost invariably set up on the basis of issuing new ordinary shares to the investors.

Qualifying company

The 'qualifying company', in which a relevant investment is made, must be a company which:

(a) exists *solely* for the purposes of the production and distribution of one, and only one, qualifying film;

(b) is incorporated and resident in the State or is carrying on a trade in the State through a branch or agency; and

(c) does not have in its name the words 'Ireland', 'Irish', 'Éireann', 'Eire' or 'National' where those words are registered under the Companies Acts 1963 to 1999 and/or the Registration of Business Names Act 1963, or where they are registered under the law of the territory in which the company is incorporated (TCA 1997, s 481(1)).

Condition (a) limiting the qualifying company definition to a company set up solely for one qualifying film means that it is necessary to form a separate company for each qualifying film that is to be produced with s 481 funding.

A company which distributes a film which it has not produced is not a qualifying company. A company which produces part of a film may, in certain circumstances, be a qualifying company, but the condition that it must exist solely for the production (and distribution) of that one qualifying film has to be met.

Disqualifying circumstances

Further, a company shall not be regarded as a qualifying company:

(a) unless the company, in relation to a qualifying film, notifies the Revenue Commissioners in writing immediately when the principal photography has commenced, the first animation drawings have commenced or the first model movement has commenced, as appropriate;

(b) if the financial arrangements which the company enters into in relation to the qualifying film are:

(i) financial arrangements of any type with a person resident, registered or operating in a territory other than:

(I) a Member State of the European Communities, or

(II) a State with which Ireland has a double tax agreement,

(ii) financial arrangements under which funds are channelled, directly or indirectly, to, or through, a territory other than a territory referred to in clause (I) or (II) of sub paragraph (i);

(c) unless the company provides, when requested to do so by the Revenue Commissioners, for the purposes of verifying compliance with the provisions governing the relief or with any condition specified in a certificate issued by them, evidence to vouch each item of expenditure in the State or elsewhere on the production and distribution of the qualifying film, whether expended by the qualifying company or by any other person engaged, directly or indirectly, by the qualifying company to provide goods, services or facilities in relation to such production or distribution and, in particular, such evidence shall include:

(i) records required to be kept or retained by the company by virtue of TCA 1997, s 886 (see **2.606**), and

(ii) records, in relation to the production and distribution of the qualifying film, required to be kept or retained by that other person by virtue of TCA 1997, s 886, or which would be so required if that other person were subject to the provisions of that section;

and

(d) unless the company, within such time as is specified in the accompanying regulations:

(i) notifies the Revenue Commissioners in writing of the date of completion of the production of the qualifying film,

(ii) provides to the Revenue Commissioners and to the Minister, such number of copies of the film in such format and manner as may be specified in those regulations, and

(iii) provides to the Revenue Commissioners, a compliance report, in such format and manner as is specified in those regulations, which proves to the satisfaction of the Revenue Commissioners that:

(I) the provisions of this section in so far as they apply in relation to the company and a qualifying film have been met, and

(II) any conditions attaching to a certificate issued to the company in relation to a qualifying film have been fulfilled (TCA 1997, s 481(2C)).

With effect from 1 January 2012, where the company fails to provide a compliance report within the deadline set by the regulations, an obligation to provide that report within two months following that deadline falls on any director (as defined extensively for the purposes of the close company legislation by TCA 1997, s 433(4) or secretary of the company (TCA 1997, s 481(2F)).

It is possible to have a qualifying company which is not resident in the State but which is carrying on its production and distribution trade through a branch or agency in the State.

TCA 1997, s 481(2CA) provides for approval by the Revenue Commissioners of certain

financial arrangements involving territories outside the EU with which Ireland does not have a double taxation treaty, in limited circumstances. The arrangements must relate to an investment in a qualifying film and/or the filming of part of film in the territory. Requests for approval must be made before the arrangements are effected and the Revenue Commissioners must be satisfied with the arrangements and the ability of the qualifying company to provide records. The Revenue Commissioners may seek information in relation to the arrangements and any person directly or indirectly involved. Where approval is given, money expended as part of the arrangements cannot be treated as money expended on the employment of eligible individuals or on the provision of eligible goods, services and facilities.

Qualifying film

For the film to be a qualifying film (to the company producing it to be a qualifying company), the following conditions must be met:

(a) the film must be of a kind which is included in the categories of eligible films as laid down by the accompanying regulations authorised by sub-s (2E);

(b) the film must be one which is produced:

(i) on a commercial basis with a view to the realisation of profit, and

(ii) wholly or principally for exhibition to the public in cinemas or on television,

but a *film made for exhibition* as an advertising programme or as a commercial is not a qualifying film;

(c) the Revenue Commissioners must have issued a certificate in accordance with the provisions of TCA 1997, s 481(2A) to the effect that the film may be treated as a qualifying film; and

(d) the certificate must not have been revoked by the Revenue Commissioners under TCA 1997, s 481(2D) (see below).

The real definition of a qualifying film is, therefore, in effect contained in the rules of TCA 1997, s 481(2), (2A) which prescribe the circumstances in which the Revenue Commissioners may issue a qualifying film certificate. In order to obtain a certificate in respect of any film, the company intending to produce the film must make the appropriate application to the Revenue Commissioners. The Revenue Commissioners are obliged to refer the application to the Minister for Tourism, Culture and Sport (the 'Minister') who may authorise the Revenue Commissioners to issue a certificate subject to meeting the criteria laid down in sub-s (2A) (see below). The Minister must have regard to the accompanying regulations and also the following matters:

(a) the categories of films eligible for certification by the Revenue Commissioners, as specified in the accompanying regulations; and

(b) any contribution which the production of the film is expected to make to either or both the development of the film industry in the State and the promotion and expression of Irish culture.

Where such authorisation is given, the Minister, having regard to those matters, shall specify in the authorisation such conditions, as the Minister may consider proper, including a condition:

In relation to:

(a) the employment and responsibilities of the producer, and the producer company, of a film for the production of that film; and

(b) the employment of personnel, including trainees, (other than the producer) for the production of that film (TCA 1997, s 481(2)).

Subject to authorisation by the Minister, the Revenue Commissioners may issue a certificate. However:

(a) nothing shall be construed as obliging the Revenue Commissioners to issue a certificate and in any case where, in relation to a film, the principal photography has commenced, the first animation drawings have commenced or the first model movement has commenced, as the case may be, before application is made by a qualifying company, the Revenue Commissioners shall not issue a certificate;

(b) an application for a certificate under paragraph (a) shall be in the form prescribed by the Revenue Commissioners and shall contain such information as may be specified in the accompanying regulations;

(c) in considering whether to issue a certificate the Revenue Commissioners shall, in respect of the proposed production of the film, examine all aspects of the qualifying company's proposal;

(d) The Revenue Commissioners may refuse to issue a certificate if they are not satisfied with any aspect of the qualifying company's application and, in particular, the Revenue Commissioners may refuse to issue a certificate:

   (i) if they have reason to believe that the budget or any particular item of proposed expenditure in the budget is inflated, or

(ii) where:

(I) they are not satisfied that there is a commercial rationale for the corporate structure proposed:

(A) for the production, financing, distribution or sale of the film, or

(B) for all of those purposes, or

(II) they are of the opinion that the corporate structure proposed would hinder the Revenue Commissioners in verifying compliance with any of the provisions governing the relief;

and

(e) a certificate issued by the Revenue Commissioners shall be subject to such conditions specified in the certificate as the Revenue Commissioners may consider proper, having regard, in particular, to the examination referred to in (c) above and any conditions specified in the authorisation given by the Minister, and in particular the Revenue Commissioners shall specify in the certificate a condition:

(i) in relation to the matters specified by the Minister in the authorisation by virtue of (2)(b)(II) above,

(ii) that the amount per cent of the total cost of production of the film which may be met by relevant investments shall not exceed the *specified percentage* (see below),

(iii) in relation to the minimum amount of money to be expended on the production of the qualifying film:

(I) directly by the qualifying company on the employment by the company of eligible individuals (as defined below) in so far as those individuals exercise their employment in the State in the production of the qualifying film, and

(II) directly or indirectly by the qualifying company on the provision of certain goods, services and facilities, as set out in regulations made under sub-s (2E). (Effectively this provision will ensure that the amount expended in the State on the production of a qualifying film is at least equal to, or exceeds, the amount of relevant investments raised under TCA 1997, s 481 for the film.)

Finance (No 2) Act 2013 substituted the following for the definition of 'eligible individual'. 'Eligible individual means an individual employed by a qualifying company for the purposes of the production of a qualifying film'. This amendment removes the residence requirement that had existed so that the amount spent on an eligible individual qualifies for relief regardless of where the individual is resident. Prior to this amendment an 'eligible individual' meant an individual who is a citizen of Ireland or of another Member State of the European Communities, or an individual domiciled, resident or ordinarily resident in the State or in another Member State of the European Communities. This had limited qualifying expenditure to amounts spent on EU citizens. As a consequence of the amendment Finance (No 2) Act 2013, s 25 inserted a new Ch 1A (ss 529B to 529M) to provide for withholding tax on payments made by companies qualifying for film relief to performing artistes who are resident outside of EU and EEA Member States. SI 18/2015 was published on 21 January 2015. The withholding tax applies at the standard rate, currently 20 per cent on any payments exclusive of value-added tax. The payments may be made directly or indirectly by a qualifying company in respect of artistic services provided by an artiste including any payment relating to the exploitation of or compensation for any rights held by or on behalf of or in respect of the artiste but excludes emoluments subject to PAYE. Allowable expenses notified by Revenue to the qualifying company incurred by the performing artiste will not be subject to the withholding tax. Artistic service means the services of an individual, when provided within the State, in giving a performance in audio-visual works of any kind, including films and television content, which is or may be made available to the public or any section of the public. A deduction certificate is to be issued by the company when a payment is made and tax is deducted. Electronic returns and payments are to be made by the qualifying company on ROS. The tax deducted is not available for a refund except where a deduction in respect of expenditure, which was not reimbursed or is not reimbursable, incurred in the provision of artistic services to a qualifying company. The above amendment is subject to a Ministerial Commencement Order.

The Revenue Commissioners, having consulted with the Minister as appropriate, may amend or revoke any condition (including a condition added by them) specified in the certificate, or add to such conditions, by giving notice in writing to the qualifying company concerned of the amendment, revocation or addition, and this section shall apply as if:

(a) a condition so amended or added by the notice was specified in the certificate; and
(b) a condition so revoked was not specified in the certificate.

Where a company fails to comply with the requirements outlined in Qualifying Circumstances above or fails to satisfy the Revenue Commissioners under criteria (d) and (e) immediately above, the Revenue Commissioners may revoke the certificate in writing, served by registered post (TCA 1997, s 481(2D)).

In carrying out their functions in relation to s 481 the Revenue Commissioners may:

(a) consult with any person, agency or body of persons, as in their opinion may be of assistance to them; and
(b) notwithstanding any obligation as to secrecy or other restriction on the disclosure of information imposed by, or under, the Tax Acts or any other statute or otherwise, disclose any detail in a qualifying company's application which they consider necessary for the purposes of such consultation.

TCA 1997, s 481(2E) provides for the making of statutory regulations in respect of the administration of the relief by the Revenue Commissioners and also (subject to the consent of the Minister) in relation to the matters to be considered by the Minister in granting authorisation to the Revenue Commissioners to potentially issue a certificate. These regulations are now contained in SI 869/2004. The regulations may include provision:

(a) governing the application for certification and the information and documents to be provided in or with such application;
(b) specifying the categories of films eligible for certification by the Revenue Commissioners;
(c) prescribing the form of such application;
(d) governing the records that a qualifying company shall maintain or provide to the Revenue Commissioners;
(e) governing the period for which, and the place at which, such records shall be maintained;

(f) specifying the time within which a qualifying company shall notify the Revenue Commissioners of the completion of the production of a qualifying film;

(g) specifying the time within which, and the format, number and manner in which, copies of a qualifying film shall be provided to the Revenue Commissioners and to the Minister;

(h) specifying the form and content of the compliance report to be provided to the Revenue Commissioners, the manner in which such report shall be made and verified, the documents to accompany the report and the time within which such report shall be provided;

(i) governing the type of expenditure which may be accepted by the Revenue Commissioners as expenditure on the production of a qualifying film;

(j) governing the provision of the goods, services and facilities referred to (e)(iv)(II) above, including the place of origin of those goods, services and facilities, the place in which they are provided and the location of the supplier;

(k) specifying the currency exchange rate to be applied to expenditure on the production of a qualifying film; and

(l) specifying the criteria to be considered by the Minister, in relation to the categories of films eligible for certification and the contribution expected to be made by the film to the Irish film industry and/or Irish culture (see above):

  (i) in deciding whether to give the relevant authorisation to the Revenue Commissioners,

  (ii) in specifying conditions in such authorisation, noted above,

  and the information required for those purposes to be included in the application made to the Revenue Commissioners by a qualifying company;

(m) governing financial arrangements approved in accordance with sub-s (2C)(ba); and

(n) the employment of eligible individuals and the circumstances in which expenditure by a qualifying company would be regarded as being on the employment of those individuals in the production of a qualifying film.

Authorised officers

With effect from 1 January 2006, references to the Revenue Commissioners performing or discharging functions under the film relief provisions include also references to an authorised officer (FA 2006, s 18).

Limit to relief

TCA 1997, s 481(2)(c) prescribes an upper limit to the percentage of the total cost of production of a film (the 'film budget') which may be met by investments qualifying for relief (whether held by individual and/or company investors). The maximum percentage of s 481 funding allowed for any film – referred to as the 'specified percentage' determined under the rules now discussed – must be stated in the certificate for the film in question. The amount of the specified percentage for any film varies with the total film budget:

Total film budget	*Maximum*
Up to €5,080,000	66%
Over €5,080,000 to €6,350,000 (see below)	55% to 66%
Over €6,350,000	55%

Where the film has a budget in excess of €5.08m and up to €6.35m, the maximum amount of relevant investments is determined by a formula which, in effect, reduces the maximum percentage from 66 per cent (budget not exceeding €5.08m) to 55 per cent (budget €6.35m) at the rate of 1.1 per cent per €127,000 of budget increase (and pro rata for less than €127,000).

In cases where the budget exceeds €6.35m, the total cost of production which may be met by relevant investments cannot exceed €15,000,000 (increased from €10,480,000 by FA 2004, s 28 from 1 January 2005 (ie the stated maximum percentage – 55 per cent – is subject to an overall cap of €15,000,000 where the production cost is €6.35m or greater) (TCA 1997, s 481(2)(c)).

With effect from 18 May 2006, the maximum specified percentage is increased to 80 per cent in all cases, subject to an overall cap of €35,000,000 on the total amount of production costs which may be met by relevant investments (FA 2006, s 18; SI 256/2006). FA 2008 provided for an increase in the overall cap from €35,000,000 to €50,000,000.

18.403 Claims by individuals

TCA 1997, s 481(6) entitled a qualifying individual to claim film relief in respect of a relevant investment (the qualifying film investment) made prior to 31 December 2014. As mentioned there was a limited extension for films where they went into the production company prior to 13 February 2015. The claim must be accompanied by a certificate issued in a prescribed form by the company (a 'Film 3 certificate'). The Film 3 certificate certifies that the conditions for the s 481 relief, so far as they apply to the film company and the qualifying film, are or will be satisfied in relation to that investor's relevant investment (TCA 1997, s 481(12)). Before issuing the Film 3 certificate, the company must furnish the Revenue Commissioners with a statement that that it does or will satisfy the conditions for the relief together with any such other information as the Revenue Commissioners may reasonably require (TCA 1997, s 481(13)). The Film 3 Certificate may not be issued without the approval of the Revenue Commissioners. TCA 1997, s 481(14) provides that the Revenue Commissioners may refuse to approve the issue of a Film 3 certificate to a film company if they are not satisfied that they have received adequate information, or if they have reason to believe that the conditions for granting the relief will not be complied with. The Revenue must issue a notice of determination to that effect, which is subject to the same rights of appeal as apply in relation to claims for reliefs and repayments under TCA 1997, s 864.

The certificate issued to each investor specifies the details of that person's investment including the name of the film company, the investor's name, the date of the investment, the numbers of shares acquired and the amount invested for them. The certificate is also required to state that the Revenue Commissioners have authorised the issue of the certificate.

In addition to the condition that the individual is not connected with the film company, certain further conditions must be met if the relief is to be given, namely:

(a) the investment must be one made for genuine commercial reasons and not as part of a scheme or arrangement the main purpose or one of the main purposes of which is the avoidance of tax;

(b) the investment must be made at the risk of the investor;

(c) the money invested has been, or will be, used in the production of a qualifying film; and

(d) neither the investor nor any person connected with the investor is entitled to receive any payment, in money or money's worth, or other benefit, directly or indirectly borne by, or attributable to, the film company, except that the relief is not denied through either:

(i) a payment made on an arm's length basis for goods or services supplied, or

(ii) a payment out of the proceeds of exploiting the film to which the investor is entitled under the terms subject to which the investment is made (TCA 1997, s 481(18)).

In relation to condition (c), this should be read in conjunction with the rule contained in the definition of *Relevant investment* (see **18.402**) that the qualifying company in which the investment is made must use the money invested in the production of the qualifying film within two years of its receipt by that company. If the qualifying company fails to use the money within this deadline, the investor loses the entitlement to the relief.

How relevant deduction given and limit to deduction

Film relief under TCA 1997, s 481 is given to an individual by allowing a 'relevant deduction' from his total income for the year of assessment in which the qualifying film investment is made. Subject to the individual's total income being sufficient to cover it, the amount of the relevant deduction for a tax year is an amount equal to the lower of the amount invested or deemed to be invested in the year and €50,000 (TCA 1997, s 481(7)). The reference to an amount deemed to be invested in a tax year refers to a case where there is an amount of unused relevant deduction carried forward from a previous year (see *Carry forward of unused relevant deduction* below).

If an individual makes two or more relevant investments in the same tax year, the aggregate of those investments is taken in applying the €50,000 relevant deduction limit. In the case of a husband and wife, each spouse is entitled to a relevant deduction in the tax year in respect of his own relevant investment(s), with the same limit being applied separately to the investment (or aggregate of the investments) made by the spouse in question. This applies whether the husband and wife are taxed jointly for the year or are taxed as single individuals.

It follows that a husband and wife may together obtain relevant deductions totalling €100,000 in a tax year, provided that each has sufficient income and if each makes separate qualifying film investments. This maximum total assumes that each spouse invests a minimum of €50,000 in qualifying investments. If either or both spouses invests less than €50,000, their relevant deduction is, of course, limited to the amount of the investing spouse's own film investment(s). If one spouse invests more than €50,000 and the other spouse less than €50,000, there is no facility for the former picking up the latter's unused limit – even where the husband and wife are taxed jointly.

Before any film relief may be given to any individual, the film production company must have obtained the qualifying film certificate for the film from the Minister, and must have complied with various other formalities, so as to be able to issue to the investor the 'film 3' certificate to be submitted by the individual with his claim.

De minimis rule

TCA 1997, s 481(6), provides a *de minimis* rule which provides that an individual is not entitled to a relevant deduction in respect of a relevant investment in a qualifying company in a year of assessment unless the amount so invested in the film production company in that year is at least €250. This minimum investment requirement has to be applied separately to each qualifying company in which an investment is made. For example, if Mr A invests €250 in 2012 in film company R Limited and €195 in film company S Limited, Mr A can claim a relevant deduction for the investment in R Limited, but is not entitled to any relevant deduction for the investment in S Limited.

However, in applying this *de minimis* rule in the case of a husband and wife assessed jointly for the tax year in which a relevant investment (or investments) is (or are) made, the amount of either spouse's investment may be deemed to have been made by the other spouse.

Carry forward of unused relevant deduction

TCA 1997, s 481(8), (9) entitled an individual to carry forward the relevant deduction for any relevant investment which could not be fully utilised in the year in which the investment is made to future years, but no later than the tax year 2014. The carry forward may arise either because the amount of the relevant investment exceeds the annual limit of €50,000 or the total income of the individual is not sufficiently great to cover the relevant deduction. The carry forward is granted by treating the amount of the unused relevant deduction as if it were a relevant investment made in the subsequent tax year(s), taking the earliest following years first.

A relevant deduction in any tax year is to be given firstly in respect of notional relevant investments referable to carry forward unused relevant deductions in priority to actual relevant investments made in that tax year; where the notional relevant investments refer to unused relevant deductions of two or more prior tax years, the relevant deduction must be given by reference to the earliest of those years first (TCA 1997, s 481(10)).

Procedure for claiming relief

An individual normally claims the relevant deduction to which he is entitled under TCA 1997, s 481 for a year of assessment by including details of the relevant investment(s) made in that year in his tax return for that year.

In the case of an individual liable to PAYE on Sch E income who wishes to include the relief in his tax-free allowances, the claim may be made by letter to the appropriate PAYE district accompanied by the Film 3 certificate.

When determining if an adequate amount of preliminary tax has been paid by reference to the liabilities of the preceding or pre-preceding tax years as appropriate, those liabilities must be recomputed if necessary in order to disregard any relief obtained under the scheme (see **2.104**).

18.404 Withdrawal of relief

If, following the grant of relief to an investor, the film production company fails to meet any of the statutory requirements or any of the conditions subject to which the qualifying film certificate is issued, or the Revenue Commissioners revoke the company's certificate (see above), the investor ceases to be entitled to that relief and any relief already given is withdrawn. The relief is withdrawn by means of an assessment under Sch D case IV for the year of assessment in which the relief was originally granted; notwithstanding any other provisions to the contrary, such an assessment may be made at any time (TCA 1997, s 481(19)).

18.5 Mid-Shannon Tourism Infrastructure Pilot Scheme

18.501 Introduction

TCA 1997, Pt 10, Ch 12 contains a tax incentive scheme for tourism facilities in the mid-Shannon area, ie alongside the Shannon River in Counties Clare, Galway, Tipperary, Offaly, Roscommon and Westmeath. The scheme is aimed at encouraging the development of new tourism infrastructure, or the refurbishment of existing tourism infrastructure, namely holiday camps and associated facilities, in that area. Restaurants, but not public houses or gaming establishments are eligible for relief. The qualifying period for the scheme is the period from 1 June 2008 to 31 May 2013. This qualifying period may be extended for a two-year period to 31 May 2015 subject to the issue of a Ministerial Order. This Ministerial Order has not yet been issued and at the time of writing is very unlikely to issue. For this reason the contents which follows is for academic interest. In the case of refurbishment the qualifying expenditure must exceed 20 per cent of the market value of the property before work commences. An upper cap is also placed on qualifying expenditure on accommodation facilities. Where the relevant building or structure is wholly situated in an area listed in TCA 1997, Sch 8B Pt 1 or Pt 5 (see **18.507**), only 80 per cent of construction and refurbishment expenditure will qualify for relief. There are extensive approval, certification and administrative conditions to be satisfied.

Relief will be granted by way of accelerated capital allowances over seven years for qualifying construction and refurbishment expenditure incurred in the qualifying period (15 per cent in years one to six and 10 per cent in year seven). There will be a potential clawback of allowances on the disposal of a qualifying building or structure within a 15-year time frame. Investors may only claim allowances in excess of their rental income up to a ceiling of €31,750 and the relief is subject to the restrictions applicable to high income individuals discussed at **3.111**. The FA 2012 restrictions on carry forward of unused capital allowances (discussed at **6.107**) apply to this scheme.

18.502 Key definitions

A number of terms are defined for the purposes of the scheme by TCA 1997, s 372AW, as follows:

'accommodation building', in relation to a project (see definition below) means a building or structure or part of a building or structure which consists of accommodation facilities or which is to be used or is suitable for use for the provision of such facilities;

'market value', in relation to a building or structure, means the price which the unencumbered fee simple of the building or structure would fetch if sold in the open market in such manner and subject to such conditions as might reasonably be calculated to obtain for the vendor the best price for the building or structure, less the part of that price which would be attributable to the acquisition of, or of rights in or over the land on which the building or structure is constructed;

'mid-Shannon corridor' means the corridor of land comprising all qualifying mid-Shannon areas;

'mid-Shannon Tourism Infrastructure Board' ('the Board' hereafter) means a board consisting of not more than 5 persons selected for the purposes of the scheme by the Minister (see definition below) in consultation with the Minister for Finance;

'Minister' means the Minister for Arts, Sport and Tourism;

'project' means the construction or refurbishment of buildings and structures comprising:

(a) a qualifying holiday camp (see below), or
(b) one or more qualifying tourism infrastructure facilities,

the site or sites of which is or are wholly within a qualifying mid-Shannon area

'property developer' means a person carrying on a trade which consists wholly or mainly of the construction or refurbishment of buildings or structures with a view to their sale;

'qualifying mid-Shannon area' means any area described in TCA 1997, Sch 8B (see **18.507** below);

'qualifying tourism infrastructure facilities' means such class or classes of buildings and structures as may be approved for the purposes of the scheme by the Minister, in consultation with the Minister for Finance, and published in the relevant guidelines;

'refurbishment', in relation to a building or structure, means any work of construction, reconstruction, repair or renewal, including the provision or improvement of water, sewerage or heating facilities, carried out in the course of:

(a) the repair or restoration, or
(b) maintenance in the nature of repair or restoration,

of the building or structure;

'relevant guidelines' mean guidelines issued for the purposes of the scheme.

18.503 Qualifying period

TCA 1997, s 372AW(1) provides that 'qualifying period' means the period commencing on 1 June 2008. Finance Act 2010, s 27(1)(a) provided for an extension of the qualifying period to 31 May 2015. However, this extension was subject to a Ministerial Order which has never issued.

In determining to what extent, capital expenditure is incurred in the qualifying period, so much of that expenditure as is properly attributable to work on the construction or refurbishment of the premises actually carried out during the qualifying period shall (notwithstanding any other provision of the Tax Acts as to the time when any capital expenditure is or is to be treated as incurred) be treated as having been incurred in that period (TCA 1997, s 372AY(5)).

18.504 Qualifying expenditure on buildings and structures

General

Capital expenditure on the construction or *refurbishment* (as defined: see **18.502** above) of qualifying holiday camps and qualifying tourism infrastructure facilities (see below) will generally be eligible for capital allowances, but under certain scenarios the expenditure will be excluded from relief (see below). The relief is granted subject to meeting certain procedural preconditions (see below). There is also a 20 per cent threshold in relation to refurbishment expenditure and an upper cap on allowable expenditure in relation to accommodation buildings (see below). In addition, only 80 per cent of construction and refurbishment expenditure in respect of sites wholly situated in an area listed in TCA 1997, Sch 8B Pt 1 or Pt 5 will qualify for relief (see **18.507**).

Excluded expenditure

No capital allowances will be available on expenditure where:

(a) a property developer (as defined above: see **18.502**) or a person connected (within TCA 1997, s 10) with the property developer is entitled to the relevant interest (see **6.403**) in respect of the expenditure concerned and either the developer, that person or any other person connected to the developer (within TCA 1997, s 10) incurred that expenditure;

(b) where any part of the expenditure concerned has been, or is to be met, directly or indirectly, by grant assistance or any other assistance which is granted by or through the State, any board established by statute, any public or local authority or any other agency of the State;

(c) the potential capital allowances in relation to the building or structure concerned and the project in which it is comprised fail to comply with either:

  (i) the requirements of the Guidelines on National Regional Aid for 2007–2013 (OJ No C54, p 13) prepared by the European Commission on 4 March 2006, or

  (ii) the National Regional Aid for Ireland for the period 1 January 2007 to 31 December 2013 (OJ No C292, p 11) prepared by the European Commission on 24 October 2006; or

(d) the person entitled to the relevant interest (see **6.403**) in respect of the expenditure concerned is subject to an outstanding recovery order following a previous decision by the European Commission declaring that State Aid received by that person was illegal and incompatible with the Common Market.

(TCA 1997, s 372AZ(1) as amended by FA 2008, ss 27, 29).

Procedural Preconditions

In all cases, the Board must have:

(i) granted approval in principle in relation to the construction or refurbishment of the building or structure concerned prior to any expenditure being incurred, *and*

(ii) after the expenditure is incurred, certified in writing that the construction or refurbishment which was carried out is in accordance with the criteria specified in the relevant guidelines, having regard to any relevant conditions and requirements imposed by the Board in the approval. A fully completed application for approval must have been received by the Board within a period of two years from the start of the qualifying period (1 June 2008). This period was to have been extended by a further two years by the Finance Act 2010, s 27(1)(b) but the extension was subject to a ministerial order which has never issued. (TCA 1997, s 372AW(2)).

Threshold for allowable refurbishment expenditure

Relief will only apply to refurbishment expenditure if the total amount incurred is not less than 20 per cent of the market value (as defined: see **18.502** above) of the building or structure immediately before that expenditure was incurred (TCA 1997, s 372AX(3); s 372AY(3)).

Restrictions on accommodation buildings

The Board may only grant approval and certification for the construction or refurbishment of one or more *accommodation buildings* (see definition above) in a *project* (see definition above), to the extent that such expenditure exceeds (or, where an application for approval is involved, is projected to exceed) the '*limit amount*', ie the lesser of:

(i) 50 per cent, or such lower percentage as may be specified in the relevant guidelines for the type of project involved, of the total amount of the capital expenditure on all the buildings or structures in the project, and

(ii) the amount of the capital expenditure incurred on the construction or refurbishment of buildings and structures in the project apart from accommodation buildings.

Where there is more than one accommodation building in a project, and the aggregate expenditure exceeds the *limit amount*, then the limit amount must be apportioned on a just and reasonable basis between all those buildings. Expenditure in excess of the limit amount will not be eligible for capital allowances (TCA 1997, s 372AW(4)).

Restriction of allowances in Clare and Tipperary areas

Where the relevant site is wholly situated in an area described in either Pt 1 (Clare) or Pt 5 (Tipperary) of Sch 8B (see **18.507**), then only 80 per cent of the capital expenditure actually incurred will be taken into account in computing capital allowances and any balancing adjustments (TCA 1997, s 372AZ(4)).

Qualifying holiday camp

This is defined as a building or structure which meets the following qualifying conditions:

(a) the site is wholly within a qualifying mid-Shannon area;

(b) it is in use as a holiday camp which is:

  (i) registered in the register of holiday camps kept under the Tourist Traffic Acts 1939 to 2003, and

  (ii) it meets the requirements of the relevant guidelines;

(c) the *prescribed data* (see below) has been provided to the Board in respect thereof; and

(d) the Board has given the requisite certificate in respect thereof (see *Certification* below) (TCA 1997, s 372AX(1)).

Qualifying tourism infrastructure facilities

This is defined as a building or structure which meets the following qualifying conditions:

(a) the site is wholly within a qualifying mid-Shannon area;

(b) it is not, or is not deemed to be an industrial building;

(c) it is in use for the purposes of the operation of one or more qualifying tourism infrastructure facilities;

(d) it does not include a building or structure thereof which is a licensed premises (as defined in the Intoxicating Liquor Act 1988, s 2), other than a restaurant (as defined in s 6 of the Intoxicating Liquor Act 1988) in relation to which:

  (I) a wine retailer's on-licence, within the meaning of the Finance (1909–10) Act 1910, is currently in force, or

  (II) a special restaurant licence, within the meaning of the Intoxicating Liquor Act 1988, has been granted under section 9 of that Act;

(e) it does not include a building or structure or part of a building or structure in use as a facility in which gambling, gaming or wagering of any sort is carried on for valuable consideration or which supports the carrying on of such activities;

(f) the *prescribed data* (see below) has been provided to the Board in respect thereof; and

(g) the Board has given the requisite certificate in respect thereof (see *Certification* below) (TCA 1997, s 372AY(1)).

Prescribed data

This consists of the following details to be provided to the Board for onward transmission to the Minister and the Minister for Finance and:

(i) (I) the amount of the capital expenditure actually incurred in the qualifying period on the construction or refurbishment of the building or structure, and

  (II) where relevant the amount of expenditure which is eligible for certification in relation to an accommodation building (see above);

(ii) the number and nature of the investors that are investing in the building or structure;

(iii) the amount to be invested by each investor; and

(iv) the nature of the structures which are being put in place to facilitate the investment in the building or structure, together with such other information as may be specified in the relevant guidelines as being of assistance to the Minister for Finance in evaluating the costs, including but not limited to exchequer costs, and the benefits arising from the operation of tax relief for buildings and structures under this Chapter (TCA 1997, s 372AX(1)(c); s 372AY(1)(f)).

Certification

The Board must give a certificate in writing after the building or structure is first used or, where capital expenditure is incurred on the refurbishment of a building or structure, first used subsequent to the incurring of that expenditure:

(i) stating that it is satisfied that the qualifying conditions have been met and

(ii) confirming the date of first use or, as the case may be, first use after refurbishment, and

(iii) which includes certification in accordance with the preconditions noted above or a copy of such certification (if previously issued) (s 372AX(1)(d); s 372AY(1)(g)).

18.505 Capital allowances available on qualifying buildings and structures

General

For the purposes of granting capital allowances, qualifying tourism infrastructure facilities are treated as if they were an industrial building in which a trade is being carried on (irrespective of whether any trade is in fact being carried on therein). Qualifying holiday camps will already be entitled to be treated as industrial buildings by virtue of TCA 1997, s 268(3). In both cases, enhanced allowances are granted at a rate of 15 per cent pa for the first six years (commencing with the date of first use or in the case of refurbishment the date of first use following the refurbishment) and 10 per cent in the seventh year. The tax life of the building will be 15 years from date of the first use (or the date of first use following refurbishment) so a sale etc of the building within that period will potentially trigger off a balancing adjustment (s 372AX(2); s 372AY(2)).

Buildings purchased unused etc

The provisions of TCA 1997, s 279 (see **6.408**) are adapted to take into account the restrictions on allowable expenditure which may arise in respect of accommodation buildings and also expenditure incurred in certain areas (see **18.504** above) (TCA 1997, s 372AZ(5)(b)). For these purposes, the definition of 'net price paid' is re-defined as:

$$B \times C / (D + E)$$

Where:

- B is the amount paid by a person on the purchase of the relevant interest (see **6.403**) in the building or structure;
- C is the amount of the expenditure actually incurred on the construction of the building or structure as reduced in accordance with either or both of the above-mentioned restrictions;
- D is the amount of the expenditure actually incurred on the construction of the building or structure; and
- E is the amount of any expenditure actually incurred which is disqualified under TCA 1997, s 270(2).

The broad effect is to scale down the amount of the net price paid in proportion to the restrictions imposed on allowable expenditure under the scheme. Where the purchaser acquires the building etc from a builder, he will be deemed to incur expenditure on the relevant interest equal to the lesser of the net price (as calculated above) and the actual expenditure (as restricted). Where the purchaser acquires the building etc from a non-builder, he will be deemed to incur expenditure on the relevant interest equal to the lesser of the net price (as calculated above) and the actual expenditure (as restricted).

No double relief

Where relief is given under the scheme, relief shall not be given in respect of the expenditure concerned under any other provision of the Tax Acts, TCA 1997, s 372AZ(2)).

Limits on claims

Investors may only claim allowances in excess of their rental income up to a ceiling of €31,750 and the relief is subject to the restrictions applicable to high income individuals (discussed at **3.111**).

18.506 Relevant guidelines

The Minister must in consultation with the Minister for Finance, issue guidelines to which the Board shall have regard in deciding whether to grant approval in principle or to issue certification in relation to any building or structure (TCA 1997, s 372AW(3)). These guidelines may include criteria in relation to all or any one or more of the following:

(a) the nature and extent of the contribution which the project, in which the building or structure is comprised, makes to tourism development in the mid-Shannon corridor or the qualifying mid-Shannon area;
(b) coherence with national tourism strategy;
(c) environmental sensitivity, having particular regard to any area which is:
  (i) a European site within the meaning of the European Communities (Natural Habitats) Regulations 1997 (SI 94/1997), or
  (ii) a natural heritage area, a nature reserve or a refuge for fauna for the purposes of the Wildlife Acts 1976 and 2000;
(d) the amenities and facilities required to be provided in each type of project;
(e) the nature of and maximum extent to which accommodation buildings (if any) are allowable in each type of project;
(f) specific standards of design and construction in relation to buildings and structures which may qualify for relief under the scheme;
(g) relevant planning matters, including the need for consistency with the requirements of a development plan or a local area plan within the meaning of those terms in the Planning and Development Act 2000;
(h) the details and information required to be provided in an application for approval or certification; and
(i) matters relating to the provision of prescribed data (see **18.504**).

together with such other matters as the Minister, in consultation with the Minister for Finance, may consider are required to be included.

18.507 Mid-Shannon areas

TCA 1997, Sch 8B prescribes the qualifying mid-Shannon areas as follows:

Part 1: Description of qualifying mid-Shannon areas of Clare

The District Electoral Divisions of Ayle, Ballynahinch, Boherglass, Caherhurley, Cappaghabaun, Carrowbaun, Cloonusker, Coolreagh, Corlea, Derrynagittagh, Drummaan, Fahymore, Feakle, Inishcaltra North, Inishcaltra South, Killaloe, Killokennedy, Killuran, Kilseily, Lackareagh, Loughea, Mountshannon, O'Briensbridge, Ogonnelloe and Scarriff.

Part 2: Description of qualifying mid-Shannon areas of Galway

The District Electoral Divisions of Abbeygormacan, Abbeyville, Balinasloe Rural, Ballinasloe Urban, Ballyglass, Ballynagar, Bracklagh, Clonfert, Clontuskert, Coos, Derrew, Drumkeary, Drummin, Eyrecourt, Kellysgrove, Killimor (Portumna rural area), Kilmacshane, Kilmalinoge, Kilquain, Kiltormer, Kylemore, Laurencetown, Leitrim, Lismanny, Loughatorick, Marblehill, Meelick, Moat, Pallas, Portumna, Tiranascragh, Tynagh and Woodford.

Part 3: Description of qualifying mid-Shannon areas of Offaly

The District Electoral Divisions of Ballycumber, Banagher, Birr Rural, Birr Urban, Broughal, Cloghan, Clonmacnoise, Derryad, Doon, Drumcullen, Eglish, Ferbane, Gallen, Hinds, Hunston, Killyon, Lumcloon, Lusmagh, Mounterin, Moyclare, Shannonbridge, Shannonharbour, Srah and Tinamuck.

Part 4: Description of qualifying mid-Shannon areas of Roscommon

The District Electoral Divisions of Athleague East, Athleague West, Athlone West Rural, Ballydangan, Ballynamona, Castlesampson, Caltragh, Cams, Carnagh, Carrowreagh, Cloonburren, Cloonown, Crannagh, Creagh, Culliagh, Drumlosh, Dysart, Fuerty, Kilcar, Kiltoom, Lackan, Lecarrow, Lismaha, Moore, Mote, Rockhill, Roscommon Rural, Roscommon Urban, Scregg, Taghmaconnell, Thomastown and Turrock.

Part 5: Description of qualifying mid-Shannon areas of Tipperary

The District Electoral Divisions of Aglishcloghane, Ardcrony, Ballina, Ballingarry (in Borrisokane rural area), Ballygibbon, Ballylusky, Ballymackey, Ballynaclogh, Birdhill, Borrisokane, Burgesbeg, Carrig, Carrigatogher, Castletown, Cloghprior, Clohaskin, Cloghjordan, Derrycastle, Finnoe, Graigue (in Borrisokane rural area), Greenhall, Kilbarron, Kilcomenty, Killoscully, Kilkeary, Kilmore, Kilnarath, Knigh, Lackagh, Lorrha East, Lorrha West, Mertonhall, Monsea, Nenagh East Urban, Nenagh Rural, Nenagh West Urban, Newport, Rathcabban, Redwood, Riverstown, Terryglass, Uskane and Youghalarra.

Part 6: Description of qualifying mid-Shannon areas of Westmeath

The District Electoral Divisions of Athlone East Rural, Athlone East Urban, Athlone West Urban, Ardnagragh, Auburn, Ballymore, Bellanalack, Carn, Castledaly, Doonis, Drumraney, Glassan, Killinure, Moate, Mount Temple, Moydrum, Muckanagh, Noughaval, Templepatrick, Tubbrit, Umma and Winetown.

18.6 Living City Initiative

18.601 Introduction

TCA 1997, Pt 10 Ch 13 contains the Living City Initiative tax incentive scheme. The Living City Initiative is aimed at the regeneration of Georgian areas. It does so by providing an annual 10 per cent allowance for owner occupiers of residential units on refurbishment and conversion expenditure. It also provides for capital allowances at 15 per cent per annum on the conversion or refurbishment of retail premises. The areas covered will be in Cork, Dublin, Galway, Kilkenny, Limerick and Waterford. The initiative was commenced by SI No 171/2015 with 5 May 2015 appointed as the day the initiative is to come into operation. SI Nos 182–187 outline the areas specified as special regeneration areas for the purposes of the relief.

18.602 Owner occupier relief

The relief is available to an individual who incurs refurbishment or conversion expenditure on a qualifying premises in the five-year period which commences from the date that this section is enacted by way of Ministerial Order. Provided the individual meets the conditions of the relief, he or she is entitled to claim a deduction of 10 per cent per annum of the qualifying expenditure against their total income. The qualifying premises must be their main or only residence in each year that the deduction is claimed. If the dwelling ceases to be their only or main residence, the deduction is no longer available but there is no clawback of deductions previously given. There is no definition of main residence.

'Qualifying premises' is a relevant house within a special regeneration area which is used solely as a dwelling and which is first used as the individual's main or only residence after the expenditure has been incurred. A relevant house is defined as a building constructed prior to 1915. Prior to Finance Act 2014, only buildings of at least two storeys qualified for the relief. Since Finance Act 2014, the relief has been extended to single storey buildings. In practice this change has no effect as the legislation has yet to become operative. It does not have to be a Georgian building to qualify. In order to be a qualifying premises the individual entitled to the relief must receive a letter of certification from the relevant local authority stating that:

(a) planning permission if required was received for the refurbishment or conversion work;
(b) the house complies with certain standards including relating to water and sewerage;
(c) the costs of the expenditure is reasonable.

'Qualifying expenditure' is expenditure on the conversion or refurbishment of a qualifying premises after deducting from the amount of the expenditure incurred any grant aid which the individual has received or is entitled to receive. Conversion is defined as work converting a building or buildings, not used as a dwelling, into a house(s) and includes any expenditure on construction, repairs and renewals and the provision or improvement of water, sewerage or heating facilities. Refurbishment work is widely defined to include construction, reconstruction work or repairs in the restoration of the building and the provision or improvement of water, sewerage or heating facilities. The qualifying expenditure must be equal to at least 10 per cent of the market value of the house immediately before the expenditure was incurred. Market value for this purpose is the market value of the freehold excluding that part which relates to the value of the land. The above '10 per cent' requirement was removed by FA 2016, s 15 and replaced with a requirement that qualifying expenditure must exceed €5,000.

Finance Act 2014 amended TCA 1997, s 372AAB to exclude relief under this section unless certain information is provided to the Revenue as part of the relevant claim made. The information required to be provided as part of the claim includes the name and PPS number (as defined in TCA 1997, s 477B(1)) of the individual claiming the relief, the address of the qualifying premises in respect of which the expenditure has been incurred, the unique identification number (if any) assigned to the qualifying premises under the Finance (Local Property Tax) Act 2012, s 27; and details of the aggregate of all qualifying expenditure incurred by the individual in respect of the qualifying premises. Finance Act 2014 also stipulates that the relevant claim should be made by electronic means. The Revenue will need to revert on how such electronic filings are to be made.

Example 18.602.1

John Murphy purchased a relevant house built in 1906 in a special regeneration area. The cost of the house is €300,000 and it was estimated that the value of the site at the date of purchase was €50,000. John spends €150,000 on modernising the house. This comprised of restoring period plaster, doors, windows, roof repairs and a new heating system. It also included €30,000 for a new modern kitchen.

It is unlikely that the new modern kitchen would qualify for the relief. However, the remaining €120,000 should qualify. Provided Mr Murphy receives his letter of certification and occupies the house as his main or only residence he will be entitled to a deduction of €12,000 per annum against his total income or the total income of his spouse or civil partner.

A qualifying premises means a house built prior to 1915.

18.603 Capital allowances for commercial premises

Capital allowances are available in respect of qualifying expenditure (ie capital expenditure) on the refurbishment or conversion of a building in a qualifying special regeneration area in the five-year period commencing on the date that this initiative comes into operation (SI 171/2015 appointed 5 May 2015 as the day of coming into operation). (TCA 1997, s 372AAC). The building must not otherwise be an industrial building and must be in use either for a retail trade or, a trade which involves the provision of services within the State. A qualifying building can also include a building which is let on bona fide commercial terms for the purposes of the retailing of goods or the provision of services within the State. However, a qualifying building does not include any part of a building or structure in use as or as part of a dwelling house. It is only conversion or refurbishment work that qualifies, construction work does not qualify for relief. It is interesting that the expenditure must be capital expenditure to qualify for relief yet it includes maintenance in the nature of repair.

the building is seven years and there is no balancing adjustment if the building is sold outside this seven-year period.

For the purposes of determining in relation to a claim for an allowance whether and to what extent eligible expenditure incurred on the conversion or refurbishment of a special qualifying premises is incurred or not in the relevant qualifying period then only such an amount of that eligible expenditure as is properly attributable to work on the conversion or refurbishment of the premises actually carried out during the relevant qualifying period shall (notwithstanding any other provision of the Tax Acts as to the time when any capital expenditure is or is to be treated as incurred) be treated as having been incurred in that period. Expenditure in respect of which a person is entitled to this relief shall not include any expenditure in respect of which that person is entitled to a deduction, relief or allowance under any other provision of the Tax Acts.

Relief under TCA 1997, s 372AAD shall not be given unless the following information is provided to the Revenue Commissioners as part of the first claim made by the person:

(a) the name and PPS number or tax reference number of the person making the claim;

(b) the address of the special qualifying premises in respect of which the eligible expenditure was incurred;

(c) the unique identification number (if any) assigned to the special qualifying premises under s 27 of the Finance (Local Property Tax) Act 2012; and

(d) details of the aggregate of all eligible expenditure incurred by the person in respect of the special qualifying premises.

Any claim made, or information required to be provided, to the Revenue Commissioners under this relief, is to be made or provided by electronic means. Qualifying expenditure is to be reduced by an amount equal to three times the sum received or receivable where it has been met by grant assistance. Capital allowances are also not available to a property developer or persons connected with the property developer. Further relief is not available while the claimant is regarded as an undertaking in difficulty for the purposes of the Commission Guidelines on State Aid for rescuing and restructuring non-financial undertakings in difficulty. Those guidelines (referenced in FA 2016, s 15 – OJ No C249, 31.7.2014, p 1) note that an undertaking is considered to be in difficulty when, '…without intervention by the State, it will almost certainly be condemned to going out of business in the short or medium term'. The guidelines outline various indicators as to when such difficulty is in point.

18.7 Property Tax Incentives

18.701 Property tax incentives

Full details of the various property incentive schemes may be found in Division 19 of the 2009 and earlier editions of this book. It should be noted that the FA 2012 restrictions on carry forward of unused capital allowances (discussed at **6.107**) apply to allowances and reliefs granted under these schemes.

Index

[*all references are to paragraph number*]